The Complete Works
of
Oswald Chambers

Discovery House Publishers

Books, music, and videos that feed the soul with the Word of God

Box 3566 Grand Rapids, MI 49501

The Complete Works
of
Oswald Chambers

The Complete Works of Oswald Chambers
Copyright © 2000 by
Oswald Chambers Publications Association, Limited

Discovery House Publishers is affiliated with
RBC Ministries, Grand Rapids, Michigan 49512

Discovery House books are distributed to the trade exclusively by
Barbour Publishing, Inc., Uhrichsville, Ohio 44683

Cover portrait and design by Jim Connelly Studios, © 2000.

Library of Congress Cataloging-in-Publication Data

Chambers, Oswald, 1874–1917.
    [Works. 2000]
    The complete works of Oswald Chambers / by Oswald Chambers.
        p. cm.
    Includes bibliographical references (p.   ) and index.
    ISBN 1-57293-039-X
    1. Christian life. 2. Spiritual life. I. Title.
BV4501.2 .C462 2000
242--dc21

00-060118

Printed in the United States of America

01 02 03 04 05 06 / RRD / 9 8 7 6 5 4 3 2

Contents

Introduction

The Complete Works of Oswald Chambers

Contents

For the first time, all the published books of Oswald Chambers have been collected in one volume. Also included are notes on Isaiah, Jeremiah, and Ezekiel previously unpublished in book form.

Each book is prefaced by a brief introduction, noting the time and place when the lectures were given and a history of their publication.

The text of the books in this volume is taken from the editions published in the United Kingdom by the Oswald Chambers Publications Association. British spelling has been retained throughout.

Footnotes

Oswald Chambers urged his students at the Bible Training College to read and study with a dictionary at hand. "Never intend to look up a word," he said. *"Do it now."*

In the spirit of Chambers and his philosophy of education, we have not robbed the reader of the opportunity to learn by personal effort.

If a name, word, or term appears in *Merriam Webster's Collegiate Dictionary,* Tenth Edition, it is not footnoted. In some cases, a person not fully identified in the text has been footnoted.

Scripture Index

Those readers possessing the CD ROM version of this volume may trace any verse or passage of Scripture throughout the teaching of Chambers. The CD ROM is located in the envelope at the back of the book and uses the popular Logos software.

Poetry and Other Quotations

Many of the quotations from poetry and other writings were not identified in the original text. The editors have not provided any identification of sources that did not appear in the books as originally published by Mrs. Chambers.

General Index

A general index of people, places, and terms is provided for those wishing to locate specific information contained in this volume.

The editors have not attempted to reference every appearance of words such as Holy Spirit, obedience, prayer, sanctification, and so on. That would require a concordance almost as large as the book itself! Readers may use the CD ROM version of this volume to locate all occurrences of words in Chambers' books by using their computer's search function.

Bibliography

This complete list of the books in this volume, with a brief summary of content, will aid readers in searching for Chambers' teaching on various themes such as prayer, sanctification, ethics, and others.

Publication Information

In the years before tape recording, it was common for sermons and speeches to be taken down in shorthand by stenographers, then published in newspapers and magazines. Chambers' early messages in Britain and the U.S. would have been recorded in this way. After his marriage in 1910, virtually all of his lectures and sermons were recorded in shorthand and transcribed for publication by his wife, Biddy.

The following periodicals are mentioned throughout this volume:

- *God's Revivalist and Bible Advocate,* published by God's Bible School, Cincinnati, Ohio, USA (1900–present). This publication was originally called *The Revivalist* and published by Martin Wells Knapp prior to his founding of God's Bible School in 1900.

For information on this publication, contact God's Bible School, 1810 Young Street, Cincinnati, OH 45210, USA.

- *Tongues of Fire,* published by the Pentecostal League of Prayer. In 1916, the magazine changed its name to *Spiritual Life.*

  Tongues of Fire, numbers 1–300, January 1891– December 1915

  Spiritual Life , numbers 301–692, January 1916– December 1950

  A complete set of this publication is held in the British Newspaper Library, Colindale, London.

- *The Bible Training Course* (B.T.C.) *Monthly Journal* (April 1932–March 1952)

  Published by Mrs. Chambers as "A Journal for the continuance of the teaching given by Oswald Chambers, as Principal of the Bible Training College, Clapham, London, 1911–1915; and in the Y.M.C.A. Huts Zeitoun, etc., Egypt, 1915–1917."

Mrs. Chambers saw this publication primarily as a means of keeping in touch with the hundreds of people whose lives had been touched during their ministry, many of whom were serving as missionaries overseas. It began as a monthly publication, but wartime restrictions and paper shortages caused the change to a bimonthly and finally quarterly journal. Although subscriptions were sold, Mrs. Chambers generously provided scores of complimentary copies.

Throughout the 1930s and 1940s, many of the Oswald Chambers works first appeared in article form and upon completion of the series were published as books. Since the Bible Training College ceased to exist in 1916, Mrs. Chambers used the familiar initials B.T.C., simply changing the last word to reflect the new phase of continuing her husband's teaching in this way.

A complete set of this publication is held in the British Library, St. Pancras, London.

A WORD ABOUT OSWALD CHAMBERS

Oswald Chambers was not famous during his lifetime. At the time of his death in 1917 at the age of forty-three, only three books bearing his name had been published. Among a relatively small circle of Christians in Britain and the U.S., Chambers was much appreciated as a teacher of rare insight and expression, but he was not widely known.

Chambers was born in Aberdeen, Scotland, in 1874, the youngest son of a Baptist minister. He spent his boyhood years in Perth, then his family moved to London when Oswald was fifteen. Shortly after the move to London, Oswald made his public profession of faith in Christ and became a member of Rye Lane Baptist Church. This marked a period of rapid spiritual growth, along with an intense struggle to find God's will and way for his life.

A gifted artist and musician, Chambers trained at London's Royal Academy of Art, sensing God's direction to be an ambassador for Christ in the world of art and aesthetics. While studying at the University of Edinburgh (1895–96), he decided, after an agonizing internal battle, to study for the ministry. He left the university and entered Dunoon College, near Glasgow, where he remained as a student, then a tutor for nine years.

In 1906, he traveled to the United States, spending six months teaching at God's Bible School in Cincinnati, Ohio. From there, he went to Japan, visiting the Tokyo Bible School, founded by Mr. and Mrs. Charles Cowman. This journey around the world in 1906–07 marked his transition from Dunoon College to full-time work with the Pentecostal League of Prayer.

During the last decade of his life, Chambers served as:

- Traveling speaker and representative of the League of Prayer, 1907–10
- Principal and main teacher of the Bible Training College, London, 1911–15
- Y.M.C.A. chaplain to British Commonwealth soldiers in Egypt, 1915–17

He died in Cairo on November 15, 1917, of complications following an emergency appendectomy. The complete story of his life is told in *Oswald Chambers: Abandoned to God* (1993), available from Discovery House Publishers, Box 3566, Grand Rapids, MI 49501.

During the seven years of their marriage, his wife, Gertrude (Biddy) Hobbs, took verbatim shorthand notes of nearly all his lectures and sermons. After his death, she spent the rest of her life publishing her husband's spoken words. His best-known book, *My Utmost for His Highest,* has been continuously in print since it was first published in 1927.

From the earliest days of publication following World War I, Mrs. Chambers was advised and assisted by a small group of personal friends. In later years, this group became known as the Oswald Chambers Publications Association, which was incorporated in 1942, and exists today as a Registered British Charity. It oversees the publication and distribution of Oswald Chambers' material around the world.

Through the years, one of the Association's goals has been to keep all of Oswald Chambers' books in print. This has often meant the amalgamation of smaller books and booklets into single volumes for greater cost efficiency. The publication of this volume fulfills a goal held by Mrs. Chambers and the Association. By presenting the Complete Works in a single volume, it is hoped to preserve Chambers' words for future generations.

We commend this work to the reader with the prayer that you will be spiritually strengthened and encouraged as you encounter the person of Jesus Christ through the words of His servant, Oswald Chambers.

Approved unto God

including

Facing Reality
Oswald Chambers

INTRODUCTION

Source

These lectures were given to students in the sermon class at the Bible Training College,[1] London, from 1911 to 1915.

Publication History

- As articles: These lectures were published in the *BTC Monthly Journal,* May 1932–March 1934.[2]
- As a book: The material was first published in 1936.
- *Facing Reality* (© 1939) was incorporated in the 1946 and later editions.

Chambers limited the BTC[3] sermon classes to enrolled students only and allowed no visitors. Since sermon preparation and delivery were course requirements, he wanted all class members on an equal footing as participants, with no idle observers and critics. Much more than a course on how to prepare and deliver sermons, these lectures reveal Chambers' heart concerning being a worker for God.

To these students Chambers said: "Here in this College, God can break or bend or mould, just as He chooses. You do not know why He is doing it; He is doing it for one purpose only, that He may be able to say, 'This is My man, My woman.'"

---

1. Residential school near Clapham Common in SW London, sponsored by the League of Prayer. Oswald Chambers was Principal and main teacher; Biddy Chambers was Lady Superintendent. Known as the BTC, it closed in July 1915 because of World War I.

2. *Bible Training Course Journal:* published from 1932 to 1952 by Mrs. Chambers, with help from David Lambert.

3. Bible Training College, London, 1911–1915.

CONTENTS

FOREWORD

"Study to show thyself approved unto God, a workman that needeth not to be ashamed" (2 Timothy 2:15), makes a big demand upon a worker for God, and these God-given messages, spoken to the students at the Bible Training College, London, by the Principal, the late Oswald Chambers, help us to meet that Divine requirement. One clear note in them is "that the servant of God has to go through the experience of things before he is allowed to go through a study of them." So the worker is required to enter voluntarily into that discipline of his life that will bring him into line with God's way for him. Here there is as much insistence upon spiritual fitness as right mentality, and upon intellectual discipline as upon spiritual well-being. The worker for God is a unity, spirit, soul and body, and needs to be brought by God's grace and by personal choice and concentration into a harmoniously working whole. Mere intellectualism can be a great snare and mere pietism is not enough. The man of God to be thoroughly furnished unto every good work must accept the spiritual discipline of reproof and correction and training in righteousness that the Scriptures convey, and also the mental discipline which a right understanding of the Scripture demands. These Talks in a striking manner put us in the way of becoming competent servants of Jesus Christ, spiritually fit, and mentally fitted, for the great task entrusted to us. Do not read this book unless you mean business, but if you do you will find wisdom and understanding on every page.

David Lambert[4]

4. David Lambert (1871–1961): Methodist minister and friend of Oswald Chambers. Assisted Mrs. Chambers with OC publications from 1917–1961.

THE WORKER
1 Corinthians 9:11–27

The Matter
Plant every man on the Rock, and plant the whole man there.

(a) Amid a Crowd of Paltry Things
(1 Corinthians 9:11–15)

The first thing a worker has to learn is how to be God's noble man or woman amid a crowd of paltry things. A Christian worker must never make this plea—"If only I were somewhere else!" The only test that a worker is Christ's witness is that he never becomes mean[5] from contact with mean people any more than he becomes sinful from contact with sinful people.

We are not workers for God by our own choice (see John 15:16). Many deliberately choose to be workers for God, but they have no matter of God's mighty grace in them, no matter from God's mighty word. The pattern for God's worker is that he is entrusted with a mission—for example, Moses and the Apostle Paul. We have to be in God's hand so that He can plant men on the Rock as He has planted us, not by our testimony only, but because we are being made co-workers with God.

(b) Amid a Creed of Powerful Things
(1 Corinthians 9:16–17)

Unless we have the right matter in our minds intellectually and in our hearts affectionately, we will be hustled out of usefulness to God. Keep the note of greatness in your creed: Whom do I believe Jesus Christ is? What do I believe sin is? What do I believe God can do with sin? What do I believe is God's purpose for the human race? Face yourself with one central Fact only, the Lord Jesus Christ, His Life and Death and Resurrection.

Every Christian must testify, testimony is the nature of the life; but for preaching there must be the agonising grip of God's hand, something akin to verse 16. The whole of my life, says Paul, is in the grip of God for this one thing, I cannot turn to the right hand or to the left, I am here for one purpose, to preach the gospel. How many of us are held like that? The note of the majority is verse 17, that is why there is so much mediocrity, so much lazy work for God. "*I have chosen you*"—that is where the note of greatness is struck out of your creed.

The Manner
However things move, they do not change us.

(a) The External Crush of Things
(1 Corinthians 9:18–19)

God buries His men in the midst of paltry things, no monuments are erected to them, they are ignored, not because they are unworthy but because they are in the place where they cannot be seen. Who could see Paul in Corinth? Paul only became marvellous after he had gone. All God's men are ordinary men made extraordinary by the matter He has given them. God puts His workers where He puts His Son. This is the age of the humiliation of the saints.

Manner is the outcome of matter. Paul's whole soul and mind and heart were taken up with the great matter of what Jesus Christ came to do, he never lost sight of that one thing (see 1 Corinthians 2:2).

(b) The Ethical Character of Things
(1 Corinthians 9:20–27)

"I am become all things to all men, that I may by all means save some" (1 Corinthians 9:22 RV). The worker who is not chosen by God says, "I am all things to all men, and nothing in particular to any man." The stamp of the worker gripped by God is that, slowly and surely, one here and another there is being won for God.

The worker chosen by God has to believe what God wishes him to believe, though it cost agony in the process; the worker who chooses to work for God may believe what he likes. It is the latter class who exploit the Bible.

Here, in this College, God can break or bend or mould, just as He chooses. You do not know why He is doing it; He is doing it for One purpose only, that He may be able to say, "This is My man, My woman." Never choose to be a worker, but when once God has put His call on you, woe be to you if you turn to the right hand or to the left. God will do with you what He never did with you before the call came; He will do with you what He is not doing with other people. Let Him have His way.

---

5. mean: ordinary, common, low, or ignoble, rather than cruel or spiteful

THE BASE
1 Timothy 1:12

The Real Thanks of the Worker

And I thank Christ Jesus our Lord . . .

Everything that God has created is like an orchestra praising Him. "All Thy works shall praise Thee." In the ear of God everything He created makes exquisite music, and man joined in the paean of praise until he fell, then there came in the frantic discord of sin. The realisation of Redemption brings man by way of the minor note of repentance back into tune with praise again. The angels are only too glad to hear that note, because it blends man into harmony again (see Luke 15:10).

Praising God is the ultimate end and aim of all we go through. "Whoso offereth praise glorifieth Me." What does it matter whether you are well or ill! whether you have money or none! It is all a matter of indifference, but one thing is not a matter of indifference, and that is that we are pleasing to the ears of God.

Paul had got back again by way of repentance into tune with God (cf. 1 Timothy 1:13), and now he has his base as a worker in thanksgiving to Christ Jesus; his whole life has been brought into perfect relation to God.

The Realised Test of the Worker

who hath enabled me . . .

The test of the worker is that he knows he has been enabled by the Lord Jesus, therefore he works and learns to do it better all the time. The realisation that my Lord has enabled me to be a worker keeps me strong enough never to be weak. Conscious obtrusive weakness is natural unthankful strength; it means I refuse to be made strong by Him. When I say I am too weak it means I am too strong; and when ever I say "I can't" it means "I won't." When Jesus Christ enables me, I am omnipotently strong all the time. Paul talks in paradoxes, "for when I am weak, then am I strong."

The Recognised Truth by the Worker

for that He counted me faithful . . .

To recognise that my Lord counts us faithful removes the last snare of idealising natural pluck. If we have the idea that we must face the difficulties with pluck, we have never recognised the truth that He has counted us faithful; it is His work in me He is counting worthy, not my work for Him. The truth is we have nothing to fear and nothing to overcome because He is all in all and we are more than conquerors through Him. The recognition of this truth is not flattering to the worker's sense of heroics, but it is amazingly glorifying to the work of Christ. He counts us worthy because He has done everything for us. It is a shameful thing for Christians to talk about "getting the victory"; by this time the Victor ought to have got us so completely that it is His victory all the time, not ours. The overcoming referred to in the Book of the Revelation is not the personal overcoming of difficulties but the overcoming of the very life of God in us while we stand resolutely true to Him.

The Responsible Trust of the Worker

. . . putting me into the ministry.

The ministry is, the "glorious gospel of the blessed God, which was committed to my trust." If I am going to be loyal to that trust, it will mean I must never allow any impertinent sensitiveness to hinder my keeping the trust. My trust is the glorious gospel for myself and through me to others, and it is realised in two ways: in the perfect certainty that God has redeemed the world, and in the imperative necessity of working on that basis with everyone with whom I come in contact (cf. Colossians 1:28–29).

THE WORKER'S SPIRITUAL LIFE

Communication of the Life of God
(Galatians 2:20)

As a worker, watch the "sea-worthiness" of your spiritual life; never allow a spiritual leakage. Spiritual leakage arises either by refusing to treat God seriously, or by refusing to do anything for Him seriously. Bear in mind two things: the pressure of God on your thought from without, and the pressure of God on your attention from within.

There are three ways in which we can responsibly receive communications from God: by giving deliberate thoughtful attention to the Incarnation; by identifying ourselves with the Church, and by means of Bible revelation. God gave Himself in the Incarnation; He gives Himself to the Church; and He gives Himself in His Word; and these are the ways He has ordained for conveying His life to us. The mere reading of the Word of God has power to communicate the life of God to us mentally, morally and spiritually. God makes the words of the Bible a sacrament, i.e., the means whereby we partake of His life, it is one of His secret doors for the communication of His life to us.

Co-Ordination of Our Capacities for God
(Ephesians 3:16–19)
Our whole being, not one aspect of it, has to be brought to comprehend the love of God. We are apt to co-ordinate our spiritual faculties only; our lack of co-ordination is detected if we cannot pass easily from what we call the secular to the sacred. Our Lord passed from the one to the other without any break; the reason we cannot is that we are not pressed on to the life of God. We have made "a world within the world" of our own which we have to guard jealousy: "I must not do this and that"; "I must keep myself entirely here." That is not the life of God at all, it is not genuine enough; it is artificial and cannot stand the strain of actual life. There is no room in the New Testament for sickly piety, but room only for the robust, vigorous, open-air life that Jesus lived—*in* the world but not *of* it, the whole life guided and transfigured by God. Beware of the piety that is not stamped by the life of God, but by the type of a reli-

gious experience. Be absolutely and fiercely godly in your life, but never be pious. A "pi" person does not take God seriously, he only takes himself seriously, the one tremendous worship of his life is his experience.

Concentrated Centring on God
(Romans 8:3)
If we would concentrate on God we must mortify our religious self-will. Our Lord refused to be self-willed religiously, and it was this that staggered the Pharisees. We are self-willed religiously, consequently we tell God we do not intend to concentrate on Him, we only intend to concentrate on our idea of what the saintly life should be, and before long we find that the pressing in of the life of God ceases and we begin to wilt. We are living a religiously self-centred life and the communication of life from God comes no longer. We must beware of turning away from God by grubbing amongst our own experiences.

God does not expect us to *imitate* Jesus Christ: He expects us to allow the life of Jesus to be manifested in our mortal flesh. God engineers circumstances and brings us into difficult places where no one can help us, and we can either manifest the life of Jesus in those conditions, or else be cowards and say, "I cannot exhibit the life of God there." Then we deprive God of glory. If you will let the life of God be manifested in your particular human edition—where God cannot manifest it, that is why He called you, you will bring glory to God.

The spiritual life of a worker is literally, God manifest in the flesh.

THE WORKER AND THE WORD

Aspect of Sacred Authority (Matthew 21:23)
Authority means a rule to which the worker is bound in loyalty. It is not sufficient to say, "Because Jesus Christ says so, therefore you must obey," unless we are talking to people who know Who Jesus Christ is. Authority must be of a moral, not a superstitious character. In the old days it was the authority of the Church, or the authority of the Bible; both these were external authorities, not indigenous to man. Nowadays people are saying, "Bother[6] external authority; why should I accept external authority?" Immediately a man becomes spiritual by being born from above (RV mg), the Bible becomes his authority, because he discerns a law in his conscience that has no objective resting place save in the Bible; and when the Bible is quoted, instantly his intu-

ition says, "Yes, that must be the truth"; not because the Bible says so, but because he discerns what the Bible says to be the word of God for him. When a man is born from above (RV mg) he has a new internal standard, and the only objective standard that agrees with it is the word of God as expressed in the Bible.

What is needed to-day is not a new gospel, but live men and women who can re-state the Gospel of the Son of God in terms that will reach the very heart of our problems. To-day men are flinging the truth overboard as well as the terms. Why should we not become workmen who need not to be ashamed, rightly dividing the word of truth to our own people? The majority of orthodox ministers are hopelessly useless, and the unorthodox seem to be the only ones

---

6. bother (verb): forget, disregard.

who are used. We need men and women saturated with the truth of God who can re-state the old truth in terms that appeal to our day.

Aspect of Social Authority *(John 18:36)*

Christianity is in its essence social. When once we begin to live from the otherworldly standpoint, as Jesus Christ wants us to live, we shall need all the fellowship with other Christians we can get. Some of us can do without Church fellowship because we are not Christians of the otherworldly order. Immediately a man dares to live on Jesus Christ's line, the world, the flesh and the devil are dead against him in every particular. "The only virtue you will have in the eyes of the world as My disciples," says Jesus, "is that you will be hated." That is why we need to be knit together with those of like faith; and that is the meaning of the Christian Church.

In the old days the ecclesiastics used to dictate, now they are ignored, and instead we have a society of men as they are. In the present day we have to face a brotherhood of men apart from Jesus Christ. If a man stands on the present system of civilisation as one of the general brotherhood of men, and yet proclaims a different brotherhood, that of the disciples of Jesus Christ, John 16:2 will be the result, "they shall put you out of the synagogues." According to Jesus Christ, Christianity is a society based on the brotherhood of men who have been lifted into a right relationship with God by regeneration. "My kingdom is not of this world," said Jesus, and yet we are more inclined to take our orders from the world than from Jesus Christ.

Aspect of Personality (John 17:22)

The conception which Jesus Christ had of society was that men might be one with Him as He was one with the Father. The full-orbed meaning of the term "personality" in its fundamental aspect is a being created by God who has lived on this earth and formed his character. The majority of us are not personalities as yet, we are beginning to be, and our value to God in His Kingdom depends on the development and growth of our personality. There is a difference between being saved and sanctified by the sheer sovereign grace of God and choosing to be the choice ones, not for heaven, but down here. The average view of Christianity, that we only need to have faith and we are saved, is a stumbling block. How many of us care anything about being witnesses to Jesus Christ? How many of us are willing to spend every ounce of energy we have, every bit of mental, moral and spiritual life for Jesus Christ? That is the meaning of a worker in God's sense. God has left us on earth, what for? To be saved and sanctified? No, to be at it for Him. If we are "footing it"[7] bit by bit, and living in the otherworldly spirit while in the world, we are developing our personality, and are of far more worth to Jesus Christ than those who have entered into the experience of sanctification but have never gone on any farther.

Are we willing to be broken bread and poured-out wine in Jesus Christ's hands for others? to be spoilt for this age, for this life, this time, spoilt from every standpoint saving as we can disciple men and women to Him? My life as a worker is the way I say "Thank you" to God for His unspeakable salvation. The hatred and the indignation of the world does not come when we are sanctified; it comes when we try to live our daily life according to the rule of sanctification. It is not preaching sanctification that awakens resentment, but living the life to which sanctification introduces us, the life of oneness with Jesus Christ, and insisting that that oneness be manifested in our practical life. "Except ye eat the flesh of the Son of man. . . . From that time many of His disciples went back, and walked no more with Him." It is quite possible for anyone to be cast out as reprobate silver, "lest that by any means, . . . I myself should be a castaway."

THE RIGHT LINES OF WORK
1 Timothy 6:20–21

What to Concentrate On *(2 Timothy 1:13–14)*
To concentrate is not to be absorbed or carried away with a subject; concentration is the sternest physical effort. There is nothing spiritual about the brain. Control over associated ideas must be acquired, it is not a natural gift. Never garrison an infirmity with indifference—"Oh, I can't." DO IT!

Paul gives Timothy indications of the right lines of work: he is to concentrate on the deposit of truth conveyed by the words of Scripture. As a preacher never have as your ideal the desire to be an orator or a beautiful speaker; if you do, you will not be of the slightest use. Read Matthew 23, and Mark 7, and see the rugged, taste-shattering language of Our Lord. An orator moves men to do what they are indifferent

---

7. footing it: walking; taking it one step at a time.

about; a preacher of the Gospel has to move men to do what they are dead-set against doing, viz., giving up the right to themselves. The one calling of a New Testament preacher is to uncover sin and reveal Jesus Christ as Saviour, consequently he cannot be poetical, he has to be surgical. We are not sent to give beautiful discourses which make people say, "What a lovely conception that is," but to unearth the devil and his works in human souls. We have to probe straight down where God has probed us, and the measure of the probing is the way God has probed us.

Be keen in sensing those Scriptures that contain the truth which comes straight home, and apply them fearlessly. The tendency nowadays is to get a truth of God and gloss it over. Always keep the sense of the passage you expound. For example, in Malachi 2:13 the prophet tells the people that God will not regard their offerings, though they cover "the altar of the LORD with tears, with weeping, and with crying out." The context gives the reason: there is a wrong temper of mind and secret immorality. Never sympathise with a soul whose case makes you come to the conclusion that God is hard. God is tenderer than anyone we can conceive of, and if a man cannot get through to Him it is because there is a secret thing he does not intend to give up. It is impossible to deal poetically with a case like that, you have to go right down to the root of the trouble until there is antagonism and pain and resentment against the message. The Gospel of Jesus awakens a tremendous craving but also a tremendous resentment. People want the blessing of God, but they will not stand the probing and the humiliation. As workers, our one method is merciless insistence on the one line, cutting down to the very root, otherwise there will be no healing.

Always carry out the significance of your text with as many details as possible. To the majority of men, holiness is all in the clouds, but take this message, "Holiness, without which no man shall see the Lord,"

and drive it home on every line until there is no refuge from the terrific application. Holy not only in my religious aspirations, but holy in my soul life, in my imagination and thinking; holy in every detail of my bodily life. Let your text get such hold of you that you never depart from its application. Never use your text as a title for a speculation of your own, that is being an impertinent exploiter of the word of God.

What to Concentrate For *(2 Timothy 2:23–26)*
Remember that the underlying principles upon which God has built human nature and the underlying principles of the Bible go together, and learn to bring the meaning of your text to bear on those principles. Leave your text alone apparently until you get men to realise in the sphere of their own lives where they lack. Then erect the standard of Jesus Christ for their lives and say for them—"But we never can be that!" Then drive it home—"But God says you must be." "How can we be?" "You cannot, unless you have a new spirit, and Jesus says that God will give you the Holy Spirit if you ask Him" (see Luke 11:13).

There must be a sense of need before your message is of any use. For example, if you present John 3:16 to a crowd of moral upright men and women, it has no application to them, the subject is not alive to them, they are in a different domain. Men are "dead in trespasses and sins," not necessarily blackguards, but their minds are blinded by the god of this world. That is the crowd we have to get in amongst, and it can only be done by relying on the Holy Spirit to awaken conviction where as yet there is none. Behind the preaching of the Gospel the creative Redemption of God is at work in the souls of men, and when the Spirit of God begins to work on their hearts they see a standard they never saw before. "I, if I be lifted up from the earth, will draw all men unto Me." Once let Jesus Christ be lifted up, and the Spirit of God creates the need for Him.

THE STUDENT
2 Timothy 2:15

Practical Sphere of Work *(2 Corinthians 11:9; 1 Timothy 4:13; 1 Thessalonians 2:9)*
The difficulty in Christian work to-day is that we put it into a sphere that upsets the reasoning of things— this sphere for sacred and that for secular; this time for activity and that for study. God will never allow us to divide our lives into sacred and secular, into study and activity. We generally think of a student as one who shuts himself up and studies in a reflective

way, but that is never revealed in God's book. A Christian's thinking ought to be done in activities, not in reflection, because we only come to right discernment in activities. Some incline to study naturally in the reflective sense, others incline more to steady active work; the Bible combines both in one life. We are apt to look on workers for God as a special class, but that is foreign to the New Testament. Our Lord was a carpenter; Paul was a weaver. If you try and live in compartments, God will tumble up the time. Acknowledge Him in all your ways, and He will bring you into the circumstances that will develop the particular side of your life that He wants developed, and be careful that you do not upset His plans by bringing in your own ideas.

Another danger in work for God is to make natural temperament the line of service. The gifts of the Spirit are built on God's sovereignty, not on our temperament. We are apt to limit God by saying, "Oh, I'm not built like that"; or, "I have not been well educated." Never limit God by those paralysing thoughts, it is the outcome of unbelief. What does it matter to the Lord Almighty of heaven and earth what your early training was like! What does matter to Him is that you don't lean to your own understanding, but acknowledge Him in all your ways. So crush on the threshold of your mind any of those lame, limping "I can'ts,"—"you see I am not gifted." The great stumbling-block that prevents some people being simple disciples of Jesus is that they *are* gifted—so gifted that they won't trust in the Lord with all their hearts. You have to learn to break by the power of the Holy Spirit the fuss and the lethargy which alternate in your life, and remember that it is a crime to be weak in His strength.

Poverty and Work *(2 Corinthians 8:9)*
Our Lord Jesus Christ became poor for our sakes not as an example, but to give us the unerring secret of His religion. Professional Christianity is a religion of possessions that are devoted to God; the religion of Jesus Christ is a religion of personal relationship to God, and has nothing whatever to do with posses-

sions. The disciple is rich not in possessions, but in personal identity. Voluntary poverty was the marked condition of Jesus (see Luke 9:58), and the poverty of God's children in all ages is a significant thing. Today we are ashamed and afraid to be poor. The reason we hear so little about the inner spiritual side of external poverty is that few of us are in the place of Jesus, or of Paul. The scare of poverty will knock the spiritual backbone out of us unless we have the relationship that holds. The attitude of Our Lord's life was that He was disconnected with everything to do with things that chain people down to this world, consequently He could go wherever His Father wanted Him to.

Providential Will of God *(Proverbs 3:5–6)*
Remember you are accountable to no one but God; keep yourself for His service along the line of His providential leading for you, not on the line of your temperament. The servant of God has to go through the experience of things before he is allowed to go through the study of them. When you have had the experience God will give you the line for study; the experience first, and then the explanation of the experience by the Spirit of God. Each one of us is an isolated person with God, and He will put us through experiences that are not meant for us at all, but meant to make us fit stuff to feed others.

How much time have you given to wondering what God is doing with you? It is not your business. Your part is to acknowledge God in all your ways, and He will blend the active and the spiritual until they are inseparable, and you learn to live in activities knowing that your life is hid with Christ in God.

WHERE AM I?
A Spiritual Stock-Taking

Why Do I Want to Work? *(Romans 10:15)*
The Christian worker must be sent; he must not elect to go. Nowadays that is the last thing thought of; it is a determination on the part of the individual—"This is something I can do, and I am going to do it." Beware of demanding that people go into work, it is a craze; the majority of saved souls are not fit to feed themselves yet. How am I to know I have been sent of God? Firstly, by the realisation that I am utterly weak and powerless and if I am to be of any use to God, God must do it all the time. Is this the humiliating certainty of my soul, or merely a sentimental phrase? Secondly, because I know I have to point men to Jesus Christ, not to get them to think what a holy man I am. The only way to be sent is to let God lift

us right out of any sense of fitness in ourselves and place us where He will. The man whose work tells for God is the one who not only realises what God has done for him but who realises his own utter unfitness and overwhelming unsuitability—the impossibility of God ever calling *me*. God allows us to scrutinise ourselves in order to understand what Paul said: "We also are weak in him."

Occasionally it may happen in your life as a worker that all you have been trying honestly and eagerly to do for God falls about your ears in ruins, and in your utterly crushed and discouraged condition God brings slowly to your mind this truth—"I have been using your work as scaffolding to perfect you to be a worker for Myself; now arise, shake off the dust, and it shall be told you what you must do." Before ever God can use us as workers He has to bring us to a place of entire poverty, where we shall have no doubt as to where we are, "Here I am, absolutely no good!" Then God can send us, but not until then. We put hindrances in the way of God's working by trying to do things for Him. The impatience of modern life has so crept into Christian work that we will not settle down before God and find out what He wants us to do.

Where Do I Live? *(Psalm 91:1)*

No one can tell you where the shadow of the Almighty is, you must find that out for yourself. When you have found out where it is, stay there; under that shadow no evil can ever befall you. The intensity of the moments spent under the shadow of the Almighty is the measure of your usefulness as a worker. Intensity of communion is not in feelings or emotions or in special places, but in quiet, fixed, confident centring on God. Never allow anything to hinder you from being in the place where your spiritual life is maintained. The expression of our lips must correspond with our communion with God. It is easy to say good and true things without troubling to live up to them; consequently the Christian talker is more likely to be a hypocrite than any other kind of worker. In all probability you will find you could express things better a few months or years ago than you can now, because the Spirit of God has been making you realise since then what you are talking about, and through the consequent distress that laid hold of mind and heart you have been driven to find out the secret place of the Most High. The strange thing is that a worker will more often exhibit ugly characteristics than one who is not a worker. There is an irritability and an impatience and a dogmatism about the average Christian worker that is never seen in those who are not engaged in that kind of work.

What Do I Know about Judgement? *(1 Peter 4:17)*

Peter is talking about suffering, and he says "the time is come that judgement must begin at the house of God." Where is the house of God? My body. As a child of God I have no right to go through a dispensation of suffering without asking my Father the reason for it. It may be suffering because of a purpose of God which He cannot explain to you, but He makes you know in your inmost heart that all is well (see verse 19). Or it may be suffering for chastisement and discipline. An undisciplined saint is inclined either to despise the chastening and say it is of the devil, or else to faint when he is rebuked, and cave in. The writer to the Hebrews says: "If you are a saint you will be chastened, be careful, see that you don't despise it." Or it may be suffering as Jesus suffered (see Hebrews 5:8; 2 Corinthians 1:5). In all these ways we have to learn how to let judgement begin at "the house of God." We escape judgement in a hundred and one ways, consequently we do not develop.

If you are a worker whom God has sent, and have learned to live under His Shadow, you will find that scarcely a day goes by without your Father revealing the need of further chastening. If any child of God is free from the goads of God, he is not in the line of the succession of Jesus Christ. If we suffer as He suffered, we are in the right line (see 1 Peter 4:13). We have to learn to bring the scrutiny of God's judgement upon ourselves. When we talk about suffering we are apt to think only of bodily pain, or of suffering because we have given up something for God, which is paltry nonsense. Joy and peace and delight all come into the life of the saint but they are so on the surface that he never heeds them; they are simply complements. The one central point for the saint is being absolutely right with God, and the only way he gets there is by this personal experience of judgement.

THE MASTERING MISSION
2 Corinthians 5:11, 14

The Obligation of Master Persuasion
(2 Corinthians 5:11)

Whenever Paul talks about his call to preach the gospel, it is a "woe is unto me, if I preach not the gospel!" It is not a calm, quiet choice, but a necessity laid upon him, an overmastering sense of call. The great note of Paul's life is that he is mastered by his mission, he cannot get away from it.

First Corinthians 9:22–23 is the exposition of Paul's sense of unrelieved obligation—"To the weak

became I as weak, that I might gain the weak: I am made all things to all men, that I might by all means save some. And this I do for the gospel's sake." Paul's persuading was by no means always successful (see Acts 17:32) but he never allowed that to deter him (see Acts 28:23–24). Paul's very earnestness for Jesus was made the subtle ground of accusing him of madness, and the strange thing is that among a section of the more fanatical they called him too sober (see 2 Corinthians 5:13).

A worker for God must be prepared to endure hardness; he must learn how to "sop up" all the bad and turn it into good, and nothing but the supernatural grace of God and his sense of obligation will enable him to do it. As workers we will be brought into relationship with people for whom we have no affinity; we have to stand for one thing only, "that I might by all means save some." The one mastering obligation of our life as a worker is to persuade men for Jesus Christ, and to do that we have to learn to live amongst facts: the fact of human stuff as it is, not as it ought to be; and the fact of Bible revelation, whether it agrees with our doctrines or not.

The Overruling Majesty of Personal Power
(2 Corinthians 5:14)
Paul says he is overruled, overmastered, held as in a vice, by the love of Christ. The majority of us are held only by the constraint of our experience. Very few of us know what it is to be held as in a grip by the sense of the love of God. "For the love of Christ constraineth us." Once that note is heard, you can never mistake it; you know that the Holy Spirit is having unhindered way in that man or woman's life. Abandon to the love of Christ is the one thing that bears fruit. Personal holiness may easily step over into sanctified Pharisaism, but abandon to the love of God will always leave the impression of the holiness and the power of God.

When we are born again of the Spirit the note of our testimony is what God has done for us, and rightly so; but the baptism of the Holy Ghost obliterates that for ever. God will never answer our prayer to be baptised by the Holy Ghost for any other reason than to be a witness for Jesus. "Ye shall receive power, after that the Holy Ghost is come upon you: and ye shall be witnesses unto Me" (RV). Not witnesses of what Jesus can do, that is an elementary witness, but "witnesses unto Me"; you will be instead of Me, you will take everything that happens, praise or blame, persecution or commendation, as happening to Me." No one can stand that unless he is constrained by the majesty of the personal power of Jesus. Paul says, "I am constrained by the love of Christ, held as in a fever, gripped as by a disease, that is why I act as I do; you may call me mad or sober, I do not care; I am after only one thing—to persuade men of the judgement seat of Christ and of the love of God."

The great passion in much of the preaching of to-day is to secure an audience. As workers for God our object is never to secure our audience, but to secure that the Gospel is presented to men. Never presume to preach unless you are mastered by the motive born of the Holy Ghost: "For I determined not to know any thing among you, save Jesus Christ, and Him crucified."

THE COMPLETE CHRISTIAN

Conformed to the Master's Standard
(Luke 6:40)
Jesus Christ's standard for the worker is Himself. Am I allowing His standard to obsess me? Am I measuring my life by His all the time? The one standard put before us is Our Lord Himself; we have to be saturated in this ideal in thinking and in praying, and allow nothing to blur the standard. We must lift up Jesus Christ not only in the preaching of the Gospel but to our own souls. If my mind and heart and spirit are getting fixed with one Figure only, the Lord Jesus Christ, and other people and other ideas are fading, then I am growing in grace. The one dominant characteristic in the life of the worker is that Jesus Christ is coming more into the ascendant. The motive is not a sentiment but a passion, the blazing passion of the Holy Ghost in the soul of the worker; not—"because Jesus has done so much for me," that is a sickening, unscriptural statement. The one attitude of the life is Jesus Christ *first, second, and third,* and nothing apart from Him. The thing that hinders God's work is not sin, but other claims which are right, but which at a certain point of their rightness conflict with the claims of Jesus Christ. If the conflict should come, remember it is to be Jesus first (see Luke 14:26).

Consecrated to the Master's Sovereignty
(2 Timothy 2:21)
The vessels in a household have their honour from the use made of them by the head of the house. As a worker I have to separate myself for one purpose—for Jesus Christ to use me for what He likes. Imitation, doing what other people do, is an unmitigated curse. Am I allowing anyone to mould my ideas of Christian service? Am I taking my ideas from some servant of God or from God Himself? We are here for one thing only—to be vessels "meet for the Master's use." We are not here to work for God because we have chosen to do so, but because God has apprehended us. Natural ability has nothing to do with service; consequently there is never any thought of, "Oh, well, I am not fitted for this."

One student a year who hears God's call would be sufficient for God to have called this College into existence. This College as an organisation is not worth anything, it is not academic; it is for nothing else but for God to help Himself to lives. Is He going to help Himself to your life, or are you taken up with your conception of what you are going to do? God is responsible for our lives, and the one great keynote is reckless reliance upon Him.

Complete for the Master's Service
(2 Timothy 3:14, 17)

Am I learning how to use my Bible? The way to become complete for the Master's service is to be well soaked in the Bible, some of us only exploit certain passages. Our Lord wants to give us continuous instruction out of His word; continuous instruction turns hearers into disciples. Beware of "spooned meat"[8] spirituality, of using the Bible for the sake of getting messages; use it to nourish your own soul. Be a continuous learner, don't stop short, and the truth will open to you on the right hand and on the left until you find there is no problem in human life with which the Bible does not deal. But remember that there are certain points of truth Our Lord cannot reveal to us until our character is in a fit state to bear it. The discernment of God's truth and the development of character go together.

The life God places in the Christian worker is the life of Jesus Christ, which is continually changing spiritual innocence into glorious practical character.

KEEP BRIGHT BY USE

General Maxims—
   (a) If you lack education, first realise it; then cure it.
   (b) Beware of knowing what you don't practise.

Cultivate Mental Habits
Give attendance to reading.
(1 Timothy 4:13)

If we wish to excel in secular things, we concentrate; why should we be less careful in work for God? Don't get dissipated; determine to develop your intellect for one purpose only—to make yourself of more use to God. Have a perfect machine ready for God to use. It is impossible to read too much, but always keep before you why you read. Remember that "the need to receive, recognise, and rely on the Holy Spirit" is before all else.

Constantly Aim at the Highest
Take heed unto thyself, and unto the doctrine.
(1 Timothy 4:16)

Remember that preaching is God's ordained method of saving the world (see 1 Corinthians 1:21). Take time before God and find out the highest ideal for an address. Never mind if you do not reach the ideal, but work at it, and never say fail. By work and steady application you will acquire the power to do with ease what at first seemed so difficult. Avoid the temptation to be slovenly in your mind and be deluded into calling it "depending on the Spirit." Don't misapply Matthew 10:19-20. Carelessness in spiritual matters is a crime.

Concentrate on Personal Resources
Neglect not the gift that is in thee. (1 Timothy 4:14)

In immediate preparation don't call in the aid of other minds; rely on the Holy Spirit and on your own resources, and He will select for you. Discipline your mind by reading and by building in stuff in private, then all that you have assimilated will come back. Keep yourself full to the brim in reading; but remember that the first great Resource is the Holy Ghost Who lays at your disposal the Word of God. The thing to prepare is not the sermon, but the preacher.

Constrain Yourself to Be Spiritually Minded
Follow after righteousness. (1 Timothy 6:11)

It is possible to have a saved and sanctified experience and a stagnant mind. Learn how to make your mind awake and fervid, and when once your mind is awake never let it go to sleep. The brain does not need rest, it only needs change of work. The intellect works with the greatest intensity when it works continuously; the more you do, the more you can do. We must work hard to keep in trim for God. Clean off the rust and keep bright by use.

Commune with God Continuously
Be instant in season, out of season. (2 Timothy 4:2)

You cannot always be in conscious glowing touch with God, but don't wait for ecstasy. See that you make all else secondary to the one purpose of your life. "My one aim is to preach Jesus by lip and life, and I will allow no other interest to dominate," then every other thing will be related to that purpose. "Instant in season, out of season"; never give way to discouragement.

---

8. spooned meat: liquefied food that requires no chewing or effort—baby food

THE PREACHER'S OBLIGATIONS
1 Corinthians 1:26

In other callings you have to work with men, but in this calling you work upon men; you come with the authority men crave for and yet resent.

A preacher must remember that his calling is different from every other calling in life; his personality has to be submerged in his message (cf. John 3:30). An orator has to work *with* men and enthuse them; a New Testament preacher has to come *upon* men with a message they resent and will not listen to at first. The Gospel comes in with a backing of Divine authority and an arrestment which men resent. There is something in every man that resents the interference of God. Before a man can be saved, the central citadel of his being has to be stormed and taken possession of by the Holy Spirit. It is easy to tell men they must be saved and filled with the Holy Ghost; but we have to live amongst men and show them what a life filled with the Holy Ghost ought to be. A preacher has to come upon men with a message and a testimony that go together. The great pattern for every witness is the abiding Witness, the Lord Jesus Christ. He came down on men from above; He stood on our level, with what men never had, in order to save men.

To the Gospel *(1 Peter 1:25)*
The Gospel is too profound for the lazy public; too positive[9] for discursive thinkers.

We have no right to preach unless we present the Gospel; we have not to advocate a cause or a creed or an experience, but to present the Gospel, and we cannot do that unless we have a personal testimony based on the Gospel. That is why so many preach what is merely the outcome of a higher form of culture. Until men get into a right relationship with God the Gospel is always in bad taste. There is a feeling of silent resentment, "Don't talk about being born again and being sanctified; be vague." "Do remember the people you are talking to." "Preach the simple Gospel, the thing that keeps us sound asleep." If you take the people as a standard, you will never preach the Gospel, it is too positive. Our obligation to the Gospel is to preach it.

To the Church *(Ephesians 5:27)*
The Church does not lead the world nor echo it; she confronts it. Her note is the supernatural note.

The Church confronts the world with a message the world craves for but resents because it comes through the Cross of Christ. The central keystone for all Time and Eternity on which the whole purpose of God depends is the Cross (see Galatians 6:14). When the world gets in a bad way, she refers to the Church; when she is prosperous, she hates it. If men could blot out the standard of the Christian Church they would do so; but in a crisis they find a need in their own heart. As preachers we are privileged by God to stand steadfast against any element that lowers His standard. We are called upon to confront the world with the Gospel of Christ, not to start off on side tracks of our own.

The Church owns a mastery the world can neither ignore nor do without, the mastery of the Lord Jesus Christ.

To the Community *(1 John 5:19)*
You must tell men they cannot be right with each other except as they are right with God in Christ and in the atoning work of Christ.

Our Lord taught that men could only be right with each other as they are right with Him, and Jesus Christ can take any man and place him in right relationship with God.

Never water down or minimise the mighty Gospel of God by considering that people may be misled by certain statements. Present the Gospel in all its fullness and God will guard His own truth.

---

9. positive: independent; unrelated to anything else.

DON'TS AND DO'S ABOUT TEXTS

Don't be Clever.	Do be Careful.
Don't be Controversial.	Do be Consecrated.
Don't be Conceited.	Do be Concentrated.

Don't Be Clever

Never choose a text, let the text choose you. Cleverness is the ability to do things better than anyone else. Always hide that light under a bushel. The Holy Ghost is never clever. In a child of God the Holy Spirit works as naturally as breathing, and the most unostentatious choices are His choices. Unless your personal life is hid with Christ in God, natural ability will continually lead you into chastisement from God. When a text has chosen you, the Holy Spirit will impress you with its inner meaning and cause you to labour to lead out that meaning for your congregation.

Do Be Careful

Nothing that has been discovered by anyone else is of any use to you until you re-discover it. Be careful to use your own mental eyes, and the eyes of those who can help you to see what you are looking at. Drummond[10] said that Ruskin taught him to *see*. Be careful to develop the power of perceiving what you look at, and never take an explanation from another mind unless you see it for yourself.

Don't Be Controversial

Never choose disputed texts; if you do, you are sure to cut yourself. The spirit that chooses disputed texts is the boldness born of impudence, not the fearlessness born of morality. Remember, God calls us to *proclaim the Gospel.* A man may increase his intellectual vim by controversy, but only one in a thousand can maintain his spiritual life and controvert. Never denounce a thing about which you know nothing.

Do Be Consecrated

Never forget who you are, what you have been, and what you may be by the grace of God. When you try and re-state to yourself what you implicitly feel to be God's truth, you give God a chance to pass that truth on to someone else through you.

Don't Be Conceited

Conceit means my own point of view and I don't care what anyone else says. "Be not wise in your own conceits," says Paul. Conceit makes the way God deals with me personally the binding standard for others. We are called to preach the Truth, Our Lord Jesus Christ, and we get decentralised from Him if we become specialists.

Do Be Concentrated

Strenuous mental effort to interpret the word of God will fag us out physically, whereas strenuous mental effort that lets the word of God talk to us will re-create us. We prefer the spiritual interpretation to the exegetical because it does not need any work. We are to be *"workmen"* for God, not take God's word to feed ourselves. The preacher has to concentrate on what God's word says; he is dealing with a written revelation, not an unwritten one. The reason we have no "open vision" is that in some domain we have disobeyed God. Immediately we obey, the word is opened up. The atmosphere of the Christian is God Himself, and in ordinary times as well as exceptional times He brings words to us. When He does not, never deceive yourself, something is wrong and needs curing, just as there would be something wrong if you could not get your breath. Supernatural manifestations of guidance are exceptional. The normal way of the Spirit of God is the way He worked in the life of Jesus Christ. Maintain your personal relationship with God at all costs. Never allow anything to come between your soul and God, and welcome anyone or anything that leads you to know Him better.

FIRST THINGS FIRST

The Absoluteness of Christ *(Philippians 2:8)*

As a preacher, allow no quarter to anyone who pretends he can give any other explanation of Jesus Christ than He gives of Himself. Jesus Christ calls Himself "the Son of Man," i.e., Representative Man. Never make the Absoluteness of Christ mean the Absoluteness of God; they are not the same. The holiness of God Almighty is Absolute, it knows no

---

10. Henry Drummond (1851–97), Scottish writer and evangelist.

development by antagonism; the holiness exhibited by the Son of Man expresses itself by means of antagonism. The words Our Lord uses of Himself show that His obedience was of a moral nature, it was not a mechanical obedience.

We must look upon Christ as a real historic figure, a real man, not a magical prodigy. He shared in the life of limited man, the life of His age and the life of His land. The limitation of His consciousness was no limitation of His moral power but its exercise.

In presenting Jesus Christ never present Him as a miraculous Being Who came down from heaven and worked miracles and Who was not related to life as we are; that is not the Gospel Christ. The Gospel Christ is the Being Who came down to earth and lived our life and was possessed of a frame like ours. He became Man in order to show the relationship man was to hold to God, and by His death and resurrection He can put any man into that relationship. Jesus Christ is the last word in human nature.

The Absoluteness of the New Testament
(1 Peter 1:16–21)

The doctrines of the New Testament as applied to personal life are moral doctrines, that is, they are understood by a pure heart, not by the intellect. "I want to know God's will in this matter," you say, and your next step is into a fog! because the only way to understand the will of God is to obey from the heart, it is a moral discernment (see Romans 12:2). My spiritual character determines the revelation of God to me.

In the New Testament we deal not with the shrewd guesses of able men, but with a supernatural revelation, and only as we transact business on that revelation do the moral consequences result in us. The danger is to preach a subjective theology, i.e. that something wells up on the inside. The Gospel of the New Testament is based on the absoluteness of revelation, we cannot get at it by our common sense. If a man is to be saved it must be from outside, God never pumps up anything from within. As a preacher, base on nothing less than revelation, and the authenticity of the revelation depends on the character of the one who brings it. Our Lord Jesus Christ put His impress on every revelation from Genesis to Revelation.

The Absoluteness of Immorality and Holiness *(Revelation 21:7–8)*

Immorality and holiness are absolute, you cannot get behind them. When Our Lord talks about the radical evil of the human heart (e.g. Mark 7:21–22), it is a revelation we know nothing of; it comes to the shores of our lives in immorality and holiness. Immorality has its seat in every one of us, not in some of us. If a man is not holy, he is immoral, no matter how good he may seem. Immorality is at the basis of the whole thing; if it does not show itself outwardly, it will show itself before God. The New Testament teaches that no man or woman is safe apart from Jesus Christ because there is treachery on the inside. "Out of the heart of men, proceed. . . ." The majority of us are grossly ignorant about the possibilities of evil in the heart. Never trust your common sense when the statements of Jesus contradict it, and when you preach see that you base your preaching on the revelation of Jesus Christ, not on the sweet innocence of human nature. When you hear a man cry out, like the publican of old, "God be merciful to me a sinner," you have the problem of the whole universe. That man has reached the realisation of himself at last, he knows that he is a guilty, immoral type of man and needs saving. Never take anyone to be good, and above all never take yourself to be good. Natural goodness will always break, always disappoint, why? Because the Bible tells us that "the heart is deceitful above all things, and desperately wicked: who can know it?" Never trust anything in yourself that God has not placed there through the regeneration of Our Lord Jesus Christ; and never trust anything saving that in anyone else.

That is the stern platform you have to stand on when you present the truth of God, and it will resolve you on to a lonely platform, because your message will be craved for but its way of being presented will be resented. The Gospel of Jesus Christ awakens an intense craving and an equally intense resentment. Base on personal love for the Lord, not on personal love for men. Personal love for men will make you call immorality a weakness, and holiness a mere aspiration; personal love for the Lord will make you call immorality devilish, and holiness the only thing that can stand in the light of God. The only safety for the preacher is to face his soul not with his people, or even with his message, but to face his soul with his Saviour all the time.

THE ORIGIN OF OUR SALVATION
2 Peter 1:16

Revelation is not primarily in my soul, but in a fact which is in the chain of history.

In preaching the Gospel remember that salvation is the great thought of God, not an experience. Experience is the gateway through which salvation comes into our conscious life, the evidence of a right relationship to Jesus Christ. Never preach experience, preach the great thought of God that lies behind. People stagnate because they never get beyond the image of their experiences into the life of God which transcends all experience. Jesus Christ Himself is the Revelation, and all our experiences must be traced back to Him and kept there.

The Supernaturalness of Our Salvation
(Ephesians 1:7; John 3:7–8)
The Gospel is a gift to our poverty, not a triumph of our resource.

Beware of a false spirituality that is not based on the rugged facts of our religion. One rugged fact is the forgiveness of sins—"we have redemption *through His blood*, the forgiveness of sins." Forgiveness is the Divine miracle of grace. Have we ever contemplated the amazing fact that God through the Death of Jesus Christ forgives us for every wrong we have ever done, not because we are sorry, but out of His sheer mercy? God's forgiveness is only natural in the supernatural domain. Another rugged fact is the need for new birth—"Marvel not that I said unto thee, Ye must be born again," that is, you must be invaded by the Spirit of God by means of a supernatural recreation. Being born again of the Spirit is an unmistakable work of God, as mysterious as the wind. Beware of the tendency to water down the supernatural in religion.

The Essence of Our Salvation
(Ephesians 4:13–16)
Man's extremity elicits the central resources of God the Saviour.

Personality sometimes hinders the Gospel, people are swept off their feet not by the truth presented but by the tremendous force of the personality that presents it. Personality is used by God to emphasise a neglected truth, but the Toms, Dicks and Harrys are the ones used to spread a knowledge of salvation amongst men. "He must increase, but I must decrease." That is the only standard for the preacher of the Gospel. John the Baptist is stating the truth that we have no right as preachers on the ground of our personality, but only because of the message we proclaim.

We have to bring an Absolute Christ to the needs of men, not to their conditions.

So many preach the human aspect of Christ, His sympathy for the bereaved and the suffering and sin-stained, and men listen whilst Christ is brought down to their conditions; but a preacher has to bring the Gospel of God to men's needs, and to do this he has to uncover their need and men resent this—"I don't want to accept the verdict on myself that Jesus Christ brings; I don't believe I am so sinful as He reveals." A man never believes what Jesus Christ says about the human heart until the Holy Ghost gives him the startling revelation of the truth of His diagnosis (see Mark 7:20–23).

Paul was never appealed to fundamentally by the distresses of men, he was appealed to only by the Cross of Christ (see 1 Corinthians 2:2). There are any number of people who awaken sympathy for the conditions of men and speak of the tragedy of human life to the one who presents the tragedy of Redemption, a broken-hearted God.

As a preacher, never remember the conditions of men, remember only the rugged facts of our salvation, and never attempt to guard them.

THE CROSS IN DISCIPLESHIP

The Cross in Discipleship That Affronts
(Matthew 8:20; Luke 9:60–61)
There is a method of making disciples which is not sanctioned by Our Lord. It is an excessive pressing of people to be reconciled to God in a way that is unworthy of the dignity of the Gospel. The pleading is on the line of: Jesus has done so much for us, cannot we do something out of gratitude to Him? This method of getting people into relationship to God out of pity for Jesus is never recognised by Our Lord. It

does not put sin in its right place, nor does it put the more serious aspect of the Gospel in its right place. Our Lord never pressed anyone to follow Him unconditionally; nor did He wish to be followed merely out of an impulse of enthusiasm. He never pleaded, He never entrapped; He made discipleship intensely narrow, and pointed out certain things which could never be in those who followed Him. To-day there is a tendency to take the harshness out of Our Lord's statements. What Jesus says *is* hard; it is only easy when it comes to those who are His disciples. Whenever Our Lord talked about discipleship He prefaced it with an "IF," never with an emphatic assertion, "You must." Discipleship carries an option with it.

The aspect of the cross in discipleship is lost altogether in the present-day view of following Jesus. The cross is looked upon as something beautiful and simple instead of a stern heroism. Our Lord never said it was easy to be a Christian; He warned men that they would have to face a variety of hardships, which He termed bearing the cross.

The time when Jesus comes to us is not so much in a revival issue, a time when He is in the ascendant, but rather at a time when we are in the ascendant, when our wills are perfectly free, when the fascination and beauty of the world on the one hand and the repelling aspect of Jesus Christ on the other is there. Our Lord never allows an allegiance which is the outcome of an impulse of enthusiasm that sweeps us off our feet, not knowing what we are doing. We must be at the balance of our wills when we choose. That is why the call of Jesus Christ awakens an immense craving and an intense resentment, and that is why as New Testament preachers we must always push an issue of will.

The Cross in Discipleship in Appreciation
(Matthew 16:24)

The next time you read those words, "If any man will come after Me, let him deny himself, and take up his cross, and follow Me," strip them of all their poetry. It is an effort to us to think of the cross as Our Lord thought of it. When Jesus said "let him deny himself, and take up his cross," He had in mind not a thing of beautiful sentiment to arouse heroism, but an ugly cruel thing, with awful nails that tore the flesh. For twenty centuries people have covered up the Cross with sentiment, and we can sit and listen to the preaching of the crucifixion of Jesus and be dissolved in tears, but very few of us have any appreciation of what our Lord conveyed when He said, "let him deny himself, and take his cross, and follow Me."

The Cross of Christ stands unique and alone; we are never called upon to carry His Cross. Our cross is something that comes only with the peculiar rela-

tionship of a disciple to Jesus Christ, it is the evidence that we have denied the right to ourselves. Our Lord was not talking about suffering for conscience' sake or conviction's sake; men suffer for conscience' sake who know nothing about Jesus Christ and own Him no allegiance; men suffer for conviction's sake, if they are worth their salt, whether they are Christians or not. The Cross of Jesus Christ is a revelation; our cross is an experience.

What the Cross was to Our Lord such also in measure was it to be to those who followed Him. The cross is the pain involved in doing the will of God. That aspect is being lost sight of, we say that after sanctification all is a delight. Was Paul's life all delight? Was Our Lord's life all delight? Discipleship means we are identified with His interests, and we have to fill up "that which is behind of the afflictions of Christ." Only when we have been identified with Our Lord in sanctification can we begin to understand what our cross means.

The Cross in Discipleship in Aggression
(Matthew 10:16–39)

These verses need to be re-read because we are apt to think that Jesus Christ took all the bitterness and we get all the blessing. It is true that we get the blessing, but we must never forget that the wine of life is made out of crushed grapes; to follow Jesus will involve bruising in the lives of the disciples as the purpose of God did in His own life. The thing that makes us whimper is that we will look for justice. If you look for justice in your Christian work you will soon put yourself in a bandage and give way to self-pity and discouragement. Never look for justice, but never cease to give it; and never allow anything you meet with to sour your relationship to men through Jesus Christ. "Love . . . as I have loved you."

In Matthew 10:34 Jesus told the disciples that they would be opposed not only in private life, but that the powers of state would oppose them and they would have to suffer persecution, and some even crucifixion. Don't say, "But that was simply meant for those days." If you stand true to Jesus Christ you will find that the world will react against you with a butt, not with a caress, annoyed and antagonistic (see John 15:18–20).

When Our Lord spoke of the cross His disciples were to bear, He did not say that if they bore it they would become holy; He said the cross was to be borne for His sake, not for theirs. He also said that they would suffer in the same way as the prophets suffered, because of the messages they spoke from God (see Matthew 5:11–12). The tendency to-day is to say, "Live a holy life, but don't talk about it; don't give your testimony; don't confess your allegiance to Jesus, and you will be left alone."

The Cross in Discipleship in Antagonism
(Matthew 5:16; 10:32)

"Whosoever therefore shall *confess* Me . . . ," i.e., confess Me by lip and by life. People are not persecuted for living a holy life, it is the confession of Jesus that brings the persecution. There is a great deal of social work done to-day that does not confess Jesus, although people may praise Him to further orders;[11] and if you confess Him there, you will find the ostracism He mentions: "Keep your religion out; don't bring your jargon of sanctification here." You must take it there, and when you do, the opposition will be tremendous. The reason for the opposition is that men have vested interests which philanthropy and kindness to humanity do not touch, but which the Spirit of Jesus testified to by human lips does touch, and indignation is awakened against the one who dares to carry the cross for his Lord there.

Self-denial and self-sacrifice are continually spoken of as being good in themselves; Our Lord never used any such affectation. He aimed a blow at the mistake that self-denial is an end in itself. He spoke of self-denial and self-sacrifice as painful things that cost and hurt (see Matthew 10:38–39). The term self-denial has come to mean giving up things; the denial Jesus speaks of is a denial right out to my right to myself, a clean sweep of all the decks to the mastership of Jesus. Some folks are so mixed up nervously that they cannot help sacrificing themselves, but unless Jesus Christ is the lodestar there is no benefit in the sacrifice. Self-denial must have its spring in personal outflowing love to Our Lord; we are no longer our own, we are spoilt for every other interest in life saving as we can win men to Jesus Christ. The one great spring of sacrifice is devotion to Jesus, "For My sake."

THE REASON WHY

The reason why the Apostle Paul was a preacher was because of his understanding of the Cross of Christ. The majority of present-day preachers understand only the blessings that come to us from the Cross, they are apt to be devoted to certain doctrines which flow from the Cross. Paul preached one thing only, the crucified Christ, "who of God is made unto us wisdom, and righteousness, and sanctification, and redemption."

The Cross of Christ for Doctrine
(1 Corinthians 1:23)

Never confuse the Cross of Christ with the benefits that flow from it. For all Paul's doctrine, his one great passion was the Cross of Christ, not salvation, nor sanctification, but the great truth that God so loved the world that He gave His only begotten Son; consequently you never find him artificial, or making a feeble statement. Every doctrine Paul taught had the blood and the power of God in it. There is an amazing force of spirit in all he said because the great passion behind was not that he wanted men to be holy, that was secondary, but that he had come to understand what God meant by the Cross of Christ. If we have only the idea of personal holiness, of being put in God's show room, we shall never come anywhere near seeing what God wants; but when once we have come where Paul is and God is enabling us to understand what the Cross of Christ means, then nothing can ever turn us (see Romans 8:35–39). If Paul had been set on his own holiness, he never would have said, "For I could wish that myself were accursed from Christ for my brethren." He cared about nothing on earth, saving one thing—the Cross of Christ. That was the great passion of his preaching, he paid no attention to what it cost him. "Woe is unto me, if I preach not the gospel!" Paul's preaching was a necessity laid upon him.

The Cross of Christ for Direction
(1 Corinthians 2:2)

The direction of Paul's sentiment, amongst saints or sinners, was never pathetic and pious, but passionately taken up with Christ crucified. What direction does my preaching take? What direction do my letters take, my dreams? What direction does the whole trend of my life take? Paul says he is determined that his life shall take no other direction than this: the emphasis on and exposition of the Cross of Christ. That is the note that is being lost sight of in our preaching to-day. We hear any amount about our cross, about what it costs us to follow Christ; but who amongst us has any inkling of what the Apostle Paul saw? He had caught an understanding of the mind of God in the Cross of Christ and grasped it, consequently he could never be exhausted or turned aside.

---

11. to further orders: ad infinitum; endlessly; the phrase, military origin, continuing present action until one receives different orders

You cannot be profoundly moved by a sentiment or by an idea of holiness, but you can be moved by a passion; and the old writers used to speak of the Cross as the Passion of Our Lord. The Cross is the great opening through which all the blood of Christian service runs. Do we bear the marks of the Lord Jesus in our preaching, or do we leave our congregations with the impression of how sweet and winsome we are? Whether Paul's words were stinging or comforting, for praise or for condemnation, the one impression left was Jesus Christ and Him crucified, not Jesus Christ risen and exalted, but *crucified*. The reason some of us have no power in our preaching, no sense of awe, is that we have no passion for God, but only a passion for Humanity. The one thing we have to do is to exhibit Jesus Christ crucified, to lift Him up all the time. "I, if I be lifted up from the earth, will draw all men unto Me." Paul had one passion only, he had seen the light of the knowledge of the glory of God in the face of Jesus Christ. Who is Jesus Christ? God exalted in Christ crucified.

The Cross of Christ for Disposition
(Galatians 6:14)
Paul disposed his whole life and all his interests in the light of his understanding of the Cross of Christ. Never take these words to mean Paul's identification with the death of Christ only. ". . . by whom the world is crucified unto me, and I unto the world"—because of my identification with the death of Jesus? No, because Jesus Christ was crucified to the world. If we deal only with our identification, we lose sight of the objective fact of Our Lord's death. The profoundest truth to us is shallow compared with the revelation given here. Most of our emphasis to-day is on what our Lord's death means to us: the thing that is of importance is that we understand what God means in the Cross. Paul did not understand the Cross in order that he might receive the life of God; but by understanding the Cross, he received the life. Study the Cross for no other sake than God's sake, and you will be holy without knowing it. The danger is to fix our eyes on our own whiteness. "I, if I be lifted up

from the earth, will draw all men unto Me." Are we lifting up what Jesus Christ can do in the place of His Cross? That snare besets us until we learn the passion of Paul's life.

The call to preach is not because I have a special gift, or because Jesus has sanctified me, but that I have had a glimpse of God's meaning in the Cross, and life can never be the same again. The passion of Paul's preaching is the suffering of God Almighty exhibited in the Cross of Christ. Many who are working for God ought to be learning in the School of Calvary. Paul says—"I determined not to know any thing among you, save Jesus Christ, and Him crucified"— not myself crucified with Christ, that is a mere *et cetera*; the one Figure left is Jesus Christ, and His Cross.

The Cross of Christ and Discipline
(Galatians 2:20)
This is not a theological statement, it is a statement of Christian experience wrought by the Holy Ghost. The Holy Ghost is the one Who regenerates us into the family to which Jesus Christ belongs; through the eternal efficacy of the Cross we are made partakers of the Divine nature. "I have been crucified with Christ" (RV). Paul's personal identification with the death of Christ is simply the presentation of how that death will work out in the life of anyone. The Cross of Christ is the Self-revelation of God, the exhibition of the essential nature of the Godhead.

Nowadays the great passion is the passion for souls, but you never find that passion mentioned in the New Testament, it is the passion for Christ that the New Testament mentions. It is not a passion for men that saves men; a passion for men breaks human hearts. The passion for Christ inwrought by the Holy Ghost goes deeper down than the deepest agony the world, the flesh and the devil can produce. It goes straight down to where Our Lord went, and the Holy Ghost works out, not in thinking, but in living, this passion for Christ. Whenever the passion for souls obscures the passion for Christ, Satan has come in as an angel of light.

BE SURE OF THE ABYSSES OF GOD

As Christian workers we must never forget that salvation is God's thought, not man's; therefore it is an unfathomable abyss. Salvation is not an experience; experience is only a gateway by which salvation comes into our conscious lives. We have to preach the great thought of God behind the experience.

Judgement on the Abyss of Love
(1 Peter 4:17)
Never sympathise with a soul who finds it difficult to get to God; God is never to blame. We have to so present the truth that the Spirit of God will show what is wrong. The element of judgement must always

come out; it is the sign of God's love. The great sterling test in preaching is that it brings everyone to judgement; the Spirit of God locates each one. Never allow in yourself or in others the phrase "I can't"; it is unconscious blasphemy. If I put my inability as a barrier, I am telling God there is something He has not taken into account. Every element of self-reliance must be slain by the power of God. The people who say "I can't" are those who have a remnant of self-reliance left; a true saint never says "I can't," because it never occurs to him that he can! Complete weakness is always the occasion of the Spirit of God manifesting His power. Never allow anything to be in you that the Cross of Christ condemns.

Conscience on the Abyss of the Cross
(2 Corinthians 5:10–1)
The most universal thing among men is conscience, and the Cross is God's conscience in supreme energy.

Conscience must be educated at the Cross. As a worker always bring the conscience of others to face the Cross of Christ. Is my life worthy of what Jesus Christ did on the Cross? Are there the elements of ability and power and peace stamped with the almightiness that comes through the Cross? If not, I am not where I should be. The Cross of Christ means that the Spirit of God can empower me almightily until

> *Every virtue we possess,*
> *And every victory won,*
> *And every thought of holiness,*
> *Are His alone.*

We imagine we have to do these things for ourselves; we have not, we have to keep steadily in the light of the Cross, relying on the Spirit of God, then we will live out the life He wants us to live. Whenever we get our eyes off Christ and His Cross and build up on our own experience, "Now God has sanctified me, I am all right," we become betrayers of the very power that saved us. When we walk in the light, with the whole of our attention taken up with Jesus Christ, there is manifested in us a holiness that glorifies God in every particular. Never get off on the intellectual line, "Think proper thoughts." *Live proper lives!* and you will think proper thoughts.

The Cross of Christ is the Self-revelation of God, the way God has given Himself. In the preaching and writing of to-day there is much brilliant stuff that passes into thin air because it is not related to this tremendous fact of the Self-bestowal of God that lifts up humanity to be in accordance with Himself.

Morality on the Abyss of the Atonement
(2 Corinthians 5:20–21)
The mind of the worker must brood much on the Atonement because every bit of our life, physical, moral and spiritual, must be judged by the standard of the Atonement, viz., holiness. Never say God's holiness does not mean what it does mean. It means every part of the life under the scrutiny of God, knowing that the grace of God is sufficient for every detail. The temptation comes along the line of compromise, "Don't be so unbendingly holy; so fiercely pure and uprightly chaste." Never tolerate by sympathy with yourself or with others any practice that is not in keeping with a holy God.

Liberty on the Abyss of the Gospel
(Galatians 5:1)
We have to present the liberty of Christ, and we cannot do it if we are not free ourselves. There is only one liberty, the liberty of Jesus Christ at work in my conscience enabling me to do what is right. If we are free with the liberty wherewith Christ makes us free, slowly and surely those whom we influence will begin to be free with the same freedom. Always keep your own life measured by the standard of Jesus Christ; bow your neck to His yoke alone and to no other yoke whatever; and see that you never bind any yoke on others that Jesus Christ Himself does not place. It takes a long time to get us out of imagining that unless people see as we do they must be wrong. That is never Jesus Christ's view. Our true sympathy lies with the One Who is absolute tenderness, and every now and again God gives us the chance of being the rugged stuff that He might be the tender One. We have to be sacramental elements in the Lord's hands.

WHAT IS FOLLOWING JESUS CHRIST?

The Still Small Voice *(Matthew 4:19)*
In the days of His flesh the invitation to follow Jesus Christ was a definite one. It meant doing as Peter said, "Lo, we have left all, and have followed Thee" (Mark 10:28). This literal following of Jesus is no longer necessary; what men are called on to forsake to-day is sin and worldliness. Never say you do not know where these things take up their abode. Get down before God and say, "Lord, why cannot I follow Thee now?" and He will show you why not in a

flash. "But," you say, "it cannot be that, it is far too small a thing." It is just that and nothing else. Never believe any being on earth if he contradicts the Holy Ghost. Whatever the Holy Ghost detects in you, trace it down, and you will find the whole disposition of sin, i.e., my claim to my right to myself, is at the basis of that infinitesimal thing of which our mind says, "But it cannot be that."

The Silent Sure Vision *(Mark 4:34; cf. Luke 10:39)*

Have you ever been alone with Jesus? The disciples enjoyed the inestimable privilege not only of hearing the truth from Our Lord's own lips, but of questioning Him in secret about everything He said. We go to John Wesley, or to Adam Clarke,[12] or some other commentator instead of going to Jesus Himself. How can we go to Him? The Holy Spirit is the Exponent of Jesus Christ's statements, and He will test whether the expositions are of God or not. Jesus Christ's teaching is involved in such a manner that only the Holy Spirit can extricate its meaning for us. "He will guide you into all truth." The Holy Spirit never witnesses to a clever interpretation; the exposition the Holy Spirit will witness to is always amazingly and profoundly simple; you feel, "That certainly is God's truth." Whenever you are without that feeling about an interpretation, hesitate, keep your judgement in abeyance. Don't force your head to argue, but get alone with Jesus and ask Him. If He keeps you waiting, He knows why He does so. Discernment of God's truth and development in spiritual character go together.

In the Sermon on the Mount Our Lord emphasises the principle that continuous instruction turns hearers into disciples (see Matthew 7:24). Irregular listeners are turned into lop-sided fanatics. Many to-day are not following Jesus Christ, they have one glowing bit of light about salvation or sanctification or healing and they say, "Follow me, I am right." Jesus says, *"Lift Me up."* We have to learn to sit at the feet of Jesus in

our disposition. The one thing needful is continuous instruction in His word. Listen to the words Jesus spoke, and let the Holy Spirit instruct you. Be at it steadily. Don't be a hearer only, but become a disciple. Experience is never your guide; experience is the doorway for you to know the Author of the experience. Get at the knowledge of God for yourself, be a continuous learner, and the truth will open on the right hand and on the left until you find there is not a problem in human life that Jesus Christ cannot deal with.

The Slow Steps in the Valley *(Luke 14:33)*

To follow Jesus Christ to-day is to follow a madman according to the ideals of present-day civilisation. We have the idea that our civilisation is God-ordained, whereas it has been built up by ourselves. We have made a thousand and one necessities until our system of civilised life is as cast iron, and then we apologise to the Lord for not following Him. "God can never mean that I have to follow Him at the cost of all I have?" But He does mean it. Instantly the clash is between our civilisation and the call of Jesus Christ. Read the Sermon on the Mount—"Seek ye first the kingdom of God"—and apply it to modern life and you will find its statements are either those of a madman or of God Incarnate.

The book entitled *Imitation of Christ* by Thomas à Kempis is exquisitely beautiful, but fundamentally twisted, because Our Lord's own message of regeneration is ignored. Many a one who has started the imitation of Christ has had to abandon it as hopeless because a strain is put on human nature that human nature cannot begin to live up to. To have attitudes of life without the life itself is a fraud; to have the life itself imitating the best Pattern of that life is normal and right (see 1 Peter 2:21–23). The teaching of Jesus Christ applies only to the life He puts in, and the marvel of His Redemption is that He gives the power of His own disposition to carry any man through who is willing to obey Him.

GOD'S

12. Adam Clarke (1762–1832), eighteenth-century Methodist leader in Britain, author of an influential six-volume commentary on the Bible.

The vows of God are on me, and I may not stay
To play with shadows, or pluck earthly flower,
Till I my work have done.
And rendered up account.

The Disciplined Life *(2 Timothy 2:3)*

The first requirement of the worker is discipline voluntarily entered into. It is easy to be passionate, easy to be thrilled by spiritual influences, but it takes a heart in love with Jesus Christ to put the feet in His footprints, and to square the life to a steady going "up to Jerusalem" with Him. Discipline is the one thing the modern Christian knows nothing of, we won't stand discipline nowadays. God has given me an experience of His life and grace, therefore I am a law unto myself. The discipline of a worker is not in order to develop his own life, but for the purposes of his Commander. The reason there is so much failure is because we forget that we are here for that one thing, loyalty to Jesus Christ; otherwise we have no business to have taken the vows of God upon us. If a soldier is not prepared to be killed, he has no business to have enlisted as a soldier. The only way to keep true to God is by a steady persistent refusal to be interested in Christian work and to be interested alone in Jesus Christ.

A disciplined life means three things—a supreme aim incorporated into the life itself; an external law binding on the life from its Commander; and absolute loyalty to God and His word as the ingrained attitude of heart and mind. There must be no insubordination; every impulse, every emotion, every illumination must be rigorously handled and checked if it is not in accordance with God and His word.

Our Lord Himself is the example of a disciplined life. He lived a holy life by sacrificing Himself to His Father; His words and His thinking were holy because He submitted His intelligence to His Father's word, and He worked the works of God because He steadily submitted His will to His Father's will; and as is the Master, so is the disciple.

The Disentangled Life *(2 Timothy 2:4; Numbers 6:2–3)*

A disciple of Jesus must know from what he is to be disentangled. The disentanglement is from things which would be right for us but for the fact that we have taken upon us the vows of God. There is a difference between disentanglement for our own soul's sake and disentanglement for God's sake. We are apt to think only about being disentangled from the things which would ensnare us—we give up this and that, not for Jesus Christ's sake, but for our own development. A worker has to disentangle himself from many things that would advantage and develop him but which would turn him aside from being broken bread and poured out wine in his Lord's hands. We are not here to develop our own spiritual life, but to be broken for Jesus Christ's sake. There is much that would advantage and develop us and make us more desirable than we are, but if we have taken the vows of God upon ourselves, those considerations must never enter in. Paul argues in this way: If anything in me, right or wrong, is hindering God's work and causing another to stumble, I will give it up, even if it is the most legitimate thing on earth (see 1 Corinthians 8:13). People say,

"Why cannot I do this?" For pity's sake do it! There is no reason why you shouldn't, there is neither right nor wrong about it; but if your love for Jesus Christ is not sufficient to disentangle you from a thousand and one things that would develop you, you know nothing about being His servant.

The appeal made in Christian work nowadays is that we must keep ourselves fit for our work, we must not; we must be in the hands of God for God to do exactly what He likes with us, and that means disentanglement from everything that would hinder His purpose. If you want to remain a full-orbed grape you must keep out of God's hands for He will crush you, wine cannot be had in any other way. The curse in Christian work is that we want to preserve ourselves in God's museum; what God wants is to see where Jesus Christ's men and women are. The saints are always amongst the unofficial crowd, the crowd that is not noticed, and their one dominant note is Jesus Christ.

The Detached Life *(2 Timothy 2:4; Leviticus 21:12)*

The worker must live a life detached to God, and the illustration of the detached life is that of a priest who intercedes. The reason so few of us intercede is because we do not understand that intercession is a vicarious work. It is not meant to develop us; it is vicarious from beginning to end.

The detached life is the result of an intensely narrow moral purity, not of a narrow mind. The mental view of Jesus Christ was as big as God's view, consequently He went anywhere—to marriage feasts, into the social life of His time, because His morality was absolutely pure; and that is what God wants of us. In the beginning we are fanatical and we cut ourselves off from external things, until we learn that detachment is the outcome of an inner moral purity, inwrought by God and maintained by walking in the light. Then God can put us where He likes, in the foreign field or anywhere, and we will never be entangled—placed there, but detached. Whenever we make our personal convictions the standard for a society or a class, we take them the first step away from Christ, and that will happen every time the light we are walking in is not the light of God. It is enough to make the heart of a stone bleed to see royal souls turning away from God in their very eagerness to serve Him, and entering into worldliness instead of standing absolutely detached.

The Discerning Life *(2 Timothy 2:6; Isaiah 28:23–28)*

The worker has to have discernment like that of a farmer, that is, he must know how to watch, how to wait, and how to work with wonder. The farmer does not wait with folded arms but with intense activity, he keeps at it industriously until the harvest.

When someone comes to you with a question which makes you feel at your wits' end, never say, "I can't make head or tail of it." Of course you cannot. Always take the case that is too hard for you to God, and to no one else, and He will give you the right thing to say. When you are being taught by God to discern, you will deal with the case in the way that God has prompted you to and you will speak with discernment. When you are used of God it is not because you discern what is wrong, but because the Holy Spirit gives you discernment, and as you speak you realise in what an amazing way the words meet the case, and you say, "I wonder why I said that?" Don't wonder any more, it was the Spirit of God inspiring you. When we are used, we never know we are used, and the times we expect to be used, we are not. We have to keep our heads out of the rush of things in order that the Spirit of God may discern through us.

The discernment for the worker himself is I am *God's,* therefore I am good for no one else; not good for nothing, but good for no other calling in life. "No man, having put his hand to the plough, and looking back, is fit for the kingdom of God." If you have taken on you the vows of God, never be surprised at the misery and turmoil that come every time you turn aside. Other people may do a certain thing and prosper, but you cannot, and God will take care you do not. There is always one fact more known only to God.

The one word to be written indelibly on each one of us is "God's." There is no responsibility in the life that is there, it is full of speechless child-like delight in God. Whenever a worker breaks down it is because he has taken responsibility upon himself which was never God's will for him to take. "Think of the responsibility it will be for you!" There is no responsibility whatever, saving that of refusing to take the responsibility. The responsibility that would rest on you if you took it would crush you to the dust; but when you know God you take no responsibility upon yourself, you are as free as a child, and the life is one of concentration on God. "Cast that He hath given thee upon the Lord" (Psalm 55:22 RV mg). The thing that interferes with the life with God is our abominable seriousness which chokes the freedom and simplicity which ought to mark the life. The freedom and simplicity spring from one point only, a heart at rest with God and at leisure from itself.

None of this is experience, it is a life; experience is the door that opens into the life. When we have had an experience the snare is that we want to go back to it. Leave experiences alone, let them come or go. God wants our lives to be absolutely centred in Himself. "We cannot kindle when we will the fire which in the heart resides," God gives us marvellous hours of insight, then He withdraws them, and we have to begin to work out "with aching hands and bleeding feet" what we saw in vision, and few understand this.

IDENTIFICATION

Identification is not experienceable; it is infinitely more fundamental than experience. Identification is a revelation, the exposition of the experience. We must get out of the way of bringing everything to the bar of personal experience. Remember two things: first, experience is not its own cause; and second, there must be a standard revelation whereby to account for our experiences. The standard revelation with regard to identification is Our Lord Jesus Christ, and the phases of our experience must always be traced back to this revelation. Jesus Christ must always be infinitely greater than any experience of Him.

Incarnation. The Word Made Weak.
God–Man (John 1:14)
Jesus Christ was not a Being Who became Divine, He was the Godhead Incarnated; He emptied Himself of His glory in becoming Incarnate. Never separate the Incarnation from the Atonement. The Incarnation was not meant to enable God to realise Himself, but that

man might realise God and gain readjustment to Him. Jesus Christ became Man for one purpose, that He might put away sin and bring the whole human race back into the oneness of identification. Jesus Christ is not an individual iota of a man; He is the whole of the human race centred before God in one Person: He is God and Man in one. Man is lifted up to God in Christ, and God is brought down to man in Christ. Jesus Christ nowhere said, "He that hath seen *man* hath seen the Father"; but He did say that God was manifest in human flesh in His own Person (John 14:9) that He might become the generating centre for the same manifestation in every human being, and the place of His travail pangs is the Incarnation, Calvary, and the Resurrection.

Identification. The Son Made Sin. *God and Man (2 Corinthians 5:21)*
What these verses express is beyond the possibility of human experience; they refer only to the experience of

Our Lord. The revelation is not that Jesus Christ was punished for our sins, but that, "He hath made Him to be sin for us, who knew no sin," that by His identification with it and removal of it, "we might be made the righteousness of God in Him." God made His own Son to be sin that He might make the sinner a saint. The Bible reveals all through that Jesus Christ bore the sin of the world by *identification,* not by sympathy. He deliberately took upon Himself and bore in His own Person the whole massed sin of the human race, and by so doing He rehabilitated the human race, that is, put it back to where God designed it to be, and anyone can enter into union with God on the ground of what Our Lord did on the Cross.

Invasion. The Sinner Made Saint. *God in Man (Galatians 2:20)*

Galatians 2:20 is the scriptural expression of identification with Jesus Christ in such a way that the whole life is changed. Paul says that his destiny is no longer self-realisation, but Christ-identity, "I live; yet not I, but Christ liveth in me."

The revelation of identification means that we are one with God in His Son, not by obedience, obedience is nothing more than the human approach to this mightiest of revelations. We enter into identification by the door of obedience and faith, but the oneness is a revelation. When we do touch God we lose all consciousness of being in conscious touch with Him, we are so absorbed with His peace and power that language cannot convey the assurance of the oneness. The experience of sanctification is simply the entrance into this relationship.

The Self-realisation of Jesus Christ—an entrancing subject to every Christian—is our Redemption; and the way in which we are to be identified experimentally with Jesus Christ is revealed in His Self-realisation. "Partakers of Christ's sufferings"; "as He is, so are we in this world"; ". . . and fill up that which is behind of the afflictions of Christ." The one absorbing passion of the life is for Him.

"Oh, but I don't feel worthy." Of course you are not worthy! Not all your praying or obedience can ever make you worthy. Leave yourself absolutely in His hands, and see that you plunge yourself deep down in faith on the revelation that you are made one with God through the Redemption of Jesus Christ.

Facing Reality

© 1939 Oswald Chambers Publications Association

INTRODUCTION

Source

Messages given at League of Prayer[13] meetings and Bible Training College classes in Britain, 1911– 1915; and to British Commonwealth troops in Egypt, 1915–1917, during World War I.

Publication History

- Most of these talks were published first as articles in *Tongues of Fire/Spiritual Life*, the magazine of the League of Prayer.

- When known, the date and location of each message is given below the chapter title.
- *Facing Reality* was first published as a booklet in 1939, then combined with *Approved unto God* in 1946 and later editions.

These talks, given to a variety of audiences, deal primarily with the theme of "belief."

CONTENTS

---

13. Pentecostal League of Prayer: founded in London in 1891 by Reader Harris (1847–1909), prominent barrister; friend and mentor of Oswald Chambers.

WHAT MUST I BELIEVE?

"WHAT MUST I BELIEVE TO BE A CHRISTIAN," DECEMBER 6, 1916,
TO BRITISH COMMONWEALTH TROOPS AT SIDI GABER CAMP, NEAR ALEXANDRIA, EGYPT

Now if any man have not the Spirit of Christ, he is none of His. Romans 8:9

There are two domains of Fact: common-sense facts and revelation facts. It is impossible to prove a fact; a fact must be accepted. We accept common-sense facts on the ground of our senses, and we accept revelation facts on the ground of our faith in God.

A Theory is the way we explain facts, an intellectual explanation of the facts we have got, and the explanation is right if there are only those facts. Your theoretical explanation won't work if you have an end to serve. The Christian Science theory says there are no such facts as pain or suffering or death, they are all imaginations; it has forgotten that there are bad facts as well as good. An hypothesis takes only those facts that agree with your theory, it works like a searchlight and life becomes amazingly simple. It is always easier to read a man's book about "life" than to live your life, because he only takes facts that agree with his view, but when you get pitchforked into the confusion of circumstances, where is your fine theory of explanation? You have come in contact with a hundred and one facts that the hypothesis had not taken into account. For the same reason, if you are religious, it is easier to read some pious book than the Bible. The Bible treats you like human life does—roughly. There are two ways of dealing with facts—one is to shut your eyes and say that they are not there, the other is to open your eyes and look at them and let them mould you.

We begin our religious life by believing our beliefs, we accept what we are taught without questioning; but when we come up against things we begin to be critical, and find out that the beliefs, however right, are not right for us because we have not bought them by suffering. What we take for granted is never ours until we have bought it by pain. A thing is worth just what it costs. When we go through the suffering of experience we seem to lose everything, but bit by bit we get it back.

It is absurd to tell a man he must believe this and that; in the meantime he can't! Scepticism is produced by telling men what to believe. We are in danger of putting the cart before the horse and saying a man must believe certain things before he can be a Christian; his beliefs are the effect of his being a Christian, not the cause of it. Our Lord's word "believe" does not refer to an intellectual act, but to a moral act.

With Him "to believe" means "to commit." "Commit yourself to Me," He says, and it takes a man all he is worth to believe in Jesus Christ. The man who has been through a crisis is more likely to commit himself to a Person, he sees more clearly; before the crisis comes we are certain, because we are shallow.

According to the Apostle Paul the essential ingredient in being a Christian is that a man has the Spirit of Christ, no matter what his "tag" may be. Human strength and earnestness cannot make a man a Christian any more than they can make him an angel; he must receive something from God, and that is what Jesus Christ calls being born from above (John 3:3 RV mg; see Luke 11:13). The supreme test of a Christian is that he has the Spirit of Jesus Christ in his actual life.

The Fact of the Bible and the Theory of Inspiration

The Bible is a world of revelation facts, and when you explain the Bible, take into account all the record of it. The Bible nowhere says we have to believe it is the Word of God before we can be Christians. The Bible is not the Word of God to me unless I come at it through what Jesus Christ says, it is of no use to me unless I know Him. The key to my understanding of the Bible is not my intelligence, but personal relationship to Jesus Christ. I begin my theories after I have got on the inside. You may believe the Bible is the Word of God from Genesis to Revelation and not be a Christian at all.

(a) The Mystery of the Bible
Holy men of God spake as they were moved by the Holy Ghost. (2 Peter 1:21)

What does the Bible say about itself? That it is inspired of the Holy Ghost, but through men, not through mechanisms. It is not that the Holy Ghost took up men in a miraculous way and used them as channels; the chief item is the man, and each Book bears the stamp of the man. The mystery of the Bible is that its inspiration was direct from God, not verbally inspired, but the inspired Word of God—the Final Word of God; not that God is not saying anything now, but He is not saying anything different from the Final Word, Jesus Christ. All God says is expounding that Word. The Final Word and the only Word are very different. Be reverent with the Bible explanation of itself.

(b) The Message of the Bible
And they are they which testify of Me. (John 5:39)

Jesus Christ says the message of the Bible is about Himself—we cannot interpret it according to any other key . . ." ". . . no prophecy of the scripture is of any private interpretation." We can prove anything we choose from the Bible once we forget the message Jesus says it contains. "The test that you know the Bible is that you understand what it is driving at, it is expounding Me, giving the exposition of what I am after."

(c) The Meaning of the Bible
All scripture is given by inspiration of God. (2 Timothy 3:16)

The Bible instructs us in righteousness, in the rightness of practical living; its meaning is to keep us living right. Most people like to use the Bible for anything other than that, for a kind of jugglery to prove special doctrines.

The Fact of Christ and the Dogma of the Trinity

Dogma means the things we say in the creed, systematised theology. There is no dogma of the Trinity in the Bible. I am not asked to believe this and that about Jesus Christ, His birth and resurrection, before I am a Christian, but when I am a Christian I begin to try and expound to myself Who Jesus Christ is, and to do that I must take into consideration the New Testament explanation of Him. The Deity of Jesus Christ does not come to a man's intellect first, but to his heart and life. Nowhere in the New Testament are you asked to believe these facts before you are a Christian. They are Christian doctrines, and the Bible is the illustration of the Christian faith. The New Testament is not written to prove that Jesus Christ was the Son of God, but written for those who believe He is. There are no problems in the New Testament.

(a) His Condition
And all bare Him witness, and wondered at the gracious words which proceeded out of His mouth. (Luke 4:22)

The condition in which Jesus Christ lived was a remarkably ordinary one, and every time people got startled in listening to Him, they came back to practical realities—He is extraordinary, but "Is not this Joseph's son? Don't we know all about Him?" Our Lord's first public sermon is an instance of how it is possible to choke the witness of the heart by the prejudice of the head.

(b) His Character
A man approved of God among you by miracles and wonders and signs. (Acts 2:22; see John 18:20; Acts 10:38)

The character of Jesus Christ is exhibited in the New Testament, and it appeals to us all. He lived His life straight down in the ordinary amalgam of human life, and He claims that the character He manifested is possible for any man if he will come in by the door He provides (see Luke 11:13).

(c) His Claims
He that hath seen Me hath seen the Father. (John 14:9)

Is the philosophic explanation I have been given of Jesus Christ the right one? Is the essential nature of Deity omniscience, omnipotence and omnipresence? The essential nature of Deity is holiness, and the power of God is proved in His becoming a Baby. That is the staggering proposition the Bible gives—God became the weakest thing we know. What does Jesus Christ say about Himself? He claims to be equal with God—"He that hath seen me hath seen the Father." The Christian revelation is not that Jesus Christ represents God to me, but that He *is* God. If Jesus Christ is not God, then we have no God. I am an agnostic; that is why I am a Christian. I could not find out anything about God, all I know about Him I accepted in the revelation given by Jesus Christ. I know no other God than Jesus Christ.

Jesus Christ is a Fact; He is the most honourable and the holiest Man, and two things necessarily follow—first, He is the least likely to be deceived about Himself, second, He is least likely to deceive anyone else. He said, "God will give the very disposition that is Mine to you, if you ask Him." Had He any right to say it—to say God would give me the disposition that ruled Him if I asked? If I say I have nothing in me to prove that Jesus Christ is real, am I willing to ask for the Holy Spirit? If I refuse to try a line Jesus Christ points out because I do not like it, my mouth is shut as an honest doubter. Let me try it and see if it works. An intellectualist never pushes an issue of will. God comes to any man instanter when he is willing to ask, and he will notice a difference in his actual experience, in his attitude to things, and he will be amazed at the change that has been wrought.

If you feel yourself being riddled and say "I don't know what to believe," go to God on the authority of Jesus Christ and ask Him to give you the Holy Spirit, and experience what the New Testament means by regeneration. It means receiving a new heredity. Jesus Christ never asks anyone to define his position or to understand a creed, but—"Who am I to you?" Has Jesus Christ made any difference at all to me in my actual life? Jesus Christ makes the whole of human destiny depend on a man's relationship to Himself.

The Fact of the Creed and the Doctrines of the Church

A creed means the ordered exposition of the Christian faith, an attempt to explain the faith you have, not the thing that gives you the Christian faith. It is the most mature effort of the human intellect on the inside, not on the outside. The churches make the blunder when they put the creed as the test on the outside, and they produce parrots who mimic the thing.

"You must believe a creed!" A man says, "I cannot, and if it is essential, then I cannot be a Christian." A creed is necessary, but it is not essential. If I am a devotee of a creed, I cannot see God unless He comes along that line.

(a) The Gift of Instructors

And He gave some, apostles; . . . and some, pastors and teachers. (Ephesians 4:11)

The test of an instructor in the Christian Church is that he is able to build me up in my intimacy with Jesus Christ, not that he gives me new ideas, but I come away feeling I know a bit more about Jesus Christ. To-day the preacher is tested, not by the building up of saints but on the ground of his personality.

(b) The Growth of Institutions *(Acts 6:1–4)*

The institutions of Churchianity are not Christianity. An institution is a good thing if it is second; immediately an institution recognises itself it becomes the dominating factor. When the war[14] struck us in civilised Britain we were members of certain churches and institutions, and were called Christians because we held certain doctrines and creeds. The bedrock of membership of the Christian Church is that we know Who Jesus Christ is by a personal revelation of Him by the Spirit of God. The essence of Christianity is not a creed or a doctrine, but an illumination that emancipates me—"I see who Jesus Christ is." It is always a surprise, never an intellectual conception.

(c) The Grasp of Intellect

Be ready always to give an answer to every man that asketh you a reason of the hope that is in you with meekness and fear. (1 Peter 3:15)

Peter does not say "give an explanation," but "a reason of the hope that is in you"—be ready to say what you base your hope on. Faith is deliberate confidence in the character of God Whose ways you cannot understand at the time. "I don't know why God allows what He does, but I will stick to my faith in His character no matter how contradictory things look." Faith is not a conscious thing, it springs from a personal relationship and is the unconscious result of believing someone. My faith is manifested in what I do, and I am able to explain slowly where I put my confidence. The faith that swallows is not faith, but credulity or fatalism. I have to get a grasp of the thing in my intellect, but that is second, not first.

Paul puts everything down to the words of Jesus Christ; if He is not what He claims, there is nothing in religion, it is pure fiction. If, however, Jesus Christ is not a humbug, and not a dreamer, but what He claims to be, then Christianity is the grandest fact that ever was introduced to any man.

VESTED INTERESTS OF THE FLESH

But ye are not . . . , if so be . . . Romans 8:9

When we are born from above (RV mg) the dominating spirit in us is the Spirit of God; the mind of the flesh is self-realisation, and the first thing that happens in a man's conscious spiritual life is a divorce between the two. The initial experience is a conflict on the inside. "For the flesh lusteth against the Spirit, and the Spirit against the flesh: and these are contrary the one to the other: so that ye cannot do the things that ye would" (Galatians 5:17).

Dominant Interest versus Interesting Details

For the law of the Spirit of life in Christ Jesus hath made me free from the law of sin and death. (Romans 8:2)

We can estimate our life on the spiritual line by our dominant interest. How do we know what is our dominant interest? It is not the thing that occupies most time. The dominating interest is a peculiarly personal one, viz., the thing that is really fundamentally ours in a crisis. In sorrow or joy we reveal our

---

14. World War I (1914–18).

dominating interest. We are taken up with interesting details; Jesus Christ was not. His insulation was on the inside, not the outside; His dominating interest was hid with God. His kingdom was on the inside, consequently He took the ordinary social life of His time in a most unobtrusive way. His life externally was oblivious of details, He spent His time with publicans and sinners and did the things that were apparently unreligious. But one thing He never did—He never contaminated His inner kingdom.

God may be dealing with you on the line of considering the lilies, He is causing you to take deeper root and meanwhile you do not bear flowers. For a time your experience is—"What I tell you in darkness, that speak ye in light." The only ones who knew who Jesus was and what He came to do, were a handful of fishermen. After He had died and risen again, He distinctly told them to wait in Jerusalem until they were endued with power from on high. According to ordinary reason they would have said, "That is absurd, this is not the time to wait; we are the only ones who know these things, we ought to be proclaiming the truth." Jesus said: "Tarry . . . until . . . ."

Don't get impatient with yourself; your dominating interest is taking deeper root. In all probability in your time of active service you were living from hand to mouth on spooned meat, you nourished your life by the interesting details of religious life, you had no nutritious root, and your work proved to be an elaborate way of evading concentration on God. There are far more people interested in consecration than concentration. It is easier to fuss around at work than to worship; easier to pay attention to details, to say our prayers or conduct a meeting, than to concentrate on God. Has God put you on the shelf deliberately? Why cannot He be glorified by a man in the dust as well as in the sunshine? We are not here to tell God what to do with us, but to let Him use us as He chooses. Remember, God's main concern is that we are more interested in Him than in work for Him. Once you are rooted and grounded in Christ the greatest thing you can do is to *be.* Don't try and be useful; be yourself and God will use you to further His ends.

Denominating Inspiration versus Individual Desire

For they that are after the flesh do mind the things of the flesh; but they that are after the Spirit the things of the Spirit. (Romans 8:5)

A denominating inspiration is a distinct expression of the character. There are all sorts and conditions of inspirations which come to a man's life. For instance, in St. Matthew 16:16–25 it is recorded that Peter had two inspirations, one was from God and the other from Satan, but he did not know where either came

from until they denominated themselves. Jesus said of one: "This is the voice of God"; of the other: "This is the voice of Satan." The denominating inspiration that is Christian has the characteristics of the Holy Spirit. Jesus said the Holy Spirit would glorify Him, "and bring all things to your remembrance, whatsoever I have said unto you." The Holy Spirit does not talk from or about Himself. When a person does extraordinary things and says, "God told me to do them," it may have been an inspiration, but its denomination had not the characteristic of Jesus Christ. The character of Jesus Christ is the inspiration of the Holy Spirit, and holiness is transfigured morality. People are inspired to do the wildest things and have no control over the inspiration. The inspiration of the Spirit of God denominates itself at once. If you are impulsively led to do a thing, examine it and see what it means. Has it the characteristics of Jesus Christ? "For as many as are led by the Spirit of God, they are the sons of God."

Pure Worship versus Power of Will

Which things have indeed a shew of wisdom in will worship. . . . (Colossians 2:23)

If we desire self-glorification we can have inspirations which have not the denomination of Jesus Christ. Worship is giving to God the best He has given us, and He makes it His and ours for ever. What is the best God has given you? Your right to yourself. "Now," He says, "sacrifice that to Me." If you do, He will make it yours and His for ever. If you do not, it will spell death to you. That is the meaning of Abraham's offering of Isaac. Isaac was the gift of God to Abraham, but God said, "Offer him . . . for a burnt offering." Abraham obeyed, and in the end received the illumination of true sacrifice and true worship of God. The best I have is my claim to my right to myself, my body. If I am born again of the Spirit of God, I will give up that body to Jesus Christ. "I beseech you therefore, brethren, by the mercies of God, that ye present your bodies a living sacrifice, holy, acceptable unto God, which is your reasonable service" (Romans 12:1).

The power of will is a different thing entirely. It says, "I see that on the line of honesty being the best policy, being a Christian is rather a good thing"—a dastardly thing to believe or say. Individual desires may smatter of the right thing, but if they have not the dominating inspiration of the Spirit of God they are dead. That is why Jesus said to the Scribes and Pharisees, "Woe unto you, . . . for ye are like unto whited sepulchres"; and to His disciples, "Do not ye after their works: for they say, and do not." There is always a twist about every one of us until we get the dominating inspiration of the Spirit of God. It makes us condemn the sins we are not inclined to while we make any amount of excuses for those we have a mind to, and they may be ten times worse. If we are inspired by the Spirit of God our lives are lived unobtrusively; we do not take the attitude of ascetics, but live perfectly natural lives in which the dominating interest is God.

Dwelling Identification versus Inevitable Death

But ye are not in the flesh, but in the spirit, if so be that the Spirit of God dwell in you. Now if any man have not the Spirit of Christ, he is none of His. (Romans 8:9)

Our true life is not intellect or morality or bodily eating and drinking; our true life is our relationship to Jesus Christ. If once we recognise that and take care to be identified with Him in the crises of life, God will look after all the rest. If we try to draw our inspiration from elsewhere we will die in the attempt.

New Creation versus Consecrating Nature

Therefore if any man be in Christ, he is a new creature: old things are passed away; behold, all things are become new. (2 Corinthians 5:17)

When we are indwelt by the Spirit of Christ we are in a new creation (RV mg). A man in love and a man convicted of sin are in the same external world, but in totally different creations. Both may be in the desert, but one has a disposition which makes him interpret the desert as a desolating piece of God's territory, while to the other the desert literally blossoms as the rose. The disposition of the one is mad, he sees no light in the sun, no sweetness in anything; his ruling disposition is one of misery, while to the other—

> *Heaven above is brighter blue,*
> *Earth around is sweeter green;*
> *Something lives in every hue*
> *Christless eyes have never seen.*

Consecrating natural gifts is popular but a snare. "I have the gift of a voice and I will consecrate it to God and sing 'Always, only, for my King.'" If a man or woman is devoted to God, they can sing anything with the blessing of God; but if they are not right they may sing "Take my life," and serve the devil in doing it. It is not the external things that tell, but the ruling disposition. There is no indication in God's Word that we should consecrate natural gifts, although we find many such indications in hymns. The only thing we can consecrate is our bodies. If we consecrate them to God, He takes them.

Immediately consecration is taken on the other line, the indwelling identification is not with Jesus Christ but with ourselves, which spells death. If we have the dwelling identification with Jesus Christ, then we are alive, and more and more alive. In the Christian life the saint is ever young; amazingly and boisterously young, certain that everything is all right. A young Christian is remarkably full of impulse and delight, because he realises the salvation of God; but this is the real gaiety of knowing that we may cast all our cares on Him and that He careth for us. This is the greatest indication of our identification with Jesus Christ.

INTEREST AND IDENTIFICATION

We did esteem Him stricken, smitten of God and afflicted. But He was wounded for our transgressions . . . and the Lord hath made to light on Him the iniquity of us all. Isaiah 53:4–6 (RV mg)

Immediately we face Jesus Christ two issues reveal themselves: first, the issue of interest, second, the issue of identification. Which issue are we caught up with? "Therefore leaving the principles of the doctrine of Christ, let us go on unto perfection; not laying again the foundation of repentance from dead works, and of faith toward God" (Hebrews 6:1).

Interest

"And sitting down they watched Him there" (Matthew 27:36). The name of those interested is legion. Thank God for interest; the fascination of our Lord Jesus Christ is on the interested, and by pious performances and personal penances, and seasons of waiting on God, they sit and watch Him there, dissolved in mists of sentiment and self-depreciating conventions. It is a gracious state to be in, as an introductory stage, but a place of imminent peril to remain in.

From positions of sitting in solemn silence, this stage of interest may reach a development like that indicated in Mark 15:39—"The centurion, which stood . . . , saw . . . , said, Truly this man was the Son of God." The attitude has changed to a standing, and speculative statements are the result. Our Lord is inferred to be a sublime martyr, good beyond any goodness of man or woman yet witnessed on this earth. His life and ideals were so far beyond His time and age that all the reward they gave Him was to crucify Him. "Truly this man was the Son of God." He is stated to be from this stage of standing interest, the very first of all martyrs, of all prophets, of all priests.

There is still another development of the issue of interest and that is indicated in John 1:38–39—"Rabbi, . . . where dwellest Thou? He saith unto them, Come and see. They came and saw . . . , and abode with Him that day." This may represent the sympathetic souls who follow our Lord Jesus Christ out of the natural affinity of their natural hearts. They "follow His steps" just as the disciples did in the days of His flesh, growing more and more perplexed at His teaching, more and more strained in their comprehension; becoming overwhelmed with their own sorrow in Gethsemane till they all forsook Him, and fled, and He went alone to His place for us—the Cross.

So many abide with Him "that day"—the day of natural devotion and interest; honest, earnest souls whose sense of the heroic, like Peter, or of the holy, like John, and the honest, like Thomas, has made them leave all and follow Him, but only to heartbreak and faltering; slowly but surely they break for retreat and return to their own (see John 16:32). All around us are these sad, spirituelle people wandering and wondering, too fascinated by our Lord Jesus Christ to turn again willingly to the "beggarly elements" of the world; all the pleasures of sin are not possible because of their interest in Him.

This inward disaster and unsatisfactoriness they scarcely dare confess to themselves, let alone to others. Where have they failed? Are you there, reader? Then you are on the way of the Cross. You must go to the Cross. Read John 20:22 and couple it with Luke 11:13, and then as a destitute soul receive the gift of the Holy Spirit on the ground of what Jesus did on the Cross, and He will identify His life with yours. "I will not leave you desolate: I come unto you" (John 14:18 RV).

Intermediate

And they stood still, looking sad. . . . And they said unto Him, . . . But we hoped. . . . Yea and beside all this, . . . Moreover certain women of our company amazed us. . . . But Him they saw not. (Luke 24:17–24 RV)

The literature produced by the interested is most prolific and enervating. This literature may deal with the statements of Jesus Christ before His Cross, and strange and fantastic are the doctrines that are woven, and no wonder, as the only exegete of our Lord's Word and doctrines is the Holy Spirit, and He is not given to any man who is blind to the Atonement of the Cross. The Holy Spirit is a gift, remission of sins is a gift, eternal life is a gift, on the ground of the Cross of our Lord and Saviour Jesus Christ. Ignore that, and life is a wayless wilderness, where all our ideals fade and falter, leaving us only a grey, uncertain outlook, gathering to an eternal night.

The literature of the unregenerated intellect in a final analysis ends where Matthew Arnold's[15] words place it.

> *Thou waitest for the spark from heaven! and we,*
> *Light half-believers of our casual creeds,*
> *Who never deeply felt, nor clearly willed,*
> *Whose insight never has borne fruit in deeds,*
> *Whose vague resolves never have been fulfilled;*
> *For whom each year we see*
> *Breeds new beginnings, disappointments new;*
> *Who hesitate and falter life away,*
> *And lose to-morrow the ground won today—*
> *Ah! do not we, wanderer, await it too?*

How one's whole being yearns to get such men and women to see that our Lord Jesus Christ by the gift of His Spirit in mighty regeneration, ends this night of sorrow. Reader, if your counterpart is in any of the sentiments already expressed, seek God now on the merits of the Cross, and ask Him for the gift of the Holy Spirit, and receive Him in faith.

Identification

I have been crucified with Christ, . . . and that life which I now live in the flesh I live in faith, the faith which is in the Son of God, Who loved me, and gave Himself up for me. (Galatians 2:20 RV)

What is imperatively needed is that emotional impressionisms and intellectual and moral interest be violently made by each individual into a moral verdict against our self-interest, our right to ourselves, determinedly letting go of all and signing the death warrant of the disposition of sin in us.

Paul says, "I have been crucified with Christ"; not "I have determined to imitate Him," or "I endeavour to follow Him," but, "I have been identified with Him." This is the point of vital godliness—the individual deciding, something after this manner: "My God, I should be there on that bitter cross."

> *My sin, my sins, my Saviour,*
> *How sad on Thee they fall.*

All that Jesus Christ wrought *for* us is worked *in* us whenever we come to such a violent moral decision and act on it, for this is the free committing that

---

15. Matthew Arnold (1822–1888), English scholar, poet, and critic.

gives the Spirit of God His chance to impart the mighty substituted holiness of God to us.

"I live; and yet no longer I, but Christ liveth in me." The individual remains, but the mainspring, the ruling disposition, is radically different; the same human body remains, but the old Satanic right to myself is gone. A lamp takes up very little room, but its burning and shining light streams far and penetrates wide, consumed in a glorious effulgence by the indwelling light. No wonder the Scriptures exclaim: "our God is a consuming fire." "Wherefore, if any man is in Christ, there is a new creation" (RV mg), and, "we have this treasure in earthen vessels."

"The life which I now live"—not the life which I long to live or pray to live, but which I live, the life which is seen in my mortal flesh, "I live by the faith of the Son of God. . . ."

This is not Paul's faith in the Son of God, but the faith that the Son of God has imparted to him. This is no longer faith in faith, but faith that has overleapt all self-conscious bounds and is the identical faith of the Son of God (see 1 Peter 1:8).

SELF-REALISATION V. CHRIST-REALISATION
Matthew 16:24

Self-realisation is a modern phrase—"Be moral, be religious, be upright in order that you may realise yourself." Nothing blinds the mind to the claims of Jesus Christ more effectually than a good, clean-living, upright life based on self-realisation (see 2 Corinthians 4:3–4). The issue with us to-day is not with external sins, but with the ideal of self-realisation, because Jesus Christ reveals that that ideal will divide clean asunder from Him. If we are going to be His disciples our ideal must be *Christ*-realisation.

The Desire
If any man will come after Me, let him deny himself . . .

There is no man awake to life but feels the attraction of Jesus Christ. There He stands, and all men are attracted to Him, whether or not they accept statements about His Deity or theories about the Atonement. What is your desire? Is it to be a fine, sterling, moral, upright character? A grand and noble desire; but watch how Jesus Christ sifts it. Two of the early disciples had the desire to follow Jesus, it was the consuming passion of their lives to come after Jesus, and when He asked them if they were able to drink of His cup and be baptised with His baptism, they said, "We are able." They were not conceited or proud, they were devout, humble-minded men, but they were perfectly ignorant about themselves. There are many people to-day who say, "Yes, Lord, I'll go with Thee all the way." But there are conditions: "If any man will come after Me, let him deny himself." What is the meaning of these words from the lips of Jesus? He is not teaching us to deny one part of ourselves in order to benefit another part of ourselves, which is what self-denial has come to mean. The full force of our Lord's words is—"let him deny his right to himself; let him give up his right to himself to Me." Jesus laid down that condition to a clean-living, sterling young man of His day, with what result? His countenance was sad, and he went away grieved; for he had great possessions. "If any man will come after Me," said Jesus, "the condition is that he must leave something behind," viz. his right to himself. Is Jesus Christ worth it, or am I one of those who accept His salvation but thoroughly object to giving up my right to myself to Him?

The Devotion
and take up his cross . . .

There is a difference between devotion to principles and devotion to a person. Hundreds of people to-day are devoting themselves to phases of truth, to causes. Jesus Christ never asks us to devote ourselves to a cause or a creed; He asks us to devote ourselves to Him, to sign away the right to ourselves and yield to Him absolutely, and take up that cross daily. The cross Jesus asks us to take up cannot be suffering for conviction's sake, because a man will suffer for conviction's sake whether he is a Christian or not. Neither can it be suffering for conscience' sake, because a man will go to martyrdom for his principles without having one spark of the grace of God in his heart. Paul says, "Though I give my body to be burned, and have not [love], it profiteth me nothing." What then is our cross? Our cross is something that comes only with the peculiar relationship of a disciple to Jesus. It is the sign that we have denied our right to ourselves and are determined to manifest that we are no longer our own, we have given away for ever our right to ourselves to Jesus Christ.

The characteristic of the cross we carry daily is that we have been "crucified with Christ." Galatians 2:20 does not refer merely to the fact that our "old man" has been crucified with Christ; it refers to the glorious liberty we have of sacrificing ourselves for Jesus Christ every day we live. What is sacrifice? Giving back to

God the best I have in order that He may make it an eternal possession of His and mine for ever.

But something must happen first. The meaning of salvation and sanctification is not only the removal of the wrong disposition, but the radical alteration of identity. Paul says that his destiny is no longer self-realisation, but Christ-identity: I live; and yet no longer I, but Christ liveth in me. We need to remember that we cannot train ourselves to be Christians; we cannot discipline ourselves to be saints; we cannot bend ourselves to the will of God: we have to be broken to the will of God. There must be a break with the dominant ruler. We may be clean and upright and religious, we may be Christian workers and have been mightily used of God; but if the bedrock of self-realisation has not been blasted out by our own free choice at the Cross of Christ, shipwreck is the only thing in the end. We enter into the Kingdom of God through the Cross of Jesus Christ, and self-realisation cannot get through with us, it must be left outside. We must be broken from self-realisation, immediately that point is reached the reality of the supernatural identification with the death of Jesus Christ takes place, and the witness of the Spirit is unmistakable—"I have been crucified with Christ" (RV).

Jesus Christ can take the man who has been broken by sin and twisted with wrong-doing and can reinstate him, not as an angel, thank God, but as a man, and present him before the throne of God without blemish, through the sheer omnipotence of His Atonement.

The Direction
. . . and follow Me.

We must not dictate to Jesus as to where we are going to serve Him. There is a theory abroad to-day that we have to consecrate our gifts to God. We cannot, they are not ours to consecrate; every gift we have has been given to us. Jesus Christ does not take my gifts and use them; He takes me and turns me right about face, and realises Himself in me for His glory. The one dominant note in the life of a disciple is—

> *Jesus only, Jesus ever,*
> *Jesus all in all I see.*

There is no devotion to principles or to a cause there; nothing but overwhelming, absorbing love to the Person of Jesus Christ.

"If any man will come after Me, let him deny himself, and take up his cross, and follow Me."

> *God grant we may answer—*
> *I have made my choice for ever,*
> *I will walk with Christ my Lord;*
> *Naught from Him my soul shall sever*
> *While I'm trusting in His word.*
> *I the lonely way have taken,*
> *Rough and toilsome though it be,*
> *And although despised, forsaken,*
> *Jesus, I'll go through with Thee.*

WHICH?

ADDRESS GIVEN AT THE ANNUAL AUTUMNAL GATHERING OF THE LEAGUE OF PRAYER
IN CAXTON HALL, LONDON, NOVEMBER 5, 1913.

But God forbid that I should glory, save in the cross of our Lord Jesus Christ, by whom the world is crucified unto me, and I unto the world. Galatians 6:14

God or Sin

God or sin must die in me. The one elementary Bible truth we are in danger of forgetting is that the Gospel of God is addressed to men as sinners, and nothing else. In tracing the experimental line of Church history one notices a significant thing—whenever a voice has been raised, like John Wesley's, on behalf of God's great power to deliver from sin, instantly a reacting wave of piety occurs, which takes the form of devotion and sentimental religious activity while the real message of the Gospel is lost by obliteration. After John Wesley's teaching a protest was lodged strongly against his emphasis on a second definite work of grace, and the consequence was a revival of that wave

of sentimental higher life not rooted and grounded in a changed life by God's grace.

Christ or Barabbas
And they crucified Him. (Matthew 27:35)

Christ versus Barabbas—we have to choose. For a long while we can ignore sin and dwell on the fact that God is our Father, but if we mean by that that He forgives sin because He is loving, we make the Atonement a huge blunder and Calvary a mistake. What does Barabbas represent? The expedient to Jesus Christ, something less radical, less emphatic, less against what we want. What is the "Barabbas" in your life and mine? Shall we give our vote for Christ or Barabbas to be crucified? Most of us have voted at one time in our history with God against Christ. The choice is always put when we are in the ascendant, when we are not being over-swayed either by Christ or Barabbas, but when we are in full possession of our powers; then God's providence puts the choice suddenly in front of us—Christ or Barabbas?

Christ or the Old Man

Knowing this, that our old man is crucified with Him. . . . (Romans 6:6)

What is our "old man"? The disposition of sin in us discovered by the incoming Spirit of God when we are born from above (RV mg). A Christian experiencing the first work of God's regenerating grace begins to discern this disposition, and the issue is clear that that old disposition must be crucified or the Spirit of Christ must be crucified, the two cannot remain long together. Paul states triumphantly, "knowing this, that our old man was crucified with Him . . ." (RV). It was not a divine anticipation on the part of the Apostle Paul, it was a very radical, definite experience. Are those of us who have experienced God's regenerating grace prepared to go the whole length with Jesus Christ? Are we prepared to let the Holy Spirit search us until we know what the disposition of sin is, the thing that rules and works its own way, that lusts against the Spirit of God that is in us? will we agree with God's verdict that that disposition should be identified with the death of Jesus? If so, then thank God, it will be as dead in us as the dead Christ was as a crucified body. Beware of going on the line of—I am reckoning myself to be "dead indeed unto sin"—unless you have been through the radical issue of will with God. Are we willing to be so identified with the death of Jesus Christ that we know with no apology that our old man was crucified with Him?

Christ or I

I have been crucified with Christ; yet I live; and yet no longer I, but Christ liveth in me. (Galatians 2:20 RV)

Christ or "I"? I mean the religious "I," the spiritual "I," the pride of spiritual possession. Have we learned the glorious, unmistakable privilege of being crucified with Christ until all that is left is Christ's flesh and Christ's blood in our flesh and in our blood where once the world, the flesh and the devil had their way? These are tremendous things to say in the light of the way the modern mind looks at things, but not too tremendous in the light of the Gospel.

Christ or the World

. . . by whom the world is crucified unto me, and I unto the world. (Galatians 6:14)

What is the world? The set of people with the ambitions, religious or otherwise, that are not identified with the Lord Jesus Christ. Paul says, "I am crucified to that world, and that world is crucified to me." When the world comes before us with its fascination and its power, it finds us dead to it, if we have agreed with God on His judgement about sin and the world.

These are not only statements made in God's Book, they are meant to be real, definite experiences in our lives. If the issue is put before you in your own life just now—Barabbas or Christ? you can no longer debate the question, you must decide; but let me plead with you to decide for Christ and have "Barabbas" crucified.

If you have been born from above and the Spirit of God is discerning in you the "old man," the disposition of sin, then make it an issue of will with Him, tell Him that you want to be identified with the death of Christ until you know that your "old man" is crucified with Christ. If you have gone through that issue of will, then stand clear for Christ and Christ only, until "I have been crucified with Christ" is not a sentiment, but a sensible fact in daily living, walk and conversation, stamped with the otherworldliness of the life hid with Christ in God.

THE ONE RIGHT THING TO BE

Believe also in Me. John 14:1

We do not now use the old evangelical phrase "a believer," we are apt to think we have something better, but we cannot have. "A believer in Jesus Christ" is a phrase that embraces the whole of Christianity. The history of the word is interesting, but what will hold our attention now by the aid of the Holy Spirit is the vital experimental meaning of the phrase "a believer in Jesus Christ."

To believe in Jesus means much more than the experience of salvation in any form, it entails a men-tal and moral commitment to our Lord Jesus Christ's view of God and man, of sin and the devil, and of the Scriptures.

Belief and the Scriptures

And they are they which testify of Me. (John 5:39)

For had ye believed Moses, ye would have believed Me: for he wrote of Me. (John 5:46)

How much intellectual impertinence there is to-day among many Christians relative to the Scriptures, because they forget that to "believe also" in Jesus means that they are committed beforehand to His attitude to the Bible. He said that He was the context of the Scriptures, ". . . they are they which testify of Me." We hear much about "key words" to the Scriptures, but there is only one "key word" to the Scriptures for a believer, and that is our Lord Jesus Christ Himself. All the intellectual arrogance about the Bible is a clear proof of disbelief in Jesus. How many Sunday school teachers to-day believe as Jesus believed in the Old Testament? How many have succumbed to the insolence of intellectual partisanship about the Person of our Lord and His limitations, and say airily, "Of course, there is no such thing as demon possession or hell, and no such being as the devil." To "believe also" in Jesus means that we submit our intelligence to Him as He submitted His intelligence to His Father. This does not mean that we do not exercise our reason, but it does mean that we exercise it in submission to Reason Incarnate. Beware of interpreters of the Scriptures who take any other context than our Lord Jesus Christ.

Belief and the Saviour
Dost thou believe on the Son of God? (John 9:35)

The number of insidious and beautiful writers and speakers to-day whose final net result will be found to be anti-Christ, is truly alarming. The writers I mean are those who examine psychologically the Person of our Lord on the ground of facts discoverable in unregenerate human consciousness, and effectually dissolve away the Person of Jesus Christ so marvellously revealed in the New Testament. John writes of this very spirit of mind and emphasises it as anti-Christ—"Every spirit which confesseth that Jesus Christ is come in the flesh is of God: and every spirit which annulleth Jesus [RV mg] is not of God" (1 John 4:2–3). To believe our Lord's consciousness about Himself commits us to accept Him as God's last endless Word. That does not mean that God is not still speaking, but it does mean that He is not saying anything different from "This is My beloved Son: hear Him."

To be a believer in Jesus Christ means that we realise that what Jesus said to Thomas is true—"I am the way, the truth, and the life," not the road we leave behind as we travel, but the Way itself. By believing, we enter into that rest of peace, holiness and eternal life. Let us maintain ourselves abiding in Him.

Belief and the Spirit
And when He is come, He will reprove the world of sin, and of righteousness, and of judgement: of sin, because they believe not on Me. (John 16:8–9)

Sin is not measured by a creed or a constitution or a society, but by a Person. The Gospels were not written to prove anything, they were written to confirm in belief those who were already Christians by means of the death and resurrection of our Lord Jesus Christ, and their theological meaning. The Holy Spirit in the mighty phases of initial quickening in spiritual regeneration (see John 20:22; Luke 11:13) and of the baptism (see Acts 1:8), does one thing only, viz. glorify Jesus. A great and glorious fact—to believe in Jesus Christ is to receive God, Who is described to the believer as "eternal life." Eternal life is not a gift *from* God, but the gift of God, that is, God Himself (see John 6:47; 17:2–3; Romans 6:23).

Belief in Service
He that believeth on Me, as the scripture hath said, out of his belly shall flow rivers of living water. (John 7:38)

How anxious we are to serve God and our fellow men to-day! Jesus Our Lord says we must pay attention to the Source—belief in Him, and He will look after the outflow. He has promised that there shall be "rivers of living water," but we must not look at the outflow, nor rejoice in successful service. "Notwithstanding in this rejoice not, that the spirits are subject unto you; but rather rejoice, because your names are written in heaven" (Luke 10:20). The source, belief in Jesus, is the thing to heed; and through that famous, for-ever binding commission, believers in Jesus are to make disciples—"Go ye therefore, and make disciples of all the nations." Are we doing it?

The great Pentecostal phrase, "witnesses unto Me" is the same thing stated for all believers in unforgettable words, witnesses not so much of what Jesus can do, but witnesses unto Him, a delight to His own heart, ". . . when He shall come to be glorified in His saints."

May God save us from Christian service which is nothing more than the reaction of a disappointed, crushed heart, seeking surcease from sorrow in social service. Christian service is the vital, unconscious result of the life of a believer in Jesus. We have much need to bear in mind Paul's warning, "But I fear, lest by any means, as the serpent beguiled Eve through his subtlety, so your minds should be corrupted from the simplicity that is in Christ" (2 Corinthians 11:3).

Pentecost makes bondslaves for Jesus Christ our Lord, not supernatural manifestations that glorify men. The Christian Church should not be a secret society of specialists, but a public manifestation of believers in Jesus.

The one right thing to be is a believer in Jesus.

ARE YOU INDEPENDENT OR IDENTIFIED?
John 21:18

Devotional Following

Verily, verily, I say unto thee, When thou wast young, thou girdest thyself, and walkedst whither thou wouldest . . .

Jesus is not rebuking Peter, He is revealing a characteristic of us all. Peter had given up everything for the Lord, and the Lord was everything to Peter, but he knew nothing whatever about the following that Jesus is referring to. Three years before, Jesus had said "Follow Me," and Peter followed easily, the fascination of Jesus was upon him; then he came to the place where he denied Jesus and his heart broke. Now Jesus says again "Follow thou Me." Peter follows now in the submission of his intelligence, his will, and his whole being. There is no Figure in front save the Lord Jesus Christ.

When we are young in grace we go where we want to go, but a time comes when Jesus says "another shall gird thee," our will and wish is not asked for. This stage of spiritual experience brings us into fellowship with the Spirit of Jesus, for it is written large over His life that "even Christ pleased not Himself." There is a distinct period in our experience when we cease to say—"Lord, show me Thy will," and the realisation begins to dawn that we *are* God's will, and He can do with us what He likes. We wake up to the knowledge that we have the privilege of giving ourselves over to God's will. It is a question of being yielded to God.

Death Following

. . . but when thou shalt be old, . . . another shall gird thee, and carry thee whither thou wouldest not.

When we are young in grace there is a note of independence about our spiritual life—"I don't intend anyone to tell me what to do, I intend to serve God as I choose." It is an independence based on inexperience, an immature fellowship; it lacks the essential of devotion. Some of us remain true to the independent following and never get beyond it; but we are built for God, Himself, not for service for God, and that explains the submissions of life. We can easily escape the submissions if we like to rebel against them, but the Spirit of God will produce the most ghastly humiliation if we do not submit. Since we became disciples of Jesus we cannot be as independent as we used to be. "I do wish Jesus did not expect so much of me." He expects nothing less than absolute oneness with Himself as He was one with the Father. ". . . That they may be one, even as We are one." That is the "hope of His calling" and it is the great light on every problem. "And for their sakes I sanctify Myself" said Jesus. Jesus makes us saints in order that we may sacrifice our saintship to Him, and it is this sacrifice which keeps us one with our Lord.

In the natural world it is a real delight to be faced with risk and danger, and in the spiritual world God gives us the "sporting chance." He will plant us down amongst all kinds of people and give us the amazing joy of proving ourselves "a living sacrifice" in those circumstances. "Thou art My beloved Son; in Thee I am well pleased"; the Father's heart was thrilled with delight at the loyalty of His Son. Is Jesus Christ thrilled with delight at the way we are living a sacrificial life of holiness? The disciple has no programme, only a distinguished passion of devotion to his Lord.

PROCESS OF BELIEF
AFTERNOON ADDRESS GIVEN AT THE ANNUAL AUTUMNAL GATHERING OF THE LEAGUE OF PRAYER IN LONDON, NOVEMBER 1911

But as many as received Him, to them gave He power to become the sons of God, even to them that believe on His name. John 1:12

According to the New Testament, belief arises from intellectual conviction and goes through moral self-surrender to identification with the Lord Jesus Christ.

Mind Reception

To as many as received Him . . .

What place has the Lord Jesus Christ in your intellectual outlook? Until the Lord Jesus Christ has been received as the highest and only Authority, Bible explanations are beside the mark because they lack the one efficient seal of the Holy Spirit Who is the only interpreter of the Bible revelation, and the Holy Spirit does not seal Bible interpretation to any man who has not accepted the Lord Jesus Christ as the final Authority for his life, for his mind, and for his whole outlook. John 1:12 represents the whole work of an individual soul in relationship to Jesus Christ.

Have I accepted Jesus Christ for my head as well as for my heart? Jesus Christ must be realised and accepted as the Authority as far as man is concerned.

Whether or not we are inside the pale of Christian experience, have we solved the problem of who is the final authority for our intellect? Is Jesus Christ? Is He the finest, the holiest Man that ever lived? If so, then our attitude of mind leads us to the position where we have the privilege of becoming sons of God.

If I have the right mental attitude to Jesus Christ the next step is easy: I will necessarily be led to accept what He says, and when He says, "If ye then, being evil, know how to give good gifts unto your children: how much more shall your heavenly Father give the Holy Spirit to them that ask Him?" then I will ask and receive.

Will I give a moral surrender to Jesus Christ's authority? If so, the privilege of becoming a child of God will be a moral fact for me because the Holy Spirit will teach me how to apply the Atonement of Jesus Christ to my own life, and how to be identified in obedience to Him with the life of Jesus Christ in the experience of entire sanctification.

Moral Reception

To them gave He power to become the sons of God . . .

But there is another class of people to whom the practical comes first. It is not the intellectual problem that bothers them but the personal one: conviction of sin, perplexity arising from a wrong disposition. Will you in that condition receive the Lord Jesus Christ as the Way, the Truth, and the Life? If once Jesus Christ is clear to the vision of the heart, everything else is simple. To as many as received Him, to them gave He the privilege (or the right) to become the sons of God.

I accept Him not only as my Authority, I accept Him as my Saviour. I pin my faith implicitly to what He says; and looking to Him in implicit confidence, I ask God to give me the Holy Spirit according to the word of Jesus and receive Him in faith.

Faith means implicit confidence in Jesus, and that requires not intellect only but a moral giving over of myself to Him. How many of us have really received from God the Spirit that ruled Jesus Christ and kept His spirit, soul and body in harmony with God? The Holy Spirit will bring conviction of sin, He will reveal Jesus Christ, and He will bring in the power verse 13 describes—"which were born . . . of God," begotten of God. He will do all that on one condition—that we surrender morally to Jesus Christ.

It is this point of moral surrender that nearly every man "shies off." We sentimentally believe, and believe, and believe, and nothing happens. We pray "Lord, increase our faith," and we try to pump up the faith, but it does not come. What is wrong? The moral surrender has not taken place. Will I surrender from the real centre of my life, and deliberately and wilfully stake my confidence on what Jesus Christ tells me?

Mystic Reception

. . . even to them that believe on His name.

From intellectual conviction and moral surrender to identification with the very life and joy of Jesus. A great thinker has said, "The seal and end of true conscious life is joy," not pleasure, nor happiness. Jesus Christ said to His disciples, "These things have I spoken unto you, that My joy might remain in you, and that your joy might be full"—identity with Jesus Christ and with His joy.

What was the joy of the Lord Jesus Christ? His joy was in having completely finished the work His Father gave Him to do; and the same type of joy will be granted to every man and woman who is born of God the Holy Ghost and sanctified, when they fulfil the work God has given them to do. What is that work? To be a saint, a walking, talking, living, practical epistle of what God Almighty can do through the Atonement of the Lord Jesus Christ—one in identity with the faith of Jesus, one in identity with the love of Jesus, one in identity with the Spirit of Jesus until we are so one in Him that the high-priestly prayer not only begins to be answered, but is clearly manifest in its answering—"that they may be one, even as We are."

God grant that from intellectual insubordination and moral insubordination and spiritual insubordination we may prove that we are made one with the Lord Jesus Christ by the marvellous gift of the Holy Spirit through the Atonement of Jesus Christ, so that, as Paul says, when our Lord comes He may be "marvelled at in all them that believed."

THE GREAT LIFE

SPOKEN TO BRITISH COMMONWEALTH TROOPS AT ZEITOUN[16] YMCA CAMP
NEAR CAIRO, EGYPT. SUNDAY MORNING SERVICE, MAY 13, 1917

. . . believeth all things. 1 Corinthians 13:7

It is a great thing to be a believer, but easy to misunderstand what the New Testament means by it. It is not that we believe Jesus Christ can *do* things, or that we believe in a plan of salvation; it is that we believe *Him;* whatever happens we will hang in to the fact that He is true. If we say, "I am going to believe He will put things right," we shall lose our confidence when we see things go wrong. We are in danger of putting the cart before the horse and saying a man must believe certain things before he can be a Christian; whereas his beliefs are the result of his being a Christian, not the cause. Our Lord's word "believe" does not refer to an intellectual act, but to a moral act; with our Lord to believe means to commit. "Commit yourself to Me," and it takes a man all he is worth to believe in Jesus Christ.

The Great Life is to believe that Jesus Christ is not a fraud. The biggest fear a man has is never fear for himself but fear that his Hero won't get through; that He won't be able to explain things satisfactorily; for instance, why there should be war and disease. The problems of life get hold of a man and make it difficult for him to know whether in the face of these things he really is confident in Jesus Christ. The attitude of a believer must be, "Things do look black, but I believe Him; and when the whole thing is told I am confident my belief will be justified and God will be revealed as a God of love and justice." It does not mean that we won't have problems, but it does mean that our problems will never come in between us and our faith in Him. "Lord, I don't understand this, but I am certain that there will be an explanation, and in the meantime I put it on one side." Our faith is in a Person Who is not deceived in anything He says or in the way He looks at things. Christianity is personal, passionate devotion to Jesus Christ as God manifest in the flesh.

The Genesis of the Great Life
Jesus answered and said unto them, This is the work of God, that ye believe on Him whom He hath sent. (John 6:29)

The Great Life is begun when we believe, belief cannot be pumped up. If we in our hearts believe in Jesus Christ, not *about* Him, but *in* Him, "*He* is all right anyway," it is an evidence that God is at work in our souls. "Abraham believed God" (Galatians 3:6). "Though He slay me, yet will I trust in Him" (Job 13:15). Every abortion and wrong-doing in spiritual life begins when we cease believing in Jesus Christ. If we believe in a state of mind He produces in us, we will be disappointed, because circumstances will come in our lives when these works of Jesus Christ are shadowed over; but if we believe in Him, no matter how dark the passage is we shall be carried right through, and when the crisis is passed our souls will have been built up into a stronger attitude towards Him.

What counts in a man's life is the disposition that rules him. When God begins His work in us He does not make a mighty difference in our external lives, but He shifts the centre of our confidence; instead of relying on ourselves and other people, we rely on God, and are kept in perfect peace. We all know the difference it makes if we have someone who believes in us and in whom we believe, there is no possibility of being crushed. The Great Life is not that we believe for something, but that when we are up against things in circumstances or in our own disposition, we stake our all on Jesus Christ's honour. If we have faith only in what we experience of salvation, we will get depressed and morbid; but to be a believer in Jesus Christ is to have an irrepressible belief and a life of uncrushable gaiety.

The Growth of the Great Life
Let not your heart be troubled: ye believe in God, believe also in Me. (John 14:1)

Jesus Christ is talking here about what no man knows but Himself viz. the day after death, and He says, "Don't be troubled about it." We grow in this Great Life by making room for Jesus Christ in our outlook on everything. Before you seal your opinion on any matter, find out what He has said about it—about God, about life, about death. Men discuss matters of heaven and hell, of life and death, and leave Jesus Christ out altogether; He says, "Before you finally seal your mind, Believe *also* in Me." If the bit we do know about Jesus Christ is so full of light, why cannot we leave the matters of heaven and hell, of life and death,

---

16. *Zeitoun* (zay TOON). An area 6 miles NE of Cairo. Site of YMCA camp, Egypt General Mission compound and a large base area for British, Australian and New Zealand troops. Site of the Imperial School of Instruction (1916–19).

in His hand and stake our confidence in Him? "God is light," and one day everything will be seen in that light. "I am the light of the world: he that followeth Me shall not walk in darkness, but shall have the light of life." To be a believer in Jesus Christ means we are committed to His way of looking at everything, not that we are open to discuss what people say He taught; that is the way difficulties have arisen with regard to Christian faith. Theology ought to be discussed; it does not follow, however, that our faith is assailed, but that in the meantime we stake our all in Jesus Christ. The great lodestar of our life is—"I believe in Jesus Christ, and in everything on which I form an opinion I make room for Him and find out His attitude."

The Grandeur of the Great Life

Verily, verily, I say unto you, he that believeth on Me hath everlasting life. (John 6:47)

We often hear it put as if God gave us a present called "eternal life." What Jesus Christ says is, "he that committeth himself to Me *hath* eternal life," i.e., the life that was characteristic of Himself (see John 17:3; Romans 6:23; 1 John 5:11). If we commit ourselves to Jesus He says, "Stake your all on Me and I will see you through, don't worry about anything but your relationship to Me." "The Best is yet to be." We shall yet see everything brought into subjection to the one in Whom we believe.

Watch carefully how you begin to get away from believing in Jesus. When we mistake darkness for sin, or when we get into moods and hang fire, we choke the work of God in us. "This is the work of God," not that you believe you are turned into a child of God, but "that ye believe on Him whom He hath sent." What does it matter what happens to us? The thought of ourselves ought never to come in at all! The one thing that tells is the great fundamental rock: "Believe also in Me." Many know a good deal about salvation, but not much about this intense patience of "hanging in" in perfect certainty to the fact that what Jesus Christ says is true.

"... believeth all things." That is the greatest courtesy in the whole of human life. If we believe in Jesus Christ we will determine to make our relationship to men what Jesus Christ's was to us. He believed that He could save every man irrespective of his condition. Do we believe He can? or do we get small and sceptical and cynical about some men? If we do, we are hindering them from being right. There are some people we feel the better for meeting, their ruling disposition is a generous one, they are not frost-bitten and mean; they are not necessarily good, but they have hold of the right relationship to things. That is true in the spiritual world; when we meet a man or woman who believes in Jesus Christ, we feel we can tell them anything. The thing for us to examine is: Are we really living the Great Life, or are we living in a bandbox[17] with a priggish notion that Jesus Christ is tied up in some formula? Jesus Christ is God manifest in the flesh, and He says, "This is the work of God that you believe in Me." The full growth in the Great Life is to "Believe *also* in Me" about everything. "Make room for Me, especially in matters where you cannot go; bring the child's mind to what I have said about them." We want to be our own Lord and master, to get everything solved for ourselves, Jesus says, "Look unto Me, and be ye saved." To commit his life and reasoning to Jesus Christ's attitude takes a man right out of himself and into Jesus Christ. This is not rational, it is redemptive. How many saw Jesus Christ as the Son of God? He was nothing more than a Carpenter to the majority. It comes with a rush of revelation, "I see Who He is!" and He gives us the life which is inherent in Himself.

Many Christians get depressed over mean,[18] despicable things they find in themselves; I feel glad, because it is a justification of what Jesus said, "Without Me ye can do nothing." If we stake our all in Him, He will see us through as Saviour or as Deliverer just where we need Him. It is a great thing to have a God big enough to believe in. To believe in a God whom "to be God is not fit" makes a man immoral. The God revealed in Jesus Christ is grand enough for every problem of life. "I am the way, the truth, and the life." Let us carry away the Great Life of joy and simplicity.

---

17. bandbox: a small, round box made to hold neckbands or collars for shirts; metaphorically, something small, narrow, cloistered, self-contained

18. mean: ordinary, common, low, or ignoble, rather than cruel or spiteful

IRRESISTIBLE DISCIPLESHIP

TALK GIVEN AT SUNDAY WORSHIP SERVICE, FAMILY AND YMCA WORKERS,
ZEITOUN CAMP NEAR CAIRO, EGYPT. JUNE 18, 1916

Watch ye, stand fast in the faith, quit you like men, be strong. 1 Corinthians 16:13

By a "disciple" we mean one who continues to be concentrated on our Lord. Concentration is of much more value than consecration, because consecration is apt to end in mere religious sentiment. Concentration is the gist of the Sermon on the Mount—"Be carefully careless about everything saving your relationship to Me," our Lord says.

"Irresistible," not in the sense of being exquisitely charming, or of being irresistible in war, but irresistible in the sense of not being deflected.

The Practice of Alert Detachment
Watch ye . . .

There is a detachment that is fanatical. Detachment without discretion is delusive, so when the New Testament uses the term "watch" (and the New Testament has a great deal to say about watching), it means an alert detachment which comes from a discreet understanding of the Lord's will (see Romans 12:1–2).

One continually finds an encroachment of beliefs and of attachment to things which is so much spiritual overloading. Every now and again the Spirit of God calls on us to take a spiritual stock-taking in order to see what beliefs we can do without. The things our Lord asks us to believe are remarkably few, and John 14:1 seems to sum them up—"Ye believe in God, *believe also in Me.*" We have to keep ourselves alertly detached from everything that would encroach on that belief; we all have intellectual and affectionate affinities that keep us detached from Jesus Christ instead of attached to Him. We have to maintain an alert spiritual fighting trim.

"Let us lay aside every weight, and the sin which doth so easily beset us" (Hebrews 12:1). This does not refer to indwelling sin, but to the spirit of the age, literally—the sin "which doth closely cling to us," or "which is admired of many," the thing that hinders us in running and keeps us attached. We have to see that we run alertly and run watching, run with patience, continually readjusting ourselves and determinedly holding loosely to all other things. Detachment without discretion leads us astray, but detachment with the discretion that is able to discern the Lord's will in daily occurrences will make us irresistible disciples.

Our Lord said to His disciples, "Behold, we go up to Jerusalem." There are a great many things that are quite legitimate, but if they are not on our way to Jerusalem, we do not do them.

The Practice of Attentive Decisiveness
stand fast in the faith . . .

We hear a great deal about decision of character; in irresistible discipleship we have to learn an attentive decisiveness. There is a decisiveness that is destructive, a pig-headed decisiveness that decides without deliberation. "Stand fast in the faith" gives the idea of deliberate attentive decisiveness—"I will take the time to go through the drill in order to understand what it means to stand fast" (cf. Ephesians 6:13). It is a great deal easier to fight than to stand, but Paul says our conflict is not so much a fight as a standing on guard. Our Lord requires us to believe very few things, because the nature of belief is not mathematical, but something that must be tested, and there are a number of insidious things that work against our faith. A famous preacher once said he found in his actual circumstances he did not believe half so much as he did when he was preaching. He meant he found it difficult to "stand fast in the faith" in daily circumstances.

It is possible to preach and to encourage our own souls and to appear to have a very strong faith, while in actual circumstances we do not stand fast at all, but rather prove what Herbert Spencer said to be true. Herbert Spencer said people were trained to think like pagans six days a week and like Christians the remaining day; consequently in the actual things of life we decide as pagans, not as Christians at all. The way of irresistible discipleship is to practise not only alert detachment, but also attentive decisiveness; after having deliberated on the relationship of our faith to certain things, we decide. Jesus said that the Holy Spirit would "bring all things to your remembrance, whatsoever I have said unto you." We hear some word of our Lord's and it sinks into the unconscious mind; then we come into certain circumstances and the Holy Spirit suddenly brings back that word to our conscious minds. Are we going to obey our Lord in that particular, or take the ordinary common-sense way of moral decisiveness? Are we going to stand fast in the faith, or take the easier way of decision without deliberation? To think along this line will give the death blow to the dangerous method of making principles out of our Lord's statements. To do that we do not need to maintain a detached life with Him; all we need is, to gain an intellectual grasp of His principles and endeavour to live our life in accordance with them.

We can never tell how we shall have to decide in certain circumstances, but we have to see that we stand fast in the faith. We know what "the faith" is when we have gone through with God in any particular. "The faith" is faith in the Redemption and in the indwelling Spirit of God; faith that God is love, and that He will see after us if we stand steadfast to our confidence in Him. It is easy to stand fast in the big things, but very difficult in the small things. If we do stand fast in faith in Him we shall become irresistible disciples.

The Practice of Comprehending Determination
quit you like men . . .

When we are children we are impulsive. Impulsiveness grows up with us from childhood's state; we do not quit ourselves like men. If we have been in the habit of discerning the Lord's will and love and have to decide on the spur of the moment, our determination will be comprehending, that is, we shall decide not from the point of view of self-interest, or because of the good of a cause, but entirely from our Lord's point of view.

One of the finest characteristics of a noble humanity is that of mature patience, not that of impulsive action. It is easy to be determined, and the curious thing is that the more small-minded a man is the more easily he makes up his mind. If he cannot see the various sides of a question, he decides by the ox-like quality of obstinacy. Obstinacy simply means—"I will not allow any discernment in this matter; I refuse to be enlightened." We wrongly call this strong-mindedness. Strength of mind is the whole man active, not discernment merely from an individual standpoint. The determination in a disciple

is a comprehending one. "For I determined not to know any thing among you, save Jesus Christ, and Him crucified," says Paul.

The Practice of Actual Dependability
. . . be strong.

We can depend on the man or woman who has been disciplined in character, and we become strong in their strength. When we depend on someone who has had no discipline, we both degenerate. We are always in danger of depending on people who are undisciplined, and the consequence is that in the actual strain of life they break down and we do too. We have to be actually dependable.

When we are young a hurricane or thunderstorm impresses us as being very powerful, yet the strength of a rock is infinitely greater than that of a hurricane. The same is true with regard to discipleship. The strength there is not the strength of activity but the strength of *being*. Activity may be a disease of weariness, or of degeneration; to be dependable means to be strong in the sense of disciplined reliability. To convey "stayability" is the work of the Spirit of God, not the product of convincing controversy.

These considerations convey the characteristics that the Apostle wanted the Corinthian Christians to develop in themselves. If we keep practising, what we practise becomes our second nature, then in a crisis and in the details of life we shall find that not only will the grace of God stand by us, but also our own nature. Whereas if we refuse to practise, it is not God's grace but our own nature that fails when the crisis comes, because we have not been practising in actual life. We may ask God to help us but He cannot, unless we have made our nature our ally. The practising is ours, not God's. He puts the Holy Spirit into us, He regenerates us, and puts us in contact with all His Divine resources, but He cannot make us walk and decide in the way He wants; we must do that ourselves. Paul says "I do not frustrate [i.e., make void, RV] the grace of God."

ALWAYS NOW
2 Corinthians 6:1–10

Behold, now is the accepted time; behold, now is the day of salvation. 2 Corinthians 6:2

"We . . . intreat also that ye receive not the grace of God in vain" (RV). The grace we had yesterday won't do for to-day. "The grace of God"—the overflowing favour of God; we can always reckon it is there to

draw on if we don't trust our own merits (see 2 Corinthians 5:18–21).

Conditions of Saintliness in Private Trials
But in everything commending ourselves as ministers of God, in much patience, in afflictions, in necessities, in distresses, ... (2 Corinthians 6:4 RV)

Our private life is disciplined by the interference of people in our own matters; the people who do not mean to be a trial *are* a trial; that is where the test for patience comes. Have we failed the grace of God there? Are we saying, "Oh, well, I won't count this time"? It is not feeling the grace of God, it is drawing on it *now*. Whatever is our particular condition we are sure to have one of these things Paul mentions—afflictions, necessities, distresses. It is not praying to God and asking Him to help us in these things, it is taking the grace of God now. Many of us make prayer the preparation for work, it is never that in the Bible. Christianity is drawing on the overflowing favour of God in the second of trial.

Conditions of Saintliness in Public Tribulations

In stripes, in imprisonments, in tumults, in labours, in watchings, in fastings. (2 Corinthians 6:5)

These verses are Paul's spiritual diary, they describe the outward hardships which proved the hotbed for the graces of the Spirit—the working together of outward hardships and inward grace. Imprisonments, tumults, labours—these are all things in the external life. "In tumults"—watch a porridge pot boiling and you will know what tumult means; in that condition draw on the grace of God now. Don't say "I will endure it till I can get away and pray"; draw now, it is the most practical thing on earth. Whenever you are going through any tribulation that tears, don't pray about it, but draw on the grace of God now. The exercise of prayer is the work of drawing now.

Conditions of Saintliness in Pure Temperance

In pureness, in knowledge, in long-suffering, in kindness, in the Holy Ghost, in love unfeigned. (2 Corinthians 6:6 RV)

These are the inner characteristics of the temperate life—pureness, knowledge, long-suffering, kindness, love unfeigned. There is no room for extravagant impulse there; you cannot be pure and impulsive, you can be innocent and impulsive, because that is the nature of a child. Purity is something that has been tried and found unspotted. We are always inclined to be intemperate about our religion, it is the last thing for which we learn to draw on the grace of God. In our praying we draw on our memories, on our past experiences, on our present desires. We only learn to draw on the grace of God by pureness, by knowledge, by long-suffering. How many of us have to learn that temperance is knowledge? We want to get short cuts to knowledge and because we cannot take them we rush off into intemperate work. Notice the disproportion between the modern disease called Christian

work and the one characteristic of the fruit of the Spirit. The craze in everyone's blood nowadays is a disease of intemperate work, external activities.

"In long-suffering"—long-suffering is being drawn out until you can be drawn out no more, and not snapping. God puts His saints into places where they have to exhibit long-suffering. Let circumstances pull and don't give way to any intemperance whatever, but in all these things manifest a drawing on the grace of God that will make you a marvel to yourself and to others.

"In kindness"—be perfectly clear and emphatic with regard to your preaching of God's truth, but amazingly kind in your treatment of people. Some of us have a hard, metallic way of dealing with people which never has the stamp of the Holy Ghost on it. The word of God is "sharper than any two-edged sword" but when you deal with people, deal with them in kindness; remember yourself that you are where you are by the grace of God. Don't make God's word what it is not.

"In the Holy Ghost"—it is not the tones of a man's speech or the passion of a man's personality, it is the pleading power of the Holy Ghost coming through him. ". . . as though God were intreating by us" (RV): this is the entreaty that is learned at Calvary and made real in the worker by the Holy Ghost.

"In love unfeigned." Love feigned is this: "I love you very much, but . . ." Love unfeigned never thinks or looks at things like that. If love has to give stern rebuke it never prefaces it with remarks like that; the one great thing that moves us is the love of God which has been shed abroad in our hearts, and that love is described in 1 Corinthians 13.

Proclaiming Testimony

In the word of truth, in the power of God, by the armour of righteousness on the right hand and on the left. (2 Corinthians 6:7 RV)

"In the word of truth"—draw on the grace of God for testimony. Not, "Oh, Lord, I am going to give testimony, please help me": draw on the grace of God while you testify, proclaiming the truth in the presence of God. The first motive of testimony is not for the sake of other people but for our own sake; we realise that we have no one but God to stand by us. Always give your testimony in the presence of God, and ever remember God's honour is at stake. "In the word of truth" in our testimony; "in the power of God" working in us, and "by the armour of in-the-rightness" of our public and private life shielding us. You cannot draw on the grace of God for testimony if these three things are not there—the word of God, the power of God, and the consciousness that you are walking in the integrity of that testimony in private, if they are there, then there is an unfaltering certainty. Am I "in the rightness" all round? Testimony frequently stops short because the armour of righteousness is not on the right hand and on the left. Keep drawing on the grace of God, then there will be the power of the proclaimed testimony.

Personal Temperament
By glory and dishonour, by evil report and good report; as deceivers, and yet true. (2 Corinthians 6:8 RV)

Each of these contrasts puts our natural temperament "out of it." Let circumstances bring you where they will, keep drawing on the grace of God. Our temperament is not our disposition, temperament is the tone our nature has taken from the ruling disposition. When we had the disposition of sin our temperament took its tone from that disposition; when God alters the disposition the temperament begins to take its tone from the disposition He puts in, and that disposition is like Jesus Christ's.

Perfect Trustfulness
As unknown, and yet well known; as dying, and behold, we live; as chastened, and not killed. (2 Corinthians 6:9)

"I know both how to be abased, and I know how to abound: every where and in all things I am instructed both to be full and to be hungry, both to abound and to suffer need" (Philippians 4:12)—drawing on the grace of God in every conceivable condition. One of the greatest proofs that we are drawing on the grace of God is that we can be humiliated without the slightest trace of anything but the grace of God in us. Draw on the grace of God *now*, not presently. The one word in the spiritual vocabulary is "NOW."

Poverty Triumphant
As sorrowful, yet alway rejoicing; as poor, yet making many rich; as having nothing, and yet possessing all things. (2 Corinthians 6:10)

As we draw on the grace of God He increases voluntary poverty all along the line. Always give the best you have got every time; never think about who you are giving it to, let other people take it or leave it as they choose. Pour out the best you have, and always be poor. Never reserve anything, never be diplomatic and careful about the treasure God gives.
Always now is the secret of the Christian life.

Baffled to Fight Better

Job and the Problem of Suffering
Oswald Chambers

First published in 1917
This edition ©1931 Oswald Chambers Publications Association
Scripture versions quoted: KJV; RV

INTRODUCTION

Source

These were talks given by Oswald Chambers to soldiers during the evening classes at Zeitoun,[1] March 10–April 4, 1917.

Publication History

- This material was first published as a book in December 1917. It was printed by the Nile Mission Press[2] in Cairo, and shortly thereafter was published in England.
- Subsequent editions were published in Britain and the US.

In the autumn of 1916, Chambers had just begun his second year as YMCA secretary to British Commonwealth troops at Zeitoun Camp, near Cairo.

For several weeks during the months of October and November, Chambers' personal Bible reading each morning centered in the book of Job. Excerpts from Oswald's personal diary best express the impact of Job on him and his vision of what Job would mean to people after the war.

October 7, 1916: *How profoundly in harmony with fundamental life the third chapter of Job is in its actually apparent discord. How many a man and woman could say in deepest anguish—"Wherefore is light given to him that is in [deep] misery, and life unto the bitter in soul?" Deeper and deeper grows the conviction that Tragedy is the basis of things and Redemption the way out.*

October 8, 1916: *The fourth and fifth chapters of Job make most stately reading. The searching of vv. 3–6, chap. 4, read with Romans 2:21–24, is a most beneficial thing for those of us who are always talking to others. It is easy to become an intolerable prig, a dogmatic superior person, without knowing it.*

October 10, 1916: *Job 6 is a fine full expression to multitudes in the valley of agony and sorrow just now. I believe of all the books of consolation none will be so great or grand as the Book of Job because an expression to sorrow, as to joy, means a great rising to face life again as its master.*

October 14, 1916: *Job . . . as I read him this morning . . . is not affected or sentimental, but gripped by the real and appalling agony of mystery and pain, free from spite, and yet so honest in expression of pain and distress.*

October 28, 1916: *Job 23 is surely the classic of deep woe rolling out across the very universe: "Oh that I knew where I might find Him!" All through the Book of Job there is a heartbreaking devotion to God in the midst of inexplicable complexity of sorrow. I feel growingly sure that Job is the Book of consolation for the sorrow-tossed and bereaved and broken by the war, for not only is the voice of human suffering expressed here better*

---

1. Zeitoun (zay TOON). An area 6 miles NE of Cairo. Site of YMCA camp, Egypt General Mission compound and a large base area for British, Australian and New Zealand troops. Site of the Imperial School of Instruction (1916–19).

2. Nile Mission Press was established by the Egypt General Mission in 1905 to print Christian materials primarily for outreach to Muslims.

than anywhere, but the very breath is drawn in the fear of the Lord, and the heart is strong in the hope that grades higher than faith.

October 30, 1916: *Job 24 reminds me of Ibsen's plays more than of any recent thing. Ibsen's clear-sightedness and his sense of the inexorable results of sin without any sense of forgiveness, seem to me most massively expressed in this chapter.*

November 1, 1916: *There was nothing of the Pharisee about Job, he sticks to it that he is not a sinner, and he also sticks to it that God is just, knowing implicitly that a lie could never justify God, even if it apparently justified "Bildad & Co." And of chapters 29–31, what can one say—it is a never-to-be-equalled expression of vast personal sorrow and agony. Chapter 31:35–37 is Job's autobiography, written in tears and blood. And now "the words of Job are ended," and still no light and no "way" yet.*

November 3, 1916: *The remaining chapters of Job keep my mind and heart in a glow of lifted wonder and worship.*

Oswald gave these talks to British troops in the spring of 1917. Because the men were always in training and transition, few could attend all the classes. This, along with their heartfelt response to the messages,

undoubtedly caused Oswald and Biddy to consider publishing all of the talks in this series. Almost as soon as the talks on Job were ended, Biddy was working to transcribe her shorthand notes and prepare them for publication. On April 5, 1917, OC wrote to a friend in England, "Hope to send you a book on Job soon (at least Biddy does, I take no more responsibility after having spoken my mind)."

In a diary entry for August 13, 1917, OC noted: "I am at present, with Biddy's help, getting the last sheets of my talks on Job read for the printer, the book is to be entitled *Baffled to Fight Better.*"

When Chambers died suddenly and unexpectedly in November 1917, *Baffled* had already been sent to press in Egypt.

Baffled to Fight Better is one of only three books compiled and printed before Chambers' death. The other two are *Biblical Psychology* (1912) and *Studies in the Sermon on the Mount* (1915).

The title comes from Robert Browning's "Asolando":
One who never turned his back but
        marched breast forward,
Never doubted clouds would break,
Never dreamed though right were
        worsted, wrong would triumph,
Held we fall to rise, are baffled to fight better
        Sleep to wake.

CONTENTS

FOREWORD TO THE FIRST EDITION (1917)

This book is comprised of talks given nightly by Reverend Oswald Chambers to the men at the Imperial School of Instruction,[3] Zeitoun, Egypt, during the Spring of 1917.

The one who spoke the words is now in the presence of the King, "serving Him day and night in His temple," and our prayer is that this book may serve to quicken in us all "a personal passionate devotion to Jesus Christ." Our Lord Himself was the one Lodestar in the life of my husband, and every recalling of him is an incentive to "follow his ways in Christ."

For himself
So shadowed forth in every look and act
Our Lord, without Whose name he seldom spoke,
One could not live beside him and forget.

B.C.[4] Egypt, 1917

CENTRAL HALL, WESTMINSTER, LONDON, S.W.

It is with sincere pleasure that I write a few prefatory words to this last message from Reverend Oswald Chambers.

The Church of Christ has sustained a great loss in the Passing of our dear gifted Friend.

Reverend Oswald Chambers was a scholar, a burning Evangelist, a teacher of the Word of God, who taught in faith and verity.

He was full of the Holy Ghost, and turned many to the Lord. There is pathetic interest in these musings on the great drama of sorrow, which was also a true history.

Many will read them with tearful eyes as they recall their departed Author.

All, I am sure, will read with profit: may our Friend's lessons be messages of God to us all.

May we live in full consecration as he did, and whether we "fall asleep in Jesus," or remain till the Lord's return, may we be absolutely faithful!

Dinsdale T. Young[5]

FOREWORD TO THE THIRD EDITION (1924)

These talks were given in the Y.M.C.A. Huts, Zeitoun, Egypt, to the men in the Egyptian Expeditionary Force during the early part of 1917. They were not given with the thought of publication, and the book is compiled from my own verbatim notes.

In November, 1917, God's call came to my husband for other service in His presence, and the idea came to me that to publish the talks he had been giving to the men in Egypt (and previously at the Bible Training College, London), would serve some purpose of God's, and the work was started with the prayer that the written messages might bring a knowledge of His truth to many as the spoken messages had ever done. This book was the first one to be published and was widely circulated amongst the men in Egypt and Palestine, many of whom had heard the talks given, an edition being also published in England at the same time.

I have a practically inexhaustible supply of notes, and other books will be published from time to time. *By his faith, he is speaking to us still. (Hebrews 11:4, MOFFATT).*

B.C.
200 Woodstock Road, Oxford
October 1923

---

3. The Imperial School of Instruction was established at Zeitoun in September 1916 by the British Command to train troops primarily in infantry weapons and tactics.

4. Biddy Chambers: although Mrs. Chambers was editor, compiler, and often publisher, she never identified herself by name in any of the books.

5. Dinsdale T. Young (1861–1938), noted Methodist minister who influenced Chambers, especially during Oswald's years at Dunoon Theological College in Dunoon, Scotland, 1897–1906.

THE UNSEEN UNIVERSE
Job 1:1–12

Man is not God but hath God's end to serve,
A master to obey, a course to take,
Somewhat to cast off, somewhat to become.
Grant this, then man must pass from old to new,
From vain to real, from mistake to fact,
From what once seemed good, to what now
     proves best.

                              Robert Browning

(1) The Record of the Natural (Job 1:1–5)
     The Greatest Man in the East
          (a) His Goodness (Job 1:l)
          (b) His Grandeur (Job 1:2–4)
          (c) His Graciousness (Job 1:5)
(2) The Record of the Supernatural (Job 1:6–12)
     The Scenery Behind the Seen
          (a) Sons of God (Job 1:6)
          (b) Satan and God (Job 1:7–8)
          (c) Satanic Sneer about God (Job 1:9–12)

It is in such a book as Job that many suffering souls will find consolation and sustaining, and this because no attempt is made to explain the *why* of suffering, but rather an expression is given to suffering which leaves one with the inspiration of an explanation in the final issue. The problem in connection with suffering arises from the fact that there is seemingly no explanation of it.

To say that Job was perfected by means of his sufferings is begging the question, for Job was perfect in moral and religious equipment before suffering touched his life. "Hast thou considered My servant Job, that there is none like him in the earth, a perfect and upright man, one that . . . escheweth evil?" (Job 1:8). Job suffered "according to the will of God"; he never knew the preface to his story.

Verses 6–12 are a record of the supernatural; there is nothing familiar to our minds in them. The Bible deals with what no ordinary mind sees—the scenery behind the things that are seen. We have means of inferring the existence of a supernatural world only when it interferes with us. These verses refer to something that happened in the supernatural world, and it is what happened there that accounts for Job's sufferings; therefore the upset which came into the life of this great and good man is not to be laid to his account.

There is a difference between Satan and the devil which the Bible student should note. According to the Bible, man is responsible for the introduction of Satan: Satan is the result of a communication set up between man and the devil (see Genesis 3:1–5).

When Jesus Christ came face to face with Satan He dealt with him as representing the attitude man takes up in organising his life apart from any consideration of God. In the Temptation the devil is seen in his undisguised character; only once did Our Lord address the devil as "Satan"—"Then said Jesus unto him, Get thee hence, Satan . . ." (Matthew 4:10). On another occasion Jesus said that self-pity was satanic—"But He turned, and said unto Peter, Get thee behind Me, Satan . . ." (Matthew 16:23).

The devil is the adversary of God in the rule of man and Satan is his representative. Because a thing is satanic does not mean that it is abominable and immoral; Our Lord said that "that which is highly esteemed among men is abomination in the sight of God" (Luke 16:15). Satan rules this world under the inspiration of the devil and men are peaceful—"when a strong man armed keepeth his palace, his goods are in peace"—there is no breaking out into sin and wrongdoing. One of the most cunning travesties is to represent Satan as the instigator of external sins. The satanically-managed man is moral, upright, proud and individual; he is absolutely self-governed and has no need of God.

Satan counterfeits the Holy Spirit. The Holy Spirit represents the working of God in a human life when it is at one with God through the Redemption; in other words, "Holy Spirit" is the heredity brought into human nature at regeneration. When a man is born from above he has granted to him the disposition of Jesus, *Holy Spirit*, and if he obeys that disposition he will develop into the new manhood in Christ Jesus. If by deliberate refusal a man is not born again he is liable to find himself developing more and more into the satanic, which will ultimately head up into the devil.

"Then Satan answered the LORD, and said, Doth Job fear God for nought?" Job 1:9–12 might be paraphrased in this way: Satan is represented as saying to God, "You are infatuated with the idea that man loves You for Your own sake; he never has and never will. Job, for instance, simply loves you because You bless and prosper him, but touch any one of his blessings and he will curse You to Your face and prove that no man on earth loves You for Your own sake."

It must be remembered what Job's creed was. Job believed that God prospered and blessed the upright man who trusted in Him, and that the man who was not upright was not prospered. Then came calamity after calamity, everything Job believed about God was contradicted and his creed went to the winds. Satan's sneer is the counterpart of the devil's sneer in Genesis 3; there, the devil's object is to sneer about God to man; here, Satan's object is to sneer about man to God, he is "the accuser of our brethren."

To-day there is in our midst a crop of juvenile sceptics, men who up to the time of the war had had no tension in their lives, and as soon as turmoil embroiled them they flung over their faith and became cheap and easy sceptics. The man who knows that there are problems and difficulties in life is not so easily moved. Most of us get touchy with God and desert Him when He does not back up our creed (cf. John 6:60, 66). Many a man through this war[6] has lost his form of belief in God and imagines that he has thereby lost God, whereas he is in the throes of a conflict which ought to give birth to a realisation of God more fundamental than any statement of belief.

There are things in our heavenly Father's dealings with us which have no immediate explanation. There are inexplicable providences which test us to the limit, and prove that rationalism is a mere mental pose. The Bible and our common sense agree that the basis of human life is tragic, not rational, and the whole problem is focused for us in this Book of Job. Chapter 13:15 is the utterance of a man who has lost his explicit hold on God, but not his implicit hold— "Though He slay me, yet will I trust in Him" (RV,

"wait for Him"). That is the last reach of the faith of a man. Job's creed is gone; all he believed about God has been disproved by his own experiences, and his friends when they come say, in effect, "You are a hypocrite, Job, we can prove it from your own creed." But Job sticks to it—"I am not a hypocrite, I do not know what accounts for all that has happened, but I will hold to it that God is just and that I shall yet see Him vindicated in it all."

God never once makes His way clear to Job. Job struggles with problem after problem, and Providence brings more problems all the time, and in the end Job says, ". . . now mine eye seeth Thee." He saw that all he had hung in to in the darkness was true, and that God was all he had believed Him to be, loving and just and honourable. The explanation of the whole thing lies in the fact that God and Satan had made a battleground of Job's soul without Job's permission. Without any warning, Job's life is suddenly turned into desperate havoc and God keeps out of sight and never gives any sign whatever to Job that He is. The odds are desperately against God and it looks as if the sneer of Satan will prove to be true; but God wins in the end, Job comes out triumphant in his faith in God, and Satan is completely vanquished.

Will I trust the revelation given of God by Jesus Christ when everything in my personal experience flatly contradicts it?

DAZED AND AMAZED
Job 1:13–2:13

Jesus, Whose lot with us was cast,
Who saw it out, from first to last: . . .
Would I could win and keep and feel
That heart of love, that spirit of steel.

I would not to Thy bosom fly
To slink off till the storms go by,
If you are like the man you were
You'd turn with scorn from such a prayer.

Wilfrid Brinton

1. In the Whirlwind of Disaster
(a) The Onslaught of Destruction (Job 1:13–19)
God gave Satan authority to interfere with all that Job possessed—"Behold, all that he hath is in thy power." All that a man possesses is at times not in the hand of God, but in the hand of the adversary, because God

has never withdrawn that authority from Satan. The disasters that attend a man's possessions are satanic in their origin and not of the haphazard order they seem to be. When Jesus Christ talked about discipleship He indicated that a disciple must be detached from property and possessions, for if a man's life is in what he possesses, when disaster comes to his possessions, his life goes too (cf. Luke 12:15).

Satan had been allowed to attack Job's possessions; now his power is increased, and he is free to attack Job's personal inheritance direct. When a man is hit by undeserved destruction, the immediate result is a slander against God—"Why should God allow this thing to happen?"

There are people to-day who are going through an onslaught of destruction that paralyses all our platitudes and preaching; the only thing that will bring

---

6. this war: World War I (1914–1918)

relief is the consolations of Christ. It is a good thing to feel our own powerlessness in the face of destruction, it makes us know how much we depend upon God. In these days the outstanding marvel is the way mothers and wives have gone through sorrow, not callously, but with an extraordinary sense of hopefulness. One thing the war has done is to knock on the head all such shallow optimism as telling people to "look on the bright side of things"; or that "every cloud has a silver lining": there are some clouds that are black all through.

(b) The Ordeal of Despair (Job 1:20–21)

Naked came I out of my mother's womb, and naked shall I return thither: the LORD gave, and the LORD hath taken away; blessed be the name of the LORD. (Job 1:21)

Facing facts as they are produces despair, not frenzy, but real downright despair, and God never blames a man for despair. The man who thinks must be pessimistic; thinking can never produce optimism. The wisest man that ever lived said that "he that increaseth knowledge increaseth sorrow." The basis of things is not reasonable, but wild and tragic, and to face things as they are brings a man to the ordeal of despair. Ibsen presents this ordeal, there is no defiance in his presentation, he knows that there is no such thing as forgiveness in Nature, and that every sin has a Nemesis following it. His summing up of life is that of quiet despair because he knows nothing of the revelation given of God by Jesus Christ.

"Blessed are they that mourn." Our Lord always speaks from that basis, never from the basis of the "gospel of temperament." When a man gets to despair he knows that all his thinking will never get him out, he will only get out by the sheer creative effort of God, consequently he is in the right attitude to receive from God that which he cannot gain for himself.

(c) The Ordination of Discretion Job 1:22)

"In all this Job sinned not, nor charged God foolishly." The Apostle James talks about "the patience of Job," but "patience" is surely the last word we would have applied to Job! He "skins" his friends with his terrific criticisms. Yet Job was never fundamentally impatient with God; he could not understand what God was doing, but he did not charge God with foolishness; he hung in to the certainty that God would yet be cleared, and so would he. Our Lord said that He was "meek and lowly in heart," yet meekness is not the striking feature in the Temple when He drove out those that sold and bought in the temple, and overthrew the tables of the moneychangers. Our Lord was meek towards His Father's dispensations for Him, but not necessarily meek towards men when His Father's honour was at stake.

2. In the Wickedness of Desolation
(a) The Sieve of Satan (Job 2:1–6)

In chapter 2 the veil is lifted from behind the seen and the tragedy is explained. Job's possessions have gone, but he still holds to his integrity; now Satan conducts his sneer one bit nearer. The first sneer was to God— "Man only loves You because You bless him"; now Satan obtains permission to interfere with Job's intimate possessions, his sense of integrity and his health—"Behold, he is in thine hand; but save his life." The last stake of Satan is in a man's flesh. There are times when a man's intimate personal possessions are under Satan's domination. The Apostle Paul calls Satan "an angel of light," he comes to a man whose personal possessions are being attacked and says— "You have lost the sense of the presence of God, therefore you must have backslidden." There is a wicked inspiration in it; the thing underneath is the wickedness of desolation. Desolation is never a right thing; wrong things happen *actually* because things are wrong really. One of the dangers of fanaticism is to accept disaster as God's appointment, as part of His design. It is not God's design, but His permissive will. There is a vital moral difference between God's order and His permissive will. God's order is—no sin, no Satan, no sickness, no limitations. The unaided intellect of man recognises this and says, "I will cut out sin and the Redemption and Jesus Christ, and conduct my life on rational lines." Then comes the permissive will of God—sin, Satan, difficulty, wrong and evil, and when desolation and disaster strike a man there is a wicked sting at the heart of it, and if he does not allow for the real thing behind it all he is a fool. We have to grasp God's order through His permissive will. A Christian must not lurk in the bosom of Christ because his thinking gives him a headache. It is moral and spiritual cowardice to refuse to face the thing and to give in and succumb. The greatest fear a Christian has is not a personal fear, but the fear that his Hero won't get through, that God will not be able to clear His character. God's purpose is to bring "many *sons* unto glory." Right through all the turmoil that is produced, and in spite of all Satan can do, this Book of Job proves that a man can get through to God every time.

(b) The Scourge of Suffering (Job 2:7–10)
The first outer court of a man's life is his flesh, and Job was smitten "with sore boils from the sole of his foot unto his crown." Then the wife of his bosom counselled him to "renounce God, and die. But he said unto her, Thou speakest as one of the foolish [impious, RV mg] speaketh. What? shall we receive good at the hand of God, and shall we not receive evil? In all this did not Job sin with his lips." That is

where the scourge of suffering lies. When I suffer and feel I am to blame for it, I can explain it to myself; when I suffer and know I am not to blame, it is a harder matter; but when I suffer and realise that my most intimate relations think I am to blame, that is the limit of suffering. That is where the scourge of suffering lashed Job, the power of the sneer of Satan has come now into his most intimate relationships.

(c) The Solitariness of Sorrow (Job 2:11–13)

Now when Job's three friends heard of all this evil that was come upon him, they came every one from his own place. . . . And when they lifted up their eyes afar off, and knew him not, they lifted up their voice, and wept . . . So they sat down with him upon the ground seven days and seven nights, and none spake a word unto him: for they saw that his grief was very great.

Job's friends were hit desperately by the calamities that had overtaken Job because their creed was the same as his had been, and now if Job was a good man, as their own hearts told them he was, where was their creed? They were dumbfounded with agony, and Job was left without a consoling friend. The friends came slowly to the conclusion that their view of God was right, therefore Job must be wrong. They had the ban of finality[7] about their views, which is always the result of theology being put before God. The friends suffered as well as Job, and the suffering which comes from having outgrown one's theological suit is of an acute order. Job's attitude is—"I cannot understand why God has allowed these things to happen; what He is doing hurts desperately, but I believe that He is honourable, a God of integrity, and I will stick to it that in the end it will be made absolutely clear that He is a God of love and justice and truth."

Nothing is *taught* in the Book of Job, but there is a deep, measured sense of Someone understanding. This man was buffeted and stripped of all he held dear, but in the whirlwind of disaster he remained unblameable, that is, undeserving of censure by God.

THE PASSION OF PESSIMISM
Job 3

*The world sits at the feet of Christ
Unknowing, blind, and unconsoled;
It yet shall touch His garment's fold,
And feel the heavenly Alchemist
Transform its very dust to gold.*

Whittier

Optimism is either a matter of accepted revelation or of temperament; to think unimpeded and remain optimistic is not possible. Let a man face facts as they really are, and pessimism is the only possible conclusion. If there is no tragedy at the back of human life, no gap between God and man, then the Redemption of Jesus Christ is "much ado about nothing." Job is seeing things exactly as they are. A healthy-minded man bases his life on actual conditions, but let him be hit by bereavement, and when he has got beyond the noisy bit and the blasphemous bit, he will find, as Job found, that despair is the basis of human life unless a man accepts a revelation from God and enters into the Kingdom of Jesus Christ.

1. The Irreparable Birth (Job 3:1–7)

After this opened Job his mouth, and cursed his day. . . . Let the day perish wherein I was born. (Job 3:1, 3)

It is a sad thing that Job is facing, and it seems that the only reasonable thing he can do is to mourn the day of his birth. With some people suffering is imaginary, but with Job it has actually happened, and his curse is the real deep conviction of his spirit—"Would to God I had never been born!" The sense of the irreparable is one of the greatest agonies in human life. Adam and Eve entered into the sense of the irreparable when the gates of Paradise clanged behind them. Cain cried out—"My punishment is greater than I can bear." Esau "found no place of repentance, though he sought it diligently with tears." There are things in life which are irreparable; there is no road back to yesterday.

Job's sense of the irreparable brought him face to face with the thing God was face to face with, and when a man gets there he begins to see the meaning of the Redemption. The basis of things is not rational,

---

7. ban of finality: the limitation or "curse" of having one's mind made up, unwilling to consider new information

common sense tells him it is not; the basis of things is tragic, and the Bible reveals that the only way out is through the Redemption. In Job's case it was not a question of his being over-satiated with the pleasures of life, he was suddenly hit without any explanation; his days of prosperity and conscious integrity came to an abrupt end, and, worst of all, his belief in God was assailed.

Real suffering comes when a man's statement of his belief in God is divorced from his personal relationship to God. The statement of belief is secondary, it is never the fundamental thing. It is always well to note the things in life that your explanations do not cover. Job is facing a thing too difficult for him to solve or master; he realises that there is no way out.

2. The Irresponsible Blunder *(Job 3:8–13)*
If you read a book about life by a philosopher and then go out and face the facts of life, you will find the facts do not come within the simple lines laid down in the book. The philosopher's line works like a searchlight does, lighting up what it does and nothing more, daylight reveals a hundred and one facts which the searchlight had not taken into account. There is nothing simple under heaven saving a man's relationship to God on the ground of the Redemption; that is why the Apostle Paul says, "I fear, lest by any means, . . . your minds should be corrupted from the simplicity that is in Christ" (2 Corinthians 11:3).

Reason is our guide among the facts of life, but it does not give us the explanation of them. Sin, suffering, and the Book of God all bring a man to the realisation that there is something wrong at the basis of life, and it cannot be put right by his reason. Our Lord always dealt with the "basement" of life, i.e., with the real problem; if we only deal with "the upper storey" we do not realise the need of the Redemption; but once we are hit on the elemental line, as this war has hit men, everything becomes different. There are many men to-day who for the first time in their lives find themselves in the midst of the elemental with no civilised protection, and they go through appalling agony.

The war has put an end to a great deal of belief in our beliefs. Coleridge's criticism of many so-called Christians was that they did not believe in God, but only believed their beliefs about Him. A man up against things as they are feels that he has lost God, while in reality he has come face to face with Him. It is not platitudes that tell here, but great books, like the Book of Job, which work away down on the implicit line. There are many things in life that look like irresponsible blunders, but the Bible reveals that God has taken the responsibility for these things, and that Jesus Christ has bridged the gap which sin made between God and man; the proof that He has done

so is the Cross. God accepts the responsibility for sin, and on the basis of the Redemption men find their personal way out and an explanation.

3. The Invincible Blackness *(Job 3:13–22)*
These verses are not an indication of pain and suffering, but simply of blackness and a desire for quietness. *Wherefore is light given to him that is in misery, and life unto the bitter in soul; which long for death, but it cometh not; and dig for it more than for hid treasures; which rejoice exceedingly, and are glad, when they can find the grave? (Job 3:20–22)*

In the invincible blackness caused by Job's condition death seems the only way out. In every age which has seen a great upheaval the initial stage has always been marked by the advocacy of suicide, which is an indication of the agony produced by facing things as they are. The basis of things is wild. The only way you can live your life pleasantly is by being either a pagan or a saint; only by refusing to think about things as they are can we remain indifferent.

4. The Inherited Baffling *(Job 3:23–26)*
The sense of being baffled is common, and Job is feeling completely baffled by God's dealings with him. *Why is light given to a man whose way is hid, and whom God hath hedged in? [RV] . . . I was not in safety, neither had I rest, neither was I quiet; yet trouble came. (Job 3:23, 26)*

We may not experience the sense of being baffled by reason of any terrific sorrow, but if we really face the teachings of Jesus Christ in the Sermon on the Mount honestly and drastically, we shall know something of what Job was going through. The teachings of Jesus Christ must produce despair, because if He means what He says, where are we in regard to it? "Blessed are the pure in heart"—blessed is the man who has nothing in him for God to censure. Can I come up to that standard? Yet Jesus says only the pure in heart can stand before God. The New Testament never says that Jesus Christ came primarily to teach men: it says that He came to reveal that He has put the basis of human life on Redemption, that is, He has made it possible for any and every man to be born into the Kingdom where He lives (see John 3:3). Then when we are born again His teaching becomes a description of what God has undertaken to make a man if he will let His power work through him. So long as a man has his morality well within his own grasp he does not need Jesus Christ— "For I came not to call the righteous, but sinners," said Jesus. When a man has been hard hit and realises his own helplessness he finds that it is not a cowardly thing to turn to Jesus Christ, but the way out which God has made for him.

There is a passion of pessimism at the heart of human life and there is no "plaster" for it; you cannot say, "Cheer up, look on the bright side"; there is no bright side to look on. There is only one cure and that is God Himself, and God comes to a man in the form of Jesus Christ. Through Jesus Christ's Redemption the way is opened back to yesterday, out of the blunders and blackness and baffling into a perfect simplicity of relationship to God. Jesus Christ undertakes to enable a man to withstand every one of the charges made by Satan. Satan's aim is to make a man believe that God is cruel and that things are all wrong; but when a man strikes deepest in agony and turns deliberately to the God manifested in Jesus Christ, he will find Him to be the answer to all his problems.

THE LIGHT THAT FAILED
Job 4–5

We live in deeds, not years; in thoughts, not breaths;
In feelings, not in figures on a dial.
We should count time by heart-throbs. He most lives
Who thinks most—feels the noblest—acts the best.
Life's but a means unto an end—that end,
Beginning, mean and end to all things—God.

Philip James Bailey[8]

It is not what a man does that is of final importance, but what he is in what he does. The atmosphere produced by a man, much more than his activities, has the lasting influence.

1. The Premise of Precedent *(Job 4:1–6)*
Eliphaz is the first of the friends to emerge from their dumbfounded silence, and he starts out with the premise that God will never act any differently from the way He has always acted, and that man must not expect He will. The opening verses are a stately introduction to his theme—

> *Behold, thou hast instructed many, and thou hast strengthened the weak hands. Thy words have upholden him that was falling, and thou hast strengthened the feeble knees. But now it is come upon thee, and thou faintest; it toucheth thee, and thou art troubled. (Job 4:3–5)*

The precedent from which Eliphaz argues is that although Job has instructed many and been an upholder of the weak, now that he himself is going through such terrific suffering he must be wrong somewhere. Eliphaz reasons on the ground that Job is experiencing the same kind of trouble as those whom he had previously comforted. This is not true. Job is suffering because God and Satan have made a battleground of his soul, without giving him any warning or any explanation. It is an easy thing to argue from precedent because it makes everything simple, but it is a risky thing to do. Give God "elbow room"; let Him come into His universe as He pleases. If we confine God in His working to religious people or to certain ways, we place ourselves on an equality with God. Job's suffering is not according to precedent; the thing that has struck Job had struck none of those whom he had instructed and comforted. It is a good thing to be careful in our judgement of other men. A man may utter apparently blasphemous things against God and we say, "How appalling"; but if we look further we find that the man is in pain, he is maddened and hurt by something. The mood he is talking in is a passing one and out of his suffering will come a totally different relationship to things. Remember, that in the end God said that the friends had not spoken the truth about Him, whilst Job had.

We are in danger of doing the same thing as Eliphaz; we say that a man is not right with God unless he acts on the line of the precedent we have established. We must drop our measuring-rods for God and for our fellow men. All we can know about God is that His character is what Jesus Christ has manifested; and all we know about our fellow men presents an enigma which precludes the possibility of the final judgement being with us.

2. The Presentation of Preconception *(Job 4:7–21)*
Eliphaz goes on to reason on a preconception, viz. that God blesses the good man, but does not bless the bad man.

> *Remember, I pray thee, who ever perished, being innocent? or where were the righteous cut off? Even as I have seen, they that plow iniquity, and sow wickedness, reap the same. (Job 4:7–8)*

---

8. Philip James Bailey (1816–1902), English poet, author of "Festus," 1839.

Eliphaz takes his argument from Nature: "For whatsoever a man soweth, that shall he also reap"—that God does not punish the upright, and that the innocent do not perish. That simply is not true, and it is this preconception which distorted Eliphaz' point of view. Preconceptions exist in our own head; if we start out with the preconception that God will never allow the innocent to perish and then we see a righteous man perishing, we will have to say, "You cannot be a righteous man, because my preconception tells me that if you were, God would never allow you to suffer; therefore you are proved to be a bad man." When Jesus Christ came on the scene the preconception of the historic people of God was this—"We are the constitution of God, Judaism is God's ordination, therefore You cannot be," and they crucified Him. Our Lord said that His Church would be so completely taken up with its precedents and preconceptions that when He came it would be "as a thief in the night"; they would not see Him because they were taken up with another point of view.

There are people who can silence you with their logic while all the time you know, although you cannot prove it, that they are wrong. This is because the basis of things is not logical, but tragic. Logic and reasoning are only methods of dealing with things as they are; they give no explanation of things as they are.

3. The Preaching from Prejudice *(Job 5:1–16)*

Prejudice means a judgement passed without sufficiently weighing the evidence. We are all prejudiced, and we can only see along the line of our prejudices. The way a prejudice works is seen clearly in Eliphaz: he knows God, and he knows how He will work— God will never allow the righteous to suffer, consequently when he sees the disasters in Job's life he passes judgement right off on Job and says he is not righteous. There is a saying of Bacon's to the effect that if prosperity is the blessing of the Old Testament, adversity is the blessing of the New;[9] and the Apostle Paul says that "all that will live godly in Christ Jesus shall suffer persecution" (2 Timothy 3:12).

In every life there is one place where God must have "elbow room." We must not pass judgement on others, nor must we make a principle of judging out of our own experience. It is impossible for a man to know the views of Almighty God. Preaching from prejudice is dangerous, it makes a man dogmatic and certain that he is right. The question for each of us to ask ourselves is this: Would I recognise God if He came in a way I was not prepared for—if He came in the bustle of a marriage feast, or as a Carpenter? That

is how Jesus Christ appeared to the prejudices of the Pharisees, and they said He was mad. To-day we are trying to work up a religious revival while God has visited the world in a moral revival, and the majority of us have not begun to recognise it. The characteristics that are manifested when God is at work are self-effacement, self-suppression, abandonment to something or someone other than myself, and surely there has never been more evidence of these characteristics than on the part of the men engaged in this war.

4. The Pedagogue of Priggishness *(Job 5:17–27)*

Eliphaz is not only certain what God will do, but he asserts that what Job is going through is chastisement at the hand of God—

Behold, happy is the man whom God correcteth: therefore despise not thou the chastening of the Almighty: for He maketh sore, and bindeth up: He woundeth, and His hands make whole.

—whereas chastisement is a much slighter thing than the real problem of Job's life. The chief ingredient in chastening is that it is meant to develop us, and is a means of expression. The greatest element in the suffering of Job was not chastisement, but the supernatural preface to his story of which he knew nothing. If Eliphaz is right his evidence would prove that Job was a hypocrite; his attitude is that of a pedagogue of priggishness. Beware of priggishness as you would of poison. The danger of pseudo-evangelism is that it makes the preacher a "superior person," not that he is necessarily a prig, but the attitude is produced by the way he has been taught. When Our Lord said to the disciples, "Follow Me, and I will make you fishers of men," His reference was not to the skilled angler, but to those who use the drag-net—something which requires practically no skill; the point being that you have not to watch your "fish," but to do the simple thing and God will do the rest. The pseudo-evangelical line is that you must be on the watch all the time and lose no opportunity of speaking to people, and this attitude is apt to produce the superior person. It may be a noble enough point of view, but it produces the wrong kind of character. It does not produce a disciple of Jesus, but too often the kind of person who smells of gunpowder and people are afraid of meeting him. According to Jesus Christ, what we have to do is to watch the Source and He will look after the outflow: "He that believeth on Me, . . . out of his belly shall flow rivers of living water" (John 7:38). Who are the people who have really benefited you? They are never the ones who think they do, but those who are like the stars or the lilies, no notion of the prig about

---

9. *Essays* (1625) "Of Adversity," by Francis Bacon.

them. It was this form of pseudo-evangelism, so unlike the New Testament evangelism, that made Huxley[10] say—"I object to Christians: they know too much about God." Eliphaz can tell Job everything about God, but when we come to the facts of the case we find that the man who is criticising Job is not fit to sit down beside him. Eliphaz was in a much better condition at the beginning when he did not open his mouth, then he was not a prig, but a man facing facts which had no explanation as yet.

If the study of the Book of Job is making us reverent with what we don't understand, we are gaining insight. There is suffering before which you cannot say a word; you cannot preach "the gospel of temperament"; all you can do is to remain dumb and leave room for God to come in as He likes. The point for us is—Do I believe in God apart from my reasoning about Him? Theology is a great thing, so is a man's creed; but God is greater than either, and the next greatest thing is my relationship to Him.

DE PROFUNDIS
Job 6–7

Oh the regret, the struggle and the failing!
Oh the days desolate and useless years!
Vows in the night, so fierce and unavailing!
Stings of my shame and passion of my tears!

How have I knelt with arms of my aspiring
Lifted all night in irresponsive air,
Dazed and amazed with overmuch desiring,
Blank with the utter agony of prayer!

F. W. H. Myers[11]

At this stage of his suffering Job portrays the terrific despair that can lay hold of a man; yet Job is not interested in himself, his is not the art of expressing the consciousness of every symptom of mind and heart characteristic of so many introspectionists to-day.

1. The Anatomy of Melancholy (Job 6:1–14)
Oh that my grief were throughly weighed, and my calamity laid in the balances together! (Job 6:2).

As previously stated, no sane man who thinks and who is not a Christian can be optimistic. Optimism, apart from a man's belief and his acceptance of Christianity, may be healthy-minded, but it is blinded; when he faces the facts of life as they are, uncoloured by his temperament, despair is the only possible ending for him. There is a melancholy that is insane, it comes from having a fixed idea about things and is the result of a diseased brain; but Job's melancholy is the result of an intense facing of the things that have happened to him, and of his refusal to allow his religious beliefs to blind him to what he sees. Job refuses to tell a lie either for the honour of God or for his own comfort. When a man gets within the outskirts of the

experience of Job's suffering and perplexity and is in touch with the problems at the heart of life, he will probably do one of two things—either tell a lie for the honour of God and say, "I must be much worse than I thought I was," or else accept a form of belief which does away with thinking. Most of us take our salvation much too cheaply. There is no hope for Job, and no hope for anyone on the face of the earth, unless God does something for him. One result of the war will be just this, that when a man faces things he knows despair is inevitable unless there is room for God to perform His almighty acts. This line of things may sound foreign to us because we do not think, we are too contented with what we are; we have not been desperately hit. Job's melancholy is occasioned by his acceptance of the worst point of view, not a temperamental point of view.

2. The Anger against Misunderstanding (Job 6:15–30)
My brethren have dealt deceitfully as a brook, and as the stream of brooks they pass away. (Job 6:15)

Job complains that his friends have "dealt deceitfully as a brook," i.e., they have answered his words and not his meaning (cf.—"wilt Thou indeed be unto me as a deceitful brook, as waters that are not sure?" RV mg.) A Quaker friend of mine referring to a certain man said he did not like him because he did not hate properly. Job's anger seems to be of the order the Apostle Paul mentions—"Be ye angry, and sin not" (Ephesians 4:26); his anger was against the misunderstanding of his friends, he had a right to expect that they would not misunderstand. The reason they misunderstood was that they took Job's words and deliberately denied

---

10. Most likely Thomas Henry Huxley (1825–95), English biologist and teacher.
11. F. W. H. Myers (1843–1901), British poet and educator.

the meaning which they knew must be behind them, and that is a misunderstanding not to be easily excused. It is possible to convey a wrong impression by repeating the exact words of someone else, to convey a lie by speaking the truth, and this is the kind of misunderstanding Job indicates his friends are guilty of. They have stuck steadfastly to his literal words and taken their standpoint not from God, but from the creed they have accepted; consequently they not only criticise Job and call him bad, but they totally misrepresent God. Job's complaint is not the shallow expression often heard—"No one understands me"; he is complaining of misunderstanding based on a misconstruction. He says in effect, "You have given me counsel when I did not ask for it; I am too greatly baffled and can only hold to what I am persuaded of, viz., that I have not done wrong; but I am indignant with you for not understanding."

In a crisis people quote the advice of Gamaliel— "For if this counsel or this work be of men, it will come to nought: but if it be of God, ye cannot overthrow it; lest haply ye be found even to fight against God" (Acts 5:38–39), that is, there is no use fighting against it; whereas the Christian standpoint should be one of positive anger when anyone is made to stumble. To remain indifferent when there is injustice abroad is to come under the curse of Meroz, who "came not to the help of the LORD . . . against the mighty" (Judges 5:23). A conscientious objector is not necessarily a Christian. Conscience is a constituent in a natural man, but a Christian is judged by his personal relationship to God, not by his conscience.

3. The Anguish of Misery *(Job 7:1–11)*

My days are swifter than a weaver's shuttle, and are spent without hope. . . . Therefore I will not refrain my mouth; I will speak in the anguish of my spirit; I will complain in the bitterness of my soul. (Job 7:6, 11)

Misery is an exquisite degree of torture from which there seems no relief; it is very rare. Job suffered in this way, and many people are doing so to-day on account of the war. We all experience these things in a passing mood, but with Job it is no mood, he is facing the real basis of life. That is why the Book of Job is included in the Bible. His words are not the expression of ordinary misery and melancholy, they are the expression of a man face to face with the foundation of human life, which is tragic. Every time Job opens his mouth he proves that the "bottom board" of rationalism is gone, there is nothing reasonable about what he is going through.

The war has proved that the basis of things is what Job discovered it to be—tragic, and men are being driven to realise the need for the Redemption. Facing things as they are will reveal the justification of God in the Redemption. No amount of sacrifice on the part of man can put the basis of human life right: God has undertaken the responsibility for this, and He does it on redemptive lines. Job's suffering comes from seeing the basis of things as they are; and, diseased and wild as Nietzsche was, his madness was probably from the same source. Imagine a man seeing hell without at the same time perceiving salvation through Jesus Christ— his reason must totter. Pseudo-evangelism makes an enormous blunder when it insists on conviction of sin as the first step to Jesus Christ. When we have come to the place of seeing Jesus Christ, then He can trust us with the facing of sin.

In dealing with men like Job or the Apostle Paul we must remember that we are dealing with men whom God uses to give us an estimate of things which we have never experienced. We cannot interpret Job in the light of our own moods; the problem of the whole world is mirrored for us in Job's experiences.

4. The Appeal For Mercy *(Job 7:12–21)*

Job gives utterance to a mood which is not foreign to us when he says, "Am I a sea, or a whale, that Thou settest a watch over me?" In certain moods of anguish the human heart says to God, "I wish You would let me alone, why should I be used for things which have no appeal to me?" In the Christian life we are not being used for our own designs at all, but for the fulfilment of the prayer of Jesus Christ. He has prayed that we might be one with Him as He is one with the Father, consequently God is concerned only about that one thing, and He never says "By your leave." Whether we like it or not, God will burn us in His fire until we are as pure as He is, and it is during the process that we cry, as Job did, "I wish You would leave me alone." God is the only Being who can afford to be misunderstood; we cannot, Job could not, but God can. If we are misunderstood we "get about" the man as soon as we can. St. Augustine prayed, "O Lord, deliver me from this lust of always vindicating myself." God never vindicates Himself, He deliberately stands aside and lets all sorts of slanders heap on Him, yet He is not in any hurry.

We have the idea that prosperity, or happiness, or morality, is the end of a man's existence; according to the Bible it is something other, viz., "to glorify God and enjoy Him for ever." When a man is right with God, God puts His honour in that man's keeping. Job was one of those in whom God staked His honour, and it was during the process of His inexplicable ways that Job makes his appeal for mercy, and yet all through there comes out his implicit confidence in God. "And blessed is he, whosoever shall not be offended in Me," said Our Lord.

THE INTERROGATIVE PLASTER
Job 8

If thou couldst empty all thyself of self.
Like to a shell dishabited,
Then might He find thee on the Ocean shelf,
And say—"This is not dead,"—
And fill thee with Himself instead.
But thou art all replete with very thou,
And hast such shrewd activity,
That, when He comes, He says:—"This is enow
Unto itself—'Twere better let it be:
It is so small and full, there is no room for Me."
T. E. Brown[12]

Bildad differs from Eliphaz in his condemnation of Job: Eliphaz declares straight off that Job is wrong, while Bildad takes another line—that of asking questions; neither of them come anywhere near the reason for Job's suffering. There is an element of "Yes—but" in us all, and for most of us the problems that are nearly strangling a man have no meaning, they seem extravagant and wild. Bildad did not begin to detect where the real problem of Job's suffering lay, and we must beware in our attitude toward people who are suffering that we do not blunder by imagining our point of view to be the only one. Bildad tries the application of the interrogative plaster, he puts Job off by asking questions. That is generally the way of the man who refuses to face problems.

1. The Plaint of "How" *(Job 8:1–2)*
Then answered Bildad the Shuhite and said, How long wilt thou speak these things? and how long shall the words of thy mouth be like a strong wind?

Bildad turns attention away from what is making Job speak to his actual words—"Why do you talk so much?"—but he does not take the trouble to find out the reason. When we come across a foul-mouthed, blasphemous man any number of us are ready to reprove him for the one who will try to discover why he speaks thus. Job is looking for someone who will understand what lies behind his talk, but he finds only those who are far removed from his problem.

To say that because Job lived in another dispensation therefore what he went through does not apply to us, is an easy, artificial shifting of the ground. There are characteristics which are different, but the problems manifested in the Book of Job remain the same to this day. According to consistent argument, the

New Testament saint should be leagues ahead of the Old Testament saint, but in reality no character in the New Testament is superior to those in the Old Testament. The revelation of Redemption given through our Lord Jesus Christ is retrospective in our day; in the Old Testament it is prospective. Job goes down to the heart of the problems that make the Redemption necessary, while Bildad, with his interrogative plaster and pious dealing with the problems, is really shirking the whole thing.

2. The Place of "Doth" *(Job 8:3)*
Doth God pervert judgement? or doth the Almighty pervert justice?

The trick of the sincere shirker is indicated in Bildad, which is always the result of being hit unexpectedly. We are all sincere shirkers, more or less; when we find ourselves suddenly discerned we turn the discernment off to something else for the time being (cf. John 4:16–20). In putting these abstractions before Job, Bildad is implying that Job's problem is not so difficult to understand: his suffering is caused by his own wrong-doing, and God's judgement is perfectly right. It is a trying thing to continue with a man who persists in giving an abstract supposition as a concrete fact.

3. The Philosophy of "If" *(Job 8:4–6)*
If thy children have sinned against him, . . . if thou wouldest seek unto God betimes, . . . if thou wert pure and upright. . . .

The implication behind all these suppositions is: "Even if you are as wrong as Eliphaz has made out, you are not suffering so much as you imagine, and there is no big problem at the heart of things. God is not unjust, but you are, and that is the reason for it all." When problems are pressing very hard there is always someone who brings a suggestion of "if," or "but," or "how," to take us off the track. If our problems can be solved by other men, they are not problems but simply muddles. When we come to the real downright problems of life, which have no explicit answer saving by the Designer of life, we are exactly where Job was, and we can understand his petulance with those who tried to answer him. If Job's friends had remained dumb and reverent with what they did

12. Thomas Edward Brown (1830–97), British poet.

not understand, as they did during the first seven days, they would have been a great sustaining to him, and they too would have approached the place Job ultimately reached and would not have been rebuked by God.

The "gospel of temperament" works very well if you are suffering only from psychical neuralgia, so to speak, and all you need is a cup of tea; but if you have a real deep complaint, the injunction to "Cheer up" is an insult. What is the use of telling a woman who has lost her husband and sons in the war to "Cheer up and look on the bright side"? There *is* no bright side, it is absolute blackness, and if God cannot come to her help, truly she is in a pitiable condition. It is part of the role of a man to be honest enough to know when he is up against cases like this. A gospel based on preconceived notions is merely an irritant. Bildad had his creed and his notion of God: Job does not fit into these, therefore it is a bad look out for Job—"My point of view of God cannot be wrong, therefore you must be."

4. The Pose of Platitude *(Job 8:7–10)*
For enquire, I pray thee, of the former age, and prepare thyself to the search of their fathers: . . . shall not they teach thee, and tell thee, and utter words out of their heart?

The line Bildad takes up in these verses is like a man telling the inmates of an asylum that it is better being sane than mad—but meantime they are mad! Bildad denies that Job is facing a problem never faced by his fathers. We are apt to forget that there is always an element in human suffering never there before. Tennyson puts this finely in "In Memoriam":

> *One writes that, "Other friends remain"*
> *That "Loss is common to the race"—*
> *And common is the commonplace,*
> *And vacant chaff well meant for grain*
> *That loss is common would not make*
> *My own less bitter, rather more:*
> *Too common! Never morning wore*
> *To evening, but some heart did break.*

There is a great deal in both joy and sorrow that is similar in everyone's case, but always one element entirely different; the platitudinarian evades this. On the human side the only thing to do for a man who is up against these deeper problems is to remain kindly agnostic. The biggest benediction one man can find in another is not in his words, but that he implies: "I do not know the answer to your problem, all I can say is that God alone must know; let us go to Him." It would have been much more to the point if the friends had begun to intercede for Job; if they had said, "This is a matter for God, not for us; our creed cannot begin to touch it"; but all they did was to take to "chattermagging"[13] and telling Job that he was wrong. When God emerged, He put His imprint on what Job had said of Him, and His disapproval on what the friends had said.

If Redemption is not the basis of human life, and prayer man's only resource, then we have "followed cunningly devised fables." Over and over again during this war men have turned to prayer, not in the extreme of weakness, but of limitation; whenever a man gets beyond the limit he unconsciously turns to God. Eliphaz claimed to know exactly where Job was, and Bildad claims the same thing. Job was hurt, and these men tried to heal him with platitudes. The place for the comforter is not that of one who preaches, but of the comrade who says nothing, but prays to God about the matter. The biggest thing you can do for those who are suffering is not to talk platitudes, not to ask questions, but to get into contact with God, and the "greater works" will be done by prayer (see John 14:12–13). Job's friends never once prayed for him; all they did was to try and make coin for the enrichment of their own creed out of his sufferings. We are not intended to understand Life. Life makes us what we are, but Life belongs to God. If I can understand a thing and can define it, I am its master. I cannot understand or define Life; I cannot understand or define God; consequently I am master of neither. Logic and reason are always on the hunt for definition, and anything that cannot be defined is apt to be defied, Rationalism usually defies God and defies life; it will not have anything that cannot be defined on a rational basis, forgetting that the things that make up elemental human life cannot be defined. There are teachers to-day who play the fool on these elemental lines; they declare that they can give guidance, but they only succeed in doing a fathomless amount of harm. A man is a criminal for knowing some things, he has no right to know them. The primal curse of God was on Adam when he ate the fruit of the tree of the knowledge of good and evil. Adam was intended to know good and evil, but not by eating of the fruit of the tree; God wanted him to know good and evil in the way Jesus Christ knew it, viz., by simple obedience to His Father. None of us by nature knows good and evil in this way, and when we are born from above we have to take care that we deal with reverence with the elemental things underlying life.

---

13. chattermagging: jabbering; spouting off; rambling on.

5. The Point of "Can" *(Job 8:11)*
Can the rush grow up without mire? can the flag grow without water?

Bildad uses an argument from Nature and he tries to make his argument consistent with his illustration. We are apt to run an illustration to death in logical sequence; the Bible never does. An illustration should simply be a window which does not call attention to itself. If you take an illustration from Nature and apply it to a man's moral life or spiritual life, you will not be true to facts because the natural law does not work in the spiritual world. In the first place, a law is not a concrete thing, but a constructive mental abstraction whereby the human mind explains what it sees. God says, "And I will restore to you the years that the locust hath eaten . . ."; that is not a natural law, and yet it is what happens in the spiritual world. In the natural world it is impossible to be made all over again, but in the spiritual world it is exactly what Jesus Christ makes possible. "Verily, verily, I say unto thee, Except a man be born again, he cannot see the kingdom of God" (John 3:3). What is true is that as there *is* a law in the natural world so there *is* a law in the spiritual world, i.e., a way of explaining things, but the law is not the same in both worlds. Bildad takes his illustration from the rush and the flag and applies it to Job, but he is more concerned about being consistent with his illustration than with the facts of Job's experience. If you are a logician you may often gain your point in a debate and yet feel yourself in the wrong. You get the best of it in disputing with some people because their minds are not clever, but when you get away from your flush of triumph you feel you have missed the point altogether; you have won on debate, but not on fact. You cannot get at the basis of things by disputing. Our Lord Himself comes off sec-ond best every time in a logical argument, and yet you know that He has in reality come off "more than conqueror." Jesus Christ lived in the moral domain and, in a sense, the intellect is of no use there. Intellect is not a guide, but an instrument.

6. The Practice of Piousness *(Job 8:12–22)*
Behold, God will not cast away a perfect man, neither will He help the evil doers. (Job 8:20)

Bildad is cultivating the margin of his eyesight, so to speak. This is a trick of the piousness not based on a personal relationship to God. Bildad is apparently speaking of an abstraction while all the time he is criticising Job—it is Job who is the hypocrite and the fraud. It is not meanness in Bildad that makes him do this, but "limitedness"—he is "all replete with very thou." Bildad has never seen God, while Job is getting near the place where he will see Him. All the god Bildad has is his creed; if he had known the real God he would have prayed to Him, and would have recognised the facts that were too big for him. Whenever we put belief in a creed in place of belief in God, we become this particular kind of humbug. To "imply wrong by my right" is the trick of every man who puts his creed before his relationship to God.

During this war many a man has come to find the difference between his creed and God. At first a man imagines he has backslidden because he has lost belief in his beliefs, but later on he finds he has gained God, i.e., he has come across Reality. If Reality is not to be found in God, then God is not found anywhere. If God is only a creed or a statement of religious belief, then He is not real; but if God is, as the Book of Job brings to light, One with whom a man gets into personal contact in other ways than by his intellect, then any man who touches the reality of things, touches God.

AGNOSTICISM
Job 9–10

Pour forth and bravely do your part,
O knights of the unshielded heart!
Forth and forever forward!—out
From prudent turret and redoubt,
And in the mellay charge amain,
To fall but yet to rise again.

R. L. Stevenson

Agnosticism is not always the deplorable thing it is imagined to be. An acknowledged intellectual agnosticism is a healthy thing; the difficulty arises when agnosticism is not acknowledged. To be an agnostic means I recognise that there is more than I know, and that if I am ever to know more, it must be by revelation.

1. The Cosmic Refraction of God *(Job 9:1–12)*
If you accept Jesus Christ's presentation of God and then look at the present order of the material universe you will find what is meant by the phrase, "the cosmic refraction of God." Whenever God presents Himself in the present order of things, He appears refracted, that is, distorted to our reason; we cannot understand Him. When a man comes face to face with Nature, God seems to be almighty against all his

conceptions. God allows things in the cosmic world which are a refraction, they do not continue in the straight, simple line my mind tells me they ought to take. Job says, in effect, "If God chooses to be almighty against me, where am I? If he will contend with Him, he cannot answer Him one of a thousand." The eccentric old poet, George Herbert, has a poem in which this phrase recurs—

> *Be not Almightie, let me say*
> *Against, but for me.*

The reason for Job's agony and distress is not a temperamental one; he has been brought to the heart of things and finds tragedy there, and a gap. The only way out is by means of the Redemption; in the meantime Job is stating the perplexity as it appears to a man who is really beginning to think. Every one of us in our day and generation whether we have ever thought deeply or not, has faced this problem: If God is love, why does He allow the hawk to kill the sparrow? As Tennyson puts it—". . . Nature, red in tooth and claw." Why does He allow one animal to feed on another? Why are nations allowed to fight each other? These are not passing perplexities but real puzzles, and the only thing to do is either to deny the facts or to confess we are agnostic. Job is up against the problem that things do not look as they should if God is the kind of God his implicit belief constrains him to declare He ought to be. Job's friends deny the facts; they won't have it that there is any perplexity, and they say to Job, "The reason God appears refracted is because you yourself are refracted."

The cosmic force makes God appear indifferent and cruel and remote, and if you become a special pleader of any particular creed you have to shut your eyes to facts. The only revelation which gives a line of explanation is that there is something wrong at the basis of things, hence the refraction. The Apostle Paul says that creation is all out of gear and twisted; it is waiting "for the manifestation of the sons of God." In the meantime, the problem remains.

Look at the world through either a microscope or a telescope and you will be dwarfed into terror by the infinitely minute or the infinitely great; both are appalling. When you touch the cosmic force, apart from the blinkers of intellect, there is a wild problem in it. Nature is wild, not tame. No man is capable of solving the riddle of the universe because the universe is mad, and the only thing that will put it right is not man's reason, but the sagacity of God which is manifested in the Redemption of Jesus Christ. A Christian is an avowed agnostic intellectually; his attitude is, "I have reached the limit of my knowledge, and I

humbly accept the revelation of God given by Jesus Christ."

2. The Conscious Resurgence of Goodness (*Job 9:13–20*)

How much less shall I answer Him, and choose out my words to reason with Him? Whom though I were righteous, yet would I not answer, but I would make supplication to my judge. (Job 9:14–15)

"Resurgence" is used here to mean the re-consideration of a former judgement. The majority of us start out with the belief that God is good and kind, and that He prospers those who trust in Him. Job believed this, but he has a conscious resurgence against that belief now, and it is Job's goodness, not his badness, which makes him reconsider things. There are things in the experience of us all which call for a revision of our credal findings about God; there are other elements that will not come into our declaration as to the kind of Being He is.

Eliphaz and Bildad have no problem along this line; their one aim is to convict Job of being a blackguard. The sign of dishonesty in a man's creed is that he finds out defects in everyone save himself—"It is not possible for me to be mistaken in my view of God." Bildad and Eliphaz would not admit that they could be wrong; they had the ban of finality[14] about their views. Trouble always arises when men will not revise their views of God. Bildad tells Job that if he was upright he would not suffer as he did. Job maintains—"I am upright, and yet everything has gone wrong with me." Job stuck steadily to facts, not to consistency to his creed. Over and over again a man is said to be a disbeliever when he is simply outgrowing his creed. It is a most painful thing for a man to find that his stated views of God are not adequate. Never tell a lie for the honour of God; it is an easy thing to do. Job refuses a presentation of God which does not face the facts; he has no scepticism about God, no hesitation about His existence, but he does tirade all the time against the way in which He is being presented.

3. The Concentrated Reaction of Grief (*Job 9:21–35*)

For He is not a man, as I am, that I should answer Him, and we should come together in judgement. Neither is there any daysman betwixt us, that might lay his hand upon us both. (Job 9:32–33)

Job is giving expression to a new conception of God; his hope is that an umpire, a daysman, will arise who will not only justify God, but also justify him. "My

---

14. ban of finality: the limitation or "curse" of having one's mind made up, unwilling to consider new information

creed does not do this," he says, "neither does my experience, or my way of looking at things." It was grief that brought Job to this place, and grief is the only thing that will; joy does not, neither does prosperity, but grief does. The great factor in the life of Jesus Christ, the Redeemer of the world, is this very thing—". . . Yet it pleased the LORD to bruise Him" (Isaiah 53:10). Once grief touches a man he is full of reaction, he says spiteful things because he is hurt, but in the end grief leads a man to the right point of view, viz. that the basis of things is tragic. As long as I am happy and things go well, I say what a famous philosopher said—"This is the best of all possible worlds." It plainly is not, and the Bible reveals why it is not. The world as God originally designed it, was the best of all possible worlds, but it has now become the worst of all possible worlds; in fact, the Bible reveals that it could not be any worse than it is. Individual men who take the wrong line get worse, but the world itself cannot get worse. Grief brings a man to see this more quickly than anything else, and he longs for an umpire who will hold the scales.

There is no use telling Job that there is no God or that he has not suffered: he has had too much experience of God and of suffering. It is useless to tell him that his creed is the umpire that arbitrates between himself and God: it leaves too much unsolved. Job is the type of man who could never rest in the Church, or in the Scriptures; he needs living Reality. The man who rests in a creed is apt to be a coward and refuse to come into a personal relationship with God. The whole point of vital Christianity is not the refusal to face things, but a matter of personal relationship, and it is the kind of thing that Job went through which brings a man to this issue.

4. The Conceptions for Rejection
(Job 10:1–17)
Job's utterances are the last word in the expression of certain forms of grief. These particular verses are stately and terrific; Job is trying to state to his own mind why God seems to have rejected him, and also why he should reject the way God is being presented to him—

> *Thou knowest that I am not wicked; and there is none that can deliver out of Thine hand. Thine hands have made me and fashioned me together round about; yet Thou dost destroy me. (Job 10:7–8)*

All along Job bases his conceptions on the facts which he knows, and this is the only thing to do, although

many of us would rather tell a lie for the honour of God than face the facts. A fanatic is one who entrenches himself in invincible ignorance. Job will not accept anything that contradicts the facts he knows; he is not splenetic, he does not say God is cruel, he simply states the facts—"It looks as though God is rejecting me without any reason, all the facts go to prove this and I am not going to blink them." Job will not lay a flattering unction to his soul on the line of expediency. No man ever puts a stumbling-block in the way of others by telling the truth; to tell the truth is more honouring to God than to tell a lie. If God has done something for you, you will know it unmistakably, but if He has not, never say He has for the sake of other people. Job sticks to facts, that is what confuses his friends; but in the end Job is brought face to face with God.

5. The Case for Refuge *(Job 10:18–22)*
Are not my days few? Cease then, and let me alone, that I may take comfort a little, before I go whence I shall not return, even to the land of darkness and the shadow of death. (Job 10:20–21)

"I see no way out," says Job. He lies down, not in weakness, but in absolute exhaustion. Job is not talking in a petted mood, but saying that unless God will be a Refuge for him, there is no way out, death is the only thing. In every crisis of life, as represented in the Old Testament as well as in the teaching of Our Lord, this aspect of God is emphasised—"God is our Refuge"; yet until we are hit by sorrow, it is the last thing we seek for God to be. There is a difference between the weakness of refusing to think and the weakness that comes from facing facts as they really are. Job is seeing for the first time that God is the only Refuge, the only way out for him; yet he cannot get at Him through his creed, it is all confusion; the only thing to do is to fling himself on God.

It is this aspect of God which is at the basis of the Redemption. When a man gets convicted of sin (which is the most direct way of knowing that there is a problem at the basis of life), he knows that he cannot carry the burden of it; he also knows that God dare not forgive him; if He did, it would mean that man's sense of justice is bigger than God's. If I am forgiven without being altered, forgiveness is not only damaging to me, but a sign of unmitigated weakness in God. Unless it is possible for God's forgiveness to establish an order of holiness and rectitude, forgiveness is a mean[15] and abominable thing.

The human problem is too big for a man to solve, but if he will fling himself unperplexed on God he

---

15. mean: ordinary, common, low, or ignoble, rather than cruel or spiteful

will find Him to be the kind of Refuge Job is referring to. We know nothing about the Redemption or about forgiveness until we are enmeshed by the personal problem; then we begin to understand why we need to turn to God, and when we do turn to Him He becomes a Refuge and a Shelter and a complete Rest. Up to the present Job has had no refuge anywhere; now he craves for it. When a man receives the Holy Spirit, his problems are not altered, but he has a Refuge from which he can deal with them; before, he was out in the world being battered, now the centre of his life is at rest and he can begin, bit by bit, to get things uncovered and rightly related.

BOMBAST
Job 11

I have not knowledge, wisdom, insight, thought.
Or understanding, fit to justify
Thee in thy work, O Perfect. Thou hast brought
Me up to this—and, lo! what thou hast wrought,
I cannot call it good. But I can cry—
"O enemy, the maker hath not done:
One day thou shalt behold, and from the sight
*   wilt run."*

George MacDonald

1. Stirring of Self-Respecting Indignation (Job 11:1–4)
Then answered Zophar the Naamathite and said,
Should not the multitude of words be answered? And
should a man full of talk be justified (Job 11:1–2)

Zophar is manifesting the linguistic characteristic of Job. He begins by accusing Job of using a "multitude of words," thus blinding his mind to the point at stake. If you are annoyed with someone, notice how uncomfortably conscious you are that there is an element in him you cannot reach, and rather than allow the recognition of that element you work yourself up into self-respecting indignation. Zophar has come to the conclusion that Job is wrong, his creed is wrong, and "I alone am justified." This trick of stirring up self-respecting indignation is a very common subterfuge when we are embarrassed by a problem involving our self-respect. The temptation comes to yield to the bombastic mood, and we use terms of righteous indignation to condemn the thing we are not guilty of, while all the time we may be guilty of tenfold worse.

2. Schemes of Spurious Invocation (Job 11:5–10)
But oh that God would speak, and open His lips
against thee; and that He would show thee the secrets
of wisdom. . . . Canst thou by searching find out God?
Canst thou find out the Almighty unto perfection (Job
11:5–7)

Another trick of bombastic religion is to appeal to God in order to back up a position which is obviously questionable. Here, Zophar calls God in as his ally in his attack on Job. We do it in our way of praying; our invocations and iterations often spring from false emotions; they are not spontaneous. Most of us mouth diction before God; we do not pray; we say in prayer what we ought to say, not what is actually natural to us to say. It may sound very interesting and noble, but it is not our own, it is mere sounding brass and clanging cymbals, there is no reality in it.

Another form of spurious invocation affects the idea that God is punishing our nation for certain wrongs, instead of feeling the presence of something more profound. When we are facing problems we must see to it that we are reverent and silent, for the most part, with what we do not understand. The invocation of God is an exercise of the finest spiritual mood, and we are rarely in a sufficiently exalted state of mind for it. To invocate on the assumption that we know God, comes near to blasphemy.

3. Self-Consciousness of Serious Instruction (Job 11:11–15)
If iniquity be in thine hand, put it far away, and let
not wickedness dwell in thy tabernacles. For then shalt
thou lift up thy face without spot; yea, thou shalt be
steadfast, and shalt not fear. (Job 11:14–15)

Zophar tries to instruct Job on an entirely false basis; he declares that Job will never get wisdom. "For vain man would be wise, though man be born like a wild ass's colt." This is all the length Zophar gets in dealing with a man who towers leagues above him! First, he stirs up self-respecting indignation, then he takes a religious turn, then an instructive turn, which puts the wrong self on top at once. The characteristic of this kind of instruction is that it is self-conscious. The most valuable instruction in moral life never comes from people who consciously instruct us, for we are not taught morally as we are intellectually. Confusion always results if we take the method of instruction used in intellectual life and apply it to moral life, and make certain people moral instructors. It is an abortion for any human being to dare to put himself in the position of a moral superior to another man, and this is what Zophar did with Job. No man is consciously a moral superior to another man; if he is superior intellectually that is largely a matter of upbringing. The real basis of moral instruction lies much deeper down, viz. in God, and God instructs us along the line symbolised by the Christian sacrament, which means the real presence of God being conveyed to us through the common elements. God uses children, and books, and flowers in the spiritual instruction of a man, but He seldom uses the self-conscious prig who consciously instructs. The "Zophar" type has recurred all through the Christian centuries—the man who assumes he knows, and frequently the average man is led to say, "If experts in spiritual matters do not know these things, who am I that I should?" There are no experts in spiritual matters as there are in scientific matters. The spiritual expert is never so consciously because the very nature of spiritual instruction is that it is unconscious of itself; it is the life of a child, manifesting obedience, not ostentation. Our Lord describes the spiritual expert in Matthew 18:4—"Whosoever therefore shall humble himself as this little child, the same is greatest in the kingdom of heaven."

4. Self-Complacency of Sentimental Integrity *(Job 11:16–20)*

. . . because thou shalt forget thy misery, and remember it as waters that pass away: and thine age shall be clearer than the noonday; thou shalt shine forth, thou shalt be as the morning. (Job 11:16–17)

Zophar is the type of a demagogue, the man who rules with his tongue. Any kind of absolute creed ends where Zophar ended—on the sentimental line, where things reach a pitch of enthusiastic presentation not based on facts. The sentimental line blinds man's thinking by an ecstasy of thought; it enables an orator to awaken human sentiment and sympathy, but in dealing with trouble it proves a false line; it gives impertinent advice to a man who is broken-hearted. Zophar implies that he knows exactly the kind of integrity that will stand before God and before man.

Self-respecting indignation nowadays is not on the "Zophar" line, but on the anti-Zophar, i.e., the anti-religious. Before the war it was not religious but irreligious humbug that was prevalent. Men pretended they were not religious while secretly they were.

If you are a religious person of the "Zophar" type and can work up sufficient religious indignation, you will come to the conclusion that you and God must go together, it is quite impossible for you to be mistaken; then you will begin to instruct others on the same line, and will inevitably end by placing things in a totally false light.

ON THE TRAIL
Job 12–14

True religion is betting one's life there is a God.

Donald Hankey

1. The Charge of Inveterate Intolerance *(Job 12:1–5)*

And Job answered and said, No doubt but ye are the people, and wisdom shall die with you. But I have understanding as well as you; I am not inferior to you; yea, who knoweth not such things as these. (Job 12:1–3)

Job is speaking in a mood of annoyance, he rebels against the intolerance of his friends who do not give him credit for having any common-sense. If we talk with a man who is dealing with the fundamentals, he may appear to pay no attention to any common-sense explanation we offer because his deep is beyond our deep, so we instantly credit him with having no common sense and get back to our own shallows. The

friends charge Job with a lack of seeing the obvious, and Job replies, "I am facing things you have not begun to dream about; why don't you either plunge into the deeps with me, or else keep silent, if you cannot tell me what to do?" A religious view which causes a man to deal only with the shallow side has the ban of finality about it.

2. Common Sense of Irrefutable Inference *(Job 12:6–25)*

Who knoweth not in all these that the hand of the LORD hath wrought this? In whose hand is the soul of every living thing, and the breath of all mankind. (Job 12:9–10)

Job accuses the friends of telling lies for the honour of God. That is the danger of putting theology first; it leads a man to tell a lie in order to be consistent with his point of view. Job is speaking not with the view of disproving God, but of proving that the religious conceptions of these men are not right. The things Job states are commonsense, obvious things, and they flatly contradict the creed he had believed, and which his friends are pushing down his throat. Are we going to remain true to our religious convictions or to the God who lives behind them?—true to our denominational view of God or to the God who gave the denomination its initial inspiration? Are we going to be mere sticklers for the theological statement? In the ecclesiastical history of Scotland many a man has gone to martyrdom rather than let his theology go. The organised Church is up against these things to-day.

Theology is tested by history and logic; religion must be tested by experience.

Job's creed has crumbled into ruins, "therefore," he says, "I leave my creed, but I deny that I have left God." In a theological dispute the theologian is apt to put his point of view in the place of God. "But if any man seem to be contentious, we have no such custom," says St. Paul. Only one man in a thousand can maintain his spiritual life and controvert; he may increase his intellectual vim, but he does not increase his spiritual grasp of things. Dr. Alexander Whyte[16] put this better than any other when he said:

Oh, the unmitigated curse of controversy! Oh, the detestable passions that corrections and contradictions kindle up to fury in the proud heart of man! Eschew controversy, my brethren, as you would eschew the entrance to hell itself. Let them have it their way; let them talk; let them write; let them correct you; let them traduce you; let them judge and condemn you; let them slay you. Rather let the truth of God suffer itself, than that love suffer. You have not enough of the divine nature in you to be a controversialist. "He was oppressed and He was afflicted yet He opened not His mouth; He is brought as a lamb to the slaughter, and as a sheep before its shearers is dumb, so He openeth not His mouth." "Who when He was reviled, reviled not again when He suffered, He threatened not; . . . by whose stripes ye were healed." "Heal me," prays Augustine, again and again, "of this lust of mine of always vindicating myself."

We start out with the notion that God is an almighty piece of ourselves, but God can never be on the side of any individual; the question to ask is—"Am I on God's side?" In 2 Thessalonians 2, Paul talks about the invincible ignorance of fanaticism and he says that

if a man is deluded, he is to blame. On the other hand Job says, "I am not going to say that my former definition of God is true; God must be true. but I find that the way I have expounded Him is not true." This put Job on the right track to find God. Are we on the trail of God, or on the obstinate, intolerant line, where we argue for our statements instead of for the truth? Does our religion put us on the line of understanding the revelation of God, or is it merely a blind authority? It is a good thing to take stock of the things which commonsense inferences and religion cannot explain.

3. The Conception of Invincible Ignorance (Job 13:1–12)
What ye know, the same do I know also. (Job 13:2)

This verse is a description of the fanaticism which builds on one point of view only and is determinedly ignorant of everything else. This is the thing Job rages against all the time—"God must be other than you have stated because of what I have experienced," and Job is right. It is possible to build logical edifices on a theological position and at the same time to prove in practical life that the position is wrong. For example, on the metaphysical line the predestinations of God seem clear, but our conception of those predestinations may prove dangerously false when we come to the actual facts of life.

The theological view ought to be constantly examined; If we put it in the place of God we become invincibly ignorant, that is, we won't accept any other point of view, and the invincible ignorance of fanaticism leads to delusions for which we alone are to blame. The fundamental things are not the things which can be proved logically in practical life.

Watch where you are inclined to be invincibly ignorant, and you will find your point of view causes you to break down in the most vital thing. An accepted view of God has caused many a man to fail at the critical moment, it has kept him from being the kind of man he ought to be, and only when he abandons his view of God for God Himself, does he become the right kind of man.

4. The Consecration of Instinctive Integrity (Job 13:13–28)
Hold your peace, let me alone, that I may speak, and let come on me what will. Wherefore do I take my flesh in my teeth, and put my life in mine hand! Though He slay me, yet will I trust in Him. (Job 13:13–15)

Job feels that in spite of all that is happening, God's integrity remains, and his own integrity. He cannot

---

16. Alexander Whyte (1836–1921), Scottish minister who influenced Chambers during Oswald's time at Edinburgh University, 1895–96.

explain his sufferings by saying, "I am being punished because I have done wrong," or, "I am suffering because I needed to be perfected." The friends have accused Job of being a hypocrite and imply that he is also an atheist, but just at this very time Job gives expression to the most sublime utterance of faith in the whole of the Old Testament—"Though He slay me, yet will I trust in Him." "Though He, whom you are misrepresenting, and whom I cannot state in words—though He slay me, I will trust in the fact that He is full of the integrity I believe Him to be, and I will wait for Him. I will face my own common-sense integrity, and dedicate my instinctive sense of God's integrity, and in the end I know that both will work out into one."

Always remain true to facts and to the intuitive certainty that God must be just, and do not try to justify Him too quickly. The juggling trick tries to justify God for allowing sin and war. Sin and war are absolutely unjustifiable, and yet the instinct of every Christian is—"I know that in the end God will justify Himself." Meantime you can only justify Him by a venture of faith which cannot be logically demonstrated.

5. The Consciousness of Implicit Infirmity (Job 14)

O that Thou wouldest hide me in the grave, that Thou wouldest keep me secret, until Thy wrath be past, that Thou wouldest appoint me a set time, and remember me! If a man die, shall he live again? all the days of my appointed time will I wait, till my change come. (Job 14:13–14)

Job has discovered that the basis of things is tragic, not logical. "I know I am weak and there are facts in my life and in human history which I cannot explain, but because of my conscious infirmity I know that God will see me through it all and out the other side; meanwhile I refuse to accept a creed which misrepresents God, and also misrepresents me." To get there means a man is on the right trail.

Job's integrity remains as well as his conscious infirmity, and also the sense that he is not entirely to blame for his sinfulness. No man is held responsible by God for having an heredity of sin: what God holds a man responsible for is refusing to let Jesus Christ deliver him from it when he sees that that is what He came to do (see John 3:19).

Judged by average theology, many of Job's utterances sound far from right, yet in reality they are full of reverence. He is saying that in any statement about God there must be some indication that will justify Him in allowing human beings to be infirm—"Your statement of God is not only untrue to man, but blasphemously untrue to God." Job states the facts of human experience, and that there seems to be an unsatisfactory end to life—"Just when I was going to grasp the thing and find the fulfilment of all my desires, I am cut off." There are countless men like that to-day; just when life was at its best and highest, suddenly they are swept clean off.

We get an expression of Job's meaning in verses 13–22 when we say of a man—"Well, he is dead now, and although he did not come up to the standard of our orthodox religion. we will leave him in the hands of a merciful God!" That is a subterfuge. Job states the facts and he is strong on the point that he will get to the place where he will see God justified in what He has allowed to happen. Never take a suspended judgement as final, but watch for the chance of getting fresh light on the matter. It is never sufficient to take a mental safety valve as the end of the matter. Many problems which arise from a man's instinctive integrity have not been answered; no theological statement can make answer to them, and we have to watch that we do not accept any statement which our instinctive nature tells us is a lie. We have our guide in Jesus Christ; we must never accept a view of God which contradicts what He manifested—"I am the Way, the Truth and the Life." The vital thing is to get on the trail of a personal relationship to God, and then use the facts of experience and of revelation to bring us to a consideration of things which satisfies our nature, and until it is satisfied, don't say it is. "I will stick to it that God is a God of love and justice, and I look forward to the time when I shall see it manifestly." We have no business to say piously, "Oh, I leave it with God." God will have us discern what He is doing, but it takes time because we are so slow to obey, and only as we obey do we perceive morally and spiritually.

PONDEROSITY
Job 15

A pill to cure an earthquake. . . .
                                    G. K. Chesterton

There is nothing more ludicrous than the way in which some folk try to soothe sorrow and deal with trouble in other lives. Eliphaz makes out that Job's problems are not what he thinks they are; he tries to wear down Job's opposition by sheer ponderosity, i.e., saying nothing with terrific emphasis. One can almost hear him choking with indignation: "What knowest thou, that we know not? . . ." (Job 15:9). Then follows the revealing of the unconscious egotism of the orthodox credist, dictatorially asserting the character of God (Job 15:14–16). Then, like a theological buzzard, he sits on the perch of massive tradition and preens his ruffled feathers and croaks his eloquent platitudes. There is no trace of the fraud in Eliphaz, he vigorously believes his beliefs, but he is at a total loss to know God. Eliphaz represents the kind of humbug that results from remaining true to conviction instead of to facts which dispute the conviction. The difference between an obstinate man and a strong-minded man lies just here: an obstinate man refuses to use his intelligence when a matter is in dispute, while a strong-minded man makes his decision after having deliberately looked at it from all standpoints, and when opposed, he is willing to give reasons for his decision.

1. The Weapons of the Temporising Mind *(Job 15:1–6)*

Then answered Eliphaz the Temanite and said, Should a wise man suffer vain knowledge, and fill his belly with the east wind? Should he reason with unprofitable talk? or with speeches wherewith he can do no good? (Job 15:1–3).

A temporising mind is one that takes its position from immediate circumstances and never alters that position. Eliphaz says that Job is simply bombastic; he sees in Job what he is himself. The weapon of a temporising mind is sarcasm. There is a difference between sarcasm and irony (cf. Job 12:1–3). Sarcasm is the weapon of the weak man; the word literally means to tear flesh from the bone. Both Isaiah and the Apostle Paul make free use of irony, but they never use sarcasm. If a weak man is presented with facts he cannot understand, he invariably turns to sarcasm.

Eliphaz addresses a "man of straw," but all the time he purports to be talking to Job. First, he takes the scolding turn—"All you say about the suffering you are going through is much ado about nothing." Scolding is characteristic of the mind which is in a corner and does not see the way out; it falls back therefore to its own entrenched position. No one damns like an theologian, nor is any quarrel so bitter as a religious quarrel. If God can be summed up in a phrase—and Eliphaz and every man with a creed holds that He can be—then there is the ban of finality about the view: "What I say is God"; and this is the essential nature of religious tyranny. Up to the time of the war, God, to many a man, was merely his own theological statement of Him; but now his religious forms of belief have been swept away and for a while he says—"I have lost my faith in God." What has happened is that though he has lost his faith in his statement of God, he is on the way to finding God Himself. Never be afraid if your circumstances dispute what you have been taught about God; be willing to examine what you have been taught, and never take the conception of an theologian as infallible; it is simply an attempt to state things.

2. The Weight of the Traditional Manner *(Job 15:7–13)*

Art thou the first man that was born? Or wast thou made before the hills? Hast thou heard the secret of God? and dost thou restrain wisdom to thyself? What knowest thou, that we know not? What understandest thou, which is not in us? (Job 15:7–9).

When once the sledge-hammer of tradition is brought to bear there is nothing more to say—"With us are both the grey-headed and the very aged men, much elder than thy father." Eliphaz says to Job—"Do you imagine that you have a setting of the problem which has never been dealt with before?" The Pharisees adopted this method with Jesus. Our Lord claimed that the law and the prophets were until Himself. "Ye have heard that it was said by them of old time, . . . but I say unto you . . . ." The Pharisees said, "We have all the weight of history behind us and the lore of tradition, consequently the constitution of God is with us and not with You; You are devil-possessed and a sinner," and they put Him to death. That is the traditional manner at its worst.

The "Eliphaz" method has hindered more souls in developing the life with God than almost any other thing, because very few men are willing to say: "Yes, I have a re-statement of the problem which has never been dealt with traditionally." When once the weight of what was known in the past is brought to bear, it crushes the life out of what is going on in the present. If the traditional manner has any weight at all, it should make men courteous with the problems which are recent. Paul's advice to Timothy was—"Let no man despise thy youth." "Don't try to make up for your youth by dogmatism and talk, but see that you walk in such a manner that you are an example to the believers." No really wise, liberal-minded person ever needs to say, "Remember how old I am."

Traditional belief has the root of the matter in it, but its form is often archaic. We begin our religious life by believing our beliefs, we accept what we are taught without questioning; then when we come up against things we begin to be critical and we find that however right those beliefs are, they are not right for us because we have not bought them by suffering. Job's experiences and his suffering made him re-state his beliefs. It is absurd to tell a man he must believe this and that; in the meantime he cannot. The traditional manner sits on the safety valve of every new type of experience. After the war, the Redemption will need to be re-stated theologically. Redemption must be seen to be God's "bit," not man's. A man cannot redeem himself. At present "Redemption" is not in the vocabulary of the average earnest Christian man. When the traditional believer hears men talk as they are doing, he is apt to get scared and to squash the life out of what, behind its insufficient expression, is going to be a re-illumination of traditional truth. If Eliphaz had been wise he would have seen what Job was getting at—"Job is facing something I do not see; I don't understand his problem, but I will treat him with respect." Instead of that he said, "According to my traditional belief, you are a hypocrite, Job."

3. The Ways of the Theological Method
(Job 15:14–16)
Behold, He putteth no trust in His saints; yea, the heavens are not clean in His sight. How much more abominable and filthy is man, which drinketh iniquity like water? (Job 15:15–16)

Theology is the science of religion, an intellectual attempt to systematise the consciousness of God. If we take the doctrine of the Trinity (which is a noble attempt of the mind of man to put into an theological formula the Godhead as revealed in the Bible) and say—"That is God," every other attempt at a statement of the Godhead is met by a sledge-hammer blow of finality. My theology has taken the place of God and I have to say—"That is blasphemy." Theol-ogy is second, not first; in its place it is a handmaid of religion, but it becomes a tyrant if put in the first place. The great doctrines of predestination and election are secondary matters, they are attempts at definition, but if we take sides with the theological method we will damn men who differ from us without a minute's hesitation. Is there any form of belief which has taken the place of God with me? We only believe along the line of what we conceive of God, and when things happen contrary to that line, we deny the experience and remain true to our theological method. Job is on the right trail.

4. The Words of the Tragedy-Monger
(Job 15:17–35)
I will shew thee, hear me; and that which I have seen I will declare. . . . (Job 15:17)

Eliphaz empties all the vials of his wrath on Job, he takes the facts of Job's life and colours them, then states them again as "a man of straw." He pictures the terrific tragedy which is likely to happen to his "man of straw," and drives it home with—"Thou art the man." If Job is right, Eliphaz must be wrong, so he has to come to the conclusion that Job is a hypocrite, the worst of bad men, because what his creed declares to be the portion of a bad man, has come to Job. This accounts for the tirade of Eliphaz.

As a product of shallow evangelical teaching, people are led to "cod" themselves into believing that they are what they know perfectly well they are not; whereas the New Testament says if a man has the Holy Spirit it will show itself in fruit—"Wherefore by their fruits ye shall know them." There are any number of men who suddenly realise the shallowness of persuading themselves that they are what they are not, and they long for Reality.

The standard for God cannot be experience; the standard is what Jesus Christ has revealed about God. If anything we may be told about God contradicts the manifestation given by Jesus Christ, we are at liberty to say, "No, I cannot believe that." Things have been taught about God which are seen to be diabolical when viewed in the light of Our Lord's revelation of Him. Remain steadfastly true to what you have learned, and when you have to suspend your judgement, say it is suspended. This was Job's attitude all through. "Your creed distorts the character of God, but I know in the end He will prove to be all that I trust Him to be, a God of love and justice, and absolutely honourable."

THE FRONTIERS OF DESPAIR
Job 16–17

Then as I weary me and long and languish,
Nowise availing from that pain to part
Desperate tides of the whole great world's anguish
Forced thro' the channels of a single heart,
Straight to thy presence get me and reveal it,
Nothing ashamed of tears upon thy feet,
Show the sore wound and beg thine hand to heal it,
Pour thee the bitter, pray thee for the sweet.
F. W. H. Myers

Up till now we have seen Job as a sane pessimist, but now we find him on the frontiers of despair. A man may get to the point of despair in a hundred and one different ways, but when he does get there, there is no horizon. In everything else there is hope that a dawn may come, but in despair there is no hope of anything brighter, it is the most hopeless frontier a human mind can enter without becoming insane. An insane person is never despairing, he is either immensely melancholy or immensely exalted. Despair is the hopelessness that overtakes a sane mind when it is pushed to the extreme in grief.

1. The Revolt against Pose *(Job 16:1–5)*
Then Job answered and said, I have heard many such things: miserable comforters are ye all. (Job 16:1–2)

Job ironically takes on the pose which Eliphaz adopted, the pose of the superior person. Eliphaz has scolded Job and said that he is suffering because he is a bad man and a hypocrite. Job recognises that Eliphaz does not begin to understand his problem, and he revolts against pose. It is difficult to evade pose in religious life because it is of the nature of unconscious priggishness. If you have the idea that your duty is to catch other people, it puts you on a superior platform at once and your whole attitude takes on the guise of a prig. This too often is the pose of the earnest religious person of to-day. Of all the different kind of men one meets the preacher takes the longest to get at, for this very reason; you can get at a doctor or any professional man much more quickly than you can a professionally religious man.

The religious pose is based, not on a personal relationship to God, but on adherence to a creed. Immediately we mistake God for a creed, or Jesus Christ for a form of belief, we begin to patronise what we do not understand. When anyone is in pain the thing that hurts more than anything else is pose, and that is what Job is fighting against here. No one revolts against a thing without a reason for doing so, not nec-

essarily a wrong reason, because revolt is of a moral order. If we come across a counterfeit, reality is sure to be found somewhere. Job is up against the religious pose of men who do not begin to understand where his sorrow lies.

2. The Recapitulation of Pain *(Job 16:6–22)*
Job's honesty and his freedom from cowardice come out very clearly; he would not say he was guilty of what he knew he was not guilty. He says, "I am not suffering because I have committed sin; I do not know why I am suffering, but I know that is not the reason." The majority of us would have caved in and said, "Oh, well, I suppose I am worse than I thought I was." What looks like revolt against God may really be not against God at all, but against the presentation being given of Him.

(a) The Psychology of It (Job 16:6–8)
Though I speak, my grief is not assuaged: and though I forbear, what am I eased? But now He hath made me weary: Thou hast made desolate all my company. (Job 16:6–7)

Many forms of grief find relief in expression—"the garment of words expressing the thing," but Job says that he cannot get any assuagement of his grief through expressing it. Not one of his friends can endure him; they believe he is desolate because God has left him. Every line of Job's experience seems psychologically to justify their judgement of him, and yet Job knows that what they say is not the explanation.

(b) The Providence of It (Job 16:9–15)
God hath delivered me to the ungodly, and turned me over into the hands of the wicked. I was at ease, but He hath broken me asunder. (Job 16:11–12)

These verses describe in Oriental terms the providence of Job's pain; everything has come out against him. "God seems to have engineered everything dead against me; the inner circumstances and the outer are all the same—God has beset me behind and before like a wild beast; everything in my providential setting and my human life goes to prove that my pain is the outcome of my sin."

(c) The Pathos of It (Job 16:16–22)
O earth, cover thou not my blood, and let my cry have no place.... My friends scorn me: but mine eye poureth out tears unto God. O that one might plead for a man

with God, as a man pleadeth for his neighbour! When a few years are come, I shall go the way whence I shall not return. (Job 16:18, 20–22)

This is not the pathos of a whining beggar who "puts it on" in order to awaken sympathy. Job's recounting of his suffering is not the expression of self-conscious pathos; he is stating for his own sake that he is sane, that he is in despair, and, so far as he can see, he is perfectly justified in being pessimistic.

There are many things like this as the outcome of this war, and we have to be careful lest we take on the religious pose, or the evangelical pose, or the denominational pose, or any pose that is not real, when we come across suffering in which there is no deliverance and no illumination. The only thing to do is to be reverent with what we do not understand. The basis of things is tragic; therefore God must find the way out, or there is no way out. Human reasoning and a human diagnosis of things will do exactly what Job's friends did, viz: belittle the grief.

3. The Recognition of Pre-Destiny *(Job 17)*
If we look for understanding from a person and do not get it, the first feeling is one of revolt and indignation against him; but when we begin to examine things, we may find that after all he is not to blame for his density. It is this element that increases the suffering of Job, while at the same time it clears him from condemnation. Everything at the back of his life and of his creed, goes to justify the conclusion he has come to.

(a) In the Density of Men *(Job 17:1–4)*
For Thou hast hid their heart from understanding. (Job 17:4)

When we look for our friends to understand, and find they do not, we accuse them of being dense. In grief the sufferer frequently declares that no one on earth can assist him. This is sometimes a pose, but Job is seeing that his friends' density does not lie with them, but with the fact of predestination. There are some kinds of suffering and temptation and sorrow no one can sympathise with, and by means of them a man gets on to the solitary way of life. It is not the suffering of a man who has done wrong and knows it; it is an isolation in which no one can sympathise, God alone can come near.

The suffering of Job is accounted for by the fact that God and Satan had made a battleground of his life, and he is beginning to discover that it is God who has closed up the understanding of his friends. Satan

has declared that Job does not love God for Himself, but only for His blessings, and now everything in the way of shelter and comradeship and sympathy has been completely stripped from Job, and he sees that God must have allowed it. This is the deepest line Job has come to as yet, but he still clings to it that God is honourable. "I have lost my family, my wealth, my friends, the consolation of my creed—I have lost everything to which a man can at all look for comfort; yet, though He slay me, I will trust in Him." This is supreme despair, along with extraordinary confidence in God who meantime looks like a moloch.[17]

(b) In the Discretion of Men *(Job 17:5–10)*
Upright men shall be astonied at this, and the innocent shall stir up himself against the hypocrite. . . . But as for you all, do ye return, and come now; for I cannot find one wise man among you. (Job 17:8, 10)

Job is recounting the fact that his experiences of sorrow and difficulty have so come about that the wise element of discretion in men must make them pass judgement against him. Everything seems against him: not only his creed, but the ordinary sagacity of men. There is nothing more agonising to a man who knows his own integrity than to find that the best people leave him alone, not because they do not know why he suffers, but because they are sure he is more in the wrong than he says, and their view is backed by their own discretion and knowledge. As in the case of the density of men, this discretion must not be laid at the door of men, but at the predestiny of the way human wisdom is fixed. The predestiny of human wisdom is rationalism. Any number of things happen which are not reasonable, and human discretion is apt to say that the man who suffers unreasonably is to blame; and when it is pointed out that the basis of things is without reason, men say that is only a passing difference. The Bible reveals that the basis of things is not reasonable, but tragic. When a man is driven to the bottom board, he gets to the tragedy, not to the reason; he is alone with God, and if God does not see him through, despair is the only place for him. The more deeply and earnestly and directly a man thinks, the more he finds what Solomon says is true—"He that increaseth knowledge increaseth sorrow." It is not Job's humour[18] that brings him to a pessimist's point of view, but his plain sanity; he refuses to say that his pessimism is a mood; optimism *is* a mood. If God does not see Job through, Satan has won his wager; if God does not come on the scene somewhere, it is a forlorn hope, and Satan will have proved that no one loves God for His own sake. Everything

---

17. moloch: a tyrannical power requiring sacrifice in order to be appeased
18. humour: mood, temperament, or disposition.

a man can rely upon has disappeared, and yet Job does not curse God; he admits that his former creed is not right, neither are his friends right, yet he declares steadily that in the end God will be justified.

(c) In the Despair before Men (Job 17:11–16)

Job cannot hide his despair. For unfathomable pathos, verse 11 is unequalled in any language under heaven:

My days are past, my purposes are broken off, even the possessions of my heart. (Job 17:11 RV mg)

A certain type of religious hypocrisy makes men hide what they feel, but Job has come to the place where he cannot hide it—"I cannot pretend that I am comforted of God," he says. If only Job could have taken on the pose that he had the comfort of God, his friends would not have challenged him, but he says, "I have no comfort; I do not see God, neither can I talk to Him; all I know is that my creed and former belief must be wrong. I do not know what to accept, but I am certain God will prove that He is just and true and right, and I refuse to tell a lie in order to help Him out."

This attitude of religious faith is finely expressed by the Psalmist—"Then will I go unto the altar of God, unto God my exceeding joy"(Psalm 43:4). This is sublime faith, the faith that Jesus demanded of John the Baptist. ". . . And blessed is he, whosoever shall not be offended in Me." Will I stick to it, without any pretence or humbug, that God is righteous, although everything in my actual experience seems to prove that He is cruel? Most of us are hypocrites, we are too afraid to state the thing as Job did. We say right out, "God is cruel to allow me to go through this, and I refuse to believe in Him any more." Job stuck to his point that when everything was known it would not be to God's dishonour, but to His honour.

Because of this war, a great number of men in lesser degree have arrived at the place Job has got to, their creeds about God have gone, and it would be the height of absurdity to pretend that their former beliefs of God are true as they see Him now. It does not follow because a man has lost belief in his beliefs that therefore he has lost faith in God. Many a man has been led to the frontiers of despair by being told he has backslidden, whereas what he has gone through has revealed that his belief in his beliefs is not God. Men have found God by going through hell, and it is the men who have been face to face with these things who can understand what Job went through. All the impatience and irritation against the religious life, so called, is accounted for on the same line as Job's revolt against religious pose—"If they would only stop their pose and face facts as they are; be reverent with what they don't understand, and assist me in my faith in God." Job's friends were in the right place when they sat with him dumbfounded for seven days; they were much nearer God then than afterwards. Immediately they took up the cudgels for God,[19] they took on a religious pose, lost touch with the reality of actual experience, and ended in being bombastic.

THE BITTEREST HURT IN LIFE
Job 18–20

Nay but much rather let me late returning
Bruised of my brethren, wounded from within.
Stoop with sad countenance and blushes burning.
Bitter with weariness and sick with sin,—

. . . .

Safe to the hidden house of thine abiding
Carry the weak knees and the heart that faints,
Shield from the scorn and cover from the chiding,
Give the world joy, but patience to the saints.
                                          F. W. H. Myers

The bitterest hurt in life is to be wounded in the house of your friends; to be wounded by an enemy is bad enough, but it does not take you unawares, you expect it in a measure. "My kinsfolk have failed, and my familiar friends have forgotten me. . . . All my inward friends abhorred me: and they whom I loved are turned against me" (Job 19:14, 19).

1. The Removal of the Atmosphere of Comradeship *(Job 18)*
There is always an intangible something which makes a friend, it is not what he does, but what he is. You feel the better for being in the presence of some men. Job is suffering because his friends have turned against him; he has lost the atmosphere of comradeship. He has no explanation for what he is going through, no line of exonerating God.

(a) The Dignity of Withdrawal (Job 18:1–4)
Then answered Bildad the Shuhite, and said, How long will it be ere ye make an end of words? Mark, and afterwards we will speak. (Job 18:1–2)

In this withdrawal of comradeship there is an acuteness of suffering which is difficult to state. Job is hurt, and his friends not only tackle his belief, but they have withdrawn all support from him. The sympathy which is reverent with what it cannot understand is worth its weight in gold. The friends have stopped giving this kind of sympathy to Job, instead they say, "We know why it is you suffer." By sticking to his creed a man is able to withdraw with dignity simply because there is so much he does not see.

Bildad is certain that Job is wrong and he is right, and the puzzling thing is that Bildad can prove his statements, while Job has to remain silent. This is one of the biggest stings in life. When a man gets to Reality he has to get there alone, there is no comradeship. He may have had comradeship up to a certain point, then he is told, "Now we have to leave you, you are outside the pale." The men who act like this have the logic of it on their side, but the man who is face to face with facts knows that logic is only an attempt to explain facts, it does not give us the facts. The man who does not believe that the basis of things is tragic may get the best of it in argument, but the man who gets the best of it in fact is the one who believes in God yet has to remain inarticulate.

Bildad describes the worst man he can think of, and Job says, "All this has happened to me, and you say therefore I must be a bad man, but I say I am not. You have the logic of your creed, while I have the reality of my experience. The God of your creed is One who would make me an atheist. The God who will explain my experience I have not yet found, but I am confident there is such a God, and meantime I refuse to accept your counterfeit of Him."

There are countless experiences like Job's to-day; men are being called atheists who are not atheists at all but are simply rebelling against the presentation of God which is being thrust upon them. If to accept a presentation of God means the denial of things he knows to be facts, a man is in a better case who says with Job, "I will not accept an explanation of God which makes me call a fact not a fact."

(b) The Discourse in the Withdrawal (Job 18:5–21)
Yea, the light of the wicked shall be put out, and the spark of his fire shall not shine. . . . Surely such are the dwellings of the wicked, and this is the place of him that knoweth not God. (Job 18:5, 21)

A man has to cover his retreat somehow, and Bildad withdraws in a cloud of rhetoric; his description of the wicked man is a covert description of Job in his present condition. He recounts what Job has gone through and makes it the experience of a thorough-paced hypocrite—"I have satisfied my mind that you are a hypocrite; you are suffering because you are bad." Bildad airs his complete knowledge of the psychology of wickedness as God must deal with it, but evidently with as complete an ignorance of God as of man. His indignation with Job is petty, you can almost hear him puffing with righteous annoyance. The friends' speeches prove that when Providence or suffering contradicts any form of credal belief, the holder of the creed becomes vindictive in trying to justify what is threatened, and no longer discerns the truth.

2. The Reaction of the Affection of Courage (Job 19)
(a) The Appeal of Discouragement (Job 19:1–5)
Then Job answered and said, How long will ye vex my soul, and break me in pieces with words? (Job 19:1–2)

"Discouragement is disenchanted egotism" (Mazzini), i.e., the heart knocked out of self-love. Job had been in love with his creed, now belief in his creed is gone and he is completely at his wits' end, and from the centre of his discouragement he makes his appeal to the men whom he had a right to expect would stand by him. "You take the side of the Providence of God," he says, "which undoubtedly seems my enemy." This chapter is not only an expression of real agony and sorrow, but also of the stout integrity which will not allow itself to tell a lie for the honour of God. "God seems to be my enemy providentially," says Job, "and you say it is because I am bad; but I say that that is not the reason."

(b) The Account of Desolateness (Job 19:6–20)
Know now that God hath overthrown me, and hath compassed me with His net. Behold, I cry out of wrong, but I am not heard: I cry aloud, and there is no judgement. (Job 19:6–7)

Job's statements are not coloured, he simply states what has happened to him—everything has gone and no explanation has been given him. There is no bright side to some troubles. There is no reasonable hope for countless lives on account of this war, and it is shallow nonsense to tell them to "cheer up"; life to them is a hell of darkness of the most appalling order. The one who preaches at such a time is an impertinence, but the one who says "I don't know why you are going through this, it is black and desperate, but I will wait with you," is an unspeakable benediction and sustaining. Job has no one to do this for him, his one-time friends simply add to his bitterness; they too have been hit along the line of their creed, and they are indignant and talk only on the religious line.

(c) *The Agony of Dereliction* (Job 19:21–29)
Have pity on me, have pity on me, O ye my friends; for the hand of God hath touched me. . . . For I know that my redeemer liveth, and that He shall stand at the latter day upon the earth. . . . Job 19:21, 25)

The question of immortality is not necessarily implied in Job's words; he is stating that he believes a time will come when an umpire will arise who will expound to him what he is going through—to the justification of God as well as of himself. It is heroism almost unequalled to say, as Job did, "Though He slay me, I will stick to it that God is a God of love and justice and truth. I see no way out at all, but I will remain true to my belief that when the whole thing is known God will not be condemned." All through Job refuses to take the easy way out along the line of his former creed.

3. The Recession of the Apprehension of Communion *(Job 20)*
The withdrawal of your most intimate friend with the conviction that you are wrong, means the loss of the atmosphere of comradeship and all that is represented by the closer intimacies of communion.

(a) *The Disdain of the Offended* (Job 20:1–3)
Then answered Zophar the Naamathite, and said, . . . I have heard the check of my reproach, and the spirit of my understanding causeth me to answer. (Job 20:1, 3)

Zophar speaks with dignity, but dignity is not an indication of discernment. Zophar has listened to Job's words but not to the spirit of them; he is ashamed of the attitude his former friend has taken. A retreat from comradeship is nearly always covered by a terrific amount of utterance either in writing or speech. Bildad withdraws with descriptions; Zophar gives a disquisition as to why he turns on Job with disdain.

(b) *The Disquisition of the Offensive* (Job 20:4–29)
Knowest thou not this of old, since man was placed upon earth, that the triumphing of the wicked is short, and the joy of the hypocrite but for a moment? (Job 20:4–5)

One point of mercy is that the friends do not put the curse on Job directly. Cursing with us is only profane language, an expression and no more, but in the case of the curse of an Arab or a Hebrew the curse lies in the words themselves: if the curse is uttered it is impossible, according to their conviction, but that it shall fall. Zophar is uttering this kind of curse, only indirectly, and it gives his words tremendous power. The power of the spoken word accounts for the prominent place given in the Bible to prophesying and preaching.

Job's strong utterances are not against God, but against the statements of his former creed. The man who will stand true to God behind the expression of his creed is true to his belief *in God*, instead of to the presentation of Him which is in dispute. If you listen to a man who has been sorely hit, he may utter what, to you who have not been hit, sounds blasphemous. Job's claim is that his friends ought to have known that it was not imagination made him speak as he did, but the fact that he had been desperately hard hit. The only way out for Job is not on the line of reason, but on the line of implicit confidence, such as he expresses in chapter 13—"Though He slay me, yet will I trust in Him."

THE PRIMAL CLASH
Job 21–25

If we are going to understand the ordinary run of human life we must take into account the extraordinary experiences and tragedies. One reason for the futility of pseudo-evangelism is that we have taken the mediocre man, the average man, as the one best able to expound Christian experience. Christianity does embrace the weakest and the feeblest, but it is the men of exceptional experiences, such as Job or the Apostle Paul, who make clear the basis of things. The "Primal Clash" means that we are down to the foundation of things.

1. The Realising Sense of Perverseness *(Job 21)*

What is the Almighty that we should serve Him? and what profit should we have, if we pray unto Him? . . . God layeth up His iniquity for His children: He rewardeth him, and he shall know it. . . . Behold, I know your thoughts and the devices which ye wrongfully imagine against me. . . . How then comfort ye me in vain, seeing in your answers there remaineth falsehood? (Job 21:15, 19, 27, 34)

It is soul certainty that the world needs, even more than sound principles—not soul facility, but soul certainty, not ready religion, but sure.

Dr. Forsyth[20]

Job persists in stating that the basis of things is not clear or easy to understand. "It is absurd to say, as you are doing," he says, "that God punishes the evil man and looks after the good, there is so much perversity at the basis of things that that explanation won't do." The friends give this explanation because they are true to their creed, and Job says, "I held the same creed as you do until I came to my great trouble." Their creed was based on sound principles, but what is needed is a sound relationship at the basis of things. When things are suddenly altered by bereavement or by some tension in personal experience, we find ourselves wonderfully at home with what Job says. There is a wildness about things, and we revolt against the people who explain everything on the basis of sound principles. They have everything ready to hand, and can tell you just where everyone goes wrong; but Job's contention is that when a man is face to face with things as they are, easy explanations won't do, for things are not easy; there is a perverseness all through. If Job is not right in his contention, then the Redemption is "much ado about nothing."

2. The Reasoning Severity of Pharisaism
(Job 22)

Then Eliphaz the Temanite answered and said, Can a man be profitable unto God, as he that is wise may be profitable unto himself? . . . Acquaint now thyself with Him, and be at peace: thereby good shall come unto thee. (Job 22:1–2, 21)

Many a gross Pharisee is a mighty moralist and he believes himself sincere with it. The deadliest Pharisaism is not hypocrisy, it is the unconscious Pharisaism of unreality.

Dr. Forsyth

The nature of Pharisaism is that it must stand on tiptoe and be superior. The man who does not want to face the foundation of things becomes tremendously stern and keen on principles and on moral reforms. A man who is hyper-conscientious is nearly always one who has done something irregular or who is morbid; either he is close on the verge of lunacy, or he is covering up something wrong by tremendous moral earnestness along certain lines of reform. A Pharisee shuts you up, not by loud shouting, but by the unanswerable logic he presents; he is bound to principles,

not to a relationship. There is a great amount of Pharisaism abroad to-day, and it is based on "devotee-ness" to principles. Devotion to a cause is the great mark of our day, and in religion it means being devoted to the application of religious principles. A disciple of Jesus Christ is devoted to a Person, not to principles.

Job's experience flatly contradicts the creed of this particular Pharisee, Eliphaz, so he jumps on Job. His words are eloquent and his charges terrific; he sums up all the facts and informs Job that he has maltreated the innocent, wronged the widow, and starved the orphan—

Is not thy wickedness great? And thine iniquities infinite? For thou hast taken a pledge from thy brother for nought, and stripped the naked of their clothing. Thou hast not given water to the weary to drink, and thou hast withholden bread from the hungry. (Job 22:5–7)

This is always the dodge of a Pharisee, whether he is a demagogue or a religious man, he must make a moral issue somewhere. If he can rouse up a passion for a neglected principle, it is exactly what he wants, but there is no reality in it. The Pharisaism of Our Lord's day was based on the principles of Judaism, and when Jesus Christ came the Pharisees did not recognise Him but said, "You are a hypocrite, we can prove it." Many of the religious phases of to-day do not touch reality, but only the Pharisaic insistence on a certain form of sound doctrine, and the man who is up against things finds nothing but chaff. Every denominationalist is certain that the crowd who does not agree with what "we" call our sound principles must be wrong; he never imagines that the "Job" type of man can be right with God. When God spoke to Eliphaz, as He did at the close, it would be the last humiliation for Eliphaz to find that after all from God's standpoint Job was the only one among them who was right. In the meantime it is far easier to stand by the utterances of Eliphaz than by the utterances of Job.

The Pharisee is an intense moralist (see John 16:2; Hebrews 13:13). When Jesus Christ came He was found to be unresolvable by every set of religious principles, that was His "reproach." To "go forth therefore unto Him without the camp, bearing His reproach," does not mean going outside the worldly crowd; it means being put outside the religious crowd you belong to. One of the most poignant bits of suffering for a disciple comes along that line. If you remain true to Jesus Christ there are times when you will have to go through your convictions and out the other side, and most of us shrink from such a step

---

20. Peter Taylor Forsyth (1848–1921), British Congregationalist minister and theologian. Chambers read many of Forsyth's books and valued his insights.

because it means going alone. The "camp" means the religious set you belong to; the set you do not belong to does not matter to you.

Eliphaz is certain that Job is so bad that he wonders at the patience of God with him. If Eliphaz had been in the position of God, he would have excommunicated Job right away; and yet Job is the one who is face to face with Reality. To-day men are not asking, "Is the thing true?" but "Is it real?" It is a matter of indifference whether a thing is true; any number of things can be demonstrated to be true which do not matter to us. Have I a real God, or am I trying to produce a Pharisaic cloak for myself? Job would not accept a Pharisaic cloak; he would not grant that he was wrong, neither would he say that the friends' creed was right. He was in a quandary, but he knew that God was real, and therefore he would wait until He appeared.

3. The Revolutionary Struggle of Prayer
(Job 23–24)

Oh that I knew where I might find Him! that I might come even to His seat! I would order my cause before Him, and fill my mouth with arguments. (Job 23:3–4)

There is no reality without struggling. If you are not called to wrestle, it is only because the wrestling is being done for you.

Dr. Forsyth

The reason the experience of Redemption is so easy is because it cost God so much. If my religion slips easily into my life it is because someone else has paid the price for it. If, however, the simple experience is taken as true to the whole of life, we will be misled; only if we take the experience of those who have paid the price for us, do we get to Reality. It is men like Job and the Apostle Paul who bring us to the basis of things, not the average Christian among us, who knows no more why the basis of his salvation is Redemption than the average common-sense man knows the basis of ordinary human life. We must get hold of the great souls, the men who have been hard hit and have gone to the basis of things, and whose experiences have been preserved for us by God, that we may know where we stand. One of the reasons for the futility of pseudo-evangelism is that it bases its doctrine on the shallow weak things it has saved. Thank God, Christianity does save the shallow weak things, but they are not the ones to diagnose Christianity, they are the expression of the last reach of Christianity. Paul said—". . . not many mighty, not many noble, are called"—he did not say "not *any* mighty, not *any* noble." It is Our Lord Himself, and men like Job in the Old Testament and Paul in the New who give us the indication of where we are to look for the foundation of our faith when it is being shaken.

Job's cry, "Oh that I knew where I might find Him!" is the birth of evangelical prayer on the basis of Redemption. The "finding" cannot be by reasoning or by religious faith; the only way to find God is through prayer. In the religious life of the Pharisee, prayer becomes a rite, a ceremony. In all religion based on sound principles prayer is an exercise, a ceremony, it is not blood or passion, not actual from the whole manhood. In such prayers there is magnificently beautiful diction which one needs to be in a calm, quiet state of mind to appreciate. The most beautiful prayers are prayers that are rites, but they are apt to be mere repetition, and not of the nature of Reality. There is no sting in them, no tremendous grip of a man face to face with things. There is no way out by rites or by religious beliefs, but only, as Jesus Christ indicates, by prayer.

It takes a tremendous amount of reiteration on God's part before we understand what prayer is. We do not pray at all until we are at our wits' end. ". . . their soul fainted in them. *Then* they cried unto the LORD in their trouble" (Psalm 107:5–6). During this war many a man has prayed for the first time in his life. When a man is at his wits' end it is not a cowardly thing to pray, it is the only way he can get in touch with Reality. "Oh that I knew where I could get into touch with the Reality that explains things!" There is only one way, and that is the way of prayer (see 1 John 5:14–15).

There are undoubtedly things which present a puzzle, e.g., the presentation of the basis of Redemption; how am I going to understand whether the Redemption covers everything, or only partially covers? Never by reasoning, only by prayer; and as sure as God is God you will get the answer and know of a certainty. If we take the line of disputing and spitting fire like Eliphaz did, we will get at nothing. We do not get insight by struggling, but by going to God in prayer. Most of us are wise in our own conceits, we have notions of our own which we want to see through. There is nothing to be valued more highly than to have people praying for us; God links up His power in answer to their prayers.

Redemption is easy to experience because it cost God everything, and if I am going to be regenerated it is going to cost me something. I have to give up my right to myself. I have deliberately to accept into myself something that will fight for all it is worth, something that will war against the desires of the flesh, and that will ask me to go into identification with the death of Jesus Christ, and these things produce a struggle in me. The majority of us prefer to get up and ride rather than to "get out and shove." It is only the people who "get out and shove" who really make things go. The men who are up against things just now and who are determined to get at Reality at all costs, and will not accept a thing on the religious line unless that line states Reality—these are the men who are paying the price for the next generation. The reason we are here in the natural world is because our mothers struggled for our existence, and the more unhindered the birth pangs the stronger and healthier the child. A thing is worth just what it costs.

4. The Redundant Sonorousness of Position (Job 25)

Then answered Bildad the Shuhite, and said, Dominion and fear are with Him, He maketh peace in His high places. Is there any number of His armies? And upon whom doth not His light arise? (Job 25:1–3).

We have the modern and insidious type of Pharisaism, the unconscious hypocrite, the man or woman not of fraud, but of pose, not of deep and dark design, but of subtle egotism, prompt certainty and facile religiosity.

Dr. Forsyth

Bildad's utterances here are inadvertent and wildly away from the theme. The modern Pharisee of the "Bildad" type is the man who has a pose to keep up; he is not touched by any problem himself, and when there is trouble on he comes out with these redundant phrases. Job does not get annoyed with Bildad, he is full rather of pity for him. Eliphaz stings Job because he takes up a superior position; he knows why Job suffers; he stands strong for his set of principles, but he is not in touch with Reality. Bildad is in touch with nothing, he is courageously heartless; he never thinks when he talks, but simply pours it out. The "Bildad" type is often met with in the pulpit; men roll out phrases and talk the most ponderous stuff with nothing in it. It is like a roll of thunder over your head when what you want is real nourishment. These men continually brought things to the surface and said to Job, "This is what you want." What a man wants is somewhere to rest his mind and heart, and the only place to rest in is God, and the only way to come to God is by prayer. Much of our praying has nothing in it; it is not the talk of a child to his Father when he has come up against things or is hurt. "Ask, and it shall be given you," Jesus says. We do not ask, we worry, whereas one minute in prayer will put God's decree at work, viz., that He answers prayer on the ground of Redemption. Jesus Christ did not say, "Ask what you like, and it shall be done unto you," but "ask what you will, ask when your will is in the thing that is a real problem to you," and God has pledged His honour that you will get the answer every time.

PARABLES
Job 26–31

Be near me when my light is low,
When the blood creeps, and the nerves prick
And tingle; and the heart is sick,
And all the wheels of Being slow.

Be near me when the sensuous frame
Is rack'd with pangs that conquer trust;
And Time, a maniac scattering dust,
And Life, a Fury slinging flame.

Be near me when my faith is dry,
And men the flies of latter spring,
That lay their eggs, and sting and sing
And weave their petty cells and die.

Be near me when I fade away,
To point the term of human strife.
And on the low dark verge of life
The twilight of eternal day.

Tennyson

A parable is an earthly story which does not explain itself. Every one of us has an earthly story and the explanation of it is not to be found in its own expression, but only in the domain of the Designer of life. Job says that the explanation his friends give of his earthly story is hopeless, they are nowhere near understanding it; God alone is the Source from whence will come the explanation of all he is going through.

1. God and the Sublimities (Job 26)

Lo, these are parts of His ways: but how little a portion is heard of Him? But the thunder of His power who can understand? (Job 26:14)

The sublime things in Nature swamp our intelligent understanding of them; rugged mountain scenery, for instance, will awaken a sense of the sublime. The man who has never had the sense of the sublime awakened in him is scarcely born. The story of the earth itself is so full of sublimities that it requires God, not man, to expound it. If a man cannot expound the sublimities of Nature, he need not expect to be able to expound the sublimity of the human soul. The sublimities of Nature cannot be explained on the line of reason, but only on the line of the a-logical, that which goes beyond and underneath the logical. Job recognises this, and he implies, "If you imagine you can explain the deeper sublimities of a man's soul, you have not pondered human life enough." The Psalmist puts it in this way— "My God, Thou art the God of the mountains and of the fathomless deep, the God of the early mornings and late at nights; but there are deeper depths than these in me, my God; more mysterious things in my soul, and I cannot fathom my own way, therefore search me, O God" (see Psalm 139). Job is on the same line.

"Lo, these are but the outskirts of His ways: and how small a whisper do we hear of Him!" (Job 26:14 RV). In the Book of Job Nature is always referred to as being wild; this is a point of view we have forgotten nowadays. We talk about laws and findings, we give scientific explanations of thunder and of a sunset, and come to the conclusion that there is no unexplained sublimity in Nature at all. The wildness of Nature has to be recognised, there are forces in the earth and air and sea which baffle attempts at explanation or of control; all we can do is to give a direction for thought along certain lines.

Neither logic nor science can explain the sublimities of Nature. Supposing a scientist with a diseased olfactory nerve says that there is no perfume in a rose, and to prove his statement he dissects the rose and tabulates every part, and then says, "Where is the perfume? It is a fiction; I have demonstrated that there is none." There is always one fact more that science cannot explain, and the best thing to do is not to deny it in order to preserve your sanity, but to say, as Job did, "No, the one fact more which you cannot explain means that God must step in just there, or there is no explanation to be had."

2. God and the Subtleties *(Job 27)*

Moreover Job continued his parable, and said, . . . God forbid that I should justify you: till I die I will not remove mine integrity from me. My righteousness I hold fast, and will not let it go: my heart shall not reproach me so long as I live. (Job 27:1, 5–6)

God is never subtle in His revelations, but always elemental and simple. The "simple Gospel" does not mean simple to understand, but simple in the way God Himself is simple. Job says, "I have no explanation as yet of what I am going through; your explanation on the line of your creed is irritating nonsense, because it makes you leave out the facts which I know, while you try to explain the One none of us can get at, viz., God." Job is not speaking in spite, but in honesty—"If I were to justify you in your explanation I should sin against my

conscience, and say that you have told the truth whereas in reality you have told a lie."

There is a difference between the subtlety of Eliphaz and the subtlety of Job. Eliphaz sums up the history of the wicked man and says that God does all these things to punish him, whereas Job recognises that the history of any man cannot be accounted for on the surface, and that God alone can explain His own dealings. The description Elpihaz gives of the wicked man is a covert condemnation of Job; he takes the facts of Job's present condition and puts them as the picture of a wicked man, while all the time he implies, "Thou art the man." "That is not the way to comfort me, or bring me any help," says Job. He does not brag and say he is a good man, but he does maintain that the reason he suffers is not because he is bad. "You pretend to know the attitude of God to things, but all that you describe as the experience of a wicked man I can give as my experience of being a good man."

The explanation of Job's suffering is the fact that God and Satan had made a battleground of his soul. It was not for Job's chastening or his perfecting, but for an ulterior purpose which he did not know, but his intuition made him stick to the fact that the only One who could explain the sublimities of Nature was the One who could explain what he was going through. "Though He slay me, though my creed goes and everything is destroyed, "yet I will trust in Him"—not trust Him to deliver me, but trust that He is honourable and just and true, and that I shall yet be justified in sticking to my faith in His honour, though meantime it looks as if He is deliberately destroying me.

There is a lot of cheap-jack talk just now regarding the British Empire, viz., that God is punishing us for our sins—a hopeless misrepresentation. The Cross of Calvary and the Redemption have to do with the sins of the world. If God began to punish the nations for their sins there would be no nation left on the face of the earth. Job takes the right line, that the difficulties are produced by a conflict of wills.

Beware of the subtleties which twist facts. It is possible to torture a man with a delicate type of mind, as in the case of Ugo Bassi,[21] torture him not physically, but by suggesting that he has been guilty of base motives and deeds. The sensitiveness of Ugo Bassi's mind was such that after a while he began to believe he had been guilty unconsciously of the things he was accused of. Job's friends said to him, "We have all these facts about you, and they are only explainable along the line that you are a bad man; you may not be conscious of your badness, nevertheless you are a hypocrite, because our creed says that if a man trusts God, God will bless him; and instead of being blessed, you have

---

21. Ugo Bassi, central figure in H. E. Hamilton King's epic, *The Disciples,* published in 1873.

been cursed in every way and have lost everything: therefore must be a bad man." If Job had been of the Ugo Bassi stamp with a hypersensitive mind and not the robust spirit he was, he would have said, "Oh, well, I must be much worse than I imagined; and I must be guilty." But he stuck to it, "No, I have not been dishonourable and bad, you may say of me what you like, but that is not the reason why I suffer."

3. God and the Sublunary *(Job 28)*
Surely there is a vein for the silver, and a place for gold where they fine it. Iron is taken out of the earth, and brass is molten out of the stone. (Job 28:1–2)

Careful examination of every reference Job makes to geology or meteorology reveals that there is no significant or insignificant blunder in all he says; every reference is a piece of consummate accuracy. This in passing.

Every common-sense fact requires something for its explanation which common-sense cannot give. The facts of every day and night reveal things our own minds cannot explain. When a scientific man comes across a gap in his explanations, instead of saying, "There is no gap here," let him recognise that there is a gap he cannot bridge, and that he must be reverent with what he cannot understand. The tendency is to deny that a fact has any existence because it cannot be fitted into any explanation as yet. That "the exception proves the rule" is not true: the exception proves that the rule won't do; the rule is only useful in the greatest number of cases. When scientists treat a thesis as a fact they mean that it is based on the highest degree of probability. There are no "infallible" findings, and the man who bows down to scientific findings may be as big a fool as the man who refuses to do so. The man who prays ceases to be a fool, while the man who refuses to pray nourishes a blind life within his own brain and he will find no way out that road. Job cries out that prayer is the only way out in all these matters—

> *Whence then cometh wisdom? and where is the place of understanding? . . . Behold, the fear of the LORD, that is wisdom: and to depart from evil is understanding. (Job 28:20, 28)*

4. God and the Shadows *(Job 29)*
Oh that I were as in months past, as in the days when God preserved me; when His candle shined upon my head, and when by His light I walked through darkness. (Job 29:2–3)

Truth for ever on the scaffold, Wrong for ever on the throne,—Yet that scaffold sways the Future, and, behind the dim unknown. Standeth God within the shadow, keeping watch above his own.

The "shadows" depict what Job is describing, viz., the things in human history and in personal experience that are shadowed by mystery and cannot be explained by reason or religious creeds, but only by belief in God who will make all plain in His own way. Job is saying that there is nothing in life you can reckon on with any certainty. We may say that if a man has been well brought up and has developed his own integrity and lived rightly, success will be sure to attend him, but you cannot calculate along that line. Never ignore the things that cannot be explained, put them on one side, but remember they are there and have to be reckoned with. There is a gap and a wildness in things and if God does not step in and adjust it, there is no hope; but God has stepped in by the Redemption, and our part is to trust confidently in Him. Either the pessimist is right when he says we are autumn leaves driven by the blast of some ultimate power without mind, or else the way out is by the Redemption of Jesus Christ.

5. God and the Scurrilous *(Job 30)*
And now I am their song, yea, I am their byword. . . . They flee far from me, and spare not to spit in my face. (Job 30:9–10)

Jesus Christ was in the case Job is describing, He was placed alongside the most scurrilous immorality of His day—"Behold, a gluttonous man, and a winebibber, a friend of publicans and sinners!" And He was put to death between two malefactors. It is impossible to calculate on the line that virtue will bring a man to honour, and that uprightness will escape the punishment which falls on men who are not upright. Any explanation at all leaves a gap which cannot be bridged as yet.

6. God and the Scrupulous *(Job 31)*
If I have walked with vanity, or if my foot hath hasted to deceit; let me be weighed in an even balance that God may know mine integrity. (Job 31:5–6)

Job examines the statements of the creed and its moral findings, and then disputes it from his own experience—"Do you think I am trying to make out before God that I am what I have not been? would I talk to God with what would be blatant insolence if I had not the facts to back me up? The inference from the facts of my life is that I have been beyond reproach, and in my approach to God I will not say I have been guilty of what I know I have not been. I stand clear before God on every one of these lines, and though I do not see Him or know Him, I will stick to it that He is other than you say, and that when I do see Him He will not say that I deceived myself when I spoke the truth."

It is foolish to say that this chapter refers to a past dispensation and that we are in advance of it. We are in another dispensation, but not necessarily a better one. What man among us can come anywhere near the standard of integrity of Job? That kind of statement comes from accepting principles for guidance instead of a personal relationship. If I worship God from fear or superstition, then I am wrong, my heart has been "secretly enticed." Job's point of view is that if I do anything in order to appease God, I am committing iniquity. The only reason for my approach to God must be that He is what I believe Him to be, a God of honour and justice, not a God of coercive necromancy who demands that we do things without any reason. To-day we are dealing with the very thing for which the friends have pulled Job to pieces. There are people who say, "I will not, I dare not, accept the God you are presenting because He is not a moral God; there is something wrong in such a presentation, my whole being cries out against it, I cannot go to such a God as a Deliverer."

In these chapters Job is insisting that God must be other than his former creed said He was, and that it must be acknowledged that there are facts which the creed had not taken into account. Thank God for theology, but theology is second, not first; if we put it first, we will do what the friends did, refuse to look at facts and remain consistent to certain ideas which pervert the character of God. In the final run God will not have us say an untrue thing for the sake of His honour.

THE PASSION FOR AUTHORITY
Job 32–37

In Elihu the passion for authority is represented. The average man in Job's condition is apt to break away from all authority. A lesser man than Job would have become a sophist and said that every man is a law unto himself, i.e., his own inner consciousness is sufficient law. Job was not of this order, neither was Elihu. The passion for authority is a noble one, but Elihu missed out the fact that authority to be worthy arises out of the nature of a superior moral integrity, and not simply from one who happens to be higher up in the scale than ourselves. Elihu comes with the idea that because God has said a thing, therefore it is authoritative: Job wants to know what kind of God it was who said it, is He a being whose character does not contradict the moral basis of life? Authority must be of a moral, not a superstitious character. Elihu's contention is, "Because God has said so," that is sufficient; or, "Because the creed says so," therefore it must be blindly accepted. To be without any authority is to be lawless, but to have only an internal authority is as bad as having a blind external authority; the two must meet together somehow.

1. The Inspiration of Autocratic Authority
(Job 32)
Autocratic authority means to rule by right of insistence, not necessarily by right of personal integrity. Napoleon said of Jesus Christ that He had succeeded in making every human soul an appendage of His own because He had the genius of holiness. Other men exercised authority by coercive means, Jesus Christ never did, His authority was *worthy*. He proved Himself worthy not only in the domain of God, which we do not know, but in the domain of man, which we do know; He is worthy there, consequently He prevails to open the Book (see Revelation 5). Authority to be lasting must be of the same order as that of Jesus Christ, not the authority of autocracy or coercion, but the authority of worth, to which all that is worthy in a man bows down. It is only the unworthy in a man that does not bow down to worthy authority.

The Superior Conceit of Shyness (Job 32:1–22)
And Elihu the son of Barachel the Buzite answered and said, I am young, and ye are very old; wherefore I was afraid, and durst not shew you mine opinion. . . . Behold, I waited for your words; I gave ear to your reasons, while ye searched out what to say. Yea, I attended unto you, and behold, there was none of you that convinced Job, or that answered his words. (Job 32:6, 11–12)

There is a fine apparent modesty about Elihu. He says, "I waited for you to speak, but all I have listened to has made me angry, because Job has justified himself at the expense of God, and you have stopped short without challenging him in the right way, and now I will speak."

Then was kindled the wrath of Elihu . . . against Job was his wrath kindled, because he justified himself rather than God. (Job 32:2)

Elihu exhibits the superior conceit of shyness. There is quite possibly a superior conceit in a shy or quiet man. A man may keep silent not because he is really modest, but he does not intend to speak until he gets a proper audience—"I do not intend to bring out my notion of things until people are prepared to listen; I do not wish what I say to go into the mere rush of ordinary conversation, so I shall wait for a suitable opportunity." This does not altogether diagnose Elihu, but he certainly exhibits this characteristic.

Elihu says that the inspiration of authority comes from God simply because He is God, and not from any sense of right in Himself. Job stands up against this; he says, in effect, "I will not accept any authority on the ground of superstition; I must know the moral ingredient in the authority." This is the element Elihu loses sight of altogether.

2. The Insistence of Autocratic Authority (Job 33)

The Spiritual Consciousness of Submission

Behold, in this thou art not just: I will answer thee, that God is greater than man. Why dost thou strive against Him? For He giveth not account of any of His matters. (Job 33:12–13)

The antagonism of the friends in battling for their creed was an indication that they were getting shaky regarding it. But Elihu is not shaky, he does not accept the creed of the other three, he has a notion of his own based on the conception of autocratic authority, viz., that no man has any right to enquire whether God is good; it is a question of His supreme authority, and submission is the only line to take. It is dangerous to be conscious of submission to a spiritual power. The difference between fatalism and faith lies just here. Fatalism means, "My number's up; I have to bow to the power whether I like it or not; I do not know the character of the power, but it is greater than I am, and I must submit." The submission of faith is that I do know the character of the Power, and this was the line Job took—"Though He slay me, yet I will trust the fact that His character is worthy." This is the attitude of faith all through—I submit to One whose character I know but whose ways are obscured in mystery just now." We do know the character of God, if we are Christians, because we have it revealed to us in Jesus Christ—"He that hath seen Me hath seen the Father." Anything that contradicts the manifestation given in and through the Lord Jesus Christ cannot be true of God. Therefore we know that the character of God is noble and true and right, and any authority from God is based, not on autocracy or mere blind power, but on worthiness which everything in me recognises as worthy, therefore I submit. Elihu was moved with indignation because Job said, "I cannot submit to the fact that God has decreed such things as you say; you must give me room to say that your credal exposition of God is wrong. By your creed you prove me to be wrong where I know I am right; therefore if the facts I do know are disproved by you, how can I accept your explanation of the facts I do not know?" Elihu says God does not explain Himself, and you have no right to try and find Him out, it is sufficient to know that the autocratic authority of the Omnipotent has spoken, therefore you must submit. Job's sufferings have produced in him this attitude—"I want to know where what you call the supreme authority of the Almighty gets hold on the moral line of things, where it agrees, in part at least, with what I understand as worthy."

The same thing occurs in matters of religious controversy. Am I going to submit to the authority of a Church, or a Book or to the authority of a Person? If I submit to the authority of a Person it must be demonstrated that that Person is greater than I am on the "worthy" line, the line which is recognised as worthy by the majority of sane humanity; if He is greater there, then I will bow down to His authority at once.

3. The Indictment of Autobiographic Antagonism (Job 34–35)

(a) The Suffering Chastisement of Sinfulness (Job 34:35–37)

Job hath spoken without knowledge, and his words were without wisdom. My desire is that Job may be tried unto the end because of his answers for wicked men. For he addeth rebellion unto his sin, he clappeth his hands among us, and multiplieth his words against God.

Elihu sums up the autobiographic side, the subjective side. The great phase at present is the sophistic conception that a man is a law unto himself. Elihu is in advance of that: he says there is an authority other than myself. Job is looking for an authority, and he gives his own subjective experiences as the reason for disbelieving the presentation of God which has been given. On the ground of what he was going through, he was indignant at this presentation. Elihu says, "Your experiences are explainable on the line that you are a sinful man, not a hypocrite, as the others have said, but sinful, and God is chastising you. You have spoken rashly and wildly, and this is the way God is answering." This kind of view presents a conception not really based on facts, but which easily melts down any opposition by its sentimental presentation.

(b) The Sentimental Conception of the Supreme (Job 35:10–11)

But none saith, Where is God my maker, who giveth songs in the night; who teacheth us more than the beasts of the earth, and maketh us wiser than the fowls of the heaven?

There is no pretence about Elihu; he says some sublime things, but in his tirade against experience he introduces a line that stirs up human sympathies without the basis of facts underneath. The sentimental line stirs up a conception of things which overlooks both the actual and the real facts and sweeps a man off his feet. It is all very well to have experiences, but there must be a standard for measuring them, and a standard more worthy than my own on the line on which I know I am worthy. The standard for Christian experience is not the experience of another Christian, but God Himself. "Be ye therefore perfect, even as your Father which is in heaven is perfect." "If you are My disciple," says Jesus, "the standard by which you are to measure your experiences as a regenerated saint is the character of God." "They took knowledge of them, that they had been with Jesus." The Apostles bore a strong family likeness to Jesus Christ, their experience and their character were being brought up to God's standard.

There must be an authority which is internal as well as external. The tendency nowadays is to have no authority at all. A man says, "I will have no Church, no Bible, no God, nothing but my own self-realisation." This is the modern phase of sophistic religion. Every bit of morality a man has demands that there should be, not a coercive or autocratic authority, but a worthy authority. Elihu is speaking to Job on the subjective line as though Job were saying that there was no authority whatever binding upon him; whereas Job is getting at the right relationship to the real standard, and his protest is against a presentation of the standard which is not worthy.

4. The Interpretation of Absolute Authority (*Job 36–37*)
Elihu also proceeded, and said, Suffer me a little, and I will shew thee that I have yet to speak on God's behalf. . . . (Job 36:1–2)

If one may say it reverently, Almighty God is nothing but a mental abstraction unless He becomes concrete and actual, because an ideal has no power unless it can be realised. The doctrine of the Incarnation is that God did become actual, He manifested Himself on the plane of human flesh, and "Jesus Christ" is the name not only for God and Man in one, but the name of the personal Saviour who makes the way back for every man to get into a personal relationship with God. Jesus Christ declares that He is the exclusive way to the Father—". . . neither knoweth any man the Father, save the Son, and he to whomsoever the Son will reveal Him." Any theology which ignores Jesus Christ as the supreme Authority ceases to be Christian theology. "I am the Way," said Jesus, not the road we leave behind us, but the Way we stay in: "no man

cometh unto the Father, but by Me." On the ground of His absolute, not coercive, authority, every man recognises sooner or later that Jesus Christ stands easily first.

(a) The Supreme Character of the Sublime (Job 36:22–26)
Behold, God exalteth by His power: who teacheth like Him? (Job 36:22)

Job's contention is that he has proved by experience that what he has been told about God cannot be true, "because," he says, "when you try to explain the facts I know in the light of the One whom you call God, you have to deny those facts; therefore I must conclude that your exposition of God is wrong." Elihu goes back to the position that it is no use trying to find out whether God is worthy; it is sufficient to know that He is supreme, a Being who issues His orders without the remotest regard to moral right; and the man who dares to try and discover whether the authority of God is morally right is a blasphemer and a dangerous man. Voltaire's scurrilous talk about God was mainly tremendous indignation at the presentation of God then prevailing.

There is always a tendency to produce an absolute authority; we accept the authority of the Church, or of the Bible, or of a creed, and often refuse to do any more thinking on the matter; and in so doing we ignore the essential nature of Christianity which is based on a personal relationship to Jesus Christ, and works on the basis of our responsibility. On the ground of the Redemption I am saved and God puts His Holy Spirit into me, then He expects me to react on the basis of that relationship. I can evade it by dumping my responsibility on to a Church, or a Book or a creed, forgetting what Jesus said—"Ye search the Scriptures, because ye think that in them ye have eternal life; and these are they which bear witness of Me; and ye will not come to Me, that ye may have life" (John 5:39–40, RV). The only way to understand the Scriptures is not to accept them blindly, but to read them in the light of a personal relationship to Jesus Christ. If we insist that a man must believe the doctrine of the Trinity and the inspiration of the Scriptures before he can be saved, we are putting the cart before the horse. All that is the effect of being a Christian, not the cause of it; and if we put the effect first we produce difficulties because we are putting thinking before life. Jesus says, "Come unto Me, and if you want to know whether My teaching is of God, do His will." A scientist can explain the universe in which common-sense men live, but the scientific explanation is not first; life is first. The same with theology; theology is the systematising of the intellectual expression of life from God; it is a mighty thing, but it is second, not first.

(b) The Sorrowful Condemnation of Sanity (**Job 37:23–24**)

Touching the Almighty, we cannot find Him out: He is excellent in power, and in judgement, and in plenty of justice; He will not afflict. Men do therefore fear Him: He respecteth not any that are wise of heart.

Elihu condemns Job sorrowfully, but absolutely; he declares that not only has Job made shipwreck of his faith, but he has become defiant in silencing the friends.

Job will not accept anything blindly, he says, "I must see that it does not contradict what I know." The Apostle Paul speaks of "the foolishness of God" as pitted against the wisdom of men, and the wisdom of men when it saw Jesus Christ said, "That cannot be God." When the Judaic ritualists saw Jesus Christ, they said, "You are a blasphemer; You do not express God at all." Anna and Simeon were the only two of the descendants of Abraham who recognised who Jesus was, hence the condemnation of the other crowd. If two who had lived a life of communion with God could detect Jehovah as the Babe of Bethlehem within the symbolism, the others who did not recognise Him are to be condemned. They did not see Him because they had become blinded on the line of absolute authority, the line of symbolism or creed, and when that which was symbolised appeared, they could not see Him.

Every phase of this Book, with the exception of Job's own utterances, takes up the challenge of Satan—"No man, no matter how good he is, loves You for Your own sake. You call Job perfect, but touch the things You have given him, destroy his blessings, and he will curse You to Your face." Job's blessings were destroyed, and yet he clings to it, "I don't know the reason why I suffer; the reason you give is not the one, God alone can explain it to me, and I will wait for Him." Part of the gamble was that God must keep out of sight, and that Job must not be aided, and he was not. The exposition of Job's sufferings must be given in the light of this preface, which was never made known to him. Job never knew that Satan and Jehovah had made a battleground of his soul.

The problem in the Book of Job represents the problem of the whole world. No matter what a man's experiences may be, whether slight or terrific, there is something in this Book which gives him an indication as to why the Redemption was necessary, and also a line of explaining the otherwise inexplicable things of human experience.

THE PASSION FOR REALITY
Job 38–41

*We cannot kindle when we will
The fire which in the heart resides;
The spirit bloweth and is still,
In mystery our soul abides.
    But tasks in hours of insight will'd
    Can be through hours of gloom fulfill'd
With aching hands and bleeding feet
We dig and heap, lay stone on stone;
We bear the burden and the heat
Of the long day, and wish 'twere done,
    Not till the hours of light return.
    All we have built do we discern.*

Matthew Arnold[22]

The word "Reality" is used to represent the realm of God and the whole of mankind in correspondence. The creeds give us a theological statement of God, but Job's experience proves that a statement of belief does not give us God. The only way we get at God is through conscience, because through conscience we get at the moral relation to things. We have seen that Job would not bow down to an authority which had not its basis in what was right in actual life. God has to clear Himself from the wrong presentation given of Him by the friends, and although Job is right in repudiating their presentation, God rebukes him for remaining too much of an agnostic, and He leads him out along the line indicated when he said, "Though He slay me, yet will I trust in Him," i.e., "I will trust that God is what my innate manhood tells me He must be." The authority we blindly grope after is God Himself, not a tendency making for righteousness, not a set of principles. Behind Reality is God Himself, and the final authority is a personal relationship. Christianity is a personal relationship to a personal God on the ground of the Redemption. The reason Jesus Christ is our Lord and Master is not first because He is God Incarnate, but because He is easily first in the human domain.

---

22. Matthew Arnold (1822–1888), English scholar, poet, and critic.

1. The Still Small Voice of God *(Job 38:1–4a)*
Then the LORD answered Job out of the whirlwind, and said, Who is this that darkeneth counsel by words without knowledge? Gird up now thy loins like a man; for I will demand of thee, and answer thou Me. Where wast thou when I laid the foundations of the earth? . . . (see also Job 40:6–7)

God arraigns both Elihu and Job, He appeals to them to come before Him on the basis of their actual knowledge, and while being true to the facts they know, to leave room for facts they do not know. The still small voice is an appeal not to a superstitious belief in God, but to the actuality of God to man. God disposes altogether of a relationship to Himself born of superstitious dread—"No, stand like a man, and listen to facts as they are." God counsels Job—"Don't come to too hasty a conclusion, but gird up your loins like a man and wait. You have done right so far in that you would not have Me misrepresented, but you must recognise that there are facts you do not know, and wait for Me to give the revelation of them on the ground of your moral obedience." Job would not bow before God on the basis of superstition; he could not conceive such a God to be worthy. The ground of appeal is not that God says I must do a certain thing, but that the manhood in me recognises that what God says is likely to be right. Jesus Christ never coerced anyone; He never used the apparatus of sacerdotalism or of supernatural powers, or what we understand by revivals; He faced men on the ground on which all men stood, and refused to stagger human wits into submission to Himself.

2. The Sub-Scientific Value of Immanence *(Job 38:4b–41)*
"Immanence" means the notion of the immediate presence of God pervading everything, and the pantheist says that this view explains everything. Elihu is stating with enormous airs that "Humanity" is another name for God; whereas one of the big Bible doctrines is that Humanity is not God, and was created to be distinctly not God. There is evidence that God is in the facts of Nature, but also evidence that He is other than Nature. We may make a working definition of the laws of Nature, "but, remember," says God, "behind those laws I come."

Scientific dogmatism is as dangerous as religious dogmatism. Religious dogmatism takes a man's experience and tells him why everything has happened; but every now and again things happen outside human experience which cannot be explained. It is well to note what can be known, but no one has any right to be dogmatic about the things which cannot be known saving by revelation. We can state scientific laws so far as we have been able to discover them, but we are outside our domain if we say that those laws govern regions we know nothing about. Inferences based on the facts I know will never enable me to find God. I may study all the facts of geology and natural history, but where does the note of authority come in it all? The note of authority comes only through conscience. Laws are effects, not causes. If we can know God by means of our intellect, then Jesus Christ's claim to reveal God is a farce, and the Redemption nonsense.

Job declared that he could not know God—"I do not know God," he says, "but I do know that the God you describe in your creed cannot be God, because in order to make Him God you have to deny facts which I know." The friends said that the way out was to accept the agnostic position and become a fatalist—"Don't try to find out whether God's character is noble and right," and they ended in telling an untruth about God. God says, "When I reveal Myself it will be as the God of the morality you know," and yet we must never tie God up along the line of subjective experience.

The only reality in life is moral reality, not intellectual or aesthetic. Religion based on intellectualism becomes purely credal, Jesus Christ is not needed in it. The intellect does not get us at Reality, neither do the emotions alone, but conscience does, as soon as it relates itself to these two. The basis of things is not rational. Reason and intellect are our guides among things as they are, but they cannot explain things as they are. For instance, it is not rational that Christian nations should be at war. The basis of things is tragic, and intellect makes a man shut his eyes to this fact and become a superior person. One of the great crimes of intellectual philosophy is that it destroys a man as a human being and turns him into a supercilious spectator; he cuts himself off from relationship with human stuff as it is and becomes a statue.

A moral man, i.e., the man who will do the right and be the right thing in actual life, is more likely than any other kind of man to recognise God when He manifests Himself. If I become a devotee of a creed I cannot see God unless He comes along my line. It takes the whole man—conscience, intellect, will and emotions, to discover God as Reality. The man who is standing well within his own right, whose conscience is not yet awakened, feels no need of God. "I did not come to call him," said Jesus. But let a man come up against things, and he will find not a creed or a doctrine, but the Reality of God. The elemental facts a man comes up against transform his stubbornness into amenableness to Reality.

3. The Supernormal Vindication of Morality *(Job 39–41)*
Wilt thou also disannul My judgement? Wilt thou condemn Me that thou mayest be righteous? (Job 40:8)

In these chapters the whole of the universe is symbolised, and whatever the universe is, it is not tame. A certain type of modern science would have us believe it is, that we can harness the sea and air and earth. Quite true, you can, if you only read scientific manuals and deal with successful experiments; but before long you discover elements which knock all your calculations on the head and prove that the universe is wild and unmanageable. And yet in the beginning God intended man to control it; the reason he cannot is because he twisted God's order; instead of recognising God's dominion over himself, man became his own god, and by so doing lost control of everything else (see Genesis 3).

When Jesus Christ came He was easily Master of the life in the air and earth and sky, and in Him we see the order God originally intended for man. If you want to know what the human race is to be like on the basis of the Redemption, you will find it mirrored in Jesus Christ—a perfect oneness between God and man, no gap; in the meantime there is a gap, and the universe is wild, not tame. Every type of superstition pretends it can rule the universe, the scientific quack proclaims he can control the weather, that he has occult powers and can take the untameable universe and tame it. God says it cannot be done.

4. The Strangely Stirred Valley of Job *(Job 40)*

Then Job answered the LORD, and said, Behold I am vile; what shall I answer Thee? I will lay mine hand upon my mouth. Once have I spoken; but I will not answer: yea, twice; but I will proceed no further. (Job 40:3–5)

There is nothing cringing in Job's attitude, it is the bowing down of a man strangely stirred in humiliation by the realisation that he is face to face with that which is superior to himself.

The revelation given by Jesus Christ of God is not the revelation of Almighty God, but of the essential nature of Deity—unutterable humility and moral purity, utterly worthy in every detail of actual life. In the Incarnation God proves Himself worthy in the sphere in which we live, and this is the sphere of the revelation of the Self-giving of God. Job recognises this; he knows it is no superstition-monger, or creed-monger, or theology-monger, speaking to him, but the voice of God, because this Voice does not contradict what he knows, but leads him straight out to what he could never discover for himself. And so Job bows his head in true humility before God and listens—"I am on the right track at last."

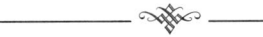

LOCKS V. KEYS
Job 42:1–6

You tell me, doubt is Devil-born
I know not: one indeed I knew
In many a subtle question versed,
Who touch'd a jarring lyre first,
But ever strove to make it true:

Perplext in faith, but pure in deeds,
At last he beat his music out.
There lives more faith in honest doubt,
Believe me, than in half the creeds.

He fought his doubts and gather'd strength
He would not make his judgement blind.
He faced the spectres of the mind
And laid them: thus he came at length

To find a stronger faith his own;
And Power was with him in the night,
Which makes the darkness and the light,
And dwells not in the light alone,

But in the darkness and the cloud,
As over Sinai's peaks of old,
While Israel made their gods of gold,
Altho' the trumpet blew so loud.

Tennyson

Everything a man takes to be the key to a problem is apt to turn out another lock. For instance, the theory of evolution was supposed to be the key to the problem of the universe, but instead it has turned out a lock. Again, the atomic theory was thought to be the key; then it was discovered that the atom itself was composed of electrons, and each electron was found to be a universe of its own, and that theory too becomes a lock and not a key. Everything that man attempts as a simplification of life, other than a personal relationship to God, turns out to be a lock, and we should be alert to recognise when a thing turns from a key to a lock. The creed Job held, which pretended to be a key to the character of God, turned out to be a lock, and Job is realising that the only key to life is not a statement of faith in God, nor an intellectual conception of God, but a personal relationship to Him. God Himself is the key to the riddle of the universe, and the basis of things is to be found only in Him. If a man leaves out God and takes any scientific explanation as the key, he only succeeds in finding another lock.

1. The Rehabilitation of Faith in God
As the Source and Support of All Existence
Then Job answered the LORD, *and said, I know that Thou canst do every thing, and that no thought can be withholden from Thee. (Job 42:1–2)*

To rehabilitate means to reinstate, to restore to former rank. The problem all through the Book of Job is that the teaching of the creed and Job's implicit faith in God do not agree, and it looks as if he is a fool to hang in to his belief in God. In this last chapter we see everything rehabilitated, put back into rank, by means of Job's personal relationship to God. That is what will happen as the result of this war—many a man's faith in God will be rehabilitated. The basis of things must always be found in a personal relationship to a personal God, never in thinking or feeling.

Job says, "I cannot find any rest in your reasonings or in my own, and I refuse to blink the facts in order to make a rational statement." Job had perfect confidence in the character of God though he did not understand the way He was taking. "Though He slay me, yet will I trust in Him." We sometimes wrongly illustrate faith in God by the faith of a business man in a cheque. Faith commercially is based on calculation, but religious faith cannot be illustrated by the kind of faith we exhibit in life. Faith in God is a terrific venture in the dark; I have to believe that God is good in spite of all that contradicts it in my experience. It is not easy to say that God is love when everything that happens actually gives the lie to it. Everyone's soul represents some kind of battlefield. The point for each one is whether we will hang in, as Job did, and say "Though things look black, I will trust in God."

"Then Job *answered* the LORD. . . ." This does not mean that Job saw the Lord standing before him as a man; but that he had a trained ear as the result of his faith in God. The basis of a man's faith in God is that God is the Source and Support of all existence, not that He *is* all existence. Job recognises this, and maintains that in the end everything will be explained and made clear. Have I this kind of faith—not faith in a principle, but faith *in God*, that He is just and true and right? Many of us have no faith in God at all, but only faith in what He has done for us, and when these things are not apparent we lose our faith and say, "Why should this happen to me? Why should there

be a war? Why should I be wounded and sick? Why should my 'cobber' be killed? I am going to chuck up my faith in God."

2. The Re-Establishment of Truth in Life and Personality
As the Source and Support of All Real Experience
Who is he that hideth counsel without knowledge? Therefore have I uttered that I understood not; things too wonderful for me, which I knew not. (Job 42:3)

There is a great difference between Christian experience and Christian faith. The danger of experience is that our faith is made to rest in it, instead of seeing that our experience is simply a doorway to God Himself. The reason many of us refuse to think and discover the basis of true religion is because evangelical Christianity has been stated in such a flimsy way. We get at Truth through life and personality, not by logic or scientific statements. "Therefore have I uttered that I understood not; things too wonderful for me, which I knew not." In refusing to stand by what was not true, Job uttered bigger things than he understood at the time. That is the way God uses men when they are rightly related to Him; He conveys His real presence as a sacrament through their commonplace lives. Our Lord Himself becomes real in the same way that life and personality are real. Intellect asks, "What is truth?" as if truth were something that could be stated in words. "I am . . . the Truth," said Jesus. The only way we get at Truth is by life and personality. When a man is up against things it is no use for him to try and work it out logically, but let him obey, and instantly he will see his way through. Truth is moral, not intellectual. We perceive Truth by doing the right thing, not by thinking it out. "If any man will do His will, he shall know of the doctrine. . . ." Men have tried to get at the truth of Christianity head-first, which is like saying you must think how you will live before you are born. We instantly see the absurdity of that, and yet we expect to reason out the Christian life before we have been born into the realm of Jesus Christ. "Except a man be born again, he cannot see the kingdom of God." If ever we are to see the domain where Jesus lives and enter into it, we must be born again, become regenerated by receiving the Holy Spirit; then we shall find that Truth is not in a creed or a logical statement, but in Life and Personality. This is what Job is realising.

3. The Religious Basis of Science and Philosophy
As the Source and Support of All Abiding Exposition
Hear, I beseech Thee, and I will speak: I will demand of Thee, and declare Thou unto me. (Job 42:4)

We have not to bring God into our system of philosophy, but to found our philosophy on God. The source and support of all abiding exposition is a man's personal relationship to God. If we base our philosophy on reason, we shall produce a false philosophy; but if we base it on faith in God, we can begin to expound life rightly. Actual conditions come into account, but underneath lies the Redemption.

Sin is not man's problem, but God's. God has taken the problem of sin into His own hands and solved it, and the proof that He has is the Cross of Calvary. The Cross is the Cross of God. On the ground of the Redemption I can wash my robes, and make them "white in the blood of the Lamb." Pseudo-evangelism has twisted the revelation and made it mean—"Now that God has saved me, I do not need to do anything." The New Testament revelation is that now I am saved by God's grace, I must work on that basis and keep myself clean. It does not matter what a man's heredity is, or what tendencies there are in him, on the basis of the Redemption he can become all that God's Book indicates he should be. The essential truth of Christianity in thinking is that I can wash my robes, and make them clean in the blood of the Lamb. That is the exposition of the Redemption in actual experience. Are we thinking along this line, or on the pagan line which makes out that the basis of things is rational, and leaves out God, and Jesus Christ, and the Redemption altogether?

4. Repentance and the Dawn of God's Humanity

As the Source and Support of a "Second Chance"

I have heard of Thee by the hearing of the ear; but now mine eye seeth Thee. Wherefore I abhor myself, and repent in dust and ashes. (Job 42:5–6)

Because a man has altered his life it does not necessarily mean that he has repented. A man may have lived a bad life and suddenly stop being bad, not because he has repented, but because he is like an exhausted vol-cano. The fact that he has become good is no sign of his having become a Christian. The bedrock of Christianity is repentance. The Apostle Paul never forgot what he had been; when he speaks of "forgetting those things which are behind," he is referring to what he has attained to; the Holy Spirit never allowed him to forget what he had been (see 1 Corinthians 15:9; Ephesians 3:8; 1 Timothy 1:13–15). Repentance means that I estimate exactly what I am in God's sight and I am sorry for it, and on the basis of the Redemption I become the opposite. The only repentant man is the holy man, i.e., the one who becomes the opposite of what he was because something has entered into him. Any man who knows himself knows that he cannot be holy, therefore if he does become holy, it is because God has "shipped" something into him; he is now "presenced with Divinity," and can begin to bring forth "fruits meet for repentance."

A man may know the plan of salvation, and preach like an archangel, and yet not be a Christian (cf. Matthew 7:21–22). The test of Christianity is that a man lives better than he preaches. The reality of the heredity of Jesus Christ comes into us through regeneration, and if ever we are to exhibit a family likeness to Him it must be because we have entered into repentance and have received something from God. If the disposition of meanness and lust and spite shows itself through my bodily life, when the disposition of Jesus Christ is there, it will show through my bodily life too, and no one need ever be afraid that he will be credited with the holiness he exhibits. "Now mine eye seeth Thee," said Job. "Wherefore I abhor myself ["I loathe my words," RV mg], and repent in dust and ashes." When I enthrone Jesus Christ I say the thing that is violently opposed to the old rule. I deny my old ways as entirely as Peter denied his Lord.

Jesus Christ's claim is that He can put a new disposition, His own disposition, Holy Spirit, into any man, and it will be manifested in all that he does. But the disposition of the Son of God can only enter my life by the way of repentance.

DISGUISE OF THE ACTUAL
Job 42:7–17

That low man seeks a little thing to do,
Sees it and does it:
This high man, with a great thing to pursue,
Dies ere he knows it.
That low man goes on adding one to one,
His hundred's soon hit:
This high man, aiming at a million,

Misses an unit.
That, has the world here—should he need the
*   next*
Let the world mind him!
This, throws himself on God, and unperplexed,
Seeking shall find him.

Robert Browning

Our actual life is a disguise, no one expresses what he really is. Job could not express actually, either before or after his suffering, what he really was. The "great Divine event" to which we look forward is when the earth will actually express itself as the work of God, and saints will actually express themselves as the sons of God. Meanwhile, actual appearances do not express the real things.

All through Job has maintained his belief that God is honourable; he declares that the friends' credal statement of God was not adequate because they have said things he could disprove from his own experience. "Why I am suffering, I do not know; but your explanation does not satisfy me. Though He slay me, though I am knocked to pieces really, I believe that God is honourable, a God of love and justice, and I will wait for Him, and one day it will be proved, that my faith was right." That is the sublime reach of Job's faith. Now God takes it in hand to deal with the friends.

1. The Scourge of Eternal Reality
The LORD said to Eliphaz the Temanite, My wrath is kindled against thee, and against thy two friends: for ye have not spoken of Me the thing that is right, as My servant Job hath. (Job 42:7)

Everyone who poses as a religious teacher is faced sooner or later by Eternal Reality. The friends had posed as religious teachers, they said they knew God, and their criticism of Job was along this line; but God says, "Ye have not spoken of Me the thing that is right, as My servant Job hath." In reading what Job says we should probably have come to the conclusion that a man who talked as he did could not be a good man, he said such wild, extravagant things; and yet in the end God, who is Eternal Reality, said that he had spoken rightly of Him. A man may utter wild things which seem to us all wrong, but it will be a humiliation to find that he has spoken of God more truly than we have. When Eternal Reality strikes, pose is no good, religious humbug is no good. The voice of God is scathing Eliphaz and the others, not because they had spoken untruths—they had spoken what was logically true all the time, but because they had misrepresented Him. Christianity does not consist in telling the truth, or walking in a conscientious way, or adhering to principles; Christianity is something other than all that, it is adhering in absolute surrender to a Person, the Lord Jesus Christ.

If the Reality of God is a scourge to a man who has never pretended to be religious, it must be ten times more so to a man who has been a religious teacher, who has said to people, "I can tell you why you suffer." "I can tell you why God has allowed this war, and what He is doing with the British Empire." When such a man comes up against eternal realities and hears God say, "You have not spoken the thing

which is true of Me," the scourge must be appalling (cf. John 15:2–6). Eliphaz had spoken the truth abstractly, but he had misrepresented God all through. God is not an abstract truth; He is the Eternal Reality, and is discerned only by means of a personal relationship.

When one is found out by Eternal Reality the danger is to become defiant or despairing. When the friends were scourged by God they took the right attitude and did not get into despair. If the scourge of Eternal Reality comes, see that it leaves you face to face with God, not with yourself.

2. The Surgery of Events Reacting
Therefore take unto you now seven bullocks and seven rams, and go to My servant Job, and offer up for yourselves a burnt offering; and My servant Job shall pray for you: for him will I accept. (Job 42:8a)

We only see along the line of our prejudices—our evangelical or un-evangelical prejudices, the prejudices of our belief or of our agnosticism; we cannot see otherwise until events operate on us. The surgery of events is a most painful thing. It has taken a devilish thing like this war to root up the prejudices of men who were misrepresenting God to themselves. A prejudice is a foreclosed judgement without having sufficiently weighed the evidence. Not one of us is free from prejudices, and the way we reveal them most is by being full of objection to the prejudices of other people. If we stick obstinately to any line of prejudice, there will come the surgery of events that will shift us out of it. Watch that you do not make an issue with God; it is a dangerous thing to do.

The surgery of events brought the friends out of their prejudices. All along they had said to Job, "You are wrong, we can prove it, you are a bad man, and it is a wonder to us that God does not strike you dead." But the surgery of events brings them to their knees in utter humiliation. "Go to My servant Job," God says, "and he shall pray for you." "Go through the issue, or you will never get to Me." Think of the humiliation of it!

> *. . . lest I deal with you after your folly, in that ye have not spoken of Me the thing which is right, like My servant Job. (Job 42:8)*

What is it to speak "the thing that is right" about God? I have never seen God; to call Him omnipotent and omnipresent and omniscient means nothing to me; I do not care one bit for an Almighty Incomprehensible First Cause. To speak the thing which is right about God, I must be in living personal relationship with Him. God is riddling the friends because while preaching the right thing, they have misrepresented Him and told a lie about the Author of Truth. If I preach the right thing but do not live it, I am telling an untruth about God. This is one of the cardinal truths of Christianity (see Romans 2:17–23). "But," a man says, "how am I going to live the truth?" The Sermon on the Mount says we must have a disposition which is never lustful or spiteful or evil; where are we going to begin? Unless Jesus Christ can put into us His own heredity, it is impossible. But that is just what He claims He can do. By regeneration Jesus Christ can put into any man the disposition that will make him the living example of what he preaches. The baptism of the Holy Ghost did not add anything to the Apostles' doctrine, it made them specimens of what they taught (see Acts 1:8).

3. The Sacrament of Experimental Repentance
So Eliphaz the Temanite and Bildad the Shuhite and Zophar the Naamathite went, and did according as the LORD commanded them. (Job 42:9)

The friends accepted the humiliation, and did a repentant thing.

Strictly speaking, repentance is a gift of God. No man can repent when he chooses. A man can be remorseful when he chooses, but remorse is a lesser thing than repentance. Repentance means that I show my sorrow for the wrong thing by becoming the opposite. The old Puritans used to pray for "the gift of tears." A man has the power to harden himself against one of God's greatest gifts. If in order to dissolve a piece of ice, you take a hammer and smash it up, you simply break it into so many pieces of ice; but put the ice out in the sunshine and it quickly disappears. That is just the difference between man's handling of wrong and God's. Man's handling may cause it to crumble, but it is only so much crumbled-up wrong; when God handles it, it becomes repentance, and the man turns to God and his life becomes a sacrament of experimental repentance.

These men did not say, "No, we will not go to Job"; they did not attempt to justify themselves, they did exactly what God told them to, and in so doing they did a grand and noble thing, and took the only chance of getting to know God.

4. The Supplication of Emancipating Religion
And the LORD turned the captivity of Job, when he prayed for his friends. (Job 42:10a)

Have you come to "when" yet? If you are in the position of Job and have shipped some trouble on board that makes you taken up with yourself, remember that when Job prayed for his friends, God emancipated him. Pray for your friends, and God will turn your

captivity also. The emancipation comes as you intercede for them; it is not a mere reaction, it is the way God works. It is not a question of getting time for Bible study, but of spontaneous intercession as we go about our daily calling, and we shall see emancipation come all along, not because we understand the problems, but because we recognise that God has chosen the way of intercession to perform His moral miracles in lives. Then get to work and pray, and God will get His chance with other lives; you do not even need to speak to them. God has based the Christian life on Redemption, and as we pray on this basis God's honour is at stake to answer prayer.

5. The Society of Enlarged Friendship *(Job 42:10–17)*
. . . also the LORD gave Job twice as much as he had before. (Job 42:10b)

Job's actual life looked exactly the same after his suffering as before to anyone who does not know the inner history. That is the disguise of the actual. There is always this difference in the man who has been through real trouble—his society is enlarged in every direction, he is much bigger minded, more generous and liberal, more capable of entertaining strangers. One of the greatest emancipators of personal life is sorrow. After the war there will be the society of enlarged friendship in many a life; men will never be as estranged from one another as they used to be. One thing which has gone by the board entirely is the conceit that we know men. Men do not live in types; there is always one fact more in every life that no one knows but God. The last thing to go is the religious category. A man will stick to his religious categories of men until he receives a shaking up from Eternal Reality, as these men did. Eliphaz and the others maintained the conception that unless a man held to the particular shibboleth of their religious creed, he was lost. The one thing that will cause the conceit that we know men to disappear is the surgery of events, the Eternal Reality of God shaking the nonsense out of us. This has happened in many a life through the cataclysm of war, and men find they have a different and a broader way of looking at things. There is no room for veneer and pretence in camp life.

> *Then came there unto him all his brethren, and all his sisters, and all they that had been of his acquaintance before, and did eat bread with him in his house: and they bemoaned him, and comforted him over all the evil that the LORD had brought upon him. (Job 42:11a)*

There was a larger, grander society in Job's actual life after his suffering. In his Epistle Peter refers to the people who have plenty of time for you, they are those who have been through suffering, but now seem full of joy (see 1 Peter 4:12–19). If a man has not been through suffering he will snub you unless you share his interests, he is no more concerned about you than the desert sand; but those who have been through things are not now taken up with their own sorrows, they are being made broken bread and poured-out wine for others. You can always be sure of the man who has been through suffering, but never of the man who has not.

> *. . . every man also gave him a piece of money, and every one an earring of gold. (Job 42:11b)*

Job accepted the gifts from his friends and brethren, which is an indication of a generous spirit. The majority of us prefer to give, but Job was big enough to accept all that his friends brought him.

> *So the LORD blessed the latter end of Job more than his beginning. (Job 42:12)*

Biblical Ethics

Oswald Chambers

INTRODUCTION

Source

These lectures were given by Oswald Chambers at:
The Bible Training College,[1] 1911–1915.
League of Prayer meetings in Britain, 1909–1915.
Zeitoun YMCA Huts, classes for soldiers in Egypt, 1917.[2]

Publication History

- This material was first published as articles in the *Bible Training Course* (BTC) *Monthly Journal,*[3] 1932–1945.
- It was first published as a book in 1947.

Shortly after the Bible Training College opened in January 1911, Oswald Chambers began teaching a class on biblical ethics. The class was open to resident and visiting students alike, and reflected Chambers' deep belief in the importance of thinking.

"We must never forget that God is a great deal bigger than our experience of Him; that Jesus Christ is a great deal bigger than our experience of Him," Oswald said. "It is because people won't take the labour to think, that the snare gets hold of them; and remember thinking is a tremendous labour" ("Thinking," *Tongues of Fire,* January 1914, p. 5).

Noted London pastor Dr. G. Campbell Morgan[4] spoke at the College's first anniversary celebration and made special mention of the classes on biblical ethics and biblical philosophy, saying that such classes were unusual in a Bible college of that day.

Throughout the years of the BTC[5] (1911–1915), Biblical Ethics remained a part of the syllabus, with Chambers sometimes using James Stalker's[6] book *The Ethic of Jesus according to the Synoptic Gospels* (1909) as a text.

Additional material on ethics and thinking appears in *The Moral Foundations of Life* in this volume.

---

1. Residential school near Clapham Common in SW London, sponsored by the League of Prayer. Oswald Chambers was Principal and main teacher; Biddy Chambers was Lady Superintendent. Known as the BTC, it closed in July 1915 because of World War I.

2. Zeitoun (zay TOON). An area 6 miles NE of Cairo. Site of YMCA camp, Egypt General Mission compound and a large base area for British, Australian and New Zealand troops. Site of the Imperial School of Instruction (1916-19).

3. The *Bible Training Course Journal* was published from 1932 to 1952 by Mrs. Chambers, with help from David Lambert.

4. G. Campbell Morgan (1863–1945), British preacher, writer, internationally known Bible teacher. Pastor of Westminster Chapel from 1904 to 1917, and from 1933 to 1943.

5. Bible Training College.

6. James Stalker (1848–1927), Scottish theologian, scholar, pastor, writer.

CONTENTS

FOREWORD
(to the original 1947 edition)

This latest book of Talks, Lectures, Addresses, given by Oswald Chambers at different times and in varied circumstances—as when the New Theology was making its shallow appeal in 1909, or in the strenuous days of the Bible Training College in London, or when speaking to the soldiers in Egypt in 1917 (just before his own Home-call)—covers a wide range of religious thinking.

The earlier chapters on Biblical Ethics remind us that the *ultimate* aim of Christ's Atonement is that God may readjust man to Himself. That calls for a moral response on our part, involving thought and feeling and will. And we need to recognise the ethical demands made in the Scriptures on God's people.

Our Lord gave us the Sermon on the Mount; it appears in the beginning of St. Matthew's Gospel. He also taught what appears later in the Gospel, that "the Son of Man must suffer many things . . . and be killed, and the third day be raised up" (Matthew 16:21; and that His Life would be "a ransom for many" (Matthew 20:28). The former without the latter would mock us. Oswald Chambers based all on the Atonement.

I have found in this book some of the most arresting truths I have yet met with. Those who have been most helped by the O.C. literature already published will find fresh pastures here. For he was indeed a scribe bringing forth "out of his treasure things new and old," whose ideas never become obsolete or stale, as he is divinely enabled to see old and precious things in new relationships. May God make this book to be a blessing to many.

David Lambert[7]

THE MORAL IMPERATIVE—I
(i.e., a law universal and binding on every rational will)
How Can I Do What I Ought to Do?

Strictly speaking, there is no disobedience possible to an imperative law, the only alternative being destruction. In this sense the moral law is not imperative, because it can be disobeyed and immediate destruction does not follow. And yet the moral law never alters, however much men disobey it; it can be violated, but it never alters. Remember, at the back of all human morality stands God.

1. God's "Oughts"—Old Testament
The Ten Commandments were not given with any consideration for human ability or inability to keep them; they are the revelation of God's demands made of men and women who had declared that if God would make His law known, they would keep it. "And all the people answered together, and said, All that the LORD hath spoken we will do" (Exodus 19:8). "And God spake all these words saying, . . . Thou shalt . . . Thou shalt not . . ." (Exodus 20:1–17). The com-

mandments were given with the inexorable awfulness of Almighty God; and the subsequent history of the people is the record of how they could not keep them.

The moral law ordained by God does not make itself weak to the weak, it does not palliate our shortcomings, it takes no account of our heredity and our infirmities; it demands that we be absolutely moral. Not to recognise this is to be less than alive. The Apostle Paul said, "I was alive without the law once: but when the commandment came, sin revived, and I died" (Romans 7:9). Undress yourself morally and see how much you owe to your upbringing, to the circumstances you are in; when you have got rid of all that, there is little to stand before God in, certainly nothing to boast of. Immediately we come into actual human conditions we find inability with regard to the keeping of God's law, then comes in the equivocation—"Of course God won't demand it." "Of course God will make allowances." God's laws are not

---

7. David Lambert (1871–1961): Methodist minister and friend of Oswald Chambers. Assisted Mrs. Chambers with OC publications from 1917–1961.

watered down to suit anyone; if God did that He would cease to be God. The moral law never alters for the noblest or the weakest; it remains abidingly and eternally the same.

Every man has an imperative something within him which makes him say "I ought," even in the most degraded specimens of humanity the "ought" is there, and the Bible tells us where it comes from—it comes from God. The modern tendency is to leave God out and make our standard what is most useful to man. The utilitarian says that these distinct laws of conduct have been evolved by man for the benefit of man—the greatest use to the greatest number. That is not the reason a thing is right; the reason a thing is right is that God is behind it. God's "oughts" never alter; we never grow out of them. Our difficulty is that we find in ourselves this attitude—"I ought to do this, but I won't"; "I ought to do that, but I don't want to." That puts out of court the idea that if you teach men what is right they will do it—they won't; what is needed is a power which will enable a man to do what he knows is right. We may say "Oh I won't count this time"; but every bit of moral wrong is counted by God. The moral law exerts no coercion, neither does it allow any compromise. "For whosoever shall keep the whole law, and yet offend in one point, he is guilty of all" (James 2:10). Once we realise this we see why it was necessary for Jesus Christ to come. The Redemption is the Reality which alters inability into ability.

2. Christ's Principles—New Testament
If the "Oughts" of the Old Testament were difficult to obey, Our Lord's teaching is unfathomably more difficult. Remember, the commandments were given irrespective of human ability or inability to keep them; then when Jesus Christ came, instead of doing what we all too glibly say He did—put something easier before men, He made it a hundredfold more difficult, because He goes behind the law to the disposition. There is an idea abroad to-day that because as Christians we are not under law, but under grace, therefore the Ten Commandments have no meaning for us—what did Jesus say? "Think not that I am come to destroy the law ...: I am not come to destroy, but to fulfil" (Matthew 5:17). The teaching of the Sermon on the Mount is overwhelmingly and disastrously penetrating. Jesus Christ does not simply say, "Thou shalt not do certain things"; He demands that we have such a condition of heart that we never even think of doing them, every thought and imagination of heart and mind is to be unblameable in the sight of God. Who is sufficient for these things—an unsullied purity that never lusts, a forgiving disposition that loves its enemies, a generous spirit that "taketh not account of evil" (RV)? That standard can produce only one thing in an open-eyed man, absolute despair.

What is the use of saying, "All we need is to know what Jesus Christ teaches and then live up to it": where are you going to begin? If we are Christians we have to live according to the teaching of the Sermon on the Mount; and the marvel of Jesus Christ's salvation is that He puts us in the place where we can fulfil all the old law and a great deal more.

Be careful not to be caught up in the clap-trap of to-day which says, "I believe in the teachings of Jesus, but I don't see any need for the Atonement." Men talk pleasant, patronising things about Jesus Christ's teaching while they ignore His Cross. By all means let us study Christ's teaching, we do not think nearly enough along New Testament lines, we are swamped by pagan standards, and as Christians we ought to allow Jesus Christ's principles to work out in our brains as well as in our lives; but the teaching of Jesus apart from His Atonement simply adds an ideal that leads to despair. What is the good of telling me that only the pure in heart can see God when I am impure? of telling me to love my enemies when I hate them? I may keep it down but the spirit is there. Does Jesus Christ make it easier? He makes it a hundred-fold more difficult! The purity God demands is impossible unless we can be re-made from within, and that is what Jesus Christ undertakes to do through the Atonement. Jesus Christ did not come to tell men they ought to be holy—there is an "ought" in every man that tells him that, and whenever he sees a holy character he may bluster and excuse himself as he likes, but he knows that is what he ought to be: He came to put us in the place where we can be holy, that is, He came to *make* us what He teaches we should be, that is the difference.

Our Lord's first requirement is a personal relationship to Himself, and then obedience to His principles. Tolstoi blundered in applying the Sermon on the Mount practically without insisting on the need to be born again of the Spirit first, and he had an enormous following of intellectual faddists, mere "spring-cleaners." It is not a question of applying Jesus Christ's principles to our actual life first of all, but of applying them to our relationship to Himself, then as we keep our souls open in relation to Him our conscience will decide how we are to act out of that relationship. The principles of Jesus Christ go to the very root of the matter, they have an intensely practical application to our moral life. "For I say unto you, That except your righteousness shall exceed the righteousness of the scribes and Pharisees, ye shall in no wise enter into the kingdom of heaven" (Matthew 5:20).

We said that the teaching of Jesus Christ apart from His Atonement leads to despair; but if it produces the pauper condition, it is the right kind of despair. "Blessed are the poor in spirit...." Conviction of sin will bring a man there, and so will the realisation of God's demands. The best expression for us is the 139th Psalm, "Search me, O God"; I cannot make my heart pure, I cannot alter my heredity, I cannot alter the dreams of my mind; "Search me, O God, and know my heart." That is the poverty of spirit Jesus says is blessed; if you are in that condition, He says you can easily enter the kingdom of heaven. Why? Because God gives the almighty gift of salvation from sin to paupers; He gives the Holy Spirit to paupers (see Luke 11:13).

3. The New Man—Present Day

Jesus Christ, as Representative Man, accepted the responsibility of exhibiting on the human plane the absolute holiness of God; He lived up to God's standard in every detail of holy living and holy speaking and holy working, and His claim is that through the Atonement He can put us in the place where we can do the same. The very disposition that was in Him is put into me—is it there? If it is not, I will have to answer for it. It is not that God puts the life of Jesus in front of us and says, "Do your best to follow Him," but that "the life also of Jesus" is to "be made manifest in our mortal flesh." When "Christ is formed" in us by regeneration (Galatians 4:19), we have to see that our human nature puts on the "clothing" that is worthy of the Son of God. That is where our responsibility comes in—not in being absolutely holy, but in seeing that we allow Jesus Christ to be absolutely holy in us. Regeneration does not resolve a human being into imbecility, it lifts him powerfully into oneness with God in Christ Jesus.

We shall come to find that being "not under the law, but under grace" does not mean we are so free from the law that it does not matter now what we do; it means that in our actual lives we can fulfil all the requirements of the law of God.

THE MORAL IMPERATIVE—II
(i.e., a law universal and binding on every rational will)

Why Should I Do What I Ought to Do?

Authority in the final sense must spring from within. To begin with, we are educated by means of authority on the outside—"thou shalt" and "thou shalt not"; but that authority does not treat us as men. The ultimate aim imbedded in all external authority is to produce a standard of authority within ourselves. The authority our Lord obeyed was an internal authority, not an external one, that is, His inner life and the life He exhibited were one and the same, and the purpose of all external authority is to bring us there. We only realise the moral law when it comes with an IF, that means, I have the power not to obey it.

We imagine that if we obey authority we limit ourselves, whereas obedience to authority is not a limitation but a source of power; by obeying we *are* more. Naturally we are built to command, not to obey; man was originally constituted by God to have dominion—"And God said, Let us make man in our image, after our likeness: and let them have dominion . . ." (Genesis 1:26); consequently there is the natural desire to want to explain things, because everything we can explain we can command. Spiritually, we are built not to command, but to obey. Always beware of the tendency to want to have things explained; you may take it as an invariable law that when you demand an explanation in connection with a moral problem it means you are evading obedience.

1. Authority and Humanity—Conditional

The first standard of authority the Bible reveals is the authority of innocence, a conditional authority (see Genesis 2:16–17). Innocence means the absence of legal guilt. As long as Adam obeyed God he was in this state of innocence; God placed him in an external setting so that he might transform his innocence into moral character by a series of choices. It was to be a natural progress of development, not from evil to good, but from the natural to the spiritual. This Adam failed to do; the temptation came—Take dominion over yourself, "and ye shall be as God"; he took dominion over himself, and by so doing lost dominion over everything else, and the disposition of sin—my claim to my right to myself, I will do what I like—became the inheritance of the whole human race. "Therefore, as through one man sin entered into the world . . ." (Romans 5:12 RV). Children born of natural generation are not innocent in the same way that Adam was innocent, neither does the innocence of a child contain conditional authority; the innocence of Regeneration alone corresponds to Adam's innocence.

Some people maintain that innocence should be the only standard of authority; the idea works out magnificently on paper or in thinking, but it does not work out in practical life. If we were all born with the right disposition, development along this line would have been all right; but we quickly find out that there is something drastically wrong, the disposition of sin is at work, this opposing principle which is not true to human nature as God created it. It sounds very delightful to talk about the innocence of children and "living the simple life"; but try it in actual experience, and you will find it works out the wrong way every time. Authority based on innocence soon becomes ignorance, not ignorance of ourselves, but a determined being without the knowledge of God, and ignorance quickly corrupts into iniquity (see Genesis 3–4).

Another standard of authority is that of conscience, or "the inner light"—what Socrates called "the presiding dæmon," an un-get-at-able, indefinable spirit which gives liberty or check to whatever a man feels impelled to do. Every man has a conscience, although every man does not know God. If God had never made known His demands we might have said that every man was a law to himself—"Whatever I think is right according to my own inner light, must be right." As soon as a man becomes a law to himself he begins to do what he likes, and if you teach development along the line of obedience to a man's inner light, what about the man who is born with damnable tendencies—where will it lead him? to a moral pigsty. The final standard of authority must be one that can be owned by all men.

2. Authority As Happiness—Corrupt

Happiness is the portion of a child, children ought to be thoughtless and happy, and woe be to the people who upset their happiness; but if you take happiness as the end and aim for men and women you have to make its basis a determined ignorance of God, otherwise men will, like Job, remember God and be troubled (see Job 23:15). Read the Seventy-third Psalm, it is the description of the man who has made happiness his aim—he is not in trouble as other men, neither is he plagued like other men, he has more than heart could wish; but once let his moral equilibrium be upset by conviction of sin and all his happiness is destroyed. The end and aim of human life is not happiness, but "to glorify God and enjoy Him for ever." Holiness of character, chastity of life, living communion with God—that is the end of a man's life, whether he is happy or not is a matter of moonshine.[8] Happiness is no standard for men and women because happiness depends on my being determinedly ignorant of God and His demands. Whenever the Spirit of God disturbs a man, He brings him back to the Decalogue. The point is that anything that relieves us from the individual responsibility of being personally related to God is corrupt.

Immorality will produce happiness very quickly—the duration of the happiness is another matter; if you go on doing wrong long enough you will be happy doing wrong and miserable doing right—therefore quit doing right! Immorality may be physically clean, but at its heart is this thought—"All I am concerned with is the happiness of the greatest number, and I don't care anything at all about God." Once remove personal accountability to God and you will get immorality, whether it is bestial or not is a matter of accident. The Bible talks very unvarnishedly, it calls things by the hideous names that belong to them (e.g., Colossians 3:5; Galatians 5:19–21). Beware of being cute enough to detect immorality only in a moral pigsty, learn to detect it in your own spiritual imaginations.

3. Authority As Holiness—Correct

The commandments of God exhibit not His consideration for man, but His authoritative demands of man. Man has to fulfil God's laws in his physical life, in his mental and moral life, in his social and spiritual life, and to offend in one point is to be guilty of all (see James 2:10). Until we realise that God cannot make allowances, the Gospel has no meaning for us; if God made allowances He would cease to be God. All through the Bible the authority of God's law is unflinchingly revealed, together with man's responsibility to meet its demand; but the problem of problems is—how is it going to be done? When a man reads the teachings of Jesus he is obliged to say, "Yes, that is right, but His teaching destroys my peace; I believe that is what I ought to be, but where am I going to begin?"

Holiness is the agreement between a man's disposition and the law of God, as expressed in the life of Jesus. According to the Bible there are only two Men, Adam and Jesus Christ; both came into the world directly by the hand of God, innocent. Jesus Christ, the last Adam, did what the first Adam failed to do; He transformed innocence into holy character. The law of God was incarnated in Jesus Christ, He walked this earth in human guise and lived the perfect life which God desired. Never think of Jesus Christ as an individual, He is the Federal Head of the race; He not only fulfilled all God's demands, but He made the way for every imperfect son of man to live the same kind of life. Jesus Christ does not put us back where Adam was, He puts us where Adam never was: He puts us where He is Himself; He presences us with Divinity, viz., the Holy Spirit. The meaning of the Redemption is that any man can be regenerated into the life Jesus lived and can have the holiness of God imparted to him, not the power to imitate His holiness, but the very nature of God—". . . that we

---

8. moonshine: insignificant or meaningless

may be partakers of His holiness." Holiness is the characteristic of the man after God's own heart.

The holiness which God demands is impossible unless a man can be re-made from within, and that is what Jesus Christ has undertaken to do. Jesus Christ does not merely save people from hell: "thou shalt call His name JESUS; for it is He that shall save His people from their sins," i.e., make totally new moral men. Jesus Christ came from a holy God to enable men, by the sheer might of His Redemption, to become holy. "Ye shall be holy: for I the LORD your God am holy."

N.B.—NOTES OF THIS LECTURE ARE INCOMPLETE.

MORAL INSTITUTIONS—I
In Precept

By "In Precept" is meant necessary principles laid down beforehand.

God has ordained that man is to govern man, whether he wants to or not. This keeps socialism from being "it"; the socialistic scheme falls to pieces because it ignores the fact that human institutions are not utilitarian, that is, they do not spring from the ingenuity of man, but were deliberately ordained by God for the government of man by man. Peter brings this out when he says, "Be subject to every ordinance of man," but he is careful to add "for the Lord's sake" (1 Peter 2:13 RV).

Man is responsible to God for the government of the whole world, but if a man succumbs to the temptations of his official position, that very position will have the effect of hardening his heart away from God. We read in the Old Testament that Pharaoh hardened his heart (Exodus 7:14, et seq.); and we read also that God hardened his heart (Exodus 4:21, et seq.). The difficulty of this apparent contradiction is purely superficial. It must not be interpreted to mean that God hardened a man's heart and then condemned him for being hardened. The hardening of Pharaoh's heart by himself and by God is the expression of the working of one of God's laws, and God's laws do not alter. Any ruler or ordinary man who refuses to obey the right law will find himself distinctly hardened away from God. If a man is to govern rightly he must see that the institutions he builds up are based on the stabilities of human nature as God created it; otherwise havoc will be produced.

One of the first general principles to be borne in mind is that we must never think of men and women in the mass. We talk about "the struggling mass of humanity"—there is no such thing, the mass is made up of separate individuals. The danger of thinking of people in the mass is that you forget they are human beings, each one an absolutely solitary life. Everyone has something or someone to govern, the most ignominious slave has an influence somewhere, and God is going to hold us responsible for the way we govern.

Another thing to be borne in mind is the incalculable element in every life. In the government of man by man you are not dealing with a mathematical problem, but with human beings, and you can never be sure how they will act, any more than you can always be sure how you yourself will act.

These are simply indications of the problems a man has to face in the government of other men, and yet God has so constituted things that man has to govern man and to answer to God for the way he governs.

DESIRE. One of the biggest ingredients in a man's make-up is what he desires, or regards as good. Discouragement or any kind of "sulks" is accounted for by the fact that the good a man aims at is not good enough. A man of character will set himself at nothing less than the highest.

The remarkable thing about the "universe of desire" is that at any second it may alter. Every now and again a tumult comes into a man's life and alters what he desires. For instance, death has an amazing power of altering what a man desires, because death profoundly affects his outlook; or the experience of new birth will do it. When a man is born again he stops desiring the things he used to desire, not gradually, but suddenly; things begin to matter that did not matter before, and the things that used to matter no longer do so. He experiences a conflict of desire; at one time he wants to do the old things, at another, the new, and for a while he is in an unbalanced state. That is the result ethically and morally of conviction of sin, and is exactly what Jesus meant when He said, "Think not that I came to cast peace on the earth: I came not to cast peace, but a sword" (Matthew 10:34 RV mg).

This sudden alteration in the universe of desire is one of the perplexities in the government of man by man. You cannot be sure that the man you are dealing with will always be the same, at any second he may alter. You see someone set on a line you know to be wrong, but remember, at any second the universe of his desire may change. To remember this will bring a tremendous hopefulness and cure us of our unbelief about any life.

Another thing to bear in mind is the difference between a young life and a mature life. A boy or girl just emerging from the "teens" is always chaotic; if a young life is normal it is a chunk of chaos; if it is not, there is something wrong, there ought to be the chaotic element. A precocious young life rarely ends well, it becomes ordered too soon. God holds us responsible for the way we judge a young life; if we judge it by the standards by which we would judge a mature life, we will be grossly unjust. As you watch the life it seems sometimes to lean towards the good, sometimes towards the wrong, and you find yourself getting either excited or depressed over it; but there is one main trend coming out, and that trend can be guarded by prayer. This emphasises the importance of intercessory prayer. Much misjudgement of young life goes on in the reli-

gious domain. There is a stage when a young life manifests a sudden interest in everything to do with religion, but never bank on these awakenings because they are not necessarily awakenings by the Spirit of God, and when the intense stage passes—and it certainly will pass if it is not born of the Spirit—the one who is judging is apt to say that the boy or girl has backslidden. What has happened is that they have passed through a dangerous stage of development. The defects of a growing life are one thing; the vices of a mature life are another. Be as merciless as God can make you towards the vices of a mature life, but be very gentle and patient with the defects of a growing life.

These things make us understand how careful we have to be to recognise God in our government of other lives. If the government of our own life is "upon His shoulder," we will be careful to rely on Him in connection with the lives we are called on to influence and govern.

MORAL INSTITUTIONS—II
In Practice

By "In Practice" is meant fitness through regular exercise. If we do not fit ourselves by practice when there is no crisis, we shall find that our nature will fail us when the crisis comes. The grace of God never fails, but we may fail the grace of God. Unless our nervous system is made the ally of the new life from God it becomes a humiliation to us, and we sit down under a tyranny of nerves. Once we have received the Holy Spirit we must sit down to nothing. In these distinctly personal matters it must be borne in mind that the moral institutions ordained by God take no account whatever of nervous disabilities, they take account only of God Himself and the way He has designed man. When your nervous system, which has been ruled by the wrong disposition, is inclined to say "I can't," you must say, "You must," and to your amazement you find you can!

1. Righteousness—Conformity to a Right Standard
—where no one but God sees us. That is where very few of us are Christians.

(a) In Intention
Little children, let no man deceive you: he that doeth righteousness is righteous. . . . (1 John 3:7)

Jesus Christ demands of His disciples that they live in conformity to the right standard in intention. We say, "Though I didn't do well, I meant well'; then it is

absolutely certain you did not mean well. Jesus Christ makes no allowance for heroic moods; He judges us by the diligently applied bent of our disposition. Concentration on the part of a Christian is of more importance than consecration.

". . . he that *doeth* righteousness is righteous." There are different kinds of intention, e.g., outer and inner; immediate and remote; direct and indirect. The righteous man is the one whose inner intention is clearly revealed in his outer intention, there is no duplicity, no internal hypocrisy. A man's outer intention is easily discernible by other people; his inner intention needs to be continually examined. The marvel of the grace of God is that it can alter the mainspring of our make-up; then when that is altered we must foster in ourselves those intentions which spring from the Spirit of Jesus and make our nervous system carry them out. The Holy Spirit will bring us to the practical test, it is not that I *say* I am righteous, but that I prove I am in my deeds.

(b) In Individuals
For I say unto you, That except your righteousness shall exceed the righteousness of the scribes and Pharisees, ye shall in no wise enter into the kingdom of heaven. (Matthew 5:20 RV)

Take Saul of Tarsus as an example of Pharisaism; he says of himself in writing to the Philippians, "as touching the law, a Pharisee; . . . touching the righteousness which is in the law, blameless . . ." (Philippians 3:5–6): Jesus Christ says as disciples we have to exceed that. No wonder we find His statements absolutely shattering. Our righteousness has to be in excess of the righteousness of the man whose external conduct is blameless according to the law—what does that produce? despair straightaway. When we hear Jesus say, "Blessed are the pure in heart," our answer, if we are awake is, "My God, how am I going to be pure in heart? If ever I am to be blameless down to the deepest recesses of my intentions, You must do something mighty in me." That is exactly what Jesus Christ came to do. He did not come to *tell us* to be holy, but to *make* us holy, undeserving of censure in the sight of God. If any man or woman gets there it is by the sheer supernatural grace of God. You can't indulge in pious pretence when you come to the atmosphere of the Bible. If there is one thing the Spirit of God does it is to purge us from all sanctimonious humbug, there is no room for it.

(c) In Institutions
Submit yourselves to every ordinance of man for the Lord's sake. . . . (1 Peter 2:13; see 2 Peter 2:13–18)

Peter's statements in these verses are remarkable, and they are statements the modern Christian does not like. He is outlining what is to be the conduct of saints in relation to the moral institutions based on the government of man by man. No matter, he says, what may be the condition of the community to which you belong, behave yourself as a saint in it. Many people are righteous as individuals, but they ignore the need to be righteous in connection with human institutions. Paul continually dealt with insubordination in spiritual people. Degeneration in the Christian life comes in because of this refusal to recognise the insistence God places on obedience to human institutions. Take the institution of home life. Home is God's institution, and He says, "Honour thy father and thy mother"; are we fulfilling our duty to our parents as laid down in God's Book? Guard well the central institutions ordained by God, and there will be fewer problems in civilised life. We have to maintain spiritual reality wherever we are placed by the engineering of our circumstances by God; as servants we are to be subject to our masters, to the froward master as well as to the good and gentle. That is where the shoe pinches, and whenever you feel the pinch it is time you went to the death of something.

2. Rights—What One Has a Just Claim To
Every right brings with it an obligation. Legally, a man can do what he likes with his own; morally, he is under obligation to use it for the general good; spiritually, he is bound to devote it to God.

(a) Of Life
Whoso sheddeth man's blood, by man shall his blood be shed. (Genesis 9:6)

Every man in the sight of God has an equal right to life, and if a man takes away the life of another, his own life shall be taken away. The right of life is insisted on all through the Bible. As long as I do not murder anyone outright the law cannot touch me, but is there someone dependent on me to whom in the tiniest way I am not giving the right to live? someone for whom I am cherishing an unforgiving dislike? "whosoever hateth his brother is a murderer," says John (1 John 3:15). One of the terrors of the Day of Judgement will be our indifference to the rights of life.

(b) Of Land
When ye come into the land which I give you, then shall the land keep a sabbath unto the LORD. . . . In the seventh year shall be a sabbath of solemn rest for the land, a sabbath unto the LORD. (Leviticus 25:2, 4, RV; see Leviticus 25:1–7)

The twenty-fifth chapter of Leviticus is the great classic on the rights of the land. The establishment of men's rights on the earth is limited by the rights of the earth itself. If you keep taking from the land, never giving it any rest, in time it will stop giving to you. We talk about the rights of the land, and make it mean our right to grab as much from it as we can. In God's sight the land has rights just as human beings have, and many of the theories which are being advanced to-day go back to God's original prescription for the land. When God ordained "a sabbath of solemn rest for the land," it was a reiteration of the instructions given to Adam in the Garden of Eden— "Be fruitful, and multiply, and replenish the earth, and subdue it" (Genesis 1:28). Man was intended to replenish the earth by looking after it, being its lord not its tyrant; sin has made man its tyrant (cf. Romans 8:19). The rights of the land will probably only be fully realised in the Millennium, because in this dispensation men ignore obedience to God's laws.

In the teaching of Jesus the earth is never confounded with the world. "Blessed are the meek: for they shall inherit the earth" (Matthew 5:5). The meek, i.e., those who have the disposition of the Son of God and are practising righteousness in accordance with that disposition, are to inherit the earth. The world is the system of things which man has erected on God's earth. To-day people belong to various "isms" and "ites" and they say, "We are going to inherit the earth; we are the favoured people of God," but that characteristic is not meekness, it is rather the spirit of the devil. Jew or Gentile, lost tribe or found, none of it is of any account unless it is based on the principles Jesus

Christ lays down. He says that the meek, those who obey the laws of God, shall inherit the earth. The material earth is God's, and the way men treat it is a marvellous picture of the long-suffering of God.

(c) Of Liberty
All things are lawful for me, but not all things are expedient. (1 Corinthians 6:12 RV)

We call liberty allowing the other fellow to please himself to the same extent as we please ourselves. True liberty is the ability earned by practice to do the right thing. There is no such thing as a gift of freedom; freedom must be earned. The counterfeit of freedom is independence. When the Spirit of God deals with sin, it is independence that He touches, that is why the preaching of the Gospel awakens resentment as well as craving. Independence must be blasted right out of a Christian, there must be only liberty, which is a very different thing. Spiritually, liberty means the ability to fulfil the law of God, and it establishes the rights of other people.

The teaching of the Sermon on the Mount is the exact opposite of the modern jargon about "equal rights"; "Why shouldn't I do this? I'm within my rights." Of course you are, but never call yourself a Christian if you reason like that because a Christian is one who sacrifices his liberty for the sake of others, for Jesus Christ's sake. Paul's whole argument is based on this (see 1 Corinthians 8; Romans 14). Don't use your liberty "as an occasion to the flesh," he says. When we receive the Holy Spirit we receive the nature of God, and He expects us to keep our nervous system obedient to the dictates of the Holy Spirit. All through these studies we have emphasised the principle of obedience to the highest; it is one of the most practical guides for our conduct as individuals. Paul continually dealt with people who under the guise of religion were libertines; they talked about liberty when what they really meant was, "I insist on doing what it is my right to do, and I don't care a jot about anyone else." That is not liberty, that is lawlessness. The only liberty a saint has is the liberty not to use his liberty. There is nothing more searching than what the New Testament has to say about the use of liberty. It is never your duty to go the second mile, to give up your possessions or property to someone else, but Jesus says if we are His disciples, that is what we will do.

THE MORAL INDIVIDUAL—I
Individuality

Individuality is the husk of the personal life, it is all "elbows"; it separates and isolates. The husk of individuality is God's created natural covering for the protection of the personal life, but unless individuality gets transfigured it becomes objectionable, egotistical and conceited, interested only in its own independence. Individuality is the characteristic of a child and rightly so, but if we mistake individuality for the personal life we will remain isolated. It is the continual assertion of individuality that hinders our spiritual development more than anything else; individuality must go in order that personality may emerge and be brought into fellowship with God.

1. Independence
. . . a fugitive and a wanderer shalt thou be in the earth. (Genesis 4:12 RV)

Individuality is natural, but when individuality is indwelt by sin it destroys personal communion and isolates individuals, like so many crystals, and all possibility of fellowship is destroyed. The characteristics of individuality are independence and self-assertiveness. There is nothing dearer to the heart of the natural man than independence, and as long as I live in the outskirts of my prideful independence Jesus Christ is nothing to me.

Personality, not individuality, is the great Christian doctrine, but we misunderstand the teaching of Our Lord when we confound the natural with the spiritual, and individuality with sin. Independence of one another is natural; independence of God is sin. When natural independence of one another is wedded with independence of God it becomes sin, and sin isolates and destroys, and ultimately damns the life. Positive[9] individuality in any form is not only anti-Christian, but antihuman, because it instantly says, "I care for neither God nor man, I live for myself."

Cain stands for positive individuality—"not as Cain was of the evil one, and slew his brother. And wherefore slew he him? Because his works were evil, and his brother's righteous" (1 John 3:12 RV). (It is not the act of murder only that is taken into account—Our Lord said *"out of the heart proceed . . . murders."* The state-

---

9. positive: independent; unrelated to anything else.

ments of Jesus at times startle us painfully awake.) Cain was the first isolated individual; Adam was not an isolated individual. Before the Fall Adam was in relationship with God and with the world; when he was driven out from the Garden he was still in relationship with the world. Cain's sin shattered him into absolute solitariness. Being alone is not solitariness; it is the loneliness with an element of moral dis-esteem in it which is solitariness. There is no comrade for a murderer, he is isolated by the very success of his sin. It is instructive to notice what associates itself with God and what with the sinner: nothing associates itself with the sinner but his sin. The sinner is absolutely solitary on God's earth, and as long as he remains proud in his solitariness he goes against everything that is anything like God; he goes against man, who is likest God, and against the earth, which is also like God, and both man and earth cry out to God against him all the time. "The voice of thy brother's blood crieth unto Me from the ground" (Genesis 4:10).

For an individual to be isolated is either a sign of sin or of a transition stage, i.e., a person in the making. The most dangerous stage in a soul's development is the "No one understands me" stage—of course they don't! "I don't understand myself"—of course you don't! If this stage develops unduly the boy or girl will find when they get out into the world that they cannot work with others, and they become more and more impossible until the unwholesome idea that they are different from everyone else is knocked out of them. It is well to remember that our examination of ourselves can never be unbiased, so that we are only safe in taking our estimate of ourselves from our Creator instead of from our own introspection which makes us either depressed or conceited. The oft-repeated modern phrase "self-mastery" is misleading; profoundly speaking, a man can never master what he does not understand, therefore the only master of a man is not man himself, or another man, but God. Because introspection cannot profoundly satisfy, it does not follow that introspection is wrong; it is right, because it is the only way in which we will discover our need of God. It is the introspective power that is made alert by conviction of sin.

2. Interdependence

And not one of them said that aught of the things which he possessed was his own; but they had all things common. (Acts 4:32 RV)

And let us consider one another to provoke unto love and good works; not forsaking the assembling of ourselves together. . . . (Hebrews 10:24–25)

These two passages serve to indicate the main characteristic of Christianity, viz., the "together" aspect; false religions inculcate an isolated holy life. Try and develop a holy life in private, and you find it cannot be done. Individuals can only live the true life when they are dependent on one another. After the Resurrection Our Lord would not allow Mary to hold a spiritual experience for herself, she must get into contact with the disciples and convey a message to them—"Touch Me not; . . . but go unto My brethren, and say to them, I ascend unto My Father and your Father, and My God and your God." After Peter's denial the isolation of misery would inevitably have seized on him and made him want to retire in the mood of "I can never forgive myself," had not Our Lord forestalled this by giving him something positive to do—". . . and when thou art converted, strengthen thy brethren." Immediately you try to develop holiness alone and fix your eyes on your own whiteness, you lose the whole meaning of Christianity. The Holy Spirit makes a man fix his eyes on his Lord and on intense activity for others. In the early Middle Ages people had the idea that Christianity meant living a holy life apart from the world and its sociability, apart from its work and citizenship. That type of holiness is foreign to the New Testament; it cannot be reconciled with the records of the life of Jesus. The people of His day called Him "the friend of publicans and sinners" because He spent so much time with them.

The danger of the Higher Christian Life movements[10] is that the emphasis is put not on the regenerating power of the grace of God, but on individual consecration, individual fasting and prayer, individual devotion to God. The Apostle Paul sums up individual human effort under the guise of religion as things which have "a shew of wisdom in will worship, and humility, and neglecting of the body" (Colossians 2:23). It is simply individualism veneered over with religious phraseology—"What has Jesus done for me? I have done it all for myself; I did it by prayer, by fasting, by consecration." To reason like that is to put Our Lord "out of it" as Saviour and Sanctifier. We do not come to Jesus Christ, we come to our own earnestness, to our own consecration; what happens when we do come to Jesus is the miracle of a new creation. The Christian life is stamped all through with impossibility. Human nature cannot come anywhere near Jesus Christ's demands, and any rational being facing those demands honestly, says, "It can't be done, apart from a miracle." Exactly. In our modern Christianity there is no miracle; it is—"You must pray more"; "you must

---

10. Higher Christian Life movements refers to various groups and organizations that emphasized sanctification and personal holiness.

give up this and that"—anything and everything but the need to be born into a totally new kingdom.

In these talks we have traced all through the insistence that we are brought up in families, and families form communities, and communities institutions, and institutions are under governments, and governments are answerable to God—all for one purpose, that we might develop together. In the external aspects of Christianity in civilised life individuality is not lost, but it is not positive,[11] it is interdependent. Beware of becoming a positive individual in your Christian community, and saying,—"I must separate myself and start a little place of my own." "If we walk in the light, as He is in the light," we have fellowship with everyone else who is in the light. Natural affinity does not count here at all.

3. Identification

". . . that they may be one, even as we are one." (John 17:22)

Christianity is personal, therefore it is un-individual. An individual remains definitely segregated from every other individual; when you come to the teaching of Our Lord there is no individuality in that sense at all, but only personality, "that they may be *one.*" Two *individuals* can never merge; two *persons* can become one without losing their identity. Personality is the characteristic of the spiritual man as individuality is the characteristic of the natural man. When the Holy Spirit comes in He emancipates our personal spirit into union with God, and individuality ultimately becomes so interdependent that it loses all its self-assertiveness. Jesus Christ prayed for our identification with Himself in His oneness with the Father—"that they may be one, *even as we are one.*" That is infinitely beyond experience. Identification is a revelation—the exposition of the experience. The standard Revelation with regard to identification is Our Lord Himself, and you can never define Him in terms of individuality, but only in terms of personality. When Jesus Christ emancipates the personality individuality is not destroyed, it is transfigured, and the transfiguring, incalculable element is love, personal passionate devotion to Himself, and to others for His sake.

THE MORAL INDIVIDUAL—II

THE WORLD	*WORLDLY*	*OTHERWORLDLY*
In It	*Of It*	*In It but Not of It*

1. The World—*In It*

The term "world" is used to mean the material world, and the men and women in it—we are all "in it" in this sense. The Bible says that "God *so loved the world.* . . ."—and the unfathomable depth of His love is in that word "so"—yet it also says that "whosoever would be *a friend of the world* maketh himself an enemy of God" (James 4:4). The apparent contradiction can be explained like this—God's love for the world is the kind of love that makes Him go all lengths in order to remove the sin and evil from it. Love to be anything at all must be personal; to love without hating is an impossibility, and the stronger and more emphatic the love, the more intense is its obverse, hatred. God loves the world so much that He hates with a perfect hatred the thing that switched men wrong; and Calvary is the measure of His hatred. The natural heart of man would have argued—"God so loves the world that of course He will forgive its sin": God so loved the world that He could not forgive its sin. There is no such thing as God overlooking sin, therefore if He does

forgive there must be a reason that justifies Him in doing so.

To be "a friend of the world" means that we take the world as it is and are perfectly delighted with it—the world is all right and we are very happy in it. Never have the idea that the worldling is unhappy; he is perfectly happy, as thoroughly happy as a Christian. The people who are unhappy are the worldlings or the Christians if they are not at one with the principle which unites them. If a worldling is not a worldling at heart, he is miserable; and if a Christian is not a Christian at heart he carries his Christianity like a headache instead of something worth having, and not being able to get rid of his head, he cannot get rid of his headache. A worldling is not immoral, he is one who wisely keeps within the bounds of the disposition which the Bible alone reveals as sinful, viz., my claim to my right to myself. The Bible reveals the solidarity of sin, a bond of union that keeps men together, it is the mutual inheritance of the human race—"Wherefore, as by one man sin entered into the

---

11. positive: independent, not related to anything else.

world, and death by sin; and so death passed upon all men, for that all have sinned:" (Romans 5:12). Satan is anxious to keep that solidarity intact because whenever it breaks out into immoral acts it disintegrates his kingdom. Two things disintegrate the solidarity of sin—the breaking out into overt acts of sin, and the conviction of the Spirit of God. This will be found to be the solution of a number of moral problems.

To love the world as it is is the wrong kind of love, it is that sentiment which is "the enemy of God," because it means I am the friend of the system of things which does not take God into account. We are to love the world in the way God loves it, and be ready to spend and be spent until the wrong and evil are removed from it. When Jesus said "I pray not for the world, . . ." it did not mean He was indifferent to the world, or despised it: His work for the world is to save it. In thinking about the world we are apt to overlook the greatest factor of all from the Bible standpoint, viz., that man belongs to a fallen race. In our intellectual conceptions the Fall has no place at all; the human race is looked upon as a crowd of innocent babes in the wood. The Bible looks upon the human race as it is as the result of a mutiny against God; consequently you find in the Bible something you find in no other book or conception. The modern view of man is— What a marvellous promise of what he is going to be! The Bible looks at man and sees the ruin of what he once was. In the Bible everything is based on the fact that there is something wrong at the basis of things.

2. Worldly—*Of It*

To be "of" the world means to belong to the set that organises its religion, its business, its social life and pleasures without any concern as to how it affects Jesus Christ, as to whether He lived or died matters nothing at all. When Our Lord said "Be of good cheer; I have overcome *the world.*" He obviously did not mean the world in the material physical sense, the rocks and trees, the seasons, and the beautiful order of Nature, the sea and sky; it was not these He overcame, but the world in its ordered system of religion and morality, with all its civilisations and progress, which system reveals in the final analysis that it is organised absolutely apart from any consideration of God. A clean cut from everything that savours of the world in this sense is essential for the Christian. No one can decide the matter for you; you may have to draw the line in one place; I may have to draw it in another, while the Holy Spirit is educating us down to the scruple.[12] If I have for my religious ideal a good social life lived among the societies of men, that is to be "of" the world, no matter how religious it may be in terms.

It is easy to denounce wrong in the world outside me—anyone without a spark of the grace of God can do that; easy to denounce the sins of others while all the time I may be allowing all sorts of worldly things in my own religious life. We must be continually renewed in the spirit of our mind so that the slightest beginning of compromise with the spirit of the world is instantly detected. "Well, what's the harm; there's nothing wrong in it," when you hear that you know you have the spirit of the world, because the spirit that comes from Jesus says, "Does this glorify God?" The only way we are going to overcome the world as Jesus overcame it is by experimental sanctification. We are to live in heavenly places in Christ Jesus while on this earth and among worldly people. That is the glorious discipline of the sanctified life. The Apostle Paul in writing to the Corinthians says, I don't say you are to have no dealings with those that are without—"for then must ye needs go out of the world"; but I do say you are to have nothing to do with those who practise wrong doing within the Christian community. Outside the Christian community, we must bear the shame and humiliation of contact with bad men vicariously, like Jesus did, and we may win them to God. "Do not ye judge them that are within? But them that are without God judgeth" (see 1 Corinthians 5:10–13).

"As He is, so are we in this world." Our Lord's own life proved that in the midst of the world where we are placed we can be holy men and women, not only talking rightly, but living rightly. The greatest insult you can offer God is pious talk unless it is backed up by holy actions. The attitude of a Christian towards the providential order in which he is placed is to recognise that God is behind it for purposes of His own. For example, in our own country the dominance of State machinery stops occasionally and things are reconsidered and readjusted by means of a General Election. Then is the time for Christians to work and make their voice heard. As soon as the machinery is at work again, the counsel abides—subjection to the higher powers: "the powers that be are ordained of God."

3. Otherworldly—*In It but Not of It*

"Otherworldly" is simply a coined word to express what Our Lord prayed for in John 17—"I pray not that Thou shouldest take them out of the world, but that Thou shouldest keep them from the evil"—"I don't ask You to take them out of the world, away from the society of men, but to keep them out of compromise with the evil one who works in the world." The counsel of the Spirit of God to the saints is that they must allow nothing worldly in themselves

---

12. down to the scruple: to the smallest item.

while living among the worldly in the world. Those who live otherworldly in this world are the men and women who have been regenerated and who dare to live their life according to the principles of Jesus. When once the protest is made where your Lord requires you to make it, you will soon find where you stand—exactly where Jesus said you would, outside the synagogue, called purist, narrow and absurd.

"I have given them Thy word; and the world hated them, because they are not of the world, even as I am not of the world" (John 17:14 RV). The hatred of the world is its intense objection to the principles exhibited by the saint, and frequently it is the best specimens of the worldly spirit who positively hate and detest the otherworldly spirit of the saint. It is not that they hate you personally, they may be very kind to you, but they hate what you represent of Jesus Christ. Remember what sin is, fundamental independence of God, the thing in me that says, I can do without God, I don't need Him. The hatred of the world has its source there. When you meet the hatred of the whole world-system unspiritual people around you will laugh to scorn the idea that you have a struggle on hand, but you realise that you are wrestling not against flesh and blood, but against the spiritual hosts of wickedness in the heavenly places.

Most of us live our life in the world without ever discovering its hatred, but it is there, and a crisis may suddenly arise and bring it to a head, then we are appalled to find the meaning of Our Lord's words, "And ye shall be hated of all men for My name's sake." I have no business to stir up the hatred of the world through a domineering religious opinionativeness—that has nothing whatever to do with the spirit of Jesus; I am never told to rejoice when men separate me from their company on that account; but when in all modesty I am standing for the honour of Jesus Christ and a crisis arises when the Spirit of God requires that I declare my otherworldliness, then I learn what Jesus meant when He said, men will hate you. It is the hatred of the world expressed to the otherworldly standpoint once it is made clear.

This Age is the last of the ordered ages which condition man's life on this earth, and the New Testament writers look on to the time when creation's thraldom ends in deliverance and in the manifestation of the sons of God. "We . . . look for new heavens and a new earth"; nowadays people have got tired of the preaching about a future heaven and they have gone to the other extreme and deal only with what is called the practical, consequently they rob themselves of the unfathomable joy of knowing that everything God has said will come to pass. The Redemption covers more than men and women, it covers the whole earth; everything that has been marred by sin and the devil has been completely redeemed by Jesus Christ. ". . . new heavens and a new earth, wherein dwelleth righteousness"—nothing that defiles can be on it at all; at present that is absolutely inconceivable to us. The world and the earth are not the same; the world represents the societies of men on God's earth, and they do as they like; the earth remains God's. "Blessed are the meek: for they shall inherit the earth." The meek bide God's time.

THE MORAL INDIVIDUAL—III
Conversion

The literal meaning of "conversion" is a change of mind after watching certain facts, e.g., we read in Acts 28 that the barbarians *"changed their minds"* about Paul (Acts 28:6). We are dealing with conversion here not so much on the religious side as the ethical. Beware of making conversion synonymous with regeneration. Conversion is simply the effort of a roused human being; the sign of regeneration is that a man has *received* something. When a man fails in Christian experience it is nearly always because he has never received anything. There are books which set out to give the psychology of new birth by saying that suddenly something bursts up from a man's unconscious personality and alters him: a man is never born again by a subliminal uprush, but only by receiving something that was never there before, viz., the Holy Spirit. Certain forms of sin exhaust themselves and we may say of a man "Now he is saved," but he may be nothing of the sort. According to the New Testament the only evidence of new birth is not merely that a man lives a different life, but that the basis of that different life is repentance. The bedrock in the classic experience of the Apostle Paul was not only his enthroning of Jesus Christ as Lord, but His enthronement on the basis of a real ringing repentance wrought in him by the Holy Ghost.

1. Mental Conversion
A double minded man is unstable in all his ways. (James 1:8)

Instability is an appalling snare in the natural life, and is disastrous spiritually—"for let not that man think that he shall receive anything of the Lord," says James. There may be conversions of heart which are not conversions of mind; the last thing a man comes to is the conversion of his mind. Our Lord refers to this instability in His parable of the sower and the seed—they receive the word gladly, but they have no root in themselves—quicksilver Christians. They may have as many conversions as there are days in the year, and at the end of the year they remain the same unreliable emotional people, utterly incapable of resting in a stable point of truth, and they become eager adherents of every new interest. The main characteristic of young modern life to-day is an intense craving to be interested—literature, amusements, all indicate this tendency, and in religion the Church is apt to pander to the demand to be interested; consequently men won't face the rugged facts of the Gospel, because when the Holy Spirit comes in He challenges a man's will, demands a reconstruction of his whole life, and produces a change of mind which will work havoc in his former complacency.

2. Moral Conversion

"Except ye . . . become as little children." (Matthew 18:3)

Our Lord teaches that moral progress must start from a point of moral innocence, and is consequently only possible to a man when he has been born again. A child's life is implicit, not explicit. To become "as little children" means to receive a new heredity, a totally new nature, the essence of which is simplicity and confidence towards God. In order to develop the moral life innocence must be transformed into virtue by a series of deliberate choices in which the present pleasure is sacrificed for the ultimate joy of being good. This aspect of truth is familiar in all Paul's Epistles, viz., that the natural has to be transformed into the spiritual by willing obedience to the word and will of God. Such passages as Romans 12:2 (". . . be ye transformed by the renewing of your mind:") and Ephesians 4:23 ("be renewed in the spirit of your mind") apply directly to the moral life of those who have been supernaturally saved by the grace of God, those in whom the Holy Spirit dwells and is at work. To renew means to transform to new life. These passages make it clear that we can be renewed in our mind when we choose. We have no choice about being born into this world, but to be born again, if we will but come to Jesus and receive His Spirit, is within our own power. This is true all along in the Christian life, you can be renewed in the spirit of your mind when you choose, you can revive your mind on any line you like by sheer force of will. Always remember that Jesus Christ's statements force an issue of will and conscience first, and only as we obey is there the understanding with the mind (see John 7:17). The challenge to the will comes in the matter of study, as long as you remain in the "stodge" state there is no mental progress—"I am overwhelmed by the tremendous amount there is to know and it's no use my going on." If you will forge through that stage you will suddenly turn a corner where everything that was difficult and perplexing becomes as clear as a lightning flash, but it all depends on whether you will forge ahead. When people say, "Preach us the simple Gospel," what they mean is, "Preach us the thing we have always heard, the thing that keeps us sound asleep, we don't want to see things differently"; then the sooner the Spirit of God sends a thrust through their stagnant minds the better. Continual renewal of mind is the only healthy state for a Christian. Beware of the ban of finality[13] about your present views.

3. Mystical Conversion

. . . to whom God would make known what is the riches of the glory of this mystery among the Gentiles: which is Christ in you, the hope of glory. (Colossians 1:27)

"Mystical" is a word that is easily abused; it means the type of mind the Holy Spirit develops in us whereby we see things by intuition. Intuition in the natural world is the power to see things at a glance without reasoning, and the Spirit of God develops that power in the saint. The accuracy of intuitive judgement is in proportion to the moral culture of the one who judges. A child and a good woman are the best examples of intuitive judgement. It is a bad look-out when anything blurs intuition because it is an indication that something is wrong with the moral character. All this is common to human beings apart from the Holy Spirit; spiritual intuition lives in the same sphere as natural intuition *plus* the Holy Spirit. "My sheep hear My voice," said Jesus. Keep the intuitive secret life clear and right with God at all costs; never blunt intuition. Whenever a man comes into personal contact with Jesus Christ he knows at once whether he is good or bad; he does not reason it out, he knows it intuitively. These are the moments "when the spirit's true endowments stand out plainly from its false ones. . . ."

"If a man love Me, he will keep My words: . . . and We will come unto him, and make our abode with him" (John 14:23)—the Triune God, Father, Son, and Holy Ghost, abiding with the saint. These words of Our Lord refer to mystical communion with God in all matters of mental and moral judgement, and imply sympathy with all that the heart of God holds dear.

---

13. ban of finality: the limitation or "curse" of having one's mind made up, unwilling to consider new information

SPIRITUAL EVOLUTION

Evolution means a gradual working out or development. There is a difference between natural evolution and spiritual evolution: in natural evolution we do not know the final goal; in spiritual evolution the goal is given before the start—". . . till we all come in the unity of the faith . . . unto a perfect man, unto the measure of the stature of the fulness of Christ" (Ephesians 4:13).

1. Spiritual Biogenesis
In Him was life; and the life was the light of men. (John 1:4)

Verily, verily, I say unto you, Except ye eat the flesh of the Son of man, and drink His blood, ye have no life in you. (John 6:53)

No man by nature has the life of the Son of God in him; he has in him the life which God creates in all men, but before he can have in his actual life the life that was in the Son of God, he must be born from above. "Ye have not [this] life in yourselves" (RV), said Jesus, i.e., the life He had. The life of Jesus is imparted to us on the ground of the Redemption, but we have to come to Him for it. A man may say, "I have the life of God in me by nature, all I have to do is to develop it, Jesus will assist me; He is the great type-Christian." If you take that view, viz., that a man becomes spiritual as he pays attention to the best elements in himself, you make the Atonement unnecessary. "Except a man be born again, he cannot see the kingdom of God." Unless my personal life so assimilates the life of Jesus that I can manifest it, I have not got the life which characterised Him. Life can only come from pre-existing life: I must get the life of God from the One who has it. "He that hath the Son hath the life; he that hath not the Son of God hath not the life" (1 John 5:12 RV). ". . . and ye will not come to Me, that ye may have life" (John 5:40 RV).

2. Spiritual Birth
Marvel not that I said unto thee, Ye must be born again. (John 3:7)

Drummond's[14] thesis in his *Natural Law in the Spiritual World* makes it too easy, it does not recognise the factor of sin, and consequently does not cover all the facts. According to the New Testament, a man can only be lifted into the Kingdom of God by being born into it. Here Drummond's illustration holds good,* but remember, it was the tragedy caused by sin that made new birth necessary. It sounds much more sensible to say that if a man goes on evolving and developing he will become a spiritual being; but once get a dose of "the plague of your own heart" and you will find that things are as the Bible says they are, tragically wrong. As long as men have no experience of tragedy in their own life they remain ignorant of the need for the Redemption. "I was alive without the law once," says the Apostle Paul in that little-understood chapter, Romans 7, which deals with his alternating experiences. When once a man recognises the gap sin has made between God and man, the meaning of the Atonement is clear—that in the Cross Jesus Christ bridged the gap and made it possible for any man to be lifted to where the whole human race was designed to be, viz., in perfect communion with God.

God formed Adam of the dust of the ground, *a* son of God. *The* Son of God was born of the Holy Ghost. If I am ever going to have the heredity of the Son of God I must have a similar experience, I must be "born of the Spirit"; my personal life must be impregnated by the Holy Ghost—"My little children, of whom I am again in travail until Christ be formed in you" (Galatians 4:19 RV). You cannot illustrate new birth by natural birth. Natural birth is by means of a process of procreation; new birth is not in the least like it. The only symbol for being born "from above"

---

14. Henry Drummond (1851–1897), Scottish writer and evangelist. His book, *Natural Law in the Spiritual World,* was published in 1883.

    *The exclusion of the spiritually inorganic from the Kingdom of the spiritually organic is not arbitrary. Nor is the natural man refused admission on unexplained grounds. His admission is a scientific impossibility. Except a mineral be born "from above"—from the Kingdom just *above* it—it cannot enter the Kingdom just above it. And except a man be born "from above," by the same law, he cannot enter the Kingdom just above him. . . . The breath of God, blowing where it listeth, touches with its mystery of Life the dead souls of men, bears them across the bridgeless gulf between the natural and the spiritual, between the spiritually inorganic and the spiritually organic, endows them with its own high qualities, and develops within them these new and secret faculties, by which those who are born again are said to *see the kingdom of God* (pp. 72–3).

    The first law of biology is this; That which is Mineral is Mineral; that which is Flesh is Flesh; that which is Spirit is Spirit. The mineral remains in the inorganic world until it is seized upon by a something called Life outside the inorganic world: the natural man remains the natural man, until a Spiritual Life from without the natural life seizes upon him, regenerates him, changes him into a spiritual man (pp. 380–1). *[This footnote was in the original text]* is the advent of Jesus Christ into this world. Jesus Christ entered into the human race from outside it; He entered it through the door of the Virgin's womb by the conception of the Holy Ghost—"Therefore also that holy thing which shall be born of thee shall be called the Son of God" (Luke 1:35).

Adam was created a son of God, that is, he was innocent in relation to God, and God intended him to take part in his own development by a series of moral choices whereby he was to sacrifice the natural life to the spiritual. If Adam had done this there would have been no death, but transfiguration, as in Jesus Christ, the last Adam. But Adam refused to let God be his Ruler; he took his right to himself and became his own god, thereby cutting himself off from the domain of God. The New Testament phrase is that we are "dead in trespasses and sins," dead towards all that Jesus Christ stands for.

The two realms, the natural and the spiritual, ought to be one and the same: to be born a man, should be to be a son of God, as Adam was in the beginning. But God's original order for mankind was broken into—"sin entered into the world, and death by sin"; consequently the necessity of the new birth is insisted on all through. "Marvel not that I said unto thee, Ye must be born again." It is a statement of foundation fact. The words were spoken not to a sinner, as men count sin, but to an upright, godly man. Before any man can be in the realm of God he must be born into it.

New birth is not the working of a natural law. The introduction of anything into this world is cataclysmic: before a tree can grow it must be planted; before a human being can evolve he must be born— a distinct and emphatic crisis. Every child born into the world involves a cataclysm to someone, the mother has practically to go through death. The same thing is true spiritually. Being "born from above" is not a simple easy process; we cannot glide into the Kingdom of God. Common sense reasoning says we ought to be able to merge into the life of God, but according to the Bible, and in actual experience, that is not the order. The basis of things is not rational, it is tragic, and what Jesus Christ came to do was to put human life on the basis of Redemption whereby any man can receive the heredity of the Son of God and be lifted into the domain where He lives.

The historic Jesus represents the personal union of God and man. He lived on the human plane for thirty-three years and during that time He presented what God's normal Man was like. When we are regenerated we enter into the Kingdom of God, we begin to grow, and the goal is certain—". . . we know

that, when He shall appear, *we shall be like Him;* for we shall see Him as He is." But before I can begin to see what Jesus Christ stands for I have to enter into another domain— "Except a man be born again, *he cannot . . . enter into the kingdom of God."* I enter into the life of God by its entering into me, that is, I deliberately undertake to become the home of the life of the Son of God. "Bethlehem." I do not draw my life from myself, I draw it from the One who is the Source of life.

3. Spiritual Breath
And the spirit of the LORD shall rest upon Him, . . . and shall make Him of quick understanding in the fear of the LORD. (Isaiah 11:2–3)

—literally, "He shall draw his breath in the fear of the LORD." Most of us draw our breath from the ordinary human life we all live. The time a Christian gives to prayer and communion with God is not meant for his natural life, but meant to nourish the life of the Son of God in him. God engineers the circumstances of His saints in order that the Spirit may use them as the praying-house of the Son of God. If you are spiritual the Holy Spirit is offering up prayers in your bodily temple that you know nothing about, it is the Spirit making intercession in you (see Romans 8:26–27). We hear it said that "Prayer alters things"; prayer not so much alters things as alters the man who prays, and he alters things. When I am born from above the life of the Son of God is born in me, and I have to take time to nourish that life. The essential meaning of prayer is that it nourishes the life of the Son of God in me and enables Him to manifest Himself in my mortal flesh.

The secret of our Lord's life is given us in His own words—"Verily, verily, I say unto you, Except a corn of wheat fall into the ground and die, it abideth alone: but if it die, it bringeth forth much fruit" (John 12:24). Spiritual life is always of that order: just when you think it is going to be successful, it disappears; it is not time for it yet, it will appear in another order. Ultimately the meek shall inherit the earth, and then we shall have a system of national life without any of the materialistic crudities seen everywhere to-day. There are views abroad of a federation of nations, but it can only be brought about by the Lord Jesus Christ, by our adherence entirely to Him. Whenever a religious community begins to get organised it ceases to "draw [its] breath in the fear of the LORD"; the old way of talking is kept up, but the life is not there, and men who used to be keen on proclaiming the Gospel are keen now only on the success of the organisation.

SPIRITUAL CONSTRUCTION—I
Nehemiah 4:1–6

So we built the wall. (Nehemiah 4:6)

The first essential in spiritual construction is to clear away the rubbish. Nehemiah could not begin to build until the rubbish had been dealt with (see Nehemiah 4:2). Rubbish is waste matter, and there is the moral equivalent of rubbish which must be dealt with before we can begin to build a spiritual character. We do not start with a clean sheet, we start with a sheet that is like a palimpsest, a manuscript that has been written on twice, and if the right chemical is used, the first writing is seen. We all have hereditary writing in us which is so much rubbish to be removed.

1. Destruction by Neglect
Mortify therefore your members which are upon the earth; fornication, uncleanness, passion, evil desire, and covetousness, the which is idolatry. (Colossians 3:5 RV)

In this passage Paul mentions things that are of the nature of rubbish, and he mentions them in their complete ugliness. They are the abortion of the stuff human nature is made of, and he says, "Mortify them, destroy them by neglect." Certain things can only be dealt with by ignoring them; if you face them you increase their power. It is absurd to say, Pray about them; when once a thing is seen to be wrong, don't pray about it, it fixes the mind on it; never for a second brood on it, destroy it by neglect. We have no business to harbour an emotion which we can see will end in any of the things Paul mentions. No man or woman on earth is immune, each one of us knows the things we should not think about, or pray about, but resolutely neglect. It is a great thing for our moral character to have something to ignore. It is because these things are not understood that there is so much inefficiency in spiritual life. What Christianity supplies is "the expulsive power of a new affection." We cannot destroy sin by neglect; God deals with sin, and we can get the effective measure of His dealing with it in our actual life.

2. Direction by Sacrifice
And if thy right eye causeth thee to stumble, pluck it out, and cast it from thee: for it is profitable for thee that one of thy members should perish, and not thy whole body be cast into hell. (Matthew 5:2 RV)

Sacrifice is spoken of in the Bible in its disciplinary, chastening aspect as well as in its worshipping aspect.

The worshipping aspect means that I give back to God the best He has given me and in this way He makes it His and mine for ever. What is the best God has given me? My right to myself. Jesus Christ is always unyielding on one point, viz., that I must give up my right to myself to Him. He does not teach the annihilation of self, He shows how self can be rightly centred in personal passionate devotion to God. Self-sacrifice may be a disease; we are not to sacrifice for our own sake, or for the sake of anyone else, but for God's sake. Why should God make it that the natural had to be sacrificed to the spiritual? God did not: God intended the natural to be transformed into the spiritual by obedience; sin made it necessary to sacrifice the natural. It was God's permissive will, not His order. Sanctification means not only that we are delivered from sin, but that we start on a life of stern discipline. It is not a question of praying but of performing, of deliberately disciplining ourselves. There is no royal road there; we each have it entirely in our own hands. It is not wrong things that have to be sacrificed, but right things. "The good is the enemy of the best," not the bad, but the good that is not good enough. The danger is to argue on the line of giving up only what is wrong; Jesus Christ selected things essential to a full-orbed life—the right hand and the eye, these are not bad things, they are creations of God. Jesus Christ talked rugged unmitigated truth, He was never ambiguous, and He says it is better to be maimed than damned. There was never a saint yet who did not have to start with a maimed life. Anyone will give up wrong things if he knows how to, but will I give up the best I have for Jesus Christ? If I am only willing to give up wrong things, never let me talk about being in love with Him! We say, "Why shouldn't I do it, there is no harm in it?" For pity's sake, go and do it, but remember that the construction of a spiritual character is doomed once you take that line.

3. Designed by Desires
Delight thyself also in the LORD, and He shall give thee the desires of thine heart. (Psalm 37:4)

If ye abide in Me, and My words abide in you, ask whatsoever ye will, and it shall be done unto you. (John 15:7 RV)

We have any number of instincts, but very few desires. Desire is what you determine in your mind and settle in your heart and set yourself towards as good, and that is the thing God will fulfil if you delight in Him—that is the condition. God deals with us on the line of character building—"Ye shall ask what ye *will*," said Jesus, not what you like, but what your will is in; and we *ask* very few things. If our desires are distorted we are apt to say that God gave us a stone when we asked for bread, whereas God always hears our prayers, but He answers them according to His own nature.

The basis of spiritual construction is implicit faith in Jesus Christ. If I stake all on His astute Mind I will find I have struck bedrock. The majority of us only believe in Jesus Christ as far as we can see by our own wits. If we really believed Him what a mighty difference there would be in us! we would trust His Mind instead of our own; we would stop being "amateur providences" over other lives, and we would be fit to do our twenty-four hours' work like no one else. "Except ye . . . become as little children"—simple-hearted, trusting and not being afraid.

You can never become a Christian by thinking, you can only become a Christian by receiving something from God; but you must think after you are a Christian. Some folks have a cowardly fear of intellect in spiritual matters. After the war the most energetic thinking will have to be done by Christians; we must think as we have never thought before, otherwise we will be outstripped by those who think on lines which ignore Jesus Christ and endeavour to prove that the Redemption is not necessary.

SPIRITUAL CONSTRUCTION—II
The Alloy

1. The Divine and the Human

But we have this treasure in earthen vessels, that the excellency of the power may be of God, and not of us. (2 Corinthians 4:7)

In spiritual reconstruction after the war the purely spiritual line, if it ignores the human, will be useless; and the purely human will not be any good; there must be the amalgam, i.e., the pure Divine and the pure human mixed—not Divine and sinful, but Divine and human. Paul is not despising the earthen vessel, it is in the earthen vessel that the excellency of God's power is to be manifested.

In the Incarnation we see the amalgam of the Divine and the human. Pure gold cannot be used as coin, it is too soft; in order to make gold serviceable for use it must be mixed with an alloy. The pure gold of the Divine is of no use in human affairs; there must be an alloy, and the alloy does not stand for sin, but for that which makes the Divine serviceable for use. God Almighty is nothing but a mental abstraction to me unless He can become actual, and the revelation of the New Testament is that God did become actual: "the Word was made flesh." Jesus Christ was not pure Divine, He was unique: Divine and human.

The Christian doctrine of the Incarnation is not only that "God was manifest in the flesh," but that the same thing will take place in anyone who receives the Holy Spirit: he receives from God a totally new heredity, the life of the Son of God, "until Christ be formed in you." Human nature is the home where the Divine manifests itself. Holiness Movements are apt to ignore the human and bank all on the Divine; they tell us that human nature is sinful, forgetting that Jesus Christ took on Him our human nature, and "in Him is no sin." It was God who made human nature, not the devil; sin came into human nature and cut it off from the Divine, and Jesus Christ brings the pure Divine and the pure human together. Sin is a wrong thing altogether and is not to be allowed for a moment. Human nature is earthly, it is sordid, but it is not bad, the thing that makes it bad is sin. Sin is the outcome of a relationship set up between man and the devil whereby man becomes "boss" over himself, his own god (see Genesis 3:8). No man was ever created to be his own master, or the master of other men; there is only one Master of men, and that is Jesus Christ. We can be fanatical and ignore the human, or sinful and ignore the Divine, or we can become the mixture of the Divine and the human. No man is constituted to live a pure Divine life on earth; he is constituted to live a human life on earth presenced with Divinity. When the pure Divine comes into us we have the difficulty of making our human nature the obedient servant of the new disposition, it is difficult, and thank God it is! God gives us the fighting chance. A saint is not an ethereal creature too refined for life on this earth; a saint is a mixture of the Divine and the human that can stand anything.

2. The Preacher and the Philosopher

. . . it was God's good pleasure through the foolishness of the thing preached to save them that believe. (1 Corinthians 1:21 RV mg)

The preacher is there not by right of his personality or oratorical powers, but by right of the message he proclaims. Who is the man that attracts us to-day? The man with a striking personality and we don't care about his message. Paul said, "Yea, woe is unto me, if I preach not the gospel!" An orator rouses human nature to do what it is asleep over: the New Testament preacher has to move men to do what they are dead-set against doing, viz., giving up the right to them-selves to Jesus Christ; consequently the preaching of the Gospel awakens a terrific longing, but an equally intense resentment. The aspect of the Gospel that awakens desire in a man is the message of peace and goodwill—but I must give up my right to myself to get there. The basis of human life has been put on Redemption, and on the ground of that Redemption any man can be lifted into right relationship with God. The Gospel is "the power of God unto salvation to everyone that believeth." There is no room for despair on the part of any man if he will only believe what the New Testament preacher proclaims—but it takes some believing. No thinking will ever make me a Christian; I can only become a Christian through listening to what is preached and accepting salvation as a gift; but I must think after I am a Christian.

The shaking through this war[15] has revealed the shallowness of our Christianity, there is no moral power in it—not sufficient moral power to make a man live as a disciple of Jesus Christ in his home life, let alone his business life or his camp life. The conse-quence is the moral emphasis has been coming from the world, not from the Church. There needs to be a radical change in many of us who name the Name of Christ if we are going to measure up to the nobility and self-sacrifice exhibited by men and women of the world. Now is the time when the preaching of the Cross will have a chance it never had before. The war has hit rationalism a severe blow, but rationalism will gather itself together and take its revenge. Rational-ism fundamentally is rotten. The boldness of ratio-nalism is not in what it does, but in the way it criticises. The basis of things is not rational, it is tragic; there is something wrong at the heart of life that reason cannot account for. According to ratio-nalism there is no need to be born again—"develop the best in yourself." That was God's original design for the human race, viz., that man should take part in his own development by a series of moral choices whereby he would transfigure the natural into the

spiritual; but sin entered and there came an hiatus, a break, and man's development is not now based on the rational progression God designed, but on the Redemption, which deals with the tragedy caused by sin. No man can get at God as Jesus Christ presents Him by philosophy. The philosopher has vision, so has the poet, but neither of them has any memory; the preacher of the Gospel has vision and memory; he realises there is a gap between God and man, and knows that the only way that gap can be bridged is by Jesus Christ making the Divine and the human one. The goal of human life is to be one with God, and in Jesus Christ we see what that oneness means.

In spiritual construction after the war the emphasis must be laid on what the preacher proclaims, not on what the philosopher reasons about. The great message of the Incarnation is that there the Divine and the human became one, and Jesus Christ's claim is that He can manifest His own life in any man if he will co-oper-ate with Him. If I am going to nourish the pure Divine in my human life I must first of all let God deal drasti-cally with sin; by my own willing agreement I must let Him put His axe to the root of sin, and then when His life has come into me, I must obey it. Do I as a preacher of the Gospel really believe the Gospel I preach? The test is in the soul of the preacher himself, in the one who says he believes the Gospel. For instance, do I believe that that man who did me a cruel wrong, that man who thwarted me, can be presented "perfect in Christ Jesus"?

We are rarely taught to think along these lines. Thinking is not of first importance, but it is of mighty importance secondarily. The man who prefers to be lazy in his spiritual life may do well enough, but it is the man who has thought on the basis of things who is able to give intelligent help to those who are up against it. Men have been hit during the war and few of us have been able to help them, we are inarticulate, we don't know how to put things because we have not thought about them. "My people doth not consider," says God, they do not think. We are not called on to preach a philosophy of thought, which is the tendency nowadays—but to preach "Jesus Christ, and Him cru-cified," because that preaching enables God to create His miracles in human lives. If I prefer to preach my philosophy I prevent God creating His miracles, but when I am simple enough to preach the Cross, God performs His miracles every time.

15. this war: World War I (1914–1918)

SPIRITUAL CONSTRUCTION—III
Do It!
John 13:13–18

We have to recognise that we are one half mechanical and one half mysterious; to live in either domain and ignore the other is to be a fool or a fanatic. The great supernatural work of God's grace is in the incalculable part of our nature; we have to work out in the mechanical realm what God works in in the mysterious realm. People accept creeds, but they will not accept the holy standards of Jesus Christ's teaching. To build on the fundamental work of God's grace and ignore the fact that we have to work it out in a mechanical life produces humbugs, those who make a divorce between the mysterious life and the practical life. In John 13 the mysterious and the mechanical are closely welded together.

1. The Lordship of Jesus

Ye call Me Master and Lord: and ye say well; for so I am. If I then, your Lord and the Master, have washed your feet, ye also ought to wash one another's feet. (John 13:14)

Verse 13 refers to the spiritual mastery of Jesus over His disciples; verse 14 states how that mastery is to be expressed in the mechanical life. You can't wash anybody's feet mysteriously; it is a purely mechanical, matter-of-fact job; you can't do it by giving him devotional books or by praying for him; you can only, wash anybody's feet by doing something mechanical. Our Lord did not tell the disciples *how* they were to do it: He simply says—"Do it." He is not questioning whether or not they can do it; He is saying that they must do what the mastery of His ruling shows them they should do. Our bodily habits are purely mechanical, and the revolution caused in individual lives by our Lord's salvation is that He enables us to do what He commands us to do, if we will but practise the doing. Habits are built up, not by theory, but by practice. The one great problem in spiritual life is whether we are going to put God's grace into practice. God won't do the mechanical; He created us to do that; but we can only do it while we draw on the mysterious realm of His divine grace. "If ye love Me, ye will keep My commandments." We have to remember that there is a domain of our life that is handed over to mechanism; God will not work it for us, but if we obey His Spirit we shall find we can make this mechanism work out God's will exactly. Beware of any spiritual emotion that you do not work out mechanically; whenever in devotion before God His Spirit gives a clear indication of what He wants you to do, *do it.*

The way to examine whether we are doing what Jesus Christ wants us to do is to look at the habits of our life in three domains—physical, emotional, and intellectual. The best scrutiny we can give ourselves is along this line: Are my bodily habits chaste? is my emotional nature inordinate? is my intellectual life insubordinate? When we begin to work out what God has worked in, we are faced with the problem that this physical body, this mechanism, has been used by habit to obeying another rule called sin; when Jesus Christ delivers us from that rule, He does not give us a new body, He gives us power to break and then re-mould every habit formed while we were under the dominion of sin. Much of the misery in our Christian life comes not because the devil tackles us, but because we have never understood the simple laws of our make-up. We have to treat the body as the servant of Jesus Christ: when the body says "Sit," and He says "Go," go! When the body says "Eat," and He says "Fast," fast! When the body says "Yawn," and He says "Pray," pray!

Education is for the purpose of behaviour, and habits are the stuff out of which behaviour is formed. The difference between an educated and an uneducated person lies just here—when an educated person is put into new circumstances, he always knows how to behave because his mind is stored with examples of right behaviour. When an uneducated person comes into a new situation he does not know what to do and behaves in an ignorant manner. Spiritual education and habit go together in this connection, that I learn to make my body act quickly along the line of education the Holy Spirit has given me, then when I find myself in new circumstances I shall not be helpless because I have educated myself according to the laws of God's grace.

2. The Example of Jesus

For I have given you an example, that ye should do as I have done to you. (John 13:15)

Jesus did not tell the disciples to imitate Him in washing one another's feet; the one thing He condemned was imitation before the life was there. For instance, when He set before them a little child and said "Except ye . . . become as little children," He did not mean they were to act like babies; He was telling them to be as simple and artless in their relationship to God as a child is in relation to his father. If we try to imitate Jesus Christ we produce a mechanical exhibition of what we are ourselves, the life is not there, we are spiritual frauds, and everybody knows it. But our Lord's teaching is clear—"If I am your Lord and Master, it means you have received My Spirit, then you will do what I do," and our habits are copies of the true indwelling Spirit of Jesus.

The disciples had not always been in the relation of disciples to Jesus, but now they are His disciples and as such He says to them, *"do as I have done to you."* When you see a thing should be done, the command of Jesus is always—Do it. Beware of saying, "I must go and tell Mrs. So-and-so to do that, she is just suited for it"; it is for you to do. There must be a mechanical outlet for spiritual inspiration. You must do what you see, or become blind in that particular.

In order to obey our Lord we must accumulate all possible circumstances to reinforce the right motive. It is easy to sit in a drawing-room and think about the terrible condition of things in the world, and pray and sentimentalise over it to further orders;[16] but Jesus says, "I have given you an example, that you should go and do to others what I have done to you." If all Jesus Christ had done was to have sat before His Father's throne and prayed for us, we would have been exonerated for leaving things undone, but He has given us an example to follow. Never allow that your circumstances exonerate you from obeying any of the commands of Jesus. The lessons which have to be repeated are those we have not bothered our heads to learn.

3. The Warning of Jesus
I speak not of you all: I know whom I have chosen: but that the scripture may be fulfilled, He that eateth My bread lifted up his heel against Me. (John 13:18 RV)

Any one of us can lift our "heel," our mechanical life, against Jesus Christ's dominion, and while eating His bread play the traitor to Him in private. No one preaches more earnestly, talks more earnestly, than we do, we are absolutely sincere, but we are not real because we have never acted when the opportunity occurred along the line Jesus Christ wants us to. The thing the world is sick of to-day is sincerity that is not real.

So much depends on a simple understanding of the mechanical laws of our nature. The only One who knows the mysterious, unfathomable depths of our personality is God; we have to deal with the practical part, and see that we have faith in God with regard to the mysterious part while we obey Him in the practical domain. Jesus Christ lived the only sane life that ever was lived. In His life the mysterious and the mechanical were wrought into one wonderful unique Personality, and it is His life that is to be "manifested in our mortal flesh."

"Now is the day of salvation," and to *do it now* is the "thank you" of our acceptance of that salvation.

APRIL 9, 1917 — ZEITOUN YMCA HUTS, EGYPT

THE FUNDAMENTAL OFFENCE

And apart from shedding of blood there is no remission. Hebrews 9:22

1. Christ is the Blood of God
   The cross is the blood of Christ (1 John 2:2)

When we speak of the blood of Christ we mean that what He did drew upon what was the very citadel of His personality and involved His total self.

2. Sin is the Blood of Satan
   Self-realisation is the blood of sin (1 John 3:8)

What in us harrows the heart, in Him harrowed Hell. He revolutionises the eternal foundations of our moral world.

3. Sanctification Is the Blood of the Saint
   Repentance is the blood of sanctification (1 John 1:7)

The sinner could only be saved by something that damned his sin.

Dr. P. T. Forsyth[17]

1. Christ Is the Blood of God
And He is the propitiation for our sins; and not for ours only, but also for the whole world. (1 John 2:2 RV)

The expression "the blood of Christ" means not only that Christ shed His blood, but that He poured out His

---

16. to further orders: ad infinitum; endlessly; the phrase, military origin, continuing present action until one receives different orders

17. Peter Taylor Forsyth (1848–1921), British Congregationalist minister and theologian. Chambers read many of Forsyth's books and valued his insights.

very life before God. In the Old Testament the idea of sacrifice is that the blood, which is the life (see Genesis 4:4), is poured out to God, its Giver. When Jesus Christ shed His blood on the Cross it was not the blood of a martyr, or the blood of one man for another; it was the life of God poured out to redeem the world. It is easy to be thrilled by the sacrifices men make: it takes the Spirit of Almighty God to get us even interested in the cost of our redemption to God. There is a good deal of talk to-day to the effect that the men who sacrifice their lives are thereby redeemed. It is said in an earnest mood, but it reveals a total lack of understanding of the Cross, which is not the cross of a man, but the Cross of God, i.e., the offering of God for the purpose of bringing back the human race into fellowship with Himself. Either the Cross is the only way there is of explaining God, the only way of explaining Jesus Christ, and of explaining the human race, or there is nothing in it at all. If the human race apart from the Cross is all right, then the Redemption was a useless waste.

Our Lord did not sacrifice Himself for a cause: He poured out His life for a purpose in the Mind of God. We will sacrifice ourselves to further orders for another part of ourselves, but the meaning of Jesus Christ's passion is that He poured out His total Self. The Cross is the expression of the very heart of God, and when my eyes are opened I see that Jesus Christ has made the basis of life Redemptive, and it cost Him everything to do it. The death of Christ was not the death of a martyr, it was God manifesting Himself in the heart of the human race when the human race was saying, "Crucify Him."

The Christian revelation is not that Jesus Christ stands to us as the Representative of God, but that He *is* God. If He is not, then we have no God. "... *God was in Christ,* reconciling the world unto Himself." We do not worship an austere, remote God, He is here in the thick of it. The Cross is a Reality, not a symbol—at the wall of the world stands God with His arms outstretched. There is nothing more certain in Time or Eternity than what Jesus Christ did on the Cross: He switched the whole human race back into right relationship to God and made the basis of human life Redemptive, consequently any member of the human race can get into touch with God *now*. It means not simply that men are saved from hell and put right for heaven, but that they are freed from the wrong disposition and can have imparted to them the very disposition of the Son of God, viz., Holy Spirit. The dangerous tendency of to-day is not so much the anti-religious tendency as the pietistic tendency, that by prayer and consecration, by giving up things and devoting ourselves to God, He will recognise us. We can never get to God in that way; we can get to God instanter irrespective of what we are on the basis of the Redemption. On that

basis I can be forgiven, and through the forgiveness I can be turned into another man.

2. Sin Is the Blood of Satan
For this purpose the Son of God was manifested, that He might destroy the works of the devil. (1 John 3:8)

The Bible makes a distinction between the devil and Satan, only occasionally are the terms used synonymously, e.g., Revelation 20:2. The devil is the antagonist of God: Satan is the result of a relationship set up between man and the devil. God took on Himself the responsibility of having created the being who became the devil and the being who became the sinner, and the proof that He did so is the Cross. God never lays the sin of the human race on anyone saving Himself; the revelation is not that God punished Jesus Christ for our sins, but that "Him who knew no sin He made to be sin on our behalf. . . ." The relationship set up between Adam and the devil was self-realisation, not immorality and vice, but, my claim to my right to myself, whether it is manifested in clean living or unclean living is a matter of indifference; sin is the fundamental relationship underneath. Sin is not wrong doing, it is wrong being, independence of God; God has undertaken the responsibility for its removal on the ground of the Redemption. The condemnation is not that a man is born with an heredity of sin; a man begins to get the seal of condemnation when he sees the Light and prefers the darkness (see John 3:19).

The great miracle of the Redemption is that I can receive an absolutely new heredity, viz., Holy Spirit; and when that heredity begins to work out in me, I manifest in my mortal flesh the disposition of the Son of God. The result of the Redemption in my life must be that I justify God in forgiving me. I can "mouth" my salvation, I can thank God for it, but if I do not produce "goods up to sample" my religious life is a travesty. Always beware of the presentation of Redemption which produces a dangerous state of priggishness in moral life—that I can receive forgiveness and yet go on being bad; if I do, God is not justified in forgiving me. "If you are justified by faith, show it by your works," says the Apostle James (see James 2:14–24); in what way are you different in your life? does the reality of the Redemption at work in you justify God in having forgiven you? A man has to clear the conscience of God in forgiving him. Present-day evangelism is inclined to go much more strongly on the line of the "passion for souls" than "the passion for sanctification"; everyone has gone a-slumming to save the lost; it suits our religious passion to help the men and women who are down and out. Saving souls is God's work, man's work is discipling those souls (see Matthew 28:18–20). When Jesus Christ faced men with all the forces of evil born in them and men who were cleanliving and moral and upright, He did not look at the immorality of the one or the morality of the other, He looked at something we do not see—self-realisation. If my religion is based on my right to myself, that spells "Satan" in my soul; I may be right-living, but I am anti-God. "If you are going to be My disciple," Jesus says, "you must give up your right to yourself." Jesus Christ came to do what I could not do, viz., alter my heredity, and the point for me is, am I going to let Him do it? "And apart from shedding of blood there is no remission." God redeemed the world by shedding His blood, by putting the whole passion of the Godhead into it. He did not become interested and put one arm in to help the human race up, He went into the Redemption absolutely, there was nothing of Himself left out. Am I willing to put my whole self into becoming His? or am I one of those who accept His salvation, but thoroughly object to giving up my right to myself to Him? Unless I am willing to shed my blood for Him my Christianity is not worth anything. The trouble is that we have never come to the realisation of what sin is, we confound it with sins. *Sin* has to be cleansed, *sins* must be forgiven; the Redemption of Jesus Christ deals with *sin*. Do I agree with God's judgement on sin and self-realisation on the Cross? If so, I see where that judgement hits me and I agree that God is right. Self-realisation and God cannot live together. In the history of the human race when God appeared in the Person of Jesus Christ, they crucified Him. When I am born from above I realise that if I am going to obey the Holy Spirit I must enter into identification with Jesus Christ, otherwise I will kill the life of God in me. If I agree with God's judgement on self-realisation, then

the salvation of Jesus Christ will be manifested in me. It is a moral decision. There is no shirking the point and saying, "Oh, I'm not so bad as other people"; it is a question of agreeing with God's verdict on sin. Will I go through the condemnation now? If I will, there is no more condemnation for me, the salvation of Jesus Christ is made actual.

3. Sanctification Is the Blood of the Saint

But if we walk in the light, as He is in the light, . . . the blood [the essential life] of Jesus Christ His Son cleanseth us from all sin. (1 John 1:7)

The one condition is that we walk in the light as God is in the light. God does not give a man a clean thing to look after, He puts a life within him that keeps him clean as long as he walks in the light—a superabounding life, "a well of water springing up into everlasting life."

Repentance is the blood of sanctification, the exhibition of a real gift of God; not only am I sorry for my sin, that is human, but in the sorrow for sin God slips in something else—the power never to do the thing again. Many a man is kept away from Jesus Christ by a sense of honour—"I don't deny what you say, that God is able to save, but it can't mean me—if you only knew me! the mistakes I have made, the wrong things I have done, the blundering things; I would be a perfect disgrace to Him." There are more men in that attitude than is commonly supposed; but when a man realises what Jesus Christ undertakes to do—not tell him to do his best, but to surrender to Him and He will put into him the power to do right, he is emancipated right away.

YMCA Hut, Zeitoun, Egypt, April 10, 1917

IS CHRISTIANITY WORTHY OF GOD?
2 Corinthians 5:18–21

The Redemption is God's battle unto death with sin.

Dr. Forsyth

There is a presentation of Christianity which is sentimental and weak and unworthy of God; the Christianity of the New Testament is something "angels desire to look into." God has paid the price of redeeming a race that had become degenerate; He is not *going to* redeem it, He *has* redeemed it. The Gospel is just that—good news about God, that He has redeemed the human race. "God was in Christ, reconciling the world unto Himself. . . ." Is the

Gospel, as it is popularly presented, good news about God, or is it a misrepresentation of God? It is not good news about God unless it presents the revelation that God has put the basis of human life on Redemption. The Redemption means a great deal more than my personal salvation and yours, that is a mere outcome; pseudo-evangelism is apt to make it the great thing. The great thing according to the New Testament is not that the Redemption touches *me*, but that it avails for the whole human race. The Cross is not the cross of a martyr: it is the mirror of the nature of God focused in one point of history. If I want to know what God is like, I see it in the Cross. Jesus Christ is not Someone who leads me to God: either He is God, or I have none.

1. Christ's Cross the Conscience of the Human Race

How much more shall the blood of Christ, who through the eternal Spirit offered Himself without blemish unto God, cleanse your conscience from dead works to serve the living God? (Hebrews 9:14 RV)

If we do not take as much pains that our conscience is true, the pains we take to be true to our conscience is wasted.

Dr. Forsyth

Christianity is not consistency to conscience or to convictions; Christianity is being true to Jesus Christ. Over and over again a man's personal relationship to Jesus Christ gets into his convictions and splits them, like new wine put into old wine-skins, and if he sticks to his convictions before long he will become anti-Christ. The standard for my conscience and for the conscience of the whole human race is the Cross, and if I do not take care to rectify my individual conscience by the Cross I become "persnickety" and end in criticising God. The standard for the Christian is never—Is this thing right or wrong? but, is it related to the blood and passion and agony of the Cross of Christ? does it identify itself with the death of self-realisation?

Wherever Christianity has ceased to be vigorous it is because it has become Christian *ethics* instead of the Christian *evangel*. People will listen more readily to an exposition of the Sermon on the Mount than they will to the meaning of the Cross; but they forget that to preach the Sermon on the Mount apart from the Cross is to preach an impossibility. What is the good of telling me to love my enemies—and that "Blessed are the pure in heart"? You may talk like that to further orders, but it does not amount to anything. Jesus Christ did not come to teach men to be or do any of these things: He did not come primarily to teach, He came to make a man the possessor of His own disposition, the disposition portrayed in the Sermon on the Mount.

The conscience of the race, i.e., the standard whereby men are judged, is the Cross. I do not make my own conscience the standard, or the Sermon on the Mount the standard; the Cross of Christ, not His teaching, is the central thing, and what God condemns in the Cross is His standard for me. My conscience may be a competitor against Jesus Christ; I may be conscientious to the backbone, as Saul of Tarsus was, and be anti-Christ. ("I verily thought with myself, that I ought to do many things contrary to the name of Jesus of Nazareth." Acts 26:9). The conscientious objector takes as his standard, not the Cross—which is a cruel thing, a thing which sheds blood and blasts life—but the teachings of Jesus, which have no meaning apart from His Cross, consequently he is in danger of becoming a bloodless kind of individual. Immediately you come face to face with realities there has to be war to the death. It is absurd to call Christianity a system of non-resistance; the great doctrine of Christianity is resistance "unto blood" against sin. If a man does not resist physically it is only in order that he may resist all the more morally; where moral resistance does not tell, then physical resistance must. Take Our Lord Himself, we read that He went into the Temple and cast out them that sold and bought, overthrew the tables of the money-changers, and in a voice of thunder ordered the whole crowd out. Is He the "meek and mild and gentle Jesus" there? Up to the time of the war we had a Christianity that had lost the element of fight, the element of grit and judgement; the war has brought back these elements. There is something appalling about human life, and if we make our own private conscience the standard and remain in the offing on the conscientious line, we shall come under the curse of Meroz who "came not to the help of the LORD . . . against the mighty." My aim is not to be the saving of my own soul, getting myself put right for heaven, but battling to the death for what the Cross of Christ stands for. The great thing is not the teaching of Jesus, but what He came to do for the human race, viz., to make the way back to God. It cost Him His life to do it, and the writer to the Hebrews says, "Consider Him . . . lest ye be wearied and faint in your minds. Ye have not yet resisted unto blood, striving against sin." Have I got the iron of the Cross of Christ into my conscience, or am I a weak sentimentalist, kind and generous, but with nothing of the nature of the Cross in me? Is there anything in me that would go to the death for Jesus Christ's sake, or do I easily knuckle under because I base all on the teachings of Jesus instead of on His Cross? Conscientiousness is an ingredient in human nature, but the first and foremost relationship in Christianity is the sovereign preference for Jesus Christ.

2. Christ's Cross the Consecration of the Human Race

For what the law could not do, in that it was weak through the flesh, God sending His own Son in the likeness of sinful flesh, and for sin, condemned sin in the flesh. (Romans 8:3)

The process and progress of the Kingdom of God in history only unfolds this final achievement of His universal person.

Dr. Forsyth

The Cross of Christ consecrated the human race to God, and the human race cannot be run with success on any other line—we are certain it can. It cannot be run on imperial lines or democratic lines, it can only be run on the lines on which Jesus Christ consecrated it.

Where it touches my individual life is that in the Cross God "condemned *sin* in the flesh," not sins. Sins I look after; sin God looks after. The Redemption deals with sin. When the disposition of sin rules in my body it takes my organs and uses them for lust. Lust means, I will satisfy myself; whether I satisfy myself on a high or a low level makes no difference, the principle is the same. It is the exercise of my claim to my right to myself, and that has to go; in the final wind-up of the human race there won't be a strand of it left. Where we blunder is in confounding regeneration with the Redemption; the experience of regeneration is rare, the majority of men don't come anywhere near it, but that does not alter the fact of the Redemption. The meaning of regeneration is that in my actual life I become of some account to Jesus Christ, I become His disciple, and recognise that my body is the temple of the Holy Ghost. We say we can do what we like with our bodies, we cannot. If I try to satisfy any appetite on the basis of my right to myself, it means there is a spirit of antagonism to Jesus Christ at work in me; if I recognise that my body is the temple of the Holy Ghost, it is a sign that my life is based on the Cross.

3. Christ's Cross the Concentration of the Human Race

Knowing this, that our old man is crucified with Him, that the body of sin might be destroyed. (Romans 6:6)

Mankind's acquirement of its soul is Christ's moral and bloody victory worked into detail; His justice made to triumph and sin made to yield its opposite.

Dr. Forsyth

There are two Mystical Bodies, the Body of Christ and the body of sin, both are outside me. The disposition of sin inside me, called the "old man," connects me with the body of sin; when I am born from above I have the disposition of holiness imparted to me, and this connects me with the Body of Christ and I go to the death of the "old man" and in this way the body of sin is going to be destroyed. Sanctification is not a question of being delivered from hell, but of identifying myself with the death of Christ. Am I based in the moral centre of my life on the Cross of Christ? have I ever been moved for one second by the Cross? Those of us who are Christians ought to give a great deal more time to thinking on the fundamentals of our religion. Take it in your actual life, if you are not delivered from any particular element of sin, the reason is either you don't believe God can deliver you or you don't want Him to. Immediately you want Him to deliver you, the power of God is yours and it is done, not presently, but now, and the manifestation is wonderful. Let a man give up the right to himself to Jesus Christ, and the efficacy of His Redemption works out instanter.

THE ETHICS OF ENTHUSIASM
Ephesians 5

Enthusiasm means, to use the phrase of a German mystic, "intoxicated with God"; the word has come down in the world and popularly means anything that enthuses. Christianity takes all the emotions, all the dangerous elements of human nature, the things which lead us astray, all feelings and excitabilities, and makes them into one great power for God. Other religions either cut out dangerous emotions altogether or base too much on them. The tendency is in us all to say, "You must not trust in feelings"; perfectly true, but if your religion is without feeling, there is nothing in it. If you are living a life right with God, you will have feeling, most emphatically so, but you will never run the risk of basing your faith on feelings. The Christian is one who bases his whole confidence in God and His work of grace, then the emotions become the beautiful ornament of the life, not the source of it.

1. The Excitable Course of Personal Energy
(Ephesians 5:1–13)
Anything that awakens the strong emotions of a man will alter his mental outlook, e.g., the incoming of the Holy Spirit breaks every habit and every arranged set of ideas he has, and if he will obey the Spirit, he can re-make himself according to God's plan.

(a) The Drift of Ideas
If a man is unexcited his ideas are dull, he drifts impersonally; but let the excitement of anger, or of love, or hate, or jealousy come in, or let the Holy Spirit come in, and the drift stops and his whole mind is concentrated at once along one line. Human nature, if it is healthy, demands excitement, and if it does not obtain its thrilling excitement in the right way, it will take it in the wrong. That is a law of human nature which the Spirit of God does not contradict, but exalts. Every

false religion and false order of culture tries to make out that we ought to be absolutely unmoved—the passionlessness of exhaustion; but a healthy, full-orbed life is continually seeking excitement. God never makes us bloodless stoics, He makes us passionate saints. The word used of Jesus Christ has in it the very essence of Christianity—our Lord's "passion"; you could never speak of His passionlessness, the one characteristic of our Lord's life was its condensed intensity.

(b) The Direction of Ideas

Obedience to the Holy Spirit will mean that we have power to direct our ideas. It is astonishing how we sit down under the dominance of an idea, whether a right or wrong idea, and saints have sat down under this idea more than any other, that they cannot help thoughts of evil. Thank God that's a lie, we can. If you have never realised this before, put it to the test and ask yourself why the Spirit of God through the Apostle Paul should say, ". . . bringing every thought into captivity to the obedience of Christ" if we cannot do it? Never sit down under ideas that have no part or lot in God's Book; trace the idea to its foundation and see where it comes from. The Bible makes it plain that we can help thoughts of evil; it is Satan's interest to make us think we cannot. God grant the devil may be kept off the brains of the saints!

(c) The Divine Inhibition of Ideas

The Holy Spirit not only instructs us, but as we obey Him He inhibits our ideas. Those of you who have been a while in grace, examine yourselves and you will be astonished to find how much has been shed off your life, like autumn leaves. Ideas you never imagined you could get rid of have gone completely because God's Spirit has been definitely selecting out of your mind the ideas He can use, and as you obey Him and keep on that line the other ideas die out. It is only done by obedience, not by impulses, but by keeping at it.

2. The Emotional Centre of Personal Energy (Ephesians 5:14–20)

(a) The Scarcity of Emotions
Awake, thou that sleepest, and arise from the dead. (Ephesians 5:14)

The Bible reveals that apart from the Spirit of God men have no moving emotion towards God, they are described as "dead"; the preaching of the Gospel, the reading of the Word of God, has no answering emotion. Religious enterprise that has not learned to rely on the Holy Spirit makes everything depend on the human intellect—"God has said so-and-so, now believe it and it will be all right," but it won't. The basis of Jesus Christ's religion is the acceptance of a new Spirit, not a new creed, and the first thing the Holy Spirit does is to awaken us out of sleep. We have to learn to rely on the Holy Spirit because He alone gives the Word of God life. All our efforts to pump up faith in the Word of God is without quickening, without illumination. You reason to yourself and say, "Now God says this and I am going to believe it," and you believe it, and re-believe it, and re-re-believe it, and nothing happens, simply because the vital power that makes the words living is not there. The Spirit of God always comes in surprising ways—"The wind bloweth where it listeth, . . . so is every one that is born of the Spirit." No creed or school of thought or experience can monopolise the Spirit of God. The great snare of some aspects of presenting the Gospel is that everything is put in the head, everything must be rational and logical, no room is left for the great power of life which shows itself in surprising ways. In natural life people without any emotions are undesirable to have as friends, and a Christian life that is without the continual recurrence of Divine emotion is suffering from spiritual sleeping-sickness.

(b) The Successive Emotions
See then that ye walk circumspectly. (Ephesians 5:15)

Emotions in nature and in grace succeed one another very rapidly and need a strong controlling power. In natural life people who have successive emotions are in danger of becoming sentimentalists; in spiritual life successive emotions lead to being driven about by every wind of doctrine that savours of piety. A sentimentalist is one who likes to live in a great swim of emotions, but he is unfit to meet the facts of life, and when real trouble comes his way he tries to hide himself away from it and becomes intensely selfish. The anxiety lest you should suffer—"It is such a distress to me to see you in pain"—is really anxiety lest he should suffer. In spiritual life successive emotions are more dangerous. If you are without the control of the Spirit of God, devotional emotion and religious excitement always end in sensuality. Emotions that stir feelings must act themselves out, whether rightly or wrongly will depend on the person. If you feel remarkably generous, then be generous at once, act it out; if you don't, it will react and make you mean.[18] If you have a time of real devotion before God and see what God wants you to do and you do not work it out in your practical life, it will react in secret immorality. That is not an exceptional law, it is an eternal law, and I wish it could be blazed in letters of fire into the mind of every Christian. Very often you will find that

---

18. mean: ordinary, common, low, or ignoble, rather than cruel or spiteful

God paralyses your emotional nature and allows you to feel nothing; it is a sure sign that He is guiding, because your life has been too full of emotions you have not been working out.

(c) The Sovereign Emotions
. . . be filled with the Spirit. (Ephesians 5:18)

The sovereign emotions are guided and controlled by love, but bear in mind that love in its highest moral meaning is the preference of one person for another person. A Christian's love is personal passionate devotion to Jesus Christ, and he learns to grip on the threshold of his mind as in a vice every sentiment awakened by wrong emotions. God holds the saints responsible for emotions they have not got and ought to have as well as for the emotions they have allowed which they ought not to have allowed. If we indulge in inordinate affection, anger, anxiety, God holds us responsible; but He also insists that we have to be passionately filled with the right emotions. The emotional life of a Christian is to be measured by the exalted energy exhibited in the life of our Lord. The language applied to the presence of the Holy Spirit in the saint is descriptive of the energy of emotion that keeps the inner and outer life like our Lord's own life. We must find out for ourselves the particular "psalms and hymns and spiritual songs" (Ephesians 5:19) which will keep our emotional life right with God, and we shall find that the Holy Spirit insists on intellectual fasting as well as on intellectual control. The Apostle Paul continually urges the saints to stir up their minds; we have no right to be stagnant and dull. If we have no emotional life, then we have disobeyed God. "Be filled with the Spirit"; it is as impossible to be filled with the Spirit and be free from emotion as it is for a man to be filled with wine and not show it. The reason some of us are so amazingly dull and get sleeping-sickness is that we have never once thought of paying attention to the stirring up the Spirit of God gives the mind and our emotional nature. How many of us are terrified out of our wits lest we should be emotional! Jesus Christ demands the whole nature, and He demands that part of our nature the devil uses most, viz., the emotional part. We have to get the right bed-rock for our nature, the life of Jesus Christ, and then glean the things which awaken our emotions, and see that those emotions are expressed in ways like the character of our Lord.

3. The Expansive Character of Personal Energy *(Ephesians 5:21–33)*

(a) Transformation of Self-hood
submitting yourselves one to another in the fear of God. (Ephesians 5:21)

When the Holy Spirit first comes into us He seems to put us into a prison house; then He opens our eyes and causes us to expand in the realisation that "all things are yours," from the tiniest flower that blooms to God on His throne. When we have learnt the secret that God Himself is the Source of our life, then He can trust us with the expansion of our nature. Every expansion of our nature transforms self-hood into unselfishness. It is not peculiar to Christians, it is true of human nature apart altogether from the grace of God. Inspiration, either true or false, unites the personality, makes a man feel at one with himself and with everyone else, and he is unselfish as long as the inspiration lasts. Paul says, "Don't be drunk with wine," which is the counterfeit of the true transformation, "but be filled with the Spirit," and all self-interested considerations are transformed at once, you will think only, without trying to, of the good of others and of the glory of God. Be careful what you allow to unite you and make you feel unselfish; the only power we must allow as Christians is the Holy Spirit who will so transform us that it will be easy to submit one to another in the fear of God.

(b) Transfiguration of Self-hood
Wives, submit yourselves unto your own husbands, as unto the Lord. (Ephesians 5:22)

With a sudden abruptness Paul mentions the closest practical relationships in life, and immediately it becomes clear why he does so. If the expansive character of the Holy Spirit is at work in us as saints, it will transfigure the life in all these relationships. The Holy Spirit keeps us on the line of the transfiguration of self-hood and the thought of good to ourselves never enters in, unless it is introduced by someone else.

(c) Tenderness of Sainthood
The characteristic of the expansive power of the Holy Ghost in a saint appears in a tenderness just like Jesus Christ's—". . . even as Christ also loved the church, and gave Himself for it" (Ephesians 5:25). These characteristics never come by impulse. Impulse is the impertinence of human nature keeping on tiptoe to try and look as big as God. The Holy Spirit always checks impulse, and the saint learns through humiliation to bring it to heel. Watch how Jesus Christ not only checked, but rebuked impulse in the disciples. The vagaries of modern spiritual life come in because our impulses are insubordinate—"No, I won't submit, I have illumination." The Holy Spirit never works like that. Be "being filled with the Spirit," and as we walk in the light the life of God is worked out moment by moment—a life of glorious discipline and steady obedience.

PERSONALITY—I

Personality is the perplexing fact of my self which is continually changing and yet remains the same. Personality is an enigma; its only answer is God. Never confound personality with consciousness; all that can be dealt with psychologically is consciousness, but a man's salvation is not limited to his consciousness.

1. The Disposition of Darkness

The natural man receiveth not the things of the Spirit of God: for they are foolishness unto him. (1 Corinthians 2:14)

The word "disposition" is used here in the sense of the mainspring that moves me. Apart from a knowledge of Jesus Christ, and apart from being crumpled up by conviction of sin, men have a disposition which keeps them perfectly happy and peaceful. The natural man is not in distress, not conscious of any disharmony in himself; he is not "in trouble as other men," and is quite content with being once-born; the things Jesus Christ stands for have no meaning for the natural man. The Bible refers to this disposition as one of darkness—". . . being darkened in their understanding" (Ephesians 4:18 RV). We preach to men as if they were conscious of being dying sinners, they are not, they are having a good time, and all our talk about the need to be born again is from a domain they know nothing about; because some men try to drown unhappiness in worldly pleasures it does not follow all are like that. There is nothing attractive about the Gospel to the natural man; the only man who finds the Gospel attractive is the man who is convicted of sin. Conviction of sin and being guilty of sins are not the same thing. Conviction of sin is produced by the incoming of the Holy Spirit because conscience is promptly made to look at God's demands and the whole nature cries out, in some form or other. "What must I do to be saved?"

For a man to be undisturbed and in unity with himself is a good condition, not a bad one, because a united personality means freedom from self-consciousness; but if his peace is without any consideration of Jesus Christ it is simply the outcome of this disposition of darkness which keeps men alienated from the life of God. When Jesus Christ comes in He upsets this false unity; He comes not as a Comforter, but as a thorough Disturber. "If I had not come . . . , they had not had sin"—then why did He come? If I was peaceful and happy, living a clean upright life, why should Jesus Christ come with a standard of holiness I never dreamt of? Simply because that peace was the peace of death, a peace altogether apart from God. The coming of Jesus Christ to the nat-ural man means the destruction of all peace that is not based on a personal relationship to Himself.

2. The Disposition Divided

For we know that the law is spiritual: but I am carnal, sold under sin. For that which I do I allow not: for what I would, that do I not; but what I hate, that do I. (Romans 7:14–15)

Romans 7 is the classic for all time of the conflict a man experiences whose mind is awakened by the incoming of the light of God. Never say "We must get out of the 7th of Romans," some of us will never get into it; if we did, we would be in hell in two minutes. The 7th of Romans represents the profound conflict which goes on in the consciousness of a man without the Spirit of God, facing the demands of God. Only to one in a thousand can God lift the veil to show what the 7th of Romans means. It is the presentation by a man who stands now as a saint, looking back on the terrific conflict produced by his conscience having been awakened to the law of God, but with no power to do what his mind assigns he should. A lot of tawdry stuff has been written on this chapter simply because Christians so misunderstand what conviction of sin really is. Conviction of sin such as the Apostle Paul is describing does not come when a man is born again, nor even when he is sanctified, but long after, and then only to a few. It came to Paul as an apostle and saint, and he could diagnose sin as no other. Knowledge of what sin is is in inverse ratio to its presence; only as sin goes do you realise what it is; when it is present you do not realise what it is because the nature of sin is that it destroys the capacity to know you sin.

The problem in practical experience is not to know what is right, but to do it. My natural spirit may know there are a great many things I ought to do, but I never can do what I know I should until I receive the Life which is life indeed, viz., Holy Spirit. "For the good that I would I do not: but the evil which I would not, that I do" (Romans 7:19). That is the picture of a man conscious of a dislocation within himself. "O wretched man that I am! who shall deliver me from the body of this death?" The consciousness of a personality at this stage is that of a house divided against itself; it is the stage technically known as conviction of sin. "For I was alive without the law once"—at peace till I saw what Jesus Christ was driving at, "but when the commandment came, sin revived, and I died" Romans 7:9. "If all God can do for me is to destroy the unity I once had, make me a divided personality, give me light that makes me morally insane with longing to do what I cannot do, I would rather be without His salvation, rather remain happy and peaceful without Him." But if this experience is only a stage towards a life of union with God, it is a different matter.

3. The Disposition Divorced

For the flesh lusteth against the Spirit, and the Spirit against the flesh: and these are contrary the one to the other: so that ye cannot do the things that ye would. (Galatians 5:17)

After being born again a man experiences peace, but it is a militant peace, a peace maintained at the point of war.

The wrong disposition is no longer in the ascendant, but it is there, and the man knows it is. He is conscious of an alternating experience, sometimes he is in ecstasy, sometimes in the dumps; there is no stability, no real spiritual triumph. To take this as the experience of full salvation is to prove God not justified in the Atonement.

"For the flesh lusteth against the Spirit, and the Spirit against the flesh." The Spirit of God entering into a man wars against "the flesh," not flesh and blood, but the disposition of sin. Paul calls the product of this friction between the Spirit and the flesh, "carnality." A worldly man has no carnality; he is not conscious of any conflict between the Spirit and his flesh; when he is born again the conflict begins, and there is a disclosure of the carnal mind, which is "enmity against God." No man knows he has that enemy on the inside until he receives the Holy Spirit.

The carnal mind is not something which has to be removed: it either is, or is not. Immediately you agree to the dethronement of the disposition which lusts against the Spirit, the carnal mind is not. The flesh and the Spirit are daggers drawn, so to speak, and I have to decide which shall rule. If I am going to decide for the Spirit, I will crucify the flesh; God cannot do it, I must do it myself. To "crucify" means to put to death, not counteract, not sit on, not whitewash, but kill. If I do not put to death the things in me which are not of God, they will put to death the things that are of God. To belong to Christ means I have deliberately chosen to depose the disposition of the flesh and be identified with Christ—"Yes, I agree with the Spirit, and go to the death of the old disposition; I agree with God's condemnation in the Cross of self-interest and self-realisation, though these things have been dearer to me than life." Jesus Christ is merciless to self-realisation, to self-indulgence, pride, unchastity, to everything that has to do with the disposition you did not know you had till you met Him. The Redemption does not tinker with the externals of a man's life; it deals with the disposition. "And they that are of Christ Jesus have crucified the flesh with the passions and the lusts thereof" (Galatians 5:24 RV). No one is really Christ's till that is done.

4. The Disposition Divine

... that by these [exceeding great and precious promises] ye might be partakers of the divine nature. (2 Peter 1:4)

At this stage a man's personality is again united into peace. Jesus Christ's one aim is to bring us back into oneness with God. The whole purpose of the Redemption is to give back to man the original source of life, and in a regenerated man this means "Christ ... formed in you." Am I willing that the old disposition should be crucified with Christ? If I am, Jesus Christ will take possession of me and will baptise me into His life until I bear a strong family likeness to Him. It is a lonely path, a path of death, but it means ultimately being "presenced with Divinity." The Christian life does not take its pattern from good men, but from God Himself, that is why it is an absolutely supernormal life all through. "Ye therefore shall be perfect, as your heavenly Father is perfect."

PERSONALITY—II
Self-Realisation versus Christ-Realisation

Self-realisation is a modern phrase—"Be moral, be religious, be upright, in order that you may realise yourself." Nothing blinds the mind to the claims of Jesus more effectually than a good moral life based on the disposition of self-realisation. Paul says, "If our gospel is veiled, it is veiled in them that are perishing: in whom the god of this world hath blinded the minds of the unbelieving ..." (2 Corinthians 4:3–4 RV). The issue is not with external sins and wrong-doing, but with the ideal of self-realisation, because it is this disposition that divides clean asunder from all Jesus Christ stands for. In using Bible terms, remember they are used from God's standpoint, not man's. From man's standpoint, self-realisation is full of light and wisdom; from God's standpoint, it is the dark night of the soul. Romans 7 describes the giving way of the foundations of self-realisation.

1. Separate Self-Consciousness

The notion that we conceive of ourselves as separate from everyone else is erroneous, it is the rarest thing—unless we have done wrong, then immediately we realise not our oneness with others, but our separateness. The guilty man is the one who wants to be alone, the man who is right with God does not; neither does a child. Separate self-consciousness is the realisation that I am other than what I see and am troubled by all that is not "me." The "I" of separate self-consciousness is the manifestation of sin; the final curse of a disobedient soul is that it becomes a separate, self-conscious individual.

God did not create Adam holy. He created him innocent, that is, without self-consciousness (as we understand the word) before God; Adam was conscious of himself only in relation to the Being whom he was to glorify and enjoy. Consciousness of self was an impossibility in the Garden until something happened, viz., the introduction of sin. To begin with Adam was not afraid of God; he was not afraid of the beasts of the field, or of anything, because there was no consciousness of himself apart from God. Immediately he disobeyed, he became conscious of himself and he felt afraid—"I heard Thy voice in the garden, and I was afraid . . ." (Genesis 3:10); he had ceased to be a child and had become a sinner. That is why our Lord says we have to become children all over again. Through the miracle of regeneration we are placed back into a state of innocence. "Sin kills the child out of us and creates the bitter sinner in us." In other words, God's right to me is killed by the incoming of my self-conscious right to myself—"I can do without God." Sin is not a creation, it is a relationship set up between the devil (who is independent entirely of God) and the being God made to have communion with Himself. Disobey God, separate yourself from Him, and you will be "as God, knowing good and evil" (Genesis 3:5 RV; see Genesis 3:22). The entrance of sin meant that the connection with God was gone and the disposition of self-realisation had come in its place.

Our Lord never denounced wrong-doing and immorality so strongly as He denounced self-realisation. Have you ever been puzzled by His attitude to the people of His day—why He told the chief priests that "the publicans and the harlots go into the kingdom of God before you"? He could not have meant that social sins were not abominable: He was looking at something we do not see, viz., the disposition at the basis of right and wrong-doing. If either my goodness or my badness is based on the disposition of self-realisation, I am anti-Christ. Modern culture and much of the "Higher Christian Life"[19] type of teaching goes on the line of perfecting my natural individual self until I am in such a condition that God will say, "Now you have done so well I will call you My child." Could anything be more alien to the New Testament? Our Lord's teaching is always *anti*–self-realisation. "He that findeth his life shall lose it . . ." Why do we ignore what Jesus said? When we come across something we don't like we say we don't understand it; it is too plain not to be understood. Jesus Christ says that the relationship to Himself is to be supreme. ". . . and he that loseth his life *for My sake* shall find it."

We know experimentally what it is to be born again, but we do not *think* along that line, consequently barriers come in the way, e.g., self-conscious piety, sanctimonious sincerity. Anything that makes me conscious of myself or of my experience is of the nature of sin and brings the bondage of self-consciousness. In a religious person self-consciousness dresses itself up in the guise of piety; you can't be "pi" without feeling self-conscious. The truly godly person is one who is entirely sanctified, and he or she is never sanctimonious, but absolutely natural. The characteristic of a saint is freedom from anything in the nature of self-consciousness. Our Lord was conscious of only one thing—"I and My Father are one."

2. Solidarity in Christ

If I am prepared to have the disposition of self-realisation destroyed and the disposition of Christ-realisation put in its place, I get to the bedrock of identification with the death of Jesus, and there begins the possibility of my being something which will show my gratitude for His Redemption. Identification with the death of Jesus is a most powerfully practical experience. The dominating principle at work now is towards Christ-realisation; experimentally it means that I am ruled by the very disposition of Jesus. Once we are reinstated in the life of God through the Redemption self-consciousness gets feebler and feebler until it disappears altogether, and we are conscious only of personality as a means of knowing God.

The beginning of the Christian life is characterised by an abomination of self-interest; it is "what the Lord said to me" and "what I said to Him"; it is a stage through which many a life goes, but it is not in agreement with the life Jesus pictures, not the life of a child. There is never any trace of self-conscious sainthood in abandonment to Jesus, there is only one consciousness—

Jesus only, Jesus ever,
Jesus all in all I see.

Some people are everlastingly badgered by self-consciousness, full of nervous troubles, but let some-

19. The Higher Christian Life emphasized sanctification and personal holiness.

thing like war or a bereavement strike the life and all the morbid self-interest is gone, and the abandonment of concern for others marks the beginning of real life. That is an ordinary natural law and has nothing to do with the Spirit of God. Apply it to what our Lord teaches about discipleship—He makes abandonment to Himself the condition (see Luke 14:26).

Whenever our Lord talked about the relation of a disciple to Himself it was in terms of mystical union: "I am the vine [not the root of the vine, but the vine itself], ye are the branches." We have not paid enough attention to the illustrations Jesus uses. This is the picture of sanctification in the individual, a completeness of relationship between Jesus Christ and myself. Pharisaic holiness means that my eyes are set on my own whiteness and I become a separate individual. I have the notion that I have to be something; I have not, I have to be absolutely abandoned to Jesus Christ, so one with Him that I never think of myself apart from Him. Love is never self-conscious.

We are one with God only in the manner and measure we have allowed the Holy Spirit to have way with us. The fruit of the Spirit is the fruit of a totally new disposition, the disposition of Christ-realisation. Instead now of self-realisation, self-consciousness and sin, there is sanctity and spiritual reality, bringing forth "fruit unto holiness."

PERSONALITY—III
Psalm 139
Intercessory Introspection

1. The Supernatural Intimacy of God *(Psalm 139:1–6)*

O LORD, Thou hast searched me, and known me. . . . (Psalm 139:1)

The 139th Psalm ought to be the personal experience of every Christian. My own introspection, or exploration of myself, will lead me astray, but when I realise not only that God knows me, but that He is the only One who does, I see the vital importance of intercessory introspection. Every man is too big for himself, thank God for everyone who realises it and, like the Psalmist, hands himself over to be searched out by God. We only know ourselves as God searches us. "God knows me" is different from "God is omniscient"; the latter is a mere theological statement; the former is a child of God's most precious possession—"O LORD, Thou hast searched *me*, and known *me*."

No matter what our Christian experience may be the majority of us are nowhere near where the Psalmist was; we will rest in our experience instead of seeing that the experience is meant to bring us to the place of knowing God's supernatural intimacy.

"Thou compassest my path and my lying down, and art acquainted with all my ways. For there is not a word in my tongue, but, lo, O LORD, Thou knowest it altogether." To say "Of course God is omniscient and knows everything" makes no effect on me, I don't care whether God is "omni" anything; but when by the reception of the Holy Spirit I begin to realise that God knows all the deepest possibilities there are in me, knows all the eccentricities of my being, I find that the mystery of myself is solved by this besetting God. Do I really believe I am too big a mystery to solve by myself? or am I so desperately ignorant that I imagine I understand myself thoroughly? If so, I am likely to have a rude awakening. The Psalmist implies—"Thou art the God of the early mornings, the God of the late at nights; the God of the mountain peaks, the God of the sea; but, my God, my soul has further horizons than the early mornings, deeper darkness than the nights of earth, higher peaks than any mountain, greater depths than any sea—Thou who art the God of all these, be my God. I cannot search to the heights or to the depths; there are motives I cannot trace, dreams I cannot get at; my God, search me out and explore me, and let me know that Thou hast." Look back over your past history with God and you will see that this is the place He has been bringing you to—"God knows me, and I know He does." You can't shift the man who knows that; there is the sanity of almighty God about him. It is an interpretation of what Jesus Christ said—"The very hairs of your head are all numbered. Fear ye not therefore. . . ."

> *Never shall I think*
> *Of anything that thou might'st overlook:—*
> *In faith born triumph at thy feet I sink.*
>
>   George MacDonald

2. The Surprising Presence of God *(Psalm 139:7–12)*

Whither shall I go from Thy Spirit? or whither shall I flee from Thy presence? (Psalm 139:7)

The Psalmist states further that the presence of God is the secure accompaniment of His knowledge; not only does God know everything about him, but He is with him in the knowledge. Where is the place that God is not?—hell? No, hell is God; if there were no God, there would be no hell. "If I make my bed in hell, behold, Thou art there." The first thing "the fool" does is to get rid of God ("The fool hath said in his heart, There is no God." (Psalm 14:1); then he gets rid of heaven and hell; then he gets rid of all moral consequences—no such thing as right and wrong. The Psalmist is stating that wherever he may go in accordance with the indecipherable Providence of God, there the surprising presence of God will meet him. Immediately you begin to forecast and plan for yourself God will break up your programme, He delights to do it, until we learn to live like children based on the knowledge that God is ruling and reigning and rejoicing, and His joy is our strength. When we say—"even there shall Thy hand lead me, and Thy right hand shall hold me," there is no foreboding anxiety, because "His love in times past" enables us to rest confidentially in Him. The only rest there is is in abandon to the love of God. There is security from yesterday—"Thou hast beset me behind"; security for to-morrow—"and before"; and security for to-day,

"and laid Thine hand upon me." It was this knowledge that gave our Lord the imperturbable peace He always had. We must be like a plague of mosquitoes to the Almighty, with our fussy little worries and anxieties, and the perplexities we imagine, all because we won't get into the elemental life with God which Jesus came to give.

This Psalm is the expression of the Atonement at work in human experience, at-one-ment with God. The marvel of the Atonement is that Jesus Christ can create endlessly in lives the oneness which He had with the Father. When the Holy Spirit emancipates my personality no attention is paid to my individuality, to my temperament or prejudices; He brings me into oneness with God entirely when once I am willing to waive my right to myself and let Him have His way. No man gets there without a crisis, a crisis of a terrific nature in which he goes to the death of something.

God is never far enough away from His saints to think about them: He *thinks* them, we are taken up into His consciousness. This is expressed in the life of our Lord. How we get there we cannot say, but it is by the processes of God's training of us. God won't leave us alone until the prayer of His Son is answered, that we may be one with the Father even as He is one.

PERSONALITY—IV

I am crucified with Christ: nevertheless I live; yet not I, but Christ liveth in me: and the life which I now live in the flesh I live by the faith of the Son of God, who loved me, and gave Himself for me. Galatians 2:20

1. The Sacrifice of Soul

... when Thou shalt make His soul an offering for sin. (Isaiah 53:10)

Galatians 2:20 is a complete statement of "the life hid with Christ in God" in personal experience, and the prophecy in Isaiah that the soul of our Lord was made "an offering for sin" has exactly the same idea. The sacrifice of body may be an un-Christian sacrifice— "and though I give my body to be burned, and have not charity [love, RV] it profiteth me nothing"; but the sacrifice of soul is a willing love-offering.

"I am crucified with Christ ..." The teaching of self-realisation is the great opponent of the doctrine of sanctification—"I have to realise myself as a separate individual, educate and develop myself so that I fulfil the purpose of my being." Self-realisation and self-consciousness are ways in which the principle of sin works out, and in Galatians 2:20 Paul is referring

to the time and the place where he got rid of his "soul" in this respect. There is nothing in the nature of self-realisation or of self-consciousness in our Lord.

People will say glibly, "Oh yes, I have been crucified with Christ," while their whole life is stamped with self-realisation; once identification with the death of Jesus has really taken place self-realisation does not appear again. To be "crucified with Christ" means that in obedience to the Spirit granted to me at regeneration, I eagerly and willingly go to the Cross and crucify self-realisation for ever. The crucifixion of the flesh is the willing action of an obedient regenerate man or woman. "And they that are Christ's have crucified the flesh with the affections and lusts" (Galatians 5:24). Obey the Spirit of God and the Word of God, and it will be as clear as a sunbeam what you have to do; it is an attitude of will towards God, an absolute abandon, a glad sacrifice of the soul in unconditional surrender. Then comes the marvellous revelation—"I have been crucified with Christ"—not, "I am being crucified," or, "I hope to be crucified by and by"; not, "I am getting nearer to the place where I shall be crucified with Christ," but, *"I have been crucified with Christ,"* I realise it and know it.

2. The Surprise of Sacrifice

For to me to live is Christ. (Philippians 1:21)

"*. . . nevertheless I live; yet not I, but Christ liveth in me.*" Paul still says "I," but the "I" is so taken up with Christ that all he sees is Christ-realisation, not self-realisation. "Knowing this, that our old man is crucified with Him"—the "old man" is the scriptural name for self-realisation, and it is my "old man" that connects me with the body of sin. Sin is infinitely more than my "old man"; there is a supernatural body of sin which backs me up in wrong, it is an impulsion to wrong on the outside which is far more powerful than the disposition to sin on the inside. By the identification with the death of Christ Paul refers to, the "old man," self-realisation in me, is crucified, and in this way the body of sin is "done away," not crucified, but destroyed. There are two mystical bodies—the body of sin ruled over by Satan, and the Body of Christ built up of the men and women who have been made one in Him. That is why Paul refers to our Lord as "the last Adam," He is the Federal Head of a totally new conception of Humanity. When I am lifted by the Atonement into oneness with God I do not lose my personal identity, my identity becomes that of conscious union with God. Man's relationship with God in the beginning was such that the consciousness of union with Him was a delight: as soon as sin entered that went and man became *self*-conscious: he realised he was no longer in union with God and tried to hide himself from His presence.

Paul says, "I have been crucified with Christ: *nevertheless I live*"—"my personal identity as created by God and restored in Christ Jesus, is still there, but the "I" is no longer ruled by the disposition of sin, that has been identified with the Cross, and it is Christ who lives in me." Paul's whole life was so identified with Christ that it was not only not untrue for him to say "Christ liveth in me," it was the only truth. When he says, in writing to the Corinthians, "I fear, lest . . . your minds should be corrupted from the simplicity

that is in Christ," he is referring to the fundamental simplicity of this relationship. Our Lord Himself continually reminded His disciples of this simplicity—"Verily I say unto you, Except ye be converted, and *become as little children, . . .*" (Matthew 18:3); "I thank Thee, O Father, . . . *because Thou . . . hast revealed [these things] unto babes*" (Matthew 11:25)—out of the complication, out of the torture of self-consciousness, out of the strenuousness and effort, into the simplicity of the life hid with Christ in God, where God is at liberty to do with us what He likes, even as He did with His own Son.

3. The Summit of Substitution

He that eateth My flesh, and drinketh My blood, dwelleth in Me, and I in him. (John 6:56)

"*. . . and the life which I now live in the flesh I live by the faith of the Son of God.*" The doctrine of substitution in the Bible is "Christ *for* me" that it may be "Christ *in* me," until the personal oneness can only be expressed in the language of our Lord in John 6. "The life which I *now* live," says Paul, not hereafter, but the life you can see, the life I live in the flesh, the life exhibited through my tongue, through all the organs of my body, the way I eat and drink, and the way I do my work. That is the life Paul has the audacity to say he lives "by the faith of the Son of God." It is the life of the Spirit made manifest in the flesh, and that is always the test of identification with Christ, not prayer meetings and times of devotion. If I have been identified with the Cross of Christ it must show through my finger-tips.

"*. . . who loved me and gave Himself for me.*" Paul is identified for ever with the interests of the Son of God in other lives, he attracted to Jesus Christ all the time, never to himself; he became a sacramental personality, wherever he went Jesus Christ helped Himself to his life. "Unto me, who am less than the least of all saints, was this grace given, to preach [i.e., sacramentally express] unto the Gentiles the unsearchable riches of Christ" (Ephesians 3:8 RV).

WHERE JESUS CHRIST TELLS

1. In the Domain of Struggle and Sin

If Jesus Christ does not mean anything to you it is because you have not entered into the domain where He tells; you may have to enter that domain through a ruthless doorway. Immediately you go through the bottom board of self-complacency and come to the elemental you enter the domain of struggle and sin, and Jesus Christ begins to tell at once. Men are alive

physically and intellectually apart from Jesus Christ, and as long as they are satisfied with that attitude to life Jesus Christ is not a necessity; the wholesome-minded type is totally oblivious to Jesus Christ. "I did not come for the whole," said Jesus, "but for they that are sick" (see Luke 5:31–32).

There are numbers of men and women who are materially satisfied, their reach does not exceed their grasp; they are not moral renegades, but they remain outside the domain in which Jesus Christ figures. They have no disrespect for Jesus Christ, but they have no use for Him, He seems to be untouched by the reality of things. It is quite possible to live in that domain and never come across the need for Jesus Christ; in fact you can work out a better philosophy of life without Him because He comes in as an interruption. But when once a man realises that his actual life spits at his creed, then begins the struggle. A boy in his teens thinks higher and nobler than at any other time, then he begins to find that his actual life comes nowhere near his ideal—"I can't begin to be actually what I see I ought to be." The struggle represented by that type of mind is an agony, and that is the first domain where Jesus Christ begins to tell. If a man has got this struggle on there is only one way out—"Come unto Me, all ye that labour and are heavy laden, and I will give you rest." If you are not struggling, you don't need to bother your head; but if it is a struggle worthy of the name, remember the only way out is by coming to Jesus. So long as I have no struggle, no sense of sin, I can do well enough without Him.

2. In the Domain of Suffering and Sorrow

Another domain in which Jesus Christ tells is the domain of suffering and sorrow. You cannot think of a home to-day that is without suffering. The war has knocked on the head the stupid temperamental idea that "every cloud has a silver lining"; there are clouds in countless lives with an inkier lining inside than outside. It is an insult to tell such people to "Cheer up and look on the bright side"; their lives are blasted for all time from every standpoint saving Jesus Christ's. The remarkable thing is that it is rarely the one who suffers who turns against God; it is the lookers-on who turn against God because they do not see the one fact more in the life which gives God room to work. Those who look on are apt to come to the conclusion either that the one who suffers is a sinner, or that God is cruel; they take the line of Job's comforters. Why there should be suffering we do not know; but we have to remain loyal to the character of God as revealed by Jesus Christ in the face of it.

There is a type of suffering caused because we do not see the way out. A man may say that the basis of things is rational—"Get to the bottom of things and you will find it all simple and easy of explanation"— well, that simply is not true. The basis of things is not rational, but tragic, and when you enter the domain of suffering and sorrow you find that reason and logic are your guide amongst things as they are, but nothing more. Is it rational that I should be born with an heredity over which I have no control? Is it rational that nations that are nominally Christian should be at war? The basis of things is tragic, and the only way out is through the Redemption. Many a man in mental stress of weather is driven to utter what sounds like blasphemy, and yet he may be nearer God than in his complacent acceptance of beliefs that have never been tried. Never be afraid of the man who seems to you to talk blasphemously, he is up against problems you may never have met with; instead of being wrathful, be patient with him. The man to be afraid of is the one who is indifferent, what morality he has got is well within his own grasp, and Jesus Christ is of no account at all.

3. In the Domain of Spirit and Sublimity

It is in the implicit domains that Jesus Christ tells. By "implicit" is meant the thing you can't put into words but which makes you "you." It is in the moments when the implicit is awakened that Jesus Christ becomes the only One who does tell. You cannot get there when you like, there are moral conditions. Jesus Christ makes Himself the great Decider of human destiny—"But who say ye that I am?" Beware of the subtlety that likes to listen to the teaching of Jesus but says, "There is no need for all this talk about the Atonement and the Cross, all that is necessary is to live out the Sermon on the Mount, to follow in the steps of Jesus." If Jesus Christ came to teach a man to be what he never can be, would He had never come! He is the greatest tantaliser of mankind if all He came to do was to tell us to be pure in heart, to be so holy that when God scrutinises us He can see nothing to censure. But what He came to do was to make it possible for any man to receive the disposition that ruled Him, viz., the Holy Spirit. When a man is born again what happens is that he receives the heredity of Jesus Christ. That is the meaning of Regeneration. There is only one disposition that can live out the teaching of Jesus, and that is His own disposition. When I have received the disposition of Jesus Christ, God does not shield me from any requirements of a son; I have the opportunity of proving actually worthy of His great Redemption. "If the Son . . . shall make you free, ye shall be free indeed," said Jesus—free from the inside, free in essence; there will be no pretence, no putting yourself on a pedestal and saying "This is what God has done for me," you will *be* free, the thing will be there ostensibly.

WITH CHRIST IN THE SCHOOL OF PHILOSOPHY

1. The New Thinking of Pentecost
. . . the things of the Spirit of God. (1 Corinthians 2:14)

Everywhere the charge is made against Christian people, not only the generality of Christians, but really spiritual people, that they think in a very slovenly manner. Very few of us in this present dispensation live up to the privilege of thinking spiritually as we ought. This present dispensation is the dispensation of the Holy Ghost. The majority of us do not think according to the tremendous meaning of that; we think ante-Pentecostal thoughts, the Holy Spirit is not a living factor in our thinking; we have only a vague impression that He is here. Many Christian workers would question the statement that we should ask for the Holy Spirit (Luke 11:13). The note struck in the New Testament is not "Believe in the Holy Spirit," but "Receive the Holy Spirit." That does not mean the Holy Spirit is not here; it means He *is* here in all His power, for one purpose, that men who believe in Him might receive Him. So the first thing we have to face is the reception of the Holy Spirit in a practical conscious manner.

Always distinguish between yielding to the Spirit and receiving the Spirit. When the Spirit is at work in a time of mighty revival it is very difficult not to yield to the Spirit, but it is quite another thing to receive Him. If we yield to the power of the Spirit in a time of revival we may feel amazingly blessed, but if we do not receive the Spirit we are left decidedly worse and not better. That is first a psychological fact and then a New Testament fact. So as Christians we have to ask ourselves, does our faith stand "in demonstration of the Spirit and of power"? Have we linked ourselves up with the power of the Holy Ghost, and are we letting Him have His way in our thinking?

(a) Material of This Thinking
Ye shall know them by their fruits. Matthew 7:16; see Matthew 7:15–20)

The touchstone of truth is not a big intellect but a pure heart—a holy man; but an unholy man can test the reality of a man's holiness. Jesus told His disciples to test preachers and teachers not by the fact that they prophesied in His name, but by their fruits. How many of us do? How many of us know experimentally what Jesus meant when He said: "My sheep hear My voice," but "they know not the voice of strangers"? We

must never test our teachers by our spiritual prejudices. Jesus laid down as the one principle for testing teachers, not that God was at work through them, but by their fruits. God will honour His word whether a saint or a bad man preaches it; this is one of the startling things that our Lord says (see Matthew 7:21–23). Jesus demands that we submit our teachers to the test He Himself submitted to (see John 18:20). A teacher sent from God never teaches in secret, or teaches the special esoteric line of things which only the initiated few can get into.

Take it individually, are we thinking on the sane, vigorous lines we have indicated generally? Do the things we teach demonstrate themselves in practical living? "Wherefore by their fruits ye shall know them." If a man's character does not back up what he teaches, we must brand him as a false prophet. We all know the boomerang effect of messages; after we have preached the Spirit of God comes and says, "What about you?" It is this kind of thinking that puts the death-blow to the sentimental evangelism and "Higher Lifeism"[20] that is not robust enough to pay its debts, or to be clean and upright, to be absolutely beyond suspicion in every detail of the life.

(b) The Method of This Thinking
Prove all things. (1 Thessalonians 5:21)

The only way we can prove spiritual things is by experience. Are we thinking along ante-Pentecostal lines? are we thinking, that is, without making room for the supernatural? Much of the thinking of to-day belongs to a day before Pentecost; the majority of us are out of date. To think along Pentecostal lines means that we have received the Holy Spirit, and this should be sufficient for us to see that we have the ability to do the things that are demanded by God. It is a crime for a saint to be weak in God's strength. "For this is the will of God, even your sanctification." Have we thought about that? Have we proved it by experience? We can prove it only by having the mind of the Person Who said it put into us. It is no use enquiring of John Wesley or of saved and sanctified saints, we must come to one place only, viz., five minutes' concentration before God—"Lord, I want to prove this thing, I am willing to go the whole length." That is the only way we can prove spiritual things, the only way we become vigorous New Testament thinkers, not working signs and wonders—that is child's play, froth, it may indicate the

---

20. Higher Spiritual Life.

tremendous ocean underneath or it may not. The great thing that the Holy Spirit reveals is that the supernatural power of God is ours through Jesus Christ, and if we will receive the Holy Spirit He will teach us how to think as well as how to live. Always refer back to the *receiving* of the Holy Spirit, we receive Him to do His work in us. Just as Jesus glorified God, so the Holy Spirit glorifies Jesus; He makes us written epistles not only in living, but in thinking.

(c) The Mind of the Thinker
Let this mind be in you, which was also in Christ Jesus. (Philippians 2:5)

To have the Spirit of Christ is one thing, to form His mind is another. To have the mind of Christ means that we are willing to obey the dictates of the Holy Spirit through the physical machines of our brains and bodies till our living bears a likeness to Jesus. Every Christian ought to be living in this intense, vigorous atmosphere, no sentimental weaknesses. The majority of us scorn self-pity along physical and moral lines, but I am not so sure that we scorn self-pity along spiritual lines. We must form the mind of Christ till it works out in a strong family likeness to Jesus. Every time we come in contact with a Christian of this sort we feel as if we are brought face to face with the Lord Himself. That alone is the evidence of the Holy Spirit. The great glorious power of the Holy Ghost, if He has been received by us, manifests itself in the way we think. It is not sufficient to know God said a thing, but relying on the Holy Ghost we must prove it. God brings us into circumstances where we have to "prove all things," where we form the mind of Christ and make our thinking like His—robust, vigorous and strong, right towards God, not because we are in earnest, but because we have received the earnest Holy Ghost.

2. The New Thinking about Christ
But Christ as a Son over His own house. (Hebrews 3:6)

(a) The Reminiscent Christ
though we have known Christ after the flesh . . . (2 Corinthians 5:16)

Pentecost made Christ spiritual to us. We mean by reminiscent what Paul implies here, trying to picture by desperate efforts of imagination what Christ was like, searching the Bible records and trying by sheer effort of mind to bring back to our minds what Christ would tell us if He were here now. All that belongs to a dispensation we have no business to be living in. The Holy Ghost makes Jesus Christ both present and real. He is the most real Being on earth, "closer is He than breathing, and nearer than hands and feet." Sim-

ply receive the Holy Spirit, rely upon Him and obey Him and He will bring the realisation of Christ.

(b) The Realisation of Christ
Lo, I am with you alway. (Matthew 28:20)

When the Lord Jesus shall be revealed from heaven . . . (2 Thessalonians 1:7)

The Scriptures make a distinction between the *Parousia* and the *Apokalupsis*. The *Parousia* is spiritual and invisible; the *Apokalupsis* is a hope. We rejoice in the presence of the Lord, we wait in hope for the revelation of the Lord Jesus Christ from heaven. Are any of us struggling to remember what Christ was like, saying, "I wish that His hands had been placed on my head"? By receiving the Holy Spirit we may know Him ten thousand-fold better! The very life of Jesus will be in us by the sheer supernatural grace of God. That is the marvel of this present dispensation. The Holy Ghost is seeking to awaken men out of lethargy; He is pleading, yearning, blessing, pouring benedictions on men, convicting and drawing them nearer, for one purpose only, that they may receive Him so that He may make them holy men and women exhibiting the life of Jesus Christ. How the devil does rob Christians who are not thinking on Pentecostal lines of the tremendous power of the Presence of Jesus made real by the Holy Spirit!

(c) The Revelation of Christ
. . . and He shall give you another Comforter. (John 14:16)

The Holy Spirit is not a substitute for Jesus, the Holy Spirit is all that Jesus was, and all that Jesus did, made real in personal experience now. The Holy Spirit alone makes Jesus real, the Holy Spirit alone expounds His Cross, the Holy Spirit alone convicts of sin; the Holy Spirit alone does *in* us what Jesus did *for* us. It is thinking along these lines that makes it a burden insuperable when one sees men and women who ought to be princes and princesses with God bound up in a "show of things," taken up with duties which are not the supreme duty. Instead of applying the supreme law, which we ought to do in every case of conflict, viz., "Thou shalt love the Lord Thy God with all thy heart. . . ." the second commandment is put first, "Thou shalt love thy neighbour as thyself." Whenever Jesus dealt with the closest relationships and with our own self-interest, He always put Himself first. His meaning is perfectly clear, that if His claims clash with those relationships, it must be instant obedience to Him (see Luke 14:26). Men and women who ought to be living in the glorious privileges of this Pentecostal dispensation are very often bound up by duties that are right from every standpoint but one, the standpoint of the

Holy Ghost; right according to the logic of morality and common sense and justice, but not according to the logic of Pentecost, the Spirit does not witness, His illumination does not come. Some people spend their lives sacrificing themselves for other people, with the only result that the people for whom the sacrifice is made become more and more selfish. Whenever the Holy Ghost inspires the sacrifice, it is the sacrifice of ourselves for Jesus' sake, and that never blights, but always blesses. Half the heart-breaks and difficulties which some of us have hurried ourselves into would have been prevented if we had only dared to obey God in the power of the Spirit.

3. The New Thinking about God
No man hath seen God at any time. (John 1:18)

(a) The Eternal God
He that hath seen Me hath seen the Father. (John 14:9)

Pentecost has made God spiritual to us. Jesus Christ was God Incarnate; Pentecost is God come in the Spirit. The essential nature of God the Father, of God the Son and of God the Spirit is the same. The characteristics that marked God the Father in the old dispensation, and that marked God the Son when He lived on this earth, mark God the Holy Ghost in this present dispensation. "God is a Spirit." Apart from the Spirit of God we cannot think about anything that has not its basis in space and time, consequently when people without the Spirit think of God, they think of a Being sitting somewhere or ruling somewhere. We cannot think about God until we have received the Spirit, our natural hearts are atheistic. We have a dumb blind instinct that feels after God (see Acts 17:27), but it leads nowhere. When we receive the Holy Spirit He opens the eyes of our understanding, convicts of sin and shows us what Jesus came to do. "The things of God knoweth no man, but the Spirit of God." Is it not astounding the amount of persuasion that is necessary before some of us will receive the Holy Spirit—we will argue and debate and do everything under heaven before we will waive aside our preconceived notions, our doctrinal points of view, and come as simple children and ask for the Holy Spirit. "If thou knewest the

gift of God, . . . thou wouldest have asked of Him, and He would have given thee living water" (John 4:10). Jesus did not speak these words to a learned man, but to a sinful woman. He told her to ask for the Holy Spirit, and there would be done in that woman of Samaria what was done at Pentecost for the disciples, and that is where we ought to be living to-day.

(b) The Eternal Spirit (Universal)
I will pour out of My Spirit upon all flesh. (Acts 2:17)

The dispensation of Pentecost is not confined to the Jews, not confined to Christendom, it is confined nowhere, it is absolutely universal, the sweep and sway and majesty of the power of the Holy Ghost is at work in every crook and cranny of the universe. For what purpose? That men may receive Him. We imagine that God has special favourites, and by trying to prescribe the movements of the Holy Ghost we exploit Him. We do not say so, but we are apt to think that unless people come the way we came, the Holy Ghost will not teach them. The great truth is that God's Spirit in this dispensation is absolutely universal for one purpose, that the life of Jesus may be made manifest in our mortal flesh.

(c) The Eternal Spirit (Ubiquitous)
Whither shall I flee from Thy presence? (Psalm 139:7)

If we try to drown God's presence in the depths of iniquity, it is there; if we go to the heights and speculate, it is there—insisting, wooing, drawing; the hand of Christ knocking at the door, for one purpose, to get in. The Spirit of God is everywhere, would that men would yield to Him! The reason we do not yield is that in the deep recesses of our hearts we prefer the captaincy of our own lives, we prefer to go our own way and refuse to let God govern. A human being cannot alter us; God Almighty Himself cannot alter us. Jesus Christ Himself stood absolutely powerless before people with the spiritual "nod." Do you know what the spiritual "nod" is? Disbelief in anything but my own point of view. "And He did not many mighty works there because of their unbelief."

Have you received the Holy Spirit? If not, why not receive Him now?

I. HOW TO THINK ABOUT GOD

Lord, shew us the Father, and it sufficeth us.

. . . He that hath seen Me hath seen the Father; and how sayest thou then, Shew us the Father? John 14:8–9

How do we think about God habitually? Jesus said, "He that hath seen Me hath seen the Father." In the face, in the character, in the walk and the work of Jesus, we have God the Father revealed. The Christian faith affirms the existence of a personal God Who reveals Himself. Pseudo-Christianity departs from this, we are told we cannot know anything at all about God, we do not know whether He is a personal Being, we cannot know whether He is good. The Christian revelation is that God is a personal Being and He is good. By "good," I mean morally good. Test all beliefs about God by that; do they reveal clearly that God is a good God, and that all that is moral and pure and true and upright comes from God?

1. Instinct and Revelation

For as I passed by, and beheld your devotions, I found an altar with this inscription, To The Unknown God. Whom therefore ye ignorantly worship, him declare I unto you. (Acts 17:23)

The evangelical teaching about this intuition and instinct in human nature is that it is to be recognised as being there, but requiring a revelation from outside to discover to it what it wants. The Christian affirmation is that this instinct and intuition is not God, but a dumb, inarticulate feeling after God. "That they should seek God, if haply they might feel after Him, and find Him, though He is not far from each one of us" (Acts 17:27 RV). That is the first point of divergence of the modern tendency from the Christian affirmation. We see at once how it works out in practical religious life; it means that we have the Spirit of God in us by nature, we do not need to be born again of the Spirit. This line of thinking could not be more diametrically opposed to the New Testament conception. The New Testament reveals that the deepest instinct in us is to feel after God, but that instinct is never to be taken for the Spirit of God.

Honeycombing all our Christian teaching to-day is the idea that the instinct in us is God and that as we allow the deepest instinct in us expression, we reveal ourselves as more or less God, and that the Being in whom this instinct had its greatest expression was the Lord Jesus Christ; therefore He stands in the modern movements and to everyone who follows that line of thinking, as the best expression of God. The New Testament reasoning is that if we are going to enter into contact with the God Whom the Bible reveals we must be born from above, be lifted into a totally new realm by means of the Atonement. "Marvel not that I said unto thee, Ye must be born again" (John 3:7). Jesus Christ is a distinct break in our order and not the product of our order. Just as Our Lord came into human history from the outside, so He must come into us from the outside. The meaning of new birth is that we know God in a vital relationship (see John 1:12–13).

Paul puts as the Christian attitude to God that we are "the offspring of God." The term "the fatherhood" of God is rarely used nowadays in the New Testament sense, it is only used in the sense of God as Creator, not in the sense that Jesus Christ used it; the consequence is great havoc is produced in our Lord's teaching. If God is our Father by creation in the sense Jesus says He is by the experience of regeneration, then the Atonement is nonsense. What was the good of Jesus Christ living and dying and rising again? Where is the need for all this teaching that we have to be born again? If our instinct is God, we need only be sufficiently well-educated to allow the instinct which is in us to come out. But does this satisfy you and me regarding ourselves? Are we consciously, solemnly and satisfyingly confident that if we let the deepest instinct in us have expression, we are letting God express Himself? According to the Bible, the very essence of Satan is self-rule, and there are two mighty forces at work, one against and one for God.

Paul argues, "who among men knoweth the things of a man, save the spirit of the man, which is in him? even so the things of God none knoweth, save the Spirit of God" (1 Corinthians 2:11 RV). It is the same insistence on the need to be born from above, and if any man will take Jesus Christ's way and face facts as He asks us to face them, he will find all the mystery of doing right amid entrancing wrong, all the mystery of attaining the highest when the lowest is the most attractive, all the mystery of complete deliverance from the disposition of sin, opened up and made possible. Doctrine is expounded not by our intelligence, not by our searching, but by the indwelling of a completely new Spirit imparted to us by the Lord Jesus Christ.

It is necessary to give a note of warning against the tyranny of abstractions. An ideal has no power over us until it becomes incarnate. The idea of beauty lies unawakened until we see a thing we call beautiful. God may be a mere mental abstraction; He may be spoken of in terms of culture or poetry or philosophy, but He has not the slightest meaning for us until He becomes incarnate. When once we know that God has "trod this earth with naked feet, and woven with human hands the creed of creeds," then we are arrested. When once we know that the Almighty Being Who reigns and rules over His creation does not do so in calm disdain, but puts His back to the wall of the world, so to speak, and receives all the downcast, the outcast, the sin-defiled, the wrong, the wicked and the sinful into His arms, then we are arrested. An intellectual conception of God may be found in a bad vicious character. The knowledge and vision of God is dependent entirely on a pure heart. Character determines the revelation of God to the individual. The pure in heart see God. Jesus Christ changes the worst into the best and gives the moral readjustment that enables a man to love and delight in the true God. Of a great almighty incomprehensible Being we know nothing, but of Our Lord

Jesus Christ we do know, and the New Testament reveals that the Almighty God is nothing that Jesus was not.

2. Ideas and Revelation

For in Him we live, and move, and have our being. . . . Being then the offspring of God . . . (Acts 17:28–2 RV)

Our ideas of God are no greater than ourselves, and we ought to receive from God other ideas by revelation, so that the working mind of man may receive the power to live a larger, grander life than lies in any of his own ideas. Our ideas of God are indistinct, and when we make those ideas in their indistinctness the ground of our understanding of God, we are hopelessly at sea. We are never told to walk in the light of our convictions or instinctive ideas; according to the Bible, we have to walk in the light of Our Lord. Nothing is known about God saving in and through Our Lord Jesus Christ. "Neither doth any know the Father, save the Son, and he to whomsoever the Son willeth to reveal Him"

(Matthew 11:27 RV). I can only have a personal, passionate love for a Being who is not myself, and the whole meaning of the Atonement is to destroy the idolatry of self-love, to extract the pernicious poison of self-interest, and presence us with the Divinity which enables us to love God with all our heart, and soul, and mind, and strength. The New Testament reveals that we are not ultimately to be absorbed into God; we are distinctly and eternally to be the passionate lovers of God. No man was ever created to be his own god, and no man was ever created to be the god of another man, and no system of ideas was ever made to dominate man as god. There is "one God," and that God was Incarnate in the Lord Jesus Christ. And as that marvellous Being has His dominant sway over us, the whole of Time, the whole of Eternity, and the threshold between the two, will be shot through with the dawn of an endless day that shall never end in night. when "God shall wipe away all tears from their eyes" and Heaven prove the complement of earth.

II. HOW TO THINK ABOUT THE LORD JESUS CHRIST

All things have been delivered unto Me of My Father: and no one knoweth the Son, save the Father. Matthew 11:27 (RV)

In Matthew 11:27 the unique position of Jesus Christ to His own consciousness is clearly exhibited. The mystery of the Person of Jesus resides in its nature from the beginning; before we begin to understand His Person we must be quickened from above by the Holy Spirit. That is where the battle rages to-day—around the Person of Jesus Christ (cf. 1 John 4:2–3). The call for every Christian worker is to thoroughly equip himself with right thinking about Jesus Christ.

The Bible has no respect for mental abstractions. Jesus Christ did not talk about "the Infinite" or "the Incomprehensible"; whenever He talked about God He brought it down to concrete reality—"He that hath seen Me hath seen the Father." Unless God has become a concrete reality in Jesus Christ, He has no meaning for us at all. Jesus nowhere said, "He that hath seen *man* hath seen the Father": He emphatically states that He is the only medium God has for revealing Himself. The trend of thought at the heart of all the modern ethical movements is based on the idea that God and Humanity are one and the same. Jesus nowhere taught that God was in man, but He did teach that God was manifest in human flesh in

His Person that He might become the generating centre for the same thing in every human being, and the place of His travail pangs is Bethlehem, Calvary, and the Resurrection.

"I and My Father are one." Do we accept Jesus Christ's thinking about Himself? According to His own thinking He was equal with God, and He became Incarnate for the great purpose of lifting the human race back into communion with God, not because of their aspirations, but because of the sheer omnipotence of God through the Atonement. The life of Jesus Christ is made ours not by imitation, but by means of His death on Calvary and by our reception of His Spirit. Our Lord's marvellous message for all time is the familiar one: "Come unto Me, . . . and I will give you rest."

"The wayfaring men, yea fools, shall not err therein." When a man does err in the way of God, it is because he is wise in his own conceits. When the facts of life have humbled us, when introspection has stripped us of our own miserable self-interest and we receive a startling diagnosis of ourselves by the Holy Spirit, we are by that painful experience brought to the place where we can hear the marvellous message—profounder than the profoundest philosophies earth ever wove, "Come unto Me, all ye that labour and are heavy laden, and I will give you rest." Until this experience comes men may patronise Jesus Christ, but they do not come to Him for salvation. The only solution is the one given by Jesus Christ Himself to a good upright man of His day: "Marvel not that I said unto thee, Ye must be born again."

"Howbeit when He, the Spirit of truth, is come . . . He shall glorify Me" (John 16:13–14). There is abroad to-day a vague, fanatical movement which bases everything on spiritual impulse—"God gave me an impulse to do this, and that," and there are the strangest outcomes to such impulses. Any impulse which does not lead to the glorification of Jesus Christ has the snare of Satan behind it. People say, "How am I to know whether my impulse is from the Holy Spirit or from my own imagination?" Very easily. Jesus Christ gave us the simplest, most easy-to-be-understood tests for guidance—"The Holy Ghost . . . shall teach you all things, and bring all things to your remembrance, whatsoever I have said unto you"; the Holy Spirit "will guide you into all truth: for He shall not speak of Himself." Beware of any religious experience which glorifies you and not Jesus Christ. It may use the right phrasing, it may praise Jesus Christ and praise the Atonement—that is one of the subtlest powers of the insinuations of Satan, but the life does not glorify Jesus, it does not magnify and uplift the crucified Son of God. Living much in the presence of Jesus, coming in contact with His mind, simplifies life to a believer, and makes him an unflurried sceptic of everything that is not true to the nature of God.

The central citadel of Christianity is the Person of our Lord Jesus Christ. The final standard for the Christian is given at the outset—"to be conformed to the image of His Son."

III. HOW TO THINK ABOUT MAN

What is man, that Thou are mindful of him? And the son of man, that Thou visitest him? Psalm 8:4

The Christian faith declares the spiritual nature and dignity of man, that his creation is in the Divine image and his destination is to bear the likeness of God in a perfected relation of sonship—". . . to be conformed to the image of His Son" (Romans 8:29). In reading the history of the race our thought must fit itself into one of two fundamental categories: either we are wonderful beings in the making, or we are wonderful ruins of what we once were. The latter is the view of the Bible. In John 3 we find our Lord recognised the un-making of man so keenly that He told Nicodemus not to marvel when he was told he must be born again. A man never grows out of a natural into a spiritual man without being re-created. The Apostle Paul bases his reasoning entirely on this fundamental revelation; he argues, "Wherefore if any man is in Christ, *there is a new creation*" (2 Corinthians 5:17 RV mg). According to the Bible, we do not evolve into better manifestations of God, or even into nearness to God; but only by a violent readjustment to God through regeneration are we re-made to bear the family likeness to God which we were at first designed to have. It is much easier to live a holy life than to think on Jesus Christ's lines. Are we traitors intellectually to Jesus Christ while professing to be His disciples?

1. Man's Creation
So God created man in His own image. (Genesis 1:27; see Colossians 1:16–17)

The modern view is that man is continually evolving and developing, each phase being better than the last and the last gives us the best revelation of God; from this standpoint Jesus Christ is looked upon as the manifestation of all the best in the evolutionary processes of man. The evolutionary conception starts from something un-get-at-able, incalculable, with a power within itself to evolve endlessly. The great word we bow down and worship to-day is "progress"; we are progressing and developing, and the consequence is we are blind to the facts of history and blind to moral facts. The Bible revelation about man is that man as he is, is not as God made him.

Immediately we get the idea that we are part of God, and the universe is His thought about Himself, we are unable to accept the idea that God created us. It is far more natural for us to suppose ourselves emanations from the Being of God, time-manifestations of God, as Jesus was, all of the same kindred. Such conceptions have a wonderful element of truth in them when applied to regenerated humanity, but the Bible reveals the presence in unregenerated humanity of a positive anarchy against God (see Romans 8:7). It is possible to be so full of love and sympathy for unregenerate man as to be red-handed anarchists against God. This is exactly what the New Testament states, especially in the reasonings of St. Paul regarding the "old man," the disposition of self-interest that entered into human nature and un-made God's creation so that man's likeness to God in disposition was blotted out. The New Testament reveals that this disposition cannot be educated, it cannot be disciplined or altered, it must be removed and a new mainspring to human nature put in its place. The marvel of the Atonement is that any man or woman who will make the moral decision that the "old man" ought to be crucified, and will accept the gift of the Holy Spirit which was manifested in Jesus Christ, will receive the new disposition which introduces him into the kingdom of God, and raises him to sit in heavenly places in Christ Jesus, which surely means a present experience, not a future one.

It is always fascinating to follow an intellectual process that more or less blinds one to facts, because whatever hinders that intellectual process must either be absorbed or removed. In practical experience when the deep within us calls to the deep without, there is tumult and upset, and we find a tremendous force that works away from God and will never work in harmony with Him. When in the experience of individuals or of nations the upburst of this disintegrating power occurs, we turn with wistful glance to the Book that has been discarded; and to the one Being who has the key to all the problems of life and death, first things and last things, the beginning and ending of things, viz., the Lord Jesus Christ.

2. Man's Calling

The Bible reveals that man's calling is to stand before God and develop by obedience from the lowest point of conscious innocence to the highest reach of conscious holiness, with no intermediaries. This is man's calling as God created him, and that is why God will never leave us alone until the blaze and pain of His fire has burned us as pure as He is Himself (cf. Matthew 3:11).

It is the moment of unique crisis when a man realises for the first time the hiatus between himself and God, when the cry goes out from the depths of his nature, "Oh, that I knew where I might find Him!" or, My God, "what must I do to be saved?" This is not the cry of a man crumpled up by moral irregularities, it is the cry wrung from the depths of human nature. In this crisis, which is the immortal moment of a man's conscious life, the meaning of the Gospel first comes into play (see Matthew 1:21; 1 John 3:8). Jesus Christ claims that He can do in human nature what human nature cannot do for itself, viz., "destroy the works of the devil," remove the wrong heredity and put in the right one. He can satisfy the last aching abyss of the human heart, He can put the key into our hands which will give the solution to every problem that ever stretched before our minds. He can soothe by His pierced hands the

wildest sorrow with which Satan or sin or death ever racked humanity. There is nothing for which Jesus Christ is not amply sufficient and over which He cannot make us more than conquerors. The New Testament does not represent Jesus Christ as coming to us in the character of a celestial lecturer; He is here to re-create us, to presence us with Divinity in such a way that He can re-make us according to God's original plan, eternal lovers of God Himself, not absorbed into God, but part of the great Spirit-baptised humanity—"Till we all attain unto the unity of the faith, and of the knowledge of the Son of God, unto a fullgrown man, unto the measure of the stature of the fulness of Christ" (Ephesians 4:13 RV).

3. Man's Communion

And Enoch walked with God. (Genesis 5:24; see John 14:23)

The Bible reveals man's communion to be consciously with God, not in spasms or ecstasies, but under the figure of a walk in the Old Testament, and the abiding inmates[21] of a home in the New Testament; it is not absorption, but communion. In the Bible man is revealed as a created being, intended to be God's lover, not a part of God, but to be brought back into the relationship of conscious, passionate devotion to God even as our Lord Himself expressed it. Jesus Christ showed us during a life of thirty-three years what a normal man should be; in what He did and said, and in what He was, He showed us how to think about man, viz., that he is to be the companion and lover of God.

Many to-day are seeking reconciliation between the modern views and the New Testament views. It is being attempted ably, but it is a perfectly useless attempt, as useless as trying to make black, white; as trying to make wrong, right; as trying to make the "old man" the "new man" by whitewash. It can never be done. There is only one solution, and that solution comes along the line of the Personality of truth, not the abstraction of truth. "*I* am the Way, the Truth, and the Life"—the Way in the waylessness of this wild universe; the Truth amidst all the contending confusions of man's thought and existence; the Life amidst all the living deaths that sap men's characters and their relationships and connections with the highest. Only by being re-created and re-adjusted to God through the Atonement of our Lord Jesus Christ can we understand the marvellous unity between God and man for which God destined man. "That they may all be one; even as Thou, Father, art in Me, and I in Thee, that they also may be in us: that the world may believe that Thou didst send Me" (John 17:21 RV).

---

21. inmates: people living under one roof as members of a family or group. Not used to mean those who are institutionalised or imprisoned.

IV. HOW TO THINK ABOUT SIN

Then the lust, when it hath conceived, beareth sin: and the sin, when it is full grown, bringeth forth death. James 1:15 (RV)

How do we think about sin habitually, as Christians? If we have light views about sin we are not students in the school of Christ. The fact of sin is the secret of Jesus Christ's Cross; its removal is the secret of His risen and ascended life. Do we think along these lines? It is quite possible to be living in union with God through the Atonement and yet be traitors mentally. It is easy to be traitors unless we are disciplined along the lines that Jesus taught, viz., the need to submit our intellect to Him as He submitted His intellect to His Father. Do we think along the line that salvation is only possible through the Cross? We do not think, and we do not like to think, along Jesus Christ's line, we are told it is old-fashioned and ugly, and so it is; it is awful, it is so awful that it broke God's heart on Calvary.

Every subject we have touched on during this series of talks has been important, but the subject of sin is the vital pivot on which all the rest turn. The slightest deflection from the real truth about sin, and all the rest of the reasoning goes wrong. Once placed fundamentally right regarding the doctrine of sin, and the reasoning follows in good order. If you read carefully the modern statements regarding sin you will be amazed to find how often we are much more in sympathy with them than with the Bible statements. We have to face the problem that our hearts may be right with God while our heads have a startling affinity with a great deal that is antagonistic to the Bible teaching. What we need, and what we get if we go on with God, is an intellectual re-birth as well as a heart re-birth.

The trouble with the modern statements regarding sin is that they make sin far too slight. Sin according to the modern view simply means selfishness, and preachers and teachers are as dead against selfishness as the New Testament is. Immediately we come to the Bible we find that sin is much deeper than that. According to the Bible, sin in its final analysis is not a defect but a defiance, a defiance that means death to the life of God in us. Sin is seen not only in selfishness, but in what men call unselfishness. It is possible to have such sympathy with our fellow-men as to be guilty of red-handed rebellion against God. Enthusiasm for humanity as it is, is quite a different thing from the enthusiasm for the saints which the Bible reveals, viz., enthusiasm for readjusted humanity.

Sin intellectually viewed is never anything else than defective development, because the intellect will not allow for gaps that destroy its main principle of outlook. The Bible supplies the facts for the gaps which intellect will not accept. According to the Bible, sin is doing without God. Sin is not wrong doing, it is wrong *being*, deliberate and emphatic independence of God. That may sound remote and far away from us, but in individual experience it is best put in the terms of "my claim to my right to myself." Every one of us, whether we have received the Holy Spirit or not, will denounce selfishness, but who amongst us will denounce "my right to myself"? As long as my right to myself remains, I respect it in you, you respect it in me, and the devil respects it in the whole crowd, and amalgamates humanity under one tremendous rule which aims at blotting the one true God off His throne. The Bible shows that human nature as it is is one vast "strike" against God. Paul states that "through one man sin entered into the world" (Romans 5:12 RV); but we must remember that that man was not a man like you or me, he was the federal head of the human race. Sin entered into the world through that man's disobedience to God's rule (see Genesis 3). From that moment the "strike" against God began and has gone on all down the dispensations, and never was there such a big, massive, organised "strike" as there is to-day against God and God's rule.

All the great movements of the modern mind are on the line of a combine that swamps individual value. Men detest the doctrine of individual responsibility, and react against a doctrine of salvation through Jesus Christ because it fixes on the value of the individual. The Bible reveals that the losing of the sense of personal responsibility is the result of sin (see Genesis 4:8–9). The characteristic of sin is to destroy the capacity to know we sin, and the Bible talks about unregenerate men as "dead," not dead physically, but dead towards God (see Ephesians 2:1).

The recovery of the Bible affirmation about sin is what is needed. The Bible distinctly states that sin is not the natural result of being a finite being, but a definite stepping aside from what that finite being knew to be right. How one wishes that people who read books about the Bible would read the Bible itself! Read the 18th chapter of Ezekiel—"the soul that sinneth, it shall die"; and again—"for the wages of sin is death" (Romans 6:23). The Bible does not deal with sin as a disease; it does not deal with the outcome of sin, it deals with the disposition of sin itself. The disposition of sin is what our Lord continually faced, and it is this disposition that the

Atonement removes. Immediately our evangelism loses sight of this fundamental doctrine of the disposition of sin and deals only with external sins, it leaves itself open to ridicule. We have cheapened the doctrine of sin and made the Atonement a sort of moral "lavatory" in which men can come and wash themselves from sin, and then go and sin again and come back for another washing. This is the doctrine of the Atonement: "Him who knew no sin" (not sins)—Him who had not the disposition of sin, who refused steadfastly, and to the death on Calvary, to listen to the temptations of the prince of this world, who would not link Himself on with the ruling disposition of humanity, but came to hew a way single-handed through the hard face of sin back to God—"He made to be sin on our behalf; that we might become the righteousness of God in Him."

The disposition of sin that rules our human nature is not suppressed by the Atonement, not sat on, not cabined and confined, it is removed. Human nature remains unaltered, but the hands and eyes and all our members that were used as the servants of the disposition of sin can be used now as servants of the new disposition (see Romans 6:13). Then comes the glorious necessity of militant holiness. Beware of the teaching that allows you to sink back on your oars and drift; the Bible is full of pulsating, strenuous energy. From the moment a man is readjusted to God then begins the running, being careful that "the sin which doth so easily beset us" does not clog our feet.

I believe that God so radically, so gloriously, and so comprehensively copes with sin in the Atonement that He is more than master of it, and that a practical experience of this can take place in the life of anyone who will enter into identification with what Jesus Christ did on the Cross. What is the good of saying, "I believe in Jesus Christ as the Saviour of the world" if you cannot answer the blunt question, "What has He saved you from?" The test is not in theories and theologies, but in practical flesh and blood experience. Jesus Christ is our Saviour because He saves us from sin, radically altering the ruling disposition. Anyone who has been in contact with the Lord when He alters the ruling disposition knows it, and so do others. But there is a painful, tremendous repentance first. The whole teaching of the Bible on the human side is based on repentance. The only repentant man is the holy man, and the only holy man is the one who has been made so by the marvel of the Atonement. And here comes the wonder—let the blunders of lives be what they may, let hereditary tendencies be what they like, let wrongs and evils crowd as they will, through the Atonement there is perfect readjustment to God, perfect forgiveness, and the gift of a totally new disposition which will manifest itself in the physical life just as the old disposition did (see Romans 6:19). Jesus Christ comes as the last Adam to take away the abnormal thing (which we call natural), the disposition of my right to myself, and He gives us a new disposition, viz., His own heredity of unsullied holiness, *Holy Spirit*.

V. HOW TO THINK ABOUT THE ATONEMENT

God was in Christ, reconciling the world unto Himself. . . . 2 Corinthians 5:19 (see 2 Corinthians 5:18–21)

The modern view of the Atonement is that it simply reveals the oneness of God and man; immediately we turn to the New Testament we find that the doctrine of the Atonement is that God can readjust man to Himself, indicating that there is something wrong, something out of joint, something that has to be put right. The Bible reveals that there is anarchy somewhere, real thorough going anarchy in the heart of men against God; therefore the need is strong that something should come into us from the outside to readjust us, to reconcile us, to turn us round, to put us right with God. The doctrine of the Atonement is the explanation of how God does that. The doctrine of the Atonement is that "while we were yet sinners, Christ died for us." All heaven is interested in the Cross of Christ, all hell terribly afraid of it, while

men are the only beings who more or less ignore its meaning.

No one can believe in the teaching of Jesus unless he believes in the Cross. A man who says, "I believe in the Sermon on the Mount" means that he gives his mental assent to it—"it is a good ideal for whoever can come up to it." But if all Jesus came to do was to tell me I must have an unsullied career, when my past has been blasted by sin and wickedness on my own part, then He but tantalises me. If He is simply a teacher, He only increases our capacity for misery, for He sets up standards that stagger us. But the teaching of Jesus Christ is not an ideal, it is the statement of the life we will live when we are readjusted to God by the Atonement. The type of life Jesus lived, the type of character He expressed, is possible for us by His death, and only by His death, because by means of His death we receive the life to which His teaching applies.

"Him who knew no sin he made to be sin on our behalf; that we might become the righteousness of God in Him" (2 Corinthians 5:21 RV). The idea of substitution popularly understood is that Jesus Christ was punished for me, therefore I go scot-free. The doctrine of substitution in the Bible is always two-fold: Christ for me, that He might be substituted in me. There is no Christ *for* me if there is no Christ *in* me. The doctrine of substitution is the most practical, radically working thing in the world; it is the very essence of our Lord's teaching. "Except ye eat the flesh of the Son of man and drink His blood, ye have not life in yourselves" (John 6:53 RV). When the Apostle John says "He that doeth righteousness is righteous," he is not talking of the righteousness of good moral conduct, but the righteousness that is impossible to a man unless he has been readjusted to God. "When it pleased God . . . to *reveal His Son in me* . . ." says Paul. That is the doctrine of substitution; not, "I believe in God the Father, God the Son, and God the Holy Ghost," and remain the same miserable, selfish, crooked sinner all the time.

How are we to get to the place where the mighty efficacy of the Lord's life is ours? Immediately we are willing to recognise that God condemned sin for ever in the death of His Son. If we will accept His verdict and go to God just as we are, the Holy Spirit will apply the Atonement to us personally, and we will know with a knowledge that passes knowledge that we have been born again from above into the realm where Jesus lives, and all the marvellous efficacy of His life comes into our mortal frame. The consequence is we can do all that God commands. The only sign of a readjusted life to God is not a head-belief at all, but a manifestation in our mortal flesh that we can keep the commandments of God.

Now examine the Sermon on the Mount. Can a man by praying, by letting the generous impulse of his nature have its way, produce a heart so pure that it sees God? Can a man by doing those things that are easily within the reach of morality, produce a life unblameable in holiness before God? Paul says *He* is "made unto us . . . righteousness." That is the doctrine of the Atonement—that we are made undeserving of censure in God's sight, so that God looking down into the motives of our heart can see nothing to blame. Will I let God identify me with the Cross of Christ until I can say, not merely with my lips, but by my life—"I have been crucified with Christ; yet I live; and yet no longer I, but Christ liveth in me: and that life which I now live in the flesh I live in faith, the faith which is in the Son of God, Who loved me, and gave Himself up for me"? From that position it becomes possible for God to take us into His counsels regarding His redemptive purpose. Our understanding of the Atonement depends on our spiritual growth, not on our Bible study or on our praying. As we "grow up into Him in all things" the one thing about which we get more and more understanding is the mystery of Redemption, and we understand why Jesus said, "Blessed are *the pure in hear:* for they shall see God."

VI. HOW TO THINK ABOUT THE SCRIPTURES

For the word of God is quick, and powerful, and sharper than any two-edged sword, piercing even to the dividing asunder of soul and spirit, and of the joints and marrow, and is a discerner of the thoughts and intents of the heart. Hebrews 4:12

"Why should I believe a thing because it is in the Bible?" That is a perfectly legitimate question. There is no reason why you should believe it, it is only when the Spirit of God applies the Scriptures to the inward consciousness that a man begins to understand their living efficacy. If we try from the outside to fit the Bible to an external standard, or to a theory of verbal inspiration or any other theory, we are wrong. "Ye search the scriptures, because ye think that in them ye have eternal life; and these are they which bear witness of Me; and ye will not come to Me, that ye may have life" (John 5:39–40 RV).

There is another dangerous tendency, that of closing all questions by saying, "Let us get back to the external authority of the Bible." That attitude lacks courage and the power of the Spirit of God; it is a literalism that does not produce "written epistles," but persons who are more or less incarnate dictionaries; it produces not saints but fossils, people without life, with none of the living reality of the Lord Jesus. There must be the Incarnate Word and the interpreting word, i.e., people whose lives back up what they preach, written epistles, "known and read of all men." Only when we receive the Holy Spirit and are lifted into a total readjustment to God do the words of God become "quick, and powerful" to us. The only way the words of God can be understood is by contact with the Word of God. The connection between our Lord Himself, who is the Word, and His spoken words is so close that to divorce them is fatal. "The words that I speak unto you, they are spirit, and they are life."

The Bible does not reveal all truth, we have to find out scientific truth and common-sense truth for ourselves, but knowledge of the Truth, our Lord Himself, is only possible through the reception of the Holy Spirit. "Howbeit when He, the Spirit of truth, is come, He will guide you into all truth." The Holy Spirit alone makes the Word of God understandable. The regenerating and sanctifying work of the Holy Spirit is to incorporate us into Christ until we are living witnesses to Him. S. D. Gordon[22] put it well when he said, "We have the Bible bound in morocco, bound in all kinds of beautiful leather; what we need is the Bible bound in shoe leather." That is exactly the teaching of our Lord.

After the disciples had received the Holy Spirit they became witnesses to Jesus, their lives spoke more eloquently than their lips—"and they took knowledge of them, that they had been with Jesus." The Holy Spirit being imparted to us and expressed through us is the manifested exhibition that God can do all that His Word states He can. It is those who have received the Holy Spirit who understand the will of God and "grow up into Him in all things." When the Scriptures are made quick and powerful by the Holy Spirit, they fit every need of life. The only interpreter of the Scriptures is the Holy Spirit, and when we have received the Holy Spirit we learn the first golden lesson of spiritual life, which is that God reveals His will according to the state of our character (cf. Psalm 18:25–26).

VII. HOW TO THINK ABOUT OUR FELLOW-MEN

A new commandment I give unto you, that ye love one another; as I have loved you, that ye also love one another. John 13:34

There is no subject more intimately interesting to modern people than man's relationship to man; but men get impatient when they are told that the first requirement is that they should love God first and foremost. "The first of all the commandments is, . . . thou shalt love the Lord thy God with all thy heart, and with all thy soul, and with all thy mind, and with all thy strength: this is the first commandment." In every crisis in our lives, is God first in our love? in every perplexity of conflicting duties, is He first in our leading? "And the second is like, namely, this, Thou shalt love thy neighbour as thyself." Remember the standard, *"as I have loved you."* I wonder where the best of us are according to that standard? How many of us

have turned away over and over again in disgust at men, and when we get alone with the Lord Jesus He speaks no word, but the memory of Him is quite sufficient to bring the rebuke—"as I have loved you." It takes severe training to think habitually along the lines Jesus Christ has laid down, although we act on them impulsively at times.

How many of us are letting Jesus Christ take us into His school of thinking? The saint who is thoughtful is like a man fasting in the midst of universal intoxication. Men of the world hate a thoughtful saint. They can ridicule a living saint who does not think, but a thinking saint—I mean of course, one who lives rightly as well—is the annoyance, because the thinking saint has formed the Mind of Christ and re-echoes it. Let us from this time forth determine to bring into captivity every thought to the obedience of Christ.

---

22. Samuel Dickey Gordon (1859–1936), American writer and lecturer; his Quiet Talks book series sold more than 1.5 million copies.

Biblical Psychology

A Series of Preliminary Studies

Oswald Chambers

Text for this volume is from the Second Edition, copyright 1936, Oswald Chambers
Publications Association.
Scripture versions quoted: KJV; RV

INTRODUCTION

Source

These lectures were given at the Bible Training College, London, during 1911.[1]

Publication History

- As articles: In *God's Revivalist Magazine,* March 1911–January 1912.
- As a book: Published in 1912 by God's Revivalist Press, Cincinnati, Ohio.
- Mrs. Chambers reprinted the book in Britain in 1921 and issued a second edition (revised) in 1936. In the years following, various editions were published in Britain and the U.S.

Oswald and Biddy spent their honeymoon in America during the summer of 1910. As they traveled to Oswald's speaking engagements at camp meetings in Ohio, Maryland, Massachusetts, and Maine, they often pondered what God had in store for them. Two dreams that fired Oswald's imagination were a collaboration together in publishing and a shared ministry through a residential Bible training college.

When they returned to Britain in September, they faced a full schedule of League of Prayer classes in Manchester, Blackpool, and Stoke-on-Trent. Instead of preaching or lecturing, Oswald had decided to teach, requiring study and participation from the students. The topic for the classes was biblical psychology.

During the next few years, the Biblical Psychology material was used for correspondence courses, evening classes, and a core class at the Bible Training College.

Biblical Psychology is one of only three Oswald Chambers books compiled and printed before his death. The other two are *Studies in the Sermon on the Mount* (1915) and *Baffled to Fight Better* (1917).

Prefatory and introductory remarks to the earlier editions of *Biblical Psychology* are included on the following pages.

Chambers' Use of "Atoms" and "Molecules"

In chapter 18, "The Mundane Universe," it may appear to the modern reader that Chambers had his atoms and molecules mixed up, but a look at an earlier

---

1. Residential school near Clapham Common in SW London, sponsored by the League of Prayer. Oswald Chambers was Principal and main teacher; Biddy Chambers was Lady Superintendent. Known as the BTC, it closed in July 1915 because of World War I.

edition of this book reveals that he understood both modern and ancient science. The 1920 edition of *Biblical Psychology* read:

> *Away in the earlier days, when the Greeks tried to explain the material world, they said it was made of atoms, then down the ages they found they could split up the atoms, and they called those split-up elements molecules, then they found they could split up the molecules, and that the split-up molecules were made of electrons, then they discovered that the electron is like a solar system, and that behind it all is force.*

In OC's 1911 lectures at the Bible Training College, he was referring to the Greek understanding of science during the fifth century B.C., specifically their theory of "atomism." The atomists believed that the basic elements of reality were atoms—indivisible and indestructible particles of matter.

In this case, a slight revision of the text made in 1936 to increase clarity resulted in some confusion for a later generation of readers.

Chambers' understanding of atomic theory, within the limits of his day, is revealed in this statement from *Baffled to Fight Better,* lectures given in Egypt in 1917: "Again, the atomic theory was thought to be the key; then it was discovered that the atom itself was composed of electrons, and each electron was found to be a universe of its own, and that theory too becomes a lock and not a key."

PREFATORY NOTE
(1st Edition)

This book is compiled from verbatim reports of my lectures on Biblical Psychology, delivered at the Bible Training College, 45, North Side, Clapham Common, London, during 1911.

The reports were taken by my wife and sent on to the editors of the *Revivalist* who now, out of the generosity of their hearts, are publishing them in book form.

May this "Introduction to the Study of Biblical Psychology" stir up the minds of the saints, lest Satan as an angel of light instil error (2 Peter 1:12–13).

1912, Oswald Chambers

INTRODUCTION TO THE 1920 EDITION

This book was originally published in America in 1912. That edition is now exhausted, and a second one has been found necessary.

The book was used as a text book at the evening study classes held in the Y.M.C.A., Zeitoun, Egypt,[2] after my husband had entered into Life. Numbers of the men found it a great stimulus to the study of God's word, and realised the need to bring their thinking "into line with the living Spirit of God."

That God may continue to use the book to this end in many other lives is our prayer in sending out this new edition.

B. Chambers
London, 1920

---

2. Zeitoun (zay TOON). An area 6 miles NE of Cairo. Site of YMCA camp, Egypt General Mission compound and a large base area for British, Australian and New Zealand troops. Site of the Imperial School of Instruction (1916–19).

PREFACE TO THE 2ND EDITION (1936)

This is a revised edition of a very remarkable book. The first edition of *Biblical Psychology* was compiled from reports of lectures on that subject, given by Oswald Chambers at the Bible Training College, London. It was used as a text-book at the evening study classes at the Y.M.C.A., Zeitoun, Egypt, after Mr. Chambers entered into Life in November 1917; and another edition was published later on. The book ended with these lines by the author himself, "The whole book is merely a verbatim report of the lectures, and we have decided to let it go for what it is worth— a mere effort to arouse the average Christian worker to study the wealth of Scripture, and to become better equipped for dividing the Word of Truth."

This New Edition has been most carefully revised in the direction of increased lucidity and concentration of statement. It is a great book, and presents the Bible Psychology of profound thinkers like Delitzsch and Beck and others, through the media of modern psychological expressions. It is based so surely on Scripture that the homeliest mind who studies the Word of God can follow it. Yet there are also depths of thought in it for minds of finest training. It is a treasure of wealth for every kind of Christian worker, helping them to understand their own psychological experiences, and enabling them to present the Truth of God effectively to many minds perplexed by moral problems of their own inner life of feeling, thought, and will.

David Lambert[3]

---

3. David Lambert (1871–1961): Methodist minister and friend of Oswald Chambers. Assisted Mrs. Chambers with OC publications from 1917–1961.

CONTENTS

A small book of Outline Studies has been prepared based on this volume and published at 6d., which can be used for guided Study by individual students or by Classes. The aim has been to simplify these great truths, and link them with illuminating Scripture passages, while yet retaining the deep psychological teaching of *Biblical Psychology*.

  (Booklet of outline studies prepared by David Lambert)

Chapter I

MAN: HIS CREATION, CALLING AND COMMUNION

ALTHOUGH THE PASSAGES QUOTED APPEAR AS TEXTS, THEY ARE
REALLY PORTIONS OF CONNECTED REVELATION.

1 Conditions before Man's Creation
   (Genesis 1:1)
   (a) Celestial Creations (Job 38:4–7)
   (b) Celestial Catastrophe (Isaiah 14:12;
       Luke 10:18)
   (c) Celestial Condemnation (John 8:44;
       Jude 6)

2. Conditions Leading to Man's Creation
   (Nehemiah 9:6)
   (a) Terrestrial Chaos (Genesis 1:2)
   (b) Terrestrial Creations (Genesis 1:2–25)
   (c) Terrestrial Cosmos (Genesis 1:4, 10, 12, 18,
       21, 25, 31)

3. Climax of Creation. (Genesis 1:26–27)
   (a) The Son of God (Genesis 1:27;
       Luke 3:38)
   (b) The Six Days' Work (Genesis 1:28–31)
   (c) The Sabbath Rest (Genesis 2:1–3)

1. Conditions before Man's Creation

*In the beginning God created the heaven and the earth.
And the earth was without form, and void; and darkness was upon the face of the deep. And the Spirit of God
moved upon the face of the waters. (Genesis 1:1–2)*

Between verses 1 and 2 of the first chapter of Genesis, there is a great hiatus. Verse 1 refers to an order
of things before the reconstruction referred to in 2.

(a) Celestial Creations

We mean by celestial creations the creations that were
before men and the system of things as we understand
them. These celestial creations belong to a period
before man. The creations first alluded to, then, are not
men, but something other than man. Job 38:4–7 refers
to a time when "the sons of God shouted for joy."
Who were these "sons of God"? They were not men;
they were unquestionably angels and archangels, and
the indirect inference is that God had put that former
world under the charge of an archangel, Lucifer.

(b) Celestial Catastrophe

The Bible also alludes to a catastrophe before man was
created, which makes the first two verses of Genesis 1

understandable. God gave the rule of this universe to
Lucifer, who opposed himself to God's authority and
rule. In falling, he dragged everything down with him,
and consequently called forth on this earth a tremendous judgement which resulted in chaos: "and the
earth was without form, and void." This catastrophe is
referred to in such passages as Isaiah 14:12, How art
thou fallen from heaven, O Lucifer, son of the morning!" and "Luke 10:18, "I beheld Satan as lightning fall
from heaven." When did our Lord behold this? Surely
it is legitimate to suggest that this refers to the period
before our Lord's Incarnation, when He was with
God, in the beginning, before all things. (This particular verse is frequently thought to refer to the time yet
to be and that our Lord annihilated time by His
forelook.) These verses are like mountain peaks revealing a whole table-land of God's revelation of the order
of things before man was created.

This interpretation is of the nature of a legitimate
speculation and would seem to account for a great
number of indications in the Bible. Beware, however,
of making too much of these indications, because
although as has been hinted, chaos may have been the
result of judgement, a careful reading of Genesis
1:1–2 does not necessarily imply it.

(c) Celestial Condemnation

Then comes the condemnation of the angels, a celestial condemnation, the condemnation of Lucifer and
all his angels, nothing whatever to do with man, "And
the angels which kept not their first estate, but left
their own habitation, He hath reserved in everlasting
chains under darkness unto the judgement of the
great day" (Jude 6).

When Jesus Christ uses the phrase "from the
beginning" He does not mean the beginning of man,
but the beginning of creation of God, which was long
enough before man was created (see John 8:44). Hell
is the place of angelic condemnation. It has nothing
to do primarily with man. God's Book never says that
hell was made for man, although it is true that it is
the only place for the man who rejects God's salvation. Hell was the result of a distinct condemnation
passed by God on celestial beings, and is as eternal as
those celestial anarchists.

These three amazing episodes indicate the conditions before the creation of man, viz.: that the archangels and the angels governed a wonderful world which God created in the beginning, and which God's Spirit alludes to in that phrase in Job, "When the morning stars sang together, and all the sons of God shouted for joy." Lucifer fell, and with him all his angels in a tremendous ruin. "And the earth was without form, and void; and darkness was upon the face of the deep. And the Spirit of God moved upon the face of the waters" (Genesis 1:2). Without some such explanation, verse 2 is unintelligible. To say that "In the beginning God created the heaven and the earth," and then to say that "the earth was without form, and void" is a confusion. The inference is that between the epochs referred to in these verses there occurred a catastrophe which the Bible does not say much about, the evident purpose of the Bible being to tell what God's purpose is with man. Roughly outlining that purpose, we might say that God created man in order to counteract the devil.

These sections refer to the strange unfamiliar background of the life we live at present. Such things are not to be made too much of, nor on the other hand are they to be ignored. It is necessary to note them in Biblical Psychology because they have a distinct part to play in man's present existence.

2. Conditions Leading to Man's Creation

Thou, even Thou, art LORD alone; Thou hast made heaven, the heaven of heavens, with all their host, the earth, and all things that are therein, the seas, and all that is therein, and Thou preservest them all; and the host of heaven worshippeth Thee. (Nehemiah 9:6)

(a) Terrestrial Chaos (Genesis 1:2)
Satan was the means of the ruin of the first created order, and now God begins to create another order out of the confusion of ruin. "Void" means the aftermath of destruction by judgement, or the result of Divine judgement.

(b) Terrestrial Creations
God began to create things. Genesis 1:2–25 gives a detailed account of the creation of the earth and the life upon it. The Bible nowhere says that God set processes to work and out of those processes evolved the things which now appear. The Bible says that God created things by a distinct act. If the Bible agreed with modern science, it would soon be out of date, because, in the very nature of things, modern science is bound to change. Genesis 1 indicates that God created the earth and the life on the earth in order to fit the world for man.

(c) Terrestrial Cosmos
The order and beauty of this world were created by God for man. Genesis 1, verses 4, 10, 12, 18, 21, 25 and 31, all say that "God saw that it was good." After the judgement by God on the previous order, God created a new thing, for a totally new being whom no angel had ever seen. This new being, man, stood at the end of the six days' work as a creation of earth, and he stood at the threshold of God's Sabbath Day. God created a unique being, not an angel, and not God Himself; He created man. Man was created out of the earth, and related to the earth, and yet he was created in the image of God, whereby God could prove Himself more than a match for the devil by a creation a little lower than the angels, the order of beings to which Satan belongs. This is, as it were, God's tremendous experiment in the creation of man. God put man at the head of the Terrestrial Creation. The whole meaning of the creation of the world was to fit and prepare a place for the wonderful being called Man that God had in mind. There is nothing in the Bible about the evolution and development of man as a "survival of the fittest," or about the "process of natural selection." The Bible reveals that we are earth and spirit, a combination of the two. The devil is spirit, just as God is; the angels are spirit; but when we come to man, man is earth and spirit.

3. Climax of Creation
(a) The Son of God (Luke 3:38)
Adam is called the son of God. There is only one other "Son of God" in the Bible, and He is Jesus Christ. Yet we are called "sons of God," but how? By being reinstated through the Atonement of Jesus Christ. This is an important point. We are not the sons of God by natural generation. Adam did not come into the world as we do; neither did Adam come into the world as Jesus Christ came. Adam was not "begotten"; Jesus Christ was. Adam was "created." God created Adam, He did not beget him. We are all generated, we are not created beings. Adam was the "son of God," and God created him as well as everything else that was created.

In Genesis 1:27 we read, "So God created man in His own image, in the image of God created He him; male and female created He them." This is a point of importance. Adam and Eve are both needed before the image of God can be perfectly presented. God is, as it were, all that the best manhood presents us with, and all that the best womanhood presents us with.

(This aspect will be dealt with in subsequent lectures.)

(b) The Six Days' Work (Genesis 1:28–31)
This word "day" means roughly what we understand by twenty-four hours, and has no such meaning as the Day of Atonement or the Day of Judgement. Devotion to the ephemeral scientific doctrine of evolution is responsible for the endeavour to make out that the Bible means a period of years instead of a solar day. The

particular unparabolic use of the term "evening and morning" in Genesis distinctly indicates a solar day.

Man was the climax of the six days' work; in God's plan the whole of the six days' work of creation was for man. The tendency nowadays is to put the six days' work of creation above man. Some people are far more concerned about dogs and cats than about human beings.

There is not only the tendency to exalt animals above man, but there is the speculation of the superman, which holds that man, as we understand him and as the Bible reveals him, is not the climax of creation, but that there is a higher being yet to be, called "the superman," and that man is as inferior to this being that is going to be as the ape is to him. All through the New Testament the Spirit of God has foretold that we are going to have the worship of man installed, and it is in our midst to-day. We are being told that Jesus Christ and God are ceasing to be of importance to the modern man, and what we are worshipping more and more now is "Humanity," and this is slowly merging into a new phase; all the up-to-date minds are looking towards the manifestation of this "superman," a being much greater than the being we know as man. Second Thessalonians 2 gives us a picture of the head of this great expectation. ". . . the son of perdition; who opposeth and exalteth himself above all that is called God, or that is worshipped; so that he as God sitteth in the temple of God, shewing himself that he is God" (2 Thessalonians 2:3–4). He is to be the darling of every religion; there is to be a consolidation of religions, and of races and of everything on the face of the earth, a great socialism. The ethical standard of the "superman" claims to be higher than Jesus Christ's standard. The tendency is noticeable already in the objection of some people to Jesus Christ's teaching, such as "Thou shalt love thy neighbour as thyself"; they say, "That is selfish, you must love your neighbour and not think of yourself." The doctrine of the superman is absolute sinless perfection. We are going to evolve a being, they say, who has reached the place where he cannot be tempted. This is all an emanation from Satan.

Man is the climax of creation. He is on a stage a little lower than the angels, and God is going to overthrow the devil by this being who is less than angelic. God has, as it were, put man in the "open field," and He is allowing the devil to do exactly what he likes up to a certain point, "because," He says, "greater is He that is in you, than he that is in the world." This is also the explanation of our own spiritual setting. Satan is to be humiliated by man, by the Spirit of God in man through the wonderful regeneration of Jesus Christ.

Man, then, is the head and the purpose of the six days' creation. Man's body has in it those constituents that connect it with the earth; it has fire and water and all the elements of animal life, consequently God keeps us here. The earth is man's domain, and we are going to be here again after the terrestrial cremation. "Here-after," without the devil, without sin and wrong. We are going to be here, marvellously redeemed in this wonderful place which God made very beautiful, and with which sin has played havoc, and creation itself is waiting "for the manifestation of the sons of God."

(c) The Sabbath Rest (Genesis 2:1–3)

Not only is Man the head and climax of the six days' work, but he is the beginning of, and stands at the threshold of, the Sabbath of God. God's heart is, as it were, absolutely at rest now that He has created man; even in spite of the fact of the fall, and all else, God is absolutely confident that everything will turn out as He said it would. The devil has laughed at God's hope for thousands of years, and has ridiculed and scorned that hope, but God is not upset or alarmed about the final issue; He is certain that man will bruise the serpent's head. This has reference to those who are born again through Jesus Christ's amazing Atonement.

Chapter II
MAN: HIS CREATION, CALLING
AND COMMUNION
Man's Making

1. The Man of God's Making (Genesis 2:4–25)
   (a) The Image of God (John 4:24)
   (b) The Image of God in Angels (Genesis 6:2;
      Psalm 89:6; Job 1:6; Job 38:7)
   (c) The Image of God in Man (Genesis 1:26;
      Psalm 8:4–5)
2. The Manner of Man's Making. (John 1:3)
   (a) Man's Body (Genesis 2:7)
   (b) Man's Soul (Acts 17:28)
   (c) Man's Self-Consciousness (Proverbs 20:27;
      1 Corinthians 2:11)

N.B.—Visible creations that surround
man are not in the image of God.

Some notes will be given on
the appearances of angels in our
material universe.

Some notes also on the human
representations of God.

1. The Man of God's Making *(Genesis 2:4–25)*
God's heart is, so to speak, at rest now that He has created man.

(a) The Image of God
God is a Spirit. (John 4:24)

This is a mountain-peak text which reveals a whole tableland of God's revelation about Himself.

(b) The Image of God in Angels
Now there was a day when the sons of God came to present themselves before the Lord, and Satan came also among them. (Job 1:6; see also Genesis 6:2; Psalm 89:6; Job 38:7)

The phrase "sons of God" in the Old Testament always refers to angels, and we have to find out from the context whether they are fallen angels or not. Angels have no physical frame, they are not like man, and they are not manifested after this order of things; since, however, they are called "sons of God," the inference is clear that they bear the image of God.

(c) The Image of God in Man
And God said, Let Us make man in Our image, after Our likeness. (Genesis 1:26; see Psalm 8:4–5)

In its primary reference the image of God in man is to the hidden or interior life of man. The image of God in man is primarily spiritual, yet it has to be manifested in his body also. "Thou hast made him but little lower than God" (RV) or "than the angels" (Psalm 8:5). Man's chief glory and dignity is that he was made "of the earth, earthy" to manifest the image of God in that substance. We are apt to think that to be made of the earth is our humiliation, but it is the very point of which God's Word makes most. God "formed man of the dust of the ground," and the Redemption is for the dust of the ground as well as for man's spirit. Man's body before he degenerated must have been dazzling with light. We get this by inference from Genesis 3:7, "And the eyes of them both were opened, and they knew that they were naked; and they sewed fig leaves together, and made themselves aprons." Man was obviously naked before his disobedience, and the death of his union with God was instantly revealed in his body. (We shall deal with this point in the next chapter.)

From these revelation facts in God's Book, men have reasoned backwards; they have said that because men have bodies, therefore God has a corporeity too. This error began centuries ago and is continually being revived. The Bible does speak of the "form" of God—"Who, being in the form of God" (Philippians 2:6); but the error has arisen from our too readily inferring that "form" means physical body. In the Old Testament there are allusions over and over again to what is called the anthropomorphic view of God; that is, God is represented as having hands and limbs and looking like a man, and from this it is easy to draw the inference that God has a body like man. All these Old Testament pictures of God are forecasts of the Incarnation. There are passages in the Book of Isaiah which reveal apparently conflicting statements about God, He is represented in many contradictory phrases; but all these contradictions blend in that unique Being, Jesus Christ, the last Adam.

The great Triune God has "form," and the term that is used for describing that form is "glory." "And now, O Father, glorify Thou Me with Thine own self with the glory which I had with Thee before the world was" (John 17:5). Our word "Trinity" is an attempt to convey the externally disclosed Divine nature, and "glory" is the Bible term for conveying the idea of the external form of that Triune Being. (This will be alluded to several times in the course of our studies in Biblical Psychology, and we shall thus become familiar with this profound revelation.)

God is sometimes referred to as the sun, but the sun is never stated to be made in the image of God, although there are illustrations of God in God's Book drawn from the sun. But nowhere, is it stated that God made the sun in His own image.

In the Bible record angels certainly did appear to men. We may take it from the revealed facts in God's Word that angels have the power of will to materialise and to appear to human beings when human beings are in suitable subjective conditions. This power is given to good and bad angels alike. It is probably to this that Paul refers Ephesians 6:12: "For we wrestle not against flesh and blood, but against principalities, against powers, against the rulers of the darkness of this world, against spiritual wickedness in high places." This inference is a great guide in regard to Spiritualism. Spiritualism, according to the Bible, is not a trick; it is a fact. Man can communicate with beings of a different order from his own, and can put himself into a state of subjectivity in which angels can appear.

2. The Manner of Man's Making

All things were made by Him; and without Him was not any thing made that was made. (John 1:3)

God did not create man by direct fiat; He moulded him by His own deliberate power (see Genesis 1:26–27). A common mistake is to infer that the soul was made along with the body; the Bible says that the body was created prior to the soul. Man's body was formed by God "of the dust of the ground"; which means that man is constituted to have affinity with everything on this earth. This is not man's calamity but his peculiar dignity. We do not further our spiritual life in spite of our bodies, but in and by means of our bodies. Then we read that God "breathed into his nostrils the breath of life; and man became a living soul," i.e., a soul-enlivened nature.

There is another "breathing" mentioned in John 20:22, when our Risen Lord breathed on the disciples and said, "Receive ye the Holy Ghost." This has not the same meaning as Genesis 2:7, where God breathed into man's nostrils the breath of life which became, not God's Spirit, but man's. Jesus Christ breathed into His disciples Holy Spirit, and man's spirit became energised by the Spirit of the Son of God. When God breathed into man's nostrils the breath of life, man did not become a living God, he became "a living soul." Consequently in man, regenerate or degenerate, there are three aspects—spirit, soul and body. The uniting of men's personality, spirit,

soul and body, may be brought about in various ways. The Bible reveals that sensuality will do it (Ephesians 5:5); that drunkenness will do it (Ephesians 5:18); and that the devil will do it (Luke 11:21); but the Holy Spirit alone will do it rightly, this is the only true at-one-ment. When our personality is sanctified, it is not God's Spirit that is sanctified, it is our spirit. "And the very God of peace sanctify you wholly; and I pray God your whole spirit and soul and body be preserved blameless unto the coming of our Lord Jesus Christ" (1 Thessalonians 5:23). Paul's injunction to "cleanse ourselves from all filthiness of the flesh and spirit" refers to man's spirit.

God's inbreathing into man's nostrils the breath of life called into actual existence his soul, which was potentially in the body, i.e., existing in possibility. Man's soul is neither his body nor his spirit, it is that creation which holds his spirit and his body together, and is the medium of expressing his spirit in his body. It is not true to state that man's soul moulds his body; it is his spirit that moulds his body, and soul is the medium his spirit uses to express itself.

It is impossible for us to conceive what Adam was like as God made him—his material body instinct with spiritual light, his flesh in the likeness of God, his soul in absolute harmony with God, and his spirit in the image of God. In the personal life of a man who has fallen away from God, his soul and his spirit gravitate more and more to the dust of the earth, more and more to the brutish life on one side and the Satanic life on the other. The marvellous revelation is that in and through Jesus Christ, our personality in its three aspects of body, soul and spirit, is sanctified and preserved blameless in this dispensation; and in another dispensation, body, soul and spirit will be instinct with the glory of God. Whenever an Old Testament character succeeded in perfectly doing God's will, earth seemed to lose its hold on him, e.g., Enoch, Elijah. Again, why did not Jesus Christ go straight back to Heaven from the Mount of Transfiguration? He was standing in the full blaze and glory of His pre-incarnate glory; but He "emptied Himself" (RV) a second time of the glory of God, and came down from the Mount to the humiliation of the Cross. When Jesus Christ comes again, those who are saved and sanctified will be "changed, in a moment, in the twinkling of an eye"; all disharmony will cease and a new order will begin.

What does glorification mean? Adam is never spoken of as being glorified in the first decades of creation. Glorification is Christ enthroned in fullness of consummating power, when having subdued all things unto Himself, He enters back into Absolute Deity as "in the beginning" before any creations were (see 1 Corinthians 15:28). That is where our vocabulary will not go.

To sum up: God made man in His own image and breathed into his nostrils the breath of life, and man became, not a living God, but a living soul, a soul-enlivened nature; his whole bodily temple, every corpuscle of blood, every nerve, every sinew, was the temple which could manifest harmony with God, i.e., manifest the image of God in the form of man, through faith and love. The angels can manifest the image of God only in bodiless spirits; only one being can manifest God on this earth, and that is man. Satan thwarted God's purpose, and then laughed his devilish laugh against God, but the Bible says that God will laugh last. "The Lord shall laugh at him: for He seeth that His day is coming" (Psalm 37:13).

Chapter III
MAN: HIS CREATION, CALLING AND COMMUNION
Man's Unmaking

1. The Primal Anarchy (Genesis 3; Romans 5:12)
   (a) The Serpent (Genesis 3:1)
   (b) The Serpent and Eve (2 Corinthians 2:3)
   (c) The Serpent, Eve and Adam (1 Timothy 2:14)

   ORIGINAL SIN—DOING WITHOUT GOD

2. The Pre-Adamic Anarchy (Ezekiel 28:12–15)
   (a) Satanic Pretensions. Implied (Matthew 4:8; 2 Corinthians 4:4)
   (b) Satanic Perversions (Genesis 3:5; implied, Job 1:9)
   (c) Satanic Perils (Jude 6; Matthew 16:23; 2 Thessalonians 2:9)

   ORIGIN OF SIN—DETHRONING OF GOD

3. The Punished Anarchists (Genesis 3:23–24)
   (a) Destitution and Death (Genesis 2:17)
   (b) Division from Deity (Genesis 3:8, 13)
   (c) Divine Declaration (Genesis 3:15)

   ORIGIN OF SALVATION—
   DARING WAY BACK TO GOD

Now we come to the revelation statement of how sin was introduced into this world.

1. The Primal Anarchy
(a) The Serpent
Now the serpent was more subtil than any beast of the field which the LORD God had made. (Genesis 3:1)

This creature was evidently a beautiful creation of God's and we must beware of imagining that it was in the beginning as it was after being cursed. After the fall, God cursed this beautiful creature into the serpent, to feed on dust and to crawl. The serpent in the physical domain is a picture of Satan in the spiritual domain. In our universe of physical things we shall find many which picture spiritual things. (This line of thought belongs to Biblical Philosophy, so it is only alluded to in passing.)

(b) The Serpent and Eve
But I fear, lest by any means, as the serpent beguiled Eve through his subtilty, so your minds should be corrupted from the simplicity that is in Christ. (2 Corinthians 11:3)

Why did Satan come *via* the serpent, and to Eve?—why did he not go direct to Adam? In thinking of man and woman as they were first created, it is extremely difficult, especially nowadays, to present the subject without introducing small, petty and disreputable ideas relative to the distinctions between man and woman. In Adam and Eve we are dealing with the primal creations of God. Adam was created immediately by the hand of God; Eve was created mediately. Eve stands for the soul side, the psychic side, of the human creation; all her sympathies, and affinities were with the other creations of God around. Adam stands for the spirit side, the kingly, Godward side. Adam and Eve together are the likeness of God, "And God said, Let Us make man in Our image. . . . Male and female created He them." The revelation made here is not that woman stands as inferior to man. but that she stands in quite a different relation to all things, and that both man and woman are required for the complete creation of God referred to by the big general term "Man."

(c) The Serpent, Eve and Adam
And Adam was not deceived, but the woman being deceived was in the transgression. (1 Timothy 2:14)

Eve, having this affinity and sympathy with the other creations around, would naturally listen with more unsuspecting interest to the suggestions which came through the subtle creature which spoke to her. The Bible says that Eve was deceived, it does not say that Adam was deceived; consequently Adam is far more responsible than Eve because he sinned deliberately. There was no conscious intention to disobey in Eve's heart, she was deceived by the subtle wisdom of Satan *via* the serpent. Adam, however, was not deceived, he sinned with a deliberate understanding of what he was doing; so the Bible associates "sin" with Adam ("Wherefore, as by one man sin entered into the world . . ." Romans 5:12) and "transgression" with Eve ("And Adam was not deceived, but the woman being deceived was in the transgression") .

In this connection it is of importance to note that the Bible reveals that our Redeemer entered into the world through the woman. Man, as man, had no part whatever in the Redemption of the world; it was "the seed of the woman." In Protestant theology and in the Protestant outlook we have suffered much from our opposition to the Roman Catholic Church on this one point, viz. intense antipathy to Mariolatry, and we have lost the meaning of the woman side of the revelation of God. All that we understand by womanhood and by manhood, all that we understand by fatherhood and motherhood, is embraced in the term "El Shaddai" (Genesis 17:1 RV mg). (This is a mere hint at a line of thought that cannot be taken up here.)

A distinction may legitimately be made between transgression and sin (cf. Matthew 6:12–15). Transgression is nearly always an unconscious act, there is no conscious determination to do wrong. Sin is never an unconscious act, as far as culpability is concerned, it is always a conscious determination. Adam was the introducer of sin into this order of things (see Romans 5:12). Original sin is doing without God. A noticeable feature in the conduct of Adam and Eve is that when God turned them out of the garden, they did not rebel. The characteristic of sin in man is fear and shame. Sin in man is doing without God, but it is not rebellion against God in its first stages.

2. The Pre-Adamic Anarchy
(a) Satanic Pretensions
The pretensions of Satan are clear. He is the god of this world and he will not allow relationship to the true God. Satan's attitude is that of a pretender to the throne, he claims it as his right. Wherever and whenever the rule of God is recognised by man, Satan proceeds to instil the tendency of mutiny and rebellion and lawlessness.

(b) Satanic Perversions
Satan ever perverts what God says. Genesis 3:5 is one of the revelation facts concerning Satan ("For God doth know that in the day ye eat thereof, then your eyes shall be opened and ye shall be as gods, knowing good and evil"). Remember, the characteristics of man's union with God are faith in God and love for Him. This union was the first thing Satan aimed at in Adam and Eve, and he did it by perverting what God had said. In the case of Job, Satan goes the length of trying to pervert God's idea of man. That is an amazing revelation of the power of Satan! He is represented as presenting himself with the sons of God in the very presence of God and trying to pervert God's mind about Job. We might apply personally (not exegetically) this statement from Isaiah: "A bruised reed shall He not break, and the smoking flax shall He not quench." Satan is called "the accuser of our brethren"; he not only slanders God to us, but accuses us to God. It is as if he looked down and pointed out a handful of people and insinuated to God, "Now, that woman is a perfect disgrace to You, she has only one spark of grace amongst all the fibres of her life; I advise You to stamp out that spark." What is the revelation? "He will raise it to a flame." Or, he points out a man and says, "That man is a disgrace to You, he is a 'bruised reed,' I wonder You build any hope on him whatever, he is a hindrance and an upset to You, break him!" But no, the Lord will bind him up and make him into a wonderful instrument. The old reeds were used to make wonderful musical instruments, and instead of crushing out the life that is bruised and wrong, God heals it and discourses sweet music through it.

In the revelation in Genesis 3 Satan implies that God is jealous—"God knows that if you disobey Him you will become as God." Satan perverted God's statement. he did not say that God had said it, he was too wise for that, he said, "Hath God said . . . ?" insinuating "You do not know what God meant, but I do; He means that if you disobey Him and eat of the tree, you will become as He is." I do not think that Eve accepted this suggestion about God, because, if you watch, Satan's words worked in her as a deception unconsciously, all she saw was that the fruit was "a delight to the eyes." Our discernment of what Eve did is given to us by the Spirit of God. We are not ignorant of Satan's devices (2 Corinthians 2:11). Satan's pretension is that he is equal with God. His perversion is two-fold: he tries to pervert what God says to us, and also to pervert God's mind about us.

(c) Satanic Perils
And the angels which kept not their first estate, but left their own habitation, he hath reserved in everlasting chains under darkness unto the judgement of the great day. (Jude 6)

What are Satanic perils? The Satanic perils spring straight out of the way we are made, and in Matthew

16:22–23 we come to where we live. Have you ever noticed the remarkable identification Jesus Christ makes in this passage? When Peter said, "Be it far from Thee, Lord," what did our Lord reply?—"Get thee behind Me, *Satan*." Our Lord then told Peter that what he had said belonged to the wrong disposition in man, which He identifies with Satan. Beware of Satanic perils when they are taken to be merely natural tendencies. Remember, Satan is an awful being, he is able to deceive us on the right hand and on the left, and the first beginnings of his deceptions are along the lines of self-pity. Self-pity, self-conceit, and self-sympathy will make us accept slanders against God. Satanic perils arise out of the wrong disposition which was introduced into the human race, and that wrong disposition shows itself in self-pity and self-sympathy. Beware of slandering the "old man," as is often done; I mean, beware of making the "old man" appear ugly. The "old man" does not appear ugly to anyone but the Holy Ghost. The "old man," i.e., the disposition that connects me with the mystical body of sin, is a highly desirable thing until I am quickened by the Spirit of God and born from above; it makes me consider my rights, it makes me look after myself and consider what is good for me. "Ye are they that justify yourselves in the sight of men; but God knoweth your hearts: for that which is exalted among men is an abomination in the sight of God" (Luke 16:15 RV).

"Then shall that Wicked be revealed . . . even him, whose coming is after the working of Satan with all power and signs and lying wonders" (2 Thessalonians 2:8–9). This verse reveals another peril, viz. that there are tremendous and appalling external manifestations of Satan. The curious thing nowadays is that people are watching eagerly for these manifestations of Satanic power while they allow other Satanic perils, e.g., spiritualism, to have their way. Once the disposition is altered, we shall never be deluded by any of the Satanic powers which manifest themselves in the external world. The great peril is the peril within, which men never think of as a peril. My right to myself, self-pity, self-conceit, consideration for my progress, my ways of looking at things, those things are the Satanic perils which will keep us in perfect sympathy with Satan.

Satanic anarchy is conscious and determined opposition to God. Wherever God's rule is made known, Satan will put himself alongside and oppose it. Satan's sin is at the summit of all sins; man's sin is at the foundation of all sins, and there is all the difference in the world between them. Satan's sin is conscious, emphatic, and immortal rebellion against God; he has no fear, no veneration, and no respect for God's rule. Whenever God's law is stated, that is sufficient,

Satan will break it, and his whole purpose is to get man to do the same. Satanic anarchy is a conscious, tremendous thing. Satan is never represented in the Bible as being guilty of doing wrong *things:* he is a wrong *being*. Men are responsible for doing wrong things, and they do wrong things because of the wrong disposition in them. The moral cunning of our nature makes us blame Satan when we know perfectly well we should blame ourselves; the true blame for sins lies in the wrong disposition in us. In all probability Satan is as much upset as the Holy Ghost is when men fall in external sin, but for a different reason. When men go into external sin and upset their lives, Satan knows perfectly well that they will want another Ruler, a Saviour and Deliverer; as long as Satan can keep men in peace and unity and harmony apart from God, he will do so (see Luke 11:21–22). Remember, then, Satan's sin is dethroning God.

3. The Punished Anarchists
We have seen in Chapter II how God punished Satan; He has reserved for him what is revealed as the eternal hell. Now we come to the punishment of Adam and Eve. "Therefore the LORD God sent him forth from the garden of Eden, to till the ground from whence he was taken. So He drove out the man. . . ." (Genesis 3:23–24). It is a familiar revelation fact to us that there was no rebellion in Adam and Eve. They did not fight against God, they simply went out of the Garden covered with fear and shame. Satan was the originator of sin; Adam was not. Adam accepted the way Eve had been deceived and sinned with his eyes open, and instantly an extraordinary thing happened:. "they knew that they were naked." There is quite sufficient to indicate that when Adam's spirit, soul and body were united in perfect faith and love to God, his soul was the medium through which the marvellous life of the Spirit of God was brought down. The very image of God was brought down into his material body and it was clothed in an inconceivable splendour of light until the whole man was in the likeness of God. The moment he disobeyed, the connection with God was shut off, and spirit, soul and body tumbled into death that instant. The fact of dissolving into dust in a few years' time is nothing more than death visible. Do not bring the idea of time in at all. Death happened instantly in spirit, soul and body, spiritually and psychically. The connecting link with Deity was gone, and man's spirit, soul and body tumbled into disintegrating death; and when they "heard the voice of the LORD God walking in the garden," they were terrified and hid themselves. By the term "Death" is meant that the body crumbles back into dust, the soul disappears, and the spirit goes back to God Who gave it (see Ecclesiastes 12:7). Spirit is the immortal part

of man. The spirit of man is not absorbed into God, it goes back to God, Who breathed into his nostrils the breath of life, with the characteristics upon it which he has developed for either the judgement or the praise of God.

God turned man out of the garden of Eden into destitution, but in turning him out He put him on the way to become an infinitely grander and nobler being than even Adam was at the first. The whole Bible, from Genesis to Revelation, instead of being a picture of despair is the very opposite. The worst is always "bettered" by God. God as it were, took His hand off man and let Satan do the very worst that diabolical spiritual genius could do. Satan knew what would happen, he knew that God would have to punish man, and God did punish him, but with the perfect certainty that the being that was to come out of the ordeal of the fall would be greater than the first Adam.

Adam and Eve went out from the garden covered with fear and shame. In the New Testament the characteristics of the wrong disposition are fearfulness and unbelief; what does the Atonement do? It takes away fearfulness and unbelief, and brings us back again into the relationship of faith and love to God. ". . . faith and love which is in Christ Jesus" (1 Timothy 1:14). Regeneration means that the Holy Spirit lifts man out of the slough he is in through sin and death into a totally new realm, and by sudden intuitions and impulses the new he is able to lift up soul and body. The soul must obey the union with God which the new life has given, or it may ultimately fall away. The new birth will bring us to the place where spirit, soul and body are identified with Christ, sanctified here and now and preserved in that condition, not by intuitions now, not by sudden impulses and marvellous workings of the new life within, but by a conscious, superior, moral integrity, transfigured through and through by our union with God through the Atonement.

When Adam sinned his union with God was cut off, and God turned him out of the garden and guarded the way to the tree of life, that is to say, God prevented Adam from getting back as a fallen being. If Adam had got back to the tree of life as a fallen being, he would have become an incarnate devil, and God would have been finally thwarted with man; but when Adam was driven out, God placed cherubim and a gleaming sword to keep the way of the tree of life. If Adam had become an incarnate devil, there would have been the same havoc on this earth as when the angels fell; but Adam did not sin as Satan sinned. Adam was covered with fear and shame, and the light that had glistened all through his physical body faded out because of sin. Jesus Christ is going to change "the body of our humiliation" and conform it "to the body of His glory," and the result will be not an intuitive innocency only, but a conscious manly and womanly holiness. Holiness is the expression of the new disposition God has given us maintained against all odds. Holiness is militant, Satan is continually pressing and ardent, but holiness maintains itself. It is morality on fire and transfigured into the likeness of God. Holiness is not only what God gives me, but what I manifest that God has given me. I manifest this coruscating holiness by my reaction against sin, the world, and the devil. Wherever God's saints are in the world they are protected by a wall of fire which they do not see, but Satan does. "That wicked one toucheth him not." Satan has to ask and plead for permission; as to whether God grants him permission is to do with the sovereignty of God and is not in our domain to understand. All we know is that Jesus Christ taught us to pray, "Lead us not into temptation."

Man was turned out into destitution, and was thus divided from Deity; God disappeared from him, and he disappeared from God. As mentioned before, there are three false unities possible in a man's experience, viz., sensuality, drunkenness, and the devil, whereby man's spirit, soul and body are brought into harmony and he is quite peaceful, quite happy, with no sense of death about him. A drunken man has no self-consciousness, he is perfectly delivered from all the things which disintegrate and upset. Sensuality and Satan will do the same; but each of these unities is only possible for a time. When Satan rules, men's souls are in peace, they are not troubled or upset like other men, but quite happy and peaceful. There is only one right at-one-ment, and that is in Jesus Christ; only one right unity, and that is when body, soul and spirit are united to God by the Holy Ghost through the marvellous Atonement of the Lord Jesus Christ.

The origin of salvation is a daring way back to God. How did Jesus Christ make a way back to God? Through every worst onslaught of Satan. By the sheer force of the tremendous integrity of His Incarnation, Jesus Christ hewed a way straight through sin and death and hell right back to God, more than conquerorover all.

As in chapters I and II, we are dealing here more properly with theology than with psychology, but it is these fundamental theological facts which must safeguard our psychological studies.

Chapter IV
MAN: HIS CREATION, CALLING AND COMMUNION
Readjustment by Redemption

1. Incarnation. Word Made Weak (John 1:14) God-Man
   (a) Self-Surrender of Trinity (John 17:5; Mark 13:32: Ephesians 4:10)
   (b) Self-same with Trinity (Matthew 2:27; John 14:9)
   (c) Self-sufficiency of Trinity (Proverbs 8:22–32)

2. Identification. Son Made Sin (2 Corinthians 5:20–21) God and Man
   (a) Day of His Death (Matthew 16:21; Mark 9:31; Romans 6:3)
   (b) Day of His Resurrection (Romans 6:5; Philippians 3:10)
   (c) Day of His Ascension (Matthew 28:18; 2 Corinthians 5:16)

3. Invasion. Sinner Made Saint (Galatians 2:20) God in Man
   (a) The New Man (2 Corinthians 5:17)
   (b) The New Manners (Ephesians 4:22–32)
   (c) The New Mankind (Ephesians 4:13; 2 Peter 3:10)

1. Incarnation. *Word Made Weak*
And the Word was made weak, and dwelt among us . . . (see John 1:14).

The word "Trinity" is not a Bible word. Over and over again in the Bible the Triune God is revealed, so that the idea conveyed by the Trinity is thoroughly Scriptural. The following distinctions have existed from all eternity:

- The Essence of Godhead (*esse*) usually known as God the Father;
- The Existence of Godhead (*existere*) usually known as God the Son;
- The Proceeding of Godhead (*procedere*) usually known as God the Holy Ghost.

One thing we have to guard against is the teaching that God became incarnate in order to realise Himself; it is an un-Biblical statement. God was Self-sufficient before the Son became Incarnate. What is

known as New Theology springs from this fundamental error—that God had to create something in order to realise Himself; consequently we are told that we are essential to God's existence, that apart from us, God is not. If we start with that theory, then all that goes by the name of "New Theology" follows easily. The Bible has nothing to do with such conceptions. The Creation and the Incarnation are the outgoings of the overflowing life of the Godhead. Another aspect of New Theology is that God is all; the Bible reveals that God is not all. The Bible distinctly states that our universe is pluralistic, not monistic; that means there are other forces at work beside God, viz., man and the devil. These are not God, and never will be. Man is meant to come back to God and to be in harmony with Him through Jesus Christ; the devil will be at enmity with God for ever.

In Philippians 2:6 the form of God is mentioned. What is the form of God? In chapter II we found that men have reasoned that because man was made in the image of God, therefore God had a body. We stated that this did not mean God had a corporeal form; and that whenever bodily members are mentioned in connection with God, the reference is to the Incarnation. The Godhead had a form originally, and that "form" is best implied by the term "glory." The Bible reveals that the Godhead was absolutely Self-sufficient. God did not need to be incarnated in order to realise Himself; neither was the creation needed to enable God to realise Himself.

Jesus Christ is not a Being one-half God and one-half Man. When George Eliot[4] translated Strauss's *Life of Christ*,[5] this impossibility to human reason was presented to her mind, and it was along this line that she made shipwreck of her faith. The Bible reveals that Jesus Christ is God-Man, viz., God Incarnate, the Godhead existing in flesh and blood.

(a) The Self-Surrender of the Trinity
The Incarnation is part of the self-surrender of the Trinity. John 17:5 refers to this. "And now, O Father, glorify Thou Me with Thine own self with the glory

---

4. George Eliot, pen name of Mary Ann Evans (1819–1880), English novelist.
5. David Friedrich Strauss (1808–1874), German theologian who wrote *Jesu Leben* (Life of Jesus) in 1835. Translated into English by George Eliot.

which I had with Thee before the world was." Jesus Christ was not a Being Who became Divine; He was the Godhead incarnated, the Word made weak. Jesus Christ emphatically alludes to His own limitations, and Paul says He "emptied Himself," i.e., of the form of God, "taking the form of a servant, being made in the likeness of men."

In Mark 13:32 we see another indication of the limitations of our Lord. "But of that day and that hour knoweth no man, no, not the angels which are in heaven, neither the Son, but the Father." I am aware of the danger of attempting to sketch out the Self-consciousness of Jesus; we cannot do it. We have to remember what the Scriptures say about Him—that He was the Godhead Incarnate, and that He emptied Himself of His glory in becoming Incarnate. In the Redemption, it was not God the Son paying a price to God the Father: it was God the Father, God the Son and God the Holy Ghost surrendering this marvellous Being, the Lord Jesus Christ, for one definite purpose. Never separate the Incarnation from the Atonement. The Incarnation is for the sake of the Atonement. In dealing with the Incarnation, we are dealing with a revelation fact, not with a speculation.

We find another allusion to the limitations of Jesus through His Incarnation in the Epistle to the Hebrews. To say that Jesus Christ could not be tempted flatly contradicts the Word of God—He was "in all points tempted like as we are, yet without sin." (Hebrews 4:15).

(b) Self-Same with Trinity
All things are delivered unto Me of My Father: and no man knoweth the Son, but the Father; neither knoweth any man the Father, save the Son, and he to whomsoever the Son will reveal Him. (Matthew 11:27)

Jesus says here, in effect, "I am the only medium for revealing the Father; you cannot know the Father through Nature, or through the love of your friends, you cannot know the Father in any other way than through Me." Couple with that verse our Lord's words in John 14:6, 9, ("Jesus saith unto him, I am the way, the truth, and the life: no man cometh unto the Father, but by Me"—"he that hath seen Me hath seen the Father; and how sayest thou then, Shew us the Father?"), where He makes the same statement. No one knows anything about the Father unless he accepts the revelation made of Him by Jesus Christ. These statements come over and over again, and if we examine our Lord's teaching closely we shall find that He makes the final destiny of man depend on his relationship to Himself.

(c) The Self-Sufficiency of the Trinity (Proverbs 8:22–32)
Read in the light of the Incarnation this passage is amazing. What Solomon calls "Wisdom" is the same word as "Logos" in John 1, it means God's Word expressing His thought. The Trinity was Self-sufficient; the Incarnation was not meant to satisfy God, but for another purpose altogether. The thought is exactly the opposite, viz., instead of man being necessary to complement God so that He might realise Himself, the Incarnation was in order that man might realise God and gain adjustment to Him. The whole purpose of the Incarnation is the Redemption, viz., to overcome the disasters of the fall and produce a being more noble than the original Adam.

At the climax of everything, the Son resumes His original position in the Trinity; the Son gives up all to the Father, and the Trinity thus resolves itself again into this absolute Self-sufficient Deity (see 1 Corinthians 15:28).

2. Identification. *Son Made Sin*
. . . we pray you in Christ's stead, be ye reconciled to God. For He hath made Him to be sin for us, Who knew no sin; that we might be made the righteousness of God in Him. (2 Corinthians 5:20–21)

These verses reveal why God became Incarnate, why the Word was made weak, why the "Logos" became possessed of a weak human frame, viz. that the Son might be identified with sin. The revelation is not that Jesus Christ was punished for our sins, that is a slighter aspect. The statement in verse 21 is astounding: He was made to be sin for us. Jesus Christ became identified not only with the disposition of sin, but with the very body of sin. He Who had no sin, no connection in Himself with the body of sin, became identified with sin, Him who knew no sin, He made to be sin. Language can hardly bear the strain put upon it, but it may nevertheless convey the thought that Jesus Christ went straight through identification with sin in order that every man and woman on earth might be freed from sin through the Atonement. He went through the depths of damnation, through the deepest depths of death and hell, and came out more than conqueror; consequently anyone and everyone who is willing to be identified with Him will find that he is freed from the disposition of sin, freed from his connection with the body of sin, and that he too can come out "more than conqueror" because of what Jesus Christ has done.

(a) The Day of His Death
For He taught His disciples, and said unto them, The Son of Man is delivered into the hands of men, and they shall kill Him; and after that He is killed, He shall rise the third day. (Mark 9:31; see also Matthew 16:21; Romans 6:3)

By "day" we mean the period of time covered by our Lord's life on earth. Why was He born as a Babe in such conditions that the mightiest empires of the world were simply not able to detect His existence? why did He live those thirty years in Nazareth, and those three years of popularity, scandal and hatred, and why did He say He came on purpose to lay down His life? Our Lord never presented His death as that of a martyr. He said "I have power to lay [My life] down, and I have power to take it again." He laid down His life because of the great purpose behind in the mind of God.

The only way we can explain Jesus Christ is the way He explains Himself—and He never explains Himself away. Why did Jesus Christ live and die? The Scriptures reveal that He lived and died and rose again that we might be readjusted to the Godhead, i.e., that we might be delivered from sin and be brought back into the relationship of favour with God. If we teach that Jesus Christ cannot deliver from sin we shall end in nothing short of blasphemy. Present that line of thinking before God, tell Him that the Atonement cannot deliver us from sin but can only give us a Divine anticipation, and the danger and un-scripturalness of it will soon appear. The Bible reveals that Jesus Christ became identified with sin in order that "we might become the righteousness of God in Him." Forgiveness is a tremendous thing from our standpoint, but it is not the whole experimental meaning of the Atonement for us. We can become so identified with Jesus Christ until we know that "our old man is crucified with Him," i.e., that our connection with the body of sin is severed, and we may become "the righteousness of God in Him." This means we are readjusted to God and are free to fulfil all His commands.

(b) The Day of His Resurrection
For if we have been planted together in the likeness of His death, we shall be also in the likeness of His resurrection. (Romans 6:5; see also Philippians 3:10)

By His resurrection, Jesus Christ has power to impart to us the Holy Spirit, which means a totally new life. The Holy Ghost is the Deity in proceeding power Who applies the Atonement of the Son of God in our experience. Jesus Christ laid all the emphasis on the coming of the Holy Spirit—"When He . . . is come, He will guide you into all truth," and shall "bring all things to your remembrance, whatsoever I have said unto you"; He will not only be with you, but He "shall be in you." We hear on the right hand and on the left that this is the age of the Holy Spirit. Thank God it is, and the Holy Spirit is with all men that they might receive Him. Just as God the Father was rejected and spurned in the Old Testament dispensation, and Jesus Christ the Son was despised and spurned in His dispensation, so God the Holy Ghost is despised (as well as flattered), in this dispensation. He is not given His right, we praise Him and say that we rely on His

power, but the question of receiving Him that He may make real *in* us all that Jesus Christ did *for* us, is a rare experience. Immediately the Holy Spirit comes in as life and as light, He will chase through every avenue of our minds; His light will penetrate every recess of our hearts; He will chase His light through every affection of our souls, and make us know what sin is. The Holy Spirit convicts of sin, man does not.

The Holy Spirit is that marvellous Spirit that kept our Lord when He was incarnate, spirit, soul and body, in perfect harmony with absolute Deity. When Jesus said "Ye have no life in you," He meant the life He lived; and we cannot have that life saving through Him. "He that believeth on the Son hath eternal life"—the life Jesus lived, Holy Spirit life. The Holy Spirit will take us, spirit, soul and body, and bring us back into communion with God; and if we obey the light He gives, He will lead us into identification with the death of Jesus, until we know experimentally that our old man, my right to myself, is crucified with Him and our human nature is free now to obey the commands of God. The word "substitution" is never used in the Bible, although the idea is a Scriptural one. Substitution is always two-fold—not only is Jesus Christ identified with my sin, but I am so identified with Him that the disposition which ruled Him is in me.

(c) The Day of His Ascension
And Jesus came and spake unto them, saying, All power is given unto me in heaven and in earth. (Matthew 28:18; see also 2 Corinthians 5:16)

At His Ascension our Lord became omnipresent, omniscient and omnipotent. This means that all He was in the days of His flesh, all that He was able to impart in the Day of His Resurrection, He is now almighty to bestow without measure on all obedient children of men. Jesus Christ makes us one in holiness with Himself, one in love with Himself and ultimately one in glory with Himself. He is the supreme Sovereign, and He is able to give to His people a supreme sovereignty. In the days of our flesh, He says, "Lo, I am with you alway, even unto the end of the world." He is with us in all power and in all wisdom, guiding, directing, controlling and subduing. He is King of kings and Lord of lords from the day of His Ascension until now.

3. Invasion. *Sinner Made Saint*
I have been crucified with Christ; yet I live; and yet no longer I, but Christ liveth in me: and that life which I now live in the flesh I live in faith, the faith which is in the Son of God, Who loved me, and gave Himself up for me. (Galatians 2:20 RV)

Through the identification of Jesus Christ with sin we can be brought back again into perfect harmony with God; but God does not take away our responsibility;

He puts upon us a new responsibility. We are made sons and daughters of God through the Atonement and we have a tremendous dignity to maintain; we have no business to bow our necks to any yoke saving the yoke of the Lord Jesus Christ. There ought to be in us a holy scorn whenever it comes to being dictated to by the spirit of the age in which we live. The age in which we live is governed by the prince of this world who hates Jesus Christ. His great doctrine is self-realisation, We ought to be free from the dominion of the prince of this world; only one yoke should be upon our shoulders, the yoke of the Lord Jesus. Our Lord was meek towards His Father, He let God Almighty do what He liked with His life and never murmured; He never awakened self-pity, nor brought down sympathy for Himself. "Take My yoke upon you, and learn of Me; for I am meek and lowly in heart: and ye shall find rest unto your souls. For My yoke is easy, and My burden is light" (Matthew 11:29–30).

Galatians 2:20 is the Scriptural expression of identification with Jesus Christ in such a way that the whole life is changed. The destiny was getting wonderfully like the destiny of Satan, viz. self-realisation; now, Paul says, it is no longer the destiny of self-realisation for me, but the destiny of Christ-realisation, ("and that life which I now live in the flesh I live in faith, the faith which is in the Son of God, . . .") that is, the very faith which governed Jesus Christ now governs him. Paul is not talking of elementary faith in Jesus, of *the faith which is in the Son of God,* the very faith that was in Jesus is in me, he says. "Let this mind be in you, which was also in Christ Jesus." There is only one kind of holiness, and that is the holiness of the Lord Jesus. There is only one kind of human nature, and that is the human nature of us all, and Jesus Christ by means of His identification with our human nature can give us the disposition that He had. We have to see to it that we habitually work out that disposition through our eyes and ears and tongue, through all the organs of our body and in every detail of our life. The Apostle Paul has been identified with the death of Jesus Christ, his whole life has been invaded by a new spirit, he has been "by one spirit . . . baptized into one body," and now he has no longer any connection with the body of sin, that mystical body which ultimately ends with the devil. We are made part of the mystical Body of Christ by sanctification.

We have used the term "invasion" because it gives the idea better than any other. The illustration our Lord uses of the vine and the branches in John 15 is the most satisfactory one, because it indicates that every bit of the life in the branch which bears fruit is the result of an invasion from the parent stem: "I am the vine, ye are the branches." Our life is drawn from the Lord Jesus, not only the spring and the motive of the life, but our actual thinking and living and doing. This is what Paul means when he talks about the new man in Christ Jesus. After sanctification that is where the life is drawn from. "All my springs are in Thee." Notice how God will wither up every other spring you have. He will wither up your natural virtues, He will break up confidence in your natural powers, He will wither up your confidence in brain and spirit and body, until you learn by practical experience that you have no right to draw your life from any source other than the tremendous reservoir of the resurrection life of Jesus Christ. Thank God if you are going through a drying-up experience!

Our Lord never patches up our natural virtues, He replaces the whole man from within, until the new man is shown in the new manners. God does not give new manners; we make our own, but we have to make them out of the new life (Ephesians 4:22–32). Every detail of our physical life is to be absolutely under the control of the new disposition which God planted in us by means of identification with Jesus Christ, and we shall no longer be allowed to murmur "can't." There is no such a word as "can't" in a Christian's vocabulary if he is rightly related to God; there is only one word and that is "I can." "I know how to be abased, and I know also how to abound: in everything and in all things have I learned the secret both to be filled and to be hungry, both to abound and to be in want [RV]. I can do all things through Christ which strengtheneth me" (Philippians 4:12–13). And watch the kind of things Paul said he could do.

Manners refer to Christian character, and we are responsible for our manners. God works the alteration within us now, says Paul, "Work out what God works in," and we shall find when we are right with Him that God uses the machinery of our circumstances to enable us to do it. God is not after satisfying us and glorifying us; He wants to manifest in us what His Son can do. "When He shall come to be glorified in His saints, and to be admired in all them that believe" (1 Thessalonians 2:10). The invasion of the life of Jesus Christ makes us sons and daughters of God. These are things that the angels desire to look into. It is as if they look down on us and say, "Look at that woman, how wonderfully like Jesus Christ she is; she used not to be, but look at her now. We know Jesus Christ did it, but we wonder how?" Or, "Look at that man, he is just like his Master, how did Jesus Christ do it?"

Thank God we are not going to be angels, we are going to be something tenfold better. By the Redemption of Jesus Christ there is a time coming when our bodies will be in the image of God. The "body of our humiliation" is to be "conformed to the body of His glory," and our body will bear the image of God as our spirit does.

Chapter V
SOUL: THE ESSENCE, EXISTENCE
AND EXPRESSION

1. The Term Soul (Generally)
   (a) Applied to Men and Animals (Genesis 1:20–21, 24, 30)
   (b) Applied to Men, Not Animals (Genesis 2:7; 1 Corinthians 15:45)
   (c) Applied to Men Individually (Genesis 12:13; 1 Samuel 18:1)

   N.B. (1) NEVER APPLIED TO ANGELS OR TO GOD. (COMP. 2 CORINTHIANS 4:7)
   (2) NEVER APPLIED TO PLANTS. (SEE JOB 14:8–9.)

2. The Truth about the Soul (Specifically)
   (a) And Spirit (Genesis 2:7)
   (b) And Body (James 2:26)
   (c) And Personality (Isaiah 29:24; Romans 8:16)

   N.B.—THE SPIRIT IS THE ESSENTIAL FOUNDATION OF MAN; THE SOUL HIS PECULIAR ESSENTIAL FORM; THE BODY HIS ESSENTIAL MANIFESTATION."

We take first of all the term Soul Generally and Specifically. The next chapter deals with "The Fundamental Powers" of the soul, which means the soul as it is influenced either by a degenerate intelligence or by the Spirit of God; there we shall deal with the varied powers of the soul. Then "The Fleshly Presentation of the Soul" will be considered, which means the soul manifesting and expressing itself in the bodily life: and finally, we shall deal with the "Past, Present and Future" of the Soul, and with the theses that have gathered round the doctrine of the soul, which are quite scriptural and yet lead to conclusions most unscriptural.

In the Old Testament the word "soul," i.e., animal soul, the soul that is present only in this order of beings, is mentioned about 460 times. In the New Testament the word "soul" is mentioned about 57, with the same meaning. When the Bible mentions a thing over five hundred times, it is time that Christians examined the teaching about it with care.

1. The Term Soul (Generally)
The term "soul" generally, is used in three distinct ways. First, as applied to men and animals alike as distinct from all other creations; second, the more particular use of the word as applied to men distinguished from animals; and third, as applied to one man as distinct from another.

(a) Applied to Men and Animals (Genesis 1:20–21, 24, 30)
The term "soul" here includes animals and men to distinguish them from every other form of creation.

The Bible nowhere says that God has a soul; the only way in which the soul of God is referred to is prophetically in anticipation of the Incarnation. Angels are never spoken of as having souls, because soul has reference to this order of creation and angels belong to another order. Our Lord emphatically had a soul, but of God and of angels the term "soul" is not used. The term "soul" is never applied to plants. A plant has life, but the Bible never speaks of it as having soul.

For there is hope of a tree, if it be cut down, that it will sprout again, and that the tender branch thereof will not cease. Though the root thereof wax old in the earth, and the stock thereof die in the ground; yet through the scent of water it will bud, and bring forth boughs like a plant. But man dieth, and wasteth away: yea, man giveth up the ghost, and where is he? (Job 14:7–10)

The distinction there is very clear; you can cut off a piece of a plant and the cut off part will grow; but if you cut off the limb of an animal and plant it, it will not grow, the reason being that a plant has no soul, but an animal has. There is nothing said in the Bible about the immortality of animals. The Bible says that there will be animals in the regenerated earth, but nowhere does it say that the animals which we see now are immortal and that when they die they are raised again. The Bible indicates that everything which partakes of the curse through the Fall will be restored by God's mighty Redemption; nothing will be lost.

(b) Applied to Men, Not Animals
And the LORD God formed man of the dust of the ground, and breathed into his nostrils the breath of life; and man became a living soul. (Genesis 2:7)

And so it is written, The first man Adam was made a living soul; the last Adam was made a quickening spirit. (1 Corinthians 15:45)

Soul, then, is something peculiar to men and animals, that God has not, that angels have not, and that plants have not. Man has soul, and brute has soul. What kind of spirit has a brute? Soul is the holder of spirit and body together, then it follows that there must be a spirit in the brute, otherwise we must revise our statement about soul. There is certainly a spirit in the brute, for the Bible reveals that when an animal dies, its spirit "goeth downward." The spirit of the brute is part of the spirit of entire nature, and when the brute dies its spirit goes back again into entire nature. The spirit of entire nature is manifestly a creation of God. The spirit in man which holds his soul and body together is entirely different from the spirit of a brute; it is the human spirit which God created when He breathed into man's nostrils the breath of life. God did not make man a little god; He breathed into his nostrils the spirit which became man's distinct spirit, "and man became a living soul."

Where does man's spirit go when he dies? "The spirit of man . . . goeth upward, and the spirit of the beast . . . goeth downward to the earth" (Ecclesiastes 3:21). Scientists tell us that death is a molecular disturbance, that when we die we are distributed into the spirit of entire nature. The Bible says that the spirit of a man goes back to God. This does not imply that man's spirit is absorbed into God; but that man's spirit goes back to God with the characteristics on it for either judgement or praise. When we deal more narrowly with this subject later on, we shall find that the nature of man's spirit, whether it be sensual or spiritual, is to express itself in soul. The whole effort of the spirit is to try and express itself through the soul, that is, in ordinary physical life.

(c) Applied to Men Individually

Say, I pray thee, thou art my sister, that it may be well with me for thy sake; and my soul shall live because of thee. (Genesis 12:13)

And it came to pass, when he had made an end of speaking unto Saul, that the soul of Jonathan was knit with the soul of David, and Jonathan loved him as his own soul. (1 Samuel 18:1)

These passages describe the use of the term "soul" as an individual personal soul distinct from every other soul. An individual soul cannot be divided or cut up. In popular language we speak of a person expressing soul in music, or in literature or art; or we refer to him as being hard and mechanical and soul-less, and it is to this aspect of soul we are referring here. The phrases "beautiful soul" and "mean soul"[6] refer to the individual aspect of soul. When demon possession is

referred to in the Scripture (e.g. Luke 8:26–39), the body is the location or habitation of other spirits besides the man's own spirit. Thought takes up no room, spirit partakes of the nature of thought, and there is no limit to the number of spirits a man's body may hold during demon possession.

2. The Truth about the Soul (Specifically)
(a) The Soul and Spirit (Genesis 2:7)

What is the relationship between spirit and soul? where did the soul come from? The soul has no existence until the spirit and the body come together; it holds its existence *in fee* entirely by spirit, which statement is the needed complementary truth of what has already been stated, that soul is the holder of spirit and body together.

What is the spirit in a fallen man? "For what man knoweth the things of a man, save the spirit of man which is in him? even so the things of God knoweth no man, but the Spirit of God" (1 Corinthians 2:11). We must approach this subject by making a distinction between sensual man and spiritual man. The spirit in a fallen or sensual man is his mind, which has a vast capacity for God, to Whom, however, he is dead, and the spirit of a fallen man is imprisoned in his soul and degraded by the body. A sensual person may have marvellous ideas, wonderful intelligence, and yet his whole life may be corrupt and rotten. Take Oscar Wilde for instance. It would be difficult to find a more flagrant example of gross immorality, and yet while in prison, after a life of unthinkable immorality, Oscar Wilde wrote a most amazing book entitled *De Profundis,* a book which shows a wonderful grasp of our Lord's teaching. The spirit in Oscar Wilde was nothing more than an intellectual spirit, a spiritual capacity that had no life in itself and was enslaved by the body through the soul. Instead of a fallen man's intelligence being able to lift up his body, it does exactly the opposite; a fallen man's intelligence severs his intellectual life more and more from his bodily life and produces inner hypocrisy. In the case of the lives of certain poets and literary men and geniuses, the exception is to find a man who has a clean life as well as a good mind. You can never judge a man by his intellectual flights. You may hear the most magnificent and inspiring diction from a man who his sunk lower than the beasts in his moral life. He has a sensual spirit; that is, instead of his soul allowing his spirit to lift up his body, it drags it down, and there is a divorce between the man's intellectual life and his practical life.

A spiritual man is quite different. Jesus Christ was a spiritual Personality; the Holy Spirit filled His spirit and kept His soul and body in perfect harmony with God. The meaning of the Atonement is that Jesus

---

6. mean: ordinary, common, low, or ignoble, rather than cruel or spiteful

Christ has power to impart to us the Holy Spirit. Holy Spirit has "life in itself," and immediately that life is manifested in our souls, it wars against what we have been describing. Slowly and surely if we "mind" the Holy Spirit Who fills our spirit and re-energises it, we shall find that He will lift our soul, and with our soul our body, into a totally new unity until the former divorce is annulled. In a spiritual personality the Spirit of Jesus Christ enables the material body of a man to show His nature. The spirit of a man cannot do this for it has not life in itself. Never judge a man by the fact that he has good ideas; and never judge yourself by the fact that you have stirring visions of things. We are told that a man cannot teach the doctrine of entire sanctification unless he is entirely sanctified himself, but he can. The devil can teach entire sanctification if he pleases. This power is one of the most dangerous powers of the soul. There are "spiritual" persons and "sensual" persons. A sensual person is one in whom the divorce between mental conception and practical living is discernible. The only solution of the problem lies in receiving the Holy Spirit, not believing Him, or complimenting Him; but *receiving* Him. When we receive the Holy Spirit, He so energises our spirit that we are able to detect the things that are wrong, and we are enabled to rectify them if we "mind" the Holy Spirit. This is the Scotch use of the term "mind," and it means "remember to obey." It carries with it the meaning of another Scotch word, "lippen," that is, "trust." Mind the Holy Spirit, mind His light, mind His convictions, mind His guidance, and slowly and surely the sensual personality will be turned into a spiritual personality.

(b) The Soul and Body
For as the body without the spirit is dead, so faith without works is dead also. (James 2:26)

The body has the earth as its ancestor. "The being of man plants its foot on the earth and the being of earth culminates in man, for both are destined to the fellowship of one history." We have insisted all through these studies that from God's standpoint man's chief glory is his body. "But we have this treasure in earthen vessels, that the excellency of the power may be of God, and not of us" (2 Corinthians 4:7). The "treasure" is God's Spirit being manifested in a human spirit. God's Spirit cannot be manifested in angels, or in animals, or in plants; it can only be manifested in human "earthen vessels." Do not make that mean that Paul is pouring contempt on the "earthen vessel"; it is exactly the opposite. Jesus Christ took on Him the nature of the "earthen vessel," not the nature of angels. "Of the earth, earthy," is man's glory, not his shame, and it is in the earth, earthy, that Jesus Christ's full regenerating work is to have its ultimate reach. Man's body and the earth on which he treads are to partake

in the final restitution. Our soul's history is not furthered "in spite of our bodies," but because of our bodies. Nothing can enter the soul but through the senses, God enters into the soul through the senses. "The words that I speak unto you, they are spirit, and they are life." Beware of the absorption type of mysticism, it is never presented in the Bible. All that the soul retains comes through its bodily senses, and when the Holy Spirit is finding His way into a man's spirit it is through the bodily senses on the physical side. "He shall glorify Me," said Jesus; in my mind, my imagination, in and through my body. And again, He shall "bring all things to your remembrance, whatsoever I have said unto you." This can only be done by the material brain working through the body. Beware of all inward impressions. Beware of all instincts which you cannot curb by the wisdom taught in God's Book. If you take every impression as a call of the Spirit of God, you will end in hallucinations (see 2 Thessalonians 2:10–12). Test every movement by the tests Jesus Christ has given, and they are all tangible, sensible tests. The way to test men, Jesus says, is "by their fruits." We say that the fruit of the Spirit has altogether to do with the spiritual, but the Bible reveals that the spiritual must show itself in the physical. God knows no divorce whatever between the three aspects of a man's nature, spirit, soul and body, they must be at one, and they are at one either in damnation or in salvation. If a man has not the Holy Spirit of God energising his spirit, he will come to be judged more and more by the judgement passed on his bodily life. Beware of the people who teach that though a man's body may sin, his soul does not. No such distinctions are taught in God's Word. In God's judgement, body, soul and spirit go together. If a man is not enlivened by the Holy Spirit, his intelligence has no power to lift him; he cannot lift himself by his ideas, or intelligent notions, or knowledge. That is why intelligence is never the primary thing from God's standpoint. "If any man will know My doctrine," says Jesus, "let him do the will" (see John 7:17)—performance of the will before perception of the doctrine always in spiritual matters. Immediately we receive the Holy Spirit and are energised by God, we shall find our bodies are the first place of attack for the enemy, because the body has been the centre which ruled the soul and divided it from spiritually intelligent standards; consequently the body is the last "stake" of Satan. The body is the "margin of the battle" for you and me. Health is simply the perfect balance of the body with the outer world; when anything upsets that balance we become diseased. Immediately the Holy Spirit comes in, disturbance occurs, physically, morally and spiritually, and the balance is upset. Jesus Christ said, "I came not to send peace, but a sword." What balance will the Holy Spirit give back?

The old one? No! We can never get back the old balance of health again; we have to get a new balance, viz., that of holiness, which means the balance of our disposition with God's laws. We shall find the "choppy waters" come just there. So many misunderstand why it is their bodies are attacked now that they are spiritual in a way they never were attacked before they were spiritual. We shall deal later with the difference between natural sickness and demoniacal sickness. The Bible has a great deal to say about them both. The Bible is the only Book that throws light on our physical condition, on our soul condition, and on our spiritual condition. In the Bible the sense of smell and sight, etc., are not used as metaphors only; they are identified with the nature of the soul's life. This accounts for what people are apt to call the vulgar teaching of the Bible.

God has safeguarded us in every way. Spiritualism is the great crime; it pushes down God's barriers and brings us into contact with forces we cannot control. On the other hand, if we give ourselves over to Jesus Christ and are ruled by Him, the Holy Spirit can do through us anything He chooses. "I beseech you, therefore, brethren . . . present your bodies a living sacrifice," and "bodies" means "faculties" as well. Why should we expect God to deal with less than the devil deals with? A good man is a flesh and blood good man, not an impression. The body is the "vessel" of the soul, and it enables the soul to turn its inward life into an outward life.

Chapter VI
SOUL: THE ESSENCE, EXISTENCE AND EXPRESSION
Fundamental Powers of the Soul

1. Contraction
   (a) First Power. Self-comprehending (Deuteronomy 13:6–7; 1 Samuel 18:1)
   (b) Second Power. Stretching Beyond Itself (Psalm 27:12)

2. Expansion
   (c) Third Power. Self-living (Job 2:6; John 10:11)
   (d) Fourth Power. Spirit-penetrated (Isaiah 26:9; Jude 19)

3. Rotation
   (e) Fifth Power. Stirred Sensually or Spiritually (Exodus 23:9; 1 Peter 2:11)
   (f) Sixth Power. Speaking the Spirit's Thoughts (Genesis 41:40)
   (g) Seventh Power. Sum Total in Unity (Jeremiah 38:16)

1. Contraction

We mean by fundamental, the powers that work in the interior of the soul. The soul's existence has its origin in the spirit and in its struggle to realise itself. This is the counterpart of the statement made in the last chapter, viz., that the soul is the holder of the body and spirit together.

By Contraction, we mean that the soul has power to contract into itself. By Expansion, we mean that the soul has power to strive away from itself, reaching beyond itself; and by Rotation we mean that the soul has the power of expressing itself by the restlessness of becoming.

This mechanical division is merely an arbitrary way of presenting a complex truth. All scientific laws exist in men's heads and are simply attempts to explain observed facts. For instance it is a dangerous mistake to talk about the law of gravitation as if it were a thing. The law of gravitation is the explanation given by scientific men of certain observed facts, and to say that Jesus Christ "broke the law of gravitation" when He walked on the sea, and when He ascended, is a misstatement. He brought in a new series of facts for which the law of gravitation, so-called, could not account.

(a) First Power. Self-Comprehending

If . . . thy friend, which is as thine own soul, entice thee secretly, saying, Let us go and serve other gods, which thou hast not known . . . (Deuteronomy 13:6–7; see also 1 Samuel 18:1)

These verses indicate the power of the soul to comprehend itself as an individual separate from every other individual. Watch your own experience, and you will recognise this soul power at once. When a child begins to be self-conscious, it is this power that is awakening, the power to contract into itself and to realise that it is different from its father and mother and from all other children, and the tendency to shut up the life to itself increases. This power shows itself in feelings of isolation and separation, alternating between pride and shyness. Self-consciousness drags down the harmony of the soul. In some people it lasts a long time; some never get beyond the manifestation of this power of soul, viz., the power to contract into themselves, the power to be different from everybody else; they have not gone on to realise that they have the power to expand, that is, to come into contact with other souls without being afraid or timid.

That is the first power in a natural soul. Now take it in a soul born again of the Spirit of God, how does this power of the soul express itself? The power of self-comprehension in a born-again soul shows itself in opposition to sinfulness. Watch the swing of the pendulum, as it were, in your own life, and in the life of anybody newly born again of the Spirit; the life goes to the opposite extreme of the way it lived when in the world, e.g., if it was given to finery and dress when in the world, it will go to the opposite extreme on its introduction to the new life. This is the first recognisable power of an individual soul.

(b) Second Power. Stretching beyond Itself
Deliver me not over unto the will of mine enemies: for false witnesses are risen up against me, and such as breathe out cruelty. (Psalm 27:12)

This power of the soul causes a person to find out first not the forces in agreement with it, but those that are different from it. Other souls seem to be in opposition to it. The boy who has become self-conscious always imagines every other boy is his enemy, and he suspects any boy who wants to become his friend. This power of the soul also makes a man realise that he can do pretty well what he likes with his body—a dangerous moment in a human life. Or again it makes a man realise he is able to deceive everyone else. There is no restriction at all when this power first dawns. I realise I can satisfy my bodily appetites as I choose; I can also cunningly deceive everyone else. If I am a servant, I can easily defraud my master or mistress; if I am a business man, I can easily defraud the public. This power of the soul can be seen worked out to its complete issue in the life of the world.

In a spiritual nature this power of the soul shows itself in opposition to sinful craving. Jesus Christ says, in effect: "If you are My disciple, you will easily be defrauded, but you will not allow yourself to be defrauded from the simplicity of the Gospel." Knowledge of evil broadens a man's mind, makes him tolerant, but paralyses his action. Knowledge of good broadens a man's mind, makes him intolerant of all sin, and shows itself in intense activity. A bad man, an evil-minded man, is amazingly tolerant of everything and everyone, no matter whether they are good or bad, Christian or not, but his power of action is paralysed entirely. he is tolerant of everything—the devil, the flesh, the world, sin, and everything else. Jesus Christ never tolerated sin for one moment, and when His nature is getting its way in a soul the same intolerance is shown, and it manifests itself "not with eye service." If I am a servant I won't serve my master or mistress with this power of my soul realising I have power to

deceive. I will use it to show that I belong to Jesus Christ. Neither shall I use this power of my soul to do what I like with my body. "Not with eye-service, as menpleasers; but as the servants of Christ, doing the will of God from the heart" (Ephesians 6:6). "Servants, obey in all things your masters according to the flesh; not with eye-service as menpleasers; but in singleness of heart, fearing God" (Colossians 3:22).

In a spiritual soul this power of the soul will show itself in intense opposition to all sinful cravings. A soul that is born again does everything, from sweeping a room to preaching the Gospel, from cleaning streets to governing a nation, for the glory of God. This second power of the soul enables it to stretch beyond itself; the whole mainspring of the soul's life is altered.

2. Expansion
(c) Third Power. Self-Living
I am the good shepherd: the good shepherd giveth His life for the sheep. (John 10:11)

And the LORD said unto Satan, Behold, he is in thine hand; but save his life. (Job 2:6)

These passages refer to the one power in a man that neither God nor the devil can touch without the man's sanction. The devil has power up to a certain point, but he cannot touch a man's life, and whenever Jesus Christ presents the Gospel of God to a soul, it is always on the line of "Are you willing?" There is never any coercion. God has so constituted us that there must be a free willingness on our part. This power is at once the most fearful and the most glorious power. A human soul can withstand the devil successfully, and it can also withstand God successfully. This self-living power is the essence of the human spirit, which is as immortal as God's Spirit and as indestructible; whether the human spirit be good or bad, it is as immortal as God. This power of the soul enables it to put itself on a par with God; this is the very essence of Satan. The power that can make a man either a compeer of the Lord or a compeer of the devil is the most terrible power of the soul. Jesus Christ is referring to this power when He says, "I lay down My life. . . . No man taketh it from Me, but I lay it down of Myself."

When the soul is born again and lifted into the domain our Lord lives in, this power shows itself in opposition to sinful passionateness. Passionateness means something that carries everything before it. The prince of this world is intense, and the Spirit of God is intense. When Paul talks about the flesh and the Spirit working in a man's soul, he expresses the intensity by using the word "lust." The Spirit lusts, passionately desires the whole life for God; and the mind of the flesh lusts, passionately longs, for the whole life back again in the service of the world. In the spiritual realm passionateness also means something that overcomes every obstacle. When the writer to the Hebrews talks about perfection, he means this overwhelming passion which carries a soul right on to all God has for it. "Be filled with the Spirit," this is the key word of life. The Bible indicates that we overcome the world not by passionlessness, not by the patience of exhaustion, but by passion, the passion of an intense and all-consuming love for God. This is the characteristic in a born-again soul—opposition to every sinful passionateness. Do insist in your own mind that God does not work in vague, gentle impressions in a human soul, but in violent oppositions which rend and tear the soul, making it, instead of a place of harmonious happiness, exactly the opposite for a season. This experience is true in every soul that is going on with God. When we are first introduced to the life of God there is violent opposition to everything that used to be prevalent, and that it is so is not a mistake, it is what God intends, because there is the force of a totally new life.

(d) Fourth Power. Spirit Penetrated
With my soul have I desired Thee in the night; yea, with my spirit within me will I seek Thee early. (Isaiah 26:9; see also Jude 19)

We mean by "Spirit-Penetrated" the spiritual power in man which struggles to express itself in soul. The spirit of man in an unregenerate nature is the power of mind not energised by the Holy Spirit which has no "life in itself." It proves utterly futile in lifting the body, and produces a great divorce between the ideal and the real. Every kind of intellectual excellence is a snare of Satan unless the spirit of the man has been renewed by the incoming of the Spirit of God. A man's intellect may give him noble ideas and power to express them through his soul in language but it does not give him power to carry them into action. The charge of idolatry is very apt here. We are apt to ridicule, or pass over with a smile, the descriptions given of idolatry in, say, the Book of Isaiah, where the writer refers to a tree being taken and one part of it used to cook the man's food and the other part carved into an idol before which the man bows and worships; yet this is exactly what men do with their ideas. The intellect forms ideas for guiding a man's physical life, and then takes other ideas and worships them as God, and if a man has made his own ideas his god, he is greater than his own god. This is not such a terrible power, perhaps, as the self-living power of the soul, but it is a power that will work havoc unless the soul is right with God. It is the power that produces internal hypocrisy, the power that makes me able to think good thoughts while I live a bad life, unconvicted.

How does this power show itself in those who are born again of the Spirit of God? This power shows itself in opposition to secularity. Take your own experience, those of you who are spiritual—spiritual in the Bible sense, identified with the Lord Jesus Christ in a practical way—you cannot make a distinction now between secular and sacred, it is all sacred; but in the first realisation of this power the line is drawn clearly and strongly between what is called secular and what is called sacred. In the life of Jesus Christ there was no division into secular and sacred, but with us when this power begins to be realised it always manifests itself in a line of cleavage. There are certain things we won't do; certain things we won't look at; certain things we won't eat; certain hours we won't sleep. It is not wrong, it is the Spirit of God in a soul beginning to utilise the powers of the soul for God; and as the soul goes on it comes to a full-orbed condition, where it manifests itself as in the life of the Lord Jesus and all is sacred.

If you obey the Spirit of God and practise in your physical life all that God has put in your heart by His Spirit, when the crisis comes you will find your nature will stand by you. So many people misunderstand why they fall. It comes from this idea, "Now I have received the grace of God, I am all right." Paul says he did not "frustrate the grace of God," i.e., receive it in vain. If we do not go on practising day by day and week by week, working out what God has worked in, when a crisis comes God's grace is there right enough, but our nature is not. Our nature has not been brought into line by practice and consequently does not stand by us, and down we go and then we blame God. We must bring our bodily life into line by practice day by day, hour by hour, moment by moment, then when the crisis comes we shall find not only God's grace but our own nature will stand by us, and the crisis will pass without any disaster at all, but exactly the opposite will happen, the soul will be built up into a stronger attitude towards God.

3. Rotation
(e) Fifth Power. Stirred Sensually or Spiritually
Also thou shalt not oppress a stranger: for ye know the heart of a stranger, seeing ye were strangers in the land of Egypt. (Exodus 23:9)

Dearly beloved, I beseech you as strangers and pilgrims, abstain from fleshly lusts, which war against the soul. (1 Peter 2:11)

Remember that the soul is manifested as the spirit struggles to make itself expressed. Exodus 23:1–9 is a magnificent passage; it is intensely, movingly practical in every detail, and there this power of the soul is clearly recognisable. It fits itself on with the second power, viz., the power we have to deceive everybody else, to do cunning things, to defraud, to utilise other people for our own ends; and the warning is, be careful not to be stirred in your soul by the wrong spirit. If the soul can be stirred by its own cunning, the cunning of a man's own inner nature, it can be stirred by vileness and abominable sensuality through the senses (1 Peter 2:11).

How does this power show itself in a regenerate soul? It shows itself in opposition to worldly bondage. You will find in your own experience, and in all recorded experiences, that when the life is going on along God's line, God puts the fear of you on those who are on the outside because of the scorn you have of worldly bondages. The Spirit of God in you will not allow you to bow your neck to any yoke but the yoke of the Lord Jesus Christ. When you stand on this platform of God's grace, you see instantly that the bondage is in the world. The etiquette and standards of the world are an absolute bondage, and those who live in them are abject slaves, and yet the extraordinary thing is that when a worldly person sees anyone emancipated and under the yoke of the Lord Jesus Christ, he says they are in bondage, whereas exactly the opposite is true. True liberty exists only when the soul has this holy scorn in it, "I will bow my neck to no yoke but the yoke of the Lord Jesus Christ." Our Lord was meek to all that His Father did, but intolerant to all the devil did; He would not suffer compromise with the devil in any shape or form. This power of the soul, then, when the soul is born again, manifests itself in opposition to all worldly bondage.

(f) Sixth Power. Speaking the Spirit's Thoughts
Thou shalt be over my house, and according unto thy word shall all my people be ruled: only in the throne will I be greater than thou. (Genesis 41:40)

We are now dealing with Rotation, the restlessness of becoming. That is how all these powers are going to manifest themselves in a fully matured soul. Genesis 41:40 is a picture of a soul right with God; but remember there is a corresponding picture. A man in whom all the powers of the soul are developing will come to a place where he shows literally, not only with his mouth, but with his eyes and every power of his body, who is on the throne of his life. If it is the prince of this world, the man is prime minister of his own body under the devil. When the full powers of the soul are developed I am obliged to carry out the behests of the ruling monarch.

How does this power show itself when a soul is born again of the Spirit of God? It shows itself in opposition to worldly thoughts and customs. "Only in the throne will I be greater than thou." Take Pharaoh as a picture of Jesus Christ; the soul that is born again and is going on with God, who has been identified with Jesus Christ in practical sanctification and has the full powers of the soul developed and manifested, that soul is prime minister of his own body under Jesus Christ's dominion. That is the ideal, and it is not an ideal only, but an ideal which Jesus Christ expects us to carry out—all the powers of the

soul working through the body in an express personality, revealing the Ruler to be the Lord Jesus Christ.

(g) Seventh Power. Sum Total in Unity
As the LORD liveth, that made us this soul, I will not put thee to death, neither will I give thee into the hand of these men that seek thy life. (Jeremiah 38:16)

The sum total is a perfect unity of badness or a perfect unity of goodness. "All the souls that came with Jacob into Egypt . . ." (Genesis 46:26 RV). The word "soul" there refers to the full maturity of the powers manifested in the bodily life. This is the description of a full-grown man, whether he is a bad man or a good man, and when a soul gets into full maturity of expression, the chances are he will never alter. In Jeremiah 38:16, soul is mentioned in the same way. This is not the soul in its beginnings, in its chaotic state; but the soul absolutely mastered by the ruling spirit and expressing itself through the body.

How does this perfection of soul life show itself in a born-again man who is living the life God wants him to live? It shows itself in opposition to all other powers, and manifests itself in its bodily life in "the wisdom that is from above." It is literally the uncrushable loveliness of a soul manifesting God's rule, all its powers now in harmony. This is not in Heaven, but on earth. It is not mental perfection, nor bodily perfection: it is the perfection of a soul's attitude when all its powers are under the control of the Spirit of God. All the "corners" have been chipped away; all the extreme swinging of the pendulum has been regulated; all the chaotic turmoil has become ordered, and the life is now manifesting the life of the Lord Jesus in its mortal flesh.

By way of revision, we find that these powers of the soul show themselves in every one of us more or less. For instance, we would never think of judging a boy or girl by the same standard of judgement we would pass on them when they are mature, because a boy or a girl is not in full grip of a character; but when once a soul is matured, the character which is manifested meets with severe judgement. There is no excuse to be made for it now; all its powers are consolidated and the wrong it does is not the wrong of an impulse, it is the wrong of a dead set. When the soul is consolidated and is right with God, the whole character manifests something which bears a strong family likeness to Jesus Christ. There is, however, a chaotic period in Christian experience. Read the Apostle Paul's earnest, almost motherlike, solicitation over his young converts; he almost seems to "croon" over them, to use an old Scotch word, to agonise in heart over them, because of the chaotic state of their souls. Jesus Christ commissioned Peter, and the other disciples through him to "feed My lambs."

Chapter VII

SOUL: THE ESSENCE, EXISTENCE AND EXPRESSION
Fleshly Presentation of the Soul

1. In Embryo
   - (a) Before Consciousness (Psalm 139:15; Hosea 12:3; Genesis 25:22; Luke 1:41)
   - (b) Breath Consciousness (Genesis 2:7; Isaiah 2:22)
   - (c) Blood Circulation (Genesis 9:4; Leviticus 17:10, 14)

2. In Evolution
   - (d) "Hub" of Life (Proverbs 4:23)
   - (e) "Hubbub" of Life
     - (1) Sense of Sight (Psalm 119:37)
     - (2) Sense of Hearing (Job 12:11)
     - (3) Sense of Taste (Psalm 119:103)
     - (4) Sense of Smell (Genesis 8:21; 2 Corinthians 2:14–16)
     - (5) Sense of Touch (Acts 17:27; 1 John 1:1)

3. In Expression
   - (f) Hilarity of Life (Ecclesiastes 11:9; Luke 6:45)
   - (g) Himself (Judges 8:18; Luke 2:40, 52; Ephesians 4:13)

By the word "fleshly" we do not mean what the Apostle Paul meant when he uses the word in his Epistles; we are using the word to denote this natural body. Paul's use of the word, unless prefaced with "mortal," means a disposition of mind.

The subject is divided under three headings: in Embryo, in Evolution, and in Expression. In Embryo means in the beginning; Evolution means growth, the growth of the human soul. Evolution is a fact both scientific and scriptural, that is, if we mean by Evolution that there is growth in every species; but not growth from one species into another. There is growth in a plant, in an animal and in a man; and that is the only way in which we use the word. The last division simply means the Expression of the soul in and through the body.

1. In Embryo
(a) Before Consciousness
And it came to pass, that, when Elisabeth heard the salutation of Mary, the babe leaped in her womb; and Elisabeth was filled with the Holy Ghost. (Luke 1:4; see also Genesis 25:22; Hosea 12:3)

In the very beginning of human life, body, soul and spirit are together. "My substance was not hid from Thee, when I was made in secret, and curiously wrought in the lowest parts of the earth" (Psalm 139:15). Modern tendencies of thought which are working great havoc indicate that a child has not a soul until it is born into this world. The Bible says that body, soul and spirit develop together. This may not appear to the majority of us as being of any importance, but it will do so when we come in contact with the views that are abroad to-day, even amongst some who call themselves Christian teachers, but who are really wolves among the sheep and whose teaching comes from the bottomless pit.

(b) Breath Consciousness
And the LORD God formed man of the dust of the ground, and breathed into his nostrils the breath of life; and man became a living soul. (Genesis 2:7; see also Isaiah 2:22)

In a multitude of verses in the Bible, the soul life and the breath of the body are identified. The Bible teaches that it is not the body that breathes, but the soul. The body did not breathe in the beginning before God breathed into man's nostrils the breath of life; so as far as conscious soul life is concerned, it depends on our breathing. All through God's Book the soul life is connected with the breathing; in fact, it is incorporated into our idea of life that when breath is suspended, life is gone. "The soul is departed" is the popular phrase.

(c) Blood Circulation
But flesh with the life thereof, which is the blood thereof, shall ye not eat. (Genesis 9:4; see also Leviticus 17:10–14)

In the Bible the soul is connected and identified with breath and blood—two fleshly, physical things. In Genesis 9:4 blood and soul are alternate terms, they are identified completely, and the verses in God's Book that prove this are innumerable. When the blood is spilt, the soul is gone; when the breath is taken, the soul is gone. The whole life of a man consists physically in his breath and in his blood. The soul in working itself into the blood never fails to impart to it the peculiar character of its own life. This psychologically is brought out very clearly by our Lord's statement in John 6:53, "Except ye eat the flesh of the Son of man, and drink His blood, ye have no life in you." An unobvious revelation is that when I eat and drink and discern the Lord's body, or, in other words, receive my food and drink from Him, the physical nourishment thus derived enables my Lord to manifest Himself in my flesh and blood. If I do not discern the Lord's body, and do not receive my food from Him, my physical nourishment will humiliate Him in me. The ruling disposition of the soul shows itself in the blood, the physical blood. In every language, good blood and bad blood is referred to; merciful blood and tender blood, hot or cold blood, and this is based on Scriptural teaching. Jesus Christ insists on the fact that if we are His disciples it will be revealed in the blood, i.e., the physical life. The old soul tyranny and disposition, the old selfish determination to seek our own ends, manifests itself in our body, through our blood; and when that disposition of soul is altered, the alteration shows itself at once in the blood also. Instead of the old tempers and the old passions being manifested in our physical blood, the good temper reveals itself. It never does to remove Jesus Christ's spiritual teaching into the domain of the inane and vague, it must come right down where the devil works; and just as the devil works not in vague ways but through flesh and blood, so does the Lord, and the characteristics of the soul for better or worse are shown in the blood.

The first fundamental reference in the verse, "And without shedding of blood is no remission" of sins, is unquestionably to our Lord's Atonement; and yet there is a direct reference to ourselves. Do we begin to know what the Bible means by "the blood of Jesus Christ"? Blood and life are inseparable. In the Bible the experiences of salvation and sanctification are never separated as we separate them; they are separable in experience, but when God's Book speaks of being "in Christ" it is always in terms of entire sanctification. We are apt to look upon the blood of Christ as a kind of magic-working thing, instead of an impartation of His very life. The whole purpose of being born again and being identified with the death of the Lord Jesus is that His blood may flow through our mortal body; then the tempers and the affections and the dispositions which were manifested in the life of the Lord will be manifested in us in some degree. Our present-day "wise talk" is to push all the teaching of Jesus Christ into a remote domain, but the New Testament drives its teaching straight down to the essential necessity of the physical expression of spiritual life; that just as the bad soul life shows itself in the body, so the good soul life will show itself there too. There are two sides to the Atonement—it is not only the life of Christ *for* me but His life *in* me for

my life; no Christ *for* me if I do not have Christ *in* me. All through there is to be this strenuous, glorious practising in our bodily life of the changes which God has wrought in our soul through His Spirit, and the only proof that we are in earnest is that we work out what God works in. As we apply this truth to ourselves, we shall find in practical experience that God does alter passions and nerves and tempers. God alters every physical thing in a human being so that these bodies can be used now as slaves to the new disposition. We can make our eyes, and ears, and every one of our bodily organs express as slaves the altered disposition of our soul. Remember, then, that blood is the manifestation of the soul life, and that all through the Bible God applies moral characteristics to the blood. The expressions "innocent blood," and guilty blood, have reference to the soul, and the soul life must show itself in the physical connection.

2. In Evolution
(d) Hub of Life
Keep thy heart with all diligence; for out of it are the issues of life. (Proverbs 4:23)

"Hub" literally means the centre of a wheel, and the word is used here to indicate the centre of the soul life, of the personal life and the spirit life. This will be dealt with more fully when we come to the chapters on "Heart." The Bible places in the heart everything that the modern psychologist places in the head.

(e) Hubbub of Life
By "hubbub" we mean exactly what the word implies, a tremendous confusion. The confusion in the soul life is brought about by the exercise of our senses. "In the Bible, psychological terms are not merely metaphors, but reflect the organic condition of the soul." The body makes itself inward by means of the soul, and the spirit makes itself outward by means of the soul. The soul is the binder of these two together. There is not one part of the human body left out in God's Book; every part is dealt with and made to have a direct connection either with sin or with holiness. It is not accidental but part of the Divine revelation. The five senses do not seem to the majority of us to have any spiritual meaning, but in the Bible they have. In the Bible the senses are dealt with in anything but a slight manner; they are dealt with as being expressions of the soul life. The Bible reveals that every part of man's physical life is closely connected with sin or with salvation, and that anything that sin has put wrong, Jesus Christ can put right. We are dealing with soul as it expresses itself through the body. The organs of the body are used as indicators of the state of the spiritual life. We mentioned previously in connection with breathing, that the internal part of a man's being

is affected by his spiritual relationships. If his spiritual connections are not right with God, his bodily condition will, sooner or later, manifest the disorganisation. This is proved over and over again in the case of mental diseases. In most insane persons a bodily organ is seriously affected, and the old method of dealing with insanity was to try and get that organ healed. The modern method is simply to leave the organ alone and concentrate on the brain. When the mind is right, the disease in the organ disappears.

(1) Sense of Sight

Turn away mine eyes from beholding vanity; and quicken Thou me in Thy way. (Psalm 119:37)

How am I going to have my eyes kept from beholding vanity? By having the disposition of my soul altered. God controls the whole thing, and you will find that you can control it too when once He has given you a start. That is the marvellous impetus of the salvation of Jesus Christ. Our eyes record to the brain what they look at, but our disposition makes our eyes look at what it wants them to look at, and they will soon pay no attention to anything else. When the disposition is right, the eyes, literally the body, may be placed wherever you like and the disposition will guard what it records. This is not a figure of speech; it is a literal experience. God does alter the desire to look at the things we used to look at; and we find our eyes are guarded because He has altered the disposition of our soul life.

(2) Sense of Hearing

Doth not the ear try words? (Job 12:11)

Jesus Christ continually referred to hearing: "He that hath ears to hear, let him hear." We say that He means the ears of our heart, but that is very misleading. He means our physical ears which are trained to hear by the disposition of our soul life. God spoke to Jesus once and the people said it thundered, Jesus did not think it thundered; His ears were trained by the disposition of His soul to know His Father's voice (see John 12:28–30). We can elaborate this thought endlessly all through God's Book. I will always hear what I listen for, and the ruling disposition of the soul determines what I listen for, just as the ruling disposition either keeps the eyes from beholding vanity or makes them behold nothing else. When Jesus Christ alters our disposition, He gives us the power to hear as He hears. A telegraph operator does not hear the ticking of the machine, his ears are trained to detect the message; we detect only the jingle and tapping of the machine and can make nothing of it. You hear people say, "Thank God, I heard His voice!" How did they hear it? The disposition of the soul enabled the ears to hear something which the soul interpreted at once. It is always true that we only hear what we want to hear, and we shout the other sounds down by controversy and dispute. "Who hath believed our report?"—literally, "that which we have heard"—"and to whom hath the arm of the LORD been revealed?" (Isaiah 53:1 RV). We have either a disposition of soul that can discern the arm of the Lord, or we are just like the beasts of the field who take things as they come and see nothing in them. "I was as a beast before Thee," said the Psalmist—without any spiritual intelligence. The disposition of my soul determines what I see, and the disposition of my soul determines what I hear.

(3) Sense of Tasting

How sweet are Thy words unto my taste! yea, sweeter than honey to my mouth! (Psalm 119:103)

We are getting more and more remote and more difficult to understand from the ordinary, unspiritual standpoint. We have entirely divorced tasting and smelling, seeing and hearing and touching, from spiritual conditions, because the majority of Christian workers have never been trained in what the Bible has to say about ourselves. It can be proved over and over again, not only in personal experience, but all through God's Book, that He does alter the taste, not merely mental tastes, but physical tastes, the taste for food and drink; but there is something far more practical even than that, the blessing of God on our soul life gives us an added sensitiveness of soul akin to taste or to sight or healing.

(4) Sense of Smell

And the LORD smelled a sweet savour; and the LORD said in His heart, I will not again curse the ground any more for man's sake. . . . (Genesis 8:21; see also 2 Corinthians 2:14–16)

The Bible has a great deal to say about the sense of smell, and yet it is the one sense we make nothing of. This sense to the majority of us has only one meaning, viz., an olfactory nerve that makes us conscious of pleasant things or of exactly the opposite; but the Bible deals with the sense of smell in another way. Read the following quotation from a book written by Helen Keller, entitled *The World I Live In*, the chapter is entitled, "Smell, the Fallen Angel." Remember, Helen Keller writes as one who can neither see nor hear nor speak.

For some inexplicable reason the sense of smell does not hold the high position it deserves among its sisters. There is something of the fallen angel about it. When it woos us with woodland scents and beguiles us with the fragrance of lovely gardens, it is admitted frankly to our discourse. But when it gives us warning of something noxious in our vicinity, it is treated as if the demon had the upper hand of the angel, and is relegated to outer darkness, punished for its faithful service. It is most difficult to keep the true significance of words when one discusses the prejudices of mankind and I find it hard to give an account of odour perceptions which shall at once be dignified and truthful.

In my experience. smell is most important, and I find that there is high authority for the nobility of the sense which we have neglected and disparaged. It is recorded that the Lord commanded that incense be burnt before Him continually with a sweet savour. I doubt if there is any sensation arising from sight more delightful than the odours which filter through sun-warmed, wind-tossed branches, or the tide of scents which swells, subsides, and rises again wave on wave, filling the wide world with invisible sweetness. A whiff of the universe makes us dream of worlds we have never seen, recalls in a flash entire epochs of our dearest experiences. I never smell daisies without living over again the ecstatic mornings that my teacher and I spent wandering in the fields, while I learned new words and the names of things. Smell is a potent wizard that transports us across a thousand miles and all the years we have lived. The odour of fruits wafts me to my Southern home, to my childish frolics in the peach orchard. Other odours, instantaneous and fleeting, cause my heart to dilate joyously or contract with remembered grief. Even as I think of smells, my nose is full of scents that start awake sweet memories of summers gone and ripening grain-fields far away.

In Helen Keller the sense of smell takes the place of sight. This is a case which brings the Bible idea more home to us. Let this subject be revised in our Bible study, and let us see whether we are not treating whole tracts of our sense-life indifferently, not understanding that we can develop and cultivate our eyes, and nose, and mouth, and ears, and every organ of the body to manifest the disposition which Jesus Christ has put into us. Every sense that has been disorganised can be reorganised; not only the senses that we are dealing with, but other senses, every one of them, is mentioned in God's Book and is regulated either by the Spirit of God or by the spirit of Satan. When Paul refers to lust he never places it in the body, but in the disposition of the soul. "Let not sin therefore reign in your mortal body, that ye should obey it in the lusts thereof." Jesus Christ had a fleshly body as we have, but He was never tempted by lust, because lust resides in the ruling disposition, not in the body. When God changes the ruling disposition, the same body that was used as the instrument of sin to work all manner of uncleanness and unrighteousness, can now be used as

the slave of the new disposition. It is not a different body; it is the same body, with a new disposition.

(5) Sense of Touch
That they should seek the Lord, if haply they might feel after Him, and find Him, though He be not far from every one of us. (Acts 17:27)

That which . . . our hands have handled, of the Word of life. (1 John 1:1)

These passages refer not to mental feeling, but to real, downright, bodily feeling. The disciples had "felt" God Incarnate in Jesus Christ. This is where the issue is so strong between New Testament teaching and the Unitarian teaching. God does not ignore feeling and the sense of touch; He elevates them. The first effort of the soul towards bringing the body into harmony with the new disposition is an effort of faith. The soul has not yet got the body under way, therefore in the meanwhile feeling has to be discounted. When the new disposition enters the soul, the first steps have to be taken in the dark, without feeling; but immediately the soul has gained control, all bodily organs are brought into physical harmony with the ruling disposition.

3. In Expression
(f) Hilarity of Life
Rejoice, O young man, in thy youth; and let thy heart cheer thee in the days of thy youth, and walk in the ways of thine heart, and in the sight of thine eyes: but know thou, that for all these things God wilt bring thee into judgement. (Ecclesiastes 11:9)

For out of the abundance of the heart his mouth speaketh. (Luke 6:45)

These passages refer to the physical hilarity of life. Remember, a bad man whose life is wrong has a hilariously happy time, and a good man whose life is right has a hilarious time. All in between are more or less diseased and sick, there is something wrong somewhere: the healthy pagan and the healthy saint are the only ones who are hilarious. The New Testament writers, especially the Apostle Paul, are intense on the hilarity of life. Enthusiasm is the idea, intoxicated with the life of God. Watch nature—if men do not get thrilled in the right way, they will get thrilled in the wrong way. If they are not thrilled by the Spirit of God, they will try to get thrilled with strong drink. "Be not drunk with wine, wherein is excess," says Paul, "but be filled with the Spirit." We have no business to be half-dead spiritually, to hang like clogs on God's plan; we have no business to be sickly, unless it is a preparatory stage for something better, or God is nursing us through some spiritual illness: but if it is the main characteristic of the life, there is something wrong somewhere. Psalm 73 describes the bad man as having all that heart can desire; this is the expression of soul satisfaction without God. When Solomon says that to fear the Lord shall be "marrow to thy bones" (Proverbs 3:8), he is talking about the physical bones which are affected amazingly by the condition of the soul life. In Luke 11 our Lord gives a description of the bad man: "When a strong man armed keepeth his palace, his goods are in peace," i.e., when Satan, the prince of this world, guards this world, his goods—the souls of men—are in peace; they are quite happy, hilarious and full of life. One of the most misleading statements is that worldlings have not a happy time; they have a thoroughly happy time. The point is that their happiness is on the wrong level, and when they come across Jesus Christ, Who is the enemy of all that happiness, they experience annoyance. People must be persuaded that Jesus Christ has a higher type of life for them, otherwise they feel they had better not have come across Him. When a worldly person who is happy, moral and upright comes in contact with Jesus Christ, Who came to destroy all that happiness and peace and put it on a different level, he has to be persuaded that Jesus Christ is a Being worthy to do this, and instead of the Gospel being attractive at first, it is the opposite. When the Gospel is presented to an unsaved, healthy, happy, hilarious person, there is violent opposition straight away. The gospel of Jesus Christ does not present what men want, it presents exactly what they need. As long as you talk about being happy and peaceful, men like to listen to you; but talk about having the disposition of the soul altered, and that the garden of the soul has first of all to be turned into a wilderness and afterwards into a garden of the Lord, and you will find opposition right away.

(g) Himself

We mean by "himself," not God, but man.

Till we all come in the unity of the faith, and of the knowledge of the Son of God, unto a perfect man, unto the measure of the stature of the fulness of Christ. (Ephesians 4:13; see also Judges 8:18; Luke 2:40, 52)

In these passages we have a description splendidly given of a full-orbed man. A full-orbed bad man or woman (bad in God's sight) is a wonderful being to look at and a full-orbed man or woman who is right with God is also a wonderful being to look at. The rest of us are simply beings in the making. There is a tremendous fascination about a completely "bad" man; there is nothing more desirable from the standpoint of this world than a thoroughly well-trained bad man or woman, but they are the opponents of Jesus Christ, they hate Him with every power of the soul; I mean the Jesus Christ of the New Testament.

God grant that the ruling disposition of our souls may be so altered that we work out the alteration practically. If we have come into experimental touch with the grace of God and have received His Spirit, are we working it out? Is every organ of our body enslaved to the new disposition? or are we using our eyes for what we want to see, and our bodies for our right to ourselves? If so, we have received the grace of God in vain. God grant that we may determine to work out through our bodies the life which Jesus Christ has put into us by His Spirit.

Chapter VIII

SOUL: THE ESSENCE, EXISTENCE AND EXPRESSION
Past, Present and Future of the Soul

1. Pre-Existence
   (a) Spurious Speculations (Deuteronomy 29:29; Revelation 5:3)
   (b) Startling Scriptures (Jeremiah 1:5; Malachi 3:1; Romans 9:11, 13; Luke 1:41)
   (c) Steadying Scriptures
      (1) No Soul before Body (Genesis 1–2)
      (2) No Soul Destiny Pre-Adamic (Romans 5:12)
      (3) No Soul but by Procreation (Genesis 5)

N.B.—NOTE THE PRE-EXISTENCE OF OUR LORD JESUS CHRIST. JOHN 17:5.

2. Present Existence
   (a) Satisfaction of the Soul (Psalm 66:9, 12, 16, Isaiah 55:3)
   (b) Sins and Surroundings of the Soul (Proverbs 18:7; Psalm 6; Ezekiel 18:4; 1 Peter 1:9)
   (c) Supernatural Setting for the Soul (Luke 9:54–56; Ephesians 6:12; 1 Corinthians 10:20–21)

N.B. SPIRITUALISM IS THE GREAT SOUL
CRIME. SICKNESS, NATURAL AND
DEMONIACAL, WILL BE EXAMINED.

3. Perpetual Existence
   (a) Mortal Aspect of the Soul (Job 14:2; James
       4:14)
   (b) Immortal Aspect of the Soul (Luke 16:19,
       31; 23:43)
   (c) Eternal Life and Eternal Death of the Soul
       (Matthew 10:28; Romans 5:21; 6:23)

In concluding our general survey of this great
theme of the Soul, we purpose to sketch in outline the
Past, Present and Future state of the soul.

1. Pre-Existence
—i.e. the speculation that souls existed in a former
world.

(a) Spurious Speculations
The student cannot be too careful about these speculations. There is no book which lends itself more
readily to speculation than the Bible, and yet all
through the Bible warns against it. By speculation we
mean taking a series of facts and weaving all kinds of
fancies round them. In Deuteronomy 29:29 ("The
secret things belong unto the LORD our God: but
those things which are revealed belong unto us and
to our children for ever . . ."), and Revelation 5:3
("And no man in heaven, nor in earth, neither under
the earth, was able to open the book, neither to look
thereon"), the bounds of human knowledge with
regard to Bible revelation are fairly well marked.
What is revealed in God's Book is for us; what is not
revealed is not for us. Speculation is searching into
what is not revealed. The subject of pre-existence as
it is popularly taught is not revealed in God's Book; it
is a speculation based on certain things said in God's
Book. Theosophy lends itself largely to speculation,
and all theosophic and occult speculations are ultimately dangerous to the mental, moral and spiritual
balance. Speculate if you care to, but never teach any
speculation as a revelation from the Bible.

Speculation comes right down to our lives in very
enticing ways. Telepathy is one enticing way in which
the speculation of transmigration and pre-existence is
introduced to our minds. Telepathy means being able
to discern someone else's thought by my own. This
opens up the line of auto-suggestion. If one man can
suggest thoughts to another man, then Satan can do
the same, and the consciousness of auto-suggestion
on the human side opens the mind to it diabolically.
Telepathy is mentioned because all these occult things
come down to our lives in seemingly harmless phases.
For instance, spiritualism comes by way of palmistry,

reading fortunes in tea-cups or in cards, by planchette,
and so on, and people say there is no harm in any of
these things. There is all the harm and the "backing
up" of the devil in them. Nothing awakens curiosity
more quickly than reading fortunes in tea-cups or by
cards. The same is true of all theosophic speculations,
they come right down to our lives on the line of things
which is wrongly called "psychology" and awaken an
insatiable curiosity.

It has already been stated that the Bible does not
teach pre-existence and yet we have—

(b) Some Startling Scriptures
—which appear to contradict that statement (Jeremiah 1:5; Romans 9:11–13; Luke 1:41).

We have called these startling Scriptures for the
obvious reason that they look as if the Bible did teach
pre-existence. There is, however, what may be termed
a false and a true idea of pre-existence. The false idea
of pre-existence is that we existed as human beings
before we came into this world; the true idea is pre-
existence in the mind of God. It is not an easy subject
to state, but it is one which is revealed in Scripture,
viz., the pre-existence in the mind of God not only
with regard to the great fact of the human race, but
with regard to individual lives. Individual lives are the
expression of a pre-existing idea in the mind of God;
this is the true idea of pre-existence. Call it ideal, or
call it what you like, but it is revealed in God's Book.
In the few passages given, and in a great many more,
the idea of pre-existence in the Divine mind is clearly
revealed.

There is one other thing in regard to individual
spiritual experience, viz. that our individual lives can
be, and ought to be, manifest answers to the ideas in
God's mind. "Man's goings are of the LORD; how can
a man then understand his own way?" (Proverbs
20:24). This gives a lofty dignity as well as a great
carefulness to human lives. The expression of it in the
life of our Lord is becoming familiar to us, viz., that
He never worked from His right to Himself; He
never performed a miracle because He wanted to
express how able He was; He never spoke in order to
show how wonderful was His insight into God's
truth. He said, "The Son can do nothing of Himself."
He always worked from His Father (see John 14:10).

There are racial memories which obtrude themselves into our consciousness whereby a person may be
distinctly conscious of a form of life he never lived, it
may be a form of life centuries past. The explanation
of this does not lie in the fact that that particular individual lived centuries ago, but that his progenitors did,
and there are traces in his nerve substance which by
one of the incalculable tricks of individual experience
may suddenly emerge into consciousness.

(c) The Steadying Scriptures

By this we mean those Scriptures which hold our minds to some steady line of interpretation.

(1) No Soul before Body (Genesis 1–2)

In the creation of man the Bible reveals that his body was created first, not his soul. The body existed before the soul in creation; so we cannot trace the history or the destiny of the human soul before the creation of the human race. This is the first main general line of revelation. We have in Genesis 1:26 a splendid example of true pre-existence. God deliberately said what was in His mind before He created man—"Let Us make man in Our image, after Our likeness"—the pre-existence of man in the mind of God.

(2) No Soul Destiny Pre-Adamic

Wherefore, as by one man sin entered into the world, and death by sin; and so death passed upon all men, for that all have sinned. (Romans 5:12)

Soul destiny began with the human race, not before it. Take any passage which deals with individual destiny—Ezekiel 18, for instance—and you will find that destiny is determined in the lifetime of the individual soul. All speculations regarding the transmigration of soul are alien to the teaching of the Bible.

(3) No Soul but by Pro-Creation

We are not created directly by the hand of the Almighty as Adam was; we are pro-created, generated, and our spirit, soul and body, all come together in embryo, as related elsewhere.

The pre-existence of our Lord. "And now, O Father, glorify Thou Me with Thine own self with the glory which I had with Thee before the world was" (John 17:5). This pre-existence is quite different from the phase of pre-existence previously mentioned. This is the existence of a Being Who was known before He came here, and the reason of His coming here is explained by what He was before He came. This is the only case of the pre-existence of a Person in a former life. The Bible nowhere teaches that individuals existed in a world before they came here; the only pre-existence is in the Divine mind.

2. Present Existence

Now we come down to simple ground where we are at home. In the last chapter we dealt with something of the nature of the complex characteristics of the soul, more perplexing and whirling and confusing the more we think of them. When we begin to think of the possibilities of the human soul, no clear thought is possible at first. We come now to the possibilities and capacities of the soul. Can these be satisfied here and now? The Bible says they can. The claim of the salvation of Jesus Christ is that the Spirit of God can satisfy the last aching abyss of the human soul, not only hereafter, but here and now. Satisfaction does not mean stagnation; satisfaction is the knowledge that we have gained the right type of life for our souls.

(a) Satisfaction of the Soul

O bless our God, ye people, . . . [Who] holdeth our soul in life, and suffereth not our feet to be moved. (Psalm 66:8–9; see also Psalm 66:12, 16; Isaiah 55:3)

These are indications from innumerable passages in God's Book which prove that this complex soul which we have been examining can be satisfied and placed in perfect harmony with itself and with God in its present existence. The thought that a human soul can fulfil the predestined purpose of God is a great one. The human soul, however, can also be stagnated by ignorance. In the beginning, we do not know the capabilities of our souls and are content to be ignorant; but when we come under conviction of sin, we begin to understand the awful, unfathomable depths of our nature and the claim of Jesus Christ that He can satisfy this abyss. Every man who knows what his soul is capable of, knows its possibilities and terrors, but knows also the salvation of God, will bear equal testimony with the written Word of God that Jesus Christ can satisfy the living soul. Isaiah 55:3 is our Lord's message to the age in which we live—"Incline your ear, and come unto Me: hear, and your soul shall live; and I will make an everlasting covenant with you, even the sure mercies of David." Bear in mind that the devil does satisfy for a time. "Their eyes stand out with fatness: they have more than heart could wish" (Psalm 73:7). "They have no changes, therefore they fear not God" (Psalm 55:19).

(b) Sins and Surroundings of the Soul

Psalm 6 refers to the surroundings of the soul in bodily sickness and perplexity and the inward results of these. The Psalmist's first degree of prayer is, "Heal me; for my bones are vexed"; the second degree is, Heal me, "for my soul is also sore vexed," and the third degree is, "Save me for Thy mercies' sake." These are three degrees of perplexity arising from the soul's surroundings: because of pain; because the mental outlook is cloudy, and because God has not said a word. When the soul is perplexed—and it certainly will be if we are going on with God, because we are a mark for Satan—and the sudden onslaught comes, as it did in the life of Job, we cry, "Heal me because of my pain," but there is no answer. Then we cry, "Heal me, not because I am in pain, but because my soul is perplexed; I cannot see any way out of it or why this thing should be"; still no answer; then at last we cry, "Heal me, O Lord, not because of my pain, nor because my soul is sick, but for Thy mercies' sake." Then we have the answer, "The LORD hath heard my supplication." The surroundings of the soul, the scenes which arise from our doings, do produce perplexity in the soul. The soul cannot be separated from the body, and bodily perplexities produce difficulties in the soul, and these difficulties go inward and at times intrude right to the very throne of God in the heart.

"Behold, all souls are Mine; . . . the soul that sinneth, it shall die" (Ezekiel 18:4). In this passage the soul life and the sin that is punished are connected. The inherited disposition of sin must be cleansed, but for every sin we commit we are punished. "Receiving the end of your faith, even the salvation of your souls" (1 Peter 1:9). "Salvation" refers to the whole gamut of a man, spirit, soul and body; "Christ the firstfruits," with the ultimate reach in the hereafter of our spirit, soul and body being like His in a totally new relationship. The soul in the present life can be satisfied in all its perplexities, and in all onslaughts and dangers it is kept by the power of God. Sin destroys the power of the soul to know its sin, punishment brings awakening, self-examination brings chastisement and saves the soul from sleeping sickness, and brings it into a healthy satisfaction.

In 1 Corinthians 11:30 ("For this cause many are weak and sickly among you, and many sleep"), Paul alludes to sickness which has a moral and not a physical source. The immediate connection is the obscene conduct at the Lord's Supper of former heathen converts, and Paul says that that is the cause of their bodily sickness. The truth laid down abides, that certain types of moral disobedience produce sicknesses which physical remedies cannot touch; obedience is the only cure. For instance nothing can touch the sicknesses produced by tampering with spiritualism; there is only one cure—yielding to the Lord Jesus Christ.

(c) The Supernatural Setting for the Soul
. . . Lord, wilt Thou that we command fire to come down from heaven and consume them? (Luke 9:54)

The disciples knew Jesus Christ well enough to know that He had intimacy with supernatural powers, but they had yet to learn that it is possible to scathe sin and at the same time serve one's self. "But He turned, and rebuked them, and said, Ye know not what manner of spirit ye are of." It is possible to do right in the wrong spirit. These were the very men who a little while afterwards asked that they might sit, "one on Thy right hand, and the other on Thy left hand, in Thy glory"; and one of them (see Acts 8) was sent down by God to Samaria, where he realised what the fire was that God was to send, viz., the fire of the Holy Ghost.

"For we wrestle not against flesh and blood, but against principalities, against powers . . ." (Ephesians 6:12). This has to do not with the bodily side of things, but with the supernatural. We are surrounded immediately by powers and forces which we cannot discern physically.

". . . I would not that ye should have fellowship with devils. Ye cannot drink the cup of the Lord, and the cup of devils . . ." (1 Corinthians 10:20–21). You can always tell whether Christians are spiritually minded by their attitude to the supernatural. The modern attitude to demon possession is very instructive; so many take the attitude that there is no such thing as demon possession, and infer that Jesus Christ Himself knew quite well that there was no such thing, not seeing that by such an attitude they put themselves in the place of the superior person, and claim to know all the private opinions of the Almighty about iniquity. Jesus unquestionably did believe in the fact of demon possession. The New Testament is full of the supernatural; Jesus Christ continually looked on scenery we do not see, and saw supernatural forces at work. "Try the spirits whether they are of God" (1 John 4:1). The soul of man may be vastly complicated by interference from the supernatural; but Jesus Christ can guard us there.

Sickness, natural and demoniacal. By "natural" sickness we mean that which comes from natural causes, not through the interference of any supernatural force. Demoniacal sickness comes from certain parts of the body being infested by demons. Read the records of our Lord casting out demons. Sometimes He said "Thou dumb and deaf spirit, I charge thee, Come out," (e.g., Mark 9:25); at other times He said nothing about demons when He healed the deaf and dumb (e.g., Matthew 9:32). In addressing the demon-possessed our Lord frequently mentioned the particular organ affected, but in the case of the man of Gadara, he was possessed by demons not only in a particular organ but through the whole of his body. How much room does thought take up? None! How many thoughts can we have in our brain? Why, countless! How much room does personality take up? None! How many personalities can there be in one body? Take this man of Gadara. "And Jesus asked him, What is thy name? And he said, Legion; for many devils were entered into him" (Luke 8:30 RV).

The case of Judas instances the identification of a human soul with the devil himself; just as a man may become identified with Jesus Christ so he can be identified with the devil. Just as a man can be born again into the kingdom where Jesus Christ lives and moves and has His being and can become identified with Him in entire sanctification, so he can be born again, so to speak, into the devil's kingdom and be entirely consecrated to the devil. "Then entered Satan into him" (John 13:27 RV). "Have not I chosen you twelve," said Jesus, "and one of you is a devil?" (John 6:70). This subject awakens tremendous terrors, but these are facts revealed in God's Book. There are supernatural sicknesses of the body and soul in this present life, but Jesus Christ can deal with them all.

3. Perpetual Existence
(a) Mortal Aspect of the Soul
What is your life? It is even a vapour, that appeareth for a little time, and then vanisheth away. (James 4:14; see also Job 14:2)

By mortal is meant in this order of things only. All through God's Book the soul and man as he appears now is described as mortal in one aspect. The soul is the holder of the body and spirit together, and when the spirit goes back to God Who gave it, the soul disappears. In the resurrection there is another body, a body impossible to describe in words, either a glorified body or a damnation body (". . . for the hour is coming, in the which all that are in the graves shall hear His voice, and shall come forth; they that have done good, unto the resurrection of life; and they that have done evil, unto the resurrection of damnation" (John 5:28–29), and instantly the soul is manifested again. We have not a picture of the "resurrection unto damnation"; yet our Lord states that there will be such a thing (see also Luke 16:19–31). We have a picture of the "resurrection unto life" in the resurrected body of our Lord. "Who shall change our vile body, that it may be fashioned like unto His glorious body . . ." (Philippians 3:21).

The soul life, then, is entirely dependent upon the body. The indelible characteristics of the individual are in his spirit: and our Lord, Who is "the firstfruits" (1 Corinthians 15:23), was spirit, soul and body. Therefore resurrection does not refer to spirit, i.e., personality—that never dies, but to body and soul. "It is sown a natural body; it is raised a spiritual body." God raises an incorruptible glorified body like His own Son's—"every man in his own regiment," and Jesus Christ leading. just as the glorified body of our Lord could materialise during those forty days, so will our body be able to materialise in the day yet to be.

(b) Immortal Aspect of the Soul (Luke 16:19, 31; 23:43)
The mortal aspect is strong in the Bible, and the immortal aspect is just as strong. The annihilationists build all their teaching on the mortal aspect; they give proof after proof that because the soul and body are mortal only those who are born again of the Spirit are immortal. The Bible reveals that there is everlasting damnation as well as everlasting life. Nothing can be annihilated. In Scripture the word "destroy" never means "annihilate." In this present bodily aspect the soul

is mortal, but in another aspect it is immortal, for God sees the soul in its final connection with spirit in the resurrection. See Luke 16:25–26 ("Son, remember . . ."), and Luke 23:43 ("And Jesus said unto him, Verily I say unto Thee, To-day shalt thou be with Me in paradise"). Both these passages refer to the state immediately after death, and reveal that man's spirit, i.e., personality, never sleeps and never dies in the sense that body and soul do. The "soul-sleep" heresy creeps in here. The Bible nowhere says the soul sleeps; it says that the body sleeps but never the personality; the moment after death, unhindered consciousness is the state.

(c) Eternal Life and Eternal Death of the Soul
For the wages of sin is death; but the gift of God is eternal life through Jesus Christ our Lord. (Romans 6:23; see also Matthew 10:28; Romans 5:21)

We have no more ground for saying that there is eternal life than we have for saying there is eternal death. If Jesus Christ means by "eternal life," unending conscious knowledge of God, then eternal death must be never-ending conscious separation from God. The destruction of a soul in Hades, or Hell, is the destruction of the last strand of likeness to God. Mark uses a strange phrase: "salted with fire," i.e., preserved in eternal death. In Romans 8:6, Paul tells us what death is—"to be carnally minded is death." The people who say that eternal damnation is not personal but that eternal life is, put themselves in an untenable position. We know no more about the one than we do about the other, and we know nothing about either saving what the Bible tells us. Probably the greatest book on this subject, apart from the Bible, is the one entitled *Human Personality and Its Survival of Bodily Death* (by Dr. F. W. H. Myers[7]) It was written during the last few years by a great man who tried to prove, not from God's Book, but simply from speculation, that the human soul is immortal, and he ends exactly where he begins, viz., with his intuitions.

All we know about eternal life, about hell and damnation, the Bible alone tells us. If we say that God is unjust because He reveals perennial death and imply that the Bible therefore does not teach it, we put ourselves under the condemnation of those passages (i.e., in the Books of Deuteronomy and in the Revelation) to which we have already referred. These things transcend reason, but they do not contradict Incarnate Reason, our Lord Jesus Christ, and He is the final authority.

All we can have hoped to do in these studies of the human soul is to have suggested lines of research for the Bible student.

---

7. F. W. H. Myers (1843–1901), British poet and educator.

Chapter IX
HEART: THE RADICAL REGION OF LIFE

1. Centre of Physical Life
    (a) Lifeless Objects (Deuteronomy 4:11; Matthew 12:40; Jonah 2:3; Ezekiel 26:5; 27:6)
    (b) Lowest Life-Power (Genesis 18:5; Judges 19:5)
    (c) Life-Power (Psalm 38:10; Luke 21:34)
    (d) Life of the Whole Person (Acts 14:17; James 5:5)

2. Centre of Practical Life
    (a) Emporium (Psalm 5:9; 49:11; 1 Peter 3:4)
    (b) Export (Mark 7:21; Esther 7:5)
    (c) Import (Acts 5:3; 16:14; 2 Corinthians 4:6)

N.B.—THE RELATIVE POSITION OF HEAD AND HEART IN THE BIBLE AND MODERN THOUGHT WILL BE EXPLAINED. THE HEAD IS TO THE EXTERNAL APPEARANCE WHAT THE HEART IS TO THE INTERNAL AGENCY OF THE SOUL.

1. Centre of Physical Life

In the Bible the heart, and not the brain, is revealed to be the centre of thinking. For a long time science maintained a steady opposition to the Bible standpoint; but modern psychologists are now slowly coming to find it necessary to revise their previous un-Biblical findings in order to explain the facts of conscious life.

The heart is the first thing to live physically, and the Bible puts in the heart all the active factors we have been apt to place in the brain. The head is the exact outward expression of the heart. In the Mystical Body of Christ, Christ is the Head, not the heart. "Christ is the head of the church . . ." (Ephesians 5:23; see also Colossians 2:19; 1 Corinthians 11:3). Then how can people who are not rightly related to God, whose inward disposition has not been changed, be part of that Body, if Christ is the Head, i.e., the true expression of the Body, especially in the centre of its life?

In the Old Testament the head has the prominence of blessing given to it because it is the outward expression of the condition of the heart. "Blessings are upon the head of the just" (Proverbs 10:6; see also Genesis 48:14; 49:26; Leviticus 8:12; Psalm 133:2).

The other passages refer to "the countenance," meaning not only the face and front of the head, but the whole carriage which is an external expression of the person. The countenance becomes the true mirror of the heart, when the heart has had time to manifest its true life. ". . . Moses wist not that the skin of his face shone while he talked with Him" (Exodus 34:29). "The shew of their countenance doth witness against them; and they declare their sin as Sodom, they hide it not" (Isaiah 3:9; see also Matthew 17:2; 2 Corinthians 3:13; 1 Samuel 16:7).

The Bible puts the head in the prominent position, not the central position; the head is the "finish off," the manifestation of what the heart is like; the outward expression of the heart, as a tree is the outward expression of the root. This is the relationship between the head and the heart which the Bible reveals.

Materialistic scientists say that "the brain secretes thinking as the liver does bile," they make the brain the centre of thinking. The Bible makes the heart the centre of thinking, and the brain merely the machinery the heart uses to express itself. This point is very vital in our judgement of men. Carlyle,[8] for instance, represents the judgement of men by those who do not accept the Bible standpoint on this matter. He judged men by their brains, and came to the conclusion that the majority of the human race were fools. God never judges men by their brains; He Judges them by their hearts.

The use of the Bible term "heart" is best understood by simply saying "me." The heart is not merely the seat of the affections, it is the centre of everything. The heart is the central altar, and the body is the outer court. What we offer on the altar of the heart will tell ultimately through the extremities of the body.

The heart, then, is the centre of living, the true centre of all vital activities of body and soul and spirit. When the Apostle Paul says "with the heart man believeth" he means by the word "heart" more than we are apt to mean. The Bible always means more than we are apt to mean. The term "heart" in the Bible means the centre of everything. The human soul has the spirit in and above it and the body by and about it; but the vital centre of all is the heart. When we speak of the heart, figuratively or actually, we mean

---

8. Thomas Carlyle (1795–1881), Scottish-born literary figure in nineteenth-century England, a writer, biographer, essayist, historian, and critic.

the midmost part of a person. The Bible teaching differs from that of science in that it makes the heart the soul centre and the spirit centre as well.

In dealing with the Bible the danger is to come to it with a preconceived idea, to exploit it, and take out of it only what agrees with that idea. If we try, as has been tried by psychologists, to take out of the Bible something that agrees with modern science, we shall have to omit many things the Bible says about the heart. According to the Bible the heart is the centre: the centre of physical life, the centre of memory, the centre of damnation and of salvation, the centre of God's working and the centre of the devil's working, the centre from which everything works which moulds the human mechanism.

(c) Life Power
And take heed to yourselves, lest at any time your hearts be overcharged with surfeiting, and drunkenness, and cares of this life. . . . Luke 21:34; see also Psalm 38:10)

These passages are typical of many others where the heart is revealed to be the centre of all life power, physical and otherwise. Anything that makes the heart beat more quickly works towards a higher or lower manifestation of the life; our Lord produces the kind of life that instantly alters the heart life. There are people you come in contact with who "freeze" you, you cannot think, things do not "go," everything feels tight and mean;[9] you come into the zone of other people and all those bands disappear, you are surprised at how clearly you can think, everything seems to "go" better. You take a deep breath and say, "Why, I feel quite different; what has happened?" The one personality brought an atmosphere that froze the heart not only physically, but psychically; kept it cold, kept it down, kept it back; the other personality gave the heart a chance to expand and develop and surge throughout the whole body. Taken in the physical domain, if people knew that the circulation of the blood and quickening of the heart life would remove distempers from the body, there would be a great deal less medicine taken and a great deal more walking done. The heart is the centre of all physical life and of all the imaginations of the mind. Anything that keeps the physical blood in good condition and the heart working properly, benefits the soul life and spirit life as well. That is why Jesus Christ said, "Take heed to yourselves, lest at any time your hearts be overcharged with surfeiting. . . ." Whenever Paul mentions certain kinds of sins he calls them idolatry. Covetousness is called idolatry because every drop of blood in the life of a covetous man is drawn away

from God spiritually. And so it is by sensuality and drunkenness and vengeance. Vengeance is probably the most tyrannical passion of the carnal mind. The first wonderful thing done by the new life given to us by the Holy Spirit is to loosen the heart, and as we obey the Spirit the manifestation in the life becomes easier. Satan, however, is as subtle as God is good, and he tries to counterfeit everything God does, and if he cannot counterfeit it, he will limit it. Do not be ignorant of his devices!

(d) Life of the Whole Person
Nevertheless He left not Himself without witness, in that He did good, and gave us rain from heaven, and fruitful seasons, filling our hearts with food and gladness. (Acts 14:17; see also James 5:5)

These passages refer to the power of the heart life. If our hearts are right with God, we realise what is mentioned in Acts 14:17, that everything nourishes and blesses the life. James 5:5 indicates the other side of this truth ("Ye have lived in pleasure on the earth, and been wanton; ye have nourished your hearts, as in a day of slaughter"). We can develop in the heart life whatever we will; there is no limit to the possible growth and development. If we give ourselves over to meanness and to Satan, there is no end to the growth in devilishness; if we give ourselves over openly to God, there is no end to our development and growth in grace. Our Lord has no fear of the consequences when once the heart is open towards Him. No wonder the Bible counsels us to guard our *heart* "with all diligence; for out of it are the issues of life"; Solomon prayed for "an understanding *heart*," and Paul says that the peace of God will "garrison our *hearts*."

2. Centre of Practical Life
(a) The Emporium
For there is no faithfulness in their mouth; their inward part is very wickedness. (Psalm 5:9)

The phrase "inward part" is simply another phrase for heart, and in Psalm 49:11 the phrase "inward thought" means heart. "Whose adorning . . . let it be the hidden man of the heart, in the incorruptible apparel of a meek and quiet spirit, which is in the sight of God of great price" (1 Peter 3:3–4 RV). The heart is the exchange and mart; our words and expressions are simply the coins we use, but the "shop" resides in the heart, the emporium where all the goods are, and that is what God sees but no man can see. That is why Jesus Christ's judgements always confuse us until we learn how to receive, recognise and rely on the Holy Spirit. The way people judged Jesus in His

---

9. mean: ordinary, common, low, or ignoble, rather than cruel or spiteful

day is the way we judge Him to-day. The way the Bible is judged and Jesus Christ is judged is an indication of what the heart is like if we have not received the Holy Spirit. When we receive the Holy Spirit we are in the condition of the disciples after the Resurrection: their eyes were opened and they had the power to discern. Before they received the Holy Spirit they could not perceive correctly, they simply recorded physically; they saw that Jesus Christ was a marvellous Being Whom they believed to be the Messiah; but after they had received the Holy Spirit, they discerned what they had seen and heard and handled, because their hearts had been put right; the whole "shop" inside had been renovated and re-stocked by the Holy Spirit.

Notice the difference in the characteristics of the man who makes the head the centre and the man who makes the heart the centre. The man who makes the head the centre becomes an intellectual being, he does not estimate things at all as the Bible does. Sin is a mere defect to him, something to be overlooked and grown out of, and the one thing he despises is enthusiasm. Take the Apostle Paul, or any of the New Testament saints, the characteristic of their life is enthusiasm; the heart is first, not second. This is the antipodes of modern intellectual life. Mere intellectuality leads to bloodlessness and passionlessness, to stoicism and unreality. The more merely intellectual a person becomes the more hopelessly useless he is, until he degenerates into a mere criticising faculty, passing the strangest and wildest verdicts on life, on the Bible, and on our Lord.

(b) Export
For from within, out of the heart of men, proceed evil thoughts, adulteries, fornications, murders. . . . (Mark 7:21)

This passage is detestable to an unspiritual person, it is in absolutely bad taste, nine out of every ten people do not believe it because they are grossly ignorant about the heart. In these verses Jesus Christ says, to put it in modern language,

"No crime has ever been committed that every human being is not capable of committing." Do I believe that? Do you? If we do not, remember we pass a verdict straight off on the Lord Jesus Christ, we tell Him He does not know what He is talking about. We read that Jesus "knew what was in man," meaning that He knew men's hearts; and the Apostle Paul emphasises the same thing—"Don't glory in man; trust only the grace of God in yourself and in other people." No wonder Jesus Christ pleads with us to give over the keeping of our hearts to Him so that He can fill them with a new life! Every characteristic seen in the life of Jesus Christ becomes possible in our lives when once we hand over our hearts to Him to be filled with the Holy Spirit.

(c) Import
But Peter said, Ananias, why hath Satan filled thine heart to lie to the Holy Ghost?. . . (Acts 5:3)

A Pentecostal liar. That is a terrible statement, a statement with a shudder all through it. Such a lie has never been mentioned in this particular profundity before, but it is mentioned here because it is actually possible for the heart to try and deceive the Holy Ghost. "Thou hast not lied unto men, but unto God." "Why hath Satan filled thine heart to lie to the Holy Ghost?"

Our Lord undertakes to fill the whole region of the heart with light and holiness. "For God, Who commanded the light to shine out of darkness, hath shined in our hearts, to give the light of the knowledge of the glory of God in the face of Jesus Christ" (2 Corinthians 4:6). Can He do it? Do I realise that I need it done? Or do I think I can realise myself? That is the great phrase to-day, and it is growing in popularity—"I must realise myself." (If I want to know what my heart is like, let me listen to my mouth, in an unguarded frame, for five minutes!) Thank God for everyone who has been saved from this perilous path by yielding himself to the Lord Jesus, and asking Him to give him the Holy Spirit and obeying the light He gives!

Chapter X

HEART: THE RADICAL REGION OF LIFE
The Radiator of Personal Life

1. Voluntary
    (a) Determination (Exodus 35:21; Esther 7:5; Ecclesiastes 8:11; 2 Corinthians 9:7; Romans 6:17)
    (b) Design (1 Kings 8:17–18; 10:2; Psalm 21:2; Proverbs 6:18; Isaiah 10:7; Acts 11:23; Romans 10:1)

2. Versatility
    (a) Perception (Deuteronomy 29:4; Proverbs 14:10; Isaiah 32:4; Acts 16:14)
    (b) Meditation (Nehemiah 5:7; Luke 2:19; Isaiah 33:18; Psalm 49:3; Psalm 19:14)

   THIS INCLUDES DELIBERATION AND REFLECTION.

    (c) Estimation (Proverbs 16:1, 9; 19:21; Psalm 33:10–11
    (d) Inclination (Deuteronomy 32:46; Joshua 24:23; Deuteronomy 11:18; Proverbs 3:3)

3. Virtues and Vices
    (a) All Degrees of Joy (Isaiah 65:14; 66:5; Acts 2:46)
    (b) All Degrees of Pain (Proverbs 25:20; Psalm 109:22; Acts 21:13; John 16:6)
    (c) All Degrees of Ill-will (Proverbs 23:17; Deuteronomy 19:6; Acts 7:54; James 3:14)

A radiator is a body that emits rays of light and heat. We have used a purely mechanical term in order to picture what the heart is, viz., the centre that emits rays of light and heat in the physical frame, in the soul, and in the spirit. The heart physically is the centre of the body; the heart sentimentally is the centre of the soul; and the heart spiritually is the centre of the spirit.

By Voluntary we mean acting by choice; choice is made in the heart, not in the head. By Versatility we mean the power to turn easily from one thing to another. By Virtues we mean moral excellencies; by Vices, immoral conduct.

1. Voluntary
The Bible reveals that the power of choice springs from the heart, and there are two things to be looked at, Determination and Design.

(a) Determination
But God be thanked, that ye were the servants of sin, but ye have obeyed from the heart that form of doctrine which was delivered you. (Romans 6:17; see also Exodus 35:21)

These passages are typical of many which prove that the act of choice is in the heart, not in the brain. Impulse in anyone but a child is dangerous; it is the sign of something unstable and unreliable. Determination means to fix the form of our choice, and God demands that we use this power when we pray. The majority of us waste our time in mere impulses in prayer. There are many verses in God's Book which refer to this power in the heart to choose voluntarily. Impulse is not choice; impulse is very similar to instinct in an animal. It is the characteristic of immaturity and ought not to characterise men and women. In spiritual matters take it as a safe guide never to be guided by impulse; always take time and curb your impulse, bring it back and see what form a choice based on that particular impulse would take.

"Bringing into captivity every thought to the obedience of Christ"—that means the harnessing of impulse. We have the power in our hearts to fix the form of our choice either for good or for bad. No wonder the Bible says, "Keep thy heart with all diligence; for out of it are the issues of life." We never get credit spiritually for impulsive giving. If suddenly we feel we should give a shilling to a poor man, we get no credit from God for giving it, there is no virtue in it whatever. As a rule, that sort of giving is a relief to our feelings; it is not an indication of a generous character, but rather an indication of a lack of generosity. God never estimates what we give from impulse. We are given credit for what we determine in our hearts to give; for the giving that is governed by a fixed determination. The Spirit of God revolutionises our philanthropic instincts. Much of our philanthropy is simply the impulse to save ourselves an uncomfortable feeling. The Spirit of God alters all that. As saints our attitude towards giving is that we give for Jesus Christ's sake, and from no other motive. God holds us responsible for the way we use this power of voluntary choice.

(b) Design
Design means planning in outline.

Whereas it was in thine heart to build an house unto My name, thou didst well that it was in thine heart. (1 Kings 8:18)

This is a typical instance of the fact that God gives us credit, not for our impulses, but for the designs of our hearts. God may never allow the design to be carried out, but He credits us with it. When we have had a good dinner and feel remarkably generous, we say, "If only I had a thousand pounds, what I would do with it!" We do not get credit for that until what we do with what we have is considered. The proof that the design for the thousand pounds would be worked out is what we do with the twopence-halfpenny[10] we have. David planned in his heart what he would do for God, and although he was not allowed to carry it out, God credited him with having the design in his heart. God deals with the designs of our hearts, either for good or for bad. Character is the whole trend of a man's life, not isolated acts here and there, and God deals with us on the line of character building.

Remember, then, that we have the power to fix the form of our choice. "Delight thyself also in the LORD; and He shall give thee the desires of thine heart." Desire embraces both determination and design. Some people when they read this verse, behave before God as people do over a wishing-bone at a Christmas dinner. They say, "Now I have read this verse, I wonder what shall I wish for?" That is not desire. Desire is what we determine in outline in our minds and plan and settle in our hearts; that is the desire which God will fulfil as we delight ourselves in Him.

2. Versatility

Versatility is the power to turn from one thing to another; in the natural world it is called humour.[11] The power to turn from one thing to another is due to a sense of proportion. A self-righting lifeboat gives the idea. Sin destroyed this power in the people of God. Read Psalm 106: "We have sinned with our fathers." How did they sin? They forgot what God had done in the past, they had no power to turn from their present trying circumstances to the time when their circumstances were not trying, consequently they sinned against God by unbelief. We have the power to turn from deep anguish to deep joy: "O my God, my soul is cast down within me: therefore will I remember Thee. . . ." Some people take on the characteristic of always being merry and think they must always keep up that role. Others take on the role of being great sufferers, and never turn from it.

In the life of our Lord we find the basal balance of this power; look also at Paul's argument in Romans 8:28: "And we know that to them that love God all things work together for good" (RV). We have to take the "all things" when put "together," not in bits. If your circumstances are trying just now, remember the time when they were not trying, and you will be surprised at the self-righting power in the human heart to turn from one thing to another. How much misery a human heart can stand, and how much joy! If we lose the power of turning from one to the other, we upset the balance. God's Spirit restores and keeps the balance right.

(a) Perception
. . . an heart to perceive, and eyes to see, and ears to hear . . . (Deuteronomy 29:4; see also Proverbs 14:10)

Perception means the power to discern what we hear and see and read; the power to discern the history of the nation to which we belong, the power to discern in our personal lives. This power is also in the heart. How many of us have the power to "hear with our ears"? Jesus said, "He that hath ears to hear, let him hear." We must have the power of perception in order to interpret what we hear. Isaiah 53:1 (mg) puts it in this way: "Who hath believed that which we have heard? and to whom hath the arm of the LORD been revealed?" We all see the common occurrences of our daily life, but which of us is able to perceive the arm of the Lord behind them? Who can perceive behind the thunder the voice of God? We read in John 12 that when there came a voice out of heaven, the people that stood by said it thundered; but Jesus recognised His Father's voice. The One had perception, the others had not. The light which smote Saul of Tarsus on the way to Damascus staggered and amazed the men who journeyed with him, but they heard not the voice; Saul knew it to be the Lord and answered, "Who art Thou, Lord?" The one had the power of perception, the others had not. The characteristic of a man without the Spirit of God is that he has no power of perception, he cannot perceive God at work in the ordinary occurrences. The marvellous, uncrushable characteristic of a saint is that he does discern God. You may put a saint in tribulation, amid an onslaught of principalities and powers, in peril, pestilence or under the sword, you may put a saint anywhere you like, and he is "more than conqueror" every time. Why? Because his heart being filled with the love of God, he has the power to perceive and understand that behind all these things is God making them "work together for good."

---

10. two pence and a half penny, 1 percent of a British pound prior to 1971; "tuppence ha'penny" is a colloquial expression meaning next to nothing, or nothing at all.

11. humour: mood, temperament or disposition.

"Turn away mine eyes from beholding vanity." This does not mean "keep my eyes shut," but, "give me the power to direct my eyes aright." A sheet of white paper can be soiled, a sunbeam cannot be soiled, and God keeps His saints like light. Oh, the power of full-orbed righteousness! Thank God for the sanity of His salvation! He takes hold of our hearts *and* our heads!

(b) Meditation

Meditation means getting to the middle of a thing; not being like a pebble in a brook letting the water of thought go over us; that is reverie, not meditation. Meditation is an intense spiritual activity, it means bringing every bit of the mind into harness and concentrating its powers; it includes both deliberation and reflection. Deliberation means being able to weigh well what we think, conscious all the time that we are deliberating and meditating. "My heart consulted in me" (Nehemiah 5:7 mg)—that is exactly the meaning of meditation; also—"But Mary kept all these things, pondering them in her heart" (Luke 2:19 RV mg).

A great many delightful people mistake meditation for prayer; meditation often accompanies prayer, but it is not prayer, it is simply the power of the natural heart to get to the middle of things. Prayer is asking, whereby God puts processes to work and creates things which are not in existence until we ask. It is not that God withholds, but He has so constituted things on the ground of Redemption that they cannot be given until we ask. Prayer is definite talk to God, around which God puts an atmosphere, and we get answers back. Meditation has a reflex action; men without an ounce of the Spirit of God in them can meditate, but that is not prayer. This fundamental distinction is frequently obscured. Mary "pondered" these things in her heart, i.e., she meditated on them, got right to the centre of the revelations about her Son, but as far as we know, she did not utter a word to anyone. But read St. John's Gospel, and a wonder will occur to you. St. Augustine has called John's Gospel "the Heart of Jesus Christ." Recall what Jesus said to His Mother about John: "Woman, behold, thy son!" and to John about Mary, "Behold, thy mother! And from that hour that disciple took her unto his own home." It is surely quite legitimate to think that Mary's meditations found marvellous expression to John under the guidance of the Spirit of God, and found a place in his Gospel and Epistles.

(c) Estimation
The preparations of the heart in man, and the answer of the tongue, is from the LORD. (Proverbs 16:1; see also verse 9)

To estimate means to reckon the value. Estimates are made in the heart, and God alters our estimates. To put it practically—those of you who have received God's Spirit and know His grace experimentally, watch how He has altered your estimate of things. It used to matter a lot what your worldly crowd thought about you: how much does it matter now? You used to estimate highly the good opinion of certain people: how do you estimate it now? You used to estimate that immoral conduct was the worst crime on earth, but how do you estimate it now? We are horrified at immoral conduct in social life, but how many of us are as horrified at pride as Jesus Christ was? Do we begin to understand what Jesus meant When He used such words as "ye are like unto whited sepulchres," or, "ye offspring of vipers" (RV)? To whom was He talking? To the Scribes and Pharisees!

God alters our estimates, and we shall find that God gives us a deeper horror of carnality than ever we had of immorality; a deeper horror of the pride which lives clean amongst men but lifts itself against God, than of any other thing. Pride is the central citadel of independence of God.

God will also alter our estimate of honour. Every man has an honour of some sort; a thief has an honour, a gambling man has an honour, everybody has an honour of some kind. Jesus Christ had an honour; they called Him "a man gluttonous, and a winebibber"; they said He was "beside Himself"; "hath a devil," and he never opened His mouth. He "made Himself of no reputation." But once let His Father's honour be touched and all was different. Watch His first public ministry in Jerusalem—a scourge of small cords in His hands overturning the moneychangers' tables, and driving men and cattle out! Where is the meek and mild and gentle Jesus now? His Father's honour was at stake.

Our estimate of honour measures our growth in grace. What we stand up for proves what our character is like. If we stand up for our reputation it is a sign it needs standing up for! God never stands up for His saints, they do not need it. The devil tells lies about men, but no slander on earth can alter a man's character. Once let God's honour be slandered, and instantly there is something else to deal with in your "meek" saint. You cannot arouse him on his own account, but once begin to slander God and a new sense of honour is awakened, a new estimate has been put in. God enables us to have the right perspective, to come to the place where we understand that the things which are seen are temporal, and to estimate them accordingly and hold a right scale of judgement.

3. Virtues and Vices
(a) All Degrees of Joy (Isaiah 65:14; 66:5)
The Bible talks plentifully about joy, but it nowhere speaks about a "happy" Christian. Happiness depends

on what happens; joy does not. Remember, Jesus Christ had joy, and He prays "that they might have My joy fulfilled in themselves."

I want to give one warning concerning Christian Science. There is no objection to what Christian Science does to people's bodies, but there is a tremendous objection to its effect on people's minds. Its effect on people's minds is to make them intolerably indifferent to physical suffering, and in time it produces the antipodes of the Christian character, viz., a hardness and callousness of heart.

All degrees of joy reside in the heart. How can a Christian be full of happiness (if happiness depends on the things that happen) when he is in a world where the devil is doing his best to twist souls away from God, where people are tortured physically, where some are downtrodden and do not get a chance? It would be the outcome of the most miserable selfishness to be happy under such conditions; but a joyful heart is never an insult, and joy is never touched by external conditions. Beware of preaching the gospel of temperament instead of the Gospel of God. Numbers of people to-day preach the gospel of temperament, the gospel of "cheer up." The word "blessed" is sometimes translated "happy," but it is a much deeper word; it includes all that we mean by joy in its full fruition. Happiness is the characteristic of a child, and God condemns us for taking happiness out of a child's life; but as men and women we should have done with happiness long ago, we should be facing the stern issues of life, knowing that the grace of God is sufficient for every problem the devil can present.

(b) All Degrees of Pain
. . . . as vinegar upon nitre, so is he that singeth songs to an heavy heart. (Proverbs 25:20)

This is simply what has been stated already—preaching the gospel of temperament, the gospel of "cheer up," when a person cannot cheer up; telling him to look on the bright side of things when there is no bright side. It is as ridiculous as telling a jelly-fish to listen to one of Handel's Oratorios, it would have to be made over again first. It is just as futile to tell a man convicted of sin to cheer up; what he needs is the grace of God to alter him and put in him the wellspring of joy.

Pain exists in the heart and nowhere else. We try to measure pain in the aggregate; but we cannot. When hundreds are killed in a great accident, we are horrified, much more horrified than when one man is killed. There is no such thing as pain in the mass, pain is individual; nobody can feel more pain than the acme of nerves will give, and the more physical expression there is in pain, the less pain there is. It is by refusing to estimate things in their right light that we misunderstand the direction of pain.

(c) All Degrees of Ill-Will (Proverbs 23:17; Deuteronomy 19:6; Acts 7:54; James 3:14)
The deepest-rooted passion in the human soul is vengeance. Drunkenness, sensuality, and covetousness go deep, but not so deep as vengeance. Some such thought as this explains Judas; it says that he "kissed Him much" (Mark 14:45 RV mg). We read of the remorse of Judas, but there was no repentance in it; the end of his life was reached, there was nothing more to live for. There are records of men committing murder after a long line of vengeance and then dying of a broken heart, not because they are penitent, but because there was nothing more to live for.

Vengeance is the most deeply rooted passion in the human soul, and the impersonation of it is the devil. The devil has an absolute detestation of God, an immortal hatred of God. Satan's sin is at the summit of all sins; our sin is at the base of all sins. If sin has not reached its awful height in us, it may do so unless we let God alter the springs of our heart.

Thank God He does alter the heart, and when His new life is in our heart, we can work it out through our head and express it in our lives.

Chapter XI

HEART: THE RADICAL REGION OF LIFE
The Radiator of Personal Life (continued)

1. Voluntary
    (c) Love (1 Timothy 1:5; Proverbs 23:26; Judges 5:9; Philippians 1:7; 2 Corinthians 7:3)
    (d) Hate (Leviticus 19:17; Psalm 105:25)

2. Versatility
    (e) Memory (Isaiah 65:17; Jeremiah 3:16; 2 Chronicles 7:11; Acts 7:23; 1 Corinthians 2:9; Luke 1:66; 21:14)
    (f) Thinking (Genesis 8:21; 17:17; 24:45; Ecclesiastes 1:16; Matthew 24:48; Hebrews 4:12)
    (g) Birthplace of Words (Job 8:10; Psalm 15:2; Matthew 12:34; Exodus 28:3)

3. Virtues and Vices
    (d) All Degrees of Fear (Proverbs 12:25; Ecclesiastes 2:20; Deuteronomy 28:28; Psalm 143:4; Jeremiah 32:40)
    (e) All Degrees of Anguish (Joshua 5:1; Jeremiah 4:19; Leviticus 26:36; Psalm 102:4)
    (f) All Conscious Unity (1 Chronicles 12:38; Jeremiah 32:39; Ezekiel 11:19; Acts 4:32)

1. Voluntary

(c) Love
But the end of the charge is love out of a pure heart and a good conscience and faith unfeigned. (1 Timothy 1:5 RV; see also Judges 5:9; Proverbs 23:26; Philippians 1:7; 2 Corinthians 7:3)

Love is the sovereign preference of my person for another person, and we may be astonished to realise that love springs from a voluntary choice. Love for God does not spring naturally out of the human heart; but it is open to us to choose whether we will have the love of God imparted to us by the Holy Spirit. ". . . the love of God is shed abroad in our hearts by the Holy Ghost which is given unto us" (Romans 5:5; see also Luke 11:13). We are emphasising just now the need of voluntary choice. It is of no use to pray, "O Lord, for more love! give me love like Thine; I do want to love Thee better," if we have not begun at the first place, and that is to choose to receive the Holy Spirit Who will shed abroad the love of God in our hearts.

Beware of the tendency of trying to do what God alone can do, and of blaming God for not doing what we alone can do. We try to save ourselves, but God only can do that; and we try to sanctify ourselves, but God only can do that. After God has done these sovereign works of grace in our hearts, we have to work them out in our lives. ". . . work out your own salvation with fear and trembling. For it is God which worketh in you both to will and to do of His good pleasure" (Philippians 2:12–13).

The love of God is the great mainspring, and by our voluntary choice we can have that love shed abroad in our hearts, then unless hindered by disobedience, it will go on to develop into the perfect love described in 1 Corinthians 13.

We have, then, to make the voluntary choice of receiving the Holy Spirit Who will shed abroad in our hearts the love of God, and when we have that wonderful love in our hearts, the sovereign preference for Jesus Christ, our love for others will be relative to this central love. "We preach not ourselves, but Christ Jesus the Lord; and ourselves your servants *for Jesus' sake*" (2 Corinthians 4:5).

(d) Hate
Thou shalt not hate thy brother in thine heart. (Leviticus 19:17; see also Psalm 105:25)

(The passages quoted are chosen from an innumerable number which mention hate.) The exact opposite to love is hate. We do not hear much about hatred in connection with Christianity nowadays. Hatred is the supreme detestation of one personality for another, and the other person ought to be the devil. The Word of God clearly shows the wrong of hating our brother men; but Paul says, "we wrestle not against flesh and blood," i.e., against bad men, "but against principalities, against powers, . . . against spiritual wickedness" behind men. Bad men are simply the manifestation of the power of Satan.

If the love of God were presented as having no hatred of wrong and of sin and the devil, it would simply mean that God's love is not so strong as our love. The stronger and higher and more emphatic the love, the more intense is its obverse, hate. God loves the world so much that He hates with a perfect hatred the thing that is twisting men away from Him. To put it crudely, the two antagonists are God and the devil.

A good way to use the "cursing" Psalms is in some such way as this—"Do not I hate them, O Lord, that hate Thee? . . . I hate them with perfect hatred." Ask yourself what is it that hates God? Nothing and no one hates God half so much as the wrong disposition in you does. The carnal mind is *"enmity against God"*; what we should hate is this principle that lusts against the Spirit of God and is determined to have our bodies and minds and rule them away from God. The Spirit of God awakens in us an unmeasured hatred of that power until we are not only sick of it, but sick to death of it, and we will gladly make the moral choice of going to its funeral. The meaning of Romans 6:6 is just this put into Scriptural language—"Knowing this, that our old man is crucified with Him." The "old man" is the thing the Spirit of God will teach us to hate, and the love of God in our hearts concentrates our soul in horror against the wrong thing. Make no excuse for it. The next time you read those Psalms, which people think are so terrible, bring this interpretation to bear on them.

One other thing, the Bible says that "God so loved the world, that He gave His only begotten Son, . . ." and yet it says that if we are friends of the world we are enemies of God. "Know ye not that the friendship of the world is enmity with God?" (James 4:4). The difference is that God loves the world so much that He goes all lengths to remove the wrong from it, and we must have the same kind of love. Any other kind of love for the world simply means that we take it as it is and are perfectly delighted with it. The world is all right and we are very happy in it; sin and evil and the devil are so many Orientalisms. It is that sentiment which is the enemy of God. Do we love the world in this sense sufficiently to spend and be spent so that God can manifest His grace through us until the wrong and the evil are removed?

Thank God, these voluntary choices are in our hearts, and they will work out tremendous purposes in our lives. Have I made the voluntary choice to receive the love of God? Have I come to the end of myself? Am I really a spiritual pauper? Do I realise, without any cunning, that I have no power at all in myself to be holy? Do I deliberately choose to receive from God the sovereign grace that will work these things in me? If so, then I must work them out with glad activity.

2. Versatility

In a previous study we explained Versatility as the power to turn easily from one thing to another. When you are in difficult circumstances, remember the time when they were not so trying. God has given us this power to turn ourselves by remembrance; if we lose the power, we punish ourselves and it will lead on to melancholia and the peril of fixed ideas.

(e) Memory

As expressive of this great and surprising power, take memory, which resides not in the brain, but in the heart.

Thus Solomon finished the house of the LORD . . . *and all that came into Solomon's heart to make in the house of the* LORD . . . *he prosperously effected. (2 Chronicles 7:11; see also Isaiah 65:17; Jeremiah 3:16; Acts 7:23; 1 Corinthians 2:9)*

The brain is not a spiritual thing, the brain is a physical thing. Memory is a spiritual thing and exists in the heart; the brain recalls more or less clearly what the heart remembers. In our Lord's parable (see Luke 16:25) when Abraham said to the rich man, "Son, remember," He was not referring to a man with a physical brain in this order of things at all. There are other passages which refer to the marvellous power of God to blot certain things out of His memory. Forgetting with us is a defect; forgetting with God is an attribute. "I have blotted out, as a thick cloud, thy transgressions, and, as a cloud, thy sins" (Isaiah 44:22). "All these sayings were noised abroad throughout all hill country of Judaea. And all they that heard them laid them up in their hearts. . . ." (Luke 1:65–66; see also Luke 21:14). In these passages memory is placed in the heart. We never forget save by the sovereign grace of God; the problem is that we do not recall easily. Recalling depends upon the state of our physical brain, and when people say they have a bad memory, they mean they have a bad power of recalling. Paul says, "Forgetting those things which are behind" (Philippians 3:13), but notice the kind of things he forgot. Paul never forgot that he was "before a blasphemer, and a persecutor, and injurious" (1 Timothy 1:13); he is referring to his spiritual attainments: "I forget to what I have attained because I am pressing on to something ahead." Immediately you begin to "rest on your oars" over your spiritual experience, and say, "Thank God I have attained to this," that moment you begin to go back. Forget to what you have attained, keep your eyes fixed on the Lord Jesus, and press on. People say God helps us to forget our past, but is that true? Every now and again the Spirit of God brings us back to remember who we are, and the pit from whence we were digged, so that we understand that all we are is by the sovereign grace of God, not by our own work, otherwise we would be uplifted and proud.

In the case of people with an impaired memory, as it is termed, some say it would be better to remove them; to put them to sleep if that were legal. Why do they say this? Because they estimate wrongly; they estimate according to the perfection of the machine. God looks at what we cannot see, viz., at the heart. God does not look at the brain, at what man looks at, neither does He sum men up in the way we do. The wonderful thing is that if we will hand our lives over to God by a voluntary choice and receive His Spirit, He will purify us down to deeper depths than we can ever go. Then how foolish people are not to hand over their lives to

Him! "He will keep the feet of His saints." He will keep your heart so pure that you would tremble with amazement if you knew how pure the Atonement of the Lord Jesus can make the vilest human heart, if we will but keep in the light, as God is in the light. "But if we walk in the light, as He is in the light, we have fellowship one with another, and the blood of Jesus Christ His Son cleanseth us from all sin" (1 John 1:7). We use this verse much too glibly; it is simply God letting the plummet right straight down to the very depths of the experience of a redeemed heart and saying, "That is how I see you"—made pure by the marvellous Atonement of Jesus, the last strand of memory purified through the blood of His Son.

(f) Thinking
Thinking takes place in the heart, not in the brain. The real spiritual powers of a man reside in the heart, which is the centre of the physical life, of the soul life, and of the spiritual life. The expression of thinking is referred to the brain and the lips because through these organs thinking becomes articulate. "For the word of God . . . is a discerner of the thoughts and intents of the heart" (Hebrews 4:12; see also Genesis 8:21; 17:17; 24:45; Ecclesiastes 1:16; Matthew 24:48).

According to the Bible, thinking exists in the heart, and that is the region with which the Spirit of God deals. We may take it as a general rule that Jesus Christ never answers any questions that spring from a man's head, because the questions which spring from our brains are always borrowed from some book we have read, or from someone we have heard speak; but the questions that spring from our hearts, the real problems that vex us, Jesus Christ answers those. The questions He came to deal with are those that spring from the implicit centre. These problems may be difficult to state in words, but they are the problems Jesus Christ will solve.

(g) Birthplace of Words
The heart is the first thing to live in physical birth and in spiritual birth. It is a wonderful thing that God can cleanse and purify the thinking of our hearts. That is why our Lord says, "Of the abundance of the heart his mouth speaketh" (Luke 6:45). The Bible says that words are born in the heart, not in the head. "Shall not they teach thee, and tell thee, and utter words out of their heart?" (Job 8:10; see also Matthew 12:34).

Jesus Christ said He always spoke as His Father wished Him to. Did His Father write out the words and tell Him to learn them by heart? No, the mainspring of the heart of Jesus Christ was the mainspring of the heart of God the Father, consequently the words Jesus Christ spoke were the exact expression of God's thought. In our Lord the tongue was in its right place; He never spoke from His head, but always from His heart. "If any man among you seem to be religious, and bridleth not his tongue . . . this man's religion is vain" (James 1:26), there is nothing in it. The tongue and the brain are under our control, not God's.

Look at the history of words in the different countries of the human race, or take our words to-day—the words, for instance, at the head of these studies, they are all technical, there is no "heart" in them. Compare the language of the Authorised Version of the Bible, which was translated into the language the people spoke. Our modern speech is a great aid to inner hypocrisy, and it becomes a snare because it is easy to talk piously and live iniquitously. Speaking from the heart does not mean refinement of speech merely; sometimes Jesus Christ's speech sounded anything but nice to natural ears, e.g., Matthew 23. Some of the words He used, and some applications He made of His truth were terrible and rugged. Read our Lord's description of the heart: "Out of the heart," says Jesus, "proceed . . ."—and then comes the ugly catalogue (Matthew 15:19). Upright men and women of the world simply do not believe this. Jesus Christ did not speak as a man there. He spoke as the Master of men, with an absolute knowledge of what the human heart is like. That is why He so continually pleads with us to hand the keeping of our hearts over to Him.

There is a difference between innocence and purity. Innocence is the true condition of a child; purity is the characteristic of men and women. Innocence has always to be shielded; purity is something that has been tested and tried and has triumphed; something that has character at the back of it, that can overcome, and has overcome. Jesus Christ by His Spirit can make us men and women fit to face the misery and wrong and discordance of life if we will keep in tune with Him.

3. Virtues and Vices
All degrees of Fear, all degrees of Anguish, and all Conscious Unity reside in the heart. Notice how the natural virtues break down, the reason being that our natural virtues are not promises of what we are going to be, but remnants of what we were designed to be. God does not build up our natural virtues and transfigure them. You will often find that when a good, upright worldling is born again, his natural virtues fail, and confusion is the first result of the Spirit of God coming in. Jesus Himself said, "I came not to send peace, but a sword," i.e., something that would divide a man's own personal unity.

There is a difference between the modern way life looking at men and the way the Bible looks at men. The modern way of looking at man and his virtues is to say, "What a wonderful promise of what man is going to be; given right conditions, he will develop and be all right." The Bible looks at man and says, "He must be born again; he is a ruin, and only the Spirit of God can re-make him." We cannot patch up our natural virtues and make them come up to Jesus Christ's standard. No natural love, no natural patience, no natural purity, no natural forgiveness, can come anywhere near what Jesus Christ demands. The hymn has it rightly:

> And every value we possess,
> And every victory won,
> And every thought of holiness,
> Are His alone.

As we bring every bit of our bodily machine into harmony with the new life God has put within, He will exhibit in us the virtues that were characteristic of the Lord Jesus; the supernatural virtues are made natural. That is the meaning of learning to draw on the life of God for everything.

(d) All Degrees of Fear
Therefore is my spirit overwhelmed within me; my heart within me is desolate. (Psalm 143:4)

And I will make an everlasting covenant with them, . . . I will put my fear in their hearts, that they shall not depart from Me. (Jeremiah 32:40; see also Proverbs 12:25; Ecclesiastes 2:20; Deuteronomy 28:28)

Fear resides in the heart. Take it physically, if you take a deep breath, you cause your heart to pump the blood faster through your veins, and physical fear goes; and it is the same with the spirit. God expels the old fear by putting in a new Spirit and a new concern. What is that concern? The fear lest we grieve Him.

(e) All Degrees of Anguish
I am pained at my very heart; . . . I cannot hold my peace. . . . (Jeremiah 4:19; see also Joshua 5:1; Leviticus 26:36; Psalm 102:4)

There again we find that the physical and spiritual centre is the heart. All anguish is in the heart. What we suffer from proves where our hearts are. What did Jesus Christ suffer from? The anguish of our Lord's heart was on account of sin against His Father. What causes the anguish of our hearts? Can we "fill up that which is behind of the afflictions of Christ"? Are we shocked only at social evils and social wrongs, or are we as profoundly shocked at pride against God? Do we feel as keenly as Jesus Christ did the erecting of mine self-will against God? The centre of true anguish is in the heart, and when God puts our hearts right, He brings us into fellowship with Jesus Christ and we enter into fellowship with His sufferings.

(f) All Conscious Unity
All these men of war, that could keep rank, came with a perfect heart to Hebron, to make David king over all Israel and all the rest also of Israel were of one heart to make David king. (1 Chronicles 12:38; see also Jeremiah 32:39; Ezekiel 11:19; Acts 4:32)

The heart is the place where God works, and there all conscious unity resides; when once the Spirit of God is in the heart He will bring spirit, soul and body into perfect unity. Other powers can do this beside God, viz: the world, the flesh, and the devil. The world can give a conscious unity to man's heart; so can the flesh and the devil. The man who gives way to sensuality, to worldliness, to devilishness, or to covetousness, is perfectly satisfied without God. God calls that idolatry.

We have to watch and see with what our hearts are getting into unity; what our hearts are bringing our souls and bodies into line with. "O LORD our God, other lords beside Thee have had dominion over us."

Chapter XII

HEART: THE RADICAL REGION OF LIFE
The Rendezvous of Perfect Life

1. The Inner
   (a) Highest Love (Psalm 73:26; Mark 12:30–31)
   (b) Highest Licence (Ezekiel 28:2)
   (c) Darkened (Romans 1:21; Ephesians 4:18)
   (d) Hardened (Isaiah 6:10; Jeremiah 16:12; 2 Corinthians 3:14)

2. The Inmost
   (a) The Laboratory of Life (Mark 7:20–23)
   (b) Lusts (Mark 4:15–19; Romans 1:24)
   (c) Law of Nature (Romans 2:15)
   (d) Law of Grace (Isaiah 51:7; Jeremiah 31:33)
   (e) Seat of Conscience (Hebrews 10:22; 1 John 3:19–21)
   (f) Seat of Belief and Disbelief (Romans 10:10; Hebrews 3:12)

3. The Innermost
   (a) Inspiration of God (2 Corinthians 8:16)
   (b) Inspiration of Satan (John 13)
   (c) Indwelling of Christ (Ephesians 3:17)
   (d) Indwelling of Spirit (2 Corinthians 1:22)
   (e) Abode of Peace (Colossians 3:15)
   (f) Abode of Love (Romans 5:5)
   (g) Abode of Light (2 Peter 1:19)
   (h) Abode of Communion (Ephesians 5:19)

A Rendezvous is an appointed place of meeting. The heart is the appointed place of meeting not only for all the life of the body physically, but for all the life of the soul and of the spirit. We have seen that the heart is the centre of the bodily life physically, the centre of the soul life, and the centre of the spirit life, and that the Bible places in the heart what modern science puts in the brain.

All through these studies we have insisted on what the Bible insists on, viz., that our body is the most gracious gift God has given us, and that if we hand over the mainspring of our life to God we can work out in our bodily life all that He works in. It is through our bodily lives that Satan works and, thank God, it is through our bodily lives that God's Spirit works. God gives us His grace and His Spirit; He puts right all that was wrong, He does not suppress it nor counteract it, but readjusts the whole thing; then begins our work. We have to work out what God has worked in, and we have to beware of the snare of blaming God for not doing what we alone can do. When Paul says, "Be renewed in the spirit of your mind," he is referring to the heart, which is renewed by the Spirit of God The expression of the heart is made through the mechanism of the brain, and the marvellous emancipation which comes, slowly and surely, is that when God has altered the heart and filled it with a new Spirit, we have the power to will and to do all that He wants us to do.

Jesus Christ puts the test this way: "If ye love Me, ye will keep My commandments," not some of them, but all of them. No man can keep Jesus Christ's commandments unless God has done a radical work in his heart; but if He has, this is the practical, common-sense proof—he keeps the commandments of Jesus.

1. The Inner
The Inner, the Inmost, and the Innermost—we now come right to the very centre of our personality, where we know nothing except what God reveals. God's Book counsels: "Keep thy heart with all diligence; for out of it are the issues of life" (Proverbs 4:23). We are far too complex to understand ourselves; we must hand over the keeping of our hearts to God. If we think that we are simple and easy to understand, we shall never ask God to save us or keep us; but if we

have come to the condition of the psalmist, we will hand the keeping of our souls right over to Him and say, "Search me, O God, and know my heart: try me, and know my thoughts" (Psalm 139:23).

(a) Highest Love
We must put the emphasis where the Bible puts it: "*God* is the strength of my heart" (Psalm 73:26). "Thou shalt love the Lord thy God with all thy heart, and with all thy soul, and with all thy mind, and with all thy strength: this is the first commandment. And the second is like, namely this, Thou shalt love thy neighbour as thyself" (Mark 12:30–31). According to the Bible, the highest love of the human heart is not for our kind, but for God. Our Lord distinctly taught His disciples that if they were going to live the spiritual life, they must barter the natural for it; that is, they must forgo the natural life. We mean by the "natural" life, the ordinary, sensible, healthy, worldly-minded life. The highest love is not natural to the human heart. Naturally, we do not love God, we mistrust Him; consequently in thinking we are apt to apply to God what should be applied to Satan. Satan uses the problems of this life to slander God's character; he tries to make us think that all the calamities and miseries and wrongs spring from God.

We have defined love, in its highest sense, as being the sovereign preference of my person for another person. The surest sign that God has done a work of grace in my heart is that I love Jesus Christ best, not weakly and faintly, not intellectually, but passionately, personally and devotedly, overwhelming every other love of my life.

In Romans 5:5 ("The love of God is shed abroad in our hearts by the Holy Ghost which is given unto us"), Paul does not say that the capacity to love God is shed abroad in our hearts, he says "*the love of God* is shed abroad." The Bible knows only one love in this connection, and that is the supreme, dominating love of God. Jesus Christ teaches that if we have had a work of grace done in our hearts, we will show to our fellow-men the same love God has shown to us. "A new commandment I give unto you, that ye love one another; as I have loved you, that ye also love one another" (John 13:34).

The natural heart, we cannot repeat it too often, does not want the Gospel. We will take God's blessings and His loving-kindnesses and prosperity, but when it comes to close quarters and God's Spirit informs us that we have to give up the rule of ourselves and let Him rule us, then we understand what Paul means when he says the "carnal mind" (which resides in the heart) "is enmity against God." Are we willing for God not to suppress or counteract, but to totally alter the ruling disposition of our heart? The wonderful work of the grace of God is that through the Atonement God can alter the centre of my life, and put there a supreme, passionate devotion to God Himself.

The natural man does not like God's commands; he will not have them, he covers them over and ignores them. Jesus said that the first commandment is: "Thou shalt love the Lord thy God with all thy heart, and with all thy soul, and with all thy mind, and with all thy strength." Men put the second commandment first: "Thou shalt love thy neighbour as thyself." The great cry to-day is "love for mankind." The great cry of Jesus is "love for God first," and this love, the highest love, the supreme, passionate devotion of the life, springs from the inner centre.

What a rest comes when the love of God has been shed abroad in my heart by the Holy Spirit! I realise that God is love, not loving, but love, something infinite greater than loving, consequently He has to be very stern. There is no such thing as God overlooking sin. That is where people make a great mistake with regard to love; they say, "God is love and of course He will forgive sin": God is holy love and He *cannot* forgive sin. Jesus Christ did not come to forgive sin; He came to save us from our sins. The salvation of Jesus Christ removes the "sinner" out of my heart and plants in the "saint." That is the marvellous work of God's grace.

That the natural heart of man does not want the Gospel of God is proved by the resentment of the heart against the working of the Spirit of God, "No, I don't object to being forgiven, I don't mind being guided and blessed, but it is too much of a radical surrender to ask me to give up my right to myself and allow the Spirit of God to have absolute control of my heart." That is the natural resentment. But oh, the ineffable, unspeakable delight when we are made one with God, one with Jesus Christ, and one with every fellowbeliever in this great, overwhelming characteristic of love, when life becomes possible on God's plan!

(b) Highest Licence
In Ezekiel 28:2 ("Say unto the Prince of Tyrus, Thus saith the Lord GOD; Because thine heart is lifted up, and thou hast said, I am a God, . . . yet thou art a man, and not God. . . .") we have the presentation of the personality of sin, not the picture of the wrong disposition, which we have all inherited, but of the being who is the instigator behind the wrong disposition inciting to licence. Licence simply means—"I will not be bound by any laws but my own." This spirit resents God's law and will not have anything to do with it— "I shall rule my body as I choose, I shall rule my social relationships and my religious life as I like, and I will not allow God or any creed or doctrine to rule me." That is the way licence begins to work.

Watch how often the Apostle Paul warns us not to use our liberty "for an occasion to the flesh," i.e.,

don't use your liberty for licence. What is the difference between liberty and licence? Liberty is the ability to perform the law, perfect freedom to fulfil all the demands of the law. To be free from the law means that I am the living law of God, there is no independence of God in my make-up. Licence is rebellion against all law. If my heart does not become the centre of Divine love, it may become the centre of diabolical licence. Do people believe that nowadays? The majority of us do not accept Jesus Christ's statements. Immediately we look at them, their intensity and profundity make us shrink.

A very profitable and solemn study is the connection of the phrase "children of the devil" as used by Jesus. "Ye are of your father the devil, and the lusts of your father ye will do" (John 8:44). He is not referring to ordinary sinners, but to religious sinners. Natural sinners are called "children of wrath," but when our Lord used the phrase, "children of the devil," He was referring to religious disbelievers, viz., those who had seen the light and refused to walk in it, they would not have it.

Remember the two alternatives: our heart may be the centre of the Divine rule making us one with God's thoughts and purposes, or it may be the centre of the devil's rule making us one with the prince of this world, the being who hates God, one with the natural life which barters the spiritual.

(c) Darkened
. . . when they knew God, they glorified Him not as God . . . but became vain in their imaginations, and their foolish heart was darkened. Romans 1:21; see also Ephesians 4:18)

These are striking passages, quite at home in the New Testament, but at home nowhere else. This is not the darkness which comes from intensity of light, it is the refusal to allow any light at all. Read John 3:19 and you will see how our Lord uses the word "darkness." "This is the judgement," He says, i.e., the critical moment, "that the light is come into the world, and men loved the darkness rather than the light; for their works were evil" (RV). On another occasion Jesus said, "If therefore the light that is in thee be darkness, how great is that darkness!" Darkness is my own point of view; when once I allow the prejudice of my head to shut down the witness of my heart, I make my heart dark.

When Jesus Christ preached His first public sermon in Nazareth "where He had been brought up," the hearts of the people witnessed to Him wonderfully, then their prejudices got in the way and they closed down the witness of their hearts, broke up the service and tried to kill Him. That is an instance of how it is possible to choke the witness of the heart by the prejudice of the head. In John 3 Jesus was talking to a man who was in danger of closing down the witness of his heart because of his Jewish prejudice. Is there any light for which some of us have been thanking God, as the Psalmist puts it "God is the LORD, which hath shewed us light: bind the sacrifice with cords . . ." (Psalm 118:27), and is there a prejudice coming in and closing down the witness of the heart? If so, that is where the darkened heart begins; the light does not shine because it cannot. Until the Holy Spirit comes in we see only along the line of our prejudices. when we let the Holy Spirit come in, He will blow away the lines of our prejudices with His dynamic power, and we can begin to "go" in God's light.

A darkened heart is a terrible thing, because a darkened heart may make a man peaceful. A man says—"My heart is not bad, I am not convicted of sin; all this talk about being born again and filled with the Holy Spirit is so much absurdity." The natural heart needs the Gospel of Jesus, but it does not want it, it will fight against it, and it takes the convicting Spirit of God to make men and women know they need to experience a radical work of grace in their hearts.

(d) Hardened
But their minds were hardened: for until this very day . . . the same veil remaineth unlifted; which veil is done away in Christ. (2 Corinthians 3:14)

The characteristic of the hardened heart is familiar in the Bible but not anywhere else. For instance, we read in Exodus that God hardened Pharaoh's heart (Exodus 4:21, *et seq*). This must not be interpreted to mean that God hardened a man's heart and then condemned him for being hard. It means rather that God's laws, being God's laws, do not alter, and that if any man refuses to obey God's law he will be hardened away from God, and that by God's own decree. No man's destiny is made for him, he makes his own; but the imperative necessity that a man must make his own destiny is of God.

Whenever a man comes into an exalted position, it is a position in which he can either show the marvellous grace of God, or the hardening of his heart away from God. This is true of the prejudiced heart and the hardened heart, but not so true of the darkened heart. In a hardened heart there is no witness being crushed down, the heart is simply hard and untouched, and when God's love and God's works are abroad, it remains like ice; it may be smashed and broken by judgements, but it is simply breaking ice. The only way to alter the hardened heart is to melt it, and the only power that can melt it is the fire of the Holy Ghost.

The heart is so truly central that God alone knows it, and the illustrations the Bible uses are varied figures in order that we may understand how God deals with the heart.

2. The Inmost
(a) The Laboratory of Life
A laboratory is the place where things are prepared for use. The heart never dies, it is as immortal as God's Spirit because it is the centre of man's spirit. Memory never dies, mind never dies; our bodily machine dies, and the manifestation of our heart and life in the body dies, but the heart never dies. "Son, remember," these words were spoken to a man out of the body.

The things prepared for use are prepared in the heart. "For from within, out of the heart of man, proceed evil thoughts. . . ." (Mark 7:20). These are staggering words, and they spring from the lips of the Master of the human heart. They are not the shrewd guesses of a scientist, or the simple intimations of an apostle, they are the revelation of God Almighty through Jesus Christ. Look at them and see whether they not awaken resentment in you unless you have received the Spirit of God. These verses mean that no crime has ever been committed by a human being that every human being is not capable of committing. How many people believe that? "It is absurd, morbid nonsense," they say, which means that Jesus Christ did not know what He was talking about. To-day people are willingly and eagerly and all-embracingly accepting Christian Science, that popularisation of the belief that there is no such thing as sin or suffering or death, they are all imagination. The consequence is people are preaching the gospel of temperament—"Cheer up and look on the bright side of things." How can a man look on the bright side of things when the Spirit of God has shown him the possibilities of hell within? The majority of us are shockingly ignorant about ourselves simply because we will not allow the Spirit of God to reveal the enormous dangers that lie hidden in the centre of our spirit. Jesus Christ taught that dangers never come from outside, but from within. If we will accept Jesus Christ's verdict and receive the Spirit of God, we need never know in conscious life that what He says about the human heart is true, because He will re-relate the heart from within.

Perfect life does not mean perfection. Perfection means perfect attainment in everything. Perfect life means the perfect adjustment of all our relationships to God, nothing out of joint, everything rightly related; then we can begin to have the perfect life, that is, we can begin to attain. A child is a perfect human being, so is a man; what is the difference? The one is not yet grown and matured, the other is. Paul puts the two perfections very clearly in Philippians 3:12–15. When you are sanctified you have become perfectly adjusted to God; but remember, he implies, that you have attained to nothing yet; the whole life is right, undeserving of censure, now then begin to attain in your bodily life and prove that you are perfectly adjusted to Him.

(b) Lusts
Wherefore God also gave them up to uncleanness through the lusts of their own hearts. (Romans 1:24)

What is lust? "I must have it at once!" That is lust. Jesus said that lust would destroy the work of grace He has begun in us; "the lusts of other things entering in, choke the word" (Mark 4:19). The word "lust" is also used in other connections, viz., of the Spirit of God, "the Spirit [lusteth] against the flesh" (Galatians 5:17). The Spirit of God Who comes in at new birth lusts after this body, must have it at once, for God, and He will not tolerate the carnal mind for one second; consequently when a person is born again of the Spirit, there is a disclosure of enmity against God. No man knows he has that enmity inside until he receives the Holy Spirit. Immediately he receives the Spirit the carnal mind is aroused, and the carnal mind clamours and will not yield to the Spirit. This war is described in Galatians 5:17, the flesh lusting against the Spirit, and the Spirit against the flesh, both demanding "I must have this body at once." To which power are we going to give our body? Thank God for everyone who says, "Lord, I want to be identified with the death of Jesus until I know that my 'old man' was crucified with Him."

But watch lust on the other side—watch where it begins. "Ye did run well; who did hinder you?" Think what simple things Jesus Christ says will choke His word—"the cares of this world, . . . the lusts of other things." Once become worried and the choking of the grace of God begins. If we have really had wrought into our hearts and heads the amazing revelation which Jesus Christ gives that God is love and that we can never remember anything He will forget, then worry is impossible. Notice how frequently Jesus Christ warns against worry. The "cares of this world" will produce worry, and the "lusts of other things" entering in will choke the word God has put in. Is the thing which claims my attention just now the one thing for which God saved and sanctified me? If it is, life is all the time becoming simpler, and the crowding, clamouring lusts have no hold.

(c) The Law of Nature, (d) the Law of Grace, (e) the Seat of Conscience and (f) the Seat of Belief and Disbelief are all in the heart.

Conscience is the "eye of the soul," and the orbit of conscience, that marvellous recorder, is the heart. "Having our hearts sprinkled from an evil conscience." God puts the law of grace where the law of nature works, viz., in the heart. Thank God for His sovereign grace which can alter the mainspring of life!

(f) The Seat of Belief and Unbelief
Take heed, brethren, lest there be in any of you an evil heart of unbelief, in departing from the living God. (Hebrews 3:12)

There the distinction is made perfectly clear—the heart must never be agnostic, the head, if you like, may be. Every Christian is an avowed agnostic. Have you ever thought of that? How do I know God? All I know of God I have accepted as a revelation, I did not find it out by my head. "Canst thou by searching find out God?" Next time you meet some agnostic friend, say something like that to him and see if it does not alter the problem for him. We have to keep our minds open about a great many things. The reason people disbelieve God is not because they do not understand with their heads—we understand very few things with our heads, but because they have turned their hearts in another direction. Why was Jesus Christ so stern against disbelief? Because disbelief never springs from the head but from the wrong direction of the heart. Can I have the evil heart of unbelief taken out and a heart of belief put in? Thank God, the answer is "Yes!" "A new heart also will I give you, and a new spirit will I put within you . . ." (Ezekiel 36:26). Can I have an impure, defiled heart made pure, so pure that it is pure in God's sight? The answer is "Yes!" ". . . the blood of Jesus Christ His Son cleanseth us from all sin" (1 John 1:7). Can I be filled with the Holy Ghost until every nook and cranny is exactly under the control of God? Again the answer is "Yes!" "He that cometh after me is mightier than I, . . . He shall baptize you with the Holy Ghost and with fire: Whose fan is in His hand, and He will throughly purge His floor . . ." (Matthew 3:11–12).

Jesus Christ's salvation works first at the centre, not at the circumference. No one is capable of thinking about being born, or of how they will live when they are born, until they are born; we have to be born into this world first before we can think about it. "Marvel not that I said unto thee, Ye must be born again"—"you must be born into a new world first, and if you want to know My doctrine, do My will" said Jesus. A right relation to God first is essential. How are we to have a right heart relationship to God? By accepting His Spirit, and He will bring us where we can understand how God's grace works. If any man will receive the Spirit of God, he will find He will lead him into all truth.

3. The Innermost
(a) The Inspiration of God
The inspiration of God may dwell in the innermost recesses of my heart. "But thanks be to God, which put the same earnest care into the heart of Titus for you" (2 Corinthians 8:16). You may be surprised at the seeming slightness of this passage. The inspiration for benevolence and philanthropy springs from God, and God's Book has some stern revelations to make about philanthropy and benevolence, it reveals that they may spring from a totally wrong motive.

The inspiration of God does not patch up my natural virtues; He re-makes the whole of my being until we find that "every virtue we possess is His alone." God does not come in and patch up our good works, He puts in the Spirit that was characteristic of Jesus; it is His patience, His love, and His tenderness and gentleness that are exhibited through us. "Whoso eateth My flesh, and drinketh My blood . . . ." When God alters a man's heart and plants His Spirit within, his actions have the inspiration of God behind them; if they have not, they may have the inspiration of Satan.

(b) Inspiration of Satan
And supper being ended, the devil having now put into the heart of Judas Iscariot . . . to betray Him. . . . (John 13:2)

(c) The Indwelling of Christ
The indwelling of Christ—an unspeakable wonder! "That Christ may dwell in your hearts by faith . . ." (Ephesians 3:17). This figure of the indwelling of Christ is very remarkable; we are made part of the mystical Body of Christ that Christ may indwell us. The New Testament gives three pictures of Jesus: first, the historic Jesus; second, God Incarnate; and third, the mystical Body of Christ, which is being made up now of sanctified believers. By the sovereign work of God and the indwelling Christ, we can show through our lives, through our bodily relationships, the very same characteristics that were seen in the Lord Jesus, so that men may take knowledge of us that we have been with Jesus, and, as our Lord said, men seeing your good works, may "glorify your Father which is in heaven."

The thought is unspeakably full of glory, that God the Holy Ghost can come into my heart and fill it so full that the life of God will manifest itself all through this body which used to manifest exactly the opposite. If I am willing and determined to keep in the light and obey the Spirit, then the characteristics of the indwelling Christ will manifest themselves.

(d) The Indwelling of the Spirit
This is something more explainable. The spirit, soul and body of the Man Christ Jesus were kept in perfect oneness with God the Father by the Holy Spirit. Study Jesus Christ's life: His up-look to God, i.e., His prayer life, was always right; His out-look on men was always right, and His down-look on sin and the devil and hell was always right. He did not ignore any of these facts, as a great many people are doing to-day, and His Spirit energising our spirit will produce in us the same characteristics and lift us by His marvellous Atonement into the same at-one-ment with God. "That they may be one, even as We are one," not by absorption, but by identification. This is not the

teaching which is prevalent nowadays that we are to be absorbed into one great, infinite Being; we are to be made one in identity with Jesus Christ, to have a disposition like His; consequently we are interested only in the things in which He is interested, we cannot be appealed to on any other line.

(e) The Abode of Peace
"*And let the peace of God rule in your hearts*" (Colossians 3:15). This is the peace *of* God, not peace *with* God. Thank God, there is a peace with God, but this is a different peace. "Peace I leave with you, *My* peace I give unto you," said Jesus, i.e., the peace that characterised Jesus Christ is to characterise His saints.

(f) The Abode of Love
"The love of God is shed abroad in our hearts" (Romans 5:5), not the capacity to love God, but the very love of God. That is what Paul means by those words with which we are so familiar—"I have been [RV] crucified with Christ: nevertheless I live; yet not I, but Christ liveth in me: and the life which I now live in the flesh I live by the faith of the Son of God." This is not faith *in* Jesus, but "*the faith of the Son of God,*" i.e., the faith that was in Jesus is in me; I am identified with Jesus to such an extent that you cannot detect a different spring of life, because there is not one! It is no longer the old disposition that rules me, says Paul, but the disposition that is in Jesus Christ. If you have not the Spirit of God, you will think the Apostle is straining language beyond its limit in his effort to express what the Spirit of God does, viz., He alters the ruling disposition, and a man shows himself as entirely changed.

(g) The Abode of Light
". . . a light that shineth in a dark place" (2 Peter 1:19). We have a wonderful picture of light in James 1:17, ". . . the Father of lights, with Whom can be no variation, neither shadow that is cast by turning" (RV), nothing to hide. That is the characteristic of God, and St. Paul counsels us to "Walk as children of light."

(h) The Abode of Communion
St. John says, "If we walk in the light, as He is in the light, we have fellowship one with another." That is a wonderful description of the communion we shall have. Natural affinity does not count here at all. Watch how God has altered our affinities since we were filled with the Spirit; we have an affinity of fellowship with people for whom we have no natural affinity at all, we have fellowship with everyone who is in the light, no matter who they are, or to what nation they belong, or anything else—a most extraordinary alteration.

Chapter XIII

OURSELVES: I; ME; MINE

Ourselves As "Knower." I the "Ego"

1. Some Distinctions of Importance
   (a) Individuality
   (b) Personality
   (c) Egotism and Egoism

2. Some Determinations of Interest (John 3:2)
   (a) The Ego Is Inscrutable (Isaiah 26:9; Psalm 19:12)
   (b) The Ego Is Introspective (Psalm 139; Proverbs 20:27)
   (c) The Ego Is Individual (Ezekiel 18:1–4)

3. Some Delusions of Importance (2 Thessalonians 2:7–12)
   (a) The Ego in Delusions of Insanity
   (b) The Ego in Delusions of Alternating Personalities
   (c) The Ego in Delusions of Mediums and Possessions

We have divided this subject of Ourselves into two: the part that knows, the Ego; and the part that is known, the Me.

1. Some Distinctions of Importance

First of all we will take these distinctions generally—Individuality and Personality, Egotism and Egoism, and we shall find that the Bible gives us wonderful insight into these distinctions.

(a) Individuality

Individuality is a smaller term than Personality. We speak of an individual animal, an individual man, an individual thing. An individual man is one by himself, he takes up so much space, requires so many cubic feet of air, etc.

(b) Personality

Personality is infinitely more. Possibly the best illustration we can use is that of a lamp. A lamp unlighted will illustrate individuality; a lighted lamp will illustrate personality. The lighted lamp takes up no more room, but the light permeates far and wide; so the influence of personality goes far beyond that of individuality. "Ye are the light of the world" said our Lord. Individually we do not take up much room, but our influence is far beyond our calculation. When we use the term "personality," we use the biggest mental conception we have, that is why we call God a Person,

because the word "person" has the biggest import we know. We do not call God an individual we call God a Person. He may be a great deal more, but at least He must be that. It is necessary to remember this when the personality of God is denied and He is taken to be a tendency. If God is only a tendency, He is much less than we are. Our personality is always too big for us. When we come to examine the next sections and trace the Bible teaching we shall find that we are much too complex to understand ourselves.

Another illustration of personality, more often used, is the following: an island may be easily explored, yet how amazed we are when we realise that it is the top of a mountain, whose greater part is hidden under the waves of the sea and goes sheer down to deeper depths than we can fathom. The little island represents our conscious personality. The part of ourselves of which we are conscious is a very tiny part, there is a greater part underneath about which we know nothing; consequently there are upheavals from beneath that we cannot account for. We cannot grasp ourselves at all. We begin by thinking we can, but we have to come to the Bible standpoint that no one knows himself; the only One Who knows him is God. "There is a way that seemeth right unto a man, but the end thereof are the ways of death" (Proverbs 16:25).

Individuality, then, is a smaller term than personality. Personality means that peculiar, incalculable being that is meant when you speak of "you" as distinct from everybody else. People say, "Oh, I cannot understand myself"; of course you can't! "Nobody else understands me"; of course they don't! There is only one Being Who understands us, and that is our Creator.

(c) Egotism and Egoism

It is necessary to have a proper distinction in our minds regarding egotism and Egoism. Egotism is a conceited insistence on my own particular ways and manners and customs. It is an easily discernible characteristic, and fortunately is condemned straightway by right thinking people. We are inclined to overlook egotism in young people and in ignorant people, but even in them it is of the detestable, vicious order. Of egoism only good things can be said. It is that system of thinking which makes the human personality the centre. The thinking that starts from all kinds of abstractions is contrary to the Bible. The Bible way of thinking brings us right straight down to man as the centre. That which puts man right and keeps man right is the revelation we have in God's Book. For instance, the teaching of our Lord and of the Apostle Paul continually centres around "I," yet there is no egotism about it; it is egoism. Everything in the Bible is related to man, to his salvation, to his sanctification, to his keeping, etc. Any system of thinking which has man for its centre and as its aim and purpose is rightly called Egoism.

2. Some Determinations of Interest
The personality of man is his inmost nature; it is distinct from spirit, soul and body and yet embraces all; it is the innermost centre of man's spirit, soul and body. There are three things to be said about the "Ego."

(a) Inscrutable
It is inscrutable, i.e., we cannot understand it or search it out. The Bible says that a man is incapable of searching himself out satisfactorily. "With my soul have I desired Thee in the night; yea, with my spirit within me will I seek Thee early" (Isaiah 26:9). There the distinction is made clearly between the inmost personality called "I" and spirit, soul and body; and this distinction is maintained all through God's Book. I can search my spirit to a certain point. I can search my soul, but only to a certain point. Immediately man comes to examine himself he begins to find that he is inscrutable, he cannot examine himself thoroughly. He may make certain arbitrary distinctions and call himself body, soul and spirit, but he instantly finds that that is not satisfactory. Those of you who are familiar with books dealing with this subject will find the word "subliminal" (below the threshold) constantly occurring. Something from below the threshold of consciousness every now and again emerges and upsets our teaching about ourselves. Our Lord's dealings with the disciples made them conscious of things in themselves of which they had been hitherto unconscious. For instance, in Matthew 16 we read that Jesus said to Peter, "Blessed art thou," and shortly afterwards He said to him, "Get thee behind Me, Satan." Peter had not the slightest notion that God Almighty had lifted him up as a trumpet and blown a blast through him, which Jesus Christ recognised as the voice of His Father; or that a little while afterwards Satan took him up and blew a blast through him, which Jesus recognised as the voice of Satan. Again, if Peter had been told that he would deny his Lord with oaths and curses, he would have been unable to understand how anyone could think it possible. There are possibilities below the threshold of our lives which no one but God knows. Jesus Christ brought His disciples through crises in order to reveal to them that they were much too big to understand themselves; there were forces within them which would play havoc with every resolution they made. "Who can understand his errors? Cleanse Thou me from secret faults" (Psalm 19:12). This verse is simply a type of the revelation running all through God's Book. We cannot understand ourselves, we do not know the beginnings of our dreams or of our motives; we do not know our secret errors, they lie below the region we can get at.

(b) Introspective
Not only are we inscrutable, but we are so built that we are obliged to examine ourselves; that is the meaning of introspective. Introspection means the direct observation of the processes of our mind. Along this line people become insane. If you cut a tree in half you can tell by the number of rings inside how old it is; and people try to do this psychically, that is, they try to cut their consciousness in half and find out how it is made. We are so built that we must introspect. Immediately a man realises he is incalculable, he wants to understand himself, and consequently he begins to introspect. The great chapter in the Bible on wise introspection is the 139th Psalm; it is a Psalm of Intercessory Introspection. The words are a contradiction in terms, but they exactly convey the meaning of the Psalm. The tendency in me which makes me want to examine myself, and know the springs of my thoughts and motives takes the form of prayer, "O Lord explore me." The Psalmist talks of the great *Creator*. Who knows the beginnings of the morning and the endings of the evening, Who knows the fathomless deep and the tremendous mountains, but he does not end with vague abstractions; these things are all very well, but they are useless for his purpose: he asks this great Creator to come and search *him*. "My God there are beginnings of mornings and endings of evenings in me that I cannot understand; there are great mountain peaks I cannot scale; such knowledge is too wonderful for me, I cannot attain unto it, explore me, search me out." Or again, he means, "Search out the beginnings of my dreams, get down below where I can go, winnow out my way until You understand the beginnings of my motives and my dreams, and let me know that You know me; and the only way I shall know that You know me is that You will save me from the way of grief, from the way of self-realisation, from the way of sorrow and twistedness, and lead me in the way everlasting." The Greek philosophers used to tell us to know ourselves, and Socrates' teaching is exactly along the line of this Psalm, but from a different standpoint. Socrates' wisdom consisted in finding out that he knew nothing of himself, and that is why he was called by the Oracle the wisest man on earth. We have to be avowed agnostics about ourselves. We begin by thinking that

we know all about ourselves, but a quarter of an hour of the "plague of our own heart" upsets all our thinking, and we understand the meaning of the Psalmist, "O Lord, search me!"

Mark you, God does not search us without our knowing. "The spirit of man is the candle of the LORD, searching all the inward parts of the belly" (Proverbs 20:27). The word translated by the old Saxon word "belly" means the innermost part. God makes a man know that He is searching him. When we come to our Lord, this line explains His attitude towards the human soul, "If I had not come, . . . they had not had sin." If Jesus Christ had not come with His light, and the Holy Ghost had not come with His light men had not known anything about sin. It takes the Apostle Paul to use the phrase "sold under sin," and to know the meaning of it Paul had been searched clean through by the penetration of the Spirit of God.

We are inscrutable, but we are so built that we must introspect. Introspection without God leads to insanity. We do not know the springs of our thinking, we do not know by what we are influenced, we do not know all the scenery psychically that Jesus Christ looked at. Our Lord continually saw things and beings we do not see. He talked about "Satan" and "demons" and "angels." We don't see Satan or demons or angels, but Jesus Christ unquestionably did, and He sees their influence upon us. The man who criticises Jesus Christ's statements about demon possession does not realise what he is doing. The people with no tendency to introspect are those described in the New Testament as "dead in trespasses and sins," they are quite happy, quite contented, quite moral, all they want is easily within their grasp, everything is all right with them; but they are dead to the world to which Jesus Christ belongs, and it takes His voice and His Spirit to awaken them.

(c) Individual

By the term individual, we mean, first, what we stated at the beginning in distinguishing between individuality and personality; and second, that every man is judged before God as an individual being; what he has done, he alone is responsible for. "The word of the LORD came unto me again, saying What mean ye, that ye use this proverb concerning the land of Israel, saying, The fathers have eaten sour grapes, and the children's teeth are set on edge? As I live, saith the Lord GOD, ye shall not have occasion any more to use this proverb in Israel. Behold, all souls are Mine; as the soul of the father, so also the soul of the son is Mine: the soul that sinneth, it shall die" (Ezekiel 18:1–4). This line of revelation runs all through God's Book, and it shows the absurdity of the criticism arising from the fictitious conception that we are punished for Adam's

sin. The Bible does not say so. The Bible says that men are punished for their own sins, that is, for sins committed culpably. The Bible says that sin entered into the world by one man, but sin is not an act on my part at all. Sin is a disposition, and I am in no way responsible for having the disposition of sin; but I am responsible for not allowing God to deliver me from the disposition of sin when once I see that that is what Jesus Christ came to do. The wrong things I do I shall be punished for and whipped for, no matter how I plead. For every wrong that I do, I shall be inexorably punished and shall have to suffer. The inexorable law of God is laid down that I shall be held responsible for the wrong that I do, I shall smart for it and be punished for it, no matter who I am. The Atonement has made provision for what I am not responsible for, viz., the disposition of sin. John 3:19 sums it up: "This is the judgement" (the crisis, the critical moment), "that the light is come into the world, and men loved the darkness rather than the light; for their works were evil" (RV). What is light? Jesus says, "I am the light of the world," and He also said, "If therefore the light that is in thee be darkness, how great is that darkness!" Darkness is my own point of view.

In Regeneration God works below the threshold of our consciousness; all we are conscious of is a sudden burst up into our conscious life, but as to when God begins to work no one can tell. This emphasises the importance of intercessory prayer. A mother, a husband, or a wife, or a Christian worker, praying for another soul has a clear indication that God has answered their prayer; outwardly the one prayed for is just the same, there is no difference in his conduct, but the prayer is answered. The work is unconscious as yet, but at any second it may burst forth into conscious life. We cannot calculate where God begins to work any more than we can say when it is going to become conscious; that is why we have to pray in reliance on the Holy Spirit (see Romans 8:26–27). The path of peace for us is to hand ourselves over to God and ask Him to search us, not what we think we are, or what other people think we are, or what we persuade ourselves we are or would like to be, but, "Search *me* out, O God, explore *me* as I really am in Thy sight."

3. Some Delusions of Importance
(2 Thessalonians 2:7–12)

There are supernatural powers and agencies of which we are unconscious which, unless we are garrisoned by God, can play with us like toys whenever they choose. The New Testament continually impresses this on us. "For we wrestle not against flesh and blood, but against principalities, against powers, against the rulers of the darkness of this world, against spiritual wickedness in high places" (Ephesians 6:12). All that is outside the realm of our consciousness. If we only look for results in the earthlies when we pray, we are ill-taught. A praying saint performs far more havoc amongst the unseen forces of darkness than we have the slightest notion of. "The effectual fervent prayer of a righteous man availeth much." We have not the remotest conception of what is done by our prayers, nor have we the right to try and examine and understand it; all we know is that Jesus Christ laid all stress on prayer. "And greater works than these shall he do; because I go unto My Father. And whatsoever ye shall ask in My name, that will I do."

It is only when these speculations and terrors are awakened in us that we begin to see what the Atonement of Jesus Christ means. It means safeguarding in the unseen, safeguarding from dangers we know nothing about. "Kept by the power of God"! The conscious ring of our life is a mere phase, Jesus Christ did not die and rise again to save that only; the whole personality of man is included. We have to beware of estimating Jesus Christ's salvation by our experience of it. Our experience is a mere indication in the conscious life of an almighty salvation that goes far beyond anything we ever can experience.

Second Thessalonians 2:7–12 represents the borderland realm of things which it is difficult to trace. The theme is not an isolated one, it runs all through the Bible and indicates a borderland we cannot step over.

(a) Delusions of Insanity

What is insanity? One of the greatest mistakes being made to-day is the statement that the cases of demon possession in the Bible were cases of insanity. The distinction between the two is made perfectly clear; the symptoms are not even the same. Insanity simply means that a man is differently related to affairs from the majority of other men and is sometimes dangerous. Paul was charged with madness (Acts 26:24–25), and the same charge was brought against Jesus Christ—"For they said, He is beside himself." Have you ever noticed the wisdom of the charge? Both Jesus Christ and Paul were unquestionably mad, according to the standard of the wisdom of this world; they were related to affairs differently from the majority of other men, consequently, for the sake of self-preservation, they must be got rid of. Our Lord was crucified, and Paul was beheaded. When we are imbued with Jesus Christ's Spirit and are related to life as He was, we shall find that we are considered just as mad according to the standard of this world.

Another thing said about insane people is that they have lost their reason; this is technically untrue. An insane person is one who has lost everything but his reason. According to the universal standard, an insane person has lost the relation of the body to his reason, lost the relation of the outside world to his reason, yet he can find a reason for everything. Anyone who knows anything about the diagnosis of insanity knows that this is true.

Read the expositions of the Sermon on the Mount to-day and you will find some of the cleverest dialectics that have ever been written. The writers try to prove that Jesus is not mad according to the standards of this world; but He is mad, absolutely mad, and there is no apology needed for saying it. Either the modern attitude to things must alter, or it must pronounce Jesus Christ mad. "Seek ye first the kingdom of God, and His righteousness; and all these things shall be added unto you." Volumes have been written to prove that the Lord did not mean that; but He did. Common sense says, "That is nonsense, I must seek my living first, then I will devote myself to the kingdom of God." In 1 Corinthians 1 Paul reasons that in the view of God it is the world that is mad, and that man only becomes sane in God's sight when he is readjusted to God through the Atonement.

(b) The Delusion of Alternating Personalities (see Mark 5:1–15)

That is, one body being the arena of more than one personality. This is not demon possession entirely, although the case we are taking is such. The incident recorded in Mark 5 is not a case of insanity. You wonder first of all who is speaking; the man with the unclean spirit bows down before Jesus and worships Him, he knows perfectly well that Jesus can deliver him; but as soon as he gets there, the other personality cries out against Jesus Christ, and pleads with Him to deal mercifully with him.

There are cases of alternating personalities to-day, amazing records of people suddenly disappearing from one part of the country and living a totally different life in another part of the country. The delusions arising from alternating personalities cannot be dealt with by science; but Jesus Christ can deal with them.

(c) Delusions of Mediums and Possessions

And it came to pass, as we went to prayer, a certain damsel possessed with a spirit of divination met us, which brought her masters much gain by soothsaying. (Acts 16:16)

Paul was grieved because this girl was a medium. A spiritualistic medium commits the greatest psychical crime in the world, that is, the greatest crime against the soul. Drunkenness and debauchery are child's play compared with spiritualism. According to the Bible, it is possible for a man or woman to make himself or herself a medium through which unseen spirits can talk to seen men and women. Beware of using the phrase "Yield, give up your will." Be perfectly certain to whom you are yielding. No one has any right to yield himself to any impression or to any influence or impulse; immediately you yield, you are susceptible to all kinds of supernatural powers and influences. There is only one Being to whom you must yield, and that is the Lord Jesus Christ; but be sure it is the Lord Jesus Christ to Whom you yield. In religious meetings it is the impressionable people who are the dangerous people. When you get that type of nature to deal with, pray as you never prayed, watch as you never watched, and travail in communion as you never travailed in communion, because the soul that is inclined to be a medium between any supernatural forces and himself will nearly always be caught up by the supernatural forces belonging to Satan instead of by God. Insanity is a fact, demon possession is a fact, and mediumship is a fact. The Bible says regarding the false Christs ". . . if it were possible, they shall deceive the very elect" (Matthew 24:24). So beware to whom you yield. When once a nature is laid hold of by the sovereign power of God and recognises to Whom he is yielding, then that nature is safeguarded for ever. Beware of impressions and impulses unless they wed themselves to the standards given by Jesus Christ.

"All power is given unto Me," said Jesus; "and I give unto you power . . . over all the power of the enemy."

Chapter XIV

OURSELVES: I; ME; MINE
Ourselves As "Known." "Me"

1. The Sensuous "Me" (Ecclesiastes 12:13)
   (a) My Body (Romans 12:1)
   (b) My Bounty (Hebrews 13:15)
   (c) My Blessings (Romans 12:13)

2. The Social "Me" (Ecclesiastes 7:29)
   (a) My Success (Matthew 5:13–16)
   (b) My Sociability (John 5:40–44)
   (c) My Satisfaction (Matthew 10:17–22)

3. The Spiritual "Me" (Ephesians 2:6)
   (a) My Mind (Romans 12:2)
   (b) My Morals (Matthew 5:20)
   (c) My Mysticism (Colossians 2:20–23)

The Sensuous "Me." By "Sensuous" we mean bodily, material consciousness. My Body represents one aspect of "Me." Under the heading of My Bounty, we shall consider our "flesh and blood relations," and under the heading of My Blessings, our home, property, and wealth.

The Social "Me." Under the Social "Me" we shall consider all that my "set" means: if you insult my "set," you insult "Me." It is important to impress upon ourselves that God recognises that this is the way He has made us. Our Lord insists on the social aspect of our lives: He shows very distinctly that we cannot further ourselves alone.

The Spiritual "Me." This means my religious convictions—my Mind, my Morals, and my Mysticism.

To go back to our first statement. If my body is hurt, I look upon it as a personal hurt; if my home or my people are insulted, it is a personal insult; if my "set" and my society are hurt, I consider it a personal hurt; and if my religious convictions are hurt or upset or scandalised, I consider myself as being hurt and scandalised.

The normal "Me," from the Scriptural standpoint, is not the average man. "Normal" means regular, exact, perpendicular, everything according to rule. "Abnormal" means irregular, away from the perpendicular; and "super-normal" means that which goes beyond regular experience, not contradicting it, but transcending it. Our Lord represents the "supernormal." Through the salvation of Jesus Christ we partake of the normal, regular, upright; apart from His salvation we are abnormal.

We mean by the term "Me" the sum total of all that a man calls his. That means there is no real practical distinction between "me" and "mine." My personality identifies "mine" with my self so completely that it is not necessary to make a distinction between "me" and mine.

1. The Sensuous "Me"

"*Let us hear the conclusion of the whole matter: Fear God, and keep His commandments: for this is the whole duty of man*" (Ecclesiastes 12:13). This verse is the conclusion from the point of view of human and Divine wisdom as to what is the whole end of life, viz., to "fear God, and keep His commandments."

"Sensuous" means that which is affected through our senses, or that which we get at through our senses. The first thing we get at through our senses is the body.

The Bible has a great deal to tell us about our bodies. The main point to emphasise is that the Bible reveals that our body is the medium through which we develop our spiritual life. In the Middle Ages the body was looked upon as a clog, a hindrance, an annoyance, something that kept us back and upset our higher calling; something which had sin in the very corpuscles of its blood, in the cells of its make-up. The Bible entirely disproves this view; it tells us that our body is "the temple of the Holy Ghost," not a thing to be despised. The Bible gives the body a very high place indeed.

(a) My Body
"*I beseech you therefore, brethren, by the mercies of God, that ye present your bodies a living sacrifice*" (Romans 12:1). The Apostle does not say, "Present your "all"; the "Higher Life"[12] hymns do that, consequently they are unsatisfactory for you can never know when you have given your "all." Look at it in the light of the last chapter, if our personality is too big for us to understand, how are we to know when we have presented our all? The Bible never says any thing so vague as "present your all," but "present your bodies." There is nothing ambiguous or indefinite about that statement, it is definite and clear. The body means only one thing to us all, viz., this flesh and blood body.

Ask yourself this practical question: Who is the ruling person that is manifested through my body, through my hands, through my tongue, through my eyes, through my thinking and loving? Is it a self-realising person, or a Christ-realising person? Our body is to be the temple of the Holy Ghost, the medium for manifesting the marvellous disposition of Jesus Christ all through. Instead of our body being a hindrance to our development, it is only through our body that we are developed. We express our character through our body: you cannot express a character without a body. When we speak of character, we think of a flesh and blood thing; when we speak of disposition, we think of something that is not flesh and blood. Through the Atonement God gives us the right disposition; that disposition is inside our body, and we have to manifest it in character through our body and by means of our body. The meaning of bodily control is that the body is the obedient medium for expressing the right disposition. The Bible, instead of ignoring the fact that we have a body, exalts it. "What, know ye not that your body is the temple of the Holy Ghost which is in you?" "If any man defile the temple of God, him shall God destroy." Instead of the Bible belittling the laws of health and bodily uprightness and cleanliness, it insists on these by implication far more than modern science does by

explicit statement. Go back again to our first subject, viz., The Making of Man, and you will recall that the chief glory of man is not that he is in the image of God spiritually, but that he is made "of the earth, earthy." This is not man's humiliation but his glory, because through his mortal body is to be manifested the wonderful life and disposition of Jesus Christ. "Christ in you, the hope of glory."

(b) My Bounty
By Him therefore let us offer the sacrifice of praise to God continually, that is, the fruit of our lips giving thanks to His name. (Hebrews 13:15)

This verse comes in a chapter which is intensely practical, and which deals with our relationship to strangers as well as our relationships in the most intimate and practical matters of life. The next relationship of my body is my blood relations, my father and mother, my sister and brother, my wife, etc. Have you ever noticed that these are the relationships Jesus Christ refers to most often? Over and over again when Our Lord tells about discipleship, that is the sphere He deals with; He puts the relationships in this sphere as crucial. Read Luke 14:26–27, 33, there our Lord places our love for Himself away beyond our love for father and mother; in fact, He uses a tremendous word: "If any man come to Me, and *hate* not his father, and mother, . . . he cannot be My disciple." That word "hate" appears to be a stumbling-block to a great number of people. It is quite conceivable that many persons have such a slight regard for their fathers and mothers that it is nothing to them to separate from them; but the word "hate" shows by contrast the kind of love we ought to have for our parents, an intense love; yet, says Jesus, our love for Him is to be so intense that every other relationship is "hatred" in comparison if it should conflict with His claims.

Love for the Lord is not an ethereal, intellectual, dream-like thing; it is the intensest, the most vital, the most passionate love of which the human heart is capable. The realisation of such a fathomless love is rarely conscious, saving in some supreme crisis akin to martyrdom. In the generality of our days our love for God is too deeply imbedded to be conscious; it is neither joy nor peace, it is "me" obsessed by God in the unconscious domain. Love, to be love, is deeper than I am conscious of, and is only revealed by crises. This intense personal love is the only kind of love there is, not Divine *and* human love.

Jesus preached His first sermon in Nazareth, "where He had been brought up," and He told His disciples they were to begin "in Jerusalem." Did Jesus

---

12. The Higher Spiritual Life, concep emphasized sanctification and personal holiness.

Christ have such great success in Nazareth where He was known? No, He had exactly the opposite. When they heard Him speak they were so filled with wrath that they broke up the service and tried to kill Him. Our Lord insists that we begin at Jerusalem for the sake of our own character, and our "Jerusalem" is unquestionably among the bounties of our own particular flesh and blood relations. It is infinitely easier to offer the "sacrifice of praise" before strangers than amongst our own flesh and blood. That is where the "*sacrifice* of praise" comes in, and that is what young converts want to skip. It is by testifying to our own flesh and blood that we are confirmed in our own character and in our relationship to Jesus Christ. It is recorded in Luke 4:23–27, that Jesus spoke words which maddened His own people; He said, in effect, "It is God's way to send His message through strangers before that message is accepted." They would not accept it from Him. Why? Because they knew Him, and if we look into that statement we shall find that it revolutionises a great many of our conceptions. We should naturally have said that if Jesus had testified amongst His own people, they would have gladly received Him: the only place in which they did not receive Him, the place in which He could not do many mighty works, was the place where He was brought up. The place in which Jesus tells us as His disciples to begin our work is amongst our own flesh and blood, that is our "Jerusalem"; there we shall get consolidated and know where the true basis of our life lies. We do not often put together the words "sacrifice" and "praise." Sacrifice means giving the best we have, and it embraces an element of cost. Our own flesh and blood relationships have to be the scene of the sacrifice of praise on our part, whether It is accepted or not. That is where the *sacrifice* of praise comes in.

(c) My Blessings

By "Blessings" we mean our homes and our property.

Distributing to the necessity of saints; given to hospitality" (Romans 12:13).

The Bible has a great deal to say about "hospitality" and "entertaining strangers." God recognises the enormous importance of our immediate circle. The term "blessings" includes my home and my property, all that I distinctly look upon as mine, and I have to use it with this outlook of hospitality, and immediately I do, I find how personal it is. If any stranger finds fault with my home or insults it, my resentment is intense. My home is guarded in exactly the same way as my body is guarded. It is mine, therefore it is part of the very make-up of my personality, and God will not allow me to be exclusive over it, I must keep it open, be "given to hospitality." In the East they know a great deal more about hospitality than we do. By "home" we mean what we Britishers specially think of when we mention the word, viz., the most intimate relationships; that is the scene where we are to be given to hospitality. The point is that we are to be "given to hospitality" from God's standpoint; not because other people deserve it, but because God commands it. This principle runs all through our Lord's teaching. My body, my blood relationships, my home—I have to keep all these intimate and right, recognising the first duty in each one. My body is the temple of the Holy Ghost, not for me to disport myself in or to realise myself. My blood relationships unquestionably have to be recognised, but they are to be held in subjection; my first duty in them is to God; and my home is to be given to hospitality. Have you ever noticed how God's grace comes to those who are given to hospitality, if they are His children? Prosperity in home, in business, and in every way comes from following God's instructions in each detail.

2. The Social "Me"

Lo, this only have I found, that God hath made man upright; but they have sought out many inventions. (Ecclesiastes 7:29)

The word "inventions" is a quaint one. it means devices arising from man's self-love. God made man upright, normal, perpendicular, regular; but he has sought out many devices, many ingenious twistings away from the normal. The Social "Me" means recognition by my set, and this is a wonderful influence with us all. For instance, a boy who is good and mild to his father and mother at home may swear like a trooper when he is with the other set, not because he is bad or evil, but because he wants to be recognised by his set. This is true all through life, and the Spirit of God recognises the principle and regenerates it. We must be moulded by the set to which we belong whether we like it or not, and God may often alter our special setting. We may affect any amount of individuality, but it remains true that we either grovel or strut, according to our realisation of how we are recognised by the set to which we belong. The Book of God is insistent on this; we cannot develop a holy life alone, it would be a selfish life, without God in it and wrong. Jesus Christ was charged with being "a man gluttonous, and a winebibber" because He lived so sociably amongst men; and in His High-priestly prayer, He prays ". . . not that Thou shouldest take them from the world, but that Thou shouldest keep them from the evil one." The first place to which Jesus Christ led His disciples after He had said "Follow Me," was to a marriage feast. "We will come unto him, and make our abode with him," fellowship with the Trinity, that is the Set the Christian is placed in.

Therefore our concern is to see that we live according to the recognition of that Set, and do those things which please God.

(a) My Success (Matthew 5:13–16)

Success means to end with advantage. What is the Christian standard of success? Jesus Christ distinctly recognises that we have to succeed, and He indicates the kind of success we must have. The advantage with which we are to end is that we become preserving salt and shining lights; not losing our savour but preserving health, and not covering our light with a bushel but letting it shine. If salt gets into a wound, it hurts, and if God's children get amongst those who are "raw" towards God—every immoral person is an open wound towards God, their presence hurts. The sun, which is a benediction to eyes that are strong, is an agony of distress to eyes that are sore. The illustration holds with regard to the man who is not right with God; he is like an open wound, and when "salt" has got into it, the pain stirs him first to annoyance and distress, and then to spite and hatred. That is why Jesus Christ was hated; He was a continual annoyance. Again, nothing is cleaner or grander or sweeter than light. Light cannot be soiled; a sunbeam may shine into the dirtiest puddle, but it is never soiled. A sheet of white paper can be soiled, so can almost any white substance, but you cannot soil light. Men and women who are rightly related to God can go and work in the most degraded slums of the cities, or in the vilest parts of heathendom where all kinds of immorality are practised, without being defiled because God keeps them like the light, unsullied.

(b) My Sociability

Sociability means good fellowship. How insistent God is that we keep together in fellowship! In the natural world it is only by mixing with other people that we get the corners rubbed off. It is the way we are made naturally, and God takes this principle and transfigures it. "Not forsaking the assembling of ourselves together" is a Scriptural injunction.

In John 5:40–44 our Lord distinctly indicates that He can have nothing to do with a certain class of men, viz., with the men who "receive honour one of another." He says, in effect, "It is a moral impossibility for that man to believe in Me." Our Lord is exceedingly good company to the saints—"where two or three are gathered together in My name, there am I in the midst." Beware of isolation; beware of the idea that you have to develop a holy life alone. It is impossible to develop a holy life alone, you will develop into an oddity and a peculiarism, into something utterly unlike what God wants you to be. The only way to develop spiritually is to go into the society of God's own children, and you will soon find how God alters your set. God does not contradict our social instincts, He alters them. Jesus said, "Leap for joy" when they shall "separate you from their company and cast out your name as evil, *for the Son of man's sake,*" not for some crotchety notion or faddy idea of your own, or for some principle you have wedded yourself to, but, *for My sake.* When we are true to Jesus Christ, our sociability is lifted to a different sphere.

"And hath raised us up together, and made us sit together in heavenly places in Christ Jesus" (Ephesians 2:6). We are not raised up alone, but together. All through the social instinct is God-given. From the Bible standpoint, whenever a man gets alone, it is always in order to fit him for society. Getting alone with God is such a dangerous business that God rarely allows it unless it means that we come into closer contact with people afterwards. It is contact with one another that keeps us full-orbed and well-balanced, not only naturally but spiritually.

(c) My Satisfaction

These things are applicable in the natural and the spiritual world alike. Satisfaction means comfortable gratification. There are people who say that if you like a particular thing you must not have it, they think that any satisfaction is a sin. Satisfaction, comfortable gratification, is a good thing, but it must be satisfaction in the highest. Jesus said: "Blessed are they which do hunger and thirst after righteousness: for they shall be filled," i.e., satisfied.

Matthew 10:17–22 may seem an extraordinary passage to be taken in this connection. The reason it is taken is that it indicates the only place where satisfaction is found, viz., in doing God's will. These verses are often applied to methods people adopt when they speak at meetings. I remember hearing a man say, "I have not had much time to prepare for this morning's address, so I am going to give you what the Holy Spirit gives me; I hope to be better prepared this evening," and he used this very passage as his justification. When we seek satisfaction from God in the world of men, we shall come in contact with "open wounds," and Jesus says men will hate you, systematically vex and persecute you "for My sake." You will be put in all kinds of difficult places, but don't be alarmed, the Spirit of God will bring to your remembrance in those moments what you should say.

So we end where we began, that the social setting of our lives is The Highest. In secret or in public the one Set we are anxious to please is God the Father, God the Son, and God the Holy Spirit; and the only ones with whom we have real communion are those who have the same dominant note in their life. "Whosoever shall do the will of My Father which is in heaven, the same is My brother, and sister, and mother."

3. The Spiritual "Me"

And hath raised us up together, and made us sit together in heavenly places in Christ Jesus. (Ephesians 2:6)

This verse refers to now, not to hereafter.

(a) My Mind

My mind means my particular cast of thought and feeling; if you ridicule that, you hurt me. Whenever a certain type of thought is ridiculed, someone is hurt. "And be not conformed to this world: but be ye transformed by the renewing of your mind that ye may prove what is that good, and acceptable and perfect, will of God" (Romans 12:2). A wonderful thing in our spiritual experience is the way God alters and develops our sensitiveness. At one time we were amazingly sensitive to what certain people thought; then God altered that and made us indifferent to what they thought but amazingly sensitive to what other people thought, and finally we are sensitive only to what God thinks. "But with me it is a very small thing that I should be judged of you, or of man's judgement: yea, I judge not mine own self. . . . But He that judgeth me is the Lord" (1 Corinthians 4:3–4). We have to be renewed in the spirit of our minds for one purpose, viz., that we "may prove what is that good, and acceptable, and perfect, will of God."

(b) My Morals

My morals, i.e., my standard of moral conduct.

Except your righteousness shall exceed the righteousness of the scribes and Pharisees, ye shall in no case enter into the kingdom of heaven. (Matthew 5:20)

The practical outcome of these words is astonishing; it means that my standard of moral conduct must exceed the standard of the most moral, upright man I know who lives apart from the grace of God. Think of the most upright man, the most worthy person you know who has had no experience whatever of receiving the Spirit of God, Jesus Christ says, in effect, that we have to exceed his rectitude. Instead of our Lord lowering the standard of moral conduct, He pushes it to a tremendous extreme. We have not only to do right things, but our motives have to be right, the springs of our thinking have to be right; we have to be so unblameable that God Himself can see nothing to censure in us. That is the standard of moral conduct when we are born again of the Spirit of God and are obeying Him. What is my standard of moral conduct? Is it God's standard, or the modern one? The modern standard is summed up in one phrase, self-realisation. The two are diametrically opposed to one another, there is no point of reconciliation between them.

(c) My Mysticism (Colossians 2:20–23)

My Mysticism means my direct and immediate communion with God.

Everyone, whether he is religious or not, has something of this sort whereby he goes directly to God. Mysticism is a natural ingredient in everybody's make-up, whether they call themselves "atheist," or "agnostic," or "Christian." God does not alter the need of our nature, He fulfils the need on a totally different line. We are so mysterious in personality, there are so many forces at work in and about us which we cannot calculate or cope with, that if we refuse to take the guidance of Jesus Christ, we may, and probably shall be, deluded by supernatural forces far greater than ourselves. Jesus Christ's way exalts everything about us, it exalts our bodies, exalts our flesh and blood relationships, exalts our homes, exalts our social standing, exalts all the inner part of our life, our mind and morals and mysticism, until we have at-one-ment with God in them all.

Chapter XV

OURSELVES: I; ME; MINE
Ourselves As "Ourselves." "Self"

THE PASSAGES ALLUDED TO IN THIS OUTLINE ARE EXCLUSIVELY FROM THE NEW TESTAMENT;
THE STUDENT CAN SUPPLY OLD TESTAMENT ILLUSTRATIONS FOR HIS OWN USE.

1. Self (Luke 18:9–14)
   (a) Greatness (Mark 12:31;
       comp. 2 Thessalonians 2:3)
   (b) Grovelling (Luke 15:19; Luke 5:8)

2. Self-Seeking (Romans 15:1–3)
   (a) Honour (John 5:41–44; John 8:49)
   (b) Humility (Matthew 18:4; Philippians
       2:1–4)

3. Self-Estimation (John 13:13–17)
   (a) Superiority (Philippians 2:5–11)
   (b) Inferiority (Matthew 5:19)

N.B. IMPORTANT DEFINITIONS:

(1) SELF MEANS THE SUM TOTAL OF ALL A
    MAN CAN CALL "ME" AND "MINE."

(2) SELFISHNESS MEANS ALL THAT GIVES
    ME PLEASURE WITHOUT CONSIDERING
    CHRIST'S INTERESTS.

(3) SIN MEANS INDEPENDENCE OF GOD.

My self is my conscious personality. "My total self
includes the whole succession of my personal experiences, and it therefore includes that special phase of
my conscious life in which I think of myself." There
are three divisions to guide our treatment of this subject: Self; Self-Seeking; Self-Estimation.

1. Self

Greatness and Grovelling. (Luke 18:9–14). In the final
analysis, both attitudes are wrong; one grovels and
the other swells in greatness, both are expressive of
abnormal conditions. Our Lord never teaches the
annihilation of self; He reveals how self can be rightly
centred, the true centre being perfect love towards
God (see 1 Corinthians 13:4–8). Until self is rightly
related there, we either grovel or swell in greatness;
both attitudes are untrue and need to be put right.
The true centre for self is Jesus Christ.

(a) Greatness
*The first of all the commandments is . . . thou shalt love
the Lord thy God with all thy heart, and with all thy
soul, and with all thy mind, and with all thy strength.
(Mark 12:29–30)*

This commandment is at the heart of all the revelations made by Jesus Christ. He reveals the right centre for self to be God. personal, passionate devotion
to Him; then I am able to show to my fellow-men the
same love that God has shown to me. Until I get
there, I take the position of the Pharisee or of the
publican; I either thank God that I am not an out-
and-out sinner and point out certain people who are
worse than I am, or else I grovel to the other extreme.
Both attitudes are wrong because they are not truly
centred. How could the Pharisee in our Lord's parable possibly love his neighbour as himself? It was
impossible, he had not found the true centre for himself. His centre was self-realisation, and instead of loving the publican he increased his own conceit in every
detail of comparison. Immediately I become rightly
related to God and have perfect love toward Him, I
can have the same relationship to my fellow-men that
God has to me, and can love my fellow-men as I love
myself. When a man gets rightly related to God by
the Atonement of Jesus Christ, he understands what
the Apostle Paul meant when he said, "We preach not
ourselves,"—i.e., self-realisation—"but Christ Jesus
the Lord; and ourselves your servants for Jesus' sake."

This is the one thing that keeps a man from taking account of evil. If my love is first of all for God, I
shall take no account of the base ingratitude of others, because the mainspring of my service to my fellow-men is love to God. The point is very practical
and clear. if I love someone and he treats me unkindly
and ungenerously, the very fact that I love him makes
me feel it all the more, and yet Paul says love "taketh
not account of evil," because self is absorbed and
taken up with love for Jesus Christ. If you are going
to live for the service of your fellow-men, you will certainly be pierced through with many sorrows, for you
will meet with more base ingratitude from your fellow-men than you would from a dog. You will meet
with unkindness and "two-facedness," and if your
motive is love for your fellow-men, you will be
exhausted in the battle of life. But if the mainspring
of your service is love for God, no ingratitude, no sin,
no devil, no angel, can hinder you from serving your
fellow-men, no matter how they treat you. You love
your neighbour as yourself, not from pity, but from
the true centring of yourself in God.

(b) Grovelling

I am no more worthy to be called thy son: make me as one of thy hired servants. (Luke 15:19 RV)

When Simon Peter saw it, he fell down at Jesus' knees, saying, Depart from me; for I am a sinful man, O Lord. (Luke 5:8)

Everyone goes through this stage when convicted of sin; we always have a wrong estimate of ourselves when we are under conviction of sin. The prodigal's estimate of himself went beyond his father's estimate of him, and when we are convicted of sin by the Holy Spirit the same thing happens. The balance is upset, the health of the body is upset, the balance is pushed right out by conviction of sin. Sin puts man's self altogether out of centre, and he becomes eccentric. When the Spirit of God convicts a man, he is wrongly related to everything; he is wrongly related to God, to his own body, to everything round about him, and he is in a state of abject misery. The picture of a man not convicted of sin is exactly the opposite. If you watch the tendencies all around us to-day you will notice this tendency—"Ignore sin, deny its existence; if you make mistakes, forget them: live the healthy-minded, open-hearted, sunshiny life; don't allow yourself to be convicted of sin, realise yourself, and as you do, you will attain perfection." There is no conviction of sin, no repentance, no forgiveness of sin, in that outlook. The Holy Spirit opens not only my eyes, but my heart and my conscience to the horror of the thing that is wrong within, and immediately He does, I get to the grovelling stage. The Psalmist says that conviction of sin makes man's beauty "to consume away like a moth" (Psalm 39:11). "Beauty" means the perfectly ordered completeness of a man's whole nature. The pharisee does not grovel, there is a certain beauty of order about a conceited man, a conformity with himself; he is of the nature of a crystal, clear and compact and hard. Immediately the Spirit of God convicts him, all that "beauty" crumbles and he goes to pieces, as it were. Jesus Christ takes the man who has been broken on the wheel by conviction of sin and rendered plastic by the Holy Spirit, and re-moulds him and makes him a vessel fit for God's glory.

Self, then, is not to be annihilated, but to be rightly centred in God. *Self*-realisation has to be turned into *Christ*-realisation. Our Lord never taught—"Deeper death to self"; He taught death right out to my right to myself, to self-realisation. He taught that the principal purpose of our creation is "to glorify God and to enjoy Him forever"; that the sum total of my self is to be consciously centred in God.

2. Self-Seeking *(Romans 15:1–3)*

"The reproaches of them that reproached Thee fell on *Me*." What reproaches fell on Jesus? Everything that was hurled in slander against God hurt our Lord. The slanders that were hurled against Himself made no impression on Him; His suffering was on account of His Father. On what account do you suffer? Do you suffer because men speak ill of you? Read Hebrews 12:3: "For consider Him that hath endured such gainsaying of sinners against [Himself, KJV], that ye wax not weary, fainting in your souls" (RV). Perfect love takes no account of the evil done unto it. It was the reproaches that hit and scandalised the true centre of His life that Jesus Christ noticed in pain. What was that true centre? Absolute devotion to God the Father and to His will; and as surely as you get Christ-centred you will understand what the Apostle Paul meant when he talks about filling up "that which is lacking of the afflictions of Christ." Jesus Christ could not be touched on the line of self-pity. The practical emphasis here is that our service is not to be that of pity, but of personal, passionate love to God, and a longing to see many more brought to the centre where God has brought us.

(a) Honour

Jesus answered, . . . I honour My Father, and ye do dishonour Me. (John 8:49; see also John 5:41–44)

The central honour in our Lord's life was His Father's honour; He "made Himself of no reputation." Every kind of scandal it was possible for men to think of was heaped upon Him, and He never attempted to clear Himself; but let anyone show an attitude of dishonour towards His Father and instantly Jesus Christ was ablaze in zeal; and "as He is, so are we in this world." Jesus Christ changes the centre of our self-love. Is my honour God's honour? Are they identically the same, as they were in Jesus Christ? Let these statements analyse us: we are scandalised at immorality, why? Is it because God's honour is at stake? or is it not rather because our social honour is upset and antagonised? As saints, we should smart and suffer keenly whenever we see pride and covetousness and self-realisation, because these are the things that go against the honour of God. "Ye have not the love of God in you," said Jesus Christ to the Pharisees, and He pointed out that it was therefore a moral impossibility for them to believe (see John 5:44). No man with a standard of honour other than Jesus Christ's can believe in Him. Jesus Christ exalts the standard of honour and puts it alongside God's throne. The real underlying meaning of our Lord being "moved with indignation in the spirit" (John 11:33 RV mg) was because Martha and her sister had accepted a scandal against His Father. As soon as death came on the scene, they accepted an interpretation that went against the goodness and the love of God. The only thing that roused Jesus Christ was for His Father's honour to be brought into disrepute. In the Temple, instead of seeing "a meek and gentle Jesus," we see a terrible Being with a whip of small cords in His hand, driving out the money-changers. Why could not He have driven them out in a gentler way? Because passionate zeal, an enthusiasm and detestation of everything that dared to call His Father's honour into disrepute, had eaten Him up; and exactly the same characteristic is seen in the saints. You cannot rouse them on the line of personal interest, of self-pity or of self-realisation; but when once anything is contrary to Jesus Christ's honour, instantly you find your meek and gentle saint becomes a holy terror. The phrase, "the wrath of the Lamb," is understandable along this line. The obverse side of love is hate.

(b) Humility
Whosoever therefore shall humble himself as this little child, the same is greatest in the kingdom of heaven. (Matthew 18:4; see also Philippians 2:1–4)

These two passages are a wonderful revelation; they show that the true disposition of a saint in this order of things is humility. When the disciples were discussing who should be the greatest, Jesus took a little child in His arms and said, "Unless you become like that, you will never see the kingdom of heaven." He did not put up a little child as an ideal; if He had, He would have destroyed the whole principle of His teaching. If humility were put up as an ideal it would serve only to increase pride. Humility is not an ideal, it is the unconscious result of the life being rightly related to God and centred in Him. Our Lord is dealing with ambition, and had He put up a little child as a standard, it would simply have altered the manifestation of ambition. What is a little child? We all know what a child is until we are asked, and then we find we do not know. We can mention his extra goodness or his extra badness, but none of this is the child himself. We know implicitly what a child is, and we know implicitly what Jesus Christ means, but as soon as we try to put it into words it escapes. A child works from an unconscious principle within, and if we are born again and are obeying the Holy Spirit, we shall unconsciously manifest humility all along the line. We shall easily be the servant of all men, not because it is our ideal, but because we cannot help it. Our eye is not consciously on our service, but on our Saviour.

There is nothing more awful than conscious humility, it is the most Satanic type of pride. To consciously serve is to be worse than the Pharisee who is eaten up with conceit. Jesus Christ presented humility as a description of what we shall be unconsciously when we have become rightly related to God and are

rightly centred in Jesus Christ. Our humility amongst men can only be understood by those who are Christ-centred in the same way. This is portrayed over and over again in the New Testament. Peter says, "They think it strange that ye run not with them to the same excess of riot" (1 Peter 4:4), and our Lord says, "Leap for joy" when "they shall separate you from their company, . . . for the Son of man's sake" (Luke 6:22–23). The centre of the life is altered, and the worldling is hopelessly at sea[13] in trying to find out the centre from which the Christian works. The analysis of a Christian from a worldly standpoint results at first not in attraction, but in ridicule. The Apostle Paul said that what he preached was foolishness, unutterable stupidity to the Greeks, to those who seek after wisdom; and that is the attitude towards the saints in this dispensation. A saint arouses interest for a little while, when things go ill he arouses deep interest; but when things go well, the interest gradually changes into ridicule, and then into his being absolutely ignored, because he is centred in Someone the world does not see, viz., in God. As long as a Christian complies with the standards of this world, the world recognises him; but when he works from the real standard, which is God, the world cannot understand him, and consequently it either ignores or ridicules him. Jesus Christ and the Spirit of God in the Epistles point out this antagonism between the spirit of the world and the Spirit of God, it is a deeply rooted antagonism, and as Christians we have to realise that if we obey the Spirit of God, we are going to be detested and ridiculed and ignored by those whose centre is self-realisation.

Our attitude in this dispensation manifests itself in a humility that cannot sting us into action on our own account. That is the thing that maddens the prince of this world. When the prince of this world and his minions scandalise Jesus Christ and misrepresent Him, the weakest saint becomes a giant, he is ready to go to martyrdom any time and anywhere all the world over for the Lord Jesus Christ. We hear it said that the spirit of martyrdom has died out; the spirit of martyrdom is here. If scandal should arise against Jesus Christ, there would be many to-day who would stand true to the honour of the Lord Jesus Christ where in the past there would have been but one.

What is self-seeking? I must have self-seeking, and if my self is truly centred, my seeking is God's honour. God's honour is at stake in my eyes, in my hands and feet; His honour is at stake wherever I take my body. My body is the temple of the Holy Ghost, therefore I have to see that it is the obedient slave of the disposition Jesus Christ has put in to stand for Him. The

---

13. at sea: in a state of confusion or perplexity; at a loss.

centre of my self should be God and love for Him. This question often arises—"I believe I ought to love God, but how am I to do it? How am I to have this tremendous love towards God? I agree that I ought to love Him, but how can I?" Romans 5:5 is the solution: "The love of God hath been shed abroad in our hearts through the Holy Ghost which was given unto us" (RV). Have you received the Holy Spirit? If not, Luke 11:13 will help you: "If ye then, being evil, know how to give good gifts unto your children: how much more shall your heavenly Father give the Holy Spirit to them that ask Him?" Also John 17:26: "That the love wherewith Thou lovedst Me may be in them, and I in them" (RV). Ask God to answer the prayer of Jesus Christ. There is no excuse for any of us not having the problem answered in our own life. Our natural heart does not love God; the Holy Ghost is the only Lover of God, and immediately He comes in, He will make our hearts the centre of love for God, the centre of personal, passionate, overwhelming devotion to Jesus Christ. (God and Jesus Christ are synonymous terms in practical experience.) When the Holy Spirit comes in and sin and self-interest are in the road, He will instantly detect them and clear them out as soon as we give our consent, until we become incandescent with the very love of God. "Keep yourselves in the love of God" (Jude 21). That does not mean keep on trying to love God, it means something infinitely profounder, viz., "Keep the windows of your soul open to the fact that God loves you"; then His love will continually flow through you to others.

There are two terms used in modern psychology which are of importance in this connection—*Projective* and *Ejective*. Projective means that I see in other people the qualities I want but am without. Ejective means that I attribute my qualities or my defects to other people. The ejective method is seen in the matter of judging; when somebody has trespassed against me, I instantly impute to him every mean[14] motive of which I would have been guilty had I been in his circumstances. "Wherefore thou art without excuse, O man, whosoever thou art that judgest: for wherein thou judgest another, thou condemnest thyself" (Romans 2:1 RV). In Matthew 6:15 Jesus Christ puts the forgiveness of our trespasses on the ground that we forgive those who trespass against us. If we take the ejective method, we do not forgive them, we simply attribute to others what we should be capable of in the way of meanness in similar circumstances. The statement that we only see what we bring with us the power of seeing, is perfectly correct. If I see meanness and wrong and evil in others, let me take the self-judgement at once—that is what I would be guilty of

if I were in their circumstances. The searching light of the Scriptures comes over and over again on this line, and we come to find that there is no room in a Christian for cynicism.

3. Self-Estimation *(John 13:13–17)*
This is a reiteration of the same point, viz., that self must be centred in God. Is my self Christ-centred or self-centred? When I am in difficult circumstances. does the disposition in me make me say, "Why should this happen to me?" That disposition was never in the Lord Jesus Christ. Whenever His consciousness was revealed, it was His Father's honour that occupied Him, not His own honour. My self is a human edition for God to be glorified in. "Let this mind be in you, which was also in Christ Jesus" (Philippians 2:5). Could anything be more practical, or more profound than that command? The mind of Christ showed itself in His actions and in His speech, and our mind is shown in our speech and in our actions. What was it that Satan antagonised in Jesus Christ? God-realisation. Satan wanted to alter that centre: "Do God's work in Your own way; You are His Son, then work from that centre." At the heart of each of our Lord's answers to Satan's temptations is this—"I came . . . not to do Mine own will, but the will of Him that sent Me." Jesus Christ was tempted, and so shall we be tempted when we are rightly related to God. "I have somewhat against thee, because thou hast left thy first love" (Revelation 2:4). All the rest becomes of no account. To get eccentric, off the centre, is exactly what Satan wants. He does not tempt to immorality; the one thing he makes his business is to dethrone God's rule in the heart. The superiority of Jesus Christ's Self was that He was God-centred. "He that gathereth not with Me scattereth," said our Lord; and all morality, all goodness, all religion, and all spirituality that is not Christ-centred is drawing away from Jesus Christ all the time. All the teaching of Jesus weaves round the question of self. It is not "Oh, to be nothing, nothing!" but "Oh, to be something, something!" Aggressively and powerfully something, uncrushably something, something that stands next to God's throne, on the Rock; to be those in whom God can walk and talk and move and do what He likes with, because self is personally, passionately in love with God, not absorbed into God; but centred in God.

Selfishness means that which gives me pleasure without considering Jesus Christ's interests. Talk about selfishness on its bad side, and you will have everyone's sympathy; but talk about selfishness from Jesus Christ's standpoint and you will arouse the interest of very few and the antipathy of a great many.

---

14. mean: ordinary, common, low, or ignoble, rather than cruel or spiteful

Sympathy for my fellow-men is quite likely to rouse antagonism to God. Unless my relationship to God is right, my sympathy for men will lead me astray and them also; but when once I am right with God, I can love my neighbour as God has loved me. How has God loved me? God has loved me to the end of all my sinfulness, the end of all my self-will, all my selfishness, all my stiff-neckedness, all my pride, all my self-interest; now He says—"love one another, as I have loved you." I am to show to my fellow-men the same love that God showed to me. That is Christianity in practical working order.

Chapter XVI
OURSELVES: I; ME; MINE
Ourselves and Conscience

CONSCIENCE is the innate law in nature whereby man knows he is known.

N.B. THE HALF TRUTH AND HALF ERROR OF SUCH PHRASES AS "CONSCIENCE IS THE VOICE OF GOD" AND "CONSCIENCE CAN BE EDUCATED" WILL BE DEALT WITH.

1. Conscience before the Fall (Genesis 2:16–17; 3:2–3)
   (a) Consciousness of Self
   (b) Consciousness of the World (Genesis 3:1–24)
   (c) Consciousness of God

   > THESE THREE ARE THE SEVERAL SIDES OF MAN'S PERSONAL LIFE.

2. Conscience after the Fall (John 3:19–21)
   (a) The Standard of the Natural Person (Romans 2:12–15)
   (b) The Standard of the Nations—Pagan (Matthew 25:31–46)
   (c) The Standard of the Naturally Pious (Acts 26:9; John 16:2)

3. Conscience in the Faithful (1 Corinthians 8:7, 12)
   (a) Conscience and Character in the Saint (Romans 9:1; John 17:22)
   (b) Conscience and Conduct in the Saint (2 Corinthians 1:12)
   (c) Conscience and Communion of the Saints (1 John 1:7; Ephesians 4:13; Hebrews 9:14)

"Conscience is the innate law in human nature whereby man knows he is known." From every standpoint that is a safeguarded definition of conscience.

If conscience were the voice of God, it would be the most contradictory voice man ever heard. For instance, a Hindoo mother obeys her conscience when she treats her child cruelly, and a Christian mother obeys her conscience when she sends her child to Sunday school and brings it up generally "in the nurture and admonition of the Lord." If conscience were the voice of God, contrasts of this kind would never occur. "Conscience attaches itself to that system of things which man regards as highest," consequently conscience records differently in different people. The conscience of the Hindoo mother attaches itself to the highest she knows, viz., the Hindoo religion; the conscience of the Christian mother attaches itself to the highest she knows, viz., the revelation of God in the Lord Jesus Christ.

Probably the best illustration of conscience is the human eye. The eye records what it looks at, and conscience may be pictured as the eye of the soul recording what it looks at, and, like the eye, it will always record exactly what it is turned towards. We are apt to lose what Ruskin called the "innocence of sight." The majority of us know what we look at, and we try to tell ourselves what our eyes see. An artist does not use his logical faculties, he records exactly from the innocence of sight. When art students are being trained to sketch from nature, you will find that in looking at a distant hill draped in blue mist, with little touches of white or colour here and there, the beginner will sketch not what he sees, but what he knows those blotches indicate, viz., houses; while the artist gives you the presentation of what he sees, not of what he knows he sees. Something very similar happens with conscience. The recording power of conscience may be distorted or perverted, and conscience itself may be seared. "Some shall depart from the faith, . . . having their conscience seared with a hot iron" (1 Timothy 4:1–2).

Then, again, if you throw a white light on trees, the eye records that the trees are green; if you throw a yellow light on the trees, the eye records that the trees are blue; if you throw a red light on trees, the eye records that the trees are brown. Your logical faculties will tell you all the time that the trees are green, but the point of the illustration is that the eye has no business other than to record what it looks at; and it is the same with conscience.

To go back to the illustration of the Hindoo mother and the Christian mother. The conscience of the Hindoo mother looks out on what her religion teaches her to be God and records accordingly, and reasoning on the records of her conscience, she behaves cruelly. The conscience of the Christian mother looks out on God as He is seen in the "white light" of Jesus Christ, and reasoning on what her conscience records, she behaves as a Christian mother should. So it can never be true to call conscience the voice of God. The difference in the records of conscience is accounted for by the varieties of traditional religions, etc. Whether a person is religious or not, conscience attaches itself to the highest he or she knows, and reasoning on that, the life is guided accordingly.

The phrase, "Conscience can be educated," is a truth that is half error. Strictly speaking, conscience cannot be educated. What is altered and educated is a man's reasoning. A man reasons not only on what his senses bring him, but on what the record of his conscience brings him. Immediately you face a man with the "white light" of Jesus Christ (white is pure, true light, and embraces all shades of colour), his conscience records exactly what he sees, his reason is startled and amazed, and his conscience condemns him from every standpoint.

1. Conscience before the Fall *(Genesis 2:16–1; 3:2–3)*

The words "consciousness" and "conscience" meant the same thing originally; they do not now. In Conscience before the Fall we take the three aspects of a man's personal life, viz., Consciousness of Self, Consciousness of the World, and Consciousness of God.

"And the LORD God commanded the man, saying, Of every tree of the garden thou mayest freely eat: but of the tree of the knowledge of good and evil, thou shalt not eat of it: for in the day that thou eatest thereof thou shalt surely die" (Genesis 2:16–17). "And the woman said unto the serpent, We may eat of the fruit of the trees of the garden: but of the fruit of the tree which is in the midst of the garden, God hath said, Ye shall not eat of it, neither shall ye touch it, lest ye die" (Genesis 3:2–3).

In these passages the three aspects are clear-consciousness of self, of the world, and of God. It is the consciousness of God which has been most conspicuously blurred by the Fall.

(a) Consciousness of Self

This takes us back to the general subject of Man. When the other creations were passed before Adam in procession "to see what he would call them. . . . There was not found an help meet for him." Man has no affinity with the brutes; this instantly distinguishes man clearly and emphatically from the brute creation around him. There is no evidence that a brute is ever conscious of itself, but man is ostensibly self-conscious.

(b) Consciousness of the World

We mean by "the world" the thing that is not my self-"continuum," that which continues to exist outside me. By realising how we come into contact with that which is not ourselves we realise our barriers and limitations. For instance we can never understand the consciousness of an angel, or the consciousness of a dog, because both these creations are constituted differently from the way in which we are constituted.

How do we come in contact with what is not ourselves? By means of a nervous system; consequently we can always say, up to a certain point, how another human being sees things outside himself. How do angels come in contact with that which is not angelic? Certainly not by a nervous system; therefore we have no possibility of knowing how an angel comes in contact with what is not angelic. Read the records in the Bible of angelic appearances, and of the appearances of our Lord after His Resurrection; physical barriers simply did not exist to Him or to them. Physical barriers exist to us because of our nervous system. Angels can come and go through rocks and doors, can appear and disappear in a way we cannot understand. Their consciousness is above ours, different from it. When anyone tries to explain to you how an angel sees and knows things, say to yourself, "private speculation." You will always find that God's Book puts the barrier clearly, "Thus far and no farther." Jesus Christ did not take on Him the consciousness of an angel; He came down to where man was, into the world we live in, and He took on Him a body and a nervous system like our own. Jesus Christ saw the world as we see it, and He came in contact with it as we do (see Hebrews 2:16–18).

We are only conscious of ourselves and of what is outside us by means of a nervous system: our conscious life depends altogether on our nerves. When we are asleep we are not conscious at all. What happens when we sleep? The world "goes out"; the nervous system is not working. An anaesthetic makes the world "go out." The reason we shut up a lunatic in an asylum is because his nervous system relates him to the world differently from the majority of men. He does not record what he sees outside as we do, consequently he becomes so different and possibly dangerous that he has to be confined.

Now think of the lower animals. A great deal is said about the intelligence of dogs, and a great amount of talk about insight, falsely so called, into the nature of a dog. A dog is the most human of all animals, but yet we have no means of knowing how a dog sees what is not itself. We have no more means of knowing how a dog sees than we have of knowing how an angel sees; we simply take our own consciousness and transfer it to the dog. The recognition of these barriers above us and below us is essential to knowledge, and keeps us aware of our limitations. Spiritualists deny that there are any barriers: they claim that we can come in contact with angels, and understand how angels see things.

Remember, the body of man is his glory, not his drawback. It is through the body that man's character is made and manifested. The body is essential to the order of creation to which we belong; "Your body is the temple of the Holy Ghost," says Paul, and we are held responsible for the way we manifest this fact to the world. When a man experiences a great alteration inwardly, his nervous system is altered. This explains what Paul says in 2 Corinthians 5:17: "If any man is in Christ, he is a new creature: the old things are passed away; behold, they are become new" (RV). Wherever the grace of God works effectually in a man's inner nature, his nervous system is altered and the external world begins to take on a new guise. Why? Because he has a new disposition. "If any man is in Christ Jesus," his nervous system will prove that he is a "new creature," and he will begin to see things differently.

Heaven above is brighter blue.
Earth around is sweeter green.
Something lives in every hue
Christless eyes have never seen;
Birds with gladder songs o'erflow.
Flowers with deeper beauties shine.
Since I know, as now I know.
I am His and He is mine.

That is not only poetry, it is a fact.

(c) Consciousness of God

These three types of consciousness are clearly manifest in the way Eve talked to the serpent (see Genesis 3:2–3). Eve was conscious of herself, she was conscious of her surroundings, and conscious of God. In our Lord Jesus Christ these three aspects of consciousness were perfectly clear. With us, the consciousness of God has become obliterated, and we miscall all kinds of things "God." The system of things a man considers highest he is apt to call "God." In Adam the consciousness of God was different from our natural consciousness, it was the same as in our Lord. Jesus Christ restores the three aspects of a man's personal life to their pristine vigour: we come into real, definite communion with God through Jesus Christ; we come to a right relationship with our fellow-men and with the world outside, and we come to a right relationship with ourselves, we become God-centred instead of self-centred.

2. Conscience after the Fall *(John 3:19–21)*

That is where we live to-day, viz., a mixture of Christian and non-Christian, and a great deal that is neither one nor the other. John 3:19–21 is the fundamental analysis: ". . . Light is come into the world, and men loved the darkness rather than the light; for their works were evil" (RV). What is light? Jesus said, "I am *the* Light." He also said, "If therefore the light that is in thee be darkness, how great is that darkness!" Darkness, in this connection, is my own point of view. Immediately a man sees Jesus Christ and understands Who He is, that instant he is criticised and self-condemned; there is no further excuse. Our Lord is the final Standard.

(a) The Standard of the Natural Person

Under this heading we deal with the standard of the natural person—i.e., the one who has never seen or heard of Jesus Christ. In Romans 2:12–15 the contrast is drawn clearly and emphatically between what we may call religious and irreligious people. What is the standard of judgement? The Gentiles knew nothing about Jesus Christ or about the law of God as an external standard, and they were judged according to their conscience. Take the grossest case you can think of—nowhere is there any record of a cannibal tribe thinking it right to eat a man; they always try to conceal it.

(b) The Standard of the Nations

The Standard of the Nations—i.e., pagan nations, who likewise know nothing about Jesus Christ (Matthew 25:31–46). These verses are often applied to Christians, but their primary reference is to the judgement of the nations. The standard for Christians is not these verses in the twenty-fifth chapter of Matthew; the standard for Christians is our Lord Jesus Christ. In the twenty-fifth chapter of Matthew God's magnanimous interpretation of the acts of certain people is revealed, and they are amazed and astounded—"When saw we Thee an hungered? . . . When saw we Thee sick?" We never heard of Thee before. "Inasmuch as ye have done it unto one of the least of these My brethren, ye have done it unto Me." The standard of judgement for the natural person is conscience; and the standard of judgement for the nations is conscience.

(c) The Standard of the Naturally Pious
I verily thought with myself [i.e., according to conscience], that I ought to do many things contrary to the name of Jesus of Nazareth. (Acts 26:9)

If conscience is the voice of God, we have a nice problem to solve! Saul was the acme of conscientiousness. Our Lord refers to the same thing: "They shall put you out of the synagogues: yea, the hour cometh, that whosoever killeth you shall think that he offereth service unto God," they will think they serve God in putting you to death (John 16:2 RV). That is the outcome of obedience to what is understood as conscience. No one who has read the life of the Apostle Paul and his records of himself could accuse him of not being conscientious—he was hyper-conscientious. Conscience is the standard by which men and women are to be judged until they are brought into contact with the Lord Jesus Christ. It is not sufficient for a Christian to live up to the light of his conscience; he must live in a sterner light, the light of the Lord Jesus Christ. Conscience will always record God when once it has been faced by God.

3. Conscience in the Faithful *(1 Corinthians 8:7–12)*

These verses show that we can be "spectacles" to other Christians. When the natural sight is wrong, spectacles are worn to adjust the vision. We have to be as spectacles to others. So many Christians are shortsighted, so many are long-sighted, and so many have not the right kind of sight; be spectacles to them! A very humble position, but a very useful one. In 1 Corinthians 7 Paul makes a distinction between equal rights and equal duties. The Corinthians have been criticising Paul, and from this chapter onwards he is dealing with their questions, and evidently the whole point is the matter of equal rights. Paul says, "No! equal duties, but not equal rights." We all have equal duties to perform towards God, but not equal rights. Paul deals with the matter in a statesmanlike manner.

There is a difference between "offence" and "stumbling." "And they were offended in Him. But Jesus said unto them, A prophet is not without honour, save in his own country . . ." (Matthew 13:57). "But Jesus knowing in Himself that His disciples murmured at this, said unto them, Doth this cause you to stumble?" (John 6:61 RV; see also Matthew 5:29; 11:6; 13:41; 16:23; 17:27; 18:6–7). Offence means going contrary to someone's private opinion, and it is sometimes our moral duty to give offence. Did Jesus Christ know that He was offending the private opinion of the Pharisees

when He allowed His disciples to pluck the ears of corn and eat them on the Sabbath day? Did He know that He was offending them when He healed the sick on the Sabbath day? Certainly He did; and yet our Lord never put an occasion of stumbling in anyone's way. The passage which alludes to Him as "a stone of stumbling and a rock of offence" has another reference.

Stumbling, then, is different from offence. For example, someone who does not know God as well as you do, loves you and continually does what you do because he loves you, and as you watch him, you begin to discern that he is degenerating spiritually, and to your amazement you find it is because he is doing what you are doing. No offence is being given, but he is stumbling, distinctly stumbling. Paul works this out from every standpoint in 1 Corinthians 8 and 9: "As long as I live," he says, "I will never again do those things whereby my brother is made to stumble; I reserve the right to suffer the loss of all things rather than be a hindrance to the gospel: I will not insist on my rights, on my liberty of conscience, but only on my right to give up my rights." Waive aside your own liberty of conscience if it is going to be the means of causing someone to stumble. The application of this is what our Lord teaches in the Sermon on the Mount in practical experience. To put it crudely, the Sermon on the Mount simply means that if you are a disciple of Jesus Christ, you will always do more than your duty, you will always be doing something equivalent to going the second mile. People say, "What a fool you are! Why don't you insist on your rights?" Jesus Christ says, "If you are My disciple, you will insist only on your right to give up your rights."

God educates every one of us from the great general principles down to the scruples.[15] People who are right with God are often guilty of the most ugly characteristics and you are astounded that they do not see it: but wait; if they go on with God, slowly and surely God's Spirit will educate them from the general principles to the particular items, until after a while they are as careful as can be down to the "jots" and "tittles"[16] of their life, thereby proving their sanctification in the growing manifestation of the new disposition God has given them. No wonder the Book of God counsels us to be patient with ourselves and with one another!

(a) Conscience and Character in the Saint
I say the truth in Christ, I lie not, my conscience also bearing me witness in the Holy Ghost. (Romans 9:1; see also John 17:22)

---

15. down to the scruple(s): to the smallest item(s).
16. jots and tittles: smallest details; minute things. See Matthew 5:18.

Character is the sum total of a man's actions. You cannot judge a man by the good things he does at times; you must take all the times together, and if in the greater number of times he does bad things, he is a bad character, in spite of the noble things he does intermittently. You cannot judge your character by the one time you spoke kindly to your grandmother if the majority of other times you spoke unkindly. The fact that people say of a man, "Oh well, he does do good things occasionally," proves that he is a bad character; the very statement is a condemnation. Character in a saint means the disposition of Jesus Christ persistently manifested. You cannot appeal to a saint on the line of self-interest; you can only appeal to him on the line of the interests of Jesus Christ. The feeblest, weakest saint becomes a holy terror immediately Jesus Christ is scandalised. Whose honour are we seeking?

(b) Conscience and Conduct in the Saint

For our rejoicing is this, the testimony of our conscience, that in simplicity and godly sincerity, not with fleshly wisdom, but by the grace of God, we have had our conversation in the world, and more abundantly to youward. (2 Corinthians 1:12)

The point there is an important one; viz., that the knowledge of evil which came through the Fall gives a man a broad mind but paralyses his action. The restoration of a man by our Lord gives him simplicity, and simplicity always shows itself in actions. Do not mistake simplicity for stupidity. By "simplicity" is meant the simplicity that was in Jesus Christ. Paul says, "I fear, lest by any means . . . your minds should be corrupted from the simplicity that is in Christ" (2 Corinthians 11:3). There are men and women of the world whose minds are poisoned by all kinds of evil, they are marvellously generous in regard to their notions of other people, but they can *do* nothing, every bit of their knowledge and broadmindedness paralyses them. The essence of the Gospel of God working through conscience and conduct is that it shows itself at once in action. God can make simple, guileless people out of cunning, crafty people; that is the marvel of the grace of God. It can take the strands of evil and twistedness out of a man's mind and imagination and make him simple towards God, so that his life becomes radiantly beautiful by the miracle of God's grace.

(C) Conscience and Communion of the Saint

But if we walk in the light, as He is in the light, we have fellowship one with another. . . . (1 John 1:7; see also Ephesians 4:13; Hebrews 9:14)

These references emphasise the "together" aspect. Nowhere is "Enthusiasm for Humanity" mentioned in the Bible, that is a modern phrase. "Enthusiasm for the communion of saints" is frequently mentioned, and the argument in these verses and many others is that if we keep our conscience open towards God as He is revealed in Jesus Christ, we shall find He will bring other souls into oneness with Himself through us.

In 1 Corinthians 4:3–4 ("But with me it is a very small thing that I should be judged of you, or of man's judgement: Yea, I judge not mine own self. For I know nothing against myself; yet am I not hereby justified: but He that judgeth me is the Lord" RV). Paul mentions three standards of judgement which he has left behind: 1. Judgement according to the standard of the "special set"—"It is a very small thing that I should be judged of you." 2. The standard of universal human judgement—"or of man's judgement." 3. The standard of conscience—"Yea, I judge not mine own self."

The standard Paul accepts as the final one is our Lord. "But He that judgeth me is the Lord."

One of the greatest disciplines in spiritual life is the darkness that comes not on account of sin, but because the Spirit of God is leading you from walking in the light of your conscience to walking in the light of the Lord. Defenders of the faith are inclined to be bitter until they learn to walk in the light of the Lord. When you have learned to walk in the light of the Lord, bitterness and contention are impossible.

Chapter XVII
SPIRIT: THE DOMAIN AND DOMINION OF SPIRIT
Process of the Trinity

N.B. "The entire province of life, both in its lowest forms
or stages and in its highest, is the province of spirit."

1. An Instructive Parallel (1 Corinthians 2:1–14)

2. What The Bible Says about the Godhead
   (John 4:24)
   The Essential Nature of God the Father, God
   the Son and God the Holy Ghost
   Will (Exodus 3:14; John 10:17–18; 16:8–11)
   Love (1 John 4:8; Revelation 1:5; Romans
   5:5)
   Light (1 John 1:5; John 8:12; John 16:13)

The Spirit is the first power we practically experience but the last power we come to understand. The working of the Spirit of God is much easier to experience than to try and understand, the reason being that we form our ideas out of things we have seen and handled and touched; but when we come to think about the Godhead and the Spirit, language is strained to its limit, and all we can do is to use pictures to try and convey our ideas. Yet in spite of the difficulty, it is very necessary that we should think as Christians as well as live as Christians. It is not sufficient to experience the reality of the Spirit of God within us and His wonderful work; we have to bring our brains into line with our experience so that we can think and understand along Christian lines. It is because so few do think along Christian lines that it is easy for wrong teaching and wrong thinking to come in, especially in connection with the Spirit.

1. An Instructive Parallel *(1 Corinthians 2:11–14)*

In these verses the Apostle Paul is referring to the basis of how to think. The way we understand the things of a man, he says, is by the spirit of man; and the way we understand the things of God is by the Spirit of God; that just as the spirit of man knows the things of a man, so the Spirit of God alone knows the things of God. This is the first principle that the Apostle Paul lays down, and we must see that we grasp and clearly understand it. The next step is clear, viz., that we cannot expound the things of God unless we have the Spirit of God. There is an analogy, Paul says: as there is a law in the natural world whereby we reason and think and argue about natural things, so there is a law in the spiritual world; but the law which runs through the natural world is not the same as in the spiritual world. We can only discern the spiritual world by the Spirit of God, not by our own spirit; and if we have not received the Spirit of God we shall never discern spiritual things or understand them; we shall move continually in a dark world, and come slowly to the conclusion that the New Testament language is very exaggerated. But when we have received the Spirit of God, we begin to "know the things that are freely given to us of God," and to compare "spiritual things with spiritual," "not in the words which man's wisdom teacheth, but which the Holy Ghost teacheth."

The Apostle Paul here is at the very heart of things as he always is, because he is not only inspired by the Spirit of God in the way inspiration is generally understood, but he is "moved by the Holy Ghost" in a special manner to expound the basis of Christian doctrine.

The things of God cannot be expounded by the spirit of man, but only by the Spirit of God. "But the natural man receiveth not the things of the Spirit of God: for they are foolishness unto him: neither can he know them, because they are spiritually discerned" (1 Corinthians 2:14). For example, take the attitude of the "master in Israel" to Jesus Christ. Nicodemus believed that the germ of life was in him and in all men like him; but Our Lord brought before him this truth which Paul is expounding, viz., "That which is born of the flesh is flesh; and that which is born of the Spirit is spirit. Marvel not that I said unto thee, Ye must be born again."

Let us get this fundamental distinction clearly in our minds: we cannot penetrate the things of God and understand them by our intelligence: the only way we can understand the things of God is by the Spirit of God. Every Christian unquestionably is mentally agnostic; that is, all we know about God we have accepted by revelation, we did not find it out for ourselves. We did not worry it out by thinking. Or work it out by reasoning. We did not say, "Because so and so is true in the natural world, therefore it must be true in the spiritual world." We cannot find out God in that way. Jesus said, "If you would know My doctrine," i.e., My logic, My reasoning and My thinking, "first do My will, believe in Me, commit yourself to Me, obey Me; then you will know whether My doctrine is of God, or whether I speak of Myself" (see John 7:17).

There is a great deal of teaching abroad to-day which says that we have the Spirit of God in us and all that is needed is for it to be developed; if people are placed into the right conditions, the spirit in them will develop and grow and in that way they will come to understand God. This is contrary to all that Jesus Christ taught, and contrary to the New Testament all through. We have to come to the stage of realising that we are paupers in our own spirit; we have no power to grasp God, we cannot begin to understand Him. If ever we are going to understand God, we must receive His Spirit, then He will begin to expound to us the things of God. We understand the things of the world by our natural intelligence, and we understand the things of God by "the spirit which is of God."

2. What the Bible Says about the Godhead
God is a Spirit: and they that worship Him must worship Him in spirit and in truth. (John 4:24)

Jesus Christ is not implying that I must worship God sincerely; "in spirit" does not refer to my spirit, i.e. to human sincerity, but to the Spirit of God. I must have the same Spirit in me before I can worship God.

"God is a Spirit." What is spirit? Instantly we find insuperable barriers to thought. Did you ever try for one minute to think of God? We cannot think of a Being Who had no beginning and Who has no end; consequently men without the Spirit of God make a god out of ideas of their own. It is a great moment in our lives when we realise we must be agnostic about God, that we cannot get hold of Him. Then comes the revelation that Jesus Christ will give to us the Holy Spirit, Who will lift us into a new domain and enable us to understand all that He reveals, and to live the life God wants us to live.

The Essential Nature of God the Father, God the Son, and God the Holy Ghost:
> **Will** (Exodus 3:14; John 10:17–18; 16:8–11)
> **Love** (1 John 4:8; Revelation 1:5; Romans 5:5)
> **Light** (1 John 1:5; John 8:12; 16:13)

The first thing to notice is that what is true of God the Father is true also of God the Son and of God the Holy Ghost, because They are one. The main characteristics which are the same in the Father and in the Son and in the Holy Ghost are Will, Love and Light. The point to emphasise is that the essential nature of One Person of the Trinity is the essential nature of the other Persons of the Trinity. If we understand God the Holy Ghost, we shall understand God the Son and God the Father (see Matthew 11:27): therefore the first thing for us to do is to receive the Holy Ghost (see Luke 11:13).

The essential nature of God the Father is Spirit. In order to show the difficulty of putting this into words, ask yourself how much room does thinking take up? Why, no room at all because thought is of the nature of spirit. It is by means of our spirit that we understand the things with which we come in contact. "God is a Spirit," therefore if we are going to understand God, we must have the Spirit of God. Man's spirit takes up no room and the Spirit of God takes up no room, they work and interwork. My spirit has no power in itself to lay hold of God; but when the Spirit of God comes into my spirit, He energises my spirit, then the rest depends upon me. If I do not obey the Spirit of God and bring into the light the wrong things He reveals and let Him deal with them, I shall grieve Him, and may grieve Him away.

"And God said unto Moses, I AM THAT I AM: and he said, Thus shalt thou say unto the children of Israel, I AM hath sent me unto you" (Exodus 3:14). The first fundamental characteristic of God the Father, or God Almighty, is that of pure free will. There is no such thing as pure free will in man; God Almighty is the only Being Who has the power of pure free will. By His will He created what His breath sustains. The Bible revelation is that the essential nature of God is this power of free will.

What is the characteristic of God the Son? "I lay down My life, that I might take it again. No man taketh it from Me, but I lay it down of Myself. I have power to lay it down, and I have power to take it again. This commandment have I received of My Father" (John 10:17–18). No man has the power to lay down his life in the way Jesus Christ is referring to. Remember, Jesus Christ is God Incarnate, and the fundamental characteristic of God the Father is the fundamental characteristic of God the Son. Our Lord says, in effect, "I lay down My life because I choose to lay it down, and I take it again because I choose to."

"And when He is come, He will reprove the world of sin, and of righteousness and of judgement" (John 16:8). The subject of human free will is nearly always either overstated or understated. There is a pre-determination in man's spirit which makes him will along certain lines; but no man has the power to make an act of pure free will. When the Spirit of God comes into a man, He brings His own generating will power and causes him to will with God, and we have the amazing revelation that the saint's free choices are the pre-determinations of God. That is a most wonderful thing in Christian psychology, viz., that a saint chooses exactly what God pre-determined he should choose. If you have never received the Spirit of God this will be one of the things which is "foolishness" to you: but if you have received the Spirit and are obeying Him, you find He brings your spirit into complete harmony with God and the sound of your goings and the sound of God's goings are one and the same.

New Theology, Christian Science and Theosophy all teach that God created the Being called His Son in order to realise Himself. They say, in fact, that the term "Son of God" means not only our Lord Jesus Christ, but the whole creation of man. God is All, and the creation of man was in order to help God to realise Himself. The practical outcome of this line of thinking is to make men say, "It is absurd to talk about sin and the fall; sin is merely a defect, and to talk about the need of an atonement is nonsense." The Bible nowhere says that God created the world in order to realise Himself. The Bible reveals that God was absolutely Self-sufficient, and that the manifestation of the Son of God was for another purpose altogether, viz., for the solution of the gigantic problem caused by sin. The marvel of the creation of man is that he is made "of the earth, earthy." God allowed the enemy to work on this creation of man in a way he cannot work on any other creation, but ultimately God is going to overthrow the rule of His enemy by a being "a little lower than the angels," viz., man. When God came into this order of things, He did not come as an angel, He came as a Man, He took upon Him our human nature. This is the marvel of the Incarnation.

We know nothing about God the Father saving as Jesus Christ has revealed Him. "Philip saith unto Him, Lord, shew us the Father. . . . Jesus saith unto him, Have I been so long time with you and yet hast thou not known Me, Philip? He that hath seen Me hath seen the Father." The characteristics of God Almighty are mirrored for us in Jesus Christ; therefore if we want to know what God is like, we must study Jesus Christ.

The first fundamental characteristic of the mighty nature of God is will; consequently when God's Spirit comes into our spirit, we can will to do what God wants us to do. "For it is God which worketh in you both to will and to do of His good pleasure" (Philippians 2:13). Will is not a faculty. We talk of a person having a weak will, or a strong will; that is misleading. "Will" means the whole nature active, and when we are energised by the Spirit of God, we are enabled to do what we could not do before; that is, we are able to obey God.

The next great fundamental characteristic of God the Father is Love. "God is love" (1 John 4:8). The Bible does not say that God is loving, but that God is love. The phrase "the lovingkindness of God" is frequently used, but when the nature of God is revealed, the Bible does not say God is a loving Being, it says, "God is love."

The same characteristic is revealed in God the Son, viz., love, and instantly the kind of love is shown: He "loved us, and washed us from our sins in His own blood" (Revelation 1:5): not a love that overlooks sin, but a love the essential nature of which is that it delivers from sin.

". . . the love of God is shed abroad in our hearts by the Holy Ghost which is given unto us" (Romans 5:5). This does not mean that when we receive the Holy Spirit He enables us to have the capacity for loving God, but that He sheds abroad in our hearts *the love of God*, a much more fundamental and marvellous thing. It is pathetic the number of people who are piously trying to make their poor human hearts love God! The Holy Spirit sheds abroad in my heart, not the power to love God, but the very nature of God; and the nature of God coming into me makes me part of God's consciousness, not God part of my consciousness. I am unconscious of God because I have been taken up into His consciousness. Paul puts it in Galatians 2:20 (a verse with which we are perfectly familiar, but which none of us will ever fathom, no matter how long we live, or how much we experience of God's grace): "I am crucified with Christ: nevertheless I live; yet not I, but Christ liveth in me." Again in Galatians 1:15–16, Paul refers to the receiving of the very nature of Jesus Christ: "When it pleased God, Who separated me from my mother's womb, and called me by His grace, to reveal His Son in me." This is the true idea of a saint. A saint is not a human being who is trying to be good, trying by effort and prayer and longing and obedience to attain as many saintly characteristics as possible; a saint is a being who has been re-created. "If any man is in Christ, he is a new creation" (RV mg).

We have to be solemnly careful that we do not travesty and belittle the work of God and the Atonement of the Lord Jesus Christ. If we belittle it in the tiniest degree, although we may do it in ignorance, we shall surely suffer. The first thing which will make is belittle the Atonement is getting out of sympathy with God into sympathy with human beings, because when we do this we begin to drag down the tremendous revelation that the essential nature of God is Will and Love and Light, and that it is these characteristics which are imparted to us by the Holy Ghost. We have not these characteristics naturally. By nature our hearts are darkened away from God; we have no power to generate will within ourselves; we have no power to love God when we like, and our hearts are darkened.

Again, the essential nature of God the Father is Light. "This then is the message which we have heard of Him, and declare unto you, that God is light, and in Him is no darkness at all" (1 John 1:5). There is no variableness in God, no "shadow that is cast by turning" (RV). We are told that where there is light and substance, there must be shadow; but there is no shadow in God, none whatever.

What does Jesus Christ say of Himself? "I am the Light of the world" (John 8:12): no shadow in Jesus Christ. And of the Holy Spirit, Jesus said, "Howbeit when He, the Spirit of truth, is come, He will guide you into all truth: for He shall not speak of Himself; but whatsoever He shall hear, that shall He speak: and He will shew you things to come" (John 16:13).

Active Will, pervading Love showing itself as Light in God the Father; active Will, pervading Love showing itself as Light in the Lord Jesus Christ; all-pervading energy and Will and all-pervading Love showing itself as Light in the Holy Ghost. These are the fundamental characteristics of the Godhead.

To revise, "God is love." No man who is wide-awake naturally ever believes that unless he has received the Spirit of God, it is foolishness to him. In the Sermon on the Mount Jesus Christ says, in effect, that when as His disciples we have been initiated into the kind of life He lives, we are based on the knowledge that God is our heavenly Father and that He is love. Then there comes the wonderful working out of this knowledge in our lives, it is not that we *won't* worry, but that we have come to the place where we *cannot* worry, because the Holy Spirit has shed abroad the love of God in our hearts, and we find that we can never think of anything our heavenly Father will forget. Although great clouds and perplexities may come, as they did in the case of Job, and of the Apostle Paul, and in the case of every saint, yet they never touch "the secret place of the Most High." "Therefore will not we fear, though the earth be removed, and though the mountains be carried into the midst of the sea." The Spirit of God has so centred us in God and everything is so rightly adjusted that we do not fear.

We cannot give ourselves the Holy Spirit; the Holy Spirit is God Almighty's gift if we will simply become poor enough to ask for Him. "If ye then, being evil, know how to give good gifts unto your children: how much more shall your heavenly Father give the Holy Spirit to them that ask Him?" (Luke 11:13). But when the Holy Spirit has come in, there is something we can do and God cannot do, we can obey Him. If we do not obey Him, we shall grieve Him. "And grieve not the Holy Spirit of God" (Ephesians 4:30). Over and over again we need to be reminded of Paul's counsel, "Work out your own salvation with fear and trembling. For it is God which worketh in you both to will and to do of His good pleasure." Thank God, it is gloriously and majestically true that the Holy Spirit can work in us the very nature of Jesus Christ if we will obey Him, until in and through our mortal flesh may be manifested works which will make men glorify our Father in heaven, and take knowledge of us that we have been with Jesus.

Light is the most marvellous description of clear, beautiful moral character from God's standpoint. "If we walk in the light, as He is in the light, we have fellowship one with another, and the blood of Jesus Christ His Son cleanseth us from all sin" (1 John 1:7). "If we walk in the light . . ." What light? ". . . *as God is in the light*"! What light? "*I am the Light of the world*"! What light?—*the light of the Holy Spirit!* "And this is the condemnation," said Jesus, "that light is come into the world, and men loved darkness rather than light, because their deeds were evil" (John 3:19). "Darkness" is my own point of view, my prejudices and preconceived determinations; if the Spirit of God agrees with these, well and good; if not, I shall go my own way.

The "weaning" that goes on when a soul is being taken out of walking in the light of its own convictions into walking in the light of God is a time of peril. When a child is being weaned, it is fractious, and when God is trying to wean us from our own ways of looking at things in order to bring us into the full light of the Holy Spirit, we are fractious too. If we persist in sticking to our own convictions, we shall end in darkness; but if we walk in the light, as God is in the light, recognising and relying on the Holy Spirit, we shall be brought into a complete understanding of God's way and we shall have "fellowship one with another" i.e., with all those who are walking in the same light.

Then comes this wonderful thing—we shall have a purity of life in God's sight that is too pure for us to begin to understand; "and the blood of Jesus Christ His Son cleanseth us from all sin." Anything less than that—I say it measuring every word—anything less than that would be blasphemous. If God cannot cleanse us from all sin and make us "holy and without blame" in His sight, then Jesus Christ has totally misled us, and the Atonement is not what it claims to be. Oh, if we would only get into the way of bringing our limitations before God and telling Him He cannot do these things, we should begin to see the awful wickedness of unbelief, and why our Lord was so vigorous against it, and why the Apostle John places fearfulness and unbelief at the head of all the most awful sins (see Revelation 21:8). When the Holy Spirit comes in, unbelief is turned out and the energy of God is put into us, and we are enabled to will and to do of His good pleasure. When the Holy Spirit comes in He sheds abroad the love of God in our hearts, so that we are able to show our fellows the same love that God has shown to us. When the Holy Spirit comes in He makes us as "light," and our righteousness will exceed the righteousness of the most moral upright natural man because the supernatural has been made natural in us.

Chapter XVIII
SPIRIT: THE DOMAIN AND DOMINION OF SPIRIT
Mundane Universe

Spirit As Physical Force
    1. World of Matter (Psalm 104:30; 33:6;
       2 Peter 3:5)
    2. World of Nature (Genesis 1:2; Job 26:13)
    3. World of Self (John 6:63; James 2:25;
       Ezekiel 1:20; Revelation 11:11)

The student will find that we claim that the Bible gives the working explanation of all things. We found in the last chapter that the fundamental characteristics of the Godhead are Will, Love and Light; that God is the only Being Who can will pure will, and that when we receive the Holy Spirit He energises our spirits so that we are able to do the will of God. The present day is the dispensation of the Holy Spirit. We are familiar with the phrase, but do we understand sufficiently Who the Holy Spirit is? The Holy Spirit is identical with God the Father and with God the Son; and being a Person, He must exercise an influence. The more pronounced a person, the more powerful is his influence; but we have to recognise that nowadays the majority of people do not know the Holy Ghost as a Person, they know Him only as an influence.

Spirit As Physical Force

By the Mundane Universe is meant the terrestrial world in which we live, the earth and rocks and trees, and the people we come in contact with. When we dealt with the physical world, we found that everything leads us back to the Bible revelation, viz., that at the back of all is spirit force, not matter and material things, but spirit. What is this tremendous force? The Bible reveals that the force behind everything is the great Spirit of God. A great change has come over what is called material science, and scientists are coming back to the Bible point of view, viz., that at the back of everything is spirit; that the material world holds itself in existence by spirit. In the early days when men tried to explain the material world, they said that it was made up of atoms; then they found that those atoms could be split up, and the split-up elements were called molecules; then they found that the molecules could be split up, and that the split-up

molecules were made of electrons; then they discovered that the electron itself is like a solar system.[17]

These facts are significant because they point out the absurdity of the cry that the Bible and modern science do not agree; how could they? If the Bible agreed with modern science, in about fifty years both would be out of date. All scientific findings have at one time been modern. Science is simply man's attempt to explain what he knows.

An important aside—do not belittle the Bible and say that it has only to do with man's salvation. The Bible is a universe of revelation facts which explains the world in which we live, and it is simply "giving a sop to Satan"[18] to say, as some modern teachers do, that the Bible does not pretend to tell us how the world came into existence. The Bible claims to be the only exposition of how the world came into being and how it keeps going, and the only Book which tells us how we may understand the world.

1. The World of Matter
By the word of the LORD were the heavens made; and all the host of them by the breath of His mouth. (Psalm 33:6; see also Psalm 104:30; 2 Peter 3:5)

These passages simply express what is revealed all through the Bible, viz., that God created the world out of nothing. The Bible does not say God "emanated" the world. The exponents of the clever modern idea of emanation say that God evolved the world out of Himself. The Bible says that God created the world "by the breath of His mouth." Meditate for a moment on the word "creation," and see what a supernatural word it is. No philosopher ever thought of it, no expounder of natural history ever imagined such a word. We can understand "evolution" and "emanation," but we simply do not know what "creation" means. There is only one Being Who knows, and that is God Himself, and the Bible says that God *created* the heaven and the earth.

What is the world of matter? For instance, I am looking at a book, I see it is bound in a red cover, it is flexible, and has black marks on it. I can account by my senses for the redness and the blackness and the

---

17. See an explanation of Chambers' use of "atoms" and "molecules" in the introduction to this book.
18. giving a sop to Satan: pacifying, appeasing, buying off with a present or bribe.

flexibility, but the one thing I cannot describe is what it is that awakens those sensations. I see a clock, and I should probably describe it in the same way as you would—that it is hard and smooth, and brown and white; I can hear a sound, and see its face, and so on; all of which can be described as the result of my sensations, but what is it makes me have those sensations? The way we see things depends on our nerves, but what the thing is in itself that makes us see things in a particular way we do not know; that is, we do not know what matter is. The Bible says the world of matter was created by God; the way we interpret it will depend on what spirit we have.

2. The World of Nature

The world of nature (Genesis 1:2; Job 26:13)—i.e., the order in which material things appear to me. I explain the world outside me by thinking; then if I can explain the world outside me by my mind, there must have been a Mind that made it. That is logical, simple and clear; consequently atheism is what the Bible calls it, the belief of a fool. "The fool hath said in his heart, There is no God" (Psalm 53:1). An atheist is one who says, "I can explain by my mind to a certain extent what things are like outside, but there is not a mind behind that created them."

"In the beginning" God created things out of nothing; matter did not exist before God created it. It was God Who created it, out of nothing; not out of Himself. "And the earth was without form, and void; and darkness was upon the face of the deep. And the Spirit of God moved upon the face of the waters" (Genesis 1:2). This verse refers to the reconstruction of things out of chaos. As we pointed out in dealing with the subject of Man, in all probability there was a former order of things, which was ruined by disobedience, thereby producing the chaos out of which God reconstructed the order of things which we know, and which we so differently interpret.

"For by Him were all things created, that are in heaven, and that are in earth, visible and invisible, whether they be thrones, or dominions, or principalities, or powers: all things were created by Him" (Colossians 1:16). We hear it said that if God created everything that was created, then He is responsible for the presence of sin. The Bible reveals all through that God has taken the responsibility for sin. What is the proof that He has? Calvary! God created everything that was created; God created the being who became Satan and He created the being who became the sinner. But sin is not a creation; sin is the outcome of a wrong relationship set up between two of God's creations. From the very beginning God holds Himself responsible for the possibility of sin (cf. Revelation 13:8). Nowhere does the Bible say that God holds man responsible for having the disposition of sin; but what God does hold man responsible for is refusing to let Him deliver him from that heredity the moment he sees and understands that that is what Jesus Christ came to do. John 3:19 is the final word on condemnation, "And this is the condemnation, that light is come into the world, and men loved darkness rather than light, because their deeds were evil."

We have seen that God is responsible for the established order of Nature; but there are conflicting views about the world of Nature. If you read the Book of Job carefully you will find there that the world of Nature is a wild contradiction; you cannot explain it satisfactorily at all. If you start out and say that God is good, you will come across some facts which seem to prove He is not good. How is it that we come to different conclusions about the world: one man sees everything as bad as bad can be, while another man sees everything as good as good can be? It all depends on the spirit within a man. There may be as many accounts of the world of Nature as there are human beings. That is why the world of Nature seems such a contradiction. The spirit within a man accounts for the way he interprets what he sees outside; and if I have not the Spirit of God, I shall never interpret the world outside as God interprets it; I shall continually have to shut my eyes and deny certain facts. I shall do what the Christian Scientist does, deny that facts are facts.

Along this line we see the limitations of trying to dispute with a man who says there is no God, you cannot disprove it to him; but get him to receive the Holy Spirit and his logic will alter immediately. That is Paul's argument in 1 Corinthians 2—that the spirit of man understands the things of a man, but that the spirit of man cannot understand the things of God. If I have not the Spirit of God, I shall never interpret the world of Nature in the way God does; the Bible will be to me simply an Oriental tradition, a "cunningly devised fable." If I am to understand the Bible, I must have the Spirit of God.

As Christians, we recognise that we must have the Spirit of God for practical living, but do we realise the need of the Spirit of God for thinking? Christian workers use dangerous weapons against what they take to be the enemies of Christianity (but in reality against our Lord Himself) simply because they are not renewed in the spirit of their mind; they won't think on God's line; they refuse to make their minds work. We have no business to be ignorant about the way God created the world, or to be unable to discern "the arm of the LORD" behind things. When the Holy Spirit has transformed our practical life, He begins to stir up our minds, and the point is, will we bring our minds into harmony with the new way of living? Jesus Christ laid down a remarkable principle for practical living and for practical thinking, that is, He taught His disciples how to think by "correspondences." "I am the true Vine." Is the natural vine false? No, the natural vine is the shadow of the real. "My Father giveth you the true Bread from heaven." Is the bread we eat false? No, it is the shadow of the real bread. "I am the Door," and so on.

If we have the Spirit of God within, we shall be able to interpret in the light of God what we see with our eyes and hear with our ears and understand with our minds. "The sun shall be no more thy light by day; neither for brightness shall the moon give light unto thee; but the Lord shall be unto thee an everlasting light" (Isaiah 60:19). May this not mean that the ordinary days and nights bring before us facts which we cannot explain, but that when we receive the Spirit of God we get a line of explanation? For instance, we cannot explain life, yet it is a very commonplace fact that we are alive. We cannot explain love; we cannot explain death; we cannot explain sin; yet these are all everyday facts. The world of Nature is a confusion; there is nothing clear about it; it is a confusing, wild chaos. Immediately we receive the Spirit of God, He energises our spirits not only for practical living but for practical thinking, and we begin to "the arm of the LORD," i.e., to see God's order in and through all the chaos.

"I thank Thee, O Father, Lord of heaven and earth, because Thou hast . . . revealed [these things] unto babes" (Matthew 11:25). Our Lord thanked His Father that He was the only Medium the Father had for revealing Himself; and the invitation "Come unto Me" is given to disciples, not to sinners. Watch your own mind if you have been born again of the Spirit of God, and you will understand the condition of mind Jesus Christ is alluding to—"all ye that labour and are heavy laden"; trying to think out what cannot be thought out, and Jesus Christ's message to all such is, "Come unto Me, . . . and I will give you rest." "I am the Way." "If My Spirit is imparted to you, you will begin to see. things as I do." "Marvel not that I said unto thee, Ye must be born again," i.e., born again for practical thinking as well as for practical living.

It is a strange thing the indiscriminate way we are taught to think as pagans and live as Christians. So much of our thinking explanations are pagan; men who are being trained to teach others are taught to think as pagans, and the consequence is what we are seeing. We have to bring our thinking into line with the living Spirit of God, to take laborious trouble to think, to "meditate on these things," "bringing into captivity every thought to the obedience of Christ." Never allow your mind to run off on wild speculations, that is where danger begins, "I want to find out this and that." The sin of Eve begins whenever the mind is allowed to run off at a tangent on speculations. "Come unto Me," says Jesus. "I am the Way," not only the way to be saved and sanctified and to live as a Christian, but the way to think as a Christian. "Neither knoweth any man the Father, save the Son, and he to whomsoever the Son will reveal Him," and Jesus will reveal the Father to anyone who will come to Him.

3. The World of Self

It is the Spirit that quickeneth; the flesh profiteth nothing: the words that I speak unto you, they are spirit, and they are life. (John 6:63; see also James 2:26; Ezekiel 1:20; Revelation 11:11)

Can Jesus Christ speak to me to-day? Certainly He can, through the Holy Spirit; but if I take the words of Jesus without His Spirit, they are of no avail to me. I can conjure with them, I can do all kinds of things with them, but they are not "spirit" and "life." When the Holy Spirit is in me, He will bring to my remembrance what Jesus has said and make His Words live. The Spirit within me enables me to assimilate the words of Jesus. The Holy Spirit exercises a remarkable power in that He will frequently take a text out of its Bible context and put it into the context of our life. We have all had the experience of a verse coming to us right out of its Bible setting and becoming alive in the setting of our own life, and that word becomes a precious, secret possession. See that you keep it a secret possession, don't "cast ye your pearls before swine"—those are the strong words of our Lord.

To use an ingenious symbol—we read that when Jesus was led away to be crucified, they "were come unto a place called Golgotha, that is to say, a place of a skull," and that is where Jesus Christ is always crucified; that is where He is put to shame to-day, viz., in the heads of men who won't bring their thinking into line with the Spirit of God. If men are inspired by the Holy Spirit, their words are built on the Word of God. Paul urges us to be renewed in the spirit of our mind; and the way we are renewed is not by impulses or impressions, but by being gripped by the Word of God. The habit of getting a word from God is right; don't give up till you get one. Never go on an impression, that will pass, there is nothing in it; there is nothing lasting until a word becomes living, when it does it is the Holy Spirit bringing back to your remembrance some word of Jesus Christ.

In this way we are able to discern "the arm of the LORD," and the World of Self becomes what Jesus Christ wants it to be, but if we are ruled by a spirit other than the Spirit of God, e.g., the spirit of "my right to myself," we shall explain the world of Self according to that spirit. We shall never explain things as Jesus Christ explains them, we will begin to patronise Him; or if we do not dare to patronise Jesus Christ, we will patronise the Apostle Paul. Anything to appear "up to date," because the spirit that is in man, no matter how cultured and moral and religious, or how favourable it may appear to men, if it is not indwelt by the Spirit of God, must be scattering away from Jesus Christ. "He that gathereth not with Me scattereth abroad."

"Whithersoever the spirit was to go, they went, thither was their spirit to go; and the wheels were lifted up over against them: for the spirit of the living creature was in the wheels" (Ezekiel 1:20). This is a picture of the ultimate working of everything in harmony with God by His Spirit. "And when the cherubim went, the wheels went by them: and when the cherubim lifted up their wings to mount up from the earth, the same wheels also turned not from beside them" (Ezekiel 10:16). The cherubim are an Old Testament figure of the Mystical Body of Christ. Moses was told to make two cherubim: "And thou shalt make two cherubim of gold, of beaten work shalt thou make them, in the two ends of the mercy seat" (Exodus 25:18–22); and yet God had said, "Thou shalt not make unto thee any graven image, or any likeness of anything that is in heaven above, or that is in the earth beneath, or that is in the water under the earth" (Exodus 20:4). The cherubim are not like anything in heaven above or in the earth beneath, but like something which is now being made, viz., the Mystical Body of Christ. This is prefigured in Genesis; when Adam and Eve were driven out of the garden of Eden there was placed "at the east of the garden of Eden Cherubim, and a flaming sword which turned every way, to keep the way of the tree of life" (Genesis 3:24). The cherubim are the guardians into the holiest of all, and when the Mystical Body of Christ is complete, all the "machinery" of this earth will be moved and directed by the Spirit of God.

To be saved and sanctified means to be possessed by the Spirit, not only for living, but for thinking. If we will bring our thinking into captivity to the Holy Spirit, we form what is termed "Nous." *Nous* is a Greek word meaning responsible intelligence. Whenever we get to this point of responsible intelligence, we have come to a sure line of thinking. Until the nous is formed in natural life and in spiritual life, we get at things by intuition, by impulse, but there is no responsible intelligence. The writer to the Hebrews refers to this, "By this time you ought to be teachers, but you want "spooned meat"[19] again: by this time you ought to be robust and mature, no longer either children or fools, but men and women able to distinguish between right and wrong, between good and bad, with a thoroughly informed, responsible intelligence" (see Hebrews 5:12–14). How many of us have allowed the Spirit of God to bring us there and enabled us to think along Jesus Christ's line? Or do we have to say when these subjects are referred to,

"Oh, I leave those things for other people"? We have no business to talk like that, we ought to be at our best for God. We have not only to be good lovers of God, but good thinkers, and it is only along this line that we can "try the spirits whether they are of God."

How are we going to test the teaching that is abroad to-day? A man or a woman may have a real Christian experience, but if their minds are not informed and disciplined, their intelligence becomes a hotbed for heresy. Our thinking would be revolutionised if we would bring our imagination into line with the Bible context, viz., the heart of God. The Bible not only explains God, it explains the world in which we live, it explains not only things that are right, but things that are wrong. If we start out with the idea that everything is going well and all is bright and happy and then there is an earthquake, or someone is killed by lightning, or there are tremendous floods, or a shocking murder, or worse crime, the idea with which we started out will be flatly contradicted by the world outside, that is, by the facts we see and know. The Bible and the outside world agree, but both the Bible and the outside world are an absolute puzzle to us until we receive the Spirit of God. When we receive the Spirit of God, we are lifted into a totally new realm, and if we will bring our minds into harmony with what the Spirit of God reveals, begin to discipline ourselves and bring every thought into captivity, we shall not only begin to discern God's order in the Bible, but our eyes will be opened and the secrets of the world will be understood and grasped. When we read the records of history we shall begin to discover the way in which God has been at work; and we shall discover when we look at our own lives, not a number of haphazard chances, but some preconceived idea of God which we did not know being worked out. We shall begin to find to our amazement that our lives are answers to the prayers of the Holy Ghost, and that at the back of everything is the mind of God.

"But we have the mind of Christ," says Paul. To have the mind of Christ means a great deal more than having the Spirit of Christ. To have the mind of Christ means to think as Jesus thought, and He always thought from one centre, viz., God. "For I have not spoken of Myself; but the Father which sent Me, He gave Me a commandment, what I should say, and what I should speak" (John 12:49). Where did our Lord get His words from? From the Spirit that was in Him. The tongue in our Lord Jesus Christ got to its right place because He never spoke from the spirit of His right to Himself; and our tongue and our brain will only be in the right place when we learn to obey the Spirit of God in thinking. Thank God we are

---

19. spooned meat: liquefied food that requires no chewing or effort—baby food.

given a line of explanation for everything under heaven. When we receive the Holy Spirit and obey Him, we find that Jesus Christ does satisfy the last aching abyss of our minds as well as our hearts. The one word ringing out over our mental life is "Obey! Obey!" Those of you who know what obedience means in the moral realm, bring it into the intellectual realm. Are you bringing into captivity every thought to the obedience of Christ? Are you continually being renewed in the spirit of your mind? Is your thinking in absolute harmony with Jesus Christ's thinking?

The day we live in is a day of wild imaginations everywhere, unchecked imaginations in music, in literature, and, worst of all, in the interpretation of Scripture. People are going off on wild speculations, they get hold of one line and run clean off at a tangent and try to explain everything on that line, then they go off on another line: none of it is in accordance with the Spirit of God. There is no royal road for bringing our brains into harmony with the Spirit God has put in our hearts; we do not get there all at once, but only by steady discipline.

Chapter XIX

SPIRIT: THE DOMAIN AND DOMINION OF SPIRIT
Man's Universe
Job 12:10

NATURAL NOUS
BEWILDERED NOUS
SPIRITUAL NOUS

1. Spirit As Soul-Making Power
    (a) Particular Form (Genesis 2:7; 6:17)
    (b) Personal Form (Numbers 16:22; 27:16; Zechariah 12:1; Isaiah 19:3; Psalm 2:10)
    (c) Physical Form (Job 32:8; Genesis 7:22; Hebrews 2:19; Revelation 13:15; Job 34:14–15)

2. Spirit in the Flesh
    (a) Independent (1 Corinthians 2:12–14)
    (b) Dependent (Psalm 32:2; 2 Corinthians 7:1; James 3:15)
    (c) Death (Romans 7:18–23; 8:5–7; 1 Peter 3:19)

    N.B. WE DEAL HERE PARTICULARLY WITH
    SPIRIT IN THE NATURAL MAN.

First of all we will deal with "Nous." As already stated, nous means responsible intelligence both in a natural man and a spiritual man. Jesus Christ is the expression of the responsible intelligence of God. He is "Logos," the Word of God Incarnate. There is the same thing in man, that is, there is spirit.

Natural Nous

The moment when responsible intelligence begins in the natural life differs; some people never seem to reach it at all, they live as children and die as children, or more as simpletons than children. They have impulses and imaginations and fancies, but they never

come to a responsible intelligence. A child is not responsible, but the statements of persons of mature intelligence are responsible; consequently we are judged by our words. It is quite true that there are times when we have to say, "answer my meaning, not my words," but those times are exceptional. The things we express, the statements we make, and the thoughts we form, are all stamped with responsibility.

There is a capacity in man apart from the Spirit of God to know that there is a God. "For the invisible things of Him from the creation of the world are clearly seen, being understood by the things that are made, even His eternal power and Godhead" (Romans 1:20). We are speaking of natural nous apart altogether from the work of grace. As soon as a man becomes responsibly intelligent, he comes to the conclusion that there must be responsible intelligence not less than his own behind everything there is, and God holds every man responsible for knowing that. ". . . he that cometh to God must believe that He is" (Hebrews 11:6).

The ordinance of God is placed in the natural make-up of a man, and when a man becomes responsibly intelligent he is able to discern a great many things, things which he calls justice and righteousness, and the Apostle Paul states that the heathen are judged by conscience (see Romans 1:20–21). We are getting very near the point where conscience becomes the responsible power working in a man's life. When we dealt with conscience, we called it the "eye of the soul," which looks out towards God, and how it records depends entirely upon the light thrown upon God. Nous, or responsible intelligence, which is nearly the same as conscience, discerns the ordinance of God written in man's spirit; therefore to say that men are not responsible for doing wrong is untrue to experience and to revelation. The Bible says that a man knows by the way he is made that certain things are wrong, and as he obeys or disobeys the ordinance of God written in his spirit, he will be judged.

"Through faith we understand that the worlds were framed by the word of God, so that things which are seen were not made of things which do appear" (Hebrews 11:3). It is not a question of swallowing a revelation, but of understanding with responsible intelligence how the world was made. This is simply a fresh emphasis on what has been emphasised all through, viz., the responsibility of those of us who are Christians in experience for being Christians in responsible intelligence. If we can form responsible intelligence as natural men, we must form it also as spiritual men. The Bible does not only teach the way of salvation, but the way of spiritual sanity.

Bewildered Nous
In 2 Corinthians 11:3 Paul is referring to the devil beguiling Eve through his subtlety, and so bewildering her that she could not understand God's will or obey it, and he says, "I fear lest by any means . . . your minds should be corrupted from the simplicity that is in Christ"; and in writing to the Galatians he says, "Who hath bewitched you, that ye should not obey the truth?" This confusion of the responsible intelligence takes place at the beginning of the Christian life and people are in danger of becoming legal. "I am afraid of you, lest I have bestowed upon you labour in vain," says Paul— lest you become all wrong, because you are going back to the old legal notions and trying to make yourselves perfect in that way (Galatians 4:11). It is along these lines that the subtlety of Satan bewitches away from God a life that was coming under His dominion. Our Lord alludes to the same thing when He says, "the cares of this world, and the deceitfulness of riches, and the lusts of other things entering in, choke the word," i.e., bewilder you. No wonder the first law of a born again soul is concentration. We hear a great deal about consecration, but not so much about concentration.

"A double minded man is unstable in all his ways" (James 1:8). A double-minded man is a "switherer," that is the description of a bewildered soul, the responsible intelligence of the natural man pulling and the responsible intelligence of the Spirit of Christ also pulling, and he does not know which way to take. "Let not that man think that he shall receive anything of the Lord." A man must decide whether he will be identified with the death of the Lord Jesus Christ,

which will mean the turning out not only of the "old man," but of the old responsible intelligence, the old bondage, the old legalism, the things which used to guide the life before, and the forming of a totally new mind. It works out in this way: in your practical life you come to a crisis where there are two distinct ways before you, one the way of ordinary, strong, moral, common sense and the other the way of waiting on God until the mind is formed which can understand His will. Any amount of backing will be given you for the first line, the backing of worldly people and of semi-Christian people, but you will feel the warning, the drawing back of the Spirit of God, and if you wait on God, study His Word, and watch Him at work in your circumstances, you will be brought to a decision along God's line, and your worldly "backers" and your semi-Christian "backers" will fall away from you with disgust and say, "It is absurd, you are getting fanatical."

"For to be carnally minded is death; but to be spiritually minded is life and peace" (Romans 8:6). We are familiar with the carnal mind in the moral aspect, its enmity against God, its wrong longings and seekings; but it takes a good deal of courage to face the fact that the mind of the natural man is wrong in its responsible thinking, that is, it will give verdicts against what Jesus Christ says; it will decide straightaway that His responsible intelligence is that of a madman, or the irresponsible intelligence of a mere dreamer. We are using the phrase "carnally minded" in this connection to mean what is called common sense, i.e., the mature responsible intelligence of an unregenerate human being, and over and over again we find how this clashes with the teaching of Jesus before it harmonises with it. We are bridging now between the bewildered and the spiritual nous. When the Holy Spirit comes in it confuses a man's reasonable intelligence and turns his thinking upside down, and he gets thoroughly bewildered (cf. Matthew 10:34). We are not dealing with the carnal mind here in the deep moral sense, but with the responsible intelligence which sets itself against the spiritual understanding and refuses to be reconciled to it, in the same way that it may refuse to be reconciled to it morally; and until common sense becomes sanctified sense (not "sanctified common sense," which is not a Bible phrase, nor has it a Bible meaning), and the responsible intelligence has been re-formed by the Spirit of God, this antagonism will go on. When we begin to think along God's line, we come up with an amazing clash against certain things which we have accepted as being inalienable rights for everyone, because Jesus Christ's teaching works from another standpoint, and this clash brings confusion and bewilderment for a time, until we resolve to remove ourselves altogether from the old ways of looking at things and to look at everything from the standpoint of the mind of Christ. "If any man is in

Christ, he is a new creation" (RV mg), not his spirit alone, but spirit, soul and body, and slowly the new creation is seen all through.

Spiritual Nous

For who hath known the mind of the Lord, that he may instruct Him? But we have the mind of Christ. (1 Corinthians 2:16)

The great benediction of the grace of God is that those who seem to have no natural nous are enabled to construct nous in the spiritual realm by the Spirit of God, and use it aright in the temple of the Holy Ghost. To begin with, a child has no responsible intelligence, and the same is true in the spiritual domain. When we begin the spiritual life we have the Spirit of Christ but not the mind of Christ. To have the mind of Christ means much more than having His Spirit, it means to have the responsible understanding of Christ. When we are born again, we find every now and then that the Spirit of God within us is struggling to get us to understand as God understands, and we are very stupid in the way we mistake the things the Spirit of God is trying to teach us; but when, in entire sanctification, the Son of God is formed in us (see Galatians 4:19), we understand with a responsible intelligence even as Jesus Christ did; consequently we are held responsible for doing through our bodies all that we understand God wishes us to do. Jesus Christ spoke what He knew His Father wished Him to speak, and He spoke nothing else; we must do the same if we have the mind of Christ. Jesus Christ worked only those works which He knew were the exact expression of His Father, "My Father worketh hitherto, and I work" (John 5:17). We must do the same. To form a spiritual nous means not only that the Holy Spirit energises our spirit but that we allow Him to work out in a responsible intelligence in us.

"And we know that the Son of God is come, and hath given us an understanding, that we may know Him that is true . . ." (1 John 5:20). The word "understanding" does not mean anything necromantic; it means that we understand with a responsible intelligence that which comes from God; and God holds us responsible for not knowing it. It is not a question of any uncanny spiritual influence, or of a flashing spiritual intuition, but of having the nous, our responsible intelligence, so obedient to the Holy Spirit that we can understand what is of God and what is not. In this way we begin to form a responsible spiritual intelligence, and we must take care not to grieve the Spirit of God along these lines.

"For this is the covenant that I will make, . . . saith the Lord; I will put My laws into their mind, and write them in their hearts: and I will be to them a God, and they shall be to Me a people" (Hebrews 8:10). That embraces everything—a full, mature, understanding intelligence on the part of the people of God, not being at the mercy of spiritual impulses, driven about by every wind of doctrine, but becoming mature, vigorous minded people who not only understand what the will of God is, but who do it.

1. Spirit As Soul-Making Power

We are dealing here particularly with spirit in the natural man.

Remember, the whole meaning of the soul is to express the spirit, and the struggle of spirit is to get itself expressed in the soul. In the natural life when an immature mind is trying to express itself, there are tremendous struggles and all kinds of physical exertions and efforts. It has no responsible intelligence, no vocabulary; when a child gets into tempers, it is often an attempt to express itself. When a young life is trying to express itself, it experiences exquisite suffering; music is run to, theatres are run to, literature is run to—anything to try and get the power to express what is there in longing; and if a life goes on too long on these lines, it will never form a responsible intelligence, but will become most unpractical. The discipline of the machinery of life enables us to get the power to express what is in us. That is the value of language. There is a great difference in languages; for instance, take the language of the Authorised Version of the Bible and the language we use to-day. The words of the Bible express the inner soul; the words we use to-day are nearly all technical, borrowed from somewhere else, and our most modern words do not express the spirit at all, but cunningly cloak it over and give no expression.

This kind of phrase is often heard from a young person, "Oh, I don't understand myself"; or, "Nobody understands me!" Why, of course they don't; but we are responsible for not having a responsible intelligence as to where we can be understood (see Psalm 139). The meaning of education is not to pack in something alien, but the drawing out of what is in for the purpose of expression. One of the greatest benefits when a young life is trying to express itself is to have something to work at with the hands, to model in wax, to paint, or write, or dig, anything that will give an opportunity of expression.

If it is true in the natural life that the mind goes through all this turmoil in trying to express itself, it is just as true in the spiritual life. When the Spirit of God comes into me the same kind of struggle goes on. The Spirit of God tries to get me out of the natural "ruts" into line with Him and to obey Him so that He can express Himself through my responsible intelligence. These are the throes and the growing pains of a life after being born again, and they go on until the mind of Christ is formed, and the old carnal antagonism is no more. The value of a spiritual teacher is that he expresses for us what we have been trying to express for ourselves but could not. Whenever a person or a book expresses for us what we have been trying to express for ourselves, we feel unspeakably grateful, and in this way we learn how to express for ourselves. Tribulation will teach us how to express things, our circumstances will teach us, temptations of the devil will teach us, difficult things will teach us. All these things will develop the power of expression until we become responsible in expression of the Spirit of God as Jesus Christ was the responsible expression of the mind of God Almighty.

(a) Particular Form

And the LORD God formed man of the dust of the ground, and breathed into his nostrils the breath of life; and man became a living soul. (Genesis 2:7; see 6:17)

The particular forms of nature, i.e., rocks and trees, animals and men, are all the outcome of the breathing of the Spirit of God. There is a true law of correspondence between the things which we see and the Mind that is behind them. When we have in us the Mind behind the things we see, we begin to understand how these things manifest that Mind, but if we have not that Mind we shall never understand them.

(b) Personal Form

Let the LORD, the God of the spirits of all flesh, set a man over the congregation. (Numbers 27:16; see 16:22; Zechariah 12:1; Isaiah 19:3; Psalm 51:10)

These passages make it clear that man has a distinct responsibility of his own, that is, he can express the spirit of the prince of this world in a responsibly intelligent way, or he can express the Spirit of God in a responsibly intelligent way. This is what we mean when we say a man shows "soul" in his writings or speaking, he shows "soul" in his prayers and in his manner of living; we mean that he has the power to express his spirit, the personal note comes out all the time. God is a Person, and He expresses the peculiar stamp of His Person in all that He creates. When we have the Spirit of God and are forming a responsible intelligence spiritually, we begin to think God's thoughts after Him and to see His meaning, not by our natural intelligence, but by the Spirit of God.

(c) Physical Form

But there is a spirit in man: and the inspiration of the Almighty giveth them understanding. Great men are not always wise: neither do the aged understand judgement. (Job 32:8; see Genesis 7; Habakkuk 2:19; Revelation 13:15; Job 34:14–15)

Our physical life is meant to express all that is in the spirit. The soul struggles in travail of birth until the zone of expression in the body is reached. Paul is stating just this idea when he says, "My little children, of whom I travail in birth again until Christ be formed in you" (Galatians 4:19). To begin with we have not our own body, but probably a body which is very much like that of our grandmother or grandfather, but every few years the physical form alters, and it alters into the shape of the ruling spirit. We may find a beautifully moulded face begin to take on a remarkably un-beautiful moral expression as it grows older, or we may find an ugly face begin to take on a remarkably beautiful moral expression. Sooner or later, through the turmoil in the soul, the physical life must express the ruling spirit. We grow exactly like our spirit. If that spirit is the spirit of man, we shall grow further and further away from the image of God; but if we have the Spirit of God within, we shall grow more and more "into the same image from glory to glory."

2. Spirit in the Flesh

(a) Independent (1 Corinthians 2:11–14)

For what man knoweth the things of a man, save the spirit of man which is in him? even so the things of God knoweth no man, but the Spirit of God. (1 Corinthians 2:11)

The expression of the spirit is independent of the flesh to begin with, consequently there is a divorce between the spirit in a born-again person and the expression of the spirit in the life. Beware of saying there is no difference in the external life of a person who is born again and one who is sanctified. It is untrue to revelation and to experience alike; there is a tremendous difference. The spirit in a born-again person does not express itself in the flesh in the same degree that it does when the point of sanctification has been reached, because the body has not yet learned obedience to God. In the beginning the Spirit of God works in independence of the flesh and conviction of sin is produced. When the Spirit of God comes into a soul there is darkness and difficulty because He produces discernment of the wrong disposition, and this discernment makes the spirit yearn and long after being made like God, and nothing and no one but God can comfort the soul that is born of the Spirit. The only hope for that life is concentration on and obedience to the Spirit of God.

(b) Dependent (Psalm 32:2; 2 Corinthians 7:1; James 3:15)

Blessed is the man unto whom the LORD imputeth not iniquity, and in whose spirit there is no guile. (Psalm 32:2)

When the Spirit of God comes into me, He does not express Himself straightaway in my flesh; He works independently of my flesh, and I am conscious of the divorce. I gain slow, sure, steady victories, but I am conscious of the turmoil. The soul is the birthplace of the new spirit, and the soul struggles while the spirit tries to express itself through the body. If I do not obey the Spirit of God, my spirit will become enchained to my flesh and be absolutely dependent upon it, and the clamouring of the wrong mind through the avenues of the flesh will gradually crush and grieve the Spirit of God. "Having therefore these promises, dearly beloved, let us cleanse ourselves from all filthiness of the flesh and spirit, perfecting holiness in the fear of God" (2 Corinthians 7:1). The Spirit of God works independently in me to begin with, just as my natural spirit does, and if I do not obey the Spirit of God the insistence of the flesh, of "the carnal mind," will gradually defile everything He has been trying to do. When we are being brought into harmony with the Spirit of God and are learning to form the mind of Christ the flesh "lusteth against the Spirit, and the Spirit against the flesh"; nevertheless we can, slowly and surely and victoriously, claim the whole territory for the Spirit of God, until at entire sanctification, the only thing there is, is the Spirit of God, Who has enabled us to form the mind of Christ, and now we can begin to manifest that growth in grace which will express the life of Jesus in our mortal flesh.

(c) Death

For I know that in me (that is, in my flesh,) dwelleth no good thing: for to will is present with me; but how to perform that which is good I find not. (Romans 7:18; see 8:5–7)

Romans 8:6 ("To be carnally minded is death") is very direct, and puts an end to all the absurd squabbles as to what is spiritual death. To be given over to an ordinary responsible intelligence which has not been re-formed by the Spirit of God, is death, and that intelligence in its manifestation will develop further and further away from God, until a man can sink so low as to be perfectly happy without God. Psalm 73 describes this condition: "There are no bands in their death. . . . They are not in trouble as other men. . . . Their eyes stand out with fatness: they have more than heart could wish." The extraordinary thing is that that kind of man is the only man that worldly people call "alive"! When a person has the Spirit of God in him and is slowly manifesting the life of Christ in his life, the world says he is "half dead." "They think it strange that ye run not with them to the same excess of riot" (1 Peter 4:4). "If any man be in Christ, he is a new creature: old things are passed away; behold, all things are become new" (2 Corinthians 5:17).

Where are we with regard to this responsible spiritual intelligence? How many of us as Christians with a definite spiritual experience, realise that we have to be continually renewed in the spirit of our mind so that we are able to discern what the will of God is—the thing which is "good, and acceptable, and perfect"? All the childish clamours, the "being driven from pillar to post" by every wind of doctrine, must cease, and the mature, sensible, strong, stable life begin. Nothing can upset that life, neither death, nor life, nor things to come, nor height, nor depth, nor any other creature. Every power such a life comes up against, whether it be a material power or a human or a diabolical power, will be but another occasion for the forming of a deeper and more intelligent grasp of the mind of God. The only way we develop intelligence in the natural world is by coming in contact with things that are irrational and un-intelligent, and in the things of God we form the mind of Christ by subduing all to a spiritual understanding.

Chapter XX

SPIRIT: THE DOMAIN AND DOMINION OF SPIRIT
Man's Universe (continued)
1 Corinthians 15:45

N.B. WE DEAL HERE PARTICULARLY WITH SPIRIT IN THE SPIRITUAL MAN.

1. Spirit in Its Freedom from the Flesh (Extraordinary)
   (a) Ecstasy (Acts 10:10; 22:17; 2 Corinthians 12:2–4; Revelation 4:2; Sometimes with the body: Acts 8:39; 2 Corinthians 12:2–4; 1 Thessalonians 4:17; Revelation 12:5; Matthew 4:1)
   (b) Emancipation
   (1) Death (Luke 16:25; 23:43; Hebrews 12:23)
   (2) Deliverance (Hebrews 4:12; Galatians 5:24; Colossians 2:11; Romans 6:6; Galatians 6:8; John 3:8; 20:22)

2. Spirit Operating in Sense (Exodus 6:9; Proverbs 15:13; 2 Corinthians 2:13; Acts 17:16; John 11:33)

3. Spirit Operating Inwardly (Luke 10:21; 1 Corinthians 2:4; 14:2, 14–16)

4. Spirit Operating Morally (Exodus 35:21; Acts 19:31; 20:22; Proverbs 16:18; Isaiah 11:2)

And so it is written, The first man Adam was made a living soul; the last Adam was made a quickening spirit. (1 Corinthians 15:45)

The contrast in 1 Corinthians 15:45 is not a contrast of moral worth, but of revelation. The phrase "the first man Adam was made a living soul" refers to the great fact of God's creation; the phrase "the last Adam was made a quickening spirit," refers to God's regenerating work in the soul. Man's spirit has not "life in itself," i.e., man cannot will pure will, or love pure love. The Holy Spirit has life in Himself, and when He comes in He energises our spirit and enables us "to will and to do of His good pleasure." "Adam" does not mean the "old man," but our human nature. Never confound the "old man" with Adam, they are not synonymous terms: and never confound the "old man" with the devil.

1. Spirit in Its Freedom from the Flesh (Extraordinary)

We mean by Extraordinary, away from the ordinary, not contrary to it or against it, but out of it. We have to bear in mind that there are facts revealed in God's Book which are not common to our experience, and a great moment is reached in the mental life when our minds are opened to the fact that there are states of experience, either for good or bad, about which the majority of us know nothing. It is easy to ridicule these experiences, but ridicule may be a sign of ignorance; it may simply mean—I know everything that everybody can experience, and if a man says he has seen things I have not seen, then I take him to be a fool and laugh at him. It is I who am the fool. Paul uses this argument in 1 Corinthians 1, he says the preaching of the Cross is foolishness to those that seek after wisdom. Again, in connection with the testimony to sanctification people will tell you point blank that no man ever was sanctified, and if you say that you are sanctified, you are a liar, or you suffer from hallucinations. It is quite possible that many of us may have this attitude to the extraordinary experiences recorded in God's Book.

(a) Ecstasy

And he [Peter] became very hungry, and would have eaten: but while they made ready, he fell into a trance. (Acts 10:10)

And it came to pass, that, when I was come again to Jerusalem, even while I prayed in the temple, I was in a trance. (Acts 22:17)

And immediately I was in the Spirit: and, behold, a throne was set in heaven, and One sat on the throne. (Revelation 4:2)

I knew a man in Christ above fourteen years ago, (whether in the body, I cannot tell; or whether out of the body, I cannot tell: God knoweth;) such an one caught up to the third heaven.... (2 Corinthians 12:2)

Ecstasy is a word applied to states of mind marked by temporary mental aberration and altered consciousness, a state in which a man is taken out of his ordinary setting into an extraordinary state where he sees and hears things apart from the bodily organs. Remember, this power may be for good or bad. A necromancer can take a man's personality right out of his bodily setting and put him into another setting where he sees and hears altogether apart from his body.

In these extraordinary conditions the body is sometimes taken with the spirit. "And when they were come up out of the water, the Spirit of the Lord caught away Philip, that the eunuch saw him no more" (Acts 8:39). In this phase of ecstasy the body is taken with the soul by extraordinary transportation, by a supernatural "aeroplane," something absolutely unusual. First Thessalonians 4:17 ("Then we which are alive and remain shall be caught up together with them in the clouds to meet the Lord in the air: and so shall we ever be with the Lord") refers to the instantaneous change of a material body into a glorified body (cf. Revelation 12:5; Matthew 4:1). After the Resurrection our Lord appeared to His disciples during the forty days before He ascended; that is, He had power to materialise whenever He chose. "He said unto them, Have ye here any meat? And they gave Him a piece of a broiled fish, and of an honeycomb. And He took it, and did eat before them" (Luke 24:41–43). In the Millennium we shall have exactly the same power as saints; we are to "meet the Lord in the air." Is that conceivable to you? If it is, it certainly is not conceivable to me. I do not know how I am going to stay up "in the air" with the Lord; but that is no business of mine, all I know is that God's Book reveals that we shall do so. The marvellous power which the glorified resurrection body will have is pictured in the Lord Jesus Christ. He could materialise whenever He chose, He proved that He could, and He could disappear whenever He chose; and we shall do exactly the same. Just think of the time when our thinking will be in language as soon as we think it! If we have the idea that we are to be penned up for ever in a little physical temple, we are twisted away from the Bible revelation. Just now in this order of things we are confined in this bodily temple for a particular reason, but at any second, "in the twinkling of an eye," God can change this body into a glorified body.

All we are arguing for is the need to have an open mind about things we can know nothing of as yet. If when an experience is recorded, I say it is nonsense because I have never had it, I put myself in the place of the superior person, an attitude I have no business to take.

The state of ecstasy, something that lifts a man right out of his ordinary setting, and the transportation at times of body as well as spirit, then is revealed in the Bible. A miracle? Yes, but not more of a miracle than the fact that I am alive. Why should it be thought more of a miracle for God to transform me into the image of His Son than for me to be alive now? How is it that I am alive now? How is it that the material wood of this table and the fleshly material of my hand are different? If we can explain the one, we can explain the other; God Who has made the one made the other. The point we are emphasising is that we have to remember that at any moment God may turn a man's calculations upside down concerning what He will do and what He will not do. Scientists reached the conclusion long ago that they dare not produce their "experimental curve" into the inferential region beyond. They say, according to the record of common experience such and such is the case, and any isolated experience is put by itself. They do not say it cannot be, but that it does not come into their line of explanation. No true scientist says because the majority of human beings have never had a particular experience, therefore it is untrue.

All this is part and parcel of the subject of personality. As long as we are flippant and stupid and shallow and think that we know ourselves, we shall never give ourselves over to Jesus Christ; but when once we become conscious that we are infinitely more than we can fathom, and infinitely greater in possibility either for good or bad than we can know, we shall be only too glad to hand ourselves over to Him.

Mystery there must be, but the remarkable thing about the mysteries which the Bible reveals is that they never contradict human reason, they transcend it. The mysteries of other religions contradict human reason. The miracles which our Lord performed (a miracle simply means the public power of God) transcend human reason, but not one of them contradicts human reason. For example, our Lord turned water into wine, but the same thing is done every year all over the world in process of time: water is sucked up through the stem of the vine and turned into grapes. Why, should it be considered more of a miracle when it is done suddenly by the same Being Who does it gradually? When Jesus Christ raised a man from the dead, He simply did suddenly what we all believe implicitly He is going to do by and by.

Have any of us a sealed mind about these facts in God's Book which we have never experienced? Do we try and apologise for them, try to make out, for instance, that Philip was not caught away suddenly by the Spirit; that the Apostle Paul was not "caught up to the third heaven"; that Peter did not fall into a trance and see the things he did see? There is always the danger of doing this. Accept these revelations as facts, and you will find your understanding illuminated as to how marvellously things can happen when the great mighty God is at work.

(b) Emancipation

(1) Death
We are dealing here with the spirit in its freedom from the flesh. We mean by "flesh," this body we are in, not the "mind of the flesh." It is possible for the spirit to exist apart altogether from man's body.

"And Jesus said unto him, Verily I say unto thee, To day shalt thou be with Me in paradise" (Luke 23:43; see also Luke 16:25; Hebrews 12:23). These passages refer to the place where the body is not—the unseen. The Bible points out that man's spirit is immortal, whether or not he is energised by the Spirit of God; that is, spirit never sleeps. Instead of the spirit sleeping at what we call death, at the breaking away of spirit from the body, the spirit is ten thousand-fold more awake. With the majority of us our spirits are half-concealed while we are in this body. Remember, spirit and personality are synonymous, but as long as a man is in the body his personality is obscured. Immediately he dies his spirit is no more obscured, it is absolutely awake; no limitations now, man is face to face with everything else that is of spirit "Son, remember. . . ."

Soul and body depend upon each other, spirit does not, spirit is immortal. Soul is simply the spirit expressing itself in the body. Immediately the body goes, the soul is gone, but the moment the body is brought back, soul is brought back, and spirit, soul and body will again be together. Spirit has never died, can never die, in the sense in which the body dies; the spirit is immortal, either in immortal life or in immortal death. There is no such thing as annihilation taught in the Bible. The separation of spirit from body and soul is temporary. The resurrection is the resurrection of the body.

Our Lord never speaks of the resurrection of spirit—the spirit does not need resurrecting; He speaks of a resurrection body for glorification and a resurrection body for damnation. "The hour is coming, in the which all that are in the graves shall hear His voice, and shall come forth; they that have done good, unto the resurrection of life; and they that have done evil, unto the resurrection of damnation" (John 5:28–29). We know what the resurrection body for glorification will be like: it will be like "His glorious body"; but all we know about the resurrection of the bad is that Jesus Christ (Who ought to know what He is talking about) says that there will be a resurrection to damnation. The question of eternal punishment is a fearful one, but let no one say that Jesus Christ did not say anything about it, He did. He said it in language we cannot begin to understand and the least thing we can do is to be reverent with what we do not understand.

(2) Deliverance

For the word of God is quick, and powerful, and sharper than any two-edged sword, piercing even to the dividing asunder of soul and spirit, and of the joints and marrow, and is a discerner of the thoughts and intents of the heart. (Hebrews 4:12)

Many teachers make spirit and soul one and the same; when the word of God comes into my heart it instantly divides between the two, that is how the Spirit of God convicts of sin. "And they that are Christ's have crucified the flesh with the affections and lusts" (Galatians 5:24). What is flesh? Paul is not talking to disembodied spirits, to a lot of corpses, he is talking to living men and women, so he certainly does not mean "mortal flesh"; he is referring to a disposition within which he calls "the flesh." When Paul speaks of the body, he speaks of it as "mortal flesh"; when he refers to the old disposition, he calls it "the flesh."

"In Whom also ye are circumcised with the circumcision made without hands, in putting off the body of the sins of the flesh by the circumcision of Christ" (Colossians 2:11; see also Romans 6:6; Galatians 6:8; John 3:8). Emancipation means deliverance while I am in the flesh, not counteraction or suppression; it may begin in counteraction, but blessed be God, emancipation is possible here and now. According to the Apostle Paul, and according to the whole of the teaching of the New Testament, we can be delivered from the old disposition—"knowing this, that our old man is crucified with Him. . . ." Crucifixion means death. The majority of testimonies contradict what the New Testament reveals. With whom are we going to side? "Let God be true, but every man a liar" (Romans 3:4)

Emancipation does not remove the possibility of disobedience; if it did, we should cease to be human beings. To make the removal of the wrong disposition mean that God removes our human nature is absurd. God does remove the wrong disposition, but He does not alter our human nature. We have the same body, the same eyes, the same imperfect brain and nervous system, but Paul argues—you used to use this body as an obedient slave to the wrong disposition, now use it as an obedient slave to the new disposition. ". . . for as ye have yielded your members servants to uncleanness and to iniquity unto iniquity; even so now yield your members servants to righteousness unto holiness" (Romans 6:19).

2. Spirit Operating in Sense

We have been dealing with the emancipation of spirit from slavery of sin, now we come to the Bible teaching that the spirit can operate through our senses, so that we can express in our lives that we are delivered: no "reckoning" or hoodwinking ourselves, no pretending we are emancipated when we are not, but the manifestation through every cell of our bodies that God has done what we testify with our mouth He has done.

The children of Israel . . . hearkened not unto Moses for anguish of spirit, and for cruel bondage. (Exodus 6:9)

Their anguish of spirit had so distorted their senses that they could not listen. "A merry heart maketh a cheerful countenance: but by sorrow of the heart the spirit is broken" (Proverbs 15:13). When a man is happy, he cannot pull a long face, he may try to, but it is the face of a clown; when he is happy inside he shows it on the outside. If you hear a Christian with a sad face saying, "Oh, I am so full of the joy of the Lord," well, you know it is not true. If I am full of the joy of the Lord, it will pour out of every cell of my body. "I had no rest in my spirit, because I found not Titus my brother . . ." (2 Corinthians 2:13). "While Paul waited for them at Athens, his spirit was stirred in him, when he saw the city wholly given to idolatry" (Acts 17:16). "When Jesus therefore saw her weeping . . . He was moved with indignation in the spirit and troubled Himself" (John 11:33 RV mg). All these passages refer to spirit showing itself instantly in the flesh. The spirit of wrong shows itself in the flesh, and, thank God, the Spirit of God does the same.

As soon as we become rightly related to God, the prince of this world has his last stake in the flesh, he will suck every bit of your physical life out of you if he can. Many Christian workers do not know this, and Satan will seek to wear them out to the last cell; but if they know this "trick" of his and also know God's grace, every time they are exhausted in work for God, they will get supernatural physical recuperation, and the proof that it is God's work is the experience of this supernatural recuperation. If you become exhausted in doing work in the world, what have you to do? You have to take an iron tonic and have a holiday, but if you are exhausted in God's work, all the iron tonics in the world will never touch you, the only thing that will recuperate you is God Himself. Paul said he did not count his life dear unto himself so that he might finish his course with joy; and when the dear sisters and brothers say to you, "You must not work so hard," simply say, "Get thee behind me, Satan!" Remember, Satan's last stake is in the flesh, and when once you know that all your fresh springs are in God, you will draw on Him. Beware of laying off before God tells you to; if you lay off before God tells you to, you will rust, and that leads to "dry rot" always.

3. Spirit Operating Inwardly

The spirit operates outwardly through our senses, and operates inwardly towards God.

In that hour Jesus rejoiced in spirit, and said, I thank Thee, O Father, Lord of heaven and earth, that Thou hast hid these things from the wise and prudent, and hast revealed them unto babes. (Luke 10:21)

Our Lord was talking to God inwardly by His Spirit. "And my speech and my preaching was not with enticing words of man's wisdom, but in demonstration of the Spirit and of power" (1 Corinthians 2:4). If you have the Spirit of God in you, the preaching of the Cross is according to the wisdom of God: if you have not the Spirit of God in you, the preaching of Christ crucified is foolishness.

"For if I pray in an unknown tongue, my spirit prayeth, but my understanding is unfruitful . . ." (1 Corinthians 14:14). The question of tongues here is not a question of foreign languages, but what is called "glossalalia," i.e., spiritual gibberish, nothing intelligible in it. Such phrases as "Hallelujah!" and "Glory be to God!" come about in this way. Just as a baby "blethers" for expression before its human spirit has worked through its soul, so a soul when being born of the Holy Ghost is apt to be carried away with emotional ecstasy. Try and understand a baby's blether, you cannot, unless you are its mother, then possibly you may.

In dealing with the Corinthians, Paul tells them to form a spiritual *nous*, an understanding whereby the spirit can be expressed. When a soul is first introduced to the heavenly domain by the Spirit of God, there is a tremendous bursting up of new life in the soul and there is no language for it. Paul urges the Corinthians to form a spiritual nous as soon as they can, to come to the point of understanding whereby the spirit can be expressed. "If you don't watch what you are doing, this will produce disgraceful mockery among the nations. If they come into your meetings and see you jabbering, you will give an occasion to the enemy to blaspheme" (see 1 Corinthians 14:23). In the modern Tongues movement the responsibility is with the teachers. May God have mercy on them!

When we are introduced by the Spirit of God into a new domain, we have no language; we are in a phase of spiritual babyhood; we have sighings and groanings and tears, but no language. Paul counsels us to be instructed, and one of the wisest ways of instruction is to let the Psalms express for you. When you are worked up to a pitch emotionally, read some of the Psalms, and the Spirit of God will gradually teach you how to form a spiritual nous, a mind whereby you will not only understand but will slowly and surely get to the place where you can express your spirit, you will have a totally new language. We read that "when the day of Pentecost was fully come . . . they were all filled with the Holy Ghost, and began to speak with other tongues, as the Spirit gave them utterance" (Acts 2:1, 4). This was not "glossalalia," it was the gift of new language.

4. Spirit Operating Morally

And they came, every one whose heart stirred him up, and every one whom his spirit made willing, and they brought the Lord's offering to the work of the tabernacle of the congregation, and for all His service, and for the holy garments. (Exodus 35:21; see also Acts 19:21; 20:22; Proverbs 16:18; Isaiah 11:2)

The Spirit working through the senses and working inwardly to God, produces a morality and an uprightness just like Jesus Christ's. The worthiness of our Lord Jesus Christ is moral worth in the Divine and in the human sphere, and our moral worth is to be of the same order.

God grant we may ever "walk in the Spirit, and ye shall not fulfil the lust of the flesh."

This book ends abruptly, but we leave it so. The whole book is merely a verbatim report of lectures given at the Bible Training College, and we have decided to let it go for what it is worth—a mere effort to rouse up the average Christian worker to study the wealth of the Scriptures, and thus become better equipped for rightly dividing the word of truth.

God bless all who care to read the book!

Bringing Sons unto Glory

Studies in the Life of Our Lord

Oswald Chambers

For it became Him, for whom are all things, and through whom are all things, in bringing many sons unto glory, to make the author of their salvation perfect through sufferings. For both He that sanctifieth and they that are sanctified are all of one: for which cause He is not ashamed to call them brethren. Hebrews 2:10–11 (RV)

INTRODUCTION

Source

Lectures given at the Bible Training College[1] and evening classes in London (1911–1915).

Publication History

- As articles: In the *Bible Training Course* (BTC) *Monthly Journal,*[2] April 1939–March 1940.
- As a book: 1944.

When the Bible Training College opened in January 1911, it had great potential but no students. While Oswald Chambers worked and prayed for resident students at the College, he followed an aggressive program of correspondence courses and extension classes. The latter took him throughout greater London several times a week to teach core classes of the BTC curriculum. Even after the College reached its capacity of resident students, Chambers continued to teach evening classes at key locations in London. In so doing, he multiplied the outreach of the BTC and touched thousands of people who were able to take only one or two courses.

This book parallels and complements the study of Christ presented in OC's book *The Psychology of Redemption*, published in 1930.

---

1. Residential school near Clapham Common in SW London, sponsored by the League of Prayer. Oswald Chambers was Principal and main teacher; Biddy Chambers was Lady Superintendent. Known as the BTC, it closed in July 1915 because of World War I.

2. The *Bible Training Course Journal* was published from 1932 to 1952 by Mrs. Chambers, with help from David Lambert.

CONTENTS

FOREWORD

These Studies in the Life of Our Lord were given by Oswald Chambers at the Bible Training College, Clapham, and to groups of evening students in various parts of London. They interpret the Life of Our Lord as presented in the four-fold Gospel record. They take the same line as in the earlier book, *The Psychology of Redemption.* But in these Talks there is the "something else" which brings to the earnest reader a yet deeper spiritual insight into the meaning of Our Lord's Life for us. It is required of us that we walk even as He walked. Jesus Christ is the Firstborn of many brethren, the Elder Brother of a vast family of brothers, and it is our privilege to bear the family likeness of Jesus Christ. In Him we see the Son of God—the exact expression of Almighty God; and also the Son of Man—the presentation of God's normal Man. At times Jesus Christ lifts the veil from His own consciousness and we are permitted to gaze with awe into the depths of that sacred Personality. But the end is to be that we become partakers of the Divine nature, and build up ourselves on our most holy faith, and so grow up into Him in all things, Who is the Head, even Christ. Those who have been helped by earlier books will welcome this one as carrying us a stage further in each one becoming by the grace of God a disciple of Jesus Christ.

D. L. (David Lambert)[3]

---

3. David Lambert (1871–1961): Methodist minister and friend of Oswald Chambers. Assisted Mrs. Chambers with OC publications from 1917–1961.

HIS HUMANITY AND INCARNATION

The only "Life" of the Lord Jesus is the New Testament. There are phases of the Life of Our Lord presented in the New Testament that no other Life, so-called, deals with. If you start with the theory that Jesus Christ was a man who became God, you have to leave out any number of New Testament facts; if you say that Jesus Christ was God and His manhood a seeming phase, you have to miss out other facts. The Person of Jesus Christ revealed in the New Testament is unique—God-Man. In Him we deal with God as Man, the God-Man, the Representative of the whole human race in one Person. Jesus Christ is not a Being with two personalities; He is *Son of God*—the exact expression of Almighty God, and *Son of Man*—the presentation of God's normal Man.

A great many of the books written on what is called "the Psychology of Jesus" are an attempt to understand the Person of Jesus through an understanding of ourselves. That is fatally misleading because Jesus Christ does not begin where we begin. "All things have been delivered unto Me of My Father: and no one knoweth the Son, save the Father . . ." (Matthew 11:27 RV). The basis of the Person of Jesus is not the basis of ours unless we have been born again of the Holy Ghost. The tendency to-day to "annul," i.e. "dissolve by analysis," the Person of Jesus, does untold damage to moral and spiritual understanding (see 1 John 4:1–3). Immediately we introduce a rationalism that does not accept the New Testament revelation, we get confused. We will not bring to the subject the innocence of mind which the Spirit of God demands; we bring objections which spring from preconceived notions.

Analogy of the First Adam and Last Adam (Romans 5:12, 19)
There are only two Men in the Bible: Adam and Jesus Christ, "with all humanity hanging at their girdles."

And the LORD God formed man of the dust of the ground, and breathed into his nostrils the breath of life; and man became a living soul. (Genesis 2:7)

The Holy Ghost shall come upon thee, and the power of the Highest shall overshadow thee: therefore also that holy thing which shall be born of thee shall be called the Son of God. (Luke 1:35)

The New Testament reveals that the birth of Jesus was an advent, not a beginning—an advent that put Him on the plane, humanly speaking, that Adam was on. The first Adam and the last Adam came direct from the hand of God.

God did not create Adam holy, He created him innocent, without self-consciousness (as we understand the word) before God; the one thing Adam was conscious of was God and only of himself in relation to the Being Whose commands he was to fulfil; the main trend of his spirit was towards God. Adam was intended by God to take part in his own development by a series of moral choices whereby he would transform innocence into holiness. Adam failed to do this, Jesus Christ came on the same platform as Adam and did not fail. Supposing Adam had transformed the natural life into the spiritual by obedience, what would have happened? Transfiguration; he would have "spiritualised" the natural life and made it all that God wanted it to be. The natural life is neither good nor bad, moral nor immoral; it is the principle within that makes it good or bad, moral or immoral.

"And the child grew, and waxed strong, filled with wisdom: and the grace of God was upon Him" (Luke 2:40 RV). The innocence of Jesus was not the innocence of a babe born into our order of things, it was the innocence of Adam as God created him, the innocence of an untried possibility of holiness. Innocence is never safe, it is simply full of possibility. The holiness of God is absolute, not progressive; that is, it knows no development by antagonism. Man's holiness must be progressive. The holiness of Jesus developed through antagonism because He revealed what a holy man should be.

Our Lord transformed innocence into holiness by a series of moral choices. Satan tempted Him along this line: "Do God's will according to Your own understanding; don't sacrifice the life of nature to the will of God." Jesus made invariably one answer—"For I am come down from heaven, not to do Mine own will, but the will of Him that sent Me" (John 6:38).

How are we to "follow His steps"? By imitating Jesus? We cannot begin to. How are we going to have the innocence that Jesus had? In one way only, by being born again from above. "Marvel not that I said unto thee, Ye must be born again" (John 3:7). We can be brought into a state of pristine childlike innocence before God by the regenerating work of His grace. God does something infinitely grander than give a man a new start: He re-makes him from the inside. We have the power, because we have received it, to transform the natural into the spiritual even as Jesus did, because the life generated into us is His own life.

(a) Resources of Life

God created Adam to "have dominion over the fish of the sea, and over the fowl of the air, and over every living thing that moveth upon the earth" (Genesis 1:28); the one thing Adam was not to have dominion over was himself. God was to have dominion over him, and Adam had to partake in his own development by obeying God's rule over him, not his own wisdom. The source of life in Adam was his obedience to God.

Jesus Christ, the last Adam, states over and over again—"I can of Myself do nothing" (John 5:19, 30; see 7:16; 8:28; 12:49; 14:10).

The birth of Jesus throws a striking light on our regeneration. Our new birth is the birth of the Son of God into our human nature, and our human nature has to be transfigured by the indwelling life of the Son of God. We have the power now to sacrifice the life of nature to the will of God, keeping our minds dependent on Jesus Christ as He was dependent on God. To-day the characteristic is spiritual insubordination; we will not bring "every thought into captivity to the obedience of Christ."

(b) Retrogression from Life

When the Apostle Paul says that "sin entered into the world through one man," he did not mean a man like ourselves; he was speaking of the Federal Head of the human race, the noble being that God created. The third chapter of Genesis reveals how sin was introduced into the world. Watch the subtlety of Satan's reasoning: "And he said unto the woman, Yea, hath God said . . . ?" The one thing he was aiming at was the dominion of God over man. "For God doth know that in the day ye eat thereof, then your eyes shall be opened, and ye shall be as God, knowing good and evil" (RV), i.e. you will become god over yourself. Sin is not a creation, it is a relationship. The essential nature of sin is my claim to my right to myself.

When Our Lord confronts men, He confronts them on that basis. Read the New Testament, and you will find that Jesus Christ did not get into a moral panic over the things that rouse us. We are staggered at immorality, but Jesus faced those things in the most amazingly calm way (see Matthew 21:31). When He was roused to a state of passionate indignation it was by people who were never guilty of such things. What Our Lord continually faced was the disposition behind either the morality or the immorality. "If I had not come and spoken unto them, they had not had sin . . ." (John 15:22). Any man would have known without His coming that it was wrong to take life, the law is written in him; any man would have known that immorality was wrong; but no man apart from Jesus Christ would believe that "my right to myself" is the very essence of sin. When we realise what Jesus means when He says, "If you would be My disciple,

give up your right to yourself to Me," we begin to understand that "the carnal mind is enmity against God." "I will not give up my right to myself; I will serve God as I choose." Jesus Christ came to remove this disposition of self-realisation.

(c) Readjustment into Life

Sin interrupted the normal development of man, and it required another Man to take up the story where it was broken off and complete it, without the sin. "Ye have not [this] life in yourselves," said Jesus (John 6:53 RV). What life? His life He had, the life that is at the true Source. Eternal Life means the life Jesus lived. "And this is the record, that God hath given to us eternal life, and this life is in His Son" (1 John 5:11). Eternal life is the life Jesus lived; the life of God in a mortal being, transformed by God's regenerating power into harmony with Himself.

"In Him was life; and the life was the light of men" (John 1:4). Why did Jesus live thirty-three years if all He came to do was to die for sin? He lived thirty-three years because He had to show what a normal man after God's pattern was like. He died that through His death we might have the source of life that was in Him (see Romans 5:17). That is why it is so absurd to say, "I accept Jesus as a Teacher only." Try to apply the teachings of Jesus to your life without an understanding of His Death and you will find it cannot be done; it would either make you commit suicide or take you to the Cross and give you an understanding of why it was necessary for Him to die.

Preaching about the life of Jesus awakens an immense craving, but it leaves us with the luxury of sympathy with ourselves—"Oh well, I know that is very high and holy, but I was not born that way and God cannot expect that kind of life from me." We like to hear about the life of Jesus, about His teaching and His words, about His sympathy and tenderness, but when we stand face to face with Him in the light of God and He convicts us of sin, we resent it. Men crave for what the Gospel presents but they resent the way it is presented by Jesus. That is a point that has been lost sight of nowadays, and every now and again the Church succumbs to the temptation to which Jesus Christ did not succumb—the temptation of putting man's needs first, with the result that certain features of the Gospel are eliminated. Never separate the Incarnation and the Atonement. The Incarnation was not for the Self-realisation of God, but for the purpose of removing sin and reinstating humanity into communion with God. Jesus Christ became Incarnate for one purpose, to make a way back to God that man might stand before Him as he was created to do, the friend and lover of God Himself. The Atonement means infinitely more than we can conceive, it means that we can be morally identified with Jesus Christ until we understand what the Apostle Paul meant when he said, "I live; yet not I, but Christ liveth in me." All the mighty efficacy of the Death of Jesus, of His Resurrection and Ascension to the right hand of the throne of God, is implanted into us by regeneration. And the lowest and most sin-stained can go that way. The measure of the salvation of Jesus is not that it does for[4] the best man we know, but that it does for the worst and most sin-stained. There is no son of man that need despair, Jesus Christ can reproduce His saving work in any and every man, blessed be the Name of God!

Do we know anything about this sublime innocence which is the outcome of regeneration, and are we developing along that line? Are we transforming innocence into holiness by a series of moral choices, or are we paying too much attention to the natural life? When we are rightly related to God as Jesus was, the spiritual life becomes as natural as the life of a child. The one dominant note of the life after sanctification is the simplicity of a child, full of the radiant peace and joy of God. "Except ye . . . become as little children . . ."

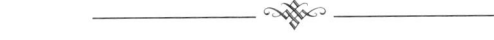

THE SILENT YEARS TO THIRTY
Luke 2:40–52

A child's life has no dates, it is free, silent, dateless. A child's life ought to be a child's life, full of simplicity. By "the silent years to thirty" we mean to picture forth the experience of the sanctified soul; we have attained to nothing yet, we are simply perfectly adjusted to God. By sanctification we are placed in the condition of Our Lord at Bethlehem, and we have the life of Jesus as our Example. We are apt to mistake the sovereign works of Grace in salvation and sanctification as being final—they are only beginnings.

1. His Evolution in Mind and Ours
We mean by "evolution" growth and development. In the child the body is put first, "And the child grew" (Luke 2:40); in the young man the mind is put first, "And Jesus advanced in wisdom" (Luke 2:52 RV). During those silent years from twelve to thirty there is nothing recorded saving that "Jesus advanced in wisdom and stature, and in favour with God and men"— nothing precocious or necromantic, a slow, steady, sane progress till He reached maturity.

"And Jesus Himself . . . was about thirty years of age" (Luke 3:23 RV). That is the age from the Jewish standpoint at which physical maturity and soul maturity are supposed to be reached. Up to that age a man was looked upon as almost a child and dependent, after thirty he was shielded from no requirements of a full grown-man. Up to the age of thirty life is full of promise and expectation, the powers are untried, they are more or less chaotic and immature. The majority of the works of genius are done before thirty. After thirty, or what is represented by that age, there is no more promise, no more vision, the life has to be lived now in accordance with all the visions it has had.

Spiritual maturity is a different matter, Spiritual maturity is not reached by the passing of the years, but by obedience to the will of God. Some people mature into an understanding of God's will more quickly than others because they obey more readily, they more readily sacrifice the life of nature to the will of God, they more easily swing clear of little determined opinions. It is these little determined opinions, convictions of our own that won't budge, that hinder growth in grace and makes us bitter and dogmatic, intolerant, and utterly un-Christlike.

(a) Willing Zone
"And He went down with them, and came to Nazareth" (Luke 2:51). Will is not a faculty but the whole man active. Our Lord sacrificed His own natural desire to the will of His Father. His natural desire would have been to stay in the temple, but "He went down with them and came to Nazareth," and stayed there eighteen years. This is an illustration of the way Jesus used His will all through His life (see John 6:38). He "advanced in wisdom" by applying His will to the will of His Father. "For Christ also pleased not Himself." To do what we like always ends in immorality; to do what God would have us do always ends in growth in grace.

(b) Wonder Zone
"How is it that ye sought Me? wist ye not that I must be in My Father's house?" (Luke 2:49 RV). This incident is the one glimpse given to us of those twelve years so full of wonder, so full of sky-lights open towards God. Think of the pure wonder of the Child Jesus in the temple when He realised with spiritual

---

4. does for: suffices; meets the needs of.

intuition that He was in His Father's house; don't picture a precocious intellectual prig. Jesus was amazed that His mother did not know what He knew, or understand what He understood. A child's mind exhibits the innocence of intelligence, and in the life of Jesus this innocence never became conceited. The starting-point of every heresy is the corrupting of the innocence of intelligence by conceit. Conceit means to have a point of view; a point of view takes the wonder out of life. It is only when we are born again and sanctified that we enter into an understanding of the life of Jesus. His life is the type of life that the Spirit forms in us when we obey Him, full of innocent wonder. (Cf. Matthew 11:25)

(c) Waiting Zone

"And He was subject unto them" (Luke 2:51 RV). Have we ever caught the full force of the thirty silent years, of those three years wandering in Palestine? Have we ever caught the full force of those ten days of waiting in the upper room? If we measure those periods by our modern way of estimating we will put it down as waste of time; but into the life of Our Lord, and into the lives of the early disciples, were going to come elements that would root and ground them on a solid foundation that nothing could shake. The waiting time is always the testing time. How we hurry people into work for God! A thrilling experience, an ecstasy of spiritual emotion, a heavenly vision, and, "I am called of God to preach"! Are you? Get back to God's Book. If you are called to preach, God will put you through mills you never dreamed of. To testify for God is absolutely essential, but never open your mouth as a preacher unless you are called of God. If you are, it is a "woe is unto me, if I preach not," not a delight. One of the worst sins amongst us is that we are more interested in the most recent views on sanctification than we are in the testimonies in God's Book. Any excitable, hysterical testimony from a tide of revival is apt to be more welcome to the majority of sanctified people than the bedrock teaching of the New Testament. With what result? ". . . because they had no root, they withered away." Picture those silent years in the life of Our Lord, shielded by His Father, until all the tremendous forces of His life were developed and grasped.

2. His Evolution in Body and Ours
(a) Organic Soul

"And Jesus advanced in . . . stature" (Luke 2:52). The spirit is soul expressing itself in the body. The body has an enormous influence on the soul, and the soul on the body. When the body is developing into manhood or womanhood there is a sudden awakening of the soul to religious influences, and it is always a dangerous time. What is looked upon as evidence of the grace of God at work is merely the opening up of the soul in the process of development. God never places any importance on that phase. Over and over again people have built up hope on the religious promise of boys and girls in their teens and after a while it fades away and the unwise say, he, or she, has backslidden. May God have mercy on the parents who develop precocity in a child! What happens physically in children who show amazing signs of wisdom is that the grey matter of the brain is being used as quickly as it is formed. Precocity is something that ought to be checked. We are apt to place our faith on the years when we are in the making, whereas lives ought to be allowed to develop along a right line to the point of reliability.

If this is true in the physical and psychical domain, it is much more so in the spiritual. There are stages in spiritual development when God allows us to be dull, times when we cannot realise or feel anything. It is one of the greatest mercies that we have those blank spaces, for this reason, that if we go on with spiritual perception too quickly we have no time to work it out; and if we have no time to work it out it will react in stagnation and degeneration. Work out what God works in—work it out through your fingertips, through your tongue, through your eyes; then when that is worked out, God will flood your soul with more light. Beware of curiosity in spiritual matters (see 2 Corinthians 11:3). If once you begin to push God's restrictions on one side and say "I wonder what this Movement is; I wonder if I should have this or that experience," you may find yourself getting perilously near the condition of the prodigal son, taking the law into your own hands and going clean off at a tangent. Unless religious emotions spring from the indwelling grace of God and are worked out on the right level, they will always, not sometimes, react on an immoral level. The time when these dangers begin is in this stage of development.

It is a wonderful point of illumination that Our Lord's soul was in a body like ours, and that for thirty silent years He exhibited a holy life through all the stages of development that our life goes through.

(b) Organic Self-Sacrifice

"I lay down My life. . . . I lay it down of Myself" (John 10:17–18). Our Lord is referring to the power He has of Self-sacrifice. Have we that power? Thank God we have. After sanctification we have the power to deliberately take our sanctified selves and sacrifice them for God. It is an easy business to be self-sacrificing in mind—"I intend to do this and that," that is, I estimate what it is going to cost me. Paul says he not only estimated the cost, he experienced it. ". . . for Whom I suffered the loss of all things" (RV). As you go on towards maturity watch the by-path meadows—"I have been so blessed of God here, this is where I ought to stay." Read the life of Jesus, He kept His eye fixed on the one purpose His Father had for His life, which He calls going "up to Jerusalem," and we have to go with Him there. One of the greatest snares is the number of good things we might do. Jesus Christ never did the good things He might have done, He did everything He ought to do because He had His eye fixed on His Father's will and He sacrificed Himself for His Father. It is not done once for all, it can only be done once for always, day by day, day by day, the sacrifice of ourselves to the will of Jesus, that is, self-realisation is gone and Christ-realisation has come in. Difficult? Nothing is ever attained in the natural world without difficulty and the same thing applies in the spiritual world. How many of us have learned the A B C of concentration? "This one thing I do," our face set like a flint towards the purposes of God, not fanatically doing our duty, but going steadfastly on with the sacrifice of ourselves for Jesus as He sacrificed Himself for His Father.

(c) Organic Spirit
"Father, into Thy hands I commend My spirit" (Luke 23:46). All through the life of Jesus there is a clear realisation of His authority over body, soul and spirit. He matured to that authority in those silent years. "Oh but," you say, "Jesus was the Son of God": He said He was the *Son of Man*, that is, He exhibited what we are to be when we become sons of God, and if He "learned obedience by the things which He suffered" (RV) are we going to rebel because we have to go the same way?

What are we doing with our brains since we entered into the experience of sanctification? Are we allowing the Holy Spirit to get hold of this bodily machine until we construct an expression of the mind of Christ? The Spirit of Jesus is given to us in new birth, but we have not the mind of Christ until we form it. How our minds express themselves depends entirely on the way we use our brains. I mean by "mind" not the spiritual mind, but the mind as it expresses itself in the bodily life. "But we have the mind of Christ." It is not true to say that God gives us our ideas, that notion is the starting-point of all heresies. God never gave anyone their ideas, God makes a man use his ideas in order to convey His mind; otherwise responsibility is destroyed. "Glean your thinking," says Paul, and we have to do it by will. The Holy Spirit energises the will to complete mastery of the brain. Don't be a mental wool-gatherer.

3. His Evolution in Maturity and Ours
Being "about thirty years of age . . ."—the period of maturity. Who was it reached maturity? The Son of God as Man—the maturity of all physical powers, all soul powers, all spiritual powers, and not until that point was reached did God thrust Him out into the three years of service. "I do always those things that are pleasing to [My Father]" (RV). Where did Jesus learn that power? In those thirty silent years.

Can God say of us—"That soul is learning, 'precept upon precept; line upon line'; it is not nearly so petulant and stupid as it used to be, it no longer sulks in corners, it no longer murmurs against discipline, it is getting slowly to the place where I shall be able to do with it what I did with My own Son"? What was that? God took His hand off, as it were, and said to the world, the flesh and the devil, "Do your worst"—". . . greater is He that is in you, than he that is in the world." God shielded His Son from no requirements of a son, and when we are rightly related to God He will not shield us from any requirements of sons.

In spiritual maturity all our powers are thoroughly adjusted into a calm poise, rightly balanced, and God can begin to trust us with His work. "If a man love Me, . . . he will keep My words," said Jesus; He is referring to the freedom of the disciple to keep His commandments. No natural man is free to keep the commandments of God, he is utterly unable to unless he is born again of the Holy Spirit. Freedom means ability to keep the law; every kind of freedom has to be earned. "And My Father will love him, and We will come unto him, and make Our abode with him"—an unspeakable, unstateable communion, God the Father, God the Son and God the Holy Ghost, and the sinner saved and sanctified by grace, communing together. That is the sheer sovereign work of the Lord Jesus Christ.

THE SELF-CONSCIOUSNESS OF JESUS—I
His Baptism

All things are delivered unto Me of My Father: and no man knoweth the Son, but the Father; neither knoweth any man the Father, save the Son, and he to whomsoever the Son will reveal Him. Matthew 11:27

There is a self-consciousness that is more or less of a disease, arising from unstrung nerves or from personal conceit; we cannot apply the term to Our Lord in that sense. By the term "the Self-Consciousness of Jesus" is meant the state of being conscious of His personal Self. I would like to warn against the modern literature which says that we can understand the Self-consciousness of Jesus Christ by examining our own. Jesus says emphatically, "No one knoweth the Son, save the Father." Any teaching regarding the Personality of Jesus that gives the lie to what He says about Himself is anti-Christ, it "dissolves by analysis" (see 1 John 4:1–3).

In attempting to deal with the Self-consciousness of Jesus we must remember that we are dealing with a revelation, something we have not as natural men, although through the experience of regeneration, we can have "the mind of Christ"; but the experience of new birth must take place first. "Let this mind be in you, which was also in Christ Jesus" (Philippians 2:5). "But we have the mind of Christ" (1 Corinthians 2:16).

In these studies, the birth of Jesus at Bethlehem stands for a presentation of the experience of sanctification in which the soul is put into a state of spiritual innocence before God, a state of untried, untested innocence; then we have to develop that innocence into holiness by a series of moral choices whereby we sacrifice the life of nature to the will of God. The majority of us only know the experience of sanctification, we do not press on to transform innocence into holiness until all our powers are matured for God. Insubordination too often marks the beginnings of the sanctified life because we will not submit to the normal development that God demands; as soon as we enter the sanctified life we expect we are going to be giants for God. We are in danger of becoming fanatical instead of developing along the great, sane, majestic lines that Jesus developed on.

The distinction between a saved soul and a disciple is fundamental. The stern conditions laid down by Our Lord for discipleship are not the conditions of salvation; discipleship is a much closer and more conscious relationship (see Luke 14:26–27, 33). The secret of discipleship is the Cross of Our Lord Jesus Christ (Galatians 6:14; 1 Corinthians 2:2).

Just when maturity is reached spiritually we cannot say, all we know is it depends entirely on obedience. After they were baptised with the Holy Ghost, the early disciples evidently reached the point of spiritual maturity, for we read that they rejoiced "that they were counted worthy to suffer shame for His Name." They could not be appealed to on any other line than that marked out for them by Jesus, it could not be tyrannised out of them or martyred out of them. The Baptism of Our Lord represents this point of amazing maturity; we are faced with a revelation we cannot understand, but must accept.

1. The Innate Realisation to Jesus Himself
(John 1:26–34)

The experience of Jesus at His Baptism is as foreign to us as His Incarnation. Read the so-called "Lives" of Jesus, and see how little is made of His baptism, the reason being that most of the writers take the Baptism to be something to teach us, or as an illustration of the rite of baptism. In the New Testament the Baptism of Jesus is not taken as an illustration of anything which we experience, it is recorded as a manifestation of Who Jesus was. He stands forth consciously—Son of God, Son of Man, God-Man—having come for one purpose, to bear away the sin of the world.

We have been dealing with Our Lord's Childhood, and with the silent years of which nothing is recorded; now at His Baptism He emerges, a full outstanding personality with a tremendous maturity of power that never wilted for one moment. There was no ambiguity in Our Lord's mind as to Who He was, or as to the meaning of the step He was taking; He was no longer maturing, He was mature. He is not manifested here as our Example, but as God Incarnate for one purpose—to be identified with the sin of the world and to bear it away. Jesus fully felt Himself to be all that John the Baptist expected He would be. Take time to find out from the Old Testament what John did expect Him to be, and then realise that Jesus was consciously that and you will understand why He said, "No man knoweth the Son, save the Father." The reason we have no counterpart in our experience of the Baptism of Jesus is because of His innate realisation of Who He was. The Jesus of the New Testament is a Being Who made Napoleon say, "I know men, and Jesus Christ is not a man." What he meant was that in Jesus Christ he had come across a preeminent Master of men.

2. The Extraordinary Revelation (Mark 1:9–11)

Beware of bringing to the study of Jesus anything that does not belong to the New Testament. If we bring preconceived notions of our own we shall never look at the facts. If we are being taught "as the truth in Jesus," we shall accept the revelation that His Baptism was an extraordinary experience to Our Lord, extraordinary even to Him. When Jesus came from Galilee to the Jordan to be baptised by John, it was a tremendous epoch in the purpose of God Almighty. Who among us could presume to say what Jesus experienced when He was baptised? Jesus came forth at the threshold of His public ministry in the full consciousness of Who He was; from that moment He manifested Himself as being here for one purpose only, to be identified with the sin of the world and to bear it away. "God was in Christ, reconciling the world unto Himself." Who was Jesus? God Incarnate. Watch what He says of Himself—"I do not work from My right to Myself" (see John 5:19, 30); "I do not think or speak from My right to Myself" (see John 8:28; 12:49); "I do not live from My right to Myself" (see John 6:38): "I work and think and live from My Father's right to Me." "Lo, I come . . . to do Thy Will, O God."

3. The Enduement Regally (Luke 3:21–22)

We read that Jesus was in communion with His Father at the time of His baptism— "Jesus also having been baptised, and praying" (RV), an inconceivable communion, and what happened?—"the heaven was opened, and the Holy Ghost descended in a bodily shape like a dove upon Him, and a voice came from heaven, which said, Thou art My beloved Son; in Thee I am well pleased." It was a purely personal experience. The Holy Ghost descended upon Jesus, and the voice of the Father spake to Him—"Thou art my beloved Son." This Man, Who was known to men as the humble Nazarene Carpenter, is Almighty God presented in the guise of a human life.

Opened heaven to Our Lord means opened heaven to every man. The Holy Ghost descending as a dove is symbolical of the Holy-Spirit life that Jesus can communicate to every man. The New Testament records two personal descents of the Holy Ghost: one on Our Lord as Son of Man at His baptism, the other on the Day of Pentecost—"Therefore being by the right hand of God exalted, and having received of the Father the promise of the Holy Ghost, He hath shed forth this, which ye now see and hear" (Acts 2:33). By right of His Death and Resurrection and Ascension Our Lord can impart Holy Spirit to any and every man (see Luke 11:13; John 20:22).

4. The Eminent Redeemer (Matthew 3:13–15)

"Then cometh Jesus from Galilee to the Jordan unto John, to be baptised of him" (RV). What was John's baptism? The baptism of repentance for the remission of sins. Jesus was baptised by that baptism, not by a baptism like it. What did John regard Jesus as? "The Lamb of God, which taketh away the sin of the world." At His baptism Jesus took on Him His vocation; it was the public manifestation that He became part of fallen humanity; that is why He was baptised with John's baptism of repentance. Beware of saying that Jesus took on the sin of the human race by sympathy. It is being said nowadays that Jesus had such a profound sympathy for the human race, He was such a pure noble character and realised so keenly the shame and horror of sin, that He took our sin on Himself by sympathy. All through the Bible it is revealed that Our Lord bore the sin of the world by *identification*, not by sympathy. If Jesus only took on the sin and wrong of human nature by sympathy, I can only take on His holiness by sympathy, All I can say is, "Yes, I mourn over my sin and wrong doing and I wish I were better; I do accept the life of Jesus as very beautiful and holy, but that holiness is not mine." The New Testament says Jesus became literally identified with the sin of the human race. "Him Who knew no sin" (here language almost fails) *"He made to be sin* on our behalf" for one purpose only—"that we might become the righteousness of God in Him" (RV). Repentance to be true must issue in holiness, or it is not New Testament repentance. Repentance means not only sorrow and distress for the wrong done, but the acceptance of the Atonement of Jesus which will make me what I have never been—holy.

Ask God to awaken in your heart and conscience a realisation of what identification with sin on the part of Jesus meant. He did not come to manifest what God was like only; He came to put away sin by the sacrifice of Himself so that men might see God in Him— "He that hath seen Me hath seen the Father." The manifestation of Jesus as God Incarnate and in His holy Manhood are incidents connected with the one great purpose of His coming, which was a vicarious identification with sin.

As saved and sanctified saints, have we ever realised that our vocation is a vicarious identification with the life of the world that is not right? One of the subtlest snares is the idea that we are here to live a holy life of our own, with our eyes fixed on our own whiteness; we are here to carry out God's will as Jesus carried it out. Jesus carried out the will of God as the Saviour of the world; we are to carry out His will as saints. Jesus Christ was a vicarious Sufferer for the sin of the world, and we have to be vicarious sufferers, filling up "that which is lacking of the afflictions of Christ." Have we ever realised that through the Atonement we can take on ourselves a vicarious attitude before God, a vicarious penitence, knowing "the fellowship of His sufferings"? Take it on the line of intercession, have we ever realised that we can hold off the curse and the terror of evil and sin from people who do not know God? May God save us from the selfish meanness of a sanctified life which says, "I am saved and sanctified, look what a wonderful specimen I am." If we are saved and sanctified we have lost sight of ourselves absolutely, self is effaced, it is not there. The sacrifice of the sanctified self is the lesson to be learned. We are saved and sanctified for God, not to be specimens in His showroom, but for God to do with us even as He did with Jesus, make us broken bread and poured-out wine as He chooses. That is the test— not spiritual fireworks or hysterics, not fanaticism, but a blazingly holy life that "confronts the horror of the world with a fierce purity," chaste physically, morally and spiritually, and this can only come about in the way it came about in the life of Our Lord.

Beware of the subtle insinuations which come in the guise of light, that we are to be like Jesus in the sense of sharing in His great mediatorial work; we are not. Jesus Christ came into the world to deliver men from sin; we do not. He was God Incarnate; we are not. Jesus said that He came to do the will of His Father, and He sends us to do His will. "As My Father hath sent Me, even so send I you." What is the will of Jesus? That we make disciples, after we ourselves have become disciples. The emphasis to-day is being put on the fact that we have to save men; we have not. We have to exalt the Saviour Who saves men, and then make disciples in His Name. Jesus says, "I, if I be lifted up from the earth, will draw all men unto Me." If I lift up Jesus where the New Testament lifts Him up, on the Cross, i.e. if I present Him as being made sin and putting it away by the sacrifice of Himself, Jesus says He will draw all men unto Him, and there will come the surprising illumination of the Spirit ". . . *so* is every one that is born of the Spirit." The "so" refers to the infinite surprise of the Spirit of God at work in the souls of men bringing the amazing revelation—"I know Who Jesus is." We have unconsciously usurped the place of the Holy Ghost; we present a series of argumentative doctrines and say, "If you believe this and accept that, something will happen." It never happens in that way, but always as a tremendous surprise.

The touchstone of the Holy Spirit's work in us is the answer to our Lord's question: "Who do men say that the Son of Man is?" Our Lord makes human destiny depend on that one thing, Who men say He is, because the revelation of Who Jesus is is only given by the Holy Spirit. The sign that we have received the Holy Spirit is that we think rightly of Jesus. Jesus bases membership in His Church on the revelation of Who He is—"Thou art the Christ, the Son of the living God." That is the "rock" on which Jesus builds His Church, viz. the revelation of Who He is and the public confession of it. (Cf. 1 Corinthians 12:3)

THE SELF-CONSCIOUSNESS OF JESUS—II
His Temptation
Matthew 4:1–11

In the silent years Our Lord learned how to *be;* at His Baptism He had revealed to Him what He had to *do;* in the Temptation what to *avoid.* Always remember that what is exhibited in the life of Our Lord is for our instruction when once we have been readjusted to God through the Atonement.

"Then was Jesus led up of the Spirit into the wilderness to be tempted of the devil" (Matthew 4:1). Immediately after His Baptism Jesus was driven by the Spirit (not by the devil) into the wilderness to be tempted of the devil. The Spirit submitted Jesus to the tremendous onslaught of a supernatural being next to God in power. We talk much too glibly about the devil. If Our Lord was led into temptation, it behoves us not to rush into it. "Resist the devil," not attack him. Our Lord taught us to pray—"Lead us not into temptation." When once we know that we are stronger through testing, the danger is real to seek it.

"And He was there in the wilderness forty days, tempted of Satan; and was with the wild beasts" (Mark 1:13). It was not because Jesus spent forty days in solitude that He was strong, but because of the power which He matured in the wilderness of living not by earthly, but by heavenly law. Solitude is bad unless the life is driven there by God. "Whosoever delighteth in solitude is a wild beast or a god" (Plato). Solitude may come after God's supreme call, as it came to the Apostle Paul (see Galatians 1:15–16); but the main characteristic of Christianity is to drive us out of solitude; other religions earn it as a reward.

The word "temptation" is built on a Latin word meaning "to stretch." Every nature brings the setting of its own temptation; it is the thing held that is strained. If you are not holy, you will not be tempted to be unholy, because you do not hold holiness. Temptation is no temptation at all if it is clearly to evil. "God cannot be tempted with evil," says James, "and He Himself tempteth no man" (RV); but immediately we come to man, and in the case of Our Lord, the Son of God Incarnate as Man, temptation is possible. He "was in all points tempted like as we are, yet without sin."

Temptation is the test by an alien power of the possessions held by a personality. What did Jesus hold? He held in His Person His own unspotted sanctity and the fact that He was to be the King of men and the Saviour of the world; and the Spirit of God drove Him into the wilderness to be tested and strained on these points. Steel can be "tired" in the process of testing, and in this way its strength is measured. Everything on earth, animate and inanimate, can be fatigued; but Satan could not begin to fatigue Our Lord; He retained the possessions of His personality intact. The affinities of a man after a period of temptation prove whether or not he has yielded. "And behold, angels came and ministered unto Him." If Jesus had failed in any degree, the angels would have had no affinity with Him. It was in the temptation that Jesus met the strong man and overcame him (see Luke 11:21–22). It was in the temptation that Our Lord bruised the head of the serpent (see Genesis 3:15, cf. Romans 16:20). Every temptation of Satan is perfectly wise. The wisest, shrewdest, subtlest things are said by Satan, and they are accepted by everybody as the acme of human philosophy; but when the Spirit of God is at work in a man, instantly the hollow mockery at the heart of what Satan is trying to do, is seen. When we understand the inwardness of the temptation we see how Satan's strategy is turned into confusion by the Spirit of God.

1. The Possibility of the Public Ministry
Matthew 4:1–4)
If Thou art the Son of God, command that these stones become bread. (Matthew 4:3 RV)

Jesus Christ came to be the Saviour of the world and the King of men; no one could ever have such an understanding of the condition of men or of their needs as He had. Now watch what Satan says—"Put man's needs first, heal their bodies, give them bread, and they will crown You King; Your chance is symbolised in Your own particular need, satisfy Your own requirements first, and then the needs of every other man." Was Satan right? Read John 6:15. After He had fed the five thousand the temptation was repeated, but "Jesus therefore perceiving that they were about to come and take Him by force, to make Him king, withdrew again into the mountain Himself alone" (RV). He would not realise His Kingship of men along that line.

What is the attitude of the Church to-day? Christ on the throne of God? No, Man on the throne of God! The tendency is to reverse the order of the commandments (see Mark 12:29–31). The temptation which beset Our Lord with such fascination and power is the very temptation which is besetting the modern Christian—"Heal bodies, cast out devils, feed the poor, and men will crown You King." The temptation is more powerful to-day than ever it has been in the history of the Church, to put men's needs first, not God; to spell God in the term "humanity"; to make God an etcetera for blessing humanity. If you heal men and give them bread, what do they care about the claims of Jesus Christ? Health and happiness is what is wanted to-day and Jesus Christ is simply exploited. We who name the Name of Christ, are we beginning to discern what Satan is after? He is trying to fatigue out of us what God has put in, viz., the possibility of being of value to God. Our only safety is to watch Our Lord and Saviour. "For in that He Himself hath suffered being tempted, He is able to succour them that are tempted" (Hebrews 2:18).

2. The Possibility of the Powerful Mastery
(Matthew 4:5–7)
If Thou art the Son of God, cast Thyself down. . . . (Matthew 4:6 RV)

Remember that temptation, literally, is to try the strength of the thing held. Satan did not tempt Jesus to sin, as we think of sin; he knew better. The one thing Satan aims at is that we put ourselves as master instead of God (see Genesis 3:5); and now he comes to the Son of God and says, "You are the King and the Saviour of mankind, why not use Your power? Use apparatus, startle people out of their wits and then say, 'Believe in Me.'" Could Jesus Christ have manifested His mastery over men in that way? Of course He could, but the Son of God as Son of Man is showing what a normal holy man is like. At His Baptism Our Lord accepted His vocation to bear away the sin of the world, and in this place of absolute loneliness He is being tested by all the powers that are against God; but He went through the temptation without fatigue.

There are plenty of Christians to-day who are not appealed to on the "bread" line, but the "signs and wonders" line does appeal to them. What is the cunning thing that is rending the Church to-day? Where it is not socialism, it is supernaturalism.—"Ask God for manifestations to prove you are a child of His." Satan's one aim is to thwart God's purpose, and he can easily do it if he succeeds in making us take this line—"Now that I am baptised with the Holy Ghost, there must be marvellous manifestations so that people will be amazed at what God has done for me." Jesus said, When the Holy Ghost is come, *"He shall glorify Me,"* not glorify you. The error of the "signs and wonders" movement is that the eye is fixed not on Jesus, but on our own whiteness, or on the amazing of those around us because of what God has done. Jesus Christ never went on that line, and the unobtrusive kind of life He lived is exactly the type of life the saints are to live. There was no "show business" with the Son of God, and there is to be no "show business" with the saints. "Thinkest thou that I cannot beseech My Father, and He shall even now send Me more than twelve legions of angels?" (Matthew 26:53 RV). Why did Jesus refuse the supernatural intervention? It was not His Father's will for Him. That is the only reason. "How then should the scriptures be fulfilled, that thus it must be?" (RV). "He was *crucified through weakness*"—the strongest Being Who ever trod this earth, because He knew what He could do and did not do it. "He saved others, Himself He cannot save." Think of the miserable little "struts" we exhibit—"I must insist on my rights." Then take them! But if you are a saint, you have a glorious opportunity of following the example of Jesus and being strong enough to decline to exercise your rights. An infallible sign of error spiritually is when all you can say about a man or woman of God is that they are so sweet, so beautiful, so gentle; they have never been true to the Lord. If the Holy Ghost is indwelling a man or woman, no matter how sweet, how beautiful, how Christ-like they are, the lasting thought you go away with is—What a wonderful Being the Lord Jesus Christ is.

3. The Possibility of Political Messiahship (Matthew 4:8–11)

All these things will I give Thee, if Thou wilt fall down and worship me. (Matthew 4:9)

This is the most subtle temptation of all—"You are the Son of God, You are here to fulfil all the promises of God, and You know perfectly well that if You compromise judiciously with the powers of evil, You can easily overcome them and will pull the whole world round to Your flag." Is Satan right? He certainly is. The first sign of the dethronement of God is the apparent absence of the devil and the peaceful propaganda that is spread abroad. The great cry to-day is "Be broad; accommodate yourself with evil so diplomatically that the line of demarcation is gone. Run up the white flag, say to the prince of this world, "We have been too puritanical in the past, there has been too clear a division between us, now we will go arm-in-arm." Is that the order? Never! "And the devil said unto Him, To Thee will I give all this authority, and the glory of them: for it hath been delivered unto me; and to whomsoever I will I give it" (Luke 4:6 RV). Satan is the prince of this world, and during this dispensation he has power to give authority to those who

will yield to him and compromise. We are here to stand true to God, not to attack men. No prophet ever lived by his message; immediately he tries to, he must accommodate his message to the standards of the people. The messenger of God has to stand where Jesus Christ stood, steadfast in obedience to God first. One of the most curious phases to-day is that people are expecting the devil to do things. Let us keep our eyes on God, and remember that behind the devil is God, and that the Son of God has bruised Satan's head. There is a wonderful symbolism about the place of the crucifixion; Jesus was crucified at "a place called Golgotha, that is to say, a place of a skull." That is where He has always been put to shame, in the thinking part of man, and only when the thinking part of a man is swayed by the Holy Ghost will he find an answer to every one of the temptations that Satan brings. The temptation to the first Adam was to ignore the supremacy of God over the individual, to make man his own god. What was it Satan tried to make the last Adam do? To do God's will according to His own discernment—"You are the Son of God, assert Your prerogative of Sonship." Jesus was led into the wilderness to see whether what He held in His Person, viz. His unique Saviourhood and His unspotted sanctity, would stand the test. The first Adam did not stand the strain for very long; but the last Adam did not begin to give way under the strain. Adam was innocent, not holy; that is, he had no wrong disposition in him, yet he was tempted. Jesus was holy, yet He was tempted. It was impossible to tempt Jesus with evil. The first obedience of Jesus was not to the needs of man but to the will of His Father, and at the heart of every one of Our Lord's answers is this—"I came to do God's work in His way, not in My own way, though I am the Son of God."

When we are sanctified we get our first introduction into what God calls temptation, viz. the temptation of His Son. We imagine that when we are sanctified we are delivered from temptation; we are not, we are loosened into it; we are not free enough before to be tempted. Immediately we are sanctified, we are free, and all these subtleties begin to work. God does not shield us from any requirements of a full-grown man or woman, because His aim is to bring many "sons unto glory"; not emotional, hysterical people, but men and women who can withstand and overcome and manifest not only innocence, but holiness. We cannot be innocent in the sense that the first Adam was until we are re-made by regeneration; and we cannot be holy in the sense that the last Adam was holy until we are made one with Him, then the same temptations that betook Our Lord will betake us when we have become His brethren (see Hebrews 2:11).

THE TRANSFIGURATION
The Great Divide

The "Great Divide" is the name given to the ultimate height of land in the Rocky Mountains where the waters separate and run one way to the Atlantic, the other to the Pacific. The Mount of Transfiguration is the "Great Divide" in the life of Our Lord.

1. Toward the Summit *(Matthew 16:13–17:8)*
When holy character was fully matured in Our Lord, earth lost its hold on Him and He was transfigured. In all probability if Adam had transformed his innocence into holy character by obeying God's voice, transfiguration would have been the way out of this order of things, there would have been no death. The entering in of sin made that impossible. "Wherefore, as by one man sin entered into the world, and death by sin; and so death passed upon all men, for that all have sinned" (Romans 5:12). "For the wages of sin is death" (Romans 6:23). Adam was intended by God to partake in his own development by sacrificing the life of nature to the will of God, and in that way to transform innocence into holiness. Our Lord came on the same plane as Adam and He did all that Adam failed to do; He transformed innocence into holy character, and when He had reached the full purpose of His Manhood He was transfigured.

The characteristic of the holiness of Almighty God is that it is absolute, it is impossible to antagonise or strain it. The characteristic of the holiness of Jesus is that it manifested itself by means of antagonism, it was a holiness that could be tested (see Hebrews 4:15). The Son of God as Son of Man transformed innocence into holy character bit by bit as things opposed; He did not exhibit an immutable holiness but a holiness of which we can be made partakers—"that we might be partakers of His holiness" (Hebrews 12:10). Jesus Christ revealed what a normal man should be and in so doing showed how we may become all that God wants us to be. When we are sanctified we do not get something like a landslide of holiness from heaven; we are introduced into a relationship of one-ness with God, and as Our Lord met antagonistic forces and overcame them, so must we. The life Jesus lived is the type of our life after sanctification. We are apt to make sanctification the end; it is only the beginning. Our holiness as saints consists in the exclusive dedication to God of all our powers.

One thing that is not sufficiently noticed is the place of the Transfiguration in the life of Our Lord; it came at the climax of His public ministry. In Matthew 16 we read that Jesus asked His disciples, first, "Who do men say that the Son of man is?" (RV) and then, "But who say *ye* that I am (RV) and in a flashing, revolutionary moment of discernment Peter confessed, "Thou art the Christ, the Son of the living God." Then Our Lord laid down the basis of membership in His Church—"upon this rock," i.e. the revelation of Who Jesus is and the public confession of it, "I will build My church." "From that time forth began Jesus to shew unto His disciples, how that He must go unto Jerusalem, and suffer many things of the elders and chief priests and scribes, and be killed, and be raised again the third day." Our Lord had made mystical allusions to His death earlier (see John 2:19–22 but the disciples did not know what He meant; here He tells them plainly why He came—to be killed. And now we read that He took three of the disciples into a high mountain apart, "and He was transfigured before them" (RV).

Another thing we are apt to overlook is what led up to the Transfiguration in Our Lord's own life. The Gospels reveal these three things—first, Jesus Christ's deliberate free submission of Himself to His Father: "I can of Mine own self do nothing." Second, the subordination of His intelligence to His Father: "The words that I speak unto you, I speak not of Myself." Third, the submission of His will (not the subjugation of His will) to His Father: "But the Father that dwelleth in Me, He doeth the works." All through, Jesus manifested a strong personal identity, but the dominant note was the submission of it all to His Father. He separated His holy Self for God's purposes, "For their sakes I sanctify Myself." Before He spoke, He listened with the inner ear to His Father; He never allowed thought to originate from Himself. "For I spake not from Myself; but the Father which sent Me, He hath given Me a commandment, what I should say, and what I should speak" (RV). That is the meaning of communion, an intelligent determined submission. "Verily, verily, I say unto you, The Son can do nothing of Himself, but what He seeth the Father do."

When we are sanctified, our spiritual education goes along the same lines—the deliberate sacrifice to God of the self God has sanctified; the determined subordination of our intelligence to God, and the determined submission of our will to God. What a glorious opportunity there is for Jesus Christ in our lives! We testify to salvation and sanctification, but are we proving day by day that Jesus Christ is "made unto us . . . sanctification" in all holy living, in all holy speaking, and all holy thinking? Are we doing the "greater works" that Jesus said we should do because our wills are submitted to Him as He submitted His will to His Father?

2. Transformation on the Summit *(Luke 9:29)*
And as He prayed, the fashion of His countenance was altered, and His raiment was white and glistering.

We say, "No cross, no crown"; in the life of Our Lord the crown of the glory of the Transfiguration came before the Cross. You never know Jesus Christ, and Him crucified unless you have seen Him transfigured in all His transcendent majesty and glory; the Cross to you is nothing but the cross of a martyr. If you have seen Jesus glorified, you know that the Cross is the revelation of God's judgement on sin, that on the Cross Our Lord bore the whole massed sin of the human race. "Him Who knew no sin He made to be sin on our behalf" (RV). No wonder we say:

> *Since mine eyes have looked on Jesus*
> *I've lost sight of all beside.*

Have we seen Him, "crowned with glory and honour"?

When the Transfiguration took place Our Lord as Son of Man had fulfilled all the requirements of His Father for His earthly life and He was back in the glory which He had with the Father before the world was. Why did He not stay there? Supposing Jesus had gone straight to heaven from the Mount of Transfiguration, what would have happened? He would have gone alone. No one would ever have been able to follow Him; His life would have been only a glorious ideal to lash humanity to despair. If Jesus Christ had gone to heaven from the Mount of Transfiguration we might have worshipped Him, but we would have had no power to live the kind of life He lived. But Jesus did not come to show us what a holy life was like: He came *to make us holy by means of His death.* The only way in which Our Lord does become our Example is when His life has been imparted to us. When we partake of His life through the experience of regeneration we are put into a state of innocence towards God, and we have then to do what Jesus did, viz. transform that innocence into holy character by a series of moral choices.

All that transpired in the life of Our Lord after the Transfiguration is altogether vicarious, we are without a guide to it in our own experience. Up to the Transfiguration we can understand His holy life and follow in His steps when we have received the Holy Spirit; after the Transfiguration there is no point of similarity, everything is unfamiliar to us. Jesus Christ has a consciousness about which we know nothing. We have come to the place where He is completing the will of God for the salvation of fallen humanity.

Beware of the teaching that makes out that Jesus Christ suffered because He was so noble, so pure, so far beyond the age in which He lived, that men put Him to death; it is not true. No martyr ever said what He said— "I lay it [My life] down of Myself." As workers, you will find that people like to listen as long as you talk about the holiness of Jesus and exalt Him as a marvellous character; but immediately you speak of His death and say that He became identified with sin that we might be delivered from it, you find resentment. In the New Testament everything centres in the Cross. The Cross did not *happen* to Jesus: He came on purpose for it.

3. Transition from the Summit *(Luke 9:30–43)*
"And behold, there talked with Him two men . . . who . . . spake of His decease which He was about to accomplish at Jerusalem" (RV). They spake not of His glory, but of His death. Who were the glorified visitants? One was Moses, whom the rabbis said died of the embraces of God, God kissed him into eternity; an ecstasy of Divine delight. The other visitant was Elijah, who was taken up to heaven in a mighty whirlwind with the accompaniment of horses and a chariot of fire; a marvellous ecstasy. Here on the Mount Our Lord Jesus Christ was back in His pre-Incarnate glory, and what did He do? He turned His back on the glory and came down from the Mount into the demon-possessed valley to be identified with sin on the Cross. The Bible is full of anti-climaxes. Over and over again we are brought up to a sublime height and then rushed down to earth. This is an anti-climax no human mind could have dreamed of. The Son of God was transfigured before His disciples—we were "eyewitnesses of His majesty," says Peter in his Epistle; the voice of the Father came with the Divine approval, "This is My beloved Son, in whom I am well pleased; hear ye Him"; then He came down from the Mount and was crucified in obscurity. At His baptism Our Lord took upon Him His vocation, viz. to take away the sin of the world by identification, and from the Transfiguration onward He fulfils that vocation. Between the Baptism and the Transfiguration there is no mention made of Jesus Christ being made sin; during that time He was perfecting holiness, i.e. living the kind of life God requires us to live. After the Transfiguration we see Him dealing with sin—"put away sin by the sacrifice of Himself."

The completion of the Transfiguration is the Ascension, not the Resurrection. The Transfiguration is a glimpse of glory—but not yet. "For the Holy Ghost was not yet given; because that Jesus was not yet glorified" (John 7:39).

We find here an explanation why God sends His servants into difficult places after the experience of sanctification; He sends them where He sent His Son. Transfiguration is the necessary result of obeying God, and there are moments when the glory does shine through, but we have to come down into all that is symbolised by the demon-possessed valley, into the toil and turmoil of the world for His sake. The Church of Jesus Christ is in danger of forgetting this nowadays; she is seeking favour in the eyes of the world, seeking signs and wonders, and Christ stands without the door knocking. Have you ever caught a glimpse of what going "without the campbearing His reproach" means? What camp? The "camp" that does not put Jesus first. After the glorious vision in the heavenlies—

what? Filling up "that which is lacking of the afflictions of Christ" (RV). Few of us get there because we stop short at sanctification. The emphasis is put on the subjective side, "Can Jesus Christ make me holy?" The dominant note with the Apostle Paul was not sanctification, but Jesus Christ, and Him crucified. When we are baptised with the Holy Ghost self is effaced in a glory of sacrifice for Jesus and we become His witnesses. Self-conscious devotion is gone, self-conscious service is killed, and one thing only remains, Jesus Christ first, second, and third.

THE KENOSIS

The Self-Limitation on the Part of the Logos in the Act of Incarnation

At one time the subject of the Kenosis was always being discussed by theologians—What was it that Jesus emptied Himself of? how did He limit Himself? or did He limit Himself at all? Nowadays, the subject is scarcely touched upon; according to the modern standpoint Jesus Christ was simply a great, noble and good man. It is not stated in so many words, but we are brought to that conclusion. We are told that by understanding our own consciousness, we can understand the consciousness of Jesus Christ. The New Testament reveals that to be false. Jesus distinctly said, "No one knoweth the Son, save the Father" (RV), and over and over again our Lord makes statements regarding Himself which reveal Him to be a unique Being.

The doctrine of the Kenosis is clear first to our heart, not to our head; it is a spiritual fact, not a thought-out fact. When a man's heart is right with God the mysterious utterances of the Bible are spirit and life to him. Spiritual truth is discernible only to a pure heart, not to a keen intellect. It is not a question of profundity of intellect, but of purity of heart.

1. Self-Disglorification

Have this in mind in you, which was also in Christ Jesus: Who, being in the form of God, counted it not a prize to be on an equality with God, but emptied Himself, taking the form of a servant. . . . (Philippians 2:5–7 RV)

Paul does not tell us what Jesus emptied Himself of: He emptied Himself of what He was in His former existence. That is a revelation fact, and we must beware of any explanation that explains it away. The Apostle Paul does not say that Jesus thought nothing

of Himself; He thought truthfully of Himself, He knew Who He was, but there was no self-assertion. Paul connects the two—"being on an equality with God" and not counting it "a thing to be grasped" (AV). That means Jesus never presumed on His equality with God, He did not continually assert it. There was only one brilliant moment in the life of Jesus, and that was on the Mount of Transfiguration. We do not know what the glory was which He had with the Father before the world was, but if we stand with Him on the Mount we see what He emptied Himself of. On the Mount the voice of the Father expressed the Divine approval—"This is My beloved Son, in whom I am well pleased"; yet it was a step on to the Cross—a way none ever went before, or has ever had to go since.

Recall the temptation of Our Lord; Satan tempted Him on this very line, viz. to assert Himself. "Remember Who You are, the Son of God, assert your prerogative as Son." At the heart of every one of our Lord's answers is this—"I did not come here to assert Who I am, I came here for God's will to be done through Me in His way."

The same temptation comes to us as God's children—"If you are sanctified, presume on it, think of it as something to be grasped." Whenever we get our thoughts fixed on our experience instead of on the God who gave us the experience, it is impossible to form the mind which was in Christ Jesus. It is not a question of sanctification, but of what happens after sanctification. The steadfast habit of the Christian life is the effacement of self, letting Jesus work through us without let or hindrance[5] as the Father worked through Him.

---

5. without let or hindrance: legal phrase meaning "without obstacle or impediment."

Whenever we are told by the Spirit of God to follow the example of Jesus, the following is emphatically prescribed to a particular point:

> *For hereunto were ye called: because Christ also suffered for you, leaving you an example, that ye should follow His steps: Who did no sin, neither was guile found in His mouth: Who, when He was reviled, reviled not again; when He suffered, threatened not. . . . (1 Peter 2:21–23 RV)*

Peter makes it perfectly clear and unambiguous how we are to "follow His steps," viz. in the way we suffer as Christians. "Who did no sin, neither was guile found in His mouth: . . . when He suffered, threatened not." "Follow His example there," says Peter; just as Christ exhibited an unthreatening spirit when He suffered, we are to do the same. No human being can suffer wrongfully without finding the spirit of threatening awakened in him, a spirit which if put into words would be—"I'll make that person smart! The idea of saying that about me!" If we are born again of the Holy Ghost the disposition of Jesus in us will enable us to "follow His steps" so that when we suffer wrongfully, we do not threaten. The following is distinctly limited to that one point. "Learn of Me; for I am meek and lowly in heart." We are never told to be like the unique Being the Lord Jesus Christ who came into the world as God Incarnate to put away sin, but when sin has been put away through the Atonement, we are to be conformed to His image. To "follow His steps" does not mean we have the belittling idea that we are to be Jesus Christ over again. It is not a question of "What would Jesus do?" but, "What would Jesus have me do?" We have to exhibit over again the life He exhibited; in this particular instance, in the circumstance of suffering wrongfully. Suffering is the touchstone of saintliness, just as temptation is, and suffering wrongfully will always reveal the ruling disposition because it takes us unawares.

"Have this mind in you, which was also in Christ Jesus" (RV). In this verse Paul indicates the type of mind we are to form, viz. the mind of true humility, the mind of Christ which He exhibited when He was on earth—utterly self-effaced and self-emptied, not the mind of Christ when He was in glory. If you are a saint, says Paul, manifest it by having the mind which was in Christ who said, "I am among you as He that serveth." One of the essential elements of Deity is the humility expressed in a baby and in Jesus Christ. "And He called to Him a little child, and set him in the midst of them, and said, Verily I say unto you, Except ye . . . become as little children, ye shall in no wise enter into the kingdom of heaven" (RV). To interpret these words to mean that we are to have as our ideal being servants of all, would end in mock humility. We cannot form the mind of Christ if we

have not got His Spirit, nor can we interpret His teaching apart from His Spirit. Our spiritual destitution and entire dependence upon God, and our despair of ever attaining to this kind of life, is in reality the most glorious chance for God. The Spirit of God never allows the thought that is apt to crop up now and again in spiritual teaching, that we are to be specimens of what God can do. That thought is inspired by the devil, never by the Spirit of God. I am not here to be a specimen of what God can do; I am here to live the life so hid with Christ in God that what Jesus said will be true, Men will "see your good works, and glorify your Father which is in heaven."

2. Self-Renunciation
And the Word became flesh . . . . (John 1:14 RV)

Him who knew no sin He made to be sin on our behalf; that we might become the righteousness of God in Him. (2 Corinthians 5:21 RV)

The Word, the Logos, became flesh for one purpose, to be identified with sin and put it away. At His Baptism Our Lord took on Him His vocation, which was to bear away the sin of the world, and it was along that line that He narrowed and limited and confined Himself. We miss the mark when we think on the æsthetic line and take Our Lord as a specimen of a highly strung, superbly fine nature, suffering from contact with coarse natures; we are talking nonsense if we put His suffering there. He never paid the remotest attention to that kind of suffering, nor is there any allusion made to it in the New Testament. His suffering is not the suffering of a man of refined sensibilities among brutes, or a holy character among unholy characters; His suffering is in a totally different domain and along a different line from anything from which we suffer, it is the suffering of a Saviour. "Though He were a Son, yet He learned obedience by the things which He suffered." Jesus Christ was God Incarnate for one purpose, not to reveal God to us, that is simply one of the outcomes of the Incarnation; the one great purpose of His coming was to bring back the whole human race into oneness with God. He who was originally "in the form of God," on an equality with God—that was His right, not a thing to be grasped—renounced it all, and took upon Him the form of a slave, and became obedient unto death, even the death of the cross, in order that He might deliver the weak and the ungodly and the sinful from sin. (See Romans 5:6–8)

In presenting the life of Jesus Christ we are not presenting an example, but an historic Fact essential to our soul's salvation, A sinner saved by grace will always refer in his testimony to the moment at which he experienced new birth. People who have never been convicted of sin say that what we call saintliness is simply the evolution of the finer qualities in man; there is no room whatever for that thinking in the New Testament. The finer qualities of man are remnants and ruins of what he once was, not the promise of what he is going to be, and the only way a man can fulfil God's purpose is by being born from above. "Marvel not that I said unto thee, Ye must be born from above" (RV mg).

We have to be careful of the teaching which is built on the idea that Jesus Christ is a great, high and wonderful Figure for us to imitate; there is no place in the New Testament for that idea. Unless we come to know Him as Saviour we are left amazingly unsatisfied—a beautiful influence, a wonderful life, that is all. "I came not to call the righteous, but sinners." A sinner, i.e. one convicted of sin, is the only one who is in a fit state to understand why Jesus came. When God became Incarnate in Jesus Christ for the purpose of removing sin, men saw nothing in Him to desire. Jesus Christ is "disadvantaged" in the eyes of everyone not convicted of sin: "He hath no form nor comeliness; and when we see Him, there is no beauty that we should desire Him" (RV); but when once the heart of a sinner is reached, that is a state of heart and mind able to understand why it was necessary for God to become Incarnate. The worst state a man could be in is never to have had a twinge of conviction of sin, everything happy and peaceful, but absolutely dead to the realm of things Jesus represents.

3. Self-Expenditure

For ye know the grace of our Lord Jesus Christ, that, though He was rich, yet for your sakes He became poor, that ye through His poverty might become rich. (2 Corinthians 8:9 RV)

"Grace" is a theological word and is unfortunately used, because we usually mean by theology something remote that has to do with controversy, something whereby our mind is tied up in knots and our practical life left alone. In the Bible theology is immensely practical. "Grace" means the overflowing nature of God; we see it in Nature, we have no words to describe the lavishness of God. "The grace of our Lord Jesus Christ" is the overflowing of God's nature in entire and absolute forgiveness through His own sacrifice. Do we discern that grace? We talk about the sacrifice of the Son of God and forget that it was the sacrifice of God Himself. *"God was in Christ, reconciling the world unto Himself."*

"... that ye through His poverty might become rich." Rich in what? Not in possessions, but in personal identity. Our Lord Jesus Christ became poor, not as an example, but to give us the secret of His religion. The religion of Jesus Christ is a religion of personal relationship to God and has nothing to do with possessions. Professional Christianity is a religion of possessions that are devoted to God. The disciple realises that his life does not consist in the abundance of things he possesses, because what we possess often possesses us—we are possessed by possessions. "This is mine, you must not touch it!" When we become rich towards God it will show in the details of our actual life. "Without shedding of blood is no remission," is true of the marvellous Redemption of our Lord Jesus, and true also of us as saints. The blood of the majority of Christians flows in hard cash. If ever we are to be loosened from the thing which keeps us poor in relation to God, we must shed our blood right out. "As having nothing, and yet possessing all things." The poverty of God's children in all ages is a significant thing, and the poverty has to come through calamity.

FOR FURTHER NOTES ON THE KENOSIS SEE "THE MIND OF CHRIST"
IN MORAL FOUNDATIONS OF LIFE.

IT IS FINISHED
John 19:30

The Transfiguration was the "Great Divide" in the life of Our Lord. He stood there in the perfect, spotless holiness of His Manhood; then He turned His back on the glory and came down from the Mount to be identified with sin, that through His death fallen humanity might not only be redeemed, but be enabled to have a conscious entrance into the life He lived. The Church of God is in danger of forgetting what Jesus Christ came for and He is being presented as a mere example. When the conscience of the Church is awakened and made to face the Cross of Christ, and to take Our Lord at His own estimate of Himself, she will realise the meaning of Paul's words—"For I determined not to know anything among you, save Jesus Christ,"—"and Him risen"? No. "And Him glorified"? No. "Save Jesus Christ, *and Him crucified.*" The Resurrection and glorification through the Ascension are understandable only by the Cross. The death of Jesus Christ holds the secret of the mind of God.

1. The Vicarious Visitation of God

The next day John seeth Jesus coming unto him, and saith, Behold the Lamb of God, which taketh away the sin of the world. (John 1:29)

At the outset of Our Lord's public ministry He accepted His vocation, which was to "bear away the sin of the world" (RV mg); we must never forget that. John's baptism was a baptism of repentance for the remission of sins, and that was the baptism with which Jesus was baptised. "Suffer it to be so now: for thus it becometh us to fulfil all righteousness"; and right through to the end Our Lord was identified with that one thing, viz. sin. The agony in Gethsemane reveals the last reach of the unfathomable depths to which Our Lord went in that identification. "Christ hath redeemed us from the curse of the law, *being made a curse for us*"; "Behold the Lamb of God, which taketh away the sin of the world"; these were almost the first words John the Baptist spoke about Jesus, and almost the last words Jesus spoke were to a criminal—"To-day shalt thou be with Me in paradise." The last possible reach of faith is the cry of a sinner who begins to realise that God can save him. Immediately he cries out to God he will find the marvel of Jesus Christ's salvation wrought out in his personal experience.

The death of Jesus Christ was not the death of a martyr; it was the death of God (cf. Acts 20:28). The Son of God was put to death by humanity based on self-realisation; through the Redemption self-realisation is turned into Christ-realisation, that is, a man enters into a relationship which puts to death, not the Son of God, but the disposition of sin. The essence of sin is my claim to my right to myself.

2. The Vanishing Vision of God

My God, My God, why hast Thou forsaken Me? (Matthew 27:46)

This is a cry from the depths, it is unfathomable; it is recorded by the Spirit of God, and we are meant to look into all that is recorded. God has nothing to conceal in His great purpose for the salvation of man, and we are meant to look into the depths that this cry represents.

Who is it that experiences God-forsakenness? Is it the lonely missionary with no comradeship? He is the one who knows the nearness of God. The ones who understand the experience of God-forsakenness are men like Cain—"Mine iniquity is greater than can be forgiven" (Genesis 4:13, RV mg); men like Esau—" . . . an exceeding great and bitter cry" (RV); men like Saul—"God is departed from me, and answereth me no more."

If Our Lord had never known the "vanishing vision of God" He could not have been a complete Saviour. Agony which has God behind it can be turned into triumph; but think of agony in which there is no God, neither in Heaven above nor earth beneath, only the terror of an accusing conscience. No human sympathy can touch that desolation. In all probability the man is to blame for it, and just because he is, no human sympathy can reach him. Anyone can have a fellow-feeling for a poor unfortunate being and can sympathise with him, but who among us can understand agony which goes deeper down than can be put into words? Who but Jesus Christ?

" . . . holiness, without which no man shall see the Lord." God cannot look on sin, and on the Cross, the world's sin and the world's punishment met in the person of the Son of Man. The Cross of Christ means that the salvation of God goes deeper down than the deepest depths of iniquity man can commit. No man can get beyond the reach of Jesus: He made a way back to the throne of God from the very heart of hell by His tremendous Atonement.

There is a conception abroad to-day that the Incarnation is something altogether apart from the idea of Atonement. According to the Bible, the Son of God became incarnate in order to bear away the sin of the human race. Before a man can take on him the sin of a family, he must be a member of it; and Jesus Christ took on Him the form of the human family that was cursed with sin, and in that human form He lived a spotlessly holy life, and by means of His death He can introduce the shamed members of the human family into the life He lived. Our Lord made human solidarity His own: He represents the vilest sinner out of hell and the purest saint out of heaven. He stands as the one great Representative of the human race, atoning for its sin. It beggars language to describe what He did—He went into identification with the depths of damnation that the human race might be delivered. "When Thou shalt make His soul an offering for sin. . . ." We praise God for our salvation, but have we ever once thought how it came to us? Through the deep shadows, deeper than any human mind can ever go.

Beware of saying that Jesus Christ took on Him the sin of the world by sympathy; that would mean that we can only take on His righteousness by sympathy. Jesus Christ took on the sin of the world by being identified with it, and we take on His righteousness by being identified with it. "But of Him are ye in Christ Jesus, who was made unto us . . . righteousness" (RV).

3. The Victorious Voice for God

And when Jesus had cried with a loud voice, He said, Father, into Thy hands I commend My spirit. (Luke 23:46)

The Cross is a tragedy to man, but a tremendous triumph to God, an absolute triumph. Listen to the clear, ringing voice—"Father, into Thy hands I commend

My spirit"! The spirit of the Son of God only? No, the spirit of the whole human race incarnated in the Saviour of the world. My spirit was there, your spirit was there; and by God's mighty grace and the gift of His Spirit which Our Lord shed forth after He ascended, we can know experimentally His complete salvation for body, soul and spirit.

Never put it on the shallow line that on the Cross the physical sufferings of Jesus were so great that His mind was blinded and He imagined His Father had gone from Him; that line does not touch the depths of identification with sin to which Our Lord went. Neither is it true to say that God was angry and hid His face from Him; if one may put it so—God was never more pleased with His Son than when He bridged the gulf between God and man by the sacrifice of Himself. When the New Testament speaks of the sufferings of Christ, it is suffering in connection with our salvation and in no other connection—"Ought not Christ to have suffered these things, and to enter into His glory?" He suffered "according to the will of God." It is not the suffering of a man; this is the Eternal Christ of God tasting "death for every man." The agony in Gethsemane represents the incomprehensible mystery of 2 Corinthians 5:21. "For He hath made Him to be sin for us. . . ."

It is only by thinking along these lines, baresouled, and humbled before God, that we can understand what a wonderful thing our salvation is. Salvation is an immense marvel to me—I, a sinner, can be made into a saint; but it is only possible because of what Jesus Christ did. Are the unfath-omable depths of suffering through which Our Lord went to mean less than entire deliverance from sin for us? The reason sanctification is so easy for us is because of Gethsemane. The Holy Spirit received as a gift into our personal life brings the supernatural marvel of the salvation wrought out by Our Lord. That is the message the Spirit of God has given to be proclaimed to the world. It matters not how sinstained a man may be, through the death of Jesus Christ on the Cross he can partake of that wondrous salvation.

"I have finished the work which Thou gavest Me to do." What was finished? The rehabilitation of the human race back to where God desired it to be. It was not the salvation of individual men and women like you and me that was being finished, but the whole human race was put on the basis of Redemption. Redemption is not going to be finished: it is finished. Believing does not make a man redeemed; believing enables him to realise that he is redeemed. To any man who thinks, the basis of life is not reason, but Redemption. The miracle of the work of God is performed when he places himself on the "It is finished" side of the Cross. We take our salvation and our sanctification much too cheaply. We ought to rejoice when a man says he is saved, but remember what it cost God to make His grace a free gift. It cost agony we cannot begin to understand. The Christian faith means that the historic Cross of Christ is the pinhole in actual history through which we get a view of the purpose of God all through. Jesus Christ is "the Lamb slain from the foundation of the world."

THE PLEROSIS
The Self-Fulfilling of Jesus

We have to place the Lord Jesus Christ to our faith where the New Testament places Him. We are apt to look upon Jesus Christ as some marvellous power of God with no identity of its own, forgetting altogether that the New Testament Jesus Christ, Who transforms human lives by the miracle of regeneration, retains His own identity all through. Our Lord had a Self-conscious existence built on exactly the same basis as our human personality. What is true of the conscious and unconscious mind is true also of personality. The part of our personality of which we are conscious is the tiniest bit; underneath are the deep realms of unconscious life known only to God. Our Lord can never be defined in terms of individuality, but only in terms of personality. "I and My Father are one." Every bit of the personality of Jesus, conscious and unconscious, fulfilled the purpose of God.

1. His Sovereign Self-Identification
That they may be one, even as We are one. (John 17:22)

(a) The Joy of Personality
These things have I spoken unto you, that My joy might remain in you, and that your joy might be full. (John 15:11)

You can never use the word "happiness" in connection with Jesus or His disciples. It is an insult to God and to human nature to have as our ideal a happy life. Happiness is a thing that comes and goes, it can never be an end in itself; holiness, not happiness, is the end of man. The great design of God in the creation of man is that he might "glorify God and enjoy Him forever." A man never knows joy until he gets rightly related to God. Satan's claim is that he can make a man satisfied without God, but all he succeeds in doing is to give happiness and pleasure, never joy. Our lives mean much more than we can tell, they fulfil some purpose of God about which we know nothing; our part is to trust in the Lord with all our heart and not lean to our own understanding. Earthly wisdom can never come near the threshold of the Divine; if we stop short of the Divine we stop short of God's purpose for our lives.

". . . that My joy might remain in you." What was the joy of Jesus? The joy of Jesus was the absolute Self-surrender and Self-sacrifice of Himself to the will of His Father, the joy of doing exactly what the Father sent Him to do. "I delight to do Thy will," and He prays that His disciples may have this joy fulfilled in themselves.

There is no joy in a personality unless it can create. The joy of an artist is not in the fame which his pictures bring him, but that his work is the creation of his personality. The work of Jesus is the creation of saints; He can take the worst, the most misshapen material, and make a saint. "Wherefore if any man is in Christ, there is a new creation" (RV mg). The fullest meaning of sanctification is that Jesus Christ is "made unto us . . . sanctification," that is, He creates in us what He is Himself. The Apostle Paul alludes to the joy of creating when he says, "For what is our hope, or joy, or crown of glorying? Are not even ye . . . ? For ye are our glory and our joy" (1 Thessalonians 2:19–20 RV).

"Who for the joy that was set before Him endured the cross, . . ." It was not reward Our Lord looked forward to, but joy. "Reward" is our lame word for joy. When we want a child to do well, we do not say "You will have joy"; we say "You will have a reward, a prize." The way the joy of Jesus manifests itself is that there is no desire for praise. As Bergson has pointed out, we only want praise when we are not sure of having done well; when we are certain we have done well, we don't care an atom whether folk praise us or not.

(b) The Peace of Personality

"My peace I give unto you" (John 14:27). The idea of peace in connection with personality is that every power is in perfect working order to the limit of activity. That is what Jesus means when He says *"My peace."* Never have the idea of jadedness or stagnation in your mind in connection with peace. Health is physical peace, but health is not stagnation; health is the perfection of physical activity. Virtue is moral peace, but virtue is not innocence; virtue is the perfection of moral activity. Holiness is spiritual peace, but holiness is not quietness; holiness is the intensest spiritual activity.

It is easy to conceive of a personality full of joy and peace, but isolated. The striking thing about Our Lord is that He was never isolated. "If a man love Me . . . ," He says, "We will come unto him, and make Our abode with him." The conception is that of perfect converse and union; the abiding of the Trinity with the saint. The destiny of mankind in the purpose of God is not to do something, but to *be* something— "that they may be one, even as We are one."

Jesus had joy and peace to the last reach of His personality. With us it is possible to have joy and peace in one domain and disturbance and unrest in another; we have spells of joy and spells that are the opposite of joy, tribulation that brings distress; but there is a time coming when there will be no more tribulation, no more distress, when every part of our personality will be as full of joy and peace as was the File Leader[6] of our faith. Have we got the unfathomable comfort of knowing that in and above all the clouds and mysteries the joy of Jesus is unsullied? "Now unto Him that is able to keep you from falling, and to present you faultless before the presence of His glory *with exceeding joy*" (Jude 24It is a good thing to let the Spirit of God kindle our imagination as to what Jesus Christ is able to do.

2. His Sovereign Self-Fulfilment
Therefore being by the right hand of God exalted . . . (Acts 2:33)

The Ascension placed Jesus Christ back in the glory which He had with the Father before the world was. The Ascension, not the Resurrection, is the completion of the Transfiguration. The two visitants on the mount, who might well have come to usher Him back into heaven, instead spake with Him "of His decease which He should accomplish at Jerusalem.""And it came to pass, while He blessed them, He was parted from them, and carried up into heaven," and the angels told the watching disciples that "this Jesus, which was received up from you into heaven, shall so come in like manner as ye beheld Him going into heaven." Our Lord does now, without any hesitation, go back into His primal glory; but He does not go alone. Through His Death and Resurrection He has made the way for the whole human race to get to the very throne of God.

The Death of Jesus was a revelation in act of the judgement of God upon the sin of the human race; the Resurrection is the absolution of God pronounced upon the human race, the abolishing of death which is the wages of sin. By His Resurrection Our Lord not only

---

6. File Leader: Leader of mountain expedition or military unit; person with absolute authority.

has the right to give His own life to anyone who will take it, but power to "fashion anew the body of our humiliation, that it may be conformed to the body of His glory . . ." (RV). That does not take place in this dispensation. Beyond our comprehension, you say? Only beyond the comprehension of intellect. There is all the difference between the comprehension of intellect and the comprehension of spirit. We comprehend a thing by our spirit and feel we know it but cannot express it; it is a knowledge "which passeth knowledge."

(a) Supreme Power

"All power is given unto Me in heaven and in earth" (Matthew 28:18). All power is given—unto whom? To the Being who lived a humble, obscure life in Nazareth; the One who says "Come unto Me, all ye that labour and are heavy laden, and I will give you rest." If all power is given to Jesus Christ, what right have I to insult Him by worrying? If we will let these words of Jesus come into our heart, we shall soon see how contemptible our unbelief is. Jesus Christ will do anything for us in keeping with His own character; the power that comes from Him is stamped with His nature. Will I say sceptically, "What does Jesus Christ know about my circumstances? Is His power and understanding sufficient to manage things for me?" To talk like that is the way to realise the size of our unbelief, and to see why Jesus Christ was so stern in condemning it.

"All power is given unto Me," and yet Paul says "He was crucified through weakness," and, he adds, "we also are weak in Him." Am I powerful enough to be weak? Any weak man can strike another back, it takes a strong man to take it meekly; the omnipotence of Jesus at work in a man means that neither the world, the flesh or the devil can make him show anything but Christ-likeness. The Self-identification of Jesus with His servants through all the ages is along this line. "They took knowledge of them, that they had been with Jesus." The meaning of salvation in experience is that we are enabled to manifest in our mortal flesh the family likeness that Jesus had to God. There is only one type of humanity, and only one type of holiness, the holiness that was manifested in the life of the Lord Jesus, and it is that holiness which He gives to us. It is not that we are put in a place where we can begin to be like Him: we are put in a place where we are like Him. In Galatians 2:20 the Apostle Paul is referring to the fact that the very disposition of holiness which was in Jesus is in him by means of his identification with His death. It is not sentiment, it is a fact; not poetry, but a practical working out of this marvellous likeness to Jesus Christ. "We know that, when He shall appear, we shall be like Him; for we shall see Him as He is" (1 John 3:2).

(b) Supreme Wisdom

"Whatsoever ye shall ask in My name, that will I do" (John 14:13). When you pray, remember that it is Jesus Christ who carries out the answer, God hands over this marvellous power to Him. By His Ascension Our Lord becomes omniscient, all-wise; have we ever had a glimpse of what that means? The wisdom which He exercised in a limited sphere and in complete dependence upon His Father while on earth, He can now exercise in an unlimited sphere. The revelation of our spiritual standing is what we ask in prayer; sometimes what we ask is an insult to God; we ask with our eyes on the possibilities or on ourselves, not on Jesus Christ. Get on to the supernatural line, remember that Jesus Christ is omniscient, and He says, "If ye shall ask anything in My name, I will do it."

(c) Supreme Presence

"And lo, I am with you alway." Don't refine this revelation fact away by taking it to mean a spiritual presence by the Holy Spirit; it is a grander, more massive revelation than that, "I am with you alway." Through His Ascension the glorified Lord is with us always. May God lift the veil as to what this means. Who was it saw Jesus after the Resurrection? Only those who had spiritual insight. When the Spirit of God opens our spiritual eyes, we see Jesus, "crowned with glory and honour."

By His Ascension Our Lord raises Himself to glory, He becomes omnipotent, omniscient and omnipresent. All the splendid power, so circumscribed in His earthly life, becomes omnipotence; all the wisdom and insight, so precious but so limited during His life on earth, becomes omniscience; all the unspeakable comfort of the presence of Jesus, so confined to a few in His earthly life, becomes omnipresence, He is with us all the days (RVmg).

What kind of Lord Jesus have we? Is He the All-powerful God in our present circumstances, in our providential setting? Is He the All-wise God of our thinking and our planning? Is He the Ever-present God, "closer than breathing, nearer than hands or feet"? If He is, we know what it means to "abide under the shadow of the Almighty." No one can tell us where the shadow of the Almighty is, we have to find it out for ourselves. When by obedience we have discovered where it is, we must abide there—"there shall no evil befall thee, neither shall any plague come nigh thy dwelling." That is the life that is more than conqueror because the joy of the Lord has become its strength, and that soul is on the way to entering ultimately into the joy of the Lord.

OUR LORD'S VIEW OF HIMSELF AND HIS WORK—I
The Fact of Christ

"But who say ye that I am?" (RV). Jesus Christ is not a Being with a dual personality, He is a unique Personality with two manifestations: Son of God and Son of Man. He gives clear indication of how He lived a holy life, of how He thought and spoke, and He also gives clear expositions of God. Those expositions were given in a human body like ours, and the New Testament reveals how it is possible for us to live the same kind of life that Jesus lived through the marvel of the Atonement because the disposition which ruled Him is ruling us. What God demands of us is the very holiness that Jesus Christ exhibited in His life. We can "follow His steps" by recognising the wonderful work He has done, and manifest daily the marvel of His grace.

The first thing we have to do is to clear away the difficulties that have gathered round the Fact of Christ.

1. Difficulties of an Intellectual Kind
(a) Pre-conceptions
Being the son (as was supposed) of Joseph. (Luke 3:23 RV)

There were many pre-conceptions about our Lord in His day, and this was a prevalent one. We do not bring with us those pre-conceptions, but we bring others; we have made up our mind that God will only come along certain lines, and like the religious people of His day, when He comes on another line, we do not recognise Him. It is difficult for anyone brought up with religious conceptions to get rid of them in the right way. What mental conception do we bring with us when we come to study the Lord Jesus Christ? If, for instance, a man has an agnostic pre-conception, it will obscure everything the New Testament says about God becoming Incarnate. This pre-conception may not trouble us, but it is as well to recognise that it is there. An agnostic says, "I cannot accept anything about Deity, I can only accept facts about human nature," then if you tell him he must accept the fact that Jesus Christ is the Son of God, you will never get near him; but if you go on this line—"Do you believe that Jesus Christ was the best, the holiest Man who ever lived?" he is obliged to listen. You cannot expect a man to accept an abstract proposition that the Bible is the Word of God; that is not the first thing to bring before him, the first thing is—

"What about Jesus Christ? If He was the best, the holiest Man who ever lived, He was least likely to be deceived about Himself or to tell a lie; then will you ask for what He says God will give, viz. the Holy Spirit?" A man ceases to be an honest doubter the moment he refuses one way of getting at the truth because he does not like that way. The Apostle Peter, when he preached to the Gentiles, spoke of Jesus not as "the Son of God" but as "Jesus of Nazareth, a man approved of God." That reveals the way in which the Holy Ghost brought Jesus Christ on to the platform on which men lived, and we have to do the same to-day. We have to be so controlled by the Holy Spirit, to so submit our intelligence to Him, that Jesus Christ is presented along the line that appeals to those to whom we talk.

(b) Prejudice
How can ye believe, which receive glory one of another, and the glory that cometh from the only God ye seek not? (John 5:44 RV)

These words of Jesus bring out the very essence of prejudice, viz. to foreclose judgement without sufficiently weighing the evidence. "It is a moral impossibility for you to believe in Me," Jesus says, "not because you are bad, but because you have another standard in view, you seek honour one of another." Remember, we only see along the line of our prejudice, and prejudice means ignorance; we are always prejudiced over what we know least about and we foreclose our judgement about it—"I have sealed the question, docketed it and put it into a pigeon-hole and I refuse to say anything more about it" (cf. John 9:22). Then it is impossible for you to see along any other line until you are willing to take the packet out of the pigeon-hole, unseal it and open the question again. Every point of view which I hold strongly makes me prejudiced and I can see nothing else but that point of view, there is a ban of finality[7] about it which makes me intolerant of any other point of view.

Up to the time of the Resurrection the disciples saw only along the line of their old narrow Jewish prejudices; when they received the Holy Spirit from the risen Lord, the operation that was performed on the inside enabled them to see along the line of Christ's revelation (see Luke 24:31, 45). What takes place at new birth is an "explosion" on the inside (a literal

---

7. ban of finality: the limitation or "curse" of having one's mind made up, unwilling to consider new information

explosion, not a theoretical one) that opens all the doors which have been closed and life becomes larger, there is the incoming of a totally new point of view.

The way a searchlight works is a very good illustration for prejudice. A searchlight illuminates only what it does and no more; but let daylight come, and you find there are a thousand and one things the searchlight had not revealed. Whenever you get the light of God on salvation it acts like a searchlight, everything you read in the Bible teaches salvation and you say, "Why, it is as simple as can be!" The same with sanctification, and the Second Coming. When you come to the place where God is the dominant light you find facts you never realised before, facts which no one is sufficient to explain saving the Lord Jesus Christ. Christianity is not walking in the light of our convictions but walking in the light of the Lord, a very different thing. Convictions are necessary, but only as stepping stones to all that God wants us to be. The Apostle Paul puts it in 1 Corinthians 4:3–4—"But with me it is a very small thing that I should be judged of you, or of man's judgement: yea, I judge not mine own self. For I know nothing by myself; yet am I not hereby justified: but He that judgeth me is the Lord." We have to get into the white light of Jesus Christ where He is easily first, not our experience of Him first, but Jesus Christ Himself first, and our experience the evidence that we have seen Him.

2. Difficulties of a Doctrinal Kind
(a) Distortions
Ye search the scriptures, because ye think that in them ye have eternal life . . . And ye will not come to Me that ye may have life. (John 5:39–40 RV)

These verses reveal how a knowledge of the Scriptures may distort the mind away from Jesus Christ. Unless we know the Living Word personally first, the literal words may lead us astray. The only way we can understand the Bible is by personal contact with the Living Word, then the Holy Spirit expounds the literal words to us along the line of personal experience. "The words that I speak unto you, they are spirit, and they are life." The Jews knew the Scriptures thoroughly, yet their minds were so distorted that when they saw Jesus Christ they said, "He hath a devil." There is a context to the Bible, and Jesus Christ is that Context. The right order is personal relationship to Him first, then the interpretation of the Scriptures according to His Spirit. Difficulties come because beliefs and creeds are put in the place of Jesus Christ.

(b) Direction by Belief (Philippians 3:18; cf. Colossians 2:8, 18–23)
"For many walk, of whom I have told you often, and now tell you even weeping, that they are the enemies of the cross of Christ. . . ." Who are the enemies of the cross of Christ? First of all, what was the Cross of Christ to Paul? The cross of a martyr? No. The Cross to Paul was the Cross of God whereby He readjusted humanity to Himself. "But God forbid that I should glory, save in the cross of our Lord Jesus Christ, by whom the world is crucified unto me, and I unto the world" (Galatians 6:14). "If any one preaches ordinances, the precepts and doctrines of men, and ignores the Cross," Paul says, "I tell you even weeping, that they are the enemies of the revelation which God gave through Jesus Christ." You can always detect the right kind of belief by a flesh-and-blood testimony. How many of us can say "The life which I now live in the flesh" (the life you know and see), "I live by the faith of the Son of God"? Christian doctrines are the explanation of how Jesus Christ makes us saints, but all the doctrine under heaven will never make a saint. The only thing that will make a saint is the Holy Ghost working in us what Jesus Christ did in the Atonement. Jesus Christ demands absolute devotion to Himself personally, then the application of His principles to our lives. For what purpose? That we may understand Him better. To be devoted to doctrines will twist us away from the Centre; devotion to Jesus Christ relates our doctrines to the one Centre, Jesus Christ. Read the words of the Spirit to the Church in Ephesus—"Nevertheless I have somewhat against thee, because thou hast left thy first love." "The doctrines you teach are all right, but they have become un-centred, they are not centred in love for Me." "Remember therefore from whence thou art fallen, and repent, and do the first works" (Revelation 2:5).

Am I prepared to accept Jesus Christ's view of Himself, or have I a point of view? Will I come to Jesus Christ just as I am and face the fact that He says certain astounding things about Himself? Jesus Christ did not preach a gospel of hope: He came to re-organise humanity from the inside through a tremendous tragedy in His own life called the Cross, and through that Cross every member of the human race can be reinstated in God's favour and enter into a conscious inheritance of the Atonement.

Jesus Christ is the only medium God Almighty has for revealing Himself—"And no man knoweth the Son, but the Father; neither knoweth any man the Father, save the Son. . . ." Our Lord knows nothing about God being revealed in Nature, in the love of our friends, etc. The poet talks about God being revealed in Nature, but the poet does not remember that there is sin in the world: he sees clearly what God's idea is for man, but he forgets that we belong to a fallen race, consequently his poetry is only a vision, it cannot be worked out on Mother Earth.

". . . And he to whomsoever the Son will reveal Him" (Matthew 11:27). Who are the ones to whom

Jesus Christ will reveal God? Jesus Christ will reveal God to all who come to Him, not those who accept certain creeds or doctrines, but those who come to Him, with beliefs or without them, if they will only get straight through to Him. "Come unto Me, all ye that labour and are heavy laden, and I will give you rest." "And him that cometh to Me I will in no wise cast out."

OUR LORD'S VIEW OF HIMSELF AND HIS WORK—II
The Force of the Fact of Christ on Thinking and Living

It is a tremendous thing to know that there are higher heights than we can scale, deeper depths than we can fathom. The reason why average Christian workers remain average Christian workers is that they are grossly ignorant about things for which they see no immediate use. The majority of us are brought up on spooned meat[8] —"for when by reason of the time ye ought to be teachers, ye have need again that some one teach you the rudiments of the first principles of the oracles of God; and are become such as have need of milk, and not of solid food" (Hebrews 5:12 RV).

1. Method of Christian Thinking
Have this in mind in you, which was also in Christ Jesus. (Philippians 2:5 RV)

The method of thinking for a Christian is first of all to become rightly related to Jesus Christ and then to begin to think in accordance with His mind. There is nothing simple under heaven saving the personal relationship to Jesus Christ, and Paul is concerned lest any philosophy should come in to corrupt that simplicity, the simplicity of an understanding relationship between God and our own soul. "But I fear, lest by any means, as the serpent beguiled Eve in his craftiness, your minds should be corrupted from the simplicity and the purity that is toward Christ" (2 Corinthians 11:3 RV). To-day any number of religious books set out to expound Jesus Christ from a philosophical point of view; they are entrancing and apparently helpful, but in reality they do a great deal of harm because instead of helping us to form the mind of Christ and understand His point of view, they serve to confuse our mind. When people use the phrase "Preach us the simple Gospel," they generally mean, "Preach us the thing we have always listened to, the thing that keeps us sound asleep; don't present us with anything new." That means the mind is not open to accept facts, not open to entering into relationship with God.

The Cross is the symbol of Christian living and it is also the symbol of Christian thinking. Until a man is born again his thinking goes round and round in a circle and he becomes intoxicated with his own importance. When he is born again there is a violent readjustment in his actual life, and when he begins to think along Jesus Christ's line there is just as tremendous a revolution in his thinking processes. To ignore the Cross in either living or thinking is to become a traitor to Jesus Christ. The Apostle Paul tells us how our thinking as saints is to be conducted, viz. by "casting down imaginations [reasonings], and every high thing that is exalted against the knowledge of God, and bringing every thought into captivity to the obedience of Christ" (RV). To bring every thought into captivity is the last thing we do, and it is not done easily; in the beginning we have to do violence to our old ways of thinking just as at sanctification we had to do violence to our old ways of living. Intellect in a saint is the last thing to become identified with Jesus Christ. Paul urges, "Have this mind in you, which was also in Christ Jesus" (RV). Many a Christian who loves Jesus Christ in his heart denies Him in his head.

The method of thinking for the saint is not to think along the line of Christian principles, but after he has become rightly related to Jesus Christ to see that he allows nothing to corrupt the profound simplicity of that relationship. That will mean we shall only have those experiences which Jesus Christ sanctions. If you go on the line of accepting whatever can be experienced, you will find you have to accept the wildest, vaguest, most indeterminate things. For example, a man may come and tell you that he has had communication with departed friends; well, he is no more likely to be untruthful than you are—how are you going to judge whether his experience is right or not? The only guide is your personal relationship to Jesus Christ. Jesus Christ prohibits it, and that shuts the door straight off for you from tampering with

---

8. spooned meat: liquefied food that requires no chewing or effort—baby food

spiritualism, therefore you refuse to have anything to do with what He will not allow. It is imperative to estimate the danger abroad to-day in books which deal with Christian thinking, particularly those which have the word "psychology" tacked on; be sure what kind of psychology it is—unless it is the psychology of the Bible it may be the psychology of agnosticism pure and simple; it may sound all right but in the final result it dethrones Jesus Christ.

The Christian method of thinking has its source in a personal relationship to Jesus Christ, and this means we have to take into account Our Lord's view of Himself. In reading the New Testament the first thing that strikes you with overwhelming clarity is that Our Lord's fundamental view of Himself was His oneness with the Father. The first and foremost consciousness of Jesus was not the needs of manhood, not the pitiable condition of men, but His relationship to His Father whose Name He had to hallow before all else. Our Lord's holy living was produced by submitting Himself to His Father: "Verily, verily, I say unto you, The Son can do nothing of Himself, but what He seeth the Father doing" (John 5:19 RV); His holy speaking was produced by submitting His intellect to His Father: "For I spake not from Myself; but the Father which sent Me, He hath given Me a commandment, what I should say, and what I should speak" (John 12:49 RV); and His holy miracle working was produced by submitting His will to His Father: "the Father abiding in Me doeth His works" (John 14:10 RV).

That is Our Lord's view of Himself, and when we become identified with Him He relates us to Himself as He was related to His Father. " . . . that they may be one, even as We are one." As saints, are we submitting our intellect to the revealed will of God and refusing to be corrupted from the simplicity of that relationship? The insistence all through the Epistles is on being transformed by the renewing of our mind; on having our minds stirred by being put in remembrance, and on building ourselves up on our most holy faith. We are called upon not only to be right in heart, but to be right in thinking. When we have become personally related to Jesus Christ we have to do the thing that is in our power to do, viz. think aright. In Philippians 4:8–9 Paul gives the rule for the thinking life of the Christian. Have we ever given our brains the task of concentrated thinking along that line? "Finally, brethren, whatsoever things are true, whatsoever things are honest, whatsoever things are just, whatsoever things are pure, whatsoever things are lovely, whatsoever things are of good report; if there be any virtue, and if there be any praise, *think on these things*." It is because we will not bring every thought into captivity to the obedience of Christ that all the perplexities are produced regarding methods of thinking which look like Christianity—strands are taken out of Jesus Christ's teaching, the Bible is exploited to agree with certain principles, but The Truth, Our Lord Jesus Christ, is ignored. If we base our thinking on principles instead of on a Person we shall go wrong, no matter how devout or honest we are. The one great Truth to keep stedfastly before us is the Lord Jesus Christ; He is the Truth. Only the whole truth is The Truth, any part of the truth may become an error. If you have a ray of light on The Truth never call it the whole truth; follow it up and it will lead you to the central Truth, the Lord Jesus Christ.

2. Method of Christian Living
For hereunto were ye called: because Christ also suffered for you, leaving you an example, that ye should follow His steps. . . . (1 Peter 2:21 RV)

The life of a Christian is stamped by a strong family likeness to Jesus. When we become rightly related to God on the ground of the Redemption our brains have to begin to think along the lines Jesus Christ thought on, and in our bodily life there will be produced a likeness to Him, so that people take knowledge of us, that we have "been with Jesus." The piety which is not built on a personal relationship to Jesus Christ is simply religious egotism, and the scunner that most of us have against "pi" people is wholesomely right. A "pi" person is simply overweeningly conceited religiously; he substitutes prayer and consecration for devotion to Jesus—"I am going to give so much time to prayer, so much time to Bible study, and by doing these things I shall produce the type of life which will please God." Where does Jesus Christ come in? He does not come in anywhere. The first thing the Holy Spirit does is to take away all sense of our own importance and produce in us a state of true humility. The test of all doctrine is, does it produce a likeness to Jesus Christ? The final test is how a man's thinking works out in his life. The Apostle Paul warns about the thinking which says that by sheer will power a man can do what he likes: " . . . which things have indeed a show of wisdom in will-worship, . . . but are not of any value against the indulgence of the flesh" (Colossians 2:23 RV). The test of this "will to power" method of thinking is, has it any element of power over the wrong thing, over the disposition of sin? Jesus Christ alone can deal with that.

Take another method of thinking, the æsthetic—and here I am on the ground that I know better than any other, saving my soul's salvation. An æsthete bases all his thinking on the principle that anything that produces joy is justifiable for him. Æstheticism may be all very well for the kingdom of heaven, but it is the doctrine of the devil himself for the kingdom of earth. If once you base your thinking on the principles of æstheticism, you can justify any kind of vile corruption. The test of every system of thinking is not how it works in the best case, but how it works in the worst case. If the test were the best cases, that is, if everyone were well brought up, if men and women had not a moral twist, then any of these philosophies would work out quite well. The miracle of the Redemption of Jesus Christ is that He can take the worst and the vilest of men and women and make saints out of them.

Another method of thinking is egoistical. The egoist is one who makes all his thinking centre around human personality. The number of books written from this standpoint is legion. "Our greatest work," they say, "is to get straight down to the one important thing, viz. man, his dignity and nobility, and to look after his needs." What is the practical outworking of this? That God and man are one and the same. All we have to do is to let our inmost personality have expression—and what are we doing? We are expressing God. Is that line of thinking unfamiliar to-day? It is becoming more and more familiar.

The Christian method of thinking puts the intellect second, not first; the modern view puts intellect on the throne. God does not sum up a man's worth by his thinking, but by the way he expresses his thinking in actual life, that is, by his character. It is possible for there to be a tremendous divorce between a man's thinking and his practical life; the only thing that tells in the sight of God is a man's character.

Beware of putting principles first instead of a Person. Jesus Christ puts personal relationship first—"Be rightly related to Me, then work out your thinking."

In these methods of thinking which contrast with the Christian method, certain aspects of Christianity are stressed whilst other aspects are ignored, and in this way men's minds are corrupted from the simplicity which is in Christ Jesus. The presentation given of Jesus Christ in these methods of thinking is of one who has a little more breath than the rest of us; He is in the same "swim," but able to turn round and give us a helping hand. Is that the view the New Testament gives of Jesus Christ? Jesus said, "Upon this rock I will build My church"—the rock of personal revelation of who Jesus Christ is—"the Son of the living God." This is the invincible fact against which nothing can prevail. Along this line we see the profundity of the Apostle Paul's words, "For I determined not to know any thing among you, save Jesus Christ, and Him crucified" (1 Corinthians 2:2). According to the New Testament the historic Jesus and the Eternal Christ are one and the same. The glorified Lord who appeared to the Apostle in all His ascended majesty is "this same Jesus" Who "trod this earth with naked feet, and wove with human hands the creed of creeds." The Jesus who saves our souls and identifies us with Himself is "this same Jesus" who went to sleep as a Babe on His mother's bosom; and it is "this same Jesus," the almighty, powerful Christ, with all power in heaven and on earth, who is at work in the world to-day by His Spirit.

OUR LORD'S VIEW OF HIMSELF AND HIS WORK—III
The Finality of the Person of Jesus Christ

By "Finality" is meant that there is nothing to be added. In our previous studies we have been clearing the ground for studying the Person of Our Lord Jesus Christ, and warning ourselves of the danger of bringing to that study a mental point of view which we have no right to bring. We must be prepared to accept facts and not try to build facts into our preconceived fancies.

"The Word became flesh . . ." (RV). What Word? The explaining Word about God, about Creation, about man, became Incarnate, became a flesh and blood Fact, and trod this earth with human feet, and worked with human hands, and thought with a human brain. Now perplexities and fogs have gone for ever! The Bible never asks us to try and find out God, the human mind can never work along that line; the

Bible is dictated by the Holy Ghost and He knows exactly the lines along which human minds can work. "All things are delivered unto Me of My Father: and no man knoweth the Son, but the Father; neither knoweth any man the Father, save the Son, and *he to whomsoever the Son will reveal Him*" (Matthew 11:27). Every other line of finding out God is atheistic impertinence, and trying to think about man is presumption, as long as we ignore the one Fact we can find out, the Lord Jesus Christ, and the interpreting fact about Him which is the Bible.

1. The Original Position of Man *(Genesis 2:7; Romans 5:12)*

When we read that "the LORD God formed man of the dust of the ground," remember, that that man was the Federal Head of the race, not a member of the degenerate race to which we belong, but man as he came direct from the hand of God; "and breathed into his nostrils the breath of life; and man became a living soul." God breathed into man that which, going forth from God and entering into man, became the spirit of man, that spirit is essentially man's spirit, and never ceases to be man's spirit. This is an insistent revelation all through the Bible. In John 20:22 another "breathing" is mentioned. After the Resurrection Jesus "breathed on them and saith unto them, Receive ye the Holy Ghost"—man's spirit became energised by the Spirit of the Son of God. We must keep this distinction in mind in order to understand the difference between the Christian belief and the beliefs of other religions, which are reviving all over our land, viz. that man's spirit is simply a drop whipped out of the ocean of God's Spirit, that individuality is a mistake, and man is going to drop back again into God's Being and cease to be. The points of view are fundamentally different. Man's spirit is as immortal as God's Spirit; God can no more annihilate man's spirit than He can annihilate Himself.

Soul is the expression of spirit in the body; soul has no existence apart from spirit and body. Immediately body goes, the spirit returns to God who gave it, and soul is not. The resurrection is of body, not of spirit or soul. Spirit is the immortal, indestructible part of a man, and it goes back to God who gave it, with all the characteristics that marked it while it was on this earth. When the Bible speaks of the resurrection body of a good man, it says it is to be like Jesus Christ's glorious body (Philippians 3:21). Our Lord does not give the picture of the resurrection body of a bad man, but He does say there will be a "resurrection of damnation" (John 5:29).

The fundamental basis of the life of man was the life of God and communion with God, and until he fell Adam's spirit and soul and body were in absolute harmony with God. What do we mean by the Fall? God intended man to progress from innocence to holiness by a series of deliberate moral choices in which he was to sacrifice the life of nature to the will of God. Adam refused to do this, and that constitutes the Fall. When Adam fell the Spirit of God was withdrawn instantly, not after a time. The real seat of death is in man's spirit, the dissolution of the body is a mere incident; the point God's Book emphasises is the instant withdrawal of life, the withdrawal of the Spirit which held man's spirit, soul and body in living communion with God. "Wherefore, as by one man sin entered into the world, and death by sin; and so death passed upon all men, for all have sinned" (Romans 5:12).

Up to the time of the Fall man drew all his sustenance from God; when he fell, he lost that harmony completely; and the danger now is that although man's spirit is as immortal as God, it receives no sustenance from God. The first thing that happened was that man became his own god, exactly what the devil said would happen. Read Genesis 3, and you will find the devil insinuates—"God knows that if you eat of the fruit of the tree, and take the rule of yourself into your own hands, you will become as He is," and verse 22 is the confirmation from God's standpoint that man has become as He is. "Behold, the man is become as one of Us, to know good and evil." Man obliterated God from the throne and claimed that he was god. That is the essential principle of sin—"my claim to my right to myself." Insubordination is the characteristic of the fallen spirit of man, he will not sacrifice the natural life for the spiritual.

Personality, which in the Bible is synonymous with spirit, reveals itself in bodily life more or less clearly. The Spirit of God alone knows the full limit of our personality; therefore the Psalmist's attitude is the right one— "Search me, O God"; I am too deep to understand myself. Unless I have received the Holy Spirit my personality is dead to all God has to say, I have no affinity with anything God wants, I am my own god; but through the Atonement I can receive the Holy Spirit who imparts to me the life of Jesus and I am lifted into the domain where He is, and by obedience I can be led to the place of identification with His death.

Soul in fallen man is the expression of his personality, either in morality or in immorality. When Jesus Christ judges men He judges them according to the spirit, not according to soul, i.e., the fleshly presentation of their personality. He saw what we do not see, viz. the spirit behind. The spirit of fallen man has not the life of God in it, it has no power within it to discern God (cf. 1 Corinthians 2:10–14). The meaning of the Atonement is that man's spirit can be restored into harmony with God. It is not human nature that needs altering, it is man's spirit that needs to be brought back into right relationship with God, and before that can be done the disposition of sin has to be dealt with.

The gift of God to every fallen son of Adam is the gift of the Holy Spirit, that is, the essential power and nature of God coming into a man and lifting him to a totally new kingdom; and that power can be had for the asking—"If ye then, being evil, know how to give good gifts unto your children: how much more shall your heavenly Father give the Holy Spirit *to them that ask Him?*" (Luke 11:13). Yet is it not strange that men should go through seas of trouble before they get to the length of asking? If a man says, "I have this power in myself, all that is necessary is to develop it," then he will never be in agreement with Jesus Christ. Jesus says, "Ye have not [this] life in yourselves (RV)—the Fall obliterated it entirely; the gift of life was withdrawn, and "death reigned." Death is not annihilation: we exist in a kingdom of death (cf. Ephesians 2:1). In the Bible the term "life" is used only of the life of God; death is all that is not God. Man lives—to use a seeming contradiction of terms—in the kingdom of death, and only when he is born from above by the Holy Ghost does he enter into the kingdom of Life (see John 3:3). When man is right with God he is filled with God's Spirit. Whenever Jesus speaks about life He is referring to the life which is in Himself, and it is this life which He imparts by means of His death.

2. The Original Position of Jesus Christ

And now, O Father, glorify Thou Me with Thine own self with the glory which I had with Thee before the world was. (John 17:5)

In these words the essence of the personality of Jesus is made known, it is identified as being exactly the same as Almighty God's. The snare of the modern tendency is in saying that we can know all about Jesus Christ if we will simply examine ourselves; Jesus says we cannot. *"No man knoweth the Son, but the Father ..."* Jesus Christ makes the distinction perfectly clear between His personality and our human personality. Jesus Christ had a two-fold personality: He was Son of God revealing what God is like, and Son of Man revealing what man is to be like. When our Lord talks about His own personality He identifies Himself with God Almighty—"I and My Father are one." For any man to say that would be blasphemy, we are not one with Almighty God; through the Atonement we become one with Jesus Christ, and He brings us into union with God, " . . . that they may be one, even as We are one." That is the meaning of the At-one-ment.

"Who, being [originally] in the form of God, . . . emptied Himself, . . . being made in the likeness of men" (RV). Our Lord might have taken on Him the form of an angel (see Hebrews 2:10), but He could not take the form of anything lower than man, because man is the last reach of creation in the image of God. Angels belong to a different realm; man was made in the likeness of God (see Genesis 1:26). In the Incarnation Jesus Christ came down to the lowest rung possible, He came on to the plane where

Adam was originally, and He lived on that plane in order to show what God's normal man was like. And then He did what no man could ever do—He made the way for man to get back to the position he had lost. By the sheer might of the Atonement we can be reinstated in God's favour—that is the marvel. After we are identified with the death of Jesus the life of Jesus becomes the pattern for our walk in this world. Jesus Christ transformed innocence into holiness by sacrificing Himself to God; when we are rightly related to God the golden rule for our life is the sacrifice of our will to Jesus Christ. It has to be submission of the intellect all along the line, and in these mortal bodies of ours, impaired and damaged through sin though they are, we are to manifest the life of Jesus. The same body which used to be the seat of a soul which expressed the wrong disposition can make itself the seat of a soul that expresses a strong family likeness to Jesus.

The sacrifice of Jesus is the essence of renunciation, it was "a sacrifice to God for a sweetsmelling savour." The death of Jesus was not a satisfaction paid to the justice of God—a hideous statement which the Bible nowhere makes. The death of Jesus was an exact revelation of the justice of God. When we read of the sacrifice of Jesus Christ, it is the sacrifice of God also. ". . . God was in Christ, reconciling the world unto Himself." When Jesus Christ lifts the veil from His own consciousness He makes it clear that His death was not the death of a martyr. "I lay it [My life] down of MyselfI have power to lay it down, and I have power to take it again." Our Lord laid down His life for one purpose, the express purpose in the mind of God; He is "the Lamb of God, which taketh away the sin of the world"; "the Lamb that hath been slain from the foundation of the world" (RV).

There is nothing obscure about these revelations, but they are so deep that only the Holy Ghost can reveal them. Where are we with regard to understanding these mysteries of our faith? Along with the craving to be right with God, there is also a deep resentment, born of our laziness, that we should be expected to understand these things, and the urgency all through the New Testament is that we should stir up our minds to search out these things, and build ourselves up on our most holy faith. We are called upon not only to be right in heart, but to be right in thinking.

Called of God

Extracts from
My Utmost for His Highest
on the Missionary Call

Oswald Chambers

INTRODUCTION

Source
These readings were selected from *My Utmost for His Highest*, © 1927.

Publication History
Compiled and published as a book in 1936.

Oswald and Biddy Chambers both had great hearts for missions. This can be seen in their life together and in Oswald's emphasis at the Bible Training College[1] in London, 1911–1915. Oswald firmly believed that a missionary must be called by God—but he saw it first as a call to "be" and second as a call to "do."

Mrs. Chambers arranged and published these selections from *My Utmost* as a topical collection on the call of God. Her reasoning is explained in the foreword.

Throughout her years of publishing her husband's spoken words, Mrs. Chambers was constantly making the material available in different formats to make it more accessible to people with a variety of interests.

In this volume, the editors have included the date of each selection in *My Utmost*. These dates were not present in the book first published by Mrs. Chambers.

---

1. Residential school near Clapham Common in SW London, sponsored by the League of Prayer. Oswald Chambers was Principal and main teacher; Biddy Chambers was Lady Superintendent. Known as the BTC, it closed in July 1915 because of World War I.

CONTENTS

FOREWORD TO THE FIRST EDITION (1936)

Called of God is selected from *My Utmost for His Highest,* by Oswald Chambers, and is made up of those portions which bear very largely upon the Missionary Call. There are many who desire to have them in this separate form, both for personal use, and use in Study Circles when that theme is being considered.

The whole subject is dealt with in fuller form in *So Send I You.* Those in charge of Young People's Classes will be glad to have these vital messages in this form for circulation among the members in preparation for corporate study.

CALLED OF GOD

Whom shall I send, and who will go for us? Then said I, Here am I; send me. Isaiah 6:8

God did not address the call to Isaiah; Isaiah overheard God saying—"Who will go for us?" The call of God is not for the special few, it is for everyone. Whether or not I hear God's call depends upon the state of my ears; and what I hear depends upon my disposition. "Many are called but few are chosen," that is, few prove themselves the chosen ones. The chosen ones are those who have come into a relationship with God through Jesus Christ whereby their disposition has been altered and their ears unstopped, and they hear the still small voice questioning all the time—"Who will go for us?" It is not a question of God singling out a man and saying, "Now, *you* go." God did not lay a strong compulsion on Isaiah; Isaiah was in the presence of God and he overheard the call, and realised that there was nothing else for him but to say, in conscious freedom—"Here am I; send me."

Get out of your mind the idea of expecting God to come with compulsions and pleadings. When Our Lord called His disciples there was no irresistible compulsion from outside. The quiet, passionate insistence of His "Follow Me" was spoken to men with every power wide awake. If we let the Spirit of God bring us face to face with God, we too will hear something akin to what Isaiah heard, the still small voice of God; and in perfect freedom will say—"Here am I; send me."

THE VOICE OF THE NATURE OF GOD

I heard the voice of the Lord, saying, Whom shall I send? Isaiah 6:8

When we speak of the call of God, we are apt to forget the most important feature, viz., the nature of the One Who calls. There is the call of the sea, the call of the mountains, the call of the great ice barriers; but these calls are only heard by the few. The call is the expression of the nature from which it comes, and we can only record the call if the same nature is in us. The call of God is the expression of God's nature, not of our nature. There are strands of the call of God providentially at work for us which we recognise and no one else does. It is the threading of God's voice to us in some particular matter, and it is no use consulting anyone else about it. We have to keep that profound relationship between our souls and God.

The call of God is not the echo of my nature; my affinities and personal temperament are not considered. As long as I consider my personal temperament and think about what I am fitted for, I shall never hear the call of God. But when I am brought into relationship with God, I am in the condition Isaiah was in. Isaiah's soul was so attuned to God by the tremendous crisis he had gone through that he recorded the call of God to his amazed soul. The majority of us have no ear for anything but ourselves, we cannot hear a thing God says. To be brought into the zone of the call of God is to be profoundly altered.

THE VOCATION OF THE NATURAL LIFE

But when it pleased God . . . to reveal His Son in me. . . . Galatians 1:15–16

The call of God is not a call to any particular service; my interpretation of it may be, because contact with the nature of God has made me realise what I would like to do for Him. The call of God is essentially expressive of His nature; service is the outcome of what is fitted to my nature. The vocation of the natural life is stated by the Apostle Paul—"When it pleased God to reveal His Son in me, that I might *preach* Him" (i.e., *sacramentally express* Him) "among the Gentiles" (RV).

Service is the overflow of superabounding devotion; but, profoundly speaking, there is no *call* to that, it is my own little actual bit, and is the echo of my identification with the nature of God. Service is the natural part of my life. God gets me into a relationship with Himself whereby I understand His call, then I do things out of sheer love for Him on my own account. To serve God is the deliberate love-gift of a nature that has heard the call of God. Service is expressive of that which is fitted to my nature: God's call is expressive of His nature; consequently when I receive His nature and hear His call, the voice of the Divine nature sounds in both and the two work together. The Son of God reveals Himself in me, and I serve Him in the ordinary ways of life out of devotion to Him.

DO YOU SEE YOUR CALLING?

Separated unto the Gospel. Romans 1:1

Our calling is not primarily to be holy men and women, but to be proclaimers of the Gospel of God. The one thing that is all important is that the Gospel of God should be realised as the abiding Reality. Reality is not human goodness, nor holiness, nor heaven, nor hell, but Redemption; and the need to perceive this is the most vital need of the Christian worker today. As workers we have to get used to the revelation that Redemption is the only Reality. Personal holiness is an effect, not a cause, and if we place our faith in human goodness, in the effect of Redemption, we shall go under when the test comes.

Paul did not say he separated himself, but—"when it pleased God who separated me. . . ." Paul had not a hypersensitive interest in his own character. As long as our eyes are upon our own personal whiteness we shall never get near the reality of Redemption. Workers break down because their desire is for their own whiteness, and not for God. "Don't ask me to come into contact with the rugged reality of Redemption on behalf of the filth of human life as it is; what I want is anything God can do for me to make me more desirable in my own eyes." To talk in that way is a sign that the reality of the Gospel of God has not begun to touch me; there is no reckless abandon to God. God cannot deliver me while my interest is merely in my own character. Paul is unconscious of himself, he is recklessly abandoned, separated by God for one purpose—to proclaim the Gospel of God (cf. Romans 9:3).

THE CALL OF GOD

For Christ sent me not to baptize, but to preach the Gospel. 1 Corinthians 1:17

Paul states here that the call of God is to preach the Gospel; but remember what Paul means by "the Gospel," viz., the reality of Redemption in our Lord Jesus Christ. We are apt to make sanctification the end-all of our preaching. Paul alludes to personal experience by way of illustration, never as the end of the matter. We are nowhere commissioned to preach salvation or sanctification; we are commissioned to lift up Jesus Christ (see John 12:32). It is a travesty to say that Jesus Christ travailed in redemption to make *me* a saint. Jesus Christ travailed in Redemption to redeem the whole world, and place it unimpaired and rehabilitated before the throne of God. The fact that Redemption can be experienced by us is an illustration of the power of the reality of Redemption, but that is not the end of Redemption. If God were human, how sick to the heart and weary He would be of the constant requests we make for our salvation, for our sanctification. We tax His energies from morning till night for things for ourselves—something for *me* to be delivered from! When we touch the bedrock of the reality of the Gospel of God, we shall never bother God any further with little personal plaints.

The one passion of Paul's life was to proclaim the Gospel of God. He welcomed heart-breaks, disillusionments, tribulation, for one reason only, because these things kept him in unmoved devotion to the Gospel of God.

THE CONSTRAINT OF THE CALL

Woe is unto me, if I preach not the Gospel! 1 Corinthians 9:16

Beware of stopping your ears to the call of God. Everyone who is saved is called to testify to the fact; but that is not the call to preach, it is merely an illustration in preaching. Paul is referring to the pangs produced in him by the constraint to preach the Gospel. Never apply what Paul says in this connection to souls coming in contact with God for salvation. There is nothing easier than getting saved because it is God's sovereign work—"Come unto Me and I will save you." Our Lord never lays down the conditions of discipleship as the conditions of salvation. We are condemned to salvation through the Cross of Jesus Christ. Discipleship has an option with it—"IF any man . . ."

Paul's words have to do with being made a servant of Jesus Christ, and our permission is never asked as to what we will do or where we will go. God makes us broken bread and poured-out wine to please Himself. To be "separated unto the Gospel" means to hear the call of God; and when a man begins to overhear that call, then begins agony that is worthy of the name. Every ambition is nipped in the bud, every desire of life quenched, every outlook completely extinguished and blotted out, saving one thing only—*"separated unto the Gospel."* Woe be to the soul who tries to put his foot in any other direction when once that call has come to him. This College exists to see whether God has any man or woman here who cares about proclaiming His Gospel; to see whether God grips you. And beware of competitors when God does grip you.

THE RECOGNISED BAN OF RELATIONSHIP

We are made as the filth of the world. 1 Corinthians 4:13

These words are not an exaggeration. The reason they are not true of us who call ourselves ministers of the Gospel is not that Paul forgot the exact truth in using them, but that we have too many discreet affinities to allow ourselves to be made refuse. Filling up "that which is behind of the afflictions of Christ" is not an evidence of sanctification, but of being "separated unto the Gospel."

"Think it not strange concerning the fiery trial—which is to try you," says Peter. If we do think it strange concerning the things we meet with, it is because we are craven-hearted. We have discreet affinities that keep us out of the mire "I won't stoop; I won't bend."

You do not need to, you can be saved by the skin of your teeth if you like; you can refuse to let God count you as one separated unto the Gospel. Or you may say—"I do not care if I am treated as the offscouring of the earth as long as the Gospel is proclaimed." A servant of Jesus Christ is one who is willing to go to martyrdom for the reality of the Gospel of God. When a merely moral man or woman comes in contact with baseness and immorality and treachery, the recoil is so desperately offensive to human goodness that the heart shuts up in despair. The marvel of the Redemptive Reality of God is that the worst and the vilest can never get to the bottom of His love. Paul did not say that God separated him to show what a wonderful man He could make of him, but *"to reveal His Son in me."*

THE OVERMASTERING MAJESTY
OF PERSONAL POWER

For the love of Christ constraineth us. 2 Corinthians 5:14

Paul says he is overruled, overmastered, held as in a vice, by the love of Christ. Very few of us know what it means to be held in a grip by the love of God; we are

held by the constraint of our experience only. The one thing that held Paul, until there was nothing else on his horizon, was the love of God. "The love of Christ constraineth us"—when you hear that note in a man or woman, you can never mistake it. You know that the Spirit of God is getting unhindered way in that life.

When we are born again of the Spirit of God, the note of testimony is on what God has done for us, and rightly so. But the baptism of the Holy Ghost obliterates that for ever, and we begin to realise what Jesus meant when He said—"Ye shall be witnesses unto Me" (RV). Not witnesses to what Jesus can do—that is an elementary witness—but *"witnesses unto Me."* We will take everything that happens as happening to Him, whether it be praise or blame, persecution or commendation. No one can stand like that for Jesus Christ who is not constrained by the majesty of His personal power. It is the only thing that matters, and the strange thing is that it is the last thing realised by the Christian worker. Paul says he is gripped by the love of Christ; that is why he acts as he does. Men may call him mad or sober, but he does not care; there is only one thing he is living for, and that is to persuade men of the judgement seat of God, and of the love of Christ. This abandon to the love of Christ is the one thing that bears fruit in the life, and it will always leave the impression of the holiness and of the power of God, never of our personal holiness.

THE CONSCIOUSNESS OF THE CALL

For necessity is laid upon me; yea, woe is unto me, if I preach not the Gospel! 1 Corinthians 9:16

We are apt to forget the mystical, supernatural touch of God. If you can tell where you got the call of God and all about it, I question whether you have ever had a call. The call of God does not come like that, it is much more supernatural. The realisation of it in a man's life may come with a sudden thunder-clap or with a gradual dawning, but in whatever way it comes, it comes with the undercurrent of the supernatural, something that cannot be put into words, it is always accompanied with a glow. At any moment there may break the sudden consciousness of this incalculable, supernatural, surprising call that has taken hold of your life—"I have chosen you." The call of God has nothing to do with salvation and sanctification. It is not because you are sanctified that you are therefore called to preach the Gospel; the call to preach the Gospel is infinitely different. Paul describes it as a necessity laid upon him.

If you have been obliterating the great supernatural call of God in your life, take a review of your circumstances and see where God has not been first, but your ideas of service, or your temperamental abilities. Paul said—"Woe is unto me, if I preach not the Gospel!" He had realised the call of God, and there was no competitor for his strength.

If a man or woman is called of God, it does not matter how untoward circumstances are, every force that has been at work will tell for God's purpose in the end. If you agree with God's purpose He will bring not only your conscious life, but all the deeper regions of your life which you cannot get at, into harmony.

THE COMMISSION OF THE CALL

Who now rejoice in my sufferings for you, and fill up that which is behind of the afflictions of Christ in my flesh for His body's sake. Colossians 1:24

We make calls out of our own spiritual consecration, but when we get right with God He brushes all these aside, and rivets us with a pain that is terrific to one thing we never dreamed of, and for one radiant, flashing moment we see what He is after, and we say— "Here am I, send me."

This call has nothing to do with personal sanctification, but with being made broken bread and poured-out wine. God can never make us wine if we object to the fingers He uses to crush us with. If God would only use His own fingers, and make me broken bread and poured-out wine in a special way! But when He uses someone whom we dislike, or some set of circumstances to which we said we would never submit, and makes those the crushers, we object. We must never choose the scene of our own martyrdom. If ever we are going to be made into wine, we will have to be crushed; you cannot drink grapes. Grapes become wine only when they have been squeezed

I wonder what kind of finger and thumb God has been using to squeeze you, and you have been like a marble and escaped? You are not ripe yet and if God *had* squeezed you, the wine would have been remarkably bitter. To be a sacramental personality means that the elements of the natural life are presented by God as they are broken providentially in His service. We have to be adjusted to God before we can be broken

bread in His hands. Keep right with God and let Him do what He likes, and you will find that He is producing the kind of bread and wine that will benefit His other children.

SOMETHING MORE ABOUT HIS WAYS

He Comes Where He Commands Us to Leave
When Jesus had made an end of commanding His twelve disciples, He departed thence to teach and to preach in their cities. Matthew 11:1

If when God said "Go," you stayed, because you were so concerned about your people at home, you robbed them of the teaching and preaching of Jesus Christ Himself. When you obeyed and left all consequences to God, the Lord went into your city to teach; as long as you would not obey, you were in the way. Watch where you begin to debate and to put what you call duty in competition with your Lord's commands. "I know God told me to go, but then my duty was here"; that means you do not believe that Jesus means what He says.

He Teaches Where He Instructs Us Not To
Master, . . . let us make three tabernacles.

Are we playing the spiritual amateur providence in other lives? Are we so noisy in our instruction of others that God cannot get anywhere near them? We have to keep our mouths shut and our spirits alert. God wants to instruct us in regard to His Son, He wants to turn our times of prayer into mounts of transfiguration, and we will not let Him. When we are certain of the way God is going to work, He will never work in that way any more.

He Works Where He Sends Us to Wait
Tarry ye . . . until. . . .

Wait on God and He will work, but don't wait in spiritual sulks because you cannot see an inch in front of you! Are we detached enough from our own spiritual hysterics to wait on God? To wait is not to sit with folded hands, but to learn to do what we are told.

These are phases of His ways we rarely recognise.

THE BIG COMPELLING OF GOD

Behold, we go up to Jerusalem. Luke 18:31

Jerusalem stands in the life of Our Lord as the place where He reached the climax of His Father's will. "I seek not Mine own will, but the will of the Father which hath sent Me." That was the one dominating interest all through Our Lord's life, and the things He met with on the way, joy or sorrow, success or failure, never deterred Him from His purpose. "He stedfastly set His face to go to Jerusalem."

The great thing to remember is that we go up to Jerusalem to fulfil God's purpose, not our own. Naturally, our ambitions are our own; in the Christian life we have no aim of our own. There is so much said to-day about our decisions for Christ, our determination to be Christians, our decisions for this and that, but in the New Testament it is the aspect of God's

compelling that is brought out. "Ye have not chosen Me, but I have chosen you." We are not taken up into conscious agreement with God's purpose, we are taken up into God's purpose without any consciousness at all. We have no conception of what God is aiming at, and as we go on it gets more and more vague. God's aim looks like missing the mark because we are too short-sighted to see what He is aiming at. At the beginning of the Christian life we have our own ideas as to what God's purpose is—"I am meant to go here or there"; "God has called me to do this special work"; and we go and do the thing, and still the big compelling of God remains. The work we do is of no account, it is so much scaffolding compared with the big compelling of God.

"He took unto Him the twelve." He takes us all the time. There is more than we have got at as yet.

THE BRAVE COMRADESHIP OF GOD

Then He took unto Him the twelve. Luke 18:31

The bravery of God in trusting us! You say—"But He has been unwise to choose me, because there is nothing in me; I am not of any value." That is why He chose you. As long as you think there is something in you, God cannot choose you because you have ends of your own to serve; but if you have let Him bring you to the end of your self-sufficiency, then He can choose you to go with Him to Jerusalem, and that will mean the fulfilment of purposes which He does not discuss with you.

We are apt to say that because a man has natural ability, therefore he will make a good Christian. It is not a question of our equipment but of our poverty; not of what we bring with us, but of what God puts into us; not a question of natural virtues, of strength of character, knowledge, and experience—all that is of no avail in this matter. The only thing that avails is that we are taken up into the big compelling of God and made His comrades (cf. 1 Corinthians 1:26–30). The comradeship of God is made up out of men who know their poverty. He can do nothing with the man who thinks that he is of use to God. As Christians we are not out for our own cause at all, we are out for the cause of God, which can never be our cause. We do not know what God is after, but we have to maintain our relationship with Him whatever happens. We must never allow anything to injure our relationship with God; if it does get injured, we must take time and get it put right. The main thing about Christianity is not the work we do, but the relationship we maintain and the atmosphere produced by that relationship. That is all God asks us to look after, and it is the one thing that is being continually assailed.

THE BAFFLING CALL OF GOD

And all things that are written by the prophets concerning the Son of man shall be accomplished. . . . And they understood none of these things. Luke 18:31, 34

God called Jesus Christ to what seemed unmitigated disaster. Jesus Christ called His disciples to see Him put to death; He led every one of them to the place where their hearts were broken. Jesus Christ's life was an absolute failure from every standpoint but God's. But what seemed failure from man's standpoint was a tremendous triumph from God's, because God's purpose is never man's purpose.

There comes the baffling call of God in our lives also. The call of God can never be stated explicitly; it is implicit. The call of God is like the call of the sea, no one hears it but the one who has the nature of the sea in him. It cannot be stated definitely what the call of God is to, because His call is to be in comradeship with Himself for His own purpose, and the test is to believe that God knows what He is after. The things that happen do not happen by chance, they happen entirely in the decree of God. God is working out His purposes.

If we are in communion with God and recognise that He is taking us into His purposes, we shall no longer try to find out what His purposes are. As we go on in the Christian life it gets simpler because we are less inclined to say—"Now why did God allow this and that?" Behind the whole thing lies the compelling of God. "There's a divinity that shapes our ends." A Christian is one who trusts the wits and the wisdom of God, and not his own wits. If we have a purpose of our own it destroys the simplicity and the leisureliness which ought to characterise the children of God.

THE "GO" OF PREPARATION

Therefore if thou bring thy gift to the altar, and there rememberest that thy brother hath ought against thee; leave there thy gift before the altar, and go thy way; first be reconciled to thy brother, and then come and offer thy gift. Matthew 5:23–24

It is easy to imagine that we shall get to a place where we are complete and ready, but preparation is not suddenly accomplished, it is a process steadily maintained. It is dangerous to get into a settled state of experience. It is preparation *and* preparation.

The sense of sacrifice appeals readily to a young Christian. Humanly speaking, the one thing that attracts to Jesus Christ is our sense of the heroic, and the scrutiny of Our Lord's words suddenly brings this tide of enthusiasm to the test. "First be reconciled to thy brother." The "go" of preparation is to let the word of God scrutinise. The sense of heroic sacrifice is not good enough. The thing the Holy Spirit is detecting in you is the disposition that will never work in His service. No one but God can detect that disposition in you. Have you anything to hide from God? If you have, then let God search you with His light. If there is sin, *confess* it, not *admit* it. Are you willing to obey your Lord and Master, whatever the humiliation to your right to yourself may be.

Never discard a conviction. If it is important enough for the Spirit of God to have brought it to your mind, it is that thing He is detecting. You were looking for a great thing to give up. God is telling you of some tiny thing; but at the back of it there lies the central citadel of obstinacy: "I will not give up my right to myself"—the thing God intends you to give up if ever you are going to be a disciple of Jesus Christ.

THE "GO" OF RELATIONSHIP

And whosoever shall compel thee to go a mile, go with him twain. Matthew 5:41

The summing up of Our Lord's teaching is that the relationship which He demands is an impossible one unless He has done a supernatural work in us. Jesus Christ demands that there be not the slightest trace of resentment even suppressed in the heart of a disciple when he meets with tyranny and injustice. No enthusiasm will ever stand the strain that Jesus Christ will put upon His worker, only one thing will, and that is a personal relationship to Himself which has gone through the mill of His spring-cleaning until there is only one purpose left—"I am here for God to send me where He will." Every other thing may get fogged, but this relationship to Jesus Christ must never be.

The Sermon on the Mount is not an ideal, it is a statement of what will happen in me when Jesus

Christ has altered my disposition and put in a disposition like His own. Jesus Christ is the only One Who can fulfil the Sermon on the Mount.

If we are to be disciples of Jesus, we must be made disciples supernaturally; as long as we have the dead-set purpose of being disciples we may be sure we are not. *"I have chosen you."* That is the way the grace of God begins. It is a constraint we cannot get away from; we can disobey it, but we cannot generate it. The drawing is done by the supernatural grace of God, and we never can trace where His work begins. Our Lord's making of a disciple is supernatural. He does not build on any natural capacity at all. God does not ask us to do the things that are easy to us naturally; He only asks us to do the things we are perfectly fitted to do by His grace, and the cross will come along that line always.

THE "GO" OF RENUNCIATION

Lord, I will follow Thee whithersoever Thou goest. Luke 9:57

Our Lord's attitude to this man is one of severe discouragement because He knew what was in man. We would have said—"Fancy losing the opportunity of winning that man!" "Fancy bringing about him a north wind that froze him and turned him away discouraged!" Never apologise for your Lord. The words of the Lord hurt and offend until there is nothing left to hurt or offend. Jesus Christ has no tenderness whatever toward anything that is ultimately going to ruin a man in the service of God. Our Lord's answers

are based not on caprice, but on a knowledge of what is in man. If the Spirit of God brings to your mind a word of the Lord that hurts you, you may be sure that there is something He wants to hurt to death.

Verse 58. These words knock the heart out of serving Jesus Christ because it is pleasing to me. The rigour of rejection leaves nothing but my Lord, and myself, and a forlorn hope. "Let the hundredfold come or go, your lodestar must be your relationship to Me, and I have nowhere to lay My head."

Verse 59. This man did not want to disappoint Jesus, nor to hurt his father. We put sensitive loyalty to relatives in place of loyalty to Jesus Christ and Jesus has to take the last place. In a conflict of loyalty, obey Jesus Christ at all costs.

Verse 61. The one who says—"Yes, Lord, but . . ." is the one who is fiercely ready, but never goes. This man had one or two reservations. The exacting call of Jesus Christ has no margin of good-byes, because good-bye, as it is often used, is pagan, not Christian. When once the call of God comes, begin to go and never stop going.

THE "GO" OF UNCONDITIONAL IDENTIFICATION

One thing thou lackest: . . . come, take up the cross, and follow Me. Mark 10:21

The rich young ruler had the master passion to be perfect. When he saw Jesus Christ, he wanted to be like Him. Our Lord never puts personal holiness to the fore when He calls a disciple; He puts absolute annihilation of my right to myself and identification with Himself—a relationship with Himself in which there is no other relationship. Luke 14:26 has nothing to do with salvation or sanctification, but with unconditional identification with Jesus Christ. Very few of us know the absolute "go" of abandonment to Jesus

"Then Jesus beholding him loved him." The look of Jesus will mean a heart broken for ever from allegiance to any other person or thing. Has Jesus ever looked at you? The look of Jesus transforms and trans-

fixes. Where you are "soft" with God is where the Lord has looked at you. If you are hard and vindictive, insistent on your own way, certain that the other person is more likely to be in the wrong than you are, it is an indication that there are whole tracts of your nature that have never been transformed by His gaze.

"One thing thou lackest. . . ." The only "good thing" from Jesus Christ's point of view is union with Himself and nothing in between.

"Sell whatsoever thou hast. . . ." I must reduce myself until I am a mere conscious man I must fundamentally renounce possessions of all kinds, not to save my soul, (only one thing saves a man—absolute reliance upon Jesus Christ) but in order to follow Jesus. "Come, . . . and follow Me." And the road is the way He went.

THE METHOD OF MISSIONS

Go ye therefore, and teach [disciple, RV] all nations. Matthew 28:19

Jesus Christ did not say—"Go and save souls" (the salvation of souls is the supernatural work of God), but—"Go and teach," i.e., disciple, "all nations," and you cannot make disciples unless you are a disciple yourself. When the disciples came back from their first mission, they were filled with joy because the devils were subject to them, and Jesus said— "Don't rejoice in successful service; the great secret of joy is that you are rightly related to Me." The great essential of the missionary is that he remains true to the call of God, and realises that his one purpose is to disciple men and women to Jesus. There is a passion for souls that does not spring from God, but from the desire to make converts to our point of view.

The challenge to the missionary does not come on the line that people are difficult to get saved, that backsliders are difficult to reclaim, that there is a "wadge" of callous indifference; but along the line of his own personal relationship to Jesus Christ. "Believe ye that I am able to do this?" Our Lord puts that question steadily, it faces us in every individual case we meet. The one great challenge is—Do I know my risen Lord? Do I know the power of His indwelling Spirit? Am I wise enough in God's sight, and foolish enough according to the world, to bank on what Jesus Christ has said; or am I abandoning the great supernatural position, which is the only call for a missionary, viz., boundless confidence in Christ Jesus? If I take up any other method, I depart altogether from the method laid down by Our Lord—"All power is given unto Me. . . . *Go ye therefore.*"

WHAT IS A MISSIONARY?

As My Father hath sent Me, even so send I you. John 20:21

A missionary is one sent by Jesus Christ as He was sent by God. The great dominant note is not the needs of men, but the command of Jesus. The source of our inspiration in work for God is behind, not before. The tendency to-day is to put the inspiration ahead, to sweep everything in front of us and bring it all out to our conception of success. In the New Testament the inspiration is put behind us, the Lord Jesus. The ideal is to be true to Him, to carry out *His* enterprises.

Personal attachment to the Lord Jesus and His point of view is the one thing that must not be overlooked. In missionary enterprise the great danger is that God's call is effaced by the needs of the people until human sympathy absolutely overwhelms the meaning of being sent by Jesus. The needs are so enormous, the conditions so perplexing, that every power of mind falters and fails. We forget that the one great reason underneath all missionary enterprise is not first the elevation of the people, nor the education of the people, nor their needs; but first and foremost the command of Jesus Christ—"Go ye therefore, and teach all nations."

When looking back on the lives of men and women of God the tendency is to say—"What wonderfully astute wisdom they had! How perfectly they understood all God wanted!" The astute mind behind is the Mind of God, not human wisdom at all. We give credit to human wisdom when we should give credit to the Divine guidance of God through childlike people who were foolish enough to trust God's wisdom and the supernatural equipment of God.

MISSIONARY PREDESTINATIONS

And now, saith the LORD that formed me from the womb to be His servant. Isaiah 49:5

The first thing that happens after we have realised our election to God in Christ Jesus is the destruction of our prejudices and our parochial notions and our patriotisms; we are turned into servants of God's own purpose. The whole human race was created to glorify God and enjoy Him for ever. Sin has switched the human race on to another tack, but it has not altered God's purpose in the tiniest degree; and when we are born again we are brought into the realisation of God's great purpose for the human race, viz., I am created for God, He made me. This realisation of the election of God is the most joyful realisation on earth, and we have to learn to rely on the tremendous creative purpose of God. The first thing God will do with us is to "force thro' the channels of a single heart" the interests of the whole world. The love of God, the very nature of God, is introduced into us, and the nature of Almighty God is focused in John 3:16, *"God so loved the world."*

We have to maintain our soul open to the fact of God's creative purpose, and not muddle it with our own intentions. If we do, God will have to crush our intentions on one side however much it may hurt. The purpose for which the missionary is created is that he may be God's servant, one in whom God is glorified. When once we realise that through the salvation of Jesus Christ we are made perfectly fit for God, we shall understand why Jesus Christ is so ruthless in His demands. He demands absolute rectitude from His servants, because He has put into them the very nature of God.

Beware lest you forget God's purpose for your life.

THE KEY TO THE MISSIONARY

All power is given unto Me in heaven and in earth. Go ye therefore, and teach all nations. Matthew 28:18–19

The basis of missionary appeals is the authority of Jesus Christ, not the needs of the heathen. We are apt to look upon Our Lord as One Who assists us in our enterprises for God. Our Lord puts Himself as the absolute sovereign supreme Lord over His disciples. He does not say the heathen will be lost if we do not go; He simply says—"Go ye therefore, and teach all nations." Go on the revelation of My sovereignty; teach and preach out of a living experience of Me.

"Then the eleven disciples went . . . into a mountain where Jesus had appointed them" (Matthew 28:16). If I want to know the universal sovereignty of Christ, I must know Him for myself, and how to get alone with Him; I must take time to worship the Being Whose Name I bear. "Come unto Me"—that is the place to meet Jesus. Are you weary and heavy laden? How many missionaries are! We banish those marvellous words of the universal Sovereign of the world to the threshold of an aftermeeting; they are the words of Jesus to His disciples.

"Go ye therefore. . . ." "Go" simply means live. Acts 1:8 is the description of how to go. Jesus did not say—Go into Jerusalem and Judaea and Samaria, but, "Ye shall be witnesses unto Me" (RV) in all these places. He undertakes to establish the goings.

"If ye abide in Me, and My words abide in you . . . ."—that is the way to keep going in our personal lives. Where we are placed is a matter of indifference; God engineers the goings.

"None of these things move me. . . ." That is how to keep going till you're gone!

THE KEY TO THE MISSIONARY MESSAGE

And He is the propitiation for our sins: and not for ours only, but also for the sins of the whole world. 1 John 2:2

The key to the missionary message is the propitiation of Christ Jesus. Take any phase of Christ's work—the healing phase, the saving and sanctifying phase, there is nothing limitless about those. "The Lamb of God, which taketh away the sin of the world"!—that is limitless. The missionary message is the limitless significance of Jesus Christ as the propitiation for our sins, and a missionary is one who is soaked in that revelation.

The key to the missionary message is the remissionary aspect of Christ's life, not His kindness and His goodness, and His revealing of the Fatherhood of God; the great limitless significance is that He is the propitiation for our sins. The missionary message is not patriotic, it is irrespective of nations and of individuals, it is for the whole world. When the Holy Ghost comes in He does not consider my predilections, He brings me into union with the Lord Jesus.

A missionary is one who is wedded to the charter of his Lord and Master; he has not to proclaim his own point of view, but to proclaim the Lamb of God. It is easier to belong to a coterie which tells what Jesus Christ has done for me, easier to become a devotee to Divine healing, or to a special type of sanctification, or to the baptism of the Holy Ghost. Paul did not say—"Woe is unto me, if I do not preach what Christ has done for me," but—"Woe is unto me, if I preach not the Gospel!" This is the Gospel—"The Lamb of God, which taketh away the sin of the world"!

THE KEY TO MISSIONARY DEVOTION

For His name's sake they went forth. 3 John 7

Our Lord has told us how love to Him is to manifest itself. "Lovest thou Me . . . Feed My sheep"—identify yourself with My interests in other people, not, identify *Me* with *your* interests in other people. 1 Corinthians 13:4–8 gives the character of this love, it is the love *of God* expressing itself. The test of my love for Jesus is the practical one, all the rest is sentimental jargon.

Loyalty to Jesus Christ is the supernatural work of Redemption wrought in me by the Holy Ghost Who shed abroad the love of God in my heart, and that love works efficaciously through me in contact with everyone I meet. I remain loyal to His Name although every commonsense fact gives the lie to Him, and declares that He has no more power than a morning mist.

The key to missionary devotion means being attached to nothing and no one saving Our Lord Himself, not being detached from things externally. Our Lord was amazingly in and out among ordinary things; His detachment was on the inside towards God. External detachment is often an indication of a secret vital attachment to the things we keep away from externally.

The loyalty of a missionary is to keep his soul concentratedly open to the nature of the Lord Jesus Christ. The men and women Our Lord sends out on His enterprises are the ordinary human stuff, plus dominating devotion to Himself wrought by the Holy Ghost.

THE KEY TO THE MASTER'S ORDERS

Pray ye therefore the Lord of the harvest, that He will send forth labourers into His harvest. Matthew 9:38

The key to the missionary problem is in the hand of God, and that key is prayer, not work, that is, not work as the word is popularly understood to-day, because that may mean the evasion of concentration on God. The key to the missionary problem is not the key of common sense, nor the medical key, nor the key of civilisation or education or even evangelisation. The key is prayer. "Pray ye therefore the Lord of the harvest." Naturally, prayer is not practical, it is absurd; we have to realise that prayer is stupid from the ordinary commonsense point of view.

There are no nations in Jesus Christ's outlook, but *the world*. How many of us pray without respect of persons, and with respect to only one Person, Jesus Christ? He owns the harvest that is produced by distress and conviction of sin, and this is the harvest we have to pray that labourers may be thrust out to reap. We are taken up with active work while people all round are ripe to harvest, and we do not reap one of them, but waste our Lord's time in over-energised activities. Suppose the crisis comes in your father's life, in your brother's life, are you there as a labourer to reap the harvest for Jesus Christ? "Oh, but I have a special work to do." A Christian is called to be Jesus Christ's own, one who is not above his Master, one who does not dictate to Jesus Christ what he intends to do. Our Lord calls to no special work: He calls to Himself. "Pray ye therefore the Lord of the harvest," and He will engineer circumstances and thrust you out.

THE MISSIONARY'S GOAL

Behold, we go up to Jerusalem. Luke 18:31

In the natural life our ambitions alter as we develop; in the Christian life the goal is given at the beginning, the beginning and the end are the same, viz., Our Lord Himself. We start with Christ and we end with Him—until we all attain to the stature of the manhood of Christ Jesus, not to our idea of what the Christian life should be. The aim of the missionary is to do God's will, not to be useful, not to win the heathen; he *is* useful and he *does* win the heathen, but that is not his aim. His aim is to do the will of his Lord.

In Our Lord's life Jerusalem was the place where He reached the climax of His Father's will upon the Cross, and unless we go with Jesus there, we shall have no companionship with Him. Nothing ever discouraged Our Lord on His way to Jerusalem. He never hurried through certain villages where He was persecuted, or lingered in others where He was blessed. Neither gratitude nor ingratitude turned Our Lord one hair's breadth away from His purpose to go up to Jerusalem.

"The disciple is not above his Master." The same things will happen to us on our way to our Jerusalem. There will be the works of God manifested through us, people will get blessed, and one or two will show gratitude and the rest will show gross ingratitude, but nothing must deflect us from going up to our Jerusalem. "There they crucified Him." That is what happened when Our Lord reached Jerusalem, and that happening is the gateway to our salvation. The saints do not end in crucifixion: by the Lord's grace they end in glory. In the meantime our watchword is—I, too, go up to Jerusalem.

THE MISSIONARY'S MASTER

Ye call Me Master and Lord: and ye say well; for so I am. John 13:13

To have a master and to be mastered is not the same thing. To have a master means that there is one who knows me better than I know myself, one who is closer than a friend, one who fathoms the remotest abyss of my heart and satisfies it, one who has brought me into the secure sense that he has met and solved every perplexity and problem of my mind. To have a master is this and nothing less—"One is your Master, even Christ."

Our Lord never enforces obedience; He does not take means to make me do what He wants. At certain times I wish God would master me and make me do the thing, but He will not; in other moods I wish He would leave me alone, but He does not.

"Ye call me Master and Lord"—but is He? Master and Lord have little place in our vocabulary, we prefer the words Saviour, Sanctifier, Healer. The only word to describe mastership in experience is love, and we know very little about love as God reveals it. This is proved by the way we use the word *obey*. In the Bible obedience is based on the relationship of equals, that of a son with his father. Our Lord was not God's servant, He was His Son. *"Though He were a Son,* yet learned He obedience. . . ."

If our idea is that we are being mastered, it is a proof that we have no master; if that is our attitude to Jesus, we are far away from the relationship He wants. He wants us in the relationship in which He is easily Master without our conscious knowledge of it, all we know is that we are His to obey.

THE MISSIONARY WATCHING

Watch with Me. Matthew 26:38

"Watch with Me"—with no private point of view of your own at all, but watch entirely with Me. In the early stages we do not watch with Jesus, we watch for Him. We do not watch with Him through the revelation of the Bible; in the circumstances of our lives. Our Lord is trying to introduce us to identification with Himself in a particular Gethsemane, and we will not go; we say—"No, Lord, I cannot see the meaning of this, it is bitter." How can we possibly watch with Someone Who is inscrutable? How are we going to understand Jesus sufficiently to watch with Him in His Gethsemane, when we do not know even what His suffering is for? We do not know how to watch

with Him; we are only used to the idea of Jesus watching with us.

The disciples loved Jesus Christ to the limit of their natural capacity, but they did not understand what He was after. In the Garden of Gethsemane they slept for their own sorrow and at the end of three years of the closest intimacy "they all forsook Him, and fled."

"They were all filled with the Holy Ghost"—the same "they," but something wonderful has happened in between, viz., Our Lord's Death and Resurrection and Ascension, and the disciples have been invaded by the Holy Spirit. Our Lord had said— "Ye shall receive power after that the Holy Ghost is come upon you," and this meant that they learned to watch with Him all the rest of their lives.

HIS!

Thine they were, and Thou gavest them Me. John 17:6

The missionary is one in whom the Holy Ghost has wrought this realisation—"Ye are not your own." To say "I am not my own," is to have reached a great point in spiritual nobility. The true nature of the life in the actual whirl is the deliberate giving up of myself to another in sovereign preference, and that other is Jesus

Christ. The Holy Spirit expounds the nature of Jesus to me in order to make me one with my Lord, not that I might go off as a showroom exhibit. Our Lord never sent any of the disciples out on the ground of what He had done for them. It was not until after the Resurrection, when the disciples had perceived by the power of the Holy Spirit Whom He was, that Jesus said "Go."

"If any man come to Me, and hate not . . ., he cannot be My disciple," not—he cannot be good and upright, but—he cannot be one over whom Jesus writes the word "Mine." Any one of the relationships Our Lord mentions may be a competitive relationship. I may prefer to belong to my mother, or to my wife, or to myself; then, says Jesus, you cannot be My disciple. This does not mean I will not be saved, but it does mean that I cannot be "His."

Our Lord makes a disciple His own possession, He becomes responsible for him. "Ye shall be witnesses unto Me" (RV). The spirit that comes in is not that of *doing* anything for Jesus, but of being a perfect delight to Him. The secret of the missionary is—I am His, and He is carrying out His enterprises through me.

Be entirely His.

AFTER OBEDIENCE—WHAT?

And straightway He constrained His disciples to get into the ship, and to go to the other side. . . . Mark 6:45

We are apt to imagine that if Jesus Christ constrains us, and we obey Him, He will lead us to great success. We must never put our dreams of success as God's purpose for us; His purpose may be exactly the opposite. We have an idea that God is leading us to a particular end, a desired goal; He is not. The question of getting to a particular end is a mere incident. What we call the process, God calls the end.

What is my dream of God's purpose? His purpose is that I depend on Him and on His power now. If I can stay in the middle of the turmoil calm and unperplexed, that is the end of the purpose of God. God is not working towards a particular finish; His end is the process—that I see Him walking on the waves, no shore in sight, no success, no goal, just the absolute certainty that it is all right because I see Him walking on the sea. It is the process, not the end which is glorifying to God.

God's training is for now, not presently. His purpose is for this minute, not for something in the future. We have nothing to do with the afterwards of obedience; we get wrong when we think of the afterwards. What men call training and preparation, God calls the end.

God's end is to enable me to see that He can walk on the chaos of my life just now. If we have a further end in view, we do not pay sufficient attention to the immediate present; but if we realise that obedience is the end, then each moment as it comes is precious.

READINESS

God called unto him. . . . And he said, Here am I. Exodus 3:4

When God speaks, many of us are like men in a fog, we give no answer. Moses' reply revealed that he was somewhere. Readiness means a right relationship to God and a knowledge of where we are at present. We are so busy telling God where we would like to go. The man or woman who is ready for God and His work is the one who carries off the prize when the summons comes. We wait with the idea of some great opportunity, something sensational, and when it comes we are quick to cry— "Here am I." Whenever Jesus Christ is in the ascendant, we are there; but we are not ready for an obscure duty.

Readiness for God means that we are ready to do the tiniest little thing or the great big thing, it makes no difference. We have no choice in what we want to do; whatever God's programme may be we are there, ready. When any duty presents itself we hear God's voice as Our Lord heard His Father's voice, and we are ready for it with all the alertness of our love for Him. Jesus Christ expects to do with us as His Father did with Him. He can put us where He likes, in pleasant duties or in mean[2] duties, because the union is that of the Father and Himself. "That they may be one, even as We are one."

Be ready for the sudden surprise visits of God. A ready person never needs to get ready. Think of the time we waste trying to get ready when God has called! The burning bush is a symbol of everything that surrounds the ready soul, it is ablaze with the presence of God.

---

2. mean: ordinary, common, low, or ignoble, rather than cruel or spiteful

VISION

I was not disobedient unto the heavenly vision. Acts 26:19

If we lose the vision, we alone are responsible, and the way we lose the vision is by spiritual leakage. If we do not run our belief about God into practical issues, it is all up with the vision God has given. The only way to be obedient to the heavenly vision is to give our utmost for God's highest, and this can only be done by continually and resolutely recalling the vision. The test is the sixty seconds of every minute, and the sixty minutes of every hour, not our times of prayer and devotional meetings.

"Though it tarry, wait for it." We cannot attain to a vision, we must live in the inspiration of it until it accomplishes itself. We get so practical that we forget the vision. At the beginning we saw the vision but did not wait for it; we rushed off into practical work, and when the vision was fulfilled, we did not see it. Waiting for the vision that tarries is the test of our loyalty to God. It is at the peril of our soul's welfare that we get caught up in practical work and miss the fulfilment of the vision.

Watch God's cyclones. The only way God sows His saints is by His whirlwind. Are you going to prove an empty pod? It will depend on whether or not you are actually living in the light of what you have seen. Let God fling you out, and do not go until He does. If you select your own spot, you will prove an empty pod. If God sows you, you will bring forth fruit.

It is essential to practise the walk of the feet in the light of the vision.

THE VISION AND THE VERITY

Called to be saints. 1 Corinthians 1:2

Thank God for the sight of all you have never yet been. You have had the vision, but you are not there yet by any means. It is when we are in the valley, where we prove whether we will be the choice ones, that most of us turn back. We are not quite prepared for the blows which must come if we are going to be turned into the shape of the vision. We have seen what we are not, and what God wants us to be, but are we willing to have the vision "batter'd to shape and use" by God? The batterings always come in commonplace ways and through commonplace people.

There are times when we do know what God's purpose is; whether we will let the vision be turned into actual character depends upon us, not upon God.

If we prefer to loll on the mount and live in the memory of the vision, we will be of no use actually in the ordinary stuff of which human life is made up. We have to learn to live in reliance on what we saw in the vision, not in ecstasies and conscious contemplation of God, but to live in actualities in the light of the vision until we get to the veritable reality. Every bit of our training is in that direction. Learn to thank God for making known His demands.

The little "I am" always sulks when God says *do*. Let the little "I am" be shrivelled up in God's indignation—"I Am That I Am" hath sent thee. He must dominate. Is it not penetrating to realise that God knows where we live, and the kennels we crawl into! He will hunt us up like a lightning flash. No human being knows human beings as God does.

VISION AND REALITY

And the parched ground shall become a pool. Isaiah 35:7

We always have visions before a thing is made real. When we realise that although the vision is real, it is not real in us, then is the time that Satan comes in with his temptations, and we are apt to say it is no use to go on. Instead of the vision becoming real, there has come the valley of humiliation.

> *Life is not as idle ore,*
> *But iron dug from central gloom,*
> *And battered by the shocks of doom*
> *To shape and use.*

God gives us the vision, then He takes us down to the valley to batter us into the shape of the vision, and it is in the valley that so many of us faint and give way. Every vision will be made real if we will have patience. Think of the enormous leisure of God! He is never in a hurry. We are always in such a frantic hurry. In the light of the glory of the vision we go forth to do things, but the vision is not real in us yet; and God has to take us into the valley, and put us through fires and floods to batter us into shape, until we get to the place where He can trust us with the veritable reality. Ever since we had the vision God has been at work, getting us into the shape of the ideal, and over and over again we escape from His hand and try to batter ourselves into our own shape.

The vision is not a castle in the air but a vision of what God wants you to be. Let Him put you on His wheel and whirl you as He likes, and as sure as God is God and you are you, you will turn out exactly in accordance with the vision. Don't lose heart in the process. If you have ever had the vision of God, you may try as you like to be satisfied on a lower level, but God will never let you.

THE PASSION OF PATIENCE

Though it tarry, wait for it. Habakkuk 2:3

Patience is not indifference; patience conveys the idea of an immensely strong rock withstanding all onslaughts. The vision of God is the source of patience, because it imparts a moral inspiration. Moses endured, not because he had an ideal of right and duty, but because he had a vision of God. He "endured, as seeing Him Who is invisible." A man with the vision of God is not devoted to a cause or to any particular issue; he is devoted to God Himself. You always know when the vision is of God because of the inspiration that comes with it; things come with largeness and tonic to the life because everything is energised by God. If God gives you a time spiritually, as He gave His Son actually, of temptation in the wilderness, with no word from Himself at all, endure; and the power to endure is there because you see God.

"Though it tarry, wait for it." The proof that we have the vision is that we are reaching out for more than we have grasped. It is a bad thing to be satisfied spiritually. "What shall I render unto the LORD?" said the Psalmist. "I will *take* the cup of salvation." We are apt to look for satisfaction in ourselves—"Now I have got the thing; now I am entirely sanctified; now I can endure." Instantly we are on the road to ruin. Our reach must exceed our grasp. "Not as though I had already attained, either were already perfect." If we have only what we have experienced, we have nothing; if we have the inspiration of the vision of God, we have more than we can experience. Beware of the danger of relaxation spiritually.

COULD THIS BE TRUE OF ME?

But none of these things move me, neither count I my life dear unto myself. Acts 20:24

It as easier to serve God without a vision, easier to work for God without a call, because then you are not bothered by what God requires; common sense is your guide, veneered over with Christian sentiment. You will be more prosperous and successful, more leisure-hearted, if you never realise the call of God. But if once you receive a commission from Jesus Christ, the memory of what God wants will always come like a goad; you will no longer be able to work for Him on the commonsense basis.

What do I really count dear? If I have not been gripped by Jesus Christ, I will count service dear, time given to God dear, my life dear unto myself. Paul says he counted his life dear only in order that he might fulfil the ministry he had received; he refused to use his energy for any other thing. Acts 20:24 states Paul's almost sublime annoyance at being asked to consider himself; he was absolutely indifferent to any consideration other than that of fulfilling the ministry he had received. Practical work may be a competitor against abandonment to God, because practical work is based on this argument—"Remember how useful you are here," or—"Think how much value you would be in that particular type of work." That attitude does not put Jesus Christ as the Guide as to where we should go, but our judgement as to where we are of most use. Never consider whether you are of use; but ever consider that you are not your own but His.

IS HE REALLY LORD?

. . . so that I might finish my course with joy, and the ministry, which I have received of the Lord Jesus. Acts 20:24

Joy means the perfect fulfilment of that for which I was created and regenerated, not the successful doing of a thing. The joy Our Lord had lay in doing what the Father sent him to do, and He says—"As My Father hath sent Me, even so am I sending you." Have I received a ministry from the Lord? If so, I have to be loyal to it, to count my life precious only for the fulfilling of that ministry. Think of the satisfaction it will be to hear Jesus say—"Well done, good and faithful servant"; to know that you have done what He sent you to do. We have all to find our niche in life and spiritually we find it when we receive our ministry from the Lord. In order to do this we must have companied with Jesus; we must know Him as more than a personal Saviour. "I will shew him how great things he must suffer *for My name's sake.*"

"Lovest thou Me?" Then—"Feed My sheep." There is no choice of service, only absolute loyalty to Our Lord's commission; loyalty to what you discern when you are in closest contact with God. If you have received a ministry from the Lord Jesus, you will know that the need is never the call: the need is the opportunity. The call is loyalty to the ministry you received when you were in real touch with Him. This does not imply that there is a campaign of service marked out for you, but it does mean that you will have to ignore the demands for service along other lines.

FELLOWSHIP IN THE GOSPEL

Fellow-labourer in the Gospel of Christ. 1 Thessalonians 3:2

After sanctification it is difficult to state what your aim in life is, because God has taken you up into His purpose by the Holy Ghost. He is using you now for His purposes throughout the world as He used His Son for the purpose of our salvation. If you seek great things for yourself—"God has called me for this and that," you are putting a barrier to God's use of you. As long as you have a personal interest in your own character, or any set ambition you cannot get through into identification with God's interests. You can only get there by losing for ever any idea of yourself and by letting God take you right out into His purpose for the world and because your goings are of the Lord, you can never understand your ways.

I have to learn that the aim in life is God's, not mine. God is using me from His great personal standpoint, and all He asks of me is that I trust Him, and never say—"Lord, this gives me such heart-ache." To talk in that way makes me a clog. When I stop telling God what I want, He can catch me up for what He wants without let or hindrance.[3] He can crumple me up or exalt me, He can do anything He chooses. He simply asks me to have implicit faith in Himself and in His goodness. Self-pity is of the devil; if I go off on that line I cannot be used by God for His purpose in the world. I have "a world within the world" in which I live, and God will never be able to get me outside it because I am afraid of being frost-bitten.

---

3. without let or hindrance: legal phrase meaning "without obstacle or impediment."

WHAT IS THAT TO THEE?

Lord, what shall this man do? . . . What is that to thee? Follow thou Me. John 21:21–22

One of our severest lessons comes from the stubborn refusal to see that we must not interfere in other people's lives. It takes a long time to realise the danger of being an amateur providence, that is, interfering with God's order for others. You see a certain person suffering, and you say—"He shall not suffer, and I will see that he does not." You put your hand straight in front of God's permissive will to prevent it, and God says—"What is that to thee?" If there is stagnation spiritually, never allow it to go on, but get into God's presence and find out the reason for it. Possibly you will find it is because you have been interfering in the life of another; proposing things you had no right to propose; advising when you had no right to advise.

When you do have to give advice to another, God will advise through you with the *direct* understanding of His Spirit; your part is to be so rightly related to God that His discernment comes through you all the time for the blessing of another soul.

Most of us live on the borders of consciousness—consciously serving, consciously devoted to God. All this is immature, it is not the real life yet. The mature stage is the life of a child which is never conscious; we become so abandoned to God that the consciousness of being used never enters in. When we are consciously being used as broken bread and poured-out wine, there is another stage to be reached, where all consciousness of ourselves and of what God is doing through us is eliminated. A saint is never consciously a saint; a saint is consciously dependent on God.

SACRAMENTAL SERVICE

Who now rejoice in my sufferings for you, and fill up that which is behind of the afflictions of Christ. Colossians 1:24

The Christian worker has to be a sacramental "go-between," to be so identified with his Lord and the reality of His Redemption that He can continually bring His creating life through him. It is not the strength of one man's personality being superimposed on another, but the real presence of Christ coming through the elements of the worker's life. When we preach the historic facts of the life and death of Our Lord as they are conveyed in the New Testament, our words are made sacramental; God uses them on the ground of His Redemption to create in those who listen that which is not created otherwise. If we preach the effects of Redemption in human life instead of the

revelation regarding Jesus, the result in those who listen is not new birth, but refined spiritual culture, and the Spirit of God cannot witness to it because such preaching is in another domain. We have to see that we are in such living sympathy with God that as we proclaim His truth He can create in souls the things which He alone can do.

"What a wonderful personality!" "What a fascinating man!" "Such marvellous insight!" What chance has the Gospel of God through all that? It cannot get through, because the line of attraction is always the line of appeal. If a man attracts by his personality, his appeal is along that line; if he is identified with his Lord's personality then the appeal is along the line of what Jesus Christ can do. The danger is to glory in men; Jesus says we are to lift *Him* up.

DESERTER OR DISCIPLE?

From that time many of His disciples went back, and walked no more with Him. John 6:66

When God gives a vision by His Spirit through His word of what He wants, and your mind and soul thrill to it, if you do not walk in the light of that vision, you will sink into servitude to a point of view which Our Lord never had. Disobedience in mind to the heavenly vision will make you a slave to points of view that are alien to Jesus Christ. Do not look at someone else and say—"Well, if he can have those views and prosper, why cannot I?" You have to walk in the light of the vision that has been given to you and not compare yourself with others or judge them, that is between them and God. When you find that a point of view in which you have been delighting clashes with the heavenly vision and you debate, certain things will begin to develop in you—a sense of property and a sense of personal right, things of which Jesus Christ made nothing. He was always against these things as being the root of everything alien to Himself. "A man's life consisteth not in the abundance of the things which he possesseth." If we do not recognise this, it is because we are ignoring the undercurrent of Our Lord's teaching.

We are apt to lie back and bask in the memory of the wonderful experience we have had. If there is one standard in the New Testament revealed by the light of God and you do not come up to it, and do not feel inclined to come up to it, that is the beginning of backsliding, because it means your conscience does not answer to the truth. You can never be the same after the unveiling of a truth. That moment marks you for going on as a more true disciple of Jesus Christ, or for going back as a deserter.

YE ARE NOT YOUR OWN

Know ye not that . . . ye are not your own? 1 Corinthians 6:19

There is no such thing as a private life—"a world within the world"—for a man or woman who is brought into fellowship with Jesus Christ's sufferings. God breaks up the private life of His saints, and makes it a thoroughfare for the world on the one hand and for Himself on the other. No human being can stand that unless he is identified with Jesus Christ. We are not sanctified for ourselves, we are called into the fellowship of the Gospel, and things happen which have nothing to do with us, God is getting us into fellowship with Himself. Let Him have His way, if you do not, instead of being of the slightest use to God in His Redemptive work in the world, you will be a hindrance and a clog.

The first thing God does with us is to get us based on rugged Reality until we do not care what becomes of us individually as long as He gets His way for the purpose of His Redemption. Why shouldn't we go through heartbreaks? Through these doorways God is opening up ways of fellowship with His Son. Most of us fall and collapse at the first grip of pain; we sit down on the threshold of God's purpose and die away of self-pity, and all so-called Christian sympathy will aid us to our death-bed. But God will not. He comes with the grip of the pierced hand of His Son, and says—"Enter into fellowship with Me; arise and shine." If through a broken heart God can bring His purposes to pass in the world, then thank Him for breaking your heart.

A BOND-SLAVE OF JESUS

I am crucified with Christ; nevertheless I live: yet not I, but Christ liveth in me. Galatians 2:20

These words mean the breaking of my independence with my own hand and surrendering to the supremacy of the Lord Jesus. No one can do this for me, I must do it myself. God may bring me up to the point three hundred and sixty-five times a year, but He cannot put me through it. It means breaking the husk of my individual independence of God, and the emancipation of my personality into oneness with Himself, not for my own ideas, but for absolute loyalty to Jesus.

There is no possibility of dispute when once I am there. Very few of us know anything about loyalty to Christ—*"For My sake."* It is that which makes the iron saint.

Has that break come? All the rest is pious fraud. The one point to decide is—Will I give up, will I surrender to Jesus Christ, and make no conditions whatever as to how the break comes? I must be broken from my self-realisation, and immediately that point is reached, the reality of the supernatural identification takes place at once, and the witness of the Spirit of God is unmistakable "I have been crucified with Christ" (RV).

The passion of Christianity is that I deliberately sign away my own rights and become a bond-slave of Jesus Christ. Until I do that, I do not begin to be a saint.

One student a year who hears God's call would be sufficient for God to have called this College into existence. This College as an organisation is not worth anything, it is not academic; it is for nothing else but for God to help Himself to lives. Is He going to help Himself to us, or are we taken up with our conception of what we are going to be?

WHERE THE BATTLE'S LOST AND WON

If thou wilt return, O Israel, saith the LORD. . . . Jeremiah 4:1

The battle is lost or won in the secret places of the will before God, never first in the external world. The Spirit of God apprehends me and I am obliged to get alone with God and fight the battle out before Him. Until this is done, I lose every time. The battle may take one minute or a year, that will depend on me, not on God; but it must be wrestled out alone before God, and I must resolutely go through the hell of a renunciation before Him. Nothing has any power over the man who has fought out the battle before God and won there.

If I say—"I will wait till I get into the circumstances and then put God to the test," I shall find I cannot. I must get the thing settled between myself and God in the secret places of my soul where no stranger intermeddles, and then I can go forth with the certainty that the battle is won. Lose it there, and calamity and disaster and upset are as sure as God's decree. The reason the battle is not won is because I try to win it in the external world first. Get alone with God, fight it out before Him, settle the matter there once and for all.

In dealing with other people, the line to take is to push them to an issue of will. That is the way abandonment begins. Every now and again, not often, but sometimes, God brings us to a point of climax. That is the Great Divide in the life; from that point we either go towards a more and more dilatory and useless type of Christian life, or we become more and more ablaze for the glory of God—"My Utmost for His Highest."

Christian Disciplines

Volume 1
The Discipline of Divine Guidance
The Discipline of Suffering
The Discipline of Peril

Oswald Chambers

INTRODUCTION

Source
Talks and lectures given in Great Britain and the United States from 1907 to 1915.

Publication History
The six "Disciplines" were published individually as articles and booklets before being issued as a two-volume book in 1965.

The Discipline of Divine Guidance: OC's messages on divine guidance, published in *God's Revivalist* magazine, March/April 1909, and February 1911, were most likely given at summer camp meetings in Cincinnati. They were also published as a pamphlet by God's Revivalist Press.

The Discipline of Suffering: This material was delivered as a sermon at God's Bible School, Cincinnati, Ohio, during early 1907. It was published as two articles in *God's Revivalist* magazine (May 1907) and later that same year as a pamphlet by God's Revivalist Press.

The Discipline of Peril: The first of these messages was given in the autumn of 1914, immediately following Britain's entry into World War I. Chambers was forty years old with a wife and a one-year-old daughter. As the country mobilized for all-out war, men were joining the army at the rate of thirty thousand a day, people were asked to sell their automobiles and farm horses to the government, and lists of the dead and wounded began appearing in daily newspapers. Uncertainty was the order of the day. Chambers was addressing fearful people facing a very real threat of personal and national peril. The messages in "The Discipline of Peril" appeared as articles in *Tongues of Fire* magazine, September 1914–May 1915 and were published by OC as a booklet in 1915. The message "The Day of the Lord" is very specifically related to Britain during the days of war and probably for that reason was not included in the 1965 book *Christian Disciplines*. The editors have chosen to include it in this collection:

"The Discipline of Peril," *Tongues of Fire*, September 1914

"Christian Seemliness," *Tongues of Fire*, October 1914

"Slighted Security," *Tongues of Fire*, November 1914

"Fitness," *Tongues of Fire*, December 1914

"First and Last," League of Prayer[1] New Years' Convention, Friday, January 1, 1915, in Pontefract, W. Yorkshire

"God's Parenthesis," *Tongues of Fire,* March 1915

"Are You Ever Disturbed?" is a talk given at a BTC[2] devotional meeting, May 27, 1914

"Radiant in the Thick of It" is a talk given in Hawes, Yorkshire September 12, 1915, at the Sunday evening service, Wesleyan Methodist Chapel

"The Day of the Lord," *Tongues of Fire,* May 1915

The Discipline of Prayer: This material was published by OC as a pamphlet in the summer of 1915.

The Discipline of Loneliness: These were sermons given, most likely, during the summer of 1908 at the annual camp meeting at God's Bible School, Cincinnati. The material was published as two articles in *God's Revivalist,* January 1909.

The Discipline of Patience: These were lectures given, most likely, to League of Prayer audiences during spring 1909. This material was first published in *Tongues of Fire* magazine as three articles, in July, August, and September 1909.

Christian Disciplines incorporates some of the earliest published lectures of Oswald Chambers, some dating back to 1907. In D. W. Lambert's book *Oswald Chambers: An Unbribed Soul* (1968), Lambert says of *The Discipline of Suffering, The Discipline of Loneliness,* and *The Discipline of Guidance:* "These three booklets based on talks given in America before the war, were first issued by the Cincinnati Bible School. These, unlike the later books, bear the marks of having been edited by Chambers; one feature is the prolific use of apt poetic quotations." All of the Oswald Chambers books originated with his spoken words, but most were published after Chambers died in 1917. In only a few cases did he personally edit his spoken material before it was published.

Because Chambers was primarily a teacher, it should be remembered that he gave the same lectures and sermons on many occasions in various places and always altered his presentation to address the unique character and needs of his audience. Mrs. Chambers had shorthand notes of several versions of some messages. Because she used all the notes in her possession to prepare the final copy for print, the book versions of his messages often differ from the earlier articles and pamphlets.

Just before Chambers left the Bible Training College in July 1915, a friend persuaded him to publish some of his messages in Britain. Any proceeds from their sale were designated for OC's work as a YMCA chaplain in Egypt. By the summer of 1915, *The Discipline in the Cure of Souls* (later expanded into the book *Workmen of God*) and *The Discipline of Peril* were in print. *The Discipline of Prayer* was in the press.

All of the six "Disciplines" were printed first as pamphlets, then in the 1930s were issued as individual booklets in a series. In 1965, they were combined into two books, *Christian Disciplines, Volume 1* and *Volume 2.*

Where possible, the date and place of individual messages has been added in this volume.

---

1. Pentecostal League of Prayer: founded in London in 1891 by Reader Harris (1847–1909), prominent barrister; friend and mentor of Oswald Chambers.

2. BTC: Bible Training College, residential school near Clapham Common in SW London, sponsored by the League of Prayer. Oswald Chambers was Principal and main teacher; Biddy Chambers was Lady Superintendent. Known as the BTC, it closed in July 1915 because of World War I.

CONTENTS

FOREWORD TO "THE DISCIPLINE OF PERIL"

This booklet is composed of articles by Oswald Chambers written during the Great War,[3] with two added messages that have appeared in leaflet form. In the main they stand as they were first prepared. They are full of that penetrating insight into those principles underlying our human lives which explains much that happens in the days of personal or national tragedy. The heart that knows and loves Jesus Christ will not yield to panic. But such will hear the call to keep awake and pray. "When the veil is lifted we shall find that the seemly conduct of prayer wrought the things of God in man." Our Lord foresaw days of crisis in the lives of men and nations, and bid us be ready for them. Always Jesus Christ is to be lifted up as an Atoning Saviour, and always we are called to intercessory prayer on the basis of His wonderful Redemption. We commend this vital booklet to all thoughtful people in these days of international uncertainty and strain.

David Lambert[4]
London, *October* 1938

---

3. The Great War: World War 1 (1914–1918).

4. David Lambert (1871–1961): Methodist minister and friend of Oswald Chambers. Assisted Mrs. Chambers with OC publications from 1917–1961.

THE DISCIPLINE OF DIVINE GUIDANCE

God is not a supernatural interferer; God is the everlasting portion of His people. When a man "born from above" (RV mg) begins his new life he meets God at every turn, hears Him in every sound, sleeps at His feet, and wakes to find Him there. He is a new creature in a new creation, and tribulation but develops his power of knowing God, till on some transfiguration morning, he finds himself entirely sanctified by God; and from that unspeakable bliss God loosens him from Heaven, a "pilgrim of eternity," to work a work for Him among men. Out he goes, a man any may take advantage of, but none dare. His child-like simplicity excites the ridicule of men, but a wall of fire encircles him. His ignorance of the way he takes makes the cunning of the age laugh at the ease with which they think they can utilise him for their own ends, but lo! they are caught in their own snare, and their wisdom is turned to sorrow and foolishness. Such a man becomes a spectacle to angels and to men. Nothing can daunt him, nothing affright him, nothing deflect him. He may be tried by cruel mockings and scourgings, by bonds and imprisonment; he may be stoned or sawn asunder, tempted, or slain with the sword; he may wander about in sheepskins and goatskins; he may be destitute, afflicted, tormented; he may home in deserts, and in mountains, and in dens and caves of the earth, but ever, by some mysterious mystic touch, we know he is one "of whom the world was not worthy." All Heaven and earth and hell are "persuaded, that neither death, nor life, nor angels, nor principalities, nor powers, nor things present, nor things to come, nor height, nor depth, nor any other creation, shall be able to separate us from the love of God, which is in Christ Jesus our Lord."

The child-mind is the only mind to which God can appeal, and our Lord went deeper than the profoundest philosophy in the incident recorded in Mark 9:36–37—"And He took a little child, and set him in the midst of them: and taking him in His arms, He said unto them, Whosoever shall receive one of such little children in My name, receiveth Me: and whosoever receiveth Me, receiveth not Me, but Him that sent Me" (RV). As soon as the gates of the head are closed on our experiences we limit God, and by sealing our minds we limit our growth and the possibility of graduating in Divine guidance. The child-heart is open to any and all avenues; an angel would no more surprise it than a man. In dreams, in visions, in visible and invisible ways, God can talk and reveal Himself to a child; but this profound yet simple way is lost for ever immediately we lose the open, child-like nature.

By every standard we know, saving one, the God of the Bible is a confusing contradiction to Himself. The God Who caused to be written: "Thou shalt not kill," commanded Abraham to offer "thine only son, whom thou lovest, even Isaac, . . . for a burnt offering" (Genesis 22:2 RV). The God Who said: "Thou shalt not commit adultery," commanded His servant Hosea to marry a harlot (see Hosea 1:2). Jesus Christ Himself presents a similar dilemma to every standard, saving one. He tells the seventy: "Behold, I have given you authority to tread upon serpents and scorpions, and over all the power of the enemy: and nothing shall in any wise hurt you" (Luke 10:19 RV). Again He tells His disciples: "They shall put you out of the synagogues: yea, the hour cometh, that whosoever killeth you shall think that he offereth service unto God" (John 16:2 RV). And the Apostle Paul, who said he had "the mind of Christ," wrote to the Corinthians: "why not rather take wrong? why not rather be defrauded?" (1 Corinthians 6:7 RV); and yet when being tried himself, he said, "I appeal unto Caesar" (Acts 25:11).

God Himself, our Lord Jesus Christ and the saints, are examples of contradiction judged by every standard saving one, viz., the standard of personal responsibility to God on the basis of personal character.

In testing circumstances saints decide differently—may all the different decisions be correct? Unquestionably they may, for the decisions are made on the basis of personal character in its responsibility to God. The blunder of the saint lies in saying, "Because I decide thus in this crisis, therefore that is the rule for all." Nonsense! God is Sovereign, and His ways are discernible according to the attainment of the particular character. One of the most fallacious lines of reasoning is on the line of an hypothesis in the matter of God's will. No saint knows what he will do in circumstances he has never been in. "I would have you without carefulness," says the Apostle Paul. A saint is a creature of vast possibilities, knit into shape by the ruling personality of God.

Supernatural voices, dreams, ecstasies, visions and manifestations, may or may not be an indication of the will of God. The words of Scripture, the advice of the saints, strong impressions during prayer, may or may not be an indication of the will of God. The one test given in the Bible is discernment of a personal God and a personal relationship to Him, witnessed to ever after in walk and conversation. A striking line of demarcation discernible just here between the guidance of God and all other guidance is that all other supernatural guidance loses sight of human personality and of Divine personality, and ends in a swoon into absolute nothingness. In every stage of Divine Guidance which the Bible records, these two elements become ever clearer: God and myself. The most intense statement of this is made by our Lord:

Jesus answered, The first [commandment] is, Hear, O Israel; The Lord our God, the Lord is one: and thou shalt love the Lord thy God from all thy heart, and from all thy soul, and from all thy mind, and from all thy strength. The second is this, Thou shalt love thy neighbour as thyself. There is none other commandment greater than these. (Mark 12:29–31 RV mg)

The eternal truth is that God created me to be distinctly not Himself, but to realise Him in perfect love. If I allow that God teaches me to walk in His will, I shall allow my neighbour, whom I love as myself, the same certainty, although his way may seem so different. "What is that to thee? follow thou Me."

Professor W. James[5] in "The Varieties of Religious Experience," says:

Among the visions and messages some have always been too patently silly; among the trances and convulsive seizures some have been too fruitless for conduct and character, to pass themselves off as significant, still less as divine. In the history of Christian mysticism the problem how to discriminate between such messages and experiences as were really divine miracles, and such others as the demon in his malice was able to counterfeit, thus making the religious person twofold more the child of hell than he was before, has always been a difficult one to solve, needing all the sagacity and experience of the best directors of conscience. In the end it had to come to our Imperialist Criterion. "By their fruits ye shall know them," not by their roots. Jonathan Edwards' "Treatise on Religious Affections" is an elaborate working out of this thesis. The roots of a man's virtue are inaccessible to us. No appearances whatever are infallible proofs of grace. Our practice is the only sure evidence, even to ourselves, that we are genuine Christians.

When all religions and philosophies and philologies have tried to define God, one and all sink inane and pass, while the Bible statements stand like eternal monuments, shrouded in ineffable glory: God Is Light; God Is Love; God Is Holy. Every attempted definition of God other than these sublime inspirations negates God, and we find ourselves possessed of our own ideas with never a glimpse of the living God. When the flatteries, the eulogies, the enthusiasms and the extravagances regarding Jesus Christ have become enshrined sentiments in poetry and music and eloquence, they pass, like fleeting things of mist, coloured but for a moment by reflected splendours from the Son of God, and our Lord's own words come with the sublime staying of the simple gentleness of God: "I am the way, and the truth, and the life." When art has fixed her ideals, and contemplation has cloistered her choicest souls, and devotion has traced her tremulous records, quivering with the unbearable pathos of martyrdom, we realise that all these miss the portrayal of the saint; and again the severe adequacy of Scripture, undeflected by earth's heart-breaks, or griefs, or sorrows, remains the true portraiture of the saint: Saved, and Sanctified, and Sent.

It is when silenced by some such considerations as these that we can behold the child-heart nestling in the arms of God, or playing about the path of the Lord Jesus Christ, or hasting with willing feet to souls perishing in the wilderness. It is only thus, with chastened, disciplined, stilled hearts that we whisper out before His throne, "I had heard of Thee by the hearing of the ear, but now mine eye seeth Thee, wherefore I loathe my words, and repent in dust and ashes" (Job 42:5–6 RV mg).

And Moses said unto the LORD, See, Thou sayest unto me, Bring up this people: and Thou hast not let me know whom Thou wilt send with me. Yet Thou hast said, I know thee by name, and thou hast also found grace in My sight. Now therefore, I pray thee, if I have found grace in Thy sight, shew me now Thy ways, that I may know Thee, to the end that I may find grace in Thy sight: and consider that this nation is Thy people. And He said, My presence shall go with thee, and I will give thee rest. (Exodus 33:12–14 RV)

Little lamb, who made thee?
Dost thou know who made thee,
Gave thee life, and bid thee feed
By the stream and o'er the mead,
Gave thee clothing of delight.
Softest clothing, woolly, bright,
Gave thee such a tender voice,
Making all the vale rejoice?
Little lamb, who made thee?
Dost thou know who made thee?

Little lamb, I'll tell thee:
Little lamb, I'll tell thee:
He is called by thy name,

---

5. William James (1842–1910): American philosopher, psychologist, and teacher.

For He calls Himself a Lamb,
He is meek, and He is mild,
He became a little child.
I a child, and thou a lamb,
We are called by His name.
Little lamb, God bless thee!
Little lamb, God bless thee!

First Stage. *By God's Sayings*

How often in the Bible we read such words as those in Genesis 12:1: "Now the LORD said unto Abram . . ." (RV), and in Ezekiel 1:3, "the word of the LORD came expressly unto Ezekiel . . ." and in Matthew 7:24: "Every one therefore which heareth these words of Mine, and doeth them, shall be likened unto a wise man, which built his house upon the rock . . ." (RV).

What is the word of God? Where are the sayings of God? The answer is readily given: "The Bible is the Word of God." But we must ask again, because we have all known battlers for the Bible as the Word of God whom we should hesitate to call saints, for many have proved logically what never came to pass from the Bible; consequently the answer is given more cautiously: "The Bible contains the word of God." This is a most ingenious fallacy and leads to a mystical type of religious life which by being "special," speedily becomes spurious (see 2 Peter 1:20).

The Bible is the Word of God only to those who are born from above and who walk in the light. Our Lord Jesus Christ, the *Word* of God, and the Bible, the *words* of God, stand or fall together, they can never be separated without fatal results. A man's attitude to our Lord determines his attitude to the Bible. The "sayings" of God to a man not born from above are of no moment; to him the Bible is simply a remarkable compilation of literature—"that it is, and nothing more." All the confusion arises from not recognising this. But to the soul born from above, the Bible is the universe of God's revealed will. The Word of God to me is ever according to my spiritual character; it makes clear my responsibility to God as well as my individuality apart from Him.

A quotation from an able article in the *Spectator* for April 13, 1907, entitled "The Mind of Christ" will serve well:

If we refuse to look at the Gospel as a whole and to use our reason; if we insist on making of Christ what He distinctly refused to be, a ruler and a judge, instead of the Light of the World, we may set up tyrannies as bad as, or worse than, those instituted by Roman dogmatism. There will be no new Torquemadas, but how much suffering may not be caused by a new Tolstoy. Upon isolated sentences of Jesus absolutely conflicting systems may be erected, and a measure of fanaticism is natural to man. . . .

But we may not forget that there is an indifference which plumes itself on its moderation, and is even more opposed to the mind of Christ than fanaticism.

What applies to our present dispensation is exactly the same in principle as applied to the hoary antiquity, viz., that the pure in heart see and hear God. The stupendous profundities of God's will, surging with unfathomable mysteries, come down to the shores of our common life, not in emotions and fires, nor in aspirations and vows, and agonies and visions, but in a way so simple that the wayfaring men, yea fools, cannot make a mistake, viz., in words.

It is recorded in Deuteronomy 32:46–47: "And he said unto them, Set your heart unto all the words which I testify unto you this day; which ye shall command your children, to observe to do all the words of this law. For it is no vain thing for you; because it is your life, and through this thing ye shall prolong your days upon the land, whither ye go over Jordan to possess it" (rv). And our Lord in Mark 4:14, states that "The sower soweth the word."

As soon as any soul is born from above, the Bible becomes to him the universe of revelation facts, just as the natural world is the universe of common-sense facts. These revelation facts are *words* to our faith, not *things*. The stage of Divine guidance by God's sayings is reached when a soul understands that, by the tribulations of the providential life, God's Spirit speaks an understanding of His Word never known before. For any soul to teach what he has not bought by suffering is almost sure to bring tribulation which will either destroy or lead to personal understanding of the word taught. Divine guidance by the Word indicates a profound and personal preparation of heart. God's sayings are sealed to every soul saving as they are opened by the indwelling Spirit of God. How often the individual soul has to learn by a bitter and, in some sense, an altogether uncalled for experience, that—

He placed thee mid this dance
Of plastic circumstance.
This Present, thou, forsooth, wouldst fain arrest:
Machinery just meant
To give thy soul its bent
Try thee and turn thee forth, sufficiently
impressed.

To search for a word of God to suit one's case is never Divine guidance, but guidance by human caprice and inclination. The Holy Spirit Who brings to our remembrance what Jesus has said and leads us into all truth, does so to glorify Jesus Christ. Divine guidance by the Word always makes us realise our responsibility to God. In the tribulations, God brings the Divine guidance by His Word and as we go on we begin to understand what our Lord said: "The words that I have spoken unto you are spirit, and are life" (John 6:63 RV). Every interpretation of the sayings of God that does not reveal this fundamental responsibility to God, and a realisation that we are to be for the praise of His glory, is a private interpretation, and is severely condemned by God.

> *. . . We abide*
> *Not on this earth; but for a little space*
> *We pass upon it: and while so we pass,*
> *God through the dark hath set the Light of Life,*
> *With witness for Himself, the Word of God,*
> *To be among us Man, with human heart,*
> *And human language, thus interpreting*
> *The One great Will incomprehensible,*
> *Only so far as we in human life*
> *Are able to receive it.*

How often have our misunderstandings of God's Word proved to us the need for the penetrating words of our Lord: "I have yet many things to say unto you, but ye cannot bear them now." In our prayers, in our desirings, in our patience, does our knowledge of God enable us to say and really mean, "Speak, LORD; for Thy servant heareth"? Would we really hear God's Word, or are we not rather in this immediate tribulation waiting for God to persuade us that our own way is right after all? Oh, the bliss of that disciplined child-heart, which when He speaks, says, "Yes, Lord," and simply obeys.

> *Pining souls! come nearer Jesus,*
> *   And oh come not doubting thus,*
> *But with faith that trusts more bravely*
> *   His huge tenderness for us.*
> *If our love were but more simple,*
> *   We should take Him at His word;*
> *And our lives would be all sunshine*
> *   In the sweetness of our Lord.*

The school of the Divine Guidance by God's Sayings is one of severe discipline. It will mean great heart-searchings, great patience, and great simplicity to be guided in this way.

Second Stage. *By God's Symbols*

And the LORD went before them by day in a pillar of cloud, to lead them the way; and by night in a pillar of fire, to give them light; that they might go by day and by night: the pillar of cloud by day, and the pillar of fire by night, departed not from before the people. (Exodus 13:21–22 RV)

When ye see the ark of the covenant of the LORD your God, and the priests the Levites bearing it, then ye shall remove from your place, and go after it. (Joshua 3:3)

And a man shall be as an hiding place from the wind, and a covert from the tempest; as rivers of water in a dry place, as the shadow of a great rock in a weary land. (Isaiah 32:2)

And the Holy Ghost descended in a bodily form, as a dove, upon Him, and a voice came out of heaven, Thou art My beloved Son; in Thee I am well pleased. (Luke 3:22 RV)

The cloudy pillar, the fiery pillar, the ark, the man, the dove, are all God's symbols. This way of Divine guidance by symbols is a deep and blessed one. God does not leave us to the vague, ungraspable intuitions of the mind of some great man for guidance, or to our own vain imaginings. He has made a world of things, other than ourselves, the safeguard and inspiration of our common-sense reasonings; and He has made a world of spiritual realities the safeguard and inspiration of our discernment. It is on this God-created ingredient in our nature that every great organisation, good or bad, is based. The revolt against error on one side is ever apt to enter into error on the other. The revolt, for instance, against Roman Catholicism has developed into an irresponsible individualism which is equally un-Biblical.

How often our Lord Jesus Christ emphasises the guidance by symbols—"*I am* the door"; "*I am* the bread of life"; "*I am* the true vine"; "*I am* the way." A right understanding of this Biblical conception is essential to all Christian thinking. The Bible order seems to be—the absolute Truth; the symbolic Truth; the False.

All that we see on this earth is symbolic reality, and only as our inward heart is purged from sin can we see the symbolism. That is why when a man is in Christ Jesus he is a new creation, and he sees everything in the common world as symbols—unseeable realities. (Remember, there are symbols of the devil and of the kingdom of evil just as there are symbols of God and of the kingdom of heaven). How simply and clearly our Lord teaches this: "If thine eye be evil, thy whole body shall be full of darkness. If therefore the light that is in thee be darkness, how great is that darkness!" And vice versa: "If therefore thine eye be single, thy whole body shall be full of light." When Jesus heard His Father speak, ("the multitude therefore, that stood by, and heard it, said that it had thundered" RV). Again, when Saul of Tarsus was met by Jesus on the way to Damascus and heard His voice, the men that journeyed with him saw only sudden lightning and physical collapse.

> *Earth's crammed with heaven,*
> *And every common bush afire with God;*
> *But only he who sees, takes off his shoes;*
> *The rest sit round it and pluck blackberries,*

And daub their natural faces unaware
More and more from the first similitude!

One is made to turn with weary exhaustion from the unthinking, hand to mouth experience of much of the religious literature of the day. To *think* as a Christian is a rare accomplishment, especially as the curious leaven which puts a premium on ignorance works its sluggish way. To speak of Plato to the majority of Christian preachers, particularly holiness preachers, would be to meet not a consciousness of ignorance, but a blatant pride which boasts of knowing nothing outside the Bible, which, in all probability, means knowing nothing inside it either. Christian thinking is a rare and difficult thing; so many seem unaware that the first great commandment according to our Lord is, "Thou shalt love the Lord thy God . . . from all thy mind. . . ." (RV mg).

No mind, other than the Mind of our Lord, has so profoundly expounded this line of Guidance by Symbols as Plato. He saw with a clearness of vision second only to the inspired prophets of God. No wonder many in the early thoughtful days of Christianity wanted to class him as a Father of the Church. It is impossible for men to be guided by absolute Truth. God, Who is Absolute Truth, said to Moses: "Thou canst not see My face: for man shall not see Me and live" (Exodus 33:20 RV). God guides us stage by stage, and the most marvellous stage of His guidance is by symbols.

What are we to understand by a symbol? A symbol represents a spiritual truth by means of images or properties of natural things. A symbol must not be taken as an allegory, an allegory is simply a figurative discourse with a meaning other than that contained in literal words. A symbol is sealed until the right spirit is given for its understanding, and God's symbols are undetected unless His Spirit is in His child to enable him to understand. What did the cloudy pillar by day or the fiery pillar by night signify to the hordes in the desert? Nothing more than the mystery of ever-varying cloud forms. To the children of God, they meant the manifested guidance of God. How a man interprets God's symbols reveals what manner of man he is. How often we have to say with the Psalmist, "I was as a beast before Thee," i.e., without understanding. How often the ass recognises that one of God's angels is speaking before the so-called prophet on its back detects it.

All that meets the bodily sense I deem
Symbolical—one mighty Alphabet

For infant minds! And we in this low world
Placed with our backs to bright Reality
That we may learn with young, unwounded ken
The Substance from the Shadow!

God shifts His symbols and we know not why; but God is ever only good, and the shifting of one symbol means surely that another symbol is to guide us to a nearer grasp of Himself. When God, so to speak, has left a symbol, it becomes transparent, and has no further binding force. How sad it is under the sun to see men worshipping a symbol which has been abandoned by God. How degenerate, how idolatrous, how ensnaring it becomes when God's voice sounds to the spirit of a child of His—"Behold, your house is left unto you desolate." We are not to worship reminiscences; this is the characteristic of all other religions, saving the Bible religion. The Bible religion is one of eternal progress, an intense and militant going on. A perilous time ensues for the individual and for the religious world whenever God shifts His symbols. Obedience to the voice of the Spirit within, the Word of God without and the suffering of the tribulation around, enable the child of God to hear God's voice and recognise His changing symbols. This discipline of Divine guidance by symbols is a serious, momentous discipline, and God never leaves His children alone in such times, for,

. . . behind the dim unknown
Standeth God within the shadows,
Keeping watch upon His own.

The worship of a past symbol is not a whit more dangerous than the irresponsible individualism that refuses to have any symbol. Both are contrary to God's Word and God's ways. Where do we stand today with regard to God's great symbols? Is it a selfish isolation, an unholy "come-out-ism"?[6] Then may God hand us the wine-cup from the hand of a despised Church member until our spiritual dullness is discerned and our spiritual pride humbled. Or is it a dead symbolism, cast aside in the economy of God, a moribund ritualism? If so, may the Spirit sting our traditional "churchianity" into going "without the camp, bearing His reproach."

Blind me with seeing tears until I see!
Let not fair poetry, science, art, sweet tones,
Build up about my soothed sense a world
That is not Thine, and wall me up in dreams;
So my sad heart may cease to beat with Thine,
The great World-heart, whose blood forever shed
Is human life; whose ache is man's dumb pain.

---

6. "Come-out-ism": belief among some holiness groups that true Christians should leave "dead" churches and form their own fellowships. Chambers agreed with the League of Prayer's position that Spirit-filled believers should remain in their churches to pray and work for revival.

As year by year the thrills of spring-tide shoot
Through earth's dull veins, with fresh, magnetic
*   might,*
Nor fail, for frosts that nip and winds that
*   blight,*
So, Lord, who erst didst stir with quickening
*   power*
My answering soul, achieve what Thou hast
*   aimed:*
Draw, for Thou has drawn; hold, what Thou
*   hast claimed.*

Draw through all failure to the perfect Flower;
Draw through all darkness to the perfect Light.
Yea, let the rapture of Thy springtide thrill
Through me, beyond me, till its ardour fill
The lingering souls that know not Thee aright;
That Thy great love may make of me, even me,
One added link to bind the world to Thee.

Third Stage. *By His Servants*

Behold, I have given him for a witness to the people, a leader and commander to the people. (Isaiah 55:4)

Guidance by God's sayings has to bring the soul into the surgery of events before a new harkening attitude can be gained to those sayings. At first the soul hears in one direction only, viz., that of its prejudices. Guidance by God's symbols makes it clear to the heart that outward vision is only possible as the inward eye is opened; and as God touches the eye with eye-salve, the soul realises that the changing symbols give deeper and more penetrating visions of God.

Guidance by His servants gives a yet more intimate nearness to God Himself. It is during this discipline that we learn that no ideal is of any practical avail unless it be incarnated. If the mystic spell of Nature in her rolling air, her eternal uplands and abiding plains, her sunrise dawnings and setting glories, her perennial springs and summer nights languishing to autumn, the strenuous grip of her icy colds—if these awaken a sense of the sublime and the unreached, it ends but in a spontaneous ache when the deep within calls to the deep outside! If the imprisoned soul of sound makes the human spirit weep tears from too deep a well to be reached by individual suffering—if music turns the human heart into a vast capacity for something as yet undreamt of till all its being aches to the verge of infinity; if the minor reaches of our music have awakened harmonies in spheres we know not, till with dumb yearnings we turn our sightless orbs, "crying like children in the night, with no language but a cry"; if painters' pictures stop the ache which Nature started, and fill for one amazing moment the yearning abysses discovered by the more mysterious thing than joy in music's moments—it is but for a moment, and all

seems but to have increased our capacity for a crueller sensitiveness, a more useless agony of suffering. But when God's servants guide us to His heart, then the first glorious outlines of the meaning of it all pass before us.

If we trace the lineaments of the servants of God in the Bible, we find a servant of God to be altogether different from an instrument of God. An instrument of God is one whom God takes up and uses and puts down again. A servant of God is one who has given up for ever his right to himself, and is bound to his Lord as His slave. "For he that was called in the Lord, being a bondservant, is the Lord's freedman: likewise he that was called, being free, is Christ's bondservant" (1 Corinthians 7:22 RV).

An instrument is one who shows God's Sovereignty, an unaccountable sovereignty may be, but unchallengeable ever. A servant is one who, recognising God's *sovereign will*, leaps to do that will of his own *free choice.*

What shall we say then? Is there unrighteousness with God? God forbid. For He saith to Moses, I will have mercy on whom I have mercy, and I will have compassion on whom I have compassion. So then it is not of him that willeth, nor of him that runneth, but of God that hath mercy. For the scripture saith unto Pharaoh, For this very purpose did I raise thee up, that I might shew in thee My power, and that My name might be published abroad in all the earth. So then He hath mercy on whom He will, and whom He will He hardeneth.

Thou wilt say then unto me, Why doth He still find fault? For who withstandeth His will? Nay but, O man, who art thou that repliest against God? Shall the thing formed say to Him that formed it, Why didst thou make me thus? Or hath not the potter a right over the clay, from the same lump to make one part a vessel unto honour, and another unto dishonour? (Romans 9:14–21 RV)

Guidance by His servants! What a blessed guidance, but oh, it is stern. "A servant of God"—the meaning of this phrase is largely lost to-day. The phrase that suits our modern mood better is, "a servant of men." Our watch-cry to-day is, "The greatest good for the greatest number." The watch-cry of the servant of God is, "The greatest obedience to my Lord." How many of us know a servant of God who has a right understanding of the science of God, and can introduce us to Him, and to His thoughts and His hopes? We are over-satiated with sympathisers with men, and with that mystic-sounding shibboleth, "Humanity." To quote G. K. Chesterton, whose insurgent mind is the best cure for any complacent stoicism:—

And the same antithesis exists about another modern religion, I mean the religion of Comte, generally known as Positivism, or the worship of humanity. Such men as Mr. Frederick Harrison,[7] that brilliant and chivalrous philosopher, who still, by his mere personality, speaks for the creed, would tell us that he offers us the philosophy of Comte, but not all Comte's fantastic proposals for pontiffs and ceremonials, the new calendar, the new holidays, and saints' days. He does not mean that we should dress ourselves up as priests of humanity or let off fireworks because it is Milton's birthday. To the solid English contrast all this appears, he confesses, to be a little absurd. To me it appears the only sensible part of Comteism. As a philosophy it is unsatisfactory. It is evidently impossible to worship humanity just as it is impossible to worship the Savile Club;[8] both are excellent institutions to which we may happen to belong. But we perceive clearly that the Savile Club did not make the stars and does not fill the universe. And it is surely unreasonable to attack the doctrine of the Trinity as a piece of bewildering mysticism, and then to ask men to worship a being who is ninety million persons in one God, neither confounding the persons nor dividing the substance.

An eminent difference is discernible between biographic studies in the Bible and outside the Bible. When men write studies of the servants of God, they are apt to drop out the uncouth and the unlovely, and out of their devotion state only the elements that idealise the servant. But the Bible reveals the blunderings and the sins and the uncouthness of the servants of God, and leaves only one idea dominant—that these men were for the glory of God. How deeply is written over the lives of the servants of God in the Bible record, ("Wherefore let no one glory in men" RV). The servants of God in the Bible are spoilt for earth, they live and speak backed by Jehovah. What kind of a bosom companion would Abraham have made? or Moses, or Jeremiah? What sort of a bedfellow would Elijah or Ezekiel have been? How sick we are over and over again with the vain sentimentalism about the servants of God. No wonder God lifts His servants up at times and shakes them and flings the parasites off.

The servants of God in the Bible never stole hearts to themselves, but handed them over to God. There is a ruggedness and an intolerable isolation about the servants of God in the Bible. They each one seem to do without you. There is nothing in the world saving God to these servants of His; all else is as a shadow. The lure the servants of God are made but attracts men to a wilderness wherein God woos men to Himself. Oh, the wild wail of the heart of the man or woman who mistook the fascination of God in His servant for God Himself, and clasped to his or her heart "a man of like passions as we are" (RV)! Oh for that man of God who will hand over to God the hearts God has called through him! It is not *you* who awakened that mighty desire in the heart; it is not *you* who called forth that longing in that spirit; it is God in you. Are you a servant of God? Then point them to Him. Down on your face, down in the dust, oh man of God, if those arms clasp you, and that heart rests on you! If that longing, loving heart awakens and finds you instead of God, what a passion of despair will blight you with the curse of solitariness and silence!

Oh, there are sad cries all over the spiritual world entering into the heart of God, and He will avenge them. Oh that we could hear it—"You have taken the East from me; you have taken the West from me; you have taken what is before me; and what is behind me; you have taken the moon, you have taken the sun from me, and, my fear is great, you have taken God from me."

Are all servants of God like that? No, thank God! The sheep are many and the shepherds are few, for the fatigue is staggering, the heights are giddy and the sights are awful. It is no wonder our Lord said "the sheep follow Him: for they know His voice. And a stranger will they not follow, but will flee from him: for they know not the voice of strangers" (John 10:4–5).

One of the greatest of these servants of God said he was a voice that cried but one thing, "Repent," and that pointed in one direction, "Behold the Lamb of God!" That is what a servant of God is for. Aye, and what a school God puts His servant through! Its years of graduation are—Separation, Sorrow, Supreme Sanctification and Suffering.

Is there one man in disenchanted days
Who yet has feet on earth and head in Heaven?
One viceroy yet to whom his King hath given
The fire that kindles and the strength that sways?
Is there a wisdom whose extremest ways
Lead upward still? For us who most have striven
Made wise too early and too late forgiven,
Our prudence palsies and our seeing slays.
We are dying; is there one alive and whole,

---

7. Frederick Harrison (1831–1923): English writer and positivist philosopher.

8. The Savile Club: founded in 1868, a private club in London whose membership has long been drawn largely from the world of the arts.

A hammer of the Lord, a simple soul,
Man with the men and with the boys a boy?
We are barren, let a male and conquering voice
Fill us and quicken us and make rejoice,
Even us who have so long forgotten joy.

God guides by His servants, and it is a guidance that disciplines heart and mind and spirit. Watch this guidance through the records of Holy Writ; the careers of Abraham, of Moses, of Joshua, of Gideon, of Deborah, and trace the discipline of their apprenticeship and mastership. Grasp the loneliness of Abraham, "the Friend of God." Enter into and imagine the rugged discipline of Moses, who esteemed "the reproach of Christ greater riches than the treasures in Egypt." Bow before the winnowing of the unworldly heart of Joshua. Marvel as you see how God took timid Gideon as His wardrobe, and clothed Himself with him. And be silent before Deborah, that sibyl of God's sanctity, as she leads God's army. And marking their self-effacement and other-worldliness, bow your face before God and learn the strangeness of His guidance by His servants.

Scarcely have we paid enough attention to the prefiguring of our Lord Himself in the prophets and servants of God, and perhaps we have over-emphasised His prefiguring in the signs and symbols of the dispensations surrounding those prophets and servants. How strangely the writers of the Psalms launch out into a definite prefiguring of our Lord! How wonderfully the sorrows of these servants of God take on new meaning when we see Jesus! The anthropomorphism of the Old Testament can never be despatched by the statement that it is man trying to state God in terms of his own ignorance. It is rather God prefiguring the stupendous mystery of the Incarnation.

'Tis the weakness in strength, that I cry for! my flesh, that I seek
In the Godhead! I seek and I find it. O Saul, it shall be
A Face like my face that receives thee; a Man like to me,
Thou shalt love and be loved by, for ever: a Hand like this hand
Shall throw open the gates of new life to thee!
See the Christ stand!

Fourth Stage. *By His Sympathy*

I will make mention of the lovingkindnesses of the LORD, and the praises of the LORD, according to all that the LORD hath bestowed on us; and the great goodness toward the house of Israel, which He hath bestowed on them according to His mercies, and according to the multitude of His lovingkindnesses. For He said, Surely, they are My people, children that will not deal falsely: so He was their Saviour. In all their affliction He was

afflicted, and the angel of His presence saved them: in His love and in His pity He redeemed them; and He bare them, and carried them all the days of old. (Isaiah 63:7–9 RV)

He found him in a desert land, and in the waste howling wilderness; He compassed him about, He cared for him, He kept him as the apple of His eye: as an eagle that stirreth up her nest, that fluttereth over her young, He spread abroad His wings, He took them, He bare them on His pinions: the LORD alone did lead him, and there was no strange god with Him. (Deuteronomy 32:10–12 RV)

Thou hast also given me the shield of Thy salvation: and Thy right hand hath holden me up, and Thy gentleness hath made me great. Thou hast enlarged my steps under me, and my feet have not slipped. (Psalm 18:35–36 RV)

The Sympathy of God

God having feeling for us! The very heart of the phrase is given in Hebrews 4:15–16, "For we have not a high priest that cannot be touched with the feeling of our infirmities; but one that hath been in all points tempted like as we are, yet without sin. Let us therefore draw near with boldness unto the throne of grace, that we may receive mercy, and may find grace to help us in time of need" (RV).

It is in the mystic tenderness of the guidance by His sympathy that God gives a love like His own. Oh, how can language put it—when the soul, the individual soul, knows God has marked all sorrows and has kept all tears till not one drop is lost, knows that "He knoweth our frame; He remembereth that we are dust," when the first great surprise of the light of His sympathy bursts on our tear-dimmed soul and turns it into radiant rainbows of promise; when no *sayings* of His resound on our ears with thrilling clarion call; when no visible *symbol* disciplines our faltering steps; when no *servant* of God is near to help us discern His will; when the cloud gathers round us, and we fear as we enter the cloud, and lo! a mystic touch is on our spirits, a coolness and balm, "as one whom his mother comforteth" so the Lord comforts us. Oh, the tenderest touch of a mother's love is nothing compared to our blessed Father's sympathy! It is there, couched in His arms, that we are guided into that secret of secrets, that it is not men's sins we have to deal with, but their suffering, it is ensphered in the nights when He gives us the treasures of darkness, that discipline us to be staying powers in the alarm moments of other lives. What an atmosphere there breathes about the life God is guiding by His sympathy! We feel a larger horizon, an expanding heart and brain and spirit grasping us and uplifting us. Nothing seems changed yet a kiss, as if the kiss of God, touches our care, and we smilingly wonder how things have altered, and life is never the same again. From guidance by His sympathy, we learn that God heeds not our faults nor our mistakes, He looks at our hearts. This point, so blessed, so rare, perhaps we could never see before. How gladly, how nobly, how purely we grow under the guidance by God's sympathy!

And yet it would be dangerous if God guided us by His sympathy too soon. Look again at Isaiah 63 for the sad sequel to such guidance: "But they rebelled, and grieved His holy Spirit: therefore He was turned to be their enemy, and Himself fought against them" (v. 10 RV). And again at the sequel in Deuteronomy 32: "But Jeshurun waxed fat, and kicked . . . then he forsook God which made him, and lightly esteemed the Rock of his salvation" (v. 15).

Clearly, sympathy may be dangerous in its effects on men. In undisciplined, self-centred lives it seems to engender a self-confident vanity that abuses the end and meaning of God's sympathy, and the goodness of God, which ought to lead to repentance, leads rather to blatant presumption. But to a nature disciplined and chastened by self-knowledge, whose cynicism (which ever arises from the narrow view of personal limitations) has long since given way to larger, more generous, more self-effacing views—to such a nature, guidance by God's sympathy is an unspeakable boon, ever leading the soul out into deep adoration of God and devotion to Him.

This aspect of guidance by God's sympathy is rarely spoken of by expounders of God's ways with men, partly because of the definite indefinableness of the guidance, and partly because so few understand it, or have learned to partake in such guidance by those mystic touches which endear the soul to God and God to that soul beyond all words.

Guidance by sympathy amongst ourselves is often questionable, because a man may sympathise out of self-sentiment, which is nothing more than disguised selfishness and has an enervating, unennobling effect. Sympathy to benefit and brace and ennoble, must spring from a higher source than the one who is suffering has reached as yet. The purpose and heart of our Lord's sympathy is that it does not make us submissive to a broken heart and to degenerate hereditary bondage; but guides us to where He will bind up the broken-hearted and set at liberty the captives. There is a distressing snare which besets a certain type of saint, the snare of a morbid desire for sympathy, which simply makes them craving spiritual sponges, so to speak, to mop up sympathy. God's criticism of us, strange to say, does not hurt, for the soul understands that it springs from a deep well of sympathy. Criticism without sympathy is cruel, but criticism that springs from sympathy is blessed—faithful wounds and goads and rousings!

The discipline of guidance by God's sympathy leads to a clearer, better understanding of God's ideas and hopes and aims. In this way He makes known to us His *ways;* otherwise we simply know His *acts* (Psalm 103:7). Through guidance by His sympathy we understand that "*He doeth all things well,*" and though He slay, that soul cannot fear. The language of the soul guided by God's sympathy is an amazed rebuke to those who do not know God! For he says by his life—"It is the LORD: let Him do what seemeth Him good."

The guidance by God's sympathy keeps the soul and heart in a rare atmosphere of blessed spiritual love. It is along this line of Divine guidance that God takes us into counsel with Himself, as it were, saying as He did about Abraham, "Shall I hide from Abraham that thing which I do . . . ?"

Before we take our final meditation and musing on those serene thoughts of guidance by God Himself, let our hearts lie open before that marvel of revelation in the fourteenth chapter of St. John's Gospel.

And I will pray the Father, and He shall give you another Comforter, that He may be with you for ever, even the Spirit of truth: whom the world cannot receive; for it beholdeth Him not, neither knoweth Him: ye know Him; for He abideth with you, and shall be in you. I will not leave you desolate: I come unto you.

Call the Comforter by the term you think best—Advocate, Helper, Paraclete, the word conveys the indefinable blessedness of His sympathy; an inward, invisible kingdom that causes the saint to sing through every night of sorrow. This Holy Comforter represents the ineffable Motherhood of God. Protestantism has lost for many generations this aspect of the Divine revelation because of its violent antipathy to Mariolatry as practised by the Roman Catholic Church; and it behoves us to remember that Protestantism is not the whole Gospel of God, but an expression of a view of the Gospel of God specially adapted to the crying needs of a particular time.

George MacDonald in his book entitled *Sir Gibbie,* writes as follows (and by the way it is a striking indication of the trend and shallowness of the modern reading public that George MacDonald's books have been so neglected)—

See revelation culminate in Elizabeth and Mary, the mothers of John the Baptist and Jesus. Think how much fitter that it should be so; that they to whom the Word of God comes should be women bred in the dignity of a natural life, and familiarity with the large ways of the earth; women of simple and few wants, without distraction, and with time for reflection—compelled to reflection, indeed, from the enduring presence of an unsullied consciousness, for wherever there is a humble, thoughtful nature, into that nature the divine consciousness, that is, the Spirit of God, presses as into its own place. Holy women are to be found everywhere, but the prophetess is not so likely to be found in the city as in the hill country.

We quote this simply for the purpose of suggesting how we limit ourselves and our conceptions of God by ignoring the side of the Divine Nature best symbolised by womanhood, and the Comforter, be it reverently said, surely represents this side of the Divine Nature. It is the Comforter Who sheds abroad the love of God in our hearts. It is the Comforter Who baptises us into oneness with Jesus, in the amazing language of Scripture, until we are indwelt by a mysterious union with God. It is the Comforter Who brings forth the fruit of love, joy, peace, long-suffering, kindness, goodness, faithfulness, meekness, temperance. Guidance by His sympathy leads by a blessed discipline into an understanding of God which passeth knowledge.

> *. . . that whatsoever spark*
> *Of pure and true in any human heart*
> *Flickered and lived, it burned itself towards Him*
> *In an electric current, through all bonds*
> *Of intervening race and creed and time,*
> *And flamed up to a heat of living faith.*
> *And love, and love's communion, and the joy*
> *And inspiration of self-sacrifice;*
> *And drew together in a central coil,*
> *Magnetic, all the noblest of all hearts,*
> *And made them one with Him, in a live flame*
> *That is the purifying and the warmth*
> *Of all the earth even to these latter days.*

Fifth Stage. *By Himself*
For in all the world there is none but Thee, my God, there is none but Thee.

After these things the word of the LORD came unto Abram in a vision, saying, Fear not, Abram: I am thy shield, and thy exceeding great reward. (Genesis 15:1)

And He said, My presence shall go with thee, and I will give thee rest. (Exodus 33:14)

If there arise in the midst of thee a prophet, or a dreamer of dreams, and he give thee a sign or a wonder, and the sign or the wonder come to pass, whereof he spake unto thee saying, Let us go after other gods, which thou hast not known, and let us serve them; thou shalt not hearken unto the words of that prophet, or unto that dreamer

of dreams: for the LORD your God proveth you, to know whether ye love the LORD your God with all your heart and with all your soul. Ye shall walk after the LORD your God, and fear Him, and keep His commandments, and obey His voice, and ye shall serve Him, and cleave unto Him. (Deuteronomy 13:1–4 RV)

The LORD is my shepherd; I shall not want. He maketh me to lie down in green pastures: He leadeth me beside the waters of rest. He restoreth my soul: He guideth me in the paths of righteousness for His name's sake. (Psalm 23:1–3 RV mg)

This is the goal on earth. In all we have touched upon we have not approached the goal of the Hereafter. God is never in a hurry, and His guidance is so severe and so simple, so sweet and so satisfying, that nothing but the child-spirit can discern it. But this is the goal—God Himself.

> *. . . not joy, nor peace,*
> *Nor even blessing, but Himself, my God.*

How true is the word of the Apostle Paul's: "strengthened with all power, according to the might of His glory, unto all patience and longsuffering with joy" (Colossians 1:11 RV). Our Lord Himself strikes the same note of patience: "In your patience ye shall win your souls" (Luke 21:19 RV) and the Apostle John writes: "I John, your brother and partaker with you in the tribulation and kingdom and patience which are in Jesus . . ." (Revelation 1:9 RV). Oh, the discipline of patience! How His guidance hastens us, sweetens us, and quickens us, until without let or hindrance[9] He can guide us by Himself.

> *Go thou into thy closet, shut thy door—*
> *And pray to Him in secret: He will hear.*
> *But think not thou, by one wild bound, to clear*
> *The numberless ascensions, more and more*
> *Of starry stairs that must be climbed, before*
> *Thou comest to the Father's likeness near.*
> *And bendest down to kiss His feet so*
> *That, step by step, their mounting flights passed o'er.*
> *Be thou content if on thy weary need*
> *There falls a sense of showers and of the Spring;*
> *A hope that makes it possible to fling*
> *Sickness aside, and go and do the deed:*
> *For highest aspiration will not lead*
> *Unto the calm beyond all questioning.*

From earliest childhood there has hovered over us in a vast o'erarching the "Over Soul," the blessed Presence that is indefinable. But it is only to the soul dis-

---

9. without let or hindrance: legal phrase meaning "without obstacle or impediment."

ciplined by suffering, by loneliness, and by Divine guidance, that "our Father's feet" appear among the dusty clouds. In the days and years of the preparation of our moral and spiritual characters, the vision tarried and we wearied waiting for it. How often it seemed like some vagrant will-o'-the-wisp, and all our life grew sick with longing. But ever and anon a vision came, perhaps in the rapt spell of prayer, when one felt if he put out his hand he might, nay, he would, touch God Himself. Perhaps it was in a holy spell of contemplation that God Himself enfolded us, till fear was impossible, and God was all in all, beyond all language and all thought. But these all passed:

> God's fashion is another; day by day
> And year by year He tarrieth; little need
> The Lord should hasten; whom he loves the most
> He seeks not oftenest, nor woos him long,
> But by denial quickens his desire,
> And in forgetting best remembers him.
> Till that man's heart grows humble and reaches out
> To the least glimmer of the feet of God,
> Grass on the mountain-tops or the early note
> Of wild birds in the bush before the day,—
> Wherever sweetly in the ends of the earth
> Are fragments of a peace that knows not man.

What is the meaning of all the pain, the longing and the questioning? Why does God not tell us plainly of Himself? Ah! our God is a Master-workman in perfecting His ideas in us; He never hastens. So often we mistake Him and His purpose, and sinking into quietism and contemplation we begin to repose in a sanctified stagnation, when suddenly He ruthlessly uproots us, and when at last we are agreed with Him and His ways, He dazes and confounds us with His own questions. (All this is put for our instruction in the last chapters of the Book of Job.) We do so want God to realise that we take ourselves very seriously. But some of the questions God asks us destroy this seriosity:

> Where wast thou when I laid the foundations of the earth?... Hast thou commanded the morning since thy days began, and caused the dayspring to know its place?... Hast thou entered into the springs of the sea? or hast thou walked in the recesses of the deep? Have the gates of death been revealed unto thee? or hast thou seen the gates of the shadow of death? Hast thou comprehended the breadth of the earth? . . . Canst thou bind the sweet influences [mg] of the Pleiades, or loose the bands of Orion? Canst thou lead forth the signs of the Zodiac[mg] in their season? or canst thou guide the Bear with her train? Knowest thou the ordinances of the heavens? canst thou establish the dominion thereof in the earth?(RV)

Oh, these terrible questions when God seems to laugh at the soul, destroying its serious self-importance, even while He upholds that soul.

> Then Job answered the LORD, and said, Behold, I am of small account; what shall I answer Thee? I lay mine hand upon my mouth. Once have I spoken, and I will not answer, yea twice, but I will proceed no further.... I know that Thou canst do all things, and that no purpose of Thine can be restrained. Who is this that hideth counsel without knowledge? therefore have I uttered that which I understood not.... I had heard of Thee by the hearing of the ear; but now mine eye seeth Thee, wherefore I loathe my words [mg], and repent in dust and ashes. (RV)

It is by these processes, for the most part unstateable, that God by His Divine guidance destroys that awful barrier of taking ourselves too seriously.

> Lord, what I once had done with youthful might,
> Had I been from the first true to the truth,
> Grant me, now old, to do—with better sight.
> And humbler heart, if not the brain of youth;
> So wilt thou, in thy gentleness and truth
> Lead back thy old soul, by the path of pain,
> Round to his best—young eyes and heart and brain.
> . . . .
> Come to me, Lord:
> I will not speculate how,
> Nor think at which door I would have thee appear,
> Nor put off calling till my floors be swept.
> But cry, "Come, Lord, come anyway, come now."
> Doors, windows, I throw wide; my head I bow,
> And sit like some one who so long has slept
> That he knows nothing till his life draws near.

God is a light so bright that the first vision of Himself is dark with excess of light. In Genesis 15, we read that "the word of the LORD came unto Abram in a vision," (mark, it was a vision—God's order is, first vision, then humiliation, then reality) "saying, Fear not, Abram: I am thy shield, and thy exceeding great reward. . . . And when the sun was going down, a deep sleep fell upon Abram; and, lo, an horror of great darkness fell upon him"—a darkness through excess of light.

There is much that changes during this discipline of Divine guidance, but one thing grows clearer and clearer, the revelation of God Himself. Moses, the servant of God, was guided first by the cloudy pillar, i.e., by an outward mysterious method; then by guidance from Mount Sinai with its inner understanding of the words uttered there; then we see the God of the cloudy pillar, the God of mount Sinai's law, revealing Himself to him, and saying, "My presence shall go with thee, and I will give thee rest." The unspeakable rapture of it all made the heart of Moses plead, "Shew me, I pray Thee, Thy glory" (RV), and God in overflowing graciousness and condescension did so—"Behold, there is a place by Me, and thou shalt stand upon the rock. . . . and I will take away Mine hand, and thou shalt see My back: but My face shall not be seen" (RV).

"*There is a place by Me*," a place of unapproachable safety. Affliction and tribulation may destroy all else, but the saint abiding in this secret place of the Most High is untouchable. There is no self-consciousness there, no uncertainty, but only Rest, unfathomable rest in God Himself, not in a vision of God, but in God Himself as a Reality, a living, bright Reality. Walking with God, and talking to Him as friend with friend, knowing that God knows He can do what He likes with us; there are no questions and no perplexities because He knows. Here, in the heart of this way of guidance by Himself, does God convey to us "the secret of the LORD."

> *Within this place of certain good*
> *Love evermore expands her wings,*
> *Or nestling in Thy perfect choice,*
> *Abides content with what it brings.*
> *Oh, lightest burden, sweetest yoke!*
> *It lifts, it bears my happy soul,*
> *It giveth wings to this poor heart;*
> *My freedom is Thy grand control.*
> *Upon God's will I lay me down,*
> *As child upon its mother's breast;*
> *No silken couch, nor softest bed*
> *Could ever give me such deep rest.*
> *Thy wonderful, grand will, my God,*
> *With triumph now I make it mine;*
> *And faith shall cry a joyous Yes!*
> *To every dear command of Thine.*

A dear little friend of mine, not four years old, facing one day some big difficulty to her little heart, with a very wise shake of her head, said, "I'll go and tell my papa." Presently she came back, this time with every fibre of her little body strutting with the pride that shone in her eye, "Now, my papa's coming!" Presently her papa came, she clasped her little hands and screamed with delight, and danced round about him, unspeakably confident in her papa. Child of God, does something face you that terrifies your heart? Say, "I'll

tell my Father." Then come back "boasting" in the Lord, "Now my Father's coming." And when He comes, you too will clasp your hands in rapture, your mouth will be filled with laughter, and you will be like one that dreams, when your Father comes.

And all this seems unmeasurable bliss here and now. What will it be when this order has passed away? If all this is but as His back, not His face, oh, what will it be! It hath not entered into the heart of man to conceive!

Conclusion

The deep secret of God is Love, and only the child-heart and the child-spirit can find the way to learn this secret. Jesus Christ satisfies the last aching abyss of the human spirit, and until He does there is a great element of the precarious in our life. Half the heart-breaks in life are caused by the lack of understanding that

> *We needs must love the highest when we see it,*
> *Not Lancelot, nor another.*

Half the wasted days and languid reveries and immortal contemplations that embarrass human relationships and obliterate individual responsibility arise from the same lack of understanding. God is not an outward gush of sentiment, not a vague abstraction of impersonal good nature: God is a living, intense Reality, and until this truth is grasped, the puzzles and the questions are more than can be met. But when by the discipline of His Divine guidance, we know Him, and He going with us gives us Rest, then Time and Eternity are merged and lost in that amazing vital relationship. The union is one not of mystic contemplation, but of intense perfection of activity, not the Rest of the placid peace of stagnation, but the Rest of perfect motion.

> *Only, my God, see thou that I content thee—*
> *Oh, take thy own content upon me.*
> *God! Ah, never, never, sure, wilt thou repent thee*
> *That thou hast called thy Adam from the clod!*
> *Yet must I mourn that thou shouldst ever find me*
> *One moment sluggish, needing more of the rod*
> *Than thou didst think when thy desire designed*
> *me.*

> *No less than thou, O Father, do we need*
> *A God to friend each lonely one of us.*

THE DISCIPLINE OF SUFFERING

Beloved, think it not strange concerning the fiery trial among you, which cometh upon you to prove you, as though a strange thing happened unto you. . . . Wherefore let them also that suffer according to the will of God commit their souls in well-doing unto a faithful Creator. 1 Peter 4:12, 19 (RV)

The awful problem of suffering continually crops up in the Scriptures, and in life and remains a mystery. From Job until now, and from before Job, the mystery of suffering remains. And always, after the noisy clamour of the novice in suffering, and after the words of weight of the veteran; after the sarcasm and cynicism and bitterness of more or less pained people, aye, and after the slander of Satan against God—the voice of the Spirit sounds clear, "Hast thou considered My servant Job?"

Perhaps to be able to explain suffering is the clearest indication of never having suffered. Sin, suffering, and sanctification are not problems of the mind, but facts of life—mysteries that awaken all other mysteries until the heart rests in God, and waiting patiently knows "He doeth all things well." Oh, the unspeakable joy of knowing that God reigns! that He is our Father, and that the clouds are but "the dust of His feet"! Religious life is based and built up and matured on primal implicit trust, transfigured by Love; the explicit statement of that life can only be made by the spectator, never by the saint.

Some years ago the wife of a murdered missionary in China told me of the blank amazed agony of those days—"We did not feel, we did not pray, we were dazed with sorrow." She was shown a lock of her little child's golden hair, and told that both husband and child had been discovered murdered, beheaded and naked in a godless Chinese town. Shattered and undone, the widow returned with the little ones spared to her to Britain. She did not doubt God, but—"He did not answer prayer." "Oh, how many prayed for my husband, good valued servant of God, but all to no avail." In those days of dull dreary reaction the people who nearly drove her wild with distress were those who knew chapter and verse, the "why" and "wherefore" of her suffering and grief. She said, "I used to beat a tattoo on the floor with my foot while they chattered, crying in my heart 'How long, O Lord, how long?'" One day as she lay prostrate on the sofa the old minister who had known her husband in the glad other days, entered the room softly, he did not speak but came gently over to her and kissed her on the forehead and went out without saying a word. "From that moment," she said, "my heart began to heal."

The unexplained things in life are more than the explained. God seems careless as to whether men understand Him or not; He scarcely vindicates His saints to men. Martha and Mary tell Jesus of the sickness of Lazarus—"Lord, behold, he whom Thou lovest is sick"; but Jesus sends no word, nor does He go. Lazarus dies, is buried, and four days afterwards Jesus appears. If you do not understand Martha as she exclaims, in effect, "Oh, I know that my brother will rise again at the last day, but that does not explain why You did not come when I sent for You; he need not have died if You had come"—if you do not understand Martha, and are satisfied with any explanation to be deduced from this incident, you are unaware of the problem of suffering, unaware of the poignant agony of God's silences.

An informal consideration of 1 Peter 4:12–19 will serve to knit into some kind of order what we consider the Bible indicates and implies with regard to the Discipline of Suffering.

The Springs of Suffering
For let none of you suffer as a murderer, or a thief, or an evil-doer, or as a meddler in other men's matters. (1 Peter 4:15 RV)

The first spring of suffering from the Bible point of view is two-fold—Wrong Doing and Wrong Temper.

(a) Wrong Doing
For let none of you suffer as a murderer, or a thief, or an evil-doer. . . .

The blasting blight of wrong-doing finds its expression in the literature of all the ages; it is a suffering that works as cruelly as the grave, and is as undying as the eternal ages. By way of expression to the suffering that springs from wrong-doing, Myers's[10] words are final—

> *When this man's best desire and highest aim*
> *Had ended in the deed of traitorous shame.*
> *When to his bloodshot eyes grew wild and dim*
> *The stony faces of the Sanhedrim,—*
> *When in his rage he could no longer hear*
> *Men's voices nor the sunlight nor the air,*
> *Nor sleep, nor waking, nor his own quick breath,*

---

10. F. W. H. Myers (1843–1901): British poet and educator.

Nor God in Heaven, nor anything but death,—
I bowed my head, and through my fingers ran
Tears for the end of that Iscariot man,
Lost in the hopeless struggle of the soul
To make the done undone, the broken whole.

The sense of the irrevocable wrings the human spirit with the awful suffering of "what might have been." It begins its records in the far past, hoary with the ages, when Paradise was lost, and the cherubim with the circling fiery sword branded the life of Adam and Eve with "Nevermore, nevermore." It embraces that lonely murderer Cain, who in his undying pain cried out, "My punishment is greater than I can bear." It pauses around Esau when, too late, remorse seized that strong man and made him weep those tears of bitter repentance, all in vain; and its records of the unspeakable suffering of the wrong-doer remain till today—

Oh, brother! howsoever, whereso'er
Thou hidest now the hell of thy despair
Hear that one heart can pity, one can know
With thee thy hopeless, solitary woe.

F. W. H. Myers

(b) Wrong Temper

There is also suffering that springs from the wrong temper—"For let none of you suffer . . . as a meddler in other men's matters" (RV). From talking in the wrong mood springs a suffering so keen, so stinging, so belittling, so hopeless, that it debases and drives the suffering one still lower. The old song from the ancient pilgrim's Song Book has this thorn at the heart of its suffering—

Deliver my soul, O LORD, from lying lips, and from
a deceitful tongue. What shall be given unto thee,
and what shall be done more unto thee, thou deceit-
ful tongue? It is as the sharp arrows of the mighty
man [mg], with coals of juniper. (Psalm 120:2–4
RV)

The suffering which springs from being "a meddler in other men's matters" ("a busybody") is humiliating to the last degree. A free translation of 1 Thessalonians 4:11 might well read: "Study to shut up and mind your own business," and among all the texts we hang on our walls, let this be one. The suffering that arises from a wrong temper has no refining side, but only a humiliating side. "Therefore take heed to your spirit." A blameworthy temper of mind is the most damning thing in the human soul. Peter, as a meddler in other men's matters, received a deserved rebuke from Our Lord: "Peter therefore see-

ing him saith to Jesus, Lord, and what shall this man do? Jesus saith unto him, If I will that he tarry till I come, what is that to thee? Follow thou Me" (RV). And surely the rebuke contained in our Lord's answer to Martha is of the same nature—"Martha, Martha, thou art anxious and troubled about many things: but one thing is needful: for Mary hath chosen the good part, which shall not be taken away from her" (RV), i.e., "she is taking her orders from Me."

How will sad memory point where, here and
    there,
    Friend after Friend, by falsehood or by fate,
From him or from each other parted were,
    And love sometimes becomes the nurse of hate!
. . .
Rather, he thinks he held not duly dear
    Love, the best gift that Man on Man
    bestows,
While round his downward path, recluse and
    drear,
    He feels the chill indifferent shadows close.
"Why did I not," his spirit murmurs deep,
    "At every cost of the momentary pride,
Preserve the love for which in vain I weep;
    Why had I wish or hope or sense beside?
O cruel issue of some selfish thought!
    O long, long echo of some angry tone!
O fruitless lesson, mercilessly taught,
    Alone to linger—and to die alone!"

Houghton[11]

The wreck of many friendships has started in this mutiny of busybody meddlesomeness. Suffering "as a busybody" (KJV) and listening to slander ends in pitiable pain. This wrong temper slanders the Almighty, and men believe the busybody gossip of the devil and sever friendship with God. Oh, the damnable pangs caused by that arch busybody, "the accuser of our brethren."

This then is the first spring of suffering, and the Spirit warns men lest they drink of this spring and endure a suffering that is neither grand nor ennobling.

(c) Suffering as a Christian

But if a man suffer as a Christian, let him not be ashamed; but let him glorify God in this name. (1 Peter 4:16 RV)

The suffering that arises from superiority, from an essential difference from the societies around, is an ennobling and God-glorifying thing. Our designation of "Christian" is of Divine appointment, whether it

---

11. Baron Richard Moncton Milnes Houghton (1809–1885): English poet.

comes from the versatile wit of Antioch, or from the reverent respect of the Gentile; to live worthily of the name of Christian is to suffer persecution. To suffer because of meekness is an exalting, refining and God-glorifying suffering. And mark this and mark it well, to suffer "as a Christian" is a shameful thing in the eyes of the societies of this world. The friends who in your hour of trial and slander, gather round to support and stand with you, are first amazed, then dazed, and then disgusted, when they find that you really do not mean to stand up for yourself, but meekly to submit. In that hour when your friends pity you (Oh, the shame of being pitied, says the world; but what a God-glorifying thing it is, for to be pitied by the world is to be pitied by God) He Himself will come and whisper to your spirit—"Blessed are ye, when men shall hate you, and when they shall separate you from their company, and reproach you, and cast out your name as evil, for the Son of man's sake. Rejoice in that day, and leap for joy: for behold, your reward is great in heaven" (Luke 6:22–23 RV).

To "suffer as a Christian" is not to be marked peculiar because of your views, or because you will not bend to conventionality; these things are not Christian, but ordinary human traits from which all men suffer irrespective of creed or religion or no religion. To "suffer as a Christian" is to suffer because there is an essential difference between you and the world which rouses the contempt of the world, and the disgust and hatred of the spirit that is in the world. To "suffer as a Christian" is to have no answer when the world's satire is turned on you, as it was turned on Jesus Christ when He hung upon the cross, when they turned His words into jest and jeer; they will do the same to you. He gave no answer, neither can you.

"... but if a man suffer as a Christian, let him not be ashamed" (RV). It was in the throes of this binding, amazing problem that Peter staggered. Peter meant to go with his Lord to death, and he did go; but never at any moment did he imagine that he would have to go without Him—that he would see Jesus taken by the power of the world, "as a lamb that is led to the slaughter" (RV), and have no answer, no word to explain—that froze him to the soul. That is what it means to "suffer as a Christian"—to hear men taunt Him, see them tear His words to pieces, and feel you cannot answer; to smart under their merciless, pitying sarcasm because you belong to that contemptible sect of "Christians." When the heart is stung in the first moments of such suffering, the language of the poet may suit it—

I can simply wish I might refute you,
Wish my friend would,—by a word, a wink,—
Bid me stop that foolish mouth,—you brute, you!

He keeps absent,—why, I cannot think.
Never mind! Though foolishness may flout me,
One thing's sure enough: 'tis neither frost,
No, nor fire, shall freeze or burn from out me
Thanks for truth—though falsehood,
gained—
though lost.

Browning

But when you have been comforted by His rod and His staff, you count it all joy to go through this God-glorifying suffering. "... but let him glorify God in this name." Suffering "as a Christian" is the second great spring of suffering, whose waters purify and ennoble the soul.

How very hard it is to be
A Christian! Hard for you and me,
. . . .
And the sole thing that I remark
Upon this difficulty, this;
We do not see it where it is,
At the beginning of the race:
As we proceed, it shifts its place,
And where we looked for crowns to fall,
We find the tug's to come,—that's all.
. . . .
... and I find it hard
To be a Christian, as I said!
Still every now and then my head
Raised glad, sinks mournful—all grows drear
Spite of the sunshine, ...
. . . .
But Easter-Day breaks! But
Christ rises! Mercy every way
Is infinite,—and who can say?

Browning

(d) Suffering According to the Will of God
Wherefore let them also that suffer according to the will of God commit their souls in well-doing unto a faithful Creator. (1 Peter 4:19 RV)

If the springs of suffering we have been considering arise in mystery, this spring overwhelms its own source in mystery, as well as the soul it covers. The great tides lift here, the splendid solitude of God's purpose transfigures agony into Redemption, and the baffling hurricanes speed the soul like a flaming arrow on to God's great Day. G. K. Chesterton, writing on Job, says in his own individual, sufficient way—

But God comforts Job with indecipherable mystery, and for the first time Job is comforted. Eliphaz gives one answer, Job gives another answer, and the question still remains an open wound. God simply refuses to answer, and somehow the question is settled. Job flings at God one riddle, God flings back at

Job a hundred riddles, and Job is at peace; he is comforted with conundrums.

When all the trite things, the sentimental things, the poetic things and the explanatory things have been said, the still small voice of the Spirit introduces the perpetual conundrum—"Hast thou considered My servant Job?" And after a pause, when our commonplace shoes are off our feet and we stand before the Cross, the conundrum is put still more deeply and more perplexingly—"Thou art My beloved Son; in Thee I am well pleased." "Yet it pleased the LORD to bruise Him; He hath put Him to grief," and we bow our head while our spirit murmurs, "Who hath believed our report" (or, "that which we have heard?") "and to whom hath the arm of the LORD been revealed?"

This spring of suffering, suffering "according to the will of God," is a great deep. Job did not know the preface to his own story, neither does any man. Job was never told that God and the devil had made a battleground of his soul. Job's suffering was not for his own sake, not for his perfecting or purifying, that was incidental; Job suffered "according to the will of God."

When shall we learn that God's great work is the production of saints? It is humbling beyond words to be told by our Father that it was not for love of the Truth that we had been bold, but that the great labour allowed us was the means of releasing our imprisoned hearts and was for our own peace. God seems careless over what men do at times.

The words of our Lord sound from those blessed Palestinian days with a deeper, truer significance: "If any man would come after Me, let him deny himself, and take up his cross, and follow Me," (RV), that is, I must never do God's will according to my will. That surely is the very essence of Satan's temptation of our Lord, and of every sanctified soul—"Take your right to yourself and do God's will according to your own sanctified understanding of it." "Never!" said Jesus, "For I am come down from heaven, not to do Mine own will, but the will of Him that sent Me"; and in the hour when dilemma perplexes him, the waves and the billows overwhelm him, and the noise of the water-spouts deafen him, the disciple learns the meaning of his Master's "Follow Me."

In the course of a sermon preached by Father Frere in St. Paul's Cathedral some years ago on "The Fourfold Attitude towards Suffering," he said this— "Have you, I wonder, ever had to do something to a pet dog in order to get it well, something which hurt it very much—pulled a thorn out of its foot, or washed out a wound, or anything of that sort? If so,

you will remember the expression of dumb eloquence in the eyes of the dog as he looked at you; what you were doing hurt him tremendously and yet there seemed to speak from his eyes such a trust of you as if he would say, 'I don't in the least understand what you are doing, what you are doing hurts, but go on with it.'"

That is an apt illustration of suffering "according to the will of God." It is very necessary to be brought to the stage of trust in our experience of suffering; perhaps we are brought to it most acutely when in the case of someone we love we have to look up mutely to God and say, "I don't understand it at all, but go on with what You are doing." That marks a real stage of learning to trust in God, and it is a step towards something still further on. Spiritual experience has begun; suffering has already deepened the soul. To look on at suffering with eyes that know not God is to make the mouth slander the Highest. To sympathise with men who suffer, without first knowing God, is to hate Him.

Therefore gird up thyself, and come to stand
Unflinching under the unfaltering hand.
That waits to prove thee to the uttermost.
It were not hard to suffer by His hand
If thou couldst see His face;—but in the dark!
That is the one last trial:—be it so.
Christ was forsaken, so must thou be too—
How couldest thou suffer but in seeming, else?
Thou wilt not see the face nor feel the hand,
Only the cruel crushing of the feet,
When through the bitter night the Lord comes
*   down*
To tread the winepress.—Not by sight, but
*   faith,*
Endure, endure,—be faithful to the end!

H. E. Hamilton King[12]

The Signs of Suffering

In the cruel fire of Sorrow
*   Cast thy heart, do not faint or wail!*
Let thy hand be firm and steady,
*   Do not let thy spirit quail!*
But wait till the trial is over
*   And take thy heart again;*
For as gold is tried by fire
*   So a heart must be tried by pain.*

I shall know by the gleam and glitter
*   Of the golden chain you wear*
By your heart's calm strength in loving,

---

12. Harriet Eleanor Hamilton King (1840–1920): English poet; author of *The Disciples* (1873), an epic poem much quoted and loved by Chambers.

Of the fire they have had to bear.
Beat on, true heart, for ever!
* Shine bright, strong golden chain,*
And bless the cleansing fire
* And the furnace of living pain!*

A. Procter[13]

Men and women betray their suffering in different ways—by threatening and evil doing; by sullenness and quietism; or by active well doing.

Suffering, when the heart knows nothing of trust in God and love for the Highest, shows itself in rancorous spite and evil deeds. The sarcasms, the cynicisms, the satires, the slanders, the murders, the wars, the law suits, all these spring from this source, and are usually, although not always, the sign of suffering which springs from wrong-doing. When we sum up the history of the various civilisations whose records are available we find it made up mostly of these forms of suffering, and we are reminded of the voice of the Ancient of Days echoing down the ages—"In sorrow shalt thou eat of it all the days of thy life" (Genesis 3:17). It is caught up in the reflections of the wisest man that ever lived—"For all his days are but sorrows, and his travail is grief; yea, even in the night his heart taketh no rest" (Ecclesiastes 2:23 RV); and uttered again in connection with God's servant Job, who remains the incarnation of the problem of suffering—"For affliction cometh not forth of the dust, neither doth trouble spring out of the ground; but man is born unto trouble, as the sparks fly upward" (Job 5:6–7 RV).

Suffering is the heritage of the bad, of the penitent, and of the Son of God. Each one ends in the cross. The bad thief is crucified, the penitent thief is crucified, and the Son of God is crucified. By these signs we know the widespread heritage of suffering.

Judge not! the workings of his brain
* And of his heart thou canst not see;*
What looks to thy dim eyes a stain,
* In God's pure light may only be*
A scar, brought from some well-won field—
Where thou wouldst only faint and yield.

The look, the air that frets thy sight
* May be a token, that below*
The soul has closed in deadly fight
* With some infernal fiery foe,*
Whose glance would scorch thy smiling grace,
And cast thee shuddering on thy face!

The fall thou darest to despise;—
* May be the Angel's slackened hand*
Has suffered it, that he may rise
* And take a firmer, surer stand;*
Or, trusting less to earthly things,
May henceforth learn to use his wings.

So judge none lost but wait and see,
* With hopeful pity, not disdain!*
The depth of the abyss may be
* The measure of the height of pain,*
And love and glory that may raise
This soul to God in after days.

A. Procter

Another sign of suffering among men is characterised by sullenness and quietism. There is a luxury of suffering that fosters the growth of the most dangerous isolation of pride, and produces a kind of human sphinx, shrouded in mystery, which seems more profound than it is. This luxury of suffering is pre-eminently cowardly as well as proud, its habit is the habit of the cloister or nunnery. According to the character of the individual it is sullen and gloomy in its expression, or mystical and remote in its quietism. The portrayal of the sullen type is well expressed in Psalm 106:24–25. "Yea, they despised the pleasant land, they believed not His word: but murmured in their tents, and hearkened not unto the voice of the LORD."

Bishop Paget[14] in a remarkable essay on "The Sin of Accidie" deals with this suffering in a unique exposition of the sullen temperament; and the Apostle Paul uses a significant phrase in the same connection ". . . but the sorrow of the world worketh death" (2 Corinthians 7:10). The ultimate result of this kind of suffering is a hatred of holier lives—"But all the congregation bade stone them with stones" (Numbers 14:10); envy and murmuring at the messengers of God—"They envied Moses also in the camp, and Aaron the saint of the LORD" (Psalm 106:16), and sullen contempt of God's word. Dante places these souls in the fifth circle, tormented in the Stygian lake—

Fix'd in the slime, they say: "Sad once were we,
In the sweet air made gladsome by the sun,
Carrying a foul and lazy mist within:
Now in these murky settlings are we sad."

The other aspect of this sign of suffering is different in character and quality, viz. quietism, a life spent in

---

13. Adelaide Anne Procter (1825–1864): English poet.
14. Francis Paget (1851–1926): English theologian; bishop of Oxford, 1901–1911.

the luxury of reverie and contemplation. This type of suffering was very common in mediaeval Christianity, it produces a quietness apart, and flatly contradicts the very spirit of Christianity. The Psalmist of old tried to be a quietist, but he found himself too robust, it would not work with him—"I said, I will take heed to my ways, that I sin not with my tongue: I will keep my mouth with a bridle, while the wicked is before me. I was dumb with silence, I held my peace, even from good; and my sorrow was stirred. My heart was hot within me; while I was musing the fire kindled: then spake I with my tongue . . ." (Psalm 39:1–3 RV). This kind of sanctity, so called, is highly esteemed in all religions, but it engenders a pseudo-mysticism that inevitably ends in private illuminations apart from the written word and prayer, and actually spells "strong delusion." The true element in evangelical mysticism, which is easily distinguishable from Quietism, is the mystery of a human life visibly manifesting the life of the Lord Jesus in its mortal flesh.

This brings us to the third sign of Suffering—active well-doing. "Wherefore let them also that suffer according to the will of God commit their souls in well-doing unto a faithful Creator" (1 Peter 4:19 RV). The New Testament idea of a saint is not a cloistered sentiment gathering around the head of an individual like a halo of glory, but a holy character reacting on life in deeds of holiness. "I am the true vine, and My Father is the husbandman. Every branch in Me that beareth not fruit, He taketh it away: and every branch that beareth fruit, He cleanseth it, that it may bear more fruit" (John 15:1–2 RV). The cleansing of the individual branch is here made the sign of well-doing.

When a soul experiences suffering caused by the cleansing process and the pruning knife, he knows he is bearing fruit. A subtle law, which is ever and anon lost sight of by Christian teachers, is that an emotion which does not react in a proper manner will find an outlet in an improper manner. How often religious fervour and emotion, not finding reaction in its proper sphere, has sought an outlet in a lower, baser form. How sad and sordid and sorrowful is the connection between high spiritual emotions and sensual disaster. The hugging to one's self of any spiritual emotion is eminently dangerous.

This line of thought throws an important sidelight on our Lord's interview with Mary Magdalene on the Resurrection morning. Mary thought to hold Jesus to herself, to have Him again as a blessed Companion for herself, but Jesus said to her—"Take not hold on Me [mg]; for I am not yet ascended unto the Father: but go unto My brethren, and say to them, I ascend unto My Father and your Father, and My God and your God" (John 20:17 RV) There, as ever, the emphasis is on doing, not on contemplation. Du Bose says—

In the first place, Jesus took definite part with the West against the East in making the distinctive note of life not apatheia but energia. Thought, desire, will were not to be abjured and disowned in despair, through the overpowering sense of their futility. Life was not to be reduced to zero through their renunciation, but raised to infinity through their affirmation and satisfaction. The life of Christianity is a life of infinite energy because it is a life of infinite faith and hope. (The Gospel in the Gospels, p. 19)

The essential difference between the stoic and the saint is just at the point where they seem most alike. Dr. George Matheson[15] points this out in his book entitled *Studies in the Portrait of Christ*. A stoic overcomes the world by passionlessness; the saint's overcoming is by passion. This suffering in active well-doing results in a blessed and beneficent reaction on life.

> *Arise! this day shall shine for evermore,*
> * To thee a star divine on Time's dark shore!*
> *Till now thy soul has been all glad and gay;*
> * Bid it awake and look at Grief to-day! . . .*
> *But now the stream has reached a dark, deep sea;*
> * And Sorrow, dim and crowned, is waiting*
> *   thee.*
> *Each of God's soldiers bears a sword divine:*
> * Stretch out thy trembling hands to-day for*
> *   thine! . . .*
> *Then with slow, reverent step, and beating*
> *   heart,*
> * From out thy joyous day thou must depart,—*
> *And leaving all behind come forth alone.*
> * To join the chosen band around the throne:—*
> *Raise up thine eyes!—be strong!—nor cast away*
> * The crown that God has given thy soul to-day!*
> A. Procter

Suffering "according to the will of God"—To be "in the will of God" is not a matter of intellectual discernment, but a state of heart. To a sanctified soul the will of God is its implicit life, as natural as breathing. It is the sick man who knows intellectually what health is, and a sinful man knows intellectually what the will of God is; but a sanctified heart is the expres-

---

15. George Matheson (1842–1906): Scottish minister and writer known as the blind poet-preacher; wrote "Oh Love That Wilt Not Let Me Go," Chambers' favorite hymn.

sion of the will of God. Its motto is—"My Father can do what He likes with me, He may bless me to death, or give me a bitter cup; I delight to do His will."

"... as unto a faithful Creator." The sovereignty of God is the greatest comfort to the saint. The soul of the sanctified saint is *en rapport* with God, he has no responsibility, he is "without carefulness" because his Father cares, God's predestinations are that soul's voluntary choosings. The pre-eminent mystery in this thought is the mystery of the nature of Love: the saint knows, with a knowledge "which passeth knowledge." This truth is never discerned by the powerful in intellect, but only by the pure in heart.

> *Therefore to whom turn I but to thee, the ineffable Name?*
> > *Builder and maker, thou, of houses not made with hands!*
> *What, have fear of change from thee who art ever the same?*
> > *Doubt that thy power can fill the heart that thy power expands?*
> *There shall never be one lost good! What was, shall live as before;*
> > *The evil is null, is nought, is silence implying sound;*
> *What was good shall be good, with, for evil, so much good more;*
> > *On the earth the broken arcs; in the heaven, a perfect round.*
> *All we have willed or hoped or dreamed of good shall exist;*
> > *Not its semblance, but itself; no beauty, nor good, nor power*
> *Whose voice has gone forth, but each survives for the melodist*
> > *When eternity affirms the conception of an hour.*
> *The high that proved too high, the heroic for earth too hard,*
> > *The passion that left the ground to lose itself in the sky,*
> *Are music sent up to God by the lover and the bard;*
> > *Enough that he heard it once: we shall hear it by-and-by.*
>
> > Browning

This brings us to the grand finale of the Discipline of Suffering, viz.:

The Sublimity of Suffering

It is not possible to define life, or love, or suffering, for the words are but names for incalculable elements in human experience, the very essence of which is implicit, not explicit. To quote G. K. Chesterton again—

A critic who takes a scientific view of the Book of Job is exactly like a surgeon who should take a poetical view of appendicitis; he is simply an old "muddler."

Suffering is grand when the heart is right with God. But for the night "the moon and the stars, which Thou hast ordained," would never be seen. And so God giveth to His own "the treasures of darkness."

The Sublimity of Suffering can be indicated in three glorious outlines—Friendship with God, Fellowship with Jesus, and Freedom in the Highest.

(a) Friendship with God

Greater love hath no man than this, that a man lay down his life for his friends. Ye are My friends, if ye do the things which I command you. . . . (John 15:13–14 RV)

The relationship of a soul to Jesus Christ is capable of being interpreted in varying ways, but our Lord seems to imply that there is an end to discipleship, an end to learning the pace, and a point is reached where the disciple emerges as the friend of God, carrying with him the swinging stride of the mountains of God, and the atmosphere of the eternal hills. In such glimpses one recalls how in the dawnlight of the ages "Enoch walked with God," and so fascinating, so exhilarating, so entrancing, were those walks that one day he did not return—"and he was not; for God took him." Again, we read of Abraham, who has been known through all the ages as the "Friend of God," the father of all those who have become or will yet become the friends of God.

It is not possible to express what Jesus Christ has done for us in better words than those of the writer to the Hebrews—"For it became Him, for whom are all things, and through whom are all things, in bringing many sons unto glory, to make the Captain of their salvation perfect through sufferings. For both He that sanctifieth and they that are sanctified are all of one: for which cause he is not ashamed to call them brethren . . ." (Hebrews 2:10–11 RV). Oh, unspeakably blessed is the suffering of the sanctified that leads them step by step to this sublime friendship with God!

> *But whoso wants God only and lets life go,*
> *Seeks him with sorrow and pursues him far,*
> *And finds him weeping, and in no long time*
> *Again the High and Unapproachable*
> *Evanishing escapeth, and that man*
> *Forgets the life and struggle of the soul,*
> *Falls from his hope, and dreams it was a dream.*
>
> > *Yet back again perforce with sorrow and shame*
> *Who once hath known him must return, nor long*

Can cease from loving, nor endures alone
The dreadful interspace of dreams and day,
Once quick with God; nor is content as those
Who look into each other's eyes and seek
To find one strong enough to uphold the earth,
Or sweet enough to make it heaven: aha,
Whom seek they or whom find? for in all the
*   world*
There is none but thee, my God, there is none
*   but thee.*

                F. W. H. Myers

Lest you who are suffering under the call to supreme sanctification should faint or wail, you will presently hear Him say, "Fear not, . . . I am thy shield, and thy exceeding; great reward." Do you catch the majesty, the might, the awe, the unspeakable satisfaction of those words?

My goal is God Himself, not joy, nor peace,
*   Nor even blessing, but Himself, my God:*
'Tis His to lead me there, not mine, but His—
*   "At any cost, dear Lord, by any road."*

                F. Brook[16]

Oh, that men would not degrade and belittle what our Lord Jesus Christ has done for us by morbid introspective sympathy with one another! How many of us can hear Him say: "These things have I spoken unto you in parables [mg]: the hour cometh, when I shall no more speak unto you in parables, but shall tell you plainly of the Father. In that day ye shall ask in My name: and I say not unto you, that I will pray the Father for you; for the Father Himself loveth you, because ye have loved Me, and have believed that I came forth from the Father" (John 16:25–27 RV) Friendship with God is not a legal fiction; it is a reality in time. "In Thy presence is fulness of joy; in Thy right hand there are pleasures for evermore" (Psalm 16:11).

And all this is ours by the sheer might of the Atonement of Jesus, who gave Himself for us to cleanse and recreate us, to baptise us with the Holy Spirit and fire, till looking at us as we tread this earth among the common round and tasks of men, Jesus will see of the travail of His soul, and being satisfied, will say, "Father, this have I done; here is another soul." That soul incandescent with the Holy Spirit, walks and talks with God, as friend with friend, letting God do as He wills with him. This, and nothing less and nothing else, constitutes the suffering of the sanctified. Oh, the sublimity of the sufferings of the sanctified! Suffering according to the will of God, not so much for personal perfecting as to enable God to express His ideas in the life.

(b) Fellowship with Jesus.

But if, impatient, thou let slip thy cross,
Thou wilt not find it in this world again,
Nor in another; here, and here alone
Is even thee to suffer for God's sake.
In other worlds we shall more perfectly
Serve Him and love Him, praise Him, work
*   for Him,*
Grow near and nearer Him with all delight;
But then we shall not any more be called
To suffer, which is our appointment here
Couldst thou not suffer then one hour,—or two
If He should call thee from thy cross to-day,
Saying, It is finished!—that hard cross of thine
From which thou prayest for deliverance,
Thinkest thou not some passion of regret
Would overcome thee? Thou wouldst say,
*   "So soon?*
Let me go back, and suffer yet awhile
More patiently;—I have not yet praised God."
And He might answer to thee,—"Never more.
All pain is done with." Whensoe'er it comes,
That summons that we look for, it will seem
Soon, yea too soon. Let us take heed in time
That God may now be glorified in us;
And while we suffer, let us set our souls
To suffer perfectly: since this alone,
The suffering, which is this world's special grace,
May here be perfected and left behind.

              H. E. Hamilton King

The Cross of Jesus Christ stands unique and alone. His Cross is not our cross. Our cross is that we manifest before the world the fact that we are sanctified to do nothing but the will of God. By means of His Cross, our cross becomes our divinely appointed privilege. It is necessary to emphasise this because there is so much right feeling and wrong teaching abroad on the subject. We are never called upon to carry Christ's Cross: His Cross is the centre of Time and Eternity; the answer to the enigmas of both.

"For hereunto were ye called: because Christ also suffered for you, leaving you an example, that ye should follow His steps" (1 Peter 2:21 RV). This is the essence of fellowship with His sufferings. He suffered for you. Are you suffering on account of someone else, or for someone else? Are your agonising prayers and suffering before the Lord on behalf of that "distressing case" because it hurts you, discomforts you, makes you long for release? If so, you are not in fellowship with His suffering, nor anything like it. But if your soul, out of love for God, longs for others and bears

---

16. Frances Brook (born 1870): English hymnwriter.

with them in a voluntary, vicarious way, then you have a fellowship Divine indeed.

When your work suffers eclipse do you wail before God because the work of your hands is ruined? Do you say, "I looked upon this as my life-work, now it is broken and blighted and shattered"? If so, you do not know what fellowship with His sufferingmeans. But if, when you see men defiling the house of God, making His courts a place for traffic in worldly business, for engendering false affections, a home for vagrant beasts, you agonise before the Lord with alternate zeal and tears, then you have fellowship with Him in His sufferings. "Now I rejoice in my sufferings for your sake, and fill up on my part that which is lacking of the afflictions of Christ in my flesh for His body's sake, which is the church" (Colossians 1:24 RV).

For as the sufferings of Christ abound unto us, even so our comfort also aboundeth through Christ. (2 Corinthians 1:5 RV)

That I may know Him, and the power of His resurrection, and the fellowship of His sufferings, becoming conformed unto His death. (Philippians 3:10 RV)

This fellowship with His sufferings is a mystery only understood by the saint. But not all suffering leads to this sublime fellowship. To suffer from the hatred of men, to be separated from their company, to be reproached of men, to be considered as having an evil name, is not necessarily to have fellowship with His sufferings. We only have fellowship with Him if we suffer "for the Son of man's sake." To suffer martyrdom, to lose your life, to leave father and mother, houses and lands, is not to have fellowship with His sufferings unless it is done because of Him and for His sake.

This same thing thins the ranks of the suffering ones who claim fellowship with Him, and it humbles us to the dust. To drink of His cup, to be baptised with His baptism, is a thing so rare that few of us ever see it, or enter into it. Have you begun the solitary way with Him and has the clamour of father or mother made you quail? or does love for them pale into insignificance before your love for Him? Does wife arise, and with face and hands too tender, seek to prevent you from your course for Him? or does your love for Him in that supreme moment rise so high that your love for her appears hatred in comparison? Have your children's baby fingers bowed your head to earth again? or has your love for Him prevailed, and commending them, bone of your bone, and flesh of your flesh, to God, have you gone forth? Have brothers and sisters scathed and scandalised you, shamed you by their just and righteous indignation? or has love for Him prevailed even over that?

Has self-culture impeded your solitary way with Him? or has love for Him been so passionate that you love not your own life? Then you have become a disciple of Jesus indeed.

All this is not yet fellowship with His sufferings; it is the first lesson learned towards that fellowship: "If any man cometh unto Me, and hateth not his own father, and mother, and wife, and children, and brethren, and sisters, yea, and his own life also, he cannot be My disciple" (Luke 14:26 RV). "Doth this cause you to stumble? . . . From that time [KJV] many of His disciples went back, and walked no more with Him. Jesus said therefore unto the twelve, Would ye also go away?" (John 6:61, 66–67 RV).

Oh, the sublimity of the suffering that gains us fellowship with Jesus!

To abandon all, to strip one's self of all, in order to seek and follow Jesus Christ naked to Bethlehem, where He was born, naked to the hall where He was scourged, and naked to Calvary where He died on the cross, is so great a mystery that neither the thing, nor the knowledge of it, is given to any but through faith in the Son of God.

John Wesley

Wherever this finds you, my beloved sister or brother, can you hear, in imagination at least, our Lord say to you at the last, knowing all, "Well done, good and faithful servant"?

But if Himself He come to thee, and stand
Beside thee, gazing down on thee with eyes
That smile, and suffer; that will smite thy heart,
With their own pity, to a passionate peace;
And reach to thee Himself the Holy Cup
(With all its wreathen stems of passion-flowers
And quivering sparkles of the ruby stars),
Pallid and royal, saying, "Drink with Me";
Wilt thou refuse? Nay, not for Paradise!
—The pale brow will compel thee, the pure hands
Will minister unto thee; thou shalt take
Of that communion through the solemn depths
Of the dark waters of thine agony,
With heart that praises Him, that yearns to Him
The closer through that hour. Hold fast His hand,
Though the nails pierce thine too! take only care
Lest one drop of the sacramental wine
Be spilled, of that which ever shall unite
Thee, soul and body to thy living Lord!

For the glory and the passion of this midnight
   I praise Thy name, I give Thee thanks.
      O Christ!
Thou that hast neither failed me nor forsaken,
   Through these hard hours with victory
      overpriced;

Now that I too of Thy passion have partaken,
   For the world's sake called, elected, sacrificed.

Thou wast alone through Thy redemption-vigil,
   Thy friends had fled;
The angel at the garden from Thee parted,
   And solitude instead
More than the scourge, or cross, O tender-hearted,
   Under the crown of thorns bowed down
     Thy head.
But I, amid the torture, and the taunting,
   I have had Thee!
Thy hand was holding my hand fast and faster,
   Thy voice was close to me
And glorious eyes said, "Follow Me, Thy Master,
   Smile as I smile thy faithfulness to see."
                 H. E. Hamilton King

(c) Freedom in the Highest

Freedom is that implicit life which fulfils all the law of God, and transfigures the fulfilment in loving devotion. Oh, the sublimity of that Freedom in the Highest, wherein suffering has freed us from being the dupes of ourselves, of our convictions and our temperaments, and we realise that "our fellowship is with the Father, and with His Son Jesus Christ." Let it be said with reverence, even with bated breath, and in the atmosphere of the deepest humility, that suffering "according to the will of God" raises us to a freedom and felicity in the Highest that baffles all language to express. As ever, the only sufficient language is the language of Scripture. "If a man love Me, he will keep My word; and My Father will love him, and we will come unto him, and make our abode with him" (John 14:23 RV). "If any man hear My voice, and open the door, I will come in to him, and will sup with him, and he with Me" (Revelation 3:20). This is verily the apotheosis of freedom and felicity. This mirrors the incomprehensible mystery of the abiding of the Trinity in every suffering soul raised to the sublimity of fellowship. "If therefore the Son shall make you free, ye shall be free indeed" (John 8:36 RV). "I delighted and [RV mg] sat down under His shadow with great delight, and His fruit was sweet to my taste. He brought me to the banqueting house, and His banner over me was love" (Song of Solomon 2:3–4). "To day I must abide at thy house" (Luke 19:5).

Do you know the unspeakable bliss of Father, Son, and Holy Spirit abiding with you, feasting with you, and making you one with Them? This is the sublime height of suffering "according to the will of God."

Surely we gaze now at the mystery of godliness. No wonder "angels desire to look into" these things! A poor, evilly-disposed sinner, cleansed, saved, wholly sanctified, walking as the friend of God, in commu-

nion with the Lord in suffering, and the Trinity abiding with him as Companions daily and hourly and momentarily. This truly is a height from which the soul can look into the depths of the pain that our Saviour and Sanctifier went through to bring us there. This gives us a key to understand the shame and agony, the mock trial, the Crucifixion, the Resurrection, the Ascension and Pentecost.

There is a way for man to rise
   To that sublime abode;
An offering and a sacrifice,
A Holy Spirit's energies,
   An advocate with God.

No wonder St. Paul prays ". . . that the God of our Lord Jesus Christ, the Father of glory, may give unto you a spirit of wisdom and revelation in the knowledge of Him; having the eyes of your heart enlightened, that ye may know what is the hope of His calling, what the riches of the glory of His inheritance in the saints" (Ephesians 1:17–18 RV). This is the hope of His calling; we are part of the glory of His inheritance. This unveils to our hearts an understanding of our Lord's great prayer ". . . that they may be one, even as We are one." One in holiness, one in love, one for ever with God the Father, God the Son and God the Holy Ghost.

Servants of God!— or sons
Shall I not call you? because
Not as servants ye knew
Your Father's innermost mind,
His, who unwillingly sees
One of His little ones lost—
Yours is the praise, if mankind
Hath not as yet in its march
Fainted, and fallen, and died.

. . . .

Then, in such hour of need
Of your fainting, dispirited race,
Ye, like angels appear
Radiant with ardour divine.
Beacons of hope, ye appear!
Languor is not in your heart,
Weakness is not in your word,
Weariness not on your brow.
We alight in our van! at your voice,
Panic, despair, flee away.
Ye move through the ranks, recall
The stragglers, refresh the outworn,
Praise, re-inspire the brave.

Order, courage, return;
Eyes rekindling, and prayers,
Follow your steps as ye go.

Ye fill up the gaps in our files,
Strengthen the wavering line,
Stablish, continue our march,
On, to the bound of the waste,
On, to the City of God.

Matthew Arnold[17]

But, marvel of marvels, the outward and visible sign of the Sublimity of Friendship and Fellowship and Freedom in the Highest is in being the humblest servant of all—"Have this mind in you, which was also in Christ Jesus: who, being in the form of God, counted it not a prize to be on an equality with God, but emptied Himself, taking the form of a servant, being made in the likeness of men . . ." (Philippians 2:5–7 RV). "By this shall all men know that ye are My disciples . . ." (John 13:35).

It is a strange thing, a unique thing, that in this hierarchy of suffering, those nearest the throne are willingly, eagerly, the humblest; and the King Himself is Servant of all. "But I am in the midst of you as He that serveth" (Luke 22:27 RV).

"Its way of suffering is the witness which a soul bears to itself" (Amiel).[18]

The production of a saint is the grandest thing earth can give to Heaven. A saint is not a person with a saintly character: a saint *is* a saintly character. Character, not ecstatic moods, is the stuff of saintliness. A saint is a living epistle written by the finger of God, known and read of all men. A saint may be any man, any wastrel or vagabond, who discovering himself at Calvary, with the nature of sin uncloaked to him, lies in despair; then discerning Jesus Christ as the Substitute for sin and rising in the glamour of amazement, he cries out—"Jesus, *I* should be there." And to his astonished spirit, he receives justification from all his sinfulness by that wondrous Atonement. Then, standing in that great light, and placing his hands, as it were, over his Saviour's crucified hands, his feet over

His crucified feet, he crucifies for ever his right to himself, and the baptises him with the Holy Ghost and fire, substituting in him a new principle of life, an identity of holiness with Himself, until he bears unmistakably a family likeness to Jesus Christ.

God, who at sundry times in manners many
*   Spake to the fathers and is speaking still,*
Eager to find if ever or if any
*   Souls will obey and hearken to his will;—*

Who that one moment has the least descried him,
*   Dimly and faintly, hidden and afar,*
Doth not despise all excellence beside him.
*   Pleasures and powers that are not and that are,*

Ay amid all men bear himself thereafter
*   Smit with a solemn and a sweet surprise,*
Dumb to their scorn and turning on their laughter
*   Only the dominance of earnest eyes?*

. . . .

This hath he done and shall we not adore him?
*   This shall he do and can we still despair?*
Come let us quickly fling ourselves before him,
*   Cast at his feet the burthen of our care,*

Flash from our eyes the glow of our
*   thanksgiving,*
*   Glad and regretful, confident and calm,*
Then thro' all life and what is after living

Thrill to the tireless music of a psalm.

Yea thro' life, death, thro' sorrow and thro'
*   sinning*
*   He shall suffice me, for He hath sufficed:*
Christ is the end, for Christ was the beginning,
*   Christ the beginning, for the end is Christ.*

F. W. H. Myers

---

17. Matthew Arnold (1822–1888): English scholar, poet, and critic.
18. Henri Frederic Amiel (1821–1881): Swiss professor and writer; known for his self-analytical *Journal*, published in 1883.

THE DISCIPLINE OF PERIL

("The Discipline of Peril," *Tongues of Fire*, September 1914)

And when you hear of wars and disturbances, do not be scared; these have to come first, but the end is not at once. Luke 21:9 (MOFFATT)

The Discipline of Peril

Our Lord talks so much about peril and disaster and we deliberately shut our eyes and hearts and minds to it, and then when these things come, if we think at all, we are at our wits' end, we do not know what to make of them.

But these things have I told you, that when the time shall come, ye may remember that I told you of them. (John 16:4)

This question is on the lips of people to-day: Is war of the devil or of God? It is of neither. It is of man, though God and the devil are both behind it. War is a conflict of wills, either in individuals or in nations, and just now there is a terrific conflict of wills in nations. If I cannot make my will by diplomacy bear on other people, then the last resort is war, and always will be until Jesus Christ brings in His kingdom.

The Inevitableness of Peril
War and disturbances . . . have to come first.

Our Lord insists on the inevitableness of peril. Right through His talks with His disciples, without panic and without passion and without fear, He says: "You must lay your account with this sort of thing, with war, with spite, with hatred, with jealousy, with despisings, with banishment, and with death. I have told you these things, that when they happen, you may remember that I told you of them, and not be scared."

Have we realised that the worst must happen? And yet Jesus says, "When ye hear of wars and disturbances do not be terrified." We are not only hearing of wars and commotions, they are here right enough. It is not imagination, it is not newspaper reports, the thing is here, there is no getting away from it. War, such as the history of the world has never known, has now begun.

Jesus Christ did not say, "You will understand why war has come," but "Do not be scared, do not be put in a panic." It is astonishing how we ignore what Jesus Christ tells us. He says that the nations will end in war and bloodshed and havoc; we ignore what He says, and when war does come we lose faith in God, we lose our wits and exhibit panic. The basis of panic is always cowardice.

The Impulse of Panic
Do not be scared. There is one thing worse than war, and that is sin. The thing that startles us is not the thing that startles God. We get tremendously scared when our social order is broken up, and well we may. We get terrorised by hundreds of men being killed, but we forget that there is something worse—sinful, dastardly lives being lived day by day, year in and year out, in our villages and towns—men without one trace of cleanness in their moral lives. That is worse.

How many of us in times of peace and civilisation bother one iota about the state of men's hearts towards God? Yet these are the things that produce pain in the heart of God, not the wars and the devastation that so upset us. The human soul is so mysterious that in the moment of a great tragedy men get face to face with things they never gave heed to before, and in the moment of death it is extraordinary what takes place in the human heart towards God.

Are the terrors that are abroad producing panic—panic born of cowardice and selfishness? You never saw anybody in a panic who did not grab for themselves, whether it was sugar or butter or nations. Jesus would never allow His disciples to be in a panic. The one great crime on the part of a disciple, according to Jesus Christ, is worry. Whenever we begin to calculate without God we commit sin.

"Fret not thyself, it tendeth only to evil-doing" (Psalm 37:8 RV). Face facts. Very few of us will face facts, we prefer our fictions. Our Lord teaches us to look things full in the face and He says: "When you hear of wars and disturbances, do not be scared." It is the most natural thing in the world to be scared. There is no natural heart of man or woman that is not scared by these things, and the evidence that God's grace is at work amongst us is that we do not get terrified.

Our attitude must be: "Father, I do not know what these things mean: it looks like starvation and distress, but Thou hast said, 'Do not be scared,' so I will not be; and Thou hast said, 'Let not your heart be troubled,' so I will not let it be; and I stake my confidence in Thee." That is the real testimony.

It is very easy to trust in God when there is no difficulty, but that is not trust at all, it is simply letting the mind rest in a complacent mood; but when there is sickness in the house, when there is trouble, when there is death, where is our trust in God? The clearest evidence that God's grace is at work in our hearts is that we do not get into panics.

Christian Seemliness

("Christian Seemliness," *Tongues of Fire*, October 1914)

And take heed to yourselves. . . . Watch ye therefore, and pray always, that ye may be accounted worthy to escape all these things that shall come to pass. . . . (Luke 21:34, 36)

Seemliness is conduct in accordance with the highest standard recognised. Our Lord in these verses describes the character of Christian conduct in the confusion at the end of this dispensation, that is, the day in which we live.

In verse 34 Our Lord warns against the subtleties of indulgence; in verse 35 He describes the snare of war and confusion as inevitable, and in verse 36 He urges Christians to strenuously maintain their integrity.

Subtleties of Indulgence
And take heed to yourselves, lest. . . . (v. 34)

The most startling thing about this verse is that the Lord should have considered it necessary to warn Christians lest they sought distraction in these times of confusion by dissipation or drunkenness.

And take heed to yourselves, lest at any time your hearts be overcharged with surfeiting, and drunkenness, and cares of this life, and so that day come upon you unawares.

This verse is another indication of how our Lord will not allow Christians to build their conduct on suppositions based on ignorant innocence, but only on the revelation facts which He Himself gives. For instance, we should feel quite sure that we were not at all likely to seek distraction in these ways: but let us not forget that our Lord said, "*Take heed to yourselves, lest. . . .*"

In this present war there have been many attempts to inculcate seemliness of conduct in the British Empire according to the highest standard of nobility accepted by our nation, and it behoves us as saints to see that we conduct ourselves according to the plan laid down for us by our Lord.

Although our Lord talks of distraction in its final stages, we must remember that He condemns it in its initial stages. The beginning of surfeiting is indifference to present conditions from self-indulgence. We must take heed that in the present calamities, when war and devastation and heart-break are abroad in the world, we do not shut ourselves up in a world of our own and ignore the demand made on us by our Lord and our fellow-men for the service of intercessory prayer and hospitality and care.

This same line of things holds good with regard to the dissipation of drunkenness and the cares of this life.

The latter distraction to Christians is the most dangerous of all. A Christian must see to it that his interest in his possessions is not of such vital order that he is distracted from God in this present confusion.

Our Lord says that if these things are not heeded that day will come upon us unawares. If in that day any Christian finds himself in a panic, that is a sin which must be confessed and the burden of criminal carefulness laid at our Lord's feet, with a determination to follow a course more seemly according to God's standard for His saints.

Snare of the Inevitable
. . . for as a snare shall it come on all them that dwell on the face of the whole earth. (v. 35)

This verse states that the sudden arriving of this day of confusion will ensnare the whole world. It is not stated as a probability but as an inevitable certainty, and Christians are counselled by our Lord to lay their account with the inevitable. Civilisation and its amenities are made possible by Christianity, but they are not Christianity, and it is these amenities which ensnare and devastate in the time in which we live, and if we by unspiritual self-indulgence have been living our life in the externals, we shall be caught by this crisis and whirled into confusion.

There is a false sense of security produced by considering that there is safety in numbers, but our Lord in this verse states that the consternation will embrace "all them that dwell on the face of the whole earth," so that instead of numbers proving a security it proves an added element of terror. Have we taken heed and laid our account with these stern certainties, or are we as Christians indulging in the infatuation of any false security?

Strenuousness of Integrity
Watch ye therefore, and pray always, that ye may be accounted worthy to escape. . . . (v. 36)

The striking thing about these words is that the escape is not the free gift of God, but the result of Christian integrity. This verse is positive in its counsel as the other verses are positive in their commands. The counsel is to keep awake and pray. That our Lord should think fit to counsel prayer in time of war when practical common sense would place active doing first, reveals how totally different man's conceptions are from our Lord's. Prayer seems suitable for old men and women and sentimental young people, but for all others it is apt to be looked upon as a religious weakness.

There are many things in the minds of Christians which are not yet brought into captivity to the obedience of Christ. Prayer is always answered rightly by God, our Lord says; no wonder we have to keep awake and pray, for thousands of men are being hurled into eternity during this war. Are we keeping awake and praying, or are we amazed at the magnitude of the slaughter? Countries are devastated, cities are sacked, commerce is tied up, hundreds are bankrupt, millions out of work, innumerable homes are blighted and broken; are we keeping awake and praying?

When the veil is lifted we shall find that the seemly conduct of prayer wrought the things of God in men. Let us keep awake and readjust ourselves to our Lord's counsel. He counsels His children to keep alert, to be pure, to yield to no temptation to panic, to false emotion, to illegitimate gain, or to a cowardly sense of futility. We can never be where we are not, we are just where we are; let us keep alert and pray just there for His sake. Then our Lord says we shall be accounted worthy to escape all these things that shall come to pass, and to stand before the Son of Man—stand, not lie, nor grovel, nor cry, but stand upright, in the full integrity of Christian manhood and womanhood before the Son of Man.

The seemliness of Christian conduct is not consistent adherence to a mere principle of peace, but standing true to Jesus Christ. Let us stop all futile wailings that express themselves in such statements as "War ought not to be." War *is*, and we must not waste our time or our Lord's by giving way to any surfeit of screaming invective for or against any one or any thing; but "casting down imaginations, and every high thing that is exalted against the knowledge of God" (RV) in connection with ourselves, let us face life as it is, not as we feel it ought to be, for it never will be what it ought to be until the kingdom of this world is become the kingdom of our Lord, and of His Christ.

Let us gird up our loins, watch and be sober, and behave in the seemly manner of those that look for their Lord.

Slighted Security
("Slighted Security," *Tongues of Fire*, November 1914)

If thou hadst known . . . the things which belong unto thy peace! But now they are hid from thine eyes. . . . Thou knewest not the time of thy visitation. (Luke 19:42, 44)

The Burdened Sense
From the end of the earth will I cry unto Thee, when my heart is overwhelmed. (Psalm 61:2)

The feeling of bewilderment, of burden and perplexity is busy with the margins of many minds to-day; although the heart remains stout in its confidence in God, yet the senses are burdened with perplexity and misgiving. We shall be wise to let these things lead us to the Rock that is higher than we are.

Incredible Things Do Happen
The kings of the earth believed not, neither all the inhabitants of the world, that the adversary and the enemy should enter into the gates of Jerusalem. (Lamentations 4:12 RV)

That ancient peril is apt to repeat itself to-day, viz. a proud arrogancy arising from intellectual confidence in God's prophetic word, irrespective of the heart's condition. God has not any favourites outside faithfulness. God's order is the beginning and the end, His permissive will is the middle. God's eternal purposes will be fulfilled, but His permissive will allows Satan, sin and strife to produce all kinds of misconceptions and false confidences until we all, individually as well as collectively, realise that His order is best. It is possible to build up a false security, as Israel and Judah did of old, based on God's own prophetic word, but which ignores heart purity and humility before Him. The destruction of a certain class of prophetic student is stated by our Lord:

Many will say to Me in that day, Lord, Lord, have we not prophesied in Thy name? . . . And then will I profess unto them, I never knew you. (Matthew 7:22–23)

It was not that what they prophesied was not true, but it was not participated in by any whose hearts are unregenerated by God's spirit, no matter what their nationality may be. The ancient city of Jerusalem stands for all time as the symbol of destructive infatuation based on God's word, whereas God's word is only interpreted by and fulfilled in regenerated hearts and lives.

There Is No Road Back to Yesterday
He found no place of repentance, though he sought it carefully with tears. (Hebrews 12:17)

There are irreparable things. To God alone there is no irreparable past. We are delivered from sin by our Lord Jesus Christ, but He alone is the sinless One; we can never be as though we had not sinned. The gates of Paradise were irreparably closed to Adam and Eve and were never entered again by them (cf. Revelation 2:7). ". . . the years that the locust hath eaten, the cankerworm, and the caterpillar, and the palmerworm . . ." shall be restored, but only to a regenerated community (Joel 2:25).

What we need to heed in these days of war is that the unregenerated heart can never perceive the rule of God: "Except a man be born again, he cannot see the kingdom of God" (John 3:3); and that an unadjusted intellect, no matter if the heart be regenerated, will work itself untold destruction: ". . . in which are some things hard to be understood, which they that are unlearned and unstable wrest, as they do also the other scriptures, unto their own destruction" (2 Peter 3:16).

We do well to insist carefully for ourselves on the fact that although the Kingdom-Revelation may be the key-word to our Lord's teaching, the key-word to the Life to which alone that teaching applies is the Cross. The disciples were not told that by the interpretation of prophecy would all men be drawn to God, but—

I, if I be lifted up from the earth, will draw all men unto Me. (John 12:32)

When ye have lifted up the Son of man, then shall ye know that I am He, and that I do nothing of Myself; but as My Father hath taught Me, I speak these things. (John 8:28)

The Bland Satisfaction
If thou hadst known, even thou, at least in this thy day....

The tears of the Redeemer over Jerusalem are without parallel for significance and teaching. Our Lord said to the daughters of Jerusalem, who were undergoing paroxysms of tears over Him:

Daughters of Jerusalem, weep not for Me, but weep for yourselves, and for your children. (Luke 23:28)

The tears of our Lord embrace the Divine knowledge of Jerusalem's irreparable past: "O Jerusalem, Jerusalem, thou that killest the prophets, and stonest them which are sent unto thee" (Matthew 23:37); the Divine knowledge of God's order: "And I John saw the holy city, new Jerusalem, coming down from God out of heaven, prepared as a bride adorned for her husband" (Revelation 21:2); and the Divine knowledge of God's permissive will: ". . . how often would I have gathered thy children together, even as a hen gathereth her chickens under her wings, and ye would not! Behold, your house is left unto you desolate" (Matthew 23:37–38).

It is too late now. The bland satisfaction, that smooth, mild infatuation which arises from pride and arrogance, has not only perverted her knowledge and her power of reading events, but given her a great sense of security. This is of great significance to-day.

If there is bland satisfaction in the conscience of any nation, then disillusionment and sudden destruction is certain. But are we quite free individually from this bland satisfaction? It is perilously possible to be fatally ignorant of our true relationship to things and to God, and for that ignorance to be culpable. Are we blandly

satisfied that it is all right and yet we are not born from above? Are we still stiff-necked? Then sudden destruction cometh. It is too late now to mourn over our indifference, but wake up, call on God and be saved!

The Belittled Security
. . . the things which belong unto thy peace!

Jerusalem and Jesus! What a contrast! With what an amazed stare of contempt the personal powers of Jerusalem confronted Jesus, the despised and rejected! Yet He was their Peace for time and eternity, and the things that belonged to their peace were all connected with Him. He said to His disciples:

"These things have I spoken unto you, that in Me ye may have peace. In the world ye have tribulation: but be of good cheer; I have overcome the world" (John 16:33 RV). The parallels in this great European war of belittled security may be many, but our aim here is more personal. Are we belittling our own security? It is easy to do it. Just as nations place their confidence for security in armaments or arbitration (as the whim takes them) and neglect the worship of God as the only security, so individuals may easily place confidence in the amenities of society, in civilised entrenchments, in a good home and a good situation, and belittle the one abiding security—IN GOD!

To be indifferent to our Lord's claims is to belittle our security and remain in infatuation, out of which it will one day be too late to deliver us.

Rouse yourselves; it is too late now to mourn over the days and years in which you did not watch with your Lord, but wake up now!

The Blind Spot
. . . but now they are hid from thine eyes . . . because thou knewest not the time of thy visitation.

Like Nelson,[19] when he put the telescope to his blind eye that he might not see the order to retreat, so Jerusalem saw only in the direction of her prejudices. Here among them stood God Incarnate, a visitation from God Himself, but pride and arrogance and self-sufficiency blinded them and they saw Him not; they called Him "a man gluttonous, and a winebibber," they called Him "a sinner," "a Samaritan," they said that He was "beside Himself," and that He was demon-possessed. And this fatal blindness arose from merely not wanting to see certain things.

An immediate danger to-day is to apply all this to nations and to feel a sense of peculiar national security by noting the blind spot in Germany's outlook[20]; but

---

19. Horatio Nelson (1758–1805): British admiral and naval hero.
20. Germany's outlook: lecture given during World War I (1914–1918).

our aim must be to see that we have no blind spot ourselves, no spot of obtuse obstinacy which has slowly formed itself into a blind spot in which we too cannot see the day of our visitation, the day in which God is visiting us. Nay, let us apply it personally—Have I a blind spot? Am I purposely, even judiciously, blind whenever I hear anyone testifying to deliverance from sin, or to the baptism of the Holy Spirit, or to the amazing positive things that happen when God is seen?

The Blessed Sense

Behold, your house is left unto you desolate. For I say unto you, Ye shall not see Me henceforth, till ye shall say, Blessed is He that cometh in the name of the Lord. (Matthew 23:38–39)

Just as it is too late now with regard to this war, so it is too late to mourn in futile fashion over days of sin and pride and self-interest. Just as it is certain that desolation and havoc and misery will come in the wake of this war, so it is certain that desolation and havoc are in your life because of sin. But what a day of rejoicing it will be when you say, "Blessed is He that cometh in the name of the Lord!" Why not now, in a humbling sense of confessed sin, bow down under the mighty hand of God that where sin abounded, He may make grace much more abound. God hasten the day when "the kingdom of the world is become the kingdom of our Lord, and of His Christ" (RV).

Fitness

("Fitness," *Tongues of Fire,* December 1914)

I am crucified with Christ: nevertheless I live; yet not I, but Christ liveth in me: and the life which I now live in the flesh I live by the faith of the Son of God, Who loved me and gave Himself for me. (Galatians 2:20)

There are three things in this verse about personal fitness in this day for what the Lord requires of us, all full of pressing personal importance.

- The Relinquished Life—"I am crucified with Christ"
- The Distinguished Life—"nevertheless I live; yet not I, but Christ liveth in me"
- The Extinguished Life—"and the life which I now live in the flesh I live by the faith of the Son of God, who loved me and gave Himself for me"

These are three aspects of the one great theme of personal identification with our Lord.

The Relinquished Life. Fitness to Fly

"I am crucified with Christ." No one is ever united with the Lord Jesus Christ until he is willing to relinquish all of the life he held before. This does not only mean relinquishing sin, it means relinquishing the whole way of looking at things. To be born from above (RV mg) of the Spirit of God means that we must let go before we lay hold.

There are many people who believe in Jesus Christ but they have not relinquished anything, consequently they have not received anything; there is still the realisation of a life that has not been relinquished, and this great word of the Apostle Paul's is a foreign language altogether, it is not practical to them, it is "in the clouds," literally there is "nothing in it." But, blessed be the Name of God, there is something in it!

In the first stages it is a relinquishing of pretence. What our Lord Jesus Christ wants us to present to Him is not our goodness, or our honesty, or our endeavour, but our real solid sin, that is all He can take. "For He hath made Him to be sin for us, Who knew no sin." And what does He give in exchange for our solid sin? Great solid righteousness—"that we might be made the righteousness of God in Him"; but we must relinquish all pretence of being anything, we must relinquish in every way all claim to being worthy of God's consideration. That is the meaning of conviction of sin.

A word to those who have been quickened by the Spirit of God and introduced into His Kingdom—they have had their eyes opened and know something of what our Lord said to Nicodemus, "Except a man be born again, he cannot see the kingdom of God." If we can say, "I have been quickened by the Spirit and I do perceive the rule of God," then in us the Spirit of God will show what further there is to relinquish. There must be the relinquishing of my right to myself in every phase and condition of it. Am I willing to relinquish my hold on my life, my hold on all I possess, my hold on all my affections, my hold on everything? Am I willing to be God's child, and to be so identified with the death of the Lord Jesus Christ that I too know I have been crucified with Him?

There may be a sharp, painful disillusionment to go through before we do relinquish. When once a man really sees himself as the Lord Jesus Christ sees him, it is not the abominable social sins of the flesh that shock him, it is the awful nature of the pride of his own heart against the Lord Jesus Christ—the shame, the horror, the desperate conviction that comes when we realise ourselves in the light of Jesus Christ as the Spirit of God reveals Him to us. That is the true gift of repentance and the real meaning of it.

Are you hoodwinking your own soul by an intellectual comprehension of God's prophetic truth while you are perfectly unfit in moral life, in spiritual life and in domestic life, to meet Him? God grant that to-day the Spirit of God may come to you and to me and make us know whether we are living this relinquished life.

If we are going to fly, things that would prevent must not have any hold on us. Lusts of the flesh, desires of the mind, possessions, must all go. One thing we are realising to-day is that to the majority of us, civilised life is an elaborate way of doing without God. We have not been living a life hid with Christ in God, we have been living the abundance of the things which we possess. Now they are shaken, and terror, panic and mental imbecility have laid hold on people who a little while ago were very strong-minded and disdainful with regard to the phase of truth presented by the Pentecostal League of Prayer or by the Salvation Army; but the shattering of the pillars of their refuge has come. Thank God, He still leaves His mighty, winning, wooing Spirit with us. "I am crucified with Christ"—it is a real definite personal experience.

The Distinguished Life. Fitness to Fight
. . . nevertheless I live; yet not I, but Christ liveth in me.

This life has marked characteristics entirely of its own. Paul is stating that the relinquished life has found him identified with his Lord, and now all the great power of God is distinguishing him as a different man from the man he was before. He does not hate what he used to hate. He used to persecute and despise the followers of Jesus Christ; he despises them no longer. Not only does he not despise them, but he is identified with them and with their Lord. After Pentecost we read that "they took knowledge of them, that they had been with Jesus." They saw the strong, distinguished family likeness in them and recognised it at once as the Lord Jesus Christ.

One great characteristic in the life of a man whose life is hid with Christ in God is that he has received the gift Jesus Christ gives. What gift does Jesus Christ give to those who are identified with him? The gift His Father gave him, The Father gave Him the Cross, and He gives us our cross: "If any man will come after Me, let him deny himself, and take up his cross daily, and follow Me." "Let him relinquish, give up his right to himself"—distinguished by one thing, ". . . ye are not your own? For ye are bought with a price." To take up our cross daily means that we take now what otherwise would go on to Jesus Christ. The distinguished life means that we "fill up that which is behind of the afflictions of Christ in [our] flesh for His body's sake, which is the church." That means practically the fulfilment of Matthew 11:29, "Take My yoke upon you, and learn of Me; for *I am meek and lowly in heart.*" There is nothing to fill up of that which remains of the afflictions of Christ for the purposes of Redemption, that is complete; but we can fill up that which remains behind of His sufferings for His Body's sake. Are we distinguished as the ones in whom Christ lives, meeting things as He did? If so, we are fit for flying, for fighting and for following.

The Extinguished Life. Fitness for Following
And the life which I now live in the flesh I live by the faith of the Son of God, Who loved me, and gave Himself for me.

—that is, there is no more of the old disposition manifested in this man, Paul the Apostle. There is no "Saul of Tarsus" disposition manifested; that has been extinguished, died right out! This is much more than sin, mark you, it is all the old way of reasoning; what is manifested now, Paul says, is the faith which was in the Son of God. Do you remember what this man said— "When it pleased God, who separated me from my mother's womb, and called me by His grace, to reveal His Son in me"? The characteristic that is manifested is the faith of the Son of God, the Lord Jesus Christ seeing the full purpose and meaning of His own life working through the Apostle Paul.

Is that altogether beside the mark? It is the practical clear direct message of God to your heart and mine to-day—a perfect fitness by the wonderful Redemption of our Lord Jesus Christ being realised in us as we relinquish.

You will find the supreme crisis in your life is "will-issues" all the time. *Will* I relinquish? *Will* I abandon? It is not that God won't make us fit, it is that He cannot. God cannot make us fit to meet Him in the air unless we are willing to let Him. He cannot make us fit as the dwellings of His Son unless we are willing, because He wants sons and daughters. If you are up against a crisis, go through with it, relinquish all, and let Him make you fit for all He requires of you in this day.

First and Last
("First and Last," League of Prayer New Years' Convention, Friday, January 1, 1915, in Pontefract, W. Yorkshire)

I am the way, the truth, and the life: no man cometh unto the Father, but by Me. (John 14:6)

The words of our Lord come to one as those that alone can be welcomed on the threshold of 1915. Other people's words are too fraught with personal prejudice or clouded by personal pain to convey a message for this New Year. There are thousands of hearts and minds too distracted by this terrible war to receive with meekness any other words than those of our Lord Jesus Christ.

The Way
I am the way.

Thomas's depressed exclamation, "Lord, we know not whither Thou goest; and how can we know the way?" is the language of many a heart to-day, and if all the saints and all the suffering and sorrowing ones would only listen to our Lord's reply, we would all be strong to bear, and rejoicing to do in the strength of the Lord.

Our Lord said, "*I am the way*," not the way to any one or anything; He is not a road we leave behind us, He is the Way to the Father in which we abide (see John 15:4). He is the Way, not He was the Way, and there is not any way of living in the Fatherhood of God except by living in Christ. Whoso findeth himself in Christ findeth life. The Way to the Father is not by the law, nor by obedience, or creed, but Jesus Christ Himself, He is the Way of the Father whereby any and every soul may be in peace, in joy, and in divine courage during the days of this coming year. In any assailing tribulation our Lord says, "that in Me ye might have peace." When imagination brooding on wars and rumours of wars is apt to affright the souls of men, Christ Jesus is the Way of the Fatherhood of God, sustaining, and comforting and joyous.

To all those who are in the Way let me urge you by abiding in Jesus to let the rivers of living water pour through you to the binding up of the broken-hearted, the setting at liberty of the captives, and the proclaiming of the acceptable year of the Lord.

The Truth
I am . . . the truth.

Amid all the whirling contentions and confusions produced in men's minds by what is called truth, again our Lord's word to Thomas abides, "*I* am . . . the truth." Truth is not a system, not a constitution, nor even a creed; the Truth is the Lord Jesus Christ Himself, and He is the Truth about the Father just as He is the Way of the Father. Our tendency is to make truth a logical statement, to make it a principle instead of a Person. Profoundly speaking there are no Christian principles, but the saint by abiding in Christ in the Way of the Fatherhood of God discerns the Truth of God in the passing moments. Confusion arises when we disassociate ourselves from our Lord and try to live up to a standard merely constructed on His word.

In John 14:8–11, our Lord distinctly says that He and the Father are one. Would that men who name the Name of Christ realised that He is the Truth, not the proclaimer of it; that He is the Gospel, not the preacher of the Gospel; that He is the Way of the Fatherhood of God. What men and women need is the "Fathering" of God, so that from all affright and fear they may be held steady by the gentleness of God, and that is only realised in Christ. Those of us who do know it have a gracious ministry to maintain, so abiding in Him that we reveal the truth as it is in Jesus in our going in and out among the devastated and distracted.

The Life
I am . . . the life.

Many start this year crying to God from weariness of life that they might die. The light of their eyes has been taken from them, the prospects of life have been extinguished and all they held most dear has been shattered, and this in no sentimental but in a very real sense. Again the superb declaration of our Lord, "I am . . . the life," comes with eternal succour. He is the Life of the Father just as He is the Father's Way and the Father's Truth. "The gift of *God* is eternal life"; not the gift *from* God, as if eternal life were a present given by God: it is Himself. The life imparted by our Lord is the Life of God, and the sacrament of the Lord's Supper is the visible commemoration of this ever-abiding fact. "For as often as ye eat this bread, and drink this cup, ye do shew the Lord's death till He come."

Let us remember that Jesus Christ is Life, and our life, all our fresh springs are in Him (PBV),[21] so that whether we eat or drink, or whatsoever we do, let us do all to the glory of God. May this be a year in which those of us who are God's children manifest the life of God in our mortal flesh.

We are near the end of the present order, and the throes and weariness of exhausted turmoil are concentrated in many hearts and lives. What is needed is the Life of the Father which is ours in Jesus Christ. He said, "I am come that they might have life"; and He also said, "Ye will not come to Me, that ye might have life." Let those of us who are God's children be the conductors of the Life of God to exhausted men and women till they too are made one in Him.

The Exclusive One
No man cometh unto the Father, but by Me.

Many to-day are realising the futility of beautiful sentimental phrases about the Fatherhood of God; they are finding them beautiful untruths. The words of our Lord, "*no man cometh unto the Father, but by Me*," reveal the error and at the same time open the way to the Father. Our Lord Jesus Christ is the Exclusive Way to the Father. By His Cross alone a man enters into the adoption of a son of God. Our Lord did not say, "No man cometh unto God, but by Me." There are many ways of coming to God other than by the Lord Jesus Christ, but no man ever came to *the Father*, but by Jesus Christ. He is the Exclusive Way

---

21. PBV: Prayer Book Version. The *Book of Common Prayer* of the Church of England.

there, the constant active medium to our intercourse with the Father.

This war, which for a time has made men in pain say petulant, unbelieving things about the creeds that are right in theory but utterly futile in practice, has at the same time prepared their hearts for the universality of the exclusive way of Christ to the Father. He is the only Way to the Father, but it is a Way that is open to any and every man, the Way that knows "neither Greek nor Jew, . . . Barbarian, Scythian, bond nor free: but Christ is all, and in all." It is the duty and privilege of those who are Christ's to proclaim this glorious revelation with lip and life, with impassioned zeal and earnestness in the closing phases of the dispensation in which we live.

God grant that 1915 may find each one of us abiding in the Way, incorporated into the Truth, infused by the Life, and manifesting the mighty Fatherhood of God in and through our Lord Jesus Christ. In the Name that is above every name we pray that this year may be the year of the First and the Last, the Beginning and the End, Our Lord Jesus Christ.

God's Parenthesis
("God's Parenthesis," *Tongues of Fire,* March 1915)
Yea, a sword shall pierce through thy own soul also. (Luke 2:35)

A parenthesis is a phrase or sentence inserted in another which is grammatically complete without it, and if you want to understand the author, pay particular attention to the parenthesis.

God puts a parenthesis in the middle flow of our lives; if you want to understand your life, read the parenthesis, if you can. There was a parenthesis in Hezekiah's life, and when he was through it, he said, "I shall go as in a solemn procession all my years." A short time after though he forgot and began to "knuckle down" and compromise with a pagan king.

Have we been paying sufficient attention to the parentheses God puts in our lives? It may have been "good fortune," it may have been "bad fortune," it may have been a delightful friendship, it may have been a heart-break. But when God sums up our lives, it is that parenthesis which really gives the heart of our life with Him.

Impaired by God
The Holy Ghost shall come upon thee, and the power of the Highest shall overshadow thee: therefore also that holy thing which shall be born of thee shall be called the Son of God. (Luke 1:35)

The Virgin Mary is not only unique as the mother of our Lord, but she stands as the type of what we must expect if we are going to be those whom our Lord calls "My brother, and sister, and mother" (Matthew 12:50).

Simeon was completely possessed, guided, and controlled by the Holy Ghost, and when he saw Mary he spoke these wonderful words:

Behold, this child is set for the fall and rising again of many in Israel, . . . (Yea, and a sword shall pierce through thy own soul also,) that the thoughts of many hearts may be revealed. (Luke 2:34–35)

When Christ is formed in us by the power of regeneration, our natural life experiences exactly the same thing, viz. a sword that we would never have had if we were not born again of God, a type of suffering that we would know nothing about if we were not born from above (RV mg), if the Son of God were not formed in us.

When the angel saluted her, Mary was amazed and staggered. After the Holy Ghost had come upon her, her life was impaired, full of embarrassment and terror. It is an abiding truth that when we are born of the Holy Ghost, instantly the life becomes impaired from every merely natural standpoint.

When we receive God's Spirit and God suddenly opens up His purpose for our lives, then when the "angel" departs we begin to realise exactly what an impaired life means if we go on with it. It means that our life will produce one or two characteristics people will sneer at, one or two characteristics people will be contemptuous over, thoroughly annoyed and angry over. It was so with Mary. The sword Simeon spoke of very soon began to pierce through her own soul.

We need to remind ourselves of the stern, heroic stuff Jesus Christ always spoke when He talked about discipleship. "If any man will come after Me, let him deny himself, and take up his cross daily, and follow Me" (Luke 9:23). Few of us do it though plenty of us talk about it. It means an impaired life:—"A sword shall pierce through thy own soul also."

You have been full of complaints these past months and have blamed everything but yourself; the reason is you were not prepared for an impaired life as far as this world was concerned. The beginnings of God's life in a man or woman are directly across the will of nature, because nature has to be transformed in your particular bodily life and mine into a spiritual life by obedience. Obedience to the Spirit of God means a maimed life, maimed in a hundred and one ways, and in the closest relationships of all (see Luke 14:26).

The Impeded Life with God
Woman, what have I to do with thee? (John 2:4)

This new life impedes us in our natural outlook and ways until we get these rightly related by putting on the new man, until the Son of God is formed in us and both the natural and the holy are the same.

The natural in us wants the Son of God to do Almighty God's work in our way. What could be better than that the Son of God should manifest the fact that He is in us? Thousands saved in a day! Ourselves transformed and held as marvellous specimens of what God can do!! Something wonderful performed at the dictates of our natural (not sinful) lives!!! We want Him to do this and that, we demand He should do it, we rush in and say, "Now this is the time," but we receive a real check from God which means that we dare not open our mouths to Him again on the subject. When our Lord's miracles are at work in us they always manifest themselves in a chastened life, utterly restrained.

Has God's parenthesis come to you by impeding some great natural impulse? You are a child of God, you started off to work for Him and expected Him to do wonderful things; in fact you demanded He should do them; then He brought you into "a corner" and you were rebuked directly by the Son of God.

Is that the parenthesis God has put in your life just now? Some purpose, some aim of yours in God's work and you were expecting Him to manifest Himself straight away by a mighty miracle, but instead there came the extinction of your naturally good impulse. Nobody heard the rebuke but you, but when the miracle was wrought you were able to understand and to listen to Him. Beware of listening to your own point of view when the Son of God has come.

The Insulated Life with God
Now there stood by the cross of Jesus His mother. . . . (John 19:25)

To insulate means to place in a detached position. The sword began to pierce very early in Mary's life, and it pierced all through. Now she stands at the Cross with her own Son, in Whom every Scripture and oracle of God has centred. He has been through His agony and His mother could do nothing for Him, she could not understand the depth of the agony of Gethsemane; now she sees Him on the Cross what happens? Jesus sees her and says, "Woman, behold thy son!" and to John, "Behold thy mother!" That is an illustration of what happens when the life of the Son of God and the full purpose of God are being worked out in us in ways we cannot understand but do not doubt.

Beware of saying, "I do not need any discipline, I am saved and sanctified, therefore everything I think is right." Nothing we think is right, only what God thinks in us is right. The Son of God revealed exactly how a man's brain and body and will were to be used if he was to live in obedience to God. Our Lord submitted His intelligence to His Father, and He submitted His will to His Father. "I came not to do Mine own will," He says over and over again.

There are great perplexities in life, but thank God, if we will trust, with the bold, implicit trust of our natural life, in the Son of God, He will bring out His perfect, complete purposes in and through our particular lives.

Are You Ever Disturbed?
("Are You Ever Disturbed?" is a talk given at a BTC devotional meeting, May 27, 1914.)

Peace I leave with you, My peace I give unto you: not as the world giveth, give I unto you. Let not your heart be troubled, neither let it be afraid. (John 14:27)

Have You Ever Received in This Way?
The disciples, like many to-day, were not in a state to provide their own inner peace. There are times when inner peace is based on ignorance; but when we awake to the troubles of life, which more than ever before surge and heave in threatening billows, inner peace is impossible unless it is received from our Lord. When our Lord spoke peace, He made peace. His words are ever spirit and life. Have you ever received what He spoke?

The peace of sins forgiven, the peace of a conscience at rest with God, is not the peace that Jesus imparts. Those are the immediate results of believing and obeying Him, but it is His own peace He gives, and He never had any sins to be forgiven or an outraged conscience to appease. Have you ever received His peace? When you are right with God, receive your peace by studying in consecrated concentration our Lord Himself; it is the peace that comes from looking at His face and remembering the undisturbed condition of our Lord in every set of circumstances. "But we all, with open face beholding as in a glass the glory of the Lord, are transformed into the same image from glory to glory" (2 Corinthians 3:18).

Are you painfully disturbed just now, distracted by the waves and billows of God's providential permission, and having turned over, as it were, the boulders of your belief, you still find no well of peace or joy or comfort—all is barren? then look up and receive the undisturbedness of our Lord Jesus Christ. Above and in the facts of war and pain and difficulties He reigns, peaceful. Reflected peace is the greatest evidence that I am right with God, for I am at liberty to turn my mind to Him. If I am not right with God I can never turn my mind anywhere but on myself. "Then will I go . . . unto God my exceeding joy" (Psalm 43:4). Am I certain that God is not miserable? Then His joy will be my strength. We are changed by looking, not by introspection. The source of peace is God, not myself; it never is my peace but always His, and if once He withdraws, it is not there. If I allow anything to hide the face, the countenance, the memory, the consideration of our Lord Jesus from me, then

I am either disturbed or I have a false security. "Consider Him . . . , that ye wax not weary, fainting in your souls" (Hebrews 12:3 RV). Nothing else is in the least like His peace. It is the peace of God, which passeth all understanding. Are you looking unto Jesus just now in the immediate pressing matter and receiving from Him peace? Then He will be a gracious benediction of peace in and through you.

Have You Ever Recognised in This Way?

The world means what it says, but it cannot impart. Our Lord imparts what He says, He does not give like the world does. Will I be absolutely confident in Jesus? What does it matter what happens to me? The thought ought never to bother us, the thing that ought to occupy us is setting the Lord always before us (cf. Acts 20:24). Jesus Christ imparts the Holy Spirit to me, and the Holy Spirit sheds abroad the love of God in my heart (see Romans 5:5). The peace of Jesus is not a cherished piece of property that I possess; it is a direct impartation from Him, and my enjoying His peace depends on my recognising this.

Have You Ever Remembered in This Way?

This kind of peace banishes trouble just now and presently. Our Lord says in effect, "Don't let your heart be troubled out of its relationship with Me." It is never the big things that disturb us, but the trivial things. Do I believe in the circumstances that are apt to bother me just now, that Jesus Christ is not perplexed at all? If I do, His peace is mine. If I try to worry it out, I obliterate Him and deserve what I get.

When we confer with Jesus Christ over other lives all the perplexity goes, because He has no perplexity, and our concern is to abide in Him. The reason we get disturbed is that we have not been considering Him. Lay it all out before Him, and in the face of difficulties, bereavement and sorrow, hear Him say, "Let not your heart be troubled." Let us be confident in His wisdom and His certainty that all will be well. "He abideth faithful; for He cannot deny Himself" (2 Timothy 2:13 RV). The angels' song is still the truth: "Glory to God in high heaven, and peace on earth for men whom He favours!" (MOFFATT).

Radiant in the Thick of It (Romans 8:33–39)

("Radiant in the Thick of It" is a talk given in Hawes, Yorkshire September 12, 1915, at the Sunday evening service, Wesleyan Methodist Chapel)

In all these things we are more than conquerors through Him that loved us. (v. 37)

The Vocation of the Saint

They looked unto Him, and were radiant. (Psalm 34:5 ASV)

There are circumstances and difficulties which can only be described as "the thick of it," and in and through all such the Apostle Paul says we are to be "more than conquerors." Paul always talked from the deep centre of things, and the majority of us do not pay much attention to him until some calamity or disaster strikes us out of the shallows, then the Bible takes on a new guise and we find that it always speaks profoundly.

The vocation of a saint is to be in the thick of it "for Thy sake." Whenever Jesus Christ refers to discipleship or to suffering, it is always, "for My sake." The deep relationship of a saint is a personal one, and the reason a saint can be radiant is that he has lost interest in his own individuality and has become absolutely devoted to the Person of the Lord Jesus Christ.

"Who shall lay anything to the charge of God's elect? Shall God that justifieth?" (v. 33 RV mg). When once a saint puts his confidence in the election of God, no tribulation or affliction can ever touch that confidence. When we realise that there is no hope of deliverance in human wisdom, or in human rectitude, or in anything that we can do, then Paul counsels us to accept the justification of God and to stand true to the election of God in Christ Jesus. This is the finest cure for spiritual degeneration or for spiritual sulks.

"Who is he that shall condemn? Shall Christ Jesus that died . . . ?" (v. 34 RV mg). "Christ died for the ungodly." Then is it a remarkable thing that after we have accepted His salvation we begin to find out our unworthiness? "Who is he that condemneth? It is Christ that died." Stake your confidence in Him! Let there be a real shifting of the whole centre of life into confidence in Jesus Christ.

"Who shall separate us from the love of Christ?" (v. 35). In the confusion and turmoil of things, there is very little we can explain; things happen which upset all our calculations, but—"Who shall separate us from the love of Christ?" Nothing! When we know that nothing can separate us from the love of Christ, it does not matter what calamities may occur, we are as unshakeable as God's throne.

The Valley of the Shadow

Yea, though I walk through the valley of the shadow of death, I will fear no evil. (Psalm 23:4)

"Who shall separate us from the love of Christ? shall tribulation, or anguish, or persecution, or famine . . .?" (RV). Can we remain true to the vocation of a saint in tribulation? Think of the thousands who have had to go through tribulation during these past years—every human hope taken from them; but yet the saint with an amazing hopefulness remains radiant in the thick of it.

". . . or nakedness, or peril, or sword?" In our own day all these things are dastardly realities. Can we maintain our vocation as a saint there? Life was going on all right when suddenly we were struck by a psychological nor'wester! Paul says we have to maintain our vocation in the midst of the most desperate things that can happen in individual life.

The Vision of Slaughter

For Thy sake we are killed all the day long; we were accounted as sheep for the slaughter. (v. 36 RV)

Every man who comes to Jesus Christ has to go through the ordeal of condemnation, he has to have his beauty "consume away like a moth," and his righteousness drop from him "as filthy rags" when he stands face to face with God.

"For I am persuaded, that neither death, nor life, nor angels, nor principalities . . ."—these are things beyond our control, and they introduce painful agonies into our experience, they slaughter our hopes: "nor things present"—things present prevail, things we cannot alter; a bereavement profoundly alters life, so does a joy, or war: "nor things to come"—think of the number of bridges we have all crossed before we come to them! Things to come are always prevailing, human wisdom cannot touch them: "nor powers," there are terrific powers that move around in total disregard of us: "nor height, nor depth, nor any other creature . . ." Can we maintain our vocation in the face of every terror? Paul says we can, because he is persuaded that none of these things "shall be able to separate us from the love of God, which is in Christ Jesus our Lord."

It all comes back to this—am I radiant in the thick of it for His sake?

THE DAY OF THE LORD

("The Day of the Lord," *Tongues of Fire,* May 1915)

The sun shall be changed into darkness and the moon into blood, ere the great, open Day of the Lord arrives. Acts 2:20 (MOFFATT)

> The Day of the Lord is at hand, at hand:
>   The storms roll up the sky:
> The nations sleep starving on heaps of gold;
>   All dreamers toss and sigh;
> The night is darkest before the morn;
> When the pain is the sorest, the child is born
>   And the Day of the Lord is at hand.
>
> Gather you, gather you, angels of God—
>   Freedom, and Mercy, and Truth:
> Come! for the Earth is grown coward and old,
>   Come down. and renew us her youth.
> Wisdom, Self-Sacrifice. Daring, and Love,
> Haste to the battle-field, stoop from above,
>   To the Day of the Lord at hand.
>
> Gather you, gather you, hounds of hell—
>   Famine, and Plague, and War;
> Idleness, Bigotry, Cant, and Misrule,
>   Gather, and fall in the snare!
> Hireling and Mammonite, Bigot and Knave,
> Crawl to the battle-field, sneak to your grave,
>   In the Day of the Lord at hand.

> Who would sit down and sigh for a lost age
>   of gold,
>   While the Lord of all ages is here?
> True hearts will leap up at the trumpet of God,
>   And those who can suffer, can dare.
> Each old age of gold was an iron age too,
> And the meekest of saints may find stern work
>   to do.
> In the Day of the Lord at hand.
>
>   Kingsley[22]

Distraction of Nations

For nation shall rise against nation, and kingdom against kingdom. (Matthew 24:7)

The words of Charles Kingsley quoted above are rousingly appropriate for that day of "blood, and fire, and vapour of smoke," the Day of the Lord, so near at hand. To consider that the " flower" of the British Empire will be mown down this summer, that the "flower" of Germany is being exterminated, the "flower" of France is broken and shattered in the soil of Flanders,[23] is really appalling. Truly it is a day of "blood, and fire, and vapour of smoke." Pictures and poems inspired by broken hearts, and the dissipation of tender and beautiful ideals, have been and are being painted and written, daring almost to blasphemy, in a realisation born of agony.

---

22. Charles Kingsley (1819–1875): English cleric and writer.
23. "flower" of . . . : lecture given during World War I (1914–1918).

It is easy to criticise from the severe security of a crystallised orthodoxy, such conceptions, but we had better remember that the cry of the human heart, long blinded to God by the god of this age, when suddenly made to see by the alchemy of Hell in slaughter, sees with distorted and blurred vision, but beware lest we forget that such things may be the half-way expression to worship. Pray for them, you who have got better sight and clearer understanding. Our duty is to serve by intercession. In these days when there are wild interpretations of His words, "Greater love hath no man than this, that a man lay down his life for his friends," remember that they are His words. If in the inspiration of the terror of war, artist or poet has made the blunder of James and John when they said in early zeal that they could drink of His cup and be baptised with His baptism, why any more than these disciples should they be made out to be belittlers of the great Atonement? We who know that the love of God is revealed in that while we were yet enemies Christ died for us, ought to have more of His Spirit who redeemed us than to criticise; we are called to pray for them the effectual prayer.

Distress of Nations

Upon the earth distress of nations, in perplexity for the roaring of the sea and the billows, men expiring for fear, and for expectation of the things which are coming on the inhabited earth. (Luke 21:25–26 RV mg)

Let us not imagine that "distress of nations" is exactly war. War is the natural inspiration of a nation's challenged pride; but distress of nations is the diabolic inspiration of covetousness, leading people to revolution and mutiny and anarchy. Psalm 65:7 says, "which stilleth the roaring of the seas, the roaring of their waves, and the tumult of the peoples," and those words might well put us on to the right track for the meaning of our Lord's words quoted above—"the roaring of the sea" refers to the nations.

Those ominous mutterings before the war, those sinister sounds during the war, on the Clyde, those irregular undisciplined outbursts in neutral countries like America, and the stormy petrels which appear from time to time in Germany are all big with portent. On Wednesday, March 3rd, 1915:—

A telegram from Berlin states that on the occasion of the second reading of the Budget for the Ministry of the Interior in the Prussian Diet, Dr. Liebnecht, the Socialist member, speaking before an almost empty House, said that the bourgeois attitude on the franchise question did not mean the democratisation of Government, but more consistent plutocratisation through plural voting.

"For the National Liberals," he said, "the war is an important economical and political business.

The democratisation of foreign and domestic policy in all states would have prevented the war.

"The only salvation for the mass of the people is an international class war. Therefore away with the hypocrisy of party peace. Forward to class war against war."

These are grave indications, and just to consider that when the "flower" of our own country, of France and Germany, are gone, who will be able to restrain the lawless mobs? Truly the words of our Lord are full of fearsome warning, "men expiring for fear."

It is also opportune here to quote Abraham Lincoln in reference to a big factor in this "distress of nations." He said this just before his assassination—

I see in the near future a crisis approaching that unnerves me, and causes me to tremble for the safety of my country. Corporations have been enthroned, an era of competition in high places will follow, and the moving power of the country will endeavour to prolong its reign by working upon the prejudices of the people until the wealth is aggregated in a few hands, and the Republic is destroyed.

Much is suppressed, but we as God's children have no right to be taken unawares when our Lord speaks so plainly, let us note how history fulfils the word, and watch unto prayer. Our motto ought not to be "Business as usual," or "Victory as usual," but rather "Nothing us usual."

Delivered from Nations

But watch ye at every season, making supplication, that ye may prevail to escape all these things that shall come to pass, and to stand before the Son of man. (Luke 21:36 RV)

There is yet, thank God, ample opportunity for repentance and we children of God must beware of two extremes:—the one the "Jonah-mood" where indignation with God arises from the fact that God's judgements are conditional, like His promises, and just because the Ninevites repented, the conditional judgements of God which Jonah had pronounced seemed to fail. God's purpose is not so much to vindicate the word of His servants as to bring to pass His divine purpose. Now there is a type of prophetic study that is apt to produce just this hard defiant severity.

The other extreme is to refine all prophetic utterances relative to the end of this age into mere spiritualised imagery, and to deify the emotions of human interest. "The Day of the Lord" is an awful joy in the Scripture use of the phrase, for it is the final vindication of Goodness and the final establishment of righteousness.

Do not be ignorant of our times, "look up." Let intercession entrench itself in all our plans for those in the trenches, enwheel the vessels and embrace them below, above and around; let intercession ascend the heavens and guard the airy premise's. For it is not peace that is to be born of this war, but the Day of the vengeance of our God, the drawing nigh of Redemption.

And He saw that there was no man, and wondered that there was no intercessor: therefore His own arm brought salvation unto Him, and His righteousness, it upheld Him. (Isaiah 59:16 RV)

Devotion in Nations
Watch ye therefore, and pray always, that ye may be accounted worthy to escape all these things that shall come to pass, and to stand before the Son of man. (Luke 21:36)

The "escape" in that verse must be interpreted in its evangelical context, namely, it must be made to convey the idea, not of saving "one's skin," because it is a word of our Lord's, and He never taught such self-preservation, but escape must be made to mean deliverance from all personal forms of selfish remembrance, and to "stand before the Son of man" undisturbed, with the "heart at leisure from itself to soothe and sympathise," and with ample power to give to others through God's good grace.

You who know by His revelation in the words of the Bible, that the earth is the Lord's and His saints, and that human world systems have foisted themselves, so to speak, on God's earth and these must pass by cataclysms or otherwise because there is nothing eternal in them, and then the meek shall inherit the earth. Surely in the "blood, and fire, and vapour of smoke" we may be accounted worthy to escape from it all standing before the Son of man unsullied and uncompromised, devoted directors and helpers together with Him!

Christian Disciplines

Volume 2
The Discipline of Prayer
The Discipline of Loneliness
The Discipline of Patience
Oswald Chambers

CONTENTS

THE DISCIPLINE OF PRAYER

Introduction

The following quotation will suggest the right background for this introduction:

In the East the following phenomenon is often observed. Where the desert touches a river-valley or oasis, the sand is in a continual state of drift from the wind, and it is this drift which is the real cause of the barrenness of such portions of the desert at least as abut upon the fertile land. For under the rain, or by infiltration of the river, plants often spring through the sand, and there is sometimes promise of considerable fertility. It never lasts. Down comes the periodic drift, and life is stunted or choked out. But set down a rock on the sand, and see the difference its presence makes. After a few showers, to the lee-ward side of this some blades will spring up; if you have patience, you will see in time a garden. How has the boulder produced this? Simply by arresting the drift.

George Adam Smith[1]

And a man shall be as an hiding place from the wind, and a covert from the tempest; as rivers of water in a dry place, as the shadow of a great rock in a weary land. (Isaiah 32:2)

Our Lord Jesus Christ is just that rock to God's children.

He personally stays the drift of arduous Christian activities, of insidious mental scepticisms, of intuitive uncertainties, and produces a sanctuary within which abide perennial inspiration and wonderful ways to imitate.

How many cease from praying by indiscernible, unconscious ways! They are not those who because of intellectual barriers have determined on prayerlessness, or who have abandoned praying in favour of a cherished sin, but those who have ceased praying by more indecipherable ways. The life of God in us is manifested by spiritual concentration, not by pious self-consciousness; pious self-consciousness produces the worship of prayer, which is anti-Christian. This unscriptural piety fixes itself on the actual incidents in such verses as Mark 1:35—"And in the morning, rising up a great while before day, He went out, and departed into a solitary place, and there prayed," and disproportionately emphasises "rising up a great while before day," implying that if this actual early rising

were imitated it would produce Christ-likeness in us; whereas our Lord prayed because He was concentrated on God; that is, He did not worship prayer.

There are sure to be resurgent, periodic drifts of scepticism destructive of all such unrobust, pious sentimentality, because the worshipping of prayer is not of the nature of reality, for spiritual effects are thus construed into spiritual causes; as if a "gift of prayer" were the cause of Christ-likeness, it may be the cause of devotion, but it is the gift *from* prayer that matters, and this is the outcome of Christian concentration.

The intellectual desire to explain and thereby command is part of our natural inheritance, but it will turn into a tyrannic dictator if not kept strictly in its place as an instrument of the life of man and not the life itself; this can only be done by obedience (see Romans 12:2). The intellectual desire to dominate by explanation has so largely prevailed that prayer has become a mere borderland exercise of natural intelligence, wherein it is explained that prayer is the "reflex action" of a particular individual with the "God of All."

It is absurd to imagine anyone trying to think how they will live before they are born, yet it is this absurdity which the intellect tries to perform in connection with prayer. If the dominion of intellectual explanation is the characteristic of a naturally cultured life, dominion by obedience is the characteristic of the spiritually disciplined life. Intellectual expression in life is the effect of a naturally educated life, but is not the cause of the life; and the Christian experience of prayer is not its own cause, but the effect of the life of God in me. Prayer is the instrument of the life of worship, it is not worship itself. Intellect and prayer are united in the saint in the consciousness of Christ which we share, consequently the consciousness of self-realisation is a perversion and a snare. Our spiritual certainty in prayer is God's Divine certainty, not a side eddy of sanctimoniousness.

O patient, patient God,
Misprized, profaned God,
Grieved and wounded God,
Dooming and quickening God,
We weary of the victim faint,
The hero martyr, peasant saint,
Who stirs our love but leaves our taint,
Is balm but never rod,
Nor rends our last green sod,

---

1. George Adam Smith (1856–1942): Scottish Old Testament scholar.

Or tombs restraint.
We crave the Eternal Holy Son,
Earth's Lord and Hell's, the Living One,
Straight from His Cross, His Grave, His Throne.
With a world-pardon all our own;
With sacramental immanence
Transcending our abased sense;
With eyes of flame at which we fall
Dead men, till He out life recall,
And be Our Life, our All in all.
With all the Church's faithful folk,
This Lord, this Spirit, we invoke.

In order to present this study on the Discipline of Prayer in as direct a way as possible, it is put under headings.

The Position of Prayer

Also, when you pray, you must not be like the hypocrites, for they like to stand and pray in the synagogues and at the street-corners, so as to be seen by men; I tell you truly, they do get their reward. When you pray, go into your room and shut the door, pray to your Father who is in secret, and your Father who sees what is secret will reward you. Do not pray by idle rote like pagans, for they suppose they will be heard the more they say; you must not copy them; your Father knows your needs before you ask Him. (Matthew 6:5–9 MOFFATT)

This general heading indicates that it is important to notice that in the New Testament, and in the life of our Lord, prayer is not so much an acquired culture as the implicit nature of the spiritual life itself. Outside the New Testament prayer is apt to be presented as something entirely acquired, something placed in the position of a meritorious decoration for valiant service in piety. In other words, the position we are apt to give to prayer is too consciously an attainment of communion, and thus it is presented out of all proportion, so that in times of spiritual declension we are inclined to place the need of prayer instead of penitent approach to God in the forefront.

Yet Thou art oft most present, Lord,
In weak distracted prayer;
A sinner out of heart with self
Most often finds Thee there.
For prayer that humbles, sets the soul
From all illusions free,
And teaches it how utterly,
Dear Lord, it hangs on Thee.

The Place of Prayer
Pray without ceasing. (1 Thessalonians 5:17)

There is a quietism of devotional self-indulgence which takes the place spiritually that loafing does socially. It is easy to call it meditative prayer, but med-

itation is only attained in actual life by the strenuous discipline of brooding in the centre of a subject. God gives of His abundant grace and the Divine fire of instinctive inspiration, but we must acquire the technical skill of expressing that genius of God in our life. There are spiritual loafers who are painfully impressionable about "tones" and "moods" and "places," and they remind one of the aesthetic affectation of many persons who have not enough of the artist in them to work arduously and overcome technical difficulties, so they live a life of self-indulgent sentimental artistic indolence. An artist is never consciously artistic, and a saint is never consciously a praying one. A saint endeavours consciously and strenuously to master the technical means of expressing God's life in himself. The place of prayer in the New Testament is just this one of severe technical trying in which spiritual sympathies are sustained in unsecular strength, and manifested in the vulgar details of actual life.

The Platform of Prayer
Having therefore, brethren, boldness to enter into the holiest by the blood of Jesus. (Hebrews 10:19)

Prayer does not bring us into contact with the rationality of human existence but into accordance with eternal Reality. The great Reality is Redemption, and Redemption is the platform of prayer. The historic fact of the Death of Jesus is Redemptive Reality brought to us as a fact which creates belief in itself. Let Hebrews 10:19 be realised, and many pietistic perils of the devotional life will never appear again. Reality is not in intellect, or intuitions, but in the conscience reacting to Redemption, that is, through the whole nature. We are based on the platform of Reality in prayer by the Atonement of our Lord Jesus Christ. It is not our earnestness that brings us into touch with God, nor our devotedness, nor our times of prayer, but our Lord Jesus Christ's vitalising death; and our times of prayer are evidences of reaction on the reality of Redemption, so we have confidence and boldness of access into the holiest. What an unspeakable joy it is to know that we each have the right of approach to God in confidence, that the place of the Ark is our place, "Having therefore, brethren, boldness." What an awe and what a wonder of privilege, "to enter into the holiest," in the perfectness of the Atonement, "by the blood of Jesus."

The Purpose of Prayer
Be careful for nothing; but in every thing by prayer and supplication with thanksgiving let your requests be made known unto God. (Philippians 4:6)

To forebode is to forbid communion with God. The child of God can never think of anything the Heavenly Father will forget; then to worry is spiritual irritability with our Lord. Prayer is the evidence that I am spiritually concentrated on God, when to fore-think is but to pray about everything, and to live in actual conditions is to be thankful in anything. Prayer is not to be used as the petted privilege of a spoiled child seeking for ideal conditions in which to indulge his spiritual propensities *ad lib.*, the purpose of prayer is the maintenance of fitness in an ideal relationship with God amid conditions which ought not to be merely ideal but really actual. Actualities are not here to be idealised, but to be realised, while by prayer we lay hold on God and He unites us into His con-sciousness. The purpose of prayer is to reveal the pres-ence of God equally present all the time in every condition.

> *For perfect childlike confidence in Thee;*
> *For childlike glimpses of the life to be;*
> *For trust akin to my child's trust in me;*
> *For hearts at rest through confidence in Thee;*
> *For hearts triumphant in perpetual hope;*
> *For hope victorious through past hopes fulfilled;*
> *For mightier hopes born of the things we know;*
> *For faith born of the things we may not know;*
> *For hope of powers increased ten thousand fold;*
> *For that last hope of likeness to Thyself,*
> *When hope shall end in glorious certainty;*
> > *With quickened hearts*
> > *That find Thee everywhere,*
> > *We thank Thee, Lord!*

The Particulars of Prayer

It is of the greatest importance to think of prayer as our Lord taught in regard to it. Our Lord never referred to unanswered prayer; He taught that prayers were always answered, "For every one that asketh receiveth" (Luke 11:10). He ever implied that prayers were answered rightly because of the Heavenly Father's wisdom, "Your Father knoweth what things ye have need of, before ye ask Him." (Matthew 6:8). In regard to prayer, we are apt to be apologetic and apathetic, complex and confused; yet what a splendid audacity a childlike child has! and that is what our Lord taught us to have.

> *I thank Thee, O Father, Lord of heaven and earth, because Thou hast hid these things from the wise and prudent, and hast revealed them unto babes. (Matthew 11:25)*

> *Verily I say unto you, Except ye be converted, and become as little children, ye shall not enter into the kingdom of heaven. (Matthew 18:3)*

We may be converted, but obviously we have too often *not* become as little children.

Our Motive
And when thou prayest, thou shalt not be as the hyp-ocrites are: for they love to pray standing in the syna-gogues and in the corners of the streets, that they may be seen of men. Verily I say unto you, They have their reward. (Matthew 6:5)

Surely there is a great glow of humour in our Lord's words, "Verily, I say unto you, They have their reward," as one who should say, "That is all there is to it." Their motive is to be "seen of men"; they are seen of men, and that is their reward, placarded "pi-ness"! Watch your motive; is it a pose arising from a real enchantment? (the word "hypocrites" here is really "play-actors"). You very earnestly and solemnly tax your resources to be a praying person; people call at your house but cannot see you because it is your time for prayer. You perhaps have not noticed before that you always take care to tell those to whom it matters how early you rise in the morning to pray, how many all nights of prayer you spend; you have great zeal-ousness in proclaiming your protracted meetings. This is all pious play-acting. Jesus says, "Don't do it." Our Lord did not say it was wrong to pray in the cor-ners of the street, but He did say it was wrong to have the motive to be "seen of men." It is not wrong to pray in the early morning, but it is wrong to have the motive that it should be known. Avoid every tendency away from the simplicity of relationship to God in Christ Jesus, and then prayer will be as the breath of the lungs in a healthy body. It is at first difficult to learn a new and better way of breathing, consequently we are conscious of it for a time, but it is merely con-sciousness of what will by habit become an uncon-scious possession. So in the better and new way of breathing spiritually in prayer, we shall be conscious of forming the habit, but it will soon pass into nor-mal spiritual health, and it must never be worshipped as a conscious process.

Our Method
But when ye pray, use not vain repetitions, as the hea-then do: for they think that they shall be heard for their much speaking. (Matthew 6:7)

Beware of the trick of exposition which externalises Scripture so that we teach but never learn its lessons. That means just this—we take a description from missionary literature of the heathen prayer roll with its yards of prayers that wind and unwind, and we dextrously show how futile and pathetic this is, and so on, and by our very method remove it from its home-coming benefit. Let the words come home to us personally in their New Testament setting, "But when ye pray, use not vain repetitions." Our Lord prayed the same prayer, using the same words, three times in the Garden of Gethsemane, and He gave the disciples a form of prayer which He knew would be repeated throughout the Christian centuries; so it cannot be mere repetition or the form of words that He is referring to. The latter half of the verse comes home better for personal purposes—"for they think that they shall be heard for their much speaking"— that is, Do not rely on your earnestness as the ground for being heard. This is a much-needed caution because it is so subtle a thing, this thing called earnestness. As the Rev. John McNeill,[2] the great Scottish evangelist, said about the student of Elisha after he had lost the axe-head (2 Kings 6:1–7): "If he had been of the modern school, Elisha would have said, 'Whack awa' wi' the stump, mon; earnestness is everything!" Earnestness is not by any means everything; it is very often a subtle form of pious self-idolatry, because it is obsessed with the method and not with the Master. The phrase "pray through" often means working ourselves up into a frenzy of earnestness in which perspiration is taken for inspiration. It is a mistake to think we are heard on the ground of our earnestness; we are heard on the ground of the evangelical basis, "Having therefore, brethren, boldness to enter into the holiest by the blood of Jesus" (Hebrews 10:19).

Our Manner
After this manner therefore pray ye. (Matthew 6:9)

(At this particular point we are not dealing with what is known as the "Lord's Prayer"; that is dealt with subsequently).

Our Lord wishes us to understand that all morbid excesses must be cut off, and the simple personal relationship allowed to react. When we pray, remember we pray to a Person, "Our Father," not to a tendency, or for the resulting reflex action; and we pray for particular personal needs, which are universal. "Daily bread," "debts," "debtors," deliverances (verses 11–13), and we pray as citizens of a universal spiritual kingdom—"Thine is the kingdom" (verse 13), and the manner is bald, simple, but absolutely spiritual.

All through our Lord implies discipleship, or what we understand by an experience of regeneration. In other words, His Death is the gateway for us into the life He lives and to which His teaching applies. Therefore to take our Lord's teaching and deny the need to be born from above (RV mg), is to produce a mockery, born of the very desire to do the opposite.

This section is presented as a stirring up and away from sentimental religiosity which is injurious to a

degree that becomes immoral, because it unfits for life instead of equipping for life, the life that is ever the result of our Lord's life in us.

The Pattern Prayer
Let this be how you pray: "our Father in heaven, Thy name be revered, Thy Reign begin, Thy will be done on earth as in heaven! give us to-day our bread for the morrow, and forgive us our debts as we ourselves have forgiven our debtors, and lead us not into temptation but deliver us from evil." (Matthew 6:9–13 MOFFATT)

(This translation may serve to rouse complacent attention to re-examine the very familiar form of words).

This pattern prayer is our Lord's lesson on prayer in answer to a prayer: Luke 11:1—"One of His disciples said unto Him, Lord, teach us to pray." It is well to remember that our Lord's disciples were used to prayer and religious exercises from their earliest childhood, but contact with Jesus produced in them the realisation of the reality of free prayer other and beyond the liturgical form. How similar is our condition: after we have received spiritual quickening and illumination from our Lord, our eloquence falters, our coherent praying falters into an unsyllabled lack of utterance, and in utter confusion of mind and chaos of spirit we come as helpless babes to our Father with the first prayer, "*Lord, teach us to pray,*" and He teaches us the alphabet of all possible prayer. This sense of utter impoverishment spiritually is a blessed pain because it is pain that takes us to God and His gracious rule and kingdom. "Blessed are the poor in spirit: for theirs is the kingdom of heaven" (Matthew 5:3).

Presentation of Ideas
After this manner therefore pray ye. (Matthew 6:9)

How blessed it is to begin at the beginning, spiritual minors, stripped of our rich and verbal devotional language, and impoverished into receptive teachableness. Let our minds, made fertile by reason of genuine humility, receive the ideas our Lord presents in this familiar pattern prayer; receive in wonder and reverence the simple idea of God's personal relationship to us, "Our Father." "Your Father knoweth what things ye have need of, before ye ask Him" (verse 8). Our Father gathers us near Him in the secret place alone with our fears and apprehensions and foolishnesses and aspirations, and He rewards us. When we talk about the Fatherhood of God, let us remember that the Lord Jesus is the exclusive way to the Father. That is not an idea to be inferred, but to be received: "No

---

2. John McNeill: late-nineteenth-century Scottish evangelist brought to faith in Christ through the preaching of D. L. Moody.

man cometh unto the Father, but by Me" (John 14:6). We can get to God as Creator apart from Jesus Christ (see Romans 1:20), but never to God as our Father saving through Him. Let us receive this inspired idea of our Lord's right into our inmost willing heart, believe it, and pray in the confidence of it.

Again, let us receive the idea of praying about our Personal Requirements. What topics our Lord suggests! What emancipation and joy come to us when we receive the revelation from our Lord Himself that we pray about things which naturally we take as animals, trusting to our wits and instinct and intuition. How many of us are like the Psalmist of old who wrote a paragraph of autobiography in the words, "So foolish was I, and ignorant: I was as a beast before Thee" (Psalm 73:22). He does not mean an immoral beast, but just as a beast of the field taking its fill without the slightest apprehension of God. When we ask "grace before meat" let us remember that it is not to be a mere pious custom, but a real reception of the idea of Jesus that God enables us to receive our daily bread from Him. I sometimes wonder if there would be as much chronic indigestion as there is if we received our ideas from God as Jesus would have us do.

Again, let us receive the idea of the Personal Rule of our Lord, "Thy kingdom come" (verse 10). This does not mean bringing to Christian discipleship our natural ideas of the kingdom, but receiving our Lord's idea of the Kingdom, or Rule, or Realm of God, a heavenly and eternal kingdom, which will only be established on earth as it is in heaven by our willing reception and reverence.

Presentation of Language
When ye pray, say, Our Father which art in heaven. . . . (Luke 11:2)

Words are full of revelation when we do not simply recall or memorise them but receive them. Receive these words from Jesus—"Father," "heaven," "Hallowed be Thy Name," "kingdom," "will," there is all the vocabulary of the Deity and Dominion and Disposition of Almighty God in relation to men in these words. Or take the words—"bread," "forgiveness," "debts," "temptation," "deliverance," "evil," in these words the primary psychological colour which portray the perplexing puzzles and problems of personal life, are all spelled out before our Father.

Or, lastly, look at such words as "power," "glory," for ever, "Amen,"—in them there sounds the transcendent triumphant truth that all is well, that God reigns and rules and rejoices, and His joy is our strength. What a rapturous grammar class our Lord Jesus conducts when we go to His school of prayer and learn of Him!

Presentation of Faith
Thy will be done in earth, as it is in heaven. (Matthew 6:10)

It is not that our Lord gives us original thoughts, but that He gives spontaneous original life to all who receive from Him. Our Lord's very words, repeated by a simple receiver of His tuition, create the faith required for Christian perseverance. Receiving from Jesus and requesting Almighty God in obedience to Him, enables God, so to speak, to create the actual things prayed for. Faith worked out in this way is submissive, but how we miss the meaning of the New Testament words if we take them etymologically only, instead of in their evangelical accidence. Submission, for instance, means etymologically, surrender to another, but in the evangelical sense it means that I conduct myself actually among men as the submissive child of my Father in heaven.

There is an illustration of this subject in the pattern prayer: "For if ye forgive men their trespasses, your heavenly Father will also forgive you: But if ye forgive not men their trespasses, neither will your Father forgive your trespasses" (Matthew 6:14–15).

The forgiveness of a child of God is not placed on the ground of the Atonement of our Lord, but on the ground that the child of God shows the same forgiveness to his fellows that God his Father has shown to him.

This is submission and perseverance and faith all worked into an intensely humble, sensible, actual, human life. We are delivered from sin that we might actually live as saints amongst men who treat us as we once treated our Heavenly Father. Let us, with chastened and delighted hearts and lips, thank God that He has taught us in the pattern prayer of our Father, our Fellowship, and our Faith.

> *Oh, long and dark the stairs I trod,*
> *With stumbling feet to find my God:*
>
> *Gaining a foothold bit by bit,*
> *Then slipping back and losing it:*
>
> *Never progressing, striving still,*
> *With weakening gasp and fainting will,*
>
> *Bleeding to climb to God: while He*
> *Serenely smiled, unnoting me.*

[* Even if this clause is not in any of the oldest MSS., it is so universally used in the Christian Church that it is not wise to miss it.—*This footnote is part of Chambers' original book.*]

Then came a certain time when I
Loosened my hold and fell thereby.

Down to the lowest step my fall,
As if I had not climbed at all.

And while I lay despairing thereby.
I heard a footfall on the stair,

In the same path where I, dismayed,
Faltered and fell and lay afraid.

And lo! when hope had ceased to be,
My God came down the stairs to me.

Private Prayer

When you pray, go into your room and shut the door, pray to your Father who is in secret, and your Father who sees what is secret will reward you. (Matthew 6:6 MOFFATT)

This verse presents our Lord's Recommendation and His Revelation.

Our Lord's Recommendation naturally presents itself in these ways: A disciple should have a Special Habit, a Selected Place, a Secret Silence, and a disciple should Strenuously Pray; and our Lord's Revelation naturally presents itself in these ways: The Father's Discerning Disposition, and Delighted Doings. So we will construe all we have to consider according to this outline.

A Disciple Should Have a Special Habit
But thou, when thou prayest . . .

Beware of the impression that could be expressed something like this—"But it is so difficult to get time." Of course it is, we have to make time, and that means effort, and effort makes us conscious of the need to re-organise our general ways. It will facilitate matters to remember, even if it humbles us, that we take time to eat our breakfast and our dinner, etc. Most of the difficulty in forming a special habit is that we will not discipline ourselves. Read carefully this quotation from Professor William James's brilliant text-book of psychology,[3] and apply it to the matter of prayer:

The great thing, then, in all education, is to make our nervous system our ally instead of our enemy. It is to fund and capitalise our acquisitions, and live at ease upon the interest of the fund. For this we must make automatic and habitual, as early as possible, as many useful actions as we can, and guard against the growing into ways that are likely to be disadvantageous to us, as we should guard against the plague. . . . The first (maxim) is that in the acquisition of a new habit, or the leaving off of an old one, we must take care to launch ourselves with as strong and decided an initiative as possible. . . . The second maxim is: Never suffer an exception to occur till the mew habit is securely rooted in your life. . . . A third maxim may be added to the preceding pair: Seize the very first possible opportunity to act on every resolution you make, and on every emotional prompting you may experience in the direction of the habit you aspire to gain.

Let us apply that lesson now right away to ourselves, and take our Lord's advice home until it becomes character. You say you cannot get up early in the morning; well, a very good thing to do is to get up in order to prove that you cannot! This does not contradict at all what has already been said, viz., that we must not put earnestness in the place of God; it means that we have to understand that our bodily mechanism is made by God, and that when we are regenerated He does not give us another body, we have the same body, and therefore the way we use our wits in order to learn a secular thing is the way to learn any spiritual thing. "But thou, when thou prayest"—begin now.

A Disciple Should Have a Selected Place
enter into thy closet . . .

Did you ever say anything like this to yourself, "It is so difficult to select a place?" What about the time when you were in love, was it impossible to select a place to meet in? No, it was far from impossible; and beware of self-indulgence. Think how long our Lord has waited for you; you have seen Him in your visions, now pray to Him; get a place, not a mood, but a definite material place and resort to it constantly, and pray to God as His Spirit in you will help you. Bring to earth the promised life you have longed for, curb your impulsive undisciplined wayward nature to His use, and rule in your body like a king where now, even in strength and honesty, you walk sentenced to be a prey to baser and less spiritual things. Do not say, "If I only had so and so;" you have not got so and so; but you can, if you will, select a place where you are actually. We can always do what we want to do if we want to do it sufficiently keenly. Do it now, "enter into thy closet"; and remember, it is a place selected to pray in, not to make little addresses in, or for any other purpose than to pray in, never forget that.

A Disciple Should Have a Secret Silence
and when thou hast shut thy door . . .

---

3. *Principles of Psychology*, 1890; William James (1842–1910): American philosopher, psychologist, and teacher.

"It is so difficult to get quiet," you say, What about the time when you were ill? Oh, it can be done, but you must know how to shut the door. Remember the devil may not know what you know until you tell him, so do not say to your friends, or your household, or your landlady, as the case may be, "I am just going to pray," that's too much like the play-acting we have already been warned about. No, it is to be a selected place, a secret shut-in place, where no one ever guesses what you are doing. Quietists and Mystics are inclined to grave danger, but they say and write some very fine things. For instance, Molinos[4] says this, and it is exactly suitable for being quiet in the shut-in place:

> *The way of inward peace is in all things to be conformed to the pleasure and disposition of the divine will. Such as would have all things succeed and come to pass according to their own fancy, are not come to know this way, and therefore lead a harsh and bitter life, always restless or out of humour, without treading in the way of peace which consists in a total conformity to the will of God.*

There is another vital moral matter mentioned in Matthew 5:23–24: "Therefore if thou bring thy gift to the altar, and there rememberest that thy brother hath ought against thee; leave there thy gift before the altar, and go thy way; first be reconciled to thy brother, and then come and offer thy gift."

If you have incurred a debt and not paid it, or cared about paying it, or have spoken in the wrong mood to another, or been vindictive—these and similar things produce a wrong temper of soul and you cannot pray in secret, it is no use trying to pray until you do what the Lord says. The one thing that keeps us from doing it is pride, and pride has never yet prayed in the history of mankind.

> *I walk down the Valley of Silence,*
> *Down the dim voiceless valley alone,*
> *And I hear not a sound of a footstep*
> *Around me but God's and my own,*
> *And the hush of my heart is as holy*
> *And bowers whence angels have flown.*
> *In the hush of the Valley of Silence,*
> *I hear all the songs that I sing,*
> *And the notes float down the dim Valley*
> *Till each finds a word for a wing*
> *That to men like the dove of the deluge,*
> *The message of peace they may bring.*

A Disciple Should Strenuously Pray
pray to thy Father which is in secret . . .

The objection is easily brought forward: "It is so difficult to concentrate one's thought," yet what about the time you were working for that position, or to pass that examination? All our excuses arise from some revealing form of self-indulgence. To pray strenuously needs careful cultivation. We have to learn the most natural methods of expressing ourselves to our Father. In the beginning we may clamour for presents and for things, and our Father encourages us in these elementary petitions until we learn to understand Him better; then we begin to talk to Him in free reverent intimacy, understanding more and more His wonderful nature. "Your Father knoweth what things ye have need of, before ye ask Him" (Matthew 6:8).

The real reason for prayer is intimacy of relation with our Father. There are many ways that help. Let me give some out of my own experience, although it is unsatisfactory to do this because others are apt to imitate instead of assimilate. To re-write the Psalms into a free language of expression of one's own has proved to me a valuable treasure-house of self-expression to God. At times, though very rarely, I like a horology such as Bishop Andrews' *Devotions*; but I find a most beneficial exercise in secret prayer before the Father, is to write things down so that I see exactly what I think and want to say. Only those who have tried these ways know the ineffable benefit of such strenuous times in secret.

> *Lord, what a change within us one short hour*
> *Spent in Thy presence will prevail to make,*
> *What heavy burdens from our bosoms take,*
> *What parched grounds refresh as with a shower!*
> *We kneel, and all around us seems to lower;*
> *We rise, and all, the distant and the near*
> *Stands forth in sunny outline, brave and clear;*
> *We kneel, how weak, we rise how full of power.*
> *Why therefore should we do ourselves this wrong*
> *Or others that we are not always strong,*
> *That we are ever overcome with care*
> *That we should ever weak or heartless be*
> *Anxious or troubled, when with us is Prayer*
> *And joy and strength and courage are with Thee?*

Such, then, are our Lord's recommendations for Private Prayer, now let us look at His Revelation regarding Private Prayer.

The Father's Discerning Disposition
and thy Father which seeth in secret . . .

The revelation here is of the free kingdom of love; there is no blind creaturely subjection to a Creator, but the free kingdom in which the one who prays is

---

4. Miguel de Molinos (1640–1697): Spanish theologian and author of *A Spiritual Guide* (1675).

conscious of limit only through the moral nature of the Father's holiness. It is a revelation of pure joyousness in which the child of God pours into the Father's bosom the cares which give pain and anxiety that He may solve the difficulties. Too often we imagine that God lives in a place where He only repairs our broken treasures, but Jesus reveals that it is quite otherwise; He discerns all our difficulties and solves them before us. We are not beggars on the one hand or spiritual customers on the other; we are God's children, and we just stay before Him with our broken treasures or our pain and watch Him mend or heal in such a way that we understand Him better.

The Father's Delighted Doings
. . . shall reward thee openly.

Think of the unfathomable bliss of the revelation that we shall perceive our Father solving our problems, and shall understand Him; it is the reward of the joyous time of prayer. In all the temptations that contend in our hearts, and amidst the things that meet us in the providence of God which seem to involve a contradiction of His Fatherhood, the secret place convinces us that He is our Father and that He is righteousness and love, and we remain not only unshaken but we receive our reward with an intimacy that is unspeakable and full of glory.

> *Give me the lowest place, not that I dare*
> *Ask for the lowest place, but Thou hast died*
> *That I might give and share*
> *　　Thy glory by Thy side.*
>
> *Give me the lowest place, or if for me*
> *That lowest place too high, make one more low*
> *Where I may sit and see*
> *　　My God and love Thee so.*

Public Prayer
I tell you another thing: if two of you agree on earth about anything you pray for, it will be done for you by my Father in heaven. For where two or three have gathered in My name, I am there among them. (Matthew 18:19–20 MOFFATT)

These words are so simple, and so remarkable for guidance and instruction regarding public prayer meetings, that our departure from their counsel is a great mystery. It is comparatively easy to think or say apt things about private prayer, but it is not so easy to say things about public prayer, the reason probably being that few of us are willing to carry the cross of public prayer, or at least if we do, we repeat aloud to a large extent our own private concerns, which are much better told in secret and alone. It is easier too to evade self-consciousness in private prayer; emancipation from self-consciousness is like a deliverance from a terrible sickness, and one gets rather alarmed at the slightest symptom of it again. Probably this is the reason why many Christians, who ought to be the strength and safeguard of a public prayer meeting in a community of Christians, are not so; they keep silent and just one or two who have merely the gift of devotional language are allowed to dominate the prayer meeting; and the mid-week prayer meeting is given up and becomes the midweek service. We must remember that there is a sacrifice of prayer as well as a sacrifice of praise.

In the words of Matthew 18:19–20, Our Lord conveys simple and plain guidance in regard to the Arrangement and the Atmosphere of a Public Prayer Meeting.

The Arrangement of the Public Prayer Meeting
It is never easy to pray in public, and so few of us are willing to have our nervous equilibrium upset for the sake of fulfilling a request of our Lord's, but why should not our nervous equilibrium be upset? Why should many public prayer meetings be ruined by the long-winded brother who does not really pray but discourses on theology and insists on doctrine? We all mourn this abuse of the public prayer meeting, it is a contemptible thing because it usurps the time of the saints; yet the real rebuke ought to lie at the door of the humble saints who should pray when the opportunity is given, and thus allow no occasion to the enemy.

Agreement in Purpose on Earth
Again I say unto you, That if two of you shall agree on earth . . .

We need to know this simple, direct truth about praying in public. It is perilously easy to make public prayer the mere fringe of devotion to what we are pleased to think of as the real centre of the meeting. Agreement in purpose on earth must not be taken to mean a predetermination to agree together to storm God's fort doggedly till He yields. It is far from right to agree beforehand over what we want, and then go to God and wait, not until He gives us His mind about the matter, but until we extort from Him permission to do what we had made up our minds to do before we prayed; we should rather agree to ask God to convey His mind and meaning to us in regard to the matter. Agreement in purpose on earth is not a public presentation of persistent begging which knows no limit, but a prayer which is conscious that it is limited through the moral nature of the Holy Ghost. It is really "symphonising" on earth with our Father Who is in heaven.

Asking in Prayer on Earth
as touching any thing that they shall ask . . .

It is a very important matter of instruction to be guided in our asking in public, and to facilitate this end it is better to have numbers of short prayers than a few long ones, and numbers of short prayers not on the same subject, but on many subjects, so that the whole meeting may agree with the petitioners. There are many simple helps in this matter, such as the leader of the meeting suggesting topics, or asking the people themselves to quote a verse of Scripture, or anything that will enable the people to pronounce aloud the request that is in their heart. It is never necessary in a public prayer meeting for one to present all the petitions as it is in a public service; there one man has to make the presentation in prayer of the needs of the congregation, and of the much larger sphere of men; but that is public worship. As in private matters, our Lord's instruction on public prayer is essentially simple.

Public Prayer Is Answered in Particular from Heaven

. . . it shall be done for them of My Father which is in heaven.

This reminds us very forcibly of our Lord's statement, viz., that "every one that asketh receiveth" (Luke 11:10). Prayer to the natural man who has not been born from above (RV mg) is so simple, so stupid, and so supernatural as to be at once "taboo." Strange to say, the reasons he gives for objecting to prayer are the very reasons that give it its true nature. Prayer is simple, as simple as a child making known its wants to its parents (see Matthew 11:25); prayer is stupid, because it is not according to common sense; it is certain that God does things in answer to prayer, and this, common sense naturally says, is ridiculous (see James 5:16); prayer is supernatural because it relies entirely on God (1 John 5:14–15).

Let us then go into the hearty cultivation of public prayer, making our requests known before one another as well as before God, and thus securing the answers in particular from Heaven.

The Atmosphere of the Public Prayer Meeting

Atmosphere is not only something assimilated, but something we help to produce, and is both subjective and objective. To ask the Spirit of God to take up His abode in the atmosphere of a meeting is not at all unnecessary; the idea of "sacred places" can be easily abused, but it does not follow that there is no such thing as a sacred place. For instance, it is easier to pray in a place used only for prayer than it is to pray in a theatre.

"For where two or three are gathered together . . ." Christian secrecy when made a conscious effort is a snare and a delusion because it leads to segregation, not congregation. The "together" aspect of the Chris-

tian life is continually insisted on in the New Testament. We are raised up together, and made to "sit together in heavenly places in Christ Jesus" (Ephesians 2:6); we attain together, ". . . unto the measure of the stature of the fulness of Christ" (Ephesians 4:13), and the writer to the Hebrews warns us not to forsake "the assembling of ourselves together" (Hebrews 10:25). There is nothing of the special coterie about the Christian prayer meeting, it is not a "hole-and-corner" secret society, but a public meeting for one purpose, assembling together to pray, and the assembly must be akin to each other.

"In My Name . . ." this oft-repeated phrase means, "in My nature." It is a sad fact that through pique or self-opinionatedness a man sometimes finds himself and his self-love wounded in the prayer meeting with his brethren, so he separates himself and has a little prayer meeting in his own home. That is certainly not assembling together "in My Name," but is assembling together from a motive of defiance. "In My Name" refers to those who are born of the Spirit of God; the nature of God is imparted to the recipient so that when we pray in His Name we pray in His nature (cf. Romans 5:5).

". . . there am I in the midst of them." A wonderful picture—a group of our Lord's children around the knees of the Heavenly Father, making their requests known in familiarity, in awe and reverence, in simplicity and confidence in Him, and in humble certainty that He is there.

Our prayers should be in accordance with the nature of God, therefore the answers are not in accordance with our nature but with His. We are apt to forget this and to say without thinking that God does not answer prayer; but He always answers prayer, and when we are in close communion with Him we know that we have not been misled.

> *Stir me, oh! stir me, Lord, I care not how,*
>   *But stir my heart in passion for the world!*
> *Stir me to give, to go—but most to pray;*
>   *Stir, till the blood-red banner is unfurled*
> *O'er lands that still in heathen darkness lie,*
> *O'er deserts where no cross is lifted high.*
>
> *Stir me, oh! stir me, Lord, till prayer is pain—*
>   *Till prayer is joy—till prayer turns into praise!*
> *Stir me, till heart and will and mind—yea, all*
>   *Is wholly Thine to use through all the day.*
> *Stir, till I learn to pray "exceedingly:"*
> *Stir, till I learn to wait expectantly.*

Patient and Prevailing Prayer

So far we have been dealing with the aspects of prayer which are more or less easy of statement; we enter now into an aspect which is more difficult to state.

Prayer is the outcome of our apprehension of the nature of God, and the means whereby we assimilate more and more of His mind.

We must here remind ourselves again of the fundamental matters of our Christian relationship, viz. that in a Christian, faith and common sense are moulded in one person by devotion to the mastership of Jesus Christ. This necessitates not conscious adherence to principles, but concentrated obedience to the Master. Faith does not become its own object, that produces fanaticism; but it becomes the means whereby God unveils His purposes to us (see Romans 12:2).

Our Lord in instructing the disciples in regard to prayer presented them with three pictures (see Luke 11:1–13; 18:1–8), and strangely puzzling pictures they are until we understand their meaning. They are the pictures of an unkind friend, an unnatural father, and an unjust judge. Like many of our Lord's answers, these pictures seem no answer at all at first, they seem evasions, but we find that in answering our inarticulate questions our Lord presents His answer to the reality discernible to conscience, and not to logic.

The Unkind Friend (Luke 11:5–8)
This is plainly a picture of what the Heavenly Father does sometimes seem to be like, and the problem our Lord faced in the minds of His disciples has to be faced by us at all times. He says, in effect, "I know that to your mind the Heavenly Father will appear at times as an unkind friend, but let Me assure you He is not; and even if He were, if you went on praying long enough, He would answer you. There is a reason which He cannot explain to you just now, because the explanation only comes through the experience of discipline which you will understand some day."

It appears as if God were sometimes most unnatural; we ask Him to bless our lives and bring benedictions, and what immediately follows turns everything into actual ruin. The reason is that before God can make the heart into a garden of the Lord, He has to plough it, and that will take away a great deal of natural beauty. If we interpret God's designs by our desires, we will say He gave us a scorpion when we asked an egg and a serpent when we asked a fish, and a stone when we asked for bread. But our Lord indicates that such thinking and speaking is too hasty, it is not born of faith or reliance on God. "Every one that asketh receiveth." Our Lord says that God the Father will give the Holy Spirit much more readily than we would give good gifts to our children, and the Holy Spirit not only brings us into the zone of God's influence but into intimate relationship with Him personally, so that by the slow discipline of prayer the choices of our free will become the preordinations of His Almighty order. When we say we have no faith, we simply betray our own case, viz. that we have no confidence in God at all, for faith is born of confidence in Him.

The Unjust Judge (Luke 18:1–8)
In this illustration our Lord recognises by implication that God does seem at times utterly powerless and unjust, but He says, in effect, "God is not unjust, He is long-suffering." Our Lord does not attempt to answer our questions on our level, He lifts us up to His level and allows us to make no excuse for not continuing in prayer. The battle in prayer is against two things in the earthlies: wandering thoughts, and lack of intimacy with God's character as revealed in His word. Neither can be cured at once, but they can be cured by discipline. In mental work it takes time to gain the victory over wandering thoughts; they do not come necessarily through supernatural agents, but through lack of concentration. Concentration is only learned little by little, and the more impulsive you are, the less concentrated you will be. So when wandering thoughts come in in prayer, don't ask God to forgive you, but stop having them. It is not a bit of use to ask God to keep out wandering thoughts, you must keep them out. And in regard to God's word, see you take time to know it; God's Spirit will give you an understanding of His nature, and make His word spirit and life to you.

Our counsel for Patient Prayer is to note the importunity which our Lord insists on in each of these illustrations, and to remember it is importunity on behalf of another, not on our own account. Our importunity must be intercessory, and the whole power of our intercession lies in the certainty that prayer will be answered. Intercessory prayer based on the Redemption enables God to create that which He can create in no other way; it is a strenuous business demanding the undivided energy of mind and heart. The effect of prayer on ourselves is the building up of our character in the understanding of the character of God, that is why we need patience in prayer. We cannot "by one wild bound, clear the numberless ascensions of starry stairs." Prayer is not logical, it is a mysterious moral working of the Holy Spirit.

The Unnatural Father (Luke 11:9–13)
Just here at the conclusion of these pictures the case of Job is of peculiar significance. In Job's case there was every element to make him conceive of God as an unkind Friend, an unnatural Father, and an unjust Judge; but through everything Job stuck to his belief in the character of God. Job lost his hereditary creed, which was that God blessed and prospered physically and materially the man who trusted in Him, but his words, "though He slay me, yet will I trust in Him," prove how tenaciously he clung to God.

At the conclusion of the book of Job these striking words occur, "And the LORD turned the captivity of Job, when he prayed for his friends: also the LORD gave Job twice as much as he had before" (Job 42:10). So the question to ask yourself, which, though it may be ungrammatical, is very pointed, is—"Have you come to 'when' yet?" Have you entered into the high-priestly union of praying for your friends? When you do, God will turn your captivity.

> Go thou into thy closet; shut thy door,
>   And pray to Him in secret: He will hear.
> But think not thou, by one wild bound, to clear
> The numberless ascensions, more and more,
> Of starry stairs that must be climbed, before
>   Thou comest to the Father's likeness near;
>   And bendest down to kiss the feet so dear
> That, step by step, their mounting flights passed
>   o'er.
>
>   Be thou content, if on thy weary need
> There falls a sense of showers and of the Spring;
> A hope that makes it possible to fling
>   Sickness aside, and go and do the deed:
>   For highest aspiration will not lead
> Unto the calm beyond all questioning.

Subconscious Prayer

Under the heading of Prevailing Prayer we come really to the subject of subconscious prayer. We mean by subconscious prayer the prayer that goes on in our unconscious mind, only occasionally bursting up into the conscious. Romans 8:26–28 is the classical example of this:

> Likewise the Spirit also helpeth our infirmities: for we know not what we should pray for as we ought: but the Spirit itself maketh intercession for us with groanings which cannot be uttered. And He that searcheth the hearts knoweth what is the mind of the Spirit, because He maketh intercession for the saints according to the will of God. And we know that all things work together for good to them that love God, to them who are the called according to His purpose.

"Praying always with all prayer and supplication in the Spirit" (Ephesians 6:18). Prayer "in the Spirit" is not meditation, it is not reverie; it is being filled with the Holy Ghost Who brings us as we pray into perfect union before God, and this union manifests itself in "perseverance and supplication for all saints." Every saint of God knows those times when in closest communion with God nothing is articulated, and yet there seems to be an absolute intimacy not so much between God's mind and their mind as between God's Spirit and their spirit.

The conscious and the subconscious life of our Lord is explained perhaps in this way. Our Lord's subconscious life was Deity, and only occasionally when He was on earth did the subconscious burst up into His conscious life. The subconscious life of the saint is the Holy Ghost, and in such moments of prayer as are alluded to in Romans 8:26–28, there is an uprush of communion with God into the consciousness of the saint, the only explanation of which is that the Holy Ghost in the saint communicating prayers which cannot be uttered, acquaints us with the—

Unrealised Particulars of Prayer
Likewise the Spirit also helpeth our infirmities: for we know not what we should pray for as we ought: but the Spirit itself maketh intercession for us with groanings which cannot be uttered. (Romans 8:26)

This verse details for us our infirmities, our inability and our Intercessor. The Holy Spirit has special prayers in every individual saint which bring him or her at times under the powerful searching of God to find out what is the mind of the Spirit. This searching of the heart is bewildering at first because we are tortured by our unsyllabled lack of utterance, but we are soon comforted by the realisation that God is searching our hearts not for the convicting of sin, but to find out what is the mind of the Spirit.

> And He that searcheth the hearts knoweth what is the mind of the Spirit, because He maketh intercession for the saints according to the will of God. (verse 27)

Unrivalled Power of Prayer
This verse describes the Spirit's intercession before God, and identification with God going on in the personality of the saint, apart altogether from the saint's conscious power of understanding. This can safely be called "speechless prayer"; we wait before God, lying fallow, as it were, while He answers the prayer the Holy Spirit is praying in us. The prayer of our Lord in John 17 is closely allied with the intercession of the Holy Ghost, and this High-priestly prayer explains many, if not all, of the mysterious things a saint has to go through.

> And we know that all things work together for good to them that love God, to them who are the called according to His purpose. (Romans 8:28)

This verse presents the unrecognised providence of prayer.

Unrecognised Providence of Prayer
The shrine of our conscious life is placed in a sacredness of circumstances engineered by God whereby He secures our effectual calling. That God engineers our circumstances for us if we accept His purpose in Christ Jesus is a thought of great practical moment.

Allow yourself to think for a little that you are to be a walking, living edition of the prayers of the Holy Spirit. No wonder God urges us to walk in the light! No wonder His Spirit prays in us and makes intercessions with groanings we cannot utter. We may feel burdened or we may not; we may consciously know nothing about it; the point is that God puts us into circumstances where He can answer the prayers of His Son and of the Holy Spirit. Remember the prayer of Jesus is "that they may be one, even as We are one." That is a oneness of personality in which individuality is completely transfigured; it is independence lost and identity revealed.

It is well to remember that it is the "together" of circumstances that works for good God changes our circumstances; sometimes they are bright, sometimes they are the opposite; but God makes them work together for our good, so that in each particular set of circumstances we are in, the Spirit of God has a better chance to pray the particular prayers that suit His designs, and the reason is only known to God, not to us.

In James 5:16–18 there is instruction for everyone. This might be called Successful Prayer. We are told that the great man Elijah is as a little man, "Elias was a man subject to like passions as we are" (verse 17); and that the great man prayed just as a little man, "and he prayed earnestly"; and the great man was answered just as a little man will be answered, by God. The phrase "he prayed earnestly" is literally, "he prayed in prayer."

Intercessory prayer is part of the sovereign purpose of God. If there were no saints praying for us, our lives would be infinitely balder than they are, consequently the responsibility of those who never intercede and who are withholding blessing from other lives is truly appalling. The subject of intercessory prayer is weakened by the neglect of the idea with which we ought to start. We take for granted that prayer is preparation for work, whereas prayer is *the* work, and we scarcely believe what the Bible reveals, viz. that through intercessory prayer God creates on the ground of the Redemption; it is His chosen way of working. We lean to our own understanding, or we bank on service and do away with prayer, and consequently by succeeding in the external we fail in the eternal, because in the eternal we succeed only by prevailing prayer,

Perils of Prayer

In conclusion it is as well to note one or two points in regard to The Perils of Prayer. Luke 22:31 reveals not only the possibility of Satan praying, but of his prayers being answered, "Satan hath desired to have you, that he may sift you as wheat"; and in Psalm 106:13–15, we have the prayer of sensuality. In both these instances prayer was answered. Satan was allowed to sift Peter and

the other disciples, with the result that after the Resurrection they were ready to receive the Holy Ghost (see John 20:22), and we read that God gave the children of Israel their request, but "sent leanness into their soul."

First John 5:16 deals with Prayer and Will. "If any man see his brother sin a sin which is not unto death, he shall ask, and He shall give him life for them that sin not unto death. There is a sin unto death: I do not say that he shall pray for it." Intercessory prayer for one who is sinning prevails, God says so. The will of the man prayed for does not come into question at all, he is connected with God by prayer, and prayer on the basis of the Redemption sets the connection working and God gives life. There is, however, a distinct limitation put to intercession—"I do not say that he shall pray for it." This is also illustrated in the prayers of Abraham for Sodom (see Genesis 18:16–33). The only way in which we can discern this limit of intercession is by living in continual communion with God and not in any wise leaning to our own understanding.

There are, so to speak, two types of redemptive effect in answer to intercession; the first where souls are "saved; yet so as by fire"; and the second where they are saved and brought into requisition for God in this life. The intercession for all men is on the former line and the intercession for particular cases is on the second. Beware of the philosophy with regard to the human will bringing factors in here that are distinctly absent in God's revelation about prayer. The fundamental basis of the human will deep down is inclined towards God, and prayer works wonders fundamentally. The prayer of the feeblest saint on earth who lives in the Spirit and keeps right with God is a terror to Satan. The very powers of darkness are paralysed by prayer; no spiritualistic seance can succeed in the presence of a humble praying saint. No wonder Satan tries to keep our minds fussy in active work till we cannot think in prayer. It is a vital necessity for Christians to think along the lines on which they pray. The philosophy of prayer is that prayer is *the* work.

Jesus Christ carries on intercession for us in heaven; the Holy Ghost carries on intercession in us on earth; and we the saints have to carry on intercession for all men.

There remains one further matter it is well to note, viz., idle prayer.

Idle Prayer

This subject of idle prayer is referred to by Charles Kingsley[5] in a letter written April 25, 1852:

You have said boldly, in words which pleased me much, though I differ from them—that I ought not to ask you

---

5. Charles Kingsley (1819–1875): English cleric and writer.

to try to cure self-seeking by idle prayer—as if a man by taking thought could add one cubit to his stature. I was pleased with the words; because they show me that you have found that there is a sort of prayer which is idle prayer, and that you had sooner not pray at all than in that way. Now of idle prayer I think there are two kinds: one of fetish prayer, when by praying we seek to alter the will of God concerning us. This is, and has been, and will be common enough and idle enough. For if the will of Him concerning us be good, why should we alter it? If bad, what use praying to such a Being at all? . . . Another, of praying to oneself to change oneself;

by which I mean the common method of trying by prayer to excite oneself into a state, a frame, an experience. This too is common enough among protestants and papists, as well as among unitarians and rationalists. Indeed, some folks tell us that the great use of prayer is "its reflex" action on ourselves, and inform us that we can thus by taking thought add certain cubits to our stature. God knows the temptation to believe it is great. I feel it deeply. Nevertheless I am not of that belief.

The whole letter is well worth reading. (*Charles Kingsley: His Letters and Memories of His Life*).

THE DISCIPLINE OF LONELINESS

And I am no more in the world, and these are in the world, and I come to Thee. Holy Father, keep them in Thy name which Thou hast given Me, that they may be one even as we are. . . . I have given them Thy word; and the world hated them, because they are not of the world, even as I am not of the world. I pray not that Thou shouldest take them out of [mg] the world, but that Thou shouldest keep them from the evil one. They are not of the world, even as I am not of the world. Sanctify them in the truth: Thy word is truth. As Thou didst send Me into the world, even so sent I them into the world. John 17:11, 14–18 RV

The friendship of a soul who walks alone with God is as abiding as God Himself, and, in degree, as terrible. What a volume of meaning is in these words, so simple in statement—"And he looked upon Jesus as He walked, and saith, Behold, the Lamb of God!" (John 1:36 RV). Charles Kingsley speaks of his wife as his "dear dread." A friend whose contact and whose memory does not make us ever do our best is one in name only. Friendship to a soul undisciplined by loneliness is a precarious sea on which many have been lost, and on whose shores the wrecks of many human hearts lie rotting.

Solitude with God repairs the damage done by the fret and noise and clamour of the world. To have been on the mount with God means that we carry with us an exhilaration, an incommunicable awe. We do not descend to the valley, no matter how low the walk of the feet may have to be, no matter how perplexing the demon-tossed may be around us, no matter if the cross awaits us in the shadows.

And it came to pass, when Moses came down from mount Sinai with the two tables of the testimony in

Moses' hand, when he came down from the mount, that Moses wist not that the skin of his face shone while he talked with Him. (Exodus 34:29)

. . . they marvelled; and they took knowledge of them, that they had been with Jesus. (Acts 4:13)

The disaster of shallowness ultimately follows the spiritual life that takes not the shining way upon the Mount of God. Power from on high has the Highest as its source, and the solitudes of the Highest must never be departed from, else that power will cease.

Heart, heart, awake! The love that loveth all
*   Maketh a deeper calm than Horeb's cave:—*
God in thee;—can His children's folly gall?
*   Love may be hurt, but shall not love be brave?*
Thy holy silence sinks in dews of balm;
Thou art my solitude, my mountain-calm!

George MacDonald

Loneliness marks the child of God. In tumults, in troubles, in disasters, in pestilences, in destructions, in fightings with wild beasts, the child of God abides under the shadow of the Almighty,

Singing hymns unbidden,
Till the world is wrought
To sympathy with hopes and tears it heeded not.

Shelley[6]

The child of God who walks alone with Him is not dependent on places and moods but carries to the world the perpetual mystery of a dignity, unruffled, and unstung by insult, untouched by shame and martyrdom. Robert Browning describes him in "An Epistle containing the Strange Medical Experience of Karshish, the Arab Physician"—

---

6. Percy Bysshe Shelley (1792–1822): English poet.

I probed the sore as thy disciple should:
"How, beast," said I, "this stolid carelessness
Sufficeth thee, when Rome is on her march
To stamp out like a little spark thy town,
Thy tribe, thy crazy tale and thee at once?"
He merely looked with his large eyes on me.
The man is apathetic, you deduce?
Contrariwise, he lives both old and young,
Able and weak, affects the very brutes
And birds—how say I? Flowers of the field—
As a wise workman recognises tools
In a master's workshop, loving what they make.

. . . . .

The very God! think, Abib; dost thou think?
So, the All-Great, were the All-Loving too—
So, through the thunder comes a human voice
Saying, "O heart I made, a heart beats here!
Face, my hands fashioned, see it in myself!
Thou hast no power nor mayest conceive of mine,
But love I gave thee, with myself to love,
And thou must love me who have died for thee!"
The madman saith He said so: it is strange.
Browning

The culture of the entirely sanctified life is often misunderstood. The discipline of that life consists of Suffering, Loneliness, Patience and Prayer. How many who started with the high ecstasy of vision have ended in the disasters of shallowness! Time, the world and God fire out the fools. Our Lord was thirty years preparing for three years' service. The modern stamp is three hours of preparation for thirty years of service. John the Baptist and Paul were trained in the massive solitudes of the desert, as are all characters of God's heroic mould.

. . . not in vain His seers
Have dwelt in solitudes and known that God
High up in open silence and thin air
More presently reveals him, having set
His chiefest temples on the mountain-tops,
His kindling altar in the hearts of men,
And these I know with peace and lost with pain,
And oft for whistling wind and desert air
Lamented, and in dream; was my desire
For the flood Jordan, for the running sound
And broken glitters of the midnight moon.
F. W. H. Myers[7]

Thus does Frederick Myers make John the Baptist soliloquise in prison. And again he touches Paul in soliloquy—

Oh the regret, the struggle and the failing!
Oh the days desolate and useless years!

Vows in the night, so fierce and unavailing!
Stings of my shame and passion of my tears!

How have I seen in Araby Orion,
Seen without seeing, till he set again,
Known the night-noise and thunder of the lion:
Silence and sounds of the prodigious plain!

How have I felt with arms of my aspiring
Lifted all night in irresponsive air,
Dazed and amazed with overmuch desiring,
Blank with the utter agony of prayer!

In the momentous crisis of Entire Sanctification and the Baptism of the Holy Ghost and Fire, all Heaven is opened and the soul is drunk with ecstasy; yet that is but the introduction to a new relationship. Entirely sanctified soul, alone with God, suffering with Jesus, do you hear Him say, "Ye know not what ye ask. Are ye able to drink the cup that I drink? or to be baptized with the baptism that I am baptized with?" (RV). The world is cursed with holiness preachers who have never trembled under awesome Sinai, or lain prostrate in shame before Calvary and had the vile ownership of themselves strangled to death in the rare air heights of Pentecost. Testify to what the Lord has done for you, but at the peril of being cast away as reprobate silver, presume to preach or teach what you have not bought by suffering. Out on the disastrous shallowness that teaches and preaches *experiences!* The true holiness preacher is one whose experience has led him to know that he is charged with the oracles of God, and, backed by Jehovah, an awful woe is on him if he preaches not the Gospel.

There is a solitude of despair, a solitude of sin—a vast curse black with the wrath of God, moaning with the pride of hatred; there is a solitude which is the aftermath of spent vice and exhausted self-love. There is no God in such solitudes; only an exhausting pessimism and a great despair. These solitudes produce the wayward, wandering cries so prevalent amongst men. At one time, striking his fist at the throne of God, that lonely soul cries—

I would ne'er have striven
As thus with thee in prayer in my sore need.
Oh! lift me as a wave, a leaf, a cloud!
I fall upon the thorns of life! I bleed!

A heavy weight of hours has chained and bowed
One too like thee: tameless, and swift, and
*				proud.*

Or again, in the utter exhaustion of companionless isolation—

I could lie down like a tired child,
And weep away the life of care

---

7. F. W. H. Myers (1843–1901): British poet and educator.

Which I have borne and yet must bear,
  Till death like sleep might steal on me,
And I might feel in the warm air
  My cheek grow cold, and hear the sea
Breathe o'er my dying brain its last monotony.
                                              Shelley

But the solitude of the sanctified, the loneliness of the child of God, brings again the glimmering of his Father's feet amongst the sorrows and the haunts of men. And to the broken in heart, to the bound in hereditary prisons, and to the wounded and weak, Jesus our Saviour draws near.

Then on our utter weakness and the hush
Of hearts exhausted that can ache no more,
On such abeyance of self and swoon of soul
The Spirit hath lighted oft, and let men see
That all our vileness alters God no more
Than our dimmed eyes can quench the stars in
      heaven:—
From years ere years were told, through all the
      sins,
Unknown sins of innumerable men.
God is himself for ever, and shows to-day
As erst in Eden, the eternal hope.
                                  F. W. H. Myers

Loneliness in Preparation

And Jacob was left alone; and there wrestled a man with him until the breaking of the day. (Genesis 32:24)

. . . life is not as idle ore
But iron dug from central gloom
  And heated hot with burning fears,
  And dipt in baths of hissing tears,
  And batter'd with the shock of doom
To shape and use.
                                  Tennyson

It is so human and so like us to be attracted by Jesus, to be fascinated by His life; but what a sorrowful revulsion many of us experience when His own words repulse us and blow out the fires of our emotion; and turning away sorrowful, we leave Jesus alone. Christianity is based on heroism and manifested in martyrdom; and the preparation for being a Christian is drastic, definite and destructive.

Separation from Possessions

And as He was going forth on His way[mg], there ran one to Him and kneeled to Him, and asked Him, Good Teacher [MOFFATT], what shall I do that I may inherit eternal life? And Jesus said unto him, Why callest thou

Me good? none is good save one, even God. Thou knowest the commandments, Do not kill, Do not commit adultery, Do not steal, Do not bear false witness, Do not defraud, Honour thy father and mother. And he said unto Him, Master, all these things have I observed from my youth. And Jesus looking upon him loved him, and said unto him, One thing thou lackest: go, sell whatsoever thou hast, and give to the poor, and thou shalt have treasure in heaven: and come, follow Me. But his countenance fell at the saying, and he went away sorrowful: for he was one that had great possessions. (Mark 10:17–22 RV)

Such was the preparation necessary before this admirable soul could become a disciple of Jesus Christ. To use the language of Dr. Donald Davidson—

Strip yourself of every possession, cut away every affection, disengage yourself from all things, be as if you were a naked soul, alone in the world; be a mere man merely, and then be God's. "Sell all that thou hast and follow Me!" Reduce yourself down, if I may say so, till nothing remains but your consciousness of yourself, and then cast the self-consciousness at the feet of God in Christ.

You cannot become a disciple of Jesus Christ as a rich man, or as a landed proprietor, or as a man of splendid reputation, or as a man of good name and family. The only road to Jesus is ALONE. Will you strip yourself and separate yourself and take that lonely road, or will you too go away "sorrowful"?

If any man is in Christ he is a new creature. (RV)

Marvel not that I said unto thee, Ye must be born from above. (RV mg)

Jesus Christ always speaks from the source of things, consequently those who deal only with the surface find Him an offence.

Separation from Professions

And there came one scribe, and said unto Him, Master, I will follow Thee whithersoever Thou goest. And Jesus said unto him, The foxes have holes, and the birds of the heaven have nests; but the Son of man hath not where to lay His head. (Matthew 8:19–20 RV)

But Peter said unto Him, Although all shall be caused to stumble [mg], yet will not I. And Jesus saith unto him, Verily I say unto thee, that thou to-day, even this night, before the cock crow twice, shalt deny Me thrice. But he spake exceeding vehemently, If I must die with Thee, I will not deny Thee. And in like manner also said they all. (Mark 14:29–31 RV)

---

8. William James (1842–1910): American philosopher, psychologist, and teacher.

Professions last as long as the conditions that called them forth last, but no longer. As long as the fervid, strong attachment to Jesus lasts, the professions are the natural expression of that attachment; but when the way grows narrow, and reputations are torn, and the popular verdict is against the shameful poverty and meekness of the Son of Man, professions wither on the tongue; not through cowardice, but because the conditions that made the heart warm, and the feelings move and the mouth speak, are altered. When the way of joyfully leaving all and following Jesus in the bounding days of devotion turns into the way of sorrow, and the heroic isolation of being with Jesus ends in shadows, and Jesus seems weak before the world, and the way of following ends in the way of derision, then professions are blighted, and the heart's feelings are frozen or changed into horror and perplexity. Peter's profession ended in denial and disaster—"But he began to curse, and to swear, I know not this man of whom ye speak" (Mark 14:71 RV).

Love never professes; love *confesses*.

From all high and stirring emotions, from all exhilarating professions arising out of true human devotion, our Lord repulses with a stern, bracing rebuke. Sanctified poverty! Ah, it chills the heart and professions die. The poverty of our Lord and of His disciples is the exact expression of the nature of the religion of Jesus Christ—just man and God; man possessing nothing, professing nothing; yet when the Lord asks at some dawn, after a heart-breaking failure, "Lovest thou Me?" the soul confesses, "Yea, Lord; Thou knowest that I love Thee." And when that poverty is a disgust to the full-fed religious world, the disciple does not *profess*, but confesses, with aching hands and bleeding feet, "I love Him," and goes outside the camp, "bearing His reproach."

Prof. Wm. James[8] in his pioneer work, "The Varieties of Religious Experience," says—

> Poverty indeed is the strenuous life,—without brass bands, or uniforms, or hysteric popular applause, or lies, or circumlocutions; and when one sees the way in which wealthgetting enters as an ideal into the very bone and marrow of our generation, one wonders whether a revival of the belief that poverty is a religious vocation may not be the transformation of military courage, and the spiritual reform of which our time stands most in need.

We have grown literally afraid of being poor. We despise anyone who elects to be poor in order to simplify and save his inner life. If he does not join the general scramble, and pant with the moneymaking street, we deem him spiritless and lacking in ambition. We have lost the power of imagining what the ancient idealisation of poverty could have meant—the liberation from material attachments, the unbribed soul, the manlier indifference, the paying our way by what we are or do, and not by what we have; the right to fling away our life at any moment irresponsibly, the more athletic trim, in short, the moral fighting shape.

> For His sake those tears and prayers are offered,
>   Which you bear as flowers to His throne;
> Better still would be the food and shelter,
>   Given for HIM, and given to His own.
> Praise with loving Deeds is dear and holy,
>   Words of Praise will never serve instead;
> Lo! you offer music, hymn and incense,
>   When He has not where to lay His head. . . .
> Jesus then and Mary still are with us—
>   Night will find the Child and Mother near,
> Waiting for the shelter we deny them
>   While we tell them that we hold them dear!
>
>   A. Procter[9]

Separation from Positions

And there arose a reasoning among them, which of them should be greatest. But when Jesus saw the reasoning of their heart, He took a little child, and set him by His side, and said unto them, Whosoever shall receive this little child in My name receiveth Me: and whosoever shall receive Me receiveth Him that sent Me: for he that is least among you all, the same is great. (Luke 9:46–48 RV)

Grant unto us that we may sit, one on Thy right hand, and one on Thy left hand, in Thy glory. But Jesus said unto them, Ye know not what ye ask. Are ye able to drink the cup that I drink? or to be baptized with the baptism that I am baptized with? And they said unto Him, We are able. And Jesus said unto them, The cup that I drink ye shall drink; and with the baptism that I am baptized withal shall ye be baptized: but to sit on My right hand or on My left hand is not Mine to give: but it is for them for whom it hath been prepared. (Mark 10:37–40 RV)

How we miss it! those loyal true, human hearts, and ourselves, until we are changed by the deep upheaval of a birth from above, and the presence of an overwhelming love to our Lord in our hearts. The desire to be the "loyalest," the "faithfullest," the "holiest" disciple produces a winsome rebuke from our Lord, and our hearts feel we have missed the point but scarcely know how. It was surely natural for the disciples to

---

9. Adelaide Anne Procter (1825–1864): English poet.

imagine "who should be the greatest"; and yet when Jesus questioned them, their hearts confused and rebuked them.

> *And he called to Him a little child, and set him in the midst of them, and said, . . . Whosoever therefore shall humble himself as this little child, the same is the greatest in the kingdom of heaven. (Matthew 18:2, 4 RV)*

By means of the implicit life of a little child Jesus taught the disciples that unless they became "as this little child," they could in no wise enter into the kingdom of heaven. The true child of God is such from an inward principle of life from which the life is ordered by implicit loving devotion, as natural as breathing, and as spontaneous as the life of a little child.

> *And another of the disciples said unto Him, Lord, suffer me first to go and bury my father. But Jesus saith unto him. Follow Me; and leave the dead to bury their own dead. (Matthew 8:21–22 RV)*

To plead with Jesus to notice us and enrol us as His disciples from any position, good, bad or indifferent, will meet one of those otherwise unaccountable chills. To seek the lowest position, or the highest, or any position at all, is to miss the mark utterly. In the days of preparation from all Possessions, Professions and Positions, Jesus leads in a separating, isolating way—"What seekest thou?" "Whom seekest thou?" The sad eyes of the Son of God lure us into the wilderness alone, and these questions ring in our hearts. From all desire for position, place, power, from every pedestal of devotion, or dedication, or deed, He draws and separates us; and suddenly we discern what He wants, deeper than tongue can express, and obedience to the heavenly vision, arising from an abandonment of love to Himself, leads us to heaven. Not as faithful friends, or as moral men, or as devout souls, or as righteous men— Jesus separates us from all these positions by an unbridgeable distance when He is making clear to us that we must leave ALL. These lonely moments are given to each of us. Have we heeded them?

> *Oh, we're sunk enough here, God knows!*
> *But not quite so sunk that moments,*
> *Sure tho' seldom, are denied us.*
> *   When the spirit's true endowments*
> *   Stand out plainly from its false ones,*
> *   And apprise it if pursuing*
> *Or the right way or the wrong way,*
> *   To its triumph or undoing.*

> *There are flashes struck from midnights,*
> *   There are fire-flames noondays kindle,*
> *Where by piled-up honours perish.*
> *   Where by swollen ambitions dwindle,*
> *While just this or that poor impulse,*
> *   Which for once had play unstifled,*
> *Seems the sole work of a life-time*
> *   That away the rest have trifled.*
>
> Browning

Loneliness in Consecration

It is no wonder that preparation has to be so drastic and so deep. It is easy to say things about the necessity of preparation, but we too readily take on the pattern and print of the age, or set, or country in which we live. The emphasis to-day in spiritual domains is on the *work*, not on the *workman*. Three hours is considered sufficient preparation for thirty years' work. But when we turn to the Bible records we almost unconsciously take the deliberate stride of the hills of God, and ever after we have an unhasting and unresting heart amid the cities of men. Our Lord Jesus Christ had thirty years' preparation for three years of ostensible work. John the Baptist had a similar preparation, and the Apostle Paul spent three lonely years in Arabia. Some words from Dr. Alexander Whyte's[10] individual reading of St. Paul will serve to keep us in the right atmosphere for the consideration of this subject of the Loneliness in Consecration—

> *For it was in Arabia, and it was under the Mount of God, that Paul's apostolic ink-horn was first filled with that ink of God with which he long afterwards wrote that so little understood writing of his, which we call the seventh of the Romans. A little-understood writing; and no wonder! The Apostle came back from Arabia to Damascus, after three years' absence, absolutely ladened down with all manner of doctrines, and directions, and examples, for us and for our salvation, if we would only attend to them and receive them. Directions and the examples, of which this is one of the first. That solitude, the most complete and not short solitude, was the one thing that Paul determined to secure for himself immediately after his conversion and his baptism. . . . And thus it is that Holy Scripture is everywhere so full of apartness and aloneness and solitude: of lodges in the wilderness, and of shut doors in the city: of early mornings, and late nights, and lonely night-watches: of Sabbath-days and holidays, and all such asylums of spiritual retreat.[11]*

> *Down to Gehenna, and up to the throne,*
> *He travels the fastest who travels alone.*

---

10. Alexander Whyte (1836–1921): Scottish minister who influenced Chambers during Oswald's time at Edinburgh University (1895–1896).

11. *The Apostle Paul* (1903), pages 42–43.

. . . .

We cannot kindle when we will
*   The fire which in the heart resides!*
The Spirit bloweth and is still,—
*   In mystery our soul abides!*
But tasks in hours of insight willed
Can be through hours of gloom fulfilled

With aching hands and bleeding feet,
*   We dig and heap, lay stone on stone;*
We bear the burden and the heat
*   Of the long day, and wish 'twere done,*
Not till the hours of light return,
All we have built do we discern.

Matthew Arnold[12]

By the term Consecration is meant that human action whereby we present ourselves to God. The period of consecration may be three minutes, or thirty years, according to the individual; or the soul may degenerate during its consecration. The period of consecration may be thoroughly misused. Sanctification begins at regeneration, and goes on to a second great crisis, when God, upon an uttermost abandonment in consecration, bestows His gracious work of entire sanctification. The point of entire sanctification is reached not by the passing of the years but by obedience to the heavenly vision and through spiritual discipline. Spiritual degeneration, so keenly portrayed in the Epistle to the Hebrews, is brought about by weak and prolonged consecration, during which the soul degenerates completely. "Of whom we have many things to say, and hard of interpretation, seeing ye are become dull of hearing. For when by reason of the time ye ought to be teachers, ye have need again that one teach you which are the rudiments of the beginning [mg] of the oracles of God; And are become such as have need of milk, and not of solid food. . . . Wherefore let us cease to speak of the first principles of Christ, and press on unto perfection [full growth, mg]" (see Hebrews 5:11–12; 6:1 RV). Perfection here simply means the full maturity of a man's powers; then begins his work.

Separation from Country

Abraham! the "Pilgrim of Eternity!" "The Father of the Faithful!" These titles give a touch emphatic and decisive to that wonderful career which emphasises this Loneliness in Consecration.

> *Now the LORD said unto Abram, Get thee out of thy country, and from thy kindred, and from thy father's house, unto the land that I will shew thee. (Genesis 12:1 RV)*

> *By faith Abraham, when he was called, obeyed to go out unto a place which he was to receive for an inheritance; and he went out, not knowing whither he went. (Hebrews 11:8 RV)*

The separation from the ideals and aims and ways of looking at things peculiar to one's set, or society, or country, is a great break. To the man who is undergoing consecration for a supreme sanctification, this separation is a persistent and pressing pain until it is obeyed. To run away from one's country or one's set is cowardly and un-Christian; that is not Christianity, but cowardly selfishness. One careful glance at our Lord's prayer will kill that cunning cowardice at once—"I pray not that Thou shouldest take them out of [mg] the world, but that Thou shouldest keep them from the evil one. They are not of the world, even as I am not of the world" (John 17:15–16 RV).

In Christianity the Kingdom and its laws and principles must be put first, and everything else second, and if the holy calling demands it, there must be instant and military obedience, leaving all and rallying round the standard of Jesus Christ. The missionary of the Cross is not first a British or an American subject, but a Christian. The missionary is not a sanctified patriot, but one whose sympathies have broken all parochial bounds and whose aims beat in unison with God's own heart. A Christian is a sanctified man in his business, or legal or civic affairs, or artistic and literary affairs. Consecration is not the giving over of the calling in life to God, but the separation from all other callings and the giving over of ourselves to God, letting His providence place us where He will—in business, or law, or science; in workshop, in politics, or in drudgery. We are to be there working according to the laws and principles of the Kingdom of God, not according to the ideals or aims or ways of looking at things from the point of view of a particular set. This constitutes us fools in the eyes of our set, and the temptation is strong then to get out of our country. It will mean working according to different aims, and we must never take the pattern and print of the set to which we belong. "Business is business" is not true for the Christian. Business is a sphere of labour in the world where a man exhibits the laws and principles of the Kingdom, otherwise he is a coward, a deserter, and a traitor to that Kingdom. It is a lonely way—

> *With a thousand things that are*
> *Births of woe and food for crime:*
> *Still, to vindicate the right*
> *Is a rough and thankless game:—*
> *Still the leader in the fight*
> *Is the hindmost in the fame.*

---

12. Matthew Arnold (1822–1888): English scholar, poet, and critic.

Do you answer to the stern, bracing, heroic call in consecration—Get thee out of thy country and stand alone with Jesus? It is a foolish and a shameful thing to be a saint in business. To be a saint may be to be outcast and ridiculed. Try it. Faith is built on heroism. Consecration is the narrow, lonely way to over-flooding love. We are not called upon to live long on this planet, but we are called upon to be holy at any and every cost. If obedience costs you your life, then pay it.

There are few who care to analyse
The mingled motives, in their complex force,
Of some apparently quite simple course.
One, disentangled skein might well surprise.
Perhaps a "single heart" is never known.
Save in the yielded life that lives for God
*   alone,—*
And that is therefore doubted as a dream
By those who know not the tremendous power
Of all-constraining love!

F. R. Havergal[13]

Separation from Comrades
If any man cometh unto Me, and hateth not his own father, and mother, and wife, and children, and brethren, and sisters, yea, and his own life also, he cannot be my disciple. (Luke 14:26 RV)

You cannot consecrate yourself and your friends. If at the altar your heart imagines that loving arms are still around you, and that together, lovers as lovers, and friends as friends, can enter through this mighty gate of supreme Sanctification, it is a fond dream, doomed to disillusionment. Alone! Relinquish all! You cannot consecrate your children, your wife, your lover, your friend, your father, your mother or your own life as yours. You must abandon all and fling yourself on God as a mere conscious being, and unperplexed, seeking you'll find Him. The teaching that presents consecration as giving to God our gifts, our possessions, our comrades, is a profound error. These are all abandoned, and we give up for ever *our right to ourselves*. A sanctified soul may be an artist, or a musician; but he is not a sanctified artist or musician: he is one who expresses the message of God through a particular medium. As long as the artist or musician imagines he can consecrate his artistic gifts to God, he is deluded. Abandonment of ourselves is the kernel of consecration, not presenting our gifts, but presenting ourselves without reserve.

Our Lord uses stern words; He says it is better to be deformed than damned—

And if thy hand or thy foot causeth thee to stumble, cut it off, and cast it from thee: it is good for thee to enter into life maimed or halt, rather than having two hands or two feet to be cast into the eternal fire. And if thine eye causeth thee to stumble, pluck it out, and cast it from thee: it is good for thee to enter into life with one eye, rather than having two eyes to be cast into the Gehenna of fire [mg]. (Matthew 18:8–9 RV)

The foot and the hand and the eye are great and mighty gifts, and also means of livelihood; yet the stern principle of our Lord is clear—It is better to be deformed than damned. The inner experience of some gifted soul, some genius or orator or artist, who has undergone this test of supreme sanctification, might well expound this marvellously profound experience. Oh, the wail of the souls who have failed at the altar, and have made their consecration a wilderness experience years long. Their language wrings with pain.

I descended into the fire of Hell
And gazed until I burned;
I came, but how I came I cannot tell,
My vile heart led me, being its own spell.
I looked, was marred,—and turned.
I entered on a heritage of woe,
And never can return;
I broke the heart of God's own Son to go,
I spurned His Spirit that besought me so,
And entered Hell to burn.
And marvel ye that I must watch and pray
While ye are sweet asleep?
Lest haply from His saving grace I stray,
Enticed by things with which you play!
Sleep on! but I must weep!

This subject of Consecration has been purposely dealt with from its deepest meaning in order that its application to all domains might be made clear. Its one note is—"Ye are not your own; for ye were bought with a price: glorify God therefore in your body" (1 Corinthians 6:19–20 RV). It is the loving hands, the tender hands, that hinder most at the altar; the hands too loving that prevent. It is a lonely way; we cannot take it with comrades.

Peter began to say unto Him, Lo, we have left all, and have followed Thee. Jesus said, Verily I say unto you, There is no man that hath left house, or brethren, or sisters, or mother, or father, or children, or lands, for My sake, and for the gospel's sake, but he shall receive a hundredfold now in this time,

---

13. Frances Ridley Havergal (1836–1879): English poet and hymn writer.

houses, and brethren, and sisters, and mothers, and children, and lands, with persecutions; and in the age [mg] to come eternal life. But many that are first shall be last; and the last first. (Mark 10:28–31)

As in the case of Separation from Country, this Separation from Comrades is not a cowardly, selfish, immoral breaking away from human ties which God has ordained; but it does mean that, if Jesus demands it, nothing must stand in the way; He must be first. Oh, for more of that abandonment of consecration and fire from Heaven which would make a mighty army of saints!

Yes, without cheer of sister or of daughter,
Yes, without stay of father or of son,
Lone on the land and homeless on the water
Pass I in Patience till the work be done.

Yet not in solitude if Christ anear me
Waketh Him workers for the great employ,
Oh not in solitude, if souls that hear me
Catch from my joyaunce the surprise of joy.

Hearts I have won of sister or of brother
Quick on the earth or hidden in the sod,
Lo every heart awaiteth me, another
Friend in the blameless family of God.

F. W. H. Myers

This hour of solitude and loneliness in consecration is followed by a blessed sanctified socialism, the hidden secret of which is the heart alone in delight with God. Multitudes of men follow whenever a soul has been on the mount with God. If one might dare whisper it, the blighting suffering in lonely consecration is God's imperial way of making what we once had intermittently our eternal possession.

Separation from Comforts

Yet it was well, and Thou hast said in season
As is the Master shall the servant be:
Let me not subtly slide into the treason,
Seeking an honour which they gave not Thee:
Never at even, pillowed on a pleasure,
Sleep with the wings of aspiration furled,
Hide the last mite of the forbidden treasure,
Keep for my joys a world within the world.

F. W. H. Myers

Nevertheless I tell you the truth; It is expedient for you that I go away: for if I go not away, the Comforter will not come unto you; but if I go, I will send Him unto you.

. . . And ye therefore now have sorrow: but I will see you again, and your heart shall rejoice, and your joy no one taketh away from you. (John 16:7, 22 RV)

Interior desolations serve a vital purpose in the soul of a Christian. It is expedient that the joys of contact be removed that our idea of the Christian character may not be misplaced. In the early days of spiritual experience we walk more by sight and feelings than by faith. The comforts, the delights, the joys of contact are so exquisite that the very flesh itself tingles with the leadings of the cloudy pillar by day and the fiery pillar by night; but there comes a day when all that ceases. Madame Guyon[14] in her poem entitled, "The Dealings of God; or The Divine Love in Bringing the Soul to a State of Absolute Acquiescence," states this Separation from Comforts—

How I trembled then and fear'd,
When my Love had disappear'd!
"Wilt thou leave me thus?" I cried,
"Whelm'd beneath the rolling tide?"
Vain attempt to reach His ear!
Love was gone, and would not hear.

Ah, return and love me still;
See me subject to Thy will;
Frown with wrath, or smile with grace,
Only let me see Thy face!
Evil I have none to fear;
All is good, if Thou art near.

Yet He leaves me,—cruel fate!
Leaves me in my lost estate.
Have I sinn'd? Oh, say wherein.
Tell me, and forgive my sin!
King and Lord whom I adore,
Shall I see Thy face no more?

Be not angry,—I resign
Henceforth all my will to Thine.
I consent that Thou depart,
Though Thine absence breaks my heart.
Go, then, and forever, too
All is right that Thou wilt do.

This was just what Love intended:
He was now no more offended;
Soon as I became a child,
Love returned to me and smiled.
Never strife shall more betide
'Twixt the Bridegroom and His bride.

It is difficult to put this experience into language without making God's way seem foolish and an occasion for our petulance. The very essence of Christianity

---

14. Madame Guyon (1648–1717): French mystic and writer.

is not so much a walk *with* Jesus as a walk *like* His walk, when we have allowed Him to baptise us with the Holy Ghost and fire. As we pointed out in "The Discipline of Suffering," the disaster of sentiments and emotions indulged in for themselves is that these end in the revenge of the lower nature; so here, delight in experiences heralds the approach of a false mysticism, the characteristic of which is an inwardness of experience, developing into a private illumination apart from the written Word. Madame Guyon ran perilously near this danger of quietism. All ecstasies and experiences, all inner voices and revelations and dreams, must be tested by the pure outer light of Jesus Christ and His word. By looking to Him we are changed into the same image from glory to glory, when consecration has been made a definite transaction. Sanity in ordinary human life is maintained by a right correspondence with outer facts, and sanity in Christian life is produced by the correspondence with the facts revealed by our Lord Jesus Christ.

These experiences are not recognised at the time, but in looking back from a more mature stage one's heart comments "Amen" to the exposition of the way God has taken us. All false mysticism arises from the fact that teachers insist on an inner experience, which by the simple process of introspection ultimately kills itself. Subjective states must be tested and estimated and regulated by objective standards. This is the only safeguard against the irresponsible crowd of fanatics who live from hand to mouth in spiritual experience and get nowhere, and by reason of their own shallowness, end in contemptible disasters. This elementary state of spiritual experience ought to herald the last stage of a protracted consecration. Thank God, these isolating, separating forces may be recognised at the moment of regeneration by intuition, and, by a willing transaction, the soul may be borne on unto perfection without these distressing wilderness experiences.

To quote Madame Guyon again; she comments thus on her own experience, long after such experiences had ceased—"To complete my distress, I seemed to be left without God Himself, Who alone could support me in such a distressing state."

"The misfortune," she adds, "is that people wish to direct God instead of resigning themselves to be directed by Him. They wish to take the lead and to follow in a way of their own selection, instead of submissively and passively following where God sees fit to conduct them. And hence it is that many souls who are called to the enjoyment of God Himself and not merely to the gifts of God, spend all their lives in pursuing and in feeding on little consolations, resting in them as in their place of delights, and making their spiritual life to consist in them."

All this goes to show that the Christian life simply reconstructs the reasonings from the common-sense facts of natural life, preparing the way for that walk in faith that fears nothing because the heart is blazing with the love of God.

> *It thou wouldst have high God thy soul assure,*
> *That she herself shall as herself endure,*
> *Shall in no alien semblance, thine and wise,*
> *Fulfil her and be young in Paradise,*
> *One way I know; forget, forswear, disdain*
> *Thine own best hopes, thine utmost loss and*
>   *gain,*
> *Till when at last thou scarce rememberest now*
> *If on the earth be such a man as thou*
> *Nor hast one thought of self-surrender—no*
> *For self is none remaining to forgo,—*
> *If ever, then shall strong persuasion fall*
> *That in thy giving thou hast gained thine all,*
> *Given the poor present, gained the boundless*
>   *scope,*
> *And kept thee virgin for the further hope.*

F. W. H. Myers

An aside. Possibly the lack of recognising the human option in this Loneliness in Consecration has led teachers to blunder unconsciously into a line of teaching perilously dangerous to Christianity. There is in our midst to-day a strong revival of pagan spirituality. Many are using the terms of Hindooism or of Buddhism to expound Christianity, and they end not in expounding Christianity at all, but in expounding the very human experience of consecration, which is not peculiar to Christianity. The peculiar doctrine or Gospel of the Christian religion is Entire Sanctification, whereby God takes the most unpromising man and makes a saint of him. The teaching called "Deeper Death to Self" is a misleading form of this doctrine. The sentiments it expresses are so languid and painful, so injurious, that during the stage of consecration there is a sympathetic agreement with the introspective morbid condition that results. Our Lord does not teach a consecrated anaemia, i.e. the destruction of personality: He teaches a very positive *death for ever to my right to myself*—a positive destruction of the disposition of sin and a positive placing in, in Entire Sanctification, of the Holy Spirit, a pronounced identity that bears a strong family likeness to Jesus. Not "Deeper Death to Self," that is sanctified suicide, but the realisation of another's self in love, that other Self being God. Jesus Christ emancipates the personality and makes the individuality pronounced, and the transfiguring, incalculable element is love, personal, passionate devotion to Himself, and to others. "Deeper Death to Self" is complacent, and enervatingly encouraging to the morbid soul who having missed the first period of discipleship in consecration, is ever fainting on the *Via Dolorosa*, but never getting to the place where the "old man," "*my right to myself,*" dies right out. Entire sanctification puts a man's breast and back as either should be, places his feet on earth and his head in Heaven, and gives him the royal insignia of the saints.

Loneliness in Sanctification

And they all left Him and fled. And a certain young man followed with Him, having a linen cloth cast about him, over his naked body: and they lay hold on him; but he left the linen cloth, and fled naked. (Mark 14:50–52 RV)

Stripped for Flight or Following?

Say, could aught else content thee? which were best,
After so brief a battle an endless rest,
Or the ancient conflict rather to renew,
By the old deeds strengthened mightier deeds to do,
Till all thou art, nay, all thou hast dreamed to be
Proves thy mere root or embryon germ of thee;—
Wherefrom thy great life passionately springs,
Rocked by strange blasts and stormy
*   tempestings,*
Yet still from shock and storm more steadfast grown,
More one with other souls, yet more thine own?—
Nay, thro' those sufferings called and chosen then
A very Demiurge of unborn men—
A very Saviour, bending half divine
To souls who feel such woes as once were thine;—
For these perchance, some utmost fear to brave
Teach with thy truth, and with thy sorrows save.

F. W. H. Myers

The Loneliness of Preparation and of Consecration are more or less complicated by enfeebling interminglings of sin and sympathy and selfishness. Now we come to the loneliness of the serene uplands where the silences of God's Eternities are ever around. Oh, it is a great thing when our Father can safely leave us alone on the mountains of God, even if the darkness is unspeakable. The loneliness of a blessed personal responsibility gladly accepted—master of everything, the lover and friend of God. God takes us mighty ways; He takes us by the lonely ways of Apprenticeship, and Workmanship, and Mastership.

Separation in Sifting

And straightway the Spirit driveth Him forth into the wilderness. And He was in the wilderness forty days tempted of Satan; and He was with the wild beasts; and the angels ministered unto Him. (Mark 1:12–13 RV)

After the baptism by the Holy Ghost and fire, we emerge as masters in the sense of fitness for the work of a saint. Then God shows us His greatest mercy, for He spares us no requirement of that mastership, or saintship. We find ourselves alone with forces which are working to sift and disintegrate, to discourage and destroy; but our inward implicit communion makes us feel the confidence of God in us. It is as if God, smiling, were saying to Satan—"Do your worst; I know that He that is in him is greater than he that is against him." I can recall seeing a picture in the Royal Academy[15] some years ago, it was a picture of lesser importance, but the artist had grasped the lofty loneliness of temptation as portrayed in Mark 1:12–13. The wilderness was under a grey lowering aspect, distance and dreariness and dread was stamped on every rock and stone, and in the midst the Figure of Christ stood, alone. No devil or angel was portrayed, only a few prowling wild beasts, accentuating the wild loneliness of that supreme moment of Satanic sifting. Is that same kind of sifting given to us? Surely it is. "For we have not a high priest that cannot be touched with the feeling of our infirmities; but one that hath been in all points tempted like as we are, yet without sin" (Hebrews 4:15 RV). When our apprenticeship is ended, we are tested as our Lord and Master was. On the threshold of our Mastership—or to put it into theological terms, after regeneration and entire consecration, when we have passed the mighty crisis of the Baptism of the Holy Ghost and begin our walk and work and worship under a supreme sanctification, then we are tempted as He was. It is not our object to consider the nature of that temptation, but merely to mention its place and its loneliness. It is not the loneliness of birth pains, or growing pains, it is the loneliness of the saint. As in nature so in grace. The first period of our natural life is one of promise and vision and enthusiasm, in which the surrounding mysteries have a fascination that alternates with fears. Then there comes a time when it is—

Never again the boy-life,
Only the pain and joy life—
More the first than the last.

F. R. Havergal

and all subsequent life holds out the proving of our powers. Saintship means mastership. The order of the saintly life is—"a witness, a leader, and a commander."

The Loneliness of Sifting lays the conviction broad and deep that the saint has substituted the will of God for his individual will. The first ordeal of

---

15. The Royal Academy of Arts: association of artists in London that operates art schools and organizes exhibitions.

temptation that tries the stuff of which the saint is made is that of loneliness, and it comes on the very threshold of the super-conquering life.

> *What, if He hath decreed that I shall first*
> *Be try'd in humble state and things adverse,*
> *By tribulations, injuries, insults,*
> *Contempts, and scorns, and snares, and*
>   *violence,—*
> *Suffering, abstaining, quietly expecting,*
> *Without distrust or doubt,—that He may know,*
> *What I can suffer, how obey?*
>
>   Milton

Separation in Suffering

These things have I spoken unto you, that in Me ye may have peace. In the world ye have tribulation: but be of good cheer; I have overcome the world. (John 16:33 RV)

> *Men as men,*
> *Can reach no higher than the Son of God,*
> *The Perfect Head and Pattern of mankind.*
> *The time is short and this sufficeth us*
> *To live and die by; and in Him again*
> *We see the same first, starry attribute,*
> *"Perfect through suffering," our salvation's seal*
> *Set in the front of His humanity.*
>
> . . . .
>
> *And while we suffer, let us set our souls*
> *To suffer perfectly: since this alone,*
> *The suffering, which is this world's special grace,*
> *May here be perfected and left behind.*
>
>   H. Hamilton King[16]

The most fundamental thing that can be said about the suffering[1] [1 This subject is dealt with more fully in "The Discipline of Suffering."—*This footnote appears in Chambers' original text.*] of the supremely sanctified is that it springs from an active, unquestioning submission to the will of God, allowing God to work out in the life His idea of what a saint should be, just as He worked out in the life of Jesus Christ, not what a saint should be, but what a Saviour should be.

After all that can be said, is said, the sufferings of the saint arise, not from inbred sin, but from obedience to the will of God, which can rarely be stated explicitly. The will of God is apprehended by the Holy Spirit indwelling the saint; it is apprehended not as the mind apprehends a truth, but in the way any incalculable element is intuitively grasped. Inestimable damage is done when the will of God is made an external law to be obeyed by conscious grasp. The will of God is apprehended by an almost unconscious impelling of the indwelling Holy Spirit. It is essentially a lonely way, for the saint knows not why he suffers as he does, yet he comprehends with a knowledge that passeth knowledge that all is well. His language is that of Job—"But He knoweth the way that I take; when He hath tried me, I shall come forth as gold" (Job 23:10).

When we understand that the saints are the rich glory of Jesus Christ's inheritance, we have added light on the mystery of the suffering of the saints.

> *. . . that ye may know . . . what the riches of the glory of His inheritance in the saints. (Ephesians 1:18)*
>
> *When He shall come to be glorified in His saints, and to be marvelled at in all them that believed. (2 Thessalonians 1:10 RV)*

The suffering of the saints at heart is not what is ensnaringly known as "Deeper Death to Self"; it springs from an active submission and determination to accept the intensely individual responsibility of doing God's will. It is not absolution by loss of individuality; that destroys all possibility of suffering, and indicates the paganising of the sanctified life so prevalent to-day. It is rather the transfiguration of individuality in the mastership of God's purpose in Christ—"till we all attain unto the unity of the faith, and of the knowledge of the Son of God, unto a full grown man, unto the measure of the stature of the fulness of Christ" (Ephesians 4:13 RV).

The moment in which a man enters into the experience of supreme sanctification is the crisis that marks his evangelical perfection; all alien things that retarded and deformed him have been removed. Then begins his life as a Master Christian, and there is no other kind of Christian on this road. In this supreme sanctification he develops and attains height after height. How clearly St. Paul puts these two perfections—

> *Not that I have already obtained, or am already made perfect: but I press on, if so be that I may apprehend that for which also I was apprehended by Christ Jesus. Brethren, I count not myself yet to have apprehended: but one thing I do, forgetting the things which are behind, and stretching forward to the things which are before, I press on toward the goal unto the prize of the high calling of God in Christ Jesus. Let us therefore, as many as be perfect, be thus minded: and if in anything ye are otherwise minded, even this shall God reveal unto*

---

16. Harriet Eleanor Hamilton King (1840–1920): English poet; author of *The Disciples* (1873), an epic poem much quoted and loved by Chambers.

*you: only, whereunto we have already attained, by
that same rule let us walk. (Philippians 3:12–16
RV)*

*And I smiled as one never smiles but once,
Then first discovering my own aim's extent,
Which sought to comprehend the works of God,
And God himself, and all God's intercourse
With the human mind; I understood, no less,
My fellows' studies, whose true worth I saw,
But smiled not, well aware who stood by me.
And softer came the voice—"There is a way:
'Tis hard for flesh to tread therein, imbued
With frailty—hopeless, if indulgence first
Have ripened inborn germs of sin to strength:
Wilt thou adventure for my sake and man's,
Apart from all reward?" And last it breathed—
"Be happy, my good soldier; I am by thee,
Be sure, even to the end!"—I answered not,
Knowing him. As he spoke, I was endued
With comprehension and a steadfast will;
And when he ceased, my brow was sealed his own.
If there took place no special change in me,
How comes it all things wore a different hue
Thenceforward?—pregnant with vast
  consequence,
Teeming with grand result, loaded with fate?
So that when, quailing at the mighty range
Of secret truths which yearn for birth, I haste
To contemplate undazzled some one truth,
Its bearing and effects alone—at once
What was a speck expands into a star,
Asking a life to pass exploring thus,
Till I near craze. I go to prove my soul!
I see my way as birds their trackless way.
I shall arrive! what time, what circuit first
I ask not: but unless God send his hail
Or blinding fire-balls, sleet or stifling snow,
In some time, his good time, I shall arrive:
He guides me and the bird. In his good time!*

         Browning

Separation in Service

*Hark, hark! a voice amid the quiet intense!
It is thy Duty waiting thee without—
Rise from thy knees in hope, the half of doubt—
A hand doth pull thee—It is Providence!
Open thy door straightway and get thee hence;
Go forth into the tumult and the shout!
Work! love! with workers, lovers all about!
Of noise alone is born the inward sense
Of silence; and from Action springs alone
The inward knowledge of true love and faith.*

      George MacDonald

Work may be executed by driven slaves or by master workmen. A saint is not an instrument of God; he is a master workman for God. A man may be used as an instrument of God without being a servant of God; there is no trace of the master workman about him. We too may have found that during the days of our apprenticeship God has allowed us to do work, not for Him, but for our own perfecting. But now God takes the saints, with skilled finger, so to speak, and with tried and tested patience, into His enterprises to battle and to build. After His Resurrection Jesus said to the disciples, "As the Father hath sent Me, even so send I you" (John 20:21 RV). And again, "Go ye therefore, and make disciples of all the nations" (Matthew 28:19 RV). And in His High-priestly prayer our Lord prayed—"As Thou didst send Me into the world, even so sent I them into the world" (John 17:18 RV). And the Apostle Paul in writing to Timothy said—"Give diligence to present thyself approved unto God, a workman that needeth not to be ashamed, holding a straight course in the word of truth" (2 Timothy 2:15 RV mg). All these words breathe activity, energy, and triumphant masterwork. Jesus did not say, "Go and discourse about making disciples," but "Go and *make* disciples." The making of converts is a Satanic perversion of this strenuous workmanlike product. How many make followers of their own convictions, and how few make disciples! The production of saints, that is the work. God Almighty regenerates men's souls; we make disciples. Are we doing it? God is apparently not very careful whom He uses or what He uses for the work of regeneration; but none but the master workmen, that is, the saints, can make disciples. Does your work for God stamp the hearts of the people round about you with an enervating, sentimental love for you? or does every remembrance of you cause a strenuous stirring of hearts to do better, grander work for God? God's curse is on the spiritual nature that cannot reproduce its own kind. The Apostle Paul cries out exultingly—"For what is our hope, or joy, or crown of glorying? Are not even ye, before our Lord Jesus Christ at His coming? For ye are our glory and our joy" (1 Thessalonians 2:19–20 RV). Can you catch sight of the product? The making of saints. What are you doing with the thousands of souls that God's mighty Spirit is regenerating? Are you stripped and at work, studying, praying, suffering, to make disciples of them?

> *Get leave to work
> In this world!—'tis the best you get at all!
> For God in cursing, gives us better gifts
> Than men in benediction. God says Sweat
> For foreheads,—men say Crowns,—and so we
>   are crowned
> Ay, gashed—by some tormenting circle of steel
> Which snaps with a secret spring.—Get Work!*

Get Work!
Be sure 'tis better than what you work to get!

E. B. Browning

"Lovest thou Me? . . . Tend My sheep" (RV). Can you feed the lambs and the sheep? Do you, or are you in the show business? Listen to the voice of your Master: "As the Father hath sent me, even so send I you" (RV). Is it not time for you to present yourself before God and say, "Father, look at my hands, my heart, and my head: Jesus has cleansed me"? And He will answer, "Son, go work to day in My vineyard."

I too could now say to myself: Be no longer a chaos, but a World, or even worldkin. Produce! Produce! Were it but the pitifullest, infinitesimal fraction of a product, produce it in God's name! 'Tis the utmost that thou hast in thee: out with it then. Up, Up! Whatsoever thy hand findeth to do, do it with thy whole might. Work while it is called to-day, for the night cometh, wherein no man can work.

Carlyle[17]

This Loneliness in Service is so subtle that if we try and state it in words we almost lose it. It is so easy to coarsen this sublime theme by a word misunderstood, so difficult to put it in any language saving when the heart is in profoundest communion with God. We are so apt to consider work as something done by an individual and yet separate from him. The essential peculiarity of the work of the sanctified servant of God is that he never can be separated from his work without a violent outrage. We are ever apt to overestimate the aloneness of our Lord prefigured by the types and symbols of the old dispensation: the scapegoat, the lamb, and the shed blood; and we ignore that the true prototype of our Lord is the prophet. How continually the prophets break out with some arresting statement that seems fit only in the mouth of our Lord! How often the Psalmist bursts out with utterances of an unaccountable touch, the full meaning of which is found for us in Jesus Christ alone. These prophets, these workmen of God, foreshadowed Jesus Christ in their measure, and experienced the awful loneliness of a servant of God. Their desolation sprang from no illusion of weakness, nor from any horror-stricken doubt of God, any more than did the profound cry of our Lord—"My God, My God, why hast Thou forsaken Me?" We discern in the personal, passionate pain of the prophets the true outlines of the workman of God. The character of the prophet is essential to his work. In all other work the character of the workman is made subservient to his skill.

"But the spirit of the LORD clothed itself with Gideon" (Judges 6:34 RV mg). Before the Holy Spirit can materialise in the saints of this present age as He did in the prophets of old, a perfect holiness, physical, moral and spiritual, is necessary. This is what Jesus Christ has wrought for us in the Atonement, and this is what is meant by Entire Sanctification. On that foundation the true elements of prophecy are built. A prophet is not a sanctified gypsy telling fortunes, but one who speaks as he is moved by the Holy Spirit within.

To make disciples, then, we must have been made disciples ourselves. There is no royal road to sainthood and discipleship. The way of the Cross is the only way. We see God only from a pure heart, never from an able intellect. The elements in the lot of a workman for God are those that first of all make him a workman, and then constitute him a toiler for God. The workman for God in all probability will have to go the way his Lord and Master went. The first flush of the career of a workman for God may be in glory and acclaim, leading to blessed transfiguration; then there comes the descent into the valley, deeper and deeper, until in that lonely place, toiling unseen, unknown, unmarked, he reaches in the spirit of travail that sublime agony of loneliness when "Father" seems frozen in his heart, and he cries out, *"Why hast Thou forsaken me?"* It is not a cry of weakness, nor of imperfection; it is not a cry of doubt in God; it is a cry from the last touch of heroism on the workman for God who is being made conformable unto the death of Jesus, not for his own sake or his own perfecting, but for the work of God. It takes him to the threshold of that awful abyss of the Master Workman Himself, where He was left alone with death and became as lonely as sin, and amid the spiritual ramifications of that unshared, unfathomed experience, He cried out, "My God, My God, why hast Thou forsaken Me?" The workman for God dare not talk, he dare not speculate; but in wonder, love and awe he thanks God for "the glory and the passion of this midnight," because it has brought him to the threshold of an understanding of the loneliness of Jesus Christ Who was "made to be sin on our behalf; that we might become the righteousness of God in Him" (RV).

And that most closely we may follow Him,
By suffering, have all hearts of men allowed.
Is suffering then more near and dear to God
For its own sake than joy is? God forbid!
We know not its beginning nor its end;
Is it a sacrifice? a test? a school? . . .
We suffer. Why we suffer,—that is hid

17. Thomas Carlyle (1795–1881): Scottish-born literary figure in nineteenth-century England, writer, biographer, essayist, historian, and critic.

With God's foreknowledge in the clouds of
*   Heaven.*

H. Hamilton King

Dismiss me not Thy service, Lord,
*   But train me for Thy will:*
For even I in fields so broad
*   Some duties may fulfil;*
And I will ask for no reward,
*   Except to serve Thee still.*

Our Master all the work has done,
*   He asks of us to-day;*
Sharing His service, every one
*   Share too His sonship may:*
Lord, I would serve and be a son;
*   Dismiss me not, I pray.*

T. T. Lynch[18]

Alone with God

Still, still with Thee, when purple morning
*   breaketh,*
*   When the bird waketh, and the shadows flee;*
Fairer than morning, lovelier than daylight,
*   Dawns the sweet consciousness, I am with*
*   Thee.*
Alone with Thee, amid the mystic shadows,
*   The solemn hush of nature newly born;*
Alone with Thee, in breathless adoration,
*   In the calm dews and freshness of the morn.*

Harriet Beecher Stowe

There's not a craving in the mind
*   Thou dost not meet and still;*
There's not a wish the heart can have
*   Which Thou dost not fulfil.*

All things that have been, all that are,
*   All things that can be dreamed,*
All possible creations made,
*   Kept faithful, or redeemed;—*

All these may draw upon Thy power,
*   Thy mercy may command,*
And still outflows Thy silent sea
*   Immutable and grand.*

O little heart of mine, shall pain
*   Or sorrow make thee moan,*
When all this God is all for thee,
*   A Father all thine own?*

Faber[19]

"In Thy presence is fulness of joy; in Thy right hand there are pleasures for evermore" (Psalm 16:11 RV). This walk alone with God is an incommunicable rapture, that leads more and more through Eternal Pleasure, Eternal Prosperity, and Eternal Paradise.

Eternal Pleasure

Therefore, behold, I will allure her, and bring her into the wilderness, and speak to her heart. And I will give her vineyards from thence, and the valley of Troubling for a door of hope: and she shall sing there, as in the days of her youth, and as in the day when she came up out of the land of Egypt. And it shall be at that day, saith the LORD, that thou shalt call Me, My husband, and shalt call me no more, My master. . . . I will betroth thee unto Me for ever; yea, I will betroth thee unto Me in right-eousness, and in judgement, and in lovingkindness, and in mercies. I will even betroth thee unto Me in faithfulness: and thou shalt know the LORD. (Hosea 2:14–16, 19–20 RV mg)

All that we know of bliss and pleasure in other domains of friendship and fellowship with kindred minds, is but the faintest foreshadowing of the unspeakable pleasure of this communion with God alone. How unhesitatingly the language of Scripture mentions human relationships as the only means of suggesting the unspeakable pleasure of this eternal fellowship with God. Just as the language of lovers is inexplicable to an unloving nature, so the language of the heart in its aloneness with God is inexplicable to those not in a like relationship. There are things "not lawful for a man to utter," not because they transcend language, but because they are based on the sacred intimacy of an individual soul united to God in love. It is perilously possible to take the language of love and degrade it into a language that grovels; and it is perilously possible to take the language of the soul alone in these walks of eternal pleasure and degrade it into a wallowing horror.

The daring sufficiency of the Song of Songs is an example of how easy it is to make that sublime Song grovel in Eastern voluptuousness and sensual wallowing; but for the soul walking alone with God its language is the choicest in the whole Bible to adequately express the eternal pleasure of this blessed loneliness—

Let him kiss me with the kisses of his mouth: for thy love is better than wine. Thine ointments have a goodly fragrance; thy name is as ointment poured forth; therefore do the virgins love thee. Draw me; we will run after thee: the king hath brought me

---

18. Thomas Toke Lynch (1818–1871): English cleric and hymn writer.
19. Frederick William Faber (1814–1863): English cleric and hymn writer.

into his chambers: we will be glad and rejoice in thee, we will make mention of thy love more than of wine: in uprightness [mg] do they love thee. (Song of Solomon 1:2–4 RV)

Possibly only when we stand alone with God are we in a fit condition to understand the strong words of Jesus, and not abuse them—"Give not that which is holy unto the dogs, neither cast your pearls before the swine, lest haply they trample them under their feet, and turn and rend you" (Matthew 7:6 RV).

"And this is life eternal, that they should know Thee the only true God, and Him whom Thou didst send, even Jesus Christ" (John 17:3 RV). This constitutes eternal life—an increasing knowledge of the unfathomable God and His only begotten Son. This is Eternal Pleasure—to know Him! How far removed it is from our conceptions of rewards and crowns and heaven. The way of a soul walking alone with God, unless we know this same unspeakable fellowship, seems a way overshadowed with sadness and insane with fanaticism.

I stand upon the mount of God,
  With sunlight in my soul;
I hear the storms in vales beneath,
  I hear the thunder's roll.

But I am calm with Thee, my God,
  Beneath these glorious skies;
And to the height on which I stand
  Nor storms nor cloud can rise.

Oh! this is life! oh, this is joy!
  My God to find Thee so;
Thy face to see, Thy voice to hear,
  And all Thy love to know!

C. B. Bubier

Eternal Prosperity

The eternal God is thy dwelling place, and underneath are the everlasting arms: and he thrust out the enemy from before thee, and said, Destroy. And Israel dwelleth in safety, the fountain of Jacob alone, in a land of corn and wine; yea, his heavens drop down dew. Happy art thou, O Israel: who is like unto thee, a people saved by the LORD, the shield of thy help, and that is the sword of thy excellency! and thine enemies shall submit themselves unto thee; and thou shalt tread upon their high places. (Deuteronomy 33:27–29 RV)

A man's idea of prosperity is according to where his hopes are founded—on God or on a hearsay God; on the living God, or on ideas of God. It is in the way alone with God that the soul says with Job—"I had

heard of Thee by the hearing of the ear; but now mine eye seeth Thee, wherefore I loathe my words [mg], and repent in dust and ashes" (Job 42:5–6 RV).

Alone with God! It is there that what is hid with God is made known—God's ideals, God's hopes, God's doings. The intense individual responsibility of walking amongst men from the standpoint of being alone with the real God, is never guessed until we do stand alone with God. It is a hidden thing, so hidden that it seems not only untenable but a wild quixotic thing to do, and so it would be if God were not known to be real. This idea is put in refreshing language by Dr. Josiah Strong:[20]

The supreme need of the world is a Real God; not the Great Perhaps, but the great "I am"; not a God of yesterday; not an "absentee" God, but one who is precisely here; not a Sunday God, but an every day God. . . . Vital religion always realises God, while irreligion or worldliness is a practical denial of Him; it is living as if God were not; it is leaving out of account the greatest fact of the universe, which is of course the greatest blunder in the universe.

Accounting the reproach of Christ greater riches than the treasures of Egypt: for he looked unto the recompense of reward. . . . He endured, as seeing Him who is invisible. (Hebrews 11:26–27 RV)

Alone with God! All hope and all aspiration springs from that source, and consequently all prosperity is measured from that source, and prosperity that springs from any other source is looked upon as disastrous. The pleasure of the Lord prospered in the hand of His Son, our Lord Jesus Christ, by the disastrous way of failure, as the world measures prosperity.

Yet it pleased the LORD to bruise Him; He hath put Him to grief: when thou shalt make His soul an offering for sin, He shall see His seed, He shall prolong His days, and the pleasure of the LORD shall prosper in His hand. (Isaiah 53:10)

Going alone with God, the pleasure of Jehovah prospering in our hands! What a pleasure, and what a prosperity! Our Lord walked alone with God; He despised the shame and the bruising, because His Father was working out His good pleasure in His own inscrutable way; and now we follow in His steps, and the pleasure of the Lord shall prosper in our hands.

What is that pleasure? Making disciples. The pleasure of the Lord that prospered in our Lord and Saviour was seeing His seed, that is, all that we understand by Regeneration and Entire Sanctification. The pleasure of the Lord God is seen as we walk alone

---

20. Josiah Strong (1847–1916): American cleric and author.

with God while we live and move and have our being in this world. Unstamped by the pattern and print of the age in which we live, we present so many puzzling features that men are obliged to pause and question, and thus the pleasure of the Lord prospers in our hands.

It is a prosperity that, beginning in the innermost of the innermost, works out to the outermost. A prosperity which transfigures with the beauty of holiness; a prosperity which, as sure as it is inward, will manifest itself to the utmost limit outwardly.

> He fixed thee 'mid this dance
> Of plastic circumstance,
> This Present, thou, forsooth, wouldst fain arrest:
> Machinery just meant
> To give thy soul its bent,
> Try thee and turn thee forth, sufficiently
> impressed.
>
> Look not thou down but up!
> To uses of a cup,
> The festal board, lamp's flash and trumpet's peal,
> The new wine's foaming flow,
> The Master's lips a-glow!
> Thou, heaven's consummate cup, what need'st
> thou with earth's wheel?
>
> But I need, now as then,
> Thee, God, who mouldest men:
> And since, not even while the whirl was worst,
> Did I,—to the wheel of life
> With shapes and colours rife,
> Bound dizzily,—mistake my end, to slake Thy
> thirst:
> So, take and use Thy work:
> Amend what flaws may lurk,
> What strain o' the stuff, what warpings past the
> aim!
> My times be in Thy hand!
> Perfect the cup as planned!
> Let age approve of youth, and death complete the
> same!

> Browning

Eternal Paradise

That they may all be one; even as Thou, Father, art in Me, and I in Thee, that they also may be in us: that the world may believe that Thou didst send Me. And the glory which Thou hast given Me I have given unto them; that they may be one, even as we are one; I in them, and Thou in Me, that they may be perfected into one; that the world may know that Thou didst send Me, and lovedst them, even as Thou lovedst Me. Father, that which Thou hast given Me, I will that, where I am,

they also may be with Me; that they may behold My glory, which Thou hast given Me: for Thou lovedst Me before the foundation of the world. O righteous Father, the world knew Thee not, but I knew Thee; and these knew that Thou didst send Me; and I made known unto them Thy name, and will make it known; that the love wherewith Thou lovedst Me may be in them, and I in them. (John 17:21–26 RV)

Paradise is a beautiful word, with an emphatic meaning which no other word conveys, viz: spiritual and material.

And the city hath no need of the sun, neither of the moon, to shine upon it: for the glory of God did lighten it, and the Lamb, the lamp thereof. And the nations shall walk by the light thereof: and the kings of the earth do bring their glory into it. And the portals thereof shall in no wise be shut by day (for there shall be no night there): and they shall bring the glory and the honour of the nations into it: and there shall in no wise enter into it anything common, or he that doeth an abomination and a lie: but only they which are written in the Lamb's book of life. (Revelation 21:23–27 RV mg)

This Eternal Paradise, entered now by those who walk alone with God, must not be spiritualised by a process of abstractions into a mere inward state of soul. This Mother Earth will yet be governed by the saints. "The kingdom of the world is become the kingdom of our Lord and of His Christ" (RV). The saints, with a tested, heroic mastership of earth and air and sky, will reign in a very real concrete Paradise. Just as we infer from the tangible material world an unseen spiritual substratum, so there is to be a concrete world which will be but the manifestation of this unseen spiritual substratum, whereby we may infer its character. It is "by their fruits" that character is known, and also society. From this present order of things we infer an unseen power making for disintegration and destruction, yet in every human heart there lurks an implicit hope of a different order. These hopes ever fade and fall, and the vision tarries so long that hearts grow sick and embittered, and all seems to end in a poet's song, or a lover's passionate extravagance, or a dreamer's dream. But to the soul alone with God the secret is known and made real, and already a Paradise has begun that presages a grander and a greater blessedness than has entered into the heart of man to imagine. The Paradisaic kingdom which cannot be seen to-day by those who have never been alone with God, will one day, at a sudden catastrophic stage, alter the configuration of the globe.

The wilderness and the [parched land] shall be glad; and the desert shall rejoice, and blossom as the rose. It shall blossom abundantly, and rejoice even with joy and singing: . . . they shall see the glory of the LORD, the excellency of our God. (Isaiah 35:1–2 RV)

It is not a flimsy, false dream that springs in the human heart, but a real visible paradise of God; the hope "springs eternal in the human breast" and will be abundantly satisfied. To spiritualise it into the vague and inane is a sickly, unreal tendency.

Alone with God, we have the glory that Jesus had, here and now, the glory of His holiness; and being "transformed into the same image from glory to glory" (RV), on and on the saints go to each place of attainment, following the Lamb "whithersoever He goeth."

And wonder of wonders, that is, after all, only the end of the stages in time; but when time shall be no more, and the basal principles of our thoughts will no more be time and space—how can we conceive what it will be like!

But as is written, Things which eye saw not, and ear heard not, and which entered not into the heart of man, whatsoever things God prepared for them that love Him. (1 Corinthians 2:9 RV)

Beloved, now are we children of God, and it is not yet made manifest what we shall be. We know that, if He shall be manifested, we shall be like Him; for we shall see Him even as He is. (1 John 3:2 RV)

*There's a fancy some lean to and others hate—
    That when this life is ended, begins
New work for the soul in another state.
    Where it strives and gets weary, loses and wins:
Where the strong and the weak, this world's
        congeries,
    Repeat in large what they practised in small,
Through life after life in unlimited series;
    Only the scale's to be changed, that's all.
Yet I hardly know. When a soul has seen
    By the means of Evil that Good is best,
And, through earth and its noise, what is heaven's
    serene,—
    When our faith in the same hath stood the
        test—
Why, the child grown man, you burn the rod,
    The uses of labour are surely done;
There remaineth a rest for the people of God
    And I have troubles.*

Browning

THE DISCIPLINE OF PATIENCE

Yea, wait thou on the LORD. Psalm 27:14 RV

The subject of Patience is so largely dealt with in the Bible that it ought to have a much larger place in our Bible studies and talks.

Patience to most minds is associated with exhaustion, or with "patients," consequently anything robust and vigorous seems naturally to connect itself with all that is impatient and impetuous. Patience is the result of well-centred strength. To "wait on the LORD," and to "rest in the LORD," is an indication of a healthy, holy faith, while impatience is an indication of an unhealthy, un-holy unbelief. This well-centred strength, or Patience, forms a prominent characteristic in the Bible revelation of God, of our Lord Jesus Christ and of the saints.

*Then on our utter weakness and the hush
Of hearts exhausted that can ache no more,
On such abeyance of self and swoon of soul
The Spirit hath lighted oft, and let men see
That all our vileness alters God no more
Than our dimmed eyes can quench the stars in
    heaven:*

*From years ere years were told, through all the
    sins,
Unknown sins of innumerable men,
God is Himself for ever, and shows to-day
As erst in Eden, the eternal hope.*

The Patience of God

Hast thou not known? hast thou not heard, that the everlasting God, the LORD, the Creator of the ends of the earth, fainteth not, neither is weary? (Isaiah 40:28)

The God of patience. (Romans 15:5)

How unmoved by, while yet unremoved from, the affairs of men is our God! He changes not and yet He does not reign in remote regions away from men; He is in the thick of all men's perplexities and loves. The gods of other religions are unmoved by men's troubles simply because they do not care; but our God in His love and compassion imposes on Himself our weakness and pain, while yet He is unmoved from the well-centred strength of His mighty purposes. If we trace in the Bible with reverence the lines along which the patience of God most obviously runs, it will well enrich us. Let us trace, for instance, the Patience of God with—

The World's Ages
According to the Bible, the history of the world is divided into Ages—(1) the pre-Adamic; (2) the Eden; (3) the Antediluvian; (4) the Mosaic; (5) the Church; (6) the Kingdom; and the remarkable thing in the record of the Ages that have been, and that are, and that are going to be, is that each Age ends in apparent disaster. In this connection read carefully (1) Genesis 1:2; (2) Genesis 3:24; (3) Genesis 7:19; (4) John 19:15–16; (5) 2 Thessalonians 2:1–4; (6) Revelation 20:7–9. This is very unexpected for one would naturally suppose that the Bible would show how successful God had been with the world's Ages, successful, that is, in the way we count success, and because the Bible does not prove this, men's minds revolt and they say that all God's plans have been overthrown by the devil and God has been checkmated, so to speak; or else they say that the Bible view is simply the fancy of a few oriental religious men of genius and is not of any use to us nowadays.

Perhaps the illustration of an artist at work on a great canvas will throw more light on the attitude of the God of the Bible to the world's Ages. In the preliminary stages of his work the artist may sketch in charcoal and for days execute sketches of varying excellence, and the beauty of these sketches may win our admiration. Then one day we are perplexed to find that he has begun to confuse and obliterate with paints all his beautiful drawings; but he is really interpreting the meaning of those sketches which was hidden from us.

Or take the old-fashioned way of erecting a scaffolding and building the structure inside. The scaffolding may be so skilfully erected and admirably proportioned and be there for so long that we come to consider this the scheme in the mind of the architect. Then one day we see the loosening of ropes and planks and ladders, and the turmoil destroys for ever the skill and beautiful proportion of the scaffolding; all that is happening is but to clear the real building that it may stand nobly before all as a thing of beauty. There is something similar to the Bible revelation of the way God deals with the world's Ages.

There have been prophets and students who handle the Bible like a child's box of bricks; they explain to us the design and structure and purpose; but as time goes on things do not work out in their way at all. They have mistaken the scaffolding for the structure, while all the time God is working out His purpose with a great and undeterred patience.

The Lord is not slack concerning His promise, as some men count slackness; but is longsuffering to

usward, not willing that any should perish, but that all should come to repentance. (2 Peter 3:9)

There are no dates
In His fine leisure.

Then we might trace the Patience of God with—

The World's Anarchy
And GOD saw that the wickedness of man was great in the earth. . . . And it grieved Him at His heart. (Genesis 6:5–6)

For He said, Surely they are My people. . . . But they rebelled, and vexed His holy Spirit. (Isaiah 63:8, 10)

Every other view of sin, saving the Bible view, looks on sin as a disease, a weakness, a blunder, an infirmity; the Bible revelation shows sin to be an anarchy, not a missing of the mark merely, but a refusal to aim at the mark. Sin is that disposition of self-rule which is enmity against God (see Romans 8:7), and as one traces right away from Genesis the clear indication of God's patience with this anarchy, His working out of the Atonement which deals with the fundamental disposition of anarchy against Himself, one reaches the unfathomable, supernatural patience of God. During the ages, human history proves that sin in man makes his heart naturally atheistic. We are all atheists at heart, and the whole world is but a gigantic palace of mirrors wherein we see ourselves reflected, and we call the reflection, God.

Know ye that the LORD He is God: it is He that hath made us, and not we ourselves. . . . (Psalm 100:3)

Isaiah 63:8, 10, already quoted, exhibits the patience of God with this disposition of anarchy in His own children. In the New Testament this spirit of anarchy is called "the old man, the carnal mind," which, until it is crucified by identification with the Cross of Christ, will continually rebel and vex His Holy Spirit. It is this spirit of anarchy that has confused the interpretation of God's dealings with men.

Lastly, we might look at the Patience of God with—

The World's Acknowledgement
In returning and rest shall ye be saved; . . . and ye would not. . . . And therefore will the LORD wait, that He may be gracious unto you. (Isaiah 30:15, 18)

How long-suffering our God is until we acknowledge Him, and how full of misery and perplexity and sorrow, and worse, men are, until they do acknowledge God.

Erasmus in a wonderful passage shows the unnecessary anguish he went through before he basked in the realisation of the acknowledged love of God:

I must confess it was the very bitterness of extremity that first compelled me to love Him, though of Himself no less lovely than love itself. It was the sharp sauce of affliction that gave edge to mine affections, and sharpened mine appetite to that sweet meat that endureth to everlasting life. But now having had some little foretaste of Him, I am ever in a holy ecstasy, so ravished, so transported, with a fervent desire of Him and of His presence, that where I am, there am I not; and where I am not, there I am. The soul is where it loveth, not where it dwelleth.

But God commendeth His own love toward us, in that, while we were yet sinners, Christ died for us. (Romans 5:8 RV)

The phrase "His own love" is very beautiful; it is God's own peculiar individual love, just as the love of a mother is her own peculiar love, and the love of a father is his own peculiar love. Every different kind of love illustrates some aspect of God's love; but it must not be forgotten that the love of God is His own peculiar love. The word translated "commendeth" conveys the meaning of *recommend*. Because of the disposition arising from anarchy against God, men do not see or believe that the Cross of Christ is the expression of God's own love; but when a man is convicted of sin, he begins to discern the marvellously patient love of God, and as he looks at the Cross his heart slowly realises—"Surely now I see—He has borne *my* griefs, and carried *my* sorrows: yet I did esteem Him stricken, smitten of God, and afflicted; but He was wounded for *my* transgression." Such a moral vision is an acknowledgement of God's own patient love with a twofold verdict—first, that God is love, and second, that the natural heart of man is desperately wicked.

Until the world acknowledges God, very often the outcome of the patience of God is that His purposes are carried out in man's bad time, and not, as so many say, in God's good time. God's good time is, *Now*, and His children as well as others cause the repetition of His words in Isaiah 30:15, "In returning and rest shall ye be saved; in quietness and in confidence shall be your strength: and ye would not." Beware of going to sleep on the decrees of God. In regard to the fulfilment of some of these decrees, such as our salvation and sanctification and sacramental service, it is not a submissive waiting that is required, but the flinging up of our hands and the acknowledgement of God's right to us.

There is one solemn, unwelcome word of warning—do not despise God's patience and keep Him waiting beyond the limit.

Knowing this first, that in the last days mockers shall come with mockery, walking after their own lusts, and saying, Where is the promise of His coming? for, from the days that the fathers fell asleep, all things continue as they were from the beginning of the creation. (2 Peter 3:3–4 RV)

The Patience of Our Lord
Looking unto Jesus . . . Who . . . endured the cross, despising shame, and hath sat down at the right hand of the throne of God. For consider Him . . . that ye wax not weary, fainting in your souls. (Hebrews 12:2–3 RV)

In many sections of the Christian community to-day Enthusiasm for Humanity is the main characteristic, but it gives a sudden alteration to this point of view when we consider the life of our Lord Jesus Christ, and notice that *His* first obedience was to the will of His Father, not to the needs of Humanity. It is a difficult matter to adjust the relationship of these two callings, but the delicate adjustment is brought about by the Spirit of God, for the Spirit and the Word of God ever put first things first, the first thing is love to God and obedience to God, and the second, service to humanity.

Let us consider the subject of the Patience of our Lord under three heads: The Father's Will; the Father's Weakness, and the Father's Waiting.

The Father's Will
The underlying element in Satan's temptation of our Lord is his seeking to remove the "first thing." Satan tempted our Lord, as he tempted the first Adam, to do God's work in His own way; and the underlying point in the strenuous replies of our Lord is always in one direction—God and God's will first. "For I came down from heaven, not to do Mine own will, but the will of Him that sent Me" (John 6:38). Hebrews 10:7 emphasises this—"Then said I, Lo, I come (in the volume of the book it is written of Me,) to do Thy will, O God" (cf. Psalm 40:7), and the light thrown on the sufferings of our Lord as an individual will interpret the remarkable statement in Hebrews 5:8 (RV)—"Though He was a Son, yet learned obedience by the things which He suffered."

In speaking of our Lord Jesus Christ we must bear in mind that we are dealing with a unique Being, of Whom it is distinctly said that He "emptied Himself" to marked limitations (see Philippians 2:6–7 RV). This point is mentioned here to show that the sufferings of our Lord did not consist in a wilfulness contrary to His Father's will, but in the fact that He, without question, let God the Father express through His life what the Saviour of the world should be.

Father, if Thou be willing, remove this cup from Me: nevertheless not My will, but Thine, be done. (Luke 22:42)

The patience of our Lord with the Father's will and the Father's purpose is a wonderful topic to study, and it explains also the harsh misunderstanding criticisms that have been made during the past centuries.

The next aspect in which the patience of our Lord exhibits itself is more startling, and at the same time more illuminating, viz. the patience of our Lord with—

The Father's Weakness

The phrase, "the weakness of God," is astonishing, but scriptural. "The weakness of God is stronger than men" (1 Corinthians 1:25). Our astonishment arises from the fact that what we call strength from the natural standpoint may be weakness; and that what God calls strength is too often esteemed by men as weakness. It was so in the life of Jesus Christ judged from the standpoint of the natural man. The Father's weakness is exhibited in the aspects of the Cradle, the Cross, and the Called.

In Isaiah 7:14, the word comes—"Therefore the Lord Himself shall give you a sign; Behold, a virgin shall conceive, and bear a son, and shall call His name Immanuel."

How much attention, think you, could the mighty Roman Empire, the tramp of whose legions shook the world and whose laws girdle it till now, pay to that little Babe born of a Jewish peasant girl and laid in a cow's trough! It was beneath the possibility of that gigantic world-power's notice. As a prominent modern writer has stated:

All the empires and the kingdoms have failed, because of this inherent and continual weakness; they were founded by strong men, and upon strong men, but this one thing, the historic Christian Church, was founded upon a weak man, and for that reason it is indestructible, for no chain is stronger than its weakest link.

The writer points out the thing that we are emphasising, God's ways of working are weakness from man's standpoint.

How patient our Lord ever was with the weakness of God! And He never explains Himself to any man saving as He receives, recognises and relies on the Holy Spirit. Our Lord could have commanded twelve legions of angels to His assistance, but He did not.

Or thinkest thou that I cannot beseech My Father, and He shall even now send Me more than twelve legions of angels? (Matthew 26:53 RV)

What weakness! Our Lord lived thirty years in Nazareth with His brethren who did not believe on Him (John 7:5); He lived three years of popularity, scandal and hatred; fascinated a dozen illiterate men who at the end of three years all forsook Him and fled (Mark 14:50); and finally He was taken by the powers that be and crucified outside the city wall. Judged from every standpoint save the standpoint of the Spirit of God, His life was a most manifest expression of weakness, and the idea would be strong to those in the pagan world who thought anything about Him that surely now He and His crazy tale were stamped out.

It is this factor of weakness that alone expounds the revelation given in the Old Testament as well as in the New.

For He grew up before Him as a tender plant, and as a root out of a dry ground: He hath no form nor comeliness; and when we see Him, there is no beauty that we should desire Him. (Isaiah 53:2 RV)

Yet when man's wisdom is rendered foolishness by the breaking forth of the Spirit of God, he understands the unspeakable wisdom of God and the unspeakable strength of God to lie in what he before called foolishness and weakness.

*'Tis the weakness in strength that I cry for!
    my flesh, that I seek
In the Godhead! I seek and I find it. O Saul,
    it shall be
A Face like my face that receives thee; a Man
    like to me,
Thou shalt love and be loved by, for ever! a
    Hand like this hand
Shall throw open the gates of new life to thee!
    See the Christ stand!*

What is as weak as one baby? Another! And so our Lord Himself taught that we must all become babes. No wonder Paul says:

For ye see your calling, brethren, how that not many wise men after the flesh, not many mighty, not many noble, are called. (1 Corinthians 1:26; see also John 3:7 and Matthew 18:2–3)

It is the "baby" weakness which is so misunderstood in the New Testament teaching, and the patience of our Lord with us until we learn the absolute necessity of being born from above is only equalled by His own patience with His Father's will.

But God hath chosen the foolish things of the world . . . ; the weak things of the world . . . ; and base things of the world, and things which are despised, . . . yea, and things which are not. . . . (1 Corinthians 1:27–28)

In every age it has always been the despised crowd that have been called Christians.

The Cross, the climax of our Lord's earthly life, is likewise an exhibition of the weakness of God.

But we preach Christ crucified, unto Jews a stumblingblock, and unto Gentiles foolishness. (1 Corinthians 1:23 RV)

Probably in the Cross more than in any other aspect of our Lord's life do we see the stumblingblock presented to the wisdom of the world. Wise men of intelligence after the flesh cannot understand why God does not speak, and misunderstanding, prejudices, and unbelief prevail among all men until by receiving the Spirit of God as babes they perceive that our Lord Jesus Christ from the Cradle to the Cross is God's great Eternal Word.

Let us look at the final aspect of our Lord's patience—

The Father's Waiting
For He must reign, till He hath put all His enemies under His feet. (1 Corinthians 15:25 RV)

It is vastly important to remember that our duty is to fit our doctrines to our Lord Jesus Christ and not to fit our Lord into our doctrines. Our Lord is God-Man, not half God and half man, but a unique Being revealed from heaven, and the Holy Spirit alone can expound Him. Let us emphasise again what has been already emphasised, viz., that our Lord Incarnate distinctly subjected Himself to limitations.

> *But of that day or that hour knoweth no one, not even the angels in heaven, neither the Son, but the Father. (Mark 13:32 RV)*

Much discussion is thus foreclosed that would otherwise gather round and confuse the life of our Lord and His temptations, in so far as these are disclosed to us. The patience of our Lord with the Father's Waiting is truly a great and wonderful deep. God the Father on occasions witnessed to His Son—"This is My beloved Son: hear Him" (cf. 2 Peter 1:17–18); but yet God never vindicated His Son to the men of His own generation because it was not the Father's purpose to do so. He left Him to the supreme satire of the Jews on the Cross in silence, and our Lord too was silent, "He opened not His mouth." Read prayerfully Mark 15:29–32, and note what might be termed the "Dilemma of Golgotha" in which Christ's own words were turned into a cruel jest and hurled back into His face while He was on the Cross. The way of sorrow for our Lord was turned into a way of derision. Men laughed while God's heart broke, and thus while hard slanders rose against God and against His Christ, the Father waited, and with pure supernatural patience, the prayer arose from the lips of our Lord—"Father, forgive them; for they know not what they do" (Luke 23:34).

And the end is not yet; the Father still waits. It must be borne in mind that the mystery abides. All the poetical things and the mystical things that have been said and written about our Lord are but effusions that appear and disappear while the mind of the unregenerate man alternates between ridicule and confusion.

The patience of God and the patience of our Lord is working to one grand Divine event, and our Lord knows, as He did in the days of His flesh, how all His saints are straitened till it be accomplished.

> *But I have a baptism to be baptized with; and how am I straitened till it be accomplished! (Luke 12:50)*

> *Right for ever on the scaffold,*
> *Wrong for ever on the throne;*
> *But that scaffold sways the future,*
> *And behind the dim unknown*
> *Standeth God within the shadows,*
> *Keeping watch upon His own.*

The Patience of the Saints
We are bound to give thanks to God always for you, . . . for your patience and faith in all your persecutions and in the afflictions which ye endure. (2 Thessalonians 1:3–4 RV)

The life of faith is the life of a soul who has given over every other life but the life of faith. Faith is not an action of the mind, nor of the heart, nor of the will, nor of the sentiment, it is the centring of the entire man in God.

The Patience of Faith
The heroes of faith catalogued in the eleventh chapter of Hebrews were not men who vaguely trusted that "somehow good would be the final goal of ill," they were heroes who died "according to faith" (verse 13 RV mg)., not faith in a principle, but faith in a Person Who promises.

> *Seeing we also are compassed about with so great a cloud of witnesses, let us . . . run with patience the race that is set before us. (Hebrews 12:1)*

This cloud of witnesses is not a noble army of poets, or dreamers, or thinkers, but a noble army—

> *who through faith subdued kingdoms, wrought righteousness, obtained promises, stopped the mouths of lions, quenched the power of fire, escaped the edge of the sword, from weakness were made strong, waxed mighty in war, turned to flight armies of aliens. (Hebrews 11:33–34 RV)*

These mighty acts were not wrought by diplomacy, but by faith in God, and we are urged to run with patience this same way of faith, "looking unto Jesus."

In dealing with the patience of the saints, the subject naturally unfolds itself into the Patience of Faith, the Patience of Hope, and the Patience of Love. We have already indicated the chief matter in the Patience of Faith, viz., faith in a Person Who promises.

The proof of your faith worketh patience. And let patience have its perfect work, that ye may be perfect and entire, lacking in nothing. (James 1:3–4 RV)

Howbeit when the Son of Man cometh, shall He find the faith on the earth? (Luke 18:8 RV)

Here is the patience and the faith of the saints. (Revelation 13:10 RV)

Here is the patience of the saints, they that keep the commandments of God, and the faith of Jesus. (Revelation 14:12 RV)

These passages assuredly serve to indicate how prominent a place patience plays in God's plans for His saints. It brings again prominently to the front what was stated earlier, that patience is an indication of strong spiritual health, not of weakness and enervation.

The Patience of Hope
For by hope were we saved. . . . If we hope for that which we see not, then do we with patience wait for it. (Romans 8:24–25 RV)

Let us rejoice in hope of the glory of God . . . knowing that tribulation worketh patience; and patience, probation; and probation, hope: and hope putteth not to shame. (Romans 5:2–5 RV)

Be patient therefore, brethren, unto the coming of the Lord. . . . Be ye also patient; stablish your hearts. (James 5:7–8 RV)

I John, your brother and partaker with you in the tribulation and kingdom and patience which are in Jesus. (Revelation 1:9 RV)

The faith of the saints is, as it were, a God-given sixth sense which takes hold on the spiritual facts that are revealed in the Bible. The hope of the saint is the expectation and certainty of human nature transfigured by faith. Let it be borne in mind that hope not transfigured by faith dies. "But we hoped that it was He which should redeem Israel" (Luke 24:21 RV). Hope without faith loses itself in vague speculation, but the hope of the saints transfigured by faith grows not faint, but endures "as seeing Him Who is invisible."

The saint in the discipline of patience enters into an experimental understanding of the patience of God and the patience of our Lord. The saint has been crucified with Christ and testifies—"I live; and yet no longer I, but Christ liveth in me: and that life which I now live in the flesh I live in faith, the faith which is in the Son of God" (Galatians 2:20 RV).

The saint bears a strong family likeness to his Lord, "weak in Him" (2 Corinthians 13:4). The saint with a glad alacrity can be humiliated or emptied or despised; he can also with untainted holiness be exalted or filled or abounding (Philippians 4:12). The hope of the saint gives the true value to the things seen and temporal—in fact the real enjoyment of things seen and temporal is alone possible to the saint because he sees them in their true relationship to God, and the sickening emptiness of the worldly-minded who grasp the things seen and temporal as though they were eternal, is unknown to him. The characteristic of the saint is not so much the renunciation of the things seen and temporal as the perfect certainty that these things are but the shows of reality. The patience of hope does not turn men and women into monks and nuns, it gives men and women the right use of this world from another world's standpoint.

"Wherefore we faint not; . . . while we look not at the things which are seen, but at the things which are not seen: for the things which are seen are temporal; but the things which are not seen are eternal" (2 Corinthians 4:16, 18 RV).

The Patience of Love
The character produced by the Patience of Hope is one that exhibits the expulsive power of a new affection.

But now abideth faith, hope, love, these three; and the greatest of these is love. (1 Corinthians 13:13 RV)

That the love wherewith Thou lovedst Me may be in them. (John 17:26 RV)

Because thou didst keep the word of My patience, I also will keep thee from the hour of trial. (Revelation 3:10 RV)

There is one sovereign preference in the Bible, viz., love towards God, and that love is not a sentiment, it is the prayerful activity of a perfectly adjusted relationship between God and the saint. Love in the Bible is ONE; it is unique, and the human element is but one aspect of it. It is a love so mighty, so absorbing, so intense that all the mind is emancipated and entranced by God; all the heart is transfigured by the same devotion; all the soul in its living, working, waking, sleeping moments is indwelt and surrounded and enwheeled in the rest of this love. The saint at times soars like the eagle, he runs like the exuberant athlete, he walks with God and knows no reaction, he faints not nor falters in the largeness of the way (see Mark 12:29–31); and, like

Tennyson's Sir Galahad, his strength is as the strength of ten, because his heart is pure,

> *That ye, being rooted and grounded in love, may be strong to apprehend with all the saints what is the breadth and length and height and depth, and to know the love of Christ which passeth knowledge, that ye may be filled unto all the fulness of God. (Ephesians 3:17–19 RV)*

The Patience of Love works out in the practical true life of the saint; it is a love that suffers long and is kind. "Love envieth not" (RV).

The saint has one striking characteristic, and that is in loving with a Divine love. Its thirst is not so much to be loved as to be loveable. The characteristics in the life of the saint are the characteristics of our Lord's life. The saint bears a strong family likeness to Jesus Christ.

"The word of My patience" is a striking phrase. It cannot be the patience of pessimism because that was not the characteristic of the patience of our Lord; neither is it the patience of exhaustion, for "He shall not fail nor be discouraged." It is surely the patience of love, the patience of joyfulness, which knows that God reigns and rules and rejoices, and that His joy is our strength.

The patience of the saints may be illustrated by the figure of a bow and arrow in the hands of God. He sees the target and takes aim, He strains the bow, not to breaking-point, however severe the strain may seem to the saint, but to just that point whence the arrow will fly with surest, swiftest speed to the bull's-eye.

The patience of the saints, like the patience of our Lord, puts the sovereignty of God over all the saint's career, and because the love of God is shed abroad in our hearts by the Holy Ghost, we choose by our free will what God predestinates, for the mind of God, the mind of the Holy Spirit, and the mind of the saint are all held together by a oneness of personal passionate devotion.

> *Work, for the Day is coming!*
> *Made for the saints of light;*
> *Off with the garments dreary,*
> *On with the armour bright:*
> *Soon will the strife be ended,*
> *Soon all our toils below;*
> *Not to the dark we're tending,*
> *But to the Day we go.*
>
> *Work, then, the Day is coming!*
> *No time for sighing now!*
> *Harps for the hands once drooping,*
> *Wreaths for the victor's brow,*
> *Now morning Light is breaking,*
> *Soon will the Day appear;*
> *Night shades appal no longer,*
> *Jesus, our Lord, is near.*

Conformed to His Image

Oswald Chambers

INTRODUCTION

Source

The material in this volume is taken from notes in classes taught by Oswald Chambers at the Bible Training College,[1] London (1911–1915) and from sermons and talks delivered in Britain, America, and Egypt.

Publication History

- As articles: Like many of the OC works published after 1932, the most of the contents of *Conformed to His Image* appeared first as articles in the *BTC Journal*[2] before being compiled into a book. These were published between 1945 and 1950.
- A longer version of "Memory of Sin in the Saint" appeared as an article in *God's Revivalist* magazine, October 13, 1910. Most likely, Chambers preached this message at a camp meeting in America during the summer of 1910.
- As a book: The material was published as a book in 1950. Mrs. Chambers often made slight changes in words or phrasing between article and book publication. Her goal was always clarity of her husband's messages.

"Notes on Lamentations" appeared in the *BTC Journal* in 1947 with a note from Mrs. Chambers saying: "These studies in Lamentations were given at the Bible Training College, following on the series on Jeremiah; it was towards the close of a Session and the Chapters were not taken in detail, consequently brief notes only are available."

Chambers taught the series on Lamentations in November 1913, a time when Biddy Chambers, caring for six-month-old Kathleen,[3] may have found it difficult to fulfill all the roles of lady superintendent of the College, wife, mother, and stenographer.

Oswald preached "A Fatal Error of Indignant Integrity" on Sunday, October 29, 1916, at Zeitoun, Egypt.[4]

---

1. Residential school near Clapham Common in SW London, sponsored by the League of Prayer. Oswald Chambers was Principal and main teacher; Biddy Chambers was Lady Superintendent. Known as the BTC, it closed in July 1915 because of World War I.

2. *BTC Journal: Bible Training Course Journal,* published from 1932 to 1952 by Mrs. Chambers, with help from David Lambert.

3. Kathleen Chambers (1913–1997) was the only child of Oswald and Biddy Chambers.

4. Zeitoun (zay TOON). An area 6 miles NE of Cairo. Site of YMCA camp, Egypt General Mission compound and a large base area for British, Australian and New Zealand troops. Site of the Imperial School of Instruction (1916–19).

CONTENTS

CHRISTIAN THINKING

I cannot soar into the heights you show,
Nor dive into the deeps that you reveal;
But it is much that high things are to know,
That deep things are to feel.

Jean Ingelow[5]

The safe position in Christian thinking is to remember that there are deeper depths than we can fathom, higher heights than we can know; it keeps us reverent, keeps us from hardening off into a confined, cabined experience of our own.

Thinking is not of first importance; life is of first importance. Neither in natural nor in spiritual life do we begin by thinking. Christian thinking means thinking on the basis of things, not thinking in pious terms. With many the experience is right, the life of God is there, but there has been no thinking on the basis of things, and when things hit, there is confusion. If we are going to think along Christian lines and know where to place our individual experiences, it is time we exercised ourselves intellectually as well as spiritually.

1. Redemption

The Gospel to me is simply irresistible. Being the man I am, being full of lust and pride and envy and malice and hatred and false good, and all accumulated exaggerated misery—to me the Gospel of the grace of God, and the Redemption of Christ, and the regeneration and sanctification of the Holy Ghost, that Gospel is to me simply irresistible, and I cannot understand why it is not equally irresistible to every mortal man born of woman.

Pascal

Redemption is the great outside fact of the Christian faith; it has to do not only with a man's experience of salvation, but with the basis of his thinking. The revelation of Redemption means that Jesus Christ came here in order that by means of His Death on the Cross He might put the whole human race on a redemptive basis, so making it possible for every man to get back into perfect communion with God. "I have finished the work which Thou gavest Me to do." What was finished? The redemption of the world. Men are not *going to be* redeemed; they *are* redeemed. "It is finished." It was not the salvation of individual men and women like you and me that was finished: the whole human race was put on the basis of Redemption. Do

I believe it? Let me think of the worst man I know, the man for whom I have no affinity, the man who is a continual thorn in my flesh, who is as mean as can be; can I imagine that man being presented "perfect in Christ Jesus"? If I can, I have got the beginning of Christian thinking. It ought to be an easy thing for the Christian who thinks to conceive of any and every kind of man being presented "perfect in Christ Jesus," but how seldom we do think! If I am an earnest evangelical preacher I may say to a man, "Oh yes, I believe God can save you," while in my heart of hearts I don't believe there is much hope for him. Our unbelief stands as the supreme barrier to Jesus Christ's work in men's souls. "And He did not many mighty works there because of their unbelief" (Matthew 13:58). But once let me get over my own slowness of heart to believe in Jesus Christ's power to save, and I become a real generator of His power to men. "Neither is there salvation in any other: for there is none other name under heaven given among men, whereby we must be saved"—the solitary, incommunicable place of Jesus in our salvation! Are we banking in unshaken faith on the Redemption, or do we allow men's sins and wrongs to so obliterate Jesus Christ's power to save that we hinder His reaching them? "He that *believeth* on Me," i.e., active belief based on the Redemption—out of him "shall flow rivers of living water." We have to be so faithful to God that through us may come the awakening of those who have not yet realised that they are redeemed.

We must distinguish between the revelation of Redemption and the experience of regeneration. We don't *experience* life; we are alive. We don't *experience* Redemption; we experience regeneration, that is, we experience the life of God coming into our human nature, and immediately the life of God comes in it produces a surface of consciousness, but Redemption means a great deal more than a man is conscious of. The Redemption is not only for mankind, it is for the universe, for the material earth; everything that sin and the devil have touched and marred has been completely redeemed by Jesus Christ. There is a day coming when the Redemption will be actually manifested, when there will be "a new heaven and a new earth," with a new humanity upon it. If Redemption is confounded with regeneration, we get confused. In the majority of cases men have had an experience of regeneration, but they have not thought about what

---

5. Jean Ingelow (1820–1897) was an English poet and novelist.

produced the experience, and when the great revelation fact of the Redemption is expounded there is misunderstanding. All that a man experiences is believing in Jesus, but that experience is the gateway into the awe and wonder of the knowledge of God. "And this is life eternal, that they should know Thee the only true God" (RV).

The Bible deals with the fundamental underlying things of human life, and one of these fundamental things is the presence of a disposition of sin in every man. Solidarity means oneness of interests, and the phrase, "the solidarity of the human race" indicates that there is an underlying connection running straight through human life; on the religious side this connection is the heredity of sin, which was introduced into the world through one man, not by the devil—"Wherefore, as by one man sin entered into the world . . . for that all have sinned" (Romans 5:12), and when the Apostle Paul says, "Knowing this, that our old man was crucified with Him" (RV), he is referring to this heredity. Through the Redemption we have deliverance from the disposition of sin which is within us, and severance from the body of sin to which we are connected by our "old man"; that is, we are absolutely and completely delivered from sin both in disposition and in domination "Being then made free from sin . . ." Unless the universality of sin is recognised we will never understand the need for the Redemption. What the Redemption deals with is the sin of the whole human race, not primarily with the sins of individuals, but something far more fundamental, viz.: the heredity of sin. Pseudo-evangelism singles out the individual, it prostitutes the terrific meaning of the Redemption into an individual possession, the salvation of my soul.

The basis of Christian thinking is that God has redeemed the world from the possibility of condemnation on account of the heredity of sin, "God was in Christ, reconciling the world unto Himself, not imputing their trespasses unto them." The revelation is not that Jesus Christ was punished for our sins, but "He hath made Him to be sin for us, who knew no sin; that we might be made the righteousness of God in Him." God nowhere holds a man responsible for having inherited the disposition of sin any more than he is held responsible for being born. We have nothing to do with our birth or with what we inherit, because we had no choice in either. A man will say, "If I am not held responsible for having a wrong disposition, what am I held responsible for?" God holds a man responsible for not allowing Jesus Christ to deliver him from the wrong disposition when he sees that that is what He came to do. A man gets the seal of condemnation when he sees the Light, and prefers darkness (see John 3:19).

If you look upon Jesus Christ from the common-sense standpoint you will never discern who He is; but if you look upon Him as God "manifested in the flesh" (RV) for the purpose of putting the whole human race back to where God designed it to be, you get the meaning of Redemption. The great marvellous revelation of Redemption is that it atones for everyone; men are "condemned to salvation" through the Cross of Christ. Discipleship is another matter. There are things to be brought about in this world that can only be done through those of us who are prepared to fulfil the conditions of discipleship. On the basis of the Redemption I can, by committing myself to Jesus Christ and by receiving His Spirit as a gift, become a disciple in my actual life; that is, I can exhibit in my mortal flesh "the life also of Jesus."

2. Man

. . . what is man, that Thou art mindful of him? (Psalm 8:4)

(a) Man and Mankind
And God created man in His own image, in the image of God created He him, male and female created He them. (Genesis 1:27 RV)

There is only one *Begotten* Son of God, one *created* son of God, and multitudes of *regenerated* sons of God through the Redemption. These three stand in different categories.

The Bible speaks of only two men—Adam and Jesus Christ. "Mankind" is the term applied to the whole race of men, the mass of human beings. God did not make *us* in His own image; He made the Federal Head of the race in His image. "In the day that God created man, in the likeness of God made He him; male and female created He them; and blessed them, and called their name Adam ['Man,' mg]" (Genesis 5:1–2 RV). Both man and woman are required for the completed creation of God. Jesus Christ is the last Adam in this sense, viz.: that He reveals the characteristics of El-Shaddai, the Father-Mother God, all vested in the unique manifestation of the Incarnation.

(b) Man as He Was
And the LORD God formed man of the dust of the ground, and breathed into his nostrils the breath of life. (Genesis 2:7)

Man as God created him is a revelation fact, not a fact we get at by our common-sense. We have never seen Man. God *created* the earth and "*formed* man of the dust of the ground," that is, God did not make man's body by a creative fiat, He deliberately built it out of the dust of created matter according to a design in the Divine mind. Adam and Jesus Christ both came direct from the hand of God. We are not creations of God, we are pro-created through progenitors, the heredity of the human race is mixed; that accounts for all the perplexities. "And the LORD God formed man of the dust of the ground"—there is nothing the matter with matter; what has gone wrong is the infection of material things by sin, which is not material. Sin is not in matter and material things; if it were, it would be untrue to say that Jesus Christ, who "was made in the likeness of men," was "without sin."

Genesis 2:7 reveals that man's nature was a spiritual, sensuous nature—he was made of the dust of the ground, and God breathed into his nostrils the breath of life. These two things, dust and Divinity, make up man. It is impossible for us to conceive what Adam was like before the Fall; his body must have been dazzling with light through his spiritual communion with God. When he took his rule over himself he not only lost his communion with God, lost the covering of glory and light inconceivable to us, he lost the dominion God intended him to have had—"Thou madest him to have dominion over the works of Thy hands" (Psalm 8:6). Men who are their own masters are masters of nothing else. A man may feel he ought to be master of the life in the sea and air and earth, but he can only be master on the line God designed he should, viz.: that he recognised God's dominion over him. The only Being who ever walked this earth as God designed man should was Jesus Christ. He was easily Master of all created things because He maintained a steadfast obedience to the word and the will of His Father. "What manner of man is this, that even the winds and the sea obey Him?" (Matthew 8:27 RV). Man's personal powers are apt to be looked at as a marvellous promise of what he is going to be; the Bible looks at man as a ruin of what he was designed to be. There have come down in mankind remnants, broken remnants, of the first creation, they are evidence of the magnificent structure God made in the beginning, but not promises of what man is going to be.

(c) Man as He Is
. . . and were by nature the children of wrath. (Ephesians 2:3)

The words *"ye are of your father the devil,"* John 8:44, were not addressed by Jesus to men generally, but to persistent religious disbelievers in Himself.

"By nature the children of wrath." The love of God and the wrath of God are obverse sides of the same thing, like two sides of a coin. The wrath of God is as positive as His love. God cannot be in agreement with

sin. When a man is severed from God the basis of his moral life is chaos and wrath, not because God is angry like a Moloch,[6] it is His constitution of things. The wrath of God abides all the time a man persists in the way that leads away from God; the second he turns, he is faced with His love. Wrath is the dark line in God's face, and is expressive of His hatred of sin. Civilisation is the gloss over chaos and wrath, we are so sheltered that we are blinded to our need of God, and when calamity comes there is nothing to hold to. Over and over again in the history of the world man has made life into chaos. Men try to find their true life in everything but God, but they cannot, they find the "insistence of the Feet" behind them all the time.

> *But with unhurrying chase,*
> *And unperturbed pace,*
> *Deliberate speed, majestic instancy,*
> *They beat—and a Voice beat*
> *More instant than the Feet—*
> *"All things betray thee, who betrayest Me."*

> *The Hound of Heaven*
> Francis Thompson[7]

Every love and justice and nobility in the world is loyal to Jesus Christ, and only loyal to me when I recognise Him as their Source. The Incarnation is the very heart of God manifested on the plane of chaos and wrath; what Jesus Christ went through in a Time phase is indicated in such words as these, "My God, My God, why hast Thou forsaken Me?" Jesus Christ came right straight down into the very depths of wrath, He clothed Himself with the humanity of the race that had fallen and could not lift itself, and in His own person He annihilated the wrath until there is "no condemnation," no touch of the wrath of God, on those who are "in Christ Jesus."

(d) Man as He Will Be
. . . He also did predestinate to be conformed to the image of His Son. (Romans 8:29)

God's order is seen in the first and the last; the middle is the record of man's attempt to arrange things in his own way. Man is to be again in the image of God, not by evolution, but by Redemption. The meaning of Redemption is not simply the regeneration of individuals, but that the whole human race is rehabilitated, put back to where God designed it to be, consequently any member of the human race can have the heredity of the Son of God put into him, viz.: Holy Spirit, by right of what Jesus did on the Cross.

---

6. Moloch: a tyrannical power requiring sacrifice to be appeased.
7. Francis Thompson (1859–1907).

The task which confronted Jesus Christ was that He had to bring man, who is a sinner, back to God, forgive him his sin, and make him as holy as He is Himself; and He did it single-handed. The revelation is that Jesus Christ, the last Adam, was "made to be sin" (RV), the thing which severed man from God, and that He put away sin by the sacrifice of Himself— "that we might become the righteousness of God in Him." He lifted the human race back, not to where it was in the first Adam, He lifted it back to where it never was, viz.: to where He is Himself. "And it doth not yet appear what we shall be: but we know that, when He shall appear, we shall be like Him; for we shall see Him as He is."

3. Sin

To-day the Bible revelation of sin as a positive thing has been revolted against, and sin is dealt with only as something which is ostensibly wrong; the Bible view is that there is something profoundly wrong at the basis of things. Sin is a revelation fact, not a common-sense fact. No natural man is ever bothered about sin; it is the saint, not the sinner, who knows what sin is. If you confound *sin* with *sins,* you belittle the Redemption, make it "much ado about nothing." It is nonsense to talk about the need of Redemption to enable a man to stop committing sins—his own will power enables him to do that, a decent education will prevent him from breaking out into sinful acts, but to deny that there is *an heredity of sin* running straight through the human race aims a blasphemous blow at the Redemption. The only word that expresses the enormity of sin is "Calvary."

> *Guilt remains guilt; you cannot bully God into any such blessing as turns guilt to merit, or penalty to rewards.*
>
> Ibsen

Ibsen saw sin, but not Calvary; not the Son of God as Redeemer. If it cost God Calvary to deal with sin, we have no business to make light of it.

God created Adam innocent, that is, he was intended to develop, not from evil to good, but from the natural to the spiritual by obedience, it was to be a natural progress. Adam switched off from God's design, instead of maintaining his dependence on God he took his rule over himself, and thereby introduced sin into the world. Sin is not wrong doing, it is wrong *being,* deliberate and emphatic independence of God. "Wherefore, as by one man sin entered into the world . . . for that all have sinned" (Romans 5:12). It is not now a question of development, the problem is that an opposing force has come in which always says "I won't" and never can be made to say "I will." "I won't" is not imperfect "I will"; it never develops into "I will," its very nature is "shan't" and "won't." Sin is

mutiny against God's rule; not vileness of conduct, but red-handed anarchy. When you get sin revealed in you, you know that that phrase is not too strong. It is not that men are conscious anarchists—the devil is the only being in whom sin is conscious anarchy—but that a man perceives that that is the nature of sin once the light of God is thrown upon it; it is "enmity against God," not "at enmity," it *is* enmity. This opposing principle is abnormal, it was not in human nature as God designed it. The exposition of the nature of sin rarely enters into my human consciousness, when it does I know there is nothing in my spirit to deliver me from it, I am powerless; "sold under sin," said Paul. "Whosoever committeth sin is the servant of sin."

Bear in mind that it requires the Holy Ghost to convict a man of sin; any man knows that immorality is wrong, his conscience tells him it is; but it takes the Holy Ghost to convince a man that the thing he most highly esteems, viz.: his own self-government, is "an abomination in the sight of God" (RV). There is nothing more highly esteemed among men than self-realisation, but it is the one thing of which Jesus Christ is the enemy because its central citadel is independence of God. If a man can stand on his own feet morally—and many a man can—what does he want with Jesus Christ and His salvation? with forgiveness? Some men are driven to God by appalling conviction of sins, but conviction of sins is not conviction of *sin.* Conviction of sin never comes as an elementary experience. If you try to convict a man of sin to begin with you draw him to a plan of salvation, but not to Jesus Christ.

The essence of sin is my claim to my right to myself, it goes deeper down than all the sins that ever were committed. Sin can't be forgiven because it is not an act; you can only be forgiven for the sins you commit, not for an heredity. "If we confess our sins, He is faithful and just to forgive us our sins": *sin* must be cleansed by the miracle of God's grace. It does not awaken antipathy in a man when you tell him God will forgive him his sins because of what Jesus did on the Cross, but it does awaken antipathy when you tell him he has to give up his right to himself. Nothing is so much resented as the idea that I am not to be my own master. If any man will be My disciple, said Jesus, "let him deny himself," i.e., deny his right to himself, not give up external sins, those are excrescences. The point is, am I prepared deliberately to give up my right to myself to Jesus Christ? prepared to say, "Yes, take complete control"? If I am, Jesus Christ has gained a disciple. We don't go in for making disciples to-day, it takes too long; we are all for passionate evangelism—taken up with adding to the statistics of "saved souls," adding to denominational membership, taken up with the things which show splendid success. Jesus Christ took the long, long trail—"If any man will come after Me, let him deny himself"— "Take time to make up your mind." Men were not to be swept into the Kingdom on tidal waves of evangelism, not to have their wits paralysed by supernatural means; they were to come deliberately, knowing what they were doing. One life straight through to God on the ground of discipleship is more satisfactory in His sight than numbers who are saved but go no further. Over and over again men and women who should stand in the forefront for God are knocked clean out. When a crisis comes, the reason is not external wrong-doing, but something has never been given up, there is something in which Jesus Christ has not had His right of way, and the discipleship is marred. God will give us ample opportunity of proving whether we have ever really given up the right to ourselves to Jesus Christ. The one who has offers no hindrance to the working of the Holy Spirit through him.

4. New Birth

As soon as we begin to examine the foundations of our salvation we are up against the thoughts of God, and as Christians we ought to be busy thinking God's thoughts after Him. That is where we fall short; we are delighted with the fact that "once I was this, and now I am that," but simply to have a vivid experience is not sufficient if we are to be at our best for God. It is because of the refusal to think on Christian lines that Satan has come in as angel of light and switched off numbers of God's children in their head, with the result that there is a divorce between heart and head. There is nothing simpler under heaven than to become a Christian, but after that it is not easy; we have to leave "the word of the beginning of Christ," and "press on unto full growth" (Hebrews 6:1 RV mg).

Except a man be born again, he cannot see the kingdom of God. (John 3:3)

There is no natural law whereby a man can be born a second time—Nicodemus was right there: *How can a man be born when he is old?* No man ought to need to be born again; the fact that he does indicates that something has gone wrong with the human race. According to modern thinking, man is a great being in the making; his attainments are looked on as a wonderful promise of what he is going to be; we are obsessed with the evolutionary idea. Jesus Christ talks about a revolution—"Ye must be born again." The evolutionary idea doesn't cover all the facts. Not every man needs to be converted; conversion simply means turning in another direction, it may be a right or a wrong direction; but every man needs to be born from above if he is going to see the kingdom of God. In listening to some presentations of the Gospel you get the impression that a man has to be a blackguard

before Jesus Christ can do anything for him. It is true that Jesus Christ can make a saint out of any material, but the man down-and-out in sin is not the only class He deals with. It was to Nicodemus, a godly upright man, not to a sinner as we understand the term, that He said, "Marvel not that I said unto thee, Ye must be born again." "Class yourself with the whole human race, it is necessary for you, the Teacher of Israel, to be born again." It is easier to think about the sensational cases of men being transformed and lifted into a new realm by God's grace, but there are hundreds of men who are not sinners in the external sense. Does Jesus Christ do anything for them?

Many Christians don't seem to know what happened to them when they were born again, that is why they continually go back to the initial experience of having had their sins forgiven, they don't "press on unto full growth." In the New Testament new birth is always spoken of in terms of sanctification, not of salvation; to be saved means that a man receives the gift of eternal life, which is "the gift *of God*"; sanctification means that his spirit becomes the birthplace of the Son of God. "My little children, of whom I am again in travail until Christ be formed in you" (Galatians 4:19 RV). If Jesus Christ is going to be in me, He must come into me from the outside; He must be "formed" in me. It is not a question of being saved from hell, the Redemption has to do with that; this is the Redemption at work in my conscious life. I become a "Bethlehem" for the life of the Son of God. The part of human nature is to sacrifice itself to nourish that life, and every now and again there are things demanded by the life of the Son of God in me that my human nature neither likes nor understands. What Simeon said to Mary—"A sword shall pierce through thine own soul" (RV)—is true of my human nature. Am I willing for my human nature to be sacrificed in order that the life of the Son of God in me may be nourished, or do I only want Him to see me through certain difficulties? The way the life of the Son of God is nourished in me is by prayer and Bible revelation, and by obedience when a crisis comes.

When I am born again my human nature is not different, it is the same as before, I am related to life in the same way, I have the same bodily organs, but the mainspring is different, and I have to see now that all my members are dominated by the new disposition (see Romans 6:13, 19). There is only one kind of human nature, and that is the human nature we have all got, and there is only one kind of holiness, the holiness of Jesus Christ. Give Him "elbowroom," and He will manifest Himself in you, and other people will recognise Him. Human beings know human beings too well to mistake where goodness comes from; when they see certain characteristics they will know they come only from the indwelling of Jesus. It is not the manifestation of noble human traits, but of a real family likeness to Jesus. It is *His* gentleness, *His* patience, *His* purity, never mine. The whole art of spirituality is that my human nature should retire and let the new disposition have its way. We are told to "follow His steps," but we can't do it; the heredity in us is not the same as it is in Jesus. Anyone who reads the Sermon on the Mount with his eyes open knows that something must happen if it is going to be lived out in him, for he has not the goods on board to produce the result. There is only one Being who can live the Sermon on the Mount and that is the Son of God. If I will walk in the light as God is in the light, then the holy nature of Jesus manifests itself in me. It is not that I receive an impartation of the Divine nature and then am left to work it out by myself— Jesus Christ "is made unto us . . . sanctification," that is, *He* is the holy nature which we receive.

"Blessed are the poor in spirit," said Jesus, because it is through that poverty I enter His Kingdom; I cannot enter it as a good man or woman, I can only enter it as a complete pauper. The knowledge of my poverty brings me to the frontier where Jesus Christ works, as long as a man is sufficient for himself, God can do nothing for him. A man may be "pagan-ly" all right, in fact a pagan is a delightful man to know, he is not "out at elbows," not troubled or upset, and he cannot understand why you should talk of the need to be born again. The born-again man has been put on the basis of a new construction of humanity, consequently for a time he is chaotic, disturbed, broken, and at this stage he is not so desirable as the man who represents the climax of the natural life. Other natural virtues are our deepest inheritance, but when the miracle of new birth is experienced, the first thing that happens is the corruption of those virtues because they can never come anywhere near what God demands. Jesus Christ loved moral beauty (see Mark 10:21), but He never said it would do. The natural virtues are a delight to God because He designed them, they are fine and noble, but behind them is a disposition which may cause a man's morality to go by the board. What Jesus Christ does in new birth is to put in a disposition that transforms morality into holiness. He came to put into the man who knows he needs it His own heredity of holiness; to bring him into a oneness with God which he never had through natural birth. "That they may be one, even as We are one."

The experimental aspect of Redemption is repentance; the only proof that a man is born from above is that he brings forth "fruits meet for repentance." That is the one characteristic of New Testament regeneration, and it hits desperately hard because the Holy Spirit brings conviction on the most humiliating lines. Many a powerless, fruitless Christian life is the result of a refusal to obey in some insignificant thing—"first go." It is extraordinary what we are brought up against when the Holy Spirit is at work in us, and the thing that fights longest against His demands is my prideful claim to my right to myself. The only sign of regeneration in practical experience is that we begin to make our life in accordance with the demands of God. Jesus Christ did not only come to present what God's normal man should be, He came to make the way for everyone of us to get there, and the gateway is His Cross. I cannot begin by imitating Jesus Christ, but only by being born into His Kingdom; then when I have been regenerated and have received the heredity of the Son of God, I find that His teaching belongs to that heredity, not to my human nature.

All this means great deliberation on our part. God does not expect us to understand these things in order to be saved, salvation is of God's free grace; but He does expect us to do our bit in appreciation of His "so great salvation."

5. Repentance

Never mistake remorse for repentance; remorse simply puts a man in hell while he is on earth, it carries no remedial quality with it at all, nothing that betters a man. An unawakened sinner knows no remorse, but immediately a man recognises his sin he experiences the pain of being gnawed by a sense of guilt, for which punishment would be a heaven of relief, but no punishment can touch it. In the case of Cain (see Genesis 4:9–14) remorse is seen at its height: "Mine iniquity is greater than can be forgiven" (4:13 RV mg) Cain was in the condition of being found out by his own sin; his conscience recognised what he had done, and he knew that God recognised it too. Remorse is not the recognition that I am detected by somebody else, I can defy that; remorse comes when intellectually and morally, I recognise my own guilt. It is a desperate thing for me to realise that I am a sneak, that I am sensual and proud, that is my sin finding *me* out. The Holy Spirit never convicts of sin until He has got Jesus Christ pretty close up; a human being would like to convict of sin before Jesus Christ is there. The classic experience of Cain has all lesser experiences folded up in it; few of us are actually murderers, but we are all criminals in potentiality—"Whosoever hateth his brother is a murderer" (1 John 3:15); and one of the greatest humiliations in work for God is that we are never free from the reminder by the Holy Spirit of what we might be in actuality but for the grace of God.

When any sin is recalled with a gnawing sense of guilt this "biting again" of remorse, watch carefully that it does not make you whine and indulge in sulks about the consequences. The beginning of sulks is the blaming of everybody but yourself, and every step you take in that direction leads further away from God and from the possibility of repentance. Whenever the lash of remorse comes, never try to prevent it, every bit of it is deserved. And if you are a worker, never tell a lie out of sympathy and say, "Oh well, you don't need to feel like that, you couldn't help it." Never tell a lie to another soul. The temptation is tremendously strong to sympathise with a man and prove a traitor to his soul's true instincts; he may fling off from you at a tangent, but truth will tell in the end.

Reformation, which means to form again or renew, is a law that works in human nature apart from the grace of God as well as after regeneration; if it takes place apart from regeneration it is simply the reformation of a rebel. Certain forms of wild oats bring forth their crop and pass and a man becomes different in conduct, but he is a deeply entrenched unregenerate person. That a man stops being bad and becomes good may have nothing to do with salvation; the only one sign that a man is saved is repentance. Instances of reformation apart from the grace of God can be multiplied because there is something in human nature that reacts towards reformation when once the right influence is brought to bear at the right time, e.g., the boy who won't reform for his father's threats or his schoolmaster's punishment, will experience a reaction towards reformation through his mother's love. Again, though a bad man become worse in the presence of suspicious people, when with little children he experiences a reaction towards reformation. If being in the presence of a good man or woman does not produce a reaction towards goodness in me, I am in a bad way. The Apostle Paul sums up this law when he says, ". . . not knowing that the goodness of God leadeth thee to repentance?" (Romans 2:4).

"And Zacchaeus stood, and said unto the Lord, Behold Lord, the half of my goods I give to the poor; and if I have taken anything from any man by false accusation, I restore him fourfold" (Luke 19:8). Why did Zacchaeus say that? who had said a word about his peculations! The desire to make restitution was stirred through his coming into the presence of Jesus, and was a sign of the working of this inevitable law of reaction. Restitution means the determination to do right to everybody I have "done," and it is astonishing the things the Holy Spirit will remind us of that we have to put right. Over and over again during times of revival and great religious awakening workers are presented with this puzzle, that people do unquestionably make restitution—men who stole pay up like sheep, with no notion why they do it, and if the worker is not well taught he will mistake this for the work of the Holy Spirit and a sign that they are born again, when the fact is that the truth has been so clearly put that it caused their nature to react

towards reformation. The thing to do with people in that condition is to get them to *receive* something from God.

Luke 11:25 is a picture of clear, sweeping reformation, the house "swept and garnished"; but what our Lord points out is the peril of a moral victory unused because the heart is left empty. The man who reforms without any knowledge of the grace of God is the subtlest infidel with regard to the need of regeneration. It is a good thing to have the heart swept, but it becomes the worst thing if the heart is left vacant for spirits more evil than itself to enter; Jesus said that "the last state of that man becometh worse than the first" (RV). Reformation is a good thing, but like every other good thing it is the enemy of the best. Regeneration means filling the heart with something positive, viz., the Holy Spirit.

Repentance is the experimental side of Redemption and is altogether different from remorse or reformation. "Repentance" is a New Testament word and cannot be applied outside the New Testament. We all experience remorse, disgust with ourselves over the wrong we have done when we are found out by it, but the rarest miracle of God's grace is the sorrow that puts an end for ever to the thing for which I am sorry. Repentance involves the receiving of a totally new disposition so that I never do the wrong thing again. The marvel of conviction of sin, of forgiveness and of the holiness of God are so interwoven that the only forgiven man is the holy man. If God in forgiving me does not turn me into the standard of the Forgiver, to talk about being saved from hell and made right for heaven is a juggling trick to get rid of the responsibility of seeing that my life justifies God in forgiving me. The great element in practical Christianity—and that is the only kind of Christianity there is—is this note of repentance, which means I am willing to go all lengths so long as God's law which I have broken is cleared in my case—". . . that Thou mayest be justified when Thou speakest, and be clear when Thou judgest" (Psalm 51:4 RV). Have I ever had a moment before God when I have said, "My God, I deserve all that Thou canst bring on me as punishment for breaking Thy holy law—'against Thee, Thee only, have I sinned, and done that which is evil in Thy sight'"? The essence of repentance is that it destroys the lust of self-vindication; wherever that lust resides the repentance is not true. Repentance brings us to the place where we are willing to receive any punishment under heaven so long as the law we have broken is justified. That is repentance, and I think I am right in saying that very few of us know anything at all about it. We have the idea nowadays that God is so loving and gentle and kind that all we need do is to say we feel sorry for the wrong we have done and we will try to be better. That is not repentance;

Repentance means that I am re-made on a plane which justifies God in forgiving me.

Once get this kind of thing into your mind and you will understand what is meant by conviction of sin. The repentant man experiences the humiliating conviction that he has broken the law of God and he is willing to accept, on God's terms, the gift of a new life which will prove sufficient in him to enable him to live a holy life, not hereafter, but here and now. Strictly speaking, repentance is a gift of God; a man cannot repent when he chooses. Repentance does not spring out of the human heart, it springs from a ground outside the human heart, viz., the ground of the Redemption.

6. Reality
(a) The Will to Believe the Redeemer
. . . blessed are they that have not seen, and yet have believed. (John 20:29; cf. John 11:40)

Reality is the thing which works out absolutely solidly true in my personal life, but I must be careful not to confound the reality of my experience with Reality itself. For instance, when I am born again I am not conscious of the Redemption of my Lord, the one thing that is real to me is that I have been born again; but if I watch the working of the Holy Spirit I find that He takes me clean out of myself till I no longer pay any attention to my experiences, I am concerned only with the Reality which produced those experiences, viz., the Redemption. If I am left with my experiences, they have not been produced by the Redemption. If experience is made the only guide it will produce that peculiar type of isolated life that is never found in the New Testament.

We say "seeing is believing," but it is not; we must believe a thing is possible before we would believe it even though we saw it. Belief must be the will to believe, and I can never will to believe without a violent effort on my part to dissociate myself from all my old ways of looking at things and putting myself right over on to God. It is God who draws me, my relationship is to Him, consequently the issue of will comes in at once—Will I transact on what God says? Never discuss with anyone when God speaks; discussion on spiritual matters is impertinent. God never discusses with anyone. Let me stake my all, blindly, as far as feelings are concerned, on the Reality of the Redemption, and before long that Reality will begin to tell in my actual life, which will be the evidence that the transaction has taken place. But there must be the deliberate surrender of will, not a surrender to the persuasive power of a personality, but a deliberate launching forth on God and what He says. Remember, you must urge the will to an issue; you must come to the point where you *will* to believe the Redeemer,

and deliberately wash your hands of the consequences.

In testing for ourselves our relation to Reality we are not left in a vague fog, we have the Word of God expressing God to us, and the Word of God, our Lord Jesus Christ, expresses Himself to us through His teaching, made vitally applicable to every domain of our human life. Any attempt to divorce the words of God from the Word of God leads to unreality; the words of God are only vitally real when we are in a right relationship to God through the Word. Men worship an intellectual creed, and you can't dispute it because it is logically correct, but it does not produce saints; it produces stalwarts and stoics but not New Testament saints, because it is based on adherence to the literal words rather than on a vital relationship to God, who is the one abiding Reality. In the final issue Christian principles are found to be antichrist, i.e., an authority other than Christ Himself. It is quite possible to have an intellectual appreciation of the Redemption without any experience of supernatural grace; an experience of supernatural grace comes by committing myself to a person, not to a creed or a conviction. I can never find Reality by looking within; the only way I can get at Reality is by dumping myself outside myself on to Someone else, viz.: God, immediately I do I am brought in touch with Reality.

(b) The Will to Receive the Redeemer
But as many as received Him . . . (John 1:12)

We do not create truth, we receive it. There are things which you perceive clearly, but are they real to you? They are not real if you have never been through a transaction of will in connection with them, your perception is based on the weaving of your own brain, not on the knowledge of Someone who knows you. The Giver is God, and every gift He offers is based on His knowledge of us; our attitude is to be that of receiving from Him all the time, and in this way we become sons and daughters of God. It requires the greatest effort, and produces the greatest humility, to receive anything from God, we would much sooner earn it. Receiving is the evidence of a disciple of the Lord; reasoning about it is the indication of a dictator to God. Effective repentance is witnessed to by my receiving from God instead of reasoning why God should give it to me. When I am willing to be such a fool as to accept, that is repentance; the other is rational pride. We can only get at Reality by means of our conscience which ultimately embraces both head and heart. There is always a practical proof when we do get at Reality, viz., actuality is made in accord with it. Does your intellect make you in accord actually with what you think? Of course it does not. Read the lives of some of the most intellectual men, men whose aesthetic sensibilities are of the finest order, but their actual life won't bear looking at. I cannot get at Reality by my intellect or by emotion, but only by my conscience bringing me in touch with the Redemption. When the Holy Spirit gets hold of my conscience He convicts me of unreality, and when I respond to God I come in touch with Reality and experience a sense of wonder—"That He should have done this for me!" It is not extravagant, it is the result of a totally new adjustment, a relation to the Reality which has been created in me by means of my abandonment to Jesus Christ.

(c) The Will to Obey the Redeemer
If ye love Me, keep My commandments. (John 14:15; see vv. 21, 23; 15:11–12)

These verses are specimens of many that reveal what is to be the abiding attitude of the saint, viz.: obeying the commandments of One whom we can only believe by will, and whose gifts we can only receive by will. We will to believe Him, then we obey by will. These exercises of the will are essential to the wholesome upkeep of a saint's actual life. The effort on the human side is to maintain the childlike relation to God, receiving from Him all the time, then obedience works out in every detail. When a man is rightly related to God it is the Holy Ghost who works through him, and as long as he maintains the will to believe, the will to receive and the will to obey, the life of Jesus is manifested in his mortal flesh.

Beware of any hesitation to abandon to God. It is the meanest characteristics of our personality that are at work whenever we hesitate, there is some element of self-interest that won't submit to God. When we do cut the shore lines and launch forth, what happens is a great deal more than a vision of the indwelling of God; what happens is the positive miracle of the Redemption at work in us, and we have patiently to make it permeate everything. Our relationship to God is first that of personality, not of intellect; intellect comes in after to explain what has transpired, and it is the ordering of the mind that makes a man a teacher and an instructor. Be stably rooted in God and then begin to know, begin to use those rusty brains.

Beware of having an overweening interest in your own character so that you are inclined to believe in God on that account; at the same time be careful to allow nothing that would hinder your relationship to God, because any impairing of that relationship hinders Him in getting at other souls through you. Continually revise your relationship to God until the only certainty you have is not that you are faithful, but that He is. Priggishness is based on concern for my own whiteness, a pathetic whine—"I am afraid I am not faithful"; "I am afraid I shall never be what God wants

me to be." Get into contact with Reality and what you feel no longer matters to you, the one terrific Reality is God.

An abiding way of maintaining our relation to Reality is intercession. Intercession means that I strive earnestly to have my human soul moved by the attitude of my Lord to the particular person I am praying for. That is where our work lies, and we shirk it by becoming active workers; we do the things that can be tabulated and scheduled, and we won't do the one thing that has no snares. Intercession keeps the relationship to God completely open. You cannot intercede if you do not believe in the Reality of Redemption, you will turn intercession into futile sympathy with human beings which only increases their submissive content to being out of touch with God. Intercession means getting the mind of Christ about the one for whom we pray, that is what is meant by filling up "that which is behind of the afflictions of Christ"; and that is why there are so few intercessors. Be careful not to enmesh yourself in more difficulties than God has engineered for you to know; if you know too much, more than God has engineered, you cannot pray, the condition of the people is so crushing that you can't get through to Reality. The true intercessor is the one who realises Paul's meaning when he says, "for we know not what we should pray for as we ought: but the Spirit [Himself] maketh intercession for us with groanings which cannot be uttered" (Romans 8:26).

7. The Holy Spirit
(a) The Holy Spirit and Revelation Purpose
. . . holy men of God spake as they were moved by the Holy Ghost. (2 Peter 1:21)

Bear in mind that there is a two-fold attitude to be maintained in dealing with the Self-revelation of God—first, its historic setting; second, its value to me personally. It is essential to have an historic basis for our Christian faith: our faith must be centred in the Life and Death of the historic Jesus. Why is it that that Life and Death have an importance out of all proportion to every other historic fact? Because there the Redemption is brought to a focus. Jesus Christ was not a Man who twenty centuries ago lived on this earth for thirty-three years and was crucified; He was God Incarnate, manifested at one point of history. All before looked forward to that point; all since look back to it. The presentation of this fact produces what no other fact in the whole of history ever could produce, viz.: the miracle of God at work in human souls. The death of Jesus was not the death of a martyr, it was the revelation of the Eternal heart of God. That is why the Cross is God's last word; that does not mean God is not speaking still, it means that He is saying nothing contrary to the Cross.

The tendency abroad to-day is to do away with the historic setting of the revelation of God in Christ in the Gospels, to do away with what the apostles wrote, and say, "All that is needed is to receive the Holy Spirit and we will have a 'private interpretation' of our own." But "no prophecy of the scripture is of any private interpretation. For the prophecy came not in old time by the will of man: but holy men . . . spake as they were moved by the Holy Ghost." That makes it incumbent upon us to be reverent to a degree with what the apostles wrote. The Epistles are not the cogitations of men of extraordinary spiritual genius, but the posthumous work of the Ascended Christ and they have therefore a peculiar significance in the programme of Redemption. The Holy Ghost used these men, with all their personal idiosyncrasies, to convey God's message of salvation to the world. Our Lord, so to speak, incarnated Himself in them—the message of God must always be incarnated, but it remains the message *of God.* The Epistles are the exposition of why God became "manifest in the flesh," and when by submissive reception I commit myself to that revelation, the Holy Ghost begins to interpret to me what Jesus Christ did on the Cross.

"Neither pray I for these alone, but for them also which shall believe on Me through their word" (John 17:20). Everyone who believes on Jesus, believes on Him "through their word." In the experience of salvation all are alike; in the matter of authoritative inspiration the apostles stand alone; their word is as final as Jesus Christ's. We have no counterpart to that. The inspiration the Holy Ghost gives us is not for revelation purposes, but for insight into the revelation already given. Apostolic inspiration is not an experience, it is as great a miracle as the Incarnation. The one great need is for the Holy Spirit to be received, because He will open up to us not only our own salvation, and the whole of the New Testament revelation, He will open up the treasures of the Old Testament—"even the mystery which hath been hid from ages and from generations, but now is made manifest to His saints: . . . which is *Christ in you*, the hope of glory" (Colossians 1:26–27).

(b) The Holy Spirit and Redemptive Preaching
For the preaching of the cross is to them that perish foolishness. . . . It pleased God by the foolishness of preaching to save them that believe. (1 Corinthians 1:18, 21)

We are nowhere told to preach salvation, or sanctification, or Divine healing; we are told to lift up Jesus, who is the Redeemer, and He will produce His redemptive results in the souls of men. If I preach only the effects of the Redemption, describe in persuasive

speech what God has done for me, nothing will happen. It is only when I am humble enough, and stupid enough, to preach the Cross that the miracle of God takes place. The "preaching of the Cross" creates that which enables a man to believe in God, because the Cross is the manifestation of the Redemption. The Cross "condemns men to salvation." The "foolishness of preaching" is the way God has chosen to make the Redemption efficacious in human lives. You can't *persuade* a man to believe in God; belief in God is not an act of the intellect, it is a moral creation produced by the interaction of God's Spirit and my spirit in willing obedience; intellect comes in afterwards to explain what has happened. In preaching the Cross we use our intellect, not to prove that Jesus died, but to present the fact of His death. The danger is to give expression to subjective experiences we have had; but that will never produce the same experiences in others, it is personal testimony and has its right place, but it is not "preaching" the Cross. The bedrock permanent thing in Christian experience is not the accidental bits of God's particular manifestation of it in you and me, the bedrock permanent thing is the Redemption, and our particular experiences of it, slight or profound, are simply meant to introduce us to that Reality.

(c) The Holy Spirit and Revealing Power
Howbeit when He, the Spirit of truth, is come, He will guide you into all truth. . . . He shall glorify Me. (John 16:13–14)

If an expositor has never realised the need to receive, recognise and rely on the Holy Spirit, he takes little account of the Cross but says, "Let us come to the teachings of Jesus." Our Lord never placed the emphasis on what He taught, neither do the apostles; they place all the emphasis on the Cross. Why? Because they were shrewd and intelligent? No, because the Holy Ghost inspired them to put the emphasis there. "But God forbid that I should glory save in the Cross of our Lord Jesus Christ." Our Lord is not the great Teacher of the world, He is the Saviour of the world and the Teacher of those who believe in Him, which is a radically different matter. His teaching is of no use saving to agonise mankind with its unattainable ideals until men are made anew through the Cross. Unless I am born from above (RV mg) the only result of the teachings of Jesus is to produce despair. People say that Jesus Christ came to teach us to be good; He never did! All the teaching in the world about a man having a pure heart won't make it pure. Our Lord's teaching has no power in it unless I possess His nature. When I am born from above it is the Conscientious relationship between my individual life and Jesus Christ that keeps my conduct right. Once I am brought into contact with Reality I begin to experience the power of the Redemption as it applies to every phase of life.

For He shall receive of Mine, and shall shew it unto you. (John 16:14)

The spirit of antichrist is that spirit which "dissolves by analysis" (RV mg) the person of Jesus—"someone unique, but not what the New Testament claims." To preach the Jesus of the Gospels at the expense of the Christ of the Epistles is a false thing, such a false thing that it is antichrist to the very core, because it is a blow direct at what Jesus said the Holy Spirit would do, viz.: expound Him to the disciples, and "through their word" to innumerable lives to the end of Time. If I say "Of course God would never convey a right interpretation of Himself through a handful of men like the disciples," I am casting a slur on what Jesus said, telling Him that His reliance on God's promise of the Spirit was without justification; that His basis of confidence on the Holy Spirit's revelation of Himself to the disciples was misplaced. When our Lord told the disciples they would do "greater works," His reliance was not on them, but on the gift of the Spirit which He was to receive from the Father and shed forth on them. Everything Jesus said the Holy Spirit would do, He has done and the New Testament is the revelation of it.

(d) The Holy Spirit and Revealed Proclamation
He gave some, apostles . . . for the edifying of the body of Christ. (Ephesians 4:11–12)

Our Lord gave the disciples the gift of the Holy Spirit as their equipment for proclaiming the Gospel to the world; in the same way the Holy Spirit comes into my personal life to bring me out of my individual narrowness into the universal purpose of God. When I want to translate all God's redemptive work into the consciousness of being saved, I become a pious humbug. God does not save me in order that I may feel saved, but to take me up into His redemptive purpose. Christian experience must be expounded as it emerges in its most extraordinary and tragic form, not in order to make that form the standard, but as giving the basis to which every experience is to be traced. You say, "I have never had such profound conviction of sin, such depth of repentance, as the Apostle Paul, therefore I can't be a true Christian." We are not meant to imitate Paul in his experience, but to remember that that profound experience gives us the right direction for tracing where our own experience comes from. Paul never says, "Follow my way of getting into Christ," because no two people ever come the same way *into* Christ, yet they must follow the same ways *in* Christ. Experience is simply the doorway into Reality, if I stick in the doorway I get cold

and die, die away from Reality; I must go through the doorway, and in the classic experiences we get the door widest open.

"For the edifying of the body of Christ." The New Testament is the product of the Holy Ghost, we are literally fed into the Body of Christ by its words. "Feed My sheep," said Jesus, and all down the ages the words of the New Testament have fed the children of God; if we try to nourish ourselves in any other way we produce abortions, what the writer to the Hebrews calls "bastards." The point for me is not simply that I appreciate with my mind what the New Testament declares, but that I am brought into such a relationship with God that His words become serviceable through me to others. It sounds pathetic to talk about "drawing on the life of Jesus" to keep the needs of my physical life supplied; but that is not His meaning; it is drawing on the life of Jesus through His word that He might serve out nourishment to others through me.

8. Natural and Personal Life
Never run away with the idea that you are a person who has a spirit, has a soul and has a body; you are a person that *is* spirit, soul and body. Man is one; body, soul and spirit are terms of definition. My body is the manifest "me." Some of us are so dominated by the body that our spirit lives only in the physical domain, instead of the physical being slowly taken into the spiritual by a series of moral choices. Our spirit goes no further than we bring our body. One of the best means of spiritual progress is to learn to deny the body in a great number of unnecessary ways (cf. 1 Corinthians 9:27).

First Corinthians 15:46 ("Howbeit that was not first which is spiritual, but that which is natural; and afterward that which is spiritual") lays down the fundamental basis of the way God deals with man all through—first the natural, then the spiritual. The whole purpose of a human personality is to turn the natural life into a spiritual life by sacrifice. The Bible never speaks of the natural life as sinful, it contrasts it with the spiritual, e.g., "the natural man receiveth not the things of the Spirit of God: . . . neither can he know them, because they are spiritually discerned. But he that is spiritual [discerneth] all things" (1 Corinthians 2:14–15).

Adam, the Federal Head of the human race, was designed by God to take part in his own development, that is, he was intended to turn the natural into the spiritual by a series of choices, which would mean moral progress. The natural life is the "lamb" for sacrifice. It is not fanaticism, but the sacrificing of what is absolutely legitimate and right and making it spiritual by obedience. That is the only way personality is exhibited in its true form. It has nothing to do with sin; there would have been sacrifice whether there had been sin or not because of God's design of man. It was not a sin for our Lord to have a human body, it was not a sin for Him to eat, but it would have been sin for Him to eat during the forty days in the wilderness because His Father's will was otherwise. Our Lord stands as the presentation of God's normal Man, and when by regeneration His life is formed in us we have to transform the natural life into a spiritual life by obedience to the will of God, letting Him engineer our circumstances as He will. We are not fundamentally free, external circumstances are not in our hands, they are in God's hands, the one thing in which we are free is in our personal relationship to God. We are not responsible for the circumstances we are in, but we are responsible for the way we allow those circumstances to affect us; we can either allow them to get on top of us, or we can allow them to transform us into what God wants us to be. If we go under in circumstances we are held responsible because God has promised an absolutely overcoming Spirit to any man who will receive Him. If you are at a loss to know how to get at what God wants you to be, listen to the Lord Jesus. He says, "If you ask God He will plant in you the very Spirit that is in Me" (Luke 11:13). If you receive the Holy Spirit you find that circumstances will never have power to do anything but give you the chance of sacrificing the natural to the spiritual and proving you are a son or daughter of God.

"And the LORD God . . . breathed into his nostrils the breath of life" (Genesis 2:7), i.e., God breathed into man that which became man's spirit, that is the indestructible factor in every human being. Man is, and he will never be un-created. Man has kinship with God as no other creation of God has; his true kinship is with God and nowhere else. When I receive the Holy Spirit He lifts my personality back into its primal relationship with God. Holy Spirit coming into my spirit never becomes my spirit; He energises my spirit and enables me "to will and to do of His good pleasure."

God has put man in an experimental sphere and if he refuses to turn the natural into the spiritual he will find himself dominated by the body, it will chain him down and make him a slave. The personality of a man apart from the Spirit of God becomes enslaved to the desires of the flesh. The marvel of the life of God in a man is that he never need be dominated by anything other than spirit—"Walk in the Spirit, and ye shall not fulfil the lust of the flesh" (Galatians 5:16). But if you don't sacrifice your natural inclinations and impulses to the will and the word of God, you are likely to be tripped up by any of the things Paul mentions: "Now the works of the flesh are manifest, which are these. . . ." It will test a man to the limit to take his stand on the Redemption and the indwelling of the Holy Spirit and prove in actual life what God has put

in him by regeneration. We are taken up with the "soul-saving" line instead of the line of character-building on the basis of the Redemption, consequently you get people who are gloriously saved but they have never gone on to sacrifice the natural to the spiritual—never put the knife to the throat of an appetite, never recognised pig-headed obstinacy, never got on the track of that green-eyed monster, envy. "But those things can't be in me now that I am saved"—and they are painted in glaring colours! When the Holy Spirit begins to unearth the works of the flesh in you, don't temporise, don't whitewash them; don't call suspicion, discernment of the spirit, or ill-temper, righteous indignation; bring it to the light, come face to face with it, confess it and get it cleansedaway.

"And they that are Christ's have crucified the flesh with the affections and lusts." When a man is saved his human nature is not altered; human nature is marred by sin, but it is not bad. Deliverance from sin does not mean deliverance from human nature. By regeneration a man is perfectly adjusted to God, now he is required to do a man's bit, viz.: to take his human nature and make it serve the new disposition. The honour of Jesus Christ is at stake in my bodily life, and if I walk in the Spirit I will be ruthless to the things that won't submit to Him. To crucify the flesh "with the affections and lusts" is not God's business, it is man's.

"And afterward that which is spiritual." We are made partakers of the Divine nature through the promises (see 2 Peter 1:4), the inherent tendency of the Divine nature is implanted in us through regeneration and we become children of God; we become, that is, not only what we are by nature, creations of God, but sons and daughters of God, with a strong family likeness to Jesus. The true conception of Man is our Lord. Man got out of God's order, and we are brought back not merely into the original order, but into a much better position through our Lord, viz.: we are to be "conformed to the image of His Son." We look at the things that are expressed externally; God looks at the tendency born in us. He knows, apart from all our pious phrases and pretences, whether we have been regenerated, He sees what the life will become. Browning puts it as no other writer outside the Bible:

All I could never be,
All, men ignored in me.
—This, I was worth to God,

9. Discovering God
(a) Evangelical v. Eclectic Expression
The effort is on an individual and philanthropic scale, not on a world scale, an evangelical scale—it is unequal to the world crisis. . . . It is the climax of a generation

of genial and gentle religion, with the nerve of the Cross cut, which therefore breaks in our hands at a great historic crisis for lack of the moral note—tonic, radical, and redemptive.

Forsyth[8]

Evangelical—the belief that God was "manifested in the flesh" (RV) in the Person of His Son in order that through His death on the Cross men might be redeemed. The Apostle Paul sums up evangelical belief when he says—"For He hath made Him to be sin for us, who knew no sin; that we might be made the righteousness of God in Him": that is, Jesus Christ takes my heredity of sin, and gives me His own heredity of holiness, and I show the alteration through my skin. The emphasis is apt to be put on one phase only, viz.: justification by faith; the real centre of the action of the Redemption has to do with a man's ruling disposition. If a man takes the rational commonsense line he despises the evangelical view, but when he gets down to things as they are he finds that the rational view is on the fifteenth storey and the evangelical view is at the basis. The rational view misses out the fact that there is an hiatus between God and man; things are wild, there is a tragedy, something irrational not rational, at the heart of life and the way out is not by reason, but only through the Cross of Christ. These things are fundamental, they come straight home to the problems of a man's own heart and life. The point for me is, Do I agree with God in what He condemns in the Cross? That is where most of our Christianity is proved to be humbug. We believe in what we call the plan of salvation, but we don't do much else. We ought to be busy *thinking* as Christians. Up to the time of the war[9] religious people were taken up, not so much with the fundamental revelation of the Redemption as with expounding a certain type of saintliness, a particular presentation of the Gospel, consequently when the war struck they were not able to grasp the providential order of God at all, they were found enervated, "unequal to the world crisis."

(b) Temperamental v. True Portrayal
God so loved, so unsparingly, as to do His Son's body and soul the injury of the Cross. That is the principle on which God's love dealt with the vast evil of the world. He reserved for Himself what He forbade Abraham to do.

Forsyth

Temperamental—the way a man looks at life. My temperament is an inner disposition which influences my thoughts and actions to a certain extent, i.e., I am either pessimistic or optimistic according to the way my blood circulates. It is an insult to take the temperamental line in dealing with a human being— "Cheer up, look on the bright side"; there are some types of suffering before which the only thing you can do is to keep your mouth shut. There are times when a man needs to be handled by God, not by his fellow men, and part of the gift of man's wisdom is to know how to be reverent with what he does not understand.

To take the temperamental view of Jesus Christ will mean that I do not make the revelation of the Bible my guide, I portray Him as one who lived beyond His age and suffered in consequence; all He did was to leave us a good example which we must try to follow, so that when a man makes the supreme sacrifice and lays down his life, he thereby redeems his own soul. A more hopeless misunderstanding of the Redemption could not be. When a man lays down his life, it takes God to expound what he has done. "Greater love hath no man than this, that a man lay down his life for his friends." The love of God is seen in that He laid down His life for His enemies. The Redemption is God's "bit." "None of them can by any means redeem his brother, nor give to God a ransom for him: (for the redemption of their soul is costly, and must be let alone for ever)" (Psalm 49:7–8 RV).

What Forsyth is pointing out is that the temperamental view ignores the fact that God deliberately paid the price of dealing with sin. It is easy if I reason from the logical common-sense point of view, to say that God created the man who became a sinner, and then condemns him to hell because he sinned. The Bible says nothing of the sort. The Bible says that God Himself accepted the responsibility for sin; the Cross is the proof that He did. It cost Jesus Christ to the last drop of blood to deal with "the vast evil of the world." The true portrayal is that the Cross is not the cross of a man, but the Cross of God. The tragedy of the Cross is the hurt to God. In the Cross God and sinful man merge; consequently the Cross is of more importance than all the world's civilisations.

"He that spared not His own Son, but delivered Him up for us all, how shall He not with Him also freely give us all things?" What does that mean? It means that I can receive a new disposition the second I see my need—"If ye then, being evil, know how to give good gifts unto your children: how much more shall your heavenly Father give the Holy Spirit to them that ask Him?" It is so simple that the majority

---

8. Peter Taylor Forsyth (1848–1921), British Congregationalist minister and theologian. Chambers read many of Forsyth's books and valued his insights.

9. World War I (1914–1918).

of us blunder over it, we won't come the bairn way; but when a man is up against things the words of Jesus become the deepest philosophy in life—"Come unto Me"; "Believe also in Me." My relation to things proves whether or not I do believe in Jesus. The life of a child of God is always the life of a child, simple and open-hearted, no ulterior motive. The Bible makes more of the death of Jesus than of His life and His teaching, because the teaching of Jesus does not apply to you and me unless we have received His Spirit. What is the good of telling me to love my enemies? I hate them! to be fathomlessly pure in heart? to have no unworthy motive? The teaching of Jesus is for the life He puts in, and I receive that life by means of the Cross.

(c) Dogmatic Creed v. Deity of Christ

No man begins his Christian life by believing a creed. The man with a dogmatic creed says, "You must believe this and that." Jesus says, "Do the will," i.e., "commit yourself to Me." Truth is not in a particular statement; Truth is a person, "I am . . . the Truth." It is a mistake to attempt to define what a man must believe before he can be a Christian; his beliefs are the effect of his being a Christian, not the cause of it. Immediately you lose sight of the central, majestic Figure of Jesus Christ you are swept off your feet by all kinds of doctrine, and when big things hit you find your religion does not stand you in good stead because your creed does not agree with the Truth.

The revelation of the Deity of Christ does not come first to a man's intellect, but to his heart and life, and he says with amazement, "Thou art the Christ, the Son of the living God." The great point of the Bible revelation of God is not only that God was *in* Christ, but that Jesus Christ *is* God. If Jesus Christ is not God, then the only God we have is an abstraction of our own minds. I know no other God in Time or Eternity than Jesus Christ; I have accepted all I know of God on the authority of the revelation He gave of Him. "He that hath seen Me hath seen the Father."

We never discover God until we come to a personal need for Him, and that drives us to Jesus. The whole meaning of life is that a man discovers God for himself. It is not sin that keeps us away from Jesus, but our own goodness. "I am not come to call the righteous," Jesus said, but sinners to repentance." We don't seem to need God until we come up against things. The basis for thinking with most of us is our ordinary logical common-sense, but when a man comes up against things he has to go deeper down than his common-sense, to fall back on something else, either fatalism or God. The Christian thought is not fatalistic, it is based on the revelation of God given by Jesus Christ.

10. Common Christian Thinking
(a) The Divine Unction of Christian Teaching
But ye have an unction from the Holy One, and ye know all things. (1 John 2:20)

The Apostle John in these verses does away with the idea that there are specialists in Christian thinking as there are specialists in other domains; he says, No, the Holy Spirit is the one Teacher, and the teaching He imparts is common to us all, consequently there is no excuse for any of us, no room for saying, "I haven't had a good education"; "I haven't had time to study." The majority of us recognise the necessity of receiving the Holy Spirit for living, but we do not sufficiently recognise the need for drawing on the resources of the Holy Spirit for thinking. Many of us don't realise that we *can* think, we lie all abroad in our minds, woolgathering. When we receive the Holy Spirit He imparts the ability to see things by intuition. Spiritual intuition lives in the same sphere as natural intuition *plus* the Holy Spirit.

> *I do not like thee, Dr. Fell,*
> *The reason why I cannot tell;*
> *But this I know, and know full well—*
> *I do not like thee, Dr. Fell.*

That is natural intuition, i.e., instant perception of the truth of things without reasoning or analysis. Instruction in spiritual intuition is what we need. The Holy Spirit will curb and check natural intuition until He brings it into accord with what Jesus meant when He said, "My sheep hear My voice." When you listen to a preacher, how are you going to know whether he is teaching the truth of God? Only by spiritual intuition. You may know that God has wonderfully used a man in the past, but never make that your ground for heeding what he says now, for at any minute a man may be out of touch with God (cf. 1 Corinthians 9:27). Never pin your faith to a man's reputation as a servant of God, always watch for the Holy Spirit. If a man is talking the truth of God those who listen will meet it again whether they like it or not; if he is not talking God's truth they won't come across it any more. Whenever the grand simple sanity of the Holy Spirit's interpretation is wanting, hold the matter in abeyance. The one stamp of the right interpretation is its "warm" natural sanity, it is not fantastic or peculiar, it doesn't twist your brain, its makes you feel, "How marvellously simple and beautiful that is!"

The Holy Spirit's anointing "abideth in you," says John. At the beginning of your spiritual life you wanted to run off to this man and that, to this book and that, until you learn that "the anointing . . . abideth in you." John and Paul and Peter all insist on the superb right of the humblest believer to test the teacher by the anointing which is in him. If we put teachers over against the Holy Ghost, when God removes them we go down, we mourn and say, "What shall we do now?" Watch how Paul deals with the people who say, "I am of Paul; and I of Apollos; and I of Cephas"; he says in effect, "All teachers are yours." A teacher is simply meant to rouse us up to face the truths revealed in the Bible and witnessed to by the Holy Ghost. Watch the tendency which is in us all to try and safeguard God's truth. The remarkable thing is that God never safeguards His own truth; He leaves statements in this Book we can easily misrepresent, the only test is the Holy Spirit who leads us into all truth.

"And ye need not that any man teach you." It is here that Satan comes in as an angel of light and says, "If you are anointed by the Spirit, everything you think is right." Not at all. Only as we obey the Spirit and keep in the light does the anointing abide. Our thinking and common-sense reasoning must be rigorously subordinated to the Spirit, and if we abide true to Him He repairs the damage sin has done to conscience and mind and keeps our thinking vital and true. Notice in your own life how He works. He begins with the big general principles and then slowly educates you down to the scruple.[10]

(b) The Divine Union of Christian Thinking
But as the same anointing teacheth you of all things. (1 John 2:27)

We have perennially to rely on the one great Source of all teaching, viz.: the Holy Spirit; He puts us in an independent position towards all other teachers, and makes our dependence on Himself as the one Teacher the only basis of union there is, "the unity of the Spirit. . . . There is one body, and one Spirit, . . . one Lord, one faith, one baptism." *Be filled with the Spirit,* says Paul. We have all seen the seashore when the tide is out, with all its separate pools, how are those pools to be made one? by digging channels between them? No, wait till the tide comes in, and where are the pools? Absolutely lost, merged in one tremendous floodtide. That is exactly what happens when Christians are indwelt by the Holy Spirit. Once let people be filled with the Holy Spirit and you have the ideal of what the New Testament means by the Church. The Church is a separated band of people who are united to God by the regenerating power of the Spirit, and the bedrock of membership in the Church is that we know who Jesus is by a personal revelation of Him. The indwelling Spirit is the supreme Guide, and He keeps us absorbed with our Lord. The emphasis to-day is placed on the furtherance of an organisation; the note is, "We must keep this thing going." If we are in God's order the thing will go; if we are not in His order, it won't. Think of the works that are kept on after God wanted to rule them out of the way because they have a source of inspiration apart from Himself.

"Ye shall abide in Him." The test that we are being taught by the Holy Spirit is that our lives are proving identical with the life of the Son of God. You cannot have identity without individuality. False teaching says we lose our personality; we never do. Jesus Christ emancipates personality, and He makes individuality pronounced; but it is personality absolutely free from my right to myself, free from identity with any other personality, manifesting a strong family likeness to Jesus, and the transfiguring element is love to Himself.

THE PSYCHOLOGY OF FAITH I

1. The Constitution of Faith
And without faith it is impossible to be well-pleasing unto Him. (Hebrews 11:6 RV)

There is not possible a normal healthy human being apart from religious faith. Faith claims the whole man and all God's grace can make him.

Forsyth

The conception of faith given in the New Testament is that it must embrace the whole man. Faith is not a faculty, faith is the whole man rightly related to God by the power of the Spirit of Jesus. We are apt to apply faith to certain domains of our lives only—we have faith in God when we ask Him to save us, or ask Him for the Holy Spirit, but we trust something other than God in the actual details of our lives. "Faith claims the whole man and all that God's grace can make him," just as it claimed the whole of our Lord's life. Our Lord represents the normal man, not the average man, but the man according to God's norm. His life was not cut up into compartments, one part sacred and another secular, it was not in any way a mutilated life. Jesus Christ was concentrated on one line, viz., the will of His Father, in every detail of His life. That

---

10. down to the scruple: to the smallest item.

is the normal standard for each of us, and the miracle of the Gospel is that He can put us into the condition where we can grow into the same image. Our Lord lived His life not in order to show how good He was, but to give us the normal standard for our lives. The life He lived is made ours by means of His death; by the gift of the Holy Spirit and obedience to Him. We are put into the relationship to God that Jesus had—"that they may be one, even as We are one."

Faith is a tremendously active principle of trust in Jesus which is ready to venture on every word He speaks: "Lord, Thou hast said (e.g., Matthew 6:33: 'But seek ye first the kingdom of God, and His righteousness; and all these things shall be added unto you'); it looks mad, but I am going to venture on it; I will sink or swim on Thy word." We cannot have faith in every word of Jesus whenever we think we will. The Holy Spirit brings a word of Jesus to our remembrance and applies it to the circumstances we are in, and the point is, will we obey that particular word? We may have seen Jesus and known His power and yet never have ventured out in faith on Him. Faith must be tested because only through conflict can head-faith be turned into a personal possession. Faith according to Jesus must have its object real, no one can worship an ideal. We cannot have faith in God unless we know Him in Jesus Christ. God is a mere abstraction to our outlook until we see Him in Jesus and hear Him say, "He that hath seen Me hath seen the Father," then we have something to build upon and faith becomes boundless.

2. Faith and Confusing Issues
Even so faith, if it hath not works, is dead, being alone. (James 2:17; see vv. 17–20)

An inadequate theory of faith distorts practice.

          Forsyth

The Apostle James continually says, "If you have faith prove it by your life." Experience is never the ground of my faith; experience is the evidence of my faith. Many of us have had a marvellous experience of deliverance from sin and of the baptism of the Holy Ghost, not a fictional experience, but a real experience whereby we prove to our amazement every day that God has delivered us, then comes the danger that we pin our faith to our experience instead of to Jesus Christ, and if we do, faith becomes distorted. When the baptism of the Holy Ghost came upon the early disciples it made them the written epistles of what they taught, and it is to be the same with us. Our experience is the proof that our faith is right. Jesus Christ is always infinitely mightier than our faith, mightier than our experience, but our experience will be along the line of the faith we have in Him. Have

we faith to bear this testimony to those who know us—that we are what we are because of our faith in Jesus? We have faith in Jesus to save us, but do we prove that He has saved us by living a new life? I say I believe that Jesus can do this and that; well, has He done it? "But by the grace of God I am what I am." Are we monuments of the grace of God, or do we only experience God's supernatural power in our work for Him? Extraordinary spiritual experiences spring from something wrong in the life, you never get the exquisite simple faith in God along any special line of experience, but only along the common line of regeneration through faith in Jesus. Be sceptical of any revelation that has not got as its source the simplicity by means of which a "babe" can enter in, and which a "fool" can express.

3. Faith and Consecrated Issues
. . . work out your own salvation. (Philippians 2:12)

The normal course of all religious experience is expansion followed by concentration.

          Forsyth

When God gives a vision of what sanctification means or what the life of faith means, we have instantly to pay for the vision, and we pay for it by the inevitable law that "expansion must be followed by concentration." That means we must concentrate on the vision until it becomes real. Over and over again the vision is mistaken for the reality. God's great Divine anticipation can only be made manifest by our human participation, these two must not be put asunder. Every expansion of brain and heart that God gives in meetings or in private reading of the Bible must be paid for inevitably and inexorably by concentration on our part, not by consecration. God will continually bring us into circumstances to make us prove whether we will work out with determined concentration what He has worked in. If you have had a vivid religious experience of the baptism of the Holy Ghost, what are you going to do with it? We are sanctified by God's grace and made one with Jesus in order that we might sanctify our holiness to God as Jesus did. "And for their sakes I sanctify Myself" (John 17:19). There is no difficulty in getting sanctified if my will and affections have at their heart the earnest desire for God's glory. If I am willing for God to strangle in me the thing that makes me everlastingly hanker after my own point of view, my own interests, my own whiteness—if I am willing for all that to be put to death, then the God of peace will sanctify me wholly. Sanctification means a radical and absolute identification with Jesus until the springs of His life are the springs of my life. "Faithful is He that calleth you, who also will do it."

The great need to-day is for Christians to toe the line: "And the heathen shall know that I am the LORD, saith the Lord GOD, *when I shall be sanctified in you before their eyes*" (Ezekiel 36:23). Unless Christians are facing up to God's commands there is no use pushing forward to meet the life of our time. Jesus wants us to face the life of our time in the power of the Holy Ghost. Do we proclaim by our lives, by our thinking, by our faith in God, that Jesus Christ is sufficient for every problem life can present? that there is no force too great for Him to cope with and overcome? If our faith is not living and active it is because we need reviving; we have a faith that is limited by certain doctrines instead of being the faith of God.

The Apostle Paul is always tremendously practical, he comes right down to where we live, he says we must *work out* the salvation God has *worked in*. "All power is given unto Me," said Jesus, and by the Holy Spirit's presence we can do those things which please God— are we doing them? By the power of the indwelling

Holy Spirit we can bring every thought and imagination into captivity to the obedience of Christ, and can keep this body the chaste temple of the Holy Ghost— are we doing it? By the power of the Holy Spirit we can keep our communications with other people the exact expression of what God is working in us—are we doing it? The proof that we have a healthy vigorous faith is that we are expressing it in our lives, and bearing testimony with our lips as to how it came about.

There is no end to the life of faith; sanctification itself is only the ABC of the Christian life. The life of Jesus from Bethlehem onwards is a picture of the sanctified life, and anything that would make our souls stagnate produces a distortion. It is a continual learning, but not of the same lesson, if we have to be taught the same lesson it is because we have been very stupid. God will bring us into circumstances and make us learn the particular lessons He wants us to learn, and slowly and surely we will work out all that He works in. There is no patience equal to the patience of God.

THE PSYCHOLOGY OF FAITH II

1. Faith and the Son of God

. . . looking unto Jesus the author and perfecter of our faith. (Hebrews 12:2 RV)

He fought the battle, He proved the possibility of victory, He shewed us the place and revealed to us the secret of the power.

Forsyth

Jesus Christ is the Captain of our faith; He has gained the victory, consequently for us Satan is a conquered foe. When we are sanctified and have become "His brethren" we are put, not in the place of the first Adam, but in the place of the last Adam, where we live by the power and might of the faith of the Son of God. We have to get rid of the idea that because Jesus was God He could not be tempted. Almighty God cannot be tempted, but in Jesus Christ we deal with God as man, a unique Being—God-Man. It was as Son of Man that "He fought the battle, and proved the possibility of victory." After His Baptism, Satan, by the direct permission of the Holy Ghost, tested the faith of Jesus: "And straightway the Spirit driveth Him forth into the wilderness" (Mark 1:12 RV). Satan broke what Adam held straight off; but he could not break what Jesus held in His person though he tested Him in every conceivable way; therefore having Himself suffered being tempted, "He is able to succour them that are tempted."

When we are born again we get our first introduction into what God calls temptation. When we are sanctified we are not delivered from temptation, we are loosened into it; we are not free enough before either morally or spiritually to be tempted. Immediately we become His "brethren" we are free, and all these subtleties are at work. God does not shield any man or woman from any requirements of a full-grown man or woman. Luke 22:28 ("But ye are they which have continued with Me in My temptations") presents Our Lord's view of His life as Man, viz., as one of temptations, not triumphs. When we are born again the Son of God is submitted to temptations in our individual lives, are we remaining loyal to Him in His temptations in us? When temptation comes, stand absolutely true to God no matter what it costs you, and you will find the onslaught leaves you with affinities higher and purer than ever before. Temptation overcome is the transfiguration of the natural into the spiritual and the establishment of conscious affinity with the purest and best.

2. Faith and the Sons of God

Beloved, now are we the sons of God. (1 John 3:2)

Having been made sons of God does not absolve us from the lifelong task of actually making ourselves sons of God.

Forsyth

We have to take pains to make ourselves what God has taken pains to make us. You can take a horse to the trough, but you can't make him drink; you can send your child to school, but you can't make him study; and God can put a saint into a right relationship with Himself, but He cannot make him work out that relationship, the saint must do that himself. We must take the pains to make ourselves visibly all that God has made us invisibly. God alters our disposition, but He does not make our character. When God alters my disposition the first thing the new disposition will do is to stir up my brain to think along God's line. As I begin to think, begin to work out what God has worked in, it will become character. Character is consolidated thought. God makes me pure in heart; I must make myself pure in conduct. This point of working things out in actuality is apt to be lost sight of.

The business of faith is to convert Truth into reality. What do you really believe? take time and catalogue it up; are you converting your belief into reality? You say, "I believe God has sanctified me"—does your actual life prove He has? "I believe God has baptised me with the Holy Ghost"—why? Because you had cold shivers and visions and marvellous times of prayer? The proof that we are baptised with the Holy Ghost is that we bear a strong family likeness to Jesus, and men take knowledge of us, as they did of the disciples after Pentecost, that we have been with Jesus, they recognise the family likeness at once. True justification can only result in sanctification. By justification God anticipates that we are holy in His sight, and if we will obey the Holy Spirit we will prove in our actual life that God is justified in justifying us. Ask yourself—Is God justified in my justification? do I prove by the way I live and talk and do my work that God has made me holy? Am I converting God's purpose in justifying me into actual experience, or only delighting in God's anticipation? There is a great snare especially in evangelical circles of knowing the will of God as expressed in the Bible without the slightest practical working of it out in the life. The Christian religion is the most practical thing on earth. If the Holy Spirit has given you a vision in your private Bible study or during a meeting which made your heart glow, and your mind expand, and your will stir itself to grasp, you will have to pay to the last farthing in concentration along that line until all you saw in vision is made actual. During these past years there has been a terrific expansion in lives through bereavement and sorrow, everything in individual life has been altered, but there is the price to pay. The price is the same in national as in individual life.

The peculiar aspect of religious faith is that it is faith in a person who relates us to Himself and commits us to His point of view, not faith in a point of view divorced from relationship to a Person. "If you would know My doctrine," said Jesus, "do My will." Our Lord never teaches first by principles, but by personal relationship to Himself. When through His Redemption we become rightly related to Him personally, our hearts are unshakeably confident in Him. That is the Divine anticipation being participated in, the tremendous work of God's supernatural grace being manifested in our mortal flesh.

THE PSYCHOLOGY OF FAITH III

1. Mental Belief

But as many as received Him, to them gave He power to become the sons of God, even to them that believe on His name. (John 1:12)

John 1:12–13 is a grand, mighty, all-embracing word—"to as many as *received* Him . . ." The way mental belief works is that it leads us to understand who Jesus Christ is and what He can do for us and in us. Jesus Christ is the normal Man, the Man according to God's standard, and God demands of us the very holiness He exhibited.

A spiritually minded Christian has to go through the throes of a total mental readjustment; it is a God-glorifying process, if a humbling one. People continually say, "How can I have more faith?" You may ask for faith to further orders,[11] but you will never have faith apart from Jesus Christ. You can't pump up faith out of your own heart. Whenever faith is starved in your soul it is because you are not in contact with Jesus; get in contact with Him and lack of faith will go in two seconds. Whenever Jesus Christ came across people who were free from the ban of finality[12]

---

11. to further orders: ad infinitum; endlessly; the phrase, military origin, continuing present action until one receives different orders

12. ban of finality: the limitation or "curse" of having one's mind made up, unwilling to consider new information.

which comes from religious beliefs, He awakened faith in them at once. The only ones who were without faith in Him were those who were bound up by religious certitude. Faith means that I commit myself to Jesus, project myself absolutely on to Him, sink or swim—and you do both, you sink out of yourself and swim into Him. Faith is implicit confidence in Jesus and in His faith. It is one thing to have faith in Jesus and another thing to have faith about everything for which He has faith. Galatians 2:20 does not refer to the Apostle Paul's elementary faith in Jesus as his Saviour, but to the faith of Jesus. He says that the identical faith that was in Jesus Christ, the faith that governed His life, the faith which Satan could not break, is now in him through identification with the death of Jesus; the faith that characterised Him now characterises Paul.

2. Moral Belief
Knowing this, that our old man is crucified with Him, that the body of sin might be destroyed, that henceforth we should not serve sin. (Romans 6:6)

If we are honest and obedient, moral belief will follow mental belief very quickly. Am I poor enough, humble enough, and simple enough to believe in Jesus? Do I believe Him when He says that God will give me the Holy Spirit if I ask Him? If I do believe in Jesus and receive the Holy Spirit on the authority of His word, then I will have to make a moral decision about all that the Holy Spirit reveals. He will reveal to me what sin is, and He will reveal that Jesus Christ can deliver me from sin if I will agree with God's verdict on it in the Cross. Many of us do believe in Jesus, we have received the Holy Spirit and know we are children of God, and yet we won't make the moral decision about sin, viz., that it must be killed right out in us. It is the great moment of our lives when we decide that sin must die right out, not be curbed or suppressed or counteracted, but crucified. It is not done easily; it is only done by a moral wrench. We never understand the relation between a human life and the Cross of Christ until we perform a moral act and have the light of God thrown upon reality.

The transactions which tell in my life for God are moral decisions, not mental ones. I may think through everything there is in Christian doctrine and yet remain exactly the same; but I never make a moral decision and remain the same, and it is the moral decisions to which the Holy Spirit is always leading us on the basis of the Redemption. A moral decision is not a decision that takes time, one second is sufficient; what takes time is my stubborn refusal to come to the point of morally deciding. Here, where we sit, we can decide

whether or not the Redemption shall take its full course in us. Once I decide that it shall, the great inrush of the Redemption takes efficacious effect immediately. There are times when the Holy Spirit does touch us, times when there are "flashes struck from midnight" and we see everything clearly, and that is where the danger comes in, because we are apt to let those touches pass off in sentimental ardour instead of making a moral decision. It is a sensible delight to feel God so near, but unless a moral decision is made you will find it much harder next time to pay attention to the touch when it comes. It is better to decide without the accompaniment of the glow and the thrill—better to decide in cold blood, when your own will is in the ascendant, deliberately swayed by the rulership of Christ.

3. Mystic Belief
For ye are dead, and your life is hid with Christ in God. Colossians 3:3)

Paul is not talking to disembodied spirits, he is talking to men and women who have been through identification with the death of Jesus and know that their "old man" is crucified with Him. If we are born again of the Holy Ghost, and have made the moral decision to obey what He reveals about sin, then we must go on to believe that God can enable us to live for His glory in any circumstances He places us in. You can always detect the right kind of belief in Jesus by a flesh-and-blood testimony. "Ye shall know them by their fruits." Other people are not likely to confuse grapes with thorns, or figs with thistles. Mystic belief means that we enter into a conscious inheritance of what the Redemption has wrought for us, and daily, hourly, manifest the marvel of the grace of God in our actual lives. The majority of us "hang on" to Jesus Christ, we are thankful for the massive gift of salvation, but we don't do anything towards working it out. That is the difficult bit, and the bit the majority of us fall in, because we have not been taught that that is what we have to do, consequently there is a gap between our religious profession and our actual practical living. To put it down to human frailty is a wiggle, there is only one word for it, and that is "humbug." In my actual life I live below the belief which I profess. We can do nothing towards our salvation, but we can work out what God works in and the emphasis all through the New Testament is that God gives us sufficient energy to do it if we will. The great factor in Christian experience is the one our Lord continually brought out, viz., the reception of the Holy Spirit who does *in* us what He did *for* us, and slowly and surely our natural life is transformed into a spiritual life through obedience.

NOTES ON LAMENTATIONS

The Lamentations are not the expression of the grief of a disappointed man, the peculiar element in Jeremiah's sorrow is that he is identifying himself with an unrepentant people (cf. Daniel 9:4–20). We suffer on account of our own wrong or the wrong of others, but that is not vicarious suffering. Jeremiah's grief personifies vicariously the grief of the whole nation. Am I prepared to be a scapegoat for the sins of others for which they are still unrepentant?

Lamentations 1—*Elegy in Degradation*
How doth the city sit solitary, that was full of people! ... She weepeth sore in the night, and her tears are on her cheeks. (Lamentations 1:1–2)

The city herself is introduced weeping, and giving expression to her sorrow over the evil determined against her on account of her sins.

"How doth the city sit solitary." Being alone is not solitariness; solitariness is loneliness that has in it an element of moral dis-esteem: "Jerusalem hath grievously sinnedtherefore she is become as an unclean thing: all that honoured her despise her" (Lamentations 1:8). Cain's solitariness is typical of this loneliness; so is the loneliness of the prodigal son in the far country who starved on what the pigs throve on. Man was not created to be alone. Jesus Christ was rarely alone; the times when He was alone are distinctly stated. Solitariness to be beneficial must never be sought and must never be on account of sin. If I choose solitariness, I go back into active life with annoyance and a contempt for other people, proving that my seeking solitariness was selfish.

"He hath spread a net for my feet ..." (Lamentations 1:13). There is no choice after the choice is made, we are at the mercy of God's inexorable justice once the choice is made which leads "into the net." Our destiny is not determined for us, but it is determined by us. Man's free will is part of God's sovereign will. We have freedom to take which course we choose, but not freedom to determine the end of that choice. God makes clear what He desires, we must choose, and the result of the choice is not the inevitableness of law, but the inevitableness of God. Verse 18 gives the reason for all that is happening—"The LORD is righteous; for I have rebelled against His commandment." God will never change His character to please anyone's pleading or petulance if they have deliberately spurned His counsel.

There are irreparable losses in human life, and no amount of whining will alter it. The Garden of Eden was closed, not to naughty children, but to sinners, and is never again opened to sinners. "The way of the tree of life" is guarded, preventing man getting back as a sinner; he only gets back, and thank God he does get back, in and through the Redemption. What is prophesied with regard to Jerusalem is the attitude of the Spirit of God to the human race. The attitude of those, not indwelt by the Spirit of God is that man's capabilities are a promise of what he is going to be: the Holy Ghost sees man as a ruin of what he once was. He does not delight in his natural virtues. We are being told what a splendid race of human beings we are!—we are a race of rebels, and the rebellion has got to be destroyed. When the Holy Ghost is having His way with a man the first thing He does is to corrupt confidence in virtues which belong to a ruin. Nothing is more highly esteemed among men than pride in my virtues, i.e., self-realisation, but Jesus Christ said that "that which is highly esteemed among men is abomination in the sight of God." If this was realised we would understand the extravagant language of Scripture about sin.

Lamentations 2—*Elegy in Destruction*
How hath the Lord covered the daughter of Zion with a cloud in His anger! He hath cast down from heaven unto the earth the beauty of Israel. . . . (Lamentations 2:1 RV)

The prophets of God have always one burden when they deal with the judgements of God, and that is that they come not from the east, nor from the west, but are directly stamped as "from the Lord." The tendency to-day is to put the consequences of sin as natural consequences: the consequences of sin have a righteous God behind them. We have taken the Bible idea out of punishment and say, "Oh well, it is the inevitable result"; the Bible says the inevitable result is brought about by a personal God.

"The Lord is become as an enemy ..." (Lamentations 2:5 RV). Deliverance comes through destruction, and for a while the soul does not know whether God is a friend or an enemy. God has one purpose in destruction, and that is the deliverance of His own. God's own is not *you*, but His own *in you*. All that is saved is the work of God in a man, nothing else. Destruction means the obliteration of every characteristic of the life that is not rooted in godliness, it never means the annihilation of the life. The judgements of God are a consuming fire whereby He destroys in order to deliver; the time to be alarmed in life is when all things are undisturbed. The knowledge that God is a consuming fire is the greatest comfort to the saint, it

is His love at work on those characteristics that are not true to godliness. The saint who is near to God knows no burning, but the farther away from God the sinner gets, the more the fire of God burns him.

In verses 1–9 the wrath of God is emphasised. God's love is wrath towards wrong; He is never tender to that which hates goodness. All through the Bible reveals that when once communion with God is severed the basis of life is chaos and wrath. The chaotic elements may not show themselves at once, but they will presently. All that this Book says about corruption in connection with the flesh is as certain as God is on His throne if the life is not rightly related to God. When we speak of the wrath of God we must not picture Him as an angry sultan on the throne of heaven, bringing a lash about people when they do what He does not want. There is no element of personal vindictiveness in God. It is rather that God's constitution of things is such that when a man becomes severed from God his life tumbles into turmoil and confusion, into agony and distress, it is hell at once, and he will never get out of it unless he turns to God; immediately he turns, chaos is turned into cosmos, wrath into love, distress into peace. "Knowing therefore the terror of the Lord" we persuade men to keep in touch with Him. The world pays no attention to those who tell them how God convicted of sin and how He delivered them; the warnings of God are of no use to sinners until they are convicted of sin and the warnings become applicable to them.

"The elders of the daughter of Zion sit upon the ground, they keep silence" (Lamentations 2:10 RV). When God's destructions are abroad there is no power to move, only to sit; no power to speak, only to keep silence. It is not a time for social intercourse of any kind, but for the deepest dejection.

"Mine eyes do fail with tears . . . for the destruction of the daughter of my people." No prophet stands so close to Jesus Christ as Jeremiah, he is the one who realises human conditions more keenly than any other and identifies himself with them. Verses 11–19 are thus lamentation over the impotence of human consolation.

"Thy prophets . . . have not discovered thine iniquity" (Lamentations 2:14). The prophet with a message based on human morality excuses sin instead of detecting it—"God knows you can't help this sort of thing"—that is a lie. "Under the circumstances you will be excused." Jeremiah was indignant with those prophets who gave a wrong application to God's message: "Sin is sin; but you don't need to imagine that that is the reason for what God is doing"; Jeremiah held to it that it was the reason.

". . . the day of the LORD's anger" (Lamentations 2:22). When God's limit is reached, He destroys into salvation; He destroys the unsaveable and liberates the saveable. Judgement days are an overflowing mercy because they separate between right and wrong. To be experimental in me the salvation of Jesus Christ is always a judgement, and it brings the understanding of God's justice even in His severest judgements. If we compare our attitude with the revelations made in God's Book we find how despicably shallow we are. Our attitude is not one of sympathy of God, not a sensitive understanding of His point of view, only an amazing sensitiveness over our own calamities and those of other people, consequently we act on the principle of giving "a pill to cure an earthquake." When God is squeezing the life of a man or of a nation in order to save the remnant, what is the use of my coming and kicking at the fingers of God and saying, "I shan't allow You to do this"? If our human sympathy with the one who is suffering under the hand of God is justified, then God is cruel. Some of us are so set on our own honour that we have no time for God's honour.

"Is this the city that men called The perfection of beauty, The joy of the whole earth?" (Lamentations 2:15 RV). Jeremiah is referring to the desolation which, by God's own decree, has fallen on everything God made to be holy; he sees God's judgement on His own choicest things—Jerusalem ruined, the Temple destroyed. "See, O LORD, and behold, to whom Thou hast done this!" (Lamentations 2:20 RV). And Jeremiah's whole heart was in Jerusalem! God did not spare His people. His judgement on them was as unconquerably certain as it was on Babylon, and as it is on us. No amount of pleading will ever alter the judgements of God.

Lamentations 3—*Elegy in Desolation*
Surely against me He turneth His hand again and again all the day. . . . (Lamentations 3:3 RV)

Obedience to God will mean that some time or other you enter into desolation; if you don't obey, you won't—for a time. Jeremiah is speaking in vicarious terms of the sorrow and anguish of the people under God's chastisement; he is not cutting a cross-section through his own personal grief, not writing his own spiritual autobiography. Jeremiah is a vicarious sufferer, that is, he does not find his place in other people, he lets other people find their place in him. Our attitude too often is—"Oh, that has nothing to do with me, I have enough to bear." We will be of no use in God's service until that spirit is removed. God so loves the world that He hates the wrong in it. Do I so love men and women that I hate the wrong in them? Most of us love other people for what they are to us instead of for what God wants them to be. The distress worked in a man's heart by the Holy Ghost is never on his own account, but always on God's account.

Desperate tides of the whole great world's anguish
Forced thro' the channels of a single heart.

Have I ever shared for a moment God's concern over people, or am I putting myself in a bandage before God and saying, "I can't stand any more"?

"Wherefore doth a living man complain, a man for the punishment of his sins?" (Lamentations 3:39). The judgements of God leave scars, and the scars remain until I humbly and joyfully recognise that the judgements are deserved and that God is justified in them. The last delusion God delivers us from is the idea that we don't deserve what we get. Once we see ourselves under the canopy of God's overflowing mercy we are dissolved in wonder, love and praise. That is the meaning of repentance, which is the greatest gift God ever gives a man. As long as my heart has never been broken by conviction of sin, I don't understand the psalmist when he says, "The sacrifices of God are a broken spirit: a broken and a contrite heart, O God, Thou wilt not despise" (Psalm 51:17). When you get there God is the only Reality; but you only get there through heartbreak and sorrow. Holiness is based on repentance, and the holy man is the most humble man you can meet. My realisation of God can be measured by my humility.

Jeremiah's reliance on the justice of God breaks into a prayer in which is manifested his confidence that God will send help—"I called upon Thy name, O LORD, out of the lowest dungeon. Thou heardest my voice; hide not Thine ear at my breathing, at my cry" (Lamentations 3:55–56 RV).

Lamentations 4—*Elegy in Dispersion*
When they fled away and wandered, men said among the nations, They shall no more sojourn here. (Lamentations 4:15 RV)

"How is the gold become dim! How is the most pure gold changed!" (Lamentations 4:1 RV). It is the holiest things that are desolated. God ordained the Temple, Jerusalem was His holy city, and yet He allows them to be ruined. Flesh and blood, man's body, is meant to be "the temple of the Holy Ghost"—God's "gold," but sin renders it disreputable. The depth of possible sin is measured by the height of possible holiness. When men come under conviction of sin by the Holy Spirit their "beauty is consumed away," like as it were a moth fretting a garment. The misery which conviction brings enables a man to realise what God created him for, viz., to glorify God and enjoy Him for ever.

"For the iniquity of the daughter of my people is greater than the sin of Sodom, that was overthrown as in a moment" (Lamentations 4:6 RV). The destruction of Sodom was a sudden calamity; the destruction of Jerusalem was a terribly long, heartrending depreciation of everything of value in God's sight.

"It is because of the sins of her prophets, and the iniquities of her priests, that have shed the blood of the just in the midst of her" (Lamentations 4:13 RV). Beware of iniquity, which means conjuring yourself out of the straight; finding out reasons why you did not do what you know you should have done. The term "iniquity" is used only of the people of God. To "shed just blood" refers to more than actual murder. The Bible never deals with proportionate sin; according to the Bible an impure thought is as bad as adultery; a covetous thought is as bad as a theft. It takes a long education in the things of God before we believe that is true. Never trust innocence when it is contradicted by the word of God. The tiniest bit of sin is an indication of the vast corruption that is in the human heart. ("For from within, out of the heart of men, proceed . . ." Mark 7:21–23). That is why we must keep in the light all the time. Never allow horror at crime to blind you to the fact that it is human nature like your own that committed it. A saint is never horror-stricken because although he knows that what our Lord says about the human heart is true, he knows also of a Saviour who can save to the uttermost.

"Thine iniquity hath an end" (Lamentations 4:22 RV mg). My guilt is ended when I repent, when I stop admitting and begin confessing. Am I blaming any of my forebears for my present condition? Then my punishment will go on till I blame them no more. Am I blaming the circumstances in which I live? Then my punishment will go on till I stop blaming my circumstances. As long as I have any remnant of an idea that I can be cleared in any other way than by God through the Redemption, my punishment will go on. The instant I stop blaming everything but myself, and acquit God of injustice to me, my recognition of Him begins.

Lamentations 5—*Elegy in Devotion*
Remember, O LORD, what is come upon us: behold, and see our reproach. (Lamentations 5:1 RV)

What had Jeremiah done to deserve in the tiniest degree all that has come upon him? Nothing but obey God in every detail, and because of his obedience he was in the midst of the distress. The one man who has kept unspottedly right with God is in all the desolation, realising it more keenly than any of those who deserved it. A snare spirituality is to refuse to bear about "in the body the dying of Jesus," and prefer the gay hilarity which is only possible for long in the new heaven and new earth. We are here for one purpose: to "fill up . . . that which is lacking of the afflictions of Christ" (RV)—spoilt for this age, alive to nothing but Jesus Christ's point of view. In this order of things it is a maimed life, and few of us will have it; we prefer a full-orbed life of infinite satisfaction which makes us absolutely crass to what is happening in "Jerusalem."

We can never be marked by the angel as those who sigh and cry for the sorrows of Jerusalem.

"Our fathers have sinned, and are not; and we have borne their iniquities" Lamentations 5:7). These words are not to be understood as intimating that the speakers conceived themselves innocent—"Woe unto us! *for we have sinned"* (Lamentations 5:16 RV). The sins of the fathers are not visited on innocent children, but on children who continue the sins of their fathers (see Exodus 20:5). Distinction must be made between punishment and suffering, they are not synonymous terms. A bad man's relation to his children is in God's hand: the child's relation to the badness of his father is in his own hand. Because we see children suffering physically for the sins of their parents, we say they are being punished; they are not, there is no element of punishment in their suffering; there are Divine compensations we know nothing about. The whole subject of heredity and what is transmitted by heredity, if taken out of its Bible setting, can be made the greatest slander against God, as well as the greatest exoneration of the bitterness of a man's spirit.

"The crown is fallen from our head. . . . For this our heart is faint; for these things our eyes are dim" (Lamentations 5:16–17). These words convey the poignancy of penitence. Nothing will make a man's heart "cave in" and his eyes stop seeing, saving sin. Sorrow won't do it, misfortune won't do it, hardship won't do it; on the contrary these things, if there is no sin, make a man's heart strong. The "fallen crown" is the figurative expression for the honourable position of the people of God which they have now lost. Sin may make a man more desirable in the eyes of the world—"the sin which is admired of many" (Hebrews 12:1 RV mg), but what makes a man ugly physically, morally and spiritually is the discovery of sin by his own heart, and all attempts to justify himself spring from the depth of conviction of private sin.

The gathering in of God's salvation around a man means that he is checked at first by the merest zephyr touch, there is nothing so gentle as the check of the Holy Spirit; if he obeys, emancipation is at once, if he does not obey, the zephyr touch will turn into a destructive blow from which there is no escape. There is never any shattering blow of God on the life that pays attention to the checks of the Spirit, but every time there is a spurning of the still small voice, the hardening of the life away from God goes on until destruction comes and shatters it. When I realise that there is something between God and me, it is at the peril of my soul I don't stop everything and get it put right. Immediately a thing makes itself conscious to me, it has no business there.

To sum up the Lamentations would be to say that the words of this vicarious sufferer direct the grieving human heart, in its deep sorrow, to the only true Comfort.

DUTY OF THE HEART
Mark 12:28–34

And one of the scribes . . . asked Him, Which is the first commandment of all? Mark 12:28

In answering the scribe's question Our Lord does not say anything original, He takes two commandments from their place in the Old Testament, where they are obscured (see Deuteronomy 6:5, Leviticus 19:18) and brings them out into a startling light. "Think not," He said, "that I am come to destroy the law, or the prophets: I am not come to destroy, but to fulfil."

1. Duty of Love for God
And thou shalt love the Lord thy God with all thy heart, and with all thy soul, and with all thy mind, and with all thy strength: this is the first commandment.

Where do we find ourselves with regard to this first great duty—"Thou shalt love the Lord thy God with all thy heart"? What does that phrase mean to us? If Jesus had said, "Thou shalt love thy lover with all thy heart," we would have known what He meant. Well, He did mean that, but the Lover is to be God. The majority of us have an ethereal, unpractical, bloodless abstraction which we call "love for God"; to Jesus love for God meant the most passionate intense love of which a human being is capable.

The writer to the Hebrews states that Jesus Christ was "perfected through sufferings," but there is any amount of suffering that "im-perfects" us because it springs from unregulated passions. This fact has made some ethical teachers say that the passions themselves are evil, something human nature suffers from. Our Lord teaches that the passions are to be regulated by this first duty of love for God. The way we are to overcome the world, the flesh and the devil is by the force of our love for God regulating all our passions until every force of body, soul and spirit is devoted to this first great duty. This is the one sign of sanctification in a life; any experience of sanctification which is less than that has something diseased about it.

If my first duty is to love God, the practical, sensible question to ask is, What is God like? Aristotle taught that love for God does not exist; "it is absurd to talk of such a thing, for God is an unknown being." The Apostle Paul met with the result of his teaching in his day—"Ye men of Athens, . . . as I passed by, and beheld your devotions [the gods ye worship, mg] I found an altar with this inscription, TO THE UNKNOWN GOD. Whom therefore ye ignorantly worship, Him declare I unto you" (Acts 17:22–23). To-day the teaching in many of our own colleges and universities is being honeycombed with pagan philosophy, pagan ethics, consequently there is a state of mind produced that appreciates what Aristotle said, that we cannot know God. Then what a startling statement Jesus made when He said, "Thou shalt love the Lord thy God with all thy heart"!

"No man hath seen God at any time; the only begotten Son, which is in the bosom of the Father, He hath declared Him" (John 1:18). Jesus knew God, and He makes Him known: "He that hath seen Me hath seen the Father." Get into the habit of recalling to your mind what Jesus was like when He was here, picture what He did and what He said, recall His gentleness and tenderness as well as His strength and sternness, and then say, "That is what God is like." I do not think it would be difficult for us to love Jesus if He went in and out among us as in the days of His flesh, healing the sick and diseased, restoring the distracted, putting right those who were wrong, reclaiming backsliders—I do not think it would be difficult for us to love Him. That is to love God. The great Lover of God is the Holy Spirit, and when we receive the Holy Spirit we find we have a God whom we can know and whom we can love with all our heart because we see "the light of the knowledge of the glory of God in the face of Jesus Christ."

2. Duty of Love to Man

And the second is like, namely this, Thou shalt love thy neighbour as thyself.

Everything our Lord taught about the duty of man to man might be summed up in the one law of giving. It is as if He set Himself to contradict the natural counsel of the human heart, which is to acquire and keep. A child will say of a gift, "Is it my own?" When a man is born again that instinct is replaced by another, the instinct of giving. The law of the life of a disciple is Give, Give, Give (e.g., Luke 6:38). As Christians our giving is to be proportionate to all we have received of the infinite giving of God. "Freely ye have received, freely give." Not how much we give, but what we do not give, is the test of our Christianity. When we speak of giving we nearly always think only of money. Money is the life-blood of most of us. We have a remarkable trick—when we give money we don't give sympathy; and when we give sympathy we don't give money. The only way to get insight into the meaning for ourselves of what Jesus taught is by being indwelt by the Holy Spirit, because He enables us first of all to understand our Lord's life; unless we do that, we will exploit His teaching, take out of it only what we agree with. There is one aspect of giving we think little about, but which had a prominent place in our Lord's life, viz., that of social intercourse. He accepted hospitality on the right hand and on the left, from publicans and from the Pharisees, so much so that they said He was "a gluttonous man, and a winebibber, a friend of publicans and sinners!" He spent Himself with one lodestar all the time, to seek and to save that which was lost, and Paul says, "I am become all things to all men, that I may by all means save some" (RV). How few of us ever think of giving socially! We are so parsimonious that we won't spend a thing in conversation unless it is on a line that helps us!

"And who is my neighbour?" (Luke 10:29). Jesus gives an amazing reply, viz., that the answer to the question, "Who is my neighbour?" is not to be found in the claim of the person to be loved, but in the heart of the one who loves. If my heart is right with God, every human being is my neighbour. There is engrained in the depths of human nature a dislike of the general ruck of mankind, in spite of all our modern jargon about "loving Humanity." We have a disparaging way of talking about the common crowd: the common crowd is made up of innumerable editions of you and me. Ask the Holy Spirit to enable your mind to brood for one moment on the value of the "nobody" to Jesus. The people who make up the common crowd are nobodies to me, but it is astonishing to find that it is the nobodies that Jesus Christ came to save. The terms we use for men in the sense of their social position are nothing to Him. There is no room in Christianity as Jesus Christ taught it for philanthropic or social patronage. Jesus Christ never patronised anyone, He came right straight down to where men live in order that the supreme gift He came to give might be theirs—"The Spirit of the Lord is upon Me, because He hath anointed Me to preach the gospel to the poor." It is only by getting our mind into the state of the Mind of Jesus that we can understand how it is possible to fulfil the royal law and love our neighbour as ourselves. We measure our generosity by the standards of men; Jesus says, "Measure your love for men by God's love for them, and if you are My disciple, you will love your neighbour *as I have loved you.*"

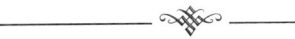

HOLINESS

1. Imitated

. . . leaving us an example, that ye should follow His steps. (1 Peter 2:21)

For one child to imitate another child only results in a more or less clever affectation; a child imitating his parents assists the expression of inherent tendencies, naturally and simply, because he is obeying a nascent instinct. It is to this form of imitation that Peter alludes. When a saint imitates Jesus, he does it easily because he has the Spirit of Jesus in him. Pharisaic holiness, both ancient and modern, is a matter of imitation, seeking by means of prayer and religious exercises to establish, seriously and arduously, but un-regeneratedly, a self-determined holiness. The only spiritually holy life is a God-determined life. "Be ye holy; for I am holy." If our best obedience, our most spotless moral walking, our most earnest prayers, are offered to God in the very least measure as the ground of our acceptance by Him, it is a fatal denial of the Atonement.

2. Imputed

. . . unto whom God imputeth righteousness without works. (Romans 4:6)

To impute means "to attribute vicariously"; it is a theological word. The revelation made by the Apostle Paul, viz., that God imputes righteousness to us, is the great truth at the basis of all our Protestant theology; we are apt to forget this to-day. Righteousness means living and acting in accordance with right and justice, that is, it must express itself in a man's bodily life. "Little children, let no man deceive you: he that *doeth* righteousness is righteous" (1 John 3:7). Imputed righteousness must never be made to mean that God puts the robe of His righteousness over our moral wrong, like a snow-drift over a rubbish heap; that He pretends we are all right when we are not. The revelation is that "Christ Jesus . . . is made unto us . . . righteousness"; it is the distinct impartation of the very life of Jesus on the ground of the Atonement, enabling me to walk in the light as God is in the light, and as long as I remain in the light God sees only the perfections of His Son. We are "accepted in the Beloved."

3. Imparted

. . . not having a righteousness of mine own, . . . but that which is through faith in Christ. (Philippians 3:9 RV)

The only holiness there is is the holiness derived through faith, and faith is the instrument the Holy Spirit uses to organise us into Christ. But do not let us be vague here. Holiness, like sin, is a disposition, not a series of acts. A man can act holy, but he has not a holy *disposition*. A saint has had imparted to him the disposition of holiness, therefore holiness must be the characteristic of the life here and now. Entire sanctification is the end of the disposition of sin, but only the beginning of the life of a saint, then comes growth in holiness. The process of sanctification begins at the moment of birth from above (RV mg) and is consummated on the unconditional surrender of my right to myself to Jesus Christ. The time that elapses between new birth and entire sanctification depends entirely on the individual. Many souls have had such a blessed vision of an entirely sanctified life during Conventions, or in times of rare communion with God, that they imagine they have the reality, and it is at this stage that that subtle heresy, "Deeper death to self" is apt to lead them astray. The vision is followed by a deep valley of humiliation, by a cross of death, before the unspeakable reality is realised. If we have reached the stage of entire sanctification and have presented our bodies to be "a living sacrifice, holy, acceptable to God," what are we doing with our holy selves? Jesus Christ gives us the key to the life of the saint—"And for their sakes I sanctify Myself" (John 17:19). We are sanctified for one purpose only, that we might "sanctify our sanctification," i.e., deliberately give it to God.

4. Habitual

Be ye transformed by the renewing of your mind. (Romans 12:2)

Practical holiness is the only holiness of any value in this world, and the only kind the Spirit of God will endorse. If we consider what Professor James[13] says in his scientific exposition of habit, it will be a great rebuke to our lazy neglect in finding out what we have to do to work out in actual life the holy disposition given us through the Atonement:

---

13. William James (1842–1910): American philosopher, psychologist, and teacher, published *The Principles of Psychology* in 1890.

(a) In the acquisition of a new habit, or the leaving off of an old one, we must launch ourselves with as strong and decided initiative as possible.

(b) Never suffer an exception to occur till the new habit is securely rooted in your life.

(c) Seize the very first possible opportunity to act on every resolution you make, and on every emotional prompting you may experience in the direction of the habits you aspire to gain.

Romans 12:2 is the Apostle Paul's passionate entreaty that we should rouse ourselves out of that stagnation which must end in degeneration, in which we are ensnared by thinking because it is "all of grace" there is no need for "gumption." Grace, Grit, Glory is the graduation course. Professor James says "we must launch ourselves with as strong and decided initiative as possible": as saints have we not a strong and decided initiative? Born again of the Spirit, cleansed from all sin, sanctified to do the will of God? "Be ye transformed by the renewing of your mind," says Paul.

It is because we have failed to realise that God requires intellectual vigour on the part of a saint that the devil gets his hold on the stagnant mental life of so many. To be transformed by the renewing of our mind means the courageous lifting of all our problems, individual, family, social and civic, into the spiritual domain, and habitually working out a life of practical holiness there. It is not an easy task, but a gloriously difficult one, requiring the mightiest effort of our human nature, a task which lifts us into thinking God's thoughts after Him.

"*That ye may prove what is the good, and acceptable, and perfect, will of God.*" God's will is only clearly understood by the development of spiritual character, consequently saints interpret the will of God differently at different times. It is not God's will that alters, but the saint's development in character. Only by intense habitual holiness, by the continual renewing of our mind, and the maintenance of an unworldly spirit, can we be assured of God's will concerning us, "even the thing which is good and acceptable and perfect" (RV mg).

THE MATURE CHRISTIAN

Ye therefore shall be perfect, as your heavenly Father is perfect. Matthew 5:48 (RV)

In Matthew 5, verses 29–30 and verse 48 respectively our Lord refers to two things which are full of vital instruction. In verses 29–30 He is referring to the necessity of a maimed life: "And if thy right eye offend thee, pluck it out, and cast it from thee"; in Matthew 5:48 He refers to the life which is not maimed, but perfect. These two statements embrace the whole of our spiritual life from beginning to end.

"Ye therefore shall be perfect, as your heavenly Father is perfect" (RV). God is so almightily simple that it is impossible to complicate Him, impossible to put evil into Him or bring evil out of Him; impossible to alter His light and His love, and the nature of the faith born in me by the Holy Ghost will take me back to the Source and enable me to see what God is like, and until I am all light and all love in Him, the things in me which are not of that character will have to pass. In the beginning of Christian experience the life is maimed because we are learning. There is the right eye to be plucked out, the right hand to be cut off, and we are apt to think that is all God means; it is not. What God means is what Jesus said, "Ye shall be perfect, as your heavenly Father is perfect." When we discern that the sword that is brought across our

natural life is not for destruction, but for discipline, we get His idea exactly.

God never destroys the work of His own hands, He removes what would pervert it, that is all. Maturity is the stage where the whole life has been brought under the control of God.

1. The Upward Look

Psalm 121 portrays the upward look—"I will lift up mine eyes unto the mountains: from whence shall my help come? My help cometh from the LORD, which made heaven and earth" (RV). The upward look of a mature Christian is not to the mountains, but to the God who made the mountains. It is the maintained set of the highest powers of a man—not star-gazing till he stumbles, but the upward gaze deliberately set towards God. He has got through the "choppy waters" of his elementary spiritual experience and now he is set on God. "I have set the LORD always before me"—but you have to fight for it.

2. The Forward Look

"Thine eyes shall see the king in his beauty: they shall behold a far stretching land ['a land of far distances,' mg]" (Isaiah 33:17 RV). The forward look is the look that sees everything in God's perspective whereby His wonderful distance is put on the things that are near.

Caleb had the perspective of God; the men who went up with him saw only the inhabitants of the land as giants and themselves as grasshoppers. Learn to take the long view and you will breathe the benediction of God among the squalid things that surround you. Some people never get ordinary or commonplace, they transfigure everything they touch because they have got the forward look which brings their confidence in God out into the actual details of life. The faith that does not react in the flesh is very immature. Paul was so identified with Jesus Christ that he had the audacity to say that what men saw in his life in the flesh was the very faith of the Son of God. Galatians 2:20 is the most audacious verse in the Bible! Paul is not referring to his own elementary faith in Jesus Christ as his Saviour, but to the faith of the Son of God, and he says that that identical faith is now in him.

Fortitude in trial comes from having the long view of God. No matter how closely I am imprisoned by poverty, or tribulation, I see "the land that is very far off," and there is no drudgery on earth that is not turned Divine by the very sight. Abraham did not always have the forward look, that is why he did a scurry down to Egypt when there was a famine in the land of promise. Why shouldn't I starve for the glory of God? Immediately I fix on God's "goods," I lose the long view. If I give up to God because I want hundredfold more, I never see God.

3. The Backward Look

And thine ears shall hear a word behind thee saying, This is the way, walk ye in it, when ye turn to the right hand, and when ye turn to the left. (Isaiah 30:21)

The surest test of maturity is the power to look back without blinking anything. When we look back we get either hopelessly despairing or hopelessly conceited. The difference between the natural backward look and the spiritual backward look is in what we forget. Forgetting in the natural domain is the outcome of vanity—the only things I intend to remember are those in which I figure as being a very fine person! Forgetting in the spiritual domain is the gift of God. The Spirit of God never allows us to forget what we have been, but He does make us forget what we have attained to, which is quite unnatural. The surest sign that you are growing in mature appreciation of your salvation is that as you look back you never think now of the things you used to bank on before. Think of the difference between your first realisation of God's forgiveness, and your realisation of what it cost God to forgive you; the hilarity in the one case has been merged into holiness, you have become intensely devoted to God who forgave you.

PERFECT LOVE

But whoso keepeth His word, in him verily is the love of God perfected. 1 John 2:5

If we love one another, God dwelleth in us, and His love is perfected in us. 1 John 4:12

1. In Abandoned Indwelling *(Romans 5:5)*

There is only one Being who loves perfectly, and that is God, yet the New Testament distinctly states that we are to love as God does; so the first step is obvious. If ever we are going to have perfect love in our hearts we must have the very nature of God in us. In Romans 5:5 the Apostle Paul tells us how this is possible; he says, "the love of God is shed abroad in our hearts by the Holy Ghost which is given unto us." He is speaking not of the power to love God, but of the very love of God itself which is "shed abroad"—a superabounding word, it means that the love of God takes possession of every crook and cranny of our nature. The practical question to ask therefore is, Have I received the Holy Spirit? has it ever come to an issue with me? There is nothing on earth like the love of God when once it breaks on the soul, it may break at a midnight or a dawn, but always as a great surprise, and we begin to experience the uniting of our whole being with the nature of God. Everything in that moment becomes easy, no command of Jesus is difficult to obey. It is not our power to love God that enables us to obey, but the presence of the very love of God in our heart which makes it so easy to obey Him that we don't even know we are obeying. As you recall to your mind the touchings of the love of God in your life they are always few—you will never find it impossible to do anything He asks.

When the love of God has been shed abroad in our hearts we have to exhibit it in the strain of life; when we are saved and sanctified we are apt to think that there is no strain, but Paul speaks of the "tribulation" which "worketh patience." I mean by strain, not effort, but the possibility of going wrong as well as of going right. There is always a risk, for this reason, that God values our obedience to Him. When

God saves and sanctifies a man his personality is raised to its highest pitch of freedom, he is free now to sin if he wants to; before, he is not free, sin is impelling and urging him; when he is delivered from sin he is free not to sin, or free to sin if he chooses. The doctrine of sinless perfection and consequent freedom from temptation runs on the line that because I am sanctified, I cannot now do wrong. If that is so, you cease to be a man. If God put us in such a condition that we could not disobey, our obedience would be of no value to Him. But blessed be His Name, when by His redemption the love of God is shed abroad in our hearts, He gives us something to do to manifest it. Just as human nature is put to the test in the actual circumstances of life, so the love of God in us is put to the test. "Keep yourselves in the love of God," says Jude, that is keep your soul open not only to the fact that God loves you, but that He is *in* you, in you sufficiently to manifest His perfect love in every condition in which you can find yourself as you rely upon Him. The curious thing is that what we are apt, too apt, to restrain is the love of God; we have to be careless of the expression and heed only the Source. Let our Lord be allowed to give the Holy Spirit to a man, deliver him from sin, and put His own love within him, and that man will love Him personally, passionately and devotedly. It is not an earning or a working for, but a gift and a receiving.

2. In Abandoned Identification

Love suffereth long, and is kind. (1 Corinthians 13:4 RV; see 1 Corinthians 13:4–7)

For the love of Christ constraineth us. (2 Corinthians 5:14)

The Holy Ghost sheds abroad the love of God in our hearts and in 1 Corinthians 13 we see how that perfect love is to be expressed in actual life. "Love suffereth long, and is kind. . . ." Substitute "the Lord" for "love," and it comes home. Jesus is the love of God Incarnate. The only exhibition of the love of God in human flesh is our Lord, and John says "as He is, even so are we in this world" (RV). God expects His love to be manifested in our redeemed lives. We make the mistake of imagining that service for others springs from love of others; the fundamental fact is that supreme love for our Lord alone gives us the motive power of service to any extent for others—"ourselves your servants for Jesus' sake." That means I have to identify myself with God's interests in other people, and God is interested in some extraordinary people, viz., in you and in me, and He is just as interested in the person you dislike as He is in you. I don't know what your natural heart was like before God saved you, but I know what mine was like. I was misunderstood and misrepresented; everybody else was wrong and I was right. Then when God came and gave me a spring-cleaning, dealt with my sin, and filled me with the Holy Spirit, I began to find an extraordinary alteration in myself. I still think the great marvel of the experience of salvation is not the alteration others see in you, but the alteration you find in yourself. When you come across certain people and things and remember what you used to be like in connection with them, and realise what you are now by the grace of God, you are filled with astonishment and joy; where there used to be a well of resentment and bitterness, there is now a well of sweetness.

God grant we may not only experience the indwelling of the love of God in our hearts, but go on to a hearty abandon to that love so that God can pour it out through us for His redemptive purposes for the world. He broke the life of His own Son to redeem us, and now He wants to use our lives as a sacrament to nourish others.

SACRAMENTAL CHRISTIANITY

The word "sacramental" must be understood to mean the real presence of Christ being conveyed through the actual elements of the speech and natural life of a Christian. "Every one therefore who shall *confess* Me before men," that is, confess with every part of me that—"Jesus Christ has come in the flesh" come, not only historically, but *in my flesh.*

1. Sacramental Service

But far be it from me to glory, save in the cross of our Lord Jesus Christ, through whom[mg] the world hath been crucified unto me, and I unto the world. (Galatians 6:14 RV)

By the Cross of Christ I am saved from sin; by the Cross of Christ I am sanctified; but I never am a sacramental disciple until I deliberately lay myself on the altar of the Cross, and give myself over emphatically and entirely to be actually what I am potentially in the sight of God, viz., a member of the Body of Christ. When I swing clear of myself and my own consciousness and give myself over to Jesus Christ, He can use me as a sacrament to nourish other lives.

Most of us are on the borders of consciousness, consciously serving, consciously devoted to God; it is all immature, it is not the life yet. Maturity is the life of a child—a child is never consciously childlike—so abandoned to God that the thought of being made broken bread and poured-out wine no longer unseals the fountain of tears.

When you are consciously being used as broken bread and poured-out wine you are interested in your own martyrdom, it is consciously costing you something; when you are laid on the altar of the Cross all consciousness of self is gone, all consciousness of what you are doing for God, or of what God is doing through you, is gone. It is no longer possible to talk about "my experience of sanctification"; you are brought to the place where you understand what is meant by our Lord's words, "Ye shall be My witnesses" (RV). Wherever a saint goes, everything he or she does becomes a sacrament in God's hands, unconsciously to himself. You never find a saint being consciously used by God; He uses some casual thing you never thought about, which is the surest evidence that you have got beyond the stage of conscious sanctification, you are beyond all consciousness because God is taking you up into His consciousness; you are His, and life becomes the natural simple life of a child. To be everlastingly on the look-out to do some work for God means I want to evade sacramental service—"I want to do what I want to do." Maintain the attitude of a child towards God and He will do what He likes with you. If God puts you on the shelf it is in order to season you. If He is pleased to put you in limited circumstances so that you cannot go out into the highways of service, then enter into sacramental service. Once you enter that service, you can enter no other.

2. Sacramental Fellowship
Except a corn of wheat fall into the ground and die, it abideth alone; but if it die, it bringeth forth much fruit. (John 12:24)

If you are wondering whether you are going on with God, examine yourself in the light of these words. The more spiritually real I become, the less am I of any account, I become more and more of the nature of a grain of wheat falling into the earth and dying in order that it may bring forth fruit. "He must increase, but I must decrease." I only decrease as He increases,

and He only increases in me as I nourish His life by that which decreases me. Am I willing to feed the life of the Son of God in me? If so, then He increases in me. There is no pathos in John's words, but delight, "Would to God I could decrease more quickly!" If a man attracts by his personality, then his appeal must come along the line of the particular work he wishes to do; but stand identified with the personality of your Lord, like John the Baptist, and the appeal is for *His* work to be done. The danger is to glory in men— "What a wonderful personality!" If when people get blessed they sentimentally "moon" around me, I am to blame because in my heart I lay the flattering unction to myself that it is because of my way of putting things they begin to idealise the one who should be being made broken bread and poured-out wine for them. Beware of stealing souls for whom Christ died for your own affectionate wealth.

3. Sacramental Responsibility
Now I rejoice in my sufferings for your sake, and fill up on my part that which is lacking of the afflictions of Christ in my flesh for His body's sake, which is the church. (Colossians 1:24 RV)

By "sacramental responsibility" understand the solemn determination to keep myself notably my Lord's, and to treat as a subtle temptation of the devil the call to take on any responsibility that conflicts with my determined identification with His interests. God's one great interest in men is that they are redeemed; am I identifying myself with that interest? Notice where God puts His disapproval on human experiences, it is when we begin to adhere to our conception of what sanctification is, and forget that sanctification itself has to be sanctified. When we see Jesus we will be ashamed of our deliberately conscious experience of sanctification, that is the thing that hinders Him, because instead of other people seeing Jesus in me, they see "me" and not Jesus. We have to be sacramental elements in His hands, not only in word but in actual life. After sanctification it is difficult to state what your aim in life is, because God has taken you up into His purposes. The design for God's service is that He can use the saint as His hands or His feet. Jesus taught that spiritually we should "grow as the lilies," bringing out the life that God blesses.

HIS CERTAIN KNOWLEDGE

. . . for He Himself [saw] what was in man. John 2:25 (RV)

Our Lord seemed to go so easily and calmly amongst all kinds of men—when He met a man who could sink to the level of Judas He never turned cynical, never lost heart or got discouraged; and when He met a loyal loving heart like John's He was not unduly elated, He never overpraised him. When we meet extra goodness we feel amazingly hopeful about everybody, and when we meet extra badness we feel exactly the opposite; but Jesus "knew what was in man," He knew exactly what human beings were like and what they needed; and He saw in them something no one else ever saw—hope for the most degraded. Jesus had a tremendous hopefulness about man.

1. How Jesus Thought about Man

Everything Jesus Christ thought about man is summed up in the parable of the two sons (see Luke 15), viz., that man had a noble origin, that he sinned wilfully, and that he has the power to return if he will. Do we accept Jesus Christ's view, or do we make excuses for ourselves? "Oh well, I am trying my best, and I am getting a little better every day"—no one ever did! numbers of us get a little worse every day. "I didn't mean to go wrong." It was not only our great forerunner who sinned wilfully, there is a wilful element in every one of us, we sin knowing it is sin. Socrates' notion was that if you tell a man what is right, he will do it, but he neglected the big factor that a man's innermost instinct is not God. There is a potential hero in every man—and a potential skunk.

Jesus Christ's thought about man is that he is lost, and that He is the only One who can find him. "For the Son of Man came to seek and to save that which was lost" (RV). Salvation means that if a man will turn—and every man has the power to turn, if it is only a look towards the Cross, he has the power for that—if a man will but turn, he will find that Jesus is able to deliver him not only from the snare of the wrong disposition within him, but from the power of evil and wrong outside him. The words of Jesus witness to His knowledge that man has the power to turn—"Come unto Me." "Him that cometh to Me I will in no wise cast out." As soon as a man turns, God finds him. The Cross of Christ spells hope for the most despairing sinner on the face of the earth. ". . . the Son of man hath power on earth to forgive sins."

2. How Jesus Treated Men

Jesus Christ treated men from the standpoint of His knowledge of them, He is the supreme Master of the human heart. Recall what He said—"For from within, out of the heart of men, proceed evil thoughts. . . ."—consequently He was never surprised, never in a panic. When He met the rich young ruler an upright-living, splendid young man, we read that "Jesus beholding him loved him," but He knew that at the back of all his morality was a disposition which could sin wilfully against God. "If thou wilt be perfect . . ." then come the conditions. Again, when Jesus met Nicodemus, a godly man, a ruler of the synagogue, He told him he must be made all over again before he could enter the kingdom of God. Or think how Jesus treated Peter. Peter loved Jesus, he declared that he was ready to lay down his life for Him, and yet he denied Him thrice. But Jesus never lost heart over him, He had told him beforehand—". . . but I made supplication for thee, that thy faith fail not: and do thou, when once thou hast turned again, stablish thy brethren" (RV). Sin never frightened Jesus; the devil never frightened Him. Face Jesus Christ with all the power of the devil: *He was manifested, that He might destroy the works of the devil.* Are you being tripped up by the subtle power of the devil? Remember, Jesus Christ has power not only to release you, but to make you more than conqueror over all the devil's onslaughts.

"For He Himself knew what was in man" (RV)—consequently He never trusted any man whether it was John, or Peter, or Thomas; He knew what was in them: they did not. How wonderfully the Apostle Paul learnt this lesson! Read his Epistles—"Don't glory in men, glory only in Jesus Christ and in His work in you." The Holy Spirit applies Jesus Christ's knowledge to me until I know that "in me, that is, in my flesh, dwelleth no good thing," consequently I am never dismayed at what I discover in myself, but learn to trust only what the grace of God does in me.

How does Jesus Christ treat me? Let me receive the Holy Spirit and I will very soon know. He will treat me as He treats every man—mercilessly with regard to sin. We say, "O Lord, leave a little bit of pride, a little bit of self-realisation." God can never save human pride. Jesus Christ has no mercy whatever when it comes to conviction of sin. He has an amazing concern for the sinner, but no pity for sin.

3. How Jesus Thought about Himself

"For in that He Himself hath suffered being tempted, He is able to succour them that are tempted. . . . [He] was in all points tempted like as we are, yet without sin"

(Hebrews 2:18; 4:15). These verses reveal that it was in His temptation our Lord entered into identification with our need. He took upon Him our human nature, our flesh and blood, and the Spirit drove Him into the wilderness to be tempted by the subtle power of the antagonist of God. Having "suffered being tempted" He knows how terrific are the onslaughts of the devil against human nature unaided; He has been there, therefore He can be touched with the feeling of our infirmities. God Almighty was never "tempted in all points like as we are," Jesus Christ was. God Almighty knows all that Jesus Christ knows; but, if I may say it reverently, *God in Christ* knows more, because *God in Christ* "suffered being tempted," and therefore He is "able to succour them that are tempted."

Those of you who have been saved by God's grace, have you accepted Jesus' thought about men and are you learning to treat them as He did? or has your soul been rushed into a moral panic as you faced a difficult case? If so, you have never begun to think in Christ's school. If you are rightly related to God there is no excuse for indulging in panic; the Holy Spirit will safe-guard you from alarm at immorality, and put you in the place where you can fill up that which remains behind of the afflictions of Christ. If you suffer from panic, you hinder the Holy Spirit working through you. It is easy to be shocked at immorality, but how much education in the school of Christ, how much reliance on the Holy Spirit, does it take to bring us to the place where we are shocked at pride against God? That sensitiveness is lacking to-day.

"And because iniquity shall abound, the love of many shall wax cold." The portrait of many of us was sketched in these words of Jesus. Think of the worst man you know, not the worst man you can think of, because that is vague, have you any hope for him? Does the Holy Spirit begin to convey to your mind the wonder of that man being presented perfect in Christ Jesus? That is the test as to whether you have been learning to think about men as Jesus thought of them. The Holy Spirit brings us into sympathy with the work Jesus has done on behalf of men in that He is "able to save them to the uttermost that come unto God by Him."

HOW THE APOSTLE PAUL RETURNS THANKS

But I have all, and abound: I am full, having received of Epaphroditus the things which were sent from you, an odour of a sweet smell, a sacrifice acceptable, wellpleasing to God. Philippians 4:18

The Apostle Paul refused to take money-help from any of the Churches he founded and over which he watched so carefully, and his reasons for this are expounded in 1 Corinthians 9 (see also a significant reference in Acts 20:34), the one exception being the Church at Philippi. Paul's imprisonment had revived their affectionate interest, and he writes to thank them for a further gift through Epaphroditus, as, "even in Thessalonica ye sent once and again unto my necessity." The Epistle is a letter of gratitude for these gifts, and along with his thanks Paul combines solicitations and teaching, and deals with some of the grandest, most fundamental truths, e.g., chapter 2.

The letter is addressed to "all the saints in Christ Jesus which are at Philippi" from "Paul and Timothy, servants of Jesus Christ" (RV). This is a wonderfully courteous touch, Paul does not call himself here "an apostle of Jesus Christ," but by a name that embraces Timothy, because he was with him when the Church was founded—bond-servants (RV mg) of Christ Jesus.

Philippians 1
But I would ye should understand, brethren, that the things which happened unto me have fallen out rather unto the furtherance of the gospel. (Philippians 1:12)

The fortune of misfortune! That is Paul's way of looking at his captivity. He does not want them to be depressed on his account, or to imagine that God's purpose has been hindered; he says it has not been hindered, but furthered. The very things that looked so disastrous have turned out to be the most opportune, so that on this account his heart bounds with joy, and the note of rejoicing comes out through the whole Letter.

"Some indeed preach Christ even of envy and strife; and some also of good will (Philippians 1:15). Paul was severity itself in dealing with those in Galatia who preached the Gospel from the wrong motive (see Galatians 1:7–8; 2:4–5, 8; 5:4–5); here, he deals with the matter more gently, what is the reason for the difference? In the first case false brethren had insinuated themselves into the Church with the set purpose of unsettling the believers and bringing them into bondage; in this case the motive, he says, was "to raise up affliction for me in my bonds" (RV). Whenever

harm is being done to the flock of God it must be tracked out and dealt with rigorously; personal injury is another matter. "Whosoever shall smite thee on thy right cheek, turn to him the other also," said our Lord, and Paul exhibits that spirit when he says, "What then? notwithstanding, every way, whether in pretence, or in truth, Christ is preached; and I therein do rejoice, yea, and will rejoice."

This brings us up against a big problem, a problem our Lord refers to in Matthew 7:21–23. Because God honours His word no matter how preached or by whom, we naturally infer that if His word is blessed, souls saved, demons cast out, mighty works done, surely the preacher must be a servant of God. It does not follow by any means. An instrument of God and a servant of God ought to be identical, but our Lord's words and Paul's are instances where they are not. It does not impair the inspiration of the Gospel to have it preached by a bad man, but the influence of the preacher, worthy or unworthy, apart altogether from his preaching, has a tremendous effect. If I know a man to be a bad man the sinister influence of his personality neutralises altogether the effect of God's message through him to me; but let me be quite sure that my intuition springs from my relationship to God and not from human suspicion.

Philippians 2
Fulfil ye my joy, that ye be like-minded, having the same love, being of one accord, of one mind. (Philippians 2:2)

In verses 1–4 Paul is arguing—"If you are rightly related to God in Christ, the life of the Son of God in you makes you identical with Him, so that the same 'comfort of love,' the same fellowship of the Spirit, the same 'mercies' that marked Him, mark you." How we water down the amazing revelation made in the New Testament, that we are made one with Christ! "I live; yet not I, but Christ liveth in me."

"Let this mind be in you, which was also in Christ Jesus" (Philippians 2:5). We are not given a fully formed reasoning Christian mind when we are born again, we are given the Spirit of Jesus, but not His mind, we have to form that. The "mind" Paul urges the Philippian Christians to form is not the mind of Almighty God, but the mind of Christ Jesus, "who, being in the form of God, thought it not robbery to be equal with God ['not a thing to be grasped,' RV mg]." This was the central citadel of the temptation— "You are the Son of God, assert your prerogative; You will bring the world to Your feet if You will remember who You are and use Your power." The answer

Jesus made was, "I did not come to do My own will, although I am the Son of God, I am here in this order of things for one purpose only, to do the will of My Father." When we are sanctified the same temptation comes to us—"You are a child of God, identified with Jesus, presume on it, think it something to be grasped, to be proud of." We are saved and sanctified for one purpose, that God's will might be done in us as it was in our Lord.

". . . work out your own salvation with fear and trembling. For it is God which worketh in you both to will and to do of His good pleasure" (Philippians 2:12–13). These verses combine all we understand by the great efficacious work of grace of God in salvation and sanctification. "You are saved," says Paul, "now *work it out:* be consistent in character with what God has worked in." The only estimate of consistent Christian character is the life of Jesus made manifest in our mortal flesh. People talk a lot about their "experience" of sanctification and too often there is nothing in it, it doesn't work out in the bodily life or in the mind, it is simply a doctrine; with Paul it was the mainspring of his life. "For it is God which worketh in you *to will*. . . ." It is nonsense to talk about a man's free will, a man's will is only fundamentally free in God, that is, he is only free when the law of God and the Spirit of God are actively working in his will by his own choice.

". . . that ye may be blameless and harmless, the sons of God, without rebuke, in the midst of a crooked and perverse nation, among whom ye shine as lights in the world" (Philippians 2:15)—that means on this earth, not in heaven. We have to shine as lights in the squalid places of earth; we can't shine in heaven, our light would be put out in two seconds. "That ye may be blameless"— if ever we are to be blameless, undeserving of censure in the sight of God who sees down to the motive of our motives, it must be by the supernatural power of God. The meaning of the Cross is just that—I can not only have the marvellous work of God's grace done in my heart, but can have the proof of it in my life. "The Higher Christian Life"[14] phraseology is apt to be nothing in the world but the expression of a futile and sorrowful struggle, adoring God for what we are in His Divine anticipation but never can be in actuality. It is only when I realise that God's anticipations for me are presented as participations through the power of the Holy Spirit, that I become that peculiarly humble person, a disciple of the Lord Jesus.

"Yea, and if I am poured out as a drink-offering [RV mg] upon the sacrifice and service of your faith, I joy, and rejoice with you all" (Philippians 2:17). Paul's conception of the altar of sacrifice is spending and being spent for the sake of the elementary children of God.

---

14. The Higher Christian Life emphasized sanctification and personal holiness.

He has no other end and aim than that—to be broken bread and poured-out wine in the hands of God that others might be nourished and fed. (Cf. Colossians 1:24) The great Saviour and His great apostle go hand-in-hand: the Son of God sacrificed Himself to redeem men; Paul, His bondservant, sacrificed himself that men might come to know they are redeemed, that they have been bought with a price and are not their own; it was no false note when Paul said, *Christ liveth in me.*

Philippians 3

. . . as touching the law, a Pharisee. (Philippians 3:5)

Saul of Tarsus did easily what all other Pharisees did, but his conscience would not allow him to be a hypocrite easily. His ardent nature tried to make his inner life come up to the standard of the law, and the tragedy of his failure is portrayed in Romans 7. No one was ever so introspective, so painfully conscious of weakness and inability to keep the law, as Paul, so when he says, "Christ is the end of the law unto righteousness" (RV) he is making an intensely practical statement. He is stating the fact that Jesus Christ has planted in him as a sheer gift of God's grace the life that enables him now to fulfil all the law of God— "not having mine own righteousness, which is of the law, but that which is through the faith of Christ, the righteousness which is of God by faith." "Imputed" means *imparted* with Paul.

"*If any other man thinketh that he hath whereof he might trust in the flesh, I more*" *(Philippians 3:4).* In verses 4–6 Paul catalogues the things that used to be "gains" to him, the things which were a recommendation to him in the eyes of the world (cf. Galatians 1:13–14); but, he says, "I fling them all overboard as refuse, that I may win Christ." The whole of Paul's life has been redetermined by regeneration, and he estimates now from an entirely different standard. The things from which we have to loose ourselves are the good things of the old creation as well as the bad, e.g., our natural virtues, because our natural virtues can never come anywhere near what Jesus Christ wants.

"*That I may know Him, and the power of His resurrection and the fellowship of His sufferings . . .*" *(Philippians 3:10).* Paul talks more about suffering than any of the apostles, but any suffering that is less than "fellowship with His sufferings" he treats very lightly— "our light affliction." Jesus suffered according to the will of God, and to be made a partaker of His sufferings destroys every element of self-pity, of self-interest, of self-anything.

"*. . . not as though I . . . were already perfect*" *(Philippians 3:12).* "Let us therefore, as many as be perfect . . ." (Philippians 3:15). Nothing but wilful perversion would make anyone misunderstand these two "perfections." In verse 12 Paul is speaking of the perfection of consummation not attainable in this life; in verse 15 he speaks of a perfection of fitness demanded now. "Remember, though you are perfectly adjusted to God, you have attained to nothing yet." The idea is that of a marathon runner, practising and practising until he is perfectly fit; when he is perfectly fit he hasn't begun the race, he is only perfectly fit to begin. By regeneration we are put into perfect relationship to God, then we have the same human nature, working along the same lines, but with a different mainspring. "Not that I am already made perfect": that is the perfection of consummation; "I haven't got there yet," says Paul; "but I follow after, if so be that I may apprehend that for which also I was apprehended by Christ Jesus." Paul was absolutely Christ-centred, he had lost all interest in himself in an absorbing passionate interest in Christ. Very few saints get where he got, and we are to blame for not getting there. We thank God for saving and sanctifying us and continually revert to these experiences: Paul reverted to one thing only—"When it pleased God . . . to reveal His Son in me," then he never bothered any more about himself. We try to efface ourselves by an effort; Paul did not efface himself by an effort, his interest in himself simply died right out when he became identified with the death of Jesus.

"*For many walk, of whom I have told you often, and now tell you even weeping, that they are the enemies of the cross of Christ*" *(Philippians 3:18).* Why did Paul say "enemies of *the cross of Christ*", and not "enemies of *Christ*"? The test all through is true-ness to the Cross. What the enemies of the cross so strenuously oppose is identification on the part of the believer with what the death of Christ on the Cross represents, viz., death to sin in every shape and form. Look at the tremendous words Paul uses, they express the agony of his heart over those who are the enemies of that moral identification. Their god is themselves—what develops "me"; not that which takes "me" right out of the road and gives the Son of God a chance to manifest Himself in me. What was it God condemned in the Cross? Self-realisation. Have I come to a moral agreement with God about that? To say that what God condemned in the Cross was social sins is not true; what God condemns in the Cross is *sin* which is away further down than any moral quirks.

Philippians 4

Therefore, my brethren, dearly beloved and longed for, my joy and crown, so stand fast in the Lord, my dearly beloved. (Philippians 4:1)

Notice Paul's earnest solicitation over those who have been saved through his ministry; he carried every convert on his heart to the end of his life, or of theirs.

"Be careful for nothing" (Philippians 4:6). The enemy of saintliness is carefulness over the wrong thing. The culture of the Christian life is to learn to be carefully careless over everything saving our relationship to God. It is not sin that keeps us from going on spiritually, but "the cares of the world, . . . the lusts of other things" (RV) that crowd out any consideration of God. We reverse the teaching of Jesus, we don't seek first the Kingdom of God we seek every other thing first, and the result accords with what Jesus said, the word He puts in is choked and becomes unfruitful.

"Finally, brethren, whatsoever things are true . . . take account of [RV mg] these things" (Philippians 4:8). "Glean your thinking"—one of the hardest things to do. For instance, it is essentially difficult to think along the lines laid down in 1 Corinthians 13: "Love . . . taketh not account of evil" (RV); apart from God we do take account of evil, we reason from that standpoint. The majority of us are not spiritual thinkers, but once we begin to think on the basis of our relationship to God through the Redemption we find it a most revolutionary thing. We are not saved by thinking, we form our nous, a responsible intelligence, by thinking, and immediately we face the application of the Redemption to the details of our lives, we find it means everything has to be readjusted bit by bit.

PROBLEMATA MUNDI

Hast thou considered My servant Job, that there is none like him in the earth, a perfect and an upright man, one that feareth God, and escheweth evil? Job 1:8

The Book of Job mirrors for all time the problem of things as they have been, as they are, and as they will be until they are altered by the manifestation of a new heaven and a new earth. When things go well a man does not want God, but when things get difficult and suffering begins to touch him, he finds the problem of the world inside his own skin. The slander of men is against God when disasters occur. If you have never felt inclined to call God cruel and hard, it is a question whether you have ever faced any problems at all. Job's utterances are those of a man who suffers without any inkling as to why he suffers; yet he discerns intuitively that what is happening to him is not in God's order, although it is in His permissive will. All through, Job stands for two things: that God is just, and that he is relatively innocent. Remember, Job was never told the preface to his own story; he did not know that he had been chosen to be the battleground between God and Satan. Satan's contention was that no man loved God for His own sake—"Doth Job fear God for nought?" "Job only loves You because You bless him, let me curse his blessings and I will prove it to You." Satan's primary concern is to sneer against God, he is after disconcerting God, putting God in a corner, so to speak, where He will have to take action along Satan's proposed lines.

There are circumstances in life which make us know that Satan's sneer is pretty near the mark. I love God as long as He blesses me, saves my soul and puts me right for heaven; but supposing He should see fit to let the worst things happen to me, would I say, "Go on, do it" and love Him still? The point is that God's honour is at stake in a man who suffers as did this "perfect and upright" man. Part of the problem was that in the bargain Satan made with God, he implied that God must keep out of sight; and God did, He never once showed Himself to Job. The presentation of the controversy between God and Satan is such that Satan has everything on his side and God nothing on His, so much so that God dare not say a word to Job till he had proved himself worthy. Job cannot answer one of the charges the friends bring against him, he tears their arguments to shreds in the fervour of his pain, yet he clings to it, "I will believe God, in spite of everything that seems to be contradicting His character."

The Apostle James talks about "the patience of Job"—Job patient! He was patient, but only to God. There is nothing logical about Job, his statements are wild and chaotic, but underneath there is an implicit understanding of God's character. He is sure of God even though He seems to be doing everything to ruin him, and he draws steadily nearer God as his friends withdraw themselves from him, heaping their anathemas upon him. They slander Job while standing up for God; but in the end God says, "Ye have not spoken of Me the thing that is right, as My servant Job hath." The citadel of true religion is personal relationship to God, let come what will.

Where does our mind rest regarding suffering? The Bible makes little of physical suffering. The modern mind looks on suffering and pain as an unmitigated curse; the Bible puts something akin to purifying in connection with suffering, e.g., "for he that hath suffered in the flesh hath ceased from sin" (1 Peter 4:1). The thing that moves us is the pathos arising from physical suffering; the anguish of a soul trying to find God we put down to lunacy. The only way traditional belief can be transformed into a personal possession is by suffering. Look at what you say you believe, not an atom of it is yours saving the bit you have proved by suffering and in no other way.

Never run away with the idea that Satan is sceptical of all virtue, he knows God too well and human nature too well to have such a shallow scepticism; he is sceptical only of virtue that has not been tried. Faith un-tried is simply a promise and a possibility, which we may cause to fail; tried faith is the pure gold. Faith must be tried, otherwise it is of no worth to God. Think of the dignity it gives to a man's life to know that God has put His honour in his keeping. Our lives mean more than we can tell, they mean that we are fulfilling some purpose of God about which we know nothing any more than Job did. God's government of the world is not for material prosperity, but for moral ends, for the production of moral characters, in the sense of holy characters. Time is nothing to God.

". . . the LORD gave Job twice as much as he had before. . . . So the LORD blessed the latter end of Job more than his beginning" (Job 42:10, 12). The charge is made that because God gave Job back his material prosperity, therefore the whole argument of the Book falls to the ground; but the blessing of God on Job was nothing more than an outward manifestation accompanying the certainty he now possessed, viz., that he loves God and that God loves him. It is the overflowing favour of God poured out on a loved son who has come through the ordeal and won his way straight through to God.

A FATAL ERROR OF INDIGNANT INTEGRITY

And he was angry, and would not go in. Luke 15:28

We get the idea that wrong views of God and of goodness arise from a life that is wrong; the Bible shows that wrong views of God and of goodness may arise out of a life that is right. The parable of the two sons is an example of this. The younger brother was a wastrel; the elder brother was a man of integrity, there was not a spot on his character—"neither transgressed I at any time thy commandment." Everything that led him to take up the position he did was perfectly justifiable, it was the protest of an upright man, but he made the fatal error of misinterpreting his father's ways and refusing to enter into a love that was too big for this earth. Many good upright people misinterpret God's ways because they do not take into account first of all the matter of personal relationship to God. They say because we are the creatures of God, we are the sons and daughters of God; Jesus Christ taught with profound insistence that we are sons and daughters of God only by an inner disposition, the disposition of love, which works implicitly. The Bible states that "love is of God." The difficulty arises out of our individuality, which is hard and tight, segregated from others; personality is never isolated, it always merges, and is characterised by an implicit understanding of things. The attitude of the elder brother is individual entirely, he is merged into nothing of the nature of love, consequently he misunderstands his father and demands that his ways ought to be more clearly justifiable to human reason. God's ways never are, because the basis of things fundamentally is not reasonable; if it were, God would be cruel to allow what He does. Our reason is simply an instrument, the way we explain things, it is not the basis of things. The problems of life are only explainable by means of a right relationship to God. If we ask for a reasonable explanation of God's ways in Providence, such as are stated in the Book of Job, or of the puzzles of Nature referred to by Paul in Romans 8:19–23, we will end in misinterpreting God; but when we receive the disposition Jesus Christ came to give us, we find our problems are explained implicitly. There is no such thing as sin to common-sense reasoning, therefore no meaning in the Cross because that view rules out what the Bible bases everything on, viz., the hiatus between God and man produced by sin and the Cross where sin is dealt with. When common-sense reasoning comes to the Cross it is embarrassed, it looks at the death of Jesus as the death of a martyr, One who lived beyond His dispensation. According to the New Testament, the Cross is the Cross of God, not of a man. The problems of Providence, the puzzles of Nature, the paradoxes of Christianity do not bother everybody, they are the problems of men who are good and upright, but distinctly individual, and their individuality causes them to misinterpret God's ways and repudiate Christianity.

". . . as soon as this thy son was come, which hath devoured thy living with harlots, thou hast killed for him the fatted calf." The elder brother is right, not wrong, according to all reasonable human standards, when he says of the prodigal, "Such a character ought not to be allowed in the home, he ought to be excluded." A bad man would have said "Oh well, it doesn't matter, he has made mistakes, we all do." Embarrassment always arises in the domain of ethics when we make the basis of Christianity adherence to principles instead of personal relationship to God. What is called Christianity, our charity and benevolence is not Christianity as the New Testament teaches it, it is simply adherence to certain principles. Jesus tells us to "give to him that asketh thee"—not because he deserves it, or because he needs it, but "because I tell you to." Ask yourself, "Do I deserve all I have got?" The teaching of Jesus revolutionises our modern conception of charity.

A false idea of God's honour ends in misinterpreting His ways. It is the orthodox type of Christian who by sticking to a crude idea of God's character, presents the teaching which says, "God loves you when you are good, but not when you are bad." God loves us whether we are good or bad. That is the marvel of His love. "I came not to call the righteous, but sinners to repentance"—whether there are any righteous is open to question. "The righteous have no need

of Me; I came for the sinful, the ungodly, the weak." If I am not sinful and ungodly and weak, I don't need Him at all.

The presentation Jesus gives of the father is that he makes no conditions when the prodigal returns, neither does he bring home to him any remembrance of the far country—the elder brother does that. It is the revelation of the unfathomable, unalterable, amazing love of God. We would feel much happier in our backslidden condition if only we knew it had altered God towards us, but we know that immediately we do come back we will find Him the same, and this is one of the things that keeps men from coming back. If God would only be angry and demand an apology, it would be a gratification to our pride. When we have done wrong we like to be lashed for it. God never lashes. Jesus does not represent the father as saying "You have been so wicked that I cannot take you back as my son, I will make you a servant"; but as saying,

Bring forth quickly the best robe, and put it on him; and put a ring on his hand, and shoes on his feet: and bring the fatted calf, and kill it, and let us eat, and make merry: for this My son was dead, and is alive again; he was lost, and is found. (RV)

DIVINE PARADOX

There is probably no more prominent feature in Bible revelation than that of paradox. In Revelation 5 the Apostle John records that in his vision he was told "the Lion of the tribe of Judah . . . hath prevailed to open the book"—and he says, "lo, in the midst of the throne . . . stood a Lamb"! We find a paradox of a similar nature in the Book of Isaiah. The prophet has been looking for some great conquering army of the Lord, and instead he sees a lonely Figure, "travelling in the greatness of his strength." If you take all the manifestations of God in the Old Testament you find them a mass of contradictions: now God is pictured as a Man, now as a Woman, now as a lonely Hero, now as a suffering Servant, and until we come to the revelation in the New Testament these conflicting characteristics but add confusion to our conception of God. But immediately we see Jesus Christ, we find all the apparent contradictions blended in one unique Person.

Drummond in his *Natural Law in the Spiritual World*,[15] surely makes a fundamental blunder by that very statement, and surely the contention in Butler's *Analogy*[16] is right—that as there is a law in the natural world so there is also a law in the spiritual world, but that they are not the same laws, the one is the complement of the other. Unless this is born in mind by the student of Scripture, and he learns to rely on the Holy Spirit to interpret the spiritual law as he relies on his own spirit to interpret the natural law, he will not only end in confusion, but will be in danger of disparaging the spiritual law in the Bible universe in favour of the natural law in the common-sense universe.

"And I saw in the right hand of Him that sat on the throne a book . . . sealed with seven seals" (Revelation 5:1). I am considering the Book in one aspect only, viz., as containing a knowledge of the future, an understanding of the Providence of God in the pre-

---

15. Henry Drummond (1851–1897): Scottish writer and evangelist. *Natural Law in the Spiritual World*, published 1883.

16. Joseph Butler (1692–1752): English philosopher and an Anglican bishop. His *Analogy of Religion*, often called a masterpiece of Christian apologetics, was published 1736.

sent, together with a grasp of the past. The deepest clamour of a man's nature once he is awake is to know the "whence" and "whither" of life—"Whence came I?" "Why am I here?" "Where am I going?" In all ages men have tried to pry into the secrets of the future, astrologers, necromancers, spiritualists, or whatever name you may call them by, have all tried to open the Book, but without success, because it is a sealed Book. "I wept much," says John, "because no one was found worthy to open the book, or to look thereon" (RV).

Because of the sealed character of the Book men become indifferent and cease to be exercised over the "whence" and "whither" of human destiny; they take no interest in Bible revelation, and are amused at our earnest solicitation on their behalf—"It is all about something we cannot know, and there is no one who can tell us." Others say, "There is nothing to know"; not, "We cannot know," but "There is nothing to know, a man lives his life, then dies, and that is all there is." The Psalmist refers to such men when he says, "The fool hath said in his heart, There is no God." There are others whose sensitive spirit gives them an implicit sense that there is more than this life; there are hidden deeps in their heart that human life and its friendships can never satisfy. The scenes of earth, its sunsets and sunrises, its "huge and thoughtful nights" all awaken an elemental sadness which makes them wonder why they were born, and they feel keenly because the Book is sealed and there is no one able to open it.

But would to God all men knew that there *is* Someone who is worthy to open the Book!

And one of the elders saith unto me, Weep not: behold, the Lion of the tribe of Juda, the Root of David, hath prevailed to open the book, and to loose the seven seals thereof. (Revelation 5:5)

Who is this Worthy One? If one may say it with reverence, realising the limitation of language, God Himself had to be proved Worthy to open the Book. In the Person of Jesus Christ God became Man, He trod this earth with naked feet,

and wrought
with human hands the creed of creeds
In loveliness and perfect deeds.

By His holy life, by His moral integrity and supreme spiritual greatness, Jesus Christ proved that He was worthy to open the Book. The Book can be opened by only one Hand, the pierced hand of the Worthy One, our Saviour Jesus Christ.

The childish idea that because God is great he can do anything, good or bad, right or wrong, and we must say nothing, is erroneous. The meaning of moral worth is that certain things are impossible to it: it is "impossible for God to lie"; it is impossible for Jesus

Christ to contradict His own Holiness or to become other than He is. The profound truth for us is that Jesus Christ is the Worthy One not because He was God Incarnate, but because He was God Incarnate on the human plane. "Being made in the likeness of men" (RV) He accepted our limitations and lived on this earth a life of perfect holiness. Napoleon said of Jesus Christ that He had succeeded in making of every human soul an appendage of His own—why? Because He had the genius of holiness. There have been great military geniuses, intellectual giants, geniuses of statesmen, but these only exercise influence over a limited number of men; Jesus Christ exercises unlimited sway over all men because He is the altogether Worthy One.

And I beheld, and, lo, in the midst of the throne . . . stood a Lamb as it had been slain. (Revelation 5:6)

Jesus Christ is the supreme Sacrifice for the sin of the world; He is "the Lamb of God, which taketh away the sin of the world!" How the Death of Jesus looms all through the Bible! It is through His death that we are made partakers of His life and can have gifted to us a pure heart, which He says is the condition for seeing God.

"Having . . . seven eyes." The Lamb is not only the supreme Sacrifice for man's sin, He is the Searcher of hearts, searching to the inmost recesses of mind and motive. It is not a curious searching, not an uncanny searching, but the deep wholesome searching the Holy Spirit gives in order to convict men of their sin and need of a Saviour; then when they come to the Cross, and through it accept deliverance from sin, Jesus Christ becomes the Sovereign of their lives, they love Him personally and passionately beyond all other loves of earth.

And He came and took the book out of the right hand of Him that sat upon the throne. (Revelation 5:7)

Jesus Christ and He alone is able to satisfy the craving of the human heart to know the "whence" and "whither" of life. He enables men to understand that they have come into this life from a deep purpose in the heart of God; that the one thing they are here for is to get readjusted to God and become His lovers. And whither are we going? We are going to where the Book of Life is opened, and we enter into an effulgence of glory (RV) we can only conceive of now at rare moments.

In the days of His flesh Jesus Christ exhibited this Divine paradox of the Lion and the Lamb. He was the Lion in majesty, rebuking the winds and demons: He was the Lamb in meekness, "who, when He was reviled, reviled not again." He was the Lion in power, raising the dead: He was the Lamb in patience—who was "brought as a lamb to the slaughter, and as a sheep before her shearers is dumb, so He openeth not His mouth." He was the Lion in authority, "Ye have heard that it hath been said, . . . *but I say unto you . . .*": He was the Lamb in gentleness, "Suffer the little children to come unto Me. . . . And He took them up in His arms, put His hands upon them, and blessed them."

In our personal lives Jesus Christ proves Himself to be all this—He is the Lamb to expiate our sins, to lift us out of condemnation and plant within us His own heredity of holiness: He is the Lion to rule over us, so that we gladly say, "the government [of this life]

shall be upon His shoulder." And what is true in individual life is to be true also in the universe at large. The time is coming when the Lion of the Tribe of Judah shall reign, and when "the kingdoms of this world" shall become "the kingdoms of our Lord, and of His Christ."

One remaining paradox—In Revelation 6:16 "the wrath of the Lamb" is mentioned. We know what the wrath of a lion is like—but *the wrath of the Lamb!*—it is beyond our conception. All one can say about it is that the wrath of God is the terrible obverse side of the love of God.

MEMORY OF SIN IN THE SAINT

. . . for that He counted me faithful, putting me into the ministry; who was before a blasphemer, and a persecutor, and injurious. 1 Timothy 1:12–13

. . . and such were some of you. 1 Corinthians 6:11

No aspect of Christian life and service is in more need of revision than our attitude to the memory of sin in the saint. When the Apostle Paul said "forgetting those things which are behind," he was talking not about sin, but about his spiritual attainment. Paul never forgot what he had been; it comes out repeatedly in the Epistles—"For I am the least of the apostles, that am not meet to be called an apostle" (1 Corinthians 15:9); "unto me who am less than the least of all saints, is this grace given" (Ephesians 3:8); ". . . sinners, of whom I am chief" (1 Timothy 1:15). And these are the utterances of a ripe, glorious servant of God.

If one wants a touchstone for the depth of true spiritual Christianity, one will surely find it in this matter of the memory of sin. There are those who exhibit a Pharisaic holiness, they thank God with an arrogant offensiveness that they are "not as other men are"; they have forgotten the horrible pit and miry clay from whence they were taken, and their feet set upon a rock through the might of the Atonement. Perhaps the reason they condemn others who have fallen and been restored is the old human failing of making a virtue out of necessity. Their lives have been shielded, the providence of God has never allowed them to be enmeshed in the subtle snares other men have encountered and whose fall has plunged them into an agony of remorse. May the conviction of God come with swift and stern rebuke upon any one who is remembering the past of another, and deliberately choosing to forget their restoration through God's

grace. When a servant of God meets these sins in others, let him be reverent with what he does not understand and leave God to deal with them.

Certain forms of sin shock us far more than they shock God. The sin that shocks God, the sin that broke His heart on Calvary, is not the sin that shocks us. The sin that shocks God is the thing which is highly esteemed among men—self-realisation, pride, my right to myself. We have no right to have the attitude to any man or woman as if he or she had sunk to a lower level than those of us who have never been tempted on the line they have. The conventions of society and our social relationships make it necessary for us to take this attitude, but we have to remember that in the sight of God there are no social conventions, and that external sins are no whit worse in His sight than the pride which hates the rule of the Holy Ghost while the life is morally clean. May God have mercy on any one of us who forgets this, and allows spiritual pride or superiority and a sense of his own unsulliedness, to put a barrier between him and those whom God has lifted from depths of sin he cannot understand.

Holiness is the only sign that a man is repentant in the New Testament sense, and a holy man is not one who has his eyes set on his own whiteness, but one who is personally and passionately devoted to the Lord who saved him—one whom the Holy Ghost takes care shall never forget that God has made him what he is by sheer sovereign grace. Accept as the tender touch of God, not as a snare of the devil, every memory of sin the Holy Ghost brings home to you, keeping you in the place where you remember what you once were and what you now are by His grace.

"This is a faithful saying, and worthy of all acceptation, that Christ Jesus came into the world to save sinners; of whom I am chief" (1 Timothy 1:15)—*sinners, of whom I am chief.* What a marvellous humility it betokens for a man to say that and mean it! In the early days of the sterner form of Calvinism a man's belief about God and about his own destiny frequently produced a wistful, self-effacing humility; but the humility Paul manifests was produced in him by the remembrance that Jesus, whom he had scorned and despised, whose followers he had persecuted, whose Church he had harried, not only had forgiven him, but made him His chief apostle: *Unto me, who am less than the least of all saints, is this grace given, that I should preach among the Gentiles the unsearchable riches of Christ.*

"Howbeit for this cause I obtained mercy, that in me first Jesus Christ might shew forth all longsuffering, for a pattern to them which should hereafter believe on Him to life everlasting." Here is the attitude of the servant of God—"since God has done this for me, I can despair of no man on the face of the earth." Show such a servant of God the backslider, the sinner steeped in the iniquity of our cities, and there will spring up in his heart an amazing well of compassion and love for that one, because he has himself experienced the grace of God which goes to the uttermost depths of sin and lifts to the highest heights of salvation.

But where sin abounded, grace did abound more exceedingly (RV).

CELEBRATION OR SURRENDER?

We begin our Christian life by believing what we are told to believe, then we have to go on to so assimilate our beliefs that they work out in a way that redounds to the glory of God. The danger is in multiplying the acceptation of beliefs we do not make our own. Every now and again we find ourselves lost in wonder at the marvel of the Redemption; it is a wholesome initial stage, but if it is made the final stage it is perilous. The difficulty of believing in the Redemption in the sense of assimilating it is that it demands renunciation. I have to give up my right to myself in complete surrender to my Lord before what I celebrate becomes a reality. There is always the danger of celebrating what Jesus Christ has done and forgetting the need on our part of moral surrender to Him; if we evade the surrender we become the more intense in celebrating what He has done.

1. The Snare of Emotional Rapture *(Mark 9:2–8)*

And Peter answered and said to Jesus, Master, it is good for us to be here. (Mark 9:5)

Be quick to notice how God brings you rapidly from emotional rapture into contact with the sordid commonplace activities of life. There are times in the Providence of God when He leads us apart by ourselves, when Jesus reveals Himself to us and we see Him transfigured. The place apart by ourselves may be a prayer meeting, a service, a talk with a friend, a sunrise or a sunset, when we are stirred to the depths and see what we are unable to utter; the snare is to imagine that that is all God means; He means much more. "And there was a cloud that overshadowed them: and a voice came out of the cloud, saying, This

is My beloved Son: hear Him"—not, "This is My beloved Son: now spend halcyon days with Him on the Mount." Beware of celestial sensuality. No matter what your experience, you may be trapped by sensuality any time. Sensuality is not sin, it is the way the body works in connection with circumstances whereby I begin to satisfy myself. Mary Magdalene was in danger of making this blunder, but Jesus said, "Touch Me not"—"Don't try and hold Me by your senses, but go and do what I say." Always thrust out into the actual, because it is there you exhibit whether your emotional rapture has seduced you, made you unfit for activities.

After a time of rapt contemplation when your mind has been absorbing the truth of God, watch the kind of people God will bring round you, not people dressed in the "castoff nimbus" of some saint, but ordinary commonplace people just like yourself. We imagine that God must engineer special circumstances for us, peculiar sufferings; He never does, because that would feed our pride; He engineers things which from the standpoint of human pride are a humiliation.

"And suddenly, when they had looked round about, they saw no man any more, save Jesus only with themselves" (Mark 9:8). Instead of its being, "no cross, no crown," spiritually, it is "no crown, no cross." We are crowned by the moment of rapture, but that is not the end, it is the beginning of being brought down into the demon-possessed valley to bear the cross for Him there. With a sudden rush we find no Moses, no Elijah, no transfiguration-glory, and we fear as we enter the cloud, till we come to the place where there is "no man, save Jesus only." As men and women we have to live in this world, in its misery and sinfulness, and we

must do the same if we are disciples. Of all people we should be able to go down into the demon-possessed valley, because once we have seen Jesus transfigured it is impossible to lose heart or be discouraged.

2. The Sincerity of Experimental Realisation

Yea doubtless, and I count all things but loss for the excellency of the knowledge of Christ Jesus my Lord. . . . (Philippians 3:8)

Paul goes on to state that he not only *estimated* the cost, he experienced it—"for whom I have suffered the loss of all things, . . . that I may win Christ and be found in Him, not having mine own righteousness. . . ." Imagine anyone who has seen Jesus Christ transfigured

saying he is sorry to find himself mean[17] and ignoble! The more I whine about being a miserable sinner, the more I am hurting the Holy Spirit. It simply means I don't agree with God's judgement of me, I think after all I am rather desirable: God thought me so undesirable that He sent His Son to save me. To discover I am what God says I am ought to make me glad; if I am glad over anything I discover in myself, I am very short-sighted. The only point of rest is in the Lord Himself.

> *Since mine eyes have looked on Jesus,*
> *I've lost sight of all beside . . .*
> *So enchained my spirit's vision*
> *Gazing on the Crucified.*

---

17. mean: ordinary, common, low, or ignoble, rather than cruel or spiteful

Disciples Indeed

Oswald Chambers

If ye continue in My word, then are ye My disciples indeed. John 8:31

INTRODUCTION

Source

These lectures were given to students in the sermon class at the Bible Training College,[1] in London, between 1911 and 1915.

Publication History

- As articles: Twenty-five articles titled "Sermon Class Notes" appeared in the *BTC Journal*[2] between April 1945 and March 1952.
- As a book: 1955.

Oswald Chambers' sermon class at the Bible Training College was a combination of lecture and practical experience. Since each student had to prepare and present a sermon before the other members of the class, no visitors were permitted. Oswald wanted everyone to be on an equal footing, as well as being sympathetic listeners, knowing their turn to speak was coming.

Because of the give and take nature of the class, Oswald's lectures were short and practical. Rather than giving a detailed process to follow in sermon preparation, he sought to motivate students to think, study, and prepare. He often stressed that the behavior and words of the person who preaches are inseparable.

From the *BTC Journal* articles, Mrs. Chambers selected thoughts on twenty-one topics and published them as *Disciples Indeed*. There is a surprising amount of material that appears here and nowhere else in the books by Oswald Chambers.

FOREWORD

Oswald Chambers was above all else a teacher of spiritual truth. Our Ascended Lord's promise was to give His Church "some to be . . . teachers; for the perfecting of the saints" (Ephesians 4:11 RV). This book contains messages spoken by such a teacher, full of wisdom and instruction in righteousness. Teachers call for learners. Some of us who heard the spoken word became humble and eager learners. Many who never saw or heard the speaker are learning from him now. In a recent letter the writer says, "It is not generally known how these books came into being, and the time seems favourable for revealing God's providence in it all." Oswald Chambers received his Home-call in 1917 when working with the YMCA

---

1. Residential school near Clapham Common in SW London, sponsored by the League of Prayer. Oswald Chambers was Principal and main teacher; Biddy Chambers was Lady Superintendent. Known as the BTC, it closed in July 1915 because of World War I.

2. *Bible Training Course Journal:* published from 1932 to 1952 by Mrs. Chambers, with help from David Lambert.

among the Troops in Egypt. It seemed like the end of a fruitful ministry. Then it was that Mrs. Chambers realised that her custom of taking down in shorthand her husband's lectures and addresses for her own profit had left her with a great store of spiritual wisdom which could be shared with the wider world by the printed page. So began a remarkable ministry of spreading in book form the original spoken words. As the writer of the above-mentioned letter says, "The whole matter is a sheer miracle, especially as the only planning has been God's."

Disciples Indeed, the latest book to be issued, speaks for itself. Other volumes show by the outlines and headings given what careful preparation was made for every spoken message. But often the spontaneous word of a Spirit-filled man, whether the subject was Christian Doctrine, Psychology, Biblical Ethics or Homiletics, would be added, and appear in the shorthand notes. Many of these not included in the earlier publications are printed here. They touch a wide range of subjects, and take us to the heart of Oswald Chambers' message. They make this book a kind of *vade mecum* of sainthood.

David Lambert[3]

CONTENTS

3. David Lambert (1871–1961): Methodist minister and friend of Oswald Chambers. Assisted Mrs. Chambers with OC publications from 1917–1961.

BELIEF

The only noble sense in which we can claim to believe a thing is when we ourselves are living in the inner spirit of that thing.

I have no right to say I believe in God unless I order my life as under His all-seeing Eye.

I have no right to say I believe that Jesus is the Son of God unless in my personal life I yield myself to that Eternal Spirit, free from all self-seeking, which became incarnate in Jesus.

I have no right to say that I believe in forgiveness as an attribute of God if in my own heart I cherish an unforgiving temper. The forgiveness of God is the test by which I myself am judged.

Belief is a wholesale committal, it means making things inevitable, cutting off every possible retreat. Belief is as irrevocable as bereavement (cf. 2 Samuel 12:21–23).

Belief is the abandonment of all claim to merit. That is why it is so difficult to believe.

A believer is one whose whole being is based on the finished work of Redemption.

It is easier to be true to our convictions than to Jesus Christ, because if we are going to be true to Him our convictions will need to be altered.

Where we blunder is in trying to expound the Cross doctrinally while refusing to do what Jesus told us to do, viz., lift Him up. "And I, if I be lifted up from the earth, will draw all men unto Myself" (John 12:32 RV).

We are not sent to specialise in doctrine, but to lift up Jesus, and He will do the work of saving and sanctifying souls. When we become doctrine-mongers God's power is not known, only the passionateness of an individual appeal.

God has a way of bringing in facts which upset a man's doctrines if these stand in the way of God getting at his soul.

Doctrine is never the guide into Christian experience; doctrine is the exposition of Christian experience.

The further we get away from Jesus the more dogmatic we become over what we call our religious beliefs, while the nearer we live to Jesus the less we have of certitude and the more of confidence in Him.

You cannot understand Jesus Christ unless you accept the New Testament revelation of Him, you must be biased for Him before you can understand Him.

Beware of coming to Jesus with preconceived notions of your own, come relying on the Holy Spirit *"He shall glorify Me,"* said Jesus (John 16:14).

Once allow that Jesus Christ is all the New Testament proclaims Him to be, and you are borne on irresistibly to believe that what He says about Himself is true.

The most conspicuous thing in the New Testament is the supremacy given to our Lord; to-day the supremacy is apt to be given to phases of the truth, to doctrines, and not to Jesus Christ.

Truth is a Person, not a proposition; if I pin my faith to a logical creed I will be disloyal to the Lord Jesus.

The most fundamental heresies which split the Christian Church are those built on what Jesus Christ can do instead of on Himself. Wreckage in spiritual experience always follows.

Many a man spurns Jesus Christ in any phase other than that of his particular religious idea.

Every partial truth has so much error in it that you can dispute it, but you can't dispute "truth as it is in Jesus."

Watch the things you say you can't believe, and then recall the things you accept without thinking, e.g., your own existence.

It is impossible to prove a fact, facts have to be swallowed and the man who swallows revelation facts is no more of a fool than the man who swallows common-sense facts on the evidence of his senses. Face facts, and play the sceptic with explanations.

The "ever-learning, and never able to come to the knowledge of the truth" stage is the cause of all spiritual epidemics; we won't realise what God has revealed.

You can't unveil Truth when you like; when the unveiling comes, beware. That moment marks your going back or your going on.

Truth is of the implicit order, you can't define Truth, and yet every man is so constituted that at times his longing for Truth is insatiable. It is not sufficient to remain with a longing for Truth, because there is something at the basis of things which drives a man to the Truth if he is honest.

When a man says he can't believe, don't argue with him on what he doesn't believe but ask him what he does believe, and proceed from that point; disbelief as often arises from temperament as from sin. Every man believes in a good character, then refer to Jesus Christ as the best character in history, and ask him to believe that what He says is likely to be true (e.g. Luke 11:13; John 3:16), and get him to transact business on that.

When once you come in contact with Jesus you are not conscious of any effort to believe in Him.

If I believe the character of Jesus, am I living up to what I believe?

The danger of pietistic movements is that we are told what we must feel, and we can't get near God because we are so hopelessly dependent on pious attitudes, consequently what is seen is not the New Testament stamp of saint, but the mixture of an insubordinate intellect along with an affected clinging to Jesus with devotion.

Whenever a Holiness Movement raises its head and begins to be conscious of its own holiness, it is liable to become an emissary of the devil, although it started with an emphasis on a neglected truth.

We must continually take stock of what is ours in Christ Jesus because only in that way will we understand what God intends us to be.

If you preach Holiness, or Sanctification, or Divine Healing, or the Second Coming, you are off the track because you de-centralise the Truth. We have to fix our eyes on Jesus Christ, not on what He does. "I *am . . . the Truth.*"

If I am going to know who Jesus is, I must obey Him. The majority of us don't know Jesus because we have not the remotest intention of obeying Him.

Our deadliest temptations are not so much those that destroy Christian belief as those that corrupt and destroy the Christian temper.

The great paralysis of our heart is unbelief. Immediately I view anything as inevitable about any human being, I am an unbeliever.

There is a difference between believing God and believing about Him, you are always conscious of the latter, it makes you a prig. If by letting your beliefs go you get hold of God Himself, let them go.

Beware of worshipping Jesus as the Son of God, and professing your faith in Him as the Saviour of the world, while you blaspheme Him by the complete evidence in your daily life that He is powerless to do anything in and through you.

The greatest challenge to a Christian is to believe Matthew 28:18—"All power is given unto Me in heaven and in earth." How many of us get into a panic when we are faced by physical desolation, by death, or war, injustice, poverty, disease? All these in all their force will never turn to panic the one who believes in the absolute sovereignty of his Lord.

THE BIBLE

"The Word" is Jesus Himself (John 1:1), therefore we must have an experimental knowledge of Him before we understand the literal words of the Bible.

The danger to-day is that people are being nourished not with the Bible so much as with conceptions which ignore Jesus Christ.

Bible facts are either revelation facts or nonsense. It depends on me which they are to me.

God does not thunder His truth into our ears, our attitude of mind must be submissive to revelation facts. Each one of us brings certain prejudices, civilised pre-judgements, which greatly hinder our understanding of revelation facts.

Our attitude to the Bible is a stupid one; we come to the Bible for proof of God's existence, but the Bible has no meaning for us until we know God does exist. The Bible states and affirms facts for the benefit of those who believe in God; those who don't believe in God can tear it to bits if they choose.

People can dispute the words of the Bible as they like, but get a soul in whom the craving for God has come, and the words of the Bible create the new life

in him. ". . . being born again, . . . by the word of God" (1 Peter 1:23).

If we understood what happens when we use the Word of God, we would use it oftener. The disablement of the devil's power by means of the Word of God conveyed through the lips of a servant of His, is inconceivable.

The main characteristic which is the proof of the indwelling Spirit is an amazing tenderness in personal dealing, and a blazing truthfulness with regard to God's Word.

There is no true illumination apart from the written Word. Spiritual impressions generated from my own experience are of no importance, and if I pay attention to them I will pay no attention to the words of Jesus.

The test of God's truth is that it fits you exactly; if it does not, question whether it is His truth.

Beware of bartering the Word of God for a
more suitable conception of your own.

Every impulse must wed itself to the express statements of the Bible, otherwise they will lead astray.

The thing to ask yourself is, "Does the Bible say it?" not, "I don't think that is a good view of God."

Profoundly speaking, it is not sufficient to say, "Because God says it," or, "Because the Bible says it," unless you are talking to people who know God and know the Bible to be His Word. If you appeal from the authority of God or of the Bible to a man not born again, he will pay no attention to you because he does not stand on the same platform. You have to find a provisional platform on which he can stand with you, and in the majority of cases you will find that the platform is that of moral worth. If Jesus Christ is proved Worthy on the plane men are on, they will be ready to put Him as the Most Worthy One, and all the rest will follow.

Whenever human nature gets driven to the end of things the Bible is the only Book, and God the only Being, in the world.

The reason some of us are not healthy spiritually is because we don't use the Bible as the Word of God but only as a text-book.

Beware of making a fetish of a word God once spoke to you; if you stick to the word God spoke you will leave Him, and the result is harshness and stagnation, a refusal to budge from the precedent you have established.

Watch every time the Word of God is made a sacrament to you through someone else, it will make you re-tune your ears to His Word.

There are saints who are being rattled out of holiness by fussy work for God, whereas one five minutes of brooding on God's truth would do more good than all their work of fuss.

*It is what the Bible imparts
to us that is of value.*

The Bible does not thrill, the Bible nourishes. Give time to the reading of the Bible and the recreating effect is as real as that of fresh air physically.

If I have disobeyed, the Word of God is dried up, there is "no open vision." Immediately I obey the Word is poured in.

To read the Bible according to God's providential order in your circumstances is the only way to read it, viz., in the blood and passion of personal life.

The statements of Scripture apart from the Holy Spirit's illumination are dull; it needs no spiritual insight to regard Jesus Christ as a Man who lived beyond His time, but when I am born again I have insight into the Person of Jesus, an insight that comes through communion with God by means of the Bible.

Beware of interpreting Scripture in order to make it suit a pre-arranged doctrine of your own.

Exegesis is not torturing a text to agree with a theory of my own, but leading out its meaning.

*Beware of reasoning about God's Word,
obey it.*

An absurd thing to say is—"Give me a text to prove it." You cannot give a text to prove any one of God's revelations, you can only give a text to prove your simplification of those revelations. A text-proof is generally used to bolster up a personal spiritual affinity of my own.

We are to be servants and handmaids of the Gospel, not devotees of the Bible, then God can make us living mediums whereby His Word becomes a sacrament to others.

THE CALL OF GOD

If you only know what God can do your talk is altogether of that, a logical exposition of doctrine, but if you have heard God's call you will always keep to the one centre, the Person of the Lord Jesus Christ.

Discard any emotion or call to work which cannot find itself at home in the absolute mastery of Jesus Christ.

If I hear the call of God and refuse to obey, I become the dullest, most common-place of Christians because I have seen and heard and refused to obey.

No experience on earth is sufficient to be taken as a call of God; you must know that the call is from God for whom you care more than for all your experiences; then nothing can daunt you.

You can never fag the life out of the one whose service springs from listening to the voice of God, its inspiration is drawn not from human sympathy, but from God Himself.

The Call is the inner motive of having been gripped by God—spoilt for every aim in life saving that of disciplining men to Jesus.

One man or woman called of God is worth a hundred who have elected to work for God.

It is an erroneous notion that you have to wait for the call of God: see that you are in such a condition that you can realise it (see Isaiah 6:8).

If God has called any man or woman in this College into His service, as He undoubtedly has, never allow anyone to interfere with your obedience to His call. Let God do what He likes, He knows exactly where you are, and when the time is fit to make you broken bread in His hands.

We need no call of God to help our fellow men, that is the natural call of humanity; but we do need the supernatural work of God's grace before we are fit for God to help Himself through us.

If a man is called to preach the Gospel, God will crush him till the light of the eye, the power of the life, the ambition of the heart, is all riveted on Himself. That is not done easily. It is not a question of saintliness, it has to do with the Call of God.

THE CHARACTER OF GOD

"No man hath seen God at any time; the only begotten Son, which is in the bosom of the Father, He hath declared Him" (John 1:18). A Christian accepts all he knows about God on the authority of Jesus Christ; he can find out nothing about God by his own unaided intellect.

The God I infer by my common sense has no power over me at all.

The vindication of God to our intelligence is the most difficult process. Only when we see righteousness and justice exhibited in the Person of Jesus Christ can we vindicate God.

In the face of problems as they are, we see in Jesus Christ an exhibition of where our faith is to be placed viz., in a God whose ways we do not understand.

Jesus Christ reveals, not an embarrassed God, not a confused God, not a God who stands apart from the problems, but One who stands in the thick of the whole thing with man.

When a so-called rationalist points out sin and iniquity and disease and death, and says, "How does God answer that?" you have always a fathomless answer—the Cross of Christ.

God's ways are "past finding out"! We often state the character of God in terms of brutal harshness while our motive is to glorify Him.

Never accept an explanation that travesties God's character.

There are some questions God cannot answer until you have been brought by obedience to be able to stand the answer. Be prepared to suspend your judgement until you have heard God's answer for yourself.

There *is* a dark line in God's face, but what we do know about Him is so full of peace and joy that we can wait for His interpretation.

God's order is clearly marked out in the first and the last; His permissive will is seen in the process in-between where everything is disorganised because of sin. The Christian is one who by the power of the indwelling Spirit sees the final issue.

The Psalmist was perplexed when he saw the prosperity of the wicked (see Psalm 73:1–12); God's final purpose is holiness, holy men and women, and He restrains none of the forces which go against that purpose.

Beware lest your attitude to God's truth reminds Him that He is very unwise. Everything worth while in life is dangerous, and yet we would have God such a tepid Being that He runs no risks!

Believe what you do believe and stick to it, but don't profess to believe more than you intend to stick to. If you say you believe God is love, stick to it, though all Providence becomes a pandemonium shouting that God is cruel to allow what He does.

Never attempt to explain God to an exasperated soul, because you cannot. Don't take the part of Job's friends and say you can explain the whole thing; if you think you can, you are very shallow. You have to take on the attitude of vicarious waiting till God brings the light.

Remember, each life has a solitary way alone with God. Be reverent with His ways in dealing with other souls because you have no notion, any more than Job had, why things are as they are. Most of us are much too desirous of getting hold of a line which will vindicate us in our view of God.

It is perilously possible to make our conceptions of God like molten lead poured into a specially designed mould, and when it is cold and hard we fling it at the heads of the religious people who don't agree with us.

God is true to the laws of His own nature, not to my way of expounding how He works.

We have to get out of the old pagan way of guiding ourselves by our heads and get into the Christian way of being guided by faith in a personal God, whose methods are a perpetual contradiction to our every preconceived notion.

We only see another in the light of what we think he is, it takes an amount of surgery on the inside to make us see other people as they really are, and it is the same with what we think about God; we take the facts revealed in the Bible and try to fit them into our own ideas of what God is like.

Am I becoming more and more in love with God as a holy God, or with the conception of an amiable Being who says, "Oh well, sin doesn't matter much"?

God never coerces, neither does He ever accommodate His demands to human compromise, and we are disloyal to Him if we do.

Watch the margins of your mind when you begin to take the view that it doesn't matter whether God is holy or not; it is the beginning of being a traitor to Jesus Christ.

Spiritual insight does not so much enable us to understand God as to understand that He is at work in the ordinary things of life, in the ordinary stuff human nature is made of.

Learn to give honour to God when good works are done, but also learn to discern whether or not they are done by God's servants. The most outrageous moment for the devil will be when he finds that in spite of himself he has done God's will; and the same with the man who has been serving his own ends.

Everything the devil does, God over-reaches to serve His own purpose.

Have I ever had a glimpse of this—that God would not be altered if all our civilised life went to pieces?

Over-refinement in civilisation turns God's order upside down.

God has no respect for our civilisations because He did not found them. While civilisation is not God's, it is His providential protection for men, generally restraining the bad, and affording His children the means of developing their life in Him.

When the present phase is over God won't have elbow-room, it will be all insurance and combine, and God won't be able to get in anywhere. What is true of civilisation will be true of us individually unless we remember to put God first.

In a time of calamity God appears to pay scant courtesy to all our art and culture, He sweeps the whole thing aside till civilisation rages at Him. It is the babe and the fool who get through in the day of God's visitation.

God cannot come to me in any way but His own way, and His way is often insignificant and unobtrusive.

Never accept an explanation of any of God's ways which involves what you would scorn as false and unfair in a man.

God does not act according to His own precedents, therefore logic or a vivid past experience can never take the place of a personal faith in a personal God.

God never crushes men beneath the fear of judgement without revealing the possibility of victorious virtue.

We say that God foresaw sin, and made provision for it: the Bible revelation is that "the Lamb that hath been slain from the foundation of the world" (RV) is the exact expression of the nature of God.

EXPERIENCE

Experiences are apt to be exalted out of all due measure whereas they are but the outward manifestation of the oneness with God made possible for us in Christ Jesus.

Get into the habit of chasing yourself out of the sickly morbid experiences that are not based on having been with Jesus (see Acts 4:13); they are not only valueless, but excessively dangerous.

The great bedrock of Christian experience is the outside fact of the Resurrection made inwardly real by the incoming of the Holy Spirit. "That I may know Him, and the power of His resurrection . . ." (Philippians 3:10).

If your experience is not worthy of the Risen, Ascended Christ, then fling it overboard.

Whenever ecstasies or visions of God unfit us for practical life they are danger signals that the life is on the wrong track.

Our identity with Jesus Christ is immediately practical or not at all, that is, the new identity must manifest itself in our mortal flesh otherwise we can easily hoax ourselves into delusions. Being "made the righteousness of God in Him" is the most powerfully practical experience in a human life.

Insubordination characterises much of what is called "The Higher Christian Life";[4] it is spiritual

---

4. The Higher Christian Life teaching emphasised sanctification and personal holiness.

anarchy based on *my* intuitions, *my* private interpretations, *my* experiences, while refusing to submit to the words of the Lord Jesus.

My experience of salvation never constitutes me an expounder of the Atonement. I am always apt to take my experience for an inclusive interpretation instead of its being merely a gateway for one into salvation.

We continually want to present our understanding of how God has worked in our own experience, consequently we confuse people. Present Jesus Christ, lift Him up, and the Holy Spirit will do in them what He has done in you.

A great deal of what we have to proclaim can never be experienced, but whenever God's standard is presented we are either exonerated or condemned by the way we ourselves carry out the dictates of the Holy Spirit.

Experience as an end in itself is a disease; experience as a result of the life being based on God is health.

Spiritual famine and dearth, if it does not start from sin, starts from dwelling entirely on the experience God gave me instead of on God who gave me the experience.

When I plant my faith on the Lord Jesus my experiences don't make me conscious of them, they produce in me the life of a child.

If my experience makes anyone wish to emulate me, I am decoying that one away from God.

"Because I have had more experience of life than you have, therefore I can discern God's will better than you can." Not at all. Whenever I put my experience of life, or my intelligence, or anything other than dependence on God, as the ground of understanding the will of God I rob Him of glory.

It is on the line of impulse that Satan leads the saints astray, in spite of Jesus Christ's warning—"so as to [lead astray, if possible, RV], even the elect." It is spiritual impulse that leads off at a tangent. Satan does not come as "an angel of light" to anybody but a saint.

Whenever we get light from God on a particular phase we incline to limit God's working to that phase forgetting that we cannot tie up Almighty God to anything built up out of our own experience.

One man's experience is as valuable as another's, but experience has nothing to do with facts. Facts pay no attention to us, facts have to be accepted, they are the real autocrats in life.

You cannot deal with facts as you like, you may object to them, but a fact is a fact, whether a commonsense fact or a revelation fact.

In spiritual experience it is not your intellect that guides you; intellect illuminates what is yours, and you get a thrill of delight because you recognise what you have been going through but could not state.

Whenever the Bible refers to facts of human experience, look to your experience for the answer; when the Bible refers to standards of revelation, look to God not to your experience.

Beware of making your religious experiences a cloak for a lack of reality.

If you have been going on with God you find He has knocked the bottom-board out of your fanaticism; where you used to be narrow and bigoted, you now exhibit His Spirit.

Would to God we got finished once for all with the experience of being adjusted to God, and let Him send us forth into vicarious service for Him!

THE HOLY SPIRIT

It is not what we feel, or what we know, but ever what we *receive* from God—and a fool can receive a gift. "If ye then, being evil, know how to give good gifts unto your children: how much more shall your heavenly Father give the Holy Spirit to them that ask Him?" (Luke 11:13). It is so simple that everyone who is not simple misses it.

Beware of telling people they must be worthy to receive the Holy Spirit; you can't be worthy, you must know you are unworthy, then you will ask for the gift —"If ye then, *being evil. . . .*"

The biggest blessing in your life was when you came to the end of trying to be a Christian, the end of reliance on natural devotion, and were willing to come as a pau-

per and receive the Holy Spirit. The humiliation is that we have to be quite sure we need Him, so many of us are quite sure we don't need Him.

It is extraordinary how things fall off from a man like autumn leaves once he comes to the place where there is no rule but that of the personal domination of the Holy Spirit.

We continually want to substitute our transactions with God for the great mystic powerful work of the Holy Spirit. "The wind bloweth where it listeth, and thou hearest the voice thereof, but knowest not whence it cometh, and whither it goeth: *so is every one that is born of the Spirit*" (John 3:8 RV).

By regeneration we are put into right relationship with God, then we have the same human nature, working on the same lines, but with a different driving power expressing itself, so that the "members" which were used for the wrong are now used for the good (see Romans 6:17–21).

The strenuous effort of the saint is not to produce holiness, but to express in actual circumstances the disposition of the Son of God which is imparted to him by the Holy Ghost.

Beware of seeking power rather than the personal relationship to Jesus Christ which is the grand avenue through which the Holy Spirit comes in His working power. "But ye shall receive power, when the Holy Ghost is come upon you: *and ye shall be My witnesses*" (Acts 1:8 RV).

The message of Pentecost is an emphasis, not on the Holy Ghost, but on the Risen and Ascended Christ (see John 16:13–15).

The Holy Spirit takes care that we fix our attention on Jesus Christ; then He will look after the presentation given of our Lord through us.

Devotion to Jesus is the expression of the Holy Spirit's work in me.

The Holy Spirit is concerned only with glorifying Jesus, not with glorifying our human generosities.

The deep and engrossing need of those of us who name the Name of Christ is reliance on the Holy Spirit.

Jesus Christ reinstates us to the position lost through sin (see Romans 5:12); we come at this knowledge experimentally, but it is never our understanding of salvation that leads to salvation. Salvation is *experienced* first, then to understand it needs the work of the Holy Spirit, which is surprising and incalculable.

We "become partakers of the divine nature" by receiving the Holy Ghost who sheds abroad the love of God in our hearts (Romans 5:5), and the oneness is manifested in a life of abandon and obedience—both unconscious.

If you are being checked by the Holy Spirit over a wrong thing you are allowing in yourself, beware of only captiously seeing the limitations in other people; you will diverge further away from God if you don't recognise that it is the still small voice of God to you.

There is nothing so still and gentle as the checks of the Holy Spirit if they are yielded to, emancipation is the result; but let them be trifled with, and there will come a hardening of the life away from God. Don't quench the Spirit.

There is no room for harsh judgement on the part of a child of God. Harsh judgement is based, not on the sternness of the Holy Ghost, but on my refusal to bear someone else's burden.

Beware of everything in which you have to justify yourself to yourself because the underlying fact is that you have cajoled yourself into taking a decision born of temperamental convictions instead of in entire reliance on the Holy Spirit.

The inspiration of the Holy Spirit is not an impulse to make me act but to enable me to interpret God's meaning; if I do act on the impulse of the inspiration, it is a mere physical reaction in myself. Impulse is God's knock at my door that He might come in, not for me to open the door and go out.

The salvation of Jesus Christ makes a man's personality intense; very few of us are real until the Holy Spirit gets hold of us.

The Holy Spirit does not obliterate a man's personality; He lifts it to its highest use, viz., for the portrayal of the Mind of God.

Beware of the "show business"—"I want to be baptised with the Holy Ghost so that I may do wonderful works." God never allows anyone to do wonderful works: *He* does them, and the baptism of the Holy Ghost prevents my seeing them in order to glory in them.

"When He ascended on high . . . He gave gifts unto men" (Ephesians 4:8 RV; cf. Acts 2:33). The only sign that a particular gift is from the Ascended Christ is that it edifies the Church. Much of our Christian work to-day is built on what the Apostle pleads it should not be built on, viz., the excellencies of the natural virtues.

Be careful to notice the difference between an offended personal prejudice which makes you feel ruffled and huffy, and the intuitive sense of bondage produced by the Holy Spirit when you are listening to something that is not God's truth.

We must distinguish between the bewilderment arising from conviction of sin and the bewilderment arising from confusion in thinking; the latter is the inevitable result in a traditionally Christian mind on first receiving the Holy Spirit; but a curious thing to note is that a heathen mind experiences no such bewilderment on receiving the Holy Spirit because there are no preconceived notions to be got rid of.

The mind that is not produced by obedience to the Holy Spirit in the final issue hates God.

If you are in danger of building on the natural virtues, which are a remnant of the former creation, the Holy Spirit will throw a searchlight and show you things that cause you to shudder. He will reveal a vindictiveness, a maliciousness, you never knew before.

Let God bring you through some midnight, when the Holy Spirit reminds you of what you once were, of your religious hypocrisies—the things the devil whispers you should forget; let God bring you to the dust before Him. This experience will always come in the path of those God is going to take up into His purposes.

The baptism of the Holy Ghost means the extinction of life-fires that are not of God, and everything becomes instinct with the life of God.

The Holy Spirit is the One who regenerates us into the Family to which Jesus Christ belongs, until by the eternal efficacy of the Cross we are made partakers of the Divine nature.

The Holy Spirit is not a substitute for Jesus. The Holy Spirit is all that Jesus was, made real in personal experience *now.*

There is one thing we cannot imitate: we cannot imitate being full of the Holy Ghost.

The mark of the Holy Spirit in a man's life is that he has gone to his own funeral and the thought of himself never enters.

The sign that the Holy Spirit is being obeyed by me is that I am not dominated by my sensualities. "And they that are of Christ Jesus have crucified the flesh with the passions and the lusts thereof" (Galatians 5:24 RV). Sensualities are not gross only, they can be very refined.

"What? know ye not that your body is the temple of the Holy Ghost which is in you . . . ?" (1 Corinthians 6:19). The indwelling of the Holy Spirit is the climax of Redemption.

The great impelling power of the Holy Spirit is seen in its most fundamental working whenever an issue of will is pushed. It is pleasanter to listen to poetical discourses, more agreeable to have your affinities appealed to, but it is not good enough, it leaves you exactly as you were. The Gospel appeal comes with a stinging grip—"Will you?" or, "Won't you?" "I will accept," or, "I'll put it off"—both are decisions, remember.

We have to distinguish between acquiring and receiving. We *acquire* habits of prayer and Bible reading and we *receive* our salvation, we *receive* the Holy Spirit, we *receive* the grace of God. We give more attention to the things we acquire; all God pays attention to is what we receive. Those things we receive can never be taken from us because God holds those who receive His gifts.

The fruit of pseudo-evangelism is different from "the fruit of the Spirit" (Galatians 5:22–23).

Guard as your greatest gift the anointing of the Holy Spirit, viz., the right of access to God for yourself. "And as for you, the anointing which ye received of Him abideth in you" (1 John 2:27 RV).

It is the fine art of the Holy Spirit to be
alone with God.

THE MORAL LAW

It has been a favourite belief in all ages that if only men were taught what good is, everyone would choose it; but history and human experience prove that that is not so. To know what good *is* is not to *be* good.

My conscience makes me know what I ought to do, but it does not empower me to do it. "For that which I do I allow not: for what I would, that do I not; but what I hate, that do I" (Romans 7:15).

To say that if I am persuaded a thing is wrong I won't do it, is not true. The mutiny of human nature is that it will do it whether it is wrong or not.

The problem in practical experience is not to know what is right, but to do it. My natural spirit may know a great many things, but I never can be what I know I ought to be until I receive the Life which has life in itself, viz., the Holy Spirit. That is the practical working of the Redemption.

"Morality is altogether based on utilitarian standards": it is not, a man's conscience will come in every time when he doesn't want it to.

Conscience resides in the essential spirit of a man, not in his reasoning faculty; it is the one thing that assists a man in his unregenerate days.

Why are men not worse than they are? The reason is the existence of the moral law of God which restrains men in spite of the impulse towards wrong, consequently you find remnants of the strivings of the moral law where you least expect it because the moral law is independent entirely of the opposition to it on the part of individual men.

When God's law is presented beware of the proud self-confidence which says, "This is good enough for me, I don't intend to soar any higher."

In dealing with the question of disease both moral and physical, we must deal with it in the light of the Redemption. If you want to know how far wrong the world has got you learn it, not in a hospital, but at the Cross. We learn by what it cost God to redeem the world how criminally out of moral order the universe has got.

The guilt abroad to-day can never be dealt with by pressing a social ethic or a moral order, or by an enfolding sympathy for man, while pooh-poohing the demands of a holy God.

Very few of us know what *love of God is,* we know what *love of moral good* is, and the curious thing is that

that leads us away from God more quickly than does a terror of moral evil; "the good is ever the enemy of the best."

Our lawlessness can be detected in relation to the words, "Come unto Me."

Liberty means ability not to violate the law; license means personal insistence on doing what I like.

If a man is not holy, he is immoral, it does not matter how good he seems, immorality is at the basis of the whole thing. It may not show itself as immoral physically, but it will show itself as immoral in the sight of God (see Luke 16:15).

Intellectual scepticism is good, but a man is to blame for moral scepticism. Every man believes in goodness and uprightness and integrity until he perverts his taste by going wrong himself.

Beware of giving way to spiritual ecstasies, it disconnects you from the great ordinances of God and shakes the very basis of sane morality God has made.

There is no such thing as a *wrong* wrong, only a *right* that has gone wrong. Every error had its start in a truth, else it would have no power.

In the moral realm if you don't do things quickly you will never do them. Never postpone a moral decision.

Second thoughts on moral matters are always deflections.

It is only when a moral act is performed and light thrown on realities that we understand the relationship between our human lives and the Cross of Christ.

PERSONALITY

Nothing in connection with our personality is so disastrously enervating as disillusionment about ourselves. We much prefer our own idea of ourselves to the stern realisation of what we really are. Paul warns, Let no man "think of himself more highly than he ought to think." Watch how God has disillusioned you over yourself and see the value of it for the future.

There is a difference between the reality of personality and its actuality, the latter is continually changing; you are sensitive now where you were indifferent before, and *vice versa*.

Individuality can never become a sacrament, it is only personality that can become a sacrament through oneness with Jesus Christ.

You often find people in the world are more desirable, easier to get on with, than people in the Kingdom. There is frequently a stubbornness, a self-opinionativeness, in Christians not exhibited by people in the world.

If there is to be another Revival[5] it will be through the readjustment of those of us on the inside who call ourselves Christians.

It is obvious that as we have grown physically we have developed into more useful human beings, but have we grown finer morally and spiritually? grown more pure and holy? We may have become broader-minded and yet not be so fine in perception as we used to be. It takes a lot of self-scrutiny to know whether we are evolving all the time in every domain of our being. "Therefore by their fruits ye shall know them" (RV).

The greatest test of Christianity is the wear and tear of daily life, it is like the shining of silver, the more it is rubbed the brighter it grows.

It is well to remember that our examination of ourselves can never be unbiased or unprejudiced, so that we are only safe in taking the estimate of ourselves from our Creator instead of from our own introspection, whether conceited or depressed.

The modern Pharisee is the one who pretends to be the publican—"Oh, I would never call myself a saint!" Exaggerated self-depreciation and exaggerated conceit are both diseased.

God has an alchemy of Providence by means of which our inner spirit precipitates itself—obliged to be holy if you are holy; obliged to be impure if you are impure. It is impossible to repress the ruling spirit when in the presence of the Spirit of God in another.

Crises reveal character. When we are put to the test the hidden resources of our character are revealed exactly.

We have to do more than we are built to do naturally; we have to do all the Almighty builds us to do.

The phrase "Self-mastery" is profoundly wrong although practically correct. Profoundly, a man can never be master of what he does not understand, therefore the only master of a man is not himself, or another man, but God. "Self-mastery" is correct if it means carrying out the edicts of God in myself.

Leave no subject connected with your own soul until you have landed at the door of the supernatural. Natural resources are liable to break down in a crisis, but if your life is based on the supernatural God His power will manifest itself, and turn the moment that might have been tragic into triumph.

Unity of self is difficult to describe, it is the state in which there is no consciousness of myself, only of unity in myself. A false unity is fictitious because at any moment it may fall to pieces in an agony of remorse.

How long it takes for all the powers in a Christian to be at one depends on one thing only, viz., obedience.

The reason self-interest is detected in us is because there are whole tracts of our nature that have never been fused by the Spirit of God into one central purpose.

If all Jesus Christ came to do is to produce disunity in me He had better never have come, because I am created to have such harmony in myself that I am unconscious of it.

Self-complacency and spiritual pride are always the beginning of degeneration When I begin to be satisfied with where I am spiritually, instantly I begin to degenerate.

There is no pride equal to spiritual pride, and no obstinacy equal to spiritual obstinacy, because they are nearest to the throne of God, and are most like the devil.

It is never our wicked heart that is the difficulty, but our obstinate will.

"Show me what to do and I'll do it"—you won't. It is easy to knock down one type of pride and erect another.

The only reason I can't get to God is pride, no matter how humble I seem.

When any personal position is credited by me to myself, God's decree is that it hardens my heart in pride.

The only sacrifice acceptable to God is "a broken and a contrite heart," not a moral upright life built on pride. When I stand on the basis of penitence, God's salvation is manifested immediately.

Note the thing which makes you say, "I don't believe it," it will prove where you are spiritually. What I resent reveals who governs me.

If excellence of character is made the test, the grace of God is "made void," because a man can develop an amazing perfection of character without a spark of the grace of God. If we put a saint or a good man as the standard, we blind ourselves to ourselves, personal vanity makes us do it; there is no room for personal vanity when the standard is seen to be God Himself.

To cling to my natural virtues is quite sufficient to obscure the work of God in me.

There is a domain of our nature which we as Christians do not cultivate much, viz., the domain of the imagination. Almost the only way we use our imagination is in crossing bridges before we come to them. The religion of Jesus embraces every part of our make-up, the intellectual part, the emotional part, no part must be allowed to atrophy, all must be welded into one by the Holy Spirit.

Learn to distinguish between what isolates you and what insulates you. God insulates; sin isolates, a gloomy, sardonic standing off from everything, the disdain of superiority; only when you are closest to God do you understand that that is its nature.

The natural virtues in some people are charming and delightful, but let a presentation of truth be given they have not seen before, and there is an exhibition of the most extraordinary resentment, proving that all their piety was purely temperamental, an unexplored inheritance from ancestors.

It is an appalling fact that our features tell our moral character unmistakably to those who can read them, and we may be very thankful there are few who can; our safety is in other people's ignorance. In spite of the disguise of refinement, sensuality, selfishness and self-indulgence speak in our features as loud as a thunder-clap. Our inner spirit tells with an indelible mark on every feature, no matter how beautiful or how ugly the features may be. Let us remember that that is how God sees us.

Nothing can hinder God's purpose in a personal life but the person himself.

In this life we must forgo much in order that we might develop a spiritual character which can be a glory to God for Time and Eternity.

In His teaching about discipleship Jesus Christ bases everything on the complete annihilation of individuality and the emancipation of personality. Until this is understood all our talk about discipleship passes into thin air.

When I am baptised with the Holy Ghost my personality is lifted up to its right place, viz., into perfect union with God so that I love Him without hindrance.

Anything that partakes of the nature of swamping my personality out of control is never of God.

PERSONAL RELATIONSHIP

The essence of Christianity is a personal relationship to Jesus Christ with any amount of room for its outworking.

The appeal of the Gospel is not that it should be preached in order that men might be saved and put right for heaven, but that they might enter into a personal relationship with Jesus Christ here and now.

Discipleship and salvation are two different things: a disciple is one who, realising the meaning of the Atonement, deliberately gives himself up to Jesus Christ in unspeakable gratitude.

The one mark of discipleship is the mastership of Jesus—His right to me from the crown of my head to the sole of my foot.

"If any man would come after Me, let him deny himself" (RV), i.e., "deny his right to himself." Jesus never swept men off their feet in ecstasy, He always talked on the line that left a man's will in the ascendant until he saw where he was going. It is impossible for a man to give up his right to himself without knowing he is doing it.

Naturally, a man regards his right to himself as the finest thing he has, yet it is the last bridge that prevents Jesus Christ having His way in a life.

The approaches to Jesus are innumerable; the result of coming to Him can be only one—the dethroning of my right to myself, or I stop short somewhere.

Jesus Christ is always unyielding to my claim to my right to myself.

The one essential element in all our Lord's teaching about discipleship is abandon, no calculation, no trace of self-interest.

Is Jesus Christ absolutely necessary to me? Have I ever shifted the basis of my reasoning on to Incarnate Reason? ever shifted my will on to His will? my right to myself on to His right to me?

What is the personal history between Jesus Christ and myself? Is there anything of the nature of "the new creation" (RV mg) in me? or is what I call my "experience" sentimental rubbish placed on top of "me" as I am?

A disciple is one who not only proclaims God's truth, but one who manifests that he is no longer his own, he has been "bought with a price."

Our service is to be a living sacrifice of devotion to Jesus, the secret of which is identity with Him in suffering, in death, and in resurrection (Philippians 3:10).

It is possible to be first in suffering for the Truth and in reputation for saintliness, and last in the judgement of the great Searcher of hearts. The whole question is one of heart-relationship to Jesus.

If you remain true to your relationship to Jesus Christ the things that are either right or wrong are never the problem; it is the things that are right but which would impair what He wants you to be that are the problem.

The mark of the saint is the good right things he has the privilege of not doing. There are a hundred and one right and good things which, if you are a disciple of Jesus, you must avoid as you would the devil although there is no devil in them. If our Lord's words in Matthew 5:29–30 were read more often we would have a healthier young manhood and womanhood.

Beware of the people who tell you life is simple. Life is such a mass of complications that no man is safe apart from God. Coming to Jesus does not simplify life, it simplifies my relationship to God.

The implicit relationship tells more than the explicit, if you put the explicit first you are apt to produce sceptics.

When Jesus Christ is bringing a son to glory, He ignores the work he has done; the work has been allowed as a discipline to perfect his relationship to the Father.

The work we do for God is made by Him a means till He has got us to the place where we are willing to be purified and made of worth to Himself.

Overmuch organisation in Christian work is always in danger of killing God-born originality; it keeps us conservative, makes our hands feeble. A false artificial flow of progress swamps true devotion to Jesus.

Whenever a spiritual movement has been true to Jesus Christ it has brought forth fruit in a hundred and one ways the originator of the movement never dreamed of.

Neither usefulness nor duty is God's ultimate purpose, His aim is to bring out the message of the Gospel, and if that can only be done by His "bruising" me, why shouldn't He? We put our intelligent fingers on God's plan.

God's idea is that individual Christians should become identified with His purpose for the world. When Christianity becomes over-organised and denominational it is incapable of fulfilling our Lord's commission; it doesn't "feed His sheep," it can't (see John 21:15–17).

"I have had visions on the mount," "wonderful times of communion with God"—but is it turning you into an individual infinitely superior to your Lord and Master? one who won't wash feet, but will only give himself up to certain types of meeting?

"If I then, the Lord and the Master, have washed your feet, ye also ought to wash one another's feet" (RV): the highest motive is the only motive for the lowliest service. Where do we stand in God's sight under that scrutiny?

A false religion makes me hyper-conscientious—"I must not do this, or that"; the one lodestar in the religion of Jesus is personal passionate devotion to Him, and oneness with His interests in other lives. Identify yourself with Jesus Christ's interests in others, and life takes on a romantic risk.

Christianity is not service for Jesus Christ, not winning souls, it is nothing less than the life of Jesus being manifested more and more in my mortal flesh.

Beware of allowing the historic Jesus Christ to be taken from you in any shape or form; make it the intensest concern of your spiritual life to accompany the disciples as He went in and out among them in the days of His flesh.

"What has my religion done for me I could not do for myself?" That is a question every man is forced to ask. Religion ostensibly is faith in Someone, or a form of belief in some power, I would be the poorer if I did not have, and I should be able to state in what way I would be poorer.

If my religion is not based on a personal history with Jesus it becomes something I suffer from, not a joyous thing, but something that keeps me from doing what I want to do.

Occasionally we have to revise our ways of looking at God's Providence. The usual way of looking at it is that God presents us with a cup to drink, which is strangely mixed. But there is another aspect which is just as true, perhaps more vitally true, viz., that we present God with a cup to drink, full of a very strange mixture indeed. God will never reverse the cup. He will drink it. Beware of the ingredient of self-will, which ought to have been dissolved by identification with the Death of Jesus, being there when you hand the cup of your life back to God.

PRAYER

God is never impressed with our earnestness, He promises to answer us when we pray on one ground only, viz., the ground of the Redemption. The Redemption of the Lord Jesus provides me with a place for intercession.

The only way to get into the relationship of "asking" is to get into the relationship of absolute reliance on the Lord Jesus. "And this is the confidence that we have in Him . . ." (1 John 5:14–16).

Remember, you have to ask things which are in keeping with the God whom Jesus Christ reveals. When you pray, what conception have you in your mind—your need, or Jesus Christ's omnipotence? (see John 14:12–13).

"Asking" in prayer is at once the test of three things—simplicity, stupidity and certainty of God. Prayer means that I come in contact with an Almighty Christ, and almighty results happen along the lines He laid down.

It is not that my prayers are so important, that is not the point; God has so made it that by means of intercession certain types of blessing come upon men. In Christian work that is where the "filling up" comes in; we are apt to bank much more on talking to people.

If I am a Christian, I am not set on saving my own skin, but on seeing that the salvation of God comes through me to others, and the great way is by intercession.

The Bible knows nothing about a gift of prayer, the only prayer the Bible talks about is the prayer that is able to bring down something from God to men.

How impatient we are in dealing with other people! Our actions imply that we think God is asleep, until God brings us to the place where we come on them from above.

The illustrations of prayer our Lord uses are on the line of importunity, a steady, persistent, uninterrupted habit of prayer.

God puts us in circumstances where He can answer the prayer of His Son (John 17), and the prayer of the Holy Ghost (Romans 8:26).

The reason for intercession is not that God *answers* prayer, but that God tells us to pray.

God never answers prayer to prove
His own might.

The answers to prayer never come by introspection but always as a surprise. We don't hear God because we are so full of noisy introspective requests.

Spiritual certainty in prayer is God's certainty, not a side-eddy of sanctimoniousness.

Prayer is the vital breath of the Christian; not the thing that makes him alive, but the evidence that he *is* alive.

The very powers of darkness are paralysed by prayer. No wonder Satan tries to keep our minds fussy in active work till we cannot think to pray.

God is not meant to answer *our* prayers, He is answering the prayer of Jesus Christ in our lives; by our prayers we come to discern what God's mind is, and that is declared in John 17.

According to the New Testament, prayer is God's answer to our poverty, not a power we exercise to obtain an answer.

Intercession does not develop the one who intercedes, it blesses the lives of those for whom he intercedes. The reason so few of us intercede is because we don't understand this.

By intercessory prayer we can hold off Satan from other lives and give the Holy Ghost a chance with them. No wonder Jesus put such tremendous emphasis on prayer!

If your crowd knows you as a man or woman of prayer, they have a right to expect from you a nobler type of conduct than from others.

If I pray that someone else may be, or do, something which I am not, and don't intend to do, my praying is paralysed.

When you put God first you will get your times of prayer easily because God can entrust them to the soul who won't use them in an irrational way and give an occasion to the enemy to enter in.

Watch God's ways in your life, you will find He is developing you as He does the trees and the flowers, a deep silent working of the God of Creation.

The enemy goes all he can against our communion with God, against our solitude with God, he tries to prevent us from drawing our breath in the fear of the Lord.

The greatest answer to prayer is that I am brought into a perfect understanding with God, and that alters my view of actual things.

We must steadfastly work out repentance in intercessory prayer.

Beware lest activity in proclaiming the Truth should mean a cunning avoidance of spiritual concentration in intercession.

The lost sight of God inevitably follows spiritual teaching that has not a corresponding balance of private prayer.

See that you do not use the trick of prayer to cover up what you know you ought to do.

The meaning of prayer is that I bring power to bear upon another soul that is weak enough to yield and strong enough to resist; hence the need for strenuous intercessory prayer.

Never try to make people agree with your point of view, begin the ministry of intercession. The only Being worth agreeing with is the Lord Jesus Christ. Remember 1 John 5:16.

The prayer of the saints is never self-important, but always God-important.

What happens when a saint prays is that the Paraclete's almighty power is brought to bear on the one for whom he is praying.

God does not give faith in answer to prayer: He reveals Himself in answer to prayer, and faith is exercised spontaneously.

PREACHING

A personal testimony feeds you from hand to mouth; you must have more equipment than that if you are to preach the Gospel.

The preacher must be part of his message, he must be incorporated in it. That is what the baptism of the Holy Ghost did for the disciples. When the Holy Ghost came at Pentecost He made these men living epistles of the teaching of Jesus, not human gramophones recording the facts of His life.

If you stand true as a disciple of Jesus He will make your preaching the kind of message that is incarnate as well as oral.

To preach the Gospel makes *you* a sacrament; but if the Word of God has not become incorporated into you, your preaching is "a clanging cymbal" (RV); it has

never cost you anything, never taken you through repentance and heartbreak.

We have not to explain how a man comes to God, instead of bringing men to God, that hinders; an explanation of the Atonement never drew anyone to God, the exalting of Jesus Christ, and Him crucified does draw men to God (see John 12:32).

Remember, you go among men as a representative of Jesus Christ.

The preacher's duty is not to convict men of sin, or to make them realise how bad they are, but to bring them into contact with God until it is easy for them to believe in Him.

No man is ever the same after listening to the

truth, he may say he pays no attention to it, he may appear to forget all about it, but at any moment the truth may spring up into his consciousness and destroy all his peace of mind.

The great snare in Christian work is this—"Do remember the people you are talking to." We have to remain true to God and His message, not to a knowledge of the people, and as we rely on the Holy Spirit we will find God works His marvels in His own way.

Live in the reality of the Truth while you preach it.

Most of us prefer to live in a particular phase of the Truth, and that is where we get intolerant and pigheaded, religiously determined that everyone who does not agree with us must be wrong. We preach in the Name of God what He won't own.

God's denunciation will fall on us if in our preaching we tell people they must be holy and we ourselves are not holy. If we are not working out in our private life the messages we are handing out, we will deepen the condemnation of our own souls as messengers of God.

Our message acts like a boomerang; it is dangerous if it does not.

A good clear emotional expression contains within it the peril of satisfactory expression while the life is miles away from the preaching. The life of a preacher speaks louder than his words.

There is no use condemning sensuality or worldly-mindedness and compromise in other people if there is the slightest inclination for these in our own soul.

It is all very well to preach, the easiest thing in the world to give people a vision of what God wants; it is another matter to come into the sordid conditions of ordinary life and make the vision real there.

Beware of hypocrisy with God, especially if you are in no danger of hypocrisy among men.

Penetration attracts hearers to God, ingenuity attracts to the preacher. Dexterity is always an indication of shallowness.

A clever exposition is never right because the Spirit of God is not clever. Beware of cleverness, it is the great cause of hypocrisy in a preacher.

Don't be impatient with yourself, because the longer you are in satisfying yourself with an expression of the Truth the better will you satisfy God.

Impressive preaching is rarely Gospel-preaching: Gospel-preaching is based on the great mystery of belief in the Atonement, which belief is created in others, not by my impressiveness, but by the insistent conviction of the Holy Spirit.

There is far more wrought by the Word of God than we will ever understand, and if I substitute anything for it, fine thinking, eloquent speech, the devil's victory is enormous, but I am of no more use than a puff of wind.

The determination to be a fool if necessary is the golden rule for a preacher.

We have to preach something which to the wisdom of this world is foolishness. If the wisdom of this world is right, then God is foolish; if God is wise, the wisdom of this world is foolishness (see 1 Corinthians 1:18–25). Where we go wrong is when we apologise for God.

If you are standing for the truth of God you are sure to experience reproach, and if you open your mouth to vindicate yourself you will lose what you were on the point of gaining. Let the ignominy and the shame come, be "weak in Him."

Never assume anything that has not been made yours by faith and the experience of life; it is presumptuous to do so. On the other hand, be ready to pay the price of "foolishness" in proclaiming to others what is really yours.

People only want the kind of preaching which does not declare the demands of a holy God. "Tell us that God is loving, not that He is holy, and that He demands we should be holy." The problem is not with the gross sinners, but with the intellectual, cultured, religious-to-the-last-degree people.

All the winsome preaching of the Gospel is an insult to the Cross of Christ. What is needed is the probe of the Spirit of God straight down to a man's conscience till his whole nature shouts at him, "That is right, and *you* are wrong.'

It is the preacher's contact with Reality that enables the Holy Spirit to strip off the sophistries of those who listen, and when He does that, you find it is the best people who go down first under conviction.

A great psychological law too little known is that the line of appeal is conditioned by the line of attraction. If I seek to attract men, that will be the line on which my aggressive work will have to be done.

To whom is our appeal? To none but those God sends you to. You can't get men to come; nobody could get you to come until you came. "The wind bloweth where it listeth, . . . so is every one that is born of the Spirit."

Many of the theological terms used nowadays have no grip, we talk glibly about sin, and about salvation; but let the truth be presented along the line of a man's deep personal need, and at once it is arresting.

Some of us are rushing on at such a headlong pace in Christian work, wanting to vindicate God in a great Revival, but if God gave a revival we would be the first to forget Him and swing off on some false fire.

" . . . not slothful in business," i.e., the Lord's business. Don't exhaust yourself with other things.

Beware as of the devil of good taste being your standard in presenting the truth of God.

"Wherefore henceforth know we no man after the flesh" (2 Corinthians 5:16); that is the way we do know men—according to our common-sense estimates. The man who knows God has no right to estimate other men according to his common-sense judgement, he has to bring in revelation facts which will make him a great deal more lenient in his judgement. To have a little bit only of God's point of view makes us immensely bitter in our judgement.

Beware lest your reserve in public has the effect of God Almighty's decree to the sea—"Hitherto shalt thou come, but no further." I have no business in God's service if I have any personal reserve, I am to be broken bread and poured-out wine in His hands.

If you are living a life of reckless trust in God the impression given to your congregation is that of the reserve power of God, while personal reserve leaves the impression that you are condescending to them.

We should give instruction unconsciously; if you give instruction consciously in a dictatorial mood you simply flatter your own spiritual conceit.

Have you never met the person whose religious life is so exact that you are terrified at coming near him? Never have an exercise of religion that blots God clean out.

Remember two things: be natural yourself, and let God be naturally Himself through you. Very few of us have got to the place of being worthily natural, any number of us are un-worthily natural, that is, we reveal the fact that we have never taken the trouble to discipline ourselves.

Don't be discouraged if you suffer from physical aphasia, the only cure for it is to go ahead, remembering that nervousness overcome is power.

Beware of being disappointed with yourself in delivery; ignore the record of your nerves.

Learn to be vicarious in public prayer. Allow two rivers to come through you: the river of God, and the river of human interests. Beware of the danger of preaching in prayer, of being doctrinal.

When you preach, you speak for God, and from God to the people; in prayer, you talk to God for the people, and your proper place is among the people as one of them. It is to be a vicarious relation, not the flinging of theology at their heads from the pulpit.

Always come from God to men; never be so impertinent as to come from the presence of anyone else.

How do interruptions affect you? If you allot your day and say, "I am going to give so much time to this, and so much to that," and God's Providence upsets your time-table, what becomes of your spirituality? Why, it flies out of the window! it is not based on God, there is nothing spiritual about it, it is purely mechanical. The great secret is to learn how to draw on God all the time.

Whenever you are discovered as being exhausted, take a good humiliating dose of John 21:15–17. The whole secret of shepherding is that someone else reaches the Saviour through your heart as a pathway.

Beware of making God's truth simpler than He has made it Himself.

By the preaching of the Gospel God creates what was never there before, viz., faith in Himself on the ground of the Redemption.

People say, "Do preach the simple Gospel," if they mean by "the simple Gospel" the thing we have always heard, the thing that keeps us sound asleep, then the sooner God sends a thrust through our stagnant minds the better.

If any man's preaching does not make me brace myself up and watch my feet and my ways, one of two things is the reason—either the preacher is unreal, or I hate being better.

- A joyous, humble belief in your message will compel attention.
- Sermons may weary, the Gospel never does.

PREPARATION

It is by thinking with your pen in hand that you will get to the heart of your subject.

"The heart of the righteous studieth to answer" (Proverbs 15:28). To give your congregation extemporaneous thinking, i.e., thinking without study, is an insult—ponderous "nothings." The preacher should give his congregation the result of strenuous thinking in un-studied, extemporaneous speech.

Extemporaneous speech is not extemporaneous thinking, but speech that has been so studied that you are possessed unconsciously with what you are saying.

Never get a studied form; prepare yourself mentally, morally, and spiritually, and you need never fear.

The great thing is not to hunt for texts, but to live in the big comprehensive truths of the Bible and texts will hunt you.

To talk about "getting a message," is a mistake. It is preparation of myself that is required more than of my message.

Don't go to your Bible in a yawning mood.

As a student of the Word of God, keep your mind and heart busy with the great truths concerning God, the Lord Jesus Christ, the Holy Spirit, the Atonement, sin, suffering, etc.

Slay on the threshold of your mind the thing that makes you sit down mentally and say, *"I can't."* Why be saved and sanctified in a rusty indolent case?

In impromptu speaking, begin naturally, and the secret of beginning naturally is to forget you are religious. Many wear a crushing religious garb.

Beware of detaching yourself from your theme in order to heed the way you present it. Never be afraid of expressing what is really you.

To develop your expression in public you must do a vast amount of writing in private. Write out your problems before God. Go direct to Him about everything

Time spent on the great fundamental revelations given by the Holy Spirit is apt to be looked upon as a waste of time—"We must get to practical work."

The work we do in preparation is meant to get our minds into such order that they are at the service of God for His inspiration.

Conscious inspiration is mercifully rare or we would make inspiration our god.

Don't chisel your subject too much. Trust the reality of your nature and the reality of your subject.

The discipline of your own powers is a very precious acquirement in the service of God; it delivers you from breathless uncertainty and possible hysterics. Learn to respect the findings of your own mind.

Always check private delight in preparation. Close your preparation with prayer and leave it with God till wanted.

When you speak, abandon yourself in confidence; don't try to recall fine points in preparation.

The burning heart while Jesus talks with us and opens up the Scriptures to us is a blessed experience, but the burning heart will die down to ashes unless we keep perennially right with God.

Spiritual insight is in accordance with the development of heart-purity.

Every domain of our life which comes under the apprehension of the Spirit of God is a call to cultivate that particular domain for Him. The trouble is that we won't break up the new soil of our lives for God.

Spiritual sloth must be the greatest grief to the Holy Ghost. Sloth has always a moral reason, not a physical one; the self-indulgent nature must be slothful.

Learn to fast over your subject in private; do the mechanical work and trust God for the inspirational in delivery.

Don't memorise what you have to say or you will serve up *"cauld kale het."*[6]

In order to expound a passage, live in it well beforehand.

Keep yourself full with reading. Reading gives you a vocabulary.

Don't read to remember; read to realise.

The speaker without notes must have two things entirely at his command—the Bible and his mother tongue.

In impromptu speaking, never try to recall, always plunge.

Let the centre of your subject grip you, then you will express its heart unconsciously.

Get moved by your message, and it will move others in a corresponding way.

Watch how God by His angels elbows you out of the hour you thought you were going to get with your Bible—only you will never call them "angels" unless you are filled with the Holy Spirit. "That objectionable person" was really an angel of God to you, saying "Get this thing worked out.'

---

6. *cauld kale het*: Scottish phrase. Literally, kale, a cheap vegetable with a strong taste, becomes almost inedible when reheated the day after being cooked. Metaphorically, something not fresh, something recycled that should have been thrown out.

REDEMPTION

God does not ask us to be good men and women He asks us to understand that we are not good; to believe that "none is good, save one, even God" (RV), and that the grace of God was manifested in the Redemption that it might cover the incompleteness of man.

When a man experiences salvation it is not his belief that saves him; teaching goes wrong when it puts a man's belief as the ground of his salvation. Salvation is God's "bit" entirely.

The danger is to preach a subjective theology, something that wells up on the inside. The Gospel of the New Testament is based on the absoluteness of the Redemption.

The great thing about the Redemption is that it deals with *sin*, i.e., my claim to my right to myself, not primarily with man's sins. It is one of the most flattering things to go and rescue the degraded, one of the social passions of mankind, but not necessarily the most Christian: it is quite another thing to tell men who are among the best of men that what Jesus Christ asks of them is that they give up the right to themselves to Him.

The great thing about the Gospel is that it should be preached. Never get distressed over not seeing immediate results. No prophet of the Old Testament, or apostle of the New (or saint of the present day), ever fully understood the import of what he said or did, hence to work for immediate results is to make myself a director of the Holy Ghost.

God is no respecter of persons with regard to salvation, but He has a tremendous respect for Christian character. There are degrees in glory which are determined by our obedience.

Salvation is a free gift through the Redemption; positions in the Kingdom are not gifts, but attainments.

There is a difference between salvation and saintliness, between being redeemed and proving myself a redeemed man. I may live a life of sordid self-seeking on the basis of the Redemption, or I may live a life which manifests the life of the Lord Jesus in my mortal flesh.

Jesus Christ did not send out the disciples to save souls, but to "make disciples" (RV), men and women who manifest a life in accordance with the life of their Redeemer.

A charge made against some methods of evangelism is that self-interest is made the basis of the whole thing: salvation is looked upon as a kind of insurance scheme whereby I am delivered from punishment and put right for heaven. But let a man experience *deliverance from sin*, and his rejoicing is not in his own interests, but that he is thereby enabled to be of use to God and his fellow men.

The bedrock permanent thing about Christianity is the forgiveness of God, not sanctification and personal holiness—the great abiding thing underneath is infinitely more rugged than that; it is all the New Testament means by that terrific word "*forgiveness*." "In whom we have our redemption through His blood, the forgiveness of sins" (Ephesians 1:7).

The virtue of our Redemption comes to us through the obedience of the Son of God—"though He were a Son, yet learned He obedience by the things which He suffered . . ." (Hebrews 5:8). Our view of obedience has become so distorted through sin that we cannot understand how it could be said of Jesus that He "learned" obedience; He was the only One of whom it could be said, because He was "without sin." He did not learn obedience in order *to be* a Son: He came *as* Son to redeem mankind.

Our Lord came to make atonement for the sin of the world, not by any impulse of a noble nature, but by the perfect conscious Self-sacrifice whereby alone God could redeem man.

Beware of the craze for unity. It is God's will that all Christians should be one with Him as Jesus Christ is one with Him (John 17:22), but that is a very different thing from the tendency abroad to-day towards a unity on a basis that ignores the Atonement.

Until we have become spiritual by new birth the Atonement of Jesus has no meaning for us; it only begins to get meaning when we live "in heavenly places in Christ Jesus."

Salvation is based on the *revelation* fact that God has redeemed the world from the possibility of condemnation on account of sin (Romans 5:12, 20–21): the *experience* of salvation means that a man can be regenerated, can have the disposition of the Son of God put into him, viz., the Holy Spirit.

Belief in the Redemption is difficult because it needs self-surrender first.

Do I believe that everything that has been touched by the consequences of man's sin is going to be put absolutely right by God through the Redemption?

Redemption is the Reality which alters inability into ability.

The mighty Redemption of God is made actual in my experience by the living efficacy of the Holy Ghost.

SANCTIFICATION

Beware of preaching Sanctification without knowing Jesus; we are saved and sanctified in order that we might know Him.

"But of Him are ye in Christ Jesus, who of God is made unto us wisdom, and righteousness, and sanctification, and redemption" (1 Corinthians 1:30). Jesus Christ is all these, they are not things He works out apart from Himself.

We cannot earn things from God, we can only take what is given us. Salvation, sanctification, eternal life, are all gifts wrought out in us through the Atonement. The question is, am I working out what God works in?

It is quite true to say "I can't live a holy life"; but you can decide to let Jesus make you holy. "I can't do away with my past"; but you can decide to let Jesus do away with it. That is the issue to push.

We use the word "consecration" before sanctification, it should be used after sanctification. The fundamental meaning of consecration is the separating of a holy thing to God, not the separating of an un-holy thing to be made holy.

". . . present your bodies a living sacrifice, holy, acceptable unto God," says the Apostle Paul. You cannot separate to God what God has not purified.

If I make personal holiness a cause instead of an effect I become shallow, no matter how profound I seem. It means I am far more concerned about being speckless than about being real; far more concerned about keeping my garments white than about being devoted to Jesus Christ.

The idea that I grow holy as I go on is foreign to the New Testament. There must have been a place where I was identified with the death of Jesus: "I have been crucified with Christ . . ." (RV). That is the meaning of sanctification. Then I grow on holiness.

Jesus Christ can make my disposition as pure as His own. That is the claim of the Gospel.

The saints have gone to sleep, "Thank God, I am saved and sanctified, it is all right now": you are simply in the right place to maintain the life which is going to confront the world and never be subdued by the world.

"Now I am sanctified the world has no attraction for me." But remember, the world is what the Holy Spirit sees, not what you see. It is not gross sins that are the attraction, but things that are part of God's creation, things "in the land of Canaan," they creep in gradually and you begin to think according to pagan standards and only in a crisis realise you have not been standing with God.

God has staked His reputation on the work of Jesus Christ in the souls of the men and women whom He has saved and sanctified.

If we are to be of any use to God in facing present-day problems we must be prepared to run the sanctification-metaphysic for all it is worth.

The great fever in people's blood to-day is, "Do something"; "Be practical." The great need is for the one who is un-practical enough to get down to the heart of the matter, viz., personal sanctification. Practical work not based on an understanding of what sanctification means is simply beating the air.

The test of sanctification is not our talk about holiness and singing pious hymns; but, what are we like where no one sees us? with those who know us best?

It is perilously possible to credit God with all our mean little prejudices even after we are sanctified.

Pious talk paralyses the power to live piously, the energy of the life goes into the talk—sanctimonious instead of sanctified. Unless your mind is free from jealousy, envy, spite, your pious words only increase your hypocrisy.

Beware of sentimentality; it means something has been aroused in me that I don't intend to work out.

Wherever there is true teaching of the Gospel there will be both salvation and sanctification taking place.

If you are called to preach, God will put you through "mills" that are not meant for you personally, He is making you suitable bread to nourish other lives. It is after sanctification you are put through these things.

If I exalt Sanctification, I preach people into despair; but if I lift up Jesus Christ, people learn the way to be made holy. "For I determined not to know anything among you, save Jesus Christ, and Him crucified" (1 Corinthians 2:2).

It is a great snare to think that when you are sanctified you cannot make mistakes; you can make mistakes so irreparably terrible that the only safeguard is to "walk in the light, as He is in the light."

When you come under the searchlight of God after sanctification, you realise much more keenly what sin is than ever you could have done before.

The deliverances of God are not what the saint delights in, but in the fact that *God* delivered him; not in the fact that he is sanctified, but that *God* sanctified him; the whole attention of the mind is on God

We are saved and sanctified not for service, but to be absolutely Jesus Christ's, the consuming passion of the life is for Him.

Never try to build sanctification on an unconfessed sin, on a duty left undone; confess the wrong, do what you ought to have done, then God will clear away all the hyper-conscientious rubbish.

In sanctification it has to be a valediction once and for ever to confidence in everyone and everything but God.

You can always test the worth of your sanctification. If there is the slightest trace of self-conscious superiority about it, it has never touched the fringe of the garment of Christ.

"I lay down My life," said Jesus; "I *lay it down of Myself.*" If you are sanctified, you will do the same. It has nothing to do with "Deeper Death to Self," it has to do with the glorious fact that I have a self, a personality, that I can sacrifice with glad alacrity to Jesus every day I live.

SIN

Sin is not man's problem, it is God's.

Beware of attempting to diagnose sin unless you have the inner pang that you are one of the worst sinners.

Whenever you talk about sin, it must be "my" sin. So long as you speak of "sins" you evade Jesus Christ for yourself.

Sin is the outcome of a relationship God never ordained, a relationship which maintains itself by means of a wrong disposition, viz., my claim to my right to myself. That is the essence of sin.

My right to myself is not merely something I claim, but something that continually makes me insist on my own way.

Whenever God touches sin it is independence that is touched and that awakens resentment in the human heart. Independence must be blasted clean out, there must be no such thing left, only freedom, which is very different. Freedom is the ability not to insist on my rights, but to see that God gets His.

There are people whose actual lives shock us, and there are those whose actual lives are speckless, but whose ruling disposition is "my claim to my right to myself." Watch Jesus Christ with them both, and you get the attitude we have lost.

Jesus Christ never faced men as we do; you may put before Him "publicans and sinners" and clean-living moral men, and you find He is much sterner with the latter. To recognise this would mean a revolution in our outlook.

Original sin is "doing without God." That phrase covers sin in its beginning in human consciousness and its final analysis in the sight of God.

"For from within, out of the heart of man proceed . . ." (see Mark 7:21–23). We should get into the habit of estimating ourselves by the rugged statements of our Lord.

The thing that makes me feel I am different from "the common herd" never came from God: I am not different. Remember, the same stuff that makes the criminal makes the saint.

A saint is "a new creation" (RV mg), made by the Last Adam out of the progeny of the first Adam no matter how degraded.

". . . Christ Jesus came into the world to save sinners" (1 Timothy 1:15). What is a sinner? Everyone who is not one with Jesus as He is one with God.

Our Lord did not scathe sin; He came to save from it.

We are apt to put the superb blessings of the Gospel as something for a special few, they are for sinners saved by grace.

A man may be magnificently saved and appallingly backward in development, or he may be a maturely developed saint, like the Apostle Paul; but neither is more than saved by God's grace.

When Jesus Christ begins to get His way He is merciless with the thing that is not of God.

As long as things are kept covered up we think God's judgement is severe, but let the Holy Ghost reveal the secret vileness of sin till it blazes out in a conspicuous glare, and we realise that His judgement is right.

The reason men enclose themselves away from the Gospel is that conviction of sin upsets the inner balance of mind, consequently of bodily health, but when once a man is convinced that holiness is of more importance than bodily health, he lets all go to get holy.

The first appeal of present-day evangelism is apt to be, not on the line of how to get rid of sin, but how to be put right for heaven, consequently men are not convicted of sin, but left with a feeling of something insufficient in life.

The only hope for a man lies not in giving him an example of how to behave, but in the preaching of Jesus Christ as the Saviour from *sin*. The heart of every man gets hope when he hears that.

Our Lord never sympathised with sin, He came to "proclaim liberty to the captives," a very different thing. We have to see that we don't preach a theology of sympathy, but the theology of a Saviour from sin.

It is not our business to convict men of sin, the Holy Ghost alone convicts of sin (RV), our duty is to lift up the One who sets free from sin. It is not a question of something being curbed, or counteracted, or sat on, it is a radical alteration on the inside, then I have to assimilate that alteration so that it is manifested in the practical relationships of my life.

The life of the Holy Spirit in a saint is fierce and violent against any tendency to sin.

The attitude of Jesus towards sin is to be our attitude towards sins.

When conviction of sin by the Holy Spirit comes it gives us an understanding of the deeps of our personality we are otherwise not conscious of (John 16:8–11).

The forgiveness of God penetrates to the very heart of His nature and to the very heart of man's nature. That is why God cannot forgive until a man realises what sin is.

- Sin is reality; sins are actuality.
- Measure your growth in grace by your sensitiveness to sin

Many a man gets to the place where he will call himself a sinner, but he does not so readily come to the place where he says, *"Against Thee, Thee only, have I sinned. . . ."*

Salvation from sin is frequently confounded with, deliverance from sins. A man can deliver himself from sins without any special work of God's grace. The bedrock of New Testament salvation is repentance, and repentance is based on relationship to a Person.

A great many people are delighted to hear about the life of Jesus, its holiness and sublimity, but when the Holy Ghost begins to convict them of sin, they resent it, and resent it deeply.

Conviction of sin in the beginning is child's play compared with the conviction the Holy Ghost brings to a mature saint. (See 1 Timothy 1:15).

Humiliation by conviction of sin is rare today. You can never be humiliated by another human being after the conviction of sin the Holy Ghost gives.

On the threshold of the Christian life people talk a lot about sin, but there is no realisation of what sin is, all that is seen is the effects of sin.

If we are ever going to come anywhere near understanding what our Lord's agony in the Garden of Gethsemane represents, we have to get beyond the small ideas of our particular religious experiences and be brought to see sin as God sees it—"For He hath made Him to *be sin* for us, *who knew no sin;* that we might be made the righteousness of God in Him."

If we eliminate the supernatural purpose of Jesus Christ's coming, viz.:, to deliver us from sin, we become traitors to God's revelation.

The Cross of Christ is God's last and endless Word. There the prince of this world is judged, there sin is killed, and pride is done to death, there lust is frozen and self-interest slaughtered, not one can get through.

It was not social crimes, but the great primal sin of independence of God, that brought the Son of God to Calvary.

STUDY

Study to begin with can never be easy; the determination to form systematic mental habits is the only secret. Don't begin anything with reluctance.

Beware of any cleverness that keeps you from working. No one is born a worker; men are born poets and artists, but we have to make ourselves "labourers."

The discipline of our mind is the one domain God has put in our keeping. It is impossible to be of any use to God if we are lazy. God won't cure laziness, we have to cure it.

More danger arises from physical laziness (which is called "brain fag") than from almost any other thing.

Inspiration won't come irrespective of study, but only because of it. Don't trust to inspiration, use your own "axe" (Psalm 74:5). Work! Think! Don't luxuriate on the mount!

The demand for inspiration is the measure of our laziness. Do the things that don't come by inspiration.

It is difficult to get yourself under control to do work you are not used to, the time spent seems wasted at first, but get at it again. The thing that hinders control is impulse.

Your mind can never be under your control unless you bring it there; there is no gift for control. You may pray till Doomsday but your brain will never concentrate if you don't make it concentrate.

In the most superficial matters put yourself under control, your own control. Be as scrupulously punctual in your private habits as you would be in a Government office.

Don't insult God by telling Him He forgot to give you any brains when you were born. We all have brains, what we need is *work*.

It is better for your mental life to study several subjects at once rather than one alone. What exhausts the brain is not using it, but abusing it by nervous waste in other directions. As a general rule, the brain can never do too much.

You can never work by impulse, you can only work by steady patient plod. It is the odd five minutes that tells.

To learn a thing is different from thinking out a problem. The only way to learn a thing is to keep at it uninterruptedly, day after day, whether you feel like it or not, and you will wake up one morning and find the thing is learned.

Beware of succumbing to failure as inevitable; make it the stepping-stone to success.

In beginning to study a new subject you do it by repeated starts until you get your mind into a certain channel, after that the subject becomes full of sustained interest.

Beware of mental lounging. Whenever we see notebooks for study, or work of any kind waiting to be done, we either go into dreamland, or we gather everything around us in an enormously bustling style, but we never do good solid work. It is nothing in the world but a habit of nerves which we have to check, and take time to see that we do.

A subject has never truly gripped you until you are mentally out of breath with it.

We have no business to go on impulses spiritually, we have to form the mind "which was also in Christ Jesus." People say their impulses are their guide—"I feel impelled to do this, or that"—that may be sufficient indication that they should not do it.

Remember, there must always be a mechanical outlet for spiritual inspiration.

We infect our surroundings with our own personal character. If I make my study a place of stern industry, it will act as an inspiration every time I go into it; but if I am lazy there, the place will revenge itself on me.

Note two things about your intelligence: first, when your intelligence feels numb, quit at once, and play or sleep; for the time being the brain must recuperate; second, when you feel a fidget of associated ideas, take yourself sternly in hand and say, "You shall study, so it's no use whining."

Mental stodge is different. Mental stodge is the result of one of three forms of over-feeding—too much dinner, too much reading, or too much meetings.

Irritation may be simply the result of not using your brain. Remember, the brain gets exhausted when it is not doing anything.

Beware of saying, "I haven't time to read the Bible, or to pray"; say rather, "I haven't disciplined myself to do these things."

Before any habit is formed you must put yourself under mechanical laws of obedience, and the higher the emotion started by the Spirit of God, the keener must be the determination to commit yourself.

If we have no system of work we shall easily come to think we are working when we are only thinking of working, that we are busy when we are only engaged.

The more we talk about work, the less we work, and the same with prayer.

We must be willing to do in the spiritual domain what we have to do in the natural domain if we want to develop, viz., discipline ourselves.

Vision is an inspiration to stand us in good stead in the drudgery of discipline; the temptation is to despise the discipline.

Enchain your body to habitual obedience.

Beware of being haunted by a suppressed dissatisfaction with the arrangements of your actual life—*get* the right programme! The secret of slacking is just here.

THE TEACHING OF JESUS

Our Lord did not come to this earth to *teach* men to be holy: He came to *make* men holy, and His teaching is applicable only on the basis of experimental Redemption.

The teaching of Jesus is not first; what *is* first is that He came to give us a totally new heredity, and the Sermon on the Mount describes the way that heredity will work out.

A good way to find out how much stodge there is in our spiritual life is to read the Sermon on the Mount and see how obtuse we are to the greater part of what Jesus Christ taught.

There is a calm deliberation about the injunctions in the Sermon on the Mount; we are not asked to obey them until the Holy Spirit brings them to our remembrance, when He does, the question is, will I exercise the disposition given me in regeneration and react in my actual life in accordance with the Mind of Christ?

Weighing the *pros and cons* for and against a statement of Jesus Christ's means that for the time being I refuse to obey Him.

We are never justified in taking any line of action other than that indicated by the teaching of Jesus and made possible for us by the grace of God.

Our Lord's teaching does not mean anything to a man until it does, and then it means everything.

Make your mind sure of what our Lord taught, and then insist and re-insist on it to the best of your ability.

Distortions of belief come because principles are put in the place of Jesus Christ. I must have a personal relationship to Him first, and then let the Holy Spirit apply His teaching.

Nothing must switch the disciple's loyalty to his Lord by loyalty to principles deduced from His teaching.

There are no infallible principles,
only an infallible Person.

All my devotion is an insult to God unless every bit of my practical life squares with Jesus Christ's demands.

Beware of being negligent in some lesser thing while being good in some spiritual thing, e.g., you may be good in a prayer meeting while not good in the matter of cleaning your boots. It is a real peril, and springs from selecting some one thing our Lord taught as our standard instead of God Himself.

Matthew 5:48 is the standard for the Christian: "Ye therefore shall be perfect, as your heavenly Father is perfect" (RV). Size yourself up with a good sense of humour—"*me*, perfect!" That is what Jesus Christ has undertaken to do.

The religion of Jesus is morality transfigured by spirituality; we have to be moral right down to the depths of our motives.

It cannot be too often emphasised that our Lord never asks us to do other than all that good upright men do, but He does ask that we do just those same things from an entirely different motive (see Matthew 5:20).

We should make less excuses for the weaknesses of a Christian than for any other man. A Christian has God's honour at stake.

When a man is regenerated and bears the Name of Christ the Spirit of God will see to it that he is scrutinised by the world, and the more we are able to meet that scrutiny the healthier will we be as Christians.

Civilised organisations were never more deadly opposed to the teaching of Jesus than in the present age.

Whenever an organisation begins to be conscious of itself, its spiritual power goes because it is living for its own propaganda. Movements which were started by the Spirit of God have crystallised into something God has had to blight because the golden rule for spiritual work has been departed from. (See John 12:24).

"I am not come to destroy, but to fulfil" (Matthew 5:17). Our Lord was not *anti* anything; He put into existing institutions a ruling principle which if obeyed would reconstruct them.

If you have never been brought close enough to Jesus to realise that He teaches things that grossly offend you as a natural man, I question whether you have ever seen Him.

Immediately you get out of touch with God, you are in a hell of chaos. That is always in the background of the teaching of Jesus. (Cf. Matthew 5:21–26). That is why the teaching of Jesus produces such consternation in the natural man.

Whenever a truth comes home to me my first reaction is to fling it back on you, but the Spirit of God brings it straight home, "Thou art the man." We always want to lash others when we are sick with our own disobedience.

The scrutiny we give other people should be for ourselves. You will never be able to cast out the mote in your brother's eye unless you have had a beam removed, or to be removed, from your own eye (Matthew 7:3–4).

It is perilously possible to do one of two things—bind burdens on people you have no intention of helping them lift, or placidly to explain away the full purport of our Lord's teaching (see Luke 11:46).

Divorced from supernatural new birth the teaching of Jesus has no application to me, it only results in despair.

Our Lord's teaching about the maimed life and the mature life has not been sufficiently recognised. You can never be mature unless you have been fanatical. (See Matthew 5:29–30, 48).

"Whosoever shall compel thee to go a mile, go with him twain" (Matthew 5:41). If you are a saint the Lord will tax your walking capacity to the limit.

It is a slow business teaching a community living below the Christian level, I have to act according to the Christian ethic while not ignoring the fact that I am dealing with a community which lives away below it. The fact that I live with a degenerate crowd does not alter my duty, I have to behave as a disciple of Jesus.

TEMPTATION

To be raised above temptation belongs to God only.

Wherever there is moral responsibility there is temptation, i.e., the testing of what a man holds in his own person.

The old Puritan idea that the devil tempts men had this remarkable effect, it produced the man of iron who fought; the modern idea of blaming his heredity or his circumstances produces the man who succumbs at once.

When we say a thing is "Satanic" we mean something abominable according to our standards: the Bible means something remarkably subtle and wise. Satanic temptations are not bestial, those temptations have to do with a man's own stupidity and wrongdoing.

The Holy Ghost is the only One who can detect the temptations of Satan, neither our common sense nor our human wisdom can detect them as temptations.

Every temptation of Satan is the acme of human wisdom, but immediately the Spirit of God is at work in a man the hollow mockery at its heart is recognised.

Jesus Christ deals with Satan as the manifestation of something for which man is held responsible. Man is nowhere held responsible for the devil.

The temptation in Christian work to-day is to turn our sympathy towards human beings, "Put man's needs first." No, sympathy with God first, let Him work as He will.

If you allow human sympathy to make you susceptible to the Satanic side of things, you instantly sever yourself from the susceptibility which in all temptation ought to be turned God-wards.

Our Lord's words to Peter, "But He turned and said unto Peter, Get thee behind Me, Satan: thou art an offence unto Me: for thou savourest not the things that be of God, but those that be of men" (Matthew 16:23) crystallise for us His authoritative view of the conclusions of man's mind, when that mind has not been formed by the Holy Spirit, viz. that it is densely and satanically incapable of understanding His form of thought.

Satan does not tempt to gross sins, the one thing he tempts to is putting myself as master instead of God.

Beware of removing our Lord into a religious wardrobe where the cast-off haloes of the saints are kept, but remember that "we have not a high priest that cannot be touched with the feeling of our infirmities; but one that hath been in all points tempted like as we are, yet without sin" (Hebrews 4:15 RV; cf. Hebrews 2:11).

How are we to face the tempter? By prayer? No. With the Word of God? No. Face the tempter with Jesus Christ, and He will apply the word of God to you, and the temptation will cease. "For in that He Himself hath suffered being tempted, He is able to succour them that are tempted" (Hebrews 2:18).

The moments of severest temptation are the moments of His divinest succour.

TESTIMONY

It is never our testimony that keeps our experience right: our experience makes us testify.

To testify is part of the life of every Christian, but because you have a personal testimony it does not follow that you are called to preach.

To say what God has done for you is testimony, but you have to preach more than you have experienced—more than anyone has ever experienced; you have to preach Jesus Christ. Present the Object of your faith, the Lord Jesus, lift Him up, and then either give your testimony, or know you have one to give.

To say a thing is the sure way to begin to believe it. That is why it is so necessary to testify to what Jesus Christ has done for you.

The false mood creeps in when you have the idea that you are to be a written epistle—of course you are! but you have not to know it.

Whenever you meet a man who is going on with God you find his testimony explains your own experience. A true testimony grips everyone who is after the Truth.

It is easier to stand true to a testimony mildewed with age, because it has a dogmatic ring about it that people agree with, than to talk from your last moment of contact with God.

Am I trying to live up to a testimony, or am I abiding in the Truth?

The danger of experience-meetings when they get outside the New Testament standard is that people don't testify to anything that glorifies God, but to experiences that leave you breathless and embarrassed. It is all on the illuminated line, on the verge of the hysterical.

People are precipitated into testifying before the vision they have had is made real—"Now I have had this experience," or, "Now I have become that." What we need to do after the vision is to examine ourselves before God and see if we are willing for all that must happen before it is made real in us.

When we get the vision of what God wants us to be, we are put to the blush by what we actually are, and that humiliation is the precursor of the coming reality, a heartpanging disgust at the realisation of what I am. That is what the Holy Spirit works in me; a disgust that will end in nothing less than death, then God can begin to make the vision real.

Never give an educated testimony, i.e., something you have taught yourself to say; wait till the elemental moves in you.

Be prepared to be unreserved in personal testimony; but remember, personal testimony must never be lowered into personal biography.

You cannot bring a knowledge of Jesus Christ to another, you can only tell him what He is to you, but until he gets where you are he will never see what you see.

If my testimony makes anyone wish to emulate me, it is a mistaken testimony, it is not a witness to Jesus.

The Holy Spirit will only witness to a testimony when Jesus Christ is exalted higher than the testimony.

THINKING

"For who among men knoweth the things of a man, save the spirit of the man, which is in him?" A man discovers intellectual things for himself but he cannot discover God by his intellect. " . . . even so the things of God none knoweth, save the Spirit of God" (1 Corinthians 2:11 RV).

Think of the labour and patience of men in the domain of science and then think of our lack of patience in endeavouring to appreciate the Atonement, and you see the need there is for us to be conscientious in our thinking, basing everything on the reality of the Atonement. We prefer to be average Christians, we don't mind it having broken God's heart to save us, but we do object to having a sleepless night while we learn to say "Thank you" to God so that the angels can hear us. We need to be staggered out of our shocking indolence.

We have no business to limit God's revelations to the bias of the human mind.

"I can't alter my thinking." You can. It is actually possible to identify your mind with the highest point of view, and to habituate yourself by degrees to the thinking and the living in accordance with it.

A man's mental belief will show sooner or later in his practical living.

If I make my life in my intellect I will certainly delude myself that I am as good as I think I am. "As [a man] thinketh *in his heart"*—that means "me," as I express my thinking in actual life, "*so is he."*

I can think out a whole system of life, reason it all out well, but it does not necessarily make any differ-

ence to my actual life, I may think like an angel and live like a tadpole.

Note the things your thinking does not account for.

Truth is discerned by moral obedience. There are points in our thinking which remain obscure until a crisis arises in personal life where we ought to obey, immediately we obey the intellectual difficulty alters. Whenever we have to obey it is always in something immensely practical.

Obedience is the basis of Christian thinking. Never be surprised if there are whole areas of thinking that are not clear, they never will be until you obey.

Every new domain into which your personal life is introduced necessitates a new form of responsible intelligence.

Watch what you say you don't understand— you understand only too clearly.

Learn to be glad when you feel yourself a chaos that makes you bitterly disappointed with yourself, because from that moment you will begin to understand that God alone can make you "order" and "beauty."

Young life must be in chaos or there is no development possible.

Until you get an answer that satisfies your best moods only, don't stop thinking, keep on querying God. The answers that satisfy you go all over you, like health, or fresh air.

Don't shut up any avenue of your nature, let God come into every avenue, every relationship, and you will find the nightmare curse of "secular and sacred" will go.

Intellectual obstinacy produces the sealed mind—"Jesus said unto them, If ye were blind, ye would have no sin: but now ye say, We see: your sin remaineth" (John 9:41 RV).

There is no jump into thinking, it is only done by a steady determined facing of the facts brought by the engineering of circumstances. God always insists that I think *where I am*. Beware of that abortion of Providence—"If I were you . . ."

With regard to other men's minds, take all you can get, whether those minds are in flesh-and-blood editions or in books, but remember, the best you get from another mind is not that mind's verdict, but its standpoint. Note the writers who provoke you to do your best mentally.

Never cease to think until you think things home and they become character.

Very few of us are real as God is real, we are only real in spots—awake morally and spiritually and dead intellectually, or *vice versa*, awake intellectually and dead morally and spiritually. It takes the shaking of God's Providence to awaken us up as whole beings, and when we are awakened we get growing pains in moral senses, in spiritual muscles we have never used. It is not the devil, it is God trying to make us appreciative sons and daughters of His.

Our thinking is often allowed to be anti-Christian while our feelings are Christian. The way I think will colour my attitude towards my fellow-men.

Always make a practice of provoking your mind to think about what it easily accepts. A position is not yours until you make it yours through suffering.

If you have ever done any thinking you don't feel very complacent after it, you get your first touch of pessimism; if you don't, you have never thought clearly and truly.

An appalling thing is that men who ignore Jesus Christ have their eyes open in a way many a preacher of the Gospel has not. Ibsen, for instance, saw things clearly: he saw the inexorable results of sin but without any deliverance or forgiveness, because he saw things apart from the Atonement.

The first thing that goes when you begin to think is your theology. If you stick too long to a theological point of view you become stagnant, without vitality.

Never try to pillory Incarnate Reason by your own petty intelligence.

"I have yet many things to say unto you, but ye cannot bear them now" (John 16:12 RV). These words are true in our mental life as well as in our spiritual life.

Doubt is not always a sign that a man is wrong, it may be a sign that he is thinking.

Keep the powers of your mind going full pace, always maintaining the secret life right with God.

If you teach anything out of an idle intellect, you will have to answer to God for it.

Never be distressed at the immediate result of thinking on the deep truths of religion because it will take years of profound familiarity with such truths before you gain an expression sufficient to satisfy you.

God never simply gives us an answer, He puts us on a line where it is possible for Truth to break more and more as we go on.

Before the mind has begun to grapple with problems it is easy to talk; when the mind has begun to grapple with problems it is a humiliating thing to talk.

Unless you think, you will be untouched, unbroken, by the truths you utter.

A logical position is satisfying to intellect, but it can never be true to life. Logic is simply the method man's intellect follows in making things definable to himself, but you can't define what is greater than yourself.

We command what we can explain, and if we bring our explanation into the spiritual domain we are in danger of explaining Jesus away—"and every spirit which annulleth Jesus is not of God" (1 John 4:3 RV mg). We have to be intelligently more than intelligent, intellectually more than intellectual, that is, we have to use all our wits in order not to worship our wits but be humble enough to worship God.

Don't run away with the idea that everything that runs contrary to your complacent scheme of things is of the devil.

As you go on with God He will give you thoughts that are a bit too big for you. God will never leave a servant of His with ideas he can easily express, He will always express through him more than he can grasp.

It takes a long time to get rid of atheism in thinking.

WORKERS FOR GOD

The worker for God must live among the common-sense facts of the natural world, but he must also be at home with revelation facts.

Be a worker with an equal knowledge of sin, of the human heart and of God.

Never take it for granted because you have been used by God to a soul that God will always speak through you, He won't. At any second you may blunt your spiritual intuition, it is known only to God and yourself. Keep the intuitive secret life clear and right with God at all costs.

Never pray for the gift of discernment, live so much in contact with God that the Holy Spirit can point out through you to others where they are wrong.

Our confidence is to be based on the fact that it is God who provides the issue in lives; we have to see that we give Him the opportunity of dealing with men by ceasing to be impressive individuals.

Beware of allowing the discernment of wrong in another to blind you to the fact that you are what you are by the grace of God.

How do I deal with a sinful soul? do I remember who I am, or do I deal with him as if I were God?

Never say, "That truth is applicable to So-and-so," it puts you in a false position. To know that the truth is applicable to another life is a sacred trust from God to you, you must never say anything about it. Restraint in these matters is the way to maintain communion with God.

How many people have you made homesick for God? The value of our work depends on whether we can direct men to Jesus Christ.

"Lovest thou Me? . . . Feed My sheep." That means giving out my life-blood for others as the Son of God gave His life-blood for me.

Christian service is not our work; loyalty to Jesus is our work.

Whenever success is made the motive of service infidelity to our Lord is the inevitable result. (Cf. Luke 10:20).

The curse of much modern Christian work is its determination to preserve itself.

This fundamental principle must be borne in mind, that any work for God before it fulfils its purpose must die, otherwise it "abideth alone." The conception is not that of progress from a seed to full growth, but of a seed dying and bringing forth what it never was. That is why Christianity is always "a forlorn hope" in the eyes of the world.

The element of faith that enables us to experience salvation is less than the faith required to make us workers for God. We have to bring into harmony all the strayed forces of our nature and concentrate them on the life of faith.

Beware of the temptation to compromise with the world, to put their interests, their needs, first—"They have kindly become interested in our Christian work, given so much time to it, now let us winsomely draw them in"—they will winsomely draw you away from God.

We constantly ask, "Am I of any use?" If you think you are, it is questionable whether you are being used by the Holy Spirit at all. It is the things you pay no attention to that the Holy Spirit uses.

Your dead-set determination to be of use never means half so much as the times you have not been thinking of being used—a casual conversation, an ordinary word, while your life was "hid with Christ in God."

As a worker, you must know how to link yourself on to the power of God; let the one you are talking to have the best of it for a time, don't try to prove that you are in the right and he is in the wrong. If we battle for a doctrinal position we will see no further spiritually.

Never interfere with God's providential dealings with other souls. Be true to God yourself and watch.

Individual responsibility for others without becoming an amateur providence, is one of the accomplishments of the Holy Spirit in a saint.

As workers for God, feed your heart and mind on this truth, that as individuals we are mere iotas in the great purpose of God. Every evangelical "craze" is an attempt to confine God to our notions, whereas the Holy Spirit constrains us to be what God wants us to be.

The greatest service you can render God is to fulfil your spiritual destiny.

Where would you be if God took away all your Christian work? Too often it is our Christian work that is worshipped and not God.

We rush through life and call ourselves practical, we mistake activity for real life, consequently when the activity stops we go out like a vapour, it has not been based on the great fundamental energy of God.

Beware of Christian *activities* instead of Christian *being*. The reason workers come to stupendous collapses is that their work is the evidence of a heart that evades facing the truth of God for itself—"I have no time for prayer, for Bible study, I must be always at it."

The lives that are getting stronger are lives in the desert, deep-rooted in God; they always remind you of God whenever you come in contact with them.

Never shrink from dealing with any life you are brought up against, but never go unless you are quite sure God wants you to, He will guide. God's permission means there is no shadow of doubt on the horizon of consciousness; when there is, wait. God never guides by fogs or by lightning flashes, He guides naturally.

Don't insult God by despising His ordinary ways in your life by saying, "Those things are beneath me." God has no special line, anything that is ordinary and human is His line.

Any worker following Paul's advice to Timothy— "Preach the word; be instant in season, out of season . . ." (2 Timothy 4:2)—will be continually surprised with new discoveries of truth, and there will be a perennial freshness about the spoken word.

You cannot be too severe with self-pity in yourself or in others. Be more merciless with yourself than you are with others.

Remember, weariness in work which is attended by spiritual weakness means you have been using your vital energy without at the same time witnessing. Natural weariness in work while you witness, produces steady and wonderful rejuvenescence.

If you obey God His order may take you into a cesspool but you will never be hurt.

If my life as a worker is right with God I am not concerned about my public pose—using discreet terms that will impress people; my one concern in public and private is to worship God.

When a worker jealously guards his secret life with God the public life will take care of itself.

Remember, in estimating other lives there is always one fact more you don't know. You don't know why some men turn to God and others don't, it is hidden in the inscrutable part of a man's nature.

If we realise the intense sacredness of a human soul in God's sight we will no longer romp in where angels fear to tread, we will pray and wait.

Never talk for the sake of making the other person see you are in the right, talk only that he may see the right, and when he does see it you will be so obliterated that he will forget to say "Thank you."

Notice carefully by what you are hurt and see whether it is because you are not being obeyed, or whether it is because the Holy Spirit is not being obeyed. If it is because you are not being obeyed, there is something desperately wrong with you.

In the majority of cases we don't care a bit about a soul rebelling against Jesus Christ, but we do care about his humiliating us.

Nothing hoodwinks us more quickly than the idea that we are serving God.

The last lesson we learn is "Hands off," that God's hands may be on.

When you are brought face to face with a case of happy indifference, pray for all you are worth, but let him alone with your tongue—the hardest thing for an earnest Christian to do.

It is much easier to do Christian work than to be concentrated on God's point of view.

Beware lest human pity pervert the meaning of Calvary so that you have more compassion for a soul than for the Saviour.

As "workers together" with God we are called upon not to be ignorant of the forces of the day in which we live. God does not alter, the truths of the Bible do not alter, but the problems we have to face do alter.

Never allow anyone to confess to you unless it is for his own soul's sake, make him tell God. The habit of confessing tends to make one person dependent on another, and the one who confesses becomes a spiritual sponge, mopping up sympathy.

The judicious weighing of what you should allow other people to tell you and what not to allow them to tell you, depends on two things: your experience of life among *men*, and your experience of life with God.

Never give a soul the help God alone should give; hand him right on to God.

Keep your mind stayed on God, and I defy anyone's heart to stop at you, it will always go on to God. Our duty is to present God, and never get in the way even in thought.

My business as a worker is to see that I am living on the basis of the Atonement in my actual life.

When you come in contact with the great destructive sins in men's lives, be reverent with what you don't understand. God says, "Leave that one to Me."

"We then, as workers together with Him. . . ." the One referred to is Almighty God, "the Creator of the ends of the earth." Think of the impregnable position it gives the feeblest saint to remember that he is a fellow-worker with God.

God's Workmanship

Oswald Chambers

For we are His workmanship, created in Christ Jesus for good works, which God afore prepared that we should walk in them. Ephesians 2:10 (RV)

INTRODUCTION

Source

Lectures and sermons given by Oswald Chambers in England and Egypt, 1910 to 1917.

Publication History

- As articles: *Tongues of Fire/Spiritual Life Magazine* and the *Bible Training Course (BTC) Journal*.[1]
- As a book: 1953.

During the 1930s and 1940s, Mrs. Chambers compiled and published most of Oswald's lectures and sermons that developed a single theme or expounded a passage of Scripture. This left many talks covering a wide variety of subjects unpublished in book form. *God's Workmanship* (1953) along with *Disciples Indeed* (1955) and *The Servant As His Lord* (1958) have preserved these miscellaneous messages. These three were among the last books compiled by Mrs. Chambers before her death in 1966.

---

1. The *Bible Training Course Journal* was published from 1932 to 1952 by Mrs. Chambers, with help from David Lambert.

CONTENTS

REALITY

The existence of a truth is nothing to me until I am brought into the current of events where that particular truth is a living reality to me because it speaks the language of my conscious life. Reality must have its source outside me; my conscious experience is the sphere of Reality in me, but I must be careful never to confound the reality of my experience with Reality itself.

1. Response to God

And without faith it is impossible to be well-pleasing unto Him: for he that cometh to God must believe that He is. . . . (Hebrews 11:6 RV)

Religion confronts God, not in scrutiny or criticism, but in response, in welcome, in obedience to His visitation. Religion is only possible to revelation. Religion is not aspiration, it is not temperament, it is not subjectivity, its roots are in God moving to man more than in man moving to God.

Forsyth[2]

We need constantly to remember that the work of God in us is the foundation of our Christian experience and faith, and as constantly do we need to remember that we never can experience the ground and spring of our Christian experience. In other words, our faith must be in the reality of the Redemption and never in what God has done in us and for us. What is experienced in our individual lives is the efficacious working of salvation, but we never can *experience* the God who gives us that experience. We are delighted with our experience, it is the thing we can talk about, but unless our faith is in the God who gives us the experience it ends in pietistic jargon; I try to pack all God's tremendous redemptive energy into a side eddy—"I have got all this to myself." If you know on what ground your experience has arisen you say, like Paul did, "I know *whom* I have believed," not "I know what I have got."

The thing to pay attention to is the miracle created in human experience, not on the ground of my reason, but on the ground of the Redemption, and it begins exactly as our Lord describes—"The wind bloweth where it listeth, and thou hearest the voice thereof, but knowest not whence it cometh, and whither it goeth: so is every one that is born of the Spirit" (John 3:8 RV). Whenever I say "I want to rea-son this thing out before I can trust," I will never trust. The reasoning out and the perfection of knowledge come after the response to God has been made. If we would learn on the threshold of our life with God to put away as impertinent, and even iniquitous, the debates as to whether or not we will trust God, we would not remain under the delusions we do; we would abandon without the slightest hesitation, cut the shore lines, burn our bridges behind us, and realise that what has happened is the positive miracle of the Redemption at work—we know with a knowledge which passeth knowledge. The whole of the New Testament exposition in the inspiration of the Holy Spirit is in order that we might know where we have been placed by Almighty God's Redemption. Immediately we come in contact with Reality our thinking is based on revelation all the time, and as we maintain our relation to Reality we will find new revelations of truth flashing out continually from the word of God.

Faith is not a faculty; if religion were the function of one particular faculty, it would claim but one side of life. Each faculty implies the rest because it is the action of the whole person.

Forsyth

Our response to God is the response of our whole nature. To speak of faith as a faculty is unfortunate; faith is not a faculty, if we mean by that something added on to what we have already got. The result of the idea that we are a bundle of separate faculties, the faculty of faith having nothing to do with the faculty of conscience, makes it possible for a man to do the most unrighteous things in his business all the week and the most devout things on Sunday. Watch the thing you are inclined to succumb over—"That will do for a knock-up job;[3] it's only that, it doesn't matter." It is never "only that," it is the same with everything you do, and is certainly what you will do in the exercise of the highest powers of your personality, viz., in your relationship to God, only it is not traced so readily there because the spiritual domain is so vast and mysterious. Bring it to the test in the ordinary everyday things of life, eating and drinking, cleaning your boots, writing an essay—is it slovenly? is it careless and indifferent? does self-indulgence come in? That little

---

2. Peter Taylor Forsyth (1848–1921): British Congregationalist minister and theologian. Chambers read many of Forsyth's books and valued his insights.

3. knock-up job: something done hastily, carelessly, or in a slipshod way.

pinhole exhibits the dry rot that runs all through everything you do, and when you trust in God, you trust in a shabby way, in a way that is defective—"I will have faith in God about this matter, but not about that"; then you don't trust God at all. If we will examine ourselves in the light of the things that can be seen we will realise that that is how God sees us all through, if only we will take the humiliating gibe to ourselves.

2. Readjustment in God

The first [commandment] is . . . thou shalt love the Lord thy God with all thy heart, and with all thy soul, and with all thy mind, and with all thy strength. (Mark 12:29–30; from all thy heart, etc., RV mg)

We do not know how good God's claim is till we have met it, and long lived in surrender to it, we must taste and see. We do not assent and then trust, that would reduce grace to persuasion, and faith to being talked over or argued down, and from grace and faith alike the divine element of miracle would disappear.

Forsyth

My relationship to God embraces every faculty, I am to love Him with *all* my heart, *all* my soul, *all* my mind, *all* my strength, every detail is instinct with devotion to Him; if it is not I am disjointed somewhere. Think what you do for someone you love! The most amazingly minute details are perfectly transfigured because your whole nature is embraced, not one faculty only. You don't love a person with your heart and leave the rest of your nature out, you love with your whole being, from

the crown of the head to the sole of the foot. That is the attitude of the New Testament all through. In 1 Corinthians 15, the Apostle Paul has been speaking about the stupendous mystery of the resurrection, and suddenly, like a swinging lamp in a mine, he rushes it right straight down and says, "Now concerning the collection. . . ." The New Testament is continually doing it—"Jesus knowing that the Father had given all things into His hands . . . began to wash the disciples' feet." It takes God Incarnate to wash feet properly. It takes God Incarnate to do anything properly.

Never limit God by remembering what you have done in the past. When you come into relation with the Reality of Redemption God creates something in you that was never there before, it is the active working of the life of God in you, consequently you can do now what you could not do before. Character is always revealed in crises. There are lives that seem selfish and self-centred until a crisis occurs and they manifest the most disinterested concern and self-effacement. On the other hand, there are lives that appear unselfish and noble and when the crisis comes they are revealed as mean[4] and despicable. In the early stages of our Christian experience we are inclined to hunt in an overplus of delight for the commandments of our Lord in order to obey them out of our love for Him, but when that conscious obedience is assimilated and we begin to mature in our life with God, we obey His commandments unconsciously, until in the maturest stage of all we are simply children of God through whom God does His will, for the most part unconsciously to us.

PARTAKERS OF GRACE

For by grace have ye been saved through faith; and that not of yourselves: it is the gift of God. Ephesians 2:8 RV

No man can be saved by praying, by believing, by obeying, or by consecration; salvation is a free gift of God's almighty grace. We have the sneaking idea that we earn things and get into God's favour by what we do—by our praying, by our repentance: the only way we get into God's favour is by the sheer gift of His grace. The first thing we consciously experience is a sense of undeserving-ness, but it does take some of us a long while to know we don't deserve to be saved. "I really am sorry for what I have done wrong"; "I really am sick of myself"—if only I am sick enough of myself, I will be sick to death; I am driven to despair,

I can do nothing; then I am exactly in the place where I can receive the overflowing grace of God.

In whom we have redemption through His blood, the forgiveness of sins, according to the riches of His grace. (Ephesians 1:7)

Think what God's forgiveness means: it means that He forgets away every sin. Forgetting in the Divine mind is an attribute, in the human mind it is a defect, consequently God never illustrates His Divine forgetfulness by human pictures, but by pictures taken from His own creation—"As far as east is from the west, so far hath He removed our transgressions from us" (Psalm 103:12); "I have blotted out, as a thick cloud, thy transgressions . . ." (Isaiah 44:22).

---

4. mean: ordinary, common, low, or ignoble, rather than cruel or spiteful

The reason God never uses the human illustration is that a human being is incapable of forgiving as God does until he is made like God through regeneration. We take the forgiveness of sins to mean something we can understand, it is such a tremendous thing that it takes the Holy Spirit to enable us to begin to understand what is made ours through the grace of God. The forgiveness of God means that we are forgiven into a new relationship with God in Christ so that the forgiven man is the holy man.

> *God is able to make all grace abound unto you. . . .*
> *(2 Corinthians 9:8 RV)*

In talking to people you will be amazed to find that they much more readily listen if you talk on the line of suffering, of the attacks of the devil; but get on the triumphant line of the Apostle Paul, talk about the super-conquering life, about God making all His Divine grace to abound, and they lose interest—"That is all in the clouds," a sheer indication that they have never begun to taste the unfathomable joy that is awaiting them if they will only take it. All the great prevailing grace of God is ours for the drawing on, and it scarcely needs any drawing on, take out the "stopper" and it comes out in torrents; and yet we just manage to squeeze out enough grace for the day—"sinning in thought, word and deed every day"! You don't find that note in the New Testament. We have to keep in the light as God is in the light and the grace of God will supply supernatural life all the time. Thank God there is no end to His grace if we will keep in the humble place. The overflowing grace of God has no limits, and we have to set no limits to it, but "grow in grace, and in the knowledge of our Lord and Saviour Jesus Christ."

HOW TO GO ON
Colossians 2:6–7 (RV)

1. How to Think of Our State
As therefore ye received Christ Jesus the Lord . . . (RV)

We all start with thinking about what we have to do; Paul goes a step further back, and says, "Think of how you stand in God's sight through receiving Jesus." It will have a tremendous influence. Have I received Christ Jesus the Lord as my Saviour? Then He is my Saviour from everything that is not of God; that I enter into this realisation is another thing. We can always claim our union with Jesus Christ in thinking: ". . . that we may present every man perfect in Christ Jesus." We know that we are not perfect yet in outer manifestation, but in thinking we have to remember what we received Jesus for, to be absolute Lord, absolute Saviour. When once we bring our minds to think of our state fundamentally, everything else becomes amazingly easy. We are apt to begin by thinking of our obedience, how we are going to work it out, and we forget the first thing, viz., that we have to receive Christ Jesus the Lord. Think what that means! It means we can go straight to the very heart of God and tell Him what we want, not because we are obedient, but because we have access into the holy place by the new and living way which Jesus dedicated (RV) for us. To think of what Jesus is to us always encourages our faith; if we begin with our obedience, our faith gets paralysed. The great basis for our thinking is, what does Jesus Christ mean to me? Have I received Him as Lord and Master, as Saviour and Sanctifier? Have I thought about Him as that?

2. How to Try Our Standing
so walk in Him . . .

Our right standing is proved by the fact that we can walk; if we are not rightly related to God in our thinking we cannot walk properly. Walk means character. If we have only our own energy and devotion and earnestness to go on we cannot walk at all; but if we are based on the revelation that if we receive Christ Jesus the Lord we are complete (RV) in Him, then we can begin to walk according to the perfection we have in Him. When God brings us up against difficult circumstances that reveal the inability of our human nature it is not that we may sink back and say, "Oh dear, I thought I should have been all right by now"; it is that we may learn to draw on our union with Jesus Christ and claim that we have sufficient grace to do this particular thing according to God's will. If we are vitally connected with God in our thinking we shall find we can walk; but if we have not been thinking rightly we will succumb—"I can't do this." If we are thinking along the line of God's grace, that He is able to make all grace abound unto us (RV), we will not only stand, but walk as a son or daughter of God and prove that His grace is sufficient. To be weak in God's strength is a crime.

God has to deal with us on the death side as well as on the life side. It is all very well to know in theory that there are things we must not trust in, but another thing to know it in fact. When God deals with us on the death side He puts the sentence of death on everything we should not trust in, and we have a miserable time until we learn never any more to trust in it, never any more to look anywhere else than to God. It sometimes happens that hardly a day passes without God saying, "Don't trust there, that is dead."

Then He deals with us on the life side and reveals to us all that is ours in Christ Jesus, and there comes in the overflowing strength of God, the unsearchable riches in Christ Jesus. Whether God is dealing with us on the death side or the life side, it is all in order to teach us how to walk, how to try our standing in Christ Jesus. God is teaching us to try our steps in faith, and it is a very tottering business to begin with, we clutch hold of everything; God gives us any amount of encouragement, "ribbons" of blessings, of feelings and touches that makes us know His presence; then He withdraws them and slowly we get strengthened on our feet and learn how to walk in Him.

3. How to Train Our Strength
rooted and builded up in Him . . .

The strength God gives us by receiving Christ Jesus the Lord is the strength He manifested when He raised the dead body of Jesus (*see* Ephesians 1:19–20). We have to train our strength by building it on that unit of measurement. When we pray for other people are we demanding more power to put them right than was wrought by God when He raised Christ from the dead? That is the measure of the exceeding greatness of His power to us-ward who believe. How am I measuring the power of God in my life?

. . . and stablished by [mg] your faith.

Think of the things you are trying to have faith for! Stop thinking of them and think about your state in God through receiving Christ Jesus; see how God has enabled you to walk where you used to totter, and see what marvellous strength you have in Him. "I can do all things in Him that strengtheneth me" (RV), says Paul. Is that mere poetry or a fact? Paul never talked only poetry. All the great blessings of God in salvation and sanctification, all the Holy Spirit's illumination, are ours not because we obey, they are ours because we have put ourselves into a right relationship with God by receiving Christ Jesus the Lord, and we obey spontaneously. As we look back we find that every time we have been blessed it was not through mechanical obedience, but by receiving from Jesus something that enabled us to obey without knowing it and life was flooded with the power of God. We make it hard for people—"Do this and that," and they obey and nothing happens. We have left out altogether the receiving of Christ Jesus the Lord; personal relationship to Jesus Christ first, then faith comes naturally. When we are standing face to face with Jesus Christ in this way and He says, "Believest thou this?"—no matter what the "this" is for—sanctification, or something further on than sanctification—faith is as natural as breathing; we say, "Why yes, Lord," and are staggered and amazed that we were so stupid as not to trust Him before. Whenever we find it hard and difficult and strengthless, we may be certain we are at the wrong place; when we get into the right thinking state through receiving Christ Jesus the Lord, it is the easiest thing in the world to have faith.

REDEMPTION

1. Not Thought but Fact
We have to *live,* thought is second. We are saved in only one way, by the supernatural efficacy of the Redemption; but to be saved and never *think* about it is a crime. "My people doth not consider," says God; they won't think. We can never become God's people by thinking, but we must think *as* God's people. It is possible to understand all about the plan of salvation without being personally related to the reality of Redemption.

My reason and my intellect are the finest instruments I have, but they are not "me," I am much more than my intellect and my reason. If I am going to get at Reality I must have my conscience at work as well as my intellect and reason, otherwise I will ignore the fact of sin, ignore all the moral perplexities, ignore the fact that God became Incarnate. Intellect is meant to be the handmaid of God, not the dictator to God. The rationalist dictates to God and dictates Him off His throne, consequently we hear it asked, "What need is there for the Redemption? for concentration on the historic fact of the life and death of Jesus?" Intellect must get into the place of receptivity, which it won't ever do if it is on the throne. All the idolatrous perversions in Nature and in grace come from exalting the instrument into the place of the life. When intellect is put in the right place it receives, then the Spirit of God creates—"Wherefore if any man is in Christ, there is a new creation" (2 Corinthians 5:17 RV mg) Then intellect comes in to explain, exactly as it does in Nature. God reveals nothing in Nature. I must use my wits, my ingenuity and common-sense, in order to discover; in the spiritual domain I only penetrate by submissive obedience. Our natural make-up is to want to have dominion; in the spiritual domain that is not the procedure, it is surrender. "Commit yourself to Me," says Jesus; get into contact with Reality and the understanding will follow.

We have to work out, not our redemption, but our human appreciation of our redemption. We owe it to God that we refuse to have rusty brains. "Why should I understand?" Because God wants intelligent sons and daughters; He is bringing "sons" to glory, not mechanisms.

Thought is not the sum-total of a man's personality, it is simply the garment personality wears. Think, for instance, of the beautiful things you write in your essays, and think of the mean scrubs you are outside your essays, proving that your beautiful thinking is not the garment that fits you yet. The only way the garment will fit you will be when you are working out your thinking in actualities. The words Jesus spoke were the exact garment of His Person, they exactly revealed Him, because He spoke out of actualities all the time. "I spake openly to the world; . . . and in secret have I said nothing."

"I can't stand coming in contact with other people"—why? Because when you do you find the beautiful conceptions and thoughts you get when you are alone, don't work. Separating myself from other people is the greatest means of producing deception because there is nothing to clash against me. Immediately people clash against me I know whether my beautiful thinking really expresses "me," or is a garment that disguises the real "me." If my actual life is not in agreement with my thinking the danger is that I exclude myself from actualities which bring home to me the knowledge of what I am, in spite of what I think. "I am a Christian worker and must put on this garb!" That is sanctimonious jargon; the only thing that will hold me right is a personal relationship to Jesus, and that life is essentially simple, there is no break into secular and sacred, the one merges into the other, exactly as it did in the life of our Lord. A false mysticism is produced if we refuse to have regard to the basal principle of our make-up, viz., that the garment of our thinking is meant to fit the actualities of life.

2. Thought and Fact United

My Christian faith must be related to the historic Jesus. The one abiding Reality is the Redemption which is focused for us in the historic event of the Life and Death of Jesus. That Fact is of more value than any other historic fact because the Holy Spirit working through it creates in me what could never be produced otherwise. It is the "preaching of the cross" that produces the crisis we call New Birth. We are in danger of preaching the new birth instead of proclaiming that which produces the new birth, viz., the preaching of Jesus Christ, and Him crucified. I cannot save a soul, or sanctify a soul, but if I will preach the Cross with all the mighty emphasis of God's Spirit on it, instantly the Holy Spirit creates the very thing which the Redemption has made possible—the miracle of God in human souls, not by magic, but by surrender. We have to preach, not the explanation of how it is done, but the Fact that does it. I have to see that I manifest in my mortal flesh the fact that the Son of God is born in me, my exposition of it is the expression in testimony that *He* did it. The danger is that I praise Jesus Christ for all I am worth while I evade the moral and essential necessity of surrendering to Him. There must be a Fact which is not "me" to be sure of before I am real.

"It was God's good pleasure through the foolishness of the thing preached [mg] to save them that believe" (1 Corinthians 1:21 RV). Those are the words of the Apostle Paul. Think of his former fiery opposition to Jesus! think of his learning, his conscientious integrity! and then tell me what power of reasoning is going to touch such a man? And by the sheer creative energy of the Spirit of God he is turned from a strong-willed intense Pharisee into a humble devoted slave of the Lord Jesus. The word of God through the Spirit is creative, not persuasive. It hinders the work of the Spirit when we try and persuade people, it puts the basis not on Redemptive Reality but on our ingenious reasoning. The Spirit of God working, by God's decree, through the historic Fact of the Life and Death of Jesus, does not convince a man's mind: He *creates* something in him, makes him "a new creation in Christ Jesus" (RV mg). The preaching of Christ crucified is a stumbling-block to the Jews and foolishness to the Greeks; but unto them which are called, both Jews and Greeks, it is "the power of God, and the wisdom of God." The presentation of the Fact of the Life and Death of Jesus creates the New Testament belief about it in me. Our certainty of salvation is realisable long before it is reasonable to our understanding. Beware of preaching a Redemption that is past; it *is* past, but it must be seen to be ever-present, and I can only make it an ever-present reality by becoming a new creation in Christ Jesus.

How is the historic Christ interpreting Himself to me? Is He to me what He undoubtedly was in His own consciousness, or something less? am I patronising Him? have I brought my curiosity, which is meant to deal with natural facts, into the domain of revelation facts and begun to let it dominate there too? I command what I can explain, and immediately I bring the natural desire to explain into the spiritual domain, I am in danger of explaining Jesus away, I "dissolve Him by analysis" (see 1 John 4:3 RV mg). There is no thinking that will explain me to myself, then how can I think to explain the Son of God? "No one knoweth the Son, save the Father" (RV), said Jesus. The only way I can begin to understand the Son of God is by receiving His Spirit through regeneration; then when I am regenerated it is my duty to think about the Son of God, that is, I must see that I put my intellect at the disposal of the Holy Spirit, who will "reveal the Son of God in me" (Galatians 1:16).

THE MINISTRY OF THE INTERIOR

I have set watchmen upon thy walls, O Jerusalem; they shall never hold their peace day nor night: ye that are the LORD's remembrancers, take ye no rest, and give Him no rest, till He establish, and till He make Jerusalem a praise in the earth. Isaiah 62:6–7 (RV)

And the LORD said unto him, Go through the midst of the city, through the midst of Jerusalem, and set a mark upon the foreheads of the men that sigh and that cry for all the abominations that be done in the midst thereof. Ezekiel 9:4

Do I know anything experimentally about this aspect of things? Have I ever spent one minute before God in intercessory importunity over the sins of other people? If we take these statements of the prophets and turn the searchlight on ourselves, we will be covered with shame and confusion because of our miserably selfish, self-centred Christianity.

How many of us have ever entered into this Ministry of the Interior where we become identified with our Lord and with the Holy Spirit in intercession? It is a threefold intercession: at the Throne of God, Jesus Christ; within the saint, the Holy Ghost; outside the saint, common-sense circumstances and common-sense people, and as these are brought before God in prayer the Holy Spirit gets a chance to make intercession according to the will of God. That is the meaning of personal sanctification, and that is why the barriers of personal testimony must be broken away and effaced by the realisation of why we are sanctified—not to be fussy workers for God, but to be His servants, and this is the work, vicarious intercession.

One of the first lessons we learn in the Ministry of the Interior is to talk things out before God in soliloquy—tell God what you know He knows in order that you may get to know it as He does.

All the harshness will go and the suffering sadness of God's Spirit will take its place, and gradually you will be brought into sympathy with His point of view.

There is an advocacy of holiness which was never born at Calvary, it is the resuscitation of the Pharisaic spirit dressed in the garb of Pentecost—an insufferable superiority. The Spirit of God must have a deep indignation at the preaching of holiness that is not the holiness of Jesus. The holiness of Jesus is the most humble thing on earth.

When God puts a weight on you for intercession for souls don't shirk it by talking to them. It is much easier to talk to them than to talk to God about them—much easier to talk to them than to take it before God and let the weight crush the life out of you until gradually and patiently God lifts the life out of the mire. That is where very few of us go.

When God brings a burden to you, never allow it to develop into carnal suspicion. In the Ministry of the Interior all we have to do is simply to take the matter before God and be made "crushed grapes" until the Holy Spirit produces such an atmosphere that the one who is wrong cannot endure it. That is God's method, and we interfere by using our own discernment.

The knowledge of where people are wrong is a hindrance to prayer, not an assistance. "I want to tell you of the difficulties so that you may pray intelligently." The more you know the less intelligently you pray because you forget to believe that God can alter the difficulties.

"Howbeit when the Son of man cometh, shall He find faith on the earth?" (RV). Which one of us would God stop at and say, "That one is My remembrancer"? or would He have to say, "That one is serving a conviction of his own, he is not My servant at all"?

I INDEED . . . BUT HE

I indeed baptize you with water unto repentance: but He . . . shall baptize you with the Holy Ghost, and with fire. Matthew 3:11

The baptism with the Holy Ghost and with fire is Jesus Christ's own peculiar right; He is the true Baptiser. "I indeed baptize you with water," said John, "but He . . . shall baptize you with the Holy Ghost, and with fire"—a strange and amazing and supernatural baptism.

I wonder if we have ever seen Jesus Christ, if we know who He is? Have we ever heard ringing in our souls these words, "Behold the Lamb of God!" There is a phrase used in America, "I want what I want when I want it." The way you will want the baptism of the Holy Ghost and fire is when you begin to see the Lord Jesus; when you see Him, the great heart-hunger, the great longing of the life will be, "I want to be like Him." But remember, you must come to Him; it is His prerogative to baptise with the Holy Ghost. It is not a blessing we gain by faith, not a blessing we merge into by devotion and fasting, it is the supernaturally natural result of coming to Jesus as the true Baptiser. One sees lives on the right hand and on the left turning sour and cynical, seeing only the frauds and disappointments in life—if they would only look to the Lord Jesus! *He* baptises with the Holy Ghost and with fire, that is, He makes us like Himself.

I want to ask a very personal question—How much do you want to be delivered from? You say, "I want to be delivered from wrong-doing"—then you don't need to come to Jesus Christ. "I want to walk in the right way according to the judgement of men"—then you don't need Jesus Christ. But some heart cries out—"I want, God knows I want, that Jesus Christ should do in me all He said He would do." How many of us "want" like that? God grant that this "want" may increase until it swamps every other desire of heart and life. Oh, the patience, the gentleness, the longing of the Lord Jesus after lives, and yet men are turning this way and that, and even saints who once knew Him are turning aside, their eyes are fixed on other things, on the blessings that come from the baptism with the Holy Ghost and have forgotten the Baptiser Himself.

Do you know what this mighty baptism will mean? It will mean being taken right out of every other setting in life but God's. Are you willing for that? It will mean that sin in you is put to death, not counteracted, but killed right out by identification with the death of Jesus; it will mean a blazing personal holiness

like His. Are you willing for that? Face Jesus Himself; other lights are fading since He grew bright. You are getting tired of life as it is, tired of yourself as you are, getting sour with regard to the setting of your life; lift your eyes for one moment to Jesus Christ. Do you want, more than you want your food, more than you want your sleep, more than you want anything under heaven, or in heaven, that Jesus Christ might so identify you with Himself that you are His first and last and for ever? God grant that the great longing desire of your heart may begin to awaken as it has never done, not only the desire for the forgiveness of sins, but for identification with Jesus Himself until you say, "I live; yet not I, but Christ liveth in me."

Another thing about this mighty baptism—it takes you out of your individual life and fits you into God's purpose. Are some of you realising the awful loneliness of being alive? You cannot mix in with the worldly crowd you used to, and there is a great hunger and longing after you know not what. Look to the Lord Jesus and say, "My God, I want to be so identified with the Lord Jesus that I am pure with His purity, empowered with His power, indwelt with His life." Do you know what will happen? God will take your lonely, isolated, individual life and fit it into a marvellous oneness, into the mystical Body of Christ. Oh, the isolated, lonely, Christian lives! What is needed is this mighty baptism with the Holy Ghost and with fire. "I have been seeking for it, fasting for it," you say; listen, "Come unto Me," says Jesus, He is the Baptiser with the Holy Ghost, and with fire.

Have you seen Jesus as "the Lamb of God, which taketh away the sin of the world"? What is the first step to take? Come to Him just as you are and ask Him to give you the Holy Spirit. As soon as you receive the Holy Spirit He begins to awaken in you the tremendous "want," overwhelming, all-absorbing, passionate in its impelling rush, to be baptised with the Holy Ghost and with fire. If you have never received the Holy Spirit, why not receive Him now? Ask God for His Spirit on the authority of Jesus, and He will lead you, as you obey Him, straight to the place where you will be identified with the death of Jesus.

Where are we in regard to the personal experience of the baptism of the Holy Ghost? If Jesus Christ had said to us, "All you need to do is to be as holy as you can, overcome sin as far as you can, and I will overlook the rest," no intelligent man under heaven would accept such a salvation. But He says—"Be ye . . . perfect;" "Love your enemies"; "Be so pure that lust is an impossibility." Instantly every heart calls back, My God, "who is sufficient for these things?" Oceans of penitential tears, mountains of good works, all powers and energy sink down till they are under the feet of the Lord Jesus, and, incarnate in John the Baptist, they all point to Him—"Behold the Lamb of God, which taketh away the sin of the world!" If Jesus Christ cannot deliver from sin, if He cannot adjust us perfectly to God as He says He can, if He cannot fill us with the Holy Ghost until there is nothing that can ever appeal again in sin or the world or the flesh, then He has misled us. But blessed be the Name of God, He can! He can so purify, so indwell, so merge with Himself, that only the things that appeal to Him appeal to you, to all other appeals there is the sentence of death, you have nothing to answer. When you come amongst those whose morality and uprightness crown them the lord of their own lives, there is no affinity with you, and they leave you alone.

When you are born again of the Spirit of God the characteristic of your testimony is this—"Once I was that, now I am this, and He did it." But when you are baptised with the Holy Ghost, there is only One you see, One you love, One you live for from early morning till late at night, One you die for. Every thought is gripped and held enthralled by the Master of human destiny, the Lord Jesus Christ, and the whole life is devoted to Him. "My witnesses," wherever we are placed He is glorified, not by the testimony of the lips only, but by the whole life.

NOW DON'T HURT THE LORD

Philip saith unto Him, Lord, shew us the Father, and it sufficeth us. John 14:8

1. You Who Regarded Christ's Command
And he findeth Philip: and Jesus saith unto him, Follow Me. (John 1:43 RV)

You may have had no reluctance in obeying the Lord's command, and yet it is probable you are hurting Him because you look for God to manifest Himself where He never can "Lord, shew us the Father." We look to God to manifest Himself to His children: God manifests Himself *in* His children, consequently the manifestation is seen by others, not by us. It is a snare to want to be conscious of God; you cannot be conscious of your consciousness and remain sane. You have obeyed Christ's command, then are you hurting Him by asking some profoundly perverse question? I believe our Lord is repeatedly astounded at the stupidity we display. It is notions of our own that make us stupid; when we are simple we are never stupid, we discern all the time. "Lord, shew us the Father"; "Shew me Thy face"; "Expound this thing to me"; and His answer comes straight back to our heart: "Have I been so long time with you, and yet hast thou not known Me?"

2. You Who Realised Christ's Character
Philip . . . saith . . . We have found Him, of whom Moses in the law, and the prophets, did write, Jesus of Nazareth. (John 1:45)

Like Philip, you know that Jesus Christ is God Incarnate, you realise His character and recognise Him in the Scriptures, then are you hurting Him by the questions you ask? Diseased, morbid questions, not the questions of a child. Jesus has said, "Let not your heart be troubled," then are you hurting Him by allowing your heart to be troubled? If your heart is troubled you are not living up to your belief. Are you trying to expound the Lord apart from Himself, bringing in ideas of your own along with your knowledge of His character? Are you taken up with considering your own perplexities, allowing some morbid question to perturb your heart? What our Lord wants is the implicit relationship to Himself which takes everything as it comes from Him.

3. You Who Recognised Christ's Claim
Philip saith unto him, Come and see. (John 1:46)

In the beginning Philip obeyed Jesus Christ readily, there was no traitorous unbelief in his heart; he realised who Jesus was, and testified of Him to others, and yet he had not perfect childlike confidence in Jesus, and it was this that hurt our Lord—"hast thou not known Me, Philip? He that hath seen Me hath seen the Father." If you know only what you have experienced, you will never see Jesus. Once put conscious experience in the road and you will hurt the Lord. You can never rely on what you believe intellectually; but once have the attitude of a perfectly simple, unsophisticated child of God and there is no trouble in believing. The questions that hurt the Lord are those that are not born of devotion to Him. Am I hurting my Lord by the kind of questions I am asking to-day? They may sound all right to others, but they hurt Him.

"Lord, shew us the Father." Philip expected the revelation of a tremendous mystery, but he did not expect it in the One whom he knew. The mystery of God is now, this minute, not in what is going to be; we look for it presently, in some cataclysmic happening. What am I asking Jesus Christ to do? "Lord, shew us the Father." He has done it: "He that hath seen Me hath seen the Father." When once I realise that everything is in Jesus Christ, I will never allow any questions that spring from without to trouble my heart. The thing that hurts Jesus is asking Him to give us experiences—"I want to be conscious of God's presence." Get rid of the morbid idea of conscious-

ness, be so completely in Jesus that His presence is salvation continually.

You have obeyed Jesus Christ's command and followed Him, you have realised His character and recognised His claims, then are you hurting Him by asking Him to show you things? "Show me Thy face"; there it is! "Show me the Father"; there He is! always just here or nowhere; He is here *now*. Once realise that and the emancipation is immediate. It is to those to "babes," to "little children," "in whom is no guile," that the revelation comes. God never guides presently, He always guides *now*. No wonder Jesus said, "Let not your heart be troubled"!

WHAT A MAN POSSESSES V.
WHAT POSSESSES A MAN

For a man's life consisteth not in the abundance of the things which he possesseth. Luke 12:15

This statement of Our Lord's needs careful consideration because we dislike it strongly. The whole teaching of Jesus is opposed to the idea of civilisation, viz., possessing things for myself—"This is mine." The sense of property is connected, not with the lasting element of our personality, but with that which has to do with sin; it is the sense of property that makes me want to gratify myself. Jesus Christ had no sense of property, there was never any attempt to gratify Himself by possessing things for Himself—"the Son of man hath not where to lay His head." What was His, He gave—"I lay down My life. . . . I lay it down of Myself." The thing that leads me wrong always and every time is what I am persuaded I possess. The thing that is mine is the thing I have with the power to give it. All that I want to possess without the power to give, is of the nature of sin. God has no possessions, consequently I cannot rob God of anything, but I rob myself of God every time I stick to what I possess. Immediately I abandon to God I get that which possesses me but has no possessions with it, there is nothing to keep. Being possessed by God means an untrammelled[5] human life.

God seems careless of His children from the standpoint of Time; when we get to the Eternal side of God's Providence we find He does not estimate a man by what he possesses; the only thing He is after is union with Himself, and He will obliterate all our possessions until He leaves only Himself. As long as

I have something from God which I possess, I have not got God. God gives us possessions in order to draw us to Himself, and when we get God we are no longer conscious of our possessions, but conscious only of God. What possesses me in a yielded life to God is God Himself.

According to Jesus Christ a man's life does not consist in the abundance of the things he possesses—not only in the way of goods and chattels, but in the way of a good name, a virtuous character; these things are a man's inheritance, but not his *life*. When the Holy Spirit begins to try and break into the house of our possessions in order to grant us the real life of God, we look on Him as a robber, as a disturber of our peace, because when He comes He reveals the things which are not of God and must go; and they are the things which constituted our life before He came in, our golden affections were carefully nested in them. The thing that hurts shows where we live. If God hurts it is because we are not living rightly related to Him, and if we say "the devil" instead of "God," it is evidence that we are living a sequestered life of our own apart from God.

Watch the opportunities of filling up "that which is behind of the afflictions of Christ." When I am possessed by God it is not that He gives me power to love like He does, but that the very nature of God loves through me, just as He put up with the things in me which were not of Him, so He puts up with the things which are not of Him in others through me, and what is manifested is the love of God, the love that suffers long and is kind, the love that does not

---

5. untrammelled: free, unhindered, not entangled.

take account of evil, the love that never fails. Just as my Lord was made broken bread and poured-out wine for me, so I must be made broken bread and poured-out wine in His hands for others. What is meant by "in His hands" is seen in the kind of things that bruise me—tyrannic powers, misunderstanding people, things that ordinarily I would have resented and said, "No, I can't allow that." Is there being produced in me, through the crushing of His disguised feet, the wine that is a real quickening of other lives? A yielded life to God becomes a doormat for men. He leaves us here to be trampled on.

THE PERSON OF OUR LORD

There is a difference between being "the offspring of God" (Acts 17:28) and being "sons of God" (John 1:12). "Offspring" means that our genus originated with God; we can only become "sons" of God by a specific act of regeneration.

Jesus Christ is the "only begotten Son"; His whole personality is Son-ship.

Every Christian knows Jesus Christ *as God*, not as the equivalent of God; the call to proclaim Him to others means that I see Him and know Him as God. There is no God that is not Father, Son and Holy Ghost—the Triune aspect of one God, from all Eternity to all Eternity. If I am ever going to get to God as Father I must come to Him through the miraculously provided way: "I am the Way," said Jesus, "no man cometh unto the Father, but by Me."

Beware of coming to the study of the Person of our Lord with preconceived ideas, e.g., that the nature of Deity is necessarily omnipotence, etc. The ultimate display of Deity is omnipotence, but the essential nature of Deity is holiness. Deity can be limited by choice. Our Lord, as Son of Man, deliberately limited omnipotence, omniscience and omnipresence in Himself, yet to His own consciousness He was "on an equality with God" (RV): *"I and My Father are one."* The great revelation the Bible gives of God is the opposite of what we are apt to imagine Him to be, it is a revelation not of the majestic power of God, but of the fact that God was "manifested in the flesh" (RV); that God became Incarnate as a Baby in the Person of His Son. That is the last reach of Self-limitation.

We have to remember what our Lord presents by His life on earth: He presents the goal to which we have to attain by means of His death on the Cross, and the progress His own life went through from Childhood to Manhood represents for us the progress our spiritual life will go through after we are born again of the Spirit. Man was not so created as to be able to reach the goal by drawing the required power from his own resources, he needed the aid of continual communications of life from God, and the reason of our Lord's coming was in order that the normal development of man, which sin had interrupted, might begin afresh.

There are two kinds of incompleteness—the incompleteness which is simply that which is growing to completeness: a child is a perfect human being in the sense of all his adjustments being right, but he is not a perfected human being in the sense of full growth and maturity, therefore the effort of a child to do a thing and not succeed, is not in the same category as failure through wilfulness, it is the limitation of his growing powers that prevents him succeeding. But alongside that is an incompleteness which comes from the presence of an opposing force, something which makes me say "I won't." A man with an impulse towards God and all that is right has also an impulse towards that which is against God, he is divided in two; it is not a question of imperfect growth but of downright opposition which not only makes for incompleteness, but makes an hiatus that cannot be bridged. No power outside God can alter that "I won't" into "I will." "I won't" is not imperfect "I will," and it will never develop into "I will."

There was no incompleteness in that sense in our Lord; He "grew, and . . . increased in wisdom and stature" (Luke 2:40, 52), and when we are born again it means that Christ is "formed" in us, then we have to "grow up in all things into Him" (RV). But that will to oppose must be dealt with before I can do that; I can't develop as Jesus did unless He takes out of me that which never was in Him. If He can do that, then I can begin to understand how He is my Example; but He is not my Example unless the Redemption has been made of practical effect in me.

When Jesus Christ, the last Adam, came He entered on the same plane as the first Adam, and from that same stage of innocence He worked out the perfect life of holiness that God required, which Adam failed to do. But He had to do more, He had to put the whole human race back, not to where Adam was, but to where Adam had never been, viz., to where He is Himself, an inconceivably higher position. Through His death on the Cross Jesus Christ not only readjusts a man in conscience and heart to God, He does something grander, He imparts to him the power to do all God wants, He presences him with Divinity, i.e., the Holy Spirit, so that he is garrisoned from within, and enabled to live without blame before God. Blameless does not mean perfection, but undeserving of censure in God's sight. That is the full meaning of being baptised with the Holy Ghost. Then, and only then, does Jesus become our Example.

We are being told nowadays how like Jesus is to ourselves—thank God He is not! The revelation of Jesus in the New Testament is that He is absolutely unlike us. Never attempt dextrously to show how altogether human Jesus is; allow the facts of Bible revelation to show you the absolute difference between ourselves and Jesus Christ, and because of this difference He is able to lift us up into likeness with Himself, to conform us to His own image.

What kind of attitude have we got to Jesus Christ? are we dictating to Him in pious phraseology what we intend to let Him do in us, or letting His life be manifested in our mortal flesh as we obey? Is my experience worth His while? If I am not a saint, it was not worth his while. I can be devout, I can put on a pious pose, religious circumspection will do all that, but has there been such an alteration in me that I know nothing at all can account for it saving the almighty grace of God working in me to will and to do of His good pleasure? The net result of the teaching of Jesus is to produce despair—if it has never produced despair in me I have not heard it aright; but that despair brings me to the place where I am willing to come, "just as I am, without one plea," and accept as an unmerited gift the Salvation wrought out by Jesus Christ.

"WHAT IS TRUTH?"
John 18:38

The Personality of Truth is the great revelation of Christianity—"I am . . . the Truth." Our Lord did not say He was "all truth" so that we could go to His statements as to a text-book and verify things; there are domains, such as science and art and history, which are distinctly man's domains and the boundaries of our knowledge must continually alter and be enlarged; God never encourages laziness. The question to be asked is not, "Does the Bible agree with the findings of modern science?" but, "Do the findings of modern science help us to a better understanding of the things revealed in the Bible?"

Again, the Bible has much to say about truth of speech, e.g., "speak ye truth each one with his neighbour" (Ephesians 4:25 RV): but this aspect, important as it is, is not what our Lord means when He says, "I am . . . the Truth." However, it is well, bearing in mind the deceitfulness and subtlety of the human heart, for us to remember that

> *The truth that's told with bad intent*
> *Beats all the lies you can invent.*

And none of us ever gets beyond the need of the warning that "lying lips are an abomination to the LORD." But we would not have needed the Bible, or the illumination of the Holy Spirit, or our Lord Himself to come and tell us about these things, our own human wisdom and ingenuity would have taught us.

1. Truth Incarnate
"And the Word became flesh" (RV)—that means not only the expression of the Mind of God, but the expression of the Mind of God *Incarnate*. God gave His final revelation in Jesus Christ; then He set processes at work for the re-organisation of the whole of humanity. Jesus Christ is the Truth, an Incarnate Ideal; to be "in Christ" means that through regeneration and sanctification that Ideal can become a reality, so that in my mortal flesh there is manifested that which is easily discerned to be "the life also of Jesus." We are to be incorporated into the truth. The ideal is not a vague end into which we evolve more or less blindly, we "grow up in all things into Him." There is a danger of seeing the truth and the true clearly with our minds, while the life and character lag woefully behind. In Christian work who has not met with clearness in verbal doctrine, almost dictatorial clearness, and wrong, almost quite wrong, attitudes in life and conduct? "He that *doeth* truth cometh to the light" (John 3:21). "Everyone that is *of the truth* heareth My voice" (John 18:37). ". . . that we know Him that is true, and *we are in Him that is true*, even in His Son Jesus Christ" (1 John 5:20). These passages make it clear that being "of the truth" refers to a condition of character. Much is written about our Lord speaking so simply that anyone could understand, and we forget that while it remains true that

the common people heard Him gladly, no one, not even His own disciples, understood Him until after the Resurrection and the coming of the Holy Spirit, the reason being that a pure heart is the essential requirement for being "of the truth.""Blessed are the pure in heart: for they shall see God."

2. Truth Interpreted

. . . no prophecy of scripture is of private interpretation. (2 Peter 1:20 RV)

We are never left with a revelation without an interpretation of it. A revelation fact needs a corresponding revelation to interpret it. Just as Jesus Christ is the final revelation of God, so the Bible is the final revelation interpreting Him. Our Lord Jesus Christ (The Word of God) and the Bible (the accompanying revelation) stand or fall together, they can never be separated without fatal results. The words of the Bible apart from being interpreted by the Word of God, are worse than lifeless, they kill (2 Corinthians 3:6). But when a soul is born from above (RV mg) and lifted to the atmosphere of the domain where our Lord lives, the Bible becomes its native air, its words become the storehouse of omnipotence, its commands and prophecies become

alive, its limitless horizons brace the heart and mind to a new consciousness, its comforts in Psalms and prayers and exhortations delight the whole man. And better than all, the Lord Jesus Christ becomes the altogether Lovely One, it is in His light that we see light, it is in Him that we become new creatures. He who is the Word of God unfolds to us the revelation of God until we say in sacred rapture, "I hold in my hands the Thought of God."

What is needed is a final court of appeal, and this we have in the Bible. It is not a question of the infallibility of the Bible, that is a side issue; but of the finality of the Bible. The Bible is a whole library of literature giving us the final interpretation of the Truth, and to take the Bible apart from that one supreme purpose is to have a book and nothing more; and further, to take our Lord Jesus Christ away from the revelation of Him given in the Bible is to be left with one who is open to all the irreverent slanders of unbelief.

"The Truth" is our Lord Himself; "the whole truth" is the inspired Scripture interpreting the Truth to us; and "nothing but the truth" is the Holy Spirit, "the Spirit of truth," efficaciously regenerating and sanctifying us, and guiding us into "all the truth" (RV).

AFTER OBEDIENCE—WHAT?
Mark 6:45–52

1. Constrained by Christ

And straightway He constrained His disciples to get into the ship, and to go to the other side. . . . (Mark 6:45)

We are apt to imagine that if Jesus Christ constrains us and we obey Him, He will lead us to great success; but He does not. We would have thought these men would have had a most successful time, but their obedience led them into a great disaster. If our Lord has ever constrained you, and you obeyed Him, what was your dream of His purpose? Never put your dream of success as God's purpose for you; His purpose may be exactly the opposite.

2. Consternation by Obedience

And He saw them toiling in rowing; for the wind was contrary unto them: and about the fourth watch of the night He cometh unto them, walking upon the sea, and would have passed by them. (Mark 6:48)

The obedience of the disciples led them into the greatest trouble they had known. Jesus did not go with them, a storm came, and they were at their wits'

end—"the ship was in the midst of the sea, and He alone on the land." They thought they were going straight to the other aide: Jesus knew they would face a storm in the centre of the lake.

Each one of us has had similar experiences—"I did obey God's voice; I am sure He led me to do this and that," and yet these very things have led to consternation in our lives. Beware of saying the devil deceived you. It is as true for saints as for anyone else that "there is a way which seemeth right unto a man, but the end thereof are the ways of death." We have nothing whatever to do with what men call success or failure. If God's command is clear, and the constraint of His Spirit is clear, we have nothing to do with the result of our obedience. The purpose of God in calling us is not something in the future, but this very minute—"Now is the accepted time," always *now;* God's training is for now, not presently. The ultimate issue will be manifested presently, but we have nothing to do with the afterwards of obedience. We get wrong when we think of the afterwards, the purpose of God is our obedience. Never have a material end in your mind and imagine that God is working towards that by means of your obedience; that is man's way of looking at things. What man calls training and preparation, God calls the end. The end God has in mind is to enable us to see that He can walk on the chaos of our lives just now. "He is there"! The first time we saw Him we were terrified; the "other side" was covered with clouds, the surroundings became wild, and the wind contrary. With how many is the wind contrary these days!

There was no point of rest for the natural mind of the disciples as to what Jesus was after—it was the deep, the dark, and the dreadful: our Lord's purpose was that they should see Him walking on the sea. We have an idea that God is leading us to a certain goal; He is not. The question of getting to a particular end is a mere incident. "For I know the plans that I am planning for you, saith the Lord, plans of welfare, and not of calamity, to give you an expected end" (see Jeremiah 29:11). What men call the process, God calls the end. If you can stay in the midst of the turmoil unperplexed and calm because you see Jesus, that is God's purpose in your life; not that you may be able to say, "I have done this and that and now it's all right." God's purpose for you is that you depend upon Him and His power *now;* that you see Him walking on the waves—no shore in sight, no success, just the absolute certainty that it is all right because you see Him.

3. Confused by Calm

And He went up unto them into the ship; and the wind ceased: and they were sore amazed in themselves beyond measure, and wondered. (Mark 6:51)

After we have obeyed there is a sudden calm, and unless we are well taught by the Spirit of God, we are afraid of this calm and imagine it is a preparation for some tremendous strain.

"For they understood not concerning [RV] the loaves: for their heart was hardened." The way our heart is hardened is by sticking to our convictions instead of to Christ. Look back at your life with God and you will find that He has made havoc of your convictions, and now the one thing that looms larger and larger is Jesus Christ and Him only, God and God only. "And this is life eternal, that they might know Thee the only true God." Convictions and creeds are always about God; eternal life is to know Him.

"Let not your heart be troubled." When we dream of ourselves in God's service our hearts do get troubled—"I think this is what God is preparing me for." God is not preparing you for anything, obedience is its own end in the purpose of God; be faithful to Him. Never say, "I wonder what God is doing with me just now." That is no business of yours, and the Spirit of God will never give you an answer. If you are spiritual I defy you to tell anyone what God is preparing you for; the preparation is His end.

Can I see Jesus in my present circumstances? Is it an obscure farther shore, with wild waves between? can I see Him walking on the waves? Is it a fiery furnace? can I see Him walking in the midst of the fire? Is it a placid, commonplace day? can I see Him there? If so, that is the perpetual mystery of the guidance of God, that is Eternal Life. We have to be transformed by the renewing of our mind, that we may "prove what is the will of God, even the thing which is good and acceptable and perfect" (RV mg), not the thing that is going to be acceptable, but which is good and acceptable and perfect *now.* If we have a further end in view we do not pay sufficient attention to the immediate minute; when we know that obedience is the end, then every moment is the most precious.

MY RELATION TO MYSELF
My Right to Myself versus My Wrong to Myself

What commandment is the first of all? . . . The first is, . . . thou shalt love the Lord thy God from all thy heart, and from all thy soul, and from all thy mind, and from all thy strength. The second is this, Thou shalt love thy neighbour as thyself. Mark 12:28–31 (RV mg)

My self is my conscious personality, the sum-total of all I call "me" and "mine." Our Lord never taught the annihilation of self, He revealed how self might be rightly centred, viz., in love to God. Love is the highest moral issue—"God is love." The Bible makes no distinction between Divine love and human love, it speaks only of "love." The majority of us have an impersonal, ethereal, vague abstraction we call love to God; Jesus says I must love God with all my heart and soul and mind and strength, then my love for my fellow men will be relative to that centre. "For the whole law is fulfilled in one word, even in this; Thou shalt love thy neighbour as thyself" (Galatians 5:14 RV; see also James 2:8). The love of self that Jesus not only justified but distinctly enjoined, is the direct product of the indwelling Holy Spirit; its perversion is the deification of my self. How is it possible for me to love my neighbour as myself? The best example of a lover of men is Jesus Christ, and the mainspring of His love for men was His love for God. Whenever you deal with a principle always take the best possible incarnation of it, never deal with it in the abstract. If I deify an abstraction called "love to God" I can jargon to further orders[6] as though I really loved my fellow men, but the crucial test when it comes will prove I don't. When I disassociate myself from God I become a law unto myself, and the first thing that happens is I don't love my neighbour as myself—I am so sure I am right and everyone else is wrong. The only way I can love my neighbour as myself is by having the love of God shed abroad in my heart, then I can love others with that same love. Self is not to be absorbed into God, it is to be centred in God.

Man was created to be the friend and lover of God and for no other end, and until he realises this he will go through turmoil and upset. Human nature must rise to its own Source, the bosom of God, and Jesus Christ by His Redemption brings it back there. God is the only One who has the right to myself and when I love Him with all my heart and soul and mind and strength, self in its essence is realised. All the teaching of Jesus is woven around self; I have a moral self-love to preserve for God; not, "Oh, I'm of no account," "a worm," that would spell self-less-ness. "I hold not my life of any account, as dear unto myself," says Paul, "so that I may accomplish my course, and the ministry which I received from the Lord Jesus, to testify the gospel of the grace of God" (RV). That is, he refused to use himself for any other interest but God's, and for what glorified God.

Fundamentally it is impossible to *love* a human being wrongly—it is possible to have an affection for a human being as a sop to my personal conceit: it is never possible to love a human being *rightly* if I love from the centre of self-interest. The love which springs from self-conceit or self-interest ends in being cruel because it demands an infinite satisfaction from another human being which it will never get. The love which has God as its centre makes no demands. Why our Lord appears to be the enemy of natural love is because we do not understand that He deals with fundamentals always. For instance, whenever He brings His challenge against the mutual relationships of life (e.g., Matthew 10:35–39; Luke 14:26), it is because the love born of those relationships is chained about by a perverted disposition which He calls sin; and where in the interests of self-love those claims are held to, He has to disillusionise me over them until the entire life is rightly related to Him. When I love Him supremely so that all other loves are hatred in comparison, then He can trust me with the hundred-fold more because the interest of self-love no longer rules. Every human relationship is put by Jesus on an eternal basis, otherwise the relationships born from the centre of what we call natural love end with this life, there is nothing more to them; but when they are rooted in the nature of God they are as eternal as God Himself.

We can easily slander God by the things we say when we are really desirous of presenting His character—Because I loved the creature God took him, or her, away. That is a lie. The only way it could be true would be if I loved in order to gratify myself, then my love, which in the sight of God was lust, was hurtful because it sprang from the centre of self-gratification. It may mean the gratification of others, but if my motive in making them happy is in order to get a better state of self-complacency, I am doing harm the more good I do. But let the lowliest soul whose influence apparently amounts to nothing get rightly related to God, and out of him will flow rivers of living water which he does not see, but one day we shall find that it is those lives which have been spreading the lasting benediction. "Love is of God"; it never came from the devil and never can go to the devil. When I am rightly related to God, the more I love the more blessing does He pour out on other lives. The reward of love is the capacity to pour out more love all the time, "hoping for nothing again." That is the essential nature of perfect love.

The true import of love is the surrender of my self, I go out of myself in order to live in and for God. To be indwelt by the Spirit of Jesus means I am willing to quit my own abode from the self-interested standpoint and live only in and for God. It is not the surrender to a conqueror, but the surrender of love, a sovereign preference for God. I surrender myself—not because it is bad, self is the best thing I have got, and I give it to God; then self-realisation is lost in God-realisation. There is a subtle form of pride which is set on *my* holiness; in sanctification there is no pride. Go to the death of independence of God and you will never be bothered about yourself because you and God are one.

"For we preach not ourselves, but Christ Jesus as Lord, and ourselves as your servants for Jesus' sake" (2 Corinthians 4:5 RV). When you are sentimentally interested in a person you are conscious of it; when you are in love with a person you are not conscious of it because the love is deeper than consciousness and is only revealed in a crisis. When you love God you become identified with His interests in other people, and He will bring around you those He is interested

---

6. to further orders: ad infinitum; endlessly; the phrase, military origin, continuing present action until one receives different orders

in—the sinners, the mean, the ungrateful, and you will soon know by your attitude to them whether you love God. The love described in 1 Corinthians 13 is impossible unless I get to the point of white-heat love for God: "Love suffereth long, . . . seeketh not its own, . . . taketh not account of evil" (RV). The discovery of whose honour I stand for is a clear revelation of who my god is. If it is my own honour that is at stake, my self is my god. The honour in the life of a saint is the honour of Jesus. When I am met by exacting and meanness, I do not say, That hurts me; I do not know it does, because I am taken up with the pain of the Holy Ghost over the hurt to Jesus. There is no greater miracle possible for a human life than that, and it can never be imitated. Our first introduction to the miracle is the realisation that we need to have it wrought in us. To "fill up on my part that which is lacking of the afflictions of Christ" (RV) is the supreme calling of a saint.

The Redemption deals not only with moral imperfections, but with every phase of self-interest. Self-interest in the spiritual domain is a demoralising force, it keeps me an individual, "all elbows";[7] keeps me looking after my "rag rights"[8] and if anyone drags them aside I am mortally offended. The only way self-interest can be effaced is by presenting my body to God as a "living sacrifice," that is, self-interest must be put to death, by my most deliberate wish, or it will never be put to death. As long as self-interest is there and has to be suppressed, the Holy Spirit will reveal that something else has to go. I may be under conscious apprehension for discipleship, and I go through the form of being willing to give up my right to myself, but the Holy Spirit reveals that I have never really done it—"I will spend myself for Jesus," "I will do everything He asks me to do"—but not one thing, and it is the only thing I can do, viz., give up my right to myself to Him. There is only one crisis and the majority of us have never been through it, we are brought up to it, and kick back every time, until God by His engineering brings us right to the one issue, "Deny for ever your right to yourself." It is a stubborn detachment, yielding bit by bit, not because the character is noble, but because it is despicably proud.

"Behold, to obey is better than sacrifice." Self-sacrifice may be simply a disease of the nerves, a morbid self-consciousness which is the obverse of intense selfishness. Our Lord never confounds selfishness and self. Whenever I make self-sacrifice the aim and end of my life, I become a traitor to Jesus; instead of placing Him as my lodestar I place Him as an example, One who helps me to sacrifice myself. I am not saved to sacrifice; I am saved to fulfil my destiny in Christ. It is much easier to sacrifice myself, to efface myself, than to do God's will in His way. Self-sacrifice is always eager to do things and then say, "That is God's will." There was no trace in our Lord's life of self-sacrifice being the idea—"For their sakes I sanctify Myself." These words give the key to the saint's life; I have deliberately to give God my self, my self which He has sanctified, that He might use me as His hands and His feet.

RIGHTEOUSNESS

Righteousness means "living and acting according to right and justice."

1. Righteousness of God
I will make mention of Thy righteousness, even of Thine only. (Psalm 71:16)

The righteousness of God must be the foundation of our life as Christians. It is easy to talk about God's righteousness and His justice, but too often we banish the revelation of His character into the limbo of the abstract; we accept His righteousness as a theological doctrine, but we do not believe it practically. In the Bible "theological" and "practical" stand for the same thing. The greatest demand God makes of us is to believe that He is righteous when everything that happens goes against that faith.

(a) In Creation
And God saw everything that He had made, and, behold, it was very good. (Genesis 1:31)

What God created is a satisfaction to God, but to no one less than God, consequently until we come to know Him there is a great deal in His creation we shrug our shoulders over; but when we come to understand God we are as delighted with His creation as He is Himself. A child enjoys what God created, everything is wonderful to him. When the Son of God came on to this earth "His own things" (RV mg)

---

7. all elbows: independent; exclusive; self-sufficient.
8. rag rights: self-righteousness; see Isaiah 64:6

recognised Him—"Who then is this, that He commandeth even the winds and the water, and they obey Him?" (Luke 8:25 RV).

The constructed world of man is not the created world of God. The sin of man has polluted the material earth, and it will have to go through a cremation, out of which will emerge "new heavens and a new earth, wherein dwelleth righteousness." That which God created can never finally be bad. God demands of His children the practical belief that all that stands for Creation is upheld by His righteousness. The One who made the world and who upholds all things by the word of His power, is the One who keeps His saints.

(b) In History (Isaiah 40:12–17)
Behold, the nations are as a drop of a bucket, and are counted as the small dust of the balance. (Isaiah 40:15)

Another demand God makes of His children is that they believe not only that He is not bewildered by the confused hubbub of the nations, but that He is the abiding Factor in the hubbub. The Bible conception of the righteousness of God at work in history is that of fire, intense blazing heat, in the flames of which the nations are seen to be tumbling into confusion as well as rising out of it. If you look at history through the medium of rational common-sense you do not see God, you see only confusion and the passions of men, and, at times, what we are seeing just now, the frantic contortions of war. Sin has not only infected material things, it is the common inheritance of the human race; but the time is coming when it will be impossible for sin to be on the earth any more, when the very material earth will be shot through with the glory of God's presence, and when man himself will be "conformed to the image of His Son." Meantime there is the conclusion and the agony which make men say, "There is no God." These things are the evidence that God is.

(c) In Providence
He leadeth me in the paths of righteousness. . . . (Psalm 23:3)

The word "righteousness" in this connection is instructive; it means that God leads His children "in the rightness," no matter in what providential dispensation they live, whether in personal cataclysms or national cataclysms. We have to accept God's purpose in the providential jumble of things, then He leads us in the paths of righteousness wherever we are placed, and continually restores our souls.

2. Righteousness before God
By His knowledge shall My righteous Servant justify many: and He shall bear their iniquities. (Isaiah 53:11 RV)

(a) In Christ
The wisdom of God is shown in that Jesus Christ is "made unto us . . . righteousness" (1 Corinthians 1:30). The meaning of the Redemption is that God can justify the unjust and remain righteous, and He does it through the Cross of Christ. It is not a thing to reason out, but a thing to have resolute faith in. I do not come before God and say, "Lord, I have prayed; I have obeyed": I stand before God without the tiniest excuse, and discover that Christ, the Just, suffered for the unjust; the Righteous for the unrighteous.

(b) In Concentration
"If ye keep My commandments, ye shall abide in My love" (John 15:10). Righteousness cannot be imitated. If I abide in Jesus, His righteousness is done through me. Nowadays the tendency is to switch away from abiding in Christ; it is—"Do this," and "Do that." You cannot do anything at all that does not become, in the rugged language of Isaiah, "as filthy rags," no matter how right it looks, if it is divorced from abiding in Christ. Haul yourself up a hundred times a day till you learn to abide. Ask yourself—Is this work, this activity, deflecting me from abiding in Christ? If so, then fling it overboard.

(c) In Communion
". . . not having a righteousness of mine own, . . . but that which is through faith in Christ" (Philippians 3:9 RV). To experience the loss of my own goodness is to enter into communion with God through Christ. Paul saw what it would mean—I must give up my right to myself, give up my boasted goodness; he estimated it exactly, and not only estimated it, but experienced it—"for whom I have suffered the loss of all things . . . that I may . . . be found in Him" (RV). If I try to be right, it is a sure sign I am wrong; the only way to be right is by stopping the humbug of trying to be and remaining steadfast in faith in Jesus Christ. "He that *doeth* righteousness is righteous, even as He is righteous."

GOD'S METHODS

Go ye, and stand and speak in the temple to the people all the words of this Life. Acts 5:20 (RV)

1. The Men of God's Method

We have to find out God's methods, not try to get God to approve our methods.

Go ye . . .

It would be an interesting study to trace out what our Lord taught in connection with the verb "to go."

The men with God's "go" in them have these three characteristics—a saving experience; the evidence of supernatural power at work, and the spiritual efficacy of success in prayer.

Unless a preacher has had a saving experience, been set free from some "prison," he has not got God's "go" in him. If this test were put to every preacher and Sunday School teacher—Has Jesus Christ done anything for you you could not do for yourself? has He set you free from the "prison" of a wrong disposition? Set you free from the tyranny of nerves? from pride? from a wrong mental outlook?—the result straightaway would be to thin the number of those who are at work for God, and those that were left would be the men of God's method. The man of God's method says—"I know I have been delivered by God; I don't know *how* He did it, but I know He did it."

How strongly spiritual efficacy in prayer is marked all through the Acts of the Apostles! It is the sign Jesus Christ gives that we believe in Him (see John 14:12–13). Prayer that is not saturated in the New Testament is apt to be based on human earnestness. God never hears prayer because a man is in earnest; He hears and answers prayer that is on the right platform—we have "boldness to enter into the holy place *by the blood of Jesus*" (RV), and by no other way. It is not our agony and our distress, but our childlike confidence in God.

2. The Manner of God's Men

and stand . . .

It takes a tremendously strong man to stand—"and having done all, to stand" (Ephesians 6:13). Not fight, but stand. The men of God's method are never hustled, never enticed, they won't allow themselves to be deflected, they know what they are there for. "None of these things move me," said Paul, "you may execrate me, or praise me, it makes no difference; I am

here for only one thing—to fulfil the ministry which I received from the Lord Jesus."

and speak to the people . . .

How few of us do speak! When we talk to a soul, we talk like a tract! When Jesus talked to the woman of Samaria He did not use a prescribed form of address, He told her Divine truth and made her aware of her sin. When He talked to the disciples on the road to Emmaus, their hearts burned within them. The characteristic of the man of God's method is that he can speak to a sinner and win him before the sinner knows where he is; he can speak to saints and make their hearts burn.

in the temple . . .

—i.e., the place where God ought to be honoured. The danger is to want to go into the show business. No man with his eyes on God ever went outside "the temple" to bear his testimony.

3. The Message of God's Men

. . . all the words of this Life.

—i.e., Jesus Christ, proclaim Him. Don't preach salvation; don't preach holiness; don't preach the baptism of the Holy Ghost; preach Jesus Christ and everything else will take its right place. The sanctification of the Bible never fixes you on the fact that you are delivered from sin: it fixes you on the One who *is* Sanctification. Sanctification is not something Jesus Christ gives me, it is Himself in me.

"And how shall they preach, except they be sent?" How am I to know I am sent? The only way we can be sent is by God deliberately lifting us out of any sense of fitness in ourselves; I realise I am utterly weak and powerless, and that if I am to be of any use for God, He must do it in me all the time. We talk about our utter unfitness, our overwhelming sense of unsuitability, but are they mere sentimental phrases, or the humble certainty of our souls? The Spirit of God allows us to scrutinise ourselves sufficiently till we know what Paul means when he said, "we . . . are weak in Him." The worker whose work tells for God is the one who realises what God has done in him.

"My word . . . shall not return unto Me void"—that is the perennial, unbreakable hope of the preacher; he knows the power of the word of God and he builds his confidence nowhere else but in God.

BLESSING AND BEATITUDE
Matthew 5:43–48

Ye therefore shall be perfect, as your heavenly Father is perfect. Matthew 5:48 (RV)

By "Blessing" we mean the great magnanimous overflowing of the heart of God to all people, whether they be good, bad, or indifferent. By "Beatitude" we mean the overflowing benediction of a life that is rightly related to God—character that lives within the frontiers where God makes Himself known. So many people think they must be right with God because He blesses them. This needs correcting, and we must get rightly related to the wonderful truths hidden in these verses.

1. The Good

In the first place, God's blessings fall, like His rain, on evil and good alike. The great blessings of health, genius, prosperity, all come from His overflowing grace, and not from the condition of the character of the recipients. For instance, if health were a sign that a man is right with God, we should lose all distinction as to what a good character is, for many bad men enjoy good health. It is humbling and illuminating to catch the profound meaning of the Apostle Paul's statement to Timothy: "If we believe not, yet He abideth faithful: He cannot deny Himself" (2 Timothy 2:13). All man's unfaithfulness, all man's sins,

> . . . alters God no more
> Than our dimmed eyes can quench the stars
> in heaven.

There is no element of the vindictive in our great and good God. But to come more personally home to our individual spiritual lives. We get a sweet, all-embracing sense and feeling of God's blessing in certain atmospheres—in churches, with certain people, in Camp meetings, in times of revival; but if we mistake that sweet sense of the blessing of God for being right with God, great harm is done to our spiritual character.

2. The Better

Or take it in the more subtle matter of private prayer. How many of us pray simply in order to feel the presence and blessing of God upon us, and mistake that for the answer? Such prayer is not transaction with God at all, it is in its final analysis an indulgence of the finer sensibilities. This idea of prayer gives rise to the thought of the present day that prayer is merely a reflex action on the life which quietens it, whereas New Testament praying is getting hold of a personal God through the opening up of a channel whereby God can deal directly with those for whom we pray. Such prayer humbles the soul always, and gives the life the benediction of being rightly related to God.

This aspect of things throws a great light on what is often a perplexity. At the outset of the Christian career the blessing of God is so sensible, so marked by feeling, that the Christian walks more by sight than by faith, God's caressings seem to be so upon him. But there comes a time in the life of the disciple when God withdraws these comforts, when joy in God is not what it used to be, when His presence is not so sweet, and when a strange dull grey (if one might say so) seems to fall over the spiritual life. For a time the soul gets into deep darkness; then he begins to realise that God is but teaching him the difference between walking in the light of blessings and entering into the experience of the Divine beatitudes; or, to put it more simply, God is taking the soul out of the realm of religious feeling and emotion into the realm of faith. "But without faith it is impossible to please Him."

3. The Best

One of the great marks that the blessings of God are being rightly used is that they lead us to repentance. ". . . not knowing that the goodness of God leadeth thee to repentance?" Repentance in the New Testament sense means just the difference between a sanctified and an unsanctified soul. The only repentant man in the New Testament sense is the holy man, one who is rightly related to God by the Atonement of Jesus and has become a written epistle, "known and read of all men." How many of us have allowed the goodness of God to lead us to repentance? Or are we so enjoying the blessings of God, like the beasts of the field, taking them as our due and not seeing behind them the great loving hand of God, whose heart is overflowing in tremendous love?

Another practical issue: if God makes no difference in His external blessings to men, who are we that we should? One of the chief stagnating influences on spiritual character is this reasoning—"Do they deserve it?" How much do any of us deserve the blessings of God? Let us ever remember that to enter into the experience of God's beatitudes is to find ourselves able to show to our fellow-men the same unmerited mercy, the same unselfish, unmerited love that God has shown to us. Jesus told His disciples that this is indeed the test: "For if ye forgive men their trespasses, your heavenly Father will also forgive you. But if ye forgive not men their trespasses, neither will your Father forgive your trespasses" (RV).

God grant we may realise more and more, with enlightened eyes and chastened hearts, "the blessing of the LORD, it maketh rich, and toil addeth nothing thereto" (RV mg); and may this external blessing of God surround the heart that has been made pure by the blood of the Lamb, that both together may witness in a life that is a blessing and a beatitude.

THE KINGDOM

1. The Prevailing Characteristics of the Kingdom

Who shall ascend into the hill of the LORD? And who shall stand in His holy place? He that hath clean hands, and a pure heart.... (Psalm 24:3–4 RV)

The prevailing characteristics of the Kingdom Jesus represents are moral characteristics. There must be an alteration in me before I can be in the Kingdom, or the Kingdom can be in me, and that can only be by means of an inner crisis, viz., regeneration. There must be something outside me which will alter me on the inside. Forgiveness is a miracle, because in forgiving a man God imparts to him the power to be exactly the opposite of what he has been: God transmutes the sinner who sinned into the saint who does not sin, consequently the only true repentant man is the holy man.

To-day we are in danger of being caught up by the lure of wrong roads to the Kingdom—"Things must be worked out at once, we cannot wait, there must be results immediately." If to benefit mankind is the whole purpose of God, quicker results could be produced apart from the Redemption, because the Redemption works appallingly slowly, according to our human standards. If all that is necessary is this hand-to-mouth business there is no need for all the teaching of Jesus, no need for patience until God's purposes are fully worked out. To look on the precepts of the Sermon on the Mount as referring to a future dispensation is to rob the Cross of its meaning. If Jesus Christ cannot alter me now, so that the alteration shows externally in my home life, in my business life, when is He going to alter me? What is going to transform me so that I can love my enemies, can pray for those that persecute me, if I cannot do it now? No suffering or discipline on my part will make me any different; the only thing that will make me different is being born again into the Kingdom of God. To look for death to make me holy is to make out that death, which is "the last enemy," is going to do what the Atonement cannot do. The Cross of Christ alone makes me holy, and it does so the second I am willing to let it.

The Kingdom of God is latent in the Cross, but don't spiritualise the Kingdom into vagueness, and don't materialise it into non-spirituality. The essential foundation of the Kingdom is the spiritual aspect, and this is apt to be forgotten. In this dispensation the emphasis is on the Kingdom within, but in another dispensation there is to be an external manifestation of the Kingdom. To say that the Kingdom is going to be brought in by the earth being swept clean through wars and cataclysms is not true; you cannot introduce the Kingdom in that way, it is impossible. Nothing can bring in the Kingdom saving the Redemption, which works in personal lives through the Cross and in no other way.

2. The Power of the Kingdom in Present Circumstances *(Luke 22:24–27)*

And He said unto them, The kings of the Gentiles have lordship over them; ... but ye shall not be so. (Luke 22:25–26 RV)

Naturally we think of a kingdom as being ruled and governed by superiors—"The kings of the Gentiles have lordship over them; ... *but ye shall not be so.*" The central meaning of the Kingdom is my personal relationship to my Lord. These words of Jesus reveal His mind regarding the Kingdom, and they also reveal the disciples' mind—"And there arose also a contention among them, which of them should be accounted the greatest" (RV). If the disciples' idea is the right one, our Lord's idea of the Kingdom is an impossibility. We have to interpret Jesus Christ's idea of the Kingdom from His nature, not from our own. One individual set over against another must insist on obedience, but in the Kingdom Jesus represents that is never the way to freedom; in His Kingdom absolute obedience is the only way to personal emancipation. Our use of the word "obedience" is that of an inferior submitting to a superior, in the New Testament the word is used as between equals (cf. Hebrews 5:8). Our Lord never takes means to make us obey Him; when we do obey it is through a oneness of spirit with Him. The reason things are found difficult is because we base everything on our natural independence, our natural morality and uprightness. Our Lord bases His Kingdom on none of these things but on the poverty of spirit which is willing to receive—"Blessed are the poor in spirit: for theirs is the kingdom of heaven" (Matthew 5:3). In the Higher Christian Life Movements[9] the Cross as the centre of the heart of God and as the centre of our personal experience, is apt to be ignored; it is, "You must pray more, you must give up this and that"; anything but the need to be born again into a totally new kingdom and to enter into a oneness of spirit with Jesus Christ. We have so insisted on the individual aspect that we have lost sight of the oneness Jesus prayed for—"that they may be one, even as We are one." It is a fundamental relationship, and we don't think on fundamental lines, but only on the line of practical efficiency.

The Christian life is stamped all through with impossibility, human nature cannot come anywhere near what Jesus Christ demands, and any rational being facing His demands honestly, says, "It can't be done, apart from a miracle." Exactly. In our modern conception of Christianity there is no miracle, the emphasis is put not on the regenerating power of the Cross, but on individual consecrations, individual fasting and prayer, individual devotion. It is simply individualism veneered over with religious phraseology. There is no need for the Cross of Christ for all that kind of thing. The only entrance into the Kingdom is the Cross; then when we are born again by means of the Cross and are in the Kingdom of God, we have to live out its laws. It is not that we take the precepts of the Sermon on the Mount and try to live them out literally, but that as we abide in Christ we live out its precepts unconsciously. Being in the Kingdom, we are fit now to live out its laws, and we obey Jesus Christ's commands because of our love for Him.

Too often the Kingdom is thought of as something to which Jesus is not at all necessary. He does not stand in relation to it where the New Testament places Him, viz., as King. It is not natural to us to think of Jesus as King; in the New Testament it is the most natural view. We are much more inclined to think of Him in a sentimental way as Saviour and sympathising Friend; in the New Testament there is something much more vigorous. He is Saviour in order that He might be King. If I am going to be of any use to Jesus Christ I must spend a great deal of time with Him as my Lord and Master, then He can reveal Himself through me to others. Christianity is not being spent in the service of men, but being spent out in the service of my Lord. What we hear about to-day is devotion to causes; the Kingdom can never be established externally as a cause.

"My kingdom is not of this world . . ." (John 18:36)—"You can have no notion of My kingdom from the kingdoms of this world." It is the duty of any upright man to oppose wrong, but Jesus Christ did not come to enable us to do that. He came to put within us a new spirit, to make us members of His Kingdom while we are in this world—not *against* the world, and not *of* it, but *in* the world, exhibiting an otherworldly spirit. The popular evangelical idea that we are to be against the world in the sense of a pitched battle with it, is simply an expression of the spirit of the world dressed up in a religious guise. Our Lord was not against the world in that sense; He submitted to its providential order of tyranny, but there was no compromise in His spirit, and the model of the Christian's spirit is Christ Himself. There is a religious cult which courts persecution. Jesus said, "Blessed are ye, when men shall revile you, and persecute you, . . . *for My sake.* Rejoice, and be exceeding glad." It is by our spiritual choices that we maintain a right relation to the world. When a man ceases conflicting the world by spiritual choices, he succumbs to it and becomes part of the world that needs saving instead of being a saviour in the world.

DON'T THINK NOW—TAKE THE ROAD

If any man would come after Me, let him deny himself. . . . Matthew 16:24 (RV)

1. Recognise, but Don't Stop to Reckon
And Peter went down from the boat, and walked upon the waters, to come to Jesus. (Matthew 14:29 RV)

We are all inclined to recognise the right thing and reckon with the wrong; inclined to recognise the real thing and reckon with the actual. In the incident recorded here the wind was actually boisterous, the water was actually water, the waves were actually high, but Peter did not see any of these at first, he did not

9. Higher Christian Life Movements: various groups and organizations that emphasized sanctification and personal holiness.

reckon with them, he simply stepped straight out in recognition of his Master and walked on the water to go to Jesus. Then he began to reckon with actual things, with the wind and the waves, and down he went instantly. Why could not our Lord have kept Peter at the bottom of the water as well as on the top of it? Only the recognition of Jesus Christ as Lord could have made either possible. If I recognise Jesus as my Lord, I have no business with where He engineers my circumstances. If He gives me the pictorial thrill of enabling me to do something ostensibly wonderful, and then suddenly alters my circumstances and puts me, so to speak, at the bottom of the ocean, what right have I to be afraid? If Jesus Christ can keep me walking on the top of the waves, He can keep me underneath them.

God often does things in order to teach us whether we are denying ourselves or only thinking about doing it. We step right out in faith on God over some matter, then self-consideration enters in and down we go. We have to learn how to rely completely on God; let actual things be what they may, we have to keep recognising Him. Whether it be walking on top of the waves or underneath them makes not the slightest difference to God, therefore it need make no difference to us. The actual things *are* but immediately we look at them we cannot recognise Jesus, we are overwhelmed, and the rebuke comes—"O thou Of little faith, wherefore didst thou doubt?" Jesus Christ is educating us to the point of giving up our right to ourselves. How can I empty myself of my self? By not thinking any more about it, but by taking the road. Recognise Jesus as Lord, obey Him, and let the next thing happen as He wills.

2. Recklessly Don't Stop to Realise

So when Simon Peter heard that it was the Lord, he girt his coat about him (for he was naked), and cast himself into the sea. (John 21:7 RV)

If you debate for a second when God has spoken, it is all up. Never try and realise more clearly and say, "I wonder if that is the Lord?" "I wonder if He did speak?" Be reckless immediately, fling it all out to Him, and you will suddenly find it is the Lord, and that He has nourishment already prepared for you; and you may also find that He has a very searching thing to say to you. God always speaks quietly, and if you try to catch an echo of His voice you will never hear it. When the moment comes and you hear, as it were from someone else, "It is the Lord," recklessly abandon immediately. If you say, "I thought it was God's voice," but you did not recklessly obey, you will find it has gone and you will have to wait now. When God's voice will come you do not know, but whenever the realisation of God comes again in the faintest way imaginable, recklessly abandon. It is only by abandon that you find Him. Never make the mistake of thinking that God speaks unmistakably clearly; He speaks in the gentlest of whispers, so unutterably quiet that it is not easy to hear Him. We only realise His voice more clearly by recklessness.

3. Relinquish, and Don't Stop to Reason

Verily, verily I say unto thee, When thou wast young, thou girdest thyself, . . . but when thou shalt be old, . . . another shall gird thee, and carry thee whither thou wouldest not. (John 21:18)

Over and over again our convictions have to be abandoned until we learn that Jesus Christ is to be All in all. When God's word becomes clear by His Spirit making it living, relinquish your own notions instantly. You have nothing whatever to do with what sits on you, all you have to do is to relinquish and be sat on—"I know how to be abased" (RV) said the Apostle Paul. Relinquish in accordance with what Jesus Christ says; don't stop to reason, but take everything that transpires as being absolutely in accordance with God's order.

One of the last things we learn is that God engineers our circumstances; we do not believe He does, we say we do. Never look for second causes; if you do, you will go wrong. We blunder when we look at circumstances as secondary, "And we know that all things work together for good to them that love God, to them who are the called according to His purpose."

Don't say—"Thy will be done," but see it is done.

MATTERS FOR MATURITY

Be not thou therefore ashamed of the testimony of our Lord, nor of me His prisoner: but be thou partaker of the afflictions of the gospel according to the power of God. 2 Timothy 1:8

This is the message of a veteran soldier to a young soldier. Timothy was constitutionally timid, and Paul had a marvellous solicitude for him, but he never allowed him to give way to self-pity. "Be instant in season, out of season," whether you feel like it or not; whether you feel well or ill, keep at it. It is a fight which means no rest till it issues in a glorious victory for God.

1. Danger of Dereliction
Be not thou therefore ashamed of the testimony of our Lord . . .

In Revelation 19:10 these striking words occur: "for the testimony of Jesus is the spirit of prophecy," and the purpose of the antagonist of God is to destroy that testimony (see Revelation 12:17). The testimony of Jesus to Himself is being explained away to-day, men and women are swerving from the Truth. The power and vigour of the Holy Spirit in lives must go further than the threshold of the experience of being right with God; bit by bit the battle for God and for His truth must be pushed, and the only way to push it is by an experimental belief in Jesus Christ's testimony regarding Himself.

If we have been allowing the silting influence of modern tendencies to overcome us, God grant we may rouse ourselves and get back again to the moral and spiritual fighting trim, free from moral nervousness and spiritual timidity, trusting in God and going steadfastly on. A derelict ship is a danger to other ships, and a derelict in the pulpit, or in the Sunday school, or in the pew, is a desperately dangerous thing to souls on their way through life.

2. Dread of Disloyalty
nor of me His prisoner . . .

Nowadays loyalty to the saints is scarcely ever thought of. The Apostle Paul is telling Timothy to be loyal to him, and he uses a remarkable phrase—"His prisoner," and yet Paul is always talking about liberty! Remaining true to Paul would be a real peril to Timothy's personal liberty. Have some of us changed our Church membership because we no longer want to know certain "out and out" people? Do we welcome the "out and out" saint as we used to, or are we a lit-

tle bit shocked when we hear the straight testimony of the saints who are "in prison"?

Some saints have to be ugly in the eyes of the world for a time. The Holy Spirit makes us understand that in spiritual things it is the good that is the enemy of the best every time. Jesus said "If thy right hand offend thee, cut it off, and cast it from thee." Off goes the right arm, out comes the right eye, and for a while the life is maimed; but slowly and surely God will bring it round to the perfected relationship. When you are in contact with saints in the maimed stage, be loyal to them. Remember the way you yourself had to go.

Intercessory prayer is the test of our loyalty. When a man stands out as a "prisoner of the Lord," the saints must garrison him by prayer. If Satan can make a servant of God bow his head in shame because of "the testimony of Jesus," or because he knows a "prisoner of Jesus," he will soon succeed in making him disloyal to Christianity altogether.

3. Discipline of Disfavour
but be thou partaker of the afflictions of the gospel . . .

The Gospel of God awakens an intense craving in men and an equally intense resentment, and the tendency is to do away with the resentment. Jesus Christ claims that He can remove the disposition of sin from every man; the only testimony worthy of the Name of Jesus is that He can make a sinner a saint. The most marvellous testimony to the Gospel is a holy man, one whose living experience reveals what God can do.

4. Divine Dynamic
. . . according to the power of God.

What is the purpose of God? That the historic Jesus should reproduce Himself by the might of His Atonement in every one who will "close" with Him, i.e., deny his right to himself and follow Him. It is not that Jesus Christ puts a permeating influence into a man; He stands outside a man and brings him to a crisis, and by means of that crisis reproduces Himself in him (see Galatians 4:19). Thank God, it is not only Timothy who had this marvellous counsel of Paul's, we have it too; and it is not only the counsel of Paul, but of the grand order of heroes right up to the present day, men and women standing for one thing, "the testimony of our Lord."

NEW CREATION

Wherefore if any man is in Christ, he is a new creature ["there is a new creation," RV mg]. 2 Corinthians 5:17

All God's direct acts are creative.

Forsyth

The creation performed by God is what the Apostle Paul calls it—a *new* creation; it is not the bringing out of something already there, but the creating of somethinqg which was never there before, an entirely new creation, as unlike anything born in a man by nature as Jesus Christ is unlike anything produced by the human race throughout its history.

1. Invasion

My little children, of whom I am again in travail until Christ be formed in you. (Galatians 4:19 RV)

We all become Christians by a miracle, not by a verdict and not by an inference, but by a decision and an obedience.

Forsyth

It is impossible for a man to become a Christian by natural reasoning effort, which is simply the working of his own mind; a man becomes a Christian by there being wrought in him "a new creation," and that new creation is the forming of the Son of God in him. "The old things are passed away; behold, they are become new" (RV): God does not discard the old, He creates that in the old which makes the old and the new one. By "old things" Paul means much more than "the old man," he means everything that was our life as natural men before we were re-created in spirit by Christ; it involves a radical alteration until the whole life is Christ-centred and you can't be roused to any other interest. Only one thing brings a man there, and that is the deliberate faith in God which will enable Him to perform the "new creation" by means of the Redemption of Jesus.

"The Holy Ghost shall come upon thee, and the power of the Most High shall overshadow thee: wherefore also that which is to be born shall be called holy, the Son of God" (Luke 1:35 RV). What happened to Mary, the mother of our Lord, historically in the conception of the Son of God has its counterpart in what takes place in every born-again soul. Mary represents the natural individual life which must be sacrificed in order that it may be transfigured into an expression of the real life of the Son of God. The individual life is the husk of the personal life, and because of the forming of the Son of God in me, the sword must go through it. ("Yea and a sword shall pierce through thine own soul," Luke 2:35 RV). It is the natural virtues that battle, not sin as we think of sin, but pride, egotism, my temperament, my affinities; all that has to have the sword run clean through it mercilessly by God, and if I stick to my natural inheritance the sword must go through me. The new creation is based on the new man in Christ (*see* Ephesians 4:24), not on the natural gifts of the first Adam. The natural life is not obliterated, when I come to God in the abandon of faith He creates supernaturally on the basis of His own nature, and the Spirit of God makes me see to it that my natural life is lived in accordance with the new life formed in me. Our Lord can never be spoken of in terms of the natural virtues, they don't apply to Him, and they don't apply to the new man in Christ; all that is taken knowledge of in those possessed by Christ is that they have been with Jesus, the dominating personality that tells is that of the Son of God, it is His life that is being manifested.

2. Incorporation

. . . Christ in you, the hope of glory. (Colossians 1:27)

. . . as God was in Christ historically, so He is in me now by the miracle of new birth. As God was manifest in Christ, so He is manifest in "Christ in me," which is the hope of glory, being the ultimate outer external manifestation of that inner hidden miracle.

Forsyth

Christ in me means ultimately "me" altogether in Christ. That is, Christ in me means that I am willing to let Christ grow in me. The obverse side of Christ in me is me in Christ; it is an incorporation. "That ye may be strengthened with power through His Spirit in the inward man; that Christ may dwell in your hearts through faith . . ." (Ephesians 3:16–17 RV)—how much of "me" is there? The only thing of "me" is "the inward man," all the rest is Christ. If my inward man is possessed and strengthened by the Spirit it means not only am I in union with Christ, but I am identical with Christ. Our Lord was not one with His Father by a union: the Father and the Son were identical. "I and My Father are one," said Jesus. The Apostle Paul mentions this identical oneness when he says, "I live; and yet no longer I, but Christ liveth in me" (RV). What sounds mystical and impractical to anyone not born again is a glorious reality to the saint.

Our Lord always speaks in terms of personality, never of individuality, and His conception of personality is His own oneness with the Father. The characteristic of my natural individual life is the opposite, it is all independence and pride, not only independent naturally, but independent of God. Christ never triumphs in my moral triumphs because they exalt that which is my inheritance by nature—that, God can only bless through sacrifice and death. The corrupting of the natural virtues is painful because it is a blow at the deepest inheritance of the natural man. The evidence of the new creation in me is that I submit to God more and more easily, surrender to Him more and more readily. "For it is God which worketh in you both to will and to do of His good pleasure" (Philippians 2:13). God does the supernatural re-creating and the setting free of the will, I have to do the *doing*. It is not that I get a new point of view—you can get a new point of view through study, but it is the same "you"; when Jesus Christ gets possession of me it is another "me"; you may search for the old "me," but you cannot find it. It is not that I consecrate my natural individual life to God, I immolate it, offer it up to God. The real burnt offering God requires is "a living sacrifice," the giving back to God the best He has given me that it might be His and mine for ever.

All this is involved in "becoming a Christian by a miracle." "If only I could understand it all, it would make me a Christian"—you can only be made a Christian by a miracle, and you can stop at any point you like. "I don't intend to go through this"—and you don't need to; but it will be a terrific awakening when you see Jesus and realise that you prevented His getting glory in your life.

3. Identification
And ye are Christ's; and Christ is God's. (1 Corinthians 3:23)

"Christ is God's" in this connection is the return back to the original with that which the original never had. The original had the intention; the return back of *Christ to God is the expression of the intention, and the expression of the intention is sinless humanity. That miraculous purpose is enacted in every individual saint's life who is obedient to God because what is true of the universal is true of the particular.*

Forsyth

When a man follows up by obedience the performing of the new creation in him, he enters into identification with Christ. Identification is not experienceable; it is infinitely more fundamental than experience. We enter into identification by the door of obedience, but the oneness is a revelation. "Every spirit which confesseth that Jesus Christ is come in the flesh is of God"—*confess,* that is, say with every corpuscle of your blood that Christ is come in your flesh and is being manifested. "And every spirit which confesseth not Jesus is not of God: and this is that spirit of antichrist . . ." (1 John 4:2–3 RV). We all have that in us which will connect us with the spirit of antichrist if we do not go through–identification with Jesus in His death so that the life we now live proves that "old things are passed away; behold, all things are become new." The miracle of becoming a Christian through the Redemption is that the Spirit of God bears us into His Kingdom, and then these things begin to be unveiled to us for our instruction; the danger is lest we refuse to "press on unto full growth" (RV mg).

The new creation is not something you can hold in your hand and say, "What a wonderful thing God has done for me"; the one indelible sign of the new creation is "My peace." It is never safe to trust in manifestations and experiences; where the miracle of the new creation touches the shores of our individual lives it is always on the line of "My peace I give unto you." That is the meaning of, "And all things are of God, who hath reconciled us to Himself by Jesus Christ."

SPASMODIC SPIRITUALITY

Your goodness is as a morning cloud, and as the early dew it goeth away. Hosea 6:4

Fits of goodness may often be seen in a base character, indicating a capacity to be noble; but apart from that, all kinds of natures are conscious of moments of unusual power and insight and excellence. These moments are wonderful and delightful episodes in both intellectual and spiritual life, yet they nearly always leave the nature with a reaction. Such emotion is no more real goodness than a dewdrop is a diamond or a meteor a star. It is a perilous thing, eminently per-

ilous, to experience "flashes struck from midnight" and not allow God to readjust the life to the level of that moment of insight. The spirituality the Spirit of God gives is entirely free from these passing episodes, the whole life is in keeping, its characteristic being persistence, which is the only sign of reality. A bird flies persistently and easily because the air is its domain and its world. A legal Christian is one who is trying to live in a rarer world than is natural to him. Our Lord said "If therefore the Son shall make you free, ye shall be free indeed," i.e., free from the inside, born from above (RV mg), lifted into another world where there is no strenuous effort to live in a world not natural to us, but where we can soar continually higher and higher because we are in the natural domain of spiritual life. One might almost say that our every effort to be good and our every effort to be holy is a sure sign that we are neither good nor holy. A child makes no effort to be the daughter or son of its parents, and a child of God born of the Spirit makes no conscious effort to be good or to be holy; but just as a child trying to imitate someone else's mother is bound to fail, so the natural man trying to imitate God is bound to fail. When the child imitates his own mother he can do it with success, because the inherent nature of the child is like the mother; and when a Christian tries to imitate Jesus Christ he can do it easily because the Spirit of Jesus is in him. The strenuous effort of the saint is not to produce holiness, but to express in every circumstance the life of Jesus which is imparted to him by the Holy Ghost. That is Paul's meaning in Philippians 2: "Work out your own salvation. . . . For it is God which worketh in you both to will and to do of His good pleasure" (Philippians 2:12–13).

The mourning of Jehovah over Ephraim and Judah is very wistful—"O Ephraim, what shall I do unto thee? O Judah, what shall I do unto thee?" I wonder if any of us are causing the same wistful yearning to the Holy Ghost? if He has to mourn over us and say "your goodness is as a morning cloud"? "Therefore," says God, "have I hewed them by the prophets; I have slain them by the words of My mouth." The first thing that will bring an unnatural natural man to his senses before God is the word of God spoken by a man of God. I mean by an un-natural natural man, one who is trying by prayer, by effort, by Bible reading, to be a saint. In the Epistle to the Galatians Paul is writing to immature Christians, and he says, "Am I therefore become your enemy, because I tell you the truth?" (Galatians 4:16). They have been disenchanted by the rugged truth of the apostle's words—"Are ye so foolish? having begun in the Spirit, are ye now made perfect by the flesh?"(Galatians 3:3). They had been reverting back to ritual and observances, trying to perfect themselves "by the flesh." Oh the emancipation of the life that has realised the fulness of God which dwells in Christ Jesus! then it is not only natural, but easy and right to "mount up with wings as eagles." No Christian has any right to be un-enthusiastic. "And be not drunk with wine, wherein is excess; but be filled with the Spirit." It is easy for many men to obey the first part of this injunction while they disobey the latter. We must be thrilled, and if human nature does not get its thrills from the right place, it will take them from the wrong. Enthusiasm means, to use the phrase of a German mystic, "intoxicated with God," filled to overflowing with God; no spasmodic spirituality about us, but a perennial source of freshness, making us a delight to our Lord, and a channel of blessing to all with whom we come in contact. The sad and serious lapsing of many immature Christians who have not got the life more abundant, must cause many a heart-pang to our Lord. Are we "filled with the Spirit"? or is our experience one that manages to draw out of God enough grace to last the day, and at its close we say with a sigh, if we remember, "Oh well, thank God I have got through the day"? Could you imagine anything more utterly unlike the superabounding life of God the New Testament talks about? is that anything like the superconquering life Paul talks about? People say they are tired of life; no man was ever tired of life; the truth is that we are tired of being half dead while we are alive. What we need is to be transfigured by the incoming of a great and new life.

Again the old message of the Psalms and the new message of the New Testament meet together—"All my fresh springs shall be in Thee" (Psalm 87:7 PBV): "Of His fulness have all we received" (John 1:16). Are all the channels of our life open to God? are the channels of our body open for Divine health to come to us through the resurrection life of Jesus? are our hearts and imaginations and spirits open for the Divine insight and comfort and sanctification of God to come to us through the Atonement? If not, we are not only starving our own lives, but are a hindrance to the lives of others and a grief to our Lord.

God grant that His Spirit may bring everyone of us to the place where the secret is learned and enjoyed that His strength is made perfect in our weakness. The realisation that my strength is always a hindrance to God's supply of life is a great eye-opener. A man who has genius is apt to rely on his genius rather than on God. A man who has money is apt to rely on money instead of God. So many of us trust in what we have got in the way of possessions instead of entirely in God. All these sources of strength are sources of double weakness. But when we realise that our true life is "hid with Christ in God," that we are "complete in Him," in whom "dwelleth all the fulness of the Godhead bodily," then His strength is radiantly manifested in our mortal flesh. God grant that every "spasmodic" saint may turn into a real sanctified saint, whose light and life and love shine more and more unto the perfect day.

THE BIBLE

The revelation of God's will has been brought down to us in words. The Bible is not a book containing communications from God, it is God's revelation of Himself, in the interests of grace; God's giving of Himself in the limitation of words. The Bible is not a faery romance to beguile us for a while from the sordid realities of life, it is the Divine complement of the laws of Nature, of Conscience and of Humanity, it introduces us to a new universe of revelation facts not known to unregenerate commonsense. The only Exegete of these facts is the Holy Spirit, and in the degree of our reception, recognition, and reliance on the Holy Spirit will be our understanding. Facts in the natural domain have to be accepted, and facts in the revelation domain have to be accepted; our explanation of facts is always open to alteration, but you cannot alter facts. The Bible does not simply explain to us the greatest number of facts, it is the only ground of understanding *all* the facts, that is, it puts into the hand of the Spirit-born the key to the explanation of all mysteries.

In dealing with revelation facts the aim is not to produce "specialists," but to make practical workers in the Bible domain. The research of specialists, both in the natural world and in the revelation world, is of the very greatest value, but remember, it is essential to be born of the Spirit before we can enter the domain of Bible revelation. The only method of Bible study is to "prove all things," not by intellect, but by personal experience.

The Context of the Bible is our Lord Jesus Christ, and personal relationship to Him. The *words* of God and The *Word* of God stand together; to separate them is to render both powerless. Any expounder of the words of God is liable to go off at a tangent if he or she does not remember this stern undeviating standard of exposition, viz., that no individual experience is of the remotest value unless it is up to the standard of The Word of God.

The Bible not only tests experience, it tests truth. "I am . . . the Truth," said Jesus. Just as the words of God and The Word of God are the counterpart of each other, so the commandments of our Lord and the conduct of His saints are the counterpart of each other; if they are not, then we are "none of His." The test of Truth is the revelation of the Son of God in me, not as a Divine anticipation, but as a delightful activity *now*. It is perilously possible to praise our Lord as Saviour and Sanctifier, and yet cunningly blind our own hearts to the necessity of His manifesting in our mortal flesh His peculiar salvation and sanctification.

The Bible tests all experience, all truth, all authority, by our Lord Himself and our relationship to Him personally; it is the confession of conduct. ". . . he that confesseth Me before men," said Jesus; the word "confess" means literally that every bit of my bodily life speaks the same truth as our Lord exhibited in the flesh. It is this scriptural scrutiny that reveals the superb standard of the grace of God: Christian experience is possible only when it is the *product of the supernatural grace of God at work in our hearts.*

SYMPATHISER OR SAVIOUR?
Isaiah 61:1

(SEE ALSO LUKE 4:18–19, RV MG)

In some ages, as with some people, the tendency is strong to make an essential out of what is a mere accompaniment. In our day this tendency is marked in the emphasising of our Lord as a sympathiser, and the direct practical effect of this is to turn spirituality into sentimentality, and to make our Lord simply a kind brother-man. To picture Jesus Christ, never so beautifully, as One who sits down beside the broken-hearted and by expression of fellow-feeling and overflowing tenderness, enables him to be resigned and submissive

to his lot, is not only thoroughly to misunderstand our Lord, but to prevent His doing what He came to do. He does come to the broken-hearted, to the captives bound by a cursed hereditary tendency, to the blind who grope for light, to the man bruised and crushed by his surroundings, but He does not come as a sympathiser—He binds up the broken-hearted, gives release to the captives, recovering of sight to the blind; He sets at liberty them that are bruised. Jesus Christ is not a mere sympathiser, He is a Saviour, and the only One, "for neither is there any other name under heaven, that is given among men, wherein we must be saved" (RV). His sympathy is the accompaniment of the work He alone can do. Again, in Hebrews 4:15–16 ("For we have not an high priest which cannot be touched with the feeling of our infirmities . . ."), the sympathy and fellow-feeling is merely the accompaniment of the deliverance wrought by coming to the throne of grace, and finding help in time of need.

Another accompaniment which is apt to be made an essential, and which even more fatally prevents men from finding Jesus Christ as Saviour, is the idea that He came to give us better social surroundings, to extend and improve our civilisations. That is a gross misreading of the Gospel our Lord said He was anointed to preach, and of the work He came to do. He did come to get things done—but what things? The things we cannot do! Social reform, political purity, progressive civilisation, is our work, not God's, and we must do it. If we don't, it will never be done. The reason we are so sluggish in the matter is because the work our Lord came to do has never been done in us. God has ordained that our work we must do, in the sweat of our brow, and through struggle and sacrifice we must work; and when the sanctified saints do the work God appoints them, then do God's work and man's work fit, and the mighty evolution with God at its heart moves on to all Eternity.

"The Spirit of the Lord is upon Me, because He anointed Me to preach the gospel to the poor . . ." (RV mg). Thank God for the deep profound note of the glorious Gospel of God, that Jesus Christ as Saviour can justify ungodly men, can set them free from their sin; and as Sanctifier He can make them into sons and daughters of God, able to love others as God has loved them, able to show others the same unconditioned mercy He has showed them.

Jesus Christ is not a sympathiser, neither is He a social reformer, He is unique—the Saviour of the world. The Atonement is God speaking to men in heart-breaking agony and long-suffering patience that they might be reconciled to His way of salvation. Beware of dragging down the Atonement into the socialistic arena. The Church is called to deliver God's message and to be for the praise of His glory, not to be a socialistic institution under the patronage of God. "Christ also loved the church, and gave Himself. up for it; . . . that He might present the church to Himself a glorious church, . . . holy and without blemish" (Ephesians 5:25, 27 RV).

PROFANING THE HOLINESS OF THE LORD

Ezekiel 36:20–29

1. The Searching of His People
. . . they profaned My holy name. (Ezekiel 36:20)

This was the characteristic of the people of God whenever they forgot whose they were and whom they served. Under the searchlight of God we realise that God's holy Name is profaned when we put before people what God's grace has wrought in us instead of God Himself. Whenever we go into work for God from any standpoint saving that of the dominance of God, we begin to patronise at once; unless we go as the bondservants of Jesus Christ we have no business to go at all. Jesus Christ became the towel-girt Servant of His own disciples. Never deal with people from the superior person's standpoint, God never blesses that; deal only by steadily presenting the Lord Jesus Christ. The characteristic of the holiness which is the outcome of the indwelling of God is a blazing truthfulness with regard to God's word, and an amazing tenderness in personal dealing.

There is only one thing to heed in Christian work, and that is God Himself and His programme.

The last thing we learn is that there is no chance happening in the saint's life, circumstances are God's, not ours, and by choosing our own way we profane God's holy Name, whatever our desire.

". . . whither they went." It is possible to profane God's holy Name in our minds where no one sees but ourselves. Our feet carry us in secret and they carry us in public; they carry us into shops and into streets, into houses and into churches; God says, "You profane My holy Name, not because of the places you went into, but by the way you went into them." Scrutinise yourself, and let God search you, as He searched these people. We forget the minuteness of God's searching; He searches us right down to the inmost recesses.

2. The Sanctifying of His People
. . . and the heathen shall know that I am the LORD, saith the Lord GOD, when I shall be sanctified in you before their eyes. (Ezekiel 36:23)

Individual sanctification is one thing; collective sanctification is another; when Paul talks about attaining "unto the measure of the stature of the fulness of Christ," he is not talking of individual saints, but of all the saints. It is the sanctification of God's people together that is required. When we isolate ourselves we hinder instead of further that end. Very few of us have got beyond the need for the searching which God gave these people. We are all too set on our own sanctification, forgetting that we are to be broken bread and poured-out wine for the lifting up of others who are not there yet. Individual sanctification has a worldwide benefit so long as the sanctified soul remains right with God. The sanctified soul keeps right with God by placing God's methods first, and God's methods are foolish to everyone who is not sanctified.

Verses 25–29 point out that purity in God's children is not the outcome of obedience to His law, but the result of the supernatural work of His grace. *"I will*

cleanse you"; *"I will give you a new heart"; "I will put My Spirit within you, and cause you to walk in My statutes"; "I will do it all."* After sanctification the first thing is to stand, as it were, with our hand in God's while He recalls to us what we once were. The memory of sin does not come before sanctification, the memory of defects and blunders comes then, but sin is only remembered and known after sanctification, and it is by the recalling of the Holy Spirit that we remember it. In the absolute humility that is produced there is never any fear of spiritual pride, never any fear of forgetting that God sends us into work for His own glory; never any fear of being harsh or unjust to others, because God has shown us what we were, and we have realised it with shame.

ARE YOU DISCOURAGED IN DEVOTION?
Luke 18:23

1. Have You Ever Heard the Master Say a Hard Word?
And when he heard this . . .

Have you ever heard the Master say a hard word?—if you have not, I question whether you have heard Him say anything. Jesus Christ says a great deal that we listen to, but do not hear. When we *do* hear it, His words are amazingly hard. These words were so hard that His very disciples were staggered—"And they that heard it said, Who then can be saved?" Jesus did not seem the least solicitous that the rich young ruler should do what He told him. He made no attempt to keep him with Him, He simply said—"Sell all that thou hast, . . . and come, follow Me." Our fuss over other souls is nearly always an evidence that we have not the slightest trust in God. Our Lord never made a fuss over anyone, and the reason He didn't could not have been that He was callous or indifferent, or that He was not tenderhearted, or that He did not understand every detail, but the fact remains that He did not make a fuss over anyone. He never pleaded, He never cajoled, He never entrapped; He simply spoke the sternest words mortal ears ever heard, and then let it alone. The rich young ruler was a clean, moral, fine, vigorous young man, with a desire for all that was noble and true, but he did not expect to hear what he did.

Have I ever heard a hard word of Jesus? Has He said something to me personally that I have deliberately listened to—not something I can expound or teach and say this and that about, but something I have deliberately heard Him say to me?

In all probability the rich young ruler was in a more wholesome state of mind towards Jesus than

were His own disciples who had left all and followed Him, because they had left all and followed Jesus without hearing one word that He said, and at the end of three years they said, "What is this that He saith? . . . We cannot tell what He saith," and then "they all forsook Him, and fled." This man did understand what Jesus said, he heard it and sized it up from height to depth, and it broke his heart. He did not go away defiant or in unbelief, he went away sorrowful, thoroughly discouraged. He had come to Jesus full of the fire of earnest desire and the word of Jesus simply froze him. Instead of the word of Jesus producing an enthusiastic devotion, it produced a heart-breaking discouragement. And Jesus did not go after him, He did not plead with him, He let him go. I wonder what we would have done? We would have written him letters, given him little booklets, asked other people to look after him, meaning by it all to get him to retrace his steps. Jesus did not do any of that, and I will tell you why He did not—our Lord has a perfect understanding that when once His word is heard, it will bear fruit sooner or later. The terrible heartbreak is that some of us prevent its bearing fruit in actual life. We hear His word, some of us heard it months ago, years ago, we heard it distinctly and in enthusiasm—not realising exactly, as this man did, what Jesus said, but more after the manner of the disciples—we said, "Yes, I will follow." Then we began to size up what it was we heard, and instead of its producing a great alacrity and devotion, it produced discouragement, and the Lord has gone on His way. I wonder what we will say when we do make up our mind to be devoted to Him on that particular point? One thing is certain—

He will never cast up anything at us, but we will be thoroughly ashamed that we actually weighed any other consideration in the balance when once we heard His word.

2. Have You Ever Been Expressionless with Sorrow?

. . . he was very sorrowful: for he was very rich.

The rich young ruler went away expressionless with sorrow, there was not a word to say; he did not go away defiant—neither did you, and neither did I; he went away sorrowful. It is a bad thing to go away cheerful from God. To say, "Oh yes, I will do it presently, God will bring His providence round," shows we have not understood anything. This man had not the slightest doubt in his mind as to what Jesus said, no debate as to what it meant, and it produced in him a sorrow that had not any words.

Have you ever got there? Has God's word come to you about something that is a very dear possession to you, something you are very rich in—temperament, personal affinity, relationships of heart and mind? Then you have very often been expressionless with sorrow, and you will be worse before you get to the end, and the Lord won't cajole, He won't caress, He won't go after you, He won't plead, He will simply repeat every time He meets you on that point, "If you mean what you say, these are the conditions . . ."

"Sell all that thou hast, and distribute unto the poor." There is a general principle here and a particular reference. We are always in danger of taking the particular reference for the general principle and evading the general principle. The particular reference here is to selling material goods. The rich young ruler had deliberately to be destitute, deliberately to distribute, deliberately to discern where his treasure was, and devote himself to Jesus Christ. The principle underlying it is that I must detach myself from everything I possess. Many of us suppress our sense of property, we don't starve it, we suppress it. Undress yourself morally before God of everything that might be a possession until you are a mere conscious human being, and then give God that. That is where the battle is fought—in the domain of the will before God, it is not fought in external things at all. Is He sovereign Lord or is He not? Am I more devoted to my notion of what Jesus Christ wants than to Himself? If so, I am likely to hear one of His hard sayings that will produce sorrow in me. What Jesus says *is* hard, it is only easy when it comes to those who really are His disciples. Beware of allowing anything to soften a hard word of Jesus.

It is a terrible thing to see how we keep Jesus Christ waiting. We serve God, but there is a drawback, and it is that drawback which Jesus gets at by His talk when once we come to Him as this man did. We twist His words and debate about their meaning, we discuss His teachings and expound His Gospel, and all the time we leave Him absolutely alone because at the centre of our heart there is the gnawing grip of one of His hard sayings that keeps us sorrowful, and He waits till we come and lay it all down. All the time in between has been utterly wasted as far as Jesus Christ is concerned, no matter how active we have been, or how much we have been a blessing to others, because none of it has sprung from devotion to Him but from devotion to an idea.

I can be so rich in poverty, so rich in the consciousness that I am nobody, that I will never be a disciple of Jesus Christ; and I can be so rich in the consciousness that I am somebody that I will never be a disciple. Am I willing to be destitute of the sense that I am destitute? This is not the application of the principle to a rich man, but to those of us who are not rich men. Am I possessed of the possibility of riches on other lines? rich in the inheritance of a particular type of temperament, and has the hard word of Jesus come against that? The thing in you and in me that other people like and esteem and laud is the very thing that makes us unable to do what Jesus says. You cannot do it unless you are willing to reduce yourself to a mere consciousness, and then give that to Him. He is bringing you to the place of resigning yourself, not of resigning things or people, there might be a sense of the heroic about that. It is not giving up outside things, but making yourself destitute to yourself and that is where the discouragement comes in. It is not a question of being willing to go straight through, but of *going* straight through. Not a question of saying, "Lord, I will do it," but of *doing* it. There must be the reckless committal of everything to Him with no regard for the consequences.

Discouragement is disenchanted self-love, and self-love may be love of devotion to Jesus. My devotion to Jesus must altogether efface my consciousness of devotion to Him.

ONE OF GOD'S GREAT DON'TS

Fret not thyself, it tendeth only to evil-doing. Psalm 37:8 (RV)

It is so easy, we think, to "rest in the LORD," and to "wait patiently for Him," until the nest is upset; until we live, as many are living to-day, in tumult and anguish—is it possible then? If this "Don't" does not work then, it will not work at any time. Resting in the Lord does not depend upon external circumstances, but on the relationship of the life of God in me to God Himself. Fussing generally ends in sin. We imagine that a little anxiety and worry is an indication of how wise we really are; it may be an indication of how wicked we really are.

1. Don't Calculate without God
Let not your heart be troubled. (John 14:1)

When you reckon things up, bring God in as the greatest factor in your calculation. How are we to have an untroubled heart? When we are well, we express the "well-ness"; but when things are not right, when circumstances are twisted upside down, can this command work then? This "don't" of our Lord's must work in days of perplexity as well as in days of peace.

God seems to have a delightful way of upsetting things which we have calculated on without Him. We get into places and circumstances He never chose, and suddenly they are shaken and we find we have been calculating on them without God; He has not entered in as a living factor. Have we learned the wonderfully practical lesson of not calculating without God? Have we got this "don't" straight home? To take God into all our calculations is the one thing that keeps us from the possibility of worrying. According to the wisdom of this world, God seems to be haphazard. He is not calculable in His providence, He works in ways we cannot estimate. If we try to work things out in logical ways, we are apt to find that suddenly in the providence of God a great upheaval comes we had never calculated on. Be silent to the Lord. There are things about which we never speak to God, because we don't need to (cf. Deuteronomy 3:26).

Fretfulness springs from a determination to get my own way. Our Lord never worried, nor was He ever anxious, because He was not "out" to realise His own ideas, He was "out" to realise God's ideas. Have I learnt to calculate upon God as the greatest factor in my common-sense decisions? "There"—in the secret place of the Most High, under the shadow of the Almighty—"shall no evil befall thee." No plague can touch that dwellingplace, no matter what happens on the outside it remains perfectly secure.

2. Don't Calculate with the Evil in View
Love . . . taketh not account of the evil. (1 Corinthians 13:4–5 RV)

Apart from God, we do reckon with evil, we reason from that standpoint. To take no account of the evil does not mean we are ignorant of its existence; it means we do not take it in as a calculable factor.

A man ought to be a quiet citadel of the Holy Ghost for prayer for all nations. The one who is suffering according to God's will is the one who has "a heart at leisure from itself." The discipline of our lives goes on in external ways, and if we are not suffering according to the will of God, we will take care to let everyone know it. People's sympathy is awakened for us, and they say, "How distressing that person's circumstances are."

"Come unto Me," says Jesus, "and I will give you rest." Do Jesus Christ's words apply to me? Does He really know my circumstances? Fretting is sinful if you are a child of God. Get back to God and tell Him with shame that you have been bolstering up that stupid soul of yours with the idea that your circumstances are too much for Him. Ask Him to forgive you and say, "Lord, I take Thee into my calculation as the biggest factor NOW!"

3. Don't Calculate with To-Morrow in View
Take therefore no thought for the morrow. (Matthew 6:34)

When we take thought for the morrow, it becomes the dominating calculation of our life. Our Lord is not saying, "Take no anxious thought," but, "Don't make to-morrow the ruling factor in to-day's work." Most of us do. To-day is lived without the power God means us to have because taking thought for the morrow is the dominating calculation, not Jesus Christ. Jesus Christ is not telling us to be careless, but to be carefully careless about everything saving one thing, seeking first the Kingdom of God and His righteousness. Many of us have no time for God and His Kingdom, we are so busy seeking other things.

SIN

Wherefore, as by one man sin entered into the world...
Romans 5:12

God intended that Adam should develop, not from evil to good, but from the natural to the spiritual, by obedience; it was to be a natural progress; but Adam stopped short, and sin entered in by his stopping short. The sin which has come down to us from Adam is not an act, but an hereditary disposition; the Bible nowhere says that a man is held responsible for having inherited a disposition in which he had no choice: the Redemption deals with sin. No man can be forgiven for a disposition, we are forgiven for acts of sin; the disposition of sin must be cleansed by the miracle of God's grace. The Son of God came to alter the basis of human life: the first Adam put it on a wrong basis, the basis of self-realisation; Jesus Christ makes the basis Redemptive. The Redemption means that God paid the price of sin. If you have never realised the impossibility of God dealing with sin on any other ground than that of the Redemption, you are living in a fool's paradise rationally.

Sin is a positive[10] thing, it is the enthronement of human independence, because man's pride must worship itself. Sin has nothing to do with circumstances or with temptation on the outside, it has to do with the bias on the inside; it is an opposing principle and has nothing to do with human nature as God constituted it. The diabolical nature of sin is that it hates God, it is not *at* enmity against God; it *is* enmity. When you get the nature of sin revealed by the Holy Spirit, you know that this phrase is not too strong—red-handed anarchy against God. None of us is conscious of this spirit of anarchy against God; the devil is the only being in whom sin is absolute, conscious anarchy. We would fly from sin in terror if we knew its nature, but it presents itself as a most desirable thing (cf. Genesis 3:6). We need never know in conscious experience that we are anarchists because we may receive the salvation of Jesus, any more than we need ever know what the human heart is like as Jesus diagnosed it if we will hand over the keeping of our heart to Him.

. . . that the body of sin might be destroyed.
(Romans 6:6)

The Bible refers to two mystical bodies—the Body of Christ and the body of sin; the Head of the one is God, the head of the other is the devil. Sin in me is a disposition of self-sufficiency which connects me with the body of sin; the connection is not in my human nature, but in my claim to my right to myself, which is the essence of sin—I'll do what I like. When I am born again I am willing to go to the crucifixion of that claim. Through the Redemption we not only have deliverance from the disposition of sin which is in us, but severance from the body of sin to which we are connected by our "old man"; that is, we are absolutely and completely delivered from sin in disposition and in domination—"Being then made free from sin. . . ."

for by the law is the knowledge of sin. (Romans 3:20)

Is the law sin? God forbid. Nay, I had not known sin, but by the law. (Romans 7:7)

Once conscience begins to be aroused it is aroused more and more till it reaches the terrible conviction that I am responsible before God for the breaking of His law; I know that God cannot forgive me and remain God; if He did I should have a clearer sense of justice than He has. There is nothing in my spirit to deliver me from sin, I am powerless—"sold under sin." Conviction of sin brings a man to this hopeless, helpless condition; until he gets there the Cross of Christ has no meaning for him.

It is of the mercy of God that no man is convicted of *sin* before he is born again; we are convicted of *sins* in order to be born again, then the indwelling Holy Spirit convicts us of sin. If God gave us conviction of sin apart from a knowledge of His Redemption, we would be driven insane. When conviction of what sin is in the sight of God comes home to me, language cannot support the strain of the verbal expression of its enormity; the only word that expresses it is "Calvary." If I see sin apart from the Cross, suicide seems the only fool's way out.

being justified freely by His grace. (Romans 3:24)

But where sin abounded, grace did much more abound. (Romans 5:20)

Justification means two things—first, that God's law is just, and second, that every sinner is unjust; therefore if God is to justify a man He can only do it by vindicating the law, and by destroying the sinner out of him. We put it that Jesus Christ came to save

---

10. positive: independent; unrelated to anything else.

sinners; He did not say so, He said, "I came to call *sinners to repentance*" (see Matthew 9:13). This phrase, "God loves the man, but hates the sinner," although not scriptural, conveys the idea. God dare not love the sinner. When God saves a sinner, profoundly speaking, and only profoundly speaking, He does not save the sinner: He saves the man who is a sinner by removing the sinner out of him. When once a man receives the humiliating conviction that he has broken God's law, and is willing to accept on God's terms the gift of forgiveness and of a new life, he will find he is brought to the place where he can live a holy life in order to vindicate God in forgiving him. This is evangelical repentance, and it is fundamentally different from the reformation which springs from remorse awakened by an overwhelming self-respect. A sinner can never stand in the presence of God; there is no justification whatever for sin in His presence, that is why a man convicted of sin has such a desperate time, he realises with the Psalmist— "Against Thee, Thee only, have I sinned, and done this evil in Thy sight." Beware of attempting to deal with sin apart from a complete reliance on the Redemption, and when you see men sinning, remember, your heart should be filled with compassion, because if you have ever had the slightest dose of conviction of sin yourself, you will know what awaits them when the recognition of sin comes home.

For He hath made Him to be sin for us, who knew no sin. . . .

Bear in mind that what makes Christ's glory is His severity, i.e., His love for God's holy law rather than His love for man: Jesus Christ stood on God's side against man. On the Cross men crucified the Son of God—and God forgave them while they did it. It is blasphemy to make little of sin. The final issue in every life is—God must kill sin in me, or sin will kill God out of me. If the Gospel is made to mean merely that "it is better being good than bad," men like to listen to it, but immediately it shows me that sin, self-realisation, self-interest, must be put to death, I resent it. If God is to be just, that is what must happen. It is the shallowest nonsense that makes people say, "God will forgive us because He is love"; once we are convicted of sin we never talk like that again. The love of God is spelt on the Cross and nowhere else; there His conscience is satisfied. God deals with every bit of sin in the light of the purest justice.

. . . that we might be made the righteousness of God in Him. (2 Corinthians 5:21)

The effect of being justified by God's grace is that He begins to entrust us with the realisation of what sin is. It is the saint who knows what sin is; it is the man who has been identified with the death of Jesus

who begins to get the first inkling of what sin is, because the only Being who knows what sin is, is not the sinner, but God. The only One who knows what the elemental human heart is like, is not the sinner, but Jesus Christ. It takes the last reach of the Atonement—the revelation of the perfections of Jesus as He is "made unto us . . . sanctification," to make us know what sin is, because sin is what He faced on Calvary. We are not always in the condition to understand the Cross, but it is of vital importance that we let God bring us at times where every commonplace mood is stripped off, and we take the shoes from off our feet and stand alone for one moment while God spells out to us the A B C of what the Cross of Christ means.

For in that He died, He died unto sin once. . . . Likewise reckon ye also yourselves to be dead indeed unto sin. (Romans 6:10–11)

The only one who can reckon he is "dead indeed unto sin" is the one who has been through identification with the death of Jesus; when he has been through that moral transaction he will find he is enabled to live according to it; but if I try the "reckoning" business without having gone through identification with the death of Jesus, I shall find myself deceived; there is no reality. When I can say, "I have been crucified with Christ" (RV), a new page of consciousness opens before me, I find there are new powers in me, I am able now to fulfil the commands of God, able to do what I never could do before, I am free from the old bondage, the old limitations; and the gateway to this new life is the death of Jesus.

This is a faithful saying, and worthy of all acceptation, that Christ Jesus came into the world to save sinners; of whom I am chief. (1 Timothy 1:15)

Before you were convicted of sin you thought the saints exaggerated in what they said about themselves; when you have been convicted of sin by the Holy Spirit you will never think it possible to exaggerate. Knowledge of what sin is is evidence that I am delivered from it; ignorance of what sin on the inside is is evidence that I have never been touched by the Atonement. Knowledge of what sin is is in inverse ratio to its presence. To mistake conscious freedom from sin for having been delivered from sin through the Atonement is to make the grand error of the Christian life. "But if we walk in the light," says John, "as He is in the light"—if we walk there, with nothing folded up, no humbug, no pretence, no end of our own to serve, if we walk there, then comes the most amazing revelation God ever gave to man—*"the blood of Jesus Christ His Son cleanseth us from all sin,"* not to our consciousness; the conscious part is walking in the light, as God is in the light.

THE GREATEST EVENT IN THE WORLD

The Lord Jesus Is Coming Again

In Bible revelation there is always a Coming Age, a Coming Day, a Coming Prophet, a Coming One—a perennial Coming.

When Thought is young, life looks simple, so does History, and man's explanation is correspondingly simple and glib. "Evolution" is the name given in our day to this young and ill-considered outlook—it is all a simple and obvious method of growth and development; to talk about the Fall is absurd, and any conception that does not recognise that the world is getting better, is discarded. Evolution is the characteristic of man's work, never of God's. God works by creation. When we infer God's methods from man's, we go wrong; we continually exalt our methods and say that is how God works.

But when Thought has passed its romantic days and has been made to face Life as it is, and History as it has been recorded, and the human soul in all its tragic features and its triumphs, it is staggered, for all these forces are wild and untameable. This way of Thought then becomes dim and perilous, and the human spirit cries out, "Oh that I knew where I might find Him! that I might come even to His seat!"

The Bible revelation presents a basis of thinking quite other. Epochs and civilisations appear after a time to be flung on the scrap-heap by God in a strangely careless manner. The remarkable thing in the record of the Ages that have been, and that are, and that are going to be, is that each Age ends in apparent disaster. The saint alone knows by spiritual intuition that "He doeth all things well," he knows that God reigns, and that the clouds are but the dust of his Father's feet and he has no need to fear. He feels assured that these catastrophic occurrences are but incidental, and that a higher peace and a purer character are to be the permanent result. He knows that "this same Jesus," who trod this earth with naked feet, "and wrought with human hands the creeds of creeds," is coming again, visibly and blessedly coming to earth again, when the petition will be fulfilled, *"Thy kingdom come."* All that men have ever dreamed of Utopias and of Golden Ages will fade into foolish fancies beside the wonder of that blessed Age, that blessed period of Christ's reign among men. We have to remain stedfastly certain in Him, not go out of Him to see when He is coming; it is to be prophetic *living* as well as prophetic study. To the saint everything is instinct with the purpose of God. History is fulfilling prophecy all the time.

ENCHANTED BUT UNCHANGED
Ezekiel 33:30–32

The thirty-third chapter of Ezekiel is a striking chapter in the career of the prophet. Hitherto it has been denunciation, but now that the great terror has fallen on Jerusalem (*see* Ezekiel 33:21–22), Ezekiel comes with a new note, and it is with this new note the people are enchanted, but, he says, they remain unchanged.

1. Pose but Not Penitence

And they come unto thee as the people cometh, and they sit before thee as My people, and they hear thy words, but do them not. (Ezekiel 33:31 RV)

There are many to-day who like to hear the word of God spoken straightly and ruggedly, they listen to, and are delighted with, the stern truth about holiness, about the baptism of the Holy Ghost, and deliverance from sin; they say to one another, "Come, I pray you, and hear what is the word that cometh forth from the

LORD." They take up a pose of religion, but they are not penitent; they change the truth God requires into a mere attitude. God not only requires us to have a right attitude to Him, He requires us to allow His truth to so react in us that we are actively related to Him. These people flocked to Ezekiel like disciples to a teacher, they looked exactly like God's children, the difference was not on the outside but on the inside, and it would take the penetration of God to see it; but it was all pose, they were not real. The real attitude of sin in the heart towards God is that of being without God; it is pride, the worship of myself, that is the great atheistic fact in human life.

I wonder if any of us are among the enchanted but unchanged crowd? We follow any man or woman who speaks the truth of God; in fact, we are so enchanted that we say, "If you come and hear this man or woman, you will hear the word of God." But has it ever altered us into an active, living relationship with God, or is it altogether pose? If any of us have got the pose of the people of God but are not real, may God deal with us until He brings us into a right relationship to Himself through the Atonement of the Lord Jesus Christ.

2. Sympathetic but Sinful

For with their mouth they shew much love, but their heart goeth after their gain. (Ezekiel 33:31 RV)

They had the right pose, the right religious attitude, but they had no desire to be changed—"they hear thy words, but do them not." "They come and listen to you as to one who is amazingly skilful in playing on an instrument, but they don't do what you say," says God; they are enraptured, but still sinful. Penitence has never struck them, the awakening of God's Spirit has never gone straight home.

This attitude is spreading amongst us to-day amazingly, people are enchanted with the truth, sympathetic with the truth of God, but remaining in sin. "Repentance" is not in their vocabulary, only regret; there is no confession of sin, only admitting. Religion is turned into education, and the Christian life is made to mean a happy life instead of a new life.

Has God been convicting us of spiritual pose before Him? Have we taken the great passion of the Atonement and made it simply mean that we must have a right attitude to God? We have to have much more than a right attitude; we have to get into an active, living relation to God, the inspiration of which is a great deep true penitence. Have we forgotten all about penitence these days? Has penitence ever rung down to our very soul, or have we only known regret? Have we ever known what it is to confess our sin, to unfold our life before God until there is nothing folded up, and God's penetrating truth has its way? If not, we shall find, as these verses reveal, that it is perilously easy to have amazing sympathy with God's truth and remain in sin.

3. Public Conformity and Private Criticism

Then said I, Ah Lord GOD! they say of me, Is he not a speaker of parables? (Ezekiel 20:49 RV)

The people indulged in unfriendly criticism, they heard the message, but their criticism of the speaker was made an excuse for not obeying the truth. "Why, he talks in parables! It is all so enigmatical and puzzling." This is not superficial criticism, but the deep subtlety of the hearers trying to get out of obeying God's truth because of the form in which it is put—

"It is too puzzling," consequently they exonerate themselves from obeying it because it is put so obscurely, so confusingly.

I do not think there is any distress to equal the distress expressed by the prophet here, viz., that people are enchanted by the truth of God, but unchanged by it. The great difficulty to many a worker and handmaid of the Lord is this very thing—"and they come unto thee as the people cometh, and they sit before thee as My people, they hear thy words, but do them not," says God. You go to God over and over again about it, you examine your own soul and say, "I know I spoke the truth of God." In our work for God we have on the one hand the enchanted but unchanged crowd, and on the other the indifferent crowd. Have you ever realised that God challenges the saints to a tremendous conflict, the conflict of believing the Gospel in the face of an indifferent world? It is easy to say we believe in God as long as we remain in the little world we choose to live in; but get out into the great world of facts, the noisy world where people are absolutely indifferent to you, where your message is nothing more than a crazy tale belonging to a bygone age, can you believe God there? Christian Science is a specimen of the way people garrison themselves around within a little world of their own. The teaching of Christian Science makes its followers deny that there are such things as sin and disease and death—they are all imagination; and they shut themselves in a little world of their own and say, "It is so easy to believe in the goodness of God"; of course it is! But let the house of their creed be taken and battered in by the gales of God; let them be driven out of the little enclosures of their preconceived notions, out into the big indifferent world, driven clean out to face the facts of sin and disease and death, and where does their belief in the goodness of God go? It cannot stand the test. The marvellous thing is that Jesus Christ prayed, not that we should be taken out of the world, but that we should be kept from evil.

God saves us and sanctifies us and places us in the circumstances He chooses, and whether it is among the enchanted but unchanged crowd, or the indifferent crowd, we have to face them, not with dismay, but with the determination to obey God, and by our faith in God to so conflict against the indifference and the sin that we produce the character that glorifies God, and the result will be that God will gain amazing glory to His own Name; enchantment will be changed by transactions with God into a changed life, and through penitence the pose will become the real life hid with Christ in God, and we shall be built up on our most holy faith.

SHOWERS OF BLESSING

For as the rain cometh down and the snow from heaven, and returneth not thither, but watereth the earth, and maketh it bring forth and bud, and giveth seed to the sower and bread to the eater; so shall My word be that goeth forth out of My mouth: it shall not return unto Me void, but it shall accomplish that which I please, and it shall prosper in the thing whereto I sent it. Isaiah 55:10–11 (RV)

". . . giveth seed to the sower." God's word is as a seed. The "seed-thought" idea is one that preachers and evangelists need to remember. We imagine we have to plough the field, sow the seed, reap the grain, bind it into sheaves, put it through the threshing machine, make the bread—all in one discourse. "For herein is the saying true, One soweth, and another reapeth" said our Lord (RV). Let each one be true to the calling given him by God. The truth is we don't believe God can do His work without us. We are so anxious about the word, so anxious about the people who have accepted the word; we need not be, if we have preached what is a word of God it is not our business to apply it, the Holy Spirit will apply it. Our duty is to sow the word, see that it is the word of God we preach, and not "huckster" it with other things, and

God says it will prosper in the thing whereto He sends it. In some cases it will be a savour of life unto life, in others a savour of death unto death; but rest assured that no individual and no community is ever the same after listening to the word of God, it profoundly alters life. The force and power of a word of God will work and work, and bring forth fruit after many days. Hence the necessity of revising much of what we preach and what we say in meetings. God has not said that the relating of my experiences, of my insight into the truth, will not return to Him void; He says *"My word . . . shall not return unto Me void."* Every temptation to exalt the human, human experiences, human interests and blessings, will fall short; the only thing that prospers in God's hands is His own word.

"As the rain cometh down . . . from heaven, . . . so shall My word be." Thank God for the sweet and radiant aspect of the falling of rain from heaven, after a time of drought it is almost impossible to describe its beauty; so when a word of God comes to a soul after a time of difficulty and perplexity, it is almost impossible to tell the ineffable sweetness of that word as it comes with the unction of the Holy Ghost.

IS HE REALLY LORD?

Jesus knowing . . . that He was come from God, . . . He riseth from supper, . . . and took a towel, . . . and began to wash the disciples' feet. John 13:3–5

Jesus Christ riddles us from all unreality. What He did shocks all affectation, pious fraud, religious pretence, sanctimoniousness, and religiosity always.

1. What Do You Know about Yourself?
Jesus knowing . . . that He was come from God . . .

Do you know you have received the Holy Spirit, know you are a child of God—are you going to be greater than Jesus Christ? Are you going to be disdainful?—"What a humiliating thing to do!" Jesus, knowing Who He was, took a towel and washed the disciples' feet; and He says, "I have given you an example, that ye should do as I have done to you." To shout "Hallelujah" is humbug unless it is genuine.

Jesus never tells you to shout "Hallelujah": He says—*"Do as I have done to you."* How much long-suffering mercy has God shown you?

2. Where Do You Place Yourself?
He riseth from supper, . . . and took a towel . . .

Do you regard yourself as a highly respectable, dignified Christian? Are you religiously self-important, placing yourself where you fancy you ought to be placed, in stately surroundings? If so, you are not following Jesus Christ's example. If you cannot do ordinary things and live as nobody anywhere, you are not a saint. Jesus left heaven and lived nowhere of any importance all His earthly life. There is a religiosity that is inspired by the devil, that gathers its skirts around it and says, "No, I cannot be in ordinary places, or in ordinary avocations; I am a servant of God." Then you will be found nowhere but in the very commonest of common places. You say you are called to be a missionary, a minister, a Christian worker: you are called to be a disciple of Jesus Christ, other things are *etceteras*. Jesus Christ did not move among transfigured things; He moved amongst prosaic, un-noteworthy things, among the most common-place things imaginable, and it was those things that He transfigured; He lived amongst them as the Servant of men, and He says, "If you are My disciple, you will do the same."

3. What Do You Do with Yourself?

. . . and began to wash the disciples' feet.

Water, a basin, feet, a towel—there is nothing Divine about those things, they are the most ordinary, common-place things one can conceive. The Lord of heaven and earth washed the feet of His disciples, He did it Himself; one of them protested, but it made no difference. "So after He . . . was set down again, He said unto them, Know ye what I have done to you? . . . I have given you an example, that ye should do as I have done to you." When the testimony and the "Hallelujah" are followed by the following of His steps in example, then comes the tremendous flow of the power of God wherever you go.

"I will make the place of My feet glorious"— among the poor, the devil-possessed, the mean,[11] the decrepit, the selfish, the sinful, the misunderstanding—that is where Jesus went, and that is exactly where He will take you if you are His disciple.

"I have given you an example, that ye should do as I have done to you." Your lips have called Him "Master," and "Lord," are you prepared to take this lesson home to yourself? What do you know about yourself? You know you have received the Holy Spirit, you know you are a child of God; then let God's providence place you where He wills, don't put yourself in special conditions. Where do you place yourself? In the common round and trivial tasks of ordinary life— supper times and ordinary people, with no pretence about it. What do you do with yourself? Exactly what Jesus did for you. He came to your house, He found your bodily temple a very unkempt and disgraceful place to come into, but He came into it and cleaned it up and is keeping it clean; now He says, "If I then, your Lord and Master, have washed your feet; *ye also ought to wash one another's feet.*"

THE STAND OF THE SAINTS
Ephesians 6:11–20

Put on the whole armour of God. . . . And, having done all, to stand. Ephesians 6:11, 13

Paul is writing from prison; he knows all about the Roman soldier whose armour he is describing, for he was chained to one of them. "I am an ambassador in chains" (RV) he says.

These verses are not a picture of how to fight, but of how not to fight. If you have not put on the armour, you will have to fight; but having put on the whole armour of God, then "*stand,*" says Paul. There are times when God's servants are sent out to attack, to storm the citadel, but the counsel given here is as to how we are to hold the position which has been gained. We need to learn this conservation of energy, "having done all, to stand," manifesting the full power of God.

"*For we wrestle not against flesh and blood*"—if we do, we are "out of it"; our warfare is against "the spiritual hosts of wickedness" (RV) which the world does not see. We are apt to forget that the enemy is unseen and that he is supernatural (cf. Daniel 10:12–13).

"Don't make any mistake," says Paul, "you are not wrestling against flesh and blood, you are wrestling against tremendous powers you will never be able to withstand unless you put on the whole armour of God. When you see men doing terrible things, remember you are not wrestling against them, they are the cat's-paw of the rulers of the darkness of this world." We are to be taken up with a much more difficult wrestling, viz., the wrestling against the spiritual hosts of wickedness in the heavenly places which prevent us from seeing God. If Satan in his malice and cunning can slander God to His own children, he will do it because that is his whole aim. Our wrestling is to be against the thoughts suggested to our mind which press down on us and make us say, "What is the good of asking God to bring peace to a broken-hearted woman? of asking God to sustain people whose lives are ruined?" If I try to describe to my own heart a bereaved home and let the sorrow of it weigh with me, instantly my faith in God is gone;

---

11. mean: ordinary, common, low, or ignoble, rather than cruel or spiteful

I am so overcome with sympathy and fellow-feeling for them that my prayer is nothing more than a wail of sympathy before God. The telepathic influence of my mind on another, whether I speak or not, is so subtle that the prince of this world will use it to prevent my getting hold of God; whereas if I remain confident in God I lift the weight off lives in a way I shall never realise till I stand before Him. We have to pray that the enemy shall not exact upon the hearts and minds of God's children and make them slander Him by worry and anxiety. As the Lord's remembrancers we are to hold off the exactings of Satan, not add to them.

Do I expect God to answer prayer? The first thing that will stagger our faith in God is the false sentiment arising out of a sympathetic apprehension of the difficulties. "Peter therefore was kept in the prison: but prayer was made earnestly of the church unto God for him" (RV): the church prayed, and God did the impossible thing, and Peter was delivered. We have to pray with our eyes on God, not on the difficulties.

"Praying always . . . for all saints." It is not always a time of triumph; there are not only times of taking strongholds by storm, but times when spiritual darkness falls, when the great powers in the heavenlies are at work, when no one understands the wiles of Satan but God; at such times we have to stand steadily shoulder to shoulder for God. How often the Spirit of God emphasises the "together-ness" of the saints!

"And for me," says Paul. Prayer is God's ordained way, the insignificant way of prayer.

SOLIDARITY OF SIN
Luke 11:21–22 (RV)

"Solidarity"—a consolidation or oneness of interests.

I mean by "sin," not sin in a particular sense, but in the big general sense, viz., a violation or neglect of the moral law. God's Book all through shows a wonderful discrimination as to the nature of sin; it reveals that there is in the threefold aspect of sin—the world, the flesh and the devil—a oneness of interest with the prince of this world. Paul refers to the same thing, the supernatural inspiration of sin, in Ephesians 6:12: "For our wrestling is not against flesh and blood, but against the principalities, against the powers, against the world-rulers of this darkness, against the spiritual hosts of wickedness in the heavenly places" (RV). We have to beware of the flood of teaching abroad which makes out that sin is a disease, a defect in the finite; in the final analysis, it is red-handed rebellion against God.

Our Lord makes it clear in this parable that "the strong man" is Satan, he is the prince of this world, and he is "fully armed" (RV). The "strong man" idea is the one that appeals to men, the strong man physically, morally, strong in every way; the kingdoms of men are to be founded on strong men and the weakest are to go to the wall.[12] History proves, however, that it is the strongest that go to the wall, not the weakest.

When the strong man fully armed guardeth his own court . . . (RV).

Satan guards on two sides—he guards from the breaking out into external sins, and from the incursion of the Spirit of God. It is not that a man guards himself, it is Satan guarding him; nothing is allowed to come into his court to disturb it. When men go into external sins and upset their life, Satan knows perfectly well that they will want a Saviour, and as long as he can keep men in peace and unity and harmony apart from God, he will do it. The greatest number of men are moral, not immoral; a clean moral life which is sufficient for itself apart from God—that is the evidence of the guarding of Satan, and we all know as workers for God the difficulty, the almost insuperable difficulty, there is in presenting the Gospel to a good-living worldling, not because his mind is obtuse or because he is insensitive, but because he is supernaturally guarded by a "fully armed strong man."

his goods [i.e., the souls of men] are in peace . . .

Psalm 73 gives a picture of the souls of men as guarded by Satan: "They are not in trouble as other men. . . . Their eyes stand out with fatness: they have more than heart could wish." It is necessary to keep in mind that this is the Bible view of the man of the world, and our Lord's parable is an amazing analogy. The analogy generally presented is that the worldling is miserable, but no one could be described as being

---

12. go to the wall: fail; lose.

"in peace" who had not got his heart's desire; he is satisfied with the world as it is, satisfied with the morality he has got. According to our Lord that kind of peace is no sign of being right with God. We talk glibly about Jesus being "the Prince of Peace," but when He comes into the world that is peaceably ruled by Satan, He comes to send a sword, not peace.

but when a stronger than he shall come upon him . . .

Satan is overcome not in a battle, but by the easy might of a power greater than his own coming upon him, and that power is none other than our Lord Himself. Every now and again when you look at life from a certain angle it seems as if evil and wrong and legalised iniquity are having it all their own way and you feel that everything must go to pieces; but it doesn't, around it is the sovereignty of God, "Hitherto shalt thou come, but no further." Blessed be the Name of God, evil shall not ultimately triumph! Let evil do its worst, let the arrogance of self-interested iniquity in all shapes and forms surge as it may, but "He that sitteth in the heavens shall laugh: the Lord shall have them in derision." The Spirit of God shatters every power of the world, the flesh and the devil, every power of sin and the domination of Satan. "The stronger than he" is Our Lord Himself. The power of Jesus rests on His holiness. No man ever successfully contends with Satan saving in the power of the Highest. We can open men's eyes by the power of the Spirit, but not all the opening of men's eyes will ever accomplish what the Spirit accomplishes, because He leads us to the Highest, our Lord Himself, and enables us to realise that it is He who has overcome.

. . . he taketh from him his whole armour wherein he trusted.

Satan is not partially overcome, he is absolutely overcome, every bit of his armour wherein he trusted is taken from him. The presence of Jesus means the total expulsion of Satan. When we are born again the Holy Spirit brings to us the realisation of what Jesus Christ has done, and the great emancipating point of personal experience is not that we have power to overcome, but that He has overcome; then the Holy Spirit instructs us all along the line how we can successfully battle against the encroachments of Satan. When by God's grace we enter into the amazing liberty of salvation and sanctification, then comes the responsibility of walking in the light, and as we keep in the light we are able to identify ourselves with Jesus Christ's victory in such a way that it is manifested in us; but this depends on our keeping in the light.

In Luke 11:24–26 Our Lord shows that a moral victory may be realised, emancipating and definite, a man recognises it, he is proud of the victory gained, and Satan recognises it too; but in that condition it is almost impossible to bring him anywhere near Jesus. To use a moral victory aright a man ought eagerly to ask for the Holy Spirit to come in, for He will bring the presence of the One who is stronger than Satan. Unless a moral victory in a man's heart means that Jesus has got right of way there, he will find that what He says is true, "the last state of that man becometh worse than the first" (RV). A man may for a shorter or longer period be master of himself, but sooner or later his will must bow to a power greater than himself.

We have to develop a saintly character by fight. Jesus Christ fits us to be overcomers. Through the forces that are against him God is making a finer type of man than the first Adam, a man more worthy to be His son. That is the meaning of His marvellous Redemption. Everything that Satan and sin have marred is going to be reconstructed and readjusted.

THINKING

. . . being ready always to give answer to every man that asketh you a reason concerning the hope that is in you. 1 Peter 3:15 (RV)

To give "a reason concerning the hope that is in you" is not at all the same thing as convincing by reasonable argument why that hope is in us. The work of the Spirit of God in us transcends reason, but never contradicts it, and when a Christian says "the reason I am so-and-so is because I have received the Holy Spirit," or, "I have received from God something which has made this possible," it does not contradict reason, it

transcends it, and is an answer concerning the hope that is in you. The line we are continually apt to be caught by is that of argumentative reasoning out why we are what we are; we can never do that, but we can always say why the hope is in us.

Reason is the faculty of mind by which man draws conclusions. Every man is always striving after a true expression of what he is. When a man is born again, his personality becomes alive to God as the Source of inspiration. Paul's words, "I live; and yet no longer I, but Christ liveth in me" (RV), are the expression of the only worthy rationalism.

The great snare is to make reason work in the circle of our experience instead of in the circle of God. As long as we use the image of our own salvation, our experience, the image of our feelings, or answers to prayer, we shall never begin to understand what Paul meant when he said, "Christ liveth in me." The exercise of man's essential reason is drawing on God as the source of life.

Those of us who have never had visions or ecstasies ought to be very thankful. Visions, or any emotions at all, are the greatest snare imaginable to spiritual life, because we are apt to build these things round our reasoning and go no further. Over and over again we find sanctified people stagnate, they do not go back and they do not go on; they get stiller and stiller, and mud-dier and muddier—spiritually, not morally—until ultimately there comes a sort of scum over the spiritual life, and you wonder what is the matter with them. They are still true to God, still true to their testimony, but they have never exercised the God-given reason in them and got beyond the image of experiences and gone on to draw their life from God, which transcends all we call experience. Never forget that the Almighty is a great deal bigger than our experience of Him; that the Lord Jesus Christ is a great deal bigger than our experience of Him. People won't go through the labour of thinking, consequently snares get hold of them, and remember, thinking is a tremendous labour. We have to labour to bring "every thought into captivity to the obedience of Christ" (RV).

NOW ARE YOU SAFEGUARDED?

Hold Thou me up, and I shall be safe. Psalm 119:117

"Kept by the power of God"—therefore you are all right *now*. There is no other time than *now* with God, no past and no future. Is your life safeguarded? If it is not, you will go under no matter what your experience is. In the Bible the men who fell, fell on their strong points, not on their weak ones, because on their strong points they were unguarded.

1. Can You See the Highest?

He sent from on high, He took me; He drew me out of many waters. (Psalm 18:16 RV; see also Ephesians 2:6; Colossians 3:2)

The Lord Jesus Christ is the Highest. Is there anyone higher to you than He is? Your life is never safeguarded until Jesus is seen to be the Highest. Past experience will not keep you, neither will deliverance from sin; the only safeguarding power is the Highest. If there is a breath of confidence anywhere else, there will be disaster, and it is by the mercy of God that you are allowed to stumble, or be pain-smitten, until you learn that He does it all—*He* keeps you from stumbling (RV), *He* raises you up and keeps you up, *He* sends from above and delivers you.

Whenever there is a complication in your circumstances, do nothing until you see the Highest, not sometimes, but always (cf. Isaiah 1:10). Can you see the Lord in your thinking? If not, suspend your judgement until you can. Can you see the face of Jesus in your affections? If not, restrain them until you can. Can you see God in your circumstances? if not, do nothing until you can. Our Lord can trust anything to the man or woman who sees Him.

"*Set* your affection on things above,"i.e., gather in your stray impulses and fix them. The spiritual life is not impulsive; we are impulsive when we are not spiritual. In every experience the safeguard is the Lord Himself, and He was not impulsive. The one thing Jesus always checked was impulse. Impulse has to be trained and turned into intuition by discipline.

Is your mind set on Jesus Christ, or have you only a principle at stake? The great simplicity of the Christian life is the relationship to the Highest. Reckless confidence in God is of far more value than personal holiness, if personal holiness is looked upon as an end in itself. When once you take any one of the great works of God as an end, or any one of the truths which depend on Jesus Christ, as *the* truth, you will go wrong, you are outside the guard of God. The safeguard is the Highest—"*I* am . . . the Truth." "*I*, if *I* be lifted up . . ." Allow nothing to take you away from Jesus Himself, and all other phases of truth will take their right place.

2. Are You Strengthened from the Highest?

Thou hast enlarged my steps under me, and my feet have not slipped. (Psalm 18:36 RV; see also Ephesians 6:15)

When first we experience the grace of God, we have the feeling that if ever we should become what Jesus Christ wants us to be, He would have to take us straight to Heaven! But when by God's grace we get there, we find we are not on a perilous mountain peak, but on a broad plateau, with any amount of room to walk—as safe and as eternal as the hills. "Thou hast enlarged my steps under me." The great note of strength is to "walk and not faint"; to "mount up with wings" is exceptional. Everywhere your foot treads; at home or abroad, should bring a preparation of the gospel of peace. Sometimes when you put down a prepared foot for God it is anything but peace! It is disturbance and upset, but that is the way God prepares for the coming of His peace. Jesus is the Prince of Peace, yet He said, "I came not to send peace, but a sword."

Are you strengthened from above mentally, physically, morally, spiritually, and "circumstantially"? Do you know how to draw on the resurrection life of Jesus? The guidance in work for God is to notice where you are exhausted without recuperation. We take on a tremendous amount of stuff which we call work for God, and God puts the sentence of death on it for we are exhausted by it without being recuperated, because our strength is drawn from somewhere other than the Highest. The sign that what we are doing is God's work is that we know the supernatural recuperation. Are we strong enough to be abject failures in the eyes of the world, or are we set upon success? Our work for God is not of any value saving as it develops us; the one thing of value in God's sight is our relationship to Jesus Christ. The branch knows nothing about its fruit, it only knows the pruning-knife (see John 15:2). "Am I a blessing?" No, certainly

not, if you are looking at the outflow. Keep rightly related to the Highest, and out of you will flow "rivers of living water."

3. Are You Succoured by the Highest?
Comfort ye, comfort ye My people, saith your God. (Isaiah 40:1; see also Philippians 2:1–2)

The things that discourage and hurt us show from whence we get our succour. Jesus Christ was never discouraged because He was succoured by the Highest. Until a worker knows the succour of God he is in danger of becoming a stumbling-block to other souls. If we are not being succoured by the Highest, of what use can we be to folks who are crushed by sorrows of which we know nothing? "The sacrifices of God are a broken spirit," broken beyond any patching up, but—"He hath sent Me to bind up the brokenhearted." The heart which has been bound up and succoured by the Lord Jesus Christ will never be caught in the train of self-interest, there is no selfishness left in it. "As one whom his mother comforteth, so will I comfort you." That is the most powerful thing God can do for us. The great note of the life which is comforted by God is—"For my Lord I live; by my Lord I am strengthened, and in my Lord I am succoured."

FRONTIERS OF THE WORKER'S LIFE
2 Corinthians 11:3

There must be two centres to our mental life as workers: the first is personal faith in Jesus Christ; the second, personal reliance on the human reason that God made. Most of us think from one centre only, the centre of human reason, consequently all that Jesus Christ stands for beyond the reach of human reason is ignored. "I fear," says Paul, "lest . . . your minds should be corrupted from the simplicity that is in Christ." Beware of making simple what the Bible does not. The line of our simplicity is in Christ—"I am the Way, the Truth, and the Life." The way the simplicity that is in Christ is corrupted is by trying to live according to a statement made by men's heads. It must be the relationship of a child all through (see Matthew 11:25). To be able to state explicitly in words what you know by faith is an impossibility; if you can state it in words, it is not faith.

The way the serpent beguiled Eve through his subtlety was by enticing her away from personal faith in God to depend on her reason alone. Confusion comes when we are consistent to our convictions

instead of to Christ. The error of the modern standard is that it begins at the wrong end, viz., with human reason. How much do we understand? The conceit of modern life is that it does understand. It reconstructs human society—and leaves out rebellion against God. It reconstructs the world by human sympathy—and leaves out love for wrong. "Canst thou by searching find out God?" (Job 11:7). We must be prepared to be led, and the way we come to an understanding is by the relationship of our personal life to the Person of Jesus Christ, then bit by bit we begin to understand.

Never have the idea that you are going to persuade men to believe in God; you can persuade them of His standard. You have to force an issue of will; but remember, along with your faithful preaching comes a thing you cannot intellectually state, the working of the Spirit of God (see John 3:8). The thing that staggers the worker is that men will not believe. How can they believe, when every spring of life is impure? The great need is to have a channel through which the grace of God can come to men and do something in their unconscious life, then slowly as that breaks into the conscious life there will come an expression of belief, because they see Jesus; but the way they see Him is through the worker who is a sacramental personality (see Acts 26:18). Christian workers rarely face men in this way. You cannot argue men into coming to Jesus, or socialise them into coming; only one thing will do it, and that is the power of the Gospel drawing men by the constraint of God's grace.

The centre of life and of thinking for the Christian worker is the Person of Jesus Christ. We get deadly respectable when we face only the problems we have been used to facing; but if we will obey the Holy Spirit He will bring us to face other problems, and as we face them through personal relationship to Jesus Christ we shall go forth with courage, confident that whether it be in the domains of heathendom or in our own land, Jesus Christ is never nonplussed, never worsted.

"I AM THE DOOR"
John 10:9

1. The Condition of Daily Salvation
By Me if any man enter in, he shall be saved . . .

This is a picture of the life we are to live as God's children—entering in by our Lord, who is the Door, not once for all, but every day, for everything. Is there trouble in the physical domain? enter in by the Door and be saved. Trouble in mental matters? enter in and be saved. A thousand and one things make up life as it is and in them all we have to learn to enter in by the Door. Entering in, in the Name of Jesus, is the condition of daily salvation, not salvation from sin only, but a salvation that keeps us manifestly the Lord's sheep.

Are you experiencing daily salvation, or are you shut out from Jesus Christ just now in your bodily life, in your mind, in your circumstances? is there any fog, any darkness, any weariness, any trouble? Every day there are things that seem to shut the way up, but you can always enter in by the Door and experience salvation. In the East it is the body of the shepherd himself that is the door of the fold.

2. The Condition of Daily Sonship
and shall go in and go out . . . (RV)

We are apt to have the idea that salvation is a kind of watertight compartment and if we enter in all our liberty will be destroyed. That is not our Lord's conception; He says we "shall go in and go out." Are we entering in by the Door for our daily work or only at a devotional meeting? The going in and out is our Lord's picture of the freedom of a son. A servant cannot go in and out as he likes, but Jesus says, "Henceforth I call you not servants; . . . but I have called you friends." Nothing is closed to you once you enter in by the Door.

3. The Condition of Daily Support
. . . and shall find pasture. (RV)

"I can't get any food out of God's Book," you say; the trouble is not in the Book, but in you. "I can't get time alone with God"—this answers the problem: "By Me if any man enter in, he shall . . . find pasture." Some people find physical nourishment in everything, air and water seem to nourish them; and there are people spiritually who get nourishment out of everything. That is our Lord's picture of the daily support of the life that is right with Him. There is no calling of any description where you cannot find ample pasturage once you learn to enter in by the Door.

Are you starving spiritually just now? have you entered in by the Door? "Nothing in my hands I bring"—don't try to be consistent to a doctrine or a creed, the Lord Jesus is the only One to whom you have to be consistent. You will find He will not allow you to have freedom in certain places, though He will always give you pasturage. There is wonderful liberty and freedom experienced among God's children, but if you try to have this freedom among those who are not God's children, He will check.

If God were to ask you "How are you?" what would you say—"I don't feel very well"? or, "I feel worried"; Or, "I feel as if I had not got hold of God"? Our Lord wants us to be filled with His life, and the only way for that is to enter in by the Door. The simplicity of it will save us from false emotion in prayer. It is easy to pray as we think we ought to pray, but we have to pray out of our personal condition. You never need to say—"But I am not in a fit condition to see my Father," the freedom is that of a child. Is there any part of your life where you are not getting nourished, not finding pasturage? Then enter in by the Door.

Have you been trying to make prayer, or faith, or the Bible, or experience, the Door? These may be ornaments about the Door, but the Door is the Lord Jesus Himself. Be absolutely loyal to Him.

"By Me if any man enter in, he shall be saved." It is an almighty salvation, salvation from darkness and dryness, from limitation and death, salvation from all that hinders you from being a healthy child of God. Can you go in and out, or are you in fear of your life when you do things, always questioning whether you should do this or that? Whenever you are in doubt as to what you should do it is because you have not entered in by the Door. Learn to enter in by the Door until it becomes the ordinary attitude of your life and you will find pasture without hunting for it, it is there. It is never a confined place, but always a door. The world, the flesh and the devil cannot imprison you, it is a life of absolute freedom.

DIVINE SACRIFICE AND DEDICATION OF THE SAINTS

I am the good shepherd: the good shepherd layeth down His life for the sheep. . . . I lay it down of Myself. John 10:11, 18 (RV)

There is an unfamiliar element in the sacrifice of Jesus compared with the sacrifices made amongst men. A man may perform a mighty act in a moment of heroism—but there is the possibility that he may escape. Our Lord pictures here the issue He is facing, "the good shepherd layeth down His life for the sheep": He deliberately laid down His life without any possibility of deliverance. There was no compulsion, it was a sacrifice made with a free mind; nor was there anything of the impulsive about it, He laid down His life with a clear knowledge of what He was doing. Jesus understood what was coming, it was not a foreboding, but a certainty; not a catastrophe which might happen, but an ordained certainty in the decrees of God, and He knew it.

Have we begun to let the Spirit of God interpret the sacrifice of Jesus to us? We have too pathetic an idea of it because we take our ideas from martyrdom, but Jesus Christ was not a martyr. There is no room for the pathetic in our Lord's attitude; it is we who take the pathetic view and look at His sacrifice from a point of view the Spirit of God never once uses. The Spirit of God never bewitches men with the strange pathos of the sacrifice of Jesus: the Spirit of God keeps us at the passion of the sacrifice of Jesus. The great passion at the back of His heart and mind in all Jesus did was devotion to His Father.

"I lay it down of Myself"; It was the sacrifice of a free personality. Jesus had the power in His own Person to prevent every evil thing that came against Him, but He never used that power. He could have performed miracles at will, but He did not. He could have asked His Father to send Him more than twelve legions of angels, but He refused to (see Matthew 26:53). The angels must have stood around Him at the end, unseen, amazed that they could not come through and minister to Him as they had done after the temptation in the wilderness, and in the Garden of Gethsemane. Finally, our Lord gave Himself up into the hands of those who tried to seize Him, yet could not (see John 18:6): "He was crucified through weakness."

How does our dedication as saints compare with the dedication of our Lord and Master? When we are identified with Jesus Christ the Spirit of God would have us sacrifice ourselves for Him, point for point, as He did for His Father. We pray and wait, and need urging, and want the thrilling vision; but Jesus wants us to narrow and limit ourselves to one thing—clearly and intelligently knowing what we are doing, we deliberately lay down our lives for Him as He laid down His life for us in the purpose of God. This is the underlying meaning of Paul's passionate pleading in Romans 12:1—"I beseech you, . . . present your bodies a living sacrifice." We want to do it in an ecstasy; Jesus Christ wants us to do it without the ecstasy. Brood on what Jesus Christ came to do, and then in the full possession of your mind, not in the excitement of a revival moment, nor in the enthusiasm of a great spiritual ecstasy, but in the calm quiet knowledge of what you are doing, say—"My life to Thee, my King, I humbly dedicate."

Jesus Christ never blinds us into devotion to Himself, never startles and staggers us. Satan as an angel of light uses the things that captivate men against their will, he uses ecstasies, visions, excitement, the things that make for unholiness, for the aggrandisement of self, for insanity; but Jesus never does. He comes to us along the line of His own dedication—*"I have power to lay it down."* Are we hindering the purpose of God in our life by seeking spiritual ecstasies in our devotions, seeking great manifestations of God's Spirit? God wants us to dedicate ourselves to Him with quiet calm intelligence, with the deep fervent passion behind of knowing what we are doing. Have we the self-dedication of that moral passion? There are a great many passions that are not moral, enthusiasms that never sprang from God. We have to hold our emotions in check and let the Spirit of God bring us into one master-worship. The one love in the Bible is that of the Father and the Son; the one passion in the Bible is the passion of Jesus to bring men into the relationship of sons to the Father, and the one great passion of the saint is that the life of the Lord Jesus might be manifested in his mortal flesh.

"This commandment received I [RV] of My Father." The great centre around which the life of Jesus moved was the will of His Father and devotion to Him. It is easy to work ourselves up into a passion of sacrifice, but that is not the true element in dedication. As a

saint I have power to refuse to give my sanctification to God; I can use that sanctification for my own selfish ends, with unutterable ruin to my own soul and to others. Our only guide is our Lord Himself: "For their sakes I sanctify Myself." In full possession of His powers Jesus dedicated Himself to God, and His call to those of us who are His disciples is to dedicate ourselves to Him with a clear knowledge of what we are doing, free from the plaintive, the sad, and the emotional. Can we only serve God when He thrills us? Can we only speak for Him when we feel His conscious touch? Cannot we have all the deep passion of our heart and spirit ablaze for God, our whole personality under control for one purpose only—to dedicate ourselves to the Lord Jesus Christ as He dedicated Himself to His Father?

Let Him make our lives narrow; let Him make them intense; let Him make them absolutely His!

"WILL YE ALSO GO AWAY?"
Notes of a Sermon
John 6

Five thousand men fed with five loaves and two fishes! The fame of the miracle-worker spreads like wildfire and the crowds blaze with enthusiasm, men and women hasten eagerly from afar to come to Him, scrambling over land and scudding over sea. "And when they had found Him on the other side of the sea, they said unto him, Rabbi, when camest Thou hither? Jesus answered them and said, Verily, verily, I say unto you, Ye seek Me, not because ye saw signs, but because ye ate of the loaves, and were filled. . . . *I am the Bread of Life.* . . . The Jews therefore murmured at Him, because He said, I am the bread which came down out of heaven" (RV). The enthusiasm begins to abate—"It is most offensive presumption." "Is not this Jesus, the son of Joseph, whose father and mother we know? how is it then that He saith, I came down from heaven?" "And the bread that I will give is My flesh, which I will give for the life of the world. . . . The Jews therefore strove among themselves, saying, How can this man give us His flesh to eat?" "Listen to Him; how can He claim such impossible things?" "Then Jesus said unto them, Verily, verily, I say unto you, Except ye eat the flesh of the Son of man, and drink His blood, ye have no life in you. . . . Many therefore of His disciples when they heard this, said, This is an hard saying; who can hear it? When Jesus knew in Himself that His disciples murmured at it, He said

unto them, Doth this offend you? . . . From that time many of His disciples went back, and walked no more with Him." The crowds have passed now, you are alone with your Lord, and He bends through the gloom of your weakness and blindness and says "You are not going away too, are you?"

Men are still offended at Jesus; they hear gladly His "Follow Me" and enthusiastically leave all to follow, but when the way becomes narrow, and to follow costs shedding of blood, they begin to waver. As long as it means peace and joy we will follow Jesus, but when it costs us dear we are tempted to go back and walk no more with Him.

1. The Offence
"Blood" was, and is, the offence. "You Christians wallow in blood," it is objected, "could no other word be used?" There is something so offensive in the word "blood." "And why talk so much about sin? Sin is but a defect, slowly being outgrown in the evolution of man." "Blood," the vital life-stream—offensive! Is there nothing offensive in sin, that devastating thing which poisons the very fountain of life, which makes the world a howling wilderness and our cities unendurable to thought—a defect! The evolutionary idea sounds all right; it is the thinker himself who is wrong. Sin has alienated man from God, and the

story of the ages is an accumulation of wrongdoing and of judgement days; there is an utter hopelessness in any attempt to meet the righteousness of God; but let a man begin to realise what sin is, then, "the blood of Jesus Christ His Son cleanseth us from all sin," will be a holy word to his soul. "The Cross" and "the blood of Jesus" are indeed names for profound mysteries, but when a soul shattered by the crushing sense of his guilt believes that through the blood of Jesus there is forgiveness for sins, he receives a new life-energy, he is purged from his old sins, and with the Spirit of Jesus in him, he begins to work out his own salvation. Then begins the true evolution of a man's soul.

2. The Offended

It is a serious thing to be offended with Jesus; it means stagnation of character. Jesus Christ can never save an offended man, because the man who is offended with Jesus shuts up his nature against Him; he will not see in Him, the Son of God, his Saviour; he will not hear His words of life. God has so constituted human nature that the man who *will not,* ultimately *cannot,* but every man who is willing to come to Jesus and is not offended in Him, is saved and receives forgiveness.

"Though all men shall be offended because of Thee, yet will I never be offended." Do you recall the time when you talked like that? Do you recall how Jesus met you after that night of bitter despairing? Do you remember most of all how He pressed the kiss of forgiveness on your brow, you feel it yet, glowing like a radiant star, and how He spoke strong words of comfort, "And when thou art converted, strengthen thy brethren"?

"Blood" is an offence not only at the beginning of the Christian career, but in the midst of it. "Except ye eat the flesh of the Son of man, and drink His blood, ye have no life in you. . . . Doth this offend you?" said Jesus: Except you are crucified with Christ until all that is left is the life of Christ in your flesh and blood, *you have no life in you.* Except your self-love is flooded away by the inrush of the love of Jesus so that you feel your blood move through you in tender charity as it moved through Him, *you have no life in you.* Except your flesh becomes the temple of His holiness, and you abide in Christ and He in you, *you have no life in you.*

3. The Offender Is Jesus Himself

"He is despised and rejected of men." Jesus offended many; His own home-folk were the first to be offended. "And when His friends heard of it, they went out to lay hold on Him: for they said, He is beside Himself"—"He assumes too much for His humble position." When He preached in the synagogue, they were astonished, but—"Is not this the carpenter? . . . And they were offended at Him." The Jews were offended at Jesus because they looked for a warrior king in their coming Messiah, and the carelessness of Jesus over temporal positions and honour did not commend itself to them. The Pharisees were offended at Him because His teaching showed up the hollow emptiness of their profession. His own disciples were offended at Him—"All ye shall be offended in Me this night" (RV)—they all forsook Him, and fled; one betrayed Him; and another denied Him.

Why did Jesus offend so many, and why does He offend so many to-day? Because men are half-blind by sin; the offence comes through their short-sightedness. Jesus offends men because He lays emphasis on the unseen life, because He speaks of motives rather than of actions; He reveals men to themselves, and because that revelation means hopelessness they turn away from Him who is their only hope. He offended men because He taught that they were lost and could only be saved through Him—"For the Son of Man is come to seek and to save that which was lost." Finally, He offended men because His own life was blameless, and His very presence disturbed their low-level contentment and

The word "blood," which offends so many, speaks of forgiveness of sins. The Carpenter, who offended so many, is the disguised Son of God, full of majestic power and condescension. We marvel, not that He performed miracles, but rather that He performed so few. He who could have stormed the citadels of men with mighty battalions of angels, let men spit upon Him and crucify Him. The faithful few, who are an offence to our great organisations, are the disguised citizens of the Kingdom of God, their step is strong with coming triumph, they walk, a mighty concourse of the redeemed; angels are their servants, the Almighty is set for their defence; Jesus Himself walks with them day by day, a constant Friend. From the East and from the West shall come multitudes who, passing through great tribulation, have "washed their robes, *and made them white in the blood of the Lamb.*"

PERSON NOT PLACE

Seek ye Me, and ye shall live. Amos 5:4

The danger of seeking places of blessing is very prevalent. Beth-el, for instance, was the place of Divine blessing historically; it was there Abraham built an altar to the Lord, there Jacob had visions of God—what place could be more suitable to seek than Beth-el, there to have the spirit of communion revived and quickened by sweet and divine meditation? and yet God says, "But seek not Beth-el, nor enter into Gilgal." Gilgal was the place of the first encampment of the children of Israel after crossing the Jordan; what could be better after sanctification than to return in memory to the place of our first encampment in the promised land? yet God says "nor enter into Gilgal, and pass not to Beersheba." Beer-sheba was the place of wonderful refreshing; Abraham dwelt there; Hagar was relieved there; Jacob was comforted there. What could be better than a pilgrimage back to our "Beershebas," the place where outcasts have been received, the discouraged encouraged, the failures revived and made successes? Yet God says, "and pass not to Beer-sheba."

At first reading of these verses one might wonder what their message is when applied spiritually, and yet very little attention will reveal that it is the old story that it is the Lord Himself and not the places of blessing the children of God are to seek. The place of former victories for God, the place that was heaven on earth in days gone by, will be places of defeat and failure if you persist in going there as a means of reviving. The message of God is "Seek ye Me, and ye shall live." It is the message that runs all through God's Book and all through the experiences of the saint's life. I wonder how many of us are trying to haunt places instead of seeking the Lord? There are places of revival to which the people of God take pilgrimages and spend hours and days and weeks there, trying to get a jaded life back again into communion with God, trying to revive by meditation and the power of association what can never be made alive apart from the living presence of God Himself. God is not confined to places, and where He once blessed, He may not bless again, it depends on the motive in seeking it.

"Seek ye Me, and ye shall live." Oh the joy of that life with God and in God and for God! It takes a sharp discipline for many of us to learn that "my goal is God Himself, not joy, nor peace, nor even blessing, but Himself my God."

THIS EXPERIENCE MUST COME
2 Kings 2:12–23

And he saw him no more. 2 Kings 2:12

"And he saw him no more"—in the way of leadership. If you have been learning a truth with a man or woman of God, there comes a time when you see him or her no more, not necessarily physically, but in your spiritual experience they stand no more to you as your guide and leader because God does not intend they should. That is the time you accuse God of making blunders—"I can't go on without Elijah." God says you must.

1. Alone at Your Jordan (2 Kings 2:13–14)—*Your Seal*

Your "Jordan" is some type of separation in which no one can have any fellowship with you, and no one can take the responsibility for you; you have to put to the test what you learned when you were in communion with your "Elijah." As a saint in God's work, your experience is that you have been to Jordan over and over again with your Elijah, he taught you wonderfully how God did things, and you saw how God worked through him, but now you are up against it alone. There is no use saying you cannot go on without him, this experience has come and you must.

What did Elisha do? He took up the mantle and did exactly what he had seen Elijah do. In the discipline of fellowship God always makes us go first as apprentices. He gives us comrades and leaders and guides whom we depend upon up to a certain stage, then there comes the experience of going alone. It is not wrong to depend on Elijah so long as God gives him to you, take all you can get from him, but remember the time will come when he will have to go. Beware then that you don't look for Elijah, don't look for any assistance, but call on God and He will give you your seal. "The spirit of Elijah doth rest on Elisha" (2 Kings 2:15). There is no sentiment here, but reality. If you want to know whether God is the real God you have faith to believe He is, then go through your Jordan alone. Jordan is taken to mean death, but here it means the threshold of life. We have to go through our Jordan as men and women who have really learned of God.

2. Alone at Your Jericho (2 Kings 2:16–22)— *Your Sin.*

Jericho is the place where you have seen your Elijah do great things. There are times in your life when Redemption and rationalism come into conflict, and your faith in God seems the most feeble and ludicrous thing there is. If you have learned well of your Elijah, you will never trust your reason, or wits, or anyone else's wits, you will remain true to what you learned with Elijah, and you will get the sign that God is with you; but you must go there alone. When you are up against your Jericho, you have a strong disinclination to take the initiative and trust in God, you want someone else to take the responsibility. While you are with your Elijah he takes the responsibility, but you come to the place where Elijah is no more use. Whether it be your Jordan or your Jericho, stand true to what you learned with your Elijah, and don't side with the clamour of the educated prophets.

3. Alone at Your Beth-El (2 Kings 2:23)— *Your Sacrament*

"And he went up from thence unto Beth-el." Beth-el stands for the house of God, the place where God revealed Himself to Jacob. Elisha had been with Elijah to all these places—"and they two went on," and now Elisha goes alone, and at Beth-el he is slandered and treated as a hypocrite. At your Beth-el you will find yourself at your wits' end and at the beginning of God's wisdom. When you get to your wits' end and feel inclined to succumb to panic, don't. In spiritual matters never do what you feel inclined to do naturally. If you knuckle down to the tyranny of physical conditions, it is all up with learning God's lesson at that particular Beth-el. Stand steadfastly true to God, and God will bring His truth out in a way that will make your life a sacrament, i.e., the abiding presence of God will come through the simple elements of your life, but you must wait for Him.

Perhaps this experience has come in your life, not in a sentimental way that makes you interested in yourself, but in reality, and you are up against it. The only thing to do is to put into vogue what you learned with your Elijah—use his cloak and pray; determine to trust in God and don't look for Elijah any more. When God removes His servants He never allows any time to mourn over them. "Moses My servant is dead; now therefore arise. . . ."

A SOUND WORKMAN

Do your utmost to let God see that you at least are a sound workman, with no need to be ashamed of the way you handle the word of the Truth. 2 Timotheus 2:15 (MOFFATT)

This advice of the Apostle's puts a sacredness on work that nothing else does.

As workers, remember that we have to be "approved unto God," not logical in our interpretation of the facts of revelation or the facts of life. Revelation transcends reason and confuses logic.

There is no royal road to becoming a worker for God. The only way is to let God in His mighty providence lift the life by a great tide, or break it from its moorings in some storm, and in one way or another get the life out to sea in reckless abandon to God. When once God's purpose is begun He seems to put His hand on the life and uproot and detach it in every way, and there is darkness and mystery and very often kicking. We can be impertinent to God's providence the moment we choose; there is no punishment, we have simply chosen not to be workers for God in that particular. We say, "Let me get back to the 'duck pond,' to its limitations, where all is so simple and placid and easy to understand." We may go back to our "duck pond" and be a success there, but God wants to launch us out into the ocean. Numbers have come within sight of an understanding of the great doctrines and have stopped short. There is no pioneer but God into the meaning of His great doctrines.

Never make an experience produced by your faithfulness to God the ground of your Christian teaching, but find in your personal experience the assurance of your relation to the Christian doctrine you have to teach. It is always easier to be a hand-to-mouth evangelist than to be a worker for God rightly expounding the evangel to the saints.

The value to God of one man or woman right out in supreme sanctification is incalculable. The value of a life can only be estimated by its spiritual relationship to God. "Every branch that beareth fruit, He cleanseth it, that it may bear more fruit" (RV). Do you feel the knife? If so, that is a sign that you are bearing fruit. The greatest service we can render God is to fulfil our spiritual destiny. It is the despised crowd God is counting on, insignificant but holy.

WHAT DO YOU SEE IN YOUR CLOUDS?

Behold, He cometh with clouds. Revelation 1:7

In the Bible clouds are always connected with God. Clouds are those sorrows or sufferings or providences without or within our personal lives which seem to dispute the empire of God. If there were no clouds we would not need faith. Seen apart from God, the clouds or difficulties are accidents, but by those very clouds the Spirit of God teaches us to walk by faith. Faith must have an autobiography; until we know God, we have no faith. Faith is the spontaneous outgoing of my person to another person whom I know.

"Behold, He cometh with clouds"—the clouds are the very sign that God is there. What a revelation it is to know that sorrow, bereavement and suffering are clouds that come along with God! God does not come near in clear shining, He comes in the clouds. "If I had not come . . . , they had not had sin." The sign that Jesus Christ has come to us is the sense of our utter unworthiness.

It is not true to say that God wants to teach us something in our trials. In every cloud He brings, God wants us to *un*learn something. God's purpose in the cloud is to simplify our belief until our relationship to Him is exactly that of a child. God uses every cloud which comes in our physical life, in our moral or spiritual life, or in our circumstances, to bring us nearer to Him, until we come to the place where our Lord Jesus Christ lived, and we do not allow our hearts to be troubled.

Christianity does not add to our difficulties, it brings them to a focus, and in the difficulties we find Jesus Himself. We must get out of the habit of misinterpreting God by saying He wants to teach us something, it is not a New Testament idea, but an idea that is as unlike the God whom Jesus revealed as could be. God is all the time bringing us to the place where we *un*learn things.

We ought to interpret all the clouds and mysteries of life in the light of our knowledge of God. In everything that happens we should be un-learning that which keeps us from a simple relationship to God. Sometimes we have to leave certain forms of religious activity and testimony alone until our relationship to God is simplified—God and my own soul, other people are shadows. Until other people become shadows, clouds and darkness will be ours every now and again. Is your relationship to God becoming simpler? The proof that it is, is that you do not bother God about yourself so much as you used to because you know Him better.

There is a connection between the strange providences of God and all that we know of God Himself. Unless we can look the darkest, blackest fact full in the face without damaging God's character, we do not know God. There are no such things as "calamities" or "accidents" to God's children—"all things work together for good." Sin and evil and the devil are not God's order; they are here by the direct permission of His providence. If we governed the universe we would clear them all out at once, but God does not work in that way. He did not work in that way with us—think how patient God has been with us! When the world, the flesh and the devil do their worst, it is for us to understand where our true life is to be lived, not in the outer courts, but "hid with Christ in God." Whatever happens, happens by God's permission.

What is your cloud just now? Is it something you cannot see through, something foggy and indefinite and perplexing that makes you shiver with fear? Are there clouds of thinking which make you afraid as you enter them? The revelation in God's Book is that the clouds are but "the dust of His feet." Then thank Him for them.

"They feared as they entered the cloud"; "Suddenly . . . they saw no man any more, save Jesus only with themselves." Have you anyone "save Jesus only" in your cloud? If you have, it will get darker. You must come to the place where there is "no man, save Jesus only," all others are shadows. Spiritual education is to know God, and nothing simplifies our life more than learning to see in the clouds the goings of His feet.

THE SUFFERING OF THE SANCTIFIED

Forasmuch then as Christ suffered in the flesh, arm ye yourselves also with the same mind; for he that hath suffered in the flesh hath ceased from sin. 1 Peter 4:1

There is suffering that is preventable, but there is an inevitable suffering that is essentially God's will for us. We do not know the preface to our own story any more than Job did; we suffer, and God alone knows why. It is beside the mark to say that it is because we deserve to suffer; Job did not deserve to suffer for he was a man "perfect and upright, and one that feared God, and eschewed evil." Neither is it at all satisfying to say that suffering develops character. There was more in Job's suffering than was required to develop his character, and so it is with the sanctified soul. The preface to Job's story lets in the light from the revelation point of view, viz., that God's honour was at stake, and the issue fought out in this man's soul vindicated God's honour.

This point of view does not deny that we receive whippings from our Father for being wilful and stupid, or that we are chastened to purity; or that any of the obvious or beautiful and sentimental things that are said and known about suffering are not true. They are true, but there is a deeper suffering in connection with sanctification that cannot be exhausted by any or all of these views.

The picture of God in the Bible is of One who suffers, and when the mask is torn off life and we see all its profound and vast misery, the suffering, sorrowing God is the only One who does not mock us. "He was despised, and rejected of men; a man of sorrows, and acquainted with grief" (Isaiah 53:3 RV).

The Cross of Christ pronounced final and irrevocable judgement against the prince of this world (see John 12:31). The cross of sanctification is not the Cross of God in the sense that the Cross of Jesus Christ was. The inevitable suffering of the sanctified is that they side with the Cross of God, and with His way against the way of the prince of this world. The prince of this world defies God at the Cross, his insidious temptation is—"Save Thyself: if Thou art the Son of God, come down from the cross." Suffering was inevitable to our Lord before God could make His Saviourhood a fact; He "learned obedience by the things which He suffered" (RV). Jesus Christ is not our Example, He is the Captain of our salvation; His position is unique. We do not suffer in order that we may become saviours; we suffer in order to enable God to fulfil His idea of saintship in us (*see* Colossians 1:24).

The evident indifference on the part of the saints in the New Testament, and since, to the experience of suffering is accounted for, not on the ground of insensitiveness or by trampling on the finer feelings, but by "the expulsive power of a new affection." When we are saved and sanctified through the Atonement we are led out into the fulfilment of the ideas of God under the Lordship of Jesus Christ. Every other aim falls into insignificance, and through earth's heart-breaks, sorrows and griefs, the sanctified soul treads calm and unwavering, unafraid even of death itself, summing up all as "our light affliction, which is for the moment . . ." (RV).

The sufferings of the sanctified are caused by growing into the idea of the will of God. God did not spare His own Son, and He does not spare His sanctified ones from the requirements of saintship. A child is a perfect specimen of the genus *homo*, so is a man. The child as it develops, suffers; it is a false mercy that spares a child any requirements of its nature to complete the full stature of manhood, and it is a false mercy that spares the sanctified child of God any of the requirements of its nature to complete "the measure of the stature of the fulness of Christ." We do not evolve into holiness, it is a gift—we evolve *in* it, attainment after attainment, becoming sons and daughters of God, brothers and sisters of the Lord Jesus. That is Paul's meaning in Philippians 3:13–14, "reaching forth unto those things which are before, I press toward the mark. . . ."

A child in the natural world is not fit for life unless it is perfectly healthy; sanctification is spiritual health, "perfect soundness."

May the God of peace sanctify us wholly so that we are no longer sickly souls retarding His purposes, but perfected through suffering. Oh, that from every heart may rise the yearning longing, as from the Apostle Paul:

Then as I weary me and long and languish,
Nowise availing from that pain to part,—

Desperate tides of the whole great world's
*   anguish*
Forced thro' the channels of a single heart.

. . . .

Oh to save these! to perish for their saving,
Die for their life, be offered for them all!

Myers[13]

---

13. F. W. H. Myers (1843–1901: British poet and educator.

VOWS, VISIONS AND VOICES

1. The Vices and Virtues of Vowing

When thou vowest a vow unto God, defer not to pay it; for He hath no pleasure in fools: pay that which thou vowest. (Ecclesiastes 5:4 RV)

At New Year time we hear much of vowing. Solomon's advice is—"Don't vow; because if you make a vow, even in ordinary matters, and do not fulfil it, you are the worse for it." To make a promise may simply be a way of shirking responsibility. Never pile up promises before men, and certainly not before God. It is better to run the risk of being considered indecisive, better to be uncertain and not promise, than to promise and not fulfil. "Better is it that thou shouldest not vow, than that thou shouldest vow and not pay" (Ecclesiastes 5:5).

The vices of vowing outweigh the virtues, because vowing is built on a misconception of human nature as it really is. If a man had the power to will pure will it would be different, but he has not. There are certain things a man cannot do, not because he is bad, but because he is not constituted to do them. We make vows which are impossible of fulfilment because no man can remain master of himself always; there comes a time when the human will must yield allegiance to a force greater than itself, it must yield either to God or to the devil.

Modern ethical teaching bases everything on the power of the will, but we need to recognise also the perils of the will. The man who has achieved a moral victory by the sheer force of his will is less likely to want to become a Christian than the man who has come to the moral frontier of his own need. It is the obstinate man who makes vows, and by the very fulfilment of his vow he may increase his inability to see things from Jesus Christ's standpoint. When a man is stirred, either by joy or sorrow, or by the seasons of the year, he is apt to make vows which are beyond the possibility of human power to keep.

Jesus Christ bases the entrance to His Kingdom not on a man's vowing and making decisions, but on the realisation of his inability to decide. Decisions for Christ fail because the bedrock of Christianity is ignored. It is not our vows before God that tell, but coming to God exactly as we are, in all our weakness, and being held and kept by Him. Make no vows at this New Year time, but look to God and bank on the Reality of Jesus Christ.

2. The Direction of Vision (Acts 26:19)

It was no passing emotion that came to Paul on the road to Damascus, the vision had very clear and emphatic direction for him, and he says, "I was not disobedient unto the heavenly vision." Paul was not given a message or a doctrine to proclaim, he was brought into a vivid, personal, overmastering relationship to Jesus Christ: "I have chosen him" (MOFFATT). There are pietistic movements started by certain forms of vision which are characterised by fasting and times of prayer and devotion, but they are the antipodes of everything Jesus Christ taught. Jesus Christ taught absolute abandonment to Himself and identification with His aims. The test of all spiritual vision is, "That I may know Him."

Recall the time when you knew without any doubt that the Spirit of God spoke to you and brought you to see what God wanted you to do; if you obeyed the vision, it has led on to emancipation in your life; but remember, every enlargement of vision has to be paid for by increased concentration. We all have moments when

> *The spirit's true endowments*
> *Stand out plainly from its false ones,*
> *And apprise it if pursuing*
> *Or the right way or the wrong way,*
> *To its triumph or undoing.*

We are inclined to be ashamed of the vision we get because it marks us out as being different from other people, and we are afraid of being considered "speckled birds."[14] The vision will mark you out as different, but if you take your direction from the vision, you will not only make a straight path for yourself but for others also.

3. The Inspiration of Voices

And I heard the voice of the Lord saying, Whom shall I send? (Isaiah 6:8)

The call of God is best heard when the soul is in a state of obedience to the known will of God, when, as it were, God's soliloquy is overheard—"Whom shall I send, and who will go for Us?" and the ready response is, "Here am I; send me." The call of God is difficult to state, it is implicit, not explicit. The call of God does not come to everyone, it comes only to the man who has the nature of God in him. For every

---

14. speckled bird: a person who stands out as abnormal, odd, or eccentric

man who is true to the call of God, there are many who are true to the call of a creed or doctrinal evangelism. There are voices that are not true to the character of Jesus Christ (see Matthew 24:23–24); the inspiration of these voices is not to glorify Jesus, but to glorify something which He does. Give time to heed the call of God. The voice of God never contradicts the character of God.

THE DISCIPLINE OF SPIRITUAL TENACITY
Psalm 46

The world as it is, is not good enough to be true. We ought not to be satisfied with it. God has prepared some better thing. But it by no means follows that what God has prepared is what we should now choose. There may be heavy sorrows and disappointments in store for us, if so it will mean that our hopes need purifying.

Forsyth

Tenacity is more than endurance, it is endurance which has at its heart the absolute certainty that what we look for is going to transpire. Spiritual tenacity is the supreme effort of the Spirit of God in a man refusing to believe that his "Hero" is going to be conquered. The greatest fear a man has is not that he will be damned, but that Jesus Christ will be worsted; that the things He stood for—love and justice, forgiveness and kindness among men, won't win out in the end. Then comes the call to spiritual tenacity, not to hang on and do nothing, but to work deliberately and tenaciously with the certainty that God is not going to be worsted.

1. In the Wildness of Nature *(Psalm 46:1–3)*

There is a wildness all through Nature and we are suddenly struck with its brutality and ask, "Why, if God is a beneficent Creator, does He allow such diabolical things to happen?" Has the Bible anything to say about this, any revelation that explains it? The Bible explanation is that Nature is in a disorganised condition, that it is out of gear with God's purposes, and will only become organised when God and man are one (see Romans 8:19).

We all have our problems, something about which we say, "Now, why is it?" Never take an explanation which is too slight.

A materialistic explanation or an evolutionary explanation cannot be final. The great thing is to remain absolutely confident in God. "Be still, and know that I am God."

2. In the Whirlwind of Nations *(Psalm 46:4–7)*

According to the Bible, the nations as we know them are the outcome of what ought never to have been. Civilisation was started by a murderer, and the whole of our civilised life is based on competition. There are grand ingredients in civilised life, but the basis is not good. In the whirlwind of nations such as is on just now, many a man has lost, not his faith in God (I have never met the man who had lost his faith in God), but belief in his beliefs. When a man's belief in his beliefs suffers a severe blow, for a while he thinks he is disbelieving in God; in reality all he has lost is the conception of God that had been presented to him and he is coming to a knowledge of God along a new line. There are those who have maintained their faith in God, and the only language they can use to express it is—"*I know* God is God, although hell seems on top all round."

3. In the Weariness of Nemesis *(Psalm 46:8–11)*

A man may sin magnificently, but he is punished drearily. The whole of our prison system is a day after day nemesis which makes men wish they had died rather than that the gates of paradise had clanged behind them.

We are apt to make the mistake of looking for God to put things ostensibly right immediately. If we dwell much on the Second Coming without having a right spiritual relationship to God, it will make us ignore the need for spiritual tenacity. Just now, Jesus says, "The kingdom of God cometh not with observation: . . . for lo, the kingdom of God is in the midst [mg] of you" (RV). When our Lord does come, He will come quickly, and we will find He has been there all the time. One of the greatest strains in life is the strain of waiting for God. "Because thou didst keep the word of My patience" (RV). God takes the saints like a bow which He stretches and at a certain point the saint says, "I can't stand any more," but God does not heed, He goes on stretching because He is aiming at His mark, not ours, and the patience of the saints is that they "hang in" until God lets the arrow fly.

If your hopes are being disappointed just now it means that they are being purified. There is nothing noble the human mind has ever hoped for or dreamed of that will not be fulfilled. Don't jump to conclusions too quickly; many things lie unsolved, and the biggest test of all is that God looks as if He were totally indifferent.

Remain spiritually tenacious.

INSIDIOUS INDIFFERENCE

And I think it right, as long as I am in this tabernacle, to stir you up by putting you in remembrance. 2 Peter 1:13 (RV)

Insidious means "advancing imperceptibly." Are you as spiritually alive and enthusiastic as you once were? Are you finding it expedient not to have so keen an edge on your discipleship as you used to have? Are you a little more inclined to sit complacently to the fashions and customs of that form of worldliness which you used to avoid with horror? Then may this word of the Apostle Peter's stir you up and preserve for you a vivid apprehension of the truth.

1. Knowledge of the Truth

Wherefore I shall be ready always to put you in remembrance of these things, though ye know them, and are established in the truth which is with you. (2 Peter 1:12 RV)

These words indicate that the warning is addressed to those who know the truth and are established in it. This may be a little startling, but it ought to prove very profitable. You are a Christian, perhaps a prominent worker, your testimony is outspoken on every occasion, you are fearless in your stand for the truth, and yet it is to such as you that these words are spoken. You would be surprised and incredulous if you were told that you were threatened with insidious indifference, and that on this enchanted ground you may sleep the fatal sleep.

Beware of your testimony when you can give it without thinking. The more decided our testimony, the more decided and growing should our thinking be. When we use the words "salvation," "sanctification," "Holy Spirit," or any of the great words, do we think more about them than we used to? or have we used them so often that we heed them little because we are established in the truth? Bear in mind that unwilled attention soon flags, but willed observation gives discernment.

2. Knowledge of Failure

For he that lacketh these things is blind, seeing only what is near, having forgotten the cleansing from his old sins. (2 Peter 1:9 RV)

Another cause of insidious indifference is from a different source, viz., the knowledge of having failed. Perhaps you have not grown in grace, you are not "stablished in the faith," you have been lazy and self-indulgent, and you have slowly become what you know you are to-day—blind, you have become "unfruitful" in your knowledge of our Lord and Saviour Jesus Christ. If this is your portrait, let these words rouse you out of your fatal sickness. Thank God it is not yet too late. Rouse up now! Add diligence to your faith, and by the grace of God you will soon begin to "add" the other things also.

3. Knowledge of Being Kept

… who by the power of God are guarded through faith unto a salvation ready to be revealed in the last time. (1 Peter 1:5 RV)

Insidious indifference is begotten not only by a knowledge of the truth, and by a knowledge of failure, but also by a knowledge of being kept. The sublime truth of the security of being kept may degenerate into a lazy drift towards destruction. The keeping power of God is a grand eternal fact; but beware of going to sleep on the decrees of God and saying, "In God's good time," when in your heart and by your habits you really mean, "In my bad time."

Let such considerations as these stir up our minds by way of remembrance. It is as if the voice of Our Master called to us saying, "BE saved!" "BE sanctified!" "BE renewed in the spirit of your mind"! taking the word "BE" to mean a steady growth "in the grace and knowledge of our Lord and Saviour Jesus Christ" (RV).

THE PRICE OF EXPANSION

Rejoice, O young man, in thy youth; and let thy heart cheer thee in the days of thy youth, and walk in the ways of thine heart, and in the sight of thine eyes: but know thou, that for all these things God will bring thee into judgement. Ecclesiastes 11:9 (RV)

Every expansion of mind, or heart, or emotion has to be paid for by additional concentration. The price is the same in national and individual life. During these years there has been a terrific expansion in lives through bereavement and sorrow, everything in individual life has been altered, but there is the price to pay. The majority of us are inclined to make little of what we feel most; it is a good thing to be inarticulate, but at the same time it is well to get an expression because others have the same experience. Up to thirty years of age life is full of promise; after that, life holds out no more promise, it holds out the test as to whether we are going to live up to what we saw in vision. The danger is to abandon the vision and say we are getting more sensible; we are, rather, getting more sordid, we have lost the moral vim, the effort to pay the price of the expansion. It is a question of "hanging in" in the dark to what we saw in the light. "While ye have light, believe in the light, that ye may be the children of light" (John 12:36).

1. Reaction of Formation *(Luke 11:24–26)*
Then goeth he, and taketh to him seven other spirits more evil than himself; and they enter in and dwell there. (Luke 11:26 RV)

There is an idea in regard to a revival that the thing is done suddenly, by a magic pill. Some things in a man's life are done suddenly, but there is always the price to pay afterwards; he has to set his face to it. To-day people are crying out for a revival and an awakening, but we have to remember that we must lay our account with the inevitable reaction. Reaction means the way I answer back to anything which impinges on me; physical health, moral and spiritual health, are all maintained by reaction. A converted man is not necessarily one God's Spirit has touched; a man may reform himself by sheer strength of will, but reaction is inevitable and unless he is willing to pay the price of the expansion, he will end worse than he began. Our Lord is not talking about the man who suddenly collapses because he has gone on in some secret sin; He is describing the man who has turned the devil out and made his heart clean by sheer will—"swept and garnished" but empty, and He

says that "the last state of that man becometh worse than the first" (RV).

Our Lord's attitude to the human will is not that frequently presented to-day; He never says that a man must make vows and decisions. "Decisions for Christ" fail, not because men are not in earnest, but because the bedrock of Christianity is left out. The bedrock of Christianity is not strength of will, but the realisation of my inability to decide: if I am ever going to be what Jesus Christ wants me to be, He must come in and do it, I am an abject pauper morally and spiritually. Fundamental free will is never possible, if it were our vowing would be omnipotent, we could do as we liked.

2. The Danger of Drifting from Ideals
Come unto Me, all ye that labour and are heavy laden, and I will give you rest. Take My yoke upon you, and learn of Me; for I am meek and lowly in heart: and ye shall find rest unto your souls. For My yoke is easy, and My burden is light. (Matthew 11:28–30)

We generally look upon an ideal as something to live up to; it is rather something to live in the inspiration of. A boy in his 'teens has clearer and purer ideals than at any future time; then when he begins to find a divorce between what he is and what he sees he ought to be, he experiences an agony of mind. We can all see visions and dream dreams, but they are not woven into the texture of our life, and unless we are willing to pay the price of expansion we will drift from our ideals. Immediately you are prepared to live in the inspiration of your ideals, you become a "speckled bird." Many a man is kept back from Jesus Christ by a sense of honour to his own crowd—"No, they will think I am becoming a superior person," and a man often chooses to drift from his ideals rather than seem disloyal to his crowd. If he goes on, ultimately his crowd will go with him, but it will test his moral calibre to the utmost.

3. The Natural Law of Emotion *(Colossians 3:5–10)*
Mortify therefore your members which are upon the earth. . . . (Colossians 3:5)

If I allow an emotion and refuse to act it out on its right level, it will react on a lower level, and the higher the emotion the deeper the reaction. The most unwholesome people spiritually are those who like to have their emotions stirred by prayer meetings and devotional readings, but they never act them out. In the natural world the one who is used to having things played before his emotions apart from actual life is as a rule the most callous, heartless person at home. My guide as to what emotion I am going to allow is to ask myself—Suppose I allow this emotion, what is its logical outcome? If it has to do with sin and Satan, then cut it clean out, allow it no more way; if it is an emotion to be generous, then *be* generous,

work it out on its right level and your moral life will be tremendously benefited. The place for discipline in both natural and spiritual life lies just here. When the Spirit of God stirs you, make as many things inevitable as possible, let the consequences be what they will. It is in such crises in spiritual life as these that Jesus says, "Come unto Me . . . and I will give you rest." He will make a man able to work out in actual life what he sees by the power of vision.

PERFECTING HOLINESS
2 Corinthians 7:1

"Having therefore these promises"—what promises? "I will dwell in them, and walk in them; and I will be their God, and they shall be My people" (2 Corinthians 6:16)—*"let us cleanse ourselves"*—no "excusing the sins we're most inclined to while condemning those we've no mind to"; there must be no moral partiality in the saint—*"from all defilement of flesh and spirit"* (RV)—nothing contrary to God's nature: "the blood of Jesus Christ His Son cleanseth us from *all* sin"—*"perfecting holiness in the fear of God."* It is perilously possible to cultivate a spurious, unhealthy holiness not "in the fear of God." There is a subtle form of carnal pride that is set on *my* holiness; it is unscriptural and morbid and ends in experience rather than in character, in taking myself more and more seriously and God less and less seriously. The cultivation of holiness is impossible without the spiritual concentration which the Holy Spirit enjoins.

"I beseech you . . . to present your bodies a living sacrifice, holy, acceptable to God" (RV). Practical holi-

ness is the only holiness of any value in this world, and the only kind God will endorse. Romans 12:1–2 is a passionate entreaty to rouse ourselves out of that stagnation in which we are ensnared by thinking that because it is all of grace there is no need for "gumption"; whereas the tremendous initiative given us to sanctification ought to rouse us to determined activity until we are transformed by the renewing of our mind and able to make out the will of God. This mental renewing means the strenuous and courageous lifting of the problems of the world, individual, family, and social, into the spiritual domain, and habitually working out a life of practical holiness. It is not an easy task, but a heroically difficult one, requiring the mightiest effort of our human nature; a task which by the grace of God lifts us into thinking God's thoughts after Him until they become our unconscious inheritance. The secret of spiritual otherworldliness is not found in adhering to a set of rules, but lies deep down in a hidden spring of life and thought which the saint continually obeys.

A MEDITATION
Job 19:25–27

For I know that my Redeemer liveth, and that He shall stand at the latter day upon the earth: and though after my skin worms destroy this body, yet in my flesh shall I see God. . . . Job 19:25–26

When a man is agitated by the Spirit of God he utters words from which he takes comfort for himself and others can do the same, but the treasure contained in the words can never be exhausted. Job did not under-

stand all the meaning of these words, yet he took a meaning of great preciousness to himself out of them. So with us, it is never possible for us to understand what we utter when we get a glimpse of God, or to express the rapture that sweeps our soul at such times. If a man's words spoken in the power of the spirit have such inexhaustible value, who can estimate the value of The Word of God, our Lord Jesus Christ Himself, who expresses to us the very thoughts of God?

God never reveals Himself in the same way to everyone, and yet the testimony of each one who has had a revelation of God is the same, viz., that God is love. If a man doubts God, he is not able to express the doubt, his lips are dumb with the pain: if a man can *say* he doubts God, the doubt is not worth heeding. Job's faith is wavering under the blows of the providence of God and the stinging cruelty of his friends; the breakdown of all his traditional belief seems like the breakdown of God, and from the delirium of his perplexity he pleads, "Have pity upon me, have pity upon me, O ye my friends; for the hand of God hath touched me." And with the utterance of his plea a new confidence seems to creep in, the Spirit of God moving through all his incoherent sadness begins to lift him to a higher plane; his consciousness of innocence is confirmed within him as God reveals Himself in a more majestic and mysterious way, there is a growing assurance that he will yet be justified in the eyes of those who now accuse him, and he repeats to himself his confidence—"though after my skin worms destroy this body, yet in my flesh shall I see God: whom I shall see for myself." The darkness, which comes from excess of light, is transformed by the never-to-be-explained rapture of his growing realisation of God. Whenever God reveals Himself to a man he instantly finds the limitation of human language and reasoning—"It is impossible! yet it shall be!"

Why is it that our faith gets contradicted by what we go through in our experience? Because of ourselves we can know nothing, we only know by God revealing Himself to us. We are in danger of taking each stage of our development in spiritual growth as final, and when a fuller flood as from God's own great life comes, overwhelming all the old traditional belief, we close down our soul over the earlier revelations—"I have the truth now," consequently we stagnate because we cut ourselves off from God. There is no limit to what God can make us are we but willing. His great love is ever overshadowing us and He waits to visit us with His saving life.

"For I know that my Redeemer liveth," Job is assured that his Redeemer (his Vindicator) will arise and will put right the wrong; and every upright soul will likewise one day be vindicated, never fear. But Job's words convey to us as Christians a deeper, more glorious truth; they mean that our Redeemer, the Lord Jesus Christ, will one day stand upon this earth and will clear *His* Name from reproach and slander! The people of God cry, "O God, how long shall the adversary reproach? shall the enemy blaspheme Thy name for ever?" The enemies of Christ are triumphant, Christianity is a failure, they say; and the Church of God herself looks on in pain at the shortcomings in her midst. But lo, at length from the very heart of the shadows appears the majestic Figure of Jesus; His countenance is as the sun shineth in his strength, around those wounds in Brow and Side and Hands and Feet—those wounds which shelter countless thousands of broken hearts—are healing rays; in that glorious Figure meets every beauty inconceivable to the imagination of man. O Christians, dry your eyes! Be not downcast, for I know that my Redeemer liveth! He is nearer than you think. Oh the speechless rapture of it, that suddenly He will appear to us! *"Yea: I come quickly. Amen: come, Lord Jesus"* (RV).

He Shall Glorify Me

Talks on the Holy Spirit
and other themes
Oswald Chambers

INTRODUCTION

Source

The lectures on the Holy Spirit were given in the Christian doctrine class at the Bible Training College,[1] London, during April and May 1915. Many of the other chapters in this volume are talks given to British Commonwealth soldiers in Egypt between 1915 and 1917. Where possible, they are identified by date and location. The YMCA camp at Zeitoun[2] was located six miles northeast of Cairo. After Oswald Chambers' death in November 1917, a number of these messages were printed as leaflet sermons and distributed widely among troops during 1918 and 1919.

Publication History

- As articles: In *Spiritual Life* magazine and the *Bible Training Course (BTC) Journal*.[3]
- As a book: 1946.

In all of these messages, the terms "the Great War" and "this war" refer to World War I (1914–1918).

---

1. Residential school near Clapham Common in SW London, sponsored by the League of Prayer. Oswald Chambers was Principal and main teacher; Biddy Chambers was Lady Superintendent. Known as the BTC, it closed in July 1915 because of World War I.

2. Zeitoun (zay TOON). An area 6 miles NE of Cairo. Site of YMCA camp, Egypt General Mission compound and a large base area for British, Australian and New Zealand troops. Site of the Imperial School of Instruction (1916–19).

3. *Bible Training Course Journal:* published from 1932 to 1952 by Mrs. Chambers, with help from David Lambert.

CONTENTS

FOREWORD

It is my privilege to have been asked to write a brief Foreword to this book, the latest addition to the treasurehouse of the Oswald Chambers literature. The idea of a Foreword is surely that some fact may be brought to light, the telling of which shall induce others to read and so share in the life-giving truth.

The writer enjoyed a close friendship with "O. C.," and there came to his own life fresh spiritual impetus and vision as he not only listened to the exposition of truths, but as he saw those same truths practised and lived out in everyday contact with men and affairs. It was indeed a life lived in abandon to God.

The whole story of the "O. C." literature is an outstanding witness of the gracious hand of God. Oswald Chambers spent the last two years of his life in YMCA work out in the desert in Egypt, in the thick of it with the men, every evening being devoted to a meeting for spiritual instruction on some vital theme. This book in particular is compiled largely from these talks, as well as from sermons delivered on Sundays. Then in November 1917 came his Home-call into God's immediate presence, and a leaflet was printed and scattered among the men in Egypt and Palestine in time for Christmas. There was little thought at the time of the number of books to which this leaflet, entitled "The Place of Help," was to be the forerunner. Other publications quickly began to follow, and each one was printed simultaneously in Egypt and in England. I have had the joy and privilege of being associated with the publishing from those early days right on until now; and with the growing demand for all the books, and for their translation into a number of languages, one feels confident that God will unfold yet more of His purpose in this great work.

So read and study and enjoy this new book, and find for yourself that *"The Best is yet to be,"* as "O. C." so frequently reminded us.

Dunstable, 1946
Percy W. Lockhart[4]

---

4. Percy Lockhart: best man at Oswald Chambers' wedding; he became a close advisor to Mrs. Chambers in publishing OC's books.

THE ADVENT OF THE HOLY SPIRIT

Howbeit when He, the Spirit of truth, is come, . . . He shall glorify Me. John 16:13–14

There are two descents of the Holy Spirit mentioned in the Bible: the first is at the baptism of our Lord, the second on the Day of Pentecost, when the Paraclete came to this earth. The power of the Holy Spirit and His personal presence are not the same; the power of the Holy Spirit was mightily present in the world before His personal advent. In this dispensation we not only have the power of the Holy Spirit, but His personal presence moving amongst us.

1. The Peace of God

And the Holy Spirit descended in a bodily shape like a dove upon Him, and a voice from heaven, which said, Thou art My beloved Son; in Thee I am well pleased. (Luke 3:22)

The first descent of the Holy Spirit was upon the Son of Man—that is, the whole human race represented in one Person, and that Person the historic Jesus Christ who was God Incarnate. It was at His baptism that the Holy Spirit descended upon Him, and we must never forget that His baptism was a baptism of repentance. It was at His baptism that Jesus Christ definitely took upon Him His vocation, which was to bear away (RV mg) the sin of the world.

John the Baptist must not be regarded as a mere individual; Jesus said of him that he was the greatest prophet that had been born of woman, and he is the last of the line of prophets. After four hundred years of absolute silence there came this lonely, mighty voice, "Prepare . . ." Jesus said to John, "for thus it becometh us to fulfil all righteousness." That could only be done by Our Lord as the Son of man accepting His vocation to bear away (RV mg) the sin of the world. Jesus is the "Prince of Peace" because only in Him can men have God's good-will and peace on earth. Thank God, through that beloved Son the great peace of God may come to every heart and to every nation under heaven, but it can come in no other way. None of us can ever have good-will towards God if we won't listen to His Son. Have we despised what the Father said about Jesus Christ at His baptism? the Mount of Transfiguration He said the same thing. The only way to peace and salvation and power, and to all that God has in the way of benedictions and blessings for us individually and for the whole world, is in the Son of Man.

2. The Power of God

And there appeared unto them cloven tongues like as of fire. (Acts 2:3)

The second mighty descent of the Holy Spirit was on the Day of Pentecost, when the power of God came in Person. The record says that they who heard were devout Jews from every nation under heaven, and the great miracle is stated "how hear we every man in our own tongue?" The Holy Spirit came not as a dove, but in cloven tongues of fire. The disciples had been told to tarry until they were endued with power from on high. As soon as Jesus Christ was glorified, the personal Holy Spirit descended, and in the decrees of God the fullness of time was reached when the Son of Man, on whom the Holy Spirit had descended as a dove ascended to the right hand of the Father and sent forth the mighty Holy Spirit. In Genesis 11 we read that God caused confusion of tongues; on the Day of Pentecost He caused a fusion of understanding by the tongues of fire, the manifestation accompanying the personal advent of the Holy Spirit. It was a far-reaching, mighty testimony to the fact that sin had been judged on the Cross.

It is one thing to believe that the Holy Spirit is given individually, but another thing to receive the revelation that He is here. He is here in personal presence in all the plenitude of His power, but His power will only work as a manifestation of what Jesus Christ has done. The Holy Spirit works in no other way than to glorify Jesus Christ. Anyone who receives the Holy Spirit receives life from the glorified Jesus, and receives also an understanding of the teaching of Jesus and complete security, provided he abides in the light the Holy Spirit sheds.

"Verily, verily, I say unto you, He that believeth on Me, the works that I do shall he do also; and greater works than these shall he do; because I go unto my Father" (John 14:12). It was this mighty Person, the Holy Spirit, who inspired the apostles to write the New Testament. The New Testament is the posthumous writing of Jesus Christ; He departed, and the Holy Spirit used these men as His pens to expound His teaching.

3. The Patience of God

For by one Spirit are we all baptized into one body. (1 Corinthians 12:13)

The baptism of the Holy Spirit delivers us from independent individuality. The one thing the Holy Spirit awakens and brings into communion with God is what is meant by personality. Individual self-assertiveness is the husk, personal identity with the Lord is the kernel. The Holy Spirit builds us into the Body of Christ.

All that Jesus Christ came to do is made experimentally ours by the Holy Spirit; He does *in* us what Jesus did *for* us. The gifts of the Spirit are not for individual exaltation, but for the good of the whole Body of Christ. The Body of Christ is an organism, not an organisation. How patient God is in forming the Body of Christ.

Our Lord's words in John 16:14 sum up the personal passion of the Holy Spirit, "He shall glorify Me." The word "passion" has come down in the world; it is generally taken to mean a distemper from which human nature suffers, but when the phrase "the Passion of our Lord" is used it means the transfiguration of peace and power and patience.

THE DOCTRINE OF THE HOLY SPIRIT—I

1. "The Beyond That Is Within"

Verily, verily, I say unto thee, Except a man be born again, he cannot see the kingdom of God. (John 3:3)

This title[5] will serve as a comment on Our Lord's words to Nicodemus. The power to see is within; what is seen is without, otherwise it is hallucination. When the Holy Spirit comes in there is a new power of perception—"And their eyes were opened, and they knew Him. . . . Then opened He their understanding, that they might understand the scriptures" (Luke 24:31, 45). The Holy Spirit regenerates my personal spirit, that is, I receive a quickening life which puts the "beyond" within, and immediately the "beyond" has come within it rises up to the "above," and I enter the domain where Jesus lives.

"Nicodemus saith unto Him, How can a man be born when he is old?" Nicodemus's question was not captious, it was a sensible, profound question arising out of the tremendously sweeping statement Jesus had made—"Except a man be born again, he cannot see the kingdom of God." The phrase "born again" was not new to Nicodemus, for the Rabbis spoke of a convert from heathenism as being "born again"; but the application Jesus made of it was absolutely amazing. "Marvel not that I said unto thee, Ye must be"—not developed, not educated, but "born again"—"fundamentally made all over again, before you can see the kingdom of God and enter into it."

Remember, Jesus is not talking to one whom men would call a sinner, there is no mention of sin; He is talking to a religious man, to "the teacher of Israel"; it is to him Jesus says, "Ye must be born again." If you define sin as external wrong doing, you miss out this class of men, men like the rich young ruler ("Master, all these have I observed from my youth"); men like Saul of Tarsus ("touching the righteousness which is in the law, blameless")—men who do not need saving from external wrong doing, they are not guilty of any. Talk about "Broken Earthenware," about going to the slums to save men and women, and every one's sympathy is with you; but Nicodemus was not "broken earthenware," he was not an outcast of society; he was a cultured Pharisee, an honoured member of the Sanhedrim, and here stands a young Nazarene Carpenter and says to him, quietly and calmly, "Ye must be born again." No wonder Nicodemus was absolutely bewildered—"I can understand how by education, religious and otherwise, I can make myself a little better; how by careful training I can keep out of sight the ugly things in my disposition; but what you say about being made all over again, I cannot understand at all."

Jesus Christ's salvation deals not only with the outcast and downtrodden, it deals with clean-living, upright, sterling men and women, and immediately you present the Gospel as Jesus presents it, it is this class you clash with. Jesus Christ came to do what no man can do for himself, viz., alter his disposition. "How can a man be born when he is old?" By receiving the gift of the Holy Spirit and allowing Him to do *in* him what Jesus did *for* him. The mighty sovereign power of God can re-make a man from within and readjust him to God. The Holy Spirit is God Himself working to make the Redemption efficacious in human lives. No wonder men leap for joy when they get saved in the New Testament way!

"Marvel not that I said unto thee, Ye must be born again." Our Lord is talking about a momentous practical experience, viz., being born from above (RV mg) while we live in the below. The conception of new birth in the New Testament is not of something that

---

5. "The Beyond That Is Within," by E. Boutroux *[Footnote included in original text.]* Étienne Émile Marie Boutroux (1845–1921) was a French philosopher and educator.

springs out of us, what modern psychology calls "a subliminal uprush," but of something that comes into us. Just as Our Lord came into the world from the outside, so He must come into us from the outside. The "washing of regeneration" comes consciously to our personal lives in and through the words of the New Testament—". . . being born again . . . by the word of God" (1 Peter 1:23). There is no authentic impulse of the Holy Spirit that is not wedded to the words of the Bible. To recognise this is the only way to be safe from dangerous delusions. To-day our beliefs are being rationalised, men are denying the supernatural element, that the Spirit of God comes in and does something which transcends human reason. A Christian is an impossible being unless a man can be made all over again. Everything hangs on this one central statement of Jesus—*"Ye must be born again."* We have lost sight of it, and we have got to get back to it.

2. The Within That Is Above

If thou knewest the gift of God, and who it is that saith to thee, Give Me to drink; thou wouldest have asked of Him, and He would have given thee living water. (John 4:10)

The idea of receiving anything as a gift from God is staggeringly original; we imagine we have to earn things by prayer and obedience. We cannot earn or win anything from God, we must receive it as a gift, like a pauper, or do without it. In this verse Our Lord is describing the essential nature of the gift—"He would have given thee living water"—a living, amazing reality. There is nothing profounder in the whole of the New Testament than this interview, it is full of the great meaning of the Gospel of God; we do not sufficiently grasp its profundity. In it we see Almighty God Incarnate stooping down to lift up a sinful woman, as a symbol of the way His salvation is at work among men.

Our Lord did not use means to attract the woman, she happened to be there—"and He must needs go through Samaria." Watch the method of His procedure, it is amazing. Our Lord does not begin by telling the woman she is a sinner, He begins by asking her to give Him something—"Give Me to drink." There is no

condescension in grace, a sinner is never afraid of Jesus; the Pharisees hated Him, that is why He said to them—"Verily I say unto you, That the publicans and the harlots go into the kingdom of God before you" (Matthew 21:31). The woman was surprised at His request not because of His personality, but because of His nationality, it was a perplexity on the surface of things. "How is it that Thou, being a Jew, askest drink of me, which am a woman of Samaria? for the Jews have no dealings with the Samaritans." "Thou, being a Jew, . . . a woman of Samaria"—both titles were absurdly insufficient. In the sight of God the woman is representative of the whole world—Jesus Christ is Almighty God Incarnate.

"If thou knewest the gift of God, . . . He would have given thee living water." The Gift of God is the Son of God; the gift from the Gift of God is the Holy Spirit. Jesus did not talk about "the gift of God" to the Master of Israel; to him He talked about the need to be born again; He talked about the gift of God to a poor, ignorant, sinful woman. To her He did not say, "Ye must be born again"; He spoke of a gift which would regenerate her, i.e., become in her "a well of water springing up into everlasting life." Our Lord gave the exposition of His salvation, not to Nicodemus, a man of sterling character, but to a sinful woman, and she understood without knowing that she did. She was plainly confused, and yet she trusted Him and asked for the gift, "Sir, give me this water. . . ." Instantly reproof followed on her request (John 4:16–18). That is always the method of the Holy Spirit; we usurp the place of the Holy Spirit when we try to convict a man of sin first.

Our Lord never talked in stages of experience, that is, He does not talk to our heads, He instructs us in our relationship to Himself. Here, He is leading a woman into the grace of God, the overflowing favour of God, it is so overflowing that we trample it under foot; it seems so humble and gentle that we ignore it. Jesus is dealing with the grace of God towards sinners, and the characteristic of the grace of God is that it wells up into everlasting life, "a fountain of living water—not merely a clean heart, but a full one, being kept clean.

THE DOCTRINE OF THE HOLY SPIRIT—II
The Bounty of Destitution
John 7:37–39

Generally speaking, Our Lord does not deal with the experimental stages of salvation, He deals with the great revelation facts; the Holy Spirit expounds the experimental stages. Our Lord makes no divisions such as conversion, regeneration, sanctification, He presents the truth in nugget form and the apostles beat out the nuggets into negotiable gold, it is in their writings that we have the stages of experience worked out. Always view the Epistles as the posthumous work of the ascended Christ; don't say, "That is only what Paul says." In the Epistles we have not got Paul's ideas or Peter's ideas; we have the ideas of the Holy Ghost, and the "pens" happen to be Paul or Peter or John. "... holy men of God spake as they were moved by the Holy Ghost" (2 Peter 1:21).

1. Christ's Infinite Patience and Human Destitution

In the last day, that great day of the feast, Jesus stood and cried, saying, If any man thirst, let him come unto Me, and drink. (John 7:37)

Our Lord begins where we would never begin, at the point of human destitution. The greatest blessing a man ever gets from God is the realisation that if he is going to enter into His Kingdom it must be through the door of destitution. Naturally we do not want to begin there, that is why the appeal of Jesus is of no use until we come face to face with realities; then the only One worth listening to is the Lord. We learn to welcome the patience of Jesus only when we get to the point of human destitution. It is not that God *will not* do anything for us until we get there, but that He *cannot*. God can do nothing for me if I am sufficient for myself. When we come to the place of destitution spiritually we find the Lord waiting, and saying, "If any man thirst, let him come unto Me, and drink." There are hundreds at the place of destitution and they don't know what they want. If I have been obeying the command of Jesus to "go . . . and make disciples" (RV), I know what they want; they want Him. We are so interested in our own spiritual riches that souls that are white unto harvest are all around us and we don't reap one for Him.

Some men enter the Kingdom of heaven through crushing, tragic, overwhelming conviction of sin, but they are not the greatest number; the greatest number enter the Kingdom along this line of spiritual destitution—no power to lay hold of God, no power to do what I ought to do, utterly poverty-stricken. Then, says Jesus, blessed are you, because you have come to the place where you can receive the gift of the Holy Spirit. We are told by some that it is foolish to tell people to ask for the Holy Spirit because this is the dispensation of the Holy Spirit. Thank God it is! God's mighty Spirit is with all men, He impinges on their lives at all points and in unexpected ways, but the great need is to receive the Holy Spirit. There stands the promise for every one who will put it to the test: "If ye then, being evil, know how to give good gifts unto your children: how much more shall your heavenly Father give the Holy Spirit to them that ask Him?" The bedrock in Jesus Christ's Kingdom is poverty, not possession; not decisions for Christ, but a sense of absolute futility—"I can't begin to do it." That is the entrance; and it does take us a long while to believe we are poor. It is at the point of destitution that the bounty of God can be given.

2. Christ's Infinite Promise and Human Dependence

He that believeth on Me, as the Scripture hath said, out of [him] shall flow rivers of living water. (John 7:38)

To the woman of Samaria, Jesus talked of the benefits to the individual personal life of the living water—"the water that I shall give him shall become [RV] in him a well of water springing up into eternal life" (4:14). Here, He is talking not of the benefits to the individual life at all, but of the rivers of living water that will flow out of the individual life. Jesus did not say, "He that believeth on Me, shall experience the fulness of the blessing of God"; but, "he that believeth on Me, out of him shall escape everything he receives." It is a picture of the unfathomable, incalculable benediction which will flow from the one great sovereign source, belief in Jesus. We have nothing to do with the outflow; we have to see to it that we are destitute enough of spiritual independence to be filled with the Holy Ghost and then pay attention to the Source, Our Lord Himself. You can never measure what God will do through you if you are rightly related to Jesus. The parenthesis in 7:39 does not apply to us: the Holy Ghost *has been* given; Jesus *is* glorified; the rivers of living water are there, and, unspeakable wonder! the sacrament may flow through our lives too. All that the one out of whom the rivers of living water are flowing is conscious of is belief in Jesus and maintaining a right relationship to Him; then day by day God is pouring the rivers of living water through you, and it is of His mercy He does not let you know it.

3. Christ's Infinite Power and Human Devotion

But this spake He of the Spirit, which they that believe in Him should receive: for the Holy Ghost was not yet given; because that Jesus was not yet glorified. (John 7:39)

The abiding vital meaning of Pentecost is not that "there were added unto them about three thousand souls"; what happened at Pentecost was that Our Lord was glorified, and that He shed forth from above the Holy Ghost in the plenitude of His power. "Therefore being by the right hand of God exalted, and having received of the Father the promise of the Holy Ghost, He hath shed forth this, which ye now see and hear" (Acts 2:33). The gift of the Holy Spirit is the impartation of a personal Spirit that blends the historic Son of God and the individual believer into

one, and the characteristic of the life is devotion to God, so much so that you don't even know you are devoted to Him until a crisis comes. When you have become united to Jesus it is impossible to talk about your experiences or to pray for yourself because you have been brought into a oneness with Him even as He was one with the Father. The "Higher Christian Life"[6] type of teaching is apt to lead us not to worshipping God and to being devoted to Jesus, but merely to pietistic experiences. The snare of experiences is that we keep coming back to the shore when God wants to get us out into the deeps. The one great thing about the salvation of Jesus is that the more you experience it the less you know what you experience; it is only in the initial stages that you know what you experience. The danger is lest we mistake the shores of our experience for the ocean. The experimental aspect of the baptism of the Holy Ghost is not defined by the historic Pentecost, but by Our Lord's words in Acts 1:8—"But ye shall receive power, after that the Holy Ghost is come upon you: and ye shall be *witnesses unto Me.*" The spirit that comes in is not that of doing anything for Jesus, but of being a perfect delight to Him.

THE DOCTRINE OF THE HOLY SPIRIT—III
The Greatest Day Yet

And when the day of Pentecost was now come [was being fulfilled, mg]. . . . Acts 2:1 (RV)

What an unspeakably wonderful day the Day of Pentecost was! There is only one Bethlehem, one Calvary, one Pentecost; these are the landmarks of Time and Eternity, everything and everyone is judged by them.

Beware of thinking of Pentecost in the light of personal experience only. The descent of the Holy Ghost can never be experimental, it is historical. The reception of the Holy Ghost into our hearts is experimental. Those who insist on the experimental line are in danger of forgetting the revelation and of putting all the emphasis on experience, while those who emphasise the revelation are in danger of forgetting the practical experience. In the New Testament the two are one; the experimental must be based on and regulated by the revelation. We imagine that we have the monopoly of the teaching about the Holy Spirit when we deal with His work in individual lives, viz., His power to transform men on the inside—the

most important phase to us, but in God's Book the tiniest phase of the work of the mighty Spirit of God.

1. The Accomplishment of the Promise of the Son *(John 14:26; 15:16; 16:7–15; cf. Matthew 3:11)*

These verses are the testimony of Jesus to the Holy Ghost, whom He calls "the Comforter," "the Paraclete." Our Lord told His disciples that it was expedient for them that He should go away because the Paraclete would not come until His work was completed. ". . . if I go, I will send Him unto you" (RV). We know the Holy Spirit first of all through the testimony of Jesus to Him, and then through the conscious enjoyment of His indwelling presence—"for He abideth with you, and shall be in you" (RV).

John 20:22 (". . . He breathed on them, and saith unto them, Receive ye the Holy Ghost.") and Acts 2:33 ("Being therefore by the right hand of God exalted, and having received of the Father the promise of the Holy

---

6. The Higher Christian Life emphasized sanctification and personal holiness.

Ghost, He hath poured forth this, which ye see and hear," RV) do not refer to the same thing. When Jesus breathed on the disciples what they received was the quickening of new life from the Risen Lord: Pentecost stands for something unrepeatable in the history of the world, viz., the personal descent of the Paraclete. The Holy Ghost came into this world on the Day of Pentecost, and He has been here ever since. He is here, but indiscernible, as Jesus was saying to the few who had the revelation that He was God Incarnate. Have we received the revelation of who the Holy Ghost is?

"Howbeit when He, the Spirit of truth is come, . . . He shall glorify Me." We lose the marvel of the indwelling of the Holy Spirit by thinking of Him as some power that does things. The most rarely recognised aspect of the Holy Spirit's work is that He causes us to do honour to Our Lord. The human spirit uninspired by the Holy Spirit only honours Jesus if He *does* things. It is easier to dishonour Jesus than we are apt to think because He never insists on being honoured. The Holy Ghost is the One who honours Jesus, and therein lies the essential necessity of receiving Him. "He shall glorify *Me,*" said Jesus. The Holy Spirit does not glorify Christ-likeness, because Christ-likeness can be imitated; He glorifies Christ. It is impossible to imitate Jesus Christ.

2. The Accomplishment of the Promise of the Father *(Luke 24:49; Acts 1:8)*
And behold, I send forth the promise of My Father upon you. (RV)

Do you say "I am waiting for my Pentecost"? Who told you to wait? "Oh, I am waiting as the disciples did in the upper room." Not all the waiting on earth will ever gain you the baptism with the Holy Ghost. The baptism with the Holy Ghost is the infallible sign that Jesus has ascended to the right hand of God and has received of the Father the promise of the Holy Ghost. We too often divorce what the New Testament never divorces: the baptism with the Holy Ghost is not an experience apart from Christ, it is the evidence that He has ascended. It is not the baptism with the Holy Ghost that changes men, it is the power of the ascended Christ coming into men's lives by the Holy Ghost that changes them.

". . . but tarry ye in the city, until ye be clothed with power from on high" (RV). "Power from on high"—the words have a fascinating sound in the ears of men; but this power is not a magical power, not the power to work miracles; it is the power that transforms character, that sanctifies faculties. "But ye shall receive power, when the Holy Ghost is come upon you" (RV), said Jesus to the disciples, and they did—the power that made them like their Lord. (Acts 4:13) It is easy to have the idea that we receive the Holy Spirit as a sort of magical power all to ourselves; the reception of the Holy Spirit is for the purpose of quickening us into identification with Our Lord. We live in utter unadulterated loyalty to the Son of God by reason of the fact that we have received His testimony regarding the Holy Ghost and have received Him into our hearts. People come piously together and ask God to baptise them with the Holy Ghost, but they forget that the first thing the Holy Ghost does is to illuminate the Cross of Christ. The emphasis in the New Testament is always on the Cross. The Cross is the secret of the heart of God, the secret of the Person of the Son of God, the secret of the Holy Ghost's work. It is the Cross alone that made it possible for God to give us the gift of eternal life, and to usher in the great era in which we live—the dispensation of the Holy Ghost.

". . . and ye shall be My witnesses" (RV). The historic Pentecost made these men the incarnation of the Holy Ghost. The apostles became written epistles, i.e., the expression of what they preached. When a man experiences salvation the note of testimony is what Jesus has done for him; when he is baptised with the Holy Ghost he becomes a witness, which means much more than a testifier to blessings received. A witness means that just as Jesus was made broken bread and poured-out wine for our salvation, so we are to be broken bread and poured-out wine in sacrificial service. The baptism with the Holy Ghost is Jesus putting the final seal on His work in you, His seal on your regenerated and entirely sanctified soul, and is your inauguration into service for Him. The Holy Spirit always works through human instrumentality, and there is never any possibility of pride when the Holy Spirit uses us. We are empowered into union with Christ by the Holy Ghost.

THE DOCTRINE OF THE HOLY SPIRIT—IV
The Spirit's Cathedral
Ephesians 2:19–22

1. The Habitation of the Holy Ghost in the Mortal Christian

What? Know ye not that your body is the temple of the Holy Ghost. . . ? (1 Corinthians 6:19)

It is one thing to have participated in regeneration and sanctification and quite another thing to enjoy the knowledge that your body is "the temple of the Holy Ghost." That is not an experience, it is a revelation, and a revelation which takes some believing, and then some obeying. Many even in the experience of entire sanctification are ignorant what the Apostle Paul is talking about. As saints our brains ought to be used to systematise and make our own the great revelations given in God's word regarding His purpose for us. People say, "I have received the Holy Spirit, therefore everything I want to do is inspired by Him." By no means; I have to see that I instruct myself regarding these revelations which are only interpreted to me by the Holy Ghost, never by my natural wisdom. There are some saints who are ideally actual, i.e., instructed as well as sanctified and living in unsullied communion with God, and there are others who are like Ephraim, "a cake not turned." Once let it dawn on your mind that your body is the temple of the Holy Ghost and instantly the impossible becomes possible; the things you used to pray about, you no longer pray about, but *do*. As in the natural world, so in the spiritual, knowledge is power. All we need to *experience* is that we have "passed out of death into life" (RV): what we need to *know* takes all Time and Eternity. "And this is life eternal, that they might know Thee the only true God . . ." (John 17:3). Begin to know Him now, and finish never!

"*. . . in whom ye also are builded together for an habitation of God through the Spirit" (Ephesians 2:22).* The conception in these verses is wonderful in its illuminating power, viz. God is building us for Himself. He does not explain why He takes us certain ways, but this passage explains it: He is building a habitation for Himself.

I am his house—for him to go in and out.
He builds me now—and if I cannot see
At any time what he is doing with me,
'Tis that he makes the house for me too grand.

George MacDonald

2. The Habitation of the Holy Ghost in the Mystic Christ *(1 Corinthians 12:13–27)*

For by one Spirit are we all baptized into one body. . . . (1 Corinthians 12:13)

God is the Architect of the human body and He is also the Architect of the Body of Christ. There are two Bodies of Christ: the Historic Body and the Mystical Body. The historic Jesus was the habitation of the Holy Ghost (*see* Luke 3:22; John 1:32–33), and the Mystic Christ, i.e., the Body of Christ composed of those who have experienced regeneration and sanctification, is likewise the habitation of the Holy Ghost. When we are baptised with the Holy Ghost we are no longer isolated believers but part of the Mystical Body of Christ. Beware of attempting to live a holy life alone, it is impossible. Paul continually insists on the "together" aspect—"God . . . hath quickened us *together*, . . . and hath raised us up *together*, and made us sit *together* . . ." (Ephesians 2:4–6). The "together" aspect is always the work of the Holy Ghost.

After the Resurrection we read that Our Lord breathed on the disciples and said, "Receive ye the Holy Ghost": i.e., He imparted to them the Holy Ghost who quickened them. On the Day of Pentecost we read that "there appeared unto them tongues distributing themselves [mg], like as of fire" (RV)—and the disciples were baptised by the personal Holy Ghost: the quickening became an equipment. "But ye shall receive power, after that the Holy Ghost is come upon you" (Acts 1:8). The baptism of the Holy Ghost is the complete uniting of the quickened believer with Christ Himself.

"For by one Spirit are we all baptized into one body." The baptism with the Holy Ghost is not only a personal experience, it is an experience which makes individual Christians one in the Lord. The only way saints can meet together as one is through the baptism of the Holy Ghost, not through external organisations. The end of all divisions in work for God is when He changes fever into white-heated fervour. Oh, the foolish fever there is these days! Organising this, organising that; a fever of intense activity for God. What is wanted is the baptism with the Holy Ghost which will mean Our Lord's prayer in John 17 is answered—"that they all may be one; as Thou, Father, art in Me, and I in Thee, that they also may be one in us" (John 17:21).

3. The Habitation of the Holy Ghost in the Militant Church

. . . and gave Him to be the head over all things to the church, which is His body. (Ephesians 1:22)

The habitation of the Holy Ghost in the Church is not yet mature, it is easy to despise or ignore it. "The habitation of God through the Spirit" refers to the Christian community as it is in this dispensation, and it is an amazing mix-up! But Christ loves the Church so patiently that He will cleanse it from every blemish, and "present it to Himself a glorious church, not having spot, or wrinkle, or any such thing . . ." (Ephesians 5:27).

The different offices of the Church are ordained of God and are based, not on the natural gifts of man, but on the spiritual gifts which Christ gave after He ascended ". . . and He gave some, apostles; and some, prophets; and some, evangelists; and some, pastors and teachers . . . for the *edifying* [*building up*, RV] of the body of Christ" (Ephesians 4:11–12); consequently the only sign that a particular gift comes from the risen Christ is that it edifies the Church. Nothing else is of any account, no flights of imagination, no spiritual fancies, only one thing is of account, viz., the building up of men and women in the knowledge of the Lord. One essential difference between before Pentecost and after Pentecost is that from God's standpoint there are no great men after Pentecost. We make great men and women, God does not. No one is called now to be an isolated lonely prophet; the prophets are a figure of the whole Christian Church which is to be isolated collectively from the world.

There is a time coming when this earth will be the habitation of God, at present it is usurped by the world systems of men; when these disappear, then God's "new heaven and new earth" will emerge (Revelation 21:1).

MAY 27, 1917, ZEITOUN, SUNDAY MORNING SERVICE

THE GLORY OF THE LORD'S DISCIPLES
Acts 1:7–8

1. The Passing of Intellectual Christianity

"It is not for you to know . . ."

Intellect is never first in spiritual life. We are not born again by thinking about it, we are born again by the power of God. Intellect comes second both in nature and in grace. The things we can express intellectually are the things that are old in our experience; the things that are recent and make us what we are, we cannot define. People say, "You must believe certain things before you can be a Christian." It is impossible. A man's beliefs are the effect of his being a Christian, not the cause of it. The evangelism which bases itself simply on justification by faith produces a hard type of mind, and when it becomes aggressive it produces the "soul-saving" type. It is impossible to locate the "soul-saving" idea in the New Testament. The glory of the Lord's disciples is not the saving of souls; but the "soul of salvation" expressed in personal lives. It is God's work to save souls: "Go ye therefore, and make disciples" (Matthew 28:19 RV). Have we been doing it? The New Testament emphasis is on living justly on the basis of salvation, i.e., expressing in our individual lives the things we believe.

2. The Power of Incarnate Christianity

But ye shall receive power, when the Holy Ghost is come upon you: and ye shall be My witnesses. (RV)

In the New Testament the emphasis is not on believing, but on receiving. The word "believe" means to commit—a commitment in order to receive. Have I ever received anything at all from God? The bedrock of Christianity is not decision for Christ, for a man who decides banks on his decision, not on God. It is the inability to decide—"I have no power to get hold of God, no power to be what I know He wants me to be." Then, says Jesus, "Blessed are you." "Blessed are the poor in spirit: for theirs is the kingdom of heaven."

"and ye shall be My witnesses"—not witnesses of what Jesus can do or of His gospel, but witnesses unto Him, that is, He is perfectly satisfied with us wherever we are. The baptism of the Holy Ghost does not mean signs and wonders, but something remarkably other—a life transfigured by the indwelling of the Holy Spirit and the realisation of the Redemption in personal experience. (See Acts 4:13; Galatians 4:19.) Historically, the baptism of the Holy Ghost added nothing to the apostles' doctrine, it made them the incarnation of what they preached. The great idea is not that we are at work for God, but that He is at work in us; not that we are devoted to a cause and doing aggressive work for God, but that He is working out a strong family likeness to His Son in us. "My witnesses"—the witness may or may not lead to martyrdom, but the indwelling of the Holy Ghost in us and the baptism of the Holy Ghost upon us, makes an

expression of the life of Jesus that perfectly satisfies Him wherever we are.

3. The Programme of Identified Christianity
... both in Jerusalem, and in all Judea and Samaria, and unto the uttermost part of the earth. (RV)

God does the arranging of our programme. At certain stages of spiritual experience we feel we could do a lot if we could arrange the scene of our own martyrdom, but the Spirit of God reminds us that we do not choose the place of our offering (Deuteronomy 12:13–14). God has the setting of the saint's life. Everyone who is born from above (RV mg) wants to be a missionary, it is the very nature of the Spirit they receive, viz., the Spirit of Jesus, and the Spirit of Jesus is expressed in John 3:16, "God so loved the world. . . ." God keeps open house for the universe. "Lovest thou Me. . . ?" said Jesus, "Feed My lambs." We prefer to build up converts to our own point of view. Are we prepared to be the disciples of the Lord Jesus in whom the glory of God is manifested? Can God see the manifestation of His Son's life in us? "Every one therefore who shall confess Me before men . . ." (RV). It is easy to be priggish and profess, but it takes the indwelling of the Holy Spirit to so identify us with Jesus Christ that when we are put in a corner we confess Him, not denounce others. "No, I cannot take part in what you are doing because it would imperil my relationship to Jesus Christ." We are afraid of being "speckled birds"[7] in the company we belong to. Jesus says, "Don't be ashamed to confess Me."

"But ye shall be baptized with the Holy Ghost . . ." (Acts 1:5). Why do we want to be baptised with the Holy Ghost? All depends on that "why." If we want to be baptised with the Holy Ghost that we may be of use, it is all up; or because we want peace and joy and deliverance from sin, it is all up. "He shall baptize you with the Holy Ghost," not for anything for ourselves at all, but that we may be witnesses unto Him. God will never answer the prayer to be baptised with the Holy Ghost for any other reason than to make us witnesses to Jesus. To be consciously desirous of anything but that one thing is to be off the main track. The Holy Ghost is transparent honesty. When we pray, "Oh Lord, baptise me with the Holy Ghost whatever it means," God will give us a glimpse of our self-interest and self-seeking until we are willing for everything to go and there is nothing left but Himself. As long as there is self-interest and self-seeking, something has to go. God is amazingly patient. The perplexity is not because of the hardness of the way, but the unwilling pride of sin, the stubborn yielding bit by bit, when it might be done any second. The acceptance of the Divine nature involves in it obedience to the Divine precepts. The commands of God are enablings. God banks entirely on His own Spirit, and when we attempt, His ability is granted immediately. We have a great deal more power than we know, and as we do the overcoming we find He is there all the time until it becomes the habit of our life.

The baptism with the Holy Ghost is the great sovereign work of the personal Holy Ghost; entire sanctification is our personal experience of it.

THE BEST IS YET TO BE
John 4

"The best is yet to be" is really true from Jesus Christ's standpoint. There is nothing noble the human mind has ever hoped for or dreamed of that will not be fulfilled, and a great deal more.

1. In Emancipating Vision
But this is that which was spoken by the prophet Joel; and it shall come to pass in the last days, saith God, I will pour out of My Spirit upon all flesh; and your sons and daughters shall prophesy, and your young men shall see visions, and your old men shall dream dreams: and on My servants and on My handmaidens I will pour

out in those days of My Spirit; and they shall prophesy. (Acts 2:16–18)

The vision of the agnostic, the socialist, the imperialist, or the Christian is the same; they all see the thing that is right—a time of peace on earth, a state of goodwill and liberty at present inconceivable. There is nothing wrong with the vision, and there is no difference in the vision, because its source is the Spirit of God. The thing to be criticised is not the vision, but the way in which the vision is to be realised. "Your sons and daughters" refers to the men and women who have no concern about the redemptive point of

---

7. speckled bird: a person who stands out as abnormal, odd, or eccentric

view. The Spirit of God sways men who do not know Him, and they talk God's mind without a knowledge of Him personally. "My servants and My handmaidens" are those who not only see the vision but have become personally related to Jesus Christ.

2. In Haphazard Ways

And He must needs go through Samaria. (John 4:4)

One great thing to notice is that God's order comes to us in the haphazard. We try to plan our ways and work things out for ourselves, but they go wrong because there are more facts than we know; whereas if we just go on with the days as they come, we find that God's order comes to us in that apparently haphazard way. The man who does not know God depends entirely on his own wits and forecasting. If instead of arranging our own programmes we will trust to the wisdom of God and concentrate all our efforts on the duty that lies nearest, we shall find that we meet God in that way and in no other. When we become "amateur providences" and arrange times and meetings, we may cause certain things to happen, but we very rarely meet God in that way; we meet Him most effectively as we go on in the ordinary ways. Where you look for God, He does not appear; where you do not look for Him, there He is—a trick of the weather, a letter, and suddenly you are face to face with the best thing you ever met. This comes out all through the life of Jesus Christ; it was the most natural thing for Him to go through Samaria.

"And we know that to them that love God all things work together for good, even to them that are called according to His purpose" (Romans 8:28 RV). It is not faith to believe that God is making things work together for good unless we are up against things that are ostensibly working for bad. God's order does come in the haphazard, but only to those who love God; the only way in which God's order is recognised in our lives is by being what Jesus calls "born from above" (RV mg). God's order comes to us in the ordinary haphazard circumstances of life, and when we are in touch with Him the sacrament of His presence comes in the common elements of Nature and ordinary people. The real meaning of the word "sacrament" is that the Presence of God comes through the common elements of the bread and the wine. If you are of a religious nature you will be inclined to put store on the symbol, but beware lest you put the symbol in the place of the thing symbolised; it is easy to do it, but once you mistake the symbol for what it symbolises, you are off the track. "Consider the lilies of the field," said Jesus; we consider motor-cars and aeroplanes, things full of energy. Jesus never drew His illustrations from these things, but always from His Father's handiwork. A lily grows

where it is put and does not fuss; we are always inclined to say "I would be all right if only I were somewhere else." If our spiritual life does not grow where we are, it will grow nowhere.

3. In Exuberant Vitality

If thou knewest the gift of God, and who it is that saith to thee, Give me to drink; thou wouldest have asked of Him, and He would have given thee living water. (John 4:10)

Jesus Christ never preached down to the level of His audience; He did not rely on human understanding, but on the interpreting power of the Holy Spirit in a human mind. The disciples frequently misunderstood what Our Lord said, but He banked everything on the work of the Holy Spirit. "Howbeit when He, the Spirit of truth, is come, He shall guide you into all the truth" (RV).

Jesus surprised the woman of Samaria by His extraordinary generosity of mind—"How is it that Thou, being a Jew, askest drink of me, which am a woman of Samaria? for the Jews have no dealings with the Samaritans." Our Lord knew who the woman was, but He did not talk with the smile of a superior person, "My poor ignorant woman, when will you understand what I say?" He let her talk about what she knew, and she talked with a growing wonder behind it. The first thing Jesus did was to awaken in her a sense of need of more than she had, and until she got the length of asking—"Sir, give me this water," He did not say a word about her sin. We don't take Jesus Christ's way, our first aim is to convict people of sin; Jesus Christ's aim was to get at them where they lived. No man can stand the revelation of what he really is in God's sight unless he is handled by Jesus Christ first. Jesus Christ takes a *Saviour's* view of what is wrong, not a sentimental view. He gently and firmly handles what is wrong in order to remove it.

"If thou knewest the gift of God, . . . thou wouldest have asked of Him, and He would have given thee living water." Jesus is referring to the gift of the Holy Spirit. Unless I receive a totally new Spirit, all the believing and correct doctrine in the world will never alter me; it is not a question of believing, but of *receiving*. The symbol Jesus uses is that of a well of water, springing up into everlasting life." "Everlasting life" is the gift of God Himself; it springs up and expresses itself in a strong family likeness to Jesus. The great sign that a man has received the Holy Spirit is that he begins to manifest the fruits of the Spirit. Life manifests itself as *life*, not as nervous hysterics. "I am come that they might have life," said Jesus, "and that they might have it more abundantly." This "well of water" is full of the ease and power of God which never exhausts itself, but continually recuperates us as we spend it out.

The message of the Gospel is not that God gives a man a clean heart, but that He gives him a pure heart. Jesus never says, "Decide for Me," but "Come to Me in your absolute emptiness and let Me fill you." Christianity is not a clean heart empty, which means a collapse sooner or later, but a life passionately full of personal devotion to Jesus Christ, and a determined identification with His interests in other men. "For the Father seeketh such to worship Him."

APRIL 8, 1917, ZEITOUN, EASTER SUNDAY, SUNDAY MORNING SERVICE

THE UNTENANTED UNIVERSE OF EASTER

He appeared to me also. 1 Corinthians 15:8 (RV)

Very few of us come to realise what is ours through the resurrected Lord, viz., that we can really draw on Him for body, soul and spirit now. We do not trust in a Christ who died and rose again twenty centuries ago; He must be a present Reality, an efficacious power now. One of the great words of God in our spiritual calendar is NOW. It is not that we gradually get to God, or gradually get away from Him; we are either there now or we are not. We may get into touch with God instanter if we will, not because of our merit, but simply on the ground of the Redemption; and if any man has got out of touch with God in the tiniest degree he can get back now, not presently; not by trying to recall things that will exonerate him for what he has done, but by an unconditional abandon to Jesus Christ, and he will realise the efficacious power of the resurrected Lord *now*.

To use the New Testament as a book of proof is nonsense. If you do not believe that Jesus Christ is the Son of God, the New Testament will not convince you that He is; if you do not believe in the Resurrection, the New Testament will not convince you of it. The New Testament is written for those who do not need convincing. After the Resurrection our Lord appeared to those only who knew Him in the days of His flesh. How many people recognised that the Carpenter of Nazareth was God Incarnate? Very few bothered their heads about Him; He was totally ignorable. The relationship to our Lord is a purely spiritual one, and the Resurrection brought out the personal relationship of each one—of Peter and John, Mary and Thomas (see John 20 and 21); and here the marvellously personal note is brought out—"He appeared to me also" (RV). Our Lord never sent out His disciples to proclaim the Gospel on the ground that He had done something for them, but only on the ground that they had seen Him.:"But go unto My brethren, and say to them . . ." (RV). Mary Magdalene was not sent on the ground that Jesus had cast seven demons out of her, but on the ground of the Resurrection. She knew now who Jesus was; before she only knew what He could do.

1. The Last Word about Myself

and that He appeared to Cephas . . . (1 Corinthians 15:5 RV)

Cephas was the man who but a little while before denied that he knew Jesus; he saw Him on the cross dead, and the last memory in his mind would be, "Yes, and I did not stand by Him, I denied Him with oaths and curses." Think of the agony of Peter's mind, and then think of this—"He appeared to Cephas." Jesus came to His heart-broken disciple after His resurrection, no record is given of what took place; all we know is that Jesus reinstated Peter in public (see John 21:15–17). But read Peter's Epistles, they are full of the kindness of the Good Shepherd to the sheep.

The great essential bedrock of relationship to the resurrected Lord is that we know the last word about ourselves. Do I really know that I am a pauper spiritually? Then Jesus says, "Blessed are you." "Blessed are the poor in spirit: for theirs is the kingdom of heaven." The Easter message is that the Lord "appeared to me also." I know Him personally for myself.

Supposing I have been delivered from sin, would that necessarily assure me that I should know Jesus if I saw Him? Not the tiniest bit. Mary Magdalene had had seven demons cast out of her, but when she saw Jesus after the Resurrection she was blinded by grief and personal sorrow and she mistook Him for the gardener. I, too, may mistake Him for "the gardener." But the Eternal Resurrected Christ may touch me through the gardener. He may touch me through a child, through a flower. If I am in living personal relationship to Jesus the things that make the common affairs of life become conveyors of the real presence of God.

If you have come to the last word about yourself, watch for the Lord; He is there all the time, and He will come to you in some supernatural way. "Lo, I am with you all the days" (RV mg). It is not an effort of faith, but a marvellous realisation.

2. The Least Witness to the Lord

And last of all, as unto one born out of due time, He appeared to me also. (RV).

"To me also"—the most unlikely! It is easy to pretend to be "less than the least" without being it, easy to be false in emotion before God, but Paul is not a pretentious humbug, he is not simply speaking out of the deep modesty of his soul, he is speaking what he believes. One of the greatest revelations is that Jesus does not appear to a man because he deserves it, but out of the generosity of His own heart on the ground of the man's need. Let me recognise I need Him, and He will appear. I believe many a man keeps away from Jesus Christ through a sense of honour—"I don't deny that God can forgive me, but I know what I am, and I don't want to let Him down." Once let that man realise that Christianity is not a decision for Christ, but a complete surrender to let Him take the lordship, and Jesus will appear to him. He will do more, He will put into him a totally new heredity, the heredity that was in Himself. That is the amazement of regeneration. "If ye then, being evil, know how to give good gifts unto your children: how much more shall your heavenly Father give the Holy Spirit to them that ask Him?" (Luke 11:13).

3. The Living Way before the Lord
Thou art the Christ, the Son of the living God. (Matthew 16:16)

It is a marvellous thing to know that Jesus Christ is the Son of God, but a more marvellous thing to know that He is the Son of God in me. "But when it pleased God, who separated me from my mother's womb, and called me by His grace, to reveal His Son in me, that I might preach Him among the heathen; immediately I conferred not with flesh and blood" (Galatians 1:15–16). My relationship to Jesus is not on the ground of Christian evidences, that I can pass an examination on the doctrine of the Person of Christ,

but suddenly by the great surprise of the indwelling Spirit of God I see who Jesus is, the Son of the Living God, absolute Lord and Master. The basis of the Christian life is an inner illumination that reveals to me who Jesus is, and on that revelation and the public confession of it, Jesus says He will build His church (Matthew 16:15–18).

The searching point is—Has Jesus appeared to me also? not simply am I saved and turned into another man, but do I know Him? Is He evidencing His marvellous presence in me? Can I bank on Him not by an effort of faith, but by a real influx of His resurrection life? One of the greatest indications as to the way the Spirit of God deals with us is to notice where we are exhausted without recuperation. When by over-energy on our part, or over-calculation of our own, we undertake more than God has sanctioned, there is the warning note of weariness. If spiritual people would only take heed, they would find God's gentle warning always comes—"Not that way; that must be left alone, this must be given up; this is the course for you."

The Living Way before the Lord is to keep in personal touch with Jesus Christ. Never take Jesus Christ as the Representative of God: He *is* God or there is none. If Jesus Christ is not God manifest in the flesh, we know nothing whatever about God; we are not only agnostic, but hopeless. But if Jesus Christ is what He says He is, then He is God to me.

Christianity is a personal history with Jesus. "and ye shall be My witnesses" (RV). The baptism of the Holy Ghost does not mean that we are put into some great and successful venture for God, but that we are a satisfaction to Jesus wherever we are placed. It is not a question of service done, but that our living relationship to Him is a witness that satisfies Him

UNCENSORED TRUTH

The twilight that I desired hath been turned into trembling unto me. Isaiah 21:4 (RV)

The Bible never deals with the domains our human minds delight to deal with. The Bible deals with heaven and hell, good and bad, God and the devil, right and wrong, salvation and damnation; we like to deal with the things in between. The Bible pays no attention to our susceptibilities. "The twilight that I desired . . ." In the Bible there is no twilight, but intense light and intense darkness.

1. The Desired Neutrality
"He that gathereth not with Me scattereth abroad" (Matthew 12:30). Neutrality in religion is always

cowardice—"I don't want to take sides." God turns the cowardice of a desired neutrality into terror: "The twilight that I desired hath been turned into trembling unto me." Our Lord makes everything depend upon a man's relationship to Himself, not upon a man's goodness or badness. Twilight is a desirable time—not too strong a light and not too dark a dark; details are not too clearly manifested, ugly lines are not visible, everything looks wonderful. We like to get into the sentimental domain of twilight spiritually.

"Little children, let no man deceive you: he that doeth righteousness is righteous, even as He is righteous" (1 John 3:7). The Apostle John won't allow "twilight" in a child of God. There is no such thing as being neutral, we are

either children of God or of the devil; we either love or we hate; the twilight is torn away ruthlessly. We are secretly unrighteous before God, not before men, we do not wish our secret sins dragged into the light of God's countenance; we object to the intense light of dawn, and desire twilight. When God's searching comes it is that kind of unrighteousness that is revealed, and we cannot say a word. We realise we have ignored God and have indulged in unrighteousness before Him.

2. The Sudden Conviction of Nemesis

"He that committeth sin is of the devil; for the devil sinneth from the beginning" (1 John 3:8). Nemesis means retributive justice, something it is impossible to escape. We recoil when we realise the inevitable things in life, and it is the things we call inevitable that make us disbelieve in God. We are not conscious anarchists against God, we worship Him to a certain point, but immediately the Spirit of God begins to point out something in us that is wrong, we are offended (cf. Matthew 11:6; John 6:66).

As long as Jesus Christ will remain the "meek and mild and gentle Jesus" I will listen to Him, but immediately He sets His face against my particular sin, my un-righteousness, my self-indulgence, I am going to have no more of Him; then the nemesis comes, and I realise that I am siding with the forces which are against Jesus Christ. Immediately God touches me or mine, I realise that I have the disposition of the devil in spite of all my religion and morality. There is a disposition in us that does not belong to human nature but to the devil, the spirit of unloving, unrighteous hatred. "Develop your deepest instinct and you will find it to be God"; Jesus says, "For from within, out of the heart of men, proceed . . ." If we live in the twilight we say, "Those things are not in my heart." The right attitude to the truth is, "Lord, Thou knowest"; otherwise we shall find to our cost that what Jesus said about the human heart is true. We are all possible saints or possible devils. "Not as Cain, who was of that wicked one, and slew his brother" (1 John 3:12). The spirit of Cain is jealousy, spite and envy. There is no hatred on earth like the hatred of a middling good man for the good man. The first civilisation was founded by a murderer. There is something worse than war, and that is the average run of commercial business life in piping times of peace; it does not destroy a man's body, but it almost damns his soul, it makes a cultured detester of the one who competes against him.

3. The Secret Condition of the Divine Nature

"In this the children of God are manifest, and the children of the devil" (1 John 3:10). Lovingkindness is the purest, rarest evidence of the indwelling of the Spirit of God—no more neutrality, no more dread of the nemesis, just the Divine nature, beautiful, pleasant beneficence, all summed up in the word "Love." When the love of God is shed abroad in our hearts it means that we identify ourselves with God's interest in other people, and God is interested in some strange people! Are we prepared to waive all our predilections and identify ourselves entirely with God's interests in other people? Is the Divine nature getting its way in us? Our actual conduct among men has to be moulded by the conduct of our Heavenly Father. When we think of the grudge we owe someone, let the Spirit of God bring back to our memory how we have treated God, and then begin to be His children. "He is kind toward the unthankful and evil" (Luke 6:35 RV). That is the actual practical climax of the teaching of the Sermon on the Mount. Never testify with your lips what your life does not back up.

NOVEMBER 19, 1916, ZEITOUN, SUNDAY MORNING SERVICE

THE LORD AS OUR "DEAR DREAD"

Then said Jesus, "It is for judgement that I have come into this world, to make the sightless see, to make the seeing blind." John 9:39 (MOFFATT)

That is one of the stiff things Jesus said. It is either nonsense, or what we believe it to be—the very wisdom of God. There is no contradiction in that verse and John 12:47—"For I came not to judge the world, but to save the world"; Jesus Christ did not come to pronounce judgement, He Himself is the judgement; whenever we come across Him we are judged instantly.

1. In the Unerring Directness of His Presence

One of the most remarkable things about Jesus Christ is that although He was full of love and gentleness, yet in His presence every one not only felt benefited, but ashamed. It is His presence that judges us; we long to meet Him, and yet we dread to. We have all known people like that; to meet them is to feel judged, not by anything they say—we are rarely judged by what people say, but by their character.

(a) The Judgement of His Language

People realised His judgement in His words, not in His pronouncements such as Matthew 23, but in His casual language, judgement came straight home. So with our friends, some casual word, a word not necessarily addressed to us at all, judges us and we feel our meanness,[8] that we have missed the mark. Jesus did not stand as a prophet and utter judgements; wherever He went the unerring directness of His presence located men. We are judged too by children, we often feel ashamed in their presence; they are much more our judges than we theirs, their simplicity and attitude to things illustrates our Lord's judgements.

(b) The Judgement of His Labours

The sense of judgement was brought home in the wonderful things Jesus did. When He told Peter to put out into the deep, and the multitude of fishes was so great that the boats began to sink, "Simon Peter . . . fell down at Jesus' knees, saying, Depart from me; for I am a sinful man, O Lord." What Jesus did judged Peter absolutely. He did not say, "You should have done what I told you without any demur," He was simply ineffably and extraordinarily kind, and that drove the judgement home.

(c) The Judgement of His Looks

It is not sentimental to say that the photograph of some people brings a sense of judgement; in certain moods we feel rebuked when we meet the look direct of someone we love, or look at their photo. If that is true of human beings, what must it have been of the looks of Jesus? "And the Lord turned, and looked upon Peter. . . . And he went out, and wept bitterly" (RV). I do not think there was any rebuke in His look—"How dare you do such a thing," but a look of absolute God-likeness, and it brought the judgement home (cf. Mark 10:21; 3:5).

It is not simply the things Jesus says to us directly, or what He does in the way of judgement particularly; it is Himself entirely, wherever He comes we are judged.

(d) The Judgement of His Life

If you look at a sheep in the summer time you would say it was white, but see it against the background of startling virgin snow and it looks like a blot on the landscape. If we judge ourselves by one another we do not feel condemned (see 2 Corinthians 10:12); but immediately Jesus Christ is in the background—His life, His language, His looks, His labours, we feel judged instantly. "It is for judgement that I have come into this world" (MOFFATT). The judgement that Jesus

Christ's presence brings makes us pronounce judgement on ourselves, we feel a sense of shame, or of missing the mark, and we determine never to do that thing again. If Jesus Christ was only like a man, with a lynx eye for seeing everything that was wrong, we might be defiant. When someone with fiendish penetration unearths all we are, it does not bring judgement home to us, it awakens resentment and we glory in our badness; but when we come across the unerring directness of Jesus Christ's presence we feel as Peter felt—"Depart from me, . . . O Lord." He felt unfit to be anywhere near Jesus.

2. In the Unexpected Discovery of His Presentations

(a) The Blindness of Human Judgement

Jesus said some astounding things. This is one of them—"I have come . . . to make the seeing blind" (MOFFATT). "For man looketh on the outward appearance. . . ." As long as we deal with things theoretically, we think that the best thing to do. I see certain facts in your life, you see certain facts in mine, and we pass judgement on one another. Jesus says that our judgement is blind, it does not *see*.

(b) The Blunders of His Judges

"Who do men say that the Son of man is? And they said, Some say John the Baptist; some, Elijah; and others, Jeremiah, or one of the prophets" (Matthew 16:13–14 RV). "He hath Beelzebub, and by the prince of the devils He casteth out devils" (Mark 3:22). "Behold, a gluttonous man, and a winebibber, a friend of publicans and sinners!" (Luke 7:34). These are some of the blunders of the human judgements of Jesus.

(c) The Astonishment of His Judgements

For instance, take Our Lord's judgement of Peter—"Thou art Simon the son of John: thou shalt be called Cephas (which is by interpretation Peter)" (John 1:42 RV), that is, "*Rock* or *Stone*"(mg). Any ordinary common-sense person would say it was absurd to call Peter a rock, he was the most impulsive, the most unreliable of all the disciples: and yet the judgement of Jesus proved to be correct. Again, Jesus saw Nicodemus alone, and although he was a cowardly disciple, He spoke the most vital truth He ever spoke to him. Again, He talked to a sinful woman about worshipping God and about the gift of the Holy Spirit.

We are apt to think the judgements of Jesus are wrong, but when they come straight home in our personal lives we judge in the same way. At first we are certain that our common-sense is wise, that we see

---

8. mean: ordinary, common, low, or ignoble, rather than cruel or spiteful

and understand; when Jesus comes. He makes that seeing blind The first coming of Jesus into a life brings confusion, not peace (see Matthew 10:34). When we receive the Holy Spirit the immediate manifestation is not peace and joy, but amazement, a sense of division instead of order, because we are being re-related to everything and seeing things differently: we had been seeing in a blind way. Before we received the Holy Spirit we used to have very clear and emphatic judgements, now in certain matters we have not even ordinary common-sense judgement, we seem altogether impoverished. The way Jesus judges makes us know we are blind. We decide what is the most sensible common-sense thing to do, then Jesus comes instantly with His judgement and confuses everything, and in the end He brings out something that proves to be the perfect wisdom of God. The judgements of Jesus are always unexpected; unexpected in every way, e.g., Matthew 25:37–40.

3. In the Unceasing Deliberateness of His Power

It is for judgement that I have come into this world. (MOFFATT

Jesus says the Father "... hath given Him authority to execute judgement also, because He is the Son of man" (John 5:27). The first of His judgements and the last, are Himself—His presence, His words, His labours, His looks, His life; these judge us all through, and it is to be the same in the end. "Judge nothing before the time, until the Lord come." Our Lord is unceasingly deliberate, the beginning and the end of His judgement is the same; He will not pass a hasty judgement on us. When He comes He will judge us straightaway, and we shall accept His judgement.

There is no vindictiveness in Our Lord's judgements; He passes judgement always out of His personal love. To my mind the thought of the last judgement is a superb comfort, because we know who is to be the judge: Jesus is to be the judge. He will not pass a judgement that scathes, we can give ourselves over to Him knowing perfectly well that there are certain things in us which must go, and we are only too willing for them

to go, but they cannot go without our feeling the pain and the shame of ever having held to them.

When we have wronged someone we love, the hard thing is not that he says something against us, but that he does not. That is the way our Lord judges, by His kindness (cf. Luke 15:21–24).

> *No! I dare not raise*
> *One prayer, to look aloft, lest it should gaze*
> *On such forgiveness as would break my heart.*

"... not knowing that the goodness of God leadeth thee to repentance" (Romans 2:4). Some passages in the New Testament are taken to refer to the Second Coming of Our Lord, but their real meaning is His presence (e.g., 1 Thessalonians 2:19; 3:13; 5:23; 1 John 2:28). He may come at any minute into our minds, or into our circumstances, and suddenly we feel a sense of shame. He is a "dear dread," we long to see Him and yet we are afraid to, because we know His presence will bring judgement on the things that are wrong.

"For every one that doeth ill hateth the light, and cometh not to the light, lest his works should be reproved" (John 3:20 RV). You instantly know when you are away from the light by the lust of vindication in yourself—"I know I am right," and you may dispute it right up to the threshold of the Lord's coming, but when He comes, instead of vindicating yourself, you will feel like Peter, "Depart from me, ... O Lord."

"If any man have not the Spirit of Christ, he is none of His" (Romans 8:9). When we have a ban of finality[9] about our views, we do not exhibit the Spirit of Jesus, but the spirit of the Pharisee. We pronounce judgements, not by our character or our goodness, but by the intolerant ban of finality in our views, which awakens resentment and has none of the Spirit of Jesus in it. Jesus never judged like that. It was His presence, His inherent holiness that judged. Whenever we see Him we are judged instantly. We have to practise the presence of Jesus and work on the basis of His disposition. When we have experienced the unfathomable forgiveness of God for all our wrong, we must exhibit that same forgiveness to others.

---

9. ban of finality: the limitation or "curse" of having one's mind made up, unwilling to consider new information

THE MIRACLE OF JOY

Joy is the great note all through the Bible. We have the notion of joy that arises from good spirits or good health, but the miracle of the joy of God has nothing to do with a man's life or his circumstances or the condition he is in. Jesus does not come to a man and say "Cheer up," He plants within a man the miracle of the joy of God's own nature. "Then will I go unto the altar of God, unto God my exceeding joy" (Psalm 43:4). The stronghold of the Christian faith is *the joy of God* not *my joy in God.* It is a great thing for a man to have faith in the joy of God, to know that nothing alters the fact of God's joy. God reigns and rules and rejoices, and His joy is our strength. The miracle of the Christian life is that God can give a man joy in the midst of external misery, a joy which gives him power to work until the misery is removed. Joy is different from happiness, because happiness depends on what happens. There are elements in our circumstances we cannot help, joy is independent of them all.

That My joy might remain in you, and that your joy might be full. (John 15:11)

What was the joy of Jesus? That He did the will of His Father, and He wants that joy to be ours. Have I got the joy of Jesus, not a pumped-up ecstasy? The joy of Jesus is a miracle, it is not the outcome of my doing things or of my being good, but of my receiving the very nature of God. In every phase of human experience apart from Jesus, there is something that hinders our getting full joy. We may have the fulfilment of our ambitions, we may have love and money, yet there is the sense of something unfulfilled, something not finished, not right. A man is only joyful when he fulfils the design of God's creation of him, and that is a joy that can never be quenched.

. . . who for the joy that was set before Him endured the cross, despising the shame. (Hebrews 12:2)

What was the joy set before Jesus? The joy of bringing many *sons* to glory, not saved souls. It cost Jesus the Cross, but He despised the shame of it because of the joy that was set before Him. He had the task of taking the worst piece of broken earthenware and making him into a son of God. If Jesus cannot do that, then He has not succeeded in what He came to do. The badness does not hinder Him, and the goodness does not assist Him.

Ask, and ye shall receive, that your joy may be full. (John 16:24)

"Ask in My Name," says Jesus, i.e., "in My nature." How can I have the nature of Jesus? By being born from above (RV mg), by the Holy Spirit coming into me on the ground of the Redemption and putting into me the disposition of Jesus. It is all done by the miracle of God's grace. "For the Father Himself loveth you," it is the wonder of a complete communion between you and the Father.

There are crushing, unspeakable sorrows in this world. To any man with his eyes open, life is certainly not worth living apart from Jesus Christ. If it is worth living, it is because he is blind (see 2 Corinthians 4:3–4). Am I going to live in a fool's paradise, or let God open my eyes?

The joy of God remained with Jesus, and He said, "I want My joy to be in you." The wonder of communion is that I know and believe that Jesus Christ has redeemed the world; my part is to get men to realise it and then devote themselves to Jesus. Am I willing to forgo every other interest and identify myself with Jesus Christ's interests in other people? ". . . that we may present every man perfect in Christ Jesus." The people who influence us are those who have stood unconsciously for the right thing, they are like the stars and the lilies, and the joy of God flows through them all the time.

"Thou wilt show me the path of life: in Thy presence is fulness of joy; at Thy right hand there are pleasures for evermore"—an eternity of gratitude. Am I grateful to God for showing me the way of life? "I am the Way," not creed, nor church, nor doctrine, but Jesus Christ. God can take any man and put the miracle of His joy into Him, and enable him to manifest it in the actual details of his life.

HIS VOICE

And the sheep follow him: for they know his voice. John 10:4

We do not use our ears to hear in the particular way our Lord means, we use them to listen to what our disposition wishes us to decipher, either from fear or desire, as the case may be. When we desire a thing we shut ourselves off from every other thing and concentrate on our desire, but the hearkening our Lord indicates springs from neither fear nor desire, but from an intense humility. When we are born again we are no longer muddled by idiosyncrasies, and we begin to listen irrespective of our disposition.

1. The Distractions of Individuality
And they heard the voice of the LORD God . . . : and Adam and his wife hid themselves from the presence of the LORD God. (Genesis 3:8)

In this verse the identification of voice with personality is clear. When individuality comes into contact with God's voice, it desires not to hear it. Adam, in taking his right to himself, made individuality lord it over personality: communion with God was lost and he became tyrannical over himself and would allow no intimation from personality. Adam and Eve are not now saying of God's voice, "Cause me to hear it"; they are hiding from His presence in fear. They have taken individuality, which is the God-created husk of personality, and made it god, and when the Creator, who speaks only in the language of personality, came, they were afraid. It is now self-realisation, not God-realisation. Self-realisation is based on individuality which is entrenched in human nature through sin, and it effectually distracts us from wanting to hear God's voice. Anything that makes for the realisation of individual relationships, individual well-being and development—that is the thing we want to hear. When the voice of God comes it disregards all that, and it produces terror. We don't want God to cause us to hear His voice, we want God to establish and deify the voices that characterise our individuality, our notions of what we ought to be. Wherever there is self-realisation, the voice of God is a continual embarrassment. Individuality ignores Jesus Christ; when He speaks our individual concerns make too much noise for us to hear His voice. "He that hath ears to hear, let him hear." Are we distracted from hearing God's voice by any form of individuality? If God says something not in accordance with my individual attitude to things, do I really want to hear His voice? Jesus Christ deals always with our personal relationship to

Him; He totally disregards individuality; it does not come into His calculations and He has no consideration for it, because individuality is simply the husk, personality is the kernel.

2. The Delight of Intimacy
Thou that dwellest in the gardens, thy companions hearken for thy voice: cause me to hear it. (RV)

The companions of God, i.e., the angels and the saints, hear His voice. In God's garden God Himself is the cultivator and the producer, the refiner of its atmosphere and flowers, of its human and animal life, and everything.

(a) The Detachment of Transfiguration
"And this voice we ourselves heard come out of heaven . . ." (2 Peter 1:18 RV). When we are really detached from individuality, detached from every form of self-realisation, we experience something which corresponds to Peter's experience on the Mount, and it is then that God says to us, "This is My beloved Son: hear ye Him" (RV). Not only do we hear God say, "This is My beloved Son: hear ye Him," but we have.

(b) The Devotion of Trustfulness
"And the sheep hear his voice. . . . And the sheep follow him: for they know his voice" (John 10:3–4). Trustfulness is based on confidence in God whose ways I do not understand; if I did, there would be no need for trust. There are many ways of following the Lamb whithersoever He goeth because we know His voice. His voice has no tone of self-realisation in it, nor of sin, but only the tone of the Holy Ghost. His voice is essentially simple; it is "a still small voice," totally unlike any other voice. The Lord is not in the wind, not in the earthquake or in the fire, but only in "a sound of gentle stillness" (RV mg).

If we have had a personal touch from Jesus it manifests itself in *the desire of inspiration.*

(c) The Desire of Inspiration
Our whole life is desirous of saying "Cause me to hear it." We discern not by faith, but by love, by intimacy with God. The Old Testament makes much of faith; the New Testament makes everything of the relationship of love; "Lovest thou Me? . . . Feed My sheep. ". . . the greatest of these is love" (RV). That is why our Lord placed Mary of Bethany's act so high; it was not an act of faith, but of absolute love. The breaking of the alabaster box revealed the unconscious sympathy of her spirit with Jesus Christ.

Have I this delight of intimacy, or am I trying to bend Almighty God to some end of my own? Am I asking Him to make me a particular type of saint? If through my love for Him I am discerning His voice, it is a proof that individuality has been effaced in the oneness of personal relationship. The real enemy to the delight of intimacy with Jesus is not sin, but individual relationships (cf. Luke 14:26). Distraction comes from intimacy with those who are not intimate with Jesus.

We can always know whether we are hearkening to God's voice by whether we have joy or not; if there is no joy, we are not hearkening. Hearkening to the voice of God will produce the joy that Jesus had. ". . . that My joy may be in you, and that your joy may be fulfilled" (RV). A life of intimacy with God is characterised by joy. You cannot counterfeit joy or peace. What is of value to God is what we *are*, not what we affect to be.

Is your life truly "hid with Christ in God"? If it is, your continual request is—"Cause me to hear Thy voice." Can we hear the voice in which there is no self-realisation, no self-interest, no individual prefer-

ence? Spiritual muddle comes because we have other interests and loyalties, and these loyalties break our intimacy with Jesus Christ. When there is the clash of self-realisation, and individual preferences come in and compete, we have to put them on one side and remain loyal to our Lord and to nothing and no one else.

There is darkness which comes from excess of light as well as darkness which is caused by sin. There are times when it is dark with inarticulateness; there is no speech, no understanding, no guide, because you are in the centre of the light. Stedfastly endure the trial and you will get direction from it. "What I tell you in the darkness, that speak ye in the light" (RV). Darkness is the time to listen, not to speak; if you do speak, you will speak in the wrong mood; you will be inclined to criticise God's providential arrangements for other lives and to tell Him He has no business to allow these things. As long as you are in the dark you do not know what God is doing; immediately you get into the light, you discover it. "Because thou hast kept the word of My patience . . ." The test always comes along the line of patience.

FEBRUARY 25, 1917, ZEITOUN, SUNDAY MORNING SERVICE

THE DOCTRINE OF THE GREAT HOUR

When it was yet dark . . . John 20:1

There is twilight before night, and an infinitely deeper dark before dawn; but there are hours in spiritual experience darker than either of these, when the new day looks like disaster, and light and illumination have not yet come. There is no possible progress in personal life or national life without cataclysms, big crises, breaks. In our ordinary life we have the idea that things should gradually progress, but there comes a time when there is a tumble-up, a mixture of God and man and fiends, of crime and abomination, and all our idea of steady progress is done for, although there may be progress in individual lives. In the Bible there is the same idea. For instance, take what our Lord says about new birth—"Verily, verily, I say unto thee, Except a man be born again, he cannot see the kingdom of God" (John 3:3). Some teachers make new birth a simple and natural thing, they say it is necessary, but a necessity along the line of natural development. When Jesus Christ talks about it He implies that the need to be born again is an indication of something radically wrong—"Marvel not that I said unto thee, Ye must be born again." It is a crisis.

We like to talk about the light of God coming like the dawn, but it never does to begin with, it comes in a lightning flash, in terrific upheaval. Things do not go unless they are started, and the start of everything in history and in men's souls proves that the basis of things is not rational but tragic; consequently there must be a crisis.

1. The Dark of the Darkest Dawn
The first day of the week cometh Mary Magdalene early, when it was yet dark. . . . (John 20:1)

Can you imagine anything more completely dark than that? Mary Magdalene had had a wonderful history with Jesus Christ, He had absolutely delivered her: "and certain women, which had been healed of evil spirits and infirmities, Mary called Magdalene, out of whom went seven devils, . . ." then she saw Him crucified before her eyes, and now she has come to mourn the biggest disaster of her life. "When it was yet dark"—no light or illumination.

Many may be going through this experience. The testimony they used to give, which was quite genuine, is not working now, they are in other conditions and it is no good; they work for all they are worth, but there is neither life nor power in it. The weakness of many a testimony is that it is based on what the Lord has done—"I have to testify to what God has done for me in order that other people may have the same thing done for them." It sounds all right, but it is not the New Testament order of testimony. Jesus Christ never sent out a disciple on the ground that He had done something for him, but only because he had seen the Lord after He had done something for him (see John 9:35–38). People testify to conversion and to the grace of God in their lives, but plainly they do not know Him. There is no question about His having emancipated them from sin and done a mighty work in them, but the great passion of the life is not Jesus Christ; their personal experience is not marked by Paul's words—"that I may know Him."

2. The Desolation of the Glorious Day
But Mary stood without at the sepulchre weeping. (John 20:11)

Mary was standing weeping in absolute distress; it was the most desolating dawn she had ever known, and yet it was the dawn of the most glorious day she was ever to know. *"And as she wept, she stooped down and looked into the sepulchre. . . ."* It is a good thing to stoop as well as weep; there is more pride in human grief and misery than in joy and health; certain elements in human sorrow are as proud as the devil himself. There are people who indulge in the luxury of misery, they are always talking of the agonising and distressing things—"No one ever suffered as I do; there is a special element in my suffering, it is isolated." At the back of it is terrific pride, it is weeping that will not stoop.

"and seeth two angels in white. . . ." Mary was not at all surprised when through her tears she saw angels; there was only One whom she wanted and that was her Lord and Master. ". . . she turned herself back, and saw Jesus standing, and knew not that it was Jesus." Mary is standing face to face with Jesus Christ and yet she does not know Him; the obsession of her grief makes her mistake Him for the gardener. Mary had had a wonderful history with Jesus, but now in her desolation she does not know Him. We only see along the line of our prejudices until the surgery of events alters our outlook. We may have had an experience of what Jesus Christ can do and yet not have known Him. Suddenly at any turn He may come—"Now I see Him." It takes all time and eternity to know God.

3. The Direction from the Great Divide
Jesus saith unto her, Mary. (John 20:16)

In the midst of her grief, Jesus said one word which had in it all her personal history with Him—"Mary." If Mary had had no past history with Jesus Christ she would not have detected Him when He spoke that word. If you have had a past history with Jesus Christ, if He has delivered and emancipated you, when He speaks, He speaks with the volume of that intimacy of personal acquaintance and you know, not by hearing only, but implicitly all through you—"It is the Lord! No one else could speak like that to me."

"She turned herself, and saith unto Him, Rabboni; which is to say, Master." Mary thought that Our Lord had come back to the old relationship—"He is back again!" But Jesus said, "Touch me not; for I am not yet ascended to My Father"—"You can no longer hold Me under the evidence of your senses, no longer hold Me as a possession of your own individual life as before; the relationship now is one you cannot begin to conceive as yet—a relationship of identity with Me through the indwelling Spirit of God, and I am going to the Father to make that possible." ". . . but go to My brethren, and say unto them, I ascend unto My Father, and your Father; and to My God, and your God."

The direction from "The Great Divide" is that it is connected instantly with the verb "to Go," never to stay and moon. As soon as we see Jesus and perceive who He is by His Spirit, He says "Go"—"Go out into actual life and tell My brethren, not what I have done for you, but that I am risen."

No one can tell another about Jesus until he has seen Him as He really is, the One who imparts His own life, i.e., Holy Spirit, an impartation from the Lord Himself.

Darkness is not synonymous with sin; if there is darkness spiritually it is much more likely to be the shade of God's hand than darkness on account of sin; it may be the threshold of a new revelation coming through a big break in personal experience. Before the dawn there is desolation; but wait, the dawn will merge into glorious day—". . . the light of dawn [mg], that shineth more and more unto the perfect day" (RV). If you are experiencing the darkness of desolation on individual lines, go through with it, and you will find yourself face to face with Jesus Christ as never before. "I am come that they might have life,"—life in which there is no death—"and that they might have it more abundantly."

DESERT DAYS

Beloved, think it not strange concerning the fiery trial which is to try you, as though some strange thing happened unto you. . . . 1 Peter 4:12

We have no faith at all until it is proved, proved through conflict and in no other way. There are things in life equivalent to the desert. This war[10] is a "fiery trial," it has come out against our faith in God's goodness and justice. Are we going to remain steadfast in our faith in God until we see all that contradicts our common sense transfigured into exactly what our faith believes it should be?

1. The Decree of the Desolating Desert

And unto Adam He said, Because thou hast hearkened unto the voice of thy wife, and hast eaten of the tree, of which I commanded thee, saying, Thou shalt not eat of it: cursed is the ground for thy sake; in sorrow shalt thou eat of it all the days of thy life. (Genesis 3:17)

In actual life there is a desolating desert, and it is there by the decree of God; the Bible knows nothing about what we call natural law. Back of the origin of the desert is the decree of God. The desolating desert is not a distress to God, it is completely within His grasp, although not within ours. The Moslems have a fine phrase for the desert—"The Garden of Allah." One characteristic of the desert is its fierce, cruel, unshielding light. "The sun shall not smite thee by day . . ." Another characteristic of the desert is its storms; these are never beneficial, they are of the sirocco order, blighting, fierce and pitiless. Jeremiah describes them—"At that time shall it be said to this people and to Jerusalem, A dry wind of the high places in the wilderness toward the daughter of My people, not to fan, nor to cleanse" (Jeremiah 4:11). The sun as seen in the desert is not a benediction, the storms are not beneficial storms; and night in the desert is a desperate thing. It is all very well to think of the night in our own land, but night in the desert is appalling. Little bits of the desert are fascinating, but the real thing is terrible—"that great and terrible wilderness" (Deuteronomy 1:19).

The characteristics of the desert are the characteristics of God to a man when he tastes life as it is. Ibsen saw very clearly the desolating desert of life, i.e., the terrific penalty of sin, and he also saw God as He appears to a man awakened to the facts of existence. We are apt to say that Ibsen was pessimistic, but every man whose thinking has not been interfered with by his temperament is a pessimist. To think fair and square is not to see goodness and purity everywhere, but to see something that produces despair. When a man sees life as it really is there are only two alternatives—the Cross of Jesus Christ as something to accept, or suicide. We are shielded by a merciful density, by a curious temperament of hopefulness that keeps us blind to the desolating desert.

The reason the desert came is that man ate of the fruit of the tree of knowledge of good and evil. God placed the tree in the garden, but He did not intend that man should eat of its fruit; He intended man to know evil only by contrast with good, as Our Lord did. It is by the decree of God that the man who knows good by contrast with evil shall find life a desolating desert. When the cosmic order of earth and the moral nature of man are in touch with God, the order of the earth is beauty, and the order of human life is love. Immediately a man gets out of touch with God, he finds the basis of things is not beauty and love, but chaos and wrath.

The first Adam, the federal head of the race, swung the race on to the basis of wrath, and Jesus Christ, the Last Adam, swung the human race back on to the basis of love. The terms "in Adam," "in Christ," are not mystical terms, but actual revelations of man's condition. When we are "in Adam" we get down to the desolating desert aspect of life. Take love—the most abiding thing about love is its tragedy; or life, the most desolating thing about life is its climax, death. When we are "in Christ" the whole thing is reversed. We read that "Jesus advanced in wisdom and stature, and in favour with God and men"(RV)—He never ate of the fruit of the tree of good and evil, He knew evil only by contrast with good. When a man is born from above (RV mg) the desolating desert aspect of life goes. There is no sadness now in natural love, it ends nowhere but in the heart of God; "in Christ" life knows no death, it goes on more and more fully. If you want to know God's original design for man, you see it in Jesus Christ; He was easily Master of the life on the earth, in the air and in the sea, not as God, but as Man; it was the human in Jesus that was master.

---

10. This war: World War I (1914–1918).

2. The Devil and the Divine in the Desert

And immediately the Spirit driveth Him into the wilderness. (Mark 1:12)

In the Bible the devil is represented as the antagonist of Deity; Satan represents the self-interest of humanity. Our Lord's words "Get thee hence, Satan" (Matthew 4:10; see also Matthew 16:23), refer to the interests of humanity in conflict with God's interests. In the temptation the devil antagonised the same thing that he antagonised in the first Adam, viz., oneness with God. Our Lord's unvarying answer was, "I came down from heaven, not to do Mine own will, but the will of Him that sent Me"—the very thing the first Adam refused to do. "Man shall not live by bread alone,"said Jesus, "but by every word that proceedeth out of the mouth of God." As long as civilisation prevents us noticing the desert and the basis of wrath, we do not need anything other than bread, and what bread means. The claim of Satan to our Lord was, "You will get your Kingship of men if You give them bread" (see John 6:15). Jesus Christ's first obedience was to the will of His Father, and it is by the obedience of Jesus Christ as Son of Man that the whole human race is swung back again to God. It was there, in the desert, that Our Lord bound the strong man and overcame him. The strong man represents the whole of humanity vested in a personal presence enthroned as God. When the strong man rules, his "goods," i.e. the souls of men, are in peace; but when "a stronger than he" comes, He upsets that rule, and "taketh from him his whole armour wherein he trusted, and divideth his spoils" (Luke 11:22 RV).

Jesus Christ is the One who upsets the humanitarian reign. That is why in certain moods of individual as well as national experience, Jesus Christ is considered the enemy of mankind. "Think not that I am come to send peace on earth: I came not to send peace, but a sword" (Matthew 10:34).

3. The Direction in the Desert *(Luke 3:2; Galatians 1:15–17)*

The word of God came to John in the desert—"The word of God came unto John the son of Zacharias in the wilderness"; and to Paul—"But when it was the good pleasure of God . . . to reveal His Son in me . . . I went away into Arabia" (RV). The nutriment of a man's life comes when he is alone with God; he gets his direction in the desert experiences. The Psalmist says, "Before I was afflicted I went astray." King Hezekiah came face to face with death and the experience made just that kind of difference to him—"I shall go softly [as in a solemn procession, RV mg] all my years in the bitterness of my soul" (Isaiah 38:15). Men learn in these ways that "man doth not live by bread alone"; there are factors in life which produce terror and distress.

4. The Divine Departure of the Desert *(Isaiah 35:1–2)*

The wilderness and the solitary place shall be glad; and the desert shall rejoice, and blossom as the rose. (Isaiah 35:1 RV)

The Divine recovers the desert for man as a Garden. The sin of man has polluted the material earth and it will have to be disinfected (Isaiah 24:1), and there will be "a new heaven and a new earth." The actual conditions of life will surpass all that Utopian dreamers have ever dreamed. "And death shall be no more; neither shall there be mourning, nor crying, nor pain, any more" (RV)—here-after, without the desert; no tears, no darkness, no sinful defect, no haunting thought, no sickness, no sorrow. *It has not entered into the heart of man to conceive "the things which God hath prepared for them that love Him."*

NOVEMBER 6, 1916, ZEITOUN, STUDY HUT

IS HUMAN SACRIFICE REDEMPTIVE?

Greater love hath no man than this, that a man lay down his life for his friends. John 15:13

But God commendeth His own love toward us, in that, while we were yet sinners, Christ died for us. Romans 5:8 (RV)

There is a vast difference between human sacrifice and Divine sacrifice. John 15:13 refers to human sacrifice, the highest height to which a human being can get; Romans 5:8 refers to Divine sacrifice, that which God has done for the human race and which no man can ever do. "Greater love hath no man than this, that a man lay down his life for his friends." It has nothing to do with a man's religion; a pagan will lay down his life for his friend, so will an atheist, and so will a Christian; it has to do with the great stuff human nature is made of, there is nothing Divine about it. We find men who have been the greatest scamps in civil life doing the most heroic things in war.

The love of God is other than that—God laid down His life for His enemies, a thing no man can do. The fundamental revelation made in the New

Testament is that God redeemed the human race when we were spitting in His face, as it were. We can all be stirred by high, noble, human sacrifice; it is much more thrilling than Calvary. Calvary is an ignoble thing, against all the ideas of human virtue and nobility; it is far more thrilling to talk about men fighting in the trenches. God's love is not in accordance with our human standards in any way.

In the generality of our thinking the Bible does not mean anything to us, other things are of more practical use, and we are apt to discard what the Bible says until we come up against things. The Bible speaks about the Redemption, viz., what God has done for the human race, not about what we can get at by our common sense. The great fundamental revelation regarding the human race is that God has redeemed us. Redemption is finished and complete; but what does it mean in our personal lives? The fact of Redemption amounts to nothing in my actual life unless I get awakened to a sense of need. It is a matter of moonshine[11] to me whether Jesus Christ lived or died until I come up against things—either sin in myself or something that ploughs deeply into me, then I find I have got beyond anything I know, and that is where the revelation of Jesus Christ comes in; if I will commit myself to Him, I am saved, saved into the perfect light and liberty of God on the ground of Redemption.

The Redemption is a revelation, not something we get at by thinking, and unless we grant that Redemption is the basis of human life we will come up against problems for which we can find no way out. I can no more redeem my own soul and put myself right with God than I can get myself upstairs by hanging on to my shoestrings—it is an impossibility; but right at the basis of human life is the Redemption. The Redemption means that God has done His "bit": men are not *going to be* redeemed, they *are* redeemed. "It is finished," said Jesus on the Cross. But the way the Redemption works in my actual life depends on my willing attitude to the revelation.

Every man is redeemed, and the Holy Spirit is here to rouse us up to the fact that we are redeemed. Once that realisation dawns, the sense of gratitude springs up in a man and he becomes of use to God in practical life.

Human sacrifice can never be redemptive. How can a man, noble or ignoble, get me nearer God? He may stir and move me till I say, "That is a magnificent deed," but he tells me no more about God. Many a man without any knowledge of God has laid down his life in the same noble manner that a Christian has done. That is the greatest love of *man*. The love of *God* is that He laid down His life for His enemies in order that He might make the basis of life redemptive. We have to reason on that basis, viz., on what God has done for the human race. Think of the worst man or woman you know; can you say to yourself, with any degree of joyful certainty, "That man, that woman—perfect in Christ Jesus"? You will soon see how much you believe in Christ Jesus and how much in common sense.

The Gospel is not good news to men, but good news about God, viz., that God has accepted the responsibility for creating a race that sinned, and the Cross is the proof that He has done so. The basis of human life is the Redemption, and on that basis God can perform His miracles in any man, i.e., He can put a new disposition into me whereby I can live an entirely new life. Think of the relief that the Gospel brings to a man's mind, and then think of the abortion that is called the Gospel and is preached to men as good news!

The test of our religious faith is not that it does for[12] us, but that it does for the worst blackguard we can think of. If the Redemption cannot get hold of the worst and vilest, then Jesus Christ is a fraud, but if this Book means anything it means that at the wall of the world stands God, and any man driven there by conviction of sin finds the arms of God outstretched to save him. God can forgive a man anything but despair that He can forgive him.

---

11. moonshine: insignificant or meaningless
12. does for: suffices, meets the needs of.

THE LIE IN THE GREATEST FEAR OF LIFE

For He must reign, till He hath put all enemies under His feet. The last enemy that shall be destroyed is death.
1 Corinthians 15:25–26

The greatest fear in life is not personal fear for myself, but fear that after all God will be worsted. We do not state it in that way until we come to one of the rare, lucid moments in our experience. The phrase "He must reign" indicates our greatest fear, viz., the fear that in the end Jesus Christ will not come out triumphant, that evil and wrong will triumph. We reveal our fear by intense assertions that of course He will win through. That is the curious way we are built; we speak as intensely of a position about which we are fearful as we do of a position we are sure of. Whenever this particular fear assails us, we assert most definitely—"Oh, yes, there is no doubt that He will get through," while our real fear is that He will not. We are familiar with it along other lines—in reading a book we turn to the end to see whether the hero gets through. Fears are facts; there is a danger of saying that because a thing is wrong, therefore it does not exist; fear is a genuine thing, there is no courage without fear. The courageous man is the one who overcomes his fear. There are things in personal experience and in national life that make us hold our breath; then in faith we look on to the end.

1. The Fearful Hour

Then said Jesus unto the twelve, Will ye also go away?
(John 6:67)

John describes the disappointment Jesus Christ was to men. The crowd on the outside gathered to Him because He did wonderful things and they would have made Him king (John 6:15), but He disappointed them. "The Jews therefore murmured concerning Him, because He said, I am the bread which came down out of heaven" (John 6:41 RV). Then there was the smaller crowd on the inside who came because they were religious and had the intellect of the time, and they listened, until He said things that offended them—"Many therefore of His disciples, when they heard this, said, This is a hard saying; who can hear it?" (John 6:60 RV). Then there was the little crowd of disciples, and of these we read—"Upon this many of His disciples went back, and walked no more with Him" (John 6:66); and Our Lord forecast the fearful hour of His being left by everybody—left by the crowd, by the Pharisees, and by the disciples, and He turns to the handful left and says, "Will ye also go away?" and Peter replies, in effect, "We have gone too far." The hearts of these disciples must have feared, not for their own sakes, but—"After all, are we mistaken in this Man? We have left our homes and our fishing, we have been thrilled by Him, He has done wonderful things, but will He win through after all?"

The question comes to us personally: "Will ye also go away?" and we say, "I believe Jesus Christ will get through," but at the same time the forces are so awful and so intense that we wonder. At the heart of the fear there is a lie, and the lie comes in because we estimate Jesus Christ in the way we would estimate any other man, viz., by success. It is significant that Jesus Christ told His disciples not to estimate themselves by success (see Luke 10:19–20). According to the ordinary standards of men Our Lord Himself is as a corn of wheat falling into the ground and becoming futile. "Except a corn of wheat fall into the ground and die, it abideth alone; but if it die, it bringeth forth much fruit" (John 12:24). Look at the history of every vigorous movement born spontaneously of the Holy Ghost, there comes a time when its true spiritual power dies, and it dies in correspondence to the success of the organisation. Every denomination or missionary enterprise departs from its true spiritual power when it becomes a successful organisation, because the advocates of the denomination or of the missionary enterprise after a while have to see first of all to the establishment and success of their organisation, while the thing which made them what they are has gone like a corn of wheat into the ground and died. One of the greatest snares of modern evangelism is this apotheosis of commercialism manifested in the soul-saving craze. I do not mean God does not save souls, but I do believe the watchword "A passion for souls" is a snare. The watchword of the saint is "A passion for Christ." The estimate of success has come imperceptibly into Christian enterprise and we say we must go in for winning souls; but we cannot win souls if we cut ourselves off from the source, and the source is belief in Jesus Christ (John 7:37). Immediately we look to the outflow, i.e., the results, we are in danger of becoming specialists of certain aspects of truth, of banking on certain things, either terror or emotionalism or sensational presentations—anything rather than remaining confident that "He must reign." If we stand true to Jesus Christ in the midst of the fearful hour we shall come to see that there is a lie at the heart of the fear which shook us. We are not called to be successful in accordance with ordinary standards, but in accordance with a corn of wheat falling into the ground and dying, becoming in that way what it never could be if it were to abide alone. After the corn is garnered into the granary it has to go through processes before it is ready for eating. It is the "broken-bread" aspect which produces the faithfulness that God looks upon as success; not the fact of the harvest, but that the harvest is being turned into nutritious bread.

2. The Forlorn Hope

And when He rose up from prayer, and was come to His disciples, He found them sleeping for sorrow. (Luke 22:45)

The disciples had given up everything for Jesus; they had followed Him for three years; now He talks to them in a significant way about buying swords (Luke 22:36), and Peter and the other disciples imagine that this is the time when He will break through and introduce His kingdom; and instead of watching and praying, they make up their minds where the struggle is to be. But what happened was the worst they had feared; instead of Jesus Christ showing any fight, He gives Himself up, and the whole thing ends in humiliating insignificance. Peter never dreamt he was going to see Jesus Christ give Himself up meekly to the power of the world, and he was broken-hearted and "followed Him afar off." To call Peter a coward for following Jesus afar off is an indication of how we talk without thinking. Peter and all the disciples were broken-hearted, everything they had hoped for with regard to Jesus Christ had deliberately failed—"We trusted in Him and were perfectly certain He would win through," and now their worst fears were realised. and "they all forsook Him and fled." Many a Christian since the day of Peter has suffered complete heartbreak, not because he fears anything personally, but because it looks as if his Lord is being worsted; the lie at the heart of the fear is almost succeeding.

The presentation of the spiritual aspect of things is that it is a forlorn hope always, and designedly so, in this order of things. We are apt to forget that we must go far enough back to find the basis on which things erect themselves. For instance, if civilised life is right and the best we can know, Christianity is a profound mistake; but if you turn back to the Bible you find that its diagnosis of civilisation is not that it is

the best we know, it is on an entirely wrong basis. Civilised life is based on the *reason* at the heart of things; Jesus Christ's teaching is based on the *tragedy* at the heart of things, and consequently the position of true spiritual life is that of the forlorn hope. It is of the nature of the earth on which we tread—The meek shall inherit *the earth,* not the "world," because the world, according to the Bible, is the system of civilised things that men place on God's earth. In the meantime God's earth is like the earth we are on now; we can do what we like with it, shovel rubbish on it, mine it and turn it into trenches; we can score it, and make it the foundation for the erections of human pride; but Jesus Christ says. "the meek . . . shall inherit *the earth.*" There is a time coming when the earth itself shall be the very garment of God, when the systems of the world and those that represent them shall call on the mountains and the rocks to hide them, but at that time the earth won't shelter them.

3. The Faith That Triumphs

Jesus saith unto him, Thomas, because thou hast seen Me, thou hast believed: blessed are they that have not seen, and yet have believed. (John 20:29)

Thomas was not an intellectual doubter, he was a temperamental doubter; there was not a more loyal disciple than Thomas, he was a loyal, gloomy-hearted man. He had seen Jesus killed; he saw them drive the nails through His hands and His feet, and he says, "Except I shall see . . . , I will not," I dare not, "believe." This is a man with a passionate desire to believe something over which he dare not allow himself to be deceived. Seeing is never believing: we interpret what we see in the light of what we believe. Faith is confidence in God before you see God emerging, therefore the nature of faith is that it must be tried. To say "Oh, yes, I believe God will triumph" may be so much credence smeared over with religious phraseology; but when you are up against things it is quite another matter to say, "I believe God will win through." The trial of our faith gives us a good banking account in the heavenly places, and when the next trial comes our wealth there will tide us over. If we have confidence in God beyond the actual earthly horizons, we shall see the lie at the heart of the fear and our faith will win through in every detail.

DISCOVERY BY DEVOTION

And I set my face unto the Lord God, to seek by prayer and supplications. Daniel 9:3

1. The Determination to Concentrate
And I set my face . . .

We discern spiritual truth not by intellectual curiosity or research, but by entreating the favour of the Lord, that is, by prayer and by no other way, not even by obedience, because obedience is apt to have an idea of merit. If we are not concentrated we affect a great many attitudes; but when we set our faces "unto the Lord God" all affectation is gone—the religious pose, the devout pose, the pious pose, all go instantly when we determine to concentrate; our attention is so concentrated that we have no time to wonder how we look. "This one thing I do. . . ." says Paul; his whole attention was fixed on God. Is my mind fixed entirely on God or on service for God? If I am only fixed on the service of God my attention is not held, I am taken up with affectation; but in a great crisis, as in this of Daniel, there is the determination to concentrate. When I set my face and determine to concentrate I am not devoted to creeds or forms of belief or to any phase of truth, not to prayer or to holiness, or to the spreading of any propaganda, but unto God. We never turn to God unless we are desperate, we turn to common sense, to one another, to helps and means and assistances, but when we do turn to the Lord it is always in desperation (see Psalm 108). The desperation of consecration is reached when we realise our indolence and our reluctance in coming to God.

2. The Desecration of Consecration
unto the Lord God . . .

Belief is not that God can do the thing, but belief *in God.* If I believe in God I pray on the ground of Redemption and things happen; it is not reasonable, it is Redemptive. Where reason says "There is a mountain, it is impossible," I do not argue and say "I believe God can remove it," I do not even see the mountain; I simply set my face unto the Lord God and make my prayer, and the mountain ceases to be (see Matthew 17:20). As long as we reason and argue and say "It is not sensible," we do not turn to the Lord but try to bolster up some conviction of our own.

Through the desperation of consecration we not only reach the limit of reason but we get a line of recognition which is other than reasonable, i.e., we discern Jesus Christ in the most ordinary people and things. "Jesus stood on the shore: but the disciples knew not that it was Jesus." He appeared to be an ordinary fisherman, but John discerned that it was the Lord (John 21:7). When we are concentrated on God we enter on a life of revelation, we begin to penetrate and discover things. "To him that overcometh . . ." Life is given as we overcome—overcome the tendency to indolence, above all the tendency not to do what we know we should, and instantly we get a revelation.

3. The Discipline of Consciousness
to seek by prayer and supplications . . .

It is easy to create a false emotion in prayer, nothing easier than to work ourselves up until we imagine we are really concerned about a thing when we are not because it has never been brought to our mind by the Holy Spirit. That kind of prayer is not natural, we let our emotions carry us away. Prayer is not only to be about big things, but talking to God about everything—"Let your requests be made known." If we try to recall something by our own effort in praying, instantly we get an atmosphere of rebuke about another person. When we concentrate on God that spirit is not present, there is no irrelevant emotion to deflect our attention and we pray about the things the Spirit of God brings most naturally to our minds. "Ye shall ask what ye will. . . ." We do not ask what our will is in, we develop false emotions, consciousnesses that are not really our own. A false emotion is one we have at rare times. What is ours is the circumstances we are in just now, the people we are with; we have to learn to school our emotions into relationship to God in all these things. The seeking by prayer is determined by the circumstances we are in and by the life we habitually live; we have to concentrate on the ordinary obvious things we are in all the time. We cannot talk to God unless we walk with Him when we are not talking. The Son of God revealed in me and the epistle of Christ written in my life day by day will give me an expression before God; if I am not walking with God I have to borrow other people's phrases when I pray. "If any man is in Christ there is a new creation" (RV mg), everything becomes amazingly simple, not easy, but simple with the simplicity of God.

LOSING OURSELVES

He that findeth his life [soul] shall lose it: and he that loseth his life [soul] for My sake shall find it. Matthew 10:39

"We *are* what we are interested in."

"Soul" refers to the way a personal spirit reasons and thinks in a human body. We talk about a man exhibiting "soul" in singing or in painting, that is, he is expressing his personal spirit. "If you are going to be My disciple," says Jesus, "you must lose your soul, i.e., your way of reasoning, and acquire another way." When the Holy Spirit energises my spirit, my way of reasoning begins to alter, and Jesus says unless I am prepared for that, I cannot be His disciple. It takes a long time to acquire a new way of reasoning, the majority of us who are inclined to be earnest Christian people simply deal with the fact of spiritual experience without any spiritual reasoning. We have to acquire the new soul with patience (Luke 21:19).

1. The Undiscovered Territory of Conscious Realisation
He that findeth his life . . .

There is nothing more highly esteemed among men than self-realisation, but Jesus says that "that which is highly esteemed among men is abomination in the sight of God." We are apt to have the notion that all Jesus Christ came to do was to deliver morally corrupt people from their corruption. A man is largely responsible for the corruption of his actual life; Jesus Christ does not deal with my morality or immorality, but with "my right to myself." Whenever our Lord talked about discipleship He always said "IF"—"*If* any man will be My disciple, let him deny himself," not deny himself things as an athlete does, but "let him give up his right to himself to Me." If I am going to know Jesus Christ as Lord and Master I must realise what I have to forgo, viz., the best thing I know, my right to myself. It is easy to say, "Yes, I am delighted to be saved from hell and put right for heaven, but I don't intend to give up my right to myself." Apart from Jesus Christ, conscious self-realisation is the great thing—the desire to develop myself. My natural self may be noble, but it is a moral earthquake to realise that if I pursue the conscious realisation of myself it must end in losing my ideal of life. It is a tremendous revelation when I realise that self-realisation is the very spirit of antichrist. Self-realisation is possible in the spiritual domain as well as the natural. Much of the "Higher Spiritual Life" teaching is simply self-realisation veneered over with Christian terms. For a man to be set on his own salvation, on his own whiteness, to want to be "the one taken," is not Christian. The great characteristic of our Lord's life is not self-realisation, but the realisation of God's purposes.

Self-realisation may keep a man full of rectitude, but it is rectitude built on a basis that ultimately spells ruin, because man is not a promise of what he is going to be, but a magnificent ruin of what human nature once was. If we go on the line of conscious self-realisation, there will be an aftermath of bitterness.

2. The Untraceable Troubles of Consecrated Renunciation
shall lose it: and he that loseth his life . . .

In certain stages of spiritual life God is dealing with us on the death side and we get the morbid conception that everything we have, we must give up—"the everlasting 'No.'" In the Bible the meaning of sacrifice is the deliberate giving of the best I have to God that He may make it His and mine for ever: if I cling to it I lose it, and so does God. We come to our renunciations in the same way that Abraham came to his. God told Abraham to offer up Isaac for a burnt offering, and Abraham interpreted it to mean that he was to kill his son; but on Mount Moriah Abraham lost a wrong tradition about God and got a right insight as to what a burnt offering meant, viz., a *living* sacrifice (Romans 12:1–2). It looks as if we had to give up everything, lose all we have, and instead of Christianity bringing joy and simplicity, it makes us miserable; until suddenly we realise what God's aim is, viz., that we have to take part in our own moral development, and we do this through the sacrifice of the natural to the spiritual by obedience, not denying the natural, but sacrificing it.

Christianity is a personal relationship to Jesus Christ made efficacious by the indwelling Holy Spirit. We take Christianity to be adherence to principles. Conscience is not peculiarly a Christian thing, it is a natural asset, it is the faculty in a man that fits on to the highest he knows. Our convictions and conscientious relationships have continually to be enlarged, and that is where the discipline of spiritual life comes in. A man who is on the grousing line has no brightness or joy, no time for other people, he is taken up with the diseases of his own mind.

3. The Unhindered Triumphs of Christ-Realisation

. . . for My sake shall find it.

The characteristic of Christianity is abandon, not consciously setting myself on my own whiteness; the one thing that matters is, is Jesus Christ getting His way? The Christianity of the New Testament is not individual, it is personal, we are merged into God without losing our identity—"that they may be one, even as We are one." Individuality is the husk of the personal life, it cannot merge; personality always merges.

Am I prepared to lose my soul, lose the miserable self-introspection as to whether I am of any use? I am never of any use so long as I try to be. If I am rightly related to Jesus Christ, He says, Out of you "shall flow rivers of living water." The people who tell are those who don't know they are telling, not the priggish people who worship work.

Am I prepared to go through death to my right to myself, to have "a white funeral"[13] and abandon myself to Jesus Christ—"for My sake"? If I am, I shall find my soul. The Holy Spirit coming into my personal spirit manifests itself in my soul, in the way I reason, consequently all my previous calculations are upset and I begin to see things differently. In the initial stages of discipleship you get "stormy weather," then you lose the nightmare of your own separate individuality and become part of the Personality of Christ, and the thought of yourself never bothers you any more because you are taken up with your relationship to God.

JUNE 24, 1917, ZEITOUN, SUNDAY MORNING SERVICE & DEVOTIONAL HUT

THE IMMENSE ATTENTION OF GOD

And when he opened the seventh seal, there followed a silence in heaven about the space of half an hour. Revelation 8:1 (RV)

If we are ever going to understand the Book of the Revelation we have to remember that it gives the programme of God, not the guess of a man. "Write the things which thou hast seen, and the things which are, and the things which shall be hereafter." The Apostle is writing what the Spirit revealed to him—that is the origin of the Book. Apocalyptic literature is never easy to understand, its language is either a revelation or fantastic nonsense. We study it and worry over it and never begin to make head or tail of it, while obedience will put us on the line of understanding. Spiritual truth is never discerned by intellect, only by moral obedience. God brings His marvels to pass in lives by means of prayer, and the prayers of the saints are part of God's programme.

The presentation of Christianity which is not based on the New Testament produces an abortion—that a man's main aim is to get saved and put right for heaven; New Testament Christianity produces a strong family likeness to Jesus Christ and a man's notions are not centred on himself. The great aim of the Holy Spirit is to get us abandoned to God.

God allows the prayers of the saints, those who have entered into an understanding of His mind and purpose, to be brought to Him. We are busy praying that our particular phase of things may succeed, that men's souls may be saved; but what is meant by "a saved soul" is frequently determined by our doctrine of salvation and not by a personal relationship to Jesus Christ. We are devotees of one tiny phase of what Jesus Christ came to do: He came not only to save men's souls, but to bring "many sons unto glory." We have lost out on that line altogether, we who are the saved souls—where has been the production of disciples? That is not our line, it has no success, it cannot be tabulated. There has been no silence in heaven over our prayers, they have not entered into the programme of God, they have not been based on the Redemption; we have had no concern for the revelation of Jesus Christ, only for a particular phase of our own.

The whole idea of the prayers of the saints is that God's holiness, God's purpose and God's wise ways may be brought about irrespective of who comes or goes. The notion has grown almost imperceptibly that God is simply a blessing machine for men—"If I link myself on to God He will see me through"; instead, the human race is meant to be the servant of God, a different thing altogether. If some of us are ever going to see God we shall have to go one step outside our particular relationship to things, religious or otherwise, and step into the revelation that Jesus Christ is our Lord and Master as well as our Saviour.

---

13. "White funeral:" a passage from one stage of life to another; leaving the past behind and moving into the future; spiritually, death to self.

God is using us in His own purposes, we have to remain true to His honour. "Though He slay me, yet will I wait for Him" (Job 13:15 RV)—that is the true nobility of the saint. Are we praying on the authority of the Redemption or on the ground of a preconceived notion of our own? Do we really believe that the basis of human life is Redemption? If we do, we shall no longer look for logical results, we shall look for God to work His own results, and His results work within certain moral frontiers (e.g., John 5:44). If we are outside those frontiers, we cannot see God; inside the frontiers we see Him at once. The prayers of the saints either enable or disable God in the performance of His wonders. The majority of us in praying for the will of God to be done say, "In God's good time," meaning "in my bad time"; consequently there is no silence in heaven produced by our prayers, no results, no performance.

Have our prayers demanded the immense attention of God? Have they been linked on to the basis of Redemption, or are we praying, for instance, on the line that God must bless the Allies in this war because they are in the right?

The result of the war will not be simply a national result. Men have not enlisted "For King and Country," but for a deeper reason, and in the final issue our prayer should be that the British Empire may be God's servant as well as His instrument.

Are we adding to the prayers of the saints or becoming sulky with God if He does not give us what we want, so taken up with the "nobility of man" that we forget what our calling is as saints? As saints we are called to go through the heroism of what we believe, not of stating what we believe, but of standing by it when the facts are dead against God. It is easy to say "God is love" when all is going well, but face a woman who has gone through bereavement and see if you find it easy to say it. There is suffering which staggers your mind as you watch it, and yet those who go through it are sustained in a way we do not understand. Every day lives are passing by us, how much of the silence of heaven have we broken up by our prayers for them? How much of our praying is from the empty spaces round our own hearts and how much from the basis of the Redemption, so that we give no thought for ourselves or for others, but only for Jesus Christ? Inarticulate prayer, the impulsive prayer that looks so futile, is the great thing God heeds more than anything else because it is along the line of His programme. A prayer offered by the humblest and most obscure saint on the ground of the Redemption of Jesus Christ demands the complete attention of God and the performance of His programme.

April 2, 1917, Zeitoun, Communion Service

HIS FACE IN THE RIDDLE OF THE UNIVERSE

But we see Jesus, . . . crowned with glory and honour.
Hebrews 2:9

Supposing there was a certain region of earth about which you knew nothing and you received a communication from someone who said "I have never been to the country but this map is a sure guide"; and you also received a communication from someone who sent you no map but who said, "I have been to this country myself and if you will trust yourself to me I will guide you straight there"; how absurd it would be to trust to the information which was not firsthand and not go with the one who had been there and knew the way. In all the problems of life there are any number of "maps," all more or less guesswork, but Jesus says, *"I am the Way."* There are people who tell us they have "maps" of what is beyond this seclusion of earth, but Jesus Christ is the only One who has not only been on this earth, but beyond it, consequently He alone is our guide. Have we confidence in Jesus, or have we only a "map"? The "maps" lead astray, Jesus Christ is the only One who knows; any number of things may confuse us, but nothing confuses Him.

1. Un-Made or Made by the Grave Seclusion (2 Corinthians 5:1–4)
We are shut up to this physical world; other planets may be inhabited, we are shut up to this one—shut up to our five senses and to this earth. Some minds are un-made when they realise this seclusion, other minds are made because they see God's purpose in it. "We that are in this bodily frame [RV mg] do groan," says Paul, "earnestly desiring to be clothed upon with our house which is from heaven. . . ." "I would rather be away from this body," he says, "but yet to abide in the flesh is more needful for your sake, so I remain with joy because it is God's will." When people get fanatical it is the barriers they go against, the barriers placed by birth and death, the barriers of sex. If we try to get out of the body by spiritualistic means or by suicide we shall have no guide; but if we get out of it in the providence of God and by faith in Jesus, there is no darkness or desperation—"O death, where is thy sting?" "Death is swallowed up in victory." When people are puzzled by the grave seclusion they are in and try to push away the barriers, they get out into the

open before they are ready and are likely to become unhinged in mind; but if "we see Jesus," there is no perplexity. Regarding the hereafter, He has said, "Let not your heart be troubled. . . . I go to prepare a place for you." Can we see Jesus in everything concerning ourselves, or are we trying to defy the barriers, wasting our time wishing we were somewhere else? The only way not to evade the problems of our grave seclusion in the body is by seeing Jesus and being devoted to Him.

The way we see the world outside us depends entirely upon our nervous system, and the marvel of God's construction of us is that we see things outside us as we do. For instance, the existence to us of beauty and colour and sound is due entirely to our nervous system: there is no colour to me when my eyes are shut, no sound when I am deaf, no sensation when I am asleep. If you want to know the most marvellous thing in the whole of creation, it is not the heavens, the moon and the stars, but—"What is man that Thou art mindful of him? . . . Thou madest him to have dominion over the works of Thy hands." The whole of creation was designed for man, and God intended man to be master of the life upon the earth, in the air and in the sea; the reason he is not master is because of sin, but he will yet be. (See Romans 8:19–22). Paul indicates that the problems of the grave seclusion we are in are accounted for by sin, yet it remains true that our nervous system is not a disease, but is designed by God to be the temple of the Holy Ghost. The greatest proof of this is that Jesus Christ became the inhabiter of a nervous system like our own; He took upon Him the likeness of man and dwelt upon the earth. "If any man is in Christ, he is a new creature" (RV); that is, he has a totally new way of looking at things because he has a new disposition and begins to see things differently. Take two men in the desert, in the same regiment—one is in love, the other has committed sin; to the one the desert blossoms as the rose, to the other there is no beauty in anything. The difference is not in external setting, but in the ruling disposition. One day we shall be changed, "in a moment, in the twinkling of an eye," and the things which we see by means of our nervous system will suddenly take on another guise.

2. Un-Daunted or Daunted by the Great Scheme *(2 Peter 3:8–13)*
The great scheme is the scheme of civilised life upon this earth. The apostle says, "Seeing that these things are all to be dissolved . . ." (RV); he does not say "destroyed," but "dissolved." What men have built upon the earth without any regard for God will be destroyed. The great scheme is that the physical universe which we see will be transfigured, i.e., become translucent with light. When our Lord was transfig-

ured we read that His garments became glistering, transfigured by indwelling light, and Peter indicates that the earth will go through its transfiguration and only what is holy will be able to live upon it. Now, we are limited to our body; then, we shall be transfigured in it. The way Jesus manifested Himself after the Resurrection is an indication of what we will be like when everything is related to God, we shall do things which seem miracles to us now. Jesus Christ was master of the elements because of His relation to God as Man, and in Him we see God's original design for man.

Nevertheless we, according to His promise, look for new heavens and a new earth, wherein dwelleth righteousness. The Apostles were not daunted by the great scheme of things because they were looking for something else, the coming of the Day of God. If you think of the great scheme apart from seeing Jesus, you will be daunted by it. When civilised life goes into the crucible, as it is doing just now, men lose their wits, Jesus said they would; but to His disciples He said, "And ye shall hear of wars and rumours of wars: *see that ye be not troubled.*" The revolution is proving that the revelation given by Jesus Christ is true. Men are finding the "maps" which they have taken as their guide are useless, they do not touch the basis of things, and as long as men refuse to take the direction of Jesus Christ wars and upheavals cannot be prevented; if they will take Him as their Guide they will find that things are slowly and definitely working toward the great scheme of "new heavens and a new earth, wherein dwelleth righteousness." Never look at actual things as if they were all; look at actual things in the light of the real, i.e., in the light of Jesus Christ.

3. Un-Demented or Demented by the Grand Society *(Revelation 3:20; John 14:23)*
The way we get demented, off our balance, is by dreaming of what is yet to be—the Utopian vision of the grand state of society when all men are going to be brothers. It is not the vision that is wrong, it is right, what is wrong is the way men are trying to bring it about, and if they don't look to Jesus Christ they easily get unbalanced. Think what the Bible says is going to be! "Death shall be no more, neither shall there be any mourning, nor crying, nor pain, any more" (RV); no more anything accursed; "but God Himself shall be with them, . . . and He shall wipe away every tear from their eyes" (RV). Meantime there are tears, and sorrow and sighing, but though "we see not yet all things put under him. But *we see Jesus, . . .* crowned with glory and honour." Tears are not going to be wiped away by our receiving pettings from God; the revelation is that through the marvel of the Redemption God is going to make it impossible for there to be any more crying or sorrow, all will be as satisfactory as God Himself.

The writers of the New Testament look forward to the grand society, but they do not become unbalanced because they are based on the Redemption. The aim of the grand society is not to be good, but to become the associates of God—"We will come unto him, and make our abode with him"; and the crown is—"they shall walk with Me in white: for they are worthy." We are to see God's face and confer with Him: "and His servants shall do Him service; and they shall see His face."

CLIMATE AND SPIRITUAL LIFE

And He awoke, and rebuked the wind, and said unto the sea, Peace, be still. And the wind ceased and there was a great calm. Mark 4:39 (RV)

This verse is a picture of our own spiritual life; there are occasions, such as this war, when it looks as if God were asleep, as if all our prayers were of no use; there are breakers ahead and it looks like destruction. But when He awakes in us, He calms the storm and rebukes our unbelief.

The life of Our Lord exhibits the influence of character on climate. It is easy to make this absurd, but looked at from the attitude of the Spirit of God you find there is an amazing connection between the storm and distresses and wild confusion of the earth just now and the waywardness and wrong of man; when the waywardness of man ceases and the sons of God are manifested, then "the creature itself also shall be delivered from the bondage of corruption into the glorious liberty of the children of God."

The Bible reveals that there is a close connection between character and climate. Ruskin is almost the only writer who recognises it, and in this respect he is akin to the great prophets. The reason for the connection is fundamental. According to the Bible revelation, God created man a mixture of dust and Deity, and when the Redemption comes to its full scope, the whole earth is going to partake in it. Because man's body and his earthly setting have been affected by sin, we are apt to think that being made of the dust of the ground is his shame; the Bible implies that it is his chief glory, because it is in that body that the Son of God was manifested.

1. The Way of God and the Dawn
And in the morning, a great while before day, He rose up and went out, and departed into a desert place, and there prayed. (Mark 1:35 RV)

Specific times and places and communion with God go together. It is by no haphazard chance that in every age men have risen early to pray. The first thing that marks decline in spiritual life is our relationship to the early morning. It is significant that before nations have been gripped by civilisation they always began their day early. (An American on visiting England after a lapse of years made this significant remark—"One thing that strikes me is the difference in the time people get up; twenty years ago everybody used to be astir early, but now I notice they rise much later.") When we are in touch with the earnestness of things, we begin soon.

(a) The Devotion of Our Lord
And it came to pass in those days, that He went out into a mountain to pray, and continued all night in prayer to God. And when it was day, He called unto Him His disciples. (Luke 6:12–13)

It is not a haphazard thing, but in the constitution of God, that there are certain times of the day when it not only seems easier, but it *is* easier, to meet God. If you have ever prayed in the dawn you will ask yourself why you were so foolish as not to do it always: it is difficult to get into communion with God in the midst of the hurly-burly of the day. George Mac-Donald said that if he did not open wide the door of his mind to God in the early morning he worked on the finite all the rest of the day—"stand on the finite, act upon the wrong." It is not sentiment but an implicit reality that the conditions of dawn and communion with God go together. When the day of God appears there will be no night, always dawn and day. There is nothing of the nature of strain in God's Day, it is all free and beautiful and fine. "And there shall be night no more" (RV).

(b) The Difference of Administration
Now late on the sabbath day, as it began to dawn toward the first day of the week, came Mary Magdalene. . . . (Matthew 28:1 RV)

Mary Magdalene thought that this dawn would be like an ordinary one, but it was the dawn of the greatest day, not only for Mary Magdalene but for the whole world. Our Lord told her that there would be a different administration—"Till now you have known Me as God manifest in the flesh, now it is to be a knowledge after the Spirit; I will be in you, an indwelling Presence." Penetration into truth comes when we choose the times God has chosen for us. All through the Old Testament the "first" is dedicated to God; whenever that was neglected the prophets rebuked the people (e.g., Malachi 3:8–9). We all know when we are at our best intellectually, and if instead of giving that time to God we give it to our own development, we not only rob God, but rob ourselves of the possibility of His life thriving in us. We heard it said that we shall suffer if we do not pray; I question it. What will suffer if we do not pray is the life of God in us; but when we do pray and devote the dawns to God His nature in us develops, there is less self-realisation and more Christ-realisation.

(c) The Direction of Our Lord
But when day was now breaking, Jesus stood on the beach. . . . And He said unto them, Cast the net on the right side of the boat, and ye shall find. (John 21:4, 6 RV)

We have special times and days when we expect God to do things, but He usually does them when we don't expect it, e.g., when we are coming back in the early morning from fishing, it is then that God gives us direction. It is not simply that it is easier to get direction in the early morning, it is a profound revelation that that is the time when direction comes.

2. The Wilderness of Temptation—The Devil and the Divine
And Jesus, full of the Holy Spirit, returned from the Jordan, and was led by the Spirit in the wilderness during forty days, being tempted of the devil. (Luke 4:1–2 RV)

When artists or poets of earlier days wanted to depict a particular type of man they painted or described in words the climatic and geographical setting agreeing with that type. For instance, if they wanted to portray a man in an angry temper, they put in the scenery of a thunderstorm. Dante does it in the "Inferno"[14] and Milton in "Paradise Lost."[15] The outward is the symbol of the inner, according to the Bible: there is a closer connection between them than we imagine. When our supreme temptation comes, the setting we are in, whether it is a city or the actual desert, brings us into contact with the foundation of things as God made them. According to Genesis, the basis of physical material life is chaos, and the basis of personal

moral life, wrath. If I live in harmony with God, chaos becomes cosmos to me, and the wrath of God becomes the love of God. If I get out of touch with God I get into hell, physically and morally; when I live in relationship to God by the inner witness of the Spirit, "Heaven above is brighter blue, earth around a sweeter green. . . ."

(a) The Desertion of a Disciple
And Satan entered into Judas who was called Iscariot, being of the number of the twelve. (Luke 22:3 RV)

There was the wilderness of temptation in the lives of the disciples; in one disciple the devil conquered absolutely and Judas became what Jesus called him, "the son of perdition." The popular idea of temptation is that it is towards evil, meaning that we can see it to be evil by our common sense, but temptation is always a short cut to good, the mind is perplexed—"I wonder if this is the way of God?" If I yield to the temptation the devil gets his way, as he did with Judas in the last extreme.

(b) The Desperation of a Disciple
And the Lord turned, and looked upon Peter. . . . And he went out, and wept bitterly. (Luke 22:61–62 RV)

The devil tried to get Peter where he got Judas, but he did not succeed; Satan did not "enter into" Peter; Peter got the length of denying Jesus, but in his wilderness of temptation he "struck" the Divine, Judas "struck" the devil; consequently Peter experienced a desperation producing tears, and those tears were the most amazing bitterness in his life. Peter with his impulsive heart would feel he could never forgive himself, he would have spent the rest of his days mourning, but Jesus had told him beforehand, "And do thou, when once thou hast turned again, establish thy brethren" (RV).

(c) The Defeat of the Devil
Then the devil leaveth Him. (Matthew 4:11)

Jesus Christ met the devil in the wilderness and defeated him. When you go through a time of trial, a wilderness of temptation in heart or mind or spirit, you feel inclined to get away out into somewhere like the desert. The reason for that is not haphazard, but because in the primal constitution of God man is connected with the dust of the earth: he is related to the elemental condition of things all through. When the sons of God are manifested the desolate place will alter at once. "The desert shall rejoice, and blossom as the rose."

---

14. "Inferno" (Hell): Part 1 of the *Divine Comedy,* written 1307–1321.
15. *Paradise Lost,* published 1667.

3. The Wall of God and the Darkness on the Deep

And it was now dark and Jesus had not yet come to them. And the sea was rising by reason of a great wind that blew. (John 6:17–18 RV)

This happens in our own lives—we are on the deep, it is dark, and Jesus is not there. It is a description of every elemental experience, such as bereavement or heart-break, or any of the big things that beset human life, there is real speechless terror and misgiving. You may have had communion with God in the dawn, you may have continued with Jesus in temptation, but this thing makes you feel helpless—there is no way out. In times of deep sorrow it is not the people who tell you why you are suffering who are of any use; the people who help you are those who give expression to your state of mind, often they do not speak at all, they are like Nature. Nature is never heartless to the one who is bereaved, but it takes a revelation to make us know this.

(a) At the Request of Jesus

And He said unto them, Let us go over unto the other side of the lake. And they launched forth. (Luke 8:22)

"If you obey Jesus you will have a life of joy and delight." Well, it is not true. Jesus said to the disciples—"Let us go to the other side of the lake," and they were plunged into the biggest storm they had ever known. You say, "If I had not obeyed Jesus I should not have got into this complication." Exactly. The problems in our walk with God are to be accounted for along this line, and the temptation is to say, "God could never have told me to go there, if He had done so this would not have happened." We discover then whether we are going to trust God's integrity or listen to our own expressed scepticism. Scepticism of the tongue is only transitional; real scepticism is wrung out from the man who knows he did not get where he is on his own account—"I was not seeking my own, I came deliberately because I believe Jesus told me to, and now there is the darkness and the deep and the desolation."

(b) The Revelation of Jesus

But Simon Peter, when he saw it, fell down at Jesus' knees, saying, Depart from me; for I am a sinful man, O Lord. (Luke 5:8 RV)

The revelation of Jesus comes in the way He walks on our deeps; He tells us to do something which in the light of our own discernment sounds ridiculous, but immediately we do it, we experience the judgement of Jesus. The judgement is not in what He says, it is Himself. "Depart from me, . . . O Lord," said Peter, but that was the last thing Peter wanted Him to do, it was the impulsive expression of his state of mind.

(c) At the Rebuke of Jesus

And He arose, and rebuked the wind, and said unto the sea, Peace, be still. . . . And He said unto them, Why are ye so fearful? how is it that ye have no faith? (Mark 4:39–40)

Our Lord rebuked the disciples for fearing when apparently they had good reason for being alarmed. The problem is—if Jesus Christ is only the Carpenter of Nazareth, then the disciples were foolish to put Him at the tiller; but if He is the Son of God, what are they alarmed about? If Jesus Christ is God, where is my trust in Him? If He is not God, why am I so foolish as to pretend to worship Him?

"And they feared exceedingly, and said one to another, What manner of man is this, that even the wind and the sea obey Him?" (Mark 4:41). Just where Jesus does not seem to be, when it looks as if the waves would overwhelm them, the Son of God comes walking on the top of those very billows. As we go on in our spiritual life we get into similar conditions, they are not symbolic, but the actual conditions of our lives. God engineers us out of our sequestered places and brings us into elemental conditions, and we get a taste of what the world is like because of the disobedience of man. We realise then that our hold on God has been a civilised hold, we have not really believed in Him at all. When we get out on to the deep and the darkness we realise what a wonderful thing the Psalmist says—"Therefore will not we fear, though the earth be removed. . . ." But it takes some confidence in God to say that when everything you trust in has gone.

4. The Word of God and Elemental Destruction (Matthew 7:24–27)

Therefore whosoever heareth these sayings of mine, and doeth them, I will liken him unto a wise man, which built his house upon a rock: and the rain descended, and the floods came, and the winds blew, and beat upon that house; and it fell not; for it was founded upon a rock. . . . (Matthew 7:24)

Our Lord reveals that the elemental destructions cannot touch us, neither death nor hell, nor all the forces of man and the devil put together, can prevail against the word of God if once we build on that; but if we build on our own discernment, then when the elemental destructions come, not only do we go, but our foundations go too. Our foundations must be rooted in God, then when the upheavals come we do not need to be afraid.

(a) The Cosmic Power of Discernment (Mark 13:24–27)

And then shall they see the Son of man coming in the clouds with great power and glory. (Mark 13:26)

The cosmic powers belong to God, and the great changes that will take place when He establishes His Kingdom will reveal that the Son of Man and the cosmic powers are identified, "The meek . . . shall inherit the earth," not the world; the world is not God's; the world is the name given to the system of things men have placed on God's earth, and the Bible foretells the time when these shall pass away; they are going into the crucible just now. Poets talk about Nature being "the garment of God," and it will be true literally. We look for God in little ways, and He is there in all the terrific powers of Nature. We shall discern Him "in the clouds," i.e., the great elemental powers, when "the heavens shall pass away . . . and the elements shall melt with fervent heat." And there will be new heavens and a new earth, wherein dwelleth righteousness.

(b) The Conscious Person and Divinity
And He was transfigured before them. And His raiment became shining, exceeding white as snow. (Mark 9:2–3)

Our Lord emptied Himself of His glory when He became Incarnate, and here on the Mount the glory which He had with the Father before the world was suddenly burst through; the material part of Him was shot through with glory, that is, God and matter became one. That is what would have happened to the human race if Adam had not sinned, there would have been no death, but transfiguration. The counterpart of the Transfiguration is not the Resurrection, but the Ascension.

(c) The Comprehensive Presence and Direction
Go ye therefore, and make disciples of all the nations, . . . and lo, I am with you alway. (Matthew 28:19–20 RV)

Jesus Christ teaches us to build our confidence in the abiding reality of Himself in the midst of everything. If a man puts his confidence in the things which must go, imagine his incomprehensible perplexity when they do go. No wonder Jesus said "men's hearts failing them for fear." These words describe the time we are in now. Our true life is not in the things which are passing, and if we build ourselves on God and His word, when they go, the marvel is that we are not scared. The thing to examine spiritually is, am I connected with Jesus Christ personally? If I have only a form of belief or a creed, all that may go when the elemental trouble comes and I shall have nothing to cling to, but if I build my "house" on the words of Jesus and do them, then no matter what happens I shall find I am founded upon the Rock.

DECEMBER 10, 1916, ZEITOUN, SUNDAY MORNING & COMMUNION SERVICE

THE NAME

And His name shall be called Wonderful. . . . Isaiah 9:6

In the New Testament "name" frequently stands for "nature." When we pray in the Name of Jesus the answers are in accordance with His nature, and if we think our prayers are unanswered it is because we are not interpreting the answer along this line.

1. The Expression of God's Thought
And the Word became flesh, and dwelt among us. . . . (John 1:14 RV)

It is easy to get vague when we think about the thought of God; the poet talks about hearing God's voice on the rolling air, or as coming to us in the love of our friends; it sounds beautiful, but it may be all nonsense. Our sense of the beautiful has to take shape somehow, an ideal is of no use to me unless it has become incarnated. Nowhere in the Bible is there any notice taken of the worship of abstractions. We may talk about God as the Almighty, the All-powerful, but He means nothing to us unless He has become incar-nated and touched human life where we touch it; and the revelation of Redemption is that God's Thought did express itself in Jesus Christ, that God became manifest on the plane on which we live.

(a) The Time-Beginning of God's Thought (Genesis 1:2)
When the mind of God thought on the chaos it was like an artist mixing the colours on his palette, and Genesis 1:2 describes the state of the "palette"—"without form, and void"; and out of that God created Cosmos; He expressed His thought in the universe we see. The earth is always spoken of in the Bible as God's. The word of God produces its own expression. And God said, Let there be light: and there was light." Our language rarely expresses us at all.

(b) The Time-Birth of God's Thought (John 1:1–3)
God's Thought expressed itself not only in the universe which He created, but in a Being called "the Word," whose name to us is "Jesus Christ." John

declares that God's Thought manifested itself in a Word, and that that Word became incarnated in a human life. We only know God's thought and the expression of it in Jesus Christ, and we only know the meaning of "God and man one" in Jesus Christ. Our conception of the Trinity is an attempt of the human mind to define how God manifested Himself.

(c) The Timeless Benediction of God's Thought (Philippians 2:9–11; Ephesians 1:21)

Jesus Christ not only has dominion now, but in the ages to come. God never says to man "You must"; He says, "You will ultimately come there." We may come in the right way or by breaking our neck, but we will come, not by compulsion but by absolute agreement that Jesus Christ alone is The Way. God has so decreed it that man must work together with Him and bring about agreement with His own expressed Thought. We are apt to make the mistake of thinking that God is going to coerce men; He never does. God is giving men ample time to do exactly what they like, both as individuals and as nations; He allows us to develop as we choose, but in the end we will come to agree with Him. The introduction of socialism into the history of civilisation is the next thing to be manifested, everything else has been tried, and socialism will end as every other human attempt has ended, in proving that man cannot establish himself in unity with God and ignore Jesus Christ, either in individual or in national life.

2. The Education in God's Thought
Ye are our epistle. (2 Corinthians 3:2)

You cannot prove that God is love if you have not been born from above (RV mg), because everything around you disproves it. Take the war and the ruination going on just now, it is absurd to say that it is just and reasonable; it is tragic and wrong; and yet when you are born from above you are able to discern the "arm of the Lord" behind it all, but it takes the nature of Jesus Christ to see it, human nature apart from Him is unable to do so. "Marvel not that I said unto thee, Ye must be born again," Jesus said to Nicodemus. I must have the nature of Jesus Christ born into me, then I shall see things as He did.

(a) The Character of the Name (Matthew 1:21)

"*. . . and thou shalt call His name Jesus: for it is He that shall save His people from their sins" (RV).* The character of the Name is that Jesus Christ is Saviour, and the evidence that I belong to Him is that I am delivered from sin; if I am not, I have a name to live, but am dead. When I become a Christian Jesus Christ exhibits the character of His own Name in me.

(b) The Curriculum of the Name (Acts 4:12)

This verse is a profound utterance, the inevitable certainty that there is no salvation under heaven, saving through the Name of Jesus. The whole of our education is to bring us to this understanding. So often we are like a man crossing a moor who obstinately refuses to take any directions, and he goes on and on only to find himself hopelessly lost; then he humbly tracks back to the signpost and looking up, sees the way to go. God does not get angry with us, He simply waits until we realise that what He says is true. "And in none other is there salvation: for neither is there any other name under heaven, that is given among men, wherein we must be saved" (RV).

(c) The Comprehension of the Name (1 Corinthians 12:3)

We blunder when we tell people they must believe certain things about Jesus Christ; a man cannot believe until he knows Him, then belief is spontaneous and natural. "No man can say, Jesus is Lord, but in the Holy Spirit" (RV). You may get a parrot recital of a creed, but when a man says, with a thrill all through him, "Thou art the Christ," he is stating an intuitive revelation, not an intellectual conception; it is a committal to a Person. When I commit myself to Jesus I begin to see properly. No man believes what he sees unless he believes before he sees. "Because thou hast seen Me, hast thou believed? [RV mg] Blessed are they that have not seen, and yet have believed."

3. The Experience as God's Thought

We become incorporated into God's Thought, and then we go on to experience it. It will take all Time and Eternity to experience God's Thought—"And this is life eternal, that they should know Thee. . . ." (RV)—a continual new wonder. The schooling we are going through just now is to develop us into an understanding of the Thought of God.

(a) The Charge of the Name (Matthew 10:32)

The charge of the Name means that I stand true to Jesus Christ, confessing Him wherever I am. It is easy to preach, nothing easier, but it is another thing to confess. Confessing means to say with every bit of me that Jesus Christ has come into my flesh. In practical outcome it means that if I say I have been saved by God's grace, I must show it, I have to be true to the Name in every detail. "By their fruits ye shall know them."

(b) The Charm of the Name (Revelation 2:17)

Think of the way God disciplines us into an experience of the phases of the Name; sometimes we are chastened into knowing Jesus Christ as the Way, at other times into knowing Him as the Truth, and the Life; but there is another and a grander Name yet—"a new name . . . , which no one knoweth but he that receiveth it" (RV).

(c) The Community of the Name (Ephesians 4:13)
We attain to the fulness of Christ in one way only, through the Name. It is not individuals who attain, but humanity as a whole. One day the whole human race will be in God's sight as the Body of Christ, completely one with God. Jesus Christ was the Word of God, the expression of God's thought, and His earthly life is a symbol of what the human race will be like when it is related to God as the Son of Man was related. ". . . till we all come in the unity of the faith, and of the knowledge of the Son of God, unto a perfect man, unto the measure of the stature of the fulness of Christ."

1916, ZEITOUN.

HAVE I TO FORGIVE MY ENEMIES?
Matthew 5:43–44

Did Jesus Christ mean it when He said "Love your enemies"? If He did, we must come to the conclusion either that He was a madman, or that there is a meaning underneath His words which we do not at first see. It is impossible to do what Our Lord says if we imagine we can do it of ourselves, and we soon discover our ignorance. Jesus Christ bases all His teaching on the fundamental fact that God can do for a man what he cannot do for himself. It is an easy business to say I love my enemies when I haven't any, but when I have an enemy, when a man has done me or those who belong to me, a desperate wrong, what is my attitude as a Christian to be? Does Jesus Christ mean that I have to ignore the rugged sense of justice which is in every man, and be a sentimentalist and say, "Oh yes, I forgive you"? What we are up against just now is the danger of not making the basis of forgiveness and peace the right kind. If it is not the basis of perfect justice, it will fail. We may succeed in calling a truce, but that is not peace, and before long we will be at it again.

1. The Matter of Forgiveness. *Repentance* (Ephesians 1:7)
In whom we have redemption through His blood, the forgiveness of sins, according to the riches of His grace.

Forgiveness is the great message of the Gospel, and it satisfies a man's sense of justice completely. The fundamental factor of Christianity is "the forgiveness of sins." But what about the man who does not care whether he is forgiven or not? That is the case with us all to begin with, we do not care whether Jesus Christ lived or died or did anything at all, and to hear about God forgiving us, why, there is nothing in it. But when a man gets convicted of sin (which is the most direct way of knowing that at the basis of life there is a problem too big for him to solve), he knows that God dare not forgive him; if He did, then man has a bigger sense of justice than God. The majority of us know nothing about the Redemption or forgiveness until we are enmeshed by the personal problem—something happens which stabs us wide awake and we get our indifferent hide pierced; we come up against things and our conscience begins to be roused. When once a man's conscience is roused he knows God dare not forgive him and it awakens a sense of hopelessness. Forgiveness is a revelation—hope for the hopeless; that is the message of the Gospel.

According to the Bible the basis of things is tragic, and the way out is the way Jesus Christ made in the Redemption. Any man, whether he be Cain or Judas, or you or I, can receive absolute forgiveness from God the moment he knows he needs it: but God cannot forgive a man unless he repents. Repentance means that we recognise the need for forgiveness—"hands up, I know it." Jesus Christ did not come to fling forgiveness broadcast; He did not come to the Pharisees, who withstood Him, and said He was possessed with a devil, and say "I forgive you": He said, "How can ye escape the damnation of hell?" We may talk as much as we like about forgiveness, but it will never make any difference to us unless we realise that we need it. God can never forgive the man who does not want to be forgiven. As long as we live in the "tenth storey" we either talk sentimental stuff or else we remain indifferent to the fact of forgiveness; only when we "strike bottom" morally do we begin to realise what the New Testament means by forgiveness. Immediately a man turns to God, the Redemption is such that forgiveness is complete.

"In whom we have redemption through His blood, the forgiveness of sins." The background of the forgiveness of God is His holiness. If God were not holy, there would be nothing in His forgiveness. The conscience of God means that He has to completely forgive and finally redeem the whole human race. Every man knows by the way he is made that there is such a thing as justice, and God forgives on the basis of *His* justice, viz., on the ground of Redemption. We are apt to say glibly that God will forgive us, but when we come up against the thing we know He dare not; if He did, He would cease to be God. There is no such thing as God overlooking sin. That is where people make a great mistake with regard to God's love; they say "God is love and of course He will forgive sin": God is *holy* love and of course He *cannot* forgive sin. Therefore if God does forgive, there must be a reason that justifies Him in doing it. Unless there is a possibility of forgiveness establishing an order of holiness and rectitude in a man, it would be a mean and abominable thing to be forgiven. If I am forgiven without being altered by the forgiveness, forgiveness is a damage to me and a sign of unmitigated weakness on the part of God. A man has to clear God's character in forgiving him. The revelation of forgiveness in the Bible is not that God puts snow over a rubbish heap, but that He turns a man into the standard of Himself, the Forgiver. If I receive forgiveness and yet go on being bad, I prove that God is not justified in forgiving me. When God forgives a man He gives him the heredity of His own Son, and there is no man on earth but can be presented "perfect in Christ Jesus." Then on the ground of the Redemption, it is up to me to live as a son of God. The reason my sins are forgiven so easily is because the Redemption cost God so much.

2. The Method of Forgiveness. *Reaction* (Matthew 6:12–15)

Jesus Christ taught His disciples to pray, "Forgive us our debts, as we forgive our debtors," that is, He taught them to recognise that God's method of forgiveness is the same as our own. Jesus Christ did not say *"because* we forgive our debtors," but *"as* we forgive our debtors," that is, as children of God we are forgiven not on the ground of Redemption, but on the ground that we show the same forgiveness to our fellows that God has shown to us. "For if ye forgive men their trespasses, your heavenly Father will also forgive you: but if ye forgive not men their trespasses, neither will your Father forgive your trespasses." God's method in forgiveness is exactly the method of our forgiveness, and is according to our human sense of justice.

Peter seemed to stand on tiptoe once and try to reach to God's forgiveness—"Lord, how oft shall my brother sin against me, and I forgive him? till seven times? Jesus saith unto him, I say not unto thee, Until seven times: but, Until seventy times seven." Yet when a man has deliberately done you a wrong, it is accord-

ing to the teaching of Jesus that you must not say you forgive him unless he turns; if he turns, forgiveness is to be complete. We may forgive easily because we are shallow, but when we are deeply roused, we cannot forgive unless our sense of justice is satisfied. The most marvellous ingredient in the forgiveness of God is that He also forgets, the one thing a human being can never do. Forgetting with God is a divine attribute; God's forgiveness forgets. We can never forget saving by the sovereign grace of God. God exhausts metaphors to show what His forgiveness means—"I, even I, am He that blotteth out thy transgressions for Mine own sake, and will not remember thy sins" (Isaiah 43:25); "I have blotted out, as a thick cloud, thy transgressions, and, as a cloud, thy sins" (Isaiah 44:22); "As far as the east is from the west, so far hath He removed our transgressions from us" (Psalm 103:12); "For Thou hast cast all my sins behind Thy back" (Isaiah 38:17); "For I will forgive their iniquity, and I will remember their sin no more" (Jeremiah 31:34).

When the prodigal son came back with words which meant, "I am sorry to the backbone for what I have done and am ashamed of myself," the father never said a word about the far country, about the harlots and the riotous living (the elder brother reminded him of all that); he did not cast up at him one thing he had done—sufficient for him that his son had returned. Is it conceivable to us that God will forget what we have done? He says He will; but the forgiveness of God does not work unless we turn; it cannot, any more than it does according to human justice. When we turn to God and say we are sorry, Jesus Christ has pledged His word that we will be forgiven, but the forgiveness is not operative unless we turn, because our turning is the proof that we know we need forgiveness.

3. The Message of Forgiveness. *Retaliation v. Retribution* (Matthew 18:15–17; 34–35)

Moreover if thy brother shall trespass against thee, go and tell him his fault between thee and him alone: if he shall hear thee, thou hast gained thy brother. (Matthew 18:15)

It would be an immoral thing to forgive a man who did not say he was sorry. If a man sins against you and you go to him and point out that he has done wrong—if he hears you, then you can forgive him; but if he is obstinate you can do nothing; you cannot say "I forgive you," you must bring him to a sense of justice. Jesus Christ said, "I say unto you, Love your enemies," but He also said the most appallingly stern things that were ever uttered, e.g., "... *neither will your Father forgive your trespasses.*" I cannot forgive my enemies and remain just unless they cease to be my enemies and give proof of their sorrow, which must be expressed in repentance. I have to remain steadfastly true to God's justice. There are times when it would be easier to say "Oh well, it does not matter, I forgive you," but Jesus insists that the uttermost farthing must be paid. The love of God is based on justice and holiness, and I must forgive on the same basis.

There is a difference between retaliation and retribution. The basis of life is retribution—"For with what judgement ye judge, ye shall be judged: and with what measure ye mete, it shall be measured to you again." This statement of our Lord's is not a haphazard guess, it is an eternal law and it works from God's throne right down. Life serves back in the coin you pay. You are paid back what you give not necessarily by the same person; and this holds with regard to good as well as evil. If you have been generous, you will meet generosity again through someone else; if you have been shrewd in finding out the defects of others, that is the way people will judge you. Jesus Christ never allows retaliation, but He says that the basis of life is retribution. If my enemy turns and gives proof of his sorrow, I am not to meet him with retaliation. Christianity is not a set of principles, but relationship to a Person, Jesus Christ, while the Holy Spirit works in us a spontaneous relationship to things on the basis of God's forgiveness of us.

The distinctive thing about Christianity is forgiveness, not sanctification or my holiness, but forgiveness—the greatest miracle God ever performs through the Redemption. Forgiveness means not merely that a man is saved from sin and made right for heaven—no man would accept forgiveness on such a level; forgiveness means that I am saved from sinning and put into the Redeemer to grow up into His image. I am forgiven into a recreated relationship, i.e., into identification with God in Christ, so that the forgiven man is the holy man. The basis of human life is Redemption. There is nothing more certain in Time or Eternity than what Jesus Christ did on the Cross. He switched the whole of the human race back into right relationship to God, and any one of us can get into touch with God *now,* not presently.

Forgiveness is the miracle of grace; it is impossible for human beings to forgive, and it is because we do not see this that we misunderstand the revelation of forgiveness. The great characteristic of God is not that He says He will pay no more attention to what we have done, but that He forgives us, and in forgiving He is able to deal with our past, with our present and our future. Do I believe that God can deal with my "yesterday" and make it as though it had never been? By means of the Redemption God undertakes to deal with a man's past, and He does it in two ways—first, He forgives it, and then He makes it a wonderful culture for the future. When God says "Don't do that any more," He instils into me the power that enables me not to do it any more, and the power comes by right of what Jesus Christ did on the Cross. That is the unspeakable wonder of the forgiveness of God, and when we become rightly related to God, we are to have the same relationship to our fellow men that God has to us. "And be ye kind one to another, tenderhearted, forgiving one another, even as God for Christ's sake hath forgiven you" (Ephesians 4:32).

July 1, 1917, Zeitoun, Sunday Morning Service & Devotional Hut

THE CALL OF GOD
Isaiah 6

It is difficult to define the call of God—it is an implicit thing, like the call of the sea or of the mountains. Not everyone hears the call of the sea and of the mountains, but only those who have the nature of the sea or the mountains in them. In the same way no man hears the call of God unless he has the nature of God in him and has got into the way of listening to the implicit leading of the call. The significant thing is that God did not call Isaiah. There are times when God does call a man to a special work, but in Isaiah's case God did not call him; he "[over]heard the voice of the Lord, saying, Whom shall I send, and who will go for us?" Isaiah had been brought by spiritual concentration as well as consecration inside the moral frontiers where he could hear God's voice. We need trained ears to hear. One man may hear the call of God and another hear nothing; it depends on what goes on within the man, not outside him.

"In the year that king Uzziah died, I saw the Lord . . ." (RV). "In the years of the Great War, I saw the Lord." That is the time when a man sees differently. It takes a crisis when the deeps are opened and life is profoundly altered before a man can say, "I saw the Lord." After Hezekiah had come face to face with death he said, "I shall go softly [as in solemn procession, RV mg] all my years, because of the bitterness of my soul" (Isaiah 38:15). There is always a difference in the man who has come face to face with certain death, when he goes through the supreme crisis the true elements come out. This war has brought tension to countless lives and people are coming to see differently because of it. When a man goes through a crisis he fears he is losing God, but instead of that he is beginning to see Him for the first time, and he sees Him as a grander, more marvellous Being than ever he imagined.

1. Comprehensiveness of the Call

The first thing that impresses us about the call of God is that it comes to the whole man, not to one part of him. The majority of us are godly in streaks, spiritual in sections; it takes a long time to locate us altogether to the call of God. We have special days and religious moods, but when we get into contact with God we are brought in touch with Reality and made all of a piece. Our Lord's life was all one reality, you could never cut it into two—shallow here and profound there. My conception of God must embrace the whole of my life. When I see the Lord truly I see Him as God of my whole being; if He is only God in sections of me, He is not God at all.

2. Consciousness of Grossness

Then said I, Woe is me! for I am undone; because I am a man of unclean lips, and I dwell in the midst of a people of unclean lips: for mine eyes have seen the King, the LORD of hosts. (Isaiah 6:5)

Isaiah's words are a confession not of sin, but of the sense of absolute grossness. "I was as a beast before Thee" said the Psalmist, not an immoral beast but— "What an incapacitated type of man I am! I have seen the Lord, but how am I going to come anywhere near His marvellous holiness?" Any man will go to God for deliverance from sin, but it is another thing to have this consciousness of grossness dealt with; it takes discipline and patience and concentration. Will I agree that I am gross—"Woe is me! for I am undone"? If so, I am coming slowly to the condition Isaiah was in. It was his consciousness of grossness that brought Isaiah into a right relationship to God, that is an illuminating point. It is never my sense of goodness that brings me into touch with God, but my sense of unworthiness: "Woe is me!" for I am undone—that brings me

into the presence of God at once. When a man knows his destitution, knows he cannot get hold of God, cannot be the things he longs to be, he begins to realise what it was Jesus Christ came to do, viz., to supply what he really lacks.

There is no obstacle, nothing in the past or the present or in his heredity, that can stand in a man's way if he will only make room for Jesus Christ. Once let him realise his need—"I can't be holy, I can't be pure in heart, I can't be the child of my Father in heaven and be kind to the unthankful and evil, I can't love my enemies"—Jesus Christ claims that He can do all that for him, but it depends on the man, i.e., upon how much he has come up against the things he cannot do for himself.

3. Character of the Commission

Isaiah saw the Lord, then he saw himself; then he overheard the voice of God saying "who will go?" and he said, "Here am I; send me"; and then God gave him a staggering message to deliver. "And He said, Go, and tell this people, Hear ye indeed, but understand not; and see ye indeed, but perceive not. Make the heart of this people fat, and make their ears heavy, and shut their eyes; lest they see with their eyes, and hear with their ears, and understand with their heart, and turn again, and be healed" (Isaiah 6:9–10 RV). "Unless the people turn, the truth will deepen their condemnation, but you must speak." God's condemnations as well as His promises are conditional; as long as we remain with the wrong disposition unremoved, every truth of God will harden us and ripen us for judgement.

Isaiah caught a sudden glimpse, terrible in its clearness, of his own sin and his people's sin. There is very little of that amongst us nowadays and a lot of gathering our spiritual skirts around us; instead of our repentance being social repentance and our intercession vicarious, we are vindictive and bitter in spirit. The sight of God deepens humiliation in a saint and lifts him into intercession. Repentance is needed not only for individual sins, but for social sins. There is a social repentance to-day, but it is repentance not for the honour of God but because of the sorrows and sufferings of the people. All through the Bible runs the idea of *national* repentance, of *social* sanctification, until the idea reaches its climax in *a holy city*.

SPIRITUAL DISENCHANTMENT AND DELIGHT

1. Disillusionment and the Furnace of Disappointment

Let no man glory in men. For all things are yours. . . . (1 Corinthians 3:21)

Enchantment in the natural realm means to be taken out of your wits by song and rhythm; spiritual enchantment comes along the line of aggressive Christian work, meetings, and the contagion of other people's joy, and it is ensnaring. If we get taken up with salvation or with holiness or Divine healing instead of with Jesus Christ, we will be disillusioned. We pin our faith to a plan of salvation that can be expressed in words and we glory in it, then we begin to find it does not work and a curious disillusionment begins. It sounds all right, but its fruit is not that which bears a family likeness to Jesus Christ, and it causes us consternation if we are conscientious and desirous of being all that God wants us to be. Many a man to-day when he is dumped down in the desert[16] has found disillusionment, he is amongst men who do not care for his religion, and he finds there is not the thrill and the joy there used to be; he realises he has been fostering a religious life which is not genuine, and spiritual cynicism may be the result. A cynic spiritually is one who cuts himself off from other people because the enchantment of service and association with others instead of producing reality has been engendering priggishness, the attitude of a superior person. Paul continually warns "Don't glory in men." If you find your spiritual character is disappointing you, you are not developing a family likeness to Jesus Christ, it is because there is no inner reality. When you come to the furnace of disappointment, beware of the swing of the pendulum. Discouragement means the heart knocked out of self-love and my estimate of what God can do. We are also impatient with the things that are neither black nor white, but immensely difficult and perplexing, not easy to decipher. We are made up of a thousand and one springs and the only One who can bring the thing out right is the One who designed it. If a man has never gone through a spell of fanaticism it is because he is not prepared to cut off anything in order to get at reality. It is essential to be maimed for a while in order to develop our life with God (see Matthew 5:29–30).

2. Detachment from the Fury of Desire

For by Him were all things created, . . . and He is before all things, and by Him all things consist. (Colossians 1:16–17)

Our natural life is a fury of desire for the things we can see. That is the meaning of lust—I must have it at once, a fury of desire without any regard for the consequences. I have to be detached from the things I can see and be brought into a living relationship with the Creator of those things. If I am taken up with the created things and forget Jesus Christ I shall find that things disappoint and I get disillusioned. If my body is "bossed" by personal self-realisation I am defiling the temple of the Holy Ghost; I may be moral and upright but I have become ruler over my own life. "Give up your right to yourself to Me," says Jesus, "let Me realise Myself in you." He quenches the fury of desire by detaching us from things so that we may know Him. In this way God brings us into the fulness of life. The majority of us are not in the place where God can give us the hundredfold more. We say, "A bird in the hand is worth two in the bush," while God is wanting to give us the bush with all the birds in it! It is necessary to be detached from things and then come back to them in a right relationship. A sense of property is a hindrance to spiritual growth, that is why so many of us know nothing about communion with Jesus Christ.

When we are detached from things on the inside the fury of desire burns itself out. The attitude is not one born of external detachment, that is atheistic, Paul told Timothy to beware of those who teach abstinence from meats and marriage. The detachment is not to be that of an æsthete but that which springs from being in perfect communion with God. Our Lord's external life was so social that the men of His day, who were externally detached, said of Him, Behold, a gluttonous man, and a winebibber." They were detached externally, but not in spirit; Jesus Christ was detached in His disposition, but not externally. Those of us who are spiritual are hopelessly blind to God's purpose; the Spirit of God is all the time trying to make us detached in mind in order to bring us into real communion with God. God is trying to educate us in inner martyrdom and we won't have it, we get tired of being educated spiritually.

---

16. in the desert: Chambers was speaking to soldiers camped in Egypt.

3. Devotion to the Face of Deity

Looking unto Jesus . . . (Hebrews 12:2)

If I want to see the Face of God I must fast from other things and concentrate on God. If in my inner life I am under apprehension by Jesus Christ for the time being I am out of touch with ordinary things. To fast is not to give up food, but to cut off the right arm, and pluck out the right eye. But that is only a stage, what we are tending towards is the perfection Jesus speaks of in Matthew 5:48—"Ye therefore shall be perfect, as your heavenly Father is perfect" (RV); but in order to get there we have to go the longest way round. The end is a relationship to God perfect and complete in every particular, but it means going through a furnace of disillusionment, and the furnace burns hard. One of the cruellest experiences is the disappointment over what we find in other lives. The last thing we learn is not to glory in men. Jesus Christ never expected from human nature what it was not designed to give; consequently He was never bitter or cynical. Unless our human relationships are based in God they will end in frantic disillusionment. The cause of it is the demand in human nature for satisfaction. No human being can ever give satisfaction, and when I demand it and do not get it I become cruel and spiteful. When we are rightly related to Jesus Christ human love is transfigured because the last aching abyss of the heart is satisfied; but if the relationship with God is cut out our relationship to others is embittered. When once the relationship with God is right the satisfaction of human love is marvellous.

Christianity is not devotion to work, or to a cause, or a doctrine, but devotion to a Person, the Lord Jesus Christ. Christianity is a personal relationship which works spontaneously by "the moral originality of the Holy Ghost," there is a perfect gaiety of delight. You could never awaken self-pity in the Apostle Paul, you might starve him or imprison him, but you could never knock out of him that uncrushable gaiety and certainty of God. A *khamseen*[17] wind knocks us out! Paul refused to take anything or anyone seriously but Jesus Christ. That is Our Lord's teaching in the Sermon on the Mount, viz., "Be carefully careless of everything saving your relationship to Me." We take everything else but that seriously. Our experience of spiritual delight depends upon whether we are getting to know Jesus Christ better, whether we have the power to make what we know real. If you are going through disenchantment, remember that is not the end, the end is the life which exhibits the spirit of Jesus—"I delight to do Thy will, O My God."

HOW TO USE VICTORY

And in the morning, rising up a great while before day, He went out, and departed into a solitary place, and there prayed. Mark 1:35

This incident in the life of Our Lord occurred after what one would call a most successful day. He had endured the fierce onslaught in the wilderness, driven there for the devil to do his worst, and had come off more than conqueror, for we read that "angels came and ministered unto Him." If after a season of temptation a saint retains the power that draws the purest spirits to him, he may feel assured that the temptation has been gone through with successfully. Our Lord had called the men who were to be His disciples, and they had promptly left all and followed Him; He had had a triumphant time in Capernaum, casting out demons and setting men and women free. The fame and success of this mysterious Being grew, and we read that "all the city was gathered together at the door." It was after this time of eminent success in relieving men and blessing them that Jesus departed into a solitary place and spent the night in prayer.

Dr. George Adam Smith,[18] in a sermon on Prayer, uses the following illustration from his own experience in Switzerland. He was an ardent mountain climber, and (I quote from memory) as he neared the top of a certain mountain his guide stepped back in order to let him have the privilege of being first on the top. He said the exhilaration of the experience made him leap and jump for joy, but instantly the guide called out, "Down on your knees! It isn't safe standing up there." Dr. Smith used the illustration in the way I want to use it. After our days of successful service are we spending too much time in exuberant joy and shouting, forgetting that the only safe place is on our knees?

---

17. *khamseen*: also *khamsin;* a hot, south wind from the Sahara.
18. George Adam Smith (1856–1942): Scottish Old Testament scholar.

"And in the morning, rising up a great while before day, He went out, and departed into a solitary place, and there prayed." I wonder what that night and early dawn hid? Our Lord went through His days with such easy power; what did He do in those solitary moments alone with God? Did He go back, in mind at least, to the glory which He had with the Father before the world was? Did He recline on the bosom of the Father and hear unspeakable words not lawful to utter? Such thoughts as these are not presumptuous but the meditation of the heart that knows what communion with God means. If that communion means so much to a human heart that has been saved and sanctified through the Atonement, what must it have meant to the Son of God? What it was Our Lord experienced is hidden from us, yet we too in our measure have had the unspeakable experience, if rare, when the dark night of Nature gives place to the dawn, when the "huge and thoughtful" silence of the night makes everything that is petty and trifling fall away, and lifts us into the larger isolation, which is no isolation but the realisation of the presence of God.

Where do we place the night of prayer and the dawn of intercession in our soul's calendar? do we place it after a day of marvellous success in work for God? If we do not, our souls are in peril. Have we ever sufficiently realised our responsibility along the line of intercession? The Apostle Paul emphasises the tremendous importance of prayer—"Praying always with all prayer and supplication in the Spirit, and watching thereunto with all perseverance and supplication for all saints; *and for me. . . .*" When our souls have been lifted into the presence of God and we have grasped some truth with new illumination, how much time have we spent in prayer for those servants and handmaids whom God has used to bless us? We allow ourselves to imagine that it would be presumptuous on our part to pray for the "Pauls"; but this is a snare of Satan.

Notice this phrase, "He departed into a solitary place"; and notice also Our Lord's instructions regarding private prayer—"But thou, when thou prayest, enter into thy closet, *and when thou hast shut thy door,* pray to thy Father which is in secret." Any soul who has not that solitary place alone with God is in supreme peril spiritually. Let us ask ourselves if we have allowed the solitary places to be broken down or built over with altars that look beautiful, and people passing by say "How religious that man or woman must be." Such an altar, if there is no other in the solitary place, is an insult to the deep work of God in our souls. God grant we may learn more and more of the profound joy of getting alone with God in the dark of the night and toward the early dawn.

THE WITNESS OF SORROW

Set a mark upon the foreheads of the men that sigh and that cry for all the abominations that be done in the midst thereof. Ezekiel 9:4

We can fathom our own natures by the things we sorrow over. In this ancient Book of Ezekiel the man clothed in linen, with a writer's inkhorn by his side, was to set a mark upon the foreheads of the men who sorrowed for the city's sin. Let us take time to wonder if such a visitant on such an errand would mark us as among the people privileged to sorrow thus. Jeremiah has been called "the weeping prophet," and in his Lamentations we find that the secret of his sorrow is Jerusalem, the city of his love. "How doth the city sit solitary, that was full of people!" (Lamentations 1:1). Instantly our minds pass on to what is recorded in Luke 19:41, "And when He drew nigh, He saw the city and wept over it" (RV), and we remember with adoring wonder that Our Lord is known throughout all generations as "a Man of sorrows."

1. Worldly Sorrow
. . . the sorrow of the world worketh death. (2 Corinthians 7:10)

It is a terrible thing to say, and yet true, that there is a sorrow so selfish, so sentimental and sarcastic that it adds to the sin of the city. All sorrow that arises from being baffled in some selfish aim of our own is of the world and works death. Those who sorrow over their own weaknesses and sins and stop short at that, have a sorrow that only makes them worse, it is not a godly sorrow that works repentance. Oh that all men knew that every sentiment has its appropriate reaction, and if the nature does not embrace that reaction it degenerates into a sullen sentimentalism that kills all good action.

How certain it is that the men in Jerusalem of old upon whose foreheads the mark was set, were working out the appropriate reaction of their sorrow. It is an appalling thing to mourn and sigh over the sins and iniquities of our city and do nothing about it.

2. Working Sorrow

For godly sorrow worketh repentance unto a salvation which bringeth no regret. (2 Corinthians 7:10 RV mg)

No one can be touched with sorrow for the sins of his city unless he has felt keen sorrow over his own sins. The Apostle Paul never forgot his past sins (see 1 Timothy 1:12–16). Scriptural repentance leads to positive salvation and sanctification; the only truly repentant man is the holy man. Every forgiven soul will love the world so much that he hates to death the sin that is damning men; to love the world in any other sense is to be an enemy of God: to love the world as God loves it is to spend and be spent that men might be saved from their sins. Godly sorrow not only works a positive godliness, but grants us the mark of the Cross in winning souls, an unsleeping sorrow that keeps us at it night, day and night, filling up "that which is behind of the afflictions of Christ."

3. Winsome Sorrow

Behold, and see if there be any sorrow like unto my sorrow. (Lamentations 1:12)

The sign for the world without God is a circle, complete in and for itself; the sign for the Christian is the Cross. The Christian knows by bitter yet blessed conviction of sin that no man is sufficient for himself, and he thereby enters into identification with the Cross of Calvary, and he longs and prays and works to see the sinful, self-centred world broken up and made the occasion for the mighty Cross to have its way whereby men may come to God and God come down to men.

4. Weakening Sorrow

What, could ye not watch with Me one hour? (Matthew 26:40)

For this cause many among you are weak and sickly, and not a few sleep. (1 Corinthians 11:30 RV)

There are many to-day who are suffering from spiritual sleeping sickness, and the sorrow of the world which works death is witnessed in all directions. If personal sorrow does not work itself out along the appropriate line, it will lull us to a pessimistic sleep. For instance, when we see our brother "sinning a sin not unto death" (1 John 5:16 RV), do we get to prayer for him, probed by the searching sorrow of his sin? Most of us are so shallow spiritually that when Our Lord in answer to some outrageous request we have made, asks us—"Are ye able to drink the cup that I drink? or to be baptized with the baptism that I am baptized with?" we say "We are able" (RV). Then He begins to show us what the cup and the baptism meant to Him—"But I have a baptism to be baptized with; and how am I straitened till it be accomplished!" (Luke 12:50). "And Jesus said unto them, Ye shall indeed drink of the cup that I drink of; and with the baptism that I am baptized withal shall ye be baptized"—and there begins to dawn for the disciple the great solemn day of martyrdom which closes for ever the day of exuberant undisciplined service, and opens the patient pilgrimage of pain and joy, with "more of the first than the last."

5. Without Sorrow

Many are in the "show business" spiritually, and the danger of this is greater than at first appears; it is a danger as old as the Book of Job, and is expressed in the character of Eliphaz who takes up the position of a superior person because of his own mysterious experience. Such an one could never have the mark set on his forehead as one who sighs and cries for the sin of his city; instead he would be an un-suffering dogmatist forgetting all about the sin of his city in his own personal experience. To-day there are in our midst many so-called Christian movements, but they bear the characteristic of being without sorrow for sin and without sympathy for suffering.

The witness of sorrow identifies us with Our Lord "who His own self bare our sins in His body" (RV); it binds us—if one may reverently put it so—into a mighty league of sin-bearers, pouring out the strenuous service of love and long-suffering akin to the love which God has shown to us. Thank God for the beauty of the Cross-crowned lives; it is the mark of the highest type of Christian life, the evidence of complete salvation.

And thus that far-off day in dim antiquity is linked with the great Day yet to be, of which it is written, "And they shall see His face; *and His name shall be in their foreheads*" (Revelation 22:4).

SINCERITY AND REALITY

Simon, I have somewhat to say unto thee. . . . Master, say on. Luke 7:40

It is quite possible to be a sincere person, to be in earnest in proclaiming the truth of God, and yet not have one iota of reality along with it. This does not mean that the sincere person is a hypocrite or a sham, but it does mean that he has never understood that God wants him to be *real.*

In Luke 7 we read that "one of the Pharisees desired Him that He would eat with him. And He entered into the Pharisee's house, and sat down to meat" (RV). Simon, his host, was no doubt sincere; he kept his own counsel, and while he said nothing openly of his disapproval of the penitent woman's presence, yet he "spake within himself, saying, This man, if He were a prophet, would have perceived who and what manner of woman this is which toucheth Him, that she is a sinner" (RV). Then Jesus proved He was a prophet indeed by telling Simon aloud all he had been thinking silently, and went on to point out that his Pharisaic standards had caused him to treat Him in a neglectful manner—"thou gavest Me no water for My feet": "thou gavest Me no kiss": "My head with oil thou didst not anoint. . . ." When Our Lord enters our homes, or our churches, or social order, and says "I have somewhat to say unto thee," many of us, like Simon, answer quite sincerely, "Master, say on," although what Jesus has to say may prove just as unpalatable to us as it must have been to Simon.

Custom in spiritual matters is apt to make us peculiarly dead to much that Jesus Christ has to say—our perfectly sincere mood blinds us to the terrible fact that we are utterly un-real. What about all our sincere talk of sanctification—are we *really* sanctified? our sincere talk about the Holy Spirit—are we *really* indwelt by the Spirit? our sincere talk about the Sermon on the Mount—are we *really* living out its teaching? Let us examine ourselves and see whether religious "use and wont"[19] has not resulted in our being perfectly sincere in our testimony for the Truth while we are quite un-real as regards a genuine living out of the Truth. We have to beware of the deadening of our conscience spiritually through familiarity with certain favourite passages of Scripture (e.g., Luke 11:13; John 3:16; Galatians 2:20). There is a kind of quiet smugness about a knowledge of Scripture which says, sincerely, "Thank God I know that now," while the life may be as un-real as a mirage, for "the letter killeth, but the Spirit gives life."

It may give us a surprising shock to have our spiritual customs broken into by some word of Jesus applied by the Spirit, but in this way the sensitiveness of our conscience, which is ever apt to go to sleep over the repetition of sincere religious customs, is quickened. We may think it a great thing to answer to Jesus, in all sincerity, "Master, say on," and yet it may piously mean that we only intend to listen to Him about the things over which we have made up our minds; it is quite a different matter to be willing, at all cost to spiritual pride and prejudice, to be willing to re-arrange everything under the authority of Jesus Christ, until we are real with the vivid reality which tells not only in our actions, but in the atmosphere we carry with us. May the Holy Spirit keep us full of the marvel of the statements of Jesus, and so renew us in the spirit of our minds that we more and more sensitively apprehend God's purpose in our lives.

The cure for this perilous divorce between sincerity and reality lies in the determined service of the mind. To say, "Master, say on," as a mere homage of the lips, while we are quietly determined to go on just as we have always done, is false and damaging, and this is bound to be the result in the most sincere soul among us unless we allow the Holy Spirit to continually renew our minds by concentration on The Truth. It is the spiritual interpretation of Our Lord's teaching which makes us real, and gives us the power to overcome the world and be the inspirers of many a lagging-behind soul. The strength of a *real* man or *real* woman cannot be estimated. There is always a great danger that the sentimental emotions which drift around every high and holy certainty may shift us from the courageous concentration on Christ's teaching which alone can make us and keep us real.

Let us with renewed concentration so obey Our Lord that He may find us hopeful, alert, wide-awake saints, determined to keep in sympathy with His words and His point of view.

"I have somewhat to say unto *thee. . . . Master, say on.*"

---

19. use and wont: custom; habit; familiarity.

DEVOTIONAL "WE" OR "ME"?
Matthew 23:8–10

"WE" meant to serve so much,
In daily life to help the poor and sad,
And by the tenderness of word and deed
To make them feel God's goodness, and be glad;
    Should "I" serve less?

"WE" meant to love so much,
To let our kindred, friends and neighbours feel
That we had been with Christ and learned of
    Him
The gentlest ways of love to help and heal;
    Dare "I" love less?

Because "WE" meant so much,
Shall I with coward heart lie down and see
Life's meaning and its service unfulfilled
My Father! Grant the strength and love to "me"
    Not to do less!

The aspect of collective discipleship and individual discipleship is frequently brought out in the New Testament. It is so easy to talk about what "we" are going to do—"we" are going to do marvellous things, and it ends in none of us doing anything. The incident in John 6:66–71 brings clearly to light the "we" aspect as emphasised by Peter, and also Our Lord's rigorous sorting of it out to the personal element—"Would ye also go away? Simon Peter answered Him, Lord, to whom shall we go? . . ." (RV). Then Jesus says something that seems irrelevant but is not—"Did I not choose you the twelve, and one of you is a devil?" (RV). We never become disciples in crowds or even in twos; discipleship is always a personal matter (see Luke 13:23–24; John 21:21–22). We are brought together by God, not by our own selecting. Let me get my "me" rightly related to Jesus Christ and I shall find others will get related in the same way.

1. Omniscient Teacher
For one is your Teacher, and all ye are brethren. (RV)

It is necessary to haul ourselves up short and ask—Do I recognise Jesus Christ as my Teacher, or am I at the mercy of vague spiritual impulses of my own? Am I accepting someone else's conception of God, or am I bringing everything I hear, every impulse, every emotion that comes to me, into line with the teaching of Christ? The test of every spiritual impulse is, does it make Jesus Christ the supreme Teacher? Jesus said, When the Holy Spirit is come, "He shall teach you all things." The Holy Spirit is the great bond of union because He keeps us united to the one Teacher. Jesus

Christ is not a great Teacher alongside Plato and other great teachers; He stands absolutely alone. "Test your teachers," said Jesus; the teachers who come from God are those who clear the way to Jesus Christ, and keep it clear. We are estimated in God's sight as workers by whether or not we clear the way for people to see Jesus.

2. Omnipresent Father
For one is your Father, which is in heaven.

George MacDonald in one of his books gives a graphic description of the wonderful simplicity a child of God has; he pictures Job opening God's private door, as it were, and flinging himself into His presence and presenting his problems. He is indicating the freedom a child of God has to come and say, "I am puzzled by this and that; why should things be so?" He is coming not to a monarch who will terrify him, but to a Father, if he is a disciple, and he can speak just like a child with perfect simplicity and freedom. Some of us seem to have the idea that we are away in a howling wilderness and we must cry and agonise before we can get God's ear. Turn to the New Testament and see what Jesus says—"Father, I thank Thee that Thou hast heard Me. And I knew that Thou hearest Me always."

"One is your Father"—your Father! Think for one minute, have you behaved to-day as though God were your Father or have you to hang your head in absolute shame before Him for the miserable, mean, unworthy thoughts you have had about your life? It all springs from one thing, you have lost hold of the idea that God is your Father. Some of us are such fussy, busy people, refusing to look up and realise the tremendous revelation in Jesus Christ's words—*"Your heavenly Father knoweth. . . ."*

3. Omnipotent Master
For one is your Master, even Christ.

There is no room in Our Lord's conception of discipleship for a disciple to say, "Now, Lord, I am going to serve You." That does not come into His idea of discipleship. It is not that we work for God, but that God works through us; He uses us as He likes, He allots our work where He chooses, and we learn obedience, even as our Lord did. ". . . though He were a Son, yet learned He obedience by the things which He suffered." Jesus said, "As the Father hath sent Me, even so send I you" (RV). How did God send Jesus? To do His will. How does Jesus send His disciples?

To do His will. "Ye shall be My witnesses" (RV), a satisfaction to Christ wherever we are placed.

"One is your Master, even Christ"; He is all-wise, stand true to Him and other saints will be true to you; if you stand true to someone else's teaching you will find you become segregated from the saints. "But if we walk in the light, as He is in the light, we have fellowship one with another. . . ." If you hide anything in your life with God, down you go, no matter what you have experienced; hide nothing.

THE MINISTRY OF THE INTERIOR

I have set watchmen upon thy walls, O Jerusalem; they shall never hold their peace day nor night: ye that are the LORD's remembrancers, take ye no rest, and give Him no rest, till He establish, and till He make Jerusalem a praise in the earth. Isaiah 62:6–7 (RV)

And the LORD said unto him, Go through the midst of the city, through the midst of Jerusalem, and set a mark upon the foreheads of the men that sigh and cry for all the abominations that be done in the midst thereof. Ezekiel 9:4

Do I know anything experimentally about this aspect of things? Have I ever spent one minute before God in intercessory importunity over the sins of other people? If we take these statements of the prophets and turn the searchlight on ourselves, we will be covered with shame and confusion because of our miserably selfish, self-centred Christianity.

How many of us have ever entered into this Ministry of the Interior where we become identified with Our Lord and with the Holy Spirit in intercession? It is a threefold intercession: at the Throne of God, Jesus Christ; within the saint, the Holy Ghost; outside the saint, common-sense circumstances and common-sense people, and as these are brought before God in prayer the Holy Spirit gets a chance to make intercession according to the will of God. That is the meaning of personal sanctification, and that is why the barriers of personal testimony must be broken away and effaced by the realisation of why we are sanctified—not to be fussy workers for God, but to be His servants, and this is the work, vicarious intercession.

One of the first lessons learnt in the Ministry of the Interior is to talk things out before God in soliloquy—tell Him what you know He knows in order that you may get to know it as He does. All the harshness will go and the suffering sadness of God's Spirit will take its place, and gradually you will be brought into sympathy with His point of view.

There is an advocacy of holiness which was never born at Calvary, it is the resuscitation of the Pharisaic spirit dressed in the garb of Pentecost—an insufferable superiority. The Spirit of God must have a deep indignation at the preaching of holiness that is not the holiness of Jesus. The holiness of Jesus is the most humble thing on earth.

When God puts a weight on you for intercession for a soul don't shirk it by talking to him. It is much easier to talk to him than to talk to God about him—much easier to talk to him than to take it before God and let the weight crush the life out of you until gradually and patiently God lifts the life out of the mire. That is where very few of us go.

When God brings a burden to you never allow it to develop into carnal suspicion. In the Ministry of the Interior all we have to do is simply to take the matter before God and be made "crushed grapes" until the Holy Spirit produces such an atmosphere that the one who is wrong cannot endure it. That is God's method, and we interfere by using our own discernment.

The knowledge of where people are wrong is a hindrance to prayer, not an assistance. "I want to tell you of the difficulties so that you may pray intelligently." The more you know the less intelligently you pray because you forget to believe that God can alter the difficulties.

"Howbeit when the Son of man cometh, shall He find faith on the earth?" (RV). Which one of us would God stop at and say, "That one is My remembrancer" (RV)? or would He have to say, "That one is serving a conviction of his own, he is not My servant at all"?

" . . . greater works than these shall he do; because I go unto the Father. *And whatsoever ye shall ask in My name, that will I do.*"

"FOR CHRIST'S CROWN AND COVENANT"

For Christ's Crown and Covenant[20] comes nearer to the New Testament conception of loyalty to Christ than any other all down the centuries of Christianity, and what we need to do is to translate it into terms which fit our own day and generation.—this motto of the Scottish Covenanters.[21]

1. Loyalty to His Royalty
Pilate therefore said unto Him, Art Thou a king then? Jesus answered, Thou sayest it, because I am a king. (John 18:37 RV mg)

Jesus Christ is not only Saviour, He is King, and He has the right to exact anything and everything from us at His own discretion. We talk about the joys and comforts of salvation; Jesus Christ talks about taking up the cross and following Him. Whenever Our Lord talks about discipleship He prefaces it with an "If"— "you need not unless you like." It is always easier in certain crises to be "Demas" than a devoted disciple. Very few of us know anything about loyalty to Jesus Christ. "For My sake"—that is what makes the iron saint. We look upon Jesus Christ as the best Example of the Christian life; we do not conceive of Him as Almighty God Incarnate, with all power in heaven and on earth. We make Him a comrade, One who in the battle of life has more breath than the rest of us and He turns round to lend a hand. We deal with Him as if He were one of ourselves; we do not take off the shoes from our feet when He speaks. Jesus Christ is Saviour, and He saves us into His own absolute and holy lordship.

2. Loyalty to His Lordship
Ye call Me, Master, and, Lord: and ye say well; for so I am. (John 13:13 RV)

From a dog to a man, the master makes the difference. "Pi" people have no master, they are always hole-and-corner folks. Whenever a man is mastered by Jesus Christ you have a man "with breast and back as either should be," no whimperer, no sentimentalist, no pietist, but a man of God. That can only be produced by the mastership of Jesus Christ. The curious thing about Our Lord is that He never insists on our obedience. When we begin to usurp authority and say, "You must" and "you shall" it is a sure sign that we are out of touch with the supreme Authority. If you are in

a position of authority and people are not obeying you, the greatest heart-searching you can have is the realisation that the blame does not lie with them, but with you; there is a leakage going on spiritually. Get right with God yourself, and every other one will get in touch with God through you.

3. Loyalty to His Rule
I am crucified with Christ: nevertheless I live; yet not I, but Christ liveth in me. (Galatians 2:20)

To imagine that Jesus Christ came to save and sanctify *me* is heresy: He came to save and sanctify me *into Himself,* to be His absolute bondslave; so completely His bondslave that when He speaks there is no possibility of dispute. "I reckon on you for extreme service, with no complaining on your part and no explanation on Mine." We begin to debate and say, "Why shouldn't I do this? I'm within my rights." That idea is so foreign to Our Lord's conception that He has made no provision for it. The passion of Christianity is that I deliberately sign away my own rights and become a bondslave of Jesus Christ. Any fool can insist on his rights, and any devil will see that he gets them; but the Sermon on the Mount means that the only right the saint will insist on is the right to give up his rights. That is the New Testament idea of sanctification, and that is why so few get anywhere near the baptism with the Holy Ghost. "I want to be baptised with the Holy Ghost so that I may be of use"—then it is all up. We are baptised with the Holy Ghost not *for* anything at all, but entirely, as Our Lord puts it, to be His witnesses, those with whom He can do exactly what He likes.

4. Loyalty to His Calling
And we know that to them that love God all things work together for good [God worketh all things with them for good, mg], even to them that are called according to His purpose. (Romans 8:28 RV)

It is only the loyal saint who believes that God engineers circumstances. We take such liberties with our circumstances, we treat the things that happen as if they were engineered by men, although we say that we believe God engineers them. To be faithful in every circumstance means that we have only one loyalty, and that is to our Lord. Most of us are too devoted to our own ideas of what God wants even to

---

20. "For Christ's Crown and Covenant." Chambers used this as the motto for the Bible Training College (BTC).
21. Scottish Covenanters (1638) refused to honor the head of state as the head of the church.

hear His call when it comes. We may be loyal to what we like, but we may find we have been disloyal to God's calling of us by not recognising Him in either the distress and humiliation or the joy and blessing. The test of loyalty always comes just there.

Loyalty to our own ideas is always the result of disloyalty to a person. God educates us by people. Any refusal to be loyal to whatever "Elijah" God sends us is detected by pious talk about being loyal to a word of God. Loyalty to the teachers God sends ends ultimately in supreme devotion to Himself. Beware how you treat the messengers of God because there is only one aim in the true messengers of God, and that is unflinching loyalty to the Lordship of Jesus Christ, and we shall have to account to God for our heedfulness of them or our heedlessness.

CLEANSED FROM SIN

1. Where Sin Ceases. "*Walk in the Light*"

But if we walk in the light, as He is in the light, we have fellowship one with another, and the blood of Jesus Christ His Son cleanseth us from all sin. (1 John 1:7)

"*. . . as He is in the light*"—God has nothing to hide: have I anything to hide from God? If I try to vindicate myself, I am not in the light; if I say "I can explain that away," I am not in the light, I have something to cover up; but if I walk in the light *as God is in the light,* then comes the amazing revelation that so that God Almighty can see nothing to censure "the blood of Jesus Christ His Son cleanseth us from all sin," in me. That is not a conscious experience, it is a revelation. If you make the experience of conscious freedom from sin the test you make hypocrites. Sin enough and you will soon be unconscious of sin. The nature of sin is that it destroys the possibility of knowing that you sin. Sin ceases when I am in the light as God is in the light, and in no other way. In my experience it works with a keen poignant knowledge of what sin is (cf. 1 Timothy 1:15–16).

"*If we confess our sins, He is faithful and just to forgive us our sins, and to cleanse us from all unrighteousness*" *(1 John 1:9)*. Watch the difference between *confessing* and *admitting*; the majority of us are quite ready to admit, it is the rarest thing to get to the place where we will confess—confess to God, not to man. It is much more difficult to confess to God than we are apt to think. It is not confessing in order to be forgiven; confession is the evidence that I am forgiven. God does not forgive me because I confess; I realise by my confession that I am forgiven. Am I willing to be brought to the place where God draws out my confession? When the Spirit of God convicts of sin it is not like a detective convicting a criminal, it is sin finding out a man's own nature and making him say, "Yes, I recognise it." When once your sin does find you out, the exquisite pain of confessing acts like the sweetest medicine—"a broken and a contrite heart, O God, Thou wilt not despise." Beware of having anything that makes your mind accept an excuse for yourself. I can step out of darkness into the light—when God is willing? No, when I am willing. "I do want to be in living communion with God"; I don't, if I did, I could be there in one second; the reason I am not there is that I won't confess, I won't submit to God's condemnation of the thing. Immediately confession is made the Atonement of Our Lord steps in with its supernatural efficacy.

2. Where Love Invades. "*Walk in Love*"

And walk in love, even as Christ also loved you. . . . (Ephesians 5:2 RV)

If I want God's light to increase in me until I am a child of the light, 1 Corinthians 13 is what I must measure up to.

"*Love suffereth long, and is kind . . .*" *(RV)*. Have you had to suffer anything? have you remained kind in heart? It is damnably easy to be kind in speech and cruel in heart. To "walk in love" means that the very breathing of my disposition is kindness. If I get the trick of the right expression of face and speech, I can harbour a spirit that is as unlike Jesus Christ as can be. Beware of affectation spiritually, it is the very paw of the devil over the saint.

"*Love envieth not . . .*" *(RV)*. Envy and jealousy may remain entirely latent until competition is launched on a certain plane and I recognise someone else's superiority; there is no getting away from it, I recognise that in the particular quality on which I prided myself, the other person is superbly my superior. How do I know when I am envious, jealous of someone being what I am not? When I am secretly rather glad, though my lips say the opposite, when that one stumbles. It springs from a jealous dislike of easily recognised superiority in the very same line of things as my own. No one can be with a superior person without having a feeling of envy and jealousy unless he is a saint; the saint knows no jealousy or envy because the life of the Lord Jesus is being manifested in him.

"seeketh not her own . . ." Self is so completely effaced that the only characteristic of the life is, "in all the world, my God, there is none but Thee." Its self does not bother its self, it is altogether devoted to God's interests in others.

"is not provoked . . ." (RV). Was Jesus Christ ever irritable? am I? God will put me in places where it would be natural for me to be provoked so that He might magnify His grace in me.

". . . taketh not account of evil" (RV). If someone has done an unkind thing to you, don't let it blot God out. Apart from God we do reckon with evil, we reason from that standpoint. To "take no account of evil" does not mean we are ignorant of its existence; it means we do not take it in as a calculable factor. When the love of God is shed abroad in my heart by the Holy Ghost there is no lurking nest of remembrance in my spirit for the evil. Always beware of suspicion, it comes from the devil and ends there. The Holy Spirit never suspects.

First Corinthians 13 is sentiment transfigured into character. Love springs spontaneously, that is, it is not premeditated: but love does not develop like that. Both naturally and spiritually love requires careful developing; love won't stay if it is not sedulously cultivated. If I am not careful to keep the atmosphere of my love right by cultivation, it will turn to lust—"I must have this thing for myself." No love of the natural heart is safe unless the human heart has been satisfied by God first. The tragedies of human lives can only be solved by an understanding of the one great fundamental truth that Jesus Christ alone can satisfy the last aching abyss of the human heart.

LEAST IN THE KINGDOM OF HEAVEN

Whosoever therefore shall break one of these least commandments, and shall teach men so, he shall be called the least in the kingdom of heaven. Matthew 5:19

John Wesley in expounding this passage said it meant that "whosoever shall break one of these least commandments, and shall teach men so, shall not be in the kingdom of heaven at all"; but Our Lord is warning that it is possible to be as "the least" in the kingdom of heaven. When the Apostle Paul says he is "less than the least of all saints," he is not referring to this standard of measurement, but to himself in his own eyes. (See Ephesians 3:8.)

What is it exactly to be "least in the kingdom of heaven"? For one thing, the words surely point out the necessity of searching the Scriptures in order to find out what the commandments and precepts of God are. As we go on in the spiritual life the Spirit of God educates us down to the scruple,[22] that is, He applies the commandments of God to all the ramifications of our being. We may see Christian people doing things that surprise us, and yet it would be untrue to say they were not Christians; as you watch their development in the ways of God you find they are becoming more and more careful over things they used to be careless over.

The writer to the Hebrews warns us about "the sin which doth closely cling to us" (RV mg), literally, the spirit of the age, the spirit which makes our minds obtuse to the commandments of God. There is a culture in the spiritual life not realised by all teachers and preachers, consequently they tell men that God does not hold certain things necessary. What an awakening awaits all such when they stand before God and find they have not glorified Him as they should have done, because they stood more for their own personal freedom and independent rights than for the careful searching out of Our Lord's commandments and teaching men regarding them. It is easy for those who are "out and out" for God to condemn such teachers and put them outside the kingdom; Our Lord puts them not outside, but as "least in the kingdom."

This warning should bring us to the place where we measure up and see whether we are growing in sensitiveness towards all God's commandments so that we tremble at the very approach of any defilement that might blur the clear vision of His truth. Our spiritual fighting trim becomes enervated by any compromise with the world's standards, and if we teach men by both word and precept to do the same, we run perilously near being those Our Lord warns.

To know how to maintain and develop the habits of the holy life according to the commandments of God is the sublime education of the soul. There are times of ignorance that God winks at and overlooks, but there are other times when He holds us responsible for being frivolous and light regarding His commandments. I wonder how many of us in our dealing with our fellow men have made it easy for them to break some of the commandments of God because it was so hard for us to appear unsympathetic with them?

---

22. down to the scruple: to the smallest item.

"he shall be called least in the kingdom of heaven," says Our Lord. What need there is that the minister of the Gospel should continually face himself with his Saviour, to know how he stands before Him, lest he fail to measure up to His standard, and having preached to others should himself become a castaway.

The argument that the keeping of certain commandments is not essential to salvation is such a mean,[23] beggarly line of argument that it need scarcely be mentioned. If my love for God is so faint and poor that I will only do what is absolutely essential and not what it is my privilege to do, it is then that I deserve not only to be "least in the kingdom of heaven," but not to be in it at all. May every faculty of heart and mind and soul be roused up to be its glorious best for God all the time for the glory of the Lord Jesus Christ.

PAUL'S WAYS IN CHRIST

For this cause have I sent unto you Timothy, . . . who shall put you in remembrance of my ways which be in Christ. 1 Corinthians 4:17 (RV)

You say—"How can I follow Paul? I was not trained at the feet of Gamaliel like he was; nor have I any of his great gifts." Watch Paul's argument in this very chapter—"For who maketh thee to differ from another? and what hast thou that thou didst not receive?" (1 Corinthians 4:7). The following has nothing to do with natural gifts, or natural ability, or natural anything; Paul says, "Follow my ways *which be in Christ.*"

1. The Way of Conversion
And he said, Who art Thou, Lord? (Acts 9:5)

When God touches a life by bereavement, or by sickness or disaster, it is always a supernatural touch. What did you do in that moment when the true attitude of your life was revealed in a flash? did you say with Saul of Tarsus, "Who art Thou, Lord?" It was not the supernatural light from heaven that made Paul tremble, but the voice that spoke to him, the voice of the despised Nazarene: "I am Jesus whom thou persecutest. . . . And he trembling and astonished said, Lord, what wilt Thou have me to do?" Paul was turned in one second from a strong-willed intense Pharisee into a humble devoted slave of the Lord Jesus. There was no mention of sin, that came later: it was a complete surrender to the lordship of Jesus.

2. The Way of Consecration
For I will shew him how great things he must suffer for My name's sake. (Acts 9:16)

There has been an absolute swing round in Saul's life, he has enthroned Jesus as Lord, and now Ananias comes and calls him "Brother Saul," and mentions again *"the Lord,* even Jesus that appeared unto thee in the way as thou camest, hath sent me, that thou mightest receive thy sight, and be filled with the Holy Ghost." When Paul received his sight, he received a spiritual insight into the Person of Jesus Christ. Martin Luther said that Paul was intoxicated with Jesus Christ; He was never out of his waking or his sleeping moments, and all through his Epistles is stamped this certainty of his knowledge of Jesus as Lord. That is the marvellous thing about the baptism of the Holy Ghost, every other spell is gone—

Since mine eyes have looked on Jesus
I've lost sight of all beside.

The baptism of the Holy Ghost makes us witnesses to Jesus, not witnesses to what He can do, that is an elementary witness, but "witnesses unto Me." The spirit that comes in is not that of *doing* anything for Jesus, but of being a perfect delight to Him. "For I will shew him how great things he must suffer *for My name's sake."* Paul gloried in his suffering, and when he sums it all up he calls it "our light affliction"! It is the triumphant phrase of a super-conqueror. You can't imagine Paul saying "I've had such a tussle with the devil but I have got the victory"; it was the Victor who had got Paul, he was absolutely Jesus Christ's.

3. The Way of Conference
But when it pleased God . . . to reveal His Son in me, . . . immediately I conferred not with flesh and blood. (Galatians 1:15–16)

When Paul realised the Divine call he did not confer with flesh and blood, his own or any one else's; imagine him in the desert alone with God, while the Holy Ghost worked in him those revelations which found expression afterwards in his Epistles, and you have a picture of his way of conference. When God speaks to you what do you do? go to the nearest saint and ask him about it? That is wrong. If God has spoken, confer with Him alone, rely on the Holy Spirit, and He

---

23. mean: ordinary, common, low, or ignoble, rather than cruel or spiteful

will soon clinch the matter. "My sheep hear My voice," said Jesus. Many go astray because they will not take Paul's way of conference. Born-again souls should be thrust out to testify, not into work; they need to soak before God until they become rooted and grounded in the revelation of God, and have learned how to submit their will and intelligence to Jesus Christ.

4. The Way of Confidence
Though I might also have confidence in the flesh. (Philippians 3:4)

If any man has reason to boast in the flesh, Paul says he is that man—"an Hebrew of the Hebrews; as touching the law, a Pharisee; concerning zeal, persecuting the church; touching the righteousness which is in the law, blameless"; but, he says, we are those who "rejoice in Christ Jesus, and have no confidence in the flesh." Paul continually counsels, "Don't glory in men." The best of men are but the best of men. Never trust the best man or woman you ever met, trust only the Lord Jesus. If when you are sanctified you turn for one second to the natural life, the sentence of death is there. Never take your guidance from the natural life, but learn to sacrifice the natural to the will of God.

5. The Way of the Cross
But none of these things move me, neither count I my life dear unto myself. . . . (Acts 20:24)

Did that sound like the modern advice—"Now do be careful, don't work so hard, you must look after yourself." Paul says there is only one dear element about his life, and that is that it can be used for Jesus Christ to be glorified in. "I keep under my body," he says; "it does not dictate to me." Paul had received a ministry from the Lord Jesus, and in comparison of accomplishing that, he held nothing else of any account. "He shall testify of Me before kings," and Paul did so in the most fearless manner. Paul is so bound up with what he preaches that you cannot separate his preaching from his testimony. His Epistles are a testimony that he is determined to know nothing among men save Jesus Christ, and Him crucified. He welcomed heartbreaks, tribulation, suffering, for one reason only, that these things kept him in unmoved devotion to the gospel of the grace of God.

God grant that being put in remembrance of Paul's ways in Christ, we may learn to follow those ways, to His glory.

DISCIPLESHIP

Christ ruined many careers and brought sorrow and death to many souls.

Dr. Forsyth[24]
(*The Christian Ethic of War*, 1916)

1. The Call to Discipleship
If any man would come after Me, let him deny himself, and take up his cross daily, and follow Me. (Luke 9:23 RV)

The call of Jesus to discipleship has a fascinating side but also a desolating side; we nearly always ignore that side of the call. There is a difference between being a disciple and being what is called "saved." It is not the bad things that are the stumbling-block to becoming a disciple, anyone will give up sin and wrong if he knows how to, but will I give up the "rightest" thing I have got, viz., my right to myself? will I crown Jesus as Lord? Whenever Our Lord talks about discipleship that is what He bases it on, the giving up of my

right to myself—". . . *let him deny himself.*" Many are called, but few prove the choice ones, that is, few of us take up the cross and follow Jesus, the reason being not that we are irreligious and bad, but we don't prefer that Jesus should be Lord. We like to hear about deliverance from hell and forgiveness of sins, but this comes a bit too close, this demands too much, and we back out. "Upon this many of His disciples went back, and walked no more with Him" (RV), they went back from following Jesus and never became actual disciples. If I do become a disciple my career may have to be ruined, am I prepared for it? is He worth it? "IF any man would come after Me . . ." "If" means, "You don't need to unless you like, but you won't be of any account to Me in this life unless you do." Wherever Christian experience is proving unsatisfactory it is because the Holy Spirit is still battling around this one point, my right to myself, and until that is deliberately given over by me to Jesus Christ I will never have the relationship to Him He asks for.

---

24. Peter Taylor Forsyth (1848–1921) was a British Congregationalist minister and theologian. Chambers read many of Forsyth's books and valued his insights.

2. The Communion of Discipleship

Rabbi, . . . where abidest Thou? . . . Come, and ye shall see. (John 1:38–39 RV)

There is something so natural and yet so supernatural about Jesus. We never read that Jesus button-holed anybody; these men came to Him and asked, "Master, where do you live?" He said "Come, and ye shall see"—obvious and simple, yet full of Divine power. The difference between the Christianity stamped by the Holy Ghost and that stamped by ecstasy and fanaticism is just here, the one makes the supernatural "spooky" and puts the natural nowhere; the other makes the supernatural natural. Jesus does not come to men in extraordinary ways, but in the most ordinary things—washing disciples' feet; preparing breakfast; at a wedding feast. The early disciples were not attracted to Jesus because of their sense of sin, they were religious men, in touch with the elemental forces of nature, simple and unconventional, and when they saw Jesus their spirit indicated at once—"This is the very One we have been looking for." There are plenty of men who have not lived lives of sin—has Jesus Christ any message for them?

3. The Crown of Discipleship

John did no miracle: but all things that John spake of this man were true. (John 10:41)

The crown of John's discipleship was that his disciples became the disciples of Jesus. "And the two disciples heard him speak, and they followed Jesus" (John 1:37). If in the final issue the souls of those I have taught do not turn to Jesus when they see Him, I have been a traitor. In the New Testament it is never the personality of the preacher that counts, what counts is whether he knows how to direct those who come to him to Jesus. If a man preaches on the ground of his personality he is apt to be a detractor from Jesus. The only reason for presenting Jesus is that He is All-in-all to me absolutely. Many of us only know devoteeness to a creed, to a phase of evangelical truth, very few know anything about personal devotion to Jesus.

The call to discipleship comes as mysteriously as being born from above (RV mg); once a man hears it, it profoundly alters everything. It is like the call of the sea, the call of the mountains, not everyone hears these calls, only those who have the nature of the sea or the mountains—and then only if they pay attention to the call. To hear the call of God or the call to discipleship necessitates education in understanding and discernment. Never be afraid of the thing that is vague, the biggest things in life are vague as far as expression goes, but they are realities.

"Go ye therefore, and make disciples of all the nations. . . ." (RV)—not "Go out and save souls," but "Go and make disciples." It is comparatively easy to proclaim salvation from sin, but Jesus comes and says, "What about you—if *you* would be My disciple, deny yourself, take up that cross daily, and follow Me." It has nothing to do with eternal salvation, it has everything to do with our temporal value to God, and most of us do not care anything about our temporal worth to God, all we are concerned about is being saved from hell and put right for heaven. There is something infinitely grander than that, and Jesus Christ gives us a marvellous chance of giving up our right to ourselves to Him in order that we might become the devoted bondslaves of the One who saves us so supernaturally.

THE WORKER'S WAY ABOUT FAITH

1. Faith and the Ancient Witness *(Hebrews 11:4–40)*

. . . And these all, having had witness borne to them through their faith . . . (Hebrews 11:39)

Faith is never defined; it is described, as in Hebrews 11:1, but never defined. Definitions can only be given of things that are perfectly understood and are inferior to the mind that defines them. It is absurd to try and put God into a definition; if I can define God I am greater than God. Intellectual definition is of no use whatever in the spiritual life. Faith cannot be intellectually defined; faith is the inborn capacity to see God behind everything, the wonder that keeps you an eternal child. What is your faith to you—a wonderful thing, or a bandbox[25] thing? Satisfaction is too often the peace of death; wonder is the very essence of life. Beware always of losing the wonder, and the first thing that stops wonder is religious conviction. Whenever you give a trite testimony the wonder is gone. The only evidence of salvation or sanctification is that the sense of wonder is developing, not at things as they are, but at the One who made them as they are. There is no set definition of faith into which you can fit these men and women, they were heroes of faith because they "endured, as seeing Him who is invisible." The acts of faith the writer

---

25. bandbox: a small, round box made to hold neckbands or collars for shirts; metaphorically, something small, narrow, cloistered, self-contained.

refers to were not performed by astute-minded men and women who made defined statements about God, they were not tortured for convictions' sake, but for the sake of their faith. There is no mention of salvation from sin, the one point insisted on is their faith, and God is training us to do what they did, viz., live a life of tenacious hold upon God in spite of everything that happens. Do we know anything about this life of confidence in God, or are we everlastingly hunting in our theological "wardrobes" for definitions to work to? Faith is the indefinable certainty of God behind every thing, and is the one thing the Spirit of God makes clearer and clearer as we go on.

2. Faith and the Abiding Witness

. . . looking unto Jesus, the author and finisher of our faith. (Hebrews 12:2)

The abiding Witness is our Lord Jesus Christ, and the writer gives three characteristics of His life—*joy, renunciation,* and *reward.* The first element in the life of faith is joy, which means the perfect fulfilment of that for which we were created. Joy is not happiness; there is no mention in the Bible of happiness for a Christian, but there is plenty said about joy—". . . that they might have My joy fulfilled in themselves," said Jesus. The next element is the realisation that we have the delight of giving our lives as a lovegift to Jesus Christ. "He that loseth his life *for My sake* shall find it." Reward is the ultimate delight of knowing that God has fulfilled His purpose in my life; it is not a question of resting in satisfaction, but the delight of being in perfect conscious agreement with God.

3. Faith and the Alert Witness *(Hebrews 12:1–3)*

Let us also . . . lay aside every weight, and the sin which doth so easily beset us, and let us run with patience the race that is set before us. . . . (Hebrews 12:1 RV)

Run light—nothing clings to us more closely (RV mg) than trying to live up to the ideas we have got from saintly people. We have nothing to do with saintly people, we have only to do with "looking unto Jesus." How much "cargo" are you carrying in the upper storey? how many definitions to fit your teaching into? No wonder people have nervous breakdowns! Avoid definitions as you would avoid the devil. Immediately your mind accepts a definition you will learn no more about that thing until the definition is smashed. Definition and human authority are the two things that kill faith; with Jesus Christ there are no definitions at all. Jesus Christ always taught vaguely; in the beginning of our Christian life we think He teaches definitely, and we get hold of trite definitions until we find the marvellous life of God is not there at all.

Run looking—Keep nothing in view but the vision of the Lord Jesus Christ. To rest in any experience apart from Him, even though He gave it you, is to be away from the main Centre. Jesus Christ is first, second and third; let the revelation of His life keep you full of wonder, love and praise.

Run learning—"Despise not . . . the chastening of the Lord, nor faint when thou art rebuked of Him." Never stop learning. People stagnate, not through backsliding, but because they stop learning and harden into a wrong mental poise. We learn through chastisement, because God is supplying heaven with sons and daughters, not with precious stones. Sons and daughters must grow, and God is never in a hurry with us. As you go on in the life of faith you find everything is becoming so simple that you are afraid it can't be true, it is so unlike what you had been taught. Beware of being in bondage to yourself or to other people. Oppression and depression never come from the Spirit of God. He never oppresses, He convicts and comforts. It is unconscious stubbornness that brings us into bondage. In the presence of Jesus we find how perverse and timid and unfaithful we have been, when God was going to enlarge our life we shrank back. The summing up of the life of faith is the teaching of Jesus in the Sermon on the Mount—*Be carefully careless about everything saving your relationship to God.*

THE CERTAINTIES OF THE KINGDOM

1. The Substratum of Certainty *(Acts 17:22–29)*

Whom therefore ye ignorantly worship, Him declare I unto you. . . . For in Him we live, and move, and have our being. (Acts 17:23, 28)

Substratum—an under stratum or layer, a fundamental element that does not appear, but on which all that does appear rests.

There is a difference between the Christian foundation and my experience of it. I can no more experience the foundation of my faith than a building can experience its foundation; but the two must be associated. Dissatisfaction in the Christian life is sure to arise if the foundations are ignored. Because men cannot experience the foundations of the Christian faith they are apt to discard them as unnecessary: they are more necessary than all the experiences which spring from them. To say "You don't need theology to save a soul" is like saying "What is the good of a foundation? what we want is a house." The good of the foundation is that when the storms come nothing can wreck the "house" that is built on the foundation (see Matthew 7:24–27).

Theology is the science of Christianity; much that is wrongly called theology is mere psychological guess-work, verifiable only from experience. Christian theology is the ordered exposition of revelation certainties. If our teaching and preaching is not based on a recognition of those things that cannot be experienced it will produce parasites, people who depend on being fed by others. We are dealing in these studies with the great fundamental certainties of the Kingdom, and it is essential to take time to soak in these certainties so that when we get out into work we find we are rooted and grounded on the right foundation. If we go into work on the ground of our experience we will soon be exhausted.

What do I know about the foundation truths which I expect to reproduce in my own experience? Experience is an effect; I must have faith in a God whom I never can experience. My experiences are accountable for only by the fact that I am based on God who is bigger than all my experiences of Him. We must take time to know Who it is we worship. We worship a Revelation, not a mystery. "Whom therefore ye ignorantly worship, Him declare I unto you." How can I know God? Jesus Christ has revealed Him: "He that hath seen Me hath seen the Father." I do not *experience* God; I relate all my experiences to the revelation of God which Jesus Christ has made.

2. The Superstructure of Cultivation
(1 Corinthians 3:10–15)
But let every man take heed how he buildeth thereupon. (1 Corinthians 3:10)

Superstructure—anything erected on a foundation. We are to be wise masterbuilders, taking care that the superstructure is built according to the foundation, and see to it that we put on the foundation only those things that will stand the fire. Self-interest cannot stand the fire, it is not of the nature of God. There is a danger in us all of ignoring the fundamental things and dealing only with the things that affect our immediate interests; what engrosses our attention actually is what we are after. The "practical" craze, anything that is efficient, is the insanity of our day— we must be at it! Do anything at all, but don't take time to sit down and think and pray, that is a waste of time; all that is required is to live right practically. If

you are living right practically it is because you have not only experienced new birth, but you are being nourished on the right foundation. ". . . and the fire shall try every man's work of what sort it is." We put on the foundation stuff built by our own human energy, consequently as soon as it is touched by the fire of the Presence of God, it fizzles up; it is not of the nature of reality, it does not belong to the foundation. In 1 Corinthians 13:1–3, the Apostle Paul is referring to the white-heat of emotional energy, the height of intellectual efficiency and competence; I can do certain things and ostensibly prove I can, but, he says, it all amounts to nothing because it is not based on the foundation. The only work that will abide is that which is built on the Foundation, "which is Jesus Christ."

3. The Supremacy of Christ
Come unto Me. . . . (Matthew 11:28)

Supremacy—highest authority or power.

God never insists on our obedience; human authority does. Our Lord does not give us rules and regulations; He makes very clear what the standard is, and if the relation of my spirit to Him is that of love, I will do all He wants me to do without the slightest hesitation. If I begin to object it is because I love someone else in competition with Him, viz., myself.

Galatians 2:20 is foundation truth and experimental truth in one—"I am crucified with Christ: nevertheless I live; yet not I, but Christ liveth in me." These words mean the breaking of my independence and surrendering to the supremacy of the Lord Jesus. No one can do this for me, I must do it myself. There is no possibility of debate when once I am there. It is not that we have to do work for God, we have to be so loyal to Jesus Christ that He does His work through us. We learn His truth by obeying it.

"Come unto Me." It is the rarest thing for us to come to Jesus; we come to our own earnestness; we come with notions of what we want. How often have you come to God with your requests and gone away with the feeling, "Oh, well, I have done it this time"! and yet you go away with nothing, while all the time God has stood with outstretched hands, not only to take you but for you to take Him. Think of the invincible, unconquerable, unwearying patience of Jesus— *"Come unto Me."* The attitude of coming is that you fling yourself entirely on Him, and that is salvation, because *He* is salvation. Stake your all on God, and never be impertinent enough to tell Him that that is what you are doing. *Come,* if you are weary and heavy laden; *ask,* if you are evil; and everything that happens after that is of God.

The Highest Good

containing also
The Pilgrim's Song Book
and
Thy Great Redemption

Oswald Chambers

The Pilgrim's Song Book 1940
The Highest Good 1938
Thy Great Redemption 1937
Combined edition: copyright 1965 By Oswald Chambers Publications Association
Scripture versions quoted: KJV and RV

The Pilgrim's Song Book
Introduction

Source
The material in *The Pilgrim's Song Book* is from talks given by Oswald Chambers in the Wensleydale district of Yorkshire during August and September 1915.

Publication History
- As articles: The material was published as a series of articles in *Spiritual Life* magazine between October 1939 and May 1940.
- As a book: *The Pilgrim's Song Book* was first published as a book in 1940. It was published in a combined volume with *The Highest Good* and *Thy Great Redemption* in 1965.

After Oswald volunteered for service as a chaplain and was accepted by the YMCA, the Bible Training College[1] closed at the end of the term in July 1915. For their August holiday, Oswald, Biddy, and Kathleen[2] stayed in a house provided by their friend and League of Prayer[3] associate Jim Skidmore, in the Yorkshire village of Askrigg. During August, they hiked the moors, picnicked with friends, and Oswald fished the clear streams. They also kept an open door to a steady stream of family, friends, and former students of the Bible Training College. At their informal evening gatherings and at Sunday chapel services in the surrounding villages, Oswald spoke from the Psalms of Ascent, 120 through 134.

---

1. Residential school near Clapham Common in SW London, sponsored by the League of Prayer. Oswald Chambers was Principal and main teacher; Biddy Chambers was Lady Superintendent. Known as the BTC, it closed in July 1915 because of World War I.

2. Kathleen Chambers (1913–1997): the only child of Oswald and Biddy Chambers.

3. Pentecostal League of Prayer: founded in London in 1891 by Reader Harris (1847–1909), prominent barrister; friend and mentor of Oswald Chambers.

It is probable that Mrs. Chambers was unable to take notes of all Oswald's talks. Psalm 121 is not included, and the series concludes at Psalm 128. (For a 1910 message given by Oswald Chambers on Psalm 121, see *The Place of Help*, chapter 1.)

During September, Chambers began his ministry to soldiers in the training camps of Wensleydale. In October 1915, he sailed for Egypt, where he was joined in December by Biddy, Kathleen, and their close friend Mary Riley.[4]

Katherine Ashe's[5] foreword to the first edition expresses the freedom and joy of those summer days in Askrigg,[6] despite the shadow of uncertainty and separation cast on all of them by World War I.[7]

FOREWORD TO THE FIRST EDITION

"Our own are our own for ever" has been said by one and another in differing words and in many languages. That is why time and distance are (in a sense) nothing in any human life that lives in the "Things unseen—Eternal" where St. Paul had his abiding place.

And just as the essential beauty and sweetness of a rose is what stays with us, and not the very rose itself so it is the personality of a beloved person or the spirit of a season of time (to put it like that) that abides with us for ever. In London's hurrying life; in the press of teeming humanity in a Chinese city; in the grinding monotony of a quiet countryside; on a parched soil under a burning sky; in deep Canadian winter snows, or in the peace of a leisured life—the Yorkshire Moor away up at Wensleydale, with its waters and streams, its rushing winds and stealing lovely airs, its lights and its shadows, its cliffs and rolling spaces; above all, its magnificence of space and sky, is as present to bless and renew as if Wensleydale itself were here—our very own.

It was at Wensleydale around Askrigg that, in the summer and autumn of 1915, a company of men and women gathered to spend some weeks in the most informal way of living, coming and going, alone or together, gathered with one implicit motive—that of seeking to enter more deeply into a personal relationship with the Redeemer of the world, and into a deeper understanding of Redemption. The two people who created this most natural time of simplicity and freedom, lived that summer in a tiny cottage with Kathleen, then a gay and bonnie baby of two, and Mary of the deep and loving heart, and these Psalms and their exposition were part of the evening hour in the cottage. Some were given in the little plain unadorned Chapels in the villages:

> *I to the hills will lift mine eyes*
> *As the hills stand round about Jerusalem,*
>   *so . . .*

The sun by day, the moon by night, and always one sensed these were "Songs of Ascent," the marching, singing crowds, the hills, the stars—that and the deep, deep life of the human race in its going through the ages of time—one did not forget.

The war came into all our lives when those days ended. War, and the years that followed War—and the world was never again as we had known it. The great Earth—yes, and her glorious and most gentle loveliness and strength—but the thought and world dream of pre-war days was for ever gone. Only the stern business of holding the eternal values in the strange world dream of these new days is left us as our task.

But the pure and vigorous life of the thought and worship of that time remains—our own for ever; and the fresh strong gladness of its setting in the moors is ours for all time—for ever ours.

> *I to the hills will lift mine eyes;*
> *From whence shall come mine aid?*
> *My help it cometh from the Lord*
> *Who heaven and earth hath made.*

Katherine Ashe
Cairo, July 1940

---

4. Mary Riley was a BTC student who had a long association with the Chambers through the League of Prayer, at the Bible Training College, and with the YMCA in Egypt.

5. Katherine Ashe (1865–1956) was converted to Christ through Oswald Chambers' influence in Ireland in 1908. Miss Ashe, as she was always known, attended the BTC as a student and as a teacher, then went to Egypt in 1916 for ministry to soldiers through the YMCA.

6. Askrigg was a village in Wensleydale, Yorkshire, England.

7. World War I (1914–1918).

CONTENTS

I

PSALM 120

We can judge a nation by its songs. The minor note is indicative of a crushed, but unconquered people. In the Bible there is nothing altogether minor; nothing, that is, of the nature of despair. The Bible deals with terrors and upsets, with people who have got into despair—in fact, the Bible deals with all that the devil can do, and yet all through there is the uncrushable certainty that in the end everything will be all right.

The Songs of Ascents are the autobiography of the children of God; they reveal their inner secrets. These psalms express not the outward, but the inward condition of the children of God, when they realise that they are pilgrims. We do not immediately realise that we are pilgrims; when a child is born into the world it is welcomed and for a time it feels perfectly happy and at home. Neither when we are born again do we realise at once that we are pilgrims; rather, we feel more at home on the earth than ever; we have come into contact with the Creator of it all, and

> *Heaven above is brighter blue,*
> *Earth around a sweeter green.*

But as we go on, this sense of at-home-ness disappears and ultimately we realise a deep alienation to all that the world represents, and we recognise that we are "strangers and pilgrims on the earth," that "here we have no continuing city." That mood is represented in these Psalms. God seems to delight to stir up our nests; it is not the devil who does it, but God; this is curiously unrecognised on our part.

The peace of this world can never be the peace of God. The peace of physical health, of mental healthy-mindedness, of prosperous circumstances, of civilisation—not one of these is the peace of God, but the outcome of the souls of men being garrisoned by the prince of this world (see Luke 11:21). When we are born again from above (RV mg) and realise that we belong to God, we begin to recognise the element of destruction that there is imbedded in many of our Lord's words, e.g., "Think not that I came to cast [mg] peace on the earth: I came not to cast [mg] peace, but a sword" (RV). We realise that the reasoning of the world is not in accordance with the Bible, and we find we are alien to it.

1. Direction in Distress
In my distress I cried unto the LORD, and He answered me. (Psalm 120:1 RV)

If I am a child of God, distress will lead me to Him for direction. The distress comes not because I have done wrong, it is part of the inevitable result of not being at home in the world, of being in contact with those who reason and live from a different standpoint. We blunder when we try to make out that the prosperity referred to in the Old Testament is intended for us in this dispensation. Plainly that prosperity has never yet been fulfilled in the history of the world; it is going to be fulfilled, but it does not refer to this dispensation, which is the dispensation of the humiliation of the saints, not of their glorification. One of Satan's greatest delusions is to decoy folks off on to blessings that are merely secondary. We become sidetracked if we make physical health our aim and imagine that because we are children of God we shall always be perfectly well; that there will be great manifestations of God's power, thousands saved, etc.

"In my distress . . ." There are elements in our circumstances if we are children of God that can only be described by the word *"distress";* it would be untruthful to say it was otherwise. *"Then* will I go unto . . . God," says the Psalmist, not "with joy," but "unto God [Who is] my exceeding joy." We go to God when we have no joy in ourselves and find that His joy is our strength. Are our hearts resting in the certainty that God is full of joy although with us it is "clouds and darkness" because we are pilgrims?

". . . I cried unto the LORD, and He answered me." It is one thing to cry to God and another thing to hear Him answer. We don't give God time to answer. We come in a great fuss and panic, but when all that is taken out of our hearts and we are silent before God, the quiet certainty comes—"I know God has heard me."

2. Deliverance from Deception
Deliver my soul, O LORD, from lying lips, and from a deceitful tongue. (Psalm 120:2)

One of the hardest things on earth to bear is deception, especially when it comes through our friends. We do not need the grace of God to stand the deception or slander of an enemy, human pride will stand that; but to be wounded in the house of our friends takes us unawares. Judas had "lying lips"; we read that he kissed Jesus much (RV mg). Are we honest with our lips? It is only Christians who can be frank with one another, because their disposition has been altered by God (cf. Ephesians 4:29).

> *What shall be given unto thee, and what shall be done more unto thee, thou deceitful tongue? (Psalm 120:3 RV)*

Most of our relationships are carried on with discreet deceit. The words "shrewdness," "diplomacy," "aye keep a bittie to yersel," express an attitude essential in the life of the world, but a Christian has no time to be a dabster[8] with his tongue, no time to

profit by being clever. The teaching of the Sermon on the Mount is never to look for justice but never to cease to give it. We waste our time looking for justice; we have to see that we always give it to others. "If you are My disciple," Jesus says, "people won't play you fair; but never mind that, see that you play fair."

> *Sharp arrows of the mighty, with coals of juniper. (Psalm 120:4)*

The Bible reveals the tongue to be the worst enemy a man has (see James 3:6–8)—"Sharp arrows of the mighty"—they never miss their mark. The same thing is true when we are born again, God sees that our words get home; but if we are not born again our words rankle and sting and annoy and spread destruction. Sarcasm is the weapon of a weak, spiteful nature, its literal meaning is to tear the flesh from the bone. The antipodes of sarcasm is irony—conveying your meaning by saying the opposite; irony is frequently used by the prophets.

3. Distraction for a Dwelling
Woe is me, that I sojourn in Meshech, that I dwell among the tents of Kedar! My soul hath long had her dwelling with him that hateth peace. (Psalm 120:5–6 RV)

Our Lord lived for thirty years in that atmosphere (see John 7:5). We sing, "There's no place like home," but the author of that song was far away from home when he wrote it. The description the Bible gives of home is that it is a place of discipline. Naturally we do not like what God makes; we prefer our friends to our God-made relations. We are undressed morally in our home life and are apt to be meaner[9] there than anywhere else. If we have been captious and mean with our relations, we will always exhibit that spirit until we become new creatures in Christ Jesus. That is why it is easier to go somewhere else, much easier often to go as a missionary than to stay at home. God alters the thing that matters.

4. In a Dilemma by the Disputers
I am for peace: but when I speak they are for war. (Psalm 120:7)

There is nothing more terrible than for people to take what you say and to turn it into dispute (cf. Psalm 109:4). We are not to keep things back, but we realise that if we stand for God there will be the dilemma of dispute. "They say: What say they? Let them say." Paul says the same thing—"But with me it is a very small thing that I should be judged of you, or of man's

---

8. dabster: proficient; expert; adept.
9. mean: ordinary, common, low, or ignoble, rather than cruel or spiteful

judgement: yea, I judge not mine own self" (1 Corinthians 4:3).

In a crisis we are always in danger of standing true to something that is acclaimed by this world rather than standing absolutely loyal to God. Had our Lord been a patriot, He would have been a traitor to His country in submitting to the Roman dominance; He ought to have led an insurrection—"This dominance is wrong, We must break it." Instead of that, He bowed His head to it. He submitted to the providential order of tyranny knowing that through it God was working out His purposes. "Knowest thou not that I have power to release Thee, and have power to crucify Thee? Jesus answered him, Thou couldest have no power against Me, except it were given thee from above" (John 19:10–11 RV).

Note:—No notes are available on Psalm 121.

II

PSALM 122

1. Gladness of Comradeship

I was glad when they said unto me, Let us go into the house of the LORD. (Psalm 122:1)

God begins with us individually in the experience of conscious salvation, then He unites us to one another. Notice the *"altogetherness"* of the saints all through the Epistles—"till we all attain unto the unity of the faith, . . . unto the measure of the stature of the fulness of Christ" (RV). None of us individually can reach the "fulness of Christ"; we reach that standard all together. "I have called you friends," said Jesus. The idea is that the presence of Jesus is the arena in which we live. A friend is one who makes me do my best.

2. Goings of a Community

Our feet shall stand within thy gates, O Jerusalem. (Psalm 122:2)

The gifts of our ascended Lord—apostles, prophets, evangelists—are "for the perfecting of the saints." If you should be in advance of the rest of the community, God will take you into "the ministry of the interior." Spiritual insight is not for the purpose of making us realise we are better than other people, but in order that our responsibility might be added to. If we neglect to go to God about our communities, our ministers, we become criticising centres instead of ministers of the interior. God expects us to be intercessors, not dogmatic fault-finders, but vicarious intercessors, until other lives come up to the same standard. Locusts in their flight over a stream may drown by the million, but others keep coming until there is a way for the live ones to go over their bodies. God uses His saints in the same way. "The blood of the martyrs is the seed of the Church." There are prominent names in works of faith, such as Müller[10] and Quarrier,[11] but there are thousands of others whose names are not known. It is the same truth our Lord uttered regarding Himself, "Except a corn of wheat fall into the ground and die, it abideth alone: but if it die, it bringeth forth much fruit." The work in a community to begin with may be a wondrous delight, then it seems to die out, and if you do not know the teaching of our Lord you will say it is dead; it is not, it has fallen into the ground and died in its old form, but by and by it will bring forth fruit which will alter the whole landscape.

3. God's Own City

Jerusalem is builded as a city that is compact together. (Psalm 122:3)

For he looked for a city which hath foundations, whose builder and maker is God. (Hebrews 11:10)

And I John saw the holy city, new Jerusalem, coming down from God out of heaven, prepared as a bride adorned for her husband. (Revelation 21:2)

What a curious anomaly—a city of God! We could have understood if it had been the *country* of God, but a holy *city* is inconceivable to us. The city of Jerusalem, like the Temple, was ordained of God, that is why the Children of Israel were so certain the

---

10. George Müller (1805–1898) was a founder of Christian orphanages in Bristol, England, which were supported by faith and complete reliance on God.

11. William Quarrier (1829–1903) was a founder of the Orphan Homes of Scotland; he was noted as a great man of faith and prayer.

prophets were wrong in saying that God would ever leave Jerusalem; but God did leave it, He left it desolate on account of the sins of the people.

There is a time coming when we shall live in God's own city: Abraham looked for it; John saw it coming down out of heaven. Our present-day communities are man's attempt at building up the city of God; man is confident that if only God will give him time enough he will build not only a holy city, but a holy community and establish peace on earth, and God is allowing him ample opportunity to try, until he is satisfied that God's way is the only way.

4. Gathering of the Clans
. . . whither the tribes go up, the tribes of the LORD, unto the testimony of Israel, to give thanks unto the name of the LORD. (Psalm 122:4)

The prophets look forward to the time when all the tribes will meet together in harmony. It is a symbol of what happens in this dispensation of grace; there is absolute harmony in Christ Jesus, no matter what the difference of nationality may be. The Bible is the Charter of the city of God, and all sorts and conditions of people have communion with one another through it. There is a gathering of the clans of all who belong to the race of the twice-born—"Now therefore ye are no more strangers and foreigners, but fellow citizens with the saints, and of the household of God." The saints find their closest unity in communion with God, but we have to be put through a great deal of discipline before the oneness for which Jesus prayed in John 17 is realised. You will find that God introduces you to teachers and friends who are just beyond you in attainment in order to keep you from stagnation.

5. Christ's Own Crown
For there are set thrones of judgement, the thrones of the house of David. (Psalm 122:5)

When our Lord stood before Pilate and he asked Him, "Art Thou a King then?" Jesus answered, "I am a King, but My Kingdom is not of this world, else would My servants fight." The Kingship of Jesus consists in the entire sanctification of individuals. "For Christ's Crown and Covenant"[12] was the motto of the Scottish Covenanters.[13] Am I eager to be saved and sanctified so that Jesus Christ is crowned King in my life? "Ye call Me Master and Lord: and ye say well; for so I am"—but is He? Is He Lord and Master of our sentiments with regard to this war? of our passions and patriotic pride? We may think He is until

we are brought into a crisis, and then we realise that there are whole domains over which He is not Lord and Master. This is true in individual life and in national life.

6. Generosity of Community
Pray for the peace of Jerusalem: they shall prosper that love thee. (Psalm 122:6)

"Pray for the peace of the city" because it will be better for us as saints if the city is in peace. It is true that in times of war people are driven to God, but the distraction of war upsets the harmony and peace which are essential conditions for the worship of God. Are we set on praying for the peace of Jerusalem only because it will bring prosperity with God to souls?

7. Goodwill in Concentration
Peace be within thy walls, and prosperity within thy palaces. For my brethren and companions' sakes, I will now say, Peace be within thee. (Psalm 122:7–8)

In times of prosperity we are apt to forget God, we imagine it does not matter whether we recognise Him or not. As long as we are comfortably clothed and fed and looked after, our civilisation becomes an elaborate means of ignoring God.

"God bless Jerusalem"—for Jerusalem's sake? No, for my companions' sake. "God bless the world with peace"—because it is deserving of peace? No, because of the Christians in it. Because God's House is here, we pray "God bless Askrigg." Because of the saints in Britain, we pray "God bless Britain."

But remember God's blessing may mean God's blasting. If God is going to bless me, He must condemn and blast out of my being what He cannot bless. "Our God is a consuming fire." When we ask God to bless, we sometimes pray terrible havoc upon the things that are not of God. God will shake all that can be shaken, and He is doing it just now.

8. Graciousness in Compensation
Because of the house of the LORD our God I will seek thy good. (Psalm 122:9)

"Inasmuch as ye have done it unto one of the least of these My brethren, ye have done it unto Me." This is not the judgement of Christians, but of the nations who have never heard of Jesus. They are amazed at the magnanimity of His words—"Lord, when saw we Thee an hungred, and fed Thee?" If that is God's attitude to the nations who do not know Him, what is

---

12. Chambers used "For Christ's Crown and Covenant," the battle cry of the Scottish Covenanters (1638) who refused to honor the head of state as the head of the church, as the motto for the Bible Training College.
13. Scottish Covenanters (1638) refused to honor the head of state as the head of the church.

His attitude toward us? We are never told to walk in the light of conscience, but to walk in the light of the Lord. If Jesus Christ has taught me to be "as He is . . . in this world," then in every particular in which I am not like Him, I shall be condemned. God engineers circumstances to see what we will do. Will we be the children of our Father in heaven, or will we go back again to the meaner,[14] common-sense attitude? Will we stake all and stand true to Him? "Be thou faithful unto death, and I will give thee a crown of life." The crown of life means I shall see that my Lord has got the victory after all, even in me.

III

PSALM 123

This Psalm represents the inner biography of faith. It is not easy to have faith in God, and it is not meant to be easy because we have to make character. God will shield us from no requirements of His sons and daughters any more than He shielded His own Son. It is an easy business to sit in an armchair and say, "Oh yes, I believe God will do this and that"; that is credulity, not faith. But let me say, "I believe God will supply all my needs," and then let me "run dry," no money, no outlook, and see whether I will go through the trial of my faith, or sink back and put my trust in something else. It is the trial of our faith that is precious. If we go through the trial, there is so much wealth laid up in our heavenly banking account to draw upon when the next test comes.

1. Direction of Aspiration

Unto Thee lift I up mine eyes, O Thou that dwellest in the heavens. (Psalm 123:1)

"Unto Thee *lift I up* mine eyes"—we have to make the effort to look up. The things that make it difficult to look up are suffering, or difficulty, or murmuring. If you are suffering, it is intensely difficult to look up. The command to the Children of Israel when they were bitten by the fiery serpent was, *"Look* to the brazen serpent." We cannot look up if we are murmuring; we are like the child who does not want to do what he is told, and the father comes and says, "Now look up," but the child won't. We behave like that with God; our circumstances are hard, we are not making progress in life, and the Spirit of God says, "Look up," but we refuse and say, "I'm not going to play this game of faith any more." The counsel given by the writer to the Hebrews is based on the effort of the saint—*"let us lay aside every weight"; "let us run with patience the race that is set before us"; "looking unto Jesus"; "Consider Him"* (Hebrews 12:1–3).

2. Description of the Attention

Behold, as the eyes of servants look unto the hand of their masters, and as the eyes of a maiden unto the hand of her mistress; so our eyes wait upon the LORD our God, until that He have mercy upon us. (Psalm 123:2)

God intends our attention to be arrested, He does not arrest it for us. The things Jesus tells us to consider are not things that compel our attention— "Consider the lilies of the field," "Behold the fowls of the air." The Spirit of God instructs us to be attentive. Are our eyes so fixed upon God that we have spiritual discernment and can see His countenance in the dreadful cloud of war? Most of us are at our wits' end, we have no inkling of what God is doing because our eyes have not been waiting upon Him. We are apt to pay more attention to our newspaper than to God's Book, and spiritual leakage begins because we do not make the effort to lift up our eyes to God. "But we all, with open face beholding as in a glass the glory of the Lord, are changed into the same image from glory to glory" (2 Corinthians 3:13). That is a description of entire reliance on God. Be careful of anything that is going to deflect your attention from God. It is easier to rely on God in big things than in little things. There is an enormous power in little things to distract our attention from God; that is why our Lord said that "the cares of this world," "the lusts of other things," would choke the word and make it unfruitful.

3. Distraction of Annoyance

Have mercy upon us, O LORD, have mercy upon us: for we are exceedingly filled with contempt. Our soul is exceedingly filled with the scorning of those that are at ease, and with the contempt of the proud. (Psalm 123:3–4)

---

14. mean: ordinary, common, low, or ignoble, rather than cruel or spiteful

The thing to heed is not so much damage to our faith in God as damage to our temper of mind. "Therefore take heed to your spirit, that ye deal not treacherously" (Malachi 2:16). The temper of mind if it is not right with God is tremendous in its effects, it is the enemy that penetrates right into the soul and distracts us from God. There are certain tempers of mind we never dare indulge in; if we do, we find that they distract us from God, and until we get back into the quiet mood before God our faith in Him is *nil* and our confidence in human ingenuity the thing that rules.

Spiritual leakage comes not so much through trouble on the outside as through imagining you have "screwed yourself a bit too high." For instance, you came to a particular crisis and made a conscientious stand for God and had the witness of the Spirit that everything was all right; but the weeks have gone by, and the months, and you are slowly beginning to come to the conclusion that you had been taking a stand a bit too high. Your friends come and say, "Now don't be a fool, you are only an ordinary human being; when you talked about this spiritual awakening we knew it was only a passing phase; you can't keep up the strain, God does not expect you to"; and you say, "Well, I suppose I was a bit too pretentious." It sounds wise and sensible, but the danger is that you do not rely on God any longer; reliance on worldly opinion has taken the place of reliance on God. We have to realise that no effort can be too high, because Jesus says we are to be the children of our Father in heaven. It must be my utmost for His highest all the time and every time.

"Have mercy upon us, O LORD, . . . for we are exceedingly filled with contempt." As God's children we have to see that we keep looking in the face of God, otherwise we shall find our souls in the condition of being filled with contempt and annoyance, with the result that we are spiritually distracted instead of spiritually self-possessed. This is true in individual circumstances as well as national crises. It is not always the cross mood that leads to the cross speech, but the cross word that makes the cross mood. If in the morning you begin to talk crossly, before long you will *feel* desperately cross. Take to God the things that perturb your spirit. You notice that certain people are not going on spiritually and you begin to feel perturbed; if the discernment turns you to intercession, it is good; but if it turns to criticism it blocks you in your way to God. God never gives us discernment of what is wrong for us to criticise it, but that we might intercede.

"Unto Thee lift I up mine eyes" (Psalm 123:1). The terrible thing is that we are likely to get to the place where we do not miss the consciousness of God's presence; we have gone on so long ignoring the lifting up of our eyes to Him that it has become the habit of our mind and it never bothers us. We go on depending on our own wits and ingenuity until suddenly God brings us to a halt and we realise how we have been losing out. Whenever there is spiritual leakage, remedy it immediately. It does not matter what you are doing, stop instantly when there is the realisation that you are losing out before God; lift up your eyes to Him and tell Him you recognise it— "Lord, this thing has been coming in between my spirit and Thee, I am not resting in faith." Get it readjusted at once. There is always a suitable place to pray, to lift up your eyes to God; there is no need to get to a place of prayer, pray wherever you are. Confess before God that you have been distracted away from faith in Him; don't vindicate yourself. The lust of vindication is a state of mind that destroys the soul's faith in God—"I must explain myself"; "I must get people to understand." The remarkable thing about our Lord is that He never explained anything to anybody. Nothing ever distracted Him out of His oneness with God, and He prays "that they may be one, *even as We are one.*"

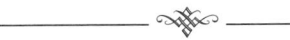

IV

PSALM 124

1. Alternative Danger

If it had not been the LORD who was on our side, now may Israel say . . . (Psalm 124:1)

Facing an alternative is not to deal in supposition, but part of wisdom and understanding; supposition is wisdom gone to hysteria. In estimating the dangers which beset us we have to remember that they are not haphazard, but things that will happen. Our Lord told His disciples to lay their account with peril, with hatred, in fact He tells them to leap for joy "when men shall hate you, and when they shall separate you from their company, and shall reproach you and cast out your name as evil, for the Son of man's sake" (Luke 6:22–23). We are apt to look at this alternative as a supposition, but Jesus says it will happen and must be estimated. It is never wise to under-estimate an enemy. We look upon the enemy of our souls as a conquered foe, so he is, but only to God, not to us.

(a) Estimate of Antagonism

*If it had not been the L*ORD *who was on our side, when men rose up against us: then they had swallowed us up quick, when their wrath was kindled against us. (Psalm 124:2–3)*

We have to lay our account with the antagonism of men, it is a danger that is always with us. ". . . when *men* rose up against us"—not tendencies, not the moods of men, but men themselves. All that makes life either honourable or terrible is summed up in the word "men." In estimating the forces against us we are slow to believe in this antagonistic element, we look at them too haphazardly, not realising that they are dead set against us. "But beware of men"—it is the last thing we do. The reason our Lord tells us to beware of men is that the human heart is "deceitful above all things, and desperately wicked," and if we put our trust in men we shall go under, because men are just like ourselves, and none of us in our wits before God would ever think of trusting ourselves; if we do it is a sign that we are ignorant of ourselves.

At heart men are antagonistic to the lordship of Jesus Christ. It is not antagonism to creeds or points of view, but antagonism encountered *for My sake.* Many of us awaken antagonism by our way of stating things; we have to distinguish between being persecuted for some notion of our own and being persecuted "for My sake." We are apt to think only of the bad things as being against Jesus, but it is the refined things, the cultured things, the religious things which are dead against Jesus Christ unless they are loyal to Him. It was the religious people of our Lord's time who withstood Him, not the worldly. "If the world hate you, ye know that it hated me before it hated you" (John 15:18). These are the deliberate words of our Lord to His disciples. In the measure in which we are loyal to Jesus Christ the same thing happens to us; we are at a loss to understand why people should have the most apparently absurd antipathy to us. Their anger is strangely unaccountable; it is not irritation, but an inspired working against.

(b) Estimate of Agony

Then the waters had overwhelmed us, the stream had gone over our soul. (Psalm 124:4)

One element in the alternative danger that attends the saints of God is the agony it produces. It is strange that God should make it that "through the shadow of an agony cometh Redemption"; strange that God's Son should be made perfect through suffering; strange that suffering should be one of the golden pathways for God's children. There are times in personal life when we are brought into an understanding of what Abraham experienced. "Get thee out of thy country. . . ." It is not so much that we are misunderstood, but that suffering is brought on others through

our being loyal to God, and it produces agony for which there is no relief on the human side, only on God's side. Then we pray "Thy Kingdom come" we have to share in the pain of the world being born again; it is a desperate pain. God's servants are, as it were, the birth-throes of the new age. "My little children, of whom I travail in birth again until Christ be formed in you" (Galatians 4:19). Many of us receive the Holy Ghost, but immediately the throes begin we misunderstand God's purpose. We have to enter into the travail with Him until the world is born again. The world must be born again just as individuals are.

(c) Estimate of Annihilation

Then the proud waters had gone over our soul. (Psalm 124:5)

The ultimate result of the danger is annihilation, our Lord leaves us in no doubt about that; He always estimated things in the final analysis. Our Lord teaches that the forces against us work for our annihilation, "And ye shall be hated of all men for My name's sake." Nowadays we do not catch the drift of these words. It is not the question of a law of nature at work, but a law of antagonism, everything that is not loyal to Jesus Christ is against us. "And Saul, yet breathing out threatenings and slaughter against the disciples of the Lord. . . ." Saul of Tarsus was spending all his educated manhood to annihilate those who were "of the Way" (RV). It is that spirit we have to estimate in the danger that besets us if we are true to God.

2. Appreciated Deliverance

*Blessed be the L*ORD, *who hath not given us as a prey to their teeth. (Psalm 124:6)*

The reason some of us are so tepid spiritually is that we do not realise that God has done anything for us. Many people are at work for God, not because they appreciate His salvation, but because they think they should be doing something for other people. Our Lord never called anyone to work for Him because they realise a need, but only on the basis that He has done something for them. The only basis on which to work for God is an esteemed appreciation of His deliverance, that is, our personal history with God is so poignant that it constitutes our devotion to Him. God's deliverance makes us His absolute debtors. Have we taken into account what God has done for us? Estimate the alternative danger, and then begin to call on your soul to bless God for His deliverance. ". . . to whom little is forgiven, the same loveth little."

(a) Entire Escape

Our soul is escaped as a bird out of the snare of the fowlers: the snare is broken, and we are escaped. (Psalm 124:7)

God does not deliver us gradually, but suddenly, it is a perfect deliverance, a complete emancipation. When the deliverance is realised, it is realised altogether, from the crown of your head to the sole of your foot, and your devotion to God is on account of that deliverance. It is a good thing to begin prayer with praising God for His attributes, and for the way those attributes have been brought to bear on our personal salvation. Let your mind soak in the deliverance of God, and then praise Him for them.

(b) Eternal Element
Our help is in the name of the LORD, who made heaven and earth. (Psalm 124:8)

Our help is not in what God has done, but in God Himself. There is a danger of banking our faith and our testimony on our experience, whereas our experience is the gateway to a closer intimacy with God. Our help is in the Name of the One who delivers. The dangers that beset us are real dangers, and if we estimate them we shall appreciate God's deliverance. Why our Lord said that self-pity was of the devil is that self-pity will prevent us appreciating God's deliverance. When we begin to say "Why has this happened to me?" "Why does poverty begin to come to me?" "Why should this difficulty come, this upset?" it means that we are more concerned about getting our own way than in esteeming the marvellous deliverance God has wrought. We read of God's people of old that "They soon forgot His works," and we are in danger of doing the same unless we continually lift up our eyes to God and bless Him for His deliverances.

V

PSALM 125

1. The Fastnesses of the Godly
They that trust in the LORD shall be as mount Zion which cannot be removed, but abideth for ever. (Psalm 125:1)

The security of the eternal God is what we are to have confidence in, and the Psalmist likens that security to the mountains, because a mountain is the most stable thing we know. There is nothing so secure as the salvation of God; it is as eternal as the mountains, and it is our trust in God that brings us the conscious realisation of this. The one thing Satan tries to shake is our confidence in God. It is not difficult for our confidence to be shaken if we build on our experience; but if we realise that all we experience is but the doorway leading to the knowledge of God, Satan may shake that as much as he likes, but he cannot shake the fact that God remains faithful (see 2 Timothy 2:13), and we must not cast away our confidence in Him. It is not our trust that keeps us, but the God in whom we trust who keeps us. We are always in danger of trusting in our trust, believing our belief, having faith in our faith. All these things can be shaken; we have to base our faith on those things which cannot be shaken (see Hebrews 12:27).

Our consciousness of God is meant to introduce us to God, not to our experience of Him. Jesus said, ". . . no man is able to pluck them out of My Father's hand" (John 10:29). No power, however mighty, is able to pluck us out of the hand of God, so long as that power is outside us. Our Lord did not say, however, that His sheep had not power to take themselves out. The devil cannot take us out, neither can man; we are absolutely secure from every kind of enemy, saving our own wilfulness. God does not destroy our personal power to disobey Him; if He did, we would become mechanical and useless. No power outside, from the devil downward, can take us out of God's hand; so long as we remain faithful, we are as eternally secure as God Himself.

2. The Frontiers of God
As the mountains are round about Jerusalem, so the LORD is round about His people from henceforth even for ever. (Psalm 125:2)

There are margins beyond which the Spirit of God does not work. Nightingales will not sing outside certain geographical areas, and that is an exact illustration of the frontiers of God. There is a place where God reveals His face, and that place has moral frontiers, not physical. We can blind our minds by perverse thinking; blind our moral life by crooked dealing in business, or by sin. We can never get away from God geographically, but we can get away from Him morally. The writer to the Hebrews mentions the moral frontier, "let thy conversation be without covetousness; and be content with such things as ye have" (Hebrews 13:5). Outside that moral frontier, God does not reveal His face. Let me become impatient, let me fix my heart on gain, and I do not see God. If I enthrone anything other than God in my life, God retires and lets the other god do what it can. The majority of us do not enthrone God, we enthrone common-sense. We make our decisions and then ask the real God to bless our god's decision. We say, "It is common-sense to do this thing," and God leaves us, because we are outside the frontier where He works. Keep yourself from the love of money, and be content. Think of the imperative haste in our spirit to wish we were somewhere else! That danger is always there, and we have to watch it. When I wish I was somewhere else I am not doing my duty to God where I am. I am wool-gathering, fooling with my own soul; if I am God's child I have no business to be distracted. If I keep myself from covetousness, content with the things I have, I remain within the frontiers of God. If I have the spirit of covetousness in my heart I have no right to say, "The Lord is my helper"—He is not, He is my destroyer. I have no right to say I am content and yet have a mood that is not contented. If I am ill-tempered, set on some change of circumstances, I find God is not supporting me at all; I have worried myself outside the moral frontier where He works and my soul won't sing; there is no joy in God, no peace in believing. We have to watch that we are not enticed outside the frontier of our own control, just as soldiers have to watch. If they get outside the frontier of their strategy they will probably be killed, and so we have to watch that we are not enticed outside God's frontier. Remember, no man can take us outside, it is our own stupidity that takes us out. When we realise that we have got outside the moral frontier, the only thing to do is to get back again and realise what the Apostle Paul says in Philippians 4:11–13.

3. The Faithfulness of Godliness
For the rod of the wicked shall not rest upon the lot of the righteous; lest the righteous put forth their hands unto iniquity. (Psalm 125:3)

The rod means two things—it is used in counting in the sheep, and it is used to destroy the wild beast that suddenly springs out on the sheep (see Psalm 23:4). The man of sin will have his rod, he will do clever tricks, he will put the mark of the beast on every business system that he sanctions, and those who do not have that mark on them can never do business under the regime of the man of sin. Suppose you find that the people who are "counted in" under the mark of the beast succeed, and you do not succeed, you may be tempted to negotiate the thing and say, "Well, I don't know, if I did this thing it would save me; I had better just compromise a bit." We must never do that. "The rod of the wicked shall not rest on the righteous," God says. There is no need to fear, if we keep within the moral frontiers of God we can say boldly, "The Lord is my helper." We do not need to mind how the wicked bluster and say, "If you don't do this

and that, you will starve." Be faithful, make holiness your aim, holiness in every relationship—money, food, clothes, friendship—then you will see the Lord in all these domains.

4. The Fitness of Goodness
Do good, O LORD, unto those that be good, and to them that be upright in their hearts. (Psalm 125:4)

Our Lord warned the disciples that they would be put out of the synagogue, and be killed (see John 16:2), but He says, "Don't mind about that, beware only of not doing your duty according to My commandments, because that will destroy both soul and body in hell" (see Matthew 10:28; Revelation 2:10). We are apt to make salvation mean the saving of our skin. The death of our body, the sudden breaking-up of the house of life, may be the salvation of our soul. In times of peace "honesty may be the best policy," but if we work on the idea that it is better physically and prosperously to be good, that is the wrong motive; the right motive is devotion to God, remaining absolutely true to God, no matter what it costs.

5. The Futility of Godlessness
But as for such as turn aside unto their crooked ways, the LORD shall lead them forth with the workers of iniquity. (Psalm 125:5 RV)

There is no reference in the Bible to natural law. We talk of certain things as the inevitable result of what a man does: the Bible says, God. The Psalmist says, "the LORD shall lead them forth." God is active in every relationship; it is not natural law or mathematical logic, but God working all through. No man has a fate portioned out to him; a man's disposition makes what people call his fate. The course of deliberately remaining independent of God ends in damnation, by God's direct decree, not as an inevitable happening; and the course of dependence upon God ends in heaven, by God's decree, not by chance. Either course has God behind it. It is the glorious risk of the Christian life. The Apostle Peter gives the warning, "Beware lest, being carried away with the error of the wicked, ye fall from your own stedfastness" (2 Peter 3:17 RV). God does not save us from facing the music, or shelter us from any of the requirements of sons and daughters (see 1 John 4:4). As long as we remain within the moral frontiers of God, watching our hearts lest we give way to ill-content, to covetousness, or self-pity, the things which take us outside God's frontier, then God says, *"I will in no wise fail thee, neither will I in any wise forsake thee"* (RV).

VI

PSALM 126

1. The Emotion of Deliverance

When the LORD turned again the captivity of Zion, we were like them that dream. (Psalm 126:1)

Religion is never intellectual, it is always passionate and emotional; but the curious thing is that it is religion that leads to emotion, not emotion to religion. If religion does not make for passion and emotion, it is not the true kind. When you realise that you are saved, that God has forgiven your sins, given you the Holy Spirit, I defy you not to be carried away with emotion. Religion which makes for logic and reason is not religion, but to try to make religion out of emotion is to take a false step. Our Lord bases everything on life as it is, and life is implicit. For instance, you cannot explicitly state what love is, but love is the implicit thing that makes life worth living. You cannot explicitly state what sin is, but sin is the implicit thing that curses life. You cannot explicitly state what death is, all the scientific jargon in the world cannot define death; death is the implicit thing which destroys life as we know it. A child is a good illustration of the implicit, you cannot imagine a child without emotion, always logical, reasonable and well-balanced, he would not be a child but a prig.

Emotion is not simply an overplus of feeling, it is life lived at white-heat, a state of wonder. To lose wonder is to lose the true element of religion. Has the sense of wonder been dying down in your religious life? If so, you need to get back to the Source. If you have lost the fervour of delight in God, tell Him so. The old Divines used to ask God for the grace of trembling, i.e., the sense of wonder. When wonder goes out of natural love, something or someone is to be severely blamed; wonder ought never to go. With a child the element of wonder is always there, a freshness and spontaneity, and the same is true of those who follow Jesus Christ's teaching and become as little children.

People have the idea that Christianity and Stoicism are alike; the writings of the stoics sound so like the teaching of Jesus Christ, but just at the point where they seem most alike, they are most divergent. A stoic overcomes the world by making himself indifferent, by passionlessness; the saint overcomes the world by passionateness, by the passion of his love for Jesus Christ.

2. The Excitement of Delight

Then was our mouth filled with laughter, and our tongue with singing: then said they among the heathen, The LORD hath done great things for them. (Psalm 126:2)

They were carried completely off their feet with amazement and delight over what God had done (cf. Genesis 17:17; Isaiah 60:5). A man will say, "I do not doubt that God can forgive sin, that He can give the Holy Spirit and make men holy, but it cannot possibly mean me! When I come before God I remember all my blunders and sins." When he realises that it does mean him, then comes this moral hysteria—"It is too good to be true!" With God a thing is never too good to be true; it is too good not to be true.

Ruskin says that early in life he could never see a hedgerow without emotion, then later on when problems of heart and life were busy with him he saw nothing in Nature; but as soon as the inner turmoil was settled, not only did he get the old joy back, but a redoubled joy. If we have no delight in God it is because we are too far away from the childlike relationship to Him. If there is an internal struggle on, get it put right and you will experience delight in Him.

3. The Ecstasy of His Doings

The LORD hath done great things for us; whereof we are glad. Turn again our captivity, O LORD, as the streams in the south. (Psalm 126:3–4)

Whenever God brings His deliverances they are so supernatural that we are staggered with amazement. It is one of the most helpful spiritual exercises to reckon what God has done for us already. When God wanted to make His ancient people realise what manner of God He was, He said, "Remember the crossing of the Red Sea," and in the New Testament Paul says, "Remember, it is the God Who raised Jesus from the dead. . . ." These two things are the unit of measurement of God's power. If I want to know what God can do, He is the God Who made a way through the sea; if it is a question of power for my life, the measurement of that is the Resurrection of Jesus.

"Turn again our captivity, O LORD. . . ." I call upon my soul to remember what God has done and it makes me bold to entreat Him to do it again. It is a crime to give way to self-pity, to be weak in God's strength when all this God is ours. We have to build ourselves up on our most holy faith. Robert Louis Stevenson asked God to forgive him if he had "shown no morning face"; and Dante places in the lowest circles of Hell those who have been gloomy in the summer air.

4. The Enlightenment of Drudgery

They that sow in tears shall reap in joy. He that goeth

forth and weepeth, bearing precious seed, shall doubt-less come again with rejoicing, bringing his sheaves with him. (Psalm 126:5–6)

We make the blunder of wanting to sow and plough and reap all at the same time. We forget what our Lord said, that "one soweth, and another reapeth." "They that sow in tears . . ."—it looks as if the seed were drowned. You can see the seed when it is in the basket, but when it falls into the ground, it disappears (see John 12:24). The same thing is true with regard to Sunday School work or meetings, it looks as if everything were flung away, you cannot see anything happening; but the seed is there. "They that sow in tears *shall reap in joy*." "Cast thy bread upon the waters: for thou shalt find it after many days." The seed is the word of God, and no word of God is ever fruitless. If I know that the sowing is going to bring forth fruit, I am blessed in the drudgery. Drudgery is never blessed, but drudgery can be enlightened. The Psalmist says, "Thou hast enlarged me . . . in distress"; the enlargement comes through knowing that God is looking after everything. Before, when I came to a difficult bit of the way I was staggered, but now through the affliction and suffering I can put my foot down more firmly (see Romans 8:35–39).

VII

PSALM 127

1. Direction by Countenancing God

Except the LORD build the house, they labour in vain that build it: except the LORD keep the city, the watch-man waketh but in vain. (Psalm 127:1)

For that ye ought to say, If the Lord will, we shall live, and do this, or that. (see James 4:13–15)

Do I countenance God like that? not have my face towards Him, but my whole person directed by that dominating thought? One of the greatest evidences that we are born again of God is that we perceive the kingdom of God. When I am born from above (RV mg) I countenance God; the arm of the Lord is revealed and I see God as the Architect, as the One Who is doing all things. God is never away off some-where else; He is always *there.* It is this fact that needs to be taken into consideration. Do I countenance the fact that God is engineering my bodily life and all that I come in contact with? I mention the body because that is the physical case in which our spirit works. If I do not countenance God in that, my faith is jargon. If I enthrone common sense as God, there are great regions of my life in which I do not countenance God.

"Except the LORD build the house . . . ," the house of the mind or heart. God is building us for Himself not for ourselves. Do I realise that my body is the temple of the Holy Ghost, or am I educating myself for myself? I have an ambition, just where that ambi-tion rules I do not countenance God, I cannot, because my ambition rules and I won't allow God to thwart it. If I do not countenance God in every rela-tionship of my life I shall end in disaster. We get the life of God all at once, but we do not learn to obey all at once; we only learn to obey by the discipline of life.

2. Distracted Man

It is vain for you that ye rise up early, and so late take rest, and eat the bread of toil: for so He giveth unto His beloved sleep. (Psalm 127:2 RV)

This verse describes an amateur providence. We are all amateur providences, until we learn better; we are most impertinent toward God, we tell Him there are certain things we will never allow to happen in other lives, and God comes and says, "Don't interfere with that life any more." Are you rising up early and sit-ting up late to try and unravel difficulties? You cannot do it. It is a great thing to get to the place where you countenance God and know He rules. It is not done by impulse but by a settled and abiding conviction based on God's truth and the discipline of life. I know that God rules; and He gives me power to perceive His rule. There is no use sitting up late or rising up early, I must do the work that lies before me, and avoid worry as I would the devil. "It is vain for you to rise up early, to sit up late. . . ." If I take time from sleep, God's punishment rests on me; or if I take time in sleep when I should be working, He punishes me. Sloth is as bad as being a fussy workman in God's sight. We have no business to be distracted.

I wonder if we have ever considered the Bible implications about sleep? It is not true to say that sleep is simply meant for physical recuperation; surely much less time than God has ordered would have served that purpose. The Revised Version suggests a deeper, pro-founder ministry for sleep than mere physical recuper-ation. "For so He giveth unto His beloved *in* sleep" (mg). The deepest concerns of our souls, whether they be good or bad, are furthered during sleep. It is not merely a physical fact that you go to bed perplexed and wake clear-minded; God has been ministering to you during sleep. Sometimes God cannot get at us until we are asleep. In the Bible there are times when in the deep slumber of the body God has taken the souls of His servants into deeper communion with Himself (e.g. Genesis 2:21, 15:12). Often when a problem or perplexity harasses the mind and there seems no solution, after a night's rest you find the solution easy, and the problem has no further perplexity. Think of the security of the saint in sleeping or in waking, "Thou shalt not be afraid for the terror by night, nor for the arrow that flieth by day." Sleep is God's celestial nurse who croons away our consciousness, and God deals with the unconscious life of the soul in places where only He and His angels have charge. As you retire to rest, give your soul and God a time together, and commit your life to God with a conscious peace for the hours of sleep, and deep and profound developments will go on in spirit, soul and body by the kind creating hand of our God.

3. Disregarded Munificence

Lo, children are an heritage of the LORD: and the fruit of the womb is His reward. As arrows in the hand of a mighty man, so are the children of youth. (Psalm 127:3–4 RV)

Things go by threes in the Bible: Father, Son and Holy Ghost; God, Church, converts; husband, wife, children. It is God's order, not man's. Whenever one of the three is missing, there is something wrong. If you have a house, the next thing the Bible counsels is hospitality— "given to hospitality" (Romans 12:13); "pursuing hospitality" (RV mg).; give your whole mind to it. "Be not forgetful to entertain strangers: for thereby some have entertained angels unawares" (Hebrews 13:2). That is the way the blessing comes. When we begin to try to economise, God puts dry rot in us instantly. I don't care what line the economy takes, it produces dry rot. When we have the lavish hand, there is munificence at once. "There is that scattereth, and increaseth yet more; and there is that withholdeth more than is meet, but it ten-

deth only to want" (Proverbs 11:24 RV). It is the "third" element being recognised. Have I got three factors in my thinking, or only two? Is it God and myself? then I am wrong. It is God and myself for God's purposes. Do I want to be saved that I may be right with God, or that God may get His purpose through me?

4. Delivering Manoeuvres

Happy is the man that hath his quiver full of them: they shall not be ashamed, when they speak with their enemies in the gate. (Psalm 127:5 RV)

It is the element of the "third" that makes a man wealthy. ". . . trained men, born in his house" (Genesis 14:14 RV). Have I been able to reproduce my own kind spiritually? If so, in a time of difficulty I will be brought through magnificently victorious; but woe be to the spiritual man who has never produced his own kind, when the difficulties come there is none to assist, he is isolated and lonely. It is the production of the "third" that returns to you in victory. When we are right with God, Jesus says, out of you will flow "rivers of living water." Immediately you are in difficulties a thousand and one come to assist in prayer; they face the enemy in the gates. That is the great basal truth of the League of Prayer, the clustering together of the children of God. It is those you have been the means of blessing who keep you from the onslaughts of the enemy. We shall be amazed to find how much we are indebted to people we never think about, simply because they were introduced to God through us, and in our difficulties they come to our aid. There is the wire of communication when the manoeuvres take place, and we are happily delivered. The kingdoms of this world are founded on strong men, consequently they go. Jesus Christ founds His Kingdom on the weakest link, a Baby. God made His own Son a Babe. We must base our thinking on the rugged facts of life according to God's Book, and not according to the finesse of modern civilisation. Let us not be so careful as to how we offend or please human ears, but let us never offend God's ears.

VIII

PSALM 128

1. Seemliness of Sanctity

Blessed is every one that feareth the LORD; that walketh in His ways. (Psalm 128:1)

The remarkable thing about fearing God is that when you fear God you fear nothing else, whereas if you do not fear God you fear everything else. "Blessed is every

one that feareth the LORD"; the writer to the Hebrews tells us to fear lest haply there should be any promise of God's of which we come short. (Hebrews 4:1). Are we alert enough along this line? ". . . that walketh in His ways." The word *walk* breathes character, it is the symbol for seemly behaviour. John "looked upon Jesus as He walked" (RV)—not in a moment of ecstasy and transfiguration but "as He walked, he saith, Behold the Lamb of God!" "Walk worthily" (RV), says the Apostle Paul, worthily, that is, towards God, not towards man, because man's standards are not God's. When a man says he is sanctified the charge is often made, and there is no reply to it, "Remember, you are not perfect." A saint is required to be perfect towards God. *"Walk before Me, and be thou perfect"*; the standard of judgement is not man's standard, but God's. Our conduct before men will be judged by whether we walk in the seemliness of sanctity before God. That means conduct according to the highest we know, and the striking thing is that the highest we know is God Himself. "Be ye therefore perfect, even as your Father which is in heaven is perfect."

There is something in human nature that enables it to go through a big crisis, but we do need help from God to walk worthily the sixty seconds of every minute. Am I behaving myself in God's sight in the seemliness of sanctity to those who are nearest to me? in my letterwriting? in my study? Is the one great lodestar of my life walking "in His ways"? The thing we have to guard against is wanting to be somewhere else. Have I sufficient of the grace of God to behave myself as His child where I am? It is one thing to feel the sufficiency of God in a prayer meeting and in times of delight and excitement, but another thing to realise His sufficiency in whatever setting we may be—in a thunderstorm or on a calm summer day, in a cottage or a College, in an antique shop or on a moor.

2. Satisfaction in Strenuousness
For thou shalt eat the labour of thine hands: happy shalt thou be, and it shall be well with thee. (Psalm 128:2)

This verse reveals the connection between the natural creation and the regenerated creation. We have to be awake strenuously to the fact that our body is the temple of the Holy Ghost, not only in the spiritual sense, but in the physical sense. When we are born from above (RV mg) we are apt to despise the clay of which we are made. The natural creation and the creation of grace work together, and what we are apt to call the sordid things, labouring with our hands, and eating and drinking, have to be turned into spiritual exercises by obedience, then we shall eat and drink, and "do all to the glory of God." There must be a uniting in personal experience of the two creations. It cannot be done all at once, there are whole tracts of life which have to be disciplined. "Your body is the temple of the Holy Ghost," it is the handiwork of God, and it is in these bodies we are to find satisfaction, and that means strenuousness. Every power of mind and heart should go into the strenuousness of turning the natural into the spiritual by obeying the word of God regarding it. If we do not make the natural spiritual, it will become sordid; but

when we become spiritual the natural is shot through with the glory of God.

3. Security of the Saint
Thy wife shall be as a fruitful vine by the sides of thine house: thy children like olive plants round about thy table. Behold, that thus shall the man be blessed that feareth the LORD. (Psalm 128:3–4)

To-day people are altogether ignoring the fact that God has anything to do with human relationships. If we get out of any setting of natural life which God has decreed we shall not be blessed. Take the commandment to "honour thy father and mother," and apply it spiritually. I believe that many a life is hindered from entering into sanctification through not being properly related in disposition to father and mother. It is one of the most practical tests. Am I allowing inordinate affection in any relationship? or envy, or jealousy? If so I am certainly not finding blessing, it is getting dried up. I must maintain the spirit and disposition of my Lord and Master in all the ordinary relationships of life, then I shall realise the marvellous security of the saint.

4. Supremacy of Sincerity
The LORD shall bless thee out of Zion: and thou shalt see the good of Jerusalem all the days of thy life. (Psalm 128:5)

Sincerity means in the straight. Am I straight in my relationship to God and to other people? If I am the Lord says He will bless me. "And thou shalt see the good of Jerusalem all the days of thy life." It is righteous behaviour that brings blessing on others, and the heart of faith sees that God is working things out well.

5. Surroundings of Sanity
Yea, thou shalt see thy children's children, and peace upon Israel. (Psalm 128:6)

It is in ordinary surroundings and among commonplace things that the blessing of God is to dwell and reveal itself. "Blessed are they that do His commandments, that they may have right to the tree of life, and may enter in through the gates into the city" (Revelation 22:14). Have I entered in through the gates? There is a time when the exceptional has to rule and the "right arm" has to go, but that is only a phase. Our Lord was brought up so much in ordinary surroundings that the religious people of His day said that He was "a gluttonous man, and a winebibber." His life was unassuming in its naturalness. Read the records of the forty days after the Resurrection, they bear the mark of superb sanity. The test is not the success of a revival meeting, that may be questionable, but the success of living in the commonplace things that make life what it is, letting God carry out His purposes as He will.

The Highest Good

Introduction

Source

The Highest Good is comprised of lectures in Oswald Chambers' Christian ethics class at the Bible Training College, London, between 1911 and 1915.

Publication History

- As articles: The lectures were published as articles in the *BTC Monthly Journal*[15] from October 1936 through March 1937.
- As a book: *The Highest Good* was first published in 1938. It was published as part of a combined volume with *The Pilgrim's Song Book* and *Thy Great Redemption* in 1965.

In Chambers' Christian ethics class at the Bible Training College, he used as a text James Stalker's book, *The Ethic of Jesus according to the Synoptic Gospels* (1909). Thus, the frequent use of quotes from Stalker in these lectures. James Stalker (1848–1927) was a Scottish scholar and pastor who served as professor of church history at the United Free Church College, Aberdeen, from 1902 to 1926.

Other material from Chambers' teaching on ethics is found in *Biblical Ethics* (1947) and *The Moral Foundations of Life* (1936).

CONTENTS

15. The *Bible Training Course Monthly Journal* was published from 1932 to 1952 by Mrs. Chambers, with help from David Lambert.

SUMMUM BONUM

In speaking of the Highest Good as the theme of Ethics, Aristotle observes: "Every art and every kind of inquiry, and likewise every act and purpose, seems to aim at some good; and, since there are many kinds of actions, and many arts and sciences, it follows that there are many ends also. . . . And, if in what we do there be some end which we wish for on its own account, choosing all the others as means to this, this will evidently be the best of all things. And surely from a practical point of view it much more concerns us to know this good; for then, like archers shooting at a definite mark, we shall be more likely to attain what we want."

—*The Ethic of Jesus According
to the Synoptic Gospels*
Stalker[16]

All books on Ethics talk about the *"Summum Bonum,"* i.e. the Greatest Good is the Highest End. In practical life we do not begin by thinking, we begin as common-sense beings without thinking; we live first, and do things right and wrong and mixed up anyhow. The first practical thing we have to face in life is duty, and the Bible begins where common sense begins, viz. in the practical domain. We have to get at what Jesus Christ taught was the Highest Good, then we can understand why He did not accept the standard of life that we accept, and why He plays havoc with all our lesser "goods" until we get to the supreme Good He had in mind.

When we are born again we see things from a totally new perspective and we think we see all, then we go on a bit further, and when we get to the top of that peak there are regions beyond we never dreamed of, and so on. When we have got exhausted with the vistas before us we are prepared to hear Jesus say, "This is life eternal, that they should know Thee the only true God" (John 17:3 RV).

Evolution is simply a working way of explaining the growth and development of anything. When evolution is made a fetish and taken to mean God, then call it "bosh"; but evolution in a species, in an idea, in teaching, is exactly what our Lord taught: born of the Spirit and going on "till we all attain . . . unto the measure of the stature of the fulness of Christ" (RV).

To understand means we can reconstruct a thing mentally and leave no element out. When we come to try and understand the Highest Good of our Lord, we must take it in His language, and it will take all time and eternity to understand what that Good is. Whether we live for the Highest Good does not depend on our understanding, but on whether we have the life of the Highest Good in us.

1. The Greatest Good Is the Highest End
(Matthew 7:4–14; 18:8–9; 19:16; 25:46)
When Aristotle and the ancient thinkers spoke of the Highest Good, their meaning was that, in this earthly life of ours, there is for everyone a single supreme attainment, which if missed, will render life a failure, but, if gained, will render it a success.

Stalker

The Shorter Catechism states, in answer to the question, "What is man's chief end?" that "Man's chief end is to glorify God and enjoy Him for ever." It is not what man puts into his body or on his body, but what he brings out of his body (cf. Matthew 15:17–20), and what he brings out of what he puts on his body, viz. his money, that reveals what he considers his chief end. A great many people imagine they have glorified God when they have given two halfpennies for a penny, or have saved a halfpenny. The highest good to them is to keep economic relations right, the highest Good from Jesus Christ's standpoint never dawns on them. The craze to-day is that the highest good is what a man has to live on: feed him, keep his body healthy, and his moral and religious life will be all right. That is the highest good according to the standard of many. As Christians it is more important to know how to live than what to live on. The attitude of the Christian is not, "I'm but a stranger here, heaven is my home," but rather "I'm not a stranger here." A stranger is exonerated from many things for which God holds us responsible. Jesus asked His Father to treat His disciples not as strangers but as inmates[17] of the world and to keep them from the evil (John 17:15). We have to live in the heavenly places while here on earth.

16. James Stalker (1848–1927) was a Scottish scholar and pastor who served as professor of church history at the United Free Church College, Aberdeen, from 1902 to 1926. Chambers used Stalker's book, *The Ethic of Jesus According to the Synoptic Gospels* (1909), as a text to teach Christian ethics at the Bible Training College.

17. inmates: people living under one roof as members of a family or group. Not used to mean those who are institutionalised or imprisoned.

2. The Greatest Good Is the Highest Evangel
(Matthew 4:23; 9:35; 11:5; 24:14; 26:13)

In the teaching of Jesus the term "The Greatest Good" is embodied in its most comprehensive sense in His use of the word "Gospel." Our Lord in no way means what we commonly mean when we say "Gospel," viz. salvation by faith in Jesus. The Bible never gives definitions, the Bible states facts, and the Gospel that Jesus brought of good news about God is the most astounding thing the world ever heard, but it must be the Gospel that Jesus brought. Whenever the Gospel of Jesus loses the note of unutterable gladness, it is like salt that has lost its savour. We are apt to think of the Gospel on the lines of spring-cleaning. We have conceived of the kingdom of God in the time of the Millennium only, consequently when we come to the parables we are confused. The kingdom of God in this dispensation is the rule of God discerned by individuals alone (see John 3:3). "Unless you are born from above [RV mg]," Jesus says, "you will never see the rule of God." It is not seen by the intellect. The rule of God which individual saints see and recognise is "without observation" in this dispensation. There is another dispensation coming when the whole world will see it as individuals have seen it.

"The kingdom of God is within you" (Luke 17:21). The blessedness of the gospel of the kingdom of God in this dispensation is that a man is born from above (RV mg) while he is below, and he actually sees with the eyes of his spirit the rule of God in the devil's territory. You will see how far we have got away from Jesus Christ's teaching. We bring in all kinds of things, we talk about salvation and sanctification and forgiveness of sins; Jesus did not mention these things to Nicodemus (He mentioned them later to the disciples), He said, "Be born from above and you will see the rule of God." It is an attitude of essential simplicity all through. Preaching what we call the Gospel, i.e. salvation from hell does not appeal to men; but once get Jesus Christ to preach His own Gospel and the Spirit of God to expound it, then men are hauled up at once.

Consideration of Several Beatitudes

The drift of the Beatitudes has often been misunderstood. They have been supposed to describe the characteristics of true Christians, pronouncing those blessed who possess such-and-such qualities. But the structure is much more complex. . . . For example, one of the Beatitudes says, "Blessed are they that mourn": and, if we stop there, the statement is almost equivalent to the absurd saying, "Happy are the unhappy." The addition, however, of the words, "for they shall be comforted," makes all the difference. . . . And the same principle applies to all the Beatitudes. . . . Thus, mourning, hungering, persecution are not in themselves and by themselves, desirable, but the reverse; yet, taken along with
what is given by Jesus to those thus circumstanced, they are blessedness itself.

Stalker

"Blessed are the meek: for they shall inherit the earth." The gift here is the heritage of the earth by being fool enough to let other people have it at present. Jesus Christ taught that any one who possesses property of any nature has got to go through a baptism of bereavement in connection with it before he can be His disciple. The rich young ruler is a good specimen of possession (see Luke 18:22–23). The craze nowadays for those of us who have no property is to take the liberty of hauling to pieces those who have; but Jesus Christ turns it round the other way—"Do you possess *anything,* any property of pride, any sense of goodness, any virtue, any gift? Then you will have to go through intolerable bereavement before you can ever be My disciple." Intellectually that is inconceivable; spiritually it is clear to everyone who is rightly related to the Lord. This is where the obstinacy is revealed all through in us as disciples; we come up against this stone wall, and it produces obstinacy. The one great enemy of discipleship to Jesus Christ is spiritual obstinacy, the emphatic "I won't" which runs all through. Jesus says, "If you are to be My disciple this and that must go"; we are at liberty to say, "No, thank you," and to go away, like the rich young ruler, with fallen countenances and sorrowful because we have great possessions, we are somebodies, we have opinions of our own, we know exactly what we intend to do.

"Blessed are the merciful: for they shall obtain mercy." As soon as we get right with God we are going to meet things that are contrary, we are going to meet un-merciful good people and un-merciful bad people, un-merciful institutions, un-merciful organisations, and we shall have to go through the discipline of being merciful to the merciless. It is much easier to say, "I won't bother my head with them"; then we shall never know the blessedness of obtaining God's mercy. Over and over again we will come up against things, and in order to get the eternal blessedness Jesus Christ refers to we shall have to go through the unhappiness of doing something that the standards of men will be contemptuous over.

"Blessed are the pure in heart: for they shall see God." How are we going to be pure in heart? We shall have to go through the humiliation of knowing we are impure. If you want to know what a pure heart is, read the life of the Lord Jesus Christ as recorded in the New Testament. His is a pure heart, anything less is not. Do you know the real panging misery of repentance? Think of the times (they are rare) when you have been in conscious touch with God—the moments when the simplicity of your heart-relationship to God, not your head, was undeterred by a sense

of property or possession on your part—that was the time and place to see God.

3. The Greatest Good Is the Healthiest Equity *(Luke 6:20–23)*

When we try to understand Jesus Christ's teaching with our heads we get into a fog. What Jesus Christ taught is only explainable to the personality of the mind in relation to the personality of Jesus Christ. It is a relationship of life, not of intellect. That is why Jesus said, "Except ye be converted, and become as little children, ye shall not enter into the kingdom of heaven." Our conception of things has to be torn to shreds until we realise that what makes a man a Christian is a simple heart-relationship to Jesus Christ, not intellectual conceptions.

This conception enlarges our horizon and enables us to understand why it took God's Son to preach the Gospel, and why Jesus said, "The poor have the gospel [mg] preached unto them" (Matthew 11:5 RV). Why not the rich? The rich did not want it. "But if our gospel be hid," says Paul, "it is hid"—from the publicans? No; "it is hid to them that are lost: in whom the god of this world hath blinded the minds of them which believe not." That is the class for whom the Gospel of Jesus has no meaning. A healthy-hided moral man does not want Jesus Christ; a ritualist does not want Jesus Christ; a rationalist does not want Jesus Christ. It is along this line we begin to understand why Jesus said, "I am not come to call the righteous," i.e. the whole and the healthy, "but sinners to repentance." I am come to those who mourn, to those who are afflicted, to those who are in a condition of insatiable thirst." Nothing will ever satisfy a man who is awakened but the supreme Good, viz. the Gospel of God. The social worker who goes into work without this supreme Good ends in heartbreak and disaster because all he succeeds in doing even while he satisfies lesser cravings is to render more intense the craving for something other, viz. the one supreme Good.

"Blessed are ye, when men shall revile you, and persecute you, and shall say all manner of evil against you falsely, for My sake. Rejoice, and be exceeding glad." That is the mark of a Christian from our Lord's standpoint. Many of us are persecuted because we have crotchety notions of our own, but the mark of a disciple is suffering "for My sake." Have you ever suffered anything for His sake? If we are foolish enough in the eyes of the world to order our life according to the rule of the kingdom of heaven, the only virtue will be, says Jesus, that men will hate you as they hated Me. Try and work your home life or your business life according to the rule of Jesus Christ and you will find that what He said is true, you will be put out of court as a fool, and we don't like to be thought fools. That is the persecution that many a man and woman has to go through if they are true to Jesus Christ, a continual semi-cultured sneering ridicule; nothing can stand that but absolute devotion to Jesus Christ, a creed will never stand it. Christianity is other-worldliness in the midst of this-worldliness. To apply the rule of the kingdom of God to our daily life is done not by our heads but by the obedience of our hearts. "If you are ever going to get the true blessedness," says Jesus, "it must be by living your life according to the rule of God." How are we going to discern the rule of God? Jesus told Nicodemus: "If you are born from above [RV mg] you will *see* the kingdom of God, and *enter into it*" (John 3:3, 5). Then after we have entered into the kingdom of God, are we going to apply its rule to our bodily life, our mental life, our spiritual life? We are at liberty to stop short at any point, and our Lord will never cast it up at us; but think what we shall feel like when we see Him if all the "thank you" we gave Him for His unspeakable salvation was an obstinate determination to serve Him in our own way, not His.

RIGHTEOUSNESS

Bear in mind that our human life viewed from a moral standpoint is a tragedy, and that preaching precepts while we ignore the Cross of Jesus Christ is like giving "a pill to cure an earthquake," or a poultice for a cancer. Our attempts to face the problems of human life apart from Jesus Christ are futile. It is good for us to use our common sense and not live tragically, but remember, immediately you touch the moral problem you find that things are damnably wrong, the Book says so; they are so far wrong that it takes the Cross of Jesus Christ to put them right, and we live in a fool's paradise if we ignore the terrific tragedy at the bottom of everything.

Blessed are they which do hunger and thirst after righteousness: for they shall be filled. (Matthew 5:6)

Blessed are they which are persecuted for righteousness' sake: for theirs is the kingdom of heaven. (Matthew 5:10)

Most people use righteousness as a term for the behaviour of man to man; and it includes this; but, when

Christ speaks of hungering and thirsting after righteousness, and of being filled with it, there can be little doubt that, in accordance with the usage of His race, the prize He has in view is the favourable verdict of God on a man's character and conduct.

Stalker

The majority of us know nothing whatever about the righteousness that is gifted to us in Jesus Christ, we are still trying to bring human nature up to a pitch it cannot reach because there is something wrong with human nature. The old Puritanism which we are apt to ridicule did the same service for men that Pharisaism did for Saul, and that Roman Catholicism did for Luther; but nowadays we have no "iron" in us anywhere; we have no idea of righteousness, we do not care whether we are righteous or not. We have not only lost Jesus Christ's idea of righteousness, but we laugh at the Bible idea of righteousness; our god is the conventional righteousness of the society to which we belong.

The claim that our Lord was original is hopelessly wrong, He most emphatically took care not to be; He states that He came to fulfil what was already here but undiscerned. "Think not that I am come to destroy the law, or the prophets: I am not come to destroy, but to fulfil." That is why it is so absurd to put our Lord as a Teacher first, He is not first a Teacher, He is a Saviour first. He did not come to give us a new code of morals: He came to enable us to keep a moral code we had not been able to fulfil. Jesus did not teach new things; He taught "as one having authority"—with power to make men into accordance with what He taught. Jesus Christ came *to make us holy*, not to tell us to be holy: He came to do for us what we could not do for ourselves.

The great tendency to-day is that we are looking for another teacher. The world is sick of teachers and of ideals, the point is, have we ever lived up to any of our ideals? It is not more ideals we want, but the power to live up to what we know we ought to and don't. It is shallowness, not ability, that makes people say we want more teaching and higher ideals—model Sunday School classes, model Bible classes; it is all model. "Do this and don't do that," but where is it being carried out? Jesus Christ does not add one burden to the lives of men; He imparts the power to live up to what we know we ought, that is the meaning of His salvation.

For I say unto you, That except your righteousness shall exceed the righteousness of the scribes and Pharisees, ye shall in no case enter into the kingdom of heaven. (Matthew 5:20)

The sympathy of Christ with the training imparted by the Old Testament, and with the passion for righteousness thereby generated, is expressed very distinctly in the Sermon on the Mount, before the Preacher proceeds to the exposition of His own ideal; the motive underlying this declaration being a fear lest His subsequent references to the Old Testament should be understood as disparaging to its authority. In order to avoid this danger, He prefaced His exposition with the statement: "Think not that I am come to destroy the law or the prophets: I am not come to destroy, but to fulfil."

Stalker

Jesus Christ contrasts His conception of righteousness with the one already familiar to His hearers. It is not a new gospel we need, that is the jargon of the hour; it is the old gospel put in terms that fit the present-day need, and for one man or one book that does that there are hundreds who tell us that what we want is a new gospel. What we want is men who have the grace of their Lord to face the present-day problems with the old Gospel. What is the good of my talking to the crowd of to-day about the conceptions men had in Luther's day? The thing is, can I make the Gospel I have meet the problems they are facing, and can I show them where other solutions are wrong? If not, I had better keep quiet, I have not been called of God to preach. The majority of us have our own idea of what the Gospel is, but we live aloof from the time we belong to and what we preach is altogether apart from the lives of the folks we talk to.

Our Lord followed the simple line which the prophets took, He took the conceptions He knew men had and compared His own interpretation with theirs and made them judge, with what result? Absolute despair for everybody. Have we ever got hold of the idea that if Jesus Christ was only a Teacher, He was the most tantalising Teacher that ever came to this earth? If Jesus Christ came to interpret to us a standard infinitely more profound than the one we already have, what is the good of it? He tells us that if we want to see God we must be pure in heart—how are we going to begin? He tells us to love our enemies, to bless them that curse us, to do good to them that hate us, to pray for those who despitefully use us, and persecute us—how can we begin to do it? If He is a Teacher only, then He is a most cruel Teacher, for He puts ideals before us that blanch us white to the lips and lead us to a hell of despair. But if He came to do something else as well as teach—if He came to re-make us on the inside and put within us His own disposition of unsullied holiness, then we can understand why He taught like He did.

It is by facing our lives with the conceptions of Jesus that we understand the meaning of His Cross. One of the most despairing things of our day is the shallow dogmatic competence of the people who tell us they believe in the teachings of Jesus but not in His Atonement. The most unmitigated piece of nonsense human ears ever listened to! Believe in the teachings of Jesus—what is the good of it? What is the good of telling me that I have to be what I know I never can be if I live for a million years—perfect as God is perfect? What is the good of telling me I have to be a child of my Father in heaven and be like Him? We must rid our minds of the idea that is being introduced by the modern trend of things that Jesus Christ came to teach. The world is sick of teachers. Teachers never can do any good unless they can interpret the teaching that is already here.

> *For I say unto you, that except your righteousness shall exceed the righteousness of the scribes and Pharisees, ye shall in no wise enter into the kingdom of heaven.* (Matthew 5:20 RV)

> *Having thus cleared the ground, the Great Teacher proceeds, in the Sermon on the Mount, to expound His conception of righteousness; and, in so doing, He adopts a method frequently resorted to by every expositor who knows his business: He contrasts the conception of the subject in His own mind with one already familiar to His hearers. . . . The righteousness of the scribes was external; that of Jesus is internal. Theirs was a righteousness in words and actions; His flows out from the innermost thoughts and feelings. Theirs was conventional—that is to say, it was intended for the eyes of society; His was a righteousness of the conscience having regard only to God.*

> Stalker

"Except your righteousness shall exceed"—not be different from but *"exceed,"* that is, we have to be all they are and infinitely more! We have to be right in our external behaviour, but we have to be as right, and "righter," in our internal behaviour. We have to be right in our words and actions, but we have to be as right in our thoughts and feelings. We have to be right according to the conventions of the society of godly people, but we have also to be right in conscience towards God. Nominal Christians are often without the ordinary moral integrity of the man who does not care a bit about Jesus Christ; not because they are hypocrites, but because we have been taught for generations to think on one aspect only of Jesus Christ's salvation, viz. the revelation that salvation is not merited by us, but is the sheer sovereign act of God's grace in Christ Jesus. A grand marvellous revelation fact, but Jesus says we have got to say "Thank you" for our salvation, and the "Thank you" is that our righteousness is to exceed the righteousness of the most moral man on earth.

Jesus not only demands that our external life is above censure but that we are above censure where God sees us. We see the meaning now of saying that Jesus is the most tantalising Teacher: He demands that we be so pure that God Who sees to the inmost springs of our motives, the inmost dreams of our dreams, sees nothing to censure. We may go on evolving, and evolving, but we shall never produce that kind of purity. Then what is the good of teaching it? Listen: "If we walk in the light, as He is in the light, we have fellowship one with another, *and the blood of Jesus Christ His Son cleanseth us from all sin."* That is the Gospel; Jesus Christ claims that He can take a man or woman who is fouled in the springs of their nature by heredity and make them as pure as He is Himself. That is why He teaches what He does, and it is His standard we are to be judged by if we are His disciples. No wonder the disciples when they heard Jesus speak, said, "Who then can be saved?" The greatest philosophy ever produced does not come within a thousand leagues of the fathomless profundity of our Lord's statements, e.g., "Learn of Me; for I am meek and lowly in heart" Matthew 11:29). If Jesus Christ cannot produce a meekness and lowliness of heart like His own, Christianity is nonsense from beginning to end, and His teaching had better be blotted out.

The crucial point of the whole matter is our personal relationship to Jesus Christ. It is far more honest to discard Him absolutely than to play the fool with your own soul and pretend you agree with His teaching while you despise the very central part of it. No wonder Jesus said to a fine godly old man, "Marvel not that I said unto thee, Ye must be born again." If we cannot be made all over again on the inside and indwelt by the Spirit of God, and made according to the teaching of the Sermon on the Mount, then fling your New Testament away, for it will put before you an ideal you cannot reach.

The only way to get out of our smiling complacency about salvation and sanctification is to look at Jesus Christ for two minutes and then read Matthew 5:43–48 and see Who He tells us we are to be like, God Almighty, and every piece of smiling spiritual conceit will be knocked out of us for ever, and the one dominant note of the life will be Jesus Christ first, Jesus Christ second, and Jesus Christ third, and our own whiteness nowhere. Never look to your own whiteness; look to Jesus and get power to live as He wants; look away for one second and all goes wrong.

"When the Son of man cometh, shall He find faith on the earth?" We all have faith in good principles, in good management, in good common sense, but who amongst us has faith in Jesus Christ? Physical courage is grand, moral courage is grander, but the man who trusts Jesus Christ in the face of the terrific problems of life is worth a whole crowd of heroes.

MISSING IT

Anything Jesus Christ revealed may be missed. The disbelief of the human mind always wastes itself in the sentimental idea that God would never let us miss the greatest good. Jesus says He will, that is why we don't like Him, and that is why the teaching of to-day is not the teaching of the Jesus Christ of the New Testament.

1. What If a Man Gain the Whole World? (Mark 8:34–35)

(a) His Point of View
Whosoever will come after Me, let him deny himself, and take up his cross, and follow Me. For whosoever will save his life shall lose it; but whosoever shall lose his life for My sake and the gospel's, the same shall save it.

However the end of life may be conceived—whether as Blessedness, or as the Kingdom of God, or as Right-eousness—one thing is indubitable in the entire teaching of Jesus—that He looks upon the end of life as capable of being missed.

Stalker

The word translated "soul" or "life" may be equally well translated "himself," and the verses mean just what they say. Jesus is not defining the great fundamental doctrine of personality, He is talking about the man himself, the person who lives, and with whom we come in contact. Jesus says if a man gains himself, he loses himself; and if he loses himself for His sake, he gains himself.

Beware of introducing the idea of time; the instant the Spirit of God touches your spirit, it is manifested in the body. Do not get the idea of a three-storied building with a vague, mysterious, ethereal upper story called spirit, a middle story called soul, and a lower story called body. We are personality, which shows itself in three phases—spirit, soul and body. Never think that what energises the spirit takes time before it gets into the soul and body, it shows itself instantly, from the crown of the head to the soles of the feet.

Jesus says that men are capable of missing the supreme good and His point of view is not acceptable to us because we do not believe we are capable of missing it. We are far removed from Jesus Christ's point of view to-day, we take the natural rationalistic line, and His teaching is no good whatever unless we believe the main gist of His gospel, viz. that we have to have something planted into us by supernatural grace. Jesus Christ's point of view is that a man may miss the chief good; we like to believe we will end all

right somehow, but Jesus says we won't. If my feet are going in one direction, I cannot advance one step in the opposite direction unless I turn right round.

(b) His Preaching from That Point of View
When He speaks of Blessedness, He at the same time utters woes which will be the portion of some instead of blessedness; when He speaks of the Kingdom, He distinctly thinks of some that will not be able to enter into it; and when He speaks of righteousness, He glances at many who are living in unrighteousness. In short, there is a considerable portion of the words of Christ occupied with the description and denunciation of sin.

Stalker

We have, as Christian disciples, to continually recognise that much of what is called Christianity to-day is not the Christianity of the New Testament; it is distinctly different in generation and manifestation. Jesus is not the fountainhead of modern Christianity; He is scarcely thought about. Christian preachers, Sunday School teachers, religious books, all without any apology patronise Jesus Christ and put Him on one side. We have to learn that to stand true to Jesus Christ's point of view means ostracism, the ostracism that was brought on Him; most of us know nothing whatever about it. The modern view looks upon human nature as pathetic: men and women are poor ignorant babes in the wood who have lost themselves. Jesus Christ's view is totally different, He does not look on men and women as babes in the wood, but as sinners who need saving, and the modern mind detests His view. Our Lord's teaching is based on something we violently hate, viz., His doctrine of sin; we do not believe it unless we have had a radical dealing with God on the line of His teaching.

Remember that a disciple is committed to much more than belief in Jesus; he is committed to his Lord's view of the world, of men, of God and of sin. Take stock of your views and compare them with the New Testament, and never get tricked into thinking that the Bible does not mean what it says when it disagrees with you. Disagree with what our Lord says by all means if you like, but never say that the Bible does not mean what it says.

(c) His Procedure and Others'
This is the point at which the ethical teaching of Jesus differs most widely from the similar teaching of philosophy. The ethics of the philosophers bear a considerable resemblance to the teaching of Jesus in so far as the setting

up of an ideal of character and conduct is concerned; but little or nothing is said by philosophers about the inability of men to attain to the standard, or of the manifold forms of failure exhibited in actual experience.

Stalker

People say, "Oh yes, the Sermon on the Mount is very beautiful, our ideals must be better than we can attain, we shall drift into the Lord's ideals in time somehow or other"; but Jesus says we won't, we will miss them. "The manifold forms of failure exhibited in actual experience" is ignored by other ethical teachers. They say it is never too late to mend—it is; that you can start again—you cannot; that you can make the past as though it had never been—it is impossible; that anyway you can put yourself in such a condition that what you have done need not count—you cannot and our Lord is the only One who recognises these things. We think because we fail and forget it, therefore it is overlooked by God—it is not. Jesus Christ's standard remains, and the entrance into His kingdom and into a totally new life is by Regeneration, and in no other way. The teachings and standards of Jesus, which are so distasteful to modern Christianity, are based on what our Lord said to Nicodemus: "Marvel not that I said unto thee, ye must be born again"; otherwise our Lord was a dreamer. The reason we do not see the need to be born from above (RV mg) is that we have a vast capacity for ignoring facts. People talk about the evolution of the race. The writers of to-day seem to be incapable of a profound understanding of history, they write glibly about the way the race is developing, where are their eyes and their reading of human life as it is? We are not evolving and developing in any sense to justify what is known as evolution. We have developed in certain domains but not in all. We are nowhere near the massive, profound intellectual grasp of the men who lived before Christ was born. What brain to-day can come near Plato, or Socrates? And yet people say we are developing and getting better, and we are laying the flattering unction to our souls that we have left Jesus Christ and His ideas twenty centuries behind. No wonder Jesus said that if we stand by Him and take His point of view, men will hate us as they hated Him.

In spite of his tendency to self-satisfaction, every man is aware some time or other of his own broken bones, and he knows that there must be death before there is any prospect of climbing the heights of moral attainment.

Stalker

Have you ever noticed that in some moods you have battled bitterly against the position you know to

be right, and all your tirade against it is born of a fear lest after all it might be wrong? That is the real attitude of men and women, they will accept any amount of subterfuges, but right down underneath they have a superb contempt for anything less than that which goes to the root of the matter, and the only One Who does is the Lord Jesus Christ. Sooner or later every human heart flings away as chaff the idea that we are developing and growing better.

2. What If a Man Lose Himself? *(Mark 8:36–37)*
(a) The Possibility of the Question
For what shall it profit a man, if he shall gain the whole world, and lose his own soul? Or what shall a man give in exchange for his soul?

Jesus habitually saw with the mind's eye the spiritual development which those around Him might have attained had their desire been fixed more steadily on the true end of life.

Stalker

The idea seems to be, that, even though it does not come to absolute loss, yet if gaining the world involve damage to the self, the moral personality—taint, lowering of the tone, vulgarising of the soul—we lose much more than we gain.

Bruce[18]

In the training of art students, the master does not merely tell them what is wrong in a design, he puts the right design beside the wrong and lets them judge for themselves, and that is exactly what Jesus Christ did all through the Sermon on the Mount.

Do I accept the possibility that I may miss the highest good? There is a sentimental notion that makes us make ourselves out worse than we think we are, because we have a lurking suspicion that if we make ourselves out amazingly bad, someone will say, "Oh no, you are not as bad as that"; but Jesus says we are worse. Our Lord never trusted any man, "for He knew what was in man"; but He was not a cynic for He had the profoundest confidence in what He could do for every man, consequently He was never in a moral or intellectual panic, as we are, because we will put our confidence in man and in the things that Jesus put no confidence in. Paul says, "Don't glory in men; don't say, I am of Paul, or I am of Apollos, and don't think of yourself more highly than you ought to think, but think according to the measure of faith, that is, according to what the grace of God has done in you." Never trust (in the fundamental meaning of the word) any other saving Jesus Christ. That will mean you will never be unkind to anybody on the face of the earth,

---

18. Alexander Balmain Bruce (1831–1899) was a Scottish theologian and teacher.

whether it be a degraded criminal or an upright moral man, because you have learned that the only thing to depend on in a man is what God has done in him. When you come to work for Jesus Christ, always ask yourself, "Do I believe Jesus Christ can do anything for that case?" Am I as confident in His power as He is in His own? If you deal with people without any faith in Jesus Christ it will crush the very life out of you. If we believe in Jesus Christ, we can face every problem the world holds.

(b) Property and Perdition
Take heed, and beware of covetousness: for a man's life consisteth not in the abundance of the things which he possesseth. (Luke 12:15)

What He thought of most frequently as impeding the growth of true manhood was the pursuit of wealth and property.

Stalker

How many people do you know who have their godliness incarnated in economy? Are you one of them? If we can save and do justly with money, we are absolutely certain we are right in the sight of God. The thing about our Lord and His teaching which puts Him immeasurably away from us nowadays is that He is opposed to all possessions, not only of money and property, but any kind of possession. That is the thing that makes Him such a deep-rooted enemy to the modern attitude to things. The two things around which our Lord centred His most scathing teaching were money and marriage, because they are the two things that make men and women devils or saints. Covetousness is the root of all evil, whether it shows itself in money matters or in any way.

(c) Poverty and Perdition
But seek ye first the kingdom of God, and His righteousness; and all these things shall be added unto you. (Matthew 6:33)

But Jesus was hardly less sensible of the danger to which the poor were exposed of missing the prize through an opposite cause—on account, not of the glamour of riches, but the pressure of poverty. . . . His was not a gospel of meat and drink, of loaves and fishes, of better clothes and better houses.

Stalker

Jesus Christ nowhere stands with the anti-property league. It is an easy business for me to mentally satirise the man who owns land and money when I don't. It is easy for me to talk about what I could do with a thousand pounds if I had it; the test is what I do with the 2½d[19] I have got. It may be hard for a rich man to enter into the kingdom of heaven, but it is just as hard for a poor man to seek first the kingdom of God. It is not eternal perdition, it is the perdition of losing the soul for this life. Jesus thought as much of the possibility of losing the highest good through poverty as through riches. His own followers were poor, yet He said to them, "Seek ye first"—bread and cheese? money? a new situation? clothing? food? No, "the kingdom of God, and His righteousness; and all these things shall be added unto you." Did He know what He was talking about, this poor Carpenter Who had not a pillow of His own and never enough money to pay a night's lodging and yet spoke like that, and Who also said that "the cares of this world, and the deceitfulness of riches, and the lusts of other things entering in, choke the word, and it becometh unfruitful"?

Have I ever tried to practise one thing that Jesus taught in the Sermon on the Mount? Tolstoi blundered in applying the Sermon on the Mount practically without insisting on the need to be born again of the Spirit of God first; but I am taking for granted that we are born again, now try putting into practice something Jesus said, and if what He said does not prove true, say so, but try it. For instance, "Give to him that asketh thee." "Yes," you say, "and be surrounded at once with a crowd of beggars!" Is the Almighty absolutely powerless? We argue like pagans and jargonise like saints. The sentimental jargon in our prayer meetings is exactly like the New Testament language, while in practice we are pagans as if Jesus had never said a word. What man who has never allowed God to lift him up would dare to stand before his fellow creatures and lift up the standard of God? There would be deep condemnation in every message he gave.

Our Lord based a man's self-realisation on his spiritual relationship to God. Carlyle[20] estimated human beings by their brains and came to the conclusion that half the human race were fools. Fancy measuring a man by the amount of grey matter in his cranium! You cannot judge a man by his head, but only by his character. One of the greatest disasters in human life is our wrong standards of judgement, we will judge men by their brains, Jesus never did. Jesus judged men and women by their relationship to His Father, an implicit relationship. The brain is nothing more than a marvellous machine for expressing a man's conception of things, and when our hearts and

---

19. 2½d equals two pence and a half penny; 1 percent of a British pound prior to 1971. "Tuppence ha'penny"—colloquial: next to nothing; nothing at all.

20. Thomas Carlyle (1795–1881) was a Scottish-born literary figure in nineteenth-century England, a writer, biographer, essayist, historian, and critic.

lives are right with God, our brains are a means of expressing a particular conception which comes from our Lord. Never partake of the cynical view of life. Jesus Christ estimates that a man's real soul life is his relationship to God and nothing else, and Paul said, "Let no man by his philosophy beguile you away from this simplicity"—the simplicity of the life "hid with Christ in God."

IRRESPONSIBILITY

Every Christian worker has to decide this question, viz. Is Jesus Christ's mind infallible, or is the modern Western mind infallible? The tendency abroad to-day is to think ourselves infallible, and the Bible a jumble up of the most extraordinary stuff, good stuff, but we cannot be expected to accept all its views. That means, we believe ourselves more likely to be infallible than Jesus Christ. We would repudiate this statement if made baldly, but we all act as if it were true, we all take for granted that Jesus Christ's teachings are non-sense; we treat them with respect and reverence, but we do not do anything else with them, we do not carry them out.

For the past three hundred years men have been pointing out how similar Jesus Christ's teachings are to other good teachings. We have to remember that Christianity, if it is not a supernatural miracle, is a sham.

1. This Life's Use Wasted

For what shall it profit a man, if he shall gain the whole world, and lose his own soul? (Mark 8:36)

The most literal meaning of losing one's life is, of course, dying by accident; . . . if a man loses his life by accident, what is the whole world to him?

Stalker

Jesus says that life is the opportunity God gives to man to do his life work; that means that God has no respect whatever for our programmes and machinery. Our Lord insists on one thing only, God's purpose for Him; He pays not the remotest attention to civilised forces, He estimates nothing but one standard. According to our standards He was idle; for three years He walked about saying things. It is only by putting these violent contrasts before our minds that we understand how different our Lord's standpoint to life is compared with ours. We bend the whole energy of our lives to machinery, and when an accident happens and the machinery breaks up we say, What a disaster. Probably it was the emancipation of the man's life. We make nests here and there, competences here and there, but God has no respect for any of them; at any minute He may send a wind and over

goes the whole thing. The one thing God is after is character.

Not only has the Creator appointed to every human being, in the constitution of his manhood, a certain stature to which he may and ought to attain; but He has appointed a corresponding task for him to fulfil, determined by the providential circumstances in which he is placed. In fact, this is his life; and not to fulfil this God-appointed purpose of his existence is to lose his life.

Stalker

It is along these fundamental lines that we understand why the Bible says, "There is a way which seemeth right unto a man, but the end thereof are the ways of death"; why Solomon said, "God made man upright; but they have sought out many inventions" (RV); and why he further said, "Trust in the LORD with all thine heart, and lean not upon thine own understanding" (RV); and why our Lord said, "Let not your heart be troubled." The characteristic of a man who is not based on the issue of his life is an incessant cunning, crafty, commercial worry. Our Lord was absolutely devoid of that. What we call responsibility our Lord never had, and what He called responsibility men are without. Men do not care a bit for Jesus Christ's notion of their lives, and Jesus does not care for our notions. There is the antagonism. If we were to estimate ourselves from our Lord's standpoint, very few of us would be considered disciples.

This idea lay near to the heart of Jesus, first of all, in relation to Himself. He thoroughly realised, from first to last, that He had a work to do, so accurately arranged and fitted to the length of His life that every hour had its own part of the whole to clear off, and He was not allowed either to anticipate or lag behind.

Stalker

To-day we hold conferences and conventions and give reports and make our programmes. None of these things were in the life of Jesus, and yet every minute of His life He realised that He was fulfilling the purpose of His Father (e.g. John 9:4). How did

He do it? By maintaining the one relationship, and it is that one relationship He insists on in His disciples, and it is the one we have lost in the rubbish of modern civilisation. If we try and live the life Jesus Christ lived, modern civilisation will fling us out like waste material; we are no good, we do not add anything to the hard cash of the times we live in, and the sooner we are flung out the better.

In St. John's Gospel this aspect of our Lord's life is more elaborately worked out than anywhere else. It is indicated in the other Gospels (see Luke 2:49; 13:32; 12:50). Jesus knew He was here for His Father's purpose and He never allowed the cares of civilisation to bother Him. He did nothing to add to the wealth of the civilisation in which He lived, He earned nothing, modern civilisation would not have tolerated Him for two minutes.

It will be remembered how frequently He represented this life as a trust or stewardship [see Luke 19:13). On one occasion Jesus manifested extraordinary irritation. . . at the sight of a tree that was barren (Mark 11:12–14); but this was a manifestation of an impatience, which beset Him always, with objects that were not answering the end of their existence.

Stalker

In our Lord's mind any created thing which fails in making anything of its purpose is contemptible. (See Luke 13:6–9) Jesus' attitude to Roman and Grecian civilisation was one of superb contempt. Our attitude to Greece and Rome is one of un-bonneted reverence, with not so much as the cast of an eye for Jesus Christ. Our Lord followed life from His Father's standpoint, to-day we are caught up in the shows of things. Take the Bible attitude to men on the whole, civilisations are despatched at a minute's notice, armies come together and annihilate one another and God seems to pay no attention. His attitude is one which makes us blaspheme and say that He does not care an atom for human beings. Jesus Christ says He does, He says He is a Father, and that He, Jesus, is exactly like His Father. The point is that Jesus saw life from God's standpoint, we don't. We won't accept the responsibility of life as God gives it to us, we only accept responsibility as we wish to take it, and the responsibility we wish to take is to save our own skins, make comfortable positions for ourselves and those we are related to, exert ourselves a little to keep ourselves clean and vigorous and upright; but when it comes to following out what Jesus says, His sayings are nothing but jargon. We name the Name of Christ but we are not based on His one issue of life, and Jesus says, "What shall it profit a man, if he shall gain the whole world"—and he can easily do it—"and lose his own soul?"

2. This Soul's Way Missed

Or what shall a man give in exchange for his soul? (Mark 8:37)

The attitude of our Lord's mind is this, that the eternal condition of a man's spirit is determined by his soul life in this order of things.

The loss of oneself in missing one's opportunities of moral and spiritual development . . . may end in the loss of the "soul" in the awful sense of being cast away for ever. On this solemn subject the teaching of our Lord is extraordinarily copious; indeed, it is to Him that the popular conceptions about a Day of Judgement and the retributions of a future existence are due.

Stalker

The modern Christian laughs at the idea of a final judgement. That shows how far we can stray away if we imbibe the idea that the modern mind is infallible and not our Lord. To His mind at least the finality of moral decision is reached in this life. There is no aspect of our Lord's mind that the modern mind detests so fundamentally as this one. It does not suit us in any shape or form. The average modern mind reads such passages as Luke 16:23–24 and says our Lord was only using figurative language. If the picture is so dreadful figuratively, what must the reality be like? The things our Lord talks about are either arrant nonsense or they are a revelation of things that the common sense of man can never guess. The attitude of Jesus is outside our standards in every way. We must face the music nowadays as we have never faced it. Christianity is a complete sham or a supernatural miracle from beginning to end; immediately we admit it is a miracle we are responsible for walking in the light of what we know Jesus Christ to be.

To our Lord's mind the definiteness of the finality of punishment was as clear as could be, and nothing but lack of intelligence ever makes us say He did not put it in that way, and if those of us who take Him to be Lord and Master, take Him to mean what He says, where ought we to be in regard to these questions? The majority of us are apologetic about the teachings of Jesus, we are much too easily cowed by modern good taste. The modern mind is the infallible god to the majority of us. A man like Blatchford, who simply puts Jesus Christ on one side, is in a much more wholesome state. It is far better to do that than accept Jesus and leave out what we don't like. That is to be a traitor and a deserter.

The parables in the 25th chapter of St. Matthew are three aspects of the Divine estimate of life. Beware of being an ingenious interpreter. You will always find at the basis of our Lord's parables and illustrations a fundamental consistency to His revelation.

The parable of the ten virgins reveals that it is fatal from our Lord's standpoint to live this life without preparation for the life to come. That is not the exegesis, it is the obvious underlying principle.

The parable of the talents is our Lord's statement with regard to the danger of leaving undone the work of a lifetime.

And the description of the last judgement is the picture of genuine astonishment on the part of both the losers and the gainers of what they had never once thought about.

To be accustomed to our Lord's teaching is not to ask, "What must I do to be good?" but, "What must I do to be saved?" How long does it take us to know what the true meaning of our life is? One half second.

> *Oh, we're sunk enough here, God knows!*
>   *But not quite so sunk that moments,*
> *Sure tho' seldom, are denied us*
>   *When the spirit's true endowments*
> *Stand out plainly from its false ones,*
>   *And apprise it if pursuing*
> *Or the right way or the wrong way,*
>   *To its triumph or undoing.*
> *There are flashes struck from midnights,*
>   *There are fire-flames noondays kindle,*
> *Whereby piled-up honours perish*
>   *Whereby swollen ambitions dwindle,*
> *While just this or that poor impulse,*
>   *Which for once had play unstifled,*
> *Seems the sole work of a life-time*
>   *That away the rest have trifled.*

There never was anyone who did not have one moment when all the machinery tumbled away and he saw the meaning of his life. God pays not the remotest attention to our civilised cultures and our attitude to things, because that is not what we are here for. We are here for one thing—to glorify God. That is where we join issue with the Lord Jesus Christ to-day, and we look at every other thing as life—"What shall we eat? or, What shall we drink? or, Wherewithal shall we be clothed?" Our Lord came for one purpose only, to reveal God, and to get men to be spiritually real.

If we would have the blunt courage of ordinary human beings and face the teachings of Jesus, we would have to come to one of two conclusions— either the conclusion His contemporaries came to, that He was devil-possessed, or else to the conclusion the disciples came to, that He is God Incarnate. Jesus Christ will not water down His teaching to suit our weakness in any shape or form; He will not allow us to cringe in the tiniest degree. Whenever there is a trace of cringing or whining, or wanting something different from what He wants, it is the stern front of the Son of God uncloaking sin every time we look at Him; but if we come as paupers, what happens? Exactly the opposite. He will lift us up and wash us whiter than snow, and put the Holy Ghost in us and place us before the Throne of God, undeserving of censure, by the sheer omnipotence of His Atonement.

What we have to get hold of in our moral lives is that Jesus Christ demands that we live His holy life out naturally. Despair is always the gateway of faith. "If Thou canst! All things are possible to him that believeth" (RV). So many of us get depressed about ourselves, but when we get to the point where we are not only sick of ourselves, but sick to death, then we shall understand what the Atonement of the Lord Jesus Christ means. It will mean that we come to Him without the slightest pretence, without any hypocrisy, and say, "Lord, if You can make anything of me, do it," and He will do it. The Lord can never make a saint out of a good man, He can only make a saint out of three classes of people—the godless man, the weak man, and the sinful man, and no one else, and the marvel of the Gospel of God's grace is that Jesus Christ can make us naturally what He wants us to be.

THE BASE IMPULSE

> *But, ah, through all men some base impulse runs*
> *The brute the father, and the men the sons*
> *Which if one harshly sets himself to subdue,*
> *With fiercer indolence it boils anew,*
> *He ends the worst who with best hopes began,*
> *How hard is this, how like the lot of man!*

Experimentally the meaning of life is to attain the excellency of a broken heart, for that alone entails repentance and acceptance, the two great poles of Bible revelation. "The sacrifices of God are a broken spirit"— why, we do not know, but God has made it so. The one thing we are after is to avoid getting broken-hearted.

The base impulse revealed itself in the time of our Lord in three great types of sin—the sin of the publicans, the sin of the Pharisees and the sin of the Sadducees.

> *In every country there is a lost class, a class that has given way to the sins of the flesh till its sin can no*

longer be concealed. What others do by stealth, they do openly. Such a class existed in our Lord's day in Palestine, and the popular names for them in that day were publicans and sinners, or publicans and harlots, or the lost sheep of the house of Israel. . . . The attitude of Jesus to this class was one of the most singular and characteristic features of His career, and, when fully understood, reveals more clearly perhaps than any other circumstance the secret of His mission.

Stalker

It is remarkable how little Jesus directed His speech against carnal and public sins, though He showed plenty of prophetic indignation against the sins of a wholly different class, He preached His grandest sermon to a bad, ignorant woman (John 4:10–14), and one of His most prominent disciples was a publican named Matthew. The one man He ever said He wanted to stay with was another publican called Zaccheus, and some of the most fathomless things He said were in connection with a notoriously bad woman (Luke 7:36–50). It is along this line that we can understand why the Pharisees were sick to the heart and disgusted with Jesus Christ, why they called Him "a friend of publicans and sinners!" We would have done exactly the same to-day in spite of all our religious sentiments. We gloss over our Lord's actions with our civilised conceptions and destroy the meaning of His Gospel.

Our Lord's conduct was not due to any insensibility to the wickedness of open and carnal sins, nor that He was lenient to those sins: He drew near to those sins to make them for ever impossible in the lives of those guilty of them. Jesus roused the conscience of the very worst of them by presenting the highest good. We are apt to forget that our Lord's parables in Luke 15 say just what they do. Never take the fifteenth chapter of St. Luke as an exposition of the Gospel first; it is our Lord's *apologia;* He is explaining to the Pharisees why He is here.

1. The Pharisaic Invincibility

In interpreting our Lord's teaching, watch carefully who He is talking to; the parable of the prodigal son was a stinging lash to the Pharisees. We need to be reminded of the presentation of Jesus in the New Testament for the Being pictured to us nowadays would not perturb anybody; but He aroused His whole nation to rage. Read the records of His ministry and see how much blazing indignation there is in it. For thirty years Jesus did nothing, then for three years He stormed every time He went down to Jerusalem. Josephus says He tore through the Temple courts like a madman. We hear nothing about that Jesus Christ to-day. The meek and mild Being pictured to-day makes us lose altogether the meaning of the Cross. We have to find out why Jesus was beside Himself with rage and indignation at the Pharisees and not with those given over to carnal sins. Which state of society is going to stand a ripping and tearing Being like Jesus Christ Who drags to the ground the highest respected pillars of its civilised society, and shows that their respectability and religiosity is built on a much more abominable pride than the harlot's or the publican's? The latter are disgusting and coarse, but these men have the very pride of the devil in their hearts.

Ask yourself, then, what is it that awakens indignation in your heart? Is it the same kind of thing that awakened indignation in Jesus Christ? The thing that awakens indignation in us is the thing that upsets our present state of comfort and society. The thing that made Jesus Christ blaze was pride that defied God and prevented Him from having His right with human hearts. Sin is the independence of human nature which God created turning against God. Holiness is this same independence turning against sin. Sin is not doing wrong things, it is wrong being. Sins are wrong acts: sin is an independence that will not bow its neck to God, that defies God and all He presents, that will not go to the excellency of a broken heart. It is that class who stand for independence in art and culture; it is not for them a question of right or wrong, but of pleasing the senses. The greatest pillars of art and culture are erected on these lines and Jesus Christ pulls down the whole temple, because we cannot build temples of art on this earth at all; they will be built in heaven when the foundations are pure. The refinements of art and culture are all in opposition to the tumbling in crisis of God in the Incarnation.

2. The Pride of Integrity

The conspicuous point of view in which the Pharisees always figure in the Gospels is incapable of repentance. Self-knowledge is the first condition of repentance. Watch Jesus Christ whenever there is the tiniest sign of repentance, He is the incarnation of forgiving and forgetting, and He says that is God's nature. "I am not come to call the righteous, but sinners to repentance." Remember, that kind of statement hits the Pharisees to the very core of their being. Could they listen patiently to a Man like that? Jesus was killed for His words, He would not have been crucified if He had kept quiet. It was the ruthless way He went straight to the very root of Pharisaism that enraged them until they became the devil incarnate and crucified the Son of God. "Calvary" means "the place of a skull," and that is where our Lord is always crucified, in the culture and intellect of men who will not have self-knowledge given by the light of Jesus Christ.

3. Sensible Rationalism

The Sadducee is the type of person who in all ages destroys the treasure of the spirit; he is a common-sense individual.

> *There are some people to whom it is never safe to show any valued possession. . . . Now and then someone with the bump of destruction will push his way into our holy of holies, and deface what he considers our idols and leave us sad. . . . Unfold a scheme, a dream, a theory, a long-cherished recollection within the reach of a man who loves destruction, and he will reduce it to nothing. Even a book, that treasure which stands half-way between the tangible and the intangible, is not safe with him, he will turn its pages into ridicule, and give it back with half its charm destroyed.*

Thomas Carlyle utterly destroyed the early faith of his wife and never gave her anything in its stead, and Mrs. Carlyle's letters, gifted with the most amazing literary ability and mentality, are wilted and sad, like her face, because he destroyed in the true spirit of the Sadducee her holy of holies and gave her nothing in its place. This line of thought makes us understand our Lord's attitude to the Sadducees, and why He said, "Don't cast your pearls before swine." There are some things we must never show to anyone. Like children, we all think that we ought to show our cherished possessions, we ought not; there are Sadducees everywhere. You rarely find them people of uncouth speech, but rather the opposite.

We have all met people who act like an east wind, our mental horizon gets lower and we feel unmitigatedly mean[21] and despicable. When Jesus Christ came near men, He convicted them of sin, but He convicted them also of this, that they could be like He was if they would only come to Him.

> *The Sadducees were the anti-Pharisaic party, and they went as far in believing too little as the Pharisees in the direction of believing too much. They were the sceptical religious party. Their beliefs lacked warmth and conviction. The weakness of the religious sentiment in them was partly the cause and partly the effect of another characteristic, viz. worldliness. The spiritual and eternal stirred them but faintly, consequently they had a more tenacious hold on the concerns of this present life.*
>
> Stalker

Watch the difference between the faces marred by sin and those marred by coming in contact with the Sadducees, who have all their inner shrines destroyed and nothing given in their place; the latter give a look of withered, mean sanity. Sin does not produce it, it is the effect of the presence of this monster—the rational, healthy-minded Sadducee; this "monster" has been inside the Christian Church for the past twenty centuries, and is one of the problems that has to be faced. There are comparatively few Pharisees to-day, the greater number are Sadducees, who back up their little bits of common sense against all that Jesus Christ said and against everything anyone says who has had a vision of things differing from common sense.

4. Sensible Ruling

The Sadducees were the ruling class and the priestly party from the date of the Babylonian exile. Such priests have continually emerged in the affairs of God, and they are much more interested in the affairs of the visible world and but faintly tinged with the hope or spirit of the world invisible.

> Stalker

This is the type that perfectly exhibits the Sadducee of our Lord's day. It is not the brutal sceptic who is the Sadducee, he does not destroy anybody's shrines, it is the religious man or woman with particularly bright conceptions of their own, but who are far more concerned with the visible success of this world than with anything else. You go to them with some insurgent doubt in your mind, and they smile at you, and say, "Oh, don't exercise your mind on those things, it is absurd." That is the Sadducee who has done more to deface in modern life what Jesus Christ began to do than all the blackguardism and drunkenness in our modern civilisation. The subtle destruction of all that stands for the invisible is what is represented by the Sadducee.

It is necessary to get the historical atmosphere and setting of our Lord's life in order to understand the historical exegesis of His teaching. Most of us only know the spiritual exegesis, we come with our spiritual illumination and take incidents out of the Bible—"I don't care about their historic exegesis, I simply take them as expressing my own spiritual condition." That is not the thing for a student to do; a student has to rightly divide the word of truth, and to find out the historic background of Jesus Christ's teaching.

In Luke 16:19–31 we get a good picture of our Lord's attitude to the Sadducees. The rich man

> *lived to dine and to wear sumptuous clothing, neither bestowing on the poor any generosity commensurate with his means nor remembering that he was an heir of eternity, and herein is the great moral principle, viz. that of not doing being as guilty as doing, and that the Judge will accept no*

---

21. mean: ordinary, common, low, or ignoble, rather than cruel or spiteful

excuse for a life not marked by unselfishness up to the means of its opportunity.

Stalker

If we know that we have received the unmerited favour of God and we do not give unmerited favour to other people, we are damned in that degree. The best and most spiritual people to-day turn Jesus Christ's teaching out of court. They say He could never have meant what He said, and, we have to use common sense. If we apply common sense we run the risk of being Sadducees. What common sense person would carry out the Sermon on the Mount? It is the Sadducee who withers up the true spirit of devotion to God in our life by a "squirt" of common sense, because the common sense comes from a background of infidelity against God's rule. We are measured by what we do according to what we have. Some people only give to the deserving, because they imagine they deserve all they have. Our Lord says, Give, not because they deserve it, but because I tell you to.

Jesus reveals in the parable of the rich man (Luke 12:16–21) that his mind and heart have been entirely absorbed with property. About his soul and eternity he has manifested no concern, he heaped up treasure but was not rich towards God.

Stalker

Treasure in heaven is the wealth of character that has been earned by standing true to the faith of Jesus, not to the faith in Jesus. Our Lord's advice to the rich young ruler was, "Sell all that thou hast and distribute unto the poor, and thou shalt have treasure in heaven: and come, follow Me." That is, have faith for the things Jesus Christ stood for, and anybody who is fool enough

to conduct his life with Jesus Christ as absolute Master will realise what Jesus said, "Men shall . . . separate you from their company . . . and cast out your name as evil." Many of us are saved by the skin of our teeth, we are comfortably settled for heaven, that is all we care for, now we can make a pile on earth. There are plenty of people who give their testimony all right in meetings, but they are Sadducees to the backbone.

The cynicism of the official who feared not God nor regarded man, administered justice in our Lord's instance from mere annoyance. For him justice had no majesty and the misfortune of the widow had no sacredness. That which he could not be got to do, either for the fear of God or out of regard to man, he yet hastened to do merely to save himself from annoyance; and this is a thoroughly Sadducean trait.

Stalker
(See Luke 18:1–8)

The spirit of "I do not wish to be annoyed" is frequently the inspiration of the administration of justice in private cases. It works into our intercession also: I want that bad person saved—because he is of so much value in the sight of God? No, because he is an annoyance to me, I cannot live my life properly with him. That spirit cannot live anywhere near Jesus Christ, because Jesus had only one point of view—His Father's will.

In any work I do for God is my motive loyalty to Jesus, or do I have to stop and wonder where He comes in? If I work for God because I know it brings me the good opinion of those whose good opinion I wish to have, I am a Sadducee. The one great thing is to maintain a spiritual life which is absolutely true to Jesus Christ and to the faith of Jesus Christ.

THE BASE IMPULSE
(Continued)

*Lord, Lord, when we are dead, remember not
All our lost sorrows and our soul's endeavour,
Better to bear the burden of our lot,
Firmer to stand how strong the storm so-ever,
Only remember all the agony
Thou bearest in the Garden silently.*

*And when the soul by death is freed again,
Thou wilt not let the rapture of her wings
Be marred by memory of this life's pain,
But lift our hearts above our sufferings.
Lord, let our soul's life after all these years
Rise stronger, wiser, cleaner for its tears.*

1. The Low Man with a Little Thing to Do
The base impulse is the way sin works into our minds and gives us a totally wrong view of God. If the base impulse does not show itself in flesh and blood sins, it will show itself in mean-mindedness. Try and imagine what Jesus meant when He said, "Preach the gospel to every creature"; He keeps "an open house" for the whole universe. It is a conception impossible of human comprehension.

(a) Moral Distinctions
We are interested in other men's lives because of a career, a profession, or an ideal we have for them, but

God does not seem to care an atom for careers or professions, He comes down with ruthless disregard of all gifts and geniuses and sweeps them on one side; He is interested only in one thing, and that thing was exhibited in the life of our Lord, viz. a balanced holiness before God. Our Lord's character is the full-orbed expression of God's ideal of a man. We can never take any one virtue and say Jesus Christ was the representative of that virtue; we cannot speak of Jesus Christ being a holy Man or a great Man or a good Man; Jesus Christ cannot be summed up in terms of natural virtues, but only in terms of the supernatural. If we can describe a man by any one virtue, he ceases to be God's idea of a man, and the characteristic of the Spirit of God in us is that He brings us "unto the measure of the stature of the fulness of Christ."

(b) Money Matters and the Master's Mind
Money is the sign and symbol of all earthly possessions; it is earthly pleasure in a solid condition, only requiring to be melted to assume any of its more volatile and usable forms; and the pursuit of it easily becomes an absorbing passion even with those who have forgotten how to turn it into these equivalents. On this subject the language of Jesus is astonishingly severe.

                                                    Stalker

Jesus saw in money a much more formidable enemy of the Kingdom of God than we are apt to recognise it to be. Money is one of the touchstones of reality. People say, "We must lay up for a rainy day." We must, if we do not know God. How many of us are willing to go the length of Jesus Christ's teaching? Ask yourself, how does the advocacy of insurance agree with the Sermon on the Mount, and you will soon see how un-Christian we are in spite of all our Christian jargon. The more we try to reconcile modern principles of economy with the teachings of Jesus, the more we shall have to disregard Jesus. Whenever we read anything that is very plain in our Lord's words, we either say that we cannot understand it or that it has another meaning. Common sense is the best gift we have, but it must be under the dominant rule of God. We enthrone common sense, we do not enthrone God. Men must reason according to their god, and the god of to-day is common sense; that is why Jesus Christ's teaching is ruled out of court. If we try and apply the principles of the Sermon on the Mount to ordinary business life to-day, we shall see where we are. Civilisation was founded by a murderer, and the very soul and genius of civilisation is competition. What we are trying to do to-day is to Christianise civilisation, and our social problems exist because Jesus Christ's teaching is being ruled out.

2. The High Man with a Great Thing to Do
Profound as is His sense of the wickedness of the world and the lostness of the individual, the ground-tone of His preaching is not despair, but hope; and the final and enduring impression left on the mind by the prolonged and sympathetic study of all His words is, that there is an essence of divine dignity and immeasurable value, which it is the task of the Saviour and of all who are inspired with His aims to rescue from the dangers to which it is exposed and to redeem to a destiny of blessedness and immortality.

                                                    Stalker

(a) Solidarity of Sin
Solidarity means oneness of interest. We are familiar with the phrase "the solidarity of the human race," but there is also a solidarity of sin (a oneness of interest in sin), and a solidarity of salvation (a oneness of interest in salvation). I mean by sin, not sin in a particular sense, but in the great big general sense which means a violation or neglect of the laws of morality or religion, and God's Book shows that there is a oneness of interest in all sin. The Psalms show a wonderful discrimination about sin (e.g. Psalms 32, 51); they refer to the same thing the Apostle Paul refers to in Ephesians 6:12, the supernatural inspiration of sin.

We have considered the three great sins of our Lord's day—the sin of the publican, of the Pharisee, and of the Sadducee, and now we must look to the fact that our Lord considered men as evil. "If ye then, being evil . . ." (Luke 11:13). Jesus Christ is made to teach the opposite of this by modern teachers; they make out that He taught the goodness of human nature. Jesus Christ revealed that men were evil, and that He came that He might plant in them the very nature that was in Himself. He cannot, however, begin to do this until a man recognises himself as Jesus sees him.

We start with the idea that some people are good and some bad; but we are all bad, everyone of us needs saving by Jesus Christ. Imagine that being believed to-day! We can hear Christendom saying, "Nonsense, human nature is not evil." The feature of to-day is the love of man that hates God. We are alienated from the standpoint of Jesus, we have become incarnated by a leaven that never came from His point of view, and if we are going to stand for Him we shall find that what He said is true: "They will turn you out of the synagogues"—not because we denounce sin, a socialist denounces sin as much as a preacher of the Gospel. The difference between a Christian worker and one who does not know Jesus Christ is just this—that a Christian worker can never meet anyone of whom he can despair. If we do despair of anyone, it is because we have never met Jesus Christ ourselves. The social worker who does not know what Jesus Christ came to do will end in absolute despair before long, because the social worker more than anyone else begins to see the enormous havoc that sin has made of human nature, and if he does not know the Saviour from sin, all his efforts will meet with as much success as attempting to empty the Atlantic Ocean with a thimble.

(b) Saviour from Sin

The great challenge in personal work is—What relationship have I to Jesus Christ? It is not simply that we realise the power of Jesus to save, but that we recognise the possibilities for evil in our own heart, discerned in us by the Holy Spirit, and know that Jesus can save unto the uttermost. Let a man be a murderer, or an evildoer, or any of the things Jesus said men could be, it can never shake our confidence if we have once been face to face with Jesus Christ for ourselves. It is impossible to discourage us because we start from a knowledge of Who Jesus Christ is in our own life. When we see evil and wrong exhibited in other lives, instead of awakening a sickening despair, it awakens a joyful confidence—I know a Saviour who can save even that one. One worker like that is of priceless worth, because through that one life the Son of God is being manifested.

It is not only necessary to have an experience of God's grace, we must have a body of beliefs alive with the Spirit of Jesus, then when we have learned to see men as He sees them, there is no form of disease or anguish or devilishness that can belch up in human life that can disturb our confidence in Him; if it does disturb us, it is because we don't know Him.

The sense of sin is in inverse ratio to its presence, that is, the higher up and the deeper down we are saved, the more pangingly terrible is our conviction of sin. The holiest person is not the one who is not conscious of sin, but the one who is most conscious of what sin is. The one who talked most about sin was our Lord Jesus Christ. We are apt to run off with the idea that a man in order to be saved from sin must have lived a vile life himself; but the One who has an understanding of the awful horror of sin is the spotlessly holy Christ, Who "knew no sin." The lower down we get into the experience of sin, the less conviction of sin we have. When we are regenerated and lifted into the light, we begin to know what sin means. There is no mention of sin in the Apostle Paul's apprehension by Christ, yet no one wrote more about sin than the Apostle Paul years after in his Epistles, because by the marvellous working of God's grace and his own repentance, he was lifted into the heavenly places where he saw what sin really was. The danger with those of us who have experienced God's perfect salvation is that we talk blatant jargon about an experience instead of banking on the tremendous revelation of God the Holy Ghost. The purer we are through God's sovereign grace, the more terribly poignant is our sense of sin. It is perilous to say, "I have nothing to do with sin now"; you are the only kind of person who can know what sin is. Men living in sin don't know anything about it. Sin destroys the capacity of knowing what sin is. It is when we have been delivered from sin that we begin to realise by the pure light of the Holy Ghost what sin is. We shall find over and over again that God will send us shuddering to our knees every time we realise what sin is, and instead of it increasing hardness in us towards the men and women who are living in sin, the Spirit of God will use it as a means of bringing us to the dust before Him in vicarious intercession that God will save them as He has saved us. Beware of the metallic, hard, unChristlike stamp of some testimonies to sanctification, they are not stamped by the Holy Ghost. The testimony to sanctification that is of God is dipped and saturated in the blood of the Son of God, and that blood sprang from the broken heart of God on account of sin. When once the soul realises what sanctification is, it is a joy unspeakable, but it is a joy in which there is the tremendous undercurrent of a chastening humiliation. Beware of any experience that is not built absolutely on the atoning merit of Jesus Christ; and remember, the measure of your freedom from sin is the measure of your sense of what sin is.

Thy Great Redemption
Introduction

Source

Thy Great Redemption is from lectures given by Oswald Chambers from October to December 1914 in Christian doctrine class at the Bible Training College.[22]

Publication History

- As articles: The lectures appeared as articles in the *BTC Journal*[23] April 1935 through March 1936.

- As a book: *Thy Great Redemption* was published in 1937. It was published in a combined volume with *The Pilgrim's Song Book* and *The Highest Good* in 1965.

More of Chambers' teaching on redemption can be found in *The Psychology of Redemption* (1930).

CONTENTS

---

22. The Bible Training College (BTC) was a residential school near Clapham Common in southwest London. It was sponsored by the League of Prayer and operated from 1911 until it closed in July 1915 because of World War I. Oswald Chambers was principal and main teacher; Biddy Chambers, his wife, was lady superintendent.

23. The *Bible Training Course Monthly Journal* was published from 1932 to 1952 by Mrs. Chambers, with help from David Lambert.

FOREWORD

Writing in the War years[24] (1917) Oswald Chambers said, "Through this war there will emerge new restatements of God and of Christ. To me there emerge two or three grand facts: First, Fathomless Redemption as the basis of human life; absolute God-like Forgiveness of Sin; with a liberty to reject that basis on the part of man. Second, That God's Name is Jesus Christ; not that He is a revelation from God, but that He is God. That means that God became the weakest thing in His creation—a Babe. Third, That He can introduce into any man the heredity of the Son of God by New Birth, in which His Nature becomes operative in human nature, along with a series of educational developments." These articles on Redemption contribute to that very end. "Everything that has been touched by sin and the devil has been redeemed; we are to live in the world immovably banked on that faith." What sure ground for our feet we have in that glorious truth as we stand for Jesus Christ, witnesses unto Him. But the in-working of Redemption in personal life is grandly brought out in these living messages. I quote another sentence, "Immediately I accept the Cross of Christ as the revelation of Redemption I am not, I must not be, the same man; I must be another man, and I must take up my cross for my Lord." So we see Redemption working inwardly, with our reactions to it, and with the resultant issues regarding sin and righteousness and judgement. The book is *more* than worth its weight in gold.

David Lambert[25]

LECTURE: OCTOBER 9, 1914

REDEMPTION

1. Redemption in Realised Revelation
(John 19:30)
We can never expound the Redemption, but we must have strong unshaken faith in it so that we are not swept off our feet by actual things. That the devil and man are allowed to do as they like is a mere episode in the providence of God. Everything that has been touched by sin and the devil has been redeemed; we are to live in the world immovably banked in that faith. Unless we have faith in the Redemption, all our activities are fussy impertinences which tell God He is doing nothing. We destroy our souls serving Jesus Christ, instead of abiding in Him. Jesus Christ is not working out the Redemption, it is complete; we are working it out, and beginning to realise it by obedience. Our practical life is to be moulded by our belief in the Redemption, and our declared message will be in accordance with our belief. If we say we believe "It is finished" we must not blaspheme God by unbelief in any domain of our practical life.

We must make a distinction in our minds between the revelation of Redemption and conscious participation in it. When we are born again we consciously enter into participation of the Redemption. We do not help God to redeem the world: we realise that God has redeemed it. Redemption is not dependent on our experience of it. The human race is redeemed; we have to be so faithful to God that through us may come the awakening of those who have not yet realised that they are redeemed.

2. Revelation and Redemption in Relation
(2 Corinthians 5:18–21)
A sinner knows what the Redemption has wrought in him, but it is only long afterwards that he begins to grasp the revelation of how that Redemption was made particularly and in detail possible in him. It is one thing to be saved by God's grace, but another thing to have a clear revelation as to how God did it. Our Lord Jesus Christ is the Revelation complete; the Bible is the revelation come down to the shores of our life in words. The grace of God can never alter; Redemption can never alter; and the evidence that we are experiencing the grace of God in Redemption is that it is manifestly working out in us in actual ways. When the words of the Bible come home to us by the Holy Spirit, the

---

24. The War years: World War I (1914–1918).

25. David Lambert (1871–1961): Methodist minister and friend of Oswald Chambers. Assisted Mrs. Chambers with OC publications from 1917–1961.

supernatural essence of the Redemption is in those words and they bring forth new life in us. If you have been saved from sin, say so; if you have been sanctified by God's grace, say so. Don't substitute some other refinement in its place. By using other words you are not testifying to God, but compromising with the atmosphere of those to whom you are talking.

The religion of Jesus Christ is not a religion of ethical truth, but of Redemption. The teachings of Jesus have not made so much difference to the world as the teachings of Socrates and Plato, but to those who are born from above (RV mg) they make all the difference. The thing that tells is not that the actual life is lived rightly, but that the motive underneath is right. The characteristic of the Redemption when it works out subjectively in accordance with Scripture is that act of devotion of Mary of Bethany. It was not useful, nor was it her duty; it was an extravagant waste, but the motive of it was the spontaneous originality which sprang from a personal passionate devotion to Jesus Christ. When a man has been profoundly moved in his spirit by the experience of Redemption, then out of him flow rivers of living water. Stop the concern of whether you are of any use in the world. "He that believeth on Me," said Jesus, out of him "shall flow rivers of living water"; whether we see it or not is a matter of indifference. Heed the Source.

3. Redemption in Objective Form *(Luke 24:44–47)*

The disciples after the Resurrection received into themselves an influx from the risen Christ—"their eyes were opened, and they knew Him" (Luke 24:31); and their minds were opened, "that they might understand the Scriptures" (Luke 24:45 RV). The characteristic of being born again is that we know Who Jesus is. The secret of the Christian is that he knows the absolute Deity of the Lord Jesus Christ. When we are saved by God's grace our minds are opened by the incoming of the Holy Spirit and we understand the Scriptures. The test of regeneration is that the Bible instantly becomes the Book of books to us.

The objective form of the Redemption comes to us through the Person of the Lord Jesus Christ, and works itself out in saving judgements. The bedrock of Christianity is repentance. There is a certain type of badness that exhausts itself, and the nature is righted by ordinary hereditary reactions, and that is frequently mistaken for the regenerating work of God. If it is the work of the Spirit of God, repentance is its basis. We can only test the experimental working of Redemption by the fruits the New Testament has taught us to expect. "Bring forth therefore fruits worthy of [your] repentance" (Luke 3:8).

LECTURE: OCTOBER 16, 1914

REDEMPTION
The Christian's Greatest Trust

1. The Cross and the Father's Heart *(John 12:28; Galatians 6:14)*

We can understand the attributes of God in other ways, but we can only understand the Father's heart in the Cross of Christ. The Cross of Christ is not the cross of a martyr, it has become the symbol of the martyr; it is the revelation of Redemption. The Cross is the crystallised point in history where Eternity merges with Time. The cry on the cross, "My God, My God, why hast Thou forsaken Me?" is not the desolation of an isolated individual: it is the revelation of the heart of God face to face with the sin of man, and going deeper down than man's sin can ever go in inconceivable heartbreak in order that every sin-stained, hell-deserving sinner might be absolutely redeemed. If the Redemption of Christ cannot go deeper down than hell, it is not redemption at all.

It is always the tragic note that is struck when once the Spirit of God gets hold of a man. The rea-

son we are so shallow and flippant in our presentation of the Cross is that we have never seen ourselves for one second in the light of God. When we do see ourselves in the light of God, there is only one of two refuges—suicide or the Cross of Christ. The great condemnation of much of our modern preaching is that it conveys no sense of the desperate tragedy of conviction of sin. When once the real touch of conviction of sin comes, it is hell on earth—there is no other word for it. One second of realising ourselves in the light of God means unspeakable agony and distress; but the marvel is that when the conviction does come, there is God in the very centre of the whole thing to save us from it. That is the meaning of the Cross of Christ as experimentally applied to us. We have to face ourselves with the revelation of the Redemption, mirrored and concentrated in the Cross of Jesus Christ as it is presented in the New Testament, before we get the shallow, pious nonsense shaken out of our religious beliefs. To be saved by God's grace is not a beautifully pathetic thing; it is a desperately tragic thing.

2. The Cross and the Saviour's Mind
(Matthew 16:24; Galatians 2:20)
The evidence that I have accepted the Cross of Christ as the revelation of Redemption is that the regenerating life of God is manifested in my mortal flesh. Immediately I accept the Cross of Christ as the revelation of Redemption I am not, I must not be, the same man, I must be another man, and I must take up my cross from my Lord. The cross is the gift of Jesus to His disciples and it can only bear one aspect: "I am not my own." The whole attitude of the life is that I have given up my right to myself. I live like a crucified man. Unless that crisis is reached it is perilously possible for my religious life to end as a sentimental fiasco. "I don't mind being saved from hell and receiving the Holy Spirit, but it is too much to expect me to give up my right to myself to Jesus Christ, to give up my manhood, my womanhood, all my ambi-

tions." Jesus said, If any man will be My disciple, those are the conditions. It is that kind of thing that offended the historic disciples, and it will offend you and me. It is a slander to the Cross of Christ to say we believe in Jesus and please ourselves all the time, choosing our own way.

Our salvation is one of unspeakable freedom for heart and mind and body, but do we sufficiently brood on what it cost God to make it ours? At certain stages of Christian experience a saint has no courtesy towards God, no sense of gratitude; he is thankful for being delivered from sin, but the thought of living for Jesus, of being recklessly abandoned to Him, has not begun to dawn on him yet. When we come to the Cross we do not go through it and out the other side; we abide in the life to which the Cross is the gateway, and the characteristic of the life is that of deep profound sacrifice to God. Social service that is not based on the Cross of Christ is the cultured blasphemy of civilised life against God, because it denies that God has done anything, and puts human effort as the only way whereby the world will be redeemed.

LECTURE: OCTOBER 23, 1914

RELATIVE REDEMPTIVE REACTIONS

An abiding snare in dealing with Christian doctrine arises from the tendency to bend the attention exclusively either to the objective or the subjective side. If we deal only with the objective, it produces the type of practical life that contradicts the creed believed in; and to deal only with the subjective side produces the moody, sickly introspective type of life, its eyes fixed on its own whiteness. The wholesome antidote to either tendency is the New Testament, which embraces both the objective and the subjective through the miracle of regeneration. Belief in the New Testament is always practical and positive, that is, it instantly manifests itself. I do not "gull" myself into believing something has happened, it is a fact; I am not only right with God but am actually proving that I am in my life. If my faith in the Redemptive work of Christ does not react in a practical life which manifests it, the reason is a wrong temper of mind in me.

How ought life from the ascended Lord to react in me? By reaction is meant not a reaction of nerves but the essential nature of the life. The danger of dealing only with the objective side is that it blinds our minds to the fact that we have to receive something

which must have a reaction, "to open their eyes, . . . that they may *receive*" (Acts 26:18). That means the will of the individual is willing to receive. Not only has Jesus Christ been seen and believed in, but accepted, and the reaction in the life is as radical as the stupendous miracle that made it possible.

1. Sympathies—Humanitarian or Evangelical
(Galatians 3:6)
If I feel sympathy with anyone because he cannot get through to God, I am slandering God; my fundamental view is not the evangelical one, but a point of view based on mere human sympathy. Trace where your sympathies arise, and be sympathetic with God, never with the soul who finds it difficult to get through to God. God is never to blame. "Remember the people." Don't! Remember the Christ Who saves you. We are not here to woo and win men to God; we are here to present the Gospel which in individual cases will mean condemnation or salvation. "Where you get the most faithful preaching, you get the most hardened sinners" *(Thos. Guthrie).*[26] It is perilous to listen to the truth of God unless I open my will to it. We have not to rouse

---

26. Thomas Guthrie (1803–1873) was a Scottish pastor and children's advocate.

people's sympathies and humanitarian conceptions— "How beautiful and dignified man is!" We have rigorously to push an issue of will, and when the issue is put you find the obstruction; men resent it, and that is the barrier to God. Immediately that barrier is down God comes in like a torrent, there is nothing to keep Him back; the one thing that keeps Him back is anarchy and rebellion, the essential nature of Satan—I won't give up my right to myself; I won't yield, and God is powerless. Immediately a man removes the barriers it is as if God romped into his soul with all His almightiness, it is a flood of blessing quite overwhelming.

2. Strenuousness—Holy or Evangelistic
(2 Corinthians 6:1–2)
Jesus Christ is not an individual Who died twenty centuries ago; He is God and mankind centred in His Cross. The Cross is the revelation of the deepest depth in Almighty God. What should be the reaction of that in my life? Holiness, rugged, fierce holiness in every detail of the life. That is the meaning of New Testament repentance. The only truly repentant man is the holy man, he has been made holy through the incoming of God by his willing reception of Him. Evangelistic effort must never forget the source from which it springs; it often does, and all that is presented is the objective side which has no practical outcome in the life.

3. Sacrifices—Homely or Extraordinary
(Luke 14:26–27, 33)
These are extraordinary sacrifices, they cut clean across everything we believe naturally. We must have

the marks in our hands and feet that are exactly like Our Lord. There must be the crucified love of grasp for myself; the crucified love of wandering in my own ways; the crucified love of the world; the wounded pride of intellect. There is no bigger word and no word made more shallow than "surrender." To say "I surrender all" may be blethering sentiment, or it may be the deep passionate utterance of the life.

4. Strongholds—Honest or Exceptional *(Acts 20:24)*
Actions that spring from obedience to Jesus Christ can never be explained on any other ground. This is where the "shame" of testifying comes in. Testimony is not a hard protestation that I have done something better than others, nor is it first a means of helping others; it means that I have ventured out on God and have no one to rely upon but Him. I have staked my all in obedience to Jesus Christ in this matter, and it is sink or swim. Try and explain why you did a certain thing, if it sprang from obedience to Christ, and you find you cannot. It is not the logical working out of a principle, and that is why the other relationships of life do not see it. "If any man cometh unto Me, and hateth not his own father, and mother, . . . he cannot be My disciple" (RV). Remember, the crisis may never come to you, and instead of the claims of father or mother clashing with the commands of Jesus Christ, you may be clashing with commands of His coming to you through them. But if the crisis does arise, it must be prompt obedience to Jesus Christ at every cost.

"THE LORD GOD OMNIPOTENT REIGNETH"

To believe that the Lord God omnipotent reigneth and redeemeth is the end of all possible panic, moral, intellectual or spiritual. We say we believe God, and give the lie to it with every breath we draw. For a man to believe in the Redemption means that no crime nor terror nor anguish can discourage him, no matter where he is placed. God is not saving the world; it is done, our business is to get men and women to realise it, and we cannot do it unless we realise it ourselves.

1. Redemptive Sanctuary *(Jeremiah 17:12)*
What needs doing is all less than has been done. What has to be done for the world is already done in God.

Dr. Forsyth[27]

We can do nothing for the redemption of the world; we have to do in the world that which proves we believe it is redeemed; all our activities are based on that unshakeable knowledge, therefore we are never

---

27. Peter Taylor Forsyth (1848–1921) was a British Congregationalist minister and theologian. Chambers read many of Forsyth's books and valued his insights.

distressed out of that sanctuary. God makes us go a solitary way until we get there, but through one life that is there, comes all the force of the Redemption. The thing that makes our hearts fall is the profound disbelief on the part of Christian workers that God has done anything, and the wearing out of life to do what is already done. All the fuss and energy and work that goes on if we are not believing in Jesus Christ and His Redemption, has not a touch of the almighty power of God about it; it is a panic of unbelief veneered over with Christian phrases. As long as we pretend to be believers in Jesus Christ and are not, we produce humbugs, and people say, "Do you call that Christianity?" "There is nothing in it!"; or what is worse, we produce frauds, and the worst type of fraud is the religious fraud. The greatest type of reality is the Christian believer—one who has been totally readjusted on the basis of his belief. When you come across a believer in Jesus, his very presence alters your outlook. It is not that you have come to someone with amazing intelligence, but that you have come into a sanctuary which is based on a real knowledge of the Redemption. When once a man really believes that the world is redeemed, his belief will manifest itself in every detail, and that is what constitutes the heroism of a believer in Jesus Christ. Our scepticism arises from the fact that we have no experimental knowledge of Redemption.

2. Redemptive Secret *(Philippians 3:13–14)*

Our Christian destiny is to fulfil "the high calling of God in Christ Jesus." When a soul comes face to face with God, the eternal Redemption of the Lord Jesus is concentrated in that little microcosm of an individual life, and through the pinhole of that one life other people can see the whole landscape of God's purpose. The point is, am I realising the Redemption in my home circle, amongst my friends, in the pecuniary circumstances I am in? It is not heroism that makes us sacrifice ourselves, but cowardice; we can't stand being considered cads for not sacrificing ourselves. That is the basis of much of the sacrifice made in the world. The believer is one who bases all on Jesus Christ's sacrifice, and is so identified with Him that he is made broken bread and poured-out wine in the hands of his Lord. "Witnesses unto Me," a satisfaction to Jesus Christ wherever we are placed. When once we get to the right centre of energy, the omnipotence of God is at work all the time.

3. Redemptive Satisfaction *(John 3:16)*

We reason in this way: "God is so loving that I know He will forgive me." God is so holy that it is much more likely He will say I must be damned. Unless God can alter me He dare not forgive me; if He did I should have a keener sense of justice and right than He has. The realisation of the nature of God's love produces in me the convulsions of repentance, and repentance fully worked out means holiness, a radical adjustment of the life. Do I know God has saved me? Have I the satisfaction of that salvation? I can easily know whether the Redemption has been made efficacious in me by the Holy Spirit by the fact that I am at one with God. The Redemption is worked out in an at-one-ment with God, in every calculation He is the One Who dominates everything.

The assurance of faith is a certainty more certain than certainty, and it always comes with an experimental knowledge of the Redemption. Belief in the Redemption is difficult because it needs surrender first. I never can believe until I have surrendered myself to God. "If any man willeth to do His will" (RV)—what is His will? "That ye believe on Him Whom He hath sent."

LECTURE: NOVEMBER 6, 1914

THE RULING ISSUES OF REDEMPTION
John 16:7–15

And He, when He is come, will convict the world in respect of sin, and of righteousness, and of judgement.(RV)

The word "convict" means moral conviction, not logical conviction. When the Holy Spirit is come, He will convict a man with a power of moral conviction beyond the possibility of getting away from it. Whenever the Holy Spirit gets us into a corner, He never convinces our intellect; He is busy with the will which expresses itself in our intellect. It is never safe to do much introspection, but it is ruinous to do none. Introspection can never satisfy us, yet introspection is not wrong, it is right, because it is the only way we discover that we need God. It is the introspective power in us that is made alert by conviction of sin.

1. The Issue Regarding Sin
Of sin, because they believe not on Me.

Note what causes you the deepest concern before God. Does social evil produce a deeper concern than the fact that people do not believe on Jesus Christ? It was not social evil that brought Jesus Christ down from heaven, it was the great primal sin of independence of God that brought God's Son to Calvary. Sin is not measured by a law or by a social standard, but by a Person. The Holy Spirit is unmistakable in His working: "and He, when He is come, will convict the world in respect of sin, . . . *because they believe not on Me*" (RV). That is the very essence of sin. The Holy Spirit brings moral conviction on that line, and on no other. A man does not need the Holy Spirit to tell him that external sins are wrong, ordinary culture and education will do that; but it does take the Holy Spirit to convict us of sin as Our Lord defined it—*"because they believe not on Me."* Sin is not measured by a standard of moral rectitude and uprightness, but by my relationship to Jesus Christ. The point is, am I morally convinced that the only sin there is in the sight of the Holy Ghost, is disbelief in Jesus?

2. The Issue Regarding Righteousness
Of righteousness, because I go to the Father. (RV)

If I am not morally convinced with regard to sin, I won't bother my head about Jesus Christ going to the Father and having all power in heaven and on earth; but once I am convicted of sin and have accepted deliverance from unbelief in Jesus, I know beyond the shadow of a doubt that Jesus Christ is the Righteous One. The wisdom of God is shown in that Jesus Christ was made unto us righteousness (1 Corinthians 1:30). That means that God can justly justify the unjust and remain righteous. In the Cross of Calvary Our Lord is revealed as the Just One making men just before God. God never justifies men outside Christ. No man can stand for one second on any right or justice of his own; but as he abides in Christ, Jesus Christ is made righteousness unto him (see Philippians 3:8–9). Nowadays the tendency is to switch away from "the righteousness which is of God by faith," and to put the emphasis on doing things. You cannot

do anything at all that does not become, in the rugged language of Isaiah, "as filthy rags," if it is divorced from living faith in Jesus Christ. If we have the tiniest hankering after believing we can be justified by what we have done, we are on the wrong side of the Cross. To experience the loss of my own goodness is the only way to enter into communion with God in Christ (2 Corinthians 5:21).

3. The Issue Regarding Judgement
Of judgement, because the prince of this world is judged.

Have I come to judgement at the foot of the Cross? Do I accept God's verdict on sin given there? What one longs to see more often is a soul shattered under the convicting blast of the Holy Ghost. It means that Jesus Christ has seen of the travail of His soul in that one, and it is one of the rarest sights. Most of us are smugly satisfied with praising Jesus Christ without ever having realised what the Cross means. We say, "O Lord, I want to be sanctified," and at any moment in answer to that prayer the Holy Ghost may rip and tear your conscience and stagger you dumb by conviction of sin, and the question is, will you accept God's verdict on sin on the Cross of Christ, or will you whine and compromise? The only test of spirituality is holiness, practical, living holiness, and that holiness is impossible unless the Holy Ghost has brought you to your "last day," and you can look back and say "That was the day when I died right out to my right to myself, crucified with Christ." That is the day from which many a rich young ruler and many a Mary of Bethany goes away sorrowful, with countenance fallen, for they have great possessions of self-respect, great possessions in the way of ideas as to how they want to serve God. The "last day" is when a soul, gripped by the power and light of the Holy Ghost, sees the meaning of the Cross of Christ, and goes to death like a sentenced criminal. To every soul who has gone through that experience, there is no more condemnation (Romans 8:1).

LECTURE: DECEMBER 18, 1914

THE CHARACTER OF REDEEMED EXPERIENCE

By Redeemed Experience is meant eternal life manifested in the fleeting moments of temporal life. What is *not* meant is the consciousness of feeling good, or the consciousness of the presence of God. If we mistake these feelings for eternal life, we shall be disillusioned sooner or later. When we are being initiated into a new experience we are conscious of it, but any

sane person is much too wise to mistake consciousness of life for life itself. It is only the initial stages of new experiences which produce consciousness of themselves, and if we hug the consciousness of God's blessings and of His presence we become spiritual sentimentalists. God began to introduce us to life, and we would not go through with it.

1. The Unique Character of This Life *(John 6:47)*

What is eternal life? "And this is life eternal, that they might know Thee the only true God" (John 17:3). "Eternal" has reference to the quality of the life. Our Lord says very distinctly what eternal life is *not*—e.g. Matthew 4:4; Luke 12:15. Whenever Our Lord speaks of "life" He means *eternal* life, and He says, "Ye have not [this] life in yourselves" (John 6:53 RV). Men have natural life and intellectual life apart from Jesus Christ.

The life which Jesus Christ exhibited was eternal life, and He says—anyone who believes in Me, i.e. commits himself to Me, has that life. To commit myself to Jesus means there is nothing that is not committed. Belief is a twofold transaction—a deliberate destroying of all roads back again, and a complete surrender to Our Lord Himself. God comes in with a rush immediately a soul surrenders to the Lord Jesus Christ. The only barrier to God's love is unbelief working sentimentally, i.e. brooding around the shores of an experience which produces consciousness of itself; the life is not there.

2. The Upward Character of the Life *(John 11:41–42)*

The upward look towards God of eternal life is an indication of the inherent nature of the life; that is, it is not attained by effort. Natural characteristics, natural virtues and natural attainments have nothing to do with the life itself. A blackguard and an upright man both commit themselves to Jesus Christ and receive eternal life; will the latter have freer access to God? No! Eternal life works the same in both. There

is no respect of persons with God. The manifestation of eternal life is, however, a different matter.

3. The Outward Character of the Life *(John 3:16)*

This verse gives the outlook man-ward of eternal life as exhibited in Our Lord. The only way to react rightly on men around is to let eternal life react through you, and if you want to know how eternal life will react you will see it in Jesus Christ. Our Lord was in no wise a hard worker; He was an intense reality. Hard workers are like midges and mosquitoes; the reality is like the mountain and the lake. Our Lord's life was one of amazing leisure, and the presentation of His life as one of rush is incorrect. The three years of public life are a manifestation of the intense reality of life (Acts 10:38). When the passion for souls obscures the passion for Jesus Christ you have the devil on your track as an angel of light. Our Lord was never in a hurry, never in a panic. "There are no dates in His fine leisure." Our Lord's life is the exhibition of eternal life in time. Eternal life in the Christian is based on redemptive certainty; he is not working to redeem men; he is a fellow worker with God among men because they are redeemed.

4. The Downward Character of This Life *(2 Corinthians 5:21)*

The downward look of eternal life is manifested by Our Lord—a fearless, clear-eyed, understanding look at sin, at death, and at the devil—that is the unmistakable characteristic of the downward look of Our Lord. The devil's counterfeit is no sin, no hell and no judgement.

LECTURE: DECEMBER 4, 1914

THE MAGNITUDE OF REDEMPTION
1 Thessalonians 5:23

We cannot be deeply moved by "nothing"; neither can we deeply move ourselves by anything we say, unless something profound has first of all entered into us. For example, it takes a great deal of realising what the Bible reveals about Redemption to enable us to walk out into our daily lives with that astonishing strength and peace that garrisons us within and without.

1. The Working of Redemptive Security

And the God of peace Himself sanctify you wholly . . . (1 Thessalonians 5:23 RV)

The working of Redemptive security in our actual practical life is the realisation that "God is my Father, I shall never think of anything He will forget—why should I worry?" When you can say that from the ground of being profoundly moved, you are astonished at the amazing security. "My peace I give unto you" (John 14:27). The peace of Christ is synonymous with His very nature, and the "type" working of that peace was exhibited in Our Lord's earthly life. "The peace of God, which passeth all understanding . . ." (Philippians 4:7). The Redemption at work in my actual life means the nature of God garrisoning me round; it is *the God of peace* Who sanctifies wholly; the security is almighty. The gift of the peace of Christ on the inside; the garrison of God on the outside, then I have to see that I allow the peace of God to regulate all that I do, that is where my responsibility comes in—"and let the peace of Christ [RV] rule," i.e. arbitrate, "in your hearts," and life will be full of praise all the time.

2. The Working of Redemptive Strength
and may your spirit and soul and body . . . (RV)

The degree in which God will work depends on me, not on God; if I refuse in any part of my being to let God work, I not only limit Him, but I begin to criticise the Redemption. The working of Redemptive strength means that "all spiritual blessings in heavenly places" are mine when I am "at home" with God. Take up your dwelling in that word "all," then do some hunting through the Bible for spiritual blessings and say, "That is mine." If you remain on the outside and say, "Lord, bless me with this spiritual blessing," He cannot do it; the only result is to make you feel miserable; but get inside Christ, and all spiritual blessings in heavenly places are yours. It is not a question of experiencing them, you don't experience what is your life; you experience gifts given to your life. Experiences are always on the threshold of the life, they are never the real centre. Life is fullness of maturity, and there is no seeking for experiences. Beware of not seeing that experiences are nothing other than gateways home. "Saved and sanctified"—Paul says, "Go on! Get into the heavenly places in Christ Jesus." You will be so hidden with Christ that you never think of anything but Him, there will be none of the things that keep the life impoverished.

3. The Working of Redemptive Safety
be preserved entire, without blame . . . (RV)

"He that dwelleth in the secret place of the Most High shall abide under the shadow of the Almighty." Dwelling under that shadow I am in the heart of Almighty God; where I dwell He manifests Himself all the time. It is an essentially natural life. When I am dwelling under the shadow of the Almighty, my life *is* the will of God; it is only through disobedience that I begin to ask what is the will of God. Any interest that would induce me away from the shadow of the Almighty is to be treated as a snare. Resolutely treat no one seriously but God. "The LORD is *my* rock, and *my* fortress, and *my* deliverer; *my* God, *my* strong rock . . . *my* shield, and the horn of *my* salvation, *my* high tower" (Psalm 18:2 RV). Note the "my's" here, and laugh at everything in the nature of misgiving for ever after!

4. The Working of Redemptive Sight
. . . be preserved entire, without blame at the coming [presence, mg] of our Lord Jesus Christ. (RV)

The working of Redemptive sight gives me the habit of an elevated mood whereby God gives the vision of Himself. "Blessed are the pure in heart," literally, "Blessed are the God in heart," i.e. in whom the nature of God is. God's nature in us reveals His features in our life. "Man shall not see Me and live" (RV). When I see God I have to die; when I am in God I have died, and the nature of God works through me transparently all the time. "We know that, if He shall be manifested, we shall be like Him; for we shall see Him even as He is" (RV).

The only way to maintain perception is to keep in contact with God's purpose as well as with His Person. I have to place myself in relation to facts—facts in nature and facts in grace. If I refuse to do this my perception will be wrong, no matter how right my disposition may be; but the two together will produce a life perfectly in accordance with the life of the Son of God when He walked this earth.

"God is able to make all grace abound toward you." Have you been saying, "I cannot expect God to do that for me"? Why cannot you? Is God Almighty impoverished by your circumstances? Is His hand shortened that it cannot save? Are your particular circumstances so peculiar, so remote from the circumstances of every son and daughter of Adam, that the Atonement and the grace of God are not sufficient for you? Immediately we ask ourselves these things, we get shaken out of our sulks into a simple trust in God. When we have the simple, childlike trust in God that Jesus exhibited, the overflowing grace of God will have no limits, and we must set no limits to it.

ACTUALLY BORN INTO REDEMPTION
John 3:4

The abiding reality is God, and He makes known His order in the fleeting moments. Redemption partakes of God's character, therefore it is not fleeting; but we have the power and the privilege of exhibiting the Redemption in the fleeting moments of our actual life. This is the real meaning of being born from above (RV mg). Civilisation is based on principles which imply that the passing moment is permanent. The only permanent thing is God, and if I put anything else as permanent, I become atheistic. I must build only on God (John 14:6). "Because God spoke to me once, I stick to that." You are a fool if you do. Stick to the God Who spoke to you. He is speaking the word all the time; it is only as we are trained by obedience that we can understand Him (see John 6:63).

1. The Standard of Actual Redemption
The standard of actual redemption simply means the manifestation of the life of God in the actual fleeting moments of my life. The eternal reality of God's Redemption is there all the time, being born from above (RV mg) means that I am partaking in it. Nicodemus' question, "How can a man be born when he is old?" (John 3:4), is an exhibition of cultured stupidity, which is denser than ignorant stupidity because it won't be enlightened. Immediately I ask "how can?" I evade the "you must." God never debates or argues.

"We know that whosoever is born of God sinneth not" (1 John 5:18). The life of God in me does not sin (see 1 John 3:9). If I am based on the Redemption, this standard will manifest itself in the actual moments of my life, viz. I must not sin. It is not something I set myself to do, but something I know I never can do, therefore I let God do it. "I know that in me (that is, in my flesh) dwelleth no good thing" Romans 7:18). Born from above (RV mg), I realise that the life of God has entered into me. God gives me "Himself": "The gift *of God* is eternal life" (Romans 6:23), and "eternal life" consciously in me is to know God (John 17:3). The life of God cannot commit sin, and if I will obey the life of God, which has come into me by regeneration, it will manifest itself in my mortal flesh. It is only when I disobey the life of God that I commit sin; then I must get back again into the light by confession (1 John 1:9). If I walk in the light as God is in the light, sin is not.

Actual Redemption is as positive as real Redemption. We never enter into the Kingdom of God by having our head questions answered, but only by commitment.

2. Statement of Actual Recognition
Christ has to unsettle the certainty of a man's pagan mind; the wind of the Spirit touches him across the fleeting moments of his life, and he gets disturbed. The need, then, is for someone sure of Christ, and sure of His Word, to patiently watch for that soul, and that kind of watching is the meaning of intercession. The Holy Spirit imparts the energy of the Redemption into human hearts by means of actual words, and it is to this that Peter refers in his Epistle: "Having been begotten again, not of corruptible seed, but of incorruptible, through the word of God . . ." (1 Peter 1:23 RV). Redemption comes to the shores of our human lives in actual words. "You must get a word from God." "Be sure you get the witness that this is so." The assurance is more positive than intellectual knowledge. The Spirit of God always works with the word of God.

3. Substance of Active Realisation
When a man is actually born from above (RV mg), he knows that the Redemption is as eternal as Almighty God. The disturbance by the Spirit of God opens a man's eyes and he turns from darkness to light, from the authority of Satan unto God; then he is ready to receive the Holy Spirit Who conveys to Him "forgiveness of sins, and inheritance among them which are sanctified . . ." (Acts 26:18). Receiving necessitates conscious poverty (cf. Matthew 20:22; Mark 14:50; John 20:22). Receiving in its elementary and in its complete stages is described in John 1:12–13, "But as many as received Him, to them gave He power to become the sons of God, even to them that believe on His name, . . ." because to receive Jesus even intellectually, means that I commit myself. If I really receive Jesus Christ with my mind, I am given the right to become a son of God. The Holy Spirit makes that right an actual possession, and I receive sonship. To receive power to become a son of God means that I realise I am not a son; if I think I am a son already, I will patronise God. The At-one-ment means being made actually one with God through the Redemption of our Lord. This is to receive a Kingdom which cannot be shaken.

DIMENSIONS OF EFFECTIVE REDEMPTION
John 3:16; Ephesians 3:18–19

By the "dimensions of effective Redemption," understand the Redemption of God expressing itself in individual experience; but beware of limiting the Redemption to our individual experience of it.

1. Breadth
For God so loved the world . . .

The world embraces things material and things evil, things suffering and sinning. Think how narrow and bigoted the love of God is made when it is tied up in less than His own words; we make God out to be exactly the opposite of all Jesus Christ said He was. The breadth of the love of God, the agony of that love, is expressed in one word, "so." If you can estimate the "so," you have fathomed the nature of God. Our love is defective because we will not get down low enough. We must get down lower than hell if we would touch the love of God; we will persist in living in the sixteenth storey when the love of God is at the basement. We speculate on God's love, and discourse on the magnificence of the Redemption, while all the time it has never been made effective in us.

> *The love of God is broader*
> *Than the measures of man's mind.*

—it embraces the whole world. Compare John 3:16 with Our Lord's prayer in John 17. Our Lord did not pray that the world might be saved, but "that the world may know that Thou hast . . . loved them." Our Lord prays for those in whom His Redemption is at work that they may live in effective contact with God—"that they may be one, even as We are one."

The same thing with regard to sin and misery. In the Bible you never find the note of the pessimist. In the midst of the most crushing conditions there is always an extraordinary hopefulness and profound joy, because God is at the heart. The effective working of Redemption in our experience makes us leap for joy in the midst of things in which other people see nothing but disastrous calamity. When the Redemption is effectually at work it always rises to its source, viz. God.

2. Length
that He gave His only begotten Son . . .

When the supreme love of God in the giving of Himself has got hold of me, I love myself in the power of His love; that means a son of God being presented to God as a result of His effectual Redemption. "bringing many sons unto glory . . ." (Hebrews 2:10). That is a gratification to God because it is the returning back to Himself of His love in expressed reality. When the Redemption is effective in me, I am a delight to God, not to myself. I am not meant for myself, I am meant for God.

3. Depth
that whosoever believeth in Him should not perish . . .

The love of God rakes the very bottom of hell, and from the depths of sin and suffering brings sons and daughters to God. To introduce the idea of merit into belief, i.e. that I have done something by believing, is to annul my belief and make it blasphemous. Belief is the abandonment of all claim to desert; that is why it is so difficult to believe in Jesus. It requires the renunciation of the idea that I am someone—"I must have this thing explained to me"; "I must be convinced first." When the Spirit of God gets hold of me, He takes the foundation of the fictitious out of me and leaves nothing but an aching cavern for God to fill. "Blessed are the poor in spirit."

We love the lovely because it is flattering to us to do so. We love our kith and kin because it is the economy of pride to do so. God loves the un-lovely, and it broke His heart to do it. The depth of the love of God is revealed by that wonderful word, "whosoever." The Bible reveals God to be the Lover of His enemies (Romans 5:6–10). We will stick to our "rag rights,"[28] until by God's engineering of our circumstances, every "rag right" is blown from us and we are left with nothing; we become abject paupers, and say, "It's all up," and we find ourselves in heaven! We will persist in sticking to the thing that must be damned.

> *Not by wrestling, but by clinging*
> *Shall we be most blessed.*

---

28. rag rights: self-righteousness; see Isaiah 64:6.

4. Height

. . . but have everlasting life.

The Redemption of Jesus Christ effectively at work in me puts me where He was, and where He is, and where we shall for ever be (John 14:23; 16:23, 26). It is the terrific lift by the sheer, unaided love of God into a precious oneness with Himself, if I will only let Him do it. It is not a magic-working necromantic thing, but the energy of His own life. The "realest" thing is the love of God by means of the effective working of Redemption. On the human plane we may have love real, but low: my love, i.e. the sovereign preference of my person for another person, is in order that *my* purpose may be fulfilled; and when Jesus Christ comes into the life, it looks as if He were the dead enemy of that love. He is not; He is the dead enemy of the low-ness. When the love of God is realised by me, the sovereign preference of my person for God enables Him to manifest *His* purpose in me.

To realise the dimensions of the love of God, its breadth, and length, and depth, and height, will serve to drive home to us the reality of God's love, and the result of our belief in that love will be that no question will ever profoundly vex our minds, no sorrow overwhelm our spirits, because our heart is at rest in God, just as the heart of our Lord was at rest in His Father. This does not mean that our faith will not be tested; if it is faith, it must be tested, but, profoundly speaking, it will be supremely easy to believe in God.

If Thou Wilt Be Perfect . . .

Talks on Spiritual Philosophy

Oswald Chambers

INTRODUCTION

Source

Lectures on biblical philosophy given at the Bible Training College,[1] London, from January to July 1912.

Publication History

As articles: First published as articles in the *Bible Training Course (BTC) Monthly Journal*[2] from October 1937 through October 1938.

As a book: First published as a book in 1939. Mrs. Chambers had planned to title it *Spiritual Philosophy* but bowed to David Lambert's[3] suggestion to use Jesus' words to the rich young ruler in Matthew 19:21—"If thou wilt be perfect."

Always a voracious reader of wide-ranging taste, Chambers included the writings of many philosophers in his personal study. During Oswald's student days at the University of Edinburgh (1895–1896), he very likely studied Metaphysics and the History of Philosophy under Professor Andrew Seth and Moral Philosophy under Professor Henry Calderwood. In addition, he may well have attended Dr. Alexander Whyte's[4] Young Men's Classes, held every Sunday evening following the service at Free St. George's Church. When Chambers arrived in Edinburgh, Dr.

Whyte was dealing with "The Mystics," including Tauler and the book, *Theologia Germanica,* which are both quoted throughout *If Thou Wilt Be Perfect.*

In 1900, Chambers was teaching philosophy at Dunoon College,[5] a small theological school across the Firth of Clyde from Glasgow, Scotland. When his students, most of whom had no university training, expressed their difficulty in making sense of existing textbooks, Chambers compiled and published his own *Outlines for the Study of Historical Philosophy* as a guide for his classes.

Of his lecture series on Biblical Philosophy at the Bible Training College in 1912, Chambers said: "The Ethics and Philosophy classes have taken a great stride in advance, and this is all the more surprising as the Bible Philosophy class is anything but a popular subject as commonly conceived; yet the numbers attending this class grow."

One of Chambers' recurring themes was the critical necessity for every Christian to think. "The reason why the average Christian worker is only the average Christian worker," Oswald told his students, "is that he or she will remain grossly ignorant about what he does not see any need for. All of you have intelligence, and you must use it for God."

---

1. Residential school near Clapham Common in SW London, sponsored by the League of Prayer. Oswald Chambers was Principal and main teacher; Biddy Chambers was Lady Superintendent. Known as the BTC, it closed in July 1915 because of World War I.

2. The *Bible Training Course Journal* was published from 1932 to 1952 by Mrs. Chambers, with help from David Lambert.

3. David Lambert (1871–1961): Methodist minister and friend of Oswald Chambers. Assisted Mrs. Chambers with OC publications from 1917–1961.

4. Alexander Whyte (1836–1921): Scottish minister who influenced Chambers during Oswald's time at Edinburgh University, 1895–1896.

5. Chambers spent 1897–1906 at Dunoon Theological College as a student, then as a tutor.

FOREWORD

On Tauler and on *Theologia Germanica*

Two names are mentioned in this book, one is a man, Tauler, and the other a volume, *Theologia Germanica*. Quotations are made from them. Both belong to pre-Reformation times. John Tauler was born in Strasbourg about 1300. He was a Dominican monk and had already achieved honour and reputation as a preacher when a great change occurred in his spiritual outlook. An unknown layman, after hearing him preach, was moved to tell him that he was allowing himself to be "killed by the letter," and was yet in darkness, and had not tasted the sweetness of the Holy Ghost. The preacher took the words in a spirit of meekness and was ready to receive helpful counsel from his unknown friend. "You must," he said, "take up your cross and follow our Lord Jesus Christ and His example in utter sincerity, humility and patience, and must let go all your proud reasoning." He advised him to cease his preaching for a while and in quiet contemplation examine his life in the mirror of our Lord's. Tauler was nearly fifty, but he took the place of abasement and self-surrender, and for nearly two years was a seeker of God's way, praying that God's life might be brought forth in him. His former friends thought him demented. When the clear light came and he knew the time had come to bear his witness in public, he found it not easy to begin, but soon wisdom and grace from the Holy Spirit were bestowed in abundant measure. So began years of wonderful work for God. In those days when salvation by simple faith in Jesus Christ was so largely hidden beneath ceremonial worship, he taught many that the way to God was by a New Birth that brought men into a vital relation to the *Living God.* His sermons greatly influenced Luther. They have ministered to many in many countries. A volume of his sermons has been published in English under the title, *The Following of Christ.*

The book, *Theologia Germanica,* belongs to the same period. Its author is unknown. That also prepared for the Reformation, as it lays stress on the Holy Spirit's application of Christ's work to the heart of a believer. God never leaves Himself without a witness, and in that bedimmed period these lights were shining and have been shining ever since.

John Wesley complained to William Law[6] that when he was an earnest inquirer he had been directed to the mystic writers, and so had missed the basic truth of salvation by faith in Jesus Christ. We all need to know the initial experience of Christ as the Propitiation for our sins, and as the One who has brought to a world of sinners the abundance of grace and the *gift* of righteousness. Afterwards we may find, as Wesley did, much light in such writers as the above upon how God works in us to will and to do of His good pleasure, and how we can work out our own salvation (Philippians 2:12–13).

The quotations made by Oswald Chambers are themselves of great value, and the expository words that follow are full of luminous and practical teaching for us to-day.

London
David Lambert
April 1939

---

6. William Law (1686–1761): English devotional writer best remembered today for his book *A Serious Call to a Devout and Holy Life* (1728).

CONTENTS

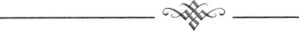

Chapter I

THE PHILOSOPHY OF PERFECTION

But when that which is perfect is come, that which is in part shall be done away. 1 Corinthians 13:10 (RV)

"That which is perfect" is a Being, who hath comprehended and included all things in Himself and His own Substance, and without whom, and besides whom, there is no true Substance, and in whom all things have their Substance.

That Which Is Perfect

The Bible reveals that "that which is perfect" is a Being. God is the only Perfect Being; no human being is perfect apart from God. We make the blunder of applying to human beings terms which the Bible applies to God only. Our Lord in replying to the rich young ruler, who used the term "Good Master," said, "None is good save One, even God" (RV). There is only one Being to whom the term "good" can be applied, and that is the Perfect Being, the term cannot be applied to good men. In the Sermon on the Mount our Lord places God as the model for Christian character; He does not say, "Be good as a man is good," but—"Ye therefore shall be perfect, as your heavenly Father is perfect" (RV). We are to be perfect as our Father in heaven is perfect, not by struggle and effort, but by the impartation of that which is Perfect.

We are accustomed to the use of the word "perfect" in connection with our relationship to God (e.g. Philippians 3:12–15), but here the word is used in a bigger sense, viz. perfect as God is perfect.

"Love" is another term we are apt to apply wrongly. We emphasise perfect love towards our fellow-men; the Bible emphasises perfect love to God. Love is an indefinable word, and in the Bible it is always used as directly characteristic of God—"God is love."Romans 5:5, Paul says that "the love of God is shed abroad in our hearts," not the power to love God, but the love of God.

Or take Truth. *The* Truth is our Lord Himself, consequently any part of the truth may be a lie unless it leads to a relation to *the* Truth. Salvation, sanctification, the Second Coming are all parts of the Truth, but none is the Truth; and they are only parts of the Truth as they are absorbed by the Truth, our Lord Himself. We are not told to expound the way of salvation, or to teach sanctification, but to lift up Jesus, i.e. to proclaim the truth.

That Which Is in Part

If any man thinketh that he knoweth anything, he knoweth not yet as he ought to know. (1 Corinthians 8:2 RV)

God wants us to lose our definitions and become rightly related to Himself, the Perfect One. If we try and state before God where we are in experience, we find we cannot do it, though we know with a knowledge "which passeth knowledge." The purpose of God is to get the part into the whole; if we remain in the part by sticking to our convictions, to that which we know, we shall fizzle off. An experience that is true and vivid cannot be stated in words, the lines of definition are gone. Our experience is only part of the Perfect. Jesus Christ is much more than we have experienced Him to be.

> But "that which is in part," or the imperfect, is that which hath its source in, or springeth from the Perfect, just as a brightness or a visible appearance floweth out from the sun or a candle, and appeareth to be somewhat, this or that. And it is called a creature, and of all these "things which are in part," none is the Perfect.

Are we resting in our experience of the Truth, or in the Truth? The part has its source in the Perfect. The experiences of salvation and sanctification spring from the perfect Source, and it is this that gives the devil his chance to come as an angel of light and make us seek experiences instead of Christ. Do we lift up Jesus, or are we busy carefully defining our religious experiences, having this measuring-rod for the Almighty and that measuring-rod for the saints, which if they do not come up to we say they are wrong? There is always a danger of doing this so long as we walk by convictions. If our experiences come from the true Source and are untouched, they will lead to one place only—to the fulness of the life of God; but if they are tampered with they will lead away from God. Satan does not tempt saints to tell lies or to steal or drink, he does not come to them in that way; he comes along the line of their experiences, he seeks to separate Christian experience from the Lord Jesus and make us want to hug a certain type of experience for ourselves.

When we have part of the Perfect nature in us and are walking in the light of the Holy Spirit, He will take us surely and certainly to the Source from which the experience sprang, viz. God—unless we prefer to stay in our experience. Are we living in the light of our convictions, prescribed and confined, or are we living the life hid with Christ in God?

To those who have had no spiritual experience it sounds absurd to talk about being one with God in Christ, absurd to talk about being guided by the Spirit, they are impatient with it; of course they are, they must be made part of the Perfect (i.e. be born from above, RV mg) before they can understand the language of the Perfect in experience.

Jesus Christ must always be much more than any Christian experience. This throws a flood of light on experiences. That which is Perfect is God, that which

is part is the creature experience. The creature experience has its source in God, but if looked at in itself it is apart altogether from God; when looked at in God it takes us straight to God Himself. When God ceases a way of guiding, when He removes the symbols of His presence, when answers to prayer do not come, it is because He is bringing us to the place where the part is merged in the Perfect, and we in our degree are becoming what Jesus wants us to be.

There is only one way to understand the Perfect and the part in relation to it, and that is by receiving the Holy Spirit; God will give us the Holy Spirit if we ask Him (Luke 11:13). We need to receive the Holy Spirit, not only for Christian experience but to bring us into perfect union with God.

That Which Is Perception (1 Corinthians 2:11–16; 1 John 2:27)

Perception means the power of discernment. "To whom hath the arm of the LORD been revealed?" (RV). We all see the common occurrences of daily life, but who amongst us can perceive the arm of the Lord behind them? who can perceive behind the thunder the voice of God? The characteristic of the man without the Spirit of God is that he has no power of perception, he cannot perceive God's working behind ordinary occurrences. The events of ordinary days and nights present facts we cannot explain, the only way to explain them is by receiving the Spirit of God Who will impart to us an interpretation that will keep the heart strong and confident in God, because it gives us an understanding of God Who is behind all things; but to the one who is not there, the explanations seem absurd.

Perception in the natural world is called intuition—I know I know, although I do not know how I know. In the spiritual world this knowledge is the "anointing" the Apostle John alludes to. When the Holy Spirit is in us He will never let us stop at the part experience. He will cause our part experience to keep us always one with the Perfect and will reveal God to us. If ever we imagine that the Spirit of God gives us an illumination apart from the written Word, Satan is twisting the truth, and it is this kind of passage that he distorts most.

> The things which are in part cannot be apprehended, known and expressed; but the Perfect cannot be apprehended, known and expressed by any creature as creature.

Peter tells us to be ready always to give an answer to every man that asketh you a reason concerning the hope that is in us. He did not say give reasonings, but a reason. We can give a reason for that we know, but we cannot reason it out with the man who has not the same spirit. We can state that we are right with God because we have received His Spirit on the word of

Jesus, but our reasonings are nonsense to the man who has not accepted the Holy Spirit.

The Coming of the Perfect *(John 17:22; Psalm 86:11)*

Now when that which is Perfect is come, then that which is in part shall be done away. But when doth it come? I say, when as much as may be, it is known, felt and tasted of the soul. . . . So also God who is the Highest Good, willeth not to hide Himself from any, wheresoever He findeth a devout soul, that is thoroughly purified from all creatures. For in what measure we put off the creature, in the same measure are we able to put on the Creator, neither more nor less.

"That they may be one"—in experience? No, "that they may be one, even as We are one." That is infinitely beyond experience, it is a perfect oneness not only in adjustment but in realisation. In our spiritual experience it means knowing that—"In all the world there is none but Thee, my God, there is none but Thee." Other people have become shadows, the creature we used to rely upon has proved a broken reed, the spiritual experience we built upon has deserted us, the methods of guidance that used to bless our souls starve us now. This is illustrated in the purifying of Abraham's faith, the purification went on until Abraham was lost in God. He did not lose his identity, he reached his identity in God. The hymns that are full of absorption in God are true of deepest spiritual experience, but only true in the fundamental sense, in the surface sense they are in error.

The Psalmist prayed, "Unite my heart to fear Thy name"—the whole spirit, soul and body so united with God that the soul does not think separately of body, soul or spirit, but only of God. There are false unities possible in a man's experience whereby man's spirit, soul and body are brought into harmony. Paul calls these things idolatry, because idolatry is the uniting of body, soul and spirit to the wrong god.

If we are despising the chastening of the Lord and fainting when rebuked of Him, it is because we do not understand what God is doing; He is weaning us from creatures to Himself, from the things we have been united to instead of being united to Him only. When God is weaning a soul from creatures, from Christian experience, from teachers and friends, then is the time that the devil begins the advocacy of self-pity. Satan tried to make Jesus realise Himself apart from God (see Matthew 16:23), but He would not— "For I am come down from heaven, not to do Mine own will, but the will of Him that sent Me" (RV). When we are filled with the Holy Spirit He unites us body, soul and spirit with God until we are one with God even as Jesus was. This is the meaning of the Atonement—at-one-ment with God.

The one perfect Personality is our Lord. When we separate ourselves from Jesus we are in part, we are not perfect but when the life of Jesus comes into us we no more think of the separating of spirit, soul and body, we think of Jesus only. Remember, we are not sanctified for our sakes, but for God's sake. How many of us are trying to exploit God with the diplomacy which the world uses? We try to exploit God when we pray—"O Lord, give me this gift, this experience." That is the spirit which springs from the devil, we are trying to ape being devout souls, trying to be like Christians, but wanting a relation to God on our own lines. We can only get rightly related to God through Jesus Christ. The coming of the Perfect means that we are made one with God by Jesus. Immediately we are rightly related to God, perfectly adjusted to Him, the Perfect life comes to us and through us.

The Conversion of the Part

. . . it is impossible to the creature in virtue of its creature-nature and qualities, that of which it saith "I" and "myself" to be perfect. For in whatsoever creature the Perfect shall be known, therein the creature-nature and qualities, I, the Self and the like, must all be lost and done away.

Our Lord told the rich young ruler to fling away all he had, to think of himself as possessing nothing— "Be a mere conscious man and give that manhood to Me. Lose altogether the sense of yourself as one who wants to be blessed and be related to God in Me" (see Matthew 19:21).

> *So long as we think much of these things, cleave to them with love, joy, pleasure or desire, so long remaineth the Perfect unknown to us.*

If we seek the baptism of the Holy Ghost in order that God may make us great servants of His, we shall never receive anything. God baptises us with the Holy Ghost that He may be All in all.

Numbers of people say, "I have asked God to sanctify me and He has not done it." Of course He has not! Do we find one word in the Bible which tells us to pray, "Lord, sanctify me"? What we do read is that God sanctifies what we give. An unconditional "give up" is the condition of sanctification, not claiming something for ourselves. This is where unscriptural holiness teaching has played so much havoc with spiritual experience. We receive from God on one condition only, viz. that we yield ourselves to Him and are willing to receive nothing. Immediately we state conditions and say, "I want to be filled with the Holy Spirit," "I want to be delivered from sin," "I want to be the means of saving souls"—we may pray to further orders,[7] but an answer will never come that way. That is all the energy of the flesh, it has no thought of the claims of Jesus on the life. Are we willing to be baptised into His death? How much struggle is there in a dead man? How much assertion of "I" and "me" and "mine"—"I have had such a wonderful experience"? The Spirit of God will never witness to testimonies along that line, they are not true to the genius of the Holy Ghost, not true to the nature of Jesus. "Whosoever shall confess *Me* before men," said Jesus. If there is a tightness and a dryness in our experience it is because we have begun to take the advice of someone other than God, have begun to try and make our experience like someone else said it should be. "But they, . . . measuring themselves by themselves, and comparing themselves with themselves, are without understanding" (RV).

The Concentration of Perception *(John 15:5; Philippians 4:13)*

That which hath flowed forth from it, is no true Substance, and hath no Substance except in the Perfect, but is an accident, or a brightness, or a visible appearance, which is no Substance, and hath no Substance except in the fire whence the brightness flowed forth, such as the sun or a candle.

"Without Me ye can do nothing." If we are not spiritual we will say that is not true, but if we are spiritual we know it is true. Our Lord said many things that are only true in the domain in which He spoke them. For instance, He said, "Ye have not life in yourselves" (John 6:53 RV). We have life, but not in the domain Jesus means. We are alive physically, alive morally and intellectually without Jesus, but we are not alive spiritually. "Ye have not *this* life in yourselves." "If any man willeth to do His will, he shall know of the teaching, whether it be of God, or whether I speak from Myself" (RV). What is God's will? That we should receive His Spirit, and God will give us the Holy Spirit if we ask. If we put ourselves in the condition of paupers and waive all right to the gift and are willing to receive, then Jesus said, God will put into us the Spirit that is in Him. When we have received the Holy Spirit we begin to realise that what Jesus said is true, "without Me ye can do nothing"—in the spiritual life. If some of us are asked to give our testimony, to speak in the open air, to take a meeting, we faint because we have not learned the lesson of drawing on the Perfect life, of drawing on Jesus. "Without Me"—nothing; but—"I can do all things through Christ which strengtheneth me."

Have we ever come to the place of saying, "Lord, do in me all Thou dost want to do?" We ask God to do much less than this and think we are asking for tremendous things; we have to come to the place of saying, "Lord, I ask that Thy will may be done in me." The will of God is the gladdest, brightest, most bountiful thing possible to conceive, and yet some of us talk of the will of God with a terrific sigh—"Oh well, I suppose it is the will of God," as if His will were the most calamitous thing that could befall us.

Are we learning to think and perceive and interpret Christian experience along this line? When people come to us, are we so relying on the Holy Spirit that He can easily lead them to Jesus, or are we trying to make their square lives fit into our round experience, trying to fit their broad experience into our poor narrow waistcoat-pocket experience? We are off our territory on those lines; we are here for one purpose only, to be taken up with Jesus.

The Principle of Sin *(1 John 5:8–12)*

The Scripture and the Faith and the Truth say, Sin is nought else, but that the creature turneth away from the unchangeable Good and betaketh itself to the changeable; that is to say, that it turneth away from the Perfect to "that which is in part" and imperfect, and most often to itself.

This is the principle of sin. Anything in spiritual life or in sensual life that makes us draw our life from anything less than God is of the essence of sin. God made man to have dominion over the life of the sea and air and earth, but God was to have dominion over man. Adam sinned by taking his claim to his right to himself. This claim to my right to myself works in those who are born again, and it is called "the carnal mind." It expresses itself like this—"I want the baptism of the Holy Ghost; I want to be sanctified; I want to be filled with the Spirit; I want to be used of God." All that springs from the wrong source, it is not drawing its life from the right place. When we receive and recognise and rely on the Holy Spirit, all that stops for ever. We have to "walk in the light, as He is in the light," the light that Jesus walked in (see John 6:38; 14:10).

The Presence of Sin *(John 5:30–32; Romans 1:25)*

When the creature claimeth for its own anything good, such as Substance, Life, Knowledge, Power, and in short whatever we should call good, as if it were that, or possessed that, or that were itself or that proceeded from it— as often as this cometh to pass, the creature goeth astray.

The one characteristic of love is that it thinks of nothing for itself, it is absorbed in God. "Love suffereth

---

7. to further orders: ad infinitum; endlessly; the phrase, military origin, continuing present action until one receives different orders.

long, and is kind; love envieth not . . . love taketh not account of the evil." We cannot live as Jesus lived by trying to imitate Him. "Jesus called a little child to Him, and set him in the midst of them, and said, Except ye . . . become as little children, ye shall in no wise enter into the kingdom of heaven." Our Lord was not setting up a child as an ideal, but as a fact. A child does not work from a conscious ambition, it obeys the law of the life that is in him without thinking. When we are born again and rightly related to God we will live the right kind of life without thinking. Immediately we begin to think about it, we fix our eyes on our own whiteness and go wrong. Much of the holiness teaching of to-day makes people fix their eyes on their own whiteness, not on Jesus Christ—"I give up this and that, I fast here, I do this and the other, I will give up anything and everything to possess a perfect life." We will never get it in that way, but only by the passion of an absolute devotion to Jesus and that is only possible by receiving the Holy Spirit and obeying Him.

The Propagation of Sin *(1 John 3:4–8; Isaiah 14:12–13; 2 Thessalonians 2:4; Colossians 2:20–23)*

What did the devil do else, or what was his going astray and his fall else, but that he claimed for himself to be also somewhat, and would have it that somewhat was his, and something was due to him? This setting up of a claim and his "I" and "me" and "mine," these were his going astray, and his fall. And thus it is to this day.

John's argument is not to do with an act of sin, but with the disposition of sin. It is this that the devil propagates in human beings. Why don't we realise what God's Book says? We talk about chopping off this, and doing that, and having times of consecration to God. The only test of holiness is that the life of Jesus is being manifested in our mortal flesh, and that we are not appealed to on the lines He was not appealed to on; nothing springs up in us and says, "Now that is mine." The perfect love is given to us freely by the grace of God, and we can hinder it when we like, no matter what our experience has been, if we cease drawing on the life of God. Anything we possess as our own, as a possession of our own personality, is the very essence and principle of sin at work. "If any man will come after Me," said Jesus, "let him deny himself"; literally, let him give up his right to himself to Me, "and take up his cross daily, and follow Me." Our Lord said this over and over again, but we have come to the conclusion that He did not mean what He said and we piously and reverently pass it over.

THE QUOTATIONS ARE FROM THE BOOK ENTITLED *THEOLOGIA GERMANICA.*

Chapter II
THE PHILOSOPHY OF THE FALL—I

Boundless Inheritance of Covetousness

What shall we say then? Is the law sin? God forbid. Nay, I had not known sin, but by the law: for I had not known lust, except the law had said, Thou shalt not covet. (Romans 7:7)

It is said, it was because Adam ate the apple that he was lost, or fell. I say, it was because of his claiming something for his own, and because of his I, Mine, Me and the like. Had he eaten seven apples, and yet never claimed anything for his own, he would not have fallen: but as soon as he called something his own, he fell, and would have fallen if he had never touched an apple.

What is true of Adam is true of every man and woman, and "not all mankind could amend his fall, or bring him back from going astray." This inheritance of covetousness is the very essence of the Fall, and no praying and no power of man, singly or banded together, can ever avail to touch it; the only thing that can touch it is the great Atonement of our Lord Jesus Christ. Lust and covetousness are summed up in the phrase, "I must have it at once and for myself." It is an absolute flood in the nature of man, it overtakes his spirit, it overtakes his soul and body. In some natures the spirit of covetousness works through the body and is seen in sordid ways; sometimes it is kept back and only in man's reason is it manifested; and sometimes it is held still further back and suppressed, but it is there. The background of the whole thing is the lust of possessing according to my affinities.

(a) Birth of Death

"For in the day that thou eatest thereof thou shalt surely die" (Genesis 2:17). Death is the inheritance of the whole human race; since Adam, no man has ever been alive to God saving by the supernatural act of re-birth. Do not get the idea that because man did not die suddenly physically, he is not dead. The manifestation of

death in the body is simply a matter of time, "For *in the day that thou eatest thereof* thou shalt surely die." The birth of death was in that moment; not the birth of death for one man, but the birth of the death of the whole human race. God's attitude revealed in the Bible towards men is that they are "dead in trespasses and sins"; no touch with God, not alive towards God at all, they are quite indifferent to God's claims.

(b) The Bye-Law of Death

"*For if by one man's offence death reigned by one . . .*" *(Romans 5:17).* A bye-law is a supplementary regulation, and the bye-law of death is a supplementary regulation on account of disobedience. "For I was alive without the law once," said the Apostle Paul, "but when the commandment came, sin revived, and I died. And the commandment, which was ordained to life, I found to be unto death" (Romans 7:9–10). We are all alive apart from God in our own consciousness, and when preachers talk about being dead in trespasses and sins, good worldly-minded men and women are amused at our being so stupid as to tell them they are dead. They say, "I am alive, my body is alive; my mind and heart and soul and spirit are alive; what do you mean by being dead?" But immediately a soul comes into contact with Jesus Christ's standard, instantly the realisation comes of what death means.

(c) Branded by Death

"*For the wages of sin is death*" *(Romans 6:23).* Every natural virtue is death-branded, because the natural virtues are remnants of a ruined humanity, they are not promises of an evolving perfection. Take the life of the intellect or of the spirit, where does it end? "He that increaseth knowledge increaseth sorrow." Love produces such pain (apart from a knowledge of God) that it makes the sensitive soul wonder if it is worth while to love. Death is everywhere, on the attainments of the mind, of the heart and spirit. When you try to approach God in prayer and draw near to Him, you find the curse of this disposition of covetousness—"I must have this for myself, I want to be right with God for my own sake"—and it saps the energy out of devotion, out of communion with God and Christian service, until the soul is almost wrung to despair. It is that kind of thing which made the Apostle Paul say—"sold under sin." We have to get down to this aspect of sin which is not familiar to us as a rule.

Talk about conviction of sin! I wonder how many of us have ever had one five minutes' conviction of sin. It is the rarest thing to know of a man or woman who has been convicted of sin. I am not sure but that if in a meeting one or two people came under the tremendous conviction of the Holy Ghost, the majority of us would not advocate they should be put in a lunatic asylum, instead of referring them to the Cross of Christ. We are unfamiliar nowadays with this tremendous conviction of sin, which Paul refers to as being "sold under sin," but it is not a bit too strong to say that when once the Spirit of God convicts a man of sin, it is either suicide or the Cross of Christ, no man can stand such conviction long. We have any amount of conviction about pride and wrong dealing with one another, but when the Holy Ghost convicts He does not bother us on that line, He gives us the deep conviction that we are living in independence of God, of a death away from God, and we find all our virtues and goodness and religion has been based on a ruinous thing, viz. the boundless inheritance of covetousness. That is what the Fall means. Let it soak into your thinking, and you will understand the marvel of the salvation of Jesus Christ which means deliverance from covetousness, root and branch. Never lay the flattering unction to your soul that because you are not covetous for money or worldly possessions, you are not covetous for anything. The fuss and distress of owning anything is the last remnant of the disposition of sin. Jesus Christ possessed nothing for Himself (see 2 Corinthians 8:9). Right through the warp and woof of human nature is the ruin caused by the disposition of covetousness which entered into the human race through the Fall, and it is this disposition which the Holy Spirit convicts of.

Beatific Incarnation *(Romans 5:1–11)*

But how shall my fall be amended? It must be healed as Adam's fall was healed, and on the self-same wise. . . . And in this bringing back and healing, I can, or may, or shall do nothing of myself, but just simply yield to God, so that He alone may do all things in me and work, and I may suffer Him and all His work and His divine will.

The Atonement means that in the Cross of Jesus Christ God redeemed the whole human race from the possibility of damnation through the heredity of sin. Jesus Christ never applied the words "children of the devil" to ordinary sinners, He applied them to religious disbelievers. Nowhere is it taught in the Bible that we are by nature children of the devil; Paul says we "were by nature the children of wrath." How many men and women do we know who have seen what Jesus Christ came to do, who really knew He came to save them from sin and who have deliberately said, "No, I won't let Him"? The majority of men are sheep, as Jesus said, and the bias of the Fall leads them astray.

(a) Ruined Race

"And I will put enmity between thee and the woman, and between thy seed and her seed; it shall bruise thy head, and thou shalt bruise his heel" (Genesis 3:15). The prophecy here does not refer to the destruction of sin in the individual, but to the destruction of what the Apostle Paul calls "the body of sin," symbolised in the first incarnation of the devil as a serpent. The body of sin stands as the counterpart of the Mystical Body of Christ. The fountain head of the body of sin is the devil; the Fountain Head of the mystical body of Christ is God. The disposition of covetousness which entered in at the Fall, connects me with the body of sin; in the personal experience of sanctification this disposition of covetousness is identified with the Cross of Christ "that the body of sin might be destroyed." The more people there are who enter into sanctification through Jesus Christ, the more is Satan's dominance ruined. The body of sin is maimed and paralysed by every being who enters into the Mystical Body of Christ through His salvation. "The carnal mind," which is "enmity against God," is my connection with the body of sin; but the body of sin is something infinitely greater than the carnal mind, it is the mystical body of sin with the devil at its head, which Jesus Christ came to destroy (1 John 3:8), and in His sanctified children is manifested the bruising of Satan and the enfeebling of the body of sin, until at the final wind-up of everything, the body of sin and the devil are absolutely removed, not only in the individual saints but from the presence of the saints. Satan is not removed now from the presence of the saints, but the saint is still kept in the world where the evil one rules, consequently the saint is continually being badgered by the evil one. Jesus prayed, not that we should be taken out of the world, but that we should be "kept from the evil one" (RV

(b) Realised Right of Saved Souls (Romans 6:12–14)

"Let not sin therefore reign in your mortal body, that ye should obey it in the lusts thereof" (Romans 6:12). Paul is strong in urging us to realise what salvation means in our bodily lives; it means that we command our bodies to obey the new disposition. That is where you find the problems on the margins of the sanctified life. Paul argues in Romans 6:19, "You are perfectly adjusted to God on the inside by a perfect Saviour, but your members have been used as servants of the wrong disposition; now begin to make those same members obey the new disposition." As we go on, we find every place God brings us into is the means of enabling us to realise with growing joy that the life of Christ within is more than a match not only for the enemy on the outside but for the impaired body that comes between. Paul urges with passionate pleading, that we present our bodies a living sacrifice, and then realise, not presumptuously, but with slow, sure, overwhelming certainty that every command of Christ can be obeyed in our bodily life through the Atonement.

(c) Restricting Remains of Sin

"What then? Shall we sin, because we are not under the law, but under grace? God forbid. Know ye not,

that to whom ye yield yourselves servants to obey, his servants ye are to whom ye obey; whether of sin unto death, or of obedience unto righteousness?" (Romans 6:15–16). A partial realisation on the part of a child of God of the salvation of Jesus Christ is the very thing Satan delights in, because it leaves within that one the remains of the sinful disposition. In regeneration a twofold experience ought to be ours: the introduction into a new kingdom by the incoming of the Holy Spirit and the realisation of forgiveness of sins; and then being borne on to a moral identification with the death of Jesus whereby we know that "our old man is crucified with Him." Impaired lives, impaired judgements and experiences—all that makes us limp and compromising, comes about because we have realised only partially what Jesus Christ came to do, and the great rouser up out of that sleep of indifference is the Apostle Paul. Read his Epistles, rely on the Spirit of God, and let Him drive home these truths to you.

Freedom for God

I am the LORD: that is My name: and My glory will I not give to another. (Isaiah 42:8)

If I call any good thing my own, as if I were it, or of myself had Power or did or knew anything, or as if anything were mine or of me, or belonged to me, or were due to me or the like, I take unto myself somewhat of honour and glory, and do two evil things: First, I fall and go astray as aforesaid; Secondly, I touch God in His honour and take unto myself what belongeth to God only. For all that must be called good belongeth to none but to the true eternal Goodness which is God only, and whoso taketh it unto himself committeth unrighteousness and is against God.

The subtlety of Satan as an angel of light comes just here, and we hear the saints, unwittingly and without any intention of doing it, taking the glory to themselves. To say a thing is the sure way to thinking it. That is why it is so necessary to testify to what Jesus Christ has done for us. A testimony gets hold of the mind as it has hold of the heart; but the same thing is true of the opposite, if we say a wrong thing often enough we begin to think it. The only way to be kept from taking glory to ourselves is to keep steadfastly faced by our Saviour and not by the needs of the people. Did you ever notice how God lets you go down when you trust good people? The best of men and women are but the best of men and women, the only good is God, and Jesus Christ always brings the soul face to face with God, and that is the one great thought we have to be soaked with. The spirit of covetousness is a flood, and when the Apostle Paul talked about the Spirit, his idea is of a flood, "Be [being] filled with the Spirit," invaded by the personal passionate Lover of God until we realise there is only one Good, and we have no time or inclination for any other kind of goodness. "In all the world there is none but Thee, my God, there is none but Thee." Are we there?

We will deal treacherously with the Bible records if we are not soaked in the revelation that God only is good. We will put the saints on the throne, not God. There is only one unshakeable goodness, and that is God. It takes time to get there because we will cling to things and to people. Those of us who ought to be princes and princesses with God cling to the shows of God's goodness instead of God Himself. The only influence that is to tell in a servant of God is God. Let people think what they like about you, but be careful that the last thought they get is God. When we have gone from them, there must be no beauty or fascination in us that makes them long for us, the only remembrance left must be, "That woman was true to God"; "That man was true to God."

THE QUOTATIONS ARE FROM THE BOOK ENTITLED *THEOLOGIA GERMANICA*.

Chapter III
THE PHILOSOPHY OF THE FALL—II

By the Fall man not only died from God, but he fell into disunion with himself; that means it became possible for him to live in one of the three parts of his nature. We want to live a spiritual life, but we forget that that life has to work out in rational expression in our souls; or we want to live a clear life in the soul and forget altogether that we have a body and spirit; or else we want to live the life of a splendid animal and forget altogether the life of the soul and spirit. When a man is born again of the Spirit of God he is introduced to life with God and union with himself. The one thing essential to the new life is obedience to the Spirit of God Who has energised our spirits; that obedience must be complete in spirit, soul and body. We must not nourish one part of our being apart from the other parts.

Margins of the Spirit *(Galatians 5:19–24)*
The margins of our spirit retain the damage done by the Fall, even after sanctification, and unless we are energised by the Spirit of God and continually draw our life from God, Satan will come in as an angel of light and deceive us, and the first way he does it is by habits of ecstasy.

(a) Habits of Ecstasy
Habits of ecstasy, that is, the tendency to live a spiritual life before God apart from the rational life of our soul and the physical life of our body. In many a life the idea that creeps in slowly is that we must develop a spiritual life altogether apart from the rational and the physical life. God is never in that type of teaching. There are people we call naturally spiritual people who devote all their time to developing the spirit, forgetting altogether the rational life and the physical life. When we look at them or read about them they seem all right, spiritual and fine, but they lack the one marvellous stamp of the religion of Jesus Christ which keeps spirit, soul and body going on together. God never develops one part of our being at the expense of the other; spirit, soul and body are kept in harmony. Remember, our spirit does not go further than we bring our body. The Spirit of God always drives us out of the visionary, out of the excitable, out of the ecstasy stages, if we are inclined that way. This blind life of the spirit, a life that delights to live in the dim regions of the spirit, refusing to bring the leadings of the Holy Spirit into the rational life, gives occasion to supernatural forces that are not of God. It is impossible to guard our spirit, the only One Who can guard all its entrances is God. Never give way to spiritual ecstasy unless there is a chance of working it out rationally, check it every time. Nights and days of prayer and waiting on God may be a curse to our souls and an occasion for Satan. So always remember that the times we have in communion with God must be worked out in the soul and in the body.

(b) Habits of Election of Days (Galatians 4:8–11)
The habits Paul refers to here are superstitious habits in which the mind fixes on "days, and months, and seasons, and years" (RV)—on certain days God will bless us, on other days He won't; if I am careful about this and that, it will bring me into the presence of God. The days, and months, and seasons, and years are appointed by God, but the Galatians were fixing on them altogether apart from God, and Paul says, "I am afraid of you, lest by any means I have bestowed labour upon you in vain" (RV). Nowadays superstition is growing again, and people are held in bondage to it. Are we in danger of fixing on means other than God for maintaining our spiritual life? Do we put the means

of grace in the place of grace itself? If we make devotional habits the source from which we draw our life, God will put us through the discipline of upsetting those times. You say, "God does not upset them in other lives, why should He in mine?" Because you are putting them in the place of God. When you put God first you will easily get your times of communion, because God can entrust them to the soul who does not use them in an irrational way and give occasion to the enemy to enter in. When our spirit is awakened by God we must bring ourselves into subordination to the Spirit of God and not fly off at a tangent, fixing on days and seasons and ritual, thus giving a chance to the mysterious background of our life that we know nothing about but which the Bible reveals, and which Satan is on the watch for all the time.

The only soul Satan cannot touch is the soul whose spiritual life and rational life and physical life is hid with Christ in God; that soul is absolutely secure.

(c) Habits of Enervation by Dreaming (Jude 8)

Ecstasy of spirit leads to external ritual in the rational life, and makes the bodily life spend its time in dreaming. The lassitude that creeps over an unhealthy soul produces the physical madness of hysteria. All animal magnetism, all the power of one person over another, and all the hysterics of self-pity that makes some people absolutely useless unless they are in the presence of certain other people, all spring from this source. It begins in a wrong relationship to God first; a real life with God was started, but instead of drawing the whole life from God and working it out through the body, the bodily life is spent in dreams, in fastings, in prayings, and slowly there develops a madness of the nerves, which is what hysteria really is. Hysteria is a physical morbid craving for sympathy from other people, which can go to such an extent that people cannot live apart from certain other people. There is no power of God in such lives. Hysteria is the actual nervous manifestation of fundamental self-pity, consequently it has been regarded for long by the medical world as a psycho-physical disease; it is more a disposition than a disease. In this domain we get the sympathy cures of Christian Science, i.e. a stronger personality coming in contact with a soul that has got out of touch with God through disobedience can soothe the hysteria of the nerves and inject a cure by its sympathy which has nothing to do with God or with the devil, but entirely to do with the influence of a strong personality over a weak one. Animal magnetism does not come from the devil, but remember that animal magnetism always gives occasion to the devil. In reading the records of French physicians, who used hypnotism in operating in the past more than they do now, case after case is recorded

where a good-living physician used hypnotism but always stated his dread and dislike of it, simply because he found that he could never be sure what would happen to the person after the cure had been effected. And to-day we find over and over again that cures are genuine, the disease disappears, but there is a derangement in the life towards God and towards men. In every case of healing by God it comes through a child-like trust in Jesus Christ.

Any man or woman who is inclined to spend their time dreaming when they should be working out actually through the finger-tips what the Spirit of God is working in, is in danger of degenerating into those who "in their dreamings defile the flesh." God never allows a Christian to carry on his life in sections—so much time for study and meditation and so much for actual work; the whole life, spirit, soul and body must progress together.

Are you forming habits of ecstasy? Beware. Are you forming habits of ritual? habits of physical dreaming, wanting to get away from the active rush of things? Beware. When we get into the healthy life of God all the margins of spirit and soul and body are merged in a complete oneness with God. ". . . that ye may be filled unto all the fulness of God" (Ephesians 3:19 RV).

(d) Habits of Envy (Proverbs 27:4)

Spiritual envy starts from having got something from God in the way of quickening and then trying to use it in our way, not God's. Spiritual envy is a terrible evil of the soul, and will always follow the tendency to develop a spiritual life apart from the rational life and the bodily life. All kinds of sour distempers will be ours spiritually, we shall be envious of people who are growing in their life with God in ways we are not, and we will have almost diabolical suggestions about them, suggestions we would never have got through our own unaided spirit. Spiritual envy is an awful possibility to any soul who does not obey the Spirit of God (cf. 1 Corinthians 13:4).

(e) Habits of Emotions of Dread (Colossians 2:18)

If we separate the life of the spirit from the rational life, we experience emotions of dread, forebodings and spiritual nightmares in the soul, which are not imaginary but real. The cause is not always to be found in the physical condition, but in the margins of our spirit life. Remember that through the Fall man fell into dis-union, spirit, soul and body were separated from one another, that means we are liable to influences from God or from the devil. It is only when we get full of dread about life apart from God that we leave ourselves in His hands. Immediately we try to live a spiritual life with God and forget our soul and body, the devil pays attention to our body, and when we pay attention to our body he begins to get at our spirit, until we learn there is only one way to keep right—to live the life hid with Christ in God, then the very life and power of God garrisons all three domains, spirit, soul and body, but it depends on us whether we allow God to do it. God cannot garrison us if we try to live a spiritual life on a life of our own, or if we go off on emotions in our rational life. God never garrisons us in bits. Whenever marrings come to our lives it is because we have got twisted off somewhere, we are not living in simple, full, child-like union with God, handing the keeping of our lives over to Him and being carefully careless about everything saving our relationship to Him; keep that right, and He will guard every avenue. "Kept by the power of God."

(f) Habits of Exceptional "Drugging" (Jude 12–13)

There are hidden perils in our life with God whenever we disobey Him. If we are not obeying God physically we experience a craving for drugs, not only physical drugs out of a bottle, but drugs in certain types of meetings and certain types of company—anything that keeps away the realisation that the habits of the bodily life are not in accordance with what is God's will. If in the providence of God, obedience to God takes me into contact with people and surroundings that are wrong and bad, I may be perfectly certain that God will guard me; but if I go there out of curiosity, God does not guard me, and the tendency is to "drug" it over—"I went with a good idea to try and find out about these things." Well, you plainly had no business to go, and you know you had no business to go because the Spirit of God is absolutely honest. The whole thing starts from disobedience on a little point. We wanted to utilise God's grace for our own purposes, to use God's gifts for our own reasoning out of things in a particular way.

(g) Habits of Enmity (Romans 8:7)

The carnal mind is a dangerous power alongside the Spirit of God in our personality before identification with Jesus Christ in His death and resurrection is reached. When a man has received the Holy Spirit, the watching of Satan is keen, his whole desire is to split up the personality. "For the flesh lusteth against the Spirit, and the Spirit against the flesh; for these are contrary the one to the other" (Galatians 5:17 RV). The carnal mind is enmity against God, and it is the carnal mind which connects us with the body of sin of which Satan is the head, and of which there is ultimately to be a new manifestation (see 2 Thessaloni-

ans 2:3). Every soul who enters into the experience of entire sanctification limits the body of sin, consequently the great yearning eagerness of the preaching of the Gospel is to get God's children to the place of sanctification where spirit, soul and body are one, one personality absolutely ruled by God, where the life of the spirit is instantly manifested in the life of the soul and body (see 1 Thessalonians 5:23). If this place of entire sanctification is not reached, there is always that in us which has a strong affinity with the devil, and this is the remarkable thing, we never knew it before we were introduced into the kingdom of God by the initial experience of regeneration; but we find after a while the strong lustful hate of something in us against what the Spirit God has put in, and the lust is for one thing—I want to dominate this personality.

(h) Habits of Earnest Devotions (Colossians 2:20–23)

Have we any helps to keep us living a godly life? That is the risk. Slowly and surely God will purify our lives from props that separate us from Him. Immediately the means of grace are taken to be grace itself, they become a direct hindrance to our life with God. The means are simply scaffolding for the time being, and as long as they are in their right place they are an assistance, immediately we put them as the source, we give occasion to the enemy. Have we helped ourselves in work for God from any other source than God? "Ye are complete in Him" (Colossians 2:10).

(i) Habits of Extraordinary Defying (2 Thessalonians 2:9–12)

A spiritual man or woman going astray can use the extraordinary powers awakened by the Spirit of God against God. The only safeguard, and it is an absolute safeguard, is to live the life hid with Christ in God. The life that steadily refuses to think from its right to itself, that steadily refuses to trust its own insight, is the only life that Satan cannot touch. Watch every time you get to a tight feeling spiritually, to a dry feeling rationally, to a hindered feeling physically, it is the Spirit of God's quiet warning that you should repair to the heavenly places in Christ Jesus. There is never any fear for the life that is hid with Christ in God, but there is not only fear, but terrible danger, for the life unguarded by God. "He that dwelleth in the secret place of the Most High"—once there, and although God's providence should take you into hell itself, you are as safe and secure as Almighty God can keep you.

Chapter IV
THE PHILOSOPHY OF DISCERNMENT

A philosopher is a lover of wisdom, and spiritual philosophy means the love of wisdom not only in our heart life, but in our heads—the last place a Christian gets to. Usually we leave our heads barren, we simply use our brains to explain our heart's experience. That is necessary, but we have to let our brains be guided by the Holy Spirit into thinking a great many things we have not experienced. That is, we are committed to Jesus Christ's view of everything, and if we only allow our brains to dwell on what we have experienced, we shut ourselves off from a great deal we ought to be exercised in. Our heart experience always outstrips our head statement, and when the experience begins to be stated explicitly, our heart witnesses to it—"Why I know that, but I never realised before how it worked." Discernment is the power to interpret what we see and hear.

The Path of Discernment
For without Me ye can do nothing. (John 15:5)

. . . man's knowledge should be so clear and perfect that he should acknowledge of a truth (that in himself he neither hath nor can do any good thing, and that none of his knowledge, wisdom and art, his will, love and good works do come from himself, nor are of man, nor of any creature, but) that all these are of the eternal God from whom they all proceed.

Have I learned to think what the testimony of my heart makes me state? We all say this kind of thing—"I know that in me . . . dwelleth no good thing," but do we *think* it? Do we really think what Jesus has taught us to know in our hearts, that apart from Him we can do nothing? We all believe it, but do we think it? Over and over again God has to take us into desert places spiritually where there is no conscious experience at all. We have probably all had this in our experience—we have had a grand time of living communion with God, we know we are sanctified, the witness of the Spirit has proved it over and over again, then all of a sudden there falls a dearth, no life, no quickness; there is no degeneration, no backsliding, but an absolute dearth. This may be the reason—the Lord is wanting to take us to a desert place apart that we may get to this path of discernment. All the noisy things that fret our lives when we are spiritual come because we have not discerned what we know in our hearts.

(a) The Discipline of Negatives (1 Corinthians 4:7)
Paul is talking about natural gifts as well as spiritual. "What hast thou that thou didst not receive? but if thou didst receive it, why dost thou glory, as if thou hadst not received it?" (RV). Have we learned to think when we see someone endowed with natural gifts, such as a fine voice, or a good brain, or any of the gifts of genius, that every one of those gifts has been received, therefore they cannot be consecrated? You cannot consecrate what is not yours. In thinking we do not really go along the scriptural lines our hearts go on. Watch your heart in relationship to God, you recognise that you cannot consecrate yourself to God: you *give* yourself to God, and yet in thinking we go along the line of consecrating our gifts to God. We have to get rid altogether of the idea that our gifts are ours, they are not, gifts are gifts, and we have to be so given over to God that we never think of our gifts, then God can let His own life flow through us. The discipline of negatives is the hardest discipline in the spiritual life, and if you are going through it you ought to shout "Hallelujah," for it is a sign that God is getting your mind and heart where the mind and heart of Jesus Christ was.

Spiritual gifts must be dealt with in the same way as natural gifts. Spiritual gifts are not glorified gifts, they are the gift of the Spirit. "Now there are diversities of gifts, but the same Spirit." None of the gifts Paul mentions in 1 Corinthians 12:8–11 are natural gifts. The danger is to say, "How highly favoured I must be if God gives me this great gift"; "what a wonderful person I must be." We never talk like that, but the slightest thought that looks upon the gifts of the Spirit as a favour to us is the first thing that will take us out of the central point of Jesus Christ's teaching. Never look at the work of God in and through you; never look at the way God uses you in His service; immediately you do, you put your mind away from where Jesus Christ wants to get it. Gifts are *gifts,* not graces.

(b) The Development of Nobility (2 Corinthians 3:5–6)
Paul is calling his own mind to a halt in order to explain to the Corinthian Church why what he says and does comes with authority. "Our sufficiency is from God; Who also made us sufficient as ministers of a new covenant" (RV). If you are right with God, you will be amazed at what other people get in the way of real spiritual help out of what you say; but never think about it. The temptation comes all along to say, "It is because I brooded that God gave me that thought." The right attitude is to keep the mind absolutely concentrated on God and never get off on the line of how you are being

used by Him. Even in the choicest of saints there is the danger. Whenever you feel inclined to say, "Well, of course that was not me, that was God," beware! you ought never to be in the place where you can think it. The teaching of Jesus is, "Be absorbed with Me, and out of you will flow rivers of living water." If we are paying attention to the Source, rivers of living water will pour out of us, but immediately we stop paying attention to the Source, the outflow begins to dry up. We have nothing to do with our "usability," but only with our relationship to Jesus Christ, nothing must be allowed to come in between.

Have we allowed this path of discernment to be trodden by our feet? Are we beginning to see where we are being led, viz. to the place where we are rooted and grounded in God? The one essential thing is to live the life hid with Christ in God.

The Pain of Deliverance

*And Jesus called a little child unto Him . . . and said,
. . . Except ye . . . become as little children . . . (Matthew
18:2–3)*

For when the ain imagination and ignorance are turned into an understanding and knowledge of the truth, the claiming of anything for our own will cease of itself.

A healthy man does not know what health is: a sick man knows what health is, because he has lost it; and a saint rightly related to God does not know what the will of God is because he *is* the will of God. A disobedient soul knows what the will of God is because he has disobeyed. The illustration Jesus gives to His disciples of a saintly life is a little child. Jesus did not put up a child as an ideal, but to show them that ambition has no place whatever in the disposition of a Christian. The life of a child is unconscious in its fullness of life, and the source of its life is implicit love. To be made children over again causes pain because we have to reconstruct our mental ways of looking at things after God has dealt with our heart experience. Some of us retain our old ways of looking at things, and the deliverance is painful. Paul urges that we allow the pain—"Let this mind be in you, which was also in Christ Jesus"; "bringing into captivity every thought to the obedience of Christ." It is hard to do it. In the beginning we are so anxious— "Lord, give me a message for this meeting," until we learn that if we live in the centre of God's will, He will give us messages when He likes and withhold them when He likes. We try to help God help Himself to us; we have to get out of the way and God will help Himself to our lives in every detail. Have we learned to form the mind of Christ by the pain of deliverance till we know we are drawing on Him for everything? Are we sacrificing our holy selves to the will of Jesus

as He did to the will of His Father? Are we beginning to speak what God wants us to speak because we are submitting our intelligence to Him? "The Son can do nothing of Himself." Our Lord never allowed such a thought as, "I have done that," in His mind. Have we spiritual discernment like that? If not, remember what the Apostle James says, "If any of you lack wisdom, let him ask of God, that giveth to all men liberally and upbraideth not; and it shall be given him."

(a) The Plunge into God (1 Corinthians 13:8–10)

Now when a man duly perceiveth these things in himself he and the creature fall behind, and he doth not call anything his own, and the less he taketh this knowledge unto himself the more perfect doth it become. So also is it with the will and love, and desire, and the like. For the less we call these things our own, the more perfect and noble and Godlike do they become, and the more we think them our own, the baser and less pure and perfect do they become.

The only way to learn to swim is to take the plunge, sink or swim; that is exactly the idea here. Will I cut loose from all moorings and plunge straight into God? It is what the New Testament is continually urging—"Let go." Life goes on in a series of coveting the best gifts, but, Paul says, "a still more excellent way shew I unto you" (RV)—take an absolute plunge into the love of God, and when you are there you will be amazed at your foolishness for not getting there before. It is not the question of the surrender of a soul for sanctification, but the unreserved surrender of a sanctified soul to God. We are so reserved where we ought to be unreserved, and so unreserved where we ought to be reserved. We ought never to be reserved towards God but utterly open, perfectly one with Him all through. After the experience of sanctification we have to present our sanctified self to God, and one of the greatest difficulties in doing this is considering the conditions other people say we have to observe. "They themselves, . . . comparing themselves with themselves, are without understanding" (RV). Watch how tied up we are with other people's notions of what we should be. The only way to get rid of it all is to take this plunge into the love of God. We have to form the mind of Christ until we are absorbed in Him and take no account of the evil done to us. No love on earth can do this but the love of God.

(b) The Participation in Godliness (Philippians 3:7–8)

We must cast all things from us, and strip ourselves of them; we must refrain from claiming anything for our own.

"*. . . for Whom I suffered the loss of all things*" (RV). To experience the loss of all things for anyone but Jesus

Christ is mental suicide. Read what Our Lord said to the rich young ruler—" "Sell whatsoever thou hast, . . . and come, follow Me—"Reduce yourself until you are a mere conscious man, and then give that manhood to Me"; and we read that "his countenance fell at the saying, and he went away sorrowful: for he was one that had great possessions" (RV). Do you possess a reputation as a Christian worker? That will be in the way when the Lord speaks to you. Are you rich in the consciousness that you are somebody spiritually? That will be in the way. You must first estimate and then experience the loss of all things and cast yourself on Jesus, then participation in godliness will be yours as it never has been.

> When we do this, we shall have the best, fullest, clearest and noblest knowledge that a man can have, and also the noblest and purest love, will and desire; for then these will be all of God alone. It is much better that they should be God's than the creature's.

The oneness Jesus Christ prayed for in John 17 is the oneness of identity, not of union. "I and My Father are one," and by the Atonement our Lord brings us into identity with Himself—"that they may be one, even as We are one."

The Plane of Delight *(2 Corinthians 4:16–18)*
While we look . . . at the things which are not seen. (2 Corinthians 4:18)

But if our inward man were to make a leap and spring into the Perfect, we should find and taste how that the Perfect is without measure, number or end, better and nobler than all which is imperfect and in part, and the Eternal above the temporal or perishable, and the foundation and source above all that floweth or can ever flow from it.

When we think of being delivered from sin, of being filled with the Spirit, we say, "Oh, I shall never get there, it is only for exceptional people like the Apostle Paul"; but when by God's grace we get there we find it is the easiest place to live; it is not a mountain-peak, but a flat tableland of delight with plenty of room for everyone. "And I pray God your whole spirit and soul and body be preserved blameless"—that is not the life we are to live hereafter, but the life God would have us live now; most of us are far too diffident about getting there.

(a) The Altitude of Love
. . . the greatest of these is love. (1 Corinthians 13:13 RV)

A Master called Bœtius said, "It is of sin that we do not love that which is Best." He hath spoken the truth. That which is best should be the dearest of all things to us.

Is it? Sometimes we crave for something less than the best, beware! We ought to love the most what is best. The spirit of God in us can teach us how to love the best, through faith, through knowledge, through everything till we are altogether in love with God, in absolute harmony with Him, absorbed in the one great purpose of God.

> And in our love of it, neither helpfulness nor unhelpfulness, advantage nor injury, gain nor loss, honour nor dishonour, praise nor blame, nor anything of the kind should be regarded.

1 Corinthians 13 is not an ideal, it is an identification which makes the ideal possible. Never put the ideal where the Spirit of God does not put it. The ideal comes after the identification.

(b) The Atmosphere of Life
But the fruit of the Spirit is love. . . . (Galatians 5:22)

Now that creature in which the Eternal Good, most manifesteth itself shineth forth, worketh, is most known and loved, is the best, and that wherein the Eternal Good is least manifested is the least good of all creatures.

In days gone by we all used to love the creatures that exhibit reflections of the Eternal Good—honour and courage and strength, but when we are made one with Jesus Christ we find we love the creatures that exhibit the fruit of the Spirit. A great alteration has come over our outlook; God is altering the thing that matters.

> Therefore when we have to do with the creatures and hold converse with them, and take note of their diverse qualities, the best creatures must always be the dearest to us, and we must cleave to them, and unite ourselves to them.

"What communion hath light with darkness?" The education God puts His children through in life is, "first that which is natural; then that which is spiritual," until we are rooted and grounded in Him, then there is no danger evermore to that life. It is always better further on—through the natural to the spiritual. No wonder the counsel of the Spirit through the writer to the Hebrews is "Ye have need of patience."

THE QUOTATIONS ARE FROM THE BOOK ENTITLED *THEOLOGIA GERMANICA*.

Chapter V

THE PHILOSOPHY OF FOLLOWING OUR LORD

First, man must consider the teaching and the life of Jesus Christ, for He hath taught poverty and lived it. And a man should follow the teaching and the life, if he wisheth to be perfect, for He saith, "Whoso loveth Me keepeth My commandments and My counsels, and heareth My word."

In every profession under heaven the great ambition of the natural heart is to be perfect. When Jesus Christ was faced with a splendid specimen of a young man, He said, "If you would be perfect, I will tell you what to do."

"If a man love Me, he will keep My words: and My Father will love him, and We will come unto him, and make our abode with him." The whole outcome of following Jesus is expressed for us in these words, viz. that the Trinity, Father, Son, and Holy Ghost, will come and make Their abode with the man who loves Jesus and keeps His word. As long as the devil can keep us terrified of thinking, he will always limit the work of God in our souls.

The Way of the Follower *Negative*
If any man will come after Me, let him deny himself, and take up his cross daily, and follow Me. (Luke 9:23)

The word "deny" embraces what the Apostle Paul meant when he said "mortify therefore," or, make dead, "your members which are upon the earth" (Colossians 3:5).

(a) Infirmity-Sins
For if ye live after the flesh, ye shall die: but if ye through the Spirit do mortify the deeds of the body, ye shall live. (Romans 8:13)

It might now be said, What is man in his selfhood, that he must deny, if he wisheth to follow after Christ? Man's selfhood consisteth in four things. First, his frailty, and that he falleth into sins; and this he must needs set aside; he must die to his defects and sins, and mortify himself.

The disposition in us is either implanted naturally through the first Adam, or implanted supernaturally through the last Adam by regeneration and sanctification. We breed our temperament out of the disposition that is in us. If we are going to follow Jesus, we must do to death infirmity-sins. God cannot do it, we have to do it ourselves. Satan takes occasion of the frailty of the bodily temple and says, "Now you know you cannot do that, you are so infirm, you cannot concentrate your mind," etc. Never allow bodily infirmities to hinder you obeying the commands of Jesus. Paul says, "But I keep under my body, and bring it into subjection." "I buffet [bruise, mg] my body, and bring it into bondage" (RV). Through the Atonement God deals with the wrong disposition in us, then He gives us the glorious privilege of making our bodies "instruments of righteousness unto God."

(b) Inordinate Affection
Mortify therefore your members which are upon the earth; . . . inordinate affection. . . . (Colossians 3:5)

Secondly, he is inclined to creatures. For man is inclined by nature to his like, and he must kill nature, and must withdraw from creatures, for God and creatures are opposites. And therefore he who wisheth to have God must leave creatures. For the soul is so narrow that God and the creature cannot dwell together in her; and therefore if God is to dwell in thy soul, the creature must remain without.

In Colossians 3:5 Paul is describing an unsanctified man, but the same man sanctified is inclined to creatures rather than to the Creator. Watch the hard things Jesus says about father, mother, wife, children, our own life (see Luke 14:26); He says if we are going to follow Him, these must be on the outside of the central citadel. The central citadel must be God and God alone. When once we are willing to "do to death" our clinging to creatures, which in certain supreme calls comes between ourselves and God, Jesus says we will receive an hundredfold, because immediately we are rightly related to God He can trust us with creaturerelationships without fear of inordinateness. With the majority of us these relationships are cut off, not by our own doing, God has to do it for us; He has to come with strange providences and cut them off, because we have professed that we are going to follow Jesus. We forget that sanctification is only the beginning; the one purpose of sanctification is that Jesus might be "marvelled at in all them that believed."

(c) Inveterate Luxury
But I keep under my body, and bring it into subjection: lest that by any means, when I have preached to others, I myself should be a castaway. (1 Corinthians 9:27)

The third point is, that man to part from selfhood should drop all sensual delight, for he must die to this and kill it in himself if he wisheth to have God's comfort. As St. Bernard saith, "The comfort of God is so noble that no one receiveth it who seeketh comfort elsewhere."

The natural life in a sanctified man or woman is neither moral nor immoral, it is the gift God has given the saint to sacrifice on the altar of love to God. Jesus Christ had a natural body, it was not a sin for Him to be hungry, but it would have been a sin for Him to satisfy that hunger when God had told Him not to, and Satan came to Him when He had fasted forty days and forty nights, and was an hungred, and said, "Satisfy that hunger *now.*" The body we have is not sinful in itself; if it were, it would be untrue to say that Jesus Christ was sinless. Paul's words have reference to the fact that our body has been ruled by a sinful disposition, a disposition which simply means I am going to find my sustaining in creature comforts. After we are sanctified we have the same body, but it is ruled by a new disposition, and we have to sacrifice our natural life to God even as Jesus did, so that we make the natural life spiritual by a series of direct moral choices.

(d) Intellectual Intemperance
And lest I should be exalted above measure . . . through the abundance of the revelations . . . (2 Corinthians 12:7)

The fourth thing a man must let go if he wisheth to follow Christ, is spiritual natural comforts, which are generated in man, by detecting the distinction between spiritual and natural knowledge. . . . Whoever tarries by this natural rational delight, hinders himself from the supernatural delight which God in His grace imparteth to the soul.

Intellectual intemperance is a great snare to a saint. Bodily fasting is child's play compared to the determined fasting from the intellectual apprehension of the teachings of Jesus that goes beyond what we are living out. The characteristic of many spiritual people to-day is intellectual intemperance, fanatical intoxication with the things of God, wild exuberance, an unlikeness to the sanity of Jesus in the very ways of God. There is a danger in the enjoyment of the delights and the power that come to us through Jesus Christ's salvation without lifting the life into keeping with His teaching, especially in spiritual people whose minds have never been disciplined and they wander off into all kinds of vagaries. That accounts for the distinction we find between spiritual sincerity and spiritual reality.

All this is the negative side of following our Lord. Have we told Jesus we will follow Him? Are we prepared to do our part in keeping under the body for one purpose only, that we may learn the fellowship of following? Are we beginning to realise that until we are born again the teachings of Jesus are simple; after

we are born again they become growingly difficult, and we find clouds and darkness are round about the things we thought we knew perfectly well once, and following our Lord is one of these things?

The Way of the Fellowship *Positive*
And he that taketh not his cross, and followeth after Me, is not worthy of Me. He that findeth his life shall lose it: and he that loseth his life for My sake shall find it. (Matthew 10:38–39)

It is possible to be grossly selfish in absorbing the salvation of Jesus, to enjoy all its benedictions, and never follow Him one step. So Jesus says, "If any man would follow Me, this is the way"— "let him deny himself, and take up his cross daily, and follow Me."

(a) Working Virtue from God
. . . for as ye have yielded your members servants to uncleanness and to iniquity unto iniquity; even so now yield your members servants to righteousness unto holiness. (Romans 6:19)

First, man should kill sin in himself through virtue; for just as man is removed from God by sin must he be brought nigh again unto God by virtue . . . but let no one believe that he is free from sins, unless he hath taken unto himself all the virtues.

The positive side is this—that we work all the virtues of Jesus in and through our members, but this can only be done when all self-reliance has come to an end (cf. 2 Corinthians 1:9). Our natural virtues are remnants of what God created man to be, not promises of what he is going to be. The natural virtues cannot be patched up to come anywhere near God's demands, and the sign that God is at work in us is that He corrupts our confidence in the natural virtues. It is simply an amplification of the old Gospel hymn—

> *Nothing in my hand I bring,*
> *Simply to Thy Cross I cling!*

(b) Willing Poverty for God
For ye know the grace of our Lord Jesus Christ, that, though He was rich, yet for your sakes He became poor, that ye through His poverty might be rich. (2 Corinthians 8:9)

The second thing that man must shun is the love for creatures. Poverty of spirit is a going out of yourself and out of everything earthly. Thereby he despiseth creatures, is despised by them, and is thus set free. A truly poor man taketh nothing from creatures, but all from God, be it bodily or spiritual. God alone will be the Giver.

To be willingly poor for God is to strip myself of all things for the sake of Jesus Christ. One of the greatest snares is built on what is really a great truth, viz. that every man has Christ in himself. The pernicious use that is made of that statement is that therefore man draws power from himself. Never! Jesus Christ never drew power from Himself: He drew it always from without Himself, viz. from His Father. "The Son can do nothing of Himself" (John 5:19, see John 5:30). Beware of being rich spiritually on earth, only be rich spiritually in heaven. Jesus said to the rich young ruler, "If you will strip yourself and have no riches here, you will lay up for yourself treasure in heaven Treasure in heaven." is faith that has been tried (cf. Revelation 3:18). Immediately we begin to have fellowship with Jesus we have to live the life of faith at all costs; it may be bitter to begin with, but afterwards it is ineffably and indescribably sweet—willing poverty for God, a determined going outside myself and every earthly thing.

(c) Watchful Purity for God
Whosoever is born of God doth not commit sin; for His seed remaineth in him: and he cannot sin, because he is born of God. (1 John 3:9)

But who knoweth, wilt thou ask, if he have all virtues? I answer to this like John, who saith, "Whosoever is born of God cannot sin." For in the same moment in which God the Father begetteth His Son in the soul, sins and all unlikeness disappear, and all virtues are born in her in a likeness to God.

According to that statement of the Apostle John no one is free from sin unless he is possessed of all the virtues. The Apostle is not teaching sinless perfection; he is teaching perfect sinlessness, which is a different matter. If as sanctified souls we walk in the light, as God is in the light, the revelation is that through the Atonement "the blood of Jesus Christ His Son cleanseth us from all sin." That does not mean cleansing from all sin in our consciousness; if it did, it would produce hypocrisy. Any number of people are not conscious of sin, but it does not follow that they are cleansed from all sin. It is not our consciousness that is referred to, but the consciousness God has of us; what we are conscious of is walking in the light with nothing to hide. The outcome of following our Lord is a holiness of character so that God sees nothing to censure because the life of His Son is working out in every particular. Our main idea is to keep steadfastly in the blazing light of God so that He can exhibit the virtues of Jesus through us unhindered. "If ye love Me, ye will keep My commandments" (RV). How many of them? All of them. Then, says Jesus, "We will come unto him, and make Our abode with him"—in heaven? No, here.

(d) Wonderful Passion for God
Forasmuch then as Christ hath suffered for us in the flesh, arm yourselves likewise with the same mind: for he that hath suffered in the flesh hath ceased from sin; that he no longer should live the rest of his time in the flesh to the lusts of men, but to the will of God. (1 Peter 4:1–2)

... and whoso would eat its fruit (the fruit of the holy cross) with profit must break it off from the cross by steadfast internal contemplation of the Passion of Our Lord.

All on the cross is full of fruit, and more than all tongues could in truth proclaim. Nay, angels' tongues could not describe the overflowing grace that is there hidden in the Passion of our Lord. Blessed are those who have found this treasure.

Steady contemplation of the Passion of our Lord will "do to death" everything that is not of God. It is only after a long while of going on with God and steady contemplation of the Cross that we begin to understand its meaning. "To day shalt thou be with Me in paradise" is said at only one place, viz. at the Cross.

This is not a message about our salvation and sanctification, but about the outcome of salvation and sanctification in our implicit life, i.e. where we live it and cannot speak it. Jesus said, "If any man would be My disciple . . ." not, "If any man would be saved and sanctified." "If any man will be My disciple—those are the conditions." Jesus Christ always talked about discipleship with an "If." We are at perfect liberty to toss our spiritual head and say, "No, thank you, that is a bit too stern for me," and the Lord will never say a word, we can do exactly what we like. He will never plead, but the opportunity is there, "If . . ."

After all, it is the great stern call of Jesus that fascinates men and women quicker than anything. It is not the gospel of being saved from hell and enjoying heaven that attracts men, saving in a very shallow mood; it is Christ crucified that attracts men; Jesus said so—"I, if I be lifted up from the earth, will draw all men unto Me." Jesus Christ never attracts us by the unspeakable bliss of Paradise; He attracts us by an ugly beam. We talk about getting down to the depths of a man's soul: Jesus Christ is the only One Who ever did. If once a man has heard the appeal of Jesus from the Cross, he begins to find there is something there that answers the cry of the human heart and the problem of the whole world. What we have to do as God's servants is to lift up Christ crucified. We can either do it as gramophones, or as those who are in fellowship with Him.

Many of us have heard Jesus Christ's first "Follow Me"—to a life of liberty and joy and gladness; how many of us have heard the second "Follow Me"—"deny your right to yourself and 'do to death' in yourself everything that never was in Me"?

Chapter VI
THE PHILOSOPHY OF HOLINESS

Verily, verily, I say unto you, He that believeth on Me, the works that I do shall he do also; and greater works than these shall he do; because I go unto My Father. John 14:12

The Way of the Working of God
Then said they unto Him, What shall we do that we might work the works of God? Jesus answered and said unto them, This is the work of God, that ye believe on Him Whom He hath sent. (John 6:28–29)

There are two kinds of work in God—a working within and a working outwardly. The working inward is God's being and nature, the outward working is the creature. . . . God worketh in souls that He may bring them to the first origin from which they have flowed, for by their works they cannot go in again.

These words of Jesus sum up the whole mystery of the work of grace, viz. that to "work the works of God" we must stop working and let God work. "This is the work of God, *that ye believe. . . .*" Un-belief is the most active thing on earth; it is negative on God's side, not on ours. Un-belief is a fretful, worrying, questioning, annoying, self-centred spirit. To believe is to stop all this and let God work.

(a) The Working Master
. . . work out your own salvation with fear and trembling, for it is God which worketh in you both to will and to do of His good pleasure. (Philippians 2:12–13)

If man is to come to God, he must be empty of all work and let God work alone. . . . Now, all that God willeth to have from us is that we be inactive, and let Him be the working Master.

Paul does not say, Work out something that will tell for your salvation; he says, Work out in the expression of your life the salvation God has worked in. If we think for a moment we shall soon know how much we are saved—What does our tongue say? what kind of things do our ears like to listen to? what kind of bodily associates do we like to be with? These things will always tell not only other people but ourselves what kind of salvation God has worked in. In regeneration God works us into relation with Himself that by our bodily expression we may prove Whose we are. If you are trying to be a Christian it is a sure sign you are not one. Fancy trying to be the daughter of your mother!

you cannot help being her daughter. But try and be the daughter of someone else's mother! Unless God has worked in us we shall hinder Him all the time by trying to be His children; we cannot, we have to be born from above (RV mg) by the will of God first, be regenerated; then our working is not working to help God, it is working to let God express through us what He has done in us so that we may prove we are the children of our Father in heaven (see Matthew 5:43–48).

So many of us put prayer and work and consecration in place of the working of God; we make ourselves the workers. God is the Worker, we work out what He works in. Spirituality is what God is after, not religiosity. The great snare in religion without genuine spirituality is that people ape being good when they are absolutely mean. There is no value whatever in religious externals, the only thing that is of value is spiritual reality, and this is spiritual reality—that I allow God to work in me to will and to do of His good pleasure, and then work out what He has worked in, being carefully careless about everything saving my relationship to God.

(b) The Workable Medium
If a man abide not in Me, he is cast forth as a branch, and is withered. (John 15:6)

If we were altogether inactive we should be perfect men. For all that is good is the work of God, and if God does not work it, it is not good.

I wonder how many of us are living on the virtues of our grandparents! The natural virtues are remnants of what the original creation of man once was, they are not promises of what man is going to be; what man is going to be is seen in the life of Jesus Christ. The workable medium is man. God takes as the medium of working the stuff we are made of, and all He requires is for us to be inactive and let Him work. When once we are rightly related to God through the Atonement we will be inactive and not in the way of His working in us as He worked in Jesus; consequently we shall be able to work out in our natural life all that God wills. It is the old twist, we will try to do what God alone can do, and then we mourn before God because He won't do what we alone can do. We put up sighing petitions—"I have tried to be good"; "I have tried to sanctify myself." All that is the work of God, and the best thing to do is to stop trying and let God do it.

What we have to do, and what God cannot do, is to work out what He has worked in. We try to do God's work for Him, and God has to wait until we are passive enough to let Him work in us. To believe in Jesus means retiring and letting God take the mastership inside. That is all God asks of us. Have we ever got into the way of letting God work, or are we so amazingly important that we really wonder in our nerves and ways what the Almighty does before we are up in the morning! We are so certain we know what is right, and if we don't always keep at it God cannot get on. Compare that view with the grand, marvellous working of God in the life of the Lord Jesus. Our Lord did not work for God; He said, "The Father that dwelleth in Me, He doeth the works." Have we any faith in God at all? Do we really expect God to work in us the good pleasure of His will, or do we expect He will only do it as we pray and plead and sacrifice? All these things shut the door to God working. What we have to ask away from, to knock at, to seek through, are these pressing strivings of our own—

> When we stay our feeble efforts,
>   And from struggling cease,
> Unconditional surrender
>   Brings us God's own peace.

—a doctrine easily travestied, but a doctrine God never safeguards. The whole basis of modern Christian work is the great impulsive desire to evade concentration on God. We will work for Him any day rather than let Him work in us. When a man or woman realises what God does work in them through Jesus Christ, they become almost lunatic with joy in the eyes of the world. It is this truth we are trying to state, viz. the realisation of the wonderful salvation of God.

(c) The Worker's Manner
And now abideth faith, hope, charity, these three; but the greatest of these is charity. (1 Corinthians 13:13)

How is a man to know if his work is of himself or from God? Shortly be it said; there are three supernatural divine virtues, Faith, Hope, and Love or Charity; whatever increaseth virtues is from God, but what diminisheth them is a sign that it is the work of man. . . . For what man worketh of himself, he applieth to himself and to time . . . but what God worketh, draweth a man away from himself to eternity, and this increaseth Faith, Hope, and Charity.

How much of faith, hope, and love is worked in us when we try to convince somebody else? It is not our business to convince other people, that is the insistence of a merely intellectual, unspiritual life. The Spirit of God will do the convicting when we are in the relationship where we simply convey God's word. We exploit the word of God in order to fit it into some view of our own that we have generated; but when it comes to the great calm peace and rest of the Lord Jesus, we can easily test where we are. To "rest in the LORD" is the perfection of inward activity. In the ordinary reasoning of man it means sitting with folded arms and letting God do everything; in reality it is being so absolutely stayed on God that we are free to do the active work of men without fuss. The times God works most wonderfully are the times we never think about it. When we work of ourselves we always connect things with time. "What is the good of faith, hope and love when I have to earn my living?" Compare that outlook with what Jesus says in the Sermon on the Mount—"Seek ye first the kingdom of God, and His righteousness; and all these things shall be added unto you." It means on our part a continual carelessness about everything but that one thing. The great curse of modern Christianity is that people will not be careless about things they have no right to be careful about, and they will not let God make them careful about their relationship to Him. Sum it up for yourself—what do you think about most, not on the surface, but in the deep centre of your centre? What is the real basal thought of your life—"what ye shall eat, or what ye shall drink; . . . what ye shall put on"? None of us are so stupid or lacking in cunning as to say we do think of these things: but if we think of what will happen to "all these things" if we put God first, we know where we are, God is not first. If He is first you know you can never think of anything He will forget.

The Way of the Working of the Godly
Therefore if any man be in Christ, he is a new creature; . . . and all things are of God. (2 Corinthians 5:17–18)

What is the divine work? It is twofold, what God worketh in the soul, one the work of grace, the other essential and divine. By the work of grace man is prepared for the essential . . . by grace God maketh man well-pleasing, it driveth him away from all defective things on to virtue, so that with it he obtaineth all virtues.

The only sign that we are new creations (RV mg) in Christ Jesus is that we know all things are of God. When we are in difficult circumstances, when we are hard up, when friends slander us, to whom do we go? If we know that "all things are of God," then we certainly are new creations in Christ Jesus. The things that upset the external life reveal where we live. If we are in Christ the whole basis of our goings is God, not conceptions of God, not ideas of God, but God Himself. We do not need any more ideas about God, the world is full of ideas about God, they are all worthless, because the ideas of God in anyone's head are of no more use than our own ideas. What we need is a real

God, not more ideas about Him. Immediately we get a real God we find that "old things are passed away; behold, all things are become new"; we are so absolutely one with God that we never think of saying we are, the whole life is hid with Christ in God.

(a) The Experimental Virtue

For by grace are ye saved through faith; and that not of yourselves: it is the gift of God. (Ephesians 2:8)

God worketh through His grace in man, when He draweth him away from sin and leadeth him on to virtue, if man leaveth sin and exerciseth virtue, this is a grace of God.

When we are first born again of the Spirit and become rightly related to God, the whole set of our life is along God's line, other people looking at us know how marvellously God has transformed us; we do things and wonder why we do them. That is experimental virtue, but it is accidental, that is, the expression in our life is that of spiritual innocence not of spiritual holiness yet; then slowly and surely the Holy Spirit leads on to the next thing—the essence of virtue.

(b) The Essence of Virtue

My little children, of whom I travail in birth again until Christ be formed in you. (Galatians 4:19)

The second work that God worketh in the soul is essential; when man cometh to this that he hath obtained all accidental virtue, and so now arriveth at the essence of virtue, then God worketh all virtue in him in an essential way, namely, the Heavenly Father begetteth His Son in the soul, and this birth raiseth the spirit above all created things into God.

"Until Christ"—not Jesus Christ, but Christ, the Son of God, Who was Incarnate once as a Man called Jesus Christ—"until Christ be formed in you." No wonder Paul talks about "the riches of the glory of this mystery; . . . which is *Christ in you*, the hope of glory." This is not an innocent state, it is a holy state, the very essence of the life is holy, and as we draw on His res-

urrection life, the life of Jesus is manifested in our mortal flesh.

(c) The Essential Vision

But God . . . hath raised us up together, and made us sit together in heavenly places in Christ Jesus. (Ephesians 2:4, 6)

Nevertheless grace leaveth not the man, but it directeth and ordereth the forces of man and cherisheth the divine birth in the essence of the soul; . . . the spirit of man hath now passed over to the Godhead.

Being seated together in heavenly places in Christ Jesus does not mean lolling about on the mount of transfiguration, singing ecstatic hymns, and letting demon-possessed boys go to the devil in the valley; it means being in the accursed places of this earth as far as the walk of the feet is concerned, but in undisturbed communion with God.

In the historic Jesus Christ the spirit of man passed over to the Godhead and Jesus saw essentially, not experimentally, and the same thing happens when Christ is formed in us. God's grace does not leave a man after an experience of grace. The common idea of how to live the right life seems to be that it is by getting continual "bouts" of God's grace, that an insight into God's grace will last us several days. As a matter of fact it won't last us any time. That is not what God's grace means.

". . . while we look not at the things which are seen"—that battle never stops. The things that are seen are not the devil, but the pressing things, the things that distract; when Christ is formed in us and the essential vision comes through looking at the things which are not seen, we find that God makes other people shadows. If my saintly friends are images of God to me, I have much further to go, yet. God alone must be my Stay and Source and everything. That is the way the godly life is lived.

What is a godly life? A life like God in my bodily edition. Imitation is the great stumblingblock to sanctification. Be yourself first, then go to your own funeral, and let God for ever after be All in all.

THE QUOTATIONS ARE FROM THE BOOK ENTITLED *THE FOLLOWING OF CHRIST,* BY JOHN TAULER.

Chapter VII
THE PHILOSOPHY OF REASON

Essence of Reason in the Saint

. . . being ready always to give answer to every man that asketh you a reason concerning the hope that is in you. (1 Peter 3:15 RV)

To give an answer concerning the hope that is in us is not the same thing as convincing by reasonable argument why that hope is in us. A line we are continually apt to be caught by is that of argumentatively reasoning out why we are what we are; we cannot argue that out. There is not a saint amongst us who can give explicit reasonings concerning the hope that is in us, but we can always give this reason: we have received the Holy Spirit, and He has witnessed that the truths of Jesus are the truths for us. When we give that answer, anyone who hears it and refuses to try the same way of getting at the truth is condemned. If a man refuses one way of getting at the truth because he does not like that way, he ceases to be an honest man.

(a) The Reach of Reason

I live; and yet no longer I, but Christ liveth in me. (Galatians 2:20 RV)

The reason . . . is always striving after this essential working. . . . By this act of hastening after the divine work, she empties herself of all created images, and with a supernatural light she presseth into the mystery of the hidden Godhead.

Reason always strives for a true expression. Soul is spirit expressing itself rationally, and whenever the work of God in a man's soul (as in the Apostle Paul's) is stated, it does not contradict the rational element, it transcends it. When a man is born again his personality becomes dead to earth as the source of its inspiration and is only alive to God. The great snare is to make reason work in the circle of our experience and not in the circle of God. As long as we use the image of our experience, of our feelings, of our answers to prayer, we shall never begin to understand what the Apostle Paul means when he says, "I live; and yet no longer I, but Christ liveth in me" (RV). The whole exercise of man's essential reason is drawing on God as the source of life. The hindrance comes when we begin to keep sensuous images spiritually in our minds. Those of us who have never had visions or ecstasies ought to be very thankful. Visions, and any emotions at all, are the greatest snare to a spiritual life, because immediately we get them we are apt to build them round our reasoning, and our reasoning round them and go no further. Over and over again sanctified people stagnate, they do not go back and they do not go on, they stagnate, they become stiller and stiller, and muddier and muddier, spiritually not morally, until ultimately there comes a sort of scum over the spiritual life and you wonder what is the matter with them. They are still true to God, still true to their testimony of what God has done for them, but they have never exercised the great God-given reason that is in them and got beyond the images of their experience into the knowledge that "God alone is life"—transcending all we call experience. It is because people will not take the labour to think that the snare gets hold of them, and remember, thinking is a tremendous labour (see 2 Corinthians 10:5).

(b) The Reaction against Reason

Be ye not as the horse, or as the mule, which have no understanding. (Psalm 32:9)

For what the creature chooseth instead of God is done by sensuality and not by the reason . . . and whoso chooseth the creature instead of God, is not a rational man, but is as an irrational beast.

We use the term rational when we should say "sensual." Sensuality is a word that has lost its meaning in the higher realm to us, we only talk of sensuality on the grovelling line, but sensuality reaches higher, it means that bodily satisfaction is taken as the source of life—what I possess, what I feel, that is not rationalism but sensuality, and when it is allowed to dominate it works out as Paul says—they "became vain in their reasonings, and their senseless heart was darkened" (RV; see Romans 1:18–23). If we will let reason act it will make itself so felt that a man has to say, "There is more than this"; the visible things he sees and knows awaken in him a sense that there is something more than these. Reason must not be prevented from reaching to God.

In the religious domain sensuality takes another guise, it becomes either pietistic or ritualistic, both are irrational. The pietistic tendency in this country is a much bigger curse than the ritualistic tendency, that is a mere excrescence that will be always as long as human beings are. The real peril is the sensual piety that is not based on a rational life with God, but on certain kinds of devotion, certain needs of consecration, certain demands of my personal life. When you come to the New Testament, particularly the writings of the Apostle Paul, you find that kind of piety is torn to shreds (e.g. Colossians 2:20–23). All fanaticism and the things that are foreign to the teachings of Jesus Christ start from spiritual sensuality, which means I have images in my mind of what I want to be, and what I am, and what I have experienced. These images hinder reason from working. Beware of any image at all in your mind but Jesus Christ, an image of sanctification, or devotion, or any other thing on earth will be the peril of your rational spiritual life. Have we any idea that it is our devotion, our consecration, the times we give to prayer, the service rendered, what we have given up, because we have been through this and that experience we are where we are?—every one of them is a hidden irrational snare. No wonder the Apostle Paul was so anxious we should get on this rational line. The essence of reason in the saint—what is it? The Holy Ghost in me being obeyed, revealing the things of Jesus.

(c) The Right Rational Man
. . . but the water that I shall give him shall become in him a well of water. . . . I am the bread of life. (John 4:14 RV; 6:35)

For the right reason seeketh God, and removes from creatures whether they be bodily or spiritual, and whoso cometh to this reason is a right, rational man, whose reason is shone through with divine light, in which you know the Godhead and forget the earthy.

The idea left in our minds by these two symbols is water measureless and bread inexhaustible. You can never be caught up by the externals of the symbols Jesus uses, He never leaves any room for sensuality, He only leaves room for the Spirit of God, consequently the symbols are uninterpretable saving to reason inspired by the Spirit of God. The Holy Spirit never swamps our personal spirit, He invades it and energises it so that the light of God in our reason gives us the power and delight of forgetting earthly things. As we take these subjects, if you are alive, your mind will say every now and again, "Oh, stop and let us think longer of this," but the Spirit of God won't stop. The reason for it is that God's Book is packed full of overwhelming riches, they are unsearchable, the more we have the more there is to have. It is a great boon to know there are deep things to know. The curse of the majority of spiritual Christians is that they are too cocksure and certain there is nothing more to know than they know. That is spiritual insanity. The more we go on with God the more amazed we are at what there is to find out, until we begin to use the power God gives us to forget earthly

things, to be carefully careless about them, but never careless about our relationship to God.

Exercise of Reason in the Saint
But desire earnestly the greater gifts. And a still more excellent way shew I unto you. (1 Corinthians 12:31 RV)

Good things will always be the bane of the spiritual life until they are wedded to and lost in the best. When God begins with us He gives us good things, He showers them down (see Matthew 5:45); God does not withhold the best, He cannot give it until we are ready to receive it. Receive the Holy Spirit and let your reason be lifted out of images and out of the good, and instantly you will be lifted into the best.

Have you ever noticed the vague indefiniteness of the Bible? Unless we are spiritual we shall say, "I do wish the Bible would talk clearly; why does it not talk as clearly as some little books I have?" If it did, the Bible would be interpretable without any knowledge of God at all. The only way we can understand whether Jesus Christ's teaching of God is by the Spirit that is in Jesus (see John 7:17).

(a) The More Excellent Way (2 Peter 1:4–7)
. . . adding on your part all diligence. (2 Peter 1:5 RV)

For virtue is never filled up in full measure, nor followed in the highest, except man strip himself of the love of all temporal possessions till he exerciseth himself in all virtue, and lose the image of all virtue, and cometh to the faculty of no longer being able to work any virtue outwardly, but only essentially and not accidentally.

Until you have stopped trying to be good and being pleased with the evidences of holiness in yourself, you will never open the wicket gate that leads to the more excellent way. The life "hid with Christ in God"— that is the more excellent way. You can never talk of Jesus Christ in the light of any one virtue, if you do, you feel you have not described Him; you can only talk of Him as the Bible does—God-Man. When we describe men we have to mention some particular virtue. People who deal with Bible characters are inclined to fix on some virtue which becomes rotten before the end of the life. When the Spirit of God has His way with us we go on till there is only one thing left—"they took knowledge of them, that they had been with Jesus." In evangelical work it is not preaching holiness, or sanctification, or bodily healing, it is preaching Christ Jesus, "I, if I be lifted up, . . . will draw all men unto Me."

Watch the corruption of the natural virtues in yourself. We have to learn that most insufferably difficult lesson that God never patches up our natural virtues, because our natural virtues can never come anywhere near what Jesus Christ wants. Over and over again men and women are so troubled at finding their natural virtues break down that they dare not say a word about it to themselves, let alone to anyone else. The reason for it is that God wants to get us out of the love of virtue and in love with the God of virtue—stripped of all possessions but our knowledge of Him.

(b) The Most Extraordinary Wonder (2 Corinthians 9:6–1
And God is able to make all grace abound unto you. (2 Corinthians 9:8 RV)

So long as a man hath he must give, and when he hath nothing more he is free. Freedom is much nobler than giving was before. for he giveth no more in accident but in essence.

Our Lord emptied Himself (RV) and had nothing all the days of His earthly life, consequently He was free for God to lavish His gifts through Him to others. Think of the rushes with which we come in front of our Heavenly Father; whenever we see an occasion we rush in and say, "I can do this, you need not trouble God." I wonder if we are learning determinedly to possess nothing? It is possessing things that makes us so conceited—"Oh yes, I can give prayer for you; I can give this and that for you." We have to get to the place about which Jesus talked to the rich young ruler where we are so absolutely empty and poor that we have nothing, and God knows we have nothing, then He can do through us what He likes. Would that we would quickly get rid of all we have, give it away till there is nothing left, then there is a chance for God to pour through in rivers for other people.

(c) The More Exceeding Worship
I beseech you therefore . . . to present your bodies a living sacrifice, . . . which is your spiritual worship [mg]. (Romans 12:1 RV)

Therefore also a teacher saith, "It is good when a man imparts his property and cometh to the help of his fellow men; but it is far better to give all and to follow Christ in a poor life."

Worship is giving the best we have unreservedly to God. Jesus Christ was entirely merciful because He kept nothing at all. We are merciful in spots, in a fragmentary way, because we will stick to our opinionettes. Whatever makes us spiritually satisfied will twist our mercy at once, because an opinionette is attached to every spot where we are satisfied, and when anyone comes in contact with that spot of satisfaction we are merciless to them. Jesus Christ was never merciless, and it is only as we draw on His life that we are like our Father in heaven. The only safety is to live the life hid with Christ in God. As long as we are consciously there, we are not there. It is only

when we are there that it never occurs to us that we are, but the evidence is strong because others are getting the blessings of God through us and are helping themselves to us, even as Jesus Christ was made broken bread and poured-out wine for us. God cannot make some of us into broken bread because there are bits of unbaked dough in us that would produce indigestion. We have to go into the furnace again to be baked properly until we are no more like Ephraim, "a cake not turned."

Expression of Resurrection Reason in the Saint
Blessed are the dead which die in the Lord. (Revelation 14:13)

(a) The Matter of Death
Except a grain of wheat fall into the earth and die, it abideth by itself alone; but if it die, it beareth much fruit. (John 12:24 RV)

Therefore we should make ourselves poor, that we may fundamentally die, and in this dying be made alive again.

Death is God's delightful way of giving us life. The monks in the early ages shut themselves away from everything to prove they were dead to it all, and when they got away they found themselves more alive than ever. Jesus never shut Himself away from things, the first place He took His disciples to was a marriage feast. He did not cut Himself off from society, He was not aloof, so much was He not aloof that they called Him "a gluttonous man, and a winebibber!" But there was one characteristic of Jesus—He was fundamentally dead to the whole thing, it had no appeal to Him. The "hundredfold" which Jesus promised means that God can trust a man anywhere and with anything when he is fundamentally dead to things.

(b) The Manner of Devotion
If thou wouldest be perfect, go, sell that thou hast, . . . and come, follow Me. (Matthew 19:21 RV)

This selling means the self-denial of man; the giving away is virtue, the following of Jesus is fundamentally to die, so that dying completely to himself God may live perfectly in him.

Immediately that is experienced we are alive with the effulgent life of God. We use the phrase "drawing on the resurrection life of Jesus," but try it, you cannot draw on it when you like. You will never get one breath of that life until you are dead, that is, dead to any desire that you want a blessing for body or soul or spirit. Immediately you die to that, the life of God is in you, and you don't know where you are with the exuberance of it. To put it in the negative way—the bits in us that won't yield to God are the bits we cling to. We are always going back to the grave and saying, "I was always respectable here; I don't need Christ there; I always had a good view of what was right and pure." Instantly the life of God in us wilts; but when the dying is gone through with and maintained (I am not talking about dying to sin, but about dying right out to my right to myself in any shape or form), then the life of Jesus can be manifested in my mortal flesh (see 2 Corinthians 4:10–12).

(c) The Method of the Discipline of Death
For ye died, and your life is hid with Christ in God. (Colossians 3:3 RV)

Blessed is the man who can die all manner of deaths, but this dying is of such a nature that no man can

rightly understand it, and he is the most rational who understandeth this dying the best. For no one understandeth it save he to whom God hath revealed it.

This secret is revealed to the humblest child of God who receives, recognises and relies on the Holy Spirit, and it leads to only one place, the effulgent life of God, while we walk in the light as He is in the light. The trouble with most of us is that we will walk only in the light of our conviction of what the light is. If you are live to God He will never take from you the amazing mercy of having something put to death. Jesus sacrificed His natural life and made it spiritual by obeying His Father's voice, and we have any number of glorious opportunities of proving how much we love God by the delighted way we go to sacrifice for Him.

THE QUOTATIONS ARE FROM THE BOOK ENTITLED *THE FOLLOWING OF CHRIST*, BY JOHN TAULER.

Chapter VIII
THE PHILOSOPHY OF LOVE
Mark 12:29–31

The Way of the Sovereign Preference of the Heart
Lovest thou Me? (John 21:15–17)

And these are the right lovers of God, who love God with their whole heart. And they who love God with their whole heart give up all bodily things for the sake of God.

Faith, hope, love (RV), the three supernatural virtues, have a two-fold aspect in the saint's life. The first is seen in the early experiences of grace when these virtues are accidental; the second, when grace is worked into us and these virtues are essential and abiding. When the work of God's grace begins, *"the love of God is shed abroad in our hearts by the Holy Ghost,"* not the power to love God, but the essential nature of God. When we experience what technically we call being born again of the Spirit of God, we have "spurts" of faith, hope, love, they come but we cannot grip them and they go; when we experience what technically we call sanctification those virtues abide, they are not accidental any more. The test of the life "hid with Christ in God" is not the experience of salvation or sanctification, but the relationship into which those experiences have led us. It is only by realising the love of God in us by His grace that we are led by His entrancing power in us whither we would not.

Love is the sovereign preference of my person for another person, and Jesus says that other Person must be Himself. Ask yourself what sort of conception you have of loving God. The majority of us have a bloodless idea, an impersonal, ethereal, vague abstraction, called "love to God." Read Jesus Christ's conception; He mentions relationships of the closest, most personal, most passionate order, and says that our love for Him must be closer and more personal than any of those (see Luke 14:26). How is it to be? Only by the work of the sovereign grace of God. If we have not realised the shedding abroad of the essential nature of God in our hearts, the words of Jesus ought to make us realise the necessity of it—"Thou shalt love the Lord thy God *from* [RV mg] all thy heart. . . ." To love God with all my heart means to be weaned from the dominance of earthly things as a guide; there is only one dominant passion in the deepest centre of the personality, and that is the love of God.

The Way of the Soul's Passion for God
Whosoever shall lose his life for My sake shall find it. (Matthew 16:25 RV)

They also love with their whole soul; that is, when they give up their life for the sake of God; for the soul giveth life to the body, and this same life they give entirely to God.

The only way to love God with all our soul is to give up our lives for His sake, not give our lives to God, that is an elemental point, but when that has been done, after our lives have been given to God, we ought to lay them down for God (see 1 John 3:16). Jesus Christ laid down His holy life for His Father's purposes, then if we are God's children we have to lay down our lives for His sake, not for the sake of a truth, not for the sake of devotion to a doctrine, but for Jesus Christ's sake—the personal relationship all through (cf. Luke 6:22–23). Have I ever realised the glorious opportunity I have of laying down my life for Jesus? It does not mean that we lay down our lives in the crisis of death; what God wants is the sacrifice *through* death, which enables us to do what Jesus did—He sacrificed His life; His death comes in as a totally new revelation. Every morning we wake, and every moment of the day, we have this glorious privilege of sacrificing our holy selves to and for Jesus Christ (see Romans 12:1).

Beware of the subtle danger that gets hold of our spiritual life when we trust in our experience. Experience is absolutely nothing if it is not the gateway only to a relationship. The experience of sanctification is not the slightest atom of use unless it has enabled me to realise that that experience means a totally new relationship. Sanctification may take a few moments of realised transaction, but all the rest of the life goes to prove what that transaction means.

The Way of the Mind's Penetration into God
(1 John 3:2–3)
... when He shall appear, we shall be like Him. (1 John 3:2)

They also love God with all their mind; that is, when their mind soareth above all created things, and penetrates into the uncreated good, which is God, and then loseth itself in the secret darkness of the unknown God. Therein it loseth itself and escapeth, so that it can no more come out.

To love God with all our mind we have to "soar above created things, and penetrate into the uncreated good," viz. God. When the Spirit of God begins to deal on this side of things we shall feel at sea,[8] if we are not spiritual, as to what is meant; when we are spiritual we feel with our hearts, not with our heads—"Yes, I begin to see what it means." When anything begins to get vague, bring yourself up against the revelation of Jesus Christ, He is a Fact, and He is the Pattern of what we ought to be as Christians (cf. Matthew 5:48). How much of our time are we giving for God to graduate us in the essential life? We know

all about the accidental life, about the sudden spurts that come to us, the sudden times of illumination and sweet inspiration from God's Book; what Our Lord is getting at is not a life of that description at all, but a life that has lost all sense of its own isolation and smallness and is taken up with God. Not only is the life hid with Christ in God, but the heart is blazing with love to God, and the mind is able to begin slowly bit by bit to bring every thought into captivity to the obedience of Christ, till we never trouble about ourselves or our conscious life, we are taken up only with thoughts that are worthy of God.

The Way of the Strength of Stillness for God
(Ephesians 3:16–19)
That He would grant you ... to be strengthened with might ... ; that Christ may dwell in your hearts by faith ... (Ephesians 3:16–17)

They further love God with all their strength; that is, they ordain all their powers according to the highest discretion, and they direct all of them to one end, and with this effort they penetrate into God.

The whole strength of the personal life, the personal spirit, is to be so gripped by the Spirit of God that we begin to comprehend His meaning. It is always risky to use a phrase with a fringe, a phrase that has a definite kernel of meaning but a fringe of something that is not definite. The way we get off on to the fringe is by ecstasy, and ecstasies may mean anything from the devil to God. An ecstasy is something which takes us clean beyond our own control and we do not know what we are doing, whether we are being inspired by God or the devil, whether we are jabbering with angels' tongues or demons'. When you come to the words of Our Lord or of the Apostle Paul the one great safeguard is the absolute sanity of the whole thing. "... that ye ... may be able to comprehend ... and to know"—there is no ecstasy there, no being carried out of yourself into a swoon, no danger of what the mystics of the Middle Ages called Quietism, no danger of losing the conditions of morality; but slowly and surely we begin to comprehend the love of Christ, i.e., the essential nature of God which the Holy Ghost has imparted to us, which enables us to live the same kind of life that Jesus lived down here through His marvellous Atonement. Anything that partakes of the nature of swamping our personality out of our control is never of God. Do we ever find a time in the life of the Lord Jesus Christ when He was carried beyond His own control? Never once. Do we ever find Him in a spiritual panic, crediting God with it? Never once; and the one great marvel of the work of the Holy Ghost is that the sanity of

---

8. at sea: in a state of confusion or perplexity; at a loss.

Jesus Christ is stamped on every bit of it. Jesus said we should know the work of the Holy Ghost by these signs—"He shall glorify Me"; "He shall teach you all things, and bring to your remembrance all that I said unto you" (RV), and, "He will guide you into all truth." The Spirit of God does not dazzle and startle and amaze us into worshipping God; that is why He takes such a long while, it is bit by bit, process by process, with every power slowly realising and comprehending "with all saints. . . ." We cannot comprehend it alone; the "together" aspect of the New Testament is wonderful. Beware of all those things that run off on a tangent spiritually. They begin by saying, "God gave me an impulse to do this"; God never gave anyone any impulse. Watch Jesus Christ, the first thing He checked in the training of the twelve was impulse. Impulse may be all right morally and physically, but it is never right spiritually. Wherever spiritual impulse has been allowed to have its way it has led the soul astray. We must check all impulses by this test—Does this glorify Jesus, or does it only glorify ourselves? Does it bring to our remembrance something Jesus said, that is, does it connect itself with the word of God, or is it beginning to turn us aside and make us seek great things for ourselves? That is where the snare comes. Nowadays, people seem to have an idea that these ecstatic, visionary, excitable, lunatic moments glorify God; they do not, they give an opportunity to the devil. The one thing Jesus Christ did when He came in contact with lunacy was to heal it, and the greatest work of the devil is that he is producing lunacy in the name of God all over the world in the spiritual realm, making people who did know God go off on tangents. What did Jesus say? ". . . so as to lead astray, if possible, even the elect" (RV). Beware of being carried off into any kind of spiritual ecstasy either in private or in public. There is nothing about ecstasy in these verses: "Thou shalt love the Lord thy God with all thy heart"—the sovereign preference of our personality for God. Can I say before God, "For in all the world there is none but Thee, my God, there is none but Thee"? Is it true? is there a woman there? is there a man there? is there a child there? is there a friend there? "Thou shalt love the Lord thy God with all thy heart." Do you say, "But that is so stern"? The reason it is stern is that when once God's mighty grace gets my heart wholly absorbed in Him, every other love of my life is safe; but if my love to God is not dominant, my love may prove to be lust. Nearly all the cruelty in the world springs from not understanding this. Lust in its highest and lowest form simply means I seek for a creature to give me what God alone can give, and I become cruel and vindictive and jealous and spiteful to the one from whom I demand what God alone can give.

". . . and with all thy soul." What are we laying down our lives for? Why do so many Christians go a-slumming? why do so many go to the foreign field? why do so many seek for the salvation of souls? Let us haul ourselves up short and measure ourselves by the standard of Jesus Christ. He said, "The Son of man is come to seek and to save that which was lost." The mainspring of His love for human souls was His love to the Father; then if I go a-slumming for the same reason, I can never do too much of it; but if my desire for the salvation of souls is the evangelical commercial craze, may God blast it out of me by the fire of the Holy Ghost. There is such a thing as commercialism in souls as there is in business. When we testify and speak, why do we?: is it out of the accident of a poor little paltry experience that we have had, or is it because the whole life is blazing with an amazing desire, planted there by the Holy Ghost, for God to glorify Himself?

> *Arrived here, all the powers keep silence and rest; this also is the highest work that the powers can perform, when they are inactive and let God only work.*

It is only when our lives are hid with Christ in God that we learn how to be silent unto God, not silent about Him, but silent with the strong restful certainty that all is well, behind everything stands God, and the strength of the soul is that it knows it. There are no panics intellectual or moral. What a lot of panicky sparrows we are, the majority of us. We chatter and tweet under God's eaves until we cannot hear His voice at all—until we learn the wonderful life and music of the Lord Jesus telling us that our heavenly Father is the God of the sparrows, and by the marvellous transformation of grace He can turn the sparrows into His nightingales that can sing through every night of sorrow. A sparrow cannot sing through a night of sorrow, and no soul can sing through a night of sorrow unless it has learned to be silent unto God—one look, one thought about my Father in heaven, and it is all right.

The Way of the Freedom of the Will *(Romans 6:21–22)*

But now being made free from sin . . . (Romans 6:22)

> *. . . Thus is the mind bound by God. To this it might be said, If this is so, the freedom of the will is taken away. I answer, the freedom of the will is not taken away but given to it, for then is the will quite free when it cannot bear anything save what God willeth.*

"Thus is the mind bound by God. . . ." The complaint of a person who is not spiritual when one talks like that, is that a man's free will is destroyed. It is not, it is given to him. The only thing that gives a personality freedom of will is the salvation of Jesus Christ. The will is not a faculty, will is the whole man active—

body, soul and spirit. Let a man get right with God through the Atonement and his activity becomes in that manner and measure akin to Jesus Christ. The whole of my will free to do God's will, that means a holy scorn of putting my neck under any yoke but the yoke of the Lord Jesus Christ. Where are Christians putting their necks nowadays? Why, nine out of every nine and a half of us are absolute cowards, we will only put our necks under the yoke of the set we belong to. It means—"without the camp, bearing His reproach." (See John 14:15; 15:9–10)

The Way of Hearing the Eternal Word

If a man love Me, he will keep My words. (John 14:23)

When now man . . . cometh to the third degree of perfection, in which he heareth, in a silent, secret speaking, the everlasting Word which God the Father speaketh in the ground of souls . . .

We all know how certain verses jump out of a page of the Bible and grip us, full of infinite sweetness and inspiration; at other times they do not. That is what people mean when they say God gave them a message—by the way, do not say that unless God does, we use phrases much too glibly. God may give you the kind of message He gave Isaiah, a blistering, burning message of the altar of God. To be able to hear "the silent, secret speaking" of the Father's voice in the words of the Bible is the essential groundwork of the soul of every saint.

"The words that I have spoken unto you are spirit, and are life" (John 6:63 RV). God makes His own word re-speak in us by His Spirit. He safeguarded that; He

uses the words His Son used, and the words those used who He determined should write them (see 2 Peter 1:21). The great insubordination of to-day is, "Who are the apostles? God spake through them, why can't He speak through me?" He will not unless we let the Spirit of God interpret to us what those men said, then He will talk through us, but in no other way. When once a man has learned to hear with the inner ear the word of God he "discardeth his self-hood," and the natural delight in God's word is lost in the realisation that it is God Who is speaking. Do you want to know how self-hood works out?—"I have such a fine message, it will do for such and such an audience"; "I have got a wonderful exposition of this text." Well, burn it and never think any more about it. Give the best you have every time and everywhere. Learn to get into the quiet place where you can hear God's voice speak through the words of the Bible, and never be afraid that you will run dry, He will simply pour the word until you have no room to contain it. It won't be a question of hunting for messages or texts, but of opening the mouth wide and He fills it.

The outcome of Mark 12:29–31 is God four times over—God the King of my heart, God the King of my soul, God the King of my mind, God the King of my strength; nothing other than God; and the working out of it is that we show the same love to our fellow-men as God has shown us. That is the external aspect of this internal relationship, the sovereign preference of my person for God. The love of the heart for Jesus, the life laid down for Jesus, the mind thinking only for Jesus, the strength given over to Jesus, the will working only the will of God, and the ear of the personality hearing only what God has to say.

THE QUOTATIONS ARE FROM THE BOOK ENTITLED *THE FOLLOWING OF CHRIST,* BY JOHN TAULER.

Chapter IX
THE PHILOSOPHY OF SACRIFICING
Matthew 16:24–26

"I Wonder if I Will or if I Won't"

God does not take the wilful "won't" out of us by salvation; at any stage we may say, "No, thank you, I am delighted to be saved and sanctified, but I am not going any further." Our Lord always prefaced His talks about discipleship with an "if"; it has no reference whatever to a soul's salvation or condemnation, but to the discipleship of the personality.

We must bear in mind that Our Lord in His teaching reveals unalterable and eternal principles. In Matthew 16:25—"For whosoever would save his life shall lose it: and whosoever shall for My sake shall find it" (RV)—Jesus says that the eternal principle of human life is that something must be sacrificed; if we won't sacrifice the natural life, we do the spiritual. Our

Lord is not speaking of a punishment to be meted out, He is revealing what is God's eternal principle at the back of human life. We may rage and fret, as men have done, against God's just principles, or we may submit and accept and go on; but Jesus reveals that these principles are as unalterable as God Himself.

"I wonder if I will or if I won't." In sanctification the freedom of the will is brought to its highest critical point. A good many people in order to express the marvellous emancipation that comes by God's salvation make the statement, "I cannot now do the things that are wrong." It is only then we have the choice; when Jesus Christ emancipates us from the power of sin, that second we have the power to disobey, before we had not the power, we were almost obliged to disobey because of the tendency in that direction. So this principle in its full meaning, "I wonder if I will or if I won't," works on the threshold of sanctification—"I wonder if I will devote myself to Jesus Christ, or to a doctrine, or a point of view of my own." Jesus says if we are to be His disciples we must sacrifice everything to that one thing.

Innocent Light under Identification
Take My yoke upon you, and learn of Me, . . . and ye shall find rest unto your souls. (Matthew 11:29)

But what use doth it bring if a man alway dieth? It bringeth a fivefold use. First, man draweth nigh thereby to his first innocence. . . . They are best in this who have most died to themselves for in that death and denial of self a new delight springeth up, for the death that man suffereth thereby openeth up the hidden joy. Christ also said, "Take My yoke upon you—that is, My Passion—and ye will find rest unto your souls."

The only place we shall find rest is in the direct education by Jesus in His Cross. A new delight springs up in any saint who suffers the yoke of Christ. Beware of dissipating that yoke and making it mean the yoke of a martyr. It is the yoke of a person who owes all he has to the Cross of Christ. Paul wore the yoke when he said, "For I determined not to know any thing among you, save Jesus Christ, and Him crucified." "Take My yoke upon you"—it is the one yoke men will not wear.

Have I taken the yoke of Christ upon me, and am I walking in the innocent light that comes only from the Spirit of God through the Atonement? When we are born again of the Spirit of God we are made totally new creatures on the inside; that means we have to live according to the new life of innocence that God has given us, and not be dictated to by the clamouring defects of the temple into which that life has been put. The danger is to become wise and prudent, cumbered with much serving, and these things choke the life God has put in (cf. Mark 4:19).

Implicit Love under Identification
Who shall separate us from the love of Christ? (Romans 8:35)

The second use is, that in each such dying a new life ariseth to man, and with this life every time a new love, so that man is overflooded with grace, and his reason is enlightened with divine light, his will is glowing with the fire of divine love . . . so that no one can any more separate him from God.

The natural life of a saint is neither pure nor impure; it is not pure necessarily because the heart is pure, it has to be made pure by the will of the person. To delight in sacrificing the natural to the spiritual means to be overflowing with the grace and love of God, and the manner and measure of the sacrificing depends on—"I wonder if I will or if I won't." Never say, if you are a thoughtful saint, "Since I have been sanctified I have done what I liked." If you have, you are immoral in that degree. If it were true, it would be true of the holiest Being Who ever lived, but it is said of Him that "even Christ pleased not Himself" (Romans 15:3; cf. John 8:28; Hebrews 5:8). There must be something to sacrifice. Jesus says, "If you would be My disciple, you must sacrifice the natural life," i.e., the life that is moral and right and good from the ordinary standpoint of man. We cannot use the terms of natural virtue in describing Jesus Christ. If you say that Jesus was a holy man you feel at once it is not sufficient; or take the terms of intense saintliness, you can never fit them on to Jesus Christ, because there is an element of fanaticism in every saint that there never was in the Lord. There is an amazing sanity in Jesus Christ that shakes the foundations of death and hell, no panic, absolute dominant mastery over everything—such a stupendous mastery that He let men take His strength from Him: "He was crucified through weakness," that was the acme of Godlike strength.

Identity of Liberty under Identification
Verily, verily, I say unto thee, except a man be born again, he cannot see the kingdom of God. (John 3:3)

Thirdly, if a man is quite pure he is emptied of all defective accident, and receptive of God alone. God is present in all things; if you accomplish all things so, then God only remaineth to us; but this purity must be sought by dying, and if the soul is freed from everything else, she is in a condition to bring forth the Son of God within her.

Bear in mind the audience of Jesus when He said these words; Jesus said them to a mature, upright, godly man, there is no mention of sin, that will come in due course, it comes in the order Jesus said it would, by the Holy Spirit (see John 16:8–9). When the Son of God is born in us He brings us into the liberty of God.

"Whosoever is begotten of God doeth no sin" (RV). The only way we can be born again is by renouncing all other good. The "old man," or the man of old, means all the things which have nothing to do with the new life. It does not mean sins, any coward among us will give up wrong things, but will he give up right things? Will we give up the virtues, the principles, the recognition of things that are dearer to the "Adam" life than the God life? The nature of the "Adam" disposition in us rebels against sacrificing natural good. Jesus says, "If you don't sacrifice natural good, you will barter the life I represent." This is the thing men resent with what Paul calls "enmity" (Romans 8:7). The preachers and teachers who have not taken on them the yoke of Christ are always inclined to exalt natural good, natural virtues, natural nobility and heroism; the consequence is Jesus Christ pales more and more into the background until He becomes "as a root out of a dry ground." Imagine a pagan who worshipped natural virtues being told that the Nazarene Carpenter was God's idea expressed in His last syllable to this order of things—it would be, as Paul said, "foolishness unto him." The same thing persists to-day.

Infusion of Likeness under Identification

If we walk in the light, as He is in the light . . . (1 John 1:7)

The fourth use ariseth if God is born in the soul, when God ravisheth the spirit from the soul and casteth her into the darkness of His Godhead, so that she becometh quite like unto God . . . so that the man becometh a son of grace, as he is a son of nature.

To be a son of God is to be free from the tyranny of the show of things. Adam preferred to take the show of things for the substance, that is, he preferred not to see that the "garment" was not the Person; he refused to listen to the voice of the Creator behind the garment, and when the Creator moved quickly, all Adam could do was to hang on to the skirts of the garment, clutch at the show of things, and the human race has been doing it ever since. Exactly what Jesus said, the spiritual has been bartered because we preferred the natural. The natural is only a manifestation of what is behind. If we walk in the light, not as holy men are in the light, but as God is in the light, we see behind the show of things—God. We become the sons of God by a regenerating internal birth, and when that regenerating principle inside takes its marvellous sway over the natural on the outside, the two are transformed into exactly what God intended them to be. That is the full meaning of the Redemption, but in order to get there the natural must be sacrificed. If I prefer to hug my Father's skirt, I must not be surprised at finding myself in darkness when He

gives it a sudden pull; but if I let my Father take me up in His arms, then He can move His skirts as He likes—"Therefore will we not fear, though the earth do change, and though the mountains be moved in the heart of the seas" (RV). I am no longer caught up in the show of things. The saints who are alive when Jesus comes will be "changed, in a moment, in the twinkling of an eye"; all the show of things will be changed instantly by the touch of God into reality.

Incorporation of Life under Identification

For as many as are led by the Spirit of God, these are sons of God. (Romans 8:14 RV; cf. Philippians 2:15)

Fifthly, if the soul be raised into God, it reigneth also with God. . . . Thus the spirit can do all things with God; he commandeth all with God, he ordereth and leadeth all with God; what God omits, he omitteth; what God doeth, he doeth with God; he worketh all things with God. This unspeakable perfection we obtain through dying.

Being born again of the Spirit is not contrary to God's original plan; for a time it has to be apparently contrary to it because Adam refused to sacrifice the life of nature to the will of God and transform it into a spiritual life by obeying the voice of God. The natural has to be sacrificed for a time, but we shall find the Redemption of Jesus works out *via* the natural in the end—"And I saw a new heaven *and a new earth.*" In the meantime to be a disciple of Jesus means to be "taboo" in this order of things.

Remember, it was not the "offscouring" that crucified Jesus, it was the highest reach of natural morality crucified Him. It is the refined, cultured, religious, moral people who refuse to sacrifice the natural for the spiritual. When once you get that thought, you understand the inveterate detestation of the Cross of Christ. Where are we with regard to this barter? Are we disciples of Jesus? Who is first, or what is first, in our lives? who is the dominating personality that is dearer to us than life, ourselves or someone else? If it is someone else, who is it? It is only on such lines as these that we come to understand what Jesus meant when He said, If any man would come after Me, let him deny himself" (RV). What He means is that He and what He stands for must be first. The enemies of the Cross of Christ, whom Paul characterises so strongly, and does it weeping, are those who represent the type of things that attract far more than Jesus Christ. Never put a false issue before men or before yourself. We begin to compare ourselves with ourselves—"Oh well, I have always had refined susceptibilities; I have always had an admiration for what is noble and true and good"; Jesus says, Die to it all. Read Philippians 3—"What things were gain to me, these have I counted loss for Christ" (RV).

"Then said Jesus unto His disciples, If any man would come after Me, let him . . . follow Me." The first "Follow Me" was a fascination for natural ideals. "Are ye able to drink the cup that I drink? . . . We are able" (RV). There is no arrogance there, only hopeless misunderstanding. We all say, "Yes, Lord, I will do anything"; but will you go to the death of that—the death of being willing to go to the death for the noble and true and right? Will you let Jesus take the sense of the heroic right out of you? will you let Him make you see yourself as He sees you until for one moment you stand before the Cross and say, "Nothing in my hands I bring"? How many of us are there to-day? Talk about getting people to hear that, they won't have it! Jesus says they won't. No crowd on earth will ever listen to that, and if under some pretence you get them and preach the Cross of Christ they will turn with a snubbing offence from the whole thing as they did in Our Lord's day (John 6:60, 66). The abominable "show business" is creeping into the very ranks of the saved and sanctified—"We must get the crowds." We must not; we must keep true to the Cross; let folks come and go as they will, let movements come and go, let ourselves be swept along or not, the one main thing is—true to the yoke of Christ, His Cross. The one thing we have to stand against is what is stated in Hebrews 12:1, "Therefore let us . . . lay aside every encumbrance [mg] and the sin which doth so easily beset us" (RV), the sin which is admired (RV mg) in many—the sin that gathers round your feet and stops you running; get stripped of the whole thing and run, with your eye on your File Leader,[9] making "straight paths for your feet, that that which is lame be not turned out of the way" (RV).

THE QUOTATIONS ARE FROM THE BOOK ENTITLED *THE FOLLOWING OF CHRIST,* BY JOHN TAULER.

Chapter X
THE PHILOSOPHY OF DISCIPLESHIP

Let no man think that sudden in a minute
All is accomplished and the work is done:—
Though with thine earliest dawn thou shouldst
*   begin it*
Scarce were it ended in thy setting sun.

Discipleship must always be a personal matter; we can never become disciples in crowds, or even in twos. It is so easy to talk about what "we" mean to do—"we" are going to do marvellous things, and it ends in none of us doing anything. The great element of discipleship is the personal one.

The disciples in the days of His flesh were in a relationship to our Lord which we cannot imagine; they had a unique relationship which no other men have had or will have. We may use the relationship of these men to Jesus as illustrative of those who are devoted to Him but not yet born from above (RV mg), or we may take them as pointing out lines of discipleship after the work of grace has been begun. Discipleship may be looked at from many aspects because it is not a dogma but a declaration. We are using discipleship in this study as an illustration of what happens after salvation. Salvation and discipleship are not one and the same thing. Whenever our Lord speaks of discipleship He prefaces what He says with an "IF."

"*If* any man come after Me . . ." Discipleship is based on devotion to Jesus Christ, not on adherence to a doctrine.

Potential Position by Grace
Then answered Peter and said unto Him, Lo, we have left all, and followed Thee; what then shall we have? (Matthew 19:27 RV; cf. 15:24)

Potential means existing in possibility, not in reality. By regeneration in its twofold phase of salvation and sanctification we are potentially able to perform all the will of God. That does not mean we are doing it, it means that we can do it if we will because God has empowered us (see Philippians 2:12–13). A man in whom the grace of God has begun its work—the grace of God does not respect persons, so I mean any kind of man you can think of—is potentially in the sight of God as Christ: the possibility of being as Christ is there. Whenever the grace of God strikes a man's consciousness and he begins to realise what he is in God's sight, he becomes fanatical, if he is healthy. We have to make allowance in ourselves and others for "the swing of the pendulum," which makes us go to the opposite extreme of what we were before. When once the grace of God has touched our hearts

9. file leader: one who leads a mountain expedition or a military unit; the person with absolute authority.

we see nothing but God, we do not see Him in relation to anything else, but only in relation to ourselves on the inside, and we forget to open the gate for gladness. Fanaticism is the insane sign of a sane relationship to God in its initial working. The joy of the incoming grace of God always makes us fanatical. It is the potential position by grace, and God leaves us in that nursery of bliss just as long as He thinks fit, then He begins to take us on another step; we have to make that possible relationship actual. We have not only to be right with God inside, we have to be manifestly rightly related to God on the outside, and this brings us to the painful matter of discipline.

Practical Path in Grace

And Jesus said unto them, Verily I say unto you, that ye which have followed Me, in the regeneration when the Son of man shall sit on the throne of His glory, ye also shall sit upon twelve thrones. (Matthew 19:28 RV; cf. Matthew 10:38)

To abandon all, to strip one's self of all, in order to seek and follow Jesus Christ naked to Bethlehem, where He was born, naked to the hall where He was scourged, and naked to Calvary where He died on the cross, is so great a mystery that neither the thing, nor the knowledge of it, is given to any but through faith in the Son of God.

John Wesley

The practical path in grace is to make what is possible actual. That is where many of us hang back; we say, "No, I prefer the bliss and the delight of the simple, ignorant babyhood of 'Bethlehem,' I like to be carried in the arms of God; I do not want to transform that innocence into holy character." The following in the steps of Jesus in discipleship is so great a mystery that few enter into it. When once the Face of the Lord Jesus Christ has broken through, all ecstasies and experiences dwindle in His presence, and the one dominant Leadership becomes more and more clear. We have seen Jesus as we never saw Him before, and the impulsion in us by the grace of God is that we must follow in His steps. As in the life of Mary, the mother of our Lord, a sword pierced through her own soul because of the Son of God, so the sword pierces our natural life as we sacrifice it to the will of God and thus make it spiritual. That is the first lesson in the practical path of grace. We go through bit by bit and realise that there are things Jesus says and the Holy Spirit applies to us, at which the natural cries out, "That is too hard."

The Practice of Pain in Grace

And every one that hath left houses . . . for My name's sake, shall receive a hundredfold. (Matthew 19:29 RV; cf. Luke 14:26–27)

"If any man come to Me, and hate not . . . , he cannot be My disciple." The word "hate" sounds harsh, and yet it is uttered by the most human of human beings because Jesus was Divine; there was never a human breast that beat with more tenderness than Jesus Christ's. The word "hate" is used as a vehement protest against the pleas to which human nature is only too ready to give a hearing. If we judge our Lord by a standard of humanity that does not recognise God, we have to put a black mark against certain things He said. One such mark would come in connection with His words to His mother at Cana, "Woman, what have I to do with thee?" Another would come in connection with John the Baptist; instead of Jesus going and taking His forerunner out of prison, He simply sends a message to him through his disciples—"Go your way, and tell John. . . . And blessed is he, whosoever shall not be offended in Me." But if we could picture the look of our Lord when He spoke the words, it would make a great difference to the interpretation. There was no being on earth with more tenderness than the Lord Jesus, no one who understood the love of a mother as He did, and if we read this into His attitude towards His mother and towards John we shall find the element of pain to which He continually alludes, that is, we have to do things that hurt the best relationships in life without any explanation. If we make our Lord's words the reply of a callous nature, we credit Him with the spirit of the devil; but interpret them in the light of what Jesus says about discipleship, and we shall see that we must sacrifice the natural in order to transform it into the spiritual. All through our Lord's teaching that comes—"If you are going to be My disciple, you must barter the natural." Our Lord is not talking about sin, but about the natural life which is neither moral nor immoral; we make it moral or immoral. Over and over again we come to the practice of pain in grace, and it is the only explanation of the many difficult things Jesus said which make people rebel, or else say that He did not say them.

Have we begun to walk the practical path in grace? Do we know anything about the practice of pain? Watch what the Bible has to say about suffering, and you will find the great characteristic of the life of a child of God is the power to suffer, and through that suffering the natural is transformed into the spiritual. The thing we kick against most is the question of pain and suffering. We have naturally the idea that if we are happy and peaceful we are all right. "I came not to send peace, but a sword," said our Lord—a striking utterance from the Prince of Peace. Happiness is not a sign that we are right with God; happiness is a sign of satisfaction, that is all, and the majority of us can be satisfied on too low a level. Jesus Christ disturbs every kind of satisfaction that is less than delight in God. Every strand of sentimental satisfaction is an indication of how much farther we have to go before we understand the life of God, it is the satisfaction of a smug self-interest which God by circumstances and pain shocks out of us as we go in the discipline of life.

Protest of Power through Grace

. . . ye also shall sit upon twelve thrones. (Matthew 19:28)

Physical power is nothing before moral power. A frail simple girl can overcome a brute who has the strength of an ox by moral superiority. Think of our Lord's life. The New Testament does not refer to the scene in the Garden as a miracle—"when therefore He said unto them, I am He, they went backward, and fell to the ground" (RV)—it was the inevitable protest of power of a pure holy Being facing unholy men from whom all power went. The wonder is not that Jesus showed His marvellous power, but that He did not show it. He continually covered it up.

> *Oh! wonderful the wonders left undone!—*
> *And scarce less wonderful than those He wrought!*
> *Oh, self-restraint, passing all human thought,*
> *To have all power and be—as having none!*

The great marvel of Jesus was that He was voluntarily weak. "He was crucified through weakness," and, says Paul, "we also are weak in Him." Any coward amongst us can hit back when hit, but it takes an exceedingly strong nature not to hit back. Jesus Christ never did. "Who, when He was reviled, reviled not again; when He suffered, He threatened not"; and if we are going to follow His example we shall find that all His teaching leads along that line. But ultimately, at the final wind-up of His great purpose, those who have followed His steps reign with Him. Those who reign with Him are not the sanctified in possibility, in ecstasy, but those who have gone through actually. Equal duties, not equal rights, is the keynote of the spiritual world; equal rights is the clamour of the natural world. The protest of power through grace, if we are following Jesus, is that we no longer insist on our rights, we see that we fulfil our duty.

That is the philosophy of a poor, perfect, pure discipleship. Remember, these are not conditions of salvation, but of discipleship. Those of us who have entered into a conscious experience of the salvation of Jesus by the grace of God, whose whole inner life is drawn towards God, have the privilege of being disciples, if we will. The Bible never refers to degrees of salvation, but there are degrees of it in actual experience. The spiritual privileges and opportunities of all disciples are equal; it has nothing to do with education or natural ability. "One is your Master, even Christ." We have no business to bring in that abomination of the lower regions that makes us think too little of ourselves; to think too little of ourselves is simply the obverse side of conceit. If I am a disciple of Jesus, He is my Master, I am looking to Him, and the thought of self never enters. So crush on the threshold of your mind any of those lame, limping "oh I can'ts, you see I am not gifted." The great stumblingblock in the way of some people being simple disciples is that they are gifted, so gifted that they won't trust God. So clear away all those things from the thought of discipleship; we all have absolutely equal privileges, and there is no limit to what God can do in and through us.

Jesus Christ never allows anywhere any room for the disciple to say, "Now, Lord, I am going to serve Thee." It never once comes into His outlook on discipleship that the disciple works for Him. He said, "As the Father hath sent Me, even so send I you" (RV). How did the Father send Jesus? To do His will. How does Jesus send His disciples? To do His will. "Ye shall be My witnesses" (RV)—a satisfaction to Me wherever you are placed. Our Lord's conception of discipleship is not that we work for God, but that God works through us; He uses us as He likes; He allots our work where He chooses, and we learn obedience as our Master did (Hebrews 5:8).

The one test of a teacher sent from God is that those who listen see and know Jesus Christ better than ever they did. If you are a teacher sent from God your worth in God's sight is estimated by the way you enable people to see Jesus. How are you going to tell whether I am a teacher sent from God or not? You can tell it in no other way than this—that you know Jesus Christ better than ever you did. If a teacher fascinates with his doctrine, his teaching never came from God. The teacher sent from God is the one who clears the way to Jesus and keeps it clear; souls forget altogether about him because the vision of Jesus is the only abiding result. When people are attracted to Jesus Christ through you, see always that you stay on God all the time, and their hearts and affections will never stop at you. The enervation that has crippled many a church, many a Sunday School class and Bible class, is that the pastor or teacher has won people to himself, and the result when they leave is enervating sentimentality. The true man or woman of God never leaves that behind, every remembrance of them makes you want to serve God all the more. So beware of stealing the hearts of the people of God in your mind. If once you get the thought, "It is my winsome way of putting it, my presentation of the truth that attracts"—the only name for that is the ugly name of thief, stealing the hearts of the sheep of God who do not know why they stop at you. Keep the mind stayed on God, and I defy anyone's heart to stop at you, it will always go on to God. The peril comes when we forget that our duty is to present Jesus Christ and never get in the way in thought. The practical certainty that we are not in the way is that we can talk about ourselves; if we are in the way, self-consciousness keeps us from referring to ourselves. The Apostle Paul looked upon himself as an exhibition of what Jesus Christ could do, consequently he continually refers to himself—"And though I am the foremost of sinners, I obtained mercy, for the purpose of furnishing Christ Jesus with a supreme proof of His utter patience, a typical illustration of it for all who were to believe in Him and gain eternal life" (1 Timothy 1:15–17 MOFFATT).

Chapter XI

THE PHILOSOPHY OF THE PERFECT LIFE
Matthew 19:16–22

The occasion of a conversation is in many respects as important to consider as its subject. The occasion of this conversation was the coming to Jesus of a splendid, upright, young aristocrat who was consumed with a master passion to possess the life he saw Jesus possessed. He comes with a feeling that there is something he has not yet, in spite of his morality and integrity and his riches, something deeper, more far-reaching he can attain to, and he feels instinctively that this Jesus of Nazareth is the One Who can tell him how to possess it. It is to this type of man that Jesus presents a most powerful attraction.

The Occasion of the Conversation of Perfection
The "What" and "May" of Matthew 19:16
"Good Master, what good thing shall I do, that I may have eternal life?

Never confound eternal life with immortality. Eternal has reference to the quality of life, not to its duration. Eternal life is the life Jesus exhibited when He was here on earth, with neither time nor eternity in it, because it is the life of God Himself (see John 17:3). Jesus said, "Ye have not [this] life in yourselves" (RV). What life? The life He had. Men have moral life, physical life and intellectual life apart from Jesus Christ. This rich young ruler felt the fascination of the marvellous life Jesus lived and asked how he might become possessed of the same life. His question was not asked in a captious spirit. Watch the atmosphere of your mood when you ask certain questions. "Good Master, what good thing shall I *do*, that I may have eternal life?" The great lesson our Lord taught him was that it is not anything he must do, but a relationship he must be willing to get into that is necessary. Other teachers tell us we have to do something—"Consecrate here; do this, leave off that." Jesus Christ always brings us back to one thing—"Stand in right relationship to Me first, then the marvellous doing will be performed in you." It is a question of abandoning all the time, not of doing.

The Obedience to the Conditions of Perfection
The "Why" and "If" of Matthew 19:17–20
Why callest thou Me good? . . . If thou wilt enter into life . . .

It looks at first as if Jesus was captious, as if the young man's question had put Him in a corner; but our Lord wishes him to understand what calling Him "good" and asking Him about "good things" meant—"If I am only a good man, there is no use coming to Me more than to anyone else; but if you mean that you are discerning Who I am," then comes the condition: "but if thou wilt enter into life, keep the commandments." The commonplace of the condition must have staggered this clean-living nobleman—"All these things have I kept from my youth up." "Then Jesus beholding him, loved him. . . ." The nobility of moral integrity and sterling natural virtue was lovely in the sight of Jesus because He saw in it a remnant of His Father's former handiwork.

In listening to some evangelical addresses the practical conclusion one is driven to is that we have to be great sinners before we can be saved; and the majority of men are not great sinners. This man was an upright, sterling, religious man; it would be absurd to talk to him about sin, he was not in the place where he could understand what it meant. There are hundreds of clean-living, upright men who are not convicted of sin, I mean sin in the light of the commandments Jesus mentioned. We need to revise the place we put conviction of sin in and the place the Spirit of God puts it in. There is no mention of sin in the apprehension of Saul of Tarsus, yet no one understood sin more fundamentally than the Apostle Paul. If we reverse God's order and refuse to put the recognition of Who Jesus is first, we present a lame type of Christianity which excludes for ever the kind of man represented by this rich young ruler. The most staggering thing about Jesus Christ is that He makes human destiny depend not on goodness or badness, not on things done or not done, but on Who we say He is.

"What lack I yet?" Jesus then instantly presses another "if": "If thou wilt be perfect . . ." The second "if" is much more penetrating than the first. Entrance into life is through the recognition of Who Jesus is, i.e., all we mean by being born again of the Spirit— "If you would enter into life, that is the way." The second "if" is much more searching—"If thou wilt be perfect . . ."—"If you want to be perfect, perfect as I am, perfect as your Father in Heaven is"—then come the conditions. Do we really want to be perfect? Beware of mental quibbling over the word "perfect." Perfection does not mean the full maturity and consummation of a man's powers, but perfect fitness for doing the will of God (cf. Philippians 3:12–15). Supposing Jesus Christ can perfectly adjust me to God, put me so perfectly right that I shall be on the footing where I can do the will of God, do I really want Him to do it? Do I want God at all costs to make me perfect? A great deal depends on what is the real deep desire of our hearts. Can we say with Robert Murray McCheyne[10]—"Lord, make me as holy as Thou canst make a saved sinner"? Is that really the desire of our hearts? Our desires come to light always when we press this "if" of Jesus—"If thou wilt be perfect . . ."

The Obliterating Concessions to Perfection
The "Go" and "Come" of Matthew 19:21
Go and sell that thou hast, . . . and come and follow Me.

After you have entered into life, come and fulfil the conditions of that life. We are so desperately wise, we continually make out that Jesus did not mean what He said and we spiritualise His meaning into thin air. In this case there is no getting out of what He meant—"If thou wilt be perfect, go and sell that thou hast, and give to the poor." The words mean a voluntary abandoning of property and riches, and a deliberate devoted attachment to Jesus Christ. To you or me Jesus might not say that, but He would say something equivalent over anything we are depending upon. Never push an experience into a principle by which to guide other lives. To the rich young ruler Jesus said, "Loosen yourself from your property because that is the thing that is holding you." The principle is one of fundamental death to possessions while being obliged to use them. "Sell that thou hast . . ."—reduce yourself till nothing remains but your

consciousness of yourself, and then cast that consciousness at the feet of Christ. That is the bedrock of intense spiritual Christianity. The moral integrity of this man made him see clearly what Jesus meant. A man who had been morally twisted would not have seen, but this man's mind was unwarped by moral damage and when Jesus brought him straight to the point, he saw it clearly.

Go and sell that thou hast. . . ." "Do you mean to say that it is necessary for our soul's salvation to do that?" Our Lord is not talking about salvation, He is saying—*"If thou wilt be perfect . . ."* Do mark the *if*s of Jesus. "If any man would be my disciple . . ." Remember, the conditions of discipleship are not the conditions for salvation. We are perfectly at liberty to say, "No, thank you, I am much obliged for being delivered from hell, very thankful to escape the abominations of sin, but when it comes to these conditions it is rather too much; I have my own interests in life, my own possessions."

The Obstructing Counterpoise to Perfection
The "When" and "Went" of Matthew 19:22
But when the young man heard that saying, he went away sorrowful: for he had great possessions.

"Counterpoise" means an equally heavy weight in the other scale. We hear a thing, not when it is spoken, but when we are in a state to listen. Most of us have only ears to hear what we intend to agree with, but when the surgical operation of the Spirit of God has been performed on the inside and our perceiving powers are awakened to understand what we hear, then we get to the condition of this young man. When he heard what Jesus said he did not dispute it, he did not argue, he did not say, "I fail to perceive the subtlety of Your meaning"; he heard it, and he found he had too big an interest in the other scale and he drooped away from Jesus in sadness, not in rebellion.

Our Lord's statements seem so simple and gentle that we swallow them and say, "Yes, I accept Jesus as a Teacher," then His words seem to slip out of our minds; they have not, they have gone into the subconscious mind, and when we come across something in our circumstances, up comes one of those words and we hear it for the first time and it makes us reel with amazement. "He that hath ears to hear, let him hear." What have we ears for?

"Go and sell that thou hast, and give to the poor." Remember, Jesus did not claim any of the rich young ruler's possessions; He did not say, "Consecrate them to Me"; He did not say, "Sell that thou hast, and give it to My service"; He said,:"Sell that thou hast, and give to the poor, and for you, you come and follow

---

10. Robert Murray McCheyne (1813–1843): Scottish minister whose short but intense life made a great impact on Scotland.

Me, and you shall have treasure in heaven." One of the most subtle errors is that God wants our possessions; they are not any use to Him. God does not want our possessions, He wants us.

In this incident our Lord reveals His profound antipathy to emotional excitement. The rich young man's powers were in unbewitched working order when Jesus called him to decide. Beware of the "seeking great things for yourself" idea—cold shivers down the back, visions of angels and visitations from God. "I can't decide in this plain, commonplace, ordinary evening as to whether I will serve Jesus or not." That is the only way Jesus Christ ever comes to us. He will never take us at a disadvantage, never terrify us out of our wits by some amazing manifestation of His power and then say "Follow Me." He wants us to decide when all our powers are in full working order, and He chooses the moment when the world, not Himself, is in the ascendant. If we chose Him when He was in the ascendant, in the time of religious emotion and excitement, we would leave Him when the moment of excitement passed, but if we choose Him with all our powers about us, the choice will abide.

"And come and follow Me." It is not only a question of "binding the sacrifice with cords to the horns of the altar," it is a rising in the might of the Holy Ghost, with your feet on the earth but your heart swelling with the love of heaven, conscious that at last you have reached the position to which you were aspiring. How long are some of us who ought to be princes and princesses for God going to be bound up in the show of things? We have asked in tears, "What lack I yet?" This is the road and no other—"Come and follow Me," "And thou shalt have treasure in heaven"—and on earth, what? "An hundredfold of all you left *for My sake.*"

The devotion to Jesus Christ of our person is the effectual working of the evangelical doctrine of Christian perfection.

Chapter XII
THE DISCIPLE AND THE LORD OF DESTINY
Revelation 3

His Divine Integrity
These things saith He that is holy, He that is true . . .
(Revelation 3:7)

(a) Harmony with God's Character
These words suggest that our Lord's unlimited sovereignty over human souls rests upon moral fitness. In Revelation 5 this aspect is again alluded to—"Who is worthy to open the book?" The appeal made to us by Jesus Christ is that He is worthy not only in the domain of God, but in the domain of man, consequently He "hath prevailed to open the book." The disciple's Lord is in absolute harmony with the highest man knows and with the highest God has revealed. The Bible is not the authority, the Church is not the authority, the Lord Jesus Christ alone is the Authority. The tendency is strong to make the statements of the Bible simpler than God makes them, the reason being that we will not recognise Jesus Christ as the Authority. It is only when we rely on the Holy Spirit and obey His leadership that the authority of Jesus Christ is recognised. The Holy Spirit will glorify Jesus only, consequently the interpretation of the Bible and of human life depends entirely on how we understand the character of Jesus Christ. If there is anything hidden from us as disciples to-day it is because we are not in a fit state to understand it. As soon as we become fit in spiritual character the thing is revealed, it is concealed at God's discretion until the life is developed sufficiently.

(b) Holiness Supreme with Man
The disciple's Lord is the supreme Authority in every relationship of life the disciple is in or can be in. That is a very obvious point, but think what it means—it means recognising it as impertinent to say, "Oh, well, Jesus Christ does not know my circumstances; the principles involved in His teachings are altogether impracticable for me where I am." That thought never came from the Spirit of God, and it has to be gripped in a vice on the threshold of the mind and allowed no way. If as we obey God such a circumstance is possible where Jesus Christ's precepts and principles are impracticable, then He has misled us. The idea insinuates itself—"Oh, well, I can be justified from my present conduct because of—so and so." We are never justified as disciples in taking any line of action other than that indicated by the teaching of Our Lord and made possible for us by His Spirit. The providence of God fits us into various settings of life to see if we will be disciples in those relationships.

(c) Highest Authority Conceivable

The highest authority conceivable for a man is that of a holy character. The holiest character is the Lord Jesus Christ, therefore His statements are never dogmas, they are declarations. In the Epistles we find the dogmas of belief stated and formulated; but Our Lord never taught dogma, He declared. There is no argument or discussion in what He says, it is not a question of the insight of a marvellous man, but a question of speaking with authority. "He taught them as one having authority" (Matthew 7:29). The disciple realises that Our Lord's statements never spring from a personal point of view; they reveal the eternal character of God as applied to the practical details of life.

His Divine Imperialism

He that hath the key of David . . . (Revelation 3:7)

(a) Abiding Sacredness of His Inheritance

The disciple's Lord has the key to every situation in heaven above or on earth beneath. Other powers that are not of Jesus Christ claim they can open the book, but the unmeasured blight of God rests on an intellectual curiosity that divorces itself from moral and spiritual worth. It is necessary to bear that in mind, for this is a day of intolerant inquisitiveness, people will not wait for the slow, steady, majestic way of the Son of God, they enter in by this door and that, and the consequence is moral, spiritual and physical insanity. All kinds of terrible and awful evils come through men having pressed open domains for themselves. They have refused to have the only authority there is, the authority of a moral, holy character. "But I fear," says Paul, "lest by any means . . . your minds should be corrupted from the simplicity that is in Christ."

(b) Antagonists Scared by His Servants

The easy supremacy of the Lord Jesus Christ in and through the life of a disciple brings the blatant terror of the synagogue of Satan to bow at his feet. "Behold, I will make them of the synagogue of Satan . . . to come and worship before thy feet, and to know that I have loved thee" (Revelation 3:9). This is the age of humiliation for the saints, just as it was the age of humiliation for Our Lord when He was on earth; we cannot stand the humiliation unless we are His disciples, we want to get into the "show business," we want to be successful, to be recognised and known; we want to compromise and put things right and get to an understanding. Never! Stand true to Jesus Christ, "in nothing terrified by your adversaries." We find the features of the synagogue of Satan everywhere, but if the disciple will obey, all that power will crumble down as bluff by the marvellous authority of Jesus Christ. "Fear not, little flock; for it is your Father's good pleasure to give you the kingdom." When once

fear is taken out, the world is humiliated at the feet of the humblest of saints, it can do nothing, it cannot touch the amazing supremacy that comes through the Divine imperialism of the saint's Lord and Master.

(c) Alpha and Omega

"I am Alpha and Omega, the first and the last." Jesus Christ is the last word on God, on sin and death, on heaven and hell; the last word on every problem that human life has to face. If you are a disciple, be loyal to Him; that means you will have to choke off any number of things that might fritter you away from the one Centre. Beware of prejudices being put in place of the sovereignty of Jesus Christ, prejudices of doctrine, of conviction or experience. When we go on Jesus Christ's way, slowly and steadily we find He builds up spiritual and moral character along with intellectual discernment, these develop together; if we push one at the expense of the other, we shall get out of touch with God. If our intellectual curiosity pushes the barriers further than God has seen fit to open, our moral character will get out of hand and we shall have pain that God cannot bless, suffering from which He cannot protect us. "The way of transgressors is hard."

"I am the first and the last." Is Jesus Christ the first and the last of my personal creed, the first and last of all I look to and hope for? Frequently the discipline of discipleship has to be delayed until we learn that God's barriers are put there not by sovereign Deity only; they are put there by a God Whose will is absolutely holy and Who has told us plainly, "Not that way" (cf. Deuteronomy 29:29).

His Divine Invincibility

. . . He that openeth, and no man shutteth; and shutteth, and no man openeth. (Revelation 3:7)

(a) Defied but Never Frustrated

The word "door" is used elsewhere in the New Testament for privileges and opportunities ("For a great door and effectual is opened unto me," 1 Corinthians 16:9); but here it means that Jesus Christ's sovereignty is effective everywhere; it is He Who opens the door and He Who shuts. "Behold, I have set before thee an open door, and no man can shut it." Behind the devil is God. God is never in a panic, nothing can be done that He is not absolute Master of, and no one in earth or heaven can shut a door He has opened, nor open a door He has shut. God alters the inevitable when we get in touch with Him. We discover the doors Our Lord opens by watching the things unsaved human nature reacts against. Everything Jesus Christ has done awakens a tremendous reaction against Him in those who are not His disciples—"I won't go that way." Insubordination is the characteristic of to-day. Men defy, but they cannot frustrate, and in the end they come to see that Jesus Christ's is the only way. The gospel gives access into privileges which no man can reach by any other way than the way Jesus Christ has appointed. Unsaved human nature resents this and tries to make out that Jesus Christ will bow in submissive weakness to the way it wants to go. The preaching of the gospel awakens an intense craving and an equally intense resentment. The door is opened wide by a God of holiness and love, and any and every man can enter in through that door, if he will. "I am the way." Jesus Christ is the exclusive Way to the Father.

(b) Divine and for Ever "Never"

Some doors have been shut by God and they will never again be opened. God opens other doors, but we find these closed doors all through the history of man.

Some people believe in an omnipotence with no character, they are shut up in a destiny of hopelessness; Jesus Christ can open the door of release and let them right out. There is no door that man or devil has closed but Jesus Christ can open it; but remember, there is the other side, the door He closes no man can open.

(c) Desired Communion

In Revelation 3:20 the metaphor is changed—"Behold, *I* stand at the door, and knock. . . ." If it is true that no man can open the doors Jesus Christ has closed, it is also true that He never opens the door for His own incoming into the heart and life of a church or an individual. ". . . IF any man . . . open the door, I will come in to him." The experience into which Jesus Christ by His sovereignty can bring us is at-one-ment with God, a full-orbed, unworrying oneness with God.

If Ye Shall Ask

Oswald Chambers

INTRODUCTION

Source

If Ye Shall Ask is from lectures given at the Bible Training College,[1] London (1911–1915); at League of Prayer[2] gatherings in Britain; to British Commonwealth troops in Egypt[3] during World War I.

Where known, date and place appear on the first page of each sermon.

Publication History

- As articles: Many of these chapters appeared first as articles in *Tongues of Fire/Spiritual Life* magazines or in the *Bible Training College (BTC) Monthly Journal.*[4]

- As a book: The material was first published as *If Ye Shall Ask* in 1937. Drawing on her store of notes from Britain and Egypt, Mrs. Chambers compiled this collection expressing the heart of Oswald's teaching on prayer and his practice of it. She selected the short prayers at the beginnings of chapters 2 through 12 from OC's personal prayer journal and from meetings at the Bible Training College.

For additional personal prayers of Oswald Chambers in this volume, see *Knocking At God's Door* (1957).

---

1. Bible Training College (BTC): residential school near Clapham Common in southwest London, sponsored and operated by the League of Prayer from 1911 until it closed in July 1915 because of World War I. Oswald Chambers was principal and main teacher; Biddy Chambers, his wife, was lady superintendent.

2. Pentecostal League of Prayer: founded in London in 1891 by Reader Harris (1847–1909), prominent barrister and friend and mentor of Oswald Chambers.

3. Zeitoun (zay TOON), Egypt: six miles northeast of Cairo; site of a YMCA camp, the Egypt General Mission compound, and, from 1916 to 1919, the Imperial School of Instruction, training base for British, Australian, and New Zealand troops during World War I.

4. *Bible Training Course Monthly Journal:* published from 1932 to 1952 by Mrs. Chambers, with help from David Lambert

FOREWORD TO THE FIRST EDITION

It is with real misgiving as to any ability to worthily express my gratitude to Almighty God for bringing me into contact with His servant Oswald Chambers, that I respond to the request that I should write a foreword to this book. Mr. Chambers was the close personal friend of my mature manhood, with whom the most intimate confidences were shared. Under God, I owe to his friendship not only the opening out of a fuller apprehension of the Redemption of our Lord Jesus Christ, but also the acquirement of the mental development necessary to enable me, in some measure, to state intelligibly to others the results of the knowledge imparted to myself. Among the many axiomatic statements that fell from his lips, the following was particularly enlightening, "Always distinguish clearly the difference between God's order and God's permissive will." And in this book he shows so concisely and simply that under God's dispensational sovereignty, deliverance from sin *now* is His expressed will, while sickness and limitation are subject to God's sovereignty active in *pre*-dispensational efficacy. Talked out with God Himself until that perfect harmony between God and our own hearts is an unshakeable fact, these lines of thought enable us to arrive at a restful explanation of most of our difficulties concerning prayer. Oswald Chambers' prayer-life was one of intercession for others. Seldom did he ask specifically for anything material for himself. His whole personal attitude towards God was that of harmonious relationship, and absolute childlike dependence upon his heavenly Father. The precious gems included in this book are more in the nature of ejaculatory response to fresh gleams of light, or fresh insight into personal needs as he enjoyed that close intercourse with his beloved Master. While many other messages on prayer have already been included in some of his other books, this is confined mainly to the talks not otherwise in book form. It will be interesting to know that the first talk was one given to the soldiers at Zeitoun, and explains the significance of the outline, also showing the kind of message the men got there. I cannot wish better for all who read these God-given messages, than that they have the effect of leading them also into that real fellowship that he himself habitually enjoyed with the Lord he loved so much.

John S. Skidmore[5]
Brimfield, Ludlow, Shropshire
18th September 1937

CONTENTS

---

5. Major John Skidmore: close friend and associate of Oswald and Biddy Chambers and was involved full-time in the League of Prayer.

GIVEN TO TROOPS, NOVEMBER 4, 1915, AND NOVEMBER 13, 1916,
YMCA CAMP, ZEITOUN, EGYPT.

Chapter I

WHAT'S THE GOOD OF PRAYER?

1 Timothy 2:1–8

Because We Need To (Luke 11:1)
    For Human Wits Have an End (Psalm 108:13, 19, 28)
    For Human Wills Have an End (Romans 8:26)
    For Human Wisdom Has an End (James 1:5)
        PRAYER ALTERS ME
Because We Must Do (James 5:16)
    If We Would Know God (Matthew 6:8)
    If We Would Help Men (John 14:12–13)
    If We Would Do God's Will (1 John 5:14–16)
        PRAYER ALTERS OTHERS
Because We Can Do (Luke 18:1)
    By Asking
    By Seeking (Luke 11:9–13; John 15:7)
    By Knocking
        PRAYER ALTERS CIRCUMSTANCES
            THROUGH ME

It is only when a man flounders beyond any grip of himself and cannot understand things that he really prays. It is not part of the natural life of a man to pray. By "natural" I mean the ordinary, sensible, healthy, worldly-minded life. We hear it said that a man will suffer in his life if he does not pray; I question it. Prayer is an interruption to personal ambition, and no man who is busy has time to pray. What will suffer is the life of God in him, which is nourished not by food but by prayer. If we look on prayer as a means of developing ourselves, there is nothing in it at all, nor do we find that idea of prayer in the Bible. Prayer is other than meditation; it is that which develops the life of God in us. When a man is born from above (RV mg), the life of the Son of God begins in him, and he can either starve that life or nourish it. Prayer is the way the life of God is nourished. Our Lord nourished the life of God in Him by prayer; He was continually in contact with His Father. We generally look upon prayer as a means of getting things for ourselves, whereas the Bible idea of prayer is that God's holiness and God's purpose and God's wise order may be brought about, irrespective of who comes or who goes. Our ordinary views of prayer are not found in the New Testament.

When a man is in real distress he prays without reasoning; he does not think things out, he simply spurts it out—"Then they cried unto the LORD in their trouble, and He saved them out of their distresses." When we get into a tight place our logic goes to the winds, and we work from the implicit part of ourselves.

"Your Father knoweth what things ye have need of, before ye ask Him." Then why ask? Very evidently our ideas about prayer and Jesus Christ's are not the same. Prayer to Him is not a means of getting things from God, but in order that we may get to know God. Prayer, that is, is not to be used as the petted privilege of a spoiled child seeking for ideal conditions in which to indulge his spiritual propensities *ad lib*.; the purpose of prayer is to reveal the Presence of God, equally present at all times and in every condition.

A man may say, "Well, if the Almighty has decreed things, why need I pray? If He has made up His mind, what is the use of me thinking I can alter His mind by prayer?" We must remember that there is a difference between God's order and God's permissive will. God's *order* reveals His character; His *permissive will* applies to what He permits. For instance, it is God's *order* that there should be no sin, no suffering, no sickness, no limitation and no death; His permissive will is all these things. God has so arranged matters that we are born into His permissive will, and we have to get at His order by an effort of our own, viz., by prayer. To be children of God, according to the New Testament, does not mean that we are creatures of God only, but that we grow into a likeness to God by our own moral character.

I question whether the people who continually ask for prayer meetings know the first element of prayer. It is often an abortion of religious hysterics, a disease of the nerves taking a spiritual twist. Jesus says we are to pray in His name, i.e., in His nature, and His nature is shed abroad in our hearts by the Holy Ghost when we are born from above (RV mg; see Luke 11:13; Romans 5:5). Again, Jesus did not promise to be at every prayer meeting, but only at those "where two or three are gathered together in My name," i.e., in His nature (Matthew 18:20). Jesus Christ does not pay any attention to the gift of "religious gab," and His words—"But when ye pray, use not vain repetitions, as the heathen do: for they think that they shall be heard for their much speaking," refer not to the mere repetition and form of words, but to the fact that it is never our earnestness that brings us into touch with God, but our Lord Jesus Christ's vitalising death. (See Hebrews 10:19)

Our Lord in His teaching regarding prayer never once referred to unanswered prayer; He said God always answers prayer. If our prayers are in the name of Jesus, i.e., in accordance with His nature, the answers will not be in accordance with our nature, but with His. We are apt to forget this, and to say without thinking that God does not always answer prayer. He does every time, and when we are in close communion with Him, we realise that we have not been misled.

"Ask, and it shall be given you." We grouse before God, and are apologetic or apathetic, but we *ask* very few things; yet what a splendid audacity a child-like child has! and our Lord says, "Except ye . . . become as little children. . . ." Jesus says, "Ask, and God will do." Give Jesus Christ a chance, give Him elbow-room, and no man ever does it until he is at his wits' end. During the war many a man prayed for the first time in his life. When a man is at his wits' end, it is not a cowardly thing to pray, it is the only way to get in touch with Reality. As long as we are self-sufficient and complacent, we don't need to ask God for anything, we don't want Him; it is only when we know we are powerless that we are prepared to listen to Jesus Christ and to do what He says.

Then again our Lord says, "If ye abide in Me, and My words abide in you, ye shall ask what ye *will*," i.e., what your will is in. There is very little our wills are in, consequently it is easy to work up false emotions. We intercede in a mechanical way, our minds are not in it. When we see a man going wrong, it is a false way to "buttonhole" him and tell him about it; Jesus Christ says, Come and tell Me, and I will give you life for him that sins not "unto death" (see 1 John 5:16).

Be yourself exactly before God, and present your problems, the things you know you have come to your wits' end about. Ask what you *will*, and Jesus Christ says your prayers will be answered. We can always tell whether our will is in what we ask by the way we live when we are not praying.

The New Testament view of a Christian is that he is one in whom the Son of God has been revealed, and prayer deals with the nourishment of that life. One way it is nourished is by refusing to worry over anything, for worry means there is something over which we cannot have our own way, and is in reality personal irritation with God. Jesus Christ says, "Don't worry about your life, don't fear them which kill the body; be afraid only of not doing what the Spirit of God indicates to you."

"In every thing give thanks." Never let anything push you to your wits' end, because you will get worried, and worry makes you self-interested and disturbs the nourishment of the life of God. Give thanks to God that *He* is there, no matter what is happening. Many a man has found God in the belly of hell in the trenches during the days of war, i.e., they came to their wits' end and discovered God. The secret of Christian quietness is not indifference, but the knowledge that God is my Father, He loves me, I shall never think of anything He will forget, and worry becomes an impossibility.

It is not so true that "Prayer changes things" as that prayer changes *me*, and then I change things; consequently we must not ask God to do what He has created us to do. For instance, Jesus Christ is not a social reformer; He came to alter us first, and if there is any social reform to be done on earth, we must do it. God has so constituted things that prayer on the basis of Redemption alters the way a man looks at things. Prayer is not a question of altering things externally, but of working wonders in a man's disposition. When you pray, *things* remain the same, but *you* begin to be different. The same thing when a man falls in love, his circumstances and conditions are the same, but he has a sovereign preference in his heart for another person which transfigures everything. If we have been born from above (RV mg) and Christ is formed in us, instantly we begin to see things differently—"If any man is in Christ, there is a new creation" (RV mg).

> Heaven above is brighter blue,
>   Earth around is sweeter green!
> Something lives in every hue
>   Christless eyes have never seen.
> Birds with gladder songs o'erflow,
>   Flowers with deeper beauties shine,
> Since I know, as now I know,
>   I am His, and He is mine.

The good of praying is that it gets us to know God and enables God to perform His order through us, no matter what His permissive will may be. A man is never what he is *in spite of* his circumstances, but *because* of them. Circumstances, as Reader Harris once said, are like feather beds—very comfortable to be on top of, but immensely smothering if they get on top of you. Jesus Christ, by the Spirit of God, always keeps us on top of our circumstances.

> How beautiful this undisturbed morning hour is with God!

---

6. Reader Harris (1847–1909): prominent British barrister, founded the Pentecostal League of Prayer in 1891; friend and mentor to Oswald Chambers.

O Lord, this day my soul would stay upon Thee as Creator of the world, and upon our Lord Jesus Christ as Creator of His life in me. Oh for the power of Thy Spirit to adore Thee in fuller measure!

. . . .

"What shall I render unto the Lord for all His benefits toward me? I take the cup of salvation. . . ." Can I think of anything so gracious and complete in sur-

render and devotion and gratitude as to take from Thee? O Lord, I would that I had a livelier sense of Thee and of Thy bounties continually with me.

. . . .

O Lord, this day may Thy beauty and grace and soothing peace be in and upon me, and may no wind or weather or anxiety ever touch Thy beauty and Thy peace in my life or in this place.

LECTURE: BIBLE TRAINING COLLEGE, APRIL 6, 1915

Chapter II

THE SECRET OF THE SACRED SIMPLICITY OF PRAYER

Watch and pray, that ye enter not into temptation: the spirit indeed is willing, but the flesh is weak. Matthew 26:41

These words were spoken in the supreme moment of our Lord's agony; we are immensely flippant if we forget that. No words our Lord ever spoke ought to weigh with us more than these words. We are dealing with the sacred simplicity of prayer. If prayer is not easy, we are wrong; if prayer is an effort, we are out of it. There is only one kind of person who can really pray, and that is the childlike saint, the simple, stupid, supernatural child of God; I do mean "stupid." Immediately you try to explain why God answers prayer on the ground of reason, it is nonsense; God answers prayer on the ground of Redemption and on no other ground. Let us never forget that our prayers are heard, not because we are in earnest, not because we suffer, but because Jesus suffered. It is because our Lord Jesus Christ went through the depths of agony to the last ebb in the Garden of Gethsemane, because He went through Calvary, that we have "boldness to enter into the holy place."

Let us take ourselves across Kedron to the Garden of Gethsemane. We can never fathom the agony in Gethsemane, but at least we need not *mis*-understand. This is not the agony of a man: this is the distress of God in Man, or rather the distress of God as Man. It is not human in any phase, it is fathomless to a human mind, but we have got several lines to go on so as not to *mis*-understand. Always beware of the tendency to think of our Lord as an extraordinary human being; He was not, He was God Incarnate.

The Line of the Undiscerned Word of Our Lord

Watch and pray . . .

"Tarry ye here, and watch with Me." Is my idea of prayer based on the keen watching that Jesus Christ asked of His disciples? He did not say, "pray for anything," or, "ask God for anything"; the whole of His attitude toward them was wrapped up in the words, "watch with Me." Our Lord did not say sentimental things or pious things about prayer He said practical and intensely real things, and this is one of them. This is a line of things that opens up nothing to us until it does, because we bring in our own ideas of prayer and do not take into account the Mastership of our Lord. Probably that is our biggest difficulty—that our Lord is not really Master. We use the phrase "Master," but we use it in a more or less pious way, we do not intend to make Him Master practically; we are much more familiar with the idea that Jesus is our Saviour, our Sanctifier, anything that puts Him in the relationship of a supernatural Comrade. We advocate anything that Jesus does, but we do not advocate Him.

(a) The Appropriate Place of Our Lord's Arranging

"Sit ye here, while I go yonder and pray . . ." It is customary, and in one sense quite right, to take our Lord as an example of how to pray, but in the fundamental sense He is not. The relationship we have to God is not the same as Jesus Christ's relationship to His Father—especially on this occasion; His is not a relationship: it is a Redemption. So until you are sure about our Lord's Redemption—"sit here, wait." People say, "Why do you waste your time in a Bible Training College? Fancy spending all your time studying the Bible! Think of the people who need to be looked after; think of the thousand and one things there are to do!" Well, they have to be done, but that is not the point. The point is, are we prepared for our Lord to say to us, "Sit ye here, while I go yonder"? Are

we prepared to give due weight to the fact that we are not our own masters? Are we devotees to a cause or disciples of the Lord Jesus Christ? He said to the disciples, "Sit ye here"; if they had been like some of us they would have said, "No, it is absurd, we must go and do something."

The more we get into the atmosphere of the New Testament the more we discover the unfathomable and unhasting leisure of our Lord's life, no matter what His agony. The difficulty is that when we do what God wants us to do, our friends say, "It is all very well, but suppose we all did that!" Our Lord did not tell all the disciples to sit there while He prayed; He told only three of them. The point is that we must take the discerning of the haphazard arrangements of our lives from God. If once we accept the Lord Jesus Christ and the domination of His Lordship, then nothing happens by chance, because we know that God is ordering and engineering circumstances; the fuss has gone, the amateur providence has gone, the amateur disposer has gone, and we know that "all things work together for good to them that love God." If Jesus says, "Sit ye here, while I go yonder and pray," the only appropriate thing we can do is to sit there.

(b) The Appointed Place of Our Lord's Associates
"And He took with Him Peter and the two sons of Zebedee . . ." Our Lord opened His sorrow to these three, as far as human beings could appreciate it. Peter may stand well for the phase of the first temptation that betook our Lord—the sensible, material side of things, for help and assistance. James may stand for the second temptation that betook our Lord—the intensely ritualistic; and John may stand for the last temptation—the temptation to compromise with everything in order to win, a great loving monopoly. These three men were taken and appointed by our Lord for one purpose—to see His agony. "Tarry ye here, and watch with Me." He did not put them there to go to sleep; He put them there to wait and watch. Remember, the twelve disciples were all He had; He knew one had gone to betray Him, and that Peter would shortly deny Him with oaths and curses, and that all of them would forsake Him and flee; but He took these three with Him to see the unveiling of His heart—and they slept for their own sorrow.

(c) The Autobiographic Place of Our Lord's Agony
". . . and began to be sorrowful and sore troubled." Our Lord said to these disciples what He never said to the others; in John 12:27, He said in soliloquy something similar ("Now is My soul troubled; and what shall I say?"), but here He really said to these three, "My soul is exceeding sorrowful, even unto death." Have we for one second watched Jesus pray? Have we ever understood why the Holy Ghost and our Lord Himself were so exceptionally careful about the recording of the agony in Gethsemane? This is not the agony of a man or a martyr; this is the agony of God as Man. It is God, as Man, going through the last lap of the supreme, supernatural Redemption of the human race. We ought to give much more time than we do—a great deal more time than we do—to brooding on the fundamental truths on which the Spirit of God works the simplicity of our Christian experience. The fundamental truths are—Redemption and the personal presence of the Holy Ghost, and these two are focused in one mighty Personality, the Lord Jesus Christ. Thank God for the emphasis laid by the Pentecostal League of Prayer on the efficacy of the Holy Ghost to make experimentally real the Redemption of Jesus Christ in individual lives.

Remember, what makes prayer easy is not our wits or our understanding, but the tremendous agony of God in Redemption. A thing is worth just what it costs. Prayer is not what it costs us, but what it cost God to enable us to pray. It cost God so much that a little child can pray. It cost God Almighty so much that anyone can pray. But it is time those of us who name His Name knew the secret of the cost, and the secret is here, "My soul is exceeding sorrowful, even unto death." These words open the door to the autobiography of our Lord's agony. We find the real key to Gethsemane in Matthew 4, which records the temptations of our Lord. Here they come again in a deeper and more appalling manner than ever before. We are not looking here (as we do when we deal with the temptations) at the type of temptation we have to go through; we are dealing here with the grappling of God as Man in the last reaches of historic Redemption.

"But these truths are so big." Why shouldn't they be? Have we to be fed with spooned meat[7] all the time? Is it not time we paid more attention to what it cost God to make it possible for us to live a holy life? We talk about the difficulty of living a holy life; there is the absolute simple ease of Almighty God in living a holy life because it cost Him so much to make it possible. Beware of placing the emphasis on what prayer costs us; it cost God everything to make it possible for us to pray, Jesus did not say to these men, "agonise"; He said, "Watch with Me." Our Lord tried to lift the veil from before these disciples that they might see what He was going through. Think Who He was—the Son of God: "My soul"—the reasoning Mind of the Lord Jesus Christ—"is exceeding sorrowful, even unto death: tarry ye here, and watch with Me."

---

7. spooned meat: liquefied food that requires no chewing or effort—baby food.

The Lure of Wrong Roads to the Kingdom
that ye enter not into temptation . . .

Whenever Jesus talked about His kingdom the disciples misinterpreted what He said to mean a material kingdom to be established on this earth; but Jesus said, "My kingdom is not of this world: if My kingdom were of this world, then would My servants fight, that I should not be delivered to the Jews." And again He said, "The kingdom of God cometh not with observation . . . for lo! the kingdom of God is within you." The only way in which we can be saved from the lure of the wrong roads to the kingdom is by doing what our Master tells us, viz., "Watch and pray, that ye enter not into temptation." If we do not watch and pray we shall be led into temptation before we know where we are. "Howbeit when the Son of man cometh, shall He find faith on the earth?" said Jesus. He will find faith in individual men and women, but the general organised form of the Christian Church has slipped almost wholesale on to wrong roads to the kingdom.

(a) The Material Road of Deliverance (Matthew 4:1–4)
"If Thou art the Son of God, command that these stones become bread" (Matthew 4:3). This temptation is profoundly human. If we could only find some means of curing everybody of disease, of feeding them and putting them on a good social basis what a marvellous thing it would be. That is the way we are being told that the kingdom of God is to be established on this earth. "We do not need any more of this talk about the Atonement, and the shedding of blood; what is needed to-day is to spend ourselves for others." That is the lure of the wrong road to the kingdom, and we cannot keep out of it if we forget to watch and pray. "Watch with Me," said Jesus; "mine is the only road to the kingdom." We have to continue with Him in His temptations. "Command that these stones become bread"—"satisfy Your own needs and the needs of men and You will get the kingship of men." Was Satan right? Read John 6:15, "When Jesus therefore perceived that they would come and take Him by force to make Him a king . . ." Why? He had just fed five thousand of them! yes, but we read that Jesus "departed again into a mountain Himself alone"; He would not be king at that price.

(b) The Mysterious Road of Devotion (Matthew 4:5–7)
Remember, we are dealing with our Lord's presentation of His own temptation; in the most sacred matters rely only on the Holy Ghost, trust no one else.

This temptation presents a wild reach of possibility—"You are the Son of God, do something super-

natural that will stagger men, and the world will be at your feet." Was Satan right? Absolutely. Is there not a lure along that road springing up to-day more than ever? There are miraculous dealings which lure to destruction, the tongues movement, the seeking for signs and wonders. Almost without exception the people who are lured on this wrong road are those who have been told to fast and concentrate for something for themselves whereby the Lord may show how marvellous He is. It does look right to human reason when it is just touched on the first outer fringe by the Holy Ghost, but it contradicts emphatically what our Lord teaches, viz., that importunity in intercession is never for ourselves but for others.

"The kingdom of God cometh not with observation": it is at work now; the manifestation of the kingdom of God externally is another thing. The disciples had still got their own ideas of the kingdom, they were blind to what Jesus Christ's kingdom meant, and they were so totally depressed that they slept for their own sorrow. "Watch with Me." How could they? They had no idea what He was after.

(c) The Mental Road of Dominion (Matthew 4:8–10)
This is the temptation to compromise—"Evil is in the world, compromise with it, work with it judiciously." "All these things will I give Thee, if Thou wilt fall down and worship me." This temptation is the most subtle of all. "Don't be so strait-laced; we have passed the day when we believe in a personal devil." May God forgive us, I am afraid we are past that stage. Will the Church that bows down and compromises succeed? Of course it will. It is the very thing that the natural man wants, but it is the lure of a wrong road to the kingdom. Beware of putting anything sweet and winsome in front of the One Who suffered in Gethsemane.

The Light of Undisciplined Vision
. . . the spirit indeed is willing, but the flesh is weak.

It is so easy when we see things in vision to start out and do them. We are caught up into the seventh heaven, far above all the grubby things of earth and it is magnificent for a time, but we have got to come down. After the Mount of Transfiguration comes the place where we have to live, viz., the demon-possessed valley. The test of reality is our life in the valley, not that we fly up among the golden peaks of the early morning.

(a) The Triumphant Minute
"*Blessed art thou, Simon Bar-jona*" (Matthew 16:17; cf. John 21:15–19). Peter had his triumphant minute, but he had to go through the mill after it; he went

through a tremendous heart-break before he was fit to hear Jesus say, "Feed My sheep." Peter would have done anything for his Lord, the spirit was willing, but the flesh was weak. We make allowances for the flesh, but we have no business to; we have to make manifest in the flesh the visions of the spirit. Thank God we are going to Heaven when we die, but thank God we are not going before we die. We get glimpses of Heaven, then we are brought down instantly into actual circumstances. Do not go too long in the light of undisciplined vision. Thank God for the triumphant minute, but we have to walk on earth according to what we saw in vision.

(b) The Transfiguration Moment
"And He was transfigured before them" (Matthew 17:2). Put alongside that moment on the Mount, Jesus standing after the Resurrection on the sea-shore in the early morning with "a fire of coals there, and fish laid thereon, and bread." Thank God for seeing Jesus transfigured, and for the almightiness of the visions He does give, but remember that the vision is to be made real in actual circumstances; the glory is to be manifested in earthen vessels. It has to be exhibited through finger-tips, through eyes and hands and feet; everywhere where Jesus exhibited it. We are so like Peter on the Mount and say, "O Lord, let me stay here."

(c) The Transcendent Moment
"Even if I must die with Thee, yet will I not deny Thee" (Matthew 26:35). Peter meant it every bit, it was a transcendent moment to him, he would have done anything for Jesus Christ; and yet he denied with oaths and curses that he ever knew Him. Peter was no hypocrite, but he did not watch and pray. Peter based his declaration on the keen generosity of his own

heart, but he did not understand that he needed to be on another basis altogether, the basis of Redemption.

Thank God for the heroic moments of life! It is comparatively easy to live in the heroic moments. We can all have haloes at times; if we stand in the right place, with stained-glass windows behind us, and have the right kind of dress on, it is not at all difficult to look remarkably fine; but there is nothing in it, not only is there nothing in it, but excessive dangers arise out of it. Beware of the transcendent moment that is a pose. A humorous sense of criticism is wholesome. Some people get to a transcendent moment and someone tells them they look remarkably fine, and everlastingly afterwards they try to live in that transcendent moment. We have to get down to the level where the reality works out, and the whole counsel comes back to this, "Watch and pray"—the secret of the sacred simplicity of prayer. Prayer imparts the power to walk and not faint, and the lasting remembrance of our lives is of the Lord, not of us.

O Lord, unto Thee do I come that I might find grace to praise and worship Thee aright. Lord lift up the light of Thy countenance upon us; send power and majestic grace.

. . . .

O Lord, how good it is for me to know Thee; how essentially necessary it is for me to draw nigh to Thee. How can I falter when Thou art my Life!

. . . .

Lord, our God, the Father of our Lord Jesus Christ, of Whom Jesus is the very image, I look to Thee and make my prayer. Bless me this hour with the feeling of Thy presence and the glow of Thy nearness, for I do trust Thee and hope only in Thee.

LECTURE: BIBLE TRAINING COLLEGE, MAY 7, 1915

Chapter III
THE SECRET OF THE SACRED STRUGGLE FOR PRAYER
Ephesians 6:12–19

Paul takes the illustration of battle and applies it at once to what goes on in a saint's life; the whole meaning of taking the armour of God is for prayer. Prayer is the position the devil is struggling for; the struggle is around the position of prayer and the simplicity of prayer. Prayer is easy to us because of what it cost God to enable us to pray. It is the Redemption of God, the

agony of our Lord, that has made our salvation so easy and prayer so simple. When we put the emphasis on the line of prayer being a cost to us, we are wrong. The cost to us is nothing, it is a supreme and superb privilege marked by supernatural ease because of what it cost God. The tendency nowadays is to worship prayer, stress is put on nights of prayer and the difficulty and cost of prayer. It is not prayer that is strenuous, but the overcoming of our own laziness. If we make the basis of prayer our effort and agony and nights of prayer, we mistake the basis of prayer. The basis of prayer is not what it costs us, but what it cost God to enable us to pray.

The Lord's Own Continuously in Practice
(Ephesians 6:12–13)

It is all very well to have vision, but we must be in continual practice so that when we find ourselves in a tight place we are perfectly fit to meet the emergency. One of the greatest difficulties in time of war is to find a man who can keep his head when everyone else is losing theirs. It is only done by steady practice. "Wherefore take unto you the whole armour of God "—not to fight, but to stand. We are not told to attack, to storm the forts of darkness; we are told to stand, unpanicky and unbudged, more than conquerors. A conqueror is one who fights and wins, a "more than conqueror" is one who easily and powerfully overcomes. The struggle is not against flesh and blood, it is against principalities and powers. We cannot touch them by intellect or organisation, by courage or foresight or forethought, we cannot touch them at all unless we are based on the Redemption.

"Wherefore take unto you the whole armour of God." It is not given, we have to take it; it is there for us to put it on, understanding what we are doing. We have the idea that prayer is for special times, but we have to put on the armour of God for the continual practice of prayer, so that any struggling onslaught of the powers of darkness cannot touch the position of prayer. When we pray easily it is because Satan is completely defeated in his onslaughts; when we pray difficult-ly it is because Satan is gaining a victory. We have not been continuously practising, we have not been facing things courageously, we have not been taking our orders from our Lord. Our Lord did not say, "Go" or "Do"; He said, "Watch and pray."

If we struggle in prayer it is because the enemy is gaining ground. If prayer is simple to us, it is because we have the victory. There is no such thing as a holiday for the beating of your heart. If there is, the grave comes next. And there is no such thing as a moral or spiritual holiday. If we attempt to take a holiday, the next time we want to pray it is a struggle because the enemy has gained a victory all round, darkness has come down and spiritual wickedness in high places has enfolded us. If we have to fight, it is because we have disobeyed; we ought to more than conquerors.

". . . and having done all, to stand"— a mental state as regards confidence, no panic. What is it puts us into a panic? The devil is a bully, but he cannot stand for a second before God. When we stand in the armour of God he pays no attention to us, but if we

tackle the devil in our own strength we are done for. If we stand in God's armour with the strength and courage of God, he cannot gain one inch of way, and the position of prayer is held, as far as we are concerned, untouched by his wiles. Confidence in the natural world is self-reliance, in the spiritual world it is God-reliance. We run away when we have not been practising, when we have not been doing anything in private, then when there is a new onslaught of the wiles of the devil we lose heart instantly. Instead of standing we scuttle, and others have to fill the gap until we are sufficiently ashamed to come back. We cannot stand against the wiles of the devil by our wits. The devil only comes along the lines that God understands, not along the lines we understand, and the only way we can be prepared for him is to do what God tells us, stand complete in His armour, indwelt by His Spirit, in complete obedience to Him. We have not to wait for some great onslaught of the enemy, he is here all the time and he is wily. The secret of the sacred struggle for prayer lies in the fact that we must stand in the armour of God, practising what God would have us do, then we can hold the position of prayer against all the attacks of the devil.

If we are struggling in prayer it is because the wiles of the enemy are getting the upper hand, and we must look for the cause of it in the lack of discipline in ourselves. There are some things we have not been strenuously practising—we used to pray in the morning, do we now? We used to commune with God over the Bible, do we now? We used to be in contact with God wherever we went, are we now? Put on the whole armour of God and keep continuously practising, then the wiles of the devil cannot get you unawares.

The Lord's Own Courageously in Preparation *(Ephesians 6:14–17)*

"Stand therefore, having your loins girt about with truth"—all active, sensible work is symbolised by girt loins—*"and having on the breastplate of righteousness;"* no inordinate fear, no questionable affinities, no tampering with winsomeness; all that breaks the armour down. Righteousness means "rightness" in my relationship to other people and their best interests.

". . . and your feet shod with the preparation of the gospel of peace." What kind of shoes do you wear? How many can say of us, "As soon as I heard your step I felt better"? Or do they say, "It was when your step came into my life that all went wrong; it was when the step of your friendship began with me that I began to lose out with God"? Put on the armour of God, keep the heart right with God, and wherever you go, you will shed the preparation of the gospel of peace. Wherever the saint goes there is the shedding of the benediction of the blessing of God, or there is the coming of the conviction of the Spirit of God.

"Above all, taking the shield of faith." Faith is unbreakable confidence in the Personality of God, not in His power. There are some things over which we may lose faith if we have confidence in God's power only. There is so much that looks like the mighty power of God that is not. We must have confidence in God over and above everything He may do, and stand in confidence that His character is unsullied. Faith stands under all tests—"Though He slay me, yet will I trust in Him." When we take the shield over-all of faith, none of these things can get through without breaking the shield, we are protected by the covering shield.

"And take . . . the sword of the Spirit." The Spirit brings to our remembrance what the Lord Jesus has said. In every onslaught of the enemy around us, that is the position he is struggling for. In order to be able to wield the sword of the Spirit, which is the Word of God, we must obey, and it takes the courageous heart to obey. If we try to apply the teaching of our Lord apart from the imparted nature of our Lord to our souls, we will make a muddle. It is not that we take the Sermon on the Mount as precepts and try to live up to them, but that when the Spirit of God brings some word of God back to our remembrance in certain circumstances—will we obey it? It will take courage, but as we obey, the wiles of the devil are withstood all the time and we stand.

The Lord's Own Competently in Place
(Ephesians 6:18–19)

That is, the place where God puts His soldiers, clad in His armour, and indwelt by His Spirit. Can we pray in prayer, or are we being beguiled by the devil? Have we been lured into a judicious winsomeness? Are we not quite so intense as we used to be? Have black and white become a neutral grey? Are we no longer so intense about sin as we used to be? Then we are out of place, we are exactly in the relationship of traitors, we can make known the position that can easily be taken by the devil unawares.

"Watch and pray," said Jesus in the centre of His own agony. If we don't, we shall slip into the lure of wrong roads without knowing it. The only way to keep right is to watch and pray. Prayer on any other basis than that on which it is placed in the New Testament is stupid, and the basis of prayer is not human earnestness, not human need, not the human will, it is Redemption, and its living centre is a personal Holy Ghost. A child can pray. Through His own agony in Redemption, God has made it as easy to pray as it sounds. There is nothing a rationally-minded being can ridicule more easily than prayer. "Praying always"—the unutterable simplicity of it! No panic, no flurry, always at leisure from ourselves on the inside.

". . . watching thereunto with all perseverance and supplication for all saints." It is all very well to have prayer meetings, but are we continually practising in the armour of God, keeping our hearts stout in the courage of God's Spirit and taking our orders from Him? Or are we making an ingenious compromise? There is only one service that has no snares, and that is prayer. Preaching has snares to the natural heart; so has public service. Prayer has no snare because it is based on the Redemption of the Lord Jesus Christ made efficacious all the time by the Holy Spirit.

". . . and for me, that utterance may be given unto me. . . ." We naturally suppose it is no use praying for "Paul," for prominent people, God will look after them all right. The prominent people for God are marked for the wiles of the devil, and we must pray for them all the time; God gives us every now and again an alarming exhibition of what happens if we don't.

Lord God Omnipotent, how my soul delights to know that Thou care for sparrows and numberest the hairs of our head! Lord, breathe on me till I am in the frame of mind and body to worship Thee.

. . . .

O Lord, I would seek Thy face now, but what avail is my seeking if Thou revealest not Thyself? Show me Thy face, O Lord. Keep me ever seeing Thee.

. . . .

O Lord, to praise Thee aright is a great desire of mine, created and fostered by Thy Spirit and grace. This morning, O Lord, I praise Thee for all the past—so wayward on my part, so wonderful and gracious and long-suffering and forgiving and tender and inspiring on Thine.

Chapter IV
THE CURRICULUM OF INTERCESSION

I will stand upon my watch, and set me upon the tower, and will watch to see what He will say unto me, and what I shall answer when I am reproved. And the LORD answered me, and said, Write the vision, and make it plain upon tables, that he may run that readeth it. Habakkuk 2:1–2

Inspired Waiting

I will stand upon my watch, and set me upon the tower . . .

How steadily all through the Old and New Testament God calls us to stand on the watch and wait for His indications, and how often God's answers to our prayers have been squandered because we do not watch and wait. My brother or sister, are you thoroughly perplexed over God's way?—you cannot reconcile God's clear way as revealed in His Book with the way He is leading you. Take the line of this prophet during his perplexity, stand and watch to see what God will say—watch at the right place.

There is a difference in the prayers of the Old and the New Testament. In chapter 3 the prophet bases his prayer on the character of God, and appeals to God's great mercies. In the New Testament, prayer is based on a relationship with God through Jesus Christ: "When ye pray, say, Our Father." There is another difference—the prayers in the Old Testament have to do with an earthly people in an earthly setting; the prayers in the New Testament have to do with a heavenly state of mind in a heavenly people while on this earth. We are continually being reminded that we wrestle not against flesh and blood, but against principalities and powers and the rulers of this world's darkness. The first thing to remember is that we watch at the right place, i.e., the place God has put us in. Watch for God's answer to your prayers, and not only watch, but wait. When God calls upon you to pray, when He gives the vision, when He gives an understanding of what He is going to do through you in your Sunday-school class, in your Church, or home—watch. How many of us have had to learn by God's reproof, by God's chastisement, the blunder of conferring with flesh and blood. Are you discouraged where you are, worker? Then get upon this tower with God, and watch and wait. The meaning of waiting in both the Old and New Testament is "standing under," actively enduring. It is not standing with folded arms doing nothing; it is not saying, "In God's good time

it will come to pass"—that often means in my abominably lazy time I let God work. Waiting means standing under, in active strength, enduring till the answer comes.

Never make the blunder of trying to forecast the way God is going to answer your prayer. When God made a tremendous promise to Abraham, he thought out the best way of helping God to fulfil His promise and did the wisest thing he knew according to flesh and blood common-sense reasoning. But for thirteen years God never spoke to him until every possibility of his relying on his own intelligent understanding was at an end. Then God came to him and said, "I am God Almighty"—El Shaddai—"walk before Me, and be thou perfect" (RV). Over and over again God has to teach us how to stand and endure, watching actively and wondering. It is always a wonder when God answers prayer. We hear people say, "We must not say it is wonderful that God answers prayer"; but it is wonderful. It is so wonderful that a great many people believe it impossible. Listen!—"Whatsoever ye shall ask in My name, that will I do." Isn't that wonderful? It is so wonderful that I do not suppose more than half of us really believe it. "Every one that asketh receiveth." Isn't that wonderful? It is so wonderful that many of us have never even asked God to give us the Holy Spirit because we don't believe He will. "If two of you shall agree on earth as touching any thing that they shall ask, it shall be done for them of My Father which is in heaven." Isn't that wonderful? It is tremendously wonderful. "The effectual fervent prayer of a righteous man availeth much." Isn't that wonderful?

Christian worker, you have had visions of how wonderfully God can answer prayer, are you watching to-day for Him to answer prayer along His line? Are you on your tower, watching stedfastly every sign of God's goings? Or are you coming under the bitter blight that came on Meroz? When the Spirit of the Lord came on Deborah, the prophetess of the Lord, what was her cry? "Curse ye Meroz, . . . curse ye bitterly the inhabitants thereof; because they came not to the help of the LORD . . . against the mighty." The first chapter of Habakkuk speaks of the tremendous devastations that are to come upon Israel (see vv. 1–11); apply it spiritually to our own day. The majority of us as saints are sound asleep to the devastation going on, and we shall come under the bitter curse of Meroz if we do not rouse ourselves up and stand with God against the mighty—spiritualism, super-naturalism, Christian Science, Millennial-dawnism[8]—all terribly wide-spread, sweeping, devouring errors. Are we thoroughly awake and watching, or are we crying in a cowardly way, "Tell us the thing that leaves us as we are; tell us the things that please us, that rouse us up and kindle us on our own lines; don't tell us about the perplexities you have as a prophet or handmaid of God regarding His work"? God grant that every child of His may get on the watch-tower and stand and watch. Immediately a difficulty comes on the horizon and clouds gather, where is the intense watching? We sulk and turn aside, we turn our backs on God and on His messengers, and say, "Thou hast not brought us into a land that floweth with milk and honey." God grant that in times of perplexity we may get back again to the watch-tower, back again to inspired waiting, back again to the wide-eyed wonder of a child at God's answers to our prayers.

Intelligent Witnessing
and will look forth to see what He will speak with me . . . (RV)

I do not think we have sufficiently the wondering spirit that the Holy Ghost gives. It is the child-spirit. A child is always wide-awake with wonder at the things it sees, and some of us as we get older are apt to forget that a child's wonder is nearer the truth than our older knowledge. When through Jesus Christ we are rightly related to God, we learn to watch and wait, and wait wonderingly. "I wonder how God will answer this prayer." "I wonder how God will answer the prayer the Holy Ghost is praying in me." "I wonder what glory God will bring to Himself out of the strange perplexities I am in." "I wonder what new turn His providence will take in manifesting Himself in my ways.'

The child-wondering Mind of the Holy Ghost, if I may say so reverently, was exhibited in the Lord Jesus Christ, everlasting wonder and expectancy at His Father's working. "For I have not spoken of Myself"; and, "the Father that dwelleth in Me, He doeth the works." Our Lord said that when the Holy Ghost is come, "He shall not speak of Himself; but whatsoever He shall hear, that shall He speak." The Lord Jesus spoke and worked from the great big Child-heart of God. God Almighty became Incarnate as a little Child, and Jesus Christ's message is, You must "become as little children." God always keeps the minds of His children open with wonder, with open-eyed expectancy for Him to come in where He likes. I wonder how many of us have been getting

our ideas and convictions and notions twisted. Thank God for the confusion if it is going to drive us straight to the watch-tower with God where our doctrines and creeds are going to be God's, not doctrines and creeds out of God's Book twisted to suit our preconceived ideas, but the doctrines of God woven into the flesh and blood tissues of our lives by the indwelling Holy Ghost—watching, waiting, wondering and witnessing.

Take all the Old Testament prophets, God never spoke with them without a corresponding wonder on their part. Over and over again the prophets were staggered with wonder at the strange things God did, and if they leaned to their own intelligence without sufficiently relying on the tremendous power of God, there was instant confusion. We have to "receive, recognise and rely on the Holy Ghost," and never get beyond that stage. God grant we may have the wonder of the child-heart which the Holy Ghost gives, and that He may keep our minds young and vigorous and un-stagnant, never asleep, but always awake with child-eyed wonder at the next wonderful thing God will do. "The LORD reigneth; let the earth rejoice"!

God grant we may get to the place where the only thing we take seriously is the place God has put us in, watching, waiting stedfastly for God's goings. Never take anything that is said by any man or woman, or in any book, without waiting and watching before God. "Try the spirits," test them, see if they be of God. I want you to beware of a mistake I have made over and over again in days gone by, of trying to interpret God's plan for other lives along the way He has led me. Never! Keep open-eyed in wonder. My brother, my sister, can God do what He likes in your life? Can He help Himself liberally to you? Can He take you up and put you down? Can He introduce His schemes through you, and never tell you the reason why? Can He make you a spectacle to men and angels, as He did Job, without giving you any explanation? Can He make you a wonder to yourself and to others, while He gives you the implicit child-like understanding that somehow or other things are working out all right?

Inviolable Walking
. . . Write the vision, and make it plain upon tables, that he may run that readeth it.

No longer watching and waiting, but actively set towards the Divine goal to which God is calling. Have you ever noticed the "wondering-ness" (if I may coin a word) of the people who go on with God? They never seem to be over-anxious or overconcerned, and

---

8. Millennial Dawnism: another name for Russellism or the Jehovah's Witnesses, founded by Charles Taze Russell.

they always seem to be getting younger. What is the characteristic of the people of this world who have not got the child-heart? They are always sighing; they have mental and spiritual rheumatism and neuralgia, moral twists and perversities, and nothing can rouse them. Why? They want the child-spirit, the Spirit that was given to the disciples after the Resurrection, and in its fullness at Pentecost, then nothing will turn them aside. After Pentecost there was the sword and great persecution and they were all scattered abroad, but nothing could stop them preaching the word. There was a hilarious shout all through these men's lives because of the mighty baptism of the Holy Ghost and fire. There was running then! No power on earth or heaven above or hell beneath could stop the tremendous strength of the child-life of the Holy Ghost in them. Have you got the wonder in your heart to-night, my brother, or are you sighing, "Thank God I have managed to squeeze enough grace out of God to last through this day"? Blessed be the Name of God, all the unsearchable riches of Christ are at your disposal!

Thank God for every life that is running in the strength of the tremendous vision. Keep your eyes on your file Leader, Jesus only, Jesus ever, "and make straight paths for your feet." Watch for His goings. When He stands and hides Himself in a cloud—stand, watch and wait. When the meaning is clear, then you will run. A vision puts enthusiasm into you, a thrilling understanding of God's Word and you soar above in a tremendous ecstasy; then you come down and run without being weary, and then you come to the grandest days and walk without fainting.

"For the vision is yet for an appointed time, but at the end it shall speak, and not lie: though it tarry, wait for it; because it will surely come, it will not tarry" (Habakkuk 2:3). "I heard the voice of the Lord, saying, Whom shall I send, and who will go for us?" That is a wonderful point—"Who will go for us?" "Lord, there is Mrs. So-and-so, she is ready, send her." Is that the answer you give "O Lord, I know there ought to be a movement in my Church, and there is Mr. So-and-so, he's just the one, send him." If you have been watching, waiting and wondering, you will say; "Here am I; send me." If God came to you to-night, would you say, "Here am I"? Do you know where you are? Some men live in a fog, they don't know where they are, but if you know anything about waiting on God and walking before Him, you will say, "Here am I, do what You like with me."

O Lord, explore down to the deepest springs of my spirit where Thy Spirit works, and read my deepest prayers I cannot pray in expression. Lord, touch my body, it is Thy temple, shine out in and through it, O Lord.

. . . .

O Lord, lift Thou up the light of Thy countenance upon us this day, and make us to fit in with Thy plans with great sweetness and light and liberty, and a lilt to Thee all day. . . . .
. . . .

O God my Father, the clouds are but the dust of Thy feet. Let me discover in every cloud of providence or nature or grace no man save Jesus only after the fear, till there be no fear.

Chapter V
AFTER GOD'S SILENCE—WHAT?

Now Jesus loved Martha, and her sister, and Lazarus. When He had heard therefore that he was sick, He abode two days still in the same place where He was.
John 11:5–6

The Absence of Audible Response
Jesus stayed two days where He was without sending a word. We are apt to say—"I know why God has not answered my prayer, it is because I asked for something wrong." That was not the reason Jesus did not answer Martha and Mary—they desired a right thing. It is quite true God does not answer some prayers because they are wrong, but that is so obvious that it does not need a revelation from God to understand it. God

wants us to stop understanding in the way we have understood and get into the place He wants us to get into, i.e., He wants us to know how to rely on Him.

God's silences are His answers. If we only take as answers those that are visible to our senses, we are in a very elemental condition of grace. Can it be said of us that Jesus so loved us that He stayed where He was because He knew we had a capacity to stand a bigger revelation? Has God trusted us with a silence, a silence that is absolutely big with meaning? That is His answer. The manifestation will come in a way beyond any possibility of comprehension. Are we mourning before God because we have not had an audible response? Mary Magdalene was weeping at the sepulchre—what was she asking for? The dead body of Jesus. Of Whom did she ask it? Of Jesus Himself, and she did not know Him! Did Jesus give her what she asked for? He gave her something infinitely grander than she had ever conceived—a risen, living impossible-to-die Lord. How many of us have been blind in our prayers? Look back and think of the prayers you thought had not been answered, but now you find God has answered them with a bigger manifestation than you ever dreamed. God has trusted you in the most intimate way He could trust you, with an absolute silence, not of despair but of pleasure, because He saw you could stand a much bigger revelation than you had at the time. Some prayers are followed by silence because they are wrong, others because they are bigger than we can understand. Jesus stayed where He was—a positive staying, because He loved them. Did they get Lazarus back? They got infinitely more; they got to know the greatest truth mortal beings ever knew—that Jesus Christ is the Resurrection and the Life. It will be a wonderful moment for some of us when we stand before God and find that the prayers we clamoured for in early days and imagined were never answered, have been answered in the most amazing way, and that God's silence has been the sign of the answer. If we always want to be able to point to something and say, "This is the way God answered my prayer," God cannot trust us yet with His silence. Here is where the devil comes in and says, "Now you have been praying a wrong prayer." You can easily know whether you have—test it by the word of God. If it has been a prayer to know God better, a prayer for the baptism of the Holy Ghost, a prayer for the interpretation and understanding of God's word, it is a prayer in accordance with God's will. You say, "But He has not answered." He has, He is so near to you that His silence is the answer. His silence is big with terrific meaning that you cannot understand yet, but presently you will. Time is nothing to God. Prayers were offered years ago and God answered the soul with silence; now He is giving the manifestation of the answer in a revelation that we are scarcely able to comprehend.

The Attitude of Awful Repose
Picture Martha and Mary waiting day after day for Jesus to come, yet not till Lazarus's body had been in the grave four days does Jesus Christ appear on the scene. Days of absolute silence, of awful repose on the part of God! Is there anything analogous to it in your life? Can God trust you like that, or are you still wanting a visible answer? "Every one that asketh receiveth." If God has given you a silence, praise Him. Think of the things you prayed to God about and tried to hold and, because of His love, He dare not let you hold

them and they went. For a time you said, "I asked God to give me bread and He gave me a stone"; He did not, and you find to-day He gave you the bread of life. You prayed that you might keep the thing that seemed to make your life as a Christian possible, you asked that it might always be preserved by God, and suddenly the whole thing went to pieces. That was God's answer. After the silence of God, if we are spiritual and can interpret His silence, we always get the trust in God that knows prayers are answered every time, not sometimes. The manifestation of the answer in place and time is a mere matter of God's sovereignty. Be earnest and eager on the line of praying. One wonderful thing about God's stillness in connection with your prayers is that He makes you still, makes you perfectly confident, the contagion of Jesus Christ's stillness gets into you—"I know He has heard me"—and His silence is the proof He has heard.

The Answer's Amazing Revelation
Could the answer that Jesus Christ gave ever have entered into the heart of Martha and Mary—a raised brother, the manifestation of the glory of God, and the understanding of Jesus Christ in a way that has blessed the Church for twenty centuries!

Remember that Jesus Christ's silences are always signs that He knows we can stand a bigger revelation than we think we can. If He gives you the exact answer, He cannot trust you yet. ".... if two of you shall agree on earth as touching any thing that they shall ask, it shall be done for them of My Father which is in heaven." That is stated for people who are not spiritual. Our Lord's revelations about prayer in Luke 11 and Luke 18 are for those who are spiritual—remain in confidence in prayer. Because Jesus Christ keeps silence it does not mean that He is displeased, but exactly the opposite, He is bringing us into the great run of His purpose, and the answer will be an amazing revelation. No wonder our Lord said, "... greater works than these shall he do.... And whatsoever ye shall ask in My name, that will I do" (John 14:12–13). That is what prayer means, not that God may bless us. As long as we have the idea only that God will bless us in answer to prayer, He will do it, but He will never give us the grace of a silence. If He is taking us into the understanding that prayer is for the glorifying of His Father, He will give us the first sign of His intimacy—silence. The devil calls it unanswered prayer; in the case of Martha and Mary the Spirit of God called it a sign that He loved them, and because He loved them and knew they were fit to receive a bigger revelation than ever they dreamed of, He stayed where He was. God will give us the blessings we want if we won't go any further, but His silence is the sign that He is bringing us into this marvellous understanding of Himself.

O Lord, for the power of Thy Spirit to adore Thee in fuller ways. Keep my spirit brightly infused by Thy Holy Spirit, O Lord, that thus energised, my Lord Jesus Christ and His perfections may be manifested in my mortal flesh.

. . . .

O Lord, breathe in me till I am one with Thee in the temper of my mind and heart and disposition,

unto Thee do I turn. How completely again I realise my lost-ness without Thee.

. . . .

O Lord, I have no inkling of Thy ways in external detail, but I have the expectancy of Thy wonders soon to be made visible. Lord, I look to Thee, how completely at rest I am, yet how free from seeing Thy way. Thou art God and I trust in Thee.

Chapter VI
NOW THIS EXPLAINS IT

As Thou, Father, art in Me, and I in Thee, that they also may be one in us. John 17:21

The Submissions of Life *(Luke 2:51; John 19:11)*

We are not built for ourselves, but for God, not for service for God, but for God; that explains the submissions of life.

"And He went down with them, . . . and He was subject unto them." An amazing submission! For thirty years Jesus lived at home with brothers and sisters who did not believe in Him, and when He began His ministry they said He was mad. "As He is, so are we in this world." We say, "When I was born again I thought it would be a time of great illumination and service, and instead of that I have had to stay at home with people who have criticised me and limited me on the right hand and on the left; I have been misunderstood and misrepresented." "The disciple is not above his master." Do we think our lot ought to be better than Jesus Christ's? We can easily escape the submissions if we like, but if we do not submit, the Spirit of God will produce in us the most ghastly humiliation before long. Knowing that Jesus has prayed for us makes us submit.

God is not concerned about your aims and mine. He does not say, "Do you want to go through this bereavement, this upset?" He allows these things for His own purpose. We may say what we like, but God does allow the devil, He does allow sin, He does allow bad men to triumph and tyrants to rule, and these things either make us fiends or they make us saints, it depends entirely on the relationship we are in towards God. If we say, "Thy will be done," we get the tremendous consolation of knowing that our Father is working everything according to His own wisdom. If we understand what God is after, we shall be saved from being mean[9] and cynical.

The things we are going through are either making us sweeter, better, nobler men and women, or they are making us more captious and fault-finding, more insistent on our own way. We are either getting more like our Father in heaven, or we are getting more mean and intensely selfish. How are we behaving ourselves in our circumstances? Do we understand the purpose of our life as never before? God does not exist to answer our prayers, but by our prayers we come to discern the mind of God, and that is declared in John 17, "That they may be one, even as We are one." Am I as close to Jesus as that? God will not leave me alone until I am. God has one prayer He must answer, and that is the prayer of Jesus Christ. It does not matter how imperfect or immature a disciple may be, if he will hang in, that prayer will be answered.

The Solitarinesses of Life *(Luke 4:1–2; 22:42)*

There was nothing to mark our Lord out from ordinary men saving that He was insulated within. He did not choose the solitary places, He was driven by the Spirit of God into the wilderness. It is not good for a man to be alone. Evil will make a man want to be alone. Jesus Christ does not make monks and nuns, He makes men and women fit for the world as it is (see John 17:15). We say, "I do wish Jesus did not expect so much of me." He expects nothing less than absolute oneness with Himself as He was one with His Father. God does not expect us to work *for* Him, but to work *with* Him.

Every man carries his kingdom within, and no one knows what is taking place in another's kingdom.

---

9. mean: as used here, something or someone ordinary, common, low, or ignoble, rather than cruel or spiteful.

"No one understands me!" Of course they don't, each one of us is a mystery. There is only One Who understands you, and that is God. Hand yourself over to Him.

Are you being subjected in this internal kingdom to tremendous temptations? Jesus was tempted of the devil, perhaps you are also, but no one guesses it. There is never any comrade for your soul when you are tempted. Temptation is the testing of the thing held; we hold from God the possibility of the answer to our Lord's prayer, and that is the line along which the temptation will come. This explains it—Jesus has prayed "that they may be one, even as We are one." Think of being one with Jesus, one in aim and purpose! Some of us are far off from this, and yet God will not leave us alone until we are one with Him, because Jesus has prayed that we may be. There is a risk in discipleship because God never shields us from the world, the flesh and the devil. Christianity is character, not a "show-business.'

If you are going through a solitary way, read John 17, it will explain exactly why you are where you are. Now you are a disciple you can never be as independent as you used to be. Jesus has prayed that you might be one with the Father as He is; are you helping God to answer His prayer, or have you another end for your life?

The Sublimity of Life *(John 17:22)*
And the glory which Thou gavest Me I have given them.

The glory of our Lord was the glory of a holy life, and that is what He gives to us. He gives us the gift of holiness, are we exercising it?

"The hope of His calling" is revealed in John 17, and it is the great light on every problem. God grant that we may remain true to that calling. "We will come unto him, and make Our abode with him," the triune God abiding with the saint. What does a man need to care after that!

> *O Lord, when I awake I am still with Thee. Quicken my mortal body with Thy mighty resurrection life; rouse me with a gracious flooding of Thy Divine life for this day.*

> *Lord, so much activity, so many things, so numberless the people, and yet Thou remainest! Bless today with largeness of heart and beauty of character for Thy glory. O Lord, unto Thee do I look up. Enlighten me, cause me to be radiant with Thy countenance. I praise Thee for Thy grace and for seeing a little of Thy marvellous doings; enable me more and more to manifest the life hid with Christ in God.*

> *Lord, through the dimness, come with dawning and drawing light. Breathe on me till I am in a pure radiant frame of body and mind for Thy work and for Thy glory this day.*

Chapter VII
PRAYING IN THE HOLY GHOST

Praying in the Holy Ghost. Jude 20

Praying always with all prayer and supplication in the Spirit. Ephesians 6:18

Praying in the Holy Ghost means the power given to us by God to maintain a simple relationship to Jesus Christ, and it is most difficult to realise this simple relationship in the matter of prayer.

Prayer Pervaded by Pentecost
We have to pray relying upon what has been revealed by the Sent-down Holy Ghost, and the first revelation is that we do not know how to pray (see Romans 8:26). We have to learn to draw on our relationship to Jesus Christ, and as we do, we realise that the Holy Ghost keeps us in simple relationship to our Lord while we pray. When we pray in the Holy Ghost we

are released from our petitions. "Your Father knoweth what things ye have need of, before ye ask Him." Then why ask? The whole meaning of prayer is that we may know God. The "asking and receiving" prayer is elementary, it is the part of prayer we can understand, but it is not necessarily praying in the Holy Ghost. Those who are not born again must ask and receive; but when we have received and have become rightly related to God, we must maintain this simplicity of belief in Him, while we pray, Our minds must be saturated by the Pentecostal revelation of prayer until we learn in every detail to pray in the Holy Ghost. Prayer is not an exercise, it is the life.

Peculiar Sense of Need
A great many people do not pray because they do not feel any sense of need. The sign that the Holy Ghost is

in us is that we realise, not that we are full, but that we are empty, there is a sense of absolute need. We come across people who try us, circumstances that are difficult, conditions that are perplexing, and all these things awaken a dumb sense of need, which is a sign that the Holy Ghost is there. If we are ever free from the sense of need, it is not because the Holy Ghost has satisfied us, but because we have been satisfied with as much as we have. "A man's reach should exceed his grasp." A sense of need is one of the greatest benedictions because it keeps our life rightly related to Jesus Christ.

Permeating Sense of Restraint

When we learn to pray in the Holy Ghost, we find there are some things for which we cannot pray, there is a sense of restraint. Never push and say, "I know it is God's will and I am going to stick to it." Beware, remember what is recorded of the children of Israel: "He gave them their request; but sent leanness into their soul" (Psalm 106:15). Let the Spirit of God teach you what He is driving at and learn not to grieve Him. If we are abiding in Jesus Christ we shall ask what He wants us to ask, whether we are conscious of doing so or not (see John 15:7).

Profound Sense of Christ's Work

When we pray relying on the Holy Ghost, He will always bring us back to this one point, that we are not heard because we are in earnest, or because we need to be heard, or because we will perish if we are not heard; we are heard only on the ground of the Atonement of our Lord (see Hebrews 10:19).

The efficacy of the atoning work of Christ is the one thing that the Holy Ghost works into our understanding, and as He interprets the meaning of that work to us we shall never bank on our own earnestness, or on our sense of need, nor shall we ever have the idea that God does not answer, we shall be so restfully certain that He always does.

The Holy Ghost will continually interpret to us that the only ground of our approach to God is "*by the blood of Jesus*," and by no other way. As we learn the spiritual culture of praying in the Holy Ghost, we shall find that the common-sense circumstances God puts us in, and the common-sense people His providence places us amongst, are used by Him to enable us to realise that the one fundamental thing in prayer is the atoning work of Jesus Christ.

Apprehension of God's Resources

When we pray in the Holy Ghost we begin to have a more intimate conception of God; the Holy Ghost brings all through us the sense of His resources. For instance, we may be called to a definite purpose for our life which the Holy Ghost reveals and we know that it means a decision, a reckless fling over on to God, a burning of our bridges behind us; and there is not a soul to advise us when we take that step saving the Holy Ghost. Our clingings come in this way—we put one foot on God's side and one on the side of human reasoning; then God widens the space until we either drop down in between or jump on to one side or the other. We have to take a leap, a reckless leap, and if we have learned to rely on the Holy Ghost, it will be a reckless leap on to God's side. So many of us limit our praying because we are not reckless in our confidence in God. In the eyes of those who do not know God, it is madness to trust Him, but when we pray in the Holy Ghost we begin to realise the resources of God, that He is our perfect heavenly Father, and we are His children.

Always keep an inner recollectedness that God is our Father through the Lord Jesus Christ.

Atmosphere for Work

Praying in the Holy Ghost gives us a true insight into why Paul said we wrestle not against flesh and blood, but against principalities and powers, against spiritual wickedness in high places.

If the Holy Spirit is having His way in us, He will charge the atmosphere round about us. There are things that have to be cleared away by the Holy Ghost. Never fight; stand and wrestle. Wrestling is not fighting, it is closing with the antagonist on your own ground, and maintaining a steady, all-embracing "stand" and "withstand." How many of us succumb to flesh and blood circumstances—"I did not sleep well"; or, "I have indigestion"; or, "I did not do quite the right thing there." Never allow any of these things to be the reason to yourself why you are not prevailing in prayer. There are hundreds of people with impaired bodies who know what it is to pray in the Holy Ghost.

In work for God never look at flesh and blood causes; meet every arrangement for the day in the power of the Holy Ghost. It makes no difference what your work is or what your circumstances are; if you are praying in the Holy Ghost He will produce an atmosphere round about you, and all these things will redound to the glory of God.

Apostolic Habit

"Pray without ceasing." Keep the child-like habit of continually ejaculating in your heart to God, recognise and rely on the Holy Ghost all the time. Inarticulate prayer, the impulsive prayer that looks so futile, is the thing God always heeds. The habit of ejaculatory prayer ought to be the persistent habit of each one of us.

Attitude of Daily Reaction

The way we react during the day will either hinder or help our praying. If we allow a state of reaction not born of a simple relationship to Jesus Christ, we shall have so much wilderness waste to get through before we can come to God, mists and shadows which come between our conscious life and the interceding Holy Ghost. The Holy Ghost is there all the time, but we have lost sight of Him by allowing things that have not sprung from our simple relationship to Jesus Christ. Anything that is so continually with us, even our religious life itself, that we never really pray in the Holy Ghost, may be a hindrance. The only one who prays in the Holy Ghost is the child, the child-spirit in us, the gay spirit of utter confidence in God. When we pray in the Holy Ghost, we bring to God the things that come quite naturally to our minds, and the Holy Ghost Who "maketh intercession for the saints according to the will of God" enables God to answer the prayer He Himself prays in your bodily temple and mine. ". . . that ye may be the children of your Father which is in heaven." The Holy Ghost cannot delight in our wisdom; it is the wisdom of God He delights in.

Have we recognised that our body is the temple of the Holy Ghost? If so, we must be careful that we keep it undefiled for Him. "My house shall be called a house of prayer," said Jesus.

Lord, how I desire to see Thee, to hear Thee, to meditate on Thee and to manifestly grow like Thee! And Thou hast said, \ "Delight thyself also in the LORD, and He shall give thee the desires of thine heart."

. . . .

O Lord, I know Thy blessing and I praise Thee, but it is the indescribable touch and enwheeling as Thy servant that I seek for—I know not what I fear for, but Thou knowest. How I long for Thee!

. . . .

Lord, I still move and live in a dim world, feeling Thee near by faith, but I will not presume. I would hide in Thee in security and patience until I am as Thou wouldst have me to be.

Chapter VIII

ST. PAUL'S INTERCESSION FOR INSTANTANEOUS INSISTENT SANCTIFICATION
1 Thessalonians 5:23–24

All through the Bible the separation of a people by God is revealed, and the individual members of that people have to separate themselves to God's service. We are set apart that we may set ourselves apart. God Who requires the separation requires also that the person be sanctified intrinsically too.

Two ideas are brought out in regard to our Lord: first, the Father separating Jesus for His redemptive work, "Say ye of Him, Whom the Father sanctified, and sent into the world, Thou blasphemest; because I said, I am the Son of God?" (John 10:36); second, Jesus sanctifying Himself for the work of God, "And for their sakes I sanctify Myself, that they also might be sanctified through the truth" (John 17:19). But our Lord was holy, why did He say "I sanctify Myself"? To coin a phrase, Jesus Christ "sanctified His sanctification," that is, He determinedly sacrificed His holy Self to His Father. Jesus Christ separated, or sanctified, Himself by sacrificing His holy Self to the will of

His Father; He sanctified His intelligence by submitting His intelligence to the word of His Father, and He sanctified His will by submitting His will to the will of His Father. As the sanctified children of God we need to bear in mind that after the experience of sanctification we have to separate our holiness to God. We are not made holy for ourselves, but for God, there is to be no insubordination about us.

The majority of us are too indifferent, too religiously sentimental, to be caught up into the sweep of the Apostle Paul's intercession. Have we a lesser idea than that God should do in us what He wants to do? Are we prepared to pray with Murray McCheyne,[10] "Lord, make me as holy as Thou canst make a sinner saved by grace"?

Some people pray and long and yearn for the experience of sanctification, but never get anywhere near it; others enter in with a sudden marvellous realisation. Sanctification is an instantaneous, continuous

---

10. Robert Murray McCheyne (1813–1843): Scottish minister whose short but intense life left a great impact on Scotland.

work of grace; how long the approach to it takes depends upon ourselves, and that leads some to say sanctification is not instantaneous. The reason why some do not enter in is because they have never allowed their minds to realise what sanctification means. When we pray to be caught up into God's purpose behind this intercession of the Apostle Paul, we must see that we are willing to face the standard of these verses. Are we prepared for what sanctification will cost? It will cost an intense narrowing of all our interests on earth, and an immense broadening of our interest in God. In other words, sanctification means an intense concentration on God's point of view— every power of spirit, soul and body chained and kept for God's purpose only. Sanctification means being made one with God, even as the Lord Jesus Christ was one—"that they may be one, even as We are one." That is much more than union, it is one in identity; the same disposition that ruled in Jesus rules in me. Am I prepared for what that will cost? It will cost everything that is not God in me. Am I prepared for God to separate me for His work in me, as He separated Jesus, and after His work is done, am I prepared to separate myself to God even as Jesus did? It is this settling down into God's truth that is needed.

The type of sanctified life is the Lord Jesus Christ, and the characteristic of His life was subordination to His Father. The only way to get right with God is to soak in the atmosphere of the life of the Lord Jesus.

The one mark of spiritual people to-day is insubordination. We have wild spiritual impulses that would give an opportunity to Satan as an angel of light to switch the very elect, if it were possible, away from God's plan. If you want to know the result of spiritual insubordination, read 1 Corinthians 12. There you will see a portrait of spiritual lunacy, absolute insubordination to the dominant sanity of the Spirit of God. The characteristic of the Holy Ghost in a man is a strong family likeness to Jesus and freedom from everything unlike Jesus.

The best of us are all too shallow and flippant in our attitude to this tremendous secret of sanctification. Are we prepared to let the Spirit of God grip us and put us under His searchlight, and then do a work in us that is worthy of God? Sanctification is not our idea of what we want God to do for us, sanctification is what God does for us, and He has to get us into the right relationship, the right attitude of mind and heart, where at any cost we let Him do it. Are we prepared to concentrate on the Holy Spirit's ministration?

The Apostle Paul is not talking about scientific truth, or intellectual truth, he is talking about spiritual truth, and the only way we can prove spiritual truth is by experience. People say, "I don't understand this doctrine of sanctification." Well, get into the experience first. You only get home by going there. You may think

about getting there, but you will never get there till you go. Am I prepared to do what Jesus said—"Come unto Me"? Am I prepared to let God make me real? Reality is the proof in my own experience that this thing is true. God grant that every worker may see the peril of not applying this spiritual logic—"Prove it." Every time we give a message that we have no experience of, the Spirit of God will bring it back to you—"Where are *you* in regard to this matter?"

The Value of Calm
And the God of peace Himself . . . (RV)

It is wonderful that by the guidance of the Holy Spirit, Paul puts the subsiding of suspicion in the first place. The very nature of the old disposition is an incurable suspicion that Jesus Christ cannot do what He came to do. Have you the tiniest suspicion that God cannot sanctify you in His Almighty way? Then you need to let the God of peace slip His great calm all through your insidious unbelief till all is quiet and there is one thing only—God and your soul; not the peace of a conscience at rest only, but the very peace of God which will keep you rightly related to God. "My peace I give unto you," said Jesus. When once you let the God of peace grip you by salvation and squeeze the suspicion out of you till you are quiet before Him, the believing attitude is born, there is no more suspicion, you are in moral agreement with God about everything He wants to do.

One of the things which we need to be cured of by the God of peace is the petulant struggle of doing things for ourselves—"I can sanctify myself; if I cut off this and that and the other I shall be all right." No, Paul says "*the very God of peace* sanctify you wholly," Has the God of peace brought you into a calm, or is there a clamour and a struggle still? Are you still hanging on to some obstinate conviction of your own?—still struggling with some particular line of things you want? "The God of peace Himself sanctify you wholly." If we are to be sanctified, it must be by the God of peace Himself. The power that makes the life of the saint does not come from our efforts at all, it comes from the heart of the God of peace. America has a phrase—"Pray through." What we have to "pray through" is all our petulant struggling after sanctification, all the inveterate suspicion in our hearts that God cannot sanctify us. When we are rid of all that and are right before God, then God lets us see how He alone does the work.

> *When we stay our feeble efforts,*
> *   And from struggling cease,*
> *Unconditional surrender*
> *   Brings us God's own peace.*

The great mighty power of the God of peace is slipped into the soul under the call for supreme sanctification. Some of us are far too turbulent in spirit to experience even the first glimpse of what sanctification means. People noisy in words are not always turbulent in spirit; excessively quiet people who have nothing to express in joy and shouting, may be suspicious in heart.

Value of Massive Truth
sanctify you wholly . . .

When once we get calm before God and are willing to let Him do what He chooses, He gives us an outline of some of His massive truths. "And the very God of peace sanctify you *wholly*" preserve you in unspotted integrity. Integrity is the unimpaired state of a thing, unblameable, undeserving of censure in God's sight. Paul's intercession is for an instantaneous and insistent sanctification that will preserve a man in unspotted integrity "unto the coming of our Lord Jesus Christ." The majority of us have never allowed our minds to dwell as they should on these great massive truths; consequently sanctification has been made to mean a second dose of conversion. Sanctification can only be named in the presence of God, it is stamped by a likeness to Christ.

"Wholly"—every detail, mystical, moral, material.

(a) Mystical
And I pray God your whole spirit . . . be preserved blameless . . .

The word "spirit" here is not the same as in verse 19. "Your whole spirit," i.e., the personality of a man imbued by the Spirit of God, the two never become identical, they become identified. A man's spirit is imbued with the Spirit of God till all the highest mystical reaches of his personality are living in God. Where are our imaginations? where are all the fancies that break through language and escape? where do they live? where are our dreams that make us afraid of ourselves? The modern psychological phrase is subconscious, super-conscious, beyond the range of what we are able to grasp. The great mystic work of the Holy Ghost is in those dim regions of personality where we cannot go. If you want to know what those regions are like, read Psalm 139. The Psalmist implies—"Thou art the God of the early mornings, the God of the late-at-nights, the God of the mountain peaks, the God of the sea; but, my God, my soul has further horizons than the early mornings, deeper darkness than the nights of earth, higher peaks than any mountain, greater depths than any sea can know. My God, Thou art the God of these, be my God! I cannot reach to the heights or depths, there are motives I cannot touch, dreams I cannot fathom, God search me, winnow out my way."

When God gives His calm, do we realise the magnitude of sanctification through His omnipotent might? Do we believe that God can garrison our imaginations, can sanctify us far beyond where we can go? Have we realised that if we walk in the light, as God is in the light, the blood of Jesus Christ cleanses us from all sin? If that means cleansing from sin in conscious experience only, God Almighty have mercy on us! The man who has become obtuse through sin is unconscious of sin. Being cleansed by the blood of Jesus means cleansing to the very heights and depths of our spirit if we walk in the light as God is in the light. None of us soak sufficiently in the terrific Godlike revelation of sanctification, and many a child of God would never have been led astray by the counterfeits of Satan if they had allowed their minds to be bent on that great conception of Paul's, "your whole spirit"—from the vague beginnings of personality known only to God, to the topmost reach, preserved entire, garrisoned by the God of peace.

(b) Moral
Your whole . . . soul preserved blameless . . .

There are those who want to form religion on mysticism—live according to your temperament. Every sanctified soul is a mystic, but he does not live in that region only, he is soul and body as well as spirit, and what is true in the mystical sphere is true in the moral sphere. Soul is man's spirit becoming rational in the body, explaining itself. When a little child wants to say something and has not a vocabulary, it speaks through gesticulations and facial workings, it has not the power of soul to express itself in words. Paul says not only "your whole *spirit* preserved blameless," but "your whole *soul*." Are we forming the mind of Christ? A man has the Spirit of Jesus given to him, but he has not His mind until he forms it. How are we to form the mind of Christ? By letting His Spirit imbue our spirit, our thinking, our reasoning faculties, then we shall begin to reason as Jesus did, until slowly and surely the very Spirit that fed the life of Jesus will feed the life of our soul.

Sanctification covers not only the narrow region where we begin the spiritual life, but the whole rational man, sanctified wholly in imagination and reasoning power. How do you read history? Do you discern the arm of the Lord behind it? How do you sum up the circumstances of your own life? "The sun shall no more be thy light by day; neither for brightness shall the moon give light unto thee; but the Lord shall be unto thee an everlasting light, and thy God thy glory." The light on the inside will guide you, a reasoning soul, to understand the facts revealed by common days and nights you cannot understand otherwise. A humble, ignorant man or woman depending on the mind of God has an explanation for things that the rational man without the Spirit of God never has.

(c) Material
. . . Your whole . . . body preserved blameless.

Man is not only mystical and moral, but material; never say because you have a body you cannot progress. According to the Apostle Paul the body is unutterably sacred. The Bible does not say that the body is a curse and a hindrance, it says it is "the temple of the Holy Ghost." "What? know ye not that your body is the temple of the Holy Ghost?" It is only when garrisoned by the God of peace that the stupendous sanctity of the Holy Ghost preserves a man, spirit, soul and body, in unspotted integrity, without blame, unto the coming of Jesus. Our whole body is preserved as we come into contact with all the different relationships of life. In the beginning of spiritual education we are apt to pay too much attention to one of these spheres and Satan gets his chance with the others. If we pay attention to the spiritual, Satan will pay attention to the nerves.

Sanctification is an instantaneous, continuous work of God; immediately we are related rightly to God it is manifested instanter in spirit, soul and body. The reason the Church as a whole does not believe it is because they will not soak in the massive truths of God, consequently every now and again in the history of the Church, God has had to raise up some servant of His to emphasise afresh this intense, vivid,

sanctification of the whole spirit, the whole soul, and the whole body, preserved blameless unto the coming of our Lord Jesus Christ.

> *O Lord, my approach to Thee is dulled because of my physical dimness, but my spirit and heart rejoice in Thee and my flesh shall rest in hope. Touch me bodily, O Lord, till I answer in thrilling health to Thy touch.*

. . . .

> *Insulate me, O Lord, from the things of sense and time, and usher me into the presence of the King.*

. . . .

> *O Lord, I am distressed at my slow manifestation of any of the beauty of holiness that might express my unspeakable gratitude for Thy salvation, such lack of the winsome. O Lord, cause me by looking to Thee to be radiant (RV).*

. . . .

> *O Lord, I would bless and praise Thee. How hard I find it to praise Thee when I am not physically fit, and yet why should it—that means that I praise Thee when it is a pleasure to me physically. O Lord, that my soul were one continual praise to Thee.*

ADDRESS AT AUTUMNAL GATHERING, LEAGUE OF PRAYER, LONDON, NOVEMBER 6, 1912

Chapter IX

THIS DAY IS THAT DAY

And in that day ye shall ask Me nothing. Verily, verily, I say unto you, Whatsoever ye shall ask the Father in My name, He will give it you. John 16:23

Unperplexed Realisation
That "day" extends from Pentecost to the day of our Lord's return. Our Lord had just been telling His disciples that He is going to His Father, and explaining to them what this going meant. It meant, as far as He was concerned, that He would be omnipresent, omnipotent and omniscient. Recall how the disciples had questioned our Lord Jesus Christ up till then, but Jesus said, "In that day ye shall ask Me no question" (RV). The day our Lord was referring to was the day we know in the annals of the Church as the Day of Pentecost, that is, the Day of the Spirit of God. What a wonderful day to live in!

Unquestioned Revelation
After the Resurrection our Lord breathed on these questioning, perplexed, confused, loyal disciples, and said, "Receive ye the Holy Ghost"; if you read the accounts in St. John and St. Luke you will find it recorded that their eyes were opened and they knew Him; their understandings were opened and they knew the Scriptures; their inner consciences were opened and they knew that they had received from their Risen Lord the very Spirit that ruled Him.

Is it possible to sit down unperplexed while lives are being blasted in the most terrible way right in our very cities? Does it mean that we are to sit with folded hands and ask no questions? No, it means something much more sublime and practical than that. It means that in the profound regions of our lives we know that God is at work, the Holy Spirit has revealed Him, and

He is taking us slowly into His counsels. "Whatsoever He shall hear, that shall He speak: and He will shew you things to come" (John 16:13).

Undeflected Reflection

This does not mean that the soul who has received the Holy Spirit can demand that God tell him His secrets, it means that he is lifted to the privilege of entering into God's counsels with Christ Jesus. Great darkness, exasperating providences, but the inner secret of the Lord is with those who have His Spirit.

Read John 16 and you will find our Lord did not mean that life would be free from external perplexities, because He says, "They shall put you out of the synagogues: yea, the time cometh, that whosoever killeth you will think that he doeth God service" (v. 2). Through it all comes the unquestioning revelation that as Christ knew His Father's mind and heart, by the mighty baptism of the Holy Ghost Jesus can lift any soul into the heavenly places with Him so that the counsel and understanding of God's mind might be revealed.

If we have been going on with Jesus Christ we have come to the day of unquestioning revelation, that is, we know what John meant when he said, "But ye have an unction from the Holy One, and ye know all things," and, "the same anointing teacheth you of all things." The meaning of that is very practical and sane—Test all you hear, all you read, by this inner anointing, by the indwelling Spirit; He will test all the truth of God.

Undisturbed Relation

Verily, verily, I say unto you, Whatsoever ye shall ask the Father in My name . . .

That day is not only a day of unquestioning revelation, but a day of undisturbed relationship between God and ourselves. Just as Jesus stood unsullied in the presence of His Father, so by the mighty efficacy of the indwelling Holy Ghost we can be lifted up into the same relationship. "That they may be one, even as We are one." "Whatsoever ye shall ask the Father in My name"—i.e., in My nature—"He will give it you."

When we are born of the Holy Ghost, when we are related to God and bear the same family likeness to God that Jesus bore—which, blessed be the Name of God, we may do by the wonderful Atonement of the Lord Jesus Christ made living and efficacious in us by this mighty Spirit of God—in that day we, too, can have this undisturbed relation to God.

Undisguised Recognition

. . . He will give it you.

Jesus said that God will recognise our prayers. What a challenge! Had Jesus any right to say it? Have we faced it for one moment? Is it possible that the Lord Jesus Christ means that by His Resurrection power, by His Ascension power, by the power of the Sent-down Holy Ghost, He can lift us into such a relationship with God that we are at one with the perfect sovereign will of God by our free choice as Jesus was? Does He mean what He says?

"Hitherto have ye asked nothing in My name"—How could they ask anything in His name when He had not yet sent forth that marvellous Holy Spirit? "Ask, and ye shall receive, that your joy may be full." Now we begin to understand why Jesus said, "Ye shall ask Me no question" (RV), because the Holy Spirit in that day glorified Jesus and revealed Him to them, and brought back to their remembrance His words and led them into their meaning.

Thank God, when clouds are around the saint knows that they are but the dust of the Father's feet, and when the shadows are dark and terrible and the soul seems to fear externally as it enters the cloud, he finds "no man any more, save Jesus only with themselves." In that wonderful position, placed there in that Day, this day, we can pray to God in the nature of Jesus Christ, gifted to us by the Holy Ghost, and Jesus Christ's sovereign character is tested by His own statement, "Verily, verily, I say unto you, whatsoever ye shall ask the Father in My name, *He will give it you.*"

O Lord, Thou art God, Holy and Almighty, and Thou doest all things well. Show Thyself to us this day. Lord, for myself I would make petition to see Thee; draw me near to Thee that I may know Thee and have rare communion with Thee.

. . . .

Lord, for the days of the past holiday I praise and thank Thee, for my lying fallow to Thy grace; for the many prayers that have surrounded me like an atmosphere of heaven.

. . . .

O Lord, save us from the murmuring spirit which with the majority of us is merely skin deep, but it is harmful, hurting the bloom of spiritual communion. Keep our life hid with Christ in God.

Chapter X

INTERCESSION
Genesis 18:23–33

And the LORD *went His way, . . . and Abraham returned unto his place. Genesis 18:33*

The great difficulty in intercession is myself, nothing less or more. The first thing I have to do is to take myself to school. My first duty is not to assert freedom, but to find an absolute Master. We think that to be without a master is the sign of a high type of life; insurgent, impertinent human beings have no master, noble beings have. I must learn not to take myself too seriously. Myself is apt to be my master, I pray to myself. We are all Pharisees until we are willing to learn to intercede. We must go into heaven backwards, that phrase means we must grow into doing some definite thing by praying, not by seeing. To learn this lesson of handling a thing by prayer properly is to enter a very severe school. A Christian's duty is not to himself or to others, but to Christ. We think of prayer as a preparation for work, or a calm after having done work, whereas prayer is the essential work. It is the supreme activity of everything that is noblest in our personality. We won't bring down to earth what we see in vision about our Master, we "moon" around it in devotional speculations, but we won't bring it straight down to mother earth and work it out in actualities.

The Strength and Self-Limitation of Intercession

If any man see his brother sin a sin which is not unto death, he shall ask, and He shall give him life for them that sin not unto death. There is a sin unto death: I do not say that he shall pray for it. (1 John 5:16)

How are we going to know when a man has sinned a sin unto death and when he has not? Only through intercession. If we make our own discernment the judge, we are wrong. We base it all on an abstract truth divorced from God, we pin our faith on what God has done and not on the God Who did it, and when the case begins to go wrong again, we do not intercede, we begin to scold God. We get fanatical, we upset the court of heaven by saying, "I must do this thing." That is not intercession, that is rushing in where angels fear to tread. It is fanatical frenzy, storming the throne of God and refusing to see His character while sticking true to our assertions of what He said He would do. Beware of making God run in the mould of His own precedent, that means, because He

did a certain thing once, He is sure to do it again, which is so much of a truth that it becomes an imperceptible error when we subtly leave God Himself out of it. Frenzy—no strength and no self-limitation. We have taken ourselves so seriously that we cannot even see God, we are dictating to God.

The Redemption of our Lord Jesus Christ mirrored in the Atonement embraces everything. Sin, sickness, limitation and death are all done away with in Redemption; but we have to remember the Atonement works under God's dispensational sovereignty. It is not a question of whether God will sovereignly permit us to be delivered from sin in this dispensation, it is His distinct expressive will that we should be delivered. When it comes to the question of sickness and limitation, it is not a question of whether we will agree with God's will, but whether God's sovereignty is active—that predispensational efficacy of the Atonement on our behalf just now. When people come to the Atonement and say—"Now I have deliverance in the Atonement, therefore I have no business to be sick," they make a fundamental confusion, because there is no case of healing in the Bible that did not come from a direct intervention of the sovereign touch of God. When it comes to deliverance from sin, it is not a question of going to God to ask Him to deliver us from sin, it is a question of accepting His deliverance. If we forget that, we take the Lord out of the Atonement and make it an abstract statement and instantly do the Pharisaic dodge of putting burdens on people that they cannot bear. Logically they are perfectly correct, it is all in the Atonement, but if it is true that in the Atonement there should be no sickness, it is also true that there should be no death, then we have no business to die! We have no business to have any human limitations, we should be in complete unbroken communion with God, and the people who teach the present resurrection are logically consistent with the folks who say the health of the body depends entirely on our acceptance of the Atonement. To say we are in resurrection bodies now means a moral pig-sty, and makes a burlesque of the whole thing; the mistake is putting an abstract truth deduced from God in the place of God Himself. Abraham had none of the fanatical in him, he did not stand true to what God said, but to God Who said it. God said, "Offer up Isaac," and then God said, "Don't." A fanatic would have said," I will stick to what God has said, this other voice is of the devil." Watch when some providence of God is going against what we have asserted God will always do. One of the most significant lessons is to see the rod of rebuke come on the people who insist on asserting that they know the meaning of the providential working of Christ's Atonement in the times in which we live. That God does give wonderful gifts of the Atonement before their dispensation is clear, there are innumerable cases of healing, but if I make that the ground on which God must work, I intercede no longer, I cannot, I become a dictator to God. When anyone is sick, I do not pray, I say, "They have no business to be sick," and that means I have destroyed altogether my contact with God.

The Sagacity and Submissiveness of Intercession

Be not ye therefore like unto them: for your Father knoweth what things ye have need of, before ye ask Him. (Matthew 6:8)

Our understanding of God is the answer to prayer; getting things from God is God's indulgence of us. When God stops giving us things, He brings us into the place where we can begin to understand Him. As long as we get from God everything we ask for, we never get to know Him, we look upon Him as a blessing-machine, that has nothing to do with God's character or with our characters. "Your Father knoweth what things ye have need of, before ye ask Him." Then why pray? To get to know your Father. It is not sufficient for us to say, "Oh yes, God is love," we have to know He is love, we have to struggle through until we do see He is love and justice, then our prayer is answered.

The nearer Abraham comes to God in his intercession, the more he recognises his entire unworthiness. There is a subtle thing that goes by the name of unworthiness which is petulant pride with God. When we are shy with other people it is because we believe we are superior to the average person and we won't talk until they realise our importance. Prayerlessness with God is the same thing, we are shy with God not because we are unworthy, but because we think God has not given enough consideration to our case, we have some peculiar elements He must be pleased to consider. We have to go to school in order to learn not to take ourselves seriously and to get the genuine unworthiness which no longer is shy before God. A child is never shy before its mother, and a child of God is not, it is conscious of its worthiness, i.e., its entire dependence.

"And he said, Oh, let not the Lord be angry, and I will speak yet but this once: Peradventure ten shall be found there. And He said, I will not destroy it for ten's sake"

(Genesis 18:32). Abraham does the interceding while the angels go for the final test, after the final test, prayer is impossible. The way Abraham reached the stopping-point is indicated by the fact that he was in complete and entire communion with God through the progress of his intercession. When we come up against things in life, are we going to cave in and say we cannot understand them? We understand them by intercession, and by our intercession God does things He does not show us just now, although He reveals more and more of His character to us. He is working out His new creations (RV) in the world through His wonderful Redemption and our intercession all the time, and we have to be sagacious, not impudent.

The Shamelessness and Strenuousness of Intercession

I say unto you, Though he will not rise and give him, because he is his friend, yet because of his importunity he will rise and give him as many as he needeth. (Luke 11:8)

Strenuousness means whipping ourselves up, and jeering at ourselves till we sit down no more. Never give yourself any encouragement, only encourage yourself in God. "And He spake a parable unto them to this end, that men ought always to pray, and not to faint" (Luke 18:1). It is a pleasant business to faint, everyone else has all the bother. "God will give it to me in His good time." He cannot until we intercede. Be at the business, use some perspiration of soul, get at the thing, and all of a sudden you will come to the place where you will say, "Now I see," but I defy you to tell anyone what you saw until they come to where you are—

Oh could I tell, ye surely would believe it!
Oh could I only say what I have seen!
How should I tell or how can ye receive it,
How, till He bringeth you where I have been?

The point is that we have come to understand God. It is never God's will for us to be dummies or babies spiritually, it is God's will for us to be sons and daughters of God, but He does not prevent us paying the price of being sons and daughters. He makes us sons and daughters potentially, and then sends us out to be sons and daughters actually. Are we prepared to go into the shameless business of prayer? that is, are we prepared to get to the right understanding of God in this matter? We can only get it by one way, not by disputing or controversy, but by prayer. Keep at it. We have no business to remain in the dark about the character of our Father when He has made His character very clear to us. The Sermon on the Mount has more to do with prayer than anything else. It means an end of self-indulgence in the body, in the mind, in the spirit, self-indulgence in anything and everything and a strenuous determination to get to understand God in this matter.

The Sacrament and Substitution of Intercession

And He cometh unto the disciples, and findeth them asleep, and saith unto Peter, What, could ye not watch with Me one hour? (Matthew 26:40)

It is a great thing to watch with God rather than put God to the trouble of watching me in case I burn myself. We tax the whole arrangement of heaven to watch us, while God wants us to come and watch with Him, to be so identified with Him that we are not causing Him any trouble, but giving Him perfect delight because He can use us now instead of taxing some other servants of heaven to look after us.

O Lord, my Lord, I come to Thee this morning with a sense of spiritual failure. Cleanse me by Thy grace and restore me to the heavenly places in Christ Jesus. O that the sweet kindness of Jesus were more and more manifest in me.

. . . .

O Lord, Thou knowest, in eager helpless trust I look up. O that in power and peace and purity and grace Thou wouldst shine forth in power, in grace and glory this day.

. . . .

O Lord, the range of Thy power, the touch of Thy grace, the breathing of Thy Spirit, how I long for these to bring me face to face with Thee; Lord, by Thy grace cause me to appear before Thee.

AFTERNOON ADDRESS AT FOUNDER'S DAY, THE ANNUAL MEETINGS OF THE PENTECOSTAL LEAGUE OF PRAYER, LONDON, MAY 5, 1915.

Chapter XI

THE KEY TO SERVICE

Pray ye therefore the Lord of the harvest, that He will send forth labourers into His harvest. Matthew 9:38

This is the key to the whole problem of Christian work. It is simple in words, but amazingly profound, because our Lord Jesus Christ said it.

Our Master's Orders

Pray ye therefore . . .

Prayer is usually considered to be devotional and more or less unpractical in ordinary life. Our Lord in His teaching always made prayer, not preparation for work, but *the* work. Thank God for all the marvellous organisation there is in Christian work, for medical missions and finely educated missionaries, for aggressive work in every shape and form; but these are, so to speak, but wards to the lock, the key is not in any of our organisations, the key lies exactly to our hand by our Lord's instruction, "Pray ye therefore."

"Verily, verily, I say unto you, He that believeth on Me, the works that I do shall he do also; and greater works than these shall he do; because I go unto My Father. And whatsoever ye shall ask in My name that will I do, that the Father may be glorified in the Son" (John 14:12–13). Have the "greater works" been done? They certainly have. The men our Lord said these words to wrote the New Testament, and the reason they wrote it is that our Lord when He was glorified sent forth the personal Paraclete, the Holy Ghost not only in His power—His power and influence were at work before Pentecost—but He sent Him forth on to this earth personally where He is to this hour, and through His might and inspiration were produced the "greater works," i.e., the New Testament.

But what does it mean for us? Have we also to do greater works than Jesus did? Certainly we have, if our Lord's words mean anything, they mean that; and the great basis of prayer is to realise that we must take our orders from our Master. He put all the emphasis on prayer, and He made prayer not preparation for the work, not a sentiment nor a devotion, but *the* work. There is a real danger of worshipping prayer instead of praying because we worship. It is easy to do it if once we lose sight of our Lord and the emphasis is put not on His command, but on the thing which He commands.

We pray on the great fundamental basis of Redemption, and our prayers are made efficacious by the wonderful presence of the personal Holy Ghost in the world. Prayer is simple, prayer is supernatural, and to anyone not related to our Lord Jesus Christ, prayer is apt to look stupid. It does sound unreasonable to say that God will do things in answer to prayer, yet our Lord said that He would. Our Lord bases everything on prayer, then the key to all our work as Christians is, "Pray ye therefore."

When we pray for others the Spirit of God works in the unconscious domain of their being that we know nothing about, and the one we are praying for knows nothing about, but after the passing of time the conscious life of the one prayed for begins to show signs of unrest and disquiet. We may have spoken until we are worn out, but have never come anywhere near, and we have given up in despair. But if we have been praying, we find on meeting them one day that there is the beginning of a softening in an enquiry and a desire to know something. It is that kind of intercession that does most damage to Satan's kingdom. It is so slight, so feeble in its initial stages that if reason is not wedded to the light of the Holy Spirit, we will never obey it, and yet it is that kind of intercession that the New Testament places most emphasis on, though it has so little to show for it. It seems stupid to think that we can pray and all that will happen, but remember to Whom we pray, we pray to a God Who understands the unconscious depths of personality about which we know nothing, and He has told us to pray. The great Master of the human heart said, "Greater works than these shall he do. . . . And whatsoever ye shall ask in My name, that will I do."

Not only is prayer the work, but prayer is the way whereby fruit abides. Our Lord puts prayer as the means to fruit-producing and fruit-abiding work; but remember, it is prayer based on His agony, not on our agony. "Ye have not chosen Me, but I have chosen you, and ordained you, that ye should go and bring forth fruit, and that your fruit should remain: that whatsoever ye shall ask of the Father in My name, He may give it you" (John 15:16).

Prayer is not only the work and the way fruit abides, but prayer is the battle. "Put on the whole armour of God, . . . Stand therefore, . . ." and then pray. Paul says, "Praying always . . . for all saints, and for me" (see Ephesians 6:11–19). Do we remember to pray on the ground of our Lord's orders for all who minister in His Name? If the Apostle Paul earnestly solicited prayer on his behalf that he might "make known with boldness the mystery of the Gospel, " (RV) surely it behoves us to remember that this is the key our Lord puts into our hands for all Christian work; not prayer because we are helpless, but prayer because God is Almighty.

Our Master's Ownership
the Lord of the harvest . . .

Jesus did not say, "Go into the field," He said, "Pray ye therefore the Lord of the harvest. . . ." That does not so much mean that the harvest is the world, it means that there are innumerable people who have reached a crisis in their life, they are "white already to harvest." We find them everywhere, not only in the foreign field, but in the people living beside us, and the way we discern it is not by intellect, not by suggestions, but by prayer. Think of the countless crises in people's lives at this time; they are at the parting of the ways, "Say not ye, There are yet four months, and then cometh harvest? behold, I say unto you, Lift up your eyes, and look on the fields; for they are white already to harvest." "Pray ye therefore the Lord of the harvest, that He will send forth labourers into His harvest."

When we read the concluding verses in St. Matthew's Gospel, we are apt to put the emphasis on the fact that Jesus said, "Go ye therefore, and teach all nations," whereas the emphasis should be on "Go" because "All power is given unto Me in heaven and in earth." Then the "going" is in perfect order, putting the emphasis where our Lord puts it. " Go ye therefore, . . . and, lo, I am with you alway," that He may work His mighty works through us.

Our Master's Option
. . . that He will send forth labourers into His harvest.

There is only one field of service that has no snares, and that is the field of intercession. All other fields have the glorious but risky snare of publicity; prayer has not. The key to all our work for God is in that one word we are apt to despise—"Pray." And prayer is "labourer" work.

The reason prayer is so important is, first because our Lord told us that prayer on the ground of His Redemption is the most mighty factor He has put into our hands, and second, because of the personal presence of the Holy Ghost in the day in which we live. We receive our knowledge of the Holy Ghost not by experience first, but by the testimony of the Lord Jesus Christ. The testimony of Jesus Christ regarding the Holy Ghost is that He is here, and the real living experience the Holy Spirit works in us is that all His emphasis is laid on glorifying our Lord Jesus Christ. We know the Holy Spirit first by the testimony of Jesus, and then by the conscious enjoyment of His presence.

"Pray ye therefore." Prayer is labour, not agony, but labour on the ground of our Lord's Redemption in simple confidence in Him. Prayer is simple to us because it cost Him so much to make it possible to us. God grant that we may work His victories for Him by taking His way about it.

> *O Lord, this morning disperse every mist, and shine clear and strong and invigoratingly. Forgive my tardiness, it takes me so long to awaken to some things.*

> *Lord God Omniscient, give me wisdom this day to worship and work aright and be wellpleasing to*

Thee. Lord, interpret Thyself to me more and more in fulness and beauty.

. . . .

Dark and appalling are the clouds of war and wickedness and we know not where to turn, but, Lord God, Thou reignest.

Chapter XII
THE UNREALISED LOGIC OF PRAYER
Romans 8:26–28

Praying always with all prayer and supplication in the Spirit. Ephesians 6:18

Praying in the Holy Ghost. Jude 20

Ephesians 6:18 and Jude 20 are not quite identical with Romans 8:26. In the former it is man praying in the atmosphere produced by the Holy Spirit indwelling and surrounding him; in the latter the Holy Spirit Himself is praying in man. The similarity is obvious, but the point of difference is often missed in thinking about prayer. We realise that we are energised by the Holy Spirit for prayer, we know what it is to pray in the atmosphere and the presence of the Holy Spirit; but we do not so often realise that the Holy Spirit Himself prays in us with prayers that we cannot utter.

The Unrealised Philosophy of Prayer
(Romans 8:26)

The great thought which we do not realise sufficiently is the interchanging action of the Divine Spirit and the human spirit. This interchanging action of the Divine and human at every stage of our religious life is vividly expressed here. The best example of the Divine Spirit working in a human spirit is seen in our Lord Jesus Christ in the days of His flesh. According to some expositors, we are so infirm that the Spirit of God brushes aside all our infirmities and prays irrespectively of us, but we find that our Lord recognised the difference between His own Spirit and the Spirit of God, and that His mind was always in subordination to the mind of God. "I can of Mine own self do nothing."

(a) The Uncovered Truth of Our Infirmities
Likewise the Spirit also helpeth our infirmities . . .

To ask how we are to get our prayers answered is a different point of view from the New Testament. According to the New Testament, prayer is God's answer to our poverty, not a power we exercise to obtain an answer. We have the idea that prayer is only an exercise of our spiritual life. "Pray without ceasing." We read that the disciples said to our Lord, "Lord, teach us to pray." The disciples were good men

and well-versed in Jewish praying, yet when they came in contact with Jesus Christ, instead of realising they could pray well, they came to the conclusion they did not know how to pray at all, and our Lord instructed them in the initial stages of prayer. Most of us can probably remember a time when we were religious, before we were born again of the Spirit of God, when we could pray fairly well; but after we were born again we became conscious of what Paul mentions here, our utter infirmity—"I do not know how to pray." We become conscious not only of the power God has given us by His Spirit, but of our own utter infirmity. We hinder our life of devotion when we lose the distinction in thinking between these two. Reliance on the Holy Spirit for prayer is what Paul is bringing out in this verse. It is an unrealised point, we state it glibly enough, but Paul touches the thing we need to remember, he uncovers the truth of our infirmity, The whole source of our strength is receiving, recognising and relying on the Holy Spirit.

(b) The Unsyllabled Torment of Our Inability
for we know not what we should pray for as we ought . . .

The only platform from which the holiest saint on earth is ever heard is the platform mentioned in Hebrews 10:19, viz., we have "boldness to enter into the holiest by the blood of Jesus." There is no other way. When we come into the presence of God, the human side of our praying makes us realise what Paul is trying to teach, that if we are ever going to approach God and pray acceptably, it must be by the "piece of God" in us which He has given us. Some of the qualities of God must be merged into us before our prayers can be fit for His acceptance. We are all familiar with Luke 11:13, but we do not always remember that our Lord spoke the words in connection with receiving the Holy Spirit for prayer. Paul in Romans 8:26 beats out into gold leaf the nugget that our Lord gives in Luke 11:13. When I realise that I cannot approach God, that I cannot see as God sees, that I am choked up with things my eyes see and my flesh wants, and the empty spaces round my heart want, then Jesus says, "If you, being evil,"—you know that is your infirmity—"if you ask God for the Holy Spirit, He will give Him to you." That is, God will be merged into me, and I can begin to think about real prayer, relying on what God has planted in me for prayer. Otherwise we could never get near Him, the crush of our infirmities would paralyse the words on our lips. We can only pray acceptably in the Spirit, that is, by the Holy Spirit in us, all the rest is being "cumbered about." The disposition of sin is removed in sanctification, there is no doubt about that; but Paul insists that the body is not changed, the body we had and which was ruled by the wrong disposition of sin still remains (see Romans 6:12–19). We have to use that body now and make it a slave to the new disposition, and we have to realise the need to do it more in prayer than in anything else.

(c) The Unutterable Tenderness of the Intercession
... but the Spirit Itself maketh intercession for us with groanings which cannot be uttered.

The spirit of a man, whether it be energised by the Spirit of God or not, is bound to try and express itself in the body, which becomes its soul manifest; if it refuses to express itself in a rational way, it will express itself in an irrational, stupid way. When the Spirit of God comes in and energises the spirit of a man, what happens is that he is taken up into the great mystery of the Holy Ghost interceding in him along a particular line. If the Holy Spirit is allowed to dwell in the human spirit He has energised, He will express the unutterable. Think what that means. It means being quickened by the incoming of the Holy Spirit Who comes in to dwell supremely, and the amazing revelation is that He intercedes in us, for us, with a tenderness exactly in accordance with the Mind of God.

Have we ever allowed our minds to dwell on this element of prayer? "The sinner out of heart with self is nearest God in prayer." It is a mistake to interpret prayer on the natural instead of on the spiritual line, to say that because prayer brings us peace and joy and makes us feel better, therefore it is a Divine thing. This is the mere accident or effect of prayer, there is no real God-given revelation in it. This is the God-given revelation: that when we are born again of the Spirit of God and indwelt by the Holy Spirit, He intercedes for us with a tenderness and an understanding akin to the Lord Jesus Christ and akin to God, that is, He expresses the unutterable for us.

The Unrivalled Power of Prayer (Romans 8:27)
(a) The Unimagined Interest of God
And He that searcheth the hearts knoweth what is the mind of the Spirit ...

The Holy Spirit when He comes in to the hidden sphere of our life applies the Atonement to us in the unconscious realm as well as in the realm of which we are conscious, that is, He works out in us the understanding of sin that God has; and it is only when we get a grasp of the unrivalled power of the Spirit in us that we understand the meaning of 1 John 1:7, "the blood of Jesus Christ His Son cleanseth us from all sin." This does not refer to conscious sin only, but to the tremendously profound understanding of sin which only the Holy Ghost in us realises, and God searches our hearts to find out what the intercession of His Spirit is.

There are tremendous thoughts expressed in God's Book, and unless we have learned to rely on the Holy Spirit we shall say, "Oh, I shall never understand that," but the Holy Spirit in us understands it, and as we recognise and rely on Him, He will work it out, whether we consciously understand or not. The point for us to remember is that we must get to the right basis of thinking spiritually as well as of living. Never close down on your personal experience, never rivet your attention on the fact that you have had the experience of salvation or sanctification, or the baptism of the Holy Ghost; these experiences are simply doorways into a life. We have to make our minds realise this great revealed thought underneath, that the Holy Spirit is working out in us the Mind of God even as He worked out the Mind of God in Christ Jesus.

(b) The Undiscovered Intercession before God
because He maketh intercession for the saints ...

Who does? The Holy Spirit in us, and God searches our hearts, not to know what our conscious prayers are, but to find out what the prayer of the Holy Spirit is in and behind all our conscious praying. In the vision of Ezekiel wings are used as the symbol of aspiration in praying, "And the sound of the wings of the cherubim was heard even to the outer court, as the voice of God Almighty when He speaketh" (Ezekiel 10:5 RV). The voice of praying in the saints is exactly identical with the voice of Almighty God, and slowly and surely God discerns in the life of the individual saint what He discerned always in His Son, Who said, "I came down from heaven not to do Mine own will, but the will of Him that sent Me." As we rely on the Holy Spirit we learn to brood along the line of His expression of the unutterable in us.

(c) The Unsurpassed Identification with God
... according to the will of God.

Look back over your own history with God in prayer, and you will find that the glib days of prayer are done. When we draw on the human side of our experience only, our prayers become amazingly flippant and familiar, and we ourselves become amazingly hard and metallic; but if along with the human element we rely on the Holy Spirit, we shall find that our prayers become more and more inarticulate; and when they are inarticulate, reverence grows deeper and deeper, and undue familiarity has the effect of a sudden blow on the face. There is something hopelessly incongruous in a flippant statement before God. We can always measure our growth in grace by what Paul is stating here. Am I growing slowly to lisp the very prayers of God? Is God gratified (if I may use the phrase) in seeing that His Spirit is having His way at last in a life, and turning that life into what will glorify His Son?

The Unrecognised Providence of Prayer
(Romans 8:28)
At the first glance this verse seems to have nothing to do with the previous verses, but it has an amazingly close connection with them.

(a) The Undefiled Shrine of Consciousness
And we know that to them that love God . . . (RV)

Do you remember how Paul never wearied of saying, "Don't you know that your body is the temple of the Holy Ghost"? Recall what Jesus Christ said about the historic temple which is the symbol of the body; He ruthlessly turned out those that sold and bought in the temple, and said, "It is written, My house shall be called the house of prayer; but ye have made it a den of thieves." Let us apply that to ourselves. We have to remember that our conscious life, though only a tiny bit of our personality, is to be regarded by us as a shrine of the Holy Ghost. The Holy Ghost will look after the unconscious part we do not know, we must see we guard the conscious part, for which we are responsible, as a shrine of the Holy Ghost. If we recognise this as we should, we shall be careful to keep our body undefiled for Him.

(b) The Undetected Sacredness of Circumstances
all things work together for good . . .

The circumstances of a saint's life are ordained by God, and not by happy-go-lucky chance. There is no such thing as chance in the life of a saint, and we shall find that God by His providence brings our bodies into circumstances that we cannot understand a bit, but the Spirit of God understands; He is bringing us into places and among people and under conditions in order that the intercession of the Holy Spirit in us may take a particular line. Do not, therefore, suddenly put your hand in front of the circumstances and say, "No, I am going to be my own amateur providence, I am going to watch this and guard that." "Trust in the Lord with all thine heart; and lean not unto thine own

understanding." The point to remember is that all our circumstances are in the hand of God. The Spirit imparts a solemnity to our circumstances and makes us understand something of the travail of Jesus Christ. It is not that we enter into the agony of intercession, it is that we utilise the common-sense circumstances into which God has put us, and the common-sense people He has put us among by His providence, to present their cases before Him and give the Holy Spirit a chance to intercede for them. We bring the particular people and circumstances before God's throne, and the Holy Spirit in us has a chance to intercede for them. That is how God is going to sweep the whole world by His saints. Are we making the Holy Spirit's work difficult by being indefinite, or by trying to do His work for Him? We must do the human side of the intercession, and the human side is the circumstances we are in, the people we are in contact with. We have to use our common sense in keeping our conscious life and our circumstances as a shrine of the Holy Ghost, and as we bring the different ones before God, the Holy Spirit presents them before the Throne all the time. The Holy Spirit does the interceding, but we must do our part; we must do the human side while He does the Divine. So never think it strange concerning the circumstances you are in.

(c) The Undeviating Security of His Calling
. . . even to them that are called according to His purpose. (RV)

To talk about our intercession for another soul being the means of doing what the Bible says, "the effectual fervent prayer of a righteous man availeth much," sounds utterly ridiculous until we get the basal thinking revealed through the Atonement and the indwelling Holy Ghost, then it is an amazing revelation of the marvellous love and condescension of God—that in Christ Jesus and by the reception of the Holy Spirit, He can take us, sin-broken, sin-diseased, wrong creatures, and re-make us entirely until we are really the ones in whom the Holy Spirit intercedes as we do our part. Are we making it easy for the Holy Spirit to work out God's will in us, or are we continually putting Him on one side by the empty requests of our natural hearts, Christians though we be? Are we learning to bring ourselves into such obedience that our every thought and imagination is brought into captivity to the Lord Jesus Christ, and is the Holy Spirit having an easy way through us more and more? Remember, your intercessions can never be mine, and my intercessions can never he yours, but the Holy Ghost makes intercession in our particular editions, without which intercession someone will be impoverished. Let us remember the depth and height and solemnity of our calling as saints.

Knocking at God's Door

A Little Book of Prayers

Oswald Chambers

INTRODUCTION

Source

The material in *Knocking at God's Door* is from the prayers Oswald Chambers recorded in his personal diary.

The prayers from January through October reflect Oswald's years as principal of the Bible Training College.[1] London (1911–1915).

The prayers from November and December reflect the final two years of Chambers' life, in which he served as a YMCA chaplain to British troops in Egypt (1915–1917).

Publication History

• First published as a book: In 1937, Mrs. Chambers was compiling Oswald's talks on prayer for the book, *If Ye Shall Ask*. Mr. C. Rae Griffin, a close friend and member of her advisory council (the Oswald Chambers Publications Association), expressed his belief that there was also a great need for a book of personal, spiritual prayers. Mrs.

Chambers turned to Oswald's diaries, in which he often wrote out his prayers at the beginning of each day. In 1938, she published *A Little Book of Prayers*, containing seventy-two of her husband's personal prayers.

• In 1957, additional prayers were added and some of the original prayers were divided to create a book with a prayer for each day of the year. It was retitled *Knocking at God's Door*.

The mention of "this house, students and the College" refers to the Bible Training College, London, during the years 1911–1915. The prayers listed in September reflect Oswald's struggle to find God's guidance early in 1915. For a more complete chronology of these events, see *Oswald Chambers: Abandoned to God*, chapter 15.

These prayers, selected and arranged by the woman who knew him best, provide a unique glimpse into the spiritual heartbeat of Oswald Chambers.

---

1. Bible Training College (BTC): a residential school near Clapham Common in southwest London, sponsored and operated by the Pentecostal League of Prayer from 1911 until it closed in July 1915 because of World War I; Oswald Chambers was principal and main teacher; Biddy Chambers, his wife, was lady superintendent.

FOREWORD

Knock, and it shall be opened unto you. Matthew 7:7

This collection of prayers, though meant for no human eye, will help many others to express themselves in love and trust and petition to God. When the disciples saw their Lord praying, one of them said, "Lord, teach us to pray," (Luke 11:1) He spoke for all of them, and the Lord's answer was for them all—and for us. They felt they needed to know that secret track to God. They wanted to pray like their Lord, and so they began to be grounded in the principles and practice of true praying.

In this Little Book of Prayers we are overhearing one of God's servants at prayer. These are some of the prayers that he breathed out to God, penning the very words in exactness of his intention, in everything by prayer and supplication with thanksgiving to let his requests be made known unto God. They can teach us much about the simplicity, the range, the power and the perseverance of Spirit-born praying, and there is no service more worthy of our deepest attention.

David Lambert[2]

Thy hand be on the latch to open the door at His first knock. Shouldst thou open the door and not see Him, do not say He did not knock, but understand that He is there, and wants thee to go out to Him. It may be He has something for thee to do for Him. Go and do it, and perhaps thou wilt return with a new prayer, to find a new window in thy soul.

George MacDonald

---

2. David Lambert (1871–1961): Methodist minister and friend of Oswald and Biddy Chambers; assisted Mrs. Chambers with OC publications from 1917 until his death in 1961.

January

1 O Lord, I praise Thee for the revelation of Thy supreme Fatherhood that dawns on me through the grace of the Lord Jesus. Oh, that I may be the child of my Father in heaven!

2 O Lord, enchain me to Thyself with great bonds of adoring love; enwheel me around with Thy Providence for Thy purposes; enlarge me until I am more and more capable of being of use to Thee.

3 "The Lord God omnipotent reigneth." Lord, the very sound of that phrase is great and inspiring. May I be full of the calm peace which comes from knowing Thou dost reign.

4 Lord, how easily the mind wanders when Thy domination is not in the ascendant! Keep the lordship of body and soul and spirit in Thy hands.

5 O Lord, grant that in sweet and gracious likeness to Thyself I might delight Thy heart this day, perfect my own life, and be an unalloyed blessing to all around me.

6 What a joyous life the life "hid with Christ in God" is! But, my God, I dare not for one moment think how far short of it I fall in spite of all Thy grace and patience. But Thou art making me, and I thank Thee.

7 "And ye yourselves like unto men that wait for their Lord—might I be like that, waiting, eager, dutiful, alert, and full of power and presence of mind.

8 Lord, unto Thee do I look up. How I know that "in me dwelleth no good thing"; and how marvellous is Thy grace that I now find in my heart no motive save for Thy glory.

9 Lord, bring the sweetness and fullness of Thy power to bear on me this day. Oh, for the big, the generous, the gracious, the grave-gay life of God!

10 Send forth Thy light, O Lord, brood over this College as Thou didst brood (RV mg) over chaos; work mightily in Thy spiritual domains, and help me to erect mountain peaks of prayer that the clouds may be rent and bring themselves down in blessing.

11 Lord, the hilarious simplicity of trust in Thee seems almost levity until I remember Thee, and dare not *not* be glad! Spread joy and gladness all around us this day.

12 Lord, this day is peculiarly Thy day; help us to remember only Thee. Bless Thy servants and handmaidens all over the world.

13 O Lord, how excellent it is to commune with Thee in the early morning hours. Enable me by patience to reproduce these exalted moments of calm into the activities of the day.

14 "Oft shall that flesh imperil and outweary"—yet what indignation does this bear in me! As I rouse myself, meet my rousing with the inspiration of Thy Spirit.

15 Lord, lift up the light of Thy countenance upon me and give me peace, Thy peace, deep as the unfathomed sea, high as the unscaled heights of heaven. Touch me now, till light and life and liberty course through me.

16 Lord, I would worship Thee in the Psalmist's words—"Unto the upright there ariseth light in the darkness": O Lord, how supreme a darkness I am! therefore Thou must be the light.

17 Lord, unto Thee I come in helplessness, yet in hopefulness inwrought by Thy Spirit, that I might be filled with Thy love, Thy Divine un-egoistic nature, Thy passionate patience, unwounded by personal considerations.

18 O Lord, this day put Thou Thy touch, great and ennobling and inspiring, upon us all. Save completely our minds from panic and our spirits from undue haste.

19 Lord, how I realise the peril of work and activity equally with that of quiet and retirement, and that the only secure haven is Thyself. Help me to be taken up altogether with Thee.

20 O Lord, I look to Thee so utterly that I am worse than useless without Thee. Be made wisdom and discernment and understanding unto me today.

21 O Lord, this day keep us so well that we never need to think of ourselves at all, but joyously spend and be spent for Thee.

22 O Lord, if I am strong in any wise it is only in Thee, and this morning my soul rejoices because of the recalling of the word—"Be strong in the Lord, and in the power of His might."

23 O Lord, in simple dependence on Thy Holy Spirit indwelling in me and uniting me with Thy nature, I look to Thee; cause me to be all Thou wouldst have me be.

24 O Lord, lift up the light of Thy countenance upon us, let Thy great and glorious voice and presence

sweep through this College. On those of us who teach send the anointing unction and gracious insight into Thy truth.

25 Lord, how dim and distant and dreary my physical life seems, and is, without Thee; fill the outer courts with Thy Divine life.

26 O Lord, as this Thy day unfolds be our peculiar treasure in everything. Permeate us with Thy Spirit that all may be transfigured with sweet complacent spiritual power.

27 O Lord, unto Thee do I come; consciously and unconsciously, I draw near in uttermost need. Lift me, lead me, fill me for Thy glory, make me harmoniously one with Thy purpose and will.

28 O God, increase my sense of Thee and my sensible understanding of Thy Son, my Lord and Master. Grant that I may more and more realise Thy dominance and rule, and more and more rejoice in simple joy in Thee.

29 O Lord, Thou art ever well, and all my fresh springs are in Thee (PBV).[3] To Thee I come; may Thy mighty life spring up in me, a veritable influx into body as well as spirit.

30 Lord, today let Thy praise abound, let joy and gladness resound everywhere. How I long for joy—great bounding liberating joy: joy in God, joy in the Holy Ghost, joy in life, and joy in love. Cause this to be a joyous house today, all day.

31 Lord, Thy ways are like Thyself—perfect: my ways are like myself—imperfect. Touch me into effectual identity with Thy consciousness, and with Thy ways for this day.

February

1 Lord God Almighty, Thou are holy; but more wonderful than praise can tell, Thou dost undertake to make me holy by Thy grace.

2 O Lord, how little I realise what it means to watch with Thee, to continue with Thee in Thy temptations. Draw me nearer this morning and insulate me by Thy mighty power until I speak and live only for Thee.

3 Lord, breathe on me until my frame is knit to Thy thought. Lift me until I see Thy face and trust Thine Almightiness without fear or insidious unbelief.

4 Lord, I praise Thee for Thy word—"In your patience possess ye your souls," and I praise Thee for Thy grace which waits while I laboriously acquire the soul Thou wouldst have me acquire.

5 O Lord, unto Thee do I turn, unto Thee. I am but a homeless waif until Thou dost touch me with the security of Thy peace, the sweet sense of Thy love.

6 Lord, Thy word comes so quietly and all-pervadingly—"If any man serve Me, let him follow Me": and, "If any man serve Me, him will My Father honour." Take me as Thy servant in this sense.

7 O Lord, how wholesome and grand a thing it is to be willing towards Thee. I am willing, eagerly willing for Thy will to be done, and I feel all deeply joyful at the prospect for nothing can be so glorious as just Thy will.

8 How I long to be so full of Thee, burning and shining and irradiating Thee, that there is no room for anything but just Thy gracious light.

9 O Lord, speak with power and graciousness in today's Services. Conduct me into the inner secret of fellowship with Thee that Thou mayest be able to convey Thyself aright.

10 O Lord, in some moods it seems so easy to slip away from Thee and Thy purposes, and yet, Lord, I do not believe it is; but I do believe it is possible to enter into Thy purposes like a beast of the field, with no discernment and no vision. Lord, I would be a son of Thine.

11 O Lord, how I need infilling and invigorating by Thy presence. Give me that buoyant, quiet confidence in Thee which is the witness of the Spirit.

12 O Lord, my soul doth praise Thee for its trust in Thee. My soul hangeth on Thy touch and smile lest any distemper of mind or imagination arise and I be corrupted from the simplicity that is in Christ.

13 O Lord, I would crave more and more to put on love like a garment, that in my contact with men that is what they will most lastingly recognise.

14 O Lord, that the most absorbing sensing of Thee might be mine, that Thy will should be done in and through me unhinderedly.

15 O Lord, how I adore Thee, but how I long for more conscious adoration and communion and

---

3. PBV: Prayer Book Version. The *Book of Common Prayer* of the Church of England includes a translation of the Psalter, or Psalms of David.

God-praising-ness. Cleanse me from the defilement of distance from Thee.

16 Here is the day, O Lord, Thy day, cause it to shine for ever in our individual lives like a jewel.

17 O Lord, I do thank Thee for the condition of heart and motive Thy grace has wrought in me, but, Oh, when in my actual life shall I express before the world the beauty of Thy peace?

18 Guard my central life from corrosion, O Lord; keep me secretly so right with Thee that I may redound to Thy glory.

19 I praise Thee for that word—"Like as a father pitieth his children, so the LORD pitieth them that fear Him." How I realise that I owe nothing to Thy severity but all to Thy love. Oh, that Thy love and gentleness and patience toward me were expressed through me to others!

20 O Lord, one thing amazes me, and that is my almost total deficiency in letting Thee manifest Thyself and Thy beauty in my outward life. Let the beauty of the Lord our God be upon me this day.

21 O Lord, with much dimness I draw nigh to Thee, clear the dimness away from me and flood me with the light of Thy countenance.

22 O Lord, I beseech Thee for sustaining strength and simple joy. Keep me humble-minded in motive and design that nothing of the superior person may be mine.

23 O Lord, how much of a lift I need this morning! Thou knowest. In my preaching, cause Thy glorious Voice to be heard, Thy lovely Face to be seen, Thy pervasive Spirit felt.

24 Cleanse me, O Lord, from all complicity of spirit, and may Thy radiant beauty be in and upon me this day.

25 How depressed and appalled I am at the prospect of sinking to the commonplace! Lord, help me to live purely and powerfully and fascinatedly Thine.

26 Oh, for one of those touches of Thy Spirit that, as the wind, quicken, and awaken, loosen and inspire!

27 How my heart and my flesh cry out for the living God! Oh, the enervation of myself! and Oh, the refreshment and joy of the Lord!

28 O Lord, in complete need I turn to Thee. Come to me physically, mentally, morally, and spiritually, and cause me to effect the manifestation of Thyself that is glorifying to Thee.

29 Oh, how I long to be all taken up by Thee, all my body, soul and spirit enthused by Thee; so many lurking things of the darkness still remain. What a gracious humiliation these things are.

March

1 I praise Thee that all I am is Thine. Oh, that I could delight Thee as the lily does, or the tree, or even the sparrows, just living the life Thou has granted!

2 O Lord God, what Thou art to me I dimly begin to discern—more than morning light, more than joy and health, more than all Thy blessings. Dawn on me afresh this morning and make me light all through with Thy light.

3 O Lord, my soul would stay upon Thee as Creator of the world, and upon our Lord Jesus Christ as Creator of His life in me. Oh, for the power of Thy Spirit to adore Thee in fuller measure!

4 "And upon the top of the pillars was lily work." O Lord, this word is in my mind, especially how devoid I am of any "lily work," so rugged and unadorned. Cause me to be Thine in the expression of Thy grace as well as in the experience of it.

5 O Lord, this new day enable me by Thy grace to full feel Thy nearness and Thy might. Keep me facing Thy glory that I may be "changed into the same image from glory to glory."

6 How manifold are the ways I need Thee! I praise Thee Thou art there to be found. Lord, be found of me; but it is only when Thou dost come Thyself that I find Thee.

7 I would, O Lord, have all my thought and emotions and words redolent with love, perfect love to Thee, and through that to men.

8 O my God, I lie in Thy fire burning and purifying—so much dross I seem to discover today, so little of Thy sweet and lovely grace in my dealing with others' faults. Lord, forgive me.

9 O Lord, soften and subdue, inspire and thrill, and raise us on to the level of such glorious communion with Thee that we may catch Thy likeness.

10 O Lord, how wonderful and great and mighty it is to turn toward Thee. Keep me from any dominance saving Thine.

11 O Lord, tone me up with Thy great power. I believe I am privileged to ask this because of the Atonement of Jesus. Make me physically all I ought to be so that Thy radiance may be on me.

12 Ah Lord, Thy Face, Thy touch, Thy blessing, I seek today. Touch me, Lord, till every part of my being vibrates and thrills with Thy gracious and powerful well-being.

13 Lord, my chief desire is to be rooted and grounded in Thee—God-centred and God-absorbed, God-enthused and God-loved. How eager my soul is to know Thee and be still!

14 O Lord, how wonderful are Thy ways! When I recall the way Thou has led me and borne with me, I am lost in wonder, love and praise.

15 Bless us here today, O Lord, so many need Thee. Go in and out amongst us, controlling and lifting with Thy saving power.

16 O Lord, what a wonder of perfect confidence it would create could I but hear some clear disposing word of Thine! Lord, speak it today.

17 O Lord, by Thy grace open my vision to Thee and Thine infinite horizons, and take me into Thy counsels regarding Thy work in this College.

18 O Lord, I would that I had a livelier sense of Thee and of Thy bounties continually with me.

19 O Lord, bless me this hour with the glow of Thy presence and sense of Thy nearness. I do trust only in Thee, yet I long for conscious delight in Thy presence, if Thou wilt vouchsafe it to me.

20 O Lord, may this day be right glorious with Thy presence and blessing. May we see Thee causing the place of Thy feet to be glorious.

21 O Lord, I do praise Thee for the mighty lines of thought that come as I think of membership in Thy Mystical Body. How I long to be quickened enough to realise the wonder of it more.

22 O Lord, Thou art my God, I know no God beside Thee. My sense of unworthiness is so great that I do not waste any time in telling Thee of it. It is to Thyself I come—yearningly, eagerly, completely.

23 O Lord, for supplies of Thy grace today, grace so Divine and mighty that many may glorify Thee through my ministry.

24 Lord God Almighty, who wast manifested in Jesus Christ, I come before Thee now with the unpretentiousness of a human being needing Thee absolutely and rejoicing in my need.

25 O Lord, when I awake, I am still with Thee. Quicken my mortal body with Thy mighty resurrection life; rouse me this hour with a gracious influx of power.

26 "Clouds and darkness are round about Him: righteousness and judgement are the foundation of His throne" (RV). Commune with me, O Lord, that I may know I am light in Thee.

27 O Lord, the "multitudes" will be coming and going today. Help me to keep, like my Master, in the lonely places and pray.

28 O Lord, visit with Thy tenderness every heart and life that has been experiencing the shattering which the penetration of Thy word brings.

29 O Lord, be such a disposer of the lot that is cast into the lap that our mouths shall be filled with laughter at what Thou wilt bring to pass!

30 O Lord, be very present today—the great joyous presence of the Holy Ghost permeating everywhere.

31 O Lord, I seem an incarnate desert before Thee, unbeautiful and arid; but, praise Thy Name, Thou canst make "the desert rejoice, and blossom as the rose."

April

1 O Lord, the truth that presses its way through all else this morning is the truth about Sanctification. Forgive me if I have imperceptibly shifted from this great purpose of Thine.

2 O Lord, blessed be the tone and power of Thy voice, its tones of tenderness and love in Grace; its tones of power in the great gales of Nature. Lord, cause Thy glorious voice to be heard in this College, and in my soul.

3 Draw me, O Lord, into vital communion with Thyself. What a difference the sun makes in the natural world: and what a difference it makes when Thou dost dawn upon us! Press through till we are thrilled with Thy presence.

4 O Lord, how niggardly is my appreciation of Thine Atonement and perfect salvation. Lord, draw me into fuller gratitude; let me ever be a passionate lover of the Lord Jesus Christ.

5 O Lord, my Lord, make this day right glorious. For myself in Thy service, I ask surcease from all distracting.

6 O Lord, I would praise Thee for Thy mighty Redemption at the heart of all our problems. By Thy great power raise us up to newness of life this Easter Day.

7 O Lord, the wonder of being one with Thee as Thou art one with the Father! Grant us this one-

ness for Thy glory, and to that end lift up the light of Thy countenance upon us and give us peace.

8   O Lord, cause my intellect to glow with Thy Holy Spirit's teaching.

9   O Lord, Thy graciousness is fresh to my soul, but how slow is my growth in Thine Almighty grace! Quicken Thou me, open my nature to grander horizons this day.

10   O Lord, I praise Thee for the prayers of the saints which have surrounded me like an atmosphere of heaven, and for the unspeakable grace which comes to me through Thy Redemption.

11   Be radiant through me, O Lord. Give me Thine approving smile and benediction, and help me to be altogether taken up with Thee.

12   How we need just Thee! Make it a day for ever memorable for intimacy with Thyself.

13   O Lord, how reluctant my nature seems to brood on the profound truths of Thy grace, and yet do not I know the power and purity of communion with Thee?

14   O Lord, bless us in this College. Today; save from indolence and spiritual sloth, and cause Thine undertakings to be almighty.

15   Lord, I make petition to see Thee, I have been pre-occupied and away from Thee in outercourt life; forgive me, and draw me near to Thyself that I may have rare communion with Thee again.

16   O Lord, I have a great implicit yearning for a token of Thy notice. Give just a sign that Thou art using me for something in Thy purpose.

17   O Lord my God, my strength, my hope, and my joy, slowly but surely I seem to be emerging into a clearer discernment of Thee. Dawn through all earth-born clouds and mists today.

18   O Lord, so many to pray for, so many in need of deliverance. Unto Thee how hungrily I look up.

19   Lord, put Thy mouth to our College life and breathe the invigorating breath of Thy recreating life through us all, putting sickness far from us.

20   O Lord, I do rejoice at Thy word, "as one that findeth great spoil." As I speak today put Thy words in my mouth; be so present that it shall be manifest to all that it is Thy word.

21   O Lord, with the coming of spring in Nature my spirit longs that Thy energising life may flow in and through me more, and still yet more. But how un-beautiful I am, how un-Christlike! and yet it is not in depression, but in amazing hope I see this.

22   O Lord, draw me to Thee; give me the glorious sensing of Thyself that makes a mere sinner like me worthy as Thy servant.

23   O Lord, "that Thine eyes may be open toward this house night and day." Keep it and guard it from all that is not in Thine order, and cause each one of us to be all that Thy secret heart desires.

24   O Lord, in humbled guise I pray this morning, full of adoration and worship, but full of humility when I remember how shielded my life is.

25   O Lord, disentangle me, I have a great longing for a simplicity of relationship with Thee that shall transfigure everything and shed blessing and benediction all around.

26   O Lord, restore the keen edge of all spiritual sensibilities; lift me into Thy light by Thine abounding grace through our Lord Jesus Christ. How slow I am to apprehend more of Thee and of thy ways!

27   O Lord, this day I have to speak in Thy Name three times, and I am un-moved and un-inspired till now. If Thou canst convey Thy mind to me in my spiritual dullness, Oh, for Jesus Christ's sake, do it.

28   O Lord my God, assist me to worship Thee. I praise Thee that Thou remainest evermore the same. Touch me, O Lord, and by Thy power renew me spiritually to keenness and appreciation of Thee and of Thy truth.

29   O Lord, dawn on us and draw us into Thyself today; begin with me. Cleanse me, O Lord, from all the imperfections which are clear to Thee though not to me.

30   "The LORD reigneth"; O Lord, let Thy reigning power be manifested this day in the bodies of Thy servants for Thy glory.

May

1   Lord, I praise Thee for this day's glad opportunity of serving Thee acceptably. I bless Thee for the revealing of the truth that Thine order comes moment by moment in the day's life.

2   "But when the kindness of God our Saviour, and His love toward man, appeared. . . ." (RV)—O Lord, that word haunts me; yet how little of Thy kindness and Thy love do I exhibit toward others!

3   May the power and tone and health of God be all-pervading this day. How I long for Thy generous-heartedness to be realised in and through all things! Keep the sense of Thy call in me fresh and vivid.

4   O Lord, I praise Thee for the Throne of Grace, and that in Jesus Christ I can draw near with boldness to receive mercy, and grace for this day's glorifying of Thee.

5   I praise Thee, O Lord, for Thy gift of salvation; for the benefit and blessing of the prayers of the saints. But how I slip into Thy favours and slowly begin to think I merit them, or act as though I did. Forgive me, Lord.

6   I would, O Lord, cleanse myself from all defilement of flesh and spirit, from every coarsening of the fibre of the spiritual life, so that I may dwell in Thee in fulness of joy.

7   O Lord, I do praise Thee that through Christ Jesus our Lord it is mercy and loving-kindness, graciousness and wonders, all along the way; I would I were more sensitive to Thee and Thy doings, more Christlike in my gratitude.

8   O Lord, by Thy grace, I see so much with my mind and speak so much—cause my heart and my conduct not only to keep pace with my mind but go far beyond it.

9   O Lord, I thank Thee for Thy word, "Not by might, nor by power, but by My Spirit, saith the LORD of Hosts." I ask for such aid of Thy Spirit that Thou mayest be satisfied with me today.

10   Lord, through all the multitudinous duties of the day keep me calm; ennoble me by Thy touch and tenderness. Settle and quieten me down in Thee.

11   O Lord, I lift up my eyes, my hopes, and my prayers to Thee. Re-energise me from Thy heights by the indwelling of Thy Holy Spirit that the light of God may arise around and in us today. Fill up the day with sweetness and glory for Thine own delight.

12   O Lord, for more love, passionate, devout and earnest love to Thee to show itself in my conscious life. Oh for grace to show and to feel patience and gentleness to those around me!

13   O Lord, Thou art what I am longing for! "My soul thirsteth for God, for the living God: when shall I come and appear before God?" Oh, for Thy touch, Thy life, Thy beauty; let it come now, Lord, even as I pray.

14   O Lord, how clearly Thou hast shown me that it is God, and God alone, who matters. May I never stumble any in this great realisation.

15   O Lord, I realise how little of the hidden life of believing in Jesus I have exercised of late, ulterior motives seem to creep in all the time. Bring the simplicity that is in Christ into my life and outlook in deeper ways—careful only of Thine approval.

16   O Lord, touch all our lives with Thine energising power and loving-kindness and beauty; make it a time of the unveiling of Thy Face. This seems to be all my prayer.

17   O Lord this day, cause Thy glorious voice to be heard, and heard by me. Oh speak to me, produce Thy stillness in my heart and mind and speak with thrilling power.

18   Lord, this Sabbath morning, insulate me from sights and sounds unusual; loosen me from the bands that bind me to the present and the recent, and fill with Thy Spirit the whole limit of this day.

19   "Like rain upon the mown grass"; "as the dew unto Israel"—O Lord, these phrases come to my mind this morning with sweet insistence. Be as rain and as dew unto us this day, refreshing, remoulding, and blessing us. Unto Thee do I come in great and glad expectancy.

20   O Lord, how complete is my need of Thee! To Thee I come, give me a gracious renewing of Thy life till my reasoning powers, my imagination, and my speaking are all of Thee. I seek Thy touch and thrilling grace today.

21   Lord, I would like to pour out my heart before Thee—my soul is not brilliant in experience just now, nor my intellect vigorous, both are jaded; but I adore Thee that Thou art never dull nor jaded, and that Thou knowest our frame.

22   O Lord, speak to me now. Inspire me for today; dullness, deep and devastating, seems to hold fast to my powers.

23   O Lord, how complete is my need of Thee! Come into our actual circumstances this day in the plenitude of thy power.

24   O Lord, how slow I am to show in my manners and ways the gracious grace of God! When shall Thy beauty be upon me for Thine honour?

25   Lord God Omnipotent, how my soul delights to know that Thou carest for sparrows, and numberest the hairs of our head! Lord, breathe on me till I am in the frame of mind and body to worship Thee.

26   O Lord, rise in grandeur into our lives and ways and goings. Be a strong presence of healing and hope and grace and beauty this day.

27 Breathe on me, Breath of God, until my mind and spirit are in suitable adjustment to Thyself. Shed abroad liberty and purity and power amongst and in us all.

28 O Lord, how all things are simple and glorious when Thou art seen! This day let me see Thy Face and be alone with Thee.

29 O Lord, make this a right royal day with Thee. Touch us, O Lord, that all our spiritual and material life may be attuned to Thy purposes. Just Thy touch, and all will be well.

30 "Whoso is wise, . . . even they shall understand the lovingkindness of the LORD." Lord, that would be beautiful! Give me this token for Thy glory. Unto Thee do I look for this day; cause the abundance of Thy bounty and beauty to be upon us.

31 O Lord, how essentially necessary it is for me to draw nigh to Thee. How can I falter when Thou art my life?

June

1 O Lord, how I realise my need of a worthier conception of Thyself. All lesser things I would merge in this petition—that I might worthily magnify Thee.

2 "Light is sown for the righteous." Lord, what a harvest! How wonderful are Thy ways.

3 O Lord, I marvel at my slowness in praise; quicken me to praise Thee aright. Give me a due sense, a powerful realisation of Thy goodness, that I might be a joyous satisfaction to Thine own heart.

4 Lord, in complete dependence I look to Thee; it is good for me to feel "wandered" till Thou dost appear.

5 O Lord, I rejoice that the "*if need be*" is Thine! and I praise Thee for the counsel to "think it not strange concerning the fiery trial," but to rejoice.

6 O Lord, for the power of Thy Spirit to adore Thee in fuller ways. Keep my spirit brightly infused by Thy Holy Spirit that thus energised, the Lord Jesus and His perfections may be manifested in my mortal flesh.

7 O Lord, with what abundant relief I turn to Thee, I need Thee in unfathomable ways, and with what amazed relief and joy I find *all* I need is Thyself.

8 O Lord, this morning disperse every mist, and shine forth clear and strong and invigoratingly.

9 "Thou hast enlarged me when I was in distress": Oh that the thoughts of my heart were more and more a well-spring of gracious treasure without ceasing!

10 Lord, Thy goodness is so beyond comparison that we are "like unto them that dream," our mouth is "filled with laughter, and our tongue with singing" (RV); we praise Thee for the time when we shall come again with joy, bringing our sheaves with us.

11 O Lord, draw near, press into my conscious possession until I am all taken up with Thee. Make this day radiant with Thy power.

12 O Lord, there is no Time with Thee for "a thousand years in Thy sight are but as yesterday when it is past"; but with me it is necessarily different. How Thou hast restored the years the cankerworm hath eaten and created me a new creature in Christ Jesus! Accept my thanksgiving.

13 O Lord, in might and majesty prevail in many more ways today. Keep me from secularisation of soul or spirit.

14 O Lord, I know Thy blessing and I praise Thee, but it is the indescribable touch and enwheeling as Thy servant that I seek for—I know not what I seek for, but Thou knowest. How I long for Thee!

15 O Lord, this day lead me into some more of Thy gracious and wondrous doings. Put Thy loving hand of grace and power upon me this day.

16 O Lord, give me the disposition of mind that delights in Thee. Cleanse me from all fog and flurry and fuss, that clear-eyed I may see Thy way this day.

17 O Lord, I do thank Thee for the relief and inspiration, the almost effulgence of joy, that has flowed into me and visited my inner kingdom. Fill me now with Thy calm peace.

18 O Lord, grant that this day may end for ever the self-consciousness that enfeebles us in Thy service, and may we be conscious only of Jesus.

19 O Lord, how I long for Thee to bring me face to face with Thyself! My soul thirsteth for Thee, for the touch of Thy grace, the breathing of Thy Spirit.

20 O Lord, anoint the College to praise Thee; anoint all of us here to praise Thee. Bring the buoyant breezes of Thy Holy Spirit upon us now.

21 O Lord, rouse and quicken me so that my mortal flesh may indeed be the obedient, docile servant of Thy Spirit.

22 Lord, what an intense need of Thee I realise this morning; supply that need according to Thy riches in Christ Jesus until I am wholly transfigured by the supply.

23 O Lord, draw Thy powerful presence around me this day as a curtain, and be the glory in the midst.

24 O Lord, remove this bondage of thought, and bring peace and purity and power. Fill me this day with Thy tenderness and compassion and grace.

25 O Lord, breathe on me till I am one with Thee in the temper of my mind and heart and disposition. Unto Thee do I turn. Again, how completely I realise my lost-ness without Thee!

26 O Lord, to praise Thee aright is a great desire of mine, created and fostered by Thy Spirit and grace.

27 Lord, so much activity, so many things, so numberless the people! Bless today with largeness of heart and beauty of character for Thy glory.

28 Lord, I would bless and praise Thee, but how hard I find it to praise Thee when I am not physically fit, yet why should it be so? This means that I praise Thee only when it is a pleasure to me. I would that my soul were one continual praise to Thee!

29 O Lord, lift up the light of Thy countenance upon us this day and make us fit in with Thy plans with great sweetness and liberty, and a lilt to Thee all day.

30 Lord, how I desire to see Thee, to hear Thee, to meditate on Thee, and manifestly grow like Thee! And Thou hast said, "Delight thyself in the LORD; and He shall give thee the desires of thine heart."

July

1 "Casting all your care upon Him; for He careth for you." O Lord, what a wonder these words are! The miasmas that at times lie around the margins of the mind need Thy constant care to keep them away. I look to Thee that I may be renewed in the spirit of my mind.

2 Keep this house,[4] O Lord, spiritually and in all ways, "exceeding magnifical." Give us the light and illumination Thou dost delight in.

3 O Lord, this day prevail to bless. These students, O Lord, into Thy hands I commend them. Thou knowest it is with a clear definite plan of my own I meet them day by day, but I thank Thee Thou

hast Thine own great plans; carry them out, O Lord, with power and grace.

4 Lord, my mind is dim in relation to _____. Lord, be Thou their strong tower; none seem to regard them or care. Prevent the enemy from exacting on them. They are as they are because of their loyalty to Thee. Lord, undertake mightily.

5 Lord, I bless Thee for this College, that in it Thou art proving "a strength to the poor, a strength to the needy in his distress, a refuge from the storm, a shadow from the heat."

6 O Lord, unto Thee do I come with praise and thanksgiving, but with a yearning for a deeper conscious appreciation of Thy goodness. Bless me this day with an enlarged capacity and power to praise.

7 "So foolish was I, and ignorant: I was as a beast before Thee." O Lord, those words express me to myself before Thee. I am ashamed of my temper of mind, so foolish, so "beast-ly," when looked at in the light of the pure and holy God-likeness our Lord demands.

8 O Lord, what great and glorious outlines have passed and are passing before the vision of our personal spirits about Thy plans. Lord, we do not see the way, but we know Thee and trust. Keep our minds and hearts strong and quiet in Thee.

9 O Lord, how much the margins of my mind are taken up with surrounding interests of late so that the surroundings seem the centre. Be Thou Thyself my strong Centre and Surrounding.

10 Bless us all this day, garrison minds and hearts from vague fancies and false emotions, from spectres of the imagination, and keep us wholesomely Thine.

11 Send us more students, O Lord, until this place is filled with men and women through whom Thou canst glorify Thyself throughout the world.

12 Touch my spirit till it be filled with Thee to overflowing. Think through my mind till I form the mind "which was also in Christ Jesus."

13 Oh, by Thy indwelling Spirit knit me together into worship and beauty and holiness. Lord, touch my body and spirit till both are sweeping in one for Thee.

14 Lord, that I might see Thee, feel Thee, "faith" Thee, and fully realise Thee in the manner and measure Thou seest I am capable of. What wait I for but Thee only?

4. this house: the Bible Training College (BTC).

15 O Lord, I would thank Thee for the nameless forebodings and spectres of the mind which hover around when not sufficient time is being given to prayer. Lord, I look up to Thee now; descend, O gracious Lord, descend, and give me grace to rejoice in Thee this day.

16 Lord, touch with energising power and sweet loving-kindness and beauty all our lives today; make it a time of the unveiling of Thy Face and power.

17 "Unite my heart to fear Thy Name." My soul is all abroad because of the meanness,[5] the self-consciousness, the less-than-the-best, which hover around and prevent me as I pray. Lord, be almighty for me!

18 O Lord, I do praise Thee that Thou art, and that by Thy Divine omnipotent grace I am learning to come into Thy presence. Touch my body and spirit with Thy grace and light and wisdom; bright and vivid make Thy touches.

19 Cause it to be light and sweetness and joy all day. Undertake with Thy easy power and might; graciously dawn on us physically and mentally and spiritually.

20 O Lord, that I might be brought into Thy presence, and see things from Thy standpoint. I have to speak to Thy people this morning, anoint me afresh, O Lord, with Thy gracious Spirit.

21 O Lord, as we consider the Fifty-third Chapter of Isaiah this morning, light it up with Thy glory; soften and subdue, inspire and thrill, and raise us on to the level of such glorious service that we may catch Thy likeness.

22 Lord, bless the Devotional Meeting today, may it break with soft beauty and sure blessing and special bounty upon us all.

23 O Lord, for greater sweetness and beauty of character; for the gift of spiritual energy and full-patienced life towards others. Thy sweetness, Thy beauty, manifest them, O Lord; instinct with Thee I would be indeed.

24 Unto Thee, O Lord, I come, may Thy beauty and grace and soothing peace be in and upon me this day, and may no wind or weather or anxiety ever touch Thy peace in my life or in this place.

25 O Lord, I would seek Thy face, but what avail is my seeking if Thou revealest not Thyself? Shew me Thy Face, O Lord. Keep me ever seeing Thee.

26 O God, my Father, the clouds are but the dust of Thy feet! Let me discover in every cloud of Providence or Nature or Grace no man save Jesus only after the fear, till there be no fear.

27 Detach me, O Lord, from the things of sense and time, and usher me into the presence of the King. Keep the precincts of my mind and heart entirely Thine.

28 O Lord, save us from the murmuring spirit which with the majority of us is merely skin-deep, but is harmful, hurting the bloom of spiritual communion.

29 Lord, the range of Thy power, the touch of Thy grace, the breathing of Thy Spirit—how I long for these to bring me face to face with Thee. Forgive my tardiness—it takes me so long to awaken to some things.

30 This morning, O Lord, I praise Thee for all the past—so wayward on my part, so gracious and long-suffering and forgiving and tender on Thine.

31 O Lord, my soul lives before Thee in adoration for Thy mighty grace bestowed on me, so that my eyes see and my ears hear and my heart understands Thy goings behind all circumstances.

August

1 "My spirit's weather"—how aptly that describes my condition today! Do Thou control it, and help me to rise in it and above it.

2 Lord, call me by name that I may thrill with that wonderful calling! What a difference a little thing for Thee to do does make—a calling by name, a passing touch, and we are in ecstasy! Oh, why dost Thou not do it oftener?

3 Lord, this day I have to preach in Thy Name; make it radiant with Thy power. Draw out my soul into the great realisation of Thyself, keep me centralised in Thee in every deep and final sense.

4 Lord, how like I am to the man who had nothing to set before the friend who came to him at midnight! So many are in need of emancipation and deliverance, undertake completely. Sweep through the whole College with Thy gracious presence.

5 O Lord, my God, how wonderfully and powerfully Thou hast caused me to know with a knowledge that passes knowledge that Redemption is the one great revelation Reality.

---

5. meanness: mean, as used here, something or someone ordinary, common, low, or ignoble, rather than cruel or spiteful.

6 Lord, I adore Thee for the past Session. How many Thou hast allowed me to see enter gloriously into a right relationship with Thee! It is too wonderful for me to praise Thee adequately.

7 Lord, extricating and beautifying are the two things my soul most needs today. To Thee I come as an incarnate need of Thee as Saviour and Lord. Repair all the loss of spiritual bloom and sensitiveness to Thee that I may be the right influence for Thee here.

8 Lord, as I speak at the Sermon Class on "The Worker's Staying Power," bring Thy light and grace to bear upon us. May we "adorn the doctrine of God our Saviour in all things."

9 Lord, how completely I need Thee and ache for Thee. Return unto me in completeness, and as Thy life fills up the limits of mind and spirit and overflows, glory will be to Thy Name.

10 With worshipping reverence I would draw nigh Thee this morning in the consciousness that Thou art my Father, and dost fully know the patience Thou hast had with me in my unreality. But, Lord, I do not seem to care now if I am real or not because Thou Thyself art the great Reality.

11 Lord, I praise Thee for this place I am in; but the wonder has begun to stir in me—is this Thy place for me? Hold me steady doing Thy will. It may be only restlessness; if so, calm me to strength that I sin not against Thee by doubting.

12 How helpless I am in bringing forth fruit, Thy kind of fruit in the world, so ungenerous and unlike Thee am I. Forgive me, and by abiding in Jesus may I bear much fruit and so glorify the Father.

13 Lord, gather my powers to Thyself, save from dissipation of energy and cure all distempers with Thy perfect health. Come and make the whole limit of this bodily temple shine with Thy presence.

14 "Holiness, without which no man shall see the Lord": Lord, I thank Thee for that word. How awful if Thou wert not holy! How easy it would seem at times to decline into a lesser, baser life; I thank Thee for the warning.

15 Lord, I feel myself longing for Thee and Thy life, and I am turning to the 91st Psalm for assurance—"Surely He shall deliver thee." Lord, I am assured of it, and would thank Thee for the sweet sense of Thy protecting care.

16 Lord, have us all completely in Thy hand, enabling us to choose Thy leading that our "God may count us worthy of our calling."

17 I would, O Lord, see Thy Face and know Thy power and thrilling grace. Draw nigh my life in full recuperation, and forgive me for the neglect of Thy ways in external details.

18 Lord, with Thy purity permeate our minds and bodies and affections; let us realise and quickly manifest the bracing and enlivening of Thy goings. Come into our circumstances in the plenitude of Thy power.

19 "If ye shall ask Me anything in My Name, that will I do" (RV). It is all so mysterious, O Lord, and all so simple—I pray, and believe that Thou dost create something in answer to and by the very means of my prayer, that was not in existence before.

20 Lord, I praise Thee Thou hast prevented my seeking things immediately for myself, but just Thy touch I do seek, a token for good; but not if it will hinder Thy welfare in me.

21 Lord, touch me physically that that well-being of Thine may lave the shores of my life and I be filled with praise.

22 Lord, I am writing "The Discipline of Prayer," instinct and inspire me, and cause the little booklet to be all Thou dost desire it should be.

23 Lord, lift me as I lift myself up to Thee. Give me the light of Thy countenance that I may irradiate it back to Thee.

24 Lord, visit us with the manifestation of Thy life today. Cause a breath of emancipation to begin and flow on unto Thee, confirming in godliness and grace each one of us here.

25 Lord, so much truth revealed, so many things to say, and so little do I feel I live up to what Thou dost show me. Lord, empower me for Thy glory.

26 Lord, I know that Thou dost abound in grace and art always well; grant me that grace and well-being. Thou knowest how much our spiritual life depends on our feeling well physically.

27 Fill the College with Thy glorious benediction and blessing. Go in and out among us today, charging the atmosphere with Thy gracious presence.

28 Lord, how complete and entire and absolute is my need of Thee in every way and in all ways. I am a vast cavity for Thee to fill; fill me to overflowing with Thy glory and beauty.

29 Lord, bring mighty showers of grace and glory upon all the Classes today, and for the Men's Meeting tonight, I beseech Thee make it a time of great power and blessing.

30 Bless the whole College with waves of health and power. Show us more love that radiantly in Thy care we may go forth this day. Bless the strangers within our gates.

31 Lord, unto Thee I look up, help me to worship Thee aright. I praise Thee that my nature does worship Thee, but my conscious life is slow to respond to Thee and Thy beauty as it might. Lord, help me.

September

1 Lord, I have decided before Thee to offer for work with the Forces; undertake and guide me in each particular. I know Thou wilt, but I am fearful of my own precipitate judgement.

2 O Lord, swamp me with Thy grace and glory that the ample tide of Thyself may be all in all.

3 Lord, be unto me a place of broad rivers, full of life and restful activity. Show each one of us more love and gentleness today, and to me, because so many are influenced directly by me.

4 Lord, cause Thy loving-kindness to be known by me this day by Thine inevitably powerful touches, and use me in Thy gentle almightiness for Thy purposes.

5 For the Devotional Meeting, make it a time, I pray Thee, of the unveiling of Thy Face. We need just Thee, and Thine ineffable sweetness and beauty.

6 How unrelieved my mind has been about the future, I praise Thee that this is not always so, or scarcely ever so. How there is nothing to hold to but just Thyself! Keep me from flagging and slacking.

7 Lord, I feel myself craving for the external sense of Thy presence, the hundredfold more of Thy joyous benediction. Lord, I leave this desire with Thee, grant it as Thou seest best.

8 My mind is still vague regarding the way I am to take, Lord; so much has gone beyond my own discernment in this decision. It is not that I doubt Thee, but all is so completely shrouded.

9 Lord, a vague desolation seems around my life, it is nebulous, I cannot define it. I have no misgiving over my decision for I have done what Thou didst indicate I should do, but still the sense of uncertainty remains. Touch this nebulous nimbus and turn it into a firmament of ordered beauty and form.

10 Lord, as we begin "Intercession for our Country" at our Morning Prayers, I ask that Thy Spirit will direct us.

11 Lord, Thou knowest the strangeness of the lull in the opening up of the future; nothing manifests itself. Such a great need just now for exaltation of mood and mind and manner. Bring confirmation to my mind.

12 My soul's horizon reports, like Elijah's servant, "There is nothing." Every door of opportunity seems closed. Keep me unhurried.

13 How complete must be my hold on Thee else through sheer futility I wilt and wander and am only weak. In my present mood I am inclined to give way to the feeling of having missed the mark. Lord, deal with my mind and outlook.

14 O Lord, I turn to Thee, nothing to perceive but just Thee. Take the elaborate and the heroic and the impulsive, and give me quietly to wait on Thee.

15 Lord, yesterday the Y.M.C.A. accepted me for their work in the Desert Camps in Egypt, and Thy word came this morning with great emphasis—Sent "before His face into every city and place whither He Himself was about to come."

16 Lord, how I praise Thee for this College. It has been four years of unique loveliness, and now I give it up because I believe I do so in answer to Thy call.

17 Lord, guide our hearts into Thy purposes. So many have come into the glorious, but perilous condition of open-ness towards Thee. Lord, inwork with a mighty influx of Thy power in correcting and health-giving fulness of life.

18 Lord, for the College, permeate it today with Thy presence and salvation from the top room to the basement. Bless with vigour and keenness mentally and spiritually.

19 Lord, what manner of man ought I to be! The graciousness of my life under Thy rule is so marvellous, and yet I find myself so ungenerous and ungracious. Lord, what shall I say?

20 Lord, come and touch all our lives and the atmosphere of the College with energising power and sweetness.

21 How I need to see Thee working in majesty and might and glory! We all need just that touch of Thine making all things new and wonderful, countering any influence or standard other than Thine own. Purify and empower us with Thy presence.

22 O Lord, the sternness, the unrelieved sternness, of my morning subject with the students [Jeremiah]. Soften the truths to our understanding, and keep us strong in Thee.

23 Lord, I would thank Thee for the profound and eager joy with which I find myself looking for Thy Second Coming! Oh that I might find grace in Thy sight, and behave more worthily of Thy great salvation!

24 O Lord, I thank Thee for the fulness of tone and health Thou dost give us these days. Continue it, O Lord. Save from all false emotion and sentimentality and sadness, and with vigour and gladness bless each one of us this day.

25 O Lord, for the days of this holiday I praise and thank Thee—for the majesty of this crowded isolation, the leagues of moor, the radiant air, the tonic of naturalness, and the sweet tonic of spiritual instruction as I lie fallow to Thy grace.

26 Lord, of late I feel a dim uncertainty as if Thou art leading me into a domain of Truth that as yet I have not entered or penetrated. Lord, lift me up till I see Thee; hold me till I fulfil Thy purpose.

27 Lord, this day glorify Thyself. Light up this house, my body, with Thy glory so that from all windows Thou mightest look forth unhindered and radiant.

28 Lord, bring me closer and nearer to Thee until I am more and more useful to Thee in Thine enterprises.

29 Lord, touch me again in body, soul and spirit. If my food and drink are hindering Thy ways in and through me, reveal this to me and keep me Thine, so that whether I eat or drink, or whatsoever I do, may be to Thy glory.

30 Lord, when I remember all Thy goodness, thy wonders and Thy grace, I alternate between praise and apprehension. O Lord, that all Thou seekest in me should be carried out in experimental life is my prayer.

October

1 Lord, carry me into Thy counsels and use me for Thy glory. For this College, may no fever of energy obstruct Thy working. Correct us in measure and in tenderness till we make it easy for Thee to carry out Thy plans through us.

2 "When He hideth His face, who then can behold Him?" There is so little sign of Thy being with us in these days of waiting. I pray not for any sign of outward success, but I do seek the sense of Thy blessing and approval.

3 Lord, I have no inkling of Thy ways in external details, but I have the expectancy of Thy wonders soon to be made visible. How completely at rest I am, and how free from seeing Thy way.

4 Lord, I praise Thee for the joy of my life here—for the love of wife and child, for the students, for the favours of the Holy Spirit. What a wonder of joy and radiant blessing this place has been!

5 Lord God Omnipotent, give me wisdom this day to worship Thee aright and be well-pleasing to Thee. Interpret Thyself to me more and more in Thy fulness and beauty.

6 Lord, how wondrous is the thought of Thee! but when shall I find my willing heart all taken up by Thee? I seem to be paralysed by my own littleness and meanness and sinfulness.

7 But surely, Lord, I do not need more verification of the truth of Thy words concerning the human heart; if it be Thy will, I do not want to know any more along that line: I want to know more of the great and gracious Reality of Thy Redemption.

8 "Lo, these are but the outskirts of His ways. . . . But the thunder of His power who can understand?" (RV). So many homeless moods float through my soul; I have no wisdom, no understanding of things pertaining to Thee until Thou dost lighten my darkness.

9 Lord, the present position presses most on my consciousness this morning. Cause my mind, my emotions, my whole nature, to want what Thou has ordained for me, that thereby I may know I have done aright.

10 "Clear Thou me from hidden faults. Keep back Thy servant also from presumptuous sins" (RV). Oh that I could find Thee exhibiting in me Thy peace and purity!

11 Lord, I praise Thee for the sense of well-being which is mine this morning. How I praise Thee for the deep revelation of Redemption! Shine with unclouded ray upon us all.

12 Lord, Thy servant's words state my inmost prayer—

My God, I look to Thee for tenderness
Such as I could not seek from any man,
Or in a human heart fancy or plan.

13 Lord, increase my certainty that I am taken up into Thy consciousness, and not that I take Thee into mine. "For in all the world there is none but Thee, my God, there is none but Thee."

14 Lord, I come to Thee this morning with a sense of spiritual failure. Cleanse me by Thy grace, and restore me to the heavenly places in Christ Jesus.

15 Lord, cause it to be proven that I shall be "like a tree planted by the streams of water," bringing forth its fruit in its season.

16 Lord, I praise Thee that Thou art, and that Thou performest Thy perfect will in and through the lives of individual men.

17 Lord, let me see Thee today fully and freely. Keep a clear space between Thee and me that I may see the way whereby I should go.

18 Lord, give me discernment and inspiration for today's Classes, especially for "The Soul of a Christian" talk this afternoon. Bless this day and make it radiant with Thy power.

19 O Lord, I have to preach in Thy Name today. Shall I, must I, speak on "God is love"? Am I to do it without Thy mighty inspiration and thrilling power? Nay, Lord, forbid it.

20 Lord, what need is mine! what weaknesses lurk in hidden places and mar my whole being. O Lord, I turn to Thee. How I need to realise that apart from Thee I can do nothing.

21 Lord, I thank Thee for the word this morning— "The Lord upholdeth him with His hand." Ah Lord, and Thou dost talk to me with the pressure of Thy hand.

22 O Lord, restore the unique joy of Thy presence to me and make me Thine and of Thee in this place. I seem unsuited for anything but just waiting on Thee. Show me a token for good, O Lord.

23 "Ye shall not fear them: for the LORD your God, He it is that fighteth for you" (RV). Lord, this word came to me insistently in my reading this morning. How entirely I look to Thee!

24 Lord, dawn on me this day, draw me, direct me into all the beauty of Thy Divine purposes; touch my senses that I may see Thy ways and delight in them.

25 O Lord, unto Thee do I come with an overwhelming sense of spiritual dryness and dearth; quicken me, O Lord, for Thy Name's sake. I will not mourn before Thee, but be filled with Thy Spirit.

26 Lord, with praise and adoration I come to Thee this Sunday morning. I bless Thee for the inspiring association of my life and upbringing with Sunday.

27 Lord, this day be God, so great, so kind, so full of life and liberty; come in grace and power. I praise Thee for the beauty of the morning.

28 Lord, I thank Thee for the past night's sleep; I bless Thee that Thou dost neither slumber nor sleep, but dost keep us by day and by night.

29 Lord, unto Thee do I come. Give me a gracious incoming of Thy life till my reasoning, my imagination, and my speaking are all of Thee. How grandly Thou hast renewed my spirit and restored to me the joy of Thy salvation!

30 Lord, what powerful words come in "Daily Light" this morning: "Be strong and of a good courage; be not afraid, neither be thou dismayed: for the LORD thy God is with thee whithersoever thou goest." Amen! Hallelujah!

31 We thank Thee that there is no Good-bye. We ask Thee that Thy Crown and Seal may be upon us every one until we see Thee face to face.

November

1 Lord, this day be the restraining One in the midst of these thousands of men; many of them are godless—Thou didst die for "the ungodly." Cause them to turn to Thee.

2 O Lord, I would beseech Thee to bring me into living union with Thy purpose for these Huts I am in charge of. Anoint me afresh for this day in all its opportunity. Let me see Thy salvation at work.

3 Lord, these words come with the dawning power of Thy Spirit's might—"He taketh away the first, that He may establish the second." How I praise Thee for every remembrance of the College, it is never far from my thoughts—that is "the first," and what will be "the second?"

4 Today, O Lord, cleanse me from flurried busyness, and keep me calmly and purely Thine. Make this Hut the house of God, and the gate of heaven to men's souls.

5 Lord, I do praise Thee for the inestimable privilege of this early morning communion with Thee; so work in me that I may both will and work (RV) for Thy good pleasure this day.

6 In all matters, O Lord, I would acknowledge Thee. Keep us in tune with Thee that others may catch the joyousness and gladness of God.

7 Lord, quicken my sense of Thee, my discernment of Thee, my concentration on Thee, so that I am carefully careless about every relationship saving that in which I stand to Thee.

8 Lord, be manifest in our midst today, give us the great objective certainty of Thy presence. This bungalow, make it Bethany indeed, a house beautiful with God.

9 O Lord, fill this Hut, our bodies, this encampment, the whole Earth, with Thy glorious Self this day. Bless with flooding tides of spiritual life all of us today, just for the delight of it!

10 Lord, cause this day to be filled with Thy praise. Give me release from this medley of distractions, from attentiveness of nerves to all the details that press. I praise Thee that my mind *is* stayed on Thee, but I do desire Thy beauty to be upon me.

11 Lord, bless this day with great evidence of Thy thoughts to us-ward. I praise Thee for Thy word this morning— "For I know the thoughts that I think towards you, saith the LORD, thoughts of peace, and not of evil."

12 Lord, lift me up to Thee so that the bloom, the radiant joy of Thy salvation, visits me and shines forth for Thy glory. Keep me in flowing intercession with Thee.

13 O Lord, how completely true of me is the Psalmist's word—"My soul cleaveth unto the dust." My soul is very dust-y, Lord, quicken me according to Thy word. One word made living by Thy Spirit and how exquisite is the life that comes! Lord, speak it now.

14 Lord, I seem to drift around, just living dimly before Thee until Thou dost spring up within me. I adore Thee that I have faith in Thy mighty Redemption, but Oh, it makes such a difference to realise Thy touch!

15 O Lord, be so really present here in this Hut that every man coming in may realise that it is God's house in deed and in truth.

16 O Lord, this sense of being choked with immediately present things is suffocating to our realisation of Thyself; come and deliver and delight us.

17 O Lord, I thank Thee for yesterday, and for the fleeting realisation of Thy deeps in me; enable me this day to join heart and mind to Thee in steady and constant prayer.

18 Lord, bless with significant blessing the opening of the Study Classes tonight. Bring keenness of interest and spiritual power to bear strongly and mightily upon us all.

19 Lord, I thank Thee for the counsel in the text this morning ("And let it be . . . that thou do as occasion serve thee; for God is with thee") not to fret myself into conscious usefulness, but just do as the occasion Thou hast engineered shall serve.

20 Lord, today give me the intuitive, instinctive inspiration of Thy Holy Spirit that I may discern Thee in all things. Fill the whole day with Thy gracious presence and peace.

21 "Let me hear Thy voice"—that is my prayer. I am willing beyond all my expression to hear Thee, to perceive Thee, to be thrilled with Thy presence.

22 Lord, this day give me the most supreme absorption in Thee—such deflections, such leakages! I would return home to Thee, living again the life of entire dependence on Thee.

23 Lord, how little nourishment I have been giving to the indwelling Christ in me; O Lord, forgive me. Fill me with the ample sense of Thy forgiveness that I may not only joy in Thy salvation, but be filled with Thy Spirit for the work here.

24 O Lord, I fully realise that "I am but a little child, I know not how to go out or come in"; give me therefore "an understanding heart," and increase my sense of Thee this day.

25 "Thy touch has still its ancient power"; touch me, Lord, into fellowship with Thyself till my whole being glows with Thy peace and joy.

26 O Lord, unto Thee do I come for this day. The degenerating tendencies of this Country are subtle to a degree of amazement! Restore the joy of life which makes all around radiant.

27 Lord, I am conscious of a lack of proportion— things that are the merest trifles loom, and the glorious things retire. Give me a way out that I may be to Thy glory.

28 Lord, I do thank Thee for the touch Thou hast given me this morning—but what amazing lethargy has been mine, what un-beautifulness! Yet this is only a revelation of what I know myself to be apart from Thy life in me.

29 Lord, give me a fresh anointing of Thy Spirit for today, in prayer, in worship, and in work, so that in all things Thou mightest have the pre-eminence.

30 Lord, unto Thee do I come, absolutely come. I feel so entire a sense of need of Thyself that I just wait for Thee to speak to me, for what can I say to Thee? Let me lie spread out before Thee even as the desert sand beneath the sun.

December

1 Lord, how dense and foggy it still is on my spiritual, or rather my mental horizon, so that details take portentous dimensions and crowd out the great issues of life. Emancipate me with Thy deliverance.

2 O Lord, cause this "rod" to bud. Make the Study Classes in this new Marquee flourish before Thee, even as "the rod of Aaron . . . put forth buds, and bloomed blossoms" (RV).

3 How often I find it is the "ass" in me rather than my intelligence that "turns aside and sees the angel of the Lord." Lord, increase my spiritual sensitiveness that I may detect Thy slightest goings and drawings.

4 Lord, unto Thee do I come, entrench me around with Thyself as a wall of fire and be the glory in the midst. This sounds entirely selfish, but I know not how else to put it. O Lord, Thou knowest.

5 Lord, not with any sense of unworthiness (how can unworthiness indulge in any sense of worthiness?), not any thought of my insufficiency, nor any thought of myself at all, I come just because Thou art Thyself.

6 O Lord, explore down to the deepest springs of my spirit where the Spirit maketh intercession for us, and read the prayers I cannot utter.

7 I praise Thee, O Lord, for the word this Sabbath morning—"And when Moses went into the tent of meeting to speak with Him, then he heard the Voice speaking unto him from above the mercy-seat, . . . and he spake unto Him" (RV).

8 Lord, for all who are taxed physically, undertake with Thy sustaining. Prevent the exacting of the enemy, and may the joy of the Lord be their strength in a marvellous manner.

9 Lord, I rejoice that with Thee, the Father of lights, there can be "no variableness, neither shadow that is cast by [RV] turning." Give me to discern Thy rule and government.

10 Lord, in my consciousness this morning a crowd of little actual things press and I bring them straight to Thy presence. In Thy wisdom, say, "Peace, be still!" and may our ordered lives confess the beauty of Thy peace.

11 "But now, O God, strengthen Thou my hands"— Lord, *now!* Come to me, fill me with Thyself, then there will be no yearning unsatisfied.

12 Lord, I do praise Thee for this sense of joyful fellowship with Thee again. Give me calmness of mind and keenness of purpose; keep me Thine, undoubtedly and undeflectedly.

13 Lord, unto Thee do I turn, and on the ground of Thy mighty Redemption I pray great triumphing prayers with "the boldness which we have toward Him, that, if we ask anything according to His will, He heareth us" (RV).

14 Lord, I look to Thee, touch my body till it is all radiant with Thy life. Bless the morning Service with the men, make it right glorious with Thy presence.

15 Lord, I turn implicitly to Thee. Be such an atmosphere in and around us that we may be those out of whom the rivers of living water flow.

16 Lord, how eager is my growing desire for Thee, not in any small parochial manner, but in the glorious manner of a fuller realisation of Thy holiness.

17 Lord, my approach to Thee is dulled because of physical dimness, but my heart is glad, and my flesh also shall rest in hope.

18 "Great is our Lord, and mighty in power; His understanding is infinite" (RV). How certainly all might and wisdom is Thine, and how certainly by Thy grace I am eager for Thee to have Thy way through me.

19 Lord, this one thing—my utterable and unutterable need of Thee. *"Poor in spirit"* describes my certain knowledge of myself. In entire necessity I come to Thee.

20 Speak, Lord, that I may hear and understand. There seems so much outwardness in my spiritual life, so little gracious power realised; quicken me until I am incandescent with Thee.

21 Lord, be such a reviving and refreshing Presence in our midst today that we can only rejoice as fresh hopes of Eternity walking the actual ways of Time open before our eyes.

22 O Lord, I thank Thee for the verse this morning—"Therefore turn thou to thy God; keep mercy and judgement, and wait on thy God continually." Fill all this vast encampment with Thy glorious presence; restrain, and inspire godliness.

23 Lord Jesus, in Thee dwelleth "*all* the fulness of God"; "*all* things" have been delivered unto Thee; "*all* power" is given unto Thee in heaven and in earth—O God, my heavenly Father, supply my every need according to Thy riches in glory in Christ Jesus.

24 Lord, the word that strikes me so intimately in my reading this morning is this—"Thus did Moses; as the Lord commanded him, so did he."

25 Lord Jesus, nineteen centuries ago Thou wast here on this earth, "manifested in the flesh" (RV). Be here again today, manifested in *my* flesh—"Christ in you, the hope of glory."

26 O Lord, my Lord and Master, may I be so consciously Thine today that I am at home with Thee, and joyous in my childlike delight in Thy possession of me.

27 Lord, fill every space around us with Thyself this day. Control everything right marvellously by Thy guiding hand; lift us up into Thy wonderful purposes, and keep us from impulsive precipitancy.

28 O Lord, this is Thy Day, and I beseech Thee to bless me with Thy exceeding great blessing and benediction. How wonderful it is to be able to approach Thee!

29 "After these things the word of the Lord came saying, Fear not, I am thy shield, and thy exceeding great reward." O Lord, "*after these things!*" How I praise Thee.

30 It is time, O my God, for a touch from Thee, one of those great transfiguring touches in which Thou dost stand out plainly and clearly from all else, brilliant moments in which I see Thee and worship and wonder.

31 Lord, in this land of brooding silences, of great generating winds, and fiercely-killing sun, I seem to be brooded over by Thee—and what will be the result? Keep me watching and waiting at Thy threshold.

The Love of God

a combined volume including
The Love of God
The Ministry of the Unnoticed
The Message of Invincible Consolation
The Making of a Christian
Now Is It Possible—
The Graciousness of Uncertainty

Oswald Chambers

INTRODUCTION

Source
The material in *The Love of God* is taken from lectures and sermons given during nearly two decades of Oswald Chambers' life.

Publication History
The messages in this book were originally published as articles, leaflet sermons, and individual booklets. In 1965, six booklets were combined in a single volume and published as a hardcover book titled *The Love of God*.

- **The Love of God (1938):** David Lambert[1] identifies the first two chapters as messages given during Chambers' years in Dunoon, Scotland[2] (1897–1906), and the final chapter "If God Is Love—Why?" as a message given to soldiers at Zeitoun, Egypt,[3] in 1917. This final chapter was printed as a leaflet sermon in 1918 and distributed in Egypt and in England.

- **The Ministry of the Unnoticed (1936):** These are three talks that were given to students at the Bible Training College,[4] London, between 1911 and 1915, most likely during the weekly devotional hour. They were published individually as leaflet sermons before being issued as a booklet in 1936.

- **The Message of Invincible Consolation (1931):** Lambert identifies the material in *The Message of Invincible Consolation* as "two talks given at an Annual Meeting of the League of Prayer,[5] on 2 Corinthians 4:16–18." Also included is "The Worker and Things As They Are," likely spoken to a League audience as well.

- These appeared as articles in *Spiritual Life* magazine from September through November 1930.

- **The Making of a Christian (1918; 1935):** *The Making of a Christian* was used as a topic in Chambers' Bible correspondence course series, for which Oswald wrote the following introduction:

  The object of these studies is to stimulate thinking along Christian lines. So many among us have a good spiritual experience, but have never thought things out on Christian lines. It is just as true that a man may LIVE a Christian life without THINKING it as that a man may THINK a Christian life without LIVING it; but to combine the two means that great help may be rendered during times of confusion, turmoil and tension like the present. Bear in mind that Christian growth is based on the regeneration of a man's soul through Redemption.

- These studies were also delivered as blackboard talks to the troops stationed at the Imperial School of Instruction, Zeitoun, Egypt, during July 1917. Chambers, ever the teacher, frequently lettered the complete outline of his lecture on a blackboard before launching into his subject. *The Making of a Christian* was printed in Egypt in 1918 as a small booklet and made available to the soldiers. In 1935, Mrs. Chambers published a new edition of the book, edited for reading rather than for study.

- **Now Is It Possible (1934):** This material is from three talks given to students at the Bible Training College, London, between 1911 and 1915.

- **The Graciousness of Uncertainty (1938):** Chambers preached "The Graciousness of Uncertainty" at a Sunday morning communion service, Zeitoun YMCA Camp, Egypt, on October 15, 1916. This sermon was omitted when *The Love of God* was printed as a paperback in 1973; it is included here, along with the foreword to the first edition.

1. David Lambert (1871–1961): Methodist minister and friend of Oswald and Biddy Chambers. He assisted Mrs. Chambers with OC publications from 1917 until his death in 1961.

2. Dunoon, Scotland: small town west of Glasgow; Chambers spent 1897–1906 at Dunoon Theological College as a student, then as a tutor.

3. Zeitoun (zay TOON), Egypt: six miles northeast of Cairo; site of a YMCA camp, the Egypt General Mission compound, and, from 1916 to 1919, the Imperial School of Instruction, training base for British, Australian, and New Zealand troops during World War I.

4. Bible Training College (BTC): a residential school near Clapham Common in southwest London; sponsored by the League of Prayer; operated from 1911 until it closed in July 1915 because of World War I. Oswald Chambers was principal and main teacher; Biddy Chambers, his wife, was lady superintendent.

5. Pentecostal League of Prayer: founded in 1891 in London by Reader Harris (1847–1909), prominent barrister and friend and mentor of Oswald Chambers.

CONTENTS

The Love of God

God is Love.

God is love. No one but God could have revealed *that* to the world, for men, and we all indeed, see nothing but its contradiction in our own limited world of experience. It needs but little imagination to construe the life of hundreds of this great city's inhabitants into a vehement laughter at such a declaration as "God is love." From shattered, broken lives, from caverns of despair where fiends seem living rather than men, comes the existing contradiction to any such statement. No wonder the carnal mind, the merely intellectually cultured, consider us infatuated, mere dreamers, talking of love when murder and war and famine and lust and pestilence, and all the refinement of selfish cruelty is abroad in the earth. But, oh the sublimity of the Abraham-like faith that dares to place the centre of its life and confidence and action and hope in an unseen and apparently unknown God, saying, "God is love," in spite of all appearances to the contrary; saying "Though He slay me, yet will I trust in Him." Such faith is counted to a man for righteousness.

Look back over your own history as revealed to you by grace, and you will see one central fact growing large—God is love. No matter how often your faith in such an announcement was clouded, no matter how the pain and suffering of the moment made you speak in a wrong mood, still this statement has borne its own evidence along with it most persistently—God is love. In the future, when trial and difficulties await you, do not be fearful, whatever and whoever you may lose faith in, let not this faith slip from you—God is Love; whisper it not only to your heart in its hour of darkness, but here in your corner of God's earth and man's great city, live in the belief of it; preach it by your sweetened, chastened, happy life; sing it in consecrated moments of peaceful joy, sing until the world around you

> is wrought
> To sympathy with hopes and fears it heeded not.

The world does not bid you sing, but God does. Song is the sign of an unburdened heart; then sing your songs of love unbidden, ever rising higher and higher into a fuller conception of the greatest, grandest fact on the stage of Time—God is Love.

But words and emotions pass, precious as their influence may be for the time, so when the duller moments come and the mind comes to require something more certain and sure to consider than the memory of mere emotions and stirring sentiments—consider this revelation, the eternal fact that God is Love, not, God is loving. God and love are synonymous. Love is not an attribute of God, it is God; whatever God is, love is. If your conception of love does not agree with justice and judgement and purity and holiness, then your idea of love is wrong. It is not love you conceive of in your mind, but some vague infinite foolishness, all tears and softness and of infinite weakness.

1. God Is Love—In His Very Nature

Some exceptionally gifted men may derive their conception of God from other sources than the Bible, but all I know of God I have got from the Bible, and those who taught me got what they taught from the Bible. In all my dreams and imaginings and visions I see God, but it is the God of the Bible that I see, and I feel Him to be near me. I see ever amid the mysteries of Providence and Grace and Creation "a Face like my face," and "a Hand like this hand," and I have learned to love God Who gave me such a sure way of knowing Him and left me not to the vain imaginations of my own sin-warped intellect.

In Creation. The love of God gives us a new method of seeing Nature. His voice is on the rolling air, we see Him in the rising sun, and in the setting He is fair; in the singing of the birds, in the love of human hearts, the voice of God is in all. Had we but ears to hear the stars singing, to catch the glorious pealing anthem of praise echoing from the hills of immortality by the heavenly hosts!

In His Wisdom. God did not create man as a puppet to please a despotic idea of His own, He created us out of the superabundant flow of overflowing love and goodness, He created us susceptible of all the blessedness which He had ordained for us. He "thought" us in the rapture of His own great heart, and lo, we are! Created in the image of God were we, innocent of evil, of great God-like capacities.

In His Power. The whole world moves but to His great inscrutable will, animate and inanimate creation, the celestial bodies moving on their orbits, the globe

with all its diversified issues and accompaniments, are all subservient to this end.

> Yes, God is good, in earth and sky,
>   In ocean depth and swelling wood,
> Ten thousand voices ever cry,
>   God made us all, and God is good.

In His Holiness. God walked with man and talked with him, He told him His mind, and showed him the precise path in which he must walk in order to enjoy the happinesses He had ordained for him; He rejoiced in the fulness of His nature over man as His child, the offspring of His love. He left nothing unrevealed to man; He loved him. Oh, the joy and rapture of God the Father over man His son!

In His Justice. God showed to man that compliance with His dictates would ever mean eternal bliss and joy unspeakable and life and knowledge for evermore, but that ceasing to comply would mean loss of life with God and eternal death.

That was in the world's bright morning when the morning stars sang together and all creation leapt in joy, but the wild, wild desolation of sin and disobedience and pride and selfish sinfulness entered and drave a great gulf between God's children and Himself. But, as ever, Love found a way, God came to us and for us, and we this day with chastened hearts and quivering lips and glistening eyes, yet with love deep and strong in our hearts, say all afresh with deep adoration, God is Love.

If God exhibits such glorious love in His Nature, what, oh what, shall we say of the glories of the dispensation of His Grace! That God would have walked this earth had sin never entered is very likely, yet sin did not refrain Him from graciously walking and revealing Himself in communion with men. No, still He came. But men were so blinded by sin that they saw Him not, they knew Him not, while He hewed a way back through the hard face of sin to the heavenly shores.

2. The Gift of God's Only Begotten Son

The gift of God's only begotten Son surely reveals His love in an amazing degree—"He that spared not His own Son"—till now it matters not how bad a man is, if he will but lift his eyes to the Cross he shall be saved. But yet so blinded and infatuated and imbecile has man become by sin that he can see nothing in the life of Christ save the evidence of a beautiful, good life, the best of human beings, living misunderstood, suffering, dying as a martyr. To meet this difficulty Love itself gave another gift—the gift of the Holy Spirit.

3. The Gift of the Holy Spirit

When He shines on the Historic Christ, all the great and grey outlines spring into glorious relief and colour and beauty, and the soul amazed, calls out, "My Lord and my God."

When the Holy Spirit has begun His gracious work in your soul and heart by making it tremulously expectant, you see a new light on the Cross and the "martyr" becomes the Saviour of the world. "Surely He hath borne our griefs, and carried our sorrows: yet we did esteem Him stricken, smitten of God, and afflicted. But He was wounded for *our* transgressions, He was bruised for *our* iniquities: the chastisement of *our* peace was upon Him; and with His stripes we are healed" (RV).

Though it is too difficult, nay impossible, to trace that God is love by mere unaided human intellect, it is not impossible to the intuitions of faith. Lift up your eyes and look abroad over the whole earth, and in the administration of God's moral government you will begin to discern that God is love, that over sin and war and death and hell He reigns supreme, that His purposes are ripening fast. We must by holy con-templation of all we have considered keep ourselves in the love of God, then we shall not be able to despond for long. The love of God performs a mira-cle of grace in graceless human hearts. Human love and lesser loves must wither into the most glorious and highest love of all, viz., the love of God. Then we shall see not only each other's faults, we shall see the highest possibilities in each other, and shall love each other for what God will yet make of us. Nothing is too hard for God, no sin too difficult for His love to overcome, not a failure but He can make it a success.

God is Love—one brief sentence, you can print it on a ring: it is the Gospel. A time is coming when the whole round world will know that God reigns and that God is Love, when hell and heaven, life and death, sin and salvation, will be read and understood aright at last.

God is Love—a puzzle text, to be solved slowly, as with tears and penitence, by prayer and joy, by vision and faith, and, last, by death.

KEEP YOURSELVES IN THE LOVE OF GOD
Jude 20–21

Keep yourselves in the love of God.

The love of God! We have lost it to-day; we have turned our back on the ocean and are looking out over barren colourless hills for the ocean's fulness. We need converting again—turning round, and there basks the ocean's fulness, whose waves sparkle and ripple on fath-omless deeps and fulnesses. We are too introspective to-day, we mourn and wonder, then lifted on waves of feeling, we glow and say we love God, but again our feelings ebb and flow and we mourn. Christianity is not a thing of times and seasons, but of God and faith. Drink deep and full of the love of God and you will not demand the impossible from earth's loves, and the love of wife and child, of husband and friend, will grow holier and healthier and simpler and grander.

But there are initial stages to be considered before we come to the glorious exhortation. The love of God is not revealed by intellectual discernment, it is a spir-itual revelation. What ups and downs we experience because we build not on faith but on feeling, not on the finished work of Christ but on our own work and endeavour and experience.

"But ye, beloved, building up yourselves on your most holy faith . . ." Is that what *you* are doing every day? Do you have family worship? Do you have private devo-tions? Do you read your Bible more and more? Can you answer "Yes" to these questions, or is an hesitant "No" given by your spirit to God? Family worship is so far off, so remote, you remember your father and mother who prayed and talked of sin and righteous-ness and judgement to come, but you have other things to heed; you, forsooth, are more enlightened, you read sceptical books, controversial books, that attack the foundations of your faith. If these things have crept in unawares into our hearts, let us get back in penitence and consider what is the foundation on which we must build our most holy faith, viz., that "God so loved the world, that He gave His only begotten Son, that whosoever believeth on Him should not perish, but have everlasting life" (RV). Let us get down to the Cross, to the broken heart of our God, down to the propitiation for our sins; let us put away the books that have sapped our faith; let us cut off the interests and the companionships that have weighed our lives down to the dust, and looking to Jesus, let us build ourselves up on our most holy faith.

"praying in the Holy Ghost . . ." That is the next step after laying the foundation of faith. Nothing is so hard as to pray aright. Do *you* pray for God's servants till your heart glows? Do you ask for your minister that he may be set ablaze with Divine fire? Do you pray Sunday after Sunday that souls may be converted to God? "Praying in the Holy Ghost"—have you ever asked for the Holy Spirit? We can only keep ourselves

in the love of God by building up ourselves on our most holy faith and by Holy Ghost praying, and by nothing else. If we try to fight God's battles with our own weapons, in our own moral resisting power, we shall fail, and fail miserably; but if we use the spiritual weapons of implicitly trusting in God and maintaining a simple relationship to Jesus Christ by praying in the Holy Ghost, we shall never fail.

"*. . . keep yourselves in the love of God.*" We know how to keep ourselves in health, how to keep ourselves in knowledge, and so on; but to keep ourselves in the love of God is a big order, and our minds are exercised to know what Jude means by this exhortation. Does it mean by relaxing all stringency and carefulness to slip out into a broad, humanitarian spirit—"God is love": "God's in His heaven—all's right with the world"? No, it cannot mean anything so natural as that, otherwise we had no need of an inspired writer to tell us to do it, and beside, Jude strikes terrible notes of warning (see vv. 17–19). "Keep yourselves in the love of God" refers very clearly to something distinct and special, something revealed in the direct will of God; a spiritual endeavour that we must consider, and consider carefully with the Holy Spirit's help.

"Keep" means work. It is not a lazy floating, it is work. Work, or you will depart from the love of God.

Begin to trace the finger of God and the love of God in the great calamities of earth, and in the calamities that have befallen you. In sweat of brain and spirit, work, agonise at times, to keep yourself in the love of God. It is our wisdom, our happiness, our security to keep ourselves in the love of God. How do I keep myself in any sphere but by using every means to abide in it? If I wish to keep in the spiritual sphere of the love of God I must use the great organ of the spiritual realm, faith. "God loves me"—say it o'er and o'er and o'er, heedless of your feelings that come and go. Do not live at a distance from God, live near Him, delighting yourself in Him. Remove all barriers of selfishness and fear, and plunge into the fathomless love of God.

"Keep yourselves in the love of God," not "keep on loving God," none can do that. When once you have understood the truth about your own heart's sinfulness, think not again of it, but look at the great, vast, illimitable magnificence of the love of God. Oh may we be driven, driven further and further out into the ocean fulness of the love of God! only taking care that nothing entices us out again.

"Who shall separate us from the love of Christ?" Oh, the fulness of peace and joy and gladness when we are persuaded that nothing "shall be able to separate us from the love of God, which is in Christ Jesus our Lord."

DECEMBER 14, 1916, ALEXANDRIA, EGYPT. ALSO GIVEN AT ZEITOUN.

IF GOD IS LOVE—WHY?

It is easy to say "God is love" when there is no war and when everything is going well; but it is not so easy to say when everything that happens actually gives the lie to it. For instance, when a man realises he has an incurable disease, or a severe handicap in life, or when all that is dear has been taken from a man, for that man to say, as he faces these things, "God is love," means he has got hold of something the average man has missed.

Love is difficult to define, but the working definition I would like to give is that "Love is the sovereign preference of my person for another person, embracing everyone and everything in that preference."

Run your idea for all it is worth. When we are young we think things are simpler than they are; we have an idea for every domain. A man says he is a materialist, or an agnostic, or a Christian, meaning he has only one main idea, but very few will run that idea for all it is worth, yet this is the only way to discover whether it will work, and the same thing is true in the idea of the Christian religion that God is Love.

1. Nature of God's Love

But God commendeth His own love toward us, in that, while we were yet sinners, Christ died for us. (Romans 5:8 RV)

The love of God is different from the love of everyone else. "God commendeth His *own* love toward us" (RV); it is not the love of a father or mother, or a wife or lover, it is of such a peculiar stamp that it has to be recommended to us, we do not believe God's love.

(a) The Foundation of God's Love

The foundation of God's love, i.e., holiness—"without which no man shall see the Lord." God's love then must be the justification of His holiness. Remember our definition—love is the sovereign preference of my person for another person, embracing everyone and everything in that preference. If God's nature is holy, His love must be holy love, seeking to embrace everyone and everything until we all become holy.

(b) The Features of God's Love

The features of God's love, i.e., the way His love as revealed in the Bible manifests itself in common life, are unfamiliar to us; the average common-sense man is completely puzzled by such a verse as John 3:16. The revelation of Christianity has to do with the foundation of things, not primarily with actual life, and when the Gospel is proclaimed it is proclaimed as the foundation. The features of God's love are that if we will commit ourselves to Him, He will impart to us the very nature of His Son. "The *gift of God* is eternal life."

(c) The Fact of God's Love (2 Corinthians 5:18–21)

"God was in Christ, reconciling the world unto Himself" (2 Corinthians 5:19). These are subjects that have no weight with us in our ordinary way of looking at things, they do not live in the same street, because they are not in the street, but in the foundation of things. When war or some other thing hits us hard and knocks us out of the commonplace, we are prepared to listen to what the Bible has to say, and we discover the Bible deals with the foundation of things that lie behind our common-sense life. The Bible does not deal with the domain of commonsense facts, we get at those by our senses; the Bible deals with the world of revelation facts which we only get at by faith in God.

2. Nature and God's Love

For the earnest expectation of the creation waiteth for the revealing of the sons of God. (Romans 8:19 RV)

Does Nature exhibit the Creator as a God of love? If so, then why is Nature a scene of rapine and murder? Has the Bible anything to say about it, any revelation that explains it? Try and weave a conception of God out of Jesus Christ's presentation of Him and then look at life as it is, and you will find that God, as He is revealed in Jesus Christ, is flatly contradicted in the natural world. God is the only Being Who can afford to be misunderstood; He deliberately stands aside and lets Himself be slandered and misrepresented; He never vindicates Himself.

When we touch the cosmic force apart from the "blinkers" of intellect, there is a wild problem in it. Nature is wild not tame. Modern science would have us believe it is tame, that we can harness the sea and the air. Quite true, if we only read scientific manuals, and deal with successful experiments; but after a while we discover that there are elements which knock men's calculations on the head and prove that the universe is wild and unmanageable and yet God in the beginning created man to have dominion over it! The reason he cannot is because he has twisted the order and become master of himself, instead of recognising God's dominion over him. Jesus Christ belonged to the order of things God originally intended for mankind; He was easily Master of the life of the sea and air and earth. If we want to know what the human race will be like on the basis of Redemption, we shall find it mirrored in Jesus Christ, a perfect oneness between God and man. In the meantime there is a gap, and the universe is wild. Paul says that creation is out of gear and twisted, that it is waiting for the manifestation of the sons of God. The New Testament view of Nature is that it is subject to bondage, that it is in a disorganised condition, out of gear with God's purpose; it is twisted and will only be right when God and man are again one.

God is responsible for the established order of nature, so if God created Nature and we have not the Spirit of God, we shall never interpret the order of Nature as God does.

(a) The Indifference of Nature

"Thorns also and thistles shall it bring forth to thee; and thou shalt eat the herb of the field; in the sweat of thy face shalt thou eat bread, till thou return unto the ground . . . (Genesis 3:18–19). This needs an explanation no man can reach by common sense. The Bible says the reason Nature is indifferent is because it became disorganised through the disobedience of the Federal Head of the human race. The indifference of nature hits us sorely when our hearts are stirred by bereavement—the inscrutable sadness of nature on the human spirit. The early mornings, the late at nights, sea scenes and mountain scenes, awaken in the sensitive human spirit not in touch with God, an ineffable sadness, ages weary, ages sad, ages worn out, pointing to this very fact that God is amazingly remote from man because man has externalised himself.

(b) The Iniquity of Nature

"And I saw a new heaven and a new earth: for the first heaven and the first earth were passed away; and there was no more sea" (Revelation 21:1). There is nothing more cruel than the sun, or more blasting than the desert. There is an element of twisted spite in the sea, in certain aspects of human life; a sailor's wife, for instance, has reason to have a deep fear and hatred of the sea. In the jungles of vast continents the most cruel and unspeakable horrors take place. These are some things that make it the height of impertinence to say glibly, "God is love."

(c) The Infidelity of Nature

"The wolf also shall dwell with the lamb, . . . they shall not hurt nor destroy in all My holy mountain: for the earth shall be full of the knowledge of the LORD, as the waters cover the sea" (Isaiah 11:6, 9). Isaiah is speaking of a time when all the indifference and iniquity and infidelity of Nature will be gone, when "the wolf shall dwell with the lamb"—a relationship will exist which

now is inconceivable; at present the lamb lies down inside the wolf! Earth is man's domain, but the Bible talks about a "hereafter" without the sin and iniquity, "a new heaven and a new earth." We are going to be here, marvellously redeemed, in this wonderful place which God made very beautiful, and which has been played havoc with by sin.

3. Nations and God's Love

The kingdoms of this world are become the kingdoms of our Lord, and of His Christ; and He shall reign for ever and ever. (Revelation 11:15)

We talk about a Christian nation—there never has been such a thing. There are Christians in the nations, but not Christian nations. The constitution of nations is the same as that of a human being. There is a difference between individuality and personality: individuality is all elbows and must stand alone; personality is something that can be merged and blended. Individuality is the husk of the personal life; when personal life is emancipated, individuality goes. So with nations. The kingdoms of this world have become intensely individualistic, with no love for God, or care for one another. The insistence of nations is that they must keep the national peace—in the way they have been doing it! In the whirlwind of nations, such as is on just now many men have lost—not their faith in God (I never met a man who lost his faith in God), but their belief in their beliefs, and for a while they think they have lost their faith in God. They have lost the conception which has been presented to them as God, and are coming to God on a new line.

(a) The Origin of Nations (Genesis 11:1–9)

"And the whole earth was of one language, and of one speech. . . . Therefore is the name of it called Babel; because the LORD did there confound the language of all the earth: and from thence did the LORD scatter them abroad upon the face of all the earth" (Genesis 11:1, 9). According to the Bible, nations as we know them are the outcome of what ought never to have been. Civilisation was founded on murder, and the basis of our civilised life is competition. There are grand ingredients in civilisation, it is full of shelter and protection, but its basis is not good. We each belong to a nation, and each nation imagines that God is an Almighty representative of that nation. If nations are right, which is *the* right one?

(b) The Object of Nations

"From whence come wars and fightings among you? . . . Ye fight and war, yet ye have not, because ye ask not" (James 4:1–2). The question is on the lips of people to-day, "Is war of the devil or of God?" It is of neither, it is of men, though both God and the devil are behind it. War is a conflict of wills, either in individ-

uals or in nations. As sure as there is will *versus* will, there must be punch *versus* punch. This is the object of nations. They will assert their rule and independence and refuse to be downtrodden. If we cannot by diplomacy make our wills bear on other people, then the last resort is war, and always will be until Jesus Christ brings in His Kingdom.

There is one thing worse than war and that is sin, the thing that startles us is not the thing that startles God. We are scared and terrorised when our social order is broken, when thousands of men are killed, and well we may be, but how many of us in times of peace and civilisation bother one iota about the state of men's hearts towards God? Yet that is the thing that produces pain in the heart of God, not the wars and devastations that so upset us.

(c) The Obliteration of Nations

"And there followed great voices in heaven, and they said [RV], The kingdoms of this world are become the kingdoms of our Lord, and of His Christ; and He shall reign for ever and ever" (Revelation 11:15). In these last days there is an idea that we are going to dominate everything by a perfect brotherhood. Any mind that expresses its view of the future says we are heading up into a federation of religions and nations when distinctions will be obliterated and there will be a great and universal Brotherhood. The quarrels of nations make men look forward to the time when nations will be federated out of independent existence. That is a revolt which is a mental safety valve only. Peter says God is "longsuffering to us-ward." At present He is giving men opportunity to try every line they like in individual life as well as in the life of the nations at large. Some things have not been tried yet, and if God were to cut us off short we would say, "If You had left us a bit longer we could have realised our ideal of society and national life." God is allowing us to prove to the hilt that it cannot be done in any other way than Jesus Christ said, viz., by a personal relationship to God through Jesus Christ Who is *God and Man—One.* When sooner or later we come to the end of our tether, we hear Jesus Christ say: "Blessed are the poor in spirit"—"If you ask God, He will give you the Holy Spirit," i.e., an unsullied heredity through Jesus Christ.

That is how the love of God comes in, and why it has to be such a long way round is because He is "bringing many *sons* unto glory," not mechanisms, but men, full-orbed and sensible all through. Jesus Christ never used a revivalistic meeting to take a man off his guard and then say, "Believe in Me." He always puts the case to a man in cold blood, He even seemed to spurn men when they wanted to follow Him (see Luke 9:57–62). "Another convert to My cause." Not a bit. "Take time and consider what you are doing, are you ready to hear what I have to say?"

The love of God is going to embrace everyone and everything in the sovereign preference of His person, which is for His Son. God purposes that everyone of us shall partake of the very essential nature of Jesus Christ and stand in complete union with Himself, even as Jesus did. Faith in God is a terrific venture in the dark, we have to believe that God is love in spite of all that contradicts it. Every soul represents some kind of battlefield. The great point for the Christian is to remain perfectly confident in God. Paul says that when the sons of God are manifested, and everything is in a right relationship with God and expressed in devotion to Jesus Christ, all the wildness and contradiction in Nature and in nations will cease, and the Love of God will be the great Reality.

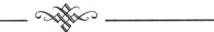

The Ministry of the Unnoticed

I will be as the dew unto Israel: he shall blossom as the lily. Hosea 14:5 (RV)

The New Testament notices things which from our standpoint do not seem to count. For instance, Our Lord called only twelve disciples, but what about all those other disciples of His who were not specially called? The twelve disciples were called for a special purpose; but there were hundreds who followed Jesus and were sincere believers in Him who were unnoticed. We are apt to have a disproportionate view of a Christian because we look only at the exceptions. The exceptions stand out *as* exceptions. The extraordinary conversions and phenomenal experiences are magnificent specimen studies of what happens in the life of everyone, but not one in a million has an experience such as the Apostle Paul had. The majority of us are unnoticed and unnoticeable people. If we take the extraordinary experience as a model for the Christian life, we erect a wrong standard without knowing it, and in the passing of the years we produce that worst abortion, the spiritual prig—an intolerant un-likeness to Jesus Christ. The man or woman who becomes a spiritual prig does so by imperceptible degrees, but the starting-point is a departure from the evangel of the New Testament and a building up on the evangel of Protestantism.

1. The Unaffected Loveliness of the Commonplace
Blessed are the poor in spirit. (Matthew 5:3)

Literally: "Blessed are the paupers in spirit." (A pauper is exceedingly commonplace! The average type of preaching emphasises strength of will, beauty of character—the things that can be easily noticed. The phrase "Decide for Christ" which we so frequently hear is too often an emphasis on the thing Our Lord never trusted. Our Lord never asks us to *decide for Him:* He asks us to *yield to Him*—a very different matter.

At the basis of Our Lord's Kingdom is this unaffected loveliness of the commonplace. The thing in which I am blessed is my poverty. If I know I have no strength of will, no nobility of disposition, then, says Jesus, "Blessed are you," because it is through that poverty that I enter into the Kingdom of Heaven. I cannot enter the Kingdom of Heaven as a good man or woman; I can only enter the Kingdom of Heaven as a complete pauper.

(a) The Influence of Disadvantage
As the lily among thorns, so is my love among the daughters. (Song of Solomon 2:2)

The lily Solomon refers to is as common as our daisy, but a perfume pervades it. The illustration is as if a traveller were passing a field and suddenly a fragrant aroma was wafted to him from a bush; marvelling at the sweetness, he looked into the bush and found a lily growing in its bosom. People come to a good but worldly home, and say, "What a beautiful influence comes from that home!" But begin to draw aside the ordinary commonplace things of the home, and you discover that tucked away somewhere is a mother or a daughter who is really a "lily" of the Lord. Or take it in connection with individual lives, we may see a man who is generally disadvantaged in appearance or in education, a thoroughly commonplace man, yet a marvellous influence radiates from him. Our Lord is spoken of as "a root out of a dry ground"—thoroughly disadvantaged, that is what Isaiah says the Hero of God will be like.

The true character of the loveliness that tells for God is always unconscious. Conscious influence is priggish and un-Christian. When we begin to wonder whether we are of any use, we instantly lose the bloom of the touch of the Lord. Jesus says—"He that believeth on Me," out of him "shall flow rivers of living water." If we begin to examine outflow, we lose touch with the Source. We have to pay attention to the Source and God will look after the outflow.

The same thing is true with regard to the "passion for souls," the great craze for successful service. Our

Lord told the disciples not to rejoice in successful service, but to rejoice because they were rightly related to Him (see Luke 10:18–20). The danger in all these things is that we are apt to make the effect the cause. Who are the people who have influenced us most? Certainly not the priggish men and women, but our mothers, our fathers, our sisters—the ones who had not the remotest idea that they were influencing us.

(b) The Inspiration of Detail
And the capitals that were upon the top of the pillars were of lily work.... (1 Kings 7:19)

The lily work added nothing to the strength of the building; many would notice the strength and the majesty of the whole building, but the inspiration of it all was in the detail, in the "lily work." In architecture it is not so much the massive strength that counts as the finely proportioned ornament, and that is never obtrusive. If we look at men and women who have been long at work for God and have been going through chastening, we notice that they have lost their individual harshness, lost a great deal of their apparent go-aheadness for God; but they have acquired something else, viz. the most exquisite "lily work" in their lives, and this after all is the thing most like Jesus Christ. It is the quiet, undisturbable Divinity that is characteristic of Jesus, not aggressiveness, and the same is true of God's children. This does not mean that Our Lord is not aggressive, or that God's children are not aggressive, but it does mean that there is a danger of making so much of the aggressive that we neglect the more important aspect, viz. the ministry of the unnoticed.

God will use any number of extraordinary things to chisel the detail of His "lily work" in His children. He will use people who are like hedgehogs, He will use difficult circumstances, the weather; He will use anything and everything, no matter what it is, and we shall always know when God is at work because He produces in the commonplace something that is inspiring.

(c) The Implicitness of Distinction
Consider the lilies.... (Matthew 6:28)

When Our Lord described the spiritual life, He always took His illustrations from His Father's handiwork, never from man's work. We take our illustrations from motor-cars, or aeroplanes, or electric light, or something go-ahead and self-advertising. We illustrate by means of things which compel our attention; Jesus mentions things we are not compelled to look at, things which we would pass by. How many of us notice sparrows and daisies and grass? They are so plentiful that we ignore them, yet it is these things Jesus tells us to consider. The characteristic of each of these things is implicitness, not explicitness. Imagine a lily, if it could speak, saying, "I am going to be a lily!" A lily obeys the law of its life where it is placed, it is unconscious in its growth. In Isaiah 47:7, we read: "And thou saidst, I shall be a lady for ever." The characteristic of a lady is implicitness, not explicitness, and in the same way a Christian is one in whom the indwelling Spirit of God shines out all the time. In the Christian life the implicit is never conscious; if it becomes conscious, it ceases to have the unaffected loveliness which is the characteristic of the life of Jesus Christ. Prudery is the outcome of obedience to a principle; whereas, according to Our Lord, purity is the outcome of an implicit relationship. If we look upon purity as the outcome of obedience to a particular standard, we produce the opposite of what Our Lord intends. He said, "Except ye ... become *as little children ...*"

2. The Unconscious Light in Circumstances
If I then, your Lord and Master, have washed your feet; ye also ought to wash one another's feet. (John 13:14)

What were the circumstances here? A supper table, a dozen fishermen, a basin of water, a towel, and Our Lord washing the feet of the fishermen. Notice the extraordinary climax to John 13:3—"Jesus knowing that the Father had given all things into His hands, and that He was come from God, and went to God ..." Had the Transfiguration scene followed on, we would have felt it to be the right order; but—"He riseth from supper, and laid aside His garments; and took a towel, and girded Himself. After that He poureth water into a basin, and began to wash the disciples' feet." Could anything be more sordid and commonplace? But it takes God Incarnate to do the most menial task properly. We may often use a towel to exhibit a characteristic totally unlike Jesus Christ. Whatever Our Lord touched became wonderful. Some people do a certain thing and the way in which they do it hallows that thing to us for ever afterwards. When Our Lord does anything, He always transfigures it. Notice the words that Our Lord glorified. A word that was scorned when He came was the word "servant," yet Jesus said: "I am among you as He that serveth," and, "whosoever of you will be the chiefest, shall be servant of all." Our Lord took words that were despised and transfigured their meaning; He did things that were commonplace and sordid and ordinary and transfigured them. Our Lord was the unconscious light in the midst of the most ordinary circumstances conceivable.

Many who knew Our Lord while He was on earth saw nothing in Him; only after their disposition had been altered did they realise Who He was. Our Lord lived so ordinary a life that no one noticed Him. The disciples were first attracted to Jesus by their sense of the heroic and the holy, but it was not until they had received the Holy Spirit that "their eyes were opened, and they knew Him." Could anything more startling be imagined than for someone to point out a Nazarene carpenter and say, "That man is God Incarnate"? It would sound blasphemous to a Pharisee.

Our Lord did not say to His disciples: "I have had a most successful time on Earth, I have addressed thousands of people and been the means of their salvation; now you go and do the same kind of thing." He said: "If I then, your Lord and Master, have washed your feet; *ye also ought to wash one another's feet.*" We try to get out of it by washing the feet of those who are not of our own set. We will wash the heathen's feet, the feet in the slums; but fancy washing my brother's feet! my wife's! my husband's! the feet of the minister of my church! Our Lord said *"one another's feet."* It is in the ordinary commonplace circumstances that the unconscious light of God is seen.

(a) The Trackless Waste
Ye are the light of the world. (Matthew 5:14)

In the New Testament "world" means the system of things which has been built on God's earth, the system of religion or of society or of civilisation that never takes Jesus Christ into account. Jesus says we are to be the light there. We need to take on us the pattern and print of Jesus Christ, not the pattern and print of the world, and immediately we try to be what Jesus wants us to be, we shall find the truth of what He said— "they shall . . . cast out your name as evil." The "camp" to which we belong will do it, not the world. It is easier to remain true to our camp than to Jesus, easier to be loyal to our convictions than to Him.

"Ye are the light of the world." We have the idea that we are going to shine in heaven, but we are to shine down here, "in the midst of a crooked and perverse nation" (Philippians 2:15). We are to shine as lights in the world in the squalid places, and it cannot be done by putting on a brazen smile, the light must be there all the time.

"*Ye* are the light of the world." We ourselves are to be the light wherever we go; but if ever we became conscious of it, we should be amazed, as Mary of Bethany must have been amazed at Jesus Christ's interpretation of her act of devotion. Mary simply discharged her over-burdened heart in a demonstration of affection for Jesus Christ, and He said that "wheresoever this gospel shall be preached throughout the whole world, this also that she hath done shall be spoken of for a memorial of her."

(b) The Trifling Ways
It giveth light unto all that are in the house. (Matthew 5:15)

The light is to be shown in all the trifling ways of home life. The average evangelical presentation is apt to produce a contempt for the trifling ways. A preacher of the Gospel may be a most objectionable being at home instead of giving light in the ordinary ways. Our Lord tells us to judge the preacher or the teacher "by his fruits." Fruit is not the salvation of souls, that is God's work; fruit is "the fruit of the Spirit," love, joy, peace, etc. We get much more concerned about not offending other people than about offending Our Lord. Our Lord often offended people, but He never put a stumbling-block in anyone's way.

(c) The Truthful Witness
. . . that they may see your good works. (Matthew 5:16)

Our Lord did not say "that you may preach the right thing." It is an easy business to preach, an appallingly easy thing to tell other people what to do; it is another thing to have God's message turned into a boomerang—"You have been teaching these people that they should be full of peace and of joy, but what about yourself? Are *you* full of peace and joy?" The truthful witness is the one who lets his light shine in works which exhibit the disposition of Jesus; one who *lives* the truth as well as preaches it.

3. The Unadvertised Life for the Community
And we ought to lay down our lives for the brethren. (1 John 3:16)

A mother lays down her life for her child and for her home, but there is nothing advertised in her doing it. If the mother were to tell her child what she was doing, it would be an abortion of motherhood. The child will never recognise what the mother has done until in years to come the child herself is in the same place, then she will recognise the unadvertised substitution of the mother's life and love. This is what Jesus Christ has done in His redemptive work— "Hereby perceive we the love of God, because He laid down His life for us: and we ought to lay down our lives for the brethren." Jesus Christ was made broken bread and poured-out wine for us, and He expects us to be made broken bread and poured-out wine in His hands for others. If we are not thoroughly baked, we will produce indigestion because we are dough instead of bread. We have to be made into good nutritious stuff for other people. The reason we are going through the things we are is that God wants to know whether He can make us good bread with which to feed others. The stuff of our lives, not simply of our talk, is to be the nutriment of those who know us.

(a) The Submissive Days
And He went down with them, . . . and was subject unto them. (Luke 2:51)

An extraordinary exhibition of submissiveness! and "the disciple is not above his master." Think of it: thirty years at home with brothers and sisters who did not believe in Him! We fix on the three years which were extraordinary in Our Lord's life and forget altogether the earlier years at home, thirty years of absolute submission. Perhaps something of the same kind is happening to you, and you say—"I don't know why I should have to submit to this." Are you any better than Jesus Christ? "As He is, so are we in this world." The explanation of it all is Our Lord's prayer—"that they may be one, even as We are one." If God is putting you through a spell of submission, and you seem to be losing your individuality and everything else, it is because Jesus is making you one with Him.

(b) The Solitary Desertions
And He was there in the wilderness forty days, tempted of Satan; and was with the wild beasts. (Mark 1:13)

The Divine, the desert, the devil, and utter desolation—"with the wild beasts." If Our Lord endured solitary desolation, why should we consider it strange when we are solitary externally and without comradeship internally? Thank God we have a shallow life, but we also have a solitary life, and it is in the solitary life that we prove whether we are willing to be made the unadvertised life for the community to which we belong—whether we are willing to be made bread or to be simply the advertisement for bread? If we are to be made bread, then we must not be surprised if we are treated in the way Our Lord was treated.

(c) The Substitution Devotion
Greater love hath no man than this, that a man lay down his life for his friends. Ye are My friends, if ye do whatsoever I command you. (John 15:13–14)

For a man to lay down his life is not to lay it down in a sudden crisis, such as death, but to lay it down in deliberate expenditure as one would lay out a pound note. Not—"Here it is, take it out in one huge martyrdom and be done with it." It is a continual substitution whereby we realise that we have another day to spend out for Jesus Christ, another opportunity to prove ourselves His friends.

CAN YOU COME DOWN?
Mark 9:2–29

The test of spiritual life is the power to descend; if we have power to rise only, there is something wrong. We all have had times on the mount when we have seen things from God's standpoint and we wanted to stay there; but if we are disciples of Jesus Christ, He will never allow us to stay there. Spiritual selfishness makes us want to stay on the mount; we feel so good, as if we could do anything—talk like angels and live like angels, if only we could stay there. But there must be the power to descend; the mountain is not the place for us to live, we were built for the valleys. This is one of the hardest things to learn because spiritual selfishness always wants repeated moments on the mount.

1. The Sphere of Exaltation
And Peter answered and said to Jesus, Master, it is good for us to be here: and let us make three tabernacles; one for Thee, and one for Moses, and one for Elias. (Mark 9:5)

When God gives us a time of exaltation it is always exceptional. It has its meaning in our life with God, but we must beware lest spiritual selfishness wants to make it the only time. The sphere of exaltation is not meant to teach us anything. We are apt to think that everything that happens to us is to be turned into useful teaching; it is to be turned into something better than teaching, viz. into character. We shall find that the spheres God brings us into are not meant to teach us something but to *make* us something. There is a great danger in asking, "What is the use of it?" There is no *use* in it at all. If you want a life of usefulness, don't be a Christian after Our Lord's stamp; you will be much more useful if you are not. The cry for the standard of usefulness knocks the spiritual Christian right out, he dare not touch it if he is going to remain true to his Master. Take the life of Our Lord: for three years all He did was to walk about saying things and healing sick people—a useless life, judged from every standard of success and of enterprise. If Our Lord and His disciples had lived in our day, they would have been put down as a most unuseful crowd. In spiritual matters we can never calculate on the line of—"What is the use of it?" "What is the use of being at a Bible Training College? Of learning Psychology and Ethics? *Do* something." Great danger lies along that line. "The good is ever the enemy of the best." The mountaintop experiences are rare moments, but they are meant for something in the purposes of God. It was not until Peter came to write his Epistles that he realised the full purpose of his having been on the Mount of Transfiguration.

2. The Sphere of Humiliation

And one of the multitude answered and said, Master, I have brought unto Thee my son, which hath a dumb spirit; And wheresoever he taketh him, he teareth him: and he foameth, and gnasheth with his teeth, and pineth away: and I spake to Thy disciples that they should cast him out; and they could not. (Mark 9:17–18)

The first thing the disciples met in the valley was a demon-possessed boy, and we have to live in the demon-possessed valley. God did not create Adam to live on the mountain; He made him of the dust of the earth, that was his glory. The mountaintop is an exceptional type of experience, we have to live down in the valley. After every time of exaltation we are brought down with a sudden rush into things as they are, where things are neither beautiful nor poetic nor spiritual nor thrilling. The height of the mountaintop is measured by the drab drudgery of the valley. We never live for the glory of God on the mount, we *see* His glory there, but we do not live for His glory there; it is in the valley that we live for the glory of God. Our Lord came down from the Mount into the valley and went on to the Cross where He was glorified; and we have to come down from the mount of exaltation into the drab life of the valley. It is in the sphere of humiliation that we find our true worth to God, and that is where our faithfulness has to be manifested. Most of us can do things if we are always at the heroic pitch; but God wants us at the drab, commonplace pitch, where we live in the valley according to our personal relationship to Him. We can all be thrilled by appeals to do things in an ecstatic way, by moments of devotion, but that is never the work of God's grace, it is the natural selfishness of our own hearts. We can all do the heroic thing, but can we live in the drab humiliating valley where there is nothing amazing, but mostly disaster, certainly humiliation, and emphatically everything drab and dull and mean?[6] That is where Jesus Christ lived most of His life. The reason we have to live in the valley is that the majority of people live there, and if we are to be of use to God in the world we must be useful from God's standpoint, not from our own standpoint or the standpoint of other people.

"If Thou canst do any thing, have compassion on us, and help us" (Mark 9:22). That is our condition when we are in the valley; we do not know God, we are full of scepticism. The great point of our life with God, and of our service for Him in the world is that we get the scepticism rooted out of us, and it takes the valley of humiliation to root it out. Look back at your own experience and you will find that until you learned Who Jesus Christ was, you were a cunning sceptic about His power. When you were on the mount you could believe anything, because it was in accordance with the selfishness of your nature, but what about the time when you were up against facts in the valley, up against questions which could not be answered? You may be perfectly able to give a testimony to sanctification, but what about the thing that is a humiliation to you? If you are without something that is a humiliation to you, I question whether you have ever come into a personal relationship with Jesus Christ. We are called to fellowship with His sufferings, and some of the greatest suffering lies in remaining powerless where He remained powerless. Had our Lord been a man, He would have healed the boy at first, but He waited until the father was in the last ebb of despair— "If Thou canst do any thing, have compassion on us, and help us." Am I patient enough in my faith in Jesus Christ to allow people to get to the last ebb of despair before they see what He can do? We step in in a thousand and one ways God never tells us to; we say we cannot bear to see God appear cruel, but God has to appear cruel from our standpoint. As disciples of Jesus we have to learn not only what Our Lord is like on the Mount of Transfiguration, but what He is like in the valley of humiliation, where everything is giving the lie to His power, where the disciples are powerless, and where He is not doing anything.

3. The Sphere of Ministration

And He said unto them, This kind can come forth by nothing, but by prayer and fasting. (Mark 9:29)

The last time you were on the mount with God you saw that all power has been given unto Jesus in heaven and on earth, are you going to be sceptical in the valley of humiliation? You have gone to God about the thing that is perplexing you over and over again and nothing has happened, "Why could not we cast him out?" Our Lord never gives an answer to questions of that description, because the answer lies in a personal relationship to Himself. "This kind can come forth by nothing, but by prayer and fasting," i.e., by concentration and redoubled concentration on Me. Prayer and fasting means concentration on God. That is the one purpose for which we are in the world. Do get out of your ears the noisy cries of the Christian world we are in—"Do this and do that." Never! *"Be* this and that, then I will do through you," says Jesus. "If Thou canst" (RV)—Is that what you say to Me?—"All things are possible to him that believeth." At last the father got to the point of personal relationship with Jesus—

---

6. mean: as used here, something or someone ordinary, common, low, or ignoble, rather than cruel or spiteful.

"Lord, I believe; help Thou mine unbelief." We slander God by our very eagerness to work for Him without knowing Him.

We must be able to mount up with wings as eagles, but we must know also how to come down. It is the coming down and the living down that is the power of the saint. Paul said, "I can do all things through Christ which strengtheneth me"; watch the things he said he could do, they were all humiliating things. We have the idea that we are meant to work for God along the heroic line; we are meant to do un-heroic work for God in the martyr spirit. The sphere of humiliation is always the place of more satisfaction to Jesus Christ, and it is in our power to refuse to be humiliated, to say, "No, thank you, I much prefer to be on the mountaintop with God." Do I believe that God engineers my circumstances, that it is He who brings me each day into contact with the people I meet? Am I faithful enough to Him to know that all I meet with in the ordinary machinery of every day by chance or haphazard is absolutely under His dominance and rule? Do I face the humiliation which sometimes comes in my contact with people with a perfect knowledge that God is working out His own will?

You are brought face to face with difficult cases, and nothing happens externally, yet you know that emancipation has been given, because *you* are concentrated on Jesus Christ. Our line of service is to see that there is nothing between Jesus and ourselves. Is there? If there is you must get through it, not by mounting up, not by ignoring it in irritation, but by facing it and going clean through it straight into the presence of Jesus. Then that very thing and all you have been through in connection with it, glorifies Jesus in a way you will never know till you see Him face to face.

When we look at our lives in this way, we understand what Jesus meant when He said, "He that believeth in Me," out of him "shall flow rivers of living water." Why should we ignore what Jesus Christ says? Why should we take our stamp of Christian service from any one other than Himself? We have to maintain our personal relationship to Jesus Christ, the attitude of a child, and to maintain the same attitude in everything and to everyone, towards every individual and circumstance we meet, and never be deflected. That is the meaning of "prayer and fasting."

THE DEDICATION OF FOLLOWING

1. The Followers of God's Life
Be ye therefore followers of God. . . . (Ephesians 5:1)

The one striking thing about following is we must not find our own way, for when we take the initiative we cease to follow. In the natural world everything depends upon our taking the initiative, but if we are followers of God, we cannot take the initiative, we cannot choose our own work or say what we will do; we have not to find out at all, we have just to follow.

"Jesus saith unto him, . . . follow thou Me" (John 21:22). Everything Our Lord asks us to do is naturally frankly impossible to us. It is impossible for us to be the children of God naturally, to love our enemies, to forgive, to be holy, to be pure, and it is certainly impossible to us to follow God naturally; consequently the fundamental fact to recognise is that we must be born again. We recognise it fundamentally, but we must recognise it actually, that in spiritual matters we must not take the initiative. We must not make decisions of our own, we must "follow the Lamb whithersoever He goeth," and when He does not go anywhere, then we do not.

In following Our Lord Jesus Christ we are not following His followers. When Paul said, "who shall bring you into remembrance of my ways," he was careful to add, "which be in Christ" (1 Corinthians 4:17). We are not called to follow in all the footsteps of the saints, but only in so far as they followed their Lord. The great meaning of following is that we imitate as children, not as monkeys.

"In Him was life . . ." (John 1:4). We are not left to anything vague. It does sound vague to say "be followers of God," but when we realise that Jesus Christ is the life of God, then we know where we are. He is the One Whom we have to imitate and follow, but we must first of all be born again and receive His Spirit, and then walk in the Spirit. "If any man have not the Spirit of Christ, he is none of His" (Romans 8:9).

(a) In Joy
These things have I spoken unto you, that My joy might remain in you, and that your joy might be full. (John 15:11)

If Jesus Christ is the life of God and we have to follow Him, we must find out what His joy was. It certainly was not happiness. The joy of the Lord Jesus Christ lay in doing exactly what He came to do. He did not come to save men first of all, He came to do

His Father's will. The saving of men was the natural outcome of this, but Our Lord's one great obedience was not to the needs of men but to the will of His Father, and He says, "as My Father hath sent Me, even so send I you." We are never told to consecrate our gifts to God, but we are told to dedicate ourselves.

The joy of anything, from a blade of grass upwards, is to fulfil its created purpose. ". . . that we should be to the praise of His glory" (Ephesians 1:12). We are not here to win souls, to do good to others, that is the natural outcome, but it is not our aim, and this is where so many of us cease to be followers. We will follow God as long as He makes us a blessing to others, but when He does not we will not follow. Suppose Our Lord had measured His life by whether or not He was a blessing to others! Why, He was a "stone of stumbling" to thousands, actually to His own neighbours, to His own nation, because through Him they blasphemed the Holy Ghost, and in His own country "He did not many mighty works there because of their unbelief" (Matthew 13:58). If Our Lord had measured His life by its actual results, He would have been full of misery.

We get switched off when instead of following God we follow Christian work and workers. We are much more concerned over the passion for souls than the passion for Christ. The passion for Christ is the counterpart of His passion for God. The life of God is manifested in Our Lord Jesus Christ, He came to do His Father's will; then when we are following Him, it will be a matter of indifference whether God puts us in the forefront or in the back seat. When we realise this, then the joy of the Lord is ours because we are fulfilling our regenerated purpose. The passion for souls is not a New Testament idea at all, but religious commercialism. When we are taken up with this passion the joy of the Lord is never ours, but only an excitable joy which always leaves a snare behind.

God engineers our circumstances as He did those of His Son; all we have to do is to follow where He places us. The majority of us are busy trying to place ourselves. God alters things while we wait for Him. Are we fulfilling the purpose of our recreation, viz. to glorify God? The sign that we are glorifying God is not that we are happy; happiness is childish, individual and pagan. It is natural for a child to be happy because a child does not face facts, but a Christian who is merely happy is blind.

The way God's life manifests itself in joy is in a peace which has no desire for praise. When a man delivers a message which he knows is the message of God, the witness to the fulfilment of the created purpose is given instantly, the peace of God settles down, and the man cares for neither praise nor blame from anyone. That is the joy of the life of God; it is uncrushable life, and there is never life without joy.

(b) In Judgement (John 3:16–21)
He that doeth truth cometh to the light. (v. 21)

In actual life we must be always in the light, and we cease to be in the light when we want to explain why we did a thing. The significant thing about Our Lord is that He never explained anything; He let mistakes correct themselves because He always lived in the light. There is so much in us that is folded and twisted, but the sign that we are following God is that we keep in the light. "I have been saved and sanctified, therefore I am all right"—that brings darkness at once.

When we are walking in the light there is never any lust of vindication, no saying before God, "I did not mean this," or, "I did not intend to do that," or, "I made a mistake there," but always coming to the light and keeping in the light all the time, with nothing folded before God. We keep in the judgement of God, consequently there is no condemnation going on in our lives. "There is therefore now no condemnation to them which are in Christ Jesus" (Romans 8:1) means keeping in the light all the time.

One danger is to go off in work, and another danger is to go off on doctrine. Doctrine is the mere statement of the life of God for the purposes of teaching. Always beware of following your own convictions in doctrine instead of following the life of God. Our Lord says, "Judge not," and yet Paul says, "we shall judge angels." Our Lord means, Do not judge by ordinary reasoning, or weighing up by carnal suspicion, but keep in the light. By keeping in the light we judge even angels. It is done by following God's life in judgement.

(c) In Jerusalem
Behold, we go up to Jerusalem. . . . (Luke 18:31)

Jerusalem was the place in the life of Our Lord where He actually fulfilled the climax of His Father's will. He did not stay long in the villages where the people were blessed abundantly, He went steadily through everything, successful service or shame, it never affected Him, and we have to do the same. We have to fulfil the purpose of God in our lives actually. We are here to be followers of the life of God. The counterpart is taking God's life for ourselves instead of giving ourselves to God. "I want God's life for my body"—at once we are off the track. Our bodies are to be entirely at God's disposal, and not God at our disposal. God does give Divine health, but not in order to show what a wonderful being a divinely healed person is. The life of God has to be followed by us, not utilised; we must not allow the life of God to stagnate in us, or imagine that we are to be put as specimens in a showcase. If God has healed us and keeps us in health, it is not that we might parade it, but that we might follow the life of God for His purposes.

We do not know where our "Jerusalem" is, but we have to go up to it, and the only way to go up to it is not by trying to find out where it is, but by being followers of God's life.

2. The Followers of God's Love

For I am persuaded, that neither death, nor life, nor angels, nor principalities, nor powers, nor things present, nor things to come, nor height, nor depth, nor any other creature, shall be able to separate us from the love of God, which is in Christ Jesus our Lord. (Romans 8:38–39)

Jesus Christ is the love of God incarnated. The love of God is not to be looked for in justice, right, truth, and purity; the love of God *is* Jesus Christ.

(a) In Loyalty

Stand fast therefore in the liberty wherewith Christ hath made us free, and be not entangled again with the yoke of bondage. (Galatians 5:1)

Loyalty is not to be to loving God, or to the love of God, but to Jesus Christ's redemption of us. "Mortify therefore your members which are upon the earth; fornication, uncleanness, inordinate affection, evil concupiscence, and covetousness, which is idolatry" (Colossians 3:5). "Since I have been saved and sanctified none of these things dwell in me." These things are only possible in the saint, because the saint's body is the temple of the Holy Ghost and may be utilised as an occasion to the flesh. Saints have to become absolutely loyal to the disposition of Jesus Christ in their lives. To mortify means to destroy by neglect. It is easy to detect whenever inordinacy comes in. "How then can I do this great wickedness?" (Genesis 39:9). God's love restrained him—that is Joseph's meaning.

The only way to keep following the love of God is by being loyal to the Lord Jesus Christ. If we make sin a theological question and not a question of actual deliverance, we become adherents to doctrine, and if we put doctrine first, we shall be hoodwinked before we know where we are; or if we take an actual experience and deposit that as a truth on which we rest our souls, we go wrong at once. In stating holiness doctrinally we are apt to make it appear harsh and vindictive; it is technically right, but without the love of God in it. Paul's phrase, "the holiness of truth" (RV), is the right one.

(b) In Liberty

If the Son therefore shall make you free, ye shall be free indeed. (John 8:36)

"Free indeed," i.e., free from the inside. The freedom of Jesus is never license, it is always liberty, and liberty means ability to fulfil the law of God. The law of

God was fulfilled in the life of Jesus Christ, therefore He is the Expression of the love of God. If I am following God's love as exhibited in the Lord Jesus Christ and He has made me free from within, I am so taken up with following Him that I will never take advantage of another child of God.

(c) In Lowliness

But made Himself of no reputation, and took upon Him the form of a servant, and was made in the likeness of men. (Philippians 2:7)

In following God's love we must do so in lowliness. "Let this mind be in you, which was also in Christ Jesus . . ." (Philippians 2:5). That is a command. God does not give us the mind of Christ, He gives us the Spirit of Christ, and we have to see that the Spirit of Christ in us works through our brains in contact with actual life and that we form His mind. Jesus Christ did not become humbled—"He humbled Himself." He was "in Some of us make a virtue of modesty and it becomes the worst form of pride. Self-assertive initiative has nothing to do with the love of God, and was never exhibited in the life of Jesus Christ.

We are all thrilled by high, human, noble pagan sacrifice; it is much more thrilling than Calvary, there is something shameful about that, it is against all human ideas of nobility. The love of God is not in accordance with human standards in any way.

3. The Followers of the Lamb

These are they which follow the Lamb whithersoever He goeth. (Revelation 14:4)

(a) In Purity

And every man that hath this hope in him purifieth himself, even as He is pure. (1 John 3:3)

We are to follow Jesus Christ down here in the actual world where there is any amount of impurity, but we have this hope, that "we shall be like Him," consequently we purify ourselves. The possibility of being impure means that there is some value to Jesus Christ in our being pure. God gives us His supernatural life, but we have to keep entirely free from the world with a purity which is of value to God; we have to grow in purity. Unless a man realises that when he is indwelt by the Spirit of God he must also walk according to the pattern of Jesus Christ, his flesh will take occasion to ensnare him. One of the most besmirching impurities lies in money matters; do we follow the Lamb in these matters? If we do, we shall purify ourselves "even as He is pure"; not only is the purity of the Holy Ghost in us, but we are working it out in every detail. We have to be God's workmanship, not to work for God. "But ye shall receive power, after that the Holy Ghost is come upon you: and ye shall be witnesses unto Me" (Acts 1:8), i.e., "those in whom I am delighted."

If Jesus Christ were manifested now, would we be like Him? or would we have a hundred and one things to do before we could be as He is? We have not been taking time to purify ourselves as He is pure because we have been restless and annoyed; we have imagined that we have things to do that no one can do but ourselves. It may be true, but immediately we think it, we lose out. There is only one lodestar to the saint, the Lord Jesus Christ. We have no business to get into circumstances God does not put us into. Faith means keeping absolutely specklessly right with God, He does all the rest. We are only what we are in the dark; all the rest is reputation. What God looks at is what we are in the dark—the imaginations of our minds; the thoughts of our heart; the habits of our bodies; these are the things that mark us in God's sight.

(b) In Patience
Because thou hast kept the word of My patience. (Revelation 3:10)

Patience has the meaning of testing—a thing drawn out and tested, drawn out to the last strand in a strain without breaking, and ending in sheer joy. The strain on a violin string when stretched to the uttermost gives it its strength; and the stronger the strain, the finer is the sound of our life for God, and He never strains more than we are able to bear. We say, "sorrow, disaster, calamity"; God says, "chastening," and it sounds sweet to Him though it is a discord in our ears. Don't faint when you are rebuked, and don't despise the chastenings of the Lord. "In your patience possess ye your souls." If God has given you a time of rest, then lie curled up in His leaves of healing.

(c) In Power
For though He was crucified through weakness, yet He liveth by the power of God. For we also are weak in Him, but we shall live with Him by the power of God toward you. (2 Corinthians 13:4)

The power of God was exhibited in Jesus Christ—that insignificant Nazarene Carpenter whom Roman paganism did not notice. In the eyes of the world pagan virtues are admirable: Christian virtues are contemptible. Are we prepared to be "weak in Him"? If so, we shall be weaklings in the eyes of men, but we shall "live with Him by the power of God."

Do we "follow the Lamb whithersoever He goeth"? He will take us through darkness, through the valley of the shadow, through the strange dark things—we must follow Him "whithersoever He goeth."

For the Lamb which is in the midst of the throne shall feed them, and shall lead them unto living fountains of waters: and God shall wipe away all tears from their eyes. (Revelation 7:17)

The Message of Invincible Consolation

KATHLEEN'S DAILY PRAYER

Father lead me day by day,
Ever in Thine own sweet way;
Teach me to be good and true,
Show me what I ought to do.

In Loving Memory of
Kathleen Mary Cheal Clarke[7]
From God 27th December, 1924
To God 29th September, 1930

Again I shall behold thee, daughter true;
The hour will come when I shall hold thee fast
In God's name, loving thee all through and through.
Somewhere in His grand thought this waits for us.
Then shall I see a smile not like thy last—
For that great thing which came when all was past,
Was not a smile, but God's peace glorious.
—George MacDonald

---

7. Kathleen Mary Cheal Clarke (1924–1930: daughter of Louis R. S. Clarke, a British soldier influenced by Chambers at Zeitoun. After the war ended, her father became a long-time member of the council assisting Mrs. Chambers in publishing the OC books.

For which cause we faint not; but though our outward man perish, yet the inward man is renewed day by day. For our light affliction, which is but for a moment, worketh for us a far more exceeding and eternal weight of glory; while we look not at the things which are seen, but at the things which are not seen: for the things which are seen are temporal; but the things which are not seen are eternal. 2 Corinthians 4:16–18

In these verses the Apostle Paul is interpreting the most sacred realities of a saint's life. We deal so much with the joyful and the happy and the exuberant in our experience that we are apt to forget that life externally is continually full of the things Paul mentions here. Paul's own life was one of the most distracting and tumultuous and terribly "spilt" lives ever recorded in history.

1. The Beyond Within

Wasting Outward Man—Winged Inner Man (2 Corinthians 4:16)

"For which cause we faint not [the word 'faint' is used in the sense of cowardly surrender]; *but though our outward man perish, yet the inward man is renewed day by day."* Paul puts the great emphasis on what God has put within; he builds up his confidence in that. The perishing of the outward man is not always indicative of old age. Look at your own life; you have had the experience of sanctification and have been lifted into the heavenly places in Christ Jesus, and yet God's hand has been laid upon you. He has allowed the finger of decay to come to your body and lay you completely aside, and you begin to see what a slight hold you have on life, and the thought comes—"Well, I expect I will have to 'cave in,' I have not the strength I once had; I can never do the things I thought I would for God." This message is for *you*—*"though* our outward man perish, yet *the inward man is renewed day by day."*

The experience may not come with years but in the ordinary circumstances of life. It may come in a hundred and one ways and you realise that the outward man is wasting, that you have not the might you once had, and this is where the cowardly surrender is apt to come in—only we give it another name. The great craze to-day is—Be healthy, be sane; "a sound mind in a sound body." Very often the soundest minds have not been in sound bodies, but in very shaky tabernacles, and the word comes—*"though our outward man perish, yet the inward man is renewed day by day."*

Paul faces the possibility of old age, of decay, and of death, with no rebellion and no sadness. Paul never hid from himself the effect which his work had upon him, he knew it was killing him, and, like his Master, he was old before his time; but there was no whining and no retiring from the work. Paul was not a fool, he

did not waste his energy ridiculously, neither did he ignore the fact that it was his genuine apostolic work and nothing else that was wearing him out. Michelangelo said a wonderful thing—"the more the marble wears, the better the image grows," and it is an illustration of this very truth. Every wasting of nerve and brain in work for God brings a corresponding uplift and strengthening to spiritual muscle and fibre.

A good test for a worker is to ask this question: Does my inner life wing itself higher with every wearing of the body in work for God? If we are going to walk in the experimental knowledge of sanctification and live where God wants us to live, we must be willing to spend and be spent to the last ebb. But if the outward man is perishing because of an injudicious waste of physical strength or because of wrong habits, then it will always make us faint, i.e., "cave in"; and if we give up prayer and communion with God, then the decay goes on to a terrible extent; there is no corresponding inward weight of glory, no inner winging.

The Apostle Paul continuously had external depression, he had agonies and distresses, terrible persecution and tumults in his life, but he never had the "blues," simply because he had learned the secret that the measure of the inner glory is the wasting of the outward man. The outer man was being wasted, Paul knew it and felt it, but the inner man was being renewed, every wasting meant a corresponding winging on the inside. Some of us are so amazingly lazy, so comfortably placed in life, that we get no inner winging. The natural life, apart altogether from sin, must be sacrificed to the will and the word of God, otherwise there is no spiritual glory for the individual. With some of us the body is not wearing away, our souls are stagnant, and the vision spiritually is not getting brighter; but once we get into the heavenlies, live there, and work from that standpoint, we find we have the glorious opportunity of spending all our bodily energies in God's service, and a corresponding weight of moral and spiritual glory remains all the time.

One of the most enervating things that can come across your life as a saint is the sympathy of others who do not understand the vision of your heart, and they say—"Poor woman, you do suffer; so many people misunderstand you; you are put in such awkward circumstances." The thing to realise is that God enlarges us on the inside, not externally, and that every bit of nervous energy spent by us in God's work means a grander weight of glory and spiritual insight. No matter how wearied or expended the body may be in God's work, there is the winging of the inner man into a higher grasp of God.

We have to beware of the pagan notion that our spirit develops in spite of our body, it develops *with* our body, and the way that spiritual insight develops in the worker is, as Paul states here, in the wasting of energy for God, because in this way the inner man is renewed. It is not a question of saying—"Oh, my body is so lazy, I must drag it up to do something," but a question of working on God's line to the last lap, spending and being spent for one purpose only, and that purpose God's. If we put the body and the concerns of the body before the eternal weight of glory, we will never have any inner winging at all, we will always be asking God to patch up this old tabernacle and keep it in repair. But when the heart sees what God wants, and knows that the body must be willing to spend and be spent for that cause and that cause alone then the inner man gets wings.

2. The Beautifying Work
Balancing the Ways (2 Corinthians 4:17)
The Apostle Paul soars above the things which were wearing out his physical life, not by sublime indifference, but by realising the weight of glory which these very afflictions are working in him. Have you got hold of this secret that if you are right with God, the very thing which is an affliction to you is working out an eternal weight of glory? The afflictions may come from good people or from bad people, but behind the whole thing is God. Whenever Paul tries to state the unfathomable joy and glory which he has in the heavenlies in Christ Jesus, it is as if he cannot find words to express his meaning. In order to try to express it here he balances his words—for instance, "affliction" is matched with "glory"; "light" is matched with "weight"; and "moment" is matched with "eternal." I wonder if we balance our words like that?

In Romans 8:18 ("For I reckon that the sufferings of this present time are not worthy to be compared with the glory which shall be revealed in us") Paul is stating that it is the standpoint of the worker which determines everything. If you think of suffering affliction you will begin to write your own epitaph, begin to dream of the kind of tombstone you would like. That is the wrong standpoint. Have your standpoint in the heavenlies, and you will not think of the afflictions but only of the marvellous way God is working out the inner weight of glory all the time, and you will hail with delight the afflictions which our Lord tells us to expect (John 16:33), the afflictions of which James writes (James 1:2), and of which Peter writes (1 Peter 4:12). Our Lord presented truth in "nugget" form, and in the Epistles the Apostles beat out these "nuggets" into negotiable gold.

"For our light affliction, which is but for a moment, worketh for us a far more exceeding and eternal weight of glory"; the apostle seems to be putting things the

wrong way round. Surely the affliction is the heavy thing and the glory the light thing! No, Paul is putting it in the right way; he puts the emphasis on the weight of glory resulting from the light affliction. Again, everything is determined by the standpoint you take. Stand in the heavenly places in Christ Jesus and when the afflictions come you will praise the Lord, not with a sickly smile but with every bit of you, because you have learned the secret of the eternal weight of glory, and you know that His yoke is easy.

"For our light affliction, which is but for a moment. . . ." Paul seems to say—"Even if it were all tribulation it would not matter, because the glory beginning already and the glory to come would make amends for it all." This law of glory working out of decay is God's beautifying work in a saint. The soother of all affliction is the steadfast thought of the glory which is being worked out by the afflictions. Paul here beats out the nugget of truth in our Lord's rebuke to Peter: Pity thyself, Lord: this shall not be unto Thee. "But He turned, and said unto Peter, Get thee behind Me, Satan." Self-pity is taking the wrong standpoint, and if self-pity is indulged in, before long we will take part in the decaying thing instead of in that which grows more and more into the glory of God's presence.

3. The Blessed Vision
The Watchword of Other-Worldliness (2 Corinthians 4:18)
The sanctified saint has to alter the horizon of other people's lives, and he does it by showing that they can be lifted on to a higher plane by the grace of God, viz., into the heavenly places in Christ Jesus. If you look at the horizon from the sea shore you will not see much of the sea, but climb higher up the cliff, and as you rise higher the horizon keeps level with your eye and you see more in between. Paul is seated in the heavenly places and he can see the whole world mapped out in God's plan. He is looking ahead like a watchman, and his words convey the calm, triumphant contemplation of a conqueror. Some of us get distracted because we have not this world-wide outlook, we see only the little bit inside our own "bandbox."[8] The Apostle Paul has burst his bandbox, he has been lifted up on to a new plane in Christ Jesus and he sees now from His standpoint. The preacher and the worker must learn to look at life as a whole. When we are lifted up to where Jesus is, it is not as if we were standing on a high pinnacle like a spiritual acrobat, balancing on one leg for two seconds and then tumbling. God lifts us up to a totally new plane where there is plenty of room to live and to grow, and

---

8.bandbox: in Chambers' day, a small, round box made to hold neckbands or collars for shirts; metaphorically, something small, narrow, cloistered, self-contained.

to understand things from His standpoint and we see life as a whole; we see not only the glory which now is, but the glory which is yet to be.

"While we look not at the things which are seen, but at the things which are not seen." The things "not seen" refer not only to the glorious reward and the life yet to be, but to the invisible things in our present life around which our Lord's teaching centres, and around which the afflictions centre. So many of us think only of the visible things, whereas the real concentration, the whole dead-set of the life, should be where our Lord put it in the huge "nugget" of truth which we call the Sermon on the Mount. There our Lord says, in effect, "Take no thought for your life; be carefully careless about everything saving one thing, your relationship to God." Naturally, we are apt to be carefully careless about everything saving that one thing. The afflictions tackle these unseen centres of our life and we have to face them in the power of the indwelling Spirit of God, and if we have been lifted up into the heavenlies we shall find that the battlings are bringing out more and more the eternal weight of glory, while we look at the things which are not seen. Do not think only of what is yet to be; think of the invisible things which are here and now. Think of the weight of glory that may be yours by means of that difficult person you have to live with, by means of the circumstances you are in, the people you come in con-

tact with day by day. The phrase "a means of grace" comes with a wonderfully new meaning when we think of it in this light.

These words of the Apostle Paul bring to us a message of invincible consolation. If you are a child of God and there is some part of your circumstances which is tearing you, if you are living in the heavenly places you will thank God for the tearing thing; if you are not in the heavenly places you cry to God over and over again—"O Lord, remove this thing from me. If only I could live in golden streets and be surrounded with angels, and have the Spirit of God consciously indwelling me all the time and have everything wonderfully sweet, then I think I might be a Christian." That is not being a Christian! A Christian is one who can live in the midst of the trouble and turmoil with the glory of God indwelling him, while he steadfastly looks not at the things which are seen, but at the things which are not seen. We have to learn to think only of things which are seen as a glorious chance of enabling us to concentrate on the things which are not seen. God engineers external things for the purpose of revealing to us whether we are living in this imperturbable place of unutterable strength and glory, viz., the life hid with Christ in God. If we are, then let the troubles and difficulties work as they may on the outside, we are confident that they are working out a grander weight of glory in the heavenlies.

THE WORKER AND THINGS AS THEY ARE
2 Corinthians 6:1–10

We have an idea that we have to alter things, we have not; we have to remain true to God in the midst of things as they are, to allow things as they are to transmute us. "Things as they are" are the very means God uses to make us into the praise of His glory. We have to live on this sordid earth, amongst human beings who are exactly like ourselves, remembering that it is on this plane we have to work out the marvellous life God has put in us. Holiness in a human being is only manifested by means of antagonism. Physically, we are healthy according to our power of fight on the inside; morally, we are virtuous according to our moral calibre—virtue is always acquired; and spiritually, if we are drawing on the resurrection life of Jesus, spiritual stamina comes as we learn to "score off" the things that come against us, and in this way we produce a holy character.

The life of a worker is not a hop, skip and a jump affair, it is a squaring of the shoulders, then a steady, steadfast tramp straight through until we get to under-

stand God's way. It takes the energy of God Himself to prepare a worker for all He wants to make him. We need a spiritual vision of work as well as a spiritual vision of truth. It is not that we go through a certain curriculum and then we are fit to work; preparation and work are so involved that they cannot be separated. The Apostle Paul always comes right down to the practical. One of the outstanding miracles of God's grace is to make us able to take any kind of leadership at all without losing spiritual power. There is no more searching test in the whole of Christian life than that.

1. The Worth to God
We then, as workers together with Him ... (2 Corinthians 6:1)

When a worker has led a soul to Christ his work has only just begun. Our attitude is apt to be—So many saved; so many sanctified, and then we shout "Hallelujah." But it is only then that the true work of the worker begins. It is then that we have to be held in God's hand and let the word of God be driven through us. It is then that we have to be put under the millstone and ground, put into the kneading trough and be mixed properly, and then baked—all in order to be made broken bread to feed God's children. "Go ye therefore, and make disciples" (RV). How many disciples have you made? Have you made one? Discipling is our work. When God's great redemptive work has issued in lives in salvation and sanctification, then the work of the worker begins. It is then that we find the meaning of being "workers together with Him," and the meaning of the Apostle Paul's agony of heart and mind over his converts—"My little children, of whom I travail in birth again until Christ be formed in you"—waiting and watching and longing and praying and working, until he can see them rooted and grounded in God. Look at the laborious way of a scientist in finding out the secrets of Nature, and then look at our own slipshod ignorance with regard to God's Book. If the worker will obey God's way he will find he has to be everlastingly delving into the Bible and working it out in circumstances, the two always run together. It requires all the machinery of circumstances to bring a worker where God wants him to be—"co-workers with God."

We are apt to say—"Now I am fitted for this particular work because of my natural temperament and I intend to work only along this line." An exclusive worker is excluded by God, because God does not work in that way. The gifts of the Spirit are divided "to every man severally as He will"; they are entirely of God and they all work together with God. The worth of a worker to God is just the worth of a man's own fingers to his brain.

2. The Wooing of God
. . . beseech you also that ye receive not the grace of God in vain . . .

The wooing of God is not the wooing of man. The wooing of a man's personality may often hinder the wooing of God. The Apostle Paul's pleading is caught up into the entreaty of the Spirit of God so that it is the wooing of God that is working through him—"as though God did beseech you by us." This is the entreaty that is learned at Calvary and made real in the worker by the Holy Ghost. It is not the tones of a man's speech, or the passion of a man's personality, it is the pleading power of the Holy Ghost coming through him; consequently the worker has no sympathy with things with which God's Spirit has no sympathy. We are in danger of being stern where God is tender, and of being tender where God is stern. The Apostle Paul so identifies his own beseeching and passion with the entreaty of God that the two are

identical. He is afraid "lest by any means . . . [their] minds should be corrupted from the simplicity that is in Christ" (2 Corinthians 11:3).

3. The World's Coarse Thumb
Giving no offence in any thing . . . (2 Corinthians 6:3)

The worldling is annoyed at the worker because the worker is always dealing with a crisis that he does not see and does not want to see. No matter what he touches on, the worker always comes back to the claim of God, and the worldling gets annoyed at this. The man of the world analyses the easy parts of life and tells you that these are all quite obvious, all the practical outcomes of life are within his reach; but when the worker begins to touch on God's message he says, "That is nonsense, you are up in the clouds and unpractical." That is why the worker's voice is always an annoyance to the worldling.

"that the ministry be not blamed . . ." The world is glad of an excuse not to listen to the Gospel message, and the inconsistencies of Christians is made the excuse. "Woe unto the world because of offences!" said our Lord. "For it must needs be that offences come; but woe to that man by whom the offence cometh!" Offence means something to strike up against, and the world is on the watch for that kind of thing. If a worker is tripped in private life, the world strikes against that at once and makes it the excuse for not accepting the Gospel. The perilous possibility of being an occasion of stumbling is always there. Paul never forgot the possibility of it in his own life—". . . lest that by any means, when I have preached to others, I myself should be a castaway." The only safeguard is living the life hid with Christ in God, and a steady watchfulness that we walk in the light as God is in the light.

4. The Wheel of Circumstances
(2 Corinthians 6:4–6)
. . . but in all things approving ourselves as the ministers of God. (v. 4)

Read the life of the Apostle Paul and you find that he drank to the last dregs the experience of every one of the things mentioned in these verses. Paul is not indulging in oratory, he is stating the things God put him through. All his experiences called for patience. Holiness can only be worked out in and through the din of things as they are. God does not slide holiness into our hearts like a treasure box from heaven and we open the lid and out it comes, holiness works out in us as it worked out in our Lord. The holiness of God Almighty is Absolute; that is, it knows no development by antagonism. The holiness exhibited by the Son of God, and by God's children, is the holiness which expresses itself by means of antagonism.

There are some wonderful words in verses 4 and 5—"in much *patience.*" Patience is the result of well-centred strength; it takes the strength of Almighty God to keep a man patient. No one can remain under and endure what God puts a servant of His through unless he has the power of God. We read that our Lord was "crucified through weakness," yet it took omnipotent might to make Him weak like that. Where is the impulsive enthusiasm which was manifested at the start of the Christian life, has it all gone? No, it has been transmuted into the strength that can be weak. *"in afflictions"*—affliction is something that crushes like a weight until you have not a word to say. *"in necessities"*—the loss of liberty, confinement. A happy heart and an unpaid salary; a high head and an empty pocket! That is the way it works out in reality. *"in distresses"*—perplexities such as sickness, the loss of friends, the inscrutable ways of God's providence; but through it all the grace of God comes, it is an inner unconquerableness. *"in stripes, in imprisonments, in tumults, in labours, in watchings, in fastings"*—in all these things manifest the drawing on the grace of God that makes you a marvel to yourself and to others. Draw now, not presently. The one word in the spiritual vocabulary is NOW. Let circumstances bring you where they will, keep drawing on the grace of God. One of the greatest proofs that you are drawing on the grace of God is that you can be humiliated without manifesting the slightest trace of anything but His grace in you.

Verses 4–10 are Paul's spiritual diary, they describe the outward hardships which proved the hot-bed for the graces of the Spirit—the working together of outward hardships and inward grace. You have been asking the Lord to give you the graces of the Spirit and then some set of circumstances has come and given you a sharp twinge, and you say—"Well, I have asked God to bring out in me the graces of the Spirit, but every time the devil seems to get the better of me." What you are calling "the devil" is the very thing God is using to manifest the graces of the Spirit in you.

"By honour and dishonour, by evil report and good report." The worker learns the secret of the "camp fires" where he can recount with other Christians the great hours when the Son of God walked with him in the fiery furnace. The thing that keeps us off enchanted ground is to remember that we are on God's campaigns, that we have no certain place of abode, no nesting place here.

> He fixed thee midst this dance
> Of plastic circumstance,
> This Present, thou, forsooth, would'st fain arrest:
> Machinery just meant
> To give thy soul its bent,
> Try thee and turn thee forth, sufficiently impressed.

The fiery furnaces are there by God's direct permission. It is misleading to imagine that we are developed in spite of our circumstances, we are developed because of them. It is mastery *in* circumstances that is needed, not mastery over them. We have to manifest the graces of the Spirit amongst things as they are, not to wait for the Millennium.

5. The Wine of God *(2 Corinthians 6:7–10)*

In these verses the Apostle Paul is giving out golden truths from his own experience. Paul's external life had been spilt and rent, and crushed and broken, then out of it came the wine of God. Wine comes only from crushed grapes, and the things Paul is mentioning here are the things which bring out the wine that God likes. You cannot be poured-out wine if you remain a whole grape; you cannot be broken bread if you remain whole grain. Grapes have to be crushed, and grain has to be ground; then the sweetness of the life comes out to the glory of God. Watch the circumstances of life; we get them fairly well mixed, and if we are getting more than enough of one kind, let us thank the Lord for it; it is producing the particular grace that God wants us to manifest.

The Making of a Christian
I

The ascendancy which He exercised in thus drawing men away from worldly callings and hopes into association with Himself is quite indefinite, and even in yielding to it, the disciples could have no distinct idea what it involved.
Dr. Denney[9]

1. Days of His Flesh
The Dominating Sentiment (Matthew 4:18–22; Mark 1:16–20; John 1:35–42)
The average preaching of Redemption deals mainly with the "scenic" cases, i.e. those who have gone through exceptional experiences. But none of the early disciples had these scenic experiences, nor was their dominating sentiment a desire for deliverance from sin. They were elemental men in touch with the forces of nature, and there was something about Jesus Christ that fascinated them. When He said, "Follow Me," they followed Him at once; it was no cross to them. It would have been a cross not to follow, for the spell of Jesus was on them. We have come to the conclusion nowadays that a man must be a conscious sinner before Jesus Christ can do anything for him. The early disciples were not attracted to Jesus because they wanted to be saved from sin; they had no conception that they needed saving. They were attracted to Him by a dominating sincerity, by sentiments other than those which we say make men come to Jesus. There was nothing theological in their following, no consciousness of passing from death unto life, no knowledge of what Jesus meant when He talked about His Cross. It was on the plane where all was natural, although mysterious and wonderful.

The call of God comes only to the affinity of God in a man, and is always implicit. The beginnings of moral ascension in a man's life are never definite, but always away down in the depths of his personality where he cannot trace. These early disciples were not trammelled by possessions, and when the dominating sentiment of sincerity in their own lives was met by the fascination of Jesus, they yielded at once. They did not follow Jesus because they wanted to be saved, but because they could not help following. Three years later when again Jesus said, "Follow Me," it was a different matter; many things had happened during those years. The first "Follow Me" meant an external

following; now it was to be a following in internal martyrdom (see John 21:18–19).

2. Days of Our Flesh
The Dominating Sincerity (1 Peter 2:21)
The attitude of the early disciples was one of self-ignorance. Jesus Christ knew perfectly well what was in them, but He did not say to John—"You will prove to be vindictive" (see Luke 9:51–55), or to Peter—"You will end in denying Me" (see Mark 14:66–72). If you had told Peter that he would deny Jesus with oaths and curses, he would have been amazed (see John 13:36–38). Jesus Christ taught the disciples the truth, and left them with the atmosphere of His own life, and slowly they began to see things differently. The disciples approached Jesus by the way of sincerity, and He put them through crises until they discovered that they could never be disciples in that way; what they needed was to have the disposition of Jesus given to them. The disciples were fascinated by Jesus; when He said, "Follow Me," they immediately left all and followed Him, and yet after three years of the closest intimacy "they all forsook Him, and fled." Their following ended in disaster.

The majority of men are attracted to Jesus on the same line as the early disciples were. The disciples were brought to a knowledge of themselves, and we have to come to a knowledge of ourselves in the same way. We have to realise that human sincerity will never stand the strain when the ideals that fascinate a man's mind come in contact with actual life. The disaster may not be external, but in his heart a man says: "I honestly tried my best to serve Jesus Christ; I did decide for Him; in all sincerity I gave all I had to the ideals He presents, but I cannot go on; the New Testament presents ideals beyond my attainment. I won't lower my ideals, although I can never hope to make them actual." Our Lord says to such a one: "Come unto Me, . . . and I will give you rest," i.e. "I will make the ideal actual." But a sense of need must arise first. As long as we deal with abstractions, we have no sense of need.

Apart from Jesus Christ there is an unbridgeable gap between the ideal and the actual; the only way out is a personal relationship to Him. The early disciples were put through crises in order to reveal them to

---

9.James Denney (1856–1917): Scottish theologian and author whose writings were greatly appreciated by Oswald Chambers.

themselves. Jesus was never in a hurry with them; He never explained; He simply stated the truth and told them that when the Holy Ghost was come, "He shall teach you all things, and bring all things to your remembrance, whatsoever I have said unto you." To-day Jesus Christ is at work in ways we cannot tabulate; lives are being drawn to Him in a thousand and one incalculable ways; an atmosphere is being created, seeds are being sown, and men are being drawn nearer to the point where they will see Him.

II

They could do what they could not do before, because He enabled them to do it, and the sense of this is a rudimentary form of this specifically Christian consciousness.

Dr. Denney

1. Days of His Flesh

The dominating sentiment which attracted the early disciples to Jesus was not a sense of conviction of sin; they had no violent sin to turn from, and consequently no conscious need of salvation. They were not sinners in the ordinary accepted sense of the term, but honest, sincere men, and they were attracted to Jesus by something more difficult to state than the desire for deliverance from sin. The spell of Jesus was on them, and when He said, "Follow Me," they followed at once, although they could have had no idea what the following would involve. The call of God is never articulate, it is always implicit.

There was in the disciples the "one fact more" which put them in one kingdom and Jesus Christ in another kingdom. Our Lord was never impatient. He simply planted seed thoughts in their minds and surrounded them with the atmosphere of His own life. He did not attempt to convince them, but left mistakes to correct themselves, because He knew that eventually the truth would bear fruit in their lives. How differently we would have acted! We get impatient and take men by the scruff of the neck and say: "You must believe this and that." You cannot make a man see moral truth by persuading his intellect. "When He, the Spirit of truth, is come, He shall guide you into all the truth."

The Desire to Serve (Matthew 20:22)

"Jesus answered and said, . . . Are ye able to drink the cup that I am about to drink? They say unto Him, We are able" (RV). The disciples would have gone any length to prove their devotion to Jesus (cf. Matthew 26:35). It was true devotion, but it wilted because it was based on an entire ignorance of themselves. In the end they "all forsook Him, and fled," not because they wanted to, but because they did not know how to go on. Jesus put the disciples through crises to reveal them to themselves and bring them to the place of receiving the Holy Spirit. They could not see their need to receive the Holy Spirit until they found out that they were spiritual paupers. "Simon, Simon, behold, Satan asked to have you, that he might sift you as wheat" (Luke 22:31 RV). Jesus allowed Peter to go over a moral precipice and deny that he ever knew Him, before Peter realised what it was that kept him from being a disciple. It is not necessary for everyone to go through the way of Peter's sifting, but the sifting must come in some form or other. The preaching of the gospel of temperament will not do for the making of disciples; nor will Jesus shield us in the slightest degree from any of the requirements of discipleship.

The early disciples were honest, sincere, zealous men; they had given up everything to follow Jesus; their sense of the heroic was grand, but where did it all end? "They all forsook Him, and fled." They came to realise that no human earnestness or sincerity on earth can ever begin to fulfil what Jesus demands of a disciple. Then after the Resurrection, Jesus "breathed on them, and saith unto them, Receive ye the Holy Ghost." They had come now to the end of themselves and all self-sufficiency, and in their destitution they were willing to receive the gift of the Holy Spirit. "Their eyes were opened, and they knew Him"; their inner consciousness was opened, there was a totally new power on the inside. "They could do what they could not do before, because He enabled them to do it." But they had first of all to be brought within the moral frontier of need before they realised they were powerless to live and move in the kingdom where Jesus lived.

2. Days of Our Flesh

The Determination to Serve (Luke 10:20)

Natural devotion may be all very well to attract men to Jesus, to make them feel the fascination of His claims; but natural devotion will never make a disciple, it will always deny Jesus somewhere or other. To-day, as in the days of His flesh, men are being drawn to Jesus by their dominating sincerity, but human sincerity is not enough to make a man a disciple of Jesus

Christ. There are many to-day who are sincere, but they are not real; they are not hypocrites, but perfectly honest and earnest and desirous of fulfilling what Jesus wants of them, but they *really* cannot do it, the reason being that they have not received the Holy Spirit Who will make them real.

The modern phrase we hear so often, "Decide for Christ," is most misleading, because it puts the emphasis on the wrong thing, and is apt to present Jesus Christ in a false way as Someone in need of our allegiance. A decision cannot hold for ever, because a man is the same after making it as before, and there will be a reaction sooner or later. Whenever a man fails in personal experience it is because he has never *received* anything. There is always a positive difference in a man when he has received something—new powers begin to manifest themselves. Nothing has any power to alter a man save the incoming of the life of Jesus, and that is the only sign that he is born again.

The bedrock in Jesus Christ's Kingdom is not sincerity, not deciding for Christ, not a determination to serve Him, but a complete and entire recognition that we cannot begin to do it; then, says Jesus, "Blessed are you." Jesus Christ can do wonderful things for the man who enters into His Kingdom through the moral frontier of need. Decisions for Christ fail not because men are not in earnest, but because the bedrock of Christianity is ignored. The bedrock of Christianity does not lie in vowing or in strength of will; to begin with it is not ethical at all, but simply the recognition of the fact that I have not the power within me to do what my spirit longs to do. "Come unto Me," said

Jesus, not "Decide for Me." When I realise my inability to be what the New Testament tells me I should be, I have to come to Jesus "just as I am." I realise that I am an abject pauper, morally and spiritually; if ever I am going to be what Jesus wants me to be, He must come in and do it. Jesus Christ claims on the basis of His Redemption that He can put into any man who is consciously poor enough to receive it, His own disposition, i.e. the ability not only to will but to do (see Philippians 2:12–13). The knowledge of our own poverty brings us to the moral frontier where Jesus Christ works.

If you are trying to live up to a standard of belief and find you have not the power to do it, be humble enough to recognise that Jesus Christ knows more about the matter than you do. He has pledged His Father's honour to give you the Holy Spirit if you ask Him—*"If ye then, being evil, know how to give good gifts unto your children: how much more shall your heavenly Father give the Holy Spirit to them that ask Him?"* (Luke 11:13). The Holy Spirit at work in our personal lives enables us to make the ideal and the actual one, and we begin slowly to discern that we have been brought into the place where Jesus Christ tells. The beginning of spiritual life is away down where it cannot be traced; the theological explanation will emerge presently. The first thing a man needs is to be born into the Kingdom of God by receiving the Holy Spirit, and then slowly and surely be turned into a disciple. The entrance into the Kingdom of God is always through the moral frontier of need. At any turn of the road the touch may come.

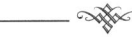

III

The Holy Spirit is the missing factor in our personality, and without it we cannot be altogether as God wants us to be. An abiding gift makes an abiding change in the person to whom the gift is made.

Selby

1. In the Days of His Resurrection
Jesus put the early disciples through crises until they discovered that they could not be disciples by means of ordinary human sincerity and devotion. Human earnestness and vowing cannot make a man a disciple of Jesus Christ any more than it can turn him into an angel; a man must receive something, and that is the meaning of being born again. When once a man is struck by his need of the Holy Spirit, God will put the Holy Spirit into his spirit. In regeneration, a man's

personal spirit is energised by the Holy Spirit, and the Son of God is formed in him (see Galatians 1:15–16; 4:19). This is the New Testament evangel, and it needs to be re-stated. New birth refers not only to a man's eternal salvation, but to his being of value to God in this order of things; it means infinitely more than being delivered from sin and from hell. The gift of the essential nature of God is made efficacious in us by the entering in of the Holy Spirit; He imparts to us the quickening life of the Son of God, and we are lifted into the domain where Jesus lives (see John 3:5).

Our creeds teach us to believe in the Holy Spirit: the New Testament says we must receive Him. The man who is crumpled up with sin is the one who most quickly comes to realise his need. It takes the upright man a long while to realise that his natural virtues are the remnants of a design which has been broken, and that the only way the design can be fulfilled is by his being made all over again. "Marvel not that I said unto thee, Ye must be born again." The bedrock in Jesus Christ's kingdom is poverty, not possession; weakness, not strength of will; infirmity of character, not goodness; a sense of absolute poverty, not decisions for Christ. "Blessed are the poor in spirit." That is the entrance, and it takes a long time to bring us to a knowledge of our own poverty. The greatest blessing we ever get from God is to know that we are destitute spiritually.

The Revelation of Christ (Luke 24:16, 31)

The disciples were with Jesus for three years, but they only once discerned Him, in the one intuitive flash recorded in Matthew 16, when it was revealed to Peter Who Jesus was. Our Lord never sent the disciples out on the ground that He had done something for them, but only on the ground that they had seen Him (cf. John 9:35–36; 10:14–18). Mary Magdalene had had seven devils cast out of her, but it was not until Jesus revealed Himself to her after His resurrection that He said—"Go tell My brethren. . . ." The man who has seen Jesus can never be daunted; the man who has only a personal testimony as to what Jesus has done for him may be daunted, but nothing can turn the man who has seen Him; he endures "as seeing Him Who is invisible."

Is my knowledge of Jesus born of inner spiritual perception, or is it only what I have learned by listening to others? Have I something in my life that connects me with the Lord Jesus as my personal Saviour? All spiritual history must have a personal knowledge for its bedrock.

2. In the Days of Our Regeneration

Every man has need of new birth. "Verily, verily, I say unto thee, except a man be born again, he cannot see the kingdom of God" (John 3:3). Jesus did not speak these words to a man down and out in sin, but to a sterling, worthy, upright man. The conception of new birth in the New Testament is not a conception of something that springs out of us, but of something that enters into us. Just as our Lord came into human history from without, so He must come into us from without. Our new birth is the birth of the life of the Son of God into our old human nature, and our human nature has to be transfigured by the indwelling life of the Son of God. Have I allowed my personal human life to become a "Bethlehem" for the Son of God? It is not that God patches up my natural virtues, but that I learn by obedience to make room for Jesus Christ to exhibit His disposition in me. It is impossible to imitate the disposition of Jesus. Am I becoming the birthplace of the Son of God (see Luke 1:35), or do I only know the miracle of God's changing grace?

The Realisation of Christ (John 20:28)

The one great characteristic of being born from above (RV mg) is that I know Who Jesus is. It is a discernment; something has happened on the inside, the surgery of events has opened my eyes. Is Jesus Christ a revelation to me, or is He simply an historical character? How are we to get the revelation of Who Jesus is? Very simply. Jesus said that the Holy Spirit would glorify Him, and we can receive the Holy Spirit by asking (see Luke 11:13); then we too shall be in the same category with Peter, and Jesus will say, "Blessed art thou, . . . for flesh and blood hath not revealed it unto thee, but My Father which is in heaven." We can only know the Father through the Son (see Matthew 11:27), and regeneration means that God puts into my spirit the Spirit of His Son. Ask God on the authority of Jesus to give you the Holy Spirit, and He will do so; but you will never ask until you have struck the bottom board of your need.

When I asked God to give me the Holy Spirit, He did so, and what a transformation took place! Life became heaven on earth after being hell on earth. Never say that Jesus has done in you what you know He has not done. God comes to any man instanter when he asks, and the man will realise the difference in his actual experience; when things happen he is amazed at the change that has been wrought, not by an effort of his will, but by banking on the new power within.

When we receive the Holy Spirit, we receive the quickening life that lifts us into the domain where Jesus lives and we have the revelation of Who He is. The secret of the Christian is that he knows the absolute Deity of Jesus Christ. Has Jesus made any difference to us in our actual life? The essence of Christianity is not a creed or a doctrine, but an illumination that emancipates us—"I see Who Jesus is." It is always a surprise, never an intellectual conception. "The wind bloweth where it listeth, . . . *so is every one that is born of the Spirit.*"

IV

*It is the true nature of the Pentecostal experience to pro-
duce a congruity between the message and the messenger.
The Gospel has to be proclaimed, it has to be commended,
it has to be announced, but it has to be adorned. The Holy
Ghost will fall on those who hear the word when it has
fallen on those who speak the word.*

Selby

My spiritual life is based on some word of God made
living in me; when I transact on that word, I step into
the moral frontier where Jesus works. He says, "Come
unto Me"; "Ask, and it shall be given you"—commitment is always required. An intellectualist never
pushes an issue of will. Our Lord uses the word
"believe" in a moral sense, not in an intellectual sense.
"Commit yourself to Me." We are to believe in a Person, not to believe for something. "This is the work
of God, that ye believe. . . ." Christianity is not a matter of deciding for Christ, nor of making vows, but of
receiving something from God on the basis of His
promise in Luke 11:13. The reception of the Holy
Spirit is the maintained attitude of the believer, Be
being filled with the Spirit. The way of His entrance
into us is the knowledge of our own poverty.

1. In the Days of His Resurrection
The Promise of the Highest (Luke 24:49–53; Acts 1:4)
The reason the disciples had to tarry until the Day of
Pentecost was not merely that they might be fitted to
receive the promise: they had to wait until the Lord
was glorified historically, for not until in the decrees
of God the fullness of time was reached that the Son
of God should be glorified and ascend to the right
hand of the Father, did the personal Holy Spirit
descend (see John 15:26; Acts 2:33). The parenthesis
in John 7:39 ("for the Holy Ghost was not yet given;
because that Jesus was not yet glorified") does not
apply to us. The Holy Spirit has been given; Jesus has
been glorified; the waiting depends upon our fitness,
not upon God's providence. The reception of the
Holy Ghost depends entirely upon moral preparation.
I must abide in the light which the Holy Ghost sheds
and be obedient to the word of God; then when the
power of God comes upon such obedience there will
be the manifestation of a strong family likeness to
Jesus. It is easier to be swayed by emotions than to live
a life shot through with the Holy Spirit, a life in
which Jesus is glorified. The Holy Spirit is absolutely
honest, He indicates the things that are right and the
things that are wrong.

"*Tarry ye . . . until. . . .*" This is the New Testament
conception of fasting, not from food only but from
everything, until the particular thing we have been told
to expect is fulfilled. Fasting means concentration in
order that the purpose of God may be developed in
our lives. . . . until ye be endued with power from on
high." There is only one "power from on high," a holy
power that transfigures morality. Never yield to a
power unless you know its character. Spiritualism is
more than trickery; it has hold of powers that are not
characterised by the holy integrity of Jesus.

Jesus Christ gives the power of His own disposition to carry us through if we are willing to obey. That
is why He is apparently so merciless to those of us
who have received the Holy Spirit, because He makes
His demands according to His disposition, not
according to our natural disposition. On the basis of
the Redemption God expects us to erect characters
worthy of the sons of God. He does not expect us to
carry on "evangelical capers," but to manifest the life
of the Son of God in our mortal flesh.

2. In The Days of Our Regeneration
The Sovereign Preference (John 21:15–17)
Our Lord here is not only reinstating Peter, but laying
down the basis of the apostolic office, and He bases it
on love. "Lovest thou Me more than these?" There is
not the slightest strand of delusion left in Peter's mind
about himself; he has come to an end of all his self-sufficiency (cf. John 13:37), and the question of his Lord
is a revelation to himself as to how much he does love
Him—"Lord, thou knowest all things; thou knowest
that I love Thee." Love is the sovereign preference of
my person for another person, and when the Holy
Spirit is in a man, that other Person is Jesus. The only
Lover of the Lord Jesus Christ is the Holy Ghost (see
Romans 5:5). When a man has entered into a personal
relationship with Jesus by means of the reception of the
Holy Spirit, the first characteristic of that relationship
is the nourishing of those who believe in Jesus. "Lovest
thou Me? . . . Feed My sheep." That is what we are
saved for, not to feed our converts, or to promulgate our
explanation of things, but to be sent out by Christ, possessed of His Spirit, to feed His sheep. There is no
release from that commission.

When we are young in grace we go where we
want to go; but Jesus says, "When thou shalt be old,
. . . another shall gird thee, and carry thee whither
thou wouldest not." The reference to Peter's death by
crucifixion has a symbolic meaning for the real inner-
ness of being fastened for discipline. It is this stage of
spiritual experience that brings us into touch with the

spirit of Jesus in that even Christ pleased not Himself." This is the crisis of discipleship. We do not object to being delivered from sin, but we do not intend to give up the right to ourselves; it is this point that is balked. Jesus will never make us give up our right to ourselves; we must do it of our own deliberate choice. Our Lord always talks about discipleship with an "IF." "If any man will be My disciple"—those are the conditions (see Luke 14:26–27, 33).

"And when He had spoken this, He saith unto him, Follow Me." When three years before Jesus said, "Follow Me," Peter did it easily; the fascination of Jesus was upon him, and he followed without any hesitation. The one being Peter did not know was himself, and he came to the place where he denied Jesus with oaths and curses, and his heart broke. Then he received the Holy Spirit; and again Jesus says, "Follow Me." There is only one lodestar in Peter's life now,

the Lord Jesus Christ; he is to follow Jesus now in the submission of his will and his intelligence to Him.

The way Jesus dealt with the disciples is the way He deals with us. He surrounded the disciples with an atmosphere of His own life and put in seed thoughts, that is, He stated His truth, and left it to come to fruition. "I have yet many things to say unto you, but ye cannot bear them now," i.e. you are not in the domain where you can understand. The disciples did not understand what Jesus taught them in the days of His flesh; but His teaching took on new meaning when once they received the Holy Spirit (see John 14:26; 16:13).

Redemption means that Jesus Christ can give me His own disposition, and all the standards He gives are based on that disposition. *Jesus Christ's teaching is for the life He puts in.*

V

The victory that overcomes the world is not human love, but Christian faith; it is not won by the natural heart, but by the re-creating cross.

Forsyth[10]

1. In the Days of His Ascension
The Promise of Authoritative Lordship (Acts 1:8)
There is only one Lord of men, the Lord Jesus Christ, and yet He never insists upon His authority; He never says "Thou shalt"; He takes the patient course with us, as He did with the early disciples. When they received the Holy Spirit, He took absolute control of them, and Jesus Christ's teachings took on new meaning. Naturally we do not pay any attention to what Jesus says unless it is in agreement with our own conceptions; we come to realise that Jesus Christ does not tell outside certain moral frontiers. The teaching of Jesus only begins to apply to us when we have received the disposition that ruled Him. Jesus Christ makes human destiny depend entirely upon a man's relationship to Himself (see John 3:36). According to our Lord, the bedrock of membership in the Christian Church is a personal revelation from God as to Who Jesus is, and a public declaration of it (cf. Matthew 15:15–19).

Our Lord taught His Lordship to His disciples, and said that after He had ascended He would send

forth the Holy Spirit, Who would be the Disposer of affairs, both individual and international. We have not made Jesus Christ Lord, we have not given up the right to ourselves to Him, consequently we continually muddle our affairs by our own intuitions and desires for our own ends. Both nations and individuals have tried Christianity and abandoned it, because it has been found too difficult; but no man has ever gone through the crisis of deliberately making Jesus Lord and found Him to be a failure. "God is no respecter of persons." Christianity cuts out a man's personal prejudices. A moral earthquake was required before Peter recognised that God was the same to the crowd outside as to those within (see Acts 10). We are apt to imagine that God will only work according to precedent. The Holy Ghost is world-wide. God says that He will pour out His spirit "upon all flesh" (Joel 2:28). Men who are not the servants of God may have a right vision in view for the human race, a vision of the time when men shall live as brothers. The difference does not lie in the vision, because the source of the vision is the Spirit of God; it lies in the way the vision is to be fulfilled. The servant of God knows that it can be fulfilled in only one way, viz. on the basis of Redemption. "Your sons and your daughters" refers to the men who have no concern about the Redemptive point of view.

10. Peter Taylor Forsyth (1848–1921): British Congregationalist minister and theologian. Chambers read many of Forsyth's books and valued his insights.

The brotherhood of the New Testament is indeed meant to cover the race at last, but it is the brotherhood of Christian faith and love, not of mankind.

Forsyth

All men are brothers, but they are not the brothers of Christ until they have become so by a moral likeness of disposition.

As our Lord ascended He stretched forth His hands; the last the disciples saw of Jesus was His pierced hands. The pierced hands are emblematic of the Atonement. "If any man shall say unto you, Lo, here is Christ, or there; believe it not." The declaration of the angel was that it is "this same Jesus" Who is to come again, with the marks of the Atonement on Him. The wounded hands and feet are a symbol of the Redeemer Who will come again. There are no marks of Atonement in the "Labour Christ," or the "Socialist Christ," or the "Christian Science Christ."

2. In the Days of Our Apprehension
The Sacramental Personality (Ephesians 4:8–12)
Up to the time of the Transfiguration, our Lord had exhibited the normal, perfect life of a Man; after the Transfiguration everything is unfamiliar to us. From the Transfiguration onwards, we are dealing not so much with the life our Lord lived as with the way in which He made it possible for us to enter into His life. On the Mount of Ascension the Transfiguration was completed, and our Lord went back to His primal glory; but He did not go back simply as Son of God: He went back *as Son of Man* as well as Son of God. That means there is freedom of access now for anyone straight to the very throne of God through the Ascension of the Son of Man. At His Ascension our Lord entered Heaven, and He keeps the door open for humanity to enter.

Our Lord told the disciples that the sign of His Ascension would be that He would send forth "the promise of My Father" upon them (Luke 24:49). The Holy Spirit is not "this same Jesus," He is the Bond-servant of the Son of God, doing *in* human lives all that Jesus did *for* them. The Holy Spirit is in complete subjection to the Person of the Redeemer for the purposes of Redemption, as our Lord was in subjection to the Father (see John 5:19; 16:13).

Notice the gifts that the Apostle Paul says Jesus sent after He ascended—viz. apostles, prophets, evangelists, pastors and teachers—"for the perfecting of the saints, for the work of the ministry, for the edifying of the body of Christ." The test of a preacher or teacher is that as we listen to him we are built up in our faith in Jesus Christ and in our intimacy with Him; otherwise he is not a gift from God. To-day we are apt to test the preacher on the ground of his personality and not by his building up of the saints. "My sheep hear My voice," said Jesus—preaching and teaching that comes from a central relationship to Himself. "Lovest thou Me? . . . Feed My sheep." Once the crisis of identification with Jesus is passed, the characteristic of the life is that we keep open house for the universe. The saint is at home anywhere on Mother Earth; he dare be no longer parochial or denominational; he belongs to no particular crowd, he belongs to Jesus Christ. A saint is a sacramental personality, one through whom the presence of God comes to others (see John 7:37–39).

"Till we all attain . . . unto the measure of the stature of the fulness of Christ" (Ephesians 4:13 RV). The personal Holy Spirit builds us up into the body of Christ. All that Jesus Christ came to do is made ours experimentally by the Holy Spirit, and all His gifts are for the good of the whole body, not for individual exaltation. Individuality must go in order that the personal life may be brought out into fellowship with God. By the baptism of the Holy Ghost we are delivered from the husk of independent individuality, our personality is awakened and brought into communion with God. We too often divorce what the New Testament never divorces. The baptism of the Holy Ghost is not an experience apart from Christ: it is the evidence of the ascended Christ. It is not the baptism of the Holy Ghost that changes men, but the power of the ascended Christ coming into men's lives by the Holy Ghost that changes them. "*Ye shall be witnesses unto Me.*" This great Pentecostal phrase puts the truth for us in unforgettable words. Witnesses not so much of what Jesus Christ can do, but *witnesses unto Me,* a delight to the heart of Jesus, a satisfaction to Him wherever He places us.

A saint's life is in the hands of God as a bow and arrow in the hands of an archer. God is aiming at something the saint cannot see; He stretches and strains, and every now and again the saint says: "I cannot stand any more." But God does not heed; He goes on stretching until His purpose is in sight, then He lets fly. We are here for God's designs, not for our own. We have to learn that this is the dispensation of the humiliation of the saints. The Christian Church has blundered by not recognising this. In another dispensation the manifestation of the saints will take place, but in this dispensation we are to be disciples of Jesus Christ, not following our own convictions but remaining true to Him.

The great lack to-day is of people who will *think* along Christian lines; we know a great deal about salvation but we do not go on to explore the "unsearchable riches of Christ." We do not know much about giving up the right to ourselves to Jesus Christ, or about the intense patience of "hanging in" in perfect certainty that what Jesus says is true.

Now Is It Possible—

And I pray God your whole spirit and soul and body be preserved blameless unto the coming of our Lord Jesus Christ. 1 Thessalonians 5:23

We never can be faultless in this life, but God's Book brings out that we must be blameless, that is, undeserving of censure from God's standpoint, and remember what His standpoint is. He can see into every crook and cranny of my spirit and soul and body, and He demands that I be blameless in all my relationships so that He Himself can see nothing worthy of censure. The revelation is one which shows the supernaturalness of the work of sanctification. It cannot be done by praying, by devoting myself, by believing; it can only be done by the supernatural power of a supernatural God.

1. To Be Blameless in My Self Life?
I pray God your whole spirit and soul and body be preserved blameless unto the coming of our Lord Jesus Christ.

Now where are we? Is there the tiniest element of the conviction of the Spirit of God? If so, yield to Him at once. We must distinguish between the working of our own suspicions and the checking of the Spirit of God who works as quietly and silently as a breeze. As He brings back to our mind our bodily life in this past week in public and in private, in eating and drinking, have we been blameless in our self life? Sanctification means that God keeps my whole spirit and soul and body undeserving of censure in His sight.

Take the soul—how have we been conducting our imaginations, our motives, our fancies, and all the working of our reasoning life; is there anything for the Spirit of God to check and censure? We must not say because we are sanctified we are sure to be right. The seal of sanctification in the practical life is that it is blameless, undeserving of censure before God. Blamelessness is not faultlessness; faultlessness was the condition of the Lord Jesus Christ. We never can be faultless in this life, we are in impaired human bodies; but by sanctification we can be blameless. Our disposition can be supernaturally altered until in the simplicity of life before God the whole limit is holy, and if that is to be done, it must be by the great grace of God. "My peace I give unto you." The Spirit of God works with an amazing zeal on Christ's words.

"I pray God your whole spirit . . . be preserved blameless." Are we spiritually affected before God? Are our petitions our own? Do we put our will into them? Do we borrow our sentiments, or are they really ours?

Paul does not say we are to be blameless in our self life in the view of other people. We never shall be; Jesus Christ was not. It was said of His bodily life—"Behold a man gluttonous, and a winebibber," of His soul life—"He . . . is mad," and of His spirit life—"He hath a devil"; but before God He was blameless. Some of us are so concerned about being blameless before men that we are to be blamed before God. The Apostle Paul prays that we may be sanctified and preserved blameless; then it is a matter of absolute indifference what anyone thinks of us, but it is not a matter of indifference what God's Holy Spirit thinks of us.

If we are sanctified by the power of the God of peace, our self life is blameless before Him, there is nothing to hide; and the more we bring our soul under the searchlight of God the more we realise the ineffable comfort of the supernatural work He has done.

Of ourselves we can never be any of the things God says we must be. We can never be blameless by thinking about it, or by praying about it, but only by being sanctified, and that is God's absolute sovereign work of grace. "Abraham believed God, and it was accounted to him for righteousness." Do I believe God can sanctify me? "Christ Jesus . . . is made unto us . . . sanctification." Have we the quiet confidence of a child that the life of Jesus Christ can be formed in us until the relationship to God of spirit, soul and body is without blame before Him? It is not the perfection of attainment in thinking, or in bodily life, or in worship, but the perfection of a blameless disposition, nothing in it to censure, and that in the eyes of God who sees everything.

Is it possible to be blameless in our self life? Paul says it is, and the writer to the Hebrews states that it is by sanctification we are made one with Jesus. "For both He that sanctifieth and they who are sanctified are all of one" (Hebrews 2:11). That is the glorious work of Jesus Christ in our life. Has He performed His work in us or has He not? Do not ask anybody else about it, the Holy Spirit will show you as clearly as can be. If you are right with God, you would not thank the angel Gabriel for telling you, because you know it. It will be the witness not of a word only, but nothing less than absolute agreement with God's standard when He brings you up against it.

2. To Be Blameless in My Social Life?
That ye may be blameless and harmless, the sons of God, without rebuke, in the midst of a crooked and perverse generation [RV], among whom ye shine as lights in the world. (Philippians 2:15)

Am I without blame in relation to my father and mother, to my wife or husband, my brothers and sisters? If the work of Jesus Christ has had its way in us, God Almighty can see nothing to censure when He scrutinises us by His Holy Spirit. The Spirit of God does not work as our minds do, that is, He does not work with suspicion, He works silently and gently as daylight. There will be a check here, an illumination there, a wonderful all-over realisation—"Thank God, He has done it!" There is no need to protest or to profess. We have to be blameless in all our social relationships before God, but that will not mean that our relations will think us blameless! We can always gauge where we are by the teachings of Jesus Christ.

Is it possible to be blameless in our social life? The Apostle Paul says it is, and if we were asked whether we believed God could make us blameless, we would all say, "Yes." Well, has He done it? If God has not sanctified us and made us blameless, there is only one reason why He has not—we do not want Him to. "This is the will of God, even your sanctification." We have not to urge God to do it, it is His will; is it our will? Sanctification is the work of the supernatural power of God.

3. To Be Blameless in My Spiritual Life?

According as He hath chosen us in Him before the foundation of the world, that we should be holy and without blame before Him in love. (Ephesians 1:4)

Wherefore, beloved, seeing that ye look for such things, be diligent that ye may be found of Him in peace, without spot, and blameless. (2 Peter 3:14)

Is it possible to be blameless in our spiritual relationship to Almighty God, to Jesus Christ and to the Holy Ghost? It is not only possible, but God's word tells us that that is what God does—"If we walk in the light, as He is in the light, . . . the blood of Jesus Christ His Son cleanseth us from all sin" (1 John 1:7). That is cleansing not from conscious sin only but from infinitely more, it is cleansing to the depths of crystalline purity so that God Himself can see nothing impure. That is the work of the Lord Jesus Christ; to make His work anything less would be blasphemous. If God Almighty cannot do that in your life and mine, we have "followed cunningly devised fables." Unless Jesus Christ can re-make Himself in us, what is the meaning of those thirty years in Nazareth, those three years of His public life? What is the meaning of the Cross of Jesus Christ, of His Resurrection and Ascension, if He cannot cleanse us from all sin? But, bless God, He can! The point is—have we let Him do it? Beware of praising Jesus Christ whilst all the time you cunningly refuse to let the Spirit of God work His salvation efficaciously in your life. Remember, the battle is in the will; whenever we say "I can't," or whenever we are indifferent, it means "I won't." It is better to let Jesus Christ uncover the obstinacy. If there is one point where we say "I won't" then we shall never know His salvation. From the moment that God uncovers a point of obstinacy in us and we refuse to let Him deal with it, we begin to be sceptical, to sneer and watch for defects in the lives of others. But when once we yield to Him entirely, He makes us blameless in our personal life, in our practical life, and in our profound life. It is not done by piety, it is wrought in us by the sovereign grace of God, and we have not the slightest desire to trust in ourselves in any degree, but in Him alone.

"Now unto Him that is able to keep you from falling, and to present you faultless before the presence of His glory with exceeding joy" (Jude 24). Can God keep me from stumbling this second? Yes. Can He keep me from sin this second? Yes. Well, that is the whole of life, you cannot live more than a second at a time. If God can keep you blameless this second, He can do it the next. No wonder Jesus Christ said "Let not your heart be troubled"! We do get troubled when we do not remember the amazing power of God.

WILL YOU GO OUT WITHOUT KNOWING?

Abraham . . . went out, not knowing whither he went.
Hebrews 11:8

That is true either of a fool or a faithful soul. One of the hardest lessons to learn is this one that Abraham's life brings out. He went out of all his own ways of looking at things and became a fool in the eyes of the world.

1. Out in Separation unto God

Now the LORD said unto Abram, Get thee out of thy country, and from thy kindred, and from thy father's house, unto the land that I will shew thee. (Genesis 12:1 RV)

Have you been "out" in that way? If you have, there is no logical statement possible if anyone asks what you are doing. Suppose you are asked why you are in this College,[11] you do not know, and you ought not to know. One of the greatest difficulties in Christian work is that everyone says—"Now what do you expect to do?" Of course you do not know what you are going to do. The only thing you know is that God knows what He is about.

Separation unto God is the first characteristic—separation unto God for food, for clothing, for money, for the next step. It is a "going out" of all your "kindred" and "house" ways of looking at things, a "going out" with nothing in view, but being perfectly certain that you are separated unto God. "Beloved, think it not strange," says Peter, "concerning the fiery trial which is to try you, as though a strange thing happened unto you: but rejoice. . . ." Whenever you have been faithful to God, you do not know you have been faithful until it is pointed out, and you say—"Why, I never thought of that as a test." It is only on looking back that you find it was. We have continually to revise our attitude towards God and see if it is a "going out," out of everything, trusting in God entirely. It is this attitude that keeps us in perpetual wonder. We know God, and we know He is a supernatural God who works miracles, and our attitude is one of childlike amazement—"I don't know what God is going to do next." A child sees giants and fairies where we see only the most prosaic things. Jesus said ". . . except ye . . . become as little children." Every morning we wake it is to be a "going out," building in confidence on God. "Therefore I say unto

you, take no thought for your life, what ye shall eat, or what ye shall drink; nor yet for your body, what ye shall put on," take no thought, that is, for anything you did take thought for before you "went out." Before you "went out" you did take thought for your life, for what you should do tomorrow, but now you belong to the crowd Jesus Christ heads, and you seek first the Kingdom of God and His righteousness.

2. Out in Surrender to God

And I will make of thee a great nation, and I will bless thee, and make thy name great; and be thou a blessing. (Genesis 12:2 RV)

It means more to surrender to God for Him to do a big thing than to surrender a big thing to God. We have to surrender our mean[12] little notions for a tremendous revelation that takes our breath away. For instance, am I humble enough to accept the tremendous revelation that God Almighty, the Lord Jesus Christ, and the Holy Ghost will come and make Their abode with me? (see John 14:23). Will I so completely surrender the sense of my own unworthiness that I go out of all my own ways of thinking and let God do exactly as He likes?

Sacrifice in the Bible means that we give to God the best we have; it is the finest form of worship. Sacrifice is not giving up things, but giving to God with joy the best we have. We have dragged down the idea of surrender and of sacrifice, we have taken the life out of the words and made them mean something sad and weary and despicable; in the Bible they mean the very opposite. To go out in surrender to God means the surrendering of the miserable sense of my own un-importance. Am I willing to surrender that mean little sense for the great big idea God has for me? Am I willing to surrender the fact that I am an ignorant, useless, worthless, too-old person? There is more hindrance to God's work because people cling to a sense of unworthiness than because of conceit. "*Who am I?*" Instantly the trend of the mind is to say—"Oh well, I have not had any education"; "I did not begin soon enough." Am I willing to surrender the whole thing, and go out in surrender to God? to go out of the carnal mind into the spiritual?—"fools for Christ's sake"?

Abraham surrendered himself entirely to the supernatural God. Have you got hold of a supernat-

---

11. Bible Training College (BTC).
12. mean: as used here, something or someone ordinary, common, low, or ignoble, rather than cruel or spiteful.

ural God? not, do you know what God is going to do? You cannot know, but you have faith in Him, and therefore He can do what He likes. Has God been trying to bring into your life the fact that He is supernatural, and have you been asking Him what He is going to do? He will never tell you. God does not tell us what He is going to do, He reveals to you who He is (cf. John 14:12–13). Do you believe in a miracle-working God, and will you go out in surrender to Him? Have you faith in your holiness or in God? faith in your obedience or in God? Have you gone out in surrender to God until you would not be an atom surprised at anything He did? No one is surprised over what God does when once he has faith in Him. Have you a supernatural God, or do you tie Him up by the laws of your own mind?

We blunder mostly on the line of surrender, not of conceit, in the continual reminders we give to God that we are small and mean. We are much worse than small and mean: Jesus said—"Without Me ye can do nothing." Let us surrender all thinking about ourselves either for appreciation or depreciation, cast ourselves confidently on God and go out like children.

3. Out in Sanctification for God

So Abram went, as the LORD had spoken unto him. (Genesis 12:4)

Sanctification means going out as God has told us. Are we going along the line God has told us in the things we have been saying and thinking, in letter-writing, to people in difficulty, in prayer? If it is a matter of our own personal sanctification, let us put God between ourselves and the difficulty.

Our Lord did not rebuke His disciples for making mistakes, but for not having faith. The two things that astonished Him were "little faith" and "great faith." Faith is not in what Jesus Christ can do, but in Himself, and anything He can do is less than Himself.

Suppose that God is the God we know Him to be when we are nearest to Him, what an impertinence worry is! Think of the unspeakable marvel of the remaining hours of this day, and think how easily we can shut God right out of His universe by the logic of our own heads, by a trick of our nerves, by remembering the way we have limited Him in the past—banish Him right out, and let the old drudging, carking care come in, until we are a disgrace to the name of Jesus. But once let the attitude be a continual "going out" in dependence on God and the life will have an ineffable charm, which is a satisfaction to Jesus Christ.

We have to learn how to "go out" of everything, out of convictions, out of creeds, out of experiences, out of everything, until so far as our faith is concerned, there is nothing between us and God.

DO YOU CONTINUE TO GO WITH JESUS?

Ye are they which have continued with Me in My temptations. Luke 22:28

We are apt to imagine that our Lord was only tempted once and that then His temptations were over. His temptations went on from the first moment of His conscious life to the last, because His holiness was not the holiness of Almighty God, but the holiness of man, which can only progress by means of the things that go against it (*see* Hebrews 2:18; 4:15). Are we going with Jesus in His temptations? It is true that He is with us in our temptations, but are we with Him in His? Many of us cease to go with Jesus from the moment we have an experience of what He can do. Like Peter, we have all had moments when Jesus has had to say to us, "What, could ye not watch with Me one hour?"

Are we lazy spiritually because we are so active in God's work? When the problems of the body face us, do we stop going with Jesus? Do we listen to the tempter's voice to put our bodily needs first—"Eat bread, be well, first look after what you are going to

wear, and then attend to God"? It is the most subtle voice any Christian ever heard, and whether it come through an archangel or through a man or woman, it is the voice of the devil. Are we going with Jesus along these lines, or are we putting our own needs and the needs of men and social reform first?

Satan does not come on the line of tempting us to sin, but on the line of making us shift our point of view, and only the Spirit of God can detect this as a temptation of the devil. It is the same in missionary enterprise and in all Christian work. The Church is apt not to go with Jesus in His temptations. The temptations of Our Lord in the days of His flesh are the kind of temptations He is subjected to in the temple of our body. Watch when God shifts your circumstances and see whether you are going with Jesus or siding with the world, the flesh and the devil. We wear His badge, but are we going with Him? "Upon this many of His disciples went back, and walked no more with Him" (RV).

The temptation may be to do some big startling thing in order to prove that we really are the children of God. Satan said to Jesus, "If Thou be the Son of God, cast Thyself down from hence," and to us he says, "If you are saved and sanctified and true to God, everyone you know should be saved too." If that were true, Jesus Christ is wrong in His revelation of God. If by our salvation and right relationship to God, we can be the means of turning our world upside down, what has Jesus Christ been doing all these years? The temptation is to claim that God does something that will prove who we are and what He has done for us. It is a temptation of the devil, and can only be detected as a temptation by the Spirit of God.

Are we taking the pattern and print of our life from some booklet or some band of Christians, or are we continuing with Jesus, standing with Him in every new circumstance of life? It is there that we understand the fellowship of His sufferings, and the broader He makes our life and our mind and circumstances, the more essential does the one thing become—to continue with Him in His temptations.

Have we given God as much "elbow room" in our lives as Our Lord gave Him in His? Have we the one set purpose, which is only born in us by the Son of God, viz., not to do our own will but the will of God? ". . . that the life also of Jesus might be made manifest in our mortal flesh." The temptations of Jesus continued all His earthly life, and they will continue all the time of His life in us. Are we going with Jesus in the life we are living now?

The temptation may be to compromise with evil—"Don't be so tremendously strong against sin and in denouncing the pleasures and interests that make up this life as it is, and the whole world will be at your feet"! Jesus Christ was tempted like His brethren (*see* Hebrews 4:15), not like men who are not born again. When we are tempted as He was, do we continue to go with Him? What are we like where nobody sees? Have we a place in our heart and mind and life where there is always open communion between ourselves and God so that we can detect the voice of the devil when he comes as "an angel of light"? Every temptation of the devil is full of the most amazing wisdom and the understanding of every problem that ever stretched before men's view. Satan's kingdom is based on wisdom, along the lines he advocates lies success, and men recognise this. Jesus Christ is not on the line of success but on the spiritual line, the holy, practical line and no other. If men and women do not continue to go with Jesus, they will begin to teach what undermines the kingdom of Jesus Christ.

"Ye are they which have continued with Me in My temptations." Are we compromising in the tiniest degree in mental conception with forces that do not continue to go with Jesus, or are we maintaining the attitude of Jesus Christ all through? Are we departing from Jesus in the slightest way in connection with the world to which we belong? Have we this past week choked the Son of God in our life by imperceptible degrees? Have the demands of the life of the Son of God in us been a bit too spiritual, too strong, too sternly holy, too sternly unworldly, too pressing, too narrow, too much in the eye of God only? or do we say "Yes, *Lord, I'll go with Thee all the way*"?

> I have made my choice for ever,
> I will walk with Christ my Lord.

Watch where Jesus went. The one dominant note in His life was to do His Father's will. His is not the way of wisdom or of success, but the way of faithfulness.

No matter what your circumstances may be, don't try to shield yourself from things God is bringing into your life. We have the idea sometimes that we ought to shield ourselves from some of the circumstances God brings round us. Never! God engineers circumstances; we have to see that we face them abiding continually with Him in His temptations. They are *His* temptations, they are not temptations to us, but to the Son of God in us. If you talk about the subtle temptations that come to you as a child of God to those who have not the life of the Son of God, they will laugh at you. We continually side with the prince of this world and have to be brought back to a spiritual stock-taking. Are we going with Jesus in His temptations in our bodies? Are we going with Him in the temptations of our mental and moral life, and of our spiritual life, abiding true to God all through? That is the one concern Jesus Christ has about us.

"Ye are they which have continued with Me in My temptations." Do you continue to go with Jesus? The way lies through Gethsemane, through the city gate, outside the camp; the way lies alone, and the way lies until there is no trace of a footstep left, only the voice—"*Follow Me.*"

"As He is, even so are we in this world" (RV). Where is Jesus in this world? There is no outward manifestation of Jesus, and we are to be as He is, hidden, true, and absolutely loyal to God. Temptations do not come in fits and starts, they abide all the time, and to continue with Jesus in them is the way the holiness of our life is going to be to the glory of God.

The Graciousness of Uncertainty
Foreword to the First Edition

Do you know the clear water of a mountain stream running the shadowy places of the trees and of the brown and green mosses? Here and there is a crystal pool, hidden beneath a rock—still it seems, like a mirror—while yet all the lovely light and life of the running stream passes through it continually. Such a shadowy living pool is my thought of the life of the beloved student of the B.T.C. whom we used to call "Lambie."[13]

Her life was spent in the quiet places, but it held the tragic sorrows and the deep joys of those who really *are* alive as human men and women created of God.

Bodily suffering and weakness were often her portion (due to a fall from her horse while still a young girl keen of all outdoor pursuits), but never her conquerors: sacrifice and duties wilfully undertaken and shared with the ones she loved best, instead of a self-chosen and deeply desired career elsewhere—these were hers. The countryside loved and trusted her, and took her teaching and her preaching to their hearts and consciences because they saw her life from day to day, and it was so very really that "outward and visible sign of the inward and spiritual grace" that the sacramental out-giving by word and prayer was to men a real and valid thing. "Greatly beloved"—might be written of her. And to those who enjoyed her inner friendship that friendship must be one of the indestructible and eternal things because in their lives and in hers it is hid with Christ in God.

One who loved her said in my hearing how beautiful her spirit would be in its manifestation when this mortal shall have put on immortality, and on those occasions when one caught it glancing out of her eyes I realised the truth of what he said.

The current of her inner life ran swiftly, controlled as well as indwelt by the Holy Spirit. She was trusted to speak often in the Name of Jesus Christ our Lord—for she never lowered His standard of truth, nor failed to set the personal knowledge of Him as *the* One essential goal for men and women in their life on earth. She preached "Jesus Christ and Him crucified" in its deep individual and racial implications. Thank God for her life. It is a gladness to think of her.

Katherine Ashe[14]
Cairo, January 1938

THE GRACIOUSNESS OF UNCERTAINTY

It is not yet made manifest what we shall be. 1 John 3:2 (RV)

We are apt to look upon uncertainty as a bad thing, because we are all too mathematical and common sense. We imagine we have to reach an end; so we have, but a particular end is easily reached, and is not of the nature of spiritual life. The nature of spiritual life is that we are certain in our uncertainty, consequently we do not make our "nests" anywhere spiritually. Immediately we make a "nest" out of an organisation or a creed or a belief, we come across the biggest of all calamities, the fact that all certainty brings death. G. K. Chesterton, that insurgent writer, pronounces all certainties "*dead certainties.*" Immediately I become certain, something dies. For instance, when I become certain that my baby is no longer a baby but a little girl, the baby is dead. When I become certain that my single life is ended in married life, something is dead—"that white funeral of the single life."[15] In the realm of belief, whenever I become certain of my creeds, I kill the life of God in my soul, because I cease to believe in God and believe

---

13. "Lambie": Ruby Lamb.

14. Katherine Ashe (1865–1956): convert to Christ through Oswald Chambers' influence in Ireland in 1908. Miss Ashe, as she was always known, came to the BTC as a student and teacher, then went to Egypt in 1916 for ministry to soldiers through the YMCA.

15. "white funeral of the single life": phrase from Tennyson's poem "To H.R.H. Princess Beatrice"; to Chambers, it meant a passage from one stage of life to another—leaving the past behind and moving into the future; he often used it to mean death to self and a complete surrender to God.

in my belief instead. All through the Bible the realm of the uncertain is the realm of joy and delight; the certainty of belief brings distress. Certainty of God means uncertainty in life; while certainty in belief makes us uncertain of God. Certainty is the mark of the common-sense life; gracious uncertainty is the mark of the spiritual life, and they must both go together. Mathematics is the rule of reason and common sense, but faith and hope is the rule of the spiritual. "It is not yet made manifest what we shall be"—we are gloriously uncertain of the next step, but we are certain of God. Immediately we abandon to God and do the duty that lies nearest, He packs our lives with surprises all the time; whereas if we become the advocates of a set creed something dies. All certainty brings death to something. When we have a certain belief, we kill God in our lives, because we do not believe Him, we believe our beliefs about Him and do what Job's friends did—bring God and human life to the standard of our beliefs and not to the standard of God. The helplessness of professional religion is that there is no room for surprise, we tie God up in His laws and in denominational doctrines and orders of services, consequently we do not see God at all. The average man is inarticulate about his belief, and the curious thing is he does not connect his belief in goodness and truth and justice with Jesus Christ and the churches because the churches have misrepresented Jesus Christ. We cannot "corner" God or spiritual life, to think we can is the curse of denominational belief—we have all the "stock" and no one can have it except in our way. Jesus Christ says, "Except ye . . . become as little children. . . ." A little child is certain of its parents, but uncertain about everything else, therefore it lives a perfectly delightful healthy life.

1. The Surprise of Real Life *(John 3:8)*

These words convey our Lord's mind, but we rarely pay any attention to His mind. He states there emphatically that the Spirit of God works in incalculable ways; we cannot say that He will work through certain denominations and channels. In times of revival people say they started in answer to prayer, but this is questionable. Revivals start entirely by the sheer surprise of the life of God. The life of God springs out on the right hand and on the left, we cannot calculate over God, and that is the immense joy of Christian life. ". . . so is everyone that is born of the Spirit." To be certain of God means that we are delightfully uncertain in all our ways, we do not know what a day may bring forth. That is generally said with a sigh of sadness, but it should be rather an expression of breathless unexpectedness. It is exactly the state of mind we should be in spiritually, a state of expectant wonder, like a child. When we are certain of God we always live in this delightful uncertainty;

whereas if we are certain of our beliefs we become even-tenored people who never expect to see God anywhere.

(a) The Frontiers of Death *(John 6:53)*

This is not a sad statement, but a joyful one. Whenever we think we can get the life of God by obedience or prayer or some kind of discipline, we are wrong. We must realise the frontiers of death, that there is no more chance of our entering into the life of God than a mineral has of entering the vegetable kingdom; we can only enter into the Kingdom of God if God will stoop down and lift us up. That is exactly what Jesus Christ promises to do. The bedrock of spiritual life as our Lord taught is poverty—"Blessed are the poor in spirit," not, "Blessed are the strong-willed, or the prayerful or the consecrated," but, "Blessed is the man who knows he is weak." When we get there the surprise of God's life may come at any time. It does not come by believing, that is a misrepresentation. Belief means committing myself to the uncertainty of God. God may spring forth at any minute in His own way in us. It is a benediction to recognise the frontiers of death—to recognise there is nothing at all of the nature of God in ourselves, then the life of God may spring forth at any minute in us. Mathematical common sense makes us think that when we reach the spiritual life we are certain. Up to the time of entering the spiritual life we are certain; afterwards we are gloriously uncertain. We do not know how the life will emerge or what it is going to be. Every now and again God leaves us behind the frontiers of death (see Isaiah 50:10–11); He deals with us on the death side and the life side all the time. The death side is the most beneficial, for when we realise we are dead and absolutely no use, we are unable to begin to do anything, then the surprise of God's real life comes to us suddenly, and the extraordinary surprise of real life is there.

(b) The Foundation of Discernment *(John 3:3)*

"Ye must be born again." That is a statement of foundation fact. We cannot be born again of ourselves any more than we can be born naturally. We cannot say we will be born again, we will believe in Jesus Christ, we will receive the Spirit; we simply cannot do it. Jesus says, "The wind bloweth where it listeth, . . . so is everyone that is born of the Spirit." Immediately we get into the attitude of knowing that we have no life in us, that we cannot re-make ourselves, then God comes in with His surprise of life. The foundation of the spiritual kingdom is, "Blessed are the poor in spirit." When we are born from above (RV mg) the first characteristic is that we begin to discern—"Except a man be born again, he cannot *see* the kingdom of God." After we are born again, we begin to discern, not in thrilling experiences, but we begin to see differently and the surprise of the spiritual life comes in all around.

(c) The Fact of Direction (1 John 2:27)

The Spirit of God directs us when we remain true to the life of God in us. The danger with all of us is to want to direct one another; we are not certain that young lives ought to be left alone, we do not believe God can manage them. "I believe God can direct me, because I am so wise, but you are certain to go wrong; I must instruct you." The fact of direction in spiritual life does not come from any human element at all, it comes entirely in the surprising manner of the life of God.

2. The Spontaneity of Real Love
(1 Corinthians 13:4–8)

Love is spontaneous, that is, not premeditated, it springs up in extraordinary ways. There is nothing mathematically certain in Paul's category of love. We cannot say, "I am going to think no evil," "I am going to believe all things"; the characteristic of love is the spontaneity of the whole thing. In everything to do with the life of God in us we never discern its nature till it is past. In looking back we find there was extraordinary disinterestedness in a particular emotion. We do not set in front of us the statements of Jesus Christ as standards, we receive the life of God and live up to the standard of His teaching without knowing it, and on looking back we are the most amazed beings on earth, which is the evidence of the spontaneity of real love being there.

(a) The Springs of Love (John 17:26)

The springs of love are in God, that means love cannot be found anywhere else. It is absurd for us to try and find the love of God in our hearts naturally, it is not there any more than the life of Jesus Christ is there. Love and life are in God and in Jesus Christ and in the Holy Spirit Whom God gives to us, not because we merit Him, but according to His own particular graciousness. We cannot say in the abstract, "I am going to love my enemies," because naturally we hate them; but when we have a real actual enemy if the love of God is in us, we find we do not hate him. The point is that the springs of love are in the Holy Spirit, not in us. We cannot order the Holy Spirit to come into us; we believe in God, He does the rest. If I try to engineer ways in which to show I love my wife, it is a certain sign I am beginning not to love her. If we try to show how much we love God it is a sure sign we do not love Him; if we love Him the evidence is absolutely spontaneous, it does not need to be worked out, it comes naturally, and if asked why we did certain things we cannot say why, they were done spontaneously according to the nature of love. Love can be simulated, we can affect it and pretend we have it; but when love is real it is spontaneous, and so is spirituality. The danger is lest common sense comes in and says, "Well, now suppose I was in that condition"—then it is all up. We cannot suppose ourselves in any condition we have never been in, therefore life is one of splendid uncertainty, we are certain only of God, and in any circumstances we are in the source of all these characteristics is the life of God in us; we cannot work them up by prayer or obedience; they are of the nature of God. "Sufficient unto the day is the evil thereof." We have to keep ourselves from being engrossed in the evil of present certainty. There are any number of things in the common-sense life which are apt to overcrowd everything else, but in spite of them all the real life of God springs up in this spontaneity of love, the springs of which are in the Holy Spirit Who is given unto us.

(b) The Strength of Life (Ephesians 3:17–19)

"That Christ may dwell in your hearts by faith," not by feeling or reckoning, but by faith. The strength of life is not in the certainty that we can do the thing, but in the perfect certainty that God will. We are certain only of the One Whom we are trusting. The strength of our life lies in knowing that our strength is in God. "And to know the love of Christ"—its breadth, and length, and depth, and height, we cannot get out of it anywhere. When we know the love of Christ, which passeth knowledge, it means that we are free from anxiety, free from carefulness, so that during the twenty-four hours of the day we do what we ought to do all the time, with the strength of life bubbling up with real spontaneous joy. How am I measuring the strength of God in my life? The greatness of God's power to me a saint is measured by the power God manifested when He raised Jesus from the dead (Ephesians 1:19).

(c) The Supremacy of Loyalty (1 Corinthians 13:13)

Greater than faith, greater than hope, greater than anything we can mention is love (RV), which is the very nature of God, and the test of the reality of our spiritual life is abandon to God, the actual condition of gracious uncertainty. Such a life can be either the most arrant piece of humbug, or the expression of the life of God, consequently a saint and a hypocrite may often look one and the same. In our actual circumstances we are based on the God Whom we love, not on our belief in anything. It is significant that Jesus Christ never says anywhere what modern evangelists say—"Believe certain things about Jesus Christ." Jesus says, "Believe also in Me"—"leave the whole thing to Me, you have nothing to do with anything but your actual life, the thing that lies nearest. It is gloriously uncertain how I will come in, but I will come." The greatest thing in our lives is to remain loyal to Jesus, and this will evidence itself as His love at work in us.

3. The Suddenness of Real Light *(Luke 24:31)*
Light is the symbol of intuitive discernment both intellectual and spiritual. Immediately we see Jesus Christ, He becomes a possession of our real life. "The inheritance of the saints in light." When once we perceive Him by the suddenness of spiritual light, we see Him in common-sense things.

(a) The Unexpected Issues (Isaiah 9:1–5)
The characteristic of this passage is the unexpectedness of the happenings. "Then was our mouth filled with laughter, and our tongue with singing." We never dreamed that such a thing would happen to us! This attitude of mind frequently comes by the way of a calamity. Many a man has had his soul restored in the valley of the shadow, not in the green pastures. There are clouds we fear to enter, but on the inside of those clouds is the suddenness of real light. We get the evidence of this on the threshold of real sorrow and difficulty, there is the suddenness of real light and a discernment of things that was unsought, which we could get in no other way.

(b) The Unrealised Interpretations (Job 42:5–6)
"Now mine eye seeth Thee, wherefore I abhor my words [RV mg]," i.e. "I abhor the things I was certain of, I abhor myself for being so obstinately certain that I knew; but now I see." In looking at Job's circumstances the curious thing is, he asks conundrum after conundrum, and instead of their being solved, the providence

of God hurls more problems at him, till at last Job says, "Now I see." He did not perceive anything in the logical line, he simply found that the interpretation lay with God. Job discerned that truth is never gained by intellect, but by moral conscientiousness. Truth is always a vision that arises in the basis of the moral nature, never in the intellect. Immediately we are rightly related to God in moral relationships, instantly we perceive. We can always tell the difference between a man with a keen intellectual discernment and the man with moral discernment; the latter always appeals to the conscience, the former simply convinces the mind and adds no power to the moral life.

(c) The Unearned Increment (Jude 24)
Our lives are enriched with things we never earned. The unearned increment is God, and the popular phrase is right—"If I do my bit, God will see it is all right." But if the statement is made to mean that God will count it as redemption, it is a devilish lie which no man in his own mind ever thought of. What the average man means is that if we do our bit, God will see to the rest. Of course He will. The basis of things is Redemption, which is finished, the point a man has to realise is that God has saved him, and what he has to do is to get into the relationship of actual salvation and be of worth to Jesus Christ here and now. Men are not *going to be* redeemed, they *are* redeemed; Redemption is complete. That is a revelation, not something we get at by thinking, and unless we grant that Redemption is the basis of human life, we will come up against problems for which we can find no way out. It is God Who redeems man; once that realisation dawns, the sense of gratitude springs up; and man becomes of use to God in practical life.

The Moral Foundations of Life

A Series of Talks on the Ethical Principles of the Christian Life

Oswald Chambers

INTRODUCTION

Source

This material is from notes of lectures at the Bible Training College,[1] London, 1911–1915.

Publication History

- As articles: in the *Bible Training Course (BTC) Monthly Journal,*[2] August 1933 September 1934.
- As a book: *The Moral Foundations of Life* was first published as a book in 1936.

One of Chambers' primary goals as a teacher was to challenge Christians to think. An equally important objective was to encourage believers to act. In Chambers' mind, the brain and the body were not enemies but allies in the effort to live a life that glorified God.

Oswald's wide reading can be seen throughout these lectures. The writers quoted range from the well-known to the now-obscure. When possible, the sources of these quotes are identified in a footnote.

Chambers' breadth of knowledge combined with his depth of biblical understanding combined to produce a potent mixture of Christ-centered theology and original thinking. His students didn't always agree with his conclusions, but it was virtually impossible for them to sit under Chambers' teaching and think only, "That was nice."

---

1. The Bible Training College (BTC) was a residential school near Clapham Common in southwest London. It was sponsored by the League of Prayer and operated from 1911 until it closed in July 1915 because of World War I. Oswald Chambers was principal and main teacher; Biddy Chambers, his wife, was lady superintendent.

2. The *Bible Training Course Journal* was published from 1932 to 1952 by Mrs. Chambers, with help from David Lambert.

CONTENTS

FOREWORD

I see sometimes in London the preparations being made for the sure foundations of one of the great modern buildings to be erected there. Far below the surface-level men and machines toil patiently on work which soon will be hidden, but which alone will make the towering building secure. These Talks on Moral Foundations take us to that depth below the surface of our everyday life where the foundations are laid for enduring sainthood. They deal profoundly with such matters as Habit, Thinking, the Will, Behaviour. The subject of Christian ethical obligation is of paramount importance in the thought life of to-day. The very basis of our religion, our moral and spiritual standing, is being challenged. Here will be found a valiant answer to the secular, sceptical and lawless questionings of our time.

The writer was one of God's saints; and also one of those sane Christian thinkers who see into the deep places of our strange, perplexing yet alluring human life. Already the chapters have proved their worth as articles in the *B.T.C. Journal*. Now in this compact form they will serve for hours of instruction in righteousness as they illumine these dim regions of the soul in the blazing light of Holy Scripture.

D. L.[3]

---

3. D. L. is David Lambert (1871–1961), a Methodist minister and friend of Oswald and Biddy Chambers. He assisted Mrs. Chambers with OC publications from 1917 until his death in 1961.

THE WILL IN DISCIPLESHIP
Luke 9:61–62

Beware of thinking of will as a faculty. Will simply means the whole nature active. We talk about people having a weak will or a strong will, it is a misleading idea. When we speak of a man having a weak will, we mean he is without any impelling passion, he is the creature of every dominating influence; with good people he is good, with bad people he is bad, not because he is a hypocrite, but because he has no ruling passion, and any strong personality knits him into shape. Will is the essential element in God's creation of a man. I cannot *give up* my will: I must exercise it.

The Want To
Lord, I will follow Thee . . .

Want is a conscious tendency towards a particular end. My wants take shape when something awakens my personal life. An invalid if left alone has no wants, he wants neither to live nor to die; but when he sees a person full of bounding physical health, a want to be like him is instantly awakened. Whatever awakens my person awakens a want. In this incident the presence of Jesus awakened a conscious want to follow Him, a want to be like Him.

(a) The Want in Conscience
The first appeal was to conscience, and could be expressed in this way: "Follow Him, He is Thy supreme Lord." The presentation of Jesus Christ always awakens that desire, the presentation of abstract ideals never does. You can present morality, good principles, the duty of loving your neighbour, and never arouse a man's conscience to want anything; but when you present Jesus Christ, instantly there is a dumb awakening; a want to be what He would like me to be. It is not conviction of sin, but an awakening out of the sleep of indifference into a want.

There are some things that are without meaning for us. For instance, to be told that God will give us the Holy Spirit if we ask Him, may be a dead proposition; but when we come in contact with a person filled with the Spirit of God we instantly awaken to a want. Or again, if you tell half a dozen clean-living, upright, sterling men that God so loved them that He gave His Son to die for them, only their good breeding will keep them from being amused—"Why should Jesus Christ die for me"? It is not a living proposition to them, not in the sphere of their life at all. Their morality is well within their own grasp, they are clean living and upright, all that can be desired; they will never be awakened in that way; but present them with Jesus Christ, or with a life that is like His life, and instantly there will awaken in them a want they were not conscious of before. That is why Jesus said, "If I had not come . . . , they had not had sin: but now they have no cloke for their sin." You can never argue anyone into the Kingdom of heaven, you cannot argue anyone any where. The only result of arguing is to prove to your own mind that you are right and the other fellow wrong. You cannot argue for truth; but immediately Incarnate Truth is presented, a want awakens in the soul which only God can meet. Conscience is that faculty of the spirit which fits itself on to the highest a man knows; and when the light of Jesus Christ is thrown on what is regarded as the highest, conscience records exactly and the reason is startled and amazed (cf. Acts 26:9).

(b) The Want in Heart
The presence of Jesus awakened a want in this man's heart. Heart is the centre of all the vital activities of body, soul and spirit. Never think of the heart in the way the old psychology thought of the will, viz., as a compartment, a kind of hat-box into which you put all your convictions and dole them out occasionally when you lift the lid. The heart is the centre of a man's personality. "For out of the heart proceed . . . ," said our Lord. You can never tell from a man's life to date what he is going to want next, because the real element of want is not logical. A man's reasoning is based on something more than reason, there is always an incalculable element.

(c) The Want in Desire
The want in conscience and in heart urges a man to immediate action: "Lord, I will follow Thee." It was the finest, profoundest element in the man that made him say it. In his conscience, in the deep depths of his personality, there was awakened the desire to follow Jesus and to be like Him. The measure of a man's want is seen in the nature of the power that awakened it. No man can stand in front of Jesus Christ and say, "I want to make money." He can stand before a successful commercial man and find the desire awakened in him to be like him and make money. This man was in contact with the Prince of persons, the Lord Jesus Christ, consequently the deep desire of his heart was for the very highest, "Lord, I want to follow Thee; and I not only want to, but I will."

The Wish To

A wish is often of an abstract character, directed towards some single element into a concrete event, without reference to accompanying circumstances.

MacKenzie[4]

When I see Jesus Christ I simply want to be what He wants me to be. A wish is more definite than a want, which is inarticulate, something I am conscious of and that is all. Contact with a personality will always harden our wishing into a clear initiative along certain lines. For example, when a boy sees a soldier he wishes to be a soldier; when he sees an engineer he wishes to be an engineer, and so on. We have to select the domain of our wishes. At a time of religious awakening when Jesus Christ is in the ascendant and I come into close contact with Him, I wish to be a Christian. I have never known conviction of sin, never seen the need for the removal of the wrong disposition and identification with Jesus, but I wish to be like Him. The "wish to" simply sees the end of the desire and takes no account of the means to that end.

(a) Re-sensitised Sympathy

Our wishes move in various domains. We cannot hold ourselves in a handful for we are never sure what is going to happen in the domain of our wishes. We may have all our wishes in a certain domain and be perfectly master of them, with everything clear and simple; then a bereavement comes, and instantly the domain of our wishing is completely altered, we are suddenly put into sensitive sympathy with things we never thought about before. When Jesus Christ is in the ascendant the wish moves in the domain in which He lives, the sensitiveness of our wishing answers to Him in a general softening of our whole nature. We are not conscious of wishing to possess any particular virtue, of wishing to be this or that; we simply wish to be in perfect sympathy with Him and His purposes. The only point of rest is for a man to have his sympathies sensitised by Jesus Christ, because the basis of our nature is always open to let us into some unsuspected "hell" until we have been dominated by Our Lord. When Our Lord speaks of discipleship He catalogues the other loves (see Luke 14:26), and says that our love to Him must be the dominant love of all, because any of those other loves may be a trap-door to something entirely removed from God's purposes.

(b) Reflection of Sublimity

Abstract principles have no more power to lift a man than a man has to lift himself; but any man, no matter how sunk in sin, will answer to Jesus Christ when He is presented. To tell a man who is down and out to get up and do the right thing can never help him; but when once Jesus Christ is presented to him there is a reflected wish to be what Jesus wants him to be. It is appalling how many books and sermons there are to-day that simply present abstract truths. Jesus Christ appeals to the highest and the lowest, to the rich young ruler type of man, and to the man whom no ethics or moral principles can touch. Always keep Jesus Christ in the front; He says Himself He is to be there. "I, if I be lifted up from the earth, will draw all men unto Me."

(c) Recession of Second Thought
Lord, I will follow Thee; but . . .

The wish ought to be followed by immediate obedience. I must take the wish and translate it into resolution and then into action; if I don't, the wish will translate itself into a corrupting power in my life instead of a redeeming power. This principle holds good in the matter of emotions. A sentimentalist is one who delights to have high and devout emotions stirred whilst reading in an arm-chair, or in a prayer meeting, but he never translates his emotions into action. Consequently a sentimentalist is usually callous, self-centred and selfish, because the emotions he likes to have stirred do not cost him anything, and when he comes across the same things in the domain where things are real and not sentimental, the revenge comes along the line of selfishness and meanness, which is always the aftermath of an unfulfilled emotion. The higher the emotion, the purer the desire, the viler is the revenge in the moral character unless the emotion is worked out on its right level. It is better never to have seen the light, better never to wish to be what you are not than to have the desire awakened and never to have resolved it into action. Always do something along the line of the emotion that has been stirred; if you do not, it will corrupt that which was good before. The curbing of the outward action revenges itself in a meaner[5] disposition on the inside, and the higher the religious emotion, the more appalling is the reaction unless it is worked out on its own level. There are those whose language and habits are coarse, yet they are not vile in their inner disposition, and suddenly they manifest graces and beauties of character that amaze you. They answer to the call given by Jesus Christ, while others of the Pharisee type do not answer (cf. Matthew 21:28–32). Jesus Christ said it was impossible for the man who is self-centred in his particular impression of himself to believe in Him (John 5:44).

---

4. John Stuart MacKenzie (1860–1935) was a British philosopher; he was the author of *Outlines of Metaphysics* (1902), the likely source of this quote.

5. The word mean as used here refers to something or someone ordinary, common, low, or ignoble, rather than cruel or spiteful.

The Will To

. . . And Jesus said unto him, no man, having put his hand to the plough, and looking back, is fit for the kingdom of God.

The will to, means I must act; it is not sufficient to want to, to wish to, I must act on the wish instantly, no matter what it costs. Whenever the conviction of God's Spirit comes there is the softening of the whole nature to obey; but if the obedience is not instant there will come a metallic hardening and a corrupting of the guidance of God.

(a) The Inspired Instinct

Whenever you stand in the presence of Jesus Christ, as He is portrayed in the Scriptures and made real to you by the Holy Spirit, the instincts of your heart will always be inspired: *let them lead*. We read that when Jesus preached His first public sermon, all the people "wondered at the gracious words which proceeded out of His mouth"; their hearts were inspired as they listened to Him, their instincts turned in the right direction; then their prejudices came in the way and they closed down the witness of their hearts, broke up the service and tried to fling Him over the brow of the hill (Luke 4:16–30). Always let the instinct that rules you in the presence of Jesus lead. That is why it is so necessary in an evangelistic meeting to push people to an issue of will. It is a terrible thing to awaken people up to a certain point and never give them the chance to act in the same atmosphere. If I preach a particularly searching discourse and never give the people a chance to act according to their inspired instincts at the time, their blood is on my head before God. If I make the issue clear and give them the opportunity to act, I clear my soul from their blood, whether they answer or not. The devil's counterfeit for this is wanting to see how many people we can get out to the penitent form. As preachers and teachers we have to bring people to the point of doing something.

(b) The Inverting Impulse

"No man, having put his hand to the plough, and looking back . . ." Never postpone a moral decision. Second thoughts in moral matters are always deflections. Give as many second thoughts as you like to matters of pru-dence, but in the presence of God never think twice—*act*. Our Lord puts it very clearly in Matthew 5:23–24, when you are at the altar, i.e., in the presence of God, and your heart answers to the conviction of the Spirit of God, you know exactly what you must do: First go. There is no mid way. If you say "I don't mind going half-way, but I was not altogether in the wrong," God's touch is gone instantly. The slightest revision of what I know God is telling me to do is the first element in the damnation of my character in that particular (see John 3:19). Immediately I see what God wants me to do when I am in His presence, I must do it and care nothing for the consequences. "Lord, suffer me first to go and bury my father." The reply of Jesus sounds harsh, but remember the man's meaning was that he must stay with his father till he died. It was a point of view that put Jesus Christ right out of court. So with the rich young ruler, the wish to be all that Jesus wanted him to be awoke as soon as he came in contact with Him, but when it came to the first step of the will in acting it out, to become a mere conscious man, sep-arated from all his wealth, dead fundamentally to the whole thing, then his countenance fell and he went away sorrowful. It is better never to have had the light than to refuse to obey it.

(c) The Intrinsic Incapacity

". . . is fit for the kingdom of God." "Not fit" does not mean, not good enough, it means out of the machine. We can never earn our place in the Kingdom of God by doing anything. Immediately we obey the instinct born in us of God's Spirit we are fitted into the Kingdom of God. Always act according to the wish that is born in you by the Spirit of God. Take the initiative to obey, never wobble spiritually. "Wobble" means that we bring in other considerations that ought never to bemean[6] the presence of God, because those considerations mean that Jesus has not thought things out properly; He has forgotten I have a duty to my father and mother; that I have this thing the matter with my body; He has forgotten my circumstances. All these things are unconscious blasphemy against the Wisdom of God. We must always get to the point of acting on the want and the wish born in us when we are in the presence of Jesus Christ.

---

6. bemean: debase; lower.

DIRECTION OF THE WILL
John 7:17

(CF. JOHN 5:19, 30)

The Will to Do
If any man willeth to do His will . . . (RV)

In John 7:17, our Lord is not so much laying down the principle that obedience is the gateway to knowledge, as specifically stating that the only way to know whether or not His teaching is of God is conditioned by obedience. The only way to *know* is to *will* to do His will.

(a) Think
The only way to progress in spiritual matters is to think voluntarily. A great amount of stuff we call thinking is not thinking, but merely reverie or meditation. Thinking is a voluntary effort, and in the initial stages it is never easy; voluntary effort must be made to keep the mind on some particular line. The teaching of some of the Higher Christian Life movements[7] is apt to put thinking out of it altogether. According to that teaching we have to be semi-swooning invalids in the power of God, letting the Spirit of God take us as so much driftwood, and all our impulses and dreams are taken to be the will of God. When we become spiritual we have to exercise the power of thinking to a greater degree than ever before. We starve our mind as Christians by not thinking. If we are going to succeed in the natural world we must think voluntarily about things, and it is the same in the spiritual world. In order to think we must stop wool-gathering, check our impulses and set the mind on one line.

(b) Think Habitually
Habit is a mechanical process of which we have ceased to become conscious. The basis of habit is always physical. A habit forms a pathway in the material stuff of the brain, and as we persist in thinking along a certain line we hand over a tremendous amount to the machine and do things without thinking. Habit becomes second nature. "Habit a second nature! Habit is ten times nature!" *(Duke of Wellington).* For instance, when you begin to use a muscle in a particular way, it hurts badly, but if you keep on using that muscle judiciously it will get beyond hurting until you are able to use it with mechanical precision. The same thing is true in regard to thinking. It is a difficult matter to begin with. If thinking gives you a headache, it is a sign that you have brains. The brain is not ethereal or mystical, it is purely a machine. The thing that is not mechanical is the power of personality which we call thought. At first we find our brains do not work well, they go in jerks, we are bothered with associated ideas; but as we persist in thinking along a particular line our brain becomes the ally of our personality. Not only is our body capable of becoming our best friend, but the places where the body has become used to thinking become a strong assistance also. We infect the places we live in by our ruling habit. If we have made our body the ally of our personality, everything works together to aid our body wherever it is placed. People complain about their circumstances because they have not begun to make their body an ally.

(c) Think Habitually to Do
Our Lord says, in effect, that if any man will habitually think, he will come to know where His teaching comes from. The only way to prove spiritual truth is by experiment. Are we willing to set our mind determinedly to work out habitually what we think is God's will? We talk about justice and right and wrong, are we prepared to act according to what we think? Are we prepared to act according to the justice and the right which we believe to be the character of God? If we are, we shall have no difficulty in deciding whether or not the teaching of Jesus Christ comes from God.

The first moment of thinking alters our life. If for one moment we have discerned the truth, we can never be the same again; we may ignore it, or forget it, but it will not forget us. Truth once discerned goes down into the subconscious mind, but it will jump up in a most awkward way when we least expect it. In the matter of intercession, when we pray for another the Spirit of God works in the unconscious domain of that one's being about which we know nothing, and about which the one we pray for knows nothing, and after a while the conscious life of the one prayed for begins to show signs of softening and unrest, of enquiry and a desire to know something. It seems stupid to think that if we pray all that will happen, but remember to Whom we pray; we pray to a Being

---

7. Higher Christian Life movements refers to various groups and organizations that emphasized sanctification and personal holiness.

Who understands the unconscious depths of a man's personality, and He has told us to pray. The great Master of the human spirit said "Greater works than these shall he do. . . . And whatsoever ye shall ask in My name, that will I do." This is true also in preaching the word. We may see no result in our congregation, but if we have presented the truth and anyone has seen it for one second, he can never be the same again, a new element has come into his life. It is essential to remember this and not to estimate the success of preaching by immediate results.

Our Lord was always stern with disbelief, i.e., scepticism, because there is always a moral twist about scepticism. Never place an agnostic in the same category as a sceptic. An agnostic is one who says, "There is more than I know, but I have not found anyone who can tell me about it." Jesus is never stern with that attitude; but He is stern with the man who objects to a certain way of getting at the truth because he does not like that way. If a man refuses to try the way Jesus Christ puts before him, he ceases from that second to be an honest doubter; he must try it and put Jesus Christ's teaching to the proof. A man cannot say he is an honest intellectual doubter if he refuses one way of getting at the truth; that is mental immorality.

The Way to Know
he shall know of the teaching . . . (RV)

If I find it hard to be a Christian it is a sign that I need the awakening of new birth. Only a spiritually ignorant person tries to be a Christian. Study the life of Jesus Christ and see what Christianity means, and you will find you cannot be a Christian by trying; you must be born into the life before you can live it. There are a great many people trying to be Christians; they pray and long and fast and consecrate, but it is nothing but imitation, it has no life in it. Immediately we have life imparted to us by the Holy Spirit, we realise that it is the very life that was in Jesus that is born into us; we are loosened from the old bondage and find that we can fulfil all the expectations of the life which has been imparted to us. It is a strenuous life of obedience to God, and God has given us bodies through which to work out the life, and circumstances to react against in order to prove its reality.

(a) Intention
Beware of praying about an intention—*act*. To pray about what we know we should do is to piously push the whole thing overboard and think no more about it. Every intention must be acted out *now*, not presently, otherwise it will be stamped out. When the intention of an honest soul is grasped by the Spirit of God he will know whether the teaching Jesus gives is of God or not. Am I going to *think*, and *think habit-*

ually, and *act on what I think*, so that the will of God may be performed in me until I know Who Jesus is, and that His teaching is the teaching of God? To know that the teaching of Jesus is of God means that it must be obeyed. It may be difficult to begin with, but the difficulty will become a joy.

(b) Intention and Insight
Intentions are born of listening to others. Whenever we obey an intention, insight into either good or bad is sure to follow. If our intention is in agreement with God and we act on it, we get insight into Who God is. The discernment of right and wrong intentions depends on how we think. There is a spasmodic type of life which comes from never really thinking about things, it is at the mercy of every stray intention. Someone makes an appeal for the Hindoo or the Chinese, and they say, "Oh yes, I will go and preach the gospel there," and they do it in intention. Then someone else says the best thing is to work in the slums, instantly their intention is to work there. Then another person says the best thing is to study in a Bible school, and they do that in intention. They are creatures of impulse, there is no real thinking along God's line, no acting on their intention. If you are sufficiently strong-minded you can generate any number of intentions in people and make them think anything you like; if they are not in the habit of thinking for themselves you can always sway them. The power of an evangelist over men and women who do not think is a dangerous thing. That is why it is so perilous to tell people to yield. *Don't* yield! Keep as stiff a neck as ever you had, and yield to nothing and to no one, unless you know it is the Lord Jesus Christ to Whom you are yielding. Once you go on the yielding line, on the surrendering line and you do not know that it is the Lord Jesus Who is calling for the yielding, you will be caught up by super natural powers that will wield you whether you like it or not. Woe be to you, if, when Jesus has asked us to yield to Him, you refuse; but be sure it is Jesus Christ to Whom you yield, and His demands are tremendous.

The insight that relates us to God arises from purity of heart, not from clearness of intellect. All the education under heaven will never give a man insight into Jesus Christ's teaching, only one thing will, and that is a pure heart, i.e., intentions that go along the right line. Education and scholarship may enable a man to put things well, but they will never give him insight. Insight only comes from a pure-heartedness in working out the will of God. That is why the subject of Divine guidance is so mysterious. "Be ye transformed by *the renewing of your mind*," says Paul, (that is what makes the thinker right), "that ye may prove what is that good, and acceptable, and perfect will of God." You cannot teach another what is the will of God. A knowledge of the will of God comes only by insight into God through acting on the right intention.

(c) Intention and Insight into Instruction

Studying our Lord's teaching will not profit us unless we intend to obey what we know is the immediate present duty. As we listen to certain interpretations of Jesus Christ's statements we do not feel warm to them, though we do not know what is wrong. Whenever the Spirit of God works in our conscious life it is like an intuition—I don't know how I know, but I know. The Holy Spirit witnesses only to His own nature, not to our reason. Jesus said "My sheep hear My voice," not because it is argued to them, but because they have His Spirit. There are statements of Jesus which mean nothing to us just now because we have not been brought into the place where we need to understand them. When we are brought there, the Holy Spirit will bring back a particular word, and as we intend to obey He gives us the insight into it. The Spirit of God never allows us to face spiritual subjects by spiritual curiosity first. We cannot say, "I am going to study the subject of Sanctification or of the Second Coming," we shall make about as much headway as a steamer in a fog. Insight into the instruction of Jesus depends upon our intention to obey what we know to be the will of God. If we have some doctrine or some end of our own to serve, we shall always find difficulty.

The Weighing of Doctrine

. . . whether it be of God, or whether I speak from Myself. (RV)

(a) Discernment

The reason the Incarnation and the Atonement are not credible to some people is that their disposition is unregenerated. A man may adopt the dogma of the Incarnation and the Atonement upon a basis of authority while his heart is unchanged, with the result that sooner or later the accumulated pride of unregenerate years will rise in revolt and secretly protest that it is incredible. That was the case with the men to whom Jesus is speaking here, and it is the case of hundreds who accept creeds but refuse to act on their belief; the consequence is they fling their creeds overboard and ignore the central test of Christianity, viz., Who is Jesus Christ to me?

The Atonement of our Lord never contradicts human reason, it contradicts the logic of human intellect that has never partaken of regeneration. The understanding of the Atonement depends not on Bible study, not on praying, but on spiritual growth. As we "grow up into Him in all things" we get moral understanding of the mystery of Redemption and understand why Jesus said "Blessed are the pure in heart: for they shall see God." The Spirit of God

brings a man to the place where he begins to discern with his heart, not with his head.

Jesus says we shall know, i.e., discern, whether His teaching is of God or not when we do what we know to be His will. We discern according to our disposition. There are moments in life when the little thing matters more than anything else, times when a critical situation depends upon our attitude of mind to another person. If a man is hesitating between obeying and not obeying God, the tiniest thing contrary to obedience is quite sufficient to swing the pendulum right away from the discernment of Jesus Christ and of God. "If thou bring thy gift to the altar, and there rememberest that thy brother hath ought against thee *. . . first be reconciled. . . .*" Distempers of mind make all the difference in the discernment of Jesus Christ's teaching. Have I a distempered view about any man or woman on earth? If I have, there is a great deal of Jesus Christ's teaching I do not want to listen to, then I shall never discern His teaching. Once let me obey God and I shall discern that I have no right to an attitude of mind to anyone other than His attitude. If I am determined to know the teaching of Jesus Christ at all costs, I must act on the intention that is stirred in me to do God's will, however humiliating it may be; and if I do, I shall discern.

(b) Discernment of Inspiration

Our Lord's teaching is God-breathed. What makes the difference between the attitude of a spiritual Christian to the teaching of Jesus and that of an unspiritual person? An unspiritual person takes the statements of Jesus to pieces as he would a man's statements, he "annulleth Jesus" (1 John 4:3 RV mg), dissolves Him by analysis; a spiritual Christian confesses "that Jesus Christ is come in the flesh." The basis of membership in the early Church was discernment of Who Jesus is by the revelation of God (see Matthew 16:17–18). All through the test is, Do I know Who Jesus Christ is; do I know that His teaching is of God?

The mystery of the Bible is that its inspiration was direct from God (2 Peter 1:21). To believe our Lord's consciousness about Himself commits me to accept Him as God's last endless Word. That does not mean that God is not still speaking, but it does mean that God is saying nothing different from the Final Word, Jesus Christ; all God says expounds that Word.

(c) Discernment of Inspiration of Christ's Teaching

Is Jesus Christ's teaching God-breathed to me? There is an intention that seeks God's blessings without obeying Jesus Christ's teaching. We are apt to say with sanctimonious piety, "Yes, Jesus Christ's teaching is of God"; but *how do we measure up to it?* Do we intend to think about it and act on it? Beware of tampering with the springs of your life when it comes to the teaching of Jesus.

Purity of heart, not subtlety of intellect, is the place of understanding. The Spirit of God alone understands the things of God, let Him indwell, and slowly and surely the great revelation facts of the Atonement begin to be comprehended. The Mind of God as revealed in the Incarnation becomes slowly and surely the mind of the spiritual Christian.

FREEDOM OF THE WILL
Psalm 27:4–6

The subject of human free will is apt to be either understated or overstated. No man has the power to act an act of pure, unadulterated, free will. God is the only Being Who can act with absolute free will. The Bible reveals that man is free to choose, but it nowhere teaches that man is fundamentally free. The freedom man has is not that of power but of choice, consequently he is accountable for choosing the course he takes. For instance, we can choose whether or not we will accept the proposition of salvation which God puts before us; whether or not we will let God rule our lives; but we have not the power to do exactly what we like. This is easily demonstrated when we think of the number of vows that are made every New Year and so quickly broken.

Man is free to choose in so far as no human force can constrain him against his will. Pope[8] is often misquoted; he did not say, "*Convince* a man against his will, he is of the same opinion still," but "*compel* a man against his will, he is of the same opinion still." God has so constituted man that it is not possible to convince him against his will; you can compel him and crush him, but you cannot convince him against his will. Only God could exercise constraint over a man which would compel him to do what in the moment of doing it is not his own will; but that God steadily refuses to do. The reason man is not free is that within his personality there is a disposition which has been allowed to enslave his will, the disposition of sin. Man's destiny is determined by his disposition; he cannot alter his disposition, but he can choose to let God alter it. Jesus said, "Whosoever committeth sin is the servant of sin"; but He also said, "If the Son therefore shall make you free, ye shall be free indeed," i.e. free in essence. We are only free when the Son sets us free; but we are free to choose whether or not we will be made free. In the experience of regeneration a man takes the step of choosing to let God alter his disposition. When the Holy Spirit comes into a man, He brings His own generating will power and makes a man free in will. Will simply means the whole nature active, and when the Holy Spirit comes in and energises a man's will, he is able to do what he never could do before, viz., he is able to do God's will (Philippians 2:13).

The Universe of the Will
Thus not only our morality but our religion, so far as the latter is deliberate, depend on the effort which we can make.
James[9]

Some propositions are alive to us and we want to work at them; other propositions are dead, they do not appeal to us at all. We have to be brought out of one universe of the will into another universe where propositions which were dead become alive. You can never tell when a proposition which up to a certain stage has been dead may suddenly become of living interest.

(a) The Live Quest of the Will
One thing have I desired of the LORD; . . . that I may dwell in the house of the LORD all the days of my life . . .

The depths of personality are hidden from our sight; we do not know anything beyond the threshold of consciousness, God is the only One Who knows. When we try to go beyond our conscious life into the depths of our personality, we do not know where we are, our only refuge is the 139th Psalm—"Search me, O God, and know my heart." Whatever rouses your will is an indication of the bias of your personality. The Bible reveals that in a man's personality there is a bias that makes him choose not the proposition of godliness, but the proposition of ungodliness. This bias is not a matter of man's deliberate choice, it is in his personality when he is born. "Wherefore, as by one man sin entered into the world . . ." (Romans 5:12). The proposition that appeals to a healthy onceborn man is that of self-realisation—"I want to

---

8. Alexander Pope (1688–1744) was an English poet.
9. William James (1842–1910) was an American philosopher, psychologist, and teacher.

develop myself." If you bring before him the proposition that he should be saved and give up his right to himself to Jesus Christ, it will be a dead proposition, without meaning for him; but let conviction of sin, or disaster, or bereavement, or any of the great surprises of God touch him, and instantly the proposition takes on a totally new aspect and he will want to act on it. Jesus Christ always puts the emphasis on the effort of obedience, there must be a live quest of the will. "If you want to know My doctrine, whether it is of God or of Myself, *do My will*," says Jesus (see John 7:17). The truth of God is only revealed to us by obedience.

(b) The Lure of the Voluntary Quest
to behold the beauty of the LORD . . .

When once the will is roused it always has a definite end in view, an end in the nature of unity. Always distinguish between will and impulse. An impulse has no end in view and must be curbed, not obeyed. Will is the whole effort of a man consciously awake with the definite end of unity in view, which means that body, soul and spirit are in absolute harmony. This end of satisfaction offers a great fascination. The characteristic of a moral hell is satisfaction, no end in view, perfectly satisfied. Moral sickness is a perilous time, it is the condition to which sin brings us, and it accounts for the unutterable disappointments in life, there is no lure, no aim, no quest, no end in view. The characteristic of the spiritual life is the delight of discerning more and more clearly the end God has in view for us. Jesus did not say that eternal life was satisfaction, but something infinitely grander: "This is life eternal, that they might know Thee." The demand for satisfaction is God-given (cf. Matthew 5:6), but it must be satisfaction in the highest.

(c) The Liberty to Question
. . . and to enquire in His temple.

When once a man has been awakened from sin to salvation, the only propositions that are alive to his will are the propositions of God. There is an insatiable inquiry after God's commands, and to every command there is a desire to act in obedience. Recall your own experience and see how true that is. The things that used to be ends in view have not only ceased to be ends, they have ceased to have any interest for you at all; they have become tasteless. This is the way God enables us to be fundamentally dead to the things of the world while we live amongst them. Jesus Christ's outward life was densely immersed in the things of the world, yet He was inwardly disconnected; the one

irresistible purpose of His life was to do the will of His Father.

If I am in right relationship to God there comes this delightful liberty of enquiring in His temple. It is not to be a Sabbath day spent in a temple, but the whole of the life, every domain of body, soul and spirit, is to be lived there. The dead set of the will is towards one end only, viz., to do the will of God. Jesus said, "My sheep hear My voice." When Jesus has not spoken there is an unutterable dullness all through, our spirit does not witness to what is being said. When once that fine balance of discernment is tampered with we give an opportunity to Satan; but if it is kept in perfect accord with God's word, He will guard. Jesus said that the Holy Spirit would bring His word to our remembrance (John 14:26). The Holy Spirit does not bring text after text until we are utterly confused; He simply brings back with the greatest of ease the words which we need in the particular circumstances we are in. Then comes in the use of the will, will I obey the word which has been brought back to our remembrance? The battle comes when we begin to debate instead of obeying. We have to obey and leave all consequences with God.

The Utmost Uses of the Will
Character exists only in so far as unity and continuity of conscious life exists, and manifests itself in systematic consistency of conduct.

Stout[10]

Will is the very essence of personality, and in the Bible will is always associated with intelligence and knowledge and desire. The will of a saint is not to be spent in dissipation in spiritual luxuries, but in concentration upon God.

(a) The Quietness of Strength
For in the time of trouble He shall hide me in His pavilion . . .

God gives us the energy of an impregnable position, the heavenly places in Christ Jesus, and we have to make the effort to be strong from that position. We have not to work up to that position, but to work *from* it with the full energy of will. It is impossible to live according to our Lord's teaching without this secret of position. We do not get to the heavenly places by struggling, or aspiring, or consecration; God lifts us there, and if we will work from that position, He keeps us in His pavilion. No wonder the life of a saint appears such an unmitigated puzzle to rational human beings without the Spirit of God. It seems so ridiculous and so conceited to say that God Almighty is our

---

10. George Frederick Stout (1860–1944), an English philosopher and psychologist, was professor of logic and metaphysics, St. Andrews University, 1903–1936.

Father and that He is looking after our affairs; but looked at from the position in which Jesus places us we find it is a marvellous revelation of truth.

(b) The Quarters of Security
He shall set me up upon a rock . . .

In our spiritual life God does not provide pinnacles on which we stand like spiritual acrobats; He provides tablelands of easy and delightful security. Recall the conception you had of holiness before you stood by the grace of God where you do to-day, it was the conception of a breathless standing on a pinnacle for a second at a time, but never with the thought of being able to live there; but when the Holy Spirit brought you there, you found it was not a pinnacle, but a plateau, a broad way, where the provision of strength and peace comes all the time, a much easier place to live than lower down.

The security of the position into which God brings His saints is such that the life is maintained without ecstasy. There is no place for ecstasy and manifestations in a normal healthy spiritual life. The emotions that are beyond the control of the will are a sign that there is something not in the secure position, something undisciplined, untrained. When we are in the quarters of security we have to will our observation of the things of God, and of the way in which He works. There are things we are obliged to observe, such as fireworks; but God uses for the training of His children the things which we have to will to observe, viz., trees and grass and sparrows.

Never allow the idea of conscious straining effort when you think of the exercise of the will spiritually. The straining effort comes in when we forget the great lines laid down by God. If you are a worker for God, Satan will try to wear you out to the last cell; but if you know God's grace you will be supernaturally recuperated physically. Recall how often you have been surprised, you thought you would have been exhausted after certain services, and instead, you became recreated whilst taking them. In this place of security there is no such thing as weariness without a corresponding recuperation if we maintain a right relationship with God.

(c) The Quality of Supremacy
. . . And now shall mine head be lifted up above mine enemies round about me.

The supremacy over our old enemies is accounted for by the fact that God makes them our subjects. What things used to be your enemies? Stodginess of head, laziness of body or spirit, the whole vocabulary of "I can'ts." When you live in the right place these things are made your subjects; the things that used to hinder your life with God become subject to you by His power. The very things that used to upset you now minister to you in an extraordinary way by reason of the spiritual supremacy God gives you over them. The life of a saint reveals a quietness at the heart of things, there is something firm and dependable, because the Lord is the strength of the life.

HABIT

In the conduct of life, habits count for more than maxims, because habit is a living maxim, become flesh and instinct. To reform one's maxims is nothing; it is but to change the title of the book. To learn new habits is everything for it is to reach the substance of life. Life is but a tissue of habits.

Amiel[11]

Man's Soul the Scene of Habit
Plasticity, then, in the wide sense of the word, means the possession of a structure weak enough to yield to influences, but strong enough not to yield all at once.

James

Beware of dividing man up into body, soul and spirit: man *is* body, soul and spirit. Soul has no entity, it depends entirely upon the body, and yet there is a subtle spiritual element in it. Soul is the rational expression of my personal spirit in my body, the way I reason and think and work. Habits are formed in the soul, not in the spirit, and they are formed in the soul by means of the body. Jesus Christ told His disciples that they must lose their soul, i.e., their way of reasoning and looking at things, and begin to estimate from an entirely different standpoint. For a while a born-again soul is inarticulate, it has no expression; the equilibrium has been upset by the incoming of a totally new spirit into the

---

11. Henri Frederic Amiel (1821–1881) was a Swiss professor and writer, known for his self-analytical *Journal*, published in 1883.

human spirit, and the reasoning faculties are disturbed. "In your patience possess ye your souls," says Jesus; that is, the new way of looking at things must be acquired with patience. On the basis of His Redemption Jesus Christ claims that He can put into my personal spirit His own heredity, Holy Spirit; then I have to form character on the basis of that new disposition. God will do everything I cannot do, but He will do nothing He has constructed me to do.

"Our virtues are habits as well as our vices." God does not give us our habits, but He holds us responsible, in proportion, for the habits we form. For instance, God does not hold a child born in the slums responsible in the same degree for its habits as He does a child born in a Christian home. The fact remains, however, that we form our own habits. God gives us a new disposition, but He gives us nothing in the shape of character. We have to work out what God works in, and the way we work it out is by the mechanical process of habit.

(a) The Mental Phase (Philippians 4:8–9; 2 Corinthians 10:5)

By the mental phase is meant, thinking that can be stated in words. There is a great deal of thinking that cannot be expressed in words, such as that which is stirred by susceptibility to the beauties of Nature, or art or music; that is spirit not yet made rational in soul. We are responsible for our habits of thinking, and Paul in these passages is dealing with the phase of mental life in which a man can choose his thinking and is able to express it in words. The old idea that we cannot help evil thoughts has become so ingrained in our minds that most of us accept it as a fact. But if it is true, then Paul is talking nonsense when he tells us to choose our thinking, to think only on those things that are true, and honourable, and just, and pure.

> We may take as an example of mental habit that of answering letters on the day on which they are received. Here what is habitual and automatic is not the process of writing the reply, but the writing of the reply on the same day on which the letter was received.
>
> Stout

The point is that we make a mental decision to do a certain thing, and the habit of doing it grows until it becomes absolutely mechanical. Remember, then, we can and we must choose our thinking, and the whole discipline of our mental life is to form the habit of right thinking. It is not done by praying, it is done only by strenuous determination, and it is never easy to begin with.

(b) The Moral Phase (Romans 6:11–19; 2 Peter 1:5–8)

The Spirit of God through the Apostles bases on the mechanism that is alike in everyone of us, the mechanism of habit. Paul says, "present your members as servants to righteousness" (RV); Peter says, "adding on your part . . ." (RV). There is something we have to do. Man's soul is "weak enough to yield to influences, but strong enough not to yield all at once." The phrase "the freedom of the will" is a catch phrase that has more of error than of truth in it. We are all so made that we can yield to an influence that is brought to bear upon us, and if we keep ourselves long enough under right influences, slowly and surely we shall find that we can form habits that will develop us along the line of those influences.

> The peculiarity of the moral habits, contradistinguishing them from the intellectual acquisitions, is the presence of two hostile powers, one to be gradually raised into the ascendant over the other. It is necessary, above all things, in such a situation, never to lose a battle. Every gain on the wrong side undoes the effect of many con quests on the right.
>
> Bain[12]

The idea is that of winding up a ball of wool. Let the ball drop, and infinitely more is undone than was wound in the same time. This is true of moral and spiritual habits. If once you allow the victory of a wrong thing in you, it is a long way back again to get readjusted. We talk on the moral and spiritual line as if God were punishing us, but He is not, it is because of the way God has constructed man's nature that "the way of transgressors is hard."

When once we begin the life with God on the moral line we must keep strictly to it. In the beginning the Holy Spirit will check us in doing a great many things that may be perfectly right for everyone else, but not right for us in the stage we are in. We have to narrow ourselves to one line, and keep ourselves narrow until our soul has gained the moral habit. The maimed life is always the characteristic to begin with (see Matthew 5:29–30), but our Lord's statements embrace the whole of the spiritual life from beginning to end, and in Matthew 5:48 (RV) He says, "*Ye therefore shall be perfect*, as your heavenly Father is perfect."

Never go contrary to your conscience, no matter how absurd it may be in the eyes of others. Conscience is to be our law in conduct, but Paul says it is not his own conscience, but the conscience of his weak brother that is his guide (1 Corinthians 8:9–13).

The characteristic of a Christian is that he has the right not to insist on his rights. That will mean that I

---

12. Alexander Bain (1818–1903) was a Scottish psychologist, educator, and author.

refuse to do certain things because they would cause my brother to stumble. To me the restrictions may be absurd and narrow-minded, I can do the things without any harm; but Paul's argument is that he reserves the right to suffer the loss of all things rather than put an occasion to fall in his brother's way. The Holy Ghost gives us the power to forgo our rights. It is the application of the Sermon on the Mount in practical life; if we are Jesus Christ's disciples we shall always do more than our duty, always do something equivalent to going "the second mile."

These are some of the moral habits we ought to form.

(c) The Mystical Phase (John 15:4)

Our Lord did not say, "Ask God that you may abide in Me"; He said "Abide in Me," it is something we have to do. Abiding in Jesus embraces physical, mental and moral phases as well as spiritual. How am I going to acquire the spiritual habit of union with Christ in God's sight? First of all by putting my body into the condition where I can think about it. We are so extraordinarily fussy that we won't give ourselves one minute before God to think, and unless we do we shall never form the habit of abiding. We must get alone in secret and think, screw our minds down and not allow them to wool-gather. Difficult? Of course it is difficult to begin with, but if we persevere we shall soon take in all the straying parts of our mental life, and in a crisis we shall be able to draw on the fact that we are one with Jesus in God's sight.

> One must first learn, unmoved, looking neither to the right nor left, to walk firmly on the strait and narrow path, before one can begin "to make one's self over again." He who every day makes a fresh resolve is like one who, arriving at the edge of the ditch he is to leap, forever stops and returns for a fresh run. Without unbroken advance there is no such thing as accumulation of the ethical forces possible, and to make this possible, and to exercise us and habituate us in it, is the sovereign blessing of regular work.
>
> Bahnsen

In the mystical life the majority of us are hopeless wool gatherers, we have never learned to brood on such subjects as "abiding in Christ." We have to form the habit of abiding until we come into the relationship with God where we rely upon Him almost unconsciously in every particular.

Mechanical Scientific Side of Habit

Man is born with a tendency to do more things than he has ready-made arrangements for in his nerve-centres.

James

(a) The Physical Side (Job 14:19)

In physical nature there is something akin to habit. Flowing water hollows out for itself a channel which grows broader and deeper, and after having ceased to flow for a time, it will resume again the path traced before. It is never as easy to fold a piece of paper the first time as after, for after the first time it folds naturally. The process of habit runs all through physical nature, and our brain is physical. When once we understand the bodily machine with which we have to work out what God works in, we find that our body becomes the greatest ally of our spiritual life. The difference between a sentimental Christian and a sanctified saint is just here. The sanctified saint is one who has disciplined the body into perfect obedience to the dictates of the Spirit of God, consequently his body does with the greatest of ease whatever God wants him to do. The sentimental type of Christian is the sighing, tear-flowing, beginning-over-again Christian who always has to go to prayer meetings, always has to be stirred up, or to be soothed and put in bandages, because he has never formed the habit of obedience to the Spirit of God. Our spiritual life does not grow *in spite of* the body, but *because* of the body. "Of the earth, earthy," is man's glory, not his shame; and it is in the "earth, earthy" that the full regenerating work of Jesus Christ has its ultimate reach.

(b) The Physiological Side (Mark 9:21)

Every nervous affection makes a groove in the brain. Dr. Carpenter,[13] the great physiologist, suffered from habitual neuralgia all the days of his life, the only time he was free from it was when he was lecturing. He said himself it was simply because the nerves had got into the habit. What a medical man aims at in the case of nervous affections is to forcibly cut short the attacks so as to give the other physical forces possession of the field. Nervous trouble can be cured by sudden calamity, by something that stops the whole nervous system and starts it again in another way; and it can be cured suddenly by the power of God. In the case of the demoniac boy our Lord did not deal with him on the medical line but on the super natural line. There was no gradual, "take a little holiday," but a sudden and emphatic breaking off, simply because our Lord recognised the way God has made the nervous system. No power on earth can touch a nervous trouble if I have submitted to it for a long time, but God can touch it if I will let Him. I may pray for ever for it to be altered but it never will be until I am willing to obey. The arresting may be terrific, a tremendous break and upset, but if I will let God have His way He will deal with it.

---

13. William Benjamin Carpenter (1813–1885).

(c) The Psychical Side (Philippians 2:12–13)

"Man is born with a tendency to do more things than he has ready-made arrangements for in his nerve centres." For instance, we are not born with a ready-made habit of dressing ourselves, we have to form that habit. Apply that spiritually; when we are born again, God does not give us a fully fledged series of holy habits, we have to make those habits. It is the application of the theological statement that we have to transform innocence into holiness by a series of moral choices. Ask yourself how much time you have taken up asking God that you may not do the things you do. He will never answer, you have simply not to do them. Every time God speaks, there is something we must obey. We should do well to revise what we pray about. Some of the things we pray about are as absurd as if we prayed, "O Lord, take me out of this room," and then refused to go. We have to revise and see whether we intelligently understand what God has done for us; if He has given us the Holy Spirit, then we can do everything He asks us to do. If our body has been the slave of wrong habits physically, mentally and morally, we must get hold of a power big enough to re-make our habits and that power lies in the word "Regeneration." "If any man be in Christ, he is a new creature," that means this marvellous thing—that I may be loosened from every wrong habit I have formed if only I will obey the Spirit of God. Immediately I do obey, I find I can begin to form new habits in accordance with God's commands, and prove physically, mentally and morally that I am a new creation (RV mg). That is why it is so necessary to receive the Holy Spirit, then when God gives a command it is sufficient to know He has told me to do it and I find I can do it. Frequently God has to say to us—"Say no more to Me on this matter; don't everlastingly cry to Me about this thing, do it yourself, keep your forces together and go forward." God is for you, the Spirit of God is in you, and every place that the sole of your foot shall tread upon, shall be yours.

Beware of the luxury of spiritual emotions unless you are prepared to work them out. God does the unseen, but we have to do the seen.

DUST AND DIVINITY
Genesis 2:7

[N.B.—ALL DIVISIONS OF THE HUMAN PERSONALITY ARE ARBITRARY.]

Genesis 2:7 reveals that man is made up of dust and Divinity. This means that in practical psychology we must always make allowance for the incalculable. You cannot exhaust man's nature by examining his "dust" qualities, nor by describing him in terms of poetic sentiment, for after you have described as much as you can, there is always an incalculable element to be taken into account. There is more than we know, therefore we cannot deal with ourselves as machines. One part of ourselves must be dealt with as a machine, and the more we deal with it as a machine the better; but to try and sum up a man as a machine only is to miss out the bigger part; or to say that man is altogether a spiritual being without anything mechanical in him is to miss out the incalculable element that cannot be summed up. These two things, dust and Divinity, make up man. That he is made of the dust is man's glory, not his shame; it has been the scene of his shame, but it was designed to be his glory.

A certain type of mind gets impatient when one talks about the incalculable element in man, and says it is nonsense to talk of man being a spiritual personality, man is nothing more than an animal. That outlook is prevalent to-day, it is called "healthy-mindedness"; it is rather blatant ignorance. We all say what is obvious until we are plunged into the deeps; but when a man is profoundly moved he instantly finds himself beyond the reach of help or comfort from the obvious. The obvious becomes trivial, it is not what his heart wants. What he needs is something that can minister to the incalculable element. When once real thought begins to trouble the mind, the disturbance goes on throughout the whole personality until the right centre is gained for thought. In the spiritual domain when a man is convicted of sin, he realises that there are deeper depths in himself than he has ever known, and the things that can be clearly explained become utterly shallow, there is no guidance whatever in them. We begin by thinking we know all about ourselves, but when a man gets a dose of "the plague of his own heart," it upsets all his thinking. Immediately man begins to examine himself, he finds he is inscrutable; there are possibilities below the threshold of his life which no one knows but God.

The Explorer of the Will *(Philippians 2:11–13)*

Psalm 139 is the classic in all literature concerning a man's personality. In this Psalm the tendency in man which makes him want to examine himself takes the form of prayer, "O Lord, explore me." The Psalmist implies: "Thou art the God of the early mornings and late at nights, the God of the mountains and the fathomless deep; but, my God, my soul has farther horizons than the early mornings, deeper darkness than the nights of earth; higher heights than any mountain peaks, greater depths than any sea in nature; search *me* out, and see if there be any way of grief in me." The Psalmist realised that God knew all about the vast universe outside him, but there was some thing more mysterious to him than the universe outside, and that was the mystery of his own heart, and he asks the great Creator to come and search him. God does not search a man without he knows it, and it is a marvellous moment in a man's life when he is explored by the Spirit of God. The great mystic work of the Holy Spirit is in the dim regions of a man's personality where he cannot go. God Himself is the explorer of man's will, and this is how He searches us.

"It is God which worketh in you both to will and to do of His good pleasure." "Will" is not a faculty; "will" is the whole man active, and the springs of will go deeper down than we can go. Paul says it is God who works in us to enable us to will, that is, the Holy Spirit, Who is the expression of God, will come into our spirit and energise our will so that we have power to actively will to do according to the standards of Jesus Christ. The Holy Spirit does not become our spirit; He invades our spirit and lifts our personality into a right relationship with God, and that means we can begin now to work out what God has worked in. The Holy Spirit enables us to fulfil all the commands of God, and we are without excuse for not fulfilling them. Absolute almighty ability is packed into our spirit, and to say "can't," if we have received the Holy Spirit, is unconscious blasphemy. We have not sufficiently realised the practical moral aspect of the Atonement in our lives. "If we walk in the light, as He is in the light"—then comes the amazing revelation, that "the blood of Jesus Christ His Son cleanseth us from all sin." Cleansing from all sin does not mean conscious deliverance from sin only, it means infinitely more than we are conscious of. The part we are conscious of is walking in the light; cleansing from all sin means something infinitely profounder, it means cleansing from all sin in the sight of God. God never bases any of His work on our consciousness.

"Do you mean to tell me that God can search me to the inmost recesses of my dreams, my inmost motives, and find nothing to blame? That God Almighty can bring the winnowing fan of His Spirit and search out my thoughts and imaginations, and find nothing to blame?" Who can stand before God and say, "My hands are clean, my heart is pure"? Who can climb that "hill of the LORD"? No man under heaven, saving the man who has been readjusted at the Cross of Christ. That man can stand before the scrutiny of God and know with a knowledge that passeth knowledge that the work of God's Son in him passes the scrutiny of God. No soul ever gets there saving by the sovereign grace of God through the Atonement.

The Expression of the Conscience *(Acts 24:16)*

Conscience is that faculty in a man that attaches itself to the highest he knows and tells him what the highest he knows demands that he does. Never be caught away with the phrase that conscience is the voice of God. If it were, it would be the most contradictory voice human ears ever listened to. Conscience is the eye of the soul and it looks out either towards God or towards what it regards as the highest, and the way conscience records is dependent entirely upon the light thrown on God (cf. Acts 26:9 and 24:16).

Take the case of a man who has had a great spiritual crisis and has entered into the experience of sanctification, his conscience is now looking towards God in the light that Jesus Christ throws upon God, what has he to do? He has to walk in that light and begin to get his bodily machine into harmony with what his conscience records, that is, he has to walk now not in the light of his convictions, but in a purer sterner light, the light of the Lord. It is something he alone can do; God cannot do it for him. Supposing we say we believe God can give us the Holy Spirit and can energise our wills "to do of His good pleasure," instantly we see that, conscience records that we must obey. Any deflection in obedience to God is a sin. We have been used to doing things in this body in accordance with the old disposition—my right to myself, my self-interest; now we have to be regulated from a different standpoint. You did use the body as a servant to the wrong disposition, says Paul, see that you use it now as a servant to the right disposition (Romans 6:19). It is never done suddenly. Salvation is sudden, but the working out of salvation in our life is never sudden. It is moment by moment, here a little and there a little. The Holy Spirit educates us down to the scruple.[14]

Paul says he exercised himself to have "a conscience void of offence toward God, and toward men." We have to endeavour to obey our conscience in our life of faith before God and in our life of fact before men.

---

14. down to the scruple: to the smallest item.

That does not mean we must not do things men will not like. Our conduct with men is measured by the way God has dealt with us, not by what men think of us. Our conscience will show us how God has dealt with us, "forgiving one another, even as God for Christ's sake hath forgiven you." That is the standard that is "void of offence toward God, and toward men." Many of us are feeble Christians because we do not heed this standard. God works in the great incalculable element of our personality; we have to work out what He works in and bring it out into expression in our bodily life. It has not sufficiently entered into us that in our practical life we must do what God says we must do, not try to do it, but *do it*, and the reason we can do it is that it is God Who works in us to will.

The Expectation of the Heart *(Psalms 27:14; 42:5)*

"Heart" is simply another term for "personality." The Bible never speaks of the heart as the seat of the affections. "Heart" is best understood if we simply say "me" (cf. Romans 10:10). When once expectation is killed out of the heart, we can scarcely walk, the feet become as lead, the very life and power goes, the nerves and everything begin to fall into decay. The true nature of a man's heart according to the Bible is that of expectation and hope. It is the heart that is strengthened by God (cf. Psalm 73:26), and Jesus Christ said that He came to "bind up the broken hearted." The marvel of the indwelling Spirit of God is that He can give heart to a despairing man. There is a difference between the human sympathy we give to a discouraged or broken-hearted man and what the Holy Spirit will do for him. We may sit down beside a broken-hearted man and pour out a flow of sympathy, and say how sorry we are for him, and tell him of other people with broken hearts; but all that only makes him more submissive to being broken-hearted. When our Lord sympathises with the heart broken by sin or sorrow, He binds it up and makes it a new heart, and the expectation of that heart ever after is from God.

The great discipline of our life spiritually is to bring other people into the realm of shadows. When God has brought other people into the realm of shadows, He can bring us into the relationship we need to be in towards Himself. The expectation of the heart must be based on this certainty: "in all the world there is none but Thee, my God, there is none but Thee." Until the human heart rests there, every other relationship in life is precarious and will end in heartbreak. There is only one Being Who can satisfy the last aching abyss of the human heart, and that is the Lord Jesus Christ. The whole history of envy and cruelty in human relationships is summed up in the demand for infinite satisfaction from human hearts, we will never get it, and we are apt to become cruel,

vindictive, bitter, and often criminal. When once the heart is right with God and the real centre of the life satisfied, we never expect or demand infinite satisfaction from a finite heart, we become absolutely kind to all other hearts and never become a snare. If our hearts are not rightly related to Jesus Christ, danger and disillusionment are on our track wherever we go, because other lives are not being led to God, they stick at us, they cannot get any further and they become enervated. But when once the heart is established in expectation on God, I defy other hearts to stick at you, they may try to, but all the time they are being led on to God Himself.

The Exhortation of the Mind *(2 Corinthians 10:5)*

Before a human spirit forms a mind it must express itself in words; immediately it expresses itself in words, it becomes a spirit of mind. In the natural man it is a spirit of mind according to the flesh, but when the Holy Spirit energises a man's spirit, the words he expresses give him a mind according to the spirit. When once the Spirit of God energises our spirit, we are responsible for forming the mind of Christ. God gives us the disposition of Jesus Christ, but He does not give us His mind, we have to form that, and we form it by the way we react on external things. "Let this mind be in you, which was also in Christ Jesus." Most of us balk forming the mind of Christ; we do not object to being delivered from sin and hell, but we do object to giving up the energy of our minds to form the mind of Christ. The Holy Spirit represents the actual working of God in a man, and He enables us to form the mind of Christ if we will. We construct the mind of Christ in the same way as we construct the natural mind, viz., by the way our disposition reacts when we come in contact with external things.

The mind is closely affiliated with its physical machine, the brain, and we are responsible for getting that machine into right habits. "Glean your thinking," says Paul (see Philippians 4:8). Never submit to the tyrannous idea that you cannot look after your mind; you can. If a man lets his garden alone it very soon ceases to be a garden; and if a saint lets his mind alone it will soon become a rubbish heap for Satan to make use of. Read the terrible things the New Testament says will grow in the mind of a saint if he does not look after it. We have to rouse ourselves up to think, to bring "every thought into captivity to the obedience of Christ" (RV). Never pray about evil thoughts, it will fix them in the mind. "Quit"—that is the only thing to do with anything that is wrong; to ruthlessly grip it on the threshold of your mind and allow it no more way. If you have received the Holy Spirit, you will find that you have the power to bring "every thought into captivity to the obedience of Christ" (RV).

BEHAVIOUR
1 Thessalonians 2:10

The Fundamental Resources of Personality

Behaviour means in its widest application every possible kind of reaction to the circumstances into which you may be brought.

There are resources of personality known only to God. Psalm 139 is the prayer of a man asking God to explore him where he cannot go, and to garrison him. In 1 Thessalonians 2:10, Paul is alluding to the working out of what God works in. The majority of us keep taking in and forget altogether that somehow we must work out what we take in: we cannot elude our destiny, which is practical. The profound nature of each one of us is created by God, but our perception of God depends entirely upon our own determined effort to understand what we come in contact with, and that perception is always coloured by the ruling disposition. If my ruling disposition is self-interest, I perceive that everything that happens to me is always for or against my self-interest; if, on the other hand, my ruling disposition is obedience to God, I perceive Him to be at work for my perfecting in everything that happens to me.

When my thought has been stirred by the Spirit of God and I understand what God wants me to be and experience the thrill that comes through the vision, I have to use my body to work out the vision. The first great psychological law to be grasped is that the brain and the body are pure mechanisms, there is nothing spiritual about them; they are the machines we use to express our personality. We are meant to use our brains to express our thought in words, and then to behave according to the way we have thought. A man's spirit only expresses itself as soul by means of words; the brain does not deal with pure thought. No thought is ours until it can be expressed in words. Immediately a thought is expressed in words, it returns to the brain as an idea upon which we can work. The type of life called the intellectual life is apt to deal only with these ideas, consequently there is a divorce from the practical life. The tyranny of intellect is that we see everything in the light of one principle, and when there is a gap, as there is in the moral development of man, the intellect has to ignore it and say these things are mere upsets. The Bible supplies the facts for the gap which the intellect will not accept. The intellect simply works on a process of logic along one line. Life is never a process of logic, life is the most illogical thing we know. The facts of life are illogical, they cannot be traced easily. Intellect is secondary, not primary. An intellectualist never pushes an issue of will.

We are not meant to spend our lives in the domain of intellectual thinking. A Christian's thinking ought never to be in reflection, but in activities. The philosopher says, "I must isolate myself and think things out"; he is like a spider who spins his web and only catches flies. We come to right discernment in activities; thinking is meant to regulate the doing. Our destiny as spiritual men and women is the same as our destiny as natural men and women, viz., practical, from which destiny there is no escape. Memory is a quality of personality; it does not exist in the brain but in the heart. The brain recalls more or less clearly what the heart remembers, and whether we can recall readily depends upon the state of our physical health. We take in through the words of others conceptions that are not ours as yet, we take them in through our ears and eyes and they disappear into the unconscious mind and become incorporated into our thinking. We say that the things we hear and read slip away from memory; they do not really, they pass into the unconscious mind. We may say at the time: "I don't agree with that"; but if what we hear is of the nature of reality we will agree with it sooner or later. A truth may be of no use to us just now, but when the circumstances arise in which that truth is needed, the Holy Spirit will bring it back to our remembrance. This accounts for the curious way in which the statements of Jesus emerge; we say: "I wonder where that word came from?" It came from the unconscious mind; the point is, are we going to obey it?

The matter of behaviour is ours, not God's. God does not make our character; character is formed by the reaction of our inner disposition to outer things through our nervous system. God does what we cannot do: He alters the mainspring and plants in us a totally new disposition; then begins our work, we must work out what God works in. The practising is ours, not God's. We have to bring the mechanism of body and brain into line by habit and make it a strong ally of the grace of God. We all know that it is never the grace of God that fails in a crisis; it is we who fail because we have not been practising. To refuse to form mental habits is a crime against the way we are made. It is no use praying, "O Lord, give me mental habits." God won't; He has made us so that we can make our own mental habits, if we will. When we are regenerated God does not give us another body, we have the same body, and we have to get the bodily mechanism into working order according to His teaching. Think of the time we waste in talking to

God and in longing to be what He has already made us instead of doing what He has told us to do!

"Be renewed in the spirit of your mind." The expression of the mind comes through the mechanism of the brain, and the marvellous emancipation that comes slowly and surely is that we have the power to do what God wants us to do. There is nothing that a man or woman energised by the Spirit of God cannot do. All the commandments of God are enablings. "If ye love Me, ye will keep My commandments," said Jesus (RV); that is the practical simple test. Our Lord did not say, "If a man *obeys* Me, he will keep My commandments"; but, "If ye *love* Me, ye will keep My commandments." In the early stages of Christian experience we are inclined to hunt with an overplus of zeal for commands of our Lord to obey; but as we mature in the life of God conscious obedience becomes so assimilated into our make-up that we begin to obey the commands of God unconsciously, until in the maturest stage of all we are simply children of God through whom God does His will for the most part unconsciously. Many of us are on the borders of consciousness—consciously serving, consciously devoted to God; all that is immature, it is not the life yet. The first stages of spiritual life are passed in conscientious carefulness; the mature life is lived in unconscious consecration. The term "obey" would be better expressed by the word "use." For instance, a scientist, strictly speaking, "uses" the laws of nature; that is, he more than obeys them, he causes them to fulfil their destiny in his work. That is exactly what happens in the saint's life, he "uses" the commands of the Lord and they fulfil God's destiny in his life. The fundamental resources of personality will always stand true to God and to the way God has made us.

The Facile Receptivity of Personality

There are endless powers of reception in the deeper realms of personality where we cannot go, and it is these realms that God guards and garrisons. Personality is built to receive, it simply absorbs and absorbs; and education gives us the facility of expressing what we have received. We are designed with a great capacity for God, and the nature of personality is that it always wants more and more. Education is the drawing out of what is in for the purpose of expression, and we have to fit ourselves by acquired habits of conduct to express what we have received. What is the difference between an educated and an uneducated person? An educated person is one whose memory is so stored with abstract conceptions that whenever he is put in new circumstances, his memory instantly comes to his aid and he knows how to conduct him-

self. An uneducated person is nonplussed in new circumstances because he has nothing to come to his aid; whereas an educated person is able to extricate himself by means of examples with which his memory is stored and by the abstract conceptions he has formed of circumstances in which he has never been placed.

Apply it spiritually: Supposing you are asked to speak in the open air—"Oh, I can't!"; to take a Sunday School class—"Oh, I can't!"; to write an essay—"Oh, I can't!"; to expound a particular passage—"Oh, I can't!" What is the matter? we have not been educated on the right line. Some of us do not know what to do in certain circumstances spiritually because we have never stored our memory with the counsels of God, never watched the way God's servants conduct themselves. If we have been storing our minds with the word of God, we are never taken unawares in new circumstances because the Holy Spirit brings back these things to our remembrance and we know what we should do; but the Holy Spirit cannot bring back to our minds what we have never troubled to put there. "My people doth not consider," God says; they live on "spooned meat"[15] spiritually, go to church on Sunday and expect to live in the strength of it all the week without doing anything. We should be so in the habit of obeying the Holy Spirit as He interprets the word of God to us that wherever we are placed, we extricate ourselves in a holy and just and unblameable manner.

These things will always come to the rescue in the nick of time to the educated mind—the memory of how we have seen others act in the same circumstances, and the conceptions we form as we study God's Word. We do not become educated all at once, nor do we form habits all at once; it is done bit by bit, and we have to take ourselves strongly in hand. The one thing that keeps us back from forming habits is laziness. The lazy person in the natural world is always captious, and the lazy person spiritually is captious with God, "I haven't had a decent chance." Never let the limitation of natural ability come in. We must get to the place where we are not afraid to face our life before God, and then begin to work out deliberately what God has worked in. That is the way the habits which will show themselves in holy and just and unblameable behaviour are formed.

The Fit Reactions of Personality

There is no reception without a reaction, and no impression without a corresponding expression. The great law regarding impressions and emotions is that if an emotion is not carried out on its own level, it will react on a lower level. The only test as to whether to allow an impression or emotion is to ask, What will

---

15. "Spooned meat" is liquefied food that requires no chewing or effort—baby food.

this emotion lead to if I let it have its way? Push it to its logical conclusion, and if the outcome is something God would condemn, grip it on the threshold of your mind as in a vice and allow it no more way. But if it is an emotion kindled by the Spirit of God, at the peril of your soul you refuse to act it out, because if you do not let that emotion have its right issue in your life, it will react on a lower level; whereas if you act an emotion out on its right level, you lift your whole life on to God's platform. Paul mentions gross immorality in close connection with sanctification because every devotional emotion not worked out on its own level will react on an immoral level secretly. This accounts for the fact that men and women whose private life is exceedingly wrong often show an amazing liking for devotional literature, for the writings of the saints, for the stirring of abstruse emotions. That is the way sentimentalists are made. Every emotion must express itself, and if it is not expressed on the right level, it will react on a lower level; and the higher the emotion, the more degraded the level on which it will react.

A saint is a bundle of specially qualified reactions. For every possible circumstance in life there is a line of behaviour marked out in advance for us; it is not stated in black and white, we have to be so familiar with God's Book that when we come to a crisis the Spirit of God brings back to our memory the things we had read but never understood, and we see what we should do. God is making characters, not mechanisms. We have to get our bodily mechanism into line with what God has worked in. The mighty work of God is done by His sovereign grace, then we have to work it out in our behaviour.

"Ye are witnesses, and God also, how holily and righteously and unblameably we behaved ourselves toward you that believe" (1 Thessalonians 2:10 RV). "Unblameable" does not mean faultless, it means a blameless disposition, undeserving of censure: that is, undeserving of censure in the sight of God Who sees everything. "Now unto Him that is able to guard you from stumbling, and to set you before the presence of His glory without blemish in exceeding joy" (Jude 24 RV).

ATTENTION
1 Timothy 4:11–16

Attention is never possible without conscious effort; interest frequently is, we can take up a book and our interest is riveted at once. Naturally we never attend to anything, we are like children, and children do not attend until they are taught to. We all have certain native interests in which we are absorbed; but attention is always an effort of will. We are held responsible by God for the culture of attention.

The Capacity to Attend
These things command and teach . . . (1 Timothy 4:11)

Interest is natural; attention must be by effort, and the great secret of a Christian's life is the attention to realities. Reality is only possible where person comes in contact with person, all the rest is a shadow of reality. That is why Jesus said, *"I am . . . the truth."* When Saint Paul told Timothy to command and teach, he was building his counsel on this capacity to attend, which must be by effort. We are always more willing to get ideas from books and from other people, which is simply an indication that we are not willing to attend but prefer to have our natural interest awakened. We scoop other people's brains either in books or in conversation in order to avoid attending ourselves. One of our greatest needs is to have a place

where we deliberately attend; that is the real meaning of prayer. "Enter into thy closet, and when thou hast shut thy door, pray to thy Father which is in secret." Prayer that is not an effort of the will is unrecognised by God. "If ye abide in Me, and My words abide in you, ye shall ask what ye will, and it shall be done unto you," said Jesus. That does not mean ask anything you like, but ask what you *will*. What are you actively willing? ask for that. We shall find that we *ask* very few things. The tendency in prayer to leave ourselves all abroad to the influence of a meeting or of a special season is not scriptural. Prayer is an effort of will, and Jesus Christ instructs us by using the word "ask." "Every one that asketh receiveth." These words are an amazing revelation of the simplicity with which God would have us pray. The other domains of prayer, the intercession of the Holy Spirit and the intercession of Christ, are nothing to do with us; the effort of our will is to do with us.

The Contemporary Attention
Let no man despise thy youth; but be thou an example of the believers . . . (1 Timothy 4:12)

To-day men's attention is being screwed down along scientific lines; that is where the effort is being made.

Think of the sweat and labour that a scientific student will expend in order to attain his end; where do we find men and women concentrating with the same intensity on spiritual realities? The majority of us are totally ignorant of the one abiding reality that demands our attention, viz., our relationship to God, which should exhibit itself in a life in accordance with that relationship. The essence of sin is the refusal to recognise that we are accountable to God at all. The relationship to God must be recognised and lived up to from the crown of the head to the soles of the feet; nothing is unimportant in this relation ship.

"Let no man despise thy youth," Paul said to Timothy. Youth is a thing to be despised, a man up to thirty ought to be shut up in a bandbox[16] and not allowed to speak. Paul is not saying, "Stand up for your rights"; not, "Let no man despise thy youth because you are as good as anybody else," but by being an example in word, in conversation, in charity, in spirit, in faith and in purity to all who believe the realities which you believe; don't be caught up by contemporary attentions. It is so easy to attend to the thing every one else is attending to, but it is difficult to attend to what no one is attending to. Paul did not say, "Pay attention to the Greek philosopher, to the history of your people," to the thousand and one things that were contemporary in his day; he said, "Screw your attention with all your effort on the one reality, your relationship to God, and be an example on that all through."

The Commiserating Attention
Give attendance to reading . . . (1 Timothy 4:13)

How many of us spend our time expecting that we will be something we are not. "Oh the time is coming when I am going to be so and so." It never will come; the time is always *now*. The amazing thing about the salvation of our Lord is that He brings us into contact with the reality that is, until we are just like children, continually seeing the wonder and beauty of things around us. The characteristic of young men and women of to-day is an affected tiredness of everything, nothing interests them. The salvation of Jesus is not a Divine anticipation, it is an absolute fact. People talk about the magnificent ideals that are yet to be; but the marvel of being born from above is that the reality is infinitely more wonderful than all we have imagined. Our Lord taught us to look at such things as grass and trees and birds; grass is not ideal, it is real; flowers are not ideal, they are real; sunrises and sunsets are not ideal, they are real. These things are all round about us, almost pressing themselves into our eyes and ears, and yet we never look at them. Jesus Christ drew all His illustrations from His Father's handiwork, from sparrows and flowers, things that none of us dream of noticing; we take our illustrations from things that compel attention. When we are born from above the Spirit of God does not give us new ideals, we begin to see how ideal the real is; and as we pay attention to the things near at hand, we find them to be the gate of heaven to our souls. The reality of the salvation of Jesus Christ is that He makes us pay attention to realities, not appearances.

The Soul's Awakening
Neglect not the gift that is in thee . . . (1 Timothy 4:14)

There is a difference between such books as Trine's *In Tune with the Infinite*[17] and the reality of life. It is possible to go dreaming through life till we are struck, not by an ideal, but by a sudden reality, and all we have ever pictured of what a man or woman should be pales before the reality we see. That is what happened when men saw Jesus Christ in the days of His flesh. The Spirit of God saves us from the absurd futility of useless tears when the near objects have become far by making us open our eyes to what is near. We weep around the graves of people and things because we have never realised that we have to pay attention to the reality that is at hand. Take a lad who has become impatient with his home, he is sick of it, he cannot stand his parents, his sisters are prosaic, and he leaves—the best thing for him. Let him come in contact with other people's fathers and mothers and sisters—Oh, yes, he much prefers them; but he will soon come to realise that the ones he has left are infinitely better. Naturally we much prefer the friends we make to our God-made relations, because we can be noble with our friends, we have no past history with them.

This principle works all through. We long for something that is not and shut our eyes to the thing that is. When the Lord Jesus awakens us to reality by new birth and brings us in contact with Himself, He does not give us new fathers and mothers and new friends; He gives us new sight, that is, we focus our eyes on the things that are near and they become wonderfully distant. "Put thy distance on the near." This craving to go somewhere else, to see the things that are distant, arises from a refusal to attend to what is near.

---

16. The bandbox of Chambers' day was a small, round box made to hold neckbands or collars for shirts. It is used metaphorically to mean something small, narrow, cloistered, self-contained.

17. Ralph Waldo Trine (1866–1958), American writer, was the author of The Life Books series, including *In Tune with the Infinite*.

Have I ever realised that the most wonderful thing in the world is the thing that is nearest to me, viz., my body? Who made it? Almighty God. Do I pay the remotest attention to my body as being the temple of the Holy Ghost? Remember our Lord lived in a body like ours. The next reality that I come in contact with by my body is other people's bodies. All our relationships in life, all the joys and all the miseries, all the hells and all the heavens, are based on bodies; and the reality of Jesus Christ's salvation brings us down to the Mother Earth we live on, and makes us see by the regenerating power of God's grace how amazingly precious are the ordinary things that are always with us. Master that, and you have mastered everything. We imagine that our bodies are a hindrance to our development, whereas it is only through our bodies that we develop. We cannot express a character without a body.

This is also true of Nature. We do not get at God through Nature, as the poets say, we get at Nature through God when once we are rightly related to Him, and Nature becomes a sacrament of His Presence. Such books as Trine's start at the wrong end, they try to bring us from the ideal to the real; it is by coming in contact with the real that we find the ideal. "Neglect not the gift that is in thee." We have to be careful not to neglect the spiritual reality planted in us by God. The first thing that contact with reality does is to enable us to diagnose our moods. It is a great moment when we realise that we have the power to trample on certain moods. Moods never go by praying, moods go by kicking. A mood nearly always has its seat in the physical condition, not in the moral, and it is a continual effort to refuse to listen to those moods which arise from a physical condition; we must not submit to them for a second. It is a great thing to have something to neglect in your life; a great thing for your moral character to have something to snub. "The expulsive power of a new affection"—that is what Christianity supplies. The Spirit of God on the basis of Redemption gives us something else to think about. Are we going to think about it?

By heeding the reality of God's grace within us we are never bothered again by the fact that we do not understand ourselves, or that other people do not understand us. If anyone understood me, he would be my god. The only Being Who understands me is the Being Who made me and Who redeems me, and He will never expound me to myself; He will only bring me to the place of reality, viz., into contact with Himself, and the heart is at leisure from itself for ever afterwards.

The first things a Christian is emancipated from is the tyranny of moods and the tyranny of feeling that he is not understood. These things are the most fruitful sources of misery. Half the misery in the world comes because one person demands of another a complete under standing, which is absolutely impossible. The only Being Who understands us is the Being Who made us. It is a tremendous emancipation to get rid of every kind of self-consideration and learn to heed only one thing, the relationship between God and ourselves. "In all the world there is none but Thee, my God, there is none but Thee." Once we get there, other people become shadows, beautiful shadows, but shadows under God's control.

The Scriptural Attitude
Meditate upon these things . . . (1 Timothy 4:15)

Meditation means getting to the middle of a thing, pinning yourself down to a certain thing and concentratedly brooding upon it. The majority of us attend only to the "muddle" of things, consequently we get spiritual indigestion, the counterpart of physical indigestion, a desperately gloomy state of affairs. We cannot see anything rightly, and all we do see is stars. "Faith is . . . the evidence of things not seen." Suppose Jesus suddenly lifted the veil from our eyes and let us see angels ministering to us, His Own Presence with us, the Holy Ghost in us, and the Father around us, how amazed we should be! We have lived in the "muddle" of things instead of in the middle of things. Faith gets us into the middle, which is God and God's purpose. Elisha prayed for his servant, "LORD, I pray Thee, open his eyes, that he may see," and when his eyes were opened he saw the hosts of God and nothing else.

We have to learn to pay attention to reality; one soul attending to reality is an emancipation to hundreds more. We are impertinently inquisitive about everything saving that one thing. Through inattention to our own true capacity we live as in a dream, when all around us and in us are the eternal realities. "Attend to these duties, let them absorb you, so that all men may note your progress." We are apt to be busy about everything but that which concerns our spiritual progress, and at the end of a profitless day we snatch up a Bible or *Daily Light*[18] and read a few verses, and it does us good for precisely three-quarters of a second. We have to take time to be diligent. Meditation is not being like a pebble in a brook, allowing the waters of thought to flow over us; that is reverie. Meditation is the most intense spiritual act, it brings every part of body and mind into harness. To

18. *Daily Light on the Daily Path* was a devotional book of selected Scripture portions for morning and evening of each day. It was first published in 1861.

be spiritual by effort is a sure sign of a false relationship to God; to be obedient by effort in the initial stages is a sure sign that we are determined to obey God at all costs. Take time. Remember we have all the time there is. The majority of us waste time and want to encroach on eternity. "Oh well, I will think about these things when I have time." The only time you will have is the day after you are dead, and that will be eternity. An hour, or half a hour, of daily attention to and meditation on our own spiritual life is the secret of progress.

The Sacred Attention
. . . Take heed unto thyself. (1 Timothy 4:16)

If we have been living in unrealities, we shall find ourselves faced with a great impatience when we do endeavour to face reality, and we are apt to behave like caged wild beasts. We have to take a grip of ourselves when we come to the true centre of things, and it means discipline *and discipline*, until we face nothing but realities. We have to exert a tremendous effort, and God is pleased to see us exert it. If you try and settle down before God in prayer when you have been dwelling in unrealities, you will recognise instantly the condition of things. As soon as you get down to pray you remember a letter you ought to write, or something else that needs to be done, a thousand and one little impertinences come in and claim your attention. When we suspend our own activities and get down at the foot of the Cross and meditate there, God brings His thoughts to us by the Holy Spirit and interprets them to us. The only mind that understands the things of God is the child mind (see Matthew 11:25); our Lord continually mentioned this simplicity (see Matthew 18:3). It is the simplicity of God, not of an imbecile, a fundamental simplicity of relationship. God has not the remotest opportunity of coming to some of us, our minds are packed full with our own thoughts and conceptions; until suddenly He comes in like the wind and blows all our thoughts right away, and thoughts come sauntering in from the Word of God. We can never get those thoughts for ourselves. They are the free gift of God for anyone and everyone who is learning to pay attention to Him.

NATURAL GROWTH IN SUPERNATURAL GRACE
1 Peter 2:7–12

Our Lord's maxims

> *Consider the lilies of the field, how they grow.*
> *Behold the fowls of the air.*
> *Become as little children.*

Our Lord did not point out wonderful sights to His disciples all the time; He pointed out things that were apparently insignificant—lilies and grass and sparrows. God does not deal with the things that interest us naturally and compel our attention; He deals with things which we have to will to observe. The illustrations Jesus Christ used were all taken from His Father's handiwork because they express exactly how the life of God will develop in us. We draw our illustrations from the works of men, consequently we get into a hustling condition and forget our Lord's maxims.

"Consider the lilies of the field, how they grow"—in the dark! We are apt to consider a lily when it is in the sunshine only, but for the greater part of the year it is buried in the ground; and we imagine that we are to be always above ground, shedding perfume and looking beautiful; or continually being cut and put into God's show-room to be admired, forgetting altogether that we cannot be as lilies unless we have spent time in the dark, totally ignored. As a disciple, Jesus says, consider your hidden life with God. When we breathe fresh air we are not consciously exhilaratingly different all the time; but if we continue to take in fresh air, it makes a profound difference. This is true of our life in Christ. If we receive the Holy Spirit and obey Him, He makes a profound difference, and it will be manifested one day as a great surprise. It is not done in a minute as far as our consciousness is concerned, but when we come to a crisis we find to our astonishment that we are not upset or perplexed, as we might have expected, but we realise that our whole outlook has been altered. The Spirit of God awaits His own time to bring the crisis, we are apt to say, "I want the crisis now." We shall never see God's point of view as long as we bring our own ideas to Him and dictate to God what we expect Him to do. We must become as little children, be essentially simple, keep our minds brooding on what God tells us to brood on, and let God do as He likes. The difficulties come because we will not be simple enough to take God at His word.

Our natural reactions are not wrong, although they may be used to express the wrong disposition. God never contradicts our natural reactions; He wants them to be made spiritual. When we are saved God does not alter the construction of our bodily life, but He does expect us to manifest in our bodily life the alteration He has made. We express ourselves naturally through our bodies, and we express the supernatural life of God in the same way, but it can only be done by the sacrifice of the natural.

How many of us are spiritual in eating and drinking and sleeping? Those acts were spiritual in our Lord; His relationship to the Father was such that all His natural life was obedient to Him, and when He saw that His Father's will was for Him not to obey a natural reaction, He instantly obeyed His Father (see Matthew 4:1–4). If our Lord had been fanatical He would have said—"I have been so long without food, I will never eat again." That would have been to obey a principle instead of God. When God is educating us along the line of turning the natural into the spiritual, we are apt to become fanatical. Because by God's grace things have been done which are miraculous, we become devoted to the miracle and forget God, then when difficulties come we say it is the antagonism of the devil. The fact is we are grossly ignorant of the way God has made us. All that we need is a little of what we understand by pluck in the natural world put into the spiritual. Don't let your body get on top and say there is nothing after all in what God said. Stand up to the difficulty, and all that you ever believed about the transforming grace of God will be proved in your bodily life.

Curiosity (1 Peter 2:7)

Curiosity is the desire to come to a full knowledge and understanding of a thing; it is a natural reaction. Imagine a child without curiosity! A child cannot sit and listen to a lecture, but let him see something bright and instantly he is curious and wants to get hold of it, whether it is the moon or a ball. The reaction is based not so much on the desire to have it for himself as on the desire to know more about it. As men and women we are curious about intellectual or philosophic or scientific things, and when a particular quality is presented our curiosity is aroused—"I want to know more about this matter, can anyone explain it to me satisfactorily?" It is the natural reaction of the way we are made, and to ignore it is fanatical. The instinct of curiosity can be used in the wrong way (see Genesis 3:6), but that does not mean that the reaction itself is wrong, it depends upon the motive. A point that is frequently missed in dealing with the questions of a child is that he asks them from a disinterested motive; a teacher can always appeal to the disinterested curiosity of a child. A child's questions are at the very heart of things, questions that scarcely occur to a philosopher.

In natural life we grow by means of curiosity, and spiritually we grow by the same power. The Spirit of God uses the natural reaction of curiosity to enable us to know more about the One Who is precious. The instinct is not denied, but lifted on to a different platform and turned towards knowing Jesus Christ. As saints our curiosity must not be all abroad; we become insatiably curious about Jesus Christ; He is the One Who rivets our attention. Think of the avidity with which you devour anything that has to do with expounding the Lord Jesus Christ—"unto you therefore which believe He is Precious."

Imitation (1 Peter 2:9)

Imitation is one of the first reactions of a child, it is not sinful. We come to a right knowledge of ourselves by imitating others. The instinct that makes us afraid of being odd is not a cowardly instinct, it is the only power of self-preservation we have. If you live much by yourself you become an oddity, you never see the quirks in yourself. Some people won't live with others spiritually, they live in holes and corners by themselves. The New Testament warns of those who "separate themselves" (Jude 19). By the grace of God we are taken out of the fashion we were in and we become more or less speckled birds.[19] Immediately you introduce a standard of imitation which the set to which you belong does not recognise, you will experience what Peter says, "they think it strange that ye run not with them to the same excess of riot" (1 Peter 4:4).

The Spirit of God lifts the natural reaction of imitation into another domain and by God's grace we begin to imitate Our Lord and shew forth His praises. It is the natural instinct of a child to imitate his mother, and when we are born again the Holy Spirit lifts this instinct into the spiritual domain and it becomes the most supernaturally natural thing for us to imitate our Lord. We grow in grace naturally, not artificially. Mimicking is the counterfeit of imitation and produces the "pi" person, one who tries his level best to be what he is not. When you are good you never try to be. It is natural to be like the one we live with most; then if we spend most of our time with Jesus Christ, we shall begin to be like Him, by the way we are built naturally and by the Spirit God puts in.

Emulation (1 Peter 2:9)

Emulation is the instinct to imitate what you see anther doing, in order not to appear inferior. A boy who accepts the place of inferiority is either lazy or is becoming heartbroken; he has no right to sit down

---

19. A "speckled bird" is a person who stands out as abnormal, odd, or eccentric.

and submit to being inferior, he is not built that way naturally. A child always admires anyone with skill, and the teacher who says, "Do this and that," has no influence over a child compared with the one who says, "Come and do this with me." When a child has seen his teacher do a thing and is asked to do it, instantly the instinct of emulation is at work.

Our Lord builds His deepest teaching on the instinct of emulation. When His Spirit comes in He makes me desire not to be inferior to Him Who called me. Our example is not a good man, not even a good Christian man, but God Himself. By the grace of God I have to emulate my Father in heaven. "Be ye therefore perfect, even as your Father which is in heaven is perfect" (Matthew 5:48). The most natural instinct of the supernatural life of God within me is to be worthy of my Father. To say that the doctrine of sanctification is unnatural is not true, it is based on the way God has made us. When we are born again we become natural for the first time; as long as we are in sin we are abnormal, because sin is not normal. When we are restored by the grace of God it becomes the most natural thing to be holy, we are not forcing ourselves to be unnatural. When we are rightly related to God all our natural instincts help us to obey Him and become the greatest ally of the Holy Spirit. We disobey whenever we become independent. Independence is not strength but unrealised weakness, and is the very essence of sin. There was no independence in our Lord, the great characteristic of His life was submission to His Father.

Emulation and imitation both centre around whatever is our ideal. When once we see Jesus, it is good-bye to all ideals; we cannot have them back again, nor do we want them back again if we are true to Him. We have to keep the one Lodestar, the Lord Jesus Christ, in front and be absorbingly taken up with Him; consequently we have to put ourselves through discipline and fast from every other type of emulation.

Ambition *(1 Peter 2:11)*

Ambition is a mixture of pugnacity and pride, a reaction of unwillingness to be beaten by any difficulty. It is a natural reaction. Think of a boy without the instinct to fight! The reaction that makes one boy punch another is not bad, although the disposition behind it may be. The natural reaction of ambition in a man or woman saved by God's grace is that they will not be beaten by anything the world, the flesh or the devil can put in the way of their fulfilling God's idea for them. By the grace of God we get to the place where we do not punch other people, but punch the devil clean out of the arena. "Resist the devil." How can we resist the devil unless we are ambitious not to be beaten by him! When we become spiritual the reac-

tion of pugnacity is lifted on to another plane and we say to our body, "It can be done and it shall be done" (cf. 1 Corinthians 9:27). Most of us are devoid of spiritual pluck. Many who are naturally plucky lose all their pluck when they get a smattering of grace and become sentimental and pathetic, every tiny ache which they would have ignored altogether before they were saved, is of the devil! God does not tell us to leave the natural life entirely alone; the natural life has to be turned into the spiritual, and it is because we do not realise this that we become whining people spiritually where we would have scorned to whine naturally.

When we are born into the kingdom of God we realise that we are not fighting against flesh and blood, but against spiritual enemies, "against spiritual wickedness in high places." The Book of the Revelation is based on the reaction to overcome. "To him that overcometh . . ." You cannot overcome if there is nothing to over come. In natural education everything is built up on difficulty, there is always something to overcome. And this is true in the spiritual world. If the world, the flesh and the devil have knocked you out once, get up and face them again, and again, until you have done with them. That is how character is made in the spiritual domain as well as in the natural. Our prayers for God's help are often nothing but incarnate laziness, and God has to say, "Speak no more unto Me of this matter. Get thee up. . . ."

The pugnacious element is a natural reaction, and as Christian teachers we have to recognise it. Ambition in the spiritual domain is the reaction which refuses to bow its neck to any yoke but the yoke of the Lord Jesus Christ. Nothing awakens scorn amongst men more than a quitter, one who funks in a game. Weakness or imbecility do not awaken contempt as much as one sign of the white feather, a refusal to face the music, the tiniest sign of the lack of pugnacity. The law of antagonism runs all through life, physical, moral, mental and spiritual. I am only healthy according to the fighting corpuscles in my blood, when the fighting millions inside get low, I become diseased and after a while I shall be snuffed out. Morally it is the same, we are not born moral, we are born innocent and ignorant; morality is the outcome of fight. Immediately I am lazy in moral matters, I become immoral. Spiritually it is the same. "In the world ye shall have tribulation"—everything that is not spiritual makes for our undoing—" but be of good cheer; I have overcome the world." Why did not our Lord say that He would help us to overcome? Because we have to imitate Him through the power He has put in us. Think of sitting in a corner before the Almighty and saying, "But my difficulties are so enormous." Thank God they are! The bigger the difficulty, the more amazing is your profit to Jesus Christ as you draw on His supernatural grace.

Ownership *(1 Peter 2:11–12)*

The instinct of ownership is seen from the first of life to the last. As soon as an infant tongue can say anything, it will say "me" and "mine.' "Is this mine?" "Yes"—then expect to see it smashed. The child wishes you to understand that he can do what he likes with his own. It is only the discipline of life that teaches us to keep things. The instinct of ownership is a right one, though the disposition expressed through it may be wrong. In a saint the idea of ownership is that we have the power to glorify God by good works (see Matthew 5:16). What we own is the honour of Jesus Christ. Have I ever realised that His honour is at stake in my bodily life? "What? know ye not that your body is the temple of the Holy Ghost which is in you?" Do I own my body for that one purpose? do I own my brain to think God's thoughts after Him? We have to be intensely and personally God's.

The Spirit of God brings us into the realisation of our ownership, and the instinct of ownership becomes a tremendous wealth in the life. "All things are yours," and Paul prays that the eyes of our understanding may be enlightened that we may know what is ours in Christ Jesus.

No personality, from a tiny child to Almighty God, is without this sense of ownership. How wonderfully sprightly a dog looks when he is owned! How weary and hang-dog we become when we are convicted of sin; but when we experience God's salvation, we straighten up immediately, everything is altered, we can fling our heads back and look the world in the face because the Lord Jesus Christ is ours and we are His. A dominant ownership, such as the ownership of the Lord means that we own everything He owns. "The meek . . . shall inherit the earth."

THE WAY OF A SOUL
Ephesians 5:14–18

The Way of the Awakening of the Soul *(Ephesians 5:14–15)*

Awake thou that sleepest, and arise from the dead . . . (Ephesians 5:14)

What is Possible in the Way of Habits. A good many of us are in the condition that St. Augustine described himself to be in, the condition of a half-awakened man who does not wish to be awakened—"a little more sleep." God smote St. Augustine with the words, "not in chambering and wantonness." When the Spirit of God brings a word of God to us, are we going to wake up and lay hold of it, or remain in the condition St. Augustine was in—"a little more worldliness; a little less intensity"? If God tells us to awake, we must get into the habit of awakening. We have to wake up physically before we can wake up spiritually. When God tells us to do a thing He empowers us to do it, only we must do the doing. Think of the number of times we say, "Oh, I can't." For the good of your own soul, say "I won't." To say, "I can't" enervates the whole life. If we really cannot, God has misled us. Jesus said "All power is given unto Me"; if He tells us to do something and we cannot, this is simply not true.

We talk about attacks of the devil—"I cannot concentrate my mind, the devil hinders me." The reason we cannot concentrate is that we are culpably ignorant about ourselves. The devil does not need to bother about us as long as we remain ignorant of the way God has made us and refuse to discipline our-

selves; inattention and our own slovenliness will soon run away with every power we have. Watch the care students take in other domains of life, and then think of our own laziness and the way we continually fall back and say, "It can't be done." All we need is grit and gumption and reliance on the Holy Spirit. We must bring the same determined energy to the revelations in God's Book as we bring to earthly professions. Most of us leave the sweat of brain outside when we come to deal with the Bible.

Anything and everything is possible in the way of habits. Habits form a pathway in the material stuff of the brain. We cannot form a habit without thinking about it; but when once the pathway in the brain is formed we can do a thing easily without thinking about it. For instance, we were not born with the ready-made habit of dressing ourselves, we had to form that habit. If we persist in using our bodies in a certain way, alterations will take place in the make-up of the brain. Spiritually we have to learn to form habits on the basis of the grace of God. What happens at new birth is that the incoming of a totally new life breaks all the old habits, they are completely dislodged by the "expulsive power of a new affection." Most of us do not realise this and we continue to obey habits when there is no need to. The incoming of the Spirit of God from without forms a disassociation physically, and new habits can be formed. Never dispute for a second when God speaks; if you debate, you give an opportunity to the old habits to reassert themselves. Launch yourself with as strong an initiative as possible on the line of obedience; it is difficult at first, but immediately you start to obey, you find you can do it. The danger is to say "I can't," or, "I will do it presently." When in your soul's vision you see clearly what God wants, let me advise you to do something physical immediately. If you accompany a moral or spiritual decision with a physical effort you give the necessary initiative to form the new habit. A physical exertion is imperative in spiritual transactions, otherwise it is in danger of passing into thin air. When God tells you to do a thing, never wait for a fitting opportunity, *do it now*. You may dream about doing it to further orders,[20] the only thing to do is to launch out at once and make things inevitable, make it impossible to go back on the decision.

Beware of divorcing the physical and the spiritual. Habits are physical, and every command of God has a physical basis. "He that hath ears to hear, let him hear." You cannot hear with your heart if you do not listen with your physical ears. Does God find me quick in the uptake to discern what He says? Am I awake enough to hear? God always locates His spiritual revelations in a physical body. The great God became Incarnate in flesh and blood; the great thoughts of God became crystallised in words. When the Spirit of God touches us, we are responsible for forming the mind of Christ. God does the wonderful indwelling part, but we have to do the expressing (see Philippians 2:12–13), and when once we understand how God has made us, it becomes not at all difficult to do it. The Spirit of God knocks and says, "Wake up, form this habit," and if you try, you find you can because you find you have a wealth of power within. It is only when we are willing to be identified with the death of Jesus that the full power of His life is able to work, and we find a new page of consciousness open in our lives. There are new forces in us and we are able now to do what we never could before; we are free from the old bondage and limitations. The gateway into this life is through the death of Jesus Christ.

Be a saint physically.

The Way of the Apprehension of the Soul
(Ephesians 5:16–17)
understanding what the will of the Lord is . . . (Ephesians 5:17)

What is possible in the Way of Intelligence
Have we begun to form the habit of thinking? Thinking is the habit of expressing what moves our spirit. In order to think we must concentrate. Thinking is a purely physical process. No one can tell us how to begin to think, all they can do is to tell us what happens when we do think. In the grey matter of the brain are multitudes of blood-vessels, distributed equally all over the brain, and when we think, the blood gathers to the one part of the brain we are using. This is called concentration. Dissipated thinking means that the blood goes back to the other parts of the brain and wakens up associated ideas. When we focus our will around certain thoughts, the blood converges to that particular part of the brain, and if we can hold our wills fixed there for five minutes, we have done a tremendous thing, we have begun to form the habit of mental concentration. The majority of us allow our brains to wool-gather, we never concentrate on any particular line. Concentration is physical, not spiritual. The brain must be brought into order by concentration, then when the Spirit of God brings a spontaneous illumination of a particular theme instantly the brain is at the disposal of God. If we have not learned to concentrate, the brain cannot focus itself anywhere, it fusses all round and wool-gathers. No one is responsible for that but ourselves.

This is true in ordinary thinking, and the same brain is used by the Holy Spirit. We have to learn to bring "every thought into captivity to the obedience of Christ" (RV); to "stay our imagination" (RV mg) on God. This can only be done by concentration, by fixing our thoughts and our imagination deliberately on God. The majority of us are unable to fix our thoughts in prayer, we lie all abroad before God and do not rouse ourselves up to lay hold of Him, consequently we have wandering thoughts continually. God will not bring every thought and imagination into captivity; we have to do it, and that is the test of spiritual concentration. The inattentive, slovenly way we drift into the presence of God is an indication that we are not bothering to think about Him. Whenever our Lord spoke of prayer, He said, "ask." It is impossible to ask if you do not concentrate. The marvel of the goodness of God is that He does so much for us; if we would only meet with physical obedience what God does for us spiritually, the whole of our body would be under such control that we should apprehend His meaning when He speaks. It is not a question of learning a thing outside but of determination inside. God gives us the Holy Spirit not only for holy living but for holy thinking, and we are held responsible if we do not think concentratedly along the right lines. To concentrate with our mind fixed on one trend of things is never easy to begin with. There never is a time when we cannot begin to concentrate.

---

20. "To further orders" means ad infinitum; endlessly; the phrase is of military origin, meaning continuing the present action until one receives different orders.

"Be ye not unwise, but understanding what the will of the Lord is." We have to use the same power of concentration spiritually as we do naturally. How are we going to find out the will of God? "God will communicate it to us." He will not. His will is there all the time, but we have to discover it by being renewed in our minds, by taking heed to His word and obeying it. If we are not going to be "conformed to this world; but . . . transformed," we must use our brains. God does the spiritual, powerful part we cannot do; but we have to work it out, and as we do the obeying we prove, i.e., "make out," "what is that good, and acceptable, and perfect, will of God." We need to make our own nature the ally of the Spirit of God. The grace of God never fails us, but we often fail the grace of God because we do not practise. If we do not practise when there is no need, we shall never do it when there is a need. When people say, "I cannot think, I have not the gift," they mean that they have never used their brains. We all have bodies and brains. When we use our brains in concentration in a way we have never done before, we will have growing pains; a headache after thinking is a sign we have brains. The more we work and get beyond the conscious stage of doing things, the more easily will we do them. We all have unconscious mental methods. Never imitate to stick to what you imitate; imitate only in order to provoke your mind to know its own mechanism.

An artist is one who not only sees but is prepared to pay the price of acquiring the technical knowledge to express what he sees. An artistic person is one who has not enough art in him to make him work at the technique of art whereby he can express himself, he indulges in moods and tones and impressions; consequently there are more artistic people than there are artists. The same is true of poetry, there are many people with poetic notions, but very few poets. It is not enough for a man to feel the divine flame burning in him; unless he goes into the concentrated, slogging business of learning the technique of expression, his genius will be of no use to anyone. Apply these illustrations spiritually: if we have not enough of the life of God in us to overcome the difficulty of expressing it in our bodies, then we are living an impoverished spiritual life. Think of the illuminations the Spirit of God has given you; He expected you to bring your physical body which He made into obedience to the vision, and you never attempted to but let it drift, and when the crisis came and God looked for you to be His mouthpiece, you crumpled all to pieces. You had not formed the habit of apprehending; your physical machine was not under control. It is a terrible thing to sit down to anything.

Beware of being side-tracked by the idea that you can develop a spiritual life apart from physical accompaniments. It is a desperately dangerous thing to allow the spiritual vision to go ahead of physical obedience.

Do some practical obeying.

The Way of Appreciation by the Soul
(Ephesians 5:18)
. . . be filled with the Spirit.

What is Possible in the Way of Inspiration
There are two ways of inspiration possible—being drunk with wine, and being filled with the Spirit. We have no business to be nondescript, drunk neither one way nor the other. A man may be sober and incapable as well as drunk and in capable. Watch human nature; we are so built that if we do not get thrilled in the right way, we will get thrilled in the wrong. If we are without the thrill of communion with God, we will try to get thrilled by the devil, or by some concoction of human ingenuity. Don't be inspired with wine, the counterfeit of the Spirit, says Paul, but be filled with the Spirit. Enthusiasm is the idea— intoxicated with the life of God. Paul puts it as a command, "Be being filled." When our Lord talked to the woman of Samaria, He said, "the water that I shall give him shall be in him a well of water springing up into everlasting life." Profoundly speaking, there is no refilling; "a well of water" is there all the time. The picture is not that of a channel, but of a fountain, a continual infilling and overflowing of the inspiration of God.

In the matter of inspiration the first thing to watch is the temper of our own soul. A blameworthy temper of mind about another soul will end in the spirit of the devil. We cannot approach God in a wrong temper of mind, it will put a shutter down between and we shall not see Him. God introduces us to people who conduct themselves to us as we have conducted ourselves to Him, and if we do not recognise what He is doing we will ride a moral hobbyhorse—"I will not be treated like that." There is no further inspiration possible from the Spirit of God until that temper of mind is gone. "Take heed to your spirit, that ye deal not treacherously." Our Lord always puts His finger unerringly on the thing that is wrong. "*First be reconciled . . .*" (Matthew 5:24). The next thing we have to watch is our private relationship with God. Are we determined to prove that God must do what we have said He must? If so, our intercession becomes frenzied fanaticism. Or are we only concerned about being brought into an understanding of God, which is the real meaning of prayer? The greatest barrier to intercession is that we take ourselves so seriously, and come to the conclusion that God is reserved with us; He is not. God has to ignore things we take so seriously until our relationship to Him is exactly that of a child. If we are watching the temper of our minds towards other people and towards God, there will be the continual incoming and outflowing of the inspiration of God, a fresh anointing of the Holy Spirit all the time. Imagine Jesus being jaded in the life of God! There was never anything jaded about Him. When we are jaded there is always a reason, and it is either the temper of our mind towards another or towards God. We have no business to be half-dead spiritually, to hang like clogs on God's plan; we should be filled with a radiant intensity of life, living at the highest pitch all the time without any reaction. "I am come that they might have life, and that they might have it more abundantly."

Be being filled with the life Jesus came to give.

WHAT TO THINK ABOUT
Philippians 4:8

Never run away with the idea that it does not matter much what we believe or think; it does. What we think and believe, we *are;* not what we say we think and believe, but what we really do think and believe, we are; there is no divorce at all. To believe, in the sense our Lord used the word, is never an intellectual act but a moral act. The following quotation from Dr. Arnold[21] of Rugby explains the way fanatics are made, and also points out the incongruity of those Christians who are sanctified and yet show an unconscionable bigotry and narrow-mindedness in their mental outlook:—

> *I am quite sure that it is a most solemn duty to cultivate our understandings to the uttermost, for I have seen the evil moral consequences of fanaticism to a greater degree than I ever expected to see them realised; and I am satisfied that a neglected intellect is far oftener the cause of mischief to a man than a perverted or over-valued one. Men retain their natural quickness and cleverness while their reason and judgement are allowed to go to ruin, and thus they do work their minds and gain influence, and are pleased at gaining it; but it is the undisciplined mind which they are exercising, instead of one wisely disciplined.*

The Freedom of Christian Thinking
Whatsoever things are true, . . . think on these things.

It is more painful to think about these things than to think about what we know, about what is old in our experience, because immediately we begin to think God's thoughts after Him we have to bring concentration to bear, and that takes time and discipline. When once the mind begins to think, the horizon is continually broadening and widening, there is a general unsettlement, and the danger is to go back to the old confined way and become fanatical and obstinate. This explains why some people who really are God's children have such an inveterate dislike of study. They do not quite call it the devil, but they come pretty near it. To give time to soak in God's truth, time to find out how to think along God's line, appears to them a snare and delusion. All the insubordination and difficulties and upsets come from the people who will not think. "Glean your thinking," says Paul, and we must do it by will. What are we doing with our brains now that we have entered into the sanctified life? The Holy Spirit energises the will to a complete mastery of the brain; then don't be a wool-gatherer mentally. If we are saved and sanctified by God's grace, it is unadulterated mental laziness on our part not to rouse ourselves up to think. It is not a question of the opportunities of learning, but of the determination to be continually renewed in the spirit of our mind.

(a) The Topic of the Things of Truth
The things of truth are things which are in keeping with the Person of Truth, the Lord Jesus Christ: "*I am . . . the Truth.*" Truth therefore means not only accuracy, but accuracy about something that corresponds with God. We must distinguish between an accurate fact and a truthful fact. The devil, sin, disease, spiritualism, are all accurate facts, but they are not truthful facts. Christian Science makes the blunder of saying that because sin is not of the nature of truth, therefore it is not a fact. But sin is a fact. The accuracy of facts and the accuracy of the facts of truth are two different things. Never say that things that are not of the truth are non-existent. There are many facts that are not of the truth, that is, they do not correspond with God, Paul says, Limit your thinking to the things that are true.

---

21. Thomas Arnold (1795–1842) was a British cleric, historian, and innovative headmaster at Rugby, the noted school for English boys.

Have you begun to discipline your mind in that way? If you have, people may pour bucket-loads of the devil's garbage over your head but it will have no more effect on you than dirt has on a crystal. Our minds are apt to be all abroad, like an octopus with its tentacles out to catch everything that comes along—newspaper garbage, spiritualistic garbage, advertisement garbage, we let them all come and make a dumping ground of our heads, and then sigh and mourn and say we cannot think right thoughts. Beware of saying you cannot help your thoughts; you can; you have all the almighty power of God to help you. We have to learn to bring every thought into captivity to the obedience of Christ, and it takes time. We want to reach it in a moment like a rocket, but it can only be done by a gradual moral discipline, and we do not like discipline, we want to do it all at once.

(b) The Topic of the Things of Honesty

Honest—"honourable" (RV), "reverend" (RV mg). The word "honest" has come down in the world, it means something noble and massive, awe-inspiring and grand, that awakens our reverence and inspires sublime thoughts, as a cathedral does. The things of honesty make a man's character sublime, and Paul counsels us to think on these things. See that there is a correspondence between a sublime piece of architecture and your character. Anything that awakens the sense of the sublime is an honourable thing. In the natural realm a sunset, a sunrise, mountain scenery, music, or poetry will awaken a sense of the sublime. In the moral world, truthfulness in action will awaken it. Truthfulness in action is different from truthfulness in speech. Truth-speaking people are an annoyance, they spank children for having imagination; they are sticklers for exact accuracy of speech and would have everyone say the same thing, like gramophone records; they drag down the meaning of truth out of its sphere. So we mean truthfulness in action, a true act all through.

Another thing that awakens the sense of the sublime is suffering that arises from the misunderstanding of those whom one esteems highest. Jesus Christ brought this suffering to the white heat of perfection; He let those He esteemed misunderstand Him foully and never once vindicated Himself, but was meek towards all His Father's dispensations for Him. That is moral sublimity. In the spiritual world, the sense of the sublime is awakened by such a life as that of Abraham, or of the Apostle Paul, or of anyone going through the trial of their faith. "Though He slay me, yet will I trust in Him." That is the most sublime utterance of faith in the Old Testament.

We are accustomed to think of honourable things in connection with the spiritual world, but there are honourable things in the natural world and in the moral world as well. We have the idea that God has only to do with the spiritual, and if the devil can succeed in keeping us with that idea, he will have a great deal of his own way; but Paul pushes the battle-line into every domain—"*whatsoever* things are honest, . . . think on these things," because behind them all is God.

(c) The Topic of the Things of Justice

Justice means rightness with God; nothing is just until it is adjusted to God. The justice of a law court is superficial exactitude between man and man. That is why we often rebel against the verdict of a law court, although its justice can be proved to the hilt. Paul is not referring to justice between man and man, but to the very essence of justice, and he knows no justice where God is ignored. The great exhibition of justice is Jesus Christ; there was no superficial exactitude in His life because He was perfectly at one with God. The standard all through the Sermon on the Mount is that of conduct arising from a right relationship to God. We say—"Oh well, I certainly would show a forgiving spirit to them if they would be right with me." Jesus said, "If ye forgive not men their trespasses, neither will your Father forgive your trespasses." Take any of the teaching of the Sermon on the Mount and you will find it is never put on the ground that because a man is right with me, therefore I will be the same to him, but always on the ground of a right relationship to Jesus Christ first, and then the showing of that same relationship to others. To look for justice from other people is a sign of deflection from devotion to Jesus Christ. Never look for justice, but never cease to give it. We think of justice in the most absurd connections—because people tread on our little notions, our sense of what is right, we call that injustice. When once we realise how we have behaved towards God all the days of our life until we became adjusted to Him through the Atonement, our attitude to our fellow men will be that of absolute humility (cf. Ephesians 4:32).

(d) The Topic of the Things of Purity

Purity is not innocence, it is much more. Purity means stainlessness, an unblemishedness that has stood the test. Purity is learned in private, never in public. Jesus Christ demands purity of mind and imagination, chastity of bodily and mental habits. The only men and women it is safe to trust are those who have been tried and have stood the test; purity is the outcome of conflict, not of necessity. You cannot trust innocence or natural goodness; you cannot trust possibilities. This explains Jesus Christ's attitude. Our Lord trusted no man (see John 2:24–25), yet He was never suspicious, never bitter; His confidence in what God's grace could do for any man was so perfect that He never despaired of anyone. If our trust is placed in human beings, we will end in despairing of every one. But when we limit our thinking to the things of purity we shall think only of what God's grace has done in others, and put our confidence in that and in nothing else. Look back over your life and see how many times you have been pierced through with wounds, and all you can say when God deals with you is, "Well, it serves me right; over and over again God taught me not to trust in myself, not to put confidence in men, and yet I have persisted in doing it." God holds us responsible for being ignorant in these matters, and the cure for ignorance is to think along the lines Paul indicates here. It will mean that we shall never stand up for our own honour, or for the honour of others; we shall stand only for the honour and the dignity of the Lord Jesus Christ. Our temperamental outlook is altered by thinking; and when God alters the disposition, temperament begins to take its tone from the new disposition. These things are not done suddenly, they are only done gradually, by the stern discipline of the life under the teaching of the Spirit of God.

(e) The Topic of the Things of Loveliness

That is, the things that are morally agreeable and pleasant. The word "lovely" has the meaning of juicy and delicious. That is the definition given by Calvin, and he is supposed to be a moloch[22] of severity! We have the idea that our duty must always be disagreeable, and we make any number of duties out of diseased sensibilities. If our duty is disagreeable, it is a sign that we are in a disjointed relationship to God. If God gave some people a fully sweet cup, they would go carefully into a churchyard and turn the cup upside down and empty it, and say, "No, that could never be meant for me." The idea has become incorporated into their make-up that their lot must always be miserable. Once we become rightly related to God, duty will never be a disagreeable thing of which we have to say with a sigh, "Oh, well, I must do my duty." Duty is the daughter of God. Never take your estimate of duty after a sleepless night, or after a dose of indigestion; take your sense of duty from the Spirit of God and the word of Jesus. There are people whose lives are diseased and twisted by a sense of duty which God never inspired; but once let them begin to think about the things of loveliness, and the healing forces that will come into their lives will be amazing. The very essence of godliness is in the things of loveliness; think about these things, says Paul.

(f) The Topic of the Things of Good Report

Literally, the things that have a fine face, a winning and attractive tone about them. What should we be like after a year of thinking on these things? We might not be fatter, but I am certain we should look pleasanter! When we do think about the things of good report we shall be astonished to realise where they are to be found; they are found where we only expected to find the opposite. When our eyes are fixed on Jesus Christ we begin to see qualities blossoming in the lives of others that we never saw there before. We see people whom we have tabooed and put on the other side exhibiting qualities we have never exhibited, although we call ourselves saved and sanctified. Never look for other people to be holy; it is a cruel thing to do, it distorts your view of yourself and of others. Could anyone have had a sterner view of sin than Jesus had, and yet had anyone a more loving, tender patience with the worst of men than He had? The difference in the attitude is that Jesus Christ never expected men to be holy; He knew they could not be: *He came to make men holy*. All He asks of men is that they acknowledge they are not right, then He will do all the rest—"Blessed are the poor in spirit." It comes back to the central message of Jesus Christ, "*I, if I be lifted up . . .*" If we preach anything other than "Jesus Christ, and Him crucified," we make our doctrines God and ourselves the judge of others. Think of the times we have hindered the Spirit of God by trying to help others when only God could help them, because we have forgotten to discipline our own minds. It is the familiar truth that we have to be stern in proclaiming God's word, let it come out in all its rugged bluntness, unwatered down and unrefined; but when we deal with others we have to remember that we are sinners saved by grace. The tendency to-day is to do exactly the opposite, we make all kinds of excuses for God's word—"Oh God does not expect us to be perfect," and when we deal with people personally we are amazingly hard.

All these things lead us back to Jesus Christ—He is the Truth; He is the Honourable One; He is the just One; He is the Pure One; He is the altogether Lovely One: He is the only One of Good Report. No matter where we start from, we will always come back to Jesus Christ.

The Frontiers of Christian Thinking

. . . if there be any virtue, and if there be any praise, think on these things.

Paul seems to come to the conclusion that he has not made the area of thinking wide enough yet, so he says, "If there is any morally excellent thing, anything whatever to praise, anything recommendable, take account of it." We are apt to discard the virtues of those who do not know Jesus Christ and call them

---

22. moloch: a tyrannical power requiring sacrifice to be appeased.

pagan virtues. Paul counsels, "If there is any virtue anywhere in the world, think about it," because the natural virtues are remnants of God's handiwork and will always lead to the one central Source, Jesus Christ. We have to form the habit of keeping our mental life on the line of the great and beautiful things Paul mentions. It is not a prescribed ground. It is we who make limitations and then blame God for them. Many of us behave like ostriches, we put our heads in the sand and forget altogether about the world outside—"I have had this and that experience and I am not going to think of anything else." After a while we have aches and pains in the greater part of ourselves, which is outside our heads, and then we find that God sanctifies every bit of us, spirit, soul and body. God grant we may get out into the larger horizons of God's Book.

Always keep in contact with those books and those people that enlarge your horizon and make it possible for you to stretch yourself mentally. The Spirit of God is always the spirit of liberty; the spirit that is not of God is the spirit of bondage, the spirit of oppression and depression. The Spirit of God convicts vividly and tensely, but He is always the Spirit of liberty. God Who made the birds never made bird-cages; it is men who make bird-cages, and after a while we become cramped and can do nothing but chirp and stand on one leg. When we get out into God's great free life, we discover that that is the way God means us to live "the glorious liberty of the children of God."

THINKING GODLINESS
Philippians 4:5–8; 3:7–14

In physical life we do best those things we have habitually learned to do, and the same is true in mental and spiritual life. We do not come into the world knowing how to do anything; all we do we have acquired by habit. Remember, habit is purely mechanical.

Thinking Habits *(Philippians 4:5)*
Our thinking processes are largely subject to the law of habit. "Let your forbearance," i.e., self-control, "be known unto all men" (RV). Self-control is nothing more than a mental habit which controls the body and mind by a dominant relationship, viz.: the immediate presence of the Lord—for "the Lord is at hand." The danger in spiritual matters is that we do not *think* godliness; we let ideas and conceptions of godliness lift us up at times, but we do not form the habit of godly thinking. Thinking godliness cannot be done in spurts, it is a steady habitual trend. God does not give us our physical habits or our mental habits; He gives us the power to form any kind of habits we like, and in the spiritual domain we have to form the habit of godly thinking.

To a child the universe is a great confusing, amazing "outsideness"; when the child grows to be a man he has the same nervous system and brain, but the will has come in and determined his tendencies and impulses. It is natural for a child to be impulsive; but it is a disgraceful thing for a man or woman to be guided by impulse. To be a creature of impulse is the ruin of mental life. The one thing our Lord checked and disciplined in the disciples was impulse; the determining factor was to be their relationship to Himself.

We are so made that our physical life gives us an affinity with every material thing; our thinking life gives us affinity with everything in the mental realm, and it is the same with our moral and spiritual life. We are held responsible by God for the way we deal with the great mass of things that come into our lives. We all have susceptibilities in every direction; everyone is made in the same way as everyone else; consequently it is not true to say we cannot understand why some people like to devote themselves to pleasure, to races and dancing, etc. If we do not understand it, it is because part of our nature has become atrophied. Whatever one human being can do, either in the way of good or bad, any human being can do. There are things we must deny, but the negation that is the outcome of ignorance is of no value whatever to the character; the denial by will is of enormous value. "If thy right eye causeth thee to stumble, pluck it out, and cast it from thee . . ." (Matthew 5:29 RV); determine to select those elements of your conscious life that are going to tell for the characteristic of godliness.

Trending Habitually *(Philippians 4:6)*
We have to watch the trend of things. The trend of our conscious life is determined by us, not by God, and Paul makes the determining factor in the conscious life of a godly person the determination to pray. Prayer is not an emotion, not a sincere desire; prayer is the most stupendous effort of the will. "Let your requests be made known unto God. And the peace of God, which passeth all understanding, shall guard your hearts and your thoughts in Christ Jesus" (RV),

the poising power of the peace of God will enable you to steer your course in the mix-up of ordinary life. We talk about "circumstances over which we have no control." None of us have control over our circumstances, but we are responsible for the way we pilot ourselves in the midst of things as they are. Two boats can sail in opposite directions in the same wind, according to the skill of the pilot. The pilot who conducts his vessel on to the rocks says he could not help it, the wind was in that direction; the one who took his vessel into the harbour had the same wind, but he knew how to trim his sails so that the wind conducted him in the direction he wanted. Never allow to yourself that you could not help this or that; and never say you reach anywhere *in spite of* circumstances; we all attain *because* of circumstances and no other way.

> Let us not always say
>   Spite of this flesh to-day
> I strove, made head, gained ground upon the whole!

Touching Habitual Fundaments *(Philippians 4:8)*

There is a difference between thinking and grinding. Such subjects as languages or mathematics require grinding, and it is no use saying we have not the mental power to grind, we have; and the more we grind the more the mechanical part of our nature will come to our aid if we keep at it uninterruptedly. When it comes to matters of imagination, different faculties are needed. Some minds are more easily put on the grind than others, and some are more easily taught on the imaginative line than others. We have to discipline ourselves along both lines. Insubordination is another name for mental laziness. Watch the difference between listening to a language lesson and to a sermon or lecture; you will be worn out in no time by the former unless you have learned to grind; but with the latter, after a few sentences, your mind is kindled through the connection of previous thinking. It is not that we are gifted in this way but that we are created in this way. Paul insists on this very law. ". . whatsoever things are true, . . . *think* on these things." Glean your thinking; don't allow your mind to be a harbourage for every kind of vagabond sentiment; resolutely get into the way of disciplining your impulses and stray thinking. The law of attention controls the mind and keeps it from shifting hither and thither.

The forming of a new habit is difficult until you get into the way of doing the thing, then everything you meet with aids you in developing along the right line. It is good practice to sit down for five minutes and do nothing; in that way you will soon discover how little control you have over yourself. In forming a new habit it is vitally important to insist on bringing the body under control first. Paul says, "I maul and

master my body, lest, after preaching to other people, I am disqualified myself" (1 Corinthians 9:27 MOFFATT). The natural man is created by God as well as the new man in Christ, and the new man has to be manifested by the natural man in his mortal flesh. Paul puts it very practically in Romans 6:19, "Your members have been used to serve the disposition of sin; now that you are made free from sin, use your members to serve the disposition of righteousness." In 1 Corinthians 10:31 he puts it still more practically: "So whether you eat or drink, or whatever you do, let it be all done for the glory of God" (MOFFATT). It is difficult to begin with, but as you go on you find it becomes easier until you are able not only to practise the presence of God in your spirit, but are able to prove by the habits of your actual life that your body is the temple of the Holy Ghost.

Native and Acquired Interests *(Philippians 3:7)*

There are some subjects that are natively interesting and other subjects for which we have to acquire an interest. A child's mind is only natively interested; an adult mind if it is well formed has voluntarily acquired an interest in other subjects. We imagine that a native interest will develop into an acquired interest all at once, but it won't. It will only become a dominant interest when it has come into the very make-up of our being. Think of the things you are interested in to-day, the things that are really forming your mind, you can remember the time when you had no affinity with them at all, they awakened no interest in you. What has happened? The Spirit of God by the engineering of God's Providence has brought some word of His and connected it with your circumstances in such a way that the whole of your outlook is altered. "The old things are passed away; behold, they are become new" (2 Corinthians 5:17 RV). *God alters the thing that matters.*

The interests of a child are altogether in the senses, and in teaching a child you must begin by interesting him. The teacher who succeeds best with children is the one who does things before them; it is no use teaching children abstract stuff. That is why it is necessary in teaching a young life, whether young in years of the flesh or the spirit, for a teacher to attend more to what he does than to what he says. The crystallising point of our Lord's teaching lies here, and the reason our Lord condemned the Pharisees was that "they say, and do not." Everyone has a perfect right to come and ask those of us who teach whether we practise what we teach. The influence of our teaching is in exact proportion to our practical doing.

In Philippians 3:7–8, Paul states that he has flung overboard the things that were natively interesting to him in order to acquire other interests which at one time were of no value to him; and now the whole of his attention is set on Jesus Christ's idea for him, "I press on, if so be that I may apprehend, seeing that also I was apprehended [mg]" (Philippians 3:12 RV). A man can go through any drudgery under heaven to attain the object he has in view. Paul's object was to win Christ, and he counted "all things to be loss" (RV), and "suffered the loss of all things," counting them but refuse, to attain his object.

Nurturing Appreciation *(Philippians 3:10)*

These words never fail to awaken a thrill of emotion in the heart of every Christian, but the question arises—"How can I become interested in these matters to the degree that the Apostle was interested in them?" The only way in which a truth can become of vital interest to me is when I am brought into the place where that truth is needed. Paul calls the people to whom the gospel is not vitally interesting, "dead"; but when once they are brought under conviction of sin, the one thing they will listen to is the thing they despised before, viz., the gospel. There is a difference between the way we try to appreciate the things of God and the way in which the Spirit of God teaches. We begin by trying to get fundamental conceptions of the creation and the world; why the devil is allowed; why sin exists. When the Spirit of God comes in He does not begin by expounding any of these subjects; He begins by giving us a dose of the plague of our own heart; He begins where our vital interests lie—in the salvation of our souls. In every Christian life spiritual sentiment is at times carried to the white heat of devotion, but the point is how can we so attend to these things that the devotion is there all the time. In spiritual life most of us progress like frogs; we jump well at times, but at other times we stay a long while in one place until God in His Providence tumbles up our circumstances. The Apostle Paul's life was not a frog jumping business, not a spasmodic life kept going by conventions and meetings, but an abiding, steadfast, attending life. If we are alive spiritually, the Spirit of God will continually prod us to attend to new phases of our salvation, and if we sit down, we sit on something that hurts. There will be always something that "bids nor sit nor stand but go!" The people who are of absolutely no use to God are those who have sat down and have become overgrown with spiritual mildew; all they can do is to refer to an experience they had twenty or thirty years ago. That is of no use whatever, we must be vitally at it all the time. With Paul it was never "an experience I once had," but *the life which I now live."*

Negotiating Associations *(Philippians 3:12–14)*

We have to build up useful associations in our minds, to learn to associate things for ourselves, and it can only be done by determination. There are ideas associated in each of our minds that are not associated in the mind of anyone else, and this accounts for the difference in individuals. For instance, learn to associate the chair you sit in with nothing else but study; associate a selected secret place with nothing but prayer. We do not sufficiently realise the power we have to infect the places in which we live and work by our prevailing habits in those places.

The law of associated ideas applied spiritually means that we must drill our minds in godly connections. How many of us have learned to associate our summer holidays with God's Divine purposes? to associate the early dawn with the early dawn on the Sea of Galilee after the Resurrection? If we learn to associate ideas that are worthy of God with all that happens in Nature, our imagination will never be at the mercy of our impulses. Spiritually, it is not a different law that works, but the same law. When once we have become accustomed to connecting these things, every ordinary occurrence will serve to fructify our minds in godly thinking because we have developed our minds along the lines laid down by the Spirit of God. It is not done once for always; it is only done *always.* Never imagine that the difficulty of doing these things belongs peculiarly to you, it belongs to every one. The character of a person is nothing more than the habitual form of his associations.

Learn to beware of marginal pre-occupations that continually provoke other associations. For instance, there are people who cultivate the margin of vision; they look at you, but out of the margin of their eye they are really occupied with something else all the time; and in the mental realm there are people who never pay attention to the subject immediately in hand, but only to the marginal subjects round about. Spiritually there is the same danger. Jesus Christ wants us to come to the place where we see things from His standpoint and are identified with His interests only. "My one thought is, by forgetting what lies behind me and straining to what lies before me, to press on to the goal . . ." (MOFFATT).

Concentration is the law of life mentally, morally and spiritually.

THE MIND OF CHRIST
Philippians 2:5–8

Have this mind in you, which was also in Christ Jesus . . . (RV)

We are apt to forget that the mind of Christ is supernatural, His mind is not a human mind at all. Never run away with the idea that because you have the Spirit of Christ, therefore you have His mind. God gives us the Spirit of Jesus, but He does not give us His mind; we have to construct the mind of Christ, and it can only be done as we work out in the habits of a holy life the things that were familiar in the life of our Lord. We cannot form the mind of Christ once for always; we have to form it *always;* that is, all the time and in everything. "Acquire your soul," i.e., the new way of looking at things, "with patience" (see Luke 21:19), and learn never to say fail! When God re-creates us in Christ Jesus He does not patch us up; He makes us *a new creation*" (RV mg). Every power of our being is no longer to be used at the dictates of our right to ourselves, but to be subordinated to the Spirit of God in us Who will enable us to form the mind of Christ.

The type of mind Paul urges us to form is prescribed clearly—the mind of true humility; the mind "which was also in Christ Jesus" when He was on this earth, utterly self-effaced and self-emptied; not the mind of Christ when He was in glory. Humility is the exhibition of the Spirit of Jesus Christ, and is the touchstone of saintliness.

His Deity and Our Dependence

Who, being [originally] in the form of God, counted it not a thing to be grasped[mg] to be on an equality with God . . . (RV)

Paul precludes the idea that Jesus thought nothing of Himself: our Lord thought truly of Himself. There was no assertion in any shape or form, and no presumption. It was along this line that Satan tempted Him—"Remember Who You are: You are the Son of God; then assert the prerogative of Sonship—command that these stones become bread; do something supernatural—cast Yourself down from hence. . . ."

It was a temptation to the fulfilment of the Incarnation by a "short cut." Each time the temptation came, our Lord "blunted" it: "I did not come here to assert Myself; I came for God's will to be done through Me in His own way" (see John 6:38). Paul connects the two things—"on an equality with God": "not a thing to be grasped." Our Lord never once asserted His dignity, He never presumed on it.

When we are sanctified, the same temptation comes to us—"You are a child of God, saved and sanctified, presume on it, think it something to be grasped." As long as our thought is fixed on our experience instead of on the God Who gave us the experience, the habit of making nothing of ourselves is an impossibility. If we think only along the line of our experience we become censorious, not humble. Sanctification is the gateway to a sanctified life, not to boasting about an experience. The habit of forming the mind of Christ will always make us obey our Lord and Master as He obeyed His Father, and there are whole domains of natural life to be brought under the control of this habit. It is not sinful to have a body and a natural life; if it were, it would be untrue to say that Jesus Christ was sinless, because He had a body and was placed in a natural life; but He continually sacrificed His natural life to the word and the will of His Father and made it a spiritual life, and we have to form the same habit. It is the discipline of a lifetime; we cannot do it all at once. We are absolutely dependent, and yet, strange to say, the last thing we learn spiritually is to make nothing of ourselves.

but emptied Himself . . . (RV)

Jesus Christ effaced the God head in Himself so effectually that men without the Spirit of God despised Him. No one without the Spirit of God, or apart from a sudden revelation from God, ever saw the true Self of Jesus while He was on earth. He was "as a root out of a dry ground," thoroughly disadvantaged in the eyes of everyone not convicted of sin. The reference in 2 Corinthians 8:9 is not to a wealthy *man* becoming poor, but to a wealthy *God* becoming poor for men. Our Lord is the time-representation of a Self-disglorified God. The purpose of the Incarnation was not to reveal the beauty and nobility of human nature, but in order to remove sin from human nature. To those who seek after wisdom the preaching of Christ crucified is foolishness; but when a man knows that his life is twisted, that the mainspring is wrong, he is in the state of heart and mind to understand why it was necessary for God to become Incarnate. The doctrine of the Self-limitation of Jesus is clear to our hearts first, not to our heads. We cannot form the mind of Christ unless we have His Spirit, nor can we understand our Lord's teaching apart from His Spirit. We cannot see through it; but when once we receive His Spirit we know implicitly what He means. Things which to the intellect may be hopelessly bewildering are lustrously clear to the heart of the humble saint (see Matthew 11:25).

taking the form of a servant . . . (RV)

Our Lord took upon Him habitually the part of a slave: "I am among you as he that serveth"; consequently He could be "put upon" to any extent, unless His Father prevented it (cf. John 19:11); or His Father's honour was at stake (cf. Mark 11:15–19). It was our Lord's right to be "in the form of God," but He renounced that right and took the form of a "bondservant" (RV mg), not the form of a noble man, but of a slave. Our Lord crowned the words that the powers of this world detest—"servant," "obedience," "humility," "service."

being made in the likeness of men . . . (RV)

That is, in "the likeness of sinful flesh" (Romans 8:3). The assimilation was as complete as our Lord's sinlessness would permit, and gave Him so truly human a life that by His fulfilling all righteousness in the face of temptation, He "condemned sin in the flesh."

> *The nature was sinless in Him because He was sinless in it, not vice versa. . . . Jesus Christ does not stand for an originally holy human nature, but a sanctified or made-holy human nature.*
>
> Du Bose

The first Adam came in the flesh, not in sinful flesh: Jesus Christ, the last Adam, came on the plane of the first Adam; He partook of our nature but not of our sin. By His mighty Atonement He can lift us into the Kingdom in which He lived while He was on this earth so that we may be able to live a life freed from sin. That is the practical point the Apostle Paul is making.

> *. . . and being found in fashion as a man, He humbled Himself, becoming obedient even unto death, yea, the death of the cross. (RV)*

Right at the threshold of His manhood our Lord took upon Him His vocation, which was to bear away the sin of the world—by *identification*, not by sympathy (John 1:29). Our Lord's object in becoming Deity Incarnate was to redeem mankind, and Satan's final onslaught in the Garden of Gethsemane was against our Lord *as Son of Man*, viz., that the purpose of His Incarnation would fail. The profundity of His agony has to do with the fulfilling of His destiny. The Cross is a triumph for *the Son of Man;* any and every man has freedom of access straight to the throne of God by right of what our Lord accomplished through His death on the Cross. *Though he was a Son*, He learned obedience *as a Saviour* by the things which He suffered, and thereby became the author of eternal salvation unto all them that obey Him.

"He was crucified through weakness." Jesus Christ represents God limiting His own power for one purpose: He died for the weak, for the ungodly, for sinners, and for no one else. "I came not to call the righteous, but sinners to repentance." No chain is stronger than its weakest link. In one aspect Jesus Christ became identified with the weakest thing in His own creation, a Baby; in another aspect He went to the depths of a bad man's hell, consequently from the babe to the vilest criminal Jesus Christ's substitution tells for salvation, nothing can prevail against Him.

The first thing the Spirit of God does in us is to efface the things we rely upon naturally. Paul argues this out in Philippians 3, he catalogues who he is and the things in which he might have confidence, "but," he says, "I deliberately renounce all these things that I may gain Christ." The continual demand to consecrate our gifts to God is the devil's counterfeit for sanctification. We have a way of saying—"What a wonderful power that man or woman would be in God's service." Reasoning on man's broken virtues makes us fix on the wrong thing. The only way any man or woman can ever be of service to God is when he or she is willing to renounce all their natural excellencies and determine to be weak in Him—"I am here for one thing only, for Jesus Christ to manifest Himself in me." That is to be the steadfast habit of a Christian's life. Whenever we think we are of use to God, we hinder Him. We have to form the habit of letting God carry on His work through us without let or hindrance[23] as He did through Jesus, and He will use us in ways He dare not let us see. We have to efface every other thought but that of Jesus Christ. It is not done once for all; we have to be always doing it. If once you have seen that Jesus Christ is All in all, make the habit of letting Him be All in all. It will mean that you not only have implicit faith that He is All in all, but that you go through the trial of your faith and prove that He is. After sanctification God delights to put us into places where He can make us wealthy. Jesus Christ counts as service not what we do for Him, but what we are to Him, and the inner secret of that is identity with Him in person. *"That I may know Him."*

His Dedication and Our Discipline

"And for their sakes I sanctify Myself" (John 17:19). How does that statement of our Lord fit in with our idea of sanctification? Sanctification must never be made synonymous with purification; Jesus Christ had

---

23. without let or hindrance: legal phrase meaning "without obstacle or impediment."

no need of purification, and yet He used the word "sanctify." In the words, "I sanctify Myself," Jesus gives the key to the saint's life. Self is not sinful; if it were, how could Jesus say "I sanctify Myself"? Jesus Christ had no sin to deny, no wrong self to deny; He had only a holy Self. It was that Self He denied all the time, and it was that Self that Satan tried to make Him obey. What could be holier than the will of the holy Son of God? and yet all through He said, "not as I will, but as Thou wilt." It was the denying of His holy Self that made the marvellous beauty of our Lord's life.

If we have entered into the experience of sanctification, what are we doing with our holy selves? Do we every morning we waken thank God that we have a self to give to Him, a self that He has purified and adjusted and baptised with the Holy Ghost so that we might sacrifice it to Him? Sacrifice in its essence is the exuberant passionate love-gift of the best I have to the one I love best. The best gift the Son of God had was His Holy Manhood, and He gave that as a love-gift to God that He might use it as an Atonement for the world. He poured out His soul unto death, and that is to be the characteristic of our lives. God is at perfect liberty to waste us if He chooses. We are sanctified for one purpose only, that we might sanctify our sanctification and give it to God.

One of the dangers of present-day teaching is that it makes us turn our eyes off Jesus Christ on to ourselves, off the Source of our salvation on to salvation itself. The effect of that is a morbid, hypersensitive life, totally unlike our Lord's life, it has not the passion of abandon that characterised Him. The New Testament never allows for a moment the idea that continually crops up in modern spiritual teaching—"I have to remember that I am a specimen of what God can do." That is inspired by the devil, never by the Spirit of God. We are not here to be specimens of what God can do, but to have our life so hid with Christ in God that our Lord's words will be true of us, that men beholding our good works will glorify our Father in heaven. There was no "show business" in the life of the Son of God, and there is to be no "show business" in the life of the saint. Concentrate on God, let Him engineer circumstances as He will, and wherever He places you He is binding up the broken-hearted through you, setting at liberty the captives through you, doing His mighty soul-saving work through you, as you keep rightly related to Him. Self-conscious service is killed, self-conscious devotion is gone, only one thing remains—"witnesses unto Me," Jesus Christ first, second and third.

"The Father abiding in Me doeth His works" (John 14:10 RV). Our Lord habitually submitted His will to His Father, that is, He engineered nothing but left room for God. The modern trend is dead against this submission; we do engineer, and engineer with all the sanctified ingenuity we have, and when God suddenly bursts in in an expected way, we are taken unawares. It is easier to engineer things than determinedly to submit all our powers to God. We say we must do all we can: Jesus says we must let God do all He can.

"As the Father taught Me, I speak these things" (John 8:28 RV). The secret of our Lord's holy speech was that He habitually submitted His intelligence to His Father. Whenever problems pressed on the human side, as they did in the temptation, our Lord had within Him self the Divine remembrance that every problem had been solved in counsel with His Father before He became Incarnate (cf. Revelation 13:8), and that therefore the one thing for Him was to do the will of His Father, and to do it in His Father's way. Satan tried to hasten Him, tried to make Him face the problems as a Man and do God's will in His own way: "The Son can do nothing of Himself, but what He seeth the Father doing" (John 5:19 RV).

Are we intellectually insubordinate, spiritually stiff-necked, dictating to God in pious phraseology what we intend to let Him make us, hunting through the Bible to back up our pet theories? Or have we learned the secret of submitting our intelligence and our reasoning to Jesus Christ's word and will as He submitted His mind to His Father?

The danger with us is that we will only submit our minds to New Testament teaching where the light of our experience shines. "If we walk in the light"—as our experience is in the light? No, "if we walk in the light *as He is in the light* . . ." We have to keep in the light that God is in, not in the rays of the light of our experience. There are phases of God's truth that cannot be experienced, and as long as we stay in the narrow grooves of our experience we shall never become Godlike, but specialists of certain doctrines—Christian oddities. We have to be specialists in devotion to Jesus Christ and in nothing else. If we want to know Jesus Christ's idea of a saint and to find out what holiness means, we must not only read pamphlets about sanctification, we must face ourselves with Jesus Christ, and as we do so He will make us face ourselves with God. "Be ye therefore perfect, even as your Father which is in heaven is perfect." When once the truth lays hold of us that we have to be God-like, it is the death-blow for ever to attempting things in our own strength. The reason we do attempt things in our own strength is that we have never had the vision of what Jesus Christ wants us to be. We have to be God-like, not good men and women. There are any number of good men and women who are not Christians.

The life of sanctification, of service and of sacrifice, is the threefold working out in our bodies of the life of Jesus until the supernatural life is the only life. These are truths that cannot be *learned*; they can only be habitually *lived*.

OUR LORD ON HOW TO THINK
Matthew 6:19–24

We so readily look upon our Lord as Saviour in the fundamental way that we are apt to forget He is much more than Saviour, He is Teacher as well. In the same way we are familiar with the fact that all Christians have the Spirit of Christ, but not all Christians have the mind of Christ. We balk this because we do not care to go into the laboriousness of forming His mind. We all have times of inspiration and ecstasy, but in these verses our Lord is not talking of times of ecstasy, but of the deliberate set of the life all through. God does His great sovereign works of grace in us and He expects us to bring all the powers under our control into harmony with what He has done. It is an arduous and difficult task, it is not done easily; and remember, God does not do it for us. We have to transform into real thinking possession for ourselves all that the Spirit of God puts into our spirits. The last reach of spirituality is the thinking power, i.e., the power to express what moves our spirit.

The Depository of Thought (Matthew 6:19–21)

Lay not up for yourselves treasures upon the earth, . . . but lay up for yourselves treasures in heaven . . . (Matthew 6:19–20 RV)

We have to lay up treasure for ourselves, it is not laid up for us; and we have to lay it up in heaven, not on earth. To begin with, we do lay up the treasure of Jesus Christ's salvation on earth, we lay it up in our bodily lives, in our circumstances; and the curse spiritually is to lay up treasure in experience. Whatever we possess in the way of treasure on earth is liable to be consumed by moth and rust. Our Lord's counsel is to lay up treasure that never can be touched, and the place where it is laid up cannot be touched. "And made us to sit with Him in the heavenly places, in Christ Jesus" (Ephesians 2:6 RV). No moth nor rust in the heavenly places, no possibility of thieves breaking through there. When we lay up treasure on earth it may go at any moment, but when we learn to lay up treasure in heaven, nothing can touch it—"therefore will not we fear, though the earth be removed. . . ." It is perfectly secure.

Our Lord kept all His treasure of heart and mind and spirit in His oneness with the Father; He laid up treasure in heaven, not on earth. Our Lord never possessed anything for Himself (cf. 2 Corinthians 8:9). The temptation of Satan was to get Him to lay up things in the earthly treasury, viz., in His own body, and to draw from that source: "You are the Son of God, command these stones to be made bread; cast Yourself down and Your Father will send His angels to take care of you." Our Lord never drew power from Himself, He drew it always from without Himself, that is, from His Father. "The Son can do nothing of Himself, but what He seeth the Father do" (John 5:19). The one great interest in our Lord's life was God, and He was never deflected from that centre by other considerations, not even by the devil himself, however subtly he came. "I and my Father are one." It was a oneness not of union, but of identity. It was impossible to distinguish between the Father and the Son, and the same is to be true of the saint and the Saviour: "that they may be one, even as We are one."

Examine your own experience as a saint and see where your treasure is: is it in the Lord, or in His blessings? In the degree that we possess anything for ourselves we are separated from Jesus. So many of us are caught up in the shows of things, not in the way of property and possessions, but of blessings, and all our efforts to persuade ourselves that our treasure is in heaven is a sure sign that it is not. If our treasure is in heaven we do not need to persuade ourselves that it is, we prove it is by the way we deal with matters of earth. The religion of Jesus Christ is a religion of personal relationship to God and has nothing to do with possessions. A sense of possessions is sufficient to render us spiritually dense because what we possess often possesses us. Whenever our Lord spoke of "life" He meant the kind of life He lived, and He says, "ye have not [this] life in yourselves" (John 6:53 RV). Are we living the kind of life Jesus lived, with the skylights always open towards God, the windows of the ground floor open towards men, and the trap-door open towards sin and Satan and hell? Nothing was hidden from Jesus, all was faced with fearless courage because of His oneness with the Father.

"For where your treasure is, there will your heart be also . . ." The Bible term "heart" is best understood if we simply say "me," it is the central citadel of a man's personality. The heart is the altar of which the physical body is the outer court, and whatever is offered on the altar of the heart will tell ultimately through the extremities of the body. "Keep thy heart with all diligence; for out of it are the issues of life."

Where do we make our depository of thinking? What do we brood on most, the blessings of God, or God Himself? Look back over your life as a saint and you will see how the weaning has gone on from the blessing to the Blesser, from sanctification to the Sanctifier. When we no longer seek God for His blessings, we have time to seek Him for Himself.

The Division of Thinking *(Matthew 6:22–23)*
The lamp of the body is the eye: if therefore thine eye be single, thy whole body shall be full of light . . . (Matthew 6:22 RV)

The eye records exactly what it looks at, and conscience may be called the eye of the soul. A "single[24] eye" is essential to correct understanding spiritually. If the spirit is illumined by a conscience which has been rightly adjusted, then, says Jesus, the whole body is full of light because body, soul and spirit are united in a single identity with Himself. Beware of mistaking domination for identity. Identity is a oneness between two distinct persons in which neither person dominates, but the oneness dominates both. The only way this can be realised is along the line of our Lord's own life. Jesus Christ's first obedience was to the will of His Father, and our first obedience is to be to Him. The thing that detects where we live spiritually is the word "obey." The natural heart of man hates the word, and that hatred is the essence of the disposition that will not let Jesus Christ rule. The characteristic of our Lord's life was submission to His Father, not the crushing down of His own will to His Father's, but the love-agreement of His will with His Father's—"I am here for one thing only, to do Thy will, and I delight to do it." When the Holy Spirit comes into us, the first thing He does is to make us men and women with a single motive, a "single eye" for the glory of God. The essential element in the life of a saint is simplicity— "thy whole body shall be full of light."

"*But if thine eye be evil, thy whole body shall be full of darkness . . .*" What is an evil eye? Thinking that springs from our own point of view. "Is thine eye evil, because I am good?" (Matthew 20:15). Jesus says that if our eye is evil, we shall misjudge what He does. If our spirits are untouched by God's Spirit, unillumined by God, the very light we have will become darkness. The disposition of the natural man, my claim to my right to myself, banks on things of which our Lord makes nothing, e.g., possessions, rights, self-realisation; and if that disposition rules, it will cause the whole body to be full of darkness. Darkness in this connection is our own point of view; light is God's point of view (cf. 1 John 1:7).

We deal much too lightly with sin; we deal with sin only in its gross actual form and rarely deal with it in its possessing form. "Howbeit, I had not known sin, except through the law: for I had not known cov-eting, except the law had said, Thou shalt not covet" (Romans 7:7 RV). This inheritance of covetousness is the very essence of sin, and the only thing that can touch it is the Atonement of our Lord Jesus Christ. It is an aspect of sin which is not familiar to us. We must never lay the flattering unction to our souls that because we are not covetous of money or worldly possessions, we are not covetous of anything. Whatever we possess for ourselves is of the nature of sin. The fuss and distress of owning anything is the last remnant of the disposition of sin; whatever we own as Christians apart from Jesus Christ is a chance for the devil.

The Decisions of the Thinker
. . . No man can serve two masters. . . . Ye cannot serve God and mammon. (Matthew 6:24)

Have we allowed these inexorable decisions of our Lord to have their powerful way in our thinking? The line of detachment runs all through our Lord's teaching: You cannot be good and bad at the same time; you cannot serve God and make your own out of the service; you cannot make "honesty is the best policy" a motive, because immediately you do, you cease to be honest. There is to be only one consideration, a right relationship with God, and we must see that that relationship is never dimmed. Never compromise with the spirit of mammon. It is easy to associate mammon only with sordid things; mammon is the system of civilised life which organises itself without any consideration of God (cf. Luke 16:15).

To be detached from our possessions is the greatest evidence that we are beginning to form the mind of Christ. If it is possible to conceive being caused sore distress through the withdrawal of any particular form of blessing, it is a sure sign that we are still trying to serve two masters. For instance, can we say, not with our lips, but with our whole souls, "For I could wish that myself were accursed from Christ for my brethren"? Have we for one second got hold of the spirit that was in Paul when he said that, the very spirit of Jesus? Neither fear of hell nor hope of heaven has anything to do with our personal relationship to Jesus Christ, it is a life hid with Christ in God, stripped of all possessions saving the knowledge of Him. The great lodestar of the life is Jesus Himself, not anything He does for us.

This kind of thinking is impossible until we are spiritual, and when we become spiritual we realise how completely our thinking has been reconstructed. Watch God's method of teaching us to think along the lines He has taken our spirits by His grace. In the initial

---

24. single: pure; unmixed.

stages we learn that we cannot serve two masters by recognising the disposition that Paul calls "the carnal mind," and are only too passionately grateful to come to the place where we know that that disposition is identified with the death of Jesus (Romans 6:6). No wonder Paul says "the carnal mind is enmity against God"; he does not say it is "at enmity," it *is* enmity against God. The carnal mind is the brother of the devil; he is all right until you bring him in contact with Jesus, but immediately you do he is a chip of the old block, he hates with an intense vehemence everything to do with Jesus Christ and His Spirit. "My right to myself" is the carnal mind in essence, and we need a clear thinking view of what it means to be delivered from this disposition. It means that just as our personality used to exhibit a ruling disposition identical with the prince of this world, so the same personality can now exhibit an identity with the Lord Jesus Christ. Sanctification means that and nothing less. Sanctification is not *once for all, but once for always*. Sanctification is an instantaneous, continuous work of grace. If we think of sanctification as an experience once for all, there is an element of finality about it; we begin the hop, skip and jump testimony, "Bless God, I am saved and sanctified," and from that second we begin to get *"scantified."* Sanctification means we have the glorious opportunity of proving daily, hourly, momentarily, this identity with Jesus Christ, and the life bears an unmistakable likeness to Him. The religion of Jesus Christ makes a man united, we are never meant to develop one part of our being at the cost of another part. When we are united with Jesus He garrisons every part, "and that wicked one toucheth him not."

Another way by which we learn that we cannot serve two masters is by putting away the aim of successful service for ever. When the seventy returned with joy, our Lord said, in effect, "Don't rejoice that the devils are subject unto you, that is My authority through you; but rejoice that you are rightly related to Me." It is sadly true that after an experience of sanctification many do try and serve two masters, they go into the joy of successful service, and slowly the eye becomes fixed on the sanctified "show business" instead of on Jesus Himself. The only illustrations our Lord used of service were those of the vine (John 15:1–6), and the rivers of living water (John 7:37–39). It is inconceivable to think of the vine delighting in its own grapes; all that the vine is conscious of is the husbandman's pruning knife. All that the one out of whom rivers of living water are flowing is conscious of is belief in Jesus, and maintaining a right relationship to Him. Are we bringing forth fruit? We certainly are if we are identified with the Lord, luscious bunches of grapes for the Husbandman to do what He likes with. Pay attention to the Source, believe in Jesus, and God will look after the outflow. God grant we may let the Holy Ghost work out His passion for souls through us. We have not to imitate Jesus by having a passion for souls like His, but to let the Holy Ghost so identify us with Jesus that His mind is expressed through us as He expressed the mind of God.

Do we recognise Jesus Christ as our Teacher, or are we being led by vague spiritual impulses of our own? We have to learn to bring into captivity every thought to the obedience of Christ, and never be intellectually insubordinate. The teaching of Jesus Christ fits every point of a saint's life, but no point of the life of a natural man. If we apply these statements—"Seek ye first the kingdom of God and His righteousness. . . ." "Take no thought for your life. . . ."—to the life of a natural man, they are open to ridicule. We reverse God's order when we put Jesus as a Teacher first instead of Saviour; but when we are rightly related to God on the basis of the Atonement and begin to put Jesus Christ's teaching into practice, the marvel of marvels is we find it can be worked out. If we as saints are strenuously seeking first the kingdom of God and His righteousness, His "in-the-rightness," all the time, we shall find not only the Divine un-reason of things, but the Divine reason of things working out beyond all our calculations—"and all these things shall be added unto you"; "for your heavenly Father knoweth that ye have need of all these things."

Never allow anything to fuss your relationship to Jesus Christ, neither Christian work, nor Christian blessing, nor Christian anything. Jesus Christ first, second and third; and God Himself by the great indwelling power of the Spirit within will meet the strenuous effort on your part, and slowly and surely you will form the mind of Christ and become one with Him as He was one with the Father. The practical test is—"Is Jesus Christ being manifested in my bodily life?"

EDUCATION IN HOLY HABIT
Psalms 86:11; 143:10

Educative Evangelism *versus* Emotional Evangelism

After a great crisis, such as an experience of salvation or sanctification, the danger is that we fix ourselves there and become spiritual prigs. A spiritual prig is one who has had an experience from God and has closed down on it, there is no further progress, no manifestation of the graces of the Spirit. The world pours contempt on that kind of Christian; they seem to have very little conscience, no judgement, and little will. We have to remember that unless we are energised by the Spirit of God, the margins of our spirits retain the damage done by the Fall.

By the Fall man not only died from God but fell into disunion with himself; that means it became possible for man to live in one of the three parts of his nature. What happens at new birth is that a man is not only introduced into a relationship to God, but into union with himself. The one thing that is essential to the new life is obedience to the Spirit of God Who energises our spirits, and that obedience must be complete in body, soul and spirit. It is not done suddenly. Salvation is sudden, but the working of it out in our lives is never sudden. It is moment by moment, here a little and there a little. God educates us down to the scruple. The area of our conscious life gradually gets broader and broader, and we begin to bring into line with the new life things we never thought of before.

We have to remember that we have a bodily machine which we must regulate, God does not regulate it for us. Until we learn to bring the bodily machine into harmony with God's Will, there will be friction, and the friction is a warning that part of the machine is not in working order. As we bring our bodily life into line bit by bit we shall find that we have God's marvellous grace on the inside enabling us to work out what He has worked in.

The Habit of a Refined Conscience *(Psalm 86:11)*

Teach me Thy way, O LORD.

Conscience is that power in a man's soul that fixes on what he regards as the highest. Never call conscience the voice of God. If it were, it would be the most contradictory voice man ever listened to. For instance, Saul of Tarsus obeyed his conscience when he hounded men and women to death for worshipping Jesus Christ, and he also obeyed his conscience when later on in his life he acted in exactly the opposite way (see John 16:2; Acts 26:9).

(a) *Regulated after Sin (1 Timothy 1:12–15)*

After the disposition of sin is removed there is the need for conscience to be regulated. The Spirit of God always begins by repairing the damage after sin. The Apostle Paul argues in Romans 6, "You did use your members as servants of the wrong disposition, now use them as servants of the right disposition." It is a long way to go and many of us faint in the way. After a great spiritual crisis a man's conscience looks out towards God in a new light, the light which Jesus Christ throws upon God, and he has to walk in that light and bring his bodily life into harmony with what his conscience records.

Sin is the disposition of my right to myself, and it is also independence of God. These two aspects of sin are strikingly brought out in the Bible. Sin has to be dealt with from the ethical and intellectual aspect as well as from the spiritual aspect. The way sin works in connection with the life of the soul is in independence of God. Many people are never guilty of gross sins, they are not brought up in that way, they are too refined, have too much good taste; but that does not mean that the disposition to sin is not there. The essence of sin is my claim to my right to myself. I may prefer to live morally because it is better for me: I am responsible to no one, my conscience is my god. That is the very essence of sin. The true characteristic of sin is seen when we compare ourselves with Jesus Christ. We may feel quite happy and contented as long as we compare ourselves with other people, because we are all pretty much the same; but when we stand before Jesus Christ we realise what He meant when He said, "If I had not come, . . . they had not had sin: but now they have no cloke for their sin."

There is a difference between a refined conscience towards God and the fussy conscience of a hyperconscientious person without the Spirit of God. Hyperconscientious people are an absolute plague to live with, they are morally and spiritually nervous, always in terror expecting something to happen, always expecting trials, and they always come. Jesus Christ was never morally or spiritually nervous any more than He was physically nervous. The refinement of conscience in a Christian means learning to walk in accordance with the life of the Lord Jesus, drawing from God as He did. It is a life of absolute largeness and freedom.

(b) *Restored after Prejudice (Acts 26:4–5)*

Prejudice means a foreclosed judgement without sufficiently weighing the evidence. When first we get right with God we are all prejudiced, ugly and distorted. When we come up against a prejudice we are stubborn and obstinate, and God leaves us alone; then the prejudice comes up again, and God waits, until at last we say "I see," and we learn how to be restored after our prejudices. Wherever there is a prejudice, the grace of God is hammering at it to break it down. The havoc in lives that are going on with God is accounted for because they are being restored after prejudice. Wherever you find a prejudice in yourself, take it to Jesus Christ. Our Lord is the only standard for prejudice, as He is the only standard for sin. Our Lord never worked from prejudice, never foreclosed His judgement without weighing the evidence. Are we letting God restore us after prejudice, or are we tied up in compartments? "I have always worshipped God in this way and I always intend to." Be careful! "I have always believed this and that, and I always shall." Be careful!

It is easier to be true to convictions formed in a vivid religious experience than to be true to Jesus Christ, because if we are going true to Jesus Christ our convictions have to be altered. Unless our experiences lead us on to a life, they will turn us into fossils; we will become mummified gramophones of convictions instead of "witnesses unto Me." Some of us are no good unless we are placed in the circumstances in which our convictions were formed; but God continually stirs up our circumstances and flings us out to make us know that the only simplicity is not the simplicity of a logical belief, but of a maintained relationship with Jesus Christ, and that is never altered in any circumstances. We must keep in unbroken touch with God by faith, and see that we give other souls the same freedom and liberty that God gives us. The duty of every Christian, and it is the last lesson we learn, is to make room for God to deal with other people direct; we will try and limit others and make them into our mould.

(c) Roused after Compromise (1 Thessalonians 2:10–12)

In the temptation of our Lord the compromise for good ends is pictured, "Don't be so stern against sin; compromise judiciously with evil and You will easily win Your Kingship of men." When we become rightly related to God our intellect is apt to say exactly the same thing, "Don't be narrow; don't be so pronounced against worldliness, you will upset your friends." Well, upset them, but never upset the main thing that God is after. There is always the tendency to compromise and we have to be roused up to recognise it. We have to walk in very narrow paths before God can trust us to walk in the wide ones. We have to be limited before we can be un-limited.

The Bible nowhere teaches us to be uncompromising in our opinions. Jesus did not say, "Leap for joy when men separate you from their company for the sake of your convictions"; He said, "Leap for joy when men cast out your name as evil, *for the Son of Man's sake.*" I may be such a pig-headed cross-patch, and have such determined notions of my own, that no one can live with me. That is not suffering for the Son of Man's sake, it is suffering for my own sake. Never compromise with anything that would detract from the honour of the Lord. Remember that the honour of Jesus is at stake in your bodily life and rouse yourself up to act accordingly.

The Habit of Reliable Judgement (Psalm 143:10)
Teach me to do Thy will.

Our conscience may be right towards God, and yet we may err in judgement. When the disposition has been perfectly adjusted towards God, it does not mean we have a perfectly adjusted body and brain; we have the same body and brain as before and we have to bring them into line until we form the judgement that is according to Jesus Christ. Many of us are impulsive spiritually and we live to be sorry for it. We have to form the habit of reliable judgement. God never gives us reliable judgement; He gives us a disposition which leads to a perfect judgement if we will work out that disposition.

(a) The Disciplined Imagination (2 Corinthians 10:5)

We have to practise the submitting of our intelligence to Jesus Christ in His word. The imagination of a saint too often is vague and intractable. We have to learn to bring every thought and imagination into captivity to the obedience of Christ. An undisciplined imagination will destroy reliable judgement more quickly even than sin. Mental and spiritual insubordination is the mark of to-day. Jesus Christ submitted His intelligence to His Father. Do I submit my intelligence to Jesus Christ and His word?

(b) The Illuminated Judgement (1 Corinthians 4:5)

We have to learn to see things from Jesus Christ's standpoint. Our judgement is warped in every particular in which we do not allow it to be illuminated by Jesus Christ. For instance, if we listen to what our Lord says about money we shall see how we disbelieve Him. We quietly ignore all He says, He is so unpractical, so utterly stupid from the modern standpoint. "Seek ye first the kingdom of God and His righteousness; and all these things shall be added unto you." Which one of us believes that? If we are the children of God He will bring us into circumstances where we will be tested on every line to see whether we will form the habit of reliable judgement. We have to learn to see things from Jesus Christ's standpoint. He says, "All power is given unto Me. . . ." The illumination of judgement comes personally when we recognise that the evil and wrong in our sphere of life is there not by accident, but in order that the power of God may come in contact with it as His power has come into us. When we come into contact with objectionable people the first natural impulse of the heart is to ask God to save them because they are a trial to us; He will never do it for that reason. But when we come to see those lives from Jesus Christ's standpoint and realise that He loves them as He loves us, we have a different relation ship to them, and God can have His way in their lives in answer to our prayer.

(c) The Resourcefulness of Tact (1 Corinthians 9:19–23)

It is instructive to notice the way our Lord dealt with different people. In every case where He did not find bigotry He won them straight away. When we first become rightly related to God we have the idea that we have to talk to everyone, until we get one or two well deserved snubs; then our Lord takes us aside and teaches us His way of dealing with them. How impatient we are in dealing with others! Our attitude implies that we think God is asleep. When we begin to reason and work in God's way, He reminds us first of all how long it took Him to get us where we are, and we realise His amazing patience and we learn to come on other lives from above. As we learn to rely on the Spirit of God He gives us the resourcefulness of Jesus.

The Habit of a Rectified Will *(Psalm 86:11)*
Unite my heart to fear Thy name.

Never look upon the will as something you possess as you do a watch. Will is the whole man active. Education in holy habit is along this line: at first we pray "Teach me Thy way, O Lord"; then we pray, "Teach me to do Thy will," and step by step God teaches us what is His will; then comes a great burst of joy, "I delight to do Thy will! There is nothing on earth I delight in more than in Thy will." When we become rightly related to God we *are* the will of God in disposition, and we have to work out God's will; it is the freest, most natural life imaginable. Worldly people imagine that the saints must find it difficult to live with so many restrictions, but the bondage is with the world, not with the saints. There is no such thing as freedom in the world, and the higher we go in the social life the more bondage there is. True liberty exists only where the soul has the holy scorn of the Holy Ghost—I will bow my neck to no yoke but the yoke of the Lord Jesus Christ; there is only one law, and that is the law of God.

(a) The Joy of Jesus (John 15:11)
The joy of Jesus lay in knowing that every power of His nature was in such harmony with His Father that He did His Father's will with delight. Some of us are slow to do God's will; we do it as if our shoes were iron and lead; we do it with a great sigh and with the corners of our mouths down, as if His will were the most arduous thing on earth. But when our wills are rectified and brought into harmony with God, it is a delight, a superabounding joy, to do God's will. Talk to a saint about suffering and he looks at you in amazement—"Suffering? Where does it come in?" It comes in on God's side along the line of interpretation; on the side of the saint it is an overwhelming delight in God; not delight in suffering, but if God's will should lead through suffering, there is delight in His will.

(b) The Bent of Obedience (John 15:14)
Each one of us has to rule, to exercise some authority. When we have learned the obedience to God which was manifested in our Lord, we shall govern the world. Self-chosen authority is an impertinence. Jesus said that the great ones in this world exercise authority but that in His Kingdom it is not so; no one exercises authority over another because in His Kingdom the King is Servant of all (see Luke 22:24–27). If a saint tries to exercise authority it is a proof that he is not rightly related to Jesus Christ. The characteristic of a saint's life is this bent of obedience, no notion of authority anywhere about it. If we begin to say "I have been put in this position and I have to exercise authority," God will soon remove us. When there is steadfast obedience to Jesus, it is the authority of God that comes through and other souls obey at once.

(c) The Stage of Rare Fruition (John 15:5, 8)
These verses refer to the stage of fruition—bringing forth fruit and the fruit remaining, that is what glorifies God and blesses others. If we as preachers or teachers are rightly related to God in obedience, God is continually pouring through us. When we stop obeying Him, everything becomes as hard and dry as a ditch in mid summer. When we are placed in a position by God and we keep rightly related to Him, He will see to the supply. Personally, whenever there is dryness I know that it is because I am forgetting some particular point in relation to my own life with God; when that is put right the flow is unhindered, and I believe this is true in every phase of work for God. If you are called to preach, preach; if you are called to teach, teach. Keep obedient to God on that line. The proof that you are on God's line is that other people never credit you with what comes through you. Jesus said, "Let your light so shine before men, that they may see your good works, and glorify your Father which is in heaven." Go on doing God's will, and you will be recreated while you do it.

My Utmost for His Highest

Selections for the Year
Oswald Chambers

INTRODUCTION

Source

These readings are selected from lectures and sermons given by Oswald Chambers from 1910 until his death in 1917.

Publication History

- As a book: *My Utmost for His Highest* was first published in 1927.

My Utmost is the best-known of the Oswald Chambers books and the one with which most people are familiar. Mrs. Chambers compiled excerpts taken from all of Oswald's spoken messages, which she recorded in shorthand during the seven years of their marriage.

Mrs. Chambers worked on the book for nearly three years while supporting herself and her daughter, Kathleen,[1] by running a boarding house for university students in Oxford, England. Many of the daily readings contain material on a single theme gleaned from two or three different messages.

Most of the material in *My Utmost* appears in the other published books, but some of it does not, particularly that from Oswald's talks during the weekly devotional hour at the Bible Training College.[2] Those messages came from his heart to the students and were neither lectures nor sermons but talks about their life of faith and their walk with God. The devotional hour talks followed no theme or pattern, and many were never published in the *BTC Journal*[3] or as books.

My Utmost for His Highest has been translated into at least twenty-five languages and has been continuously in print since it was first published in 1927.

Throughout *My Utmost*, all mentions of "this College" refer to the Bible Training College, London.

Bible references noted MOFFATT are from James Moffatt's translation of the New Testament, published in 1913.

---

1. Kathleen Chambers (1913–1997): the only child of Oswald and Biddy Chambers.
2. Bible Training College (BTC): residential school near Clapham Common in southwest London; sponsored by the League of Prayer and operated from 1911 until it closed in July 1915 because of World War I. Oswald Chambers was principal and main teacher; Biddy Chambers, his wife, was lady superintendent.
3. The *Bible Training Course Journal*: published from 1932 to 1952 by Mrs. Chambers, with help from David Lambert.

FOREWORD (TO THE FIRST EDITION)

These daily readings have been selected from various sources, chiefly from the lectures given at the Bible Training College, Clapham, during the years 1911–1915; then, from October 1915 to November 1917, from talks given night by night in the Y.M.C.A. Huts, Zeitoun, Egypt.[4] In November 1917 my husband entered God's presence. Since then many of the talks have been published in book form, and others from which these readings have been gathered will also be published in due course.

A large proportion of the readings have been chosen from the talks given during the Devotional Hour at the College.[5]

Men return again and again to the few who have mastered the spiritual secret, whose life has been hid with Christ in God. These are of the old-time religion, hung to the nails of the Cross. (Robert Murray McCheyne)[6]

It is because it is felt that the author is one to whose teaching men will return, that this book has been prepared, and it is sent out with the prayer that day by day the messages may continue to bring the quickening life and inspiration of the Holy Spirit.

B. C.[7]
200 Woodstock Road
Oxford
October 1927

To the Students of the Bible Training College

For His Name's sake they went forth. . . .
Witnesses unto Me . . . unto the uttermost part of the earth

---

4. Zeitoun (zay TOON), Egypt: six miles northeast of Cairo; site of a YMCA camp, the Egypt General Mission compound, and, from 1916 to 1919, the Imperial School of Instruction, training base for British, Australian, and New Zealand troops during World War I.

5. the College: the Bible Training College (BTC)—an hour which for many of the students marked an epoch in their life with God.

6. Robert Murray McCheyne (1813–1843): Scottish minister whose short but intense life left a great impact on Scotland.

7. B. C., Biddy Chambers; although editor, compiler, and often publisher, she never identified herself by name in any of the books.

JANUARY 1

LET US KEEP TO THE POINT

My eager desire and hope being that I may never feel ashamed, but that now as ever I may do honour to Christ in my own person by fearless courage. Philippians 1:20 (MOFFATT)

My Utmost for His Highest. "My eager desire and hope being that I may never feel ashamed." We shall all feel very much ashamed if we do not yield to Jesus on the point He has asked us to yield to Him. Paul says—"My determination is to be my utmost for His Highest." To get there is a question of will, not of debate nor of reasoning, but a surrender of will, an absolute and irrevocable surrender on that point. An over-weening consideration for ourselves is the thing that keeps us from that decision, though we put it that we are considering others. When we consider what it will cost others if we obey the call of Jesus, we tell God He does not know what our obedience will mean. Keep to the point; He does know. Shut out every other consideration and keep yourself before God for this one thing only—"My Utmost for His Highest." I am determined to be absolutely and entirely for Him and for Him alone.

My Undeterredness for His Holiness. "Whether that means life or death, no matter!" (v. 21 MOFFATT). Paul is determined that nothing shall deter him from doing exactly what God wants. God's order has to work up to a crisis in our lives because we will not heed the gentler way. He brings us to the place where He asks us to be our utmost for Him, and we begin to debate; then He produces a providential crisis where we have to decide—for or against, and from that point the "Great Divide" begins.

If the crisis has come to you on any line, surrender your will to Him absolutely and irrevocably.

JANUARY 2

WILL YOU GO OUT WITHOUT KNOWING?

He went out, not knowing whither he went. Hebrews 11:8

Have you been "out" in this way? If so, there is no logical statement possible when anyone asks you what you are doing. One of the difficulties in Christian work is this question—"What do you expect to do?" You do not know what you are going to do; the only thing you know is that God knows what He is doing. Continually revise your attitude towards God and see if it is a going out of everything, trusting in God entirely. It is

this attitude that keeps you in perpetual wonder—you do not know what God is going to do next. Each morning you wake it is to be a "going out," building in confidence on God. "Take no thought for your life, . . . nor yet for your body"—take no thought for the things for which you did take thought before you "went out."

Have you been asking God what He is going to do? He will never tell you. God does not tell you what He is going to do; He reveals to you Who He is. Do you believe in a miracle-working God, and will you go out in surrender to Him until you are not surprised an atom at anything He does?

Suppose God is the God you know Him to be when you are nearest to Him, what an impertinence worry is! Let the attitude of the life be a continual "going out" in dependence upon God, and your life will have an ineffable charm about it which is a satisfaction to Jesus. You have to learn to go out of convictions, out of creeds, out of experiences, until, so far as your faith is concerned, there is nothing between yourself and God.

JANUARY 3

CLOUDS AND DARKNESS

Clouds and darkness are round about Him. Psalm 97:2

A man who has not been born of the Spirit of God will tell you that the teachings of Jesus are simple. But when you are baptised with the Holy Ghost, you find "clouds and darkness are round about Him." When we come into close contact with the teachings of Jesus Christ we have our first insight into this aspect of things. The only possibility of understanding the teaching of Jesus is by the light of the Spirit of God on the inside. If we have never had the experience of taking our commonplace religious shoes off our commonplace religious feet, and getting rid of all the undue familiarity with which we approach God, it is questionable whether we have ever stood in His presence. The people who are flippant and familiar are those who have never yet been introduced to Jesus Christ. After the amazing delight and liberty of realising what Jesus Christ *does*, comes the impenetrable darkness of realising Who He *is*.

Jesus said: "The words that I speak unto you," not—"the words I have spoken"— "they are spirit, and they are life." The Bible has been so many words to us—clouds and darkness, then all of a sudden the words become spirit and life because Jesus re-speaks them to us in a particular condition. That is the way God speaks to us, not by visions and dreams, but by words. When a man gets to God it is by the most simple way of words.

JANUARY 4

WHY CANNOT I FOLLOW THEE NOW?

Peter said unto Him, Lord, why cannot I follow Thee now? John 13:37

There are times when you cannot understand why you cannot do what you want to do. When God brings the blank space, see that you do not fill it in, but wait. The blank space may come in order to teach you what sanctification means; or it may come after sanctification to teach you what service means. Never run before God's guidance. If there is the slightest doubt, then He is not guiding. Whenever there is doubt—*don't.*

In the beginning you may see clearly what God's will is—the severance of a friendship, the breaking off of a business relationship, something you feel distinctly before God is His will for you to do, never do it on the impulse of that feeling. If you do, you will end in making difficulties that will take years of time to put right. Wait for God's time to bring it round and He will do it without any heartbreak or disappointment. When it is a question of the providential will of God, wait for God to move.

Peter did not wait on God, he forecast in his mind where the test would come, and the test came where he did not expect it. "I will lay down my life for Thy sake." Peter's declaration was honest but ignorant. "Jesus answered him . . . The cock shall not crow, till thou hast denied Me thrice." This was said with a deeper knowledge of Peter than Peter had of himself. He could not follow Jesus because he did not know himself, or of what he was capable. Natural devotion may be all very well to attract us to Jesus, to make us feel His fascination, but it will never make us disciples. Natural devotion will always deny Jesus somewhere or other.

JANUARY 5

THE AFTERWARDS OF THE LIFE OF POWER

Whither I go, thou canst not follow Me now; but thou shalt follow Me afterwards. John 13:36

"And when He had spoken this, He saith unto him, Follow Me." Three years before, Jesus had said—"Follow Me," and Peter had followed easily, the fascination of Jesus was upon him, he did not need the Holy Spirit to help him to do it. Then he came to the place where he denied Jesus, and his heart broke. Then he received the Holy Spirit, and now Jesus says again—"Follow Me." There is no figure in front now saving the Lord Jesus Christ. The first "Follow Me" had nothing mystical in it, it was an external following; now it is a following in internal martyrdom (cf. John 21:18).

Between these times Peter had denied Jesus with oaths and curses, he had come to the end of himself and all his self-sufficiency; there was not one strand of himself he would ever rely upon again, and in his destitution he was in a fit condition to receive an impartation from the risen Lord. "He breathed on them, and saith unto them, Receive ye the Holy Ghost." No matter what changes God has wrought in you, never rely upon them, build only on a Person, the Lord Jesus Christ, and on the Spirit He gives.

All our vows and resolutions end in denial because we have no power to carry them out. When we have come to the end of ourselves, not in imagination but really, we are able to receive the Holy Spirit. "*Receive ye the Holy Ghost*"—the idea is that of invasion. There is only one lodestar in the life now, the Lord Jesus Christ.

JANUARY 6

WORSHIP

And he . . . pitched his tent, having Beth-el on the west, and Ai on the east: and there he builded an altar. Genesis 12:8 (RV)

Worship is giving God the best that He has given you. Be careful what you do with the best you have. Whenever you get a blessing from God, give it back to Him as a love gift. Take time to meditate before God and offer the blessing back to Him in a deliberate act of worship. If you hoard a thing for yourself, it will turn into spiritual dry rot, as the manna did when it was hoarded. God will never let you hold a spiritual thing for yourself; it has to be given back to Him that He may make it a blessing to others.

Bethel is the symbol of communion with God; Ai is the symbol of the world. Abraham pitched his tent between the two. The measure of the worth of our public activity for God is the private profound communion we have with Him. Rush is wrong every time; there is always plenty of time to worship God. Quiet days with God may be a snare. We have to pitch our tents where we shall always have quiet times with God, however noisy our times with the world may be. There are not three stages in spiritual life—worship, waiting and work. Some of us go in jumps like spiritual frogs, we jump from worship to waiting, and from waiting to work. God's idea is that the three should go together. They were always together in the life of Our Lord. He was unhasting and unresting. It is a discipline, we cannot get into it all at once.

JANUARY 7

INTIMATE WITH JESUS

Have I been so long with you, and yet hast thou not known Me? John 14:9

These words are not spoken as a rebuke, nor even with surprise; Jesus is leading Philip on. The last One with whom we get intimate is Jesus. Before Pentecost the disciples knew Jesus as the One Who gave them power to conquer demons and to bring about a revival (see Luke 10:18–20). It was a wonderful intimacy, but there was a much closer intimacy to come—"I have called you friends." Friendship is rare on earth. It means identity in thought and heart and spirit. The whole discipline of life is to enable us to enter into this closest relationship with Jesus Christ. We receive His blessings and know His word, but do we know Him?

Jesus said—"It is expedient for you that I go away"—in that relationship, so that He might lead them on. It is a joy to Jesus when a disciple takes time to step more intimately with Him. Fruitbearing is always mentioned as the manifestation of an intimate union with Jesus Christ (John 15:1–4).

When once we get intimate with Jesus we are never lonely, we never need sympathy, we can pour out all the time without being pathetic. The saint who is intimate with Jesus will never leave impressions of himself, but only the impression that Jesus is having unhindered way, because the last abyss of his nature has been satisfied by Him. The only impression left by such a life is that of the strong calm sanity that Our Lord gives to those who are intimate with Him.

JANUARY 8

DOES MY SACRIFICE LIVE?

And Abraham built an altar . . . and bound Isaac his son. Genesis 22:9

This incident is a picture of the blunder we make in thinking that the final thing God wants of us is the sacrifice of death. What God wants is the sacrifice *through* death which enables us to do what Jesus did, viz., sacrifice our lives. Not "I am willing to go to death with Thee," but, "I am willing to be identified with Thy death so that I may sacrifice my life to God." We seem to think that God wants us to give up things! God purified Abraham from this blunder, and the same discipline goes on in our lives. God nowhere tells us to give up things for the sake of giving them up. He tells us to give them up for the sake of the only thing worth having, viz., life with Himself. It is a question of loosening the bands that hinder the life, and immedi-

ately those bands are loosened by identification with the death of Jesus, we enter into a relationship with God whereby we can sacrifice our lives to Him.

It is of no value to God to give Him your life for death. He wants you to be a "*living* sacrifice," to let Him have all your powers that have been saved and sanctified through Jesus. This is the thing that is acceptable to God.

JANUARY 9

INTERCESSORY INTROSPECTION

And I pray God your whole spirit and soul and body be preserved blameless. 1 Thessalonians 5:23

"Your whole spirit . . ." The great mystical work of the Holy Spirit is in the dim regions of our personality which we cannot get at. Read the 139th Psalm; the Psalmist implies—"Thou art the God of the early mornings, the God of the late at nights, the God of the mountain peaks, and the God of the sea; but, my God, my soul has further horizons than the early mornings, deeper darkness than the nights of earth, higher peaks than any mountain peaks, greater depths than any sea in nature—Thou Who art the God of all these, be my God. I cannot reach to the heights or to the depths; there are motives I cannot trace, dreams I cannot get at—my God, search me out."

Do we believe that God can garrison the imagination far beyond where we can go? *The blood of Jesus Christ . . . cleanseth us from all sin*"—if that means in conscious experience only, may God have mercy on us. The man who has been made obtuse by sin will say he is not conscious of sin. Cleansing from sin is to the very heights and depths of our spirit if we will keep in the light as God is in the light, and the very Spirit that fed the life of Jesus Christ will feed the life of our spirits. It is only when we are garrisoned by God with the stupendous sanctity of the Holy Spirit, that spirit, soul and body are preserved in unspotted integrity, undeserving of censure in God's sight, until Jesus comes.

We do not allow our minds to dwell as they should on these great massive truths of God.

JANUARY 10

THE OPENED SIGHT

To open their eyes, . . . that they may receive . . . Acts 26:18

This verse is the grandest condensation of the propaganda of a disciple of Jesus Christ in the whole of the New Testament.

The first sovereign work of grace is summed up in the words—"that they may receive remission of sins" (RV). When a man fails in personal Christian experience, it is nearly always because he has never *received* anything. The only sign that a man is saved is that he has received something from Jesus Christ. Our part as workers for God is to open men's eyes that they may turn themselves from darkness to light; but that is not salvation, that is conversion—the effort of a roused human being. I do not think it is too sweeping to say that the majority of nominal Christians are of this order; their eyes are opened, but they have received nothing. Conversion is not regeneration. This is one of the neglected factors in our preaching today. When a man is born again, he knows that it is because he has received something as a gift from Almighty God and not because of his own decision. People register their vows, and sign their pledges, and determine to go through, but none of this is salvation. Salvation means that we are brought to the place where we are able to receive something from God on the authority of Jesus Christ, viz., remission of sins.

Then there follows the second mighty work of grace—"and inheritance among them which are sanctified." In sanctification the regenerated soul deliberately gives up his right to himself to Jesus Christ, and identifies himself entirely with God's interest in other men.

JANUARY 11

WHAT MY OBEDIENCE TO GOD COSTS OTHER PEOPLE

They laid hold upon one Simon, . . . and on him they laid the cross. Luke 23:26

If we obey God it is going to cost other people more than it costs us, and that is where the sting comes in. If we are in love with our Lord, obedience does not cost us anything, it is a delight, but it costs those who do not love Him a good deal. If we obey God it will mean that other people's plans are upset, and they will gibe us with it—"You call this Christianity?" We can prevent the suffering; but if we are going to obey God, we must not prevent it, we must let the cost be paid.

Our human pride entrenches itself on this point, and we say—"I will never accept anything from anyone." We shall have to, or disobey God. We have no right to expect to be in any other relation than our Lord Himself was in (see Luke 8:2–3).

Stagnation in spiritual life comes when we say we will bear the whole thing ourselves. We cannot. We are so involved in the universal purposes of God that immediately we obey God, others are affected. Are we going to remain loyal in our obedience to God and go through the humiliation of refusing to be independent, or are we going to take the other line and say—"I will not cost other people suffering"? We can disobey God if we choose, and it will bring immediate relief to the situation, but we shall be a grief to our Lord. Whereas if we obey God, He will look after those who have been pressed into the consequences of our obedience. We have simply to obey and to leave all consequences with Him.

Beware of the inclination to dictate to God as to what you will allow to happen if you obey Him.

JANUARY 12

HAVE YOU EVER BEEN ALONE WITH GOD?

When they were alone, He expounded all things to His disciples. Mark 4:34

Our Solitude with Him. Jesus does not take us alone and expound things to us all the time; He expounds things to us as we can understand them. Other lives are parables. God is making us spell out our own souls. It is slow work, so slow that it takes God all time and eternity to make a man and woman after His own purpose. The only way we can be of use to God is to let Him take us through the crooks and crannies of our own characters. It is astounding how ignorant we are about ourselves! We do not know envy when we see it, or laziness, or pride. Jesus reveals to us all that this body has been harbouring before His grace began to work. How many of us have learned to look in with courage?

We have to get rid of the idea that we understand ourselves, it is the last conceit to go. The only One Who understands us is God. The greatest curse in spiritual life is conceit. If we have ever had a glimpse of what we are like in the sight of God, we shall never say—"Oh I am so unworthy," because we shall know we are, beyond the possibility of stating it. As long as we are not quite sure that we are unworthy, God will keep narrowing us in until He gets us alone. Wherever there is any element of pride or of conceit, Jesus cannot expound a thing. He will take us through the disappointment of a wounded pride of intellect, through disappointments of heart. He will reveal inordinate affections—things over which we never thought He would have to get us alone. We listen to many things in classes, but they are not an exposition to us yet. They will be when God gets us alone over them.

JANUARY 13

HAVE YOU EVER BEEN ALONE WITH GOD?

When He was alone, . . . the twelve asked of Him. . . .
Mark 4:10

His Solitude with Us. When God gets us alone by affliction, heartbreak, or temptation, by disappointment, sickness, or by thwarted affection, by a broken friendship, or by a new friendship—when He gets us absolutely alone, and we are dumbfounded and cannot ask one question, then He begins to expound. Watch Jesus Christ's training of the twelve. It was the disciples, not the crowd outside, who were perplexed. They constantly asked Him questions, and He constantly expounded things to them; but they only understood after they had received the Holy Spirit (see John 14:26).

If you are going on with God, the only thing that is clear to you, and the only thing God intends to be clear, is the way He deals with your own soul. Your brother's sorrows and perplexities are an absolute confusion to you. We imagine we understand where the other person is, until God gives us a dose of the plague of our own hearts. There are whole tracts of stubbornness and ignorance to be revealed by the Holy Spirit in each one of us, and it can only be done when Jesus gets us alone. Are we alone with Him now, or are we taken up with little fussy notions, fussy comradeships in God's service, fussy ideas about our bodies? Jesus can expound nothing until we get through all the noisy questions of the head and are alone with Him.

JANUARY 14

CALLED OF GOD

Whom shall I send, and who will go for us? Then said I, Here am I; send me. Isaiah 6:8

God did not address the call to Isaiah; Isaiah overheard God saying—"Who will go for us?" The call of God is not for the special few, it is for everyone. Whether or not I hear God's call depends upon the state of my ears; and what I hear depends upon my disposition. "Many are called, but few are chosen," that is, few prove themselves the chosen ones. The chosen ones are those who have come into a relationship with God through Jesus

Christ whereby their disposition has been altered and their ears unstopped, and they hear the still small voice questioning all the time—"Who will go for us?" It is not a question of God singling out a man and saying, "Now, *you* go." God did not lay a strong compulsion on Isaiah; Isaiah was in the presence of God and he overheard the call, and realised that there was nothing else for him but to say, in conscious freedom—"Here am I; send me."

Get out of your mind the idea of expecting God to come with compulsions and pleadings. When Our Lord called His disciples there was no irresistible compulsion from outside. The quiet, passionate insistence of His "Follow Me" was spoken to men with every power wide awake. If we let the Spirit of God bring us face to face with God, we too will hear something akin to what Isaiah heard, the still small voice of God; and in perfect freedom will say—"Here am I; send me."

JANUARY 15

DO YOU WALK IN WHITE?

Buried with Him . . . that . . . even so we also should walk in newness of life. Romans 6:4

No one enters into the experience of entire sanctification without going through a "white funeral"[8] — the burial of the old life. If there has never been this crisis of death, sanctification is nothing more than a vision. There must be a "white funeral," a death that has only one resurrection—a resurrection into the life of Jesus Christ. Nothing can upset such a life; it is one with God for one purpose, to be a witness to Him.

Have you come to your last days really? You have come to them often in sentiment, but have you come to them *really*? You cannot go to your funeral in excitement, or die in excitement. Death means that you stop being. Do you agree with God that you stop being the striving, earnest kind of Christian you have been? We skirt the cemetery and all the time refuse to go to death. It is not striving to go to death, it is dying—"baptized into His death."

Have you had your "white funeral," or are you sacredly playing the fool with your soul? Is there a place in your life marked as the last day, a place to which the memory goes back with a chastened and extraordinarily grateful remembrance—"Yes, it was then, at that 'white funeral,' that I made an agreement with God"?

8."white funeral": phrase from Tennyson's poem "To H.R.H. Princess Beatrice"; to Chambers, it meant a passage from one stage of life to another; leaving the past behind and moving into the future; he often used it to mean death to self and a complete surrender to God.

"This is the will of God, even your sanctification." When you realise what the will of God is, you will enter into sanctification as naturally as can be. Are you willing to go through that "white funeral" now? Do you agree with Him that this is your last day on earth? The moment of agreement depends upon you.

JANUARY 16

THE VOICE OF THE NATURE OF GOD

I heard the voice of the Lord saying, Whom shall I send? Isaiah 6:8

When we speak of the call of God, we are apt to forget the most important feature, viz., the nature of the One Who calls. There is the call of the sea, the call of the mountains, the call of the great ice barriers; but these calls are only heard by the few. The call is the expression of the nature from which it comes, and we can only record the call if the same nature is in us. The call of God is the expression of God's nature, not of our nature. There are strands of the call of God providentially at work for us which we recognise and no one else does. It is the threading of God's voice to us in some particular matter, and it is no use consulting anyone else about it. We have to keep that profound relationship between our souls and God.

The call of God is not the echo of my nature; my affinities and personal temperament are not considered. As long as I consider my personal temperament and think about what I am fitted for, I shall never hear the call of God. But when I am brought into relationship with God, I am in the condition Isaiah was in. Isaiah's soul was so attuned to God by the tremendous crisis he had gone through that he recorded the call of God to his amazed soul. The majority of us have no ear for anything but ourselves, we cannot hear a thing God says. To be brought into the zone of the call of God is to be profoundly altered.

JANUARY 17

THE VOCATION OF THE NATURAL LIFE

But when it pleased God . . . to reveal His son in me . . . Galatians 1:15–16

The call of God is not a call to any particular service; my interpretation of it may be, because contact with the nature of God has made me realise what I would

like to do for Him. The call of God is essentially expressive of His nature; service is the outcome of what is fitted to my nature. The vocation of the natural life is stated by the Apostle Paul—"When it pleased God to reveal His Son in me that I might *preach* Him [i.e., *sacramentally express* Him] among the Gentiles."

Service is the overflow of superabounding devotion; but, profoundly speaking, there is no *call* to that, it is my own little actual bit, and is the echo of my identification with the nature of God. Service is the natural part of my life. God gets me into a relationship with Himself whereby I understand His call, then I do things out of sheer love for Him on my own account. To serve God is the deliberate love-gift of a nature that has heard the call of God. Service is expressive of that which is fitted to my nature: God's call is expressive of His nature; consequently when I receive His nature and hear His call, the voice of the Divine nature sounds in both and the two work together. The Son of God reveals Himself in me, and I serve Him in the ordinary ways of life out of devotion to Him.

JANUARY 18

IT IS THE LORD!

Thomas answered and said unto Him, My Lord and my God. John 20:28

"Give Me to drink." How many of us are set upon Jesus Christ slaking our thirst when we ought to be satisfying Him? We should be pouring out now, spending to the last limit, not drawing on Him to satisfy us. "Ye shall be witnesses unto Me"—that means a life of unsullied, uncompromising, and unbribed devotion to the Lord Jesus, a satisfaction to Him wherever He places us.

Beware of anything that competes with loyalty to Jesus Christ. The greatest competitor of devotion to Jesus is service for Him. It is easier to serve than to be drunk to the dregs. The one aim of the call of God is the satisfaction of God, not a call to do something for Him. We are not sent to battle for God, but to be used by God in His battlings. Are we being more devoted to service than to Jesus Christ?

JANUARY 19

VISION AND DARKNESS

An horror of great darkness fell upon him. Genesis 15:12

Whenever God gives a vision to a saint, He puts him, as it were, in the shadow of His hand, and the saint's duty is to be still and listen. There is a darkness which comes from excess of light, and then is the time to listen. Genesis 16 is an illustration of listening to good advice when it is dark instead of waiting for God to send the light. When God gives a vision and darkness follows, wait. God will make you in accordance with the vision He has given if you will wait His time. Never try and help God fulfil His word. Abraham went through thirteen years of silence, but in those years all self-sufficiency was destroyed; there was no possibility left of relying on commonsense ways. Those years of silence were a time of discipline, not of displeasure. Never pump up joy and confidence, but stay upon God (cf. Isaiah 50:10–11).

Have I any confidence in the flesh? Or have I got beyond all confidence in myself and in men and women of God, in books and prayers and ecstasies; and is my confidence placed now in God Himself, not in His blessings? "I am the Almighty God"—El-Shaddai, the Father-Mother God. The one thing for which we are all being disciplined is to know that God is real. As soon as God becomes real, other people become shadows. Nothing that other saints do or say can ever perturb the one who is built on God.

JANUARY 20

ARE YOU FRESH FOR EVERYTHING?

Except a man be born again, he cannot see the kingdom of God. John 3:3

Sometimes we are fresh for a prayer meeting but not fresh for cleaning boots!

Being born again of the Spirit is an unmistakable work of God, as mysterious as the wind, as surprising as God Himself. We do not know where it begins, it is hidden away in the depths of our personal life. Being born again from above (RV mg) is a perennial, perpetual and eternal beginning, a freshness all the time in thinking and in talking and in living, the continual surprise of the life of God. Staleness is an indication of something out of joint with God—"I must do this thing or it will never be done." That is the first sign of staleness. Are we freshly born this minute, or are we stale, raking in our minds for something to do? Freshness does not come from obedience but from the Holy Spirit; obedience keeps us in the light as God is in the light.

Guard jealously your relationship to God. Jesus prayed "that they may be one, even as We are one"—nothing between. Keep all the life perennially open to Jesus Christ, don't pretend with Him. Are you drawing your life from any other source than God Himself? If you are depending upon anything but Him, you will never know when He is gone.

Being born of the Spirit means much more than we generally take it to mean. It gives us a new vision and keeps us absolutely fresh for everything by the perennial supply of the life of God.

JANUARY 21

RECALL WHAT GOD REMEMBERS

I remember . . . the kindness of thy youth. Jeremiah 2:2

Am I as spontaneously kind to God as I used to be, or am I only expecting God to be kind to me? Am I full of the little things that cheer His heart over me, or am I whimpering because things are going hardly with me? There is no joy in the soul that has forgotten what God prizes. It is a great thing to think that Jesus Christ has need of me—"Give Me to drink." How much kindness have I shown Him this past week? Have I been kind to His reputation in my life?

God is saying to His people—"You are not in love with Me now, but I remember the time when you were." "I remember . . . the love of thine espousals." Am I as full of the extravagance of love to Jesus Christ as I was in the beginning, when I went out of my way to prove my devotion to Him? Does He find me recalling the time when I did not care for anything but Himself? Am I there now, or have I become wise over loving Him? Am I so in love with Him that I take no account of where I go? or am I watching for the respect due to me, weighing how much service I ought to give?

If, as I recall what God remembers about me, I find He is not what He used to be to me, let it produce shame and humiliation, because that shame will bring the godly sorrow that works repentance.

JANUARY 22

WHAT AM I LOOKING AT?

Look unto Me, and be ye saved. Isaiah 45:22

Do we expect God to come to us with His blessings and save us? He says—"*Look unto Me, and be* saved." The great difficulty spiritually is to concentrate on God, and it is His blessings that make it difficult. Troubles nearly always make us look to God; His blessings are apt to make us look elsewhere. The teaching of the Sermon on the Mount is, in effect—Narrow all your interests until the attitude of mind and heart and body is concentration on Jesus Christ.

Many of us have a mental conception of what a Christian should be, and the lives of the saints become a hindrance to our concentration on God. There is no salvation in this way, it is not simple enough. "Look unto Me" and—not "you will be saved," but "you *are* saved." The very thing we look for, we shall find if we will concentrate on Him. We get preoccupied and sulky with God, while all the time He is saying—"Look up and be saved." The difficulties and trials, the casting about in our minds as to what we shall do this summer, or to-morrow, all vanish when we look to God.

Rouse yourself up and look to God. Build your hope on Him. No matter if there are a hundred and one things that press, resolutely exclude them all and look to Him. "Look unto Me," and salvation *is,* the moment you look.

JANUARY 23

TRANSFORMED BY INSIGHT

We all, with open face, beholding as in a glass the glory of the Lord, are changed into the same image. 2 Corinthians 3:18

The outstanding characteristic of a Christian is this unveiled frankness before God so that the life becomes a mirror for other lives. By being filled with the Spirit we are transformed, and by beholding we become mirrors. You always know when a man has been beholding the glory of the Lord, you feel in your inner spirit that he is the mirror of the Lord's own character. Beware of anything which would sully that mirror in you; it is nearly always a good thing, the good that is not the best.

The golden rule for your life and mine is this concentrated keeping of the life open towards God. Let everything else—work, clothes, food, everything on earth—go by the board, saving that one thing. The rush of other things always tends to obscure this concentration on God. We have to maintain ourselves in the place of beholding, keeping the life absolutely spiritual all through. Let other things come and go as they may, let other people criticise as they will, but never allow anything to obscure the life that is hid with Christ in God. Never be hurried out of the relationship of abiding in Him. It is the one thing that is apt to fluctuate but it ought not to. The severest discipline of a Christian's life is to learn how to keep "beholding as in a glass the glory of the Lord."

JANUARY 24

THE OVERMASTERING DIRECTION

I have appeared unto thee for this purpose. Acts 26:16

The vision Paul had on the road to Damascus was no passing emotion, but a vision that had very clear and emphatic directions for him, and he says—"I was not disobedient to the heavenly vision." Our Lord said, in effect, to Paul—"Your whole life is to be overmastered by Me; you are to have no end, no aim, and no purpose but Mine." *"I have chosen him."*

When we are born again we all have visions, if we are spiritual at all, of what Jesus wants us to be, and the great thing is to learn not to be disobedient to the vision, not to say that it cannot be attained. It is not sufficient to know that God has redeemed the world, and to know that the Holy Spirit can make all that Jesus did effectual in me; I must have the basis of a personal relationship to Him. Paul was not given a message or a doctrine to proclaim, he was brought into a vivid, personal, overmastering relationship to Jesus Christ. Verse 16 is immensely commanding—"to make thee a minister and a witness." There is nothing there apart from the personal relationship. Paul was devoted to a Person not to a cause. He was absolutely Jesus Christ's; he saw nothing else; he lived for nothing else. "For I determined not to know any thing among you, save Jesus Christ, and Him crucified."

JANUARY 25

LEAVE ROOM FOR GOD

But when it pleased God . . . Galatians 1:15

As workers for God we have to learn to make room for God—to give God "elbow room." We calculate and estimate, and say that this and that will happen, and we forget to make room for God to come in as He chooses. Would we be surprised if God came into our meeting or into our preaching in a way we had never looked for Him to come? Do not look for God to come in any particular way, but *look for Him.* That is the way to make room for Him. Expect Him to come, but do not expect Him only in a certain way. However much we may know God, the great lesson to learn is that at any minute He may break in. We are apt to overlook this element of surprise, yet God never works in any other way. All of a sudden God meets the life—"When it was the good pleasure of God . . ." (RV).

Keep your life so constant in its contact with God that His surprising power may break out on the right hand and on the left. Always be in a state of expectancy, and see that you leave room for God to come in as He likes.

JANUARY 26

LOOK AGAIN AND CONSECRATE

If God so clothe the grass of the field, . . . shall He not much more clothe you? Matthew 6:30

A simple statement of Jesus is always a puzzle to us if we are not simple. How are we going to be simple with the simplicity of Jesus? By receiving His Spirit, recognising and relying on Him, obeying Him as He brings the word of God, and life will become amazingly simple. "Consider," says Jesus, "how much more your Father Who clothes the grass of the field will clothe you, if you keep your relationship right with Him." Every time we have gone back in spiritual communion it has been because we have impertinently known better than Jesus Christ. We have allowed the cares of the world to come in, and have forgotten the "much more" of our Heavenly Father.

"Behold the fowls of the air"—their one aim is to obey the principle of life that is in them and God looks after them. Jesus says that if you are rightly related to Him and obey this Spirit that is in you, God will look after your "feathers."

"Consider the lilies of the field"—they grow where they are put. Many of us refuse to grow where we are put, consequently we take root nowhere. Jesus says that if we obey the life God has given us, He will look after all the other things. Has Jesus Christ told us a lie? If we are not experiencing the "much more," it is because we are not obeying the life God has given us, we are taken up with confusing considerations. How much time have we taken up worrying God with questions when we should have been absolutely free to concentrate on His work? Consecration means the continual separating of myself to one particular thing. We cannot consecrate once and for all. Am I continually separating myself to consider God every day of my life?

JANUARY 27

LOOK AGAIN AND THINK

Take no thought for your life. Matthew 6:25

A warning which needs to be reiterated is that the cares of this world, the deceitfulness of riches, and the lust of other things entering in, will choke all that God puts in. We are never free from the recurring tides of this encroachment. If it does not come on the line of clothes and food, it will come on the line of money or lack of money; of friends or lack of friends; or on the line of difficult circumstances. It is one steady encroachment all the time, and unless we allow the Spirit of God to raise up the standard against it, these things will come in like a flood.

"Take no thought for your life." "Be careful about one thing only," says our Lord—"your relationship to Me." Common sense shouts loud and says—"That is absurd, I *must* consider how I am going to live, I *must* consider what I am going to eat and drink." Jesus says you must not. Beware of allowing the thought that this statement is made by One Who does not understand our particular circumstances. Jesus Christ knows our circumstances better than we do, and He says we must not think about these things so as to make them the one concern of our life. Whenever there is competition, be sure that you put your relationship to God first.

"Sufficient unto the day is the evil thereof." How much evil has begun to threaten you to-day? What kind of mean[9] little imps have been looking in and saying—"Now what are you going to do next month—this summer?" "Be anxious for nothing," Jesus says. Look again and think. Keep your mind on the "much more" of your Heavenly Father.

JANUARY 28

BUT IT IS HARDLY CREDIBLE THAT ONE COULD SO PERSECUTE JESUS!

Saul, Saul, why persecutest thou Me? Acts 26:14

Am I set on my own way for God? We are never free from this snare until we are brought into the experience of the baptism of the Holy Ghost and fire. Obstinacy and self-will will always stab Jesus Christ. It may hurt no one else, but it wounds His Spirit. Whenever we are obstinate and self-willed and set

9. mean: as used here, something or someone ordinary, common, low, or ignoble, rather than cruel or spiteful.

upon our own ambitions, we are hurting Jesus. Every time we stand on our rights and insist that this is what we intend to do, we are persecuting Jesus. Whenever we stand on our dignity we systematically vex and grieve His Spirit; and when the knowledge comes home that it is Jesus Whom we have been persecuting all the time, it is the most crushing revelation there could be.

Is the word of God tremendously keen to me as I hand it on to you, or does my life give the lie to the things I profess to teach? I may teach sanctification and yet exhibit the spirit of Satan, the spirit that persecutes Jesus Christ. The Spirit of Jesus is conscious of one thing only—a perfect oneness with the Father, and He says "Learn of Me; for I am meek and lowly in heart." All I do ought to be founded on a perfect oneness with Him, not on a self-willed determination to be godly. This will mean that I can be easily put upon, easily over-reached, easily ignored; but if I submit to it for His sake, I prevent Jesus Christ being persecuted.

JANUARY 29

BUT IT IS HARDLY CREDIBLE THAT ONE COULD BE SO POSITIVELY IGNORANT!

Who art Thou, Lord? Acts 26:15

"The LORD spake thus to me with a strong hand." There is no escape when Our Lord speaks. He always comes with an arrestment of the understanding. Has the voice of God come to you directly? If it has, you cannot mistake the intimate insistence with which it has spoken to you in the language you know best, not through your ears, but through your circumstances. God has to destroy our determined confidence in our own convictions. "I know this is what I should do"— and suddenly the voice of God speaks in a way that overwhelms us by revealing the depths of our ignorance. We have shown our ignorance of Him in the very way we determined to serve Him. We serve Jesus in a spirit that is not His, we hurt Him by our advocacy for Him, we push His claims in the spirit of the devil. Our words sound all right, but our spirit is that of an enemy. "He . . . rebuked them, and said, Ye know not what manner of spirit ye are of." The spirit of Our Lord in an advocate of His is described in 1 Corinthians 13.

Have I been persecuting Jesus by a zealous determination to serve Him in my own way? If I feel I have done my duty and yet have hurt Him in doing it, I may be sure it was not my duty, because it has not fostered the meek and quiet spirit, but the spirit of self-satisfaction. We imagine that whatever is unpleasant is our duty! Is that anything like the spirit of our Lord—"I *delight* to do Thy will, O My God."

JANUARY 30

THE DILEMMA OF OBEDIENCE

And Samuel feared to shew Eli the vision. 1 Samuel 3:15

God seldom speaks to us in startling ways, but in ways that are easy to misunderstand, and we say, "I wonder if that is God's voice?" Isaiah said that the Lord spake to him "with a strong hand," that is, by the pressure of circumstances. Nothing touches our lives but it is God Himself speaking. Do we discern His hand or only mere occurrence?

Get into the habit of saying, "Speak, Lord," and life will become a romance. Every time circumstances press, say, "Speak, Lord"; make time to listen. Chastening is more than a means of discipline, it is meant to get me to the place of saying, "Speak, Lord." Recall the time when God did speak to you. Have you forgotten what He said? Was it Luke 11:13, or was it 1 Thessalonians 5:23? As we listen, our ear gets acute, and, like Jesus, we shall hear God all the time.

Shall I tell my "Eli" what God has shown to me? That is where the dilemma of obedience comes in. We disobey God by becoming amateur providences— I must shield "Eli," the best people we know. God did not tell Samuel to tell Eli; he had to decide that for himself. God's call to you may hurt your "Eli"; but if you try to prevent the suffering in another life, it will prove an obstruction between your soul and God. It is at your own peril that you prevent the cutting off of the right hand or the plucking out of the eye.

Never ask the advice of another about anything God makes you decide before Him. If you ask advice, you will nearly always side with Satan: "Immediately I conferred not with flesh and blood."

JANUARY 31

DO YOU SEE YOUR CALLING?

Separated unto the Gospel. Romans 1:1

Our calling is not primarily to be holy men and women, but to be proclaimers of the Gospel of God. The one thing that is all important is that the Gospel of God should be realised as the abiding Reality. Reality is not human goodness, nor holiness, nor heaven, nor hell, but Redemption; and the need to perceive this is the most vital need of the Christian worker to-day. As workers we have to get used to the revelation that Redemption is the only Reality. Personal holiness is an effect, not a cause, and if we place our faith in human goodness, in the effect of Redemption, we shall go under when the test comes.

Paul did not say he separated himself, but—"when it pleased God, who separated me. . . ." Paul had not a hypersensitive interest in his own character. As long as our eyes are upon our own personal whiteness we shall never get near the reality of Redemption. Workers break down because their desire is for their own whiteness, and not for God. "Don't ask me to come into contact with the rugged reality of Redemption on behalf of the filth of human life as it is; what I want is anything God can do for me to make me more desirable in my own eyes." To talk in that way is a sign that the reality of the Gospel of God has not begun to touch me; there is no reckless abandon to God. God cannot deliver me while my interest is merely in my own character. Paul is unconscious of himself, he is recklessly abandoned, separated by God for one purpose—to proclaim the Gospel of God (cf. Romans 9:3).

FEBRUARY 1

THE CALL OF GOD

For Christ sent me not to baptize, but to preach the gospel. 1 Corinthians 1:17

Paul states here that the call of God is to preach the gospel; but remember what Paul means by "the gospel" viz., the reality of Redemption in our Lord Jesus Christ. We are apt to make sanctification the end-all of our preaching. Paul alludes to personal experience by way of illustration, never as the end of the matter. We are nowhere commissioned to preach salvation or sanctification; we are commissioned to lift up Jesus Christ (John 12:32). It is a travesty to say that Jesus Christ travailed in Redemption to make *me* a saint. Jesus Christ travailed in Redemption to redeem the whole world, and place it unimpaired and rehabilitated before the throne of God. The fact that Redemption can be experienced by us is an illustration of the power of the reality of Redemption, but that is not the end of Redemption. If God were human, how sick to the heart and weary He would be of the constant requests we make for our salvation, for our sanctification. We tax His energies from morning till night for things for ourselves—something for *me* to be delivered from! When we touch the bedrock of the reality of the Gospel of God, we shall never bother God any further with little personal plaints.

The one passion of Paul's life was to proclaim the Gospel of God. He welcomed heart-breaks, disillusionments, tribulation, for one reason only, because these things kept him in unmoved devotion to the Gospel of God.

FEBRUARY 2

THE CONSTRAINT OF THE CALL

Woe is unto me, if I preach not the gospel! 1 Corinthians 9:16

Beware of stopping your ears to the call of God. Everyone who is saved is called to testify to the fact; but that is not the call to preach, it is merely an illustration in preaching. Paul is referring to the pangs produced in him by the constraint to preach the Gospel. Never apply what Paul says in this connection to souls coming in contact with God for salvation. There is nothing easier than getting saved because it is God's sovereign work—"Come unto Me and I will save you." Our Lord never lays down the conditions of discipleship as the conditions of salvation. We are condemned to salvation through the Cross of Jesus Christ. Discipleship has an option with it—"IF any man . . ."

Paul's words have to do with being made a servant of Jesus Christ, and our permission is never asked as to what we will do or where we will go. God makes us broken bread and poured-out wine to please Himself. To be "separated unto the gospel" means to hear the call of God; and when a man begins to overhear that call, then begins agony that is worthy of the name. Every ambition is nipped in the bud, every desire of life quenched, every outlook completely extinguished and blotted out, saving one thing only—*"separated unto the gospel."* Woe be to the soul who tries to put his foot in any other direction when once that call has come to him. This College exists to see whether God has any man or woman here who cares about proclaiming His Gospel; to see whether God grips you. And beware of competitors when God does grip you.

FEBRUARY 3

THE RECOGNISED BAN OF RELATIONSHIP

We are made as the filth of the world. 1 Corinthians 4:13

These words are not an exaggeration. The reason they are not true of us who call ourselves ministers of the gospel is not that Paul forgot the exact truth in using them, but that we have too many discreet affinities to allow ourselves to be made refuse. "Filling up that which is behind of the afflictions of Christ" is not an evidence of sanctification, but of being "separated unto the gospel."

"Think it not strange concerning the fiery trial which is to try you," says Peter. If we do think it strange concerning the things we meet with, it is because we are craven-hearted. We have discreet affinities that keep us out of the mire—"I won't stoop; I won't bend." You do not need to, you can be saved by the skin of your teeth if you like; you can refuse to let God count you as one separated unto the gospel. Or you may say—"I do not care if I am treated as the offscouring of the earth as long as the Gospel is proclaimed." A servant of Jesus Christ is one who is willing to go to martyrdom for the reality of the gospel of God. When a merely moral man or woman comes in contact with baseness and immorality and treachery, the recoil is so desperately offensive to human goodness that the heart shuts up in despair. The marvel of the Redemptive Reality of God is that the worst and the vilest can never get to the bottom of His love. Paul did not say that God separated him to show what a wonderful man He could make of him, but *"to reveal His son in me."*

FEBRUARY 4

THE OVERMASTERING MAJESTY OF PERSONAL POWER

For the love of Christ constraineth us. 2 Corinthians 5:14

Paul says he is overruled, overmastered, held as in a vice, by the love of Christ. Very few of us know what it means to be held in a grip by the love of God; we are held by the constraint of our experience only. The one thing that held Paul, until there was nothing else on his horizon, was the love of God. "The love of Christ constraineth us"—when you hear that note in a man or woman, you can never mistake it. You know that the Spirit of God is getting unhindered way in that life.

When we are born again of the Spirit of God, the note of testimony is on what God has done for us, and rightly so. But the baptism of the Holy Ghost obliterates that for ever, and we begin to realise what Jesus meant when He said—"Ye shall be witnesses unto Me." Not witnesses to what Jesus can do—that is an elementary witness—but *"witnesses unto Me."* We will take everything that happens as happening to Him, whether it be praise or blame, persecution or commendation. No one can stand like that for Jesus Christ who is not constrained by the majesty of His personal power. It is the only thing that matters, and the strange thing is that it is the last thing realised by the Christian worker. Paul says he is gripped by the love of Christ; that is why he acts as he does. Men may call him mad or sober, but he does not care; there is only one thing he is living for, and that is to persuade men of the judgement seat of God, and of the love of Christ. This abandon to the love of Christ is the one thing that bears fruit in the life, and it will always leave the impression of the holiness and of the power of God, never of our personal holiness.

FEBRUARY 5

ARE YOU READY TO BE OFFERED?

Yea, and if I be offered upon the sacrifice and service of your faith, I joy, and rejoice with you all. Philippians 2:17

Are you willing to be offered for the work of the faithful—to pour out your life blood as a libation on the sacrifice of the faith of others? Or do you say—"I am not going to be offered up just yet, I do not want God to choose my work. I want to choose the scenery of my own sacrifice; I want to have the right kind of people watching me and saying, 'Well done.'"

It is one thing to go on the lonely way with dignified heroism, but quite another thing if the line mapped out for you by God means being a door-mat under other people's feet. Suppose God wants to teach you to say, "I know how to be abased"—are you ready to be offered up like that? Are you ready to be not so much as a drop in a bucket—to be so hopelessly insignificant that you are never thought of again in connection with the life you served? Are you willing to spend and be spent; not seeking to be ministered unto, but to minister? Some saints cannot do menial work and remain saints because it is beneath their dignity.

FEBRUARY 6

ARE YOU READY TO BE OFFERED?

I am already being poured out as a drink offering. 2 Timothy 4:6 (RV mg)

"I am now ready to be offered"(KJV). It is a transaction of will, not of sentiment. *Tell* God you are ready to be offered; then let the consequences be what they may, there is no strand of complaint now, no matter what God chooses. God puts you through the crisis in private, no one person can help another. Externally the life may be the same; the difference is in will. Go through the crisis in will, then when it comes externally there will be no thought of the cost. If you do not transact in will with God along this line, you will end in awakening sympathy for yourself.

"Bind the sacrifice with cords, even unto the horns of the altar." The altar means fire—burning and purification and insulation for one purpose only, the destruction of every affinity that God has not started and of every attachment that is not an attachment in God. *You do not destroy it, God does;* you bind the sacrifice to the horns of the altar; and see that you do not give way to self-pity when the fire begins. After this way of fire, there is nothing that oppresses or depresses. When the crisis arises, you realise that things cannot touch you as they used to do. What is your way of fire?

Tell God you are ready to be offered, and God will prove Himself to be all you ever dreamed He would be.

FEBRUARY 7

THE DISCIPLINE OF DEJECTION

But we trusted . . . and beside all this, to-day is the third day. . . . Luke 24:21

Every fact that the disciples stated was right; but the inferences they drew from those facts were wrong. Anything that savours of dejection spiritually is always wrong. If depression and oppression visit me, I am to blame; God is not, nor is anyone else. Dejection springs from one of two sources—I have either satisfied a lust or I have not. Lust means—I must have it at once. Spiritual lust makes me demand an answer from God, instead of seeking God Who gives the answer. What have I been trusting God would do? And to-day—the immediate present—is the third day, and He has not done it, therefore I imagine I am justified in being dejected and in blaming God. Whenever the insistence is on the point that God answers prayer, we are off the track. The meaning of prayer is that we get hold of God, not of the answer. It is impossible to be well physically and to be dejected. Dejection is a sign of sickness, and the same thing is true spiritually. Dejection spiritually is wrong, and we are always to blame for it.

We look for visions from heaven, for earthquakes and thunders of God's power (the fact that we are dejected proves that we do), and we never dream that all the time God is in the commonplace things and people around us. If we will do the duty that lies nearest,

we shall see Him. One of the most amazing revelations of God comes when we learn that it is in the commonplace things that the Deity of Jesus Christ is realised.

FEBRUARY 8

INSTANTANEOUS AND INSISTENT SANCTIFICATION

And the very God of peace sanctify you wholly. 1 Thessalonians 5:23–24

When we pray to be sanctified, are we prepared to face the standard of these verses? We take the term sanctification much too lightly. Are we prepared for what sanctification will cost? It will cost an intense narrowing of all our interests on earth, and an immense broadening of all our interests in God. Sanctification means intense concentration on God's point of view. It means every power of body, soul and spirit chained and kept for God's purpose only. Are we prepared for God to do in us all that He separated us for? And then after His work is done in us, are we prepared to separate ourselves to God even as Jesus did? "For their sakes I sanctify Myself." The reason some of us have not entered into the experience of sanctification is that we have not realised the meaning of sanctification from God's standpoint. Sanctification means being made one with Jesus so that the disposition that ruled Him will rule us. Are we prepared for what that will cost? It will cost everything that is not of God in us.

Are we prepared to be caught up into the swing of this prayer of the Apostle Paul's? Are we prepared to say—"Lord make me as holy as You can make a sinner saved by grace"? Jesus has prayed that we might be one with Him as He is one with the Father. The one and only characteristic of the Holy Ghost in a man is a strong family likeness to Jesus Christ, and freedom from everything that is unlike Him. Are we prepared to set ourselves apart for the Holy Spirit's ministrations in us?

FEBRUARY 9

ARE YOU EXHAUSTED SPIRITUALLY?

The everlasting God . . . fainteth not, neither is weary. Isaiah 40:28

Exhaustion means that the vital forces are worn right out. Spiritual exhaustion never comes through sin but only through service, and whether or not you are exhausted will depend upon where you get your supplies. Jesus said to Peter—"Feed My sheep," but He gave him nothing to feed them with. The process of being made broken bread and poured-out wine means that *you* have to be the nourishment for other souls until they learn to feed on God. They must drain you to the dregs. Be careful that you get your supply, or before long you will be utterly exhausted. Before other souls learn to draw on the life of the Lord Jesus direct, they have to draw on it through you; you have to be literally "sucked," until they learn to take their nourishment from God. We owe it to God to be our best for His lambs and His sheep as well as for Himself.

Has the way in which you have been serving God betrayed you into exhaustion? If so, then rally your affections. Where did you start the service from? From your own sympathy or from the basis of the Redemption of Jesus Christ? Continually go back to the foundation of your affections and recollect where the source of power is. You have no right to say—"Oh Lord, I am so exhausted." He saved and sanctified you in order to exhaust you. Be exhausted for God, but remember that your supply comes from Him. "All my fresh springs shall be in Thee" (PBV).[10]

FEBRUARY 10

IS YOUR IMAGINATION OF GOD STARVED?

Lift up your eyes on high, and behold who hath created these things. Isaiah 40:26

The people of God in Isaiah's day had starved their imagination by looking on the face of idols, and Isaiah made them look up at the heavens; that is, he made them begin to use their imagination aright. Nature to a saint is sacramental. If we are children of God, we have a tremendous treasure in Nature. In every wind that blows, in every night and day of the year, in every sign of the sky, in every blossoming and in every withering of the earth, there is a real coming of God to us if we will simply use our starved imagination to realise it.

The test of spiritual concentration is bringing the imagination into captivity. Is your imagination looking on the face of an idol? Is the idol yourself? Your work? Your conception of what a worker should be? Your experience of salvation and sanctification? Then your imagination of God is starved, and when you are up against difficulties you have no power, you can only endure in darkness. If your imagination is starved, do not look back to your own experience; it is God Whom you need. Go right out of yourself, away from the face of your idols, away from everything that has been starving your imagination. Rouse yourself, take the gibe that Isaiah gave the people, and deliberately turn your imagination to God.

One of the reasons of stultification in prayer is that there is no imagination, no power of putting ourselves deliberately before God. We have to learn how to be broken bread and poured-out wine on the line of intercession more than on the line of personal contact. Imagination is the power God gives a saint to posit himself out of himself into relationships he never was in.

FEBRUARY 11

IS YOUR HOPE IN GOD FAINT AND DYING?

Thou wilt keep him in perfect peace whose imagination is stayed on Thee. Isaiah 26:3 (RV mg)

Is your imagination stayed on God or is it starved? The starvation of the imagination is one of the most fruitful sources of exhaustion and sapping in a worker's life. If you have never used your imagination to put yourself before God, begin to do it now. It is no use waiting for God to come; you must put your imagination away from the face of idols and look unto Him and be saved. Imagination is the greatest gift God has given us, and it ought to be devoted entirely to Him. If you have been bringing every thought into captivity to the obedience of Christ, it will be one of the greatest assets to faith when the time of trial comes, because your faith and the Spirit of God will work together. Learn to associate ideas worthy of God with all that happens in Nature—the sunrises and the sunsets, the sun and the stars, the changing seasons, and your imagination will never be at the mercy of your impulses, but will always be at the service of God.

"We have sinned with our fathers . . . [and] remembered not"—then put a stiletto in the place where you have gone to sleep. "God is not talking to me just now," but He ought to be. Remember Whose you are and Whom you serve. Provoke yourself by recollection, and your affection for God will increase tenfold; your imagination will not be starved any longer, but will be quick and enthusiastic, and your hope will be inexpressibly bright.

---

10. PBV: Prayer Book Version. The *Book of Common Prayer* of the Church of England includes a translation of the Psalter, or Psalms of David.

FEBRUARY 12

MUST I LISTEN?

And they said unto Moses, Speak thou with us and we will hear: but let not God speak with us, lest we die. Exodus 20:19

We do not consciously disobey God, we simply do not heed Him. God has given us His commands; there they are, but we do not pay any attention to them, not because of wilful disobedience but because we do not love and respect Him. "If ye love Me, ye will keep My commandments" (RV). When once we realise that we have been "disrespecting" God all the time, we are covered with shame and humiliation because we have not heeded Him.

"Speak thou with us . . . : but let not God speak with us." We show how little we love God by preferring to listen to His servants only. We like to listen to personal testimonies, but we do not desire that God Himself should speak to us. Why are we so terrified lest God should speak to us? Because we know that if God does speak, either the thing must be done or we must tell God we will not obey Him. If it is only the servant's voice we hear, we feel it is not imperative, we can say, "Well, that is simply your own idea, though I don't deny it is probably God's truth."

Am I putting God in the humiliating position of having treated me as a child of His while all the time I have been ignoring Him? When I do hear Him, the humiliation I have put on Him comes back on me— "Lord, why was I so dull and so obstinate?" This is always the result when once we do hear God. The real delight of hearing Him is tempered with shame in having been so long in hearing Him.

FEBRUARY 13

THE DEVOTION OF HEARING

Speak; for Thy servant heareth. 1 Samuel 3:10

Because I have listened definitely to one thing from God, it does not follow that I will listen to everything He says. The way in which I show God that I neither love nor respect Him is by the obtuseness of my heart and mind towards what He says. If I love my friend, I intuitively detect what he wants, and Jesus says, "Ye are My friends." Have I disobeyed some command of my Lord's this week? If I had realised that it was a command of Jesus, I would not consciously have disobeyed it; but most of us show such disrespect to God that we do not even hear what He says, He might never have spoken.

The destiny of my spiritual life is such identification with Jesus Christ that I always hear God, and I know that God always hears me (John 11:41). If I am united with Jesus Christ, I hear God by the devotion of hearing all the time. A lily, or a tree, or a servant of God, may convey God's message to me. What hinders me from hearing is that I am taken up with other things. It is not that I will not hear God, but that I am not devoted in the right place. I am devoted to things, to service, to convictions, and God may say what He likes but I do not hear Him. The child attitude is always "Speak, LORD, for Thy servant heareth." If I have not cultivated this devotion of hearing, I can only hear God's voice at certain times; at other times I am taken up with things—things which I say I must do, and I become deaf to Him, I am not living the life of a child. Have I heard God's voice to-day?

FEBRUARY 14

THE DISCIPLINE OF HEEDING

What I tell you in darkness, that speak ye in light; and what ye hear in the ear, that preach ye upon the house-tops. Matthew 10:27

At times God puts us through the discipline of darkness to teach us to heed Him. Song birds are taught to sing in the dark, and we are put into the shadow of God's hand until we learn to hear Him. "What I tell you in darkness"—watch where God puts you into darkness, and when you are there, keep your mouth shut. Are you in the dark just now in your circumstances, or in your life with God? Then remain quiet. If you open your mouth in the dark, you will talk in the wrong mood: darkness is the time to listen. Don't talk to other people about it; don't read books to find out the reason of the darkness, but listen and heed. If you talk to other people, you cannot hear what God is saying. When you are in the dark, listen, and God will give you a very precious message for someone else when you get into the light.

After every time of darkness there comes a mixture of delight and humiliation (if there is delight only, I question whether we have heard God at all), delight in hearing God speak, but chiefly humiliation—"What a long time I was in hearing that! How slow I have been in understanding that! And yet God has been saying it all these days and weeks." Now He gives you the gift of humiliation which brings the softness of heart that will always listen to God now.

FEBRUARY 15

AM I MY BROTHER'S KEEPER?

None of us liveth to himself. Romans 14:7

Has it ever dawned on you that you are responsible for other souls spiritually before God? For instance, if I allow any private deflection from God in my life, everyone about me suffers. We "sit *together* in heavenly places." "Whether one member suffer, all the members suffer with it." When once you allow physical selfishness, mental slovenliness, moral obtuseness, spiritual density, everyone belonging to your crowd will suffer. "But," you say, "who is sufficient for these things, if you erect a standard like that?" Our sufficiency is of God, and of Him alone.

"Ye shall be My witnesses" (RV). How many of us are willing to spend every ounce of nervous energy, of mental, moral and spiritual energy we have for Jesus Christ? That is the meaning of a *witness* in God's sense of the word. It takes time, be patient with yourself. God has left us on the earth—what for? To be saved and sanctified? No, to be at it for Him. Am I willing to be broken bread and poured-out wine for Him? To be spoilt for this age, for this life, to be spoilt from every standpoint but one—saving as I can disciple men and women to the Lord Jesus Christ. My life as a worker is the way I say "thank you" to God for His unspeakable salvation. Remember it is quite possible for anyone of us to be flung out as reprobate silver—". . . lest that by any means, when I have preached to others, I myself should be a castaway."

FEBRUARY 16

THE INSPIRATION OF SPIRITUAL INITIATIVE

Arise from the dead. Ephesians 5:14

All initiative is not inspired. A man may say to you— "Buck up, take your disinclination by the throat, throw it overboard, and walk out into the thing!" That is ordinary human initiative. But when the Spirit of God comes in and says, in effect, "Buck up," we find that the initiative is inspired.

We all have any number of visions and ideals when we are young, but sooner or later we find that we have no power to make them real. We cannot do the things we long to do, and we are apt to settle down to the visions and ideals as dead, and God has to come and say—"Arise from the dead." When the inspiration of God does come, it comes with such miraculous power that we are able to arise from the dead and do the impossible thing. The remarkable thing about spiri-

tual initiative is that the life comes after we do the "bucking up." God does not give us overcoming life; He gives us life *as we overcome*. When the inspiration of God comes, and He says—"Arise from the dead," we have to get up; God does not lift us up. Our Lord said to the man with the withered hand—"Stretch forth thy hand," and as soon as the man did so, his hand was healed, but he had to take the initiative. If we will do the overcoming, we shall find we are inspired of God because He gives life immediately.

FEBRUARY 17

THE INITIATIVE AGAINST DEPRESSION

Arise and eat. 1 Kings 19:5

The angel did not give Elijah a vision, or explain the Scriptures to him, or do anything remarkable; he told Elijah to do the most ordinary thing, viz., to get up and eat. If we were never depressed we should not be alive; it is the nature of a crystal never to be depressed. A human being is capable of depression, otherwise there would be no capacity for exaltation. There are things that are calculated to depress, things that are of the nature of death; and in taking an estimate of yourself, always take into account the capacity for depression.

When the Spirit of God comes He does not give us visions; He tells us to do the most ordinary things conceivable. Depression is apt to turn us away from the ordinary commonplace things of God's creation, but whenever God comes, the inspiration is to do the most natural simple things—the things we would never have imagined God was in, and as we do them we find He is there. The inspiration which comes to us in this way is an initiative against depression; we have to do the next thing and to do it in the inspiration of God. If we do a thing in order to overcome depression, we deepen the depression; but if the Spirit of God makes us feel intuitively that we must do the thing, and we do it, the depression is gone. Immediately we arise and obey, we enter on a higher plane of life.

FEBRUARY 18

THE INITIATIVE AGAINST DESPAIR

Rise, let us be going. Matthew 26:46

The disciples went to sleep when they should have kept awake, and when they realised what they had done it produced despair. The sense of the irreparable is apt to make us despair, and we say—"It is all up now, it is no use trying any more." If we imagine that this kind of despair is exceptional, we are mistaken, it is a very ordinary human experience. Whenever we realise that we have not done that which we had a magnificent opportunity of doing, then we are apt to sink in despair, and Jesus Christ comes and says—"Sleep on now, that opportunity is lost for ever, you cannot alter it, but arise and go to the next thing." Let the past sleep, but let it sleep on the bosom of Christ, and go out into the irresistible future with Him.

There are experiences like this in each of our lives. We are in despair, the despair that comes from actualities, and we cannot lift ourselves out of it. The disciples in this instance had done a downright unforgivable thing; they had gone to sleep instead of watching with Jesus, but He came with a spiritual initiative against their despair and said—"Arise and do the next thing." If we are inspired of God, what is the next thing? To trust Him absolutely and to pray on the ground of His Redemption.

Never let the sense of failure corrupt your new action.

FEBRUARY 19

THE INITIATIVE AGAINST DRUDGERY

Arise, shine. Isaiah 60:1

We have to take the first step as though there were no God. It is no use to wait for God to help us, He will not; but immediately we arise we find He is there. Whenever God inspires, the initiative is a moral one. We must do the thing and not lie like a log. If we will arise and shine, drudgery becomes divinely transfigured.

Drudgery is one of the finest touchstones of character there is. Drudgery is work that is very far removed from anything to do with the ideal—the utterly mean,[11] grubby things; and when we come in contact with them we know instantly whether or not we are spiritually real. Read John 13; we see there the Incarnate God doing the most desperate piece of drudgery, washing fishermen's feet, and He says—"If I then, your Lord and Master, have washed your feet, ye also ought to wash one another's feet." It requires the inspiration of God to go through drudgery with the light of God upon it. Some people do a certain thing, and the way in which they do it hallows that thing for ever afterwards. It may be the most com-

monplace thing, but after we have seen them do it, it becomes different. When the Lord does a thing through us, He always transfigures it. Our Lord took on Him our human flesh and transfigured it, and it has become for every saint the temple of the Holy Ghost.

FEBRUARY 20

THE INITIATIVE AGAINST DREAMING

Arise, let us go hence. John 14:31

Dreaming about a thing in order to do it properly is right; but dreaming about it when we should be doing it is wrong. After Our Lord had said those wonderful things to His disciples, we might have expected that He would tell them to go away and meditate over them all; but Our Lord never allowed "mooning." When we are getting into contact with God in order to find out what He wants, dreaming is right; but when we are inclined to spend our time in dreaming over what we have been told to do, it is a bad thing and God's blessing is never on it. God's initiative is always in the nature of a stab against this kind of dreaming, the stab that bids us "neither sit nor stand but go."

If we are quietly waiting before God and He has said—"Come ye yourselves apart," then that is meditation before God in order to get at the line He wants; but always beware of giving over to mere dreaming when once God has spoken. Leave Him to be the source of all your dreams and joys and delights, and go out and obey what He has said. If you are in love, you do not sit down and dream about the one you love all the time, you go and do something for him; and that is what Jesus Christ expects us to do. Dreaming after God has spoken is an indication that we do not trust Him.

FEBRUARY 21

HAVE YOU EVER BEEN CARRIED AWAY FOR HIM?

She hath wrought a good work on Me. Mark 14:6

If human love does not carry a man beyond himself, it is not love. If love is always discreet, always wise, always sensible and calculating, never carried beyond

---

11. mean: as used here, something or someone ordinary, common, low, or ignoble, rather than cruel or spiteful.

itself, it is not love at all. It may be affection, it may be warmth of feeling, but it has not the true nature of love in it.

Have I ever been carried away to do something for God not because it was my duty, nor because it was useful, nor because there was anything in it at all beyond the fact that I love Him? Have I ever realised that I can bring to God things which are of value to Him, or am I mooning round the magnitude of His Redemption whilst there are any number of things I might be doing? Not Divine, colossal things which could be recorded as marvellous, but ordinary, simple human things which will give evidence to God that I am abandoned to Him? Have I ever produced in the heart of the Lord Jesus what Mary of Bethany produced?

There are times when it seems as if God watches to see if we will give Him the abandoned tokens of how genuinely we do love Him. Abandon to God is of more value than personal holiness. Personal holiness focuses the eye on our own whiteness; we are greatly concerned about the way we walk and talk and look, fearful lest we offend Him. Perfect love casts out all that when once we are abandoned to God. We have to get rid of this notion—"Am I of any use?" and make up our minds that we are not, and we may be near the truth. It is never a question of being of use, but of being of value to God Himself. When we are abandoned to God, He works through us all the time.

FEBRUARY 22

THE DISCIPLINE OF SPIRITUAL TENACITY

Be still, and know that I am God. Psalm 46:10

Tenacity is more than endurance, it is endurance combined with the absolute certainty that what we are looking for is going to transpire. Tenacity is more than hanging on, which may be but the weakness of being too afraid to fall off. Tenacity is the supreme effort of a man refusing to believe that his hero is going to be conquered. The greatest fear a disciple has is not that he will be damned, but that Jesus Christ will be worsted, that the things He stood for—love and justice and forgiveness and kindness among men—will not win out in the end; the things He stands for look like will-o'-the-wisps. Then comes the call to spiritual tenacity, not to hang on and do nothing, but to work deliberately on the certainty that God is not going to be worsted.

If our hopes are being disappointed just now, it means that they are being purified. There is nothing noble the human mind has ever hoped for or dreamed of that will not be fulfilled. One of the greatest strains in life is the strain of waiting for God. "Because thou hast kept the word of My patience."

Remain spiritually tenacious.

FEBRUARY 23

THE DETERMINATION TO SERVE

The son of Man came not to be ministered unto, but to minister. Matthew 20:28

Paul's idea of service is the same as our Lord's: "I am among you as He that serveth"; "ourselves your servants for Jesus' sake." We have the idea that a man called to the ministry is called to be a different kind of being from other men. According to Jesus Christ, he is called to be the "door-mat" of other men; their spiritual leader, but never their superior. "I know how to be abased," says Paul. This is Paul's idea of service—"I will spend myself to the last ebb for you; you may give me praise or give me blame, it will make no difference. So long as there is a human being who does not know Jesus Christ, I am his debtor to serve him until he does." The mainspring of Paul's service is not love for men, but love for Jesus Christ. If we are devoted to the cause of humanity, we shall soon be crushed and broken-hearted, for we shall often meet with more ingratitude from men than we would from a dog; but if our motive is love to God, no ingratitude can hinder us from serving our fellow men.

Paul's realisation of how Jesus Christ had dealt with him is the secret of his determination to serve others. "I was before a blasphemer, and a persecutor, and injurious"—no matter how men may treat me, they will never treat me with the spite and hatred with which I treated Jesus Christ. When we realise that Jesus Christ has served us to the end of our meanness, our selfishness, and sin, nothing that we meet with from others can exhaust our determination to serve men for His sake.

FEBRUARY 24

THE DELIGHT OF SACRIFICE

I will very gladly spend and be spent for you. 2 Corinthians 12:15

When the Spirit of God has shed abroad the love of God in our hearts, we begin deliberately to identify ourselves with Jesus Christ's interests in other people, and Jesus Christ is interested in every kind of man there is. We have no right in Christian work to be guided by our affinities; this is one of the biggest tests of our relationship to Jesus Christ. The delight of sacrifice is that I lay down my life for my Friend, not fling it away, but deliberately lay my life out for Him and His interests in other people, not for a cause. Paul spent himself for one purpose only—that he might win men to Jesus Christ. Paul attracted to Jesus all the time, never to himself. "I am made all things to all men, that I might by all means save some." When a man says he must develop a holy life alone with God, he is of no more use to his fellow men: he puts himself on a pedestal, away from the common run of men. Paul became a sacramental personality; wherever he went, Jesus Christ helped Himself to his life. Many of us are after our own ends, and Jesus Christ cannot help Himself to our lives. If we are abandoned to Jesus, we have no ends of our own to serve. Paul said he knew how to be a "door-mat" without resenting it, because the mainspring of his life was devotion to Jesus. We are apt to be devoted not to Jesus Christ but to the things which emancipate us spiritually. That was not Paul's motive: "I could wish that myself were accursed from Christ for my brethren"—wild, extravagant—is it? When a man is in love it is not an exaggeration to talk in that way, and Paul is in love with Jesus Christ.

FEBRUARY 25

THE DESTITUTION OF SERVICE

Though the more abundantly I love you, the less I be loved. 2 Corinthians 12:15

Natural love expects some return, but Paul says—"I do not care whether you love me or not, I am willing to destitute myself completely, not merely for your sakes, but that I may get you to God." "For ye know the grace of our Lord Jesus Christ, that, though He was rich, yet for your sakes He became poor." Paul's idea of service is exactly along that line—"I do not care with what extravagance I spend myself, and I will do it gladly." It was a joyful thing to Paul.

The ecclesiastical idea of a servant of God is not Jesus Christ's idea. His idea is that we serve Him by being the servants of other men. Jesus Christ outsocialists the socialists. He says that in His Kingdom he that is greatest shall be the servant of all. The real test of the saint is not preaching the gospel, but washing disciples' feet, that is, doing the things that do not count in the actual estimate of men, but count everything in the estimate of God. Paul delighted to spend himself out for God's interests in other people, and he did not care what it cost. We come in with our economical notions—"Suppose God wants me to go there—what about the salary? What about the cli-

mate? How shall I be looked after? A man must consider these things." All that is an indication that we are serving God with a reserve. The Apostle Paul had no reserve. Paul focuses Jesus Christ's idea of a New Testament saint in his life, viz.: not one who proclaims the Gospel merely, but one who becomes broken bread and poured-out wine in the hands of Jesus Christ for other lives.

FEBRUARY 26

INFERIOR MISGIVINGS ABOUT JESUS

Sir, Thou hast nothing to draw with. John 4:11

"I am impressed with the wonder of what God says, but He cannot expect me really to live it out in the details of my life!" When it comes to facing Jesus Christ on His own merits, our attitude is one of pious superiority—"Your ideals are high and they impress us, but in touch with actual things, it cannot be done." Each of us thinks about Jesus in this way in some particular. These misgivings about Jesus start from the amused questions put to us when we talk of our transactions with God—"Where are you going to get your money from? How are you going to be looked after?" Or they start from ourselves when we tell Jesus that our case is a bit too hard for Him. "It is all very well to say 'Trust in the Lord,' but a man must live, and Jesus has nothing to draw with—nothing whereby to give us these things." Beware of the pious fraud in you which says—"I have no misgivings about Jesus, only about myself." None of us ever had misgivings about ourselves; we know exactly what we cannot do, but we do have misgivings about Jesus. We are rather hurt at the idea that He can do what we cannot.

My misgivings arise from the fact that I ransack my own person to find out how He will be able to do it. My questions spring from the depths of my own inferiority. If I detect these misgivings in myself, let me bring them to the light and confess them—"Lord, I have had misgivings about Thee, I have not believed in Thy wits apart from my own; I have not believed in Thine Almighty power apart from my finite understanding of it.

FEBRUARY 27

THE IMPOVERISHED MINISTRY OF JESUS

From whence then hast Thou that living water? John 4:11

"The well is deep"—and a great deal deeper than the Samaritan woman knew! Think of the depths of human nature, of human life, think of the depths of the "wells" in you. Have you been impoverishing the ministry of Jesus so that He cannot do anything? Suppose there is a well of fathomless trouble inside your heart, and Jesus comes and says—"Let not your heart be troubled"; and you shrug your shoulders and say—"But, Lord, the well is deep; You cannot draw up quietness and comfort out of it." No, He will bring them down from above. Jesus does not bring anything up from the wells of human nature. We limit the Holy One of Israel by remembering what we have allowed Him to do for us in the past, and by saying—"Of course I cannot expect God to do this thing." The thing that taxes almightiness is the very thing which as disciples of Jesus we ought to believe He will do. We impoverish His ministry the moment we forget He is Almighty; the impoverishment is in us, not in Him. We will come to Jesus as Comforter or as Sympathiser, but we will not come to Him as Almighty.

The reason some of us are such poor specimens of Christianity is because we have no Almighty Christ. We have Christian attributes and experiences, but there is no abandonment to Jesus Christ. When we get into difficult circumstances, we impoverish His ministry by saying—"Of course He cannot do any thing," and we struggle down to the deeps and try to get the water for ourselves. Beware of the satisfaction of sinking back and saying—"It can't be done"; you know it can be done if you look to Jesus. The well of your incompleteness is deep, but make the effort and look away to Him.

FEBRUARY 28

DO YE NOW BELIEVE?

By this we believe. . . . Jesus answered . . . , Do ye now believe? John 16:30–31

"Now we believe." Jesus says—"Do you? The time is coming when you will leave Me alone." Many a Christian worker has left Jesus Christ alone and gone into work from a sense of duty, or from a sense of need arising out of his own particular discernment. The reason for this is the absence of the resurrection life of Jesus. The soul has got out of intimate contact with God by leaning to its own religious understanding. There is no sin in it, and no punishment attached to it; but when the soul realises how he has hindered his understanding of Jesus Christ, and produced for himself perplexities and sorrows and difficulties, it is with shame and contrition he has to come back.

We need to rely on the resurrection life of Jesus much deeper down, to get into the habit of steadily referring everything back to Him; instead of this we make our commonsense decisions and ask God to bless them. He cannot, it is not in His domain, it is severed from reality. If we do a thing from a sense of duty, we are putting up a standard in competition with Jesus Christ. We become a "superior person," and say—"Now in this matter I must do this and that." We have put our sense of duty on the throne instead of the resurrection life of Jesus. We are not told to walk in the light of conscience or of a sense of duty, but to walk in the light *as God is in the light.* When we do anything from a sense of duty, we can back it up by argument; when we do anything in obe- dience to the Lord, there is no argument possible; that is why a saint can be easily ridiculed.

FEBRUARY 29

WHAT DO YOU WANT THE LORD TO DO FOR YOU?

Lord, that I may receive my sight. Luke 18:41

What is the thing that not only disturbs you but makes you a disturbance? It is always something you cannot deal with yourself. "They rebuked him, that he should hold his peace: but he cried so much the more." Persist in the disturbance until you yet get face to face with the Lord Himself; do not deify common sense. When Jesus asks us what we want Him to do for us in regard to the incredible thing with which we are faced, remember that He does not work in com- monsense ways, but in supernatural ways.

Watch how we limit the Lord by remembering what we have allowed Him to do for us in the past: "I always failed there, and I always shall"; consequently we do not ask for what we want, "It is ridiculous to ask God to do this." If it is an impossibility, it is the thing we have to ask. If it is not an impossible thing, it is not a real disturbance. God will do the absolutely impossible.

This man received his sight. The most impossible thing to you is that you should be so identified with the Lord that there is nothing of the old life left. He will do it if you ask Him. But you have to come to the place where you believe Him to be Almighty. Faith is not in what Jesus says but in Himself; if we only look at what He says we shall never believe. When once we see Jesus, He does the impossible thing as natu- rally as breathing. Our agony comes through the wil- ful stupidity of our own heart. We *won't* believe, we *won't* cut the shore line, we prefer to worry on.

MARCH 1

THE UNDEVIATING QUESTION

Lovest thou Me? John 21:17

Peter declares nothing now (cf. Matthew 26:33–35). Natural individuality professes and declares; the love of the personality is only discovered by the hurt of the question of Jesus Christ. Peter loved Jesus in the way in which any natural man loves a good man. That is temperamental love; it may go deep into the individuality, but it does not touch the centre of the person. True love never professes anything. Jesus said— "Whosoever shall *confess* Me before men," i.e., confess his love not merely by his words, but by everything he does.

Unless we get hurt right out of every deception about ourselves, the word of God is not having its way with us. The word of God hurts as no sin can ever hurt, because sin blunts feeling. The question of the Lord intensifies feeling, until to be hurt by Jesus is the most exquisite hurt conceivable. It hurts not only in the natural way but in the profound personal way. The word of the Lord pierces even to the dividing asunder of soul and spirit, there is no deception left. There is no possibility of being sentimental with the Lord's question; you cannot say nice things when the Lord speaks directly to you, the hurt is too terrific. It is such a hurt that it stings every other concern out of account. There never can be any mistake about the hurt of the Lord's word when it comes to his child; but the point of the hurt is the great point of revelation.

MARCH 2

HAVE YOU FELT THE HURT OF THE LORD?

He said unto him the third time, Lovest thou Me? John 21:17

Have you felt the hurt of the Lord to the uncovered quick, the place where the real sensitiveness of your life is lodged? The devil never hurts there, neither sin nor human affection hurts there, nothing goes through to that place but the word of God. "Peter was grieved, because Jesus said unto him the third time. . . ." He was awakening to the fact that in the real true centre of his personal life he was devoted to Jesus, and he began to see what the patient questioning meant. There was not the slightest strand of delusion left in Peter's mind, he never could be deluded

again. There was no room for passionate utterance, no room for exhilaration or sentiment. It was a revelation to him to realise how much he did love the Lord, and with amazement he said—Lord, Thou knowest all things." Peter began to see how much he did love Jesus; but he did not say—"Look at this or that to confirm it." Peter was beginning to discover to himself how much he did love the Lord, that there was no one in heaven above or upon earth beneath beside Jesus Christ; but he did not know it until the probing, hurting questions of the Lord came. The Lord's questions always reveal me to myself.

The patient directness and skill of Jesus Christ with Peter! Our Lord never asks questions until the right time. Rarely, but probably once, He will get us into a corner where He will hurt us with His undeviating questions, and we will realise that we do love Him far more deeply than any profession can ever show.

MARCH 3

THE UNRELIEVED QUEST

Feed My sheep. John 21:17

This is love in the making. The love of God is unmade, it is God's nature. When we receive the Holy Spirit He unites us with God so that His love is manifested in us. When the soul is united to God by the indwelling Holy Spirit, that is not the end; the end is that we may be one with the Father as Jesus was. What kind of oneness had Jesus Christ with the Father? Such a oneness that the Father sent him down here to be spent for us, and He says—"As the Father hath sent Me, even so send I you" (RV).

Peter realises now with the revelation of the Lord's hurting question that he does love Him; then comes the point—Spend it out. Don't testify how much you love Me, don't profess about the marvellous revelation you have had, but—"Feed My sheep." And Jesus has some extraordinarily funny sheep, some bedraggled, dirty sheep, some awkward butting sheep, some sheep that have gone astray! It is impossible to weary God's love, and it is impossible to weary that love in me if it springs from the one centre. The love of God pays no attention to the distinctions made by natural individuality. If I love my Lord I have no business to be guided by natural temperament; I have to feed His sheep. There is no relief and no release from this commission. Beware of counterfeiting the love of God by working along the line of natural human sympathy, because that will end in blaspheming the love of God.

MARCH 4

COULD THIS BE TRUE OF ME?

But none of these things move me, neither count I my life dear unto myself. Acts 20:24

It is easier to serve God without a vision, easier to work for God without a call, because then you are not bothered by what God requires; common sense is your guide, veneered over with Christian sentiment. You will be more prosperous and successful, more leisure-hearted, if you never realise the call of God. But if once you receive a commission from Jesus Christ, the memory of what God wants will always come like a goad; you will no longer be able to work for Him on the commonsense basis.

What do I really count dear? If I have not been gripped by Jesus Christ, I will count service dear, time given to God dear, my life dear unto myself. Paul says he counted his life dear only in order that he might fulfil the ministry he had received; he refused to use his energy for any other thing. Acts 20:24 states Paul's almost sublime annoyance at being asked to consider himself; he was absolutely indifferent to any consideration other than that of fulfilling the ministry he had received. Practical work may be a competitor against abandonment to God, because practical work is based on this argument—"Remember how useful you are here," or—"Think how much value you would be in that particular type of work." That attitude does not put Jesus Christ as the Guide as to where we should go, but our judgement as to where we are of most use. Never consider whether you are of use; but ever consider that you are not your own but His.

MARCH 5

IS HE REALLY LORD?

. . . so that I might finish my course with joy, and the ministry, which I have received of the Lord Jesus. Acts 20:24

Joy means the perfect fulfilment of that for which I was created and regenerated, not the successful doing of a thing. The joy Our Lord had lay in doing what the Father sent Him to do, and He says—"As My Father hath sent Me, even so am I sending you." Have I received a ministry from the Lord? If so, I have to be loyal to it, to count my life precious only for the fulfilling of that ministry. Think of the satisfaction it will be to hear Jesus say—"Well done, good and faithful servant"; to know that you have done what He sent you to do. We have all to find our niche in life, and spiritually we find it when we receive our ministry from the Lord. In order to do this we must have companied with Jesus; we must know Him as more than a personal Saviour. "I will shew him how great things he must suffer *for My sake.*"

"Lovest thou Me?" Then—"Feed My sheep." There is no choice of service, only absolute loyalty to Our Lord's commission; loyalty to what you discern when you are in closest contact with God. If you have received a ministry from the Lord Jesus, you will know that the need is never the call: the need is the opportunity. The call is loyalty to the ministry you received when you were in real touch with Him. This does not imply that there is a campaign of service marked out for you, but it does mean that you will have to ignore the demands for service along other lines.

MARCH 6

AMID A CROWD OF PALTRY THINGS

. . . in much patience, in afflictions, in necessities, in distresses. 2 Corinthians 6:4

It takes Almighty grace to take the next step when there is no vision and no spectator—the next step in devotion, the next step in your study, in your reading, in your kitchen; the next step in your duty, when there is no vision from God, no enthusiasm and no spectator. It takes far more of the grace of God, far more conscious drawing upon God to take that step, than it does to preach the Gospel.

Every Christian has to partake of what was the essence of the Incarnation, he must bring the thing down into flesh-and-blood actualities and work it out through the finger-tips. We flag when there is no vision, no uplift, but just the common round, the trivial task. The thing that tells in the long run for God and for men is the steady persevering work in the unseen, and the only way to keep the life uncrushed is to live looking to God. Ask God to keep the eyes of your spirit open to the Risen Christ, and it will be impossible for drudgery to damp you. Continually get away from pettiness and paltriness of mind and thought out into the thirteenth chapter of St. John's Gospel.

MARCH 7

UNDAUNTED RADIANCE

Nay, in all these things we are more than conquerors through Him that loved us. Romans 8:37

Paul is speaking of the things that might seem likely to separate or wedge in between the saint and the love of God; but the remarkable thing is that nothing *can* wedge in between the love of God and the saint. These things can and do come in between the devotional exercises of the soul and God and separate individual life from God; but none of them is able to wedge in between the love of God and the soul of the saint. The bedrock of our Christian faith is the unmerited, fathomless marvel of the love of God exhibited on the Cross of Calvary, a love we never can and never shall merit. Paul says this is the reason we are more than conquerors in all these things, super-victors, with a joy we would not have but for the very things which look as if they are going to overwhelm us.

The surf that distresses the ordinary swimmer produces in the surf-rider the super joy of going clean through it. Apply that to our own circumstances, these very things—tribulation, distress, persecution, produce in us the super joy; they are not things to fight. We are more than conquerors through Him *in* all these things, not in spite of them, but in the midst of them. The saint never knows the joy of the Lord in spite of tribulation, but *because* of it. "I am exceeding joyful in all our tribulation," says Paul.

Undaunted radiance is not built on anything passing, but on the love of God that nothing can alter. The experiences of life, terrible or monotonous, are impotent to touch the love of God, which is in Christ Jesus our Lord.

MARCH 8

THE RELINQUISHED LIFE

I am crucified with Christ. Galatians 2:20

No one is ever united with Jesus Christ until he is willing to relinquish not sin only, but his whole way of looking at things. To be born from above (RV mg) of the Spirit of God means that we must let go before we lay hold, and in the first stages it is the relinquishing of all pretence. What Our Lord wants us to present to Him is not goodness, nor honesty, nor endeavour, but real solid sin; that is all He can take from us. And what does He give in exchange for our sin? Real solid righteousness. But we must relinquish all pretence of being anything, all claim of being worthy of God's consideration.

Then the Spirit of God will show us what further there is to relinquish. There will have to be the relinquishing of my claim to my right to myself in every phase. Am I willing to relinquish my hold on all I possess, my hold on my affections, and on everything, and to be identified with the death of Jesus Christ?

There is always a sharp painful disillusionment to go through before we do relinquish. When a man really sees himself as the Lord sees him, it is not the abominable sins of the flesh that shock him, but the awful nature of the pride of his own heart against Jesus Christ. When he sees himself in the light of the Lord, the shame and the horror and the desperate conviction come home.

If you are up against the question of relinquishing, go through the crisis, relinquish all, and God will make you fit for all that He requires of you.

MARCH 9

THE TIME OF RELAPSE

Will ye also go away? John 6:67

A penetrating question. Our Lord's words come home most when He talks in the most simple way. We know Who Jesus is, but in spite of that He says— "Will ye also go away?" We have to maintain a venturing attitude toward Him all the time.

"From that time many of His disciples went back, and walked no more with Him." They went back from walking with Jesus, not into sin, but they relapsed. Many to-day are spending and being spent in work for Jesus Christ, but they do not walk with Him. The one thing God keeps us to steadily is that we may be one with Jesus Christ. After sanctification the discipline of our spiritual life is along this line. If God gives a clear and emphatic realisation to your soul of what He wants, do not try to keep yourself in that relationship by any particular method, but live a natural life of absolute dependence on Jesus Christ. Never try to live the life with God on any other line than God's line, and that line is absolute devotion to Him. The certainty that I know I do not know—that is the secret of going with Jesus.

Peter only saw in Jesus Someone to minister salvation to him and to the world. Our Lord wants us to be yoke-fellows with Him.

Verse 70: Jesus answers the great lack in Peter. We cannot answer for others.

MARCH 10

HAVE A MESSAGE AND BE ONE

Preach the word. 2 Timothy 4:2

We are not saved to be "channels only," but to be sons and daughters of God. We are not turned into spiritual mediums, but into spiritual messengers; the message must be part of ourselves. The Son of God was His own message, His words were spirit and life; and as His disciples our lives must be the sacrament of our message. The natural heart will do any amount of serving, but it takes the heart broken by conviction of sin, and baptised by the Holy Ghost, and crumpled into the purpose of God, before the life becomes the sacrament of its message.

There is a difference between giving a testimony and preaching. A preacher is one who has realised the call of God and is determined to use his every power to proclaim God's truth. God takes us out of our own ideas for our lives and we are "batter'd to shape and use," as the disciples were after Pentecost. Pentecost did not teach the disciples anything; it made them the incarnation of what they preached—"Ye shall be witnesses unto Me."

Let God have perfect liberty when you speak. Before God's message can liberate other souls, the liberation must be real in you. Gather your material, and set it alight when you speak.

MARCH 11

VISION

I was not disobedient unto the heavenly vision. Acts 26:19

If we lose the vision, we alone are responsible, and the way we lose the vision is by spiritual leakage. If we do not run our belief about God into practical issues, it is all up with the vision God has given. The only way to be obedient to the heavenly vision is to give our utmost for God's highest, and this can only be done by continually and resolutely recalling the vision. The test is the sixty seconds of every minute, and the sixty minutes of every hour, not our times of prayer and devotional meetings.

"Though it tarry, wait for it." We cannot attain to a vision, we must live in the inspiration of it until it accomplishes itself. We get so practical that we forget the vision. At the beginning we saw the vision but did not wait for it; we rushed off into practical work, and when the vision was fulfilled, we did not see it. Waiting for the vision that tarries is the test of our loyalty to God. It is at the peril of our soul's welfare that we get caught up in practical work and miss the fulfilment of the vision.

Watch God's cyclones. The only way God sows His saints is by His whirlwind. Are you going to prove an empty pod? It will depend on whether or not you are actually living in the light of what you have seen. Let God fling you out, and do not go until He does. If you select your own spot, you will prove an empty pod. If God sows you, you will bring forth fruit.

It is essential to practise the walk of the feet in the light of the vision.

MARCH 12

ABANDONMENT

Then Peter began to say unto Him, Lo, we have left all, and have followed Thee. . . . Mark 10:28

Our Lord replies, in effect, that abandonment is for Himself, and not for what the disciples themselves will get from it. Beware of an abandonment which has the commercial spirit in it—"I am going to give myself to God because I want to be delivered from sin, because I want to be made holy." All that is the result of being right with God, but that spirit is not of the essential nature of Christianity. Abandonment is not for anything at all. We have got so commercialised that we only go to God for something from Him, and not for Himself. It is like saying—"No, Lord, I don't want Thee, I want myself; but I want myself clean and filled with the Holy Ghost; I want to be put in Thy showroom and be able to say—'This is what God has done for me.'" If we only give up something to God because we want more back, there is nothing of the Holy Spirit in our abandonment; it is miserable commercial self-interest. That we gain heaven, that we are delivered from sin, that we are made useful to God—these things never enter as considerations into real abandonment, which is a personal sovereign preference for Jesus Christ Himself.

When we come up against the barriers of natural relationship, where is Jesus Christ? Most of us desert Him—"Yes, Lord, I did hear Thy call; but my mother is in the road, my wife, my self-interest, and I can go no further." "Then," Jesus says, "you cannot be My disciple."

The test of abandonment is always over the neck of natural devotion. Go over it, and God's own abandonment will embrace all those you had to hurt in abandoning. Beware of stopping short of abandonment to God. Most of us know abandonment in vision only.

MARCH 13

THE ABANDONMENT OF GOD

God so loved the world, that He gave. . . . John 3:16

Salvation is not merely deliverance from sin, nor the experience of personal holiness; the salvation of God is deliverance out of self entirely into union with

Himself. My experimental knowledge of salvation will be along the line of deliverance from sin and of personal holiness; but salvation means that the Spirit of God has brought me into touch with God's personality, and I am thrilled with something infinitely greater than myself; I am caught up into the abandonment of God.

To say that we are called to preach holiness or sanctification, is to get into a side-eddy. We are called to proclaim Jesus Christ. The fact that He saves from sin and makes us holy is part of the effect of the wonderful abandonment of God.

Abandonment never produces the consciousness of its own effort, because the whole life is taken up with the One to Whom we abandon. Beware of talking about abandonment if you know nothing about it, and you will never know anything about it until you have realised what John 3:16 means, that God gave Himself absolutely. In our abandonment we give ourselves over to God just as God gave Himself for us, without any calculation. The consequence of abandonment never enters into our outlook because our life is taken up with Him.

MARCH 14

OBEDIENCE

His servants ye are to whom ye obey. Romans 6:16

The first thing to do in examining the power that dominates me is to take hold of the unwelcome fact that I am responsible for being thus dominated because I have yielded. If I am a slave to myself, I am to blame for it because at a point away back I yielded myself to myself. Likewise, if I obey God I do so because I have yielded myself to Him.

Yield in childhood to selfishness, and you will find it the most enchaining tyranny on earth. There is no power in the human soul of itself to break the bondage of a disposition formed by yielding. Yield for one second to anything in the nature of lust (remember what lust is: "I must have it at once," whether it be the lust of the flesh or the lust of the mind, once yield and though you may hate yourself for having yielded, you are a bond-slave to that thing. There is no release in human power at all, but only in the Redemption. You must yield yourself in utter humiliation to the only One Who can break the dominating power, viz., the Lord Jesus Christ. "He hath anointed Me . . . to preach deliverance to the captives."

We find this out in the most ridiculously small ways—"Oh, I can give that habit up when I like." You cannot, you will find that the habit absolutely dominates you because you yielded to it willingly. It is easy

to sing—"He will break every fetter," and at the same time be living a life of obvious slavery to yourself. Yielding to Jesus will break every form of slavery in any human life.

MARCH 15

THE DISCIPLINE OF DISMAY

And as they followed, they were afraid. Mark 10:32

At the beginning we were sure we knew all about Jesus Christ, it was a delight to sell all and to fling ourselves out in a hardihood of love; but now we are not quite so sure. Jesus is on in front and He looks strange. "Jesus went before them: and they were amazed."

There is an aspect of Jesus that chills the heart of a disciple to the core and makes the whole spiritual life gasp for breath. This strange Being with His face set like a flint and His striding determination strikes terror into me. He is no longer Counsellor and Comrade, He is taken up with a point of view I know nothing about, and I am amazed at Him. At first I was confident that I understood Him, but now I am not so sure. I begin to realise there is a distance between Jesus Christ and me; I can no longer be familiar with Him. He is ahead of me and He never turns round; I have no idea where He is going, and the goal has become strangely far off.

Jesus Christ had to fathom every sin and every sorrow man could experience, and that is what makes Him seem strange. When we see Him in this aspect we do not know Him, we do not recognise one feature of His life, and we do not know how to begin to follow Him. He is on in front, a Leader Who is very strange, and we have no comradeship with Him.

The discipline of dismay is an essential necessity in the life of discipleship. The danger is to get back to a little fire of our own and kindle enthusiasm at it (cf. Isaiah 50:10–11). When the darkness of dismay comes, endure until it is over, because out of it will come that following of Jesus which is an unspeakable joy.

MARCH 16

THE MASTER ASSIZES

For we must all appear before the judgement seat of Christ. 2 Corinthians 5:10

Paul says that we must all, preacher and people alike, "appear before the judgement seat of Christ." If you learn to live in the white light of Christ here and now, judgement finally will cause you to delight in the work of God in you. Keep yourself steadily faced by the judgement seat of Christ; walk now in the light of the holiest you know. A wrong temper of mind about another soul will end in the spirit of the devil, no matter how saintly you are. One carnal judgement, and the end of it is hell in you. Drag it to the light at once and say—"My God, I have been guilty there." If you don't, hardness will come all through. The penalty of sin is confirmation in sin. It is not only God who punishes for sin; sin confirms itself in the sinner and gives back full pay. No struggling or praying will enable you to stop doing some things, and the penalty of sin is that gradually you get used to it and do not know that it is sin. No power save the incoming of the Holy Ghost can alter the inherent consequences of sin.

"But if we walk in the light *as He is in the light.*" Walking in the light means for many of us walking according to our standard for another person. The deadliest Pharisaism to-day is not hypocrisy, but unconscious unreality.

MARCH 17

THE WORKER'S RULING PASSION

Wherefore we labour, that . . . we may be accepted of Him. 2 Corinthians 5:9

"Wherefore we *labour*. . . ." It is arduous work to keep the master ambition in front. It means holding one's self to the high ideal year in and year out, not being ambitious to win souls or to establish churches or to have revivals, but being ambitious only to be "accepted of Him." It is not lack of spiritual experience that leads to failure, but lack of labouring to keep the ideal right. Once a week at least take stock before God, and see whether you are keeping your life up to the standard He wishes. Paul is like a musician who does not heed the approval of the audience if he can catch the look of approval from his Master.

Any ambition which is in the tiniest degree away from this central one of being "approved unto God" may end in our being castaways. Learn to discern where the ambition leads, and you will see why it is so necessary to live facing the Lord Jesus Christ. Paul says—Lest my body should make me take another line, I am constantly watching so that I may bring it into subjection and keep it under (see 1 Corinthians 9:27).

I have to learn to relate everything to the master ambition, and to maintain it without any cessation.

---

12. down to the scruple: to the smallest item.

My worth to God in public is what I am in private. Is my master ambition to please Him and be acceptable to Him, or is it something less, no matter how noble?

MARCH 18

SHALL I ROUSE MYSELF UP TO THIS?

Perfecting holiness in the fear of God. 2 Corinthians 7:1

"Having therefore these promises." I claim the fulfilment of God's promises, and rightly, but that is only the human side; the Divine side is that through the promises I recognise God's claim on me. For instance, am I realising that my body is the temple of the Holy Ghost, or have I a habit of body that plainly will not bear the light of God on it? By sanctification the Son of God is formed in me, then I have to transform my natural life into a spiritual life by obedience to Him. God educates us down to the scruple.[12] When He begins to check, do not confer with flesh and blood, cleanse yourself at once. Keep yourself cleansed in your daily walk.

I have to cleanse myself from all filthiness of the flesh and spirit until both are in accord with the nature of God. Is the mind of my spirit in perfect agreement with the life of the Son of God in me, or am I insubordinate in intellect? Am I forming the mind of Christ, Who never spoke from His right to Himself, but maintained an inner watchfulness whereby He continually submitted His spirit to His Father? I have the responsibility of keeping my spirit in agreement with His Spirit, and by degrees Jesus lifts me up to where He lived—in perfect consecration to His Father's will, paying no attention to any other thing. Am I perfecting this type of holiness in the fear of God? Is God getting His way with me, and are other people beginning to see God in my life more and more?

Be serious with God and leave the rest gaily alone. Put God first literally.

MARCH 19

THE WAY OF ABRAHAM IN FAITH

He went out, not knowing whither he went. Hebrews 11:8

In the Old Testament, personal relationship with God showed itself in separation, and this is symbolised in the life of Abraham by his separation from his country and from his kith and kin. To-day the separation is more of a mental and moral separation from the way that those who are dearest to us look at things, that is, if they have not a personal relationship with God. Jesus Christ emphasised this (see Luke 14:26).

Faith never knows where it is being led, but it loves and knows the One Who is leading. It is a life of *faith*, not of intellect and reason, but a life of knowing Who makes us "go." The root of faith is the knowledge of a Person, and one of the biggest snares is the idea that God is sure to lead us to success.

The final stage in the life of faith is attainment of character. There are many passing transfigurations of character; when we pray we feel the blessing of God enwrapping us and for the time being we are changed, then we get back to the ordinary days and ways and the glory vanishes. The life of faith is not a life of mounting up with wings, but a life of walking and not fainting. It is not a question of sanctification; but of something infinitely further on than sanctification, of faith that has been tried and proved and has stood the test. Abraham is not a type of sanctification, but a type of the life of faith, a tried faith built on a real God. *"Abraham believed God."*

MARCH 20

FRIENDSHIP WITH GOD

Shall I hide from Abraham that thing which I do? Genesis 18:17

Its Delights. This chapter brings out the delight of real friendship with God as compared with occasional feelings of His presence in prayer. To be so much in contact with God that you never need to ask Him to show you His will, is to be nearing the final stage of your discipline in the life of faith. When you are rightly related to God, it is a life of freedom and liberty and delight, you *are* God's will, and all your commonsense decisions are His will for you unless He checks. You decide things in perfect delightful friendship with God, knowing that if your decisions are wrong He will always check; when He checks, stop at once.

Its Difficulties. Why did Abraham stop praying when he did? He was not intimate enough yet to go boldly on until God granted his desire, there was something yet to be desired in his relationship to God. Whenever we stop short in prayer and say— "Well, I don't know; perhaps it is not God's will"— there is still another stage to go. We are not so intimately acquainted with God as Jesus was, and as He wants us to be—"That they may be one, even as We are one." Think of the last thing you prayed

about—were you devoted to your desire or to God? Determined to get some gift of the Spirit or to get at God? "Your Heavenly Father knoweth what things ye have need of before ye ask Him." The point of asking is that you may get to know God better. "Delight thyself also in the LORD; and He shall give thee the desires of thine heart." Keep praying in order to get a perfect understanding of God Himself.

MARCH 21

INTEREST OR IDENTIFICATION?

I have been crucified with Christ. Galatians 2:20 (RV)

The imperative need spiritually is to sign the death-warrant of the disposition of sin, to turn all emotional impressions and intellectual beliefs into a moral verdict against the disposition of sin, viz., my claim to my right to myself. Paul says—"I have been crucified with Christ"; he does not say, "I have determined to imitate Jesus Christ," or, "I will endeavour to follow Him," but, "I have been *identified* with Him in His death." When I come to such a moral decision and act upon it, then all that Christ wrought for me on the Cross is wrought *in* me. The free committal of myself to God gives the Holy Spirit the chance to impart to me the holiness of Jesus Christ.

". . . *nevertheless I live*. . . ." The individuality remains, but the mainspring, the ruling disposition, is radically altered. The same human body remains, but the old satanic right to myself is destroyed.

"And the life which I now live in the flesh, . . ." not the life which I long to live and pray to live, but the life I now live in my mortal flesh, the life which men can see, "I live by the faith of the Son of God." This faith is not Paul's faith in Jesus Christ, but the faith that the Son of God has imparted to him—"the faith *of the Son of God.*" It is no longer faith in faith, but faith which has overleapt all conscious bounds, the identical faith of the Son of God.

MARCH 22

THE BURNING HEART

Did not our heart burn within us? Luke 24:32

We need to learn this secret of the burning heart. Suddenly Jesus appears to us, the fires are kindled, we have wonderful visions; then we have to learn to keep the secret of the burning heart that will go through anything. It is the dull, bald, dreary, commonplace day, with commonplace duties and people, that kills the burning heart unless we have learned the secret of abiding in Jesus.

Much of our distress as Christians comes not because of sin, but because we are ignorant of the laws of our own nature. For instance, the only test as to whether we ought to allow an emotion to have its way is to see what the outcome of the emotion will be. Push it to its logical conclusion, and if the outcome is something God would condemn, allow it no more way. But if it is an emotion kindled by the Spirit of God and you do not let that emotion have its right issue in your life, it will react on a lower level. That is the way sentimentalists are made. The higher the emotion is, the deeper the degradation will be if it is not worked out on its proper level. If the Spirit of God has stirred you, make as many things inevitable as possible, let the consequences be what they will. We cannot stay on the mount of transfiguration, but we must obey the light we received there; we must act it out. When God gives a vision, transact business on that line, no matter what it costs.

> *We cannot kindle when we will*
> *The fire which in the heart resides,*
> *The spirit bloweth and is still,*
> *In mystery our soul abides;*
> *But tasks in hours or insight will'd*
> *Can be through hours of gloom fulfill'd.*[13]

MARCH 23

AM I CARNALLY MINDED?

Whereas there is among you jealousy and strife, are ye not carnal? 1 Corinthians 3:3 (RV)

No natural man knows anything about carnality. The flesh lusting against the Spirit that came in at regeneration, and the Spirit lusting against the flesh, produces carnality. "Walk in the Spirit," says Paul, "and ye shall not fulfil the lusts of the flesh"; and carnality will disappear.

Are you contentious, easily troubled about trifles? "Oh, but no one who is a Christian ever is!" Paul says they are, he connects these things with carnality. Is there a truth in the Bible that instantly awakens petulance in you? That is a proof that you are yet carnal. If sanctification is being worked out, there is no trace of that spirit left.

If the Spirit of God detects anything in you that is wrong, He does not ask you to put it right; He asks you to accept the light, and He will put it right. A child of the light confesses instantly and stands bared before God; a child of the darkness says—"Oh, I can explain that away." When once the light breaks and the conviction of wrong comes, be a child of the light, and confess, and God will deal with what is wrong; if you vindicate yourself, you prove yourself to be a child of the darkness.

What is the proof that carnality has gone? Never deceive yourself; when carnality is gone it is the most real thing imaginable. God will see that you have any number of opportunities to prove to yourself the marvel of His grace. The practical test is the only proof. "Why," you say, "if this had happened before, there would have been the spirit of resentment!" You will never cease to be the most amazed person on earth at what God has done for you on the inside.

MARCH 24

DECREASING INTO HIS PURPOSE

He must increase, but I must decrease. John 3:30

If you become a necessity to a soul, you are out of God's order. As a worker, your great responsibility is to be a friend of the Bridegroom. When once you see a soul in sight of the claims of Jesus Christ, you know that your influence has been in the right direction, and instead of putting out a hand to prevent the throes, pray that they grow ten times stronger until there is no power on earth or in hell that can hold that soul away from Jesus Christ. Over and over again, we become amateur providences; we come in and prevent God, and say—"This and that must not be." Instead of proving friends of the Bridegroom, we put our sympathy in the way, and the soul will one day say—"That one was a thief, he stole my affections from Jesus, and I lost my vision of Him."

Beware of rejoicing with a soul in the wrong thing, but see that you do rejoice in the right thing. "The friend of the Bridegroom . . . rejoiceth greatly because of the Bridegroom's voice: this my joy therefore is fulfilled. He must increase, but I must decrease." This is spoken with joy and not with sadness—at last they are to see the Bridegroom! And John says this is his joy. It is the absolute effacement of the worker, he is never thought of again.

Watch for all you are worth until you hear he Bridegroom's voice in the life of another. Never mind what havoc it brings, what upsets, what crumblings of health, rejoice with divine hilarity when once His

---

13. Matthew Arnold, *Morality* (1852)

voice is heard. You may often see Jesus Christ wreck a life before He saves it. (Cf. Matthew 10:34)

MARCH 25

THE MOST DELICATE MISSION ON EARTH

The friend of the Bridegroom. John 3:29

Goodness and purity ought never to attract attention to themselves, they ought simply to be magnets to draw to Jesus Christ. If my holiness is not drawing towards Him, it is not holiness of the right order, but an influence that will awaken inordinate affection and lead souls away into side-eddies. A beautiful saint may be a hindrance if he does not present Jesus Christ but only what Christ has done for him; he will leave the impression—"What a fine character that man is!"— that is not being a true friend of the Bridegroom; *I* am increasing all the time, He is not.

In order to maintain this friendship and loyalty to the Bridegroom, we have to be more careful of our moral and vital relationship to Him than of any other thing, even of obedience. Sometimes there is nothing to obey, the only thing to do is to maintain a vital connection with Jesus Christ, to see that nothing interferes with that. Only occasionally do we have to obey. When a crisis arises we have to find out what God's will is, but the greater part of the life is not conscious obedience but the maintenance of this relationship— the friend of the Bridegroom. Christian work may be a means of evading the soul's concentration on Jesus Christ. Instead of being friends of the Bridegroom, we become amateur providences and may work against Him whilst we use His weapons.

MARCH 26

VISION BY PERSONAL PURITY

Blessed are the pure in heart: for they shall see God. Matthew 5:8

Purity is not innocence, it is much more. Purity is the outcome of sustained spiritual sympathy with God. We have to grow in purity. The life with God may be right and the inner purity remain unsullied, and yet every now and again the bloom on the outside may be sullied. God does not shield us from this possibility, because in this way we realise the necessity of maintaining the vision by personal purity. If the spiritual bloom of our life with God is getting impaired

in the tiniest degree, we must leave off everything and get it put right. Remember that vision depends on character—*the pure in heart* see God.

God makes us pure by His sovereign grace, but we have something to look after, this bodily life by which we come in contact with other people and with other points of view; it is these that are apt to sully. Not only must the inner sanctuary be kept right with God, but the outer courts as well are to be brought into perfect accord with the purity God gives us by His grace. The spiritual understanding is blurred immediately the outer court is sullied. If we are going to retain personal contact with the Lord Jesus Christ, it will mean there are some things we must scorn to do or to think, some legitimate things we must scorn to touch.

A practical way of keeping personal purity unsullied in relation to other people is to say to yourself— That man, that woman, *perfect in Christ Jesus!* That friend, that relative, *perfect in Christ Jesus!*

MARCH 27

VISION BY PERSONAL CHARACTER

Come up hither, and I will shew thee things. Revelation 4:1

An elevated mood can only come out of an elevated habit of personal character. If in the externals of your life you live up to the highest you know, God will continually say—"Friend, go up higher." The golden rule in temptation is—"Go higher." When you get higher up, you face other temptations and characteristics. Satan uses the strategy of elevation in temptation, and God does the same, but the effect is different. When the devil puts you into an elevated place, he makes you screw your idea of holiness beyond what flesh and blood could ever bear. It is a spiritual acrobatic performance, you are just poised and dare not move; but when God elevates you by His grace into the heavenly places, instead of finding a pinnacle to cling to, you find a great table-land where it is easy to move.

Compare this week in your spiritual history with the same week last year and see how God has called you up higher. We have all been brought to see from a higher standpoint. Never let God give you one point of truth which you do not instantly live up to. Always work it out, keep in the light of it.

Growth in grace is measured not by the fact that you have not gone back, but that you have an insight into where you are spiritually; you have heard God say "Come up higher," not to you personally, but to the insight of your character. "Shall I hide from Abraham that thing which I do?" God has to hide from us what

He does until by personal character we get to the place where He can reveal it.

MARCH 28

ISN'T THERE SOME MISUNDERSTANDING?

Let us go into Judea again. His disciples say unto Him, . . . Goest Thou thither again? John 11:7–8

I may not understand what Jesus Christ says, but it is dangerous to say that therefore He was mistaken in what He said. It is never right to think that my obedience to a word of God will bring dishonour to Jesus. The only thing that will bring dishonour is not obeying Him. To put my view of His honour in place of what He is plainly impelling me to do is never right, although it may arise from a real desire to prevent Him being put to open shame. I know when the proposition comes from God because of its quiet persistence. When I have to weigh the *pros* and *cons*, and doubt and debate come in, I am bringing in an element that is not of God, and I come to the conclusion that the suggestion was not a right one. Many of us are loyal to our notions of Jesus Christ, but how many of us are loyal to Him? Loyalty to Jesus means I have to step out where I do not see anything (cf. Matthew 14:29); loyalty to my notions means that I clear the ground first by my intelligence. Faith is not intelligent understanding, faith is deliberate commitment to a Person where I see no way.

Are you debating whether to take a step in faith in Jesus or to wait until you can see how to do the thing yourself? Obey Him with glad reckless joy. When He says something and you begin to debate, it is because you have a conception of His honour which is not His honour. Are you loyal to Jesus or loyal to your notion of Him? Are you loyal to what He says, or are you trying to compromise with conceptions which never came from Him? "Whatsoever He saith unto you, *do it.*"

MARCH 29

OUR LORD'S SURPRISE VISITS

Be ye therefore ready also. Luke 12:40

The great need for the Christian worker is to be ready to face Jesus Christ at any and every turn. This is not easy, no matter what our experience is. The battle is not against sin or difficulties or circumstances, but against being so absorbed in work that we are not ready to face Jesus Christ at every turn. That is the one great need, not facing our belief, or our creed, or the question whether we are of any use, but to face *Him.*

Jesus rarely comes where we expect Him; He appears where we least expect Him, and always in the most illogical connections. The only way a worker can keep true to God is by being ready for the Lord's surprise visits. It is not service that matters, but intense spiritual reality, expecting Jesus Christ at every turn. This will give our life the attitude of child-wonder which He wants it to have. If we are going to be ready for Jesus Christ, we have to stop being religious (that is, using religion as a higher kind of culture) and be spiritually real.

If you are looking off unto Jesus, avoiding the call of the religious age you live in, and setting your heart on what He wants, on thinking on His line, you will be called unpractical and dreamy; but when He appears in the burden and the heat of the day, you will be the only one who is ready. Trust no one, not even the finest saint who ever walked this earth, ignore him, if he hinders your sight of Jesus Christ.

MARCH 30

HOLINESS V. HARDNESS TOWARDS GOD

And He . . . wondered that there was no intercessor. Isaiah 59:16

The reason many of us leave off praying and become hard towards God is because we have only a sentimental interest in prayer. It sounds right to say that we pray; we read books on prayer which tell us that prayer is beneficial, that our minds are quieted and our souls uplifted when we pray; but Isaiah implies that God is amazed at such thoughts of prayer.

Worship and intercession must go together, the one is impossible without the other. Intercession means that we rouse ourselves up to get the mind of Christ about the one for whom we pray. Too often instead of worshipping God, we construct statements as to how prayer works. Are we worshipping or are we in dispute with God—"I don't see how You are going to do it." This is a sure sign that we are not worshipping. When we lose sight of God we become hard and dogmatic. We hurl our own petitions at God's throne and dictate to Him as to what we wish Him to do. We do not worship God, nor do we seek to form the mind of Christ. If we are hard towards God, we will become hard towards other people.

Are we so worshipping God that we rouse ourselves up to lay hold on Him, that we may be brought into contact with His mind about the ones for whom we pray? Are we living in a holy relationship to God, or are we hard and dogmatic?

"But there is no one interceding properly"—then be that one yourself, be the one who worships God and who lives in holy relationship to him. Get into the real work of intercession, and remember it is a work, a work that taxes every power; but a work which has no snare. Preaching the gospel has a snare; intercessory prayer has none.

MARCH 31

HEEDFULNESS V. HYPOCRISY IN OURSELVES

If any man see his brother sin a sin which is not unto death, he shall ask, and He shall give him life for them that sin not unto death. 1 John 5:16

If we are not heedful of the way the Spirit of God works in us, we shall become spiritual hypocrites. We see where other folks are failing, and we turn our discernment into the gibe of criticism instead of into intercession on their behalf. The revelation is made to us not through the acuteness of our minds, but by the direct penetration of the Spirit of God, and if we are not heedful of the source of the revelation, we shall become criticising centres and forget that God says—"... he shall ask, and he shall give him life for them that sin not unto death." Take care lest you play the hypocrite by spending all your time trying to get others right before you worship God yourself.

One of the subtlest burdens God ever puts on us as saints is this burden of discernment concerning other souls. He reveals things in order that we may take the burden of these souls before Him and form the mind of Christ about them, and as we intercede on His line, God says He will give us "life for them that sin not unto death." It is not that we bring God into touch with our minds, but that we rouse ourselves until God is able to convey His mind to us about the one for whom we intercede.

Is Jesus Christ seeing of the travail of His soul in us? He cannot unless we are so identified with Himself that we are roused up to get His view about the people for whom we pray. May we learn to intercede so whole-heartedly that Jesus Christ will be abundantly satisfied with us as intercessors.

APRIL 1

HEARTINESS V. HEARTLESSNESS TOWARDS OTHERS

It is Christ ... who also maketh intercession for us.... The Spirit ... maketh intercession for the saints. Romans 8:34, 27

Do we need any more argument than this to become intercessors—that Christ "ever liveth to make intercession"; that the Holy Spirit "maketh intercession for the saints"? Are we living in such vital relationship to our fellow men that we do the work of intercession as the Spirit-taught children of God? Begin with the circumstances we are in—our homes, our business, our country, the present crisis as it touches us and others—are these things crushing us? Are they badgering us out of the presence of God and leaving us no time for worship? Then let us call a halt, and get into such living relationship with God that our relationship to others may be maintained on the line of intercession whereby God works His marvels.

Beware of outstripping God by your very longing to do His will. We run ahead of Him in a thousand and one activities, consequently we get so burdened with persons and with difficulties that we do not worship God, we do not intercede. If once the burden and the pressure come upon us and we are not in the worshipping attitude, it will produce not only hardness toward God but despair in our own souls. God continually introduces us to people for whom we have no affinity, and unless we are worshipping God, the most natural thing to do is to treat them heartlessly, to give them a text like the jab of a spear, or leave them with a rapped-out counsel of God and go. A heartless Christian must be a terrible grief to Our Lord.

Are we in the direct line of the intercession of our Lord and of the Holy Spirit?

APRIL 2

THE GLORY THAT EXCELS

The Lord ... hath sent me, that thou mightest receive thy sight. Acts 9:17

When Paul received his sight he received spiritually an insight into the Person of Jesus Christ, and the whole of his subsequent life and preaching was nothing but Jesus Christ—"I determined not to know any thing among you, save Jesus Christ, and Him crucified." No attraction was ever allowed to hold the mind and soul of Paul save the face of Jesus Christ.

We have to learn to maintain an unimpaired state of character up to the last notch revealed in the vision of Jesus Christ.

The abiding characteristic of a spiritual man is the interpretation of the Lord Jesus Christ to himself, and the interpretation to others of the purposes of God. The one concentrated passion of the life is Jesus Christ. Whenever you meet this note in a man, you feel he is a man after God's own heart.

Never allow anything to deflect you from insight into Jesus Christ. It is the test of whether you are spiritual or not. To be unspiritual means that other things have a growing fascination for you.

> *Since mine eyes have looked on Jesus,*
> *I've lost sight of all beside,*
> *So enchained my spirit's vision,*
> *Gazing on the Crucified.*

APRIL 3

IF THOU HADST KNOWN!

If thou hadst known . . . in this thy day, the things which belong unto thy peace! but now they are hid from thine eyes. Luke 19:42

Jesus had entered into Jerusalem in triumph, the city was stirred to its foundations; but a strange god was there, the pride of Pharisaism; it was religious and upright, but a "whited sepulchre."

What is it that blinds me in this *my* day? Have I a strange god—not a disgusting monster, but a disposition that rules me? More than once God has brought me face to face with the strange god and I thought I should have to yield, but I did not do it. I got through the crisis by the skin of my teeth and I find myself in the possession of the strange god still; I am blind to the things which belong to my peace. It is an appalling thing that we can be in the place where the Spirit of God should be getting at us unhinderedly, and yet increase our condemnation in God's sight.

"If thou hadst known"—God goes direct to the heart, with the tears of Jesus behind. These words imply culpable responsibility; God holds us responsible for what we do not see. "Now they are hid from thine eyes"—because the disposition has never been yielded. The unfathomable sadness of the "might have been"! God never opens doors that have been closed. He opens other doors, but He reminds us that there are doors which we have shut, doors which need never have been shut, imaginations which need never have been sullied. Never be afraid when God brings back the past. Let memory have its way. It is a minister of God with its rebuke and chastisement and sorrow. God will turn the "might have been" into a wonderful culture for the future.

APRIL 4

THOSE BORDERS OF DISTRUST

Behold, the hour cometh . . . that ye shall be scattered. John 16:32

Jesus is not rebuking the disciples, their faith was real, but it was disturbed; it was not at work in actual things. The disciples were scattered to their own interests, alive to interests that never were in Jesus Christ. After we have been perfectly related to God in sanctification, our faith has to be worked out in actualities. We shall be scattered, not into work, but into inner desolations and made to know what internal death to God's blessings means. Are we prepared for this? It is not that we choose it, but that God engineers our circumstances so that we are brought there. Until we have been through that experience, our faith is bolstered up by feelings and by blessings. When once we get there, no matter where God places us or what the inner desolations are, we can praise God that all is well. That is faith being worked out in actualities.

". . . and shall leave Me alone." Have we left Jesus alone by the scattering of His providence? Because we do not see God in our circumstances? Darkness comes by the sovereignty of God. Are we prepared to let God do as He likes with us—prepared to be separated from conscious blessings? Until Jesus Christ is Lord, we all have ends of our own to serve; our faith is real, but it is not permanent yet. God is never in a hurry; if we wait, we shall see that God is pointing out that we have not been interested in Himself, but only in His blessings. The sense of God's blessing is elemental.

"Be of good cheer; I have overcome the world." Spiritual grit is what we need.

APRIL 5

HIS AGONY AND OUR FELLOWSHIP

Then cometh Jesus with them unto a place called Gethsemane, and saith unto the disciples, . . . tarry ye here, and watch with Me. Matthew 26:36, 38

We can never fathom the agony in Gethsemane, but at least we need not misunderstand it. It is the agony of God and Man in one, face to face with sin. We know nothing about Gethsemane in personal experience. Gethsemane and Calvary stand for something unique; they are the gateway into Life for us.

It was not the death on the cross that Jesus feared in Gethsemane; He stated most emphatically that He came on purpose to die. In Gethsemane He feared lest He might not get through as Son of Man. He would get through as Son of God—Satan could not touch Him there; but Satan's onslaught was that He would get through as an isolated Figure only; and that would mean that He could be no Saviour. Read the record of the agony in the light of the temptation: Then the devil "departed from Him for a season." In Gethsemane Satan came back and was again overthrown. Satan's final onslaught against Our Lord *as son of Man* is in Gethsemane.

The agony in Gethsemane is the agony of the Son of God in fulfilling His destiny as the Saviour of the world. The veil is drawn aside to reveal all it cost Him to make it possible for us to become sons of God. His agony is the basis of the simplicity of our salvation. The Cross of Christ is a triumph for the *son of Man*. It was not only a sign that Our Lord had triumphed, but that He had triumphed to save the human race. Every human being can get through into the presence of God now because of what the Son of Man went through.

APRIL 6

THE COLLISION OF GOD AND SIN

Who His own self bare our sins in His own body on the tree. 1 Peter 2:24

The Cross of Jesus is the revelation of God's judgement on sin. Never tolerate the idea of martyrdom about the Cross of Jesus Christ. The Cross was a superb triumph in which the foundations of hell were shaken. There is nothing more certain in Time or Eternity than what Jesus Christ did on the Cross: He switched the whole of the human race back into a right relationship with God. He made Redemption the basis of human life, that is, He made a way for every son of man to get into communion with God.

The Cross did not *happen* to Jesus: He came on purpose for it. He is "the Lamb slain from the foundation of the world." The whole meaning of the Incarnation is the Cross. Beware of separating *God manifest in the flesh* from *the Son becoming sin*. The Incarnation was for the purpose of Redemption. God

became incarnate for the purpose of putting away sin; not for the purpose of Self-realisation. The Cross is the centre of Time and of Eternity, the answer to the enigmas of both.

The Cross is not the cross of a man but the Cross of God, and the Cross of God can never be realised in human experience. The Cross is the exhibition of the nature of God, the gateway whereby any individual of the human race can enter into union with God. When we get to the Cross, we do not go through it; we abide in the life to which the Cross is the gateway.

The centre of salvation is the Cross of Jesus, and the reason it is so easy to obtain salvation is because it cost God so much. The Cross is the point where God and sinful man merge with a crash and the way to life is opened—but the crash is on the heart of God.

APRIL 7

WHY ARE WE NOT TOLD PLAINLY?

He charged them that they should tell no man what things they had seen, till the Son of man were risen from the dead. Mark 9:9

Say nothing until the Son of man is risen in you—until the life of the risen Christ so dominates you that you understand what the historic Christ taught. When you get to the right state on the inside, the word which Jesus has spoken is so plain that you are amazed you did not see it before. You could not understand it before, you were not in the place in disposition where it could be borne.

Our Lord does not hide these things; they are unbearable until we get into a fit condition of spiritual life. "I have yet many things to say unto you, but ye cannot bear them now." There must be communion with His risen life before a particular word can be borne by us. Do we know anything about the impartation of the risen life of Jesus? The evidence that we do is that His word is becoming interpretable to us. God cannot reveal anything to us if we have not His Spirit. An obstinate outlook will effectually hinder God from revealing anything to us. If we have made up our minds about a doctrine, the light of God will come no more to us on that line, we cannot get it. This obtuse stage will end immediately His resurrection life has its way with us.

"Tell no man...."—so many do tell what they saw on the mount of transfiguration. They have had the vision and they testify to it, but the life does not tally with it, the Son of man is not yet risen in them. I wonder when He is going to be formed in you and in me?

APRIL 8

HIS RESURRECTION DESTINY

Ought not Christ to have suffered these things, and to enter into His glory? Luke 24:26

Our Lord's Cross is the gateway into His life: His Resurrection means that He has power now to convey His life to me. When I am born again from above (RV mg), I receive from the risen Lord His very life.

Our Lord's Resurrection destiny is to bring "many sons unto glory." The fulfilling of His destiny gives Him the right to make us sons and daughters of God. We are never in the relationship to God that the Son of God is in; but we are brought by the Son into the relation of sonship. When Our Lord rose from the dead, He rose to an absolutely new life, to a life He did not live before He was incarnate. He rose to a life that had never been before; and His resurrection means for us that we are raised to His risen life, not to our old life. One day we shall have a body like unto His glorious body, but we can know now the efficacy of His resurrection and walk in newness of life. I would know Him in *"the power of His resurrection."*

"As Thou hast given Him power over all flesh, that He should give eternal life to as many as Thou hast given Him." "Holy Spirit" is the experimental name for Eternal Life working in human beings here and now. The Holy Spirit is the Deity in proceeding power Who applies the Atonement to our experience. Thank God it is gloriously and majestically true that the Holy Ghost can work in us the very nature of Jesus if we will obey Him.

APRIL 9

HAVE I SEEN HIM?

After that He appeared in another form unto two of them. Mark 16:12

Being saved and seeing Jesus are not the same thing. Many are partakers of God's grace who have never seen Jesus. When once you have seen Jesus, you can never be the same, other things do not appeal as they used to do:

Always distinguish between what you see Jesus to be, and what He has done for you. If you only know what He has done for you, you have not a big enough God; but if you have had a vision of Jesus as He is, experiences can come and go, you will endure, "as seeing Him Who is invisible." The man blind from his birth did not know Who Jesus was until He appeared and revealed Himself to him. Jesus appears to those for whom he has done something; but we cannot dictate when He will come. Suddenly at any turn He may come—"Now I see Him!"

Jesus must appear to your friend as well as to you; no one can see Jesus with your eyes. Severance takes place where one and not the other has seen Jesus. You cannot bring your friend unless God brings him. Have you seen Jesus? Then you will want others to see Him too. "And they went and told it unto the residue: neither believed they them." You must tell, although they do not believe.

> *O could I tell, ye surely would believe it!*
> *O could I only say what I have seen!*
> *How should I tell or how can ye receive it,*
> *How, till He bringeth you where I have been?*

APRIL 10

MORAL DECISION ABOUT SIN

Knowing this, that our old man is crucified with Him, that the body of sin might be destroyed, that henceforth we should not serve sin. Romans 6:6

Co-Crucifixion. Have I made this decision about sin—that it must be killed right out in me? It takes a long time to come to a moral decision about sin, but it is the great moment in my life when I do decide that just as Jesus Christ died for the sin of the world, so sin must die out in me, not be curbed or suppressed or counteracted, but crucified. No one can bring any one else to this decision. We may be earnestly convinced, and religiously convinced, but what we need to do is to come to the decision which Paul forces here.

Haul yourself up, take a time alone with God, make the moral decision and say—"Lord, identify me with Thy death until I know that sin is dead in me." Make the moral decision that sin in you must be put to death.

It was not a divine anticipation on the part of Paul, but a very radical and definite experience. Am I prepared to let the Spirit of God search me until I know what the disposition of sin is—the thing that lusts against the Spirit of God in me? Then if so, will I agree with God's verdict on that disposition of sin—that it should be identified with the death of Jesus? I cannot reckon myself "dead indeed unto sin" unless I have been through this radical issue of will before God.

Have I entered into the glorious privilege of being crucified with Christ until all that is left is the life of Christ in my flesh and blood? "I am crucified with Christ; nevertheless I live; yet not I, but Christ liveth in me."

APRIL 11

MORAL DIVINITY

For if we have been planted together in the likeness of His death, we shall be also in the likeness of His resurrection. Romans 6:5

Co-Resurrection. The proof that I have been through crucifixion with Jesus is that I have a decided likeness to Him. The incoming of the Spirit of Jesus into me readjusts my personal life to God. The resurrection of Jesus has given Him authority to impart the life of God to me, and my experimental life must be constructed on the basis of His life. I can have the resurrection life of Jesus now, and it will show itself in holiness.

The idea all through the Apostle Paul's writings is that after the moral decision to be identified with Jesus in His death has been made, the resurrection life of Jesus invades every bit of my human nature. It takes omnipotence to live the life of the Son of God in mortal flesh. The Holy Spirit cannot be located as a Guest in a house, He invades everything. When once I decide that my "old man" (i.e., the heredity of sin) should be identified with the death of Jesus, then the Holy Spirit invades me. He takes charge of everything, my part is to walk in the light and to obey all that He reveals. When I have made the moral decision about sin, it is easy to reckon actually that I am dead unto sin, because I find the life of Jesus there all the time. Just as there is only one stamp of humanity, so there is only one stamp of holiness, the holiness of Jesus, and it is His holiness that is gifted to me. God puts the holiness of His Son into me, and I belong to a new order spiritually.

APRIL 12

MORAL DOMINION

Death hath no more dominion over Him . . . in that He liveth, He liveth unto God. Likewise reckon ye also yourselves to be dead indeed unto sin, but alive unto God. Romans 6:9–11

Co-Eternal Life. Eternal life was the life which Jesus Christ exhibited on the human plane, and it is the same life, not a copy of it, which is manifested in our mortal flesh when we are born of God. Eternal life is not a gift from God, eternal life is the gift *of God.* The energy and the power which were manifested in Jesus will be manifested in us by the sheer sovereign grace of God when once we have made the moral decision about sin.

Ye shall receive the power of the Holy Ghost—not power as a gift from the Holy Ghost; the power *is* the Holy Ghost, not something which He imparts. The life that was in Jesus is made ours by means of his Cross when once we make the decision to be identified with Him. If it is difficult to get right with God, it is because we will not decide definitely about sin. Immediately we do decide, the full life of God comes in. Jesus came to give us endless supplies of life: "that ye might be filled with all the fulness of God." Eternal Life has nothing to do with Time, it is the life which Jesus lived when He was down here. The only source of Life is the Lord Jesus Christ.

The weakest saint can experience the power of the Deity of the Son of God if once he is willing to "let go." Any strand of our own energy in ourselves will blur the life of Jesus. We have to keep letting go, and slowly and surely the great full life of God will invade us in every part, and men will take knowledge of us that we have been with Jesus.

APRIL 13

WHAT TO DO UNDER THE CONDITIONS

Cast thy burden upon the LORD. Psalm 55:22

We must distinguish between the burden-bearing that is right and the burden-bearing that is wrong. We ought never to bear the burden of sin or of doubt, but there are burdens placed on us by God which He does not intend to lift off, He wants us to roll them back on Him. "Cast what He hath given thee upon the LORD" (RV mg). If we undertake work for God and get out of touch with Him, the sense of responsibility will be overwhelmingly crushing; but if we roll back on God that which He has put upon us, He takes away the sense of responsibility by bringing in the realisation of Himself.

Many workers have gone out with high courage and fine impulses, but with no intimate fellowship with Jesus Christ, and before long they are crushed. They do not know what to do with the burden, it produces weariness, and people say—"What an embittered end to such a beginning!"

"Roll thy burden upon the LORD" (see Psalm 37:5 RV mg)—you have been bearing it all; deliberately put one end on the shoulders of God. "The government shall be upon His shoulder." Commit to God "what He hath given thee" (RV mg); not fling it off, but put it over on to Him and yourself with it, and the burden is lightened by the sense of companionship. Never dissociate yourself from the burden.

APRIL 14

INSPIRED INVINCIBILITY

Take My yoke upon you, and learn of Me. Matthew 11:29

"Whom the Lord loveth He chasteneth." How petty our complaining is! Our Lord begins to bring us into the place where we can have communion with Him, and we groan and say—"Oh Lord, let me be like other people!" Jesus is asking us to take one end of the yoke—"My yoke is easy, get alongside Me and we will pull together." Are you identified with the Lord Jesus like that? If so, you will thank God for the pressure of His hand.

"To them that have no might He increaseth strength." God comes and takes us out of our sentimentality, and our complaining turns into a psalm of praise. The only way to know the strength of God is to take the yoke of Jesus upon us and learn of Him.

"The joy of the Lord is your strength." Where do the saints get their joy from? If we did not know some saints, we would say—"Oh, he, or she, has nothing to bear." Lift the veil. The fact that the peace and the light and the joy of God are there is proof that the burden is there too. The burden God places squeezes the grapes and out comes the wine; most of us see the wine only. No power on earth or in hell can conquer the Spirit of God in a human spirit, it is an inner unconquerableness.

If you have the whine in you, kick it out ruthlessly. It is a positive crime to be weak in God's strength.

APRIL 15

THE RELAPSE OF CONCENTRATION

But the high places were not taken away out of Israel; nevertheless the heart of Asa was perfect all his days. 2 Chronicles 15:17

Asa was incomplete in his external obedience, he was right in the main but not entirely right. Beware of the thing of which you say—"Oh, that does not matter much." The fact that it does not matter much to you may mean that it matters a very great deal to God. Nothing is a light matter with a child of God. How much longer are some of us going to keep God trying to teach us one thing? He never loses patience. You say—"I know I am right with God"; but still the "high places" remain, there is something over which you have not obeyed. Are you protesting that your heart is right with God, and yet is there something in your life about which He has caused you to doubt? When-

ever there is doubt, quit immediately, no matter what it is. Nothing is a mere detail.

Are there some things in connection with your bodily life, your intellectual life, upon which you are not concentrating at all? You are all right in the main, but you are slipshod; there is a relapse on the line of concentration. You no more need a holiday from spiritual concentration than your heart needs a holiday from beating. You cannot have a moral holiday and remain moral, nor can you have a spiritual holiday and remain spiritual. God wants you to be entirely his, and this means that you have to watch to keep yourself fit. It takes a tremendous amount of time. Some of us expect to "clear the numberless ascensions" in about two minutes.

APRIL 16

CAN YOU COME DOWN?

While ye have light, believe in the light. John 12:36

We all have moments when we feel better than our best, and we say—"I feel fit for anything; if only I could be like this always!" We are not meant to be. Those moments are moments of insight which we have to live up to when we do not feel like it. Many of us are no good for this workaday world when there is no high hour. We must bring our commonplace life up to the standard revealed in the high hour.

Never allow a feeling which was stirred in you in the high hour to evaporate. Don't put your mental feet on the mantelpiece and say—"What a marvellous state of mind to be in!" Act immediately, do something, if only because you would rather not do it. If in a prayer meeting God has shown you something to do, don't say—"I'll do it"; *do it!* Take yourself by the scruff of the neck and shake off your incarnate laziness. Laziness is always seen in cravings for the high hour; we talk about working up to a time on the mount. We have to learn to live in the grey day according to what we saw on the mount.

Don't cave in because you have been baffled once, get at it again. Burn your bridges behind you, and stand committed to God by your own act. Never revise your decisions, but see that you make your decisions in the light of the high hour.

APRIL 17

NECK OR NOTHING

Now when Simon Peter heard that it was the Lord, he girt his fisher's coat unto him, . . . and did cast himself into the sea. John 21:7

Have you ever had a crisis in which you deliberately and emphatically and recklessly abandoned everything? It is a crisis of will. You may come up to it many times externally, but it amounts to nothing. The real deep crisis of abandonment is reached internally, not externally. The giving up of external things may be an indication of being in total bondage.

Have you deliberately committed your will to Jesus Christ? It is a transaction of will, not of emotion; the emotion is simply the gilt edge of the transaction. If you allow emotion first, you will never make the transaction. Do not ask God what the transaction is to be, but make it in regard to the thing you do see, either in the shallow or the profound place.

If you have heard Jesus Christ's voice on the billows, let your convictions go to the winds, let your consistency go to the winds, but maintain your relationship to Him.

APRIL 18

READINESS

God called unto him. . . . And he said, Here am I. Exodus 3:4

When God speaks, many of us are like men in a fog, we give no answer. Moses' reply revealed that he was somewhere. Readiness means a right relationship to God and a knowledge of where we are at present. We are so busy telling God where we would like to go. The man or woman who is ready for God and His work is the one who carries off the prize when the summons comes. We wait with the idea of some great opportunity, something sensational, and when it comes we are quick to cry—"Here am I." Whenever Jesus Christ is in the ascendant, we are there; but we are not ready for an obscure duty.

Readiness for God means that we are ready to do the tiniest little thing or the great big thing, it makes no difference. We have no choice in what we want to do; whatever God's programme may be we are there, ready. When any duty presents itself we hear God's voice as Our Lord heard His Father's voice, and we are ready for it with all the alertness of our love for Him. Jesus Christ expects to do with us as His Father did with Him. He can put us where He likes, in pleasant duties or in mean[14] duties, because the union is that of the Father and Himself. "That they may be one, even as We are one."

Be ready for the sudden surprise visits of God. A ready person never needs to get ready. Think of the time we waste trying to get ready when God has called! The burning bush is a symbol of everything that surrounds the ready soul, it is ablaze with the presence of God.

APRIL 19

IS IT NOT IN THE LEAST LIKELY?

For Joab had turned after Adonijah, though he turned not after Absalom. 1 Kings 2:28

Joab stood the big test, he remained absolutely loyal and true to David and did not turn after the fascinating and ambitious Absalom, but yet towards the end of his life he turned after the craven Adonijah. Always remain alert to the fact that where one man has gone back is exactly where any one may go back (see 1 Corinthians 10:13). You have gone through the big crisis, now be alert over the least things; take into calculation the "retired sphere of the leasts."

We are apt to say—"It is not in the least likely that having been through the supreme crisis, I shall turn now to the things of the world." Do not forecast where the temptation will come; it is the least likely thing that is the peril. In the aftermath of a great spiritual transaction the "retired sphere of the leasts" begins to tell; it is not dominant, but remember it is there, and if you are not warned, it will trip you up. You have remained true to God under great and intense trials, now beware of the undercurrent. Do not be morbidly introspective, looking forward with dread, but keep alert; keep your memory bright before God. Unguarded strength is double weakness, because that is where the "retired sphere of the leasts" saps. The Bible characters fell on their strong points, never on their weak ones.

"Kept by the power of God"—that is the only safety.

APRIL 20

CAN A SAINT SLANDER GOD?

For all the promises of God in Him are yea, and in Him Amen. 2 Corinthians 1:20

Jesus told the parable of the talents recorded in Matthew 25 as a warning that it is possible for us to

---

14. mean: as used here, something or someone ordinary, common, low, or ignoble, rather than cruel or spiteful.

misjudge our capacity. This parable has not to do with natural gifts, but with the Pentecostal gift of the Holy Ghost. We must not measure our spiritual capacity by education or by intellect; our capacity in spiritual things is measured by the promises of God. If we get less than God wants us to have, before long we will slander Him as the servant slandered his master: "You expect more than You give me power to do; You demand too much of me, I cannot stand true to You where I am placed." When it is a question of God's Almighty Spirit, never say "I can't." Never let the limitation of natural ability come in. If we have received the Holy Spirit, God expects the work of the Holy Spirit to be manifested in us.

The servant justified himself in everything he did and condemned his lord on every point—"Your demand is out of all proportion to what you give." Have we been slandering God by daring to worry when He has said: "Seek ye first the Kingdom of God, and His righteousness; and all these things shall be added unto you"? Worrying means exactly what this servant implied—"I know You mean to leave me in the lurch." The person who is lazy naturally is always captious—"I haven't had a decent chance," and the one who is lazy spiritually is captious with God. Lazy people always strike out on an independent line.

Never forget that our capacity in spiritual matters is measured by the promises of God. Is God able to fulfil His promises? Our answer depends on whether we have received the Holy Spirit.

APRIL 21

NOW DON'T HURT THE LORD!

Have I been so long time with you, and yet hast thou not known Me, Philip? John 14:9

Our Lord must be repeatedly astounded at us—astounded at how un-simple we are. It is opinions of our own which make us stupid; when we are simple we are never stupid, we discern all the time. Philip expected the revelation of a tremendous mystery, but not in the One Whom he knew. The mystery of God is not in what is going to be, it is now; we look for it presently, in some cataclysmic event. We have no reluctance in obeying Jesus, but it is probable that we are hurting Him by the questions we ask. "Lord, shew us the Father." His answer comes straight back—"There He is, always here or nowhere." We look for God to manifest Himself to His children: God only manifests Himself *in* His children. Other people see the manifestation, the child of God does not. We want to be conscious of God; we cannot be conscious

of our consciousness and remain sane. If we are asking God to give us experiences, or if conscious experience is in the road, we hurt the Lord. The very questions we ask hurt Jesus because they are not the questions of a child.

"Let not your heart be troubled"—then am I hurting Jesus by allowing my heart to be troubled? If I believe the character of Jesus, am I living up to my belief? Am I allowing anything to perturb my heart, any morbid questions to come in? I have to get to the implicit relationship that takes everything as it comes from Him. God never guides presently, but always now. Realise that the Lord is here *now*, and the emancipation is immediate.

APRIL 22

THE LIGHT THAT FAILS

We all with open face beholding . . . the glory of the Lord. 2 Corinthians 3:18

A servant of God must stand so much alone that he never knows he is alone. In the first phases of Christian life disheartenments come, people who used to be lights flicker out, and those who used to stand with us pass away. We have to get so used to it that we never know we are standing alone. "All men forsook me: . . . notwithstanding the Lord stood with me" (2 Timothy 4:16–17). We must build our faith, not on the fading light, but on the light that never fails. When "big" men go we are sad, until we see that they are meant to go; the one thing that remains is looking in the face of God for ourselves.

Allow nothing to keep you from looking God sternly in the face about yourself and about your doctrine, and every time you preach see that you look God in the face about things first, then the glory will remain all through. A Christian worker is one who perpetually looks in the face of God and then goes forth to talk to the people. The characteristic of the ministry of Christ is that of unconscious glory that abides. "Moses wist not that the skin of his face shone while He talked with him."

We are never called on to parade our doubts or to express the hidden ecstasies of our life with God. The secret of the worker's life is that he keeps in tune with God all the time.

APRIL 23

THE WORSHIP OF THE WORK

Labourers together with God. 1 Corinthians 3:9

Beware of any work for God which enables you to evade concentration on Him. A great many Christian workers worship their work. The one concern of a worker should be concentration on God, and this will mean that all the other margins of life, mental, moral and spiritual, are free with the freedom of a child—a worshipping child, not a wayward child. A worker without this solemn, dominant note of concentration on God is apt to get his work on his neck; there is no margin of body, mind or spirit free, consequently he becomes spent out and crushed. There is no freedom, no delight in life; nerves, mind and heart are so crushingly burdened that God's blessing cannot rest. But the other side is just as true—when once the concentration is on God, all the margins of life are free and under the dominance of God alone. There is no responsibility on you for the work; the only responsibility you have is to keep in living, constant touch with God, and to see that you allow nothing to hinder your co-operation with Him. The freedom after sanctification is the freedom of a child, the things that used to keep the life pinned down are gone. But be careful to remember that you are freed for one thing only—to be absolutely devoted to your co-Worker.

We have no right to judge where we should be put, or to have preconceived notions as to what God is fitting us for. God engineers everything; wherever He puts us our one great aim is to pour out a whole-hearted devotion to Him in that particular work. "Whatsoever thy hand findeth to do, do it with thy might."

APRIL 24

THE WARNING AGAINST WANTONING

Notwithstanding in this rejoice not, that the spirits are subject unto you. Luke 10:20

As Christian workers, worldliness is not our snare, sin is not our snare, but spiritual wantoning is, viz.: taking the pattern and print of the religious age we live in, making eyes at spiritual success. Never court anything other than the approval of God, go "without the camp, bearing His reproach." Jesus told the disciples not to rejoice in successful service, and yet this seems to be the one thing in which most of us do rejoice. We have the commercial view—so many souls saved and sanctified, thank God, now it is all right. Our work begins where God's grace has laid the foundation; we are not to save souls, but to disciple them. Salvation and sanctification are the work of God's sovereign grace; our work as His disciples is to disciple lives until they are wholly yielded to God. One life wholly devoted to God is of more value to God than one hundred lives simply awakened by His Spirit. As workers for God we must reproduce our own kind spiritually, and that will be God's witness to us as workers. God brings us to a standard of life by His grace, and we are responsible for reproducing that standard in others.

Unless the worker lives a life hidden with Christ in God, he is apt to become an irritating dictator instead of an indwelling disciple. Many of us are dictators, we dictate to people and to meetings. Jesus never dictates to us in that way. Whenever Our Lord talked about discipleship, He always prefaced it with an "IF," never with an emphatic assertion—"You must." Discipleship carries an option with it.

APRIL 25

INSTANT IN SEASON

Be instant in season, out of season. 2 Timothy 4:2

Many of us suffer from the morbid tendency to be instant "out of season." The season does not refer to time, but to us. "Be instant in season, out of season," whether we feel like it or not. If we do only what we feel inclined to do, some of us would do nothing for ever and ever. There are unemployables in the spiritual domain, spiritually decrepit people, who refuse to do anything unless they are supernaturally inspired. The proof that we are rightly related to God is that we do our best whether we feel inspired or not.

One of the great snares of the Christian worker is to make a fetish of his rare moments. When the spirit of God gives you a time of inspiration and insight, you say—"Now I will always be like this for God." No, you will not, God will take care you are not. Those times are the gift of God entirely. You cannot give them to yourself when you choose. If you say you will only be at your best, you become an intolerable drag on God; you will never do anything unless God keeps you consciously inspired. If you make a god of your best moments, you will find that God will fade out of your life and never come back until you do the duty that lies nearest, and have learned not to make a fetish of your rare moments.

APRIL 26

THE SUPREME CLIMB

Take now thy son, . . . and offer him there for a burnt offering upon one of the mountains which I will tell thee of. Genesis 22:2

Character determines how a man interprets God's will (cf. Psalm 18:25–26). Abraham interpreted God's command to mean that he had to kill his son, and he could only leave this tradition behind by the pain of a tremendous ordeal. God could purify his faith in no other way. If we obey what God says according to our sincere belief, God will break us from those traditions that misrepresent Him. There are many such beliefs to be got rid of, e.g., that God removes a child because the mother loves him too much—a devil's lie! and a travesty of the true nature of God. If the devil can hinder us from taking the supreme climb and getting rid of wrong traditions about God, he will do so; but if we keep true to God, God will take us through an ordeal which will bring us out into a better knowledge of Himself.

The great point of Abraham's faith in God was that he was prepared to do anything for God. He was there to obey God, no matter to what belief he went contrary. Abraham was not a devotee of his convictions, or he would have slain Isaac and said that the voice of the angel was the voice of the devil. That is the attitude of a fanatic. If you will remain true to God, God will lead you straight through every barrier into the inner chamber of the knowledge of Himself; but there is always this point of giving up convictions and traditional beliefs. Don't ask God to test you. Never declare as Peter did—I will do anything, I will go to death with Thee. Abraham did not make any such declaration, he remained true to God, and God purified his faith.

APRIL 27

WHAT DO YOU WANT?

Seekest thou great things for thyself? Jeremiah 45:5

Are you seeking great things for yourself? Not seeking to be a great one, but seeking great things from God for yourself. God wants you in a closer relationship to Himself than receiving His gifts, He wants you to get to know Him. A great thing is accidental, it comes and goes. God never gives us anything accidental. Nothing is easier than getting into a right relationship with God except when it is not God Whom you want but only what He gives.

If you have only come the length of asking God for things, you have never come to the first strand of abandonment, you have become a Christian from a standpoint of your own. "I did ask God for the Holy Spirit, but He did not give me the rest and the peace I expected." Instantly God puts His finger on the reason—you are not seeking the Lord at all, you are seeking something for yourself. Jesus says—"Ask, and

it shall be given you." Ask God for what you want, and you cannot ask if you are not asking for a right thing. When you draw near to God, you cease from asking for things. "Your Father knoweth what things ye have need of, before ye ask Him." Then why ask? That you may get to know Him.

Are you seeking great things for yourself—"O Lord, baptise me with the Holy Ghost"? If God does not, it is because you are not abandoned enough to Him, there is something you will not do. Are you prepared to ask yourself what it is you want from God, and why you want it? God always ignores the present perfection for the ultimate perfection. He is not concerned about making you blessed and happy just now; He is working out His ultimate perfection all the time—"that they may be one, even as We are."

APRIL 28

WHAT YOU WILL GET

Thy life will I give unto thee for a prey in all places whither thou goest. Jeremiah 45:5

This is the unshakeable secret of the Lord to those who trust Him—I will give thee thy life. What more does a man want than his life? It is the essential thing. "Thy life . . . for a prey" means that wherever you may go, even if it is into hell, you will come out with your life, nothing can harm it. So many of us are caught up in the show of things, not in the way of property and possessions, but of blessings. All these have to go; but there is something grander that never can go—the life that is "hid with Christ in God."

Are you prepared to let God take you into union with Himself, and pay no more attention to what you call the "great things"? Are you prepared to abandon entirely and let go? The test of abandonment is in refusing to say—"Well, what about this?" Beware of suppositions. Immediately you allow—"What about this?" it means you have not abandoned, you do not really trust God. Immediately you do abandon, you think no more about what God is going to do. Abandon means to refuse yourself the luxury of asking any questions. If you abandon entirely to God, He says at once, "Thy life will I give unto thee for a prey." The reason people are tired of life is because God has not given them anything, they have not got their life as a prey. The way to get out of that state is to abandon to God. When you do get through to abandonment to God, you will be the most surprised and delighted creature on earth; God has got you absolutely and has given you your life. If you are not there, it is either because of disobedience or a refusal to be simple enough.

APRIL 29

THE GRACIOUSNESS OF UNCERTAINTY

It doth not yet appear what we shall be. 1 John 3:2

Naturally, we are inclined to be so mathematical and calculating that we look upon uncertainty as a bad thing. We imagine that we have to reach some end, but that is not the nature of spiritual life. The nature of spiritual life is that we are certain in our uncertainty, consequently we do not make our nests anywhere. Common sense says—"Well, supposing I were in that condition. . . ." We cannot suppose ourselves in any condition we have never been in.

Certainty is the mark of the commonsense life: gracious uncertainty is the mark of the spiritual life. To be certain of God means that we are uncertain in all our ways, we do not know what a day may bring forth. This is generally said with a sigh of sadness; it should be rather an expression of breathless expectation. We are uncertain of the next step, but we are certain of God. Immediately we abandon to God, and do the duty that lies nearest, He packs our life with surprises all the time. When we become advocates of a creed, something dies; we do not believe God, we only believe our belief about Him. Jesus said "Except ye . . . become as little children." Spiritual life is the life of a child. We are not uncertain of God, but uncertain of what He is going to do next. If we are only certain in our beliefs, we get dignified and severe and have the ban of finality[15] about our views; but when we are rightly related to God, life is full of spontaneous, joyful uncertainty and expectancy.

"Believe also in Me," said Jesus, not—"Believe certain things about Me." Leave the whole thing to Him, it is gloriously uncertain how He will come in, but He will come. Remain loyal to Him.

APRIL 30

THE SPONTANEITY OF LOVE

Love suffereth long, and is kind. . . . 1 Corinthians 13:4 (RV)

Love is not premeditated, it is spontaneous, that is, it bursts up in extraordinary ways. There is nothing of mathematical certainty in Paul's category of love. We cannot say—"Now I am going to think no evil; I am going to believe all things." The characteristic of love is spontaneity. We do not settle statements of Jesus in front of us as a standard; but when His Spirit is having His way with us, we live according to His standard without knowing it, and on looking back we are amazed at the disinterestedness of a particular emotion, which is the evidence that the spontaneity of real love was there. In everything to do with the life of God in us, its nature is only discerned when it is past.

The springs of love are in God, not in us. It is absurd to look for the love of God in our hearts naturally, it is only there when it has been shed abroad in our hearts by the Holy Spirit.

If we try to prove to God how much we love Him, it is a sure sign that we do not love Him. The evidence of our love for Him is the absolute spontaneity of our love, it comes naturally. In looking back we cannot tell why we did certain things, we did them according to the spontaneous nature of His love in us. The life of God manifests itself in this spontaneous way because the springs of love are in the Holy Ghost. (Romans 5:5)

MAY 1

INSIGHT NOT EMOTION

I have to lead my life in faith, without seeing Him. 2 Corinthians 5:7 (MOFFATT)

For a time we are conscious of God's attentions, then, when God begins to use us in His enterprises, we take on a pathetic look and talk of the trials and the difficulties, and all the time God is trying to make us do our duty as obscure people. None of us would be obscure spiritually if we could help it. Can we do our duty when God has shut up heaven? Some of us always want to be illuminated saints with golden haloes and the flush of inspiration, and to have the saints of God dealing with us all the time. A gilt-edged saint is no good, he is abnormal, unfit for daily life, and altogether unlike God. We are here as men and women, not as half-fledged angels, to do the work of the world, and to do it with an infinitely greater power to stand the turmoil because we have been born from above (RV mg).

If we try to re-introduce the rare moments of inspiration, it is a sign that it is not God we want. We are making a fetish of the moments when God did come and speak, and insisting that He must do it again; whereas what God wants us to do is to walk by faith. How many of us have laid ourselves by, as it were, and said—"I cannot do any more until God appears to me." He never will, and without any inspiration, without any sudden touch of God, we will have to get up. Then comes the surprise—"Why, He

---

15. "ban of finality": the limitation or curse of having one's mind made up; unwilling to consider new information.

was there all the time, and I never knew it!" Never live for the rare moments, they are surprises. God will give us touches of inspiration when He sees we are not in danger of being led away by them. We must never make our moments of inspiration our standard; our standard is our duty.

MAY 2

THE PASSION OF PATIENCE

Though it tarry, wait for it. Habakkuk 2:3

Patience is not indifference; patience conveys the idea of an immensely strong rock withstanding all onslaughts. The vision of God is the source of patience, because it imparts a moral inspiration. Moses endured, not because he had an ideal of right and duty, but because he had a vision of God. He "endured, as seeing Him Who is invisible." A man with the vision of God is not devoted to a cause or to any particular issue; he is devoted to God Himself. You always know when the vision is of God because of the inspiration that comes with it; things come with largeness and tonic to the life because everything is energised by God. If God gives you a time spiritually, as He gave His Son actually, of temptation in the wilderness, with no word from Himself at all, endure; and the power to endure is there because you see God.

"Though it tarry, wait for it." The proof that we have the vision is that we are reaching out for more than we have grasped. It is a bad thing to be satisfied spiritually. "What shall I render unto the LORD?" said the Psalmist, "I will *take* the cup of salvation." We are apt to look for satisfaction in ourselves—"Now I have got the thing; now I am entirely sanctified; now I can endure." Instantly we are on the road to ruin. Our reach must exceed our grasp. "Not as though I had already attained, either were already perfect." If we have only what we have experienced, we have nothing; if we have the inspiration of the vision of God, we have more than we can experience. Beware of the danger of relaxation spiritually.

MAY 3

VITAL INTERCESSION

Praying always with all prayer and supplication in the Spirit. Ephesians 6:18

As we go on in intercession we may find that our obedience to God is going to cost other people more than we thought. The danger then is to begin to intercede in sympathy with those whom God was gradually lifting to a totally different sphere in answer to our prayers. Whenever we step back from identification with God's interest in others into sympathy with them, the vital connection with God has gone; we have put our sympathy, our consideration for them, in the way, and this is a deliberate rebuke to God.

It is impossible to intercede vitally unless we are perfectly sure of God, and the greatest dissipater of our relationship to God is personal sympathy and personal prejudice. Identification is the key to intercession, and whenever we stop being identified with God, it is by sympathy, not by sin. It is not likely that sin will interfere with our relationship to God, but sympathy will, sympathy with ourselves or with others which makes us say—"I will not allow that thing to happen." Instantly we are out of vital connection with God.

Intercession leaves you neither time nor inclination to pray for your own "sad sweet self." The thought of yourself is not kept out, because it is not there to keep out; you are completely and entirely identified with God's interests in other lives.

Discernment is God's call to intercession, never to fault finding.

MAY 4

VICARIOUS INTERCESSION

Having therefore, brethren, boldness to enter into the holiest by the blood of Jesus. Hebrews 10:19

Beware of imagining that intercession means bringing our personal sympathies into the presence of God and demanding that He does what we ask. Our approach to God is due entirely to the vicarious identification of our Lord with sin. We have "boldness to enter into the holiest *by the blood of Jesus.*"

Spiritual stubbornness is the most effectual hindrance to intercession, because it is based on sympathy with that in ourselves and in others that we do not think needs atoning for. We have the notion that there are certain right and virtuous things in us which do not need to be based on the Atonement, and just in the domain of "stodge" that is produced by this idea we cannot intercede. We do not identify ourselves with God's interests in others, we get petulant with God; we are always ready with our own ideas, and intercession becomes the glorification of our own natural sympathies. We have to realise that the identification of Jesus with sin means the radical alteration of all our sympathies. Vicarious intercession means that we deliberately substitute God's interests in others for our natural sympathy with them.

Am I stubborn or substituted? Petted or perfect in my relationship to God? Sulky or spiritual? Determined to have my own way or determined to be identified with Him?

MAY 5

JUDGEMENT ON THE ABYSS OF LOVE

For the time is come that judgement must begin at the house of God. 1 Peter 4:17

The Christian worker must never forget that salvation is God's thought, not man's; therefore it is an unfathomable abyss. Salvation is the great thought of God, not an experience. Experience is only a gateway by which salvation comes into our conscious life. Never preach the experience; preach the great thought of God behind. When we preach we are not proclaiming how man can be saved from hell and be made moral and pure; we are conveying good news about God.

In the teachings of Jesus Christ the element of judgement is always brought out, it is the sign of God's love. Never sympathise with a soul who finds it difficult to get to God; God is not to blame. It is not for us to find out the reason why it is difficult, but so to present the truth of God that the Spirit of God will show what is wrong. The great sterling test in preaching is that it brings everyone to judgement. The Spirit of God locates each one to himself.

If Jesus ever gave us a command He could not enable us to fulfil, He would be a liar; and if we make our inability a barrier to obedience, it means we are telling God there is something He has not taken into account. Every element of self-reliance must be slain by the power of God. Complete weakness and dependence will always be the occasion for the Spirit of God to manifest His power.

MAY 6

LIBERTY ON THE ABYSS OF THE GOSPEL

Stand fast therefore in the liberty wherewith Christ hath made us free. Galatians 5:1

A spiritually minded man will never come to you with the demand—"Believe this and that"; but with the demand that you square your life with the standards of Jesus. We are not asked to believe the Bible, but to believe the One Whom the Bible reveals (cf. John 5:39–40). We are called to present liberty of conscience, not liberty of view. If we are free with the liberty of Christ, others will be brought into that same liberty—the liberty of realising the dominance of Jesus Christ.

Always keep your life measured by the standards of Jesus. Bow your neck to His yoke alone, and to no other yoke whatever; and be careful to see that you never bind a yoke on others that is not placed by Jesus Christ. It takes God a long time to get us out of the way of thinking that unless everyone sees as we do, they must be wrong. That is never God's view. There is only one liberty, the liberty of Jesus at work in our conscience enabling us to do what is right.

Don't get impatient, remember how God dealt with you—with patience and with gentleness; but never water down the truth of God. Let it have its way and never apologise for it. Jesus said, "Go . . . and make *disciples*" (RV) not—make converts to your opinions.

MAY 7

BUILDING FOR ETERNITY

For which of you, intending to build a tower, sitteth not down first, and counteth the cost, whether he have sufficient to finish it? Luke 14:28

Our Lord refers not to a cost we have to count, but to a cost which He has counted. The cost was those thirty years in Nazareth, those three years of popularity, scandal and hatred; the deep unfathomable agony in Gethsemane, and the onslaught at Calvary—the pivot upon which the whole of Time and Eternity turns. Jesus Christ has counted the cost. Men are not going to laugh at Him at last and say—"This man began to build, and was not able to finish."

The conditions of discipleship laid down by Our Lord in verses 26–27 and 33 mean that the men and women He is going to use in His mighty building enterprises are those in whom He has done everything. "If any man come to Me, and hate not . . . , *he cannot be My disciple.*" Our Lord implies that the only men and women He will use in His building enterprises are those who love Him personally, passionately and devotedly beyond any of the closest ties on earth. The conditions are stern, but they are glorious.

All that we build is going to be inspected by God. Is God going to detect in His searching fire that we have built on the foundation of Jesus some enterprise of our own? These are days of tremendous enterprises, days when we are trying to work for God, and therein is the snare. Profoundly speaking, we can never work for God. Jesus takes us over for *His* enterprises, *His* building schemes entirely, and no soul has any right to claim where he shall be put.

MAY 8

THE PATIENCE OF FAITH

Because thou hast kept the word of My patience.
Revelation 3:10

Patience is more than endurance. A saint's life is in the hands of God like a bow and arrow in the hands of an archer. God is aiming at something the saint cannot see, and He stretches and strains, and every now and again the saint says—"I cannot stand any more." God does not heed, He goes on stretching till His purpose is in sight, then He lets fly. Trust yourself in God's hands. For what have you need of patience just now? Maintain your relationship to Jesus Christ by the patience of faith. "Though He slay me, yet will I wait for Him" (RV).

Faith is not a pathetic sentiment, but robust vigorous confidence built on the fact that God is holy love. You cannot see Him just now, you cannot understand what He is doing, but you know *Him*. Shipwreck occurs where there is not that mental poise which comes from being established on the eternal truth that God is holy love. Faith is the heroic effort of your life, you fling yourself in reckless confidence on God.

God has ventured all in Jesus Christ to save us, now He wants us to venture our all in abandoned confidence in Him. There are spots where that faith has not worked in us as yet, places untouched by the life of God. There were none of those spots in Jesus Christ's life, and there are to be none in ours. "This is life eternal, that they might know Thee." The real meaning of eternal life is a life that can face anything it has to face without wavering. If we take this view, life becomes one great romance, a glorious opportunity for seeing marvellous things all the time. God is disciplining us to get us into this central place of power.

MAY 9

GRASP WITHOUT REACH

Where there is no vision, the people cast off restraint.
Proverbs 29:18 (RV)

There is a difference between an ideal and a vision. An ideal has no moral inspiration; a vision has. The people who give themselves over to ideals rarely *do* anything. A man's conception of Deity may be used to justify his deliberate neglect of his duty. Jonah argued that because God was a God of justice and of mercy, therefore everything would be all right. I may have a right conception of God, and that may be the very

reason why I do not do my duty. But wherever there is vision, there is also a life of rectitude because the vision imparts moral incentive.

Ideals may lull to ruin. Take stock of yourself spiritually and see whether you have ideals only or if you have vision.

Ah, but a man's reach should exceed his grasp,
Or what's a heaven for?

"Where there is no vision. . . ." When once we lose sight of God, we begin to be reckless, we cast off certain restraints, we cast off praying, we cast off the vision of God in little things, and begin to act on our own initiative. If we are eating what we have out of our own hand, doing things on our own initiative without expecting God to come in, we are on the downward path, we have lost the vision. Is our attitude to-day an attitude that springs from our vision of God? Are we expecting God to do greater things than He has ever done? Is there a freshness and vigour in our spiritual outlook.

MAY 10

TAKE THE INITIATIVE

Add to your faith virtue ["Furnish your faith with res-
olution," MOFFATT]. . . . 2 Peter 1:5

"Add" means there is something we have to do. We are in danger of forgetting that we cannot do what God does, and that God will not do what we can do. We cannot save ourselves nor sanctify ourselves, God does that; but God will not give us good habits, He will not give us character, He will not make us walk aright. We have to do all that ourselves, we have to work out the salvation God has worked in. "Add" means to get into the habit of doing things, and in the initial stages it is difficult. To take the initiative is to make a beginning, to instruct yourself in the way you have to go.

Beware of the tendency of asking the way when you know it perfectly well. Take the initiative, stop hesitating, and take the first step. Be resolute when God speaks, act in faith immediately on what He says, and never revise your decisions. If you hesitate when God tells you to do a thing, you endanger your standing in grace. Take the initiative, take it yourself, take the step with your will now, make it impossible to go back. Burn your bridges behind you—"I *will* write that letter"; "I *will* pay that debt." Make the thing inevitable.

We have to get into the habit of hearkening to God about everything, to form the habit of finding out what God says. If, when a crisis comes, we instinctively turn to God, we know that the habit has been formed. We have to take the initiative where we *are*, not where we are not.

MAY 11

YOU WON'T REACH IT ON TIPTOE

Add . . . to your brotherliness . . . love. 2 Peter 1:5, 7 (see MOFFATT)

Love is indefinite to most of us, we do not know what we mean when we talk about love. Love is the sovereign preference of one person for another, and spiritually Jesus demands that that preference be for Himself (cf. Luke 14:26). When the love of God is shed abroad in our hearts by the Holy Ghost, Jesus Christ is easily first; then we must practise the working out of these things mentioned by Peter.

The first thing God does is to knock pretence and the pious pose right out of me. The Holy Spirit reveals that God loved me not because I was loveable, but because it was His nature to do so. "Now," He says to me, "show the same love to others"—"*Love as I have loved you.*" "I will bring any number of people about you whom you cannot respect, and you must exhibit My love to them as I have exhibited it to you." *You won't reach it on tiptoe.* Some of us have tried to, but we were soon tired.

The Lord "suffereth long. . . ." Let me look within and see His dealings with me. The knowledge that God has loved me to the uttermost, to the end of all my sin and meanness[16] and selfishness and wrong, will send me forth into the world to love in the same way. God's love to me is inexhaustible, and I must love others from the bedrock of God's love to me. Growth in grace stops the moment I get huffed. I get huffed because I have a peculiar person to live with. Just think how disagreeable I have been to God! Am I prepared to be so identified with the Lord Jesus that His life and His sweetness are being poured out all the time? Neither natural love nor Divine love will remain unless it is cultivated. Love is spontaneous, but it has to be maintained by discipline.

MAY 12

MAKE A HABIT OF HAVING NO HABITS

For if these things are yours and abound, they make you to be not idle nor unfruitful. 2 Peter 1:8 (RV)

When we begin to form a habit we are conscious of it. There are times when we are conscious of becoming virtuous and patient and godly, but it is only a stage; if we stop there we shall get the strut of the spiritual prig. The right thing to do with habits is to lose them in the life of the Lord, until every habit is so practised that there is no conscious habit at all. Our spiritual life continually resolves into introspection because there are some qualities we have not added as yet. Ultimately the relationship is to be a completely simple one.

Your god may be your little Christian habit, the habit of prayer at stated times, or the habit of Bible reading. Watch how your Father will upset those times if you begin to worship your habit instead of what the habit symbolises—"I can't do that just now, I am praying; it is my hour with God." No, it is your hour with your habit. There is a quality that is lacking in you. Recognise the defect, and then look for the opportunity of exercising yourself along the line of the quality to be added.

Love means that there is no habit visible, you have come to the place where the habit is lost, and by practice you do the thing unconsciously. If you are consciously holy, there are certain things you imagine you cannot do, certain relationships in which you are far from simple; that means there is something to be added. The only supernatural life is the life the Lord Jesus lived, and He was at home with God anywhere. Is there anywhere where you are not at home with God? Let God press through in that particular circumstance until you gain Him, and life becomes the simple life of a child.

MAY 13

THE HABIT OF A GOOD CONSCIENCE

A conscience void of offence toward God, and toward men. Acts 24:16

God's commands are given to the life of His Son in us, consequently to the human nature in which His Son has been formed, His commands are difficult, but immediately we obey they become divinely easy.

Conscience is that faculty in me which attaches itself to the highest that I know, and tells me what the highest I know demands that I do. It is the eye of the soul which looks out either towards God or towards what it regards as the highest, and therefore conscience records differently in different people. If I am

---

16. mean: as used here, something or someone ordinary, common, low, or ignoble, rather than cruel or spiteful.

in the habit of steadily facing myself with God, my conscience will always introduce God's perfect law and indicate what I should do. The point is, will I obey? I have to make an effort to keep my conscience so sensitive that I walk without offence. I should be living in such perfect sympathy with God's Son, that in every circumstance the spirit of my mind is renewed, and I "make out" (MOFFATT) at once "what is that good, and acceptable, and perfect, will of God." God always educates us down to the scruple. Is my ear so keen to hear the tiniest whisper of the Spirit that I know what I should do? "Grieve not the Holy Spirit." He does not come with a voice like thunder; His voice is so gentle that it is easy to ignore it. The one thing that keeps the conscience sensitive to Him is the continual habit of being open to God on the inside. When there is any debate, quit. "Why shouldn't I do this?" You are on the wrong track. There is no debate possible when conscience speaks. At your peril, you allow one thing to obscure your inner communion with God. Drop it, whatever it is, and see that you keep your inner vision clear.

MAY 14

THE HABIT OF ENJOYING THE DISAGREEABLE

That the life also of Jesus might be made manifest in our mortal flesh. 2 Corinthians 4:11

We have to form habits to express what God's grace has done in us. It is not a question of being saved from hell, but of being saved in order to manifest the life of the Son of God in our mortal flesh, and it is the disagreeable things which make us exhibit whether or not we are manifesting His life. Do I manifest the essential sweetness of the Son of God, or the essential irritation of "myself" apart from Him? The only thing that will enable me to enjoy the disagreeable is the keen enthusiasm of letting the life of the Son of God manifest itself in me. No matter how disagreeable a thing may be, say—"Lord, I am delighted to obey Thee in this matter," and instantly the Son of God will press to the front, and there will be manifested in my human life that which glorifies Jesus.

There must be no debate. The moment you obey the light, the Son of God presses through you in that particular; but if you debate you grieve the Spirit of God. You must keep yourself fit to let the life of the Son of God be manifested, and you cannot keep yourself fit if you give way to self-pity. Our circumstances are the means of manifesting how wonderfully perfect and extraordinarily pure the Son of God is. The thing that ought to make the heart beat is a new way

of manifesting the Son of God. It is one thing to choose the disagreeable, and another thing to go into the disagreeable by God's engineering. If God puts you there, He is amply sufficient.

Keep your soul fit to manifest the life of the Son of God. Never live on memories; let the word of God be always living and active in you.

MAY 15

THE HABIT OF RISING TO THE OCCASION

That ye may know what is the hope of His calling. . . . Ephesians 1:18

Remember what you are saved for—that the Son of God might be manifested in your mortal flesh. Bend the whole energy of your powers to realise your election as a child of God; rise to the occasion every time.

You cannot do anything for your salvation, but you must do something to manifest it, you must work out what God has worked in. Are you working it out with your tongue, and your brain and your nerves? If you are still the same miserable crosspatch, set on your own way, then it is a lie to say that God has saved and sanctified you.

God is the Master Engineer, He allows the difficulties to come in order to see if you can vault over them properly—"By my God have I leaped over a wall." God will never shield you from any of the requirements of a son or daughter of His. Peter says—"Think it not strange concerning the fiery trial which is to try you." Rise to the occasion; do the thing. It does not matter how it hurts as long as it gives God the chance to manifest Himself in your mortal flesh.

May God not find the whine in us any more, but may He find us full of spiritual pluck and athleticism, ready to face anything He brings. We have to exercise ourselves in order that the Son of God may be manifested in our mortal flesh. God never has museums. The only aim of the life is that the Son of God may be manifested, and all dictation to God vanishes. Our Lord never dictated to His Father, and we are not here to dictate to God; we are here to submit to His will so that He may work through us what He wants. When we realise this, He will make us broken bread and poured-out wine to feed and nourish others.

MAY 16

THE HABIT OF WEALTH

Partakers of the divine nature. 2 Peter 1:4

We are made partakers of the Divine nature through the promises; then we have to "manipulate" the Divine nature in our human nature by habits, and the first habit to form is the habit of realising the provision God has made. "Oh, I can't afford it," we say—one of the worst lies is tucked up in that phrase. It is ungovernably bad taste to talk about money in the natural domain, and so it is spiritually, and yet we talk as if our Heavenly Father had cut us off with a shilling! We think it a sign of real modesty to say at the end of a day—"Oh, well, I have just got through, but it has been a severe tussle." And all the Almighty God is ours in the Lord Jesus! And He will tax the last grain of sand and the remotest star to bless us if we will obey Him. What does it matter if external circumstances are hard? Why should they not be! If we give way to self-pity and indulge in the luxury of misery, we banish God's riches from our own lives and hinder others from entering into His provision. No sin is worse than the sin of self-pity, because it obliterates God and puts self-interest upon the throne. It opens our mouths to spit out murmurings and our lives become craving spiritual sponges, there is nothing lovely or generous about them.

When God is beginning to be satisfied with us, He will impoverish everything in the nature of fictitious wealth, until we learn that all our fresh springs are in Him (PBV).[17] If the majesty and grace and power of God are not being manifested in us (not to our consciousness), God holds us responsible. "God is able to make all grace abound," then learn to lavish the grace of God on others. Be stamped with God's nature, and His blessing will come through you all the time.

MAY 17

HIS ASCENSION AND OUR UNION

And it came to pass, while He blessed them, He was parted from them, and carried up into heaven. Luke 24:51

We have no corresponding experience to the events in Our Lord's life after the Transfiguration. From then onwards Our Lord's life was altogether vicarious. Up to the time of the Transfiguration He had exhibited the normal perfect life of a man; from the Transfiguration onwards—Gethsemane, the Cross, the Resurrection—everything is unfamiliar to us. His Cross is the door by which every member of the human race can enter into the life of God; by His Resurrection He has the right to give eternal life to any man, and by His Ascension Our Lord enters heaven and keeps the door open for humanity.

On the Mount of Ascension the Transfiguration is completed. If Jesus had gone to heaven from the Mount of Transfiguration, He would have gone alone; He would have been nothing more to us than a glorious Figure. But He turned His back on the glory, and came down from the Mount to identify Himself with fallen humanity.

The Ascension is the consummation of the Transfiguration. Our Lord does now go back into His primal glory; but He does not go back simply as Son of God: He goes back to God as *Son of Man* as well as Son of God. There is now freedom of access for anyone straight to the very throne of God by the Ascension of the Son of Man. As Son of Man Jesus Christ deliberately limited omnipotence, omnipresence and omniscience in Himself. Now they are His in absolute full power. As Son of Man Jesus Christ has all power at the throne of God. He is King of kings and Lord of lords from the day of His Ascension until now.

MAY 18

CAREFUL UNREASONABLENESS

Behold the fowls of the air. . . . Consider the lilies of the field. Matthew 6:26, 28

Consider the lilies of the field, how they grow, they simply *are!* Think of the sea, the air, the sun, the stars and the moon—all these *are*, and what a ministration they exert. So often we mar God's designed influence through us by our self-conscious effort to be consistent and useful. Jesus says that there is only one way to develop spiritually, and that is by concentration on God. "Do not bother about being of use to others, believe on Me"—pay attention to the Source, "and out of you will flow rivers of living water." We cannot get at the springs of our natural life by common sense, and Jesus is teaching that growth in spiritual life does not depend on our watching it, but on concentration on our Father in heaven. Our heavenly Father knows the circumstances we are in, and if we keep concentrated on Him we will grow spiritually as the lilies.

The people who influence us most are not those who buttonhole us and talk to us, but those who live their lives like the stars in heaven and the lilies in the field, perfectly simply and unaffectedly. Those are the lives that mould us.

---

17. PBV: Prayer Book Version. The *Book of Common Prayer* of the Church of England includes a translation of the Psalter, or Psalms of David.

If you want to be of use to God, get rightly related to Jesus Christ and He will make you of use unconsciously every minute you live.

MAY 19

"OUT OF THE WRECK I RISE"

Who shall separate us from the love of Christ? Romans 8:35

God does not keep a man immune from trouble; He says—"I will be with him in trouble." It does not matter what actual troubles in the most extreme form get hold of a man's life, not one of them can separate him from his relationship to God. We are "more than conquerors *in* all these things." Paul is not talking of imaginary things, but of things that are desperately actual; and he says we are super-victors in the midst of them, not by our ingenuity, or by our courage, or by anything other than the fact that not one of them affects our relationship to God in Jesus Christ. Rightly or wrongly, we are where we are, exactly in the condition we are in. I am sorry for the Christian who has not something in his circumstances he wishes was not there.

"*Shall tribulation . . . ?*" Tribulation is never a noble thing; but let tribulation be what it may—exhausting, galling, fatiguing, it is not able to separate us from the love of God. Never let cares or tribulations separate you from the fact that God loves you.

"*Shall . . . anguish . . . ?*" *(RV)*—can God's love hold when everything says that His love is a lie, and that there is no such thing as justice?

"*Shall . . . famine . . . ?*"—can we not only believe in the love of God but be more than conquerors, even while we are being starved?

Either Jesus Christ is a deceiver and Paul is deluded, or some extraordinary thing happens to a man who holds on to the love of God when the odds are all against God's character. Logic is silenced in the face of every one of these things. Only one thing can account for it—the *love of God in Christ Jesus.* "Out of the wreck I rise" every time.

MAY 20

THE REALM OF THE REAL

In your patience possess ye your souls. Luke 21:19

When a man is born again, there is not the same robustness in his thinking or reasoning for a time as formerly. We have to make an expression of the new life, to form the mind of Christ. "Acquire your soul

with patience" (RV). Many of us prefer to stay at the threshold of the Christian life instead of going on to construct a soul in accordance with the new life God has put within. We fail because we are ignorant of the way we are made, we put things down to the devil instead of our own undisciplined natures. Think what we can be when we are roused!

There are certain things we must not pray about—moods, for instance. Moods never go by praying, moods go by kicking. A mood nearly always has its seat in the physical condition, not in the moral. It is a continual effort not to listen to the moods which arise from a physical condition; never submit to them for a second. We have to take ourselves by the scruff of the neck and shake ourselves, and we will find that we can do what we said we could not. The curse with most of us is that we *won't.* The Christian life is one of incarnate spiritual pluck.

MAY 21

DIVINE REASONINGS OF FAITH

But seek ye first the kingdom of God, and His righteousness; and all these things shall be added unto you. Matthew 6:33

Immediately we look at these words of Jesus, we find them the most revolutionary statement human ears ever listened to. "Seek ye *first* the kingdom of God." We argue in exactly the opposite way, even the most spiritually-minded of us—"But I *must* live; I *must* make so much money; I *must* be clothed; I *must* be fed." The great concern of our lives is not the kingdom of God, but how we are to fit ourselves to live. Jesus reverses the order: Get rightly related to God first, maintain that as the great care of your life, and never put the concern of your care on the other things.

"*Take no thought for your life. . . .*" Our Lord points out the utter unreasonableness from His standpoint of being so anxious over the means of living. Jesus is not saying that the man who takes thought for nothing is blessed—that man is a fool. Jesus taught that a disciple has to make his relationship to God the dominating concentration of his life, and to be carefully careless about everything else in comparison to that. Jesus is saying—Don't make the ruling factor of your life what you shall eat and what you shall drink, but be concentrated absolutely on God. Some people are careless over what they eat and drink, and they suffer for it; they are careless about what they wear, and they look as they have no business to look; they are careless about their earthly affairs, and God holds them responsible. Jesus is saying that the great care of the life is to put the relationship to God first, and everything else second.

It is one of the severest disciplines of the Christian life to allow the Holy Spirit to bring us into harmony with the teaching of Jesus in these verses.

MAY 22

NOW THIS EXPLAINS IT

That they all may be one; as Thou, Father, art in Me, and I in Thee, that they also may be one in Us. John 17:21

If you are going through a solitary way, read John 17, it will explain exactly why you are where you are—Jesus has prayed that you may be one with the Father as He is. Are you helping God to answer that prayer, or have you some other end for your life? Since you became a disciple you cannot be as independent as you used to be.

The purpose of God is not to answer our prayers, but by our prayers we come to discern the mind of God, and this is revealed in John 17. There is one prayer God must answer, and that is the prayer of Jesus—"that they may be one, even as We are one." Are we as close to Jesus Christ as that?

God is not concerned about our plans; He does not say—"Do you want to go through this bereavement; this upset?" He allows these things for His own purpose. The things we are going through are either making us sweeter, better, nobler men and women; or they are making us more captious and fault-finding, more insistent upon our own way. The things that happen either make us fiends, or they make us saints; it depends entirely upon the relationship we are in to God. If we say—"Thy will be done," we get the consolation of John 17, the consolation of knowing that our Father is working according to His own wisdom. When we understand what God is after we will not get mean and cynical. Jesus has prayed nothing less for us than absolute oneness with Himself as He was one with the Father. Some of us are far off it, and yet God will not leave us alone until we *are* one with Him, because Jesus has prayed that we may be.

MAY 23

CAREFUL INFIDELITY

Take no thought for your life, what ye shall eat, or what ye shall drink; nor yet for your body, what ye shall put on. Matthew 6:25

Jesus sums up commonsense carefulness in a disciple as infidelity. If we have received the Spirit of God, He will press through and say—"Now where does God come in in this relationship, in this mapped-out holiday, in these new books?" He always presses the point until we learn to make Him our first consideration. Whenever we put other things first, there is confusion.

"Take no thought . . ."—don't take the pressure of forethought upon yourself. It is not only wrong to worry, it is infidelity, because worrying means that we do not think that God can look after the practical details of our lives, and it is never anything else that worries us. Have you ever noticed what Jesus said would choke the word He puts in? The devil? No, the cares of this world. It is the little worries always. I will not trust where I cannot see, that is where infidelity begins. The only cure for infidelity is obedience to the Spirit.

The great word of Jesus to His disciples is *abandon*.

MAY 24

THE DELIGHT OF DESPAIR

And when I saw Him, I fell at His feet as dead. Revelation 1:17

It may be that like the Apostle John you know Jesus Christ intimately, when suddenly He appears with no familiar characteristic at all, and the only thing you can do is to fall at His feet as dead. There are times when God cannot reveal Himself in any other way than in His majesty, and it is the awfulness of the vision which brings you to the delight of despair; if you are ever to be raised up, it must be by the hand of God.

"He laid His right hand upon me." In the midst of the awfulness, a touch comes, and you know it is the right hand of Jesus Christ. The right hand not of restraint nor of correction nor of chastisement, but the right hand of the Everlasting Father. Whenever His hand is laid upon you, it is ineffable peace and comfort, the sense that "underneath are the everlasting arms," full of sustaining and comfort and strength. When once His touch comes, nothing at all can cast you into fear again. In the midst of all His ascended glory the Lord Jesus comes to speak to an insignificant disciple, and to say—"Fear not." His tenderness is ineffably sweet. Do I know Him like that?

Watch some of the things that strike despair. There is despair in which there is no delight, no horizon, no hope of anything brighter; but the delight of despair comes when I know that "in me (that is, in my flesh) dwelleth no good thing." I delight to know that there is that in me which must fall prostrate before God when He manifests Himself, and if I am ever to be raised up it must be by the hand of God. God can do nothing for me until I get to the limit of the possible.

MAY 25

THE TEST OF SELF-INTEREST

If thou wilt take the left hand, then I will go to the right; or if thou depart to the right hand, then I will go to the left. Genesis 13:9

As soon as you begin to live the life of faith in God, fascinating and luxurious prospects will open up before you, and these things are yours by right; but if you are living the life of faith you will exercise your right to waive your rights, and let God choose for you. God sometimes allows you to get into a place of testing where your own welfare would be the right and proper thing to consider if you were not living a life of faith; but if you are, you will joyfully waive your right and leave God to choose for you. This is the discipline by means of which the natural is transformed into the spiritual by obedience to the voice of God.

Whenever *right* is made the guidance in the life, it will blunt the spiritual insight. The great enemy of the life of faith in God is not sin, but the good which is not good enough. The good is always the enemy of the best. It would seem the wisest thing in the world for Abraham to choose, it was his right, and the people around would consider him a fool for not choosing. Many of us do not go on spiritually because we prefer to choose what is right instead of relying on God to choose for us. We have to learn to walk according to the standard which has its eye on God. *"Walk before Me."*

MAY 26

THINK AS JESUS TAUGHT

Pray without ceasing. 1 Thessalonians 5:17

We think rightly or wrongly about prayer according to the conception we have in our minds of prayer. If we think of prayer as the breath in our lungs and the blood from our hearts, we think rightly. The blood flows ceaselessly, and breathing continues ceaselessly; we are not conscious of it, but it is always going on. We are not always conscious of Jesus keeping us in perfect joint with God, but if we are obeying Him, He always is. Prayer is not an exercise, it is the life. Beware of anything that stops ejaculatory prayer. "Pray without ceasing," keep the childlike habit of ejaculatory prayer in your heart to God all the time.

Jesus never mentioned unanswered prayer; He had the boundless certainty that prayer is always answered. Have we by the Spirit the unspeakable certainty that Jesus had about prayer, or do we think of the times when God does not seem to have answered prayer? "Every one that asketh receiveth." We say— "But, . . . but . . ." God answers prayer in the best way, not sometimes, but every time, although the immediate manifestation of the answer in the domain in which we want it may not always follow. Do we expect God to answer prayer?

The danger with us is that we want to water down the things that Jesus says and make them mean something in accordance with common sense; if it were only common sense, it was not worth while for Him to say it. The things Jesus says about prayer are supernatural revelations.

MAY 27

THE LIFE THAT LIVES

Tarry ye in the city of Jerusalem, until ye be endued with power from on high. Luke 24:49

The disciples had to tarry until the day of Pentecost not for their own preparation only; they had to wait until the Lord was glorified historically. As soon as He was glorified, what happened? "Therefore being by the right hand of God exalted, and having received of the Father the promise of the Holy Ghost, He hath shed forth this, which ye now see and hear." The parenthesis in John 7:39 ("For the Holy Ghost was not yet given; because that Jesus was not yet glorified") does not apply to us; the Holy Ghost *has been* given, the Lord *is* glorified; the waiting depends not on God's providence, but on our fitness.

The Holy Spirit's influence and power were at work before Pentecost, but *He* was not here. Immediately Our Lord was glorified in Ascension, the Holy Spirit came into this world, and He has been here ever since. We have to receive the revelation that He is here. The reception of the Holy Spirit is the maintained attitude of a believer. When we receive the Holy Spirit, we receive quickening life from the ascended Lord.

It is not the baptism of the Holy Ghost which changes men, but the power of the ascended Christ coming into men's lives by the Holy Ghost that changes them. We too often divorce what the New Testament never divorces. The baptism of the Holy Ghost is not an experience apart from Jesus Christ: it is the evidence of the ascended Christ.

The baptism of the Holy Ghost does not make you think of Time or Eternity, it is one amazing glorious NOW. "This is life eternal, that they might know Thee." Begin to know Him now, and finish never.

MAY 28

UNQUESTIONED REVELATION

And in that day ye shall ask Me nothing. John 16:23

When is "that day"? When the Ascended Lord makes you one with the Father. In that day you will be one with the Father as Jesus is, and "in that day," Jesus says, "ye shall ask Me nothing." Until the resurrection life of Jesus is manifested in you, you want to ask this and that; then after a while you find all questions gone, you do not seem to have any left to ask. You have come to the place of entire reliance on the resurrection life of Jesus which brings you into perfect contact with the purpose of God. Are you living that life now? If not, why shouldn't you?

There may be any number of things dark to your understanding, but they do not come in between your heart and God. "And in that day ye shall ask Me no question"—you do not need to, you are so certain that God will bring things out in accordance with His will. John 14:1 has become the real state of your heart, and there are no more questions to be asked. If anything is a mystery to you and it is coming in between you and God, never look for the explanation in your intellect, look for it in your disposition, it is that which is wrong. When once your disposition is willing to submit to the life of Jesus, the understanding will be perfectly clear, and you will get to the place where there is no distance between the Father and His child because the Lord has made you one, and "in that day ye shall ask Me no question."

MAY 29

UNDISTURBED RELATIONSHIP

At that day ye shall ask in My name. . . . The Father Himself loveth you. John 16:26–27

"At that day ye shall ask in My name," i.e., in My nature. Not—"You shall use My name as a magic word," but—"You will be so intimate with Me that you will be one with Me." "That day" is not a day hereafter, but a day meant for here and now. "The Father Himself loveth you"—the union is so complete and absolute. Our Lord does not mean that life will be free from external perplexities but that just as He knew the Father's heart and mind, so by the baptism of the Holy Ghost He can lift us into the heavenly places where He can reveal the counsels of God to us.

"Whatsoever ye shall ask the Father in My name . . ." "That day" is a day of undisturbed relationship between God and the saint. Just as Jesus stood unsullied in the presence of His Father, so by the mighty efficacy of the baptism of the Holy Ghost, we can be lifted into that relationship—"that they may be one, even as We are one."

". . . He will give it you." Jesus says that God will recognise our prayers. What a challenge! By the Resurrection and Ascension power of Jesus, by the sent-down Holy Ghost, we can be lifted into such a relationship with the Father that we are at one with the perfect sovereign will of God by our free choice even as Jesus was. In that wonderful position, placed there by Jesus Christ, we can pray to God in His name, in His nature, which is gifted to us by the Holy Ghost, and Jesus says—"Whatsoever ye shall ask the Father in My name, He will give it you." The sovereign character of Jesus Christ is tested by His own statements.

MAY 30

"YES—BUT . . . !"

Lord, I will follow Thee; but . . . Luke 9:61

Supposing God tells you to do something which is an enormous test to your common sense, what are you going to do? Hang back? If you get into the habit of doing a thing in the physical domain, you will do it every time until you break the habit determinedly; and the same is true spiritually. Again and again you will get up to what Jesus Christ wants, and every time you will turn back when it comes to the point, until you abandon resolutely. "Yes, but—supposing I do obey God in this matter, what about . . . ?" "Yes, I will obey God if He will let me use my common sense, but don't ask me to take a step in the dark." Jesus Christ demands of the man who trusts Him the same reckless sporting spirit that the natural man exhibits. If a man is going to do anything worth while, there are times when he has to risk everything on his leap, and in the spiritual domain Jesus Christ demands that you risk everything you hold by common sense and leap into what He says, and immediately you do, you find that what He says fits on as solidly as common sense. At the bar of common sense Jesus Christ's statements may seem mad; but bring them to the bar of faith, and you begin to find with awe-struck spirit that they are the words of God. Trust entirely in God, and when He brings you to the venture, see that you take it. We act like pagans in a crisis, only one out of a crowd is daring enough to bank his faith in the character of God.

MAY 31

GOD FIRST

Put God First in Trust

Jesus did not commit Himself unto them, . . . for He knew what was in man. (John 2:24–25)

Our Lord trusted no man; yet He was never suspicious, never bitter, never in despair about any man because He put God first in trust; He trusted absolutely in what God's grace could do for any man. If I put my trust in human beings first, I will end in despairing of everyone; I will become bitter, because I have insisted on man being what no man ever can be—absolutely right. Never trust anything but the grace of God in yourself or in anyone else.

Put God's Needs First

Lo, I come to do Thy will, O God. (Hebrews 10:9)

A man's obedience is to what he sees to be a need; Our Lord's obedience was to the will of His Father. The cry to-day is—"We must get some work to do; the heathen are dying without God; we must go and tell them of Him." We have to see first of all that God's needs in us personally are being met. "Tarry ye until. . . ." The purpose of this College is to get us rightly related to the needs of God. When God's needs in us have been met, then He will open the way for us to realise His needs elsewhere.

Put God's Trust First

And whoso receiveth one such little child in My name receiveth Me. (Matthew 18:5)

God's trust is that He gives me Himself as a babe. God expects my personal life to be a "Bethlehem." Am I allowing my natural life to be slowly transfigured by the indwelling life of the Son of God? God's ultimate purpose is that His Son might be manifested in my mortal flesh.

JUNE 1

THE STAGGERING QUESTION

Son of man, can these bones live? Ezekiel 37:3

Can that sinner be turned into a saint? Can that twisted life be put right? There is only one answer: "O Lord, Thou knowest, I don't." Never trample in with religious common sense and say—"Oh, yes, with a little more Bible reading and devotion and prayer, I see how it can be done."

It is much easier to *do* something than to trust in God; we mistake panic for inspiration. That is why there are so few fellow-workers with God and so many workers for Him. We would far rather work for God than believe in Him. Am I quite sure that God will do what I cannot do? I despair of men in the degree in which I have never realised that God has done anything for me. Is my experience such a wonderful realisation of God's power and might that I can never despair of anyone I see? Have I had any spiritual work done in me at all? The degree of panic is the degree of the lack of personal spiritual experience.

"Behold, O my people, I will open your graves." When God wants to show you what human nature is like apart from Himself, He has to show it you in yourself. If the Spirit of God has given you a vision of what you are apart from the grace of God (and He only does it when His Spirit is at work), you know there is no criminal who is half so bad in actuality as you know yourself to be in possibility. My "grave" has been opened by God and "I know that in me (that is in my flesh) dwelleth no good thing." God's Spirit continually reveals what human nature is like apart from His grace.

JUNE 2

WHAT ARE YOU HAUNTED BY?

What man is he that feareth the Lord? Psalm 25:12

What are you haunted by? You will say—"By nothing," but we are all haunted by something, generally by ourselves, or, if we are Christians, by our experience. The Psalmist says we are to be haunted by God. The abiding consciousness of the life is to be God, not thinking about Him. The whole of our life inside and out is to be absolutely haunted by the presence of God. A child's consciousness is so mother-haunted that although the child is not consciously thinking of its mother, yet when calamity arises, the relationship that abides is that of the mother. So we are to live and move and have our being in God, to look at everything in relation to God, because the abiding consciousness of God pushes itself to the front all the time.

If we are haunted by God, nothing else can get in, no cares, no tribulation, no anxieties. We see now why Our Lord so emphasised the sin of worry. How can we dare be so utterly unbelieving when God is round about us? To be haunted by God is to have an effective barricade against all the onslaughts of the enemy.

"His soul shall dwell at ease." In tribulation, misunderstanding, slander, in the midst of all these things, if our life is hid with Christ in God, He will keep us at ease. We rob ourselves of the marvellous revelation of this abiding companionship of God. "God is our Refuge"—nothing can come through that shelter.

JUNE 3

THE SECRET OF THE LORD

The secret ["friendship," RV] of the LORD is with them that fear Him. Psalm 25:14

What is the sign of a friend? That he tells you secret sorrows? No, that he tells you secret joys. Many will confide to you their secret sorrows, but the last mark of intimacy is to confide secret joys. Have we ever let God tell us any of His joys, or are we telling God our secrets so continually that we leave no room for Him to talk to us? At the beginning of our Christian life we are full of requests to God, then we find that God wants to get us into relationship with Himself, to get us in touch with His purposes. Are we so wedded to Jesus Christ's idea of prayer—"Thy will be done" — that we catch the secrets of God? The things that make God dear to us are not so much His great big blessings as the tiny things, because they show His amazing intimacy with us; He knows every detail of our individual lives.

". . . *him shall He teach in the way that He shall choose.*" At first we want the consciousness of being guided by God, then as we go on we live so much in the consciousness of God that we do not need to ask what His will is, because the thought of choosing any other will never occur to us. If we are saved and sanctified God guides us by our ordinary choices, and if we are going to choose what He does not want, He will check, and we must heed. Whenever there is doubt, stop at once. Never reason it out and say—"I wonder why I shouldn't?" God instructs us in what we choose, that is, He guides our common sense, and we no longer hinder His Spirit by continually saying—"Now, Lord, what is Thy will?"

JUNE 4

THE NEVER-FAILING GOD

For He hath said, I will never leave thee, nor forsake thee. Hebrews 13:5

What line does my thought take? Does it turn to what God says or to what I fear? Am I learning to say not what God says, but to say something after I have heard what He says? "He hath said, I will never leave

thee, nor forsake thee. So that we may boldly say, The Lord is my helper, and I will not fear what man shall do unto me."

"I will in no wise fail thee" (RV)—not for all my sin and selfishness and stubbornness and wayward-ness. Have I really let God say to me that He will never fail me? If I have listened to this say-so of God's, then let me listen again.

"Neither will I in any wise forsake thee" (RV). Sometimes it is not difficulty that makes me think God will forsake me, but drudgery. There is no Hill Difficulty to climb, no vision given, nothing wonder-ful or beautiful, just the commonplace day in and day out—can I hear God's say-so in these things?

We have the idea that God is going to do some exceptional thing, that He is preparing and fitting us for some extraordinary thing by and by, but as we go on in grace we find that God is glorifying Himself here and now, in the present minute. If we have God's say-so behind us, the most amazing strength comes, and we learn to sing in the ordinary days and ways.

JUNE 5

GOD'S SAY-SO

He hath said . . . so that we may boldly say . . . Hebrews 13:5–6

My say-so is to be built on God's say-so. God says— "I will never leave thee," then I can with good courage say—"The Lord is my helper, I will not fear"—I will not be haunted by apprehension. This does not mean that I will not be tempted to fear, but I will remem-ber God's say-so. I will be full of courage, like a child "bucking himself up" to reach the standard his father wants. Faith in many a one falters when the appre-hensions come, they forget the meaning of God's say-so, forget to take a deep breath spiritually. The only way to get the dread taken out of us is to listen to God's say-so.

What are you dreading? You are not a coward about it, you are going to face it, but there is a feeling of dread. When there is nothing and no one to help you, say—"But the Lord is my Helper, this second, in my present outlook." Are you learning to say things after listening to God, or are you saying things and try-ing to make God's word fit in? Get hold of the Father's say-so, and then say with good courage—"I will not fear." It does not matter what evil or wrong may be in the way, He has said—"I will never leave thee."

Frailty is another thing that gets in between God's say-so and ours. When we realise how feeble we are in facing difficulties, the difficulties become like giants, we become like grasshoppers, and God becomes a nonentity. Remember God's say-so—*"I will in no wise fail you"* (RV). Have we learned to sing after hearing God's key-note? Are we always possessed with the courage to say—"The Lord is my helper," or are we succumbing?

JUNE 6

WORK OUT WHAT GOD WORKS IN

Work out your own salvation. Philippians 2:12

Your will agrees with God, but in your flesh there is a disposition which renders you powerless to do what you know you ought to do. When the Lord is presented to the conscience, the first thing conscience does is to rouse the will, and the will always agrees with God. You say—"But I do not know whether my will is in agreement with God." Look to Jesus and you will find that your will and your conscience are in agreement with Him every time. The thing in you which makes you say "I shan't" is something less profound than your will; it is perversity, or obstinacy, and they are never in agreement with God. The profound thing in man is his will, not sin. Will is the essential element in God's creation of man: sin is a perverse disposition which entered into man. In a regenerated man the source of will is almighty, "For it is God which worketh in you both to will and to do of His good pleasure." You have to work out with concentration and care what God works in; not *work* your own salvation, but *work it out*, while you base resolutely in unshaken faith on the complete and perfect Redemption of the Lord. As you do this, you do not bring an opposed will to God's will, God's will is your will, and your natural choices are along the line of God's will, and the life is as natural as breathing. God is the source of your will, therefore you are able to work out His will. Obstinacy is an unintelligent "wedge" that refuses to be enlightened; the only thing is for it to be blown up with dynamite, and the dynamite is obedience to the Holy Spirit.

Do I believe that Almighty God is the source of my will? God not only expects me to do His will, but He is in me to do it.

JUNE 7

DON'T SLACK OFF

Whatsoever ye shall ask in My name, that will I do. John 14:13

Am I fulfilling this ministry of the interior? There is no snare, or any danger of infatuation or pride in inter-

cession, it is a hidden ministry that brings forth fruit whereby the Father is glorified. Am I allowing my spiritual life to be frittered away, or am I bringing it all to one centre—the Atonement of my Lord? Is Jesus Christ more and more dominating every interest in my life? If the one central point, the great exerting influence in my life, is the Atonement of the Lord, then every phase of My life will bear fruit for Him.

I must take time to realise what is the central point of power. Do I give one minute out of sixty to concentrate upon it? "If ye abide in Me"—continue to act and think and work from that centre—"ye shall ask what ye will, and it shall be done unto you." Am I abiding? Am I taking time to abide? What is the greatest factor of power in my life? Is it work, service, sacrifice for others, or trying to work for God? The thing that ought to exert the greatest power in my life is the Atonement of the Lord. It is not the thing we spend the most time on that moulds us most; the greatest element is the thing that exerts most power. We must determine to be limited and concentrate our affinities.

"Whatsoever ye shall ask in My name, that will I do." The disciple who abides in Jesus *is* the will of God, and his apparently free choices are God's foreordained decrees. Mysterious? Logically contradictory and absurd? Yes, but a glorious truth to a saint.

JUNE 8

WHAT NEXT?

Determine to know more than others
If ye know these things, happy are ye if ye do them. John 13:17

If you do not cut the moorings, God will have to break them by a storm and send you out. Launch all on God, go out on the great swelling tide of His purpose, and you will get your eyes open. If you believe in Jesus, you are not to spend all your time in the smooth waters just inside the harbour bar, full of delight, but always moored; you have to get out through the harbour bar into the great deeps of God and begin to know for yourself, begin to have spiritual discernment.

When you know you should do a thing, and do it, immediately you know more. Revise where you have become "stodgy" spiritually, and you will find it goes back to a point where there was something you knew you should do, but you did not do it because there seemed no immediate call to, and now you have no perception, no discernment; at a time of crisis you are spiritually distracted instead of spiritually self-possessed. It is a dangerous thing to refuse to go on knowing.

The counterfeit of obedience is a state of mind in which you work up occasions to sacrifice yourself; ardour is mistaken for discernment. It is easier to sacrifice yourself than to fulfil your spiritual destiny, which is stated in Romans 12:1–2. It is a great deal better to fulfil the purpose of God in your life by discerning His will than to perform great acts of self-sacrifice. "To obey is better than sacrifice." Beware of harking back to what you were once when God wants you to be something you have never been. "If any man will *do . . . , he shall know . . .*"

JUNE 9

THE NEXT BEST THING TO DO

Ask if You Have Not Received

For every one that asketh receiveth. Luke 11:10

There is nothing more difficult than to ask. We will long and desire and crave and suffer, but not until we are at the extreme limit will we *ask.* A sense of unreality makes us ask. Have you ever asked out of the depths of moral poverty? "If any of you lack wisdom, let him ask of God. . . ."—but be sure that you do lack wisdom. You cannot bring yourself up against Reality when you like. The next best thing to do if you are not spiritually real, is to ask God for the Holy Spirit on the word of Jesus Christ (see Luke 11:13). The Holy Spirit is the One Who makes real in you all that Jesus did for you.

"For every one that asketh receiveth." This does not mean you will not get if you do not ask (cf. Matthew 5:45), but until you get to the point of asking you won't *receive* from God. To receive means you have come into the relationship of a child of God, and now you perceive with intelligent and moral appreciation and spiritual understanding that these things come from God.

"If any of you lack wisdom . . ." If you realise you are lacking, it is because you have come in contact with spiritual reality; do not put your reasonable blinkers on again. People say—Preach us the simple gospel: don't tell us we have to be holy, because that produces a sense of abject poverty, and it is not nice to feel abjectly poor. "Ask" means *beg.* Some people are poor enough to be interested in their poverty, and some of us are like that spiritually. We will never receive if we ask with an end in view; if we ask, not out of our poverty but out of our lust. A pauper does not ask from any other reason than the abject panging condition of his poverty, he is not ashamed to beg. Blessed are the *paupers* in spirit.

JUNE 10

THE NEXT BEST THING TO DO

Seek if You Have Not Found

Seek, and ye shall find. Luke 11:9

"Ye ask, and receive not, because ye ask amiss." If you ask for things from life instead of from God, you ask amiss, that is, you ask from a desire for self-realisation. The more you realise yourself the less will you seek God. "Seek, and ye shall find." Get to work, narrow your interests to this one. Have you ever sought God with your whole heart, or have you only given a languid cry to Him after a twinge of moral neuralgia? Seek, concentrate, and you will find.

"Ho, every one that thirsteth, come ye to the waters." Are you thirsty, or smugly indifferent—so satisfied with your experience that you want nothing more of God? Experience is a gateway, not an end. Beware of building your faith on experience, the metallic note will come in at once, the censorious note. You can never give another person that which you have found, but you can make him homesick for what you have.

"Draw nigh to God." "Knock, and it shall be opened unto you." Knock—the door is closed, and you suffer from palpitation as you knock. "Cleanse your hands"—knock a bit louder, you begin to find you are dirty. "Purify your heart"—this is more personal still, you are desperately in earnest now—you will do anything. "Be afflicted"—have you ever been afflicted before God at the state of your inner life? There is no strand of self-pity left, but a heartbreaking affliction of amazement to find you are the kind of person that you are. "Humble yourself"—it is a humbling business to knock at God's door—you have to knock with the crucified thief. "To him that knocketh, *it shall be opened.*"

JUNE 11

GETTING THERE

Where the Sin and the Sorrow Cease and the Song and the Saint Commence

Come unto Me. Matthew 11:28

Do I want to get there? I can now. The questions that matter in life are remarkably few, and they are all answered by the words—"Come unto Me." Not—"Do this, or don't do that"; but—"Come unto Me." If

I will come to Jesus my actual life will be brought into accordance with my real desires; I will actually cease from sin, and actually find the song of the Lord begin.

Have you ever come to Jesus? Watch the stubbornness of your heart, you will do anything rather than the one simple childlike thing—"Come unto Me." If you want the actual experience of ceasing from sin, you must come to Jesus.

Jesus Christ makes Himself the touchstone. Watch how He used the word "Come." At the most unexpected moments there is the whisper of the Lord—"Come unto Me." and you are drawn immediately. Personal contact with Jesus alters everything. Be stupid enough to come and commit yourself to what He says. The attitude of coming is that the will resolutely lets go of everything and deliberately commits all to Him.

"and I will give you rest," i.e., I will stay you. Not—I will put you to bed and hold your hand and sing you to sleep; but—I will get you out of bed, out of the languor and exhaustion, out of the state of being half dead while you are alive; I will imbue you with the spirit of life, and you will be stayed by the perfection of vital activity. We get pathetic and talk about "suffering the will of the Lord"! Where is the majestic vitality and might of the Son of God about that?

JUNE 12

GETTING THERE

Where the Self-Interest Sleeps and the Real Interest Awakens

Master, where dwellest Thou?. . . Come and see. . . . John 1:38–39

Come *with* Me

"They . . . abode with Him that day." That is about all some of us ever do, then we wake up to actualities, self-interest arises and the abiding is passed. There is no condition of life in which we cannot abide in Jesus.

"Thou art Simon . . . : thou shalt be called Cephas." God writes the new name on those places only in our lives where He has erased the pride and self-sufficiency and self-interest. Some of us have the new name in spots only, like spiritual measles. In sections we look all right. When we have our best spiritual mood on, you would think we were very high-toned saints; but don't look at us when we are not in that mood. The disciple is one who has the new name written all over him; self-interest and pride and self-sufficiency have been completely erased.

Pride is the deification of self, and this to-day in some of us is not of the order of the Pharisee, but of the publican. To say "Oh, I'm no saint," is acceptable to human pride, but it is unconscious blasphemy against God. It literally means that you defy God to make you a saint. "I am much too weak and hopeless, I am outside the reach of the Atonement." Humility before men may be unconscious blasphemy before God. Why are you not a saint? It is either that you do not want to be a saint, or that you do not believe God can make you one. It would be all right, you say, if God saved you and took you straight to heaven. That is just what He will do! "We will come unto Him, and make our abode with Him." Make no conditions, let Jesus be everything, and He will take you home with Him not only for a day, but for ever.

JUNE 13

GETTING THERE

Where the Selective Affinity Dies and the Sanctified Abandon Lives

Come ye after Me. Mark 1:17

One of the greatest hindrances in coming to Jesus is the excuse of temperament. We make our temperament and our natural affinities barriers to coming to Jesus. The first thing we realise when we come to Jesus is that He pays no attention whatever to our natural affinities. We have the notion that we can consecrate our gifts to God. You cannot consecrate what is not yours; there is only one thing you can consecrate to God, and that is your right to yourself (Romans 12:1). If you will give God your right to yourself, He will make a holy experiment out of you. God's experiments always succeed. The one mark of a saint is the moral originality which springs from abandonment to Jesus Christ. In the life of a saint there is this amazing wellspring of original life all the time; the Spirit of God is a well of water springing up, perennially fresh. The saint realises that it is God Who engineers circumstances, consequently there is no whine, but a reckless abandon to Jesus. Never make a principle out of your experience; let God be as original with other people as He is with you.

If you abandon to Jesus, and come when He says "Come," He will continue to say "Come" through you; you will go out into life reproducing the echo of Christ's "Come." That is the result in every soul who has abandoned and come to Jesus.

Have I come to Jesus? Will I come *now*?

June 14

GET A MOVE ON

In the Matter of Determination

Abide in Me. John 15:4

The Spirit of Jesus is put into me by the Atonement, then I have to construct with patience the way of thinking that is exactly in accordance with my Lord. God will not make me think like Jesus, I have to do it myself; I have to bring every thought into captivity to the obedience of Christ. "Abide in Me"—in intellectual matters, in money matters, in every one of the matters that make human life what it is. It is not a bandbox[18] life.

Am I preventing God from doing things in my circumstances because I say it will hinder my communion with Him? That is an impertinence. It does not matter what my circumstances are, I can be as sure of abiding in Jesus in them as in a prayer meeting. I have not to change and arrange my circumstances myself. With Our Lord the inner abiding was unsullied; He was at home with God wherever His body was placed. He never chose His own circumstances, but was meek towards His Father's dispensations for Him. Think of the amazing leisure of Our Lord's Life! We keep God at excitement point, there is none of the serenity of the life hid with Christ in God about us.

Think of the things that take you out of abiding in Christ—"Yes, Lord, just a minute, I have got this to do; Yes, I will abide when once this is finished; when this week is over, it will be all right, I will abide then." *Get a move on;* begin to abide *now.* In the initial stages it is a continual effort until it becomes so much the law of life that you abide in Him unconsciously. Determine to abide in Jesus wherever you are placed.

June 15

GET A MOVE ON

In the Matter of Drudgery

And beside this, . . . add . . . 2 Peter 1:5

You have inherited the Divine nature, says Peter (v. 4), now screw your attention down and form habits, give diligence, concentrate. "Add" means all that character means. No man is born either naturally or super-naturally with character; he has to make character. Nor are we born with habits; we have to form habits on the basis of the new life God has put into us. We are not meant to be illuminated versions, but the common stuff of ordinary life exhibiting the marvel of the grace of God. Drudgery is the touchstone of character. The great hindrance in spiritual life is that we will look for big things to do. "Jesus . . . took a towel, . . . and began to wash the disciples' feet."

There are times when there is no illumination and no thrill, but just the daily round, the common task. Routine is God's way of saving us between our times of inspiration. Do not expect God always to give you His thrilling minutes, but learn to live in the domain of drudgery by the power of God.

It is the "adding" that is difficult. We say we do not expect God to carry us to heaven on flowery beds of ease, and yet we act as if we did! The tiniest detail in which I obey has all the omnipotent power of the grace of God behind it. If I do my duty, not for duty's sake, but because I believe God is engineering my circumstances, then at the very point of my obedience the whole superb grace of God is mine through the Atonement.

June 16

WHAT DO YOU MAKE OF THIS?

Greater love hath no man than this, that a man lay down his life for his friends. . . . I have called you friends. John 15:13, 15

Jesus does not ask me to die for Him, but to lay down my life for Him. Peter said—"I will lay down my life for Thy sake," and he meant it; his sense of the heroic was magnificent. It would be a bad thing to be incapable of making such a declaration as Peter made; the sense of our duty is only realised by our sense of the heroic. Has the Lord ever asked you—"Wilt thou lay down thy life for My sake?" It is far easier to die than to lay down the life day in and day out with the sense of the high calling. We are not made for brilliant moments, but we have to walk in the light of them in ordinary ways. There was only one brilliant moment in the life of Jesus, and that was on the Mount of Transfiguration; then He emptied Himself the second time of His glory, and came down into the demon-possessed valley. For thirty-three years Jesus laid out His life to do the will of His Father, and, John says,

---

18. bandbox: in Chambers' day, a small, round box made to hold neckbands or collars for shirts; metaphorically, something small, narrow, cloistered, self-contained.

"we ought to lay down our lives for the brethren." It is contrary to human nature to do it.

If I am a friend of Jesus, I have deliberately and carefully to lay down my life for Him. It is difficult, and thank God it is difficult. Salvation is easy because it cost God so much, but the manifestation of it in my life is difficult. God saves a man and endues him with the Holy Spirit, and then says in effect—"Now work it out, be loyal to Me, whilst the nature of things round about you would make you disloyal." "I have called you friends." Stand loyal to your Friend, and remember that His honour is at stake in your bodily life.

JUNE 17

THE UNCRITICAL TEMPER

Judge not, that ye be not judged. Matthew 7:1

Jesus says regarding judging—*Don't*. The average Christian is the most penetratingly critical individual. Criticism is a part of the ordinary faculty of man; but in the spiritual domain nothing is accomplished by criticism. The effect of criticism is a dividing up of the powers of the one criticised; the Holy Ghost is the One in the true position to criticise, He alone is able to show what is wrong without hurting and wounding. It is impossible to enter into communion with God when you are in a critical temper; it makes you hard and vindictive and cruel, and leaves you with the flattering unction that you are a superior person. Jesus says, as a disciple, cultivate the uncritical temper. It is not done once and for all. Beware of anything that puts you in the superior person's place.

There is no getting away from the penetration of Jesus. If I see the mote in your eye, it means I have a beam in my own. Every wrong thing that I see in you, God locates in me. Every time I judge, I condemn myself (see Romans 2:17–20). Stop having a measuring rod for other people. There is always one fact more in every man's case about which we know nothing. The first thing God does is to give us a spiritual spring-cleaning; there is no possibility of pride left in a man after that. I have never met the man I could despair of after discerning what lies in me apart from the grace of God.

JUNE 18

DON'T THINK NOW, TAKE THE ROAD

And Peter . . . walked on the water, to go to Jesus. But when he saw the wind boisterous, he was afraid. Matthew 14:29–30

The wind was actually boisterous, the waves were actually high, but Peter did not see them at first. He did not reckon with them, he simply recognised his Lord, and stepped out in recognition of Him and walked on the water. Then he began to reckon with the actual things, and down he went instantly. Why could not our Lord have enabled him to walk at the bottom of the waves as well as on the top of them? Neither could be done saving by recognition of the Lord Jesus.

We step right out on God over some things, then self-consideration enters in and down we go. If you are recognising your Lord, you have no business with where He engineers your circumstances. The actual things *are*, but immediately you look at them you are overwhelmed, you cannot recognise Jesus, and the rebuke comes: Wherefore didst thou doubt?" Let actual circumstances be what they may, keep recognising Jesus, maintain complete reliance on Him.

If you debate for a second when God has spoken, it is all up. Never begin to say—"Well, I wonder if He did speak?" Be reckless immediately, fling it all out on Him. You do not know when His voice will come, but whenever the realisation of God comes in the faintest way imaginable, recklessly abandon. It is only by abandon that you recognise Him. You will only realise His voice more clearly by recklessness.

JUNE 19

THE SERVICE OF PASSIONATE DEVOTION

Lovest thou Me? . . . Feed My sheep. John 21:17

Jesus did not say—Make converts to your way of thinking, but look after My sheep, see that they get nourished in the knowledge of Me. We count as service what we do in the way of Christian work; Jesus Christ calls service what we are to Him, not what we do for Him. Discipleship is based on devotion to Jesus Christ, not on adherence to a belief or a creed. "If any man come to Me, and hate not . . . , he cannot be My disciple." There is no argument and no compulsion, but simply—"If you would be My disciple, you must be devoted to Me." A man touched by the Spirit of God suddenly says—"Now I see Who Jesus is," and that is the source of devotion.

To-day we have substituted credal belief for personal belief, and that is why so many are devoted to causes and so few devoted to Jesus Christ. People do not want to be devoted to Jesus, but only to the cause He started. Jesus Christ is a source of deep offence to the educated mind of to-day that does not want Him in any other way than as a Comrade. Our Lord's first obedience was to the will of His Father, not to the needs of men; the saving of men was the natural out-come of His obedience to the Father. If I am devoted to the cause of humanity only, I will soon be exhausted and come to the place where my love will falter; but if I love Jesus Christ personally and passionately, I can serve humanity though men treat me as a door-mat. The secret of a disciple's life is devotion to Jesus Christ, and the characteristic of the life is its unobtrusiveness. It is like a corn of wheat, which falls into the ground and dies, but presently it will spring up and alter the whole landscape (see John 12:24).

JUNE 20

HAVE YOU COME TO "WHEN" YET?

And the LORD turned the captivity of Job, when he prayed for his friends. Job 42:10

The plaintive, self-centred, morbid kind of prayer, a dead-set that I want to be right, is never found in the New Testament. The fact that I am trying to be right with God is a sign that I am rebelling against the Atonement. "Lord, I will purify my heart if You will answer my prayer; I will walk rightly if You will help me." I *cannot* make myself right with God, I *cannot* make my life perfect; I can only be right with God if I accept the Atonement of the Lord Jesus Christ as an absolute gift. Am I humble enough to accept it? I have to resign every kind of claim and cease from every effort, and leave myself entirely alone in His hands, and then begin to pour out in the priestly work of intercession. There is much prayer that arises from real disbelief in the Atonement. Jesus is not beginning to save us, He has saved us, the thing is done, and it is an insult to ask Him to do it.

If you are not getting the hundredfold more, not getting insight into God's word, then start praying for your friends, enter into the ministry of the interior. "The Lord turned the captivity of Job *when he prayed for his friends.*" The real business of your life as a saved soul is intercessory prayer. Wherever God puts you in circumstances, pray immediately, pray that His Atonement may be realised in other lives as it has been in yours. Pray for your friends *now;* pray for those with whom you come in contact *now.*

JUNE 21

THE MINISTRY OF THE INTERIOR

But ye are . . . a royal priesthood. 1 Peter 2:9

By what right do we become "a royal priesthood"? By the right of the Atonement. Are we prepared to leave ourselves resolutely alone and to launch out into the priestly work of prayer? The continual grubbing on the inside to see whether we are what we ought to be, generates a self-centred, morbid type of Christianity, not the robust, simple life of the child of God. Until we get into a right relationship to God, it is a case of hanging on by the skin of our teeth, and we say—"What a wonderful victory I have got!" There is nothing indicative of the miracle of Redemption in that. Launch out in reckless belief that the Redemption is complete, and then bother no more about yourself, but begin to do as Jesus Christ said—pray for the friend who comes to you at midnight, pray for the saints, pray for all men. Pray on the realisation that you are only perfect in Christ Jesus, not on this plea—"O Lord, I have done my best, please hear me."

How long is it going to take God to free us from the morbid habit of thinking about ourselves? We must get sick unto death of ourselves, until there is no longer any surprise at anything God can tell us about ourselves. We cannot touch the depths of meanness in ourselves. There is only one place where we are right, and that is in Christ Jesus. When we are there, we have to pour out for all we are worth in the ministry of the interior.

JUNE 22

THE UNDEVIATING TEST

For with what judgement ye judge, ye shall be judged: and with what measure ye mete, it shall be measured to you again. Matthew 7:2

This statement is not a haphazard guess, it is an eternal law of God. Whatever judgement you give, it is measured to you again. There is a difference between retaliation and retribution. Jesus says that the basis of life is retribution—"with what measure ye mete, it shall be measured to you again." If you have been shrewd in finding out the defects in others, remember that will be exactly the measure given to you. Life serves back in the coin you pay. This law works from God's throne downwards (cf. Psalm 18:25–26).

Romans 2 applies it in a still more definite way, and says that the one who criticises another is guilty of the very same thing. God looks not only at the act, He looks at the possibility. We do not believe the statements of the Bible to begin with. For instance, do we believe this statement, that the things we criticise in others we are guilty of ourselves? The reason we see hypocrisy and fraud and unreality in others is because they are all in our own hearts. The great characteristic of a saint is humility—"Yes, all those things and other evils would have been manifested in me but for the grace of God; therefore I have no right to judge."

Jesus says—"Judge not, that ye be not judged"; if you do judge, it will be measured to you exactly as you have judged. Who of us would dare to stand before God and say—"My God, judge me as I have judged my fellow men"? We have judged our fellow men as sinners; if God should judge us like that we would be in hell. God judges us through the marvellous Atonement of Jesus Christ.

JUNE 23

ACQUAINTANCE WITH GRIEF

A Man of sorrows, and acquainted with grief. Isaiah 53:3

We are not acquainted with grief in the way in which Our Lord was acquainted with it; we endure it, we get through it, but we do not become intimate with it. At the beginning of life we do not reconcile ourselves to the fact of sin. We take a rational view of life and say that a man by controlling his instincts, and by educating himself, can produce a life which will slowly evolve into the life of God. But as we go on, we find the presence of something which we have not taken into consideration, viz., sin, and it upsets all our calculations. Sin has made the basis of things wild and not rational. We have to recognise that sin is a fact, not a defect; sin is red-handed mutiny against God. Either God or sin must die in my life. The New Testament brings us right down to this one issue. If sin rules in me, God's life in me will be killed; if God rules in me, sin in me will be killed. There is no possible ultimate but that. The climax of sin is that it crucified Jesus Christ, and what was true in the history of God on earth will be true in your history and in mine. In our mental outlook we have to reconcile ourselves to the fact of sin as the only explanation as to why Jesus Christ came, and the explanation of the grief and sorrow in life.

JUNE 24

RECONCILING ONE'S SELF TO THE FACT OF SIN

This is your hour, and the power of darkness. Luke 22:53

It is not being reconciled to the fact of sin that produces all the disasters in life. You may talk about the nobility of human nature, but there is something in human nature which will laugh in the face of every ideal you have. If you refuse to agree with the fact that there is vice and self-seeking, something downright spiteful and wrong in human beings, instead of reconciling yourself to it when it strikes your life, you will compromise with it and say it is of no use to battle against it. Have you made allowance for this hour and the power of darkness, or do you take a recognition of yourself that misses out sin? In your bodily relationships and friendships do you reconcile yourself to the fact of sin? If not, you will be caught round the next corner and you will compromise with it. If you reconcile yourself to the fact of sin, you will realise the danger at once—"Yes, I see what that would mean." The recognition of sin does not destroy the basis of friendship; it establishes a mutual regard for the fact that the basis of life is tragic. Always beware of an estimate of life which does not recognise the fact that there is sin.

Jesus Christ never trusted human nature, yet He was never cynical, never suspicious, because He trusted absolutely in what He could do for human nature. The pure man or woman, not the innocent, is the safeguarded man or woman. You are never safe with an innocent man or woman. Men and women have no business to be innocent; God demands that they be pure and virtuous. Innocence is the characteristic of a child; it is a blameworthy thing for a man or woman not to be reconciled to the fact of sin.

JUNE 25

RECEIVING ONE'S SELF IN THE FIRES OF SORROW

What shall I say? Father, save me from this hour?[mg] But for this cause came I unto this hour. Father, glorify Thy name. John 12:27–29 (RV)

My attitude as a saint to sorrow and difficulty is not to ask that they may be prevented, but to ask that I may preserve the self God created me to be through every fire of sorrow. Our Lord received Himself in the fire of sorrow, He was saved not *from* the hour, but *out of* the hour.

We say that there ought to be no sorrow, but there *is* sorrow, and we have to receive ourselves in its fires. If we try and evade sorrow, refuse to lay our account with it, we are foolish. Sorrow is one of the biggest facts in life; it is no use saying sorrow ought not to be. Sin and sorrow and suffering *are*, and it is not for us to say that God has made a mistake in allowing them.

Sorrow burns up a great amount of shallowness, but it does not always make a man better. Suffering either gives me my self or it destroys my self. You cannot receive your self in success, you lose your head; you cannot receive your self in monotony, you grouse. The way to find your self is in the fires of sorrow. Why it should be so is another matter, but that it is so is true in the Scriptures and in human experience. You always know the man who has been through the fires of sorrow and received himself, you are certain you can go to him in trouble and find that he has ample leisure for you. If a man has not been through the fires of sorrow, he is apt to be contemptuous, he has no time for you. If you receive yourself in the fires of sorrow, God will make you nourishment for other people.

JUNE 26

ALWAYS NOW

We . . . beseech you also that ye receive not the grace of God in vain. 2 Corinthians 6:1

The grace you had yesterday will not do for to-day. Grace is the overflowing favour of God; you can always reckon it is there to draw upon. "In much patience, in afflictions, in necessities, in distresses"— that is where the test for patience comes. Are you failing the grace of God there? Are you saying— "Oh, well, I won't count this time"? It is not a question of praying and asking God to help you; it is taking the grace of God *now*. We make prayer the preparation for work, it is never that in the Bible. Prayer is the exercise of drawing on the grace of God. Don't say—"I will endure this until I can get away and pray." Pray *now;* draw on the grace of God in the moment of need. Prayer is the most practical thing, it is not the reflex action of devotion. Prayer is the last thing in which we learn to draw on God's grace.

"In stripes, in imprisonments, in tumults, in labours"—in all these things manifest a drawing upon the grace of God that will make you a marvel to yourself and to others. Draw now, not presently: The one word in the spiritual vocabulary is *Now*. Let circumstances bring you where they will, keep drawing on the grace of God in every conceivable condition you may be in. One of the greatest proofs that you are drawing on the grace of God is that you can be humiliated without manifesting the slightest trace of anything but His grace.

"Having nothing. . . ." Never reserve anything. Pour out the best you have, and always be poor. Never be diplomatic and careful about the treasure God gives. This is poverty triumphant.

JUNE 27

THE OVERSHADOWING PERSONAL DELIVERANCE

I am with thee to deliver thee, saith the LORD. Jeremiah 1:8

God promised Jeremiah that He would deliver him personally—"Thy life will I give unto thee for a prey." That is all God promises His children. Wherever God sends us, He will guard our lives. Our personal property and possessions are a matter of indifference, we have to sit loosely to all these things; if we do not, there will be panic and heartbreak and distress. That is the inwardness of the overshadowing of personal deliverance.

The Sermon on the Mount indicates that when we are on Jesus Christ's errands, there is no time to stand up for ourselves. Jesus says, in effect, "Do not be bothered with whether you are being justly dealt with or not." To look for justice is a sign of deflection from devotion to Him. Never look for justice in this world, but never cease to give it. If we look for justice, we will begin to grouse and to indulge in the discontent of self-pity—"Why should I be treated like this?" If we are devoted to Jesus Christ we have nothing to do with what we meet, whether it is just or unjust. Jesus says—"Go steadily on with what I have told you to do and I will guard your life. If you try to guard it yourself, you remove yourself from My deliverance." The most devout among us become atheistic in this connection; we do not believe God, we enthrone common sense and tack the name of God on to it. We do lean to our own understanding, instead of trusting God with all our hearts.

JUNE 28

APPREHENDED BY GOD

If that I may apprehend that for which also I am apprehended. Philippians 3:12

Never choose to be a worker; but when once God has put His call on you, woe be to you if you turn to the right hand or to the left. We are not here to work for God because we have chosen to do so, but because God has apprehended us. There is never any thought of—"Oh well, I am not fitted for this." What you are to preach is determined by God, not by your own natural inclinations. Keep your soul steadfastly related to God, and remember that you are called not to bear testimony only, but to preach the gospel. Every Christian must testify, but when it comes to the call to preach, there must be the agonising grip of God's hand on you. Your life is in the grip of God for that one thing. How many of us are held like that?

Never water down the word of God; preach it in its undiluted sternness. There must be unflinching loyalty to the word of God; but when you come to personal dealing with your fellow men, remember who you are—not a special being made up in heaven, but a sinner saved by grace.

"I count not myself to have apprehended: but *this one thing I do. . . .*"

JUNE 29

DIRECTION OF DISCIPLINE

And if thy right hand offend thee, cut it off, and cast it from thee: for it is profitable for thee that one of thy members should perish, and not that thy whole body should be cast into hell. Matthew 5:30

Jesus did not say that everyone must cut off the right hand, but—"If your right hand offends you in your walk with Me, cut it off." There are many things that are perfectly legitimate, but if you are going to concentrate on God you cannot do them. Your right hand is one of the best things you have, but Jesus says if it hinders you in following His precepts, cut it off. This line of discipline is the sternest one that ever struck mankind.

When God alters a man by regeneration, the characteristic of the life to begin with is that it is maimed. There are a hundred and one things you dare not do, things that to you and in the eyes of the world that knows you are as your right hand and your eye, and the unspiritual person says—"Whatever is wrong in that? How absurd you are!" There never has been a saint yet who did not have to live a maimed life to start with. But it is better to enter into life maimed and lovely in God's sight than to be lovely in man's sight and lame in God's. In the beginning Jesus Christ by His Spirit has to check you from doing a great many things that may be perfectly right for everyone else but not right for you. See that you do not use your limitations to criticise someone else.

It is a maimed life to begin with, but in v. 48 Jesus gives the picture of a perfectly full-orbed life—"Ye shall be *perfect*, as your heavenly Father is perfect."

JUNE 30

DO IT NOW

Agree with thine adversary quickly. Matthew 5:25

Jesus Christ is laying down this principle—Do what you know you must do, now, and do it quickly; if you do not, the inevitable process will begin to work and you will have to pay to the last farthing in pain and agony and distress. God's laws are unalterable; there is no escape from them. The teaching of Jesus goes straight to the way we are made up.

To see that my adversary gives me my rights is natural; but Jesus says that it is a matter of eternal and imperative importance to me that I pay my adversary what I owe him. From our Lord's standpoint it does not matter whether I am defrauded or not; what does matter is that I do not defraud. Am I insisting on my rights, or am I paying what I owe from Jesus Christ's standpoint?

Do the thing quickly, bring yourself to judgement now. In moral and spiritual matters, you must do it at once; if you do not, the inexorable process will begin to work. God is determined to have His child as pure and clean and white as driven snow, and as long as there is disobedience in any point of His teaching, He will prevent none of the working of His Spirit. Our insistence in proving that we are right is nearly always an indication that there has been some point of disobedience. No wonder the Spirit so strongly urges to keep steadfastly in the light!

"Agree with thine adversary quickly." Have you suddenly turned a corner in any relationship and found that you had anger in your heart? Confess it quickly, quickly put it right before God, be reconciled to that one—*do it now*.

JULY 1

THE INEVITABLE PENALTY

Verily I say unto thee, Thou shalt by no means come out thence, till thou have paid the uttermost farthing. Matthew 5:26 (RV)

"There is no heaven with a little of hell in it." God is determined to make you pure and holy and right; He will not allow you to escape for one moment from the scrutiny of the Holy Spirit. He urged you to come to judgement right away when He convicted you, but you did not; the inevitable process began to work and now you are in prison, and you will only get out when you have paid the uttermost farthing. "Is this a God of mercy, and of love?" you say. Seen from God's side, it is a glorious ministry of love. God is going to bring you out pure and spotless and undefiled; but He wants you to recognise the disposition you were showing— the disposition of your right to yourself. The moment you are willing that God should alter your disposition, His re-creating forces will begin to work. The moment you realise God's purpose, which is to get you rightly related to Himself and then to your fellow men, He will tax the last limit of the universe to help you take the right road. Decide it now—"Yes, Lord, I *will* write that letter to-night"; "I *will* be reconciled to that man now."

These messages of Jesus Christ are for the will and the conscience, not for the head. If you dispute the Sermon on the Mount with your head, you will blunt the appeal to your heart.

"I wonder why I don't go on with God"! Are you paying your debts from God's standpoint? Do *now* what you will have to do some day. Every moral call has an "ought" behind it.

JULY 2

THE CONDITIONS OF DISCIPLESHIP

If any man come to Me, and hate not . . . , he cannot be My disciple. Luke 14:26, see also 27, 33

If the closest relationships of life clash with the claims of Jesus Christ, He says it must be instant obedience to Himself. Discipleship means personal, passionate devotion to a Person, Our Lord Jesus Christ. There is a difference between devotion to a Person and devotion to principles or to a cause. Our Lord never proclaimed a cause; He proclaimed personal devotion to Himself. To be a disciple is to be a devoted love-slave of the Lord Jesus. Many of us who call ourselves Christians are not devoted to Jesus Christ. No man on earth has this passionate love to the Lord Jesus unless the Holy Ghost has imparted it to him. We may admire Him, we may respect Him and reverence Him, but we cannot love Him. The only Lover of the Lord Jesus is the Holy Ghost, and He sheds abroad the very love of God in our hearts. Whenever the Holy Ghost sees a chance of glorifying Jesus, He will take your heart, your nerves, your whole personality, and simply make you blaze and glow with devotion to Jesus Christ.

The Christian life is stamped by "moral spontaneous originality," consequently the disciple is open to the same charge that Jesus Christ was, viz., that of inconsistency. But Jesus Christ was always consistent to God, and the Christian must be consistent to the life of the Son of God in him, not consistent to hard and fast creeds. Men pour themselves into creeds, and God has to blast them out of their prejudices before they can become devoted to Jesus Christ.

JULY 3

THE CONCENTRATION OF PERSONAL SIN

Woe is me! for I am undone; because I am a man of unclean lips. Isaiah 6:5

When I get into the presence of God, I do not realise that I am a sinner in an indefinite sense; I realise the concentration of sin in a particular feature of my life. A man will say easily—"Oh yes, I know I am a sinner," but when he gets into the presence of God he cannot get off with that statement. The conviction is concentrated on—"I am this, or that, or the other." This is always the sign that a man or woman is in the presence of God. There is never any vague sense of sin, but the concentration of sin in some personal particular. God begins by convicting us of one thing fixed on in the mind that is prompted by His Spirit; if we will yield to His conviction on that point, He will lead us down to the great disposition of sin underneath. That is the way God always deals with us when we are consciously in His presence.

This experience of the concentration of sin is true in the greatest and the least of saints as well as in the greatest and the least of sinners. When a man is on the first rung of the ladder of experience, he may say—"I do not know where I have gone wrong, but the Spirit of God will point out some particular definite thing." The effect of the vision of the holiness of the Lord on Isaiah was to bring home to him that he was a man of unclean lips. "And he laid it upon my mouth, and said, Lo, this hath touched thy lips; and thine iniquity is taken away, and thy sin purged." The cleansing fire had to be applied where the sin had been concentrated.

JULY 4

ONE OF GOD'S GREAT DON'TS

Fret not thyself, it tendeth only to evil doing. Psalm 37:8 (RV)

Fretting means getting out at elbows mentally or spiritually. It is one thing to say "Fret not," but a very different thing to have such a disposition that you find yourself able not to fret. It sounds so easy to talk about resting in the Lord and waiting patiently for Him, until the nest is upset—until we live, as so many are doing, in tumult and anguish, is it possible then to rest in the Lord? If this "don't" does not work there, it will work nowhere. This "don't" must work in days of perplexity as well as in days of peace, or it never will work. And if it will not work in your particular case, it will not work in anyone else's case. Resting in the Lord does not depend on external circumstances at all, but on your relationship to God Himself.

Fussing always ends in sin. We imagine that a little anxiety and worry are an indication of how really wise we are; it is much more an indication of how really wicked we are. Fretting springs from a determination to get our own way. Our Lord never worried and He was never anxious, because He was not "out" to realise His own ideas; He was "out" to realise God's ideas. Fretting is wicked if you are a child of God.

Have you been bolstering up that stupid soul of yours with the idea that your circumstances are too much for God? Put all "supposing" on one side and dwell in the shadow of the Almighty. Deliberately tell God that you will not fret about that thing. All our fret and worry is caused by calculating without God.

JULY 5

DON'T CALCULATE WITHOUT GOD

Commit thy way unto the LORD; trust also in Him; and He shall bring it to pass. Psalm 37:5

Don't calculate without God. God seems to have a delightful way of upsetting the things we have calculated on without taking Him into account. We get into circumstances which were not chosen by God, and suddenly we find we have been calculating without God; He has not entered in as a living factor. The one thing that keeps us from the possibility of worrying is bringing God in as the greatest factor in all our calculations.

In our religion it is customary to put God first, but we are apt to think it is an impertinence to put Him first in the practical issues of our lives. If we imagine we have to put on our Sunday moods before we come near to God, we will never come near Him. We must come as we are.

Don't calculate with the evil in view. Does God really mean us to take no account of the evil? "Love . . . taketh not account of evil" (RV). Love is not ignorant of the existence of the evil, but it does not take it in as a calculating factor. Apart from God, we do reckon with evil; we calculate with it in view and work all reasonings from that standpoint.

Don't calculate with the rainy day in view. You cannot lay up for a rainy day if you are trusting Jesus Christ. Jesus said—"Let not your heart be troubled." God will not keep your heart from being troubled. It

is a command—"*Let not. . . .*" Haul yourself up a hundred and one times a day in order to do it, until you get into the habit of putting God first and calculating with Him in view.

JULY 6

VISION AND REALITY

And the parched ground shall become a pool. Isaiah 35:7

We always have visions before a thing is made real. When we realise that although the vision is real, it is not real in us, then is the time that Satan comes in with his temptations, and we are apt to say it is no use to go on. Instead of the vision becoming real, there has come the valley of humiliation.

> *Life is not as idle ore,*
> *But iron dug from central gloom,*
> *And batter'd by the shocks of doom*
> *To shape and use.*

God gives us the vision, then He takes us down to the valley to batter us into the shape of the vision, and it is in the valley that so many of us faint and give way. Every vision will be made real if we will have patience. Think of the enormous leisure of God! He is never in a hurry. We are always in such a frantic hurry. In the light of the glory of the vision we go forth to do things, but the vision is not real in us yet; and God has to take us into the valley, and put us through fires and floods to batter us into shape, until we get to the place where He can trust us with the veritable reality. Ever since we had the vision God has been at work, getting us into the shape of the ideal, and over and over again we escape from His hand and try to batter ourselves into our own shape.

The vision is not a castle in the air, but a vision of what God wants you to be. Let Him put you on His wheel and whirl you as He likes, and as sure as God is God and you are you, you will turn out exactly in accordance with the vision. Don't lose heart in the process. If you have ever had the vision of God, you may try as you like to be satisfied on a lower level, but God will never let you.

JULY 7

ALL NOBLE THINGS ARE DIFFICULT

Enter ye in at the strait gate . . . : because strait is the gate, and narrow is the way. . . . Matthew 7:13–14

If we are going to live as disciples of Jesus, we have to remember that all noble things are difficult. The Christian life is gloriously difficult, but the difficulty of it does not make us faint and cave in, it rouses us up to overcome. Do we so appreciate the marvellous salvation of Jesus Christ that we are our utmost for His highest?

God saves men by His sovereign grace through the Atonement of Jesus; He works in us to will and to do of His good pleasure; but we have to work out that salvation in practical living. If once we start on the basis of His Redemption to do what He commands, we find that we can do it. If we fail, it is because we have not practised. The crisis will reveal whether we have been practising or not. If we obey the Spirit of God and practise in our physical life what God has put in us by His Spirit, then when the crisis comes, we shall find that our own nature as well as the grace of God will stand by us.

Thank God He does give us difficult things to do! His salvation is a glad thing, but it is also a heroic, holy thing. It tests us for all we are worth. Jesus is bringing many "sons unto glory," and God will not shield us from the requirements of a son. God's grace turns out men and women with a strong family likeness to Jesus Christ, not milksops. It takes a tremendous amount of discipline to live the noble life of a disciple of Jesus in actual things. It is always necessary to make an effort to be noble.

JULY 8

THE WILL TO LOYALTY

Choose you this day whom ye will serve. Joshua 24:15

Will is the whole man active. I cannot *give up* my will, I must exercise it. I must *will* to obey, and I must *will* to receive God's Spirit. When God gives a vision of truth it is never a question of what He will do, but of what we will do. The Lord has been putting before us all some big propositions, and the best thing to do is to remember what you did when you were touched by God before—the time when you were saved, or first saw Jesus, or realised some truth. It was easy then to yield allegiance to God; recall those moments now as the Spirit of God brings before you some new proposition.

"Choose you this day whom ye will serve." It is a deliberate calculation, not something into which you drift easily; and everything else is in abeyance until you decide. The proposition is between you and God; do not confer with flesh and blood about it. With every new proposition other people get more and more "out of it," that is where the strain comes. God allows the opinion of His saints to matter to you, and yet you are brought more and more out of the certainty that others understand the step you are taking. You have no business to find out where God is leading, the only thing God will explain to you is Himself.

Profess to Him—"I will be loyal." Immediately you choose to be loyal to Jesus Christ, you are a witness against yourself. Don't consult other Christians, but profess before Him—"I will serve Thee." *Will* to be loyal—and give other people credit for being loyal too.

JULY 9

THE GREAT PROBING

Ye cannot serve the LORD. Joshua 24:19

Have you the slightest reliance on any thing other than God? Is there a remnant of reliance left on any natural virtue, any set of circumstances? Are you relying on yourself in any particular in this new proposition which God has put before you? That is what the probing means. It is quite true to say—"I cannot live a holy life"; but you can decide to let Jesus Christ make you holy. "Ye cannot serve the Lord God"—but you can put yourself in the place where God's Almighty power will work through you. Are you sufficiently right with God to expect Him to manifest His wonderful life in you?

"Nay; but we will serve the LORD." It is not an impulse, but a deliberate commitment. You say—"But God can never have called *me* to this, I am too unworthy, it can't mean *me*." It does mean you, and the weaker and feebler you are, the better. The one who has something to trust in is the last one to come anywhere near saying—"I will serve the Lord."

We say—"If I really could believe!" The point is—If I really *will* believe. No wonder Jesus Christ lays such emphasis on the sin of unbelief. "And He did not many mighty works there because of their unbelief." If we really believed that God meant what He said—what should we be like! Dare I really let God be to me all that He says He will be?

JULY 10

THE SPIRITUAL SLUGGARD

Let us consider one another to provoke unto love and to good works: not forsaking the assembling of ourselves together. Hebrews 10:24–25

We are all capable of being spiritual sluggards; we do not want to mix with the rough and tumble of life as it is, our one object is to secure retirement. The note struck in Hebrews 10 is that of provoking one another and of keeping together—both of which require initiative, the initiative of Christ-realisation, not of self-realisation. To live a remote, retired, secluded life is the antipodes of spirituality as Jesus Christ taught it.

The test of our spirituality comes when we come up against injustice and meanness and ingratitude and turmoil, all of which have the tendency to make us spiritual sluggards. We want to use prayer and Bible reading for the purpose of retirement. We utilise God for the sake of getting peace and joy, that is, we do not want to realise Jesus Christ, but only our enjoyment of Him. This is the first step in the wrong direction. All these things are effects and we try to make them causes.

"I think it meet," said Peter, ". . . to stir you up by putting you in remembrance." It is a most disturbing thing to be smitten in the ribs by some provoker of God, by someone who is full of spiritual activity. Active work and spiritual activity are not the same thing. Active work may be the counterfeit of spiritual activity. The danger of spiritual sluggishness is that we do not wish to be stirred up, all we want to hear about is spiritual retirement. Jesus Christ never encourages the idea of retirement—"Go tell My brethren. . . ."

JULY 11

THE SPIRITUAL SAINT

That I may know Him. Philippians 3:10

The initiative of the saint is not towards self-realisation, but towards knowing Jesus Christ. The spiritual saint never believes circumstances to be haphazard, or thinks of his life as secular and sacred; he sees everything he is dumped down in as the means of securing the knowledge of Jesus Christ. There is a reckless abandonment about him. The Holy Spirit is determined that we shall realise Jesus Christ in every domain of life, and He will bring us back to the same point again and again until we do. Self-realisation leads to the enthronement of work; whereas the saint enthrones Jesus Christ in his work. Whether it be eating or drinking or washing disciples' feet, whatever it is, we have to take the initiative of realising Jesus Christ in it. Every phase of our actual life has its counterpart in the life of Jesus. Our Lord realised His relationship to the Father even in the most menial work. "Jesus knowing . . . that He was come from God, and went to God; . . . took a towel, . . . and began to wash the disciples' feet."

The aim of the spiritual saint is "that I may know Him." Do I know Him where I am to-day? If not, I am failing Him. I am here not to realise myself, but to know Jesus. In Christian work the initiative is too often the realisation that something has to be done and I must do it. That is never the attitude of the spiritual saint, his aim is to secure the realisation of Jesus Christ in every set of circumstances he is in.

JULY 12

THE SPIRITUAL SOCIETY

Till we all come . . . unto the measure of the stature of the fulness of Christ. Ephesians 4:13

Rehabilitation means the putting back of the whole human race into the relationship God designed it to be in, and this is what Jesus Christ did in Redemption. The Church ceases to be a spiritual society when it is on the look-out for the development of its own organisation. The rehabilitation of the human race on Jesus Christ's plan means the realisation of Jesus Christ in corporate life as well as in individual life. Jesus Christ sent apostles and teachers for this purpose—that the corporate Personality might be realised. We are not here to develop a spiritual life of our own, or to enjoy spiritual retirement; we are here so to realise Jesus Christ that the Body of Christ may be built up.

Am I building up the Body of Christ, or am I looking for my own personal development only? The essential thing is my personal relationship to Jesus Christ—"That *I* may know *Him.*" To fulfil God's design means entire abandonment to him. Whenever I want things for myself, the relationship is distorted. It will be a big humiliation to realise that I have not been concerned about realising Jesus Christ, but only about realising what He has done for me.

> *My goal is God Himself, not joy nor peace,*
> *Nor even blessing, but Himself, my God.*

Am I measuring my life by this standard or by anything less?

JULY 13

THE PRICE OF VISION

In the year that king Uzziah died, I saw also the Lord. Isaiah 6:1

Our soul's history with God is frequently the history of the passing of the hero. Over and over again God has to remove our friends in order to bring Himself in their place, and that is where we faint and fail and get discouraged. Take it personally: In the year that the one who stood to me for all that God was, died—I gave up everything? I became ill? I got disheartened? or—I saw the Lord?

My vision of God depends upon the state of my character. Character determines revelation. Before I can say "I saw also the Lord," there must be something corresponding to God in my character. Until I am born again and begin to see the Kingdom of God, I see along the line of my prejudices only; I need the surgical operation of external events and an internal purification.

It must be God first, God second, and God third, until the life is faced steadily with God and no one else is of any account whatever. "In all the world there is none but Thee, my God, there is none but Thee."

Keep paying the price. Let God see that you are willing to live up to the vision.

JULY 14

THE ACCOUNT WITH PERSECUTION

But I say unto you, That ye resist not evil: but whosoever shall smite thee on thy right cheek, turn to him the other also. Matthew 5:39, etc.

These verses reveal the humiliation of being a Christian. Naturally, if a man does not hit back, it is because he is a coward; but spiritually if a man does not hit back, it is a manifestation of the Son of God in him. When you are insulted, you must not only not resent it, but make it an occasion to exhibit the Son of God. You cannot imitate the disposition of Jesus; it is either there or it is not. To the saint personal insult becomes the occasion of revealing the incredible sweetness of the Lord Jesus.

The teaching of the Sermon on the Mount is not—Do your duty, but—Do what is not your duty. It is not your duty to go the second mile, to turn the other cheek, but Jesus says if we are His disciples, we shall always do these things. There will be no spirit of—"Oh well, I cannot do any more, I have been so misrepresented and misunderstood." Every time I insist upon my rights, I hurt the Son of God; whereas I can prevent Jesus from being hurt if I take the blow myself. That is the meaning of filling up that which is behind of the afflictions of Christ. The disciple realises that it is his Lord's honour that is at stake in his life, not his own honour.

Never look for right in the other man, but never cease to be right yourself. We are always looking for justice; the teaching of the Sermon on the Mount is—Never look for justice, but never cease to give it.

JULY 15

THE POINT OF SPIRITUAL HONOUR

I am debtor both to the Greeks, and to the Barbarians. Romans 1:14

Paul was overwhelmed with the sense of his indebtedness to Jesus Christ, and he spent himself to express it. The great inspiration in Paul's life was his view of Jesus Christ as his spiritual creditor. Do I feel that sense of indebtedness to Christ in regard to every unsaved soul? The spiritual honour of my life as a saint is to fulfil my debt to Christ in relation to them. Every bit of my life that is of value I owe to the Redemption of Jesus Christ; am I doing anything to enable Him to bring His Redemption into actual manifestation in other lives? I can only do it as the Spirit of God works in me this sense of indebtedness. I am not to be a superior person amongst men, but a bondslave of the Lord Jesus. "Ye are not your own." Paul sold himself to Jesus Christ. He says—"I am a debtor to everyone on the face of the earth because of the Gospel of Jesus; I am free to be an absolute slave only." That is the characteristic of the life when once this point of spiritual honour is realised. Quit praying about yourself and be spent for others as the bondslave of Jesus. That is the meaning of being made broken bread and poured-out wine in reality.

JULY 16

THE NOTION OF DIVINE CONTROL

How much more shall your Father which is in heaven give good things to them that ask Him? Matthew 7:11

Jesus is laying down rules of conduct for those who have His Spirit. By the simple argument of these verses He urges us to keep our minds filled with the notion of God's control behind everything, which means that the disciple must maintain an attitude of perfect trust and an eagerness to ask and to seek.

Notion your mind with the idea that God is there. If once the mind is notioned along that line, then when you are in difficulties it is as easy as breathing to remember—Why, my Father knows all about it! It is not an effort, it comes naturally when perplexities press. Before, you used to go to this person and that, but now the notion of the Divine control is forming so powerfully in you that you go to God about it. Jesus is laying down the rules of conduct for those who have His Spirit, and it works on this principle—God is my

Father, He loves me, I shall never think of anything He will forget, why should I worry?

There are times, says Jesus, when God cannot lift the darkness from you, but trust Him. God will appear like an unkind friend, but He is not; He will appear like an unnatural Father, but He is not; He will appear like an unjust judge, but He is not. Keep the notion of the mind of God behind all things strong and growing. Nothing happens in any particular unless God's will is behind it, therefore you can rest in perfect confidence in Him. Prayer is not only asking, but an attitude of mind which produces the atmosphere in which asking is perfectly natural. "Ask, and it shall be given you."

JULY 17

THE MIRACLE OF BELIEF

My speech and my preaching was not with enticing words. 1 Corinthians 2:4

Paul was a scholar and an orator of the first rank; he is not speaking out of abject humility, but saying that he would veil the power of God if, when he preached the gospel, he impressed people with his "excellency of speech." Belief in Jesus is a miracle produced only by the efficacy of Redemption, not by impressiveness of speech, not by wooing and winning, but by the sheer unaided power of God. The creative power of the Redemption comes through the preaching of the Gospel, but never because of the personality of the preacher. The real fasting of the preacher is not from food, but rather from eloquence, from impressiveness and exquisite diction, from everything that might hinder the gospel of God being presented. The preacher is there as the representative of God—"as though God did beseech you by us." He is there to present the Gospel of God, not human ideals. If it is only because of my preaching that people desire to be better, they will never get anywhere near Jesus Christ. Anything that flatters me in my preaching of the Gospel will end in making me a traitor to Jesus; I prevent the creative power of His redemption from doing its work.

"*I, if I be lifted up . . . , will draw all men unto Me.*"

JULY 18

THE MYSTERY OF BELIEVING

And he said, Who art Thou, Lord? Acts 9:5 (RV)

By the miracle of Redemption Saul of Tarsus was turned in one second from a strong-willed, intense Pharisee into a humble, devoted slave of the Lord Jesus.

There is nothing miraculous about the things we can explain. We command what we are able to explain, consequently it is natural to seek to explain. It is not natural to obey; nor is it necessarily sinful to disobey. There is no moral virtue in obedience unless there is a recognition of a higher authority in the one who dictates. It is possibly an emancipation to the other person if he does not obey. If one man says to another—"You must," and "You shall," he breaks the human spirit and unfits it for God. A man is a slave for obeying unless behind his obedience there is a recognition of a holy God. Many a soul begins to come to God when he flings off being religious, because there is only one Master of the human heart, and that is not religion but Jesus Christ. But woe be to me if when I see Him I say—"I *will* not." He will never insist that I do, but I have begun to sign the death-warrant of the Son of God in my soul. When I stand face to face with Jesus Christ and say—"I will not," He will never insist; but I am backing away from the re-creating power of His Redemption. It is a matter of indifference to God's grace how abominable I am if I come to the light; but woe be to me if I refuse the light (see John 3:19–21).

JULY 19

MASTERY OVER THE BELIEVER

Ye call Me Master and Lord: and ye say well; for so I am. John 13:13

Our Lord never insists on having authority; He never says—"Thou shalt." He leaves us perfectly free—so free that we can spit in His face, as men did; so free that we can put Him to death, as men did; and He will never say a word. But when His life has been created in me by His Redemption, I instantly recognise His right to absolute authority over me. It is a moral domination—"Thou art *worthy. . . .*" It is only the unworthy in me that refuses to bow down to the worthy. If when I meet a man who is more holy than myself, I do not recognise his worthiness and obey what comes through him, it is a revelation of the unworthy in me. God educates us by means of people who are little better than we are, not intellectually, but "holily," until we get under the domination of the Lord Himself, and then the whole attitude of the life is one of obedience to Him.

If Our Lord insisted upon obedience He would become a taskmaster, and He would cease to have any authority. He never insists on obedience, but when we do see Him we obey Him instantly. He is easily Lord, and we live in adoration of Him from morning till night. The revelation of my growth in grace is the way in which I look upon obedience. We have to rescue the word "obedience" from the mire. Obedience is only possible between equals. It is the relationship between father and son, not between master and servant. "I and My Father are one." "Though He were a Son, yet learned He obedience by the things which He suffered." The Son's obedience was as Redeemer, *because He was Son,* not in order to be Son.

JULY 20

DEPENDENT ON GOD'S PRESENCE

They that wait upon the LORD . . . shall walk, and not faint. Isaiah 40:31

There is no thrill in walking; it is the test of all the stable qualities. To "walk and not faint" is the highest reach possible for strength. The word "walk" is used in the Bible to express the character—John, "looking upon Jesus *as He walked,*" said, Behold the Lamb of God!" There is never anything abstract in the Bible, it is always vivid and real. God does not say—"Be spiritual," but—"*Walk before Me.*"

When we are in an unhealthy state physically or emotionally, we always want thrills. In the physical domain this will lead to counterfeiting the Holy Ghost; in the emotional life it leads to inordinate affection and the destruction of morality; and in the spiritual domain if we insist on getting thrills, on mounting up with wings, it will end in the destruction of spirituality.

The reality of God's presence is not dependent on any place, but only dependent upon the determination to set the Lord always before us. Our problems come when we refuse to bank on the reality of His presence. The experience the Psalmist speaks of— "Therefore will we not fear, though. . . ."—will be ours when once we are based on Reality; not the consciousness of God's presence but the reality of it— "Why, He has been here all the time."

At critical moments it is necessary to ask guidance, but it ought to be unnecessary to be saying always—"Oh Lord, direct me here, and there." Of course He will! If our commonsense decisions are not God's order, He will press through them and check; then we must be quiet and wait for the direction of His presence.

JULY 21

THE GATEWAY TO THE KINGDOM

Blessed are the poor in spirit. Matthew 5:3

Beware of placing Our Lord as a Teacher first. If Jesus Christ is a Teacher only, then all He can do is to tantalise me by erecting a standard I cannot attain. What is the use of presenting me with an ideal I cannot possibly come near? I am happier without knowing it. What is the good of telling me to be what I never can be—to be pure in heart, to do more than my duty, to be perfectly devoted to God? I must know Jesus Christ as Saviour before His teaching has any meaning for me other than that of an ideal which leads to despair. But when I am born again of the Spirit of God, I know that Jesus Christ did not come to *teach* only: He came to *make me what He teaches I should be.* The Redemption means that Jesus Christ can put into any man the disposition that ruled His own life, and all the standards God gives are based on that disposition.

The teaching of the Sermon on the Mount produces despair in the natural man—the very thing Jesus means it to do. As long as we have a self-righteous, conceited notion that we can carry out Our Lord's teaching, God will allow us to go on until we break our ignorance over some obstacle, then we are willing to come to Him as paupers and receive from Him. "Blessed are the paupers in spirit," that is the first principle in the kingdom of God. The bedrock in Jesus Christ's kingdom is poverty, not possession; not decisions for Jesus Christ, but a sense of absolute futility—"I cannot begin to do it." Then Jesus says— "Blessed are you." That is the entrance, and it does take us a long while to believe we are poor! The knowledge of our own poverty brings us on to the moral frontier where Jesus Christ works.

JULY 22

SANCTIFICATION

This is the will of God, even your sanctification. 1 Thessalonians 4:3

The Death Side
In sanctification God has to deal with us on the death side as well as on the life side. Many of us spend so

much time in the place of death that we get sepulchral. There is always a battle royal before sanctification, always something that tugs with resentment against the demands of Jesus Christ. Immediately the Spirit of God begins to show us what sanctification means, the struggle begins. "If any man come to Me, and hate not . . . his own life, he cannot be My disciple."

The Spirit of God in the process of sanctification will strip me until I am nothing but "myself," that is the place of death. Am I willing to be "myself," and nothing more—no friends, no father, no brother, no self-interest, simply ready for death? That is the condition of sanctification. No wonder Jesus said: "I came not to send peace, but a sword." This is where the battle comes, and where so many of us faint. We refuse to be identified with the death of Jesus on this point. "But it is so stern," we say; "He cannot wish me to do that." Our Lord *is* stern; and He does wish me to do that.

Am I willing to reduce myself simply to "me," determinedly to strip myself of all my friends think of me, of all I think of myself, and to hand that simple naked self over to God? Immediately I am, He will sanctify me wholly, and my life will be free from earnestness in connection with everything but God.

When I pray—"Lord, show me what sanctification means for me," He will show me. It means being made one with Jesus. Sanctification is not something Jesus Christ puts into me: it is *Himself* in me.

JULY 23

SANCTIFICATION

Of Him are ye in Christ Jesus, who of God is made unto us . . . sanctification. 1 Corinthians 1:30

The Life Side
The mystery of sanctification is that the perfections of Jesus Christ are imparted to me, not gradually, but instantly when by faith I enter into the realisation that Jesus Christ is made unto me sanctification. Sanctification does not mean anything less than the holiness of Jesus being made mine manifestly.

The one marvellous secret of a holy life lies not in imitating Jesus, but in letting the perfections of Jesus manifest themselves in my mortal flesh. Sanctification is "Christ in you." It is *His* wonderful life that is imparted to me in sanctification, and imparted by faith as a sovereign gift of God's grace. Am I willing for God to make sanctification as real in me as it is in His word?

Sanctification means the impartation of the holy qualities of Jesus Christ. It is His patience, His love, His holiness, His faith, His purity, His godliness, that

is manifested in and through every sanctified soul. Sanctification is not drawing from Jesus the power to be holy; it is drawing from Jesus the holiness that was manifested in Him, and He manifests it in me. Sanctification is an impartation, not an imitation. Imitation is on a different line. In Jesus Christ is the perfection of everything, and the mystery of sanctification is that all the perfections of Jesus are at my disposal, and slowly and surely I begin to live a life of ineffable order and sanity and holiness "Kept by the power of God."

JULY 24

DISPOSITION AND DEEDS

Except your righteousness shall exceed the righteousness of the scribes and Pharisees, ye shall in no case enter into the kingdom of heaven. Matthew 5:20

The characteristic of a disciple is not that he does good things, but that he is good in motive because he has been made good by the supernatural grace of God. The only thing that exceeds right *doing* is right *being*. Jesus Christ came to put into any man who would let Him a new heredity which would exceed the righteousness of the scribes and Pharisees. Jesus says—"If you are My disciple you must be right not only in your living, but in your motives, in your dreams, in the recesses of your mind." You must be so pure in your motives that God Almighty can see nothing to censure. Who can stand in the Eternal Light of God and have nothing for God to censure? Only the Son of God, and Jesus Christ claims that by His Redemption He can put into any man His own disposition, and make him as unsullied and as simple as a child. The purity which God demands is impossible unless I can be re-made within, and this is what Jesus has undertaken to do by His Redemption.

No man can make himself pure by obeying laws. Jesus Christ does not give us rules and regulations; His teachings are truths that can only be interpreted by the disposition He puts in. The great marvel of Jesus Christ's salvation is that He alters heredity. He does not alter human nature; He alters its mainspring.

JULY 25

AM I BLESSED LIKE THIS?

Blessed are . . . Matthew 5:3–10

When we first read the statements of Jesus they seem wonderfully simple and unstartling, and they sink unobserved into our unconscious minds. For instance, the Beatitudes seem merely mild and beautiful precepts for all unworldly and useless people, but of very little practical use in the stern workaday world in which we live. We soon find, however, that the Beatitudes contain the dynamite of the Holy Ghost. They explode, as it were, when the circumstances of our lives cause them to do so. When the Holy Spirit brings to our remembrance one of these Beatitudes we say—"What a startling statement that is!" and we have to decide whether we will accept the tremendous spiritual upheaval that will be produced in our circumstances if we obey His words. That is the way the Spirit of God works. We do not need to be born again to apply the Sermon on the Mount literally. The literal interpretation of the Sermon on the Mount is child's play; the interpretation by the Spirit of God as He applies Our Lord's statements to our circumstances is the stern work of a saint.

The teaching of Jesus is out of all proportion to our natural way of looking at things, and it comes with astonishing discomfort to begin with. We have slowly to form our walk and conversation on the line of the precepts of Jesus Christ as the Holy Spirit applies them to our circumstances. The Sermon on the Mount is not a set of rules and regulations: it is a statement of the life we will live when the Holy Spirit is getting His way with us.

JULY 26

THE ACCOUNT WITH PURITY

Out of the heart proceed ... Matthew 15:18–20

We begin by trusting our ignorance and calling it innocence, by trusting our innocence and calling it purity; and when we hear these rugged statements of Our Lord's, we shrink and say—"But I never felt any of those awful things in my heart." We resent what Jesus Christ reveals. Either Jesus Christ is the supreme Authority on the human heart, or He is not worth paying any attention to. Am I prepared to trust His penetration, or do I prefer to trust my innocent ignorance? If I make conscious innocence the test, I am likely to come to a place where I find with a shuddering awakening that what Jesus Christ said is true, and I shall be appalled at the possibility of evil and wrong in me. As long as I remain under the refuge of innocence, I am living in a fool's paradise. If I have never been a blackguard, the reason is a mixture of cowardice and the protection of civilised life; but when I am undressed before God, I find that Jesus Christ is right in His diagnosis.

The only thing that safeguards is the Redemption of Jesus Christ. If I will hand myself over to Him, I need never experience the terrible possibilities that are in my heart. Purity is too deep down for me to get to naturally: but when the Holy Spirit comes in, He brings into the centre of my personal life the very Spirit that was manifested in the life of Jesus Christ, viz. *Holy* Spirit, which is unsullied purity.

JULY 27

THE WAY TO KNOW

If any man will do His will, he shall know of the doctrine.... John 7:17

The golden rule for understanding spiritually is not intellect, but obedience. If a man wants scientific knowledge, intellectual curiosity is his guide; but if he wants insight into what Jesus Christ teaches, he can only get it by obedience. If things are dark to me, then I may be sure there is something I will not do. Intellectual darkness comes through ignorance; spiritual darkness comes because of something I do not intend to obey.

No man ever receives a word from God without instantly being put to the test over it. We disobey and then wonder why we don't go on spiritually. "If when you come to the altar," said Jesus, "there you remember your brother hath ought against you... don't say another word to Me, but first go and put that thing right." The teaching of Jesus hits us where we live. We cannot stand as humbugs before Him for one second. He educates us down to the scruple. The Spirit of God unearths the spirit of self-vindication; He makes us sensitive to things we never thought of before.

When Jesus brings a thing home by His word, don't shirk it. If you do, you will become a religious humbug. Watch the things you shrug your shoulders over, and you will know why you do not go on spiritually. *First go*—at the risk of being thought fanatical you must obey what God tells you.

JULY 28

AFTER OBEDIENCE—WHAT?

And straightway He constrained His disciples to get into the ship, and to go to the other side.... Mark 6:45; see verses 45–52

We are apt to imagine that if Jesus Christ constrains us, and we obey Him, He will lead us to great success. We must never put our dreams of success as God's purpose for us; His purpose may be exactly the opposite. We have an idea that God is leading us to a particular end, a desired goal; He is not. The question of getting to a particular end is a mere incident. What we call the process, God calls the end.

What is my dream of God's purpose? His purpose is that I depend on Him and on His power now. If I can stay in the middle of the turmoil calm and unperplexed, that is the end of the purpose of God. God is not working towards a particular finish; His end is the process—that I see Him walking on the waves, no shore in sight, no success, no goal, just the absolute certainty that it is all right because I see Him walking on the sea. It is the process, not the end, which is glorifying to God.

God's training is for now, not presently. His purpose is for this minute, not for something in the future. We have nothing to do with the afterwards of obedience; we get wrong when we think of the afterwards. What men call training and preparation, God calls the end.

God's end is to enable me to see that He can walk on the chaos of my life just now. If we have a further end in view, we do not pay sufficient attention to the immediate present; but if we realise that obedience is the end, then each moment as it comes is precious.

JULY 29

WHAT DO YOU SEE IN YOUR CLOUDS?

Behold, He cometh with clouds. Revelation 1:7

In the Bible clouds are always connected with God. Clouds are those sorrows or sufferings or providences, within or without our personal lives, which seem to dispute the rule of God. It is by those very clouds that the Spirit of God is teaching us how to walk by faith. If there were no clouds, we should have no faith. The clouds are but the dust of our Father's feet. The clouds are a sign that He is there. What a revelation it is to know that sorrow and bereavement and suffering are the clouds that come along with God! God cannot come near without clouds, He does not come in clear shining.

It is not true to say that God wants to teach us something in our trials; through every cloud He brings, He wants us to *unlearn* something. God's purpose in the cloud is to simplify our belief until our relationship to Him is exactly that of a child—God and my own soul, other people are shadows. Until other people become shadows, clouds and darkness will be mine every now and again. Is the relationship between myself and God getting simpler than ever it has been?

There is a connection between the strange providences of God and what we know of Him, and we have to learn to interpret the mysteries of life in the light of our knowledge of God. Unless we can look

the darkest, blackest fact full in the face without damaging God's character, we do not yet know Him.

"They feared as they entered the cloud. . . ." Is there anyone "save Jesus only" in your cloud? If so, it will get darker; you must get to the place where there is "no one any more save Jesus only."

JULY 30

THE DISCIPLINE OF DISILLUSIONMENT

Jesus did not commit Himself unto them . . . for He knew what was in man. John 2:24–25

Disillusionment means that there are no more false judgements in life. To be undeceived by disillusionment may leave us cynical and unkindly severe in our judgement of others, but the disillusionment which comes from God brings us to the place where we see men and women as they really are, and yet there is no cynicism, we have no stinging, bitter things to say. Many of the cruel things in life spring from the fact that we suffer from illusions. We are not true to one another as *facts;* we are true only to our *ideas* of one another. Everything is either delightful and fine, or mean and dastardly, according to our idea.

The refusal to be disillusioned is the cause of much of the suffering in human life. It works in this way—if we love a human being and do not love God, we demand of him every perfection and every rectitude, and when we do not get it we become cruel and vindictive; we are demanding of a human being what he or she cannot give. There is only one Being Who can satisfy the last aching abyss of the human heart, and that is the Lord Jesus Christ. Why Our Lord is apparently so severe regarding every human relationship is because He knows that every relationship not based on loyalty to Himself will end in disaster. Our Lord trusted no man, yet He was never suspicious, never bitter. Our Lord's confidence in God and in what His grace could do for any man was so perfect that He despaired of no one. If our trust is placed in human beings, we shall end in despairing of everyone.

JULY 31

TILL YOU ARE ENTIRELY HIS

Let your endurance be a finished product, so that you may be finished and complete, with never a defect. James 1:4 (MOFFATT)

Many of us are all right in the main, but there are some domains in which we are slovenly. It is not a question of sin, but of the remnants of the carnal life which are apt to make us slovenly. Slovenliness is an insult to the Holy Ghost. There should be nothing slovenly, whether it be in the way we eat and drink, or in the way we worship God.

Not only must our relationship to God be right, but the external expression of that relationship must be right. Ultimately God will let nothing escape, every detail is under His scrutiny. In numberless ways God will bring us back to the same point over and over again. He never tires of bringing us to the one point until we learn the lesson, because He is producing the finished product. It may be a question of impulse, and again and again, with the most persistent patience, God has brought us back to the one particular point; or it may be mental wool-gathering, or independent individuality. God is trying to impress upon us the one thing that is not entirely right.

We have been having a wonderful time this Session[19] over the revelation of God's Redemption, our hearts are perfect towards Him; His wonderful work in us makes us know that in the main we are right with Him; now, says the Spirit, through St. James, "Let your endurance be a finished product." Watch the slipshod bits—"Oh, that will have to do for now." Whatever it is, God will point it out with persistence until we are entirely His.

SOMETHING MORE ABOUT HIS WAYS

He Comes Where He Commands Us to Leave

When Jesus had made an end of commanding His twelve disciples, He departed thence to teach and to preach in their cities. (Matthew 11:1)

If when God said "Go," you stayed, because you were so concerned about your people at home, you robbed them of the teaching and preaching of Jesus Christ Himself. When you obeyed and left all consequences to God, the Lord went into your city to teach; as long as you would not obey, you were in the way. Watch where you begin to debate and to put what you call duty in competition with your Lord's commands. "I know God told me to go, but then my duty was here"; that means you do not believe that Jesus means what He says.

He Teaches Where He Instructs Us Not To

Master, . . . let us make three tabernacles.

Are we playing the spiritual amateur providence in other lives? Are we so noisy in our instruction of others that God cannot get anywhere near them? We have to keep our mouths shut and our spirits alert. God wants to instruct us in regard to His Son, He wants to turn our times of prayer into mounts of transfiguration, and we will not let Him. When we are certain of the way God is going to work, He will never work in that way any more.

He Works Where He Sends Us to Wait

Tarry ye . . . until . . . .

Wait on God and He will work, but don't wait in spiritual sulks because you cannot see an inch in front of you! Are we detached enough from our own spiritual hysterics to wait on God? To wait is not to sit with folded hands, but to learn to do what we are told.

These are phases of His ways we rarely recognise.

THE DISCIPLINE OF DIFFICULTY

In the world ye shall have tribulation: but be of good cheer; I have overcome the world. John 16:33

An average view of the Christian life is that it means deliverance from trouble. It is deliverance *in* trouble, which is very different. "He that dwelleth in the secret place of the Most High . . . *there* shall no evil befall thee"—no plague can come nigh the place where you are at one with God.

If you are a child of God, there certainly will be troubles to meet, but Jesus says do not be surprised when they come. "In the world ye shall have tribulation: but be of good cheer; I have overcome the world," there is nothing for you to fear. Men who before they were saved would scorn to talk about troubles, often become "fushionless"[20] after being born again because they have a wrong idea of a saint. God does not give us overcoming life: He gives us life as we overcome. The strain is the strength. If there is no strain, there is no strength. Are you asking God to give you life and liberty and joy? He cannot, unless you will accept the strain. Immediately

---

19. this Session: talk given at BTC devotional hour, June 23, 1915.
20. fushionless: insipid; lacking energy; mentally or spiritually dull.

you face the strain, you will get the strength. Overcome your own timidity and take the step, and God will give you to eat of the tree of life and you will get nourishment. If you spend yourself out physically, you become exhausted; but spend yourself spiritually, and you get more strength. God never gives strength for tomorrow, or for the next hour, but only for the strain of the minute. The temptation is to face difficulties from a commonsense standpoint. The saint is hilarious when he is crushed with difficulties because the thing is so ludicrously impossible to anyone but God.

AUGUST 3

THE BIG COMPELLING OF GOD

Behold, we go up to Jerusalem. Luke 18:31

Jerusalem stands in the life of Our Lord as the place where He reached the climax of His Father's will. "I seek not Mine own will, but the will of the Father which hath sent Me." That was the one dominating interest all through Our Lord's life, and the things He met with on the way, joy or sorrow, success or failure, never deterred Him from His purpose. "He steadfastly set His face to go to Jerusalem."

The great thing to remember is that we go up to Jerusalem to fulfil God's purpose, not our own. Naturally, our ambitions are our own; in the Christian life we have no aim of our own. There is so much said today about our decisions for Christ, our determination to be Christians, our decisions for this and that, but in the New Testament it is the aspect of God's compelling that is brought out. "Ye have not chosen Me, but I have chosen you." We are not taken up into conscious agreement with God's purpose, we are taken up into God's purpose without any consciousness at all. We have no conception of what God is aiming at, and as we go on it gets more and more vague. God's aim looks like missing the mark because we are too short-sighted to see what He is aiming at. At the beginning of the Christian life we have our own ideas as to what God's purpose is—"I am meant to go here or there"; "God has called me to do this special work"; and we go and do the thing, and still the big compelling of God remains. The work we do is of no account, it is so much scaffolding compared with the big compelling of God. "He took unto Him the twelve," He takes us all the time. There is more than we have got at as yet.

THE BRAVE COMRADESHIP OF GOD

Then He took unto Him the twelve. Luke 18:31

The bravery of God in trusting us! You say—"But He has been unwise to choose me, because there is nothing in me; I am not of any value." That is why He chose you. As long as you think there is something in you, God cannot choose you because you have ends of your own to serve; but if you have let Him bring you to the end of your self-sufficiency, then He can choose you to go with Him to Jerusalem, and that will mean the fulfilment of purposes which He does not discuss with you.

We are apt to say that because a man has natural ability, therefore he will make a good Christian. It is not a question of our equipment but of our poverty; not of what we bring with us, but of what God puts into us; not a question of natural virtues, of strength of character, knowledge, and experience—all that is of no avail in this matter. The only thing that avails is that we are taken up into the big compelling of God and made His comrades (cf. 1 Corinthians 1:26–30). The comradeship of God is made up out of men who know their poverty. He can do nothing with the man who thinks that he is of use to God. As Christians we are not out for our own cause at all, we are out for the cause of God, which can never be our cause. We do not know what God is after, but we have to maintain our relationship with Him whatever happens. We must never allow anything to injure our relationship with God; if it does get injured, we must take time and get it put right. The main thing about Christianity is not the work we do, but the relationship we maintain and the atmosphere produced by that relationship. That is all God asks us to look after, and it is the one thing that is being continually assailed.

THE BAFFLING CALL OF GOD

And all things that are written by the prophets concerning the Son of man shall be accomplished. . . . And they understood none of these things. Luke 18:31, 34

God called Jesus Christ to what seemed unmitigated disaster. Jesus Christ called His disciples to see Him put to death; He led every one of them to the place where their hearts were broken. Jesus Christ's life was an absolute failure from every standpoint but God's. But what seemed failure from man's standpoint was a tremendous triumph from God's, because God's purpose is never man's purpose.

There comes the baffling call of God in our lives also. The call of God can never be stated explicitly; it is implicit. The call of God is like the call of the sea, no one hears it but the one who has the nature of the sea in him. It cannot be stated definitely what the call of God is to, because His call is to be in comradeship with Himself for His own purpose, and the test is to believe that God knows what He is after. The things that happen do not happen by chance, they happen entirely in the decree of God. God is working out His purposes.

If we are in communion with God and recognise that He is taking us into His purposes, we shall no longer try to find out what His purposes are. As we go on in the Christian life it gets simpler, because we are less inclined to say—"Now why did God allow this and that?" Behind the whole thing lies the compelling of God. "There's a divinity that shapes our ends." A Christian is one who trusts the wits and the wisdom of God, and not his own wits. If we have a purpose of our own, it destroys the simplicity and the leisureliness which ought to characterise the children of God.

AUGUST 6

THE CROSS IN PRAYER

At that day ye shall ask in My name. John 16:26

We are too much given to thinking of the Cross as something we have to get through; we get *through* it only in order to get into it. The Cross stands for one thing only for us—a complete and entire and absolute identification with the Lord Jesus Christ, and there is nothing in which this identification is realised more than in prayer.

"Your Father knoweth what things ye have need of, before ye ask Him." Then why ask? The idea of prayer is not in order to get answers from God; prayer is perfect and complete oneness with God. If we pray because we want answers, we will get huffed with God. The answers come every time, but not always in the way we expect, and our spiritual huff shows a refusal to identify ourselves with Our Lord in prayer. We are not here to prove God answers prayer; we are here to be living monuments of God's grace.

"I say not that I will pray the Father for you: for the Father Himself loveth you." Have you reached such an intimacy with God that the Lord Jesus Christ's life of prayer is the only explanation of your life of prayer? Has Our Lord's vicarious life become your vital life? "At that day" you will be so identified with Jesus that there will be no distinction.

When prayer seems to be unanswered, beware of trying to fix the blame on someone else. That is always a snare of Satan. You will find there is a reason which is a deep instruction to you, not to anyone.

AUGUST 7

PRAYER IN THE FATHER'S HOUSE

Wist ye not that I must be in My Father's house? Luke 2:49 (RV)

Our Lord's childhood was not immature manhood: our Lord's childhood is an eternal fact. Am I a holy innocent child of God by identification with my Lord and Saviour? Do I look upon life as being in my Father's house? Is the Son of God living in His Father's house in me?

The abiding Reality is God, and His order comes through the moments. Am I always in contact with Reality, or do I only pray when things have gone wrong, when there is a disturbance in the moments of my life? I have to learn to identify myself with my Lord in holy communion in ways some of us have not begun to learn as yet. "I must be about My Father's business" (KJV)—live the moments in My Father's house.

Narrow it down to your individual circumstances—are you so identified with the Lord's life that you are simply a child of God, continually talking to Him and realising that all things come from His hands? Is the Eternal Child in you living in the Father's house? Are the graces of His ministering life working out through you in your home, in your business, in your domestic circle? Have you been wondering why you are going through the things you are? It is not that *you* have to go through them, it is because of the relation into which the Son of God has come in His Father's providence in your particular sainthood. Let Him have His way, keep in perfect union with Him.

The vicarious life of your Lord is to become your vital simple life; the way He worked and lived among men must be the way He lives in you.

AUGUST 8

PRAYER IN THE FATHER'S HONOUR

That holy thing which shall be born of thee shall be called the Son of God. Luke 1:35

If the Son of God is born into my mortal flesh, is His holy innocence and simplicity and oneness with the

Father getting a chance to manifest itself in me? What was true of the Virgin Mary in the historic introduction of God's Son into this earth is true in every saint. The Son of God is born into me by the direct act of God; then I as a child of God have to exercise the right of a child, the right of being always face to face with my Father. Am I continually saying with amazement to my commonsense life—"Why do you want to turn me off here? Don't you know that I must be about my Father's business?" Whatever the circumstances may be, that Holy, Innocent, Eternal Child must be in contact with His Father.

Am I simple enough to identify myself with my Lord in this way? Is He getting His wonderful way in me? Is God realising that His Son is formed in me, or have I carefully put Him on one side? Oh the clamour of these days! Everyone is clamouring—for what? For the Son of God to be put to death. There is no room here for the Son of God just now, no room for quiet holy communion with the Father.

Is the Son of God praying in me or am I dictating to Him? Is He ministering in me as He did in the days of His flesh? Is the Son of God in me going through His passion for His own purposes? The more one knows of the inner life of God's ripest saints, the more one sees what God's purpose is—filling up "that which is behind of the afflictions of Christ." There is always something to be done in the sense of "filling up."

AUGUST 9

PRAYER IN THE FATHER'S HEARING

Father, I thank Thee that thou hast heard Me. John 11:41

When the Son of God prays, He has only one consciousness, and that consciousness is of His Father. God always hears the prayers of His Son, and if the Son of God is formed in me the Father will always hear my prayers. I have to see that the Son of God is manifested in my mortal flesh. "Your body is the temple of the Holy Ghost," the "Bethlehem" of the Son of God. Is the Son of God getting His chance in me? Is the direct simplicity of the life of God's Son being worked out exactly as it was worked out in His historic life? When I come in contact with the occurrences of life as an ordinary human being, is the prayer of God's Eternal Son to His Father being prayed in me? "In that day ye shall ask in My name . . ." (RV). What day? The day when the Holy Ghost has come to me and made me effectually one with my Lord.

Is the Lord Jesus Christ being abundantly satisfied in your life or have you got a spiritual "strut" on? Never let common sense obtrude and push the Son of God on one side. Common sense is a gift which God gave to human nature; but common sense is not the gift of His Son. Supernatural sense is the gift of His Son; never enthrone common sense. The Son detects the Father; common sense never yet detected the Father and never will. Our ordinary wits never worship God unless they are transfigured by the indwelling Son of God. We have to see that this mortal flesh is kept in perfect subjection to Him and that He works through it moment by moment. Are we living in such human dependence upon Jesus Christ that His life is being "manifested in our mortal flesh" (RV)?

AUGUST 10

THE SACRAMENT OF THE SAINT

Let them that suffer according to the will of God commit the keeping of their souls to Him in well-doing. 1 Peter 4:19

To choose to suffer means that there is something wrong; to choose God's will even if it means suffering is a very different thing. No healthy saint ever chooses suffering; he chooses God's will, as Jesus did, whether it means suffering or not. No saint dare interfere with the discipline of suffering in another saint.

The saint who satisfies the heart of Jesus will make other saints strong and mature for God. The people who do us good are never those who sympathise with us, they always hinder, because sympathy enervates. No one understands a saint but the saint who is nearest to the Saviour. If we accept the sympathy of a saint, the reflex feeling is—"Well, God is dealing hardly with me." That is why Jesus said self-pity was of the devil (see Matthew 16:23). Be merciful to God's reputation. It is easy to blacken God's character because God never answers back, He never vindicates Himself. Beware of the thought that Jesus needed sympathy in His earthly life; He refused sympathy from man because He knew far too wisely that no one on earth understood what He was after. He took sympathy from His Father only, and from the angels in heaven. (Cf. Luke 15:10.)

Notice God's unutterable waste of saints. According to the judgement of the world, God plants His saints in the most useless places. We say—"God intends me to be here because I am so useful." God puts His saints where they will glorify Him, and we are no judges at all of where that is.

AUGUST 11

THIS EXPERIENCE MUST COME

And he saw him no more. 2 Kings 2:12

It is not wrong to depend upon Elijah as long as God gives him to you, but remember the time will come when he will have to go; when he stands no more to you as your guide and leader, because God does not intend he should. You say—"I cannot go on without Elijah." God says you must.

Alone at your Jordan (2 Kings 2:14). Jordan is the type of separation where there is no fellowship with anyone else, and where no one can take the responsibility for you. You have to put to the test now what you learned when you were with your Elijah. You have been to Jordan over and over again with Elijah, but now you are up against it alone. It is no use saying you cannot go; this experience has come, and you must go. If you want to know whether God is the God you have faith to believe Him to be, then go through your Jordan alone.

Alone at your Jericho (v. 15). Jericho is the place where you have seen your Elijah do great things. When you come to your Jericho you have a strong disinclination to take the initiative and trust in God, you want someone else to take it for you. If you remain true to what you learned with Elijah, you will get the sign that God is with you.

Alone at your Bethel (v. 23). At your Bethel you will find yourself at your wits' end and at the beginning of God's wisdom. When you get to your wits' end and feel inclined to succumb to panic, don't; stand true to God and He will bring His truth out in a way that will make your life a sacrament. Put into practice what you learned with your Elijah, use his cloak and pray. Determine to trust in God and do not look for Elijah any more.

AUGUST 12

THE THEOLOGY OF REST

Why are ye fearful, O ye of little faith? Matthew 8:26

When we are in fear we can do nothing less than pray to God, but Our Lord has a right to expect that those who name His Name should have an understanding confidence in Him. God expects His children to be so confident in Him that in any crisis they are the reliable ones. Our trust is in God up to a certain point, then we go back to the elementary panic prayers of those who do not know God. We get to our wits' end, showing that we have not the slightest con-fidence in Him and His government of the world; He seems to be asleep, and we see nothing but breakers ahead.

"O ye of little faith"! What a pang must have shot through the disciples—"Missed it again!" And what a pang will go through us when we suddenly realise that we might have produced downright joy in the heart of Jesus by remaining absolutely confident in Him, no matter what was ahead.

There are stages in life when there is no storm, no crisis, when we do our human best; it is when a crisis arises that we instantly reveal upon whom we rely. If we have been learning to worship God and to trust Him, the crisis will reveal that we will go to the breaking point and not break in our confidence in Him.

We have been talking a great deal about sanctification—what is it all going to amount to? It should work out into rest in God which means oneness with God, a oneness which will make us not only blameless in His sight but a deep joy to Him.

AUGUST 13

QUENCH NOT THE SPIRIT

Quench not the spirit. 1 Thessalonians 5:19

The voice of the Spirit is as gentle as a zephyr, so gentle that unless you are living in perfect communion with God, you never hear it. The checks of the Spirit come in the most extraordinarily gentle ways, and if you are not sensitive enough to detect His voice you will quench it, and your personal spiritual life will be impaired. His checks always come as a still small voice, so small that no one but the saint notices them.

Beware if in personal testimony you have to hark back and say—"Once, so many years ago, I was saved." If you are walking in the light, there is no harking back, the past is transfused into the present wonder of communion with God. If you get out of the light you become a sentimental Christian and live on memories, your testimony has a hard, metallic note. Beware of trying to patch up a present refusal to walk in the light by recalling past experiences when you did walk in the light. Whenever the Spirit checks, call a halt and get the thing right, or you will go on grieving Him without knowing it.

Suppose God has brought you up to a crisis and you nearly go through but not quite, He will engineer the crisis again, but it will not be so keen as it was before. There will be less discernment of God and more humiliation at not having obeyed; and if you go on grieving the Spirit, there will come a time when that crisis cannot be repeated, you have grieved Him away. But if you go through the crisis, there will be the psalm of praise to God. Never sympathise with the thing that is stabbing God all the time. God has to hurt the thing that must go.

AUGUST 14

CHASTENING

Despise not thou the chastening of the Lord, nor faint when thou art rebuked of Him. Hebrews 12:5

It is very easy to quench the Spirit; we do it by despising the chastening of the Lord, by fainting when we are rebuked by Him. If we have only a shallow experience of sanctification, we mistake the shadow for the reality, and when the Spirit of God begins to check, we say—"Oh, that must be the devil."

Never quench the Spirit, and do not despise Him when He says to you—"Don't be blind on this point any more; you are not where you thought you were. Up to the present, I have not been able to reveal it to you, but I reveal it now." When the Lord chastens you like that, let Him have His way. Let Him relate you rightly to God.

"Nor faint when thou art rebuked of Him." We get into sulks with God and say—"Oh well, I can't help it; I did pray and things did not turn out right, and I am going to give it all up." Think what would happen if we talked like this in any other domain of life!

Am I prepared to let God grip me by His power and do a work in me that is worthy of Himself? Sanctification is not my idea of what I want God to do for me; sanctification is God's idea of what He wants to do for me, and He has to get me into the attitude of mind and spirit where at any cost I will let Him sanctify me wholly.

AUGUST 15

SIGNS OF THE NEW BIRTH

Ye must be born again. John 3:7

The answer to the question "How can a man be born when he is old?" is—When he is old enough to die—to die right out to his "rag rights,"[21] to his virtues, to his religion, to everything, and to receive into himself the life which never was there before. The new life manifests itself in conscious repentance and unconscious holiness.

"As many as received Him" (John 1:12). Is my knowledge of Jesus born of internal spiritual perception, or is it only what I have learned by listening to others? Have I something in my life that connects me with the Lord Jesus as my personal Saviour? All spiritual history must have a personal knowledge for its bedrock. To be born again means that I see Jesus.

"Except a man be born again, he cannot see the kingdom of God" (John 3:3). Do I seek for signs of the Kingdom, or do I perceive God's rule? The new birth gives a new power of vision whereby I begin to discern God's rule. His rule was there all the time, but true to His nature; now that I have received His nature, I can see His rule.

"Whosoever is born of God doth not commit sin" (1 John 3:9). Do I seek to stop sinning or have I stopped sinning? To be born of God means that I have the supernatural power of God to stop sinning. In the Bible it is never—Should a Christian sin? The Bible puts it emphatically—*A Christian must not sin.* The effective working of the new birth life in us is that we do not commit sin, not merely that we have the power not to sin, but that we have stopped sinning. First John 3:9 does not mean that we *cannot* sin; it means that if we obey the life of God in us, we *need not* sin.

AUGUST 16

DOES HE KNOW ME?

He calleth . . . by name. John 10:3

When I have sadly misunderstood Him? (John 20:17). It is possible to know all about doctrine and yet not know Jesus. The soul is in danger when knowledge of doctrine outsteps intimate touch with Jesus. Why was Mary weeping? Doctrine was no more to Mary than the grass under her feet. Any Pharisee could have made a fool of Mary doctrinally, but one thing they could not ridicule out of her was the fact that Jesus had cast seven demons out of her; yet His blessings were nothing in comparison to Himself. Mary "saw Jesus standing, and knew not that it was Jesus"; immediately she heard the voice, she knew she had a past history with the One who spoke. "Master"!

When I have stubbornly doubted? (John 20:27). Have I been doubting something about Jesus—an experience to which others testify but which I have not had? The other disciples told Thomas that they had seen Jesus, but Thomas doubted—"Except I shall see . . . , I will not believe." Thomas needed the personal touch of Jesus. When His touches come, or how they come, we do not know; but when they do come

---

21. rag rights: self-righteousness; see Isaiah 64:6.

they are indescribably precious. "My Lord and my God"!

When I have selfishly denied Him? (John 21:15–17). Peter had denied Jesus Christ with oaths and curses, and yet after the Resurrection Jesus appeared to Peter alone. He restored him in private, then He restored him before the others. "Lord, Thou knowest that I love Thee."

Have I a personal history with Jesus Christ? The one sign of discipleship is intimate connection with Him, a knowledge of Jesus Christ which nothing can shake.

AUGUST 17

ARE YOU DISCOURAGED IN DEVOTION?

Yet lackest thou one thing; sell all that thou hast . . . and come, follow Me. Luke 18:22

"And when he heard this . . ." Have you ever heard the Master say a hard word? If you have not, I question whether you have heard Him say anything. Jesus Christ says a great deal that we listen to, but do not hear; when we do hear, His words are amazingly hard.

Jesus did not seem in the least solicitous that this man should do what He told him, He made no attempt to keep him with Him. He simply said— "Sell all you have, and come, follow Me." Our Lord never pleaded, He never cajoled, He never entrapped; He simply spoke the sternest words mortal ears ever listened to, and then left it alone.

Have I ever heard Jesus say a hard word? Has He said something personally to me to which I have deliberately listened? Not something I can expound or say this and that about, but something I have heard Him say to me? This man did understand what Jesus said, he heard it and he sized up what it meant, and it broke his heart. He did not go away defiant; he went away sorrowful, thoroughly discouraged. He had come to Jesus full of the fire of earnest desire, and the word of Jesus simply froze him; instead of producing an enthusiastic devotion, it produced a heart-breaking discouragement. And Jesus did not go after him, He let him go. Our Lord knows perfectly that when once His word is heard, it will bear fruit sooner or later. The terrible thing is that some of us prevent it bearing fruit in actual life. I wonder what we will say when we do make up our minds to be devoted to Him on that particular point? One thing is certain, He will never cast anything up at us.

AUGUST 18

HAVE YOU EVER BEEN EXPRESSIONLESS WITH SORROW?

And when he heard this, he was very sorrowful: for he was very rich. Luke 18:23

The rich young ruler went away expressionless with sorrow; he had not a word to say. He had no doubt as to what Jesus said, no debate as to what it meant, and it produced in him a sorrow that had not any words. Have you ever been there? Has God's word come to you about something you are very rich in—temperament, personal affinity, relationships of heart and mind? Then you have often been expressionless with sorrow. The Lord will not go after you, He will not plead, but every time He meets you on that point He will simply repeat—"If you mean what you say, those are the conditions."

"Sell all that thou hast" —undress yourself morally before God of everything that might be a possession until you are a mere conscious human being, and then give God that. That is where the battle is fought—in the domain of the will before God. Are you more devoted to your idea of what Jesus wants than to Himself? If so, you are likely to hear one of His hard sayings that will produce sorrow in you. What Jesus says *is* hard, it is only easy when it is heard by those who have His disposition. Beware of allowing anything to soften a hard word of Jesus Christ's.

I can be so rich in poverty, so rich in the consciousness that I am nobody, that I shall never be a disciple of Jesus; and I can be so rich in the consciousness that I am somebody—that I shall never be a disciple. Am I willing to be destitute of the sense that I am destitute? This is where discouragement comes in. Discouragement is disenchanted self-love, and self-love may be love of my devotion to Jesus.

AUGUST 19

SELF-CONSCIOUSNESS

Come unto Me. Matthew 11:28

God means us to live a fully-orbed life in Christ Jesus, but there are times when that life is attacked from the outside, and we tumble into a way of introspection which we thought had gone. Self-consciousness is the first thing that will upset the completeness of the life in God, and self-consciousness continually produces wrestling. Self-consciousness is not sin; it may be produced by a nervous temperament or by a sudden dumping down into new circumstances. It is never God's will that we should be anything less than absolutely complete in Him. Anything that disturbs rest in Him must be cured at once, and it is not cured by being ignored, but by coming to Jesus Christ. If we come to Him and ask Him to produce Christ-consciousness, He will always do it until we learn to abide in Him.

Never allow the dividing up of your life in Christ to remain without facing it. Beware of leakage, of the dividing up of your life by the influence of friends or of circumstances; beware of anything that is going to split up your oneness with Him and make you see yourself separately. Nothing is so important as to keep right spiritually. The great solution is the simple one—"Come unto Me." The depth of our reality, intellectually, morally and spiritually, is tested by these words. In every degree in which we are not real, we will dispute rather than come.

AUGUST 20

COMPLETENESS

And I will give you rest. Matthew 11:28

Whenever anything begins to disintegrate your life with Jesus Christ, turn to Him at once and ask Him to establish rest. Never allow anything to remain which is making the dis-peace. Take every element of disintegration as something to wrestle against, and not to suffer. Say—"Lord, prove Thy consciousness in me," and self-consciousness will go and He will be all in all. Beware of allowing self-consciousness to continue because by slow degrees it will awaken self-pity, and self-pity is Satanic. "Well, I am not understood; this is a thing they ought to apologise for; that is a point I really must have cleared up." Leave others alone and ask the Lord to give you Christ-consciousness, and He will poise you until the completeness is absolute.

The complete life is the life of a child. When I am consciously conscious, there is something wrong. It is the sick man who knows what health is. The child of God is not conscious of the will of God because he *is* the will of God. When there has been the slightest deviation from the will of God, we begin to ask—"What is Thy will?" A child of God never prays to be conscious that God answers prayer, he is so restfully certain that God always does answer prayer.

If we try to overcome self-consciousness by any commonsense method, we develop it tremendously.

Jesus says "Come unto Me . . . and I will give you rest," i.e., Christ-consciousness will take the place of self-consciousness. Wherever Jesus comes He establishes rest, the rest of the perfection of activity that is never conscious of itself.

AUGUST 21

THE MINISTRY OF THE UNNOTICED

Blessed are the poor in spirit. Matthew 5:3

The New Testament notices things which from our standards do not seem to count. "Blessed are the poor in spirit," literally—Blessed are the paupers—an exceedingly commonplace thing! The preaching of to-day is apt to emphasise strength of will, beauty of character—the things that are easily noticed. The phrase we hear so often, "Decide for Christ," is an emphasis on something Our Lord never trusted. He never asks us to decide for Him, but to yield to Him, a very different thing. At the basis of Jesus Christ's Kingdom is the unaffected loveliness of the commonplace. The thing I am blessed in is my poverty. If I know I have no strength of will, no nobility of disposition, then Jesus says—Blessed are you, because it is through this poverty that I enter His Kingdom. I cannot enter His Kingdom as a good man or woman, I can only enter it as a complete pauper.

The true character of the loveliness that tells for God is always unconscious. Conscious influence is priggish and un-Christian. If I say, "I wonder if I am of any use," I instantly lose the bloom of the touch of the Lord. "He that believeth on Me, out of [him] shall flow rivers of living water." If I examine the outflow, I lose the touch of the Lord.

Which are the people who have influenced us most? Not the ones who thought they did, but those who had not the remotest notion that they were influencing us. In the Christian life the implicit is never conscious; if it is conscious, it ceases to have this unaffected loveliness which is the characteristic of the touch of Jesus. We always know when Jesus is at work because He produces in the commonplace something that is inspiring.

AUGUST 22

"I INDEED . . . BUT HE"

I indeed baptize you with water . . . but He . . . shall baptize you with the Holy Ghost and with fire. Matthew 3:11

Have I ever come to a place in my experience where I can say—"I indeed . . . but He"? Until that moment does come, I will never know what the baptism of the Holy Ghost means. *"I indeed"* am at an end, I cannot do a thing: *"but He"* begins just there—He does the things no one else can ever do. Am I prepared for His coming? Jesus cannot come as long as there is anything in the way either of goodness or badness. When He comes am I prepared for Him to drag into the light every wrong thing I have done? It is just there that He comes. Wherever I know I am unclean, He will put His feet; wherever I think I am clean, He will withdraw them. Repentance does not bring a sense of sin, but a sense of unutterable unworthiness. When I repent, I realise that I am utterly helpless; I know all through me that I am not worthy even to bear His shoes. Have I repented like that? Or is there a lingering suggestion of standing up for myself? The reason God cannot come into my life is because I am not through into repentance.

"He . . . shall baptize you with the Holy Ghost and with fire." John does not speak of the baptism of the Holy Ghost as an experience, but as a work performed by Jesus Christ, *"He* shall baptise you." The only conscious experience those who are baptised with the Holy Ghost ever have is a sense of absolute unworthiness.

"I indeed" was this and that; *"but He"* came, and a marvellous thing happened. Get to the margin where He does everything.

AUGUST 23

PRAYER CHOICE AND PRAYER CONFLICT

When thou prayest, enter into thy closet, and when thou hast shut thy door, pray to thy Father which is in secret. Matthew 6:6

Jesus did not say—"Dream about thy Father in secret," but *"pray* to thy Father in secret." Prayer is an effort of will. After we have entered our secret place and have shut the door, the most difficult thing to do is to pray. We cannot get our minds into working order, and the first thing that conflicts is wandering thoughts. The great battle in private prayer is the overcoming of mental wool-gathering. We have to discipline our minds and concentrate on wilful prayer.

We must have a selected place for prayer and when we get there the plague of flies begins—This must be done, and that. "Shut thy door." A secret silence means to shut the door deliberately on emotions and remember God. God is in secret, and He sees us from the secret place; He does not see us as other people see us, or as we see ourselves. When we live in the secret place it becomes impossible for us to doubt God, we become more sure of Him than of anything else. Your Father, Jesus says, is in secret and nowhere else. Enter the secret place, and right in the centre of the common round you find God there all the time. Get into the habit of dealing with God about everything. Unless in the first waking moment of the day you learn to fling the door wide back and let God in, you will work on a wrong level all day; but swing the door wide open and pray to your Father in secret, and every public thing will be stamped with the presence of God.

AUGUST 24

THE SPIRITUAL INDEX

Or what man is there of you, whom if his son ask bread, will he give him a stone? Matthew 7:9

The illustration of prayer that Our Lord uses here is that of a good child asking for a good thing. We talk about prayer as if God heard us irrespective of the fact of our relationship to Him (cf. Matthew 5:45). Never say it is not God's will to give you what you ask, don't sit down and faint, but find out the reason, turn up the index. Are you rightly related to your wife, to your husband, to your children, to your fellow-students—are you a "good child" there? "Oh, Lord, I have been irritable and cross, but I do want spiritual blessing." You cannot have it, you will have to do without until you come into the attitude of a good child.

We mistake defiance for devotion; arguing with God for abandonment. We will not look at the index. Have I been asking God to give me money for something I want when there is something I have not paid for? Have I been asking God for liberty while I am withholding it from someone who belongs to me? I have not forgiven someone his trespasses; I have not been kind to him; I have not been living as God's child among my relatives and friends.

I am a child of God only by regeneration, and as a child of God I am good only as I walk in the light. Prayer with most of us is turned into pious platitude, it is a matter of emotion, mystical communion with God. Spiritually we are all good at producing fogs. If we turn up the index, we will see very clearly what is wrong—that friendship, that debt, that temper of mind. It is no use praying unless we are living as children of God. Then, Jesus says—"Every one that asketh receiveth."

AUGUST 25

THE FRUITFULNESS OF FRIENDSHIP

I have called you friends. John 15:15

We never know the joy of self-sacrifice until we abandon in every particular. Self-surrender is the most difficult thing—"I will if . . . !" "Oh well, I suppose I must devote my life to God." There is none of the joy of self-sacrifice in that.

As soon as we do abandon, the Holy Ghost gives us an intimation of the joy of Jesus. The final aim of self-sacrifice is laying down our lives for our Friend. When the Holy Ghost comes in, the great desire is to lay down the life for Jesus; the thought of sacrifice never touches us because sacrifice is the love passion of the Holy Ghost.

Our Lord is our example in the life of self-sacrifice—"I delight to do Thy will, O My God." He went on with His sacrifice with exuberant joy. Have I ever yielded in absolute submission to Jesus Christ? If Jesus Christ is not the lodestar, there is no benefit in the sacrifice; but when the sacrifice is made with the eyes on Him, slowly and surely the moulding influence begins to tell.

Beware of letting natural affinities hinder your walk in love. One of the most cruel ways of killing natural love is by disdain built on natural affinities. The affinity of the saint is the Lord Jesus. Love for God is not sentimental; to love as God loves is the most practical thing for the saint.

"I have called you friends." It is a friendship based on the new life created in us, which has no affinity with our old life, but only with the life of God. It is unutterably humble, unsulliedly pure, and absolutely devoted to God.

AUGUST 26

ARE YOU EVER DISTURBED?

Peace I leave with you, My peace I give unto you. John 14:27

There are times when our peace is based upon ignorance, but when we awaken to the facts of life, inner peace is impossible unless it is received from Jesus. When Our Lord speaks peace, He makes peace, His words are ever "spirit and life." Have I ever received what Jesus speaks? *"My peace I give unto you"*—it is a peace which comes from looking into His face and realising His undisturbedness.

Are you painfully disturbed just now, distracted by the waves and billows of God's providential per-

mission, and having, as it were, turned over the boulders of your belief, are you still finding no well of peace or joy or comfort; is all barren? Then look up and receive the undisturbedness of the Lord Jesus. Reflected peace is the proof that you are right with God because you are at liberty to turn your mind to Him. If you are not right with God, you can never turn your mind anywhere but on yourself. If you allow anything to hide the face of Jesus Christ from you, you are either disturbed or you have a false security.

Are you looking unto Jesus now, in the immediate matter that is pressing, and receiving from Him peace? If so, He will be a gracious benediction of peace in and through you: But if you try to worry it out, you obliterate Him and deserve all you get. We get disturbed because we have not been considering Him. When one confers with Jesus Christ the perplexity goes, because He has no perplexity, and our only concern is to abide in Him. Lay it all out before Him and in the face of difficulty, bereavement and sorrow, hear Him say—"Let not your heart be troubled."

AUGUST 27

THEOLOGY ALIVE

Walk while ye have the light, lest darkness come upon you. John 12:35

Beware of not acting upon what you see in your moments on the mount with God. If you do not obey the light, it will turn into darkness. "If therefore the light that is in thee be darkness, how great is that darkness!" The second you waive the question of sanctification or any other thing upon which God gave you light, you begin to get dry rot in your spiritual life. Continually bring the truth out into actuality; work it out in every domain, or the very light you have will prove a curse.

The most difficult person to deal with is the one who has the smug satisfaction of an experience to which he can refer back, but who is not working it out in practical life. If you *say* you are sanctified, *show it.* The experience must be so genuine that it is shown in the life. Beware of any belief that makes you self-indulgent; it came from the pit, no matter how beautiful it sounds.

Theology must work itself out in the most practical relationships. "Except your righteousness shall *exceed* the righteousness of the scribes and Pharisees, . . ." said Our Lord, i.e., you must be more moral than the most moral being you know. You may know all about the doctrine of sanctification, but are you running it out into the practical issues of your life? Every bit of our life, physical, moral and spiritual, is to be judged by the standard of the Atonement.

AUGUST 28

WHAT'S THE GOOD OF PRAYER?

Lord, teach us to pray. Luke 11:1

It is not part of the life of a natural man to pray. We hear it said that a man will suffer in his life if he does not pray; I question it. What will suffer is the life of the Son of God in him, which is nourished, not by food, but by prayer. When a man is born from above (RV mg), the life of the Son of God is born in him, and he can either starve that life or nourish it. Prayer is the way the life of God is nourished. Our ordinary views of prayer are not found in the New Testament. We look upon prayer as a means of getting things for ourselves; the Bible idea of prayer is that we may get to know God Himself.

"Ask, and ye shall receive." We grouse before God, we are apologetic or apathetic, but we *ask* very few things. Yet what a splendid audacity a childlike child has! Our Lord says—"Except ye . . . become as little children." Ask, and God will do. Give Jesus Christ a chance, give Him elbow room, and no man will ever do this unless he is at his wits' end. When a man is at his wits' end it is not a cowardly thing to pray, it is the only way he can get into touch with Reality. Be yourself before God and present your problems, the things you know you have come to your wits' end over. As long as you are self-sufficient, you do not need to ask God for anything.

It is not so true that "prayer changes things" as that prayer changes *me* and I change things. God has so constituted things that prayer on the basis of Redemption alters the way in which a man looks at things. Prayer is not a question of altering things externally, but of working wonders in a man's disposition.

AUGUST 29

SUBLIME INTIMACY

Said I not unto thee, that, if thou wouldest believe, thou shouldest see the glory of God? John 11:40

Every time you venture out in the life of faith, you will find something in your commonsense circumstances that flatly contradicts your faith. Common sense is not faith, and faith is not common sense; they stand in the relation of the natural and the spiritual. Can you trust Jesus Christ where your common sense cannot trust Him? Can you venture heroically on Jesus Christ's statements when the facts of your commonsense life shout "It's a lie"? On the mount it is easy to say—"Oh yes, I believe God can do it"; but

you have to come down into the demon-possessed valley and meet with facts that laugh ironically at the whole of your mount-of-transfiguration belief. Every time my programme of belief is clear to my own mind, I come across something that contradicts it. Let me say I believe God will supply all my need, and then let me run dry, with no outlook, and see whether I will go through the trial of faith, or whether I will sink back to something lower.

Faith must be tested, because it can be turned into a personal possession only through conflict. What is your faith up against just now? The test will either prove that your faith is right, or it will kill it. "Blessed is he, whosoever shall not be offended in Me." The final thing is confidence in Jesus. Believe steadfastly on Him and all you come up against will develop your faith. There is continual testing in the life of faith, and the last great test is death. May God keep us in fighting trim! Faith is unutterable trust in God which never dreams that He will not stand by us.

AUGUST 30

AM I CONVINCED BY CHRIST?

Notwithstanding in this rejoice not, . . . but rather rejoice, because your names are written in heaven. Luke 10:20

Jesus Christ says, in effect, Don't rejoice in successful service, but rejoice because you are rightly related to Me. The snare in Christian work is to rejoice in successful service, to rejoice in the fact that God has used you. You never can measure what God will do through you if you are rightly related to Jesus Christ. Keep your relationship right with Him, then whatever circumstances you are in, and whoever you meet day by day, He is pouring rivers of living water through you, and it is of His mercy that He does not let you know it. When once you are rightly related to God by salvation and sanctification, remember that wherever you are, you are put there by God; and by the reaction of your life on the circumstances around you, you will fulfil God's purpose, as long as you keep in the light as God is in the light.

The tendency to-day is to put the emphasis on service. Beware of the people who make usefulness their ground of appeal. If you make usefulness the test, then Jesus Christ was the greatest failure that ever lived. The lodestar of the saint is God Himself, not estimated usefulness. It is the work that God does through us that counts, not what we do for Him. All that Our Lord heeds in a man's life is the relationship of worth to His Father. Jesus is bringing many *sons* to glory.

AUGUST 31

MY JOY . . . YOUR JOY

That My joy might remain in you, and that your joy might be full. John 15:11

What was the joy that Jesus had? It is an insult to use the word happiness in connection with Jesus Christ. The joy of Jesus was the absolute self-surrender and self-sacrifice of Himself to His Father, the joy of doing that which the Father sent Him to do. "I delight to do Thy will." Jesus prayed that our joy might go on fulfilling itself until it was the same joy as His. Have I allowed Jesus Christ to introduce His joy to me?

The full flood of my life is not in bodily health, not in external happenings, not in seeing God's work succeed, but in the perfect understanding of God, and in the communion with Him that Jesus Himself had. The first thing that will hinder this joy is the captious irritation of thinking out circumstances. The cares of this world, said Jesus, will choke God's word. Before we know where we are, we are caught up in the shows of things. All that God has done for us is the mere threshold; He wants to get us to the place where we will be His witnesses and proclaim Who Jesus is.

Be rightly related to God, find your joy there, and out of you will flow rivers of living water. Be a centre for Jesus Christ to pour living water through. Stop being self-conscious, stop being a sanctified prig, and live the life hid with Christ. The life that is rightly related to God is as natural as breathing wherever it goes. The lives that have been of most blessing to you are those who were unconscious of it.

SEPTEMBER 1

DESTINY OF HOLINESS

Ye shall be holy; for I am holy. 1 Peter 1:16 (RV)

Continually restate to yourself what the purpose of your life is. The destined end of man is not happiness, nor health, but holiness. Nowadays we have far too many affinities, we are dissipated with them; right, good, noble affinities which will yet have their fulfilment, but in the meantime God has to atrophy them. The one thing that matters is whether a man will accept the God Who will make him holy. At all costs a man must be rightly related to God.

Do I believe I need to be holy? Do I believe God can come into me and make me holy? If by your preaching you convince me that I am unholy, I resent your preaching. The preaching of the gospel awakens an intense resentment because it must reveal that I am unholy; but it also awakens an intense craving. God has one destined end for mankind, viz., holiness. His one aim is the production of saints. God is not an eternal blessing-machine for men; He did not come to save men out of pity: He came to save men because He had created them to be holy. The Atonement means that God can put me back into perfect union with Himself, without a shadow between, through the Death of Jesus Christ.

Never tolerate through sympathy with yourself or with others any practice that is not in keeping with a holy God. Holiness means unsullied walking with the feet, unsullied talking with the tongue, unsullied thinking with the mind—every detail of the life under the scrutiny of God. Holiness is not only what God gives me, but what I manifest that God has given me.

SEPTEMBER 2

THE SACRAMENT OF SACRIFICE

He that believeth on Me, . . . from within him shall flow. . . . John 7:38 (RV mg)

Jesus did not say—"he that believeth in Me shall realise the blessing of the fullness of God," but—"he that believeth in Me, out of him shall escape everything he receives." Our Lord's teaching is always *anti*–self-realisation. His purpose is not the development of a man; His purpose is to make a man exactly like Himself, and the characteristic of the Son of God is self-expenditure. If we believe in Jesus, it is not what we gain, but what He pours through us that counts. It is not that God makes us beautifully rounded grapes, but that He squeezes the sweetness out of us. Spiritually, we cannot measure our life by success, but only by what God pours through us, and we cannot measure that at all.

When Mary of Bethany broke the box of precious ointment and poured it on Jesus' head, it was an act for which no one else saw any occasion; the disciples said it was a waste. But Jesus commended Mary for her extravagant act of devotion, and said that wherever His gospel was preached "this also that she hath done shall be spoken of for a memorial of her." Our Lord is carried beyond Himself with joy when He sees any of us doing what Mary did, not being set on this or that economy, but being abandoned to Him. God spilt the life of His Son that the world might be saved; are we prepared to spill out our lives for Him?

"He that believeth on Me," out of him, "shall flow rivers of living water," that is, hundreds of other lives will be continually refreshed. It is time now to break the life, to cease craving for satisfaction, and to spill the thing out. Our Lord is asking who of us will do it for Him?

THE WATERS OF SATISFACTION SCATTERED

. . . nevertheless he would not drink thereof, but poured it out unto the LORD. 2 Samuel 23:16

What has been like water from the well of Bethlehem to you recently—love, friendship, spiritual blessing? Then at the peril of your soul, you take it to satisfy yourself. If you do, you cannot pour it out before the Lord. You can never sanctify to God that with which you long to satisfy yourself. If you satisfy yourself with a blessing from God, it will corrupt you; you must sacrifice it, pour it out, do with it what common sense says is an absurd waste.

How am I to pour out unto the Lord natural love or spiritual blessing? In one way only—in the determination of my mind. There are certain acts of other people which one could never accept if one did not know God, because it is not within human power to repay them. But immediately I say—"This is too great and worthy for me, it is not meant for a human being at all, I must pour it out unto the Lord"; then these things pour out in rivers of living water all around. Until I do pour these things out before the Lord, they endanger those I love as well as myself because they will turn to lust. We can be lustful in things which are not sordid and vile. Love has to get to its transfiguration point of being poured out unto the Lord.

If you have become bitter and sour, it is because when God gave you a blessing you clutched it for yourself; whereas if you had poured it out unto the Lord, you would have been the sweetest person out of heaven. If you are always taking blessings to yourself and never learn to pour out anything unto the Lord, other people do not get their horizon enlarged through you.

HIS!

Thine they were, and Thou gavest them Me. John 17:6

The missionary is one in whom the Holy Ghost has wrought this realisation—"Ye are not your own." To say "I am not my own," is to have reached a great point in spiritual nobility. The true nature of the life in the actual whirl is the deliberate giving up of myself to another in sovereign preference, and that other is Jesus Christ. The Holy Spirit expounds the nature of Jesus to me in order to make me one with my Lord, not that I might go off as a showroom exhibit. Our Lord never sent any of the disciples out on the ground of what He had done for them. It was not until after the Resurrection, when the disciples had perceived by the power of the Holy Spirit Whom He was, that Jesus said "Go."

"If any man come to Me, and hate not . . . , he cannot be My disciple," not—he cannot be good and upright, but—he cannot be one over whom Jesus writes the word "Mine." Any one of the relationships Our Lord mentions may be a competitive relationship. I may prefer to belong to my mother, or to my wife, or to myself; then says Jesus, you cannot be My disciple. This does not mean I will not be saved, but it does mean that I cannot be "His."

Our Lord makes a disciple His own possession, He becomes responsible for him. "Ye shall be witnesses unto Me." The spirit that comes in is not that of *doing* anything for Jesus, but of being a perfect delight to Him. The secret of the missionary is—I am His, and He is carrying out His enterprises through me.

Be entirely His.

THE MISSIONARY WATCHING

Watch with Me. Matthew 26:40

"Watch with Me"—with no private point of view of your own at all, but watch entirely with Me. In the early stages we do not watch with Jesus, we watch for Him. We do not watch with Him through the revelation of the Bible; in the circumstances of our lives. Our Lord is trying to introduce us to identification with Himself in a particular Gethsemane, and we will not go; we say—"No, Lord, I cannot see the meaning of this, it is bitter." How can we possibly watch with Someone Who is inscrutable? How are we going to understand Jesus sufficiently to watch with Him in His Gethsemane, when we do not know even what His suffering is for? We do not know how to watch with Him; we are only used to the idea of Jesus watching with us.

The disciples loved Jesus Christ to the limit of their natural capacity, but they did not understand what He was after. In the Garden of Gethsemane they slept for their own sorrow, and at the end of three years of the closest intimacy they "all forsook Him, and fled."

"They were all filled with the Holy Ghost"—the same "they," but something wonderful has happened in between, viz., Our Lord's Death and Resurrection and Ascension, and the disciples have been invaded by the Holy Spirit. Our Lord had said—"Ye shall receive power after that the Holy Ghost is come upon you," and this meant that they learned to watch with Him all the rest of their lives.

SEPTEMBER 6

DIFFUSIVENESS OF LIFE

Rivers of living water. John 7:38

A river touches places of which its source knows nothing, and Jesus says if we have received of His fulness, however small the visible measure of our lives, out of us will flow the rivers that will bless to the uttermost parts of the earth. We have nothing to do with the outflow—"This is the work of God, that ye *believe*. . . ." God rarely allows a soul to see how great a blessing he is.

A river is victoriously persistent, it overcomes all barriers. For a while it goes steadily on its course, then it comes to an obstacle and for a while it is balked, but it soon makes a pathway round the obstacle. Or a river will drop out of sight for miles, and presently emerge again broader and grander than ever. You can see God using some lives, but into your life an obstacle has come and you do not seem to be of any use. Keep paying attention to the Source, and God will either take you round the obstacle or remove it. The river of the Spirit of God overcomes all obstacles. Never get your eyes on the obstacle or on the difficulty. The obstacle is a matter of indifference to the river which will flow steadily through you if you remember to keep right at the Source. Never allow anything to come between yourself and Jesus Christ, no emotion, or experience; nothing must keep you from the one great sovereign Source.

Think of the healing and far-flung rivers nursing themselves in our souls! God has been opening up marvellous truths to our minds, and every point He has opened up is an indication of the wider power of the river He will flow through us. If you believe in Jesus, you will find that God has nourished in you mighty torrents of blessing for others.

SEPTEMBER 7

SPRINGS OF BENIGNITY

The water that I shall give him shall be in him a well of water. John 4:14

The picture Our Lord gives is not that of a channel but a fountain. Be being filled, and the sweetness of vital relationship to Jesus will flow out of the saint as lavishly as it is imparted to him. If you find your life is not flowing out as it should, you are to blame; something has obstructed the flow. Keep right at the Source, and—you will be blessed personally? No, out of you will flow rivers of living water, irrepressible life.

We are to be centres through which Jesus can flow as rivers of living water in blessing to everyone. Some of us are like the Dead Sea, always taking in but never giving out, because we are not rightly related to the Lord Jesus. As surely as we receive from Him, He will pour out through us, and in the measure He is not pouring out, there is a defect in our relationship to Him. Is there anything between you and Jesus Christ? Is there anything that hinders your belief in Him? If not, Jesus says, out of you will flow rivers of living water. It is not a blessing passed on, not an experience stated, but a river continually flowing. Keep at the Source, guard well your belief in Jesus Christ and your relationship to Him, and there will be a steady flow for other lives, no dryness and no deadness.

Is it not too extravagant to say that out of an individual believer, rivers are going to flow? "I do not see the rivers," you say. Never look at yourself from the standpoint of—"Who am I?" In the history of God's work you will nearly always find that it has started from the obscure, the unknown, the ignored, but the steadfastly true to Jesus Christ.

SEPTEMBER 8

DO IT YOURSELF

Determinedly Demolish Some Things

Casting down imaginations, and every high thing that exalteth itself against the knowledge of God. 2 Corinthians 10:5

Deliverance from sin is not deliverance from human nature. There are things in human nature, such as prejudices, which the saint has to destroy by neglect; and other things which have to be destroyed by violence, i.e., by the Divine strength imparted by God's Spirit. There are some things over which we are not to fight, but to stand still in and see the salvation of God; but every theory or conception which erects itself as a rampart against the knowledge of God is to be determinedly demolished by drawing on God's power, not by fleshly endeavour or compromise (2 Corinthians 10:4).

It is only when God has altered our disposition and we have entered into the experience of sanctification that the fight begins. The warfare is not against sin; we can never fight against sin: Jesus Christ deals with sin in Redemption. The conflict is along the line of turning our natural life into a spiritual life, and this is never done easily, nor does God intend it to be done easily. It is done only by a series of moral choices. God does not make us holy in the sense of character; He makes us holy in the sense of innocence, and we have to turn that innocence into holy character by a series of moral choices. These choices are continually in antagonism to the entrenchments of our natural life, the things which erect themselves as ramparts against the knowledge of God. We can either go back and make ourselves of no account in the Kingdom of God, or we can determinedly demolish these things and let Jesus bring another son to glory.

SEPTEMBER 9

DO IT YOURSELF

Determinedly Discipline Other Things

Bringing into captivity every thought to the obedience of Christ. 2 Corinthians 10:5

This is another aspect of the strenuous nature of sainthood. Paul says—"I take every project prisoner to make it obey Christ" (MOFFATT). How much Christian work there is to-day which has never been disciplined, but has simply sprung into being by impulse! In Our Lord's life every project was disciplined to the will of His Father. There was not a movement of an impulse of His own will as distinct from His Father's—"The Son can do nothing of Himself." Then take ourselves—a vivid religious experience, and every project born of impulse put into action immediately, instead of being imprisoned and disciplined to obey Christ.

This is a day when practical work is over-emphasised, and the saints who are bringing every project into captivity are criticised and told that they are not in earnest for God or for souls. True earnestness is found in obeying God, not in the inclination to serve Him that is born of undisciplined human nature. It is inconceivable, but true nevertheless, that saints are not bringing every project into captivity, but are doing work for God at the instigation of their own human nature which has not been spiritualised by determined discipline.

We are apt to forget that a man is not only committed to Jesus Christ for salvation; he is committed to Jesus Christ's view of God, of the world, of sin and of the devil, and this will mean that he must recognise the responsibility of being transformed by the renewing of his mind.

SEPTEMBER 10

MISSIONARY MUNITIONS

Worshipping as Occasion Serves

When thou wast under the fig tree, I saw thee. John 1:48

We imagine we would be all right if a big crisis arose; but the big crisis will only reveal the stuff we are made of, it will not put anything into us. "If God gives the call, of course I will rise to the occasion." You will not unless you have risen to the occasion in the workshop, unless you have been the real thing before God there. If you are not doing the thing that lies nearest, because God has engineered it, when the crisis comes instead of being revealed as fit, you will be revealed as unfit. Crises always reveal character.

The private relationship of worshipping God is the great essential of fitness. The time comes when there is no more "fig-tree" life possible, when it is out into the open, out into the glare and into the work, and you will find yourself of no value there if you have not been worshipping as occasion serves you in your home. Worship aright in your private relationships, then when God sets you free you will be ready, because in the unseen life which no one saw but God you have become perfectly fit, and when the strain comes you can be relied upon by God.

"I can't be expected to live the sanctified life in the circumstances I am in; I have no time for praying just now, no time for Bible reading, my opportunity hasn't come yet; when it does, of course I shall be all right." No, you will not. If you have not been worshipping as occasion serves, when you get into work you will not only be useless yourself, but a tremendous hindrance to those who are associated with you.

The workshop of missionary munitions is the hidden, personal, worshipping life of the saint.

SEPTEMBER 11

MISSIONARY MUNITIONS

Ministering as Opportunity Surrounds Us

If I then, your Lord and Master, have washed your feet; ye also ought to wash one another's feet. John 13:14

Ministering as opportunity surrounds us does not mean selecting our surroundings, it means being very selectly God's in any haphazard surroundings which

He engineers for us. The characteristics we manifest in our immediate surroundings are indications of what we will be like in other surroundings.

The things that Jesus did were of the most menial and commonplace order, and this is an indication that it takes all God's power in me to do the most commonplace things in His way. Can I use a towel as He did? Towels and dishes and sandals, all the ordinary sordid things of our lives, reveal more quickly than anything what we are made of. It takes God Almighty Incarnate in us to do the meanest duty as it ought to be done.

"I have given you an example, that ye should do as I have done to you." Watch the kind of people God brings around you, and you will be humiliated to find that this is His way of revealing to you the kind of person you have been to Him. Now, He says, exhibit to that one exactly what I have shown to you.

"Oh," you say, "I will do all that when I get out into the foreign field." To talk in this way is like trying to produce the munitions of war in the trenches—you will be killed while you are doing it.

We have to go the "second mile" with God. Some of us get played out in the first ten yards, because God compels us to go where we cannot see the way, and we say—"I will wait till I get nearer the big crisis." If we do not do the running steadily in the little ways, we shall do nothing in the crisis.

SEPTEMBER 12

BY SPIRITUAL CONFUSION

Ye know not what ye ask. Matthew 20:22

There are times in spiritual life when there is confusion, and it is no way out to say that there ought not to be confusion. It is not a question of right and wrong, but a question of God taking you by a way which in the meantime you do not understand, and it is only by going through the confusion that you will get at what God wants.

The Shrouding of His Friendship (Luke 11:5–8). Jesus gave the illustration of the man who looked as if he did not care for his friend, and He said that that is how the Heavenly Father will appear to you at times. You will think He is an unkind friend, but remember He is not; the time will come when everything will be explained. There is a cloud on the friendship of the heart, and often even love itself has to wait in pain and tears for the blessing of fuller communion. When God looks completely shrouded, will you hang in in confidence in Him?

The Shadow on His Fatherhood (Luke 11:11–13). Jesus says there are times when your Father will appear as if He were an unnatural father, as if He were callous and indifferent, but remember He is not; I have told you—"Every one that asketh receiveth." If there is a shadow on the face of the Father just now, hang into it that He will ultimately give His clear revealing and justify Himself in all that He permitted.

The Strangeness of His Faithfulness (Luke 18:1–8). "When the Son of Man cometh, shall He find faith on the earth?" Will He find the faith which banks on Him in spite of the confusion? Stand off in faith believing that what Jesus said is true, though in the meantime you do not understand what God is doing. He has bigger issues at stake than the particular things you ask.

SEPTEMBER 13

AFTER SURRENDER—WHAT?

I have finished the work which Thou gavest Me to do. John 17:4

Surrender is not the surrender of the external life, but of the will; when that is done, all is done. There are very few crises in life; the great crisis is the surrender of the will. God never crushes a man's will into surrender, He never beseeches him, He waits until the man yields up his will to Him. That battle never needs to be re-fought.

Surrender for Deliverance. "Come unto Me, . . . and I will give you rest." It is after we have begun to experience what salvation means that we surrender our wills to Jesus for rest. Whatever is perplexing heart or mind is a call to the will—"Come unto Me." It is a voluntary coming.

Surrender for Devotion. "If any man will come after Me, let him deny himself." The surrender here is of my self to Jesus, my self with His rest at the heart of it. "If you would be My disciple, give up your right to yourself to Me." Then the remainder of the life is nothing but the manifestation of this surrender. When once the surrender has taken place we never need "suppose" anything. We do not need to care what our circumstances are, Jesus is amply sufficient.

Surrender for Death (John 21:18–19). ". . . another shall gird thee." Have you learned what it means to be bound for death? Beware of a surrender which you make to God in an ecstasy; you are apt to take it back again. It is a question of being united with Jesus in His death until nothing ever appeals to you that did not appeal to Him.

After surrender—what? The whole of life after surrender is an aspiration for unbroken communion with God.

SEPTEMBER 14

IMAGINATION V. INSPIRATION

The simplicity that is in Christ. 2 Corinthians 11:3

Simplicity is the secret of seeing things clearly. A saint does not think clearly for a long while, but a saint ought to *see* clearly without any difficulty. You cannot think a spiritual muddle clear, you have to obey it clear. In intellectual matters you can think things out, but in spiritual matters you will think yourself into cotton wool. If there is something upon which God has put His pressure, obey in that matter, bring your imagination into captivity to the obedience of Christ with regard to it and everything will become as clear as daylight. The reasoning capacity comes afterwards, but we never see along that line, we see like children; when we try to be wise we see nothing (Matthew 11:25).

The tiniest thing we allow in our lives that is not under the control of the Holy Spirit is quite sufficient to account for spiritual muddle, and all the thinking we like to spend on it will never make it clear. Spiritual muddle is only made plain by obedience. Immediately we obey, we discern. This is humiliating, because when we are muddled we know the reason is in the temper of our mind. When the natural power of vision is devoted to the Holy Spirit, it becomes the power of perceiving God's will and the whole life is kept in simplicity.

SEPTEMBER 15

WHAT TO RENOUNCE

But have renounced the hidden things of dishonesty. 2 Corinthians 4:2

Have you "renounced the hidden things of dishonesty"—the things that your sense of honour will not allow to come to the light? You can easily hide them. Is there a thought in your heart about anyone which you would not like to be dragged into the light? Renounce it as soon as it springs up; renounce the whole thing until there is no hidden thing of dishonesty or craftiness about you. Envy, jealousy, strife—these things arise not necessarily from the disposition of sin, but from the make-up of your body which was used for this kind of thing in days gone by (see Romans 6:19 and 1 Peter 4:1–2): Maintain a continual watchfulness so that nothing of which you would be ashamed arises in your life.

"Not walking in craftiness," that is, resorting to what will carry your point. This is a great snare. You know that God will only let you work in one way, then be careful never to catch people the other way; God's blight will be upon you if you do. Others are doing things which to you would be walking in craftiness, but it may not be so with them; God has given you another standpoint. Never blunt the sense of your Utmost for His Highest. For you to do a certain thing would mean the incoming of craftiness for an end other than the highest, and the blunting of the motive God has given you. Many have gone back because they are afraid of looking at things from God's standpoint. The crisis comes spiritually when a man has to emerge a bit farther on than the creed he has accepted.

SEPTEMBER 16

THE DIVINE REGION OF RELIGION

But thou, when thou prayest, enter into thy closet, and when thou hast shut thy door, pray to thy Father which is in secret. Matthew 6:6

The main idea in the region of religion is—Your eyes upon God, not on men. Do not have as your motive the desire to be known as a praying man. Get an inner chamber in which to pray where no one knows you are praying, shut the door and talk to God in secret. Have no other motive than to know your Father in heaven. It is impossible to conduct your life as a disciple without definite times of secret prayer:

"But when ye pray, use not vain repetitions. . . ." (Matthew 6:7). God is never impressed by our earnestness. He does not hear us because we are in earnest, but only on the ground of Redemption. Prayer is not simply getting things from God, that is an initial form of prayer; prayer is getting into perfect communion with God. If the Son of God is formed in us by regeneration, He will press forward in front of our common sense and change our attitude to the things about which we pray.

"Every one that *asketh* receiveth." We pray pious blether, our will is not in it, and then we say God does not answer; we never asked for anything. "Ye shall ask what ye *will*," said Jesus. Asking means our will is in it. Whenever Jesus talked about prayer, He put it with the grand simplicity of a child; we bring in our critical temper and say—"Yes, but. . ." Jesus said—*"Ask."* But remember that we have to ask of God things that are in keeping with the God Whom Jesus Christ revealed.

SEPTEMBER 17

WHAT'S THE GOOD OF TEMPTATION?

There hath no temptation taken you but such as is common to man. 1 Corinthians 10:13

The word "temptation" has come down in the world; we are apt to us it wrongly: Temptation is not sin, it is the thing we are bound to meet if we are men. Not to be tempted would be to be beneath contempt. Many of us, however, suffer from temptations from which we have no business to suffer, simply because we have refused to let God lift us to a higher plane where we would face temptations of another order.

A man's disposition on the inside, i.e., what he possesses in his personality, determines what he is tempted by on the outside. The temptation fits the nature of the one tempted, and reveals the possibilities of the nature. Every man has the setting of his own temptation, and the temptation will come along the line of the ruling disposition.

Temptation is a suggested short cut to the realisation of the highest at which I aim—not towards what I understand as evil, but towards what I understand as good. Temptation is something that completely baffles me for a while, I do not know whether the thing is right or wrong. Temptation yielded to is lust deified, and is a proof that it was timidity that prevented the sin before.

Temptation is not something we may escape, it is essential to the full-orbed life of a man. Beware lest you think you are tempted as no one else is tempted; what you go through is the common inheritance of the race, not something no one ever went through before. God does not save us from temptations; He succours us in the midst of them (Hebrews 2:18).

SEPTEMBER 18

HIS TEMPTATION AND OURS

For we have not an high priest which cannot be touched with the feeling of our infirmities; but was in all points tempted like as we are, yet without sin. Hebrews 4:15

Until we are born again, the only kind of temptation we understand is that mentioned by St. James—"Every man is tempted, when he is drawn away of his own lust, and enticed." But by regeneration we are lifted into another realm where there are other temptations to face, viz., the kind of temptations Our Lord faced. The temptations of Jesus do not appeal to us, they have no home at all in our human nature. Our Lord's tempta-

tions and ours move in different spheres until we are born again and become His brethren. The temptations of Jesus are not those of a man, but the temptations of God as Man. By regeneration the Son of God is formed in us, and in our physical life He has the same setting that He had on earth. Satan does not tempt us to do wrong things; he tempts us in order to make us lose what God has put into us by regeneration, viz., the possibility of being of value to God. He does not come on the line of tempting us to sin, but on the line of shifting the point of view, and only the Spirit of God can detect this as a temptation of the devil.

Temptation means the test by an alien power of the possessions held by a personality. This makes the temptation of Our Lord explainable. After Jesus in His baptism had accepted the vocation of bearing away the sin of the world (RV mg), He was immediately put by God's Spirit into the testing machine of the devil; but He did not tire. He went through the temptation "without sin," and retained the possessions of His personality intact.

SEPTEMBER 19

DO YOU CONTINUE TO GO WITH JESUS?

Ye are they which have continued with Me in My temptations. Luke 22:28

It is true that Jesus Christ is with us in our temptations, but are we going with Him in His temptations? Many of us cease to go with Jesus from the moment we have an experience of what He can do. Watch when God shifts your circumstances, and see whether you are going with Jesus, or siding with the world, the flesh and the devil. We wear His badge, but are we going with Him? "From that time many of His disciples went back, and walked no more with Him." The temptations of Jesus continued throughout His earthly life, and they will continue throughout the life of the Son of God in us. Are we going with Jesus in the life we are living now?

We have the idea that we ought to shield ourselves from some of the things God brings round us. Never! God engineers circumstances, and whatever they may be like we have to see that we face them while abiding continually with Him in His temptations. They are *His* temptations, not temptations to us, but temptations to the life of the Son of God in us. The honour of Jesus Christ is at stake in your bodily life. Are you remaining loyal to the Son of God in the things which beset His life in you?

Do you continue to go with Jesus? The way lies through Gethsemane, through the city gate, outside the camp; the way lies alone, and the way lies until there is no trace of a footstep left, only the voice, *"Follow Me."*

SEPTEMBER 20

THE DIVINE RULE OF LIFE

Be ye therefore perfect, even as your Father which is in heaven is perfect. Matthew 5:48

Our Lord's exhortation in these verses is to be generous in our behaviour to all men. In the spiritual life beware of walking according to natural affinities. Everyone has natural affinities; some people we like and others we do not like. We must never let those likes and dislikes rule in our Christian life. If we "walk in the light," as God is in the light, God will give us communion with people for whom we have no natural affinity.

The Example Our Lord gives us is not that of a good man, or even of a good Christian, but of God Himself. "Be ye therefore perfect, even as your Father in heaven is perfect"—show to the other man what God has shown to you; and God will give us ample opportunities in actual life to prove whether we are perfect as our Father in heaven is perfect. To be a disciple means that we deliberately identify ourselves with God's interests in other people. "That ye love one another; as I have loved you. . . ."

The expression of Christian character is not good doing, but Godlikeness: If the Spirit of God has transformed you within, you will exhibit Divine characteristics in your life, not good human characteristics. God's life in us express itself as *God's* life, not as human life trying to be godly. The secret of a Christian is that the supernatural is made natural in him by the grace of God, and the experience of this works out in the practical details of life, not in times of communion with God. When we come in contact with things that create a buzz, we find to our amazement that we have power to keep wonderfully poised in the centre of it all.

SEPTEMBER 21

MISSIONARY PREDESTINATIONS

And now, saith the LORD that formed me from the womb to be His servant. Isaiah 49:5

The first thing that happens after we have realised our election to God in Christ Jesus is the destruction of our prejudices and our parochial notions and our patriotisms; we are turned into servants of God's own purpose. The whole human race was created to glorify God and enjoy Him for ever. Sin has switched the human race on to another tack, but it has not altered God's purpose in the tiniest degree; and when we are born again we are brought into the realisation of God's great purpose for the human race, viz., I am created for God, He made me. This realisation of the election of God is the most joyful realisation on earth, and we have to learn to rely on the tremendous creative purpose of God. The first thing God will do with us is to "force thro' the channels of a single heart" the interests of the whole world. The love of God, the very nature of God, is introduced into us, and the nature of Almighty God is focused in John 3:16—*"God so loved the world. . . ."*

We have to maintain our soul open to the fact of God's creative purpose, and not muddle it with our own intentions. If we do, God will have to crush our intentions on one side however much it may hurt. The purpose for which the missionary is created is that he may be God's servant, one in whom God is glorified. When once we realise that through the salvation of Jesus Christ we are made perfectly fit for God, we shall understand why Jesus Christ is so ruthless in His demands. He demands absolute rectitude from His servants, because He has put into them the very nature of God.

Beware lest you forget God's purpose for your life.

SEPTEMBER 22

THE MISSIONARY'S MASTER

Ye call Me Master and Lord: and ye say well; for so I am. John 13:13

To have a master and to be mastered is not the same thing. To have a master means that there is one who knows me better than I know myself, one who is closer than a friend, one who fathoms the remotest abyss of my heart and satisfies it, one who has brought me into the secure sense that he has met and solved every perplexity and problem of my mind. To have a master is this and nothing less—"One is your Master, even Christ."

Our Lord never enforces obedience; He does not take means to make me do what He wants. At certain times I wish God would master me and make me do the thing, but He will not; in other moods I wish He would leave me alone, but He does not.

"Ye call me Master and Lord"—but *is* He? Master and Lord have little place in our vocabulary, we prefer the words Saviour, Sanctifier Healer. The only word to describe mastership in experience is love, and we know very little about love as God reveals it. This is proved by the way we use the word obey. In the Bible obedience is based on the relationship of equals, that of a son with his father. Our Lord was not God's servant, He was His son. *"Though He were a Son,* yet learned He obedience. . . ."* If our idea is that we are being mastered, it is a proof that we have no master; if that is our attitude to Jesus, we are far away from the relationship He wants. He wants us in the relationship in which He is easily Master without our conscious knowledge of it, all we know is that we are His to obey.

SEPTEMBER 23

THE MISSIONARY'S GOAL

Behold, we go up to Jerusalem. Luke 18:31

In the natural life our ambitions alter as we develop; in the Christian life the goal is given at the beginning, the beginning and the end are the same, viz., Our Lord Himself. We start with Christ and we end with Him—until we all attain (RV) to the stature of the manhood of Christ Jesus, not to our idea of what the Christian life should be. The aim of the missionary is to do God's will, not to be useful, not to win the heathen; he *is* useful and he *does* win the heathen, but that is not his aim. His aim is to do the will of his Lord.

In Our Lord's life Jerusalem was the place where He reached the climax of His Father's will upon the Cross, and unless we go with Jesus there, we shall have no companionship with Him. Nothing ever discouraged Our Lord on His way to Jerusalem. He never hurried through certain villages where He was persecuted, or lingered in others where He was blessed. Neither gratitude nor ingratitude turned Our Lord one hair's breadth away from His purpose to go up to Jerusalem.

"The disciple is not above his Master." The same things will happen to us on our way to our Jerusalem. There will be the works of God manifested through us, people will get blessed, and one or two will show gratitude and the rest will show gross ingratitude, but nothing must deflect us from going up to our Jerusalem.

"There they crucified Him." That is what happened when Our Lord reached Jerusalem, and that happening is the gateway to our salvation. The saints do not end in crucifixion: by the Lord's grace they end in glory. In the meantime our watchword is—I, too, go up to Jerusalem.

SEPTEMBER 24

THE "GO" OF PREPARATION

Therefore if thou bring thy gift to the altar, and there thou rememberest that thy brother hath ought against thee; leave there thy gift before the altar, and go thy way; first be reconciled to thy brother, and then come and offer thy gift. Matthew 5:23–24

It is easy to imagine that we shall get to a place where we are complete and ready, but preparation is not suddenly accomplished, it is a process steadily maintained. It is dangerous to get into a settled state of experience. It is preparation *and* preparation.

The sense of sacrifice appeals readily to a young Christian. Humanly speaking, the one thing that attracts to Jesus Christ is our sense of the heroic, and the scrutiny of Our Lord's words suddenly brings this tide of enthusiasm to the test. "First be reconciled to thy brother." The "go" of preparation is to let the word of God scrutinise. The sense of heroic sacrifice is not good enough. The thing the Holy Spirit is detecting in you is the disposition that will never work in His service. No one but God can detect that disposition in you. Have you anything to hide from God? If you have, then let God search you with His light. If there is sin, *confess* it, not *admit* it. Are you willing to obey your Lord and Master, whatever the humiliation to your right to yourself may be?

Never discard a conviction. If it is important enough for the Spirit of God to have brought it to your mind, it is that thing He is detecting. You were looking for a great thing to give up. God is telling you of some tiny thing; but at the back of it there lies the central citadel of obstinacy: "I will not give up my right to myself"—the thing God intends you to give up if ever you are going to be a disciple of Jesus Christ.

SEPTEMBER 25

THE "GO" OF RELATIONSHIP

And whosoever shall compel thee to go a mile, go with him twain. Matthew 5:41

The summing up of Our Lord's teaching is that the relationship which He demands is an impossible one unless He has done a supernatural work in us. Jesus Christ demands that there be not the slightest trace of resentment even suppressed in the head of a disciple when he meets with tyranny and injustice. No enthusiasm will ever stand the strain that Jesus Christ will put upon His worker, only one thing will, and that is a personal relationship to Himself which has gone through the mill of His spring-cleaning until there is only one purpose left—"I am here for God to send me where He will." Every other thing may get fogged, but this relationship to Jesus Christ must never be.

The Sermon on the Mount is not an ideal, it is a statement of what will happen in me when Jesus Christ has altered my disposition and put in a disposition like His own. Jesus Christ is the only One Who can fulfil the Sermon on the Mount.

If we are to be disciples of Jesus, we must be made disciples supernaturally; as long as we have the dead-set purpose of being disciples we may be sure we are not. *"I have chosen you."* That is the way the grace of God begins. It is a constraint we cannot get away from; we can disobey it, but we cannot generate it. The drawing is done by the supernatural grace of God, and we never can trace where His work begins. Our Lord's making of a disciple is supernatural. He does not build on any natural capacity at all. God does not ask us to do the things that are easy to us naturally; He only asks us to do the things we are perfectly fitted to do by His grace, and the cross will come along that line always.

SEPTEMBER 26

THE UNBLAMEABLE ATTITUDE

If thou . . . rememberest that thy brother hath ought against thee . . . Matthew 5:23

If when you come to the altar, there you remember that your brother has anything against you, not—If you rake up something by a morbid sensitiveness, but—"If thou . . . rememberest," that is, it is brought to your conscious mind by the Spirit of God: "first be reconciled to thy brother, and then come and offer thy gift." Never object to the intense sensitiveness of the Spirit of God in you when He is educating you down to the scruple.

"First be reconciled to thy brother. . . ." Our Lord's direction is simple—"first be reconciled." Go back the way you came, go the way indicated to you by the conviction given at the altar; have an attitude of mind and a temper of soul to the one who has something against you that makes reconciliation as natural as breathing. Jesus does not mention the other person, He says—*you* go. There is no question of your rights.

The stamp of the saint is that he can waive his own rights and obey the Lord Jesus.

"And then come and offer thy gift." The process is clearly marked. First, the heroic spirit of self-sacrifice, then the sudden checking by the sensitiveness of the Holy Spirit, and the stoppage at the point of conviction; then the way of obedience to the word of God, constructing an unblameable attitude of mind and temper to the one with whom you have been in the wrong; then the glad, simple, unhindered offering of your gift to God.

SEPTEMBER 27

THE "GO" OF RENUNCIATION

Lord, I will follow Thee whithersoever Thou goest. Luke 9:57

Our Lord's attitude to this man is one of severe discouragement because He knew what was in man. We would have said—"Fancy losing the opportunity of winning that man!" "Fancy bringing about a north wind that froze him and turned him away discouraged!" Never apologise for your Lord. The words of the Lord hurt and offend until there is nothing left to hurt or offend. Jesus Christ has no tenderness whatever toward anything that is ultimately going to ruin a man in the service of God. Our Lord's answers are based not on caprice, but on a knowledge of what is in man. If the Spirit of God brings to your mind a word of the Lord that hurts you, you may be sure that there is something He wants to hurt to death.

Verse 58. These words knock the heart out of serving Jesus Christ because it is pleasing to me. The rigour of rejection leaves nothing but my Lord, and myself, and a forlorn hope. "Let the hundredfold come or go, your lodestar must be your relationship to Me, and I have nowhere to lay My head."

Verse 59. This man did not want to disappoint Jesus, nor to hurt his father. We put sensitive loyalty to relatives in place of loyalty to Jesus Christ and Jesus has to take the last place. In a conflict of loyalty, obey Jesus Christ at all costs.

Verse 61. The one who says—"Yes, Lord, but . . ." is the one who is fiercely ready, but never goes. This man had one or two reservations. The exacting call of Jesus Christ has no margin of good-byes, because good-bye, as it is often used, is pagan, not Christian. When once the call of God comes, begin to go and never stop going.

SEPTEMBER 28

THE "GO" OF UNCONDITIONAL IDENTIFICATION

One thing thou lackest: . . . come, take up the cross, and follow Me. Mark 10:21

The rich young ruler had the master passion to be perfect. When he saw Jesus Christ, he wanted to be like Him. Our Lord never puts personal holiness to the fore when He calls a disciple; He puts absolute annihilation of my right to myself and identification with Himself—a relationship with Himself in which there is no other relationship. Luke 14:26 has nothing to do with salvation or sanctification, but with unconditional identification with Jesus Christ. Very few of us know the absolute "go" of abandonment to Jesus.

"Then Jesus beholding him loved him." The look of Jesus will mean a heart broken for ever from allegiance to any other person or thing. Has Jesus ever looked at you? The look of Jesus transforms and transfixes. Where you are "soft" with God is where the Lord has looked at you. If you are hard and vindictive, insistent on your own way, certain that the other person is more likely to be in the wrong than you are, it is an indication that there are whole tracts of your nature that have never been transformed by His gaze.

"One thing thou lackest. . . ." The only "good thing" from Jesus Christ's point of view is union with Himself and nothing in between.

"Sell whatsoever thou hast. . . ." I must reduce myself until I am a mere conscious man, I must fundamentally renounce possessions of all kinds, not to save my soul, (only one thing saves a man—absolute reliance upon Jesus Christ) but in order to follow Jesus. "Come, and follow Me." And the road is the way He went.

SEPTEMBER 29

THE CONSCIOUSNESS OF THE CALL

For necessity is laid upon me; yea, woe is unto me, if I preach not the gospel! 1 Corinthians 9:16

We are apt to forget the mystical, supernatural touch of God. If you can tell where you got the call of God and all about it, I question whether you have ever had a call. The call of God does not come like that, it is much more supernatural. The realisation of it in a man's life may come with a sudden thunder-clap or with a gradual dawning, but in whatever way it comes, it comes with the undercurrent of the supernatural, something that cannot be put into words, it is always accompanied with a glow. At any moment there may break the sudden consciousness of this incalculable, supernatural, surprising call that has taken hold of your life—"I have chosen you." The call of God has nothing to do with salvation and sanctification. It is not because you are sanctified that you are therefore called to preach the gospel; the call to preach the gospel is infinitely different. Paul describes it as a necessity laid upon him.

If you have been obliterating the great supernatural call of God in your life, take a review of your circumstances and see where God has not been first, but your ideas of service, or your temperamental abilities. Paul said—"Woe is unto me, if I preach not the gospel!" He had realised the call of God, and there was no competitor for his strength.

If a man or woman is called of God, it does not matter how untoward circumstances are, every force that has been at work will tell for God's purpose in the end. If you agree with God's purpose He will bring not only your conscious life, but all the deeper regions of your life which you cannot get at, into harmony.

SEPTEMBER 30

THE COMMISSION OF THE CALL

Who now rejoice in my sufferings for you, and fill up that which is behind of the afflictions of Christ in my flesh for His body's sake. Colossians 1:24

We make calls out of our own spiritual consecration, but when we get right with God He brushes all these aside, and rivets us with a pain that is terrific to one thing we never dreamed of, and for one radiant, flashing moment we see what He is after, and we say—"Here am I, send me."

This call has nothing to do with personal sanctification, but with being made broken bread and poured-out wine. God can never make us wine if we object to the fingers He uses to crush us with. If God would only use His own fingers, and make me broken bread and poured-out wine in a special way! But when He uses someone whom we dislike, or some set of circumstances to which we said we would never submit, and makes those the crushers, we object. We must never choose the scene of our own martyrdom. If ever we are going to be made into wine, we will have to be crushed; you cannot drink grapes. Grapes become wine only when they have been squeezed.

I wonder what kind of finger and thumb God has been using to squeeze you, and you have been like a marble and escaped? You are not ripe yet, and if God *had* squeezed you, the wine would have been remarkably bitter. To be a sacramental personality means that the elements of the natural life are presenced by God as they are broken providentially in His service. We have to be adjusted to God before we can be broken bread in His hands. Keep right with God and let Him do what He likes, and you will find that He is producing the kind of bread and wine that will benefit His other children.

OCTOBER 1

THE SPHERE OF EXALTATION

Jesus . . . leadeth them up into a high mountain apart by themselves. Mark 9:2

We have all had times on the mount, when we have seen things from God's standpoint and have wanted to stay there; but God will never allow us to stay there. The test of our spiritual life is the power to descend; if we have power to rise only, something is wrong. It is a great thing to be on the mount with God, but a man only gets there in order that afterwards he may get down among the devil-possessed and lift them up. We are not built for the mountains and the dawns and aesthetic affinities, those are for moments of inspiration, that is all. We are built for the valley, for the ordinary stuff we are in, and that is where we have to prove our mettle. Spiritual selfishness always wants repeated moments on the mount. We feel we could talk like angels and live like angels, if only we could stay on the mount. The times of exaltation are exceptional, they have their meaning in our life with God, but we must beware lest our spiritual selfishness wants to make them the only time.

We are apt to think that everything that happens is to be turned into useful teaching, it is to be turned into something better than teaching, viz., into character. The mount is not meant to *teach* us anything, it is meant to *make* us something. There is a great snare in asking—"What is the use of it?" In spiritual matters we can never calculate on that line. The moments on the mountain top are rare moments, and they are meant for something in God's purpose.

OCTOBER 2

THE SPHERE OF HUMILIATION

If Thou canst do any thing, have compassion on us, and help us. Mark 9:22

After every time of exaltation we are brought down with a sudden rush into things as they are, where it is neither beautiful nor poetic nor thrilling. The height of the mountain top is measured by the drab drudgery of the valley; but it is in the valley that we have to live for the glory of God. We *see* His glory on the mount, but we never *live* for His glory there. It is in the sphere of humiliation that we find our true worth to God, that is where our faithfulness is revealed. Most of us can do things if we are always at the heroic pitch because of the natural selfishness of our hearts, but God wants us at the drab commonplace pitch, where we live in the valley according to our personal relationship to Him. Peter thought it would be a fine thing for them to remain on the mount, but Jesus Christ took the disciples down from the mount into the valley—the place where the meaning of the vision is explained.

"If Thou canst do any thing . . ." It takes the valley of humiliation to root the scepticism out of us. Look back at your own experience, and you will find that until you learned Who Jesus was, you were a cunning sceptic about His power. When you were on the mount, you could believe anything, but what about the time when you were up against facts in the valley? You may be able to give a testimony to sanctification, but what about the thing that is a humiliation to you just now? The last time you were on the mount with God, you saw that all power in heaven and in earth belonged to Jesus—will you be sceptical now in the valley of humiliation?

OCTOBER 3

THE SPHERE OF MINISTRATION

This kind can come forth by nothing, but by prayer and fasting. Mark 9:29

"Why could not we cast him out?" The answer lies in a personal relationship to Jesus Christ. This kind can come forth by nothing but by concentration and redoubled concentration on Him. We can ever remain powerless, as were the disciples, by trying to do God's work not in concentration on His power, but by ideas drawn from our own temperament. We slander God by our very eagerness to work for Him without knowing Him.

You are brought face to face with a difficult case and nothing happens externally, and yet you know that emancipation will be given because *you* are concentrated on Jesus Christ. This is your line of service—to see that there is nothing between Jesus and yourself. Is there? If there is, you must get through it, not by ignoring it in irritation, or by mounting up, but by facing it and getting through it into the presence of Jesus Christ. Then that very thing, and all you have been through in connection with it, will glorify Jesus Christ in a way you will never know till you see Him face to face.

We must be able to mount up with wings as eagles; but we must also know how to come down. The power of the saint lies in the coming down and the living down. "I can do all things through Christ which strengtheneth me," said Paul, and the things he referred to were mostly humiliating things. It is in our power to refuse to be humiliated and to say—"No, thank you, I much prefer to be on the mountain top with God." Can I face things as they actually are in the light of the reality of Jesus Christ, or do things as they are efface altogether my faith in Him, and put me into a panic?

OCTOBER 4

THE VISION AND THE VERITY

Called to be saints. 1 Corinthians 1:2

Thank God for the sight of all you have never yet been. You have had the vision, but you are not there yet by any means. It is when we are in the valley, where we prove whether we will be the choice ones, that most of us turn back. We are not quite prepared for the blows which must come if we are going to be turned into the shape of the vision. We have seen what we are not, and what God wants us to be, but are we willing to have the vision "batter'd to shape and use" by God? The batterings always come in commonplace ways and through commonplace people.

There are times when we do know what God's purpose is; whether we will let the vision be turned into actual character depends upon us, not upon God. If we prefer to loll on the mount and live in the memory of the vision, we will be of no use actually in the ordinary stuff of which human life is made up. We have to learn to live in reliance on what we saw in the vision, not in ecstasies and conscious contemplation of God, but to live in actualities in the light of the vision until we get to the veritable reality. Every bit of our training is in that direction. Learn to thank God for making known His demands.

The little "I am" always sulks when God says *do*. Let the little "I am" be shrivelled up in God's indignation—"I AM THAT I AM . . . hath sent me." He must dominate. Is it not penetrating to realise that God knows where we live, and the kennels we crawl into! He will hunt us up like a lightning flash. No human being knows human beings as God does.

OCTOBER 5

THE BIAS OF DEGENERATION

Wherefore, as by one man sin entered into the world, and death by sin; and so death passed upon all men, for that all have sinned. Romans 5:12

The Bible does not say that God punished the human race for one man's sin; but that the disposition of sin, viz., my claim to my right to myself, entered into the human race by one man, and that another Man took on Him the sin of the human race and put it away (Hebrews 9:26)—an infinitely profounder revelation. The disposition of sin is not immorality and wrong-doing, but the disposition of self-realisation—I am my own god. This disposition may work out in decorous morality or in indecorous immorality, but it has the one basis, my claim to my right to myself. When Our Lord faced men with all the forces of evil in them, and men who were clean living and moral and upright, He did not pay any attention to the moral degradation of the one or to the moral attainment of the other; He looked at something we do not see, viz., the disposition.

Sin is a thing I am born with and I cannot touch it; God touches sin in Redemption. In the Cross of Jesus Christ God redeemed the whole human race from the possibility of damnation through the heredity of sin. God nowhere holds a man responsible for having the heredity of sin. The condemnation is not that I am born with a heredity of sin, but if when I realise Jesus Christ came to deliver me from it, I refuse to let Him do so, from that moment I begin to get the seal of damnation. "And this is the judgement" (the critical moment) "that the light is come into the world, and men loved the darkness rather than the light."

OCTOBER 6

THE BENT OF REGENERATION

When it pleased God . . . to reveal His son in me. Galatians 1:15–16

If Jesus Christ is to regenerate me, what is the problem He is up against? I have a heredity I had no say in; I am not holy, nor likely to be; and if all Jesus Christ can do is to tell me I must be holy, His teaching plants despair. But if Jesus Christ is a Regenerator, One Who can put into me His own heredity of holiness, then I begin to see what He is driving at when He says that I have to be holy. Redemption means that Jesus Christ can put into any man the hereditary disposition that was in Himself, and all the standards He gives are based on that disposition: *His teaching is for the life He puts in.* The moral transaction on my part is agreement with God's verdict on sin in the Cross of Jesus Christ.

The New Testament teaching about regeneration is that when a man is struck by a sense of need, God will put the Holy Spirit into his spirit, and his personal spirit will be energised by the Spirit of the Son of God—"until Christ be formed in you." The moral miracle of Redemption is that God can put into me a new disposition whereby I can live a totally new life. When I reach the frontier of need and know my limitations, Jesus says—"Blessed are you." But I have to get there. God cannot put into me, a responsible moral being, the disposition that was in Jesus Christ unless I am conscious I need it.

Just as the disposition of sin entered into the human race by one man, so the Holy Spirit entered the human race by another Man; and Redemption means that I can be delivered from the heredity of sin and through Jesus Christ can receive an unsullied heredity, viz., the Holy Spirit.

OCTOBER 7

RECONCILIATION

For He hath made Him to be sin for us, who knew no sin; that we might be made the righteousness of God in Him. 2 Corinthians 5:21

Sin is a fundamental relationship; it is not wrong doing, it is wrong *being*, deliberate and emphatic independence of God. The Christian religion bases everything on the positive,[22] radical nature of sin. Other religions deal with sins; the Bible alone deals with sin. The first thing Jesus Christ faced in men was the heredity of sin, and it is because we have ignored this in our presentation of the Gospel that the message of the Gospel has lost its sting and its blasting power.

The revelation of the Bible is not that Jesus Christ took upon Himself our fleshly sins, but that He took upon Himself the heredity of sin which no man can touch. God made His own Son to be sin that He might make the sinner a saint. All through the Bible it is revealed that Our Lord bore the sin of the world by *identification*, not by *sympathy*. He deliberately took upon His own shoulders, and bore in His own Person, the whole massed sin of the human race—

"He hath *made Him to be sin for us,* who knew no sin," and by so doing He put the whole human race on the basis of Redemption. Jesus Christ rehabilitated the human race; He put it back to where God designed it to be, and anyone can enter into union with God on the ground of what Our Lord has done on the Cross.

A man cannot redeem himself; Redemption is God's "bit," it is absolutely finished and complete; its reference to individual men is a question of their individual action. A distinction must always be made between the revelation of Redemption and the conscious experience of salvation in a man's life.

OCTOBER 8

THE EXCLUSIVENESS OF CHRIST

Come unto Me. Matthew 11:28

Is it not humiliating to be told that we must come to Jesus! Think of the things we will not come to Jesus Christ about. If you want to know how real you are, test yourself by these words—"Come unto Me." In every degree in which you are not real, you will dispute rather than come, you will quibble rather than come, you will go through sorrow rather than come; you will do anything rather than come the last lap of unutterable foolishness—"Just as I am." As long as you have the tiniest bit of spiritual impertinence, it will always reveal itself in the fact that you are expecting God to tell you to do a big thing, and all He is telling you to do is to "come."

"Come unto Me." When you hear those words you will know that something must happen in you before you can come. The Holy Spirit will show you what you have to do, anything at all that will put the axe at the root of the thing which is preventing you from getting through. You will never get further until you are willing to do that one thing. The Holy Spirit will locate the one impregnable thing in you, but He cannot budge it unless you are willing to let Him.

How often have you come to God with your requests and gone away with the feeling—"Oh well, I have done it this time!" And yet you go away with nothing, whilst all the time God has stood with outstretched hands not only to take you, but for you to take Him. Think of the invincible, unconquerable, unwearying patience of Jesus—"*Come unto Me.*"

---

22. positive: independent; unrelated to anything else.

OCTOBER 9

PULL YOURSELF TOGETHER

Yield your members servants to righteousness unto holiness. Romans 6:19

I cannot save and sanctify myself; I cannot atone for sin; I cannot redeem the world; I cannot make right what is wrong, pure what is impure, holy what is unholy. That is all the sovereign work of God. Have I faith in what Jesus Christ has done? He has made a perfect Atonement, am I in the habit of constantly realising it? The great need is not to *do* things, but to *believe* things. The Redemption of Christ is not an experience, it is the great act of God which He has performed through Christ, and I have to build my faith upon it. If I construct my faith on my experience, I produce that most unscriptural type, an isolated life, my eyes fixed on my own whiteness. Beware of the piety that has no presupposition in the Atonement of the Lord. It is of no use for anything but a sequestered life; it is useless to God and a nuisance to man. Measure every type of experience by our Lord Himself. We cannot do anything pleasing to God unless we deliberately build on the presupposition of the Atonement.

The Atonement of Jesus has to work out in practical, unobtrusive ways in my life. Every time I obey, absolute Deity is on my side, so that the grace of God and natural obedience coincide. Obedience means that I have banked everything on the Atonement, and my obedience is met immediately by the delight of the supernatural grace of God.

Beware of the piety that denies the natural life, it is a fraud. Continually bring yourself to the bar of the Atonement—where is the discernment of the Atonement in this thing, and in that?

OCTOBER 10

WHEREBY SHALL I KNOW?

I thank Thee, O Father, . . . because Thou hast hid these things from the wise and prudent, and hast revealed them unto babes. Matthew 11:25

In spiritual relationships we do not grow step by step, we are either there or we are not. God does not cleanse us more and more from sin, but when we are in the light, walking in the light, we *are* cleansed from all sin. It is a question of obedience, and instantly the relationship is perfected. Turn away for one second out of obedience, and darkness and death are at work at once.

All God's revelations are sealed until they are opened to us by obedience. You will never get them open by philosophy or thinking. Immediately you

obey, a flash of light comes. Let God's truth work in you by soaking in it, not by worrying into it. The only way you can get to know is to stop trying to find out and by being born again. Obey God in the thing He shows you, and instantly the next thing is opened up. We read tomes on the work of the Holy Spirit, when one five minutes of drastic obedience would make things as clear as a sunbeam. "I suppose I shall understand these things some day!" You can understand them now. It is not study that does it, but obedience. The tiniest fragment of obedience, and heaven opens and the profoundest truths of God are yours straight away. God will never reveal more truth about Himself until you have obeyed what you know already. Beware of becoming "wise and prudent."

OCTOBER 11

AFTER GOD'S SILENCE— WHAT?

When He had heard therefore that he was sick, He abode two days still in the same place where He was. John 11:6

Has God trusted you with a silence—a silence that is big with meaning? God's silences are His answers. Think of those days of absolute silence in the home at Bethany! Is there anything analogous to those days in your life? Can God trust you like that, or are you still asking for a visible answer? God will give you the blessings you ask if you will not go any further without them; but His silence is the sign that He is bringing you into a marvellous understanding of Himself. Are you mourning before God because you have not had an audible response? You will find that God has trusted you in the most intimate way possible, with an absolute silence, not of despair, but of pleasure, because He saw that you could stand a bigger revelation. If God has given you a silence, praise Him, He is bringing you into the great run of His purposes. The manifestation of the answer in time is a matter of God's sovereignty. Time is nothing to God. For a while you say—"I asked God to give me bread, and He gave me a stone." He did not, and to-day you find He gave you the bread of life.

A wonderful thing about God's silence is that the contagion of His stillness gets into you and you become perfectly confident—"I know God has heard me." His silence is the proof that He has. As long as you have the idea that God will bless you in answer to prayer, He will do it, but He will never give you the grace of silence. If Jesus Christ is bringing you into the understanding that prayer is for the glorifying of His Father, He will give you the first sign of His intimacy—silence.

GETTING INTO GOD'S STRIDE

Enoch walked with God. Genesis 5:24

The test of a man's religious life and character is not what he does in the exceptional moments of life, but what he does in the ordinary times, when there is nothing tremendous or exciting on. The worth of a man is revealed in his attitude to ordinary things when he is not before the footlights. (Cf. John 1:36.) It is a painful business to get through into the stride of God, it means getting your "second wind" spiritually. In learning to walk with God there is always the difficulty of getting into His stride; but when we have got into it, the only characteristic that manifests itself is the life of God. The individual man is lost sight of in his personal union with God, and the stride and the power of God alone are manifested.

It is difficult to get into stride with God, because when we start walking with Him we find He has outstripped us before we have taken three steps. He has different ways of doing things, and we have to be trained and disciplined into His ways. It was said of Jesus, "He shall not fail nor be discouraged," because He never worked from His own individual standpoint but always from the standpoint of His Father, and we have to learn to do the same. Spiritual truth is learned by atmosphere, not by intellectual reasoning. God's Spirit alters the atmosphere of our way of looking at things, and things begin to be possible which never were possible before. Getting into the stride of God means nothing less than union with Himself. It takes a long time to get there, but keep at it. Don't give in because the pain is bad just now, get on with it, and before long you will find you have a new vision and a new purpose.

INDIVIDUAL DISCOURAGEMENT AND PERSONAL ENLARGEMENT

Moses . . . went out unto his brethren, and looked on their burdens. Exodus 2:11

Moses saw the oppression of his people and felt certain that he was the one to deliver them, and in the righteous indignation of his own spirit he started to right their wrongs. After the first strike for God and for the right, God allowed Moses to be driven into blank discouragement, He sent him into the desert to

feed sheep for forty years. At the end of that time, God appeared and told Moses to go and bring forth His people, and Moses said—"Who am I, that I should go?" In the beginning Moses realised that he was the man to deliver the people, but he had to be trained and disciplined by God first. He was right in the individual aspect, but he was not the man for the work until he had learned communion with God.

We may have the vision of God and a very clear understanding of what God wants, and we start to do the thing; then comes something equivalent to the forty years in the wilderness, as if God had ignored the whole thing, and when we are thoroughly discouraged God comes back and revives the call, and we get the quaver in and say—"Oh, who am I!" We have to learn the first great stride of God—"I AM THAT I AM . . . hath sent me." We have to learn that our individual effort for God is an impertinence; our individuality is to be rendered incandescent by a personal relationship to God (see Matthew 3:11). We fix on the individual aspect of things; we have the vision—"This is what God wants me to do"; but we have not got into God's stride. If you are going through a time of discouragement, there is a big personal enlargement ahead.

THE KEY TO THE MISSIONARY

All power is given unto Me in heaven and in earth. Go ye therefore, and teach all nations. Matthew 28:18–19

The basis of missionary appeals is the authority of Jesus Christ, not the needs of the heathen. We are apt to look upon Our Lord as One Who assists us in our enterprises for God. Our Lord puts himself as the absolute sovereign supreme Lord over His disciples. He does not say the heathen will be lost if we do not go; He simply says—"Go ye therefore, and teach all nations." Go on the revelation of My sovereignty; teach and preach out of a living experience of Me.

"Then the eleven disciples went . . . into a mountain where Jesus had appointed them" (v. 16). If I want to know the universal sovereignty of Christ, I must know Him for myself, and how to get alone with Him; I must take time to worship the Being Whose Name I bear. "Come unto Me"—that is the place to meet Jesus. Are you weary and heavy laden? How many missionaries are! We banish those marvellous words of the universal Sovereign of the world to the threshold of an after-meeting; they are the words of Jesus to His disciples.

"Go ye therefore. . . ." "Go" simply means live. Acts 1:8 is the description of how to go. Jesus did not say—Go into Jerusalem and Judea and Samaria, but, "Ye shall be witnesses unto Me" in all these places. He undertakes to establish the goings.

"If ye abide in Me, and My words abide in you . . ."—that is the way to keep going in our personal lives. Where we are placed is a matter of indifference; God engineers the goings. "None of these things move me. . . ." That is how to keep going till you're gone!

OCTOBER 15

THE KEY TO THE MISSIONARY MESSAGE

And He is the propitiation for our sins: and not for ours only, but also for the sins of the whole world. 1 John 2:2

The key to the missionary message is the propitiation of Christ Jesus. Take any phase of Christ's work—the healing phase, the saving and sanctifying phase; there is nothing limitless about those. "The Lamb of God, which taketh away the sin of the world!"—that is limitless. The missionary message is the limitless significance of Jesus Christ as the propitiation for our sins, and a missionary is one who is soaked in that revelation.

The key to the missionary message is the remissionary aspect of Christ's life, not His kindness and His goodness, and His revealing of the Fatherhood of God; the great limitless significance is that He is the propitiation for our sins. The missionary message is not patriotic, it is irrespective of nations and of individuals, it is for the whole world. When the Holy Ghost comes in He does not consider my predilections, He brings me into union with the Lord Jesus.

A missionary is one who is wedded to the charter of his Lord and Master; he has not to proclaim his own point of view, but to proclaim the Lamb of God. It is easier to belong to a coterie which tells what Jesus Christ has done for me, easier to become a devotee to Divine healing, or to a special type of sanctification, or to the baptism of the Holy Ghost. Paul did not say—"Woe is unto me, if I do not preach what Christ has done for me," but—"Woe is unto me, if I preach not the gospel!" This is the Gospel—"The Lamb of God, which taketh away the sin of the world!"

OCTOBER 16

THE KEY TO THE MASTER'S ORDERS

Pray ye therefore the Lord of the harvest, that He will send forth labourers into His harvest. Matthew 9:38

The key to the missionary problem is in the hand of God, and that key is prayer, not work, that is, not work as the word is popularly understood to-day, because that may mean the evasion of concentration on God. The key to the missionary problem is not the key of common sense, nor the medical key, nor the key of civilisation or education or even evangelisation. The key is prayer. "Pray ye therefore the Lord of the harvest." Naturally, prayer is not practical, it is absurd; we have to realise that prayer is stupid from the ordinary commonsense point of view.

There are no nations in Jesus Christ's outlook, but *the world.* How many of us pray without respect of persons, and with respect to only one Person, Jesus Christ? He owns the harvest that is produced by distress and conviction of sin, and this is the harvest we have to pray that labourers may be thrust out to reap. We are taken up with active work while people all round are ripe to harvest, and we do not reap one of them, but waste our Lord's time in over-energised activities. Suppose the crisis comes in your father's life, in your brother's life, are you there as a labourer to reap the harvest for Jesus Christ? "Oh, but I have a special work to do!" No Christian has a special work to do. A Christian is called to be Jesus Christ's own, one who is not above his Master, one who does not dictate to Jesus Christ what he intends to do. Our Lord calls to no special work: He calls to Himself. "Pray ye therefore the Lord of the harvest," and He will engineer circumstances and thrust you out.

OCTOBER 17

GREATER WORKS

And greater works than these shall he do; because I go unto My Father. John 14:12

Prayer does not fit us for the greater works; prayer *is* the greater work. We think of prayer as a commonsense exercise of our higher powers in order to prepare us for God's work. In the teaching of Jesus Christ prayer is the working of the miracle of Redemption in me which produces the miracle of Redemption in others by the power of God. The way fruit remains is by prayer, but remember it is prayer based on the agony of Redemption, not on my agony. Only a child gets prayer answered; a wise man does not.

Prayer is the battle; it is a matter of indifference where you are. Whichever way God engineers circumstances, the duty is to pray. Never allow the thought—"I am of no use where I am"; because you certainly can be of no use where you are not. Wherever God has dumped you down in circumstances, pray, ejaculate to Him all the time. "Whatsoever ye shall ask in My name, that will I do." We won't pray unless we get thrills, that is the intensest form of spiritual selfishness. We have to labour along the line of God's direction, and He says *pray*. "Pray ye therefore the Lord of the harvest, that He will send forth labourers into His harvest."

There is nothing thrilling about a labouring man's work, but it is the labouring man who makes the conceptions of the genius possible; and it is the labouring saint who makes the conceptions of his Master possible. You labour at prayer and results happen all the time from God's standpoint. What an astonishment it will be to find, when the veil is lifted, the souls that have been reaped by you, simply because you had been in the habit of taking your orders from Jesus Christ.

OCTOBER 18

THE KEY TO THE MISSIONARY DEVOTION

For His name's sake they went forth. 3 John 7

Our Lord has told us how love to Him is to manifest itself. "Lovest thou Me? . . . Feed My sheep"—identify yourself with My interests in other people, not, identify *Me* with *your* interests in other people. 1 Corinthians 13:4–8 gives the character of this love, it is the love *of God* expressing itself. The test of my love for Jesus is the practical one, all the rest is sentimental jargon.

Loyalty to Jesus Christ is the supernatural work of Redemption wrought in me by the Holy Ghost Who sheds abroad the love of God in my heart, and that love works efficaciously through me in contact with everyone I meet. I remain loyal to His name although every commonsense fact gives the lie to Him, and declares that He has no more power than a morning mist.

The key to missionary devotion means being attached to nothing and no one saving Our Lord Himself, not being detached from things externally. Our Lord was amazingly in and out among ordinary things; His detachment was on the inside towards God. External detachment is often an indication of a secret vital attachment to the things we keep away from externally. The loyalty of a missionary is to keep his soul concentratedly open to the nature of the Lord Jesus Christ. The men and women Our Lord sends out on His enterprises are the ordinary human stuff, plus dominating devotion to Himself wrought by the Holy Ghost.

OCTOBER 19

THE UNHEEDED SECRET

My kingdom is not of this world. John 18:36

The great enemy to the Lord Jesus Christ in the present day is the conception of practical work that has not come from the New Testament, but from the systems of the world in which endless energy and activities are insisted upon, but no private life with God. The emphasis is put on the wrong thing. Jesus said, "The kingdom of God cometh not with observation; . . . for, behold, the kingdom of God is within you," a hidden, obscure thing. An active Christian worker too often lives in the shop window. It is the innermost of the innermost that reveals the power of the life.

We have to get rid of the plague of the spirit of the religious age in which we live. In Our Lord's life there was none of the press and rush of tremendous activity that we regard so highly, and the disciple is to be as his Master. The central thing about the kingdom of Jesus Christ is a personal relationship to Himself, not public usefulness to men. It is not its practical activities that are the strength of this Bible Training College, its whole strength lies in the fact that here you are put into soak before God. You have no idea of where God is going to engineer your circumstances, no knowledge of what strain is going to be put on you either at home or abroad, and if you waste your time in over-active energies instead of getting into soak on the great fundamental truths of God's Redemption, you will snap when the strain comes; but if this time of soaking before God is being spent in getting rooted and grounded in God on the un-practical line, you will remain true to Him whatever happens.

OCTOBER 20

IS GOD'S WILL MY WILL?

This is the will of God, even your sanctification. 1 Thessalonians 4:3

It is not a question of whether God is willing to sanctify me; is it *my* will? Am I willing to let God do in me all that has been made possible by the Atonement? Am I willing to let Jesus be made sanctification to me, and to let the life of Jesus be manifested in my mortal flesh? Beware of saying—"Oh, I am longing to be sanctified." You are not, stop longing and make it a matter of transaction—"Nothing in my hands I bring." Receive Jesus Christ to be made sanctification to you in implicit faith, and the great marvel of the Atonement will be made real in you. All that Jesus made possible is made mine by the free loving gift of God on the ground of what He performed. My attitude as a saved and sanctified soul is that of profound humble holiness (there is no such thing as proud holiness), a holiness based on agonising repentance and a sense of unspeakable shame and degradation; and also on the amazing realisation that the love of God commended itself to me in that while I cared nothing about Him, He completed everything for my salvation and sanctification (see Romans 5:8). No wonder Paul says nothing is "able to separate us from the love of God, which is in Christ Jesus our Lord." Sanctification makes me one with Jesus Christ, and in Him one with God, and it is done only through the superb Atonement of Christ. Never put the effect as the cause. The effect in me is obedience and service and prayer, and is the outcome of speechless thanks and adoration for the marvellous sanctification wrought out in me because of the Atonement.

OCTOBER 21

DIRECTION BY IMPULSE

Building up yourselves on your most holy faith. Jude 20

There was nothing either of the nature of impulse or of cold-bloodedness about Our Lord, but only a calm strength that never got into panic. Most of us develop our Christianity along the line of our temperament, not along the line of God. Impulse is a trait in natural life, but Our Lord always ignores it, because it hinders the development of the life of a disciple. Watch how the Spirit of God checks impulse, His checks bring a rush of self-conscious foolishness which makes us instantly want to vindicate ourselves. Impulse is all right in a child, but it is disastrous in a man or woman; an impulsive man is always a petted man. Impulse has to be trained into intuition by discipline.

Discipleship is built entirely on the supernatural grace of God. Walking on the water is easy to impulsive pluck, but walking on dry land as a disciple of Jesus Christ is a different thing. Peter walked on the water to go to Jesus, but he followed Him afar off on the land. We do not need the grace of God to stand crises, human nature and pride are sufficient, we can face the strain magnificently; but it does require the supernatural grace of God to live twenty-four hours in every day as a saint, to go through drudgery as a disciple, to live an ordinary, unobserved, ignored existence as a disciple of Jesus. It is inbred in us that we have to do exceptional things for God; but we have not. We have to be exceptional in the ordinary things, to be holy in mean streets, among mean people, and this is not learned in five minutes.

OCTOBER 22

THE WITNESS OF THE SPIRIT

The Spirit Himself beareth witness with our spirit.... Romans 8:16 (RV)

We are in danger of getting the barter spirit when we come to God, we want the witness before we have done what God tells us to do. "Why does not God reveal Himself to me?" He cannot; it is not that He will not, but He cannot, because you are in the road as long as you won't abandon absolutely to Him. Immediately you do, God witnesses to Himself; He cannot witness to you, but He witnesses instantly to His own nature in you. If you had the witness before the reality, it would end in sentimental emotion. Immediately you transact on the Redemption and stop the impertinence of debate, God gives you the witness. As soon as you abandon reasoning and argument, God witnesses to what He has done, and you are amazed at your impertinence in having kept Him waiting. If you are in debate as to whether God can deliver from sin, either let Him do it, or tell Him He cannot. Do not quote this and that person, try Matthew 11:28—"Come unto Me." *Come,* if you are weary and heavy laden; *ask* if you know you are evil (Luke 11:13).

The simplicity that comes from our natural commonsense decisions is apt to be mistaken for the witness of the Spirit, but the Spirit witnesses only to His own nature and to the work of Redemption, never to our reason. If we try to make Him witness to our reason, it is no wonder we are in darkness and perplexity. Fling it all overboard, trust in God, and He will give the witness.

OCTOBER 23

NOT A BIT OF IT!

If any man be in Christ, he is a new creature: old things are passed away. 2 Corinthians 5:17

Our Lord never nurses our prejudices, He mortifies them, runs clean athwart them. We imagine that God has a special interest in our particular prejudices; we are quite sure that God will never deal with us as we know He has to deal with other people. "God must deal with other people in a very stern way, but of course He knows that my prejudices are all right." We have to learn—"Not a bit of it!" Instead of God being on the side of our prejudices, He is deliberately wiping them out. It is part of our moral education to have our prejudices run straight across by His providence, and to watch how He does it. God pays no respect to anything we bring to Him; there is only one thing He wants of us, and that is our unconditional surrender. When we are born again, the Holy Spirit begins to work His new creation in us, and there will come a time when there is not a bit of the old order left; the old solemnity goes, the old attitude to things goes, and "all things are of God." How are we going to get the life that has no lust, no self-interest, no sensitiveness to pokes, the love that is not provoked, that thinketh no evil, that is always kind? The only way is by allowing not a bit of the old life to be left, but only simple perfect trust in God, such trust that we no longer want God's blessings, but only want Himself. Have we come to the place where God can withdraw His blessings and it does not affect our trust in Him? When once we see God at work, we will never bother our heads about things that happen, because we are actually trusting in our Father in Heaven Whom the world cannot see.

OCTOBER 24

THE VIEWPOINT

Now thanks be unto God, which always causeth us to triumph in Christ. 2 Corinthians 2:14

The viewpoint of a worker for God must not be as near the highest as he can get, it must be *the* highest. Be careful to maintain strenuously God's point of view, it has to be done every day, bit by bit; don't think on the finite. No outside power can touch the viewpoint.

The viewpoint to maintain is that we are here for one purpose only, viz., to be captives in the train of Christ's triumphs. We are not in God's showroom, we are here to exhibit one thing—the absolute captivity of our lives to Jesus Christ. How small the other points of view are—"I am standing alone battling for Jesus"; "I have to maintain the cause of Christ and hold this fort for Him." Paul says—"I am in the train of a conqueror, and it does not matter what the difficulties are, I am always led in triumph." Is this idea being worked out practically in us? Paul's secret joy was that God took him, a red-handed rebel against Jesus Christ, and made him a captive, and now that is all he is here for. Paul's joy was to be a captive of the Lord, he had no other interest in heaven or on earth. It is a shameful thing for a Christian to talk about getting the victory. The Victor ought to have got us so completely that it is His victory all the time, and we are more than conquerors through Him. "For we are unto God a sweet savour of Christ." We are enwheeled with the odour of Jesus, and wherever we go we are a wonderful refreshment to God.

OCTOBER 25

THE EXTERNAL CRUSH OF THINGS

I am made all things to all men, that I might by all means save some. 1 Corinthians 9:22

A Christian worker has to learn how to be God's noble man or woman amid a crowd of ignoble things. Never make this plea—"If only I were somewhere else!" All God's men are ordinary men made extraordinary by the matter He has given them. Unless we have the right matter in our minds intellectually and in our hearts affectionately, we will be hustled out of usefulness to God. We are not workers for God by choice. Many people deliberately choose to be workers, but they have no matter in them of God's almighty grace, no matter of His mighty word. Paul's whole heart and mind and soul were taken up with the great matter of what Jesus Christ came to do, he never lost sight of that one thing. We have to face ourselves with the one central fact—Jesus Christ, and Him crucified.

"I have chosen you." Keep that note of greatness in your creed. It is not that you have got God, but that He has got you. Here, in this College, God is at work, bending, breaking, moulding, doing just as He chooses. Why He is doing it, we do not know; He is doing it for one purpose only—that He may be able to say, "This is My man, My woman." We have to be in God's hand so that He can plant men on the Rock as He has planted us.

Never choose to be a worker, but when God has put His call on you, woe be to you if you turn to the right hand or to the left. He will do with you what He never did with you before the call came; He will do with you what He is not doing with other people. Let Him have His way.

OCTOBER 26

WHAT IS A MISSIONARY?

As My Father hath sent Me, even so send I you. John 20:21

A missionary is one sent by Jesus Christ as He was sent by God. The great dominant note is not the needs of men, but the command of Jesus. The source of our inspiration in work for God is behind, not before. The tendency to-day is to put the inspiration ahead, to sweep everything in front of us and bring it all out to our conception of success. In the New Testament the inspiration is put behind us, the Lord

Jesus. The ideal is to be true to Him, to carry out *His* enterprises.

Personal attachment to the Lord Jesus and His point of view is the one thing that must not be overlooked. In missionary enterprise the great danger is that God's call is effaced by the needs of the people until human sympathy absolutely overwhelms the meaning of being sent by Jesus. The needs are so enormous, the conditions so perplexing, that every power of mind falters and fails. We forget that the one great reason underneath all missionary enterprise is not first the elevation of the people, nor the education of the people, nor their needs; but first and foremost the command of Jesus Christ—"Go ye therefore, and teach all nations."

When looking back on the lives of men and women of God the tendency is to say—"What wonderfully astute wisdom they had! How perfectly they understood all God wanted!" The astute mind behind is the Mind of God, not human wisdom at all. We give credit to human wisdom when we should give credit to the Divine guidance of God through childlike people who were foolish enough to trust God's wisdom and the supernatural equipment of God.

OCTOBER 27

THE METHOD OF MISSIONS

Go ye therefore, and teach [disciple] all nations. Matthew 28:19

Jesus Christ did not say—"Go and save souls" (the salvation of souls is the supernatural work of God), but—"Go and teach," i.e., disciple, "all nations," and you cannot make disciples unless you are a disciple yourself. When the disciples came back from their first mission, they were filled with joy because the devils were subject to them, and Jesus said—"Don't rejoice in successful service; the great secret of joy is that you are rightly related to Me." The great essential of the missionary is that he remains true to the call of God, and realises that his one purpose is to disciple men and women to Jesus. There is a passion for souls that does not spring from God, but from the desire to make converts to our point of view.

The challenge to the missionary does not come on the line that people are difficult to get saved, that backsliders are difficult to reclaim, that there is a "wadge" of callous indifference; but along the line of his own personal relationship to Jesus Christ. "Believe ye that I am able to do this?" Our Lord puts that question steadily, it faces us in every individual case we meet. The one great challenge is—Do I know my risen Lord? Do I know the power of His indwelling

Spirit? Am I wise enough in God's sight, and foolish enough according to the world, to bank on what Jesus Christ has said; or am I abandoning the great supernatural position, which is the only call for a missionary, viz., boundless confidence in Christ Jesus? If I take up any other method, I depart altogether from the method laid down by Our Lord—"All power is given unto Me. . . . *Go ye therefore.*"

OCTOBER 28

JUSTIFICATION BY FAITH

For if, when we were enemies, we were reconciled to God by the death of His Son, much more, being reconciled, we shall be saved by His life. Romans 5:10

I am not saved by believing; I realise I am saved by believing. It is not repentance that saves me; repentance is the sign that I realise what God has done in Christ Jesus. The danger is to put the emphasis on the effect instead of on the cause—"It is my obedience that puts me right with God, my consecration." Never! I am put right with God because prior to all, Christ died. When I turn to God and by belief accept what God reveals I can accept, instantly the stupendous Atonement of Jesus Christ rushes me into a right relationship with God, and by the supernatural miracle of God's grace I stand justified, not because I am sorry for my sin, not because I have repented, but because of what Jesus has done. The spirit of God brings it with a breaking, all-over light, and I know, though I do not know how, that I am saved.

The salvation of God does not stand on human logic, it stands on the sacrificial Death of Jesus. We can be born again because of the Atonement of Our Lord. Sinful men and women can be changed into new creatures, not by their repentance or their belief, but by the marvellous work of God in Christ Jesus which is prior to all experience. The impregnable safety of justification and sanctification is God Himself. We have not to work out these things ourselves; they have been worked out by the Atonement: The supernatural becomes natural by the miracle of God; there is the realisation of what Jesus Christ has already done—*"It is finished."*

OCTOBER 29

SUBSTITUTION

He hath made Him to be sin for us, . . . that we might be made the righteousness of God. . . . 2 Corinthians 5:21

The modern view of the death of Jesus is that He died for our sins out of sympathy. The New Testament view is that He bore our sin not by sympathy, but by identification. He was *made to be sin.* Our sins are removed because of the death of Jesus, and the explanation of His death is His obedience to His Father, not His sympathy with us. We are acceptable with God not because we have obeyed, or because we have promised to give up things, but because of the death of Christ, and in no other way. We say that Jesus Christ came to reveal the Fatherhood of God, the loving-kindness of God; the New Testament says He came to bear away the sin of the world (RV mg). The revelation of His Father is to those to whom He has been introduced as Saviour: Jesus Christ never spoke of Himself to the world as one Who revealed the Father, but as a stumbling-block (see John 15:22–24). John 14:9 was spoken to His disciples.

That Christ died for me, therefore I go scot free, is never taught in the New Testament. What *is* taught in the New Testament is that "He died for all" (not—He died my death), and that by identification with His death I can be freed from sin, and have imparted to me His very righteousness. The substitution taught in the New Testament is twofold: "He hath made Him to be sin for us, who knew no sin; *that we might be made the righteousness of God in Him."* It is not Christ *for* me unless I am determined to have Christ formed *in* me.

OCTOBER 30

FAITH

Without faith it is impossible to please Him. Hebrews 11:6

Faith in antagonism to common sense is fanaticism, and common sense in antagonism to faith is rationalism. The life of faith brings the two into a right relation. Common sense is not faith, and faith is not common sense; they stand in the relation of the natural and the spiritual; of impulse and inspiration. Nothing Jesus Christ ever said is common sense, it is revelation sense, and it reaches the shores where common sense fails. Faith must be tried before the reality of faith is actual. "We know that all things work together for good," then no matter what happens, the alchemy of God's providence transfigures the ideal faith into actual reality. Faith always works on the personal line, the whole purpose of God being to see that the ideal faith is made real in His children. For every detail of the commonsense life, there is a revelation fact of God whereby we can prove in practical experience what we believe God to be. Faith is a tremendously active principle which always puts Jesus

Christ first—"Lord, Thou hast said so and so" (e.g., Matthew 6:33), "it looks mad, but I am going to venture on Thy word." To turn head faith into a personal possession is a fight *always,* not sometimes. God brings us into circumstances in order to educate our faith, because the nature of faith is to make its object real. Until we know Jesus, God is a mere abstraction, we cannot have faith in Him; but immediately we hear Jesus say—"He that hath seen Me hath seen the Father," we have something that is real, and faith is boundless. Faith is the whole man rightly related to God by the power of the Spirit of Jesus Christ.

OCTOBER 31

DISCERNMENT OF FAITH

Faith as a grain of mustard seed . . . Matthew 17:20

We have the idea that God rewards us for our faith, it may be so in the initial stages; but we do not earn anything by faith. Faith brings us into right relationship with God and gives God His opportunity. God has frequently to knock the bottom board out of your experience if you are a saint in order to get you into contact with Himself. God wants you to understand that it is a life of *faith,* not a life of sentimental enjoyment of His blessings. Your earlier life of faith was narrow and intense, settled around a little sun-spot of experience that had as much of sense as of faith in it, full of light and sweetness; then God withdrew His conscious blessings in order to teach you to walk by faith. You are worth far more to Him now than you were in your days of conscious delight and thrilling testimony.

Faith by its very nature must be tried, and the real trial of faith is not that we find it difficult to trust God, but that God's character has to be cleared in our own minds. Faith in its actual working out has to go through spells of unsyllabled isolation. Never confound the trial of faith with the ordinary discipline of life. Much that we call the trial of faith is the inevitable result of being alive. Faith in the Bible is faith in God against every thing that contradicts Him—"I will remain true to God's character whatever He may do." "Though He slay me, yet will I trust Him"—this is the most sublime utterance of faith in the whole of the Bible.

NOVEMBER 1

YE ARE NOT YOUR OWN

Know ye not that . . . ye are not your own? 1 Corinthians 6:19

There is no such thing as a private life—"a world within the world"—for a man or woman who is brought into fellowship with Jesus Christ's sufferings. God breaks up the private life of His saints, and makes it a thoroughfare for the world on the one hand and for Himself on the other. No human being can stand that unless he is identified with Jesus Christ. We are not sanctified for ourselves, we are called into the fellowship of the Gospel, and things happen which have nothing to do with us, God is getting us into fellowship with Himself. Let Him have his way, if you do not, instead of being of the slightest use to God in His Redemptive work in the world, you will be a hindrance and a clog.

The first thing God does with us is to get us based on rugged Reality until we do not care what becomes of us individually as long as He gets His way for the purpose of His Redemption. Why shouldn't we go through heartbreaks? Through these doorways God is opening up ways of fellowship with His Son. Most of us fall and collapse at the first grip of pain; we sit down on the threshold of God's purpose and die away of self-pity, and all so-called Christian sympathy will aid us to our death-bed. But God will not. He comes with the grip of the pierced hand of His Son, and says—"Enter into fellowship with Me; arise and shine." If through a broken heart God can bring His purposes to pass in the world, then thank Him for breaking your heart.

NOVEMBER 2

AUTHORITY AND INDEPENDENCE

If ye love Me, ye will keep My commandments. John 14:15 (RV)

Our Lord never insists upon obedience; He tells us very emphatically what we ought to do, but He never takes means to make us do it. We have to obey Him out of oneness of spirit. That is why when Our Lord talked about discipleship, He prefaced it with an IF—you do not need to unless you like. "If any man will be My disciple, let him deny himself"; let him give up his right to himself to Me. Our Lord is not talking of eternal positions, but of being of value to Himself in this order of things, that is why He sounds so stern (cf. Luke 14:26). Never interpret these words apart from the One who uttered them.

The Lord does not give me rules, He makes His standard very clear, and if my relationship to Him is

that of love, I will do what He says without any hesitation. If I hesitate, it is because I love someone else in competition with Him, viz., myself. Jesus Christ will not help me to obey Him, I must obey Him; and when I do obey Him, I fulfil my spiritual destiny. My personal life may be crowded with small petty incidents, altogether unnoticeable and mean,[23] but if I obey Jesus Christ in the haphazard circumstances, they become pinholes through which I see the face of God, and when I stand face to face with God I shall discover that through my obedience thousands were blessed. When once God's Redemption comes to the point of obedience in a human soul, it always creates. If I obey Jesus Christ, the Redemption of God will rush through me to other lives, because behind the deed of obedience is the Reality of Almighty God.

NOVEMBER 3

A BOND-SLAVE OF JESUS

I am crucified with Christ: nevertheless I live; yet not I, but Christ liveth in me. Galatians 2:20

These words mean the breaking of my independence with my own hand and surrendering to the supremacy of the Lord Jesus. No one can do this for me, I must do it myself. God may bring me to the point three hundred and sixty-five times a year, but He cannot put me through it. It means breaking the husk of my individual independence of God, and the emancipation of my personality into oneness with Himself, not for my own ideas, but for absolute loyalty to Jesus. There is no possibility of dispute when once I am there. Very few of us know anything about loyalty to Christ—"*For my sake.*" It is that which makes the iron saint.

Has that break come? All the rest is pious fraud. The one point to decide is—Will I give up, will I surrender to Jesus Christ, and make no conditions whatever as to how the break comes? I must be broken from my self-realisation, and immediately that point is reached, the reality of the supernatural identification takes place at once, and the witness of the Spirit of God is unmistakable—"I have been crucified with Christ" (RV).

The passion of Christianity is that I deliberately sign away my own rights and become a bond-slave of Jesus Christ. Until I do that, I do not begin to be a saint.

One student a year who hears God's call would be sufficient for God to have called this College into existence. This College as an organisation is not worth anything, it is not academic; it is for nothing

---

23. mean: as used here, something or someone ordinary, common, low, or ignoble, rather than cruel or spiteful.

else but for God to help Himself to lives. Is He going to help Himself to us, or are we taken up with our conception of what we are going to be?

NOVEMBER 4

THE AUTHORITY OF REALITY

Draw nigh to God, and He will draw nigh to you. James 4:8

It is essential to give people a chance of acting on the truth of God. The responsibility must be left with the individual, you cannot act for him, it must be his own deliberate act, but the evangelical message ought always to lead a man to act. The paralysis of refusing to act leaves a man exactly where he was before; when once he acts, he is never the same. It is the foolishness of it that stands in the way of hundreds who have been convicted by the Spirit of God. Immediately I precipitate myself over into an act, that second I live; all the rest is existence. The moments when I truly live are the moments when I act with my whole will.

Never allow a truth of God that is brought home to your soul to pass without acting on it, not necessarily physically, but in will. Record it, with ink or with blood. The feeblest saint who transacts business with Jesus Christ is emancipated the second he acts; all the almighty power of God is on his behalf. We come up to the truth of God, we confess we are wrong, but go back again; then we come up to it again, and go back; until we learn that we have no business to go back. We have to go clean over on some word of our redeeming Lord and transact business with Him. His word "come" means "transact." "Come unto Me." The last thing we do is to come; but everyone who does come knows that that second the supernatural life of God invades him instantly. The dominating power of the world, the flesh and the devil is paralysed, not by your act, but because your act has linked you on to God and His redemptive power.

NOVEMBER 5

PARTAKERS OF HIS SUFFERINGS

Rejoice, inasmuch as ye are partakers of Christ's sufferings. 1 Peter 4:13

If you are going to be used by God, He will take you through a multitude of experiences that are not meant for you at all; they are meant to make you useful in His hands, and to enable you to understand what transpires in other souls so that you will never be surprised at what you come across. "Oh, I can't deal with that person." Why not? God gave you ample opportunity to soak before Him on that line, and you "barged off" because it seemed stupid to spend time in that way.

The sufferings of Christ are not those of ordinary men. He suffered "according to the will of God," not from the point of view we suffer from as individuals. It is only when we are related to Jesus Christ that we can understand what God is after in His dealings with us. It is part of Christian culture to know what God's aim is. In the history of the Christian Church the tendency has been to evade being identified with the sufferings of Jesus Christ; men have sought to procure the carrying out of God's order by a short cut of their own. God's way is always the way of suffering, the way of the "long, long trail."

Are we partakers of Christ's sufferings? Are we prepared for God to stamp our personal ambitions right out? Are we prepared for God to destroy by transfiguration our individual determinations? It will not mean that we know exactly why God is taking us that way; that would make us spiritual prigs. We never realise at the time what God is putting us through; we go through it more or less misunderstandingly; then we come to a luminous place and say—"Why, God has girded me, though I did not know it!"

NOVEMBER 6

PROGRAMME OF BELIEF

Believest thou this? John 11:26

Martha believed in the power at the disposal of Jesus Christ; she believed that if He had been present He could have healed her brother. She also believed that Jesus had a peculiar intimacy with God and that whatever He asked of God, God would do; but she needed a closer personal intimacy with Jesus. Martha's programme of belief had its fulfilment in the future; Jesus led her on until her belief became a personal possession, and then slowly emerged into a particular inheritance—"Yea, Lord: I believe that Thou art the Christ. . . ."

Is there something like that in the Lord's dealings with you? Is Jesus educating you into a personal intimacy with Himself? Let Him press home His question to you—"Believest thou *this?*" What is your ordeal of doubt? Have you come, like Martha, to some overwhelming passage in your circumstances where your programme of belief is about to emerge into a personal belief? This can never be until a personal need arises out of a personal problem.

To believe is to commit. In the programme of mental belief I commit myself, and abandon all that is not related to that commitment. In personal belief I commit myself morally to this way of confidence and refuse to compromise with any other; and in particular belief I commit myself spiritually to Jesus Christ, and determine in that thing to be dominated by the Lord alone.

When I stand face to face with Jesus Christ and He says to me—"Believest thou this?" I find that faith is as natural as breathing, and I am staggered that I was so stupid as not to trust Him before.

NOVEMBER 7

THE UNDETECTED SACREDNESS OF CIRCUMSTANCES

All things work together for good to them that love God. Romans 8:28

The circumstances of a saint's life are ordained of God. In the life of a saint there is no such thing as chance. God by His providence brings you into circumstances that you cannot understand at all, but the Spirit of God understands. God is bringing you into places and among people and into conditions in order that the intercession of the Spirit in you may take a particular line. Never put your hand in front of the circumstances and say—"I am going to be my own providence here; I must watch this, and guard that." All your circumstances are in the hand of God, therefore never think it strange concerning the circumstances you are in. Your part in intercessory prayer is not to enter into the agony of intercession, but to utilise the commonsense circumstances God puts you in, and the commonsense people He puts you amongst by His providence, to bring them before God's throne and give the Spirit in you a chance to intercede for them: In this way God is going to sweep the whole world with His saints.

Am I making the Holy Spirit's work difficult by being indefinite, or by trying to do His work for Him? I must do the human side of intercession, and the human side is the circumstances I am in and the people I am in contact with. I have to keep my conscious life as a shrine of the Holy Ghost, then as I bring the different ones before God, the Holy Spirit makes intercession for them.

Your intercessions can never be mine, and my intercessions can never be yours, but the Holy Ghost makes intercession in our particular lives, without which intercession someone will be impoverished.

NOVEMBER 8

THE UNRIVALLED POWER OF PRAYER

We know not what we should pray for as we ought: but the Spirit itself maketh intercession for us with groanings which cannot be uttered. Romans 8:26

We realise that we are energised by the Holy Spirit for prayer; we know what it is to pray in the Spirit; but we do not so often realise that the Holy Spirit Himself prays in us prayers which we cannot utter. When we are born again of God and are indwelt by the Spirit of God, He expresses for us the unutterable.

"He," the Spirit in you, "maketh intercession for the saints according to the will of God," and God searches your heart not to know what your conscious prayers are, but to find out what is the prayer of the Holy Spirit.

The Spirit of God needs the nature of the believer as a shrine in which to offer His intercession. "Your body is the temple of the Holy Ghost." When Jesus Christ cleansed the temple, He "would not suffer that any man should carry any vessel through the temple." The Spirit of God will not allow you to use your body for your own convenience. Jesus ruthlessly cast out all them that sold and bought in the temple, and said—"My house shall be called the house of prayer; but ye have made it a den of thieves."

Have we recognised that our body is the temple of the Holy Ghost? If so, we must be careful to keep it undefiled for Him. We have to remember that our conscious life, though it is only a tiny bit of our personality, is to be regarded by us as a shrine of the Holy Ghost. He will look after the unconscious part that we know nothing of; but we must see that we guard the conscious part for which we are responsible.

NOVEMBER 9

SACRAMENTAL SERVICE

Who now rejoice in my sufferings for you, and fill up that which is behind of the afflictions of Christ . . . Colossians 1:24

The Christian worker has to be a sacramental "go-between," to be so identified with his Lord and the reality of His Redemption that He can continually bring His creating life through him. It is not the strength of one man's personality being superimposed on another, but the real presence of Christ coming through the elements of the worker's life. When we preach the historic facts of the life and death of Our

Lord as they are conveyed in the New Testament, our words are made sacramental; God uses them on the ground of His Redemption to create in those who listen that which is not created otherwise. If we preach the effects of Redemption in human life instead of the revelation regarding Jesus, the result in those who listen is not new birth, but refined spiritual culture, and the Spirit of God cannot witness to it because such preaching is in another domain. We have to see that we are in such living sympathy with God that as we proclaim His truth He can create in souls the things which He alone can do.

"What a wonderful personality!" "What a fascinating man!" "Such marvellous insight!" What chance has the Gospel of God through all that? It cannot get through, because the line of attraction is always the line of appeal. If a man attracts by his personality, his appeal is along that line; if he is identified with his Lord's personality, then the appeal is along the line of what Jesus Christ can do. The danger is to glory in men; Jesus says we are to lift *Him* up.

NOVEMBER 10

FELLOWSHIP IN THE GOSPEL

Fellow labourer in the gospel of Christ. 1 Thessalonians 3:2

After sanctification it is difficult to state what your aim in life is, because God has taken you up into His purpose by the Holy Ghost. He is using you now for His purposes throughout the world as He used His Son for the purpose of our salvation. If you seek great things for yourself—"God has called me for this and that," you are putting a barrier to God's use of you. As long as you have a personal interest in your own character, or any set ambition, you cannot get through into identification with God's interests. You can only get there by losing for ever any idea of yourself and by letting God take you right out into His purpose for the world, and because your goings are of the Lord, you can never understand your ways.

I have to learn that the aim in life is God's, not mine. God is using me from His great personal standpoint, and all He asks of me is that I trust Him, and never say—"Lord, this gives me such heartache." To talk in that way makes me a clog. When I stop telling God what I want, He can catch me up for what He wants without let or hindrance.[24] He can crumple me up or exalt me, He can do anything He chooses. He simply asks me to have implicit faith in Himself and in His goodness. Self-pity is of the devil; if I go off

on that line I cannot be used by God for His purpose in the world. I have "a world within the world" in which I live, and God will never be able to get me outside it because I am afraid of being frost-bitten.

NOVEMBER 11

THE SUPREME CLIMB

Take now thy son. . . . Genesis 22:2

God's command is—Take *now*, not presently. It is extraordinary how we debate! We know a thing is right, but we try to find excuses for not doing it at once. To climb to the height God shows can never be done presently, it must be done now. The sacrifice is gone through in will before it is performed actually.

"And Abraham rose up early in the morning, . . . and went unto the place of which God had told him" (v. 3). The wonderful simplicity of Abraham! When God spoke, he did not confer with flesh and blood. Beware when you want to confer with flesh and blood, i.e., your own sympathies, your own insight, anything that is not based on your personal relationship to God. These are the things that compete with and hinder obedience to God.

Abraham did not choose the sacrifice. Always guard against self-chosen service for God; self-sacrifice may be a disease. If God has made your cup sweet, drink it with grace; if He has made it bitter, drink it in communion with Him. If the providential order of God for you is a hard time of difficulty, go through with it, but never choose the scene of your martyrdom. God chose the crucible for Abraham, and Abraham made no demur; he went steadily through. If you are not living in touch with Him, it is easy to pass a crude verdict on God. You must go through the crucible before you have any right to pronounce a verdict, because in the crucible you learn to know God better. God is working for His highest ends until His purpose and man's purpose become one.

NOVEMBER 12

THE TRANSFIGURED LIFE

If any man be in Christ, he is a new creature: old things are passed away; behold, all things are become new. 2 Corinthians 5:17

What idea have you of the salvation of your soul? The experience of salvation means that in your actual life things are really altered, you no longer look at things

---

24. without let or hindrance: legal phrase meaning "without obstacle or impediment."

as you used to; your desires are new, old things have lost their power. One of the touchstones of experience is—Has God altered the thing that matters? If you still hanker after the old things, it is absurd to talk about being born from above (RV mg), you are juggling with yourself. If you are born again, the Spirit of God makes the alteration manifest in your actual life and reasoning, and when the crisis comes you are the most amazed person on earth at the wonderful difference there is in you. There is no possibility of imagining that *you* did it. It is this complete and amazing alteration that is the evidence that you are a saved soul.

What difference has my salvation and sanctification made? For instance, can I stand in the light of 1 Corinthians 13, or do I have to shuffle? The salvation that is worked out in me by the Holy Ghost emancipates me entirely, and as long as I walk in the light as God is in the light, He sees nothing to censure, because His life is working out in every particular, not to my consciousness, but deeper than my consciousness.

NOVEMBER 13

FAITH AND EXPERIENCE

The Son of God, who loved me, and gave Himself for me. Galatians 2:20

We have to battle through our moods into absolute devotion to the Lord Jesus, to get out of the hole-and-corner business of our experience into abandoned devotion to Him. Think Who the New Testament says that Jesus Christ is, and then think of the despicable meanness[25] of the miserable faith we have—"I haven't had this and that experience!" Think what faith in Jesus Christ claims—that He can present us faultless before the throne of God, unutterably pure, absolutely rectified and profoundly justified. Stand in implicit, adoring faith in Him, *He* is "made unto us wisdom, and righteousness, and sanctification, and redemption." How can we talk of making a sacrifice for the Son of God! Our salvation is from hell and perdition, and then we talk about making sacrifices!

We have to get out into faith in Jesus Christ continually; not a prayer meeting Jesus Christ, nor a book Jesus Christ, but the New Testament Jesus Christ, Who is God Incarnate, and Who ought to strike us to His feet as dead. Our faith must be in the One from Whom our experience springs. Jesus Christ wants our absolute abandon of devotion to Himself.

We never can *experience* Jesus Christ, nor ever hold Him within the compass of our own hearts, but our faith must be built in strong emphatic confidence in Him.

It is along this line that we see the rugged impatience of the Holy Ghost against unbelief. All our fears are wicked, and we fear because we will not nourish ourselves in our faith. How can anyone who is identified with Jesus Christ suffer from doubt or fear! It ought to be an absolute psalm of perfectly irrepressible, triumphant belief.

NOVEMBER 14

DISCOVERING DIVINE DESIGNS

I being in the way, the LORD led me. . . . Genesis 24:27

We have to be so one with God that we do not continually need to ask for guidance. Sanctification means that we are made the children of God, and the natural life of a child is obedience—until he wishes to be disobedient, then instantly there is the intuitive jar. In the spiritual domain the intuitive jar is the monition of the Spirit of God. When He gives the check, we have to stop at once and be renewed in the spirit of our mind in order to make out what God's will is. If we are born again of the Spirit of God, it is the abortion of piety to ask God to guide us here and there. "The Lord led me," and on looking back we see the presence of an amazing design, which, if we are born of God, we will credit to God.

We can all see God in exceptional things, but it requires the culture of spiritual discipline to see God in every detail. Never allow that the haphazard is anything less than God's appointed order, and be ready to discover the Divine designs anywhere. Beware of making a fetish of consistency to your convictions instead of being devoted to God. "I shall never do that"—in all probability you will have to, if you are a saint. There never was a more inconsistent Being on this earth than Our Lord, but He was never inconsistent to His Father. The one consistency of the saint is not to a principle, but to the Divine life. It is the Divine life which continually makes more and more discoveries about the divine mind. It is easier to be a fanatic than a faithful soul, because there is something amazingly humbling, particularly to our religious conceit, in being loyal to God.

---

25. mean: as used here, something or someone ordinary, common, low, or ignoble, rather than cruel or spiteful.

NOVEMBER 15

WHAT IS THAT TO THEE?

Lord, and what shall this man do? . . . What is that to thee? Follow thou Me. John 21:21–22

One of our severest lessons comes from the stubborn refusal to see that we must not interfere in other people's lives. It takes a long time to realise the danger of being an amateur providence, that is, interfering with God's order for others. You see a certain person suffering, and you say—"He shall not suffer, and I will see that he does not." You put your hand straight in front of God's permissive will to prevent it, and God says—"What is that to thee?" If there is stagnation spiritually, never allow it to go on, but get into God's presence and find out the reason for it. Possibly you will find it is because you have been interfering in the life of another; proposing things you had no right to propose; advising when you had no right to advise. When you do have to give advice to another, God will advise through you with the direct understanding of His Spirit; your part is to be so rightly related to God that His discernment comes through you all the time for the blessing of another soul.

Most of us live on the borders of consciousness—consciously serving, consciously devoted to God. All this is immature, it is not the real life yet. The mature stage is the life of a child which is never conscious; we become so abandoned to God that the consciousness of being used never enters in. When we are consciously being used as broken bread and poured-out wine, there is another stage to be reached, where all consciousness of ourselves and of what God is doing through us is eliminated. A saint is never consciously a saint; a saint is consciously dependent on God.

NOVEMBER 16

STILL HUMAN!

Whatsoever ye do, do all to the glory of God. 1 Corinthians 10:31

The great marvel of the Incarnation slips into ordinary childhood's life; the great marvel of the Transfiguration vanishes in the devil-possessed valley ; the glory of the Resurrection descends into a breakfast on the sea-shore. This is not an anticlimax, but a great revelation of God.

The tendency is to look for the marvellous in our experience; we mistake the sense of the heroic for

being heroes. It is one thing to go through a crisis grandly, but another thing to go through every day glorifying God when there is no witness, no limelight, no one paying the remotest attention to us. If we do not want medieval haloes, we want something that will make people say—"What a wonderful man of prayer he is!" "What a pious, devoted woman she is!" If you are rightly devoted to the Lord Jesus, you have reached the sublime height where no one ever thinks of noticing you, all that is noticed is that the power of God comes through you all the time.

"Oh, I have had a wonderful call from God!" It takes Almighty God Incarnate in us to do the meanest[26] duty to the glory of God. It takes God's Spirit in us to make us so absolutely humanly His that we are utterly unnoticeable. The test of the life of a saint is not success, but faithfulness in human life as it actually is. We will set up success in Christian work as the aim; the aim is to manifest the glory of God in human life, to live the life hid with Christ in God in human conditions. Our human relationships are the actual conditions in which the ideal life of God is to be exhibited.

NOVEMBER 17

THE ETERNAL GOAL

By Myself have I sworn, saith the LORD, for because thou hast done this thing, . . . that in blessing I will bless thee. . . . Genesis 22:16–17

Abraham has reached the place where he is in touch with the very nature of God, he understands now the reality of God.

My goal is God Himself. . .
At any cost, dear Lord, by any road.

"At any cost, by any road" means nothing self-chosen in the way God brings us to the goal.

There is no possibility of questioning when God speaks if He speaks to His own nature in me; prompt obedience is the only result. When Jesus says—"Come," I simply come; when He says—"Let go," I let go; when he says—"Trust in God in this matter," I do trust. The whole working out is the evidence that the nature of God is in me.

God's revelation of Himself to me is determined by my character, not by God's character.

Tis because I am mean,
Thy ways so oft look mean to me.

By the discipline of obedience I get to the place where Abraham was, and I see Who God is. I never

---

26. mean: as used here, something or someone ordinary, common, low, or ignoble, rather than cruel or spiteful.

have a real God until I have come face to face with Him in Jesus Christ, then I know that "in all the world, my God, there is none but Thee, there is none but Thee."

The promises of God are of no value to us until by obedience we understand the nature of God. We read some things in the Bible three hundred and sixty-five times and they mean nothing to us; then all of a sudden we see what God means, because in some particular we have obeyed God, and instantly His nature is opened up. All the promises of God in Him are yea, and in Him Amen." The "yea" must be born of obedience; when by the obedience of our lives we say "Amen" to a promise, then that promise is ours.

NOVEMBER 18

WINNING INTO FREEDOM

If the Son therefore shall make you free, ye shall be free indeed. John 8:36

If there is any remnant of individual conceit left, it always says—"I can't." Personality never says—"I can't," but simply absorbs and absorbs. Personality always wants more and more. It is the way we are built. We are designed with a great capacity for God; and sin and our individuality are the things that keep us from getting at God. God delivers us from sin: we have to deliver ourselves from individuality, i.e., to present our natural life to God and sacrifice it until it is transformed into a spiritual life by obedience.

God does not pay any attention to our natural individuality in the development of our spiritual life. His order runs right across the natural life, and we have to see that we aid and abet God, not stand against Him and say—"I can't do that." God will not discipline us, we must discipline ourselves. God will not bring every thought and imagination into captivity; we have to do it. Do not say—"O Lord, I suffer from wandering thoughts." *Don't* suffer from wandering thoughts. Stop listening to the tyranny of your individuality, and get emancipated out into personality.

"If the Son . . . shall make you free . . ." Do not substitute "Saviour" for "Son." The Saviour set us free from sin; this is the freedom of being set free *by the Son.* It is what Paul means in Galatians 2:20—"I have been crucified with Christ" (RV), his natural individuality has been broken and his personality united with his Lord, not merged but united; "ye shall be free indeed," free in essence, free from the inside. We will insist on energy, instead of being energised into identification with Jesus.

NOVEMBER 19

WHEN HE IS COME

And He, when He is come, He will convict the world in respect of sin . . . John 16:8 (RV)

Very few of us know anything about conviction of sin; we know the experience of being disturbed because of having done wrong things; but conviction of sin by the Holy Ghost blots out every relationship on earth and leaves one relationship only—"Against Thee, Thee only, have I sinned." When a man is convicted of sin in this way, he knows with every power of his conscience that God dare not forgive him; if God did forgive him, the man would have a stronger sense of justice than God. God does forgive, but it cost the rending of His heart in the death of Christ to enable Him to do so. The great miracle of the grace of God is that He forgives sin, and it is the death of Jesus Christ alone that enables the Divine nature to forgive and to remain true to itself in doing so. It is shallow nonsense to say that God forgives us because He is love. When we have been convicted of sin we will never say this again. The love of God means Calvary, and nothing less; the love of God is spelt on the Cross and nowhere else. The only ground on which God can forgive me is through the Cross of my Lord. There, His conscience is satisfied.

Forgiveness means not merely that I am saved from hell and made right for heaven (no man would accept forgiveness on such a level); forgiveness means that I am forgiven into a recreated relationship, into identification with God in Christ. The miracle of Redemption is that God turns me, the unholy one, into the standard of Himself, the Holy One, by putting into me a new disposition, the disposition of Jesus Christ.

NOVEMBER 20

THE FORGIVENESS OF GOD

In whom we have . . . the forgiveness of sins. Ephesians 1:7

Beware of the pleasant view of the Fatherhood of God—God is so kind and loving that of course He will forgive us. That sentiment has no place whatever in the New Testament. The only ground on which God can forgive us is the tremendous tragedy of the Cross of Christ; to put forgiveness on any other ground is unconscious blasphemy. The only ground on which God can forgive sin and reinstate us in His favour is through the Cross of Christ, and in no other way. Forgiveness, which is so easy for us to accept, cost the agony of Calvary. It is possible to take the forgiveness of sin, the gift of the Holy Ghost, and our sanctification with the simplicity of faith, and to forget at what enormous cost to God it was all made ours.

Forgiveness is the divine miracle of grace; it cost God the Cross of Jesus Christ before He could forgive sin and remain a holy God. Never accept a view of the Fatherhood of God if it blots out the Atonement. The revelation of God is that He cannot forgive; He would contradict His nature if He did. The only way we can be forgiven is by being brought back to God by the Atonement. God's forgiveness is only natural in the super-natural domain.

Compared with the miracle of the forgiveness of sin, the experience of sanctification is slight. Sanctification is simply the marvellous expression of the forgiveness of sins in a human life, but the thing that awakens the deepest well of gratitude in a human being is that God has forgiven sin. Paul never got away from this. When once you realise all that it cost God to forgive you, you will be held as in a vice, constrained by the love of God.

NOVEMBER 21

IT IS FINISHED

I have finished the work which Thou gavest Me to do. John 17:4

The death of Jesus Christ is the performance in history of the very mind of God. There is no room for looking on Jesus Christ as a martyr; His death was not something that happened to Him which might have been prevented. His death was the very reason why He came.

Never build your preaching of forgiveness on the fact that God is our Father and He will forgive us because He loves us. It is untrue to Jesus Christ's revelation of God; it makes the Cross unnecessary, and the Redemption "much ado about nothing." If God does forgive sin, it is because of the death of Christ. God could forgive men in no other way than by the death of His Son, and Jesus is exalted to be Saviour because of His death. "We see Jesus . . . because of the suffering of death, crowned with glory and honour" (RV). The greatest note of triumph that ever sounded in the ears of a startled universe was that sounded on the Cross of Christ—*"It is finished."* That is the last word in the Redemption of man.

Anything that belittles or obliterates the holiness of God by a false view of the love of God, is untrue to the revelation of God given by Jesus Christ. Never allow the thought that Jesus Christ stands with us against God out of pity and compassion; that He

became a curse for us out of sympathy with us. Jesus Christ became a curse for us by the Divine decree. Our portion of realising the terrific meaning of the curse is conviction of sin, the gift of shame and penitence is given us; this is the great mercy of God. Jesus Christ hates the wrong in man, and Calvary is the estimate of His hatred.

NOVEMBER 22

SHALLOW AND PROFOUND

Whether therefore ye eat, or drink, or whatsoever ye do, do all to the glory of God. 1 Corinthians 10:31

Beware of allowing yourself to think that the shallow concerns of life are not ordained of God; they are as much of God as the profound. It is not your devotion to God that makes you refuse to be shallow, but your wish to impress other people with the fact that you are not shallow, which is a sure sign that you are a spiritual prig. Be careful of the production of contempt in yourself, it always comes along this line, and causes you to go about as a walking rebuke to other people because they are more shallow than you are. Beware of posing as a profound person; God became a Baby.

To be shallow is not a sign of being wicked, nor is shallowness a sign that there are no deeps; the ocean has a shore. The shallow amenities of life, eating and drinking, walking and talking, are all ordained by God. These are the things in which Our Lord lived. He lived in them as the Son of God, and He said that "the disciple is not above his Master."

Our safeguard is in the shallow things. We have to live the surface commonsense life in a commonsense way; when the deeper things come, God gives them to us apart from the shallow concerns. Never show the deeps to anyone but God. We are so abominably serious, so desperately interested in our own characters, that we refuse to behave like Christians in the shallow concerns of life.

Determinedly take no one seriously but God, and the first person you find you have to leave severely alone as being the greatest fraud you have ever known, is yourself.

NOVEMBER 23

DISTRACTION OF ANTIPATHY

Have mercy upon us, O LORD, have mercy upon us: for we are exceedingly filled with contempt. Psalm 123:3

The thing of which we have to beware is not so much damage to our belief in God as damage to our Christian temper. "Therefore take heed to thy spirit, that ye deal not treacherously." The temper of mind is tremendous in its effects, it is the enemy that penetrates right into the soul and distracts the mind from God. There are certain tempers of mind in which we never dare indulge; if we do, we find they have distracted us from faith in God, and until we get back to the quiet mood before God, our faith in Him is *nil*, and our confidence in the flesh and in human ingenuity is the thing that rules.

Beware of "the cares of this world," because they are the things that produce a wrong temper of soul. It is extraordinary what an enormous power there is in simple things to distract our attention from God. Refuse to be swamped with the cares of this life.

Another thing that distracts us is the lust of vindication. St. Augustine prayed—"O Lord, deliver me from this lust of always vindicating myself." That temper of mind destroys the soul's faith in God. "I must explain myself; I must get people to understand." Our Lord never explained anything; He left mistakes to correct themselves.

When we discern that people are not going on spiritually and allow the discernment to turn to criticism, we block our way to God. God never gives us discernment in order that we may criticise, but that we may intercede.

NOVEMBER 24

DIRECTION OF ASPIRATION

Behold, as the eyes of servants look unto the hand of their masters, . . . so our eyes wait upon the LORD *our God. Psalm 123:2*

This verse is a description of entire reliance upon God. Just as the eyes of the servant are riveted on his master, so our eyes are up unto God and our knowledge of His countenance is gained (cf. Isaiah 53:1 RV). Spiritual leakage begins when we cease to lift up our eyes unto Him. The leakage comes not so much through trouble on the outside as in the imagination, when we begin to say—"I expect I have been stretching myself a bit too much, standing on tiptoe and trying to look like God instead of being an ordinary humble person." We have to realise that no effort can be too high.

For instance, you came to a crisis when you made a stand for God and had the witness of the Spirit that all was right, but the weeks have gone by, and the years maybe, and you are slowly coming to the conclusion, "Well, after all, was I not a bit too pretentious? Was I not taking a stand a bit too high?" Your rational friends come and say—"Don't be a fool, we knew when you talked about this spiritual awakening that it was a passing impulse, you can't keep up the strain, God does not expect you to." And you say—"Well, I suppose I was expecting too much." It sounds humble to say it, but it means that reliance on God has gone and reliance on worldly opinion has come in. The danger is lest, no longer relying on God, you ignore the lifting up of your eyes to Him. Only when God brings you to a sudden halt, will you realise how you have been losing out. Whenever there is a leakage, remedy it immediately. Recognise that something has been coming between you and God, and get it readjusted at once.

NOVEMBER 25

THE SECRET OF SPIRITUAL COHERENCE

But God forbid that I should glory. . . . Galatians 6:14

When a man is first born again, he becomes incoherent, there is an amount of unrelated emotion about him, unrelated phases of external things. In the Apostle Paul there was a strong steady coherence underneath, consequently he could let his external life change as it liked and it did not distress him, because he was rooted and grounded in God. Most of us are not spiritually coherent because we are more concerned about being coherent externally. Paul lived in the basement; the coherent critics live in the upper storey of the external statement of things, and the two do not begin to touch each other. Paul's consistency was down in the fundamentals. The great basis of his coherence was the agony of God in the Redemption of the world, viz., the Cross of Jesus Christ.

Re-state to yourself what you believe, then do away with as much of it as possible, and get back to the bedrock of the Cross of Christ. In external history the Cross is an infinitesimal thing; from the Bible point of view it is of more importance than all the empires of the world. If we get away from brooding on the tragedy of God upon the Cross in our preaching, it produces nothing. It does not convey the energy of God to man; it may be interesting but it has no power. But preach the Cross, and the energy of God is let loose. "It pleased God by the foolishness of preaching to save them that believe. . . . We preach Christ crucified."

NOVEMBER 26

THE CONCENTRATION OF SPIRITUAL ENERGY

. . . save in the cross of our Lord Jesus Christ. Galatians 6:14

If you want to know the energy of God (i.e., the resurrection life of Jesus) in your mortal flesh, you must brood on the tragedy of God. Cut yourself off from prying personal interest in your own spiritual symptoms and consider bare-spirited the tragedy of God, and instantly the energy of God will be in you. Look unto *Me,*" pay attention to the objective Source and the subjective energy will be there. We lose power if we do not concentrate on the right thing. The effect of the Cross is salvation, sanctification, healing, etc., but we are not to preach any of these, we are to preach Jesus Christ and Him crucified. The proclaiming of Jesus will do its own work. Concentrate on God's centre in your preaching, and though your crowd may apparently pay no attention, they can never be the same again. If I talk my own talk, it is of no more importance to you than your talk is to me; but if I talk the truth of God, you will meet it again and so shall I. We have to concentrate on the great point of spiritual energy, the Cross, to keep in contact with that centre where all the power lies, and the energy will be let loose. In holiness movements and spiritual experience meetings the concentration is apt to be put not on the Cross of Christ, but on the effects of the Cross.

The feebleness of the churches is being criticised to-day, and the criticism is justified. One reason for the feebleness is that there has not been this concentration of spiritual energy; we have not brooded enough on the tragedy of Calvary or on the meaning of Redemption.

NOVEMBER 27

THE CONSECRATION OF SPIRITUAL ENERGY

By whom the world is crucified unto me, and I unto the world. Galatians 6:14

If I brood on the Cross of Christ, I do not become a subjective pietist, interested in my own whiteness; I become dominantly concentrated on Jesus Christ's interests. Our Lord was not a recluse nor an ascetic, He did not cut Himself off from society, but He was inwardly disconnected all the time. He was not aloof, but He lived in another world. He was so much in the ordinary world that the religious people of His day called Him a glutton and a winebibber. Our Lord never allowed anything to interfere with His consecration of spiritual energy.

The counterfeit of consecration is the conscious cutting off of things with the idea of storing spiritual power for use later on, but that is a hopeless mistake. The Spirit of God has spoiled the sin of a great many, yet there is no emancipation, no fullness in their lives. The kind of religious life we see abroad to-day is entirely different from the robust holiness of the life of Jesus Christ. "I pray not that Thou shouldest take them out of the world, but that Thou shouldest keep them from the evil." We are to be *in* the world but not *of* it; to be disconnected fundamentally, not externally.

We must never allow anything to interfere with the consecration of our spiritual energy. Consecration is our part, sanctification is God's part; and we have deliberately to determine to be interested in that only in which God is interested. The way to solve perplexing problems is to ask—"Is this the kind of thing which Jesus Christ is interested in, or the kind of thing the spirit that is the antipodes of Jesus is interested in?"

NOVEMBER 28

THE BOUNTY OF THE DESTITUTE

Being justified freely by His grace . . . Romans 3:24

The Gospel of the grace of God awakens an intense longing in human souls and an equally intense resentment, because the revelation which it brings is not palatable. There is a certain pride in man that will give and give, but to come and accept is another thing. I will give my life to martyrdom, I will give myself in consecration, I will do anything, but do not humiliate me to the level of the most hell-deserving sinner and tell me that all I have to do is to accept the gift of salvation through Jesus Christ.

We have to realise that we cannot earn or win anything from God; we must either receive it as a gift or do without it. The greatest blessing spiritually is the knowledge that we are destitute; until we get there Our Lord is powerless. He can do nothing for us if we think we are sufficient of ourselves; we have to enter into His Kingdom through the door of destitution. As long as we are rich, possessed of anything in the way of pride or independence, God cannot do anything for us. It is only when we get hungry spiritually that we receive the Holy Spirit. The gift of the nature of God is made effectual in us by the Holy Spirit; He imparts to us the quickening life of Jesus, which puts "the beyond" within, and immediately the beyond has come within, it rises up to "the above," and we are lifted into the domain where Jesus lives. (John 3:5)

THE ABSOLUTENESS OF JESUS CHRIST

He shall glorify Me. John 16:14

The pietistic movements of to-day have none of the rugged reality of the New Testament about them; there is nothing about them that needs the death of Jesus Christ, all that is required is a pious atmosphere, and prayer and devotion. This type of experience is not supernatural nor miraculous, it did not cost the passion of God, it is not dyed in the blood of the Lamb, not stamped with the hall-mark of the Holy Ghost. It has not that mark on it which makes men say, as they look with awe and wonder—"That is the work of God Almighty." That and nothing else is what the New Testament talks about.

The type of Christian experience in the New Testament is that of personal, passionate devotion to the Person of Jesus Christ. Every other type of Christian experience, so called, is detached from the Person of Jesus. There is no regeneration, no being born again into the Kingdom in which Christ lives, but only the idea that He is our Pattern. In the New Testament Jesus Christ is Saviour long before He is Pattern. To-day He is being despatched as the Figurehead of a religion, a mere Example. He is that, but He is infinitely more; He is salvation itself. He *is* the Gospel of God.

Jesus said—"When He, the Spirit of truth, is come, . . . He shall glorify Me." When I commit myself to the revelation made in the New Testament, I receive from God the gift of the Holy Spirit Who begins to interpret to me what Jesus did, and does in me subjectively what Jesus Christ did for me objectively.

BY THE GRACE OF GOD I AM WHAT I AM

His grace which was bestowed upon me was not in vain. 1 Corinthians 15:10

The way we continually talk about our own inability is an insult to the Creator. The deploring of our own incompetence is a slander against God for having over-

looked us. Get into the habit of examining in the sight of God the things that sound humble before men, and you will be amazed at how staggeringly impertinent they are. "Oh, I shouldn't like to say I am sanctified; I'm not a saint." Say that before God; and it means—"No, Lord, it is impossible for You to save and sanctify me; there are chances I have not had; so many imperfections in my brain and body; no, Lord, it isn't possible." That may sound wonderfully humble before men, but before God it is an attitude of defiance.

Again, the things that sound humble before God may sound the opposite before men. To say—"Thank God, I know I am saved and sanctified," is in the sight of God the acme of humility, it means you have so completely abandoned yourself to God that you know He is true. Never bother your head as to whether what you say sounds humble before men or not, but always be humble before God, and let Him be all in all.

There is only one relationship that matters, and that is your personal relationship to a personal Redeemer and Lord. Let everything else go, but maintain that at all costs, and God will fulfil His purpose through your life. One individual life may be of priceless value to God's purpose, and yours may be that life.

THE LAW AND THE GOSPEL

For whosoever shall keep the whole law, and yet offend in one point, he is guilty of all. James 2:10

The moral law does not consider us as weak human beings at all, it takes no account of our heredity and infirmities, it demands that we be absolutely moral. The moral law never alters, either for the noblest or for the weakest, it is eternally and abidingly the same. The moral law ordained by God does not make itself weak to the weak, it does not palliate our shortcomings, it remains absolute for all time and eternity. If we do not realise this, it is because we are less than alive; immediately we are alive, life becomes a tragedy. I was alive without the law once: but when the commandment came, 'sin revived, and I died." When we realise this, then the Spirit of God convicts us of sin. Until a man gets there and sees that there is no hope, the Cross of Jesus Christ is a farce to him. Conviction of sin always brings a fearful binding sense of the law, it makes a man hopeless—*"sold under sin."* I, a guilty sinner, can never get right with God, it is impossible. There is only one way in which I can get right with God, and that is by the death of Jesus Christ. I must get rid of the lurking idea that I can ever be right with God because of my obedience—which of us could ever obey God to absolute perfection!

We only realise the power of the moral law when it comes with an "if." God never coerces us. In one mood we wish He would make us do the thing, and in another mood we wish He would leave us alone. Whenever God's will is in the ascendant, all compulsion is gone. When we choose deliberately to obey Him, then, with all His almighty power, He will tax the remotest star and the last grain of sand to assist us.

DECEMBER 2

CHRISTIAN PERFECTION

Not as though I had already attained, either were already perfect . . . Philippians 3:12

It is a snare to imagine that God wants to make us perfect specimens of what He can do; God's purpose is to make us one with Himself. The emphasis of holiness movements is apt to be that God is producing specimens of holiness to put in His museum. If you go off on this idea of personal holiness, the dead-set of your life will not be for God, but for what you call the manifestation of God in your life. "It can never be God's will that I should be sick," you say. If it was God's will to bruise His own Son, why should He not bruise you? The thing that tells for God is not your relevant consistency to an idea of what a saint should be, but your real vital relation to Jesus Christ, and your abandonment to Him whether you are well or ill.

Christian perfection is not, and never can be, human perfection. Christian perfection is the perfection of a relationship to God which shows itself amid the irrelevancies of human life. When you obey the call of Jesus Christ, the first thing that strikes you is the irrelevancy of the things you have to do, and the next thing that strikes you is the fact that other people seem to be living perfectly consistent lives. Such lives are apt to leave you with the idea that God is unnecessary, by human effort and devotion we can reach the standard God wants. In a fallen world this can never be done. I am called to live in perfect relation to God so that my life produces a longing after God in other lives, not admiration for myself. Thoughts about myself hinder my usefulness to God. God is not after perfecting me to be a specimen in His show-room; He is getting me to the place where He can use me. Let Him do what He likes.

DECEMBER 3

NOT BY MIGHT NOR BY POWER

And my speech and my preaching was not with enticing words of man's wisdom, but in demonstration of the Spirit and of power. 1 Corinthians 2:4

If in preaching the Gospel you substitute your clear knowledge of the way of salvation for confidence in the power of the Gospel, you hinder people getting to Reality. You have to see that while you proclaim your knowledge of the way of salvation, you yourself are rooted and grounded in faith in God. Never rely on the clearness of your exposition, but as you give your exposition see that *you* are relying on the Holy Spirit. Rely on the certainty of God's redemptive power, and He will create His own life in souls.

When once you are rooted in Reality, nothing can shake you. If your faith is in experiences, anything that happens is likely to upset that faith; but nothing can ever upset God or the almighty Reality of Redemption; base your faith on that, and you are as eternally secure as God. When once you get into personal contact with Jesus Christ, you will never be moved again. That is the meaning of sanctification. God puts His disapproval on human experience when we begin to adhere to the conception that sanctification is merely an experience, and forget that sanctification itself has to be sanctified (see John 17:19). I have deliberately to give my sanctified life to God for His service, so that He can use me as His hands and His feet.

DECEMBER 4

THE LAW OF ANTAGONISM

To him that overcometh . . . Revelation 2:7

Life without war is impossible either in nature or in grace. The basis of physical, mental, moral, and spiritual life is antagonism. This is the open fact of life.

Health is the balance between physical life and external nature, and it is maintained only by sufficient vitality on the inside against things on the outside. Everything outside my physical life is designed to put me to death. Things which keep me going when I am alive, disintegrate me when I am dead. If I have enough fighting power, I produce the balance of health. The same is true of the mental life. If I want to maintain a vigorous mental life, I have to fight, and in that way the mental balance called thought is produced.

Morally it is the same. Everything that does not partake of the nature of virtue is the enemy of virtue in me, and it depends on what moral calibre I have whether I overcome and produce virtue. Immediately I fight, I am moral in that particular. No man is virtuous because he cannot help it; virtue is acquired.

And spiritually it is the same. Jesus said—"In the world ye shall have tribulation," i.e., everything that is not spiritual makes for my undoing, but—"be of good cheer, I have overcome the world." I have to learn to score off the things that come against me, and in that way produce the balance of holiness; then it becomes a delight to meet opposition.

Holiness is the balance between my disposition and the law of God as expressed in Jesus Christ.

DECEMBER 5

THE TEMPLE OF THE HOLY GHOST

Only in the throne will I be greater than thou. Genesis 41:40

I have to account to God for the way in which I rule my body under His domination. Paul said he did not "frustrate the grace of God"—make it of no effect. The grace of God is absolute, the salvation of Jesus is perfect, it is done for ever. I am not being saved, I am saved; salvation is as eternal as God's throne; the thing for me to do is to work out what God works in. "Work out your own salvation"; I am responsible for doing it. It means that I have to manifest in this body the life of the Lord Jesus, not mystically, but really and emphatically. "I keep under my body, and bring it into subjection." Every saint can have his body under absolute control for God. God has made us to have government over all the temple of the Holy Spirit, over imaginations and affections. We are responsible for these, and we must never give way to inordinate affections. Most of us are much sterner with others than we are in regard to ourselves; we make excuses for things in ourselves whilst we condemn in others things to which we are not naturally inclined.

"I beseech you," says Paul, "present your bodies a living sacrifice." The point to decide is this—"Do I agree with my Lord and Master that my body shall be His temple?" If so, then for me the whole of the law for the body is summed up in this revelation, that my body is the temple of the Holy Ghost.

DECEMBER 6

THE BOW IN THE CLOUD

I do set my bow in the cloud, and it shall be for a token of a covenant between Me and the earth. Genesis 9:13

It is the will of God that human beings should get into moral relationship with Him, and His covenants are for this purpose. "Why does not God save me?" He has saved me, but I have not entered into relationship with Him. "Why does not God do this and that?" He has done it, the point is—Will I step into covenant relationship? All the great blessings of God are finished and complete, but they are not mine until I enter into relationship with Him on the basis of His covenant.

Waiting for God is incarnate unbelief, it means that I have no faith in Him; I wait for Him to do something in me that I may trust in that. God will not do it, because that is not the basis of the God-and-man relationship. Man has to go out of himself in his covenant with God as God goes out of Himself in His covenant with man. It is a question of faith in God—the rarest thing; we have faith only in our feelings. I do not believe God unless He will give me something in my hand whereby I may know I have it, then I say—"Now I believe." There is no faith there. *"Look unto Me, and be ye saved."*

When I have really transacted business with God on His covenant and have let go entirely, there is no sense of merit, no human ingredient in it at all, but a complete overwhelming sense of being brought into union with God, and the whole thing is transfigured with peace and joy.

DECEMBER 7

REPENTANCE

For godly sorrow worketh repentance to salvation. 2 Corinthians 7:10

Conviction of sin is best portrayed in the words—

My sins, my sins, my Saviour.
How sad on Thee they fall.

Conviction of sin is one of the rarest things that ever strikes a man. It is the threshold of an understanding of God. Jesus Christ said that when the Holy Spirit came He would convict of sin, and when the Holy Spirit rouses a man's conscience and brings him into the presence of God, it is not his relationship with men that bothers him, but his relationship with God—"against Thee, Thee only, have I sinned, and done this evil in Thy sight." Conviction of sin, the marvel of forgiveness, and holiness are so interwoven that it is only the forgiven man who is the holy man, he proves he is forgiven by being the opposite to what he was, by God's grace. Repentance always brings a man to this point: "I have sinned." The surest sign that God is at work is when a man says that and means it. Anything less than this is remorse for having made blunders, the reflex action of disgust at himself.

The entrance into the Kingdom is through the panging pains of repentance crashing into a man's respectable goodness; then the Holy Ghost, Who produces these agonies, begins the formation of the Son of God in the life. The new life will manifest itself in conscious repentance and unconscious holiness, never the other way about. The bedrock of Christianity is repentance. Strictly speaking, a man cannot repent when he chooses; repentance is a gift of God. The old Puritans used to pray for "the gift of tears." If ever you cease to know the virtue of repentance, you are in darkness. Examine yourself and see if you have forgotten how to be sorry.

DECEMBER 8

THE IMPARTIAL POWER OF GOD

For by one offering He hath perfected for ever them that are sanctified. Hebrews 10:14

We trample the blood of the Son of God under foot if we think we are forgiven because we are sorry for our sins. The only explanation of the forgiveness of God and of the unfathomable depth of His forgetting, is the Death of Jesus Christ. Our repentance is merely the outcome of our personal realisation of the Atonement which He has worked out for us. "Christ Jesus. . . is made unto us wisdom, and righteousness, and sanctification, and redemption." When we realise that Christ is made all this to us, the boundless joy of God begins; wherever the joy of God is not present, the death sentence is at work.

It does not matter who or what we are, there is absolute reinstatement into God by the death of Jesus Christ and by no other way, not because Jesus Christ pleads, but because He died. It is not earned, but accepted. All the pleading which deliberately refuses to recognise the Cross is of no avail; it is battering at another door than the one which Jesus has opened. "I don't want to come that way, it is too humiliating to be received as a sinner." "There is none other Name . . . ." The apparent heartlessness of God is the expression of His real heart, there is boundless entrance in His way. "We have forgiveness through His blood."

Identification with the death of Jesus Christ means identification with Him to the death of everything that never was in Him.

God is justified in saving bad men only as He makes them good. Our Lord does not pretend we are all right when we are all wrong. The Atonement is a propitiation whereby God through the death of Jesus makes an unholy man holy.

DECEMBER 9

THE OFFENCE OF THE NATURAL

And they that are Christ's have crucified the flesh with the affections and lusts. Galatians 5:24

The natural life is not sinful; we must be apostatised from sin, have nothing to do with sin in any shape or form. Sin belongs to hell and the devil; I, as a child of God, belong to heaven and God. It is not a question of giving up sin, but of giving up my right to myself, my natural independence and self-assertiveness, and this is where the battle has to be fought. It is the things that are right and noble and good from the natural standpoint that keep us back from God's best. To discern that natural virtues antagonise surrender to God, is to bring our soul into the centre of its greatest battle. Very few of us debate with the sordid and evil and wrong, but we do debate with the good. It is the good that hates the best, and the higher up you get in the scale of the natural virtues, the more intense is the opposition to Jesus Christ. "They that are Christ's have crucified the flesh"—it is going to cost the natural in you everything, not something. Jesus said—If any man will be My disciple, "let him deny *himself,*" i.e., his right to himself, and a man has to realise Who Jesus Christ is before he will do it. Beware of refusing to go to the funeral of your own independence.

The natural life is not spiritual, and it can only be made spiritual by sacrifice. If we do not resolutely sacrifice the natural, the supernatural can never become natural in us. There is no royal road there; each of us has it entirely in his own hands. It is not a question of praying, but of performing.

DECEMBER 10

THE OFFERING OF THE NATURAL

Abraham had two sons, the one by a bondmaid, the other by a freewoman. Galatians 4:22

Paul is not dealing with sin in this chapter of Galatians, but with the relation of the natural to the spiritual. The natural must be turned into the spiritual by sacrifice, otherwise a tremendous divorce will be produced in the actual life. Why should God ordain the natural to be sacrificed? God did not. It is not God's order, but His permissive will. God's order was that the natural should be transformed into the spiritual by obedience; it is sin that made it necessary for the natural to be sacrificed.

Abraham had to offer up Ishmael before he offered up Isaac. Some of us are trying to offer up spiritual sacrifices to God before we have sacrificed the natural. The only way in which we can offer a spiritual sacrifice to God is by presenting our bodies a living sacrifice. Sanctification means more than deliverance from sin, it means the deliberate commitment of myself whom God has saved, to God, and I do not care what it costs.

If we do not sacrifice the natural to the spiritual, the natural life will mock at the life of the Son of God in us and produce a continual swither. This is always the result of an undisciplined spiritual nature. We go wrong because we stubbornly refuse to discipline ourselves, physically, morally or mentally. "I wasn't disciplined when I was a child." You must discipline yourself now. If you do not, you will ruin the whole of your personal life for God.

God is not with our natural life while we pamper it; but when we put it out in the desert and resolutely keep it under, then God will be with it; and He will open up wells and oases, and fulfil all His promises for the natural.

DECEMBER 11

INDIVIDUALITY

If any man will come after Me, let him deny himself. Matthew 16:24

Individuality is the husk of the personal life. Individuality is all elbows, it separates and isolates. It is the characteristic of the child and rightly so; but if we mistake individuality for the personal life, we shall remain isolated. The shell of individuality is God's created natural covering for the protection of the personal life; but individuality must go in order that the personal life may come out and be brought into fellowship with God. Individuality counterfeits personality as lust counterfeits love. God designed human nature for Himself; individuality debases human nature for itself.

The characteristics of individuality are independence and self-assertiveness. It is the continual assertion of individuality that hinders our spiritual life more than anything else. If you say—"I cannot believe," it is because individuality never can believe. Personality cannot help believing. Watch yourself when the Spirit of God is at work. He pushes you to the margins of your individuality, and you have either to say—"I shan't," or to surrender, to break the husk of individuality and let the personal life emerge. The Holy Spirit narrows it down every time to one thing (cf. Matthew 5:23–24). The thing in you that will not be reconciled to your brother is your individuality. God wants to bring you into union with Himself, but unless you are willing to give up your right to yourself, He cannot. "Let him deny himself"—deny his independent right to himself, then the real life has a chance to grow.

DECEMBER 12

PERSONALITY

That they may be one, even as We are one. John 17:22

Personality is that peculiar, incalculable thing that is meant when we speak of ourselves as distinct from everyone else. Our personality is always too big for us to grasp. An island in the sea may be but the top of a great mountain. Personality is like an island; we know nothing about the great depths underneath, consequently we cannot estimate ourselves. We begin by thinking that we can, but we come to realise that there is only one Being Who understands us, and that is our Creator.

Personality is the characteristic of the spiritual man as individuality is the characteristic of the natural man. Our Lord can never be defined in terms of individuality and independence, but only in terms of personality, "I and My Father are one." Personality merges, and you only reach your real identity when you are merged with another person. When love, or the Spirit of God, strikes a man, he is transformed, he no longer insists upon his separate individuality. Our Lord never spoke in terms of individuality, of a man's "elbows" or his isolated position, but in terms of personality—"that they may be one, even as We are one." If you give up your right to yourself to God, the real true nature of your personality answers to God straight away. Jesus Christ emancipates the personality, and the individuality is transfigured; the transfiguring element is love, personal devotion to Jesus. Love is the out-pouring of one personality in fellowship with another personality.

DECEMBER 13

WHAT TO PRAY FOR

Men ought always to pray, and not to faint. Luke 18:1

You cannot intercede if you do not believe in the reality of the Redemption; you will turn intercession into futile sympathy with human beings which will only increase their submissive content to being out of touch with God. In intercession you bring the person, or the circumstance that impinges on you, before God until you are moved by His attitude towards that person or circumstance. Intercession means filling up "that which is behind of the afflictions of Christ," and that is why there are so few intercessors. Intercession is put on the line of—"Put yourself in his place." Never! Try to put yourself in God's place.

As a worker, be careful to keep pace with the communications of reality from God or you will be crushed. If you know too much, more than God has engineered for you to know, you cannot pray, the condition of the people is so crushing that you cannot get through to reality.

Our work lies in coming into definite contact with God about everything, and we shirk it by becoming active workers. We do the things that can be tabulated, but we will not intercede. Intercession is the one thing that has no snares, because it keeps our relationship with God completely open.

The thing to watch in intercession is that no soul is patched up, a soul must get through into contact with the life of God. Think of the number of souls God has brought about our path and we have dropped them! When we pray on the ground of Redemption, God creates something He can create in no other way than through intercessory prayer.

DECEMBER 14

THE GREAT LIFE

Peace I leave with you, My peace I give unto you. . . . John 14:27

Let not your heart be troubled. John 14:1

Whenever a thing becomes difficult in personal experience, we are in danger of blaming God, but it is we who are in the wrong, not God, there is some perversity somewhere that we will not let go. Immediately we do, everything becomes as clear as daylight. As long as we try to serve two ends, ourselves and God, there is perplexity. The attitude must be one of complete reliance on God. When once we get there, there is nothing easier than living the saintly life; difficulty comes in when we want to usurp the authority of the Holy Spirit for our own ends.

Whenever you obey God, His seal is always that of peace, the witness of an unfathomable peace, which is not natural, but the peace of Jesus. Whenever peace does not come, tarry till it does or find out the reason why it does not. If you are acting on an impulse, or from a sense of the heroic, the peace of Jesus will not witness; there is no simplicity or confidence in God, because the spirit of simplicity is born of the Holy Ghost, not of your decisions. Every decision brings a reaction of simplicity.

My questions come whenever I cease to obey. When I have obeyed God, the problems never come between me and God, they come as probes to keep the mind awake and amazed at the revelation of God. Any problem that comes between God and myself springs out of disobedience; any problem, and there are many, that is alongside me while I obey God, increases my ecstatic delight, because I know that my Father knows, and I am going to watch and see how He unravels this thing.

DECEMBER 15

APPROVED UNTO GOD

Study to shew thyself approved unto God, a workman that needeth not to be ashamed, rightly dividing the word of truth. 2 Timothy 2:15

If you cannot express yourself on any subject, struggle until you can. If you do not, someone will be the poorer all the days of his life. Struggle to re-express some truth of God to yourself, and God will use that expression to someone else. Go through the winepress of God where the grapes are crushed. You must struggle to get expression experimentally, then there will come a time when that expression will become the very wine of strengthening to someone else; but if you say lazily—"I am not going to struggle to express this thing for myself, I will borrow what I say," the expression will not only be of no use to you, but of no use to anyone. Try to re-state to yourself what you implicitly feel to be God's truth, and you give God a chance to pass it on to someone else through you.

Always make a practice of provoking your own mind to think out what it accepts easily. Our position is not ours until we make it ours by suffering. The author who benefits you is not the one who tells you something you did not know before, but the one who gives expression to the truth that has been struggling for utterance in you.

DECEMBER 16

WRESTLING BEFORE GOD

Wherefore take unto you the whole armour of God. . . . praying always . . . Ephesians 6:13, 18

You have to wrestle *against* the things that prevent you from getting to God, and you wrestle in prayer for other souls; but never say that you *wrestle with God* in prayer, it is scripturally untrue. If you do wrestle with God, you will be crippled all the rest of your life. If, when God comes in some way you do not want, you take hold of Him as Jacob did and wrestle with Him, you compel Him to put you out of joint. Don't be a hirpler[27] in God's ways, but be one who wrestles before God with things, becoming more than conqueror through Him. Wrestling before God tells in His Kingdom. If you ask me to pray for you and I am not complete in Christ, I may pray but it avails nothing; but if I am complete in Christ, my prayer prevails all the time. Prayer is only effective when there is completeness—"Wherefore take unto you the whole armour of God."

Always distinguish between God's order and His permissive will, i.e., His providential purpose towards us. God's order is unchangeable; His permissive will is that with which we must wrestle before Him. It is our reaction to the passive will of God that enables us to get at His order. "All things work together for good to them that love God"—to those who remain true to God's order, to His calling in Christ Jesus. God's permissive will is the means whereby His sons and daughters are to be manifested. We are not to be like jelly-fish saying—"It's the Lord's will." We have not to put up a fight before God, not to wrestle with God, but to wrestle before God *with things*. Beware of squatting lazily before God instead of putting up a glorious fight so that you may lay hold of His strength.

DECEMBER 17

REDEMPTION CREATES THE NEED IT SATISFIES

But the natural man receiveth not the things of the Spirit of God: for they are foolishness unto him. 1 Corinthians 2:14

The Gospel of God creates a sense of need of the Gospel. Paul says—"If our gospel be hid, it is hid"—to those who are blackguards? No, "to them that are lost: in whom the god of this world hath blinded the minds of them which believe not." The majority of people have their morality well within their own grasp, they have no sense of need of the gospel. It is God Who creates the need of which no human being is conscious until He manifests Himself. Jesus said—"Ask, and it shall be given you," but God cannot give until a man asks. It is not that He withholds, but that that is the way He has constituted things on the basis of Redemption. By means of our asking, God gets processes into work whereby He creates the thing that is not in existence until we do ask. The inner reality of Redemption is that it creates all the time. As the Redemption creates the life of God in us, so it creates the things belonging to that life. Nothing can satisfy the need but that which created the need. This is the meaning of Redemption—it creates and it satisfies.

"I, if I be lifted up from the earth, will draw all men unto Me." We preach our own experiences and people are interested, but no sense of need is awakened. If Jesus Christ is lifted up, the Spirit of God will create a conscious need of Him. Behind the preaching of the Gospel is the creative Redemption of God at work in the souls of men. It is never personal testimony that saves men. "The words that *I* speak unto you, they are spirit, and they are life."

DECEMBER 18

THE TEST OF LOYALTY

And we know that all things work together for good to them that love God. Romans 8:28

It is only the loyal soul who believes that God engineers circumstances. We take such liberties with our circumstances, we do not believe God engineers them, although we say we do; we treat the things that happen as if they were engineered by men. To be faithful in every circumstance means that we have only one loyalty, and that is to our Lord. Suddenly God breaks up a particular set of circumstances, and the realisation comes that we have been disloyal to Him by not recognising that He had organised them. We never saw what He was after, and that particular thing will never be repeated all the days of our life. The test of loyalty always comes just there. If we learn to worship God in the trying circumstances, He will alter them in two seconds when He chooses.

Loyalty to Jesus Christ is the thing that we "stick at" to-day. We will be loyal to work, to service, to anything, but do not ask us to be loyal to Jesus Christ. Many Christians are intensely impatient of talking about loyalty to Jesus. Our Lord is dethroned more

---

27. hirpler: one who walks with a limp or hobble.

emphatically by Christian workers than by the world. God is made a machine for blessing men, and Jesus Christ is made a Worker among workers.

The idea is not that we do work for God, but that we are so loyal to Him that He can do His work through us—"I reckon on you for extreme service, with no complaining on your part and no explanation on Mine." God wants to use us as He used His own Son.

DECEMBER 19

WHAT TO CONCENTRATE ON

I came not to send peace, but a sword. Matthew 10:34

Never be sympathetic with the soul whose case makes you come to the conclusion that God is hard. God is more tender than we can conceive, and every now and again He gives us the chance of being the rugged one that He may be the tender One. If a man cannot get through to God it is because there is a secret thing he does not intend to give up—"I will admit I have done wrong, but I no more intend to give up that thing than fly." It is impossible to deal sympathetically with a case like that: we have to get right deep down to the root until there is antagonism and resentment against the message. People want the blessing of God, but they will not stand the thing that goes straight to the quick.

If God has had His way with you, your message as His servant is merciless insistence on the one line, cut down to the very root, otherwise there will be no healing. Drive home the message until there is no possible refuge from its application. Begin to get at people where they are until you get them to realise what they lack, and then erect the standard of Jesus Christ for their lives—"We never can be that!" Then drive it home: "Jesus Christ says you must." "But how can we be?" "You cannot, unless you have a new Spirit" (see Luke 11:13).

There must be a sense of need before your message is of any use. Thousands of people are happy without God in this world. If I was happy and moral till Jesus came, why did He come? Because that kind of happiness and peace is on a wrong level; Jesus Christ came to send a sword through every peace that is not based on a personal relationship to Himself.

DECEMBER 20

THE RIGHT LINES OF WORK

I, if I be lifted up, . . . will draw all men unto Me. John 12:32

Very few of us have any understanding of the reason why Jesus Christ died. If sympathy is all that human beings need, then the Cross of Christ is a farce, there was no need for it. What the world needs is not "a little bit of love," but a surgical operation.

When you are face to face with a soul in difficulty spiritually, remind yourself of Jesus Christ on the Cross. If that soul can get to God on any other line, then the Cross of Jesus Christ is unnecessary. If you can help others by your sympathy or understanding, you are a traitor to Jesus Christ. You have to keep your soul rightly related to God and pour out for others on His line, not pour out on the human line and ignore God. The great note to-day is amiable religiosity.

The one thing we have to do is to exhibit Jesus Christ crucified, to lift Him up all the time. Every doctrine that is not imbedded in the Cross of Jesus will lead astray. If the worker himself believes in Jesus Christ and is banking on the Reality of Redemption, the people he talks to *must* be concerned. The thing that remains and deepens is the worker's simple relationship to Jesus Christ; his usefulness to God depends on that and that alone.

The calling of a New Testament worker is to uncover sin and to reveal Jesus Christ as Saviour, consequently he cannot be poetical, he must be sternly surgical. We are sent by God to lift up Jesus Christ, not to give wonderfully beautiful discourses. We have to probe straight down as deeply as God has probed us, to be keen in sensing the Scriptures which bring the truth straight home and to apply them fearlessly.

DECEMBER 21

EXPERIENCE OR REVELATION

We have received . . . the spirit which is of God; that we might know the things that are freely given to us of God. 1 Corinthians 2:12

Reality is Redemption, not my experience of Redemption; but Redemption has no meaning for me until it speaks the language of my conscious life. When I am born again, the Spirit of God takes me right out of myself and my experiences, and identifies me with Jesus Christ. If I am left with my experiences, my experiences have not been produced by Redemption. The proof that they are produced by Redemption is that I am led out of myself all the time; I no longer pay any attention to my experiences as the ground of Reality, but only to the Reality which produced the experiences. My experiences are not worth anything unless they keep me at the Source, Jesus Christ.

If you try to dam up the Holy Spirit in you to produce subjective experiences, you will find that He will burst all bounds and take you back again to the historic Christ. Never nourish an experience which has not God as its Source, and faith in God as its result. If you do, your experience is anti-Christian, no matter what visions you may have had. Is Jesus Christ Lord of your experiences, or do you try to lord it over Him? Is any experience dearer to you than your Lord? He must be Lord over you, and you must not pay attention to any experience over which He is not Lord. There comes a time when God will make you impatient with your own experience—"I do not care what I experience; I am sure of Him."

Be ruthless with yourself if you are given to talking about the experiences you have had. Faith that is sure of itself is not faith; faith that is sure of God is the only faith there is.

DECEMBER 22

THE DRAWING OF THE FATHER

No man can come to Me, except the Father which hath sent Me draw him. John 6:44

When God draws me, the issue of my will comes in at once—will I react on the revelation which God gives; will I come to Him? Discussion on spiritual matters is an impertinence. Never discuss with anyone when God speaks. Belief is not an intellectual act; belief is a moral act whereby I deliberately commit myself. Will I dump myself down absolutely on God and transact on what He says? If I will, I shall find I am based on Reality that is as sure as God's throne.

In preaching the gospel, always push an issue of will. Belief must be the *will* to believe. There must be a surrender of the will, not a surrender to persuasive power; a deliberate launching forth on God and on what He says until I am no longer confident in what I have done, I am confident only in God. The hindrance is that I will not trust God, but only my mental understanding. As far as feelings go, I must stake all blindly: I must *will* to believe, and this can never be done without a violent effort on my part to dissociate myself from my old ways of looking at things, and by putting myself right over on to Him.

Every man is made to reach out beyond his grasp. It is God Who draws me, and my relationship with Him in the first place is a personal one, not an intellectual one. I am introduced into the relationship by the miracle of God and my own will to believe, then I begin to get an intelligent appreciation and understanding of the wonder of the transaction.

DECEMBER 23

HOW CAN I PERSONALLY PARTAKE IN THE ATONEMENT?

But God forbid that I should glory, save in the cross of our Lord Jesus Christ. Galatians 6:14

The Gospel of Jesus Christ always forces an issue of will. Do I accept God's verdict on sin in the Cross of Christ? Have I the slightest interest in the death of Jesus? Do I want to be identified with His death, to be killed right out to all interest in sin, in worldliness, in self—to be so identified with Jesus that I am spoilt for everything else but Him? The great privilege of discipleship is that I can sign on under His Cross, and that means death to sin. Get alone with Jesus and either tell Him that you do not want sin to die out in you; or else tell Him that at all costs you want to be identified with His death. Immediately you transact in confident faith in what Our Lord did on the Cross, a supernatural identification with His death takes place, and you will know with a knowledge that passeth knowledge that your "old man" is crucified with Christ. The proof that your "old man" has been crucified with Christ is in the amazing ease with which the life of God in you enables you to obey the voice of Jesus Christ.

Every now and again, Our Lord lets us see what we would be like if it were not for Himself; it is a justification of what He said—"Without Me ye can do nothing." That is why the bedrock of Christianity is personal, passionate devotion to the Lord Jesus. We mistake the ecstasy of our first introduction into the Kingdom for the purpose of God in getting us there; His purpose in getting us there is that we may realise all that identification with Jesus Christ means.

DECEMBER 24

THE HIDDEN LIFE

Your life is hid with Christ in God. Colossians 3:3

The Spirit of God witnesses to the simple, almighty security of the life hid with Christ in God, and this is continually brought out in the Epistles. We talk as if it were the most precarious thing to live the sanctified life; it is the most secure thing, because it has Almighty God in and behind it. The precarious thing is to try and live without God. If we are born again it is the easiest thing to live in right relationship to God and the most difficult thing to go wrong, if only we will heed God's warnings and keep in the light.

When we think of being delivered from sin, of being filled with the Spirit, and of walking in the light, we picture the peak of a great mountain, very high and wonderful, and we say—"Oh, but I could never live up there!" But when we do get there by God's grace, we find it is not a mountain peak, but a plateau where there is ample room to live and to grow. "Thou hast enlarged my steps under me."

When you really see Jesus, I defy you to doubt Him. When He says—"Let not your heart be troubled," if you see Him I defy you to trouble your mind, it is a moral impossibility to doubt when He is there. Every time you get into personal contact with Jesus, His words are real. "My peace I give unto you," it is a peace all over from the crown of the head to the sole of the feet, an irrepressible confidence. "Your life is hid with Christ in God," and the imperturbable peace of Jesus Christ is imparted to you.

DECEMBER 25

HIS BIRTH AND OUR NEW BIRTH

Behold, a virgin . . . shall bring forth a son, and they shall call His name Emmanuel, which being interpreted is, God with us. Matthew 1:23

His Birth in History. "Therefore also that holy thing which shall be born of thee shall be called the Son of God" (Luke 1:35). Jesus Christ was born *into* this world, not *from* it. He did not evolve out of history; He came into history from the outside. Jesus Christ is not the best human being, He is a Being Who cannot be accounted for by the human race at all. He is not man becoming God, but God Incarnate, God coming into human flesh, coming into it from outside. His life is the Highest and the Holiest, entering in at the lowliest door. Our Lord's birth was an advent.

His Birth in Me. "Of whom I travail in birth again until Christ be formed in you" (Galatians 4:19). Just as Our Lord came into human history from outside, so He must come into me from outside. Have I allowed my personal human life to become a "Bethlehem" for the Son of God? I cannot enter into the realm of the Kingdom of God unless I am born from above (RV mg) by a birth totally unlike natural birth. "Ye must be born again." This is not a command, it is a foundation fact. The characteristic of the new birth is that I yield myself so completely to God that Christ is formed in me. Immediately Christ is formed in me, His nature begins to work through me.

God manifest in the flesh—that is what is made profoundly possible for you and me by the Redemption.

DECEMBER 26

PLACED IN THE LIGHT

If we walk in the light, as He is in the light, . . . the blood of Jesus Christ His Son cleanseth us from all sin. 1 John 1:7

To mistake conscious freedom from sin for deliverance from sin by the Atonement is a great error. No man knows what sin is until he is born again. Sin is what Jesus Christ faced on Calvary. The evidence that I am delivered from sin is that I know the real nature of sin in me. It takes the last reach of the Atonement of Jesus Christ, that is, the impartation of His absolute perfection, to make a man know what sin is.

The Holy Spirit applies the Atonement to us in the unconscious realm as well as in the realm of which we are conscious, and it is only when we get a grasp of the unrivalled power of the Spirit in us that we understand the meaning of 1 John 1:7, *"the blood of Jesus Christ cleanseth us from all sin."* This does not refer to conscious sin only, but to the tremendously profound understanding of sin which only the Holy Ghost in me realises.

If I walk in the light as God is in the light, not in the light of my conscience, but in the light of God—if I walk there, with nothing folded up, then there comes the amazing revelation—the blood of Jesus Christ cleanses me from all sin so that God Almighty can see nothing to censure in me. In my consciousness it works with a keen poignant knowledge of what sin is. The love of God at work in me makes me hate with the hatred of the Holy Ghost all that is not in keeping with God's holiness. To walk in the light means that everything that is of the darkness drives me closer into the centre of the light.

DECEMBER 27

WHERE THE BATTLE'S LOST AND WON

If thou wilt return, O Israel, saith the LORD . . . Jeremiah 4:1

The battle is lost or won in the secret places of the will before God, never first in the external world. The Spirit of God apprehends me and I am obliged to get alone with God and fight the battle out before Him. Until this is done, I lose every time. The battle may take one minute or a year, that will depend on me, not on God; but it must be wrestled out alone before God, and I must resolutely go through the hell of a renunciation before Him. Nothing has any power over the man who has fought out the battle before God and won there. If I say—"I will wait till I get into the circumstances and then put God to the test," I shall find I cannot. I must get the thing settled between myself and God in the secret places of my soul where no stranger intermeddles, and then I can go forth with the certainty that the battle is won. Lose it there, and calamity and disaster and upset are as sure as God's decree. The reason the battle is not won is because I try to win it in the external world first. Get alone with God, fight it out before Him, settle the matter there once and for all.

In dealing with other people, the line to take is to push them to an issue of will. That is the way abandonment begins. Every now and again, not often, but sometimes, God brings us to a point of climax. That is the Great Divide in the life; from that point we either go towards a more and more dilatory and useless type of Christian life, or we become more and more ablaze for the glory of God—"My Utmost for His Highest."

DECEMBER 28

CONTINUOUS CONVERSION

Except ye be converted, and become as little children . . . Matthew 18:3

These words of Our Lord are true of our initial conversion, but we have to be continuously converted all the days of our lives, continually to turn to God as children. If we trust to our wits instead of to God, we produce consequences for which God will hold us responsible. Immediately our bodies are brought into new conditions by the providence of God, we have to see our natural life obeys the dictates of the Spirit of God. Because we have done it once is no proof that we shall do it again. The relation of the natural to the spiritual is one of continuous conversion, and it is the one thing we object to. In every setting in which we are put, the Spirit of God remains unchanged and His salvation unaltered but we have to "put on the new man." God holds us responsible every time we refuse to convert ourselves, our reason for refusing is wilful obstinacy. Our natural life must not rule, God must rule in us.

The hindrance in our spiritual life is that we will not be continually converted, there are "wadges" of obstinacy where our pride spits at the throne of God and says—"I won't." We deify independence and wilfulness and call them by the wrong name. What God looks on as obstinate weakness, we call strength. There are whole tracts of our lives which have not yet

been brought into subjection, and it can only be done by this continuous conversion. Slowly but surely we can claim the whole territory for the Spirit of God.

DECEMBER 29

DESERTER OR DISCIPLE?

From that time many of His disciples went back, and walked no more with Him. John 6:66

When God gives a vision by His Spirit through His word of what He wants, and your mind and soul thrill to it, if you do not walk in the light of that vision, you will sink into servitude to a point of view which Our Lord never had. Disobedience in mind to the heavenly vision will make you a slave to points of view that are alien to Jesus Christ. Do not look at someone else and say—"Well, if he can have those views and prosper, why cannot I?" You have to walk in the light of the vision that has been given to you and not compare yourself with others or judge them, that is between them and God. When you find that a point of view in which you have been delighting clashes with the heavenly vision and you debate, certain things will begin to develop in you—a sense of property and a sense of personal right, things of which Jesus Christ made nothing. He was always against these things as being the root of everything alien to Himself. "A man's life consisteth not in the abundance of the things which he possesseth." If we do not recognise this, it is because we are ignoring the undercurrent of Our Lord's teaching.

We are apt to lie back and bask in the memory of the wonderful experience we have had. If there is one standard in the New Testament revealed by the light of God and you do not come up to it, and do not feel inclined to come up to it, that is the beginning of backsliding, because it means your conscience does not answer to the truth. You can never be the same after the unveiling of a truth. That moment marks you for going on as a more true disciple of Jesus Christ, or for going back as a deserter.

DECEMBER 30

"AND EVERY VIRTUE WE POSSESS"

All my fresh springs shall be in Thee. Psalm 87:7 (PBV)[28]

---

28. PBV: Prayer Book Version. The Book of Common Prayer of the Church of England includes a translation of the Psalter, or Psalms of David.

Our Lord never patches up our natural virtues, He remakes the whole man on the inside. "Put on the new man"—see that your natural human life puts on the garb that is in keeping with the new life. The life God plants in us develops its own virtues, not the virtues of Adam but of Jesus Christ. Watch how God will wither up your confidence in natural virtues after sanctification, and in any power you have, until you learn to draw your life from the reservoir of the resurrection life of Jesus. Thank God if you are going through a drying-up experience!

The sign that God is at work in us is that He corrupts confidence in the natural virtues, because they are not promises of what we are going to be, but remnants of what God created man to be. We will cling to the natural virtues, while all the time God is trying to get us into contact with the life of Jesus Christ which can never be described in terms of the natural virtues. It is the saddest thing to see people in the service of God depending on that which the grace of God never gave them, depending on what they have by the accident of heredity. God does not build up our natural virtues and transfigure them, because our natural virtues can never come anywhere near what Jesus Christ wants. No natural love, no natural patience, no natural purity can ever come up to His demands. But as we bring every bit of our bodily life into harmony with the new life which God has put in us, He will exhibit in us the virtues that are characteristic of the Lord Jesus.

And every virtue we possess
Is His alone.

YESTERDAY

The God of Israel will be your rereward. Isaiah 52:12 (RV)

Security from Yesterday. "God requireth that which is past." At the end of the year we turn with eagerness to all that God has for the future, and yet anxiety is apt to arise from remembering the yesterdays. Our present enjoyment of God's grace is apt to be checked by the memory of yesterday's sins and blunders. But God is the God of our yesterdays, and He allows the memory of them in order to turn the past into a ministry of spiritual culture for the future. God reminds us of the past lest we get into a shallow security in the present.

Security for To-morrow. "For the LORD will go before you." This is a gracious revelation, that God will garrison where we have failed to. He will watch lest things trip us up again into like failure, as they assuredly would do if He were not our rereward. God's hand reaches back to the past and makes a clearing-house for conscience.

Security for To-day. "For ye shall not go out with haste." As we go forth into the coming year, let it not be in the haste of impetuous, unremembering delight, nor with the flight of impulsive thoughtlessness, but with the patient power of knowing that the God of Israel will go before us. Our yesterdays present irreparable things to us; it is true that we have lost opportunities which will never return but God can transform this destructive anxiety into a constructive thoughtfulness for the future. Let the past sleep, but let it sleep on the bosom of Christ.

Leave the Irreparable Past in His hands, and step out into the Irresistible Future with Him.

Not Knowing Whither

The Steps of Abraham's Faith

A Series of Studies in the Life of Abraham
Oswald Chambers

> *Father, the narrow path*
> *To that far country show;*
> *And in the steps of Abraham's faith*
> *Enable me to go.*
> *A cheerful sojourner*
> *Where'er Thou bidst me roam,*
> *Till, guided by Thy Spirit here.*
> *I reach my heavenly home.*

INTRODUCTION

Source

The material in *Not Knowing Whither* is taken from lectures in Old Testament studies class at the Bible Training College,[1] London, January through April 1915, covering Genesis 12:1 through 25:10.

Publication History

*   As articles: The lectures were first published as articles in the *BTC Monthly Journal*[2] between April 1932 and July 1933.
*   As a book: *Not Knowing Whither* was published in 1934.

This is one of one only five Oswald Chambers books that expounds a section of scripture rather than developing a theme. The others are *Our Portrait in Gene-* *sis*, on Genesis 1 through 9 and 26 through 50; *Baffled to Fight Better*, on Job; *Shade of His Hand*, on Ecclesiastes; and *Studies in the Sermon on the Mount*, on Matthew 5 through 7.

During the months Oswald Chambers gave these lectures on the life of Abraham, he was struggling to find God's leading for the next step in his own life. Should he remain at the Bible Training College, or should he volunteer for military service in the British forces then fighting World War I? By the time he concluded this series, he had offered to serve as a chaplain and within a few weeks was selected for duty with the YMCA in Egypt. On October 28, 1915, he began his work with the troops at Zeitoun,[3] just outside Cairo.

---

1. Bible Training College (BTC): a residential school near Clapham Common in southwest London. Sponsored by the League of Prayer; operated from 1911 until it closed in July 1915 because of World War I. Oswald Chambers was principal and main teacher; Biddy Chambers, his wife, was lady superintendent.

2. *Bible Training Course Monthly Journal:* published from 1932 to 1952 by Mrs. Chambers, with help from David Lambert.

3. Zeitoun (zay TOON), Egypt: six miles northeast of Cairo; site of a YMCA camp, the Egypt General Mission compound, and, from 1916 to 1919, the Imperial School of Instruction, training base for British, Australian, and New Zealand troops during World War I.

Throughout these talks, Chambers quotes from many writers and poets, particularly from his favorite, Robert Browning.

Lectures on some of the earlier and later chapters in Genesis were published in 1957 as *Our Portrait in Genesis,* which is also included in this volume. *Gems from Genesis* (1989) combined *Not Knowing Whither* and *Our Portrait in Genesis* into one volume, with a chapter on the Tower of Babel added by Arthur Neil, long-time OC scholar and editor of the Oswald Chambers Publications Association.

For this collection, we have presented *Not Knowing Whither* and *Our Portrait in Genesis* separately, in the form in which they were originally published.

To Our Mother[4] whose interest in sending forth of my husband's messages has been an unfailing source of inspiration.

B. C.[5]

CONTENTS

---

4. Our Mother: Emily Amelia Hobbs (1850-1934), mother of Biddy Chambers and her sister, Edith Hobbs. Mrs. Hobbs died shortly before this book was published; Edith was a long-time council member of the Oswald Chambers Publications Association.

5. B. C.: Biddy Chambers; although Mrs. Chambers was editor, compiler, and often publisher, she never identified herself by name in any of the books.

PREFACE (TO THE FIRST EDITION)

These studies, from the lips of the late Oswald Chambers, are as wonderful as anything published by him hitherto. They concern the life of the great pioneer of the life of faith in which we see faith's reactions to God's call, to clashing circumstances, to the claims of companions, and to the terrific cost of God's Friendship. Herein we see linked up, in a wonderful way, the experience of grace under the New Covenant with the eternal purpose of God made plain under the Old Covenant. Abraham is studied as a forerunner of modern saints in their faith-walk.

The book is replete with spiritual wisdom. The very chapter titles betray that touch of genius, as men call it, which sparkles in the pages.

If great books are the life-blood of the world's master spirits, then such a book as this is the lifeblood of one who by grace was brought to the fulness of the stature of Christ . The studies first appeared in the *B.T.C. Journal*. In book form they will make possible a term of guided reading on this outstanding example of the walk of faith in this world of men.

David Lambert[6]

CROSSING THE BAR
Genesis 12:1–3

Sunset and evening star,
    And one clear call for me!
And may there be no moaning of the bar
    When I put out to sea.

But such a tide as moving seems asleep,
    Too full for sound and foam,
When that which drew from out the boundless deep
    Turns again home.

Twilight and evening bell,
    And after that the dark!
And may there be no sadness of farewell,
    When I embark;

For tho' from out our bourne of Time and Place
    The flood may bear me far,
I hope to see my Pilot face to face
    When I have crost the bar.

Tennyson

Now the Lord had said unto Abram, Get thee out. . . .
Genesis 12:1

"Crossing the Bar" is indicative of what happens whenever we act in faith in God. Whatever the faith is in connection with, we have to launch right out on God. To debate with God and trust common sense is moral blasphemy against God. The call of God embarrasses us because of two things—it presents us with sealed orders, and urges us to a vast venture. When God calls us He does not tell us along the line of our natural senses what to expect; God's call is a command that *asks* us, that means there is always a possibility of refusal on our part. Faith never knows where it is being led, it knows and loves the One Who is leading. It is a life of *faith*, not of intelligence and reason, but a life of knowing Who is making me "go."

The personal private life of faith of each one of us has its source and explanation in the life of the Father of the Faithful, Abraham. Abraham's call, with his limitations as well as his obedience, is full of minute instruction with regard to the life of faith.

1. The Call of God
The call of God can never be stated explicitly, it is implicit. The call of God is like the call of the sea, or of the mountains; no one hears these calls but the one who has the nature of the sea or of the mountains; and no one hears the call of God who has not the nature of God in him. It cannot be definitely stated what the call of God is to, because it is a call into comradeship with God Himself for His own purposes, and the test of faith is to believe that God knows what He is after. The call of God only becomes clear as we obey, never as we weigh the *pros* and *cons*

---

6. David Lambert (1871–1961): Methodist minister; friend of Oswald and Biddy Chambers. Assisted Mrs. Chambers with OC publications from 1917 until his death in 1961.

and try to reason it out. The call is God's idea, not our idea, and only on looking back over the path of obedience do we realise what is the idea of God; God sanctifies memory. When we hear the call of God it is not for us to dispute with God, and arrange to obey Him if He will expound the meaning of His call to us. As long as we insist on having the call expounded to us, we will never obey; but when we obey it is expounded, and in looking back there comes a chuckle of confidence—"He doeth all things well." Before us there is nothing, but overhead there is God, and we have to trust Him. If we insist on explanations before we obey, we lie like clogs on God's plan and put ourselves clean athwart His purpose.

To do our best is one part, but to wash our hands smilingly of the consequences is the next part of any sensible virtue.

Robert Louis Stevenson

When Jesus Christ says "Follow Me," He never says to where, the consequences must be left entirely to Him. We come in with our "buts," and "supposings," and "what will happen if I do?" (cf. Luke 9:57–62). We have nothing to do with what will happen if we obey, we have to abandon to God's call in unconditional surrender and smilingly wash our hands of the consequences. Until we get through all the shivering wisdom that will not venture out on God, we will never know all that is involved in the life of faith. Fate means stoical resignation to an unknown force. Faith is not resignation to a power we do not know; faith is committal to One Whose character we do know because it has been revealed to us in Jesus Christ. As we live in contact with God, His order comes to us in the haphazard, and we recognise that every detail of our lives is engineered for us by our Heavenly Father. If we are going to live a life of faith, we must rest nowhere until we see God and know Him in spite of all apparent contradictions.

I have to take care not to settle on the sandbank of selfishness, but to leave all for the Lord to order it. If I then make shipwreck, it will be in the wide sea of God's love, the depths of which are as welcome to me as the surest haven. But nature fights against the thought of venturing forth we know not where, out of self, into unknown regions.

Tersteegen[7]

2. The Calling of Abraham
Now the Lord had said unto Abram, Get thee out . . .

". . . and he went out, not knowing whither he went." This is true of a fool or of a faithful soul. One of the hardest lessons to learn is the one brought out by Abraham's obedience to the call of God. He went "out" of all his own ways of looking at things and became a fool in the eyes of the world. In the beginning faith is always uncertain, because every broad view is at first an uncertain view of particulars. We hear the call of God while we listen to a sermon, or during a time of prayer, and we say—"Yes, I will give myself to God unreservedly." Then something happens in our immediate circumstances which does not seem to fit into the vision we have had, and the danger is that we compromise and say we must have been mistaken in the vision. We have to stand true to the fact of God's call and smilingly wash our hands of the consequences. We have nothing to do with the afterwards of obedience. It is easy to want to be always on the mount, but when we come down to the devil-possessed valley we get annoyed or exhausted, we cannot go on with God there. We have perfect faith in God as long as He keeps us on the mount, but not the slightest atom of faith when He takes us into the valley. We have to be careful that the things which are really impertinent actualities do not find us either ignoring them or abandoning our faith in God. We have to go through the trial of our faith in these particulars, because it is the trial of our faith that makes us wealthy towards God.

"And from thy kindred . . ." Personal acquaintance with God shows itself in separation, symbolised by Abraham's physical separation from his country and his kindred. Nowadays it means much more a moral separation from the way those nearest and dearest to us think and look at things, if, that is, they have not a personal relationship with God. Jesus emphasised this (see Luke 14:26). Arguers against obeying the call of God will arise in the shape of country and kindred, and if you listen to them you will soon dull your ears to God's call and become the dullest, most commonplace Christian imaginable, because you have no courage in your faith; you have seen and heard, but have not gone on. If you accept sympathy from those who have not heard the call of God, it will so blunt your own sense of His call that you become useless to Him. Every saint must stand out absolutely alone. Beware lest the sympathy of others competes with God for the throne of your life. Don't look for a comrade other than God when God speaks to you; through *you* will come His purpose.

---

7. Gerhard Tersteegen (1697–1769): Prussian-born spiritual teacher and hymn writer.

ON WITH GOD
Genesis 12:4–9

Not of the sunlight,
Not of the moonlight,
Not of the starlight!
O young Mariner,
Down to the haven,
Call your companions,
Launch your vessel,
And crowd your canvas,
And, ere it vanishes
Over the margin,
After it, follow it,
Follow The Gleam.

                        Tennyson

So Abram departed. Genesis 12:4

It is not sin or disobedience only that keeps us from obeying the call of God, but the good, right, natural things that make us hesitate. The natural can only be transformed into the spiritual by obedience, and the beginnings of God's life in a man or woman cut directly across the will of nature. The sword has to go through the natural (cf. Luke 2:35). The call of God comes with a realisation that what God says is true, but that does not prevent us from going through the trial of our faith in connection with actual details, and it is when we touch actual details that we begin to dispute with God and say—"But if I obeyed God here my sense of justice and right would be injured." To talk in that way means we do not believe God one atom, although we say we do. The knowledge of God's will is not in the nature of a mathematical problem; as we obey, we make out what is His will, it becomes as clear as daylight. We have to be continually renewed in the spirit of our minds, refusing to be conformed to the spirit of the age in which we live, then we shall "prove"—literally, make out in obedience—"what is that good, and acceptable, and perfect will of God." We have to beware of giving credit to man's wisdom for the way he has taken, when all the time it is the perfect wisdom of God that is manifested through the simple obedience of the man. It is never the acute ability of the saint that is exhibited, but the astute wisdom of God.

1. The Concession of Abraham's Faith
(Genesis 12:4)
We must remember that faith in God always demands a concession from us personally. "So Abram departed," that is, he went on with God as God had commanded him, "not knowing whither he went." Watch the debates

that go on in our minds when God speaks, whether it is in a big or a little matter, we won't launch out on God's word, we will hug the shore line. "But it is so unwise to trust God in this matter"—that implies that God has no wisdom at all. If we are going to obey God there must be a concession made on our part; we have deliberately to trust the character of God as it has been revealed to us in the face of all obstacles. "If God would only come down and explain everything to me, I would have faith in Him," we say; and yet how little trust we are inclined to have in God, even when we have had an experience of His grace and a revelation of Himself. We sink back to the experience instead of being confident in the God Who gave us the experience. Experience is never the ground of our trust, it is the gateway to the One Whom we trust. The work of faith is not an explanation to our minds, but a determination on our part to obey God and to make a concession of our faith in His character; immediately we do what God says, we discern what He means. Naturally, man is made to have dominion, therefore he insists on explanations, because everything we can explain we can command. In the spiritual domain nothing is explained until we obey, and then it is not so much an explanation as an instant discernment. "If any man *will do* . . . he shall *know*. . . ." If we say "I want to know why I should do this," it means we have no faith in God, but only sordid confidence in our own wits. "If God would only give me supernatural touches, I would trust Him." No, we would idolise ourselves. "I do not mind being a saint if I can remain natural and be a saint entirely on my own initiative. If I can instruct God about my upbringing and my particular temperament and affinities, and construct my own scenery, then I would like to be a saint." All along it is the hesitation of the natural refusing to be transformed into the spiritual. In Abraham there was no hesitation, although there were misinterpretations. In the life of Our Lord there was no hesitation and no misinterpretations; He combined the great vision of faith with the actual details. The Apostle Paul always applies the great eternal truths to actual details, because that is where faith has to work. The characteristic of Abraham's faith was that he did not select his affinities, he made a concession of his faith to God, and "went out, not knowing whither he went."

2. The Companions of Abraham's Faith
(Genesis 12:5)
If God has given you a personal revelation of Himself and you have made a distinct concession on your part of

faith in His character, you will make a great blunder if you look to see whether others see the same thing. God will undertake to instruct them if you remain faithful to the immediate connections in which He has put you. To live a life alone with God does not mean that we live it apart from everyone else. The connection between godly men and women and those associated with them is continually revealed in the Bible, e.g., 1 Timothy 4:10. If you are going on with God, says Paul, your attitude is to "labour and suffer reproach" from those who because of apparently accidental relationships go with you, so that by your labour you may bring them to be among the conscious believers. There is a difference between conscious and unconscious salvation. To be consciously saved means that we become of immense practical value to God in this order of things.

3. The Consecration of Abraham's Faith
(Genesis 12:6–9)
Notice the significance of v. 8—"there he builded an altar unto the LORD." Worship is the tryst of sacramental identification with God, that is, I deliberately give back to God the best He has given me that I may be identified with Him in it. Whenever Abraham neglected to build an altar after God had made a promise to him, he fell into sin. Every act of worship to be effective must be a public testimony to those who in God's providence are with us for worship; it is at once the most public and the most personally sacred act that God demands of His faithful ones. Whenever God has given you a blessing, take time to meditate beside the blessing and offer it back to God in a deliberate ecstasy of worship. God will never allow you to hold a spiritual blessing for yourself, it has to be given back to Him that He may make it a blessing to others. If you hoard it, it will turn to spiritual dry rot. If God has blessed you, erect an altar and give the blessing back to God as a love-gift.

Abraham "pitched his tent, having Beth-el on the west and Hai on the east." Beth-el is the symbol of communion with God; Hai is the symbol of the world: Abraham pitched his tent between the two. The measure of the worth of our public activity to God is the private, profound communion we have with Him. Rush is always wrong; there is plenty of time to worship God. There are not three stages— worship, waiting and work; some of us go in jumps like spiritual frogs, we jump from worship to waiting and from waiting to work. God's idea is that the three should go together; they were always together in the life of Our Lord, He was unhasting and unresting. It is a discipline, we cannot get there all at once.

THE DANCE OF CIRCUMSTANCES
Genesis 12:10–13

Not for such hopes and fears
  Annulling youth's brief years,
Do I remonstrate: folly wide the mark!
  Rather I prize the doubt
  Low kinds exist without,
Finished and finite clods, untroubled by a spark.

Then, welcome each rebuff
  That turns earth's smoothness rough,
Each sting that bids nor sit nor stand but go!
  Be our joy three-parts pain!
  Strive, and hold cheap the strain;
Learn, nor account the pang; dare, never grudge the throe!

Browning

And there was a famine in the land. Genesis 12:10

There is a difference between circumstances and environment. We cannot control our circumstances, but we are the deciders of our own environment. Environment is the element in our circumstances which fits the disposition. A man convicted of sin and a man in love may be in the same external circumstances, but the environment of the one is totally different from that of the other. Our environment depends upon our personal reaction to circumstances. "Circumstances over which I have no control" is a perfectly true phrase, but it must never be made to mean that we cannot control ourselves in those circumstances. No matter into what perplexing circumstances God's providence may lead us or allow us to go, we have to see to it that in our reaction to those circumstances, which dance around us so perplexingly, we exhibit a personal relation to the highest we know. It is only by living in the presence of God that we cease to act in an ungodlike manner in perplexing circumstances.

1. The Famine in the Land of Promise
(Genesis 12:10)
This must have been a severe test to Abraham's faith. Take it personally: we hear God's word on the mount, but when it comes to the dance of circumstances we are "knocked out," because we forget that we have to react in those circumstances in accordance with our

faith in God. In going down to Egypt, Abraham declined from this standard.

The element of discipline in the life of faith must never be lost sight of, because only by means of the discipline are we taught the difference between the natural interpretation of what we call good and what God means by "good." We have to be brought to the place of hearty agreement with God as to what He means by good, and we only reach it by the trial of our faith, never by a stoical effort, such as saying— "Well, I must make up my mind that this is God's will, and that it is best,"

At times it appears as if God has not only forsaken His word, but has deliberately deceived us. We asked Him for a particular thing, or related ourselves to Him along a certain line, and expected that it would mean the fulness of blessing, and actually it has meant the opposite—upset, trouble and difficulty all around, and we are staggered, until we learn that by this very discipline God is bringing us to the place of entire abandonment to Himself.

Never settle down in the middle of the dance of circumstances and say that you have been mistaken in your natural interpretation of God's promise to you because the immediate aftermath is devastation; say that God did give you the promise, and stick to it, and slowly God will bring you into the perfect, detailed fulfilment of that promise. When and where the fulfilment will take place, depends upon God and yourself, but never doubt the absolute fulfilment of God's word, and remember that the beginning of the fulfilment lies in your acquiescence in God's will. Remain true to God, although it means the sword going through the natural, and you will be brought into a supernaturally clear agreement with God. We are not introduced to Christianity by explanations, but we must labour at the exposition of Christianity until we satisfactorily unfold it through God's grace and our own effort.

2. The Foreboding on the Line of Peace
(Genesis 12:11–13)
In the beginning of the life of faith the first element is that of fanaticism. There must be the cutting off, and the maiming, and the separation. There is nothing fascinating about any of that, but when the life has become imbedded in God, and the maiming has disappeared into the full-orbed perfection of a child of God, then that perfection has a tremendous fascination for others even though they do not care anything about God. Then comes the danger of this subterfuge—"I won't tell other people the whole truth, I won't say I am delivered from all sin, or sanc-

tified wholly, that is too rugged, it will offend them; I will cover up the vital testimony and say I am religiously inclined, then I shall be able to preserve my influence with them." Whenever that cunning rascal "expediency" comes in, it will bring in its train a foreboding anxiety, which is a sure sign that in that particular we are ceasing to obey God. Our testimony must be unmistakably to the whole of the truth, not to part of it only. It is impossible to go on in our life with God if the element of personal testimony is left out; we will begin to get dextrous with a dexterity that is more or less doubtful, we say the truth but not the whole truth. Whenever God reveals something which we have never seen before and which affects others, a public testimony must be made, and the peril is lest we say—"But if I stand up and give that testimony, other people will be stumbled." Whenever we start this doubtful weighing of things we are acting not in accordance with our reliance on God, but in presumptuous confidence that God will see us through if we trust our wits: God will see us through only if we stand stedfastly true to what He has told us. Another danger is to imagine that it is my particular presentation of things that will attract people. It may attract them, but never to God. The line of attraction is always an indication of the goal of the attracted; if you attract by personal impressiveness, the attracted will get no further than you. Our Lord said—"*I*, if *I* be lifted up, will draw all men unto Me."

Verse 13 reveals a weakness in Abraham's faith, he does not yet perfectly rely upon the help of God in God's own way and time. This weakness arises from the inability to apply our faith in God to the actual circumstances we are in. We have to be true to God. not true only to our idea of God.

The failures of the chosen men of God upon a closer examination reveal them as sins of weakness arising from unguarded strength, which failures on the one hand do not destroy the personal standing with God, but on the other hand render necessary in him a purifying and providential training.

Foster's Essay on "The Aversion of Men of Taste to Evangelical Religion"

If we imagine we have strength apart from God, we shall have to break the neck of our strength over some obstacle before we are willing to rely upon God. Our own strength is the backbone of the natural life. but if the backbone of the strength of the natural man is removed without planting in the backbone of the life of God, there will be the "wobble," which persists until the vision of faith and the reality are one and the same.

BLANK ASTONISHMENT
Genesis 12:14–20

Pure faith indeed—you know not what you ask!
Naked belief in God the Omnipotent,
Omniscient, Omnipresent, sears too much
The sense of conscious creatures to be borne.
It were the seeing him, no flesh shall dare.

. . . .

No, when the fight begins within himself,
A man's worth something. God stoops o'er his
head,
Satan looks up between his feet—both tug—
He's left, himself, i' the middle: the soul wakes
And grows. Prolong that battle through his life!
Never leave growing till the life to come!

Browning

What is this that thou hast done unto me? Genesis 12:18

When we sin directly, we are never blankly astonished at the result. We may be defiant, we may tell lies; or, what is better, we may accept God's forgiveness. Blank astonishment always comes because of failure to do God's will by our very desire to do it. There is no word of censure on Abraham in the Bible for his distinct failure in going down to Egypt on account of the famine in the land God had promised him; but the blank astonishment which it caused is implied all through. Beware of saying what Abraham ought to have done—firstly, because he did not do it; and secondly, because you increase the severity of your own condemnation. This incident is not related for the dishonour of Abraham, but for the honour of God. Abraham did not attempt to vindicate himself.

Beware of thinking (no matter what you say) that God guided you in your decisions; the thought leads to spiritual hypocrisy. God holds His children responsible for the way in which they interpret His will. We only discern God's will by being renewed in the spirit of our minds in every circumstance we are in. We must learn to tell ourselves the truth on the basis of God's word, not on the basis of independent spiritual impulse, although by our blunders of impulse we are chastened as God's sons and daughters.

1. The Saint's Guilt in the Worldling's Sin
(Genesis 12:14–16)
The result of Abraham's going down to Egypt was perplexity to himself, and he was also responsible for bringing a direct occasion of sin to Pharaoh. Pharaoh

treats Abraham with a generosity which must have put Abraham to shame.

Get alarmed when your desire to serve God brings you into such a position that you have to accept, because you cannot refuse, the magnanimous treatment of worldlings who do not know your Lord; because to be in that position means you have transgressed God's order by the very keenness of your desire to do His will; and when you withdraw, as you must do ultimately, it will be with the knowledge that you have been the direct occasion of sin to them.

Christian work is apt to lead individual saints into blank astonishment, because it springs from an eager desire to do God's will. To say—"I want to do God's will," is to put myself outside God altogether. The striking thing in Our Lord's life was that He was not more eager to do the will of His Father than His Father was for Him to do it. He was the Saviour of the world, everything depended upon Him, and yet for thirty years He did nothing wonderful. "His doing nothing wonderful was in itself a kind of wonder" (Bonaventura). Our Lord's life is the exhibition of *the will of God*, not of *doing* the will of God.

Beware in your judgement either on Abraham or on yourself that you do not transfer the judgement to a stage of moral development not yet reached. It is easy to exaggerate. For example, an act that would be criminal in a man is not criminal in a boy. Abraham's transgression must never be classed as a sin morally. He transgressed through eagerness to do the right thing. Transgression is nearly always an unconscious act, there is no conscious determination to do wrong; sin is never an unconscious act. We blunder when we refuse to discern between these two.

2. The Saint's Gifts from the Worldling's Sincerity *(Genesis 12:16)*
The Egyptian maid Hagar, who became so important an influence in the lives of Abraham and Sarah, was probably amongst the gifts which came to Abraham in Egypt. The friendships and gifts of the world are perfectly sincere, but the saint soon realises that these friendships and gifts are embarrassing and hindering if he is to remain loyal to God. Then begins the blank astonishment of real perplexity, and God never shields us from anxiety on this score. It is not a case of right and wrong, but of learning through chastening what Abraham learned, that we cannot come eagerly and find out God's will by guessing. We must be renewed in our minds in every circumstance we are in, and

beware of suspicions and considerations and suggestions that make themselves seem right to us. Beware of despising the chastening of the Lord, or of fainting when you are rebuked of Him. The only thing to do is to take your blank astonishment, be silent about it, and go on to the next thing.

3. The Saint's Groaning and the Worldling's Scorn *(Genesis 12:17–18)*

Pharaoh is a better man than those around him, and he concludes directly that the judgement on his house is from God on account of Sarah, whose person God is guarding as the true mother of Israel. Abraham did not tell a lie, he told a half-truth (see Genesis 20:12).

To say that if a man is committing sin he will hinder the purpose of God, is not true; if a *leader* is trying to serve his own ends, he will hinder the purpose of God. For instance, if I were to try and utilise this house of God[8] for my own ends, the atmosphere of the house would be damaged instantly. Personal sin does not present a barrier in God's house, although it does put a barrier between the one who is sinning and God; but immediately anyone tries to utilise God's house, or God's people, or God's things for his own purposes and ends, then the atmosphere is altered at

once. Then the thoughts of many hearts are revealed and there is produced the groaning of the saints and the scorn of the worldling, and the humiliating thing is that in such a case the worldling is right.

4. The Saint's Grade in the Worldling's Separation *(Genesis 12:19–20)*

Abraham was dismissed by Pharaoh—a most unspeakable humiliation. If you have made a compromise out of your eagerness to stand for God's honour, you will have to endure to the last limit, as Abraham did, the scorn of the honourable worldling. Instead of your breaking from the world, the world will come with all its courtesy and say—Will you go? By your very desire to stand up loyally for God, you have put yourself in a position where you cannot stand up for Him. The discipline of our lives is to become as little children. A little child would have stayed in the land whether there was a famine or not.

Abraham's going down to Egypt, and his "dumbfoundering" there, is the reason for all the complexity that came afterwards, and accounts for the continual recurrence of Egypt in the history of the Kingdom of God, until at last Egypt is to be united into the great, full purpose of God.

UNPERPLEXED
Genesis 13

Yea, this in him was the peculiar grace
    (Hearten our chorus!)
That before living he'd learn how to live—
    No end to learning:
Earn the means first—God surely will contrive
    Use for our earning.
Others mistrust and say, "But time escapes:
    Live now or never!"
He said, "What's time? Leave Now for dogs and
    apes!
    Man has Forever."

                         Browning

. . . unto the place of the altar, which he had made there at the first. Genesis 13:4

When we come to study the lives of the saints, the confusing thing is that from one standpoint they are a jumble of inconsistencies, whilst from another standpoint they are an exhibition of the boundless

consistency of God. This needs to be heeded, because if we study the life of a saint in order to find out what God is like, we shall finish up in the dumps and say— It is enough; whereas if we study God Himself, we shall find that He manifests His amazing consistency in the weakest and feeblest saint. At one time we find Abraham in a blank and sordid muddle; at another, we find him unperplexed and noble. The point is that God remains the same whether Abraham is unperplexed or muddled.

1. The Tryst of Sacramental Identification *(Genesis 13:1–4)*

Abraham went with God, and Lot "went with Abraham." Lot went down to Egypt with Abraham, and came back with Abraham, and the abundance of their possessions nearly brought about strife. A life of *faithfulness* is devotion to a servant or handmaid of God; a life of *faith* is devotion to God. Lot continually went to pieces; Abraham never did.

---

8. this house of God: reference to Bible Training College (BTC).

The Way. We have to keep tryst with God in contact with the peculiar ways of everyone, and this can only be done by sacramental identification. The one thing Our Lord heeded was His tryst with God in connection with everyone, whether it was Judas or Peter or John; He took no account of the evil. We get huffed in no time—"No, they did not treat me rightly";—they did not consider that I ought to have been considered." Will I keep my tryst with God in contact with the blackguard or the traitor or the saint? Whoever it is, is nothing to do with me. I have not to fit other people into my ideas, but to keep tryst with God in relation to them. I am not to ignore them, but to refuse to look at them from my idea of what they ought to be, and to look at them only as facts in relation to my tryst with God.

The Wealth. Abraham came back exceedingly wealthy, but he kept tryst with God over his possessions. Beware of not keeping tryst with God over your possessions, whether they be material or not. It is perilously possible not to, but to make your spiritual life depend on the abundance of things you possess. If God has given you the wealth of Divine healing for your body, keep tryst with Him over it. When you are learning to trust God, He gives you at first certain things you lean on; then He withdraws, and you say it is the devil. No, it is the chastening of the Lord because He sees that you are possessing those things. You can only possess your possessions by being detached from them to God Who is the Source. If you are drawing your life from God and begin to take a wrong line, God will withdraw His life. This is also true with regard to money. We have only one Source, and that is God. One of the biggest snares is the idea that God is sure to lead us to success.

The Worship. All commentators notice one interesting point in Abraham's life, viz. the times he erected an altar and the times he did not; whenever he neglected to erect an altar, he went astray. This fact is one of great significance because worship is the tryst of sacramental identification. In worship I deliberately give back to God the best He has given me that I may be identified with Him in it. If Abraham had erected an altar, he would not have gone down to Egypt, but would have identified himself with God over the famine in the land of promise. Selfishness in spiritual matters produces delusion rapidly. If in every case of blank astonishment, we go back to the place where we first built an altar to God, we will be delivered from the delusion of obtuse independent certainty. Worship is the sacramental element in the saint's life.

2. The Test of Self Interest *(Genesis 13:5–13)*

As surely as we begin our life of faith with God, fascinating, luxurious and rich prospects will open to us, which are ours by right, but if we are living the life of

faith we will exercise the right to waive our rights and give them away, letting God choose for us. It is the discipline of transforming the natural into the spiritual by obedience to God's voice. In the life of faith God allows us to get into a place of testing where the consideration of our own welfare would be the right and proper thing if we were not living the life of faith; but if we are living the life of faith, we will heartily waive our own rights in favour of those whose right it is not, and leave God to choose for us. Whenever we make "right" our guidance, we blunt our spiritual insight. The greatest enemy of the life with God is not sin, but the good that is not good enough. It would seem the wisest thing in the world for Abraham to choose, it was his right, and the people round him would consider him a fool for not choosing. Many of us do not go on in our spiritual life because we prefer to choose what is our right instead of relying upon God to choose for us. We have to learn to walk according to the standard that has its eye on God.

The Tax of Riches (vv. 5–7). Abraham's riches were in a great measure a tax to him. Every possession is tainted with a want; in this case the want was for sufficient pasturage. When Jesus Christ came He possessed nothing; the only symbol for our Lord is the symbol of poverty (Luke 9:58; 2 Corinthians 8:9) and this is true of the saint—"having nothing, and yet possessing all things." Every possession produces an appetite that clings.

The Touch of Rectitude. Lot forgot the place of communion, he thought only of the world. But Abraham, unperplexed, instantly exhibited forbearance as the result of his tryst with God, he walked in the moral atmosphere of the Sermon on the Mount. Abraham's rectitude was not the rectitude of honour, but of holiness. This rectitude is exhibited in the life of Jesus Christ, of Whom it is recorded that He "pleased not Himself." This gives the deathblow to subjectivity, that is, to the subjective experiences based on what is pleasing to my holy self; of the holiest Being Who ever trod this earth it is recorded that He pleased not Himself.

The Tarnish of Reasonableness (vv. 10–13). Lot chose what he considered the best for his possessions. This is the tarnish of reasonableness of a mind that has neglected its tryst with God.

3. The Type of Supreme Integrity *(Genesis 13:14–18)*

We must distinguish between the times when God revealed Himself to Abraham and the times when He concealed Himself. In the former, Abraham's faith is elevated; in the latter it sinks.

The Manifestation of God (v. 14). The first manifestation of God to Abraham was in his migration to

Canaan; the first concealing when he went down to Egypt. Abraham did not have another manifestation of God until after his noble act of faith toward Lot.

The Message of God (vv. 15–16). The promises of God correspond to the acts and conduct of faith in Abraham. Only when Abraham acts in accordance with his real faith in God, does God speak to him.

There is a connection throughout between the providence of God and the conduct of Abraham.

The Man of God (v. 18). Paul takes Abraham as a type of the life of faith, not as the type of a saint, but of a tried faith built on a real God. The sanctification of our faith, as distinct from the sanctification of our heart, is the unfathomable, supernatural blessing from God.

WAR
Genesis 14:1–16

Let it go or stay, so I wake to the higher aims
Of a land that has lost for a while her lust of gold,
And love of a peace that was full of wrongs and
    shames,
Horrible, hateful, monstrous, not to be told;
And hail once more to the banner of battle
    unroll'd!
Tho' many a light shall darken, and many shall
    weep
For those that are crush'd in the clash of jarring
    claims. . . .
Let it flame or fade, and the war roll down like a
    wind,
We have proved we have hearts in a cause, we are
    noble still,
And myself have awaked, as it seems, to the better
    mind;
It is better to fight for the good than to rail at the
    ill;
I have felt with my native land, I am one with
    my kind,
I embrace the purpose of God, and the doom
    assign'd.

                            Tennyson

. . . and [one] told Abram the Hebrew; . . . he armed his trained servants. Genesis 14:13–14

In the study of Abraham, as in the study of all Bible characters, principles are no guide. The inconsistencies which we find in Abraham reveal the consistency of God, and the thing to note is that Abraham remained true to God both before and after his lapses. Beware, however, what you call lapses in Abraham. For instance, there is no lapse on Abraham's part in connection with this war, but rather the presentation of the inspiration of God. Error lies in making the basis of truth an abstraction, or a principle, instead of a personal relationship. Reality is not found in logic; Reality is a Person. *"I am . . . the Truth."* Spiritual life is based on a personal relationship to

Jesus Christ, and on the consequent responsibility of that relationship.

1. The War of Violence *(Genesis 14:1–8)*
This is the first war mentioned in Scripture, and its cause was the lust for dominion. The war of the world against the world is portrayed in this chapter, and it is full of the most intense spiritual interpretation. Life without conflict is impossible, either in nature or in grace. This is an open fact of life. The basis of physical, mental, moral and spiritual life is antagonism. Physical life is maintained according to the power of fight in the corpuscles of the blood. If I have sufficient vital force within to overcome the forces without, I produce the balance of health. The same is true of mental life. If I want to maintain a clear, vigorous, mental life, I have to fight, and in this way I produce the balance of thought. Morally it is the same. Virtue is the result of fight; I am only virtuous according to the moral stability I have within. If I have sufficient moral fighting capacity, I produce the moral balance of virtue. We make virtue out of necessity, but no one is virtuous who is good because he cannot help it. Virtue is the outcome of conflict. And spiritually it is the same. "In the world ye shall have tribulation"; i.e., everything that is not spiritual makes for my undoing; "but be of good cheer; I have overcome the world." When once this is understood it is a perfect delight to meet opposition, and as we learn to score off the things that come against us, we produce the balance of holiness. Faith must be tried, and it is the trial of faith that is precious. If you are faint-hearted, it is a sign you won't play the game, you are fit for neither God nor man because you will face nothing.

2. The War of Faint-Hearted Defence *(Genesis 14:9–12)*
When God's providence involves us unexpectedly in all sorts of complications, the test comes on two lines—Will I have faith in God; and will I ally myself with those who rescue the down-trodden irrespective

of their beliefs? It is instructive to note in the Bible that faint-heartedness arises whenever self-interest begins to get luxurious. The sign of faint-heartedness in individuals is in the languid talk of "someone else" when there is anything to be done.

Whenever there is the experience of fag or weariness or degradation, you may be certain you have done one of two things—either you have disregarded a law of nature, or you have deliberately got out of touch with God. There is no such thing as weariness in God's work. If you are in tune with the joy of God, the more you spend out in God's service, the more the recuperation goes on, and when once the warning note of weariness is given, it is a sign that something has gone wrong. If only we would heed the warning, we would find it is God's wonderfully gentle way of saying—"Not that way; that must be left alone; this must be given up." Spiritual fatigue comes from the unconscious frittering away of God's time. When you feel weary or are exhausted, don't ask for hot milk, but get back to God. The secret of weariness and nervous disease in the natural world is the lack of a dominating interest, and the same is true in spiritual life. Much of what is called Christian work is veneered spiritual disease; it is Christian activity that counts—dominating life from God, and every moment is filled with an energy that is not our own, a super-abounding life that nothing can stand before.

3. The War of Divine Inspiration *(Genesis 14:13–16)*

In chapter 13 Abraham was put through the test of self-interest, and here he is put through the test of self-complacency. The occasion for self-complacency would be in seeing that what befell Lot was just, and that God was proving Abraham to be in the right. But Abraham did not go under in the test; he did not sit down, as it were, with a sanctified smirk and say, "Perhaps he will learn wisdom now." Abraham entered into the war with the light and cheerful heroism of heaven.

". . . servants, born in his own house." This phrase is of great spiritual significance. Whenever a conflict takes place, such as is pictured here, the successful fighters are the faithful children of the faithful saints. In spiritual warfare may God have mercy on the barren saint who has never produced his own kind but has to rely upon the converts of others. In the rugged details of the Old Testament regarding marriage, there is always a spiritual revelation. In the natural world there are three—father, mother and child; and in the spiritual world there are three—God, Church and converts. If a spiritual nature cannot reproduce its own kind, it will have to answer to God for it. If you have to rely in times of stress upon the converts of others, the conflict drags out desperately; you can always rely on your own converts, those whom you have been the means of leading into the truth.

MORE THAN CONQUEROR
Genesis 14:17–24

Why have we yet no great deliverance wrought,
Why have we not truth's banner yet unfurled,
High floating in the face of all the world,—
Why do we live and yet accomplish nought?

What time the years pass from us of our youth,
And we unto the altar of high truth
As yet no worthy offering have brought.
But now we bid these restless longings cease;

If Heaven has aught for us to do or say,
Our time will come; and we may well hold peace,
When He, till thrice ten years had passed away,
In stillness and in quietness upgrew,
Whose word once spoken should make all things
new.

Trench[9]

Now consider how great this man was, unto whom even the patriarch Abraham gave the tenth of the spoils. Hebrews 7:4

We have to live perfectly actual lives, not actually perfect lives. This fact makes all the difference between religious faith and religious farce, and is very clearly brought out in the life of Abraham. God is not actual, He is real, and He bears into me His Holy Spirit Who enables me to live a perfectly actual life, kept by the reality of the love of God. "I don't feel this and that"—how can you when God is not actual, but real? Feeling has to do with actualities and will come later. Right feeling is produced by obedience, never vice versa. I am brought into contact with actuality by my senses, and into contact with reality by my faith. The test in actual things is—Am I living a life of faith, or a life of com-

---

9. Richard Chenevix Trench (1807–1886): poet; Anglican archbishop of Dublin.

mon sense which denies faith? Faith does not make me *actually perfect*; faith makes me *perfectly actual*.

1. When the Victory Is Won *(Genesis 14:17)*

The supreme test in the perfectly actual life of faith comes after a victory has been gained, because in the expansive hour of relaxation the ruling disposition of the heart is instantly manifested. We read of Our Lord that after a day when "all the city was gathered together at the door," He rose up a great while before day in order to pray, not to praise (Mark 1:32–35). In Abraham the victory revealed that he was more than conqueror over himself. To say "I have got the victory" is a selfish testimony; the testimony of the Spirit of God is that the Victor has got me. If we can notify victories for ourselves, we are not in right relationship to God at that particular time. Instead of worshipping God we are conscious only of what He has done through us, and we triumph in the experience He has brought us. My actual life is given me by God, and I can live in it either as an atheist or as a worshipper. Abraham stands as one who worships God after a victory.

2. Where the Victor Is a Worshipper *(Genesis 14:18–20)*

Just where Abram stands as the most striking character, Melchizedek enters and towers above him.

> *What better type or symbol could there be of the absolute, the everlasting, the divine, high priesthood and kingship than that phenomenal figure of Melchizedek? He comes out of the invisible, timeless eternity of the past; he belongs to the timeless assured eternity of the future; he is High Priest forever.*
>
> Du Bose

Melchizedek is a type of Christ; Abraham is never taken as a type of Christ, he is a type of the perfectly actual children of God. Melchizedek represents the Incarnation of God; Abraham represents the life of faith in the God Who became Incarnate. "Christ in me" and "I in Christ"; "Christ the Lord" and "Christ the Servant"—all become simple when we understand the relationship of Melchizedek and Abraham.

The supreme lesson of the perfectly actual life of faith is to learn how to worship. Faith brings me into personal contact with God before Whom I must ever bow. I have to maintain a worshipful relationship to God in everything, and in the beginning this is difficult. I am all right at meetings, at anything that is

illuminated, but when it comes to actual life, I am actually of no use. I can talk till further orders,[10] but don't ask me to live the life.

We have to contend for God in our actual circumstances, and our contention for God lies in seeing that we rely upon Him absolutely while we carry out the dictates of our faith in Him. Melchizedek brings bread and wine to refresh the heroes of the perfectly actual life. Christ never takes part in the perfectly actual mix-up of our human lives; therefore to ask "What would Jesus do?" is not the question of faith, but of Pharisaism, The question to ask is—*"What would Jesus have me do?"* It is impossible for Christ to be where you are, that is why He has put you there. You have to put on the new man in the actual circumstances you are in and manifest Him. It is arrogant humbug to imagine we are to be God Almighty on this earth. We are to be the sons and daughters of God, to live actual lives and put on the new man by deliberate acts of faith all the time, not denying the actual life. We have to remember that our bodies are the temples of the Holy Ghost, and to see that God is manifested in our mortal flesh by our worship; and that can only be done as we take the nourishment, the bread and the wine, which will sustain us in our actual contentions for God. "For in that He Himself hath suffered being tempted, He is able to succour them that are tempted," i.e., succour us with His bread and wine in the hour of our temptation (Hebrews 2:18; 4:15).

It is dangerous to take Abraham as the picture of sanctification. Sanctification means the perfection of Jesus Christ manifesting itself in actual experience. If you take Abraham as a picture of sanctification, you will have to chop his life up and say—This part is sanctification, and that is not; and you will produce a false spiritual interpretation. Abraham is a picture of the life of faith, not the result of faith. He portrays for all time the ups and downs, the haphazards and the tests, the nobilities and the blunders of the perfectly actual life of faith.

3. While the Victorious Is Worthy *(Genesis 14:21–24)*

Abraham renounces any advantage for himself, but he preserves the rights of those with him. We have the perfect right not to insist on our rights, it is the privilege of a Christian to waive his rights; but we do not always recognise that we must insist on those associated with us getting their rights. If they prefer to take the line of faith that we take, that is their responsibility, but we are not exonerated from seeing that they get their rights.

---

10. "till further orders": ad infinitum; endlessly; of military origin, meaning continuing the present action until one receives different orders.

A STAR-HITCHED WAGON
Genesis 15:1–6

Be near me when my light is low,
*   When the blood creeps, and the nerves prick*
*   And tingle; and the heart is sick,*
And all the wheels of Being slow.

Be near me when the sensuous frame
*   Is rack'd with pangs that conquer trust;*
*   And Time, a maniac scattering dust,*
And Life, a Fury slinging flame.

Tennyson

And he believed in the LORD. *Genesis 15:6*

The title represents the wildness of God's expectations. If only He had told us to hitch our wagon to a mule, we could see how it might be done; but to tell us to hitch our natural lumbering wagons to the star of Almighty God makes us wonder whether we have understood Him aright. Faith sticks to the wagon and the star; fanaticism jumps from the wagon to the star and breaks its neck. A saint is not an angel and never will be; a saint is the flesh and blood theatre in which the decrees of God are carried to successful issues. All of which means that God demands of us the doing of common things while we abide in Him,

1. The Vision in the Valley of Afterwards *(Genesis 15:1)*
The meaning of the valley of afterwards is that there must be an interchange between actualities and realities, it is the successful interchange between the two that keeps the life healthy. There is no "afterwards" to the one who lives his life mystically only; a life that produces no results is an intensely selfish life. There must be the interchange between my real standing before God and my life on the earth, i.e., my wagon must be hitched to the star, and hitched to it by faith.

The afterwards of success for God produces the feeling—Was it worthwhile? The coward fears before danger; the heroic spirit fears afterwards. It was after the victory, when Abraham went into the valley of the afterwards, that God said to him—"Fear not, Abram: I am thy shield, and thy exceeding great reward." If you say, "My goal is God Himself" before you have been to school, it is merely a nursery rhyme; but say it after winning a victory that tells for God, and the victory does not seem such a glorious thing after all, until you find that the goal is not a prize, but the fulfilment of a decree of God in and through you.

2. The Veil on the Vision of Abraham *(Genesis 15:2–3)*
Abraham is not rebellious, but he is not hilarious. He believes that Eliezer must be his heir, and he acquiesces in the purpose of God and only wants light as to the meaning of it. The phrase—"Behold, to me Thou hast given no seed" is not a murmur against God, but a pious exclamation of weakness. It is not a challenge to God, but an expression of resignation; Abraham is blaming himself for misinterpreting God—"Excuse me for being so disappointed, Lord, but I find that all my hopes and ideas have been wrong"; but he came to find that they were not wrong.

Beware of being sorry for God's reputation in your particular case. Self-pity is Satanic; but pity for God is the betrayal of your affections. Here Abraham is in the condition not of pitying himself, but of pitying God's reputation in himself; he cannot understand how God is going to fulfil what He has said—no heir other than Eliezer, the idea of having a child must have been a misinterpretation. The veil on the vision of Abraham makes him say: It can't be done—I want an explanation as to Your meaning. When God's promise refers to fertility in mud, we must not think it refers to birds of paradise in heaven, and because we see the mud only and no sign of fertility, say we are mistaken. If any promise of God that has emphatically to do with this earth and with flesh and blood people, is not being fulfilled, beware of saying—Oh well, I must have misinterpreted what God meant. We forget that we have to build in absolute confidence on God. There is nothing more heroic than to have faith in God when you can see so many better things in which to have faith. It is comparatively easy to have faith in God in a pathetic way in the starvation of things round about you, but a different matter to have faith in God after a tremendous victory has been won, and then in the aftermath that follows to think that there is to be no realisation of that for which God had caused you to hope.

3. The Voice and the Vastness of Altitude *(Genesis 15:4–5)*
In this chapter we fathom the depths of all that the New Testament unfolds. Abraham the childless is to become the father of nations—How mad the promise sounds! "And He brought him forth abroad, and said, Look now toward heaven, and tell the stars: . . . So

shall thy seed be." God points Abraham away from his wagon in the mud to the starry night, and hitches the two together by His own word. God's appeal to the stars is not to furnish proof for a doubting mind, but to provide nourishment for a faltering faith. Nature to the saint is a sacrament of God, not merely a series of facts; not symbols and signs, but the real evidence of the coming of God as a sacrament to His faithful children.

The whole discipline of the life of faith is to mix together the light of heaven and the sordid actuality of earth. Contemplation and consideration must go together, i.e., take your plan for what you do on earth from the altitude of heaven; let contemplation of the stars be mixed with what you build on earth.

In personal life despise these two things—dumps and hurry; they are worse than the devil, and are both excessively culpable. Dumps is an absolute slur against God—I won't look up, I have done all I could but it is all up, and I am in despair. Hurry is the same mood expressed in an opposite way—I have no time to pray, no time to look to God or to consider anything, I must do the thing. Perspiration is mistaken for Inspiration. Consequently I drive my miserable little wagon in a rut instead of hitching it to a star and pulling according to God's plan. God hitched the wagon of Abraham to the stars which He had created, by His word. In our personal lives the great solution is always found in the words of Our Lord when we have His Spirit. Jesus Christ is God Incarnate, and He makes His words spirit and life to us; our little human wagons are hitched to the star of God's sacramental purpose by the words of Jesus and in no other way. Whenever we indulge in hurry or in the dumps and refuse to pay attention to His words, we smash the connecting line and go off on our own.

4. The Veracity and Virtue of Attitude (Genesis 15:6)

"And he believed in the LORD." This is the act by which Abraham goes out of himself and relies upon God for righteousness and grace. Abraham had manifested many noble qualities of heart and many virtues in his walk of faith, but he is not made righteous before God by these. The lack in Abraham is supplied through his living confidence in God. The justification of every sinner is by faith and by faith alone, and when a man walks in that faith his justification appears in his flesh and justifies God (*see* Psalm 51:4).

This verse is the first germ of the great doctrine of "The LORD our Righteousness." Righteousness must never be made to mean less than a guiltless position in the presence of justice and right. God justifies me by my supernatural faith in Him, but it is my just walk that proves Him just in saving me; if I do not walk in the life of faith, I am a slander to God.

GOOD VERSUS BEST
Genesis 16:1–6

How the world is made for each of us!
 How all we perceive and know in it
 Tends to some moment's product thus,
When a soul declares itself—to wit,
 By its fruit, the thing it does!

Be hate that fruit or love that fruit,
 It forwards the general deed of man.
And each of the Many helps to recruit
 The life of the race by a general plan;
Each living his own, to boot.

         Browning

She fled from her face. Genesis 16:6

In the spiritual life we do not go from good to better, and from better to best; because there is only One to Whom we go, and that One is The Best, viz., God Himself. There can be no such thing as God's second best. We can perversely put ourselves out of God's order into His permissive will, but that is a different matter. In seeking the Best we soon find that our enemy is our good things, not our bad. The things that keep us back from God's best are not sin and imperfection, but the things that are right and good and noble from the natural standpoint. To discern that the natural virtues antagonise surrender to God is to bring our soul at once into the centre of our greatest battlefield. Very few of us debate with the sordid and the wrong, but we do debate with the good; and the higher up we go in the scale of the natural virtues, the more intense is the opposition to Jesus Christ, which is in inverse ratio to what one would naturally imagine (cf. Matthew 23:31).

1. The Fanaticism of Self–Denial (Genesis 16:1–2)

The childless state of Abraham's house was its great sorrow, and was a constant trial to Abraham's faith.

Everything to do with Abraham's call was dependent upon his having seed. It is instructive to note where both Abraham and Sarah began to go wrong. They did their best to fulfil God's command, but in so doing they got out of God's order into His permissive will. The fanatical passionate desire to fulfil God's will led them into desperate error. Beware of the fanaticism of self-denial, it will lead to error lasting in its effects. When we go off on that line we become devoted to our interpretation of our destiny. Destiny is never abstract. The destiny of a human being is vested in personal relationship to God. Abraham learned this lesson later; on Mount Moriah he distinctly proved that he knew the difference between obeying what God said and obeying God Who said it. Fanaticism is sticking true to my interpretation of my destiny instead of waiting for God to make it clear. The fanatical line is—*Do* something; the test of faith lies in *not* doing. Fanaticism is always based on the highest I believe; a sordid being is never fanatical. Our Lord taught His disciples to pray—"Lead us not into temptation." To say—"Lord, I will do whatever You tell me to do; I will stand loyal to You," is deliberately to disobey this caution of Our Lord.

Natural impulse in a saint leads to perdition every time unless it is brought into obedience to the destiny of God, then it is turned into inspiration. It is not that impulse is wrong, but it will lead to wrong unless it is brought into obedience to the spiritual destiny of the life, and this can only be done by devotion to the One Who founds our destiny for us, Our Lord Himself. Beware of trying to forestall God's programme by your own impulse.

2. The Falsity of Sagacious Discernment (Genesis 16:4)

Abraham and Sarah both adhered to their sagacious discernment in acting in accordance with the practice of the time in which they lived. Beware of discerning according to your own sagacity how God must do some things, because it means that you dictate to God—That word of God must be fulfilled; I cannot allow that I have been deluded, therefore there is only one thing left to do. That is leaning to your own understanding instead of trusting in the Lord with all your heart. Never say—God must do this thing. He must not; God will fulfil His own word. You have no business to dictate to Him, you have to remain true to God and when His word is fulfilled, you will know He has fulfilled it because it is a supernatural fulfilment. Always beware of being more eager to do God's will than God is for you to do it. The remarkable thing about the life of Our Lord was not that He was eager to do God's will, but that He was *obedient* to do it. He never put His fingers across the threads of His Father's providential order for Him and gave a tug saying—"Now I will help You," and pulled the thing right out of His Father's hands. He simply obeyed, leaving His Father's wisdom to arrange all for Him. We rush in and say—I see what God wants and I will do it, and we wound our own souls and injure other lives.

3. The Frenzy of Spent Devotion (Genesis 16:5)

Sarah's appeal in which she demands that the wrong should be upon Abraham—"My wrong be upon thee"—is a passionate outbreak. The whole thing is the consequence of the wrong into which Abraham has allowed himself to be drawn. It is significant to note that both Adam and Abraham receive the severe judgement of God; they heeded the voice of their wives and they had no business to. The full force of God's judgement comes on the man, not on the woman. All through it is man who is held responsible, he may escape from man's judgement but never from God's judgement ultimately. Nothing in the way of judgement is visited by God on the woman (cf. 1 Timothy 2:14); in human judgement it is the opposite. In this case the punishment fell distinctly on Abraham, although the instigation came from the fanatical self-denial of Sarah. God never holds a woman responsible in the same way as He does a man.

4. The Fanaticism of Sensual Dominion (Genesis 16:6)

Sarah through her harsh treatment of Hagar evidently thrust her back into the position of a mere slave; Hagar believed that she had grown above that position, and fled. Hagar does not stand for sin, but for the natural life when it gets out of place and up against the spiritual life. Hagar and her son received real protection and blessing from God. Sin can never be in a subordinate position. My natural life must be in subordination and under the absolute control of the spiritual. The natural must be turned into the spiritual by obedience, whatever sword has to go through its heart. The natural life must be "spiked" for the glory of God. The characteristic of the natural life is the independent passion for free dominion over itself. Immediately the natural life fights to get away, it comes into opposition. It is the *good* that hates the *best*. It is not only sin that produces the havoc in life, but the natural determination to "boss the show" for God and everyone else.

CONTINUOUS CONVERSION
Genesis 16:7–16

Lord, I have fallen again—a human clod!
Selfish I was, and heedless to offend;
Stood on my rights. Thy own child would not send
Away his shreds of nothing for the whole God!
Wretched, to thee who savest, low I bend:
Give me the power to let my rag-rights go
In the great wind that from thy gulf doth blow.

Keep me from wrath, let it seem ever so right:
My wrath will never work thy righteousness.
Up, up the hill, to the whiter than snow-shine,
Help me to climb, and dwell in pardon's light.
I must be pure as thou, or ever less
Than thy design of me—therefore incline
My heart to take men's wrongs as thou tak'st mine.

George MacDonald

Whence camest thou? . . . Return, . . . and submit.
Genesis 16:8–9

Hagar represents the natural life, she does not represent sin; sin cannot be converted. I have continually to convert the natural life into submission to the Spirit of God in me and not say—I will never do anything natural again; that is fanatical. When by the providence of God my body is brought into new conditions, I have to see that my natural life is converted to the dictates of the Spirit of God in me. Because it has been done once is no proof that it will be done again. "Except ye be converted, and become as little children . . ." is true for all the days of the saintly life, we have continually to turn to God. The attitude of continuous conversion is the only right attitude towards the natural life, and it is the one thing we object to. Either we say the natural is wrong and try to kill it, or else we say that the natural is all there is, and that everything natural and impulsive is right. Neither attitude is right. The hindrance in spiritual life is that we will not be continuously converted, there are "wadges" of obstinacy where our pride spits at the throne of God and says—"I shan't; I am going to be boss." We cannot remain boss by the sheer power of will; sooner or later our wills must yield allegiance to some force greater than their own, either God or the devil.

1. The Angel of the Lord and Wrecked Passion *(Genesis 16:7)*

Hagar in her helpless condition is in a fit state for the angel of the Lord to appear to her. Sarah's fanatical self-denial and vindictive spite are far from right, but they do not justify Hagar for her passionateness. I alone am responsible for the wrong I do. Hagar desired to be the mother of the seed of Abraham, but she was not to be; in her own mind she insisted on being not only the equal of Sarah but her displacer. Beware of passion that makes you reach for position, because it will end in spiritual infamy. Passion is the combination of desire and pride with a wild reach of possibility. The desire may be for a big or a little thing, but the instant result of anything done at the spur of passion lands you in a wilderness of disgust, nursing wounded pride.

The right relationship of Hagar to Sarah is to be the relationship of my natural life to the domination of the Holy Ghost. My natural life must not rule, the spiritual must rule, and it must rule over the natural life, which is represented by Hagar. I have to convert my natural life continually into submission to the Spirit of God in me, otherwise I shall produce the divorce which ends in hell.

2. The Angel of the Lord and Wounded Pride *(Genesis 16:9)*

The angel of the Lord and conscience say the same thing—Return and submit—yet they stand distinct. If the voice of God does not correspond with what conscience says, I need pay no attention to it; but when it says the same thing as conscience, I must either obey or be damned in that particular. Return from assumed responsibility and submit—to the old oppression? Yes, but without the element of passion and of pride, and the result will be according to the will of God.

Natural pride has to do with my standing before men, not before God—I shall not bow, I will make others bow to me. That is natural domination, and represents the antagonism of the natural life to the domination of the Holy Spirit. Wherever there is natural pride the Lord must inevitably be put to open shame.

3. The Angel of the Lord and the Word of Promise *(Genesis 16:10–12)*

"The LORD hath heard thy affliction." Throughout the Bible this is the revelation of the personal attitude of God to the miseries of the world. He is not indifferent, the cry does not go up to the ears of a deaf God.

Hagar's great desire is to be the mother of the believing children of Abraham; the angel says—No, Hagar is to be the mother of Ishmael, and Ishmael is to be blessed. The limitation of the promise is connected with the promise itself. Do not miss the point of Hagar's mistake. Hagar must be cured of the delusion that she is destined to become the mother of the believing seed of Abraham—"Cast out the bondwoman and her son": i.e. cast them out of the position they have no right to be in (*see* Galatians 4:30).

The attitude of Our Lord towards anything to do with the natural is that of unflinching, patient sternness; He is not cruel, but He is stern, just as He was stern with His mother (John 2:4), and just as the Apostle Paul was stern with his own body (1 Corinthians 9:27).

When we are born again we enthrone Ishmael, that is, we consecrate our natural gifts and say these are the things with which God is going to do His work: they are the things God makes His servants, and I have to see that they are put in the position of servants. If I put them on the throne, I start a mutiny within my own soul. The bondwoman and her child have to be cast out; the natural has to be sacrificed in order that it may be brought into perfect at-home-ness with the Spirit of God. If we make our natural life submit and obey the Holy Spirit within us, we will hasten the time for the manifestation of the sons of God (Romans 8:21). It is the man who can rule his natural spirit that is able to take the city . It is only when we have learned to bring the natural life into perfect submission to the ruling personality of God that God dare turn His saints loose. It is of no use to turn out a lot of half-baked Ephraims into unlimited power. If I enthrone natural pride or natural virtue, I am in total insubordination to God in just that particular and cannot be His son or daughter.

4. The Appearing of the Lord and Waiting Patience *(Genesis 16:13–16)*

"Thou art a God that seeth" (RV). We *see* for the first time when we do not look. We see actual things, and we say that we see them, but we never really see them until we see God; when we see God, everything becomes different. It is not the external things that are different, but a different disposition looks through the same eyes as the result of the internal surgery that has taken place. We see God, and then we see things actually as we never saw them before.

THE RESERVATIONS OF GOD
Genesis 17:1

Oh, we're sunk enough here, God knows!
But not quite so sunk that moments,
Sure tho' seldom, are denied us,
When the spirit's true endowments
Stand out plainly from its false ones,
And apprise it if pursuing
Or the right way—or the wrong way,
To its triumph or undoing.
There are flashes struck from midnights,

There are fire-flames noondays kindle,
Whereby piled-up honours perish,
Whereby swollen ambitions dwindle.
While just this or that poor impulse,
Which for once had play unstifled,
Seems the sole work of a life-time
That away the rest have trifled.

Browning

I am the Almighty God. Genesis 17:1

God is a perplexing Being to man because He is never in the wrong, and through the process of allowing every bit of man's wrongdoing to appear right at the time, He proves Himself right ultimately. Beware of the conception that God has to use His wits to keep Himself from being outwitted by man and the devil. God will never have more power than He has now; if He could have, He would cease to be God. Individually we may thwart God's purpose in our lives for a time, but God's purpose will be fulfilled, wherever we end. Human free will is God's sovereign work, and God not only respects it in man but He delights to posit it in him. I have perfect power not to do God's will, and I have that power by the sovereign will of God; but I can never thwart God's will ultimately. God allows ample room for man and the devil to do their worst; He allows the combination of other wills to work out to the last lap of exhaustion so that that way need never be tried again, and men will have to confess, either reluctantly or willingly, that God's purpose was right after all. And this holds true in the individual lives of God's children. I am at liberty if I choose to try every independent plan of my own, but I shall find in the end (whether too late or not is another matter), that what God said I had better do at the beginning was the right thing, if only I had listened to Him.

Every blunder Abraham made was repeated in his descendants by the inevitableness of God's providence. The consequence of doing wrong is brought out in the life of Abraham in great prominence, but the abiding truth remains the same for each one of us. It is not cause and effect, but because God is God.

1. The Rigour of the Everlasting No

The LORD appeared to Abram . . .

Compare Genesis 15:1—"The word of the LORD came unto Abram *in a vision*." God's method all through seems to be vision first and then reality. So many mistake the vision for the reality, but in between the vision and the reality there is often a deep valley of humiliation, cf. 15:12—"Lo, an horror of great darkness fell upon him." How often has a faithful soul been plunged into a like darkness; after the vision has come the test and the darkness. Whenever God gives a vision to a saint, He puts the saint, as it were, in the shadow of His hand, and the saint's duty is to be still and listen. Genesis 16 is an illustration of the danger of listening to good advice when it is dark instead of waiting for God to send the light (cf. Galatians 1:15–16). When God gives a vision and darkness follows, wait; God will bring you into accordance with the vision He has given if you will wait His time. We try to do away with the supernatural in God's undertakings. Never try and help God fulfil His word. There are some things we cannot do, and that is one of them.

Never try to anticipate the actual fulfilment of a vision; you transact some business spiritually with God on your mount of transfiguration and by faith see clearly a vision of His purpose, and immediately afterwards there is nothing but blank darkness. You trust in the Lord, but you walk in darkness; the temptation is to work up enthusiasm, you have to stay on God and wait (Isaiah 50:10–11). If darkness turns to spiritual doldrums, you are to blame. When God puts the dark of "nothing" into your experience, it is the most positive something He can give you. If you do anything now it is sure to be wrong, you have to remain in the centre of nothing, and say "thank you" for nothing. It is a very great lesson, which few of us learn, that when God gives us nothing it is because we are inside Him, and by determining to do something we put ourselves outside Him. Abraham would not stay in the land when the famine came because there was nothing; he would not trust God for a child because there was not one. God kept giving Abraham "nothing," i.e., Himself, and by determining to do something Abraham jumped outside God, and came to find that he was putting himself in the relationship of the Everlasting No. There are things God tells us to do without any light or illumination other than just the word of His command, and if we do not obey it is because we are independently strong enough to wriggle out of obeying. All God's commands are enablings, therefore it is a crime to be weak in His strength.

The phrase "When Abram was ninety years old and nine" is of immense significance. Thirteen years have rolled by in between Genesis 16:16 and Genesis 17:1. Abraham had anticipated the purpose of God and had to pass through a long time of discipline. The act of Abraham and Sarah produced a complexity in God's plan all down the ages. So Moses had to wait forty years after his presumptuous attempt to reach his destination. Adam and Eve did the same thing, they took the "short cut" (which is the meaning of temptation) and anticipated their destination to be *actually* what they were *potentially*—"as God" (Genesis 3:5 RV), and thereby they went wrong. Our destination is to be as God, that is what we are here to become, and in Jesus Christ we do become so. Beware of estimating the temptation of a child of God to be less royal than it really is. The temptation of a child of God does not spring from selfish lust, but from a passionate desire to reach God's destination.

Abraham emerged out of this stage of discipline with one determination, viz., to let God have His way. There is no indication that he is relying on the flesh any longer, his reliance is on God alone. All self-sufficiency has been destroyed in every shape and form, there is not one common sense ray left as to how God is going to fulfil His word. God never hastens and He never tarries. He works His plans out in His own way, and we either lie like clogs on His hands or we assist Him by being as clay in the hands of the potter.

"*The LORD appeared to Abram*"—the real God now, not a vision. The knowledge of the real God is reached when my confidence is placed in God and not in His blessings. Paul takes Abraham as the type of the life of faith; not of sanctification, but of a tried faith built on a real God.

2. The Reality of the Everlasting Yea

I am God Almighty . . . (RV)

"I am God Almighty"—El Shaddai, the Father-Mother God, God proved as sufficient for everything. The wonder of El Shaddai (the power to create new things in the old world) runs through the whole kingdom of grace. Remember, Isaac was born of dead parents (Romans 4:19). If I think I am going to produce the Son of God in myself by prayer, or obedience, or consecration, I am making exactly the same blunder that Sarah and Abraham made over Hagar. ". . . which were born, not . . . of the will of the flesh, nor of the will of man, but of God." Immediately I realise that the thing is impossible, then God will do it. To be brought to the verge of the impossible is to be brought to the margin of the reservations of God. When God is bringing us there we indulge in sulky misbehaviour—"I don't want to go that way; I want

Your blessings," and when God asks if we have to come to the end of ourselves, we sit resigned and say—"It is all up now"; then suddenly we are in Paradise because we have come to the end of the thing God could not bring in. The Everlasting Yea is reached when we perceive that God is El Shaddai, the All-Sufficient God. There is no need so far as God is concerned for the years of silence and discipline if we will only be stupid enough to hear the everlasting No and not try to make it Yea—"Oh yes, I am going to try and make my natural virtues pleasing to God"; God says you cannot do it. God does not discard the old and create something entirely new; He creates something in the old until the old and the new are made one. To call conversion new birth is an impoverishment. Because a man who has lived in sin stops sinning, it is no sign that he is born from above (RV mg). Jesus did not talk about new birth to a sinner, but to a religious man, a godly man full of rectitude; but Nicodemus worshipped God as a reminiscence, he had not the creation of El Shaddai in him. The creation of El Shaddai is what is made possible by the Lord Jesus (Galatians 4:19).

3. The Reasonableness of the Everlasting Way
Walk before Me . . .

Abraham's faith is to be permanent, that is, he must walk continually before the eyes of the Almighty in the conscious unconsciousness of His presence. We won't walk before God because we are not confident in Him, and the proof that we are not confident in God is that occasionally we get into the sulks. If you are walking with God it is impossible to be in the sulks. Never have the idea that you have disobeyed when you know you have not, the reason you say so is because you are not walking in the permanent light of faith. Suppose Job had said—"If I were trusting in God I should not be treated like this"; he *was* trusting in God, and he *was* treated like that. Faith is not that I see God, but that I know God sees me; that is good enough for me, I will run out and play—a life of absolute freedom. Watch the spiritual sulks that arise because we want something other than God; we want God to give us something, to make us feel well, to give us wonderful insight into the Bible. That is not the attitude of a saint but of a sinner who is trying to be a saint, and who is coming to God to get things from Him. Unless we give to God the things we get from Him, they will prove our perdition.

4. The Rectitude of the Everlasting Day
. . . and be thou perfect.

"And be perfect," free from blame, or guiltless. Abraham was still lacking in the development of his faith and was therefore not blameless as yet. Had Abraham stayed in the land of promise, no matter though he starved to death, he would have been blameless, but he went down to Egypt and so was not blameless. We must beware lest we ignore what the old theologians called prevenient grace, that is, receiving beforehand the grace of God which will keep us worshipping Him instead of trusting in our wits. If we put moral wits in the place of mystic worship, we will go wrong. The life of Abraham does not stand for the life of a saint but for the life of the Father of the Faithful, consequently every error he committed, as well as every glorious thing he did, is recorded and traced out in its consequences through the history of his people. We are not to follow all the steps of Abraham, but to follow the steps of his faith (cf. 1 Corinthians 4:17).

We try to scrape our defects off and say—I think I am all right now. That is not walking blamelessly before God, but walking in determined opposition to faith in God. If I walk in faith in God there will be no specks to rub off; but if I don't walk in faith in God, everything is a defect and a stain, however good I am. It is a snare to continually think about defects, things which we really think should not be there. Imagine anyone who has seen himself in the light of Jesus Christ thinking of his defects! Why we are too filthy for words, and to be concerned because of the spots upon us is absurd. Leave the whole miserable thing alone; we have the sentence of death in ourselves that we should not trust in ourselves but in God, and there are no specks in God. I have determinedly to take no one seriously but God, and the first person I have to leave severely alone as being the greatest fraud I have ever known is myself. "Oh I am sick of myself"—if you really were sick of yourself you would go to your own funeral and for ever after let God be all in all. Until you get to that point you will never have faith in God.

Beware of the thing that makes you go down before God and sway from side to side spiritually—"I don't know what to do"; then don't do anything. "I don't see anything"; well, don't look for anything. "I thought by this time I should see something"; if you don't, be foolish enough to trust in God. It is the height of madness from common-sense standpoints to have faith in God. Faith is not a bargain with God—I will trust You if You give me money, but not if You don't. We have to trust in God whether He sends us money or not, whether He gives us health or not. We must have faith in God, not in His gifts. Let us walk before God and be perfect, you in your circumstances and I in mine, then we will prove ourselves true children of Abraham.

AWE
Genesis 17:2–14

I faced a future all unknown,
No opening could I see,
I heard without the night wind moan.
The days were dark to me—
I cannot face it all alone
O be Thou near to me!

He has, He will, He worketh still,
In ways most wonderful.
He drew me from the miry clay,
He filled my cup quite full.
And while my heart can speak I'll tell
His love unspeakable.

John Oxenham[11]

And Abram fell on his face. Genesis 17:3

It is significant to note the times when Abraham did not speak to God but remained silent before Him, not sullen, but silent. Awe is just that—reverential dread and wonder. Beware of its imitation; the pose of reverential awe is the greatest cloak for unbelief. Awe is the condition of a man's spirit realising Who God is and what He has done for him personally. Our Lord emphasises the attitude of a child, no attitude can express such solemn awe and familiarity as that of a child. In the Apocalypse the attitude of St. John is that of an awe-struck child of God.

1. The Personal Relation in Faithfulness
(Genesis 17:2)
The covenant with the Father of the Faithful is applicable to every man when once faith (i.e. a relationship between the individual and God) is born. We make covenants with ourselves, or with our experiences, or with our transactions—I came out to the penitent form; or, I surrendered to God. That is a covenant of self-idolatry, an attempt to consecrate our earnest consecration to God. It is never a question of covenanting to keep our vows before God, but of our relationship to God Who makes the covenant with us. In the matter of salvation it is God's honour that is at stake, not our honour. Few of us have faith in God, the whole thing is a solemn vow with our religious selves. We promise that we will do what God wants; we vow that we will remain true to Him, and we solemnly mark a text to this effect; but no human being can do it. We have to steadily refuse to promise anything and give ourselves over to God's promise, flinging ourselves entirely on to Him, which is the only possible act of the faith that comes as God's gift. It is a personal relation to God's faith—"between Me and thee." *"Come unto Me,"* said Jesus. The thing that keeps us from coming is religious self-idolatry; we will not let God make a covenant with us, we will make vows with God. Vowing means I can do it if I pledge myself to do it (cf. Exodus 19:3–5). We have to stake ourselves on the truthfulness of God's character; what He does with us is a matter of indifference. Beware of trusting in your trust and see that you trust in the Lord, and you will never know you trust Him because you are taken up into His certainty.

2. The Profound Realisation of Fruition
(Genesis 17:3)
And Abram fell on his face . . .

This is an expression of deep humility and trustful confidence and pure joy; these are always the characteristics of faith in God. Every time you say—I feel I haven't got the witness, pack up and get out—out of the compartment of yourself and into the compartment of God, and stay there. Whenever you make a transaction with God, it is real instantly and you have the witness; when there is no witness, no humility, no confidence or joy, it is because you have made a transaction with your religious self and you say—I must wait for God's witness. That is self-idolatry; there is no trust in God in it, but just the mewling of a sick infant. The relation is to be that of a child; fling yourself clean over on to God and wash your hands of the consequences, and John 14:27—"My peace I give unto you"—becomes true at once. The profound realisation of God makes you too unspeakably peaceful to be capable of any self-interest.

3. The Precious Recognition of Fellowship
(Genesis 17:3–4)
. . . and God talked with him.

The faith that is the creation of God's Spirit in the human soul is never private and personal. When once that faith is created we are caught up into the terrific universal purpose of God, "Thou shalt be a father of many nations." The Holy Spirit destroys our personal private life and turns it into a thoroughfare for God.

---

11. John Oxenham: pseudonym of William Arthur Dunkerley (1861–1941), English businessman and writer.

Faith is not the means whereby we take God to ourselves for our select coterie; faith is the gift of God whereby He expresses His purposes through us. God wants to take us up into His purpose so that we no more keep for our joys "a world within the world," but God can do with us exactly what He likes without saying—By your leave. God does not ask permission to use us any more than we ask permission to use our hands, but we have to keep in joint with God. Full power cannot be put into a machine that is out of gear. (Cf. 1 John 1:7.)

4. The Promised Royalty of Fatherhood *(Genesis 17:4)*

This amazing promise is exactly expressive of the power of God and it produces moral hysterics. When it begins to dawn in my conscious life what God's purpose is, there is the laughter of the possibility of the impossible. The impossible is exactly what God does. The sure sign that we have no faith in God is that we have no faith in the supernatural. No man can believe God unless God is in him. The promises to Abraham are God all over from beginning to end. Don't only make room for God, but believe that God has room enough for you.

5. The Peculiar Recognition of Regeneration Familiarity *(Genesis 17:5)*

The new name "Abraham" announces a new disposition, and circumcision represents the renewal of the whole into a more noble nature by the presence of a new disposition within until the two are made one (cf. Matthew 5:48). Hagar represents not the sinful but the natural, which must first go through the pain of being a willing slave and be turned into oneness with the purpose of God. The difficulty in personal life is that the natural in us says to God in spiteful irritation—"I shan't; I won't go back to Sarah; I won't submit to any rule at all, I will boss the whole thing myself." But you cannot; you will either have to come to the death of the natural willingly, or be dragged there by the providential tyranny of God.

6. The Physical Sign of Spirituality *(Genesis 17:6–14)*

Circumcision, or sanctification which it symbolises, is the decision to cut away all self-idolatry and abandon to God entirely. The old nature and the new have to be made one, and the sign that they are one is circumcision in the Old Testament and sanctification in the new. The point to remember is that the new creation is made by El Shaddai in the old world. When the Holy Spirit comes in the two natures are there distinctly, and they have to be amalgamated into one nature. The old has to be turned into a noble nature by the incoming of God; we are not to be fanatical and turn our noses up at the old. The new disposition is the one in which God is all. The Judaisers taught that all those who were of the direct historic seed of Abraham were all right. The Apostle John says No, it is not by physical generation but by supernatural generation (see John 1:12–13). Then came the spiritualising people who denied that God had anything to do with the physical generation. The Apostle says No. Jesus Christ came that way (see 1 John 4:2), which is a proof that everything that has been defiled is to be made holy through Christ. Beware of insulting God by being a pious prude instead of a pure person.

ECSTASIED
Genesis 17:15–27

Though dim as yet in tint and line,
We trace Thy picture's wise design,
And thank Thee that our age supplies
Its dark relief of sacrifice.
    Thy will be done!
Strike, Thou the Master, we Thy keys,
The anthem of the destinies!
The minor of Thy loftier strain,
Our hearts shall breathe the old refrain,
    Thy will be done!

               Whittier

Then Abraham fell upon his face, and laughed. Genesis 17:17

There are certain phases of the life of faith which look so much like cant and humbug that we are apt to grieve God's Spirit by our religious respectability in regard to them, and ecstasy is just one of those phases. An ecstasied man is one whose state of mind is marked by mental alienation from his surroundings, and his very consciousness is altered into excessive joy. These states are open gateways for God or for the devil. If they are worked up by thrills of our own seeking, they are of the devil; but when they come unsought in faithful performance of duties, they are the gateway into direct communication with God. Ecstasy is not a state in which to live; keep your ecstatic times dark. You have no business to show the depths to anyone but yourself and God.

We are all so abominably serious, so interested in our own characters, that we refuse to behave like Christians in the shallow concerns of life. Our safeguard is the God-given shallowness. It is the attitude of a spiritual prig to go about with a countenance that is a rebuke to others because you have the idea that they are shallower than you. Live the surface commonsense life in a common-sense way, and remember that the shallow concerns of life are as much of God as the profound concerns. It is not our devotion to God or our holiness that makes us refuse to be shallow, but our wish to impress others that we are not shallow, which is a sure sign that we are prigs. We are to be of the stamp of Our Lord and Master, and the prigs of His day called Him a glutton and a winebibber, they said He was not dealing with the profound things. Beware of the production of contempt for others by thinking that they are shallow. To be shallow is not a sign of being wicked; the ocean has a shore. The shallow amenities of life are appointed of God and are the things in which Our Lord lived, and He lived in them as the Son of God. It is easier for personal pride not to live in them. Beware of posing as a profound person; God became a Baby.

1. The Princess of God In Human Expression (*Genesis 17:15–16*)
The name "princess" is not earned by piety on the part of the woman, it is the new thing which has been created in her by faith in God. When we find unfortunate ingredients in Abraham and Sarah, and in ourselves, we have to realise that God's designations refer to what He redemptively creates in us, and not to our decorations of ourselves. The treasure is "in earthen vessels." A princess in God's sense is not a princess when she prides herself on her own initiative. When Our Lord says, "the same is My sister, and mother," note the condition of His designation, viz., "whosoever shall *do* the will of My Father which is in heaven"; not whosoever has done the will of God once. Doing the will of God is instantaneously continuous. Am I doing the will of God *now?* Faith does not give us a feeling of eternal life upon which we draw; faith is a fountain of living water overflowing. If I keep living the life of faith then I shall be a sister of the Lord Jesus. There is only one way to live the life of faith, and that is to *live it.*

2. The Paradoxes of God and Human Emotion (*Genesis 17:17*)
This is the first time laughter is mentioned in the Bible, and the first mention of a thing in the Bible colours its meaning all the way through. Abraham's laughter had in it no intermixture of wrong. Laugh-ter and weeping are the two intensest forms of human emotion, and these profound wells of human emotion are to be consecrated to God. The devil is never said to laugh. Laughter that is not the laughter of a heart right with God, a child heart, is terrible; the laughter of sin is as the crackling of burning thorns. Whenever the angels come to this earth they come bursting with a joy which instantly has to be stayed (cf. Luke 2:13). This earth is like a sick chamber, and when God sends His angels here He has to say—"Now be quiet; they are so sick with sin that they cannot understand your hilarity." Whenever the veil is lifted there is laughter and joy. These are the characteristics that belong to God and God's order of things; sombreness and oppression and depression, are the characteristics of all that does not belong to God.

The promise was so great that Abraham sank reverently upon the ground, and so paradoxical that he ecstatically laughed—"Is it to be now at this late day even as Thou didst assure me it was to be?" There was no doubt, but amazement; the thing was so completely impossible that Abraham believed it absolutely, so absolutely that his equilibrium was upset. We have all experienced ecstasy in minor degrees. Every time we have transacted business with God on His covenant and have let go entirely on God, there is no sense of merit in it, no human ingredient at all, but such a complete overwhelming sense of being a creation of God's that we are transfigured by peace and joy.

3. The Purpose of God and Human Expectation (*Genesis 17:18–21*)
Abraham was all this time contented with the supposition that Ishmael was the child of promise, but in this new revelation he receives the definite statement of God that Sarah shall bear to him the true heir, and the promise is revealed even in regard to time. Up till now there had been the mingling of doubt with Abraham's faith, he did not trust God completely because he did not see how He was going to fulfil His word (cf. Luke 24:41). In v. 20 the promise is still more clearly revealed, and with this revelation God withdraws—"and God went up from Abraham."

4. The Programme of God and Human Exercise (*Genesis 17:22–27*)
These verses state how Abraham complies with the prescribed rite of circumcision. God uses circumcision (as He did the rainbow) and makes it a sign and symbol for something it never was until He made it so. Circumcision becomes with the historic people of God a real sign of the covenant with God that they are His people, but there must be an accompanying sign of our agreement with God. For instance, the

physical exertion of coming to a penitent form has a more emphatic meaning than we imagine, and it is against those exertions that human nature protests— "But it is so humiliating." Of course it is! If you sit tight against the monitions of the Holy Ghost, you will make yourself obtuse to the voice of God. The thing that keeps you back from obeying is the domination of natural human pride that will not bow to God. Salvation will never be actual until you physically commit yourself to it (Romans 10:10).

FRIEND OF GOD
Genesis 18:1–15

Nor hope to find
A Friend but what has found a Friend in thee!—
All like the purchase; few the price will pay;
And this makes Friends such miracles below.
*   But since Friends grow not thick on every*
*   bough,*
Nor ev'ry Friend unrotten at the core;
First on Thy Friend, delib'rate with thyself!
Pause—ponder—sift! not eager in the choice
Nor jealous of the chosen:—fixing, fix!
Judge before Friendship, then confide till death.

Young

Pass not away, I pray Thee, from Thy servant. Genesis 18:3

The Apostle James calls Abraham "the Friend of God." The foundations of friendship with God are laid in inborn qualities; Abraham has that in him now which makes it possible for him to be the friend of God. Never confound "Saviour" with "friend," Our Lord said "Ye are My friends" to His disciples, not to sinners. Friendship with God means that there is now something of the nature of God in a man on which God can base His friendship. These inborn qualities are formed in me by the incoming of the Holy Spirit, they are not there by natural generation; then as I obey the revelation granted to me, friendship with God begins, based on the new life which has been created in me. That new life has no affinities on the old lines, but only on the line of God, and is unutterably humble and holy, unsulliedly pure, and absolutely devoted to God. "El Shaddai"—the One Who creates something *in* the old world, and transfigures it.

Friendship with God is faith in action in relation to God and to our fellow men. "A new commandment I give unto you, that ye love one another; even as I have loved you" (RV). I love others as God has loved me, and I see in the ingratitude of others the ingratitude which I have exhibited to God. The fellowship which arises out of such a friendship is a delight to the heart of God.

1. The Altar of Fellowship *(Genesis 18:1–5)*
This manifestation of God to Abraham is the most striking sign in the old Covenant of the Incarnation. The Incarnation in practical identification means the manifestation of God in mortal flesh in every detail of human life. Our Lord was not an ascetic like John the Baptist, He was not limited, or proscribed and fanatical. In Our Lord's life the natural and the supernatural were reconciled, the natural was not violently discarded. There was no ostensible preparation for the coming of the Son of God. How many knew that Jesus was God Incarnate? (John 1:11–12). It was only when the surgery of events had taken place that their eyes were opened and they knew Him (Luke 24:31). Our Lord comes in the most casual way, and we will miss Him unless we are prepared in our nature to discern Him. The most amazing evidence of a man's nature being changed is the way in which he sees God, to say "God led me here"; "God spoke to me"; is an everyday occurrence to him.

The altar of fellowship means that in every occurrence of life I offer myself in devotion to God. Abraham had difficulty at first in bringing the actual details of his life into touch with his real faith in God. Our Lord's actual life was a continual manifestation of His real faith in God, every detail—washing disciples' feet, fasting, praying, marriage feasts—manifested the altar of fellowship.

2. The Discipline of Fellowship *(Genesis 18:6–8)*
The reality of God being our Guest is the most awful joy in the discipline of fellowship. The spirit of hospitality consists in this, that in or with the stranger, we receive the Lord Himself. If Abraham could have done more for God actually than he would for any other, his fellowship with God was imperfect; but Abraham did no other for God than he would have done for a stranger, and this is the essential of readiness for God. We do our best to dress ourselves up, we put on behaviour that is not ours, moods that have

nothing to do with us, all in order to offer God suitable accommodation. The only way in which we can have God as our Guest is by receiving from Him the Holy Spirit Who will turn our bodies into His house. It is not that we prepare a palace for God, but that He comes into our mortal flesh and we do our ordinary work, in an ordinary setting, amongst ordinary people, as for Him. Our Lord teaches that we have to receive those He sends as Himself (Matthew 10:40). When therefore we receive hospitality from others in His name, we have to remember that it is being offered to our Master, not to us. It is easier to receive the rebuffs and the spurnings than to receive the hospitality and welcome really offered to Our Lord. We say—"But I cannot accept this"; if we are identified with our Lord we will have to go through the humiliation of accepting things of which we feel ourselves unworthy.

Times of feasting reveal a man's master like nothing else in human life, and it is in those times that Our Lord reveals Himself to be Master. My treatment of Jesus Christ is shown in the way I eat and drink, I am either a glutton and put Jesus Christ to shame, or else I am an ascetic and refuse to have fellowship with Him in eating and drinking; but when I become a humble saint I reveal Him all the time in the ordinary common ways of life. The ordinance of the Lord's Supper is a symbol of what we should be doing all the time. It is not a memorial of One Who has gone, but of One Who is always here, "This do in remembrance of Me"—be in such fellowship with Me that you show My death until I manifest Myself again. It is in the common things of life that evidence of the discipline of fellowship is given.

3. The Illumination of Fellowship *(Genesis 18:9–15)*

"Sarah laughed within herself." Abraham's laughter was that of joyful faith (chapter 17:17); Sarah's laughter was that of doubting little faith. Sarah had to come to the place where her faith was as active as Abraham's, where she was certain that what God had said would happen, would happen. There are times when God seems to overlook certain forms of unbelief, at the other times He brings our unbelief out suddenly into the light and makes us cringe with shame before it. It is not because He wants to show how miserable and mean[12] we are, but because our particular form of un-faith is hindering the expression of His purpose in and through us.

A child of faith must never limit the promise of God by what seems good to him, but must give to the power of God the preference over his own reason. God never contradicts reason, He transcends it always. We "limit the Holy One of Israel" by remembering what we have allowed Him to do for us in the past; this hinders God and grieves His Spirit. In a time of communion God brings to us a real illumination of His word and we feel thoroughly exhilarated, then we begin to bring in our "Buts." Whenever you are severely rebuked by God for indulgence in unbelief, take it as an honour from God, because prompt obedience on your part will mean the expression of God's purpose in and through you. The things that burden us either make us laugh at their absurdity, or else make us realise that God is burdening us for His own purpose.

In verses 9–14 we have a record of the most remarkable table-talk in the world, the table-talk of God with Abraham and his wife.

GETTING THERE
Genesis 18:16–33

If we with earnest effort could succeed
*   To make our life one long connected Prayer,*
As lives of some perhaps have been and are:—
If—never leaving Thee—we had no need
Our wandering spirits back again to lead
*   Into Thy presence, but continued there,*
*   Like angels standing on the highest stair*

Of the sapphire throne—this were to pray indeed!
*   But if distractions manifold prevail,*
*   And if in this we must confess we fail,*
Grant us to keep at least a prompt desire,
*   Continual readiness for Prayer and Praise—*
An altar heaped and waiting to take fire
*   With the least spark, and leap into a blaze!*

Trench

---

12. mean: as used here, something or someone ordinary, common, low, or ignoble, rather than cruel or spiteful.

And Abraham drew near, and said . . .

"Getting there" means coming into intimate relationship with God without impertinence or lack of reverence. The meaning of intercession is that we see what God is doing, consequently there is an intimacy between the child and the Father which is never impertinent. We must pour into the bosom of God the cares which give us pain and anxiety in order that He may solve for us, and before us, the difficulties which we cannot solve. We injure our spiritual life when we dump the whole thing down before God and say—You do it. That spirit is blind to the real union with God. We must dump ourselves down in the midst of our problems and watch God solve them for us. "But I have no faith"—bring your problems to God and stay with Him while He solves them, then God Himself and the solution of your problems will be for ever your own. Watch the tendency to pathetic humbug in your approach to God. If we could see the floor of God's immediate presence, we would find it strewn with the "toys" of God's children who have said—This is broken, I can't play with it any more, please give me another present. Only one in a thousand sits down in the midst of it all and says—I will watch my Father mend this. God must not be treated as a hospital for our broken "toys," but as our Father.

1. The Actual and Real in Union *(Genesis 18:16–19)*

Verse 16 reveals the union of vision and actual life. Abraham sees Jehovah, but he also does his duty to his guests; he does not forget the courtesy of seeing his sublime visitors on their way as if they were ordinary men. The union of the actual and the real was an habitual condition in the life of Our Lord; it is not so with us until we learn to make it so. We have a wonderful time of communion with God, then comes the spiritual pout—I have to go and clean boots, or write an essay! In Our Lord's life there was no divorce between the actual and the real, He never gave Himself "continually to prayer." Beware of the tendency that makes you wish that God would pretend you are someone special, it is a childish make-believe, standing on spiritual tiptoe to look as big as God—others can do this and that, but I must give myself to prayer. The great secret of the obedient life of faith is that the actual conditions of bodily life are transfigured by real communion with God.

"Shall I hide from Abraham that which I do?" (RV). Notice the communing of God with Himself before He gives the revelation to Abraham. God cannot reveal Himself to anyone; the revelations of God are determined by the condition of individual character (cf. Psalm 18:24–26); God takes up the man who is worthy to be the recipient of a revelation. Abraham by his own obedience was fitted to receive the revelation, and this is recognised by God when He brings him into union with Himself, not into absorption, but into complete union.

2. The Awful Reckoning Ultimately *(Genesis 18:20–22)*

The moral demand is for the punishment of sin. Every grain of sand cries out for its punishment (cf. Genesis 4:10). Human beings do not echo the cry, only one or two echo it in intercession, and the cry of Nature is joined by the man who knows God.

"I will know." This is the introduction of the final decision. It must become evident in the last trial whether the limit of the long-suffering patience of God has been reached. Verse 22: "And the men . . ." must be connected with Genesis 19:1. They were two angels who accompanied Jehovah, and in the form of men they depart to introduce the final test; they depart, but Abraham stands "yet before the Lord."

3. The Appealing Reverence to the Uttermost *(Genesis 18:23–33)*

There is no impertinence in Abraham's attitude, only profound humility and intensest intimacy. Abraham is not questioning God, but bringing himself to see how God will solve the matter. God allows Abraham to come out with his full intercession until Abraham begins to grasp the essential conditions by which God governs all things. Abraham goes on from step to step, and Jehovah grants him step by step, without once going before his request. The stopping point is reached by reason of the fact that Abraham was in complete communion with God throughout the progress of his intercession. After the final test prayer is impossible (cf. 1 John 5:16).

By means of intercession we understand more and more the way God solves the problems produced in our minds by the conflict of actual facts and our real faith in God. Whenever temptations contend in our minds, and things meet us in the providence of God which seem to involve a contradiction of what we believe, let the conviction of God's righteousness remain unshaken.

It is an insult to sink before God and say "Thy will be done" when there has been no intercession. That is the prayer of impertinent unbelief—There is no use in praying, God does whatever He chooses. The saying of "Thy will be done" is born of the most intimate relationship to God whereby I talk to Him freely. There is in this prayer of Abraham a distinction between the begging which knows no limit and the prayer which is conscious that there are limits set by the holy character of God. Repetition in intercessory importunity is not bargaining, but the joyous insistence of prayer.

The nearer Abraham came to God in his intercession the more he recognised his entire unworthiness—"Behold now, I have taken upon me to speak unto the Lord, which am but dust and ashes." Genuine unworthiness is never shy before God any more than a child is shy before his mother. A child of God is conscious only of his entire dependence upon God.

In the beginning of our spiritual life our prayers are not of faith but of fretfulness. But when you get into the inner place I defy you to go on praying for yourself, it never occurs to you to do so because you are brought into relationship with God Who makes your spirit partake of His own. Whenever Our Lord spoke of importunity in intercession it was never for ourselves but for others. When by imperceptible degrees we stop praying for ourselves, we are "getting there." Prayer is the supreme activity of all that is noblest in our personality, and the essential nature of prayer is faith.

SCARCELY SAVED
Genesis 19:1–29

Better in bitterest agony to lie,
Before Thy throne,
Than through much increase to be lifted up on high,
And stand alone.

Yet best—the need that broke me at Thy feet,
In voiceless prayer,
And cast my chastened heart, a sacrifice complete,
Upon Thy care.

John Oxenham

Escape for thy life. Genesis 19:17

It is such chapters as these that enable us to understand the essential nature of God's Redemption.

1. Prepared by Gracious Experiences *(Genesis 19:1–3)*
The manifestation which was given to Lot corresponds to that given to Abraham (see Genesis 18:2). Lot was not a noble man of God like Abraham, but the fact that he bowed himself to the ground before the angels shows that he retained the power to know when God was near. In comparison with his generation, Lot was righteous, and his contact with Abraham made his manners similar to Abraham's. This preparation by gracious experiences occurs in our personal lives, and such experiences should be cherished for they enable us to do the right thing when we might otherwise do wrong. Beware of not heeding the angel of God in whatever form he comes to you.

"They entered into his house." The entrance of God into a house does not secure anything, but reveals that there is something there with which God has affinity. It is never our merit God looks at but our faith. If there is only one strand of faith amongst all the corruption within us, God will take hold of that one strand.

After every temptation notice where your affinities lie. If you have gone through the temptation successfully, your affinities will be with the highest and purest (cf. Matthew 4:11); but if you have not the same affinity with the highest, it is a sign that you have become blunted in your spiritual susceptibilities. The seal of doom in a man is that he cannot believe in purity, and this can only be accounted for by an internal twist; no man gets there easily. What is true in individual lives has become appallingly true in Sodom.

God has given us a precious gift in that looking at other Christians we see not them but the Lord. If you see only where others are *not* the Lord, it is you who are wrong, not they; you have lost the bloom of spirit which keeps you in touch with Jesus Christ. If I cannot see God in others, it is because He is not in me. If I get on my moral high horse and say it is they who are wrong, I become that last of all spiritual iniquities, a suspicious person, a spiritual devil dressed up as a Christian. Beware of mistaking suspicion for discernment, it is the biggest misunderstanding that ever twisted Christian humility into Pharisaism. When I see in others things that are not of God, it is because the Spirit of God has revealed to me my own meanness[13] and badness; when I am put right with God on the basis of His Redemption and see those things in others, it is in order that God may restore them through my intercession. Be careful never to lose the bloom of your spiritual susceptibilities.

2. Proposals of Great Evil *(Genesis 19:4)*
The history of Sodom reveals that sin is the beginning of the most appalling corruption. Always distinguish between what we are apt to call sin and what the Bible calls sin. The Bible does not call the cor-

---

13. mean: as used here, something or someone ordinary, common, low, or ignoble, rather than cruel or spiteful.

ruption of Sodom sin; sin is a disposition, not a deed; the corruption of Sodom is the criminal result of sin. It is because this distinction has been lost sight of that pseudo-evangelical preaching has been to the effect that only moral blackguards can be saved. When Our Lord faced men not guilty of moral blackguardism, but worthy, upright men, He did not deal with them in the way He did with sinners; He seemed to be infinitely sterner with the Pharisees than with the publicans (*see* Matthew 21:31). He looked at something we do not see, viz., the disposition.

Lot was the only one who stood as a representative of God in Sodom, and while he was free from the abominations of Sodom, he was not far from its worldly mind. His was the doubting heart which soon turns to double ways. Lot's position arises from having borrowed most of his piety (Genesis 12:4). Weak faith chooses the visible things instead of enduring as seeing Him Who is invisible, and slowly and surely such faith settles down between mammon and righteousness. In the supreme test Lot trusted his wits; Abraham worshipped and waited.

3. Perils of Grievous Emotion *(Genesis 19:5–9)*

In the history of Sodom, independence of God reaches the limit of blasphemy. The way to get there in personal life is to indulge in sentimental spirituality. If you indulge in a spiritual sentiment you do not intend to obey, the exact opposite of that emotion will come in its wake. Beware of panic, because panic always advocates doing wrong that right may result. In fact, the tendency to *do* instead of to devote one's self to God, is nearly always the sign of a smudged purity of relationship to God.

4. Performance of God's Ends *(Genesis 19:10–29)*

Abraham standing alone with God is the key to the rescue of Lot and his family, out they come whether they like it or not. The angels are insistent in answer to Abraham's intercession (*see* v. 16). Yet Lot was rescued with the greatest difficulty because of his vacillation. Vacillation in a crisis is the sign of an unabandoned nature. An abandoned nature never can vacillate because there is nothing to weigh; such a nature is completely abandoned to another. Lot's fear was culpable because it was indicative of a stultified judgement.

See to it that you do not profane the holiness of God by refusing to abandon yourself away from your experience of what He has done for you to God Himself. Whenever you do not come in contact with God for yourself, you will begin to watch your own whiteness—I dare not say this or do that. It is a cabined, confined life and when difficulties come like a wall of fire, God has to come and rescue you; and He does it by means of intercession on the part of some one else. Beware of accepting the blessings and visions of God as an indication of your goodness and not of the mercy and purpose of God—"the LORD being merciful unto him."

WRECKED IN HARBOUR
Genesis 19:30–38

A Chequer-Board of mingled Light and Shade?
And We the Pieces on it deftly laid?
Moved and removed, without a word to say,
By the Same Hand that Board and Pieces made?

No Pieces we in any Fateful Game,
Nor free to shift on Destiny the blame;
Each Soul doth tend its own immortal flame,
Fans it to Heaven, or smothers it in shame.

John Oxenham

And he dwelt in a cave. Genesis 19:30

The phrase "wrecked in harbour" describes the character that has gone through great storms and has made the harbour, and yet is wrecked as the result of an inward, persisting defect.

I am very sorry for the failures at Christchurch of which you tell. I suspect that cleverness was at the bottom of the failure, for it is a character of mind the exercise of which is so instantly and pleasantly rewarded, that the temptation to cultivate it is always present.

Sir James Paget in a letter to his son

Spiritual cleverness is the cause of much of our failure. We may not have much mental cleverness, but some of us are dextrously clever spiritually. We have so many memories of the times when God came in and did the thing that we determinedly "loaf" on God—only we call it "relying on the Holy Ghost." There are times when God does give real spiritual insight and times when He does not, and if between the times of inspiration you do not work but "loaf," you are leading up to tremendous failure one day. The moments of light and inspiration are an indication of the standard which we must work to keep up. If between the times of inspiration we refuse to practise, we shall fail spiritually exactly where Paget's son failed intellectually. He failed because he trusted to the clever moments of his genius, and we fail because we trust to the monuments of spiritual cleverness.

1. The Natural History of the Prudence Peril

The prudence which appears in the life of Abraham as sinful prudence (e.g., Genesis 12:10) appears again in the lives of his kindred, and is the persisting defect in the character of Lot. No man can do things and leave them with himself. He may not see the result, but he will have to answer for it generations after. The prudence peril is traceable first of all in Adam, then in Noah, then in Abraham, and right on to the end of the chapter until it becomes the most dominant characteristic of Israel and Judah. The terror of the prudence peril is that it can end in such a deed as this. These things are written for our instruction. "But I never could do such things." What any man has ever done, any man can do if he does not watch.

The error is putting prudence in competition with God's will, weighing *pros* and *cons* before God when He has spoken. Always beware when you want other people to commend the decision you have made, because it is an indication that you have trusted your wits instead of worshipping God. If you say "But I can prove I was right," you may be sure you are wrong, because you have to use your ingenuity to prove you are right. When you act in faith in God it is not logical proof that you are right that matters, but the certainty of the Divine approval, and this keeps you from seeking the approval of others. We have to watch that we use our wits to assist us in worshipping God and carrying out His will, not in carrying out our own will and then asking God very piously to bless the concoction. Put communion with God on the throne, and then ask God to direct your common sense to choose according to His will. Worship first and wits after.

2. The Natural History of Panic Perversity

Sensual passion always follows spent panic. It is easy to fall into the sins of the flesh when once the ideals of life lose their power. All you have to do is to get into a panic on any line, and you will be as perverse as can be because you have committed a sin against your own nature. Not only so, but you have given an opportunity to the devil over your body. There was an entire absence of panic in the life of Our Lord, consequently nothing of the nature of perversity. Notice how Our Lord continually curbed Peter on the line of impulse, because impulse is apt to lead to panic, and anything of the nature of panic opens the door to perversity and sensuality. A saint has no right to give way to a panic of nerves, it is a deliberate giving way and has to be hauled up instantly. When we give way to a panic of nerves we give the temple of the Holy Ghost over to the devil. Beware of the "panickiness" which takes the form of hysteria, because on the borders of hysteria lurk all the demons that can possess human nature. Never sympathise with anyone who is giving way to hysteria; if you do, you aid and abet Satan in thrusting the temple of the Holy Ghost into the clutches of the devil.

Never allow an emotion which you know you dare not carry out on its own level; grip it on the threshold of your mind in a vice of blood and allow it no more way. Few of us realise the power we have of doing this. I am a criminal in the sight of God for allowing an emotion with regard to anyone which I know I dare not carry out on its logical level. If once we got hold of the psychological law that an emotion not carried out on its legitimate level will react on a lower level, it would bring the wind of rugged reality into devotional meetings. It is possible to step from devotion to God into a moral cesspool in one second, and we are to blame before God for not knowing these things. God's word is as rugged and unvarnished as can be on this line, and it is the cunning and abominable nonsense of what is called good taste that prevents these things being stated. I have no business to allow false emotions before God, emotions that are not "me" at all, and that I have not the remotest intention of carrying out. Our Lord requires not only chastity of body, He requires chastity of thought.

The law that every extraordinary expansion or satisfaction of heart or brain or will is paid for, paid for inevitably without the possibility of putting off or transferring the payment, is one of the truths about which no human being with a soul a little above the brute has the slightest doubt. . . . It is an eternal and immutable verity and the soul of man is a witness to it.

"The Law of Nemesis," Prof. Saintsbury

PHILISTINISM
Genesis 20:1–7

When the powers of hell prevail
  O'er our weakness and unfitness,
Could we lift the fleshly veil,
  Could we for a moment witness
    Those unnumbered hosts that stand
    Calm and bright on either hand—
Oh! what joyful hope would cheer!
  Oh! what faith serene would guide us!
Great may be the danger near,
  Greater are the friends beside us.

And Abraham journeyed . . . and sojourned in Gerar.
Genesis 20:1

The term "Philistinism" owes its popularity to Matthew Arnold[14] and is used to-day in reference to uncultured people. It is used here because this is the first meeting of the house of Abraham with the Philistines, and also because at this stage Abraham lapsed into uncultured confidence in himself and into compromise with spiritually uncultured people. To say "I can't understand how Abraham could do it" is self-deception. If you will look inside your own heart, provided you do not love yourself too much, you will never say such a thing. We have to be careful lest we blind ourselves by putting up our own standards instead of looking at the standard God puts up. If we put a saint up as a standard, we blind ourselves to ourselves; it is personal vanity makes us do it. When we put God's standard up, viz., Himself, there is no room for personal vanity. It is self-deception to say— "Because I am saved and sanctified, therefore all I do is sure to be right." As long as I establish myself amongst people who agree with me and am consciously "bigger" than them all, it is easy to be complacent; but when circumstances oust me out amongst another set of people who do not accept my standards, my complacency is upset and I am nowhere. The grace of God makes us honest with ourselves. We must be humorous enough to see the shallow tricks we all have, no matter what our profession of Christianity. We are so altogether perverse that God Almighty had to come and save us! Whenever we forget this and begin to set up little standards of our own, imbedded in some favourite saint, we are sure to go wrong. We have to get rid of all notions about ourselves and our own standards, and keep in front what God puts in front, viz., Our Lord Himself, then we will not be tempted to delusion about ourselves. Our eye must be on God, not on ourselves.

1. The Disposition of Reaction *(Genesis 20:1)*
When the Bible records facts of experience, look in your own experience for the answer; when the Bible reveals standards of revelation, look to God, not to experience.

The reaction from a state of great spiritual excitement is revealed in Abraham as well as in Lot, and as on a former occasion (*see* Genesis 12:10) Abraham decides to change his residence—"and he sojourned in Gerar." If we bring the light of experience to this reaction on the part of Abraham, we shall understand how even such a believer as he fell the second time into the same sin. We are apt to say—I won't do that thing again now that God has warned me." But you will, you will do it as certainly as Abraham did if you trust to your vows instead of to God. The one thing to do is to look steadfastly to God. Always beware when you are perfectly certain you are right, so certain that you do not dream of asking God's counsel. God never puts the judgement with our wits, but entirely with Himself, consequently we must never depend on our moral judgement or our intellectual discernment, or on our sense of right and justice. All these are right in themselves but not right in us, we can only be right as we remain absolutely confident in God. When we realise that we have repeated a sin, the danger is to lie down in the mud and refuse to get up. There is no refuge in vowing or in praying, but only in one place, in absolute confidence in God. The child attitude is the only right one.

2. The Discretion of Reason *(Genesis 20:2)*
Judged from every standpoint, it would seem the right thing for Abraham to get away from the blasted country of Sodom and go to Gerar. It was not wrong from any standpoint, it was the act of a wise, sensible, reasoning man of God; but Abraham was not God's man in going because immediately he goes God rebukes him. In going to Gerar, as in going down to Egypt, Abraham thought he was justified, but in each case an entirely different thing happens from what he intended, viz., Sarah is taken from him. Whenever we bring in our ordinary wisdom as a factor of decision on any point, we are "out of it," not morally or with

---

14. Matthew Arnold (1822–1888): English scholar, poet, and critic.

human beings (it will end with a wrong relation to human beings ultimately), but our relationship to God is injured. Abraham had no notion that he was doing wrong to Abimelech, but the record proves that he did, and also that he injured his relationship to God as a faithful soul. Beware of being other than a simple child of God. The only safeguard is dependence upon God, not on godly decisions.

Beware whenever your logical moral right puts you in a wrong relation to God. "If God will only prove that my right is right"—it is the one thing over which we are stubbornly jealous of God. "I know I am right," we say, and it has to be proved to us that from the standpoint of the Holy Ghost we are wrong. If I can prove to my own mind that I am right, by that very act I am wrong in disposition towards God.

3. The Dream of Realisation *(Genesis 20:3)*
The fact that God makes good come out of my wrong does not make my wrong any better, I have simply utilised God's permissive will to go in a circle when I should have gone straight. There are times when you see what God wants and you begin to obey with the simple direct obedience of a child; then comes the "choppy waters" of friends' advice or of considerations of yourself, and for a while you wobble because you have become discreet and shrewd and wise, instead of being a child of God. Then when after the passing of days, or longer, according to your stubbornness, God brings you out of all the turmoil, the devil comes and says it was a good thing after all. It was not, it was a bad thing. You prevented God's order being worked out directly through you, and He had to allow you to go in a circle and only brought you back after having grieved you through with sorrows.

Beware of justifying yourself when God alone is the justifier. If ever I can justify myself, I make God unjust. If I am right and morally based in all I do and say, I do not need a Saviour, and God is not justified in the extravagant waste of sending Jesus Christ to die for me. If God judges me a sinner who needs saving, and I can prove that I am just, I make God unjust (cf. Psalm 51:4). Every kind of upholding I give to myself, whether I be saint or sinner, is a blow in the face of God, and is a proof that I am on the wrong basis. If in any detail I take the justice of God and make it mean my own justice, I thereby prove God to be unjust. This is part of the mystery of godliness and can only be understood by the intuition of faith (Matthew 11:25).

4. The Dilemma of Rectitude *(Genesis 20:4–7)*
God stepped in and delivered Abimelech from committing sin because of His sheer mercy—"I also withheld thee from sinning against Me." There is a difference between deliverance from sin by God's sovereign act, which is an occasion for praise, and the defiance of sin by personal integrity, which tells in the building up of character. There are times in personal life when God by His sovereign act prevented us from committing sin, and when we look back and see how He preserved us, the danger is to say it must have been because of our innocence. No, it was of the mercy of God.

We have to learn to utilise a right reliance on circumstances in the spiritual domain, to discern that it is God Who engineers circumstances. Abraham refused to see this, and every now and again he stepped in and engineered circumstances for himself, and every time he did this, he upset everything. Reverent humility and moral pride are ultimately brought out very clearly—the former in Abraham and the latter in Abimelech. The believer in his weakness is exalted above the man of the world in his strength.

HUMILIATION
Genesis 20:8–18

Sink in thou blessed sign!
  Pass all my spirit through
And sever with thy sacred touch
  The hollow from the true.

Through my heart's very ground
  Thy ploughshare must be driven,
Till all are better loved than self,
  And yet less loved than heaven.

And Abraham said, Because . . . Genesis 20:11

Humiliation and humility must not be confounded. Humility can never be humiliated. To be humiliated means to be lowered in condition. The word as applied to our Lord has no reference whatever to His personal calibre, but to the lowering of His external form from *"being in the form of God"* to *"taking the form of a servant."* Humiliation as applied to us means a lowering of condition in the sense of being mortified. Whenever we pride ourselves on anything as being of real acceptance to God and realise that He absolutely ignores that thing, we will experience the ghastly humbling of humiliation.

1. The Humility and Honour of Abimelech
(Genesis 20:8–10)
Abimelech's true humility is revealed in the way he humbles himself in communicating the events of his dream to his courtiers, he deliberately makes known before his whole court the compromising position he is in. Verse 8 describes the intense publicity of his confession, and verses 9–11 his rigorous, yet not vindictive talk with Abraham—although there is stinging irony in what he says to Sarah (v.16).

In nine cases out of ten, reserve is simply personal pride, which will turn to insolence or iniquity at a moment's notice. One of the most delicate issues in the history of the human soul is that of concealing what ought to be made known and of making known what ought to be concealed. When concealing is a great relief, question it; when revealing is a great relief, question it. The only guiding factor is obedience to the highest we know. The wriggling we indulge in to escape from being humiliated prevents our being right with God. For instance, you have a wrong attitude of mind towards another, and the Spirit of God tells you to put it right between yourself and that one (cf. Matthew 5:24), and you say—No, I will put it right between myself and God. You cannot do it; it is impossible. Instead of deliberately obeying God, irrespective of what it costs, we use the trick of prayer to cover our own cowardice. It is a very subtle subterfuge to prevent ourselves being humiliated, but God will bring us into a place of humiliation externally, and others will see we are humiliated. If, on the other hand, there is something between yourself and God, and you feel it would be an enormous relief to tell someone else about it, *don't*. "Immediately I conferred not with flesh and blood." It is never a question of giving an explanation to someone else, but of maintaining obedience to the highest we know at all costs.

Personal misconduct will never bring bondage on others unless the misconduct springs from an independent attitude of mind towards God. Wrong doing on the part of any student here will never interfere with the atmosphere unless along with the misconduct there is a deliberate defiance of mind against God, then the whole atmosphere of the College will be charged with antagonism, and the antagonism will last as long as that one remains at "loggerheads" with God spiritually. It is not wrong doing but a wrong attitude of mind towards God spiritually that damages the atmosphere.

It was independence of God on the part of Abraham that brought the trouble on the house of Abimelech. Abraham repeated the mistake of a former occasion because of a wrong attitude to God; he was so wrong that he thought he was doing right. Abimelech had reason to complain of the conduct of Abraham in the same way that Pharaoh had reason to complain of it (cf. Genesis 12:13–20), and Abimelech does not shrink from declaring his injured sense of truth and justice. Imagine the humiliation it would be to Abraham when he realised what he had done.

2. The Humiliation and Honour of Abraham
(Genesis 20:11–18)
The way in which Abraham offers his apologies reveals clearly that he was ashamed. The fear of man which had determined him earlier (Genesis 12:11–13) was awakened afresh in him by what he had so recently seen in Sodom, and he was suspicious of human nature everywhere—"Because I thought, Surely the fear of God is not in this place." Abraham ashamedly explains his motive and gives his explanation for his equivocation. In verse 12 he explains that what he said of Sarah was not untrue, but he also indicates that his reason for saying she was his sister has deservedly brought him into humiliation. There was none of the sneakish element in Abraham as there was in Jacob, his reason for denying his wife was that through her God had promised him a child, and he was trying to guard her for God.

We are always in danger of mistaking personal predilections for Christian perfection, and we have to learn to take the veil off our moral quirks. Over and over again it works like this: we begin to be cunning and think—Now, if I am not careful that man will utilise my position for his own purposes. The real reason we say it is that we do not like that particular man and imagine therefore that God does not like him either. Or else it works in this way: when someone whom we like comes, we say—Oh yes, that is of God's order; but I can't be bothered with those other people, I do not think God guided them to come. It is the same old trick, and we have to be excessively careful that we do not lean to our own understanding and try to conserve God's order in our way instead of allowing God to conserve His order in His own way.

There was never any element of fear or cunning or diplomacy in Our Lord in any shape or form. Our Lord was never suspicious of anyone; yet He trusted no one saving His Father, consequently He was never vindictive, nor was He ever humiliated. It is only possible to be humiliated when we are serving our own pride.

Abraham's defects are clear and his sins obvious, but his nobility is extraordinary. Abraham is never presented as a saint or as a type of sanctification. Phases of his life may be used to present these, but Abraham himself is the type of the life of faith in its failures and in its successes. Sanctification is not something Our Lord does in me; sanctification is *Himself* in me. "Of Him are ye in Christ Jesus, who . . . is made unto us . . . sanctification" (1 Corinthians 1:30).

GOD IS GOOD
Genesis 21:1–8

*Never to be again! But many more of the kind
As good, nay, better perchance: is this your comfort
        to me?
To me, who must be saved because I cling with
        my mind
To the same, same self, same love, same God: ay,
        what was, shall be.*

*There shall never be one lost good! What was,
        shall live as before;
The evil is null, is nought, is silence implying
        sound;
What was good shall be good, with, for evil, so
        much good more;
On the earth the broken arcs; in the heaven, a
        perfect round.*

                                                            Browning

God hath made me to laugh. Genesis 21:6

One of the greatest demands of God on the human spirit is to believe that God is good when His providence seems to prohibit the fulfilment of what He has promised. The one character in the Bible who sustains this strain grandly is Abraham. Paul in summing up the life of Abraham points to it as his greatest quality—"Abraham believed God."

1. God's Performance of His Own Promise *(Genesis 21:1)*
No one can fulfil a promise but the one who made it. These words contain the whole autobiography of the godly ups and downs of the life of faith. During the years when everything seemed to contradict the fulfilment of the promise, Abraham continually forgot this fundamental fact and tried to help God fulfil it. God alone can fulfil His promise, and we have to come to the place of perfect reliance upon God (cf. 1 Thessalonians 5:23–24).

"The LORD visited Sarah as He had said, and the LORD did unto Sarah as He had spoken." God visits the believer with the word of promise and visits him again with the word of fulfilment. Abraham endured for twenty-five years without any sign of fulfilment. The majority of us know nothing about waiting, we don't wait, we endure. Waiting means that we go on in the perfect certainty of God's goodness—no dumps or fear. The attitude of the human heart towards God Who promises should be to give Him credit for being as honest as He ought to be, and then to go on in the actual life as if no promise had been made. That is faithful waiting.

2. God's Presentation of His Own Performance *(Genesis 21:2)*
The presentation of God's performance here is in the actual details of the birth of an ordinary child, extraordinary only to the eye of faith. We come to God not with faith in His goodness but with a conception of our own, and we look for God to come to us in that way. God cannot come to me in my way. He can only come in His own way—in ways man would never dream of looking for Him. In the Incarnation the Eternal God was so majestically small that He was not detected, the world never saw Him. And this is true in regard to us, God is so insignificant providentially, that we never see Him. We cry out—"Oh God, I wish You would come to me," when He is there all the time, and suddenly we see Him and say "Surely the LORD is in this place; and I knew it not." We looked for desolation and anguish, and instead there is the laughter and hilarity of realising that we see God. This astonishment at the performance of God is brought out over and over again until we learn to be humiliated at our despicable disbelief. "I don't know what I am going to do after Easter."[15]—But I thought you knew God! Have all these days and weeks gone by and has God shown you nothing? Your

---

15. after Easter: end of that term at the Bible Training College; lecture of March 18, 1915.

anxiety proves that you do not believe in the goodness of God an atom, and it postpones the time of His performance.

3. God's Programme for His Progeny *(Genesis 21:3–8)*

What Abraham did for his son was in accordance with God's programme for him, not according to Abraham's ways for him (cf. Proverbs 22:6). God has a distinct programme for every child born into this world, legitimately or illegitimately. If the programme is unheeded, the reason is that parents do not care about God's programme being fulfilled, but it will be fulfilled all the same. In spiritual matters be careful to note God's programme for His progeny in you. Is the Son of God formed in me? Have I heard God's promise about Him? He "shall be called the Son of God" (Luke 1:35), that is, He has nothing to do with my natural abilities. There is no relation between the promise of God for the life He forms in us by regeneration and our personal private ambitions, those ambitions are completely transfigured. I have to heed the promise of God for my child, be it a child of nature or of grace, and see that I do not try and make God's gift fulfil my own ends. If I do, I become cruel in my judgement of God and God has to be very severe with me.

Suppose that God sees fit to put you into desolation when He begins the forming of His Son in you, what does it matter to you, and what ought it to matter? God's programme was to look after Sarah only until the child of His promise was born, and all He is after in you and me is the forming of His Son in us. When He drives the sword through the natural, we begin to whine and say "Oh, I can't go through that," but we must go through it. If we refuse to make our natural life obedient to the Son of God in us, the Son of God will be put to death in us. We have to put on the new man in our human nature to fit the life of the Son of God in us, and see that in the outer courts of our bodily lives we conduct our life for Him.

"God hath made me to laugh." Sarah's hilarity is the joy of God sounding through the upset equilibrium of a mind that scarcely expected the promise to be fulfilled. The son of Sarah is himself a type of the Son of Mary, and in each case the promise is limited through a particular woman, and through an apparently impossible, yet actual birth. Fancy making everything depend on that haughty, inclined-to-be unstable, not amazingly-superb-in-rectitude Sarah! How haphazard God seems, not sometimes but always. God's ways turn man's thinking upside down.

Verse 7 is indicative of the amazement that comes when God's promise is fulfilled. What is known as the dark side of Christian experience is not really Christian experience at all, it is God putting the rot of sacramental death through the natural virtues in order to produce something in keeping with His Son, and all our whining and misery ought to be the laughter of Sarah—Now I see what God wants! Instead of that, we moon in corners and gloom before God, and say "I am afraid I am not sanctified." If you fight against the desolation, you will kill the life of God in you; yield to it, and God's fulfilment will amaze you. It is in the periods of desolation that the sickly pietists talk about "What I am suffering!" They are in the initial stages and have not begun to realise God's purpose. God is working out the manifestation of the fulfilment of His promise, and when it is fulfilled there is never any thought of self or of self-consideration anywhere.

WHICH?
Genesis 21:9–21

Profit?—Loss?
Who shall declare this good—that ill?
When good and ill so intertwine
But to fulfil the vast design
Of an Omniscient Will?—
When seeming gain but turns to loss,—
When earthly treasure proves but dross,—
And what seemed loss but turns again
To high, eternal gain?

John Oxenham

And God said, . . . Let it not be grievous in thy sight.
Genesis 21:12

The dilemmas of our personal life with God are few if we obey and many if we are wilful. Spiritually the dilemma arises from the disinclination for discipline; every time I refuse to discipline my natural self, I become less and less of a person and more and more of an independent, impertinent individual. Individuality is the characteristic of the natural man; personality is the characteristic of the spiritual man. That is why Our Lord can never be defined in terms of individuality, but only in terms of personality. Individuality is the characteristic of the child, it is the husk of the personal life. It is all "elbows," it separates and isolates; personality can merge and be blended. The shell of individuality is God's created covering for the protection of the personal life, but individuality must go in order that the personal life may be brought out into fellowship with God—"that they may be one, even as We are one."

1. The Offence of the Natural *(Genesis 21:6–10)*

Sarah is full of indignation when she sees the mocking of Ishmael, and begs Abraham to "cast out this bondwoman and her son." God tells Abraham to hearken to what Sarah says, and Ishmael is cast out. We have to remember, however, that Sarah gave Hagar to Abraham to be his wife; we always become anxious when we take our own self-chosen ways. In the Epistle to the Galatians the Apostle Paul makes his great revelation regarding that which was "born after the flesh" and that which was "born after the Spirit." He is dealing not with sin, but with the relationship between the natural and the spiritual. The natural must be disciplined and turned into the spiritual by sacrifice (cf. Galatians 5:24), otherwise it will produce a tremendous divorce in the life. Why did God make it necessary for the natural to be sacrificed to the spiritual? God did not. God's order was that the natural should be transformed into the spiritual by obedience; sin made it necessary for the natural to be sacrificed to the spiritual, and that after sanctification, remember. We have the idea that sanctification means deliverance from sin only; it means much more, it means that we start on a life of discipline such as nine out of every ten of us will have nothing to do with.

The offence of the natural is its robust ridicule of the spiritual, and if the natural is not "cast out" it will not only perish itself but will lead the whole personal life astray. "I was not disciplined when I was a child." You must discipline yourself now, if you do not, you will ruin your life for God. If the natural is not sacrificed to the spiritual by me, not by God, it will mock at the life of the Son of God in me and produce a continual "swither," which is always the result of an undisciplined nature. Instead of "I can't," say *"I won't,"* and you have it exactly, it is the Ishmael jeer. People go wrong spiritually because they stubbornly refuse to discipline themselves physically, mentally or in any way, and after a while they become that most contemptible and objectionable thing, a petted man or woman, and their own greatest cause of suffering. There is no suffering to equal the suffering of self-love arising from independent individuality which refuses to submit either to God or to its nobler self.

2. The Offering of the Natural *(Genesis 21:11–13)*

The casting out of the bondwoman and her son was necessary not only for the line of promise but for the welfare of Ishmael himself. All the problems regarding civilisation and organisation and the natural virtues arise along this line. If I put the civilised organisation to which I belong, or my natural virtues, on the throne, they will make a mock of the Son of God Who is formed in me . These things are the outcome of the natural life and I have to resolutely put them under, not because they are wrong, but because they are individual protests against the life of the Son of God in me. The natural life is not spiritual, it can only be made spiritual by deliberately casting it out and making it the slave instead of the ruler. My business is to make independent individuality conform to the Son of God in me by severity. We are apt to deify wilfulness and independence and call them by the wrong name; what we call strength of will God looks upon as contemptible weakness. The Being with the greatest will who ever lived on the earth was Our Lord Jesus Christ, and yet He never exercised His will, as We think of will; His life was one of meekness and submission (see John 5:19, 30). Our Lord was the antipodes of the individual, there was nothing independent or wilful or self-assertive about Him, and He says "Learn of Me; for I am meek and lowly in heart." Jesus Christ cannot give me a meek and quiet spirit, I have to take His yoke upon me; that is, I have to deliberately discipline myself. The teaching of the Sermon on the Mount is the destruction of individuality and the exaltation of personality. When the personal life is merged with God, it will manifest the characteristics of God. Individuality never exhibits the characteristics of God but natural characteristics, the characteristics of Ishmael, or of Esau, or of Saul of Tarsus, that mock at the meek and lowly Son of God. What is it that begins to mock in you? "Meek? Do you think I am going to bow my neck to that? Be loyal there, in my home? Obey a passing sentiment that came to me in a prayer meeting?" Cast out "the bondwoman and her son"—the natural life and all that nourishes it, or it will lead your personal life to ruin. The casting out must be done by you, then God will bring it back into its rightful inheritance. The natural life can only be brought into union by being cast out (cf. Matthew 5:29, 48).

If we do not resolutely cast out the natural, the supernatural can never become natural in us. There are some Christians in whom the supernatural and the natural seem one and the same, and you say— Well, they are not one with me, I find the natural at "loggerheads" with the spiritual. The reason is that the other life has gone through the fanatical stage of cutting off the right arm, gone through the discipline of maiming the natural, completely casting it out, and God has brought it back into its right relationship with the spiritual on top, and the spiritual manifests itself in a life which knows no division into sacred and secular. There is no royal road there, each one has it entirely in his own hands; it is not a question of praying but of performing.

3. The Ostracism of the Natural *(Genesis 21:14)*

The casting out of Hagar and Ishmael is necessary, but Hagar is not divorced. Divorce stands for apostasy (cf. Isaiah 1:1). We must be *divorced* from sin, not separated from sin. Sin belongs to hell and the devil; I, as a child of God, belong to heaven and God, and I must have nothing to do with sin in any shape or form. The separation which goes on all through the life of faith is alluded to by Paul in Galatians 2:20 — "I have been crucified with Christ" (RV); and again in Romans 12:1—"Present your bodies a living sacrifice"—go to the funeral of your own independence. It is not a question of giving up sin, but of giving up my right to myself, my natural independence and self-assertiveness. Immediately I do, the natural cries out and goes through terrific suffering. There are things in me which must go through death or they will abide alone and ruin the personal life (cf. John 12:24). But if I sternly put them through death, God will bring them back into the right inheritance. Jesus says If any man will be My disciple, "let him deny himself," i.e., deny his right to himself, and a man has to realise Who Jesus Christ is before he will do it. It is the things that are right and noble and good from the natural standpoint that keep us back from God's best. To discern that the natural virtues antagonise surrender to God, is to begin to see where the battle lies. It is going to cost the natural everything, not something.

4. The Ordeal of the Natural *(Genesis 21:15–16)*

Beware of blaspheming the Creator by calling the natural sinful. The natural is not sinful, but un-moral and un-spiritual. It is the home of all the vagrant vices and virtues, and must be disciplined with the utmost severity until it learns its true position in the providence of God. Remember, Abraham had to offer up Ishmael before he offered up Isaac. Some of us are trying to offer spiritual sacrifices before we have sacrificed the natural. The only way we can offer a spiritual sacrifice to God is to do what He tells us to do, discipline what He tells us to discipline. Under no consideration must we dictate to God on the basis of the natural life. When God's Son tells me to do a thing, I have no business to allow the natural to dictate and say—I cannot do that because I get so tired. What does it matter if it kills the natural? God's purpose for the natural will be fulfilled, I have to be absolutely stern with it and not make God wait on my natural inclinations.

5. The Outrance of the Natural *(Genesis 21:19–21)*

"Outrance"—the utmost extremity or bitter end. Verse 20 is striking—"God was with the lad," as long as he remained in the straits of the desert, and he found his home in the oases and by the wells. After Ishmael had learned by experience that he was not a fellow heir with Isaac, he was richly endowed by Abraham, and he also remained in friendly relationship with Isaac (Genesis 25:6, 9). God is not with my natural life as long as I pamper it and pander to it, but when I put it out in the desert, resolutely cast it out and keep it under, then God is with it and He opens up wells and oases, and fulfils His promise for it. It must be stern discipline, rigorous severity to the last degree on my part (cf. 1 Corinthians 9:27), then God will be with the natural life and bring it to its full purpose.

CONDITIONS
Genesis 21:22–34

Now, who shall arbitrate?
   Ten men love what I hate,
Shun what I follow, slight what I receive;
   Ten, who in ears and eyes
   Match me: we all surmise,
They this thing, and I that: whom shall my soul
     believe?

But I need, now as then,
   Thee, God, who mouldest men;
And since, not even while the whirl was worst,
Did I,—to the wheel of life
   With shapes and colours rife,
Bound dizzily,—mistake my end, to slake Thy
     thirst.

Browning

Thus they made a covenant at Beer-sheba. Genesis 21:32

The life of faith as portrayed in the life of Abraham is a detailed presentation of its majesties and its muddles. We have detected Abraham's blunder in the actual conditions in working from his wits, but we must not forget that by far the most striking thing about Abraham is his worship of God.

In this chapter the right relation between common sense and faith is exhibited. Common sense is not faith and faith is not common sense; they stand in the relation of Ishmael and Isaac, of the natural and the spiritual, of individuality and personality, of impulse and inspiration. Faith in antagonism to common sense is fanaticism, and common sense in antagonism to faith is rationalism. The life of faith brings the two into right relationship. No one can solve the difficulty of making them one for me, I must do it for myself, and I can only solve it by life not by thinking, just as the natural can only be made spiritual in life, not in thinking. We have the idea that the body, individuality, and the natural life are altogether of the devil; they are not, they are of God, designed by God, and it is in the human body and in the natural order of things that we have to exhibit our worship of God. The danger is to mistake the natural for the spiritual, and instead of worshipping God in my natural life to make my natural life God.

How am I going to find out what the will of God is? In one way only, by not trying to find out. If you are born again of the Spirit of God, you *are* the will of God, and your ordinary common-sense decisions are God's will for you unless He gives an inner check. When He does, call a halt immediately and wait on Him. Be renewed in the spirit of your mind that you may make out His will, not in your mind, but in practical living. God's will in my common-sense life is not for me to *accept* conditions and say—"Oh well, it is the will of God," but to *apprehend* them for Him, and that means conflict, and it is of God that we conflict. Doing the will of God is an active thing in my common-sense life.

1. The Arbitration between Abraham and Abimelech *(Genesis 21:22–24)*
Abimelech does not stand for the sinful, but for the noble and upright and perfectly natural. The blessing of God is recognised by the natural, but never recognised by the sinful. Abimelech stands as the type of civilisation with its organisations and culture and good sense. Between the Church, which is an organism, and organisation which is pagan, there must be arbitration. Much of our organisation in the Church is pagan, and it is our salvation to see that it is pagan. Immediately we forget this and compromise instead of arbitrate, we have sold the Son of God to the world.

The attitude of faith to organisation is illustrated in Our Lord's attitude to Pilate. Our Lord did not compromise with Pilate, He arbitrated with him— "You have to decide this matter because God has put you in the position where you must. You stand there on your dignity as proconsul: I stand here on My dignity as Son of God. If you put Me to death as your duty, I go to death because it is My duty." There is no compromise there. "If My kingdom *were* of this world, then would My servants fight" (John 18:36); but there is no fight, there is arbitration, and the reason for it is God's order behind the whole thing.

2. The Apprehension of Abimelech by Abraham *(Genesis 21:25–26)*
Abraham distinguishes clearly between political and private rights in this matter of the well, and now he in his turn administers a rebuke to Abimelech. In verse 26 Abimelech throws back the reproof on Abraham on the plea that he had not been told that the well had been taken away. This of course is mere natural shrewdness, and is the ground of their first arbitration. It is instructive to notice that Abraham always takes his rebukes magnificently, he never once shows individuality but always personality.

When first we become spiritual we arbitrate with our bodies until we say—I will put the natural into absolute subjection and have no more arbitration (*see* 1 Corinthians 9:27). The same kind of thing is taking place in the history of the world to-day. At present there is arbitration between the children of God and the natural forces of civilisation. We arbitrate between the two by recognising the present claims of each without compromising either. When the Lord Jesus comes again there will be no more arbitration, all the natural forces of civilisation will instantly be put in subjection to Him, in the same way that those who enter into the sanctified life deliberately put the natural in themselves into subjection to Jesus Christ. In the meantime there is arbitration, no compromise and no fight, but deliberate arbitration between the two.

As Abimelech rebuked Abraham when he was in the wrong (*see* Genesis 20), and Abraham in his turn rebuked Abimelech, so in the same way the children of men from time to time rebuke the children of God, and the children of God rebuke the politics of natural men. Compromise with each other or unity between them is immoral. Arbitration until He comes whose right it is to reign is the God-ordained programme.

Abimelech exhibits the characteristic of natural, noble, worldly civilisation which recognises the blessing of God attached to the people of God, and shrewdly realises the value of having the people of God in the midst of civilised life. No man on earth "pooh-poohs" the people of God, although he himself does not intend to become one of them. Our Lord did not pray that His disciples should be taken out of the world, but that they should be kept from the evil (John 17:10).

3. The Agreement of Abraham and Abimelech *(Genesis 21:27–34)*

The Old Testament Scriptures always regard the oath as a peculiar sacrament. If you read what the Bible says about vowing you will see how culpably negligent we are in the way we promise. If we do not fulfil a promise, we damage our moral and spiritual life. It is infinitely better to refuse to promise anything, even in the most superficial relationships, than to promise and not perform. Spiritual leakages are accounted for in this way. Always do what you ought to do, but be careful of promising anything, because a promise puts the blood of God on your character.

If you make a promise you must see that it is fulfilled, no matter what it costs you. The glib way we promise is indicative of the slipshod ways we have got into, and of our laziness and indifference. The word of a natural man is his bond; the word of a saint binds God. It is a question of relationship to God all through.

The origin of the phrase "business is business" is in the fact that business must not be carried on as a matter of faith but as a matter of covenant. Business is the go-between between the children of God and natural civilised life, and must be carried on by bonds.

By means of this arbitration Abraham's faith develops more fully into faith in the eternal truth of Jehovah's covenant (v. 33).

THE SUPREME CLIMB
Genesis 22:1–3

Thy prayer shall be fulfilled; but how?
   His thoughts are not as thine,
While thou wouldst only weep and bow,
   He saith, "Arise and shine!"
Thy thoughts were all of grief and night,
But His of boundless joy and light.
Thy Father reigns supreme above,
   Thy glory of His name
Is Grace and Wisdom, Truth and Love,
   His Will must be the same.
And thou hast asked all joys in one
In whispering forth, "Thy will be done."

Frances Ridley Havergal[16]

Take . . . , get . . . , offer . . . upon one of the mountains which I will tell thee of. Genesis 22:2

In the life of Abraham we deal with the failures and the triumphs of the life of faith, and this chapter records the perfecting of the obedience of faith in Abraham. His obedience was not merely in the sacrifice of Isaac, but in his readiness to perceive a revelation even when it seemed to contradict what God had told him (cf. Genesis 22:11–12). The very nature of faith is that it must be tried; faith untried is only ideally real, not actually real. Faith is not rational, therefore it cannot be worked out on the basis of logical reason; it can only be worked out on the implicit line by living obedience. God proves Abraham's faith by placing him in the most extreme crisis possible, because faith must prove itself by the inward concession of its dearest objects, and in this way be purified from all traditional and fanatical ideas and misconceptions.

1. The Crucible for Abraham
God did tempt Abraham. (Genesis 22:1)

These are startling words, for centuries later the Holy Ghost caused it to be written that God tempteth no man (James 1:13). Again, Our Lord taught us to pray "lead us not into temptation"; and He Himself was deliberately "led up of the Spirit into the wilderness to be tempted of the devil." The reason for the apparent contradiction is that there is a difference between the providence of God's rule and the providence of God's grace. The providence of God's grace is wrought out in the development of faith, and Paul refers to this when he says "we know that all things work together for good to them that love God"—everything that happens transforms ideal faith into actual reality by the alchemy of God's providence (cf. Hebrews 12:11). The providence of God's grace is worked out in and through the arrangement of His rule, but is conditioned by the individual life of the one with whom He is dealing, e.g., God placed Abraham in a position He would not have placed Sarah or Lot. When we learn

---

16. Frances Ridley Havergal (1836–1879): English poet and hymn writer.

not to trust in our wits, we will never put ourselves where we have no business to be.

God does not further our spiritual life in spite of our circumstances, but in and by our circumstances. The whole purpose of God is to make the ideal faith actually real in the lives of His servants. God is working for His highest purpose until it and man's highest good become one.

God sits "as a refiner and purifier of silver"—the crucible of testing is placed by God, not by man. It is easy to pass a crude verdict on God if you are not living in touch with Him. If you look at God through the mist of the heat of the crucible, you will say God is cruel. You must go through the crucible before you have any right to pronounce a verdict. On the off-side of the crucible a great many things are said which prove to be misconceptions—"God took away my child because I loved her too much." Go through the crucible, and you will find that in it you learned to know God better.

2. The Concentration of Abraham
Behold, here I am. (v. 1)

These words express the greatest application of the human mind. To say "Here I am" when God speaks, is only possible if we are in His presence, in the place where we can obey. To understand where I am in the sight of God means not only to listen but to obey promptly all He says. I can always know where I am. Whenever I want to debate about doing what I know to be supremely right, I am not in touch with God.

3. The Command to Abraham
Take now thy son, thine only son Isaac, whom thou lovest . . . (v. 2)

God's words are, as it were, blows aimed against the incrustations of natural individual life in order that Abraham's personal faith might be emancipated into fellowship with God. The blows are aimed at individuality because individuality will not come into fellowship with God; personality always does. Individuality is the husk of the personality, the home of independence and pride; but when God is developing the faith of a man all that must be sacrificed. It is the chrysalis developing into a butterfly, a winged creature of personal life. If you are not in the crucible yourself, the blows seem cruel; but if you are, you find the ecstasy of being brought into personal fellowship with God. Faith always works on the personal line (cf. Job 1:12).

God's command is—"Take *now*," not presently. To go to the height God shows can never be done presently, it must be done now. Every mother who gives her son in war-time climbs to the height instantly, there may be any amount of protest, but she climbs to the height and buries her son; her woman's heart goes through the bereavement long before it comes actually.

4. The Climb for Abraham
. . . and offer him there for a burnt offering upon one of the mountains which I will tell thee of. (v. 2)

The mount of the Lord is the very height of the trial into which God brings His servant. There is no indication of the cost to Abraham, his implicit understanding of God so far out-reaches his explicit knowledge that he trusts God utterly and climbs the highest height on which God can ever prove him, and remains unutterably true to God. There was no conflict, that was over, Abraham's confidence was fixed; he did not consult with flesh and blood, his own or anyone else's, he instantly obeyed. The point is that though all other voices should proclaim differently, obedience to the dictates of the Spirit of God at all costs is to be the attitude of the faithful soul. This mountain is not a mountain of sacrifice, but the mountain of proof that Abraham loved God supremely (*see* Genesis 22:12).

It is extraordinary how we debate with right. We know a thing is right but we try to seek excuses for not doing it now. Always beware when you want to confer with your own flesh and blood, i.e., your own sympathies, your own insight. These things are based on individuality, not on personal relationship to God, and they are the things that compete with God and hinder our faith. When Our Lord is bringing us into personal relationship with Himself, it is always the individual relationships He breaks down. He comes with a sword rap on the husks that will not break, that will not let the life out for God (Matthew 10:34). "If any man comes to Me, and hate not . . . , he cannot be My disciple" (Luke 14:26). If you are outside the crucible you will say that Jesus Christ is cruel, but when you are in the crucible you see that it is a personal relationship with Himself that He is after all the time. He is after the true gold, and the devil is after it too.

5. The Consecration of Abraham
And Abraham rose up early in the morning . . . and went unto the place of which God had told him. (v. 3)

Verse 3 reveals the wonderful simplicity of Abraham. This is the sacrifice of *Abraham*, not of Isaac. Always guard against self-chosen service for God; self sacrifice may be a disease. God chose the crucible for Abraham, and Abraham made no demur, he went steadily through. If God has made your cup sweet, drink it with grace; if He has made it bitter, drink it in communion with Him. If it is a hard time of difficulty in the providential order of God, go through with it, but never choose your own service. If God has given the command, He will look after everything; your business is to get up and go, and smilingly wash your hands of the consequences.

Beware of pronouncing any verdict on the life of faith if you are not living it.

ISOLATION
Genesis 22:3–6

Let no man think that sudden in a minute
  All is accomplished and the work is done;
Though with thine earliest dawn thou shouldst
    begin it,
  Scarce were it ended in thy setting sun.

How have I knelt with arms of my aspiring
  Lifted all night in irresponsive air,
Dazed and amazed with overmuch desiring,
  Blank with the utter agony of prayer!

Myers[17]

The place afar off. Genesis 22:4

Verse 1 states that God "did tempt Abraham," and the context proves that the word "tempt" has the underlying meaning of purifying: God had to lift Abraham's faith into an understanding of Himself. The life of Abraham is a life of faith, and faith in its actual working out has to go through spells of unsyllabled isolation (cf. Romans 8:26). Temptations in the life of faith are not accidents, each temptation is part of a plan, a step in the process of faith. Faith is not logical, it works on the line of life and by its very nature must be tried. Never confound the trial of faith with the ordinary discipline of life. Much that we call the trial of our faith is the inevitable result of being alive. The problem lies in the clearing of God's character with regard to what He allows. Faith according to the Bible is confidence in God when He is inscrutable and apparently contradictory in His providences.

1. The Duty of Diligence
And Abraham rose up early in the morning. (v. 3)

This phrase is characteristic not only of men and women in the Bible, but of God Himself. The revelation of God in the Old Testament is that of a working God. No other religion presents God either as diligent or as suffering, but as an all-in-all principle, ruling in lofty disdain. The God Who reveals Himself to Abraham is One ever intent on the fulfilment of His great designs; and like God, like people. If God is diligent, surely we ought to be diligent in doing our duty to Him. Think how patient and how diligent God has been with us! Over and over again God gets us near the point, and then by some petty individual sulk we spoil it all, and He patiently begins all over again. Think of the vision, "whiter than snow shine," God gave of what He wanted us to be—where has it gone this Easter time?[18] Has God had to begin all over again from where we left off last time, or have we said—I will be true to God at all costs, no matter what the isolation?

2. The Direction of Duty
And went unto the place of which God had told him. (v. 3)

Abraham took the direction of his duty from God's word, not from his own discernment (cf. Genesis 12:4; Hebrews 11:6). Our danger is to water down God's word to suit ourselves. God never fits His word to suit me; He fits me to suit His word. The discernment of God's call does not come in every moment of life, but only in rare moments; the moments Our Lord spoke of as "the light" (John 12:35–36). We have to remain true to what we see in those moments; if we do not, we will put back God's purpose in our life. The undercurrent of regret arises when we confer with those who have not heard the call of God, and if we listen to them we get into darkness. The life of Abraham is an illustration of two things: of unreserved surrender to God, and of God's complete possession of a child of His for His own highest end.

It is never the consecration of our gifts that fits us for God's service. Profoundly speaking, we are not here to work for God. Absorption in practical work is one of the greatest hindrances in preventing a soul discerning the call of God. Unless active work is balanced by a deep isolated solitude with God, knowledge of God does not grow and the worker becomes exhausted and spent out. Our Lord said that the only men He will use in His enterprises are those in whom He has done everything (Luke 14:26, 27, 33); otherwise we would serve our own ends all the time. Many have begun well but have gone off on doctrine, all their energy is spent furthering a cause, Jesus Christ is not the dominating ruler. The direction of duty lies not in doing things for God, but in doing what God tells us to do, and God's order comes to us in the haphazard moments. We do not make the haphazard moments, God is the arranger of the haphazard. The

---

17. F. W. H. Myers (1843–1901): British poet and educator.
18. lecture, April 13, 1915.

direction of duty is loyalty to God in our present circumstances.

3. The Discipline of Distance
Then on the third day . . . (v. 4)

God is never in a hurry. We say, "I see what God wants and it seems so easy, I wish I could do it now." Abraham had to travel many long hours to the place of sacrifice, a deed was to be done after days of reflection, not on the impulse of the moment, and during the journey not a look or a word betrayed his secret. Isaac never guessed at the isolation in his father's mind. Never reveal to anyone the profound depths of your isolation; when the life is going on profoundly with God, conceal it. "Appear not unto men to fast." It was this about Our Lord that staggered the Pharisees, no one know what He was going through in the profoundest concerns of His life. And at the end when He might easily have been absorbed in the tremendous issue which He knew was at hand, He revealed no concern about Himself, only for His disciples—"Let not your heart be troubled."

4. The Deception of Determination
I and the lad will . . . come again to you. (v. 5)

The strength of Abraham's faith appears in that he held to God's promise while he promptly went to do what seemed to prevent its fulfilment. He believed that God would fulfil all He had promised and did not stay to question. To take God at His word may mean expecting God to come up to my standard; whereas true faith does not so much take God at His word as take the word of God as it is, in the face of all difficulties, and act upon it, with no attempt to explain or expound it.

5. The Devotion of the Devoted
And Abraham took the wood of the burnt offering, and laid it upon Isaac his son. (v. 6)

This verse is sublime. There is nothing more wonderful than the picture of this thoughtful, obedient boy going with his father, and even when he knew what the purpose was (v. 9), he was willing to relinquish the joy of life (cf. John 21:18).

THE PATH OF GOD
Genesis 22:7–14

My God, my God, let me for once look on thee
As though nought else existed, we alone!
And as creation crumbles, my soul's spark
Expands till I can say,—Even from myself
I need thee and I feel thee and I love thee.
I do not plead my rapture in thy works
For love of thee, nor that I feel as one
Who cannot die: but there is that in me
Which turns to thee, which loves or which should
    love.

                                        Browning

God will provide Himself . . . Genesis 22:8

The life of Abraham provides the pattern spiritual biography in which the life ascends from the rational and accountable to the personally traced footsteps of the soul's path to God. The turning points in the spiral ascent of faith are, first, obedience to the effectual call of God (Genesis 12); and second, the culmination of unreserved resignation to God (Genesis 22). Our difficulties spiritually arise from unrecognised spiritual hysterics, in which mood we unconsciously select God to watch us and our symptoms. The only cure for that is to get hold of God and have no symptoms.

1. The Speech of Silent Spirituality (*Genesis 22:7–8*)
The speech of Abraham and Isaac reveals that they are spiritually silent—the son is silent before the father as the father is silent before God, and thus God elevates them both above unspiritual human nature. That is, both father and son have gone one step beyond the limit of the possible because they are on the path of God. To talk easily about spiritual experiences is an indication that I have only a devout nodding acquaintance with the experiences of others, and am devoid of all such experiences myself.

In the life of faith the pressure of forethought is transferred to God by the faith which fulfils His behests; I have faith in God's accountable rationality, not in my own. If I have never heard the call of God, all I see is the accountability that I can state to myself. Practical work is nearly always a determination to think for myself, to take the pressure of forethought on myself: I see the need, therefore I must do something. That is not the effectual call of God, but the call of my sympathy with conditions as I see them. When God's call comes, I learn to do actively what He tells me and take no thought for the morrow. Take a step in faith in God, and your rational friends will say: "Very beautiful, but suppose We all did it. . . !" You are not living on the line of accountable rationality, but a life of agreement with God's effectual call, and have therefore no reply to make.

In Hebrews 11:19 we get an insight into Abraham's spirituality—"Accounting that God was able to raise him up, even from the dead." It was not Abraham's common sense but his spiritual illumination that made him know it. Beware of turning a commonsense somersault and make God appear foolish by saying that Abraham knew all about it and it was not a sacrifice at all. Abraham did not know all about it; he believed that God would give Isaac back to him, but how, he had no notion; he surrendered himself entirely to the supernatural God. God never tells us what He is going to do. He reveals Who He is.

So, "they went both of them together" in the obedience of faith. Abraham stood in the midst of the most appalling personal controversy, the controversy between natural love and faith, and Isaac was worthy of his father. The path to God is never the same as the path of God. When I am going on with God in His path, I do not understand, but God does; therefore I understand God, not His path. When you take a step in faith in God and fulfil His behests, God does the forethinking for you. When you do it for yourself. God has to take second place. If you are going through the discipline of transferring your forethought to God and actively fulfilling His behests, you have to be silent; and when you do speak your speech is shallow, it does not convey where you are. People must never guess what you are going through. Piety always pretends to be going through what it is not.

2. The Sacrifice of Surrendered Sonship (*Genesis 22:9–10*)

God is the ruling factor in all our transaction (cf. Proverbs 20:24). When we commit ourselves to God He arranges the haphazard, and we have to see that we actively fulfil His behests where He places us.

The binding of Isaac is a prefiguring of the fulfilment and the perfection of the Death of Christ. The emphasis of the so-called Higher Christian Life[19] is to look at Christ as our Example, not as our sacrifice: by prayer and consecration we come into God's favour. We do not, that is blasphemy. God never accepts us because we obey; He can only accept us on the ground of sacrifice, which cost death. Therefore our approach to God can never be on the ground of our merit—that I am being bound by Another; that is the effect of the sacrifice of Christ in me. Personal

holiness is never the ground of my acceptance with God; the only ground of acceptance is the Death of the Lord Jesus Christ.

3. The Sympathy of Supreme Spirit (*Genesis 22:11–12*)

Abraham had a rational understanding of what God's command meant and he had to step out of it. Abraham was not a fanatic, the instant the voice of God came he surrendered himself in devotion to the voice, although it seemed an arrest of obedience to the Divine command. The essence of true religious faith is devotion to a Person. Beware of sticking to convictions instead of to Christ; convictions are simply the clothes of your growing life.

The great point of Abraham's faith in God was that he was prepared to do anything for God. Mark the difference between that and doing anything to prove your love to God. Abraham was there to obey God, no matter to what he went contrary. Abraham was not a pledged devotee of his own convictions, or he would have slain his son and said the voice of the angel was the voice of the devil. There is always the point of giving up convictions and traditional beliefs. If I will remain true to God, He will lead me straight through the ordeal into the inner chamber of a better knowledge of God. Our Lord taught us to pray "lead us not into temptation." Don't ask God to test you. Don't declare as Peter did, I will do anything, I will go to death for You. Abraham did not make any such declaration, he remained true to God, and God purified his faith.

Abraham is taught by the ancient ritual what Paul clearly expressed in Romans 12:1. Genesis 22:9 is a picture of the blunder of thinking that the sacrifice of death is the final thing God wants: what God wants is the sacrifice through death which enables a man to do what Jesus did, viz. sacrifice his life. Many of us think that God wants us to give up things; we make Christianity the great apotheosis of giving up! God purified Abraham from this blunder, and the same discipline goes on in our lives. "Oh well, I expect God will ask me to give that up." God nowhere tells us to give up things for the sake of giving them up; He tells us to give them up for the sake of the only thing worth having, viz. life with Himself. It is a question of loosening the bands that hinder our life, and immediately those bands are loosened by identification with the death of Jesus, we enter into a relationship with God whereby we sacrifice our life to God. To give God my life for death is of no value; what is of value is to let Him have all my powers that have been saved

---

19. The Higher Christian Life: concept taught by various groups and organizations that emphasized sanctification and personal holiness.

and sanctified, so that as Jesus sacrificed His life for His Father, I can sacrifice my life for Him. "Present your bodies a living sacrifice," says Paul.

4. The Substitution of Sacramental Service (*Genesis 22:13–14*)

Abraham did not receive a positive command to sacrifice the ram, he recognised in the ram caught by his horns in a thicket behind him a Divine suggestion. Until we get into fellowship with God His suggestions are no good to us. When people are intimate with one another suggestions convey more than words, and when God gets us into oneness with Himself we recognise His suggestions. Abraham offers the ram as a substitute for his son; he does not withhold his son in intention, although in fact he offers a substitute. The entire system of sacrifice is an extension of the sacrifice of the ram. The spiritual sacrifice of Isaac and the physical sacrifice of the ram are made one, the natural and the spiritual are blended. That Christ is the substitute for me and therefore I go scot free, is never taught in the New Testament. If I say that Christ suffered instead of me, I knock the bottom board out of His sacrifice. Christ died *in the stead of me. I*, a guilty sinner, can never get right with God, it is impossible. I can only be brought into union with God by identification with the One Who died in my stead. No sinner can get right with God on any other ground than the ground that Christ died *in his stead*, not *instead of him*.

THE ETERNAL GOAL
Genesis 22:15–19

My goal is God Himself, not joy, nor peace.
Nor even blessing, but Himself, my God;
'Tis His to lead me there, not mine, but His—
"At any cost, dear Lord, by any road!"

One thing I know, I cannot say Him nay;
One thing I do, I press towards my Lord;
My God my glory here, from day to day,
And in the glory there my Great Reward.

F. Brook[20]

In blessing I will bless thee . . . because thou hast obeyed My voice. Genesis 22:17–18

The spirit of obedience gives more joy to God than anything else on earth. Obedience is impossible to us naturally, even when we do obey, we do it with a pout in our moral underlip, and with the determination to scale up high enough and then "boss my boss." In the spiritual domain there is no pout to be removed because the nature of God has come into me. The nature of God is exhibited in the life of Our Lord, and the great characteristic of His life is obedience. When the love of God is shed abroad in my heart by the Holy Ghost (Romans 5:5), I am possessed by the nature of God, and I know by my obedience that I love Him. The best measure of a spiritual life is not its ecstasies, but its obedience. "To obey is better than sacrifice."

1. The Supreme Call of God (*Genesis 22:15*)

When God first called to Abraham there was still a dim gulf between them, God had to call and Abraham to answer (v. 1). Now that gulf is bridged. "The angel of the Lord called a second time out of heaven, . . ." i.e., an inward state of soul, and Abraham is so near to God that he does not need to reply; he is in the place of unimpeded listening. Is there any impediment between my ears and God's voice?

The call of God is a call in accordance with the nature of God, not in accordance with my idea of God. At first, Abraham did not interpret the call along the line of the nature of God because he did not know it; he interpreted it along the line of the Chaldaic tradition and took it to mean he was to kill his son. The supreme crisis in Abraham's faith has now been reached, all his imperfect conceptions of God have been left behind and he has come now to understand God. Always beware of self-assertiveness, it bruises our relationship to God, and distorts the manifestation of His nature in us. Abraham was neither an amateur providence nor a moral policeman, he simply believed God.

2. The Supreme Reality of God (*Genesis 22:16*)

Abraham has come to the place where he is in touch with the very nature of God, he understands the real-

---

20. Frances Brook (b. 1870): English hymn writer.

ity of God, and God, as it were, unveils Himself to him in a burst of enthusiasm. There is no possibility of questioning on my part when God speaks, if He is speaking to His own nature in me; prompt obedience is the only result. When Jesus says "Come unto Me," I simply come; when He says "Trust in God in this matter," I do not try to trust, I *do* trust. An alteration has taken place in my disposition which is an evidence that the nature of God is at work in me.

3. The Supreme Character of God *(Genesis 22:17–18)*

The promise of God stands in relation to Abraham's tried and willing obedience. The revelation of God to me is determined by my character, not by God's (Psalms 25–26). If I am mean,[21] that is how God will appear to me.

> *'Tis because I am mean, Thy ways so oft*
> *Look mean to me.*

By the discipline of obedience, I come to the place Abraham reached and see God as He is. The promises of God are of no use to me until by obedience I understand the nature of God. We read some things in the Bible three hundred and sixty-five times and they mean nothing to us, then all of a sudden we see what they mean, because in some particular we have obeyed God, and instantly His character is revealed. "For how many soever be the promises of God, in Him is the yea" (RV). The "yea" must be born of obedience; when by the obedience of our life, we say "Amen," "So let it be," to a promise, then that promise is made ours.

4. The Supreme Reward *(Genesis 22:19)*

The more we have to sacrifice for God, the more glorious is the reward presently. We have no right to choose our sacrifice, God will let us see where the sacrifice is to come, and it will always be on the line of what God has given us, our "Isaac," and yet His call is to sacrifice it. God is always at work on the principle of lifting up the natural and making it and the spiritual one, and very few of us will go through with it. We will cling to the natural when God wants to put a sword through it. If you go through the transfiguration of the natural, you will receive it back on a new plane altogether. God wants to make eternally our own what we only possessed intermittently.

In the beginning we do not train for God, we train for work, for our own aims, but as we go on with God we lose all our own aims and are trained into God's purpose. Unless practical work is appointed by God, it will prove a curse (cf. John 17:13). "At any cost, by any road," means nothing self-chosen. The Bible does not say that God blessed Abraham and took him to heaven; but that He blessed him and kept him on earth. The maturity of character before God is the personal channel through which He can bless others. If it takes all our lifetime before God can put us right, then others are going to be impoverished. We need to hurry and climb our Mount Moriah, come to the place where God can put an end to the dim gulf between Him and ourselves, then He will be able to bless us as He did Abraham.

No language can express the ineffable blessedness of the supreme reward that awaits the soul that has taken its supreme climb, proved its supreme love, and entered on its supreme reward. What an imperturbable certainty there is about the man who is in contact with the real God! Thank God, the life of the Father of the Faithful is but a specimen of the life of every humble believer who obediently follows the discipline of the life of faith. What a depth of transparent rightness there must be about the man who walks before God, and the meaning of the Atonement is to place us there in perfect adjustment to God. "Walk before Me, and be thou perfect," not faultless, but blameless, undeserving of censure in the eyes of God.

---

21. mean: as used here, something or someone ordinary, common, low, or ignoble, rather than cruel or spiteful.

STILL HUMAN
Genesis 22:20–24

*For some may follow truth from dawn to dark
As a child follows by his mother's hand,
Knowing no fear, rejoicing all the way;
And unto some her face is as a star
Set through an avenue of thorns and fires,
And waving branches, black without a leaf.
And still it draws them, though the feet must
    bleed,
Though the garments must be rent and eyes be
    scorched;
And if the valley of the shadow of death
Be passed, and to the level road they come,
Still with their faces to the polar star,
It is not with the same looks, the same limbs,
But halt and maimed and of infirmity.*

And it came to pass . . . that it was told Abraham.
Genesis 22:20

1. God's Omniscience and Human Life
What the natural reason would call an anti-climax is the very climax of God's supernatural grace whereby a man having gone through the most wonderful experience, emerges and lives an unwonderful, ordinary life. That is the difference between the fanatic and the faithful soul. You find it all through the New Testament. The wonder of the Incarnation slips into the life of ordinary childhood; the marvel of the Transfiguration descends to the valley and the demon-possessed boy, and the glory of the Resurrection merges into Our Lord providing breakfast for His disciples on the sea shore in the early dawn. The tendency in early Christian experience is to look for the marvellous. We are apt to mistake the sense of the heroic for being heroes. It is one thing to go through a crisis grandly, but a different thing to go through every day glorifying God when there is no witness, no limelight, and no one paying the remotest attention to you. If we don't want medieval haloes, we want something that will make people say—What a wonderful man of prayer he is! What a pious, devoted woman she is! If anyone says that of you, you have not been loyal to God. If you are rightly devoted to Jesus Christ, you have reached the sublime height where no one thinks of noticing you, all that is noticed is that the power of God comes through all the time. It is along some such line as this that we are to understand the omniscience of God and human life. "Oh, I have had a wonderful call from God!" It takes Almighty God Incarnate in you to peel potatoes properly, and to wash heathen

children for the glory of God. *Anyone* cannot do these things; anybody can do the shining in the sun and the sporting in the footlights, but it takes God's incarnated Spirit to make you so absolutely humanly His that you are utterly unnoticeable.

2. God's Object and Human Nature
The history of the life of Abraham does not close abruptly with his greatest act of faith, but from that act of faith there is a natural human progress to a sanctified life. Human nature likes to read about the heroic and the intense: it takes the Divine nature to be interested in grass and sparrows and trees, because they are so unutterably commonplace, and also because God happens to have made them. God's order is the human; the devil's is the spectacular. The object of the crisis is that we may live the human life in perfect relation to God.

Abraham is not the type of a saint or of sanctification, but of the life of faith. Our human relationships are the actual conditions in which the ideal life of God is to be exhibited. Any sordid being can sit in a cathedral in the twilight and listen to beautiful music and feel divine; Abraham lived as God's man in the earthly conditions of his life. If the indwelling of God cannot be manifested in human flesh, then the Incarnation and the Atonement are of no avail. All our Christian work may be merely scaffolding poles to prepare us so that God may do what He likes with us, unobtrusively. The test of the life of a saint is not success, but faithfulness as a steward of the mysteries of God in human life as it actually is (cf. Luke 6:40). We will put up success as the aim in Christian work; the one thing glorifying to God is the glory of God manifested in human lives unobtrusively. The "show business" belongs to the pagan order of things; devotion to God in actual human conditions belongs to the Redemptive order. A Christian is one who has learned to live the life hid with Christ in God in human conditions.

3. God's Order and Human Haphazard
(Genesis 22:20)
The message which Abraham received was providential and came at the right moment. The message was apparently haphazard, but it was all in the order of God. It is a great moment in the life of a child of God when letters and messages are seen to be under the direction of Divine providence. When God brings me a word on occasions and I obey it, He will look

after everything else. There is nothing haphazard to a child of God (Romans 8:28).

4. God's Opportunity and Human Forethought *(Genesis 22:21–23)*

Abraham must soon think of Isaac's marriage, and the message from his kindred causes him to hope that he may find in his brother's family a bride for Isaac. Remain true to God in your obscurity, and remember you are not the designer of your destiny. You hear the call of God and realise what He wants, then you begin to find reasons why you should not obey Him. Well, obey Him, because away in some other part of the world there are other circumstances being worked by God, and if you say—"I shan't, I wasn't made for this," you get out of touch with God. Your "goings" are not according to your mind, but according to God's mind. Remain true at all costs to what God is doing with you and don't ask why He is doing it. Don't loaf along like a strayed poet on the fringes of God's providence; the Almighty has got you in hand, leave yourself alone and trust in Him. Half the sentimental pious folks that strew the coasts of emotional religious life are there because we will engineer our own circumstances. We have to be for God's purpose, and God cannot explain His purpose until it happens. God's omniscience, God's order, and God's opportunity in my individual life all work together, and Jesus Christ enters into my life just at the point of the haphazard circumstances I am in. Sanctification is not the end of Redemption, it is the gateway to the purpose of God. No Christian experience is the end and purpose of Redemption. God's own plans are the purpose of Redemption.

When the call of Jesus Christ comes, it comes to *you*, it cannot come to your father or your mother, or to your wife, or to your own self-interest; it comes entirely to your personal life. Instantly the clamour begins. Father and mother say No, the claims of my own life say No; Jesus Christ says Yes. Think—could Jesus Christ's call mean that I hurt my father and mother irrevocably? Certainly it could not; then if I obey Him, even though it looks like bringing the sword and the upset into lives, in the final wind up God will bring His wisdom out perfectly, and I shall find that every one of those human relationships have been brought in in the wake of my obedience. The point is—will I trust God, or lean to my own convictions? Obedience to the supremacy of the Lord Jesus is the only legitimate outcome of sanctification. Thank God, He wants us to be human, not spooks!

HUMAN GREATNESS
Genesis 23

We cannot kindle when we will
*   The fire which in the heart resides;*
The spirit bloweth and is still,
*   In mystery our soul abides.*
*   But tasks in hours of insight will'd*
*   Can be through hours of gloom fulfill'd.*

With aching hands and bleeding feet,
*   We dig and heap, lay stone on stone;*
We bear the burden and the heat
*   Of the long day, and wish 'twere done.*
*   Not till the hours of light return*
*   All we have built do we discern*

                                        Matthew Arnold

Thou art a prince of God. Genesis 23:6 (RV)

1. In the Place of Sorrow *(Genesis 23:1–2)*

The Old Testament relates the end of no other woman's life so particularly as it does the end of Sarah's life. Abraham's personal sorrow is recorded in the words—"to weep for her." It is a farce to make nothing of death; the natural expressions of the heart are not suppressed, but tempered and transfigured. It is no part of faith to affect insensibility to sorrow, that is stoical humbug. In certain stages of religious experience we have the idea that we must not show sorrow when we are sorrowful. That idea is an enemy to the Spirit of Jesus Christ, because it leads to heartlessness and hypocrisy. Not to sorrow is not even human, it is diabolical. The Spirit of God hallows sorrow.

In dealing with the life of Abraham as the Father of the Faithful neither faith nor common sense must be our guide, but God Who unites both in the alchemy of personal experience. To be guided by common sense alone is fanatical; both common sense and faith have to be brought into relation to God. The life of faith does not consist of acts of worship or of great self-denial and heroic virtues, but of all the daily conscious acts of our lives.

2. In the Place of Sojourning *(Genesis 23:3–4)*

The phrase Abraham uses, "a stranger and sojourner," is the inner meaning of the term "Hebrew." Abraham could never say that he was at home in Canaan, he left his home never to find another on earth. The thought of pilgrimage sank deep into the Hebrew mind, and the note of the sojourner is, essentially the note of the Christian. Instead of being pilgrims and strangers on the earth, we become citizens of this order of things and entrench ourselves here, and the statements of Jesus have no meaning. The genius of the Spirit of God is to make us pilgrims, consequently there is the continual un-at-home-ness in this world (cf. Philippians 3:20). It is a matter of indifference to the Spirit of God where we are, and it ought to be equally indifferent to us. As saints, we are cursed, not blessed, by patriotism. The idea of nations is man's, not God's. When Our Lord establishes His Kingdom there will be no nations, only the great Kingdom of God. That is why His Kingdom is not built up on civilised life.

3. In the Place of Sentiment *(Genesis 23:8–9)*

Sentiment is thought occasioned by feeling; sentimentality is feeling occasioned by thought. Sentiment plays an important part in human affairs. and no sentiment is more sacred than that connected with our dead. Sentimentality is produced by watching things we are not in. Go through a disaster or bereavement, and the emotions produced are the bedrock of feeling which makes human life worthy. As Christians we should conduct our lives on the high sentiment which is the outcome of a transaction with the Lord Jesus Christ. If our testimony is hard, it is because we have gone through no crisis with God, there is no heartbroken emotion behind it. If we have been through a crisis in which human feeling has been ploughed to its inner centre by the Lord, our testimony will convey all the weight of the greatness of God along with human greatness. It is essential to go through a crisis with God which costs you something, otherwise your devotional life is not worth anything. You cannot be profoundly moved by nothing, or by doctrine; you can only be profoundly moved by devotion.

Verses 8–9. The story of Abraham's palaver with the Hittites conveys the idea that they had respect for the true greatness of Abraham.

> *Bending before men is a recognition that there does dwell in that presence of our brother something divine.*
>
> Carlyle[22]

We all recognise human trappings; only one in a thousand recognises human greatness. We bow not to greatness, but to the trappings of money and of birth. If I bow because I must, I am a conventional fraud; if I bow because I recognise true greatness, it is a sign that I am being emancipated. The greatest humiliation for a Christian is to recognise that he has ignored true greatness because it was without trappings. If the Pharisees had been reverent towards true greatness, they would not have treated the Nazarene Carpenter as they did.

4. In the Place of Scrupulosity *(Genesis 23:17–18)*

The details of this palaver must not be passed over. We are apt to say that religion is religion, and business is business; but there is no cleavage in the life of faith. Slovenliness is an insult to the Holy Ghost. Our Lord is scrupulous in His saving of us, surely we can be scrupulous in the conduct of His temple, our bodies and our bodily connections. That will mean God's greatness coming down into our human setting, and we see to it that we do everything in keeping with the greatness of God.

5. In the Place of Sublimity *(Genesis 23:6)*

The Hittites had no word for "gentleman," so they called Abraham "a prince of God." Abraham kept company with God until he became a partaker of the Divine nature. It is impossible for a saint, no matter what his experience, to keep right with God if he will not take the trouble to spend time with God. In order to keep the mind and heart awake to God's high ideals you have to keep coming back again and again to the primal source. If you do not, you will be crushed into degeneracy. Just as a poet or an artist must keep his soul brooding on the right lines, so a Christian must keep the sense of God's call always awake. Spend plenty of time with God; let other things go, but don't neglect Him. And beware of practical work. We are not here to do work *for* God, we are here to be workers *with* Him, those through whom He can do His work.

---

22. Thomas Carlyle (1795–1881): Scottish-born literary figure in nineteenth-century England, a writer, biographer, essayist, historian, and critic.

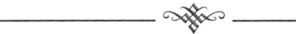

BEATIFIC BETROTHAL
Genesis 24

Warp and Woof and Tangle,—
  Weavers of Webs are we.
Living and dying—and mightier dead,
For the shuttle, once sped, is sped—is sped;—
  Weavers of Webs are we.

White, and Black, and Hodden-gray,—
  Weavers of Webs are we.
To every weaver one golden strand
Is given in trust by the Master-Hand;—
  Weavers of Webs are we.

And that we weave, we know not,—
  Weavers of Webs are We.
The threads we see, but the pattern is known
To the Master-Weaver alone, alone;—
  Weavers of Webs are we.

John Oxenham

Come in, thou blessed of the LORD; wherefore standest thou without? Genesis 24:31

Nothing can exceed the dignity and beauty of this chapter in the Bible. It reveals God's providential workings in the lives of several elemental, upright people, and clearly conveys God's order for each one. In the case of Abraham we see sublime sentiment (thought born in profound feeling) being worked out in plain common-sense details, yet with the natural sensibilities alive at once to human conditions and to the demands of God.

1. Sentiment, Sense and Sensibility
As already stated, there is a difference between sentiment and sentimentality. We cannot be profoundly moved by thought; we can only be profoundly moved by a personal crisis with God in which our usual equilibrium is disturbed, and our subsequent conceptions of life must be taken from the emotions stirred by the crisis. If the disturbance comes to you from outside, you will be exactly the same after it; but if you go through a personal crisis, such as Our Lord insists on, the personal crisis of devotion to Himself in discipleship, then all your conceptions of life will take colour from that moment. People are called backsliders who are merely sentimental pious people, they have had no crisis, all they have is the affectation of sentimentality. Recall the depths of feeling through which God has taken Abraham, and now in this chapter we see him being led rightly in the actual concerns of life.

Right views on profound subjects will always be the spring of right relationships in shallow matters. To be guided by common sense is as foolish as being guided by faith. God is the One Who welds both faith and common sense into one practical personality.

By "Sense" understand matters of practical human existence, and remember that any feature of actual life not brought under the severe control of the conception born of your crisis with God will leave a loophole for the devil. For instance, if you ignore certain aspects of your natural life as it has been constructed by God—take too much sleep, or not enough sleep, forego meals—you will give occasion to the enemy straightaway, no matter how great a saint you are. We have no business to leave out any part of our being from the control of the conceptions born of our crisis with God. The difficulty with us as Christians is that we will not think in accordance with the crisis we have had; consequently when we come to the things of sense and meet with people who have not had a crisis with God, it is an easy business to climb down. If we remain true to the sentiment produced in us by our crisis with God, those who meantime protest against us will ultimately come up to the same standard; but if we succumb, everything will go down.

By "Sensibility" understand the natural intuitive power usually called tact, which makes it possible for us to live with other people without annoying them. These three, sentiment, sense and sensibility, must be welded into one in our personal lives by devotion to the Lord Jesus Christ.

2. Solemn Sacredness of Serving
Eliezer in many respects stands as a picture of a disciple of the Lord; the whole moulding of his life is his devotion to another, not to a sense of right or duty, but to his master (cf. John 13:13–14). We know very little about devotion to Jesus Christ. We know about devotion to right and to duty, but none of that is saintly, it is purely natural. My sense of duty and of right can never be God's. If I can state what my duty is, I have become my god in that particular. There is only One Who knows what my duty is as a Christian, and that is God. The Sermon on the Mount nowhere tells us what our duty is; it tells us the things a saint will do—things that are not his duty, e.g., Matthew 5:39–42. Be renewed in the spirit of your mind, says Paul, not that you may do your duty, but that you may make out what God's will is.

All the reward Eliezer seeks is the happiness of his master, self-remembrance in him is dead. He is shrewd and practical, yet as guileless as a child, the exact embodiment of 1 Corinthians 4:2—"It is required in stewards, that a man be found *faithful*."

3. Self–Forgetfulness in Stewards of Secrets

One significant thing to notice is that Rebecca came alone and unveiled, and conversed freely with a stranger. The self-forgetfulness of Eliezer and Rebecca's own intuition made her know that she was safe with him. "Man's virtue and woman's liberty go hand in hand." There are those who talk like angels, yet they smudge the soul; there are others who may not talk sweetly yet they exhilarate the soul. Guard your intuition as the gift of God. You cannot judge virtue by its obverse; you can only judge virtue by intuition. Woe be to any woman who ignores her intuition, ignores the warning which says—Now draw back. For God's sake and your own womanhood's sake, draw back, it matters not who the person is.

4. Sweet Supremacy of Singleness

Rebecca's brother and mother recognise God's hand in the whole matter (Genesis 24:50), and Those words are the answer to Eliezer's prayer. Rebecca felt the thrill which always passes through any pure young heart in the presence of a saint. A soul's trust in a saint in the providence of God is something more precious even than love. Few of us know anything about it because we are too sordidly selfish, we want things for ourselves all the time. Eliezer had only one conception, loyalty to his master, and in the providence of God he brought Rebecca straight to Isaac. This marriage, like all true marriages, concerns the Kingdom of God.

DISCOVERING DIVINE DESIGNS
Genesis 24

Let us not always say
　　"Spite of this flesh to-day
I strove, made head, gained ground upon the
　　　　whole!"
　　As the bird wings and sings,
　　Let us cry "All good things
Are ours, nor soul helps flesh more, now, than
flesh helps soul!"

He fixed thee mid this dance
　　Of plastic circumstance,
This Present, thou, forsooth, wouldst fain arrest:
　　Machinery just meant
　　To give thy soul its bent,
Try thee and turn thee forth, sufficiently
impressed.

　　　　　　　　　　　　　Browning

And the man bowed down his head and worshipped the LORD. *Genesis 24:26*

The whole discipline of the life of faith is to make the ideal visions of faith and the actual performance of life one in personal possession. Only one Being can enable us to make the ideal and the actual one in personal life, viz., the Holy Spirit. In art and literature the ideal and the actual are only made one in a picture or a poem or book. The temple of the Holy Ghost is our personal life.

1. Human Forethought and Divine Design (*Genesis 24:1–9*)

Abraham's motive is clearly stated here. Never speak of human motives as if they were opposed to the Divine. In the life of a child of God the human motive is the disguised Divine. Sanctification means that I become a child of God, consequently my common-sense decisions are God's will unless He gives the check of His Spirit. I decide things in perfect fellowship with God, knowing that if my decisions are wrong, He will check. When He checks, I must stop at once. It is the inner check of the Spirit that prevents common sense being our god. There are times of crisis when we must wait on God, but they are rare. It is the abortion of piety to ask God to guide us here and there, of course He will! Such asking is not real. Remember our Lord's injunction—"Except ye . . . become as little children."

If God is not recognised by His blessings in the details of actual life in the beginning, He will be recognised in the end by His destructions. Human forethought in a faithful soul such as Abraham is the manifestation of the Divine design. In looking back you see not the haphazard, but an amazing design which, if you are born of God, you will credit to God; otherwise you credit it to the extraordinary wisdom of men and women.

2. Human Appointments and Divine Discoveries *(Genesis 24:10–21)*

It is our wisdom to follow providence, but folly to force it. By earnest human effort Eliezer makes his appointments, and these are not only recognised by God, but become also discoveries of the Divine mind. Unless you are a saint, your praying is pious humbug; but if you are a saint, you soon realise that you discover the Divine by energetically doing the human, provided you are maintaining a personal relationship to God. The fanatical element in the saint is the element that is devoted to a principle instead of to consistent conduct before God. For instance, I may become a devotee to the doctrine of Divine healing which means I must never be sick, and if I am sick then I say I must have gone wrong. The battle all through is against the absurdity of being consistent to an ideal instead of to God. The vital point about Eliezer is not his asking for signs, but that *Eliezer* asked for signs. Eliezer was a man who related everything entirely to God, consequently his human appointments, which are easy to ridicule, were God's way of enabling him to discover His mind. Beware of making a fetish of consistency to convictions instead of developing your faith in God. "I shall never do that"—in all probability you will have to if you are a saint. Whenever we take what God has done and put it in the place of Himself, we instantly become idolaters. If Our Lord had been fanatically consistent, He would have said after the temptation —I have not eaten for forty days, therefore I will never eat food again. He did not eat for forty days because it was His Father's will for Him not to. Judged on the line of logical consistency there was no more inconsistent being than Our Lord. He said—"Resist not evil"; and then He cleansed the temple in Jerusalem (Mark 11:15–16). But Our Lord was never inconsistent to His Father. The saint is to be consistent to the Divine life within him, not logically consistent to a principle. A fanatic is concerned not about God but about proving his own little fanatical ideas. It is a danger peculiar to us all. It is easier to be a fanatic than a faithful soul, because there is something amazingly humbling, particularly to our religious conceit, in being loyal to God.

3. Human Astonishment and Divine Details *(Genesis 24:21–33)*

The details of these verses are commonplace to Eastern custom, but Eliezer sees God in them. It is easy to see God in exceptional things or in a crisis, but it requires the culture of spiritual discipline to see God in every detail. Never allow that the haphazard is anything less than God's appointed order.

One other thing to note in these verses is the characteristic of the hospitality, it is an incurious, generous hospitality, which is the rarest type. Hospitality is characteristic not only of the East but of God's programme. To be curious about another person's affairs is an impertinence and is never Christian.

4. Human Affinities and Divine Directions *(Genesis 24:34–49)*

Eliezer gives a simple account of his journey, but his speech is an example of great wisdom. When the Spirit of God guides a man's human affairs, his speech indicates not human shrewdness, but the frankness of Divine skill. Ever note that we must be ready to discover the Divine designs *anywhere*.

5. Human Abandon and Divine Devotion *(Genesis 24:50–67)*

The custom according to which the brother must interest himself in the affairs of the sister is the explanation of much in these verses. They recognised the will of God in the whole matter, and have neither good nor ill to say. The consent of Rebecca is not sought in the betrothal, but only in the less important point of immediate departure.

When a soul abandons to God, God will not abandon it. But let that soul trust its wits and become its own amateur providence and a dextrous muddle will be the result. When once you have the amateur providence idea, it will prevent your doing the thing God tells you to do—"I must not tell my parents about my call; I want to prevent them suffering." Your plain duty before God is to tell them. If you are abandoned to God and do the duty that lies nearest, God will not abandon you; but if you trust in your wits and bring in the amateur providence idea, He will have to abandon you, and there will be heartbreaks and distresses that He is not in at all. Present the whole thing where it ought to be presented—in abandonment to God, and He will engineer everything in His own way.

SUNSET
Genesis 25:1–10

That low man seeks a little thing to do,
*   Sees it and does it:*
This high man, with a great thing to pursue,
*   Dies ere he know it.*
That low man goes on adding one to one,
*   His hundred's soon hit:*
This high man, aiming at a million,
*   Misses an unit.*
That, has the world here—should he need the next,
*   Let the world mind him!*
This, throws himself on God, and unperplexed,
*   Seeking shall find him.*

Browning

And his sons Isaac and Ishmael buried him. Genesis 25:9

It is not what a man achieves, but what he believes and strives for that makes him noble and great. Hebrews 11 impresses this aspect of the life of faith over against the life of human perfection. The first thing faith in God does is to remove all thought of relevant perfection. Some lives may seem humanly perfect and yet not be relevant to God and His purpose. The effect such lives leave is not of a reach that exceeds its grasp, but of a completed little circle of their own. It takes a man completely severed from God to be perfect in that way. There is a difference between a perfect human life lived on earth and a personal life with God lived on earth; the former gasps that for which it reaches, the latter is grasped by that which it never can reach. The former chains us to earth by its very completeness; the latter causes us to fling ourselves unperplexed on God. The difference is not a question of sin, but the paradox of the incomplete perfection of a right relationship to God.

1. The Region of the Irrelevant *(Genesis 25:1–4)*
One of the most striking features in Abraham's life is its irrelevancy. If we take Abraham to be the embodiment of an idea, say, of sanctification, we will have to cut out much that God puts in. The irrelevant things in Abraham's life are evidences of that half-conscious living which proves that his mind was not taken up

with himself. The greatest thing in Abraham's life is God, not "Abraham-ism." The whole trend of his life is to make us admire God, not Abraham.

The outstanding characteristic in the life of a saint is its irrelevance, an irrelevance which is amazingly relevant to the purpose of God. If you become a devotee to a principle, you become a religious lunatic; you are no longer loyal to the life of Jesus, but loyal only to the logic of your convictions about Him. A fanatic dismisses all irrelevancy in life. We say that a lunatic is a man who has lost his reason; a lunatic is a man who has lost everything but his reason. A madman's explanation of things is always complete. The main thing is life, not logic. It is the irrelevant running all through life that makes it what it is worth.

One of the dangers of the so-called Higher Christian Life movements[23] is the idea that God wants to produce specimens to put in His museum. You can often find better specimens in the world than in the Church. Think of the men and women you know who have not been through the crisis you have been through, and your human reason tells you they are infinitely better than you are, they are more unselfish, never irritable or upset, and yet they would not dream of saying what you have to say, that you are loyal to Jesus Christ. The irrelevancy of your life and the relevancy of theirs will produce perplexity in your mind until you remember that you are not called to produce one of God's specimens; you are called to live in perfect relationship to God so that the net result of your life is not admiration for you, but a longing after God. Christian perfection is not, and never can be, human perfection. Christian perfection is the perfection of a relationship to God which shows itself in the total irrelevancy of human life.

If you get off on the line of personal holiness or Divine healing or the Second Coming of Our Lord, and make any of these your end, you are disloyal to Jesus Christ. Supposing the Lord has healed your body and you make Divine healing your end, the dead set of your life is no longer for God but for what you are pleased to call the manifestation of God in your life. Bother your life! "It can never be God's will that I should be sick." If it was God's will to bruise His own Son, why should it not be His will to bruise you?

---

23. Higher Christian Life movements: various groups and organizations that emphasized sanctification and personal holiness.

The thing that tells is not relevant consistency to an idea of what a saint's life is, but abandonment abjectly to Jesus Christ whether you are well or ill.

Much of our life is irrelevant to any and every mind saving God's mind. When you obey the call of God the first thing that strikes you is the irrelevancy of the things you have to do, and you are sure to be brought up full butt against the perfect human specimens. The net result of such lives does not leave you with the "flavour" of God at all, it leaves you with the idea that God is totally unnecessary—by human effort and human devotion we can reach the standard God wants. Well, in a fallen world it cannot be done. Paul refers to this in 2 Corinthians 4:3–4—"the god of this world hath blinded the minds of the unbelieving . . ." (RV), i.e., they have the perfection of the human, but never once have they seen the perfection of God.

Beware of taking your conception of a saint from deductions from certain Scriptures, and always clarify your views by meditation on John 17. God wants to do with the saints what His Son prayed He would do—make them one with Himself (v. 21).

2. The Reign of the Irrevocable *(Genesis 25:5–7)*

Ishmael is the son born of the wrong way of doing God's will. If we try to do God's will through our own effort, we produce Ishmael. Much of our modern Christian enterprise is "Ishmael," i.e., it is born not of God, but of an inordinate desire to do God's will in our own way—the one thing Our Lord never did.

Ishmael, as we have seen, had to be dismissed and disciplined until he was willing to become subservient and be utilised for God's purposes; and the natural has to be put completely under, dismissed and denied, until it is willing to be subjected to God, not to our ideas of relevancy. We put sin in the wrong place.

Remember, we cannot touch sin. The Atonement of the Lord alone touches sin. We must not tamper with it for one second. We can do nothing with sin; we must leave God's Redemption to deal with it. Our part has to do with "Ishmael," i.e., the natural. The natural has to be denied, not because it is bad and wrong, but because it has nothing to do with our life of faith in God until it is turned into the spiritual by obedience. It is the attitude of the maimed life, which so few of us understand.

3. The Realm of the Irreproachable *(Genesis 25:8)*

The Hebrews regarded life as complete when it was full of days and riches and honour. Age was looked upon as a sign of favour. Whenever a nation becomes unspiritual, it reverses this order, the demand is not for old age but for youth. This reversal in the modern life of to-day is indicative of apostasy, not of advance.

Abraham's life wore to a tranquil sunset. He is described as "full of years," i.e., satisfied with life. He had seen, felt, believed, loved, suffered enough, earth had no more to offer him. Through God's goodness he found goodness in everything. Bitterness and cynicism are born of broken gods; bitterness is an indication that somewhere in my life I have belittled the true God and made a god of human perfection.

4. The Reunion of the Irreconcilable *(Genesis 25:9–10)*

Ishmael and Isaac are re-united at the grave of their father. Ishmael—strong, rugged, human perfection; Isaac—meditative, incomplete visionary, but on the trail of God. These two unite at the burial of Abraham, the Friend of God, whom God will not forsake. "Gathered to his people" means gathered to the unseen world. This is immortality in direct statement in the Old Testament.

containing also
Grow Up into Him
and
As He Walked
Oswald Chambers

Our Brilliant Heritage, 1929, Talks on the Gospel Mystery of Sanctification
Grow Up into Him, 1931, Talks on Christian Habits
As He Walked, 1930, Talks on Christian Experience
This edition copyright 1965, Oswald Chambers Publications Association
Combined hardback edition first published in 1965
Scripture versions quoted: KJV, RV, MOFFATT

INTRODUCTION

Source
This material is from talks and lectures given at League of Prayer[1] meetings and at the Bible Training College[2] in London between 1911 and 1915.

Publication History
The three parts that comprise *Our Brilliant Heritage* were published individually as articles and booklets before being issued as a combined volume in 1965.

- **Our Brilliant Heritage:** These lectures were most likely given to League of Prayer meetings in London. "The Gospel Mystery of Sanctification" appeared as an article in *Tongues of Fire* in November 1912. It was identified as "verbatim notes of a lecture given by Chambers at Speke Hall," the League's headquarters. It is also probable that Chambers included this subject matter in his classes on Christian doctrine at the Bible Training College between 1911 and 1915. The material was published as five articles in *Spiritual Life* magazine, from October 1925 through February 1926, then as a booklet in 1929.

- **Grow Up into Him:** These lectures on Christian habits were given at the Bible Training College, London, from October 1 through December 17, 1914. The material was published as articles in *Spiritual Life* magazine over a period of two years, from August 1926 through August 1928, then published as a booklet in 1931.

- When Oswald Chambers gave these lectures in the autumn of 1914, fear and uncertainty ruled the minds of many in Britain as World War I showed no sign of the early conclusion people had hoped for. Basic necessities were being rationed

---

1. Pentecostal League of Prayer: founded in London in 1891 by Reader Harris (1847–1909), prominent barrister and friend and mentor of Oswald Chambers.

2. Bible Training College (BTC): a residential school near Clapham Common in southwest London. Sponsored by the League of Prayer; operated from 1911 until it closed in July 1915 because of World War I. Oswald Chambers was principal and main teacher; Biddy Chambers, his wife, was lady superintendent.

and, for most BTC students, money was in short supply. On December 17, as Oswald spoke on "The Habit of Wealth," he asked, "What have we to spend this Christmas-time? We ought to be going about like multi-millionaires. Externally we may have 2½*d*.[3] only, but spiritually we have all the grace of God to spend on others."

- **As He Walked:** The material in *As He Walked* is drawn from lectures on Christian experience given at the Bible Training College, from April 30 through July 9, 1914. The talks were published as articles in *Spiritual Life* magazine from September 1929 through March 1930, and published as a booklet in 1930.

CONTENTS

---

3. 2½*d*. = Two pence and a half penny; 1 percent of a British pound prior to 1971. "tuppence ha'penny"—colloquial: next to nothing; nothing at all.

INTRODUCTORY NOTE
(FROM THE 4TH EDITION, 1937)

This Book will greatly help seekers after Holiness, because it meets us on the threshold of our life in Christ and leads us along a luminous path of Scriptural teaching, to the full measure of the believer's identification with his Risen Lord. "The candidates for sanctification are those who have the first-fruits of sanctification in the initial work of grace." They are then shown that the secret of holiness is the imparted holiness of Jesus Christ. "What a marvellous thing sanctification is. The perfections of Jesus—ours by the sheer gift of God."

As Chapter II nourishes the heart by leading us to implicit trust in Jesus; so Chapter III feeds the mind with deepest Scriptural truth. It might be described as Spiritualised Theology. And the Chapter on "in Heavenly Places" is an unveiling of the glory and strength and security of the most intimate relationship we can know with our Risen Lord. "Jesus Christ can create in us the image of God even as it was in Himself." What an arresting sentence is this—

"In illustrating the spiritual life, our tendency is to catch the tricks of the world, to watch the energy of the business man, and to apply these methods to God's work. Jesus Christ tells us to take the lessons of our lives from the things men never look at. "Consider the lilies": "Behold the fowls of the air." How often do we look at clouds, or grass, at sparrows, or flowers? Why, we have no time to look at them, we are in the rush of things—it is absurd to sit dreaming about sparrows and trees and clouds! Thank God when He raises us to the heavenly places, He manifests in us the very mind that was in Christ Jesus, unhasting and unresting, calm, steady and strong."

And the last Chapter insists on the possession of the Light, and shows its marvellous ministry in illuminating through His saints the darkness around. "Have we let God raise us up to the heavenly places in Christ Jesus, and are we learning to walk in the light as God is in the light?"

THE MYSTERY OF SANCTIFICATION

And without controversy great is the mystery of godliness: God was manifest in the flesh. 1 Timothy 3:16

By the word mystery we mean something known only to the initiated, therefore if we are going to understand the gospel mystery of Sanctification and fully experience it, we must belong to the initiated, that is, we must be born from above (RV mg) by the Spirit of God. Robert Murray McCheyne[4] said, and I would like his words engraven on my own heart, "The greatest need for my people is my personal holiness." Minister of the gospel, say that of your congregation—"The greatest need for my people is my personal holiness." Teacher, say that of your class—"The greatest need for my Sunday School class is my personal holiness."

Am I born again of the Spirit of God? What is the relation of my heart to holiness? Our Lord said, "Every tree is known by his own fruit," and I know whether I am born of the Spirit by the desires of my heart. Do I desire holiness more keenly than I desire

any other thing? Do I desire that my motives, my heart, my life, everything in me, should be as pure as God wants it to be? If so, it is a strong witness to the fact that I am amongst the initiated; I am in the place where I can understand the mystery of sanctification sufficiently to enter into it.

1. The Awakening of Desires
Be ye transformed by the renewing of your mind. (Romans 12:2)

When we are born again of the Spirit of God, the Word of God awakens great desires in us, and in times of prayer the Spirit of God renews our minds; in times of meeting with God's people the gracious sense of God's quickening comes until we know that the great desire of our hearts before God is to be as holy as God desires us to be. We do want to be baptised with the Holy Ghost so that we bear a strong family likeness to Jesus Christ. These deep desires are

---

4. Robert Murray McCheyne (1813–1843): Scottish minister whose short but intense life left a great impact on Scotland.

strong in the heart of every one who is born from above (RV mg). Paul says he speaks the mystery of God to all such, because they have the Spirit of God to enable them to understand it. We must watch and note whether these are our desires.

The candidates for sanctification are those who have the first-fruits of sanctification in the initial work of grace, those who are rightly adjusted to God through the Atonement of the Lord Jesus Christ, and who hunger and thirst after holiness, and desire to do all God's will.

Do we long for holiness? Are the deepest desires of our hearts Godward? Do we know, first of all, that we are reconciled to God? Do we know that our sins are forgiven, that God has put the life of His Spirit into us, and are we learning how to walk in the light, and are we gaining victories by the power of the Spirit? Do we realise that as we rely on God we have strength to perform our duties in accordance with God's will?

All this is grand, ordinary, Christian experience in its elementary stages. Everyone who is born again of the Spirit of God experiences these things; they are the initiated, the ones who can understand the mystery of sanctification and, God grant, may enter into the experience of it.

There is a type of Christian who says—"Yes, I have the desire for holiness, I am reading God's word, I am trying to be holy and to draw on the resurrection life of Jesus." Never will the mystery of sanctification dawn in that way; it is not God's way. Sin is a step *aside;* being born of the Spirit of God is a step *inside,* and sanctification is being built into all the perfect character of Jesus Christ *by a gift.*

Another type of Christian says—"Well, I have tried and striven and prayed, but I find it so hard to cut off my right arm, to poke out my right eye, that I have come to the conclusion that I am unworthy of this great blessing from God; I am not one of these special people who can be holy." I believe there are numbers of Christians who have laid themselves on one side, as it were, and come to the conclusion that sanctification is not meant for them; the reason being that they have tried to work sanctification out in their own way instead of in God's way, and have failed.

There are others who by strange penances, fastings and prayers, and afflictions to their bodies are trying to work out sanctification. They, too, have tried to penetrate the mystery in a way other than God's appointed way.

Are you trying to work out sanctification in any of these ways? You know that salvation is a sovereign work of grace, but, you say, sanctification is worked out by degree. God grant that the Spirit of God may put His quiet check on you, and enable you to understand the first great lesson in the mystery of sanctifi-cation which is "*Christ Jesus, who of God is made unto us . . . sanctification.*"

2. Impartation, Not Imitation

Sanctification does not put us into the place that Adam was in and require us to fulfil the will of God as He makes it known to us; sanctification is something infinitely more than that. In Jesus Christ is perfect holiness, perfect patience, perfect love, perfect power over all the power of the enemy, perfect power over everything that is not of God, and sanctification means that all that is ours in Him. The writer to the Hebrews does not tell us to imitate Jesus when we are tempted; he says—"Come to Jesus, and He will succour you in the nick of time." That is, all *His* perfect overcoming of temptation is ours in Him.

We have heard it put in this way so often—When faced with difficulties, we do not try to brace ourselves up by prayer to meet them, but by the power of the grace of God we let the perfections of Jesus Christ be manifested in us. Jesus Christ does not give us power to work up a patience like His own. *His* patience is manifested if we will let His life dwell in us. So many have the idea that in sanctification we draw from Jesus the power to be holy. We draw from Jesus the holiness that was manifested in Him, and He manifests it in us. This is the mystery of sanctification.

Sanctification does not mean that the Lord gives us the ability to produce by a slow, steady process a holiness like His; it is *His* holiness in us. By sanctification we understand experimentally what Paul says in 1 Corinthians 1:30: "Of Him are ye in Christ Jesus, who of God is *made unto us . . . sanctification.*" Whenever Paul speaks of sanctification, he speaks of it as an impartation, never as an imitation. Imitation comes in on a different line. Paul does not say, nor does the Spirit of God say anywhere, that after we are born again of the Spirit of God, Jesus Christ is put before us as an Example and we make ourselves holy by drawing from Him. Never! Sanctification is Christ formed in us; not the Christ-life, but Christ Himself. In Jesus Christ is the perfection of everything, and the mystery of sanctification is that we may have in Jesus Christ, not the start of holiness, but the holiness of Jesus Christ. All the perfections of Jesus Christ are at our disposal if we have been initiated into the mystery of sanctification. No wonder men cannot explain this mystery for the joy and the rapture and the marvel of it all, and no wonder men see it when it is there, for it works out everywhere.

3. The Mystery of Fellowship
We will come unto him, and make our abode with him. (John 14:23)

The "nuggets of gold" spoken by our Lord in the Gospels are beaten out by the apostles in the Epistles.

Jesus states that the relationship between the Father and the Son is to be the relationship between the Father and the Son and the sanctified soul. Talk about "nothing between"! There is no possible room for anything between, unless the soul steps aside. As long as the soul realises in the simplicity of faith that all that Jesus was and is, is his, then the very life, the very faith, the very holiness of Jesus is imparted to him.

Think what the fellowship of our Lord Jesus Christ with His Father was when He was here—"I knew that Thou hearest Me always." "I do always those things that please Him." This is not an example for us: it is infinitely more. It means that this fellowship is exactly what is made ours in sanctification. Jesus said "At that day . . . I say not unto you, that I will pray the Father for you: for the Father Himself loveth you." In what day? The day when we are brought into that union of fellowship with the Father and all the perfections of Jesus are made ours so that we can say with Paul—"I live; yet not I, but Christ liveth in me."

Those of you who are hungering and thirsting after holiness, think what it would mean to you to go out to-night knowing that you may step boldly into the heritage that is yours if you are born of the Spirit, and realise that the perfections of Jesus are yours by His sovereign gift in such a way that you can prove it experimentally!

4. The Mystical Union
I am the vine, ye are the branches. (John 15:5)

He that is joined unto the Lord is one spirit. (1 Corinthians 6:17)

The New Testament exhausts itself in trying to expound the closeness of this union. The Spirit of God conveys to the initiated, to those who are born again, what a marvellous thing sanctification is. The perfections of Jesus—ours by the sheer gift of God: God does not give us power to imitate Him: He gives us His very Self.

This is what sanctification means for you and me. Do you say it is too much? Do you know what it comes down to? It comes down to *faith*: our word is confidence. If we are born again of God by the Spirit, we have not the slightest doubt in our minds of Jesus Christ; we have absolute confidence in Him. But draw nearer still— Have we confidence to let the Spirit of God explain to us what sanctification means, and lead us into the experience? If so, instead of its being painful to follow the ways of wisdom, we will find that "her ways are ways of pleasantness, and all her paths are peace."

5. The Mystery of the Incarnation
Therefore also that holy thing which shall be born of thee shall be called the Son of God. (Luke 1:35)

There are three big mysteries: The Mystery of the Triune God—Father, Son and Holy Ghost; the Mystery of our Lord Jesus Christ, who is both human and Divine, and the Mystery we are dealing with—the mystery that I, a sinner, can be made into the image of Jesus Christ by the great work of His Atonement in my life.

Have you ever noticed how our Lord's death is explained and applied by the Spirit of God in the Apostle Paul's teaching? For instance, "Therefore we are buried with Him by baptism into death: that like as Christ was raised up from the dead by the glory of the Father, even so we also should walk in newness of life" (Romans 6:4) means that all that our Lord's death is stated to mean in the New Testament can be made real in our experience. We can go through identification with the death of Jesus until we are alive only to the things which He was alive to. Jesus Christ does not give us power to put the "old man" to death in ourselves: *"our old man was crucified with Him"* (Romans 6:6 RV); we can be identified with His death and know that this is true. We are not merely put into a state of innocence before God; by identification with Our Lord's death we are delivered from sin in every bit of its power and every bit of its presence.

God never removes from us the power of stepping aside; we can step aside any moment we like. Read the First Epistle of John—*If* any man step aside— John's thought is surely that it is a rare thing for a man to step aside. Our attitude seems to be that it is a rare thing to keep in the light!

"And hath raised us up together, and made us sit together in heavenly places"—like Christ Jesus? No, *"in* Christ Jesus." The very Spirit that ruled Jesus in His life now rules us. How has it come about? Read Romans 8:10. "And if Christ be in you, the body is dead because of sin; but the Spirit is life because of righteousness." John the Baptist said of Jesus—"He shall baptize you with the Holy Ghost and with fire." The Spirit of God Who wrought out that marvellous Life in the Incarnation will baptise us into the very same life, not into a life like it, but into His life until the very holiness of Jesus is gifted to us. It is not something we work out in Him, it is *in Him*, and He manifests it through us while we abide in Him. This explains why in the initial stages of sanctification we sometimes see marvellous exhibitions of Christ-like life and patience. All that was wrought out in the life of Jesus was wrought out by the Holy Ghost Whom our Lord has shed forth by His ascended right, and by the baptism of the Holy Ghost the perfections of Jesus are made ours. We are not put into the place where we can imitate Jesus; the baptism of the Holy Ghost puts us into the very life of Jesus:

Are you hungering after sanctification? Have you such confidence in Jesus that you can pray this prayer, the prayer of a child—"Father, in the Name of Jesus, baptise me with the Holy Ghost and fire until sanctification is made real in my life"?

THE GOSPEL OF THE GRACE OF GOD

Unto Me, who am less than the least of all saints, is this grace given, that I should preach among the Gentiles the unsearchable riches of Christ. Ephesians 3:8

To whom God would make known what is the riches of the glory of this mystery among the Gentiles; which is Christ in you, the hope of glory. Colossians 1:27

The mystery of sanctification is that the perfections of Jesus Christ are imparted to us, not gradually, but instantly, when by faith we enter into the realisation that Christ is made unto us sanctification. Sanctification does not mean anything less than the holiness of Jesus Christ being made ours manifestly, and faith is the instrument given us to use in order to work out this unspeakable mystery in our lives. There are two "means"; the Gospel of the Grace of God, and faith, which enables the life and liberty and power and marvel of the holiness of Jesus Christ to be wrought out in us.

1. The Instrument of Faith
Do we know anything about this mystical union whereby the unsearchable riches of Jesus Christ are made ours? If we have been born from above (RV mg) of the Spirit of God, the deep craving of our hearts is to be as holy as Jesus Christ, and just as we took the first step in salvation by faith, so we take the next step by faith. We are invited, we are commanded and pleaded with, to believe the gospel of the grace of God, which is, "Christ in you, the hope of glory."

The one marvellous secret of a holy life is not in imitating Jesus, but in letting the perfections of Jesus manifest themselves in our mortal flesh. Do we believe that? Do we believe it with the same simple trust and confidence we had when we first trusted Jesus to save us?

The way to believe it is to listen first. "So then faith cometh by hearing, and hearing by the word of God." Have we listened? Have we ever listened with the ears of our spirit to this wonderful statement— *"Christ in you"*? Do we hear that? If we are born of the Spirit of God, we do hear it, we hear it more eagerly, more passionately, more longingly than anything else that can be told. We are invited and commanded by God to believe that we can be made one with Jesus as He is one with God, so that His patience, His holiness, His purity, His gentleness, His prayerfulness are made ours. The way the gift of faith works in us and makes this real is by hearing. We first hear, and then we begin to trust. It is so simple that most of us miss the way. The way to have faith in the gospel of God's grace, in its deepest profundity as well as in its first working, is by listening to it. How many of us have brought the ears of our spirit straight down to the gospel of God's grace?

Our idea of faith has a good deal to do with the harmful way faith is often spoken of. Faith is looked upon as an attitude of mind whereby we assent to a testimony on the authority of the one who testifies. We say that because Jesus says these things, we believe in Him. The faith of the New Testament is infinitely more than that; it is the means by which sanctification is manifested, the means of introducing the life of God into us, not the effect of our understanding only. In Romans 3:24–25, Paul speaks about faith in the blood of Jesus, and faith is the instrument the Spirit of God uses. Faith is more than an attitude of the mind; faith is the complete, passionate, earnest trust of our whole nature in the Gospel of God's grace as it is presented in the Life and Death and Resurrection of our Lord Jesus Christ.

2. Implicit Trust in Jesus
Some of us have never allowed God to make us understand how hopeless we are without Jesus Christ. It was my experience of the tempter, and my knowledge of my own heart under his assaults, that made me a preacher of Paul's gospel. It was my own exceeding sinfulness of heart that ever more and more taught and compelled me to preach Jesus Christ alone, His blood and His righteousness. Everyone who is born again of the Spirit of God knows that there is no good thing outside the Lord Jesus Christ. It is no use looking for sanctification through prayer or obedience; sanctification must be the direct gift of God by means of this instrument of faith, not a half-hearted faith, but the most earnest, intense, and personal faith.

Sanctification is *"Christ in you."* Is anything we hear in testimonies to sanctification untrue of Jesus Christ? It is *His* wonderful life that is imparted to us in sanctification, and it is imparted by faith. It will never be imparted as long as we cling to the idea that we can get it by obedience, by doing this and that. We have to come back to one thing, faith alone, and after having been put right with God by sanctification, it is still a life of faith all through. Those who are in the experience of sanctification know that it means that the holiness of Jesus is imparted as a sovereign gift of God's grace. We cannot earn it, we cannot pray it down, but, thank God, we can take it by faith, "through faith in His blood."

When we have become rightly related to God, it is the trial of our faith that is precious (see 1 Peter

1:7). Satan tries to come in and make the saint disbelieve that sanctification is only by faith in God; he comes in with his "cinematograph show" and says, "You must have this and you must do that." The Spirit of God keeps us steadily to one line—faith in Jesus, and the trial of our faith, until the perfections of Jesus Christ are lived over again in our lives.

3. Identification with Jesus

God says that He will give us the desires of our heart. What are our desires? What do we desire more than anything else on earth? If we are born again of the Spirit of God, our one desire is a hunger and thirst after nothing less than holiness, the holiness of Jesus, and He will satisfy it.

"Whoso eateth My flesh, and drinketh My blood, hath eternal life." Just as we take food into our bodies and assimilate it, so, Jesus says, we must take Him into our souls. Faith is not seeing food and drink on the table; faith is taking it. So many say, "Oh, yes, I have faith that the Lord Jesus will save me." If we have faith that the Lord Jesus will save us, we *are* saved, and we know it. When by the Spirit of God Jesus is made real to us, His presence makes everything as natural as breathing. His presence is the reality.

What do we do to earn a gift? Nothing; we take it. If we have the slightest remnant of thinking we can earn it, we will never take it; if we are quite certain we do not deserve it, we will take it. We come with the sense of abject unworthiness, knowing that "in me (that is, in my flesh,) dwelleth no good thing"; if ever I am to be holy, I must be made holy by God's sovereign grace.

That is the Gospel. We receive it by faith; and the Spirit of God is the One Who makes the simple act of faith the supernatural work of God. To those outside Christian experience it sounds foolish; to those inside it is wonderfully real. Immediately we stretch out the instrument of faith with implicit trust, the Spirit of God imparts to us the holiness of Jesus Christ and all that that means; and it is on this line alone we live. Obedience is the means whereby we show the earnestness of our desire to do God's will. We receive this perfect adjustment to God as a gift, and then begin to manifest the life of Jesus Christ in our mortal flesh.

Those of you who have never had this experience of sanctification, think! The perfections of Jesus Christ made yours entirely! The Lord showing His love, His purity, His holiness through you! "I live; yet not I, but Christ liveth in me." It is not power to live like Jesus; it is Christ living in us, and it is His life that is seen, but it is only seen as by faith we walk in the light.

What does Paul say? "My little children, of whom I travail in birth again until Christ be formed in you," and again, "We are His workmanship, created in Christ Jesus unto good works." How many of us can look up into God's face by simple faith, trusting entirely in the great gospel of His grace, and say— "Lord, make the sanctification in me as real as the sanctification revealed in Thy Word"? Are we willing for Him to do it? Then we must turn from every other thing and trust in Him. Jesus Christ re-creates us by His marvellous life until we are a new creation (RV mg) in Him, and "all things are of God." The life is lived naturally as we lived the old life. Consciously? No, infinitely deeper; it is lived moment by moment by the faith of the Sons of God; only in rare moments are we conscious of it. When we come up against a crisis, for a moment we hesitate and wonder how we are going to meet the difficulty then we find that it is the perfections of Jesus Christ imparted into us that meet it, and slowly and surely we begin to live a life of ineffable order and sanity and holiness, kept by the power of God. No wonder the Apostle Paul says, "When He shall come to be glorified in His saints, and to be admired in all them that believe"!

Have you any doubt about the gospel of the grace of God? None whatever, you say. Then launch out in simple faith and say, "My God, make the sanctification of the New Testament mine; make the unsearchable riches of Jesus Christ mine till my Lord and I are one"—so much one that it never consciously occurs to you to be anything else, and in all the circumstances of life you will find that you have the perfections of Jesus Christ—at the back of you? No, dwelling in you! No wonder the Apostle John is so eager that we should walk in the light!

UNREALISED TRUTHS OF SANCTIFICATION

Therefore if any man be in Christ, he is a new creature: old things are passed away; behold, all things are become new. And all things are of God, who hath reconciled us to Himself by Jesus Christ, and hath given to us the ministry of reconciliation. 2 Corinthians 5:17–18

I want to deal with some of the unrealised truths of sanctification, the things we do not readily notice, from the standpoint of the new creation (RV mg) in Christ Jesus.

As we have seen, the idea of sanctification is not that God gives us a new spirit of life, and then puts Jesus Christ in front of us as a copy and says, "Do your best and I will help you"; but that God imparts to us the perfections of Jesus Christ. By the perfections of Jesus we do not mean His attributes as Son of God. What is imparted to us is the holiness of Jesus, not a principle of life that enables us to imitate Him, *but the holiness of Jesus* as it met life in Him.

1. Creation through Christ

For by Him were all things created, that are in heaven, and that are in earth, visible and invisible, whether they be thrones, or dominions, or principalities, or powers: all things were created by Him, and for Him. (Colossians 1:16)

And unto the angel of the church of the Laodiceans write; These things saith the Amen, the faithful and true witness, the beginning of the creation of God. (Revelation 3:14)

These verses are chosen out of a number in the Bible which reveal that God Almighty created the world and everything that was created, through the Eternal Son. Some people tell us that Revelation 3:14 means that the Son was the first Creation of God Almighty. The Bible does not say so. The Bible says, "He is before all things, and by Him all things consist." Jesus Christ was introduced into the world in this way: the Spirit of God took hold of a part of that creation, of which the Son of God was Himself the Creator, in the Virgin Mary and formed in her the Son of God—"therefore also that holy thing which shall be born of thee shall be called the Son of God" (Luke 1:35). That is the last reach of the creation of God. The Son of God was the One Whom we know as Jesus Christ, and in the life of Jesus we have the pattern life of all God desires man to be, and also the pattern life of sanctification.

2. Creation in Christ

All things were made by Him; and without Him was not anything made. That which hath been made was life in Him; and the life was the light of men. (John 1:3–4 RV mg)

By creation we are the children of God; we are not the sons and daughters of God by creation; Jesus Christ makes us sons and daughters of God by regeneration (John 1:12). The idea of the Fatherhood of Jesus is revealed in the Bible, though rarely mentioned. "Everlasting Father" refers to the Being we know as the Son of God. Paul in talking to the Athenians said, "We are the offspring of God." But the creator-power in Jesus Christ is vested in a more marvellous way even than when God created the world through Him for He has that in Himself whereby He can create His own image. God created the world and everything that was made through the Son, and "that which hath been made was life in Him" (RV mg); therefore just as God created the world through Him, the Son is able to create His own image in anyone and everyone. Have we ever thought of Jesus as the marvellous Being Who can create in us His own image? "Wherefore if any man is in Christ, there is a new creation [mg]"! (2 Corinthians 5:17 RV). We do not sufficiently realise the wonder of it. Those of us who are in the experience of God's mighty salvation do not give ourselves half enough prayerful time, and wondering time, and studying time to allow the Spirit of God to bring this marvellous truth home to us.

"Verily, verily, I say unto you, he that believeth on Me hath everlasting life." The very life that was in Jesus is the life of the soul who believes in Him, because it is created in him by Jesus. This life is only in Jesus Christ, it is not in anyone else, and we cannot get it by obeying or by praying, by vowing or by sacrificing.

"Marvel not that I said unto thee, Ye must be born again." We must have the image of God in our spirits, and Jesus will create His image in us by His sovereign right. The fullest and most gracious meaning of regeneration and sanctification is that in Christ Jesus we can be made a new creation (RV mg). Sanctification is not being given a new start, not that God wipes out the past and says it is forgiven, but something inconceivably grander, viz., that Jesus Christ has the power to create in us the image of God as it was in Himself. Paul says, "My little children, of whom I travail in birth again"—every strand of my spirit and soul and body aches—"until Christ be formed in you." "I fear," he says, "lest by any means . . . your minds should be corrupted from the simplicity that is in Christ." "Beware lest any man spoil you through philosophy." We have already dealt with this along the line of faith; we have to receive Jesus Christ in implicit confidence and let Him do His work in us.

Creation in Christ means that Jesus Christ is able to create us into His own image, not merely re-create us, because what we get in Jesus Christ is something that Adam never had. Adam was created a "son of God," an innocent being with all the possibilities of development before him; God intended him to take part in that development by a series of moral choices whereby the natural life was to be sacrificed to the will of God and turned into a spiritual life. Adam failed to do this. Jesus Christ creates in us not what was in Adam, He creates in us what He was and is. "*Christ Jesus, who of God is made unto us . . . sanctification.*" This is the meaning of the grand old evangelical hymn—

> *My hope is built on nothing less*
> *Than Jesus' blood and righteousness.*

3. Creation like Christ
As He is, so are we in this world. (1 John 4:17)

Those of us who are God's children ought to stand in determined reverence before this verse. It can mean only one thing, and that is that the image and character and holiness of Jesus Christ is ours by the sovereign right of His creation. Sanctification means that we are taken into a mystical union which language cannot define (cf. 1 John 3:2). It is Jesus Christ's holiness that is granted to us, not something pumped up by prayer and obedience and discipline, but something created in us by Jesus Christ. No wonder the New Testament puts Jesus Christ upon the throne! No wonder Jesus said that the Holy Ghost would glorify Him! And no wonder this talk is called "*unrealised* truths of sanctification"!

We are potentially sons and daughters of God through God's claim upon us in Christ, but we are only sons and daughters of God *in reality* through our will. Do we will, not to imitate Jesus, but to hand ourselves over to God until His claim is realised in us? Paul says, "We pray you," we passionately entreat you, "as though God did beseech you by us, . . . be ye reconciled to God." It is one thing to realise in speechless wonder, when the heart is attuned to an impulse of worship, what the claim of God is, and another thing to tell God that we want Him to realise His claim in us. "My God, I am Thine by creation, I am Jesus Christ's through His Atonement, and I choose that Thy claim shall be realised in me."

"Wherefore if any man is in Christ . . ." (RV). "Any man" means ourselves—men of no account. Our Lord never taught individualism; He taught the value of the individual, a very different thing. Does Paul mean that I, an ordinary man with no particular education, with ordinary common-place work, surrounded by commonplace people, can be made a new creation (RV

mg) in Christ Jesus? He does, because he says "*any man,*" and you must come in there. Will you choose to be one of the ordinary common rut, the "any man," and let God get hold of you? You are part of the creation of God, then let Jesus Christ make His creation good in you.

Jesus Christ does not make us original characters, He makes our characters replicas of His own; consequently, argues the Spirit of God, when men see us, they will not say, "What wonderful, original, extraordinary characters." No, none of that rubbish! They will say, "How marvellous God must be to take poor pieces of human stuff like those men, and turn them into the image of Jesus Christ!" ". . . which things the angels desire to look into." We are too free from wonder nowadays, too easy with the Word of God; we do not use it with the breathless amazement Paul does. Think what sanctification means—*Christ in me; made like Christ; as He is, so are we.*

4. The Transient Life
Old things are passed away.

By "old things" Paul does not mean sin and the "old man" only, he means everything that was our life as natural men before we were re-created in spirit by Christ. That means a great deal more than some of us mean. The "old things" means not only things that are wrong, any fool will give up wrong things if he can, but things that are right. Watch the life of Jesus and you will get Paul's meaning. Our Lord lived a natural life as we do, it was not a sin for Him to eat, but it would have been a sin for Him to eat during those forty days in the wilderness, because during that time His Father's will for Him was otherwise, and He sacrificed His natural life to the will of God. That is the way the "old things" pass away.

In his Second Epistle to the Corinthians Paul uses as an illustration of this the glory which came from Moses. It was a real glory, but it was a glory that was "to be done away" (3:7); and the writer to the Hebrews writes of a covenant which was doomed "to vanish away" (8:13). The natural life of man is a real creation of God, but it is meant to pass away into a spiritual life in Jesus Christ's way. Watch Paul's argument in the Epistle to the Romans—"But ye are not in the flesh, but in the Spirit . . ." (8:9). Paul was talking to flesh and blood men and women, not to disembodied spirits, and he means that the old order is passed. "You used to look at things differently from Jesus Christ," he says, "but now that you have turned to the Lord" (God grant you may if you have not) "the veil is taken away, and "where the Spirit of the Lord is, there is liberty."

5. The Transfigured Life
Behold, all things are become new.

Have those of us who are in the experience of sanctification learned the practical insistent habit of realising that the "old things are passed away," and that "all things are become new"? In their testimony people put it in this way—"God alters the thing that matters; it used to matter to me what certain people thought, now it does not matter at all." "Old things" are passed away, not only sin and the old disposition, but the whole old order of things, and "behold, all things are become new."

Paul is trying to get us to an amazed state of mind—*"Therefore if any man be in Christ, he is a new creature"*! Some of us talk about sanctification as if we were talking of a new book, or an article in the newspaper. With Paul the wonder never ceased; however often he talked about it, each time he was more full of wonder than the last.

The great mighty work of God's grace in sanctification is a Divine work. Do we choose to walk in God's way and let Him make it real in us? Then let the things that are passed *be* passed, and when the circumstances come again that tempt us to self-pity, remember that the old things are passed away. Do we choose never to let things affect us that never affected Jesus Christ? Immediately we do, we will find it is possible because the perfections of Jesus Christ are made ours by the sovereign right of His creation. No wonder Paul talks of "the unsearchable riches of Christ"! No wonder the marvel of the revelation breaks through his language and escapes until those who are not sanctified think him mad; and John is called an old man in "the sere and yellow leaf" who talked vaguely about the possibility of living without sin! Those who talk in this way have never entered into the wonderful experience of sanctification, but, thank God, it is for "any man."

6. The Truest Life of All
All things are of God.

"Be ye therefore followers"—of good principles? Of holiness? Of the life Jesus lived on earth? No! "Be ye therefore followers of God." "Be ye therefore perfect, as your Father which is in heaven is perfect." God by sanctification creates us into the image of His Son. Do we choose to walk in the light of that life? Never make excuses, never turn to the right hand nor to the left. Keep the life concentrated on this marvellous gift of God, *"Christ Jesus, who of God is made unto us . . . sanctification."*

IN HEAVENLY PLACES

And hath raised us up together, and made us sit together in heavenly places, in Christ Jesus. Ephesians 2:6

Sanctification is the impartation to us of the holy qualities of Jesus Christ. It is His patience, His love, His holiness, His faith, His purity, His godliness that are manifested in and through every sanctified soul. The presentation that God by sanctification plants within us His Spirit, and then setting Jesus Christ before us says—"There is your Example, follow Him and I will help you, but you must do your best to follow Him and do what He did," is an error. It is not true to experience, and, thank God, it is not true to the wonderful Gospel of the grace of God. The mystery of sanctification is *"Christ in you, the hope of glory."* "That which hath been made was life in Him" (RV mg), that is, Jesus Christ can create in us the image of God even as it was in Himself.

1. The Impartial Power of God
And hath raised us up.

Who are the "us" He has raised up? We have pointed out the "any man" aspect, and it needs pointing out because we often hear a man say—"Well, it cannot mean me, I'm not a true, fine-spirited person; my past life has been very sordid; I have not had the advantages of other people, and it cannot mean me; God cannot mean that by His marvellous grace He can raise *me* up." Yes, He can, and it is just such a man He does mean. God stoops down to the very lowest, to the very weakest, to the sons of disobedience, the children of wrath, and raises them right up. In this particular instance Paul is driving home the impartiality of God with more than usual insistence; he is talking to Gentiles and he says that God by the Cross of Jesus Christ makes no distinction between Jew and Gentile in the matter of personal salvation. Thank God for the impartiality of His grace!

Any man, every man, we ourselves, may partake of this marvellous raising up whereby God puts us into the wonderful life of His Son, and the very qualities of Jesus Christ are imparted to us. There is plenty of room to grow in the heavenly places; room for the head to grow, for the heart to grow, for the bodily relationships to grow, for the spirit to grow—plenty of room for every phase of us to grow into the realisation of what a marvellous Being our Lord Jesus Christ is.

"And hath quickened us together with Christ." The illustration Paul uses is that as God raised the dead body of Jesus, so He has quickened those who were dead in trespasses and sins and has raised them up with Jesus. It means that there is a participation now in all the wonderful perfections of Jesus Christ, and that ultimately "we shall be like Him; for we shall see Him as He is."

2. The Inviolable Place of God
Heavenly places in Christ Jesus.

That is where God raises us. We do not get there by climbing, by aspiring, by struggling, by consecration, or by vows; God lifts us right straight up out of sin, inability and weakness, lust and disobedience, wrath and self-seeking—lifts us right up out of all this, "up, up to the whiter than snow shine," to the heavenly places where Jesus Christ lived when He was on earth, and where He lives to this hour in the fullness of the plenitude of His power. May God never relieve us from the wonder of it. We are lifted up into that inviolable place that cannot be defiled, and Paul states that God can raise us up there *now*, and that the wonder of sitting in the heavenly places in Christ Jesus is to be manifested in our lives while we are here on earth.

"And made us sit together." Sit? But I have to earn my living! Sit? But I am in the midst of the wild turmoil of city life! Sit? But I have my calling in life and my ambitions to fulfil! Paul says that God has raised us up and made us *sit* together in heavenly places in Christ Jesus. We must have in our minds that by "heavenly places" is meant all that Jesus Christ was when He was down here, and all that He is revealed to be now by the Word; and God raises us up to sit together with Him there. There is ample time and ample room to grow in the heavenly places.

3. The Symbols in the Heavenly Places
Have you ever noticed the kind of pictures God gives to the saints? They are always pictures of creation, never pictures of men. God speaks of the unfailing stars and the upholding of the "worm Jacob." He talks about the marvels of creation, and makes His people forget the rush of business ideas that stamp the kingdoms of this world. The Spirit of God says—"Do not take your pattern and print from those; the God Who holds you is the God Who made the world—take your pattern from Him." The marvellous characteristic of the Spirit of God in you and me when we are raised up to the heavenly places in Christ Jesus is that we look to the Creator, and see that the marvellous Being Who made the world and upholds all things by the word of His Power is the One Who keeps us in every particular.

Our Lord always took His illustrations from His Father's handiwork. In illustrating the spiritual life, our tendency is to catch the tricks of the world, to watch the energy of the business man, and to apply these methods to God's work. Jesus Christ tells us to take the lessons of our lives from the things men never look at—"Consider the lilies"; "Behold the fowls of the air." How often do we look at clouds, or grass, at sparrows, or flowers? Why, we have no time to look at them, we are in the rush of things—it is absurd to sit dreaming about sparrows and trees and clouds! Thank God, when He raises us to the heavenly places, He manifests in us the very mind that was in Christ Jesus, unhasting and unresting, calm, steady and strong.

4. The Safety of the Heavenlies
My peace I give unto you. (John 14:27)

Your life is hid with Christ in God. (Colossians 3:3)

We are familiar with these verses, but has God ever struck the marvel out of them until we are lost in wonder, love, and praise as they are applied to us as sanctified souls? "My peace I give unto you." We talk about the peace of Jesus, but have we ever realised what that peace was like? Read the story of His life, the thirty years of quiet submission at Nazareth, the three years of service, the slander and spite, backbiting and hatred He endured, all unfathomably worse than anything we shall ever have to go through; and His peace was undisturbed, it could not be violated. It is that peace that God will exhibit in us in the heavenly places; not a peace like it, but that peace. In all the rush of life, in working for our living, in all conditions of bodily life, wherever God engineers our circumstances—"My peace"; the imperturbable, inviolable peace of Jesus imparted to us in every detail of our lives. "Your life is hid with Christ in God." Have we allowed the wonder of it to enwrap us round and soak us through until we begin to realise the ample room there is to grow there? "The secret place of the Most High," absolutely secure and safe.

As we go on in life and grow in grace, we realise more and more wonderingly what the peace of Jesus means. Watch the saint who is sanctified, "in tumults," Paul says—tribulation, turmoil, trouble, afflictions all around everywhere, yet the peace of Jesus is gifted and manifests itself, and the life grows as the lily spiritually. Tolstoi made the blunder of applying the teaching of Jesus to men who were not born again of the Holy Ghost, and with what result? They found it impossible to carry it out. But when we are born again from above (RV mg), quickened and raised up by God, we find it is possible to consider the lilies because we have not only the peace of God, but the very peace that characterised Jesus Christ; we are seated in heavenly places in Christ Jesus, absolutely safe, the mind imperturbably ensphered in Christ. "For ye are dead," says Paul; that is, the old way of looking at things, the old way of doing things, the old fuss and fume are dead, and we are a new creation (RV mg) in Christ Jesus, and in that new creation is manifested the very peace that was manifested in Jesus Christ.

5. The Strength in the Heavenlies

All spiritual blessings in heavenly places in Christ. (Ephesians 1:3)

The unsearchable riches of Christ. (Ephesians 3:8)

God is able to make all grace abound toward you. (2 Corinthians 9:8)

These verses mean that just as the overflowing, omnipotent power of God was exhibited in and through our Lord, so it will be exhibited in and through us when we are raised up into the heavenly places. Get into the habit of saying—"Lord Jesus, prove Thyself sufficient in me for this thing now." Do not say—"Oh Lord, show me what to do"; let Him do it and it will be done. It is *His* perfections, not ours; His patience, His love, His holiness, His strength—"all spiritual blessings in Christ Jesus." How blind we are! There is a danger with the children of God of getting too familiar with sublime things. We talk so much about these wonderful realities, and forget that we have to exhibit them in our lives. It is perilously possible to mistake the exposition of the truth for the truth; to run away with the idea that because we are able to expound these things we are living them too. Paul's warning comes home to us—". . . lest that by any means, when I have preached to others, I myself should be a castaway."

6. The Sight in the Heavenlies

Blessed are the pure in heart. (Matthew 5:8)

What do we mean by "pure in heart"? We mean nothing less and nothing else than what the Son of God was and is. When God raises us up into the heavenly places He imparts to us the very purity that is Jesus Christ's. That is what the sanctified life means—the undisturbable range of His peace, the unshakeable, indefatigable power of His strength, and the unfathomable, crystalline purity of His holiness. There is plenty of room in the heavenly places to grow into the realisation of the unfathomable depths of the purity of Christ's heart.

"Blessed are the pure in heart: *for they shall see God.*" When the Son of God "walked this earth with naked feet, and wove with human hands the creed of creeds," He understood the revealed counsels of His Father to Him because His heart was pure, and to the sanctified soul God says—"Friend, come up higher." Jesus warns the disciple never to be afraid of the contempt of the world when he possesses spiritual discernment. Those who are in the heavenly places see God's counsels in what to the wisdom of the world is arrogant stupidity. We can never stand for one second in the heavenly places in a secular mood. Jesus never had secular moods, His heart was never defiled by secular thinking or by secular ways. What do we mean by secular ways? Secularity has to do with what we desire within, not with what happens to our bodies. What do we desire most? What the heart of Jesus wanted most was God's glory, and sanctification means that that same desire is imparted to us. The wonder of a pure heart is that it is as pure as Jesus Christ's heart. Sanctification does not mean that a purity like Jesus Christ's is gifted to us, but that *His* purity is gifted to us. Our Lord was wonderfully sensitive to the things of God, and He says—"all things that I have heard of My Father I have made known unto you." His Father distinctly revealed things to Him.

The sanctified soul realises with growing amazement what we are trying feebly to put into words, that all these things are ours if we are willing for God to realise His claim in us. "All things are yours . . . and ye are Christ's; and Christ is God's."

To be "in Christ Jesus" means that we are initiated into the position of sons. Do you know how God speaks to His sons? He softly breathes His stern messages in the heavenly places, with what result? There is never any panic in His sons. The Son of God had pre-intimations of what was to happen, and as we walk with the mind stayed where God places it by sanctification, in that way steadfastly keeping our garments white, we will find that nothing strikes us with surprise or with panic. God never allows it to; He keeps us in perfect peace while He whispers His secrets and reveals His counsels, We are struck with panic whenever we turn out of the way; when we forget to "grow up into Him in all things"; when we forget to keep the childlike weakness which never dreams it can look at things in the way Jesus does apart from His Spirit.

"Bringing into captivity every thought to the obedience of Christ." Our Lord never pried into His Father's secrets, neither will the saint. Some have made the blunder of trying to wrest God's secrets from Him. That was never Jesus Christ's way, nor is it communicated by the Spirit of God. God always gifted His intimations to His Son. How many of us have allowed God to reveal His counsels to us in this way, and how many of us are being humiliated by realising that we have been trying to probe into God's secrets some other way? When we are raised up into the heavenly places, it is a life of joy unspeakable and full of glory.

One word of warning—we must guard the life where the Spirit of God warns we should guard it, and the first thing to be guarded against is inordinate curiosity. Remember what Jesus said of Himself, and of the Holy Spirit: "I do nothing of Myself; but as My Father hath taught Me, I speak these things." "The Spirit of truth . . . shall not speak of Himself; but whatsoever He shall hear, that shall He speak." When our minds are stayed upon God and we are growing in the realisation of the purity of Christ's heart and His wonderful strength and power, we will find that that same characteristic is being worked out in us, there is no mental or intellectual insubordination, but a complete subordination to Jesus Christ, even as He was subordinated to His Father. The same thing is true of our wills; just as Jesus brought His will into subjection to His Father and said—"I seek not Mine own will, but the will of the Father which hath sent Me," when we are raised up to the heavenly places in Christ Jesus, we will manifest the same.

Whenever a decline comes, whenever there is a tendency to turn aside, we will find God is a con-suming fire: He will hold and hurt cruelly, and we may cry out to Him to let us go, but He will not let us go. God loves us too much to let us go, and He will burn and burn until there is nothing left but the purity that is as pure as He is—unless we determine to side with the impure and become as reprobate silver. Men are apt to cry to God to stop—"If only God would leave me alone!" God never will. His passionate, inexorable love never allows Him to leave men alone, and with His children He will shake everything that can be shaken till there is nothing that can be shaken any more; then will abide the consuming fire of God until the life is changed into the same image from glory to glory, and men see that strong family likeness to Jesus that can never be mistaken.

THE INHERITANCE OF THE SAINTS

Giving thanks unto the Father, which hath made us meet to be partakers of the inheritance of the saints in light. Colossians 1:12

Sanctification means the impartation to us and through us of the Lord Jesus Christ, His patience, His purity, His holiness. It is not that Jesus Christ enables us to imitate Him; not that the power of God is in us and we try our best and fail, and try again; but that the very virtues of Jesus Christ are manifested in our mortal flesh.

1. The Possession of Light
The inheritance of the saints in light.

How often God's book refers to God as light, to Jesus Christ as light, to the Spirit of God as light, and to the saints as light. By sanctification God places us in the light that He is in, the light in which our Lord Jesus lived His life. "And the life was the light of men." Our inheritance in light means that we manifest in our mortal flesh the life of the Lord Jesus Christ. The "light" means the very things He exhibited, a life full of approach to God, full of understanding of God and of man.

"He that followeth Me shall not walk in darkness, but shall have the light of life" (John 8:12). Supposing you are walking over a moor at night, you know there is a path but it is too dark and obscure for you to see; then the moon struggles through the clouds and you see the path, a clear strip of white, straight across the hill; in a little while all is obscure again, but you have seen the path and you know the way to go. There are times in our experience when life is just like that. We do not see the path though we know it is there, then the light shines and we see it, and when darkness comes again we can step boldly. Sometimes the light is as the moonlight or the dawn, or it comes as a terrifying flash of lightning, when all of a sudden we see the way we should go. "While ye have light, believe in the light, that ye may be the children of light" (John 12:36). Have we believed in the light we have had? Can we recall the time when the light of God in the Face of Jesus Christ was clearer to us than anything else has ever been, when we saw perfectly clearly and understood exactly what the Lord wanted? Did we believe in that light; and have we walked up to the light? Can we say to-night, "I was not disobedient unto the heavenly vision"? So many of us see the light, we see the way across the moor; by a sudden lightning flash of God's revealing grace we see the way to go, but we do not take it. We say, "Oh, yes, I did receive the Spirit of God, and I thought that it would be like this and that, but it has not been." The reason is that we did not believe in the light when it was given. You say, "I am a Christian, I have been born of the Spirit of God; I understand that sanctification is the qualities of the Lord Jesus being exhibited in me; only two weeks ago I had a wonderful time of communion with the Lord in the heavenly places; I saw the way so clearly, and I knew exactly what I should do in the circumstances I was in; but I failed to do it." "While ye have light, believe in the light," and slowly and surely we shall find what our Lord said is true—"he that followeth Me shall not walk in darkness, but shall have the light of life."

If we have entered into the heavenly places in Christ Jesus, the light has shone, and, this is the marvellous thing, as we begin to do what we know the

Lord would have us do, we find He does not enable *us* to do it, He simply puts through us all His power and the thing is done in His way. Thank God for everyone who has seen the light, who has understood how the Lord Jesus Christ clears away the darkness and brings the light by showing His own characteristics through us.

Did I believe the light when I had it? Is there someone who had the light a year ago, last week, you saw clearly what God wanted; did you obey the light? You answer, "No, I did not." Well, tell Him so, and thank God there is another opportunity; and those who have obeyed the light and have been going on, ask God to confirm you in the way that you may be partakers of the inheritance of the saints in light.

One remarkable thing about our Lord's life is that He always understood that His Father was right. I wonder if we always do? There is much that is obscure, much we cannot understand, but are we certain that our Father understands? Have we let Jesus Christ so manifest Himself in us that we know that the Father always does things well? When we come across a dark trial, such as war, or a trial more personal and peculiarly our own, something that is a distress and a pain and a wildness, with no light or liberty, the danger is that we begin to say, "Why should this happen to me? Why should I be plunged into this darkness?" But if we remember our possession of light, the Son of God in all His understanding of the Father takes possession of us absolutely, and we see in our hearts just as Jesus Christ saw. That is the marvel of sanctification. At the threshold of every new experience, of every new phase of the truth of God, there is a margin of darkness where we have this glorious test—will I let the Son of God manifest Himself in my mortal flesh in this thing, and will I possess the light that God has given me? If so, we shall see just as Jesus Christ saw.

2. Partakers of Light
There is a difference between this inheritance and an earthly inheritance. When we partake in an earthly inheritance it becomes a particular possession of our own that no one else can have, and not only so but by taking it we may impoverish someone else. The marvellous thing about the inheritance of the saints in light is that when we take our part of the inheritance, everyone else is blessed in the taking; but if we refuse to be partakers of the inheritance of the saints in light, we rob others of its glory and its wonder.

There is another thing about the possession of light in Jesus Christ: my possession of light is quite different from yours. Each of us has a particular possession of light that no one else can have, and if we refuse to take our possession, everyone else will suffer. In every saint's life there is a particular personal edition of the possession of light, and until that is partaken of with full-hearted confidence, all the others suffer. The difficulty is that the round person wants to be in the square hole; this shows how we become deflected from the light that is in Christ. There is a possession of light that the Spirit distributes to each one according to the perfect wisdom of God. It is Satan, not God, who makes a man say everyone must be just as he is. As we participate in the light and the Son of God is manifested in us in our particular setting, there will be marvellous blessing to all the people round about. The test for apostles and teachers is not that they talk wonderful stuff, not that they are able to expound God's word, but that they edify the saints (Ephesians 4:12). No individual can develop a holy life with God without benefiting all other saints. I wonder if we have been obedient to the heavenly vision, or have we been hankering after being like someone else?

One of the greatest dangers of Satan when he comes as an angel of light is that he tries to persuade the saint of God that he must let go the possession of what God wants him to have and take a possession belonging to someone else. If a man has a special gift for preaching God's truth, Satan will try to persuade him that preaching the gospel of Jesus Christ is not what God has called him to do, but that he has been called to live a quiet life with God in secret. Always remember that the tiniest deflection of the eye or the heart away from God in light, and from Jesus Christ in light, and from obeying the light when it is given, will mean a deflection for a long while, much sorrow and much distress. Thank God He does not leave His children alone; there is much pain and distress, but He will always bring them back.

I wonder if we have seen Jesus Christ as a possession of light—in our circumstances, in our business, in our home relations, or in whatever it may be? Have we seen clearly what God wants us to do, and have we done it? As surely as we begin to put ourselves into the path of obedience, the perfections of the Son of God are manifested through us with such a great brilliancy of light that we will never think of taking credit to ourselves for it. One step in the right direction in obedience to the light, and the manifestation of the Son of God in your mortal flesh is as certain as that God is on His throne. When once God's light has come to us through Jesus Christ, we must never hang back, but obey; and we shall not walk in darkness, but will have the light of life.

"As He is, so are we." The sanctified life is a life that bears a strong family likeness to Jesus Christ, a life that exhibits His virtues, His patience, His love, His holiness. Slowly and surely we learn the great secret of eternal life, which is to know God.

Every bit of knowledge that we have of God fills us with ineffable joy. Remember what Jesus said to His disciples—"That My joy might be in you" (RV).

What was the joy of Jesus? That He understood the Father. Do we understand God on any one point? If we do, we will know something of the joy that Jesus had. It is a wonderful possession, it is the very characteristic of Jesus. To understand the tiniest bit of truth about God is to love it with all our heart and soul and mind; all that lies dark and obscure just now is one day going to be as clear, as radiantly and joyously clear, as the bit we have seen. No wonder God counsels us to be patient. Little by little everything will be brought into the light until we understand as Jesus Christ understood. The whole of Eternity will be taken up with understanding and knowing God, and, thank God, we may begin to know Him down here. The sanctified life means that we begin to understand God and to manifest the life of the Son of God in our mortal flesh.

Before we get hold of the Spirit of God and the Spirit of God gets hold of us, we are apt to be taken up with the outside of things, we cling to them and mistake them for the essential reality until slowly they begin to dwindle from us and to turn to ashes and disappointment. But when we are made partakers of light we are wedded to God's realities behind the things that are seen, and we remain absolutely true to Him.

3. Light Indwelling
Now are ye light in the Lord: walk as children of light. (Ephesians 5:8)

What we have in the kingdom of light, we give. That is always the characteristic. If we try to picture to others the glory of communion with God without being in close contact with God ourselves, we will paralyse the imagination of those we talk to. George MacDonald, in his poem "The Disciple," pictures the sense of dreary disappointment that came to a boy when he heard it said that godly people were as pillars in the temple of God—

> *Straightway my heart is like a clod,*
> *My spirit wrapt in doubt:—*
> *A pillar in the house of God,*
> *And never more go out!*

That will always be the result when we try to portray a truth of God without being partakers of the light, without being lifted into the inheritance.

As we partake of this possession of light, it is as if the Son of God lifted the veil from the way God created things. He lifts our eyes up to the stars and says—"Do you see those? Every one of them is known to your Father in heaven," and something we cannot state in words gets hold of our souls and it means this—God is so full of light that He knows us down to the tiniest detail of our lives. Then another time He shows us the makeup of a daisy and He

says—"That was God's thought when He created a daisy," and slowly the Spirit of God makes our lives into exactly God's idea of what we ought to be.

By sanctification we are placed in the will of God. We have not to ask what the will of God is, we *are* the will of God, and as we keep in the light as He is in the light, the decisions of the mind and the natural progress of the life go on like a law, and when the decision is likely to be wrong the Spirit checks. Whenever there is the tiniest inward check, we must stop, and we will find that the Lord Jesus Christ and His perfections will be there to meet every emergency.

In prayer have we learned the wonderful power of that phrase ". . . boldness to enter into the holiest by the blood of Jesus"? It means that we can talk to God as Jesus Christ did, but only through the right of His Atonement. We must never allow the idea that because we have been obedient, because our need is great, because we long for it, therefore God will hear us. There is only one way into the holiest, and that is by the blood of Jesus. Being made partakers of the light means that we are taken into the fellowship Jesus referred to when He said, "the Father Himself loveth you."

As we are made partakers of the inheritance of the saints in light, we begin to understand that there is no division into sacred and secular, it is all one great glorious life with God as the Son of God is manifested in our mortal flesh. Paul puts it in this way: "When it pleased God . . . to reveal His Son in me." You in your shop, you in your office, you in your home, say that in your own heart—"The Son of God revealed *in me!*" That is sanctification.

4. Placed in the Light
And hath translated us into the kingdom of His dear Son.

Just as the stars are poised by God Almighty, so the Apostle says the great power of the Father lifts the saints into the light that He and His Son are in, and poises them there, as eternally established as the stars. Have we ever allowed our imagination to be kindled by the light of God? God is Light, and He lifts us up in Himself, no matter who we are, and poises us as surely as He established the stars, in the very light that He is in. He makes us meet to be partakers of that wonderful inheritance, and slowly and surely the marvel of the life of the Son of God is manifested in our mortal flesh. No wonder Paul says—"Giving thanks unto the Father"!

It was never from His right to Himself that our Lord Jesus Christ spoke; He never thought from His right to Himself; that is, He never thought or spoke from His bodily conditions or the condition of His circumstances. We do talk from our right to ourselves, from the condition of our bodies, from our personal possessions; these are the things we all reason from naturally. They are the things the Son of God never reasoned from; He thought and spoke always from His Father; that is, He expressed the thought of God in light. When we are sanctified, the Spirit of God will enable us to do the same. As we go on with God we shall find that we see things in quite a different way, we see them with the eyes of Jesus Christ.

When we shut ourselves in alone with God at night, with the stars and the great quietness round about, it is so easy and so wonderful to talk to God; but do we walk in the light of the talk we had when the morning comes? Do we allow the Son of God to manifest Himself in our walk and conversation, or do we forget and begin to work from ourselves, and at the end of the day do we have to say to God—"I am sorry, Lord, but I made a tremendous blunder, I forgot to step back and let Thee manifest Thyself."

Remember, God wants to lift us up and poise us in the light that He is in, and that everything that is dark just now will one day be as clear to us as it is to Him. Think of all the things that are dark just now. Jesus said, "There is nothing covered, that shall not be revealed." Things are dark and obscure to us because we are not in a right condition to understand them. Thank God for all that we have understood, for every bit of truth that is so full of light and liberty and wonder that it fills us with joy. Step by step as we walk in that light, and allow the Son of God to meet every circumstance by His virtues, by His power and His presence, we shall understand more and more with a knowledge "which passeth knowledge."

How many of us know anything about this Gospel Mystery of Sanctification? Are we allowing the life and liberty and power and marvel of the holiness of Jesus Christ to be wrought out in us? Do we know what it is to be made new creatures in Christ Jesus? Have we let God raise us up to the heavenly places in Christ Jesus, and are we learning to walk in the light as God is in the light?

For this is the will of God, even your sanctification.

But of Him are ye in Christ Jesus, who of God is made unto us . . . sanctification.

Grow Up into Him
Take the Initiative

Add to your faith virtue. 2 Peter 1:5 ("Furnish your faith with resolution." MOFFATT)

This love requires nothing of us but innocent and regular manners and behaviour. It would only have us do all those things for the sake of God which reason bids us practise. The thing required is not to add to the good actions we have already done, but only to do that out of love to God which men of reputation and virtuous lives do from a principle of honour and regard of themselves. We are not only to lop off evil. That we must do if we were guided by no other principle than right reason. But for everything else leave it in the order God has established in the world. Let us do all the same honest and virtuous actions, but let us do them for the sake of Him Who made us and to Whom we owe our all.

Fenelon

The question of forming habits on the basis of the grace of God is a very vital one. God regenerates us and puts us in contact with all His Divine resources, but He cannot make us walk according to His will; the practising is ours, not God's. We have to take the initiative and "add to . . . faith virtue. . . ." To take the initiative means to make a beginning, and each one of us must do it for himself: We have to acquaint ourselves with the way we have to go; and beware of the tendency of asking the way when we know it perfectly well.

To "add" means to acquire the habit of doing things, and it is difficult in the initial stages. We are in danger of forgetting that we cannot do what God does and that God will not do what we can do. We cannot save ourselves or sanctify ourselves; God only can do that; but God does not give us good habits, He does not give us character, He does not make us walk aright; we must do all that. We have to work out what God has worked in (Philippians 2:12–13). Many of us lose out spiritually, not because the devil attacks us, but because we are stupidly ignorant of the way God has made us. Remember, the devil did not make the human body; he may have tampered with it, but the human body was created by God, and its constitution after we are saved remains the same as before. For instance, we are not born with a ready-made habit of dressing ourselves; we have to form that habit. Apply it spiritually—when we are born again, God does not give us a fully fledged series of holy habits, we have to make them; and the forming of habits on the basis of God's supernatural work in our souls is the education of our spiritual life.

Many of us refuse to do it; we are lazy and we frustrate the grace of God.

1. Stop Hesitating

A doubleminded man is unstable in all his ways. (James 1:8)

We have to stop hesitating and take the first step; and the first step is to stop hesitating! "How long halt ye between two opinions?" There are times when we wish that God would kick us right over the line and *make* us do the thing; but the remarkable thing about God's patience is that He waits until we stop hesitating. Some of us hesitate so long that we become like spiritual storks; we look elegant only as long as we stand on one leg; when we stand on two we look very ungraceful.

Or we have stood so long on the verge of a promise of God's that we have grown like monuments on its edge; and if we were asked to go over the edge in the way of giving our testimony or doing something for God, we should feel very awkward. It would be a good thing for us if we could be pushed over, no matter how we sprawled. If God tells us to do something good we hesitate over obeying, we endanger our standing in grace.

"A double minded man," i.e. a discreet man, diplomatic and wise—"is unstable in all his ways." The man who does not put God first in his calculations is always double minded. "If I do," "Supposing," and "But"—these are all in the vocabulary of the double minded man. If we begin to weigh things, we let in that subtle enemy against God, viz., insinuation. When God speaks we have to be resolute and act immediately in faith on what He says. When Peter walked on the water, he did not wait for someone to take his hand; he stepped straight out, in recognition of Jesus, and walked on the water.

Never revise decisions. If you have made a wrong decision, then face the music and stand up to it; do not whimper and say—"I won't do that again." Take the initiative, take the step with your will now; burn your bridges behind you—"I *will* write that letter"; "I *will* pay that debt"; make it impossible to go back on the decision. Sentimentality always begins when we refuse to obey, when we refuse to take some stand God has told us to because of an insinuation that has come in from somewhere. If we hesitate, insinuations are sure to come.

2. Start Hearkening

Whosoever . . . heareth My sayings, and doeth them . . . (Luke 6:47)

Whether we are Christians or not, we must all build; the point is that a Christian builds upon a different basis. If we build to please ourselves, we are building on the sand; if we build for the love of God, we are building on the rock. Do we listen to what Jesus has to say? All we build will end in disaster unless it is built on the sayings of Jesus. "He that hath ears to hear, let him hear." Before we can hear certain things, we must be trained. Our disposition determines what we listen for; and when Jesus alters the disposition, He gives us the power to hear as He hears. (Cf. John 12:29–30.) If, when no one is watching us, we are building ourselves up in the word of God, then, when a crisis comes, we shall stand; but if we are not building on the word of God, when a crisis comes we shall go down, no matter what our wills are like. Have we learned the habit of listening to what God says? Have we added this resolute hearing in our practical life? We may be able to give a testimony as to what God has done for us, but does the life we live evidence that we are not listening now, but living only in the memory of what we once heard? We have to keep our ears trained to detect God's voice, to be continually renewed in the spirit of our mind. If when a crisis comes we instinctively turn to God, we know that the habit of hearkening has been formed. At the beginning there is the noisy clamour of our own misgivings; we are so taken up with what we have heard that we cannot hear any more. We have to hearken to that which we have not listened to before, and to do it we must be insulated on the inside.

"He wakeneth mine ear to hear as the learned." Once a week at least read the Sermon on the Mount and see how much you have hearkened to it—"Love your enemies, bless them that curse you"; we do not listen to it because we do not want to. We have to learn to hearken to Jesus in everything, to get into the habit of finding out what He says. We cannot apply the teachings of Jesus unless we are regenerated, and we cannot apply all His teachings at once. The Holy Spirit will bring back to our remembrance a certain word of our Lord's and apply it to the particular circumstances we are in, the point is—are we going to obey it? "Whosoever . . . heareth My sayings, and *doeth* them . . ." When Jesus Christ brings a word home, never shirk it.

3. Stand Heroically

Having done all, to stand. (Ephesians 6:13)

It is a great deal easier to fight than to stand; but spiritually our conflict is not so much a fight as a standing on guard—"having done all, *to stand.*" When we are in a frenzy, we attack; when we are strong, we stand to overcome. To-day in Christian work we are suffering from a phase of spiritual dyspepsia that emphasises *doing.* The great thing *to do* is *to be* a believer in Jesus.

With Jesus it is never "*Do, do*," but "*Be, be* and I will do through you." To stand, means to work on the level of the heroic. It would be a terrible thing to lose the sense of the heroic, because the sense of our duty is only realised by our sense of the heroic. Our Lord calls us to a joyful heroic life, and we must never relax:

"Put on the whole armour of God." If we try to put on the armour without a right relationship to God we shall be like David in Saul's armour; but when we are right with God we find that the armour fits us exactly, because it is God's own nature that is the armour. The armour God gives us is not the armour of prayer, but the armour of Himself, the armour *of God*. "That ye may be able to stand against the wiles of the devil." The devil is a bully, but when we stand in the armour of God, he cannot harm us; if we tackle him in our own strength we are soon done for; but if we stand with the strength and courage of God, he cannot gain one inch of way at all. Some of us run away instead of standing; when there is a fresh onslaught of the wiles of the devil we lose heart instantly; and instead of standing we scuttle and others have to stand until we are sufficiently ashamed to come back again. We have to take the initiative in standing against panic. One strong moral man will form a nucleus around which others will gather; and spiritually, if we put on the armour of God and stand true to Him, a whole army of weak-kneed Christians will be strengthened. Remember, we have to take the initiative where we are, not where we are not.

YOU WON'T REACH IT ON TIPTOE!

Furnish your . . . brotherliness with Christian love. 2 Peter 1:5, 7 (MOFFATT)

Love, to most of us, is an indefinite thing; we do not know what we mean when we speak of love: The love Paul mentions in 1 Corinthians 13 means the sovereign preference of my person for another person, and everything depends on who the other person is. Jesus demands that the sovereign preference be for Him. We cannot love to order, and yet His word stands— "If any come to Me, and *hate not* his father, and mother, and wife, and children, and brethren, and sisters, yea, and his own life also," (i.e., a hatred of every loyalty that would divide the heart from loyalty to Jesus) "he cannot be My disciple." Devotion to a Person is the only thing that tells; and no man on earth has the love which Jesus demands, unless it has been imparted to him. We may admire Jesus Christ, we may respect Him and reverence Him; but apart from the Holy Ghost we do not love Him. The only Lover of the Lord Jesus Christ is the Holy Ghost. In Romans 5:5, Paul says that "the love of God"—not the power to love God, but *the love of God*—"is shed abroad in our hearts by the Holy Ghost which is given unto us." The Holy Ghost is the gift of the ascended Christ. "Have I received the Holy Ghost?" Not, "Do I believe in Him?" but, "Have I received Him?" Something must come into me (Luke 11:13). When by a willing acceptance, I receive the Holy Spirit, He will shed abroad the love of God in my heart; and on the basis of that love I have to practise the working out of the things which Peter mentions here, and Paul mentions in 1 Corinthians 13. We cannot reach it on tiptoe; some of us tried to once for seven days, then we got tired! The springs of love are in God, not in us. It is absurd to look for the love of God in our natural hearts; the love of God is only there when it has been shed abroad by the Holy Ghost.

1. Love Where You Cannot Respect
But God commendeth His love toward us, in that, while we were yet sinners, Christ died for us. (Romans 5:8)

The revelation of God's love is that He loved us when He could not possibly respect us—He loved us "while we were yet sinners"; "when we were enemies." When we receive the nature of God into us, the first thing that happens is that God takes away all pretence and pious pose; and He does it by revealing that He loved us, not because we were loveable, but because it is His nature to love. "*God is love.*" The surest evidence that the nature of God has come into me is that I know I am a sinner—"I know that in me (that is, in my flesh,) dwelleth no good thing." When God has made me know what I am really like in His sight, it is no longer possible for me to be annoyed at what others may tell me I am capable of; God has revealed it to me already. When once we have had a dose of the plague of our own heart, we will never want to vindicate ourselves. The worst things that are said about us may be literally untrue; but we know that whatever is said is not so bad as what is really true of us in the sight of God.

Never try to prevent a soul feeling real disgust at what he is like in God's sight. The first thing the Holy Spirit does when He comes in is to convict, not to comfort, because He has to let us know what we are like in God's sight; and then He brings the revelation that God will fill us with His own nature if we will let Him.

The curious thing about the love of God is that it is the cruellest thing on earth to everything that is not of Him. God hurts desperately when I am far away from Him; but when I am close to Him, He is unutterably tender. Paul says that "God *commendeth* His own love toward us" (RV). God's love seems so strange to our natural conceptions that it has to be commended, i.e. recommended, to us before we see anything in it. It is only when we have been awakened by conviction to the sin and anarchy of our hearts against God that we realise the measure of His love toward us, even "while we were yet sinners." "The Son of God, Who loved me, and gave Himself for *me*"—Paul never lost the wonder of that love.

The Lord "suffereth long, and is kind. . . ." If I watch God's dealings with me, I shall find that He gives me a revelation of my own pride and bad motives towards Him, and the realisation that He loved me when He could not begin to respect me will send me forth into the world to love others as He loved me. God's love for me is inexhaustible, and His love for me is the basis of my love for others. We have to love where we cannot respect and where we must not respect, and this can only be done on the basis of God's love for us. "This is My commandment, That ye love one another, *as I have loved you.*"

Love means deliberate self-limitation; we deliberately identify ourselves with the interests of our Lord in everything. "Having loved His own which were in the world, He loved them unto the end." The revelation comes home to me that God has loved me to the end of all my meanness and my sin, my self-seeking and my wrong motives; and now this is the corresponding revelation—that I have to love others as God has loved me. God will bring around us any number of people we cannot respect, and we have to exhibit the love of God to them as He has exhibited it to us. Have we ever realised the glorious opportunity we have of laying down our lives for Jesus Christ? Jesus does not ask us to die for Him, but to lay down our lives for Him. Our Lord did not sacrifice Himself for death, He sacrificed His *life*, and God wants our life, not our death. "I beseech you," says Paul, "present your bodies a *living* sacrifice."

The greatest love of a man is his love for his friends (John 15:13); the greatest love of God is His love for His enemies (Romans 5:8–10); the highest Christian love is that a man will lay down his life for his Friend, the Lord Jesus Christ—"I have called you friends." Our Lord here connects the highest human love with the highest Divine love, and the connection is in the disciple, not in our Lord. The emphasis is laid on the deliberate laying down of the life, not in

one tragic crisis such as death, but in the grey face of actual facts illumined by no romance, obscured by the mist of the utterly commonplace—expending the life deliberately day by day because of my love for my Friend. This is the love that never fails, and it is neither human nor Divine love alone, but the at-one-ment of both being made manifest in the life of the disciple, The supreme moment of the Cross in actual history is but the concentrated essence of the very nature of the Divine love. God lays down His life for the very creation which men utilise for their own selfish ends. The Self-expenditure of the love of God exhibited in the life and death of our Lord becomes a bridge over the gulf of sin; whereby human love can be imbued by Divine love, the love that never fails.

2. Love Where You Are Not Respected (1 Peter 2:20–21)

We shall not always be respected if we are disciples of Jesus. Our Lord said—"These things have I spoken unto you, that ye should not be offended. They shall put you out of the synagogues: yea, the time cometh, that whosoever killeth you will think that he doeth God service," and that will be so again. "The disciple is not above his Master." How much respect did Jesus Christ receive when He was on this earth?

A Nazarene Carpenter, despised, rejected, and crucified. "We e'en must love the highest when we see it" is not true, for when the religious people of our Lord's day saw the Highest Incarnate before them, they hated Him and crucified Him. "Remember the word that I said unto you, The servant is not greater than his Lord. If they have persecuted Me, they will also persecute you." We are apt to think of a Christian merely as a civilised individual; a Christian is one who is identified with Jesus; one who has learned the lesson that the servant is not greater than his Lord.

If we are despised because we have extraordinary notions, we are apt to be uplifted by that; it suits our natural pride; but Jesus said—"Blessed are ye, when men shall hate you, and when they shall separate you from their company, and shall reproach you, and cast out your name as evil, *for the Son of Man's sake.*" If you want a good time in this world, do not become a disciple of Jesus. "If any man will come after Me, let him deny himself," i.e. give up his right to himself to Me. There is always an IF in connection with discipleship, and it implies that we need not unless we like. There is never any compulsion; Jesus does not coerce us. There is only one way of being a disciple, and that is by being devoted to Jesus.

3. Love Wherever Redemption Reaches (John 3:16)

What has God redeemed? Everything that sin and Satan have touched and blighted, God has redeemed;

Redemption is complete. We are not working *for* the redemption of the world, we are working *on* the Redemption, which is a very different thing. Jesus Christ's last command to His disciples was not to go and save the world; the saving is done. He told them to go and make disciples (RV). Our work is to "open their eyes, to turn them from darkness to light, from the power of Satan unto God, that they may receive forgiveness of sins," i.e., that they may receive the Redemption which is complete but which is incredible to a man until he does receive it—"I do not doubt that God saves men; nor do I doubt that He can do all the Bible says He can; but it is ridiculous to suppose it includes me!"

We have to beware of making the need the call; the Redemption is the call; the need is the opportunity, and the opportunity is in our own homes, in our work, just wherever we are, not simply in meetings. Naturally we always want to go somewhere else, but the love of God works just where we are, and His love works irrespective of persons.

Are we banking in unshaken faith on the Redemption of Jesus Christ? Is it our conviction amongst men that every man can be presented "perfect in Christ Jesus"? Are we filling up "that which is behind of the afflictions of Christ . . . for His body's sake"? That means we have to be so identified with our Lord that His love is being poured out all the time, we have to be prepared to be nothing at all so that He can pour His sweetness through us. Neither natural love nor Divine love will remain unless it is cultivated. We must form the habit of love until it is the practice of our lives.

MAKE A HABIT OF HAVING NO HABITS

For as these qualities exist and increase with you, they render you active and fruitful in the knowledge of our Lord Jesus Christ. 2 Peter 1:8 (MOFFATT)

When we are forming a habit we are conscious of it, but in the real Christian life, habits do not appear, because by practice we do the thing unconsciously. As Christians, we have to learn the habit of waiting upon God as He comes to us through the moments, and to see that we do not make common-sense our guide; we do until we have seen the Lord. When we realise that God's order comes to us in the haphazard, our life will manifest itself in the way our Lord indicates in the Sermon on the Mount. The illustrations our Lord uses there are "the fowls of the air," "the lilies of the field." Birds and flowers obey the law of their lives in the setting in which they are placed; they have no consciousness of being conscious; it is not their own thought that makes them what they are, but the thought of the Father in heaven. If our childlike trust in God is giving place to self-consciousness and self-depreciation, it is a sign that there is something wrong; and the cure for it is to reach the place where every habit is so practised that there is no conscious habit at all. Watch how God will upset our programmes if we are in danger of making our little Christian habits our god. Whenever we begin to worship our habit of prayer or of Bible reading, God will break up that time. We say—"I cannot do this, I am praying; it is my hour with God." No, it is our hour with our habit; we pray to a habit of prayer.

1. Exercising Habits until Each Habit Is Lost
For as these qualities exist and increase with you . . . (MOFFATT)

Are they existing in us? There are times when we are conscious of becoming virtuous and patient and godly, but they are only stages; if we stop there we get the strut of the "pi" person. A "pi" person is one who does his level best to be what he would like to be but knows he is not. Our Christian life continually resolves itself into consciousness and introspection because there are some qualities we have not added yet. Ultimately, the relationship is to be a completely simple one.

Consciousness of a defect is a disease spiritually; yet it is produced by the finger of God because we have neglected to add some quality. We must acknowledge the defect, and then look out for the opportunity of exercising ourselves along the line of the quality to be added—patience, godliness, love. We have to exercise the quality until the habit is merged in the simplicity of a child's life.

We have to beware of singling out one quality only. Peter says "as these qualities," faith, virtue, knowledge, temperance, patience, godliness, brotherly kindness, charity, "exist and increase with you" (MOFFATT). Our Lord is the type of all Christian experience, and He cannot be summed up in terms of natural virtues, but only in terms of the supernatural. "Come unto Me," says Jesus, "and I will give you rest," the rest of the perfection of activity that is never conscious of itself. This perfection of activity can be illustrated by the spinning of a coloured top; if the top spins quickly, all the colours merge and a musical sound is heard; but if it spins slowly, it wobbles and sighs and every colour is conspicuous. If we are conscious of a defect it is because the Lord is pointing out that there is a quality to be added; and until it is added we are conscious of a black streak here, and a coloured streak there. But when the particular quality has been added we are no longer conscious of the defect, all the qualities are merged and the whole life is at rest in the perfection of activity.

The dominant thing about a saint is not self-realisation, but the Lord Himself; consequently a saint can always be ignored because to the majority of eyes our Lord is no more noticeable in the life of a saint than He was to men in the days of His flesh. But when a crisis comes the saint is the one to whom men turn; and the life which seemed colourless is seen to be the white light of God.

2. Expressing Holiness until Conscious Holiness Is Lost

they render you active and fruitful . . .

It is an utter mistake to fix our eyes on our own whiteness, for all we are conscious of then is a passionate longing for a holy relationship to God. We have to come to the place where conscious holiness ceases to be because of the presence of the One Who is holiness. When we have been made partakers of the Divine nature we are taken up into God's consciousness, we do not take God into our consciousness. If we are consciously holy we are far from simple in certain relationships, for there will be certain things we imagine we cannot do; whereas in reality we are the only ones who ought to be able to do those things. Once we come into simple relationship with God, He can put us where He pleases and we are not even conscious of where He puts us. All we are conscious of is an amazing simplicity of life that seems to be a haphazard life externally. The only supernatural life ever lived on earth was the life of our Lord, and He was at home with God anywhere. Wherever we are not at home with God, there is a quality to be added. We have to let God press through us in that particular until we gain Him, and life becomes the simple life of a child in which the vital concern is putting God, first.

3. Experiencing Knowledge until Knowledge Is Lost

. . . in the knowledge of our Lord Jesus Christ.

"Then shall I know even as also I am known"—love abides, and knowledge is merged. Knowledge is faith perfected, and faith in turn passes into sight. We experience knowledge until knowledge is swallowed up in the fact of God's presence—"Why He is here!" Knowledge is an expression of the nature of God, and is the practical outcome of the life of God in us, but if we isolate knowledge we are in danger of criticising God. We look for God to manifest Himself to His children: God only manifests Himself *in* His children, consequently others see the manifestation, the child of God does not. You say, "I am not conscious of God's blessing now"—thank God! "I am not conscious now of the touches of God"—thank God! "I am not conscious now that God is answering my prayers"—thank God! If you are conscious of these things it means you have put yourself outside God. "That the life also of Jesus might be made manifest in our mortal flesh"—"I am not conscious that His life is being manifested," you say, but if you are a saint it surely is. When a little child becomes conscious of being a little child, the child-likeness is gone; and when a saint becomes conscious of being a saint, something has gone wrong. "Oh but I'm not good enough." You never will be good enough! that is why the Lord had to come and save you. Go to your own funeral and ever after let God be all in all, and life will become the simple life of a child in which God's order comes moment by moment.

Never live on memories. Do not remember in your testimony what you once were; let the word of God be always living and active in you, and give the best you have every time and all the time.

THE HABIT OF A GOOD CONSCIENCE

Having a good conscience. 1 Peter 3:16

We hear it said that conscience is the voice of God, but logically that is easily proved to be absurd. Paul said—"I verily thought within myself that I ought to do many things contrary to the name of Jesus of Nazareth"; Paul was obeying his conscience when he hated Jesus Christ and put His followers to death; and our Lord said that "whosoever killeth you will think that he doeth God service." If conscience were the voice of God it would be the most contradictory voice human ears ever listened to. Conscience is the eye of the soul; and how it records depends entirely upon the light thrown upon God. The God Whom Saul of Tarsus knew had the light of Judaism upon Him, and Paul's conscience recording in that light brought him to the conclusion that he should hate Jesus and persecute His followers. Immediately the white light of our Lord was thrown upon God, Saul's conscience recorded differently—"and he trembling and astonished said, Lord, what wilt Thou have me to do?" Saul had not another conscience, but it recorded differently, and the result was a tremendous disturbance in his life. Conscience is the faculty of the spirit that fits itself on to the highest a man knows, whether he be an agnostic or a Christian; every man has a conscience, although every man does not know God.

1. The Sensitive Conscience

And herein do I exercise myself, to have always a conscience void of offence toward God, and toward men. (Acts 24:16)

If I am in the habit of steadily and persistently facing myself with God, my conscience will always introduce God's perfect law to me; the question then is will I do what my conscience makes me understand clearly I should do? When conscience has been enlightened by the Son of God being formed in me, I have to make an effort to keep my conscience so sensitive that I obey that which I perceive to be God's will. I have to be so keen in the scent of the Lord, so sensitive to the tiniest touch of His Spirit, that I know what I should do. If I keep my soul inwardly open to God, then when I come in contact with the affairs of life outside, I know immediately what I should do; if I do not, I am to blame. I should be living in such perfect sensitiveness to God, in such perfect sympathy with His Son that in every circumstance I am in, the spirit of my mind is renewed, and I prove, i.e. make out, what is God's will, the thing that is good, and acceptable, and perfect.

We avoid forming a sensitive conscience when we say—"Oh well, God cannot expect me to do this thing, He has not told me to do it." How do we expect God to tell us? The word is "not in heaven . . . neither is it beyond the sea . . . but the word is very nigh unto thee, in thy mouth, and in thy heart, that thou mayest do it" (Deuteronomy 30:12–14). If we are Christians that is where the word of God is—in our hearts.

In the engineering of our circumstances, God gives us opportunities to form a sensitive conscience, and in this way He educates us down to the scruple.[5] When we come to a crisis it is easy to get direction, but it is a different matter to live in such perfect oneness with God that in the ordinary occurrences of life we always do the right thing. Is my conscience so sensitive that it needs neither terrible crime nor sublime holiness to awaken it, but the ordinary occurrences of life will awaken it? "Grieve not the Holy Spirit." He does not come with a voice of thunder, but with a voice so gentle that it is easy to ignore it. The one thing that keeps the conscience sensitive is the continual habit of seeing that I am open to God within. Whenever there is debate, quit. "Why shouldn't I do this?" You are on the wrong track. When conscience speaks there must be no debate whatever. In a crisis human nature is put on the strain, and we usually know what to do; but the sensitive conscience of the Christian is realised in the ordinary things of life, the humdrum things. We are apt to think of conscience only in connection with something outrageous. The sensitiveness of conscience is maintained by the habit of always being open towards God. At the peril of your soul you allow one thing to obscure your inner communion with God. Drop it, whatever it is, and see that you keep your inner vision clear.

2. The Seared Conscience

Having their conscience seared with a hot iron. (1 Timothy 4:2)

The conscience referred to here has been damaged by some terrific iron cramp.[6] Conscience is the eye of the

---

5. down to the scruple: to the smallest item.

6. iron cramp: same as cramp iron—device for holding or fastening things together. Metaphorically, anything that confines or hampers.

soul recording what it looks at, but if what Ruskin calls "the innocence of the eye" is lost, then the recording of conscience may be distorted. If I continually twist the organ of my soul's recording, it will become perverted. If I do a wrong thing often enough, I cease to realise the wrong in it. A bad man can be perfectly happy in his badness. That is what a seared conscience means.

Our critical faculties are given us for the purpose of self-examination, and the way to examine ourselves under the control of the Spirit of God is to ask ourselves—"Am I less sensitive than I used to be to the indications of God's will, less sensitive regarding purity, uprightness, goodness, honesty and truth?" If I realise that I am, I may be perfectly certain that something I have done (not something done to me) has seared my conscience. It has given me, so to speak, a bloodshot eye of the soul and I cannot see aright.

Conscience may be seared by means of a desperate crime as in the case of Herod. Herod ordered the voice of God to be silent in his life (see Mark 6:16–28), and when Jesus Christ stood before him we read that "He answered him nothing" (Luke 23:8–9).

The human eye may be damaged by gazing too much on intense whiteness, as in the case of snow blindness when men remain blind for months. And conscience may be damaged by tampering with the occult side of things, giving too much time to speculation; then when we turn to human life we are as blind as bats. It may be all right for angels to spend their time in visions and meditation, but if I am a Christian I find God in the ordinary occurrences of my life. The special times of prayer are of a different order. If I sequester myself and press my mind on one line of things and forget my relation to human life, when I do turn to human affairs I am morally blind. Am I trying to embrace a sensation of God spiritually for myself? When God has saved and sanctified us there is a danger that we are unwilling to let the vision fade; we refuse to take up our ordinary work, and soon we will be completely at a loss because we have hugged an experience to our souls instead of maintaining a right relationship to God Who gave us the experience.

My mortal flesh does not come in contact with God, it comes in contact with other mortal flesh, with earthly things, and I have to manifest the Son of God there by putting on the new man in connection with all these things. Am I doing it? Have I formed the habit of keeping my conscience sensitive to God on the inside and equally sensitive to man on the outside

by always working out what God works in? God engineers our circumstances and He brings across our paths some extraordinary people, viz., embodiments of ourselves in so many forms, and it is part of the humour of the situation that we recognise ourselves. Now, God says, exhibit the attitude to them that I showed to you. This is the one way of keeping a conscience void of offence toward God and man.

3. The Saintly Conscience
Having our hearts sprinkled from an evil conscience.
(Hebrews 10:22)

Can God readjust a seared conscience and make it sensitive again? He can, and it is done by the vicarious Atonement of our Lord. "How much more shall the blood of Christ . . . purge your conscience from dead works to serve the living God?" (Hebrews 9:14). When the Holy Spirit comes into me, my whole nature is in a desperate turmoil because immediately a man sees Jesus and understands Who He is, that instant he is criticised and self-condemned. If the Holy Spirit is obeyed He will make the Atonement of the Lord efficacious in me so that the blood of Christ cleanses my conscience from dead works and I become readjusted to God. The experimental element that works this transforming mystery of the Atonement becoming my vital life is repentance wrought in me by the Holy Spirit. The deepest repentance is not in the sinner, but in the saint. Repentance means not only sorrow for sin, it involves the possession of a new disposition that will never do the thing again. The only truly repentant man is the holy man. "If we confess our sins, He is faithful and just to forgive us our sins, and to cleanse us from all unrighteousness." To *admit* instead of *confess* is to trample the blood of the Son of God under foot, but immediately we allow the Holy Spirit to give us the gift of repentance, the shed blood of Christ will purge our conscience from dead works and send us into heart-spending service for God with a passionate devotion.

If I allow the saintly conscience to have way in me it will mean that I keep my own life steadfastly open towards God and keep steadfastly related to Him on the line of intercessory prayer for others. The clearing house for a guilty conscience is that by our intercession Jesus repairs the damage done to other lives, and the consolation to our conscience is amazing. The saintly conscience means that I maintain an open scrutiny before God, and that I carry out the sensitiveness gained there all through my life.

THE HABIT OF ENJOYING THE DISAGREEABLE

Whereas he who has not these by him is blind, short-sighted, oblivious that he has been cleansed from his erstwhile sins. 2 Peter 1:9 (MOFFATT)

In order to express what God's grace has done in us we have to form habits until all habits are merged in the perfect relationship of love. It is the relationship of a child wherein we realise that everything which God tells us to do we must do and not debate. God's commands are made to the life of His Son in us, not to our human nature; consequently all that God tells us to do is always humanly difficult; but it becomes divinely easy immediately we obey because our obedience has behind it all the omnipotent power of the grace of God.

The meaning of sanctification is that the Son of God is formed in us (Galatians 4:19); then our human nature has to be transfigured by His indwelling life, and this is where our action comes in. We have to put on the new man in accordance with the life of the Son of God in us. If we refuse to be sanctified, there is no possibility of the Son of God being manifested in us, because we have prevented our lives being turned into a Bethlehem; we have not allowed the Spirit of God to bring forth the Son of God in us. Are we putting on the new man in accordance with the Son of God, or are we choking His life in us? If we allow things which do not spring from the Son of God, we will put His life in us to death. The historic life of our Lord is the type of the life that will be produced in us if we take care to work out what God works in. Our human nature is meant for the Son of God to manifest Himself in, and this brings us to the margin of our responsibility. Scriptural language may seem to destroy individual responsibility, but in reality it increases it a hundredfold. For example, to say with Paul—I have been crucified with Christ; yet I live; and yet no longer I, but Christ liveth in me—does not mean that I am without responsibility; it means that I have the responsibility now of seeing that the Son of God works through me all the time. I have to see that the outer courts in which He lives are kept in perfect trim for Him to work through. I must not allow them to be choked up with prejudices or notions of my own.

1. By Keeping Yourself Fit
But he that lacketh these things is blind . . .

When Christ is formed in us we have to see that our human nature acts in perfect obedience to all that the Son of God reveals. God does not supply us with character, He gives us the life of His Son and we can

either ignore Him and refuse to obey Him, or we can so obey Him, so bring every thought and imagination into captivity, that the life of Jesus is manifested in our mortal flesh. It is not a question of being saved from hell, but of being saved in order to manifest the Son of God in our mortal flesh. Our responsibility is to keep ourselves fit to manifest Him.

Are we lacking in the things that Peter through the Spirit of God says we must add—the things which ought to mark the life of the saint? For instance, do we exhibit the virtue of self-control, the virtue of godliness, in the letters we write, in the conversations we hold? If not, then we not only give a wrong impression of the Son of God, but we hurt His life in us. If we are lacking in these things, it is because we have become short-sighted; we have forgotten that we have been cleansed from our old sins and are in imminent peril of being taken up with an experience and an illumination, and of forgetting that the life of Jesus is to be manifested in our mortal flesh.

The only way to keep yourself fit is by the discipline of the disagreeable. It is the disagreeable things which make us exhibit whether we are manifesting the life of the Son of God, or living a life which is antagonistic to Him. When disagreeable things happen, do we manifest the essential sweetness of the Son of God or the essential irritation of ourselves apart from Him? Whenever self comes into the ascendant, the life of the Son of God in us is perverted and twisted; there is irritation, and His life suffers. We have to beware of every element in human nature which clamours for attention first. Growth in grace stops the moment we get huffed. We get huffed because we have a peculiar person to live with—just think of the disagreeable person you have been to God! Every disagreeable person you ever met is an objective picture of what you were like in the sight of God. We have to learn to get in the first blow at the thing that is unlike God in ourselves. We can take in our human nature the blow that was meant for Him and so prevent the tramp of feet on Him. That is what Paul means when he speaks of filling up "that which is behind of the afflictions of Christ in my flesh for His body's sake."

It is one thing to go into the disagreeable by God's engineering, but another thing to go into it by choice. If God puts us there, He is amply sufficient. No matter how difficult the circumstances may lie, if we will let Jesus Christ manifest Himself in them, it will prove to be a new means of exhibiting the wonderful perfection and extraordinary purity of the Son of

God. This keen enthusiasm of letting the Son of God manifest Himself in us is the only thing that will keep us enjoying the discipline of the disagreeable. "Let your light so shine before men. . . ." Our light is to shine in the darkness; it is not needed in the light. It is on earth, in this condition of things, that we have to see that the life of the Son of God is manifested in us, and we must keep ourselves fit to do it.

2. By Keeping Your Sight Fit
and cannot see afar off . . .

In human sight we soon lose the innocence of sight; we know what we see, but instead of trusting the innocence of sight we confuse it by trying to state what we ought to see. Jesus restores the spiritual innocence of sight—"Except a man be born again, he cannot *see* the kingdom of God." Paul said that he was sent by God *to open men's eyes.* If you are being trained as an art student you will first of all be taught to see things as a whole, in mass outline, and then in detail. The meaning of perspective is that we keep the view of the whole whilst paying attention to the detail.

What is the thing that is pressing just now so that you cannot see aright? The reason it presses is that you have forgotten the One Who is far off to human sight, but very near to spiritual sight—God Himself. "And there we saw the giants . . . and we were in our own sight as grasshoppers, and so we were in their sight." When we see God we see neither the obstacle, nor ourselves, but, like Moses, we endure "as seeing Him Who is invisible." Can I see the Invisible One in the thing that is nearest to me—my food, my clothes, my money, my friendships? Can I see these in the light of God? Everything that came into the life of our Lord externally was transfigured because He saw always Him Who is Invisible—"I knew that Thou hearest Me always": "I do always those things that please Him."

I cannot keep my sight right if I give way to self-pity. "Why should this happen to me?" To talk in that way is a grief to Jesus because it is a deliberate refusal on my part to take His yoke upon me. He was meek towards His Father's dispensations for Him and never once murmured. The reason the thing has happened to you will only be seen when you are identified with Jesus in it; see that you remain in entire connection with Him. If you indulge in self-pity and the luxury of misery, it means that you have forgotten God, forgotten that you have been purged from your old sins,

and that you have to put on the new man, in accordance with the life of the Son of God in you.

"While we look not at the things which are seen, but at the things which are not seen." The way to keep our sight fit is by looking at the things which are not seen, and external things become a glorious chance of enabling us to concentrate on the invisible things. Once we realise that God's order comes to us in the passing moments, then nothing is unimportant. Every disagreeable thing is a new way of bringing us to realise the wonderful manifestation of the Son of God in that particular. What was the thing that obliterated God and you know it had no business to? You forget to take your heart to God and spill it. The thing that ought to make our hearts beat is a new way of manifesting the Son of God in us.

3. By Keeping Your Soul Fit
. . . and hath forgotten that he was purged from his old sins.

Jesus says that a man must lose his soul in order to find it—"whosoever will lose his life [i.e. soul] for My sake shall find it." Soul is "me," my personal spirit, manifesting itself in my body, my way of estimating things. The incoming of the Holy Spirit into my spirit enables me to construct a new way of reasoning and looking at things. "Let this mind be in you, which was also in Christ Jesus." Our Lord's way of reasoning certainly is not ours naturally; we have to *form* His mind. We cannot form the mind of Christ without having His Spirit, but we may have the Spirit of Christ and refuse to form His mind. We cannot alter our reasoning until God calls us up short. We may have been going steadily on not realising that we had to readjust our views, and then the Holy Spirit brings to our conscious mind what we knew perfectly well, but had never seen in that connection before. There must be instant obedience. The moment we obey the light the Spirit of God brings, the mind of Jesus is formed in us in that particular, and we begin to reason as He reasons; but if we debate and go back to our old way of reasoning we grieve the Spirit of God. In new circumstances there are always readjustments to be made. No matter how disagreeable things may be, say—"Lord, I am delighted to obey Thee in this matter," and instantly the Son of God presses to the front and in our human minds there is formed the way of reasoning that glorifies Jesus. We have to keep our soul fit to form the mind of Christ.

THE HABIT OF RISING TO THE OCCASION

So be the more eager, brothers, to ratify your calling and election, for as you exercise these qualities you will never make a slip. 2 Peter 1:10 (MOFFATT)

In natural life our aims shift and alter as we develop; but development in the Christian life is an increasing manifestation of Jesus Christ. Christian faith is nourished on dogma, and all young Christian life is uniform; but in the mature Christian life there are diversities. We must be careful that we do not remain children too long, but see that we "grow up into Him in all things." We have to assimilate truth until it becomes part of us, and then begin to manifest the individual characteristics of the children of God. The life of God shows itself in different manifestations, but the aim ultimately is the manifestation of Jesus Christ. "Till we all come in the unity of the faith, and of the knowledge of the Son of God, unto a perfect man, unto the measure of the stature of the fulness of Christ."

If Jesus Christ is not being manifested in my mortal flesh, I am to blame; it is because I am not eating His flesh and drinking His blood. Just as I take food into my body and assimilate it, so, says Jesus, I must take Him into my soul. "He that eateth Me, even he shall live by Me." Food is not health, and truth is not holiness. Food has to be assimilated by a properly organised system before the result is health, and truth must be assimilated by the child of God before it can be manifested as holiness. We may be looking at the right doctrines and yet not assimilating the truths which the doctrines reveal. Beware of making a doctrinal statement of truth *the* truth—"*I am . . . the* Truth," said Jesus. Doctrinal statement is our expression of that vital connection with Him. If we divorce what Jesus says from Himself, it leads to secret self-indulgence spiritually; the soul is swayed by a form of doctrine that has never been assimilated and the life is twisted away from the centre, Jesus Christ Himself.

1. The Habit of Ratifying Your Election
Wherefore the rather, brethren, give diligence to make your calling and election sure . . .

To ratify (MOFFATT) is to make sure of. I have to form the habit of assuring myself of my election, to bend the whole energy of my Christian powers to realise my calling, and to do that I must remember what I am saved for, viz.; that the Son of God might be manifested in my mortal flesh. How much attention have I given to the fact that my body is the temple of the Holy Ghost? When the Son of God is formed in me is He able to exhibit His life in my mortal flesh, or

am I a living contradiction of what my mouth professes? Am I working out what God works in or have I become divorced from Jesus Christ? I become divorced from Him immediately I receive anything apart from His indwelling. Have I a testimony to give that is not "me"? If my testimony is only a thrilling experience, it is nothing but a dead, metallic thing; it kills me and those who listen to me. But when I am in contact with Jesus Christ every testimony of mine will reveal Him.

"That ye may know what is the hope of *His* calling, and what the riches . . . of *His* inheritance in the saints." That which is taken for humility before men is blasphemy before God. To say, "Oh I'm no saint; I can't stand the folks who testify that they are sanctified," is acceptable with men; they will say it is true humility to talk in that way. But say this before God, and though it may sound humble, it is blasphemy because it means—"God cannot make me a saint." The one whom men call proud is really unutterably humble before God—"Nothing in my hands I bring."

2. The Habit of Realising Your Exercises
for if ye do these things . . .

We cannot do anything for our salvation, but we must do something to manifest it; we must work it out. Am I working out my salvation with my tongue, with my brain, and with my nerves? We are all apt to say with Rip Van Winkle—"I won't count this time." We put off the realisation that if we are going to grow up into Him in all things, there are things that we must do. "If ye know these things, happy are ye if ye *do* them." said Jesus. Character is the way we have grown to act with our hands and our feet, our eyes and our tongue; and the character we make always reveals the ruling disposition within. "If any man is in Christ, there is a new creation" (RV mg). Where is the new creation? If I am still the same miserable cross-patch, set on my own way, it is a lie to say that I am a new creature in Christ.

Have I learned to submit my will to Jesus? When we are rightly related to God we have uncovered to us for the first time the power of our own wills. Our wills are infirm through sin, but when we are sanctified there is revealed to us the pure pristine will-power with which God created us, and which the Holy Ghost calls into action. Then we have to submit our will to Jesus as He submitted His will to His Father. How was Jesus one with His Father when He was in this human frame? By complete obedience, complete dependence, and complete intercourse with Him all the time.

"If ye do these things"—am I adding resolution to my faith, self-control to my knowledge, steadfastness to my piety? We ought to be infinitely more humble in exercising ourselves in these ways. God's order for the saint is trusting imperially, and working humbly in the midst of things as they are, not thinking imperially, and contemptuously ignoring things as they are. God knows where we are, and His order comes to us moment by moment. We are not called to manifest Jesus in heaven; we have to be the light in the darkness and the squalor of earth. Our place is in the demon-possessed valley, not on the Mount of Transfiguration. It is in the valley that we have to exercise these things.

God will never shield us from any requirements of a child of His. "Think it not strange," says Peter, "concerning the fiery trial which is to try you." God is the Master Engineer; He allows difficulties to come to see if we can vault over them properly. "By my God have I leaped over a wall." *Do* the thing; it does not matter how it hurts so long as it gives God a chance to manifest Himself in our mortal flesh. May God not find the whine in us any more, but may He find us full of spiritual pluck and athleticism, ready to face anything He brings and to exercise ourselves in order that the Son of God may be manifested in our mortal flesh. Remember, we go through nothing that God does not know about.

3. The Habit of Recognising Your Expectations
. . . ye shall never fall.

What do you expect? One way to detect inordinate imagination is to try and locate to yourself what you expect God to do. One expectation you cannot have, and that is the expectation of successful service. When the Lord sent out the disciples on their first evangelical tour, they came back hilarious over their success— "Lord, even the devils are subject unto us through Thy name." That is all they thought about. Our Lord said, Don't rejoice in successful service, "but rather rejoice, because your names are written in heaven." We are not called to success but to faithfulness.

The life of our Lord is given to us that we may know the way we have to go when we are made sons and daughters of God. We must be careful not to have the idea that we are put into God's show room. God never has museums. We are to have only one aim in life, and that is that the Son of God may be manifested; then all dictation to God will vanish. Our Lord never dictated to His Father, and we are not to dictate to God; we are to submit our wills to Him so that He works through us what He wants. "I do not know why I should have to go through this"—the moment that thought is produced in us, no matter what our experience may be, we are no longer saints. It is a thought that has neither part nor lot with the life of the Son of God in us, and it must be put away instantly. We are the only ones who should go through these things, though we need not unless we like. If we refuse to, the trample will go back on the Lord, and we will never hear Him complain. We will get off scot free—"That was rather smart of me, that man thought he was going to put on me!" "What is that mark on Thy hand?" "That is the mark of the blow that should have been taken by you, but it came back on Me." Always go the second mile with God. It is never our duty to do it; but if we make duty our god we cease to be Christians in that particular. It is never our duty to go the second mile, to turn the other cheek, but it is what we shall do if we are saints. The Lord is doing it with us just now; we compel Him to go the second mile; we won't do this and that, and He has to do it for us. Are you saying to God, "I shall not accept these circumstances"? God will not punish you; but you will punish yourself when you realise that He was giving you a glorious opportunity of filling up that which is behind of the afflictions of Christ.

It is Peter, the man who denied his Lord and Master, who tells us that we "should follow His steps." Peter had come to a recognition of himself by means of a strange and desperate fall—"Simon, Simon, . . Satan hath desired to have you, that he may sift you as wheat: but I have prayed for thee, that thy faith fail not: and when thou art converted, strengthen thy brethren." Peter understands these words of Jesus now by the indwelling Spirit bringing them back to his remembrance. Are we following in the steps of His unseen feet? Where did Jesus place His feet? He placed them by the sick and the sorrowful, by the dead, by the bad, by the twisted and by the good. He placed His feet exactly where we have to place ours, either with or without Him, in the ordinary rough and tumble of human life as it is. "I will make the place of My feet glorious." As we walk in this body according to the new life that has been imparted to us by the Holy Spirit, we shall find it is no longer mounting up in ecstasy, running and not being weary, but walking with an infinite, steady, uncrushable, indescribable patience until men take knowledge that the Son of God is walking through us again.

THE HABIT OF WEALTH

You will thus be richly furnished with the right of entry into the eternal realm of our Lord and Saviour Jesus Christ. 2 Peter 1:11 (MOFFATT)

Through the promises we are made partakers of the Divine nature (v. 4); then we have to "manipulate" the Divine nature in our human nature by habits. Jesus prayed "that they may be one, even as We are one," and Paul urges, on the most practical lines, that we form in our actual lives the habits that are in perfect accordance with oneness with God. Our bodies are the temples of the Holy Ghost in which Jesus Christ is to manifest His life; and He can only do it as we put on the new man and see to it that our external conduct springs from a right relationship to Him. Verses 3–4 describe the super-natural works of grace; then we have to form the habit of working out all that God has worked in. "Add to your faith virtue. . . ." "Add" means there is something we must do.

1. The Habit of Realising the Provision

For so an entrance shall be ministered unto you . . .

The entrance is "by a new and living way," viz., our Lord Jesus Christ, and the outgoing is to God Himself —"filled with all the fulness of God." We get impoverished spiritually because we will stop at the barrier of consciousness. We will believe only in what we consciously possess; consequently we never realise the provision. If the grace and majesty and life and power and energy of God are not being manifested in us to the glory of God (not to our consciousness), God holds us responsible; we are wrong somewhere. There is always a danger of placing experience and consciousness in the wrong place. If we want something conscious from God, it means there is a reserve; the will has not been surrendered; immediately we do surrender, the tidal wave of the love of God carries us straight into all the fulness of God. "O fools, and slow of heart to believe"! We will believe only in what we have experienced. We never can *experience* Jesus Christ, that is, we can never hold Him within the compass of our own hearts. Jesus Christ must always be greater than our experience of Him, but our experience will be along the line of the faith we have in Him.

"If these things be in you, and abound." Have we formed the habit of wealth spiritually, or are we gambling with what is not ours, hoodwinking ourselves with delusions? "These things"—self-control, patience, love—are not in us if we are not born from above (RV mg). Are we trying to persuade ourselves that we are right with God when we know we are not? Earthly inheritances are particular possessions of our own, and in taking them we may impoverish others; but the marvellous thing about spiritual wealth is that when we take our part in that, everyone else is blessed; whereas if we refuse to be partakers, we hinder others from entering into the riches of God.

"Unto me . . . is this grace given, that I should preach . . . the unsearchable riches of Christ." In the natural world it is ungovernably bad taste to talk about money; one of the worst of lies is tucked up in the phrase we so often hear—"I can't afford it." The same idea has crept into the spiritual domain; and we have the idea that it is a sign of modesty to say at the close of the day—"Well, I have got through, but it has been a severe tussle!" And all the grace of God is ours without let or hindrance[7] through the Lord Jesus, and He is ready to tax the last grain of sand and the remotest star to bless us. What does it matter if circumstances are hard? Why shouldn't they be! We are the ones who ought to be able to stand them.

It is a crime to allow external physical misery to make us sulky with God. There *are* desolating experiences, such as the Psalmist describes in Psalms 42–43, and he says, "Then will I go . . unto God my exceeding joy"—not "*with* joy," but unto God *Who is my joy.* No calamity can touch that wealth. No sin is worse than self-pity because it puts self-interest on the throne; it "makes the bastard self seem in the right"; it obliterates God and opens the mouth to spit out murmurings against God; and the life becomes impoverished and mean,[8] there is nothing lovely or generous about it. Always beware of the conscious superiority that arises out of suffering—"I am so peculiarly constituted." If we indulge in the luxury of misery, we become isolated in the conception of our own sufferings; God's riches are banished and self-pity, the deeply entrenched essence of Satanhood, is enthroned in the soul.

2. Rejoicing in the Privilege

abundantly into the everlasting kingdom . . .

Jesus said, "My kingdom is not of this world: if My kingdom were of this world, then would My servants

---

7. without let or hindrance: legal phrase meaning "without obstacle or impediment."
8. mean: as used here, something or someone ordinary, common, low, or ignoble, rather than cruel or spiteful.

fight," i.e. they would do the same thing that every rational being does, but "My kingdom is not of this world"; it belongs to eternal realities. The idea of a kingdom that is not maintained by might is inconceivable to us, and the "otherworldly" aspect of Jesus Christ's Kingdom is apt to be forgotten. Jesus Christ's kingdom is not built on principles that can be discerned naturally, but on "otherworldliness," and we must never adapt principles that He did not adapt. If we have come to a dead stop spiritually, is it not because we have ceased to be "otherworldly"? Are we prepared to obey the scrutiny of the Holy Ghost when He brings the "otherworldly" standpoint of Jesus to bear upon our practical life? If we are, we shall be considered fools from every standpoint but the standpoint of the Holy Ghost. We are to be *in* the world but not *of* it. Are we letting God's light break on us as it did on Jesus? Are we showing in the prevailing bent of our lives the characteristics that were in Him? "The kingdom of God is within you." Jesus Christ is the King *and* the Kingdom. "This is life eternal, that they might know Thee." Eternal life is God and God is eternal life; and the meaning of the At-one-ment is that Jesus produces that life in us. By sanctification we enter into the kingdom of perfect oneness with Jesus Christ; everything He is, we are by faith. He is "made unto us wisdom, and righteousness, and sanctification, and redemption," we have nothing apart from Him. Have we formed the habit of rejoicing in this privilege?

3. Recognising Him Personally
. . . of our Lord and Saviour Jesus Christ.

Jesus Christ is *Saviour* and *Lord* in experience, and *Lord* and *Saviour* in discernment. "Ye call Me, Master and, Lord: and ye say well; for so I am"—but *is* He? The witness of the Holy Spirit is that we realise with growing amazement Who Jesus is to us personally, our Lord and Master. The baptism of the Holy Ghost makes us witnesses to Jesus, not wonder-workers. The witness is not to what Jesus does, but to what He is. "Ye shall be witnesses unto Me." We have had such an abundant entrance ministered unto us into His Kingdom, i.e. into oneness with Himself, that we are a delight to Him and His heart is being satisfied

with us. When God is beginning to be satisfied with us, He impoverishes every source of fictitious wealth. After sanctification God will wither up every other spring until we know that all our fresh springs[PBV][9] are in Him. He will wither up natural virtues; He will break up all confidence in our own powers, until we learn by practical experience that we have no right to draw our life from any other source than the tremendous reservoir of the unsearchable riches of Jesus Christ. Thank God if you are going through a drying-up experience! And beware of pumping up the dregs with the mud at the bottom of the well when all the Almighty power and grace of God is at your disposal. We have superabounding supplies, the unsearchable riches of Jesus Christ; and yet some of us talk as if our Heavenly Father had cut us off with a shilling!

What have we to spend this Christmas-time? We ought to be going about like multimillionaires. Externally we may have 2½*d.* only, but spiritually we have all the grace of God to spend on others.

"He that believeth on Me," out of him "shall flow rivers of living water." If you turn away from the Source and look at the outflow, at what God is doing through you, the Source will dry up and you will sit down on the outskirts of the entrance and howl—"It is dreadfully hard to live the Christian life!" Turn round and enter into the kingdom, pay attention to the Source, our Lord Himself, and you will experience the hilarity of knowing that you see God. Never be surprised at what God does, but be so taken up with Him that He may continue to do surprising things through you.

Are you sulking before God? Are the corners of your mouth, morally and spiritually, getting down and are you feeling sorry for yourself? You have turned your back upon God and are marching away from Him. Get straight to God, be abundantly stamped with His grace and His blessing will come through all the time; and when you get to heaven you will find that God has bound up the broken-hearted through you, has set at liberty the captives through you—but not if you have a murmur in your heart—"God is very hard." There is no self-pity left in the heart that has been bound up and succoured by the Lord Jesus Christ.

---

9. PBV: Prayer Book Version. The *Book of Common Prayer* of the Church of England includes a translation of the Psalter, or Psalms of David.

As He Walked
The Next Best Thing to Do

Ask, and it shall be given you; seek, and ye shall find; knock, and it shall be opened unto you. Matthew 7:7

Experience is not what a man *thinks* through, but what he *lives* through. The Bible is like life and deals with facts, not with principles, and life is not logical. Logic is simply a method of working the facts we know; but if we push the logical method to the facts we do not know and try to make God logical and other people logical, we shall find that the experience of life brings us to other conclusions. God sees that we are put to the test in the whole of life. We have to beware of selecting the portions of life only where we imagine we can live as saints and of cutting off any part of life because of the difficulty of being a Christian *there*. Christian experience means that we go to the whole of life open-eyed, wearing no doctrinal or denominational "blinkers" which shut off whole areas of unwelcome fact. Our faith has to be applied in every domain of our lives.

Our Lord's teaching is so simple that the natural mind pays no attention to it, it is only moral perplexity that heeds. For instance, Our Lord said: "Ask, and it shall be given you." These words have no meaning for us if we are wearing any kind of ecclesiastical "blinkers," and are refusing to see what we do not wish to see. "I can live beautifully in my own little religious bandbox."[10] That is not Christian experience. We have to face the whole of life as it is, and to face it fearlessly.

The difficulty of Christian experience is never in the initial stages. Experience is a gateway, not an end.

There are definite stages of conscious experience, but never pin your faith to any experience; look to the Lord Who gave you the experience. Be ruthless with yourself if you are given to talking about the experiences you have had. Your experiences are not worth anything unless they keep you at the Source, viz., Jesus Christ. It is tremendously strengthening to meet a mature saint, a man or woman with a full-orbed experience, whose faith is built in strong emphatic confidence in the One from Whom their experience springs.

The next best thing to do is to ask, if you have not received; to seek, if you have not found; to knock, if the door is not opened to you.

1. "Ask, and It Shall Be Given You"

Nothing is more difficult than to ask. We long, and desire, and crave, and suffer, but not until we are at the extreme limit will we *ask*. A sense of unreality makes us ask. We cannot bring ourselves up against spiritual reality when we like—all at once the staggering realisation dawns that we are destitute of the Holy Spirit, ignorant of all that the Lord Jesus stands for. The first result of being brought up against reality is this realisation of poverty, of the lack of wisdom, lack of the Holy Spirit, lack of power, lack of a grip of God. "If any of you lack wisdom, let him ask of God, . . ." but be sure you do lack wisdom. Have you ever asked out of the depths of moral and spiritual poverty?

If you realise you are lacking, it is because you have come in contact with spiritual reality. Don't put your reasonable "blinkers" on again—"Preach us the simple gospel"; "Don't tell me I have to be holy; that produces a sense of abject poverty, and it is not nice to feel abjectly poor." Some people are poor enough to be interested in their poverty, and some of us are like that spiritually. "Ask" means *beg*. A pauper does not ask from any desire save the abject, panging condition of his poverty.

Never deceive yourself by saying that if you do not ask you will not receive (cf. Matthew 5:45), although you'll never *receive* from God until you have come to the stage of asking. Asking means that you have come into the relationship of a child of God, and you now realise with moral appreciation and spiritual understanding that "every good gift and every perfect gift is from above, and cometh down from the Father of lights."

"Ye ask, and receive not," says the Apostle James, "because ye ask amiss." We ask amiss when we ask simply with the determination to outdo the patience of God until He gives us permission to do what we want to do. Such asking is mere sentimental unreality. And we ask amiss when we ask things from life and not from God, we are asking from the desire of self-realisation, which is the antipodes of Christian experience. The more we realise ourselves the less will we ask of God. Are we asking things of God or of

---

10. bandbox: in Chambers' day, a small, round box made to hold neckbands or collars for shirts; metaphorically, something small, narrow, cloistered, self-contained.

life? We shall never receive if we ask with an end in view, we are asking not out of our poverty, but out of our lust.

2. "Seek, and Ye Shall Find"

Get to work and seek, narrow your interests to this one thing. Have you ever really sought God, or have you only given a languid cry to Him after a twinge of moral neuralgia? "*Seek*," concentrate, and you will find. To concentrate is to fast from every other thing. "Ho, every one that thirsteth, come ye to the waters"—are you thirsty, or are you smugly indifferent, so satisfied with your experience that you want nothing more of God? If you build your faith on your experience, the censorious, metallic note comes in at once.

You can never give other people what you have found, but you can make them homesick for the same thing. That is the meaning of these words of Our Lord—"Ye shall be My witnesses"—you will exhibit

a oneness with Jesus Christ whilst He carries out His will in your life in every detail.

3. "Knock, and It Shall Be Opened unto You"

"Draw nigh to God"—the door is closed, and you suffer from palpitation as you knock. "Cleanse your hands"—knock a bit louder, you begin to discover where you are dirty. "Purify your heart, ye double-minded"—this is more personal and interior still, you are desperately in earnest now, you will do anything. "Be afflicted and mourn and weep"—have you ever been afflicted before God at the state of your inner life? When you get there, there is no strand of self-pity left, only a heart-breaking affliction and amazement at finding the kind of man you are. "Humble yourselves in the sight of the Lord." It is a humbling thing to knock at God's door, you have to knock with the crucified thief, with the cunning crafty publican, but—"to him that knocketh, *it shall be opened*."

NOT A BIT OF IT!

Therefore if any man be in Christ, he is a new creature: old things are passed away; behold, all things are become new. 2 Corinthians 5:17

Christian experience must be applied to the facts of life as they are, not to our fancies. We can live beautifully inside our own particular religious compartment as long as God does not disturb us; but God has a most uncomfortable way of stirring up our nests and of bringing in facts that have to be faced. It is actualities that produce the difficulty—the actual people we come in contact with, the actual circumstances of our lives, the actual things we discover in ourselves; and until we have been through the trial of faith in connection with actualities and have transfigured the actual into the real, we have no Christian experience. Experience is what is *lived* through.

1. The Experience of Useless Solemnity

Why do we and the Pharisees fast oft, but Thy disciples fast not? (Matthew 9:14)

When the disciples of Jesus were criticised for not fasting and being solemn, Jesus did not apologise for them, all He said was—"They are not in the mood to be gloomy." "Can the children of the bridechamber mourn, as long as the bridegroom is with them?" Our Lord was never careful not to offend the Pharisees, nor careful to warn His disciples not to offend them; but Our Lord never put a stumbling-block in the way of anyone. The one thing about Our Lord that the

Pharisees found it hard to understand was His gaiety in connection with the things over which they were appallingly solemn. And what puzzled the religious people of Paul's day was his uncrushable gaiety; he treated buoyantly everything that they treated most seriously. Paul was in earnest over one thing only, and that was his relationship to Jesus Christ. There he was in earnest, and there they were totally indifferent.

Reverence and solemnity are not the same. Solemnity is often nothing more than a religious dress on a worldly spirit. Solemnity which does not spring from reverence towards God is of no use whatever. The religious solemnity of the Pharisees was grossly offended at the social life of Our Lord (see Matthew 11:19). Our Lord paid the scantiest attention to all their solemnity; but one thing Our Lord was never lacking in, and that was reverence. The religion of Jesus Christ is the religion of a little child. There is no affectation about a disciple of Jesus, he is as a little child, amazingly simple but unfathomably deep. Many of us are not childlike enough, we are childish. Jesus said— "Except ye . . . become as *little children* . . ."

It is part of moral and spiritual education to watch how God deals with prejudices. We imagine that God has a special interest in our prejudices, and we magnify our conceptions and prejudices and put them on the throne. We are quite sure that God will never deal with our prejudices as we know He must deal with other people's. "God must deal very sternly with other people, but of course He knows that my prejudices are all right, they are from Him." We have to learn—not a bit of it! Instead of God being on the side of our prejudices, He deliberately wipes them out by ignoring them. God mortifies our prejudices, runs clean athwart them by His providence. God has no respect for anything we bring Him, He is after one thing only, and that is our unconditional surrender to Him.

2. The Experience of Useless Garments
No man putteth a piece of new cloth unto an old garment, for that which is put in to fill it up taketh from the garment, and the rent is made worse. (Matthew 9:16)

The way the Holy Spirit corrupts our natural virtue when He comes in is one of the most devastating experiences. He does not build up and transfigure what we possess in the way of virtue and goodness by natural heredity; it is corrupted to death, until we learn that we

> *. . . dare not trust the sweetest frame,*
> *But wholly lean on Jesus, name.*

It is a deep instruction to watch how natural virtues break down. The Holy Spirit does not patch up our natural virtues, for the simple reason that no natural virtue can come anywhere near Jesus Christ's demands. God does not build up our natural virtues and transfigure them, He totally recreates us on the inside. "And every virtue we possess is His alone." As we bring every bit of our nature into harmony with the new life which God puts in, what will be exhibited in us will be the virtues that were characteristic of the Lord Jesus, not our natural virtues. The supernatural is made natural. The life that God plants in us develops its own virtues, not the virtues of Adam but of Jesus Christ, and Jesus Christ can never be described in terms of the natural virtues.

Beware of the hesitation of the natural against being turned into the spiritual—"I do not mind being a saint if I can remain natural and be a saint entirely on my own initiative; if I can instruct God in regard to my temperament, my affinities, and my upbringing." If we have a religious strut about us, some prejudice, some particular refinement, some possession of natural heredity, it is like putting a piece of new cloth into an old garment. All has to go. "If any man be in Christ . . . , old things are passed away." The Holy Spirit begins to work in us the manifestation of the new creation (RV mg) until there comes a time when there is not a bit of the old order left. The old solemnity goes, the old attitude to things goes, the old confidence in natural virtues goes, and a totally new life begins to manifest itself, "and all things are of God." It is time some of us had a new set of clothes! The

outstanding characteristic of Our Lord and His disciples is moral originality.

3. The Experience of Useless Bottles
Neither do men put new wine into old bottles: else the bottles break, and the wine runneth out, and the bottles perish: but they put new wine into new bottles, and both are preserved. (Matthew 9:17)

The old systems of religion were distinctly ordained of God. All the ordinances to which the Pharisees held had been given by God, but the Pharisees had become second editions of the Almighty, they had usurped the place of God. There is always a danger of Phariseeism cropping up. In our own day its form is evangelical, man becomes a little god over his own crowd doctrinally.

The idea the Pharisees had of the Kingdom of God was that it belonged to certain favourites of God and its laws were to be worked out by the select few. According to Jesus, the Kingdom of God is love. "How sweet and simple," you say! But where are we going to begin? How are we going to have the love that has no lust in it, no self-interest, no sensitiveness to "pokes," the love that is not provoked, that thinketh no evil, is always kind? The only way is by having the love of God shed abroad in our hearts until there is not a bit of the old order left.

The love of God in us will produce an amazing sweetness in disposition towards Jesus Christ; but if we try to put that sweetness into the "bottle" we give to some earthly friend, the bottle will break and the wine will be lost. We have to be careless of the expression and heed only the Source. We say—"No, I must pay attention to the outflow, I am going to try and be a blessing there." We have to pay attention to the Source, Jesus Christ, see that we love *Him* personally, passionately and devotedly, and He will look after the outflow. Then it is not new wine in old wineskins, it is new wine creating its own wineskin. Is the love that is being exhibited by us the love of God or the love of our own natural hearts? God does not give us power to love as He loves; the love of God, the very nature of God, possesses us, and He loves through us.

How many amateur providences there are! "I must do this and that, and this one must not do this and that," and God retires and lets us go our own way. When we say—"But it is common sense to do this and that," we make our common sense almighty God, and God has to retire right out, then after a while He comes back and asks us if we are satisfied. There must not be a bit of that order left. God totally re-creates us on the inside until "all things are of God." May God enable us to stop trying to help Him, and may we let Him do what He likes with us.

GETTING THERE

Come unto Me, all ye that labour and are heavy laden, and I will give you rest. Matthew 11:28

1. Where the Sin and Sorrow Cease and the Song and the Saint Commence
Come unto Me (Matthew 11:28)

The questions that matter in life are remarkably few, and they are all answered by these words "Come unto Me." Not—"Do this" and "Don't do that," but "Come." "Come unto Me, all ye that labour and are heavy laden"—why *"labour"*? The word "labour" is a picture of the type of mind that realises that longings and ideals are not being worked out, the reality is not there, and there is an encroachment of sorrow which makes these words a description of the soul. You say—"I have thought about sanctification, and of the way God delivers from sin and gives the Holy Spirit, and alters the shadow of death to life"—but are you *actually* sanctified? Are you *actually* delivered from sin, from sorrow, from meanness—are you *actually* delivered from the things that make you un-Christlike? If you are not, you have no Christian experience. "Come unto Me," says Jesus, and by coming to Him your actual life will be brought into accordance with the reality revealed in Jesus. You will actually cease from sin and from sorrow, and actually find the song of the Lord begin; you will actually find that He has transformed you, the sinner, into a saint. But if you want this actual experience, you must come to Jesus. Our Lord makes Himself the touchstone.

Have you ever come to Jesus? Watch the stubbornness of your heart and mind, you will find you will do anything rather than the one simple, childlike thing—Come. Be stupid enough to come, and commit yourself to what Jesus says. The attitude of coming is that the will resolutely lets go of everything and deliberately commits the whole thing to Jesus. At the most unexpected moments there comes the whisper of the Lord—"Come unto Me," and we are drawn to Him. Personal contact with Jesus alters everything. He meets our sins, our sorrows, and our difficulties with the one word—"Come."

"And I will give you rest." Rest means the perfection of motion. "I will give you rest," that is, "I will stay you." Not—"I will put you to bed and hold your hand and sing you to sleep"; but—"I will get you out of bed, out of the languor and exhaustion, out of being half dead while you are alive; I will so imbue you with the spirit of life that you will be stayed by the perfection of vital activity." It is not a picture of an invalid in a bathchair, but of life at such a pitch of health that everything is at rest, there is no exhaustion without recuperation. Physical health is a delight because it is an exact balance between our physical life and outer circumstances. Disease means that outer circumstances are getting too much for the vital force on the inside. Morally it is the same. No one is virtuous naturally, we may be innocent naturally, but innocence is often a hindrance because it is nothing in the world but ignorance. Virtue can only be the outcome of conflict. Everything that does not partake of the nature of virtue is the enemy of virtue in us. Immediately we fight we become moral in that particular. Spiritually it is the same, everything that is not spiritual will make for our undoing. "In the world ye shall have tribulation," said Jesus, "but be of good cheer, I have overcome the world." Spiritual grit is what we need. We become spiritual whiners and talk pathetically about "suffering the will of the Lord." Where is the majestic vitality and might of the Son of God about that! "Come unto Me, . . . and I will give you rest," i.e.; "I will imbue you with the spirit of life so that you will be stayed by the perfection of vital activity." Jesus will produce in us the actual experience that is exactly like the reality; that means that the very life of Jesus will be manifested in our actual lives if we will face the music in His strength. Faith is not a mathematical problem, the nature of faith is that it must be tried. How many of us are laying up "gold" for a rainy day? When we go through the trial of faith we gain so much wealth in our heavenly banking account, and the more we go through the trial of faith the wealthier we become in the heavenly regions.

2. Where the Self-Interest Sleeps and the Real Interest Awakens
Come with Me (John 1:39)

"They abode with Him that day"—that is about all some of us have ever done, and then we awoke to actualities, self-interest arose, and the abiding was over. There is no condition of life in which we cannot abide in Jesus. We have to learn to abide in Him wherever we are placed.

"Thou art Simon. . . . thou shalt be called Cephas." Jesus writes the new name in those places in our lives where He has erased our pride and self-sufficiency and self-interest. Some of us have the new name in spots only—like sanctified measles. When we have our best spiritual mood on, you would think we were high-toned saints, but don't look at us when we are not in that mood! A disciple is one who has nothing but the new name written all over him; self-interest and pride have been erased entirely. Pride is the deification of myself, and that nowadays is not the order of the Pharisee, but of the publican—"Oh, I'm no saint." To talk like that is acceptable to human pride, but it is unconscious blasphemy against God. It literally means I defy God to make me a saint. The reason I am not a saint is either that I do not want to be a saint or I do not believe God can make me one. "I would be all right," we say, "if God saved me and took me straight to heaven." That is exactly what He will do! "We will come unto him, and make Our abode with him"—the Triune God abiding with the saint. Do we believe it? It is a question of will. Make your will let Jesus do everything, make no conditions, and He will take you home with Him not only for a day but for ever; self-interest will be done with, and the only thing left will be the real interest that identifies you with Jesus.

3. Where the Selective Affinity Dies and the Sanctified Abandon Lives

Come after Me (Mark 1:17)
If you do come after Jesus, you will realise that He pays no attention whatever to your natural affinities. One of the greatest hindrances to our coming to Jesus is the talk about temperament. I have never seen the Spirit of God pay any attention to a man's temperament, but over and over again I have seen people make their temperament and their natural affinities a barrier to coming to Jesus. We have to learn that Our Lord does not heed our selective natural affinities. The idea that He does heed them has grown from the notion that we have to consecrate our gifts to God. We cannot consecrate what is not ours. The only thing I can give to God is "my right to myself" (Romans 12:1). If I will give God that, He will make a holy experiment out of me, and God's experiments always succeed. The one mark of a disciple is moral originality. The Spirit of God is a well of water in the disciple, perennially fresh. When once the saint begins to realise that God engineers circumstances, there will be no more whine, but only a reckless abandon to Jesus. Never make a principle out of your own experience; let God be as original with other people as He is with you.

"Come unto Me." Have you come? Will you come *now?* If you do come and abandon yourself to Jesus, He will continue to say "Come" through you to others.

If you have come to Jesus Christ and to the truth of God through a servant or a handmaid of God, you never think of the one who brought you there, because that one is so completely one with the Lord Jesus that the thought of himself or herself is never obtruded. Other people come to Jesus not through *you*, but through His word speaking through you.

Is your life producing the echo of Christ's "come"?

GET A MOVE ON!

And beside this, giving all diligence, add . . . 2 Peter 1:5

We are made partakers of the Divine nature through the promises (see v. 4), now, says Peter, "giving all diligence, add . . . ," screw your attention down and form habits. No one is born with habit, we have to form habit, and the habits we form most easily are those which we form by imitation. When we begin to form a habit we are conscious of it. There are times when we are conscious of becoming virtuous and patient and godly, but that is only a stage; if we stop there we get the strut of the spiritual prig.

1. In the Domain of Drudgery

Jesus . . . took a towel . . . , and began to wash the disciples' feet. (John 13:3–5)

Are we refusing to enter the domain of drudgery? Drudgery is the touchstone of character. It is a "drudging" thing to be virtuous. Necessity is not virtue; virtue can only be the outcome of conflict. The virtuous man or woman is like one who has gone through the fight and has added virtue, added it on the basis of the Divine nature, not on the basis of human determination.

The greatest hindrance of our spiritual life lies in looking for big things to do; Jesus Christ "took a towel. . . ." We are not meant to be illuminated versions; we are meant to be the common stuff of ordinary human life exhibiting the marvel of the grace of God. The snare in Christian life is in looking for the gilt-edged moments, the thrilling times; there are times when there is no illumination and no thrill, when God's angel is the routine of drudgery on the level of towels and washing feet. Are we prepared to "get a move on" *there?* Routine is God's way of saving us between our times of inspiration. We are not to expect Him to give us His thrilling minutes always.

2. In the Domain of Determination

Abide in Me. (John 15:4)

The secret of bringing forth fruit is to abide in Jesus. "Abide in Me," says Jesus, in spiritual matters, in intellectual matters, in money matters, in every one of the matters that make human life what it is. Beware of putting on your religious "blinkers"—"I can live finely in this type of meeting, or with that particular set." The Christian life is not a bandbox life. We must live where we can be tested by the whole of life. Are we preventing God from doing things in our circumstances because we imagine it will hinder our communion with Him? That is impertinence. No matter what our circumstances are, we can be as sure of abiding in Him in them as in a prayer meeting. We are not to be changing and arranging our circumstances ourselves. Our Lord and Master never chose His own circumstances, He was meek towards His Father's dispensation for Him; He was at home with His Father wherever His body was placed. Think of the amazing leisure of Our Lord's life! For thirty years He did nothing. We keep God at excitement point, there is none of the serenity of the life "hid with Christ in God" about us.

"Abide in Me." Think of the things that might take you out of abiding in Christ—"Yes, Lord, I will abide when once I can get this finished; I will abide, but I must do this first; when this week is over, I shall be all right." Get a move on! Begin to abide *now!* In the initial stage abiding is a continual effort until it becomes so much of the law of our lives that we abide in Him unconsciously. Watch it in your bodily life, in your social life—are you abiding *there?* are you bringing forth fruit *there?* That is where My Father is glorified, says Jesus.

Are our minds stayed on Jesus? Do we brood and dwell on this line of abiding in Him? It takes the breathless panic out of us. Our Lord was never in a panic because with Him the abiding on the inside was unsullied. It is the "plague of flies," mental, moral and spiritual, that annoy us and take us out of abiding in Jesus. There is something in human pride that can stand big troubles, but we need the supernatural grace and power of God to stand by us in the little things.

The tiniest detail in which we obey has all the omnipotent power of the grace of God behind it. When we do our duty, not for duty's sake, but because we believe that God is engineering our circumstances in that way, then at the very point of our obedience the whole superb grace of God is ours. It is the "adding" that is difficult. We say we do not expect God to carry us to heaven on "flowery beds of ease," but we act as if we did!

We have to live in the domain of drudgery by the power of God, and to learn to abide in Him where we are placed. Remember that God gives us the Spirit of Jesus, but He does not give us the mind of Jesus; we have to form the mind of Christ. The Spirit of Jesus is given to us by the marvel of the Atonement, then we have to construct with patience that way of thinking which is exactly in accordance with the mind of our Lord. God will not make us think as Jesus thought, we have to do that ourselves, to bring "into captivity every thought to the obedience of Christ." Peter's counsel to "add," means to form habits on the basis of the new life which God has put in.

3. In the Domain of Devotion

Ye are My friends, if ye do whatsoever I command you. (John 15:14)

God created man to be His friend. If we are the friends of Jesus we have deliberately and carefully to lay down our life for Him. It is difficult, and thank God it is! When once the relationship of being the friends of Jesus is understood, we shall be called upon to exhibit to everyone we meet the love He has shown to us. Watch the kind of people God brings across your path, you will find it is His way of picturing to you the kind of person you have been to Him.—"You are My child, the friend of My Son, now exhibit to that 'hedgehoggy' person the love I exhibited to you when you were like that towards Me; exhibit to that mean, selfish person exactly the love I showed you when you were mean and selfish." We shall find ample room to eat "humble pie" all the days of our life. The thing that keeps us going is to recognise the humour of our heavenly Father in it all, and we shall meet the disagreeable person with a spiritual chuckle because we know what God is doing, He is giving us a mirror that we may see what we have been like towards Him; now we have the chance to prove ourselves His friends, and the other person will be amazed and say—"Why the more I poke her, the sweeter she gets!" and will tumble in where we tumbled in, into the grace of God.

YOU NEED NOT SIN
Romans 6:13–18

How shall we, that are dead to sin, live any longer therein? Romans 6:2

We have to build in faith on the presupposition of the perfect Atonement of Jesus Christ, not build on an experience. If we construct our faith on our experience, we produce that most unscriptural type of holiness, an isolated life, with our eyes fixed on our own whiteness. If we do not base all our thinking on the presupposition of the Atonement, we shall produce a faith conscious of itself, hysterical and unholy, that cannot do the work of the world. Beware of the piety that has no presupposition of the Atonement, it is no use for anything but leading a sequestered life; it is useless to God and a nuisance to man. We have to base resolutely in unshaken faith on the complete and perfect Atonement of Jesus Christ.

"Likewise reckon ye also yourselves to be dead indeed unto sin, but alive unto God through Jesus Christ our Lord." How many of us reckon like that, or do our prayers, our piety, come in the way? Our prayers and our piety are the evidence that we are on the right foundation. Is the Atonement the one thing that exerts a dominating influence in my life?

1. If You Obey in the Matter of Dedication

Yield ... your members as instruments of righteousness unto God. (Romans 6:13)

There is something we must do, viz., dedicate our members. Have we ever, as saved souls dedicated our bodies to God? "Present your bodies a living sacrifice, holy, acceptable unto God," not "Present your *all*," but present your *body*. If you obey in this matter of dedication, you can keep your bodily life free from vice and sin. Sin dwells in human nature, but it has no light there, it does not belong to human nature as God created it. Deny the disposition of sin, says Paul, bring it to the place of crucifixion (v. 6). Let not sin i.e., your right to yourself, rule any longer, deny that disposition and let Jesus Christ rule. Never let any member dominate and say—You must.

2. If You Obey in the Matter of Deliverance

For sin shall not have dominion over you. (Romans 6:14)

"Let not sin therefore reign in your mortal body," that is, do not let sin command your body. Sin is a monarch ruling on the outside, demanding obedience on the inside. We can add nothing to the Atonement, we can do nothing for our deliverance, but we must manifest that we are delivered from sin. If you obey in this matter of deliverance, you will realise that there is no bondage in the Atonement. "Even so reckon ye yourselves to be ... alive unto God in Jesus Christ" (RV).

3. If You Obey in the Matter of Discernment

What then? Shall we sin, because we are not under the law, but under grace? (v. 15)

Do you discern that Jesus Christ means His Atonement to be recognised *there*—in my home life, in my business? The grace of God is absolute, but your obedience must prove that you do not receive it in vain. Continually bring yourself to the bar of judgement and ask—Where is the discernment of the Atonement in this matter and in that? The grace of God in a human being is proved by the discernment of the Atonement in unobtrusive practical ways. The amateur providence element, the insistence of common-sense morality, is the great enemy of the life of Jesus in a saint because it competes with the Atonement— "Of course God does not mean that the Atonement is to be worked out through my finger-tips, in the getting of meals, in my business!" If the Atonement does not work out there, it will work out nowhere. Beware of the piety that denies the natural life, it is a fraud. We can all shine in the sun, but Jesus wants us to shine where there is no sun, where it is dark with the press of practical things.

4. If You Obey in the Matter of Debate

Know ye not, that to whom ye yield [KJV] yourselves as servants unto obedience, his servants ye are whom ye obey? (v. 16 RV)

What do you debate about in your mind? When Jesus speaks, never say: "Let us talk this matter over." Some of us obey God in prayer meetings only or in devotional times; we never think of obeying Him at mealtimes or in our offices, etc. We fail whenever we forget to do in the insignificant details those things we were delighted to see when we were looking into the law of God. (See James 1:22–25.) When things come out against us, do we sit down under them, or have we such a habit of mind that God is always first, not piously and pathetically, but actually? Prayer does not place God first; prayer is the evidence that our minds are fixed on God. We have to get our minds used to putting God first, it is conscious to begin with. The snare is putting common sense first. Jesus says—

Reverse the order, put God first. The tiniest thing that comes between you and God will blot God out. A twinge of neuralgia is sufficient to make some of us forget the Atonement.

5. If You Obey in the Matter of Delight

But ye have obeyed from the heart. (Romans 6:17)

"Obedience of the heart is the heart of obedience." Whenever we obey, the delight of the supernatural grace of God meets our obedience instantly. Absolute Deity is on our side at once every time we obey, so that natural obedience and the grace of God coincide. If we look at obedience apart from the presupposition of the Atonement, it makes it seem absurd. Obedience means that we bank everything on the Atonement, and the supernatural grace of God is a delight. We cannot do anything pleasing to God unless there is this deliberate building on the presupposition of the Atonement.

6. If You Obey in the Matter of Devotion

Being then made free from sin, ye became the servants of righteousness. (v. 18)

Thank God we can do what we ought to do—when? *NOW!* We are free to become the servants of righteousness. Sin is nothing but a big bully. Sin was killed at the Cross of Christ; it has no power at all over those who are set free by the Atonement of Jesus and are prosecuting their life in Him: ". . . in nothing terrified by your adversaries."

We have to "grow in the nurture and admonition of the Lord." The more we are taught, the more we can be taught, and the more we are taught the more the growth and the glorifying of God will go on in our souls. Have we ever been taught anything? Being taught of God is a delightful life, it means the discernment is exercised. God does not put us in His "show room," we are here for Him to show His marvellous works in us and to use us in His enterprises.

We have to prosecute our life in Christ, not be dragged in His wake or the strain will be too heavy and down we shall go. The only place to prosecute our life in Christ is just where we are, in the din of things, and the only way in which we can prosecute our life in Christ is to remember that it is God Who engineers circumstances, and that the only place where we can be of use to Him is where we are, not where we are not. God is in the obvious things.

Am I banking in faith on the Eternal Fact of the Atonement? Am I so devoted to my Lord that He is working out His purposes in me? Or am I one of those miserable individuals who is working out his own particular type of religion by himself? We have to measure every type of experience by the Lord Jesus Christ and His Atonement. We must build on the great fact of the Redemption which God has performed through Christ, and continually presuppose that Redemption. If we fail to prosecute our life in Jesus, and build our faith on our experiences only, then the further away we get from our experiences, the dimmer will Jesus Christ become.

WHAT NEXT?
Matthew 5:45–48

1. Deny Yourself More Than Others

That ye may be the children of your Father which is in heaven. (Matthew 5:45)

According to the Bible, self-seeking did not begin on earth, it began in heaven and was turned out of heaven because it was unworthy to live there, and it will never get back again. If we are to be Christian after the stamp Our Lord requires, we must deny ourselves more than others. Our Lord never taught us to deny sin: sin must be destroyed, not denied. Nothing sinful can ever be good. "If any man would come after Me, let him deny himself" (Matthew 16:24 RV). Our Lord is referring to the natural self which must be denied in order that it may be made spiritual. Our Lord does not teach "Deeper Death to Self"; He

teaches death right out to my self, death right out to self-realisation and self-seeing. Sin and self are not the same thing. Sin does not belong to human nature as God created it. Adam was innocent when God created him, and God intended him to take part in his own moral development, and to transform his natural life into a spiritual life by obedience; but Adam refused to do it. Our Lord continually denied the natural and turned it into the spiritual by obedience. With Our Lord everything was spiritual. His eating and drinking were acts of continual subordination to His Father's will (cf. Matthew 4:2–4). We have a natural life to be sacrificed and thereby turned into a spiritual, life. The meaning of sacrifice is giving the best we have to God, denying it to ourselves, that He may make it an eternal possession of His and ours.

2. Devote Yourself to Prayer More Than Others

Lord, teach us to pray. (Luke 11:1)

Pray without ceasing. (1 Thessalonians 5:17)

Never *say* you will pray about a thing; *pray about it.* Our Lord's teaching about prayer is so amazingly simple but at the same time so amazingly profound that we are apt to miss His meaning. The danger is to water down what Jesus says about prayer and make it mean something more common sense; if it were only common sense, it was not worth His while to say it. The things Jesus says about prayer are supernatural revelations.

It is not part of the life of a natural man to pray. We hear it said that a man will suffer in his life if he does not pray; I question it. What will suffer is the life of the Son of God in him, which is nourished not by food but by prayer. When a man is born from above (RV mg), the life of the Son of God is born in him, and he can either starve that life or nourish it. Prayer is the way the life of the Son of God is nourished. God has so constituted things that prayer on the basis of Redemption alters the way a man looks at things. Prayer is not a question of altering things externally, but of working wonders in a man's disposition. One great effect of prayer is that it enables the soul to command the body. By obedience I make my body submissive to my soul, but prayer puts my soul in command of my body. It is one thing to have the body in subjection, but another thing to be able to command it. When I command my body, I make it an ally, the means by which my spiritual life is furthered.

"For your Father knoweth what things ye have need of, before ye ask Him" (Matthew 6:8). If God sees that my spiritual life will be furthered by giving the things for which I ask, then He will give them, but that is not the end of prayer. The end of prayer is that I come to know God Himself. If I allow my bodily needs to get out of relationship to God, then those needs will keep me morbidly interested in myself all the time, much to the devil's enjoyment. We have to leave ourselves resolutely in God's hands and launch out into the work of intercession on the basis of faith in the perfect Redemption of Jesus.

3. Dedicate Yourself to Love More Than Others

Thou shalt love the Lord thy God with all thy heart, and with all thy soul, and with all thy mind. This is the first and great commandment. (Matthew 22:37–38)

If ye love Me, keep My commandments. (John 14:15)

Before we can love God we must have the Lover of God in us, viz., the Holy Spirit. When the Holy Spirit has shed abroad the love of God in our hearts, then that love requires cultivation. No love on earth will develop without being cultivated. We have to dedicate ourselves to love, which means identifying ourselves with God's interests in other people, and God is interested in some funny people, viz.; in you and in me! We must beware of letting natural affinities hinder our walking in love. One of the most cruel ways of killing love is by disdain built on natural affinities. To be guided by our affinities is a natural tendency, but spiritually this tendency must be denied, and as we deny it we find that God gives us affinity with those for whom we have no natural affinity. Is there anyone in your life who would not be there if you were not a Christian? The love of God is not mere sentimentality; it is a most practical thing for the saint to love as God loves. The springs of love are in God, not in us. The love of God is only in us when it has been shed abroad in our hearts by the Holy Spirit, and the evidence that it is there is the spontaneous way in which it is manifested.

4. Dispose Yourself to Believe More Than Others

Said I not unto thee, that, if thou wouldest believe, thou shouldest see the glory of God? (John 11:40)

He that believeth on Me, . . . out of [him] shall flow rivers of living water. (John 7:38)

"I am not ashamed of the gospel of Christ," said Paul, "for it is the power of God to salvation to everyone that believeth." So as long as we live in a religious compartment, make our own theology, wear doctrinal "blinkers," and live only amongst those who agree with us, we shall not see where the shame comes in; but let God shift us and bring us into contact with those who are indifferent to what we believe, and we shall realise soon the truth of what our Lord said—"therefore the world hateth you." If we really believed some phases of our Lord's teaching it would make us a laughing stock in the eyes of the world. It requires the miracle of God's grace for us to believe as Jesus taught us to.

"Said I not unto thee, that, if thou wouldest believe, thou shouldest see the glory of God?" Every time our programme of belief is clear to our minds we come across something that contradicts it. Faith, before it is real, must be tried. As we dispose ourselves to believe, we see God all the time, not in spasms. We see His arm behind all the facts in individual life and in history. Are we disposing ourselves to believe more than others?

5. Determine to Know More Than Others

If any man will do His will, he shall know of the doctrine, whether it be of God, or whether I speak of Myself.

If ye know these things, happy are ye if ye do them. (John 13:17)

If you believe in Jesus, you will not spend all your time in the smooth waters just inside the harbour, full of exhilaration and delight, but always moored; you will have to go out through the harbour bar into the great deeps of God and begin to know for yourself, begin to get spiritual discernment. If you do not cut the moorings, God will have to break them with a storm and send you out. Why not unloosen and launch all on God and go out on the great swelling tide of His purpose?

"If any man will do His will, he shall know. . . ." When you know you should do a thing and you do it, immediately you will know more. If you revise where you are stodgy spiritually, you will find it goes back to the point where there was one thing you knew you should do, but you did not do it because there seemed no immediate call to, and now you have no perception, no discernment. Instead of being spiritually self-pos-

sessed at the time of crisis, you are spiritually distracted. It is a dangerous thing to refuse to go on knowing.

When the Spirit of God has opened your mind by His incoming and you are determining to know more, you will find that external circumstances and internal knowledge go together, and by obedience you begin to fulfil your spiritual destiny. The counterfeit of obedience is the state of mind in which you work up occasions to sacrifice yourself, ardour is mistaken for the discernment built on knowledge. "To obey is better than sacrifice." It is a great deal better to fulfil the purpose of God in your life by discerning His will than it is to perform great acts of self-sacrifice.

Beware of harking back to a past knowledge when God wants to bring you into a new relationship; beware of harking back to what you once were when God wants you to be something you have never been.

PULL YOURSELF TOGETHER

If ye abide in Me, and My words abide in you, ye shall ask what ye will, and it shall be done unto you. John 15:7

In all Christian experience there must be the presupposition of the Atonement; we have to build in faith on the great work which God has performed through Christ. We cannot save ourselves, or sanctify ourselves; we cannot atone for sin; we cannot redeem the world; we cannot make right what is wrong, pure what is impure, holy what is unholy—all that is the sovereign work of God. God has made a perfect Atonement, are we in the habit of realising it? We must never put character in the place of faith, there is a great danger of doing so. Our character can never be meritorious before God: we stand before God on the basis of His grace. Character is the evidence that we are built on the right foundation. What we need is the perfect realisation of the Atonement of Jesus Christ. The need is not to *do* things, but to *believe*. "What must I *do* to be saved? . . . *Believe* on the Lord Jesus Christ, and thou shalt be saved."

1. By the Habit of Constantly Realising
If ye abide in Me . . .

If we continue to act and think and work from the centre of abiding in Jesus, then Jesus says that other things will happen, viz., we shall bring forth fruit. Are we abiding in Jesus? Do we take time to abide? What is the dominating factor of power in our lives? Is it work, service, sacrifice for others? The thing that

ought to exert the greatest power in our lives is the Atonement. Do we give one minute out of every sixty to make ourselves realise it? We must get into the habit of constantly realising the Atonement, of centralising everything there. To concentrate causes consciousness of effort to begin with. "Abide in Me," says Jesus. It is imperative on our part that we abide in Jesus. It is a responsibility for us to continually realise the Eternal Fact of the Atonement.

2. By the Habit of Constantly Remembering
and My words abide in you . . .

We maintain our relationship to Jesus by the use of the means which He gives us, viz., His words. Some of us can only hear God in the thunder of revivals or in public worship; we have to learn to listen to God's voice in the ordinary circumstances of life. It is not the length of time we give to a thing that matters, but whether the time we give opens the door to the greatest power in our life. The greatest factor in life is that which exerts most power, not the element which takes most time. The five minutes we give to the words of Jesus the first thing in the morning are worth more than all the rest of the day.

Beware of any experience that does not wed itself to the words of Jesus. Experience is simply the doorway into the great revelation of Jesus Christ. "The words that I speak unto you, they are spirit, and they are life." *Read* the Bible, whether you understand it or not, and the Holy Spirit will bring back some word of Jesus to you in a particular set of circumstances and make it living; the point is—will you be loyal to that word? Never ask anyone else what the word means, go direct to God about it. Are we in the habit of listening to the words of Jesus? Do we realise that Jesus knows more about our business than we do ourselves? Do we take His word for our clothes, our money, our domestic work; or do we think we can manage these things for ourselves? The Spirit of God has the habit of taking the words of Jesus out of their scriptural setting and putting them into the setting of our personal lives.

3. By the Habit of Constantly Requesting
ye shall ask what ye will . . .

This solves the mystery of what we should pray for. If we are abiding in Jesus, we shall ask what He wants us to ask whether we are conscious of doing so or not. "Ye shall ask what ye *will,*" i.e., what your will is in. The meaning of prayer is that we recognise we are in the relationship of a child to his father. "Your Father knoweth what things ye have need of, before ye ask Him." When once we realise that we can never think of anything our Father will forget, worry becomes impossible. Beware of getting into a panic. Panic is bad for the natural heart, and it is destructive to the spiritual life. "*Let not* your heart be troubled"—it is a command. Are we in the habit of constantly requesting, of continually talking to Jesus about everything? Where we go in the time of trial proves what the great underlying power of our lives is.

4. By the Habit of Constantly Recognising
. . . and it shall be done unto you.

If we are abiding in Jesus and His words are abiding in us, then Jesus says God will answer our prayers. Do we recognise that? "But," you say, "suppose I ask for something not according to God's will?" I defy you to, if you are fulfilling the abiding in Jesus. The disciple who is in the condition of abiding in Jesus *is* the will of God, and his apparent free choices are God's fore-ordained decrees. Mysterious? Logically absurd? But a glorious truth to a saint.

"And whatsoever ye shall ask in My Name, that will I do." Are we performing this ministry of the interior?

Do we pray for those in prominent places, for the "Pauls"? There is no snare or danger of infatuation or pride or the "show business" in prayer. Prayer is a hidden, obscure ministry which brings forth fruit that glorifies the Father. "Severed from Me you can do nothing," i.e., "you will not bear My fruit, you will bear something that did not come from Me at all"; but—"Abide in Me," and you will bring forth fruit that testifies to the nature of the vine, fruit whereby the Father is glorified. "The effectual fervent prayer of a righteous man," one who is abiding, "availeth much." Are we constantly recognising that God does answer prayer if we are abiding in Jesus? Are we building in faith on the presupposition of the Atonement and bringing everything to that one centre, or are we allowing our lives to be frittered away? Is Jesus Christ dominating every interest of our lives more and more? This does not mean that we are to be thinking about God always and giving all our time to so-called religious work, but it does mean that we are to concentrate on the great fact of the Atonement with the greatest amount of our time even to the ordinary things of life as they are engineered for us by God.

Those who use the jargon of "abiding in Christ," if not really abiding are an annoyance and an irritation. If we make the Atonement of the Lord Jesus Christ the great exerting influence of our life, every phase of our life will bear fruit for God. Take time and get to know whether the Atonement is the central point of all power for you, and remember that Satan's aim is to keep you away from that point of power. Jesus said that the cares of this world and the lust of other things would choke His word. We can choke God's word with a yawn; we can hinder the time that should be spent with God by remembering we have other things to do. "I haven't time!" Of course you have not time! *Take* time, strangle some other interests and make time to realise that the centre of power in your life is the Lord Jesus Christ and His Atonement. Paul limited his knowledge to that one thing—"I determined not to know any thing among you, save Jesus Christ, and Him crucified." We have to learn to concentrate our affinities, to determine to be limited.

DON'T SLACK OFF
2 Timothy 3:14–15

1. In What You Have Been Taught
But continue thou in the things which thou hast learned . . . (2 Timothy 3:14)

We learn very few things, because we learn that only to which we give our wits. Are we sticking to the things we have learned? We say we believe that God is love, but have we *learned* that He is? Have we assimilated it? We see truths, but we are not yet in the circumstances where we can learn them. Many things are taught, but we cannot learn them all at once. We say—"Oh yes, I would like to be that," then there comes the "stick-at-iveness"—sixty seconds every minute, sixty minutes every hour. The only way in which we learn is by the terrific iteration of the commonplace.

Experience is never the ground of our confidence; experience is the opening of the door to a new life which must be continued in. Some of us are continually having doors opened, but we will not go through them. *Don't slack off*, keep on with the thing which you have learned. We speak about testifying to the experience of sanctification; what we really testify to is not an *experience* of sanctification but to a revelation granted us by God of what sanctification is: the *experience* of sanctification is the rest of life from that moment.

2. In What You Have Tested
and hast been assured of . . . (v. 14)

Many of us believe, but we will not confess to what we believe, consequently we are assured of nothing. "I did ask God for the Holy Spirit, but I do not feel sure of anything." Confess what you believe for, and instantly the assurance of that for which you believe will be made yours. We are so terribly afraid to venture on what God says. Confession is not for the sake of other people, but for our own sake. Confession means we have trusted God for this thing and we believe on the ground of His word that the work is done. We realise by confessing that we have no one saving God to stand by us. Have we ever taken the cross of confessing? When we believe with the heart, we have to confess with our mouth what we believe to those whose business it is to know. The reason some of us lack assurance is because we do not continue in what we have tested, something has made us slack off.

3. In Loyalty to Your Teachers
knowing of whom thou hast learned them . . . (v. 14)

God brings His own particular teachers into our lives, and we have to watch that we do not slack off in our loyalty to them. Loyalty to teachers is a very rare thing. The man or woman used by God to teach me is not necessarily the one used to teach you. We must not foist our teachers on everyone else. Are we loyal, to our teachers, or are we spiritual butterflies? Does every new-comer on the highway of spiritual life switch us off on to a new line? God very rarely teaches direct from His word until the way for that has been opened by His own order—"and He gave some, apostles; and some, prophets; and some, evangelists; and some, pastors and *teachers*" (Ephesians 4:11). God makes His own teachers; we have to see that we do not slack off in our loyalty to them.

4. In the Scripture Truth
and that from a child thou hast known the holy scriptures . . .

It is not the thing on which we spend most time that moulds us, but the thing that exerts the greatest power.

Five minutes with God and His word is worth more than all the rest of the day. Do we come to the Bible to be spoken to by God, to be made "wise unto salvation," or simply to hunt for texts on which to build addresses? There are people who vagabond through the Bible, taking sufficient only out of it for the making of sermons, they never let the word of God walk out of the Bible and talk to them. Beware of living from hand to mouth in spiritual matters; do not be a spiritual mendicant.

Beware of the novel things. Some of us spiritually are independent, impudent travellers—"Oh, I can find my way all right." The thing to do is to keep on the steady track—"Honour thy father and thy mother." "Remember the sabbath day, to keep it holy," etc. God brings back what is old in order to test our loyalty. All the novel things slip away; the essential track remains.

5. In the Salvation Testimony
. . . which are able to make thee wise unto salvation through faith which is in Christ Jesus.

The Bible is not the word of God to us unless we come to it through what Jesus Christ says. The Scriptures, from Genesis to Revelation, are all revelations of Jesus Christ. The context of the Bible is Our Lord himself, and until we are rightly related to Him, the Bible is no more to us than an ordinary book. We cannot know the Holy Scriptures by intellectual exercises. The key to our understanding of the Bible is not our intelligence, but our personal relationship to Jesus Christ (cf. John 5:39–40). The New Testament was not written in order to prove that Jesus Christ is the Son of God; but written to confirm the faith of those who believe that Jesus Christ is the Son of God. There are no problems in the New Testament. We take much for granted, but nothing is ever ours until we have bought it by pain; a thing is worth just what it costs. We seem to lose everything when we go through the suffering of experience, but bit by bit we get it back. The Bible treats us as human life does—roughly.

"He wakeneth morning by morning, He wakeneth mine ear to hear as the learned." Do we allow ourselves to be arrested when we read the Holy Scriptures? The vital relationship of the Christian to the Bible is not that he worships the "letter," but that the Holy Spirit makes the words of the Bible "spirit and life" to him. When we are born from above (RV mg) the Bible becomes to us a universe of revelation facts whereby we feed our knowledge of Jesus Christ.

PRACTISING GODLINESS

Work out your own salvation. . . . For it is God which worketh in you both to will and to do of His good pleasure. Philippians 2:12–13

When Our Lord is presented to the conscience, the first thing conscience does is to rouse the will, and the will agrees with God always. You say—"I do not know whether my will is in agreement with God"—look to Jesus, and you will find that your will and your conscience are in agreement with God every time. The element in you which makes you say "I shan't" to God is something less profound than your will, it is perversity, or obstinacy, which are never in agreement with God. Obstinacy is a remnant of the disposition of sin, and it fights against that which a man's will and conscience indicate to be right. If we persist in being perverse and obstinate, we shall ultimately get to the place where the emotions of will and conscience are stultified.

Will is the essential element in the creation of man; sin is a perverse disposition that has entered into man. The profound thing in man is his will, not sin. Human nature as God made it was not sinful, and it was human nature as God made it that Our Lord took on Him. Obstinacy is an unintelligent "wodge" that refuses to be enlightened. It continually surprises you—"Why didn't I do that thing?" The only cure for obstinacy is to be blown up by dynamite, and the dynamite is obedience to the Holy Spirit. When the Holy Spirit comes into my human spirit, He makes me one with Jesus as He was one with His Father, it is an identification that raises the personality to its right place.

1. The Way of the Working of God
For it is God which worketh in you to will. . . .

Before a man is rightly related to God, his conscience may be a source of torture and distress to him, but when he is born again it becomes a source of joy and delight because he realises that not only are his will and his conscience in agreement with God, but that God's will *is* his will, and the life is as natural as breathing, it is a life of proving, or making out, what is "that good, and acceptable, and perfect, will of God."

Is it possible for human nature to get to such a standard that it can work out actually what God wills? God's word says it is. God not only gives me supernatural grace, but He is in me to will and to do of His good pleasure, and that means I can do all that God's will and my conscience indicate I should do. If I am a child of God, I realise not only that God is the source of my will, but that God is *in* me to will. I do not bring an opposed will to God's will, God's will *is* my will, and my natural choices are along the line of His will. Then I begin to understand that God engineers circumstances for me to do His will in them, not for me to lie down under them and give way to self-pity. We are called to do God's will here and now; are we doing it or are we murmuring—"Why should I be in these trying circumstances?" "Why should I have these disabilities?" That is murmuring. *Do* God's will. God not only expects me to do His will, but He is in me to do it.

Doing God's will is never hard. The only thing that is hard is *not* doing His will. All the forces of nature and of grace are at the back of the man who does God's will because in obedience we let God have His amazing way with us. If some of us were taken to be specimens of doing God's will, we should be sorry recommendations! We ought to be superabounding with joy and delight because God is working in us to will and to do of His good pleasure. The "goodest" thing there is is the will of God. God's will is hard only when it comes up against our stubbornness, then it is as cruel as a ploughshare and as devastating as an earthquake. God is merciless with the thing that tells against the relationship of a man to Himself. When once God does have His way, we are emancipated into the very life of God, i.e., into the life that Jesus lived. The only estimate of a consistent Christian character is that the life of the Son of God is being manifested in the bodily life.

2. The Way of the Working of the Godly
Work out your own salvation. . . .

If we are practising godliness, i.e., practising in our life day by day and week by week, working out what God works in, then we shall find when the crisis comes that our nature will stand by us, because we have disciplined and trained our nature to work out what God works in. We make what we practise second nature, and in the crisis as well as in the details of life we find that not only does God's grace stand by us, but also our own nature, we have made it an ally. If we have not been practising in the daily round, it is not God's grace that fails when the crisis comes, but our nature that deserts us, and we fail. God does not make our habits for us or do the practising—God alters our disposition and we are left to work out the new disposition He has put in, by practice and the forming of habits. If we have had a great illumination of God's grace, we have to go on to work out all that God has worked in; the danger is that we become stationary.

"Work out your own salvation. . . ." We have not to work out that which tells for our salvation, but to work out in the expression of our lives the salvation which God has worked in. What does my tongue say? What things do my ears like to listen to? What kind of bodily associates do I like to be with?

These things reveal whether we are working out the salvation God has worked in. The inward working is God's; the outward working is ours. In regeneration God puts us into line with Himself so that by the expression of that union in our bodily lives we may prove Whose we are. The first lesson to learn is that God works on the inside, and we have to work on the outside what He has wrought inside. The place for yielding and surrendering comes just there. We hinder God when we try to work on the inside. So many of us put prayer and consecration in place of God's work; we make ourselves the workers. God is the Worker, and He is after spirituality. God does nothing other than the profound; we have to do the practical. We have to see that we continually work out with concentration and care that which God has worked in, not *work* our own salvation, but *work it out*. We have to work out what God works in whilst we base resolutely in unshaken faith on the complete and perfect Redemption of the Lord Jesus Christ.

Our Portrait in Genesis

Oswald Chambers

INTRODUCTION

Source

The material in *Our Portrait in Genesis* is from lectures by Oswald Chambers to his Old Testament studies class at the Bible Training College,[1] London, from September 1914 to January 1915 and from April to July 1915.

Publication History

- As Articles: "Notes on Genesis," chapters 26 through 37, were published in the *BTC Journal*[2] between April 1941 and May 1943; "Notes on Genesis," chapters 1 through 6, were published between April 1951 and March 1952.

- As a book: *Our Portrait in Genesis* was first published in 1957. *Gems from Genesis* (1989) combined *Not Knowing Whither* (1934) and *Our Portrait in Genesis* in one volume. In the present collection, these books are presented as two separate volumes, the form in which they were originally published.

Chambers' lectures on Genesis were given in his Old Testament studies class at the Bible Training College between September 1914 and July 1915. Although the lectures covered Genesis chronologically, they were not published in order. The lectures on chapters 12 through 25 appeared in 1934 as *Not Knowing Whither,* Studies in the Life of Abraham. Twenty-three years elapsed before Mrs. Chambers published her notes from the other chapters as *Our Portrait in Genesis.*

Neither volume included Oswald's two lectures on Genesis 11, on the tower of Babel. It may have been simply Mrs. Chambers' editorial decision regarding material she considered of greatest interest to the reader. Or, she may have been unable to attend every class and did not have notes on chapter 11—during the eleven-month span of these lectures she had the care of their infant daughter, Kathleen,[3] and, as lady superintendent of the college, oversight of myriad daily details, as well as the taking of verbatim shorthand notes of everything her husband said.

Our Portrait in Genesis is the last book published by Mrs. Chambers from her shorthand notes. (*The Servant as His Lord,* published in 1959, combined four previously published booklets.) In 1960, Mrs. Chambers began to show evidence of severe mental illness, which virtually curtailed her work. She died in 1966.

---

1. Bible Training College (BTC): a residential school near Clapham Common in southwest London. Sponsored by the League of Prayer; operated from 1911 until it closed in July 1915 because of World War I. Oswald Chambers was principal and main teacher; Biddy Chambers, his wife, was lady superintendent.

2. *Bible Training Course Monthly Journal:* published from 1932 to 1952 by Mrs. Chambers, with help from David Lambert.

3. Kathleen Chambers (1913–1997): only child of Oswald and Biddy Chambers.

FOREWORD

Now these things were our examples. 1 Corinthians 10:6

We know nothing of the beginning of life on this planet Earth unless we accept the revealed facts recorded in the Bible. When these early stories are accepted as a true record of individual lives we can learn much about God's dealings with men and women in every age. There are flashes of light on God's relation to fallen Man which can touch a live nerve in a modern wrong-doer, and something of the Divine mercy is seen as it persists with perverse and misguided men.

Oswald Chambers brings out the moral significance of human conduct; the intrusion of sin into human affairs, and God's counter-move against sin and against the Satanic power behind the scenes. "Now these things were our examples," wrote the Apostle Paul in reference to some Old Testament incidents. This can be applied to Cain and Abel, to Noah, and to Abraham ("in these things they became figures of us"—RV margin) as we see the subtle working of sin in the unregenerate human heart; of craftiness and insincerity between man and man; of the law of retribution on the one hand or the due recompense on the other.

Here is a book for to-day. The Spirit of God is revealing the deep things of God, especially as they bear on the deep things of humanity. Above all we hear of the God of all grace, Who gave His Son to be a propitiation for our sins—yours and mine—"and not for ours only, but also for the whole world." I thank God for this gallery of portraits in Genesis, and for the Spirit's illumination through the expositor's instructed and clear-seeing mind.

David Lambert[4]

CONTENTS

4. David Lambert (1871–1961): Methodist minister; friend of Oswald and Biddy Chambers. Assisted Mrs. Chambers with OC publications from 1917 until his death in 1961.

BEGINNINGS
Genesis 1–2

In the beginning God . . . Genesis 1:1

I am Alpha and Omega, the beginning and the ending, saith the Lord, which is, and which was, and which is to come, the Almighty. Revelation 1:8

The Bible never argues or debates, it states revelation facts, and in order to understand these facts we are dependent entirely, not on intellectual curiosity, but on a relationship of faith. Our perception of Bible truth is of the nature of implicit vision granted by the Holy Spirit, and the remarkable thing about the Holy Spirit's illumination of Bible truth is that it commends itself as being the true interpretation to every child of God who is in the light.

Science (knowledge systematised) is man's intellectual effort to expound established facts, facts which all intelligent men accept as facts; it is his attempt to arrange these facts into some kind of unity which will not contradict the fundamental way man is made. When we are born again we come in contact with another domain of facts, viz., the Bible domain of revelation facts, and there must be an at-one-ment made between the two domains. Scientific "truth" is apt to be accepted readily while we are sceptical over revelations made by the Holy Spirit. Our tendency is to put truth into a dogma: Truth is a Person. "*I am . . . the Truth,*" said Jesus.

> *In the beginning God created the heaven and the earth. And the earth was without form, and void ["waste and void," RV]. (Genesis 1:1–2)*

> *Through faith we understand that the worlds were framed by the word of God, so that things which are seen were not made of things which do appear. (Hebrews 11:3)*

Fundamentally, chaos—the state of matter before it was reduced to order by the Creator—is not to be regarded necessarily as the result of Divine judgement but as the foundation of cosmos, like a painter's palette where he mixes his colours: he sees in it what you cannot. "Bairns and fools shouldn't see half-done work." We must bear in mind that the constructed world of man we see to-day is not the created world of God. The basis of man's life has had a formation put upon it which is not of God; what is needed is not the re-forming of the basis, but the removal of that which has been erected on the basis. If I build my life on the things which God did not form He will have to destroy them, shake them back into chaos. That is

why whenever a man, moral or immoral, sees for the first time the light of God in Jesus Christ it produces conviction of sin, and he cries out, "Depart from me; for I am a sinful man, O Lord." When the Holy Spirit comes into a man "his beauty is consumed away," the perfectly ordered completeness of his whole nature is broken up; then the Holy Spirit, brooding over the chaos that is produced, brings a word of God, and as that word is received and obeyed a new life is formed.

"And the Spirit of God moved upon ['was brooding upon,' RV mg] the face of the waters. And God said, Let there be light: and there was light." God's word creates, and creates by its own power. God speaks, and His word performs that which He sends it to accomplish (cf. Isaiah 55:11). "And God saw the light, that it was good": The matter of God's creation is a satisfaction to God, and when we come to know God by His Spirit we are as delighted with His creation as He is Himself. A child enjoys all that God has created, everything is wonderful to him.

As in the beginning God's word was the creative fiat, and that word's witness to itself satisfied God, so the work of Christ in a disciple witnesses to Him; it is the Living Word speaking the words, "the words that I speak unto you, they are spirit, and they are life." My value to God is that in obedience to His spoken word I present to Him in actuality His idea in sending it forth, God's word expressed in me becomes its own witness to God. God's word is clear and emphatic, and when we first hear it we are full of joy; then that word has to become its own witness and give Him satisfaction. The fanatic mistakes the vision which the word brings for its expression in actuality. Am I prepared to put God's word into its right place, into the matter of "me"? If I am, it will bring forth, not my idea, but God's idea, viz., the life according to God. It is not my faith laying hold of the word, but the life in the word laying hold on me and faith is as natural as breathing, and I say, "Why, bless God, I *know* that is true!" Strictly speaking, no seed germ contains in itself the maturer growth, it is the other forces acting outside it as well as its own inherent life that determines what it will be ultimately.

> *And God saw every thing that He had made, and, behold, it was very good. . . . And God blessed the seventh day, and hallowed it: because that in it He rested from all His work which God had created and made. (Genesis 1:31; 2:3 RV)*

Six days God laboured, *thinking* Creation, until, as He thought, so it was. On the seventh day God rested, not from fatigue, but because that work was finished which enabled Him to rest, immanent in all the laws of Nature, in constant manifestation of His overruling power, so that it were as easy for God to perform a miracle to-day as "in the beginning."

> And the Lord God formed man of the dust of the ground. (Genesis 2:7)

> The first man is of the earth, earthy. (1 Corinthians 15:47)

These verses refer to the fundamental nature of man, don't complicate their meaning by introducing the doctrine of sin at the moment. These two things, dust and Divinity, make up man. That he is made of the dust of the ground is man's glory, not his shame—it is only his shame in so far as he is a sinner, because in it he is to manifest the image of God. We are apt to think because we are "of the earth, earthy," that this is our humiliation, but it is not so; it is the very thing God's word makes most of. A doctrine which has insinuated itself right into the heart of Christianity and has a hold on it like an octopus, is the inveterate belief that sin is in matter, therefore as long as there is any "matter" about me there must be sin in me. If sin were in matter it would be untrue to say that Jesus Christ was "without sin" because He took on Him our flesh and blood, "becoming in [RV mg] the likeness of men." Sin does not belong to human nature as God designed it, it is abnormal, therefore to speak of sin being "eradicated," rooted up, is nonsense, it never was planted in. I have no business to say, "in Christ I am all right but in myself I am all wrong"; I have to see to it that everything related to my physical life is lived in harmony with and perfect obedience to the life of the Son of God in me.

The Originator and Maintainer of the new life imparted to us by the Redemption is Christ Himself, and our Lord's words in John 6:56 reveal His fathomless conception of that life—"he that eateth My flesh, and drinketh My blood, dwelleth in Me, and I in him." Before, the disposition of self-will ruled—You touch my flesh, and I hit you back; you touch my blood, and it boils in passion. Now, says Jesus, let the very corpuscles of your blood, every nerve and cell of your flesh, exhibit the new life which has been created in you. That life is exhibited in this bodily temple of the Holy Ghost "What? know ye not that your body is the temple of the Holy Ghost which is in you?"), it is a fleshly temple, not a spiritual one. The whole meaning of being born again and becoming identified with the death of Christ is that His life might be manifested in our mortal flesh. When we are born from above (RV mg) the life of the Son of God is born in us, and the perfection of that life enables us not only to "make out" (MOFFATT) what the will of God is, but to carry out His will in our natural human life.

TEMPTATION IN PARADISE
Genesis 3

There is something inconceivable to us in Adam's relationship to God, he saw God as simply as we see one another—"And they heard the voice ['sound,' RV mg] of the LORD God walking in the garden in the cool of the day" (Genesis 3:8). Until Adam fell, he was not *interested in* God, he was *one with* God in communion—a man is never interested in that which he is; when Adam fell, he became so appallingly interested in God that he was afraid of Him—"and the man and his wife hid themselves from the presence of the LORD God amongst the trees of the garden" (RV). Sin finds us severed from God and interested only in anything we can be told about Him, consequently there is an element of fear; when we become children of God, there is no fear. As long as a child has not done wrong he enjoys perfect freedom and confidence towards his parents, but let him disobey, and the one he disobeys becomes someone in whom he is interested, with an element of fear. Conscious piety springs from being interested in God—"I want to know whether I am right with God"; if you are right with God, you are so one with Him that you are unconscious of it, the relationship is deeper than consciousness because you are being disposed by the very nature of God.

When the Apostle Paul talks of a man sinning: *"Therefore, as through one man sin entered into the world" (RV),* remember who it is he refers to, viz., not to a being like you or me, but to the great Federal Head of the human race. Sin is not part of human nature as God designed it, it is extraneous. The Bible looks on sin, not as a disease, but as red-handed rebellion against the domination of the Creator. The essence of sin is—"I won't allow anybody to 'boss' me saving myself," and it may manifest itself in a morally good man as well as in a morally bad man. Sin has not to do with morality or immorality, it has to do with my claim to my right to myself, a deliberate and emphatic independence of God, though I veneer it over with Christian phraseology. If, as a saint, I allow this spirit to get back into me, I become the embodiment of heaven and hell in conflict.

"And the LORD God commanded the man, saying, Of every tree of the garden thou mayest freely eat: but of the tree of the knowledge of good and evil thou shalt not eat of it: *for in the day that thou eatest thereof thou shalt surely die*" (Genesis 2:16–17). "And the serpent said unto the woman, *Ye shall not surely die*" (3:4). Eve finds that what Satan told her is true, death does not strike them all at once: but its possibility has come in. Death has secretly begun. We transgress a law of God and expect an experience akin to death, but exactly the opposite happens, we feel enlarged, more broad-minded, more tolerant of evil, but we are more powerless; knowledge which comes from eating of the tree of the knowledge of good and evil, instead of instigating to action, paralyses.

"For the wages of sin is death"—man becomes subject to death, not because he is a finite being, but because of sin. Whenever a man touches sin, death is the inevitable result, it is the way God has constituted him; when he is "alive" in sin, he is "dead" to God. "And you did He quicken, when ye were dead through your trespasses and sins" (Ephesians 2:1 RV). What every human being inherits is not *punishment* for sin but the *disposition* of sin which entered into the world through one man, "and death through sin; and so death passed upon all men for that all have sinned." Death was not in God's purpose for man. When we are born again we have exactly the experience of going through death. "Thou canst not see My face: for man shall not see Me and live" (Exodus 33:20 RV)—and yet we do see God and live, but we only see God by going through death. I must die, die right out to my claim to my right to myself, and receive the gift of eternal life, which is "the gift of God . . . through Jesus Christ our Lord."

"And the man said, The woman whom Thou gavest to be with me, she gave me of the tree, and I did eat." Adam does not blame himself; neither does Eve blame herself: "And the woman said, The serpent beguiled me, and I did eat." They both evade the moral truth. Verbal truth is rarely moral truth. It takes a long time to bring me to the place where I will blame myself. Adam *admits,* but there is no con-

fession, he implies rather that God is to blame— "You should not have put me in a position where I could disobey; I don't deny I did wrong, but remember the extenuating circumstances, You shouldn't be so stern and holy." That is the first manifestation of the spirit of anarchy. The diabolical nature of sin is that it hates God, because when I am face to face with the holiness of God I know there is no escape, consequently there is nothing the natural heart of man hates like a holy God. We don't live deep enough down to realise this. "If only God would not be so holy as my conscience tells me He is." It is a mixed-up certainty, I know I am not right with God and I don't want to be—and yet I do. I will do anything rather than take the responsibility on myself for having done wrong: or if I do accept the responsibility, I defy God to readjust me, the one is as bad as the other. I either refuse to say I have sinned, or I admit I have sinned and refuse to let God save me; I won't allow God to have the last word; I have the last word and intend to stick to it. That is the attitude of the devil. "If we *confess* our sins, . . ." says the Apostle John. Whenever conviction of sin comes, out into the light with it, confess it, because when I realise the shame of it and accept God's forgiveness, there is an inwrought energy brought back in place of the energy which went out in the sin; with the majority of us that energy is lost, it does not come back in the fruits of repentance.

"And the LORD God said unto the serpent, . . . I will put enmity between thee and the woman, and between thy seed and her seed . . ." (Genesis 3:14–15). God does not deal with Satan direct, man must deal with Satan because man is responsible for his introduction. That is why God became Incarnate. Put it in any other way—why God could banish Satan in two seconds; but it is man who, through the Redemption, is to overcome Satan, and much more than overcome him, he is to do that which will exhibit the perfect fulfilment of this prophecy. Jesus Christ, the last Adam, took on Him our human form, and it is through His seed in that human form that Satan is to be overcome. "And the God of peace shall bruise Satan under your feet shortly" (Romans 16:20). Everything that Satan and sin have marred, God holds in an unimpaired state for every son of man who will come to Him by the way back which Jesus Christ has made.

MESSAGE OF GOD ON SIN
Genesis 4

1. "Sin Coucheth at the Door" (Genesis 4:7)

And it came to pass, when they were in the field, that Cain rose up against Abel his brother, and slew him. (v. 8)

No man can murder his brother who has not first murdered God in himself. Cain's crime is more than murdering his brother, it is a deeper crime within that crime, viz., the putting up of his whole nature against God, and, finally, accusing God for his punishment—"Of course, my sin is unpardonable if You are a holy God, but You are to blame for being a holy God."

"And the LORD said unto Cain, Why art thou wroth? and why is thy countenance fallen? If thou doest well, shalt thou not be accepted?" (vv. 6–7). These verses present God doing for Cain what He did for Adam and Eve—giving him a Divine opportunity for repentance. Remorse is never repentance, remorse is the rebellion of man's own pride which will not agree with God's judgement on sin but accuses God because He has made His laws too stern and holy. Adam and Eve *acknowledged* their sin although they never *confessed* it. Cain evades acknowledgement; first, he lies to God, then he becomes scornful of God—"And the LORD said unto Cain, Where is Abel thy brother? And he said, I know not: am I my brother's keeper?" Sin in Adam and Eve revealed itself as envy of God (see 3:5); in Cain it advances to envy of his brother—"And the LORD had respect unto Abel and to his offering: but unto Cain and to his offering He had not respect. And Cain was very wroth, and his countenance fell." Personal vindictive rage is the spirit of murder. ". . . not as Cain was of the evil one, and slew his brother. And wherefore slew he him? Because his works were evil, and his brother's righteous. . . . Whosoever hateth his brother is a murderer" (1 John 3:12, 15 RV).

"And He said, What hast thou done? the voice of thy brother's blood crieth unto Me from the ground" (Genesis 4:10). Murder may be done in a hundred and one ways, think of the number of voices that cry unto God to-day from men who have been murdered in civilised life. The cry of every murdered innocence, every perverted right, is in the ear of God, and in this sense the blood of Abel still speaks and will never be silenced.

2. The Solitariness of Guilt (Genesis 4:11–15)

And now cursed art thou from the ground . . . a fugitive and a wanderer shall thou be in the earth. (vv. 11–12 RV)

Beware of speaking of *reaction* when God says *retribution.* The man who has done wrong has such a guilty conscience that he imagines everything is against him: everything *is* against him—God is against him, every bit of earth is against him; he stands absolutely alone. Nothing associates itself with the sinner saving his sin. Once sin enters in, you are out of gear with God morally and with the universe physically.

And Cain said unto the LORD, My punishment is greater than I can bear. Behold, thou hast driven me out this day from the face of the ground; and from thy face shall I be hid; and I shall be a fugitive and a wanderer in the earth. (vv. 13–14 RV)

Cain takes God's punishment, which is His mercy, and perverts it into a penal decree making it impossible for him to come back. He entrenches himself in despair as a garment and spits back accusations against God—"See what You have done; I can't get back." When we are punished by God for wrong-doing our attitude is apt to be—"Oh well, it's no use trying to do any better, God has sent me from His presence, and I can't get back, I can do as I like now." Beware of making the despairing-sulk complaint, which is found in all of us, a threatening accusation against God. God can never forgive despair. The door is always open to God until I shut it. God never shuts it; I shut it, then I lose the key and say, "It's all up; whatever I do now God is entirely to blame."

Look for these things inside yourself; if you don't find them there, you are a humbug to find them outside you. Never disassociate yourself from anything any human being has ever done, that is the delusion of a moral lunatic. God will give you such a knowledge of yourself that you won't be able to say, "I don't know how anyone could do that," you will know humiliatingly before God how the vilest crime could be committed. You won't say, "But I could never do that"; you could. Any human being can do what any human being has ever done. When you see a criminal and feel instantly, "How horrible and vile that man is," it is a sure sign that the Lord is not in you; if He is in you, you will not only feel how horrible and vile he is, you will say, "But for God, I am that, and much worse." But don't use it as a pious phrase; if you don't mean it, never say it.

And Cain went out from the presence of the LORD, and dwelt in the land of Nod [That is, Wandering, RV mg]. (4:16)

Cain had no rest anywhere, the earth spurned him, therefore he went into the land of Wandering and constructed his own world. Men who have sinned and maintain themselves in their sin cannot endure themselves on God's earth, so they must make a world of their own and put it on God's earth. There is no place for sin on God's earth.

And he builded a city. (v. 17)

The first civilisation was founded by a murderer, and the whole basis of civilised life is a vast, complicated, more or less gilded-over system of murder. We find it more conducive to human welfare not to murder men outright, we do it by a system of competition. It is ingrained in our thinking that competition and rivalry are essential to the carrying on of civilised life; that is why Jesus Christ's statements seem wild and ridiculous. They are the statements either of a man or of God Incarnate. To carry out the Sermon on the Mount is frankly impossible to anyone but a fool, and who is the fool? The man who has been born again and who dares to carry out in his individual life the teaching of Jesus. And what will happen? The inevitable result, not the success he would otherwise have. A hard saying, but true.

THE EVOLUTION OF DEPRAVITY
Genesis 6:1–7

1. The Floods of Elemental Sin

And the LORD saw that the wickedness of man was great in the earth, and that every imagination of the thoughts of his heart was only evil continually. (Genesis 6:5 RV)

Depravity must be taken to mean much more than going wrong, it means rather to be so established in the wrong that the result is a real pleasure in it. There is an inspiration in choosing to do wrong, it means a simplification of the life. Immediately you choose to do wrong you are not only conscious that you are without excuse, you become brazenly fixed in the wrong; that is the characteristic of the devil. The revelation the Bible makes is not that men are getting worse, but that men are damnable—consequently they are saveable; the system of things he lives in may get worse, but a man can't be worse than damnable. If the mind of man persistently tries to remove the possibility of damnation he destroys the justice of God, destroys his own manhood, and leaves in its place an evolving animal-life to which God is not necessary.

Matthew 15:19 (RV): "For out of the heart come forth evil thoughts. . . ." (See also Jeremiah 17:9: "the heart is deceitful above all things, and desperately wicked: who can know it?") refers to the depravity of the human heart apart from God. The elemental fountain of depravity is there, the reason it is not manifested to my consciousness is either sheer ignorance by reason of a refusal to accept Jesus Christ's diagnosis, or because I have been saved and sanctified by God's mighty grace. According to our Lord "these things" are in the mother-heart, that deepest seat of moral character that lies below the conscious, the conscious thought, and still more the conscious purpose.

When God's Spirit comes in and opens from underneath our consciousness the abyss we are on, the only thing to do is to completely surrender to Him, and the abyss is closed for ever. It is entire rightness with Jesus Christ alone that prevents elemental depravity working in the heart and out into deeds. If I trust Jesus Christ's diagnosis and hand over the keeping of my heart to Him, I need never know in conscious experience what depravity is, but if I trust in my innocent ignorance I am likely one of these days to turn a corner and find that what He said is true. When the crisis comes and men find that what they took to be their innocent heart is really a sink of iniquity, they would be the first to say, "Why did not God tell us?" "Why were we not warned?" We are warned, perfectly clearly, in order that we need never go through the terrible experience of knowing the truth of what Jesus said—*"For from within, out of the heart of men, evil thoughts proceed . . ." (RV)*—that is the marvellous mercy of God. Jesus Christ's teaching never beats about the bush. Our stupidity is to believe only what we are conscious of and not the revelation He has made. Instead of its being a sign of good taste, it is a sign of shocking unbelief when men won't face what Jesus Christ has put so plainly, so unmistakably plainly, so brutally plainly at times, about the human heart. Again, let me urge you, never trust your innocent ignorance when Jesus Christ's statements contradict it.

Whenever any choice of ours is based on implicit disregard of God, we are depraved, and this possibility remains in every saint. "Now I am saved and sanctified all I choose is sure to be right"; not by any means. "All I think is sure to be right," not so; if our choices and our thinking do not spring from the basis of a determined recognition of God, we are depraved, no matter what our experience spiritually.

2. The Foundation of Eternal Salvation

And it repented the LORD *that He had made men on the earth, and it grieved Him at His heart. (Genesis 6:6)*

An unemotional love is inconceivable. Love for the good must involve displeasure and grief for the evil. God is not an almighty sultan reigning aloof, He is right in the throes of life, and it is there that emotion shows itself.

"And it repented the LORD. . . ." God does not repent like a man, He repents like God, that is, without change of plan or purpose. "God is not a man, that He should lie; neither the son of man, that He

should repent: hath He said, and shall He not do it?" (Numbers 23:19). If God were to say of any sin, "Oh well, he didn't mean it, I will let it go," that would be a change in God's purpose. If God overlooked one sin in me, He would cease to be God. The "repenting" of God in individual cases means that God remains true to His purpose and must mean my condemnation, and my condemnation causes Him grief and agony. It is not that God won't overlook wrong, it is that He cannot, His very love forbids it. When I am saved by God's almighty grace I realise that I am delivered completely from what He has condemned—and *that* is salvation; I don't palliate it any longer, but agree with God's verdict on it on the Cross. At the back of all the condemnation of God put "Calvary."

THE CALL OF THE FORLORN HOPE
Genesis 6:8–22

But Noah found grace in the eyes of the LORD. *. . . Noah was a righteous [*RV*] man, and perfect ["blameless," *RV* mg] in his generations: Noah walked with God. Genesis 6:8–9*

1. "Noah Found Grace"

Grace is the overflowing immeasurable favour of God; God cannot withhold, the only thing that keeps back His grace and favour is our sin and perversity.

"Noah walked with God." To walk with God means the perpetual realisation of the nature of faith, viz., that it must be tried or it is mere fancy; faith un-tried has no character-value for the individual. There is nothing akin to faith in the natural world, defiant pluck and courage is not faith; it is the *trial* of faith that is "much more precious than of gold," and the trial of faith is never without the essentials of temptation. It is to be questioned whether any child of God ever gets through the trial of his faith without at some stage being honour-stricken; what God does comes as a stinging blow, and he feels the suffering is not deserved, yet, like Job, he will neither listen to nor tell lies about God. Spiritual character is only made by standing loyal to God's character no matter what distress the trial of faith brings. The distress and agony the prophets experienced was the agony of believing God when everything that was happening contradicted what they proclaimed Him to be; there was nothing to prove that God was just and true, but everything to prove the opposite. The forlorn-hope aspect is the best, perhaps the only idea, for the godly in Time: all that has been built up on the basis of per-

sonal faith in God is contradicted by the immediate present, and it is the man who does not believe in God who has the safest, best time of it in the immediate present. The Bible is full of this attitude to things (e.g., Psalm 73). It is when we forget this aspect of godliness that we cease to walk with God and only pay court visits to Him; we cease to be His children. To walk with God means walking apart from ultimate godless reliances. There is no such thing as a *venture* of faith, only a determined *walk with God* by faith.

"And Noah begat three sons" (Genesis 6:10). Noah's sons are mentioned because in them the continuance of the human race is secure. If you are a snob you won't like the Bible genealogies because they have no respect for the aristocratic notion. Snobbery is the insistence on going far enough back—but not too far!

2. My Spirit Shall Not Strive with Man for Ever

*And God looked upon the earth, and, behold, it was corrupt; for all flesh had corrupted His way upon the earth. And God said unto Noah, . . . Behold, I will destroy them with the earth ["from the earth," *AV* mg]. (Genesis 6:12–13)*

It is God's long-suffering patience ultimately coming to the conclusion that He must let the full destruction of His righteousness have its way. "And God looked"— as if until now God had looked away, giving time through Enoch and Methuselah and Lamech, then suddenly He looks, and destruction swift and almighty comes and there is no reprieve, it means judgement, a final sentence. The pronouncement of coming doom is a combining of judgement and deliverance. When God's limit is reached He destroys the unsaveable and liberates the saveable; consequently judgement days are the great mercy of God because they separate between good and evil, between right and wrong. Salvation to be experimental in me is always a judgement inasmuch as it is concerned with some kind of separation. "The Cross condemns men to salvation." I remain indifferent to the Cross until I realise by the conviction of the Spirit of God that there are certain things in me which are damnable. I can always know the kind of disposition I have got by the sword God brings against me, I may plead and pray, but He is merciless, He saves me "so as by fire." When once I am willing to agree with God's condemnation in the Cross on those things, God in His infinite mercy, by bringing His judgement, saves. It is not judgement inaugurating salvation, but judgement that *is* salvation. The same with nations, and with the human race.

3. "Make Thee an Ark"

The ark stands as a reminder that nothing *is* until it is. Whenever we say a thing is impossible the reason is twofold—either our prejudices don't wish it to be, or we say it is too wonderful to be possible. From the building of the ark on, just make quite sure a thing is impossible, and God does it. God can only do the impossible. In the realm of our human possible we don't need God, common-sense is our God; we don't pray to God, we pray to an erection of our common-sense. It is God who is the Architect of salvation, therefore salvation is not a common-sense design; what we have to do is to get inside that salvation. If I put my faith in any erection of my own, my vows and decisions, my consecration, I am building something for myself; I must co-operate with God in His plan of salvation. Picture Noah sitting down and saying, "God has given me a wonderful plan, I will watch and see it grow"! *Thus did Noah; according to all that God commanded him* (Genesis 6:22 RV).

"And I, behold, I do bring the flood of waters upon the earth, to destroy all flesh . . ." (v. 17 RV). The initiative springs from the Mind of Almighty God, *"And I, behold, I do bring . . .";* it is not the natural consequence of cause and effect. "But I will establish My covenant with thee" (RV); with the new humanity after the flood. The "afterwards" of God is never disconnected with the "before" of His promise, and God's "afterwards" is more than the fulfilment of His promise, it is the re-expression of the fulfilment of the "before" of His purpose by my coming into living relationship with Him, if I will.

THE DARK OF FAITH
Genesis 7–9

And the flood was forty days upon the earth . . . and all the high mountains that were under the whole heaven were covered . . . : and Noah only was left, and they that were with him in the ark. And the waters prevailed upon the earth an hundred and fifty days. Genesis 7:17–24 (RV)

The ark itself is submerged, saving the top of it, no foothold anywhere. God removed hope from anywhere but Himself. That is a picture of the Kingdom of God in this dispensation, it appears to be completely submerged, yet those very things which look as if they were going to smash it are the things God uses to preserve it.

1. The Express Covenant

But I will establish My covenant with thee. (Genesis 6:18 RV)

"And God remembered Noah" (8:1). This does not mean that God had forgotten Noah; the remem-

brances of God are sure to those who will put their trust in Him. It is significant to note that whenever the Bible uses terms such as "repent," "remember," "forsake," "love," in connection with God, their human meaning does not apply, e.g., the love of God can only be illustrated by the character of God.

"And after the end of an hundred and fifty days the waters decreased . . ." (v. 3 RV). The "at last" of God is never an anticlimax, it always exceeds any possible human forecast. We must be careful never to compromise over any promise of God when by reason of human limitation there has been only a partial fulfilment. Such a compromise is easily detected whenever you feel, "Oh well, I suppose that is all God meant." Every word God has spoken will be absolutely fulfilled; to climb down from that confidence is to be disloyal to God. Beware, though, of inferring because no good word of God will fail, that I personally will necessarily partake in its fulfilment; I assuredly will not unless I have come into vital relationship with God by determined faith.

"And he stayed yet another seven days" (v. 10). Verses 10–14 indicate the prominent characteristic of Noah, viz., the humility of patience. Patience is not the same as endurance because the heart of endurance is frequently stoical, whereas the heart of patience is a blazing love that sees intuitively and waits God's time in perfect confidence. It is impossible to be patient and proud because pride weakens into lust, and lust is essentially impatient. Noah stands for all time as the embodiment of the patience of hope.

"And God spake unto Noah, saying, Go forth of the ark. . . . And Noah went forth . . ." (8:15–16, 18). As Noah went into the ark at the command of God, so at the command of God he goes forth of the ark. Had Noah been a fanatic, when God said, "Go forth of the ark," he would have said, "No, God said 'Come thou into the ark,' and this must be the voice of the devil." There is always the danger of becoming a fanatical adherent to what God has said instead of adhering to God who said it. Noah waited God's time to go out of the ark. The only way to wait for the Second Coming is to watch that you do what you should do so that *when* He comes is a matter of indifference. It is the attitude of a child, certain that God knows what He is about. When the Lord does come it will be as natural as breathing. God never does anything hysterical, and He never produces hysterics.

2. The Abiding Relationship *(Genesis 9:8–17)*
And God spake unto Noah, and to his sons with him, saying, and I, behold, I establish My covenant with you, and with your seed after you. . . . (Genesis 9:8–9)

God cannot do certain things without the co-operation of man. We continually ask, "Why doesn't God do the thing instead of waiting for me?" He cannot.

It is the same problem as the difference between God's order and His permissive will. His permissive will allows the devil to do his worst and allows me to sin as I choose, until I choose to resist the devil, quit sinning, and come to God in the right relationship of a covenant with Him through Jesus Christ. It is God's will that human beings should get into moral relationship with Him and His covenants are for that purpose. "Why doesn't God save me?" He has saved me, but I have not entered into relationship with Him. "Why doesn't God do this and that?" He has done it, the point is—will I step into covenant relationship with Him? All the great blessings of God are finished and complete, but they are not mine until I enter into relationship with Him on the basis of His covenant. Salvation is not an edict of God; salvation is something wrought out on the human plane through God becoming Man. Waiting for God is incarnate unbelief, it means I have no faith in Him, I want Him to do something in me that I may trust in that. God won't do it, because that is not the basis of the God-and-man relationship. Man has to go out of himself in his covenant with God as God goes out of Himself in His covenant with man. It is a question of faith in God, the rarest thing, we have faith only in our feelings. I don't believe God unless He will give me something in my hand whereby I may know I have it, then I say, "Now I believe." There is no faith there. *"Look unto Me, and be ye saved,"* God says. When I have really transacted business with God on His covenant and have let go entirely, there is no sense of merit, no human ingredient in it at all, but a complete, overwhelming sense of having been brought into union with God, and the whole thing is transfigured with peace and joy.

CHAPTERS 12–25 ARE DEALT WITH IN THE BOOK ENTITLED *NOT KNOWING WHITHER.*

ABIDING FACTORS
Genesis 26:1–12

1. Commencement of Destitution
And there was a famine in the land, beside the first famine that was in the days of Abraham. (Genesis 26:1)

Isaac's history commences with the same trial as Abraham's, viz., a famine in the land. Abraham acted according to his own wits, not according to his faith in God: "and Abram went down into Egypt to sojourn there; for the famine was sore in the land" (RV)—destitution in the very land of promise. Watch the desti-

tution of wits that follows quickly on the heels of a Divine revelation. Whenever you get a revelation from God you will be starved at once, starved, that is, in your wits, you can see no way out. Every time your wits compete with the worship of God you had better take a strong dose of Isaiah 30:15–16—"In returning and rest shall ye be saved; in quietness and in confidence shall be your strength: and ye would not." Beware of restlessness and wits persuading you that God has made a blunder—"God would never allow me to fall sick after giving me such a blessing"; but He has! No matter what revelations God has made to you, there will be destitution so far as the physical apprehension of things is concerned—God gives you a revelation that He will provide, then He provides nothing and you begin to realise that there is a famine, of food, or of clothes, or money, and your commonsense as well as other people's says, "Abandon your faith in God, do this, and that." Do it at your peril. Watch where destitution comes; if it comes on the heels of a time of quiet confidence in God, then thank Him for it and stay starving and He will bring a glorious issue.

2. Command in Trial

And the LORD appeared unto him, and said, Go not down into Egypt; dwell in the land which I shall tell thee of. (Genesis 26:2)

The command to Abraham was to depart; the command to Isaac is to remain. When the "Isaac" life of quietness and confidence in God is born of the "Abraham" life of strenuous separation, don't make any more separations, just be still, and know that God is God. Those who educate you in the things of God will be the first to pull you back when you obey the voice which came through them. God taught you the right thing through them, and now you are obeying they come in with their own wits and say, "Of course we didn't mean you should do that"; but God did. Beware of mixing quietness and confidence with other people's wits.

3. Confirmation of Truth *(Genesis 26:3–5)*

. . . because that Abraham obeyed My voice, and kept My charge, My commandments, My statutes, and My laws. (v. 5)

Isaac is promised Divine blessing and protection because of God's oath which He swore to Abraham on account of his obedience. Abraham's obedience was far from perfect, but its great characteristic was its unreservedness. Abandon in the profound sense is of infinitely more value than personal holiness. Personal holiness brings the attention to bear on my own whiteness, I dare not be indiscreet, or unreserved, I dare not do anything in case I incur a speck. God can't bless that sort of thing, it is as unlike His own character as could be. The holiness produced through the indwelling of His Son in me is a holiness which is never conscious of itself. There are some people in whom you cannot find a speck and yet they are not abundantly blessed of God, while others make grave indiscretions and get marvellously blessed; the reason being that the former have become devotees of personal holiness, conscientious to a degree; the latter are marked by abandonment to God. Whatever centres attention on anything other than our Lord Himself will always lead astray. The only way to be kept cleansed is by walking in the light, as God is in the light. Only as we walk in that light is the holiness of Jesus Christ not only imputed, but imparted, to us.

Abraham's aberrations sprang not from disobedience, but from trusting in his own wits. Directly God's command was made known to him, he obeyed; when there was no command he was inclined to trust in his wits, and that is where he went wrong. It is never right to do wrong in order that right may come, although it may seem justifiable from every standard saving one. In the long run you can never produce right by doing wrong, yet we will always try to do it unless we believe what the Bible says. If I tell a lie in order to bring about the right, I prove to my own conviction that I do not believe the One at the back of the universe is truthful. Judge everything in the light of Jesus Christ, who is The Truth, and you will never do the wrong thing however right it looks.

THE TENDER GRACE
Genesis 26:13–25

The only right a Christian has is the right to give up his rights. This is the tender grace which is usually looked upon as an exhibition of lack of gumption. The embarrassing thing about Christian graces is that immediately you imitate them they become nauseating, because conscious imitation implies an affected preference for certain qualities, and we produce frauds by a spurious piety. All the qualities of a godly life are characteristic of the life of God; you cannot imitate the life of God unless you have it, then the imitation is not conscious, but the unconscious manifestation of the real thing. "Pi" people try to produce the life of God by sheer imitation; they pretend to be sweet when really they are bitter. The life of God has no pretence, and when His life is in you, you do not pretend to feel sweet, you *are* sweet.

1. The External Greatness of Isaac

And the man waxed great, and grew more and more until he became very great. (Genesis 26:13 RV)

Isaac never became great in the way that Abraham did, his greatness is of a different order. Abraham was not only a great man of God, he was a great *man*. Some lives exhibit grand characteristics and yet there are curious defects; the only standard for judging the saint is Jesus Christ, not saintly qualities. Beware of the snare of taking people as types; no one is a type of anything, he may recall a particular type, but he is always something other than the type. If Abraham is taken as the type of a saint you get embarrassed because of the things in him which are not saintly. We are always inclined to remain true to our own ideas of a person, it does not matter what the facts are, we interpret all that he does according to our idea of him. If I accept you as an expression of my idea of you, I will be unjust to you as a fact; I make you either better or worse than you are, I never hit just "you" until I learn to accept facts as facts.

2. The Extraordinary Gentleness of Isaac
(Genesis 26:14–26)

And Isaac's servants digged in the valley, and found there a well of springing ["living," mg] water. And the herdsmen of Gerar strove with Isaac's herdsmen, saying, The water is ours: and he called the name of the well Esek ["Contention," mg]; because they contended with him. (vv. 19–20 RV)

The strife arose around a well of living water, and Isaac let them have it, that is, he refused to drink of the water of "Contention." Whenever a doctrinal well becomes "Esek," give it up; your life with God is more precious than proving you are right doctrinally. It is at the peril of your communion with God that you contend about a doctrine. "And they digged another well, and they strove for that also" (RV): and Isaac surrendered it, calling it Sitnah, that is, "Enmity" (RV mg). It is a great sign of grace not to break your heart because you cannot drink of the water of "Enmity." "And he removed from thence, and digged another well, and for that they strove not: and he called the name of it Rehoboth [that is, 'Broad places,' or 'Room,' RV mg]; and he said, For now the LORD hath made room for us, and we shall be fruitful in the land."

"And the LORD appeared unto him the same night, and said, I am the God of Abraham thy father: fear not, for I am with thee, and will bless thee, and multiply thy seed for My servant Abraham's sake." Isaac has come to a broad place and God appears to him, and for the first time the grand phrase, *"I am the God of Abraham"* appears. "And he builded an altar there, and called upon the name of the LORD."

When you stand up for another who has been grossly wronged and your stand to be of any avail must have the co-operation of the wronged one, there is nothing more maddening than to find that he is

without any resentment. That must have been the heart-breaking embarrassment to the disciples over our Lord; they had built up their own ideas as to how He was going to bring in His Kingdom and they were prepared to fight for Him, then they saw Jesus meekly give Himself up to the power of the world, He did nothing whatever to assert His rights. In the Christian life the problem arises not from the world, which says you are a fool, but from your friends who are prepared to stand up for you.

Inoffensiveness, which is one of the chief characteristics of Isaac, usually means to our natural minds a quality unsuited to a strong personality. We have to bear in mind that the life of our Lord portrayed just this characteristic of inoffensiveness: "As a lamb that is led to the slaughter, and as a sheep that before her shearers is dumb; yea, He opened not His mouth" (RV). "He was crucified through weakness," and, "we also are weak in Him." Anything to do with meekness and submissiveness is antagonistic to robust human nature. Our impatience gets beyond its limit because of the characteristics Jesus Christ insists upon: *"Learn of Me, for I am meek and lowly in heart...."* The natural heart builds on adventure, recklessness, independence, impulse; the characteristics God prizes are produced only in the son of sacrifice. Natural inoffensiveness may be the weakness of constitutional timidity; supernatural inoffensiveness is almighty strength scorning to use the weapons of the flesh. Inoffensiveness is self-control indwelt by the Holy Ghost, "the fruit of the Spirit is ... self-control [MOFFATT]."

3. The Eternal and the Haphazard (Genesis 26:28–33)

Let there now be an oath ... betwixt us and thee, and let us make a covenant with thee.... And he made them a feast and they did eat and drink. And they rose up betimes in the morning, and sware one to another.... And it came to pass the same day, that Isaac's servants came, and told him concerning the well which they had digged, and said unto him, We have found water. And he called it Shibah: therefore the name of the city is Beersheba [Well of the Oath] unto this day. (RV)

All the transactions entered into by both Abraham and Isaac, no matter how temporary or casual, were based on their relationship to God, that is, they used their wits in their worship of Him. This recognition of God began to be lost during Jacob's life, and the children of Israel went on ignoring it until they came to establish all their transactions on their own wits. Our Lord warns against taking an oath (see Matthew 5:33–35), because in the sight of God an oath means the recognition of God in the most temporary transaction. In the Old Testament, and in the record of the Resurrection, we find the temporary matter of eating and drinking put on the eternal foundation of relationship to God. The things which can be most easily ridiculed are the things that have most of God in them. A saint can be ridiculed because he sees haphazard happenings in the light of the eternal—"The Lord guided me here, and there." The fact that a man who is a fraud says the same thing as a saint is proof that he is counterfeiting something which is real. No actual fact has its right name unless you can worship God in it. Remember, whatever happens, God is there. It is easy to fix your mind on God in a lecture, but a different matter to fix your *mind* on Him when there is a war on.[5] You never get at God by blinking facts, but only by naming Him in the facts; whether they are devilish or not, say, "Lord, I thank Thee that Thou art here."

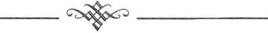

PLANS AND PROVIDENCE
Genesis 27

And Rebekah heard when Isaac spake to Esau his son. Genesis 27:5

Plans arise from the human "must"—the imperative demand of my own undisciplined nature which makes me feel, "I must do something; God is no use here." God rarely rebukes us for our impulsive plans because those plans work their own distress. Plans made apart from trusting God's wisdom are rotten. *Providence* arises from God's majesty. The wisdom of God can never be according to man's understanding, and in our regenerated lives while we are "climbing the slow ascensions" of our Heavenly Father's wisdom, He engineers our circumstances by His providence and puts within our inmost soul the childlike joy of confidence in Himself. It is always easier not to trust; if I can work the thing out for myself then I am not going to trust in God. I work out a plan whereby I say God must do the thing and I force His hand along certain lines, and when He does what I said I knew He would do, for an exhilarating moment I think I have made Him do it! Then I find I am to be punished for everything I tried to make Him do, though it looks as if my wrong had brought about His good. Beware of egging God on; possess your soul in patience.

Always beware when you can reasonably account to yourself for the action you are about to take, because the source of such clear reasoning is the enthroning of human understanding. It is this element in the personal life of a Christian that fights longest and to the last against the enthronement of Jesus Christ as Lord and Master. "Supposing I do say I will go to the foreign field, what about this, and that?" "I want a reasonable explanation." As long as you argue like that it is all up with devotion to Jesus Christ. He will have no influence over you until your plan is worked out because you have put your own wits on the throne. The reason we know so little about God's wisdom is that we will only trust him as far as we can work things out according to our own reasonable commonsense.

1. Sensitiveness to Divinely Shaped Ends (*Genesis 27:6–17*)
Now therefore, my son, obey my voice according to that which I command thee. . . . (v. 8)

Still waters run deep, but an able woman is deeper. Abraham made the supreme blunder of trying to help God fulfil His promise; Rebekah repeats the blunder. A woman with a sense of values in the end to be achieved cares nothing about herself in the accomplishing of that end. "And his mother said unto him, Upon me be thy curse, my son: only obey my voice. . . ." When a virtuous woman does wrong she does it with all the characteristic of her virtue transferred to the deception; Rebekah carried out her deception as though she were called and inspired of God to do it. In such a case the sin is not the outcome of impulse, but the deliberate perversion of integrity. In individual experience no one person is ever entirely to blame—"my father is to blame, my mother, my heredity," everybody and everything but myself. It is impossible for human wisdom to apportion the blame. Remember the one fact more which God alone knows.

2. Schemes of Discreet Expectations (*Genesis 27:18–25*)
And Rebekah took the goodly raiment of Esau her elder son, which were with her in the house, and put them upon Jacob her younger son. . . . (v. 15 RV)

This is the first pious lie enacted in the Bible. Rebekah's motive was born of the oracles of God— ". . . and the elder shall serve the younger" (25:23): her

---

5. a war on: World War I (1914–1918), underway when these lectures were given in 1914–1915.

act was entirely wrong; she enacted a lie in order to help God carry out His purpose. This is very different from the lie told for our own ends. Jacob's enunciation of the lie—"And Jacob said unto his father, I am Esau thy firstborn"—is expressive fundamentally, not of self-seeking, but of devotion to his mother, consequently there is no hesitation or bravado because he is not yet so conscious as he will be of what he is doing. Beware of obeying anyone else's obedience to God because it means you are shirking responsibility yourself.

"And his father Isaac said unto him, Come near now, and kiss me, my son. . . . Be lord over thy brethren, and let thy mother's sons bow down to thee": The whole lie is now enacted, and Jacob enters

into the fullness of the blessing. God fore-ordained that the blessing should come to Jacob, but it was not part of that fore-ordination that Jacob should enter into the blessing in the way he did. There are experiences in human lives which are not part of God's purpose, but the result of human perversity. Remember, trust in God does not mean that God will explain His solutions to us, it means that we are perfectly confident in God, and when we do see the solution we find it to be in accordance with all that Jesus Christ revealed of His character. It is nonsense to imagine that God expects me to discern all that is clear to His own mind, all He asks of me is to maintain perfect confidence in Himself. Faith springs from the indwelling of the life of God in me.

THE LONE QUEST
Genesis 28

1. The Discipline of the Unchanging Destiny (Genesis 28:1–9)

And God Almighty bless thee, . . . that thou mayest inherit the land of thy sojournings, which God gave unto Abraham. (vv. 3–4 RV)

Jacob's destiny had nothing to do with his personal character, but his personal character had everything to do with the desperate discipline he went through. God's destiny for a life will be fulfilled though the details of the fulfilment are determined by the individual. The kind of discipline Jacob went through was determined by his perversity. The "lone quest" is never pathetic unless, as in Jacob's case, it is mixed with cunning and sin in motive.

"Was not Esau Jacob's brother? saith the LORD: yet I loved Jacob; but Esau I hated" (Malachi 1:2–3 RV). In all implicit matters intuition is of more avail than logic. Naturally, we are inclined to love Esau and dislike Jacob. The most undesirable person in later life is often the one who was most desirable when young. A chaotic young life is always the most satisfactory. ". . . yet I loved Jacob"—God loves the man who needs Him. Esau was satisfied with what he was; Jacob wanted more than he was. Esau never saw visions, never wrestled with angels, although God was as near to him as to Jacob. Esau refused to sacrifice anything to the spiritual; he could never think of anything but the present. He was willing to sell the promise of the future for a mess of pottage, and thereby he wronged himself far more than Jacob did.

2. The Dream of the Unimagined Dignity (Genesis 28:10–22)

And he dreamed, and behold a ladder set up on the earth, and the top of it reached to heaven: and behold the angels of God ascending and descending on it. And, behold, the LORD stood above it ["beside him," mg], and said, I am the LORD, the God of Abraham thy father, and the God of Isaac: the land whereon thou liest, to thee will I give it, and to thy seed; and thy seed shall be as the dust of the earth, and thou shalt spread abroad to the west, and to the east, and to the north, and to the south: and in thee and in thy seed shall all the families of the earth be blessed. (vv. 12–14 RV)

Jacob's dream was a vision of the purpose of God for all the families of the earth. The destiny of the people known as "Israel" is forecast in this one lonely man. God did not *select* this people, He *elected* them. God created them from Abraham to be His servants until through them every nation came to know who Jehovah was. They mistook the election of God's purpose to be the election of God's favouritism, and the story of their distress is due to their determination to use themselves for purposes other than God's. To this day they survive miraculously, the reason for their survival is the purpose of God to be fulfilled through them. They can still wait, still see visions of God, and the time is coming when God's promise shall be fulfilled materialistically. The prophecies are frequently taken as pictures of spiritual blessings; they are much more than that.

"And he dreamed, and behold a ladder set up on the earth, and the top of it reached to heaven." The ladder symbolises communication between God and man. The only Being in whom communication with God was never broken is the Lord Jesus Christ, and His claim is that through the Redemption He can put every one of us in the place where communication with God can be re-established. Paul's phrase in Christ"—the Mystical Christ, not the Historic Christ—is a revelation of the Redemption at work on our behalf. If I am "in Christ" the angels of God are always ascending and descending on my behalf, and the voice that speaks is the voice of God. (Cf. John 1:51.) Beware of having a measuring-rod for the Almighty, of tying God up in His own laws. This pre-Incarnate vision of God was given to such a man as Jacob was. It is dangerous to have the idea that we merit these things; immediately prayer or devotion is taken as the ground of God's blessing we are off the track. Prayer and devotion are simply the evidence that we are on God's plan; to be devoid of any sense of ill-being spiritually is a sign that we are not on God's plan. Jacob is the man who represents life as it is. The world is not made up of saints or of devils, but of people like you and me, and our real home is at the foot of the ladder with Jacob. Never say that God intends a man to have a domain of dreaming, mighty visions of God, and at the same time be dead towards God in his actual life. Jesus Christ claims that He can make the real and the actual one, as they were in His own life. When the vision comes it does not come to the "Esau" type of man, he is so thick-hided that to talk to him about the nearness of God's presence is absurd, there is no meaning in it—that is absolutely true, there *is* no meaning in it, until he gets to the desolate spot. We cling to the certainty that the rational common sense life is the right one; Jesus Christ stands for the fact that a life based on the Redemption is the only right one, consequently when a man shifts from the one to the other there is a period of desolation. Remember, there is a vast moral distance between Beth-el and Peniel.

3. The Dedication of the Unparalleled Dawn (Genesis 28:16–20)

And Jacob awaked out of his sleep, and he said, Surely the LORD is in this place; and I knew it not. And he was afraid, and said, How dreadful is this place! this is none other but the house of God, and this is the gate of heaven. (vv. 16–17)

"This place" means just where it is not within the bounds of imagination to infer that God would be. "And he called the name of that place Beth-el ['The house of God,' RV mg]" because there God was revealed unto him. "Every house of God is a gate of heaven where the impossible and the miraculous become the natural breath." There is always an amazed surprise when we find what God brings with Him when He comes, He brings everything! (John 14:23).

It is in the dark night of the soul that the realisation of God's presence breaks upon us: we never see God as long as, like Esau, we are perfectly satisfied with what we are. When I am certain that "in me ... dwelleth no good thing," I begin to experience the miracle of seeing and hearing, not according to my senses, but according to the way the Holy Spirit interprets the word of God to me. Any number of people are happy without God, because happiness depends on not too profound an understanding of things; "the god of this world hath blinded their minds['thoughts,' RV mg]" (2 Corinthians 4:4). When the revelation of God's presence does come, it comes to those who are where Jacob was, in downright need and depression, knowing there is no help anywhere saving in God. As long as there is any vestige of human sufficiency it is all up with the message of God as far as we are concerned.

When we come to consider it, the phrase, "the God of Jacob," is the greatest possible inspiration; it has in it the whole meaning of the Gospel of Jesus Christ, who said ". . . for I came not to call the righteous, but sinners." Had we been left with such phrases as "the God of Joseph," or "the God of Daniel," it would have spelt hopeless despair for most of us; but "the God of Jacob" means "God is *my* God," the God not only of the noble character, but of the sneak. From the sneak to entire sanctification is the miracle of the grace of God.

LOVE
Genesis 29

Love, more than any other experience in life, reveals the shallowness and the profundity, the hypocrisy and the nobility, of human nature. In dealing with all implicit things, such as love, there is a danger of being sentimentally consistent to a doctrine or an idea while the actual life is ignored; we forget that we have to live in this world as human beings. Consistency in doctrine ought to work out into expression in actual life, otherwise it produces the humbug in us; we have the jargon of the real thing, but actually we are not there. Anything that makes a man keep up a posture is not real; e.g., it is not true to say that an understanding of the doctrine of sanctification will lead you into the experience: doctrinal exposition comes after the experience in order to bring the actual life into perfect harmony with the marvel of the work of God's grace.

1. God and the Cult of the Passing Moment *(Genesis 29:1–7)*
Then Jacob went on his journey, and came to the land of the children of the east. . . . (RV)

The true worship of God can only be maintained when the passing moments are seen as occurring in God's order. If you try to forecast the way God will work you will get into a muddle; live the life of a child and you will find that every haphazard occasion fits into God's order. "The cult of the passing moment" means that you resolutely believe that "All things work together for good to them that love God, to them who are the called according to His purpose." Don't be your own god in these matters; be concentrated, not on the haphazard, but on God, who comes to you through the haphazard. Jacob is realising God's order in the midst of the haphazard circumstances in which he finds himself; in the coming of Rachel he suddenly meets God.

2. God and the Cult of the Passionate Moment *(Genesis 29:8–14)*
And Jacob kissed Rachel, and lifted up his voice, and wept. (Genesis 29:11)

There is no safer guide in the matter of human love than the Bible, particularly the Old Testament. Solomon says a penetrating thing—"I adjure you, . . . that ye stir not up, nor awaken love, until it please"—before the time (The Song of Songs 2:7 RV), and woe be to any such awakener. Many a man has awakened love before the time, and has reaped hell into the bargain. Love is awakened before the time whenever a man or woman ignores the worship of God and becomes a mere creature of impulsive passions.

God cannot guard the natural heart that does not worship Him, it is at the mercy of every vagrant passion stirred by the nearness of another. Unless you are guarded by God in your human relationships you will get a multitude of haphazard affairs that God is not in; there are the same haphazard affairs in the life of a child of God, but God is in them. Beware of not worshipping God in your emotional history. Watch your fancies and your friends, heed who you love and who loves you, and you will be saved from many a pitfall.

3. God and the Cult of the Parenthetic Moment *(Genesis 29:15–20)*
And Jacob loved Rachel; and he said, I will serve thee seven years for Rachel. (v. 18)

Jacob was what he was—mean, yet in the most mixed human life there may come a parenthesis which is pure and unsullied. Mark well the parentheses God puts into your human life. There is not a passage in the whole of the Bible to equal verse 20 for a description of pure human love: "And Jacob served seven years for Rachel, and they seemed unto him but a few days, for the love he had to her." Sacrifice for love is never conscious; sacrifice for duty always has margins of distress. The nature of love is to give, not to receive. Talk to a lover about giving up anything, and he doesn't begin to understand you!

Love is not blind; love sees a great deal more than the actual, it sees the ideal in the actual, consequently the actual is transfigured by the ideal. That is a different thing from "halo-slinging," which means you have your own idea about other people and expect them to live up to it, and then when they don't, you blame them. An ideal is not a halo, it is reality made clear to you by intuition. If you love someone you are not blind to his defects but you see the ideal which exactly fits that one. God sees all our crudities and defects, but He also sees the ideal for us; He sees "every man perfect in Christ Jesus," consequently He is infinitely patient.

4. God and the Cult of the Paralleled Measure *(Genesis 29:25–30)*
What is this thou hast done unto me? did not I serve with thee for Rachel? wherefore then hast thou beguiled me? (v. 25)

The humour of God is sometimes tragic; He engineers across our path the kind of people who exhibit to us our own characteristics—not very flattering, is it? In this chapter we see the beguiler beguiled; Jacob was deceived, but he also was a deceiver. We say, "I wonder why this should happen to me?" Remember the Apostle Paul's words: "For he that doeth wrong shall receive again for the wrong ['receive again the wrong,' RV mg] that he hath done: and there is no respect of persons" (Colossians 3:25).

DEGENERATION

Genesis 29–30

Degeneration and backsliding are by no means one and the same. Degeneration begins in almost imperceptible ways; backsliding in the Scriptural use of the term is a distinct forsaking of what I know of God and a deliberate substitution of something other (cf. Jeremiah 2:13).

A point on which we need to be alert is that the presence of the life of the Son of God in us does not alter our human nature; God does remove the disposition of sin, but He demands of us that our human nature puts on the "new man," and no longer fashions itself according to its former natural desires. This is what the Apostle Paul means by his use of the term "mortify" (Colossians 3:5), viz., destroy by neglect. The spiritual application is that the natural must be sacrificed in order that it may be turned into the spiritual. This law works all through. Esau stands for the natural life refusing to obey. If I maintain my right to my natural self I will begin to degenerate and get out of God's purpose. What happens in my personal life when I am born from above (RV mg) is that the Son of God is born in me, then comes in the law of the sacrifice of the natural to the spiritual, and the possibility of degeneration. If I refuse to sacrifice the natural, the God-life in me is killed.

1. When the Reward of Sin Is More Sinfulness

Chapter 29 records the retribution Jacob experienced for his own deceitfulness—Jacob impersonates Esau; Laban makes Leah impersonate Rachel. Beware what you permit in your relationships because you will "be-done-by-as-you-did," and the reason for it is God. The inexorable law is stated in Matthew 7—"For with what judgement ye judge, ye shall be judged: and with what measure ye mete, it shall be measured to you again." The wrong began with Abraham and Hagar, and it works straight through "the maddening maze of things"; the only line of extrication is through the Redemption. It is one thing to deceive other people, but you have to get up very early if you want to take in God!

2. Where the Ruin of Sanctity Is Mixed Sanctity *(Genesis 30:1–24)*

Jacob's home becomes a place of friction—no man ever gave his heart to two women—yet gleams of joy come to it, every child is regarded by the Hebrew as a gift of God, and the naming of Jacob's children reveals how closely men felt God to be bound up with their history.

If you indulge in practices which the Holy Spirit condemns, or in imaginations you have no business to indulge in, the appalling lash of ruined sanctity is that my sin finds *me* out. "If I could only fling the whole thing overboard!"—but you cannot. God has made the way of transgressors hell on earth. The first mark of degeneration is to deem a wrong state permissible, and then propose it as a condition of sanctity. We only turn in disgust from the details in God's Book when we forget who we are. Nothing has ever been done by human nature that any member of the human family may not be trapped into doing; the only safeguard is to keep in the light as God is in the light.

3. Where Retribution of Selfishness Turns to Spite *(Genesis 30:25–43)*

Jacob has been robbed, and now he retaliates; his aim is to enrich himself at Laban's expense and he succeeds absolutely—"And the man increased exceedingly, and had large flocks, and maidservants and menservants, and camels and asses" (v. 43 RV). Beware of the inspiration that springs from impulse, because impulse enthrones self-lordship as God. My impulses can never be disciplined by anyone saving myself, not even by God. If my impulses are domineered over by somebody else, that one will find sooner or later that he or she has sat on a safety valve—always a risky thing to do. Unless I discipline my impulses they will ruin me, no matter how generous they may be. The revelation to ourselves in studying other people's lives ought to make us eager to realise that "in me . . . dwelleth no good thing."

THE CRISIS IN CIRCUMSTANCES
Genesis 31

And the L<small>ORD</small> *said unto Jacob, Return to the land of thy fathers. Genesis 31:3*

No man's destiny is made for him, each man makes his own. Fatalism is the deification of moral cowardice which arises from a refusal to accept the responsibility for choosing either of the two destined ends for the human race—salvation or damnation. The power of individual choice is the secret of human responsibility. I can choose which line I will go on, but I have no power to alter the destination of that line once I have taken it—yet I always have the power to get off one line on to the other.

1. Confusion in Consecration *(Genesis 31:4–10)*

Jacob would seem to think that to do things openly when you might do them obscurely is a sign of feeble intelligence; all his outwitting has not taught him wisdom. The apparent piece of humbug which these verses record is not really humbug at all, it is a repetition of what happened in the matter of the birthright, in which Isaac and Rebekah, Jacob and Esau, all did wrong, and yet out of it came the fulfilment of God's purpose. The blunder lies in trying to help God fulfil His own word. God's word will be fulfilled, but if I reach its fulfilment through committing sin, God must crush me in chastisement; the chastisement has no part in His order, it comes in under His permissive will.

2. Call To Conscience *(Genesis 31:11–13)*

Jacob has brought back to him his dream at Beth-el when God appeared to him and spoke to him—"I am the God of Beth-el, where thou anointedst a pillar, where thou vowedst a vow unto Me; now arise, get thee out from this land, and return unto the land of thy nativity" (RV). Jacob's character exhibits human nature as it is better than any other Bible character— the high mountain peaks and the cesspools, they all come out. No man is so bad but that he is good enough to know he is bad. Beware of insisting on attainments which are impossible to human nature before the possibilities of the Divine nature have come in—demanding of human nature that it should be what it never can be. Jesus Christ died for the *ungodly*, for the *weak*, for *sinners;* if we put the fruits

of the Redemption as the reason for God's forgiveness, we belittle His salvation. God's call comes, not to human nature, but to conscience, and when a man obeys what God reveals to a thoroughly awakened conscience, then begins the possibility in human nature of the expression of the life of God. To experience conviction of sin is not a cause for misgiving, but an occasion for understanding the impossible thing God has done in the Redemption.

3. Calamity in Estrangement *(Genesis 31:14–35)*
So he fled with all that he had. . . . (v. 21)

Jacob's flight and its attendant perplexities is the best unveiling of the unutterable muddle the most acute human wisdom can get into, and serves as another indication of the truth of the revelation that "A man's goings are of the L<small>ORD</small>; how then can man understand his way?" (RV). Crises reveal that we don't believe this, the only God we worship is our own wits. All through, a personal crisis ought to serve as an occasion for revealing the fact that God reigns, as well as compelling us to know our own character. You may think yourself to be generous and noble until a crisis comes, and you suddenly find you are a cad and a coward; no one else finds it out, but you do. To be found out by yourself is a terrible thing.

"Now Rachel had taken the teraphim . . ." (Genesis 31:34 RV). In the centre of the family is Rachel, and she outwits Laban and Jacob by stealing the household gods. "And Rachel stole the teraphim that were her father's" (v. 19 RV). There are only two beings a woman is not too much for, one is God, the other is the devil. A mascot is a talisman of some sort the presence of which is supposed to bring good luck. The persistence of the superstitious element is one of the most indelible stains on the character of otherwise good people, and it abounds in our own day. A re-awakening of superstition always follows on the heels of gross materialism in personal and in national life. When once the "mascot" tendency is allowed in the temple of the Holy Ghost, spiritual muddle-headedness is sure to result. Beware of excusing spiritual muddle-headedness in yourself; if it is not produced by the "Jacob" reserve, it is produced by the "Rachel" wit, and the only way out of the muddle is to walk in the light.

MAHANAIM
Genesis 32

Of all the Bible characters Jacob ever remains the best example of the recipient of God's life and power, simply because of the appalling mixture of the good and the bad, the noble and the ignoble in him. His nobility is never far to seek in the midst of it all. We have the notion that it is only when we are pure and holy that God will appear to us; that God's blessing is a sign that we are right with Him. Neither notion is true. Our Lord took care to say that God makes His sun to rise on the evil and on the good, and sends His rain on the just and on the unjust. God's blessings are not to be taken as an indication of the integrity of the character blessed, yet on the other hand the discernment of God's character is determined entirely by the individual character of the person estimating God. "With the merciful Thou wilt show Thyself merciful" (Psalm 18:25). The way I will discern God's character is determined by my own character. God remains true to His character, and as I grow in integrity I discern Him. Jacob's undeservedness, and the fact that God continually blesses him, are brought out very clearly all through his life.

1. The Venture of the Misgiving Way
And Jacob went on his way . . .

A sense of personal unworthiness is frequently the reaction of overweening conceit; genuine unworthiness has no conscious interest in itself. A genuinely unworthy nature is always possessed of sufficient nobility to face the inevitable—"And Jacob went on his way," that is the noble streak. The study of Jacob under the light of the Spirit of God is not exhilarating, but it is a wholesome cure for spiritual swagger. Whenever you get a real dose of your own unworthiness you are never conscious of it because you are so certain you are unworthy that you have the courage of despair. The first thing the Spirit of God does when He comes in is to bring this sense of unworthiness. Most of us suspend judgement about ourselves, we find reasons for not accusing ourselves entirely, consequently when we find anything so definite and intense as the Bible revelation we are apt to say it exaggerates, until we are smitten with the knowledge of what we are like in God's sight. If you can come to God without a feeling of your own contemptibility it is questionable whether you have ever come. The most humiliating thing in self-examination is that the passion of indignation we indulge in regarding others is the measure of our self detection (see Romans 2:1).

2. The Vision of the Ministering Witnesses
. . . and the angels of God met him. (Genesis 32:1)

Isn't that indiscreet of God! The appearances of God are not so much a testimony to the goodness of the individual as the revelation of God Himself. Every estimate of God must be brought to the standard of the revelation made of Him by our Lord. The appearance of the angels of God is apt to be looked upon as the result of disordered nerves, but it is only when external conditions are hopeless to the human outlook that we are in a fit state to perceive the revelation. We are content where we are as long as things have not got to the hopeless condition, and when we do get there we are sentimentally interested in our own pathos—"Whatever shall I do when this, or that, happens?" When it does happen, you will see the angels of God. There is no such thing as dull despair anywhere in the Bible, there is tragedy of the most appalling order, but an equally amazing hopefulness—always a door deeper down than hell which opens into heaven.

3. The Voice of the Mastering Wonder
And Jacob said when he saw them, This is God's host: and he called the name of that place Mahanaim. (Genesis 32:2 RV)

The sight of the two hosts, the earthly and the heavenly, is a fitting revelation of God's rule and government in this order of things. The reason so few of us see the hosts of God is that we have never let go of things as they are, never let go of our small parochial notions, of the sense of our own whiteness and respectability, consequently there is no room for God at all. Beware of the abortion of God's grace which prostitutes the Holy Spirit to the personal private use of my own whiteness, instead of allowing God by His majestic grace to keep me loyal to His character in spite of everything that transpires. Faith in God does not mean that He presents me as a museum specimen, but it does mean that however ignoble I may feel, I remain true to God's character no matter what perplexities may rage.

God's angelic hosts are like His visible mercies, countless. We are economically drunk nowadays, everybody is an economist, consequently we imagine that God is economical. Think of God in Creation! Think of the number of trees and blades of grass and flowers, the extravagant wealth of beauty no one ever sees! Think of the sunrises and sunsets we never look at! God is lavish in every degree. For God's sake, don't be economical, be God's child.

MISGIVING
Genesis 32:3–21

Misgiving is the pathetic poem of the whole of human life in a word; it signifies the destruction of confidence. Many things will destroy confidence; as in the case of Jacob, cunning and sin will do it, or cowardice; but in every experience of misgiving there is an element which it is difficult to define, and the shallow element is the most difficult. "I can't understand why I have no confidence in God"; the reason may be a matter of digestion, not enough fresh air, or sleep, too much tea—something slight. It is the shallow things that put us wrong much more quickly than the big things. The great object of the enemy of our souls is to make us fling away our confidence in God; to do this is nothing less than spiritual suicide. When we experience misgiving because we have sinned there is never any ambiguity as to its cause, the Holy Spirit brings conviction home like a lightning flash.

1. The Appointment of the Messengers
(Genesis 32:3–5)
And Jacob sent messengers before him to Esau his brother. (v. 3)

Jacob has had a vision of God's power, but now he begins to put prudent methods on foot in case God should be obliged to let him down on account of his cunning. We have all got "Uriah Heep"[6] tucked away somewhere, his original form is found in Jacob. Every one of us has the possibility of every type of meanness any human being has ever exhibited; not to believe this is to live in a fool's paradise.

2. The Apprehension of the Manœuvres
(Genesis 32:6–8)
Then Jacob was greatly afraid and was distressed. (v. 7 RV)

Jacob has still no intention of confessing his wrong, and his apprehensiveness on this account leads him to manœuvre. Beware of the "yes-but," of putting your prudence-crutch under the purpose of God when you find His engineering of things has nearly unearthed your own little bag of tricks. Whenever you debate with a promise of God, watch how you begin to manœuvre by your own prudence—but you can't sleep at night. Whenever you manœuvre it keeps up a fer-

ment because it indicates a determination not to confess where you know you are wrong, and when we experience misgiving on account of wrong-doing which we do not intend to confess we are always inclined to put a crutch under God's promise—"Now I see how I can make atonement for my wrong-doing." Nothing can act as an atonement for wrong saving an absolutely clean confession to God. To walk in the light with nothing folded up is our conscientious part, then God will do the rest.

3. The Appeal of Misgiving *(Genesis 32:9–12)*
Deliver me, I pray Thee, from the hand of my brother, from the hand of Esau: for I fear him. . . . (v. 11)

Prayer in distress dredges the soul (cf. Psalm 107). It is a good thing to keep a note of the things you prayed about when you were in distress. We remain ignorant of ourselves because we do not keep a spiritual autobiography. Jacob's misgivings while in the attitude of prayer arise from the fact that while there is that in him which causes him to obey God, he is apprehensive lest God should punish him for his wrong-doing; he has to come to the place where he willingly confesses his guilt before God. Remember. Jacob did not turn back; he was cunning and crafty, but he was not a coward. There was not a strand of the physical coward in Jacob, but he was a moral coward by reason of his guilty conscience. His misgivings arose from his misdeeds.

Beware of having plans in your petitions before God; they are the most fruitful source of misgiving. If you pray along the line of your plans misgivings are sure to come, and if the misgivings are not heeded you will pervert God's purpose in the very thing which was begun at His bidding. God begins a work by the inspiration of the Holy Spirit for His own ends entirely and we get caught up into His purpose for that thing, then we begin to introduce our own plans—"I want *this* to produce *that,*" and we storm the throne of God along that line; and the first thing God does is *not* to do it, and we say, "That must be the devil." Beware of making God an item, even the principal item, in your programme. God's ways are curiously abrupt with programmes, He seems to delight in breaking them up.

---

6. Uriah Heep: character in Charles Dickens's novel *David Copperfield;* a "detestable sneak" who hid his ambition behind a false humility.

4. The Atonement for Misdeeds *(Genesis 32:13–21)*

And he lodged there that night: and took of that which he had with him a present for Esau his brother. (v. 13 RV)

Watch your motive for giving presents; it is a good way of discerning what a mean sneak you are capable of being. The giving of presents is one of the touch stones of character. If your relationship with God is not right in your present-giving, you will find there is an abomination of self-interest in it somewhere, even though you do it out of a warm-hearted impulse; there is a serpent-insinuation in it. It creeps into all our charity unless the life is right with God.

The cunning way in which the present is made to Esau is obvious, and yet Jacob is getting near the place where "Peniel" is possible. Restitution in some form or other is as certain as that God is on His throne. Restitution on the human plane is the evidence that it was God who designed human nature. Watch the almost uncanny accuracy with which the Holy Spirit will bring a thing back—"Therefore if thou bring thy gift to the altar, and there rememberest," the Spirit of God brings it to you direct, ". . . go thy way; first be reconciled to thy brother." Beware how you deal with yourself when God is educating you down to the scruple,[7] it is nearly always some ridiculously small thing that keeps you from getting through to God. Human nature looks for something big, yet it is some little thing, but behind it is the disposition of my prideful right to myself. "First go. . . ."

PENIEL
Genesis 32:22–32

Peniel means "face of God," and the word to Moses stands—"And He said, Thou canst not see My face: for there shall no man see Me, and live" (Exodus 33:20). This gives peculiar force to Jacob's words, "I have seen God face to face, and my life is preserved," for Jacob did see God face to face, and he did die, so profound a death that God gave him a new name. "Thy name shall be called no more Jacob, but Israel."

That is always the test of the reality of sanctification, not so much that I have received something, but that I have ceased to be my old self. Through disillusionment and shattering Jacob comes out on God's side with a changed name; we drag the purpose of God through our own plans and change His name. We have to learn to distinguish between the impression made on us by a vision, and identification with the One who gave us the vision. The love of God and His forgiveness are the first things we experience, we are not prepared as yet to recognise His other attributes of holiness and justice because that will mean death to everything that does not partake of God's nature.

1. The Struggle of Anguish

And Jacob was left alone. (Genesis 32:24)

This phrase is significant because in his loneliness Jacob goes through the decisive struggle of his life. We are dealing in this chapter with Jacob the giant, not with the mean man. ". . . and there wrestled a man with him until the breaking of the day." Jacob tried to strangle the answer to his own prayer; his wrestling represents the human fighting with God. The nobler ones in God's sight are those who do not struggle but go through without demur. Abraham did not wrestle, neither did Isaac; Jacob struggles for everything. If a man has difficulty in getting through to God we are apt to imagine it is an indication of a fine character, whereas the opposite is true; he is refusing to yield and is kicking, and the only thing God can do is to cripple him. The characteristics exhibited by Jacob are those of Peter before Pentecost, of Saul of Tarsus before his conversion, a mixture of the dastardly and the heroic, the mean and the noble, all jumbled up. Jacob's wrestling is a profounder thing than the meeting with his brother, there is not one word about Esau in all that follows. Jacob is face to face with his need to acknowledge God and be blessed by Him.

2. The Surrender of All

I will not let Thee go, except Thou bless me. (v. 26)

This is the picture of Jacob's full renunciation. When the supreme crisis is reached in a mixed soul like Jacob something must die, either self-realisation or God. To the simpler nature the crisis need not come at all, but to the mean, the ambitious, and the proud, it must come, and God does not show Himself as gentleness, but as adamant. It means death without the slightest

---

7. down to the scruple: to the smallest item.

hope of resurrection. What it is that goes to death depends on me. Am I willing to let the wrong in me that cannot dwell with God go to death, or willing to let the life of God die out in me? The crisis may be reached in an apparently placid commonplace life, there may be no external sign of it, but there is an internal crumbling away from all that is pure and holy. Jacob was not like that, he did not refuse to go through the inward struggle of his own nature against the blazing holiness of God.

3. The Solicitation of Appeal

And He said unto him, what is thy name? And he said, Jacob. (v. 27)

The confession has to be made: That is my name—supplanter; sneak; there is no palliation. Jacob had to get to the place where he willingly confesses before God the whole guilt of usurping the birthright. This is full and profound and agonising repentance. "And he said, Thy name shall be called no more Jacob, but Israel: for thou hast striven with God and with men, and hast prevailed" (RV). The warrior of God is not the man of muscle and a strong jaw, but the man of un-utterable weakness, the man who knows he has not any power; Jacob is no longer strong in himself, he

is strong only in God, his life is no longer marked by striving, but by reliance on God. You cannot imitate reliance on God.

> *Not by wrestling, but by clinging*
> *Shall we be most blest;*
> . . . .
> *Unconditional surrender*
> *Brings us God's own peace.*

Jacob's wrestling means that he did not want to go through the way he knew he must, he had to come to the end of the best of his natural self, and he struggled in order not to. Then he came to the place where his wisdom was crippled for ever; "and he halted upon his thigh." The symbol is expressive of what it looks like in the eyes of shrewd worldly wisdom to cast your self unperplexed on God. When we cling to God we learn to kneel for the first time.

If you have never been to "Peniel" you are sure to come across things that will put your human wisdom into a panic; if you have seen God face to face your circumstances will never arouse any panic in you. We run off at a tangent—anywhere but Peniel, where we would see God "face to face."

THE STILL SMALL VOICE
Genesis 33–35

On the surface everything seemed right enough to Jacob in Shechem, but underneath the surface every thing was wrong. Everything is always wrong when the children of God dwell in Shechem instead of at Beth-el. This chapter is the unveiling by God of the actuality of sin.

"And Jacob came in peace to the city of Shechem" (Genesis 33:18 RV). One day the hollow "Shechem" peace was shaken by an earthquake—Dinah's fall, and her brothers' crime, rudely awakened Jacob; then God's voice was heard: "Arise, go up to Beth-el, and dwell there." To enter into peace for ourselves without becoming either tolerantly un-watchful of other lives or an amateur providence over them, is supremely difficult. God holds us responsible for two things in connection with the lives He brings around us in the apparent haphazard of His providence, viz., insistent waiting on God for them, and inspired instruction and warning from God to them. The thing that astonishes us when we get through to God is the way God holds us responsible for other lives.

1. The Awakening Voice of God

And God said unto Jacob, Arise, go up to Beth-el, and dwell there. . . . (Genesis 35:1)

This must be the voice of God; no human voice would ever have said what these words imply. Think what Beth-el meant to Jacob in memory—Beth-el was the geographical place of God to him: "How dreadful is this place! this is none other but the house of God, and this is the gate of heaven." Beth-el was the place where the Divine promises had been given, and vows made, not yet fulfilled. To go back to Beth-el meant to acknowledge error. The voice of God to an awakened soul, when it has heard the voice before, is never to go forward, but to go back. When the blood runs high and impulse worships at the shrine of the heroic, and the nerves strain for the actual doing of something, we not only do not hear God's voice, we don't want to hear it. Then when events have produced an earthquake in the personal life, we find that God was not in the earthquake, but in the still small voice, "Go to Beth-el, and stay there."

2. The Arousing Virtue of God *(Genesis 35:2–4)*

Then Jacob said unto his household, and to all that were with him, Put away the strange gods that are among you . . . (v. 2)

Now that Jacob has heard the voice of God speaking to him he is not afraid to assert his authority in his household. When you come across a man or woman who talks to you from God, you know it by the in tuition of your spirit and you obey him, scarcely realising what you are doing; on looking back you become aware that it was not a human voice at all but the voice of God. Simulated authority should be laughed at, and it is a downright sensible human duty to do so, but when the authority of God comes to you through anyone, to rebel against it would be to rebel against God. But beware of trying to be consistent to the authority that God gives you over any life on a particular occasion; you know that God used you then in that life and you say, "Now I am always going to have this authority"—that is wrong. Authority never comes from you, but from God through you, therefore let God introduce or withhold as He chooses.

3. The Appreciated Value of God

And let us arise, and go up to Beth-el; and I will make there an altar unto God . . . (v. 3)

Every expansion of heart or brain or spirit must be paid for in added concentration. In the meeting with Esau and the marvellous experience of reconciliation with him, Jacob had an expansion of heart, but he did not pay for it afterwards in concentration; he lived loosely in the exalted peace of the expanded life, and suddenly a terrible tragedy breaks up the whole thing. In our personal lives every expansion of heart, whether it is the awakening of human love, or bereavement, must be paid for by watchfulness; if it is not, looseness, the feeling of all-abroadness, ending in moral collapse, is sure to result. It is because people do not under stand the way they are made that all the havoc is produced in the lives of those who really have had times with God and experienced expansions of heart, but they have forgotten to concentrate, and the general feeling of looseness is a sure sign that God's presence has gone.

. . . who answered me in the day of my distress, and was with me in the way which I went.

The implication is, "when God answered me and brought deliverance, I forgot all about Him." Jacob settled down in the peace of Shechem, Dinah went to hell, and her brothers to the devil; then God spoke to Jacob. If you allow your mind to be expanded and forget to concentrate on God, the thing that happened in Jacob's domestic life on the big scale will happen in your bodily life on the narrow scale. The vision of what God wants must be paid for by concentration on your part, if it is not, you begin to get all abroad, and in come the "little foxes," in comes inordinate affection, in come a hundred and one things that were never there before, and down you go. It is not that these things may happen, they *will* happen as sure as God is God, unless you watch and pray, that is, concentrate until you are confirmed in the ways of God. Innocence must be transfigured into virtue by moral choices. We are all apt to be taken in by a frank nature. The man we call frank says of a wrong thing, "I'm sorry I did it," and promptly does it again, and we forgive him, while all the time the deepest deviltry goes on. The frank nature brings the glamour of virtue without its reality and stings innocence to death. Innocence is not purity, innocence is right for a child, but criminal for a man or woman. Men and women have no business to be innocent, they ought to be virtuous and pure. Character must be attained. Individuality, impulse, and innocence are the husk of personal life. Individuality, if it goes beyond a certain point, becomes pig-headedness, determined in dependence. I have to be prepared to give up my independent right to myself in order that my personality may emerge. Impulse is a subtle snare, always and every time; it may start right, but it is a short-cut to fame or infamy, and it is along the line of impulse that lust and temptation comes. Hold back the impulse and you discipline it into character, and it becomes something altogether different, viz., intuition. The same thing with innocence; innocence must be transformed into purity by a series of moral choices. There is no virtue that has not gone through a moral choice. A great many of us make virtues out of necessity.

THE BOY OF GOD
Genesis 37–50

1. Ideals of Seventeen

Joseph, being seventeen years old . . . (Genesis 37:2)

The Bible always incarnates ideals in great personalities, and Joseph stands for the magnificent integrity of boyhood; no man thinks so clearly or has such high ideals as in his teens, but unless our ideals find us living in accordance with them they become a mockery. The Bible pays no attention to intellectual and emotional conceptions, but only to the actual manifestation of the ideal. A man may have remarkable conceptions, fine intellectual views, noble ideals and his actual life be beneath contempt, proving that all the high ideals and intellectual conceptions in the world have not the slightest power to bring the life into contact with Reality. There is no room whatever in our Lord's teaching for ideals and a stumbling walk of the feet; there must be an at-one-ment between the God-inspired conceptions and actual life, and the only way this can be brought about is by "Coming to Me." Joseph was amazingly susceptible to God, and he "dreamed dreams" (see 37:5, 9). The dreams of the Old Testament are the touch of God on the spirit of a man; always reverence such dreams. "And they hated him the more for his dreams, and for his words" (37:8). The hatred produced by a sense of superiority in another is the most venomous. This gives the inner meaning of our Lord's words: "They hated Me without a cause." Beware what you brood on in secret for the fateful opportunity will come when God and the devil will meet in your soul, and you will do according to your brooding, swept beyond all your control. This is a law as sure as God is God. The fateful opportunity came to the brethren who hated Joseph—"And when they saw him afar off, even before he came near unto them, they conspired against him to slay him." Beware of saying, "Oh well, it doesn't matter much what I think about in secret"; it does, for the opportunity will come when what you think about in secret will find expression and spurt out in an act. The Bible always speaks of sin as it appears in its final analysis. Jesus does not say, "You must not covet because it will lead to stealing"; He says, "You must not covet because it *is* stealing." He does not say, "You must not be angry with your brother because it will lead to murder"; He says, "You must not be angry with your brother because it *is* murder." "Whosoever hateth his brother is a murderer" (1 John 3:15). When the climax of these things is reached we begin to see the meaning of Calvary.

2. "His Strength Was As the Strength of Ten"

And the LORD was with Joseph, and he was a prosperous man; and he was in the house of his master the Egyptian. (Genesis 39:2)

A life with presence, i.e., an uncommon spirit, redeems any situation from the commonplace. It may be cleaning boots, doing house work, walking in the street, any ordinary thing at all, but immediately it is touched by a man or woman with presence it ceases to be commonplace. The rarest asset to a godly life is to be practically conscientious in every situation. "But the LORD was with Joseph, . . . and gave him favour in the sight of the keeper of the prison" (39:21).

Joseph's adaptability was superb. Adaptability is not tact—tact is frequently nothing but the moral counterpart of hypocrisy. Adaptability is the power to make a suitable environment for oneself out of any set of circumstances. Most of us are all right if we can live in our own particular setting, with our own crowd, but when we get pitchforked somewhere else either we cannot adapt ourselves, or we adapt ourselves too easily and lose God. Joseph did not lose God; God was with Joseph in Egypt as in Canaan; with him in the prison as in the house of his master. If I simply delight in a godly atmosphere and refuse to appropriate God for myself, when I have to leave the godly atmosphere I will find myself God-less; then my natural adaptability becomes the adaptability to degenerate.

3. "Complete Steel"

How then can I do this great wickedness, and sin against God? (Genesis 39:9)

The phrase "complete steel" is Milton's definition of chastity, and is peculiarly appropriate to Joseph. Personal chastity is an impregnable barrier against evil. Like virtue, chastity is not a gift, but an attainment of determined integrity. Unsoiledness may be nothing more than necessity, the result of a shielded life, and is no more chastity than innocence is purity. Virtue and chastity are forged by me, not by God. You can't drown a cork, and you can't defile Joseph.

Four times over in this chapter is the statement made, "the LORD was with Joseph." It is the presence of God that is the secret of victory always. The fear of the Lord creates an atmosphere in which impure thoughts and unholy desires die a natural death. "But so did not I, because of the fear of God" (see Nehemiah 5:15). Joseph knew that the God whom he worshipped was "of purer eyes than to behold evil, and canst not look on iniquity." The outstanding value of the Bible is that it makes shameful things appear shameful because it never analyses them.

The discovery of the desperate recesses in the human heart is the greatest evidence of the need for the Redemption. The experiences of life awaken possibilities of evil that make you shudder, and as long as we remain under the refuge of innocence we are fools. The appalling things revealed in human lives confirm the words of the great Master of the human heart. Our Lord did not say, "*into the heart of man* 'these things' *are injected,*" but, "*from within, out of the heart of men, proceed . . .*" and then follows the terrible catalogue. We ought to get into the habit of estimating ourselves by this rugged standard. The important thing to remember is that we are better trusting the revelations of Jesus Christ than our own innocence. The only thing that safeguards is the Redemption.

> *And God sent me before you to preserve you a remnant in the earth, and to save you alive by a great deliverance. (Genesis 45:7 RV)*

That was Joseph's high vocation, to preserve life. God brings His purposes to pass in spite of all men may do, and often through what they do, and He will utilise the very things which look as if they were going dead against their fulfilment; God goes steadily on and involves us in the fulfilment.

> *So now it was not you that brought me hither, but God. (45:8)*

> *But as for you, ye meant evil against me; but God meant it unto good. (50:20 RV)*

The Place of Help

A Book of Devotional Readings
Oswald Chambers

INTRODUCTION

Source

This material is gathered from Sunday sermons in various churches in Britain between 1908 and 1915; lectures at the Bible Training College;[1] London, from 1911 to 1915; and talks to soldiers in Egypt from 1915 to 1917.

Publication History

- As a book: Many of these lectures and talks were first published as articles and pamphlets before they were combined into a book in 1935.

The origin of the first chapter, from which the book takes its name, is best described by Mrs. Chambers:

> *I recall vividly the place of the "birth" of this article; my husband dictated it to me during our stay in America in 1910, when we spent a little while in the exceedingly grand and beautiful Catskill mountains, amidst scenery which left us with the sense of worship expressed by Isaiah "The whole earth is full of His glory."*
>
> *May every thought of the one, who so continually lifted our eyes from the "hills" to God Himself, be a mighty inspiration to us all to so "dwell in the shadow of the Almighty" that our lives may be a sacrament whereby God can be revealed as our "refuge and strength and very present Help."*
>
> *As we sang the Scotch version of the Psalm at the graveside God's presence was memorably near, and we realised in a new way the reality of the truths His servant had so untiringly imparted to us by his teaching and life. The words "Greater works than these shall ye do because I go unto my Father" were among the last he spoke in this life, and our prayer is that the Lord Jesus Christ shall "see of the travail of His soul" in us and be satisfied.*

Shortly after Oswald Chambers died in November 1917, one of his close associates, Jimmy Hanson,[2] suggested to Mrs. Chambers that they print one of Oswald's messages and send it out to the soldiers to whom he had ministered in Egypt.[3] They chose "The Place of Help," and it became the forerunner of many OC messages printed and distributed without cost to the recipients.

The messages in this book provide a chronicle of Oswald Chambers' public ministry with a variety of audiences during the last decade of his life.

---

1. Bible Training College (BTC): residential school near Clapham Common, in southwest London, sponsored by the League of Prayer; operated from 1911 until it closed in July 1915 because of World War I. Oswald Chambers was principal and main teacher; Biddy Chambers, his wife, was lady superintendent.

2. Jimmy Hanson: one of the BTC students who had a long association with Oswald and Biddy Chambers through the League of Prayer, at the Bible Training College, and with the YMCA in Egypt.

3. Zeitoun (zay TOON), Egypt: six miles northeast of Cairo; site of a YMCA camp, the Egypt General Mission compound, and, from 1916 to 1919, the Imperial School of Instruction, training base for British, Australian, and New Zealand troops during World War I.

CONTENTS

FOREWORD

The honour of framing this brief foreword the writer owes to the fact of being one of the very few who heard all, or almost all, the addresses at the time they were given, and of having thus been able to sense the spirit of their setting.

In their selection no strict sequence as to dates has been observed, but they are roughly grouped as follows. The undated sermons were preached in England either to Sunday congregations in various places in country or in town (1908–15), or at the Bible Training College, Clapham Common (1911–15): the dated ones belong to the period of Oswald Chambers'

ministry under the YMCA at Zeitoun, Egypt, a centre to which men came from almost every unit of the Army in the Near East (1915–17).

The sermons entitled "Spiritual Discipleship" and "Sacramental Discipleship" were preached on the Sunday before Oswald Chambers sailed for Egypt in October 1915.

The talks at the B.T.C. were teaching talks. They lack of necessity the asides and illustrations that lit them up so delightfully, but it is easy in many cases to trace in the Scriptural references the line of Bible Study being pursued at the time each was delivered.

The sermons at Zeitoun in those years of strain and stress were the very sacrament of preaching: no one could doubt it who heard with the keen hearing of the spiritual ear the miracle of authentic stillness that falls upon an assembly of men in those rare moments when a man speaks to his hearers; spirit to spirit, and he and they alike know it. The moment passes, but the "inward and spiritual grace" abides— a sacramental permanent possession.

To all who knew Oswald Chambers, his life was the interpretation of his teaching; to those to whom it comes now in another form the meaning opens in the hidden individual ways of God. The writer believes that the Spirit of God is using this teaching in many lands to very many lives as a corrective to the wave of shallow thinking, and of shallower religious values that has swept across a section of the Christian communities everywhere.

By Oswald Chambers men's minds are thrown back upon the deep fundamental things that govern human life in its threefold aspect of spirit, soul, and body: Divine Redemption is brought down to the very shores of our daily living: the Cross of Calvary is shown to men as being the very heart and centre of the Revelation of God in the Person of Our Lord and Saviour Jesus Christ.

Now "Unto Him that loved us, . . . to Him be glory and dominion for ever and ever." Amen.

One of the B.T.C. students[4]
28th September 1935

THE PLACE OF HELP

I will lift up mine eyes unto the hills, from whence cometh my help. My help cometh from the LORD. Psalm 121:1–2

The marginal rendering puts it in the form of a question. "Shall I lift up mine eyes to the hills? from whence should my help come?" and recalls Jeremiah's statement: "In vain is help looked to from the mountains" (RV). I want to apply that statement spiritually.

Great Aspirations
Mountains stir intense hope and awaken vigour, but ultimately leave the climber exhausted and spent. Great men and great saints stir in us great aspirations and a great hopefulness, but leave us ultimately exhausted with a feeling of hopelessness; the inference we draw is that these people were built like that, and all that is left for us to do is to admire. Longfellow says: "Lives of great men all remind us we can make our lives sublime," but I question whether this is profoundly true. The lives of great men leave us with a sense of our own littleness which paralyses us in our effort to be anything else. Going back to the setting of this Psalm, one realises that the exquisite beauty of the mountain scenery awakens lofty aspirations; the limitless spaces above the highest mountain-peak, the snow-clad summit, and the scarred side ending in foliage and beauty as it sweeps to the valley below, stand as a symbol for all that is high and lofty and aspiring. When one is young this is the type of scenery most revelled in, the blood runs quicker, the air is purer and more vigorous, and things seem possible to the outlook that were not possible when we lived in the valleys; but as one gets older, and realises the limitation not only of physical life but in the inner life, the remembrance of the mountains and of mountain-top experiences leaves us a little wistful with an element of sadness, an element perhaps best expressed by the phrase, "What might have been, had we always been true to the truth, had we never sinned, had we never made mistakes!" Even such simple considerations as these bring us to the heart of the Psalmist's song in this Pilgrim Song Book[5]—"Shall I lift up mine eyes to the hills?" "Is that from whence my help is to come?" And the Psalmist answers, "No, my help cometh from the Lord Who made the hills"—and there we have the essence of the spiritual truth. Not to the great things God has done, not to the noble saints and noble lives He has made, but to God Himself does the Psalmist point.

The study of biography is always inspiring, but it has this one drawback, that it is apt to leave the life more given to sentiment and thinking and perhaps less to endeavour than is usually supposed; but when we realise what the Psalmist is pointing out and what the New Testament so strongly insists on, viz., *"the Lord* is our help," we are able to understand such a mountain character as the Apostle Paul saying "Follow my ways which be in Christ." We have not been

---

4. Most likely Jimmy Hanson or Mary Riley, two BTC students who had a long association with Chambers through the League of Prayer, at the Bible Training College, and with the YMCA in Egypt.

5. For Chambers' other messages on the Pilgrim Psalms or the Psalms of Ascent, 120–128, see *The Highest Good*.

told to follow in all the footsteps of the mountain-like characters, but in the footsteps of their faith, because their faith is in a Person.

Great Attainments

This is such an important theme that it will profit us to look at it from another aspect. This is the age when education is placed on the very highest pinnacle. In every civilised country we are told that if we will educate the people and give them better surroundings, we shall produce better characters. Such talk and such theories stir aspirations, but they do not work out well in reality. The kingdom within must be adjusted first before education can have its true use. To educate an unregenerate man is but to increase the possibility of cultured degradation. No one would wish to belittle the lofty attainments of education and culture, but we must realise we have to put them in their high, mighty, second place. Their relationship in human life is second, not first. The man whom God made is first, and the God Who made him is his only Help. God seems to point this out all through His Book—Moses, learned in all the learning of the Egyptian schools, the highest and ablest prophet-statesman conceivable, realises with a keenness and poignancy the bondage and degradation of his brethren, and sees that he is the one to deliver them: but God sends him for forty years into a wilderness to feed sheep. He removes first of all the big "I am" and then the little "I am" out of him. Read the account carefully; you will find that at the end of those forty years, when God spoke to Moses again, saying "Come now therefore, and I will send thee unto Pharaoh, that thou mayest bring forth My people," Moses said *"Who am I?"* All this points out one thing, that the ability of a man to help his brother man lies lastingly with God and is not concerned with his aspirations or his education or his attainments.

The same thing emerges in the 15th chapter of St. John's Gospel where our Lord instructs His disciples about the new dispensation "I am." "I am the Vine. . . ." If the dominant identity of the disciple is not built up by God Himself, in vain are the mountains looked to for help. There may be some who are trying by aspiration and prayer and consecration and obedience, built up from looking at the lives that stand like mountain peaks, to attain a like similarity of character, and they are woefully lagging behind; their lips, as it were, have grown pale in the intense struggle, and they falter by the way, and the characters that used to stir intense hopefulness leave the soul sighing over "what might have been," but now can never be. To such a reader let the message of this 121st Psalm come with new hope, "My help cometh from the Lord Who made the hills." A strong saintly charac-ter is not the production of human breeding or culture, it is the manufacture of God.

Great Admirations

Take it from another aspect. There are people to-day who are exalting our Lord as a Teacher, saying, in effect, that they believe in the Sermon on the Mount and its high ideals but not in the Cross; that all that is necessary is to place the pure noble ideals of the Sermon on the Mount before mankind and let men strive to attain; that there is no need for a sacrificial death. When minds and men and countries are very young in thinking, this sort of statement and teaching has a wonderful fascination, but we sooner or later learn that if Jesus Christ was merely a Teacher, He adds to the burdens of human nature, for He erects an ideal that human nature can never attain. He tantalises us by statements that poor human nature can never fit itself for. By no prayer, by no self-sacrifice, by no devotion, and by no climbing can any man attain to that "Blessed are the pure in heart," which Jesus Christ says is essential to seeing God.

When we come to the New Testament interpretation of our Lord we find He is not a Teacher, we find He is a Saviour. We find that His teaching is but a statement of the kind of life we will live when we have let Him re-make us by means of His Cross and by the incoming of His Spirit. The life of Jesus is to be made ours, not by our imitation, not by our climbing, but by means of His Death. It is not admiration for holiness, nor aspirations after holiness, but *attainment* of holiness, and this is ours from God, not from any ritual of imitation.

I would like to commend this thought for the instruction and courage of those whose hearts are fainting in the way, from whom the ideals of youth have fled, to whom life holds out no more promises. For thirty years or more it may be that life has been a boundless romance of possibilities; beckoning signs from lofty mountain peaks have lured the spirit on; but now the burden and the heat of the day have come and the mountain tops are obscured in a dazing, dazzling heat, and the road is dusty and the mileage long, and the feet are weak and the endeavour is exhausted. Let me bring the message contained in this Psalm, even as a cup of water from the clear sparkling spring of life. "My help cometh from the Lord Who made heaven and earth." He will take you up, He will re-make you, He will make your soul young and will restore to you the years that the cankerworm hath eaten, and place you higher than the loftiest mountain peak, safe in the arms of the Lord Himself, secure from all alarms, and with an imperturbable peace that the world cannot take away.

This Psalm is one of the fifteen that the people sang and chanted on their ways of weary pilgrimage to the mighty concourse and festivity of God's hosts, and it is well called one of the "Pilgrim Psalms." The Psalmist goes on to say—"The sun shall not smite thee by day, nor the moon by night. The LORD shall preserve thee from all evil," so that there be no fainting by the way. "The LORD shall preserve thy going out and thy coming in from this time forth, and even for evermore."

To whom are you looking? To some great mountainlike character? Are you even looking at the Lord Jesus Christ as a great mountain-like Character? It is the wrong way; help does not come that way. Look to the Lord alone, and come with the old pauper cry—

Just as I am, without one plea
But that Thy blood was shed for me,
And that Thou bid'st me come to Thee—
O Lamb of God, I come.

Any soul, no matter what his experience, that gets beyond this attitude is in danger of falling from grace. Oh, the security, the ineffable rest of knowing that the God Who made the mountains can come to our help! Let us hasten at once under the "shadow of the Almighty," to the "secret place of the Most High," for *there* shall no evil befall us. Jesus said, "him that cometh unto Me I will in no wise cast out."

THE WAY

The Waylessness

To the prophets and poets of the Bible, life is a wayless wilderness. In it there are many voices crying, "This is the way," many ideals with signposts claiming to point out the way. It would be interesting to trace the sadness that lays hold of the minds of those who have never known the one and true Living Way, in whose outlook the waylessness of life seems to be the dominant note. Take, for instance, Thomas Carlyle; his mighty literary genius and his instinct for God made him ask in an insurgent manner why God kept silence, why He did not manifest Himself amid all the corruption and shams of life. No wonder his mind deepened into a dark stoicism, since he never saw that God had manifested Himself in that He had pointed the way out of all the mysteries of life in the Cross of our Lord Jesus Christ. Or take our poets, those who have never known The Way—their "sweetest songs are those that tell of saddest thought." The feeling of uncertainty as to the issue, and the strange vagueness of the way is the inspiration of their thought. Or take our own personal moods when we are roused out of our commonplace equilibrium and the sense grows upon us strongly of the implicit kinship of the human spirit with the untrodden waylessness of life—until a man finds the Lord Jesus Christ, his heart and brain and spirit will lead him astray.

The Wayfarers

There are many ways in which a man's life may be suddenly struck by an immortal moment, when the true issues of his life, "the spirit's true endowments stand out plainly from its false ones," and he knows in that moment whether he is "pursuing or the right way or the wrong way, to its triumph or undoing." Such a moment may come by conviction of sin, or it may come through the opening up of the vast isolation of a man's own nature which makes him afraid. Or it may come with the feeling that somewhere he will meet One Who will put him on the way to solve his implicit questions, One Who will satisfy the last aching abyss of the human heart, and put within his hands the key to unlock the secret treasures of life. There are many gates into the Holy City, and many avenues by which God may enter the human soul.

To all whose souls have been awakened by these moods or by conviction of sin, for whom life has been profoundly altered so that it can never be the same again—to all such the voice of the Lord Jesus Christ comes as the voice of the Eternal: "I am the Way." If a man will resign himself in implicit trust to the Lord Jesus, he will find that He leads the wayfaring soul into the green pastures and beside the still waters, so that even when he goes through the dark valley of the shadow of some staggering episode, he will fear no evil. Nothing in life or death, time or eternity, can stagger that soul from the certainty of the Way for one moment.

The Wayfinder

The Way is missed by everyone who has not the childlike heart; we have to go humbly lest we miss the way of life just because it is so simple. God has hidden these things from the wise and prudent and revealed them unto babes. When a man has been found by the Lord Jesus and has given himself to Him in unconditional surrender, the fact that he has found The Way is not so much a conscious possession as an unconscious inheritance. Explicit certainty is apt to make a man proud, and that spirit can never be in the saint. The life of the saint who has discovered The Way is the life of a little child; he discerns the will of God implicitly.

One of the significant things about those who are in The Way is that they have a strong family likeness to Jesus, His peace marks them in an altogether conspicuous manner. The light of the morning is on their faces, and the joy of the endless life is in their hearts. Wherever they go, men are gladdened or healed, or made conscious of a need.

The way to the fulfilment of all life's highest ideals and its deepest longings is the Lord Jesus Christ Himself. How patiently He waits until, having battered ourselves against the impregnable bars of our universe, we turn at last, humbled and bruised, to His arms, and find that all our fightings and fears, all our wilfulness and waywardness, were unnecessary had we but been simple enough to come to Him at the first. "There is a way which seemeth right unto a man, but the end thereof are the ways of death." God grant that for our own sakes, for the sake of those near and dear to us, for the sake of the wide world, and for the sake of the Lord Jesus Christ, we may come to this New and Living Way, where "the wayfaring men . . . shall not err therein . . . but the Redeemed shall walk there . . . with songs and everlasting joy upon their heads."

TWO SIDES TO FELLOWSHIP

What I tell you in the darkness, speak ye in the light: and what ye hear in the ear, proclaim upon the housetops. Matthew 10:27 (RV)

"What I tell you in the darkness . . ." Let it be understood that the darkness our Lord speaks of is not darkness caused by sin or disobedience, but rather darkness caused from excess of light. There are times in the life of every disciple when things are not clear or easy, when it is not possible to know what to do or say. Such times of darkness come as a discipline to the character and as the means of fuller knowledge of the Lord. Such darkness is a time for listening, not for speaking. This aspect of darkness as a necessary side to fellowship with God is not unusual in the Bible (see Isaiah l:10; 5:30; 1 Peter 1:6–7). The Lord shares the darkness with His disciple—"What I tell you in the darkness . . ." He is there. He knows all about it. The sense of mystery must always be, for mystery means being guided by obedience to Someone Who knows more than I do. On the Mount of Transfiguration this darkness from excess of light is brought out—"They feared as they entered into the cloud," but in the cloud "they saw no one any more, save Jesus only with themselves."

In this side of fellowship with God the disciple must not mourn or fret for the light, nor must he put forth self-effort or any determination of the flesh or kindle a fire of his own. Many tendencies which lead to delusion arise just here. When the disciple says in his heart—"there must be a break; God must reveal Himself," he loses sight altogether that in the darkness God wants him to listen and not fuss. "In quietness and in confidence shall be your strength."

A disciple must be careful not to talk in the darkness; the listening ear is to be his characteristic, not listening to the voice of sympathising fellow disciples, or to the voice of self-pity, but listening only to the voice of the Lord, "Wherefore whatsoever ye have said in the darkness shall be heard in the light; and what ye have spoken in the ear in the inner chambers shall be proclaimed upon the housetops." Not what the disciple says in public prayer, not what he preaches from pulpit or platform, not what he writes on paper or in letters, but what he is in his heart which God alone knows, determines God's revelation of Himself to him. Character determines revelation (see Psalm 18:24–26). "With the merciful Thou wilt show Thyself merciful" (v. 25). "Say unto them, As I live, saith the LORD, surely as ye have spoken in Mine ears, so will I do to you" (Numbers 14:28 RV).

There is another side to fellowship: "What I tell you in the darkness, *speak ye in the light*." What are we speaking in the light? Many talk glibly and easily about stupendous truths which they believe, but the Lord has never revealed them to them in darkness. God's providential leadings will take the one who proclaims those glorious truths into tribulation and darkness whereby they can be made part of his own possession. Jesus tells us what we are to speak in the light: "What I tell you in the darkness."

All servants and handmaidens of the Lord have to partake in this discipline of darkness, to have the ear trained to listen to their Master's words. Our Lord never gives private illuminations to special favourites. His way is ever twofold: the development of character, and the descent of Divine illumination through the Word of God. Many are talking in the light today, and many voices have gone forth, but Jesus says, "My sheep hear My voice." "A stranger will they not follow but will flee from him: for they know not the voice of strangers." At the beginning of a disciplining spell of providential darkness, the tumult and the noise may hinder the spirit from hearing the voice of the Lord, but sooner or later the disciple, at first inclined to say it thundered and to be afraid, says, "Thy voice is on the rolling air; I see Thee in the setting sun, and in the rising, Thou art fair."

The voice of the Lord listened to in darkness is so entrancing that the finest of earth's voices are never afterwards mistaken for the voice of the Lord. Where are those in this fellowship of the Lord found to-day? "If we walk in the light, as He is in the light, we have fellowship one with another." The fellowship of the disciples is based not on natural affinities of taste but on fellowship in the Holy Ghost, a fellowship that is constrained and enthralled by the love and communion of our Lord and Saviour Jesus Christ. When both sides of this fellowship, listening in darkness and speaking in light, are realised, no darkness can terrify any more.

Thou hast done well to kneel and say,
"Since He Who gave can take away,
And bid me suffer, I obey!"
And also well to tell my heart
Thy goodness in the bitterest part,
And thou wilt profit by her smart . . .
Nor with thy share of work be vexed;
Though incomplete and e'en perplexed,

It fits exactly to the next.
What seems too dark to thy dim sight
May be a shadow, seen aright,
Making some brightness doubly bright—
The flash that struck thy tree—no more
To shelter thee—lets Heaven's blue floor
Shine where it never shone before.

Oh, the unspeakable benediction of the "treasures of darkness"! But for the night in the natural world we should know nothing of moon or stars, or of all the incommunicable thoughtfulness of the midnight. So spiritually it is not the days of sunshine and splendour and liberty and light that leave their lasting and indelible effect upon the soul but those nights of the Spirit in which, shadowed by God's hand, hidden in the dark cleft of some rock in a weary land, He lets the splendours of the outskirts of Himself pass before our gaze. It is such moments as these that insulate the soul from all worldliness and keep it in an "otherworldliness" while carrying on work for the Lord and communion with Him in this present evil world.

"Even the darkness hideth not from Thee, but the night shineth as the day; the darkness and the light are both alike to Thee."

DISSIPATED DEVOTION

Take heed to thyself that thou offer not thy burnt offerings in every place that thou seest: but in the place which the LORD shall choose in one of thy tribes, there thou shalt offer thy burnt offerings, and there thou shall do all that I command thee. Deuteronomy 12:13–14

An unusual theme, but this Old Testament ritual which refers to the people of God having too many shrines, has a lesson of penetrating importance for us in the New Testament dispensation, i.e., that there is a wilful element in our consecration that must be exterminated.

The impulse of worship is natural in the majority of human beings, and we must make the distinction very clear between the impulse of worship in an unregenerate spirit and the impulse of worship in a saint. Natural devotion chooses its own altars, its own setting, the scene of its own martyrdom. It would be very entrancing if a human being could go to martyrdom in such moods, having arranged the spectators and the scenery to suit his own ambition; but this Old Testament passage says that God chooses the place for the offering. This aims at the very root of the whole matter. We do not consecrate our gifts to God, they are not ours to have; we consecrate ourselves to God, that is, we give up the right to ourselves to Him.

Place of Consecration
A remarkable thing is that the place of the altar is not mentioned because evidently it was continually being changed. If it had been always at one place, the people would have become devoted to that place and would have made it a scene of religious festival without any indication of real devotion to God.

All through the prophets one hears the continual cry that the people have fasted or feasted for their own pleasure, they have been religious because it suited them; but the only devotion which is acceptable to God is the devotion on the part of a regenerate soul that starts from a full-hearted consecration, which by binding the sacrifice of itself to the altar of God, receives from God the supreme sanctification which identifies it for ever with the life of the Lord. The place of this devotion can never be discovered by human intelligence, or natural spirituality, but only by the Spirit of God.

It must be borne in mind that the burnt offering is not the sin offering. The Apostle Paul shows us distinctly the place of the altar, and the sacrifice God wants, "I beseech you therefore, brethren, by the mercies of God, to present your bodies a living sacrifice, . . ." literally, give up your right to yourself. That people find it extremely difficult to get to this place is true, and the reason is not difficult to find. We choose our own altars, and say, "Yes, we will devote ourselves to the foreign field," or "we will give ourselves to slum work," "to work in some orphanage" or to "rescue work." All this commends itself thoroughly to the natural heart of a man, but it is not the place the Lord chooses.

That place is discernible only by the Holy Spirit, and the offering is prompted not by devotion to duty, or devotion to a doctrine, but by devotion to a Divine Being. When our Lord talked to the woman of Samaria He pointed out that both Jews and Samaritans had begun to worship a place instead of God, but He said, "the hour cometh, and now is, when the true worshippers shall worship the Father in spirit and truth."

Purpose of Consecration

In the general aspect of consecration one is easily misled by those who are possessed of natural piety. People talk about seeing God in nature, and are in danger of mistaking the impulse that seeks after God for God Himself. Paul makes that distinction very clear in Acts 17:27, "that they should seek God, if haply they might feel after Him, and find Him, though He is not far from each one of us." The natural heart of man interprets that to mean that the instinct to worship, and to make an altar of devotion where he chooses, is the very instinct of God, whereas Paul implies that it is instinct feeling after God.

The altar of God's choosing is not approached by feelings of devotion or emotions of worship; that is why it is difficult to discover it. All natural religion reaches its climax in ritual, in the beauties of aesthetic and sensuous worship. God's altar is discerned only by the Holy Spirit when that Spirit is in a man.

The dissipation of devotion is seen over and over again in the practical issues of our lives. People give their lives to many things they have no business to. No one has any right to give up the right to himself or to herself to anyone but God Almighty, and devotion to a cause, no matter how noble or how beautiful, nowhere touches the profundity of this lesson. When we are told we must give up our right to ourselves to Jesus Christ, we are bound to ask—if we do not ask, we have not grasped the situation thoroughly—"Who is it that asks this tremendous devotion? Is there any principle, any cause, any enterprise on the face of the earth of such importance that a man has to give the very highest he has, viz., his right to himself, for it?" The only Being Who dare ask of me this supreme sacrifice is the Lord Jesus Christ.

Satan's great aim is to deflect us from the centre. He will allow us to be devoted "to death" to any cause, any enterprise, to anything but the Lord Jesus. Is any-

one roused by the Spirit of God to wonder whether the object to which he is devoting his life has been chosen in a selfish consecration or not? It is so easy for a young convert, after listening to a missionary, to say God has given him a call *there*, and deliberately to choose to consecrate his life to that place. And that sort of thing is commended all over the Christian world, but I question whether it is commended by God. The tremendous world-wide instinct is of God. No soul has ever been saved or sanctified who did not instantly lose sight of country and of kindred, of kith and kin in the determination to do God's will; but immediately the desire and ambition of the individual chooses the altar, the scene of sacrifice, his devotion is dissipated.

Whenever our Lord talked about discipleship He brought out that fundamental thought—"If any man will come after Me, let him . . . take up his cross daily and follow Me." Jesus Christ distinctly stated that He came to do the will of His Father. "I must work the works of Him that sent Me." His first obedience was not to the needs of men, but to the will of God. He nowhere chose the altar of His sacrifice, God chose it for Him. He chose to make His life a willing and obedient sacrifice that His Father's purpose might be fulfilled, and He says, "As the Father hath sent Me, even so send I you" (RV).

Position of Consecration

Are we putting the needs of mankind, heathen or otherwise, as the ground of our consecration? The amount of mistaken zeal and energy and passion and martyrdom thrown into work for God, that has to come under the category of dissipated devotion, because people have chosen the scene of their own worship, is appalling. God grant that we may accept the primary call of the saint, viz., to do the will of his Lord, and the one vivid experience in the heart is personal, passionate devotion to Jesus Christ.

Paul actually says, "If I give my body to be burned, but have not love, it profiteth me nothing" (RV). This is the place in which nine out of every ten of us are deluded. Because men and women devote themselves to martyrdom for a cause, they think they have struck the profoundest secret of religion; whereas they have but exhibited the heroic spirit that is in all human beings, and have not begun to touch the great fundamental secret of spiritual Christianity, which is wholehearted, absolute consecration of myself to Jesus, not to His cause, not to His "league of pity," but to Himself personally. "For we preach not ourselves, but Christ Jesus as Lord, and ourselves as your servants for Jesus' sake," as Paul says in 2 Corinthians 4:5 (RV). We are the servants of men, says Paul, not primarily because their needs have arrested us, but because Jesus Christ is our Lord; not because we feel the clamant needs of our age or any such sounding timbrel, but that the Lord Jesus Christ has saved and sanctified us and now He is Lord of our lives and makes us unconsciously the servants of other men, not for their sakes but for His own. This is the secret of presenting the burnt offering on the altar that God chooses.

Passion of Consecration

When the "passion for souls" has not this centre it is a dangerous passion. The socialist has a passion for souls, but the saint's passion for souls is not for man's sake primarily, but for the sake of the Lord Jesus Christ. This is the source of all evangelical missionary enterprise. The appeal is not to be put on the ground that the heathen are perishing without the knowledge of God; that appeal awakens a wilful devotion which dissipates the energies of the life. But let the preacher take back his hearer and his would-be devotee to the Garden of Gethsemane, to the still midnight in the quiet wood, to the pale moon's passionless gleam on each tree, and then in imagination again picture all

prostrate on the ground, our King, Redeemer, God, Whose bloody sweat, like heavy dew, stains the sod, and let the Holy Spirit ring through the preacher's and the hearer's heart, "This is the cost of having loved you."

And let him take the hearer and his own heart back to Calvary, to that "historic pole" of Time and Eternity, the Cross of Christ, and then let the passion and power of the Holy Ghost so seize hold of heart and brain and imagination that the sacrifice is bound with cords unto the horns of the altar and the life is entirely at the disposal of God.

It is one thing to behold the haggard, starved, sin-stained, broken-hearted faces of men, but that is not sufficient for Christian enterprise. At the back of these faces must ever be seen the "Face marred more than any man's," until the passion of the whole world's anguish that forced its way through His heart, may force its way through our hearts too, until we are His for ever, having drunk the cup of communion with His cross that shall identify us body, soul and spirit as Christ's.

SKILFUL SOUL-WINNING

He must increase, but I must decrease. John 3:30

Decreasing into His Purpose

The most delicate mission on earth is to win souls for Jesus without deranging their affections and affinities and sympathies by our own personal fascination. There is neither discouragement nor pensive humility in John's statement, but the passionate realisation of his position. As Christian workers we are about the most sacred business, seeking to win souls to the Lord Jesus, ministering to the holy relationship of Bridegroom and bride. That is our business, and we must be watchful lest any mood or disposition of our own should give a false impression of the Bridegroom and scare away the prospective bride. We are here for His sake, and we have to take care lest we damage His reputation. It may sometimes mean scaring a soul away from ourselves in order that Jesus Christ's attraction may tell.

Be jealously careful lest the impression given of our Lord in a public address is effaced when we come into the homes of the hearers. A beautiful saint may be a hindrance because he does not present Jesus Christ, but only what He has done, and the impression is left—"What a fine character!" The *worker* is increasing all the time, not Jesus Christ.

Decoying into His Power

Spiritual moods are as sensitive and delicate as the awakenings of early love; the most exquisite thing in the human soul is that early mood of the soul when it first falls in love with the Lord. By Christian courtesy to Jesus Christ, we should confirm the desire and love which has been awakened in souls wooed by our messages until we see them consorts of Him Who is the chiefest among ten thousand, the altogether lovely One. It means no rest in intercession until the soul has long lost sight of the worker, he needs him no more because he has got the Lord. We are apt to interfere in lives and produce fanatics instead of men and women devoted to Jesus because we have not been friends of the Bridegroom. We decoy them into our sect or our personal point of view instead of into His power. John's joy is this—At last they are to see the Bridegroom! "He must increase, but I must decrease"! It is said not in sadness but in joy.

The watcher of souls for God has to get them not so much out of sin and wrong as to see Jesus. If you become a necessity to a soul you have got out of God's order, your great need as a worker is to be a friend of the Bridegroom. Your goodness and purity ought never to attract attention to itself, it ought simply to be a magnet to draw others to Jesus; if it does not draw them to Him it is not holiness of the right order, it is an influence which will awaken inordinate affection and lead souls off into side issues. Over and over again we come in and prevent and say, This, or that, must not be, and instead of being friends of the Bridegroom we are sympathising snares, and the soul is not able to say, "He or she was a friend of the Bridegroom," but, "He or she was a thief and stole my affections away from Jesus Christ and located them elsewhere, and so I lost the vision."

Delighting in His Provision

When once you see a soul in sight of the claims of Jesus, you know your influence has been in the right direction, and instead of putting out a hand to withhold the throes, pray that they grow ten times stronger until no power on earth or in hell can ever hold that soul from Jesus Christ (cf. Luke 14:26). Beware of rejoicing in the wrong thing with a soul, but see that you rejoice at the right thing. "The friend of the Bridegroom, which standeth and heareth Him, rejoiceth greatly because of the Bridegroom's voice: this my joy therefore is fulfilled."

It is not sin that hinders, but our not living as friends of the Bridegroom. Suppose you talk about depending on God and how wonderful it is, and then others see that in your own immediate concerns you do not depend on Him a bit, but on your own wits, it makes them say, "Well, after all, it's a big pretence, there is no Almighty Christ to depend on anywhere, it is all mere sentiment." The impression left is that Jesus Christ is not real to you. "John indeed did no sign: but all things whatsoever John spake of this Man were true" (John 10:41 RV).

Devoted to Him Personally

In order to maintain friendship and loyalty to Christ, be much more careful of your moral and vital relationship to Him than any other thing, even obedience. Sometimes there is nothing to obey, the only thing to do is to maintain your vital connection with Jesus Christ, to see that nothing interferes with your relationship to Him. Only at occasional times do we have to obey; when a crisis arises we have to find out what God's will is, but the greater part of our life is not conscious obedience, but this maintained relationship. To have our eyes on successful service is one of the greatest snares to a Christian worker, for it has in it the peril of evading the soul's concentration on Jesus Christ, and instead of being friends of the Bridegroom we become antichrists in our domain, working against Him while we use His weapons; amateur providences with the jargon of Divine providence, and when the Bridegroom does speak we shall not hear His voice. Decreasing to the absolute effacing of the worker, till he or she is never thought of again, is the true result of devotion, and John says, That is my joy. Watch until you hear the Bridegroom's voice in the life of a soul, never mind what havoc, what upset it brings, what crumblings of health. Rejoice with divine hilarity over that soul because the Bridegroom's voice has been heard.

LOVE—HUMAN AND DIVINE

Love never faileth. 1 Corinthians 13:8 (RV)

"Love never faileth"! What a wonderful phrase that is! but what a still more wonderful thing the reality of that love must be; greater than prophecy—that vast forth-telling of the mind and purpose of God; greater than the practical faith that can remove mountains; greater than philanthropic self-sacrifice; greater than the extraordinary gifts of emotions and ecstasies and all eloquence; and it is *this* love that is shed abroad in our hearts by the Holy Ghost which is given unto us.

The Highest Human Love

Greater love hath no man than this, that a man lay down his life for his friends. (John 15:13)

This wonderful verse, quoted so often during this terrible war,[6] has suffered from contortions of belittling as well as of exaggeration; but the great words stand as those of the Lord Jesus Christ. They exhibit the highest human love, not the highest Divine love. The love that lays down the life for a man's friends is irrespective of religious faith or of lack of it. Atheists and pagans, saints and sinners alike, have exhibited this highest human love.

The revival of this greatest human love has been superb during this war, but there has not been as yet any sign of a corresponding great revival of self-sacrificing love on the part of the Church of Christ. Self-regarding love is part weakness, part selfishness, and part romance; and it is this self-regarding love that so

---

6. this . . . war: World War I (1914–1918).

counterfeits the higher love that, to the majority, love is too often looked upon as a weak sentimental thing.

"My Utmost for the Highest" was the motto of the great artist G. F. Watts, and it has very evidently been the watchword of thousands of young men whose names only figure now on the list of the killed.[7] But let it never be forgotten that the highest human love has nothing to do with religious faith, and the distortion of this mighty statement of Christ Jesus arises from the misunderstanding of this point.

Probably the finest scriptural incident illustrating the highest human love is recorded in 2 Samuel 23:15–17.

The Highest Divine Love
But God commendeth His own love toward us, in that, while we were yet sinners, Christ died for us. (Romans 5:8 RV)

This is the characteristic of the Divine love: not that God lays down His life for His friends, but that He lays down His life for His enemies (v. 10). That is not human love. It does not mean that no human being has ever laid down his life for his enemies, but it does mean that no human being ever did so without having received the Divine nature through the Redemption of our Lord.

This statement is alien to many modern minds imbued with evolutionary conceptions, because that type of intellectual thinking dislikes any break between the human and the Divine; it is easy to say that human love and Divine love are one and the same thing; actually they are very far from being the same. It is also easy to say that human virtues and God's nature are one and the same thing; but this, too, is actually far from the truth. We must square our thinking with facts. Sin has come in and made a hiatus between human and Divine love, between human virtues and God's nature, and what we see now in human nature is only the remnant and refraction of the Divine. Our Lord clearly indicates that a man needs to be born from above (RV mg) before he can possess or exhibit the oneness of the human and Divine in his own person. In theoretic conception the human and the Divine are one; in actual human life sin has made them two. Jesus Christ makes them one again by the efficacy of the Atonement. Hence the distinction is not merely theological, but experimental.

"God commendeth *His own love*" (RV). Human relationships may be used to illustrate God's love, e.g., the love of father, mother, wife, lover; but illustration is not identity. Human love may illustrate the Divine, it is not identical with the Divine love because of sin.

God's own love is so strange to our natural conceptions that we see no love in it; not until we are awakened by the conviction of our sin and anarchy do we realise God's great love towards us—"while we were yet sinners."

Tennyson's phrase, "We needs must love the highest when we see it, not Lancelot, nor another," is sufficiently true to be dangerously wrong; for when the religious people of our Lord's day saw the Highest incarnate before them, they hated Him and crucified Him.

The words of the prophet Isaiah are humiliatingly true of us. When we see the Highest, He is to us as "a root out of a dry ground: He hath no form nor comeliness; and when we see Him, there is no beauty that we should desire Him" (Isaiah 53:2 RV). The highest Divine love is not only exhibited in the extreme amazement of the tragedy of Calvary, but in the laying down of the Divine life through the thirty years at Nazareth, through the three years of popularity, scandal, and hatred, and furthermore in the long preincarnate years (cf. Revelation 13:8).

The Cross is the supreme moment in Time and Eternity, and it is the concentrated essence of the very nature of the Divine love. God lays down His life in the very creation we utilise for our own selfish ends. God lays down His life in His long-suffering patience with the civilised worlds which men have erected on God's earth in defiance of all He has revealed. The Self-expenditure of God for His enemies in the life and death of our Lord Jesus Christ, becomes the great bridge over the gulf of sin whereby human love may cross over and be embraced by the Divine love, the love that never fails (RV).

The Highest Christian Love
No longer do I call you servants; . . . but I have called you friends. (John 15:15 RV)

This is the wonderful way in which our Lord connects the highest human love with the highest Divine love; the connection is in His disciples. The emphasis is on the deliberate laying down of the life, not in one tragic crisis, but in the grey face of actual facts unillumined by romance, obscured by the mist of the utter commonplace, spending the life out deliberately day by day for my Divine Lord and His friends—this is the love that never fails (RV); and mark, the love that never fails is not human love alone, nor Divine love alone, but the at-one-ment of them in the disciples of Jesus.

We reveal the impoverished meanness[8] of our conceptions by the words we use in the actual business of life—"economy," "insurance," "diplomacy."

---

7. the killed: military personnel killed in World War I (1914–1918).
8. mean: as used here, something or someone ordinary, common, low, or ignoble, rather than cruel or spiteful.

These words cover by euphemism our ghastly disbelief in our Heavenly Father. "Be ye therefore perfect, even as your Father which is in heaven is perfect," and the connection of this perfection with its context must be observed. Its context is Matthew 5:45, "that ye may be sons of your Father which is in heaven: for He maketh His sun to rise on the evil and the good, and sendeth rain on the just and the unjust." Our Lord means by being perfect then obviously that we exhibit in our actual relationships to men as they are, the hospitality and generosity our Heavenly Father has exhibited to us. In 2 Corinthians 4:7–11 Paul makes it plain that there are no ideal conditions of life, but "My Utmost for His Highest" has to be carried out in the actual conditions of human life.

The highest Christian love is not devotion to a work or to a cause, but to Jesus Christ. In the early days of our Lord's life the grief and astonishment of Mary and Joseph was caused by this very thing, "And He said unto them, How is it that ye sought Me? wist ye not that I must be in My Father's house? And they understood not the saying which He spake unto them" (Luke 2:49–50 RV). Causes are good, and work

is good, but love in these fails. The laying down of the life for Jesus Christ's sake exhibits the Christian love that never fails. Our Lord was viewed as wild and erratic because He did not identify Himself with the cause of the Pharisees or with the Zealots, yet He laid down His life as the servant of Jehovah. "Wherefore Jesus also, that He might sanctify the people through His own blood, suffered without the gate," and the writer immediately follows it up with the injunction, "Let us therefore go forth unto Him without the camp, bearing His reproach. For we have not here an abiding city, but we seek after the city which is to come" (Hebrews 13:12–14 RV).

Thank God that we have the glorious fighting chance of identifying ourselves with our Lord's interests in other people in the love that never fails, for that love "suffereth long, and is kind; . . . envieth not; . . . vaunteth not itself, is not puffed up, doth not behave itself unseemly, seeketh not its own, is not provoked, taketh not account of evil; rejoiceth not in unrighteousness, but rejoiceth with the truth; beareth all things, believeth all things, hopeth all things, endureth all things. Love never faileth" (RV).

THE PASSION FOR CHRIST

Ye shall be witnesses unto Me. Acts 1:8

These words of our Risen Lord were spoken just before His Ascension. We have to be careful lest we make the passionate watchwords—"a passion for souls" and "a passion for Christ" into rival cries. The great passion which the Holy Ghost works in us, whereby He expresses the Redemption of our Lord in and through us in practical ways, is the passion for Jesus Christ Himself. "Ye shall be witnesses unto Me"—not witnesses only to what Jesus has done or can do, but witnesses who are an infinite satisfaction to His own heart wherever they are placed. The danger in the modern form of Christianity is its departure more and more from the great central Figure of the Lord Jesus Christ.

Christian experience does not mean we have thought through the way God works in human lives by His grace, or that we are able to state theologically that God gives the Holy Ghost to them that ask Him—that may be Christian thinking, but it is not Christian experience. Christian experience is living through all this by the marvellous power of the Holy Ghost.

The Holy Ghost working in me does not produce wonderful experiences that make people say "What a wonderful life that man lives"; the Holy Ghost work-

ing in me makes me a passionate, devoted, absorbed lover of the Lord Jesus Christ. "Passion" is a wonderful word, it is all that we mean by passive suffering and magnificent patience, and spiritually, all that is meant by human passion is lifted to the white, intense, welding heat of enthusiasm for Jesus Christ. God grant that we may be possessed by the Holy Ghost in such fullness that we may be witnesses unto Jesus Christ.

John 7:39; 14:16; 20:22, all these references to the Holy Ghost are anticipatory. The Holy Spirit's influence and power were at work before Pentecost, though He was not here. It is not the baptism of the Holy Ghost that changes men, but the power of the Ascended Christ coming into men's lives by the Holy Ghost that changes men. The baptism of the Holy Ghost is the evidence of the Ascended Christ. The Holy Ghost works along the line of the Redemption of our Lord, and along that line only. The mighty power of the Holy Ghost brings back to God the experiences of saved men and women, and ultimately, if one may put it so, will bring back to God the experiences of a totally redeemed world, a new heaven and a new earth.

"When He . . . is come, . . . He shall glorify Me." May God bring straight home to us that no human heart can love the Lord Jesus in the degree that He demands, e.g. Luke 14:26. There stands the claim of Jesus, tremendously strong, our love for Him must be overwhelmingly more passionate than every devoted earthly relationship. How is it to be done? There is only one Lover of the Lord Jesus and that is the Holy Ghost; when we receive the Holy Ghost He turns us into passionate human lovers of Jesus Christ. Then out of our lives will flow those rivers of living water that heal and bless, and we spend and suffer and endure in patience all because of One and One only. It is not the passion for men that saves men; the passion for men breaks human hearts. The passion for Christ inwrought by the Holy Ghost is deeper down than the deepest agony the world, the flesh and the devil can produce. It goes straight down to where our Lord went, and the Holy Ghost works out, not in thinking, but in living, this passion for Jesus Christ in any setting of life any human being indwelt by the Holy Ghost can get into, until Jesus can see of the travail of His soul and be satisfied.

God does not ask us to believe that men can be saved; we cannot pull men out of hell by believing that we can pull them out. When we see a man in hell, every attitude of our souls and minds are paralysed; we cannot believe he can be saved. God does not ask us to believe that he can be saved; He asks us whether we will believe that Jesus believes He can save him. The facts of life are awful, men's minds are crushed by the terrible facts of evil all around. When the Holy Ghost indwells us, He does not obliterate those facts, but slowly through all the features of crime and evil and wrong, there emerges the one great wonderful Figure, the Lord Jesus Christ, and the men possessed by the Holy Ghost, and having the Redemption of Christ inwrought in them, say "Lord, Thou knowest," and the saving work goes on.

Galatians 2:20 is not a theological statement, it is a statement of Christian experience wrought by the Holy Ghost. "I am Christ's and He is mine." It is the language of real passion, and it is not too strong an expression for stating the wonderful experience of oneness with Jesus Christ. Paul is so absorbed with Jesus that he does not think of himself apart from this marvellous identification with Jesus Christ. It is closer than a union, it is a oneness illustrated by the vine and the branches. "I am the Vine," not the root, but the Vine, "ye are the branches." The oneness is as close as that. "One, even as We are one."

Paul had one volcanic moment in his life when all his stubbornness was destroyed by the dynamite of the Holy Ghost. Some folk go through tremendous smashings and breakings, but there is no need for them to go that way. The great crashings and upsets and disappointments come because of stubbornness. Our great need is to ask for and receive the Holy Ghost in simple faith in the marvellous Atonement of Jesus Christ, and He will turn us into passionate lovers of the Lord. It is this passion for Christ worked out in us that makes us witnesses to Jesus wherever we are, men and women in whom He delights, upon whom He can look down with approval; men and women whom He can put in the shadow or the sun; men and women whom He can put upon their beds or on their feet; men and women whom He can send anywhere He chooses. God grant that our watchword may be a "passion for Christ," and that the Holy Ghost may work out in us the experience of Christ being all, so that He may do exactly what He likes with us.

PARTAKERS OF HIS SUFFERINGS

But, insomuch as ye are partakers of Christ's sufferings rejoice. 1 Peter 4:13 (RV)

If we are going to be used by God, He will take us through a multitude of experiences that are not meant for us at all, but meant to make us useful in His hands. There are things we go through which are unexplainable on any other line, and the nearer we get to God the more inexplicable the way seems. It is only on looking back and by getting an explanation from God's Word that we understand His dealings with us. It is part of Christian culture to know what God is after. Jesus Christ suffered "according to the will of God"; He did not suffer in the way we suffer as individuals. In the Person of Jesus Christ we have the universal presentation of the whole of the human race.

The Sufferings of the Long Trail of Faith
Ye are they which have continued with Me in My temptations. (Luke 22:28)

Jesus Christ looked upon His life as one of temptation; and He goes through the same kind of temptation in us as He went through in the days of His flesh. The essence of Christianity is that we give the Son of God a chance to live and move and have His being in us, and the meaning of all spiritual growth is that He has an increasing opportunity to manifest Himself in our mortal flesh. The temptations of Jesus are not those of a Man as man, but the temptations of God as Man. "Wherefore it behoved Him in all things to be made like unto His brethren" (Hebrews 2:17 RV). Jesus Christ's temptations and ours move in different spheres until we become His brethren by being born from above (RV mg). "For both He that sanctifieth and they who are sanctified are all of one: for which cause He is not ashamed to call them brethren" (Hebrews 2:11). By regeneration the,Son of God is formed in me and He has the same setting in my life as He had when on earth. The honour of Jesus Christ is at stake in my bodily life; am I remaining loyal to Him in the temptations which beset His life in me?

Temptation is a short cut to what is good, not to what is bad. Satan came to our Lord as an angel of light, and all his temptations centre around this point—"You are the Son of God, then do God's work in Your own way; put men's needs first, feed them, heal their sicknesses, and they will crown You King." Our Lord would not become King on that line; He deliberately rejected the suggested short cut, and chose the long trail, evading none of the suffering involved (cf. John 6:15).

"He answered and said, It is written, Man shall not live by bread alone, but by every word that proceedeth out of the mouth of God." It is a long time before we are able to listen to every word of God; we listen to one word—"bread" when we are hungry, but there is more than that. The fanatic hears only the word of God that comes through the Bible. The word of God comes through the history of the world, through the Christian Church, and through Nature. We have to learn to live by every word of God, and it takes time. If we try to listen to all the words of God at once, we become surfeited.

The Sorrows of the Long Fear of Hope
What, could ye not watch with Me one hour? (Matthew 26:40)

Am I watching with Jesus in my life? Am I looking for what He is looking for, or looking for satisfaction for myself? Very few of us watch with Jesus, we have only the idea of His watching with us. He is inscrutable to us because He represents a standard of things that only one or two of us enter into. We are easily roused over things that hurt us; we are scandalised at immorality because it upsets us. There is something infinitely more vital than the horror roused by social crimes, and that is the horror of God's Son at sin. In the Garden of Gethsemane the veil is drawn aside, and it reveals the suffering that realises the horror of sin. Are we more horror-struck by the pride of the human heart against God than we are by the miseries and crimes of human life? That is the test.

"If Thou art the Son of God, cast Thyself down" (RV)—"You will win the Kingship of men if You do something supernatural, use signs and wonders, bewitch men, and the world will be at Your feet." Jesus said, "Again it is written, Thou shalt not tempt the Lord thy God" (RV). Are we going to tempt Him again? "If God would only do the magical thing!" We have no right to call on God to do supernatural wonders. The temptation of the Church is to go into the "show business." When God is working the miracle of His grace in us it is always manifested in a chastened life, utterly restrained. Have I spurned the "long trail" and taken the "short cut" of self-realisation?—"Why should I not satisfy myself now? Why should I not do this or that? Why should I not devote myself to the cause I see?" I have no right to identify myself with a cause unless it represents that for which Jesus Christ died. If I allow Jesus Christ to realise Himself in me, I shall not find that I am delivered from temptation, but that I am loosened into it, introduced into what God calls temptation. Am I prepared for God to stamp my personal ambitions right out, prepared for Him to destroy by transfiguration my individual determinations, and bring me into fellowship with the sufferings of His Son? God's purpose is not seen on the surface; it looks as if He is permitting the breaking up of things; but Jesus Christ's hope is that the human race will be as He is Himself, perfectly at one with God. "When the Son of man cometh, shall He find faith on the earth?"

The Strain of the Last Terror of Love
(Matthew 12:46–50; John 19:25–27)
Who is My mother? (Matthew 12:48)

Behold thy mother! (John 19:27)

The greatest benefits God has conferred on human life, e.g., fatherhood, motherhood, childhood, home, become the greatest curse if Jesus Christ is not the Head. A home that does not acknowledge Jesus Christ as the Head will become exclusive on the line of its own affinities; related to Jesus Christ, the home becomes a centre for all the benedictions of motherhood and sonhood to be expressed to everyone—"an open house for the universe." By His Death and Resurrection our Lord has the right to give eternal life to every man; by His Ascension He enters Heaven and keeps the door open for humanity.

Through the travail of the nations just now the Spirit of God is working out His own purpose; no nation is exclusively God's. When the Holy Spirit enters a man, instantly he feels called to be a missionary; he has had introduced into him the very nature of God which is focused in John 3:16—"God so loved *the world.* . . ." The Holy Spirit sheds abroad in our hearts the love of God, a love which breaks all confines of body, soul and spirit. The Holy Spirit severs human connections and makes connections which are universal—a complete union of men and women all over the world in a bond in which there is no snare. God's call is for *the world;* the question of location is a matter of the engineering of God's providence.

Some things work suddenly and are seen; others, such as the life in a seed, work slowly and silently. There are some points of view which we do not see but they see us; that is, they take us into themselves; and some points of God's truth are like that. You say, "I don't understand this"—because you are part of it. We do not take God into our consciousness: God takes us into His consciousness, and that means we are taken up into His purpose, not into conscious agreement with His purpose; there is always more than we are conscious of. God's order comes to us in the haphazard. Things look as if they happen by chance, but behind all is the purpose of God, and the New Testament reveals what that purpose is. We are made partakers of Christ's sufferings; then, says Peter, rejoice, because when His glory is revealed you will be glad also with exceeding joy.

There is no snare of pride along any of these lines because there is no aim of our own in them; there is only the aim of God.

THE THEOLOGY OF REST
Mark 4:35–41

"Come unto Me, . . . and I will give you rest," i.e., build you up into a stable life in which there is neither weariness nor cessation from activities. The Bible never glorifies our natural conception of things; it does not use the words "rest" and "joy" and "peace" as we use them, and our common-sense interpretation of words must be keyed up to the way God uses them, otherwise we lose the "humour"[9] of God.

The incident recorded in Mark 4:35–41 is not an incident in the life of a man, but in the life of God as Man. This Man asleep in the boat is God Incarnate. Jesus had said to the disciples, "Let us go over unto the other side" (RV), but when the storm arose, instead of relying upon Him, they failed Him. The actual circumstances were so crushing that their common sense was up in alarm, their panic carried them off their feet, and in terror they awoke Him. When we are in fear, we can do nothing less than pray to God, but our Lord has the right to expect of those who name His Name and have His nature in them an understanding confidence in Him. Instead of that, when we are at our wits' end we go back to the elementary prayers of those who do not know Him, and prove that we have not the slightest atom of confidence in Him and in His government of the world: He is asleep—the tiller is not in His hand, and we sit down in nervous dread. God expects His children to be so confident in Him that in a crisis they are the ones upon whom He can rely. A great point is reached spiritually when we stop worrying God over personal matters or over any matter. God expects of us the one thing that glorifies Him—and that is to remain absolutely confident in Him, remembering what He has said beforehand, and sure that His purposes will be fulfilled.

Always beware of the thing that shuts you up but does not convince you—common sense will do that. What is common sense worth in such a crisis as is symbolised here? It simply disturbs God. In this incident our Lord answered the disciples' cry, but He rebuked them for their lack of faith, "Why are ye fearful? have ye not yet faith?" (RV). What a pang must have shot through their hearts—"Missed it again!" And what a pang will come through our hearts when we realise we have done the same thing, when we might have produced downright joy in the heart of Jesus by remaining absolutely confident in Him, no matter what was ahead. The joy that a believer can give to God is the purest pleasure God ever allows a saint, and it is very humiliating to realise how little joy we do give Him. We put our trust in God up to a certain point, then we say, "Now I must do my best." There are times when there is no human best to be done, when the Divine best must be left to work, and God expects those of us who know Him to be confident in His ability and power. We have to learn what these fishermen learned, that the Carpenter of Nazareth knew better than they did how to manage the boat. Is Jesus Christ a Carpenter, or is He God to me? If He is only man, why let Him take the tiller of the boat? Why pray to Him? But if He be God, then be heroic enough to go to the breaking-point and not break in your confidence in Him.

If we have faith at all it must be faith in Almighty God; when He has said a thing, He will perform it; we have to remain steadfastly obedient to Him. Are we learning to be silent unto God, or are we worrying Him with needless prayers? In this terrific crisis of war many of us have lost our wits, we see only breakers ahead,

---

9. humour: mood, temperament, or disposition.

with nothing for us to do but watch the whole thing go to ruin; and yet He said—"Let us go over unto the other side" (RV). Just as a general looks for the man who keeps his head in the fight, so the Lord looks for the man who will keep his faith in Him. "When the Son of man cometh, shall He find faith on the earth?" (Luke 18:8). There is no more glorious opportunity than the day in which we live for proving in personal life and in every way that we are confident in God.

The stars do their work without fuss; God does His work without fuss, and saints do their work without fuss. The people who are always desperately active are a nuisance; it is through the saints who are one with Him that God is doing things all the time. The broken and the jaded and the twisted are being ministered to by God through the saints who are not overcome by their own panic, who because of their oneness with Him are absolutely at rest, consequently He can work through them. A sanctified saint remains perfectly confident in God, because sanctification is not something the Lord gives me, sanctification is *Himself in me*. There is only one holiness, the holiness of God, and only one sanctification, the sanctification that has its origin in Jesus Christ. "But of Him are ye in Christ Jesus, Who was made unto us . . . sanctification" (1 Corinthians 1:30 RV). A sanctified saint is at leisure from himself and his own affairs, confident that God is bringing all things out well.

Spiritual realities can always be counterfeited. "Rest in the LORD" can be turned into pious "rust" in sentiment. What is all our talk about sanctification going to amount to? It should amount to that rest in God which means a oneness with Him such as Jesus had—not only blameless in God's sight, but a deep joy to Him. God grant we may be.

THE ALTAR OF FELLOWSHIP
2 Corinthians 1:8–10

For we would not have you ignorant, brethren, concerning our affliction which befell us in Asia. . . . 2 Corinthians 1:8 (RV)

Human fellowship can go to great lengths, but not all the way. Fellowship with God can go all lengths. The Apostle Paul literally fulfilled what we mean by this phrase, the altar of fellowship; he offered himself liberally and freely to God, and then offered himself at the hands of God, freely and fully, for the service of God among men, whether or not men understood him. "And I will very gladly spend and be spent for you; though the more abundantly I love you, the less I be loved." Do we know anything about this altar of fellowship whereby we offer back to God the best He has given us, and then let Him re-offer it as broken bread and poured-out wine to His other children?

Disasters of Fellowship
insomuch that we despaired even of life . . .

There are disasters to be faced by the one who is in real fellowship with the Lord Jesus Christ. God has never promised to keep us immune from trouble; He says "I will be with him in trouble," which is a very different thing. Paul was "an apostle of Jesus Christ by the will of God," and it is this fact that accounts for the crushing criticism and the spiteful treatment to which he was subjected by those who could not discern on what authority he based his apostleship.

Paul was a Pharisee of the Pharisees, he stood in the fore rank of learning until Jesus appeared to him, staggered him, blinded him, extinguished all his personal aims, and sent him out to be an apostle to the Gentiles—"I have chosen him." That was the ground Paul stood on, and that only—he was an apostle *"by the will of God"* (see Galatians 1:15–16).

If you are experiencing the disasters of fellowship, don't get into despair, remain unswervingly and unhesitatingly faithful to the Lord Jesus Christ and refuse to compromise for one second. Don't say "it can't be done" because you see a thing is going to crush your physical life. Calculate on the disaster of fellowship, because through it God is going to bring you into fellowship with His Son. This is also true of work for God—"except a corn of wheat fall into the ground and die. . . ."

Discipline of Fellowship
Yea, we ourselves have had the answer of death within ourselves . . . (RV)

If I am in fellowship with Jesus Christ and am indwelt by Him, I have the answer of death in myself, and nothing the world, the flesh or the devil can do can touch me. This divine light came to Paul out of his desperate experience in Ephesus; he realised then that nothing could any more affright him. The discipline of fellowship brought about in Paul's experience the assimilation of what he believed. We say many things which we believe, but they have never been tested. Discipline has to come through all the things we believe in order to turn them into real spiritual possessions. It is the trial of our faith that is precious. "Hang in" to Jesus Christ against all odds until He turns your spiritual beliefs into real possessions. It is heroism to believe in God.

Devotion of Fellowship
that we should not trust in ourselves . . .

Whenever we begin to note where we are successful for God, we do trust in ourselves. In Luke 10:20 our Lord says, in effect, "Don't rejoice in successful service, but rejoice that you are rightly related to Me." The Lord Jesus Christ is the beginning, the middle and the end. Many are willing to accept sanctification, but they do not want the One Who is sanctification. "I am looking to see whether I am a blessing." Supposing Paul had looked to see the result of his work amongst the Corinthians! It seemed disaster all

along the line. The devotion of fellowship means we are persuaded, like Paul, that "neither death, nor life . . . nor any other creature, shall be able to separate us from the love of God, which is in Christ Jesus our Lord." God has become to us the one vital Reality.

The Declaration of Fellowship
. . . but in God which raiseth the dead.

"According to my earnest expectation and hope, . . . Christ shall be magnified in my body" (Philippians 1:20). Paul argues—"whether that means life or death, no matter!" "I trust in God, and know He will do all He intends to do through me, and that nothing and no one can thwart His purpose."

Do I know anything about the altar of fellowship? Am I related to things, whether they be disastrous or delightful, from the standpoint of my oneness with the Lord Jesus Christ? The one dominating enthusiasm of the Apostle Paul's life was his personal, passionate devotion to Jesus Christ. "In all these things we are more than conquerors through Him that loved us."

THE EVENING TEST OF LOYALTY

For Joab had turned after Adonijah, though he turned not after Absalom. 1 Kings 2:28

Is there an equivalent to this in your life? Do you find you are turning away from loyalty to Jesus for some insignificant thing? There was a time when you stood magnificently for God, days when heart and brain and body were ablaze in absolute devotion to Jesus Christ, you would have gone anywhere for Him. The prince of this world came and found nothing in you in those days; the lusts of the world found you adamant. Has God been lifting the veil and do you find the enthusiasm is gone, the great passionate devotion to Jesus is gone? The prince of this world has begun to find something in you at last, and what a miserably insignificant thing it is that has turned you! The reason you are not so zealous for the glory of God as you used to be, not so keen about the habits of your spiritual life, is because you have imperceptibly begun to surrender morally.

Beware of the Spiritual Undertime
With freedom did Christ set us free: stand fast therefore, and be not entangled again in a yoke of bondage. (Galatians 5:1 RV)

Joab stood the big test and was not turned by the fascinations of Absalom, but towards the end of his life

he was turned by the craven Adonijah. Always remain alert to the fact that where anyone has gone back is exactly where we all may go back ("Wherefore let him that thinketh he standeth take heed lest he fall"). You have borne the burden and heat of the day, been through the big test, now beware of the undertime, the after-part of the day spiritually. We are apt to forget that there is always an afterwards, and that it comes close on the heels of the present. You made a big break with all that Absalom represents, and you are apt to say nothing will have any effect on you now, but it certainly will. You stood the big test with Absalom; don't turn after Adonijah. It is in the aftermath of a great spiritual transaction that the "retired sphere of the leasts" begins to sap. "Now that I have been through the supreme crisis, it is not in the least likely that I shall turn to the things of the world." It is the least likely thing that is the peril. The Bible characters never fell on their weak points but on their strong ones; unguarded strength is double weakness. It is in the after-part of the day spiritually that we have to be alert. This does not mean that you are to be morbidly introspective, looking forward with dread, but that you keep alert; don't forecast where the temptation will come. One of the best things for your spiritual welfare is to keep recounting the wonders God has done for you, record them in a book; mark the passage in your Bible and continually refer to it, keep it fresh in your mind. Thomas Boston[10] used to pray—"O Lord, keep me strong in the sense of Thy call." We do not keep the ideal of our attachment to Jesus constantly enough before us.

Be Alert for the Spiritual Undertow

Ye were running well; who did hinder you . . . ? (Galatians 5:7 RV)

An undertow is an undercurrent flowing in a different direction from the water at the surface. It is the undercurrent that drowns; a swimmer will never plunge into an undercurrent, a fool will. The spiritual undertow that switched away the Galatians was Judaism, formalism. It was not dominant, but hidden; it ran in exactly the opposite direction to the current of liberty into which they were being brought by Christ. Instead of going out to sea, out into the glorious liberty of the children of God, they were being switched away. "Ye were running well . . ." (RV)—they had been heading straight for the ocean, but the undercurrent of ritualism bewitched them, hindered them from obeying the truth. After a big transaction with God the current of your life heads you straight out to sea, right over the harbour bar, every sail set; now be alert for the spiritual undertow that would suck you back. The undercurrent is always most dangerous just where the river merges with the sea. The undercurrent is of the same nature as the river and will take you back into its swirling current; not out into the main stream, but back to the shipwrecks on the bank. The most pitiable of all wrecks are those inside the harbour.

Now that you have been swept out into the realisation of God's purpose, be alert over the things which used to be strong in the upper reaches of your life. The surface current, the current in which God has set your life, is the most powerful; but be alert for the spiritual undertow, the current that sets in another direction. It is after the floodtide of a spiritual transaction that the undertow begins to tell, and to tell terribly. The undercurrent for each one of us is different. It is only felt at certain stages of the tide; when the tide is full there is no undercurrent.

Be Careful of the Spiritual Undertone

For Demas forsook me, having loved this present world. . . . (2 Timothy 4:10 RV)

In music an undertone is a tone not quite in tune. When waves occur in a chord it is because the organ or piano is a half semitone out of tune. The *Vox Humana* stop, which gives the effect of the human voice, is tuned a half semitone flat to the rest of the notes, which accounts for the peculiar wave, almost a discord. It is the same spiritually. As you listen carefully to the music God is producing in your life, is there an undertone, something not in full harmony, a least thing, that you will not detect unless you are spiritually expert? The undertone was represented in Demas by his love of the world. Earlier Paul has referred to him with joy as "my fellow-worker" (Philemon 24 RV), but now the undertone of worldliness has begun to tell and is switching him off. The undertone in music is the fascinating thing that lends bewitchment; and spiritually it is the undertone that puts the tiniest tang of danger into the life. Be careful of it. The least likely thing is that we should turn away from God, but it is the least likely thing that will trip us up if we are not warned.

You have been having big transactions with God and are being taken right out into the purpose of God, now beware of the undertime, the after-part of the spiritual day. You have remained true to God under great tests, now be alert over the least things. "Mighty events turn on a straw" (Carlyle).[11] To be forewarned is to be forearmed. The way to keep alert is to keep your memory bright before God; ask Him never to allow you to forget what you have been in relation to Him. Is God saying to you—"You are not in love with Me now, but I remember the time when you were"—"I remember . . . the love of thine espousals"? If you find as you recall what God remembers about you, that He is not what He used to be to you, let it produce shame and humiliation, because that shame will bring the godly sorrow that works repentance. Don't merely accept the rebuke—receive it, and alter your conduct at once. Our only safety is to abide in Him. "Kept by the power of God."

---

10. Thomas Boston (1677–1732): Scottish Presbyterian cleric.
11. Thomas Carlyle (1795–1881): Scottish-born literary figure in nineteenth-century England, a writer, biographer, essayist, historian, and critic.

THE DISCIPLINE OF DISILLUSIONMENT
Isaiah 38:15–20

To be disillusioned means that for us there are no more false appearances in life. A disillusionised person, although all he says may be correct, is often cynical and unkindly severe about other people. The disillusionment which comes from God is just as accurate and clear and understanding, but there is no cynicism in it. "But Jesus did not trust Himself unto them, . . . for He Himself knew what was in man" (John 2:24–25 RV).

The discipline of disillusionment brings us to the place where we see men and women as they are, and yet there is no cynicism, we have no stinging, bitter things to say. Many of the cruel things in life spring from the fact that we will suffer from illusions, we are not true to one another as facts, we are only true to our ideas of one another. Everything is either delightful and fine, or else mean[12] and dastardly, according to our own ideas. Jesus Christ is the Master of the human soul, He knows what is in the human heart (see Mark 7:21–22), and He has no illusions about any man.

Few of us believe what Jesus Christ says, we prefer to trust our illusion of innocence. When we trust our own innocence, we enthrone our illusion and discard Jesus Christ, and it is likely that something will happen to awaken us to the fact that what Jesus Christ says is true. If we give our hearts to Him to be kept, we need never know this experimentally. A certain type of innocence is culpable. Innocence is the characteristic of a child, but innocence in a man or woman is culpable and wrong. It means that their own whiteness is so guarded that they are unfit for life. Men and women must be pure and virtuous, and virtue is always the outcome of conflict.

Most of the suffering in human life comes because we refuse to be disillusioned. For instance, if I love a human being, and do not love God, I demand of that man or woman an infinite satisfaction which they cannot give. I demand of them every perfection and every rectitude, and when I do not get it, I become cruel and vindictive and jealous. Think of the average married life after, say, five or ten years; too often it sinks down into the most commonplace drudgery. The reason is that the husband and wife have not known God rightly, they have not gone through the transfiguration of love, nor entered through the discipline of disillusionment into satisfaction in God, and consequently they have begun to endure one another instead of having one another for enjoyment in God. The human heart must have satisfaction, but there is only one Being Who can satisfy the last aching abyss of the human heart, and that is our Lord Jesus Christ. That is why He is apparently so severe in regard to every human relationship. He says if we are going to be His disciples, occasion may arise when we must hate both father and mother, and every closest tie there is. Our Lord has no illusions about men, and He knows that every relationship in life that is not based on loyalty to Him will end in disaster.

In Rectitude through Suffering

I shall go softly [as in solemn procession, RV mg] all my years. (Isaiah 38:15)

A peculiar nobility, a stately element, comes into the life that has had to face death; that man sees things in their real perspective. It is through suffering that we are disillusioned, but selfish suffering does not disillusionise. A man may be perfected through suffering or be made worse through suffering, it depends on his disposition. Am I in the place of disillusionment, or have I refused to be disillusioned when God has tried to talk to me through difficulties and in sufferings? If I have, it is a sign that I am still suffering from illusions; I am still culpably innocent. God is not to blame; I am to blame.

The moral calibre of a man shows itself in the way he conducts himself in the shallow things of life. Our lives are divided into two domains, the shallow and the profound. Jesus Christ was considered to be so shallow by the religious people of His day that they said He was a gluttonous man and a winebibber. His was such a full-orbed natural life that no attention was paid to Him, He was easily ignored and made of no account. Men were blind to the real profundity of His life. Our profound, solitary life is with God alone, and we have no business to obtrude it before others, unless God is bringing them there too. The shallow means the actual surface life we all live with one another. Am I prepared to let God dominate both the shallow and the profound?

The test of our spiritual life is how we behave when we ought to be shallow for God. It is easy to behave at a prayer meeting; it takes all the grace of God to behave at a marriage feast. We must not

---

12. mean: as used here, something or someone ordinary, common, low, or ignoble, rather than cruel or spiteful.

obtrude the prayer meeting conduct into the shallow things. We have to carry out our relationship with God in the shallow things, without any illusions.

No one ever became spiritual without being fanatical for a season. The shallow intercourse of our lives falls away and people object to us, because, if we are right, they are wrong. It is the swing of the pendulum to the opposite extreme of what the life used to be. My "right hand" is the thing that makes me delightful to other people, yet Jesus Christ says, "If your right hand causes you to stumble in your walk with Me, cut it off." The maimed stage is only for a season; the example for a Christian is not a maimed life, but the life of the Lord Jesus Christ (see Matthew 5:29–30, 48).

In Realisation through Salvation
Thou hast loved my soul from the pit. (Isaiah 38:17 RV mg)

This is the greatest revelation that ever struck the human life, viz., that God loves the sinner. God so loved the world when it was sinful that He sent His Son to die for it. Our Lord has no illusions about any of us. He sees every man and woman as the descendants of Adam who sinned, and with capacities in our hearts of which we have no idea. Natural ability has nothing to do with fitness for God's salvation, it may have to do with fitness for Christian work, that is a matter of civilisation.

Hezekiah begins to see himself exactly as he is in God's sight. When once a man has been "undressed" by the Holy Ghost, he will never be able to despair of anyone else. External sins are to a large extent the accident of upbringing, but when the Spirit of God comes in and probes to the depths and reveals the disposition of sin, we begin to understand what salvation is. God cannot take anything from the sinner but his solid sin, otherwise salvation would have no meaning for him (see 2 Corinthians 5:21).

Have I realised disillusionment through salvation? Think of the worst man or woman you know, do you believe that that one can be presented perfect in Jesus Christ? If you do not, it is because you are still under an illusion about yourself, you still have a notion that there is something in your virtues that will save you. There are men and women, such as the rich young ruler and Mary of Bethany, who are utterly unsullied until they receive the Spirit of God, and then a remarkable thing happens—the corruption to themselves of their natural virtues. It is a difficult thing to state because so few try to state it. When someone who is possessed of patience naturally is born again, he becomes impatient; or if someone has been pure and upright and worthy naturally, he may begin to have thoughts of evil such as he never dreamed of

before. Our natural virtues break down because they are not promises of what we are going to be, but remnants of what we once were, remnants of the man God made and sin ruined. Jesus Christ does not patch up our natural virtues. He creates a new man, "Wherefore if any man is in Christ, he is a new creature: the old things are passed away; behold, they are become new" (2 Corinthians 5:17 RV), and we find that "every virtue we possess, is His alone."

Jesus Christ cannot be spoken of in terms of the natural virtues, as a patient Man, or a pure, noble Man. He is the Man from heaven, the full-orbed Man, and the New Testament says we have to live as He lived. Our old way of reasoning and looking at things must go, and all things must become new. The way we act when we come up against things proves whether we have been disillusioned or not; do we trust in our wits or do we worship God? If we trust in our wits, God will have to repeat the same lesson until we learn it. Whenever our faith is not in God, and in Him alone, there is still an illusion somewhere.

In Revelation through Submission
They that go down into the pit cannot hope for Thy truth. (Isaiah 38:18 RV)

Submission does not mean that I submit to the power of God because I must. A stoic submits without passion, that is slavery; a saint sees God's will and submits to it with a passionate love, and in his daily life exhibits his love to God to Whom he has submitted. The real meaning of submission is seen in the Sermon on the Mount. Jesus says, "If you are rightly related to God, show that relationship to men; submit enough to live it out in your daily life." It will mean that you do not take the law into your own hands, you do not refuse to be hit. You never need be hit or hurt, but every time you refuse to be, your Lord takes the blow. Think of the honour our Lord confers on us; we have the power to prevent Him being stabbed by taking the stab ourselves. "Now I rejoice in my sufferings for your sake, and fill up on my part that which is lacking of the afflictions of Christ in my flesh for His body's sake" (Colossians 1:24 RV). When someone over-reaches us, every logical power in us says—Resent it. Morally speaking we should, but Jesus Christ says—If you are My disciple, you will go the second mile; immediately we do, men will cast out our names as evil, as He said they would.

Until we are rightly related to God, we deify pluck and heroism. We will do anything that is heroic, anything that puts the inspiration of strain on us; but when it comes to submitting to being a weak thing for God, it takes Almighty God to do it. "We are weak in Him." Some of us have still to go through disillusionment on this line, we have not learned to submit, we prefer to stand on our rights. "Take My yoke upon you, and learn of Me," says Jesus. Am I loyal to Him or am I clinging to my own rights? Is my tongue God's, or is there the poison of asps under it?

In Rejoicing through Sacrifice
Therefore we will sing my songs to the stringed instruments all the days of our life in the house of the LORD. (Isaiah 38:20 RV)

Hezekiah is not lying in a stately armchair with a sentimental atmosphere around him, he is still sick with a boil, but he says, "I will offer to Thee the sacrifice of praise." Praising costs. If you are in the dumps, sing! Sacrifice means giving up something that we mind giving up. We talk of giving up our possessions; none of them are ours to give up. "A man's life consisteth not in the abundance of the things which he possesseth." Our Lord tells us to give up the one thing that is going to hurt badly, viz., our right to ourselves.

Jesus Christ taught hypocrisy to His disciples! "But thou, when thou fastest, anoint thy head, and wash thy face, that thou be not seen of men to fast" (RV). Don't say you are fasting, or that you spent the night in prayer, wash your face; and never let your dearest friend know what you put yourself through. Natural stoicism was created by God, and when it is transfigured by the indwelling Holy Ghost, people will never think of you. "He must increase, but I must decrease." John is not saying that with a quivering mouth, or out of modesty; he is expressing the spiritual delight of his life. I am to decrease because He has come! He says it with a manly thrill. Is Jesus Christ increasing in my life, or am I taking everything for myself? When I get disillusioned I see Him and Him alone, there are no illusions left. It is a matter of indifference how I am hurt, the one thing I an concerned about is that every man may be presented "perfect in Christ Jesus."

DID JESUS CHRIST COME FOR PEACE?

His Name shall be called . . . Prince of Peace. Isaiah 9:6

The Christmas Message
Glory to God in the highest, and on earth peace among men in whom He is well pleased. (Luke 2:14 RV)

Not a Prophecy but a Proclamation
The average views of Christianity seem to be right until they are made explicit. For instance, the average view that Christianity stands for peace, for the brotherhood of men, for the peace and prosperity of nations is true generally speaking; but if you look at it narrowly you will find there is a great deal that does not fit into that view, and the critic (not necessarily a captious critic, but a man with an open mind, facing things as they are to-day) asks—"What does it all amount to? Twenty centuries have passed since Jesus, the Prince of Peace, came and the angels prophesied peace on earth, but where is peace?" The New Testament does not say that the angels prophesied peace: they proclaimed peace—"on earth peace among men in whom He is well pleased" (RV), i.e., peace to men of goodwill towards God. Jesus Christ came to manifest that God was with man, "and they shall call His Name Emmanuel, which is being interpreted, God with us" (RV). Jesus Christ is a unique Being—God-Man, and by Him any man can be made a son of God according to the pattern of Jesus Christ. This is the Christian revelation. Jesus says, "Come unto Me," and

when a man does come to Jesus he is born into another domain and his whole outlook is altered. Deliverance from sin is only part of the meaning of being born from above (RV mg), the reason it is so important to us is because we are sinners; but the meaning of new birth from God's side is that a man is brought into the viewpoint of His Son. The Christmas message crystallises the whole thing: God manifest in the flesh is what has become profoundly possible for any man on the basis of Redemption.

The Christ Menace
Think not that I came to cast[mg] peace on the earth: I came not to cast [mg] peace, but a sword. (Matthew 10:34 RV)

Not a Propaganda but a Personal Power
Is that the average view of what Jesus Christ came to do? The average view is that He came as a meek and mild and gently-dispositioned Person to spread peace and love all around and to make life infinitely more beautiful. But Jesus says here—"Do not allow yourselves to think that that is what I came to do; I did not come to fling peace abroad indiscriminately. I came to send a sword." We build our ideas on what we are taught about Jesus Christ, not on what the New Testament says. We are taught that Jesus Christ was meek and loving, and He was; but we forget the times when He was ablaze with zeal for His Father's

honour. In the Temple instead of seeing a "meek and mild and gentle Jesus," we see a terrible Being with a whip of small cords in His hand, driving out the money-changers. "I am meek and lowly in heart," says Jesus, but His meekness was towards God, not towards men. God the Father could do what He liked with His Son, and the Son received with absolute meekness the dispensations of the Father.

"I came not to cast [mg] peace, but a sword" (RV). Immediately the Holy Spirit brings you face to face with a presentation of truth which you never saw before, your peace is gone, and instead there is the sword of conviction. The coming of Jesus Christ is not a peaceful thing, it is a disturbing thing, because it means the destruction of every peace that is not based on a personal relationship to Himself. If once the moral equilibrium has been upset by conviction of sin, holiness is the only result or no peace for ever. "I was alive without the law once," says Paul. Immediately a man comes to see what Jesus Christ demands, his peace of mind is upset. "If I had not come, they had not had sin." Then why did He come? People say—"The Sermon on the Mount is good enough for me" (I should think it was!), "but I do not see the need for preaching the Atonement and the Cross of Christ." But where are you going to begin to be what the Sermon on the Mount says you must be? Jesus Christ's demand is that we be as holy as He is Himself, that we reach the "whiter than snow-shine" in our conduct, that we are unfathomably pure in heart. Are you so pure in heart that you never lust, never have a thought in the background of your mind that God could censure? If all Jesus Christ came to do was to put before us an ideal we cannot attain, we are happier without knowing it. But Jesus Christ did not come primarily to teach: He came to put within us His own disposition, viz., Holy Spirit, whereby we can live a totally new life. By conviction of sin a man is probed wide awake and made to realise that he needs to be regenerated; when he gets there, Jesus says—"Blessed are you." The one essential thing which makes a man a Christian is not what he believes in his head but what he is in disposition. Jesus Christ comes to the central part of a man's life, and the bedrock of Christianity is that Jesus Christ has done something for me I could not do for myself. Christianity is not adherence to a set of principles or to a plan of salvation, but a personal relationship to Jesus Christ; consequently the spontaneous working of the Holy Spirit in a man may make him appear inconsistent. A Christian is not consistent to hard and fast creeds, he is consistent only to the life of the Son of God in him.

The Christian Meaning
Wherefore if any man is in Christ, he is a new creature. (2 Corinthians 5:17 RV)

Not a Preaching but a Purity
If we are saved by the grace of God it means not only that we are delivered from perdition, but that we are a new creation (RV mg). The condemnation is to know a thing and not work it out. We know we have experienced the grace of God, but are we living the life of regeneration in our actual experience? We take the Christian view up to a certain point and exploit it according to our belief. The average Christian says— "Oh, yes, I am saved." Well, produce your goods! Where are the characteristics in you that Jesus Christ taught us to expect in a Christian? In what way are you different from other men? Are you just as hard in driving a bargain as they are? If Christianity does not affect my money and my marriage relationships, it is not worth anything. To-day men are asking not so much—Is Christianity true; but is it real? Does it amount to anything in actual life? If I have a personal relationship to Jesus on the basis of His Redemption, it will show in the way I live, in the way I act towards men; "old things are passed away; behold all things are become new."

Did Jesus Christ come for peace? He did; but it is a peace that is characteristic of Himself, not peace at any price. "My peace I give unto you." The peace that Jesus gives is never engineered by circumstances on the outside; it is a peace based on a personal relationship that holds all through. "In the world ye shall have tribulation: . . . in Me . . . peace."

> *Oh, the peace my Saviour gives,*
> *Peace I never knew before,*

is a Biblical thought. That peace is the deepest thing a human personality can experience, it is almighty, a peace that passes all understanding.

SPIRITUAL EDUCATION

In your patience ye shall win your souls. Luke 21:19 (RV)

Education is a bringing out of what is there and giving it the power of expression, not packing in what does not belong; and spiritual education means learning how to give expression to the Divine life that is in us when we are born from above (RV mg).

"In your patience ye shall win your souls" (RV), said Jesus to His disciples. Soul is the expression of my personal spirit in my body, the way I reason and think and act, and Jesus taught that a man must lose his soul in order to gain it; he must lose absolutely his own way of reasoning and looking at things, and begin to estimate from an entirely different standpoint. We have the Spirit of Jesus gifted to us, but we have to form the mind which was also in Christ Jesus. No man has the mind of Christ unless he has acquired it.

Dimensions of Divine Love
For God so loved the world, that He gave His only begotten Son. . . . (John 3:16)

. . . the breadth and length and height and depth, and to know the love of Christ which passeth knowledge . . . (Ephesians 3:18–19 RV)

The first thing we need to be educated in spiritually is a knowledge of the dimensions of Divine love, its length and depth and breadth and height. That God is love is a revelation. Unless I am born from above (RV mg), what is the use of telling me God is love? To me He is not love. Where is the love of God in war? in suffering? in all the inevitable inequalities of life? No one who faces facts as they are could ever prove that God is love unless he accepts the revelation of His love made by Jesus Christ. John 3:16 does not begin to have any meaning to the natural man who knows nothing whatever of the domain Jesus Christ represents; but let him come up against things and be brought to his wits' end, and then let him read John 3:16. Not until we realise that there is something tragic at the basis of human life shall we recognise the love of God.

In the Cross we may see the dimensions of Divine love. The Cross is not the cross of a man, but the exhibition of the heart of God. At the back of the wall of the world stands God with His arms outstretched, and every man driven there is driven into the arms of God. The Cross of Jesus is the supreme evidence of the love of God (Romans 8:35–39). "Who shall separate us from the love of Christ?" (v. 35).

The Cross of Christ reveals that the blazing centre of the love of God is the holiness of God, not His kindness and compassion. If the Divine love pretends I am all right when I am all wrong, then I have a keener sense of justice than the Almighty. God is a holy God, and the marvel of the Redemption is that God the Holy One puts into me, the unholy one, a new disposition, the disposition of His Son.

Direction of Divine Living *(1 Corinthians 13:4–8)*
Love is the sovereign preference of my person for another person, and Jesus demands that that other Person be Himself; and the direction of Divine living is that I deliberately identify myself with Jesus Christ's interests in other people. "Love suffereth long, and is kind; love envieth not; love . . . seeketh not its own, is not provoked, taketh not account of evil; . . . beareth all things, believeth all things, hopeth all things, endureth all things. Love never faileth" (RV). That is Christian living in actual life. If I have the disposition of a fault-finder, I am a most uncomfortable person to live with, but if the love of God has been shed abroad in my heart, I begin to see extraordinary self-sacrifice under the roughest of exteriors. I begin to see nobility where before I only saw meanness,[13] because I see only what I bring with me the power of seeing—a most humiliating thing to realise!

The direction of Divine living is that I identify myself with God's interests in other people, and He is interested in some funny people, viz., you and me! We see the humour of our Heavenly Father in the way He brings around us the type of people who are to us what we have been to Him; now He will watch how we behave to them. How did Jesus treat us? With infinite patience, with amplitude of forgiveness and generosity. "Now," He says, "treat them in the same way." "But if ye forgive not men their trespasses, neither will your Father forgive your trespasses."

Never try to be right with an abstract enemy, but get right with the enemy you have got. It is easy to talk about loving the heathen; never go off on the abstract. The direction of Divine living is that I have to be as kind to others as God has been to me, not the others I have not met, but those I have met. ". . . that ye may be the children of your Father which is in heaven."

---

13. mean: as used here, something or someone ordinary, common, low, or ignoble, rather than cruel or spiteful.

Another direction of Divine living is the realising that a Christian has the right not to insist on his rights; this is only learned by the sharpest and most severe lessons. In the Sermon on the Mount our Lord teaches us not to look for justice, but never to cease to give it. That is not common sense, it is either madness or Christianity. To look for justice is to educate myself not in the practice of Divine living, but in my "divine" right to myself. Beware of looking to see where other people come short. God expects us to be exactly what we know the other person should be— when we realise that, we will stop criticising and having a measuring rod for other people.

When the love of God is in me I must learn how to let it express itself; I must educate myself in the matter; it takes time. Acquire your soul with patience, says Jesus. Never give way to this spirit—"Oh, well, I have fallen again, I will stay down now." Have patience with yourself, and remember that this is salvation not for the hereafter, but for here and now.

Discipline of Divine Loyalty

Lovest thou Me? . . . Feed My sheep. (John 21:17)

Is that what we have been doing, feeding Jesus Christ's sheep? Take a rapid survey—have we been nourishing the lives of people in the understanding of Jesus, or has our aim been to maintain our particular deposit of doctrine? "Divine loyalty," says Jesus, "is that you feed My sheep in the knowledge of Me, not feed them with your doctrine." Peter had boasted earlier of his love for Jesus—"though all men shall be offended because of Thee, yet will I never be offended," but there is no brag left in him now— "Lord, Thou knowest all things; Thou knowest that I love Thee." "Feed My sheep." The discipline of Divine loyalty is not that I am true to a doctrine, but so true to Jesus that other people are nourished in the knowledge of Him. Get rid of the idea that you must do good things, and remember what Jesus says, if you believe on Me, out of you will flow rivers of living water. In the Christian life it is never "Do, do," but "Be, be, and I will do through you." The type of man produced by the Spirit of Jesus is the one who bears a growing family likeness to Jesus.

Am I getting nobler, better, more helpful, more humble, as I get older? Am I exhibiting the life that men take knowledge of as having been with Jesus, or am I getting more self-assertive, more deliberately determined to have my own way? It is a great thing to tell yourself the truth.

These are some of the lines of spiritual education: learning the dimensions of Divine Love, that the centre of that love is holiness; that the direction of Divine living is a deliberate surrender of our own point of view in order to learn Jesus Christ's point of view, and seeing that men and women are nourished in the knowledge of Jesus. The only way that can be done is by being loyal to Jesus myself.

THE MAKE-UP OF A WORKER
1 Timothy 1:12–17

The Service of Memory

And last of all, as unto one born out of due time, He appeared to me also. (1 Corinthians 15:8 RV)

For ye have heard of my manner of life in time past . . . how that beyond measure I persecuted the church of God. . . . (Galatians 1:13 RV)

Paul refers to himself as "one born out of due time."

Every worker for God has that feeling about himself—"If only I had known this before"; or, "If only I had made better use of my time." There is always the feeling that we have certain drawbacks. These thoughts continually recur on the threshold of the mind of the worker, and they have to be overcome. The only way we can serve God is by having "no confidence in the flesh."

When Paul says "forgetting those things which are behind," he is not referring to his past life; Paul never forgot that he had been "a blasphemer, and a persecutor, and injurious"; but he determinedly forgot all he had attained to in the Christian life, because he was always pressing on to "the things which are before." The Gospel of the grace of God takes the stain of memory from a worker, not by making him ignore the past, but by enabling him to see that God can make it of service in his work for God. A worker should never tell people to forget the past; preachers of the "gospel of temperament" do that. If we forget the past we will be hard and obtuse. If we are hard, we are of no use to God; and unless we know the Cross of Christ as the power which takes the stinging stain out of memory and transforms it, we are of no use to others. Unless a worker has had the experience of the grace of God transforming the stain of memory into a personal experience of salvation, there will be a weak-kneed-ness and a feeble-handed-ness about him that will hinder God's message. If there is no sense of sin, no stain in memory to be transformed, the trend of the teaching is apt to be the line of higher education and culture and rarely the neat line Paul was always on. The Gospel can never be preached by sinless lips, but only by the lips of those who have been saved from sin by the Atonement. Angels cannot preach the Gospel, only beings such as Paul and you and I can preach the Gospel. We say that Jesus preached the Gospel, but He did more: He came that there might be a Gospel to preach.

The first element in the make-up of a worker is that he knows the service of memory, not a memory of things that he can excuse, but a memory out of which God has taken the sting, so that he is in the place where he can become the minister of salvation to others. The Holy Spirit will bring the worker back again and again to the stained places in memory and will make them the sweetest, the most radiant portion of that one's inner life with God. The great marvel of God's grace is that "where sin abounded, grace did much more abound."

The "Seeing" of the Disciples

Then after three years I went up to Jerusalem to visit Cephas, and tarried with him fifteen days. (Galatians 1:18 RV)

Think of Paul after three years in Arabia, where he was altogether broken and then re-made by the grace of God, coming to Peter and being with him for fifteen days—can you imagine what happened? How Peter would go over the whole story, beginning with the scenes on the lake right on to the Garden of Gethsemane and the Cross; and Peter would take Paul to the Communion service, and they would see widows there, made so by Paul. Think what a memory like that would mean to a man of acute sensitiveness. It takes great courage for a forgiven man to come in contact with those whom he has wronged. Paul was ever after solicitous for the widows and orphans, remembering what he had done. It was these things that brought Paul to the place of saying—"I determined not to know anything among you, save Jesus Christ, and Him crucified." This element comes into our lives too. Every time the Spirit of God puts His finger on some wrong in the past and the tears of the soul commence, it is that He may show the marvel of His salvation.

Spiritual Appreciation

Wherefore we henceforth know no man after the flesh: even though we have known Christ after the flesh, yet now we know Him so no more. (2 Corinthians 5:16 RV)

"From the Old Testament point of view the progress is made from the knowledge of Christ to the knowledge of Jesus; from the New Testament point of view the progress is made from the knowledge of Jesus to the knowledge of Christ" (Bengel).[14] With us the progress is neither of these. It is from the standpoint of a personal emancipation that we begin to learn Who the historic Jesus Christ was. The phrase "Back to Jesus" is right only if we go back to Jesus and know Him in the way Paul knew Him, viz., after the Spirit. ". . . Who being in the form of God"—part of the Trinity—He "emptied Himself" (RV) of that form and took on Him another form, the form of a servant. Paul knew Jesus Christ in neither of these forms; he never saw Him in the form of God, because no man has ever seen God; and he never saw Him in the days of His flesh. Paul only knew Jesus Christ after He was glorified, a unique Being—God manifested in glorified flesh; consequently Paul reasons differently from the other apostles: he is the one used by the Holy Ghost to give us the doctrine of the Person of Christ. We can never know Jesus "after the flesh" as the early disciples did, we know Him only after the Spirit, hence the insistence on receiving the Spirit.

Are we putting anything that Christ has done in the place of His Cross? It is a snare that continually besets us until we learn the passion of Paul's life: the only thing I am determined to know among you is Jesus Christ, and Him crucified. What constitutes the call of God to preach? Not that I have a special gift, not that God has sanctified me; but that by the marvel of His grace I have caught God's meaning in the Cross of Christ, and life can never be the same again. Many of us who call ourselves Christian workers ought to be learners in God's school of Calvary. It is of immense value to know what the Cross of Christ can do for me, but that does not constitute a preacher: a preacher is constituted by the fact that he has seen God's heart revealed in the Cross of Christ, and says—"I am determined henceforth to preach nothing but Jesus Christ, and Him crucified," not—"myself crucified with Christ," that is a mere experience; but—"the one Figure I am determined to present is Jesus Christ, and Him crucified."

---

14. Johann Albrect Bengel (1687–1752): German Bible scholar.

LOYALTY TO THE FORLORN HOPE

If I had said, I will speak thus; behold, I had dealt treacherously with the generation of thy children. Psalm 73:15 (RV)

Loyalty to God and to God's children is the supreme test in the life of a saint. We are never free from disloyalty unless we are actually loyal. The Psalmist realised that to speak as he had been doing was to be a traitor to God's children. With whom are we standing in this generation? Are we being loyal to God and to His saints? Indignation towards every yoke but the yoke of Christ is the only attitude for the saint. Our discouragement arises from egotism. Discouragement is "disenchanted egotism"—the heart knocked out of what I want. A saint cannot be discouraged any more than Jesus Christ could be. "He shall not fail nor be discouraged." Why? Because He never wanted anything but His Father's will. We become discouraged because we do not like being told the truth; we look only for those things that will quicken and enliven us.

Faith in God Reigning over the World *(Psalm 73:1–14)*

It is easy to *say* God reigns, and then to see Satan, suffering and sin reigning, and God apparently powerless. Belief in God must be tried before it is of value to God or to a child of His. It is the trial of our faith that makes us wealthy in God's sight. We begin by saying—"I know that God is love, that He is just and holy and true"; then we come up against common-sense facts that flatly contradict what we said we believed. Are we going to succumb, as the Psalmist nearly did, to pessimistic moods of intellect and say— "After all I must abandon that view of God"? If we try to answer the problems of this world by intellectual or scientific methods we shall go mad, or else deny that the problems exist. Never get into the ostrich-like attitude of Christian Science, and say that there is no such thing as death or sin or pain. Jesus Christ makes us open our eyes and look at these things. God is the only Being Who can stand the slander that arises because the devil and pain and sin are in the world. Stand true to the life hid with Christ in God and to the facts you have to face. You will have no answer intellectually, but your faith in God will be so unshakeably firm that others will begin to see there is an answer they have never guessed. "I am the Way, the Truth, and the Life."

Metaphysically it may be true to say that suffering is the outcome of sin, but what about the problems that theory produces? What is needed is not a solution satisfying to the mind, but a moral conception, a solution that comes through a personal relationship to God Whose character we believe in but Whose ways we are unable to explain as yet. We are not true to God's character to-day, but to our creeds, to our presentations of truth, and to our experiences; but these do not cover all the facts. The question is, will the child of God in the "in between" of this life where sin and Satan are rampant, remain true to God when everything is going contrary to what he believes God's character to be?

"For I was envious at the fools [RV mg], when I saw the prosperity of the wicked." The prosperity of the wicked remains a problem to everyone who is outside the life hid with Christ in God. It is only from that centre that we come slowly by faith to a solution. The problem persists, and it cannot be answered intellectually or psychologically. Moral and spiritual integrity cannot be measured by God's blessings. God sends His favours on good and bad alike. The blessings of God are an indication that God is overflowing in grace and benediction irrespective of a man's relationship to Him. Men may partake of the blessings of God and yet never come into relationship with Him. (See Matthew 5:45–48.)

Faith in God Ruling among Worldliness *(Psalm 73:15–22)*

It is concentration on God that keeps us free from moral and spiritual panic. The one message all through the Sermon on the Mount is—Concentrate on God, and be carefully careless about everything else. To-day we are evading concentration on God and devoting ourselves to the cause of Christian work. The busyness of duties will knock us out of relationship to God more quickly than the devil. Most of us are surrounded with Christian fellowship and live such sheltered lives that we forget there are those who have to live a life of unspotted holiness in the midst of moral abominations, and God does not take them out of it. If once we lose sight of the personal relationship to God, right and wrong become relative, not absolute. "Make allowances." Never! We can only learn by the life hid with Christ in God with what a fierce purity we must confront the horror of the world. The purity of Christ is not a winsome thing, it hurts perilously everything that is not pure. "For our God is a consuming fire." If you stand true to the purity of Christ, you will have to meet problems connected with the margins of your bodily life, and if you turn for one second in public or in secret from walking in the light as God is in the light, you will lose the distinction between absolute right and wrong and make the word "affinity" an excuse to further orders.[15] Test every emotional affinity in this way—If I let this thing have its way, what will it mean? If you can see the end of it to be wrong, grip it on the threshold of your mind, and at the peril of your soul never let it encroach again upon your attention. Whenever you meet with difficulties, whether they are intellectual or circumstantial or physical, remain loyal to God. Don't compromise. If you do, everyone around you will suffer from your faithlessness, because you are disloyal to Jesus Christ and His way of looking at things. Never run away with the idea that you can ever do a thing or have an attitude of mind before God which no one else need know anything about. A man is what he is in the dark. Remain loyal to God and to His saints in private and in public, and you will find that not only are you continually with God, but that God is counting on you.

Faith in God Recognising His Own Word
(Psalm 73:23–28)

God and His promises are eternal. "The gift *of God* is eternal life." Jesus Christ came to give us eternal life,

a life in which there is neither time nor space, which cannot be marked with suffering or death; it is the life Jesus lived. Some prayers are so big, and God has such a surprising answer for us, that He keeps us waiting for the manifestation. The saint is one who knows—"Nevertheless I am continually with Thee," in Thy presence, consequently there is no perplexity or confusion if the manifestation of the answer in a particular domain is withheld. There is no logic for faith or for suffering. The region in which God deals with us is the region of implicit life that cannot be put into words.

When we try to carry out the commands of Christ it is the Christians who say—"Don't be so stupid; don't strain human nature; do you think you are a special favourite of God's?" That is the way loyalty to God is deflected. Our minds have to remain loyal to God and to His saints, and we must crucify resolutely every impression that is contrary. If we give way to a dark mood of depression, we sin against God and His saints. The purpose of God through every experience is to make us un-learn what we bring with us until we are as simple as children before Him.

SPIRITUAL EVOLUTION

The world to-day is obsessed with the idea of evolution, we hear speculations about the superman, we are told we are getting better and better; but we are tending towards we don't know what. The remarkable thing about the spiritual evolution represented by Jesus Christ is that the goal is given to us at the start, viz., Jesus Christ Himself. The natural view and the Bible view of man are different—the natural point of view is that man is a great being in the making, his achievements are a wonderful promise of what he is going to be; the Bible point of view is that man is a magnificent ruin of what God designed him to be. The Bible does not look forward to an evolution of mankind: The Bible talks of a revolution—"Ye must be born again." That is not a command but the statement of a foundation fact. There must be a break in a man's life before he enters into the spiritual realm. God and man as God created him were at one, but severance came with the introduction of sin; then Jesus Christ came, and in Him God and man are again made at one. Jesus Christ did not evolve out of history, He came into history from outside history;

He is not the best human being the world has ever seen, He is a Being who cannot be accounted for by the human race at all. Jesus Christ is the First and the Last, and Paul uses the figure of Jesus as the goal to which the whole human race is to attain—"until we all attain unto the measure of the stature of the fulness of Christ."

Struggle for Self
Strive to enter in at the strait gate. (Luke 13:24)

Everyone has to begin with this struggle for self, and striving to enter in at the strait gate is a picture of the struggle. Anything that does not enter in at the strait gate, e.g., selfishness, self-interest, self-indulgence, ends in destruction. The struggle to enter in, no matter with what it may be in connection, braces us morally. Self-indulgence is a refusal to struggle, a refusal to make ourselves fit. We must be right ourselves before we can help others to be right.

If you make a moral struggle and gain a moral victory, you will be a benefit to all you come across,

---

15. to further orders: ad infinitum; endlessly; military origin, meaning continuing the present action until one receives different orders.

whereas if you do not struggle, you act as a moral miasma. Gain a moral victory in chastity or in your emotional life, it may be known to no one but yourself, and you are an untold benefit to everyone else; but if you refuse to struggle everyone else is enervated. This is a recognised psychological law, although little known. Struggle to gain the mastery over selfishness, and you will be a tremendous assistance; but if you don't overcome the tendency to spiritual sluggishness and self-indulgence, you are a hindrance to all around you. These things are intangible, but they are there, and Jesus says to us, "Strive to enter in at the strait gate." You never get through alone. If you struggle to get through, others are the stronger and better for knowing you. The men and women who lift and inspire us are those who struggle for self, not for self-assertiveness, that is a sign of weakness, but for the development of personality. There are some people in whose company you cannot have a mean[16] thought without being instantly rebuked.

Struggle for Others

And the second [commandment] is like, namely this, Thou shalt love thy neighbour as thyself. (Mark 12:31)

Whenever you touch your own true interests, others are involved at once. No man can gain a moral or spiritual victory without gaining an interest in other men. If you struggle and overcome, you will see that the other man gets a chance to fight his own moral battle too. The danger of false moral training is that it does not allow a man the chance to fight for himself or for others. We are inclined to be amateur providences over other lives spiritually, to so shield them that they are brought up like hothouse plants instead of being where moral victories should be gained. No man or woman ought to be innocent, a woman ought to be pure and a man ought to be virtuous. Innocence has to be transformed into purity through being brought into contact with things that are impure and overcoming them, thus establishing purity. A virtuous man or a pure woman is a tremendous assistance wherever he or she goes.

"Greater love hath no man than this, that a man lay down his life for his friends"—and Jesus says—"I have called you friends." The characteristic of your life

if you are devoted to Jesus, is that you lay down your life for Him, not die for Him, but lay down your life for Him. Paul puts it—". . . ourselves as your servants for Jesus' sake" (RV). You are the servant of other men for His sake. If you are devoted to the cause of humanity, you will soon be exhausted and have your heart broken by ingratitude, but if the mainspring of your service is love for Jesus, you can serve men although they treat you as a door-mat. Never look for justice in this world, but never cease to give it. If you do look for justice, you cease to struggle for your true self.

Struggle for Co-Relation

Be ye therefore imitators of God, as beloved children; and walk in love, even as Christ also loved you. . . . (Ephesians 5:1–2 RV)

If I struggle for myself on the right line, I struggle for others also, and the struggle establishes a co-relation between God and myself, and the characteristic of the life is a strong family likeness to Jesus. A self indwelt by Jesus becomes like Him. "Walk in love, even as Christ also loved you" (RV). Jesus has loved me to the end of all my meanness[17] and selfishness and sin; now, He says, show that same love to others. "For if ye forgive men their trespasses, your heavenly Father will also forgive you"—that is, I am to ask to be forgiven, not on the ground of the Atonement, but because I forgive. "But if ye forgive not men their trespasses, neither will your Father forgive your trespasses." That is hard hitting. Am I prepared to show the man who does evil to me the love God has shown to me? I have to learn to identify myself with God's interests in other people, and God's interests are never my selfish interests, but always His interests. When the Spirit of God comes into a man, He gives him a world-wide outlook. God has no favourites. ". . . that we may present every man perfect in Christ; whereunto I labour also, striving according to His working, which worketh in me mightily" (RV). The benefit of my life to others is in proportion to whether I am making this struggle for the self God designed me to be, and my worth to God is in proportion to my getting into co-relation with Him, getting His point of view about everything.

---

16. mean: as used here, something or someone ordinary, common, low, or ignoble, rather than cruel or spiteful.
17. mean: as used here, something or someone ordinary, common, low, or ignoble, rather than cruel or spiteful.

AT GOD'S DISCRETION

It is the glory of God to conceal a thing. Proverbs 25:2

This is not an isolated phrase, the idea runs all through the Bible, see Deuteronomy 29:29: "The secret things belong unto the LORD our God: but the things that are revealed belong unto us and to our children for ever" (RV); Romans 11:33: "O the depth of the riches both of the wisdom and the knowledge of God! how unsearchable are His judgements, and His ways past tracing out!" (RV). The purpose of mystery is not to tantalise us and make us feel that we cannot comprehend; it is a generous purpose, and meant to assure us that slowly and surely as we can bear it, the full revelation of God will be made clear.

It is the glory of God to conceal His teaching in obedience: we only know as we obey. "If any man willeth to do His will, he shall know of the teaching. . . ." It is only by way of obedience that we understand the teaching of God. Bring it straight down to the commonplace things: have I done the duty that lies nearest? have I obeyed God there? If not, I shall never fathom the mysteries of God, however much I may try. When once I obey there, I receive a revelation of the meaning of God's teaching for me. How many of us have obeyed the bit of God's truth we do know?

Experience is a gateway to understanding, not an end in itself. We can be bound in other ways than by sin; we can be bound by the limits of the very experiences that were meant to lead us into the secrets of God. The faith of many really spiritual Christians is eclipsed to-day, and the reason it is eclipsed is that they tried to remain true and consistent to the narrow confines of their experience instead of getting out into the light of God. God wants to get us into the place where He holds absolutely, and experiences never bother us. Oh, the relief of it! The burden gone, the effort gone, no conscious experience left, because Jesus Christ is All and in All.

God has hidden the glory of His teaching in the experience of temptation. "Count it all joy, my brethren, when ye fall into manifold temptations" (RV), says the Apostle James. "To him that overcometh, to him will I give of the hidden manna" (RV). The feast is just beyond the fight; when you have been through the fight, there is the wondrous joy and triumph of the feast. We learn to thank God for the trial of our faith because it works patience. The thing that is precious in the sight of God is faith that has been tried. Tried faith is spendable; it is so much wealth stored up in heaven, and the more we go through the trial of our faith, the wealthier we become in the heavenly regions.

"Blessed are the pure in heart." If we go on obeying God, we shall find that "light is sown for the righteous." We are so impatient—"I thought God's purpose was to make me full of happiness and joy." It is, but it is happiness and joy from God's standpoint, not from ours. God always ignores the present perfection for the ultimate perfection. We bring God to the bar of our judgement and say hard things about Him—"Why does God bring thunderclouds and disasters when we want green pastures and still waters?" Bit by bit we find, behind the clouds, the Father's feet; behind the lightning, an abiding day that has no night; behind the thunder a still small voice that comforts with a comfort that is unspeakable.

It is the glory of God to conceal His treasures in embarrassments, i.e., in things that involve us in difficulty. "I will give thee the treasures of darkness." We would never have suspected that treasures were hidden there, and in order to get them we have to go through things that involve us in perplexity. There is nothing more wearying to the eye than perpetual sunshine, and the same is true spiritually. The valley of the shadow gives us time to reflect, and we learn to praise God for the valley because in it our soul was restored in its communion with God. God gives us a new revelation of His kindness in the valley of the shadow. What are the days and the experiences that have furthered us most? The days of green pastures, of absolute ease? No, they have their value; but the days that have furthered us most in character are the days of stress and cloud, the days when we could not see our way but had to stand still and wait; and as we waited, the comforting and sustaining and restoring of God came in a way we never imagined possible before.

God wants us to realise His sovereignty. We are apt to tie God up in His own laws and allow Him no free will. We say we know what God will do, and suddenly He upsets all our calculations by working in unprecedented ways; just when we expected He would do a certain thing, He did the opposite. There are unexpected issues in life; unexpected joys when we looked for sorrow, and sorrow when we expected joy, until we learn to say, all my expectations are from Thee.

Again, God disciplines us by disappointment. Life may have been going on like a torrent, then suddenly down comes a barrier of disappointment, until slowly we learn that the disappointment was His appointment. God hides His treasures in darkness, and many a radiant star that was not seen before comes out. In some lives you can see the treasure, there is a sweetness and beauty about them, "the ornament of a meek and quiet spirit," and you wonder where the winsome power of God came from. It came from the dark places where God revealed His sovereign will in unexpected issues. "Thou hast enlarged me when I was in distress."

"It is the glory of God to conceal a thing." God will not have us come with an impatient curiosity. Moral or intellectual or spiritual insanity must result if we push down barriers which God has placed before our spiritual progress is fit for the revelation.

This is a day of intolerant inquisitiveness. Men will not wait for the slow, steady, majestic way of the Son of God; they try to enter in by this door and that door. "And one of the elders saith unto me, Weep not: behold, the Lion that is of the tribe of Judah, the Root of David, hath overcome, to open the book and the seven seals thereof" (Revelation 5:5 RV). The barriers are placed by a Holy God, and He has told us clearly—"Not that way." God grant we may accept His clouds and mysteries, and be led into His inner secrets by obedient trust.

CELEBRATION OR SURRENDER?

But far be it from me to glory, save in the Cross of our Lord Jesus Christ, through which the world hath been crucified unto me, and I unto the world. Galatians 6:14 (RV)

We are much more ready to celebrate what Jesus Christ has done than to surrender to Him. I do not mean the initial surrender to God of a sinner, but the more glorious surrender to God of a saint.

Triviality, i.e., Taken Up with Externals
Paul is writing to really spiritual people, but they were being made the centre of a conflict of rival paths to perfection. He says—"When I 'placarded' Christ crucified before you, you were fascinated at once; now others are 'placarding' ritual and laws, and you are heeding them." If rites and ceremonies are put as a road to perfection they will become the path away from it. To put prayer, devotion, obedience, consecration, or any experience, as the means of sanctification is the proof that we are on the wrong line. In sanctification the one reality is the Lord Himself; if you know Him, you will pay no attention to experiences. Experiences are only a doorway to lead us into the awe and wonder of the revelation of God. Let experiences come and go; bank on the Lord.

The Galatians were relapsing not into sin, but into fixity; they had the jargon of sanctimoniousness, but no real vigorous life. It is easy to think that we are to be specimens of what God can do. According to the New Testament, a saint is a piece of rugged human stuff re-made by the Atonement into oneness with God by the power of the Holy Ghost. The tendency to stereotype Christian experience is an abiding danger; it leads to the amateur providence attitude—"I am not likely to go wrong, but you are." I become, as it were, god almighty over a particular doctrine and imagine that everyone else is off on a side track. For example, when I think I can define what sanctification is, I have done something God refuses to do. Books about sanctification are much clearer than the Bible. The Bible is uncommonly confusing, so is human life. There is only one thing that is simple, and that is our relationship to Jesus Christ. What is needed to-day is not so much a revival as a resurgent form of awakening, the incoming of the tremendous life of God in a new form.

The cure for triviality spiritually is a new note of greatness born of the realisation of what it cost Jesus Christ to produce His salvation in us. Only when we continually face the Cross are we safe from the danger of triviality and internal hypocrisy. To-day the clamour is "do"; but the great need is to face our souls with God until the sterling stamp and testimony of the life is—"But far be it from me to glory, save in the Cross of our Lord Jesus Christ" (RV). We are so taken up with actual happenings that we forget the one fundamental thing, viz., the Cross. Beware of any fascination that takes you away from the centre.

Temporariness, i.e., Uncertainty of Foundations *(Galatians 4:9–11)*
Paul was alarmed over these Galatian Christians because they were losing the foundation setting. He says, "I am afraid of you . . . ." (Galatians 4:11). The reason for temporariness is because we will not think. It is much easier not to think, much more peaceful. A devotee to doctrines does not need to think, but a man who is devoted to Jesus Christ is obliged to think, and to think every day of his life, and he must allow nothing to dissipate his thinking. It is not courage men lack, but concentration on Jesus Christ. We have to get out of our laziness and indifference and excuses, and rouse ourselves up to face the Cross of Christ.

The cure for uncertainty is a new note of intercessory prayer. The reason for perplexity in meeting the actual occurrences of life is because we are losing face-to-face contact with Jesus Christ through His Cross. We must get back to the place where we are concerned only about facing our own inner souls with Jesus Christ Who searches us right down to the inmost recesses. If we will face the tremendous moral earnestness at the back of the Cross, a new note will be struck in the life which will work the wonders Jesus said it would. "Whatsoever ye shall ask in My name, that will I do" (John 14:13). Prayer prevails with God for men and with men for God. Can I by the passion of my prayer, pierce the darkness of a soul and give the Holy Ghost a chance to work, or do I sit mourning on the outskirts as though God had no more power than I have to lift that life? The passionate note of intercession is born in the secret places before God. Salvation is so wonderful, so full of ease and power, because of what it cost Jesus Christ. How much of the tremendous generating power of prayer that is born at the foot of the Cross are those of us who recognise the eternal realities behind the actual happenings of life, putting in for others?

Toughness, i.e., Spiritual Self-Satisfaction

We are so happy, so sure and so satisfied, that we have lost altogether the note of surrender which marked the life of Jesus. He sacrificed His holy Self to His Father, "for their sakes I sanctify Myself"; and we have the same privilege of sacrificing ourselves to Him. Jesus Christ submitted His intelligence to the word and will of His Father; are we submitting our intelligence to Jesus Christ, or are we being caught up on the line of spiritual insubordination? False revivals come along this line. Insubordination means we will not submit our impulses and intuitions and all the forces of the inner life to Jesus Christ; we will not turn

to see the voice that speaks. "And I turned to see the voice which spake with me" (Revelation 1:12 RV). Will is the whole man active, and the whole active power and force of the saint is to be laid at the feet of Jesus Christ. We busy ourselves with work for Him while He waits for all our individual energy to be curbed and submitted to Him that He may re-direct it into the channels He wants. "He that believeth on Me," out of him "shall flow rivers of living water."

Are we more anxious to be winsome to men and women than to be loyal to God? More anxious to be friends of men than friends of God? More anxious to sympathise with men and women who are wrong than to sympathise with God? Are we getting unstable on the foundation truths of the Redemption? Beware lest it be said of us that we are "enemies of the cross of Christ." May the great note of our lives be—"In the cross of Christ I glory"; no more feeble celebrations, but the great note of surrender, "I am not my own; I am bought with a price." Keep that sterling note in front of your soul, in front of your heart and mind. In Christ's Name, what do we know about the craving for Jesus Christ's honour, the tremendous heart hunger and passion of a man like the Apostle Paul—"I could wish that myself were accursed from Christ for my brethren"? The servant of Jesus Christ has no private history other than his private history with his Lord.

"What is wanted is the re-statement of our creeds." No, what is wanted is to be brought face to face with the one abiding Reality, God Himself; to know that only through the Cross, and the efficacy of the Holy Spirit at work through the Cross, can men be lifted up. The test of Jesus Christ's salvation is that it produces Christ-likeness, a life of absolute simplicity before God. Let us be what will satisfy His heart.

THE SACRAMENT OF SILENCE
Psalm 62:5–6

My soul, wait thou only upon God ["be thou silent unto God," RV mg]. Psalm 62:5

A great deal of silence arises from sullenness or from exhaustion, but the silence the Psalmist is alluding to is the silence which springs from the absolute certainty that God knows what He is doing. The Psalmist is determined to break up the drowsiness of his own soul and to bring himself into a watchfulness before God. Silent prayer is, in reality, concentration on God. You say—"But it is not easy to concentrate on God"; it is just because it is not easy that so few learn the secret of doing it. We need to rouse ourselves

up out of our indifference, out of drifting into mere jabbering before God, and get into an attitude of fruitful vigilance. Is silent prayer to us an experience of waiting upon God, or is it a "cotton wool" experience? utterly dim and dark? a time which we simply endure until it is over? If you want discerning vision about anything, you have to make an effort and call in your wandering attention. Mental wool-gathering can be stopped immediately the will is roused. Prayer is an effort of will, and the great battle in prayer is the overcoming of mental wool-gathering. We put things down to the devil when we should put them down to our own inability to concentrate. "My soul, wait thou only upon God" i.e., "pull yourself together and be silent unto God."

MY SOUL, wait thou only upon God . . .

Soul is my personal spirit as it reasons, and thinks, and looks at things; I have to call my powers together and concentrate on God. It is possible to concentrate and yet not concentrate on God. We may have a dead set about our lives, but it may be a dead set on comfort or on money, not a dead set on God and on the wonder and majesty of His dealings. The rich fool in our Lord's parable did not ask his soul to consider God, but to consider his possessions—"Soul, thou hast much goods laid up for many years; take thine ease, eat, drink, be merry." Be careful to concentrate on a worthy object. "Wait thou only upon God." Stop all false hurry and spend time in communion with God. Think of the benediction which comes to your disposition by waiting upon God! Some of us are in such a hurry that we distort God's blessings for ourselves and for others. "Wait thou only upon God"; to do that will demand at the beginning the severest mental effort we have ever put forth.

To be "silent unto God" (RV mg) does not mean drifting into mere feeling, or sinking into reverie, but deliberately getting into the centre of things and focusing on God. When you have been brought into relationship with God through the Atonement of the Lord Jesus Christ and are concentrating on Him, you will experience wonderful times of communion. As you wait only upon God, concentrating on the glorious outlines of His salvation, there will come into you the sleeping peace of God, the certainty that you are in the place where God is doing all in accordance with His will. In this earnest life of communion with God, the stress of the life is in the right place, i.e., you are not in earnest in order that God may recognise you as His child; your earnestness is the outcome of real communion with God.

My soul, WAIT thou only upon God . . .

To wait upon God is not to sit with folded hands and do nothing, but to wait as men who wait for the harvest. The farmer does not wait idly but with intense activity, he keeps industriously "at it" until the harvest. To wait upon God is the perfection of activity. We are told to "rest in the LORD," not to rust. We talk of resting in the Lord but it is often only a pious expression; in the Bible, resting in the Lord is the patience of godly confidence. "In returning and rest shall ye be saved. . . . But ye said, No, for we will flee upon horses"; i.e., we will take the initiative. When we take the initiative we put our wits on the throne, we do not worship God. God never guides His children by their own initiative. The only initiative we have to take is the initiative of worshipping God.

For my expectation is from Him . . .

Watch the moon as it shines across the sea; there is a silver pathway of light across the billows straight from the distant horizon to the shore, a line of communication over everything between. If you are God's child, there is this expectant line of communication always between you and God. Your experience may be a dreary wilderness, a sea of despair, a dusty, sandy waste with no shade—but over all is a line of communication between you and God. "An highway shall be there, and a way." Or yours may be the experience of having to walk at the bottom of the sea—"All Thy waves and Thy billows are gone over me"; yet—"When thou passest through the waters, I will be with thee." Or it may be the extraordinarily consuming difficulties that make up the burden of life—is there a line of communication there? "The hills melted like wax at the presence of the LORD." "My expectation is from Him." Have we learned this sacrament of silence, this secret of inner communion with God?

He only is my rock . . .

A rock conveys the idea of an encircling guard, as that of a mother watching her child who is learning to walk; should the child fall, he falls into the encircling love and watchfulness of the mother's care. "The LORD is my rock," my encircling guard. Where did the Psalmist learn this truth? In the school of silent waiting upon God. The Rock of Ages is the great sheltering encirclement; we are watched over by the Mother-guardianship of God. "I am El-Shaddai," the Father-Mother God. He is my high tower and my defence. The Lord Himself is our inviolable place of safety. There is a loftiness and an inaccessibility about the heavenly places in Christ Jesus. The higher you climb the purer the air until you come to the place where the least microbe is unable to live, and spiritually there is an inaccessible place of absolute security. "Thou hast set thine house of defence very high."

. . . I shall not be moved.

God lifts us up and poises us in Himself as surely as He has established the stars.

"My soul, be thou silent unto God" (RV mg). Rouse your soul out of its drowsiness to consider God. Fix your attention on God, on the great themes of His Redemption and His holiness, on the great and glorious outlines of His character, be silent to Him there; then be as busy as you like in the ordinary affairs of life. Be like the Lord Jesus; when He was sound asleep in the fishing-boat He knew that His Father would waken Him when He wanted Him. This is a marvellous picture of confidence in God.

My soul, wait thou only upon God.

SPIRITUAL CONFUSION

Ye know not what ye ask. Matthew 20:22

At times in spiritual life there is confusion, and the usual way out is to say there ought to be no confusion. Some of us are inclined to be fanatical, we won't pay any attention to things that are not black or white, right or wrong. There are very few things that are black or white, right or wrong, and until we recognise this we are apt to be insolent or indifferent towards anything in between. A fog is as real as clear sunshine; if we don't pay any attention to the fog, we shall come to disaster. There are things in the spiritual life which are confused, not because we have disobeyed, but owing to the very nature of things. The confusion arises from being unschooled spiritually.

The Shrouding of His Friendship *(Luke 11:5–8)*
And he from within shall answer and say, Trouble me not: the door is now shut . . . (Luke 11:7)

There is a time in spiritual life when God does not seem to be a friend. Everything was clear and easily marked and understood for a while, but now we find ourselves in a condition of darkness and desolation. The parable of the importunate friend is the illustration Jesus gives of how the Heavenly Father will appear in times of spiritual confusion—as a man who does not care for his friends. We are in need, or our friends or our homes are in need, and though we go to God Who has been our Friend all through, He does nothing at all. It is as if Jesus said to His disciples—"There are times when the Heavenly Father will look like that, but don't give up, remember I have told you—*everyone that asks receives.*" In the meantime the friendship of God is completely shrouded. There are things that have no explanation, but maintain your relationship to God, "hang in" in confidence in Him, and the time will come when everything will be explained. It is only by going through the confusion that we shall get at what God wants us to get at.

Never say God has done what He has not done because it sounds better to say it; never pretend to have an answer when you have not. Jesus said "Every one that asketh receiveth"; we say—"I have asked but I have not received." It is because we ask in spiritual confusion. Jesus said to James and John: "Ye know not what ye ask"; they were brought into fellowship with Jesus Christ's cup and baptism, but not in the way they expected.

The Shadow on His Fatherhood *(Luke 11:11–12)*
And of which of you that is a father shall his son ask a loaf, and he give him a stone? (Luke 11:11 RV)

Jesus says there are times when our Heavenly Father will appear as if He were a most unnatural father, callous and indifferent—I asked for bread and He gave me a stone, and there is a shadow on His Fatherhood. But remember. says Jesus, I have told you—*everyone that asks receives.* When we get into spiritual confusion the usual way out is to say we have made a blunder, and we go back instead of forward. "I don't know what to do; I am up against a stone wall." Will you "hang in" to what Jesus said? If there is a shadow on the face of the Fatherhood of God just now, remain confident that ultimately He will give His clear issue as Jesus said. It is not a question of black or white, of right or wrong; of being in communion or out of communion; but a question of God taking us by a way which in the meantime we do not understand.

The Strangeness of His Faithfulness *(Luke 18:1–8)*
And shall not God avenge His elect, which cry to Him day and night, and He is longsuffering over them? (Luke 18:7 RV)

There are times when the Heavenly Father will look as if He were an unjust Judge, but remember, Jesus says, He is not. In the meantime there is a cloud on the friendship of the heart, and even love itself has to wait often in pain and tears for the blessing of fuller communion. The time is coming when we shall see perfectly clearly, but it is only through confusion that we can get to a clear outline.

State definitely to yourself the things that are confused; note the things that are not clear black and white. There are no problems at all over right and wrong. Human life is not made up of right and wrong, but of things which are not quite clear—"I do not know what God would have me do in this matter." Stand off in faith that what Jesus said is true—*everyone that asks receives,* and in the meantime do the duty that lies nearest, waiting and watching. If the friendship of God is shrouded and it looks as if He is not going to do anything, then remain dumb. The real problems are very heavy. Instead of God being a Father loving and kind, it looks at times as if He were totally indifferent. Remember, God has bigger issues at stake on the ground of His Redemption than the particular setting in which we ask. In the meantime we do not know what God is doing, but we are certain that what Jesus says is true. "If ye then, being evil, know how to give good gifts unto your children: how much more shall your Heavenly Father give the Holy Spirit to them that ask Him?" and when we are the possessors of the Holy Spirit we shall justify God all through.

Until we have been disciplined properly by means of spiritual confusion we shall always want to bank on God's miracles and refuse to do the moral thing ourselves. It is much easier to ask God to do our work for us than to do it ourselves—"Oh well, I will pray and ask God to clean this thing up for me." God won't.

We must do our own work. Prayer is always a temptation to bank on a miracle instead of a moral issue until we are disciplined. God will do more than we can do, but only in relationship to our spiritual growth. When we have received the gift of the Holy Spirit, we have to learn to obey God in every detail, then the shroudings will be lifted, the shadows will disappear, the strangeness will go, and we shall begin to understand the Friendship and the Fatherhood and the Faithfulness of God with regard to our lives.

"Howbeit when the Son of Man cometh, shall He find faith on the earth?"(RV). Will He find the faith that banks on Him in spite of the confusion?

THE LONG TRAIL TO SPIRITUAL REALITY

But now we see not yet all things subjected to Him. Hebrews 2:8 (RV)

When we are busy with our own outlook on life, it seems as if God were indifferent. Our human patience, as well as our impatience, gets to the point of saying—"Why does not God do things?" Redemption is complete; we believe that Our Lord has all power in heaven and on earth, then why is it such a long while before things happen? Why is God so long in making actual His answers to our prayers? When in such a state of mind we are capable of becoming bitter against God unless we are led into the inner secret of our Lord's own attitude.

The Vision of the Long Way *(Matthew 4:1)*
For thirty years Jesus had remained unknown, then He was baptised and had a wonderful manifestation of the Father's approval, and the next thing we read is that He is "led up of the Spirit into the wilderness to be tempted of the devil." The same thing puzzles us in our own spiritual experience; we have been born from above (RV mg), or have had the wonderful experience of the baptism of the Holy Ghost—surely we are fit now to do something for God; and God deliberately puts us on the shelf, amongst the dust and the cobwebs, in an utterly unaccountable way.

The agony Jesus went through in the Temptation was surely because He had the vision of the long way and saw the suffering it would entail on men through all the ages if He took His Father's way. He knew it in a way we cannot conceive. His sensitiveness is beyond anything we can imagine. If He had not been true to His Father's way, His own home would not have been upset, His own nation would not have blasphemed the Holy Ghost. The way to approach Gethsemane is to try to understand the Temptation.

Each of the temptations presented to our Lord by Satan had this as its centre: "You will get the Kingship of men and the Saviourhood of the world if You will take a 'short cut'—put man's needs first, and he will crown You King; do something extraordinarily wonderful, indicative of Your power, and man will crown You King; compromise with evil, and You will get the Kingship of men." Jesus could have brought the whole thing about suddenly (cf. John 6:15); but He did not. He withstood Satan and took the stupendously long way.

When we obey Jesus Christ it is never a question of what it costs us—it does not cost us anything, it is a delight—but of what it costs those whom we love, and there is always the danger of yielding to the temptation of the "short cut." Am I prepared to let my obedience to God cost other people something? Jesus deliberately took the long trail, and He says "the disciple is not above his Master." "Because thou hast kept the word of My patience . . ." We want to hurry things up by revivals. Over and over again we take the devil's advice and say, "It must be done quickly—the need is the call; men must be saved." An understanding of the inwardness of our Lord's temptation will throw light on the progress of Christian history as well as on personal experience.

Why does God take such a long time? Because of what He is after, viz., "bringing many sons unto glory." It takes time to make a son. We are not made sons of God by magic; we are saved in the great supernatural sense by the sovereign work of God's grace, but sonship is a different matter. I have to become a son of God by deliberate discernment and understanding and chastisement, not by spiritual necromancy, imagining I can ascend to heaven in leaps and bounds. The "short cut" would make men mechanisms, not sons, with no discernment of God. If God did not shield His only

Begotten Son from any of the requirements of sonship ("Though He was a Son, yet learned obedience by the things which He suffered"— Hebrews 5:8 RV), He will not shield us from all the requirements of being His sons and daughters by adoption.

The Valley of the Long Wait

For I reckon that the sufferings of this present time are not worthy to be compared with the glory which shall be revealed to us-ward. (Romans 8:18 RV)

It is a long wait until the sons of God appear, and they only appear by the deliberate simplicity of obedience to Him. When the Spirit of God comes into a man the first thing that happens is the corruption of the natural virtues. Natural virtues are remnants of the human race as God designed it; when a man is born again his natural virtues begin to crumble, and he is plunged into perplexity. Natural good has to die in me before the best can come. That is the keynote of spiritual reality. It is not the bad that is the enemy of God, but the good that is not good enough. We say that sin is the enemy of God—sin is *our* enemy. The enemy of God in me is morality based on a denial of Jesus, i.e., the rectitude that is not based on spiritual regeneration.

The Voice of the Living Worship *(John 14:6)*

Jesus does not take men and say—"This is the truth and if you don't believe it you will be damned." He simply shows us the truth—"I am . . . the Truth," and leaves us alone. We name His Name, but is He the Truth to us in our bodily life, in our commonsense life, in our intellectual and emotional life? It takes a long while for us to begin to see that Jesus Christ is The Truth. Truths exist that have no meaning for us until we get into the domain of their power, ". . . Verily, verily, I say unto thee, Except a man be born anew, he cannot see the kingdom of God" (John 3:3 RV). We want to get at truth by "short cuts"; the wonder is our Lord's amazing patience. He never insists that we take His way; He simply says—"I am the Way." We might as well learn to take His way at the beginning, but we won't, we are determined on our own way. Do I believe that God can only come to other men in the way He comes to me?

"Except ye . . . become as little children . . ." We won't become as little children, we have notions of our own, somewhere within us all is the "superior person." There is nothing simpler or more exquisite than a little child, and Jesus says you must become like that. We say—"But I am so and so, and I have had these experiences, and I have ideas of my own." Or we may not say it, but we think it. It takes a long time to realise what Jesus is after, and the person you need most patience with is yourself. God takes deliberate time with us, He does not hurry, because we can only appreciate His point of view by a long discipline. The grace of God abides always the same. By His grace we stand on the basis of His Redemption; but we ought to be making headway in the development of our personal sonship.

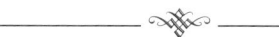

AUTOBIOGRAPHY OF COMMUNION WITH GOD

And after the earthquake a fire; but the LORD was not in the fire: and after the fire a still small voice. 1 Kings 19:12

What is mirrored in the unique, solitary figure of Elijah is not something we all experience, although it explains what we experience. An expositor must deal with exceptional cases, but we blunder if we look in our own experience for the exceptional and sensational. There are ways in our lives about which we cannot be articulate, they go beyond our exact expression, we do not know why we are moved as we are; the explanation for it is not to be found in ourselves but in the experience of some greater soul. If we study Elijah in this experience of gloom and isolation, we shall find a line of understanding for ourselves.

Interior desolation serves a vital purpose in the life of a Christian. At the beginning of the spiritual life the consciousness of God is so wonderful that we are apt to imagine our communion with God depends upon our being conscious of His presence. Then when God begins to withdraw us into Himself, and things become mysterious, we lose our faith and get into the dark, and say—"I must have backslidden," and yet we know we have not, all we know is that we have lost our consciousness of God's presence. Madame Guyon,[18] in commenting on her own experience, puts it thus—"To complete my distress I seemed to be left without God Himself Who alone could support me in such a distressing state." "The misfortune," she adds, "is that people wish to direct God instead of resigning themselves to be directed by Him." Out of this experience of desolation, Madame Guyon learned this truth, that our faith must be built on the reality of being taken up into God's consciousness in Christ, not on our taking God into our consciousness. This

---

18. Madame Guyon (1648–1717): French mystic.

means entering into a relationship with God whereby our will becomes one with the will of God. To the thought of the saints God is never far enough away to think about them, there is no separation; He thinks them. How we get there, I cannot tell you, but it is by the processes of God's training.

Conception of the Instruments of God
(1 Kings 19:11–12)

Elijah took his own initiative in telling Ahab "there shall not be dew nor rain these years, but according to my word" (1 Kings 17:1), and during the drought God made him go up and down the land and see the havoc that drought brought about. Now, when Elijah is isolated and spiritually baffled, God brings before him in miniature, a great and strong wind, an earthquake, and fire, as much as to say that these had been used as His instruments, "but the LORD was not in the wind," etc. Elijah's conception undoubtedly was that God was in them, but he had to learn that God was not there.

To-day there are colossal forces abroad and God is using them as His instruments, but He is not "in" them, that is, they are not God. It is a misconception to imagine that God is bound up in His instruments; He uses forces and powers for His own ends, but they must never be mistaken for Himself. An instrument conveys God's message, and a man used by God ought to be a holy man: but it does not always follow that he is (cf. Matthew 7:21–22).

Conscientious Introspection before God
(1 Kings 19:3–4, 10, 14)

. . . he arose, and went for his life. (1 Kings 19:3)

Elijah did an actually cowardly thing, yet he was not a coward. He ran away because he was absolutely baffled, he could not understand what God was doing. We cannot judge men by what they actually do, because the reasons of two men who do the same thing may be entirely different. Another man might have run away because he was a craven coward. Elijah fled because it seemed as if he had been let down by God in everything in which he had stood for Him. "Why is my pain perpetual, and my wound incurable, which refuseth to be healed? wilt thou indeed be unto me as a deceitful brook, as waters that fail?" (Jeremiah 15:18 RV). This sense of being baffled knocks everything out; a man is like a sparrow in a gale. It is not a question of losing his wits, but of realising that he has none. The battle in spiritual life is, on whom or on what am I building my confidence?

The striking thing about Job in his experience of being baffled was that he was strictly true to what he knew; he stuck to it all through—"I will not accept a credal statement of God that denies the facts I know."

Job would not tell a lie for the honour of God; neither would Elijah. "I have been very jealous for the LORD, the God of hosts; . . . and I, even I only, am left; and they seek my life, to take it away" (RV). "I have spent everything for Your honour, expecting You to see me through, and now I am the only one left, and I don't want the only one left standing for You to be crushed out." Elijah was conscientious before God; his baffling went deeper than discouragement, which is "disenchanted egotism." He feared that God had failed; that He had taken on too much. The greatest fear a man has is that his hero will not get through; fear for himself is child's play. Is God going to get through? Is everything going to prove a "washout"? Is my faith in God nonsense? Can Jesus Christ do what He said He could?

Consciousness of Instruction by God *(1 Kings 19:5, 7, 9, 12–13, 15)*

The angel did not give Elijah a vision, or explain the Scriptures to him, or do anything remarkable; he told Elijah to do the most ordinary thing, viz., Arise and eat." The ministrations of God come over and over again in the most commonplace manner possible. We look for some great big alteration, something marvellous like the wind, or an earthquake, or fire; and the voice of God tells us to do what the most ordinary voice we know might tell us to do. "And after the fire a still small voice"—i.e., "a sound of gentle stillness" (RV mg)—the one thing the Lord was in. Then came the command—"Go, return. . . ." God sent Elijah right back, after giving him an extraordinary heartening, to do what He had told him. The haphazard may tumble about as it likes now; Elijah has learned that God's order comes that way.

The experience of being baffled is common to us all, and the more religious and thoughtful a man is, the more intensely is he baffled. With regard to your own baffling, recognise it and state it, but don't state it dishonestly to yourself. Don't say you are not baffled if you are, and don't tell a lie in order to justify your belief in God. If you are in the dark, don't take refuge in any subterfuge which you know is not true. Never take an answer that satisfies your mind only; insist on an answer that satisfies more than your mind, an answer that satisfies by the "sound of gentle stillness" (RV mg). Jesus describes it as "My peace," the witness of God that goes all through you and produces a complete calm within. The first thing to do is the most obvious commonsense thing possible, the thing that is absolutely natural. When God has produced the "sound of gentle stillness" in your spirit, you will hear Him speak. "What I tell you in the darkness, that speak ye in the light." Then with renewed strength you go and do the thing God had already told you to do, but with the realisation that you are backed by God.

IS HE YOUR MASTER?

Ye call Me, Master, and, Lord: and ye say well; for so I am. John 13:13 (RV)

The most remarkable thing about the mastership of Jesus Christ is that He never insists on being Master. We often feel that if only He would insist, we would obey Him. Obedience to Jesus Christ is essential, but never compulsory; He will never take means to make me obey Him. Jesus Christ will always make up for my deficiencies, He always forgives my disobedience; but if I am going to be a disciple, it is essential for me to obey Him. In the early stages we have the notion that the Christian life is one of freedom, and so it is; but freedom for one thing only—freedom to obey our Master.

The Great Conception
Ye call Me, Master, and, Lord . . .

We must have our Christian conception right, and this is the right conception, that Jesus Christ is our Master. We do not give enough time to brooding on this conception of our Lord; we do not do enough at it. An artist or a musician must know how to brood on his conception. It is no use being the home of furtive ideas and having conceptions that come floating through like sunrise clouds. The artist has to go after the idea and stick to it until it is wrought into the character of his conception. It is not easy to maintain the conception of Jesus Christ as Master. Spiritual concentration is needed to do it.

    The conception of mastership which we get from our natural life is totally different from the mastership of Jesus Christ, because He never insists on our obedience. He simply says, "If ye love Me, ye will keep My commandments" (RV). That is the end of it. If I do not keep His commandments, He does not come and tell me I have done the wrong thing, I know it, there is no getting away from it. If once I have been indwelt by the Holy Spirit, He will always discern that I have done the fundamentally wrong thing when I disobey Jesus Christ. Let me disobey Him, and I am the most miserable wretch out of hell. He never punishes, yet I know that His consciousness of Himself is right, that He is Master.

    When we are born from above (RV mg) and have the Holy Spirit within, He delights to glow on the Lord Jesus Christ until His features are transfigured for us. Natural love does not grow if we do not do anything at it. It is the most ordinary business to fall in love; it is the most extraordinary business to abide there. The same thing with regard to the love of our Lord. The Holy Ghost gives us the great power to love Jesus Christ. That is not a rare experience at all; the rare experience is to get into the conception of loving Him in such a way that the whole heart and mind and soul are taken up with Him. This experience is symbolised in Mary of Bethany when she sat at the feet of Jesus. We have to sit at His feet in disposition. A thousand and one things crowd into our everyday lives, do we bring them into this conception of Jesus as Master, or have we forgotten His counsel and called ourselves master in these details? We have the conception of Him as Master with regard to a prayer meeting, but we have not the conception of Him as Master over our tongues, over our fingers, over our possessions, over everything that belongs to us. We call ourselves master in those domains, that is, we have the conception that we are responsible for them. As saints we are responsible for one thing only, viz., to maintain our conception right in relationship to God; this is the whole secret of the devotional life of a saint. The right conception is not Christian duty or service to men, but keeping Jesus as Master. How much time do I give to brooding on the conception that makes me call Him Master?

The Great Certainty
And ye say well . . .

At the beginning of the human race the conception was that Adam was to be master over everything but himself. He was to have dominion over the life on the earth and in the air and in the sea, but he was not to have dominion over himself, God was to have dominion over him. The temptation came on this line— "Disobey, and you will become as God." Man took dominion over himself and thereby lost his lordship over everything else. According to the Bible, the disposition of sin is my claim to my right to myself.

    "The disciple is not above his Master." The life of our Lord is our pattern, not a good man, and the one characteristic of our Lord's human life was that He was not His own Master. He said, in effect, "I do not speak from My right to Myself, I speak what My Father tells Me to speak. I do not work from Myself, I work the works of My Father. I do not maintain My right to Myself, I sanctify Myself to God's holy purposes." The New Testament describes how our Lord was perfected as a human being for redemptive purposes, "though He was a Son, yet learned obedience by the things which He suffered" (Hebrews 5:8 RV), and if I am a disciple of Jesus Christ, the great certainty is that I have to be perfected as my Master, and not think it strange concerning the things God puts me through.

The Great Consciousness

. . . for so I am.

We are apt to end where we begin, viz., in our own consciousness. Christianity is not my consciousness of God, but God's consciousness of me. We must build our faith on the reality that we are taken up into God's consciousness in Christ, not that we take God into our consciousness. This is the meaning of our Lord's counsel "consider the lilies," and it is also the explanation of the inordinate desire for manifestly successful Christian work. The great consciousness in our Lord's mind is that He is man's Master, and we have to get into His consciousness. The wonderful thing about our Lord is that He will not master us. He becomes the dust under our feet. He becomes less than the breath we breathe. He becomes Someone we can jeer at and utilise, Someone we can do anything we like with; yet all the time He is Master. We can crucify Him, we can spit on Him, we can slander Him, we can ignore Him, we can hurt Him; yet He is Master. And when He shows Himself at the end of the dispensation, every man will recognise Him as Master, and those who have done the cruel things to Him will be so appalled at the revelation that they will call on the rocks to cover them, and the rocks in that day will reveal that they and the earth belong to their Master.

Is He your Master? This is the true and lasting and eternal conception, and to have it will produce confusion in every other conception of Jesus. I am not a devotee of any cause, or an advocate of any creed; I am His. "Ye are not your own." I must beware of the tendency to become dissipated in my conception by false notions of Christian work, or by ideas as to what I ought to be doing. I ought to be nothing but a disciple of Jesus Christ; He will be doing through me all the time. Jesus Christ's consciousness being what it is, viz., that He is Master, if I am rightly related to God and walking in the light, no matter what happens to me, it is His look-out, not mine. I have simply to abandon to Him and smilingly wash my hands of the consequences. He will engineer my circumstances, He will dump me down where He chooses, He will give me money or give me none, as He likes; all I have to do is to keep my soul carefully in the conception of Him as Master. "For we preach not ourselves, but Christ Jesus as Lord, and ourselves as your servants for Jesus' sake" (RV).

WHY ARE WE NOT TOLD PLAINLY?

. . . He charged them that they should tell no man what things they had seen, save when the Son of man should have risen again from the dead. Mark 9:9 (RV)

Because of the Unbearable Things

I have yet many things to say unto you, but ye cannot bear them now. (John 16:12)

Our Lord does not hide things from us, but they are unbearable until we are in a fit condition of spiritual life to receive them; then the word our Lord has spoken becomes so plain that we are amazed we did not understand it before. We could not understand it before because we were not in the place either in disposition or in will where it could be borne. There must be communion with the resurrection life of Jesus before a particular word can be borne by us. "Tell the vision to no man, until the Son of man is risen from the dead" in you—until the life of the risen Christ so dominates you that you understand what the historic Christ taught.

Obtuseness is valuable sometimes. It is of God's infinite mercy that we do not understand what He says until we are in a fit condition. If God came down with His light and power, we should be witless; but our Lord never enthrals us. Satan tempted Jesus to use the power of enthralment, and false methods of service are built up on that line. When we first know the Lord we are always tempted by the "show business," our prayers are really dictation to God. God will take us out of the obtuse stage immediately we let the resurrection life of Jesus have its way with us.

Do we know anything about the impartation of the risen life of Jesus Christ? The evidence that we do is that His words are becoming interpretable to us. God cannot reveal anything to us if we have not His Spirit. If we have made up our minds about a doctrine, we cannot get any more light from God about it, light will never come to us on that line. An obstinate outlook will effectually hinder God revealing anything to us. It is not sin, but unenlightenment caused by the absence of the resurrection life of Jesus.

Because of the Unbelievable Things

By this we believe. . . . Jesus answered them, Do ye now believe? (John 16:30–31)

We need to rely much deeper down consciously on the resurrection life of Jesus; to get into the habit of steadily referring everything back to Him. Instead of that, we make our commonsense decisions and say we hope God will bless them. He cannot—they are not in His domain. "But if I do my duty, I shan't go astray." You will; it is unbelievable, but true. You will go wrong, because you have put something that can be stated in abstract form on the throne instead of our Lord. As God's children we are never told to walk in the light of conscience or of a sense of duty; we are told to walk in the light of the Lord. When we do things from a sense of duty, we can back it up by argument; but when we do things out of obedience to the Lord there is no logical argument possible. That is why a saint can easily be ridiculed.

Tell no man, till the Son of Man is risen from the dead. Is Jesus Christ risen in us? Is He getting His way? When we look back on the choice of our life work, or of our friends, or of what we call our duty, is He really the dominating One? We can soon know whether He is. We say—"Now . . . we believe. . . ." and Jesus says— "Do ye now believe? Behold, the hour cometh, . . . that ye . . . shall leave Me alone." Many a Christian worker has left his Lord alone and gone into work from a sense of duty woven out of a need, or of a call arising from his own particular discernment. There is no sin in it, and no punishment attached, but when that one realises that he has hindered his understanding of what Jesus says and produced for himself perplexities and sorrows, it is with shame and contrition he has to come back like a little child and ask the Lord to teach him all over again. "Except ye . . . become as little children." When we do a thing from a sense of duty, we become amateur providences and the child attitude is gone; the power of the resurrection life of Jesus is not there. We have put up a standard in competition with our Lord, and have got out of contact with Him by leaning to our own understanding.

"Tell the vision to no man. . . ." So many do tell, they tell what they saw on the Mount and testify to it, but the actual life does not tally with the vision; the Son of Man is not yet risen in them. The words sound all right, but He is not there. There is no communication of His life through the words, no illumination or understanding given to seeking souls, because the Son of Man is not yet risen in them. I wonder when He is going to be formed in us? "My little children, of whom I am again in travail until Christ be formed in you" (Galatians 4:19 RV). When are we going to believe that unbelievable thing, that we will leave Him alone, in spite of all we say?

Because of the Unquestioned Things

. . . the hour cometh, when I . . . shall tell you plainly of the Father. (John 16:25 RV)

And in that day ye shall ask Me nothing. (John 16:23)

When is "that day"? When the resurrection life of the Lord Jesus is the portion of our life. In that day we shall be one with the Father as Jesus said we should be, because the Holy Spirit has brought us there. No one can receive the Holy Spirit unless he is convinced of his own poverty. When we receive the Holy Spirit, He imparts the risen life of Jesus and there is no distance between the Father and His child. Have we come to this unquestioning place where there is no more perplexity of heart in regard to God? Any number of things may be dark and unexplained, but they do not come in between the heart and God. "In that day ye shall ask Me nothing"—you do not need to, you are so certain that God will bring it all out in perfect accordance with His will; John 14:1 ("Let not your heart be troubled") has become the real state of your life. Until the resurrection life of Jesus Christ is manifested, we do want to ask questions; whenever we take a new step in God's providence we want to ask this and that. When the point of entire reliance on the resurrection life of Jesus is reached, and we are brought into perfect contact with the purpose of God, we find all our questions have gone. Are we living that life now? If not, why shouldn't we?

What is it makes us say—"I wish God would tell me plainly"? Never look for an explanation from without or in your own mind, look for it in your disposition. The reason anything is a mystery and is coming in between yourself and God, is in the disposition, not in the intellect. When once the disposition is willingly submitted to the life of Jesus, the understanding becomes perfectly clear. "If any man *willeth* to do His will, he shall *know* of the teaching" (RV).

THE TRANSFIGURED EXPERIENCE OF LIFE

And suddenly looking round about, they saw no one any more, save Jesus only with themselves. Mark 9:8 (RV)

There was no other moment not even the Resurrection of our Lord, so transcendent and amazing in the experience of Peter and James and John as the moment on the Mount of Transfiguration. Peter takes care to emphasise that it was when "we were with Him in the holy mount" that he saw and heard and understood Who Jesus was, we "were eye-witnesses of His majesty." In his Epistle, James makes the practical application of this wonderful experience; and John, whilst he does not record the Transfiguration, writes his Gospel from this standpoint, the standpoint of the exceeding majesty of the Lord Jesus.

The Immortal Moments of Life

Jesus . . . bringeth them up into a high mountain apart by themselves: and He was transfigured before them. (Mark 9:2 RV)

We all have what are called "brilliant moments." We are not always dull, not always contented with eating and drinking. There are times when we are unlike our usual selves, both in the way of depression and of brilliance, when one moment stands out from every other, and we suddenly see the way which we should go. And there is the counterpart in spiritual experience of those times in the natural life. There are tides of the spirit, immortal moments, moments of amazing clearness of vision, and it is by these moments and by what we see then, that we are to be judged. "While ye have the light, believe on the light," said Jesus—do not believe what you see when you are not in the light. God is going to judge us by the times when we have been in living communion with Him, not by what we feel like to-day. God judges us entirely by what we have seen. We are not judged by the fact that we live up to the light of our conscience; we are judged by The Light, Jesus Christ. "I am the light of the world"; and if we do not know Jesus Christ, we are to blame. The only reason we do not know Him is because we have not bothered our heads about Him. Honestly, does it matter to us whether Jesus lived and died, or did anything at all? "But there are so many humbugs." There is no counterfeit without the reality. Is Jesus Christ a fraud? We are to be judged by Him. "This is the condemnation, that light is come into the world, and men loved the darkness rather than the light." We are not judged by the light we have, but by the light we have refused to accept. God holds us responsible for what we will not look at. A man is never the same after he has seen Jesus. We are judged by our immortal moments, the moments in which we have seen the light of God.

The Isolation Moments of Life

. . . they became sore afraid. And there came a cloud overshadowing them. (Mark 9:6–7 RV)

Something desolating, as well as something wonderful, happened to the disciples on the Mount of Transfiguration; they were transfixed with wonder at the sight of Who Jesus was, then an isolating shadow came over them: they do not know the Jesus Whom they are seeing now, and they are sore afraid, there is a chill over heart and life.

"For we wrestle not against flesh and blood, but against principalities, against powers, against the rulers of the darkness of this world, against spiritual wickedness in high places." There is scenery surrounding the human soul of which we are unconscious, supernatural powers and agencies we know nothing about. Many a one has come to the place of the isolation moment, where it is cloudy and overshadowed. What are we going to do in these times of isolation? It would be an appalling thing to go through life unshielded by Jesus. We are inclined to be flippant, until God lifts the veil a little, then we get terrified. Let a little puff of wind blow over us, and instantly the "terror by night" isolates us in the alarm of the spirit. It is in these periods of isolation that our Lord keeps us. The Atonement of Jesus means safeguarding in the Unseen, safeguarding from dangers of which we know nothing.

Never be afraid because you do not understand yourself, and never be sour because no one else understands you. There is only One Who understands us, and that is God (see the 139th Psalm). Our lives are lived in two compartments, the shallow and the profound, and both domains are to be God's. There is always the temptation to live only in the profound, and to despise others for not understanding our profundity. We are apt to forget that God is in the shallow as well as in the profound. We have to see that we live our shallow life in as godly a manner as we live the profound.

The Identified Meaning of Life

. . . they saw no one any more, save Jesus only with themselves (Mark 9:8 RV)

It was not that they saw no one else, but they saw no one else without seeing Jesus. The identified meaning of life is that we see "every man perfect in Christ Jesus." We do not need a transfiguration experience to see meanness, because we are mean;[19] we do not need a transfiguration experience to see sin, because we are sinners; but we do need a transfiguration experience to see Christ Jesus in the mean, in the sinner, in the all-but-lost, in the wrong and in the evil, so that it can be true of the experience of every saint—"they saw no one any more, save Jesus only with themselves." That is what contact with Jesus means. It is easy to see the specks and the wrong in others, because we see in others that of which we are guilty ourselves. "Wherefore thou art without excuse, O man, whosoever thou art that judgest: for wherein thou judgest another, thou condemnest thyself; for thou that judgest dost practise the same things" (Romans 2:1 RV). The greatest cure for spiritual conceit is for God to give us a dose of the plague of our own heart.

What a wonderful thing it will be for us if we enter into the transfigured experience of life! There is never any snare in the man or woman who has seen Jesus. Have you anyone "save Jesus only" in your cloud? If you have, then it will get darker. You must get to the place where there is "no one any more, save Jesus only."

THE DAWN THAT TRANSFIGURES TEARS

Jesus saith unto her, Woman, why weepest thou? John 20:15

"And God shall wipe away every tear from their eyes" (RV). Unless God wipes away our tears, they will always return. The day to which our Lord rose is a day in which tears are not done away with, but transfigured—a day that has no twilight, nor evening nor night. This does not mean that no more tears will be shed, but that they will never be shed again in the way they were before. We do not know what will take the place of tears, but a life in which there is no equivalent to tears would be intolerable to the imagination.

The Pressure of Pain in Termination
He is not here. (Matthew 28:6 RV)

(a) The End of the Three Years
. . . sitting over against the sepulchre. (Matthew 27:61)

Those years had been a time of marvellous delight and joy, but they are finished now, and there is the pressure of pain in the termination of them. No greater sadness than that of the disciples can be imagined. They owed everything to Jesus, and now "He is not here," and life has nothing more to hold out for them. We have all had the equivalent of those three years, a time of great joy while it lasted, but it is finished now, and we too have sat "over against the sepulchre."

(b) The End of the Thrilling Yesterdays
And he went out, and wept bitterly. (Matthew 26:75 RV)

Peter was a loyal, strong, warm-hearted man, swayed by impulse; and now all the aspirations of his life have come to an end. We have all known the thrilling yesterday—when we first entered into the realisation of love, or of friendship, or of the joy of life. If all that we have is the human, it will end in bitter tears—not sometimes, but every time. The only way in which bitter tears can be evaded is either by a man's shallowness, or by his coming into a totally new relation to the Lord Jesus Christ through His Resurrection.

(c) The End of Tender Yearnings
What communications are these that ye have one with another, as ye walk? (Luke 24:17 RV)

These words represent all we understand by tender yearnings. There are things in our lives that terminate; it is a universal human experience. Things come to an end and it produces unutterable sadness.

"He is not here." These are the saddest words on earth. Think what such words mean to mothers who have lost their sons in war, to wives who have lost their husbands. Yet in *this* connection they are extraordinarily joyful words—"He is not here, for He is risen." He is not here, in the ordinary sense of the word—not merely as One Who can sympathise with sorrow: He *is* here—but as the Risen Lord! If we pour out sympathy upon one who is bereaved, all we do is to make that one more submissive to his grief. The unique thing about Jesus is that He comes to sorrowing men as a complete Saviour from all sorrow.

---

19. mean: as used here, something or someone ordinary, common, low, or ignoble, rather than cruel or spiteful.

The Power in the Proclamation of the Impossibilities
for He is risen.

Jesus is not in the sitting by the sepulchre; He is not in the bitter tears; He is not in the sad communings. The place where we will find Jesus is just where common sense says it is impossible to find Him. It was no use for the disciples to imagine they were going to have a recurrence of those three years; it was impossible to recall the thrilling yesterdays; it was impossible for the two on the way to Emmaus to have a return of the fellowship they yearned for; but there was something infinitely better for them. "For He is risen, even as He said." Impossibility had wedded itself to what Jesus had said. The proclamation of the impossible springs from the supernatural, not from common sense. The supernatural figures largely all through the life of our Lord. At His birth the angels proclaimed that He should be called Jesus "for He shall save His people from their sins." We shall not think of our Lord as a Saviour if we look at Him in the light of our own minds, because no natural man imagines he needs to be saved. Do we make room in our faith for the impossible along the line of the supernatural? or have we reduced our religion to such commonsense platitudes that there is no need for Jesus to have lived at all?

At His Resurrection, the angels proclaimed—"He is not here; for He is risen, even as He said." The disciples' common sense would tell them that what the angel said was an impossibility. Do we believe the proclamation of the supernatural, or do we refuse to believe what we say is impossible? It is "impossible" for God to be born into human flesh; but Jesus was. It is "impossible" for a dead man to rise again; but Jesus rose. It is "impossible" for a man, even if he rose from the dead, to ascend into heaven; but Jesus did. When we reach the limit of what our common sense tells us can be done, then the word comes—"With God all things are possible." The limit of the possible means that God has a word of impossibility which He will perform in us if we have faith.

The Passing to the Path of Joy
And go quickly . . . , and lo, He goeth before you.

"He is not here"—not here in your imitations, not here in your way of looking at things; He is going before you all the time, and the rousing inspiration is—"go quickly, and tell His disciples."

Think of the unspeakable thrill that must have come to this broken-hearted woman. She had had her thrilling yesterday, Jesus had cast out of her seven devils, and all her faith and hope was in Him; but He is dead. . . . Now the angel proclaims that He is risen—"Fear not ye . . . and go quickly, and tell His disciples." All that stands for tears comes with limitation. When limitation touches us and the tears come, we are apt to say—"It is all finished now," and we are too dispirited to do anything. Then comes the inspiration—"Go quickly," get on your feet and go at once. It is not an inspiration according to common sense, but an arresting inspiration of astonishment. "Lo, He goeth before you." We take the next step in limitation and are met with limitless Divine power. We have to go as if God were not there, to take the first step without Him, and we find He is there all the time. We do not go alone, we go into the realisation of the wonder of His presence. "Lo, I have told you." The supernatural character of the angel is at stake in the accepting of the inspiration. When we talk unguardedly to a child, we speak real truth because a child sees what no one else sees; when we talk to grownup people we speak acquired common sense. We need to get back to the "angel" talk.

The Pledge of the Promise of Sight
. . . there shall ye see Him.

We shall not see Jesus if we sit still, or if we pray and long for Him, but if we go quickly, "there shall ye see Him." Go in your mind, rouse yourself up, indulge no more in reminiscent worship. That is a danger that persists until we realise that Jesus is risen not to the old life but to an inconceivably new life, and that our relationship to Him now is to be an altogether different one. "Touch Me not; . . . but go unto My brethren" (RV). We have to go on to the next thing, and there we shall see Him. We enthrone our reason and say "seeing is believing." Have we the simple childlike faith to believe that if we do the next thing we shall see Him just there? To "wash one another's feet" is a commonplace thing to do, but it is there that we see Him. Do we believe in a perfect, present, absolute Redemption—a Redemption that is complete and finished? That Redemption is the work of the Risen Lord. His Resurrection is the Dawn that transfigures tears.

THE SACRAMENT OF SACRIFICE

He that believeth on Me, . . . out of [him] shall flow rivers of living water. John 7:38

Jesus Christ did not say, "He that believeth on Me, in himself shall realise the blessing of the fulness of God," but "out of him shall escape everything he has received." Our Lord always preaches anti-self-realisation; He is not after developing a man at all, He is after making a man exactly like Himself, and the measure of the Son of God is self-expenditure. If we believe on Jesus Christ it is not what we gain but what He pours through us that counts. It is not that God makes us beautifully rounded grapes, but that He squeezes the sweetness out of us. We cannot measure our lives by spiritual success, but only by what God pours through us, and we cannot measure that at all. Who can measure the influence of a star or of a lily? Yet these are the things our Lord told us to consider. "He that believeth on Me"—"through him will I pour everything, leaving him nothing." A sacrament is the real Presence in the actual elements; in this connection the actual elements are our lives.

The Waters of Satisfaction Scattered
And the three mighty men brake through the host of the Philistines, and drew water out of the well of Bethlehem, . . . and brought it to David: but he would not drink thereof, but poured it out unto the LORD. (2 Samuel 23:16 RV)

I can never sanctify to God that with which I long to satisfy myself. If I am going to satisfy myself with the blessings of God, they will corrupt me; I have to sacrifice them, pour them out, do with them what any commonsense man would say is an absurd waste. Take it in the case of friendship, or of blessing, or of spiritual experiences, immediately I long to hold any of these for myself I cannot sanctify them to the Lord. David had the right idea when he poured out the water before the Lord.

What has been like water from the well of Bethlehem to you recently? Love, friendship, spiritual blessing? Then at the peril of your soul, you take it to satisfy yourself. If you do, you cannot pour out before the Lord. How am I to pour out spiritual gifts, or natural friendship or love? How can I give them to the Lord? In one way only—in the determination of my mind, and that takes about two seconds. If I hold spiritual blessings or friendships for myself they will corrupt me, no matter how beautiful they are. I have to pour them out before the Lord, give them to Him in

my mind, though it looks as if I am wasting them; even as when David poured the water out on the sand, to be instantly sucked up.

There are certain acts of other people one could never accept if one did not know God, because it is not within human power to repay them, all we can do is to pour it out before the Lord. If I take such a line as—"Oh, I am so winsome they have to do this for me," I have turned it into poison, and it cannot be consecrated to God. But immediately I say—"This is too great and worthy a thing for me, it is not for a human being at all, I must pour it out before the Lord," then these things pour out in rivers of living water all around. Until we do pour these things out before the Lord they will always endanger those we love, because they turn to lust. We can be lustful in things that are not sordid and vile. Love has to get to its transfiguration point of being poured out before the Lord, otherwise it will get sordid. If you have got bitter and sour, you will probably find it is because God brought you a blessing and you clutched it for yourself; whereas if you had poured it out unto the Lord, you would have been the sweetest person out of heaven. If we are craving spiritual sponges, always taking these things to ourselves, we shall become a plague; other people will not get their horizon enlarged through us because we have never learned to pour out anything unto the Lord.

The Way of Salvation
. . . because He poured out His soul unto death . . . (Isaiah 53:12 RV)

This is the greatest love of God. No man ever laid down his life for his enemies unless he was indwelt by God. By the original design of God human nature is so built that men will always answer to the heroic. John 15:13 has reference to the love of man; that sacrifice is the exhibition of the sublime height to which human nature can rise with nothing of the love of God in it. Is Jesus Christ the Saviour of the world to me, or am I so overtaken with delight and reverence at the sacrifice of men that I make the Atonement of no account? Then the pleasure of the Lord is not possible in me, it only prospers in the hands of the man who makes his soul an offering. We too often make it salvation by preaching instead of preaching salvation. We have to work on the accomplished Redemption of the world, and not for it; we are here to proclaim that God has delivered men from sin, not that a man by sacrifice can save his own soul. Our salvation comes to us so easily because it cost God so much.

The Waste of Sentiment

. . . and she brake the cruse, and poured it over His head. (Mark 14:3 RV)

It was an act no one else saw any occasion for, they said it was "a waste." It was not an extraordinary occasion, and yet Mary broke the box of ointment and spilt the whole thing. It was not a useful thing, but an act of extravagant devotion, and Jesus commended her and said wherever His gospel was preached, this also should be spoken of for a memorial of her.

God spilt the life of His Son that the world might be saved. Am I prepared to spill my life out for Him? Our Lord is carried beyond Himself with delight when He sees any of us doing what Mary did, extrav-

agantly wasting our substance for Him; not set for this or that economy, but being abandoned to Him.

In the Bible there is always a oneness between the spiritual and the material. It takes the incarnation of the Holy Ghost in a man's body to make him what Jesus Christ wants him to be. Unless the blessings of God can deal with our bodies and make them the temples of the Holy Ghost, then the religion of Jesus Christ is in the clouds. If I cannot exhibit the sentiment of the Holy Ghost in the sordid actualities of life and in doing menial things from the highest motive, I am not learning to pour out unto the Lord.

"He that believeth on Me," out of him shall flow—not, he shall gain, but hundreds of others shall be continually refreshed. It is time now to break the life, to cease craving for satisfaction, and to spill the thing out. The Lord is asking for thousands of us to do it for Him.

SPIRITUAL DISCIPLESHIP

For whosoever would save his life shall lose it: and whosoever shall lose his life for My sake shall find it. Matthew 16:25 (RV)

"Spiritual" is used here in the sense of real, i.e., that which lies behind the actual and which we cannot get at by our senses. In the beginning we call the actual things real; but when we are born again we discern that reality and actuality are not one and the same thing, and we understand the distinction Paul makes when he says—"the things which are seen are temporal; but the things which are not seen are eternal." The Redemption of our Lord Jesus Christ is the great abiding Reality; to be spiritual disciples means that we have been brought into experimental contact with Redemptive Reality by the power of the grace of God.

The Source of Spiritual Discipleship

For whosoever would save his life [soul] shall lose it . . .

Soul is my way of reasoning and looking at things, it is the expression of my personal spirit in my body. Here our Lord is saying—"If you are going to be My disciple, you must lose your soul"—am I prepared to lose my soul? When I am born from above (RV mg) and the Redemption has been made experimentally real in me by the Spirit of God, then I have to begin to reason about things as Jesus did, I have to form the mind of Christ, and it will mean a right-about face in every way. If I said I have always looked at things in this way and I always shall, then I will never become a spiritual disciple.

We are apt to confound the strong-minded man with the obstinate man. An obstinate man refuses to be reasoned with; his argument is—"I have said it and I will stick to it." Spiritually the strong-minded man is one who has learned to construct his reasoning on the basis of the Redemption, he faces every issue of life in the light of the Lord Jesus.

There is a difference between being saved and being a disciple. Some of us are saved, "yet so as through fire" (RV). We are grateful to God for saving us from sin, but we are of no use to Him in so far as our actual life is concerned. We are not spiritual disciples. Our Lord's last command was not—"Go and save men," but—"Go . . . and make disciples" (RV), we cannot make disciples of others unless we are disciples ourselves. When a man comes to Jesus it is not sin that is in the way, but self-realisation, pride, his claim to himself. "I must realise myself, I must be educated and trained, I must do those things that will help me to develop myself." Self-realisation is anti-Christian. All this is vigorous paganism, it is not Christianity. Jesus Christ's attitude is always that of *anti*-self-realisation. His purpose is not the development of man at all; His purpose is to make man exactly like Himself, and the characteristic of the Son of God is not self-realisation but self-expenditure. Spiritual selfishness must go—am I prepared for it to go? "If any man would come after Me, let him deny himself" (RV), that is, "let him give up his right to himself to Me."

"Present your bodies a living sacrifice," says Paul. He does not say "present your all." "All" is an elusive word, because no one knows what his "all" is. Paul says—"Present your bodies. . . ." Do not ask God to take your body, but give your body to God. I beseech you—I passionately entreat you—says Paul, present your bodies a living sacrifice. That is spiritual sacrifice. God does not ask us to give up things for the sake of giving them up; He asks us to sacrifice them, to give back to Him the best He has given us in order that it may belong to Him and us for ever. Sacrifice is the source of spiritual discipleship.

The Supremacy of Spiritual Discipleship

. . . and whosoever shall lose his life for My sake shall find it.

Many people lose their lives, but not for Christ's sake. "For My sake"—that is the supreme surrender. God does not transform a man's life by magic, but through the surrender of the man to Himself. The thirteenth chapter of First Corinthians is the description of the way love works out in actual life. To most of us love is a curiously useless word. The love Paul refers to is the sovereign preference of my person for another person, and that other Person Jesus Christ. That sovereign preference works out in the deliberate identification of myself with God's interests in other people, and God is interested in some strange people; He is interested in the man whom I am inclined to despise.

As a spiritual disciple I have to lose my individuality for ever. Individuality is self-assertive and independent, it is all elbows. It is natural for a child to be strongly marked by individuality, but it is a despicable thing for a man or woman to be hide-bound by individual peculiarities. It means that the personality has never been transfigured, never been filled with the Holy Ghost, never come to the source of spiritual Reality. Our Lord can only be defined in terms of personality, never in terms of individuality. "I and My Father are one," and our Lord's conception of human personality is that it can be merged and made one with God without losing its identity. If we are going to be disciples we have to break the bands of individuality which cabin and confine, and launch out in abandon to Jesus Christ.

We cannot get at Reality by thinking or by emotion, but only by conscience, and the Spirit of God working through conscience brings a man straight to the Redemptive Reality of our Lord, then there follows a life of spiritual discipleship, pouring out for others for His sake. The saint must become like his Master, utterly unobtrusive. For "we preach not ourselves, but Christ Jesus as Lord; and ourselves as your servants for Jesus' sake" (RV). If you are serving men for their sakes you will soon have the heart knocked out of you; but if you are personally and passionately devoted to the Lord Jesus Christ, then you can spend yourselves to the last ebb because your motive is love to the Lord.

We never want Jesus Christ in the actual turmoil of life unless we have found Him in the Real, but when we have found Him there He brings into actual life a transfiguring touch. He makes the Real and the Actual one. Jesus Christ is the At-one-ment, and I can only get the Atonement made real in me by being born from above (RV mg) into the realm Jesus Christ came to lift me into. God grant we may be amongst those who are prepared to be spiritual disciples. As disciples we must give up spiritual selfishness; we must make the spiritual sacrifice of presenting our bodies to God, and we must live the superlative life of being identified with God's interests in other people.

SACRAMENTAL DISCIPLESHIP
1 Corinthians 1:17–18

Christ did not send me to baptize but to preach the gospel. And to preach it with no fine rhetoric, lest the Cross of Christ should lose its power! 1 Corinthians 1:17 (MOFFATT)

The word "sacrament" is used in connection with the Lord's Supper and means the real Presence of God coming through the actual elements. The real Presence of God is brought to us also in the actual things of life by means of the sacramental element in Redemption. It is a trick of our minds to think that God and actual things are one and the same; God comes to us in actual things, but actual things are not God. "In every thing give thanks," says Paul, not— Give thanks *for* everything, but give thanks that in everything that transpires there abides the real Presence of God. God is more real than the actual things—"therefore will not we fear, though the earth be removed." We think that our actual life is profound until something happens—a war or a bereavement, and we are flung clean abroad, then through the agony of the mystery of life we cry out to God and there comes the voice of Jesus—"Come unto Me."

The Sacrament of the Historic Cross

"Christ did not send me to baptize"—to put religious rites in the front—"but to preach the gospel" (MOF-FATT). The gospel is not so much good news to man as good news about God. "And to preach it with no fine rhetoric." It is one thing to thrill an audience with fine rhetoric, or by a magnetic personality, but the New Testament order of preaching is that of John the Baptist—"He must increase, but I must decrease." The one thing for Paul was Christ and Him crucified, not Christ risen and exalted, but Christ "crucified." Paul had only one passion, and that was the exposition and the emphasis and the re-emphasis of the Cross. The New Testament emphasises the death of Christ because the Cross is the Centre that reveals the very heart of God. The death Jesus died was not the death of a martyr, it was the revelation in actual history of the very nature of God. "But we preach Christ crucified, unto Jews a stumbling-block" (RV), a distress and a humiliation; "and unto Gentiles" (those who seek wisdom), "foolishness; but unto them that are called, both Jews and Greeks, Christ the power of God, and the wisdom of God" (RV).

It seems so remote from actual things to say that the preaching of the Cross conveys the Presence of God, but God has chosen to save in this way. "It was God's good pleasure through the foolishness of the preaching to save them that believe" (RV), because behind the preaching of the Gospel is the creative Redemption of God at work in the souls of men. That is the miracle of God. If you can tell how a corn of wheat when put into the ground will bring forth what it never was before, you can also tell how the Word of God put into a man's soul will bring forth what was not there before—a new life. The same God is the Author of both. How are men born of the Spirit? By the proclaiming of the historic Cross of Christ. "The wind bloweth where it listeth . . . so is every one that is born of the Spirit." The simple proclaiming of the gospel of God creates the need for the gospel. Nothing can satisfy the need but that which creates the need. The inner reality of Redemption is that it creates all the time. "And I, if I be lifted up from the earth, will draw all men unto Myself" (RV). Once let Jesus be lifted up and the Spirit of God creates the need for Him.

Unless we are born from above (RV mg), the Cross of Christ means nothing to us; it does not matter whether Jesus lived or died; the New Testament is an exquisitely beautiful record of a life, but it *conveys* nothing. The words of Isaiah 53:2 are humiliatingly true of us all. When we see the Highest, He is to us as a root out of a dry ground, thoroughly disadvantaged. When the religious people of His day saw the Highest incarnate before them, they hated Him and crucified Him. It is only when a man gets to his wits' end and is stabbed wide awake that he realises for the first time the meaning of the Cross—"I thought that He was stricken, smitten by God and afflicted; now I see that He was wounded for my transgression."

"The Lamb that hath been slain from the foundation of the world" (RV). In the Cross God is revealed not as One reigning in calm disdain above all the squalors of earth, but as One Who suffers more keenly than the keenest sufferer—"a man of sorrows, and acquainted with grief." This rules out once and for all the idea that Jesus was a martyr. Jesus did not die the death of a martyr: He died the death not of a good man, but the death due to a bad man, with the vicarious pain of Almighty God at His heart. That pain is unfathomable to us, but we get an insight into it in the cry upon the Cross, "My God, my God, why hast Thou forsaken Me?" The death of Jesus goes away down underneath the deepest, vilest sin that human nature ever committed. Every pious mood must be stripped off when we stand before the Cross. The Cross in actual history is the point where the real Presence of God enters human history; and the point where the real Presence of God enters human life is the moment of absolute surrender, not of religious sentiment. The first step to sacramental discipleship is the crowning of Jesus as Lord.

The Sacrament of the Scriptures

Ye search the Scriptures, because ye think that in them ye have eternal life; and these are they which bear witness of me. (John 5:39 RV)

The context of the Bible is the Lord Jesus Christ. The Scriptures do not give us life unless Jesus speaks them to us. Jesus Christ makes His words spirit and life to us if we will obey them. If we are not born again the Word of God is nothing to us. When men tear this Book of God to pieces it reveals how blind they are. To the saint this Book of God is a sacrament, it conveys the real Presence of God. God by His providence puts needs in our actual life which drive us to search the Scriptures, and as we search them, the sacrament of God's Presence comes to us through the words of His Book.

The Sacrament of the Saint

Lovest thou Me? . . . Feed My sheep.

A saint must measure his life by self-expenditure, that is, by what God pours through him. Just as the real Presence of God comes through the preaching of the crucified Christ, and through the words of the Bible, so it comes through His children. "Lovest thou Me? . . . Feed My sheep"—and Jesus gave Peter nothing to feed them with. The disciple has himself to be the very bread of God by the power of the Redemption at work in him. Just as our Lord was made broken bread and poured-out wine for our salvation, so He makes us broken bread in His hands. Thank God for all those who are sacramental saints; they have been through the furnace with God, and the Presence of God comes through their actual lives.

The secret of sacramental discipleship is to be so abandoned to the disposition of God in us that He can use us as broken bread and poured-out wine for His purpose in the world, even as He broke the life of His own Son to redeem us.

SERMON AT EGYPT GENERAL MISSION, APRIL 16, 1916.

THE LIMIT OF DEDICATION

She hath done what she could. Mark 14:8

Mary Magdalene, the woman who was a sinner, and Mary of Bethany, the one who made this spontaneous dedication to Jesus, represent the three types of womanhood for whom Jesus Christ is sufficient—the tortured, the worst, and the best. Mary of Bethany stands as the noblest type of womanhood in our Lord's day. Her compeer is the rich young ruler, but he failed in relation to Jesus Christ exactly where Mary did not fail.

The Unconscious Spontaneity of Love

. . . as He sat at meat, there came a woman having an alabaster cruse of ointment of spikenard very costly; and she brake the cruse, and poured it over His head. (Mark 14:3 RV)

If human love is always discreet and calculating, never carried beyond itself, it is not of the true nature of love. The characteristic of love is that it is spontaneous, it bursts up in extraordinary ways; it is never premeditated. The reason Jesus called Mary's act a good work" was because it was wrought out of spontaneous love to Himself. It was neither useful nor her duty; it was an extravagant act for which no one else saw any occasion. "But Jesus said, Let her alone; why trouble ye her? she hath wrought a good work on Me." The disciples were indignant—"Why was this waste of the ointment made?"—"If she had only sold the ointment and given us the money, we would have used it for the poor." Money is one of the touchstones in our Lord's teaching. Nowadays we are taken up with our ideas of economy and thrift, and never see that those ideas are not God's ideas. The very nature of God is extravagance. How many sunrises and sunsets does God make?

> *Gloriously wasteful, O my Lord, art Thou!*
> *Sunset faints after sunset into the night. . . .*

How many flowers and birds, how many ineffable beauties all over the world, lavish desert blossoms, that only His eye sees? Mary's act was one of spontaneous extravagance because it sprang out of the heart of a child. When our Lord said—"Except ye . . . become as little children . . ." He was not setting up a little child as a standard, but as the exact expression of an implicit relationship to Himself.

The Unconscious Sympathy of Life

For ye have the poor always with you, and whensoever ye will ye can do them good: but Me ye have not always. She hath done what she could: she hath anointed My body aforehand for the burying. (Mark 14:7–8 RV)

Jesus is pointing out that the great note of our lives as His disciples is not sympathy with the poor, not an understanding of the needs of men, but an understanding of His point of view. *"Watch with Me"*; *"Give Me to drink"*; *"Continue with Me."* No one can understand Jesus Christ's point of view unless he has His Spirit, The need is never the call; the need is the opportunity. The call is defined in John 17:18—"As Thou didst send Me into the world, even so sent I them into the world." The first obedience of our Lord was not to the needs of men but to the will of His Father; and our first obedience is to Jesus Christ, not to the poor and the despised and afflicted. My sympathy with them is the proof that I have a loving sympathy greater than them all, viz., sympathy with my Lord. Mary of Bethany revealed in her act of extravagant devotion that the unconscious sympathy of her life was with Jesus Christ. "She hath done what she could"—to the absolute limit of what a woman can do. It was impossible to do more.

"She hath anointed My body aforehand for the burying" (RV). Mary did not know that she was anointing the body of Jesus for His burial. Her heart was bursting with love to Jesus, and she took this opportunity of giving it expression. Love is the sovereign preference of my person for another person, and if I am a disciple of Jesus, that sovereign preference is for Him. "O forgotten and neglected Jesus, mine eyes have looked on Thee." That means I am spoilt for everything saving as I can be used to glorify Him.

The Unconscious Service of Loyalty

The only thing Jesus ever commended was this act of Mary's, and He said: "Wheresoever the gospel shall be preached throughout the whole world, that also which this woman hath done shall be spoken of for a memorial of her" (RV), because in the anointing our Lord saw an exact illustration of what He Himself was about to do. He put Mary's act alongside His own Cross. God shattered the life of His own Son to save the world; are we prepared to pour out our lives for Him? Our Lord is carried beyond Himself with joy when He sees any of us doing what Mary of Bethany did. The one thing He looks for in a disciple is aban-

don. Abandon to God is of more value than personal holiness. Personal holiness focuses our eyes on our own whiteness; when we are abandoned to God, He works through us all the time. When David's three mighty men brought him the water from the well of Bethlehem, we read that "he would not drink thereof, but poured it out unto the LORD." David saw in their devotion something worthy only to be poured out before God.

Have I ever produced in the heart of the Lord Jesus what Mary of Bethany produced? "She hath done what she could"—to the absolute limit. I have not done what I could until I have done the same.

YMCA HUT, MAY 7, 1916

[THE DISTINGUISHED SERVICE ORDER (D.S.O.) IS A BRITISH MILITARY DECORATION AWARDED FOR SPECIAL SERVICES IN ACTION.]

THE SPIRITUAL "D.S.O."

If any man serve Me, let him follow Me; and where I am, there shall also My servant be: if any man serve Me, him will the Father honour. John 12:26 (RV)

The Service of Passionate Devotion

If any man serve Me, let him follow Me . . .

Our idea of service is often the outcome of devotion to a principle, but Jesus is here dealing with the service that is devotion to Him. With us, Christian service is something we do; with Jesus Christ it is not what we *do for* Him, but what we *are to* Him that He calls service. Our Lord always puts the matter of discipleship on the basis of devotion not to a belief or a creed, but to Himself. There is no argument about it, and no compulsion, simply—"If you would be My disciple, you must be devoted to Me."

(a) The Source of Devotion

"*. . . What must we do, that we may work the works of God? . . . This is the work of God, that ye believe on Him . . .*" *(John 6:28–29 RV)*. Where is the devotion to spring from? "Believe also in Me." Do I believe Jesus, not believe about Him, but believe Him? Peter, when he confessed that our Lord was the Son of God, was talking out of the spontaneous originality of his own heart. With a tremendous amazement he said, "Thou art the Christ, the Son of the living God," and instantly Jesus says, "Blessed art thou," you did not guess it, it was an intuition from My Father, and on this rock (the rock of the revelation in personal life of Who I am) I will build My Church.

Have I realised Who Jesus is to me? We substitute credal belief for personal belief. The intuitive heart of a man is suddenly touched by the Spirit of God and he says, "Now I see Who Jesus is," and that is the source of devotion.

(b) The Secret of Disaster

"*He that is a hireling . . . fleeth . . .*" *(John 10:12 RV)*. Am I out for my own? Am I utilising membership of the Christian Church to further my own ends? If a preacher uses his position to further his own ends, he is heading for disaster. There are many devoted to causes, but few devoted to Jesus Christ. If I am devoted to a particular cause only, when that cause fails I fail too. The secret of a disciple's life is devotion to Jesus Christ, and the very nature of the life is that it is unobtrusive; it falls into the ground and dies: but presently it springs up and alters the whole landscape (see John 12:24). The illustrations Jesus uses are always drawn from His Father's work—"Consider the lilies of the field—Behold the birds of the heaven"— not things with tangible external results, but lilies and trees, things with nothing pretentious about them.

(c) The Spring of Direction

"*Lovest thou Me? . . . Feed My sheep*" *(John 21:17)*. If you love Me, says Jesus, "Feed My sheep." "Don't make converts to your way of thinking, but look after My sheep, see that they are nourished in the knowledge of Me." Our Lord's first obedience was to the will of His Father, and He said, "As the Father hath sent Me, even so send I you" (RV). It sounds the right thing to say that Jesus Christ came here to help mankind: but His great desire was to do the will of His Father, and our Lord was misunderstood because He would not put the needs of men first. He said the first commandment is "Thou shalt love the Lord thy God with all thy heart, and with all thy soul, and with all thy mind, and with all thy strength."

Jesus Christ is a source of deep offence to the educated trained mind of to-day that does not want Him in any other way than as a Comrade. Many do not want to be devoted to Him, but only to the cause He started. If I am only devoted to the cause of humanity, I will be soon exhausted and come to the point where my love will falter, but if I love Jesus Christ I will serve humanity, though men and women treat me like a door-mat.

The Society of Personal Dedication
and where I am, there shall also My servant be . . .

Anywhere the man who is devoted to Jesus Christ goes, Jesus Christ is there with him.

(a) Felicity of Faithfulness
"Well done, good and faithful servant; . . . enter thou into the joy of thy Lord" (Matthew 25:23). The joy of a thing lies in fulfilling the purpose of its creation. Jesus Christ's joy is that He fulfilled the design of His Father's will, and my joy is that I fulfil God's design in calling me, viz., to make me a follower of Him.

(b) Fulness of Following
"If a man love Me, he will keep My word: and My Father will love him, and we will come unto him, and make our abode with him" (John 14:23 ASV). Here is the description of the society of a man devoted to Jesus Christ in this actual life, whether in a camp or an office or the Bush. Imagine the sublime society of a man—he has God the Father, God the Son, and God the Holy Ghost with him wherever he goes.

(c) Fruitfulness of Friendship
"I have called you friends" (John 15:15). The fruitfulness of friendship is described in verse 13, "Greater love hath no man than this, that a man lay down his life for his friends." If I am a friend of Jesus Christ, I lay down my life for Him. That does not mean that I go through the big crisis of death; it means that I lay down my life deliberately as I would lay out a pound note. I have this to lay out and expend; I have a day before me, and I am going to lay it out for Jesus Christ; I have my duty to perform, but I am going to lay it out in devotion to Jesus Christ all through. It is difficult, and thank God it is difficult. Salvation is easy because it cost God so much, but the manifestation of it in my life is difficult. God does expect a

man to be a man. God saves a man and endues him with His Holy Spirit, and says in effect, "Now it is up to you to prove it, work it out; be loyal to Me while the nature of things round about you would make you disloyal. I have called you friends, now stand loyal to your Friend." His honour is at stake in our bodily life.

The Seal of Perfect Discipline
. . . if any man serve Me, him will the Father honour.

If it were necessary for every man to lay down his life in a heroic way, as men have done in Gallipoli and in Flanders, what about the men and women who never get a chance of doing anything heroic? Everybody is not noble or generous or great; a great number of men are despicable beings. Is God going to put them on the scrap heap? "If you confess Me," Jesus says, as it were, "God Almighty will give you the D.S.O.—not if you are a good man, or have done wonderful things, but if you have served Me."

(a) The Drill in Purity
"These are they which follow the Lamb whithersoever He goeth" (Revelation 14:4). Actually pure in their natural walk, they followed the Lamb in their actual lives, and were consciously redeemed by the blood of Christ. There is a difference between innocence and purity. Innocence is the characteristic of a child, purity is the characteristic of a man or woman who knows what the tendencies and temptations to go wrong are, and who has overcome them. Virtue is not in the man who has not been tempted, neither is purity. When a man is tempted and remains steadfastly unspotted, then he is virtuous.

Jesus Christ says in effect, "If you will serve Me, you will keep your chastity," that means there has to be a fight; you realise that all the power of God is behind you as you make the fight. You may be pure and unsullied for months, when all of a sudden there will be the insinuation of an idea, grip it on the threshold of your mind in a vice instantly, and do not allow it any more. If I am to serve Jesus Christ, I have to remember that my body is the temple of the Holy Ghost. Talk about it being a "soft" thing to be a follower of Jesus Christ! It is about the sternest and most heroic thing a man ever "struck" in his life to keep himself absolutely undefiled, one who by chastity maintains his integrity. It is a discipline, and thank God for the discipline.

(b) The Duty of Patience
"Because thou didst keep the word of My patience, I also will keep thee from the hour of trial, that hour which is to come upon the whole world" (Revelation 3:10 RV). Jesus says we are to keep the word of His patience. There

are so many things in this life that it seems much better to be impatient about. The best illustration is that of an archer, he pulls the string further and further away from his bow with the arrow fixed, then, when it is adjusted, with his eye on the mark he lets fly. The Christian's life is like that. God is the archer; He takes the saint like a bow which He stretches, and we get to a certain point and say "I can't stand any more, I can't stand this test of patience any longer," but God goes on stretching. He is not aiming at our mark, but at His own, and the patience of the saints is that we hold on until He lets the arrow fly straight to His goal.

PAIN IN THE DAWN OF ETERNAL HOPE
2 Corinthians 4:16–18

For our light affliction, which is for the moment, worketh for us more and more exceedingly an eternal weight of glory. 2 Corinthians 4:17 (RV)

The basis of human life is tragedy. It is difficult to realise this until one gets through the experiences that are on the surface of life, and we discover we are built with a bigger capacity for pain than for joy, that the undertone of all our life is sorrow, and the great expression and revelation of God in the world is the revelation of the Cross, not of joy. It is one of the things which makes the Bible seem so utterly unreal so long as we are healthy and full of life and spirits. Tragedy is something in which all the forces make for disaster. Paul in writing about human life always wrote from the Bible standpoint, viz., that the basis of things is not reasonable but tragic. Sin has made a gap between God and the human race, and consequently when we try to explain our lives on the line of logic or reason, we find things don't work out that way. Then when we go through disasters such as are being produced by this war, we are more prepared to look at the Bible and its point of view. Jesus Christ stands outside the majority of our lives in the usual run because He deals with the fundamentals; we do not, we deal with the external actual, and it is only when the external actuals are ploughed into by sorrow or bereavement that we begin to find there is only one Reality—our Lord Jesus Christ, and only one Book that brings light.

Our Life in Tragedy
But though our outward man is decaying . . . (RV)

"But though our outward man is decaying"—not *may* decay, but our outward man is built that way. That in itself is a tragedy; a beautiful physical life, a beautiful child's life, is all built at present on decay. It makes us rebel and produces almost spite against the Creator, but the Bible reveals that the reason for it all is the hiatus between God and man caused by sin.

(a) Pain of Sensibility
"*I will greatly multiply thy sorrow*" (Genesis 3:16). We are introduced into this order of things by pain to someone else, not necessarily pain to ourselves but pain to our mothers. The basis of the bearing into this life of sensibility is pain. This is a fundamental revelation in God's Book.

(b) Pain of Salvation
"*Because Christ also suffered for sins once, the righteous for the unrighteous, that He might bring us to God: being put to death in the flesh, but quickened in the spirit*" (1 Peter 3:18 RV). The phrase "born from above" (RV mg) as our Lord used it does not mean being saved from hell or from sin, but that I am born into the reality in which He lives. We are born again by pain, not necessarily pain to ourselves any more than our natural birth means pain to us. We are born into the realm where our Lord lives by pain to God, and the pain of God is exhibited on Calvary.

(c) Pain of Sanctification
"*I have been crucified with Christ; yet I live; and yet no longer I, but Christ liveth in me: and that life which I now live in the flesh I live in faith, the faith which is in the Son of God, Who loved me, and gave Himself up for me*" (Galatians 2:20 RV). We are dealing with fundamental pain, the basis of which is tragedy—all the forces making for disaster. "I have been crucified with Christ"—crucifixion is a painful thing. It means, not in the theological sense, but in the spiritual sense, being made one with Jesus Christ, and that costs *me* pain. I have deliberately to be willing to give up my right to myself, that has now been put to death by mine own determination, and "that life which I now live in the flesh I live in faith, the faith which is in the Son of God," literally, the faith that was in Jesus Christ is now in me.

These are the three big fundamental things in our human life, and the basis of each is pain. They are not things to preach about, but rather matters for our consideration. In the light of this terrible tragedy of war where pain is sweeping the whole universe until there is scarcely a home that has not been touched by it, there is again a chance to witness the incoming of the quiet power of our Lord Jesus Christ. I do not believe we shall see the incoming power of denominationalism or "Churchianity" or creed; but I do believe that the Spirit of God is pushing His way into people's lives on the only line of emancipation there is, viz., through the Cross, and we are realising that the revelation given to us of God is of a God Who suffers. We see more into the real tragedy of life when we have been hit hard by bereavement or unrequited love, or by some great elemental pain that has shocked the externals. The human mind instantly says, Why should these things be? They are unreasonable. Emphatically so, we may rage as we choose, but we come to the conclusion that the Bible is right—the basis of things is tragic, not mathematical. As soon as we recognise life is based on tragedy, we won't be too staggered when tragedy emerges, but will learn how to turn to God.

Our Light in Tragedy

For our light affliction, which is for the moment, worketh for us more and more exceedingly an eternal weight of glory. (RV)

Where are we to get our light in all this appalling tragedy? It is obvious nonsense to say that suffering makes saints, it makes some people devils. Hebrews 12:11 is referring to the suffering that comes to a person who is being exercised by the Spirit of God. We all know people who have been made much meaner and more irritable and more intolerable to live with by suffering: it is not right to say that all suffering perfects. It only perfects one type of person—the one who accepts the call of God in Christ Jesus.

(a) Undiscouraged by Decay

"Wherefore we faint not; but though our outward man is decaying, yet our inward man is renewed day by day" (RV). There is nothing, naturally speaking, that makes us lose heart quicker than decay—the decay of bodily beauty, of natural life, of friendship, of associations, all these things make a man lose heart; but Paul says when we are trusting in Jesus Christ these things do not find us discouraged, light comes through them. "For we preach not ourselves, but Christ Jesus as Lord, and ourselves as your servants for Jesus' sake" (RV). That is the rock on which Paul stands, and that is where he gets his light. It does not matter what happens, there may be disasters or casualties, or wars or bereavements and heartbreaks, but the marvellous thing in the man who is rightly related to Jesus Christ is that he is not discouraged. That is supernatural, no human being can

stand these shocks and not be discouraged unless he is upheld by the supernatural grace of God. The counterfeit of true spirituality is that produced by creeds. When one has been bereaved the most trying person is the one with a creed who can come with didactic counsel with regard to suffering; but turn to a book like the Book of Job where nothing is taught at all, but wonderful expression is given to the real suffering of life, and the mere reading of it brings consolation to a breaking heart. The standards of personal relationship to Jesus Christ leave a man undiscouraged by decay. The books and the men who help us most are not those who teach us, but those who can express for us what we feel inarticulate about.

(b) Undeceived by Disillusionment

There are times in sorrow when we are disillusionised, our eyes are opened, and we see people in their true relationships, and often we get completely disheartened and feel we won't trust anyone any more. But when we are trusting to our Lord Jesus Christ, this kind of light affliction leaves us with a true discernment, we are not deceived, we see men and women in their right relationship, and light comes all through. Whatever happens, our relationship to Jesus Christ works through it. We have to learn to take up pain and weave it into the fabric of our lives.

(c) Undistracted by Discernment

"While we look not at the things which are seen, but at the things which are not seen: for the things which are seen are temporal; but the things which are not seen are eternal." The things we see are actual, but not eternal, and the curious thing about actual things is that we cannot see the real, eternal things without them. The fanatic won't have actual things at all, he pretends he can see God and God's purposes apart from actual present circumstances. That is not so, we only see by means of the actual, and when we are going through the experience of the actual we come to tragedy and sorrow and difficulty, but if we are trusting in God we are undistracted by it.

Our Love in Tragedy

While we look . . . at the things which are not seen.

That is the description of love.

(a) The Blindness of Insight

Love is not blind. Love has insight, it sees the things that are not seen. We are told that when we are in love with a person we do not see his defects: the truth is that we see what others do not see, we see him in the ideal, in the real relationship. The actual things in life are sordid and decaying and wrong and twisted, but we do not look at them, we look at the eternal things beyond, and the consequence is that in the actual tribulations and circumstances of the moment, pain works for us an eternal hope. We have all had the experience that it is only in the days of affliction that our true interests are furthered.

(b) The Blundering of Intellect
The intellect only looks for things that are seen and actual, draws its inferences from these and becomes pessimistic and loses heart.

(c) The Benediction of Inspiration
The Benediction of Inspiration—is that we know that "the things which are not seen are eternal." Love, joy, peace, these things are not seen, yet they are eternal, and God's nature is made up of these things. The Lamb breaks the seals—the eternal and abiding gentleness of God undoes everything.

"Our light affliction . . ."—To escape affliction is a cowardly thing to do; to sink under it is natural; to get at God through it is a spiritual thing. Most of us have tried the first, a good many of us have known the second, and the Spirit of God in us knows the third, getting through into the weight of glory. That means we become people of substance spiritually; we can be relied on when others are in pain or sorrow, and after this war is done there will be a call for every one of us to be of use for God in that direction, not to be didactic and set on our own views, but simply to be ourselves rightly related to our Lord Jesus Christ so that through us the presence of God may come to others. Rational common-sense talk does not deal with eternal things, and is an insult when we are dealing with the things that are not seen. We have to learn to live in the reality of the eternal things.

YMCA HUT, NOVEMBER 5, 1916

THE HONOUR OF A SAINT
Galatians 2:20

Redemption is the basis of things, it is God's "bit"; we have to live our actual life on that basis. We are apt to get a conception of the Redemption that enables us to "hang in" to Jesus mentally and do nothing else. This seems the natural outcome of the way Redemption has too often been presented. God expects us to maintain in our individual lives the honour of a saint. It is up to us to live the life of a saint in order to show our gratitude to God for His amazing salvation, a salvation which cost us nothing but which cost God everything.

In this passage Paul describes how this point of honour was reached in his life—"I have been crucified with Christ . . . and that life which I now live in the flesh . . ." (RV). The word "now" is very annoying, if only Paul had said "hereafter"—"this is the kind of life I am going to live after I am dead and in heaven; down here I am compassed about with infirmities and am a miserable sinner." But he did not, he said "now," "that life which I now live in the flesh . . ." i.e., the life men could see, ". . . I live in faith, the faith which is in the Son of God."

The Moral Death of Self-Will
I have been crucified with Christ . . . (RV)

Paul is referring to a deliberate act on his own part, he has given over to death his self-will. Will is, me, active, not one bit of me but the whole of me. Self-will is best described as the whole of myself active around my own point of view, and Paul is speaking of moral death to that,—he says, "I have deliberately identified myself with the death of Jesus, and I no longer work around my own point of view." The reference to the death of Christ is not merely to our Lord's sacrificial death with which we have nothing to do—the death of Jesus is the death of God on the plane of human history for one purpose, the justification of the holiness of God and the manifestation of the true nature of God—Paul is stating as a fact that he has morally identified himself with that death. For us it means that we deliberately and actually identify ourselves with the death of Jesus, and accept God's verdict on the things which He condemns in that death; in other words, we deliberately give up our right to ourselves to God. Whenever our Lord speaks about discipleship, it is this point He emphasises—"If any man will come after Me, let him deny himself," i.e., let him give up his right to himself. No one can bring us to this denial, even God Himself cannot, we must come there of our own accord, and the length of time it takes to do so depends entirely on whether we want to come or not. If we give way to the play of our emotions and do not intend deliberately to come to the point of identification, we will get off on to spiritual sentimentality and end nowhere.

(a) Disentangling the Inner Life

"Simon Peter answered Him, Lord, to whom shall we go? Thou hast the words of eternal life" (John 6 contains a description of the sifting out of the disciples from the crowd round about, until there were just the twelve left, and to them Jesus says—"Would ye also go away?" Some who had been following Jesus had not gone too far to turn back, and "they went back, and walked no more with Him." But Peter has gone too far to turn back and he says, "Lord, to whom shall we go?" There is a stage like that in our spiritual experience, we do not see the Guide ahead of us, we do not feel the joy of the Lord, there is no exhilaration, yet we have gone too far to go back, we are up against it now. It might be illustrated in the spiritual life by Tennyson's phrase, "a white funeral."[20] When we go through the moral death to self-will we find we have committed ourselves, there are many things that must go to the "white funeral." At the first we have the idea that everything apart from Christ is bad; but there is much in our former life that is fascinating, any amount of paganism that is clear and vigorous, virtues that are good morally. But we have to discover they are not stamped with the right lineage and superscription, and if we are going to live the life of a saint we must go to the moral death of those things, make a termination of them, turn these good natural things into the spiritual.

(b) Disciplining the Intuitive Light

"While ye have the light, believe on the light, that ye may become sons of light" (John 12:36 RV). Intuition in the nature world means that we see or discern at sight, there is no reasoning in connection with it, we see at once. When the Spirit of God is in us He gives us intuitive discernment, we know exactly what He wants; then the point is, are we going through identification with our Lord in order that that intuitive light may become the discipline of our lives? It is this practical aspect that has been ignored. We have not sufficiently emphasised the fact that we have to live as saints, and that in our lives the honour at stake is not our personal honour, but the honour of Jesus Christ.

When we are beginning to be spiritual by means of the reception of the Holy Spirit, we get moments of intuitive light. We are not always dull, there are moments when we are brilliant, and Jesus says, "While ye have the light, believe on the light" (RV). We are apt to believe what we saw in the dark, and consequently we believe wrongly. We have to believe what we saw when we were in the light, "hang in" to it, discipline the whole of our lives up to it. If the Holy Spirit is working in our hearts, all this becomes implicitly clear to us.

The Holy Spirit is honest, and we know intuitively whether we have or have not been identified with the death of Jesus, whether we have or have not given over our self-will to the holy will of God.

(c) Discovering the Inspired Loyalty (John 21:15–18)

"Lovest thou Me?. . . Feed My sheep . . ." (John 21:17). When we do decide to go to the death of self-will, we discover that the inspired loyalty of our lives is devotion to Jesus. "Lovest thou Me?" Then—"Feed My sheep." Jesus did not say—"Go out and spread propaganda," but "Feed My sheep." They are not our sheep, but His. We are apt to take loyalty to convictions to be the same as loyalty to Christ. Convictions mean a great deal in our mental make-up, but there are stages when conscience and Christ are antagonistic. Paul said, "I verily thought with myself, that I ought to do many things contrary to the name of Jesus of Nazareth" (Acts 26:9). Inspired loyalty is not loyalty to my attitude to the truth, but loyalty to The Truth—Jesus Christ. Conscience simply means that power in me that affiliates itself with the highest I know; if I do not know Jesus, then my conscience will not be loyal to God as revealed in Him. It is possible for conscience and Christ to go together, but it is not necessarily so. We see saints hard and metallic because they have become loyal to a phase of truth, instead of remembering that Jesus does not send His disciples out to advocate certain phases of truth, but to feed His sheep and tend His lambs. The inspired loyalty is to Jesus Himself.

John 21:18 is the symbol of the moral death of self-will. "When thou wast young, thou girdedst thyself, and walkedest whither thou wouldest: but when thou shalt be old, . . . another shall gird thee, and carry thee whither thou wouldest not." When we are young in the spiritual life we do practically exactly what we want to do, then there comes a time when we have to face this question of moral death to self-will. Am I determined to go through the discipline of identification with my Lord's point of view and no longer make my own point of view the centre of my life? If I am going to maintain the honour of a saint, I have deliberately to go to the death of my self-will.

The Moral Discipline of Spiritual Will

yet I live; and yet no longer I, but Christ liveth in me . . . (RV)

(a) The Blood of Christ

"But if we walk in the light, as He is in the light, we have fellowship one with another, and the blood of Jesus His Son

---

20. "white funeral of the single life": phrase from Tennyson's poem "To H.R.H. Princess Beatrice"; to Chambers, a white funeral meant a passage from one stage of life to another; leaving the past behind and moving into the future; he often used it to mean death to self and a complete surrender to God.

cleanseth us from all sin" (1 John 1:7 RV). When we speak of the blood of Jesus Christ cleansing us from all sin, we do not mean the physical blood shed on Calvary, but the whole life of the Son of God which was poured out to redeem the world. All the perfections of the essential nature of God were in that blood, and all the holiest attainments of mankind as well. It was the life of the perfection of Deity that was poured out on Calvary, ". . . the church of God, which He purchased with His own blood" (Acts 20:28 RV). We are apt to look upon the blood of Jesus Christ as a magic-working power instead of its being the very life of the Son of God poured forth for men. The whole meaning of our being identified with the death of Jesus is that His blood may flow through our mortal bodies. Identification with the death of Jesus Christ means identification with Him to the death of everything that never was in Him, and it is the blood of Christ, in the sense of the whole personal life of the Son of God, that comes into us and "cleanseth us from all sin."

(b) The Blood of Personality
"That I may know Him, and the power of His resurrection, and the fellowship of His sufferings, becoming conformed unto His death" (Philippians 3:10 RV). Paul's whole personality was passionately devoted to Jesus— "that I may know Him." As soon as that note dominates a personality everything is simplified. It is impossible for the natural man once born, to have a single motive. We know when the love of God has been shed abroad in our hearts because of this miracle of a single motive. The moral discipline of spiritual will is that I rerelate myself all through according to this motive. It is no longer my claim to my right to myself that rules my personal life—I am not dead, but the old disposition of my right to myself has gone, it is Jesus Christ's right to me that rules me now, "and that life which I now live in the flesh" I live from that centre. The attitude of a saint is that he is related to God through Jesus Christ, consequently the spring of his life is other than the world sees.

(c) The Blood of Prayer
"If ye abide in Me, and My words abide in you, ask whatsoever ye will, and it shall be done unto you" (John 15:7). ". . . and whatsoever ye shall ask in My name, that will I do" (John 14:13). "Ask whatsoever ye will," i.e., not what you like, but ask that which your personal life is in. There is very little that our personal life is in when we pray, we spell out platitudes before God and call it prayer, but it is not prayer at all. What is my personal life really in when I come before God? Jesus has pledged His honour that everything I ask with the blood of my life in, I shall have. No false emotion is necessary, we have not to conjure up petitions, they well up. The "greater works" are done by prayer because prayer is the exercise of the essential character of the life of God in us. Prayer is not meant to develop us naturally, it is meant to give the life of the Son of God in us a chance to develop that the natural order may be transfigured into the spiritual.

Moral Devotion to the Sovereign Will
. . . and that life which I now live in the flesh I live in faith, the faith which is in the Son of God, Who loved me, and gave Himself up for me. (RV)

The Gospel of Jesus always forces an issue of will. Do I accept God's verdict on sin in the death of Christ, viz., death? Do I want to be so identified with the death of Jesus that I am spoiled for everything saving Himself? The great privilege of discipleship is that I can sign on under His Cross—and that means death to sin.

(a) Sovereign Preference
"For to me to live is Christ . . ." (Philippians 1:21). Love is literally the sovereign preference of my person for another person, and Jesus says that spiritually that preference must be for Himself. When Paul said, "For me to live is Christ," he did not mean that he did not live for anything else; but that the dominant note, the great consuming passion underneath everything, was his love for Jesus Christ—it explained everything he did. We are not always conscious of the sovereign preference, but a crisis will reveal it. So many make the blunder of mistaking the ecstasy of the first introduction into the Kingdom of God for the purpose of God in getting them there; the purpose of God for us is that we realise what the death of Christ meant for *us*. When we tell God that we want at all costs to be identified with the death of Jesus Christ, at that instant a supernatural identification with His death takes place, and we know with a knowledge that passes knowledge that our "old man" is crucified with Christ, and we prove it for ever after by the amazing ease with which the supernatural life of God in us enables us to do His will. That is why the bed-rock of Christianity is personal, passionate devotion to the Lord Jesus.

(b) Sacred Presence
"And lo, I am with you alway, even unto the end of the world" (Matthew 28:20). On the threshold of every new experience of life we are conscious of it, and this is true in regard to our life with God. When we are born from above (RV mg) we are conscious of God until we get into the life of God, then we are no longer conscious of Him because our life is "hid with Christ in God." "I don't feel God's presence," you say; how can you when you are in God and God is in you? By asking God to give you "feelings" you are pressing back to the entrance into life again.

The moral honour of a saint is to recognise that "Christ touches us more deeply than our pain or our guilt." It is a question of the inner life between myself and God. If I am set on my own holiness, I become a traitor to Jesus. The note of the Christian life is abandonment to Jesus Christ. That life is not a hole-and-corner business whereby I look after my own speckless whiteness, afraid to do this and that, afraid to go anywhere in case I get soiled. The whole life is summed up in a passionate absorbing devotion to Jesus and the realisation of His presence.

(c) The Sublime Passion
"For I determined not to know anything among you, save Jesus Christ, and Him crucified" (1 Corinthians 2:2). The word "passion" has come down in the world; with us it usually means something from which human nature suffers. Passion is really the transfiguration of human plod and perseverance and patience; and when we use the word "passion" in connection with our Lord, we refer to the whole climax of His personality flashing out in an extraordinary manner, exhibiting His patience and His power and the whole personality of His life. Paul's supreme passion was for Jesus Christ. When once the Holy Spirit has come in, the thought of sacrifice never occurs to a saint because sacrifice is the love passion of the Holy Ghost. Christianity is not devotion to a cause or to a set of principles, but devotion to a Person, and the great watchword of a Christian is not a passion for souls, but a passion for Christ.

YMCA HUT, JANUARY 7, 1917

YEARNING TO RECOVER GOD
Genesis 28:10–22

Jacob was a man who could dream and wait, and that is the essential nature of a true religious life. We are not all excellent supermen, walking the earth with unsullied tread; a good many of us are "Jacobs," as mean and subtle as can be; yet Jacob is the man who had the vision, and he is taken as the type of the ancient people of God. Jacob was the man to whom God appeared, and whom God altered. "Jacob I loved" (RV). Esau is the home of all the natural vices and virtues. Perfectly contented with being once born, he does not need God, he is happy and healthy and a delight to meet; Jacob was the opposite. God loves the man who needs Him.

The Disposition of Self-Assertion
And Jacob vowed a vow, saying, If God will be with me, and will keep me in this way that I go. . . then shall the LORD be my God, . . . and of all that Thou shalt give me I will surely give the tenth unto Thee. (Genesis 28:20–22)

Our true character comes out in the way we pray. This is an assertive natural prayer, there is nothing noble or fine about it. All Jacob's prayers are selfish, self-assertive and self-centred, he cares for little else outside himself. It is this kind of thing that puts Jacob where we live. A carnal will cannot rule a corrupt heart. That is the first big lesson in spiritual life. The word "carnal" is used by St. Paul of a religious man, never of an irreligious one. The carnal mind is the result of the Spirit of God being in a man but who has not quite yielded to Him—"For the flesh lusteth against the Spirit, and the Spirit against the flesh; for these are contrary the one to the other; that ye may not do the things that ye would" (Galatians 5:17 RV). It is "enmity against God." Instead of the Spirit of God bringing you peace and joy and delight, as the shallow evangelist too often puts it, His incoming has brought disturbance. In some ways you were better off before than you are now; the incoming of the Spirit of God has brought another standard and outlook, it upsets a man. "Think not that I came to send peace on the earth: I came not to send peace, but a sword" (Matthew 10:34 RV). The natural pagan, a man whose word is as good as his bond, a moral and upright man, is more delightful to meet than the Christian who has enough of the Spirit of God to spoil his sin but not enough to deliver him from it.

Self-assertion is an indication that there is a struggle going on and we have to decide who is going to rule. We rarely take the standard of the Christian life laid down in the New Testament, viz., Jesus Christ, we make excuses. If I am yearning to recover God I have to come to the place where this disposition of self-assertion is located in me. One of the reasons we lose fellowship with God is that we will explain and vindicate ourselves; we will not let God hunt through us and chase out the interests of self-will and self-assertion. We are spiritual "Jacobs," men wrestling with God in prayer; to wrestle *before* God is another matter. Jacob tried to break the neck of God's answer to his prayer, and he hirpled[21] all the rest of his life because of the struggle. "If God will give me what I want, I will do this thing." We cannot go on spiritually if we are self-assertive.

The Dreaming of Supreme Apprehension

And he dreamed, and behold a ladder set up on the earth, and the top of it reached to heaven: and behold the angels of God ascending and descending on it. (Genesis 28:12 RV)

If the vision had come to a man like Joseph or Daniel, fine unsullied men of God, we should not have been surprised, but the vision came to a mean[22] man. The dream was a pre-Incarnation vision of God, symbolising that communication between God and man is open, there is no break now. (John 1:51 RV, "And He saith unto him, Verily, verily, I say unto you, ye shall see the heaven opened, and the angels of God ascending and descending upon the Son of man.") The only Being in Whom that ever took place was Jesus Christ, and He claims that He can put us where we can have the vision fulfilled in our own lives. Never say that God intends man to have a domain of dreaming, having mighty visions of God, and living an actual life that is dead to God at the same time. Jesus Christ claims that He can put into us the thing that connects the two. It is a great thing to be able to dream; it would be awful never to be touched by anything higher than the sordid. When we feel our deadness the consolation is that this vision came to Jacob. God transformed Jacob into "Israel," indicating one who strives with God. When a man is born again of the Spirit of God he has the nature of Jesus Christ imparted to him. If we are yearning to recover God, what we need is to get to the point of deciding against the self-assertiveness of our own hearts, and letting God teach us how to pay the price of our dreams.

The Devotion of Spiritual Aspiration (Genesis 28:19–22)

And he called the name of that place Beth-el. (v. 19)

Jacob could dream and wait; the biggest test is to wait. The difference between lust and love comes just here. Lust is—I must have it at once. Love can wait. Lust makes me impulsively impatient, I want to take short cuts, and do things right off. Love can wait endlessly. If I have ever seen God and been touched by Him and the Spirit of God has entered into me, I am willing to wait for Him; I wait in the certainty that He will come. The difference between a spiritual man and a man who is not spiritual is just in this power to wait. The best illustration of waiting upon God is that of a child at his mother's breast. We draw our nourishment from no one but God. The test of the strength of spiritual aspiration is—will I wait for God like that? Do I believe Jesus Christ can turn me into His disciple if I let Him have His way? Then I will wait for Him, and "hang in" until He does it.

In this way we may become a sacrament of the love of God. "Sacrament" means the real Presence of God coming through the common elements. A great point in the sacramental teaching of the New Testament is that God brings His real Presence through the common elements of friendship, and air, and sea, and sky. Very few of us see it. It is only when we develop in spiritual devotion to Jesus Christ that we begin to detect Him in our friendships, in our ordinary eating and drinking. The ecclesiastical doctrine of the sacraments with too many of us confines it to a particular thing, and we do not scent that it is a symbol of all life that is "hid with Christ in God." Jesus Christ teaches that He can come to us through anything, and the great sign of a Christian man is that he finds God in ordinary ways and days, and partakes of the sacrament of His Presence here.

YMCA HUT, MARCH 11, 1917

SPIRITUAL INEFFICIENCY

If ye know these things, blessed are ye if ye do them. John 13:17 (RV)

That is the big test in spiritual life. Most of us are spiritually inefficient because we cannot do certain things and remain spiritual. We can be spiritual in prayer meetings, in congenial spiritual society, in what is known as Christian work, but we cannot be spiritual in drudgery. We are all capable of being spiritual sluggards; if we live a sequestered life and continually don't do what we ought to do, we can develop a spiritual life, but in actual things we are easily knocked out. We are trying to develop a life that is sanctified and holy but it is spiritually inefficient—it cannot

---

21. hirpled: walked with a limp or hobble.
22. mean: as used here, something or someone ordinary, common, low, or ignoble, rather than cruel or spiteful.

wash feet, it cannot do secular things without being tainted. Spiritual means *real,* and the only type of spiritual life is the life of our Lord Himself; there was no sacred and secular in His life, it was all real. Jesus Christ did secular things and was God Incarnate in doing them. "Then He poureth water into the bason, and began to wash the disciples' feet, and to wipe them with the towel wherewith He was girded." If Christianity means anything, it means that He can produce that kind of life in us.

We may know all this, but, says Jesus, "you are only happy if you really do it." Very few of us are blessed; we lose the blessing immediately we have to wash feet, and all that that symbolises. It takes God Incarnate to do ordinary drudgery and maintain blessedness. The great marvel of the Incarnation is just here.

Expression and Experience *(Matthew 7:21–22)*

Not every one that saith unto Me, Lord, Lord, shall enter into the kingdom of heaven; but he that doeth the will of My Father which is in heaven. (v. 21)

It is not sufficient to have an experience. If all I can do is to preach and recount the experiences God has given me, it is dangerously insufficient. Unless my life is the exact expression of the life of Jesus Christ, I am an abortion, a bastard. Experience must be worked out into expression; the expression is a strong family likeness to Jesus, and its mark is found in the secular life, not in the sequestered life. Our Lord Himself is the one Standard, and to the people of His day He seemed unutterably secular.

Jesus Christ is infinitely bigger than any of my experiences, but if in my experiences I am coming to know Him better, then the expression will come out in the life, and its sign is the fruit of the Spirit—"love, joy, peace . . ." The fruit of the Spirit is the exact expression of the disposition of Jesus. We cannot pretend to have the fruit of the Spirit if we have not; we cannot be hypocritical over it. Expression is always unconscious. "His name shall be in their foreheads"— where everyone can see it saving the man himself. We test men spiritually by the fact that they preach the gospel, that they cast out devils, that they have an experience of these things. There are many who have these experiences, and yet Jesus said He will say of such—"I never knew you: depart from Me, ye that work iniquity." The man who is "of Me," says Jesus, is the man who is an exact expression of "your Father which is in heaven" (Matthew 5:45).

Energy and Enchantment *(Acts 1:6–8)*

But ye shall receive power, when the Holy Ghost is come upon you: and ye shall be My witnesses. . . . (v. 8 RV)

It is quite possible to be enchanted with Jesus Christ and with His truth and yet never to be changed by it. The disciples are enchanted; their Lord is risen from the dead and He is telling them wonderful things about His Kingdom; they are enthralled, enamoured, then Jesus suddenly brings them down to earth by saying— "It is not for you to know times or seasons. . . . But ye shall receive power . . . , and ye shall be My witnesses" (RV). Literally, "the Holy Ghost coming upon you will make you witnesses unto Me, not witnesses of what I can do, not recorders of what you have experienced, but witnesses who are a satisfaction to Me." The baptism of the Holy Ghost is usually illustrated by the fact that "there were added unto them in that day about three thousand souls" (RV). That was a manifestation of the power of God, but it was when the apostles were persecuted and scattered, that the real energy of the Holy Ghost showed itself. Men "took knowledge of them, that they had been with Jesus." A witness is not one who is entranced by Jesus, by the revelation He gives, by what He has done; but one who has received the energy Jesus Himself had, and is become a witness that pleases Him, wherever he is placed, whatever he is doing, whether he is known or unknown. The energy in him is the very energy of the Holy Ghost, and the expression of it in life makes a witness that satisfies Jesus Christ.

There is a real peril in being enchanted but unchanged. I may be enchanted by the truth Jesus presents, but when it comes to my life being marked in all its secular details with the disposition of the Holy Spirit, then I am out of it; I prove spiritually inefficient, of no worth at all to Jesus Christ. Experiences are good, enchantment is good, but it all makes for spiritual inefficiency unless the experience is turned into the expression of a strong family likeness to Jesus, and the enchantment is transformed into the energy of the Holy Spirit.

Epistles and Experts *(2 Corinthians 3:1–6)*

Ye are our epistle, written in our hearts, known and read of all men. (v. 2)

An "epistle of Christ" means a re-incarnation of Jesus. Thank God for experiences, for the power to be enchanted, but this is the thing that tells—"Christ in you." I may be able to expound the Word of God, I may be an expert in a great many things, but unless my experience shows in expression a strong family likeness to Jesus, it is making me spiritually inefficient; I may be enchanted with the truth, but unless my enchantment is transformed into the energy which bears the mark of the disposition of Jesus, it is making for spiritual inefficiency. I may be expert in the knowledge of Scripture and expert in Christian work, but if all this is not turning me into an epistle in which men can read "Jesus," it is making for spiritual inefficiency. Is the expression in my life more and more the expression of the indwelling Holy Ghost? Is my energy the energy that comes direct from my Risen Lord? Is my life an epistle that spells only one thing—God? Is the dominating interest in my life God? Have I any other dominating interest? If I have, then none of my energy or expert knowledge is telling in the tiniest degree for Jesus.

The spiritual life can never be lived in religious meetings, it can only be lived on sordid earth, where Jesus lived, amongst the things that make human life what it is. "If I then, the Lord and the Master, have washed your feet, ye also ought to wash one another's feet" (RV). That is the only way we can justify what we say we have experienced of the grace of God. Our visions of God, our enchantment of His power, our expert knowledge of Him, will all amount to nothing unless it is made manifest in our actual life.

WITH GOD AT THE FRONT

Behold, we go up to Jerusalem. Luke 18:31

Jerusalem stands in the life of our Lord for the place where He reached the full climax of God's will. That will was the one dominating interest all through His life, and the things He met on the way, joy or sorrow, success or failure, never deterred Him from His purpose, He steadfastly went up to Jerusalem. The same thing is true of us, there is one definite aim in every Christian life, and that aim is not ours, it is God's. In our natural life our ambitions are our own. In the Christian life we have no aim of our own, and God's aim looks like missing the mark because we are too short-sighted to see what He is aiming at. The great thing to remember is that we go up to Jerusalem to fulfil God's purpose, not our own.

The Big Compelling of God
And He took unto Him the twelve . . .

One needs to dwell on this aspect of the big compelling of God. There is so much talk about our decision for Christ, our determination to be Christians, our decisions for this and for that. When we come to the New Testament we find that the other aspect, God's choosing of us, is the one that is brought out the oftenest. "Ye did not choose me, but I chose you . . ." (John 15:16 RV). We are not taken up into conscious agreement with God's purpose, we are taken up into His purpose without any consciousness on our part at all; we have no conception of what God is aiming at, and it gets more and more vague as we go on. At the beginning of our Christian life we have our own particular notions as to what God's purpose is— we are meant to go here, or there; or, God has called us to do this or that piece of work. We go and do the thing and still we find the big compelling of God remains. The majority of the work we do is so much scaffolding to further the purpose of the big compelling of God. "He took unto Him the twelve." He takes us all the time; there is more than we have got at, something we have not seen.

As we go on in the Christian life it gets simpler, for the very reason that we get less inclined to say, "Now, why did God allow this and that?" When the Holy Spirit of God enters into a man, it is the same Spirit that was in Jesus Christ. "God so loved *the world. . . .*" and the Holy Spirit implants the same kind of love in our hearts. The thing that compels us to take the line we do is never discernible to ourselves, it is symbolised spiritually by this compelling. "And He took unto Him the twelve, and said unto them, Behold, we go up to Jerusalem." How perplexing it must have sounded to them!

The main thing about Christianity is not the work we do, but the relationship we maintain. The only things God asks us to look after are the atmosphere of our life and our relationships, these are the only things that preserve us from priggishness, from impertinence and from worry, and it is these things that are assailed all through.

Immediately I complain and say, "why does God allow this?" I am not only useless but dangerous, I am taken up with compelling God. It is rarely the big compellings of God that get hold of us in our prayers, instead we tell God what He should do, we tell Him that men are being lost and that He ought to save them. This is a terrific charge against God, it means that He must be asleep. When God gets me to realise that I am being taken up into *His* enterprises, then I get rest of soul, I am free for my twenty-four hours. Whenever I have an important fuss on, I have no room for God; I am not being taken by God, I have an aim and purpose of my own. In laying down His conditions for discipleship in Luke 14:26–33, our Lord implies—"the only men I will use in My enterprises, are those of whom I have taken charge." The illustration is that of a soldier who has forsaken all to fight. I am not out for my own end and purpose, the great campaign is God's, not mine. What man gives his life for his King and Country only? Not one man. That is a very shallow watchword. Every man who has given his life has given it for something infinitely bigger, there is something entirely other and different behind. We may try to serve our own ends, but underneath is the compelling of another purpose, and it is to be hoped that the Empire to which we belong is seeing the bigger purpose.

How can I know my way when it is God Who is planning it out for me? How can I understand the Architect's plan? To have a purpose of my own will destroy the simplicity and the gaiety of a child of God, and the leisureliness which enables me to help other people. When a man is taken up into the big compellings of God, God is responsible. Amidst all the terrors of war there is one remarkable thing, and that is, apart from grousings, the spirit of freedom and gaiety in the very bondage of it. The man who joins up has to have his individuality trampled on so that his personality might be merged into the personality of his regiment, he ceases to be of any account at all as an individual, responsibility is not his any longer.

The Brave Comradeship of God
Behold, we go up to Jerusalem . . .

The bravery of God in trusting us! It is a tremendously risky thing to do, it looks as if all the odds were against Him. The majority of us don't bother much about Him, and yet He deliberately stakes all He has on us, He stands by and lets the world, the flesh and the devil do their worst, confident we will come out all right. All our Lord succeeded in doing during His life on earth was to gather together a group of fishermen—the whole Church of God and the enterprise of our Lord on earth in a fishing boat!

We say "It seems out of all proportion that God should choose me—I am of no value"; the reason He chooses us is that we are not of any value. It is folly to think that because a man has natural ability, he must make a good Christian. People with the best natural equipment may make the worst disciples because they will "boss" themselves. It is not a question of our equipment, but of our poverty; not what we bring with us, but what He puts in us; not our natural virtues, our strength of character, our knowledge, our experience; all that is of no avail in this matter; the only thing that is of avail is that we are taken up into the big compelling of God and made His comrade (1 Corinthians 1:26–28). His comradeship is made out of men who know their poverty. God can do nothing with the men who think they will be of use to Him. "If we can only add him to our cause"—that is where the competition

comes in. We are not out for our cause at all as Christians, we are out for the cause of God, which can never be our cause. It is not that God is on our side, we must see that we are on God's side, which is a different matter. We do not know what God is after, but we have to maintain our relationship to Him whatever happens. Never allow anything to injure your relationship to God, cut it out at once; if you are getting out of touch with God, take time and get it right.

The Baffling Call of God
. . . and all the things that are written by the prophets shall be accomplished unto the son of man. (RV)

God called Jesus Christ to unmitigated disaster; Jesus Christ called His disciples to come and see Him put to death; He led every one of those disciples to the place where their hearts broke. The whole thing was an absolute failure from every standpoint but God's, and yet the thing that was the biggest failure from man's standpoint was the ultimate triumph from God's, because God's purpose was not man's.

In our own lives there comes the baffling call of God. "Let us pass over unto the other side," Jesus said to His disciples; they obeyed, but as soon as they got into the boat there arose a great storm of wind and there was a squall that nearly drowned them. The call of God cannot be stated explicitly, it is implicit. The call of God is like the call of the sea, no one hears it but the man who has the nature of the sea in him. You cannot state definitely what the call of God is to; it is to be in comradeship with God for His own purposes, and the test of faith is to believe God knows what He is after. The fact that history fulfils prophecy is a small matter compared to our maintenance of a right relationship to God Who is working out His purposes. The things that happen do not happen by chance at all, they happen entirely in the decrees of God.

To be "with God at the front" means the continual maintenance of our relationship to Him. If I maintain communion with God and recognise that He is taking me up into His purposes, I will no longer try to find out what those purposes are. The war has hit every kind of cause there is, but that does not mean it has hit God. Behind it all are the big compellings of God, and in it we see the brave comradeship of God. If God has been brave enough to trust me, surely it is up to me not to let Him down, but to "hang in." You say "God has been very unwise to choose me because there is nothing in me." As long as there is something in you He cannot choose you, because you have ends of your own to serve; but if you have let Him bring you to the end of your self-sufficiency, then He can choose you to go with Him to Jerusalem, and that means the fulfilment of His purposes which He does not discuss with you at all. We go on with Him, and in the final wind-up the glory of God will be manifested before our eyes. No wonder our way is inscrutable! "There's a divinity that shapes our ends"; we may take what ways we like, but behind them come the big compellings of God. The Christian is one who trusts the wisdom of God, not his own wits. The astute mind behind the saint's life is the mind of God, not his own mind.

THE UNSPEAKABLE WONDER

In new birth God does three impossible things, impossible, that is, from the rational standpoint. The first is to make a man's past as though it had never been; the second, to make a man all over again, and the third, to make a man as certain of God as God is of Himself. New birth does not mean merely salvation from hell, but something more radical, something which tells in a man's actual life.

Of the Road Back to Yesterday

And I will restore to you the years that the locust hath eaten, the cankerworm, and the caterpillar, and the palmerworm, my great army which I sent among you. (Joel 2:25)

Through the Redemption God undertakes to deal with a man's past, and He does it in two ways: by forgiving him, and by making the past a wonderful culture for the future. The forgiveness of God is a bigger miracle than we are apt to think. It is impossible for a human being to forgive; and it is because this is not realised that we fail to understand that the forgiveness of God is a miracle of Divine grace. Do I really believe that God cannot, dare not, must not forgive me my sin without its being atoned for? If God were to forgive me my sin without its being atoned for, I should have a greater sense of justice than God. It is not that God says in effect, "I will pay no more attention to what you have done." When God forgives a man, He not only alters him but transmutes what he has already done. Forgiveness does not mean merely that I am saved from sin and made right for heaven; forgiveness means that I am forgiven into a recreated relationship to God.

Do I believe that God can deal with my "yesterday," and make it as though it had never been? I either do not believe He can, or I do not want Him to. Forgiveness, which is so easy for us to accept, cost God the agony of Calvary. When Jesus Christ says "Sin no more," He conveys the power that enables a man not to sin any more, and that power comes by right of what He did on the Cross. That is the unspeakable wonder of the forgiveness of God. To-day men do not bank on what Jesus Christ can do, or on the miracu-lous power of God; they only look at things from their side—"I should like to be a man or a woman after God's heart, but look at the mountain of my past that is in the way." God has promised to do the thing which, looked at from the basis of our own reason, cannot be done. If a man will commit his "yesterday" to God, make it irrevocable, and bank in confidence on what Jesus Christ has done, he will know what is meant by spiritual mirth—"Then was our mouth filled with laughter, and our tongue with singing." Very few of us get there because we do not believe Jesus Christ means what He says. "It is impossible! Can Jesus Christ re-make me, with my meanness and my criminality; re-make not only my actual life, but my mind and my dreams?" Jesus said, "With God all things are possible." The reason God cannot do it for us is because of our unbelief; it is not that God *won't* do it if we do not believe, but that our commitment to Him is part of the essential relationship.

Of the Renewal of Youth

But Jesus said, Suffer the little children, and forbid them not, to come unto Me: for of such is the kingdom of heaven. (Matthew 19:14 RV)

Jesus Christ uses the child-spirit as a touchstone for the character of a disciple. He did not put up a child before His disciples as an ideal, but as an expression of the simplehearted life they would live when they were born again. The life of a little child is expectant, full of wonder, and free from self-consciousness, and Jesus said, "Except ye turn, and become as little children, ye shall in no wise enter into the kingdom of heaven" (RV). We cannot enter into the kingdom of heaven head first. How many of us thought about how we should live before we were born? Why, none. But numbers of people try to think of how to live as Christians before they are born again. "Marvel not that I said unto thee, Ye must be born anew" (RV), that is, become as little children, with open-hearted, unprejudiced minds in relation to God. There is a marvellous rejuvenescence once we let God have His way. The most seriously minded Christian is the one who has just become a Christian; the mature saint is just like a young child, absolutely simple and joyful and gay. Read the Sermon on the Mount—"Take no thought," (i.e., no care), "for your life." The word "care" has within it the idea of something that buffets. The Christianity of Jesus Christ refuses to be careworn. Our Lord is indicating that we have to be carefully careless about everything saving our relationship to Him. Fuss is always a sign of fever. A great many people mistake perspiration in service for inspiration in devotion. The characteristic of a man who has come to God is that you cannot get him to take anyone seriously but God.

Spiritually beware of anything that takes the wonder out of life and makes you take a prosaic attitude; when you lose wonder, you lose life. The Spirit of God creates the intuitions of a child in a man and keeps him in touch with the elemental and real, and the miracle of Christianity is that a man can be made young in heart and mind and spirit.

Of the Repleteness of "Yes"

And in that day ye shall ask Me nothing. Verily, verily, I say unto you, If ye shall ask anything of the Father, He will give it you in My name. (John 16:23 RV)

When once we strike the "Everlasting Yes," there is something positive all through our life. So many of us never get beyond the "Everlasting No," there is a nebulous "knockoutedness" about us—"Oh yes, I will pray, but I know what the answer will be." When we come to the repleteness of "Yes," the moral miracle God works in us is that we ask only what is exactly in accordance with God's nature, and the repleteness begins, the fulness and satisfaction of the "Everlasting Yes." "And in that day ye shall ask Me nothing." That does not mean that God will give us everything we ask for, but that God can do with us now exactly what He likes. We have no business to tell God we cannot stand any more; God ought to be at liberty to do with us what He chooses, as He did with His own Son. Then whatever happens our life will be full of joy.

Anyone who has not found the road back to yesterday, who has not experienced the renewal of youth, and the repleteness of the "Everlasting Yes," has farther to go. The unspeakable wonder is that God undertakes to do all this with the human stuff of which we are made. The emphasis put on the nobility of man is largely a matter of fiction. Men and women are men and women, and it is absurd to pretend they are either better or worse than they are. Most of us begin by demanding perfect justice and nobility and generosity from other people, then we see their defects and become bitter and cynical. Jesus Christ never trusted human nature, yet He was never cynical, never in despair about any man, because He trusted absolutely in what the grace of God could do in human nature.

YMCA HUT, JUNE 10, 1917

ACQUAINTANCE WITH GRIEF

But this is your hour, and the power of darkness. Luke 22:53

There are times when God distinctly allows the wrong thing to have its hour; every one of us more or less has had this experience in his own life. We are not "acquainted with grief" in the way our Lord was; we endure it, we get through the thing, but we do not get intimate with anything in it.

Reconciling One's Self to the Fact of Sin

The climax of sin is that it crucified Jesus Christ. When we begin our life we do not reconcile ourselves to the fact of sin; we take a rational view of life and say that a man by looking after his own instincts, educating himself, controlling the ape and the tiger in him, can produce that life which will slowly evolve into the life of God. But as we go on we find there is something that we have not taken into consideration, viz., sin, and it upsets all our calculations. Sin has made the basis of things not rational, but wild. Take the life of Jesus Christ, it seems an anticlimax that the end of that life should be a tragedy, yet it did end that way. All He succeeded in doing was to gather together a handful of fishermen as disciples, one of whom betrayed Him, another denied Him, and all of whom "forsook Him, and fled."

We do not get reconciled to the fact of sin, we do not think it should be there. Take the attitude of men's minds with regard to this war; they said that it was impossible for war to be, it was out of all reason to imagine that Christian nations would tear one another to pieces, yet that is what is actually happening. To be "acquainted with grief" and to reconcile one's self to the fact of sin is the biggest factor in our life and outlook. Men say if God had ordered the world otherwise, there would be no sin; Jesus Christ would not have been killed, men would not be at war; but men are at war, and sin is, and everywhere Jesus Christ's words are proving true: "This is your hour and the power of darkness." There is a time when the hour of sin is unhindered, it is deliberate and emphatic and clear. I have to recognise that sin is a fact, not a defect; it is red-handed mutiny against God, and acquaintance with the grief of it means that unless I withstand it to the death, it will withstand me to the death. If sin rules in me, the life of God will be killed in me; if God rules in me, sin will be killed in me. There is no possible ultimate but that.

In our mental outlook we have to reconcile ourselves to the fact that sin is the only explanation as to why Jesus Christ came, the only explanation of the grief and the sorrow that there is in life. There may be a great deal that is pathetic in a man's condition, but there is also a lot that is bad and wrong. There is the downright spiteful thing, as wrong as wrong can be, without a strand of good in it, in you and in me and in other people by nature, and we have to reconcile ourselves to the fact that there *is* sin. That does not mean that we compromise with sin, it means that we face the fact that it is there. If we try to estimate ourselves or to estimate human history and ignore sin, we are not reconciling ourselves to the fact of sin; we are not becoming acquainted with the grief produced by sin, and unless we do we shall never understand why Jesus Christ came as He did, and why He said, "this is your hour and the power of darkness."

At present in the history of the world it is the hour and the power of darkness. During the war some of the biggest intellectual juggling tricks have been performed trying to make out that war is a good thing; war is the most damnably bad thing. Because God overrules a thing and brings good out of it does not mean that in itself that thing is a good thing. We have not been getting "acquainted with grief," we have tried to juggle with the cause of it. If the war has made me reconcile myself with the fact that there is sin in human beings, I shall no longer go with my head in the clouds, or hidden in the sand like an ostrich, but I shall be wishing to face facts as they are.

It is not being reconciled to the fact of sin that produces all the disasters in life. We talk about noble human nature, self-sacrifice and platonic friendship— all unmitigated nonsense. Unless we recognise the fact of sin, there is something that will laugh and spit in the face of every ideal we have. Unless we reconcile ourselves to the fact that there will come a time when the power of darkness will have its own way, and that by God's permission, we will compromise with that power when its hour comes. If we refuse to take the fact of sin into our calculation, refuse to agree that a base impulse runs through men, that there is such a thing as vice and self-seeking, when our hour of darkness strikes, instead of being acquainted with sin and the grief of it, we will compromise straight away and say there is no use battling against it. To be "acquainted with grief" and with the fact of sin means that I will endure to the crack of doom, but will never compromise with it. The man

who accepts salvation from Jesus Christ recognises the fact of sin, he does not ignore it. Thereafter he will not demand too much of human beings.

Receiving One's Self in the Fires of Sorrow

Now is my soul troubled; and what shall I say? Father, save me from this hour. But for this cause came I unto this hour. (John 12:27)

Jesus Christ is asking God to save Him *out of* the hour, not *from* it. All through, that is the inner attitude of Jesus Christ, He received Himself in the fires of sorrow; it was never "Do not let the sorrow come." That is the opposite of what we do, we pray, "Oh, Lord, don't let this or that happen to me"; consequently all kinds of damaging and blasphemous things are said about answers to prayer. You hear of one man who has gone safely through battles, and friends tell him it is in answer to prayer; does that mean that the prayers for the men who have gone under have not been answered? We have to remember that the hour of darkness will come in every life. It is not that we are saved from the hour of sorrow, but that we are delivered in it. "But ye are they which have continued with Me in My temptations" (Luke 22:28 RV). Our Lord said He prayed for Peter, not that Satan should not sift him, but that his faith should not fail. The attitude of Jesus Christ Himself to the coming sorrows and difficulties was not to ask that they might be prevented, but that He might be saved out of them.

People say there ought to be no sorrow; but the fact remains that there *is* sorrow, there is not one family just now without its sorrow, and we have to learn to receive ourselves in its fires. If we try to evade sorrow and refuse to lay our account with it, we are foolish, for sorrow is one of the biggest facts in life, and there is no use saying it ought not to be, it is. It is ridiculous to say things ought not to be when they are. A man who wants to find an explanation of why things are as they are is an intellectual lunatic. There is nothing gained by saying, "Why should there be sin and sorrow and suffering?" They *are;* it is not for me to find out why God made what I am pleased to consider a mistake; I have to find out what to do in regard to it all.

Jesus Christ's attitude is that I have to receive myself in the fires of sorrow. It is never those who go through suffering who are in doubt, but those who watch them suffer. In the majority of cases those who have gone through the sorrow have received their "self" in its fires. That is not the same as saying that they have been made better by it; sorrow does not necessarily make a man better; sorrow burns up a great amount of unnecessary shallowness, it gives me my self, or it destroys me. If a man becomes acquainted with sorrow, the gift it presents him with is his self.

We cannot receive ourselves in success, we lose our heads; we cannot receive ourselves in monotony, we grouse; the only way we can find ourselves is in the fires of sorrow. Why it should be so I do not know, but that it is so is true not only in Scripture, but in human life. The people who have gone through the fires of sorrow in this war have not become sceptical of God; it is those who have watched others going through it who have become bitter. The letters written by friends to friends during the calamitous disasters and fires of sorrow in this war in which they have discovered themselves, will be most marvellous to read after the war is over.

Recognising One's Self in the Fulness of Sanctity

And for their sakes I sanctify Myself. (John 17:19)

Jesus Christ was holy, then why did He say "I sanctify Myself"? Jesus Christ took His holy Self and deliberately gave it to God to do what He liked with. The spiritual order of Jesus Christ in my life is that I take what God has given me and give it back to Him; that is the essence of worship. The purpose of salvation and sanctification is that we may be made broken bread and poured-out wine for others as Jesus Christ was made broken bread and poured-out wine for us. When we recognise God's purpose we hand ourselves back to God to do what He likes with. He may put me in the front of things, or He may put me on the shelf if He wants to. I separate the holy thing God has created to the Holy God.

To come back to our personal relationships. Have we made allowance there for the hour and the power of darkness, or do we take the recognition of ourselves that misses it out? In our own bodily relationships, in our friendships, do we reconcile ourselves to the fact that there is sin? If not, we will be caught round the next corner of the high-road and begin to compromise with it. If we recognise that sin is there we will not make that mistake. "Yes, I see what that means and where it would lead me." Always beware of a friendship, or of a religion, or of a personal estimate of things that does not reconcile itself to the fact of sin; that is the way all the disasters in human friendships and in human loves begin, and where the compromises start. Jesus Christ never trusted human nature, but He was never cynical, He trusted absolutely what He could do for human nature. The safeguarded man or woman is the pure man or woman. No man or woman has any right to be innocent. God demands of men and women that they be pure and virtuous. Innocence is the characteristic of a child, but it is an ignorant and blameworthy thing for a man or woman not to be reconciled to the fact that there is sin. To be forewarned is to be forearmed.

Instead of the recognition of sin destroying the basis of friendship, it establishes a mutual regard founded on the fact that the basis of life is tragedy.

Again, in sorrow—you have some personal grief, it may be a question of bereavement, of unrequited love, or of any of those things that bite desperately. Have you received your self out of it yet? or are you ignoring it? It is a foolish thing to ignore the fact that you are hurt, the only thing to do is to receive yourself in the fires of the sorrow. Am I receiving myself in sorrow, or am I getting meaner and more spiteful? If I am getting sarcastic and spiteful, it is an indication that I am being sorely bitten by the fire, but am not receiving my self in its fires. The attitude of anyone watching a person going through sorrow and becoming cynical is not to condemn that one, but to realise that he is being hurt, and badly hurt. Cynicism is never the outcome of being hurt in the fires of sorrow, but of not recognising that through the sorrow comes the chance to receive one's self.

Through the fires of suffering emerges the kind of manhood and womanhood Peter mentions in his Epistle—"Wherefore let them also that suffer according to the will of God commit their souls in well-doing unto a faithful Creator" (RV). You always know the person who has been through the fires of sorrow and has received himself; you never smell the fire on him, and you are certain you can go to him when you are in trouble. It is not the man with the signs of sorrow on him who is helpful, but the one who has gone through the fires and received himself; he is delivered from the small side of himself, and has ample leisure for others. The one who has not been through the fires of sorrow has no time for you and is inclined to be contemptuous and impatient. If I have received myself in the fires of sorrow, then I am good stuff for other people in the same condition.

What standard have I for the outcome of my life? The standard of Jesus Christ is that I may be perfect as my Father in heaven is perfect. Jesus Christ is not after making a fine character or a virtuous man; those are ingredients to another end: His end is that we may be children of our Father in heaven. The best way to know whether I am recognising myself in the fullness of sanctity is to watch how I behave towards the mean[23] folks who come around. If I am learning to behave to them as God behaved to me in Jesus Christ, then I am all right; but if I have no time for them, it means that I am growing meaner and more selfish. Our Father is kind to the unthankful, to the mean. Now, He says, you be the same. The idea of sanctity is that we must be perfect in these relationships in life.

---

23. *mean:* as used here, something or someone ordinary, common, low, or ignoble, rather than cruel or spiteful.

YMCA HUT, *JULY 22, 1917*

ENTHUSIASTIC AND CAPABLE

The Rejoicing Inspiration of Life

Be filled with the Spirit. (Ephesians 5:18)

We think that sobriety and capability go together, but it is not always so. A man may be sober and incapable as well as drunk and incapable. Paul warns against the enthusiasm according to wine, but he says we have no business to be nondescript, negative people, drunk neither one way nor the other; we must be enthusiastic. *"Be being filled."* The teaching of the New Testament presents the passion of life. Stoicism has come so much into the idea of the Christian life that we imagine the stoic is the best type of Christian; but just where stoicism seems most like Christianity it is most adverse. A stoic overcomes the world by passionlessness, by eviscerating all personal interest out of life until he is a mere submissive recording machine. Christianity overcomes the world by passion, not by passionlessness. Passion is usually taken to mean something from which human nature suffers; in reality it stands for endurance and high enthusiasm, a radiant intensity of life, life at the highest pitch all the time without any reaction. That is what Paul means by "Be being filled."

If a grain of radium is kept in a box the light will remain for a while after the radium is removed, but it becomes imperceptibly fainter, and at last fades away. The spiritual life of many Christians is like that; it is borrowed and not real; for a time it looks magnificent, but after a while it wilts clean out because it has no life in itself, it has to be kept alive by meetings and conventions.

The Radiant Intensity of Life

These things have I spoken unto you, . . . that your joy may be fulfilled. (John 15:11 RV)

The emphasis of the New Testament is on joy, not on happiness. The one thing about the Apostle Paul that staggered his contemporaries was his unaccountable gaiety of spirit: he would not be serious over anything other than Jesus Christ. They might stone him and imprison him, but whatever they did made no difference to his buoyancy of spirit. The external character of the life of our Lord was that of radiant sociability; so much so, that the popular scandalmongering about Him was that He was "a gluttonous man, and a winebibber, a friend of publicans and sinners!" The fundamental reason for our Lord's sociability was other than they knew; but His whole life was characterised with a radiant fulness, it was not an exhausted type of life. "Except ye . . . become as little children . . ." If a lit-tle child is not full of the spontaneousness of life there is something wrong. The bounding life and restlessness is a sign of health, not of naughtiness. Jesus said, "I am come that they might have life, and that they might have it more abundantly." Be being filled with the life Jesus came to give. Men who are radiantly healthy, physically and spiritually, cannot be crushed. They are like the cedars of Lebanon, which have such superabounding vitality in their sap that they intoxicate to death any parasites that try to live on them.

The Recognised Interest of Life

Awake, thou that sleepest. (Ephesians 5:14)

Have I awakened into this radiance of life, the real incoming life of God? St. Augustine said he did not want to be roused out of his sleep—"I want to live in the twilight a bit longer and not be roused up to vitality just yet." Has the twilight we desired been turned into trembling? We all like the twilight in spiritual and moral matters, not the intensity of black and white, not the clear lines of demarcation—saved and unsaved. We prefer things to be hazy, winsome and indefinite, without the clear light. When the light does come difficulty is experienced, for when a man awakens he sees a great many things. We may feel complacent with a background of drab, but to be brought up against the white background of Jesus Christ is an immensely uncomfortable thing.

"Arise from the dead, and Christ shall shine upon thee" (RV). If you arise from the dead, Christ will give you light. The one thing that Jesus Christ does for a man is to make him radiant, not artificially radiant. There is nothing more irritating than the counsel, "keep smiling"; that is a counterfeit, a radiance that soon fizzles out. The joy that Jesus gives is the result of our disposition being at one with His own disposition. The Spirit of God will fill us to overflowing if we will be careful to keep in the light. We have no business to be weak in God's strength.

"Look therefore carefully how ye walk" (RV). We have to walk in the light "as He is in the light," keep continually coming to the light, don't keep anything covered up. If we are filled with the life of Jesus we must walk circumspectly, keep the interest in life going, have nothing folded up. The evidence that we are being filled with the life of God is that we are not deceived about the things that spring from ourselves and the things that spring from Jesus Christ. "If you have sinned," says John, "confess it, keep in the light all through."

THE THROES OF THE ULTIMATE
1 Peter 1:3–9

Wherein ye greatly rejoice, though now for a little while, if need be, ye have been put to grief in manifold temptations. 1 Peter 1:6 (RV)

By "the ultimate" is meant here the real aim and end that God has in view. Once we get caught up into that life, Peter says, we will find there are throes in it, what we understand in physical life by "growing pains." When we think on unusual lines we get a headache because our brains are rusty. This accounts for the inevitable throes of getting at an ultimate end in our thinking. The same thing is true spiritually, no man can be virtuous without throes—without pangs and pains. The difference between Esau and Jacob lies here, that Esau was not concerned about virtue. The man who gets into the throes of a moral ultimate and determines to be something in his moral life, knows all about the pangs of producing a virtuous life. No man is born virtuous, we are born innocent; virtue is the outcome of conflict. Any man who lives a merely natural life is an animal, and he will know it himself better than anyone before long.

"Though for a little while, if need be, ye have been put to grief . . ." (RV). There is only one Judge of the "need be," and that is our Father in heaven. We cannot judge what seasons are best for the natural world, nor yet for our soul's life, but whatever the seasons may be, He is bringing it all out towards one end. Peter would have us remember that there are times when we are in heaviness, when it looks as if God did not answer our prayer, as if faith had no lift about it, as if everything we ever believed in was nothing at all. Then is the time to "hang in," says Peter, remember what you saw when you had the light. No matter how manifold the temptations may be, God is producing a good thing.

The Undefiled Inheritance
Unto an inheritance incorruptible, and undefiled, and that fadeth not away, reserved in heaven for you. (1 Peter 1:4 RV)

". . . reserved in heaven for you." This is a great conception of the New Testament, but it is a conception lost in modern evangelism. We are so much taken up with what God wants us to be here that we have forgotten heaven. There are one or two conceptions about heaven that have to be traced back to their home to find out whether they have their root in our faith or whether they are foreign flowers. As, for instance, during this war men are producing flowers

of scepticism which are not home-grown at all, but which are covers to hide the real throes of a man's mind, so there are conceptions of heaven which have not their root in Christianity. One of these is that heaven is a state and not a place; that is only a partial truth, for there cannot be a state without a place. The great New Testament conception of heaven is "hereafter" without the sin, "new heavens and a new earth, wherein dwelleth righteousness"—a conception beyond us. Peter is reminding every Christian that there is an undefiled inheritance awaiting us which has never yet been realised, and that it has in it all we have ever hoped or dreamed or imagined, and a good deal more. It is always *Better to come* in the Christian life until the *Best of all* comes.

There is another flower abroad to-day which has not its root in the New Testament—the idea that when a man dies for his King and Country he has thereby redeemed his soul; that is a flower which does not belong to the Christian faith. People say if a man dies in doing his duty, surely that is acceptable to God. Of course it is, but a man cannot redeem his own soul by so doing, that is God's business, and the revelation given through Jesus Christ is that the human race has been redeemed. "It is finished," and in the Cross of Jesus Christ all men are condemned to salvation. That is very different from what is called Universalism. The redemption is of universal application, but human responsibility is not done away with. Universalism looks like a Christian flower, but it has not its roots in the Christian faith. Jesus Christ is most emphatic on the fact that there are possibilities of eternal damnation for the man who positively neglects or positively rejects His redemption. In John 3:19, our Lord is talking about individual lives on the experimental line. "This is the judgement," i.e., the critical moment—not the sovereign purpose of God, nor the decree of God, but the critical moment in individual experience—"that the light," Jesus Christ, "is come into the world, and men," individual men, "loved the darkness," their own point of view, their own prejudices and preconceived determinations, "rather than the light." That, says Jesus, is the judgement.

This, then, is the basis of our faith. Peter says, despair of no man, and remember that there is an undefiled inheritance ahead. That is the ultimate, and we have to live in the light of it. It is a wonderful thing to see a man or woman live in the light of something you cannot see. You can always tell a man or woman who has a standard of life other than you can see; there is something that keeps them sweet when from every other consideration they ought to be sour. That is a mark of the Christian, he does not go under in the difficulties; the thing that keeps him is that he has an anchor that holds within the veil. The mainspring of a man's action is further in than you can see in his actual life and it accounts for his outlook. When a man has his anchorage in Jesus Christ and knows what is awaiting the human race—that there is a time coming when all things shall be explained fully, it keeps his spirit filled with uncrushable gaiety and joy.

The Unrelieved Rigours

That the proof of your faith, being more precious than gold that perisheth though it is proved by fire, might be found unto praise and glory and honour at the revelation of Jesus Christ. (1 Peter 1:7 RV)

Peter says that there are times when you won't see the vision, when you won't feel the touch of Jesus Christ, when there is no kind of inspiration at work in you, when it is all heaviness through unrelieved rigours and temptation. Jesus Christ was alone in the desert with wild beasts—the last rugged touch of human isolation. "Then the devil leaveth Him; and behold, angels came and ministered unto Him" (RV). That is the proof that you have come through the trial of your faith all right. You have no trophy, it has been a desperate time, you seem to have lost your hold on everything you can state, there has been no inspiration and no joy and you have nothing to bring away, all you can do is to dumbly "hang in" to your undefiled inheritance. The sign that you have gone through the trial rightly is that you retain your affinity with the highest. Do you feel yourself just as fond of the best as you were? Just as full of affinity with the most spiritual people when you meet them? As full of affection for those who live the highest and talk the purest? If so, you have gone grandly through.

Faith must be tried or it is not faith, faith is not mathematics nor reason. Scriptural faith is not to be illustrated by the faith we exhibit in our commonsense life, it is trust in the character of One we have never seen, in the integrity of Jesus Christ, and it must be tried. "Lay up for yourselves treasures in heaven . . . for where thy treasure is, there will thy heart be also" (RV). You have your time of unrelieved rigour when commonsense facts and your faith in Jesus Christ do not agree, and you are stepping out in the dark on His word; when you have gone through the test and are standing firm, that gives you, as it were, so many pounds in the bank, and when the next trial comes, God hands out to you a sufficient amount of your own wealth to carry you through. "Lay up for yourselves treasures in heaven," and it is the trial of faith that does

it. "Oh yes, I believe God can do everything," but, *have I proved that He can do one thing?* If so, the next time the trial comes, I can not only hold myself, but someone else. It is a great thing to meet a man who believes in God, one who has not only retained his faith in God, but is continually getting a bigger faith.

There is no evidence of God outside the moral domain. The New Testament increases and educates the faith of those who know God. I do not need anyone to tell me about Jesus Christ. I know Him on the inside. It is a wonderful thing to be able to give a hand to a man who is in the turmoil, and I cannot do it by giving him platitudes. It is easy to say "Oh yes, just trust in God." If the man sees you are not doing so yourself, it won't help him; but if he sees you are trusting God, there will come through you a tremendous assistance. When I see a person who has been through trial and who knows God, going under in some trial of his faith, I feel inclined to hang my head in shame. To see a Christian going under either in moods or in circumstances is to me a slander against Jesus Christ. It is an awful thing to see a man or woman who knows Jesus Christ begin to get sulky and dumpy under difficulties (there is a difference between this and going through the first trial of faith); begin to sink and forget the inheritance undefiled; forget that the honour of Jesus Christ is at stake in His disciple. It is dishonourable, it is caddish. Buck up and face the music, get rerelated to things. It is a great thing to see physical pluck, and greater still to see moral pluck, but the greatest to see of all is spiritual pluck, to see a man who will stand true to the integrity of Jesus Christ no matter what he is going through.

If you know a man who has a good spiritual banking account, borrow from him for all you are worth, because he will give you all you want and never look to be paid back. Here is the reason a saint goes through the things he does go through—God wants to know if He can make him good "bread" to feed other people with. The man who has gone through the crucible is going to be a tremendous support to hundreds of others.

The Unrecorded Revelation

Whom not having seen ye love; on Whom, though now ye see Him not, yet believing, ye rejoice greatly with joy unspeakable and full of glory: receiving the end of your faith, even the salvation of your souls. (1 Peter 1:8–9 RV)

"Soul" means a great deal more than we mean when we talk about a "saved soul." "Receiving the end of your faith," the issue of your faith—the whole of your reasoning and conception of things will be completely saved, saved into the perfect light and liberty of God. If you stick stedfastly, not to your faith, but to the One Who gives you the faith, there is a time coming when your whole way of being impressed, and your reasoning, will be made clear to your own satisfaction. In the meantime you have to be quiet about a good many things. You cannot stand up for Christ other than spiritually. A man slanders Jesus Christ and says "Why does not God end the war?" and you cannot say a thing; if you do, it is nonsense. At present you have one of the hardest humiliations to stand because you have a faith that apparently in the meantime is flatly contradicted, a faith marked out by your own inconsistencies and by other people's. Peter counsels, "Now you are in manifold temptations, but 'hang in,' remember the inheritance undefiled, look to Jesus, and you will receive the end of your faith." There is a time coming when everything that at present is a problem will be perfectly solved; in the meantime are you prepared to let men gibe at you, to let them have their immediate triumph over the matter, while you "hang in" to your grander horizon, to the very essence of Christianity, which is personal relationship to Jesus Christ? Look unto Him, which means spiritual discernment, remembering it is a crime to be weak in God's strength, a crime to go under in anything when Jesus Christ is what He is. If you have a trial of faith, endure it till you get through. If you have been through trials

of faith in the past God is bringing across your path immature souls, and you have no business to despise them but rather to help them through—be to them something that has to be "sucked." He perceived that virtue had gone out of Him, and you will feel the same thing: there are people who spiritually and morally have to suck the vitals out of you, and if you don't keep up the supply from the life of Jesus Christ, you will be like an exhausted volcano before long. You must keep that up and let them nourish themselves from you until they are able to stand on their own feet and take direct life from Him.

The throes of the ultimate! Carlyle said of Tennyson: "Alfred is always carrying about chaos with him and turning it into cosmos." It is a good thing to be chaotic; it means there is a terrific possibility of development. The same thing spiritually, there is chaos in our lives that God is turning into the right cosmos; in the meantime, *look unto Jesus* and take the next step as it comes. If it is unrelieved rigours, get through the thing and you will be a tremendous assistance to men who are going through the same thing. It is not for you to "lambaste" them for not being where you are, but for you to see to it that you are good nourishing stuff for them in God's hands.

YMCA hut, August 12, 1917

VOICE AND VISION

Let the redeemed of the LORD say so. Psalm 107:2

We are apt to use words without having any idea of their meaning. In a crisis a word is really an "open sesame," and in certain spiritual, moral and emotional crises if we do not say the word, emancipation will never be ours. Think of it in a simple way. When a child knows it has done something wrong and you want him to say he is sorry, the natural inclination of the child is stubbornly to refuse to say he *is* sorry; but until he does say so, there is no emancipation for him on to a higher level in his own life. This is the key to the way we are built all through; it is true not only in a child's life but in the moral domain, and emphatically true in the spiritual domain. Many of us are on the verge of a spiritual vision the realisation of which never becomes ours because we will not open our mouths to "say so." We have to "say so" before we "feel so." The writer to the Hebrews speaks of the "sacrifice of praise." If we only praise when we feel like praising, it is simply an undisciplined expression, but if we deliberately go over the neck of our disinclination and offer the sacrifice of praise, we are emancipated by our

very statements. We can slay a grousing mood by stating what we believe, and we are emancipated into a higher level of life immediately; but the "say so" must come before the emancipation is ours.

The Reserve That Ruins Spirituality
With the heart man believeth; . . . with the mouth confession is made unto salvation. (Romans 10:10)

That is, unto the realisation of the salvation for which we believe. In the Bible confession and testimony are put in a prominent place, and the test of a man's moral calibre is the "say so." I may try and make myself believe a hundred and one things, but they will never be mine until I "say so." "With the heart man believeth. . . ." "Heart" means all that is meant by "me." If I say with my self what I believe and confess it with my mouth, I am lifted into the domain of that thing. This is always the price of spiritual emancipation. If a child is to be taken out of his sulky mood he has to go across the disinclination of his reserve and *say* something; and this is true of all moral and spiritual life. If I will not confess with my mouth what I believe in my heart, that particular phase of believing will never be mine actually. Assurance of faith is never gained by reserve but only by abandonment. In the matter of human love it is a great emancipation to have it expressed; there may be intuitions of the love, but the realisation of it is not ours until it is expressed. Morally and spiritually we live, as it were, in sections, and the door from one section to another is by means of words, and until we say the right word the door will not open. The right word is always based on the killing of the disinclination which belongs to a lower section.

Reserve is an unmitigated curse, not the reserve which indicates that there is power behind, but the reserve that refuses to go over the neck of its own pride. "If I confess this thing I shall have to forgo my reserve and take a further step on." That is the reserve that ruins spirituality. Emancipation comes through the "say so"; immediately we confess, the door opens, and life rushes on to a higher platform.

The Realisation That Really Speaks
When ye pray, say, Our Father. (Luke 11:2)

"But I don't feel that God is my Father": Jesus said, "Say it"—"*say*, Our Father," and you will suddenly discover that He is. The safeguard against moral imprisonment is prayer. Don't pray according to your moods, but resolutely launch out on God, say "Our Father," and before you know where you are, you are in a larger room. The door into a moral or spiritual emancipation which you wish to enter is a word. Immediately you are prepared to abandon your reserve and say the word, the door opens and in rushes the Godward side of things and you are lifted on to another platform immediately. "Speech maketh a full man." If you want to encourage your own life in spiritual things, talk about them. Beware of the reserve that keeps to itself, that wants to develop spirituality alone; spirituality must be developed in the open. Shyness is often unmitigated conceit, an unconscious over-estimate of your own worth; you are not prepared to speak until you have a proper audience. If you talk in the wrong mood, you will remain in the wrong mood and put the "bastard self" on the throne; but if you talk in the mood which comes from revelation, emancipation will be yours. A preacher has no business to stir up emotions without giving his hearers some issue of will on which to transact.

The Revelation That Rightly Sees
Go ye, and stand and speak in the temple to the people all the words of this Life. (Acts 5:20 RV)

A man may betray Jesus Christ by speaking too many words, and he may betray Him through keeping his mouth shut. The revelation that perceives is that which recklessly states what it believes. When you stand up before your fellow-men and confess something about Jesus Christ, you feel you have no one to support you in the matter, but as you testify you begin to find the reality of your spiritual possessions, and there rushes into you the realisation of a totally new life. "Be still, and know that I am God." When a man is able to state that he believes in God, it reacts on all his relationships. The thing that preserves a man from panic is his relationship to God; if he is only related to himself and to his own courage, there may come a moment when his courage gives out.

Some of us are living on too low a level, and remember, the door is shut on our side, not on God's. Immediately we will "say so," the door opens and the salvation for which we believe is ours in actual possession. Things only become clear as we say them. Too often we are like the child who will not do anything but murmur. We grouse and refuse to say the emancipating word which is within our reach all the time. Immediately we say the emancipating word, we undo the door and there rushes into us a higher and better life, and the revelation becomes real. "I must get out of this cabined, confined place," then say the right word. If you have not received, ask; if you have not found, seek; if the door is shut, knock. When you are up against barriers, the way out is to "say so," then you will be emancipated, and your "say so" will not only be an emancipation for yourself, but someone else will enter into the light. We have to get rid of the reserve which keeps us starved and away from our fellow-men, that keeps us from getting what we should have. We have no business to live a drivelling kind of life with barely sufficient for our own needs, we ought to enter into the store-house and come out with riches for ourselves and ample to hand on to others. There are some people we are always the better for meeting, they do not talk piously, but somehow they give us a feeling of emancipation, they have a larger horizon. The reason is that they have opened the door for themselves by their "say so," and now the Word of God becomes spirit and life through them to others.

THE PLANE OF SPIRITUAL VIGOUR

Forasmuch then as Christ suffered in the flesh, arm ye yourselves also with the same mind; for he that hath suffered in the flesh hath ceased from sin. 1 Peter 4:1 (RV)

Peter is dealing with the dangers that beset the spiritual man, dangers of which the average man is unaware. As long as a man sets out to be merely healthy-minded, the further he keeps away from Jesus Christ the better. The spiritual man must deliberately enter into the zone where he suffers in the flesh. If I am to be identified with Jesus Christ in this life, I must lay my account with the fact that I am going to be troubled in the flesh in a way I would not be if I were not so related to Him, because the last stake of the enemy is in the flesh.

The Discipline in the Flesh
Forasmuch then as Christ suffered in the flesh . . .

Suffering
How did Jesus Christ suffer in the flesh? Not because He was diseased or because He was more delicately strung than we are, but because He was differently related to God, He suffered "according to the will of God," that is, He let Almighty God do His whole will in and through Him without asking His permission; He did not live His life in the flesh from the point of view of realising Himself. Any number of us suffer in the flesh who have not ceased from sin, but Peter's meaning is, "he that hath suffered in the flesh 'as Christ suffered in the flesh' hath ceased from sin."

God will not shield us from the requirements of saints. When once we are related to life as Jesus was on the basis of Redemption, He expects us to be to other people what He has been to us, and that will mean suffering in the flesh because it entails losing the aim of self-realisation and basing everything on Christ realisation, and immediately we do that, other people will wipe their feet on us. No man is designed by nature to take the wiping of other people's feet, he can only do it when he can say with the Apostle Paul, "I know how to be abased." Beware of the line of thinking which has sympathy with your sufferings but has no sympathy with Jesus Christ. Arm yourself with the mind of Christ, and the very suffering you go through will benefit others.

The Discipline in the Mind
arm ye yourselves also with the same mind . . .

Strenuousness
Some people have on an armour of innocence, like Ten-nyson's knight whose "strength was as the strength of ten because his heart was pure"; others have on an armour of love. Paul says, "Put on the whole armour of God." Don't rely on anything less than that, clothe yourself with your relationship to God, maintain it. If you do not arm yourself with the armour of God, you are open to interferences in your hidden personal life from supernatural powers which you cannot control; but buckle on the armour, bring yourself into real living contact with God, and you are garrisoned not only in the conscious realm but in the depths of your personality beneath the conscious realm. "Praying always," says Paul. Every time we pray our horizon is altered, our attitude to things is altered, not sometimes but every time, and the amazing thing is that we don't pray more. Prayer is a complete emancipation, it keeps us on the spiritual plane. When you are at one with another mind there is a telepathic influence all the time, and when born from above (RV mg) the communion is between God and yourself; "Keep that going," says Peter. "Arm ye yourselves also with the same mind."

Are you neglecting prayer? No matter what else is neglected, switch back at once, if you don't you will be a dangerous influence to the people round about you. Watch the snare of self-pity—"Why should I go through this?" Be careful, you are a danger spot. I feel as if Jesus Christ were staggered with surprise at some of us, amazed at the things we say to Him, astonished at our attitude to Him, at the sulks we get into, because we have forgotten to arm ourselves with the same mind.

The Discipline in the Experience
. . . for he that hath suffered in the flesh hath ceased from sin.

Sanctification
The characteristic of the life now that you have ceased from sin is that you no longer do the things you used to do. "For the time past may suffice to have wrought the desire of the Gentiles, . . . wherein they think it strange that ye run not with them into the same excess of riot, speaking evil of you" (1 Peter 4:3–4 RV). "Let all that finish for you," says Peter, "stand now on a new basis, on the plane of the spiritual. See that you remain in identification with the sufferings of Jesus, and fill up that which is lacking of the afflictions of Christ." That is the plane of spiritual vigour.

How am I going to maintain my relationship to God on the spiritual plane, and keep the broad horizon that will help other men? "Believe on Me," says Jesus, "and out of you will flow rivers of living water." The radiating influence from one person rightly related to God is incalculable; he may not say much, but you feel different, the pressure has gone, you are in contact with one who is on a different plane.

Arm yourselves with the mind of Christ, main-

tain your life on the plane of spiritual vigour, and you will find that other people will suck nourishment and sustenance for their life out of you. Virtue will go out of you, and if you do not remain true to Jesus, you will collapse; there must be the continual supply, the continual drawing on the unsearchable riches of Jesus.

YMCA HUT, SEPTEMBER 9, 1917

THE SENSE OF AWE

The Dread Face of His Detachment
And they that followed were afraid. (Mark 10:32 RV)

The disciples had been living in closest intimacy with Jesus, but now they begin to see that there is a dread side to His life. He has an attitude to things which is not easy to understand, and it fills them with fear. There are different kinds of fear. We know what fear is in the physical domain, and in the moral domain; but in the spiritual domain a man's fear is not for his own skin at all, but, as it were, fear that his Hero won't get through. This was the disciples' fear; it seemed as if all they had expected Jesus to do would end in nothing. Not one of them knew what Jesus was after, but still they followed, and they were afraid. Many of us are supernaturally solemn about our religion because it is not real. Immediately our religion becomes real, it is possible to have humour in connection with it. There are occasions, nevertheless, when there is not only no humour, but when humour is unfit; there is a dread sense of detachment from our ordinary attitude to things which fills us with awe. We are all apt to interpret Jesus from our own standpoint, we get too familiar with Him, and a moral surgery of events is necessary before we can understand His standpoint. We get a glimpse of what Jesus is after, and His attitude makes it look as if He were absolutely insensitive to our aims; or else He has a point of view of which we know nothing and the sense of detachment continually comes. Jesus is treating us as He treated Martha and Mary—because He loved them He stayed two days where He was, and did not come in answer to their prayer. Jesus Christ can afford to be misunderstood; we cannot. Our weakness lies in always wanting to vindicate ourselves. Jesus never takes the trouble to alter mistakes; He knows they will alter themselves.

All through our Lord's life this note continually recurs—"Behold, we go up to Jerusalem"; yet He was not in a panic to get there. He set His face like a flint to go to Jerusalem, the place where He was to reach the climax of His Father's will. There was no misun-

derstanding as to what it would mean when He got there, viz., death, with a peculiar significance. Whenever Jesus talked to His disciples about His Cross, they misunderstood Him; until at last they began to see a deeper depth than they had ever thought, a relation to things in His life about which they knew nothing. They did not know what Jesus was heading for, and as they followed they were afraid.

It is a most humiliating thing to find that we have estimated the man with whom we are familiar on too low a level; to discover that after all he has a bigger relation to things than we have ever had. If we are going to estimate another man's point of view (which is as valuable as our own), we must take the trouble to find out the kind of man he is behind his words. When we take Jesus Christ's words about His Cross, the least thing we can do is to endeavour to get at His mind behind His words. Jesus says things from a different point of view from ours, and unless we receive His Spirit, we do not even begin to see what He is driving at. "He . . . saith unto them, Receive ye the Holy Ghost" (John 20:22). ". . . the Comforter, even the Holy Spirit, . . . He shall teach you all things . . ." (John 14:26 RV).

The Disciplining Force of His Delays
I have yet many things to say unto you, but ye cannot bear them now. (John 16:12)

"Why cannot I follow Thee even now?" asked Peter. "Thou canst not follow Me now," said Jesus, "but thou shalt follow afterwards." The delays of Jesus discipline us while they continually tantalise us. "If thou art the Christ, tell us plainly" (RV). Jesus answered them, "I told you, and ye believe not" (RV); they were not in the place where they could understand. Understanding comes only by obedience, never by intellect. Our Lord does not hide things from us, but they are unbearable until we get into a fit condition of life on the inside. "Why does not God tell us these things?" we say. He is telling us all the time, but we are unable to perceive His meaning. The force of the disciplining delays lies in the fact that God is engineering our circumstances in order to bring us into a fit moral state to understand. "Before I was afflicted I went astray: but now have I kept Thy word." The delay in interpretation depends on our willingness to obey. Obedience is always the secret of understanding. For instance, if there is the tiniest grudge in our spirit against another, from that second, spiritual penetration into the knowledge of God will cease. "If therefore thou art offering thy gift at the altar, and there rememberest that thy brother hath aught against thee, leave there thy gift," says Jesus, "and go thy way; first be reconciled to thy brother, and then come and offer thy gift" (RV).

It is a great emancipation in a man's life when he learns that spiritual and moral truths can only be gained by obedience, never by intellectual curiosity. All God's revelations are sealed, and they will never be opened by philosophy, or by thinking; whereas the tiniest fragment of obedience will bring a man right through into the secret of God's attitude to things. Mere intellectual training turns a man into a psychological ostrich; his head is all right, but in actual life he is left floundering. How are we going to make plain the things which are obscure to us just now? Intellectual curiosity will not take us one inch inside moral problems, but immediately we obey, in the tiniest matter, instantly we see.

The Dawning Fear of His Deity

And when I saw Him, I fell at His feet as one dead. (Revelation 1:17 RV)

These words were uttered by the disciple who knew Jesus most intimately, the one who laid his head on Jesus' bosom, the disciple "whom Jesus loved"—when he saw Him in His unveiled Deity, he fell at His feet as one dead, paralysed with amazement; then there came the voice he had learned to know in the days of His flesh, saying, "Fear not, I am the first and the last."

Has our discipleship to Jesus a sense of awe about it, or do we patronise Him? At the beginning we were sure that we knew all about Jesus, but now we are not quite so sure; He is taken up with a point of view we know nothing about, and we can no longer be familiar with Him. Instead of walking to triumph as the disciples expected Jesus to do, He goes to disaster; instead of bringing peace, He brings a sword. In every way Jesus enters into "somewhere" that fills us with awe. A time comes when He is no longer Counsellor and Comrade. With one stride He goes deliberately in front and says, "Follow Me," and the things that lie ahead are wildly terrible to us. There is nothing familiar now about Jesus, and there is a dread sense of detachment.

It may be that in our inner life Jesus is teaching us by the disciplining force of His delays. "I expected God to answer my prayer, but He has not." He is bringing us to the place where by obedience we shall see what it is He is after. It may be that, like John, we know Jesus intimately, then suddenly He appears with no familiar characteristic at all, and the only thing we can do is to fall at His feet as one dead. There are times when God cannot reveal Himself in any other way than in His majesty. And out of the midst of the terror there comes the voice we know, saying to us personally—"Fear not." When once His touch comes like that, nothing can at all cast us into fear again.

YMCA HUT, SEPTEMBER 23, 1917

SPIRITUAL MALINGERING

O fools, and slow of heart to believe. . . . Luke 24:25

To believe is literally to commit. Belief is a moral act, and Jesus makes an enormous demand of a man when He asks him to believe in Him. To be "a believer in Jesus" means to bank our confidence in Him, to stake our soul upon His honour—"I know whom I have believed. . . ." We pray, "Lord, increase our faith," and we try to pump up faith, but it does not come. What is wrong? The moral surrender to Jesus has not taken place. Will I surrender to Jesus from the real centre of my life, and deliberately and wilfully stake my confidence in what He says? Many of us use religious jargon, we talk about believing in God, but our actual life proves that we do not really believe one tithe of what we profess.

If you can solve your problems without Jesus, then solve them, but don't blink any of the facts. "Let not your heart be troubled," says Jesus. Does Jesus really mean that He wants us to be untroubled in heart? "Believe also in Me," i.e., make room for Me, especially in the matters where you cannot go. As we bring the child mind to what Jesus says about things, we will begin to manifest the miracle of an undisturbed heart. In the Cross our Lord deals with everything that keeps a man's heart disturbed.

Unrealised Forgiveness

. . . to preach . . . the unsearchable riches of Christ. (Ephesians 3:8 RV)

"The unsearchable riches of Christ"—yet we often live

as if our Heavenly Father had cut us off with a shilling! We think it a sign of real modesty to say at the end of a day—"Oh well, I have just got through, but it has been a severe tussle." We carry our religion as if it were a headache, there is neither joy nor power nor inspiration in it, none of the grandeur of the unsearchable riches of Christ about it, none of the passion of hilarious confidence in God. And the word of our Lord comes home to us that we are half-imbecile children with regard to the things of God—"When will you believe what I say?" Instead of our life being a recommendation of Christianity it is apt to make others say—"Is that what you call Christianity? Why, I have a good deal more moral life than there is in that kind of anaemic whine!" There is nothing in it of the robust strength of confidence in God which will go through anything, and stake its all on the honour of Jesus Christ. Christianity is the vital realisation of the unsearchable riches of Christ.

"In Whom we have our redemption through His blood, the forgiveness of our trespasses . . ." (Ephesians 1:7 RV). Brood on that statement. Divine forgiveness is part of the unsearchable riches that is ours through the Redemption, and it is because we do not realise the miracle of God's forgiveness that spiritual malingering results, that is, we remain feeble and weak in Christian faith in order to evade the enormous demands that our faith makes on us. We talk glibly about forgiving when we have never been injured; when we are injured we know that it is not possible, apart from God's grace, for one human being to forgive another. "I will say no more about it, but I do not intend to forget what you have done." The forgiveness of God is altogether different. When God forgives, He never casts up at us the mean, miserable things we have done. "I have blotted out, as a thick cloud, thy transgressions, and, as a cloud, thy sins." A cloud cannot be seen when it is gone.

"But that man will take advantage of God's forgiveness." Will I take advantage of God's forgiveness? No one on earth is more mean than I am, no one more capable of doing wrong, and yet we are always more afraid of the other fellow than of ourselves. The forgiveness of God means that we are forgiven into a new relationship, viz., into identification with God in Christ, so that the forgiven man is the holy man. The only explanation of the forgiveness of God and of the unfathomable depth of His forgetting is the blood of Jesus. We trample the blood of the Son of God under foot if we think we are forgiven in any other way. Forgiveness is the Divine miracle of grace.

Unexplored Prayer Zone

Having . . . boldness to enter into the heart by the blood of Jesus. (Hebrews 10:19)

We are apt to think of prayer as an aesthetic religious exercise. The revelation made here is that we have free-

dom to go straight to the heart of God, as simply as a child going to his mother, by "the new and living way which He hath consecrated for us." Our approach is due entirely to the vicarious identification of our Lord with sin. It is not our earnestness that brings us into touch with God, not our stated times of prayer, but the vitalising death of our Lord Jesus Christ.

Unselfish Sanctification

Wherefore Jesus also, that He might sanctify the people through His own blood . . . (Hebrews 13:12)

"For their sakes I sanctify Myself." Jesus separated His holy Self to the will of His Father. The one characteristic of our Lord's human life was His submission to His Father. "The Son can do nothing of Himself." Our Lord did not come to do His own will. And we are not made holy for ourselves. Sanctification means being identified with Jesus until all the springs of our being are in Him. ". . . one, even as We are one." We do not experience sanctification for any purpose other than God's purpose.

Forgiveness of sins is the gift of God; entrance into the holiest is the gift of God; sanctification is the gift of God. A man cannot save his own soul, or forgive his sins, or get hold of God in prayer, or sanctify himself; but Jesus reveals that God has done all this in Redemption—are we going to bank on what He has done? As we do, new forces will come into our experimental life drawn entirely from the unsearchable riches, ours through the Redemption. Christian faith means putting our confidence in the efficacy of Christ's work.

When God says we have "our redemption *through His blood*" (RV), are we going to commit ourselves to Him and bank on His word? When God says; we have "boldness to enter into the holiest *by the blood of Jesus,*" are we going to draw near in faith? There is boundless entrance into the holiest by the way He has consecrated for us. When God says "Jesus also, that He might sanctify the people *through His own blood* . . ." (RV), are we going to believe Him? By sanctification we understand experimentally what Paul says in 1 Corinthians 1:30—"But of Him are ye in Christ Jesus, Who was made unto us . . . sanctification" (RV). Sanctification is an impartation, a gift, not an imitation. Sanctification means "Christ formed in you." Jesus gives us the life inherent in Himself.

"When the Son of man cometh, shall He find faith on the earth?"—the faith that banks on Him in spite of all the confusion? Or will we have to say—"No, Lord, I never trusted You for one moment, I used religious jargon, I put on a religious plaster when I was sore, but I had no confidence whatever in anything You said." We have made Christianity to mean the saving of our skins. Christianity means staking ourselves on the honour of Jesus; His honour means that He will see us through time, death and eternity. Do we credit Jesus Christ with knowing what He is talking about, or are we half imbecile with regard to these truths?

When we are standing face to face with Jesus, and He says "Believest thou this?" our faith is as natural as breathing, and we say—"Yes, Lord," and are staggered and amazed that we were so stupid as not to trust Him before.

YMCA HUT, SEPTEMBER 30, 1917

THE DEEP EMBARRASSMENTS OF GOD
Hosea 11

When a man who has known God turns away from Him, it is God Who brings out his embarrassments and engineers his enemies. There are barriers placed by God, entanglements of embarrassment, by means of which God says to the personal spirit of the man, "Not that way, My son; if you go that way, you will break your neck and be ruined." It is impossible for a man to go wrong easily; he may drift a tremendously long way easily, he may come to have different standards easily; but if a man has known better than he does now, he has not arrived there easily. "The way of transgressors is hard."

The Mothering Affection of God *(Hosea 11:1)*
When Israel was a child, then I loved him . . .

The mothering affection of God is revealed all through the Old Testament. A man won't talk of it because it is too precious. "I have nourished and brought up children" (Isaiah 1:2). "As one whom his mother comforteth, so will I comfort you" (Isaiah 66:13). "I remember for thee the kindness of thy youth" (Jeremiah 2:2 RV). When a man is born again of the Spirit of God, he does not walk by faith, but by sight, everything thrills, it is a delight to be spiritual.

We have all felt the mothering affection of God; are we departing from what we saw then? "My people are bent to backsliding from Me." Backsliding is turning away from what we know to be best to what we know is second-best. If you have known God better than you know Him to-day and are deliberately settling down to something less than the best—watch, for you will not escape, God will bring embarrassments out against you, in your private life, in your domestic life, He will enmesh you on the right hand and on the left. Compare your life with the life of one who has never known God—"they are not in trouble as other men; neither are they plagued like other men."

The Maturity of Attainment *(Hosea 11:5–7)*
And My people are bent to backsliding from Me . . . (v. 7)

Never estimate a man under thirty as you would estimate him when over forty. The vices of a man who has not reached maturity are nearly always worse than he really is and his virtues better than he really is. After maturity is reached no vice or virtue is an accident, it is a dead set of attainment. The same is true spiritually. For a while God seems to overlook the blunders and wrongdoing of His children—"The times of ignorance therefore God overlooked; but now He commandeth men that they should all everywhere repent" (Acts 17:30 RV); but when they come to maturity He makes no allowance. Spiritual maturity is not reached by the passing of the years, but by obedience. When Solomon attained to maturity, this significant thing was said of him, that his heart was turned away after other gods; God brought out his embarrassments and engineered his enemies and the things that brought him confusion and distress.

It is easy to have the attitudes of religion, but it is the temper of our mind we have to watch. It is not the wrong things, but our temper of mind in serving God that will turn us from Him. A man may have preached to others and have attained, but now the secret defects of his devotion have come to light, his heart is turned away from God. If we only believe in Jesus because He delivers us from hell, we will forsake Him in two seconds if He crosses our purposes or goes contrary to our personal disposition of mind.

It is the motive in doing right things that may be wrong. Doing a wrong thing may be a haphazard affair to a large extent, but a wrong temper of mind is never a haphazard affair. It is a determined enthronement of something other than God. A man may look all right in his ostensible religious life, he may have had a vivid religious history, but his private life may be rotten. It is a terrible thing to become blunt and insensitive. Sin destroys the power of knowing that we sin, and one of the dangerous outcomes of a mood that is not right with God is that it turns a man into a prig.

The Mastering of Antagonism *(Hosea 11:10)*
. . . the LORD, Who shall roar like a lion . . . (RV)

It will be a question of slaughter, upset and disaster, then, says God, "they shall follow Me again." If a man has reached maturity and has deliberately put something other than God before him, and is not walking humbly with God, then God will bring things out against him, his enemies will be organised by God. God brought out against His own people nations that did not know Him. Others seem to do wrong and escape, but God is gathering you round, He comes up against you on the right hand and on the left. If you have known Me, says Jesus, and pretend to be abiding in Me and yet are not bringing forth fruit, either My Father will remove you, or if you persist in masquerading, men will gather you and burn you in the fire. The exposing of hypocrisy is never a shock to the cause of God. Judgement begins at the house of God. No man is ever a stumblingblock in the way of another who does the thing he ought to do.

"While ye have light, believe in the light." Believe what you see in your best mood and not what you see in a dark mood. Watch the temper of your mind. Why do you pray? Why are you religious? Because of a consuming passion for a particular set of your beliefs to be enthroned and proved right, or because of a consuming passion for Jesus Christ? If you are religious, beware lest you are keener on the plan of salvation than on the Saviour.

Y.M.C.A. HUT, OCTOBER 7, 1917

GETTING INTO GOD'S STRIDE

Enoch walked with God. Genesis 5:24

The test of a man's religious life and character is not what he does in the exceptional moments of his life, but what he does in the ordinary times when he is not before the footlights, when there is nothing tremendous or exciting on. John looked upon Jesus "*as He walked,* and saith, Behold, the Lamb of God!" (RV). In learning to walk with God there is the difficulty of getting into His stride; when we have got into His stride, what manifests itself in the life is the characteristic of God. The idea in the Bible is not only that we might be saved, but that we might become sons and daughters of God, and that means having the attitude of God to things.

Individual Discouragement and Personal Enlargement *(Exodus 2:11–14)*
And it came to pass in those days, when Moses was grown up, that he went out unto his brethren, and looked on their burdens. (v. 11 RV)

Moses was learned in all the wisdom of the Egyptians, he was a mighty man and a great statesman, and when he saw the oppression of his people he felt that God had called him out to deliver them, and in the righteous indignation of his own spirit he started to right their wrongs. God is never in a hurry. After the first big strike for God and for the right thing, God allowed Moses, the only man who could deliver his own people, to be driven into the desert to feed sheep—forty years of blank discouragement. Then when God appeared and told him to go and bring forth the people, Moses said—"Who am I, that I should go?" The big "I am" had gone, and the little "I am" had taken its place. At first, Moses was certain he was the man, and so he was, but he was not fit yet. He set out to deliver the people in a way that had nothing of the stride of God about it. Moses was right in the individual aspect, but he was not the man for the work until he had learned communion with God, and it took forty years in the desert while God worked through him in ways of terrific personal enlargement before he recognised this.

We may have the vision of God, a very clear understanding of what God wants—wrongs to be righted, the salvation of sinners and the sanctification of believers; we are certain we see the way out, and we start to do the thing. Then comes something equivalent to the forty years in the wilderness, discouragement, disaster, upset, as if God had ignored the whole thing. When we are thoroughly flattened out, God comes back and revives the call, and we get the quaver in, and say "Oh, who am I, that I should go?" We have to learn the first great stride of God—"I AM THAT I AM . . . hath sent thee." We have to learn that our individual effort for God is an impertinence, our individuality must be rendered incandescent by a personal relationship to God, and that is not learned easily. The individual man is lost in his personal union with God, and what is manifested is the stride and the power of God. "I indeed baptise you with water unto repentance: but He that cometh after me is mightier than I, whose shoes I am not worthy to bear: He shall baptise you with the Holy Ghost and with fire" (Matthew 3:11). Moses had to learn this, and our Lord taught His disciples the same thing—"Ye did not choose Me, but I chose you, and appointed you, that ye should go and bear fruit, and that your fruit should abide: that whatsoever ye shall ask of the Father in My name, He may give it you" (John 15:16 RV), and He emphasises it in John 17:22—"that they may be one, even as *We are*."

How many of us have gone through this experience of getting into the stride of God? We have the vision, the real life is there, but we have not got into God's stride about the work and we fix on the individual aspect—"This is what God wants me to do." That is only my individual interpretation of what God wants me to do. Our efforts spring from the certainty that we understand God, and in our prayers we dictate to God what we think He ought to do. The individuality suffers terrible discouragement until we learn to get into personal union with God, then we experience an extraordinary enlargement. When the Spirit of God gets me into stride with God, He sheds abroad the love of God in my heart—"God so loved the world . . ." (John 3:16). I have my personal life, my home life, my national life, my individual attitude to things, and it takes time for me to believe that the Almighty pays no regard to any of these; I come slowly into the idea that God ignores my prejudices, wipes them out absolutely.

Inspired Direction and Personal Expression
(Ezekiel 3:12–17)
So the Spirit lifted me up, and took me away: and I went in bitterness, in the heat of my spirit, and the hand of the LORD was strong upon me (v. 14 RV)

Ezekiel was inspired of God, God's message was blazing in him—"Wait till I get to the people, I'll tell them what God has said." But when he did get there, he sat down flabbergasted and was dumb for seven days, all his message gone from him, he hadn't the heart to say a solitary word. He was inspired surely enough, directed by God, the blazing message of God was in his heart; but when he saw the condition of his fellow exiles, all he could do was to sit down amongst them in their circumstances and let their circumstances talk to him. Ezekiel had his message, but he had not the communion of God's personal attitude expressed in the particular circumstances, and he sat dumbfounded for seven days. Then his attitude was—"Have I still to give Your message?" And God said, "Yes, now you can give it free from individual spleen in a way which gives exactly My interpretation." Ezekiel had the same message, but when he had come to the inspired direction of God he understood things differently.

We have a blazing inspiration from God, we see perfectly well that certain things are wrong and we know that God will not palliate wrong, but we do not yet understand how to deal rightly with these things. We have our inspired direction, we know that God says

men are to be delivered, but we have to remember that when we sit down as Ezekiel did where people are, there is a danger lest we lose all moral distinctions and powers of judging. The danger is that we are so completely overcome with pain over the result of sin in men's lives that we forget to deliver God's message. God says—"Remember, I am a holy God, and when you have come into right relationship with Me, then give My message." When Jesus said to the scribes and Pharisees, "How can ye escape the damnation of hell?" He was speaking not out of personal vindictiveness but with a background of the inevitable—"I have exhibited God before you, yet you turn from Me and despise Me." These words were uttered by the Being Who died on Calvary, and must be read in the light of the Cross.

Inscrutable Disaster and Personal Experience
(Acts 9:9)
And he was three days without sight, and did neither eat nor drink.

Saul of Tarsus was "knocked out," and it took him three days to get his breath before he could begin to get into the stride of God. Who was Saul of Tarsus? A Pharisee of the Pharisees, a man of superb integrity and conscientiousness. If there ever was a conscientious objector it was Saul—"I verily thought with myself, that I ought to do many things contrary to the name of Jesus of Nazareth." He was conscientious when he hounded the followers of Jesus Christ to death. Then came disaster, all his world was flung to pieces. God arrests him, "he was three days without sight, and did neither eat nor drink"; but out of the inscrutable disaster and upset God brought him into a personal experience of Himself. "But when it was the good pleasure of God, Who separated me, even from my mother's womb, and called me through His grace, to reveal His Son in me, that I might preach Him among the Gentiles; immediately I conferred not with flesh and blood" (Galatians 1:15–16 RV). For three years Saul went round about Sinai while the Holy Ghost blazed into him the things that became his Epistles.

It is a painful business getting through into the stride of God, it means getting our "second wind" morally and spiritually. When I start walking with God, I have not taken three strides before I find He has outstripped me; He has different ways of doing things and I have to be trained and disciplined into His ways. It was said of Jesus, "He shall not fail nor be discouraged," because He never worked from His own individual standpoint, but always from the standpoint of His Father. Discouragement is "disenchanted egotism." We learn spiritual truth by atmosphere not by intellectual reasoning; God's spirit alters the atmosphere of our ways of looking at things and things begin to be possible which never were possible before.

If you are going through a period of discouragement there is a big personal enlargement ahead. We have the stride of Divine Healing, of Sanctification, of the Second Coming; all these are right, but the stride of God is never anything less than union with Himself.

NOTES OF THE LAST SERMON PREACHED AT ZEITOUN, OCTOBER 14, 1917

DISABLING SHADOWS ON THE SOUL

Yea, they shall be afraid of that which is high, and terrors shall be in the way; and the almond tree shall blossom, and the grasshopper shall be a burden, and the caper-berry shall fail: because man goeth to his long home, and the mourners go about the streets. Ecclesiastes 12:5 (RV)

Solomon is describing the last lap of a man's life when his nerves give way, and little things become an intolerable burden. There are things like this that come across us naturally and we have difficulty in tracing where they come from; they make us irritable or melancholy. Times when a fly or a mosquito is more annoying than the devil himself. And the same thing is true spiritually; there are times when little things pester and annoy and there is nothing in us big enough to cope with them. This verse is a picture of the shadows which come across a man's soul not because he has done wrong or has backslidden; there is nothing definite about it, but he finds himself belittling everything, there is no vision or power or grandeur in anything. Nothing has been done wrong, there is no reason why you should feel your feet like lead and your heart like ice, and yet you seem about three inches high, with the mind of an insect, irritated and annoyed over everything there is. "What is the good of anything at all? What is the good of having done my duty? of praying, or believing in God?" That aspect of things comes over and over again in the Bible and in our own experience. It happens out here physically; you suddenly feel "knocked out" and you don't know why you should. It is a symbol for what happens spiritually.

The Weariness of the Way
And let us not be weary in well-doing: for in due season we shall reap, if we faint not. (Galatians 6:9 RV)

When a man sins magnificently he is always punished monotonously, that is the ingenuity of punishment (e.g. Samson). We know about the weariness that comes from *wrong*-doing, but Paul says, "Don't be weary in *well*-doing." We all experience the weariness that comes from wrongdoing, but I want to mention the weariness which annoys us because we don't know

how it came; why our life suddenly lost all its interest. The point to note is that weariness does come in well-doing, when everything becomes listless. It has no business to be though—it is a sickness of the soul. What is the cure? The cure is that of a right vision. Every man has the power to slay his own weariness, not by "bucking up" as you do physically, but by suddenly looking at things from a different standpoint. "Why art thou cast down, O my soul? and why art thou disquieted within me? hope thou in God: for I shall yet praise Him, Who is the health of my countenance, and my God" (Psalm 42:11). It is a tremendous thing to know that God reigns and rules and rejoices, and that His joy is our strength. The confidence of a Christian is that God is never in the sulks. ". . . the Father of lights, with Whom can be no variation, neither shadow that is cast by turning" (RV).

The Wasting in the Way
Nor for the pestilence that walketh in darkness; nor for the destruction that wasteth at noonday. (Psalm 91:6)

In our modern Christian vocabulary we have lost sight of a sin the monks used to recognise, the sin of *"Accidie."* It took hold of a man at noon and he suddenly became vilely irritable. It is the inarticulate things which are the most devastating of all. Dante places in the deepest cycle of hell the people who were guilty of the sin of gloom. This wasting in the way shows itself in irritability, bad temper and melancholy; you don't seem able to "buck yourself up." If you sit down when you are in the dumps, you are a plague spot to all around you.

The Wandering from Worship
If thou turn away thy foot from the Sabbath, from doing thy pleasure on My holy day; and call the Sabbath a delight . . . (Isaiah 58:13)

If I have known God and have seen Him in my clear moments, and in any moment of lassitude have turned away from Him, instantly weariness comes. In spiritual life the danger is to make the effect the cause. Immediately I make doing right my aim, I get weary. This is the right attitude: "For we preach not ourselves, but Christ Jesus as Lord, and ourselves as your servants for Jesus' sake" (2 Corinthians 4:5 RV). When I get my eyes off Him I begin to get weary. I am kept from wasting in the way only as I abide under the shadow of the Almighty and stake my all in confidence in God. I have nothing to do with the results, but only with maintaining my relationship to Him.

"If you refrain from doing your own pleasure on My day." In every family, and in every Christian community, keeping the Sabbath day holy is a chance for ostensibly declaring to the world that we recognise that God is the Head.

Wandering from the vision you once had accounts for weariness and wasting. When you were in your best moments you saw things in a certain way. Believe what you saw then; don't believe what you saw in the lower mood (see John 12:36). The best tonic you can have comes from the man or woman who is merciless to your weariness or wandering; to pander to weariness which has no definite cause is iniquitous. If you are sick or ill that has to be handled in a different way; but if there is weariness or wasting and you cannot get at the cause of it, this is the reason—you have neglected private prayer, neglected worship, neglected doing something you know perfectly well you should have done. It hasn't yet come the length of sin; it is a defect no one notices, but sadness creeps on my soul whenever I deflect from the highest I know.

You have nothing to do with anyone else; look after the vision of your own life, and you will be a benediction to every one with whom you come in contact (John 7:38). Don't try and find out whether you are a blessing, pay attention to the Source, then out of you will flow rivers of living water that you know nothing about. But if you cut yourself off from the Source, and gloom away from God, your weariness and wasting is worse than an epidemic, it is a heavy disease to the spiritual community around.

Let me watch whether I am wandering from worship, from the highest I know; I do not wander alone. The wasting that destroys me in the noontide of my spiritual life, or the weariness that comes over me, is a thing that hinders others. Let me get back again to the place where the airs and the light and the liberty of God come, and all the time there flows through the inspiration to others.

The Psychology of Redemption

Oswald Chambers

Copyright Oswald Chambers Publications Association, 1922
Second Edition, 1930, Third Edition, 1935
Scripture versions quoted: KJV, RV, MOFFATT

INTRODUCTION

Source

The material in *The Psychology of Redemption* is taken from lectures at the Bible Training College, London,[1] from April 15 through June 31, 1915, and from talks on "Christian Psychology" given in the evening class at Zeitoun, Egypt,[2] January 24 through February 8, 1916.

Publication History

- As articles: It is unusual that the material was never published as articles, as most of the other OC books were. The publication of the book predates the existence of the *BTC Journal*,[3] which was published from 1932 to 1952, and the lectures never appeared in *Spiritual Life*, the League of Prayer[4] magazine.
- As a book: In 1919, Mrs. Chambers and her daughter, Kathleen,[5] returned to England from

Egypt. In 1922, they were living in Yarnton, in a small cottage with no electricity or running water. With financial help from friends, she had *The Psychology of Redemption* printed in Oxford, the first book after her return. The second edition was published in 1930, and the third edition in 1935.

In David Lambert's[6] foreword to the second edition, he notes that he first heard these lectures at the convention of the League of Prayer held in Perth, Scotland, in August 1914. Mrs. Chambers did not attend that convention with Oswald, so her notes came, as she states in her foreword, from the lectures at the BTC[7] and in Egypt.

The outline reproduced at the beginning of the first chapter is typical of Chambers' teaching method. Through the use of large chalkboard outlines for virtually all his lectures, he created visual and verbal keys to aid his students in remembering the content.

---

1. Bible Training College (BTC): residential school near Clapham Common in southwest London; sponsored by the League of Prayer; operated from 1911 until it closed in July 1915 because of World War I. Oswald Chambers was principal and main teacher; Biddy Chambers, his wife, was lady superintendent.

2. Zeitoun (zay TOON), Egypt: six miles northeast of Cairo; site of a YMCA camp, the Egypt General Mission compound, and, from 1916 to 1919, the Imperial School of Instruction, training base for British, Australian, and New Zealand troops during World War I.

3. *Bible Training Course Monthly Journal:* published by Mrs. Chambers, with help from David Lambert.

4. Pentecostal League of Prayer: founded in London in 1891 by Reader Harris (1847–1909), prominent barrister and friend and mentor of Oswald Chambers.

5. Kathleen Chambers (1913–1997): only child of Oswald and Biddy Chambers.

6. David Lambert (1871–1961): Methodist minister and friend of Oswald and Biddy Chambers; assisted Mrs. Chambers with OC publications from 1917 until his death in 1961.

7. BTC: the Bible Training College.

FOREWORD (TO THE FIRST EDITION)

This book is compiled from verbatim notes taken of lectures given in 1915 to the students at the Bible Training College, Clapham, and in the following year to men of the Egyptian Expeditionary force in the YMCA Hut, Zeitoun, Egypt.

"Neither pray I for these alone, but for them also which shall believe on Me *through their word*" (John 17:20). This book is just the "word" of a disciple of Jesus Christ's, and it is sent out with the prayer that it may be the "great disposing word" of God in many lives.

B. C.[8]
1922

FOREWORD TO THE SECOND EDITION

I have rough notes of these lectures as given in their first form at the Perth Convention[9] in 1914. I sat enthralled at the beauty and power of the truth being given to us. The essential message of this book was expressed then in these words: "In the Life of our Lord, as Son of Man, when He transformed innocence into holiness by a series of moral choices, He gave the pattern forever of how a holy character was to be developed." It is a basic book. It reminds me of Henry Scougal's *Life of God in the Soul of Man*, a volume that greatly influenced Whitefield and the Wesleys. That Aberdeen Professor wrote in 1668, "The power and life of religion may be better expressed in actions than in words. . . . They are perfectly exemplified in the Holy Life of our Blessed Saviour, a main part of whose business in this world was to teach by His practice what He did require of others; and to make His own conversation an exact resemblance of those rules which He prescribed. So that if ever true goodness was visible to mortal eyes it was then when His Presence did beautify and illustrate this lower world."

Oswald Chambers here shows us the parallel between our Lord's wondrous life on earth and our life lived in His Name. The psychology of the sanctified life is perfectly illustrated in our Lord's life as set forth in the Gospels. The First Adam mishandled and disarranged his human nature. The Last Adam restored Human Nature to a right working relation to God. When through the Atonement and the New Birth we are lifted into the shared life of our Risen Lord, the same laws of development operate for us as with Him. And "Christian psychology is not a knowledge of man, but a knowledge of our Lord Jesus Christ." To profit by this book demands concentrated thought, with Bible in hand, and with a humble eagerness to "act on the Word, instead of merely listening to it and deluding yourselves," James 1:22 MOFFATT. This book meets a timely need because it shows how "holiness" works out in human nature as we know it. It shows how sin has taken possession of human nature, but that sin is abnormal. Sin is the outcome of a relationship which God never ordained. Our Lord in His Human Nature cancelled that wrong relationship through His Cross; and established a new relationship. It is in that new relationship we work out that holiness of life and thought and feeling and purpose and service which is the fulfilment of the New Covenant promise, Hebrews 8:10–12.

I pray that the book may prove as great a blessing to many thoughtful students as it has been to some of us for years, bringing them to the Apostolic climax of confession, "For to me to live IS CHRIST."

David Lambert

---

8. B. C.: Biddy Chambers; although Mrs. Chambers was editor, compiler, and often publisher, she never identified herself by name in any of the books.

9. Perth Convention: annual meeting sponsored by the Pentecostal League of Prayer in Perth, Scotland.

CONTENTS

WHERE TO START THESE STUDIES
1 Corinthians 2:11–15

1 CORINTHIANS 15:45–50

First Man—Adam	Second Man—Christ	New Man—Saint
Living soul (v. 45)	Quickening Spirit (v. 45)	Earthy and heavenly image (v. 48)
Natural (v. 46)	Spiritual (v. 46)	Earthy effaced by heavenly image (v. 49)
Earthy (v. 47)	Heavenly (v. 47)	Divinely inherited kingdom of God (v. 50)

Christian Psychology is based on the knowledge of the Lord Jesus Christ, not on the knowledge of ourselves. It is not the study of human nature analysed and expounded, but the study of the new life that is born in us through the Redemption of our Lord, and the only Standard of that new life is our Lord Himself; He is formed in us by regeneration (Galatians 1:15–16). We are apt to start with the way we are made naturally and to transfer our reasonings on that to Jesus Christ, inferring that to understand ourselves is to understand Him. In Christian Psychology we have not to introspect as we do in natural psychology; we have to accept the revelations given to us in and through our Lord Jesus Christ; that is, we must take all our bearings from the Son of God, not from our natural wits. We have not to study and understand ourselves; but to understand the manifestation in us of the life of the Son of God Who became Son of Man, the Lord Jesus Christ.

According to the Bible, there are only two Men: Adam and Jesus Christ, and God deals with them as the representatives of the human race, not as individuals. All the members of the human race are grouped round these two Men. The first Adam is called "the son of God"; the last Adam is *the* Son of God, and we are made *sons* of God by the last Adam. The Christian is neither Adam nor Jesus Christ, the Christian is a new man in Christ Jesus. The first Adam and the last Adam are the only two Men according to God's norm, and they both came into this world direct from the hand of God.

First Man

Living Soul

The first man Adam was made a living soul. (1 Corinthians 15:45)

Beware of dividing man up into body, soul and spirit. Man *is* body, soul and spirit. Soul is the expression of man's personal spirit in his body. Spirit means I, myself, the incalculable being that is "me," the essence that expresses itself in the soul. The immortal part of a man is not his soul, but his spirit. Man's spirit is as indestructible as Almighty God; the expression of his spirit in the soul depends on the body. In the Bible the soul is always referred to in connection with the body. The soul is the holder of the body and spirit together, and, when the body disappears, the soul disappears, but the essential personality of the man remains. In the resurrection there is another body and instantly the soul life is manifested again (John 5:28–29). It is not a resurrection of spirit, i.e., personality, that never dies, but of body and soul.

A "living soul" means man expressing himself as God designed he should. God created man a splendid moral being, fitted to rule the earth and air and sea, but he was not to rule himself; God was to be his Master, and man was to turn his natural life into a spiritual life by obedience. Had Adam done so, the members of the human race would have gone on developing until they were transfigured into the presence of God; there would have been no death. Death to us has become natural, but the Bible reveals it to be abnormal. Adam refused to turn the natural into the spiritual; he took dominion over himself and thereby became the introducer of the heredity of sin into the human race (Romans 5:12), and instantly lost his control over the earth and air and sea. The entrance of sin means that the connection with God has gone and the disposition of self-realisation, my right to myself, has come in its place.

"For by Him were all things created . . ." (Colossians 1:16). Did God then create sin? Sin is not a creation; sin is the outcome of a relationship which God never ordained, a relationship set up between the man God created and the being God created who became the devil. God did not create sin, but He holds Himself responsible for the possibility of sin, and the proof that He does so is in the cross of our Lord Jesus Christ. Calvary is God's responsibility undertaken and carried through as Redemption. The essential nature of sin is my claim to my right to myself, and when sin entered in, the connection between man and God was instantly severed; at-one-ness was no longer possible.

Natural

Howbeit that was not first which is spiritual, but that which is natural; and afterward that which is spiritual. (1 Corinthians 15:46)

Unless we are born again, we will always be "natural" men. In John 3, our Lord is not talking about sin and hell, He is talking to a religious leader, a clean-living, upright, good, noble man —a natural man—and it was to him that He said—"Marvel not that I said unto thee, Ye must be born again." The general idea is that a man must be a blackguard before Jesus Christ can do anything for him. The average preaching of the Gospel deals mainly with the scenic cases, with people who have gone through exceptional experiences. None of the early disciples had had these exceptional experiences; they saw in Jesus Christ what they had never seen before—a Man from another realm, and they began to long after what He stood for. We preach to men as if they were conscious of being dying sinners; they are not, they are having a good time, and our talk about being born again is from a domain of which they know nothing. The natural man does not want to be born again.

Earthy

The first man is of the earth, earthy. (1 Corinthians 15:47)

This is man's glory, not his shame, because it is in a creature made of the earth that God is going to manifest His glory. We are apt to think that being made of the earth is our humiliation, but it is the very point that is made much of in God's word. In the Middle Ages it was taught that sin resided in the actual fleshly body, and that therefore the body was a clog and a hindrance. The Bible says that the body is the temple of the Holy Ghost, not a thing to be despised. Sin is not in having a body and a nature that needs to be sacrificed; sin is in refusing to sacrifice them at the call of God. Sin is a disposition which rules the body, and regeneration means not only that we need not obey the disposition of sin, but that we can be absolutely delivered from it (Romans 6:6).

Second Man

Quickening Spirit

The last Adam was made a quickening spirit. (1 Corinthians 15:45)

Jesus Christ came into the human race from the outside, and when we are born again, His life comes into us from the outside. Jesus Christ is the normal man, and in His relationship to God, to the devil, to sin and to man we see the expression in human nature of what He calls "eternal life." We try to enter the life of Jesus in the wrong way. We do not enter into His life by imitation: we enter into it by its entering into us by means of His death. Jesus Christ gives us His life, viz., Holy Spirit. When we ask God for the Holy Spirit, we receive the very nature of God, *Holy* Spirit. We become regenerate, born from above (RV mg), by the gift of life from the last Adam, then we have to live in obedience to that Spirit which has come into our spirit.

The records in the Gospels are given, not so much that we might understand the Person of our Lord from the natural standpoint, but that we might understand how to exhibit His life in us when we are born from above (RV mg). We have to take our instructions for this from Jesus Christ. The danger is lest we praise God's salvation and sovereign grace while we refuse to manifest His salvation in our human nature.

Spiritual
Howbeit that was not first which is spiritual, but that which is natural; and afterward that which is spiritual. (1 Corinthians 15:46)

That which is not earthy, but in accordance with the nature of spirit. There are counterfeit spiritualities, but the spirituality of Jesus Christ is a holy spirituality. Jesus Christ worked from a spiritual standpoint, the Spirit of God so indwelt Him that His spirituality was manifested in His ordinary soul life.

Heavenly
The second man is the Lord from heaven. (1 Corinthians 15:47)

The Second Man is the Son of God historically manifested, and the prophecy of what the human race is going to be. In Him we deal with God as Man, the God-Man, the Representative of the whole human race in one Person. Jesus Christ is not a Being with two personalities; He is Son of God (the exact expression of Almighty God), and Son of Man (the presentation of God's normal man). As Son of God, He reveals what God is like (John 14:9); as Son of Man, He mirrors what the human race will be like on the basis of Redemption—a perfect oneness between God and man (Ephesians 4:13).

New Man

Earthy and Heavenly Image
As is the earthy, such are they also that are earthy: and as is the heavenly, such are they also that are heavenly. (1 Corinthians 15:48)

The "natural" has not life in itself, therefore we must be born from above (RV mg). To be born from above

means that we are lifted into heavenly places in our personal spirit by the Holy Spirit Who comes into us, He quickens us all through. The Holy Spirit does *in* us what Jesus Christ did *for* us. Holy Spirit is essential Deity, and He energises our spirit and presences us with Deity as our Lord was presenced. Holy Spirit never becomes our spirit, He quickens our spirit, and instantly we begin to express a new soul.

When God's Spirit comes into our personality, our soul life begins to be upset, and the bodily life often gets disorganised. Health is simply the balance of our bodily life with external circumstances, anything that upsets the equilibrium on the inside upsets the bodily equilibrium on the outside, consequently when a man is convicted of sin, his "beauty consumes away like a moth" (Psalm 39:11). Beauty means the perfectly ordered completeness of a man's nature. A man into whom the Spirit of God has entered is for a while out of harmony. The Spirit of God brings upset and conviction, He throws light on what is dark, He searches the recesses of the disposition; consequently the preaching of the Gospel, while it awakens an intense craving, awakens an equally intense resentment. Conviction of sin means that we realise that our natural life is based on a disposition that will not have Jesus Christ. If the man will obey the Holy Spirit, the new balance of holiness will be set up, the balance of his disposition with the law of God. Then he must obey God's will in his body, and this will mean crucifying the flesh with its affections and lusts (Galatians 5:24).

Earthy Effaced by Heavenly Image
And as we have borne the image of the earthy, we shall also bear the image of the heavenly. (1 Corinthians 15:49)

Have you never seen the earthy effaced by the heavenly? Watch the face of a man or woman who has been born again and who is going on with God; there is a change in the features which cannot be defined. The explanation of it is that when God makes us all over again, our bodies are moulded by the new Spirit within and begin to manifest that Spirit (2 Corinthians 5:17). When we receive the Holy Spirit, He lifts us into the realm where Jesus Christ lives, and all things become new. We cannot estimate Jesus Christ along the natural line, He does not belong to this order of things, and He says that if we want to belong to His order we must be born from above (John 3:3, 7 RV mg). Tolstoi taught the principles of Jesus, but he ignored the need to be born again. Let a man receive the Holy Spirit, and Jesus Christ will do in him all that he ever imagined He would do, and he will find that it works all the time.

Nothing is born without pain, and a man cannot be born into the Kingdom of God without pain. He must have his conscience and his mind readjusted, and this will mean pain. Redemption makes a man right for heaven, but there is much more in it than that. New birth has to do with being of value to God in this present order of things.

Divinely Inherited Kingdom of God
Now this I say, brethren, that flesh and blood cannot inherit the kingdom of God; neither doth corruption inherit incorruption. (1 Corinthians 15:50)

The characteristics of the natural man, apart from sin, are independence and individuality. Individuality is the strong and emphatic and somewhat ugly husk that guards the personal life. Individuality is a right characteristic in a child, but in a man or woman it is not only objectionable but dangerous, because it means independence of God as well as of other people, and independence of God is of the very nature of sin. The only way we can get rid of the pride of individuality and become one with Jesus Christ is by being born from above (RV mg).

Sin dwells in human nature, but the Bible makes it very clear that it is an abnormal thing, it has no right there, it does not belong to human nature as God designed it. Sin has come into human nature and perverted and twisted it. The Redemption of God through our Lord Jesus Christ delivers human nature from sin, and then begins the possibility of the manifestation of the life of Jesus in our mortal flesh. We are saved by God's grace, but, thank God, we have something to do. We must take care to meet God's supernatural work of grace by our human obedience. When we have been delivered from sin, the characteristics of our natural life have to be sacrificed, not murdered, not denied in the sense of being ignored, but sacrificed, that is, transformed into agreement with the heavenly by obedience (Ephesians 4:23). We are saved from sin and readjusted to God, but we are still human beings, and we have to take the trouble to *actually* prove what God has *really* done in us. God never saves men and women the trouble of manifesting the fact that He has made them His sons and daughters. We begin all right, but it is easy to get switched off. If we do not continue to live in the right place, we will get back into "Adam" sympathies. It is on "Adam" sympathies that much of our Christian work is based, not on sympathy with Jesus Christ, the last Adam. Satan's temptations of our Lord were based on sympathy with the first Adam—"Put men's needs first." Jesus Christ says—"Do not think first of the needs of the people; think first of the commands of God" (Mark 12:29–31).

Natural individuality holds strongly to natural relationships. The natural relationships on which individuality is based are—father, mother, brothers and sisters, husband and wife, children, self-interest. These are the relationships with which our Lord says we are likely to clash if we are going to be His disciples. If the clash comes, He says it must be instant obedience to Him (Luke 14:26). Our obedience to Jesus Christ is going to cost other people a great deal, and if we refuse to go on because of the cost to them, or because of the stab and the jeer, we may find that we have prevented the call of God coming to other lives; whereas if we will go through with God, all these natural relationships will be given to our credit spiritually in the final wind-up.

HOW TO STUDY THE START

Some Things to Remember
    The Revelation of Christ (Matthew 16:16–17)
    The Records of Christ (John 5:39 RV)
    The Realisation of Christ (1 Corinthians 1:30)

Some Things to Realise
    The Evangelical Experience (The Synoptic
        Gospels and St John)
    The Examined Experience (The Epistles)
    The Exercised Experience (The Present
        Obedience)

The basis of Christian Psychology is not a knowledge of man, but a knowledge of our Lord Jesus Christ. It is easy to put up our Lord as an Example, but according to the New Testament He is much more. He is the Redeemer, One who can reproduce His own life in us. To be born from above (RV mg) means more than conversion. It means that Christ is formed in us, and the Christ in us must be exactly like the Christ outside us. The characteristics that Jesus Christ exhibited in His human life are to be exhibited in the Christian. Christian Psychology is based on our realisation of Who the Lord Jesus Christ is and on an experimental understanding of His life in us.

There is a difference between sight and the organ of sight. Most of us are quite content to see, we do not bother about the organ of sight. But when something goes wrong with the organ of sight those of us who can see only are of no use to put the eye right; we must know how the organ of sight is constructed.

The Christian worker is apt to say—"Oh, well, I have
been saved by God's grace and that is sufficient." It
may be sufficient for you, but if you are going to be "a
workman that needeth not to be ashamed," you must
do more than "be saved," you must take the trouble to
find out what the Bible says about that salvation.
Most of us are like the folks who are content with
being able to see; but the organ of sight spiritually in
many has gone wrong, and we have no knowledge of
how to deal with it, all we can do is to give our testimony. That is not good enough. The point of the
study of Christian Psychology is not only that we
might understand salvation for ourselves, but that we
might understand how to assist others.

Some Things to Remember
The Revelation of Christ
*And Simon Peter answered and said, Thou art the
Christ, the Son of the living God. And Jesus answered
and said unto him, Blessed art thou, Simon Bar jona:
for flesh and blood hath not revealed it unto thee, but
My Father which is in heaven. (Matthew 16:16–17)*

The Lord Jesus Christ is not a commonsense fact,
that is, we do not understand Him by means of our
common sense. The disciples at this stage only knew
Jesus Christ by means of their common sense—by
their eyes and ears and all the powers of common-
sense men; they had never discerned Who He was.
Our Lord is a revelation fact, and when Peter confessed, "Thou art the Christ, the Son of the living
God," Jesus Christ recognised from Whom he had
received the revelation, not from his common sense,
but from God. Is Jesus Christ a revelation to me, or is
He simply an historical character?

The Bible is the universe of revelation facts; the
natural world is the universe of common-sense facts,
and our means of communication with the two universes is totally different. We come in contact with
the natural universe by our senses, our intellect has to
be curious. Scientific knowledge, which is systematised common sense, is based on intense intellectual
curiosity. Curiosity in the natural world is right, not
wrong, and if we are not intellectually curious we shall
never know anything, God never encourages laziness.

When we come to the universe of the Bible, the
revelation facts about God, intellectual curiosity is not
of the slightest use. Our senses are no good here, we
cannot find out God by searching. We may have
inferences from our common-sense thinking which
we call God, but these are mere abstractions. We can
only get at the facts that are revealed in the Bible by
faith. Faith is not credulity; faith is my personal spirit
obeying God. The Bible does not deal in common-
sense facts; the natural universe deals in common-
sense facts, and we get at these by our senses. The

Bible deals with revelation facts, facts we cannot get
at by our common sense, facts we may be pleased to
make light of by our common sense. For instance,
Jesus Christ is a revelation fact, sin is another, the
devil is another, the Holy Spirit is another. Not one of
these is a common-sense fact. If a man were merely a
common-sense individual, he could do very well
without God.

In order to get scientific knowledge we must use
our common sense; but if we are going to know the
facts with which Jesus Christ deals, the facts which
He says belong to the Kingdom of God, we must
have them revealed to us. "Marvel not that I said unto
thee, Ye must be born again," before you can come
into contact with the domain in which I live. The
domain in which Jesus Christ lives is the domain of
Bible facts. How are we to get the revelation of Jesus
Christ? Very simply, if we want it. Jesus Christ said
that the Holy Spirit would glorify Him, and we can
receive Holy Spirit for the asking (Luke 11:13). Then
we too shall be in the same category as Peter, and
Jesus Christ will say to us, "Blessed art thou, . . . for
flesh and blood hath not revealed it unto thee, but My
Father which is in heaven." Jesus Christ is a Revelation, and we can get the revelation of Him by receiving the Holy Spirit. Jesus Christ continually said
things (such as Luke 11:13) the meaning of which
cannot be got at by common sense. Have we ever
received Holy Spirit? If we refuse any one way of getting at the truth because we do not like that way, we
are dishonest.

The Records of Christ
*Ye search the scriptures, because ye think that in them ye
have eternal life. (John 5:39 RV)*

The Scriptures, from Genesis to Revelation, are all
revelations of Jesus Christ. The context of the Bible is
our Lord Himself, and until we get rightly related to
Him, the Bible is no more to us than an ordinary
book. Common sense does not reveal Jesus Christ; to
common sense He is nothing more than a Nazarene
carpenter who lived twenty centuries ago. No natural
man can know Jesus Christ (Matthew 11:27). Higher
criticism, so called, works on the lines of common
sense, consequently when it deals with our Lord
(Whose highest sense is not common sense, but
Deity), He has to be explained away, His Person is
"dissolved by analysis" (1 John 4:1–3). The findings of
higher criticism may be logically proved, but the
biggest facts in life are not logical. If they were, we
should be able to calculate our ends and make sure of
things on rational logical lines. Logical truth is merely
the explanation of facts which common sense has
gathered. Men say, "I must have these things proved
to my reason." How much good spiritually did a man

ever get by proving things to his reason? In spiritual matters logical processes do not count. Curiosity does not count, nor argument, nor reasoning; these are of no avail for spiritual discernment. There is only one golden rule for spiritual discernment, and that is obedience. We learn more by five minutes' obedience than by ten years' study. Logic and reasoning are methods of expounding Reality, but we do not get at Reality by our intellect. Reality is only got at by our conscience. When we deal with the records of Christ we are dealing with fundamental realities, not with intellectual problems. Faith in God is the only way of coming in touch with the fundamental realities, and there is nothing logical about faith; it is of the nature of life.

After we are born again, the Bible becomes a new Book to us, and we search the Scriptures, not to get "life" out of them, but to know more about Jesus Christ. "Ye search the scriptures, because ye think that in them ye have eternal life, . . . and ye will not come to *Me* that ye might have life" (John 5:39–40 RV). The vital relationship which the Christian has to the Bible is not that he worships the letter, but that the Holy Spirit makes the words of the Bible spirit and life to him. Before we are born from above (RV mg) the Bible is only an ordinary book; after we are born from above, the Bible becomes a universe of revelation facts whereby we feed our knowledge of Jesus Christ.

The Realisation of Christ
But of Him are ye in Christ Jesus, who of God is made unto us wisdom, and righteousness, and sanctification, and redemption. (1 Corinthians 1:30)

In Proverbs 8, we read of Pre-incarnate Wisdom, and in John's Gospel that Wisdom is referred to as the Logos, or Word. Historically, the Word was called Jesus Christ. The whole wisdom of God has come down to the shores of our lives in a flesh and blood Man, and John says, we have seen Him and we know Him. How are we to realise Jesus Christ? He says "Come unto Me," and there is no profounder word in human language than that. The one thing that keeps us from coming to Jesus Christ is obstinacy; we will do anything rather than come. It is not God's will that a man should be smashed before he is saved, it is the man's obstinacy that does it. There is no need to go through the agonies and distresses that so many do go through, it is because men will not *come*. If we want to realise Jesus Christ, He says "Come unto Me," and when we do come, God makes Him "unto us wisdom, and righteousness, and sanctification, and redemption." If Jesus Christ is not revealed to us it is because we have views of our own, and we want to bend everything to those views. In order to realise Christ we must come to Him. That is, we must learn to trust Someone other than ourselves, and to do this we must

deliberately efface ourselves. Devotion and piety are apt to be the greatest opponents of Jesus Christ, because we devote ourselves to devotion instead of to Him. To surrender to God is not to surrender to the fact that we have surrendered. That is not coming at all. To come means that we come to God in complete abandonment and give ourselves right over to Him and leave ourselves in His hands. The Lord Jesus Christ is the one Person to Whom we ought to yield, and we must be perfectly certain that it is to Himself that we are yielding. Do not be sorry if other appeals find you stiff-necked and unyielding; but be sorry if, when He says "Come unto Me," you do not come. The attitude of coming is that the will resolutely lets go of everything and deliberately commits all to Him.

Some Things to Realise
The Evangelical Experience
The Synoptics are the first three Gospels; John's writings include his Epistles and the Apocalypse as well as his Gospel. Our Lord neither talked of Conversion and Regeneration and Sanctification in stages; neither does the Apostle John. If we get hold of books which talk in the stages of experience and then come to the Gospels where those stages are not marked, we are apt to get embarrassed. The Gospels always present truth in "nugget" form, and if we want to know the stages of evangelical experience, we must go to the Epistles which beat out into negotiable gold the nuggets of truth presented by our Lord. In John 3, our Lord is not talking about the stages of conversion; He is talking in the great terms of what He came to do— viz., to make Redemption the basis of human life. We can introduce other things into His words if we like, but we must not say He said them. Our Lord is not examining the evangelical experience, He is stating it. He said to Nicodemus, "Ye must be born again." That is not a command, but the statement of a foundation fact.

We mean by the Evangelical Experience an experience based on the fact that the Cross of our Lord Jesus Christ, that is, His death, is the gateway for us into His life. We delight to hear about the life of Jesus, it captivates our imagination to hear sermons on following in His steps —until we find that we cannot begin to do it. "Jesus Christ was a great Teacher." So He was, an amazing Teacher, but where are you going to begin to carry out what He says? The Sermon on the Mount is exquisitely beautiful teaching, and it fascinates us so long as we deal with it intellectually only, but when it comes down to our daily life, practical and sordid and real, we find we cannot begin to carry it out. We may give our mental assent to it, but our actual life won't walk that road. The teachings of Jesus must produce despair, because if He meant what He said, where are we in regard to it? The revelation of the New Testament is not that Jesus Christ came to teach primarily but that He came to redeem, to make us what He teaches we should be. Then the teachings of Jesus become the description of what God has undertaken to make a man if he will let the power of God work through him. Redemption means that Jesus Christ can give us His own disposition, and all the standards He gives are based on that disposition—i.e., His teaching is for the life He puts in us. We enter into the life of Jesus by means of His death, that is our only door of entrance. We may try and batter through some other way if we choose—through Bethlehem, through the teachings of Jesus, but we cannot get in. Those ways in would produce frauds and humbugs. If a teacher or preacher has not an evangelical experience himself, his preaching and teaching will degenerate into mere intellectual common sense. It may be smeared over with the teachings of Jesus and may sound beautiful, but there is no power in it to alter anything in us. We cannot get into the life of Jesus by imitation, by trying to do the right thing, because something in us will not do it. We can only enter in by identification with His death. The Cross of Jesus Christ is not the cross of a martyr, but the door whereby God keeps open house for the universe. Anyone can go in through that door. The Cross is the historical presentation of the one Reality there is, viz., Redemption, and if we come to Jesus that Reality works in us by the incoming of the Holy Spirit and we find that we are brought into a new Kingdom. There is something totally different now, we can do what we could not do before. We can show in our bodily life the disposition of Jesus Christ which we receive by means of His Cross, we can begin now to live the kind of life He lived.

The Examined Experience

The evangelical experience is stated in the Synoptics and in John's writings in its great wonderful revelation form, not in its examined stages; but if we want to have the experience examined and stated so that we can see its stages and get a grasp of it, we must turn to the Epistles. The Epistles are the posthumous writings of the Ascended Lord; He sent the Holy Ghost, and the "pens" used were the apostles, and the expositions given are from the Holy Ghost. Our Lord's teachings and the expositions given in the Epistles stand or fall together. The Epistles are our guide in finding out the stages of the experience. There we will find all about Conversion, about Regeneration, and about Sanctification. We will find the stages all carefully set forth, but we must take the trouble to find them out. Acts 26:18 gives the examined experience in condensed form better than any other passage in the New Testament. We so often try to worry out Jesus Christ's statements apart from the guidance of the Holy Spirit. It is the workman of God who can rightly divide the word of truth who becomes the expert in the things of God, and when anyone is being led astray by false doctrines, the expert can show what is wrong.

The Exercised Experience

If we have experienced regeneration, we must not only talk about the experience, we must exercise it and work out what God has worked in (Philippians 2:12–13). We have to show it in our finger-tips, in our tongue, and in our bodily contact with other people, and as we obey God we find we have a wealth of power on the inside. The question of forming habits on the basis of the grace of God is a very vital one. To ignore it is to fall into the snare of the Pharisee—the grace of God is praised, Jesus Christ is praised, the Redemption is praised, but the practical everyday life evades working it out. If we refuse to practise, it is not God's grace that fails when a crisis comes, but our own nature. When the crisis comes, we ask God to help us, but He cannot if we have not made our nature an ally. The practising is ours, not God's. God regenerates us and puts us in contact with all His divine resources, but He cannot make us walk according to His will. If we will obey the Spirit of God and practise through our physical life all that God has put in our hearts by His Spirit, then when the crisis comes we shall find that we have not only God's grace to stand by us but our own nature also, and the crisis is passed without any disaster, but exactly the opposite happens, the soul is built up into a stronger attitude towards God.

HIS BIRTH AND OUR NEW BIRTH

His Birth in History (Luke 1:35)
 The Highest. The Holiest. The Lowliest

His Birth in Me (Galatians 4:19)
 The Lowliest. The Holiest. The Highest
  Do I come to Jesus because of what they say,
   or because of what I see?
  (John 1:12–13)
  Do I seek for signs of the Kingdom of God,
   or do I see the Rule of God?
  (John 3:3)
  Do I seek to stop sinning, or have I stopped
   sinning? (1 John 3:9)

The basis of Christian Psychology is in Jesus Christ, not in Adam. Therefore, if we are to study the characteristics of the Christian soul, we must not look to Adam or to our own experience, but to Jesus Christ, the Foundation. Christian Psychology is the study of a supernatural life made natural in our human life by the Redemption. We do not know Jesus Christ by knowing ourselves; to think we do is a modern fallacy. "No man knoweth the Son, but the Father; neither knoweth any man the Father, save the Son, and he to whomsoever the Son will reveal Him" (Matthew 11:27). If we are ever going to know the Father and the Son, we must have their nature, and we are not born with it. The meaning of New Birth is that we know God by a vital relationship, not only by our intellect. "As many as received Him, to them gave He power to become the sons of God . . . which were born, not of blood, nor of the will of the flesh, nor of the will of man, but of God" (John 1:12–13). The characteristics of the new-birth life are not the characteristics of our natural life, but the supernatural characteristics of our Lord's life, which we have to see are manifested in our natural life. Jesus Christ sets the standard of God's life in us. We have not to ask what good men have experienced, but to go direct to the Lord Jesus Christ and study His exhibition of the character of God's normal man.

His Birth in History

And the angel answered and said unto her, The Holy Ghost shall come upon thee, and the power of the Highest shall overshadow thee: therefore also that holy thing which shall be born of thee shall be called the Son of God. (Luke 1:35)

Jesus Christ was born *into* this world, not *from* it. He came into history from the outside of history; He did not evolve out of history. Our Lord's birth was an advent; He did not come from the human race, He came into it from above. Jesus Christ is not the best human being, He is a Being Who cannot be accounted for by the human race at all. He is God Incarnate, not man becoming God, but God coming into human flesh, coming into it from the outside. His Life is the Highest and the Holiest entering in at the lowliest door. Our Lord entered history by the Virgin Mary.

His Birth in Me

My little children, of whom I travail in birth again until Christ be formed in you. (Galatians 4:19)

Just as our Lord came into human history from the outside, so He must come into us from the outside. Have we allowed our personal human lives to become a "Bethlehem" for the Son of God? The modern tendency is to talk of birth from beneath, not of birth from above, of something rising up out of our unconscious life into our conscious life, not of something coming into us from above. This preaching has so permeated people's views to-day that many who name the Name of Christ and are supposed to be preaching His Gospel are at the same time undermining the very foundations of their own faith.

We cannot enter into the realm of the Kingdom of God unless we are born from above (RV mg), by a birth totally unlike natural birth (John 3:5). People have the idea that because there is good in human nature (and, thank God, there is a lot of good in human nature) that therefore the Spirit of God is in every man naturally, meaning that the Spirit of God in us will become the Christ in us if we let Him have His way. Take that view if you like, but never say it is the view of the New Testament. It certainly is not our Lord's view. He said to Nicodemus, "Marvel not that I said unto thee, Ye must be born again," that is, something must come into you from the outside. To-day people are dethroning Jesus Christ and belittling the need of salvation by making new birth to mean nothing more than a rising up from beneath. The conception of new birth in the New Testament is of something that enters into us, not of something that springs out of us.

We are dealing with New Birth as our Lord presents it. The Holy Spirit, sent by Jesus after He was glorified, is the One Who expounds the various stages in the experience of new birth. Our Lord never speaks in stages of experience, and the reason people divide into stages what our Lord said to Nicodemus is that they have taken their light from the Epistles. We are not dealing just now with the stages of experience, but with the fact of new birth—Christ formed in me. This does not correspond to what is evangelically known as being saved, but rather to the Methodist doctrine of entire sanctification, which is but the beginning of the purpose of the Christian life. If we are to understand how the new birth is to work, we must look at the Epistles. Paul alludes to the new birth life at work when he says, "I travail in birth again until Christ be formed in you." It is the travailing of one who has himself been born from above (RV mg). How many of us know anything about this travailing for those who have been really quickened by the Holy Spirit until Christ is formed in them? We are apt to rejoice in the number of souls who are evangelically described as being saved, but what becomes of them all? They have been introduced into the Kingdom of God, but as yet there is no evidence that Christ is formed in them. Jesus Christ sent His disciples to "disciple" all nations. The regeneration of souls is God's work; our work as saved souls is to work under His orders on the basis of Redemption, and Galatians 4:19 is an indication of what that work is. "Pray ye therefore the Lord of the harvest, that He will send forth labourers into His harvest" (Matthew 9:38). The labour is prayer. We labour on the ground of our Lord's Redemption in simple confidence in Him.

Do I come to Jesus because of what they say or because of what I see?

But as many as received Him, to them gave He power to become the sons of God, . . . which were born, not of blood, nor of the will of the flesh, nor of the will of man, but of God. (John 1:12–13)

The Life after new birth has very simple characteristics. In order to know whether we have been born from above RV mg), we must be guided by the revelation given by our Lord. One great characteristic of new birth is that we come to Jesus not only because of what we have heard about Him, but because of what we see He is to us now. Our Lord did not send forth His disciples on the ground of what He had done for them; He sent them because they had seen Him after His resurrection, and because they knew Who He was— "Now go and tell My brethren." Mary Magdalene was His first apostle, she was the one out of whom our Lord had cast seven devils, but that was not to be the ground of her going. It was not until she had realised Who her Lord was after His resurrection, and the altered relationship in which she now stood to Him, that He said—"Go." If Christ is formed in us, the great characteristic is that we know Him and perceive Him for ourselves. We do not need anyone to tell us about Him now, He is our Lord and Master.

Another characteristic of new birth is that Jesus Christ is easily first. Where do we go in a crisis? If we are born from above (RV mg) and Jesus Christ is Lord and Master, we will go direct as a homing pigeon to Him. The reason the majority of us know so little about the Lordship of Jesus Christ is that we only know the quickening of His Spirit, we have not gone on to the experience of Christ being formed in us. We know a great deal about the evangelical doctrine of being saved from hell, but very little about Galatians 1:15–16. In Acts 1:8 our Lord said this striking thing—"Ye shall be witnesses *unto Me."* When Christ is formed in us, we are a satisfaction to our Lord and Master wherever He places us. The point of importance is to know that we are just exactly where He has engineered our circumstances. There is no "foreign field" to our Lord. The reason we feel called to foreign mission work is because God introduces His own nature into us when we are identified with Jesus Christ (John 3:16). We know what the nature of God is like, because we see it manifested in Jesus Christ. Immediately Christ is formed in us, His nature begins to work through our hearts and to alter our conceptions.

Do I seek for signs of the kingdom of God, or do I see the rule of God?

Jesus answered and said unto him, Verily, verily, I say unto thee, Except a man be born again, he cannot see the kingdom of God. (John 3:3)

Another evidence of new birth is that we see the rule of God. We no longer see the haphazard of chance or fate, but by the experience of new birth we are enabled to see the rule of God everywhere. "Who hath believed that which we have heard? And to whom hath the arm of the LORD been revealed?" (Isaiah 53:1 RV mg). Literally, "Who has the power to discern the arm of the LORD?" We all see the common occurrences of our daily life, but who amongst us can perceive the arm of the Lord behind them? The saint recognises in all the ordinary circumstances of his life the hand of God and the rule of God, and Jesus says we cannot do that unless we are born from above (RV mg). In the beginning we only discern the rule of God in exceptional things, in crises like a friendship, or marriage, or death, but that is an elementary stage. As we go on we learn to see God's rule in all the ordinary haphazard circumstances of a common-sense life, and to say, "I shall never think of anything my Heavenly Father will forget, then why should I worry?" Are we irritable and worried? Then do not let us say we are born from above, because if what Jesus says is true, how can we worry? Worry means one of two things—private sin, or the absence of new birth. Nothing happens by chance to a saint, no matter how haphazard it seems. It is the order of God, and the experience of new birth means that we are able to discern the order of God.

The Sermon on the Mount is not a set of principles to be obeyed apart from identification with Jesus

Christ. The Sermon on the Mount is a statement of the life we will live when the Holy Spirit is getting His way with us. The Holy Spirit applies the principles of Jesus to our circumstances as God engineers them, and we have to see that we exhibit the new birth life at work. Tolstoi made the blunder of applying the principles of Jesus straight away to practical circumstances while he ignored the need for the new birth. Jesus Christ does not lay down the statements in the Sermon on the Mount as principles and say, "Now work them out," He is describing what the new life is in its working from His standpoint. When circumstances arise by God's providential engineering, and the Holy Spirit brings back some word to our remembrance, are we going to obey our Lord in that particular? Never debate when the Holy Spirit brings back a word of Jesus Christ. A fanatic is one who takes the statements of Jesus and tries to live up to the standard of them while he ignores the necessity of a personal relationship with God through new birth. We have not to live according to maxim, but according to the new life in us in which Jesus Christ is manifested.

Do I seek to stop sinning, or have I stopped sinning?

Whosoever is born of God doth not commit sin; for his seed remaineth in him: and he cannot sin, because he is born of God. (1 John 3:9)

Do we seek to stop sinning, or have we stopped sinning? We are always inclined to make theoretical what God makes practical. Learned divines and others talk about the sin question, and make it a doctrinal matter of dispute. In the Bible it is never, Should a Christian sin? The Bible puts it emphatically: *A Christian must not sin.* The confusion arises when the practical experimental doctrine is made a philosophical doctrine to do with God's election. Deliverance

from sin is not a question of God's election, but of an experience in human life which God demands. The effective working of the new birth life in us is that we do not commit sin, not merely that we have the power not to sin, but that we have stopped sinning—a much more practical thing.

The one thing that will enable us to stop sinning is the experience of new birth, i.e., entire sanctification. When we are born into the new realm the life of God is born in us, and the life of God in us cannot sin (1 John 3:9). That does not mean that we *cannot* sin; it means that if we obey the life of God in us, we *need not* sin. God never takes away our power to disobey; if He did, our obedience would be of no value, for we should cease to be morally responsible. By regeneration God puts in us the power not to sin. Our human nature is just the same after new birth as before, but the mainspring is different. Before new birth we sin because we cannot help it; after new birth we need not sin. There is a difference between sin and sins; sin is a disposition, and is never spoken of as being forgiven, a disposition must be cleansed. Sins are acts for which we are responsible. Sin is a thing we are born with, and we cannot touch it; God touches sin in redemption. If we have been trying to be holy, it is a sure sign we are not. Christians are born, not made. They are not produced by imitation, nor by praying and vowing; they are produced by new birth. "By the grace of God I am what I am."

The characteristic of new birth is that we deliberately obey all that God reveals through His Spirit. We yield ourselves so completely to God that Christ is formed in us. When He is formed in us, the characteristics of His life in our mortal flesh are that we see Jesus for ourselves; we see the rule of God; and we quit sinning—all by the wonder of His supernatural new birth in us, and that is how it works all through.

HIS UNRECORDED YEARS AND OUR HIDDEN LIFE

The new birth is illustrated by the supernatural advent of our Lord, not by the birth of a child into the world. Just as our Lord came into history from the outside, so He comes into our human nature from the outside. Our new birth is the birth of the Son of God into our old human nature, and our human nature has to be transfigured by the indwelling life of the Son of God. Mary, the mother of our Lord, is the type of our natural human life, which at critical moments so misunderstands the aims and objects of the Son of God. It was so in the historic life of our Lord, and it is true in our own personal experience. We make the blunder of imagining that when we are born from above (RV mg), we cease to be ordinary human beings, whereas we become much more ordinary human beings than we were before. Our human nature goes on all the time. All through the unrecorded years of our Lord's life His ordinary human life was being lived, nothing is recorded simply because there is nothing to record. After our birth from above there is a corresponding phase in our lives when the life of God goes on in the deep unconscious part of our lives and there is nothing to record.

The new birth is not the working of a natural law. The necessity for being born again is indicative of a huge tragedy. Sin has made the new birth necessary; it was not in the original design of God. New birth does not refer simply to a man's eternal salvation, but to his being of value to God in this order of things.

The Unrecorded Years

And the child grew, and waxed strong in spirit, filled with wisdom: and the grace of God was upon Him. (Luke 2:40)

When a young life passes from early childhood into girlhood or boyhood, there is a new birth of the mind, and the boy or girl becomes interested in literature, in poetry, and usually in religion; but that is not spiritual new birth, and has nothing to do with the working of the Spirit of God; it has to do with the ordinary natural development of the life. At this stage great devotion to God and to Christian service may be manifested, and this is apt to be looked on as an evidence of the work of the Spirit of God, whereas it is the mere outcome of the natural life beginning to unfold itself in the process of development. These things always go together—physical development, an alteration in bodily organs, and mental, moral, and spiritual development. The boy or girl sees more purely and clearly than the man or woman. No man thinks so clearly at any time or is ever so thrilled as he is in his "teens." Generally speaking, thirty years of age is the age of maturity. Some reach maturity before thirty and some after, but round about thirty is the age at which all the bodily and personal powers are matured. Up to that age, or what is represented by that age, life is full of promise, of visions, of uncertainties and expectations; after that there is no more promise, no more vision, the life has to be lived now in accord with all the visions it has had. There is a stage in ordinary natural life when maturity is reached, and if it is not reached someone is to blame. That is in the physical domain. In the spiritual domain the passing of the years counts for nothing. When we are born from above (RV mg) and the Son of God is formed in us, it is not the passing of the years that matures His life in us, but our obedience.

The angel said to Mary, "The Holy Ghost shall come upon thee, and the power of the most High shall overshadow thee: wherefore also the holy thing which shall be born shall be called the Son of God" (Luke 1:35 see RV mg). That is symbolical of what happens when the Holy Ghost overshadows us: our natural life is made the mother of the Son of God. What have we done with Him? Has He grown and developed? Has He been nourished and looked after, or has He been buried? When God comes does He find something dead in us instead of the real living Son of God? We have to nourish the life of the Son of God in us, and we do it by obedience, that is, by bringing our natural life into accordance with His life and transforming it into a spiritual life.

There is another element in this new life which is often overlooked, viz., that it is unconscious in its growth When Jesus said "Consider the lilies of the field, how they grow," He was referring to the new life in us. If we make His words apply to the natural life only, we make Him appear foolish. If we are born of God and are obeying Him, the unconscious life is forming in us just where we are. God knows exactly the kind of garden to put His lilies in, and they grow and take form unconsciously. What is it that deforms natural beauty? Overmuch cultivation; and overmuch denominational teaching will deform beauty in the spiritual world. Our danger is to take the place of God in regard to the new life. Jesus said, "Disciple in My *Name,*" My nature. The new life is in Him, and we have to remember that it grows like the lily. The right atmosphere for the new life to grow in is exactly where our natural life is placed. The things we cannot touch are not things for us to pout over, but things for us to accept as God's providential order for us. As natural men, we are not inclined to like the things God makes. At certain stages of our life we much prefer the friends we make to our God-made relations, because we can be noble with our friends, we have no past history with them. We cannot be noble with our relations, because they knew us when we were mean,[10] and now when

---

10. mean: as used here, something or someone ordinary, common, low, or ignoble, rather than cruel or spiteful.

we are with them we cannot put on the pretence, it won't work.

The new life must go on and take form unconsciously. God is looking after it, He knows exactly the kind of nourishment as well as the kind of disintegration that is necessary. Be careful that you do not bury the new life, or put it into circumstances where it cannot grow. A lily can only grow in the surroundings that suit it, and in the same way God engineers the circumstances that are best fitted for the development of the life of His Son in us. It is the unconscious form that is continually alluded to in the New Testament. We must allow plenty of time for God to develop that life.

We hear it asked, "What is the good of all this study and reading of the Bible? We get no 'change' out of it." Most of us want something to show for what we do. We are not interested in God's life in us, but only in our life in God. We are not after the development of the unconscious life of the Son of God in us, but after the "small change" which enables us to say, "I did this and that." The life of the Son of God grows feebler in a life of that order.

Every mind has two storeys, the conscious and the unconscious. Most of what we hear passes out of our conscious mind into our unconscious mind and we think we have forgotten it, but we have not, we never forget anything; we cannot always recall it when we want to, but that is a different matter. We forget nothing; it is there, although not in the conscious mind, and when certain circumstances arise, suddenly the thing we thought we had forgotten is there to our amazement right enough. This is exactly what Jesus said the Holy Ghost would do, "He shall . . . bring all things to your remembrance whatsoever I have said unto you." The Holy Spirit is forming the unconscious mind all the time, and as we "mop up" His teaching—simply take it in, not try to estimate it as we would a mathematical study—we shall find God is putting in the right soil for His life to grow in. Our one concern is to keep in the right atmosphere. Where we are actually is the Almighty's business, not ours. "Consider the lilies." Our Lord knows what to do with His own lilies; if we try to transplant them they will die. We are in such a desperate hurry, but it is in the unrecorded years, the times we are apt to think are of no account, that we are developing most for the value of the Son of God. There is a time coming when He will give an unveiled year, as He did in the life of His Son, and show what has been going on all the time.

The Unveiled Year

And the child grew, and waxed strong in spirit, filled with wisdom: and the grace of God was upon Him. . . .

And Jesus increased in wisdom and stature, and in favour with God and man. (Luke 2:40, 52)

In the Temple the Child Jesus was astonished that even His mother did not understand what He was doing. The one thing in us that makes us misunderstand Jesus Christ is our "Mary" life, i.e., our natural life.

God will bring us to an unveiled year, when we will realise how we have grown without knowing it, things have altered amazingly. For example, we go through a great personal crisis in our life with God, and we conjure up all kinds of imaginary difficulties as to how things are going to fit in now with this person and with that; but when we come up to the circumstances there is no external crisis at all, only the revelation of the tremendous alteration that has gone on in us unconsciously. When a crisis does come, it reveals that a tremendous alteration has taken place in us, and if there is any astonishment, it is in the fact that those whom we had thought would have understood us do not. Crises always reveal character. A great snare about crises is that we want to live for them. If we have had one great crisis in which the revelation has come of how wonderfully God has altered us, we will want another crisis. It is a risky business to live in crises. Most of our life is lived in ordinary human affairs, not in crises. It is comparatively easy for human nature to live in a big strain for a few minutes, but that is not what human nature is called upon to do. Human nature is called upon to live a life of drudgery. The intense awful crisis of the war[11] will be followed by years of drudgery for the lives that are left—shattered nerves, maimed men, and marred lives. We get our moments of light and insight when we see what God is after, and then we come to where there is no crisis, but just the ordinary life to be lived. By and by God will give an unveiled year and reveal the wonder of what He has been doing in us all the time.

His Environment and Ours

And when they were departed, behold, the angel of the Lord appeareth to Joseph in a dream, saying, Arise, and take the young child and his mother, and flee into Egypt, and be thou there until I bring thee word: for Herod will seek the young child to destroy Him. When he arose, he took the young child and his mother by night, and departed into Egypt. . . . (Matthew 2:13–14)

We each make our own environment; it is our personality that does it. Our Lord in His historic life came up against the providential order of tyranny, to

---

11. the war: World War I (1914–1918).

which He submitted; He also met hatred and detestation and compromise; and He is born into the same kind of circumstances in our bodily lives. So beware of getting on the line of "Oh, well, if only I had better circumstances." The circumstances of our Lord were anything but ideal, they were full of difficulties. Perhaps ours are the same, and we have to watch that we remain true to the life of the Son of God in us, not true to our own aims and ends. There is always a danger of mistaking our own aim and end for the aim of the life of God in us. Take it regarding the great subject of the Call of God. The call of God is a call according to the nature of God; where we go in obedience to that call depends entirely on the providential circumstances which God engineers, and is not of any moment. The danger is to fit the call of into the idea of our own discernment and say, "God called me *there.*" If we say so and stick to it, then it is good-bye to the development of the life of God in us. We have deliberately shifted the ground of His call to fit our own conception of what He wants.

The curse of much modern religion is that it makes us so desperately interested in ourselves, so overweeningly concerned about our own whiteness. Jesus Christ was absolutely interested in God, and the saint is to be a simple, unaffected, natural human being indwelt by the Spirit of God. If the saint is paying attention to the Source, Jesus Christ, out of him and unconsciously to him are flowing the rivers of living water wherever he goes (John 7:37–39). Men are either getting better or worse because of us.

His Intimates and Ours
Is not this the carpenter's son? is not his mother called Mary? and his brethren, James, and Joses, and Simon, and Judas? And his sisters, are they not all with us? Whence then hath this man all these things? (Matthew 13:55–56; see also Mark 3:21; Luke 2:51; John 7:5)

These were the intimates our Lord grew up with in His own historic life. We say, "Oh, but the Lord must have had a sweet and delightful home life." But we are wrong. He had an exceedingly difficult home life. Jesus Christ's intimates were brothers and sisters who did not believe in Him, and He says that the disciple is not above his Master (Luke 6:40). Jesus Christ was a Man among men, a Man living in unsullied communion with God. That is the kind of man He expects us to be through His regeneration of us. He went down to Nazareth, and "was subject unto them." An amazing submission! The next time you feel inclined to grouse over uncongenial companions, remember that Jesus Christ had a devil in His company for three years.

Our Lord preached His first public sermon in the place where He was brought up, where He was most intimately known, and they smashed up His service and tried to kill Him. "Oh, but," we say, "I expected that when I was saved and sanctified, my father and mother and brothers and sisters would be made right, but instead they seem to be all wrong." If the mother of our Lord misunderstood Him, and His brethren did not believe in Him, the same things will happen to His life in us, and we must not think it strange concerning the misunderstandings of others. The life of the Son of God in us is brought into the same kind of circumstances that the historic life of Jesus Christ was brought into, and what was true of Him will be true also of His life in us.

It is not only our intimates who will misunderstand Him, but we ourselves. There is a good deal in our natural human nature that will not understand the life of the Son of God, that will say to Him, as His own mother did, "Now is Your time to work a miracle." The natural in us will always want the Son of God to work in our way. Jesus said, "Woman, what have I to do with thee? Mine hour is not yet come," and Mary accepted the rebuke. Some of the things which belong to the life of the Son of God in us do not look sane or practical to the natural man, and when Christ is formed in us by His regenerating power, our natural life experiences what Mary experienced, "A sword shall pierce through thy own soul also," a sword we should never have known if we were not born of God; a type of suffering we should have known nothing about if the Son of God had not been formed in us. A sword had to go through the heart of Mary because of the Son of God, and because of the Son of God in us, a sword must go through our natural life, not our sinful life.

His Imagination and Ours
And He said unto them, How is it that ye sought Me? wist ye not that I must be about My Father's business? (Luke 2:49; see also Colossians 3:1–3)

Our Lord was absolutely taken up with His Father, that was the inner state of His mind. To Jesus the earth was His Father's house, and His Father's concerns possessed His imagination. The teaching in the Sermon on the Mount is on this line. Jesus says— "Don't make the ambition of your life in accordance with your old human nature, but be the children of the Highest—put your concentration on the things of God." Jesus Christ is not simply making fine characters or virtuous men; His end and aim is that we may be the children of our Father in heaven (Matthew 5:48).

Where is our imagination? In Colossians 3, we are told to set our affections on things above. That means concentration, and concentration is spiritual determination to fix the mind on the things of God. Don't say, "What shall I eat? What shall I drink?" but seek first the Kingdom of God. "Oh yes, I did get born again, but . . ." "Yes, God did do something for me, but . . ." You will soon "but" the whole thing out and leave yourself as you were before. Jesus says, "Be anxious for nothing, fix your mind on Me, be carefully careless about everything saving your relationship to Me." This will take time to do. When the unveiled year came it revealed where our Lord's mind was, and He was amazed that His mother's mind was not there too. "Wist ye not that I must be about My Father's business?" It was the question of an amazed and wistful child who felt His mother should have understood. Neither have we any excuse for not understanding what Jesus Christ is after; when we are born again, we ought to know exactly why His life is born into us—for the glory of God.

His Unageing Youth

Jesus said unto them, Verily, verily, I say unto you, Before Abraham was, I am. (John 8:58; see also Matthew 18:3–5)

Spiritually we never grow old; through the passing of the years we grow so many years young. The characteristic of the spiritual life is its unageing youth, exactly the opposite of the natural life. "I am . . . the First and the Last." The Ancient of Days represents the Eternal Childhood. God Almighty became the weakest thing in His own creation, a Baby. When He comes into us in new birth we can easily kill His life in us, or else we can see to it that His life is nourished according to the dictates of the Spirit of God so that we grow "unto the measure of the stature of the fulness of Christ." The mature saint is just like a little child, absolutely simple and joyful and gay. Go on living the life that God would have you live and you will grow younger instead of older. There is a marvellous rejuvenescence when once you let God have His way. If you are feeling very old, then get born again and do more at it.

HIS BAPTISM AND OUR VOCATION

His Baptism
- The Anticipations of John (John 1:26–34)
- The Attitude of Jesus Himself (Mark 1:9–11)
- The Acceptations of Jesus for Himself (Luke 3:21–23)
- The Appointment of Jesus in Himself (Matthew 3:13–15)

Our Vocation
- The Anticipations of God (Hebrews 2:9–10)
- The Attitude of the Saint Himself (1 Corinthians 1:26–29)
- The Acceptations of the Saint for Himself (Acts 20:24)
- The Appointment of the Saint in Himself (Philippians 3:10)

The age of thirty represents the perfection of physical, mental, and spiritual powers. Jesus Christ was thirty years of age when He was baptised; all His powers were fully matured. For thirty years our Lord had done nothing in public, then at the preaching of John the Baptist He emerged and was baptised with the baptism of John, which is a baptism of repentance from sin. Our Lord's baptism is not an illustration of the Christian rite of baptism, nor of the baptism of the Holy Ghost. At His baptism our Lord accepted His vocation, which was to bear away the sin of the

world (RV mg). We have no corresponding experience to that. Jesus Christ did not come to do anything less than to bear away the sin of the world, that is His vocation as Son of Man. By His bearing away the sin of the world, the way is opened up for every human being to get to God as if there had been no sin. The revelation in the Bible is not that Jesus Christ was punished for our *sins*; but that He took on Him the *sin* of the human race and put it away—an infinitely profounder revelation (see 2 Corinthians 5:21; Hebrews 9:26). All through the Bible it is revealed that our Lord bore the sin of the world by *identification*, and not by *sympathy*. He deliberately took upon His own shoulders, and bore in His own person, the whole massed sin of the human race. Our Lord knew what He had come to do, and His baptism is the first public manifestation of His identification with sin with a conscious understanding of what He was doing. At His baptism He visibly and distinctly and historically took upon Him His vocation.

The Anticipations of John

John answered them, saying, I baptize with water: but there standeth one among you, whom ye know not; He it is, who coming after you is preferred before me, whose shoe's latchet I am not worthy to unloose. . . . And John bare record, saying, I saw the Spirit descending from heaven like a dove, and it abode upon Him. And I knew Him not: but He that sent me to baptize with water, the same said unto me, Upon whom thou shalt see the Spirit descending, and remaining on Him, the same is He which baptizeth with the Holy Ghost. And I saw, and bare record that this is the Son of God. (John 1:26–34)

The anticipations of John, which were built upon the Old Testament, begin to be fulfilled in our Lord's baptism (Matthew 3:10–12). Jesus Christ is the true Baptiser; He baptises with the Holy Ghost. He is the Lamb of God which taketh away the sin of the world, my sin (1 John 2:1). He is the One Who can make me like Himself; the baptism of John could not do that.

The Anticipations of God

But we see Jesus, who was made a little lower than the angels for the suffering of death, crowned with glory and honour; that He by the grace of God should taste death for every man. For it became Him, for whom are all things, and by whom are all things, in bringing many sons unto glory, to make the captain of their salvation perfect through sufferings. (Hebrews 2:9–10)

God's anticipations work in us because our Lord accepted His vocation. God anticipates that He is going to bring sons and daughters, not "saved souls," to glory. A saved soul is simply one who has partaken of the mighty efficacy of Redemption. A son or daughter of God is one who has not only partaken of Redemption, but has become of value to God in this order of things.

We must ever make a practical distinction in our minds between the revelation of Redemption and the conscious experience of salvation. Redemption is absolutely finished and complete, but its reference to individual men is a question of their individual action. The whole human race is condemned to salvation by the Cross of our Lord. God nowhere holds a man responsible for having the heredity of sin; the condemnation begins when a man sees and understands that God can deliver him from the heredity of sin and he refuses to let Him do it; at that moment he begins to get the seal of damnation. John 3:19 is the final word of condemnation—"This is the judgement," i.e., the critical moment, "that the light is come into the world, and men loved the darkness rather than the light; for their works were evil."

Is God realising His anticipations in our lives? Is the Son of God reaching His maturity in us? The formation of the Son of God in us and our putting on of the new man must go together. We are brooded over by the Holy Ghost (Luke 1:35), and that which is formed in us is the Holy Son of God (Galatians 1:15–16). His life is formed in our human nature and it develops quietly in the unrecorded years. We live our ordinary life as human beings, remembering that our natural life, although delivered from sin, is continually in danger of misunderstanding the Son of God, just as Mary misunderstood her own Son.

In a hundred and one ways we can prefer that the sword should go through the Son of God in us rather than through our natural life, and that our natural impressions should have the ascendancy rather than the Son of God. The putting on of the new man means that we must not allow our natural life to dictate to the Son of God, but see to it that we give Him ample chance to dominate every bit of us. He has delivered us from sin, now we must see that He dominates our natural life also, until the life of Jesus is manifested in our mortal flesh.

This is the meaning of bringing a son or daughter to glory, and it is also the meaning of the efficacy of our Lord's baptism and the acceptance of His vocation being worked out in individual lives. Our Lord's vocation, which He accepted at His baptism, was His identification with sin. Our vocation is to fulfil the anticipations of God and to become His sons and daughters. The majority of us so harp on the ordinary evangelical line that we thank God for saving us and then leave the thing alone. We cannot grow *into* holiness, but we must grow *in* it. Are we accepting our vocation and determining to let the Son of God manifest Himself in our mortal flesh? If we are, it will mean that our human nature must be perfectly obedient to the Son of God and that we must bring all our imagination and fancies and thoughts into captivity to the obedience of Christ.

The Attitude of Jesus Himself

And it came to pass in those days, that Jesus came from Nazareth of Galilee, and was baptized of John in Jordan. And straightway coming up out of the water, he saw the heavens opened, and the Spirit like a dove descending upon Him: And there came a voice from heaven, saying, Thou art my beloved Son, in whom I am well pleased. (Mark 1:9–11)

The baptism of our Lord was an extraordinary spiritual experience to Himself. "And there came a voice from heaven, saying, Thou art my beloved Son, in whom I am well pleased." We have no experience like that; it stands unique. There is only one beloved Son of God; we are sons of God through His Redemption. John's baptism was a baptism of repentance from sin, and that was the baptism with which Jesus was baptised. He was baptised into sin, *made to be sin,* and that is why His Father was well pleased with Him. When our Lord took on Him His vocation as sin-bearer the Holy Ghost descended, and the voice of the Father came. The Holy Ghost descended on Him as a dove; He comes to us as fire. The descent of the

Holy Ghost and the voice of the Father were to our Lord the seal on His accepted vocation.

The Cross of Jesus Christ and His baptism express the same thing. Our Lord was not a martyr; He was not merely a good man; He was God Incarnate. He came down to the lowest reach of creation in order to bring back the whole human race to God, and in order to do this He must take upon Him, as representative Man, the whole massed sin of the race. That is why He is called "the Lamb of God." It was in this connection also that God said, "Thou art my beloved Son." "Though He were a Son, yet learned He obedience by the things which He suffered." The Son of God alone can redeem, and because He was the Son of God, He became Man that He might bring man back to God.

We so continually run down the revelations of the New Testament to the level of our own experience. That is wrong; we must let God lift up our experience to the standard of His word.

The Attitude of the Saint Himself
For ye see your calling, brethren, how that not many wise men after the flesh, not many mighty, not many noble, are called: but God hath chosen the foolish things of the world to confound the wise; and God hath chosen the weak things of the world to confound the things which are mighty; and base things of the world, and things which are despised, hath God chosen, yea, and things which are not, to bring to nought things that are: that no flesh should glory in His presence. (1 Corinthians 1:26–29)

This is our calling as saints, and it is the only line on which the Holy Spirit will witness to us. He will never witness to our wits, or to our intelligence, or to our physical perfections, or to our insight or genius, or to anything at all that is natural to us; He will only witness to that which has been produced in us by His Redemption. Are we watching our experience, or are we estimating the witness of the Holy Ghost? The Holy Ghost witnesses only to the Son of God, and not according to our fleshly estimates of things (2 Corinthians 5:16), and if we try and estimate Jesus Christ according to the flesh, we shall find there is no reality in it.

Spiritually, God always builds upon the weakest link, never on the strong link. The empires of the world were all founded on strong men, consequently they broke, because no chain is stronger than its weakest link. God Almighty became Incarnate as a helpless Babe in Bethlehem, and Jesus Christ begins His life in us by a new birth. Do we realise that our human nature has to become the birthplace of the Son of God, or have we only realised the miracle of God's changing grace? "Bring up this child for me." How is the life of the Son of God growing in our bodily life? Are we putting on the new man in keeping with the Son of God born in us? How is the Son of God progressing in the affections of our heart and the imaginations of our mind? Have we crushed Him? The historic Son of God was put to death because the wits and wisdom of this world could not agree with Him, but blasphemed Him and crucified Him, and the same thing may happen in any individual life. Watch the barriers God puts into your life. The natural life says, "I ought to be this and that." But God has told you you cannot. Woe be to you if you hanker for a second after the thing about which God has said "No" to you. If you do, you will put to death the life of God in you. Are you willing to accept the barrier from Him? It may be a barrier with regard to personal ambition for His service. This must be our attitude to ourselves—fellowship with the things that are despised, the things that look ostensibly weak to the wise things of the world. They are not weak to God because they are based on His Redemption. When we accept our vocation of sons and daughters of God, we become identified with the Son of God, Who was Himself despised and rejected of men.

The Acceptations of Jesus for Himself
Now when all the people were baptized, it came to pass, that Jesus also being baptized, and praying, the heaven was opened, and the Holy Ghost descended in a bodily shape like a dove upon Him, and a voice came from heaven, which said, Thou art My beloved Son; in Thee I am well pleased. And Jesus Himself began to be about thirty years of age, being (as was supposed) the son of Joseph, which was the son of Heli. (Luke 3:21–23)

We read that Jesus was in communion with His Father at the time of His baptism, "Jesus also being baptized, and praying." Our Lord accepted His vocation in the centre of His spirit, consequently the temptations when they came made no appeal to Him although they were based on amazingly wise strategy. Satan could not get near Him. The vocation our Lord had accepted was that of sin-bearer, not of dominating world-lord. Satan's aim was to get Him to fulfil His vocation on another line, "There is no need *to die* for sin, You can fulfil Your vocation by a 'short cut' and evade the cross." Our Lord came here for one purpose only—to bear away the sin of the world in His own Person on the Cross. He came to redeem men, not to set them a wonderful example.

The Acceptations of the Saint for Himself
But none of these things move me, neither count I my life dear unto myself, so that I might finish my course with joy, and the ministry, which I have received of the Lord Jesus, to testify the gospel of the grace of God. (Acts 20:24)

"None of these things move me," says Paul. What things? The things that were to smash Paul's heart, crumple up his body, and extinguish all his earthly ambitions. Have we accepted that kind of vocation, or are we only concerned that we get deep conscious communion with God? The acceptation of the saint for himself is that he is concerned about nothing at all saving this one thing, "that I might finish my course with joy," not happiness. Joy is the result of the perfect fulfilment of what a man is created for. Happiness depends on things that happen, and may sometimes be an insult. It is continually necessary to revert to what the New Testament asks us to accept about ourselves. Have we received this ministry from Jesus, "As Thou hast sent Me into the world, even so have I also sent them into the world"? How did the Father send Him? For I came down from heaven, not to do Mine own will, but the will of Him that sent Me." The first obedience of Jesus was to the will of His Father, not to the needs of men. Then our first accepted vocation is not to help men, but to obey God, and when we accept that vocation we enter into relationship with the despised and the neglected. It is always easy to neglect a man or woman who deliberately accepts the aim of his life from the Lord Jesus. Many of us are imitators of other people; we do Christian work because someone has asked us to do it. We must receive our ministry, which is to testify the gospel of the grace of God, from Jesus Christ Himself, not from other Christians. Paul determined to relate everything to Jesus Christ and Him crucified (1 Corinthians 2:2). "You may do what you like with my external circumstances, but you shall not deflect me by making me consider myself, I have only one end—to fulfil the ministry I have received of the Lord Jesus." Just as our Lord accepted His vocation and Satan could not turn Him from it, so we as sons of God through His Redemption have to accept our vocation and to fulfil the ministry we receive from Him. All the onslaught of Satan gathered round the Son of God to prevent Him from fulfilling His vocation, and Jesus says the same thing will happen to us. We must beware of affections, of imaginations, of successes, of practical work, of organisations—of everything and everyone that would deflect us for one second from Jesus Christ's purpose in our life. It will mean going "without the camp," the camp that wants to dictate over the head of Jesus Christ, "bearing His reproach."

The Appointment of Jesus in Himself
Then cometh Jesus from Galilee to Jordan unto John, to be baptized of him. But John forbad Him, saying, I have need to be baptized of Thee, and comest Thou to me? And Jesus answering said unto him, Suffer it to be so now: for thus it becometh us to fulfil all righteousness. (Matthew 3:13–15)

John knew Who Jesus Christ was, viz., the One Who was to baptise with the Holy Ghost and fire, and yet that One comes to him to be baptised with the baptism of repentance. No wonder John was amazed, and he refused to baptise Jesus until Jesus said, "Suffer it to be so now: for thus it becometh us to fulfil all righteousness." John as the forerunner of the Messiah had no business to introduce his own conceptions as to what was fitting for the Messiah; John had to obey just as the Messiah did. The vocation of our Lord was His identification with sin; He became absolutely and entirely identified with sin, and His baptism is the sign before the whole world of the acceptation of His vocation "This is what I am here for." It was not a baptism into power and dominion, but a baptism into identification with sin. The disposition of sin, i.e., my claim to my right to myself, entered into the human race by one man (Romans 5:12), and the Holy Spirit entered into the human race by another Man, so that "where sin abounded, grace did much more abound." Jesus Christ by His death bore away the sin of the world (RV mg), and by our identification with His death we can be delivered from the heredity of sin and can receive a new heredity, the unsullied holiness of Jesus Christ. We receive this new heredity not by imitation, but by identification, by giving up our right to ourselves to Jesus Christ (Galatians 2:20).

The Appointment of the Saint in Himself
That I may know Him, and the power of His resurrection, and the fellowship of His sufferings, being made conformable unto His death. (Philippians 3:10)

It is one thing to recognise what God is doing with us, but another thing to deliberately accept it as His appointment. We can never accept the appointment of Jesus Christ and bear away the sin of the world (RV mg), that was His work; but He does ask us to accept our cross. What is my cross? The manifestation of the fact that I have given up my right to myself to Him for ever. Self-interest, self-sympathy, self-pity—anything and everything that does not arise from a determination to accept my life entirely from Him will lead to a dissipation of my life. How many of us have dispassionately and clearly looked at Philippians 3:10? Paul is not speaking poetically but expressing plain, blunt, simple, spiritual, heroic fact. "That I may know Him"; not what He can do, nor what I can proclaim that He has done for me, but "that I *may know Him*, and the power of His resurrection"; that I continually receive my life from Him by deliberate appointment on my own part; "and the fellowship of His sufferings"; that I enter determinedly into His relationship with things, which means going contrary to my natural intuitions, "being made conformable unto His death." It is appalling how few are willing to efface their natural nobility. Fasting from food is an easy business, but fasting in its true nature means to fast from everything that is good until the appointments of God in my soul are accepted. For instance, there are times when a preacher if he is eloquent or poetical must fast from his own conceptions of things until he has accepted the appointment of God for his life. The One Who is being hit hardest in this war is Jesus Christ, and those of us who should have been fasting in fellowship with His sufferings have been out on the "noble natural" line, and the sword that was thrust at Him we have not turned aside but have lashed into Him, and been applauded for doing it. Being made conformable unto His death"; that I may be identified with the things in which He has interests; "if by any means I might attain unto the resurrection of the dead"; that I may have a resurrection like His, not merely the resurrection of a saved soul, but of one who has proved himself a son of God by the redemption of our Lord.

Many of us are not living in the domain in which Christianity can alone be lived—the domain of deliberate identification with Jesus Christ. It takes time, and it ought to take time, and the time is not misspent for the soul who will wait before God and accept His appointment for his individual life.

HIS TEMPTATION AND OURS
Hebrews 2:18; 4:15–16

The Isolation of Mastership (Matthew 4:1–2)
    His Watch in Faith (Matthew 4:3–4)
    His Wait in Hope (Matthew 4:5–7)
    His Way of Love (Matthew 4:8–10)
    The Limit to the Devil (Matthew 4:11)

The Inner Martyrdom (1 Peter 4:12–13)
    Our Lure of Wits (Matthew 11:6)
    Our Light of Wisdom (John 12:16)
    Our Liberty of Wonders (Luke 17:21)
    The Limit to Temptation (1 Corinthians 10:13)

Temptation is not sin; we are bound to meet it if we are men. Not to be tempted would be to be beneath contempt. Temptation is a suggested short cut to the realisation of the highest at which we aim. The way steel is tested is a good illustration of temptation. Steel can be "tired" in the process of testing, and in this way its strength is measured. Temptation is the testing by an alien power of the possessions held by a personality in order that a higher and nobler character may come out of the test.

This makes the temptation of our Lord explainable. He held in His own Person His unspotted sanctity and the fact that He was to be the King of men and the Saviour of the world; and Satan was the alien power that came to test Him on these lines. The period of temptation came immediately after one of spiritual exaltation (Matthew 3:16–17; 4:1). It was a period of estimating forces, and the records reveal how our Lord faced and rejected the visions of a swift fulfilment of His vocation presented to Him by Satan. Jesus Christ in His baptism had accepted His vocation of bearing away the sin of the world, and immediately He was put by God's Spirit into the testing machine of the devil. But He did not "tire"; He retained the possessions of His personality intact. He was tempted, "yet without sin."

The temptations of our Lord have no home at all in our human nature; they do not appeal to us because they are removed from any affinity with the natural. Our Lord's temptations and ours move in different spheres until we become His brethren, by being born again (Hebrews 2:11). The temptations of Jesus are not those of Man as man, but the temptations of God as Man. The statement that our Lord was tempted as ordinary men are is readily accepted, but the Bible does not say that He was so tempted. Jesus Christ was not born with a heredity of sin; He was not tempted in all points as ordinary men are, but tempted like His brethren, those who have been born from above (RV mg) by the Spirit of God and placed in the Kingdom of God by supernatural regeneration.

The records of our Lord's temptations are given not that we might fathom Him, but that we might know what to expect when we are regenerated. When we are born again of the Spirit of God and enter into fellowship with Jesus Christ, then the temptations of our Lord are applicable to us. We are apt to imagine that when we are saved and sanctified we are delivered from temptation; we are not, we are loosened into it. Before we are born again, we are not free enough to be tempted, neither morally nor spiritually. Immediately we are born into the Kingdom of God, we get our first introduction into what God calls temptation, viz., the temptations of His Son. God does not shield any man or woman from the requirements of a full-grown man or woman. The Son of God is submitted to temptations in our individual lives, and He expects us to remain loyal to Him (Luke

22:28). The honour of Jesus Christ is at stake in our bodily life. Are we remaining loyal to the Son of God in the things, which beset His life in us? The personality of a saint holds all that God intends a man or woman to be, and the temptation to him comes along the line it came to our Lord—to fulfil what his personality holds on a line other than God intends.

The Isolation of Mastership (Matthew 4:1–11)

Then was Jesus led up of the Spirit into the wilderness to be tempted of the devil. And when He had fasted forty days and forty nights, He was afterward an hungred. (Matthew 4:1–2)

The Spirit of God drove our Lord into the wilderness for one purpose—to be tempted of the devil, not only to test Him, but to reveal what Christian mastership means. In that isolation the Lord Jesus Christ met the strong man and overcame him and bound him, and He gives us "power . . . over all the power of the enemy." The writer to the Hebrews does not say, "When you are tempted, imitate Jesus"; he says, "Go to Jesus, and He will succour you in the nick of time." That is, all His perfect overcoming of temptation is ours (Hebrews 2:18).

The Bible reveals that man is responsible for the introduction of Satan. Satan is the result of a communication between man and the devil, and man must deal with Satan; God does not deal with him direct. Satan is to be overcome and conquered by human beings. That is why God became Incarnate. It is in the Incarnation that Satan is overcome.

The Inner Martyrdom

Beloved, think it not strange concerning the fiery trial which is to try you, as though some strange thing happened unto you: but rejoice, inasmuch as ye are partakers of Christ's sufferings; that, when His glory shall be revealed, ye may be glad also with exceeding joy. (1 Peter 4:12–13)

In the history of the Church inner martyrdom and external martyrdom have rarely gone together. We are familiar with external martyrdom, but inner martyrdom is infinitely more vital. Paul deals with it in Philippians 2. "Christ Jesus . . . made Himself of no reputation"; that is, He annihilated by His own deliberate choice all His former position of glory, "and took upon Him the form of a servant." If we are to be in fellowship with Him we must deliberately go through the annihilation, not of glory, but of our former right to ourselves in every shape and form. Until this inner martyrdom is gone through, temptation will always take us unawares. Peter says, "Beloved, think it not strange concerning the fiery trial which is to try you." The internal distresses are accounted for by the fact that the saint is being taken into an understanding of what our Lord went through when He was driven by the Spirit into the wilderness to be tempted. Satan tried to put Jesus Christ on the way to becoming King of the world and Saviour of men in a way other than that pre-determined by God. The devil does not tempt us to do wrong things; he tries to make us lose what God has put into us by regeneration, the possibility of being of value to God. When we are born from above (RV mg) the central citadel of the devil's attack is the same in us as it was in our Lord—viz., to do God's will in our own way.

His Watch in Faith

And when the tempter came to Him, he said, If thou be the Son of God, command that these stones be made bread. But He answered and said, It is written, Man shall not live by bread alone, but by every word that proceedeth out of the mouth of God. (Matthew 4:3–4)

In each of the three never-to-be-forgotten pictures which our Lord has given us the temptation of Satan centres round this point—"You are the Son of God, then do God's work in Your own way; assert Your prerogative of Sonship." The first temptation was to set up a Selfish Kingdom. "You are the Son of God, then command these stones to be made bread; You do not need to be hungry; satisfy Your own needs and the needs of men, and You will get the Kingship of men." Was Satan right? Read John 6:15—"Jesus perceived that they would come and take Him by force, to make Him a king." Why? He had just fed five thousand of them! It must have been a dazzling vision that Satan presented to our Lord, for who could ever have such sympathy with the needs of men as He? For one impressive moment He must have wondered. But our Lord would not be King of men on that line. "But He answered and said, It is written, Man shall not live by bread alone, but by every word that proceedeth out of the mouth of God." He deliberately rejected the suggested "short cut," and chose the "long, long trail," evading none of the suffering involved.

In His temptation our Lord does not stand as an individual Man; He stands as the whole human race vested in one Personality, and every one of us when regenerated can find his place and fellowship in those temptations.

Our Lure of Wits

And blessed is he, whosoever shall not be offended in Me. (Matthew 11:6)

The deep dejection of John is the dejection of a great man (Matthew 11:11). John's misgivings arose from the fact that the wonderful things God had told him about the Messiah, Whom he foreran, seemed to be without application to Jesus Christ (Matthew 3:11–12). It was a case of wits *versus* revelation.

The first temptation of our Lord comes to us on this line—"Be sensible, You are here for the service of men, and surely it is the most practical thing to feed them and satisfy their needs." The clamour abroad to-day is all on this line, "Put man's needs first; never mind about the first commandment, the second commandment is the all-important one" (see Mark 12:29–31). This advice sounds sensible and right, but at its heart is the temptation of Satan to put men's needs first. The insistent demand in the world to-day to put men's needs before God's will is the outcome of the reasoning of human wits and wisdom, and who can say that the demand is a wrong one? So long as our wits and human solutions are on the throne, to satisfy the needs of men is ostensibly the grandest thing to do. Every temptation of Satan will certainly seem right to us unless we have the Spirit of God. Fellowship with our Lord is the only way to detect them as being wrong.

The conditions of our civilised life to-day ought to be realised more keenly by the Christian than by the natural man, but we must see that the worship of God is put on the throne and not our human wits. The evidence of Christianity is not the good works that go on in the world; these are the outcome of the good there is in human nature, which still holds remnants of what God designed it to be. There is much that is admirable in the civilisation of the world, but there is no promise in it. The natural virtues exhaust themselves; they do not develop. Jesus Christ is not a social reformer; He came to alter *us* first, and if any social reform is to be done on earth, we will have to do it. Social reform is part of the work of ordinary honourable humanity and a Christian does it because his worship is for the Son of God, not because he sees it is the most sensible thing to do. The first great duty of the Christian is not to the needs of his fellow-men, but to the will of his Saviour. We have to remember the counsel of our Lord, given from the centre of His own agony, "Watch and pray, that ye enter not into temptation," keep stedfastly true to what you know is God's order and listen to no suggestions from elsewhere. The one thing that will keep us watching and praying is continuing to worship God while we do our duty in the world as ordinary human beings.

His Wait in Hope
Then the devil taketh Him up into the holy city, and setteth Him on a pinnacle of the temple, and saith unto Him, If Thou be the Son of God, cast Thyself down: for it is written, He shall give His angels charge concerning thee: And in their hands they shall bear thee up, lest at any time thou dash thy foot against a stone. Jesus said unto him, It is written again, Thou shalt not tempt the Lord thy God. (Matthew 4:5–7)

This temptation presents a wild reach of possibility: "You are the Son of God, then fling Yourself off the pinnacle of the temple; do something supernatural; use signs and wonders and bewitch men so that they will be staggered out of their wits by amazement, and the world will be at Your feet. Set up a Spectacular Kingdom." Our Lord never once used signs and wonders to get a man off his guard and then say, "Now believe in Me." Jesus Christ never coerced anybody, He never used supernatural powers or the apparatus of revival; He refused to stagger human wits into submitting to Him, He always put the case to a man in cold blood, "Take time and consider what you are doing" (cf. Luke 9:57–62). Jesus Christ is engaged in making disciples in the internal sense, consequently He never entrances a man by rapture, or enamours him out of his wits by fascination. Instead, He puts Himself before a man in the baldest light conceivable, "If you would be My disciple, these are the conditions" (see Luke 14:26–27 and 33). A man must believe in Jesus Christ by a deliberate determination of his own choice. The temptation to the Church is to go into the "show business." Our Lord told His disciples they would be witnesses unto Him, a satisfaction to Him wherever they were placed (Acts 1:8).

Our Light of Wisdom
These things understood not His disciples at the first: but when Jesus was glorified, then remembered they that these things were written of Him, and that they had done these things unto Him. (John 12:16)

Our Lord's temptations are carefully presented so that we may know the kind of temptation to expect when His life is formed in us. This temptation is apt to come with tremendous lure after the experience of sanctification—"Now that I am saved and sanctified, God will surely turn the world upside down and prove what a wonderful thing He has done in me—every unsaved soul will be saved, every devil-possessed man delivered, and every sick person healed!" "You will easily get Your Kingship of men if You will use signs and wonders and stagger men's wits," said Satan to our Lord, and the same temptation comes to the Church and to individual Christians, His brethren. It sounds right to ask God to produce signs and wonders, and all through the twenty centuries of the Christian era this temptation has been yielded to, every now and again, in the most wild and inordinate manner. For the past ten years or more it has been in our midst in the Tongues movement, and hundreds of those who were really enlightened by the Spirit of God have gone off on the line of this temptation.

We are apt to have the idea that we can only estimate what God is in us by what He does through us. What about our Lord and Master, what did He do?

The marvellous thing about Him is what He did not do. Think what an ignominious failure His life was, judged from every standpoint but God's. Our Lord did not say that signs and wonders would not follow, but that the one set purpose for us is that we do God's will in His way, not in our way. All the wisdom seems to be with the temptations, but our Lord by the light of the Holy Ghost reveals where they are wrong. Are we prepared to continue with the Son of God in His temptations in us, or are we going to betray Him and say, "Now that I am saved and sanctified, I must expect God to do wonders"? It sounds right and wise, and it commends itself to our natural wisdom if once we forget our Lord's counsel to watch and pray.

His Way of Love

Again, the devil taketh Him up into an exceeding high mountain, and showeth Him all the kingdoms of the world, and the glory of them; And saith unto Him, All these things will I give Thee, if Thou wilt fall down and worship me. Then saith Jesus unto him, Get thee hence, Satan: for it is written, Thou shalt worship the Lord thy God, and Him only shalt thou serve. (Matthew 4:8–10)

Our Lord was then asked to compromise: "You will become the king of men and the Saviour of the world by judicious compromise; build Your Kingdom on broadminded lines; be judicious, You know there is evil in the world; then use it wisely, and don't be so intense against sin; don't talk about the devil and hell; don't be so extreme and say a man needs to be born from above (RV mg). Tolerate my rule of the world, call things 'necessary evils'; tell men sin is not anarchy, but a disease; fall down and worship me and my way of looking at things, and I will withdraw and the whole world will be Yours. Establish a Socialistic Kingdom." The first sign of the dethronement of Jesus is the apparent absence of the devil, and the peaceful propaganda that is spread after he has withdrawn. Will the Church that bows down and compromises succeed?

Of course it will; it is the very thing that the natural man wants. This line of temptation as revealed by our Lord is the most appallingly subtle of all.

Temptation yielded to is lust deified. In the Bible, the term "lust" is used of other things than merely of immorality. It is the spirit of, "*I must have it at once, I will have my desire gratified, and I will brook no restraint.*" Each temptation of our Lord contains the deification of lust—"You will get the Kingship of the world at once by putting men's needs first; use signs and wonders, and You will get the Kingship of men at once; compromise with evil, judiciously harmonise with natural forces, and You will get the Kingship of men at once." At the heart of every one of our Lord's answers are these words: "For I came down from heaven not to do Mine own will, but the will of Him that sent Me" (John 6:38), that is "I came to do God's work in His way, not in My own way, although I am the Son of God."

The temptation to win and woo men is the most subtle of all, and it is a line that commends itself to us naturally. But you cannot win and woo a mutiny; it is absolutely impossible. You cannot win and woo the man who, when he recognises the rule of God, detests it. The Gospel of Jesus Christ always marks the line of demarcation, His attitude all through is one of sternness, there must be no compromise. The only way in which the Kingdom of God can be established is by the love of God as revealed in the Cross of Jesus Christ, not by the lovingkindness of a backboneless being without justice or righteousness or truth. The background of God's love is holiness. His is not a compromising love, and the Kingdom of our Lord can only be brought in by means of His love at work in regeneration. Then when we are regenerated we must not insult God by imagining that in dealing with our fellow-men we can afford to ignore the need for Redemption and simply be kind and gentle and loving to all.

Our Liberty of Wonders
Neither shall they say, Lo here! or, lo there! for, behold, the kingdom of God is within you. (Luke 17:21)

"The Kingdom of God is within you"—uncompromisingly within you. We must never compromise with the kingdoms of this world; the temptation the devil presents is that we should compromise. We recognise his temptation in the teaching which proclaims that there is no such being as the devil and no such place as hell; much that is called sin is a mere defect; men and women are like poor babes lost in the wood; just be kind and gentle with them; talk about the Fatherhood of God, about Universalism and Brotherhood, the kindness of Providence and the nobility of man. Our Lord's temptations reveal where the onslaught will come. To-day, through an overplus of Christian activities, Jesus Christ is being dethroned in hearts and Christian wits and wisdom are taking His place; consequently, when trials and difficulties come most of us are at our wits' end because we have succumbed to one or another of these temptations.

The Limit to the Devil
Then the devil leaveth Him, and, behold, angels came and ministered unto Him. (Matthew 4:11)

The sign of victory is that the temptation has been gone through with successfully. If our Lord had failed in any degree, the angels would have had no affinity with Him. The affinities of a man after a period of temptation prove whether he has yielded to it or not. The practical test for us when we have been through a season of temptation is whether we have a finer and deeper affinity for the highest. Temptation must come, and we do not know what it is until we meet it. When we do meet it, we must not debate with God, but stand absolutely true to Him no matter what it costs us personally, and we will find that the onslaught will leave us with higher and purer affinities than before.

The Limit to Temptation

There hath no temptation taken you but such as is common to man: but God is faithful, who will not suffer you to be tempted above that ye are able; but will with the temptation also make a way to escape, that ye may be able to bear it. (1 Corinthians 10:13)

God does not keep us from temptation, He succours us in the midst of it. Temptation is not something we may escape; it is essential to the full-orbed life of a son of God. We have to beware lest we think we are tempted as no one else is tempted. What we go through is the common inheritance of the race, not something no one ever went through before. It is most humiliating to be taken off our pedestal of suffering and made to realise that thousands of others are going through the same thing as we are going through. Under the three pictures presented by our Lord every temptation of the devil is embraced; we must ever remember the counsel of our Lord to watch and pray lest we enter into temptation. Prayer is easy for us because of all it cost the Son of God to make it possible for us to pray. It is on the basis of His Redemption that we pray, not on the basis of our penetration, or of our wits or understanding.

HIS TRANSFIGURATION AND OUR SECRET

Our Lord's Attitude (Luke 9:28)
 Prayer always transfigures

The Attitude of the Disciples (Luke 9:32)
 The natural must sleep

Our Lord's Aspect (Luke 9:29)
 Pre-Incarnate Glory

The Aspect of the Disciples (Luke 9:32)
 Face to face with Reality

Our Lord's Attendants (Mark 9:4)
 Converse with the Glorified

The Attention of the Disciples (Luke 9:32)
 They saw His glory and His companions

Our Lord's Attention (Luke 9:31)
 His Death the Theme of Glory

The Amazement of the Disciples (Mark 9:5–6)
 Hysterical Suggestions

Almighty God's Ascription (Luke 9:35)

God Incarnate

The Awe of the Disciples (Luke 9:34)
 God's Word

As has been already stated, Christian Psychology is not the study of human nature Christianised, but the endeavour to understand the wonder and the mystery of "Christ in you, the hope of glory." Jesus Christ must ever be profoundly more than we can fathom, but we must study Him in order to get to know the characteristics of the new life which is to be manifested in our mortal flesh.

The Apostle John does not allude to the Transfiguration in his Gospel, yet his Gospel is written from that standpoint, the standpoint of the exceeding majesty of the Lord Jesus Christ.

According to the revelation of the Bible, our Lord is not to be looked upon as an individual Man, but as the One Who represents the whole human race. At His Baptism our Lord accepted His vocation as sinbearer, the Holy Ghost descended upon Him as Son of Man, and the voice of God came with the Divine approval; and at the Transfiguration the voice of God came again. The Baptism and the Transfiguration reveal Who our Lord is, and the secret of the Christian is that he knows the absolute Deity of Jesus Christ.

The Transfiguration occurs practically in the centre of our Lord's earthly ministry. The fulfilment of the Transfiguration is the Ascension. These two mountain peaks, without the Cross and the Resurrection, would portray the development of human life had there been no sin. The Cross and the Resurrection deal with sin and the need of Redemption.

Our Lord's Attitude

And it came to pass about an eight days after these sayings, He took Peter and John and James, and went up into a mountain to pray. (Luke 9:28)

In our Lord's presentation, prayer is the point where the Reality of God merges with human life. Until we are born from above (RV mg), prayer with us is honestly nothing more than a mere exercise; but in all our Lord's teaching and in His own personal life, as well as in the emphasis laid on prayer by the Holy Ghost after He had gone, prayer is regarded as *the* work (see John 14:11–13). Prayer in the Son of God as Son of Man is amazingly significant. If prayer is the highest reach of communion possible between Almighty God and the Son of Man, what part ought prayer to play in our lives? Prayer with us often becomes merely a way of patronising God. Our Lord's view of prayer is that it represents the highest reach possible to a man or woman when rightly related to God, perfectly obedient in every particular, and in perfect communion with Him. Prayer is not meant to develop us, but to develop the life of God in us after new birth.

The Attitude of the Disciples

But Peter and they that were with him were heavy with sleep. (Luke 9:32)

The natural must sleep. If we are ever going to know Who the Lord Jesus Christ is we must be born from above (RV mg) into another Kingdom, and discern by a power other than our natural wits. The natural is not sinful, but the natural is not spiritual. When the Redemption of God has dealt with sin and delivered from it, then the natural must be sacrificed. Simeon said to the mother of Jesus, "Yea, a sword shall pierce through thy own soul also," but not because of sin. Mary was the natural mother of the Son of God, and in that wonderful experience of the incoming of the Son of God into the human race she stands for our human nature. The natural has to be transfigured and subordinated to the spiritual; it must not obtrude itself.

It was required of Adam, the Federal Head of the human race, that he should turn his natural life into a spiritual life by obedience. That is, he was to have dominion over the life in the air and in the earth and in the sea, but he was not to have dominion over himself; God was to have dominion over him, and as he obeyed God his natural life would be turned into a spiritual life. Adam represented what Jesus Christ represents, viz., the whole human race, and if Adam had obeyed and transformed his innocence into holiness by a series of moral choices, the transfiguration of the human race would have happened in due course. But Adam disobeyed, and there entered in the disposition of sin, the disposition of self-realisation—I am my own God. This disposition may work out in a hundred and one different ways, in decorous morality or in indecorous immorality, but it has the one basis—my claim to my right to myself. That disposition was never in our Lord. Self-will, self-assertiveness, self-seeking were never in Him. When we become rightly related to God, we are not simply put back into the relationship Adam was in, but into a relationship Adam was never in; we are put into the Body of Christ, and then God does not shield us from any of the requirements of sons. We have the notion at first that when we are saved and sanctified by God's supernatural grace, He does not require us to do anything, but it is only then that He begins to require anything of us. God did not shield His own Son; not only did He not shield Him, but He allowed Him to be driven into the wilderness to be tempted of the devil. After the baptism of Jesus and the descent of the Holy Ghost upon Him, God took His sheltering hand off Him, as it were, and let the devil do his worst. So after the work of sanctification, when the life of a saint really begins, God lifts His hand off and lets the world, the flesh, and the devil do their worst, for He is assured that "greater is He that is in you, than he that is in the world."

The trouble comes when we forget that the Son of God is born into our old human nature. Whether we are six years old or sixty, our human nature is thousands of years old. Jesus Christ says that His Father makes His revelations, not to the virtues of human nature, not to the astute wisdom accumulated by the ages, but to "babes." Our Lord's words can only be understood by those who are born from above (RV mg), and He reveals Himself only to such. The Church of Jesus Christ is built on these two things: the Divine revelation of Who Jesus Christ is, and the public confession of it (see Matthew 16:13–19).

Our Lord's Aspect

And as He prayed, the fashion of His countenance was altered, and His raiment was white and glistening. (Luke 9:29)

Our Lord had emptied Himself of His glory for the purposes of the Incarnation, and the Transfiguration reveals His glory again. The subliminal nature of Jesus was absolute Deity, and it was that subliminal nature, the glory which He had with the Father before the world was, that suddenly burst through on the Mount of Transfiguration, and gave the manifestation of God and Man in perfect oneness—in His Son, God became His own Incarnation. The Apostle John is insistent that any tendency to dissolve the Person of Jesus by analysis is anti-Christ (1 John 4:1–3). It is this pre-Incarnate glory that is being dissolved to-day. The dissolving of the Person of Jesus by analysis is prevalent because men refuse to know Him after the Spirit, they will only know Him after the reasoning of their own minds. The test of any teaching is its estimate of Jesus Christ. The teaching may sound wonderful and beautiful, but watch lest it have at its centre the dethroning of Jesus Christ.

The Aspect of the Disciples
And when they were awake, they saw His glory, and the two men that stood with Him. (Luke 9:32)

The disciples were with Jesus Christ on the Mount, and in his Epistle, Peter records what they saw there; he says, "we were eyewitnesses of His majesty" (2 Peter 1:16). Jesus Christ is no Comrade to Peter, He is absolute King of kings. In the Apocalypse the Apostle John gives the same revelation of the appalling and sublime majesty of Jesus Christ. The disciples are fully awake now and face to face with Reality.

Intellectual thinking and reasoning never yet got a man to Reality, because these are instruments of life, and not the life itself. Our only organ for getting at Reality is conscience, and the Holy Spirit always deals with conscience first. Intellect and emotions come in afterwards as the instruments of human expression.

The disciples came down from the Mount into the demon-possessed valley, but it was not until after the Cross and the Resurrection that they began to understand what they had seen, the reason being that what they had seen in vision on the Mount had to be worked out into actual experience in their lives. By the presence of the Holy Ghost in us we know Who the Lord Jesus is. We know Him after the Spirit. The Holy Spirit glorifies the Lord Jesus to us and in us until we know Who He is, and know the exceeding majesty of Him Who said, "All power is given unto Me in heaven and in earth." We do not know this by our intellect or by our sensible reasoning, but by the real witness of the Paraclete of God. The eyes of the disciples needed to be opened by the impartation of quickening life from our Lord after the Resurrection before they knew Him (Luke 24:16, 31); and the only way in which we can know our Lord is by His Spirit.

Our Lord's Attendants
And there appeared unto them Elias and Moses: and they were talking with Jesus. (Mark 9:4)

Jesus was standing in the full blaze and glory of His pre-Incarnate glory while the two representatives of the Old Covenant talked with Him about the issue which He was about to accomplish at Jerusalem. Then He turned His back upon that glory, and came down from the Mount to be identified with fallen humanity, symbolised by the demon-possessed boy. Had He gone back into the glory which was His before the Incarnation having only reached the Mount of Transfiguration, He would have left the human race exactly where it was; His life would only have been a sublime ideal. There are many who look at the life of Jesus Christ as an ideal and nothing more—"His teachings are so fine, we do not need to have anything to do with the Atonement, or with those crude doctrines of the Apostle Paul's about the Cross and personal apprehension; it is quite enough for us to have the Sermon on the Mount." I should think it was! If Jesus Christ came to be an Example only, He is the greatest torturer of the human race. But our Lord did not come primarily to teach us and give us an example; He came to lift us into a totally new kingdom, and to impart a new life to which His teachings would apply.

The Attention of the Disciples
And when they were awake, they saw His glory, and the two men that stood with Him. (Luke 9:32)

The disciples were eye and ear-witnesses of all that transpired on the Mount. There is a curious insistence in the records on the fact that our Lord at His Transfiguration and in the Garden of Gethsemane, took His disciples to be witnesses of things which they could never experience. We see one reason why Jesus took them in Peter's Epistles and in John's Gospel. The Christian faith must stand in an Almighty Christ, not in a human being who became Divine.

Our Lord's Attention
Who appeared in glory, and spake of His decease which He should accomplish at Jerusalem. (Luke 9:31)

The visitants on the Mount talked to Jesus in all His majesty and glory of Almighty God, but they spoke of His death, not of His glory. Does not that seem an appalling anticlimax? The whole of their attention is centred on the death of the Lord Jesus. The word "death" has the meaning of "issue." They spoke of the issue He was about to accomplish at Jerusalem by His death, viz., the historic manifestation of the Redemption of the human race.

The Redemption of the human race does not necessarily mean the salvation of every individual. Redemption is of universal application, but human responsibility is not done away with. Jesus Christ states emphatically that there are possibilities of eternal damnation for the man who positively[12] neglects or positively rejects His Redemption.

Jesus Christ emptied Himself of His glory a second time; He came down from the Mount of Transfiguration and accomplished His death at Jerusalem—for what purpose? That any individual of the human race might go straight to the heart of God without the slightest fear, because of what Jesus did on the Cross. This is the great effective working of Redemption in human experience. Our Lord's death

---

12. positive: independent; unrelated to anything else.

is not the death of a martyr; it is the exhibition of the heart of God, broken in order to bring the whole human race back into perfect oneness with Himself.

The death of Jesus is the only entrance into the life He lived. We cannot get into His life by admiring Him, or by saying what a beautiful life His was, so pure and holy. To dwell only on His life would drive us to despair. We enter into His life by means of His death. Until the Holy Spirit has had His way with us spiritually, the death of Jesus Christ is an insignificant thing, and we are amazed that the New Testament should make so much of it. The death of Jesus Christ is always a puzzle to unsaved human nature. Why should the Apostle Paul say, "For I determined not to know any thing among you, save Jesus Christ, and Him crucified"? Because unless the death of Jesus has the meaning the Apostle Paul gave to it, viz., that it is the entrance into His life, the Resurrection has no meaning for us either. The life of Jesus is a wonderful example of a perfect human life, but what is the good of that to us? What is the good of presenting to us a speckless holiness that is hopeless of attainment? It would simply tantalise us. Unless Jesus Christ can put a totally new heredity into us, there is no use asking us to think about the wonderful life He lived. The revelation made by the Redemption is that God can put into us a new disposition whereby we can live a totally new life.

Now we can see why our Lord lived the life He did for thirty-three years. Before He made the entrance into that life possible for any human being, He had to show us what the life of God's normal man was like. The life of Jesus is the life we have to live here, not hereafter. There is no chance to live this kind of life hereafter, we have to live it here. Our Lord's death is not the death of a martyr, not the death of a good man; His cross is the Cross of God, whereby any human being can enter into a totally new life. The way into the life of Jesus is not by imitation of Him, but by identification with His Cross. That is the meaning of being born from above (RV mg): we enter into His life by its entering into us.

We talk about imitating Jesus, but isn't it highly absurd! Before we have taken three steps, we come across lust, pride, envy, jealousy, hatred, malice, anger—things that never were in Him, and we get disheartened and say there is nothing in it. If Jesus Christ came to *teach* the human race only, He had better have stayed away. But if we know Him first as Saviour by being born again, we know that He did not come to teach merely: He came to *make* us what He teaches we should be; He came to *make* us sons of God. He came to give us the right disposition, not to tell us that we ought not to have the wrong one; and the way into all these benedictions is by means of His death.

To Christianise human nature is simply to veneer that which is not real. The life of Jesus Christ is the Standard, and we receive His life by means of His Death. The emphasis on His death is explained when we remember that His teaching only applies to His life in us. When we preach Christ, it is not His birth that we preach, but His Cross, and we bring ourselves face to face with the wonder and the power of His resurrection life.

The Amazement of the Disciples
And Peter answered and said to Jesus, Master, it is good for us to be here: and let us make three tabernacles; one for Thee, and one for Moses, and one for Elias. For he wist not what to say; for they were sore afraid. (Mark 9:5–6)

Peter wist not what to say, then why did he say it? Have you never said things you should not have said? If we get a great grasp in vision of Who Jesus is and try to work it out in our ordinary human life by the energy of the flesh, we shall do what Peter did, talk nonsense through sheer bewilderment. When we come to Peter's Epistles, there is nothing hysterical about them. Peter has gone through disillusionment about himself; he has gone through seeing the death of his Lord and through identification with His death; through the experience of receiving from the Risen Lord the gift of the Holy Ghost, and he says, we are not hysterical, we were eyewitnesses of His majesty when we were with Him in the holy mount.

Repeatedly the vision of entire sanctification, or of the baptism of the Holy Ghost, is mistaken for the actuality. The only test of the actuality is when we are brought down into things as they are; it is then that the reality must manifest itself. When Jesus had healed the demoniac boy, the disciples asked Him, "How is it that we could not cast it out?" and Jesus said unto them, "This kind can come out by nothing, save by prayer and fasting," by spiritual concentration on Him. We can ever remain powerless, as were the disciples, by trying to do God's work through ideas drawn from our own temperament instead of by concentration on His power.

Never mistake the wonderful visions God gives you for reality, but watch, for after the vision you will be brought straight down into the valley. We are not made for the mountains, we are made for the valley. Thank God for the mountains, for the glorious spiritual realisation of Who Jesus Christ is; but can we face things as they actually are in the light of the Reality of Jesus Christ? or do things as they are efface altogether our faith in Him and drive us into a panic? When Jesus said, "I go to prepare a place for you," it was to the Cross He went. Through His Cross He prepared a place for us to "sit with Him in the heavenly places, in

Christ Jesus" *now,* not by and bye. When we get to the Cross we do not go through and out the other side, we abide in the life to which the Cross is the gateway; and the characteristic of the life is deep and profound sacrifice to God. We know Who our Lord is by the power of His Spirit, we are strongly confident in Him, and the reality of our relationship to Him works out all the time in the actualities of our ordinary life.

Almighty God's Ascription
And there came a voice out of the cloud saying, This is My beloved Son: hear Him. (Luke 9:35)

It is the same voice that spoke at our Lord's baptism. God emphatically states, "This is My beloved Son": this Man, known to men as the humble Nazarene Carpenter, is Almighty God presented in the guise of a human life; "hear Him." How many of us do hear Him? We always hear the thing we listen for, and our disposition determines what we listen for. When Jesus Christ alters our disposition, He gives us the power to hear as He hears.

The Awe of the Disciples
There came a cloud, and overshadowed them: and they feared as they entered into the cloud. (Luke 9:34)

When the clouds around are dark and terrible, thank God, the saints know that they are but "the dust of His feet," and when they fear as they enter into the cloud, they see "no man any more, save Jesus only with themselves."

HIS AGONY AND OUR FELLOWSHIP
Matthew 26:36–46
Matthew 4:1–11

His Destiny (Matthew 26:36–41; Matthew 4:1–4)
    Our Destiny as His Disciples (Matthew 20:22–23; 1 Peter 2:21)

His Dread (Matthew 26:42–43; Matthew 4:5–7)
    Our Dread as His Disciples (Philippians 3:10; John 12:27)

His Devotion (Matthew 26:44–46; Matthew 4:8–11)
    Our Devotion as His Disciples (Luke 12:49; Colossians 1:24)

We can never fathom the agony in Gethsemane, but at least we need not misunderstand it. It is the agony of God and Man in one, face to face with sin. The agony or our Lord in Gethsemane is not typical of what we go through, any more than His Cross is typical of our cross. We know nothing about Gethsemane in personal experience. Gethsemane and Calvary stand for something unique; they are the gateway into Life for us. We are not dealing here with the typical experience of the saint, but with the way the saintly life has been made possible.

We must read the record of the agony in the light of the temptation three years previously. There are three recorded temptations, and three recorded spells of agony in Gethsemane, "And when the devil had ended all the temptation, he departed from Him for a season." In Gethsemane he came back, and was again overthrown. Put away the reverential blasphemy that what Jesus Christ feared in Gethsemane was death on the cross. There was no element of fear in His mind about it; He stated most emphatically that He came on purpose for the Cross (Matthew 16:21). His fear in Gethsemane was that He might not get through as Son of Man. Satan's onslaught was that although He would get through as Son of God, it would only be as an isolated Figure; and this would mean that He could be no Saviour.

Notice again the curious insistence in the records on the fact that our Lord took His disciples with Him, not to share His agony, but to witness it.

His Destiny (Matthew 26:36–41)
Then cometh Jesus with them unto a place called Gethsemane, and saith unto the disciples, Sit ye here, while I go and pray yonder. . . . (Matthew 26:36; cf. Matthew 4:1–4)

At His Baptism the Son of God as Son of Man, i.e., as the whole human race rightly related to God, took on Himself the sin of the whole world; that is why He was baptised with John's baptism, which was a baptism of repentance from sin. It was at His Baptism that the Holy Ghost descended in the form of a dove, and God said, "This is My beloved Son, in whom I am well pleased"; and before His birth the angel proclaimed that He should be called Jesus, "for He shall save His people from their sins."

This is our Lord's destiny. No human being has a destiny like His; no human being can be a Saviour. There is only one Saviour, the Lord Jesus Christ, and the profundity of His agony has to do with the fulfilling of His destiny. The only possibility of God being satisfied with the human race is when the whole human race lives as the Son of God lived; and God became Incarnate that through His Son every one of us might be enabled to live as He lived.

In God's programme Holy Spirit and man are always identified. Adam was created to be indwelt by Holy Spirit, and God intended him to transform his innocence into holiness by a series of moral choices. But Adam refused to do this; instead, he started up a wrong relationship with the devil, and thereby became the introducer of the heredity of sin into the human race (Romans 5:12). The entering in of sin meant the departing of the Holy Spirit from the home of man's body, not the departing from him of the Spirit of God as Creator. "Elohim" has reference to God in correspondence with human flesh. When Adam sinned, this correspondence with God ceased until God became manifest in the flesh in Jesus Christ. At His Baptism the Holy Ghost came upon Him as Son of Man, and His coming was the seal of our Lord's accepted vocation. Jesus Christ represented "Elohim," God manifest in the flesh, God and man *one* in the Person of the Son of Man. The sin of the world upon the Son of God rent the Holy Ghost from Him on the Cross, and the cry on Calvary is the cry of the Holy Ghost to Jesus Christ—"My God, My God, why hast Thou forsaken Me?" It was not the cry of Jesus Christ to His Father. Jesus never spoke to God as "God"; He spoke to Him always as "Father." "Jesus knowing that all things were now accomplished, . . . He said, It is finished." These words of our Lord mean that God and the human race in the Person of the Son of Man are now one for ever in that one Person. Holy Spirit may be partaken of by any one. Anyone can enter into real fellowship with God, into fellowship as real as the communion which Jesus had with His Father, and the way into it is by means of His agony. Ephesians 4:13 is a picture of the human race redeemed by Jesus Christ. He is God's revelation in one Person of the human race as God intends it to be.

We are dealing here with revelation, not with experience. Revelation is that upon which we must nourish our faith; experience is that which encourages us that our faith is on the right track. The need to connect revelation and experience must never be overlooked.

In the temptation of our Lord, Satan's first attack was in the physical domain. In Gethsemane his onslaught is against our Lord as Son of Man, not against Him as Son of God. Satan could not touch Him as Son of God, he could only touch Him as Son of Man; and this is his final onslaught on the Son of God as Son of man. "You will get through as Son of God, I cannot touch You there, but You will never get one member of the human race through with You. Look at Your disciples, they are asleep, they cannot even watch with You. When You come to the Cross Your body will be so tortured and fatigued, so paralysed with pain, and Your soul will be so darkened and confused, that You will not be able to retain a clear understanding of what You are doing. Your whole personality will be so clouded and crushed by the weight of sin that You will never get through as Man." If Satan had been right, all that would have happened on the Cross would have been the death of a martyr only, the way into Life for us would never have been opened. But if Jesus Christ does get through as Son of Man, it means that the way is open for every one who has been born or ever will be born to get back to God. Satan's challenge to our Lord was that He would not be able to do it; He would only get through as Son of God, because Satan could not touch Him there. The fear that came upon our Lord was that He might die before He reached the Cross. He feared that as Son of Man He might die before He had opened the gate for us to get through, and He "was heard in that He feared," and was delivered from death in Gethsemane.

When our Lord came to the Cross, His body, soul, and spirit were completely triumphant, there was perfect self-possession. Did the pain of the body cloud His mind? "Father, forgive them; for they know not what they do." His mind was as clear as a sunbeam—"Woman, behold thy son!" And He was so triumphant in spirit, in His essential personality, that He cried with a loud voice, "Father, into Thy hands I commend My spirit."

The Garden of Gethsemane is the agony of Almighty God: the Cross of Christ is one terrific triumph, a triumph for the *Son of Man*. The cry, "My God, My God, why hast Thou forsaken Me?" is not the cry of the Son of God in destitution; it is the cry of the Holy Ghost being torn from the Son of God by the weight of sin upon Him. Gethsemane is the agony of the Son of God fulfilling His destiny as the Saviour of the world, and the veil is taken aside to show us what it cost Him to make it easy for us to become sons of God.

Our Destiny as His Disciples
But Jesus answered and said, Ye know not what ye ask. Are ye able to drink of the cup that I shall drink of, and to be baptized with the baptism that I am baptized with? They say unto Him, We are able. And He saith unto them, Ye shall drink indeed of My cup, and be baptized with the baptism that I am baptized with: but to sit on My right hand, and on My left, is not Mine to give, but it shall be given to them for whom it is prepared of My Father. (Matthew 20:22–23; see also 1 Peter 2:21)

Our destiny is determined by our disposition. Our Lord's destiny was determined by His disposition. Our destiny is preordained, but we are free to choose which disposition we will be ruled by. We cannot alter our disposition, but we can choose to let God alter it. If our disposition is to be altered, it must be altered by the Creator, and He will introduce us into a totally new realm by the miracle of His sovereign grace. Redemption means that Jesus Christ can give us a new disposition. At regeneration the Holy Spirit puts in us a totally new disposition, and as we obey that disposition the life of the Son of God will be manifested in our mortal flesh.

Within certain limits we have the power to choose, for instance, a man has the power to refuse to be born again, but no man has absolute free will. There comes a time when the human will must yield allegiance to a force greater than itself. God is the only Being Who can act with absolute free will, and when His Spirit comes into us, He makes us free in will, consequently our obedience becomes of value. It is not obedience when a man does a thing because he cannot help it, but when a man is made a son of God by Redemption, he has the free power to disobey, therefore the power to obey. If we have no power to disobey, we have no power to obey. Our obedience would be of no value at all if the power to sin were taken away.

Our destiny as His disciples is to be in fellowship with God as Jesus was. The cup and the baptism of our Lord are the gateways for every human being to get into perfect oneness with God. Jesus Christ gives us salvation and sanctification, but the places we take hereafter depend upon our obedience and the disposal of the Father. There is no respect of persons with God for salvation, but there are degrees of position hereafter. We are all saved by the cup and the baptism of our Lord, but the position we take individually depends entirely upon our obedience to Him. We are born again through our Lord's cup and baptism, i.e., through His fulfilling of His destiny; we do not have to agonise and suffer before we can be born from above (RV mg). All the distress and all the sacrifice in the world will never atone for sin. We must be born again through His sacrifice into the Kingdom where He lives, and when we are there we have to follow in His steps, and we find we can follow now that we have His Spirit, His nature. Our fear starts when we imagine that we have to live this new life by the energy of our human nature, because we know that it cannot be done, and every time we think of what we were before, we falter. The Bible reveals that when the Holy Spirit has come into us, every command of God is an enabling. Jesus Christ gives the power of His own disposition to anyone, that is why He is apparently so merciless on those of us who have received the Holy Spirit, because His demands on us are made according to His disposition, and not

according to our human nature. The old nature says it cannot be done. Jesus Christ says it can be done—"I did it, and I can do it in you if you will enter My life by means of My death." It is no use trying to be what we are not. We are children of God when we are born from above (RV mg), and God will never shield us from the requirements of being His children. "Follow His steps" —that is the conduct of regenerate human nature. The life of Jesus is the life of the normal man of God, but we cannot begin to live it unless we are born from above. Unless we have been taken up into His destiny, we cannot fulfil our own destiny. If we are born from above, are we trying to follow His steps, trying to work out in our mortal flesh that which God has worked in? (Philippians 2:12–13). Salvation is a sovereign gift of the Redemption of the Lord Jesus. Many will be saved through the fulfilling of the destiny of the Son of Man who have not been worth anything to God in this life, their life has been self-centred and wrong, it has not been lived on the foundation of the Son of God. Our destiny is to work out what God works in. It is not that our eternal salvation depends upon our doing it, but our value to God does, and also our position in the Kingdom of God.

His Dread

He went away again the second time, and prayed, saying, O My Father, if this cup may not pass away from Me, except I drink it, Thy will be done. (Matthew 26:42–43; cf. Matthew 4:5–7)

The disciples are the representatives of the human race in connection with Redemption, and Satan's sneer in Gethsemane is, "You will never do it, these men are the specimens of the best You have, and they are asleep. You should have gone to heaven from the Mount of Transfiguration, but instead, You came down and declared You would redeem the human race, and I am determined that You shall not." Our Lord's dread in Gethsemane was born of the knowledge that if He did not get through as Son of Man, the redemption of mankind was hopeless; we could only then have imitated Him, we could never have known Him as Saviour.

This is the agony of God as Man, not a human agony. Our Lord did not want human sympathy, His agony was infinitely profounder than human sympathy could come anywhere near. The darkness was produced because it looked as if Satan were going to triumph, and the disciples, who represented the new humanity, were without the slightest element of understanding what Jesus Christ was doing. He "offered up prayers and supplications with strong crying and tears unto Him that was able to save Him from death, and was heard in that He feared." His prayer was answered every time, and when He came to the Cross His relationship to His mother, and to John, and to His murderers, showed that His mind and His reason were triumphantly clear. It was not only a sign that our Lord had triumphed, but that He had triumphed to save the human race, so that every human being can get through into the presence of God because of all the Son of Man went through. Jesus Christ is either all that the New Testament claims Him to be—the Redeemer of the human race, or else a futile dreamer, and the only proof is in personal experience. Can God form the life that His Son lived in us? Jesus Christ claims that He can. Then have we let Him do it?

Our Dread as His Disciples
That I may know Him, and the power of His resurrection, and the fellowship of His sufferings, being made conformable unto His death. (Philippians 3:10; see also John 12:27)

Our dread as His disciples is lest we fail Jesus Christ in our service, lest in our experience of the revelation we forget the God Who gave us the experience, forget all about Jesus Christ. As disciples we have not to serve God in our own way, not to tell Him what we are going to do for Him, not to ask Him to baptise us with the Holy Ghost to make *us* something. "If you would be My disciple," says Jesus, "give up your right to yourself to Me, and take up your cross daily." No man can carry the cross of God. The Cross of God is the Redemption of the world. The cross we have to carry is that we have deliberately given up our right to ourselves to Jesus Christ, and we steadily refuse to be appealed to on any other line than He was appealed to on when He was here. With regard to all the pleasures and sciences and interests of this life, push this simple consideration, "Is this the kind of thing the Son of God is doing in the world, or is it what the prince of this world is doing?" Not, "Is it right?" but "Is it the kind of thing the Son of God would be doing in the world?" If it is not, then don't touch it. If you only give up wrong things for Jesus Christ, don't talk any more about being in love with Him. If you want to do a thing all the time, it is no virtue not to do it! Jesus Christ takes the "want to" out of us and enables us to do in this world the things He would be doing if He were here. We say, "Why shouldn't I? it isn't wrong!" What a sordid thing to say! When we love a person, do we only give up what is wrong for him? Love is not measured by what it gets, but by what it costs, and our relationship to Jesus Christ can never be on the line of, "Why shouldn't I do this?" Our Lord simply says, "If any man will be My disciple, those are the conditions" (see Luke 14:26–27 and 33). Is He worth it? Will He cast it up at us that we never gave up anything for Him? No,

He will never do that, He will never tell us what sneaks we have been, but we will find it out (Matthew 10:26). Our dread is to be lest we forget Him. Do we know Jesus Christ better to-day than ever we did?

If we have been put right with God through the agony of the Son of God, have we enthroned Him as Lord and Master as well? (Luke 6:46; John 13:13). Is He absolute Master of our body? (1 Corinthians 3:16–17). We have no business to be master of our own body. Our dread is lest we forget that our body is the temple of the Holy Ghost. We are to know Jesus Christ and the power of His resurrection in our body, to know the fellowship of His sufferings in our body. "If any man will come after Me, let him deny himself." There is no "if" in connection with salvation, only in connection with discipleship. The conditions of discipleship are found in Luke 14:26–27 and 33 . If the commands of Jesus Christ in our life clash with the most sacred relationships on earth, it must be instant obedience to Him. We must hate the claim that contends with His claim; *hate* it that is, in comparison with our love to Him. We must abandon to God at all costs. Abandon is of infinitely more value than self-scrutiny.

His Devotion
And He left them, and went away again, and prayed the third time, saying the same words. Then cometh He to His disciples, and saith unto them, Sleep on now, and take your rest: behold, the hour is at hand, and the Son of Man is betrayed into the hands of sinners. Rise, let us be going: behold, he is at hand that doth betray Me. (Matthew 26:44–46; cf. Matthew 4:8–11)

"Still sleeping? It is all right now, it is all finished, the Son of Man is betrayed into the hands of sinners." That is a joyful utterance. Our Lord is absolutely sure that as representative Man before God He will get the whole human race through, in spite of everything the devil can do, and the Cross is an absolute triumph. Our Lord, as Son of Man, has been through the depths of His agony in Gethsemane, and He has won at every point. He has won for the bodies of men, He has won for the minds and souls of men and for the spirits of men; everything that makes up a human personality is redeemed absolutely, and no matter whether a man be a vile sinner or as clean as the rich young ruler, he can enter into the marvellous life with God through the way made by the Son of Man.

"Father, into Thy hands I commend My spirit," that is, the spirit of the Son of Man, the spirit of the whole human race represented by the Son of Man getting through to God on the Cross. "Though He were a Son, yet learned He obedience by the things which He suffered" (Hebrews 5:8). He did not learn to be a Son, He was a Son, and He came to redeem as Man, and He learned obedience as Redeemer by suffering. His agony is the basis of the simplicity of our salvation. His suffering is the basis of all our light and liberty and joy. His Cross makes it simple enough for any one to get into the presence of God.

Our Lord in His agony was devoted to God's purpose. The supreme obedience of Jesus was never to the needs of men, but always to the will of His Father. The Church goes astray whenever she makes the need the call. The need is never the call; the need is the opportunity; the call is the call of God.

Our Devotion As His Disciples

I am come to send fire on the earth; and what will I, if it be already kindled? (Luke 12:49; see also Colossians 1:24)

"Our God is a consuming fire," and when God comes on to this earth in the effective working of the Redemption of Jesus Christ, He brings pain and havoc and disaster (Matthew 10:34). The first result of the Redemption of Jesus Christ in human life is havoc. If any human life can stand before God on its own basis, Calvary is much ado about nothing. If it can be proved that rationalism is the basis of human life, then the New Testament is nonsense; instead of its being a revelation, it is a cunningly devised fable. There is no need for redemption, Jesus Christ is nothing but a martyr, one of whom it was true that He was stricken, smitten of God and afflicted. If we can stand before God apart from Jesus Christ, we have proved that Calvary is not needed. Immediately Jesus Christ comes in, He produces havoc, because the whole world system is arrayed against His Redemption. It was the world system of His day, and particularly the religious system, that killed the Son of God.

"And fill up that which is behind of the afflictions of Christ in my flesh"—for Redemption's sake? No, "for His body's sake, which is the church." On the ground of Jesus Christ's Redemption, we can enter into identification with His sufferings, but we do not need to unless we like. First Corinthians 13 and Matthew 5:43–48 are practical home-coming Chris-

tian truths. "Come unto Me. . . . Take my yoke upon you, and learn of Me," "then go and bear with others for My sake." What have we suffered for Jesus Christ? Think of the passionate indignation we get into when someone slanders us!—"Consider Him." We do not need to take the blow, but if we do not, it will go back on Him. We will get off scot free, and everyone will applaud us for doing so, but the blow will fall upon Jesus Christ. If we let it come on us, it will not fall on Him. We have always the privilege of going the second mile. It is never our duty to do it, but will we go the second mile with God? Are we deliberately filling up that which remains behind of His sufferings, or becoming mere critical centres? If we have been brought into a right relationship with God by the Redemption of Jesus Christ, He expects us to put on His yoke and to learn of Him.

The devotion of the saint is to "fill up that which is behind of the afflictions of Christ for His body's sake," nothing remains behind to be filled up for Redemption's sake. How did Jesus Christ suffer? Because people misunderstood Him? Because He was persecuted? Because He could not get on with men? No, He suffered for one thing only—that men might be saved; He let Almighty God do His whole will in and through Him without asking His permission. He suffered "according to the will of God."

How can we fill up the sufferings that remain behind? First John 5:16 is an indication of one way, viz., that of intercession. Remember, no man has time to pray, he has to take time from other things that are valuable in order to understand how necessary time for prayer is. The things that act like thorns and stings in our personal lives will go instantly we pray; we won't feel the smart any more, because we have got God's point of view about them. Prayer means that we get into union with God's view of other people. Our devotion as saints is to identify ourselves with God's interests in other lives. God pays no attention to our personal affinities; He expects us to identify ourselves with *His* interests in others.

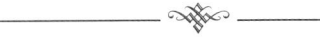

HIS CROSS AND OUR DISCIPLESHIP

The Collision of God and Sin (Acts 2:36)
  The Sacrifice to Christ of Myself (Romans
    12:1–2; Matthew 16:24; Luke 9:23)

The Contradiction of God and Satan (John
  12:31–33)
  The Suffering for Christ of Myself (Colossians
    1:24; 2 Corinthians 1:5; Philippians 3:10)

The Centre of God and Salvation (2 Corinthians
  5:14)
  The Sacrament of God in Myself (Acts 20:24;
    1 Corinthians 15:30)

There is a difference between revelation and experience. As Christians we must have an experience, but we must believe a great deal more than we can experience. For instance, no Christian can experience the Cross of Christ; but he can experience salvation through the Cross. No Christian can experience God becoming Incarnate; but he can experience the incoming of the life of God by regeneration. No Christian can experience the personal advent of the Holy Ghost on to this earth; but he can experience the indwelling of the Holy Ghost. A New Testament Christian is one who bases all his thinking on these revelations. He experiences the regenerating power of God, and then goes on to build up his mind in the most holy faith. Until a man is born again, he cannot think as a Christian. Belief of doctrine does not make a man a Christian. There are those who emphasise doctrine, they would go to martyrdom for the faith; whilst others emphasise experience, and take everything revealed in the Bible as picturing our experience. Either of these views is likely to become a dangerous side track.

Jesus Christ took thirty-three years over the historic completion of Redemption in order to exhibit what God's normal Man was like. He lived the pattern normal life of a man as God wants it to be lived, and He demands of us that we live as He did. But how are we to begin to do it? We did not come into this world as God Incarnate came. He came from pre-existing Deity; we are born with the heredity of sin. How are we to enter into the life He lived? By His Cross and by no other way. We do not enter into the life of God by imitation, or by vows, or by ceremonies, or by Church membership; we enter into it by its entering into us at regeneration. The Cross of Jesus Christ is the gateway into His life.

The Cross is not the cross of a man but the Cross of God, and the Cross of God can never be realised in human experience. Beware of saying that Jesus Christ was a martyr. Nowadays He is frequently looked upon as a martyr, His life is acknowledged to be very beautiful, but the Atonement and the Cross are not being given their rightful place, and the Bible is being robbed of its magnitude and virility. The death of our Lord was not the death of a martyr, but the exhibition of the heart of God, and the gateway whereby any member of the human race can enter into union with God. The Cross is the centre of Time and of Eternity, the answer to the enigmas of both.

The Collision of God and Sin
Therefore let all the house of Israel know assuredly, that God hath made that same Jesus whom ye have crucified, both Lord and Christ. (Acts 2:36)

The Cross of Jesus is the revelation of God's judgement on sin. It is not the cross of a martyr; it is the substitution of Jesus for sinful humanity. The Cross did not *happen* to Jesus, He came on purpose for it. The whole purpose of the Incarnation is the Cross— "the Lamb slain from the foundation of the world." The Cross is beyond Time; the actual crucifixion is the historical revelation of the heart nature of the Trinity of God. The symbolic figure of the nature of God is not a circle, complete and self-centred; God is not all. The symbol of God's nature is the Cross, whose arms stretch out to limitless reaches.

The Cross of Jesus Christ is a revelation; our cross is an experience. If we neglect for one moment the basal revelation of the Cross, we will make shipwreck of our faith, no matter what our experience is. The test of our spiritual life is our understanding of the Cross. The Cross of Jesus is often wrongly taken as a type of the cross we have to carry. Jesus did not say, "If any man will come after Me, let him take up *My* cross," but, "let him deny himself, and take up his cross, and follow Me." Our cross becomes our divinely appointed privilege by means of His Cross. We are never called upon to carry His Cross. We have so hallowed the Cross by twenty centuries of emotion and sentiment that it sounds a very beautiful and pathetic thing to talk about carrying our cross. But a wooden cross with iron nails in it is a clumsy thing to carry. The real cross was like that, and do we imagine that the external cross was more ugly than our actual one? Or that the thing that tore our Lord's hands and feet was not really so terrible as our imagination of it?

Do we agree with God's judgement upon sin in the Cross? There is a difference between sin and sins. Sin is a heredity; sins are acts for which we are responsible. Sin is a thing we are born with and we cannot touch it. God touches sin in Redemption, and the Cross reveals the clash of God and sin. If we do not put to death the things in us that are not of God, they will put to death the things that are of God. There is never any alternative, some thing must die in us—either sin or the life of God. If we agree theologically with God's condemnation of sin on the Cross, then what about sin in our own heart? Do we agree with God's verdict on sin and lust in our lives? The moment we do agree, we may be delivered from it. It is a question of agreeing with God's verdict on sin and of will. Will we go through the condemnation now? If we will, there is no more condemnation for us, and the salvation of Jesus Christ is made actual in our lives. Unless our salvation works out through our finger tips and everywhere else, there is nothing to it, it is religious humbug.

The Sacrifice to Christ of Myself

I beseech you therefore, brethren, by the mercies of God, that ye present your bodies a living sacrifice, holy, acceptable unto God, which is your reasonable service. And be not conformed to this world: but be ye transformed by the renewing of your mind, that ye may prove what is that good, and acceptable, and perfect, will of God. (Romans 12:1–2; see also Matthew 16:24; Luke 9:23)

"Present your bodies a living sacrifice." We cannot present an unholy thing at the altar, and Paul's word "brethren" means saints. It is only from the standpoint of sanctification that these verses apply. Our Lord says to those who have entered into His life by means of His Cross, "Let him deny himself, and take up his cross, and follow Me." Not, "Let him give up sin"; any man will give up sinning if he knows how to, but, "Let him deny himself," that is, "give up his right to himself to Me." Our cross is what we hold before the world, viz., the fact that we are sanctified to do nothing but God's will. We have given away our right to ourselves for ever, and the cross we take up is a sign in heaven, on earth and to hell, that we are His and our own no longer. The right to ourselves is the only thing we have to give to God. We cannot give our natural possessions, because they have been given to us. If we had not our right to ourselves by God's creation of us, we should have nothing to give, and consequently could not be held responsible.

Jesus Christ is not dealing with sin here (sin is dealt with by His Cross), but with what has been referred to as the natural life, the life symbolised by Mary, the mother of Jesus, which must be sacrificed, not annihilated. The idea of sacrifice is giving back to God the best we have in order that He may make it His and ours for ever. Have we done it? Have we as saints given up our right to ourselves to Him? or do we while accepting His salvation thoroughly object to giving up our right to ourselves to Him? Sanctification has to do with separating a holy life to God's uses. "And for their sakes I sanctify Myself, that they also might be sanctified through the truth" (John 17:19).

We are apt to imagine that the cross we have to carry means the ordinary troubles and trials of life, but we must have these whether we are Christians or not. Neither is our cross suffering for conscience' sake. Our cross is something that comes only with the peculiar relationship of a disciple to Jesus Christ; it is the evidence that we have denied our right to ourselves. "I am crucified with Christ: nevertheless I live; yet not I, but Christ liveth in me" (Galatians 2:20). It is not only that we give up our right to ourselves to Jesus Christ but that determinedly we relate ourselves to life so that we may be appealed to only by the things that appeal to Him, and do in the world only the things with which He is associated. There are myriads of right things in this world that our Lord would not touch, relationships which He described by the "eye," and the "right arm." Our right arm is not a bad thing, it is one of the best things we have, but Jesus said, "If it offends you in your walk with Me, cut it off." Most of us balk this; we do not object to being delivered from sin, but we do not intend to give up the right to ourselves to Him. The only right a Christian has is the right to give up his rights. Unless we are willing to give up good things for Jesus Christ, we have no realisation of Whom He is. "But really I cannot give up things that are quite legitimate!" Then never mention the word love again in connection with Jesus Christ if you cannot give up the best you have for Him. This is the essential nature of love in the natural life, otherwise it is a farce to call it love, it is not love, but lust; and when we come to our relationship with Jesus Christ, this is the love He demands of us. If we have entered into the experience of regeneration through His Cross, these are the conditions of discipleship (Luke 14:26–27 and 33). Always notice the "If" in connection with discipleship, there is never any compulsion. "If any man come to Me, and hate not . . . , he cannot be My disciple." He may be anything else, a very fascinating person, a most delightful asset to modern civilisation, but Jesus Christ says, "he cannot be My disciple." A man may be saved without being a disciple, and it is the point of discipleship that is always kicked against. Our Lord is not talking of eternal salvation, but of the possibility of our being of temporal worth to Himself. How many of us are of any worth to Jesus Christ? Our attitude is rather that we are much obliged to God for saving us, but the idea of giving up our chances to realise ourselves in life is too extravagantly extreme. Some of us will take all God has to give us while we take good care not to give Him anything back.

The sacrifice of myself to Christ is not a revelation, but an experience. Have I sacrificed myself to Him, or have I refused to give up my right to myself to Him because there are several things I want to do? "There are so many other interests in my life, and, of course, God will not expect it of me." Always state things to yourself in order to realise whether you ruggedly are what you sentimentally think you ought to be, and you will soon know the kind of humbug you are. Spiritual reality is what is wanted. "I surrender all"—and you feel as if you did, that is the awkward thing. The point is whether, as God engineers your circumstances, you find that you really have surrendered. Immediately you do surrender, you are made so much one with your Lord that the thought of what it cost never enters any more.

The Contradiction of God and Satan

Now is the judgement of this world: now shall the prince of this world be cast out. And I, if I be lifted up from the earth, will draw all men unto Me. This He said, signifying what death He should die. (John 12:31–33)

The prince of this world and Satan are synonymous terms. Satan is the manifestation of the devil for which man is held responsible, that is, Satan is the result of a communication between man and the devil (Genesis 3). Our Lord did not say to Peter, "Get thee behind Me, *'devil,'* but, *'Satan'*"; and then He defined Satan—"thou savourest not the things that be of God, but the things that be of men." What was it that Peter savoured? Self-pity; "Pity Thyself, Lord: this shall not be to Thee," and Jesus "turned, and said unto Peter, Get thee behind Me, *Satan:* thou art an offence unto Me." Peter's appeal was made on the ground of self-interest, and the prince of this world governs everything on that basis. Self-realisation is the essential principle of his government. "Whosoever therefore will be a friend of the world is the enemy of God." The world is that system of things which organises its life without any thought of Jesus Christ. Paul says that the lost are those whose minds are blinded by the god of this world (2 Corinthians 4:3–4). Nothing blinds the mind to the claims of Jesus Christ more effectually than a good, clean-living, upright life based on self-realisation. For a thing to be Satanic does not mean that it is abominable and immoral. The satanically managed man is moral, upright, proud, and individual; he is absolutely self-governed and has no need of God. The prince of this world is judged for ever at the Cross. If we enter into the Kingdom of God through the Cross of Christ, self-realisation cannot get through with us, it must be left outside. The Cross of Christ reveals the contradiction of God and Satan. The disposition of self-realisation is the manifestation in us of the devil as Satan, and when we come to the Cross we leave Satan outside, Satan cannot take one step inside the Cross.

The Suffering for Christ of Myself
Who now rejoice in my sufferings for you, and fill up that which is behind of the afflictions of Christ in my flesh for His body's sake, which is the church. (Colossians 1:24; see also 2 Corinthians 1:5; Philippians 3:10)

That is suffering without any notice from the world, saving its ridicule. It is not suffering like Christ, it is suffering for Christ. It is not suffering for the sake of Redemption; we have nothing to do with Redemption; that is completed. We have to fill up "that which is behind of the afflictions of Christ for His body's sake, which is the church." When by the Cross of Christ we have entered into the experience of identification with our Lord, then there comes the practical working out of Matthew 11:29, "Take My yoke upon you, and learn of Me; for I am meek and lowly in heart." When we learn of Jesus we shall not "grouse" at a dispensation of God's providence that we cannot understand; we shall not give way to self-pity and say, "Why should this happen to me?" Jesus said—"Let him . . . take up his cross, and follow Me." This means putting into exercise 1 Corinthians 13 and deliberately identifying ourselves with God's interests in others, and it involves a moral decision on our part. God will bring across our path people who embody the characteristics that we have shown to Him—stubbornness, pride, conceit, opinionativeness, sensuality, a hundred little meannesses. "Now," He says, "love them as I have loved you." It works in this way, we see that someone is going to get the better of us, and every logical power in us says—"Resent it." Morally speaking, we should, but Jesus Christ says, "When you are insulted, not only do not resent it, but exhibit the Son of God." The disciple realises that his Lord's honour is at stake in his life, not his own honour. A coward does not hit back because he is afraid to; a strong man refuses to hit back because he is strong; but in appearance they are both the same, and that is where the intense humiliation of being a Christian comes in. The Lord is asking us to go the second mile with Him, and if we take the blow, we will save Him. We can always avoid letting Jesus Christ get the blow by taking it ourselves. Be absolutely abandoned to God; it is only your own reputation that is at stake. People will not discredit God; they will only think you are a fool.

After the Resurrection, Jesus Christ did not invite the disciples to a time of communion on the Mount of Transfiguration, He said—"Feed My sheep." When God gives a man work to do, it is seldom work that seems at all proportionate to his natural ability. Paul, lion-hearted genius though he was, spent his time teaching the most ignorant people. The evidence that we are in love with God is that we identify ourselves with His interests in others, and other people are the exact expression of what we ourselves are; that is the humiliating thing! Jesus Christ came down to a most miserably insignificant people in order to redeem them. When He has lifted us into relationship with Himself, He expects us to identify ourselves with His interests in others.

The Centre of God and Salvation

For the love of Christ constraineth us; because we thus judge, that if one died for all, then were all dead. (Corinthians 5:14)

We cannot be saved by consecration, or by praying, or by giving ourselves up to God. We can only be saved by the Cross of Jesus Christ. Salvation is an absolutely free, unmerited gift of God. We would a hundred times rather that God told us to do something than we would accept His salvation as a gift. The centre of salvation is the Cross of Jesus Christ, and why it is so easy to obtain salvation is because it cost God so much; and why it is so difficult to experience salvation is because human conceit will not accept, nor believe, nor have anything to do with unmerited salvation. We have not to experience God saving the world; it is a revelation that God has saved the world through Christ, and we can enter into the experience of His salvation through the Cross. The Cross is the point where God and sinful man merge with a crash, and the way to life is opened, but the crash is on the heart of God. God is always the sufferer.

The Sacrament of God in Myself
But none of these things move me, neither count I my life dear unto myself, so that I might finish my course with joy, and the ministry, which I have received of the Lord Jesus, to testify the gospel of the grace of God. (Acts 20:24; see also 1 Corinthians 15:30)

"Neither count I my life dear unto myself." Paul was absolutely indifferent to any other consideration than that of fulfilling the ministry he had received. He could never be appealed to by those who urged him to remain in a certain place because he was being of so much use there. Watch our Lord also. He went through villages and cities where He was marvellously used, but the great characteristic of His earthly life was that He stedfastly set His face to go to Jerusalem; He never stayed in a place because He had been of use there (Mark 1:37–38). Beware of the sweet sisters and beloved brothers who say to you, "Now do consider whether you will not be of more use here than anywhere else." Probably you will, and in the passing of the months you will become mouldy bread instead of eating bread. We have nothing to do with God's purpose, but only with the sacrament of God in us, that is, the real Presence of God coming through the common elements of our lives (John 7:37–39). The measure of our service for God is not our usefulness to others. We have nothing to do with the estimate of others, nor with success in service; we have to see that we fulfil our ministry. "As Thou hast sent Me into the world, even so have I also sent them into the world" (John 17:18). Our Lord's first obedience was not to the needs of men, not to the consideration of where He was most useful, but to the will of His Father, and the first need of our life is not to be useful to God, but to do God's will. How are we to know the will of God? By living in Romans 12:1–2. By being renewed in the spirit of the mind and refusing to be conformed to this age, we shall make out "the will of God, even the thing which is good and acceptable and perfect" (RV mg).

HIS RESURRECTION AND OUR LIFE

His Resurrection Declared (Mark 16:5–8)
    Our Eternal Life (John 20:22)

His Resurrection Destiny (Luke 24:26)
    Our Experimental Life (Philippians 3:10; Romans 6:23)

His Resurrection Deity (John 20:17)
    Our Entire Life (Colossians 3:1–4)

We must always distinguish between the truths we receive as revelations and what we experience of God's grace. We experience the wonderful reality of God's salvation and sanctification in our actual lives, but we have also to receive into our minds and souls Divine revelations which we cannot experience. We cannot experience Jesus Christ rising from the dead; we cannot experience His Destiny or His Deity, but we must understand where the regenerating forces in our lives come from. The New Testament insists on an instructed mind as well as a vital experience.

His Resurrection Declared

And entering into the sepulchre, they saw a young man sitting on the right side, clothed in a long white garment; and they were affrighted. And he saith unto them, Be not affrighted: ye seek Jesus of Nazareth, which was crucified: He is risen; He is not here: behold the place where they laid Him. (Mark 16:5–8)

Our Lord died and was buried and He rose again, and this is the declaration of the Resurrection in all its incredibleness. Any question that arises in connection with the Resurrection arises in the minds of those who do not accept the necessity of being born from above (RV mg). There is always a quarrel between our common sense and the revelations made in God's Book. We must lose our soul in order to find it. We have to be born from above and receive Holy Spirit into our spirit, and then begin to construct another soul, or way of reasoning, and to do this we must accept not only the facts that come to us through our common sense, but the facts that come by revelation. We say *seeing is believing,* but it is not. We must believe a thing is possible before we should believe it even though we saw it (John 20:29).

Our Eternal Life

And when He had said this, He breathed on them, and saith unto them, Receive ye the Holy Ghost. (John 20:22)

Eternal life is the gift of the Lord Jesus Christ. "He that believeth on Me hath everlasting life (John 6:47), i.e., the life He manifested in His human flesh when He was here, and says Jesus, "Ye have not [that] life in yourselves" (John 6:53 RV). His life is not ours by natural birth, and it can only be given to us by means of His Cross. Our Lord's Cross is the gateway into His life; His Resurrection means that He has power now to convey that life to us (John 17:2).

The onslaught of Satan in Gethsemane was that Jesus Christ would never get through His agony as Son of Man. As Son of God, Satan could not prevent His getting through, but his challenge was that he would prevent Jesus Christ bringing one soul through with Him—and Satan was hopelessly defeated. By the death of the Son of Man upon the Cross, the door is opened for any individual to go straight into the presence of God; and by the Resurrection our Lord can impart to us His own life. When we are born from above (RV mg) we receive from the risen Lord His very life, our human spirit is quickened by the incoming of the life of God. That is the marvel of the power of the Lord Jesus Christ through His resurrec-tion. "I would know Him in the power of His resurrection" (Philippians 3:10 MOFFATT).

Holy Spirit, Salvation, and Eternal Life are inter-changeable terms. "Holy Spirit" is the experimental name for eternal life working in human beings here and now. The only thing that makes eternal life actual is the entrance of the Holy Spirit by commitment to Jesus Christ. Our beliefs will mock us unless some-thing comes into us from God, because nothing has any power to alter us save the incoming of the life of God. The Holy Spirit is the One Who makes exper-imentally real *in* us what Jesus Christ did *for* us. The Holy Spirit is the Deity in proceeding power Who applies the Atonement to our experience. Jesus Christ came to redeem us; to put us right with God; to deliver us from the power of death; to reveal God the Father; and when we receive the Holy Spirit He will make experimentally real in us all that Jesus Christ came to do. The great need for men and women is to receive the Holy Spirit. Our creeds teach us to believe in the Holy Spirit; the New Testament says we must *receive* Him (Luke 11:13). Are you powerless in your life? Then, for Christ's sake, get at Reality! Ask God for the Holy Spirit, i.e., His eternal life, and you will begin to manifest in your mortal flesh the life of Jesus. One day we shall have a body like His body, but we can know now the efficacy of our Lord's resurrection. We can receive the Holy Spirit and experimentally know His salvation.

His Resurrection Destiny

Ought not Christ to have suffered these things, and to enter into His glory? (Luke 24:26)

The sufferings of Jesus Christ were not an accident, they are what He came for; He knew that His life was to be a ransom for many. The men who do not suffer in this world are not worth their salt. The finest men and women suffer, and the devil uses their sufferings to slander God. God is after one thing—bringing many sons to glory, and He does not care what it costs us, any more than He cared what it cost Him. God has taken the responsibility for the possibility of sin, and the proof that He did so is the Cross. He is the suffering God, not One Who reigns above in calm disdain. "Though He were a Son, yet learned He obe-dience by the things which He suffered." He did not learn to be a Son, but because He was a Son, He deliberately chose to obey God through suffering. His resurrection destiny is to suffer and to enter into glory in order that He may bring "many sons unto glory."

We must beware lest we put the emphasis of strain and suffering on the wrong thing. Salvation and eternal life are easy for us to obtain because of what they cost God. If we find it difficult to come to God, it is because we will try to drag our human pride through. If we will only come with the simplicity of a child, there is no need for any agony at all; we can receive the marvellous revelation of salvation and experience the impartation of the life of the risen Lord Jesus; but self-realisation and self-interest and sin must all be renounced. Never sympathise with a soul who finds it difficult to get through to God. It is perilously easy to sympathise with Satan instead of with God (Matthew 16:23). No one can be more tender to men and women than God. We are slandering God if we sympathise with the wilfulness of a person and think how difficult God makes it for him. It is never hard to get to God unless our wilfulness makes it hard.

Our Lord rose to an absolutely new life, to a life He did not live before He was Incarnate, He rose to a life that had never been before. There had been resurrections before the resurrection of Jesus Christ, but they were all resuscitations to the same kind of life as heretofore. Jesus Christ rose to a totally new life, and to a totally different relationship to men and women. The resurrection of Jesus Christ grants Him the right to give His own destiny to any human being—viz., to make us the sons and daughters of God. His Resurrection means that we are raised to His risen life, not to our old life. "Like as Christ was raised up from the dead by the glory of the Father, even so we also should walk in newness of life . . . we shall be also in the likeness of His resurrection" (Romans 6:4–5).

Our Experimental Life

That I may know Him, and the power of His resurrection, and the fellowship of His sufferings, being made conformable unto His death. (Philippians 3:10; see also Romans 6:23)

Eternal life is not a present given to me by God, it is Himself. "The gift *of* God," not *from* God. How is the life of God going to work out in us? First of all, it will manifest itself in our mortal flesh in the way of death. The surging life of God instantly hates to death the things which have nothing to do with God. We experience exhaustion, a drying up of the springs of intellectual and physical life, the reason being that God is teaching us that all our life is now in the hand of God. Then the Holy Spirit will experimentally reveal the power of His resurrection. If we are right with God, physical exhaustion will always bring its own recuperation. The exhaustion does not tell because He recuperates all the time. It is not a question of being buoyed up with excitement, it is a superabounding supply of life all the time. If we live in touch with our

Lord's life experimentally, we realise that our bodies are the temples of the Holy Ghost. This comes to us first as a revelation, not as something to be experienced only. If we live on the experimental side alone, we shall get distracted. The Resurrection of Jesus Christ has given Him the right, the authority, to impart the life of God to us, and our experimental life must be constructed on the basis of His life. "All my fresh springs shall be in Thee" (Psalm 87:7 PBV).[13] Watch the things that exhaust you, and you will find you are doing something outside God's arrangement for you. There are things for which His life supplies no energy and we get spent right out. If we are doing things inside God's arrangement for us, the natural exhaustion is so quickly recuperated by the resurrection life of Jesus that we do not feel the exhaustion. We must find out whether we are instructing ourselves in the Christian revelation. Do we know the power of His resurrection? are we making that the centre of our profound life? If we are, the experimental realty will work all through.

His Resurrection Deity

Jesus saith unto her, Touch Me not; for I am not yet ascended to My Father: but go to My brethren, and say unto them, I ascend unto My Father, and your Father; and to My God, and your God. (John 20:17)

The risen Lord as Son of Man is talking to a particular representative of humanity, the woman out of whom He had cast seven devils. Our Lord is the same, yet so indefinably altered by His death and resurrection that Mary did not recognise Him at first. Then when He said to her, "Mary," she flung herself at His feet with a complete thrill of expectancy—"He is back again, and all things will be well!" Mary had to learn that the relationship she was now to be in to her Lord was not one that could be discerned by her natural senses, but a relationship based on an impartation of life from Himself. "I ascend unto My Father, and your Father." It was to be a relationship in which she was made one with Jesus Christ. His Resurrection Deity means that He can take us into union with God, and the way into that relationship of oneness is by the Cross and the Resurrection. The weakest saint can experience the power of the Deity of the Son of God if he is willing to "let go." The whole almighty power of God is on our behalf, and when we realise this, life becomes the implicit life of the child. No wonder Jesus said—"Let not your heart be troubled"! The characteristic of the saintly life is abandon to God, not a settling down on our own whiteness. God

---

13. PBV: Prayer Book Version. The *Book of Common Prayer* of the Church of England includes a translation of the Psalter, or Psalms of David.

is not making hot-house plants, but sons and daughters of God, men and women with a strong family likeness to Jesus Christ.

Our Entire Life

If ye then be risen with Christ, seek those things which are above, where Christ sitteth on the right hand of God. Set your attention on things above, not on things on the earth. For ye are dead, and your life is hid with Christ in God. When Christ, who is our life, shall appear, then shall ye also appear with Him in glory. (Colossians 3:1–4)

We starve our minds as Christians by not thinking, and we cannot think as Christians until we are born from above (RV mg). So many of us have a good spiritual experience, but we have never thought things out on Christian lines. It is just as true that a man may *live* a Christian life without thinking as that a man may *think* a Christian life without living it. We have to learn to combine the two, and to do this we must build up our minds on these great truths.

If we have been born from above (RV mg), we must seek the things that are above. To any one who is not born from above, it sounds mystical and remote, but there is nothing too profound for a saint. We can always know a saint because he discerns the revelations of God, while the unspiritual man who has not been born from above looks puzzled. Truth is not discerned intellectually, it is discerned spiritually.

The power of the Resurrection is to work out in these mortal bodies. Provided we are alive when our Lord comes again, we shall be changed, Paul says, and he goes on to expound the marvellous transformation that will take place in a flash in everything to do with the natural.

"Your life is hid with Christ in God." Christ is our entire life. When once we realise this, certain forms of doubt and perplexity vanish for ever. If we set our affection on things above, those perplexities will never trouble us any more because we know the Lord Jesus, and He is not distracted by these present perplexities. The things that are obscure to the natural man become clear to the penetration of the mind that sets itself on the things above. Such an one does not pretend not to have doubts, we know he has not got them; his is not a stoical calm. The reason is that he has been living for a long time in Colossians 3, the entire life is hid with Christ in God, the whole set of the mind is on the things above, and the things on earth are transfigured.

Thank God that the almighty power of Jesus Christ is for us. All power is vested in Him in heaven and on earth, and He says, "Lo, I am with you all the days" (RV mg). All the power of the Deity of Christ is ours through His Resurrection.

HIS ASCENSION AND OUR UNION
Luke 24:50–51; Acts 1:9–10

His Transfiguration Consummated (John 17:5)
　Our Supernatural Salvation (Acts 2:33)

His Transformation Completed (Matthew 28:18)
　Our Sanctified Security (John 14:13)

His Trustiness Continued (Acts 7:56)
　Our Simple Satisfaction (John 17:23)

All the events in our Lord's life to which we have no corresponding experience happened after the Transfiguration. From then onwards our Lord's life was altogether vicarious. Up to the time of the Transfiguration, He had exhibited the normal perfect life of a man; from the Transfiguration onwards, everything is unfamiliar to us. Gethsemane, the Cross, the Resurrection—there is nothing like these experiences in our human life. From the Transfiguration on, we are dealing not so much with the life our Lord lived as with the way He opened the door for us to enter into His life. At His Ascension our Lord enters Heaven and keeps the door open for humanity. His Cross is the door for every member of the human race to enter into the life of God. Because of His Resurrection our Lord has the right to give eternal life to every individual man (John 17:2); and by His Ascension He becomes the possessor of all power in heaven and in earth (Matthew 28:18).

His Transfiguration Consummated

And now, O Father, glorify Thou Me with Thine own self with the glory which I had with Thee before the world was. (John 17:5)

When our Lord as a Man had fulfilled all God's demands of Him, and when by obedience He had transformed His natural life into a spiritual life, He reached the place where it was all spiritual, earth had no more hold on Him, and on the Mount of Transfiguration His real nature, viz., His essential Deity, broke all through the natural and He was transfigured. He had fulfilled all the requirements of His Father for His earthly life, and God's presence, symbolised in the cloud, waited to usher Him back into the glory which He had with the Father before the world was. But He turned His back on the glory, and came down from the Mount to identify Himself with fallen humanity, because through Calvary there was to issue the newly constructed humanity. If Jesus Christ had gone to heaven from the Mount of Transfiguration, He would have gone alone. He would have been to us a glorious Figure, One who manifested the life of God's normal man and how wonderful it is for God and man to live as one, but what good would that have been to us? We can never live in the power of an ideal put before us. What is the use of Jesus Christ telling us we must be as pure in heart as He is when we know we are impure? But Jesus Christ did not go to heaven from the Mount. Moses and Elijah talked with Him, not of His glory, nor of His Deity, but of His *death*, the issue which He was about to accomplish at Jerusalem. By His death on the Cross Jesus Christ made the way for every son of man to get into communion with God.

It was on this point that the enemy of God and of man assailed our Lord in the Garden of Gethsemane: "You will never get through as Son of Man; You will get through as Deity, but not as Deity Incarnate." Our Lord's object in becoming Deity Incarnate was to redeem mankind; and He did get through as Son of Man, which means that any and every man has freedom of access straight to God by right of the Cross of Jesus Christ. That is regeneration being made effectual in human lives, and the Holy Spirit is the One Who makes this marvellous Redemption actual in us.

On the Mount of Ascension the Transfiguration is completed. There is a similarity in the details of the two scenes, because the Ascension is the consummation of the Transfiguration. Our Lord does now, without any hesitation, go back into His primal glory; He does now go straight to the fulfilment of all the Transfiguration promised. But He does not go back simply as Son of God: He goes back to God as *Son of Man* as well as Son of God. The barriers are broken down, sin is done away with, death is destroyed, the power of the enemy is paralysed, and there is now freedom of access for any one straight to the very throne of God by the Ascension of the Son of Man. As He ascended our Lord stretched out His hands, the hands that He deliberately showed to the disciples after His resurrection, and the last the disciples saw of Him was His pierced hands. Those pierced hands are emblematic of the Atonement, and the angels' declaration was that it

is "this same Jesus" Who is to come again, with the marks of the Atonement upon Him. The Atonement means that the whole of the human race has been atoned for, Redemption is complete, and any man can get straight to the throne of God without let or hindrance[14] through the wonder of all that our Lord has done. He is now at the right hand of the Father, not only as Son of God (John 1:18), but as Son of Man.

Our Supernatural Salvation
Therefore being by the right hand of God exalted, and having received of the Father the promise of the Holy Ghost, He hath shed forth this, which ye now see and hear. (Acts 2:33)

Salvation means the incoming into human nature of the great characteristics that belong to God, and there is no salvation that is not supernatural. It is easy to say that human love and Divine love are one and the same thing; actually they are very far from being the same. It is also easy to say that human virtues and God's nature are one and the same thing; but this, too, is actually far from the truth. We must square our thinking with facts. Sin has come in and made a hiatus between human and Divine love, between human virtues and God's nature, and what we see now in human nature is only the remnant and refraction of the Divine. Human virtues according to the Bible are not promises of what human nature is going to be, but remnants of what human nature once was. This explains why we so often see remnants of original nobility in men and women who have not been born again into the Kingdom of God. As Christians we must learn to trace things to their right source. God makes very distinct the difference between the qualities that are Divine and those that are human. John 15:13 has reference to human love, which lays down its life for its friends. Romans 5:8 has reference to the Divine love, which lays down its life for its enemies, a thing human nature can never do. This does not mean that human beings cannot forgive; they can and do forgive; but forgiveness is not human, it belongs entirely to the Divine nature, and is a miracle when exhibited in the human.

Beware of philosophies. It is much more satisfactory to listen to a philosopher than to a proclaimer of the Gospel, because the latter talks with the gibes and the cuts of God, and they go straight to that in man which hates the revelation of the gap there is between man and God. If we accept the revelation, it will mean that we must be born from above (RV mg), and the Gospel message is that we can be born from above the second we want to.

---

14. without let or hindrance: legal phrase meaning "without obstacle or impediment."

Intellectually, we are inclined to ignore sin. The one element in man that does not ignore sin is conscience. The Holy Spirit deals with conscience first, not with intellect or emotions. When the Holy Spirit gets hold of a man and convicts him of sin, he instantly gets to despair, for he recognises that the holiness of Jesus Christ is the only thing that can ever stand before God, and he knows there is no chance for him. When conviction of sin comes in this way there is only one of two places—either suicide or the Cross of Jesus Christ. The majority of us are shallow, we do not bother our heads about Reality. We are taken up with actual comforts, with actual ease and peace, and when the Spirit of God comes in and disturbs the equilibrium of our life we prefer to ignore what He reveals.

Salvation is always supernatural. The Holy Ghost brings me into union with God by dealing with that which broke the union. It is dangerous to preach a persuasive gospel, to try and persuade men to believe in Jesus Christ with the idea that if they do, He will develop them along the natural line. Jesus Christ said, "I did not come to send peace, but a sword"; there is something to be destroyed first. Jesus Christ does not produce heaven and peace and delight straight off, He produces pain and misery and conviction and upset, and a man says, "If that is all He came to do, then I wish He had never come." But this is not all He came to do: He came to bring us into a supernatural union with His Father. When a man believes in Jesus Christ, i.e., commits himself to Jesus Christ—belief is a moral act, not an intellectual act—then the Ascended Lord, by the Holy Ghost, brings the man into oneness with His Father, it is a supernatural union.

The two centres of Christian life are Experience and Revelation. Are we thinking along the line of the revelations Jesus Christ has given? We can never get into touch with God by our own effort; but we must maintain touch with God by our own effort (Philippians 2:12–13). Jesus Christ can take anyone, no matter who he is, and presence him with His wonderful Divine salvation. The nature of God is shed abroad in our hearts by the Holy Ghost, but we have to maintain contact with His nature by obedience. Some sections of the Christian community teach that because we are all right in the anticipation of God, therefore it does not matter how we live actually. That is not true; we must not only be right in heart towards God, our life must show that we are right. Jesus Christ's life must work through our flesh, and that is where we have to obey. So many go into raptures over God's supernatural salvation, over the wonderful fact that God saves us by His sovereign grace (and we cannot do that too much), but they forget that now He expects us to get ourselves into trim to obey Him. We have to live in this mortal flesh as sons and daughters of God; we have to bring out to our finger tips the life that is hid with Christ in God, and we can do it because our ascended Lord has all power. If our flesh and blood does not allow the Son of God to manifest Himself in us, we are actually anti-Christ, we preach what our life denies, we proclaim a creed which our practical life spits at in ridicule. It is unconscious blasphemy to deny by our life that Jesus Christ can do what He claims He can. If we are born again, we are born into the life of God, and we have to see to it that we obey His life, and the faithfulness of the Holy Spirit is shown by the way He conscientiously chases us into a corner by touching every point where we have not been obeying.

His Transformation Completed
And Jesus came and spake unto them, saying, All power is given unto Me in heaven and in earth. (Matthew 28:18; cf. Matthew 11:27)

In Matthew 11:27 our Lord states that the revelation of the Father is entirely confined to the Son, He is the only Medium for revealing the Father. In Matthew 28:18 He says, "All power is given unto Me in heaven and in earth." Then has He power to make a saint of me? If not, He has totally misunderstood Himself and has misled me. Has He all power on earth? What about this "piece of earth" I have to look after, has He power over it? Am I professing by my lips that I am a Christian while my actual "piece of earth" laughs to scorn what Jesus Christ says? He says, "All power is given unto Me"; am I demonstrating that He has no power at all?

As Son of Man Jesus Christ deliberately limited omnipotence, omnipresence, and omniscience in Himself; now they are His in absolute full power. As Deity, they were always His; now as Son of Man they are His in absolute full power. At the throne of God, Jesus Christ has all power as Son of Man. That means He can do anything for any human being in keeping with His own character.

Our Sanctified Security
And whatsoever ye shall ask in My name, that will I do, that the Father may be glorified in the Son. (John 14:13)

That is where our salvation abides in its perfect security. Couple with these words our Lord's other statement, "All power is given unto Me." You say, "Oh well, then I can ask anything I like." Try it! I defy you to do it. Our Lord says also, "Ask what you *will*," i.e., what your will is in. There is very little our wills are in, consequently it is easy to work up false emotions. When you have been touched by the Holy Spirit and have received His quickening, note what you evade in prayer. There is nothing that will detect spiritual rottenness quicker than to *ask*, i.e., with the will. We shall find we have to stop asking a number of things, and this will simplify prayer. Our Lord says, "Ask," and we will always find that we do not ask when we talk about it. "I'll pray about it"—but we won't. To say we will pray about a thing often means we are determined not to think about it. Contact with Jesus Christ made the disciples realise that they were paupers, and they said, "Lord, teach us to pray" (Luke 11:1).

If we are perplexed over the question of sanctification, or about the baptism of the Holy Ghost, we ourselves are the reason why we are bothered. God has written a Book, and the phrases "sanctification" and the "baptism of the Holy Ghost" are His, not man's; why do we not go to Him about it? We are the reason why we do not go; we dare not go. If we honestly ask God to baptise us with the Holy Ghost and fire, anything that happens is His answer, and some appalling things happen. If we accept the revelation that our body is the temple of the Holy Ghost, are we prepared to ask God to fulfil the purpose of the Holy Ghost in our body? If we are, watch the consequences—that friendship must go, that book, that association, everyone of them must decay off like a lightning flash. If anyone has a difficulty in getting through to God, it is never God who is to blame. We can get through to Him as soon as we want to, there is nothing simpler. The trouble is when we begin to sympathise with the thing that is proud and strong in independence of God.

If we have been supernaturally saved by the Redemption of Jesus Christ, we know we are unfit, therefore we do not bother any more about ourselves, and as we walk in the light we have perfect freedom of access into the very heart and presence of God. The life of communion with God that Jesus lived on earth is what He has made possible for us by His Ascension.

Do not ask others to pray for you; our Lord says, "Pray yourself, *ask*." We each have our families, our Sunday School classes, our communities, our nation; how many of us are praying for them, or are we shirking the responsibility? We have to ask the thing that our will is in, and we cannot put our will into things God has not brought before us. "Whatsoever ye shall ask in My Name, that will I do." "In My name," not in Christian jargon, or in the piety of spurious devotion, but "in My *nature*." "The effectual fervent prayer of a righteous man availeth much." The prayers of some people are more efficacious than those of others, the reason being that they are under no delusion, they do not rely on their own earnestness, they rely absolutely on the supreme authority of the Lord Jesus Christ (Hebrews 10:19).

His Trustiness Continued
And said, Behold, I see the heavens opened, and the Son of man standing on the right hand of God. (Acts 7:56)

Stephen sees our Lord after His Ascension, and He is the same Jesus (cf. Revelation 1:7–15). Some teach that the Jesus of actual history is not the Christ, and that the risen Jesus is a conception of the divinely inspired imagination of the disciples. But it was "this same Jesus" that ascended—the marks of the Atonement were upon Him. When we look for the characteristics of the ascended Lord in the accounts of the historic Jesus, we are on the right track. We will find His characteristics in the New Testament, and He will exhibit these same characteristics to us in almighty power.

Our Simple Satisfaction
That they may be made perfect in one. (John 17:23)

The baptism of the Holy Ghost delivers us from the husk of independent individuality. By personality is meant the thing in every individual that the Spirit of God awakens and brings out into real communion with God. Individual self-assertiveness is the husk, personal identity with our Lord is the kernel. Individuals can never be made one; persons can. Individuality is all "elbows," it separates and isolates. A child is an individual, and it ought to be independent. Our Lord can never be defined in terms of individuality and independence, but only in terms of personality. The thing that is marked all through His life is personality, not independence and self-assertiveness. In the natural life when two people fall in love with one another, the individuality is transfigured because the personalities are merged. Identity is not domination, but oneness between two distinct persons in which neither dominates, but the oneness dominates both. In the natural life if the individuality re-asserts itself, there will be hitches and difficulties, and the same with the spiritual life. Jesus said, "If you would be My disciple, you must deny yourself, give up your right to yourself to Me." The natural independence of individuality springs from independence of God. If I will give up my right to myself to Him, the real true nature of my personality will answer to God straight away by the indwelling Holy Ghost. Jesus prayed, "that they may be one, even as We are one"; and when Paul urges us to put on the new man, he is urging on the most practical line that we put on in our actual life the habits that are in perfect accordance with this oneness with God, and that we do it all the time. Then there will come the simple satisfaction of knowing that God is answering the prayer of Jesus Christ. If you want to know what God is after in your life, read John 17—He prays that "they may be one, even as We are one." How close to God is Jesus Christ? "I and My Father are One." That is what He asks for us, and the Father will not leave us alone until the prayer is answered. Are we hindering the power of God in our life? Then never let us blame God. We may not only be supernaturally saved, we may be supernaturally sanctified. If we will submit to God and obey Him, we shall know that all that the Lord Jesus is in Himself is ours straightaway with the greatest ease and power and satisfaction by the right of His Ascension. He is King of kings and Lord of lords from the day of His Ascension until now.

HIS GLORIFICATION AND OURS

His Former Form of God (John 17:5)
    Our Present Glorying (Galatians 6:14)

His Fulfilled Fitness In God (1 Corinthians 15:28)
    Our Prevailing Glory (Romans 8:30)

His Faithful Face of God (John 1:34)
    Our Perpetual Glory (John 17:24)

As already stated, we must have Christian experience, but we must have more. Many of us are kindly interested in Christianity and in being devoted to Jesus Christ, but we have never received anything from Him. If we told ourselves the truth, we could not say that God had regenerated us experimentally. If we are not to be merely sentimental Christians, we must know what it is to be born into the kingdom of God and to find out that God has altered the thing that matters to us. That must be made perfectly clear first, and we have the experience described in Acts 26:18. We must have the experience of the new life, and then we have to see that the new life is instructed by the facts in God's Book. There are things that we cannot experience as Christians, yet we must build our faith upon them and not choose according to the predilections which are the outcome of our own experience.

His Former Form of God
And now, O Father, glorify Thou Me with Thine own self with the glory which I had with Thee before the world was. (John 17:5)

Jesus Christ came from somewhere to here, and the "somewhere" whence He came was Absolute Deity. Jesus Christ was not a Being Who became Divine, He was the Godhead Incarnated—"Who, being in the form of God . . ." The "form" of God originally in Absolute Deity is not the form we understand by the body, but "glory," the completeness of God, a form inconceivable to our human minds, in which what we call the Trinity was an absoluteness. The term "Trinity" is not a Bible word, but a term that arose in the throes of a great conflict of minds, and is the crystallised attempt to state the Godhead in a word. One element of the Godhead became, through the Word of God, the Incarnate Son of God. Beware of separating *God manifest in the flesh* from *the Son becoming sin.* In other words, never separate the doctrine of the Incarnation and the doctrine of Redemption. The Incarnation was for purposes of Redemption. The New Testament reveals that God became Incarnate only for the purpose of putting away sin. God did not become Incarnate for the purpose of Self-revelation.

When the Son of God, Who became Son of Man, has done His work, He will be resolved back again into Absolute Deity (1 Corinthians 15:28; cf. John 17:5). This is where our vocabulary will not go. We get into difficulties over God becoming Incarnate when we bring in our own conceptions. For instance, we say that the essential nature of God is omnipotence, omnipresence, and omniscience; the New Testament reveals that the essential nature of God is holiness, and that He became the weakest thing in His own creation, viz., a Baby. Are we prepared to abandon our own conceptions? We are all idolaters, we do mentally what Isaiah ridiculed the people in his day for doing (Isaiah 24:9–20). Our ideas have no more power over us than we choose to give them. We bring God to the bar of the judgement of our ideas. Jesus Christ said that His Father made His revelations to babes. Are we modest enough, and humble enough, and regenerate enough, to accept Him as Master of our brains as well as of our souls? Are we willing to be as submissive to Incarnate Reason as we are to Incarnate God? Incarnate Reason is the Lord Jesus, and any man who exercises his reason in contradiction to Incarnate Reason is a fool. We must never take our Lord's words and interpret them by our own human reason; we must always interpret them by His life. Am I prepared to be a believer in Jesus Christ? To believe in Jesus means much more than the experience of salvation in any form, it entails a mental and moral commitment to our Lord's view of the world, of the flesh, of the devil, of God, of man, and of the Scriptures. To "believe also in Me" means that we submit our intelligence to Jesus Christ our

Lord as He submitted His intelligence to His Father. This does not mean that we do not exercise our reason, but it does mean that we exercise it in submission to Reason Incarnate.

"And now, O Father, glorify Thou Me with Thine own self with the glory which I had with Thee before the world was" (John 17:5). Our Lord is referring to the former form of God. No human being has any conception of what that is, it is a revelation. The insidious teaching abroad to-day, the heresy that dissolves the Person of Jesus Christ, has crept in everywhere. Jesus Christ asks in His prayer, from His position as Son of Man, that He might be taken back to His former glory. "I have finished the work which Thou gavest Me to do." What was that work? To rehabilitate the human race, to bring the human race back to God—that is the work which God had given Him to do. Jesus Christ made the way clear for man to get straight into at-one-ment with God. Now that that work is completed—completed in His will, and soon to be completed in actuality—our Lord prays that He may be in the former form of God. There is no human connection in His prayer, it is superbly Divine.

Is Jesus Christ to me what He is in His estimate of Himself? He makes the destiny of the whole human race depend upon their relationship to Him. It is not the Divinity but the Deity of Jesus Christ that is the important thing.

Our Present Glorying

But God forbid that I should glory, save in the cross of our Lord Jesus Christ, by whom the world is crucified unto me, and I unto the world. (Galatians 6:14)

Glorying is the experience of joy on the inside, associated with the fame of God on the outside. Paul says his glorying is in the Cross of Christ, "and God forbid that I should glory in any other thing." Joy is neither happiness nor brightness, joy is literally the nature of God in my blood, no matter what happens. The joy that Jesus exhibited in His life was in knowing that every power of His nature was in harmony with His Father's nature, therefore He did with delight what God designed Him for as Son of Man. Anything that exactly fulfils the purpose of its creation experiences joy, and Paul states that our joy is that we fulfil the purpose of God in our lives by being saints. How are we going to be saints? We all like to listen to the life of Jesus and to His teaching, but what does it all amount to? Ask the one who has been born again, and he will tell you, to the limit of his language, the difference it has made. It has made an absolute difference, because by the Cross of Jesus Christ, we enter into the life of the Son of God. What is the sign that we are born from above (RV mg)? That we see the

rule of God. Have we got in us the new power, the new life, the new disposition that actually works itself out in our actual life? Our Lord did not tell us to ask for peace or for joy or for life, He told us to ask for the Holy Spirit (Luke 11:13), and when we ask, the honour of Jesus Christ is at stake. The reason God gives us the Holy Spirit so easily is because of what His Son has done, and yet He never emphasises what it cost, that is in the background altogether.

Our glorying is in the Cross of Jesus Christ because it is through this doorway that all the new life comes in (1 Corinthians 2:2). The normal life that God wants us to live is the life of the Lord Jesus Christ; but what good does it do us to talk about the speckless perfection of Jesus Christ? It would be a tantalising thing if all Jesus Christ gave us was the example of His own life. If a man is in earnest, it produces absolute despair. What is the good of teaching the Beatitudes, the Sermon on the Mount? They are out of our reach altogether. Once we remember that the normal life, the life of perfect oneness with God, is ours by means of Jesus Christ's death, it is all explained. We can enter there by His Cross. Have we entered there? It does not matter who the man is, how degraded or how moral, he can enter in at the door of His death, and then never cease to thank God that this is the crown of his joy. It is through the Cross of Jesus Christ that we begin to fulfil all that we are created for, and the great aim of the life is for the fame of God, not for the needs of men. Human sympathy has swamped the commands of God in the average Christian. Instead of the need being the opportunity it is made to be the call. The first of all the commandments is—"Thou shalt love the Lord thy God with all thy heart, and with all thy soul, and with all thy mind, and with all thy strength."

The basis of Reality is Redemption and not reason. Reason is the basis of the way we work on reality, it is an instrument. Thank God for logic and for reason, they are instruments for expressing our life, but life itself is not reasonable. Man's intellect has no power to lead him; his intellect makes him either a polished hypocrite or, in the case of a disciple of Jesus Christ, it becomes the bond slave of the right discernment of God's will (John 7:17).

His Fulfilled Fitness In God

And when all things shall be subdued unto Him, then shall the Son also Himself be subject unto Him that put all things under Him, that God may be all in all. (1 Corinthians 15:28)

This is the fulfilment of the prayer in John 17:5. When the Redemption wrought by the Son is actually fulfilled and all things are subdued unto Him, and when the whole human race and God are at one, then the Son of Man will cease to be by resolving back again into Absolute Deity. "And when all things shall be subdued unto Him" —remember everything is not yet subdued unto Him. Redemption does not only mean personal salvation and the redemption of our body, it means the absolute and complete redemption of the whole material earth in every iota, and not only the earth, but the whole material universe—"a new heaven and a new earth." It means that all relegated authority shall pass and God will be the absolute Authority, "that God may be all in all." There is a time coming, thank God, when everything shall be under the direct rule of God in every detail. We look for new heaven and a new earth, and then shall the human race stand before God as Jesus Christ stood before Him when He was here. Jesus Christ, Son of God and Son of Man, is not a mere individual, He is the One Who represents the whole human race. In order to see the human race as God intends it to be, look at the life of Jesus; and by the Redemption the human race is to be brought there. When the human race is actually there, Jesus Christ as Son of Man ceases to be and becomes absolute Deity again. The Son becomes subject to the Father, and God remains all in all. Our Lord's prayer is answered. "And now, O Father, glorify Thou Me with Thine own self with the glory which I had with Thee before the world was." That glory is to be in God.

Our Prevailing Glory
And whom He justified, them He also glorified. (Romans 8:30)

In John 17:5 we see the transcendent revelation of the Absolute Deity of our Lord; in John 17:22 He speaks of a second glory, "and the glory which Thou gavest Me I have given them." What glory had Jesus when He became the Son of Man vicariously, when He became the whole human race in one Person? what was His glory then? Did every one who saw Him say, "That is God Incarnate"? No, Isaiah said He shall be "as a root out of a dry ground," utterly disadvantaged. Is this true? Look in your own heart and you will see it is true. "He hath no form nor comeliness; and when we shall see Him, there is no beauty that we should desire Him." It is not true that "we needs must love the highest when we see it"; the human beings of His own day saw the Highest, and they hated Him. It needs the transformation of an inward surgery, being born from above (RV mg), to see that He is the altogether lovely One. The glory of Jesus was not an external thing; He effaced the Godhead in Himself so effectually that men without the Spirit of God

despised Him. His glory was the glory of actual holiness. What is holiness? Transfigured morality blazing with in dwelling God. Any other kind of holiness is fictitious and dangerous. One of the dangers of dealing too much with the Higher Christian Life[15] is that it is apt to fizzle off into abstractions. But when we see holiness in the Lord Jesus, we do know what it means, it means an unsullied walk with the feet, unsullied talk with the tongue, unsullied thinking of the mind, unsullied transactions of the bodily organs, unsullied life of the heart, unsullied dreams of the imagination—that is the actual holiness Jesus says He has given them. This is the meaning of sanctification. Paul says, and no wonder, "My little children, of whom I travail in birth again until Christ be formed in you." The holiness of the Son of God is to be actually manifested in our ordinary bodily lives. This is the actual experience of sanctification working out in each detail.

This is our prevailing glory; Paul is not talking about being justified and glorified hereafter, but now. Thank God, the joy of the Lord is an actual experience now, and it goes beyond any conscious experience, because the joy of the Lord takes us into the consciousness of God, and the honour at stake in our body is the honour of God. Have we realised that the Son of God has been formed in us by His wonderful Redemption? Are we putting on the habits that are in keeping with Him? This is the glory of the saint here and now—the glory of actual holiness manifested in actual life. Whether it comes out in eating and drinking or in preaching, it must show in every detail straight through until the whole limit actually manifests the complete new life.

His Faithful Face of God
And the Word was made flesh, and dwelt among us, (and we beheld His glory, the glory as of the only begotten of the Father,) full of grace and truth. (John 1:14)

In Genesis 1:2–3 we read that the Spirit of God brooded, the word of God was spoken, and creation was begun. John takes us back there; see also Proverbs 8—The Word has become Incarnate in the Lord Jesus Christ. He is the Word of God Incarnated, made flesh, and in Him we see the Face of God. All that our Lord said about Himself is in perfect accordance with this. "I and My Father are One." He did not say, "I and Humanity are one." Jesus nowhere said that God and man are one; He nowhere said "He that hath seen *man* hath seen the Father." Jesus nowhere taught that God was in man; but He did teach that God was manifested in human flesh in His own Per-

---

15. the Higher Christian Life: concept taught by various groups and organizations that emphasized sanctification and personal holiness.

son that He might become the generating centre for the same thing in every human being, and the place of His travail pangs is the Incarnation and Calvary and the Resurrection. Jesus Christ did not say that human beings were all specimens of God, as some men try to prove from conceptions of their own. "Reason being God, there can be nothing unreasonable; sin is not a positive thing, it is a defect in the desire to grasp hold of God." These blasphemies start from a thing that looks so humble, "God is all." God is not all. I am not God, neither are you. Jesus Christ reveals God as the Father. "I am the Way, . . . no man cometh unto the Father, but by Me." Jesus Christ is not the way to God, not a road we leave behind us, a fingerpost that points in the right direction; He is the way itself. "Abide in Me"; consequently the Lord satisfies the last aching abyss of the human heart. Has He satisfied yours? If not, why are you in Christian work? What is the explanation of the great craving for the salvation of the souls of men? If it is not born of the Holy Ghost experimentally realised in us, it is nothing in the world but the introduction of sordid commercialism into religion (Matthew 23:15). Why do we want people to be saved? Has Jesus Christ made such a difference to us that we cannot rest day or night till by prayer we get all our friends there? That is the passion for souls born of the Holy Ghost because its experimental reality is with us every day.

If we want to know what God is like, let us study the Lord Jesus. "He that hath seen Me hath seen the Father." How did people see Him in the days of His flesh? By their natural eyes? No, after His resurrection they received Holy Spirit, and their eyes were opened and they knew Him. We do not know Him by the reasoning of our minds, but by the new life.

Jesus Christ is to us the faithful Face of God. Could anyone be in doubt any more after they had seen Jesus Christ by the Holy Ghost? Think of the absurd, painful, distressing, never-to-be-answered questions we ask—"Shall I know those whom I love after death?" Wild, vagrant, wrong, stupid, painful questions. Look at Jesus Christ, get into contact with Him by the Holy Spirit, and those questions are impossible. He says—"Let not your heart be troubled: ye believe in God, believe also in Me." The Face of God is the Lord Jesus Christ. It always comes back to the simple point, "Come unto Me."

Our Perpetual Glory
Father, I will that they also, whom Thou hast given Me, be with Me where I am; that they may behold My glory, which Thou has given Me. (John 17:24)

Now our Lord is speaking of the glory which we are only to behold. We are not to be absorbed into God as drops in an ocean, we are to be lifted into perfect oneness with Him until God and the glory of perfected human redemption are transfigured by a mutual love. "I want those whom Thou hast given Me," says Jesus, "to behold My glory." What is His glory? "The glory which I had with Thee before the world was," and our perpetual glory is not only that we are saved and sanctified and redeemed and lifted into the glory of unspeakable things as the result of our Lord's Redemption, but something other—we shall see God face to face, an inconceivable beatific vision. This is what Jesus Christ has prayed for His saints. This is not the glory we have here, but the glory we are going to have, the glory of beholding His glory.

The Philosophy of Sin

and other
Studies in the Problems of
Man's Moral Life

Oswald Chambers

INTRODUCTION

Source

The Philosophy of Sin is taken from lectures by Oswald Chambers at the Bible Training College,[1] London, and at other meetings.

Publication History

- As articles: The lectures were published in the *Bible Training Course (BTC) Journal*[2] from April 1935 through March 1936, under the topic "Talks on Moral Foundations." Two sermons on "Sin" published in *God's Revivalist* magazine in 1908

contain a number of the same concepts presented in this book.

- As a book: *The Philosophy of Sin* was published in 1937.

Although the exact dates of these talks cannot be pinpointed, the essence of the material was delivered on many different occasions. It forms the bedrock of OC's teaching about human need and the provision of God to meet it. The biblical truths that burned in the soul of Oswald Chambers are stated and restated throughout this volume.

---

1. Bible Training College (BTC): a residential school near Clapham Common in southwest London. Sponsored by the League of Prayer; operated from 1911 until it closed in July 1915 because of World War I. Oswald Chambers was principal and main teacher; Biddy Chambers, his wife, was lady superintendent.

2. *Bible Training Course Monthly Journal:* published from 1932 to 1952 by Mrs. Chambers, with help from David Lambert.

CONTENTS

FOREWORD

The Philosophy of Sin is a subject of perennial interest, because the dreadful fact of sin is always with us. In every age there are the plain signs of some disruptive force at work among men. Hearts are being broken, lives are being spoiled, humanity is overclouded. Our Christian Faith sees that the underlying cause is Man's sin—his fundamental dislocation from God, with all its bitter consequences. A book like this, dealing with sin and its remedy, is to be welcomed, for it helps us to a clearer understanding of what is wrong with humankind, and of how the basic wrong can be put right—through Christ's Atonement making possible Man's repentance and appropriating faith. The salvation that blots out sin is here disclosed. "Sin is the radical twist with a supernatural originator, and salvation is a radical readjustment with a supernatural Originator." That is Good News indeed to every sinner; and every man finds out at last that he is that, if he is a seeker after the truth. There are many other matters treated here. There are problems of conscience, of outward conduct, of the emotional life, the intellect, the bodily life, of circumstances, nerves, spiritual reality, the natural instincts, and of true inward adjustment to God. No one can ponder these themes as here treated without profit. The one great aim is to show modern Christians the way to the high levels of true holiness and righteousness, so that we may well use Dora Greenwell's[3] prayer,

And Oh, that He fulfilled may see
The travail of His soul in me
And with His work contented be,
As I with my dear Saviour!

D. L.[4]

3. Dora Greenwell (1821–1882): English writer.
4. D. L.: David Lambert (1871–1961), Methodist minister; friend of Oswald and Biddy Chambers. Assisted Mrs. Chambers with OC publications from 1917 until his death in 1961.

THE PHILOSOPHY OF SIN

Departure from God's love is the common nature of all sin; and when the departure from this love was associated with a desire to progress in the direction of a selfishly appointed end, rather than of the end divinely appointed, this was the common nature of the primal sin of the world-spirit and of humanity.

The Bible is the only Book that tells us anything about the originator of sin. There is a difference between an experimental knowledge of sin and an intellectual understanding of what sin is. We seem to be built on the following plan: at first we experience a need, then we hunt for the satisfaction of that need; when the need is supplied we turn our whole nature in the direction of an explanation of how the need was supplied. When we are convicted of sin, we are convicted of the need of a Saviour; and we seek for the Saviour intellectually and in various other ways till we meet with our Lord by the power of His Spirit and experience salvation; then comes the great need we are trying to insist on in these talks, the need of turning the whole nature to understand how God supplied the need. That is what Christians are neglecting, they have the experience but they have left their minds to stagnate, they have not turned back again and tried to find out what God reveals about sin, about salvation, and about the whole life of man. According to the Bible, God is only manifested at the last point; when a man is driven by personal experience to the last limit, he is apt to meet God. The same thing is true in thinking, we can do very well without God in thinking as long as we think only as splendid animals. As long as we are not at the last place, not facing our problems at all, but simply pleased to be in existence, pleased to be healthy and happy, we will never find God, we do not see any need for Him. But when we are driven in thinking to the last limit, then we begin to find that God manifests Himself there. To people who are satisfied on too shallow a level the Bible is a book of impertinences, but whenever human nature is driven to the end of things, then the Bible becomes the only Book and God the only Being in the world.

1. The Masked Origin of Satan's Primal Sin (*Isaiah 14:12–15*)

We are dealing not so much with the experience of sin as with the light God's Word throws on how sin began; we must have a basis for thinking. If we have been delivered from sin by the power of God within us, thank God for it; but there is something more than that, we have now to allow God to illuminate our darkness by His revelation.

We take this passage in Isaiah as the early Christian fathers did, as an exposition of Satan behind his material puppets. One of the significant things the Bible reveals about Satan is that he rarely works without being incarnated. (See Genesis 3:15 and Matthew 16:23.) God's Spirit and our Lord trace Satan behind men and women who are really time-manifestations of Satan. That is the region in which we are to look for the obscure origin of sin; it does not look as if sin came in that way at all. Only when we are driven to extremes do we realise that the Bible is the only Book that gives us any indication of the true nature of sin, and where it came from.

(a) *Marvellous Originator of Sin (Isaiah 14:12)* An angel next in power to God is revealed to be the originator of sin.

(b) *Mystic Order of Revolt (v. 13)* In this verse the Mystic Order of Satan's Revolt is revealed, it was a purely spiritual revolt against God.

(c) *Mad Outrival of God (v. 14)* A determination to outrival God.

These three points are nonsense unless we are driven to the last limit. The fact that people ridicule the belief in Satan and sin is simply an indication of the principle we have laid down, that we do not see God till we get to the last point and His Word has no meaning for us until we get there; but when the soul of man is driven to the last lap of trying to find out things, then the Bible becomes the only Book there is, and this "theory," as men call it, is seen to be the revelation of God about the origin of sin. Sin is that factor in human nature which has a supernatural originator who stands next to God in power. The sin of Satan is revealed only dimly, but the dim outline indicates that it was the summit of all sin, full, free, conscious, spiritual sin; he was not entrapped into it, he was not ensnared into it, he sinned with the full clear understanding of what he was doing. We know that much, so far the veil is transparent.

2. The Masked Outguards of Satan's Primal Snare (*Genesis 3:6–7*)

Satan guards the main body of his purpose; neither Eve nor Adam had the slightest notion who he was; he was as far removed in his first snare from his real body of intent as could possibly be. We have to remember that God created Adam a "son of God," and God required Adam to develop himself by obeying Him; that obedience necessarily involved the sacrifice of the natural life to transform it into spiritual life, and this was to be done by a series of moral choices. Satan lays his first snare there, the first out-guard[5] of his snare is away altogether from the main body of his purpose, he does not reveal what he is after in the beginning.

(a) Soul Stained by Natural Interest (Genesis 3:6)

Verse 6 reveals that Satan was part of God's natural creation, he spoke to the woman first, who represented all we understand by the affinities of a human soul for the natural life, unsuspecting, unsuspicious, sympathetic and curious. In looking at sin in its beginnings, we find its true nature in all its working. Our Lord spoke about men as sheep; a sheep has no set conscious purpose to go wrong, it simply wanders; and our Lord used the illustration for men; the majority of men wander like sheep without any conscious bad intent at all. That is the first outwork or outguard of Satan, he gets us all here like silly stupid sheep; he has never altered his way of working, and although it is written clearly in God's Book, we never seem to be forewarned that the soul is stained through natural interest.

(b) Soul Snared by Natural Intimacy (v. 6)

The two intimacies indicated in verse 6 are, first, intimacy with the object desired, and, second, intimacy with the closest vital relationship; when Eve saw the food was good she fetched her husband. To sin alone is never possible. In writing of Eve, Paul says that Satan "beguiled" her, meaning by that that there was no clear understanding on her part of the wrong she had done; but "Adam was not beguiled" (RV). "He did eat" (Genesis 3:6). Adam's sin was the perfect conscious realisation of what he was doing.

(c) Soul Sin by Natural Influence (Genesis 3:7)

Adam was required by God to take part in his own development, i.e. he had to transform the life of nature into the spiritual life by obeying God. The life of nature is neither moral nor immoral; our bodies are neither moral nor immoral, we make them moral or immoral. Our Lord had a body, and we read that He hungered; it was not a sin for Him to be hungry, but it would have been a sin for Him to have eaten during the forty days in the wilderness, because His Father's word at that time was that He should not eat. It is not a sin to have a body, to have natural appetites, but it is a sin to refuse to sacrifice them at the word of God. Satan's first fundamental outguards are in the innocence of nature. We say, "But it cannot be wrong to have a little sympathy here, a little curiosity there"; the Bible lifts the veil just enough to show there is a great supernatural force behind that entices for one purpose, to get us away from obeying God's voice.

3. The Masked Overset of Spiritual Surrender (Genesis 3:1–7)

Satan succeeded in putting his outguards so far away from the main body of his purpose that no one but God Himself knew what he was doing. Unsuspecting Eve was as far removed from understanding what Satan was doing as we are when we sin, but where both are culpable in every respect is in the refusal to obey God; and whenever there is a refusal to obey God, instantly Satan's first snare is entered into. When once the first snare has caught us we are done for, the rest is as easy as can be; once let the principle of refusing to sacrifice the life of nature to the will of God have way, and all the rest happens easily.

(a) Infused Suspicion of the Innermost (Genesis 3:1)

It was the internal region of man, the innermost, that yielded first; bodily action was last; the first thing that yielded was the mind. The Bible reveals that human nature possesses an incurable suspicion of God. Its origin is explained in the Bible; two great primal creatures of God, the angel who became Satan, and Adam, negotiated a relationship which God never sanctioned. That was how sin was introduced into the world. As long as we live on the surface of things merely as splendid animals, we shall find the Bible nonsense. We are reverent over the Bible simply because our fathers and mothers taught us to be reverent; but we find no practical reason for reverence until we get to the last lap, until we are pressed out of the outer court into the inner, then we find there is no mind among men that has ever penned words that are sufficient for us there; we begin to find that the only Book there is the Bible. When we get to the last point the only exact counterpart for our natural life is this Book.

When the Bible touches the question of sin, it always comes right down to this incurable suspicion of God which never can be altered apart from the Atonement because it is connected with a great supernatural power behind. Paul talks about it and calls it the "carnal mind," he does not say it is at enmity with God, because that might mean it could be cured; he says it *is* "enmity against God." Remember the summit of all sin was a conscious red-handed revolt against God. Adam's sin was not a conscious revolt against God; it worked out ultimately through the race as a revolt against God, but Adam's sin instead of being at the summit of all sin is at the foundation of all sin. Consequently whatever sin you take, you will get the characteristics that were in this first sin, viz., the principle and the disposition of this infused suspicion, "Yea, hath God said . . ." (Genesis 3:1). Absolute devastation awaits the soul that allows sus-

---

5. outguard: advance guard, outpost, or decoy away from the main army or site of defense.

picion to creep in. Suspicion of God is like a gap in a dike, the flood rushes through, nothing can stop it. The first thing you will do is to accept slanders against God. Because it is peculiar to you? No, because it is according to the stock that runs right straight through the human race, from this first sin of infused suspicion in the intelligence, in the innermost part of man.

The majority of us prefer to trust our innocence rather than the statements of Jesus. It is always risky to trust your innocence when the statements of Jesus are contrary to it. Jesus says that "from within, out of the heart of men, proceed . . . ," then comes the awful catalogue. You say, "Why, that is nonsense, I never had any of those things in my heart, I am innocent." Some day you will come up against a set of circumstances which will prove that your innocence was a figment, and that what Jesus said about the human heart was perfectly true.

(b) Irresistible Sensuality of the Inner (Genesis 3:5)
Once allow suspicion of God and of His goodness and justice to enter into a man's mind and the floodgates of sensuality are opened. We mean by "sensuality," the life that draws its sustenance from natural surroundings, guided by a selfishly appointed purpose. We used to mean by sensuality gross awful and shocking sins; the word means that but a great deal more. Sensuality may be refined down to the thinness of a cloud. It is quite possible to be grossly sensual and spiritual. It is possible to say, "I have one desire in being good, in being saved and sanctified, a particular end of my own"; that is sensuality. Once suspicion of God is allowed to come in, there is no limit to the flood of sensuality. Lust, too, is a word that the Bible uses in a different way. We use the word lust for the gross abominable sins of the flesh only, but the Bible uses it for a great deal more than that. Lust simply means, "I must have this at once"; it may be a bodily appetite or a spiritual possession. The principle lust works on is, "I must have it at once, I cannot wait for God's time, God is too indifferent," that is the way lust works. Watch how our Lord faced men, He always faced this disposition of sin, He never summed men up by their external conduct. He was not driven into panics by immorality and fleshly sordidness, that sort of sin never seemed to bother Him half as much as the respectable pride of men and women who never were guilty of those things. The mainspring of such lives is a wise judicious working which keeps all outward circumstances in harmony with the one ruling desire. The soul, remember, is simply the spirit of a man expressing itself. The spirit of a child can rarely express itself, the soul has not become articulate. "Soul" in the Bible nearly always refers to the fleshly nature, it is the only power a man has for expressing his true spirit. "God is always manifested in the ulti-

mates" (Goethe). That is what we mean by saying that God is only revealed at the last point. If we are only living on the surface of things the Bible line will appear stupid, but if we have had a dose of the plague of our own heart, and realise what God has delivered us from, we know much too much ever to accept man's definition of sin, we know that there is no other explanation than the Bible one, and nothing but pity is awakened when we hear people trying to explain sin apart from the Bible.

(c) Iniquitous Succumbing of the Individual (Genesis 3:7)
"Iniquitous" means an unjust and unequal twisting; and "individual" means here the whole person going out in a definite act. Suspicion first, sensuality next, and manifest ruin last. If sin is a radical twist with a supernatural originator, salvation is a radical readjustment with a supernatural Originator. To present salvation as less than that is deplorable. If all Jesus Christ can do is to run a parallel counteraction with what Satan can do, His right name is "Culture," not "Saviour"; but His revealed nature was stated by the angel to Mary, and repeated over and over again, "Thou shalt call His name Jesus; *for He shall save His people from their sins.*" The slight views of salvation, the sympathetic drifty views that all Jesus Christ can do is to put in us a principle that counteracts another principle, will cause anyone who has got to the last limit to blaspheme God for a thing like that. It all comes from a flimsy, wrong view of sin. If that is all He can do, what is the good of calling Him Saviour? No one who has ever faced sin in its reality would ever give one cent for that kind of salvation, it is nothing but the exalting of education, culture will do that, or cunning. When you come to the New Testament and to your own experience you find that salvation is as radical as sin, and if God has not radically altered your heredity, thank God you may know He can by the power of Jesus Christ's Atonement. It is only the right view of sin and right thinking about sin that ever will explain Jesus Christ's Life and Death and Resurrection. It is sin that He came to cope with; He did not come to cope with the poor little mistakes of men, they cope with their own mistakes; He came to give them a totally new stock of heredity, that is, He came to implant into them His own nature, so that Satan's power in the soul is absolutely destroyed, not counteracted.

When God has put His Spirit in you and identified you with Jesus Christ, what is to be your attitude to your bodily life? You have the same body, the same appetites and the same nature as before, your members used to be servants of sin; but Jesus Christ is your Example now. He sacrificed Himself to His Father's will, see that you do the same as a saint. He submitted His intelligence to His Father's will, see that you do the same as a saint. He submitted His will to His Father, see that you as a saint do the same. Jesus Christ did all that Adam failed to do. Satan met our Lord with his masked outguards exactly as he met Adam, and the Spirit of God drove Jesus into the wilderness to meet these outguards of Satan. "If Thou be the Son of God . . ." Satan tried to insinuate the first suspicion, but it would not work, Jesus refused to be suspicious of God. He overcame by obeying the word of His Father, that is, He transformed His natural life into a spiritual life by obeying the voice of God, and as saints we have to obey Jesus Christ and sacrifice the life of nature to His will.

EDUCATIVE INSIGHT INTO REDEMPTION

How much more shall the blood of Christ, who through the eternal Spirit offered Himself without blemish unto God, cleanse your conscience from dead works to serve the living God? Hebrews 9:14 (RV)

1. True to the Cross

As we go on with God the Holy Spirit brings us back more and more to the one absorbing theme of the New Testament, viz. the death of the Lord Jesus Christ and its meaning from His standpoint. Our right to ourselves in every shape and form was destroyed once and for ever by the death of Jesus, and we have to be educated into the realisation of what this means in all its fulness. We have to come to a relationship to the Cross in thought as well as in life.

"*How much more . . .*" How much more is there to know, for instance, after sanctification? Everything! Before sanctification we know nothing, we are simply put in the place of knowing; that is, we are led *up* to the Cross; in sanctification we are led *through* the Cross—for what purpose? For a life of outpouring service to God. The characteristic of a saint after identification with the death of Jesus is that he is brought down from the ineffable glory of the heavenly places into the valley to be crushed and broken in service for God. We are here with no right to ourselves, for no spiritual blessing for ourselves; we are here for one purpose only—to be made servants of God as Jesus was. Have we as saints allowed our minds to be brought face to face with this great truth. The death of Jesus not only gives us remission from our sins, it enables us to assimilate the very nature of Jesus until in every detail of our lives we are like Him. "How much more" does the death of Jesus mean to us to-day than it ever has before? Are we beginning to be lost in wonder, love and praise at the marvellous loosening from sin, and are we so assimilating the nature of Jesus that we bear a strong family likeness to Him?

"*shall the blood of Christ . . .*" It was not the blood of a martyr, not the blood of goats and calves, that was shed, but "the blood of Christ." The very life of God was shed for the world—"the church of God which He purchased with His own blood." (Acts 20:28 RV) All the perfections of the essential nature of God were in that blood; all the holiest attainments of man were in that blood. The death of Jesus reaches away down underneath the deepest sin human nature ever committed. This aspect of the death of Jesus takes us into a spiritual domain beyond the threshold of the thinking of the majority of us. The cry on the Cross, "My God, My God, why hast Thou forsaken Me?" is unfathomable to us. The only ones—and I want to say this very deliberately—the only ones who come near the threshold of understanding the cry of Jesus are not the martyrs, they knew that God had not forsaken them, His presence was so wonderful; not the lonely missionaries who are killed or forsaken, they experience exultant joy, for God is with them when men forsake them: the only ones who come near the threshold of understanding the experience of God-forsakenness are men like Cain—"My punishment is greater than I can bear"; men like Esau, ". . . an exceeding bitter cry"; men like Judas. Jesus Christ knew and tasted to a fuller depth than any man could ever taste what it is to be separated from God by sin. If Jesus Christ was a martyr, our salvation is a myth. We have followed cunningly devised fables if Jesus Christ is not all that this cry represents Him to be—the Incarnate God becoming identified with sin in order to save men from hell and damnation. The depth of this cry of Jesus is deeper than any man can go because it is a cry from the heart of God. The height and depth of our salvation are only measured by God Almighty on His throne and Jesus Christ in the heart of hell. The most devout among us are too flippant about this great subject of the death of Jesus Christ. When we stand before the Cross, is our every commonplace pious mood stripped off, or do we get caught up by the modern spirit and think of the Cross only as delivering us from sin, or as a type of sanctification? Thank God for salvation through the Cross, for sanctification through the Cross; but thank God also for insight into what it cost God to make that salvation and sanctification possible. God grant that the pulsing power of identification with the death of Jesus may come again into our testimony and make it glow with devotion to Him for His unspeakable salvation.

"*Who through the eternal Spirit . . .*" The life of Jesus portrays the handiwork of the Holy Spirit; we know what the Holy Spirit will be in us if we let Him have His way. The underlying consciousness of Jesus was the Eternal God Himself; the Eternal Spirit was behind all He did. It is not so with us. There is a fundamental difference as well as a similarity between the Spirit in Jesus and the Spirit in us. The Eternal Spirit was incarnated in Jesus; He never is in us. By regeneration and sanctification He energises our spirits and brings us into oneness with Jesus Christ, so that our underlying consciousness is "hid with Christ in God." We are only made acceptable to God by relying on the Eternal Spirit Who was incarnated absolutely in Jesus Christ. The Spirit in us will never allow us to forget that the death of Jesus was the death of God Incarnate. "God was in Christ, reconciling the world unto Himself" (2 Corinthians 5:19).

"*offered Himself without blemish unto God . . .*" Who offered Himself? The Son of God. He was immaculate, without blemish, yet He was crucified. This rules out once and for ever the conception that Jesus died the death of a martyr; He died a death no martyr could touch. He died the death not of a good man but of a bad man, with the vicarious pain of Almighty God in His heart.

Our hearts are wrung with pathos when we read of the offering of Isaac and the sacrifice of Jephthah's daughter, for they are unbearably pathetic. The offering of Jesus is not pathetic in the tiniest degree; it is beyond all pathos. There is something infinitely profounder than pathos in the death of Jesus; there is a mystery we cannot begin to touch. The death of Jesus is the death of God, at the hands of man, inspired by the devil. He gathered round Him the raging hate of humanity, and was crucified. He offered Himself through the Eternal Spirit—He died in the Spirit in which He lived.

Are we being true to the Cross in our preaching, putting first the holiness of God that makes men know that they are sinners? When we preach the love of God there is a danger of forgetting that the Bible reveals not first the love of God but the intense, blazing holiness of God, with His love as the centre of that holiness. When the holiness of God is preached, men are convicted of sin; it is not the love of God that first appeals but His holiness. The awful nature of the conviction of sin that the Holy Spirit brings makes us realise that God cannot, dare not, must not forgive

sin; if God forgave sin without atoning for it our sense of justice would be greater than His.

2. True to Conscience

How does all the profound thought underlying the death of Jesus touch us? The writer to the Hebrews instantly connects it with conscience—"How much more shall the blood of Christ, . . . *cleanse your conscience* from dead works to serve the living God?" (RV). Has conscience the place in our salvation and sanctification that it ought to have? Hyper-conscientious people blind themselves to the realisation of what the death of Jesus means by saying, "No, I have wronged this person and I must put the thing right." It springs from the panging remorse that we experience when we realise we have wronged another. "All you say about the Cross may be true, but I have been so mean[6] and so wrong that there are things I must put right first." It sounds noble to talk like that, but it is the essence of the pride that put Jesus Christ to death. The only thing to do is to cast the whole thing aside: "My God, this thing in me is worthy only of death, the awful death of crucifixion to the last strand of life. Lord, it is my sin, my wrong, not Jesus Christ, that ought to be on that Cross." When we get there and abandon the whole thing, the blood of Christ cleanses our conscience and the freedom is ineffable and amazing.

The greatest problems of conscience are not the wrong things we have done, but wrong relationships. We may have become born again, but what about those we have wronged? It is of no use to sit down and say, "It is irreparable now, I cannot alter it." Thank God He can alter it! We may try to repair the damage in our own way, by apologising, by writing letters; but it is not a simple easy matter of something to apologise for. Behind the veil of human lives God begins to reveal the tragedies of hell. Or we may say, "I have been atoned for, therefore I do not need to think about the past." If we are conscientious, the Holy Spirit will make us think about the past, and it is just here that the tyranny of nerves and the bondage of Satan comes in. The shores of life are strewn with ruined friendships, irreparable severances through our own blame or others', and when the Holy Spirit begins to reveal the tremendous twist, then comes the strange distress, "How can we repair it?" Many a sensitive soul has been driven into insanity through anguish of mind because he has never realised what Jesus Christ came to do, and all the asylums in the world will never touch them in the way of healing; the only thing that will is the realisation of what the death of Jesus means, viz. that the damage we have

---

6. mean: as used here, something or someone ordinary, common, low, or ignoble, rather than cruel or spiteful.

done may be repaired through the efficacy of His Cross, Jesus Christ has atoned for all, and He can make it good in us, not only as a gift but by a participation on our part. The miracle of the grace of God is that He can make the past as though it had never been; He can "restore . . . the years that the locust hath eaten, the cankerworm, and the caterpillar, and the palmerworm" (Joel 2:25).

How Jesus Christ does cleanse our conscience! It is freedom not only from sin and the damage sin has done, but emancipation from the impairing left by sin, from all the distortions left in mind and imagination. Then when our conscience has been cleansed from dead works, Jesus Christ gives us the marvellously healing ministry of intercession as "a clearing-house for conscience." Not only is all sense of past guilt removed, but we are given the very secret heart of God for the purpose of vicarious intercession (see Romans 8:26–27).

"*from dead works . . .*" What are "dead works"? Everything done apart from God. All prayer, all preaching, all testifying, all kind, sacrificial deeds done apart from God, are dead works that clog the life. Never forget for one moment that you are what you are by the grace of God. If you are not what you are by the grace of God, then may God have mercy on you! Everything we are that is not through the grace of God will be a dead clog on us. Oh believe me, the curse of the saint is his goodness! Let the whole thing go, be true to the Cross, and let Jesus Christ cleanse your conscience from dead works. Many saints misunderstand what happens to the natural virtues after sanctification. The natural virtues are not promises of what we are going to be, but remnants of what God created man to be. We have the idea that we can bank on our natural patience and truthfulness and conscientiousness; we can bank on nothing in heaven above or earth beneath but what the grace of God has wrought in us. Everything we possess in the way of moral property, of noble spiritual property, severs us from God; all must go.

"Nothing in my hands I bring. . . ." Immediately we abandon like that, we experience what Paul says in Galatians 2:20—"I have been crucified with Christ" (RV), and the reconstruction of our lives proves that God has cleansed us from all dead works.

"*. . . to serve the living God.*" This means a life laid down for Jesus, a life of narrowed interests, a life that deliberately allows itself to be swamped by a crowd of paltry things. It is not fanaticism, it is the steadfast, flint-like attitude of heart and mind and body for one purpose—spoilt for everything saving as we can be used to win souls for Jesus. It is not "a passion for souls," but something infinitely profounder than that, it is the passion of the Holy Ghost for Jesus Christ. There are things that are too humanly tender for this kind of service. There are lives prevented by claims that are not God's, prevented by the tender, passionate love of others who have come in between. Oh the amount of wasted service for God, the agonies of weeping and self-pity, the margins of mourning over wasted opportunities! Jesus Christ never spent one moment of His life mourning in that way. The kind of things we grieve over is the evidence of where our life is hid. Some of us have a social conscience, we are shocked at moral crime; some of us have a religious conscience, we are shocked at the things that go against our creeds. The conscience formed in us by the Holy Spirit makes us amazingly sensitive to the things that tell against the honour of God.

I am convinced that what is needed in spiritual matters is reckless abandonment to the Lord Jesus Christ, reckless and uncalculating abandonment, with no reserve anywhere about it; not sad, you cannot be sad if you are abandoned absolutely. Are you thankful to God for your salvation and sanctification, thankful He has purged your conscience from dead works? Then go a step further; let Jesus Christ take you straight through into identification with His death until there is nothing left but the light at the foot of the Cross, and the whole sphere of the life is hid with Christ in God.

SALVATION

Ye that have escaped the sword, go ye, stand not still; remember the LORD from afar, and let Jerusalem come into your mind. Jeremiah 51:50 (RV)

Salvation is the biggest, gladdest word in the world; it cannot mean pretence in any shape or form, therefore suppression is no element of the word, neither is counteraction. Salvation is God's grace to sinful men, and it takes a lifetime to say the word properly. Most of us restrict the meaning of salvation, we use it to

mean New Birth only, or something limited. We are dealing with the subject here practically, not theologically.

1. The Element of Destruction in Salvation
Ye that have escaped the sword . . .

The 51st chapter of Jeremiah almost burns the page, it is so full of strong and intense destruction; but it gives the keynote to the purpose of God in destruction, viz. the deliverance of the good. You will never find in the Bible that things are destroyed for the sake of destruction. Human beings destroy for the sake of destruction, and so does the devil; God never does, He destroys the wrong and the evil for one purpose only, the deliverance of the good.

(a) The Purpose of the Sword

The purpose of the sword is to destroy everything that hinders a man being delivered. The first thing in salvation is the element of destruction, and it is this that men object to. With this thought in mind, recall what our Lord said about His own mission: "Think not that I am come to send peace on earth: I came not to send peace, but a sword" (Matthew 10:34). Our Lord reveals Himself as the destroyer of all peace and happiness, and of ignorance, wherever these are the cloke for sin (cf. Matthew 3:10). It sounds a startling and amazing thing to say that Jesus did not come to send peace, but He said He did not. The one thing Jesus Christ is after is the destruction of everything that would hinder the emancipation of men. The fact that people are happy and peaceful and prosperous is no sign that they are free from the sword of God. If their happiness and peace and well-being and complacency rests on an undelivered life, they will meet the sword before long, and all their peace and rest and joy will be destroyed.

(b) The Peril of the Sword

To say that "God loves the sinner, but hates his sin" sounds all right, but it is a dangerous statement, because it means that God is far too loving ever to punish the sinner. Jesus Christ came to save us so that there should be no "sinner" left in us. The phrase "a sinner saved by grace" means that a man is no longer a sinner; if he is, he is not saved. If I refuse to let God destroy my sin, there is only one possible result—I must be destroyed with my sin. The light of the Lord's presence convicts of sin. (See John 15:22–24.) Sin is never imputed unless it is conscious. These verses reveal the very essence of the destructive element of salvation. I can easily say I am not convicted of sin; but immediately I stand face to face with Jesus Christ I know the difference between Him and myself; I have no cloke and no excuse, and if I refuse to allow the Lord to deliver me from all that He reveals, I shall be destroyed with the thing He came to destroy. "To this end was the Son of God manifested, that He might destroy the works of the devil" (1 John 3:8 RV).

(c) The Power of the Sword

An ancient legend tells of a blacksmith who became famous for the magnificent swords he made; he claimed that they could cut a coat of armour in two with one sweep. The king hearing of this boast, summoned the blacksmith to his presence and told him

to cut through his coat of armour and if he could not do it, he would be put to death for his boasting. The blacksmith swung his sword round and put it back in its sheath; the king was about to challenge him, when the blacksmith said, "Shake yourself, your majesty"; the king shook himself, and fell in two. The legend is an illustration of the tremendous power of the sword in God's hands, "the sword of the Spirit, which is the word of God." "The word of God is . . . sharper than any twoedged sword," and it deals effectually with the sin in us; for a while we may not be conscious that anything has happened, then suddenly God brings about a crisis and we realise that something has been profoundly altered. No one is ever the same after listening to the word of God, you cannot be; you may imagine you have paid no attention to it, and yet months after maybe a crisis arises and suddenly the word of God comes and grips you by the throat, so to speak, and awakens all the terrors of hell in your life, and you say, "Wherever did that word come from?" Years ago, months ago, weeks ago, it sank straight into your unconscious mind, God knew it was there though you did not, and it did its damaging work, and now it has suddenly come to light. The question is, will you allow yourself to escape the edge of the sword, or will you be destroyed with the thing the sword has pierced?

Look back over your own life and examine the points of view you have now and the points of view you once had. At one time you were violently opposed to the views you now hold; what has altered you? You cannot honestly say it was conscious study. God says that His word shall not return unto Him void (Isaiah 55:10–11)—the abiding success of the word of God! The word of God is never without power, and as a servant or handmaid of God you have nothing whatever to do with whether people dislike and reject the word of God, or "purr" over it. See you preach it no matter what they think of you, that is a matter of absolute indifference, sooner or later the effect of that word will be manifested. The great snare is to seek acceptance with the people we talk to, to give people only what they want; we have no business to wish to be acceptable to the people we teach. "Study to show thyself approved"—unto the saints? No, "unto God." I have never known a man or woman who taught God's word to be always acceptable to other people. As a worker for God truths are all the time coming into your own life which you would never have seen for yourself, and as you give other people truths they never saw before, they will say—"I don't agree with that." It is foolish to begin to argue, if it is God's truth leave it alone; let mistakes correct themselves. When a crisis comes that shakes the life, they will find the old dominating power is not there at all. What has happened? The destruction of God has gone on. Then comes the critical moment, will I go with the thing that is destroyed, or will I stay by the hand that holds the sword?

The best measure of the profundity of any religious doctrine is given by its conception of sin and its cure of sin.

Do I believe that sin needs to be corrected or killed? If sin only needed to be corrected, the symbol would have been a lash, not a sword; but God uses the symbol for killing. Beware of getting into your mind ideas which never came from God's word, the idea, for instance, that we sin a little less each day; if we do, the salvation of Jesus Christ has never touched us. If we grow in grace a little more every day, it is a sign that the destructive power of God has been at work, and that we have been delivered from the thing that hindered us growing. The view men have of sin is always the test of their view of salvation, and to-day views are creeping into God's Book that never came from Him. Sin must be destroyed, not corrected; it is the destruction of something in order to lead to emancipation. It is always God rescuing Israel from Babylon; always Jesus Christ rescuing His people from their sin.

2. The Element of Direction in Salvation
Go ye, stand not still . . .

To study the teaching of our Lord in connection with the verb "to go" would amaze us. How often do you hear in meetings the word "go," and how often do you hear the word "get"? We emphasise "get"; the New Testament emphasises "go." If you have escaped the edge of the sword, go!

(a) The Paralysis of Sin
Slaves born in slavery and suddenly freed, will often prefer to go back. When the slaves in America were freed, they did not know what to do with their freedom, they were amazed and dazed and stupid, they had never been master of themselves before, and many pleaded with their masters to be taken back. That moment of paralysis is the natural result of being suddenly delivered. A sinner when first delivered from sin has such moments, he wishes God would take him safe to heaven where he would be secure from temptation. We may not say it, but it is common to us all to look at things in this way in the implicit region, if not in the explicit—"Yes, I believe God does deliver from sin and fill with the Holy Spirit, and if He would only take me straight to heaven it would be all right, but I have to live amongst people who are wrong, in the midst of a people of unclean lips and the memory of how continually I fell in the past makes me fear I shall do it again in the

future." Satan takes advantage of these moments of paralysis; consequently there is need for direction. A snare in many evangelistic meetings is that people are taught to say, "Thank God, I am saved," or, " Thank God I am sanctified," but no line of direction is given. The counsel in God's Book is—Testify to the truth God has revealed to you, and go on. People begin to degenerate because they don't know what to do; the direction given in God's Book has never been put in its right place. The direction is summed up in this one word, *Go.*

(b) The Pain of the Saved
When a limb that has long been cramped is released, there is the experience of excessive pain, but the pain is the sign of life. The first moment of realising God's truth is usually a moment of ecstasy, the life is brimming over with joy and happiness and brightness, there is no pain, nothing but unspeakable, unfathomable joy. Then the verb "to go" begins to be conjugated, and we experience the "growing pains" of salvation, and Satan comes as an angel of light and says, "Don't go on, stand still," and, in the language of the hymn, "sing yourself away to everlasting bliss"! We do not consider enough the necessity of learning how to walk spiritually. Remember, when we are saved, we have been cramped in sin. Paul puts it in this way— "You used to use your members as servants for sin, now you are emancipated from sin, use your members as servants to righteousness," that is, use them in a different way. (See Romans 6:19.) If a man has used his arm only for writing, and then becomes a blacksmith, he will groan for days with the tremendous pain in the deltoid muscle until by practice the time comes when there is no more pain because the muscle has become rightly adjusted to its new work. The same thing happens spiritually, God begins to teach us how to walk and over and over again we begin to howl and complain. May God save us from the continual whine of spiritual babes—"Teach us the same things over and over again, don't give us the revelations of God which are painful, give us the 'simple gospel,' i.e. what we have always believed, don't tell us of things we have never thought about before, because that causes pain" (cf. Hebrews 5:12). Of course it does. Thank God there is a pain attached to being saved, the pain of growing until we come to maturity where we can do the work of a son or daughter of God.

(c) The Passion in the Saving
The application of our Lord's phrase, "Behold, we go up to Jerusalem," is this passion not to stand still, but to go on. Look back over your life in grace, whether long or short, and ask yourself which are the days that have furthered you most in the knowledge of God— the days of sunshine and peace and prosperity? Never!

The days of adversity, the days of strain, the days of sudden surprises, the days when the earthly house of this tabernacle was strained to its last limit, those are the days when you learned the meaning of this passion of "Go." Any great calamity in the natural world—death, disease, bereavement—will awaken a man when nothing else would, and he is never the same again. We would never know the "treasures of darkness" if we were always in the place of placid security. Thank God, salvation does not mean that God turns us into milksops; God's salvation makes us for the first time into men and women. The passion of the Holy Ghost means that we go on with God exactly on the lines God wants; the Holy Ghost will give the direction, and if we do not know it we are to blame. "My people doth not consider," says God; they won't heed this Book. We say, "I don't like studying these subjects, I have no affinity for them." We do not say it actually, but over and over again these thoughts keep us from going on with God. The Holy Spirit will make us face subjects for which we have no affinity naturally in order that we may become full-orbed as God's servants.

3. The Element of Discipline in Salvation
... *Remember the* LORD *from afar, and let Jerusalem come into your mind.*

In the midst of an alien land, afar off from the home of God, the remembrance of the Lord will make you strong with the strength of ten. Note carefully in this connection our Lord's use of the phrase "Do this in remembrance of Me." The ordinance of the Lord's Supper is not a memorial of One Who has gone, but of One Who is always here.

(a) The Dangerous Infatuation
Infatuation means a stupid sense of my own security. A sick person has often the dangerous infatuation that he is all right. This danger overtakes a saint on what Bunyan calls "the enchanted ground." (Cf. 2 Peter 1:12–13.) Whenever we come to the state of feeling, "Well, it's all right now and I can rest here," we are in danger. There is only one point of rest, and that is in the Lord, not in our experiences. We are never told to rest in the experience of salvation or of sanctification or in anything saving the Lord Himself. Whenever you rest in the dangerous infatuation, "Thank God, I know I am all right," you will go down as sure as Satan is Satan and you are you.

(b) The Divine Imperative
"Remember the LORD from afar." The command to remember does not simply mean to recall, but to re-identify yourself in imagination with your Lord. The passive stage is a great danger—
When obstacles and trials seem like prison walls to be,
I lay me down and go to sleep and leave it all to Thee!

That is the stage of spiritual dry rot. There is nothing more difficult to get rid of than the encroachments of this spiritual sickness; it is not physical weariness, that will come over and over again, but spiritual weariness, and spiritual weariness coins such phrases as "Once in grace always in grace, no matter how disgraceful you are." "The Lord is far too good to let me go." "I have been so much used in days gone by, I am all right." It is rather a certainty that you are spiritually sick. Jesus said, "I am come that they might have *life*," not laziness. Whenever we are in danger of nestling in spiritual armchairs, the clarion voice of the Lord comes and bids us neither "sit nor stand but go!" Look back over your life and you will see whenever there was the danger of spiritual dry rot or of getting off on to enchanted ground, God in mercy to your soul allowed an earthquake to come, and the whole thing went to pieces and you with it; for a while you were dazed and amazed, and then all of a sudden He set you on your feet again. "For we have not here an abiding city" (RV). To "remember the LORD from afar" means to remember that we have to be like Him.

(c) The Devoted Intellect
"And let Jerusalem," the God-lit city, "come into your mind." Ask yourself—"What do I let come into my mind?" If a man lets his garden alone, it pretty soon ceases to be a garden; and if a saint lets his mind alone, it will soon become a garbage patch for Satan's scarecrows. Read the terrible things that Paul says will grow in the mind of a saint unless he looks after it (e.g. Colossians 3:5). The command to let Jerusalem come into our mind means we have to watch our intellect and devote it for one purpose; let only those things come in that are worthy of the God-lit city. "*Let* . . ." it is a command. See to it by the careful watching of your mind that only those thoughts come in that are worthy of God. We do not sufficiently realise the need to pray when we lie down at night, "Deliver us from the evil one" (RV). It puts us in the attitude of asking the Lord to watch our minds and our dreams, and He will do it.

REALITY

It seems to me that somewhere in my soul
There lies a secret self as yet asleep;
No stranger hath disturbed its slumber deep,
No friend dispersed the clouds that round it roll.
But it is written on my Fortune's scroll
That should some hand the chords of being sweep
And speak a certain sound, this self would leap
To fullest life and be awake and whole.

And He said unto all, If any man would come after Me, let him deny himself, and take up his cross daily, and follow Me. Luke 9:23 (RV)

By Reality we mean that all the hidden powers of our life are in perfect harmony with themselves and in perfect harmony with God. None of us are real in the full sense of the word; we become real bit by bit as we obey the Spirit of God. It is not a question of sham and reality or of hypocrisy and reality, but of sincerity being transformed into reality. It is possible to be perfectly real to ourselves but not real to God; that is not reality. It is possible to be perfectly real to ourselves and real to other people, but not real in our relationship to God; that is not reality. The only reality is being in harmony with ourselves and other people and God. That is the one great reality towards which God is working, and towards which we are working as we obey Him.

1. Self-Realisation—Naturally
If any man would come after Me . . . (RV)

It is a painful process becoming conscious of one's self; we are not conscious of ourselves at the beginning of life. A child has no realisation of himself as distinct from those round about him, consequently he is in complete harmony. When a child begins to realise himself he becomes self-conscious and his distress begins; he begins to find he is different from everyone else and thinks that no one understands him, and he becomes either conceited or depressed.

(a) Sense of Individualism
The critical moment in a man or woman's life is when they realise they are individually separate from other people. When I realise I am separate from everyone else, the danger is that I think I am different from everyone else. Immediately I think that, I become a law to myself; that means I excuse everything I do, but nothing anyone else does. "My temptations are peculiar," I say; "my setting is very strange; no one knows but myself the peculiar forces that are in me."

When first that big sense awakens that I am different from everyone else, it is the seed of all lawlessness and all immoralities.

(b) Sense of Intuition
This sense that I know what other people do not know, that I have a special intuition that tells me things, is even more dangerous than the sense of individualism because it leads to spiritual deception in a religious nature and to hard intellectual conceit in a natural nature.

(c) Sense of Isolation
When a person realises he is alone the danger of inordinate affection arises. Have you ever noticed the remarkable phrase in the Song of Songs—". . . stir not up, nor awaken . . . love, until it [RV mg] please"? The forces of the world, the flesh and the devil are set to do that one thing, to awaken the soul's love before the true Lover of the soul, the Lord Jesus Christ, has been revealed. It would serve us well if we thought a great deal more from the ethical side of our Christian work than we do. We think of it always from the spiritual side because that is the natural way for us, but when we think of it from the ethical side we get at it from a different angle. More damage is done because souls have been left alone on the moral side than Christian workers ever dream, simply because their eyes are blinded by seeing only along the spiritual line. When once the powers of a nature, young or old, begin to awaken it realises that it is an individual; that it has a power of knowing without reasoning, and it begins to be afraid because it is alone and looks for a companion, and the devil is there always to supply the need. Remember the old proverb—"If you knock long enough at a door the devil may open it." The Bible indicates that there is a wrong as well as a right perseverance.

Self-realisation naturally means—I must develop my nature along its natural line: I am an individual, therefore I shall take care that no one who is not like me teaches me; I have gifts of soul that make me feel a strong affinity for, certain natures, those I shall foster; I feel very much alone, therefore I shall select another person or persons to comrade me. The Spirit of God counteracts these tendencies of the nature which He has created until they flow into the right channels.

There are many signs of religiosity in a young life that arise simply from natural physical development and are not spiritual at all. A boy or girl in their teens often shows amazingly religious tendencies and these are mistaken for the real work of the Spirit of God; they may or may not be. The need for spiritual discernment on this point in those of us who are workers is intense. Whenever there is real spiritual life, Jesus Christ is in the first place; when it is not the work of the Spirit of God there are vague notions about God, aspirations after this and that, and great strivings that may end anywhere, towards God or not. The great need is for the Holy Spirit to introduce Jesus Christ. The supreme moment for Our Lord in any life is when that individual life is beginning to awaken. The incalculable power of intercession comes in here. A Christian father or mother or teacher or friend can anticipate that moment in the life of their child or teacher or friend, so that when the awakening comes, the Spirit of God in answer to believing prayer holds off the world, the flesh and the devil and introduces the Friend of friends, the Lord Jesus Christ. I wish I could convey to you the imperative importance of intercessory prayer. If the devil is anxious about one thing he is anxious not to allow us to see this; if we will only say, "Well, prayer does not much matter; they are very young and inexperienced." Forestall the time; hold off the devil! We do not know when a nature begins to awaken along the line of self-realisation, it may be very early in life or later on; but I do believe that by intercessory prayer, as Jesus Himself has told us, the great power of God works in ways we cannot conceive. I think sometimes we will be covered with shame when we meet the Lord Jesus and think how blind and ignorant we were when He brought people around us to pray for, or gave us opportunities of warning, and instead of praying we tried to find out what was wrong. We have no business to try and find out what is wrong, our business is to pray, so that when the awakening comes Jesus Christ will be the first they meet. The one who meets a nature at its awakening has the opportunity of making or marring that life. As soon as Jesus Christ touches "the chords of being," the nature is fascinated by Him, as the early disciples were—no work of regeneration as yet, simply the holding of the nature entranced by Jesus Christ. The chances for the devil in that life are very poor indeed; but if the world, the flesh and the devil get the first touch, a long line of havoc may follow before Jesus Christ has His chance.

2. Christ-Realisation
let him deny himself . . .

Jesus is talking to men who have reached the point of self-realisation naturally; now He is requiring from them an identification with Himself.

It is not only that they identify themselves in a fidelity which is indistinguishable from that which is due to God alone, but that He, in the most solemn, explicit, and overpowering words, requires from them that identification, and makes their eternal destiny depend upon it.

Denney[7]

Self-realisation naturally cares nothing about God, it does not care whether Jesus lived or died or did anything at all. For ourselves we live and for ourselves we die; that is self-realisation that leads to death and despair; it is absolutely and radically opposed to Christ-realisation. True self-realisation is exhibited in the life of Our Lord, perfect harmony with God and a perfect understanding of man; and He prays "that they may be one, even as We are one."

(a) Power of Asceticism
Asceticism is the passion of giving up things, and is recognisable in a life not born again of the Spirit of God. It is all very well if it ends in giving up the one thing God wants us to give up, viz. our right to ourselves, but if it does not end there, it will do endless damage to the life. In a sanctified soul the power of asceticism shows itself in an understanding of the mighty place of martyrdom in Our Lord's programme for a disciple. "Let him deny himself." These words of Jesus reveal the line He continually worked on when He talked to the disciples; He introduced the closest ties and said that at times even these have to be severed if we are to be true to Him. That sounds harsh to anyone if he has not come into the understanding of Jesus that we get after sanctification.

Consider how great this Man is who declares that the final destiny of men depends on whether or not they are loyal to Him, and who demands absolute loyalty though it involve sacrifice of the tenderest affections, and the surrender of life in the most ignominious death.

Denney

(b) Passion of Absorption
When Jesus Christ is seen by a newly awakened nature His fascination is complete—no conviction of sin, no reception of the Holy Spirit, no believing even, but an absorbing passion for Jesus Christ. There are a great number of Christians in this immature stage, they write books and conduct meetings along the line of being absorbed in Jesus, but we have the feeling as we listen—"There is something lacking—what is it?" What is lacking is the realisation that we have to be

---

7. James Denney (1856–1917): Scottish theologian and author whose writings were greatly appreciated by Oswald Chambers.

brought by means of the death of Jesus into the relationship to God that Our Lord Himself had. The hymns that are written by people in this stage emphasise the human aspect of Jesus, but there is no real gripping power in them for the saint.

The passion of absorption is also recognisable in the initial stages of sanctification, perhaps more so than at any other stage; there is no consciousness of a separate life. To talk about suffering and cross-bearing and self-denial is not only outside the soul's vocabulary but outside the possibility of his thinking, he seems to be absolutely absorbed in Christ. This stage is excessively dangerous unless it leads to one thing, identification with the death of Jesus.

(c) Perseverance of Adoration

When Jesus touches a nature, a long series of devotional hours characterises the life—always wanting times of being alone with God, always wanting to pray and read devotional books. In some natures it goes as far as ecstasy. After sanctification the characteristic of the life is clear—Jesus Christ first, Jesus Christ second and Jesus Christ third, all that the Lord wants; the life goes on with a flood of intense energy, adoration unspeakable "I live," said Paul, "and yet no longer I, but Christ liveth in me" (RV). The identity is changed, the very faith, the very nature that was in Jesus is in us now, and we with all other saints may grow into the full realisation of God's purpose in Redemption. " . . . till we all attain unto the unity of the faith" (RV). We cannot attain to it alone.

3. Self-Realisation—Spiritually

. . . and take up his cross daily, and follow Me.

In the first experience of sanctification we lose altogether the consciousness of our own identity, we are absorbed in God; but that is not the final place, it is merely the introduction to a totally new life. We lose our natural identity and consciously gain, the identity that Jesus had, and it is when God begins to deal with sanctified souls on that line that darkness sometimes comes and the strange misunderstanding of God's ways. They are being taught what God taught Abraham:

> *My goal is God Himself, not joy, nor peace,*
> *Nor even blessing, but Himself, my God.*

Jesus said to His disciples, "I have yet many things to say unto you, but ye cannot bear them now." They could not bear them until the Holy Spirit brought them into the realisation of Who Jesus was.

(a) Patient Dedication

"and take up his cross . . ." The immature stage of the life of sanctification merges into a clear, patient dedication to Jesus Christ; free from all hurry spiritually and all panic there is a slow and growing realisation of what Jesus meant when He said, "As the Father hath sent Me, even so send I you" (RV). Our cross is the steady exhibition of the fact that we are not our own but Christ's, and we know it, and are determined to be unenticed from living a life of dedication to Him. This is the beginning of the emergence of the real life of faith.

(b) Plain Daylight

"daily . . ." The life of manifestations is a critical stage in the saint's experience. The real life of the saint on this earth, and the life that is most glorifying to Jesus, is the life that steadfastly goes on through common days and common ways, with no mountain-top experiences. We read that John the Baptist "looked upon Jesus *as He walked. . . .*"—not at Jesus in a prayer meeting or in a revival service, or Jesus performing miracles; he did not watch Him on the Mount of Transfiguration, he did not see Him in any great moment at all, he saw Him on an ordinary day when Jesus was walking in an ordinary common way, and he said, "Behold the Lamb of God!" That is the test of reality. Mounting up with wings as eagles, running and not being weary, are indications that something more than usual is at work. Walking and not fainting is the life that glorifies God and satisfies the heart of Jesus to the full—the plain daylight life, unmarked, unknown, only occasionally, if ever, does the marvel of it break on other people.

(c) Persistent Devotion

". . . and follow Me." This is the life of martyrdom with the glowing heat of perfect love at its heart. Only one figure ahead and that the Lord Jesus, other people, saints or sinners, shadows. The mark of this life of devotion is its persistence. Spasms are a sign of returning or departing life. The continual feeling, "I must wind myself up, I have been letting things go, I must screw my life up[8] and get to work," may be a sign that we are coming nearer the source of the true life or it may be exactly the opposite, it may be a sign that we are declining into death. God and ourselves are the only judges of that. The one thing to fix on is that the life Jesus lived is the pattern of what our lives will be when once we come to the place of self-realisation spiritually.

---

8. screw up: strengthen; fortify.

No one is worthy of Jesus who does not follow Him, as it were, with the rope round his neck—ready to die the most ignominious death rather than prove untrue.

Denney

The idea of martyrdom is the very essence of the saint's life. Jesus Christ always used the figure of martyrdom when He spoke of this stage of the Christian life (see John 21:18). The saint at this stage is leagues beyond the point of asking—"Am I doing God's will?" he is God's will; leagues beyond the point of saying—"I do want God to bless me here and use me there"; leagues beyond the point of saying—"I have got the victory" and praising God for it; he is in the place where God can make him broken bread and poured-out wine just as He made His Son broken bread and poured-out wine for us.

May this message make clear to our hearts and minds the purpose of God in our salvation and sanctification. God's purpose is to make us real, that is, to make us perfectly at one with all our own powers and perfectly at one with God, no longer children but understanding in our heads as well as in our hearts the meaning of the Redemption, and slowly maturing until we are a recommendation to the redeeming grace of our Lord Jesus Christ. As the angels look down on us, do they see something that makes them marvel at the wonderful workmanship of Jesus Christ—"When He shall come to be glorified in His saints, and to be marvelled at in all them that believed"? (RV).

JUDGEMENT

Oh, we're sunk enough here, God knows!
    But not quite so sunk that moments,
Sure tho' seldom, are denied us,
    When the spirit's true endowments
Stand out plainly from its false ones,
    And apprise it if pursuing
Or the right way or the wrong way,
    To its triumph or undoing.

R. B. (Robert Browning)

And this is the judgement, that the light is come into the world, and men loved the darkness rather than the light; for their works were evil. John 3:19 (RV)

The healthiest exercise for the mind of a Christian is to learn to apprehend the truth granted to it in vision. Every Christian with any experience at all has had a vision of some fundamental truth, either about the Atonement or the Holy Spirit or sin, and it is at the peril of their souls that they lose the vision. By prayer and determination we have to form the habit of keeping ourselves soaked in the vision God has given. The difficulty with the majority of us is that we will not seek to apprehend the vision, we get glimpses of it and then leave it alone. "I was not disobedient unto the heavenly vision," says Paul. It is one of the saddest things to see men and women who have had visions of truth but have failed to apprehend them, and it is on this line that judgement comes. It is not a question of intellectual discernment or of knowing how to present the vision to others, but of seeking to apprehend the vision so that it may apprehend us. Soak and soak and soak continually in the one great truth of which you have had a vision; take it to bed with you,

sleep with it, rise up in the morning with it, continually bring your imagination into captivity to it, and slowly and surely as the months and years go by God will make you one of His specialists in that particular truth. God is no respecter of persons.

1. The Master Meaning of Crisis
And this is the judgement . . . (RV)

"And this is the judgement," i.e., the critical moment. A man is not judged by his ordinary days and nights because in these he is more or less a creature of drift, but a crisis is immediately his test. A crisis is a turning-point that separates, and it will always reveal character. If, after a crisis is passed, you will take the trouble to go back, you will find there was a moment away back when a clear idea was given you of what God wanted you to do and you did not do it; the days have gone on and suddenly the crisis comes, and instantly judgement is passed. The thing that tells is the crisis. The generality of men drift along without bothering their heads about anything until a crisis comes, and it is always critical.

(a) The Critical Issue (Mark 6:16)
"But Herod, when he heard thereof, said, John, whom I beheaded, he is risen" (RV). The crisis in the case of Herod was brought about by the disciples' preaching of Jesus; when "His name had become known" (RV), Herod was mastered and made known to himself; the crisis revealed a terror-stricken conscience. Herod was a Sadducee and Sadducees said that there is no resurrection, but when the name of Jesus was noised abroad, he was superstitiously terrified and said, "John, whom I beheaded, he is risen."

(b) The Convicting Idea (Mark 6:18)

"*For John said unto Herod, It is not lawful for thee to have thy brother's wife*" (RV). The convicting idea was produced by what Herod heard; the truth had been spoken to him, he had been convicted by it—"he heard him gladly," and "did many things [RV mg]" (v. 20), but not the one thing. Herod refused to obey the light when it was given, and it was that moment that determined how he would show himself in the crisis.

(c) The Confirming Intention (Mark 6:21)

"*And when a convenient day was come . . .*" The convenient day will always come, the convenient day for the satisfaction of sin. This is a general principle which the generality of Christian workers do not seem to realise. Sin has got to be satisfied, or else strangled to death by a supernatural power. Hell is the satisfaction of all sin. Sentimentalism arises in the nature that is unused to facing realities. People will pile on Christian work, will do anything, will slave to further orders,[9] rather than let you touch the thing that is wrong. Great oceans of penitence and confession are shown, but when all that is through you find there is one fact more, one blind spot which the one you are dealing with refuses to look at or to let you look at. If you are a servant of God, you must ruthlessly rip up the sentimental humbug and go direct to the one thing.

These three things play their part in every crisis. Be careful to note, however, that a crisis does not make character; a crisis reveals character. No sane person is allowed by God to live continually in the light of his conscience. The characteristic of the life of a saint is essential elemental simplicity. Apart from moments of crisis, character is not consciously known. You can see this every day you live; we all say—"If I had been in your place, I should have done so and so." You have no means of knowing what you would have done; the nature of a crisis is that it takes you unawares, it happens suddenly, and the line you take reveals your character; it may also reveal something that amazes you. For instance, you may think a certain person selfish, self-interested and self-satisfied, but a crisis comes, bereavement or a business disaster or sickness, and to your amazement you find he or she is not the self-interested person you thought they were at all, there are whole tracts of generosity in their nature of which you knew nothing. Or you may think a person very generous and kind and loving, and when a crisis occurs, to your amazement and every one else's, they show themselves mean and selfish and cruel. The crisis is always the judgement.

2. The Moral Majesty of the Criterion

That the light is come into the world . . . (RV)

What does Jesus Christ say the standard of God's judgement is for us all? The Light that has come into the world. Who is the Light of the world? The Lord Jesus Christ, Son of God and Son of Man.

> *To judge is to see clearly, to care for what is just, and therefore to be impartial and impersonal.*
>
> Amiel[10]

A few moments' consideration will reveal what a difficult task the Holy Spirit has in bringing even the best of saints to this impersonal standard of judgement. This idea, which shows our personal way of looking at things, is always lurking about us—"Oh well, God knows I really meant to devote myself to Him and to obey Him, but so many things have upset me; I have not had the opportunities I should have had." "I don't really mean to speak and act as I do, but I shall not count it this time." All this shows how difficult it is for the Holy Spirit to bring us to apply the standard of Jesus Christ to ourselves, we will apply His standard to other people; but Jesus Christ brings it home to us. Am I willing to obey the light? We have to beware of personal interests which blur the mind from accepting Our Lord's standard. To walk in the light, as God is in the light, is the one condition of being kept cleansed from all sin.

(a) The Standard for the Heathen (Matthew 25:31–46; John 1:9; Romans 2:11–16)

The first thing to ask in regard to this standard is—what about the people who have never heard of Jesus Christ, and may never hear of Him, how are they judged? The passages given all refer to God's standard of judgement for the heathen, viz. the light they have, not the light they have never had and could not get. Conscience is the standard by which men and women are to be judged until they have been brought into contact with the Lord Jesus Christ. The call to preach the Gospel to the heathen is not the frenzied doctrine that the heathen who have never known Jesus Christ, and never had the chance of knowing Him, are going to be eternally lost, but the command of Jesus Christ—"Go ye into all the world, and preach the gospel to every creature."

(b) The Standard for Christendom (John 3:18)

"*He that believeth on Him is not judged: he that believeth not hath been judged already, because he hath not believed*

9. "to further orders": ad infinitum; endlessly; of military origin, meaning continuing the present action until one receives different orders.

10. Henri Frederic Amiel (1821–1881): Swiss professor and writer, known for his self-analytical *Journal*, published in 1883.

on the name of the only begotten Son of God." The standard for the judgement of Christendom is not the light it has received but the light it ought to have received. Every country in Christendom has had plenty of opportunity of knowing about Christ, and the doom of a soul begins the moment it consciously neglects to know Jesus Christ or consciously rejects Him when He is known. Beware of applying Our Lord's words in Matthew 25 to Christians; Matthew 25 is not the standard for the judgement of Christians, but the standard for the judgement of the nations that do not know Christ. The standard for the judgement of Christians is Our Lord.

(c) The Standard for the Church (Ephesians 4:11–13)

"And He gave some to be apostles; and some, prophets; and some, evangelists; and some, pastors and teachers; . . . till we all attain unto the unity of the faith." These verses do not refer to individual Christian lives but to the collective life of the saints. The individual saint cannot be perfected apart from others. "He gave some to be apostles . . . ," for what purpose? To show how clever they were, what gifts they had? No, "for the perfecting of the saints." In looking back over the history of the Church we find that every one of these "gifts" has been tackled. Paul says that apostles, prophets, evangelists, pastors and teachers, are all meant for one thing by God, viz. "for the perfecting of the saints, . . . unto the building up of the body of Christ." No saint can ever be perfected in isolation or in any other way than God has laid down. There are very few who are willing to apprehend that for which they were apprehended, they thank God for salvation and sanctification and then stagnate, consequently the perfecting of the saints is hindered.

3. The Making Moment of Choice

. . . And men loved the darkness rather than the light; for their works were evil. (RV)

Our choice is indelibly marked for time and eternity. What we decide makes our destiny, not what we have felt, nor what we have been moved to do, or inspired to see, but what we decide to do in a given crisis, it is that which makes or mars us. Sooner or later there comes to every life the question—Will I choose to side with God's verdict on sin in the Cross of Christ? I may say "I won't accept," or "I will put it off," but both are decisions, remember.

(a) The Prejudice for Darkness (Matthew 6:23)

"If therefore the light that is in thee be darkness, how great is that darkness!" The disposition of a man determines the way he will decide when the crisis comes, but the only One Who knows the disposition other than the man himself is God. The unaltered, natural disposition of a man is called by our Lord "darkness," that means prejudice against the light.

(b) The Persistence of Direction (Mark 6:26–27)

"And the king was exceeding sorry; but for the sake of his oaths, and of them that sat at meat, he would not reject her. And straightway the king sent forth a soldier of his guard, and commanded to bring his head . . ." (RV). John the Baptist represented the voice of God to Herod; Herod decided to silence the voice of God. He had one subsequent twinge (see Mark 6:16–18); then his conscience never bothered him again, and Jesus Christ and all He represented became a farce to him. We read in Luke 23:8–9, that "when Herod saw Jesus, he was exceeding glad: for he was of a long time desirous to see Him, . . . and he hoped to see some miracle done by Him. And he questioned Him in many words; but He answered him nothing" (RV). Herod had ordered the voice of God to be silent, and it was; and now all sails are set for perdition. His was "a ghastly smooth life, dead at heart." That is the awful condition to which a man may get where he no longer believes in goodness or purity or justice; but the Bible never allows that a man can get there without being culpable in God's sight. Whenever you see a soul in danger of closing over one sin, go at it no matter how it hurts or how annoyed that soul is with you, go at it until the sin is blasted right out, never palliate it or sympathise. Very few voices rise up against the sins that make for the seal of silence on men and women and churches. This is what is lacking to-day.

(c) Pronouncement of Destiny (Luke 23:9)

"And he questioned Him in many words; but He answered him nothing" (RV). The reason "He answered him nothing" is to be found in Mark 6:26–27. Herod decided to silence the voice of God in his life, and when the Son of God stood before him, he saw nothing in Him; there was no more compunction of conscience. Whenever a man makes the decision that Herod made—"I don't want to hear any more about the matter," it is the beginning of the silence of God in his soul. To silence the voice of God is damnation in time; eternal damnation is that for ever. "God . . . answereth me no more" (1 Samuel 28:15) is an expression of damnation in time. Divine silence is the ultimate destiny of the man who refuses to come to the light and obey it.

It is a terrible thing in the spiritual career not to be apprehended by the light that has been given; it may have been at some midday or midnight; in childhood or in the early days of your Christian life, or as recently as last week, you know exactly when it was, it is between you and God, are you going to decide along that line—"My God, I don't know all that it means, but I decide for it"? Whenever any light is given you on any fundamental issue and you refuse to settle your soul on it and apprehend it, your doom is sealed along that particular line. If when a clear emphatic vision of some truth is given you by God, not to your intellect but to your heart, and in spite of it all you decide to take another course, the vision will fade and may never come back.

There are men and women who ought to be princes and princesses with God but they are away on God's left, they may even be sanctified, but they are left at a particular stage because they chose to be left; instead of obeying the heavenly vision, the natural judicious decisions of an average Christian life have been preferred. It has nothing to do with salvation, but with lost opportunities in service for God. "Many are called, but few chosen" (RV), i.e., few prove themselves the chosen ones. Whenever the vision comes, let me plead with you, as though God were intreating by me, do not be disobedient to it, because there is only one purpose in our lives, and that is the satisfaction of the Lord Jesus Christ.

BACKSLIDING
John 6

The tendencies that make temptation possible are inherent in man as God created him, Adam and Our Lord Jesus Christ being witnesses; and we have to bear in mind that regeneration does not remove those tendencies but rather increases them. The possibility of temptation reaches its height in Jesus Christ.

1. Tendency to Repose
It takes so much effort to maintain one's self in an exceptional point of view that one falls back into prejudice by pure exhaustion.

The tendency to repose physically is a right law of our physical nature; morally and spiritually it is a tendency towards immorality and unspirituality.

(a) The Desire for Rest—The Arrest of Desire (John 6:10–15)
The desire at the heart of true spiritual life is for union with God; the tendency to rest in anything less than the realisation of this desire becomes the arrest of desire. Whenever we seek repose in any blessing spiritually, sleeping sickness begins. The tendency to rest in any of the blessings which are the natural outcome of union with God is the beginning of backsliding. Is my desire for union with God, or am I like the people who sought to make Jesus King—for what purpose? If Jesus could feed their bodies without their having to work, that was the very thing they wanted. The incident is symbolic of the tendency to repose which is inherent in human nature, but if this desire were satisfied it would be the destruction of all character.

(b) The Decay of Reality—The Dawn of Death (John 6:30–31)
Reality means that which is in perfect accord with God. If I accept any blessing of God, e.g. sanctifica-

tion, as the final end and aim of my life, from that moment decay begins in my spiritual life. Sanctification is the gateway to real union with God, which is life unutterable. Peter points out this very thing in his Epistles; he says, you know these things and are established in the truth, but you are going to sleep, you are in danger of mistaking this for the final place; it is not, it is only the introduction (2 Peter 1:12–13). Are we sufficiently well taught of the Holy Spirit to stir up souls who have got right with God, until they come to the reality of realities, absolute oneness with God?

The tendency to backslide begins right in the very secret places. No wonder Jesus urged His disciples to watch and pray, "that ye enter not into temptation." The possibility of backsliding is so full of peril that the only safety is to look to Jesus, relying on the Holy Spirit, and never to allow the repose which is a necessity physically to come into the life of the spirit. The arrest of desire begins when I want to rest in spiritual blessings; and the dawn of death in spiritual life begins when I become smugly satisfied with my attainments—"This is all God wants of me." What God wants of me is all that He has revealed in Jesus Christ. "till we all attain unto the . . . measure of the stature of the fullness of Christ" (Ephesians 4:13 RV). The rest which is the outcome of entire sanctification is not the rest of stagnation, but the rest of the reality of union with God.

(c) The Dreams of Repose—The Night of Disaster (John 6:34–35)
These words of Our Lord are a puzzle to an unspiritual mind, and an unspiritual mind is produced by allowing visions and dreams of spiritual repose which Jesus Christ continually discourages. What do I dream about and allow my mind to fancy when in communion with God? One of the greatest snares in spiritual life is to

foster dreams and fancies of our own which do not tally with the statements of Jesus, instead of bringing every thought into captivity to the obedience of Christ. People who go off at a tangent and are led astray by Satan as an angel of light are deceived just here. Disaster spiritually follows whenever the tendency to repose is yielded to. "Forgetting the things which are behind, and stretching forward to the things which are before" (RV) is the only attitude for a saint.

2. The Tendency to Revert

Is not life the test of our moral force, and all these untold waverings are they not temptations of the soul?

In all organic life there is a tendency to revert to the original type. Flowers and plants may be highly developed and cultivated, but if afterwards they are left alone year after year they will revert to the original type from which they sprang. The spiritual application of this is that there is the possibility in every child of God of reverting to the original type of self-interest; but thank God there is also the possibility of being transformed into the image of God's Son (Romans 8:29).

(a) Possibility of Offence (John 6:52)

The possibility of offence can only come when two persons have somewhat the same nature. People who have no affinity with Jesus run no risk of being offended with Him; but no Christian is ever free from that possibility (cf. Matthew 11:6). Satan comes to us with suggestions—"Surely God would never ask you to do such and such a thing? God would never guide you in such a way?" But God does. The possibility of offence is there immediately I become a child of God.

(b) The Perversity of the Offended (John 6:60–61)

Perversity means to turn away from one to whom I have been devoted because he says things that do not suit my ideas. There is a stage in spiritual experience, it may be before or after sanctification, when this perversity is possible. Someone comes with an exposition of a truth of God I have never realised before and at once the possibility of perversity is awakened and I say, "No, I am sure God would never have revealed this truth to you if He has not revealed it to me." The possibility of offence is always there, and perversity is the next step. As soon as I am offended I become perverse, my eyes are blinded and I see only along the line of my prejudices. There are saints, for instance, who resolutely shut their minds against the truth that they can draw upon the Lord's life for their bodies, or against the need for being continually renewed in their minds. This will lead not only to stagnation spiritually but to perversity. The only safety is to keep in the light as God is in the light.

(c) The Perfidy of the Offended (John 6:66)

"*Upon this many of His disciples went back, and walked no more with Him*" (RV). Reversion to self-will, and insisting on my own way of serving God, is not only utter faithlessness to Jesus Christ, but active working against the particular truth which has offended me. The people who are most perverse against the truth are those who know it. This is stated in its most extreme form in Hebrews 6:4–6.

If God were to remove from us as saints the possibility of disobedience there would be no value in our obedience, it would be a mechanical business. To say after sanctification, "Now I can do what I like," is a perilously dangerous statement. If it were true, it would never have been recorded that "even Christ pleased not Himself." The possibility of disobedience in a child of God makes his obedience of amazing value. The one who is not a child of God is the slave of the wrong disposition, he has not the power to obey; immediately God delivers him from the wrong disposition, he is free to obey, and consequently free to disobey, and it is this that makes temptation possible. Temptation is not sin; temptation must always be possible for our sonship to be of worth to God. It would be no credit for God to bring mechanical slaves to glory—"for it became Him . . . in bringing many *sons* unto glory"—not slaves, not useless channels, but vigorous, alert, wide-awake men and women, with all their powers and faculties devoted absolutely to God.

3. Tendency to Revolt

The independence which is the condition of individuality is at the same time the eternal temptation of the individual.

Spiritual revolt means the deliberately forsaking of God and signing on under another ruler. We must distinguish between degeneration and revolt. We have been dealing with the tendencies that lead to degeneration, no positive side has been taken yet, but there is a distinct disinclination to go on further—"I am thankful I am here, and here I am going to stay"—without realising that we cannot stay where we are, we must either go on or go back—and that leads ultimately to revolt, not mere declension but a deliberate signing on under another ruler. "For My people have committed two evils; they have forsaken me the fountain of living waters"—that is not backsliding; that is degeneration; "and have hewed them out cisterns, broken cisterns, that can hold no water"—these two things together constitute backsliding. The words God uses in connection with backsliding are terrible. He uses words that shock us as moral individuals in order to portray what backsliding is in His sight (e.g. Jeremiah 3:8).

(a) The Reaction of the Unattained (John 6:41, 52)

When a soul realises the truth of God and fails to attain it, there lies within him a power of reaction which not only means he will try no more but he will dissuade others. If once we have had a vision from God of His purpose for us and we leave it unattained, the tendency is to say, "Oh well, it may be meant for other people, but it isn't for me." This tendency is in every one of us, we scarcely discern it, but it is there. For anyone to leave unattained anything Our Lord has revealed as possible for him, is the beginning of Satan's chance over that soul. Our Lord makes no allowance for not attaining because by means of His Cross we have all the marvellous grace of God to draw upon, all the mighty life of the Lord Jesus Christ to enable us to attain. A great many of us try and attain without having received the life of Jesus and we are bound to fail; that is not a matter of reaction, it is inevitable. But if we have received the life of Jesus, it is unconscious blasphemy in God's sight to stop short of attaining anything He reveals as possible for us. Our Lord's illustration of salt that has lost its savour is applicable. "Ye are the salt of the earth: but if the salt have lost its savour, wherewith shall it be salted? It is thenceforth good for nothing, but to be cast out and trodden under foot of men" (RV). Savourless salt is a most cursed influence in the physical world, and a saint who has lost his saintliness is a pestilential influence in the spiritual world, We lose saintliness whenever we take our eyes for one second off the Source of our life, the Lord Jesus Christ. Whenever we do, all these errors begin to be possible. But if we keep in the light with God, our life is that of a child, simple and joyful all through. It is sufficient for a child to know that his father wishes him to do certain things and he learns to draw on a strength greater than his own and attains and attains. If he does not, he runs the risk of becoming a prodigal.

(b) The Reviling of the Unreached (John 6:61)

If a man has really tasted the life of God and knows God's purpose for him, or did know it months or years ago, but has never fulfilled that purpose through obedience, the tendency to revile the standard is irresistible. We must revile a standard we have not reached when we know we ought to have reached it. It is not something that can be prevented, it is inevitable. If once we deliberately stop short and refuse to let God's life have its way with us, we shall revile the truth because it has not been reached.

There are two things which keep us from going on with God—first, the "show business"; by the "show business" we mean the desire to appeal to the largest number: if you do that, you will have to lower the standards of Jesus Christ; and second, sympathy. Sympathy with one another that does not spring from sympathy with God's interests in that one will always end in reviling some standard of God's truth. It will not mean you use reviling language, you may use very pious and sighing language—"Oh no, *I* could never attain to that." You may preach entire sanctification and your message may be couched in beautiful language, then you say—"This is God's standard, but of course I am not there." There can be only one result in the souls of those who listen, and that is the reviling of the standard, for which you and I will be called to account. The glibness and ease with which men proclaim the great standards of Jesus Christ and then sweep them away by saying, "God forbid I should say I am there," makes one tremble, because such a statement implies, Jesus Christ cannot bring me there, it is an ideal to which I cannot attain. When we come to the New Testament there is the quiet and grandly-easy certainty that we *can* attain. All God's commands are enablings. Never sympathise with a soul who cannot get through to God on Jesus Christ's lines. The Lord is never hard nor cruel, He is the essence of tender compassion and gentleness. The reason any soul cannot get through is that there is something in him that won't budge; immediately it does, Jesus Christ's marvellous life will have its way.

(c) The Renunciation by Unbelief (John 6:70–71)

Not only is it possible for a soul to revile the standards set up by Jesus, but it is possible to do what Judas did, renounce Him by unbelief. It is easy to make Judas the arch-sinner, but he is the type of what is possible in every one of us. Thank God that the Apostle Paul is also a possible type for every one of us, but do not forget that Judas is a possible type too.

These are terrible truths, but it is the terrors of the dark night which drive us closer to the haven of unutterable security, the Lord Jesus Christ. No wonder God's Book says, "the way of transgressors is hard." Could God have made it more terrible than He has for man to go astray? Could He have put the danger signals more clearly than He has? The way is absolutely strewn with alarm signals; it is impossible to go wrong easily.

Thus in new ways we learn the profound beauty of Our Lord's words: "Come unto Me"; "*I* am the Way, the Truth, and the Life."

TEMPTATION
1 Corinthians 10:12–13

The word "temptation" has come down in the world, we use it wrongly nowadays. Temptation is not sin, it is the thing we are bound to meet if we are men; not to be tempted would be to be beneath contempt. Temptation is something that exactly fits the nature of the one tempted, and is therefore a great revealer of the possibilities of the nature. Every man has the setting of his own temptation. A good illustration of temptation is the way steel is tested. Steel can be "tired" in the process of testing, and in this way its strength is measured. Temptation means the test by an alien power of the possessions held by a personality. This makes the temptation of Our Lord explainable: He held in His Person the fact that He was to be the King of men and the Saviour of the world, and the alien power that came to test Him on these lines is called in the Bible, Satan.

Temptation is also a severe test to fulfil the possessions of personality by a short cut. Temptation trains innocence into character or else into corruption. There are some temptations, however, by which we have no business to be tempted any longer; we should be on a higher plane dealing with other temptations. We may have our morality well within our own grasp and be comparatively free from temptation, but as soon as we are regenerated by the Spirit of God we begin to understand the force of spiritual temptations of which we were unconscious before.

1. Temptation v. Sin *(James 1:12–15)*

Temptation and sin are profoundly different. Temptation is a pathway to the end desired, but it leads to a perplexing situation, inasmuch as it makes a man decide which factor he will obey in the dilemma. The possibility of sin and the inclination to sin are different things. Every man has the possibility of committing murder, but the inclination is not there. The inclination is as the deed, whether it is carried out or not (Romans 2:1; 1 John 3:15). Satan had the possibility of disobedience and when the temptation producing the dilemma came, he inclined to rebellion against God. Adam had the possibility of disobedience, and when temptation came to him producing the dilemma, he deliberately inclined to disobedience, and the disposition to disobey God became the inheritance of the whole of the human race, "Wherefore, as by one man sin entered into the world, and death by sin; and so death passed upon all men, for that all have sinned" (Romans 5:12). The disposition of sin is fundamental anarchy against God's rule over me, and as long as that disposition remains, temptation finds an inclination to sin in me; but when Our Lord delivers me from the disposition of sin, the hour of temptation discovers no inclination to sin, it tests the door of possibility only. "But now being made free from sin, and become servants to God, ye have your fruit unto holiness, and the end everlasting life" (Romans 6:22). Our Lord Jesus Christ had the possibility of disobedience, but when the temptation producing the dilemma came to Him, it found no inclination to disobedience; and everyone that is saved by Him is put in the position He was in when He was tempted (see Hebrews 2:11; 4:15–16). Until a man is regenerated and sanctified the general character of Our Lord's temptation is unguessed.

The sinless perfection heresy arises out of this confusion—it says that because the disposition of sin is removed, it is impossible to sin. The inclination to sin, thank God, is removed, but never the possibility. If the power to disobey were removed, our obedience would be of no value, for we should cease to be morally responsible. It is gloriously possible not to sin, but never impossible to sin, because we are moral agents. Morality must be militant in this order of things, but we can be "more than conquerors" every time.

The temptation James speaks of is the temptation we know naturally—"Each man is tempted, when he is drawn away by his own lust, and enticed" (RV). Until we are born again we only understand this kind of temptation, but by regeneration we are lifted into another realm and have other temptations to face, viz. the kind of temptations Our Lord faced. The temptations of Jesus have no home at all in our natural human nature, they do not appeal to us. A man's disposition on the inside, i.e. what he possesses in his personality, determines by what he is tempted on the outside, and the temptation will always come along the line of the ruling disposition. Sin is a disposition of self-love that obeys every temptation to its own lordship. Sin is literally self-centred rule, a disposition that rules the life apart from God.

Naturally we are taught by this disposition to lust for what we desire, and lust will warp character from rectitude to ruin—"drawn away by his own lust, and enticed" (RV). The destiny of lust is peculiarly fascinating. It presents a wild reach of possibility, and lust stampedes when it is not constrained by the consideration that it will lead the character to infamy, not fame. Lust means "I must have it at once, I will have my desire satisfied, and will brook no restraint." Temptation yielded to is the birth of sin in the personal life and ends in death. The verses in James 1 are the natural history of temptation. Lust is used in other ways in the Bible than merely of immorality, it is the spirit of "I must have it at once," no matter what it is. Temptation yielded to is lust deified.

The period of temptation in Our Lord's life came immediately after a time of spiritual exaltation (see Matthew 3:16–17; 4:1); it was a period of estimating forces, and the historic temptations of Jesus Christ are pictorial records of wrong ways to the kingdoms of God. At His Baptism Jesus Christ accepted the vocation of bearing away (RV mg) the sin of the world, and immediately He was put by God's Spirit into the testing machine of the devil. But He did not "tire"; He went through the temptations "without sin" and retained the possessions of His personality intact.

"Then the devil leaveth Him, and behold angels came and ministered unto Him" (Matthew 4:11). The sign that you have gone through temptation rightly is that you retain your affinity with the highest.

2. Temptation and Jesus Christ *(Matthew 4:1, 11; Hebrews 2:18; 4:15–16)*

External circumstances are made to form an exact counterpart of the internal desire, which is different in different men. For example, the temptation of Our Lord was quite different from the temptation of Judas Iscariot, because the inner disposition was different. We have to beware of saying that because Jesus was Divine, temptation to Him was not real. If that is so, then the record in the Bible of Our Lord's temptations is a mere farce and is misleading, and the writer to the Hebrews is untrue when he says of Jesus, "tempted—*yet without sin.*"

Could Jesus Christ be tempted? Undoubtedly He could, because temptation and sin are not the same thing. The temptation James speaks of, and the temptation of Jesus, are very different in character. The temptations which beset us as ordinary men gather round the disposition of sin.

In Luke 3:23 we read " . . . and Jesus Himself began to be about thirty years of age." That is the time in human life when man reaches maturity and all his powers are perfected; the time when he is spared no requirement of his manhood. Up to that time, life is full of promise, after that it is a matter of testing and attainment. After the baptism of Jesus and the descent of the Holy Ghost upon Him, God, as it were, took His sheltering hand off Him and let the devil do his worst.

Our Lord's temptation and ours move in different spheres until we are born again and become His brethren (Hebrews 2:11). The records of the temptation of Jesus are the records of how God as man is tempted, not of how man is tempted as man. The temptations of Jesus are not those of a man as man, but the temptation of God as man. Jesus Christ was not born with an heredity of sin. "Wherefore it behoved Him in all things to be made like unto His brethren" (RV). His "brethren" are those in whom He is born. It is nowhere said that Jesus Christ was "tempted like as we are" as ordinary human beings. By regeneration the Son of God is formed in us, and He has the same setting in our physical life as He had when He was on earth. Are we remaining loyal to Him in the things which beset His life in us? The devil does not need to bother about the majority of us; we have enough lust on the inside to keep us in sin, but when once a man is born from above (RV mg), the temptations alter instantly, and he realises where the temptation is aimed, viz. at the disposition.

Our Lord was tested for the fulfilment of what He held in His own personal life, viz. the Saviourhood of the world and the Kingship of men, and the temptation by Satan was that He should fulfil these by a short cut. Our Lord's temptations were set by His disposition; He could not be tempted by lust, but He was tempted to the fulfilment of His incarnation along a line other than that marked out by His Father. Satan came to Him as an "angel of light," and the central citadel of the temptations was—"You are the Son of God, then do God's work in Your own way." And at the heart of every one of Our Lord's answers is this—"I came to do My Father's work in His way, not in My own way" (see John 6:38). Satan was right every time in his promise of what would happen if Our Lord took his suggested short cuts (see John 6:15); but Our Lord would not be King of men on that line. He deliberately chose the "long, long trail," evading none of the suffering involved (see Hebrews 2:9–10).

3. Temptation, the Sinner and the Saint *(Matthew 26:41; Luke 22:28; James 1:14–15)*

We all of us suffer from temptations we have no business to be suffering from, simply because we refuse to let God lift us to a higher plane where we would have other temptations to face of another type. The temptations of Jesus are removed from any affinity with the natural; but when we are born again we realise the meaning of Our Lord's words to Peter, "Satan hath desired to have you, that he may sift you as wheat."

In our natural life we possess the possibility of self-realisation—"I am going to get the best out of myself, and train myself for my own ends." Until we are born from above (RV mg) the highest standpoint we have is that of self-realisation, and the particular possessions of our personality will be tested by the alien power to see whether that power can "tire" it. Temptation is not towards what we understand as evil, but towards what we understand as good (cf. Luke 16:15). Temptation is something that for a while completely baffles us, we do not know whether it is towards a right thing or not.

Spiritual life is attained, not by a necromantic magic pill, but by moral choices, whereby we test the thing that presents itself to us as being good. The basis of natural life and moral and spiritual life is the same. The way we maintain health in each of these domains is by fight. Health is the balance between my physical life and external nature. If the fighting force on the inside begins to dwindle or is impaired, I get diseased, things outside begin to disintegrate my vital force. The same is true of my moral life, everything that does not partake of the nature of virtue is the enemy of virtue in me, and it depends on how much moral calibre I have whether I overcome and produce virtue. The same is true spiritually; if I have enough spiritual fighting capacity, I will produce a character like Jesus Christ's. Character must be attained, it is never given to us.

The devil does not tempt to wrong things, he tries to make us lose what God has put into us by regeneration, viz. the possibility of being of value to God.

The central citadel of the devil's attack on Jesus Christ is the same in us when we are born from above (RV mg), viz. my right to myself. Satan's aim is to dethrone God, and his whole purpose through the disposition of sin is to get us to the same place. Satan is never represented in the Bible as being guilty of sins, of doing wrong things; he is *a wrong being*.

There is a limit to temptation. "God is faithful, who will not suffer you to be tempted above that ye are able." God does not save us from temptations, but He succours us in the middle of them. In Hebrews 4:15 the writer is not referring to the temptations common to man as fallen man, but to the temptations common to the sanctified soul. And when Our Lord taught His disciples to pray, "Lead us not into temptation," He is not referring to the temptation James refers to, but to the temptation He Himself was led into by the Spirit of God. After the baptism of Jesus and the descent of the Holy Ghost upon Him, God, as it were, took His sheltering hand off Him. So also after the work of sanctification, when the life of the saint really begins, God lifts His hand off us and lets the world do its worst, for He is assured that He that is in him is greater than he that is against him.

CONSCIENCE

Conscience is that innate faculty in a man's spirit that attaches itself to the highest the man knows, whether he be an atheist or a Christian. The highest the Christian knows is God: the highest the atheist knows is his principles. That "Conscience is the voice of God" is easily proved to be absurd. If conscience were the voice of God, it would be the same in everyone. "I verily thought with myself," said Paul, "that I ought to do many things contrary to the name of Jesus of Nazareth" (Acts 26:9). Paul acted according to his conscience; and Our Lord said, "Whosoever killeth you will think that he doeth God service" (John 16:2)—they will obey their conscience in putting you to death.

The eye in the body records exactly what it looks at. The eye simply records, and the record is according to the light thrown on what it looks at. Conscience is the eye of the soul which looks out on what it is taught is God, and how conscience records depends entirely upon what light is thrown upon God. Our Lord Jesus Christ is the only true light on God. When a man sees Jesus Christ he does not get a new conscience, but a totally new light is thrown upon God, and conscience records accordingly, with the result that he is absolutely upset by conviction of sin.

1. The Articles of Conscience

By the "articles" of conscience we mean the regulations of conscience in man fresh from the hand of his Creator, and those articles are—God is Love; God is Holy; God is Near. The Bible records that "God is love"; but it must be borne in mind that it is the love *of God*, and that love, which is inexpressible bliss to a Being like Jesus Christ, or to a being like Adam as God created him, is a veritable hell of pain to those of us who are not like either. To know that God is love, God is holy, God is near, is pure delight to man in his innocent relationship to God, but a terror extreme since the fall. God can never leave a man until He has burned him as pure as He is Himself. It is God's love that forbids He should let him go.

These regulations of conscience are ingrained in the spirit of fallen man as they are in the spirit of a man who is born from above (RV mg).

2. The Attitudes of Conscience

When God is revealed as Love, as Holy, and as Near, it is man's conscience that alarms him from his sleep of death; it makes hell for a man instead of a life of peace. "Think not that I am come to send peace on earth: I came not to send peace, but a sword" (Matthew 10:34).

Wherever Jesus comes He reveals that man is away from God by reason of sin, and he is terrified at His presence. That is why men will put anything in the place of Jesus Christ, anything rather than let God come near in His startling purity, because immediately God comes near, conscience records that God is holy and nothing unholy can live with Him, consequently His presence hurts the sinner. "If I had not come and spoken unto them, they had not had sin; but now they have no cloke for their sin" (John 15:22).

(a) Self-Consciousness

The first thing conscience does is to rouse up self-consciousness, and that produces embarrassment. A little child is full of winsome beauty because he is utterly free from self-consciousness; when he begins to be conscious of himself he becomes awkward and shy and does all kinds of affected things; and when once the conscience of man is roused by the presence of God, it produces a consciousness of self that makes us scuttle out of His presence like bats out of the light. Most of us know much too little about what conscience succeeds in doing when we stand in the presence of God. We talk much too lightly about sin. Stand one second in the presence of God, in the light of conscience with the Spirit of God illuminating it, without Jesus Christ, and instantly you are conscious of what is stated in Genesis 3:7, viz. your kinship with the brute creation, with no God-quality in you.

(b) World-Consciousness

One effect of the disturbance caused by the light of conscience is to drive us into the outside hubbub of things. In the early days of Christianity men brooded on their sins, nowadays psychologists tell us the more wholesome way is to forget all about sin—fling yourself into the work of the world. Rushing into work in order to deaden conscience is characteristic of the life we live today. "Live the simple life; keep a healthy body; never let your conscience be disturbed; for any sake keep away from religious meetings; don't bring before us the morbid tendency of things." We shall find that the morbid tendency of things is the conviction of the Holy Ghost.

(c) God-Consciousness

The consciousness of God will break out in spite of all our sense of uncleanness, in spite of all our rush and interest in the work of the world, and in spite of all our logic, the implicit sense of God will come and disturb our peace.

We are laying down the fundaments of the way God has constituted man. God is holy, therefore nothing that does not partake of His holiness can abide in His presence, and that means pain. When conscience begins to be awakened by God, we either become subtle hypocrites or saints, that is, either we let God's law working through conscience bring us to the place where we can be put right, or we begin to hoodwink ourselves, to affect a religious pose, not before other people, but before ourselves, in order to appease conscience—anything to be kept out of the real presence of God because wherever He comes, He disturbs.

3. The Awakening of Conscience

(a) Armoured in Sin

The majority of men are dead in trespasses and sins. Our Lord illustrates this—"When a strong man armed keepeth his palace, his goods are in peace: but when a stronger than he shall come upon him, and overcome him, he taketh from him all his armour wherein he trusted, and divideth his spoils" (Luke 11:21–22). When the prince of this world rules, men are armoured in sin, not necessarily in wrongdoing, but in a wrong attitude, consequently they have no disturbance, no trouble, no perplexity. As the Psalmist says, "They are not in trouble as other men; they have more than heart could wish. . . . There are no pangs in their death" (see Psalm 73:4–7 RV).

(b) Awakened in Sin

How is conscience in men like that to be awakened? No man can awaken another man; the Spirit of God alone can awaken him. Our Lord did not say that the strong man *battles* with the stronger man: He says, "When a stronger than he shall come upon him, and *overcome* him . . ." When once the Spirit of God shows Jesus Christ to a man in that condition, his armour is gone, and he experiences distress and pain and upset, exactly as Jesus said he would. Before, he had been armoured with the peace of "the prince of this world" and his conscience recorded that everything was all right. Immediately Jesus Christ is presented, conscience records what the man is in the light of God, and the garrison within is disturbed, his peace and joy are gone, and he is under what is called conviction of sin.

(c) Awakening to Holiness

"And He, when He is come, will convict . . . of sin" (RV). We are apt to put conviction of sin in the wrong place in a man's life. The man of all men who experienced conviction of sin was the saintly Apostle Paul. "For I was alive without the law once: but when the commandment came, sin revived, and I died" (Romans 7:9). There is no mention of conviction of sin in Paul's account of his conversion, only conviction of darkness and distress and of being out of order. But after Paul had been three years in Arabia with the Holy Ghost

blazing through him, he began to write the diagnoses of sin which we have in his Epistles. The sense of sin is in proportion to the sense of holiness. The hymn has it rightly—

And they who fain would serve Thee best
Are conscious most of wrong within.

It does not mean that indwelling sin and indwelling holiness abide together: indwelling sin can never abide with indwelling holiness; it means exactly what Paul said, "I know that in me (that is, in my flesh) dwelleth no good thing . . ." (Romans 7:18), "But we had the sentence of death in ourselves that we should not trust in ourselves . . ." (2 Corinthians 1:9). The majority of us have caught on the jargon of holiness without the tremendous panging pain that follows the awakening to holiness. The Spirit of God brings us to face ourselves steadily in the light of God until sin is seen in its true nature. If you want to know what sin is, don't ask the convicted sinner, ask the saint, the one who has been awakened to the holiness of God through the Atonement; he is the one who can begin to tell you what sin is. The man writhing at the penitent form is affected because his sins have upset him, but he has very little knowledge of sin. It is only as we walk in the light as God is in the light that we begin to understand the unfathomable depths of cleansing to which the blood of Jesus Christ goes (1 John 1:7). Every now and again the Spirit of God allows the saint to look back as the Apostle Paul did when he said, "I was before a blasphemer, and a persecutor, and injurious" (RV). Paul was a mature saint at this time, but he is looking back into what he was before Jesus Christ apprehended him.

Conscience is the internal perception of God's moral law. Have you ever been convicted of sin by conscience through the Spirit of God? If you have, you know this—that God dare not forgive you and be God. There is a lot of sentimental talk about God forgiving because He is love: God is so holy that He cannot forgive. God can only destroy for ever the thing that is unlike Himself. The Atonement does not mean that God forgives a sinner and allows him to go on sinning and receiving forgiveness; it means that God saves the sinner and turns him into a saint, i.e. destroys the sinner out of him, and through his conscience he realises that by the Atonement God has done what He never could have done apart from it. When people tes-

tify you can always tell whether they have been convicted by the Spirit of God or whether their equilibrium has been disturbed by doing wrong things. When a man is convicted of sin by the Spirit of God through his conscience, his relationship to other people is absolute child's play. If when you were convicted of sin, you had been told to go and lick the dust off the boots of your greatest enemy, you would have done it willingly. Your relationship to men is the last thing that bothers you. It is your relationship to God that bothers you. I am completely out of the love of God, out of the holiness of God, and I tremble with terror when I think of God drawing near. That is the real element of conviction of sin, and it is one of the rarest things nowadays because men are not uplifting the white light of Jesus Christ upon God, they are uplifting arbitrary standards of right. They are uplifting, for instance, the conduct of man to man; they are telling us we should love our fellow men. The consequence is the majority of us get off scot-free, we begin to feel very self-righteous, ". . . but they . . . *comparing themselves among themselves*, are not wise." But when conscience is illuminated by the Holy Ghost, these three amazing articles—God is Love, God is Holy, God is Near—are brought straight down to our inner life and we can neither look up nor down for terror. When a man begins his life with God there are great tracts of his life that he never bothers his head about, but slowly and surely the Spirit of God educates him down to the tiny little scruple.[11] Every crook and cranny of the physical life, every imagination and emotion is perfectly known to God, and He demands that all these be blameless. That brings us to absolute despair unless Jesus Christ can do what He claims He can. The marvel of the Atonement is just this very thing, that the perfect Saviour imparts His perfections to me, and as I walk in the light as God is in the light, every part of bodily life, of affectionate life and of spirit life are kept unblameable in holiness; my duty is to keep in the light, God does all the rest. That is why the life of God within the saint produces agony every now and again, because God won't leave us alone, He won't say, "Now that will do." He will keep at us, blazing and burning us, He is a "consuming fire." That phrase becomes the greatest consolation we ever had. God will consume and shake, and shake and consume, till there is nothing more to be consumed, but only Himself—incandescent with the presence of God.

11. down to the scruple: to the smallest item.

HUMANITY
Psalm 2

God does His business, do yours.

Amiel

The tendency nowadays is to take the management of the universe out of God's hands, while at the same time neglecting our business, viz. the government of our own universe within.

1. Enthusiasm for Humanity *(Psalm 2:2)*

The main line indicated in the Bible with regard to the human race and God's purpose for it is that God allows the human race full liberty, and He allows the spirit of evil, viz. Satan, nearly full liberty also. Peter says that God is longsuffering (2 Peter 3:9); He is giving us ample opportunity to try whatever line we like both in individual and in national life, but the Bible reveals that in the final end of all things, men will confess that God's purpose and His judgement are right. We must disabuse our minds of the idea that God sits like a Judge on a throne and batters humanity into shape. He is sometimes presented in that way, not intentionally, but simply because the majority of people have forgotten the principle laid down by Jesus, that "there is nothing covered that shall not be revealed; and hid, that shall not be known"; and that in the end, God's judgements will be made utterly plain and clear, and men will agree that they are right. Meantime, God is giving humanity and the devil ample opportunity to try and prove that His purposes and His judgements are wrong.

Enthusiasm means intensity of interest. Enthusiasm for Humanity is one thing; enthusiasm for saints is another, God's purpose is the latter. In order that we may see exactly the forces and the problems that are at work morally, we will look at these heads:

(a) The Master Man (Romans 5:12)

Adam stands as the Federal Head of the race, he is the master key to the virtues that still remain in sinful men. These virtues must be understood as remnants left of God's original design, and not promises of what man is going to be. The moral problem comes in this way: we inherit by nature certain strong cardinal virtues, but these are not the slightest atom of use to us, and when a man or woman is born again of the Spirit of God, these virtues are nearly always a hindrance instead of a benefit. Think of the virtues which Jesus Christ demands in His teaching and compare them with the cardinal virtues left in us as the remnants of a ruined manhood, not as promises of the new

manhood, and you will see why it is that we cannot patch up our natural virtues to come anywhere near Jesus Christ's demands. We must be re-made on the inside and develop new virtues entirely, "a new man in Christ Jesus." This is one part of the problem which no teacher outside the Bible deals with. Books on ethics and morals take the natural virtues as promises of what a man is going to be; the Bible indicates that they are remnants of what man once was, and the key to these virtues is Adam, not Jesus Christ. This accounts for our Lord's attitude, a strange perplexing attitude until we understand this point. Jesus loves the natural virtues, and yet He refers to them in a way which makes them seem utterly futile. Take the natural virtues in the rich young ruler, we read that Jesus looking on him, "loved him." Natural virtues are beautiful in the sight of Jesus, but He knows as none other could know, that they are not promises of what man is going to be, but remnants, "trailing clouds of glory," left in man, and are not of the slightest atom of practical use to him. Jesus Christ told the rich young ruler that he must strip himself of all he possessed, give his manhood to Him and then come and follow Him; in other words he must be re-made entirely.

(b) The Muddle of Men (Romans 5:12)

The "muddle of men" refers to the whole of the human race since Adam; we are all a muddle, "for that all have sinned." Since Adam, men, individually and collectively, tells us how the moral muddle has been produced, viz. by sin. In those in whom the cardinal virtues are strong and clear, there is another element which the Bible calls sin (no one else calls it sin), and it is this element which makes men and women a complete muddle; you do not know how to sort them out. In some particulars they are good, and in others they are bad, and the problem arises when you fix on one point of their personality as if it were the only point. For example, when Oscar Wilde wrote "De Profundis" in prison, he allowed one point of his personality to have way, viz. his sentimental intellectual interest in Jesus Christ, and the book was written from that point of view. He wrote sincerely, but he overlooked all the other points of his personality which contradicted that particular one, and when he came out of prison it was those other points that dominated. That is what we mean by "the muddle of men," and everyone who touches it, outside the Bible, instead of clearing it up makes it worse. The muddle is explained by one word: sin.

(c) The Mystery Man (2 Thessalonians 2:3–4)

The Bible reveals that the sin which muddles men and society is ultimately going to appear in an incarnation called the man of sin, or the Antichrist. The enthusiasm of humanity for itself in its present state simply means irrevocable disaster ultimately. Nowadays people talk about the whole human race being in the making, that our natural virtues are promises of what we are going to be; they take no account at all of sin. We have to remember that an enthusiasm for humanity which ignores the Bible is sure to end in disaster; enthusiasm for the community of saints means that God can take hold of the muddle and can re-make men, not simply in accordance with the Master man before the fall, but "conformed to the image of His Son" (Romans 8:29).

2. The Embarrassment of Humanity (Psalm 2:4–6)

(a) Bastard Solidarity (Genesis 6:5; Hebrews 12:8)

Solidarity means consolidation and oneness of interest, the solidarity of the human race means that every member of the race has one point of interest with every other member. Notice how the whole of Scripture is knit together over this false solidarity of sin. It is quite possible for the human mind to blot God out of its thinking entirely, and to work along the line of the elements which are the same in every man, and to band the whole of the human race into a solid atheistic community. The only reason this has not been done up to the present is that the human race has been too much divided, but we shall find that these divisions are gradually resolving themselves. There are elements in human nature that are the same in everybody, and if once the human mind succeeded in obliterating God, the whole of the human race would become one vast phalanx of atheism.

(b) Babel of Souls (Genesis 11:1–9)

This is the first time solidarity was attempted, away in hoary antiquity. What encumbers and embarrasses humanity is an uncomfortable feeling that God is laughing at them all the time, and in the history of men up to the present time the hindrance to perfectly organised atheism has been the saints who represent the derision of God: if they were removed, we should find perfectly organised atheism.

(c) Body of Sin (Romans 6:6)

The body of sin is this tremendous possibility of solid atheism underlying humanity; the share of individual men and women in that body is called "the old man."

Every time a man or woman by identification with Jesus enters into the experimental knowledge that his "old man" is crucified with Christ, the ultimate defeat and destruction of the body of sin becomes clearer. The body of sin is not in a man; what is in a man is "the old man," the carnal mind, which connects him with the body of sin. The Solidarity of sin forms the basis of the power of Satan, and it runs all through humanity, making it possible for the whole human race to be atheistic. Sin in its beginning is simply being without God. Paul's argument is that the purpose of "the old man" being crucified with Christ, is that the body of sin might be destroyed, i.e. that the connection with the body of sin might be severed. Everyone who becomes identified with the death of Jesus Christ aims another blow at Satan and at the great solidarity of sin. There are two mystical bodies—there is the mystical body of Christ, and the mystical body of sin which is anticipated in the man of sin. When a man begins to go wrong, he says, "I can't help it"; perfectly true. God's Book reveals the great oracle of evil, the tremendous power behind wrong, doing; it is a supernatural power antagonistic to God. We do not battle against flesh and blood but "against principalities, against powers, against the rulers of the darkness of this world, against spiritual wickedness in high places." When a man is saved and sanctified, he is severed from the body of sin, and consequently all the powers of darkness backed by Satan make a dead set for that soul. The only thing that can keep a sanctified soul is the almighty power of God through Jesus Christ, but kept by that power he is perfectly safe. When once the saints are removed, the world will be faced with the menace of the solidarity of sin and atheism.

The question of the moment is: A God that serves Humanity, or a Humanity that serves God?

Forsyth[12]

When men depart from the Bible they call humanity "God" in differing terms; the use of the term "God" means nothing to them, God is simply the name given to the general tendencies which further men's interests. This spirit is honeycombing everything, we find it coming into the way we talk of Christian experience; there is creeping in the idea that God and Jesus Christ and the Holy Ghost are simply meant to bless us, to further our interests. When we come to the New Testament we find exactly the opposite idea, that by regeneration we are brought into such harmony and union with God that we realise with great joy that we are meant to serve His interests.

---

12. Peter Taylor Forsyth (1848–1921): British Congregationalist minister and theologian. Chambers read many of Forsyth's books and valued his insights.

3. The Embroilment of Humanity *(Psalm 2:7–9)*

Embroilment means to involve in perplexity. It is the presence of the saints that upsets the calculations of Satan; and it is the presence of Jesus that involves not only Satan but humanity in all kinds of distractions. If men and Satan could only get rid of Jesus Christ, they would never be involved in perplexity, never be upset. Jesus put it very clearly: "If I had not come and spoken unto them, they had not had sin; but now they have no cloke for their sin" (John 15:22). The greatest annoyance to Satan and to humanity is Jesus Christ. Twenty centuries ago the Apostle John wrote, "every spirit which confesseth not Jesus" (RV mg, "annulleth Jesus"—dissolves Jesus by analysis) "is not of God: and this is the spirit of the Antichrist, whereof ye have heard that it cometh" (1 John 4:3 RV). Watch the tendency abroad to-day; people want to get rid of Jesus Christ, they cannot prove that He did not live, or that He was not a remarkable Man; but they set to work to dissolve Him by analysis, to say He was not really God Incarnate. Jesus Christ always upsets the calculations of humanity; that is what made Voltaire say "Crucify the wretch, stamp Him and His crazy tale out," because He was the stumbling-block to all the reasonings of men. You cannot work Jesus Christ into any system of thinking. If you could keep Him out, everything could be explained. The world could be explained by evolution, but you cannot fit Jesus Christ into the theory of evolution. Jesus Christ is an annoyance to Satan, a thorn in the side of the world at large, an absolute distress to sin in the individual. If we could crucify Him and stamp Him out, the annoyance would cease. In dealing with the carnal mind, Paul says it is *enmity against God.*

(a) *The Past Watchword*—a religion that utilises humanity. The error in the past on the part of religious teachers has been to present God as a great sovereign power Who utilises humanity without rhyme or reason.

(b) *The Present Watchword*—a humanity that utilises God—is the opposite, viz. that God is a great aimless, loving tendency that humanity utilises to forgive itself, to cleanse itself, and to justify itself.

(c) *The Persistent Word*—a Christ that unites God and Man in love—through both the errors is this, the Lord Jesus Christ, Who can unite a holy God and an un-holy humanity by means of His wonderful Redemption. In this connection, Jesus Christ stands as the type of man, and the only type of man, who can come near to God. "Christ is for the central figure of a glorified humanity to develop by Christ's aid the innate spiritual resources of a splendid race." Jesus Christ is the One Who has the power to impart His own innate spiritual life, viz. Holy Spirit, to unholy men, and develop them until they are like Himself.

That is why the devil hates Jesus Christ, and why he tries to make men calculate without Him.

(4) The Emancipation of Humanity *(Psalm 2:10–12)*

When any sinful man accepts morally the verdict of God on sin in the cross of Christ, he becomes emancipated. A moral decision is different from a mental decision, which may be largely sentiment. A moral decision means—"My God, I accept Thy verdict against sin on the cross of Jesus Christ, and I want the disposition of sin in me identified with His death"—immediately a man gets there, all that we understand by the Holy Ghost working in His tremendous power through the Redemption takes place, and the emancipation of humanity is furthered. "Christ is for the central figure of a glorious God, and Humanity's chief end is to develop from reconciliation, redemption, and subjection to God's will."

(a) The Second Man *(2 Corinthians 5:17–18)*
God emancipates the human race through this second Man, the Lord Jesus Christ. That is why Paul called Jesus Christ "the last Adam." If the first Adam is the key to the muddle of men, Jesus Christ, the last Adam, is the key to the emancipation of men. Jesus Christ stands for all that a man should be, and to the saints He stands for all that God is.

(b) Sanctified Men *(Ephesians 2:1–10)*
A sanctified man has not only had the disposition of sin crucified, but he is emancipated from his connection with the body of sin and is lifted to the heavenly places where Jesus lived when He was here. This marvellous revelation is summed up in 1 John 1:7, "But if we walk in the light, as He is in the light, we have fellowship one with another, and the blood of Jesus Christ His Son cleanseth us from all sin." This is the enthusiasm for the communion of saints in contrast to the enthusiasm for humanity. It is by thinking along these lines that we are enabled to prove experimentally what we know in our minds; and we should live with far greater power if only we would let our pure minds be stirred up by way of remembrance (2 Peter 3:1). While we are on this earth, living in alien territory, it is a marvellous emancipation to know, that we are raised above it all through Jesus Christ, and that we have power over all the power of the enemy in and through Him.

(c) Supreme Mystery *(Ephesians 5:32)*
Around the saints is the great power of God which keeps watch and ward over them so that "that wicked one toucheth them not." What is true of saints individually is true of all saints collectively, viz. that the elements which under Satan make for the solidarity of atheism, make for the solidarity of holiness under

God. "Fear not, little flock; for it is your Father's good pleasure to give you the kingdom," a tiny insignificant crowd in every age. Christianity has always been a forlorn hope because the saints are in alien territory; but it is all right, God is working out His tremendous purpose for the overthrow of everything Satan and sin can do. "He that sitteth in the heavens shall laugh." Everything that sin and Satan have ruined is going to be reconstructed and readjusted through the marvellous Redemption of our Lord Jesus Christ.

HARMONY

1. Health—Physical Harmony. *Peace of Fact* (Genesis 2:1–9, 15–17)

Harmony means a fitting together of parts so as to form a connected whole, agreement in relation. Health, or physical harmony, is God's plan from the very beginning. The first mention of any subject in the Book of Genesis colours every allusion to that subject throughout the Bible. Health (physical harmony), Happiness (moral harmony) and Holiness (spiritual harmony) are all divergent views as to what is the main aim of a man's life. Health, or physical harmony, is a perfect balance between our organism and the outer world.

(a) The Cult of the Splendid Animal (Psalm 147:10)

There always have been and always will be people who worship splendid, well-groomed health. This verse reveals that God places health, or physical harmony, in a totally different relationship from that which it is put in by man. The modern name for the worship of physical health is Christian Science. The great error of the healthy-minded cult is that it ignores a man's moral and spiritual life.

(b) The Cult of the Sick Attitude (Psalm 39:6–11)

A great many people indulge in the luxury of misery; their one worship is of anguish, agony, weakness and sensitiveness to pain. The cult of the sick attitude is well established in human history by the fact that most of the great men and women whose personalities have marked the life of their time have been to some degree deranged physically. Amiel, a highly sensitive and cultured man, almost too morbid to exist, was a lifelong invalid, and he wrote thus in his *Journal:* "The first summonses of illness have a divine value, so that evils though they seem, they are really an appeal to us from on high, a touch of God's Fatherly scourge." The healthy-minded people do not agree with that attitude, and sick people are inclined to worship it. The attitude to sickness in the Bible is totally different from the attitude of people who believe in faith-healing. The Bible attitude is not that God sends sickness or that sickness is of the devil, but that sickness is a fact usable by both God and the devil. Never base a principle on your own experience. My personal experience is this: I have never once in my life been sick without being to blame for it. As soon as I turned my mind to asking why the sickness was allowed, I learned a lesson that I have never forgotten, viz., that my physical health depends absolutely on my relationship to God. Never pin your faith to a doctrine or to anyone else's statement, get hold of God's Book, and you will find that your spiritual character determines exactly how God deals with you personally. People continually get into fogs because they will not take God's line, they will take someone else's line. God's Book deals with facts. Health and sickness are facts, not fancies. There are cases recorded in the Bible, and in our own day, of people who have been marvellously healed, for what purpose? For us to imitate them? Never, but in order that we might discern what lies behind, viz. the individual relationship to a personal God. The peace arising from fact is unintelligent and dangerous, e.g. people who base on the fact of health are at peace, but it is often a peace which makes them callous. On the other hand, people who accept the fact of being sick are inclined to have a jaundiced eye for everything healthy. For a man to make health his god is to put himself merely at the head of the brute creation.

I am purposely leaving the subject vague and without an answer; there can be no answer. The great difficulty is that people find answers which they say came from God. You cannot prove facts; you have to swallow them. The fact of health and the fact of sickness are there; we have nothing to do with choosing them, they come and go. We have to get on to another platform, the moral platform, and then the spiritual platform, before we can begin to get an explanation of these facts.

2. Happiness—Moral Harmony. *Peace of Principle*

Happiness or moral harmony is a perfect balance between our inclination and our environment. The peace of principle keeps a man's moral nature in a state of harmony.

(a) Pride of Integrity (Luke 18:11)

Integrity means the unimpaired state of anything, and pride in the integrity of a man or woman's morality will produce happiness. They have no need of prayer, or if they do pray it is a soliloquy of peace before high heaven. The Pharisee in Our Lord's parable was happy; he was not praying to God, or that others might hear; he was praying "with himself"—"God, I thank Thee that I am not as other men are, extortioners, unjust, adulterers, or even as this publican." Look at him, then put your own name behind him and you have got his portrait exactly; you know where he lives and everything about him. Beware of calling this type of happiness self-righteousness; the phrase which gives the true meaning would be "happy satisfaction with my intellectual and moral conduct." That happiness is impregnable to God and to the devil; its true emblem is ice. If you want to find an analysis of every kind of moral and immoral character, the Bible is the place to look for it. This picture in Luke 18 is not the picture of a man of the world, but of a religious man. As Christians we have to beware of Pharisaic holiness along the line of sanctification.

(b) The Pain of Iniquity (Luke 18:13)

This is the stage when the peace of principle has broken down. "When Thou with rebukes doth correct man for iniquity, Thou makest his beauty to consume away like a moth" (Psalm 39:11). According to the steadily reiterated teachings of Jesus Christ, a man who is in moral harmony with himself without being rightly related to Jesus Christ, is much nearer the devil than a bad-living man.

Harmony, both physical and moral, is God-ordained, i.e., it is God's will that a man's body with all its component parts should be in perfect harmony with themselves and with the outer world, and it is God's will that a man should be in moral harmony with himself and happy in that sense; and yet, as we have pointed out, the Bible reveals that a man can have physical health at the cost of his moral welfare, and happiness at the cost of spiritual welfare.

3. Holiness—Spiritual Harmony. *Peace of God*

Holiness, or spiritual harmony, is a perfect balance between our disposition and all the law of God. Never trust your temperament, i.e., your sensibility to things. When God makes a saint He plants a new disposition in him, but He does not alter his temperament; the saint has to mould his temperament according to the new disposition. Take your own experience, think of the time before you knew God, before God gave you the Holy Spirit, before you entered into the life of sanctification, your temperament and your sensibilities produced in you a horror for certain things which now you look at from a totally different attitude, and you begin to say, "Why, I must be getting callous!" Nothing of the sort, you have a new disposition with which your temperament is being brought into harmony, and that disposition being God-given is bringing you into sympathy with God's way of looking at things so that you are no longer the creature of your sensibilities. If you have begun to get discouraged over the difficulty of disciplining your sensibilities, don't be discouraged, get at it again. At the beginning we are apt to be tripped up by our sensibilities because they have not yet been brought into complete subjection to the Lord Jesus Christ. Remember, although Jesus Christ is on the throne, you are "prime minister" under Him.

(a) Untouched by Panic (Psalm 112:7)

Our Lord never suffered from physical or moral or intellectual panics, because He was fixed in God. "But Jesus did not commit Himself unto them, because He knew all men, . . . for He knew what was in man" (John 2:24–25). Look at your own experience and see how your sensibilities will run you into panics and try and make you believe a lie. It is through their sensibilities that Satan tries to get hold of the saints. God said to Satan about Job, "Behold, all that he hath is in thy hand [RV mg]; only upon himself put not forth thine hand" (Job 1:12). For our present argument may this not mean that Satan cannot touch the ruling disposition; but that if we are not on the watch at all the loopholes, he will get hold of the sensibilities and try to bring us into bondage? Whenever you feel bondage spiritually, smell brimstone, you are on a wrong tack. Panics are always wrong, there is nothing in them. What a blessing it is to know someone who never gets into a panic! someone you can always depend on. You go to them in a flurry, with fired and jangled nerves, brain like cotton-wool, heart panting like a butterfly nearly dead, and in two or three minutes everything is quietened. What has happened? The difference in you has come about because that one is paying no attention to his sensibilities but only to the one bedrock reality of the life, viz. God. Holiness is untouched by panic. "In tumults," says Paul. What is a tumult? Watch a porridge-pot boiling, that is a tumult; to be inside that, undisturbed, means something, and that type of character is the only one that can stand as a worker for God in this world. A man or woman with that disposition in them can stand where Jesus Christ stood, because it is His own disposition that is in them, and that disposition cannot be upset, it cannot be made to take account of the evil. In the eyes of the world the way a saint trusts God is always absurd, until there is trouble on, then the world is inclined to kneel down and worship the saint.

(b) Undeterred by Persecution (Psalm 112:10)

God's Book reveals all through that holiness will bring persecution from those who are not holy. Our Lord taught His disciples to be conspicuous. "Ye are the light of the world. A city that is set on an hill"; and He taught them never to hide the truth for fear of wolfish men (Matthew 10:16). Personal experience bears out the truth that a testimony to holiness produces either rage or ridicule on the part of those who are not holy. We are all cowards naturally; we are only not cowards when God has altered our disposition, because the disposition God puts in keeps us fixed in a right relationship to Himself. The one dominant note of the life of a saint is first of all sympathy with God and God's ideas, not with human beings. A twofold line runs all through God's Book, and especially in the Epistles of St. Paul, with regard to public preaching and teaching and dealing with people in private: Be as stern and unflinching as God Almighty in your preaching, but as tender and gentle as a sinner saved by grace should be when you deal with a human soul. To-day the order is being reversed and modern teaching is amazingly "easy-osy." Look at the standard of the preaching of to-day; sympathy with human beings is put first, not sympathy with God, and the truth of God is withheld. It must be withheld, it dare not be preached, because immediately the fullness of a personal salvation is preached—which means I must be right with God, must have a disposition which is in perfect harmony with God's laws and which will enable me to work them out, it produces conviction and resentment and upset. Jesus Christ taught His disciples never to keep back the truth of God for fear of persecution. When we come to dealing with our fellow-men, what is our attitude to be? Remember yourself, remember who you are, and that if you have attained to anything in the way of holiness, remember Who made you what you are. "But by the grace of God I am what I am," says the Apostle Paul (1 Corinthians 15:10). Deal with infinite pity and sympathy with other souls, keeping your eye on what you once were and what, by the grace of God, you are now.

In dealing with yourself be as patient as God is with you. Beware of the spiritual sulks which spring from thinking that because I, a two-year-old in sanctifying grace, am not as big and mature and strong as the twenty-year-old in grace, I can't be sanctified rightly! There is more danger there than most saints think. (See Hebrews 12:5–11.) The devil tries to make us think that when we have entered into the sanctified life, all is done; it is only begun. We have entered into Jesus Christ's finished work, but remember, says Paul, you have attained to nothing yet; everything is perfectly adjusted, now begin to attain and to "grow up into Him in all things."

These three things develop slowly together: first, the basis of spiritual holiness; second, the building of moral happiness; and third, the decoration of physical health. A full-grown man in Christ Jesus is one who has become exactly like Christ Jesus. "Till we all come . . . unto the measure of the stature of the fullness of Christ" (Ephesians 4:13).

Run Today's Race

A Word from Oswald Chambers for Every Day of the Year

Copyright © 1968 Oswald Chambers Publications Association Ltd.
Scripture versions quoted: KJV; RV

INTRODUCTION

Source

Quotations are drawn from the lectures and sermons of Oswald Chambers.

Publication History

- As a book: *Run Today's Race* was first published in 1968.

Oswald Chambers firmly believed in the concept of "seed thoughts"—brief, pithy sayings designed to arrest attention and stimulate thinking. The entry for December 9 perhaps best expresses his conviction on how to affect a person's mind and behavior:

Our Lord was never impatient. He simply planted seed thoughts in the disciples' minds and surrounded them with the atmosphere of His own life. We get impatient and take men by the scruff of the neck and say: "You must believe this and that." You cannot make a man see moral truth by persuading his intellect. "When He, the Spirit of truth is come, He shall guide you into all truth." (RV)

At the Bible Training College,[1] London, and at the Zeitoun[2] YMCA Camp in Egypt, Chambers always posted a daily thought on a centrally located notice board. The daily words ranged from a spiritual challenge to humor. After a deluge that left the Zeitoun camp flooded, the board outside Oswald's study hut read: "Closed during submarine manoeuvres!" The day before, the board had proclaimed: "Beware! there is a religious talk here each evening!"

While Mrs. Chambers was still in Egypt after her husband's death, she published the first *Seed Thoughts Calendar,* containing a brief thought from Oswald's teachings for each day of the year. The small, thin book fit easily into the breast pocket of a soldier's uniform. Other versions of the *Seed Thoughts Calendar* followed through the years.

In the two forewords included in this volume, Kathleen Chambers[3] explains the origin of the 1968 edition, and in the second, she comments for the first time on the mental illness that clouded her mother's final years.

---

1. Bible Training College (BTC): a residential school near Clapham Common in southwest London. Sponsored by the League of Prayer; operated from 1911 until it closed in July 1915 because of World War I. Oswald Chambers was principal and main teacher; Biddy Chambers, his wife, was lady superintendent.

2. Zeitoun (zay TOON), Egypt: six miles northeast of Cairo; site of a YMCA camp, the Egypt General Mission compound, and, from 1916 to 1919, the Imperial School of Instruction, training base for British, Australian, and New Zealand troops during World War I.

3. Kathleen Chambers (1913–1997): only child of Oswald and Biddy Chambers.

FOREWORD (TO THE FIRST EDITION—1968)

There's a harvest in a grain of wheat
If given to God in simple trust
For though the grain doth turn to dust
It cannot die! It lives; it must
For the power of God is behind it.

Anon.

Seed Thoughts Calendar was the name given to a small book first printed in 1918 in Egypt. That publication contained short sentences from my father's messages to the soldiers camped in the desert[4] outside Cairo.

For over twenty years it has not been reprinted. Now a similar selection appears under a new title. My mother felt, very strongly, that a new series should be prepared and in 1961 she collected and typed the first three months of these new *Seed Thoughts* and I have completed the work.

May God bless all those who read this book and may these thoughts live because "the power of God is behind them."

Kathleen Chambers
1968

FOREWORD TO THE REPRINTED EDITION (1997)

There's a harvest in a grain of wheat
If given to God in simple trust
For though the grain doth turn to dust
It cannot die! It lives; it must
For the power of God is behind it.

Anon.

Seed Thoughts Calendar was the name given to a small book first printed in 1918 in Egypt. That publication contained short sentences from my father's messages to the soldiers camped in the desert outside Cairo. My mother wanted a similar small book to be printed.

Towards the end of my mother's life, God allowed her to become very ill with a mental illness (not senility) and her mind became clouded and tormented.

She received treatment and became restored for nearly a year, before the illness returned to stay until she went into God's presence. During the time my mother's mind was freed, she typed the first three months of a Seed Thoughts Calendar. After she died, I looked up the other nine months' quotations and this book was then printed under the title Run Today's Race. It's wonderful to know that Almighty God held my mother safe in the centre of His will and His purposes were not thwarted.

May God bless all those who read this book and may these thoughts live because "the power of God is behind them."

Kathleen Chambers
1996

---

4. in the desert: Many of Chambers' talks and lectures were to soldiers during World War I at Zeitoun (zay TOON), Egypt, site of a YMCA camp, the Egypt General Mission compound, and, from 1916 to 1919, the Imperial School of Instruction, training base for British, Australian, and New Zealand troops.

January

1 God is so immediately near and so immensely strong that I get more and more joyous in my confidence in Him and less and less careful how I feel.

2 The very life of Jesus is given to us unstintedly if we will identify ourselves with His Death. At the back of us stands the Risen Life of Jesus that nothing can overcome.

3 The Spirit of God alters my dominating desires; He alters the thing that matters, and a universe of desires I had never known before, suddenly comes on the horizon.

4 It is a great moment when we realise we have the power to trample on certain moods, a tremendous emancipation to get rid of every kind of self-consciousness and heed one thing only: the relationship between God and myself.

5 Faith for my deliverance is not faith in God. Faith means, whether I am visibly delivered or not, I will stick to my belief that God is love. There are some things only learned in a fiery furnace.

6 It is easy to turn our religious life into a cathedral for beautiful memories, but there are feet to be washed, hard flints to be walked over, people to be fed. Very few of us go there, but that is the way the Son of God went.

7 Believe what you saw when you were in the light, and when you are in the ploughed field and God's moral seasons are going over you—the remainder of the cold, hard winter, the beginnings of the strange, painful stirrings of spring— keep abandoned to Him. He knows the seasons to bring to your soul as He does in the natural world.

8 The tendency is strong to say—"O God won't be so stern as to expect me to give up that!" *but He will;* "He won't expect me to walk in the light so that I have nothing to hide," *but He will;* "He won't expect me to draw on His grace for everything" *but He will.*

9 God narrows our "shan'ts" to one explosive point. I don't need to go that way, but God will have to bring me there if I persist in the little disobediences which no one knows but myself, because it is engendering in me a spirit God cannot allow.

10 The Christian life is the simplest, the gayest, the most regardless-of-consequences life, lived as it is taught by Jesus. The plan of our life comes through the haphazard moments, but behind it is the order of God.

11 Prayer with most of us is turned into pious platitude, it is a matter of emotion, mystical communion with God. It is no use praying unless we are living as children of God. Then Jesus says— "Every one that asketh receiveth."

12 Humility is the one stamp of a saint. Beware of the complacency of superiority when God's grace has done anything for you.

13 When you are brought face to face with something in God's word, watch your circumstances: the tyranny of things will either imperil your faith or increase it.

14 God has to rebuke us for our flippant, unthinking familiarity with Jesus Christ; we have forgotten Who He is.

15 Beware of the storms of spiritual misgiving. The security of the saint's life is his relationship to Jesus and obedience to His Word.

16 It is easy to trust in God when we have not to hunt for money, but immediately the penny that is not there looms large, we allow the mosquito of worry to irritate our whole life away from rest in God.

17 If you are a saint God will continually upset your programme, and if you are wedded to your programme you will become that most obnoxious creature under heaven, an irritable saint.

18 The Apostle James will have nothing to do with pious talk that is not backed by the life. Pious words without works are so much wind.

19 Reserve gives us an air of aloofness, and though it may start with being outward only, it will slowly and surely eat its way into the heart and result in a base form of self-centredness.

20 A sense of possession is sufficient to render us spiritually dense. Watch the havoc the winds of God play with possessions.

21 There is never any risk in love that is "talked." If love is reticent it becomes a secret treasure that enervates. Keep it in the open, have nothing hidden to brood over.

22 The resentment of discipline of any kind will warp the whole life away from God's purpose.

23 God always answers the stumbling questions which arise out of personal problems. We bristle with interrogation points, but we don't wait for the answer because we do not intend to listen to it.

24 When God puts His Spirit within us, we can say—"even now" it is as black as night, but I will not accept a slander against Jesus Christ.

25 "That we may know what is the hope of His calling"—have I allowed my mind to get stagnant
about Jesus Christ's hope and taken another aim
for my life? Sooner or later we must come, either
with a sense of havoc or a sense of rejoicing, to
Jesus Christ's standard for us.

26 Peter couples suffering "according to the will of
God" with active well-doing (1 Peter 4:19). The
folk who are most actively beneficent to you are
those who are being crushed with suffering that
would send you staggering.

27 "Until Christ be formed in you"—that brings me
to the margin of my responsibility. Am I allowing Him to manifest Himself, or am I saying: "I
shall not submit to that." Then the blow will fall
on the Son of God.

28 The one great enemy of discipleship is obstinacy,
spiritual obstinacy. We deify independence and
wilfulness and call them by the wrong name.

29 When we lie like fallow ground, God puts in new
seeds and the harvest is the ripe fruit of God; otherwise it is ripe fruit of naturalness only. Lying fallow is always the secret of spiritual growth.

30 When by God's grace you become possessed of a
new disposition, your nerves which have been
used to obeying the wrong disposition are sure to
say *"I can't"* and you must say *"You must,"* and to
your amazement you find you can.

31 Let me plead with you, as though Christ
besought you, do not be disobedient to the heavenly vision. There is only one purpose for your
life, and that is the satisfaction of the Lord Jesus
Christ.

February

1 Interest is natural, attention must be by effort.
One of the great needs of the Christian life is to
have a place where we deliberately attend to realities. That is the real meaning of prayer.

2 Christianity makes no allowance for heroic
moods. It is easy to feel heroic in an armchair,
when everything goes well, but Christianity deals
with God's standard in the common days when
you are out of your armchair, and when things are
not going well.

3 What we call crises, God ignores, and what God
reveals as the great critical moments of a man's
life we look on as humdrum commonplaces.
When we become spiritual we discern that God
was in the humdrum commonplace and we never
knew it.

4 Revise in your mind silences in prayer, in praise,
or for the Truth, when you were so greedy for
your own sensitiveness that you would not speak
the word which might have saved a soul from a
terrible blunder.

5 Pride, disdain for the people you talk to, will shut
your mouth quicker than anything. When you
speak, see that behind your voice is the life of
God.

6 Fearless devotion to Jesus Christ ought to mark
the saint today, but more often it is devotion to
our set that marks us. We are more concerned
about being in agreement with Christians than
about being in agreement with God.

7 You will find nothing more searching than what
the New Testament has to say with regard to the
miserable, petty line of insisting on my rights. The
Holy Ghost gives me power to forgo my rights.

8 Always beware of vowing, it is a risky thing. If
you promise to do a thing and don't do it, it
means the weakening of your moral nature. We
are all so glib in the way we promise and don't
perform and never realise that it is sapping our
moral energy.

9 How often we have faced difficulties that never
came, and every time we faced them we unfitted
ourselves for the duty that lay before us. I have
no business to be thinking about something else,
my duty is always the duty that lies nearest.

10 If you have a passion for souls is it because your
salvation has made such a practical change in you
that you would part with your right hand to get
every man there too?

11 We would never know that our spirit was wrong
unless Jesus rebuked it, because it is so emphatically right according to our reason (Luke 9:55).
The one thing to mark is the effect on our conscience—does my spirit bear the mark of native
self-assertiveness or of disciplined self-conquest?

12 The reason there is so much going off on side
issues is because of spiritual insubordination that
refuses to wed itself to Jesus Christ and His
Word.

13 It is possible for practical Christian work to be
active disobedience to God. We would rather
work for God than sit for one moment before
Him and let the Spirit riddle us through with
His light.

14 The cross of discipleship is that I daily and
hourly delight to tell my human nature that I am

not my own, I no longer claim my right to myself.

15 Insist on taking the initiative for God in every place you are in. As a worker, always determine to give God "the first foot."

16 "Trust in the LORD with all thine heart." It is this state of mind and heart which is absolutely free to do the duty that lies nearest without any flutter.

17 You will always know whether you believe in God personally by your impertinent insistence on being an amateur providence for someone else.

18 To be continually worrying—"Does God want me to say this or do that?" is to be in an infirm condition. There is no light of the knowledge of the glory of God in that, it means I am a self-conscious spiritual prig.

19 Watch spiritual hardness, if ever you have the tiniest trace of it, haul up everything else till you get back your softness to the Spirit of God.

20 Never let common sense obtrude and push the Son of God on one side. Common sense is a gift which God gave to human nature; but it is not the gift of His Son; never enthrone common sense. The Son detects the Father; common sense never yet detected the Father and never will.

21 God's providences come to you unawares and they produce flurry or faith. If they produce flurry there is no nourishment in God's Word. The tiniest touch of the wing of God's providential angel is enough to keep you from concentration on God, and the Bible is of no practical use.

22 Men do wrong things because they have no dominant interest, once a crisis comes, the vacuity is gone.

23 There was nothing secular in our Lord's life and in the saint the sacred and the secular must be all His, the one must express the other. If I have to turn consciously from the shallow to the profound, there is something radically wrong, not in the shallow, but in the profound.

24 It takes a long time to realise that God has no respect for anything I bring Him; all He wants from me is unconditional surrender.

25 There is nothing that detects spiritual rottenness so unerringly as to ask not with the lips, but with the will. "Ye shall *ask what ye will*" said Jesus.

26 The great characteristic of the supernatural grace of God in a life is put by Jesus on the line of forgiveness. Forgiveness is the supernatural manifestation of a miracle in you and me.

27 The secret of our inefficiency for God is that we do not believe what He tells us about prayer. Prayer is not rational but Redemptive. Little books of prayer are full of "buts." The New Testament says that God will answer prayer every time. The point is not—"will you believe?" but "will I, who know Jesus Christ, believe on your behalf?" (see 1 John 5:14–16).

28 A man is never the same after he has seen Jesus Christ. We are to be judged by our immortal moments.

29 In every place you are in, insist on taking the initiative for God. Every time you pray your horizon is altered, your disposition and relationship to things is altered, and you wonder why it is you don't pray more.

March

1 Grousing destroys generosity like a moth does a garment, slowly but completely.

2 If there is the tiniest grudge in your mind against any one, from that second, your spiritual penetration into the knowledge of God stops.

3 "I have chosen you." Keep that note of greatness in your creed. It is not that you have got God, but that He has got you. Why is God at work in me, bending, breaking, moulding, doing just as He chooses?—for one purpose only—that He may be able to say, "This is My man, My woman."

4 Humility is not an ideal, it is the unconscious result of the life being rightly related to God.

5 We get the idea that the best thing to do is to hurry over our work in order to get a time alone with God, and when we do get it along that line it is mildewed, not fresh and vigorous, and we feel dissatisfied instead of refreshed. Then sometimes in the midst of our work there suddenly springs up a wonderful well of inner contemplation, which is so full of recreation that we thank God for it, and we don't know how it came.

6 The only simplicity there is, is a simplicity of life which is true to Jesus, not to a theory about Him (2 Corinthians 11:3). You can't tie yourself up in anything logically consistent.

7 If you cannot express yourself on any subject, struggle 'till you can. You must struggle to get expression experimentally, then there will come a time when that expression will become the very wine of strengthening to someone else. Try to restate to yourself what you implicitly feel to be God's truth, and you give God a chance to pass it on to someone else through you.

8   Quiet trust in God is the state of mind and heart that is fittest to do the duty that lies nearest without any fluster.

9   We have judged our fellow men as sinners. If God should judge us like that we would be in hell. God judges us through the marvellous Atonement of Jesus Christ.

10 A God who did not know the last depth of sorrow and suffering would be a God "whom to be God is not fit."

11 You can never make yourself holy by external acts, but, if you are holy, your external acts will be the natural expression of holiness.

12 Don't waste time asking God to keep you from doing things—don't do them!

13 God delights to put me in a place where He can make me wealthy. Follow Me, and thou shalt have treasure in heaven.

14 It is easy to get lost in mists when we talk about the will of God, but if we don't know what it is, we are to blame.

15 The more complicated the actual conditions are, the more delightfully joyful it is to see God open up His way through.

16 When we lean to our own understanding we do away with prayer and bank all on service. Consequently by succeeding in the external we fail in the eternal. In the eternal we succeed only by prevailing prayer.

17 The world, the flesh and the devil will put imaginary grief in your way just when Jesus Christ is wanting you to enter into fellowship with His sufferings.

18 There are not three stages in spiritual life—worship, waiting and work. Some of us go in jumps like spiritual frogs, we jump from worship to waiting, and from waiting to work. God's idea is that the three should go together. They were always together in the life of our Lord.

19 God grant we may get to the place where discouragement is as impossible to us as it was to the Lord Jesus. The one dominant note of His life was the doing of His Father's will.

20 When we receive the Holy Ghost He turns us into passionate followers of Jesus Christ. Then out of our lives will flow those rivers of living water that heal and bless, and we spend and suffer and endure in patience all because of One, and One only.

21 When we try to reserve our strength it works out in weariness. Spend to the hilt all we have got and God's recreating power is greater than all the expended power.

22 "It is good that man should both hope and quietly wait for the salvation of the LORD"—quietly wait, submit to the yoke, sit silent. All these are characteristics the world ridicules. There is nothing that so quickly reveals whether we are one with Jesus as derision. If we are not one with Him, we always want to explain ourselves.

23 Beware every time you notice yourself doing a good thing, because you ruin it by the notice (Matthew 6:2).

24 Our notion of sacrifice is the wringing out of us something we don't want to give up, full of pain and agony and distress. The Bible idea of sacrifice is that I give as a love-gift the very best thing I have.

25 Unless in the first waking moment of the day you learn to fling the door wide back and let God in, you will work on a wrong level all day; but swing the door wide open and pray to your Father in secret, and every public thing will be stamped with the presence of God.

26 God comes in where my helplessness begins, that is the bedrock of entering the kingdom of heaven. "Blessed are the poor in spirit."

27 God cannot trust us with His unsearchable riches if we are not faithful in the least things. "The cares of this world" will make us put the least things as the most important.

28 Never blink facts because they don't agree with your theory.

29 "Why not rather be defrauded?" asks Paul. Who can be defrauded better than a Christian? Yet we take our standards from the world and insist on our rights.

30 "They feared as they entered the cloud." Is there anyone "save Jesus only" in your cloud? If so, it will get darker; you must get into the place where there is "no one save Jesus only."

31 "And He did not many mighty works there because of their unbelief." If we really believed that God meant what He said—what should we be like? Dare I really let God be to me all that He says He will be?

April

1 My personal life may be crowded with small, petty incidents altogether unnoticeable and mean, but if I obey Jesus Christ in the haphazard circumstances, they become pinholes through which I see the face of God and when I stand face to face with God I shall discover that through my obedience thousands were blessed.

2 To be shallow is not a sign of being wicked, nor is shallowness a sign that there are no depths; the ocean has a shore. The shallow amenities of life, eating, drinking, walking, talking are all ordained by God. These are the things in which our Lord lived. He lived in them as the Son of God, and He said that "the disciple is not above his Master."

3 Shut out every other consideration and keep yourself before God for this one thing only— "My Utmost for His Highest." I am determined to be absolutely and entirely for Him and for Him alone.

4 Whenever God's will is in the ascendant all compulsion is gone. When we choose deliberately to obey Him, then with all His almighty power He will tax the remotest star and the last grain of sand to assist us.

5 Identification with the death of Jesus Christ means identification *with* Him to the death of everything that never was in Him.

6 Intercession leaves you neither time nor inclination to pray for your own "sad sweet self." The thought of yourself is not kept out because it is not there to keep out, you are completely and entirely identified with God's interest in other lives.

7 Belief must be the *will* to believe. There must be a surrender of the will, not a surrender to a persuasive power, but a deliberate launching forth on God, and on what He says, until I am no longer confident in what I have done, I am confident only in God. The hindrance is that I will not trust God, but only my mental understanding.

8 Notion your mind with the idea that God is there. Nothing happens in any particular unless God's will is behind it, therefore you can rest in perfect confidence in Him.

9 "If God so clothe the grass of the field . . . how much more . . ." Jesus says that if we obey the life God has given us, He will look after all the other things. Has Jesus Christ told us a lie? If we are not experiencing the "much more" it is because we are not obeying the life God has given us; we are taken up with confusing considerations.

10 All I do ought to be founded on a perfect oneness with Him, not a self-willed determination to be godly. The God of Israel is He that giveth strength and power to His people.

11 There are certain tempers of mind in which we never dare indulge. If we find they have distracted us from faith in God, then until we get back to the quiet mood before God, our faith in Him is nil, and our confidence in the flesh and human ingenuity is the thing that rules.

12 Whenever the insistence is on the point that God answers prayer, we are off the track. The meaning of prayer is that we get hold of God, not of the answer.

13 One of the most amazing revelations of God comes when we learn that it is in the commonplace things that the Deity of Jesus Christ is realised.

14 Sanctification means intense concentration on God's point of view. It means every power of body, soul and spirit chained and kept for God's purpose only.

15 Remember whose you are and whom you serve. Provoke yourself by recollection and your affection for God will increase tenfold, your imagination will not be starved any longer, but will be quick and enthusiastic, and your hope will be inexpressibly bright.

16 As long as there is a human being who does not know Jesus Christ, I am his debtor until he does. The mainspring of Paul's service is not love for men but love for Jesus Christ.

17 We impoverish God's ministry to us the moment we forget He is Almighty; the impoverishment is in us, not in Him. We will come to Jesus as Comforter or as Sympathiser, but we will not come to Him as Almighty.

18 Undaunted radiance is not built on anything passing, but on the love of God that nothing can alter. The experiences of life, terrible or monotonous, are impotent to touch "the love of God, which is in Christ Jesus our Lord."

19 I claim the fulfilment of God's promises, and rightly, but that is only the human side; the Divine side is God's claim on me, which I recognise through the promises.

20 There is never any fear for the life that is "hid with Christ in God," but there is not only fear, but terrible danger, for the life unguarded by God. He that dwelleth in the secret place of the Most High"—once *there*, and although God's

providence should take you to hell itself, you are as safe and secure as Almighty God can make you.

21 We must realise the frontiers of death, that there is no more chance of our entering the life of God than a mineral has of entering the vegetable kingdom, we can only enter into the Kingdom of God if God will stoop down and lift us up. That is exactly what Jesus Christ promises to do.

22 The miracle of the grace of God is that He can make the past as though it had never been, He can "restore to you the years that the locust hath eaten, the cankerworm, and the caterpiller, and the palmerworm" (Joel 2:25).

23 As long as the devil can keep us terrified of thinking, he will always limit the work of God in our souls.

24 Never run away with the idea that it doesn't matter much what we believe or think; it does. What we believe and think, we are; not what we say we believe and think, but what we really do believe and think, we are; there is no divorce at all.

25 Don't be disturbed today by thoughts about tomorrow; leave tomorrow alone, and bank in confidence on God's organising of what you do not see.

26 God and love are synonymous. Love is not an attribute of God, it *is* God. Whatever God is, love is. If your conception of love does not agree with justice and judgement, purity and holiness, then your idea of love is wrong.

27 The springs of love are in God, that means they cannot be found anywhere else. It is absurd for us to try and find the love of God in our hearts naturally, it is not there any more than the life of Jesus Christ is there. Love and life are in God and in Jesus Christ and in the Holy Spirit whom God gives us, not because we merit Him, but according to His own particular graciousness.

28 Just as the disposition of sin entered into the human race by one man, so the Holy Spirit entered the race by another Man, and Redemption means that I can be delivered from the heredity of sin, and through Jesus Christ can receive an unsullied heredity, viz.; the Holy Spirit.

29 Obedience to Jesus Christ is essential, but never compulsory. In the early stages we have the notion that the Christian life is one of freedom, and so it is, but freedom for one thing only—freedom to obey our Master.

30 Faith is more than an attitude of mind, faith is the complete, passionate, earnest trust of our

whole nature in the Gospel of God's grace as it is presented in the Life and Death and Resurrection of our Lord Jesus Christ.

May

1 Faith is not intelligent understanding; faith is deliberate commitment to a Person where I see no way.

2 You can never measure what God will do through you if you are rightly related to Jesus Christ.

3 My worth to God in public is what I am in private. Is my master ambition to please Him and be acceptable to Him, or is it something else, no matter how noble?

4 "If we walk in the light as He is in the light." Walking in the light means walking according to His standard, which is now ours.

5 God never gives strength for tomorrow, or for the next hour, but only for the strain of the moment. . . . The saint is hilarious when he is crushed with difficulties because the thing is so ludicrously impossible to anyone but God.

6 For those who have no engineered place of holiday, God Himself becomes the mountain calm and the limitless sea spaces. By prayer and Bible reading and meditation, the drab life (drab externally) has glorious holiday hours with God in which the soul is restored even in the valley of deep darkness.

7 The stronghold of the Christian faith is the joy of God, not my joy in God. . . . God reigns and rules and rejoices, and His joy is our strength.

8 When we say "Thy will be done," do we say it with a sigh? If so, we have never realised that the character of God is holy love; nothing can ever happen outside His purposeful will.

9 Everything that Satan and sin have marred, God holds in an unimpaired state for every son of man who will come to Him by the way back which Jesus Christ has made (Romans 16:20).

10 Remember, whatever happens, God is there.

. . . You never get at God by blinking facts, but only by naming Him in the facts; whether they are devilish or not, say, "Lord, I thank Thee that Thou art here."

11 I have no right to say that I believe in forgiveness as an attribute of God if in my own heart I cherish an unforgiving temper. The forgiveness of God is the test by which I myself am judged.

12 How many of us get into a panic when we are faced by physical desolation, by death, or war, injustice, poverty, disease? All these in all their force will never turn to panic the one who believes in the absolute sovereignty of his Lord.

13 There are saints who are being rattled out of holiness by fussy work for God, whereas one five minutes of brooding on God's truth would do more good than all their work and fuss.

14 Everything the devil does, God over-reaches to serve His own purpose.

15 Naturally, a man regards his right to himself as the finest thing he has, yet it is the last bridge that prevents Jesus Christ having His way in that life.

16 Christianity is not service for Jesus Christ, not winning souls; it is nothing less than the life of Jesus being manifested more and more in my mortal flesh.

17 The very powers of darkness are paralysed by prayer. No wonder Satan tries to keep our minds fussy in active work 'till we cannot think to pray.

18 Beware of making God's truth simpler than He has made it Himself.

19 Don't shut up any avenue of your nature, let God come into every avenue, every relationship, and you will find the nightmare curse of "secular and sacred" will go.

20 If we have faith at all it must be faith in Almighty God; when He has said a thing, He will perform it; we have to remain steadfastly obedient to Him.

21 There are disasters to be faced by the one who is in real fellowship with the Lord Jesus Christ. God has never promised to keep us immune from trouble; He says "I will be with him in trouble," which is a very different thing.

22 A self indwelt by Jesus becomes like Him. "Walk in love, even as Christ also loved you." Jesus has loved me to the end of all my meanness and selfishness and sin; now, He says, show that same love to others.

23 "Why does God bring thunderclouds and disasters when we want green pastures and still waters?" Bit by bit we find, behind the clouds, the Father's feet; behind the lightening, an abiding day that has no night; behind the thunder, "a still small voice" that comforts with a comfort that is unspeakable.

24 Anywhere the man who is devoted to Jesus Christ goes, Jesus Christ is there with him.

25 Through the Redemption, God undertakes to deal with a man's past, and He does it in two ways: by forgiving him, and by making the past a wonderful culture for the future.

26 The thing that preserves a man from panic is his relationship to God; if he is only related to himself and to his own courage, there may come a moment when his courage gives out.

27 Christianity means staking ourselves on the honour of Jesus; His honour means that He will see us through time, death and eternity.

28 The great need is not to *do* things, but to *believe* things. The Redemption of Christ is not an experience, it is the great act of God which He has performed through Christ, and I have to build my faith upon it.

29 One man or woman called of God is worth a hundred who have elected to work for God.

30 Beware of interpreting Scripture in order to make it suit a pre-arranged doctrine of your own.

31 Bible facts are either revelation facts or nonsense. It depends on me which they are to me.

June

1 We must strenuously cast our ways and our burdens on Him and wait for Him in all haphazard and topsy-turvy moments.

2 The more complete our sense of need, the more satisfactory is our dependence on God.

3 Beware of paddling in the ocean of God's truth, when you should be out in it, swimming.

4 The Holy Ghost destroys my personal private life and turns it into a thoroughfare for God.

5 Be carefully careless about everything saving your relationship to God. Refuse to be swamped by the cares of this life.

6 Whenever there is the tiniest element of doubt, quit. Never say: "Why shouldn't I? There's no harm in it."

7 The pure man or woman, not the innocent, is the safeguarded man or woman. God demands that they be pure and virtuous. Innocence is the characteristic of a child, it is a blameworthy thing for a man or woman not to be reconciled to the fact of sin.

8 It is never "Do, do" with the Lord, but "Be, be" and He will "do" *through* you.

9   On the top of those very billows, which look as if they would overwhelm us, walks the Son of God.

10 The New Testament view of a Christian is that he is one in whom the Son of God has been revealed, and prayer deals with the nourishment of that life.

11 Prayer is not a question of altering things externally, but of working wonders in a man's disposition. When you pray, *things* remain the same, but *you* begin to be different.

12 In order to be able to wield the Sword of the Spirit, which is the Word of God, we must obey, and it takes a courageous heart to obey.

13 The habit of ejaculatory prayer ought to be the persistent habit of each one of us.

14 We have to form the mind of Christ until we are absorbed with Him and take no account of the evil done to us. No love on earth can do this but only the love of God.

15 Unbelief is the most active thing on earth; it is a fretful, worrying, questioning, annoying, self-centred spirit. To believe is to stop all this and let God work.

16 If God is first, you know you can never think of anything He will forget.

17 Our Lord is not the great Teacher of the world, He is the Saviour of the world and the Teacher of those who believe in Him, which is a radically different matter.

18 The suffering which springs from being "a meddler in other men's matters" (a busy-body) is humiliating to the last degree. A free translation of 1 Thessalonians 4:11 might well read, "Study to shut up and mind your own business" and among all the texts we hang on our wall let this be one.

19 God continually introduces us to people for whom we have no affinity, and unless we are worshipping God, the most natural thing to do is to treat them heartlessly, to give them a text like the jab of a spear, or leave them with a rapped-out counsel of God and go. A heartless Christian must be a terrible grief to God.

20 Let memory have its way. It is a minister of God with its rebuke and chastisement and sorrow. God will turn the "might have been" into a wonderful culture for the future.

21 "If we walk in the light" God will give us communion with people for whom we have no natural affinity.

22 "For we are unto God a sweet savour of Christ." We are enwheeled with the odour of Jesus, and wherever we go we are a wonderful refreshment to God.

23 Jesus did not say "dream about your Father in secret," but "pray to thy Father in secret." Prayer is an effort of will. After we have entered our secret place and have shut the door, the most difficult thing to do is to pray. The great battle in private prayer is the overcoming of mental woolgathering.

24 Are we detached enough from our own spiritual hysterics to wait on God? To wait is not to sit with folded hands, but to learn to do what we are told. These are phases of His ways we rarely recognise.

25 God has loved me to the end of all my sinfulness, of all my self-will, all my stiff-neckedness, all my pride, all my self-interest; now He says—"love one another, as I have loved you." I am to show to my fellow men the same love that God showed me. That is Christianity in practical working order.

26 The Bible talks plentifully about joy, but it nowhere talks about a "happy Christian." Happiness depends on what happens; joy does not. Remember, Jesus Christ had joy, and He prays "that they might have My joy fulfilled in themselves."

27 The Bible characters fell on their strong points, never on their weak ones. "Kept by the power of God"—that is the only safeguard.

28 God engineers everything; wherever He puts us, our one great aim is to pour out a wholehearted devotion to Him in that particular work. "Whatsoever thy hand findeth to do, do it with thy might."

29 Jesus said, "Go . . . and make disciples" (RV), not converts to your opinions.

30 If you want to be of use to God, get rightly related to Jesus Christ and He will make you of use unconsciously every minute you live.

July

1   I have no right to ask God for miracles when my next duty stands neglected.

2   "I will give you rest"—not a reasonable explanation, but the staying power of knowing that I am unperplexed.

3   It requires the Almighty grace of God to take the next step when there is no vision and no spectator.

4   Don't let the sense of failure corrupt your new action.

5   God's order comes in the haphazard, and never according to our scheming and planning. God takes a great delight in breaking up our programmes.

6   Zeal to serve God may be, and very often is, an insistence on God's proving that I am right.

7   God's permissive will is the means whereby His sons and daughters are to be manifested. We are not to be like jelly-fish saying—"It's the Lord's will." We have not to put up a fight before God, not to wrestle with God, but to wrestle before God with things.

8   God holds us responsible for what we won't look at. We are nowhere judged by the light we have, but by the light we have refused (John 3:19).

9   If God has made your cup sweet, drink it with grace; if He has made it bitter, drink it in communion with Him.

10   When I only do what God wants me to do, He will recuperate me all the time. Watch the things that exhaust you.

11   Wherever you make the Most High your habitation, just there you will have victory.

12   Prayer imparts the power to walk and not faint.

13   Satan has no power to dispossess God of me.

14   We must distinguish between the burden-bearing that is right and the burden-bearing that is wrong. We ought never to bear the burden of sin or doubt, but there are burdens placed on us by God which He does not intend to lift off. He wants us to roll them back on Him. "Cast what He hath given thee [mg] upon the LORD" (Psalm 55:22 RV).

15   The basis of panic is always cowardice. The clearest evidence that God's grace is at work in our hearts is that we do not get into panics.

16   To bridle the tongue does not mean to hold your tongue, that might mean "If I speak, I would say something!" It means to have the tongue under the control of a disciplined heart; that tongue need never apologise.

17   Nothing that happens can upset God or the almighty reality of Redemption.

18   The new life will manifest itself in conscious repentance and unconscious holiness, never the other way about. The bedrock of Christianity is repentance. If ever you cease to know the virtue of repentance, you are in darkness.

19   The best is always yet to be with God. Everything you have ever dreamed or longed for, will be.

20   Lack of hospitality and disbelief in holiness go together. God's Home is so sacred that He gave His only begotten Son to make it hospitable to us.

21   It is one thing to go through a crisis grandly, and another thing to go through every day glorifying God when nobody is paying any attention to you.

22   Be simply and directly and unmistakably His— today.

23   Looking for opportunities to serve God is an impertinence; every time and all the time is our opportunity of serving God.

24   Never misunderstand the shadow of God's Hand; when He leaves you alone it is assuredly to lead you into the inner meaning of Philippians 3:10.

25   When I want to debate about doing what I know to be supremely right I am not in touch with God.

26   If you once allow the victory of a wrong thing in you, it is a long way back again to get readjusted.

27   The centre of salvation is the Cross, and why it is so easy to be saved is because it cost God so much.

28   Beware of the pious fraud in you which says—"I have no misgivings about Jesus, only about myself." No one ever had misgivings about himself!

29   Measure your growth in grace by your sensitiveness to sin.

30   Don't put things down to the devil, but to your own undisciplined nervous system.

31   God never answers prayer to prove His own might.

August

1   In our own spiritual experience some terror comes down the road to meet us and our hearts are seized with a tremendous fear; then we hear our own name called, and the voice of Jesus saying, "It is I; be not afraid," and the peace of God which passeth all understanding takes possession of our hearts.

2 Jesus Christ has destroyed the dominion of death, and He can make us fit to face every problem of life, more than conqueror all along the line.

3 Jesus Christ can make the weakest man into a Divine dreadnought, fearing nothing. He can plant within him the life that Time cannot touch.

4 Never be deluded into making this statement: "I am here because I am so useful," say rather "I am here because God wants me here." The one lodestar of the saint is God Himself, not estimated usefulness.

5 Thank God for His safeguarding, for His salvation which keeps us, waking and sleeping, conscious and unconscious, in danger and out of it.

6 The love of God in Christ Jesus is such that He can take the most unfit man—unfit to survive, unfit to fight, unfit to face moral issues—and make him not only fit to survive and to fight, but fit to face the biggest moral issues and the strongest power of Satan, and come off more than conqueror.

7 The devil is a bully, but when we stand in the armour of God, he cannot harm us; if we tackle him in our own strength we are soon done for; but if we stand with the strength and courage of God, he cannot gain one inch of way at all.

8 One strong moral man will form a nucleus around which others will gather; and spiritually, if we put on the armour of God and stand true to Him, a whole army of weak-kneed Christians will be strengthened.

9 We have to love where we cannot respect and where we must not respect, and this can only be done on the basis of God's love for us. "This is My commandment, that ye love one another, as I have loved you."

10 The self-expenditure of the love of God exhibited in the life and death of our Lord becomes a bridge over the gulf of sin; human love can be imbued by Divine love, the love that never fails.

11 Whenever we begin to worship our habit of prayer or of Bible reading, God will break up that time. We say—"I cannot do this, I am praying; it is my hour with God." No, it is our hour with our habit; we pray to a habit of prayer.

12 Conscience is the faculty of the spirit that fits itself on to the highest a man knows, whether he be an agnostic or a Christian; every man has a conscience, although every man does not know God.

13 God engineers our circumstances and He brings across our paths some extraordinary people, viz., embodiments of ourselves in so many forms, and it is part of the humour of the situation that we recognise ourselves.

14 Where did Jesus place His feet? He placed them by the sick and the sorrowful, by the dead, by the bad, by the twisted and by the good. He placed His feet exactly where we have to place ours, either with or without Him, in the ordinary rough and tumble of human life as it is. "I will make the place of My feet glorious."

15 No matter what our circumstances are, we can be as sure of abiding in Him in them as in a prayer meeting.

16 There is something in human pride that can stand big troubles, but we need the supernatural grace and power of God to stand by us in the little things.

17 The need is not to *do* things, but to *believe*. "What must I *do* to be saved?" *Believe* on the Lord Jesus Christ, and thou shalt be saved."

18 Do we come to the Bible to be spoken to by God, to be made "wise unto salvation," or simply to hunt for texts on which to build addresses? There are people who vagabond through the Bible, taking out of it only sufficient for the making of sermons; they never let the word of God walk out of the Bible and talk to them.

19 It is never wise to under-estimate an enemy. We look upon the enemy of our souls as a conquered foe; so he is, but only to God, not to us.

20 There is nothing so secure as the salvation of God; it is as eternal as the mountains, and it is our trust in God that brings us the conscious realisation of this.

21 God is never away off somewhere else; He is always *there*.

22 Things go by threes in the Bible: Father, Son and Holy Ghost; God, Church, converts; Husband, wife, children. It is God's order, not man's. Whenever one of the three is missing, there is something wrong.

23 The remarkable thing about fearing God is that when you fear God you fear nothing else, whereas if you do not fear God you fear everything else. "Blessed is every one that feareth the LORD."

24 "Except your righteousness shall exceed"—not be different from but "*exceed*" that is, we have to be all they are and infinitely more! We have to be

right in our external behaviour, but we have to be as right, and "righter" in our internal behaviour. We have to be right in our words and actions but we have to be right in our thoughts and feelings.

25 It is easy for me to talk about what I could do with a thousand pounds if I had it; the test is what I do with the 2½*d*[5] I have got. It may be hard for a rich man to enter into the kingdom of heaven, but it is just as hard for a poor man to seek first the kingdom of God.

26 Work is often taken up with the absurd deification of pluck—"this thing has got to be done, and I must do it," and men damage their souls in doing it because God is not there to protect them. But when a man or a woman is called of God, the facts he or she has to face never upset the equilibrium of the life garrisoned by the presence of God.

27 Jesus Christ never says that a man is damned because he is a sinner; the condemnation is when a man sees what Jesus Christ came to do and will not let Him do it.

28 There is a purpose in every life that is in God's keeping of which we know little, but which He will fulfil if we let Him rightly relate us to Himself.

29 The whole claim of the Redemption of Jesus is that He can satisfy the last aching abyss of the human soul, not only hereafter, but here and now.

30 Thousands of people are happy without God in this world, but that kind of happiness and peace is on a wrong level. Jesus Christ came to send a sword through every peace that is not based on a personal relationship to Himself.

31 It does not matter where a man may get to in the way of tribulation or anguish, none of it can wedge in between and separate him from the love of God in Christ Jesus.

September

1 If you only know what God has done for you, you have not a big enough God; but if you have had a vision of Jesus as He is, experiences can come and go, you will endure, "as seeing Him Who is invisible."

2 "Perfect love casteth out fear," but to say "therefore will we not fear, though the earth be removed," is only possible when the love of God is having its way.

3 "Be strong *in* the Lord"—we much prefer to be strong *for* the Lord. The only way to be strong *in* the Lord is to be "weak in Him."

4 Undisciplined imagination is the greatest disturber not only of growth in grace, but of spiritual sanity.

5 Sin is not weakness, it is not a disease; it is red-handed rebellion against God, and the magnitude of that rebellion is expressed by Calvary.

6 "I suppose it's God's will"—where is the joy of the Lord about that? The conception Jesus had of the will of God was that of glad, leaping obedience to it as the most glorious thing conceivable.

7 The reason we know so little about God's wisdom is that we will only trust Him as far as we can work things out according to our own reasonable common sense.

8 How much of our security and peace is the outcome of the civilised life we live, and how much of it is built up in faith in God?

9 We impoverish God in our minds when we say there must be answers to our prayers on the material plane; the biggest answers to our prayers are in the realm of the unseen (Ephesians 6:12–13).

10 Worry is nothing in the world but personal irritation with God because I cannot see what He is after—only I don't call it that, I talk about "an overwhelming burden of care."

11 Never take your obedience as the reason God blesses you; obedience is the outcome of being rightly related to God.

12 The Christian life is stamped by "moral spontaneous originality," consequently the disciple is open to the same charge that Jesus Christ was, viz.: that of inconsistency. But Jesus Christ was always consistent to God.

13 The heredity of the Son of God is put into me at regeneration, a life neither time nor death can touch.

14 God does not do anything with us, only *through* us.

---

5. 2½*d*: two pence and a half penny, 1 percent of a British pound prior to 1971; "tuppence ha'penny": colloquial expression meaning next to nothing; nothing at all.

15 The devil would like us to believe that we are in a losing battle; nothing of the sort! We are "more than conquerors," hilariously more than victors, "through Him that loved us."

16 No power on earth or in hell can conquer the Spirit of God in a human spirit, it is an inner unconquerableness. If you have the whine in you kick it out ruthlessly. It is a positive crime to be weak in God's strength.

17 When God forgives, He never casts up at us the mean, miserable things we have done. "I have blotted out, as a thick cloud, thy transgressions, and, as a cloud, thy sins." A cloud cannot be seen when it is gone.

18 When we are standing face to face with Jesus and He says "Believest thou this?" our faith is as natural as breathing, and we say—"Yes Lord," and are staggered and amazed that we were so stupid as not to trust Him before.

19 It is a tremendous thing to know that God reigns and rules and rejoices, and that His joy is our strength. The confidence of a Christian is that God is never in the sulks ". . . the Father of lights, with Whom can be no variation, neither shadow that is cast by turning" (RV).

20 Mental wool-gathering can be stopped immediately the will is roused. Prayer is an effort of will, and the great battle in prayer is the overcoming of mental wool-gathering. We put things down to our own inability to concentrate. "My soul, wait thou only upon God," i.e., pull yourself together and be silent unto God.

21 "The LORD is my rock," my encircling guard. Where did the Psalmist learn this truth? In the school of silent waiting upon God. The Rock of Ages is the great sheltering encirclement; we are watched over by the Mother-guardianship of God.

22 When the point of entire reliance on the resurrection life of Jesus is reached, and we are brought into perfect contact with the purpose of God, we find all our questions have gone. Are we living that life now? If not why shouldn't we?

23 The secret of sacramental discipleship is to be so abandoned to the disposition of God in us that He can use us as broken bread and poured-out wine for His purpose in the world, even as He broke the life of His own Son to redeem us.

24 Buck up and face the music, get related to things. It is a great thing to see physical pluck, and greater still to see moral pluck, but the greatest to see of all is spiritual pluck, to see a man who will stand true to the integrity of Jesus Christ no matter what he is going through.

25 "Love never faileth"! (RV). What a wonderful phrase that is! but what a still more wonderful thing the reality of that love must be; greater than prophecy—that vast forth-telling of the mind and purpose of God; greater than the practical faith that can remove mountains; greater than philanthropic self-sacrifice; greater than the extraordinary gifts of emotions and ecstasies and all eloquence; and it is this love that is shed abroad in our hearts by the Holy Ghost which is given unto us.

26 A great point is reached spiritually when we stop worrying God over personal matters or over any matter. God expects of us the one thing that glorifies Him—and that is to remain absolutely confident in Him, remembering what He has said beforehand, and sure that His purpose will be fulfilled.

27 Every time you venture out in the life of faith you will find something in your common sense cares that flatly contradicts your faith. Can you trust Jesus Christ where your common sense cannot trust Him?

28 "Abide in Me," says Jesus, in spiritual matters, in money matters, in every one of the matters that make life what it is.

29 The next best thing to do is to ask, if you have not received; to seek, if you have not found; to knock if the door is not opened to you.

30 We can choke God's word with a yawn; we can hinder the time that should be spent with God by remembering we have other things to do. "I haven't time!" Of course you have time! Take time, strangle some other interests and make time to realise that the centre of power in your life is the Lord Jesus Christ and His Atonement.

October

1 Forgetting in the Divine mind is an attribute, in the human mind it is a defect, consequently God never illustrates His Divine forgetfulness by human pictures, but by pictures taken from His own creation—"As far as the east is from the west, so far hath He removed our transgressions from us" (Psalm 103:12). "I have blotted out, as a thick cloud, thy transgressions" (Isaiah 44:22).

2 We have to keep in the light as God is in the light and the grace of God will supply supernatural life all the time. Thank God there is no end to His grace if we will keep in the humble place.

The overflowing grace of God has no limits, and we have to set no limits to it, but "grow in grace, and in the knowledge of our Lord and Saviour Jesus Christ."

3   Beware of the thing of which you say—"O that doesn't matter much." The fact that it does not matter to you may mean that it matters a very great deal to God. Nothing is a light matter with a child of God. How much longer are some of us going to keep God trying to teach us one thing? He never loses patience.

4   The people who are always desperately active are a nuisance; it is through the saints who are one with Him that God is doing things all the time.

5   The essence of Christianity is that we give the Son of God a chance to live and move and have His being in us.

6   The need is never the call; God's redemption is the call, the need is the opportunity.

7   You have no right to say, because you realise a need "I must go;" if you are sanctified you cannot go unless you are sent.

8   I have to get to the implicit relationship that takes everything as it comes from God. He never guides presently, but always now. Realise that the Lord is here now, and the emancipation is immediate.

9   When you are thinking of the grudge you owe someone, let the Spirit of God bring back to your mind how you have treated God.

10 Beware of blaspheming the Creator by calling the natural sinful. The natural is not sinful, but un-moral and un-spiritual. It is the home of all the vagrant vices and virtues, and must be disciplined with the utmost severity until it learns its true position in the providence of God.

11 If a man will resign himself in implicit trust to the Lord Jesus, he will find that He leads the wayfaring soul into the green pastures and beside the still waters, so that even when he goes through the dark valley of the shadow of some staggering episode, he will fear no evil. Nothing in life or death, time or eternity, can stagger a soul from the certainty of the Way, for one moment.

12 By the "dimensions of effective Redemption" understand the Redemption of God expressing itself in the individual experience; but beware of limiting the Redemption to our individual experience of it.

13 That a Christian can smilingly do a smart trick is a staggering thing. Destruction of conscientiousness means we have lost the fierce purity of the Holy Ghost and taken on the pattern and print of the age.

14 If you are ignored because of faddy notions of your own, you are not on the right line, but if, because you stand true to your Lord and what He represents, you awaken antipathy, you are on the right line.

15 "Won't you yield to Jesus? He has done so much for you"—to talk in that way is an insult to God and a crime against human nature. It is the presentation of an overplus of human sentiment smeared over with religious jargon.

16 Don't put prayer and obedience in the place of the Cross of Christ—"Because I have obeyed, Christ will do this, or that"; He won't. The only way we are saved and sanctified is by the free grace of God.

17 Anything that obtrudes itself into my consciousness can very easily shut God out. It is not the big things that keep us from being settled in God, but the tiny things.

18 Just as Jesus Christ and His Gospel are inseparable, so the disciples were inseparable from their message. When the Holy Spirit came at Pentecost He made these men the living epistles of the teachings of Jesus, not human gramophones, recording the facts of His life; they became part and parcel of their message.

19 An appalling thing to-day is that the man of the world has his eyes open in a way many a preacher of the Gospel has not. Ibsen, for example, saw things clearly; he saw the inexorable inevitableness of God's pronouncements—no forgiveness, no deliverance, no emancipation, because he ignored Jesus Christ and His Redemption and saw facts as they are.

20 God rarely rebukes us for our impulsive plans because those plans work their own distress.

21 The bedrock permanent thing in Christianity is forgiveness not sanctification and personal holiness; the great abiding thing underneath is infinitely more rugged than that, it is all that the New Testament means by that terrific word "forgiveness."

22 If you allow anything to hide the face of Jesus Christ from you, you are either disturbed or you have a false security. "My peace I give unto you"

is a peace which comes from looking into His face and realising His undisturbedness.

23 Because a thing is impossible in a man's present moral imperfection it does not mean he is exonerated from it. God's law has nothing to do with possibility or impossibility.

24 Whenever you come in contact with the great destructive sins in other lives, be reverent with what you don't understand. There are facts in each life you know nothing about and God says: "Leave him to Me."

25 It is easier to stand true to a testimony which is mouldy with age because it has the dogmatic ring about it that people agree with, than to talk from your last moment of contact with God.

26 It is impossible to get exhausted in work for God; we get exhausted because we try to do God's work in our own way and refuse to do it in dependence on Him.

27 Beware of the sentiment that we consecrate natural gifts to God; we cannot, we can only consecrate to God the holy disposition He gives us (Romans 12:1).

28 Never try to explain God until you have obeyed Him. The only bit of God we understand is the bit we have obeyed.

29 It is the most natural thing to be like the person you live with most, therefore live most with Jesus Christ; be absorbingly taken up with Him.

30 If I am a Christian, to whom is my appeal? To none but to those God sends you to. You can't get men to come; nobody could get you to come till you came. "The wind bloweth where it listeth: . . . so is every one that is born of the Spirit."

31 To trust in the Lord is to be foolish enough to know that if we fulfil God's commands, He will look after everything.

November

1 If there is to be another revival, it will be through the readjustment of those of us on the inside who call ourselves Christians.

2 The Cross did not "happen" to Jesus. He came on purpose for it. The whole of the purpose of the incarnation is the Cross; the manifestation of it in the crucifixion is the historic revelation of the true nature of God (Revelation 13:8).

3 For one man who can introduce another to Jesus Christ by the way he lives and by the atmosphere of his life, there are a thousand who can only talk jargon about Him.

4 Nothing has any power to alter a man save the incoming of the life of Jesus, and that is the only sign that he is born again.

5 "Labour." It is the one thing we will not do. We will take open-air meetings, we will preach—but labour at prayer! There is nothing thrilling about a labouring man's work, but it is the labouring man who makes the conceptions of the genius possible; and it is the labouring saint who makes the conceptions of his Master possible.

6 The difference between a man with the Spirit of God and a man without, is that the one does the will of God by deliberate, delighted choice; the other does the will of God without knowing what he is doing, kicking and rebelling.

7 God will never begin to teach me His will in other matters until I do what I know. Theoretic knowledge becomes our condemnation—"If ye know these things blessed are ye if ye do them" (RV).

8 A man can never be the same again, I don't care who he is, after having heard Jesus Christ preached. He may say he pays no attention to it; he may appear to have forgotten all about it, but he is never quite the same, and at any moment truths may spring up into his consciousness that will destroy all his peace and happiness.

9 Am I going to live a sequestered life on the mount and never come down into the demon-possessed valley, never prove that what I saw on the mount is sufficient to enable me to face what I find in the valley?

10 It is one of the most flattering things to go and rescue the degraded, one of the social passions of mankind, but it is not the most Christian. It is quite another thing to proclaim to men who are among the best, that *they* have to give up their right to themselves to Jesus Christ.

11 Have you never met the person whose religious life is so exact that you are terrified to come near him? Never have an exercise of religion which blots God clean out.

12 To understand the tiniest bit of truth about God is to love it with all our heart and soul and mind; all that lies dark and obscure just now, is one day going to be as clear, as radiantly and joyously clear, as the bit we have seen.

13 Experiences of what God has done for me are only stepping-stones; the one great note is—I

trust in the Lord Jesus, God's providence can do with me what it likes, make the heavens like brass, earth like hell, my body loathsome (as Job's was), but the soul that is trusting in Jesus gets where Job got, "Though He slay me, yet will I trust in Him."

14 If we do only what we are inclined to do, some of us would do nothing for ever and ever! There are unemployables in the spiritual domain, spiritually decrepit people, who refuse to do anything unless they are supernaturally inspired. The proof that we are rightly related to God is that we do our best whether we feel inspired or not.

15 A great many Christian workers worship their work. The one concern of the workers should be concentration on God, and this will mean that all other margins of life are free with the freedom of a child—a worshipping child, not a wayward child.

16 God will put you through many mills that are not meant for you, mills you would not be put through but that He wants to make you good bread for His little ones to eat. You can see now the meaning of that hard place you have been in.

17 We say, "Seeing is believing," but it isn't true. Belief is necessary before we can interpret what we see; we will explain things away if we don't believe them possible. ". . . because thou hast seen Me, hast thou believed?" (John 20:29 RV mg).

18 A good way to measure our spiritual life is to ask ourselves—What is it that produces the greatest perturbation in me? Is it the sins of men against men, or is it the sins of spiritual pride against God?

19 Our attitude to the Bible is a stupid one, we come to the Bible for proof of God's existence: the Bible has no meaning for us unless we know that God *does* exist. The Bible states and affirms facts for the benefit of those who believe in God, those who don't believe in God can tear it to bits if they like.

20 Always remain alert to the fact that where one man has gone back is exactly where anyone may go back (1 Corinthians 10:13). You have gone through the big crisis, now be alert over the least things. . . . Do not forecast where the temptation will come; it is the least likely thing that is the peril.

21 By surrendering ourselves to quiet communion with God, by resting for a while from all our thinking and acting and serving, by leaving all things for once in our Heavenly father's hands, secret wounds are healed, gathering unbelief is dispelled, and displaced armour refixed.

22 Jesus Christ can put into the man, whose energy has been sapped by sin and wrong until he is all but in hell, a life so strong and full that Satan has to flee whenever he meets him. Jesus Christ can make any life more than conqueror as they draw on His Resurrection life.

23 God does not give us overcoming life: He gives life to the man who overcomes. In every case of tribulation, from gnats to the cruelty of the sword, we take the step as though there were no God to assist us, and we find He is there.

24 The afflictions after sanctification are not meant to purify us, but to make us broken bread in the Hands of our Lord to nourish others. Many Christian workers are like Ephraim, "a cake not turned"; they are faddists and cranks, and when they are given out for distribution they produce indigestion instead of giving nourishment.

25 If you sow vows, resolutions, aspirations, emotions, you will reap nothing but exhaustion (". . . and ye shall sow your seed in vain, for your enemies shall eat it," Leviticus 26:16) but sow the Word of God, and, as sure as God is God, it will bring forth fruit.

26 The greatest note of triumph that ever sounded in the ears of a startled universe was that sounded on the Cross of Christ—"It is finished." That is the last word in the Redemption of man.

27 The springs of love are in God, not in us. It is absurd to look for the love of God in our hearts naturally, it is only there when it has been shed abroad in our hearts by the Holy Spirit.

28 The first thing to do in examining the power that dominates me is to take hold of the unwelcome fact that I am responsible for being thus dominated because I have yielded. If I am a slave to myself, I am to blame for it because at a point, away back, I yielded myself to myself. Likewise, if I obey God, I do so because I have yielded myself to Him.

29 "What I tell you in darkness"—watch where God puts you into darkness, and when you are there, keep your mouth shut. When you are in the dark, listen, and God will give you a very precious message for someone else when you get into the light.

30 "Sufficient unto the day is the evil thereof." How much evil has begun to threaten you today?

What kind of mean little imps have been looking in and saying; "Now what are you going to do next month—this summer?" "Be anxious for nothing," Jesus says. Look again and think. Keep your mind on the "Much more" of your Heavenly Father.

December

1 Our Lord took words that were despised and transfigured their meaning; He did things that were commonplace and sordid and ordinary and transfigured them. Our Lord was the unconscious light in the midst of the most ordinary circumstances conceivable.

2 In the New Testament, "world" means the system of things which has been built on God's earth, the system of religion or of society or of civilisation that never takes Jesus Christ into account.

3 "Ye are the light of the world." We have the idea that we are going to shine in heaven, but we are to shine down here, "In the midst of a crooked and perverse nation" (Philippians 2:15). We are to shine as lights in the world in the squalid places, and it cannot be done by putting on a brazen smile, the light must be there all the time.

4 It is an easy business to preach, an appallingly easy thing to tell other people what to do; it is another thing to have God's message turned into a boomerang—"You have been teaching these people that they should be full of peace and joy, but what about yourself? Are you full of peace and joy?"

5 Do we "follow the Lamb whithersoever He goeth"? He will take us through the strange dark things—we must follow Him "whithersoever He goeth." "For the Lamb which is in the midst of the throne shall feed them, and shall lead them unto living fountains of waters: and God shall wipe away all tears from their eyes" (Revelation 7:17).

6 When we have a certain belief, we kill God in our lives, because we do not believe Him, we believe our beliefs about Him and do what Job's friends did—bring God and human life to the standard of our beliefs and not to the standard of God.

7 Jesus Christ says, "Except ye . . . become as little children . . ." A little child is certain of its parents, but uncertain about everything else, therefore it lives a perfectly delightful healthy life.

8 When we know the love of Christ, which passeth knowledge, it means we are free from anxiety, free from carefulness, so that, during the twenty-four hours of the day, we do what we ought to do all the time, with the strength of life bubbling up with real spontaneous joy.

9 Our Lord was never impatient. He simply planted seed thoughts in the disciples' minds and surrounded them with the atmosphere of His own life. We get impatient and take men by the scruff of the neck and say: "You must believe this and that." You cannot make a man see moral truth by persuading his intellect. "When He, the Spirit of truth, is come, He shall guide you into all the truth."

10 Nothing has any power to alter a man save the incoming of the life of Jesus and that is the only sign that he is born again.

11 The man who has seen Jesus can never be daunted; the man who has only a personal testimony as to what Jesus has done for him may be daunted, but nothing can turn the man who has seen Him; he endures "as seeing Him Who is invisible."

12 Can God keep me from stumbling this second? Yes. Can He keep me from sin this second? Yes. Well, that is the whole of life. You cannot live more than a second at a time. If God can keep you blameless this second, He can do it the next. No wonder Jesus Christ said "Let not your heart be troubled"! We do get troubled when we do not remember the amazing power of God.

13 When a so-called rationalist points out sin and iniquity and disease and death, and he says "How does God answer that?" you have always a fathomless answer—the Cross of Christ.

14 If you only take your own ideas, you will never know the truth. The whole truth is the only truth, and the whole truth is Jesus Christ—"I am . . . the Truth." Any bit of truth is an error if taken alone.

15 The majority of present day preachers understand only the blessings that come to us from the Cross, they are apt to be devoted to certain doctrines which flow from the Cross. Paul preached one thing only: the crucified Christ, "Who of God is made unto us wisdom, and righteousness, and sanctification, and redemption."

16 Who of us can see, behind chance and in chance, God? Who of us can see the finger of God in the weather? When we are in living touch with God we begin to discern that nothing happens by chance.

17 If you put your faith in your experience anything that happens—toothache, indigestion, an east

wind, incongenial work—is likely to upset the experience, but nothing that happens can ever upset God or the almighty reality of the Redemption; once based on that, you are as eternally sure as God Himself.

18 In the Cross we may see the dimensions of Divine love. The Cross is not the cross of a man, but an exhibition of the heart of God. At the back of the wall of the world stands God with His arms outstretched, and every man driven there is driven into the arms of God. The Cross of Jesus is the supreme evidence of the love of God (Romans 8:35–39).

19 "... He only is my rock and my salvation" (Psalm 62:6). A rock conveys the idea of an encircling guard, as that of a mother watching her child who is learning to walk; should the child fall, he falls into the encircling love and watchfulness of the mother's care. "The LORD is my rock," my encircling guard. Where did the Psalmist learn this truth? In the school of silent waiting upon God.

20 "Consider the lilies of the field, how they grow" (Matthew 6:28). A lily is not always in the sunshine; for the greater part of the year it is hidden in the earth. "How they grow"—in the dark, only for a short time are they radiantly beautiful and sweet. . . We can never be lilies in the garden unless we have spent time as bulbs in the dark, totally ignored. That is how to grow.

21 When it is a question of God's Almighty Spirit, never say "I can't." Never let the limitation of natural ability come in. If we have received the Holy Spirit, God expects the work of the Holy Spirit to be manifested in us.

22 Never forget that our capacity in spiritual matters is measured by the promises of God. Is God able to fulfil His promises? Our answer depends on whether we have received the Holy Spirit.

23 "Add to your faith virtue . . ." (2 Peter 1:5). "Add" means there is something we have to do. We are in danger of forgetting that we cannot do what God does, and that God will not do what we can do. We cannot save ourselves nor sanctify ourselves, God does that; and God will not give us good habits, He will not give us character, He will not make us walk aright. We have to do all that ourselves, we have to work out the salvation God has worked in.

24 Have you ever noticed what Jesus said would choke the word He puts in? The devil? No, the cares of this world. It is the little worries always. I will not trust where I cannot see, that is where infidelity begins. The only cure for infidelity is obedience to the Spirit.

25 Jesus Christ is God incarnate coming into human flesh from the outside, His Life is the Highest and the Holiest entering in at the lowliest door. Have I allowed my personal life to become a "Bethlehem" for the Son of God?

26 If I put my trust in human beings first, I will end in despairing of everyone; I will become bitter, because I have insisted on man being what no man ever can be—absolutely right. Never trust anything but the grace of God in yourself or in anyone else.

27 There are many things that are perfectly legitimate, but if you are going to concentrate on God you cannot do them. Your right hand is one of the best things you have, but Jesus says if it hinders you in following His precepts, cut it off. This line of discipline is the sternest one that ever struck mankind.

28 Put all "supposing" on one side and dwell in the shadow of the Almighty. Deliberately tell God that you will not fret about that thing. All our fret and worry is caused by calculating without God.

29 A river touches places of which its source knows nothing, and Jesus says if we have received of His fullness, however small the visible measure of our lives, out of us will flow the rivers that will bless to the uttermost parts of the earth. We have nothing to do with the out-flow—This is the work of God that ye *believe.* . . ." God rarely allows a soul to see how great a blessing he is.

30 In tribulation, misunderstanding, slander, in the midst of all these things, if our life is hid with Christ in God, He will keep us at ease. We rob ourselves of the marvellous revelation of this abiding companionship of God. God is our refuge"—nothing can come through that shelter.

31 The ideal is not that we do work for God, but that we are so loyal to Him that He can do His work through us—"I reckon on you for extreme service, with no complaining on your part and no explanation on Mine." God wants to use us as He used His own Son.

The Shadow of an Agony

Oswald Chambers

Through the Shadow of an Agony Cometh Redemption
Copyright Oswald Chambers Publications Association, First Edition 1918;
Third Edition 1933; Fourth Edition 1942
Scripture versions quoted: KJV; RV

INTRODUCTION

Source

The Shadow of an Agony is from talks on redemption given by Oswald Chambers to soldiers at the YMCA camp, Zeitoun, Egypt,[1] August 14 through 27, 1917.

Publication History

- As a book: *The Shadow of an Agony* was first published in 1918; the date of the second edition is unknown, but there was a third edition in 1933 and a fourth edition in 1942.

The title comes from the words of Ugo Bassi, central character in Harriet Eleanor Hamilton King's[2] *The Disciples* (1873), an epic poem much loved and quoted by Chambers.

> And Ugo answered, still as in a dream:
> "Yea, through the Shadow of an Agony
> Cometh Redemption—if we may but pass
> In the same footprints where our master went,
> With Him beside us;—and for me, I fear
> No evil, since He has not failed me yet,
> Nor will for ever!"
>
> *The Disciples*

During the sweltering Egyptian summer of 1918, Mrs. Chambers divided her time between caring for five-year-old Kathleen,[3] serving soldiers in the canteen at Zeitoun, and writing letters and typing sermons of her late husband in the underground dugout designed by Oswald as a refuge from the heat. On August 31, she wrote to her sister in England:

> *I feel as if I will never come to an end of my wealth of notes. The Sermon on the Mount [1915] is in hand being reprinted, and I have got the calendar of sayings [Seed Thoughts Calendar] all ready, and shall send Gertrude [Oswald's sister] a copy of it next week so that she can have them printed in England also. I feel as if that is going to mean a lot to many, I know you will like the idea. Then the next book will be Shadow of an Agony that is in the process of retyping just now. I find how much benefit I have got still from my old legal days, I mean getting into the habit of perfecting a thing by typing and retyping it, and I am glad to have had all the experience of those other days.*

Nine months after her husband's death, the pattern of Biddy Chambers' life's work was beginning to emerge.

---

1. Zeitoun (zay TOON), Egypt: six miles northeast of Cairo; site of a YMCA camp, the Egypt General Mission compound, and, from 1916 to 1919, the Imperial School of Instruction, training base for British, Australian, and New Zealand troops during World War I.

2. H. E. Hamilton King (1840–1920): English poet and author.

3. Kathleen Chambers (1913–1997): only child of Oswald and Biddy Chambers.

CONTENTS

PREFACE (TO THE FIRST EDITION)

Two classes of readers will take up this little book of Bible studies on vital questions relating to Christian character and conduct and the mystery of suffering. The one class will find in it, as did even Peter in Paul's epistles, things hard to be understood, and sentences that lull the stolid mind to sleep; the other class will read, mark, learn, and inwardly digest its contents because they challenge mind and conscience, and will do their "utmost for the Highest." The author is a lover of men's souls: he sees into the heart of things, rises above the commonplace, and goes below the surface. "The war,"[4] he says, "has upset every man's nest; we are face to face with a terrific upheaval in life; there is no civilised security anywhere on the globe. We have seen that there is no such thing as a Christian nation, we have seen the unutterable futility of the organised Christian Church, and many a man who has had no tension in his life has been suddenly obliged to face things he never intended to look at." These very things Oswald Chambers shows us in the light of the Cross. He points out that because Jesus Christ is so like unto His brethren we can face this turmoil and stress, and stand with Him in the shadow of a great agony, undiscouraged and unafraid. There is really only one mystery in the universe; it is the mystery of Redemption. The way we approach this holy ground is nearly always through suffering. Those that carry the cross after Jesus best understand why and how He first carried it, and how the nails pierced not His hands only but His heart.

To the careless and superficial this book will only appeal when they gird up the loins of their minds and are sober. Once they put on the girdle which Paul calls "sincerity" and Peter "humility," its message will grip, convince, and appeal, as it did when first delivered to the men of all ranks in the YMCA camps and huts of Egypt.

> *Great truths are greatly won,*
> *Not found by chance,*
> *Nor wafted on the breath of summer dream,*
> *But buffeting with adverse winds and tides.*

Samuel M. Zwemer[5]
Cairo, 1918

---

4. the war: World War I (1914–1918).

5. Rev. Samuel M. Zwemer (1867–1952): American missionary who served in Cairo under the United Presbyterian Mission.

COMMENT BY P. T. FORSYTH

FROM THE *BTC JOURNAL*,[6] SEPTEMBER 1933, PAGE 47:

In the Shadow of an Agony (Third Edition, ready in October)

Dr. P. T. Forsyth[7] wrote of this book:

The writer has no pi-talk, nor is he but a rouser. Not only is his manner direct and searching, but he has a real educated grasp of the moral nature of the spiritual soul and its psychology. He has a happy combination of the familiar style and the competent stuff. His is the kind of address of which we have too little—the union of moral incision and spiritual power.

I am glad to commend such teaching, and I hope the stringency of the times will develop more preachers who have this gift—not of talking about the spiritual life but of penetrating the conscience of it with some moral psychology in the name of a positive gospel. It is the kind of evangelism we deeply need, the sound modernising of Redemption. We are too familiar with ways of bringing peace to a man's mind which are not true to the fundament of things.

FOREWORD TO FOURTH EDITION

It is some years ago since a copy of "The Shadow of an Agony" came into my hands. How it did so I do not now remember. I know, however, that I started to read it with no great expectation of profit. But I soon found I had made a real discovery. The little book was a truly great book; its author a truly great man. Since then I have read and pondered every published utterance by the Rev. Oswald Chambers, and am grateful for the intellectual stimulus and spiritual quickening that have come to me from his writings. His "passing hence" was a great loss to the Christian Church.

For the times in which we live I know of no work more fitting for re-publication than "The Shadow of an Agony." It deals with root or rock principles. It comes, not from the surface, but "out of the depths." It is the work of a great brain and a great heart. It does not shirk the problems of life, but looks them straight in the face. Over against the tragedy of sin and suffering it brings us to the tragedy of the Cross of Christ.

In the hope that the book will prove to be as great a discovery and as great an inspiration to others as it has been to me, I write this Foreword.

Walter H. Armstrong
First Moderator of the Free Church
Federal Council of England and Wales
Ex-President of Methodist Conference
Norwich, *September*, 1942

---

6. *Bible Training Course Monthly Journal:* published from 1932 to 1952 by Mrs. Chambers, with help from David Lambert.

7. Peter Taylor Forsyth (1848–1921): British Congregationalist minister and theologian. Chambers read many of Forsyth's books and valued his insights.

THE AGONY OF REDEMPTION

Oh, to have watched Thee through the vineyards wander,
Pluck the ripe ears and into evening roam,
Followed and known that in the twilight yonder
Legions of angels shone about Thy home.

Ah, with what bitter triumph had I seen them,
Drops of Redemption bleeding from Thy brow,
Thieves and a culprit crucified between them,
All men forsaking Him, and that was Thou.

1. Approaching the Holy Ground (Exodus 3:5;
    Joshua 5:15; Psalm 119:67, 71, 75; Jeremiah
    31:15–19; Hebrews 12:5–11)

    The truth of Christianity cannot be proved to the
    man in the street till he comes off the street owning its
    power.

2. Apprehending the Holy Grace (Romans 5:7–9;
    Hebrews 5:7–9)

    Christianity is concerned with God's holiness before
    all else, which issues to men as love, acts upon sin as
    grace, and exercises grace through judgement.

3. Atonement by the Holy God (Matthew 1:21;
    Acts 20:28; 2 Corinthians 5:14–21)

    By centrality is meant finality for human history and
    destiny. . . . It is meant, first, that in the atonement
    we have primarily an act of God and an act of God's
    holiness; second, that it alone makes any repentance or
    expiation of ours satisfactory to God; third, that as
    regards man it is—a revolutionary act and not a mere
    stage in evolution.

                                        Dr. Forsyth

If we estimate things from the standpoint of a man's life, Redemption will seem "much ado about nothing." But when we come to a big Judgement Day like a European war, when individual lives apparently amount to nothing, and human lives are being swept away by the thousand, the "bottom board" is knocked out of our ignorance, and we begin to see that the basis of things is not rational, but wild and tragic. It is through these glimpses that we understand why the New Testament was written, and why there needed to be a Redemption made by Jesus Christ, and how it is that the basis of life is redemptive. If Jesus Christ were only a martyr, His cross would be of no significance; but if the cross of Jesus Christ is the expression of the secret heart of God, the lever by which God lifts back the human race to what it was designed to be, then there is a new attitude to things.

1. Approaching the Holy Ground

And he said, Draw not nigh hither; put off thy shoes
from off thy feet, for the place whereon thou standest is
holy ground. (Exodus 3:5)

There is a moral preparation necessary to face the truth of God. These words of God to Moses mean literally, "Stand further off and you will see better." Sometimes our moods are mean and ignoble; at other times they are lofty and good. To a large extent a man's moods are not in his own power.

We cannot kindle when we will
    The fire that in the heart resides;
The spirit bloweth and is still,
    In mystery our soul abides.
But tasks in hours of insight will'd
Can be through hours of gloom fulfilled.

"Strip off your commonplace moods," God says; "if you are going to see into this thing, you must put on the right mood for discerning it." The agony of a man's affliction is often necessary to put him into the right mood to face the fundamental things of life. The Psalmist says, "Before I was afflicted I went astray: but now have I kept Thy word." The Bible is full of the fact that there has to be an approach to the holy ground. If I am not willing to be lifted up, it is no use talking about the higher heights. In putting John the Baptist to death, Herod committed moral suicide. He ordered the voice of God to be silent in his life, and when Jesus Christ stood before him, "he questioned with Him in many words," for "he hoped to have seen some miracle done by Him"; but we read that Jesus "answered him nothing." It is quite possible for any man amongst us to get to a place where there is no such thing as truth or purity, and no man gets there without himself being to blame. Every man ought to be intellectually sceptical, but that is different from moral doubt which springs from a moral twist. No man can do wrong in his heart and see right afterwards. If I am going to approach the holy ground, I must get into the right frame of mind—the excellency of a broken heart.

The war has upset every man's nest, and we are face to face with a terrific upheaval in life; there is no civilised security anywhere on the globe. We have seen that there is no such thing as a Christian nation, and we have seen the unutterable futility of the organised Christian Church: and many a man who has had no tension in his life has been suddenly dumped "into the soup" and been obliged to face things that he never intended to look at. Consequently, there are any number of amateur sceptics, and men who are seeing the difference between "believing their beliefs," and "believing God," men, who, through the turmoil and the stress, are seeing that rationalism is not the basis of things. According to the Bible, the basis of things is tragedy, and the way out is the way made by God in Redemption. The New Testament does not say that the human race is evolving, but that the human race is a magnificent ruin of what it was designed to be. God Himself has taken the responsibility of sin, and the proof that He did so is the Cross; God holds *me* responsible if I refuse to let Him deliver me from sin. No man can redeem the world; God has done it; Redemption is complete. That is a revelation, not something we get at by thinking; and unless we grant that Redemption is the basis of human life, we will come up against problems for which we can find no way out. The thing that will need to be re-stated after the war, theologically, is Redemption; at present "Redemption" is not in the vocabulary of the average earnest man.

Through the turmoil and agony that nations and men are in, men who think are beginning to see that rationalism is not the basis of things. The basis of things is not reasonable; reason is our guide among things as they are, but it never can account for things as they are. No man ever chose his own father and mother, or his own heredity; such things go clean through the "bottom board" of rationalism; they are illogical; there is a deep, real problem at the basis of them. The basis of things, according to the Bible, is tragic, and the way out is the way made by God in Redemption, not by intellect or by reason. The revelation of New Testament Christianity deals with the basis of human life. Every one of us is shaken into the turmoil of things, caught by the last eddy, and we have to get some kind of foothold. In the meantime, don't be distressed at what men say, or at the tags they wear. "Talk to my meaning, not to my words." Don't be a debating logician and make a man mean what you mean; try and get at his mind behind the thing; and when you hear a man talk in agony, remember he is hurt. Be patient and reverent with what you don't understand.

2. Apprehending the Holy Grace (Romans 5:7–9; Hebrews 5:7–9)

"Grace"—the overflowing favour of God. The way of approach to the holy ground of God is nearly always through suffering; we are not always in the natural mood for it, but when we have been ploughed into by suffering or sorrow, we are able to approach the moral frontiers where God works. To apprehend the holy grace of God, I must remember that according to the New Testament, Jesus Christ is God manifest in the flesh. This fundamental revelation of the Christian

faith seems to be overlooked among Christians. There is only one God for the Christian, and He is Jesus Christ. The Bible only mentions two men—Adam and Jesus Christ, and it is the last Adam Who rehabilitates the human race.

During the war the stab has come to every one of us, and we are in an attitude to understand what the New Testament is talking about. Before the war it did not matter to the majority of us whether Jesus Christ lived or died, because our thinking was only within the circumference of our own lives. Now, through the war, we are seeing the need for Redemption. The grace of God which comes through Jesus Christ is revealed in that God laid down His life for His enemies. The statement that a man who gives his life for his king and country thereby redeems his soul, is a misapprehension of New Testament revelation. Redemption is not a man's bit. "Greater love hath no man than this, that a man lay down his life for his friends," has nothing to do with Christianity; an atheist will do this, or a blackguard, or a Christian; there is nothing divine about it, it is the great stuff that human nature is made of. The love of God is manifested in that He laid down His life for His enemies, something no man can do. Paul says the fundamental revelation of the New Testament is that God redeemed the whole human race when they were spitting in His face, as it were.

If you have had no tension in your life, never been screwed up by problems, your morality well within your own grasp, and someone tells you that God so loved you that He gave His Son to die for you, nothing but good manners will keep you from being amused. The majority of people who have never been touched by affliction see Jesus Christ's death as a thing beside the mark. When a man gets to his wits' end and things go hard with him, his thick hide is pierced and he is stabbed wide awake, then for the first time he begins to see something else—"At last I see; I thought that He was stricken, smitten of God and afflicted; but now I see He was wounded for my transgressions."

The great fundamental revelation regarding the human race is that God has redeemed us; and Redemption enters into our lives when we are upset enough to see we need it. There is too much common sense used, "pills to cure an earthquake" given; and "the gospel of temperament" preached. It is an insult to-day to tell some men and women to cheer up. One of the most shallow petty things that can be said is that "every cloud has a silver lining." There are some clouds that are black all through. At the wall of the world stands God with His arms outstretched; and when a man or woman is driven there, the consolations of Jesus Christ are given. Through the agonies in human life we do not make Redemption, but we see why it was necessary for God to make it. It is not necessary for every man to go through these agonies, but it takes a time of agony to get the shallow scepticism knocked out of us. It is a good thing to be reverent with what we do not understand. A moral agony gives a man "a second wind," and he runs better after it, and is a good deal more likely to win.

3. Atonement by the Holy God *(Matthew 1:21; Acts 20:28; 2 Corinthians 5:14–21)*

The Church is the new Spirit-baptised Humanity based on the Redemption of Jesus Christ. Intellectual rationalism is based on a volcano, and at any second it may be blown to pieces; but there is nothing below Redemption; it is as eternal as God's throne. Redemption is a moral thing, Jesus Christ does not merely save from hell; "He shall save his people from their sins," i.e., make totally new moral men. Jesus Christ did not come to give us pretty ideas of God, or sympathy with ourselves; He came from a holy God to enable men, by the sheer power of His Redemption, to become holy.

In the Christian faith the basis of human life is Redemption, and on that basis God can perform His miracles in any man.

So long as we live in the "tenth story" we remain indifferent to the fact of forgiveness; but when we "strike bottom" morally, we begin to realise the New Testament meaning of forgiveness. Immediately a man turns to God, Redemption is such that his forgiveness is complete. Forgiveness means not merely that I am saved from sin and made right for heaven (no man would accept forgiveness on such a level); forgiveness means that I am forgiven into a recreated relationship, into identification with God in Christ.

The background of God's forgiveness is holiness. If God were not holy there would be nothing in His forgiveness. There is no such thing as God overlooking sin; therefore if God does forgive there must be a reason that justifies His doing so. If I am forgiven without being altered by the forgiveness, forgiveness is a damage to me and a sign of the unmitigated weakness of God. When a man is convicted of sin he knows God dare not forgive him; if He did it would

mean that man has a bigger sense of justice than God. God, in forgiving a man, gives him the heredity of His own Son, i.e., He turns him into the standard of the Forgiver. Forgiveness is a revelation—hope for the hopeless; that is the message of the Gospel.

A man may say, "I don't deny that God will forgive me, but what about the folks I have put wrong? Can God give me a clearing-house for my conscience?" (Hebrews 9:14). It is because these things are neglected in the presentation of Redemption that men are kept away from Jesus Christ. Men are kept away by honesty more than by dishonesty.

Jesus Christ's revelation is the forgiveness of God, and the tremendous miracle of Redemption is that God turns me, the unholy one, into the standard of Himself, the Forgiver, by the miracle of putting into me a new disposition. The question up to me is—"Do I want Him to do it?" God's forgiveness is a bigger miracle than we are apt to think. He will not only restore to us the years the cankerworm hath eaten; not only deliver us from hell; not only make a clearing house for conscience; but He will give a totally new heredity; and many a man who has shut himself down in despair need not despair any more. God can forgive a man anything but despair that He can forgive him.

These are the fundamentals of human life. We have not been taught to *think* as Christians, and when an agony reaches us we are knocked to pieces, and only hang on by the skin of our teeth. We may have faith enough to keep us going, but we do not know where to put our feet or to tell anyone else where to put theirs. We have been taught to think as pagans, and in a crisis we act as pagans. It is a great thing to have a spiritual experience, but another thing to think on the basis of it. The great fundamental point of view in the Bible is neither rationalism nor common sense. Either it is a revelation, or it is unmitigated blether. The basis of life is not mathematical or rational; if it were we could calculate our ends, and make absolutely sure of certain things on clear, rational, logical lines. We have to take into account the fact that there is an incalculable element in every child and in every man. There is always "one fact more," and we get at it by agony.

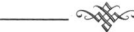

THE CONSCIENCE OF GOD
Hebrews 6:13

Thou with strong prayer and very much entreating
*   Willest be asked, and Thou shalt answer then,*
Show the hid heart beneath creation beating,
*   Smile with kind eyes and be a man with men.*

Were it not thus, O King of my salvation,
*   Many would curse to Thee and I for one;*
Fling thee Thy bliss and snatch at Thy damnation,
*   Scorn and abhor the shining of the sun.*

1. The Creator Aspect (Genesis 1:27; Psalm
   132:6; John 10:34–35; Luke 3:38)
   GOD (Intellectual): Because God is Creator
      and we are His creatures, nothing else
      matters

2. The Cosmic Aspect (Genesis 1:1; Job 38:4–7;
   Isaiah 42:5; Acts 17:24)
   GOD (Emotional): The emotions produced by
      natural actualities are no end-all.

3. The Culture Aspect (Psalm l:21; Isaiah
   44:14–17; Colossians 2:18–23)
   GOD (Educational): The refined findings of
      intellect and emotions; all else to be
      disdained.

4. The Christian Aspect (John 3:16;
   2 Corinthians 5:18–21)
   GOD (Evangelical): Complete forgiveness and
      final Redemption.

It is not necessary for a man to understand things before he can be a Christian. The understanding of the mystery of life is a secondary thing; the main thing is to be alive. Science is an understanding of life and the universe. If a man said he had no use for science, we should reckon him to be a fool. It is the same with regard to the Christian religion. The important thing is to be a born-again man. Theology is the science of religion, an intellectual attempt to systematise the consciousness of God. Intellect systematises things to a man's mind, but we do not reach reality through intellect. Theology comes second, not first, and ought always to be open to dispute. Because science and theology have been put in the wrong place, it is foolish to say we will have nothing to do with them. Redemption is not a thing we are consciously experiencing, it is a revelation given by the Christian religion of the basis of human life, and it takes some thinking about. We don't think on Christian lines at all.

"For when God made promise to Abraham, because he could swear by no greater, he swear by himself" (Hebrews 6:13). Conscience is not the voice of God; conscience is that faculty in me which appeals to the highest I know; it may or may not be religious. God has a conscience towards man and towards Himself, i.e., He has a standard to keep, and the problem He is up against is not to wipe the muddle off the slate, but to resolve it back again, and Redemption is His way of doing it. To try and explain Redemption in the span of a man's life is nonsense. Men may not feel the need of Redemption, but that does not mean it is not there. The Christian revelation is the revelation of why Redemption was necessary. God's standard is to make of man the counterpart of Himself; man has to be brought into perfect communion with God. At present there is an enormous hiatus between God and man, and God's conscience in Redemption puts man back again into the purpose for which He designed him, instead of wiping him out and saying it is all a muddle. The highest standard God has is Himself, and it is up to God to make a man as good as He is Himself; and it is up to me to let Him do it. If God is not just, the only honourable thing for a man to be is a blatant atheist.

Agony means severe suffering in which something dies—either the base thing, or the good. No man is the same after an agony; he is either better or worse, and the agony of a man's experience is nearly always the first thing that opens his mind to understand the need of Redemption worked out by Jesus Christ.

1. The Creator Aspect *(Genesis 1:27)*

God created man, the Federal Head of the human race, in His own image; we are procreated through generations of the human race; Adam was created in the image of God. The male and female together, as they were created, were in the image of God, in perfect union with God, "Adam and Eve" are both needed before the image of God can be perfectly presented.

The Creator aspect appeals to a man's intellect as long as he has no memory of the Fall and the ruin that followed when the connecting link with Deity was snapped. If you develop yourself in your brain, and say "That is 'myself,'" you have to shut yourself off from life as it actually is, and on that line you can manipulate anything, and construct the most extraordinary things. An intellectual God does not amount to "a row of old beans." The Creator aspect of God ignores everything else; it forgets that the Bible gives revelations of God on other lines. The Bible says that God created the Federal Head of the race in His own image; that means that God accepts the responsibility for the human race being put on the wrong track, and the Cross is the proof that He does so. I seal myself with damnation when I see the Light, Jesus Christ, and prefer my own standpoint. The Creator aspect of God does not amount to much. If the only aspect of God is that of Creator, to talk about a moral or spiritual life is nonsense; but the Creator aspect is not the complete Christian aspect; it is only one ingredient in it.

2. The Cosmic Aspect *(Genesis 1:1)*

Cosmic means the order of the material universe produced by actualities. The Creator aspect is a fact; the Cosmic aspect is also a fact; but there are other aspects. If I build my thinking on the Creator or the Cosmic aspect only, I have to miss some factors out. If I take an intellectual view of life only, I shall come to the conclusion that Thomas Carlyle[8] came to; he judged men by brains, and came to the conclusion that half the human race were fools. If the intellectual valuation of man be the right one, when he is insane he should be killed. The brain is the thing that makes a man express himself; but a man is more than his consciousness. The intellect says "I will have nothing to do with what I cannot explain intellectually." A man's intellect is his instrument, his guide among things as they are; but it never gave him things as they are. There is more to be taken into consideration before you get the right view of God and man.

3. The Culture Aspect *(Isaiah 44:14–17)*

This aspect says that God is the result of an educated mind, and that we get at God by abnormal means— by education, by mysticism, and aestheticism; if so, then atheism is saner. Isaiah says that a man takes a tree and cuts it in two, uses part to cook his food, and the other part he carves into an idol to worship. "None of us do that!" we say; but we *do*. There are other things which are wooden besides trees, viz. our heads! We use one half of our heads to earn our living, and the other half to worship God.

These three aspects of God amount to nothing more than a man's produces by his own nature, and have not nearly so much power over him as he has over himself. If I want to get at reality my conscience must witness as well as my emotions. I may talk like an archangel and live like a pig; I may write magnif-

icent stuff and have fine conceptions, and people may be thrilled, but that does not prove that I have touched reality. A man's intellect may give him noble ideas, and power to express them through his soul in language, but it gives him no power to carry them out in action. When a man has touched reality, he is changed into its image. Intellect has never changed a man as yet; it may have made him look different, but it will not have altered him. If intellect is the way to get to God, what about the men who have no intellect! There would be whole streaks of man's life and experience to blot out. Or if I can get at God by a fine sense of beauty only what about the men who have no sense of beauty? Some men have a magnificent heredity, while others are practically damned into existence. Rationalism is not the basis; my reason and my intellect are instruments, but there is something deeper about every human life than can be fathomed by intellect. The God constructed out of the Culture aspect does not amount to anything. Thinking is an abstraction whereby man locates the things he sees. The laws of nature have no existence outside the intellect of the scientist, and to talk about Jesus Christ transcending the laws of nature is nonsense. A law is a method of explaining things in an ordered intellect. You can dispute a man's reasoning, but you cannot dispute facts; they must be accepted. If you deal only with these three aspects, you remain out of touch with reality, because each aspect does only for the view it presents. If the aspect of God is to be coloured by refined intellect, some of us will never get there. If everybody were refined it would be all right, but everybody is not, and the Culture aspect treats the rest of the human race with disdain.

4. The Christian Aspect *(2 Corinthians 5:18–21)*

In the Christian aspect we have these three other aspects worked in with another view, viz. the Conscience of God, and the New Testament insistence on the Cross of Jesus Christ. The attitude of the Bible to the human race is not a common-sense one. The Christian aspect deals with man as a specimen of a human race which is a magnificent ruin of what it was designed to be. Supposing the view of the Bible to be right, to whom is it "up to" to right the wrong? The Creator. Has He done it? He has, and He has done it absolutely single-handed. The tremendous revelation of Christianity is not the Fatherhood of God, but the Babyhood of God—God became the weakest thing in His own creation, and in flesh and blood He levered it back to where it was intended to be. No one

---

8. Thomas Carlyle (1795–1881): Scottish-born literary figure in nineteenth-century England, a writer, biographer, essayist, historian, and critic.

helped Him; it was done absolutely by God manifest in human flesh. God has undertaken not only to repair the damage, but in Jesus Christ the human race is put in a better condition than when it was originally designed. It is necessary to understand these things if you are to be able to battle for your faith. "The deity of the Christian religion is evidenced by the variety of fools who tackle it." To-day we are erecting a man of straw, and then taking it for granted that the Author of salvation was a fool. Jesus Christ's view is that the Christian religion has been tried and abandoned, but never been tried and failed. It is not a question of whether we agree with the Bible revelation or not, but of whether we take it for what it reveals before we tackle it.

God's conscience means He has to forgive completely and finally redeem the human race. The point about Christian forgiveness is not that God puts snow over a dungheap, but that He turns a man into the standard of the Forgiver. The great thing up to God is that in forgiving me He has to give me the heredity of His Son. God Himself has answered the problem of sin and there is no man on earth but can be presented "perfect in Christ Jesus."

Redemption does not amount to anything to a man until he meets an agony; until that time he may have been indifferent; but knock the bottom board out of his wits, bring him to the limit of his moral life, produce the supreme suffering worthy of the name of agony, and he will begin to realise that there is more in Redemption than he had ever dreamed, and it is at that phase that he is prepared to hear Jesus Christ say, "Come unto Me." Our Lord said, "I did not come to call the man who is all right; I came to call the man who is at his wits' end, the man who has reached the moral frontier."

Oh could I tell, ye surely would believe it!
Oh could I only say what I have seen!
How should I tell or how can ye receive it,
How, till He bringeth you where I have been?

A man will know sooner or later; it will depend upon the pride of his intellect or the crass obstinacy of his nature how soon he gets there; but when he does he will have reached the frontier where God works. Never keep your moral nature sceptical. Never doubt that justice and truth and love and honour are at the back of everything, and that God must be all these or nothing. The Christian aspect is that God will make a man as holy as He is Himself, and this He has undertaken to do. If a man is terrified by the vastness of creation, he has never been touched by the moral problem. When he has, he knows that God created the universe for him. God created man to be master of the life in

the earth and sea and sky, and the reason he is not is because he took the law into his own hands, and became master of himself, but of nothing else. Man is a remnant of a former design. In the Conscience of God that design is restored. The "Creator" and the "Cosmic" and the "Culture" aspects are all *etceteras* to the main thing, we enter into touch with God on the frail, human experience, moral line. The Christian aspect of God represents the one Who has been in the very thick of it; and whenever a man through Nature or through conviction of sin touches the moral frontiers, then the work of Jesus Christ begins.

"If any man is in Christ, there is a new creation" (2 Corinthians 5:17 RV mg). I see the universe as a mirror of my ruling disposition. I see in sunsets and sunrises and in the whole cosmic force an exaggerated expression of the ruling disposition in myself; I do not see God, I see myself. When I am born from above (RV mg), I see the reflection of God. The disposition ruling within me determines the way I interpret outside things. A man convicted of sin and a man in love may live in the same external world, but in totally different creations. Both may be in the desert, but the disposition of the one makes him interpret the desert as a desolating piece of God's territory; while to the other the desert literally blossoms as the rose. The disposition of the one is mad; there is no light in the sun, no sweetness in anything, his ruling disposition is one of misery; while to the other:

Heaven above is brighter blue,
Earth around is sweeter green;
Something lives in every hue
Christless eyes have never seen;
Birds with gladder songs o'erflow,
Flowers with deeper beauties shine
Since I know, as now I know,
I am His and He is mine.

When you are identified with Jesus Christ you become a new creation in the same surroundings. You see life differently because of the moral transfiguration of the regeneration of the Son of God. The Conscience of God means that it is up to Him to make this possible, and any man can go through the transfiguration the second he realises his need. There are moments when you see the way you should go; don't dally with yourself then. The moments come and go, but always with a further space between. If you play the fool with yourself when they come, they get fainter; but if you heed them, they are intimations that you are stepping over into another frontier, and beginning to experience a relationship to God based on the Cross of our Lord Jesus Christ.

THE CONSCIENCE OF CHRIST

Christt! I am Christ's! and let the name suffice you,
 Ay, for me too He greatly hath sufficed;
Lo! with no winning words I would entice you—
 Paul has no honour and no friend but Christ.

Yea thro' life, death, thro' sorrow and thro' sinning
 He shall suffice me, for He hath sufficed:
Christ is the end, for Christ was the beginning,
 Christ the beginning, for the end is Christ.

1. The Character of Christ (Matthew 11:19; Acts 2:22–24)

   The New Testament never thinks that the place which Jesus has in its faith is anything else than the place which belongs to Him and truly was His.

                                                Dr. Denney[9]

2. The Consciousness of Christ (Matthew 5:21–22, 27–28, 38–39, 43–44; 11:27; John 8:46; 14:6–9)

   Jesus revealed Himself as what He was in life and works; He had to be discovered as what He was by men who associated with Him in obedience, trust, and love.

                                                Dr. Denney

3. The Cross of Christ (Matthew 16:24; 20:22; 26:12–13, 26–28; Romans 5:11)

   The Christ that we trust all to is One in whom God died for His own witness and His own work in us. God was in Christ reconciling. The prime doer in Christ's Cross was God; He was God doing the very best for man, and not man doing his very best for God.

                                                Dr. Forsyth

It is in times of intense suffering that we begin to see the reason for Redemption, and realise that Redemption is worth what it cost the original Designer. According to the New Testament, Redemption cost God everything, and that is the reason why salvation is so easy for us. The same thing happens in an agony as happens when you suddenly open your door and window during a hurricane: the wind disarranges everything. It plays havoc, and knocks things into confusion, but also brings a totally new circulation of air; and very often the man who has been knocked around by an agony begins to form a new mind, and is better able to appreciate the New Testament view of the Cross of Jesus Christ.

The basis of God's action is that it is up to Him to turn out men like Himself, and the Conscience of Christ also means just that. To say that reason is the basis of human life is absurd, but to say that the basis of human life is tragedy and that the main purpose of it as far as Jesus Christ is concerned, is holiness, is much nearer the point of view given in the Bible.

1. The Character of Christ *(Matthew 11:19; Acts 2:22–24)*

These verses portray the character of Jesus Christ as recorded in the New Testament. The New Testament is not written to prove that Jesus Christ is God Incarnate; the New Testament does not prove anything; it simply confirms the faith of those who believe beforehand. Christian evidences don't amount to anything; you can't convince a man against his will.

   The New Testament never thinks that the place which Jesus had in its faith is anything else than the place which belongs to Him and truly was His.

                                                Dr. Denney

The New Testament does not say of Jesus Christ, "This man was God Incarnate, and if you don't believe it you will be damned." The New Testament was written for the confirmation of those who believed He was God Incarnate. The man who does not believe is apt at any minute to discover by the swinging open of the door of agony, that the thing he ignored may be the way into a life he has never seen. It is quite likely that a trick of disease or war or bereavement may suddenly open the possibility of there being other things in a man's story than those he saw when he was a common-sense, robust man.

"The Son of Man came eating and drinking." One of the most staggering things in the New Testament is

---

9. James Denney (1856–1917): Scottish theologian and author whose writings were greatly appreciated by Oswald Chambers.

just this commonplace aspect. The curious difference between Jesus Christ's idea of holiness and that of other religions lies here. The one says holiness is not compatible with ordinary food and married life, but Jesus Christ represents a character lived straight down in the ordinary amalgam of human life, and His claim is that the character He manifested is possible for any man, if he will come in by the door provided for him.

There are religions in which holiness involves unusual conditions and special diet. Some forms of mysticism seem to be incompatible with married life. But the type of holiness which Jesus teaches can be achieved with an ordinary diet and a wife and five children.

The Jesus of History

T. R. Glover[10]

We must estimate the character of Jesus Christ by the New Testament, and not by our standards. Look at the ordinary commonplace things of His life—from twelve to thirty years of age He lived with brothers and sisters who did not believe in Him (John 7:5). If you had lived in His day and someone had pointed Him out and said to you, "That carpenter is God manifest in the flesh," you would have thought him mad. The New Testament is either unmitigated blether or it conveys a revelation. The majority of us make the character of God out of our own heads; therefore He does not amount to anything at all. That God is called an omnipresent, omniscient, omnipotent Being who rules the universe does not matter one iota to me. But the New Testament reveals the essential nature of God to be not omnipotence, omnipresence and omniscience, but holiness. God became the weakest thing in His own creation, viz., a Baby; He entered human history on that line. He was so ordinary that the folks of His day paid no attention to Him, and the religious people said He was making a farce of religion.

Jesus Christ is, beyond all reasonable question, the greatest Man who ever lived. The greatness of a man is to be estimated by two things; first, by the extent of his influence upon mankind, and secondly—for no one is altogether great who is not also good—by the purity and dignity of his character. Tried by both these tests, Jesus is supreme among men. He is at once the most influential and the best of Mankind.

The Fact of Christ
P. Carnegie Simpson

To refuse to try a line Jesus Christ points out because I do not like it, shuts my mouth as an honest doubter. I must try it and see if it works. As long as I am unwilling to act by any way of getting at the truth, I can say nothing.

The basis of Christ's character appeals to us all. One of the dangers of denominational teaching is that we are told that before we can be Christians we must believe that Jesus Christ is the Son of God, and that the Bible is the Word of God from Genesis to Revelation. Creeds are the effect of our belief, not the cause of it. I do not have to believe all that before I can be a Christian; but after I have become a Christian I begin to try and expound to myself Who Jesus Christ is, and to do that I must first of all take into consideration the New Testament explanation. "Blessed art thou, Simon Bar Jona: for flesh and blood hath not revealed it unto thee, but My Father which is in heaven." The *character* of Jesus Christ was lived on an ordinary plane, and exhibits one side only. To ten men who talk about the character of Jesus there is only one who will talk about His Cross. "I like the story of Jesus Christ's life, I like the things He said. The Sermon on the Mount is beautiful, and I like to read of the things Jesus did; but immediately you begin to talk about the Cross, about forgiveness of sins, about being born from above (RV mg), it is out of it." The New Testament reveals that Jesus Christ is God manifest in the flesh, not a Being with two personalities; He is Son of God (the exact expression of Almighty God) and Son of Man (the presentation of God's normal man). As Son of God He reveals what God is like (John 14:9); as Son of Man He mirrors what the human race will be like on the basis of Redemption—a perfect oneness between God and man (Ephesians 4:13). But when we come to the Cross of Jesus Christ, that is outside our domain. If Jesus Christ was only a martyr, the New Testament teaching is stupid.

2. The Consciousness of Christ *Matthew 5:21–22, 27–28, 38–39, 43–44; 11:27; John 8:46; 14:6–9)*

These verses express what Jesus Christ thought about Himself. He deliberately said "Before *I* came, Moses said: now I have come *I* say: up till now it has been so-and-so; but I interpret in a new way." If He was not God manifest in the flesh, to speak like that would have been an intoxication of conceit. Let Plato or Socrates, for instance, say, "I am the Way, the Truth, and the Life," and we see what it involves. Jesus Christ is either mad or what He claims to be, viz.: the only revelation of God Almighty that there is. Our Lord did not say, "No man cometh unto *God*, but by Me," but, "No man cometh unto *the Father*, but

---

10. Terrot Reavely Glover (1869–1943): university lecturer in ancient history, St. John's College, Cambridge; wrote *The Jesus of History*, published in 1917.

by Me." Fatherhood and Creatorship are two different things. Fatherhood refers to the moral likeness of a man's disposition.

In the Conscience of God and in the Conscience of Christ we see God accepting the responsibility for sin; He never asks man to accept it. No man is damned because he is a sinner. Jesus said, "This is the judgement" (i.e., the critical moment) "that the Light is come into the world, and men loved the darkness rather than the Light; because [KJV] their works were evil" (John 3:19 RV). If I see better than I act on, I am sealing my soul with damnation. The consciousness of Jesus Christ in the New Testament is that He and the Father are one; He did not say that the human race and God were one. The doctrine of the Trinity is not a revelation, it is an attempt to put into scientific language the fact of God. There is only one God to the Christian, and His name is Jesus Christ; any other idea of God is a matter of temperament or of refinement. The Christian is an avowed agnostic; all he knows about God has been accepted through the revelation of Jesus Christ, and to him there is only one name for the God he worships, viz. Jesus Christ. Jesus Christ manifests, on the scale we see and know, the life that makes Him say—"Almighty God is nothing that contradicts what I am; if you have seen Me you have seen the Father." Have we seen Him? We may look at a person for a long time without "seeing" him. How long did it take the men who knew Jesus Christ to perceive Who He was? (Luke 24:16, 31).

Both these themes, the Character and the Consciousness of Christ, are in the nature of speculation—interesting, but they do not amount to anything when a man is in agony. When we were plunged into the agony of the war modern Christianity was dealing with speculations, or else proclaiming a pseudo-evangelism which made salvation a moral "lavatory." Jesus Christ did not come primarily to teach; He came to make it possible for us to receive His heredity, to have put into us a new disposition whereby we can live totally new lives. Any man who uses his reason in the things he sees, and who has taken a cross section of himself, and had the conceit knocked out of him, knows he is not a strayed angel nor a noble hero; he is neither angel nor devil; he is a mixture of dust and Deity. The Sermon on the Mount is impossible to man, and yet it is what our Lord taught. Jesus Christ did not come to teach man to be what he cannot be, but to reveal that He can put into him a totally new heredity; and all He requires a man to say is—"I need it"—no shibboleth, but a recognition of his need. Jesus Christ cannot begin to do anything for a man until he knows his need; but immediately he is at his wits' end through sin or limitation or agony and cannot go any further, Jesus Christ says to him, Blessed are you; if you ask God

for the Holy Spirit, He will give Him to you. God does not give us the Holy Spirit until we come to the place of seeing that we cannot do without Him (Luke 11:13).

3. The Cross of Christ *(Matthew 16:24; 20:22; 26:12–13, 26–28; Romans 5:11)*

There are two views of Jesus Christ's death. One is that He was a martyr—that is not the New Testament view; the other is that the Cross of Jesus Christ was the Cross of God, not of a man at all—not a man doing his level best for God, but "God doing the very best for man." The Cross of Jesus Christ is the point where God and sinful man merge with a crash, and the way to life is opened; but the crash is on the heart of God. The Cross is the presentation of God having done His "bit," that which man could never do. The New Testament reveals that the basis of human life is not Rationalism, but Redemption. Just as Rationalism does not depend on individual people but on a conception of the fundament of human life, so the New Testament represents that the basis of human life is Redemption, and Christian faith and Christian thinking are to be based on that. There is much teaching abroad to-day that is veneered over as Christianity. Men preach, and undermine the very ground they stand on while they preach. The foundation of the Christian faith is that the basis of human life is Redemptive, and on that basis God performs His miracles. Jesus Christ told His disciples that He came here on purpose to die. The death of Jesus Christ is God's verdict on self-realisation and every form of sin there is. If self-realisation is to be the goal and end of the human race, then damned be God; if Jesus Christ was to be God, then damned be self-realisation—the two cannot exist together. "If you would be My disciple, give up your right to yourself."

Why should we play at being Christians? We are told that to be an experimental Christian means we understand the plan of salvation; the devil understands that, but he is not a saint. A saint is one who, on the basis of the Redemption of Jesus Christ, has had the centre of his life radically altered, and has deliberately given up his right to himself. This is the point where the moral issue comes, the frontier whereby we get in contact with God. Intellect will not bring us there, but moral obedience only, and an agony opens the door to it. To those who have had no agony Jesus says, "I have nothing for you; stand on your own feet, square your own shoulders. I have come for the man who knows he has a bigger handful than he can cope with, who knows there are forces he cannot touch; I will do everything for him if he will let Me. Only let a man grant he needs it, and I will do it for him."

This is the basis of what Jesus Christ did in Redemption, and we enter into the life of Christ by

His death, not by His birth. When Jesus Christ taught His disciples these things, and when He talked about His Cross, they misunderstood Him, just as natural minded Christians do to-day; consequently we are up against the problem already mentioned. The teaching of Jesus Christ is very fine and delightful, but it is all up in the clouds; how are we to come up to it with our heredity, with what we are with our past, with our present and with the outlook we have? How are we going to begin to do it, if all He came to do was to teach? All attempts at imitation will end in despair, in fanaticism, and in all kinds of religious nonsense. But when once we see that the New Testament emphasises Jesus Christ's death, not His life, that it is by virtue of His death we enter into His life, then we find that His teaching is for the life He puts in.

"We also joy in God through our Lord Jesus Christ, by whom we have now received the atonement" (Romans 5:11). As long as we are intellectualists and forget that we are men, our intellect tells us that God and man ought to be one, that there should be no gap between. Exactly so! But they are *not* one, and there *is* a gap, and a tragedy. Our intellect tells us that the universe ought to be the "garment of God." It ought to be, but it is not. We may hold any number of deistic and monistic theories, and theories about being one with God, but every man knows he is not God. Jesus Christ says we can only receive the at-one-ment with God on His basis, viz.: "Except a man be born again, he cannot see the kingdom of God" (John 3:3). We can enter into His Kingdom whenever the time comes for us to see it. We cannot see a thing until we do see it, but we must not be blind and say we don't see it when we do, and if we are enthusiastic saints we must not be too much disturbed about the fellow who does not see. At any second he may turn the corner of an agony and say, "I thought those other fellows were mad, but now I am prepared to see as they do."

We have been taken up with creeds and doctrines, and when a man is hit we do not know what to give him; we have no Jesus Christ, we have only theology. For one man who can introduce another to Jesus Christ by the way he lives and by the atmosphere of his life, there are a thousand who can only talk jargon about Him. Whenever you come across a man or woman who in your time of distress introduces you to Jesus Christ, you know you have struck the best friend you ever had, one who has opened up the way of life to you.

The basis of human life according to Jesus Christ is His Cross, and it is by His Cross that His conscience is manifested. He has undertaken to take the vilest piece of stuff that humanity and the devil have put together, and to transform this into a son of God. If I receive forgiveness and continue to be bad, I prove that God is immoral in forgiving me, and make a travesty of Redemption. When I accept Jesus Christ's way He transfigures me from within. "Jesus did it all," refers to Redemption; the thing is done; and if I step into it I will find the moral magic of the Redemption at work in me.

THE CHRISTIAN CONSCIENCE

Great were his fate who on the earth should linger,
   Sleep for an age and stir himself again,
Watching Thy terrible and fiery finger
Shrivel the falsehood from the souls of men.

Oh that Thy steps among the stars would quicken!
   Oh that Thine ears would hear when we are dumb!
May the hearts from which the hope shall sicken,
Many shall faint before Thy kingdom come.

N.B.—THE INTUITION IN MY NATURE WHEREBY I KNOW THAT I AM KNOWN.

THE INTUITION IN MY NATURE WHICH I REGARD AS THE HIGHEST.

THE "INNOCENCE OF SIGHT" AS AN ILLUSTRATION OF CONSCIENCE.

1. Conscience before the Racial Degeneration (Genesis 2:7–17)
   (a) Implicit Certainty of Self (v. 7)
   (b) Implicit Certainty of the World (vv. 8–15)
   (c) Implicit Certainty of God (vv. 16–17)

   The race was required to take part in its own development by a series of moral choices till transfiguration.

2. Conscience after the Racial Degeneration (Romans 1:18–27)
   (a) Standard of the Ordinary Person (Romans 2:14–16)
   (b) Standard of the Ordinary Pagan (Matthew 25:31–46)
   (c) Standard of the Ordinary Piety (John 16:2; Acts 26:9)

"Virtuous in order to secure one's self if God should be awkward."

3. Conscience in the Racial Regeneration (John 3:16–21)
   (a) Character of the Saint (John 17:22; Romans 9:1)
   (b) Conduct of the Saint (2 Corinthians 1:12)
   (c) Communion of the Saints (1 John 1:7)

Personal relation with God is to be maintained in actual experience by the spontaneous originality of the indwelling Spirit of God, interpreting the words of Christ as we obey.

"Intuition" means perception at sight; it is implicit, something I cannot express, and conscience is of the implicit order of things. "Conscience is the innate law in human nature whereby man knows he is known." Conscience is that faculty in me which fixes on what I regard as the highest; consequently conscience records differently in different people. I may be a Christian and a conscientious man, or I may be an atheist and a conscientious man. So it never can be true to call conscience the voice of God; if it were, it would be the most contradictory voice man ever heard.

Conscience is best thought of as the eye of the soul recording what it looks at; it will always record exactly what it is turned towards. We soon lose what Ruskin called "the innocence of sight." An artist does not use his logical faculties in recording what he sees; he records from the innocence of sight. A beginner sketches not what he sees, but what he knows he sees, while the artist gives the presentation of what he sees. Conscience is the eye of the soul, and how my conscience records will depend on the light that is thrown on God. Saul of Tarsus was conscientious in putting to death the followers of Jesus Christ (Acts 26:9); when he became a Christian, his conscience was not altered, but it recorded differently (Acts 24:16). When a man gets rightly adjusted to God his conscience staggers him, and his reason condemns him from all standpoints. The phrase "Conscience can be educated" is a truth that is half an error. Strictly speaking, conscience cannot be educated; what is altered and educated is a man's reasoning on what his conscience records. A man reasons not only on what his senses bring him, but on what his conscience brings him; and immediately he is faced by the white light of Jesus Christ, his conscience recording exactly, his reason is startled and amazed.

1. Conscience before the Racial Degeneration *(Genesis 2:7–17)*

In this aspect we have to consider the three facts of a man's personal life, viz. consciousness of self, consciousness of the world, and consciousness of God;

they are all brought out in the way God constituted the human race. Adam had no affinity with the brutes, and this instantly distinguished him from the brute creation around him, "but for Adam there was not found an help meet for him." There is no evidence that a brute is conscious of itself, but man is ostensibly conscious of himself.

We are conscious of ourselves and conscious of outside things only by means of a nervous system. When a man is altered inwardly by the grace of God, his nervous system is altered, and he instantly begins to see things differently. The external world around him begins to take on a new guise because he has a new disposition. "If any man is in Christ Jesus," his nervous system will prove that he is "a new creature," and the material world will appear to him as a new creation because he is now seeing it as the mirror of God's thought.

The God-consciousness in Adam was quite different from our natural consciousness; it was just like the God-consciousness shown by our Lord. In us the consciousness of God is obliterated, because that consciousness became most conspicuously blurred by the Fall; consequently, men miscall all kinds of things "God." A man is apt to call any system of things he considers highest "God."

There are three facts of our personal life that are restored by Jesus Christ to their pristine vigour. We get into real definite communion with God through Jesus Christ; we get to right relationship with our fellow-men and with the world outside; and we get into a right relationship with ourselves. We become Christ-centred instead of self-centred.

If Adam had not sinned and thereby introduced the heredity of sin into the human race, there is every reason to suppose that the human race would have been transfigured into the real presence of God; but Adam disobeyed, and sin entered in. Sin is a relationship between two of God's creations. God did not create sin; but He took the responsibility for it; and that He did so is proved in the Cross of Jesus Christ. The essential nature of sin is my right to myself. Jesus Christ, the second Adam, the second Federal Head of the race, entered into this order of things as Adam did, straight from the hand of God; and He took part in His own development until it reached its climax, and He was transfigured. Earth lost its hold on Him, and He was back in the glory which He had with the Father before the world was. But He did not go to heaven from the Mount of Transfiguration because He had Redemption to fulfil. He emptied Himself (RV) of His glory a second time, and came down into the world again to identify Himself with the sin of man (2 Corinthians 5:21).

Adam was intended by God to take part in his own development by a series of moral choices, to sacrifice his natural life to God by moral obedience and thus transform it into a spiritual thing. Instead, he took dominion over himself, and instantly lost control over the earth and air and sea, and lost also this peculiar consciousness of himself and the world and God. Poetic and intellectual types of mind recognise these factors in Adam's creation, but they ignore the fact that we have degenerated. A poet or an artist has vision and insight, but he does not see the actual. It is delightful to talk about man being in perfect accord with God and with the world about him; but we are not in that accord, and the guidance God gave to Adam is of no use to us.

We can change the world without when we change the recording instrument within. Commit sin, and I defy you to see anything beautiful without; fall in love, and you will see beauty in everything. We only know the world by a nervous system, and we infer that everyone else knows it in the same way as we do. The man who accepts things on the evidence of his senses is as wise as I am when I accept the revelation of the Bible. To accept the evidence of your senses is wise, but to say it is infallible is nonsense. It is never wise to be cocksure.

2. Conscience after the Racial Degeneration (Romans 1:18–27)

"Everyone is to blame but me; I am a strayed babe in the wood!" This attitude indicates the twist in man's nature that has come in through the Fall. A moral squint always leads to a wrong intellectual view.

(a) Standard of the Ordinary Person (Romans 2:14–16)

Every man has, implicit within himself, a standard of conduct which he accepts for life. There is an intuitive certainty in every man that there are some things that he ought not to do, and the talk about innocence is nonsense. The Bible says that a man is born with this knowledge, and that he will be judged according to his obedience to, or rejection of, the ordinance of God which is written in his spirit. The natural idea of virtue is to make a man quits with the Day of Judgement.

(b) Standard of the Ordinary Pagan (Matthew 25:31–46)

The standard for the nations is conscience, i.e., conscience attaching itself to the system of things which man regards as highest, no matter how degraded he may be. Conscience is the standard for men and women to be judged by until they have been brought into contact with the Lord Jesus Christ. The standard for Christians is not the 25th Chapter of Matthew; the standard for Christians is our Lord Jesus Christ. It is not sufficient for a Christian to walk in the light of his conscience; he must walk in a sterner light, in the light of the Lord.

(c) Standard of the Ordinary Piety (John 16:2; Acts 26:9)

Paul says, "I verily thought within myself"—i.e., according to his conscience—"I ought to do many things contrary to the name of Jesus of Nazareth." This is the length an ordinary pious conscience may take a man. Saul was the acme of conscientiousness. It is extraordinary to what an extent men may corrupt themselves if they have no real light on what they regard as the highest. There needs to be a standard for the guidance of conscience. It does not matter whether a person is religious or not, conscience attaches itself to the highest he or she knows, and reasoning according to that standard is the guide for life. Conscience will always record God whenever it has been faced by God.

3. Conscience in the Racial Regeneration (John 3:16–21)

I am not judged by the light I have, but by the light I have refused to accept. There is no man but can have the knowledge, perfectly clearly obtainable, of the standard of Jesus Christ. Whether I am a Christian or not, or whether I am conscientious or not, is not the question; it is whether I have refused the light of the finest moral character who ever lived, Jesus Christ. *This* is the condemnation, that the Light, Jesus Christ, has come into the world, and I prefer darkness, i.e., my own point of view. The characteristic of a man who begins to walk in the light is that he drags himself into the light all the time. He does not make excuses for things done in the dark, he brings everything to the light, and says, "This is to be condemned; this does not belong to Jesus Christ," and so keeps in the light. The popular view of a saint is an anaemic young man with one foot in the grave, or an old woman, or an innocent, sweet young lady—anyone who has not enough original sin to be bad. The New Testament view of a saint is a more rugged type. You and I are a mixture of dust and Deity, and God takes that sordid human stuff and turns it into a saint by Regeneration. A saint does not mean a man who has not enough sin to be bad, but a man who has received from Jesus Christ a new heredity that turns him into another man.

(a) Character of the Saint (John 17:22; Romans 9:1)

The Christian disposition keeps its balance with the law of God, which is holiness. A man's character is what he habitually is. What "glory" did Jesus Christ have? A glory that everyone could see and admit that He was a marvellous Being? No, He was so ordinary that they said He was a glutton and a winebibber; so ordinary that fishermen walked with Him, and the common people asked Him to dinner. There was no glory externally; He was not manifestly God walking in the flesh. Jesus Christ effaced the God-head in

Himself so effectually that men without the Spirit of
God despised Him. The glory our Lord had here on
earth was the glory of a holy disposition; that is, He
worked out His life in accordance with the highest
He knew—His Father; and He said "I can give men
that faculty in regeneration; I can put My Holy Spirit
in them, and He will keep them in contact with God
as I have revealed Him." Conscience and character in
the saint, then, means the disposition of Jesus Christ
persistently manifested.

(b) Conduct of the Saint (2 Corinthians 1:12)

Paul always riddled himself like that; he did not talk
to people who did not know him. He said, "The evidence of my life proves that what Jesus Christ said He
could do, He has done" (see Galatians 2:20).

"Our rejoicing is this, the testimony of our conscience, that in simplicity and godly sincerity . . . we
have had our conversation in the world." The point
there is a very important one, viz., that the knowledge
of evil that came through the Fall gives a man a broad
mind, but paralyses his action. The restoration of a
man by our Lord gives him simplicity. Paul says, "I
fear, lest by any means . . . your minds should be corrupted from the simplicity that is in Christ." There
are men and women of the world who know evil,
whose minds are poisoned by all kinds of things; they
are marvellously generous in regard to their notions
of other people, but they can do nothing, their broad-
sightedness paralyses their action. There are some
things a man is a criminal for knowing; he has no
right to know them. The knowledge of evil, instead
of instigating to action, paralyses; whereas the essence
of the Gospel of Jesus Christ working in conscience
and conduct is that it shows itself at once in action.
God can turn cunning, crafty people into simple,
guileless people. The marvel of His grace is such that
He can take out the strands of evil and twistedness
from a person's mind and imagination, and make him
single-minded and simple towards God so that his
life becomes radiantly beautiful by the miracle of His
grace.

(c) Communion of the Saints (1 John 1:7)

"But if we walk in the light, as He is in the light . . ."—
that is, don't have anything folded up, don't juggle
things, don't pretend you have not done anything
shady. John says, if you have committed sin, confess it;
walk in the light, and you will have fellowship with
everyone else who is there. Natural affinity does not
count here at all. Watch how God has altered your
affinities since you were filled with the Spirit; you have
fellowship with people you have no natural affinity for
at all; you have fellowship with everybody who is in the
light. Light is the description of clear, beautiful, moral
character from God's standpoint, and if we walk in the
light, "the blood of Jesus Christ . . . cleanses us from all
sin"; God Almighty can find nothing to censure.

We usually think of conscience as an individual
thing; the individual aspect has to be recognised, but
it is not the only aspect. The individual exercise of
conscience is never the Christian standard. The
Christian standard is the personal relationship of the
conscience in direct accord with God on the basis of
the revelation given by Jesus Christ. I do not live the
Christian life by adherence to principles; I live the
Christian life as a child lives its life. You never can calculate what a child will do, neither can you calculate
what the Spirit of God will do in you. When you are
born from above (RV mg), the Spirit of God in you
works in spontaneous moral originality. Our Lord
said, "the Holy Ghost . . . shall teach you all things,
and bring all things to your remembrance, whatsoever
I have said unto you." I do not rake around and discover some word; the Holy Spirit brings back with
the greatest of ease the word I need in a particular circumstance. Am I going to obey that word? If we keep
our individual consciences open towards God as He
is revealed in Jesus Christ, God will bring hundreds of
other souls into oneness with Himself through us.

This is the way the new racial regenerated conscience is to come about. Racial conscience is not the
conscience of the individual person, but the conscience of a whole community of people who are in
touch with God.

IN THOUGHT

Be near me when my light is low
    When the blood creeps, and the nerves prick
    And tingle; and the heart is sick,
And all the wheels of Being slow.

Be near me when the sensuous frame
    Is rack'd with pangs that conquer trust;
    And Time, a maniac scattering dust,
And Life, a Fury slinging flame.

1. In The Whirlwind of Things That Are
    (a) Quarrels of Nations (Luke 21:10–11)
    (b) Quarrels of Churches (1 Corinthians 3:1–5)
    (c) Questions of the Way On (Matthew 24:23–26)
2. Internationals of Socialism, Sacerdotalism and Spirituality
3. Federations Most Hopeful

Amid the quarrels of nations is it not wonderful that many minds, untutored either in history or in ethic, should seek to find it in some form like socialism which is indifferent to Nationality, and which overrides the concrete divisions of mankind by abstract ideas and artificial associations, while others, only too historic, find it in a Church unity over their heads.

                                        Dr. Forsyth

If we are faced with a problem, we cannot be indifferent. The greatest help we can give to another is not a positive line of things, but this warning: Don't seal up your mind too quickly.

1. In the Whirlwind of Things That Are
And ye shall hear of wars and rumours of wars; see that ye be not troubled. (Matthew 24:6)

That is either the statement of a madman or of a Being who has power to put something into a man and keep him free from panic, even in the midst of the awful terror of war. The basis of panic is always cowardice. Our Lord teaches us to look things full in the face. He says—"When you hear of wars, don't be scared." It is the most natural thing in the world to be scared, and the clearest evidence that God's grace is at work in our hearts is when we do not get into panics. Our Lord insists on the inevitableness of peril. He says "You must lay your account with war, with hatred, and with death." Men may have lived undisturbed over a volcano for a long while, when suddenly an eruption occurs. Jesus Christ did not say—"You will understand why war has come," but—"Don't be scared when it does come, do not be in a panic." It is

astonishing how we ignore Jesus Christ's words. He said that nations would end in war and bloodshed and havoc. We ignore His warnings; and when war comes we lose our wits and exhibit panic.

(a) Quarrels of Nations (Luke 21:10–11)
This question is on the lips of people to-day: "Is war of the devil or of God?" It is of neither. It is of man, though both God and the devil are behind it. War is a conflict of wills, either of individuals or of nations. National quarrels are everywhere to-day and it is these quarrels which make men say—"Well, blot out nations altogether; the only thing to do is to ignore the fact that there are nations; let us look forward to a time when there will be none." This attitude is a revolt which is a mere safety valve. The vision of a time when there will be no nations is right, but ignoring the fact that there are nations just now is not the way to establish the vision.

After the war the elemental will take its place again, and we shall recover what we had lost in over-civilisation. Civilised life will be all the better for the clearing out of some things, and there are some things we shall regret losing. We shall be driven back to the elemental; we shall be a good deal less refined, more rugged; more like our own country five hundred years ago. In the final issue some things belonging to civilisation will be found to be fine, and some disastrous. The preaching of the "gospel of temperament" and all such shallow optimism has been hit on the head by the war; there are some clouds with no "silver lining," and the injunction to "cheer up" is an insult.

(b) Quarrels of Churches (1 Corinthians 3:1–5)
It is easy to see the defects in churches. I may criticise my own church, but let me remember that her defects are those of immaturity. A person may be full of defects, but we must remember that there is a difference between the vices of a man and the failings of a boy. When we see the powerlessness and ineffectiveness of the churches, we are apt to revolt to sacerdotalism, which is priestcraft being used as an exotic over human nature. Frequently, religious peace has been brought about in this way, but it has not been a desirable peace. When men are compelled to submit to superstition, they are apt to say, "Let us have no churches at all, or else let us have a democratic church."

(c) Questions of the Way On (Matthew 24:23–26)
"If any man shall say unto you, Lo, here is Christ, or there; believe it not." To-day we have all kinds of Christs in our midst, the Christ of Labour and of

Socialism; the Mind-cure Christ and the Christ of Christian Science and of Theosophy; but they are all abstract Christs. The one great sign of Christ is not with them—there are no marks of the Atonement about these Christs. Jesus Christ is the only one with the marks of atonement on Him, the wounded hands and feet, a symbol of the Redeemer Who is to come again. There will be signs and wonders wrought by these other Christs, and great problems may be solved, but the greatest problem of all, the problem of sin, will not be touched.

The majority of us are blind on certain lines, we see only in the light of our prejudices. A searchlight lights up only what it does and no more, but the daylight reveals a hundred and one facts that the searchlight had not taken into account. An idea acts like a searchlight and becomes tyrannous. Take a man with an idea of evolution; as you listen to him the way seems perfectly clear, life is not difficult at all; but let the daylight of actual experience come across his path, and there are a thousand and one facts which the idea cannot account for, because they do not come into the simple line laid down by the evolutionist. When I am up against problems, I am apt to shut myself up in my own mind and refuse to pay any attention to what anyone says. There are many things which are neither black nor white, but grey. There is nothing simple under heaven saving a man's relationship to God on the ground of the Redemption of Jesus Christ. When Jesus Christ came on the scene, His disciples became impatient and said, "Why don't You tell us plainly who You are?" Jesus Christ could not, because He could only be discerned through moral obedience. A man who talks like a shell makes the path of a shell, that is, he makes the way straight, but destroys a good deal in doing it. There is another way of reaching the solution of a problem— the long, patient way of solving things. Jesus Christ deliberately took the "long, long trail." The temptation of Satan was that He should take the "short cut." The temptations of Satan centre round this point: "You are the Son of God, then do God's work in Your own way"; and at the heart of all our Lord's answers was this: "I came to do My Father's work in His way, not in My own way, although I am the Son of God."

A fanatic sees God's point of view but not man's. He says God ought not to allow the devil, or war, or sin. We are in the whirlwind of things that are, what is the use of wasting time and saying things ought not to be? They *are!* In the midst of the problems, what is the way out? The line of solution is not to apply the plaster of a philosophical statement or the principles of teetotalism, or of vegetarianism, but something more fundamental than these, viz., a personal relationship to God and Man as one—Jesus Christ. "Don't make principles your aim, but get rightly related to Me," Jesus Christ says.

The revelation of Christianity is that God, in order to be of use in human affairs, had to become a typical Man. That is the great revelation of Christianity, that God Himself became human; became incarnate in the weakest side of His own creation. If one can put it reverently, unless God Almighty can become concrete and actual, He is nothing to me but a mental abstraction, because an ideal has no power unless it can be realised. The doctrine of the Incarnation is that God *did* become actual, and that He manifested Himself on the plane of human flesh. Jesus Christ is not only the name of the personal Saviour Who made the way for every man to get back into that personal relationship, but He is the name for God and Man *one*. "Son of Man" means the whole human race centred in one personality. Jesus Christ declares He is the exclusive way to the Father (Matthew 11:27; John 14:6).

A religious fanatic says: "I will work from the Divine standpoint and ignore the human." You cannot do it; God Himself could not do it. He had to take upon Himself "the likeness of sinful flesh." There must be the right alloy. You cannot use pure gold as coin, it is too soft to be serviceable, and the pure gold of the Divine is no good in human affairs; there must be the alloy mixed with it, and the alloy is not sin. Sin, according to the Bible, is something that has no right in human nature at all, it is abnormal and wrong. Human nature is earthly, it is sordid, but it is not bad. The thing in human nature that is bad is the result of a wrong relationship set up between the man God created and the being God created who became the devil, and the wrong relationship whereby a man becomes absolute "boss" over himself is called sin. Sin is a wrong element, an element that has to be dealt with by God in Redemption through man's conscience.

The fanatical person is certain that human beings can live a pure Divine life on earth. But we are not so constituted, we are constituted to live the human life presenced with Divinity on earth, on the ground of Redemption. We are to have the right alloy—God and humanity one, as in our Lord Jesus Christ. That is the miracle of the Redemption when it works actually in human flesh. The way out is to remember that the alloy must be discovered in you and me, viz., the pure Divine working on the basis of my pure human. I may have the most beautiful sentiments in prayer and visions in preaching, but unless I have learned how God can mix the human and the Divine and make them a flesh and blood epistle of His grace, I have missed the point of Jesus Christ's revelation.

2. Internationals of Socialism, Sacerdotalism and Spirituality
Socialism at present is immensely vague, it is the name for something which is all right in vision, but

the point is how is the vision to get legs and walk? How are we going to establish the peace of the world so that nations will not go to war any more, or grab at each other? How are we going to arrive at an equality that will work? How is it to be done? These are the last days of a dispensation from God's standpoint. (The Bible dispensations are not things we note, they are marked off by the Spirit of God. To-day militarism has gone into hell before the eyes of the whole world.) "And it shall come to pass in the last days," saith God, "I will pour out of My Spirit upon all flesh" (irrespective of goodness or badness) ". . . and on my servants and on my handmaidens I will pour out in those days of my Spirit." What is the difference between "your sons and your daughters" and "my servants and my hand-maidens?" "Your sons and your daughters" refer to the men and women who have no concern about the Redemptive point of view: "We have the vision and we are going to do the thing in our own way." Peter says God is longsuffering, and He is giving us ample opportunity to try what ever line we like in both individual and national life. God is leaving us to prove to the hilt that it cannot be done in any other than Jesus Christ's way, or the human race will not be satisfied.

The atheist, or socialist, or Christian—all who look to the future and express a view of what ought to be, see the same vision. They see the brotherhood of man, a time of peace on earth when there will be no more war, but a state of goodwill and perfect liberty, at present inconceivable. There is nothing wrong with the vision, and there is no difference in the vision because its source is the Spirit of God; the difference is in the way it is to be reached. The vision is of the nature of a castle in the air. That is where a castle should be; who ever heard of a castle underground! The problem is how to put the foundation under your castle in the air so that it can stand upon the earth. The New Testament says that the only foundation is not Rationalism but the absolute efficacy of the Redemption of Jesus Christ. We are not prepared to see that yet; there may be individuals who are, but no nation under heaven is. It is a long process for an individual to centralise his mind on Jesus Christ's standpoint, and it must take nations a long while too. The socialist in his domain is like the fanatic in the Christian domain; he is apt to see the vision and forget the problem—forget that in the meantime we are not there! After the war we shall have to be down among the demon-possessed, and then will be the time to prove whether we can give legs to our vision. Locusts, in their flight, will tumble down in the streams and drown by the million, but others keep coming on until they bank the stream right up, and the live ones crawl over the piled-up dead. Hundreds of men in the past twenty centuries have had the vision, and given their

lives for it. No one thinks anything about them now, but it is over the lives of these men that the rest of us are beginning to crawl and find a footing.

Sacerdotalism has proved a quick way out of a good many difficulties. It says: "Put the incubus of a Church rule on the nations and say, 'You shall do this'; unite temporal and Divine power under an infallible head." It is one way of holding peace for a time, but it is a peace that does not grow from the inside of solving the problems of men; it comes from the outside, like an extinguisher, on to the problems and says, "I am the infallible Church in the line of the Apostolic Succession; you shall not doubt, I will solve all your problems." In every period when the nations have been held in peace, it has been by an external authority, such as a Church, acting like an exotic, spreading its roots over the mass of humanity and holding it together. The Roman Catholic Church is a proof of this. There is only one thing as futile as the Roman Catholic Church and that is Protestantism. In Roman Catholicism the great dominating authority is Churchianity, the Church is vested with all authority. In Protestantism it is what the Book says that is the supreme authority, and a man gets rest when he decides for either. "I am going to give up all the turmoil and let my Church do my thinking for me." If you put your faith in a Church, it will solve your problems for you. Or you may stake your faith in Bibliolatry with the same result. "Ye search the scriptures, because ye think in them ye have eternal life; and these are they which bear witness of *Me*, and ye will not come to *Me* that ye may have life" (John 5:39–40 RV). Jesus Christ says neither the Church nor the Bible is the authority, but "I am the Way, the Truth, and the Life"; the Church and the Bible are secondary. The context of the Bible is Jesus Christ, and a personal relationship with Him interprets the Bible in a man's life. There are ways of bringing peace to a man's mind which are not true to the fundament of things, and one of the most significant things during the war is the change of mental front on the part of men as they face these things.

3. Federations Most Hopeful

Another man says, "Federation is the most hopeful solution there is; not necessarily denominational union, but federations in spirit; let us look forward to the time when nations and denominations will be federated out of independent existence." This is, again, only a mental safety valve.

Another man may say: "I believe in quiet mysticism, cutting myself off from everything around and getting at things by a spiritual life of my own." The monks in the Middle Ages refused to take the responsibilities of life by shutting themselves away from the world, and people to-day seek to do the same by cutting themselves off from this and that relationship.

Paul says: "Beware of those who ignore the basis of human life." If I refuse to accept nations or churches or human beings as facts, I shall find I have nothing to help solve the problems that arise. We have to make the first footing clear. Is it possible, on the basis of Redemption, to regenerate commerce? for Jesus Christ not to ignore the fact of men and women, but to regenerate them? for nations not to be ignored, but regenerated? Jesus Christ's claim is that it is possible. Jesus Christ was not deluded, nor was He a deceiver. He is the Way, the Truth, and the Life; and the only way out is by a personal relationship to Him. We are never exonerated from thinking on the basis on which Jesus Christ has put things by Redemption.

THE DANCE OF CIRCUMSTANCES

Nay but Thou knewest us, Lord Christ, Thou
*   knowest*
*   Well Thou rememberest our feeble frame,*
Thou canst conceive our highest and our lowest,
*   Pulses of nobleness and aches of shame.*

Therefore have pity! not that we accuse Thee,
*   Curse Thee and die and charge Thee with our woe;*
Not thro' Thy fault, O Holy One, we lose Thee,
*   Nay, but our own,—yet hast Thou made us so!*

1. Personal Decisions for Christians
   (a) Sin—*destroyed* (1 John 3:8)
   (b) Sensuality—*denied* (Romans 8:13; Colossians 3:3–6)
   (c) Sentimentality—*ignored* (Luke 6:46)
   (d) Sensibilities—*controlled* (John 17:15; Romans 14:20–23)

2. Providential Discretions for Christians
   (a) The Mischief of Absorption (Galatians 4:16–20)
   (b) The Mistiness of Abstractions (1 Corinthians 5:9–13)
   (c) The Meaning of Affiliation (1 Peter 2:13–17)

Without a country ye are bastards of humanity; without a country ye have neither name, token, voice, nor, rights; no admission as brothers into the fellowship of peoples.

                                        Mazzini

"Through the shadow of an agony cometh Redemption."[11] In a supreme agony something dies, no man is the same after it. The majority of us live our lives untouched by an agony; but in war, the chances are that all are hit somewhere, and it is through a personal agony that a man is likely to begin to understand what the New Testament reveals. As long as we have our morality well within our own grasp, to talk about Jesus Christ and His Redemption is "much ado about nothing"; but when a man's thick hide is pierced, or he comes to his wits' end and enters the confines of an agony, he is apt to find that there is a great deal from which he has been shut away, and in his condition of suffering he discovers there is more in the Cross of Christ than intellectually he had thought possible.

Beware of believing that the human soul is simple; look at yourself, or read the 139th Psalm, and you will soon find the human soul is much too complex to touch. When an intellectualist says that life is simple, you may be sure he is sufficiently removed from facts to have no attention paid to him. Things look simple as he writes about them, but let him get "into the soup," and he will find they are complicated. The only simple thing in human life is our relationship to God in Christ.

Circumstances are the things that twist a man's thinking into contortions.

1. Personal Decisions for Christians

One of the first things we discover in dealing with the big universal problem is that it is mirrored in each individual life. When we are young we are all metaphysicians, we don't deal with physical things, but with things behind the physical. The young mind seems more competent than the middle-aged mind, because the latter has come the length of dealing with facts. The metaphysician and the philosopher deal only with abstractions which are supposed to explain facts. It is always the young mind that attempts to deal with the big universal problems; but when the young mind has had a dose of the plague of its own heart, the problem of the universe is obliterated by another, viz., that of its own personal life, and if a solution can be found for that, it has a solution for the problems which lie further afield. The problem of the universe is not mine but the Almighty's; the problem

---

11. "Through the shadow of an agony cometh Redemption": words of Ugo Bassi, central character in *The Disciples* (1873), epic poem much loved and quoted by Chambers, written by Harriet Eleanor Hamilton King (1840–1920).

I am up against is the muddle inside. Can I see a way out there? Is the God I have only an abstraction? If so, don't let me treat Him as anything else. Or is He one with whom I can get into a personal relationship, one who will enable me to solve my problems?

A Christian is a disciple of Jesus Christ's by the possession of a new heredity (John 3:3), one who has been brought into personal relationship with Jesus Christ by the indwelling Spirit of God, not one with certain forms of creed or doctrine; these are the effects of his relationship, not the ground of it.

The man who brings with him any conception of God (especially if he is a Scotsman), will bring a conception based on Calvinism, a God described by the "Omnis." That God does not amount to anything to me. If I start out and say that the essential nature of God can be defined as omnipotence, omniscience and omnipresence, I shall end by proving that Jesus Christ is a liar, for He was not omnipotent and omniscient and omnipresent when He was on earth; yet He claimed to be the complete revelation of God—"*He that hath seen Me hath seen the Father.*" Either my theology is wrong or Jesus Christ is. If Jesus Christ is right, I must be prepared to revise my theology and say that those terms simply express certain manifestations which I called God. But if the essential nature of God is holiness, then I can see how it is possible for Jesus Christ to be God manifest in the flesh. The doctrine of the Incarnation means that God became the weakest thing in His own creation, a Baby. The doctrine of the Trinity is not a Christian revelation, it is an attempt on the part of the mind of man to expound the Christian revelation, which is that there is only one God to the Christian, and His name is Jesus Christ.

A Christian is an avowed agnostic because he has accepted what he knows about God on the ground of revelation; he has not found it out for himself.

(a) Sin (1 John 3:8)

According to Jesus Christ, the first decision is that sin has to be destroyed. The first great moral effect of Jesus Christ's coming into the world is that He saves His people from their sins; not simply that He saves them from hell and puts them right for heaven; that is the finding of a Protestant evangel, not the New Testament view, and is only one phase of salvation. The great purpose of Jesus Christ's coming is that He might put man on a line where sin in him can be destroyed (1 John 2:1). The test of a Christian, according to the New Testament, is not that a man believes aright, but that he lives as he believes, i.e., he is able to manifest that he has a power which, apart from his personal relationship to Jesus Christ, he would not have. We all know about the power that spoils our sin, but does not take away our appetite for

it. The first great decision to be made is that the only thing to do with sin is to destroy it, and the incoming of Jesus Christ enables a man to destroy the wrong relationship in himself.

(b) Sensuality (Romans 8:13; Colossians 3:3–6)

Sensuality is not sin, it is the way my body works in connection with external circumstances whereby I begin to satisfy myself. Sensuality will work in a man who is delivered from sin by Jesus Christ as well as in a man who is not. I do not care what your experience may be as a Christian, you may be trapped by sensuality at any time. Paul says, "Mortify the deeds of the body," mortify means to destroy by neglect. One of the first big moral lessons a man has to learn is that he cannot destroy *sin* by neglect; sin has to be handled by the Redemption of Jesus Christ, it cannot be handled by me. Heredity is a bigger problem than I can cope with; but if I will receive the gift of the Holy Spirit on the basis of Christ's Redemption, He enables me to work out that Redemption in my experience. With regard to sensuality, that is my business; I have to mortify it, and if I don't, it will never be mortified. If I take any part of my natural life and use it to satisfy myself, that is sensuality. A Christian has to learn that his body is not his own. "What? know ye not that your body is the temple of the Holy Ghost . . . and ye are not your own?" Watch that you learn to mortify.

If I have an intellectual puzzle, I must see that I run it correspondingly with moral obedience. If I am perplexed about God's real universe, have I begun to make personal decisions about sin and sensuality? Every religious sentiment that is not worked out in obedience, carries with it a secret immorality; it is the way human nature is constituted. Whenever I utilise myself for my own ends, I am giving way to sensuality, and it is done not only physically, but mentally also, and one of the most humiliating things for a Christian is to realise how he does it. The impertinence of mental sensuality lies in the refusal to deny the right of an undisciplined intelligence that is contrary to Jesus Christ.

If I am going to find out a thing scientifically, I must find it out by curiosity; but if I want to find out anything on the moral line, I can only do it by obedience. God put man in a garden with the tree of knowledge of good and evil, and said, "Thou shalt not eat of it." God did not say they were not to know good and evil, but that they were not to know good and evil by eating of the tree. They were intended to know evil in the way Jesus Christ knew it, viz., by contrast with good. They did eat of the tree, consequently the human race knows good by contrast with evil. Adam knew evil positively and good negatively, and none of us knows the order God intended. No man who has eaten of the fruit of the tree knows evil by contrast with good. The curiosity of the human heart finds out the bad things first. The fruit of the tree of the knowledge of good and evil gives the bias of insatiable curiosity on the bad line, and it is only by the readjustment through Jesus Christ that the bias on the other line enters in—a tremendous thirst after God. Jesus Christ knew evil negatively by positively knowing good; He never ate of the tree, and when a man is reborn of the Spirit of God that is the order.

(c) Sentimentality (Luke 6:46)

Sentimentality is produced by watching things we are not in. We are all capable of being sentimental, i.e., of living in a state of mind which produces emotions we do not intend to carry out. A hundred and one things will produce sentimentality—a cup of tea, a concert; a letter or a novel will do it. "I like to have my emotions stirred, but don't ask me to carry them out on their own level." If I allow an emotion and refuse to act it out on its right level, it will react on a lower level. The higher the emotion, the deeper the reaction; consequently, the higher the religious emotion, unless worked out on its own level, the more debased and appalling the reaction. That is why Paul connects sanctification with immorality, and why religious men fall much more bestially. Our guide as to what emotions we are going to allow is this—What will be the logical outcome of this emotion? If it has to do with sin and Satan, then grip it on the threshold of your mind and allow it no more way. You have no business to harbour an emotion the outcome of which you can see to be bad; if it is an emotion to be generous, then be generous, or the emotion will react and make you a selfish brute.

Sentimentality has to be ignored. Jesus Christ said—"You call Me Master and Lord, but you don't do what I say." That is the gist of the failure of Christianity; it has been tried and abandoned because it has been found difficult; but it has never failed when it has been tried and gone on with honourably. There is no problem or difficulty that stretches before a man for which adherence to Jesus Christ will not give him the line of solution.

(d) Sensibilities (John 17:15; Romans 14:20–23)

"Sensibilities" means the things at the basis of life, the way we are naturally related to life. The three main sensibilities in a man's life are sex, money and food. What has he to do with them? They are not sinful, they are plain facts which can be either devilish or sublime. Whenever Jesus Christ brought His teaching to a focus it was on two points, viz., Marriage and Money. In ordaining sex God took the bigger risk and made either the most gigantic blunder or the most sublime thing. Sex has to be controlled, so have money

and food. By what? By the highest. When God created the Federal Head of the race He required him to take part in his own development by a series of moral choices, whereby he was to sacrifice his natural sensibilities to the will of God and transform them.

Our Lord says He does not pray that His disciples shall be taken out of the world, but that they shall be kept from the evil one, kept from being overwhelmed. Paul, in Romans 14, beats out into gold foil what Jesus Christ gives in nugget form. He warns all through—Beware of those who teach abstinence from marriage and from meats, they are true neither to God nor man as God made him. A false religion grew up in the Middle Ages which taught, "You must get out of the world, deny sex, and cut yourself off from everything around." The stamp of false religion is that it denies that these sensibilities have any nobility in them. It is spiritual cowardice to deny these things because they have been made sordid and bestial; if they cannot be controlled for the glory of God, Jesus Christ has misled us. Remember that we have to live a Christian life in these bodies, to get the right alloy which will produce the thing Jesus Christ stood for. The Incarnation reveals the amalgam of the Divine and the human, the right alloy, i.e., that which makes the Divine serviceable for current use.

One of the first ingredients for a man's thinking is that the Incarnation is a picture of what takes place in every man who is touched by the Spirit of God, i.e., the Son of God is formed in him by regeneration. Jesus Christ's holiness has to do with human life as it is. It is not a mystical, aesthetic thing that cannot work in the ordinary things of life, it is a holiness which "can be achieved with an ordinary diet and a wife and five children."

2. Provident Discretions for Christians

The great danger of Socialism is that it is vague, it has the right vision, but it ignores the margins and expects to come to a bigger understanding of things whilst ignoring the facts that are. Or take Sacerdotalism, which says the only way to build a governing peace over the human race is by an ecclesiastical system, such as the domination of the Pope. We can see to-day how much mischief and uselessness underlies this teaching.

These things do not seem to be a way out, but remember they are. They give rest and sustaining and peace, but not on the best line. They crush instead of developing. Another "way out" is the ultra-holiness line. There are those who go to the opposite extreme and say we must live a pure Divine life, ignoring all the claims of the natural. Jesus Christ taught that the natural must be sacrificed through obedience, and turned into the spiritual. If it is not, it will produce a tremendous divorce in the life.

(a) The Mischief of Absorption (Galatians 4:16–20)

This teaching says: There are defects in the churches, but they are not to be swept away on that account, the defects must be corrected; form the churches into an imperial Church which will dominate everything. That is what happened when Paul began to plant the Christian faith, the Judaisers came after him and said—"Now we must absorb this," and the same spirit is at work in ecclesiastical minds to-day. The only way to get peace, they say, is by a big Church that will absorb everything; an imperial power to dominate. If you do, divisions will be quieted and a peace produced such as was produced by the Roman Empire, a peace that dominates by absorption.

The divisions of the churches are to be deplored, and denominationalism is to be deplored, but we must not forget that denominations have reared up the best men we know. The defects are clear and they have to be remedied; something will have to be done, and one suggested way out is this idea of absorption which has been proved in history to be a way out.

(b) The Mistiness of Abstractions (1 Corinthians 5:9–13)

Socialism and false Christianity are both misty, they deal with the idea of absorption, that you have to run the purist line where it cannot be run, denying the fact of nations and of families as they really are. Paul says—In your own spiritual relationships you have to be "dead nuts" against sensuality, but don't be fanatical. You have to maintain your personal relationship in purity amongst those who are not pure, and see that no intermixture of impurity gets in. In your own spiritual community these things must not be. Our Lord takes the same line in Matthew 18:15–17.

Never attempt to solve outside problems first. If sin is to be destroyed in my personal life on the basis of Redemption, it is to be destroyed outside me also; if sensuality is to be mortified in my personal life, it is to be mortified outside me also. The majority of us begin with the bigger problems outside and forget the one inside. A man has to learn the "plague of his own heart" before his own problems can be solved, then he will be free to help solve the problems outside.

The mistake is that we want to take the path of a shell. Jesus Christ says—No, I have taken the long trail, and "in your patience possess ye your souls," i.e., acquire the new way of looking at things. There are problems not easy of solution, they need patient dealing with day in and day out. Take, for instance, the way some missionaries train converts with regard to marriage laws; they have tried the "hustling" dodge, and found it to be no good. It takes a long time to lift people to a cleaner "sty"; it is absurd to rush in a fine ethic of Christianity on people who have been living in polygamy, their education takes time. The danger of the visionaries is that they do not seem to know how to get their visions to walk, and they never will unless they remember and take into account these big facts of sex and money and food. Are you going to judge with the same standards, a well brought up man with generations of good, clean blood in his veins, and a man who has generations of wrong and evil in his heredity? How are you going to judge the man who boils up with bestiality? It is with him not a matter of escaping from conventions, or of taking on the colour of those he is with; there is the great fact underneath. You cannot judge him, you have to be immensely patient with him.

(c) The Meaning of Affiliation (1 Peter 2:13–17)

In the present crisis another "way out" is not to ignore facts as they are, but to affiliate them; the ultimate end is that demarcations must go. It is the affiliation of churches, not the absorption of them, that will solve the problems, and the same with nations. But, remember, we are on crutches just now and there are things to be taken into account.

Every man is up against these things to-day—socialist or imperialist, he cannot think without being touched by problems. It is not that we can offer solutions for these problems, but that the line on which personal problems are solved by Jesus Christ is the line on which the bigger problems will be solved also. But it will take a long time, and we have need of patience. Answer the problem in yourself first: How long did it take you to get your ideals actual? to stand where you are now?

There are those in the national life who are visionaries and are apt to forget that at present we are not there, just as there are visionaries in the Christian life who are apt to forget the facts of human life—I like the vision, but don't ask me how I am to make it real. I like orchids, but don't ask me to look at the miasmic swamp in which they grow; I like the fine flower of virtue, but don't show me how it was produced. No man is born virtuous, virtue and purity are the outcome of fight; innocence is natural. Man has to have enough moral muscle in him to fight against the thing that wants to make him immoral; immediately he fights, he becomes virtuous in that particular. It is a difficult thing to fight for virtue. Virtue for a man, purity for a woman, and innocence for a child, is God's order.

In all our views we must get back to facts as they are. Keep your vision, but take facts as they are; make a clean sweep of the old rubbish, the creeds and notions, and then begin to build bit by bit. You will find that the personal problems are the ones that call first for solution, and when you have solved those, you can begin to help solve the others. If the men who get back after this war will remain true to what they saw in the agonies, they ought to begin to make the new impression felt along every line.

THE PRESSURE OF THE PRESENT

The index to moral failure is to care more for a religious society than for the Church, more for a trade union than for the nation.

Dr. Forsyth

1. Findings from the Historic Christ (Luke 11:17–26)
   (a) The Kingdom of God (v. 20)
   (b) The Kingdom of Satan (v. 18)
   (c) The Kingdom of Man (vv. 21–26)

   Christ ruined many careers and brought sorrow and death to many souls.

2. Findings from Hysteric Christianity (Mark 9)
   (a) The Vision of God (v. 5)
   (b) The Valley of Godlessness (vv. 17–19)
   (c) The Verity of Gumption (v. 29)

   Don't throw on God the dirty work you are called to do.

A point of view is tyrannous, consequently when a man gets knocked about by circumstances and acquires other points of view, his findings are confused for a time.

We mean by "The pressure of the present" the things that crowd a man out from thinking on his own line. If he could only cut out the fact that he is a man, or that things are as they are, he could get on all right. We all have the trick of saying—If only I were not where I am!—If only I had not got the kind of people I have to live with! If our faith or our religion does not help us in the conditions we are in, we have either a further struggle to go through, or we had better abandon that faith and religion.

We have seen that there are ways out—the visionary way, the socialist way, or the mystical Christian way, each tending towards the brotherhood of man. The vision is all right, but how is it going to be made actual? It is easy to talk about God and holiness; humanity and love for one another; but present things must be taken into account. Jesus Christ's vision was unmistakable, and His demands from human beings were terrific, but He always took "things as they are" into account, and He insisted that in order to carry out His demands men must have the right "alloy." The Incarnation means the right alloy. For God to be of any use to human beings He must become incarnate; that means dust and Deity mixed in one. If you have merely an abstraction, the vision without the dust of the actual, you will never make the vision real. As Dr.

Forsyth points out, if in dealing with religious societies, you ignore the barriers and simply look forward to the time when there will be no barriers, you are making a mistake and you will end in failure. The vision is right, but you must take things as they are into account. Our life as disciples is not a dream, but a discipline which calls for the use of all our powers.

There are two worlds—the Actual and the Real. My personal consciousness is at home in the actual world, but not in the real; it just touches the real, it touches God. There is an inference that there is a world other than the actual, but I am not at home in it; all I can get at by my personal consciousness is a fictitious reality. Neither the actual nor the ideal is the real; according to Jesus Christ the real can only be worked out on the line of personal experience. Our Lord was at home in the ideal as well as in the actual, and consequently everything in His personal life was real. We are apt to forget that in order to get at reality we have not only to use our heads, but our consciences. No man as yet has ever reached reality by his intellect. A man may have sublime views of life and at the same time be a moral tadpole in regard to actual life. The same with emotions; a man may have any number of aesthetic susceptibilities, the finest appreciation of colour and feeling and sound, but in actual life prove that none of it touches the sordid actualities of life. There is only one thing in a man that brings him to reality, and that is his conscience. Conscience is the faculty in me that fixes on the highest I know; and it is through conscience that man touches the reality of things and becomes transformed. It is then the intellect and the emotions can come together.

1. Findings from the Historic Christ *(Luke 11:17–26)*

Christianity is not adherence to a set of principles—righteousness, goodness, uprightness—all these things are secondary. The first great fundamental thing about Christianity is a personal relationship to Jesus Christ which enables a man to work out the ideal and actual as one in his own personal life.

No man thinks so clearly at any time or is ever so thrilled as in his "teens." The tragedy begins when he finds his actual life cannot be brought up to the standard of the ideal, and he closes with an agony of his own. Then he goes to preachers who talk about the ideal, or to books, thinking he will find the real thing; but too often he does not. He finds the vision there, but not working out in actual practice; and his agony deepens. The ideal presented by Jesus Christ fascinates some men right away; there is something enthralling about Him; but inevitably, sooner or later, they come to the experience of the early disciples recorded in Mark 14:50: "They all forsook him and fled." "I gave all I had to the ideal presented by Jesus Christ, I honestly tried my best to serve Him, but I cannot go on; the New Testament presents ideals beyond my attainment. I won't lower my ideals, although I realise that I can never hope to make them actual." No man is so laboured or crushed as the man who, with the religion of ideals, finds he cannot carry them out. There are many more men in that attitude than is supposed. Men are kept away from Jesus Christ by a sense of honesty as much as by dishonesty. "I don't deny that Jesus Christ saves—but if you only knew me!—the mistakes I have made, the wrong things I have done, the blundering things—I should be a perfect disgrace to Him." Our Lord says to such a one, "Come unto Me . . . , and I will give you rest." When a man comes, he will realise that Jesus Christ does not tell him to do his best, but—Surrender to Me, and I will put into you that which will make the ideal and the actual one, and you will be able to work out in actual life what you see by the power of vision. Without Jesus Christ there is an unbridgeable gap between the ideal and the actual. The only way out is through a personal relationship to Him, a relationship with Himself whereby a man can transform the ideal and the actual into one and slowly work it out in his own experience, and then help other folks.

The thing you find to be the solution in your personal life is also the line of solution for other things. If Jesus Christ is the way for a man to make things real in his own life, He is also the way for things outside a man's personal life to be made real. It is easy to keep our intellects busy with the ideal, but the problem is how to bring the ideal and the actual together, how to make our actual life in accordance with our ideal. Jesus Christ says, "Except a man be born again, he cannot see the kingdom of God." He is not talking about deliverance from hell, but about being born into a new realm. The religion of Jesus Christ means that a man is delivered from sin into something which makes him forget all about himself. The trick of pseudo-evangelism is that it drives a man into concentrated interest in himself. The curse of much modern religion is that it makes us desperately interested in ourselves, overweeningly concerned about our own whiteness.

These findings are not part and parcel of the average Christian conception of Jesus Christ, because we do not take our findings from the New Testament, we take them from what we have been taught about Jesus Christ. Jesus Christ said, "If I had not come and spoken unto them, they had not had sin; but now they have no cloke for their sin" (John 15:22). Then why did He come? Why should He come with an ideal

that knocks the bottom out of my self-realisation? Why tell me to love my enemies when I hate them? Why tell me to be pure in heart when I am impure? Why should He taunt me with ideals? If Jesus Christ is only a Teacher, then all He can do is to tantalise us, to erect a standard we cannot attain to; but when we are born again of the Spirit of God, we know that He did not come only to teach us, *He came to make us what He teaches we should be.* These are some of the things which ought to be deduced from reading the New Testament.

(a) The Kingdom of God (Luke 11:20)
We know about the kingdom of man, but not about the other two kingdoms which belong to the domain Jesus Christ lived in.

The "strong man" is Satan; the stronger than he," Jesus Christ. The result of Jesus Christ's coming is disturbance. "Think not that I am come to send peace on earth: I came not to send peace, but a sword" (Matthew 10:34). When Satan rules, his goods, i.e., the souls of men, are in peace; there is no breaking out into sin and wrongdoing, and before God can rule man's kingdom He must first overthrow this false rule. The coming of Jesus Christ is not a peaceful thing; it is overwhelming and frantically disturbing, because the first thing He does is to destroy every peace that is not based on a personal relationship to Himself. Am I willing to be born into the realm Jesus Christ is in? If I am, I must be prepared for chaos straight away in the realm I am in. The rule which has come in between God and man has to be eclipsed. Jesus Christ's entering into me means absolute chaos in the way I have been looking at things, a turning of everything upside down.

Just as Jesus Christ produces havoc in personal lives, so He will produce it all through on every line. For instance, if Jesus Christ had not obeyed the call of His Father, His own nation would not have blasphemed against the Holy Ghost. He ruined the career of a handful of fishermen, He disappointed and crushed the hopes of many and perturbed their peace. He continually produced havoc in people's lives.

(b) The Kingdom of Satan (Luke 11:18)
There is a difference between the Devil and Satan. The Bible holds man responsible for the introduction of Satan. Adam started a communication with another of God's creations, and the result was Satan. Jesus Christ calls the self-realisation point of view, "Satan," anti-Christ (Matthew 16:23). When our Lord comes face to face with Satan, He deals with him as representing the attitude man takes up in organising his life apart from any consideration of God. For a thing to be satanic does not mean that it is an abominable and immoral thing. The satanically

managed man is moral, upright, proud, and individual; he is absolutely self-governed and has no need of God. Jesus Christ says "that which is highly esteemed among men is abomination in the sight of God" (Luke 16:15).

(c) The Kingdom of Man (Luke 11:21–26)

Jesus Christ always said, *"If* any man will be My disciple"—He did not clamour for him, or button-hole him. He never took a man off his guard, or used a revivalistic meeting to get a man out of his wits and then say, "Believe in Me," but, "Take time and consider what you are doing; if you would be My disciple, you must lose your 'soul,' i.e., your way of reasoning about things." When I am born from above (RV mg), I have to reconstruct another soul, I have to look at things from a different standpoint, viz., the standpoint of Jesus Christ. Jesus Christ taught non-resistance on the physical line in order that men might resist more on the moral line. When He was brought face to face with evil, His attitude was "Get!"—no compromise.

When Jesus Christ comes in with His standards, a man's way of looking at things is upset, and he begins to see the point of view of Jesus Christ when he strikes his own personal agony. He is brought face to face with the possibility that after all Jesus Christ knows what He is talking about, and that Rationalism may be a fools' paradise, and he himself an intellectual ostrich. We never blame our fundamental conception until we get deep enough down. Rationalism at the basis is wrong; it goes to pieces just where we expect it to prove right.

2. Findings from Hysteric Christianity (Mark 9)

That is, Christianity based on sentimentality.

(a) The Vision of God (Mark 9:5)

We are not built for mountains and dawns and artistic affinities; they are for moments of inspiration, that is all. We are built for the valley, for the ordinary stuff of life, and this is where we have to prove our mettle. A false Christianity takes us up on the mount and we want to stay there. But what about the devil-possessed world? Oh, let it go to hell! We are having a great time up here.

(b) The Valley of Godlessness (Mark 9:17–19)

The intellectualist or dreamer who by his dreams or isolation is not made fitter to deal with actual life, proves that his dreams are mere hysterical drivel. If his dreams only succeed in making him hold aloof from his fellow-men, a visionary who deals only with things belonging to the mountaintop, he is self-indulgent to a degree. No man has any right to be a spectator of his fellow-men; he ceases to be in touch with reality.

It is a great thing to be on the mount with God, and the mountains are meant for inspiration and meditation; but a man is taken there only in order that he may go down afterwards among the devil-possessed and lift them up. Our Christianity has been as powerless as dish-water with regard to things as they are; consequently the net result of Christianity is judged to be a failure. But Christianity, according to Jesus Christ, has never been tried and failed; it has been tried and abandoned in individual cases because it has been found a bit too hard, too definite and emphatic, and for the same reason it has been abandoned in nations and in Churches; but Christianity has never been tried and gone through with honourably and found to fail.

The same thing with regard to the socialistic vision; it is a great thing to have the vision, but those who have it are apt to forget the limitation of actual things as they are. Jesus Christ gives the vision of God, God's order; but He also gives us God's permissive will. God's order, according to Jesus Christ, is no sin, no sickness, no limitation, no evil, and no wrong: His permissive will allows these things, and I have to get at God's order through His permissive will by an effort of my own.

(c) The Verity of Gumption (Mark 9:29)

The disciples had the stamp of all false hysteric religion. "You work a miracle; we don't want to accept the moral responsibility." Jesus Christ said: "You cannot do these things by magic, it must be done by concentration." Peter thought it would be a fine thing to remain on the Mount, but Jesus Christ took them down from the mount and put them into the valley, i.e., the place that explains the meaning of the vision. There are times when my false religion makes me want to throw my dirty work on God. Supposing I am a slovenly workman and get saved, and I say— "Well, I will ask God to make my work fine and clean"; He won't do it, it is not His job. God's job is to alter my heredity, I cannot alter that; but when my heredity is altered, I have to manifest my altered heredity in actual circumstances. This is not only true in personal life, but in every domain. For instance, God won't clear up our social conditions; Jesus Christ is not a social Reformer, He came to alter us first, and if there is any social reform done on earth, we will have to do it. We are not to ask God to do what He has created us to do, any more than we are to attempt to do what He alone can do. Prayer is often a temptation to bank on a miracle of God instead of on a moral issue, i.e., it is much easier to ask God to do my work than it is to do it myself. Until we are disciplined properly, we will always be inclined to bank on God's miracles and refuse to do the moral thing ourselves. It is our job, and it will never be done unless we do it.

Visions are great things, but it is useless to tell a man about the vision of God on earth unless you can get down into the mire he is in and lift him up; and the marvel is that if you have got hold of the vision of God and are working it out by moral obedience in your own life, you can do the lifting. Moral insight is gained only by obedience. The second I disobey in personal bodily chastity, I hinder everyone with whom I come in contact; if in moral integrity I disobey for one second, I hinder everyone; and if as a Christian I disobey in spiritual integrity, others will suffer too.

The vision must be worked out or there is no grip in it. The majority of us who are called Christians could do nothing when the war struck us. We had our visions of God, our notions of prayer, etc., but we had no grip, we could not touch the demon-possessed. We have to deal with men who actually have done the wrong thing; can we lift them up into the place where they will become changed men? or can we only preach in a way that is equivalent to putting a snowdrift over a dung-heap? If we cannot live in the demon-possessed valley, with the hold of God on us, lifting up those who are down by the, power of the thing that is in us, our Christianity is only an abstraction.

We need to remember that the vision must be worked out in our own personal experience first. If the vision is real, the biggest test of it is that it makes God easier to believe in. Think of the men and women you know who have made it easier for you to believe in God. You go to them with your problems, and things get different, the atmosphere of your mind alters; you have come in contact with a man or woman who in his actual life is working out his vision. The best way you and I can help our fellow-men is to work out the thing in our own lives first. Unless it is backed up by our life, talking is of no use. We may talk a donkey's hind leg off, but we are powerless to do any lifting. If we look after the vision in our own life, we shall be a benediction to other people.

THE PSYCHOLOGICAL PHASE—I

But I, amid the torture and the taunting,
  I have had Thee!
Thy hand was holding my hand fast and faster,
  Thy voice was close to me;
And glorious eyes said, "Follow Me, thy Master,
Smile as I smile thy faithfulness to see."

DIVERGENT FUNDAMENTAL POINTS HEALTH HAPPINESS HOLINESS A PERFECT BALANCE BETWEEN OUR ORGANISM AND THE OUTER WORLD (PSALM 73:3–14) A PERFECT BALANCE BETWEEN OUR INCLINATION AND ENVIRONMENT (PHILIPPIANS 3:17–20) A PERFECT BALANCE BETWEEN OUR DISPOSITION AND THE LAW OF GOD (JOHN 14:27)

SOCIALISM SUPERMAN SIN (REVELATION 13:11–18) (2 THESSALONIANS 2:3–12) (1 JOHN 3:8) SPIRITUALITY SANCTIFICATION SACRAMENT (2 CORINTHIANS 4:16–18) (1 THESSALONIANS 4:3; 5:23–24; 1 JOHN 3:3) The rationalist says—"I can explain the conscious by reason, therefore all the rest is reasonable." There are chaotic elements which burst up into a man's conscious life and make him know that there are things beyond reason; not that they contradict reason, but that they are different from it. The basis of things in a man's personal life is tragedy; at any second there may come a terrific upheaval from underneath that may knock all his calculations to smithereens. Men may be good at dealing with problems on the outside but never have faced one inside their own breast-bone. The thing that knocks the conceit out of a man is to get what Solomon talked about, a dose of " the plague of his own heart," he becomes a little less certain that he can rule himself. When I receive the Spirit of God, I am lifted not out of reason, but into touch with the infinite Reason of God.

Health, Happiness, and Holiness are all divergent views as to what is the main aim of a man's life.

1. Health *(Psalm 73:3–14)*

Health means the balance between my physical life and external nature, and is maintained purely by a sufficient fighting vitality within against things outside. Health is equilibrium maintained through a terrific power of fight. Disease means that the harmony of health is gone, and a sign that the fighting corpuscles are getting weak. The things which keep you going when you are alive, disintegrate you when you are dead. Everything that is not my physical life is designed to put me to death, but if I have enough fighting power I produce the balance of health.

The same is true in my moral life; everything that does not partake of the nature of virtue is the enemy of virtue in me, and it depends on what moral calibre I have as to whether I overcome and produce virtue. I am only moral if I have sufficient moral power in me to fight; immediately I fight, I am moral in that particular. Disinclination to sin is not virtue, any more than innocence is purity. Innocence has always to be shielded, purity is something that has been tested and tried and has triumphed, something that has character at the back of it, that can overcome, and has overcome. Virtue is acquired, and so is purity. Everything that is not virtuous tries to make me immoral. Always do something you don't need to do for the sake of doing it—it keeps you in moral fighting trim.

The same thing spiritually, everything that is not my spiritual life makes for its undoing. Holiness is the balance between my disposition and the laws of God as expressed in Jesus Christ, and if I have enough spiritual fighting capacity I shall produce a character that is like Jesus Christ's. Character must be attained, it is never given to us.

The basis of physical, moral, and spiritual life is antagonism.

"A healthy mind in a healthy body," is not always true, for some of the finest minds are in diseased bodies. On the other hand the Psalmist talks about the "wicked"— "there are no bands in their death. . . . They are not in trouble as other men; neither are they plagued like other men. . . . Their eyes stand out with fatness: they have more than heart could wish." The healthy- minded cult evades anything that would be likely to upset the health of the body.

A man can make certain forms of vice or drugs necessary to himself, and the moralist who ignores the fact that a man will suffer for a time by giving them up, is nothing short of a fool. Every appetite I create demands its satisfaction; and the harmony of my body depends on its being satisfied; but not the health of my moral life. If the moral life is allowed its way, the man who has maintained his bodily health by other means has to go to rack and ruin before he gets another balance. No wonder men will do anything to avoid conviction of sin! No man can have his state of mind altered without suffering for it in his body, and that is why men will do anything rather than be upset. "I like to listen to this talk about Jesus Christ, but don't put your finger on the thing that upsets my mind. Why should I bother with a standard of things that upsets me?"

The healthy-minded cult runs through everything. If certain types of health are to be maintained, all social life will have to be re-faced, marriage will go by the board, and all the higher amenities of friendship—all the best and noblest moral relationships.

Sin is a thing that puts man's self out of centre altogether, making it ex-centric; and when the Spirit of God convicts him, the man knows he is wrongly related to God, to his own body, and to everything around him, and he is in a state of abject misery. The health of the body is upset, the balance pushed right

out, by conviction of sin. Conviction of sin makes a man's beauty "to consume away like a moth." "Beauty" means the perfectly ordered completeness of man's whole nature. When once a man's mind is upset, that beauty begins to go, the equilibrium is upset. This accounts for the characteristic tendency abroad to-day: ignore sin, deny it ever was; if you make mistakes, forget them, live the healthy minded, open-hearted, sunshiny life, don't allow yourself to be convicted of sin.

To say "Camp life has made men worse" is not true; nothing can! Camp life strips the veneer of civilised life from a man, and he comes out with what he is, he has to reveal himself, but nothing can make a man either better or worse than he is. In producing a splendid soldier you produce a splendid animal; then to be horrified because the animal gets its way is absurd. Is it our idea of a man's life, that he should be a splendid healthy animal? If so, there are several things you will have to cut out; you will have to cut out Jesus Christ, never read the New Testament, don't let the standards of Jesus Christ—never hate, never lust, always do more than your duty—come in, or you will upset your health.

Health seems to be the basis of people's outlook, but it can never account for the problems.

(a) Socialism (Revelation 13:11–18)
Numbers are used as symbols for great big generalities, and the Book of Revelation takes the number 666 to be the symbol of *humanity sufficient for itself*, it does not need God. The description given is of a great system in which humanity is its own god. (See Genesis 3:5, 22) When the Bible talks of Man, it refers to the Federal Head of the race. The remarkable point of the vision is that it says the beast (in the spiritual, the self-realising, sense) looks like a lamb, but talks like a dragon; that is, he looks like Jesus Christ, but when he talks, he talks like the old imperial dragon; when the crisis comes, he has tooth and claw exactly like the beast. The vision of Socialism is magnificent; there are benedictions and blessings for mankind on the line of Socialism which have never been yet; but if once the root is cut from Redemption, it will be one of the most frantic forms of despotic tyranny the human race has ever known. It looks like the lamb, but when the big crisis comes, it gives life to the beast. It is in the wake of Socialism that the resuscitation of Plato's ideas will come. Trace your ideas back to their roots, and you will find the root of Socialism is in Plato's teaching. You will produce healthy organisms, but will you produce noble-minded men and women after the stamp of Jesus Christ?

2. Happiness (Philippians 3:17–21)
There is a difference between environment and circumstances. Every man has his own environment; it

is that element in his circumstances which fits his disposition. We each make our own environment, our personality does it for us. Happiness means we select only those things out of our circumstances that will keep us happy. It is the great basis of false Christianity. The Bible nowhere speaks about a "happy" Christian; it talks plentifully of joy. Happiness depends on things that happen, and may sometimes be an insult; joyfulness is never touched by external conditions, and a joyful heart is never an insult. Who could be happy these days? It would be the outcome of the most miserable selfishness to be happy under such conditions as are everywhere to-day, the sign of a shallow-minded, selfish individual. Happiness is the characteristic of a child's life, and God condemns us for taking happiness out of a child's life; but we should have done with happiness long ago, we should be men and women facing the stern issues of life, knowing that the grace of God is sufficient for every problem the devil can present.

We start with the idea that prosperity or happiness or morality is the end of a man's existence; according to God, it is something other than any of these, viz., "to glorify God and enjoy Him for ever." Happiness would be all right if things were reasonable; it would be ideal if there were no self-interest, but everyone of us is cunning enough to take advantage somewhere, and after a while my inclination is to get my happiness at your cost.

(a) Superman (2 Thessalonians 2:3–12)

In Socialism there are things which look like Jesus Christ, but in the end they are more dragon-like than anything else, because one thing is evaded. The same with happiness, when once happiness and self-indulgence are allowed to rule and have their way, the end is the "Superman." If I believe I have the finest idea of happiness for my child, my child will have to come my way, and "damn the consequences." The same thing is true with a class or a nation or a state if it believes it is God. Each one of us in his own domain exhibits the tendency: in the state it is on a gigantic scale because the state is bigger than a man's individual life. The standard of happiness ends in the upset of happiness, in a tyranny and despotism of the most appalling order.

3. Holiness (John 14:27)

Holiness is the balance between our disposition and the law of God as expressed in Jesus Christ, and it is such a stern thing that the majority of us have either not begun it, or we have begun it and left it alone.

What kind of peace had Jesus Christ? A peace that kept Him for thirty years at home with brothers and sisters who did not believe in Him; a peace that kept Him through three years of popularity, hatred, and scandal; and He says, "My peace I give unto you"; "let not your heart be troubled," i.e., see that your heart does not get disturbed out of its relationship to Me.

But remember Jesus Christ has to upset the old equilibrium first. When a man is probed into by the Spirit of God, the waters of his conscious life get troubled and other ideas emerge. If I am going to follow the dictates of the Spirit of God and take up the attitude of Jesus Christ to things, it will produce an earthquake in my outlook. It will begin with the bodily life—"Know ye not that your body is the temple of the Holy Ghost?"

If you would be My disciple, says Jesus, that is the cost. No man can shift the centre of his life without being upset. "Men of good taste are averse to the teaching of Jesus Christ," because if He is right, they are wrong. Take up any attitude of Jesus Christ's and let it work, and the first thing that happens is that the old order and the old peace go. You cannot get back peace on the same level. If once you have allowed Jesus Christ to upset the equilibrium, holiness is the inevitable result, or no peace for ever (Matthew 10:34).

If happiness or health is a man's main idea, let him keep away from Jesus Christ's, for if he has any conscience at all, he will lose that health and happiness. Jesus Christ stands for holiness. At all costs a man must be rightly related to God. Redemption is the basis. When you take a point of view, watch the things it does not cover, and if you are going to think, think clean through, playing the man on every line.

(THE LATTER PART OF THE OUTLINE WAS NOT DEALT WITH,
SO THIS CHAPTER IS NECESSARILY INCOMPLETE.)

THE PSYCHOLOGICAL PHASE—II
Man Becomes What He Is

For the glory and the passion of this midnight
I praise Thy name—I give Thee thanks, O Christ!
Thou that hast neither failed me nor forsaken
Through these hard hours with victory overpriced;
Now that I too of Thy passion have partaken,
For the world's sake—called—elected—sacrificed!

N.B.—ON PERSONALITY AND INDIVIDUALITY; DISPOSITION AND CHARACTER

1. Bias of Degeneration (Romans 5:12)
   (a) Disposition of Defiance (Romans 8:7)
   (b) Destiny of Death (Romans 6:23; 7:24; 8:6; 2 Corinthians 4:4)
   (c) Battle of the Margins (Hebrews 12:14–17)

2. Bent of Regeneration (Galatians 1:15–16; 2:20)
   (a) Donation of Deity (1 Corinthians 1:30; Ephesians 2:5–6)
   (b) Disposition of Divinity (John 17:22; Philippians 2:5–8)
   (c) Borderland of the Mastery (Galatians 5:16–22)

Circumstances make a man reveal what spirit he is of. Crises reveal character more quickly than anything else.

Personality is of the nature of light, it can be merged; individuality is like a lamp which cannot merge. There may be many lamps, but only one light. Individuality cannot mix; it is all "elbows," it separates and isolates; it is the thing that characterises us naturally, in our elementary condition we are all individual. Individuality is the shell, as it were, holding something more valuable than itself—the kernel, which is personality. The shell of individuality is God's created natural coating for the protection of the personal life. It preserves the personality, and is the characteristic of the child; but if I stick to my individuality and mistake it for the personal life, I shall remain isolated, a disintegrating force ending in destruction. Individuality counterfeits personality as lust counterfeits love. God designed human nature for Himself; individuality debases human nature for itself.

Personality merges, and you only get your real identity when you are merged with another person. A man has his individuality transfigured when he falls in love. When love or the Spirit of God strikes a man or woman, they are transformed, they no longer insist on their separate individuality. Christianity is personal, therefore it is un-individual. Personality is the characteristic of the spiritual man as individuality is the characteristic of the natural man. Our Lord never spoke in terms of individuality, of a man's "elbows" or isolated position, but in terms of personality, "that they all may be *one*." Our Lord can never be defined in terms of individuality or independence, but only in terms of personality. He was the antipodes of the individual; there was nothing independent or wilful or self-assertive about Him. Jesus Christ emancipates the personality; the individuality is transfigured in the mastership of God's purpose in Christ Jesus, and the transfiguring element is love; personal, passionate devotion to Himself, and to others

Disposition is the set of my mind; character is the whole trend of my life, not what I do occasionally. Character is what we make; disposition is what we are born with. We make our characters out of the disposition we have, and when we are born again we get a new disposition, the disposition of the Son of God. We cannot imitate the disposition of Jesus Christ; it is either there or it isn't. Our destiny is determined by our disposition; pre-ordination in regard to individual life depends entirely on the disposition of the individual. If the disposition of the Son of God is in me, then heaven and God are my destination; if the disposition in me is not the disposition of God, my home is as obviously certain with the devil. Our destiny is as eternal and as certain as God's throne; it is an unalterable decree of God; but I am free to choose by what disposition I am to be ruled. I cannot alter my disposition, but I can choose to let God alter it, and Redemption means that in my practical experience Jesus Christ can give me a new heredity, a new disposition. Our destiny is something fixed by God, but determined by our disposition. We are all born with a disposition, i.e., the peculiar bent of our personal life, and it is that which determines our destiny. Praying won't alter it, nor science, nor reasoning; if the destiny of a man is going to be altered it must be altered by the Creator (John 3:3).

We are much more than we are conscious of being. Our Lord said the Holy Spirit would bring back into our conscious mind the things He had said. We never forget a thing although often we cannot recall it; we hear it and it goes into the unconscious mind. Things go on in our unconscious minds that we know nothing about, and at any second they may burst up into our conscious life and perturb us. The Spirit of God enters into a man below the threshold of his consciousness. When He will emerge into the man's conscious mind no one can say; but when He does, there is an earthquake, and the man has to read-just his life in every particular. The Spirit of God entering into the spirit of a man brings a totally new relationship to things.

1. Bias of Degeneration *(Romans 5:12)*

There are only two men according to the Bible, Adam and Jesus Christ. They are the representatives of the human race. The "image of God" was male and female together in the way God created them (Genesis 5:1–2), and sin entered into the world by that "Man." The Bible does not say that God punished the human race for one man's sin, but that the disposition of sin, i.e., my claim to my right to myself, entered into the human race by one man. The disposition of sin is not morality or wrongdoing, but my claim to my right to myself. When Jesus Christ faced men with all the forces of evil in them and men who were clean living, and moral, and upright, He did not pay any attention to the moral degradation of the one or to the moral attainment of the other; He was looking at something we do not see, viz., at the disposition in both, not at the immorality or the morality, but at the disposition—my claim to my right to myself, self-realisation, and He said: "If you would be My disciple, that must go."

(a) Disposition of Defiance (Romans 8:7)

To say that "sin is nothing but the shadow of good" is not true. Evil, according to the Bible, is the shadow of good, but sin is positive defiance. You can be educated by evil, but not by sin. Sin is the positive disposition in me that has to be removed; evil is the negative thing outside me. There is no such thing as sin outside the Bible; sin is a revelation fact, and it is the one fact that accounts for the curious twist we find in things. We must take into account that there is a bias in human nature, viz., self-interest, self-realisation; it may be refined or low, but it is there. Common sense says, what a wonderful being man is in the making! The New Testament says, what a magnificent ruin of what man was once! Which view covers the biggest number of facts?

The great element in sin is defiance against God. There is a difference between sin and sins; sin is a disposition and is never spoken of as being forgiven; sins are acts for which we are responsible. Sin is a thing we are born with, and we cannot touch sin; God touches sin in Redemption. God never laid the sin of the human race on anybody but Himself, and in Redemption He has dealt with the disposition of sin. A man cannot be forgiven for what he is not to blame, but God holds a man responsible for refusing to receive a new heredity when he sees that Jesus Christ can give it to him. In the Cross of Jesus Christ, God redeemed the whole human race from the possibility of damnation through the heredity of sin. If, when we realise that Jesus Christ came to deliver us from the wrong disposition by putting in a right one, we refuse to allow Him to do it, that is the moment when condemnation begins (John 3:19).

(b) The Destiny of Death (Romans 6:23; 7:24; 8:6; 2 Corinthians 4:4)

Many a clean-living man is in the condition these verses describe. The domain Jesus Christ represents does not awaken a tremor of sympathy, something has to stab him wide-awake, rouse him to other issues and bring him to his wits' end before the things Jesus Christ stands for are even interesting. You cannot make Jesus Christ mean anything to a man; He may be nothing to him one minute and everything the next; it depends on what happens. A man may go on well contented until something pierces his hide, or brings him up against the things which profoundly alter life; then suddenly he is within another frontier and it begins to be possible for him to see the kingdom in which Jesus Christ moves.

(c) Battle of the Margins (Hebrews 12:14–17)

There is no effort about Esau, he is content with being once born; Jacob could not be satisfied with anything less than God. Jacob tried in a hundred and one ways, cunningly to satisfy himself, but it was of no use. Esau was a man who had no battles at all, or if he had any, he fought them all on the wrong side of the margins. A man is not brought up to the margins in an ordinary way, but only through an agony. We do not come near the margins until we are hit by a form of supreme suffering, and then we see we have been shutting our lives away from a great domain. If Jesus Christ is going to regenerate us, what is the problem He is up against? We have an heredity we had no say in, we are not holy, nor likely to be; Jesus Christ had the disposition of Deity, and He says we have to be fathomlessly pure in heart. If all He can do is to tell me that I must be holy, be what I never can be, present me with an ideal I cannot come anywhere near, His teaching plants despair; He is nothing more than a tantaliser and I wish He had never come. But if He is a Regenerator, one who first of all can put into me His own heredity, then I see what He is driving at in the Sermon on the Mount—that the disposition He puts in is like His own. There is not one characteristic in the Sermon on the Mount that fits in with a man's natural disposition; we may give our mental assent to it, but our actual life won't walk that road; Jesus Christ is the only one who can carry it out. Redemption means that Jesus Christ can put into any man the hereditary disposition that was in Himself, and all the standards He gives are based on that disposition. Jesus Christ teaches that when His Spirit is in us, we shall manifest a likeness to Himself if we allow His disposition to react in us.

2. Bent of Regeneration *(Galatians 1:15–16; 2:20)*

The heredity of the Son of God is planted in me by God, a moral miracle. Pseudo-evangelism has gone wildly off the track in that it has made salvation a bag of tricks whereby if I believe a certain shibboleth, I am tricked out of hell and made right for heaven—a travesty of the most tremendous revelation of the Redemption of the human race by Jesus Christ. The New Testament's teaching about Christianity is that the Son of God is formed in me on the basis of His marvellous regeneration until, as Paul says, "the life which I now live in the flesh"—not the life I am going to live when I get to heaven, but the life I now live in this flesh, the life that all see and know—"I live by the faith of the Son of God who loved me, and gave Himself for me." What has happened to Paul? He has gone through his battle of the margins, he has gone through a moral decision with Jesus Christ, not an intellectual one; he has said— I agree with God in the things that He condemns in the Cross, self-interest, self-realisation, though these have been dearer to me than my life; "I count all *these* things but loss for the excellency of the knowledge of Christ Jesus my Lord." It may take four minutes or forty years to be identified with Jesus Christ; it depends on whether I am willing to face the music, i.e., forgo my hereditary right to my claim to myself and let Him take His claim to me. "Holy Spirit" is the name of the new disposition, and if Jesus Christ can put that into me (Luke 11:13), I see how things can happen.

(a) Donation of Deity *(1 Corinthians 1:30; Ephesians 2:5–6)*

"The kingdom of God is within you," Jesus said, i.e., without observation Spirituality is a kingdom within, a new way of looking at things. The moral miracle of Christianity is that when I know my limitations, when I reach the frontiers by weakness not by will, Jesus Christ says, Blessed are you, I will do the rest. But I have to get there; it is not that God will not do anything for me until I do, but that He cannot. God cannot put into me, a moral being, the disposition that is in Jesus Christ unless I am conscious I need it. I cannot receive that which I do not believe I need; but when I am struck by an agony, or the sense of helplessness with regard to Jesus Christ's teaching, I am ready then to receive the donation of Deity.

In the natural world I am born with an heredity for which I am not responsible, and I have a disposition through that heredity; but I have not a character through heredity. God gives disposition, but never character. Habits are not transmitted by heredity, only tendencies and qualities; habits are formed by imitation. Heredity means that the qualities or defects of the parents are manifested in the children. If I receive the Spirit of God and become a son of God by right of regeneration, God does not give me my Christian character, I have to make that. He gives me the disposition of His Son; He puts Holy Spirit into me, then He says—Now, breast and back as they should be, and work it out. My disposition tells through my body on to outward circumstances, and as I obey the Spirit of God and the word of God, I slowly form the Christian character.

(b) Disposition of Divinity *(John 17:22; Philippians 2:5–8)*

The Spirit of Christ is given us, but not the mind of Christ. Every man is born with a human spirit, but he forms his own mind by the way his human spirit reacts in the circumstances he is in, and education gives power to a man to express his personal spirit better and better. The Spirit of Christ comes into me by regeneration, then I have to begin to form the mind of Christ, begin to look at things from a different standpoint, viz., the standpoint of Jesus Christ, and to do that I must lose my soul. Soul is not a thing I have got, soul is the way a man's personal spirit manifests itself in his body, the way he reasons about things, the rational expression of his personal spirit.

If my soul has been formed on the belief that rationalism is the basis of things, that things are calculable, then when the Spirit of God enters into my spirit and the principles of Jesus burst up into my life, the former foundations quake; I discover that tragedy, and not rationalism, is the basis of things, and I have to readjust my mind. When a man is saved by God's grace, it is the beginning of the end. Some are content to be dragged into salvation by the sheer mercy of God, but Jesus Christ's conception is that a man should become His disciple and begin to mould his thinking on the basis of the Spirit of God that comes into him. That takes time; when the crisis comes, am I going to obey the word the Spirit of God recalls to me?

(c) Borderland of Mastery *(Galatians 5:16–22)*

The Holy Spirit in a Christian wars against the old heredity; the new heredity and the old war one against another. Is that all God can do for me? destroy unity in my life, make me a divided personality, and make me sick with conviction of sin? If that is all God can do, I would rather be an atheist; but if it is only a stage towards the borderland of mastery, that is a different matter. Paul says if I obey the Spirit of God, I must crucify the other mind. God cannot do that, I must do it myself. Yes, I will agree with the Spirit of God and go to the death of my old disposition (Romans 6:6). If I do not put to death the things in me that are not of God, they will put to death the things that are of God.

There are things in a man's natural life that are fine and beautiful, but when a man comes to Jesus Christ, he has to forgo them, and go to their "white funeral."[12] This is a phrase Tennyson uses in speaking of the "white funeral" of the single life; and that aspect is the only one that suits the spiritual life. Think of it in reference to babyhood, there comes a time when that phase dies and child life begins; there is a "white funeral" of the baby; and then a "white funeral" of the child and girlhood begins. Apply that spiritually. There is any amount in paganism that is good and virtuous, but if I am going on with Jesus Christ, I have to give those things a "white funeral," make a termination of them, and we very often get there through disenchantment. It is not true that everything in life apart from Christ is bad; there are many virtues that are good and moral, pride and self-interest are remarkably fine things in some aspects, "highly esteemed among men," but when I see Jesus Christ I have to go to their moral death. Any fool will give up wrongdoing and the devil,

if he knows how to do it; but it takes a man in love with Jesus Christ to give up the best he has for Him. Jesus Christ does not demand that I give up the wrong, but the right, the best I have for Him, viz., my right to myself. Will I agree to go through my "white funeral" and say I deliberately cut out my claim to my right to myself, deliberately go to the death of my self-will? If I will, instantly the Spirit of God begins to work, and slowly the new mind is formed.

These crises are reached in personal life, and we find the same thing in the life outside, and the only line of solution is this one. If we find a line of emancipation and solution for ourselves, we have also found a line of solution for problems outside ourselves. Moral problems are only solved by obedience. We cannot see what we see until we see it. Intellectually things can be worked out, but morally the solution is only reached by obedience. One step in obedience is worth years of study, and will take us into the centre of God's will for us. All our darkness comes because we will try to get into the thing head first. We must be born into the kingdom of God, Jesus says, before we can begin to think about it (John 3:3; 7:17), and when the life is there, we begin to form the masteries. We must take into account the bias of degeneration and the bent of regeneration, and our agreement with both is the only line on which we can solve the problems.

HUMANITY AND HOLINESS

PAST ERROR: A CHRISTIANITY THAT
UTILISED HUMANITY

PRESENT ERROR: A HUMANITY THAT
UTILISES CHRISTIANITY

BIBLE POINT OF VIEW: GOD AND
MAN IN UNION.

We are not suffering to-day from dogmatic theologians, but dogmatic scientists, socialists and evolutionists. To-day's cant is the cant of unspirituality.

Dr. Forsyth

*If your religion injures your intelligence, it is bad.
If your religion injures your character, it is bad.
If your religion injures your conscience, it is criminal*

Amiel[13]

1. Body of Man—Solidarity of Sin
   (2 Thessalonians 2:3–4)
   (a) Adam (Genesis 5:1–2)
   (b) Anarchy (Genesis 11:1–9)
   (c) Antichrist (1 John 4:3)

2. Body of Christ—Solidarity of Saints
   (1 Corinthians 12:12–27)
   (a) Reconciliation (1 Corinthians 5:18–21)
   (b) Repentance (Acts 2:37–40)
   (c) Regeneration (1 Corinthians 12:12–27)

In the past the error of the Christian faith was that it paid no attention to a man's actual life; it simply used human beings and made them catspaws for a religious line of things. The present error is that humanity utilises Christianity; if Jesus Christ does not coincide with our line of things, we toss Him overboard;

---

12. "white funeral": phrase from Tennyson's poem "To H.R.H. Princess Beatrice"; to Chambers, a white funeral meant a passage from one stage of life to another; leaving the past behind and moving into the future; he often used it to mean death to self and a complete surrender to God.

13. Henri Frederic Amiel (1821–1881): Swiss professor and writer, known for his self-analytical *Journal*, published in 1883.

Humanity is on the throne. In the New Testament the point of view is God and Man in union.

1. Body of Man—Solidarity of Sin
(2 Thessalonians 2:3–4)

The New Testament way of looking at humanity is not the modern way. In the New Testament *men and women* exist, there is no such thing as "Humanity," the human race as a whole.

A materialist says—Because my religious beliefs do for me, therefore they are satisfactory. Not in the tiniest degree. The test of a man's religious faith is not that it does for him, but that it will do for the worst wreck he ever knew. If every one were well brought up and had a fine heredity, then there are any number of intellectual forms of belief that would do. The materialistic line works like a searchlight, lighting up that it does and no more, but the daylight of actual experience reveals a hundred and one other facts. It does not show a clear simple path, but brings to light a multitude of facts never seen before. The evolutionist looks at man and says, What a glorious promise of what he is going to be! The New Testament looks at man's body and moral life and intelligence and says, What a ruin of what God designed him to be!

(a) Adam (Genesis 5:1–2)

Adam was created to be the friend and companion of God; he was to have dominion over all the life in the air and earth and sea, but one thing he was not to have dominion over, and that was himself. Sin, according to the Bible, is man taking his right to himself, and thereby he lost his lordship over the air and earth and sea. The only Being who ever walked this earth and was Lord of earth and air and sea as God designed man to be, was Jesus Christ. Jesus Christ and Adam, as he was first created, are the normal men, the representatives of the human race. Jesus Christ mirrors what the human race will be like on the basis of Redemption, a perfect oneness between God and man.

(b) Anarchy (Genesis 11:1–9)

This is the result in civilisation of Adam's sin. Sin is red-handed anarchy against God. Not one in a thousand understands *sin*; we understand only about sins on the physical line, which are external weaknesses. In the common-sense domain sin does not amount to much; sin belongs to the real domain. The sin the Bible refers to is a terrific and powerful thing, a deliberate and emphatic independence of God and His claim to me, *self-realisation*. Anarchy is the very nature of sin as the Bible reveals it. Other religions deal with sins; the Bible alone deals with sin. The first thing Jesus Christ faced in men was this heredity of sin, and it is because we have ignored it in our presentation of the Gospel that the message of the Gospel has lost its sting, its blasting

power; we have drivelled it into insurance tickets for heaven, and made it deal only with the wastrel element of mankind. The average preaching of Redemption deals mainly with the "scenic" cases. The message of Jesus Christ is different; He went straight to the disposition, and always said, "IF—you need not unless you like, but—IF any man will follow Me, let him give up his right to himself."

The Christian religion founds everything on the radical, positive nature of sin. Sin is self-realisation, self-sufficiency, entire and complete master-ship of myself—gain that, and you lose control of everything over which God intended you to have dominion. Sin is not an act, but an hereditary disposition. Sin must be cleansed, and the revelation of Redemption is that God through Jesus Christ has power to cleanse us from the heredity of sin. The curious thing is that we are blind to the fact of sin, and deal only with the effects of sin.

(c) Antichrist (1 John 4:3)

Every spirit that dissolves Jesus by analysis is antichrist (RV mg). What is the spirit that dissolves Him? My claim to my right to myself does it. Is Jesus Christ "boss" or am I? God's order is that He is to be absolute sovereign over me, and I am to be absolute sovereign over everything that is not God, and sin is the switch off, for the time being, that makes me my own "boss" and consequently "boss" of nothing else. I only gain the absolute control God intended me to have when I am brought back into perfect union with God. If I want to know what the human race will be like on the basis of Redemption, I shall find it mirrored in Jesus Christ, a perfect oneness between God and man, with no gap. In the meantime there is a gap. Sin, suffering, and the Book of God all bring a man to this realisation, that there is something wrong at the basis of life, and that it cannot be put right by reason. If we make Rationalism the basis of things, we shall find some great big tragedy will spit up and knock our theories to the winds. For instance, this war has taken our breath away and given all our findings a severe shaking. Before we seal up our mind on any of these matters, Jesus Christ says, *"Believe also in Me."*

Anything that puts self-realisation on top is part of the solidarity of sin, which the Bible says will head up until it gets to the terrific and marvellous figure-head Paul refers to in 2 Thessalonians, revered and respected of every race and religion and nationality. The spirit in man, however religious, however sweet and delightful it may appear to men, if it is not the Spirit of God, must be "scattering" away from Jesus. "He that gathereth not with Me scattereth."

Christianity is based on another universe of facts than the universe we get at by our common sense; it is based on the Universe of revelation facts which we only get at by faith born of the Spirit of God. The revelation which Christianity makes is that the essential nature of Deity is holiness, and the might of God is shown in that He became the weakest thing in His own creation. Jesus Christ claims that, on the basis of Redemption, He has put the whole of the human race back to where God designed it to be, and individuals begin to see this when they are awakened by their own agony.

2. Body of Christ—Solidarity of Saints
(1 Corinthians 12:12–27)

The Church of Jesus Christ is an organism; we are built up into Him, baptised by one Spirit into one body. Churchianity is an organisation; Christianity is an organism. Organisation is an enormous benefit until it is mistaken for the life. God has no concern about our organisations. When their purpose is finished He allows them to be swept aside, and if we are attached to the organisation, we shall go with it. Organisation is a great necessity, but not an end in itself, and to live for any organisation is a spiritual disaster. To-day we are hearing the crash of civilisation and the crash of organisations everywhere.

Our word "Church" is connected with civilised organisations of religious people; our Lord's attitude to the Church is different. He says it is composed of those who have had a personal revelation from God as to Who Jesus Christ is, and have made a public declaration of the same (Matthew 16:13–20).

The great conception to-day is not our being merged into God, but God being merged into us. The Christian line of things is that we are brought into union with God by love, not that we are absorbed into God. Jesus Christ maintains that this is to be brought about on the basis of His Redemption alone. Mysticism says it can be brought about by a higher refinement of nature. The stupendous difference between the religion of Jesus Christ and every other religion under heaven is that His religion is one which brings help to the bottom of hell, not a religion that can deal only with what is fine and pure.

(a) Reconciliation (2 Corinthians 5:18–21)

Sin is a fundamental relationship underneath: sin is not wrongdoing, it is wrong *being,* deliberate and emphatic independence of God. God, on the ground of Redemption, has undertaken the responsibility for sin and for the removal of it, and Jesus Christ claims that He can plant in any of us His own heredity, which will re-make us into the new order of humanity. If the human race apart from Jesus Christ is all right, then the Redemption of Jesus Christ is a useless waste.

The revelation is not that Jesus Christ was punished for our sins, but that He was made to be *sin.* "Him who knew no sin" was made to be sin, that by His identification with it and removal of it, we might become what He was. Jesus Christ became identified not only with the disposition of sin, but with the very "body" of sin. He had not the disposition of sin in Himself, and no connection with the body of sin, but, "Him who knew no sin, He made *to be sin."* Jesus Christ went straight through identification with sin so that every man and woman on earth might be freed from sin by His atonement. He went through the depths of damnation and came out more than conqueror; consequently every one of us who is willing to be identified with Him is freed from the disposition of sin, freed from the connection with the body of sin, and can come out more than conqueror too because of what Jesus Christ has done. The revelation is not that Jesus Christ took on Him our fleshly sins—a man stands or falls by his own silly weaknesses—but that He took on Him the *heredity of sin.* God Himself became sin, and removed sin; no man can touch that. God made His own Son to be sin that He might make the sinner a saint. God Almighty took the problem of the sin of the world on His own shoulders, and it made Him stoop; He rehabilitated the whole human race; that is, He put the human race back to where He designed it to be, and any one of us in our actual conditions can enter into union with God on the ground of Jesus Christ's Redemption. God has put the whole human race on the basis of Redemption. A man cannot redeem himself; Redemption is absolutely finished and complete; its reference to individual men is a question of their individual action.

(b) Repentance (Acts 2:37–40)

There is a difference between a man altering his life, and repenting. A man may have lived a bad life and suddenly stop being bad, not because he has repented, but because he is like an exhausted volcano; the fact that he has become good is no sign that he is a Christian. The bed-rock of Christianity is repentance. Repentance means that I estimate exactly what I am in God's sight, and I am sorry for it, and on the basis of Redemption I become the opposite. The only repentant man is the holy man. Any man who knows himself knows that he cannot be holy, therefore if ever he is holy, it will be because God has "shipped" something into him, and he begins to bring forth the fruits of repentance. The disposition of the Son of God can only enter my life by the road of repentance. Strictly speaking, repentance is a gift of God; no man can repent when he chooses. A man can be remorseful when he chooses, but remorse is something less than repentance. When God handles the wrong in a man it makes him turn to God and his life becomes a sacrament of experimental repentance.

(c) Regeneration (1 Corinthians 12:12–27)

When I come to the end of myself and my self-sufficiency, in my destitution I can hear Jesus Christ say,

Ask, and I will give you Holy Spirit. "Holy Spirit" is the experimental name for eternal life working in human beings here and now. Jesus Christ said, You have not that life in yourselves, and you cannot have it unless you get it through Me. He is referring to "Holy Spirit" life which by His resurrection He can impart. The Holy Spirit will take my spirit, soul and body and bring them back into communion with God, and lead me into identification with the death of Jesus Christ, until I know experimentally that my old disposition, my right to myself, is crucified with Him, and my human nature is now free to obey the commands of God.

The doctrine of substitution is twofold. Not only is Jesus Christ identified with my sin, but I am identified with Him so that His ruling disposition is in me, and the moral transaction on my part is agreement with God's verdict on sin in the Cross of Jesus Christ. Redemption means that God through Jesus Christ can take the most miserable wreck and turn him into a son of God. As long as a man has his morality well within his own grasp, Jesus Christ does not amount to anything to him, but when a man gets to his wits' end by agony and says involuntarily, "My God, what am I up against? there is something underneath I never knew was there," he begins to pay attention to what Jesus Christ says. A moral preparation is

necessary before we can believe; truth is a moral vision, and does not exist for a man until he sees it. There is a frontier outside which Jesus Christ does not tell; but when once we get over that frontier, He becomes all in all. God takes us through circumstances until we enter the moral frontiers where Jesus Christ tells.

When you come to your wits' end, remember there is a way out, viz., personal relationship to God through the Redemption of Jesus Christ.

Oh—we're sunk enough here God knows!
But not quite so sunk that moments,
Sure, though seldom, are denied us,
When the spirit's true endowments
Stand out plainly from its false ones,
And apprise it if pursuing
Or the right way or the wrong way,
To its triumph or undoing.

There are flashes struck from midnights,
There are fire-flames noondays kindle,
Whereby piled-up honours perish
Whereby swollen ambitions dwindle;
While just this or that poor impulse,
Which for once had play unstifled,
Seems the sole work of a lifetime,
That away the rest had trifled!

Shade of His Hand

Talks on the Book of Ecclesiastes
Oswald Chambers

INTRODUCTION

Source

This material is taken from talks on Ecclesiastes given by Oswald Chambers to British Commonwealth soldiers at Zeitoun, Egypt,[1] September 24 through October 17, 1917.

Publication History

- As a book: *Shade of His Hand* was published in 1924, and a second edition in 1936.

Zeitoun, six miles northeast of Cairo, was the site of the YMCA compound where Chambers spent most of his two years in Egypt. Nearby was a large military camp. For the most part, the soldiers had evenings and weekends free, and many of them regularly frequented the YMCA huts at Zeitoun for rest and recreation. Chambers taught regular classes on spiritual matters for all who were interested.

This book contains the last messages given by Oswald Chambers before his death. For a month during the autumn of 1917, he explored the meaning of life as revealed in Ecclesiastes.

Chambers completed chapters 1 through 11, but he became ill before covering the final chapter of Ecclesiastes. The first edition of *Shade of His Hand*

noted that "chapter 12 was never taken." In the 1936 edition, David Lambert[2] added his own thoughts on Ecclesiastes 12 to complete the book.

Some of Oswald Chambers' impressions of Ecclesiastes 12 can be found in the last chapter of his book *The Place of Help*. Chambers' last Sunday sermon at Zeitoun was given on October 14, 1917, titled, "Disabling Shadows on the Soul," based on Ecclesiastes 12:5.

On October 17, Chambers became ill after his evening class for soldiers at Esbekieh Gardens in Cairo. He managed to conduct the evening class at Zeitoun on Thursday, October 18, but was in such pain he had to leave all meetings to others for the next ten days.

On October 29, he underwent an emergency appendectomy at Gizeh Red Cross Hospital in Cairo. After recovering well for a week, he began to hemorrhage from the lungs. His condition fluctuated for a week before he died on the morning of November 15.

Shade of His Hand was the second book published by Mrs. Chambers after her 1919 return to England from Egypt. She compiled the book while supporting herself and her daughter, Kathleen,[3] by keeping a boarding house for four university students in Oxford.

---

1. Zeitoun (zay TOON), Egypt: six miles northeast of Cairo; site of a YMCA camp, the Egypt General Mission compound, and, from 1916 to 1919, the Imperial School of Instruction, training base for British, Australian, and New Zealand troops during World War I.

2. David Lambert (1871–1961): Methodist minister and friend of Oswald and Biddy Chambers; assisted Mrs. Chambers with OC publications from 1917 until his death in 1961.

3. Kathleen Chambers (1913–1997): only child of Oswald and Biddy Chambers.

FOREWORD TO THE FIRST EDITION

These talks on Ecclesiastes were not given with any idea of subsequent publication, and they are compiled from my own verbatim notes. It seemed fitting that the talks, the last message that God would speak through his servant, should be reproduced, outlines and all, as nearly as possible as they were delivered, and this has been done.

May the Spirit of God bring to all who read the book a vision of Our Lord Jesus Christ "in whom are hid all the treasures of wisdom."

B. C.[4]
200 Woodstock Road, Oxford
October, 1924

PREFACE (1936 EDITION)

These talks on Ecclesiastes were given by my friend Oswald Chambers at the YMCA Hut, Zeitoun, Egypt, to the Troops in October, 1917. They are a verbatim report of what really were the last lectures he ever delivered, for he was called from the midst of his happy, arduous, fruitful toil among the soldiers into the immediate Presence of his Lord on November 15, 1917. This came before Eccles. 12 had been reached, so notes on the final chapter have been added to make the book complete.[5]

These last expository talks ought to be taken in the light of his former teaching. Those who knew his other books, *Biblical Psychology, The Sermon on the Mount,* The *Discipline* Books, *The Psychology of Redemption,* etc., will profit most by this one. In the earlier books he shows the process of salvation as it works out in the inner life of a man. Here we see it in its relation to the everyday world outside us.

Does Ecclesiastes teach that life is not worth living? That gloomy tale would not be worth telling. Oswald Chambers interprets its message as being— Life is not worth living apart from Redemption. This is a Book of Wisdom for to-day. It shows how it is possible for a redeemed man to glorify God amid all the inter-play of life's forces, in work and play, in study, in recreation, in home life or social intercourse. Life apart from Redeeming Love is full of sin and sorrow, guile and cruelty, callous selfishness and numbing despair, This book takes full account of all that. It anticipates many of the problems facing the young life of today, and brings to their solution the one and only key, the realisation of the Lord Jesus Christ in every relationship of life.

David Lambert

---

4. B. C., Biddy Chambers; although Mrs. Chambers was editor, compiler, and often publisher, she never identified herself by name in any of the books.

5. Lambert's preface to the 1924 first edition said: "The final chapter is missing, as Eccl. XII was never taken."

CONTENTS

I shook the pillaring hours
And pulled my life upon me; grimed with smears,
I stand amid the dust o' the mounded years.
. . . .
       Is my gloom, after all,
Shade of His hand, outstretched caressingly?

                              The Hound of Heaven [6]

---

6. *The Hound of Heaven*, by Francis Thompson (1859–1907).

RATIONALISM HARD PRESSED
Ecclesiastes 1

Myself when young did eagerly frequent
Doctor and Saint, and heard great Argument
About it and about, but evermore
Came out by the same Door wherein I went.
With them the Seed of Wisdom did I sow,
And with mine own hand wrought to make it
     grow,
And this was all the Harvest that I reaped,
I came like Water and like Wind I go.
Omar Khayyám[7]

(N.B.—SOLOMON AND HIS SCHOOL
OF WISDOM, 1 KINGS 4:29–32)

The Wisdom of the Hebrews (Proverbs 8:22–36)
The Wisdom of the Greeks (1 Corinthians
    1:19–25)

1. Practical Experiment
   (a) Constant Obliteration of Conscious
       Effort (Ecclesiastes 1:2–4)
   (b) Continual Oblivion of Cosmic Effects
       (verses 5–6)
   (c) Common Origin of Changing
       Experiences (verses 7–9)
   (d) Counterfeit Originality of Casual
       Expressions (verses 10–11)

2. Personal Experience
   (a) Actual Condition of Thought
       (Ecclesiastes 1:12–13)
   (b) Absolute Conundrum of Thinking
       (verses 14–15)
   (c) Applied Cultures of Time (verse 16)
   (d) Ascertained Cruelty of Truth (verses
       17–18)

It is important to notice the difference between the Wisdom of the Hebrews and the Wisdom of the Greeks.

The Wisdom of the Hebrews is based on an accepted belief in God; that is, it does not try to find out whether or not God exists, all its beliefs are based on God, and in the actual whirl of things as they are, all its mental energy is bent on practical living. The Wisdom of the Greeks, which is the wisdom of our day, is speculative; that is, it is concerned with the origin of things, with the riddle of the universe, etc., consequently the best of our wits is not given to practical living.

1 Kings 4:29–32. The Book of Job was produced by Solomon and his School of Wisdom, and in it we see worked out, according to Hebrew wisdom, how a man may suffer in the actual condition of things. The sufferings of Job were not in order to perfect him (see Job 1:8). The explanation of Job's sufferings was that God and Satan had made a battleground of his soul, and the honour of God was at stake.

The sneer of Satan was that no man loved God for His own sake, but only for what God gave him. Satan was allowed to destroy all his blessings and yet Job did not curse God; he clung to it that the great desire of his heart was God Himself and not His blessings. Job lost everything he possessed, including his creed; the one thing he did not lose was his hold on God, "Though He slay me, yet will I trust Him."

The value of the Book of Job is not in what it teaches, but that it expresses suffering, and the inscrutability of suffering.

In the Book of Psalms, Wisdom is applied to things as they are and to prayer. The Book of Proverbs applies Wisdom to the practical relationships of life, and Ecclesiastes applies Wisdom to the enjoyment of things as they actually are; there is no phase of life missed out, and it is shown that enjoyment is only possible by being related to God.

The record of the whirl of things as they are is marvellously stated in these Books of Wisdom: Job—how to suffer; Psalms—how to pray; Proverbs—how to act; Ecclesiastes—how to enjoy; Song of Solomon—how to love.

The Wisdom of the Hebrews
(Proverbs 8:22–36)
The Wisdom of the Hebrews does not set out to discover whether God is, nor does it enter into speculating enquiries as to the origin of sin, etc. Belief in God is never questioned, and on that basis Hebrew Wisdom sets out to deal with practical things as they are.

The basis of things is not rational, but tragic. Reason is our guide among facts as they are, but reason cannot account for things being as they are. This does not mean that a man is not to use his reason; reason is the biggest gift he has. The rationalist says that everything in between birth and death is discernible by human reason; but the actual experience of life is that things do not run in a reasonable way, there are irrational elements to be reckoned with.

---

7. Omar Khayyam (d. 1123): Persian astronomer and poet.

The Old Testament is coming to its own just now; we have been too patronising. We always get out of touch with the Bible attitude to things when we come to it with our own conclusions. For instance, the Bible does not prove the existence of God, nor does it prove that Jesus Christ is the Son of God. The Bible was written to confirm the faith of those who already believe in God. We are apt to come to the conclusion that the Bible is tepid. Why, some of the most heroic and drastic thinking is within the covers of the Bible! St. John and St. Paul reconstructed religious thought, quoting from no one; there are no thinkers like them, yet it has been fashionable to belittle them.

The Wisdom of the Greeks
(1 Corinthians 1:19–25)
Our modern wisdom, which is the wisdom of the Greeks, is three removes from actual facts. It is mental; we are busy trying to find out the origin of things. It is a type of wisdom that does not find its home in the Bible. The intellectual order of life does not take things as it finds them, it makes us shut our eyes to actual facts and try to live only in the ideal world. The Wisdom of the Greeks tells us how things should be—there ought to be no sin, no war, no devil, no sickness, no injustice; but these things are! It is no use to turn ourselves into ostriches mentally and ignore them. Solomon is fearless in facing facts as they are. No room is allowed either in the Old or New Testament for mysticism pure and simple, because that will mean sooner or later an aloofness from actual life, a kind of contempt expressed or implied by a superior attitude, by occult relationships and finer sensibilities. That attitude is never countenanced in the Bible. The Mount of Transfiguration may serve for a symbol of mysticism—"and Peter answered and said to Jesus, Master it is good for us to be here, and let us make three tabernacles. . . ." But there quickly followed the transition to the demon-possessed valley. The test of mountain-top experiences, of mysticism, of visions of God and of solitariness is when you are "in the soup" of actual circumstances. It is not a question of living a blind life in the brain away from actuality, not of living in dawns or on mountain tops; but of bringing what you see there straight down to the valley where things are sordid, and living out the vision there.

1. Practical Experiment (Ecclesiastes 1:1–11)
In the Book of Ecclesiastes we deal with the actual condition of the things we are in, which is the arena for manifesting the hold we have on God in the unseen.

(a) Constant Obliteration of Conscious Effort
(verses 2–4)
Vanity of Vanities, saith the Preacher, vanity of vanities; all is vanity. What profit hath a man of all his labour which he taketh under the sun? One generation passeth away, and another generation cometh: but the earth abideth for ever.

"Vanity," i.e., ephemeral, not conceit, but fleeting, here and gone as a day. Everything man has ever done is constantly being obliterated; everything a man fights for and lives for passes; he has so many years to live and then it is finished. This is neither fiction nor dumps. In true thinking of things as they are, there is always a bedrock of unmitigated sadness. Optimism is either religious or temperamental. No man who thinks and faces life as it actually is, can be other than pessimistic. There is no way out unless he finds it by his religious faith or is blinded by his temperament. The summing up of all practical life is that the basis of things is tragic. Sum up your life as it actually is, and, unless you look at actual things from a religious or a temperamental or an intellectual standpoint, everything is to be said for this philosophy: Eat, drink and be merry, for to-morrow we die. If Rationalism is the basis of things, that is undoubtedly the most reasonable thing to do. But if the basis of things is tragic, then the Bible standpoint comes nearer the solution, and Nietzsche is nearer the truth than any rationalist. Nietzsche declares that the basis of things is tragic, and that the way out is by the merciless Superman; the Bible reveals that the basis of things is tragic, and that the way out is by Redemption. We say that man is in process of evolution—a magnificent promise of what he is going to be! The Wisdom of the Hebrews looks at man's history and attainments and says—What a magnificent ruin of what he was created to be!

Very few of us think unblinded by a religious or a temperamental point of view, we are not capable of it. We are blinded either by religion, or temperament, or by thick-headedness. To look at things as they are, with the superb wisdom and understanding and disillusioned eye of Solomon, takes a Solomon to do it. Another man did it with the knowledge and understanding of Solomon, and he was Ibsen. He saw facts as they are clearly, without losing his head, and without any faith in God he summed it all up—no forgiveness, no escape from penalty or retribution, it is absolutely and inexorably certain that the end of things is disaster. In Shakespeare's writings there is an under-current of faith which makes him the peculiarly valuable writer he is, and makes him more at home to those who understand the Bible point of view than to those who do not.

(b) Continual Oblivion of Cosmic Effects
(verses 5–6)
The sun also ariseth, and the sun goeth down, and hasteneth to his place where he arose. The wind goeth toward the south, and turneth about unto the north; it

*whirleth about continually, and the wind returneth
again according to his circuits.*

Everything that happens in Nature is continually
being obliterated and beginning again. What Solomon
says is not merely a poetical statement. A sunset or a
sunrise may thrill you for half a minute, so may beautiful music or a song, but the sudden aftermath is a terrific, and almost eternal sadness. Lovers always think
of what one would do if the other died; it is more than
drivel. Immediately you strike the elemental in war or
in Nature or in love, you come to the basis of ineffable sadness and tragedy. You feel that things ought to
be full of joy and brightness, but they are not. You will
never find the abiding order of joy in the haphazard,
and yet the meaning of Christianity is that God's order
comes to a man in the haphazard.

There is a difference between God's will and
God's order. Take the case of two boys born in the
slums, one determines to get out of it, and carves out
for himself an honourable career, he gets at God's
order in the middle of His permissive will. The other
sinks down in despair and remains where he is. God's
order is—no sin, no sickness, no devil, no war: His
Permissive will is things as they are.

(c) Common Origin of Changing Experiences (verses 7–9)

*All the rivers run into the sea; yet the sea is not full;
unto the place from whence the rivers come, thither they
return again. All things are full of labour; man cannot
utter it: the eye is not satisfied with seeing, nor the ear
filled with hearing. The thing that hath been, it is that
which shall be; and that which is done is that which
shall be done: and there is no new thing under the sun.*

You may try to rest in any phase of actual existence,
says Solomon, but apart from your relationship to
God, you are better dead. Unless you bank your faith
in God, you will not only be wrongly related in practical life and have your heart broken, but you will
break other things you touch. (Cf. Matthew 18:6–7.)

(d) Counterfeit Originality of Casual Expressions (verses 10–11)

*Is there anything whereof it may be said, See, this is
new? it hath been already of old time, which was before
us. There is no remembrance of former things; neither
shall there be any remembrance of things that are to
come with those that shall come after.*

It is only when we are ignorant that we believe in
originality. We have such magnificent "forgetteries"

that we obliterate the whole of human history for the
discovery we have made, and say—This is original.
Solomon says the whole thing is an incessant and
appalling weariness.

2. Personal Experience *(Ecclesiastes 1:12–18)*
These verses are not guesswork, but the conclusion of
the wisest man that ever lived. The Bible indicates
that a man always falls on his strongest point. Abraham, the man of faith, fell through unbelief; Moses,
the meek man, fell through losing his temper; Elijah,
the courageous man, fell through losing heart; and
Solomon, the most colossally wise, wealthy, luxurious,
superb king, fell through grovelling, sensual idolatry.

(a) Actual Condition of Thought (verses 12–13)

*I the preacher was king over Israel in Jerusalem. And
I gave my heart to seek and search out by wisdom concerning all things that are done under heaven: this sore
travail hath God given to the sons of man to be exercised therewith.*

These are the words of a man who has tried and experienced the things he speaks of. We say there ought
not to be war,[8] there ought to be no devil, no suffering, and we fuss and fume; but these things *are!* If we
lived in the clouds, it would be different; but we are
here. "If only I was not where I am!" It is in the present dilemma that practical wisdom is required.

I believe that the atheism of Job and of men to-
day is more wholesome than to believe in a God about
Whom you have to tell lies to prove He is God.
Voltaire tiraded against the God Who was masquer-
aded before men in his day. In a mental stress of
weather it is better not to believe in a Being Who has
not the clear sense of justice we have, than to believe
in One Who is an outrage to our sense of justice; better to "snatch at the damnation" of such a Being than
to accept His salvation.

We are driven back every time to Jesus Christ—
"I am the Way, the Truth and the Life." Have I seen
Him, or do I see only that which echoes myself? Am
I prepared to see in Jesus Christ the outlines of the
true character of God, which is holiness? We *perceive*
our friend while we only *see* the other man, and it is
the same with the perception of God. (See John 3:3.)

Jesus Christ is God-Man. God in Essence cannot
come anywhere near us. Almighty God does not matter to me, He is in the clouds. To be of any use to me,
He must come down to the domain in which I live; and
I do not live in the clouds but on the earth. The doctrine
of the Incarnation is that God did come down into our
domain. The Wisdom of God, the Word of God, the

---

8. war: World War I (1914–1918).

exact expression of God, was manifest in the flesh. That is the great doctrine of the New Testament—dust and Deity made one. The pure gold of Deity is of no use to us unless it is amalgamated in the right alloy, viz. the pure Divine working on the basis of the pure human: God and humanity one, as in Our Lord Jesus Christ. There is only one God to the Christian, and His name is Jesus Christ, and in Him we see mirrored what the human race will be like on the basis of Redemption— a perfect oneness between God and man." Jesus Christ has the power of reproducing Himself by regeneration, the power of introducing into us His own heredity, so that dust and Deity again become one.

Solomon sums up the whole thing as follows: If you try to find enjoyment in this order of things, you will end in vexation and disaster. If you try to find enjoyment in knowledge, you only increase your capacity for sorrow and agony and distress. The only way you can find relief and the right interpretation of things as they are is by basing your faith in God, and by remembering that man's chief end is to glorify God and enjoy Him for ever. Jesus Christ is the One Who can transmute everything we come across.

THE REMAINDER OF THE OUTLINE
WAS NOT DEALT WITH.[9]

IN THE THICK OF IT

Ecclesiastes 2

But whoso wants God only and lets life go,
Seeks Him with sorrow and pursues Him far,
And finds Him weeping, and in no long time
Again the High and Unapproachable
Evanishing escapeth, and that man
Forgets the life and struggle of the soul,
Falls from his hope and dreams it was a dream.
Yet back again perforce with sorrow and shame
Who once hath known him must return, not long
Can cease from loving, nor endures alone
The dreadful interspace of dreams and day,
Once quick with God, nor is content as those
Who look into each other's eyes, and seek
To find out strong enough to uphold the earth,
Or sweet enough to make it heaven: aha,
Whom seek they or whom find? For in all the world
There is none but thee, my God, there is none but thee.
                                    Myers[10]

1. The Culture of Revolt (Ecclesiastes 2:1–11)
   (a) Revolt in Every Passion (verses 1–2)
   (b) Restraint in Epicurean Appetite (verse 3)
   (c) Reconstruction in Aestheticism
       (verses 4–10)
   (d) Reaction in Each Affinity (verse 11)

2. The Culture of Restraint (Ecclesiastes 2:12–23)
   (a) Nature of Right Estimation (verses 12–14)

   (b) Nemesis of Reasonable Excellence
       (verses 15–19)
   (c) "Nihilism" of Revolving Experience
       (verses 20–23)

3. The Culture of Religion (Ecclesiastes 2:24–26)
   (a) "The Cult of the Passing Moment"
       (verse 24)
   (b) The Conception of the Prevailing Master
       (verse 25)
   (c) The Centre of Providential Mystery
       (verse 26)

If a man faces actual things as they are and thinks them right out, he must be a pessimist. Most of us are either too thick-headed, or too prejudiced, or too religious, to think right out to the bottom board of things, until the tension comes and obliges us to face them; then we find out who are the men who point the finest way of thinking.

1. The Culture of Revolt *(Ecclesiastes 2:1–11)*
(a) Revolt in every Passion (verses 1–2)
I said in mine heart, Go to now, I will prove thee with mirth, therefore enjoy pleasure: and, behold, this also is vanity. I said of laughter, It is mad: and of mirth, What doeth it?

In this chapter Solomon gives himself up to the philosophical line—Why should not a man take life as he finds it? Solomon was sick of trying to find any ratio-

---

9. Mrs. Chambers' note in the text.
10. F. W. H. Myers (1843–1901): British poet and educator.

nality at the back of things, he revolted from it, and indulged every passion and appetite without restraint. Always distinguish between the man who is naturally given to passion and appetite and the man who goes into these things from revolt. There is an irony and a bitterness and a criminality about the man who does it in revolt. In the same way there is a difference between laughter that is natural and laughter that is a revolt. There is nothing more awful than to hear laughter that is a revolt. The man who discovers that he can find no way out may go into the pigsty and let every passion have its way; but when a man has been gripped by purity and has seen God if only for one minute, he may try and live in a pigsty but he will find he cannot, there is something that produces misery and longing even while he lets loose his passions.

(b) Restraint in Epicurean Appetite (verse 3)

I sought in mine heart to give myself unto wine, yet acquainting mine heart with wisdom; and to lay hold on folly, till I might see what was that good for the sons of men, which they should do under the heaven all the days of their life.

Solomon based all his knowledge of art and education on the desire to satisfy with restraint and wisdom all the natural life of a man. If the basis of life is rational, that should be sufficient. Epicurus was a philosopher of the first order, and he tried to make the basis of life a judicious handling of the pleasures of life, especially the pleasures of the table. "I sought in mine heart to give myself unto wine, yet acquainting mine heart with wisdom," i.e., not living the life of a beast, but trying to find out whether it was possible by judiciously handling the right appetites of life to find satisfaction, but that too was vanity. This was not an experiment a man might think of trying, but an experiment that was tried, and tried by a man who had opportunities such as no one before or since has had of proving it.

(c) Reconstruction in Aestheticism (verses 4–10)

I made me great works; I builded me houses; I planted me vineyards: I made me gardens and orchards, and I planted trees in them of all kinds of fruits: I made me pools of water, to water therewith the wood that bringeth forth trees: I got me servants and maidens, and had servants born in my house; also I had great possessions of great and small cattle above all that were in Jerusalem before me: I gathered me also silver and gold, and the peculiar treasure of kings and of the provinces: I gat me men singers and women singers, and the delights of the sons of men, as musical instruments, and that of all sorts. So I was great, and increased more than all that were before me in Jerusalem: also my wisdom remained with me. And whatsoever mine eyes desired I kept not from

them, I withheld not my heart from any joy; for my heart rejoiced in all my labour: and this was my portion of all my labour.

Solomon indicates in these verses that he reconstructed his life on the aesthetic basis to try and find joy there. On the aesthetic line a man is apt to think he is of a different order from the generality of men, and that whatever pleases his senses is legitimate for him to have. "Whatsoever mine eyes desired I kept not from them." But we have to remember that the first civilisation was founded by a murderer on murder, and that all aesthetic developments are based on that level. The origin of art and poetry and music was with God, but their development has been on a wrong basis, and consequently they have been prostituted away from their true service in a man's life. Aestheticism is all very well for the kingdom of heaven, but it won't do for the kingdom of earth. This is anti-modern view.

(d) Reaction in Each Affinity (verse 11)

Then I looked on all the works that my hands had wrought, and on the labour that I had laboured to do: and, behold, all was vanity and vexation of spirit, and there was no profit under the sun.

This is deep, profound pessimism. All the books of Wisdom in the Bible prove that the only result of sheer thinking on the basis of rationalism is pessimism, fathomlessly profound. The reason most of us are not pessimistic is either that we are religious or we have a temperament that is optimistic. The basis of life is tragic, and the only way out is by a personal relationship to God on the ground of Redemption. Solomon deliberately revolted against everything and found there was no satisfaction in anything he tried.

2. The Culture of Restraint
(Ecclesiastes 2:12–23)
(a) Nature of Right Estimation (verses 12–14)

And I turned myself to behold wisdom, and madness, and folly: for what can the man do that cometh after the king? even that which hath been already done. Then I saw that wisdom excelleth folly, as far as light excelleth darkness. The wise man's eyes are in his head; but the fool walketh in darkness: and I myself perceived also that one event happeneth to them all.

If a man chooses a right path, does that mean he will find joy? No. Job, for instance, found it did not. He believed that God would bless and prosper the man who trusted in Him, but Job's beliefs were flatly contradicted by his actual experience. Solomon says he tried folly, but found it stupid; a man is an idiot to live like a beast; the best thing to do is to make a right estimate of things.

(b) Nemesis of Reasonable Excellence (verses 15–19)

Then I said in my heart, As it happeneth to the fool, so it happeneth even to me; and why was I then more wise? Then I said in my heart, that this also is vanity. For there is no remembrance of the wise more than of the fool for ever; seeing that which now is in the days to come shall all be forgotten. And how dieth the wise man? as the fool. Therefore I hated life; because the work that is wrought under the sun is grievous unto me: for all is vanity and vexation of spirit. Yea, I hated all my labour which I had taken under the sun: because I should leave it unto the man that shall be after me. And who knoweth whether he shall be a wise man or a fool? yet shall he have rule over all my labour wherein I have laboured, and wherein I have shewed myself wise under the sun. This is also vanity.

You may do the right thing, says Solomon, but it will end in disaster; reasonable excellence has the same nemesis as revolt. It is no use trying to find true joy in being either a fool or a wise man. Solomon drives us back every time to the one thing, that a man's chief end is to glorify God and enjoy Him for ever. To-day there is a revolt against the Wisdom of the Hebrews and the wisdom expressed in the New Testament. We don't think on the Bible lines, consequently we talk the most ridiculous platitudes. It is absurd to be an ostrich, Solomon would not allow himself to be one, neither will the man who sees life fair and square as it is to-day.

The only way we can enjoy our "tree of life" is by fulfilling the purpose of our creation. Jesus Christ prayed "that they may have My joy fulfilled in themselves." The thing that kept Jesus Christ all through was not that He held aloof from actual things, but that He had a kingdom within. He so did not hold aloof that when men saw Him they said, "Behold a gluttonous man, and a winebibber, a friend of publicans and sinners!" Our Lord's whole life was rooted and grounded in God, consequently He was never wearied or cynical.

(c) "Nihilism" of Revolving Experience (verses 20–23)

Therefore I went about to cause my heart to despair of all the labour which I took under the sun. For there is a man whose labour is in wisdom, and in knowledge, and in equity: yet to a man that hath not laboured therein shall he leave it for his portion. This also is vanity and a great evil. For what hath man of all his labour, and of the vexation of his heart, wherein he hath laboured under the sun? For all his days are sorrows, and his travail grief; yea, his heart taketh not rest in the night. This is also vanity.

Everything ends the same way, though I have been good and clean and respectable, my end will be the same as the brute. Though I labour all my days, I shall end the same way as the man who has not laboured. These are not wild statements, they are the statements of a man who knew what he was talking about. If Solomon is blind to the issues of life, then the teaching of Christianity is unmitigated nonsense. Some folks are persuaded that it is, they are still cocksure, and have the notion that the kingdom of God can be brought in without the Redemption—all that is needed is to put certain wise restrictions in vogue. Solomon says he tried to do that, but it all ended the same as if he had lived like a fool.

Emerging out of it all comes one Voice—"I am the Way, the Truth, and the Life." The way out is not by intellect nor by aesthetics, but through conscience in contact with Jesus Christ.

3. The Culture of Religion (*Ecclesiastes 2:24–26*)

To serve God in order to gain heaven, is not the teaching of Christianity. Satisfaction cannot be found in gain, but only in a personal relationship to God. The presentation made by a false evangelism is that Jesus Christ taught a man must have his own soul saved, be delivered from hell and get a pass for heaven, and when one is taken and the other left, he must look out that he is the one taken. Could anything be more diametrically opposed to what Jesus Christ did teach, or more unlike the revelation of God given in the Bible? A man is not to serve God for the sake of gain, but to get to the place where the whole of his life is seen as a personal relationship to God.

(a) "The Cult of the Passing Moment" (verse 24)

There is nothing better for a man, than that he should eat and drink, and that he should make his soul enjoy good in his labour. This also I saw, that it was from the hand of God.

One great essential lesson in Christianity is that God's order comes to us in the haphazard. We are men and women, we have appetites, we have to live on this earth, and things do happen by chance; what is the use of saying they do not? "One of the most immutable things on earth is mutability." Your life and mine is a bundle of chance. It is absurd to say it is fore-ordained for you to have so many buttons on your tunic, and if that is not fore-ordained, then nothing is. If things were fore-ordained, there would be no sense of responsibility at all. A false spirituality makes us look to God to perform a miracle instead of doing our duty. We have to see that we do our duty in faith in God. Jesus Christ undertakes to do everything a man cannot do, but not what a man can do. Things do happen by chance, and if we know God, we recognise that His order comes to us in that way. We live in this haphazard order of things, and we have to maintain the abiding order of God in it. The doctrine of the Sacrament teaches the conveying of God's presence to us through the common elements of bread and wine. We are not to seek success or prosperity. If we can get hold of our relationship to God in eating and drinking, we are on the right basis of things.

(b) The Conception of the Prevailing Master (verse 25)

For who can eat, or who else can hasten hereunto, more than I?

The way I eat and drink will show who I regard as my master. Do I regard the restraining wisdom in me as master, or do I regard God as Master? The note of false Christianity is abstinence from marriage and from meats—Live away up on the mount, that is, do what no human being can do. If a man cannot prove his religion in the valley, it is not worth anything. Beware of a religion which makes you neglect the basis of your ordinary life. If you can be a beast, you can also be a son of God. "The Son of man came eating and drinking. . . ." "Have ye here any meat? . . . And He took it, and did eat before them." When once a man has learned to get at God's order in the passing minute and to know that his prevailing Master is God, then he is on the right track. Every other basis ends in disaster.

(c) The Centre of Providential Mystery (verse 26)

For God giveth to a man that is good in his sight wisdom, and knowledge, and joy: but to the sinner He giveth travail, to gather and to heap up, that he may give to him that is good before God. This also is vanity and vexation of spirit.

There is a difference between God's order and God's permissive will. We say that God will see us through if we trust Him—"I prayed for my boy, and he was spared in answer to my prayer." Does that mean that the man who was killed was not prayed for, or that prayers for him were not answered? It is wrong to say that in the one case the man was delivered by prayer but not in the other. It is a misunderstanding of what Jesus Christ reveals. Prayer alters a man on the inside, alters his mind and his attitude to things. The point of praying is not that we get things from God, but that we learn by prayer to detect the difference between God's order and God's permissive will. God's order is—no pain, no sickness, no devil, no war, no sin: His permissive will is all these things, the "soup" we are in just now. What a man needs to do is to get hold of God's order in the kingdom on the inside, and then he will begin to see how to handle the riddle of the universe on the outside.

The problem of the man who deals with practical things is not the problem of the universe, but the problem within his own breast. When I can see where the beast in me will end and where the wise man in me will end; when I have discovered that the only thing that will last is a personal relationship to God; then it will be time for me to solve the problems round about me. When once a man begins to know "the plague of his own heart," it knocks the metaphysics out of him. It is in the actual circumstances of my life that I have to find out whether the wisdom of worshipping God can steer me. Solomon says nothing else can.

IN THE WHIRL

Ecclesiastes 3:1–15

He fixed thee midst this dance
  Of plastic circumstance,
This present thou forsooth would'st fain arrest,
  Machinery just meant
  To give thy soul its bent,
Try thee and turn thee forth, sufficiently impressed.
Then, welcome each rebuff
  That turns earth's smoothness rough,
Each sting that bids nor sit nor stand but go!
  Be our joys three parts pain!
  Strive and hold cheap the strain,
Learn, nor account the pang, dare, never grudge
    the throe.

R. Browning

1. Dispensational Durations (Ecclesiastes 3:1)

2. Dispositional Distresses (Ecclesiastes 3:2–8)
    (a) Personality and Ploughing, Nature and Nations (verse 2)
    (b) Precious and Pernicious Healing (verse 3)
    (c) Priestesses of Death and Delight (verse 4)
    (d) Pleasures and Pains—Domestic and Devotional (verse 5)
    (e) Profitless and Prosperous Commerce (verse 6)
    (f) Programmes of Speech and Silence (verse 7)
    (g) Requited and Unrequited Love (verse 8)

3. Decrees of Despair (Ecclesiastes 3:9–10)

4. Discretions of Deity (Ecclesiastes 3:11–15)
   (a) Reasonableness (verses 11–13)
   (b) Rehabilitation (verses 14–15)

When we are hurt we are apt to become cynical; cynicism is a sign that the hurt is recent. A mature mind is never cynical. Solomon is not speaking cynically; he goes right down to the facts of life, and comes to the conclusion that there is no way out. There is no way out through reason or intellect; the only way out is on the Bible line, viz. Redemption.

Robert Browning wrote from the standpoint of Hebrew wisdom, viz. that of unshakeable confidence in God, but he also wrote with the mind of Solomon or Ibsen or Shakespeare for the actual facts of life. He blinks nothing, yet underneath is the confidence that the basis of a right direction of things is not a man's reason but his strong faith that God is not unjust; and that the man who hangs in to the honour of God will come out all right.

1. Dispensational Durations *(Ecclesiastes 3:1)*
To every thing there is a season, and a time to every purpose under heaven.

The dispensations of God are discernible only to the Spirit of God. If we mistake the dispensations of God to mean something we can see, we are off the track. Solomon is strong on the fact that God has made certain unalterable durations, but he does not say, as St. Augustine and Calvin did, that therefore God is tied up by His own laws. There is a most penetrating criticism of Carlyle[11] by Barry[12]—he said that Carlyle was the intellectual logical result of hyper-Calvinism. Whenever we put theology or a plan of salvation or any line of explanation before a man's personal relationship to God, we depart from the Bible line, because religion in the Bible is not faith in the rule of God, but faith in the God Who rules. If we put our faith in a credal exposition of God and our creed goes to the winds, as, for instance, Job's creed went, our faith will go too. The only thing to do is to "hang in" in confidence in God. "Then will I go. . . unto God, my exceeding joy." Our joy in God depends on what happens. The thing that really sustains is not that we feel happy in God, but that God's joy is our energy, and that when we get out of this "shell" we shall find an explanation that will justify our faith in Him.

There are certain dispensational things for which God is responsible, e.g., birth and death. Inside the limits of birth and death man has liberty to produce what he likes. We base all our thinking and reasoning on space and time, hence our difficulty when we think about God or the Hereafter, we think at once of limits that will not hold after this order of things. There is no space or time with Almighty God. We cannot think beyond the limits of birth and death; if we are to know anything beyond them, it must be by revelation. Before a man can make us understand the symbols he uses, he must take ideas we already have in our minds and put them into new combinations. It is only when we receive a like apocalyptic spirit of St. John or Ezekiel that we can understand what they are talking about. Jesus Christ did not use figurative language in talking about the Hereafter. He said: "Let not your heart be troubled"—"My business is with the Hereafter." Our business is to live a godly life in the present order of things, and not to push out beyond the durations God has placed as limits.

Within the limits of birth and death I can do as I like; but I cannot make myself un-born, neither can I escape death, those two limits are there. I have nothing to do with placing the limits, but within them I can produce what my disposition chooses. Whether I have a distressful time or a joyful time depends on what I do in between the limits of the durations.

"For by Him were all things created" (Colossians 1:16). Did Jesus Christ then create sin? Sin is not a creation, sin is a relationship set up in time between the creation called man and the being who became the devil, whereby man took the rule over himself. My claim to my right to myself—that is the disposition of sin. The Bible reveals that God holds a man responsible for acts of sin he commits, but not for the disposition of sin that he has inherited (see Romans 5:12). God Himself has deliberately accepted the responsibility for sin, and the proof that He has done so is the Cross of Jesus Christ.

In dealing with practical life we find the fundament of tragedy underlying everything. Fatalism means I am the sport of a force about which I know nothing; faith is trust in a God Whose ways I do not know, but Whose character I do know. The Bible point of view is that God is ruling and reigning, and that His character is holy. Though He slay me, yet will I trust in Him"—that is the final heroism of a man's relationship to God.

2. Dispositional Distresses *(Ecclesiastes 3:2–8)*
These verses point out where distresses are produced in a man's ordinary life and the part his disposition

---

11. Thomas Carlyle (1795–1881): Scottish-born literary figure in nineteenth-century England, a writer, biographer, essayist, historian, and critic.
   12. Sir Charles Barry (1795–1860): English architect.

plays in them. Everything to do with a man's personal life, or with agricultural life, or with national life, is summed up in this chapter.

(a) Personality and Ploughing (verse 2)
A time to be born, and a time to die; a time to plant, and a time to pluck up that which is planted.

We cannot do anything without our ruling disposition instantly being marked in it. We gain our point of distress or of joy by the way we use or misuse our twenty-four hours.

(b) Precious and Pernicious Healing (verse 3)
A time to kill, and a time to heal; a time to break down, and a time to build up.

Every art, every healing, and every good, can be used for an opposite purpose. Every possibility I have of producing a fine character in time, I can use to produce the opposite; I have that liberty from the Creator. God will not prevent my disobeying Him; if He did, my obedience would not be worth anything. Some of us complain that God should have made the universe and human life like a foolproof machine, so simple that there would be no possibility of going wrong. If He had, we would have been like jelly-fish. If there is no possibility of being damned, there is no need for salvation.

In the time between birth and death, most of us are in our "shell." There is something in us which makes us peck, and when the crack comes, instead of its being the gentle light and dawn of a new day, it is like a lightning flash. The universe we awaken to is not one of order, but a great big howling confusion, and it takes time to get adjusted. The distresses we reap in between God's decrees for us, we, together with other human beings, are personally responsible for. If we make our life a muddle, it is to a large extent because we have not discerned the great underlying relationship to God.

(c) Priestesses of Death and Delight (verse 4)
A time to weep, and a time to laugh; a time to mourn, and a time to dance.

Solomon runs a contrast between animal nature and human nature. Animals are guided by instinct; human beings are not. I may weave for myself what the Scots mean when they say—"Ye must dree yer weird."[13] There is always a point where I have the power to choose. I have no power to choose whether or not I will take the consequences of my choice; no power to say whether or not I will be born; no power to choose

my "cage"; but within the cage I have power to choose which perch I will sit on. I cannot rule out the fact that between birth and death I have to choose. I have no power to act an act of pure will; to choose whether I will be born or not; but I have power to choose which way I will use the times as they come.

Solomon is indicating the times we make within God's time. This "time," this dispensation, is man's day, and in it we may do and say what we choose. Our talk may sound blatant, but we don't do much.

I can make my domestic life, my bodily life, and my agricultural life a priestess of sorrow or delight if I watch my disposition.

(d) Pleasures and Pains—Domestic and Devotional (verse 5)
A time to cast away stones, and a time to gather stones together; a time to embrace, and a time to refrain from embracing.

Take Solomon in his profundities, and don't make him out to be a beast where he is an archangel. In the Song of Songs he says an extraordinary thing which comes in like a refrain all through—"I adjure you . . . that ye stir not up, nor awaken love, until it please" (RV mg). Many a man has awakened love before the time, and has reaped hell into the bargain. That "time" is in my power, but if I set myself to awaken love before I should, I may have all hell to live with instead of all heaven.

(e) Profitless and Prosperous Commerce (verse 6)
A time to get, and a time to lose; a time to keep, and a time to cast away.

There comes a time when the only way to save what is of enormous value to a life is to cast away all its possessions. "Thy life will I give unto thee for a prey"— you will have nothing else, but you will escape with your life. There is a time when a man may have to lose everything he has got in order to save himself (see Mark 8:35).

(f) Programmes of Speech and Silence (verse 7)
A time to rend, and a time to sew; a time to keep silence, and a time to speak.

Sometimes it is cowardly to speak, and sometimes it is cowardly to keep silence. In the Bible the great test of a man's character is his tongue (see James 1:26). The tongue only came to its right place within the lips of the Lord Jesus Christ, because He never spoke from His right to Himself. He Who was the Wisdom of God Incarnate, said "the words that I speak unto

---

13. *dree yer weird*: Scottish phrase: endure your destiny; suffer your fate.

you, I speak not of Myself," i.e., from the disposition of my right to Myself, but from My relationship to My Father. We are either too hasty or too slow; either we won't speak at all, or we speak too much, or we speak in the wrong mood. The thing that makes us speak is the lust to vindicate ourselves. ". . . leaving you an example, . . . who did no sin neither was guile found in His mouth." Guile has the ingredient of self-vindication in it—My word, I'll make him smart for saying that about me! That spirit never was in Jesus Christ. The great deliverance for a man in time is to learn the programmes of speech and of silence.

(g) Requited and Unrequited Love (verse 8)
A time to love, and a time to hate; a time of war, and a time of peace.

The most painful and most crushing thing to a man or woman is unrequited love. In summing up the attitude of men to Himself, God says that that is the way men treat Him, they "un-requite" His love. To most of us it is a matter of moonshine[14] whether Jesus Christ lived or died or did anything at all; God has to "recommend" His love to us (see Romans 5:8 RV). It is only when we come to our wits' ends, or reap a distress, or feel the first twinge of damnation and are knocked out of our complacent mental agility over things, that we recognise the love of God.

Not one of these "times" are God's times, they are our times. For example, to call war either diabolical or Divine is nonsense; war is human. War is a conflict of wills, not something that can be solved by law or philosophy. If you take what I want, you may talk till all's blue,[15] either I will hit you or you'll hit me. It is no use to arbitrate when you get below into the elemental. In the time between birth and death this conflict of wills will go on until men by their relationship to God receive the disposition of the Son of God, which is holiness.

This is the Hebrew way of summing up in sentence after sentence all that makes a man's life in time. Unless a man relates his disposition to God in between birth and death, he will reap a heritage of distress for himself and for those who come after him. The man who is banked on a real relationship to a personal God will reap not the distress that works death, but the joy of life.

3. Decrees of Despair *(Ecclesiastes 3:9–10)*
What profit hath he that worketh in that wherein he laboureth? I have seen the travail, which God hath given to the sons of men to be exercised in it.

"Honesty is the best policy"; but immediately you are honest for that reason, you cease to be an honest man. "To be a good man means I shall be prosperous"; "to be rightly related to God means I shall be saved." All such considerations as these are beside the mark.

To terrorise a man into believing in God is never the work of God, but the work of human expediency. If we want to convince a congregation of a certain thing, we may use terror to frighten them into it; but never say that is God's way, it is our way. If we do not get conversions one way, then we preach hell fire and produce terror; we don't care what we preach as long as we dominate. To call that God's method is a travesty of the character of God. The methods God uses are indicated in Jesus Christ, and He never terrorised anyone. When He lifted the veil, He said, "How can you escape the damnation of hell?" The decrees of despair lie underneath everything a man does when once he rules out his relationship to God and takes rationalism as the basis of life. Solomon sums up the whole matter—unless a man is rightly related in confidence to God, everything he tries to do will end in despair.

4. Discretions of Deity *(Ecclesiastes 3:11–15)*
Underlying everything we find the discretion and the wisdom of God.

(a) Reasonableness (verses 11–13)
He hath made every thing beautiful in His time: also he hath set the world in their heart, so that no man can find out the work that God maketh from the beginning to the end. I know that there is no good in them, but for a man to rejoice, and to do good in his life. And also that every man should eat and drink, and enjoy the good of all his labour, it is the gift of God.

So that a man cannot in time find out the whole purpose of God. We begin by bringing Almighty God to the bar of judgement and saying—"Why did You make me?" "Who am I?" When we have done our jabbering and disputing we find that the implicit relationship of our personal life which we cannot get at, remains. Then we trace every kind of wisdom but find no direction in it, saving in the Wisdom of the Hebrews which reveals that the real fundamental relationship of our life is that of personal union with God. Until we get there, everything we are related to will go wrong.

"He hath made everything beautiful in His time." And when God gets His time in you and in me, things will be beautiful again. The rationalist says that the only thing for a man to do is to live a reasonable

---

14. moonshine: something insignificant or meaningless.
15. till all's blue: until you're exasperated, blue in the face.

life. A reasonable life and a philosophically rational life are totally different. Jesus Christ taught a reasonable life on the basis of faith in God—Be carefully careless about everything saving your relationship to Me. Don't be disturbed to-day by thoughts about to-morrow, leave to-morrow alone, and bank in confidence on God's organisation of what you do not see. Yesterday is past, there is no road back to it, to-morrow is not; live in the immediate present, and yours is the life of a child. God re-makes things beautiful when He gets His time in us over again. In our "teens" we begin to get into the throes of life and we lose our sense of the beauty of things, and only after the throes when we get into a personal relationship with God do we find again that everything is beautiful. By means of our relationship to God we begin to find out how God works in our lives. In His time it comes, and we begin to spell out the character of God. "This is life eternal, that they should know Thee."

(b) Rehabilitation (verses 14–15)

I know that, whatsoever God doeth, it shall be for ever: nothing can be put to it, nor any thing taken from it: and God doeth it, that men should fear before Him. That which hath been is now; and that which is to be hath already been; and God requireth that which is past.

By the incarnate power of the Son of God, God rebuilds by degree the whole relationship of things, bringing everything back into oneness with Himself. That is the meaning of Redemption—God has done His "bit." Sin is man's "bit." God's plan and design is not altered, but in the meantime man is countering it by his own design—We can bring it out in our own way. God is infinitely patient. He says over and over again—Not that way, My son, this is the way for you, a moral relationship to Myself. "He, that being often reproved hardeneth his neck, shall suddenly be destroyed, and that without remedy." God will not prevent my breaking my back; if He sees I am determined to go my own way, He won't stop me; but when my neck is broken, He lifts me up and moves me where He wants, no difficulty now. "The sacrifices of God are a broken spirit." When my heart is broken, the husk of individual relationship is merged into a personal relationship, and I find that God rehabilitates everything, i.e., He puts things back into their right fittings in me.

"There is nothing covered, that shall not be revealed: and hid, that shall not be known." There is no man but has some spot in his life where there is something dear, something that is a truth to him, a real wonderful possession full of light and liberty and joy, the finest spot in his experience. Jesus Christ says that ultimately through patience and by deliberately going on with God, everything that is now obscure will be as clear as that one spot. Will we "hang in" in patience? If we do, we shall see everything rehabilitated, and shall justify God in everything He has allowed.

Jesus Christ deliberately chose "the long, long trail"; we choose "the short cut," and continually go wrong until we understand the meaning of the 23rd Psalm, "The LORD is my shepherd, He leads me in the right paths." It looked as if the way was leading nowhere but beside still waters and green pastures; but I begin to see that it is all unfolding one thing, viz. a personal relationship to God, which is the meaning of a man's life. The Bible declares that what is true in personal life will be true in material life; there will be "new heavens and a new earth." The Utopian visions of socialists and atheists, dreamers and Christians, are all the same, there is no difference in their vision of a united human race, a perfect order of equity, everything in perfect harmony, But how is it to come about? We are all "in the soup" just now. No nation under heaven believes it is going to be brought about in Jesus Christ's way on the basis of Redemption. We all believe it will be brought about by a line of things that has yet to be tried, viz. Socialism.* We are on the verge of trying it, and it will be the nearest and the finest approach to fulfilling the vision; but at the point where it seems nearest fulfilment, it will make the biggest departure.

Where did the Christ come from historically? From the people called the Jews. The blasphemy of a Gentile like Voltaire is futile; no Gentile can blaspheme, because no Gentile knows God in the way the Jew does. It takes the race that produced Jesus to produce Judas; and it will take the race that produced Christ to produce the anti-Christ. We are on the verge of this discovery. We are insular and closed in, and are looking in the wrong direction for the great big thing to come, instead of taking the Bible revelation. Abide in your relationship to God, and you will see that the "anti" comes on the same line as the positive.

---

* "The vision of Socialism is magnificent; there are benedictions and blessings for mankind on the line of Socialism which have never been yet; but if once the root is cut from Redemption, it will be one of the most frantic forms of despotic tyranny the human race has ever known. It looks like the lamb, but when the big crisis comes, it gives life to the beast."—*The Shadow of an Agony*, p. 97. O.C.—*Footnote in original text*

IN THE DISCIPLINE OF DISCOURAGEMENT
Ecclesiastes 3:16–22

Glory of warrior, glory of orator, glory of song,
   Paid with a voice flying by to the lost on an
    endless sea
Glory of virtue, to fight, to struggle, to right the
   wrong
   Nay, but she aim'd not at glory, no lover of
    glory she:
Give her the glory of going on, and still to be.
The wages of sin is death: if the wages of Virtue
   be dust,
   Would she have heart to endure for the life of
    the worm and the fly?
She desires no isles of the blest, no quiet seats of
   the just,
   To rest in a golden grove, or to bask in a
    summer sky:
Give her the wages of going on, and not to die.
                      Tennyson

1. The Perversion of Realised Ambition
   (Ecclesiastes 3:16)

2. The Prevailing of Righteous Authority
   (Ecclesiastes 3:17)

3. The Parallel of Perishableness (Ecclesiastes
   3:18–21)

4. The Probation of Reasonable Activity
   (Ecclesiastes 3:22)

"Discouragement is disenchanted egotism" (Mazzini), i.e., the heart knocked out of self-love; I expected things to go this way and they have not, so I shall give it all up.

1. The Perversion of Realised Ambition
(Ecclesiastes 3:16)
And moreover I saw under the sun the place of judgement, that wickedness was there; and the place of righteousness, that iniquity was there.

All through history we find it frequently happen that when a man realises his ambition, he turns it into diabolical perversity right off the reel. In the Bible the conviction is that the basis of human life is in the hand of God, not in the hand of human reason, and that an exalted position, moral, mental or spiritual, makes a man either more Godlike or more devil-like, and that by the decree of God and not by chance. When a man has mounted high and has the satisfaction of having fulfilled his ambition, he is compelled to be either a great humble man or a diabolical fiend.

Solomon is pointing out that when a man realises his ambition, he may pervert it and become tyrannical. Unless kings and rulers are God-fearing men, they may become tyrants of the wildest order.

One of the great stirring truths of the Bible is that the man who looks for justice from others is a fool. In moral and spiritual life if a man has a sense of injustice, he ceases to be of value to his fellow men. Never waste your time looking for justice; if you do you will soon put yourself in bandages and give way to self-pity. Our business is to see that no one suffers from our injustice.

The man who has satisfied his ambition may suddenly become a miserable tyrant and all his joy will go. "These things have I spoken unto you," said Jesus, "that My joy may be in you" (RV). What joy did Jesus have? He failed apparently in everything He came to do; all His disciples forsook Him, He was crucified, and yet He talked of His joy. The joy of Our Lord lay in doing what the Father sent Him to do. His purpose was not to succeed, but to fulfil the design of His coming—"For I am come down from heaven not to do Mine own will, but the will of Him that sent Me" (RV).

What is the real design of man's creation? Solomon deals with every possible phase of life—metaphysics, philosophy, religion, commercial prosperity, moral integrity not as guesswork, he had been through it all, no one has the wisdom of Solomon, and his verdict is that it all ends in disaster. That is the summing up of it all unless a man sees that his "chief end is to glorify God and enjoy Him for ever," and it takes a long while to get there. To put things on any other basis will end in disaster.

2. The Prevailing of Righteous Authority
(Ecclesiastes 3:17)
I said in mine heart, God shall judge the righteous and the wicked: for there is a time there for every purpose and for every work.

"God shall judge the righteous and the wicked." But Who is God? I have never seen God, or spoken to Him. An omnipresent, omniscient, omnipotent Being does not amount to anything to me; He is an abstract finding of a man's intellect. Can God take on hands and feet and man's ways of doing things, and manifest Himself on the plane on which we live? The Bible says that that is what God did do. Jesus Christ lived a human life on this earth, and He exhibited a disposition not yours and not mine. Any man who does not

hoodwink himself knows perfectly well that he has not a disposition like Jesus Christ's. We have only to read the Sermon on the Mount and see God's demand for a fathomlessly pure heart, to know that. What Jesus Christ exhibited was not omnipotence and omniscience and omnipresence, but absolute holiness in human flesh, and He said "he that hath seen Me hath seen the Father." Jesus Christ is the Judge. "The Father . . . hath given all judgement unto the Son" (John 5:22 RV).

Would I be concerned if my "cobber" were handed over to Jesus Christ to be judged, handed over to the Being Who paid the price of Redemption, Who lived the spell of God's dispensation between birth and death on the plane on which we live, and manifested an unsulliedly holy life, the Being Who claims He can put His own disposition into me, the One Who says "I am the first and the last," the One to Whom all judgement has been given? or would I be prepared to trust His honour and stake everything on Him?

We cannot judge ourselves by ourselves or by anyone else, there is always one fact more in everyone's life that we do not know. We cannot put men into types, we are never at the balance of one another's heredity; therefore the judgement cannot lie with us. Solomon says that God's judgement is right and true and that a man can rest his heart there. It is a great thing to notice the things we cannot answer just now, and to waive our judgement about them. Because you cannot explain a thing, don't say there is nothing in it. There are dark and mysterious and perplexing things in life, but the prevailing authority at the back of all is a righteous authority, and a man does not need to be unduly concerned. When we do find out the judgement of God, we shall be absolutely satisfied with it to the last degree, we won't have another word to say—"that Thou mightest be justified when Thou speakest, and be clear when Thou judgest."

In the meantime God has something from which to clear His character when we see Him—"and God shall wipe away all tears from their eyes." There is no problem, no personal grief, no agony or distress (and God knows there are some fathomless agonies just now—awful injustices and wrongs and evils and nobility all mixed up together) but will have an overwhelming explanation one day. If we will hang in to the fact that God is true and loving and just, every judgement He passes will find us in agreement with it finally.

Solomon is saying from his pre-Incarnation standpoint that every man when he sees the judgement of God untrammelled[16] by bodily limitations, will say that God was perfectly right in all He allowed. Can any one of us say now that God's character is clear? It is ridiculous to pin our faith to a creed

about God. The experience of Job is a proof that creeds must go. Every now and again we have to outgrow our creeds. Morally it is better to be an atheist than to believe in a God whom "to be God is not fit."

3. The Parallel of Perishableness *(Ecclesiastes 3:18–21)*

I said in mine heart concerning the estate of the sons of men, that God might manifest them, and that they might see that they themselves are beasts. For that which befalleth the sons of men befalleth beasts; even one thing befalleth them: as the one dieth, so dieth the other; yea, they have all one breath; so that a man hath no preeminence above a beast: for all is vanity. All go unto one place; all are of the dust, and all turn to dust again. Who knoweth the spirit of man that goeth upward, and the spirit of the beast that goeth downward to the earth?

There is a philosophy which says that if a man wills it, he need never die; but he cannot will it! There is a limit to will; no man can will pure will. Solomon is saying you may do what you like, but you will die like a dog. He is dealing with the spell of our actual lives; we all die. It is humiliating for our predications to remember that although the spirit of man is indestructible, the phase of life which we bank on naturally passes. We may have labour in it, and delight and satisfaction in it, but it will all pass. When a beast dies, his body disappears and his soul goes downwards into entire nature; the spirit of a man goes straight back to God Who made it; it is never absorbed into God.

The essence of Christianity is not adherence to principles; but a personal relationship to God through Jesus Christ at work in the whole of my life. The people who influence us are not those who set out to do it, they are prigs; but the folk who have a real relationship to God and who never bother whether they are being of use; these are a continual assistance.

4. The Probation of Reasonable Activity *(Ecclesiastes 3:22)*

Wherefore I perceive that there is nothing better, than that a man should rejoice in his own works; for that is his portion: for who shall bring him to see what shall be after him?

The basis of things is not rational. Reason is our guide among facts but reason cannot explain facts. Reason and logic and intellect have to do with the time between birth and death, but they can give no explanation of before birth or after death. All we infer of either is speculation; it may be interesting but it is apt to blind us to the facts. Solomon deals with the expression of practical life as it is, and he finds it a sorry mess. He

---

16. untrammelled: free, unhindered, not entangled.

says it is a philosophic plaster to say that when a man gives up a thing he makes it easier for those who come after him; a man does not find his true joy in sacrificing or in sin or in labour. We may be laying the foundations for those who come after us, but "who shall bring him to see what shall be after him?" It sounds all right, but is there any enjoyment in it? True enjoyment is not in what we do but in our relationships. If a man is true to God, everything between birth and death will work out on the line of joy. If we bank on what we do, whether it is good or bad, we are off the track; the one thing that matters is personal relationship.

What, then, are we to do in our ordinary active life? It is not a question of making it easy for those who come after us, but of what a man is to do in the spell between birth and death. According to Our Lord's teaching, a man has to base his life on his relationship to God and live according to that relationship with the simple gaiety of a child. If we apply the Sermon on the Mount to our ideas of individual and national life we shall find how we ignore what Our Lord teaches. Wherever Christianity comes straight home to us, we ignore it; when it gets at others, we preach it for all we are worth. The general history of Christianity is that it has been tried and abandoned because it is found to be difficult; but wherever it has been tried and honourably gone on with, it has never failed.

Our civilisation is based on the foundation of murder—the first civilisation was founded by Cain; and civilised life is a vast, complicated, more or less gilded-over system of murder. This does not mean that civilisation can never be just and right. The Bible speaks of a "holy city," a "new earth," and reveals that it is to be brought about by the man who lives his life based on God in all his relationships and does not worry about what he is going to do later.

When we study Hebrew wisdom we see how terrifically far we have degenerated away from God and from confidence in God. Nowadays the almighty microbe has blotted God out of His heaven. When we come to the "soup" we are in just now, the catastrophic earthquake that is blasting the whole globe to bits, all we can do is to put on plasters and borrow opportunist phrases. According to Hebrew Wisdom, the thing to do is to bank on our faith in God, and where our duty lies do it like a man "and damn the consequences."

When in doubt physically, dare; when in moral doubt, stop; when in spiritual doubt, pray; and when in personal doubt, be guided by your life with God. Base all on God, and slowly and surely the actual life will be educated along the particular line of your relationship to Him.

ON WINKING THE OTHER EYE

Ecclesiastes 4

Why do they prate of the blessings of Peace?
*   we have made them a curse,*
Pickpockets, each hand lusting for all that is not
*   its own;*
And lust of gain, in the spirit of Cain, is it better
*   or worse*
Than the heart of the citizen hissing in war on
*   his own hearthstone?*
Sooner or later I too may passively take the print
Of the golden age—why not? I have neither hope
*   nor trust;*
May make my heart as a millstone, set my face as
*   a flint,*
Cheat and be cheated, and die; who knows?
*   we are ashes and dust.*
Tennyson

1. The Oppression of Tyranny (Ecclesiastes 4:1–3)

2. The Oppression of Trade (Ecclesiastes 4:4)

3. The Oppression of Idling (Ecclesiastes 4:5–6)

4. The Obsession of Solitariness (Ecclesiastes 4:7–8)

5. The Optimism of Society (Ecclesiastes 4:9–12)

6. The Occasion of Sagacity and Stubbornness (Ecclesiastes 4:13–16)

The title of this chapter indicates the treachery that is in you and in me, and consequently in the other fellow! One of the first things to develop in a boy is the realisation that he can "do" someone.

Solomon will not allow us to imagine that life is other than full of cunning and craft and deception. The "babe in the wood" idea does not hold—"I don't know how he could do it!" Not one of us has a single[17] motive; the only One Who had a single motive was Jesus Christ, and the miracle of His Redemption is that He can put a single motive into any man. There is no cunning in the Sermon on the Mount. As long as we deal on the line of craft and cunning, Jesus Christ is no good to us. We can easily make a fool of goodness. The romance of the life of a disciple is not an external fascination but an inner martyrdom.

Tennyson and Browning and Carlyle all write as men who see things without the glamour of temperament or religion or conceit. To look at life as it is, and to think of it as it is, must make a man a pessimist. If we are not pessimistic, it is either because we are generally thick-headed and do not think, or because we have temperaments that are optimistic. If we face things as they are, we shall find that true optimism comes from a source other than temperament. According to Solomon, it comes from applying Hebrew Wisdom. To-day we are bothered over finding out whether there is a God and what is the origin of things. Solomon faces facts as they are.

1. The Oppression of Tyranny *(Ecclesiastes 4:1–3)*

So I returned, and considered all the oppressions that are done under the sun: and behold the tears of such as were oppressed, and they had no comforter; and on the side of their oppressors there was power; but they had no comforter. Wherefore I praised the dead which are already dead more than the living which are yet alive. Yea, better is he than both they, which hath not yet been, who hath not seen the evil work that is done under the sun.

In this chapter Solomon deals with injustice and tyranny; over-reaching and craftiness. Verses 1–3 are a statement of things as they are. The spell between birth and death is mine, and I along with other human beings make the kind of life I live. I cannot make it independently of other wills, unless I happen to be a Napoleon or a Kaiser and bind my will on everything under my power.

The oppression of tyranny means that I drive my will on other people, and if they do not do what I want, I break them. It is an oppression in which one power crushes another. "The tears of such as were oppressed"—nothing can heal them. Think of the devastations and havoc throughout the world just now. What is going to make up to the people who are broken? To say that "every cloud has a silver lining" is a kind lie. Unless a man can get into a relationship with the God Whom the Bible reveals, life is not worth living. Most of us are mercifully shielded, we are not sensitive enough to feel or to experience the terrific things that Solomon experienced and saw in his lifetime; we see things through coloured, or cynical, glasses, but the cynic's standpoint is not a true one, it distorts things. In human life as it is, the oppression of tyranny has the biggest run. Take the things we experience out of our own circle where they are balanced by domestic affections, into a setting where these things do not count, and see if Solomon is drawing a long bow.[18] Jesus Christ in His day submitted to the providential order of tyranny represented by Pilate (see John 18:36; 19:10–11); He saw that tyranny was inevitable because the nation to which He belonged had fallen from the standard it should have lived up to.

"And God shall wipe away all tears from their eyes." There will come one day a personal and direct touch from God when every tear and perplexity, every oppression and distress, every suffering and pain, and wrong and justice will have a complete and ample and overwhelming explanation. The Christian faith is exhibited by the man who has the spiritual courage to say that that is the God he trusts in, and it takes some moral backbone to do it. It is easier to attempt to judge everything in the span between birth and death.

2. The Oppression of Trade *(Ecclesiastes 4:4)*

Again, I considered all travail, and every right work, that for this a man is envied of his neighbour. This is also vanity and vexation of spirit.

If you go back to the origin of civilisation, you find it was founded by a murderer. Among the good things, the shielding and protecting things, that are the outcome of civilisation, what Solomon mentions is always to be found, viz. the crushing of someone in order to get gain. It may be done kindly or brutally, but the basis of success must be the crushing of something or someone. There is a rivalry between men, and we have made it a good thing; we have made ambition and competition the very essence of civilised life. No wonder there is no room for Jesus Christ, and no room for the Bible. We are all so scientifically orthodox nowadays, so materialistic and certain that rationalism is the basis of things, that we make the Bible out to be the most revolutionary, unorthodox and heretical of books. Jesus Christ echoes Solomon's attitude: "For a man's life consisteth not in the abundance of the things which he possesseth."

---

17. single: pure; unmixed.
18. drawing a long bow: exaggerating, telling unlikely stories.

At the basis of trade and civilised life lie oppression and tyranny. Whether you are king or subject, says Solomon, you cannot find joy in any system of civilised life, or in trade and commerce; for underneath there is a rivalry that stings and bites, and the kindest man will put his heel on his greatest friend. These are not the blind statements of a disappointed man, but statements of facts discerned by the wisest man that ever lived.

3. The Oppression of Idling
(Ecclesiastes 4:5–6)
The fool foldeth his hands together, and eateth his own flesh. Better is an handful with quietness, than both the hands full with travail and vexation of spirit.

"The best thing to do is to be a Bohemian and have nothing to do with civilised life; to live from hand to mouth and not do a hand's turn." This has been a cult in every age of civilised life. We have seen it in our own day in Charles Wagner[19] and his plea for a simple life, and in Walt Whitman and Thoreau, who advocated the simple life on a higher line. When a man is fed up with a certain line of things, he revolts and goes to the opposite extreme. To-day tyranny and oppression have eaten into men's sense of justice, and they have revolted and gone to the other extreme.

Solomon tried first of all to get at the secret of things through philosophy and thinking; then he revolted into a reign of animal passion; then as king he insisted on good laws, but found he was oppressing the life out of the people; then he realised the tyranny of trade and tried idling, but found that that too oppressed.

In all trade and commerce there is oppression, and we try to justify it by saying that the weakest must go to the wall.[20] But is that so? Where are the mighty civilisations of other days? Where are the prehistoric animals, those colossal powerful creatures? It is they that have gone to the wall. The great blunder in all kingdoms amongst men is that we will demand strong men, consequently each kingdom in its turn goes to the wall because no chain is stronger than its weakest link. Jesus Christ founded His Kingdom on the weakest link of all—a Baby, "Marvel not that I said unto thee, Ye must be born anew" (RV). Consequently the gates of hell cannot prevail against His Kingdom.

4. The Obsession of Solitariness
(Ecclesiastes 4:7–8)
Then I returned, and I saw vanity under the sun. There is one alone, and there is not a second; yea, he hath neither child nor brother: yet is there no end of all his labour; neither is his eye satisfied with riches; neither saith he, For whom do I labour and bereave my soul of good? This is also vanity, yea, it is a sore travail.

There is such a thing as an obsession of solitariness. Hermits, ascetics and celibates cut themselves off in revolt—"Because I cannot find peace or joy or happiness in the tyranny of civilised life or in commerce, and I cannot be an idle tramp, I become a solitary and live a sequestered life." Solomon points out what history has proved that this is an experiment that ends disastrously, because a man cannot shut out what is inside by cutting himself off from the outside. Jesus Christ was not a solitary man—"The Son of man came eating and drinking, and they say, Behold, a man gluttonous and a winebibber, a friend of publicans and sinners!" John the Baptist was a solitary man—"For John came neither eating nor drinking, and they say, He hath a devil."

"Oh that I had wings like a dove! Then would I fly away, and be at rest" (RV). The desire is to be solitary—"If only I could get away and be quiet; if only I could live in a sunrise or a sunset!" We have to find our true life in things as they are with that on the inside which keeps us right. The true energy of life lies in being rightly related to God, and only there is true joy found.

It is an interesting study in psychology to watch people who are engaged in drastic social and rescue work and find out whether they are doing it for a surcease from their own troubles, to get relief from a broken heart. In a great many cases the worker wants a plaster for his own life. He takes up slum work, not because it is the great passion of his life, but because he must get something to deliver him from the gnawing pain of his own heart. The people he works amongst are often right when they say he is doing it to save his own soul.

5. The Optimism of Society (Ecclesiastes 4:9–12)
Two are better than one; because they have a good reward for their labour. For if they fall, the one will lift up his fellow: but woe to him that is alone when he falleth; for he hath not another to help him up. Again, if two lie together, then they have heat: but how can one be warm alone? And if one prevail against him, two shall withstand him; and a three-fold cord is not quickly broken.

The conclusion that Solomon comes to is that trade is better than idling; that both solitariness and society as it is are pretty bad, but that society is better than solitariness. Domestic life and married life and com-

---

19. Charles Wagner (1852–1918): Protestant cleric and writer in Paris; authored *The Simple Life*, published in 1904.
20. go to the wall: fail; lose.

radeship are all advocated by Solomon (cf. 1 Timothy 4:1–3). The Bible always emphasises the facts of life as they are. Whenever Jesus Christ applied His teaching to actual life He focused it round two points—marriage and money. If the religion of Jesus Christ and the indwelling of the Spirit of God cannot deal with these things and keep a man and woman as God wants them to be, His religion is useless.

6. The Occasion of Sagacity and Stubbornness *(Ecclesiastes 4:13–16)*

Better is a poor and a wise child than an old and foolish king, who will no more be admonished. For out of prison he cometh to reign; whereas also he that is born in his kingdom becometh poor. I considered all the living which walk under the sun, with the second child that shall stand up in his stead. There is no end of all the people, even of all that have been before them: they also that come after shall not rejoice in him. Surely this also is vanity and vexation of spirit.

It is a disastrous thing for a man never to be ragged, an appalling thing to be a privileged young man! A lad who has been his mother's pet and has been brought up like a hothouse plant is totally unprepared for the scathing of life as it is, and when he is flung out into the rugged realities of life, he suffers intolerably. Conceive the suffering of a lad who has been sheltered, never had anything go against him, never been thwarted, when the tension does come. It is better to be a wise youth who can stand being ragged and taken down. One can always recognise the lad who has not been with others, he will not be admonished, consequently you cannot warn him.

Solomon says whether you are wise or foolish, upright or not, a king or tyrannised over by a king, successful or a failure, in society or solitary, stubborn or sagacious, all alike ends the same way. All is passing,

and we cannot find our lasting joy in any element we like to touch. It is disastrous for a man to try and find his true joy in any phase of truth, or in the fulfilment of ambition, or in physical or intellectual solitariness, or in society; he will find his joy only in a personal relationship to God. That relationship was expounded by Jesus Christ when He said—"If any man cometh unto Me, and hateth not his own father, and mother, and wife, and children, and brethren, and sisters, yea, and his own life also, he cannot be My disciple" (RV). Our first concern is to be personally related to God. Jesus Christ is God manifested in human flesh, and we have to ignore to the point of hatred anything that competes with our relationship to Him.

When once a man is there, he receives a hundredfold more of all he gave up to get there, and he never demands an infinite satisfaction from those other relationships. The man or woman who does not know God demands an infinite satisfaction from other human beings which they cannot give, and in the case of the man, he becomes tyrannical and cruel. It springs from this one thing, the human heart must have satisfaction, but there is only one Being Who can satisfy the last abyss of the human heart, and that is the Lord Jesus Christ. When once a man or woman is rightly related to Him, the one never demands the impossible from the other, everything is in its right place. "If any man would come after Me, let him deny himself" (RV), i.e., deny his right to himself. The essence of sin is self-realisation, my prideful right to myself. The disposition that ought to rule is God's right to me, i.e., Christ-realisation.

It takes a long time for any one of us to realise our need of Jesus Christ personally, and it takes a nation a long time to realise that the only way things can be put right is not on the basis of rationalism, but only on the basis of Redemption. The Bible is neither obsolete nonsense nor poetic blether: it is a universe of revelation facts.

"A MAN'S REACH SHOULD EXCEED HIS GRASP"

Ecclesiastes 5:1–7

Glory about thee, without thee; and thou fulfillest
*   thy doom*
Making Him broken gleams, and a stifled
*   splendour and gloom,*
Speak to him thou for He hears, and Spirit with
*   Spirit can meet*
Closer is He than breathing, and nearer than
*   hands and feet.*

                                    Tennyson

1. The Rectitude of Ritualism v. "Rutualism" (Ecclesiastes 5:1)

2. The Rashness of Reaction v. Recollectedness of Religion (Ecclesiastes 5:2)

3. The Refrainings of Reverence (Ecclesiastes 5:3)

4. The Repudiation of Responsibility (Ecclesiastes 5:4–6)

5. Recklessness v. Resoluteness of Righteousness (Ecclesiastes 5:7)

If we try to find lasting joy in any human relationship it will end in vanity, something that passes like a morning cloud. The true joy of a man's life is in his relationship to God, and the great point of the Hebrew confidence in God is that it does not unfit a man for his actual life. That is always the test of a false religion.

1. The Rectitude of Ritualism v. "Rutualism" (Ecclesiastes 5:1)

Keep thy foot when thou goest to the house of God, and be more ready to hear, than to give the sacrifice of fools: for they consider not that they do evil.

There is a use for ritual in a man's religious life. Because a thing is necessary at one time of life, it does not follow that it is necessary all through. There may be times when ritual is a good thing and other times when it is not. Bear in mind that in the Hebrew religion there is an insistence on ecclesiasticism and ritual. In the New Testament that is finished with (see John 4:21–24); but Ezekiel prophesies that the true worship of God will yet be established on earth as it has never yet been, and there will be ritual then to an extraordinary degree.

In the present day the revolt is against ritual and form; with the average man ritual is at a discount. There is a time in a healthy religious[21] when the revolt is right. In the history of the salvation of a man's soul it may be better for him to worship in a whitewashed building, with a bare rugged simplicity of service; but while it is true that a man may go through forms and ceremonies and be a downright hypocritical humbug, it is also true that he may despise ritual and be as big a humbug. When a man is in a right relationship to God ritual is an assistance; the place of worship and the atmosphere are both conducive to worship. We are apt to ignore that ritual is essential in a full-orbed religious life, that there is a rectitude in worship only brought about by the right use of ritual. For instance, when Jesus Christ taught His disciples to pray, He gave them a form of prayer which He knew would be repeated through the Christian centuries.

2. The Rashness of Reaction Recollectedness of Religion (Ecclesiastes 5:2)

Be not rash with thy mouth, and let not thine heart be hasty to utter any thing before God; for God is in heaven, and thou upon earth: therefore let thy words be few. (RV)

When you have been through a bereavement, or have thought you would be found out in a wrong and

were not, there is the danger of reacting into a rash spell of devotion. You read your Bible and say things to God, but there is no reality in it. It is like the reaction of a man after a drinking bout, he mistakes his remorse for repentance. Repentance is not a reaction, remorse is. Remorse is—I will never do the thing again. Repentance is that I deliberately become the opposite to what I have been.

Solomon says—Beware of this kind of religiousness; don't be rash with your mouth, hold yourself in. When you go into the presence of God, remember it is not to be in a passing mood; everything a man says to God is recognised by God and held clear in his record. Solomon indicates that it is better to have nothing to do with religious life than to talk religion in rashness only. "These are they who, when they have heard the word, immediately receive it with gladness; and have no root in themselves, and so endure but for a time."

In this war there has been less of the rashness of reaction than might be supposed; it has rather been the opposite way. Many a man when he has had the "bivvers" (i.e., a mixture of fear and cowardice and a determination to go through) has said, "I feel inclined to look at my Bible; but no, I haven't read it before and I won't now." Again, a man may suddenly in the rashness of reaction pretend he is religious; but there is nothing in it. The characteristic of true religion is recollectedness; pull yourself together, stop wool-gathering, and remember that you are in the presence of God.

3. The Refrainings of Reverence (Ecclesiastes 5:3)

For a dream cometh through the multitude of business; and a fool's voice is known by the multitude of words.

If you are busy in your daily life, the dreams you have at night may be simply the refractions of the "multitude of business." Any amount of futile religion is based on this line of things—"I have been eating too much, but now Lent has come and I will fast for a time." There is nothing genuine in it, it has not the grip of God about it. When a man comes into the presence of God he refrains himself and remembers that he is not there to suffer from his own reactions, to get comfort for himself, to pray along the line of "O Lord, bless me." He is there to refrain from his own personal needs and to get into the scope of God's outlook.

4. The Repudiation of Responsibility (Ecclesiastes 5:4–6)

When thou vowest a vow unto God, defer not to pay it; for he hath no pleasure in fools: pay that which thou hast

---

21. religious (noun): a person bound by monastic vows.

vowed. Better is it that thou shouldest not vow, than that thou shouldest vow and not pay. Suffer not thy mouth to cause thy flesh to sin; neither say thou before the angel, that it was an error: wherefore should God be angry at thy voice, and destroy the work of thine hands?

At the end of the year we hear much about vowing. Solomon's advice is—Don't vow, for if you make a vow even in ordinary matters and do not keep it, you are the worse for it. If you make an engagement to meet a man and don't fulfil it, you suffer for it. It will mean a defect in your general make-up. It is better not to promise, better to be uncertain, than to promise and not fulfil. We are all apt to be like Rip Van Winkle and say—"I won't count this time." We reap terrific damage to our own characters when we vow and do not perform. You may not take account of the fact that you made an engagement and did not keep it; but your nerves do, the record is there. Solomon's counsel in practical life as well as in religious life is—never make a vow unless at all costs you carry it through. Promises are a way of shirking responsibility. We can get over an unpleasant interview by promising to do a thing; but it is an appalling thing to say "Yes, I will," and then not do it. Don't pile up vows before men, and certainly not before God.

Jesus Christ was stern along this line. "No man, having put his hand to the plough, and looking back, is fit for the kingdom of God." When Hezekiah was sick he vowed a vow before God—"I shall go softly [as in a solemn procession, RV mg], all my years"; but when he was out of danger he forgot all about his vow. To face death day in and day out, as men do in war, is a different matter from facing sickness or an accident. If you have had a narrow escape and have come through, don't be rash in reaction; don't promise and make vows, but look to God and bank on the reality of Jesus Christ.

One of the dangers in modern evangelism is that it lays the emphasis on decision for Christ instead of on surrender to Jesus Christ. That to me is a grave blunder. When a man decides for Christ he usually puts his confidence in his own honour, not in Christ at all. No man can keep himself a Christian, it is impossible; it is God Who keeps a man a Christian. Many a man is kept away from Jesus Christ by honesty—"I won't be able to keep it up." If Christianity depends on decisions for Christ, it is better to keep away from it; but Our Lord tells us to come to Him because we are not able to decide—a very different proposition. Jesus Christ came for the weak, for the ungodly and the sinful, and He says, "Blessed are the poor in spirit," not—"Blessed is the man who has the power to decide and to keep his vow." Jesus Christ calls the man who says—"I cannot do it; others may have the strength, but I haven't." Jesus Christ says to such, "Blessed are you." It is not our vows before God that tell, but our coming before God, exactly as we are in all our weakness, and being held and kept by God.

8. Recklessness v. Resoluteness of Righteousness *(Ecclesiastes 5:7)*
For in the multitude of dreams and many words there are also divers vanities: but fear thou God.

There is such a thing as being haunted on the inside of the life. It begins when a man tampers with the borders of spiritualism and communicates with supernatural powers; he opens the unconscious part of his personality to all kinds of powers he cannot control. The only cure is to fear God, to be rightly related to God, and these fears and hauntings will go. "Put on the whole armour of God." When a man is related to God through Jesus Christ, God protects not only the conscious life but the unconscious life as well. Unless a man is guarded by God, there are forces that can find their way into the unconscious domain. There are dreams and influences that tamper with a man's life and leave him a haunted man. No man has any right to make curiosity, which is his guide in intellectual life, his guide in moral life. No man ever does it without falling. It is a terrible thing to be haunted, to have your own conscience laugh at you. When we are related to God, He guards from dangers seen and unseen. The man who fears God has nothing else to fear, he is guarded in his conscious and unconscious life, in his waking and his sleeping moments.

THE TRIUNE—DUST, DRUDGERY, DEITY
Ecclesiastes 5:8–20

Ah, make the most of what we yet may spend,
Before we too into the Dust descend;
*   Dust into Dust, and under Dust to lie*
Sans Wine, sans Song, sans Singer, and—sans End!

Alike for those who for To-day prepare,
And those that after a To-morrow stare,
*   A Muezzin from the Tower of Darkness cries,*
"Fools! your reward is neither Here nor There."
Omar Khayyám

1. Providential Order of Tyranny (Ecclesiastes 5:8)
2. Profit Ordained of Tillage (Ecclesiastes 5:9)
3. Profitless Possession of Treasure (Ecclesiastes 5:10–11)
4. Peace Out of Toil (Ecclesiastes 5:12)
5. Possessions Outwitting Trust (Ecclesiastes 5:13–14)
6. Personality the Only Truth (Ecclesiastes 5:15–17)
7. Predominant Obligation in Time (Ecclesiastes 5:18–20)

God made man a mixture of dust and Deity—"And the LORD God formed man of the dust of the ground, and breathed into his nostrils the breath of life; and man became a living soul" (Genesis 2:7). The dust of a man's body is his glory, not his shame. Jesus Christ manifested Himself in that dust, and He claims that He can presence any man with His own divinity. The New Testament teaches us how to keep the body under and make it a servant. Robert Browning of all the poets is the one who insists that we make headway not in spite of the flesh, but because of the flesh, and in no other way.

Drudgery is the outcome of sin, but it has no right to be the rule of life. It becomes the rule of life because we ignore the fact that the dust of the earth belongs to God, and that man's chief end is to glorify God. Unless we can maintain the presence of Divinity in our dust, life becomes a miserable drudgery. If a man lives in order to hoard up the means of living, he does not live at all, he has no time to, he is taken up with one form of drudgery or another to keep things going.

The wisdom of to-day concerns itself chiefly with the origin of things and not with God, consequently neither the philosopher nor the mystic has time for actual life. The Wisdom of the Hebrews concerns itself with practical life, and recognises that the basis of things is tragic. The Bible attitude to practical life is at a discount with most of us because we are far away from the rooted and grounded confidence in God of the Hebrews. We do not think on Bible lines, we think on pagan lines, and only in our emotional life do we dabble in spirituality; consequently when we are hard hit, our religion finds us dumb; or if we do talk, we talk as pagans. It has been fashionable to have a contempt for anyone who believes in the Book of Genesis. But now the war has hit us a fair blow and we cannot talk so glibly, nor are we so certain that our cocksureness about things is right; we are not so insolent in our attitude to the Bible standpoint. We are beginning to be prepared to think.

The Bible has no sympathy with saying things ought not to be as they are. The practical thing is to look at things as they are. What is the use of saying there ought to be no war, in the meantime there is! There ought to be no injustice, there is! There ought to be no violence, there is! Solomon never wastes his time in that way; he says these things are. We can ignore facing them, or we can face them in a way which will lead us either to despair or to the Cross of Jesus Christ.

1. Providential Order of Tyranny (Ecclesiastes 5:8)

If thou seest the oppression of the poor, and violent perverting of judgement and justice in a province, marvel not at the matter: for he that is higher than the highest regardeth; and there be higher than they.

All through the Bible the difference between God's order and God's permissive will is brought out. God's permissive will is the things that are now, whether they are right or wrong. If you are looking for justice, you will come to the conclusion that God is the devil; and if the providential order of things to-day were God's order, then that conclusion would be right. But if the order of things to-day is God's permissive will, that is quite another matter. God's order is no sin, no Satan, no wrong, no suffering, no pain, no death, no sickness and no limitation: God's providential will is every one of these things—sin, sickness, death, the devil, you and me, and things as they are. God's permissive will is the haphazard things that are on just now in which we have to fight and make character in, or else be damned by. We may kick and yell and say God is unjust, but we are all "in the soup." It is no use saying things are not as they are; it is no use being amazed at the providential order of tyranny, it is there. In personal life and in national life God's order is reached through pain, and never in any other way. Why it should be so is another matter, but that it is so is obvious. ". . . though He were a Son, yet learned He obedience by the things which He suffered."

We have to get hold of God's order in the midst of His permissive will. God is bringing many "sons" to glory. A son is more than a saved soul; a son is one who has been through the fight and stood the test and come out sterlingly worthy. The Bible attitude to things is absolutely robust, there is not the tiniest whine about it; there is no possibility of lying like a limp jellyfish on God's providence, it is never allowed for a second. There is always a sting and a kick all through the Bible.

Solomon says when you see the providential order of tyranny, don't be amazed at it. According to the Bible the explanation is that the basis of things is tragic; things have gone wrong and they can only be put right and brought into God's order by the individual relationship of men and women. We find tyranny everywhere. Take it in a personal way—we all think we are the creatures of injustice. There never was a man who was not! Justice is an abstraction at the back of our heads. It is absurd to make abstractions entities. Justice and righteousness are emanations from a personal God, and it is His presence and ruling that gives these abstractions their meaning. We say that God is just—where is the evidence of it? Jesus Christ taught, "From him that would borrow of thee, turn not thou away"—where is the justice in that? The great lasting point is not an abstraction called justice, not a question of right or wrong, of goodness or badness, but a personal relationship to a personal God. If I expect to see everything in the universe good and right and I find it is not, I get fainthearted. Solomon won't have us go off on the limbo of the abstract and say these things ought not to be; they are! Injustice and lust and rapine and murder and crime and bestiality and grabbing are as thick as desert sand, and it is cowardly for a man to say because things are as they are, therefore he must drift. We say we had to take a particular course because the prevailing trend of God's providence was that way. It is a remarkable thing that two boats can sail in opposite directions in the same wind, they can go according to the steering skill of the pilot and not according to the prevailing wind; and in the same way a man can trim his sails and grasp hold of God's order however much it costs him.

We need to be warned against the books that pander to our weak side, and the folks who say—"Poor fellow, he couldn't help it." It may be a kindly thing to say, but some things should not be treated with kindness. There is a tyrannical order which runs all through life, and if we get slopped over with sentiment we are not only unfit for life, but are of no use whatever to lay hold of God's order in the midst of things as they are. If the Incarnation means anything to a man, it means fight, "with breast and back as either should be," indwelt by the Spirit of God. Beware of the things that are apt to lead you to a side eddy—false spirituality or intellectual contempt will do it.

2. Profit Ordained of Tillage *(Ecclesiastes 5:9)*
Moreover, the profit of the earth is for all: the king himself is served by the field.

When God created man He made him of dust and Deity; sin introduced the other element, viz. drudgery. "Cursed is the ground for thy sake; . . . thorns also and thistles shall it bring forth to thee; . . . in the sweat of thy face shalt thou eat bread." The earth is cursed because of man's apostasy, and when that apostasy ceases in actual history, the ground will no longer bring forth the curse. The final redemption includes "new

heavens and a new earth." "Instead of the thorn shall come up the fir tree"; and "the wolf shall dwell with the lamb." Instead of the savage ferocity of the beasts, there will be the strength without the savageness—an inconceivable order of things just now.

In anything like a revolution or a war, we find what Solomon refers to here is true, that to make profit you must go back to the dust you came from. The curious thing about civilisation is that it tends to take men away from the soil, and makes them develop an artificial existence away from the elemental. Civilisation has become an elaborate way of doing without God, and when civilised life is hit a smashing blow by any order of tyranny, most of us have not a leg to stand on. Solomon reminds us that king and peasant alike can only gain their profit by proper tillage of the soil. The laws given in the Bible include a scheme for the treatment of the earth and they insist on proper rest being given to the land, and make it clear that that alone will bring profit in actual existence. Leviticus 25 is the great classic on the rights of the earth.

3. Profitless Possession of Treasure *(Ecclesiastes 5:10–11)*
He that loveth silver shall not be satisfied with silver; nor he that loveth abundance with increase: this is also vanity. When goods increase, they are increased that eat them: and what good is there to the owners thereof, saving the beholding of them with their eyes.

To make treasure is different from making profit. Treasure is the thing that is esteemed for itself, not for what it brings. The Bible tirades against possession for possession's sake. "Lay up for yourselves treasures in heaven, . . . for where your treasure is, there will your heart be also." If your treasure is in gold or in land or the possessions of earth, that is where your heart will be, and when wars and rumours of wars arise, your heart will fail you for fear. If a man has his treasure vested in bonds and a war strikes, how can he keep his mind at rest? Panic and devastation and ruin are the result—profitless in every degree.

The manipulation of civilised life has not resulted in the development of the tillage of the land, but in the building up of treasure, and it is not only the miser who grabs. The sense of possession is a snare to true spiritual life. Paul uses the life of a soldier to illustrate a saint's life (2 Timothy 2:3–4). No sense of property or possession can go along with an abiding detachment. In civilised life it is the building up of possessions that is the snare—This is *my* house, *my* land; these are *my* books, and *my* things—imagine when they are touched! I am consumed with distress. Over and over again Jesus Christ drives this point home—Remember, don't have your heart in your possessions, let them come and go. Solomon warns about the same thing—whatever possessions you have will consume the nobility of the life in an appalling way. In the case of Job, Satan asked permission to play havoc with his possessions and God gave him permission, and every possession Job had, even to his bodily health, went; but Job proved that a man would remain true to his love of God though all his possessions went to rack and ruin.

4. Peace out of Toil *(Ecclesiastes 5:12)*

The sleep of a labouring man is sweet, whether he eat little or much: but the abundance of the rich will not suffer him to sleep.

The sleep of a labouring man is sweet, it recreates him. The Bible indicates that sleep is not meant only for the recuperation of a man's body, but that there is a tremendous furtherance of spiritual and moral life during sleep. The conception of sleep that Arnold Bennett or any practical man has is that we need just enough to recuperate the body. According to the Bible, a great deal more than physical recuperation happens in the sleep of any man who has done his daily toil in actual work. "He giveth unto his beloved *in* sleep" (127:2 RV mg). This is a phase that is cut out altogether, because we ignore the deeper issues.

"Whether he eat little or much." Paul's counsel is that "if any would not work, neither should he eat." There are plenty of folks who eat but don't work, and they suffer for it. If we are physically healthy, the benefit of the food we eat corresponds to the work we do, and the same is true in mental, moral and spiritual health. The prayer Our Lord taught us is full of wisdom along this line, "Give us this day our daily bread." That does not mean that if we do not pray we shall not get it. The word "give" has the sense of "receiving." When we become children of God we receive our daily bread from Him, the basis of blessing lies there, otherwise we take it as an animal with no discernment of God.

5. Possessions Outwitting Trust *(Ecclesiastes 5:13–14)*

There is a sore evil which I have seen under the sun, namely, riches kept for the owners thereof to their hurt. But those riches perish by evil travail: and he begetteth a son, and there is nothing in his hand.

If you have many possessions, it will ruin your trust and make you suspect everyone, and the better type of life is ruined. Again, you cannot hold your possessions, you may just overreach yourselves in a speculation and "mafeesh"[22] possessions; or you may die and your sons squander all you possessed. You cannot find lasting joy in these things, let them come and go, remain true to your relationship to God and don't put your trust in possessions. Live your life as a labouring man, a man rightly related to mother earth, and to the providential order of tyranny; trust in God whatever happens, and the result will be that in your heart will be the joy that every man is seeking.

6. Personality the Only Truth *(Ecclesiastes 5:15–17)*

As he came forth of his mother's womb, naked shall he return to go as he came, and shall take nothing of his labour, which he may carry away in his hand. And this also is a sore evil, that in all points as he came, so shall he go: and what profit hath he that hath laboured for the wind? All his days also he eateth in darkness, and he hath much sorrow and wrath with his sickness.

Personal relationship brings us to the truth, and it is truth that relates a man personally to God. Jesus said, "I am . . . the Truth." We have to form the mind of Christ, and it is not done at a leap. It is done by a maintained personal relationship to Jesus Christ, and slowly and surely the new mind is formed. How many of us are working things out from the basis of a personal relationship to Jesus Christ? We work things out on the abstract logic of a sense of justice or of right. It is appalling to find spiritual people when they come into a crisis taking an ordinary common-sense standpoint as if Jesus Christ had never lived or died. It is a man's personal relationship that tells. When he dies he can take nothing he has done or made in his lifetime with him. The only thing he can take with him is what he is. There is no warrant in the Bible for the modern speculation of a second chance after death. There may be a second chance. There may be numbers of interesting things—but it is not taught in the Bible. The stage between birth and death is the probation stage.

We are apt to wrongly relate ourselves to books and to people. We often hear such remarks as—"The parson is talking over the heads of the men"; or, "The Bible is all very well, but I don't understand it." It is never the thing you understand that does you good, but what is behind what is taught. If it is God's truth, you and I are going to meet it again whether we want to or not. The thing we value most in a meeting is not so much what is said, but the release that comes from the different atmosphere that is brought in, and we can begin to think. We benefit most by things over which we cannot be articulate, and if the truths we read or hear are the truths of God, they will crop up again. "A man's reach should exceed his grasp." The

---

22. mafeesh: Arabic expression meaning finished, done with, dead; to *mafeesh* possessions is to lose everything you own.

things we listen to and read ought to be beyond our comprehension, they go into our minds like seed thoughts, and slowly and surely bring forth fruit. This is good counsel for boys and girls in their teens. We should always choose our books as God chooses our friends, just a bit beyond us, so that we have to do our level best to keep up with them. If we choose our own friends, we choose those we can lord it over.

7. Predominant Obligation in Time
(Ecclesiastes 5:18–20)

Behold that which I have seen: it is good and comely for one to eat and to drink, and to enjoy the good of all his labour that he taketh under the sun all the days of his life, which God giveth him: for it is his portion. Every man also to whom God hath given riches and wealth, and hath given him power to eat thereof, and to take his portion, and to rejoice in his labour; this is the gift of God. For he shall not much remember the days of his life; because God answereth him in the joy of his heart.

These verses are an astute summing up of a man's obligations in time. If a man becomes temporarily "magnoon"[23] through anger or lust or false religion, the first thing that happens is that he will stop eating; no man can eat when he is in a rage. If you are in the habit of getting angry, you will soon get physically upset, the connection runs all through. The test that a man is right with God is in eating and drinking. Solomon says, "It is good and comely for men to eat and drink." Paul says, Beware of those who teach abstinence from meats; "Whatsoever is set before you, eat, asking no question for conscience' sake." Remain true to God in your actual life. The right thing to do with riches is to enjoy your portion, and remember that what you lay by is a danger and a snare.

Solomon had everything a man could have in life, he had every means of satisfying himself; he tried the beastly line, the sublime line, the aesthetic line, the intellectual line but, he says, you cannot find your lasting joy in any of them. Joy is only to be found in your relationship to God while you live on this earth, the earth you came from and the earth you return to. Dust is the finest element in man, because in it the glory of God is to be manifested. The Bible makes much of man's body. The teaching of Christianity on this point has been twisted by the influence of Plato's teaching, which says that a man can only further his moral and spiritual life by despising his body. The Bible teaches that the body is the temple of the Holy Ghost, it was moulded by God of the dust of the ground and is man's chief glory, not his shame. When God became Incarnate "He took not on Him the nature of angels," but was made "in the likeness of men," and it is man's body that is yet to manifest the glory of God on earth. Material things are going to be translucent with the light of God.

Jesus Christ "came eating and drinking," and from Genesis to Revelation eating and drinking, and labouring in the ordinary toil of life in the condition of things as they are, are the things in which man will find his right relationship to life and to God.

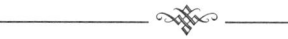

THE EDGE OF THINGS
Ecclesiastes 6:1–12

When the Soul, growing clearer.
  Sees God no nearer;
When the soul, mounting higher.
  To God comes no nigher:
But the arch-fiend, Pride,
Mounts at her side.
Foiling her high emprise.
Sealing her eagle eyes,
And, when she fain would soar,
Makes idols to adore—
Changing the pure emotion
Of her high devotion,
To a skin-deep sense

Of her own eloquence
Strong to deceive, strong to enslave—
Save oh! save.

Matthew Arnold[24]

1. Perils of Inevitable Barriers (Ecclesiastes 6:1–2)

2. Preposterous and Inveterate Brutishness (Ecclesiastes 6:3)

3. Place of Invincible Banality (Ecclesiastes 6:4–8)

4. Perdition of Individual Burning (Ecclesiastes 6:9)

5. Predisposition By Inspired Beginnings (Ecclesiastes 6:10–12)

---

23. magnoon: Scottish expression: beside himself; out of his mind.
24. Matthew Arnold (1822–1888): English scholar, poet, and critic.

To say that the basis of things is not rational does not mean that a man has not to be reasonable. A rationalist is not simply one who uses his reason, but one who says there is nothing at the basis of life that cannot be solved by ordinary reason and enlightenment. The question of tragedy, of the gap between man and God, on which the Bible bases everything, has nothing to do with the philosophy of a rationalist. To him sin is not a positive thing, it is a mere defect; consequently the need for Redemption is emphatically ruled out. There is a tragedy and an agony at the basis of things that cannot be explained by reason; it must either be explained away, or faced in the way the Bible faces it. There is something wrong, and it can only be put right by Redemption.

Many a man affects his doubts of God, they are purely intellectual. There is a phase when a man gets into tremendous stress of weather mentally, but there is also a phase when his doubts are a mere affectation. The Books of Wisdom are strong on facing facts, and yet there is no touch of despair underneath. In all other books which face things as they are, there is tremendous pessimism and abject despair, no hope whatever; but in Solomon's writings, while he maintains a ruggedness and an intensity and an unswerving truthfulness to facts, there is an extraordinary hopefulness running all through, and that without blinking anything, or getting sentimental and falling back on the kindness of God. The minor prophets also state appalling facts—slaughters and crimes on foot and foretold enough to knock hope out of any man, but the Hebrew writers never seem to despair however bad the facts may be, there is always the indefinable certainty that there is something to hope about.

1. Perils of Inevitable Barriers
(Ecclesiastes 6:1–2)
There is an evil which I have seen under the sun, and it is common among men: a man to whom God hath given riches, wealth, and honour, so that he wanteth nothing for his soul of all that he desireth, yet God giveth him not power to eat thereof, but a stranger eateth it: this is vanity, and it is an evil disease.

A man may have all these things—riches, wealth, honour—and at the same time be the victim of an incurable disease. The Hebrew mind looks upon that as an act of God, something for which the man himself is not responsible. The question of the inevitable barriers comes out very strongly in the records of Bible characters. When the inevitable strikes, there is no whine, but rather an astonishing facing of the situation. These inevitable things are outside a man's control, he is not asked about them, and when they

enter as factors into his calculations they present him with a peril. Suppose a man is very ambitious, and rightly so, then just as he has begun to attain his ambitions, he is alarmed over certain symptoms in himself and consults a doctor and the verdict of an incurable disease is passed, it is madness to think he will ever be able to fulfil his ambitions. The danger is lest the man sink into crushing despair, while the courageous thing for him is to hand over to God what belongs to Him and to wait for His solution.

As one of the results of this war men have been ruined in thousands of cases so far as their future life on this planet is concerned. To look at facts as they are and to think them right out to the bottom, makes a man a pessimist, not a despairer, but a pessimist. That means things are as bad as they can be; it is absurd to say they could be worse, it is impossible to conceive things worse. A hopeful attitude does not come by facing facts, or by not facing facts, but only by temperament or religion.

The inevitable barriers are there in every one of our lives. They may not be of an intense order, such as a terrible maiming, or blindness, or deafness, or something that knocks a man out of fulfilling his ambitions, they may be hereditary incapabilities; but the peril is lest we lie down and whine and are of no more good. The thing to do is to recognise that the barriers are inscrutable, that they are there not by chance but entirely by God's permission, and they should be faced and not ignored. Was there ever a more severely handicapped life on this earth than Helen Keller's? The peril of the inevitable barriers is that if I have not faced the facts sufficiently, I am apt to blame God for them. There is one fact more that I do not know, and that fact lies entirely with God, not with me. It is no use to spend my time saying, I wish I was not like this, I am just like it. The practical point in Christianity is—Can Jesus Christ and His religion be of any use to me as I am, not as I am not? Can He deal with me where I am, in the condition I am in?

2. Preposterous and Inveterate Brutishness
(Ecclesiastes 6:3)
If a man beget an hundred children, and live many years, so that the days of his years be many, and his soul be not filled with good, and also that he have no burial; I say, that an untimely birth is better than he.

In the Hebrew conception it was a disgrace for a man to have no burial (cf. 2 Kings 9:34–35). This conception is remote from us to-day.

Solomon says: a man has no business to be an inveterate brute, to live to breed and eat and pile up goods without the slightest idea of the kind of monument his life is erecting—for himself he lives and for himself he dies. Solomon won't have the brute aspect of human life ignored; but to remember that I am a brute and to be brutish are two different things. It is a preposterous iniquity to be a brutish man, satisfied with being once-born (cf. Psalm 73:3–9). The thing to do is to recognise that I am a brute, but I have the brute well under control. Solomon is talking of the man who will not recognise this. To ignore the fact that I am a man is the action of a fool, or of a mystic. To recognise it and see to it that I am a chaste man is the line the Bible insists on—Don't deny that you have a body, but insist on it that you can live in your body the kind of manhood that God demands. Solomon is speaking of the man who is a brute and brutish—"Yes, I am an animal, and I will glut my appetites as they come, I shall sink and not rise." Solomon says, "an untimely birth is better than he."

There is a difference between doing wicked things and being a wicked man. When Jesus Christ saw the pariahs of His day, He did not say to them, "Ye are of your father the devil"; but He did say that to the Pharisees (John 8:44). The Pharisees were play-actors, putting on what did not belong to them; but remember, too, that some of the best men in Our Lord's day were Pharisees, e.g., Nicodemus, Saul of Tarsus. Jesus said to the Pharisees: "The publicans and the harlots go into the kingdom of God before you." It was not the bad people who were guilty of the wicked things. We are apt to tone down the things Our Lord tiraded against—pride, self-realisation, etc. When a man is guilty of wrong things, he recognises instantly that there is a chance of being delivered; but the righteous man sits self-governed in his own right, he is his own god.

3. Place of Invincible Banality *(Ecclesiastes 6:4–8)*

For he cometh in with vanity, and departeth in darkness, and his name shall be covered with darkness. Moreover he hath not seen the sun, nor known any thing: this hath more rest than the other. Yea, though he live a thousand years twice told, yet hath he seen no good: do not all go to one place? All the labour of man is for his mouth, and yet the appetite is not filled. For what hath the wise more than the fool? what hath the poor, that knoweth to walk before the living?

Solomon is referring to the man who lays up for himself and for others, and he does not commend him. To-day we enthrone insurance and economy, but it is striking to recall that the one thing Jesus Christ commended was extravagance. Our Lord only called one work "good," and that was the act of Mary of Bethany when she broke the alabaster box of ointment. It was neither useful nor her duty, it sprang from her devotion to Jesus, and He said of it—"Wheresoever this gospel shall be preached throughout the whole world,

this also that she hath done shall be spoken of for a memorial of her."

The object of a man's life is not to hoard; he has to get enough for his brute life and no more; the best of his life is to be spent in confidence in God. Man is meant to utilise the earth and its products for food and the nourishment of his body, but he must not live in order to make his existence. If the children of Israel gathered more manna than they needed, it turned into dry rot, and that law still holds good.

When we learn this Wisdom of the Hebrews we shall soon see how far away we are from it and from the teaching of Jesus Christ. Our Lord taught that a man ought to be carefully careless about everything saving his relationship to Himself. We who call ourselves Christians are tremendously far, almost opposingly far, from that central point of Christianity: it is not even intimate to us. Generation after generation of civilised life have been opposed to it, and as long as we are on the line of economy and insurance, Jesus Christ cannot have His innings. In personal life, in Church life and in national life, we try Jesus Christ's teaching, but as soon as it becomes difficult we abandon it, or else we compromise. "Take no thought, saying, What shall we eat? or, What shall we drink? or, Wherewithal shall we be clothed?" Bank your faith in God, do the duty that lies nearest and "damn the consequences." Who is prepared to do this, prepared to stake his all on Jesus Christ and His word? We do it in preaching and in books, but not in practical life. We put our emphasis on the other line, trusting in our wits, and God is left out of it. When once we are related to Jesus Christ, our relation to actual life is that of a child, perfectly simple and marvellous.

4. Perdition of Individual Burning *(Ecclesiastes 6:9)*

Better is the sight of the eyes than the wandering of the desire: this is also vanity and vexation of spirit.

Lust applies not only to the bestial side of things; lust means literally—"I must have it at once, and I don't care what the consequences are." It may be a low, animal lust, or it may be a mental lust, or a moral or spiritual lust; but it is a characteristic that does not belong to the life hid with Christ in God. Love is the opposite; love can wait endlessly. "Better is the sight of the eyes, than the wandering of the desire." One of the first things Jesus Christ does is to open a man's eyes and he sees things as they are. Until then he is not satisfied with the seeing of his eyes, he wants more, anything that is hidden he must drag to the light, and the wandering of desire is the burning waste of a man's life until he finds food. His heart lusts, his mind lusts, his eyes lust, everything in him lusts until he is related to God. It is the demand for an infinite satisfaction and it ends in the perdition of a man's life.

Jesus Christ says, "Come unto Me, . . . and I will give you rest," i.e., I will put you in the place where your eyes are open. And notice what Jesus Christ says we will look at—lilies and sparrows and grass. What man in his senses bothers about these things! We consider aeroplanes and tanks and shells, because these demand our attention, the other things do not. The great emancipation in the salvation of God is that it gives a man the sight of his eyes, and he sees for the first time the handiwork of God in a daisy. No longer has he a burning lust that turns everything into a howling wilderness of wrong.

"But their eyes were holden that they should not know him. . . . And their eyes were opened, and they knew Him" (Luke 24:16, 31). We see our friend, the other man sees a fellow in a tunic, we *perceive* the man inside the tunic. When Jesus Christ asked His disciples "Who do men say that the Son of man is?" He was referring to this perception. To the majority of men Jesus Christ was only a Nazarene carpenter, but He says—"Who say *ye* that I am?" "Even though we have known Christ after the flesh, yet now we know him so no more" (2 Corinthians 5:16 RV). The salvation of Jesus Christ enables a man to see for the first time in his life, and it is a wonderful thing.

> Heaven above is brighter blue.
> Earth around is sweeter green,
> Something lives in every hue
> Christless eyes have never seen;
> Birds with gladder songs o'erflow,
> Flowers with deeper beauties shine
> Since I know, as now I know,
> I am His and He is mine.

8. Predisposition by Inspired Beginnings
(Ecclesiastes 6:10–12)

That which hath been is named already, and it is known that it is man: neither may he contend with him that is mightier than he. Seeing there be many things that increase vanity, what is man the better? For who knoweth what is good for man in this life, all the days of his vain life which he spendeth as a shadow? for who can tell a man what shall be after him under the sun?

The Hebrew Books of Wisdom are all of a piece with the first three chapters of Genesis. In order to estimate man properly in the "soup" he is in just now, we must remember what he was in the beginning. God created man in His own image, a son of God. Adam was to have control over the life in the air and on the earth and in the sea, on one condition—that he allowed God to rule him absolutely. Man was to develop the earth and his own life until he was transfigured. But instead there came the introduction of sin, man took the rule over himself, he became his own god, and thereby lost control over everything else. It is this that accounts for the condition of things as they are now.

If we are going to have a sympathetic understanding of the Bible, we must rid ourselves of the abominable conceit that we are the wisest people that have ever been on the earth; we must stop our patronage of Jesus Christ and of the Bible, and have a bigger respect for the fundamental conception of life as it is. At the basis of Hebrew wisdom first of all, is confidence in God; and second, a terrific sigh and sob over the human race as a magnificent ruin of what God designed it to be, Modern wisdom says that man is a magnificent promise of what he is going to be. If that point of view is right, then there is no need to talk about sin and Redemption, and the Bible is a cunningly devised fable. But the Bible point of view seems to cover most of the facts.

WHAT PRICE THIS?
Ecclesiastes 7:1–7

*Indeed the Idols I have loved so long
Have done my credit in Men's Eye much wrong;
Have drown'd my Honour in a shallow Cup
And sold my Reputation for a Song.
Indeed, indeed, Repentance oft before
I swore—but was I sober when I swore?
And then and then came Spring and
        Rose-in-hand
My thread-bare Penitence a-pieces tore.*

Omar Khayyám

1. The Attainment of Sagacious Character (Ecclesiastes 7:1)

2. The Advantage of a Sad Condition (Ecclesiastes 7:2)

3. The Appropriateness of Sorrow and Chastisement (Ecclesiastes 7:3)

4. The Aspects of Shallowness and Censure (Ecclesiastes 7:4–5)

5. The Atrophy of Sagacity by Clownishness
   (Ecclesiastes 7:6)
6. The Anachronism of Conscientiousness
   (Ecclesiastes 7:7)

What a man prizes highly, he prices and praises accordingly. Everything has its price and can be bought. Men and women can be bought. We are bought on the low level of swine, or bribery, or moral compromise, or spiritual insurance; and we are bought with the precious blood of Christ.

Solomon rattles the bottom board out of every piece of deception. The only true joy in life, he says, is based on a personal relationship to God. You cannot find joy in being like animals, or in art, or aestheticism, in ruling or being ruled—the whole thing is passed in survey in a most ruthless examination by a man whose wisdom is profounder than the profoundest and has never been excelled, and in summing it all up he says that joy is only found in any of these things when a man is rightly related to God.

An elemental thing to remember is that we must never read into a man's words what we mean, but just try and find out what the author of the words means. As a rule we read into his words what we mean and consequently miss his meaning altogether. Before we can criticise a man's statements we must find out his meaning, find out what kind of a genius or a fool he was who said it. If we do this with the Bible, it will put the statements made there in quite another light. If the man in the street (i.e., just you and me) is going to prove the truth of Christianity, he must "come off the street owning its power." If we do not intend to go out of our own ways of looking at things, we shall never find out the other man's ways of looking at them.

1. The Attainment of Sagacious Character
(Ecclesiastes 7:1)
A good name is better than precious ointment; and the day of death than the day of one's birth.

Solomon is speaking of character, not of reputation. Reputation is what other people think of you; "character is what you are in the dark," where no one sees but yourself. That is where the worth of a man's character lies, and Solomon says that the man who has attained a sagacious character during life is like a most refreshing, soothing, healing ointment. In the New Testament "name" frequently has the meaning of "nature." "Where two or three are gathered together in My name," i.e., My nature (Matthew 18:20). Everyone who comes across a good nature is made better by it, unless he is determined to be bad. To say a man has a good nature does not mean he is a pious individual, always quoting texts. The test of a nature

is the atmosphere it produces. When we are in contact with a good nature we are uplifted by it. We do not get anything we can state articulately, but the horizon is enlarged, the pressure is removed from the mind and heart and we see things differently.

2. The Advantage of a Sad Condition
(Ecclesiastes 7:2)
It is better to go to the house of mourning, than to go to the house of feasting: for that is the end of all men; and the living will lay it to his heart.

Solomon is not implying that it is better to grouse around in the luxury of misery than to feast; he is dealing with finding true essential joy, and he says if ever we are going to have a true estimate of life we shall have to face it at its worst. All through the books of Hebrew Wisdom there is this certainty that the basis of actual life is tragedy. Human nature is a ruin of what it once was, and a man is a fool to ignore that. If you want to know the basis of life, it is better to go to the house of mourning than to the house of pleasure. Remember, there is death, and there is worse than death—sin and tragedy and the possibility of terrible evil. Solomon does not mean us to live as some folks who seem never to be happy unless they are at a funeral. He means us to keep at the basis of things, to scrape through the veneer and face things, and we learn to do this better in mourning than in feasting. "Appear not unto men to fast." If you have had a sad dose, don't pull a long face, cover it up, don't let anyone imagine you are going through what you are.

If a man builds his life over a volcano, one day there will come terrific havoc. If we ignore the safety valves in mother earth, we will have to pay the penalty. Mount Vesuvius is one of the pumps that keeps the earth in proper order; the Creator has put His danger signals there, and yet people ignore them and plant their vineyards on its slopes, then when an eruption occurs we blame God and say how cruel He is to allow it.

No wise man will build up his life without knowing what the basis of life is, and Solomon indicates that a man can only arrive at a true view of life by brooding on the underlying tragedy.

3. The Appropriateness of Sorrow and Chastisement (Ecclesiastes 7:3)
Sorrow is better than laughter: for by the sadness of the countenance the heart is made better.

"Countenance" means more than the face; the countenance is the whole aspect of a man's nature (cf. Psalm 42:5, 11). To say "I won't countenance it" does not mean to show disapproval in my face, but that I refuse to give the thing the approval of my personal life. The man who has faced the fact that the basis of life is tragic is the one who begins to see the true relation of things, and he says "I will go softly all my years." We may find that the man who is remarkably cheerful now has gone through a hell that would make us shudder to face. The men and women who have been through things have always plenty of leisure for others, they never obtrude their own experiences. Many a man has found God in the belly of hell during the war. He has come face to face with God through having had things stripped off and having to face the fact that the basis of life is tragedy.

4. The Aspects of Shallowness and Censure
(Ecclesiastes 7:4–5)
The heart of the wise is in the house of mourning; but the heart of fools is in the house of mirth. It is better to hear the rebuke of the wise, than for a man to hear the song of fools.

Solomon says that the house of mourning is the place where a man learns wisdom, he won't be so sharp with his tongue, there are things he might have said but he won't. If you will only see your "cobber" laid out, you will shut your mouth and not say what you were going to. No man who faces the ultimate tragedy in another's life can be the cheap and easy cynic we are all apt to be without thinking. Whistler[25] wrote a book entitled *The Gentle Art of Making Enemies*—a miserably spiteful thing to do!

Go to the house of mourning and see your friend dead, and it will alter your attitude to things; don't be shallow. There is a place for the shallow, however, as well as the profound. One of the greatest defects in Christianity is that it is not shallow enough, in this respect it knows a great deal better than Jesus Christ. It is religious enough, supernormally moral, but not able to eat, drink and be merry. Jesus Christ made the shallow and the profound, the give and the take, one. The art of shallow conversation is one that is rarely learned. It is a great gift as well as a real ministration to be able to say nothing cleverly. It is an insult to be everlastingly introducing subjects that make people think on the deepest lines. It takes all the essence of Christianity to be shallow properly.

The shallowness Solomon mentions here is that of refusing to realise that there is a basis of tragedy. A man who tells his chum with a broken heart to go to a picture show is a fool. He ought to know that the house of shallowness is not the place for him, but that Jesus Christ is the only One Who can heal him. It is a question of having a wise heart through facing the reality of things. When a man has "the heart of the wise," he is able to counsel his friend in the dark way.

5. The Atrophy of Sagacity by Clownishness
(Ecclesiastes 7:6)
For as the crackling of thorns under a pot, so is the laughter of the fool: this also is vanity.

The private history of a professional clown may be one of the saddest. The man who sets himself to make others laugh has often an immensely sad life of his own behind. A man can kill his own wisdom by living apart; he can atrophy his real life by keeping up a certain role. If a man has a name for being smart, he may find it a job to keep up the role. When you take up the clownish line, you kill something that ought not to be killed, you atrophy the wisest part of your nature. It takes a tremendous amount of relationship to God for a man to be what he is.

6. The Anachronism of Conscientiousness
(Ecclesiastes 7:7)
Surely oppression [extortion, RV] maketh a wise man mad; and a gift destroyeth the heart.

Anachronism means anything out of keeping with the time. A wise man who has built his life in confidence in God will appear a fool when he is amongst people who are sleek and cunning. "Extortion" makes the wisdom of the wisest appear fools. You can ridicule anyone, even Jesus Christ. The wisdom of God is arrant stupidity to the wisdom of the world, until all of a sudden God makes the wisdom of the world foolish (1 Corinthians 1:23–25). If you stand true to your faith in God, there will be situations in which you will come across extortioners, cunning, crafty people, who use their wits instead of worshipping God, and you will appear a fool. Are you prepared to appear a fool for Christ's sake? Very few of us know anything about suffering for Christ's sake. A man who knows nothing about Christ will suffer for conscience or conviction's sake. To suffer for Christ's sake is to suffer because of being personally related to Him.

If you are going to be true to God, you will appear a fool amongst those who do not believe in God, and you must lay your account with this. Jesus said, "Every one therefore who shall confess Me before men . . ." (RV). and it tests a man for all he is worth to confess Jesus Christ, because the confession has to be made in the set he belongs to and esteems. The "shame" of the gospel. "I am not ashamed of the gospel of Christ," says Paul.

No man can confess Jesus Christ without realising the cost to others; if he states this, he rebukes them. The Spirit of God may lay hold of one man among a crowd of men to be related to God, but his sense of honour may keep him from going through—

---

25. James McNeill Whistler (1834–1903): American painter; wrote *The Gentle Art of Making Enemies,* published in 1890.

I don't want to appear different from the others; if I go through with this and relate myself to Jesus Christ, I shall be a speckled bird[26] and look superior. Many a man is kept from coming to Jesus because his own crowd is not going that road. It is a standard of honour, but a standard of honour not rightly related. In the life of a disciple it is the honour of Jesus Christ that is at stake, not our own honour. Your crowd matters to you, but your crowd does not matter to me; nor do you need to care what my crowd thinks of you. But take a step aside from your own immediate circle, and you will have to reckon with what they say about you (cf. Hebrews 13:13).

In Christian experience what stands in the way of my obedience to God is not the cost to me, but the cost to my father and mother and others. "If any man cometh unto Me, and hateth not his own father, and mother . . . he cannot be My disciple" (RV). Jesus Christ's penetration comes straight home. Think what it cost Jesus Christ's mother and His friends for Him to be true to God. If He had not been true to what He came to do, His mother would not have had the sword pierce her heart; His own nation would not have blasphemed the Holy Ghost. In going on with God this is where we find the anachronism comes in—according to the astute wisdom of the world we live in, we are made to do or say the thing at the wrong time.

This is brought home to-day by the war. It is not a question of what it costs the individual men to join up, but of the cost to those who belong to them; the strain the wives and mothers and fathers and children have to bear. That is the terrific cost to the man who goes out to fight his country's battles. No man can tell why he enlisted. The watchword "For King and Country" is too shallow. The sacrifice he makes is never intended for man, it is meant for God, and is to be poured out before the Lord, as David poured out the water from the well of Bethlehem (see 2 Samuel 23:14–17).

SOMETHING DOING
Ecclesiastes 7:8–12

And is it that the haze of grief
Makes former gladness loom so great?
The lowness of the present state,
That sets the past in this relief?
Or that the past will always win
A glory from its being far,
An orb into the perfect star
We saw not, when we moved therein.

Tennyson

1. The End Explains—and the Patient Excels the Proud (Ecclesiastes 7:8)

2. The Excitement of Exasperation—and Discretion Excels Domineering (Ecclesiastes 7:9)

3. The Religion of Reminiscence—and the Present Excels the Past (Ecclesiastes 7:10)

4. The Wisdom of the World and the World of Wisdom (Ecclesiastes 7:11–12)

There is a tendency in us all to mourn over something—to say that the past was a great deal better than the present, or that the future will be better; the worst time we ever lived in is the present—forgetting that we never lived in any other time!

Because a thing is good enough for us, or for an age, or for a nation, is not sufficient to make it the truth. It may be a statement that will do for a time, but unless we have been dumped down on to the basis of things, our experience is of no avail as a revelation of the foundation of life. It is the extraordinary thinker, the man with the extreme experience, rather than the average man, who gets at the truth at the basis of things. When we deal with great thinkers like Solomon or Shakespeare we get to the truth of things; we do not get the truth through experience. Most of us do not think; we live healthy ordinary lives and don't bother about thinking at all; but when an upheaval comes from underneath proving that the basis of things is not rational, we find the value of the Bible attitude, which is that the basis of things is tragic and not rational, and the war has proved that the Bible is right. We have to live based on our relationship to God in the actual condition of things as they are.

---

26. speckled bird: person who stands out as abnormal, odd, or eccentric.

1. The End Explains—and the Patient Excels the Proud *(Ecclesiastes 7:8)*

Better is the end of a thing than the beginning thereof: and the patient in spirit is better than the proud in spirit.

"The end explains," not "The end justifies the means"—that is never right. If you live as an animal, the end will explain that you have made a mess of things. If you live morally, the end will explain that you have lived morally. "End" has the meaning of "issue" (cf. Jeremiah 29:11 RV mg). When death ends the present order, the issue will reveal how you have lived. Only when you live in personal relationship to God does the end explain that you have the right secret of life.

In the Book of Revelation (which is the Apocalypse of the New Testament as the Song of Solomon is the Apocalypse of the Old Testament), Jesus Christ refers to Himself as "the first and the last." It is in the middle that human choices are made; the beginning and the end remain with God. The decrees of God are birth and death, and in between those limits man makes his own distress or joy.

Solomon counsels us not to be staggered when we find oppressors and tyrants around, the end will explain all. It is not enough to say that because my religious beliefs do for me, therefore they are satisfactory. If everyone were well brought up and had a good heredity, any number of intellectual forms of belief would do. The test of a man's religion is not that it does for him, but that it does for the worst man he knows.

2. The Excitement of Exasperation—and Discretion Excels Domineering *(Ecclesiastes 7:9)*

Be not hasty in thy spirit to be angry: for anger resteth in the bosom of fools.

All through the Bible, emphasis is laid steadily on patience. A man's patience is tested by three things— God, himself, and other people. An apt illustration is that of a bow and arrow in the hand of an archer. God is not aiming at what we are, nor is He asking our permission. He has us in His hands for His own purpose, and He strains to the last limit; then when He lets fly, the arrow goes straight to His goal. Acquire your soul with patience. Don't get impatient with yourself.

The Bible is a relation of facts, the truth of which must be tested. Life may go on all right for a while, when suddenly a bereavement comes, or some crisis; unrequited love or a new love, a disaster, a business collapse, or a shocking sin, and we turn up our Bibles again and God's word comes straight home, and we say, "Why, I never saw that there before." As long as you live a logical life without realising the deeper depths of your personality, the Bible does not amount to anything; but strike lower down where mathematics and logic are of no account, and you find that Jesus Christ and the Bible tell every time.

Truth is never a matter of intellect first, but of moral obedience. The great secret of intellectual progress is curiosity, but curiosity in moral matters is an abomination. Moral sophistry says—Go and find out for yourself. If I do, I am a fool. I don't care what a man's moral strength is, I defy him to start on the line of moral curiosity without instantly damning some of the finer sensibilities of his life. "But of the tree of the knowledge of good and evil, thou shalt not eat of it; for in the day that thou eatest thereof thou shalt surely die" (Genesis 2:17). We are not to know evil by eating of the fruit of the tree; if we do eat of the tree we shall die. If you are pitchforked into moral filth, you will be kept; but if you go in to it from curiosity you will not be kept, no one goes into it without coming out soiled. You may be physically clean, but you have lost something.

The essential element in moral life is obedience and submission. If you want spiritual truth, obey the highest standard you know. "If any man will do His will, he shall know of the teaching, whether it be of God or whether I speak from Myself" (John 7:17). Intellectually, curiosity is the thing; morally, obedience is what is needed. One *ounce* of chastity is worth fifty years of intellect in moral discernment. Moral truth is never reached by intellect, but only through conscience. When a fine keen intellect and moral obedience go together, we find the mind that is beginning to discover step by step where goodness and truth lie.

"Anger resteth in the bosom of fools." Solomon's warning is that a man who excites himself to exasperation is a fool, because simulated indignation produces the thing itself. For instance, if in the morning you begin to snarl, in less than half an hour you will feel thoroughly bad tempered. The man who can curb his spirit and control himself is a wise man, and is better than the man who can take a city.

Discretion excels domineering. Obstinacy and strength of will are often confounded, but they are very different. An obstinate man is unintelligent; a strong-minded man is one who has made up his mind on a matter but is prepared to listen to your arguments and deal with them, and show to your satisfaction that his decision is right. A stubborn man is always a "small potato." We may make up our minds easily, but to make up a mind of any breadth takes time, there are so many sides to every matter. If you have made up your mind on the line of strength and not of obstinacy, when you are questioned you don't domineer. Domineering is the intellectual side of stubbornness, and is a sign of moral weakness. It is absurd to mistake the expression of physical stubbornness, such as a square jaw, for strength of will;

tenacity of will may go with a jaw like a child's top. Will is not a thing I possess; will is the whole man active. Solomon is pointing out that the man who is excited into exasperation is a weak man, a fool, and if he begins to domineer it shows he has no discretion. There are some things that can be answered straight off and others that cannot.

"Be not hasty in thy spirit to be angry." Anger nearly always covers up a thing that is wrong. Suppose you have been in the wrong in a certain matter and no one knows it but yourself, and then you are wrongfully accused of something else, you are so thankful that the real thing was not discovered that you make protestations of innocence as if you were spotlessly right all through. It is an indication that there is weakness and foolishness somewhere. Never domineer, and never get exasperated unless you want to be a fool.

3. The Religion of Reminiscence—and the Present Excels the Past *(Ecclesiastes 7:10)*

Say not thou, What is the cause that the former days were better than these? for thou dost not enquire wisely concerning this.

At the beginning of the war what was called the Christian religion was mainly a cult of reminiscence. Take any denomination you like, and the religious bodies that do not consider themselves denominations—was their main object the establishment of a family likeness to Jesus Christ? No, their main object was to establish the particular creed they upheld, consequently when the crisis struck us, the religious element of the country was powerless to grip the situation. Individual spiritual people were not powerless; in every denomination there were those who were the true salt of earth, but the external phase of religion was not able to grapple with the situation. The passion of reminiscence was ruling everywhere, the old ways of doing things. A revival adds nothing, it simply brings back what had been lost and is a confession of failure. The effects of a revival may be deplorable. "Oh that we had the ancient days of simplicity and sunshine"—days of adversity and humbug! Things are bad and difficult now, but not a tithe as difficult as they used to be. It is of no use to pray for the old days; stand square where you are and make the present better than any past has been. Base all on your relationship to God and go forward, and presently you will find that what is emerging is infinitely better than the past ever was. The present excels the past because we have the wealth of the past to go on. Solomon is not talking evolution, but simple fact.

4. The Wisdom of the World and the World of Wisdom *(Ecclesiastes 7:11–12)*

Wisdom is good with an inheritance: and by it there is profit to them that see the sun. For wisdom is a defence, and money is a defence: but the excellency of knowledge is, that wisdom giveth life to them that have it.

"Wisdom is good, and so is an inheritance, but it is more excellent that both should go together. It is all very well to talk about wisdom, but the best thing is to be shrewd, to have wisdom *and* money, to balance things properly."

Solomon says that that compromise will deceive you. If a man is honest because it pays him to be, he ceases to be honest. "Ye cannot serve God and mammon." We say we can because we do not see God. If I only see you, I will wink the other eye—you trick me and I'll trick you. Civilisation is based on murder, it is wisdom with an inheritance, keep the two things going. As long as you try the juggling trick you will find the teaching of Jesus Christ is nonsense, but any man who dares to take God at His word will find it work every time. The world of wisdom is to bank all on God and disregard the consequences. Men are told to "decide for Christ"; no man can do it; what a man has to do is deliberately to commit himself to Jesus Christ. We get hold of the size of our dastardly impertinence when we say to God—"No, I can't trust Your word; I can't live the kind of life You require." Are we prepared to stake our all on the honour of Jesus Christ? Immediately a man is driven to distress and he realises that he must sink anyhow, he goes straight to Jesus Christ and finds that instead of sinking, he is lifted up and receives salvation. Stake everything on the honour of Jesus Christ, and you will find you have struck bedrock. Whenever our spiritual life is unsatisfactory it is because we have said to God—"I won't"; "You can't expect me to trust You." Then we must take the consequences. "And He did not many mighty works there because of their unbelief." If Jesus Christ has done no mighty works for me it is either because I don't believe He can, or I don't want Him to. I may say—"Oh yes, I believe Jesus Christ will give me the Holy Spirit"; but I am not prepared for Him to do it, I don't want Him to. Will you launch out on what Jesus says? If you will, you will find that God is as good as His word.

Get to the place where you make the thing inevitable, burn your bridges behind you, make retreat impossible, then go ahead. Solomon's counsel is wise— "Trust in the LORD with all thine heart; and lean not unto thine own understanding." It is leaning to our own understanding that keeps the bridges behind.

"OVER THE TOP"
Ecclesiastes 7:13–22

1. Inevitable and Attainable (Ecclesiastes 7:13)

2. Instructive and Aggregate (Ecclesiastes 7:14)

3. Irreparable and Anticlimax (Ecclesiastes 7:15)

4. Introspective and Abnormal (Ecclesiastes 7:16)

5. Iniquitous and Anarchic (Ecclesiastes 7:17)

6. Injunction and Anathema(Ecclesiastes 7:18)

7. Intelligent and Animal (Ecclesiastes 7:19)

8. Impeccable and Artificial (Ecclesiastes 7:20)

9. Invidious and Argumentative (Ecclesiastes 7:21–22)

When the time comes to act, it has to be a going over the top—over the top of everything you have been entrenched in—prejudices, beliefs, etc.

1. Inevitable and Attainable *(Ecclesiastes 7:13)*
Consider the work of God: for who can make that straight, which He hath made crooked?

All the Hebrew prophets and the New Testament apostles make a distinction between the inevitable and the attainable. There are inevitable things for which a man is not responsible. For instance, I cannot say when I will be born or when I will die; birth and death are inevitable. I have to attain within the two on the basis of things as they are. If this distinction between the inevitable and the attainable is not made, it will lead to a muddle in the presentation of evangelical religion.

When a man goes "over the top," he sees things as he never saw them before. He comes across things he cannot diagnose or understand, and he begins to flounder and wonders what he ought to do. The thing for him to do is to base on the inevitable and then find out what is attainable.

No man can redeem his own soul, or give himself a new heredity; that is the work of the sovereign grace of God. Man has nothing to do with Redemption, it is God's "bit"; but God cannot give a man a good character, that is not God's business, nor is it an inevitable thing. God will give us what we cannot give ourselves, a totally new heredity (see Luke 11:13). God will put the disposition of His Son, Holy Spirit, into any man who asks, then on that basis man has to work out a holy character. "*Work out* your own salvation with fear and trembling; for it is God which *worketh in* you. . . ."

"*Who can make that straight, which He hath made crooked?*" In our talks on the Book of Job we mentioned the refraction of God in the universe. ["Whenever God presents Himself in the present order of the material universe, He appears to go crooked, that is, crooked to our reason; we cannot understand Him. God allows things in the cosmic world which are a refraction; they do not continue in the straight simple line my mind tells me they ought to take. . . . If you try to weave a conception of God out of Jesus Christ's presentation of Him and then look at life as it is, you will find what is meant by the cosmic refraction of God—the God revealed in Jesus Christ is flatly contradicted in the natural world" (cf. Romans 8:20–22). *Baffled to Fight Better*, pp. 56–7.—*Footnote in original text.*]

What man finds it easy to explain actual facts as he sees them to-day in connection with his belief in God? Job is the expression of a man who suffered in this way. In theory God appears to be just and kind, but in actual life things seem to flatly contradict His justice and kindness. It is part of common sense to be atheistic rather than to believe in the refraction of God in the universe. Solomon says that if we try and work things out on the line of intellect, on a theory of goodness or justice, we will always find the refraction. There is something wrong at the basis of things, and it cannot be put right until another inevitable thing happens, viz. the manifestation of the sons of God. The thing to do is to place our faith in God and attain morally in the midst of things, crooked as they appear. Watch the inevitable things, and don't try to work out the riddle of the universe.

2. Instructive and Aggregate *(Ecclesiastes 7:14)*
In the day of prosperity be joyful, but in the day of adversity consider: God also hath set the one over against the other, to the end that man should find nothing after him.

The test of elemental honesty is the way a man behaves himself in grief and in joy. The natural elemental man expresses his joy or sorrow straight off. To-day in our schools boys are taught stoicism; it produces an admirable type of lad externally, but not so admirable internally. When we are rightly related to God we must let things have their way with us and not pretend things are not as they are. It is difficult not to simulate sorrow or gladness, but to remain natural and stedfastly true to God as things come. Don't deal only with the section that is sad or with the section that is joyful, deal with them together. When we accept God's purpose for us in Christ Jesus, we know that *"all things work together for good."*

Stoicism has the effect of making a man hysterical and sentimental, it produces a denseness spiritually. When you are joyful, *be* joyful; when you are sad, *be* sad. If God has given you a sweet cup, don't make it bitter; and if He has given you a bitter cup, don't try and make it sweet; take things as they come. One of the last lessons we learn is not to be an amateur providence—"I shall not allow that person to suffer." Suffering, and the inevitable result of suffering, is the only way some of us can learn, and if we are shielded God will ultimately take the one who interferes by the scruff of the neck and remove him. The fingers that caress a child may also hurt its flesh; it is the power of love that makes them hurt.

3. Irreparable and Anticlimax
((Ecclesiastes 7:15)
All things have I seen in the days of my vanity: there is a just man that perisheth in his righteousness, and there is a wicked man that prolongeth his life in his wickedness.

For a man to have doubts is not a sign that he is a bad man. David was up against things in his day—"Surely in vain have I cleansed my heart, and washed my hands in innocency; for all the day long have I been plagued, and chastened every morning" (Psalm 73:13–14 RV). Sum up the life of Jesus Christ by any other standard than God's, and it is an anticlimax of failure. "It is required in stewards, that a man be found faithful"—not successful. The anticlimax comes when we look for rewards—"If I am good, I shall be blessed." The logic of mathematics does not amount to anything in the spiritual realm. If a man has had a good beginning of splendid uprightness, and all the advantages of a good education, we may say he is sure to attain. There never was a sunnier beginning than Samson's, and yet he ended in a frantic collapse. There are irreparable things and anticlimaxes in life, and the explanation is not to be found on the rational line, but on the line of personal relationship to God. Remain true to God, and remember that certain things are irreparable. There is no road back to yesterday, it is only God on the basis of Redemption Who can get back to yesterday. Logic and reason have to do with things based on space and time, but they cannot push beyond space and time. We are all agnostic about God, about the Spirit of God, and prayer. It is nonsense to call prayer reasonable; it is the most super-reasonable thing there is.

The war has produced anticlimaxes in hundreds of lives, men are maimed and useless for fighting their ambitions. You rarely hear a man who has been through the real agony of suffering say that he disbe-lieves in God; it is the one who watches others going through suffering who says he disbelieves in God. In the suffering there is a compensation which cannot be got at in any other way. It is not seen from the outside because the compensation cannot be articulately stated.

4. Introspective and Abnormal
(Ecclesiastes 7:16)
Be not righteous over much; neither make thyself over wise: why shouldest thou destroy thyself?

Solomon is dealing with the fact that a man ought not to be either a religious fanatic or a stupid fool. Don't be fanatical, he says, remember you have an actual life to live. A fanatic sees God's order but remains invincibly ignorant about God's permissive will. The spiritual fanatic ignores the actual life and says—"Jesus Christ said there is no making and giving in marriage in heaven, so there must be none on earth." That is being over wise. If you examine yourself too much, you unfit yourself for life. There is a stage in life when introspection is necessary, but if it is pushed too far a man becomes abnormally hypersensitive, either in conceit or grovelling. Introspection is the result of love or of anything elemental. When a man falls in love, he feels he is not worthy to crawl on the earth by the side of his divinity! The same thing spiritually; when once a man sees God he is apt to forget that he has to live on this planet. Solomon's counsel is to live an earthly life on the basis of things as they are, and not to compromise or be over wise.

It is easier to cut ourselves off from actual things and to nourish a life of our own intellectually. An intellectual man sums up other men by their brains, as Carlyle[27] did, and he is apt to become contemptuous. A man is more than his brain. A man who lives a mystical life or an intellectual life frequently has an attitude of lofty contempt towards others. No man has any right to maintain such an attitude towards another human being, watching him as a spectator for purposes of his own, as journalistic copy, or as a religious specimen; if he does he ceases to be a human being by pretending to be more.

5. Iniquitous and Anarchic (Ecclesiastes 7:17)
Be not over much wicked, neither be thou foolish: why shouldest thou die before thy time?

Don't go to the opposite extreme and say, I am going to live as I choose. The right attitude is between the two—neither "over wise" nor "over much wicked."

In the Incarnation we see the right amalgam—pure Deity and the pure human mixed. The talk about pure Deity is an intellectual conceit, it sounds winning to aesthetic culture, but it has no worth in a

---

27. Thomas Carlyle.

man's practical life. An Almighty, Incomprehensible, Incognoscible Being does not amount to anything to me. It is when God becomes Incarnate that we see the right amalgam, dust and Deity made one, human flesh presenced with Divinity. That is the meaning of the Incarnation, and Jesus Christ claims He can do it for any one of us. Man cannot be pure Deity and he cannot be pure dust; he has to have the right alloy—dust and Deity, made one by drudgery, and this produces the type of life with the right balance.

6. Injunction and Anathema *(Ecclesiastes 7:18)*
It is good that thou shouldest take hold of this; yea, also from this withdraw not thine hand: for he that feareth God shall come forth of them all.

Don't be fanatically religious and don't be irreverently blatant. Remember that the two extremes have to be held in the right balance. If your religion does not make you a better man, it is a rotten religion. The test of true religion is when it touches these four things—food, money, sex and mother earth. These things are the test of a right sane life with God, and the religion that ignores them or abuses them is not right. God made man of the dust of the ground, and that dust can express either Deity or devilishness. Remember we are to be not numskulls, but holy men, full-blooded and holy to the last degree, not anaemic creatures without enough strength to be bad. The relation to life ordained by Jesus Christ does not unsex men and women, but enables them to be holy men and women. "The love of money is a root of all kinds of evil" (1 Timothy 6:10 RV). Money is a test, another thing which proves a man's religion; and the way a man treats the soil will also prove whether or not he is a son of God. A man needs to hold a right attitude to all these things by means of his personal relationship to God.

7. Intelligent and Animal *(Ecclesiastes 7:19)*
Wisdom strengtheneth the wise more than ten mighty men which are in the city.

"He that ruleth his spirit (is better) than he that taketh a city" (Proverbs 16:32). An intelligent man in a city, one who is guided by sagacity, is worth ten strong men who guard the city. In the present campaign it is the mobilisation of invention that is telling more and more. The man who is able to make use of sagacious inventions is worth a dozen men with mere strength, because he makes use of the strength of others. Our great commanders and leaders have not always been strong men physically. It is not always true that a sound mind is in a sound body; the finest of minds are often in impaired bodies, and some of the most sordid minds in healthy bodies.

8. Impeccable and Artificial *(Ecclesiastes 7:20)*
For there is not a just man upon earth, that doeth good, and sinneth not.

Impeccable—liable not to sin. The idea that because Jesus Christ was without sin therefore He could not be tempted, has become woven into religious belief. If that were so, the record of His temptation is a mere farce. Could Jesus Christ be tempted? Undoubtedly He could, because temptation and sin are not the same thing. "In all points tempted, . . . yet without sin." No good man is impeccable, that is, he never arrives at the place where it is impossible to sin. A man is able not to sin, but it never becomes impossible for him to sin. "Whosoever is born of God doth not commit sin; for his seed remaineth in him: and he cannot sin, because he is born of God" (1 John 3:9). The life of God is born in us, and the life of God cannot sin; that does not mean that we *cannot* sin; but that if we obey the life of God in us, we *need not* sin.

The best of men are but the best of men. Don't glory in men; don't say, I am of Paul; I am of Apollos. Bank your confidence in God, not in men. Unless we are damnable, we are not worth saving. If we cannot go to the devil, we cannot go to God. The measure of the depth to which a man can fall is the height to which he can rise. Virtue is the outcome of conflict, not of necessity.

9. Invidious and Argumentative *(Ecclesiastes 7:21–22)*
Also take no heed unto all words that are spoken; lest thou hear thy servant curse thee: for oftentimes also thine own heart knoweth that thou thyself likewise has cursed others.

"For with what judgement ye judge, ye shall be judged: and with what measure ye mete, it shall be measured to you again." This is an inexorable law. "I am perfectly certain So-and-so has been criticising me." Well, what have you been saying about him? Watch the process. It is as certain as God's throne, the measure you mete will be meted to you, not necessarily by the same person. Tit for tat is the inevitable law in actual life. Don't talk too much, says Solomon; if you talk too much, others will too. Don't be a busybody in other men's matters. A gossip is not always the bad person he is made out to be, those who listen and don't talk are the dangerous folk. The scandalmonger gets the blame, but the others are worse. A lie is not simply "a terminological inexactitude"; a lie is a truth told with bad intent. I may repeat the exact words of someone else and yet tell a lie because I convey a wrong meaning. Be careful, says Solomon, not to talk too much, because what you say will be taken up by others.

IN THE STY
Ecclesiastes 7:23–29

O me, why have they not buried me deep enough?
Is it kind to have made me a grave so rough,
Me, that was never a quiet sleeper?
Maybe still I am but half dead;
Then I cannot be wholly dumb;
I will cry to the steps above my head
And somebody, surely, some kind heart will come
To bury me, bury me
Deeper, ever so little deeper.

Tennyson

1. Programme and Plague of the Heart
   (Ecclesiastes 7:23–24)
2. Prospecting In Pursuit of Happiness
   (Ecclesiastes 7:25)
3. Persecution and Peril of the Hell-Cat
   (Ecclesiastes 7:26)
4. Perfidiousness of Perpetual Relation of Man
   and Woman (Ecclesiastes 7:27–28)
5. Perfection and Perversion of Humanity
   (Ecclesiastes 7:29)

The Bible deals with the worst tragedy that human nature and the devil could concoct. We seem to have forgotten this nowadays. The Atonement has been made a kind of moral "lavatory" wherein a man can wash and go out and get dirty again. But when a man like Solomon or Shakespeare or Ibsen lifts the veil from the basis of things (which most of us know nothing of because we are too dense or too remote from it), we find that the Redemption deals with tragedy of an appalling order.

When the war broke out, the ruling note in religion was being struck not by the men and women who knew the basis of things, but by those who were unfamiliar with the abominable tragedy at the basis of human life, such as is being exhibited now; consequently something feeble and ethereal and totally unlike the Bible was ruling, and being expressed in unrobust prayer meetings and in hymns and poems by anaemic people of both sexes. Our religious life was built up by people who were not dealing with tragedy. When civilised life is burst into we find what Solomon indicates, that the basis of life is tragic. No education, no culture, no sociology or government can touch the fathomless rot at the basis of human life in its deepest down storey. We live in the twenty-second storey up, and the tragedies we touch are only personal tragedies; only one in a million comes to understand the havoc

that underlies everything. This line of thinking is absolutely important, not relatively important.

1. Programme and Plague of the Heart
(Ecclesiastes 7:23–24)

All this have I proved by wisdom: I said, I will be wise; but it was far from me. That which is far on, and exceeding deep, who can find it out?

Solomon deliberately set himself to find out things and to live according to the highest possible wisdom, but, he says, "it was far from me." He discovered what every lad who has been well brought up and has had a decent amount of natural religion in his life experiences, when he finds that his ideals cannot be realised. A lad sees more clearly, dreams more purely and has higher thoughts in his teens than ever he does afterwards. Then he goes through the severest of struggles—I cannot bring my actual life up to the standard of my ideals; I won't lower my ideals, although I can never hope to make them actual. It cannot be done by prayer or by education; it can only be done in the way Jesus Christ says—"Come unto Me, all ye that labour and are heavy laden, and I will give you rest," i.e., I will make the ideal and the actual one. The only way in which ideals can be made actual is by a personal relationship to God through Jesus Christ.

Solomon was the wisest and the wealthiest of kings, yet he says that "the plague of his own heart" knocked him out (see 1 Kings 8:38). This is the first lesson everyone of us has to learn. To begin with we are not prepared to accept Jesus Christ's diagnosis of the human heart, we prefer to trust our own ignorant innocence. Jesus Christ says, "Out of the heart proceed fornication, adultery, murder, lasciviousness, thieving, lying," etc. (Mark 7:21–23). No man has ever believed that. We have not the remotest conception that what Jesus says about the human heart is true until we come up against something further on in our lives. We are apt to be indignant and say—"I don't believe those things are in my heart," and we refuse the diagnosis of the only Master there is of the human heart. We need never know the plague of our own heart and the terrible possibilities in human life if we will hand ourselves over to Jesus Christ; but if we stand on our own right and wisdom at any second an eruption may occur in our personal lives, and we may discover to our unutterable horror that we can be murderers, etc. This is one of the most ghastly and humiliating and devastating truths in the whole of human experience. Our convictions are strong on the basis of innocence, and many a man out of havoc and sin and the clanging of the gates of Paradise on the irreparable past, has to come to Jesus Christ with a life exhausted by sin. Why should he? We know what Jesus Christ can do for a man in that condition, but why cannot we see what He can do for the man who is not exhausted by sin? God does rescue the man who is down and out in sin, but there is no reason why any man should get there. Any man can get there, not one of us is immune. We may say—I don't know how he could do it. But we do. It is done by human beings just like you and just like me, without either our cowardice or our refinement. There is no virtue in not being bad on that line. It is because the vileness at the basis of the human heart has been closed over that we hear the talk nowadays of an "impossible chastity." Chastity is undesirable if I want to be a beast; but no holiness or rectitude of character is impossible; it is simply undesirable if I prefer the other way.

Education cannot deal with the plague of the heart, all our vows cannot touch it; the only Being Who can deal with it is God through a personal relationship to Him, by receiving His Spirit after accepting the diagnosis of Jesus Christ.

2. Prospecting in Pursuit of Happiness (7:25)
I applied mine heart to know, and to search, and to seek out wisdom, and the reason of things, and to know the wickedness of folly, even of foolishness and madness.

Solomon prospected to find out where the true essential enjoyment of life lay—was it in being an animal, an intellectualist, an aesthete, a governor, in being educated or uneducated? And he came to the conclusion that a man cannot find the true essential joy of his life anywhere but in his relationship to God.

Rationalism can never be the basis of things. Reason is my guide among things as they are, but reason cannot account for things being as they are. We do not think on the basis of Christianity at all. We are taught to think like pagans for six days a week and to reverse the order for one day, consequently in critical moments we think as pagans and our religion is left in the limbo of the inarticulate. Our thinking is based not on Hebrew Wisdom and confidence in God, but on the Wisdom of the Greeks which is removed from practical life, and on that basis we persuade ourselves that if a man knows a thing is wrong he will not do it. That is not true. The plague with me, apart from the grace of God, is that I know what is right, but I'm hanged if I'll do it! What I want to know is, can anyone tell me of a power that will alter my "want to"? Education will never alter the "want to," neither will high ideals nor vowing; that is where the great fundamental mistake in dealing with human problems has been made. It is only when a man is born from above (RV mg) of the Spirit of God that he finds the "want to" is altered. God does not take away the capacity to go wrong; if He did, we should not be worth anything. It is never impossible to go wrong.

We can only deal with the "sty" on the basis of Redemption, not by thinking or by education, but only by Redemption which is worked out by the Spirit of God.

3. Persecution and Peril of the Hell-Cat (Ecclesiastes 7:26)
And I find more bitter than death the woman, whose heart is snares and nets, and her hands as bands: whoso pleaseth God shall escape from her; but the sinner shall be taken by her.

The relationship of man and woman has been totally misrepresented. The revelation in the Bible is not that it is a question of the one being unequal to the other but of the two being one. "In the day that God created man, in the likeness of God made He him; male and female created He them; and blessed them, and called their name Adam, in the day when they were created" (Genesis 5:1–2). Man, the male being, took the government into his own hands and thereby introduced sin into the human race, and when God spoke He said that the Redeemer should come through the

---

* "In Adam and Eve we are dealing with the primal creations of God. . . . Eve stands for the soul side, the psychic side, of the human creation, all her sympathies and her affinities are with the other creations of God around. Adam stands for the spirit side, the kingly, Godward side. Adam and Eve together are the likeness of God, for God said: 'Let us make man in our own image, male and female created He them.' The revelation made here is that woman stands not as inferior to man, but that she stands in quite a different relation to all things, and both are required to make the complete, rounded creation of God referred to by the big general term Mankind. Eve, having this affinity and sympathy with the creation round about, would naturally listen with much more unsuspecting interest to the suggestions which came through the subtle creature that talked to her. The Bible says that Eve was deceived, the Bible does not say that Adam was deceived; consequently Adam is far more responsible than Eve, for Adam sinned deliberately. There was not the remotest conscious intention in Eve's heart of disobeying. She was deceived by the subtle wisdom of Satan via the Serpent. Adam, however, was not deceived in any shape or form; when Eve came to him he understood it was disobedience, and he sinned with a deliberate understanding of what he was doing, so the Bible associates sin with Adam (Romans 5:12), and transgression with Eve (1 Timothy 2:14). (In this connection it is of importance to note that the Bible reveals that our Redeemer entered into the world by the woman.)"—*Biblical Psychology,* Ch. III.—*Footnote in original text.*

woman (see Genesis 3:15–16). The Mother of Jesus Christ was a virgin. Redemption comes through woman, not through man.

A woman can sink lower than a man because she can rise higher; the woman who has not a right relationship to God may become a she devil, e.g., the attitude of a woman in revenge. The tragedies of human life along this line are appalling. Four things—sex, money, food, and mother earth—make a man a king and a woman a queen, or they make a man a beast and a woman a she devil.

Any lad who gets enveigled[28] by the kind of woman Solomon is describing will find that the tendrils will remain to the day of his death unless God blasts them out by Redemption. The bands round his soul will never snap otherwise, it is impossible. The terror and iniquity Solomon is speaking of is being repeated over and over again in our day. The moral nemesis runs right through, and Solomon's counsel is right, the only way a man can escape is by pleasing God. If once these relationships are started in a man's life, the only thing he can do is to go to God, to scurry to Him like a rabbit. A man may give up the practices, but he will never escape the moral nemesis, it will haunt him in his unconscious personality. There is no power in vowing or education or forgetting that can release him, but "whoso pleaseth God shall escape," that is, committing himself to Jesus Christ and being delivered.

Solomon is not "slanging" woman, but pointing out that the result of sin in the human race is to have made the feminine part of Man which ought to be directly related to God, demoniacal if not so related. The one who hauls you nearer to God is your mother or wife or sweetheart; but if your woman is not related to God, then the good Lord deliver you! No man is a match for the iniquity that is feminine when it is out of touch with God. When Pope said that "most women have no characters at all," he meant the same thing, that a woman's character comes from the essential relation of her life. If she is essentially related to God, her whole life is a sacrament for God; if not, her life may be a sacrament for the devil. The Bible reveals that the essentially feminine is meant to be the handmaid of God; but if the essentially feminine is prostitute, no man on earth can withstand her. In all Celtic races there is a terrific suspicion of women, the reason being that woman goes right back to the basis of things, which is inarticulate. A man can neither rise so high nor sink so low as a woman.

Any man or woman who falls in love comes right into God's presence, he or she instantly feels religious. Once love—my sovereign preference for another per-

son—is awakened, it always goes direct to God like a homing pigeon. It is not hypocrisy on the part of a lad when he begins to pray, he cannot help it, his love is the finest lodestar in his life. That is the contrast between love and lust. Love can wait and worship endlessly; lust says—I must have it at once. The thing that can be hellishly wrong can be marvellously right.

4. Perfidiousness of Perpetual Relation of Man and Woman *(Ecclesiastes 7:27–28)*

Behold, this have I found, saith the preacher, counting one by one, to find out the account: which yet my soul seeketh, but I find not: one man among a thousand have I found; but a woman among all those have I not found.

Solomon is not talking as a bitter disenchanted man, he is giving the Hebrew conception of things, that the counterpart of the woman is the man of God, and if she cannot find him she is either broken-hearted or she may become a woman of the devil. "I have looked for the essential wisdom in a man and have not found it; in a woman and have not found it there either." In human life as it is there is something perfidious in the perpetual relationship of man and woman.

Paul's counsel in dealing with marriage has been misrepresented—"Wives, submit yourselves unto your own husbands," because we have taken the word "submit" to mean the obedience due from a slave to his master. It is not the obedience of an inferior to a superior, but the obedience of the equality of love. In the New Testament the word "obey" is used to express the relationship of equals. ". . . though He was a Son, yet learned obedience by the things which He suffered" (RV).

"For the husband is the head of the wife, even as Christ is the head of the church." If Christ is the Head of the husband, he is easily the head of the wife, not by effort, but because of the nature of the essentially feminine. But if Jesus Christ is not the Head of the husband, the husband is not the head of the wife. Our Lord always touches the most sacred human relationships, and He says—You must be right with Me first before those relationships can be right; and if they hinder your getting right with Me, then you must hate them (see Luke 14:26).

5. Perfection and Perversion of Humanity *(Ecclesiastes 7:29)*

Lo, this only have I found, that God hath made man upright; but they have sought out many inventions.

The Bible states that God made man, i.e., the Federal Head of the race, in His own image. The only other

---

28. enveigled: to be snared by ingenuity or flattery; hoodwinked; deluded; beguiled.

Being in the image of God is Jesus Christ, the Second Adam. By eating of the fruit of the tree of knowledge of good and evil, Adam knew evil positively and good negatively. The Second Adam never ate of the fruit of the tree; He knew evil negatively by positively knowing good, and when a man is reborn of the Spirit of God he finds that that is the order God intended. Until we are born again we know good only by contrast with evil. The bias of the human heart is to find out the bad things first. How many of us are curious concerning the right way of life, concerning purity and nobility, and how many are curious to find out the borderland mysteries? The fruit of the tree of knowledge of good and evil has given human nature its bias of insatiable curiosity on the "sty" line. It is only after readjustment by Jesus Christ that the bias is on the other line, a tremendous thirst after God. "This is life eternal, that they might know Thee."

SOME PERSPECTIVE
Ecclesiastes 8

. . . life is not as idle ore,

But iron dug from central gloom,
*   And heated hot with burning fears,*
And dipped in baths of hissing tears.
*   And batter'd by the shocks of doom*
To shape and use.

                                    Tennyson

1. In the Diplomatic Service (Ecclesiastes 8:1–5)
   (a) Courtiers—Discretion (verse 1)
   (b) Consistency to Decrees (verse 2)
   (c) Character and Deportment (verse 3)
   (d) Commands of Despotism (verse 4)

2. In the Democratic Scrum (Ecclesiastes 8:6–10)
   (a) Power to Wilfulness (verses 6–7)
   (b) Powerlessness of Willingness (verse 8)
   (c) Price of Will Power (verse 9)
   (d) Perversity of Will Worship (verse 10)

3. In the Dispensational Scheme (Ecclesiastes 8:11–17)
   (a) Patience of God and Bad (verse 11)
   (b) Patience of God and Good (verses 12–13)
   (c) Preordination of God and Now (verses 14–15)
   (d) Probation of God and Worry (verse 16)
   (e) Providence of God and Faith (verse 17)

1. In the Diplomatic Service *(Ecclesiastes 8:1–5)*

It is easy to despise the man above me because I know nothing about him, but Solomon counsels us to have a wider perspective, to look at things beyond our insular notions. It is a great education to try and put yourself into the circumstances of others before passing judgement on them. Solomon's counsel in these verses lies with these who in this order of things happen to be in the diplomatic service.

(a) Courtiers' Discretion (verse 1)
Who is as the wise man? and who knoweth the interpretation of a thing? A man's wisdom maketh his face to shine, and the boldness of his face shall be changed.

In Old Testament days if a man came before an Eastern monarch with a sad countenance, he was liable to punishment (see Nehemiah 2:2). The discretion of a courtier does not make him a hypocrite, but puts him in the state of mind whereby his face indicates a strength and boldness which does not quaver. If you watch the faces of men who move much in diplomatic circles you will see exactly what Solomon indicates, an uninterpretable expression. The discretion of a courtier is to keep a bold face. Society is based on playacting, it must be. You cannot say what you really think; if you do, other people will too, and if everyone were absolutely frank there would be no room for us!

The Bible point of view about government is that God compels man to govern man for Him, whether he likes it or not. The ordinance of government, whether it is a bad or good government, does not lie with men, but is entirely in God's hands; the king or the government will have to answer to God (cf. 1 Peter 2:13–14). The conservative attitude—My king, right or wrong—is a degeneration from the one great central point of the government of man by man.

God created a certain nation from the loins of one man, to be His own people; they were not to be like the other nations of the world, but to be the bond slaves of Jehovah until every nation came to know God (see Deuteronomy 17:14–15). Israel and Judah said, "Nay, but we will have a king over us (see 1 Samuel 8:19–20). The best kings Israel and Judah ever had were David and Solomon, and yet the most troublesome conditions as well as the most prosperous came during their reigns. Whether a king is of the order of the autocratic kings of the East, or the order of the Kaiser, the explanation of kingship, according to the Bible, is that it is the result of the wrong that entered into the world by the first man taking his rule over himself.

Hell is an eternal and an abiding distress to whatever goes into it. Whatever goes into hell can never again be established as a right thing. We say that militarism is going into hell just now; but militarism will crop up again in some form or another. *Something* has gone into hell, but it is difficult to say what.

(b) Consistency to Decrees (verse 2)
I counsel thee to keep the king's commandment, and that in regard of the oath of God.

Anything bound before the king is bound as by the oath of God, and the consistency of a courtier is to abide by it. If a man lives in that order of things he must not be a traitor, he cannot take the action of a free individual man. The existence of peace and order depends entirely on this being remembered.

(c) Character and Deportment (verse 3)
Be not hasty to go out of his sight: stand not in an evil thing; for he doeth whatsoever pleaseth him.

Deportment is the way a man conducts himself. See that you neither hurry in nor out, says Solomon; your attitude must be both deliberate and careful. In the higher circles of social life this same thing is necessary.

It is an easy business for the man who deals in black and white to pass judgement on the man who deals in grey. In the diplomatic service a man never deals with black and white, only with grey. For instance, it is easy to condemn British rule in India or in Egypt, but it is another matter to recognise the vast series of complications which the rulers in these countries have to face. In politics also it is difficult to steer a course; there is a complication of forces to be dealt with which most of us know nothing about. We have no affinity for this kind of thing, and it is easy to ignore the condition of the men who have to live there, and to pass condemnation on them.

(d) Commands of Despotism (verse 4)
Where the word of a king is, there is power: and who may say unto him, What doest thou?

If a man is a courtier under a despotic king there is no possibility of replying; he has to obey to the last limit and has no right to a private opinion. The wise man is the one who knows when to speak and when to be silent.

2. In the Democratic Scrum (Ecclesiastes 8:6–10)
All this has nothing to do with us, it is outside our perspective. How a king lives is a matter of moon-shine to us; but one day we may have to pass judgement. Before long the democratic scrum may have to pass judgement on men who are not democrats, on courtiers, and on despotic kings, and before we can pass judgement we must have perspective. It is easy to condemn a state of things we know nothing about while we make excuses for the condition of things we ourselves live in.

The state of things resulting in the "democratic scrum" is better than the perfection of a machine. In our own country, rightly or wrongly, we committed regicide; France did the same. The world has never had to pay the price for either Britain or France that it has for Germany. Similarly, if I never correct my child I am making a nice mess for other folks by and by. We have lost sight of these things, but they are elements we have to come in contact with.

(a) Power to Wilfulness (verses 6–7)
Because to every purpose there is time and judgement, therefore the misery of man is great upon him. For he knoweth not that which shall be: for who can tell him when it shall be?

There is a power to wilfulness in man and when it is let loose there is the "wild ass" to account for; no matter what a man chooses, he heads towards evil.

The same problem is found in religion. One of the counterfeits of the rule of God is the Roman Catholic Church. It is a perfect system of government. After the Reformation when the people were delivered from the incubus of Roman Catholic domination, many of them went more to the devil. Whenever a man is freed from a dominance that is ostensibly wrong, he has a power of will which may make for his misery. The same thing happened in connection with the freeing of the slaves; instead of using their freedom, many went back to their masters, while others abused their freedom.

(b) Powerlessness of Willingness (verse 8)
There is no man that hath power over the spirit to retain the spirit; neither hath he power in the day of death: and there is no discharge in that war; neither shall wickedness deliver those that are given to it.

A man belonging to the democratic scrum may make up his mind that he is willingly going to do good, but no man can do it alone. The democratic rule is made up of people just like you and me, and unless we keep together, either by the right of a king or by the sway of some religious or civilised rule, we will kick things to bits, and the most willing amongst us will have the worst of it. "The divine right of kings" is a counterfeit for the true government of human life by man; at the same time it must be reckoned with.

We have to lay our account with the fact that the deepest bias in man is not towards God but away from Him, and if the individual man is allowed a right of way, he has a power of will which will increase the common misery. We have seen the hollow mockery of the diplomatic order of things under the divine right of kings, and to-day, rightly or wrongly, we are all in the democratic scrum as never before; but neither autocracy nor democracy will solve the problem.

(c) Price of Will Power (verse 9)
All this have I seen, and applied my heart unto every work that is done under the sun: there is a time wherein one man ruleth over another to his own hurt.

The man who has power over another may hurt himself by the exercise of that power unless he himself is ruled by a greater power. If I have had a vivid religious experience and have power over people by means of that experience, the danger is that I usurp the place of God and say, "You must come my way; you must have this experience." This may damage you, but it damages me more, because my spirit is far removed from the spirit of Jesus Christ, it is the spirit of a spiritual prig. Whenever I exercise will power without at the same time being dominated myself, I damage something or someone.

(d) Perversity of Will Worship (verse 10)
And so I saw the wicked buried, who had come and gone from the place of the holy, and they were forgotten in the city where they had so done: this is also vanity.

Paul warns of the things which "have indeed a show of wisdom in will-worship," the idea that you are sufficient to govern yourself. We have got out of conceit with Neitzsche's phrase, "the power to will"—if I have enough will I can do it.

The despotic rule is full of defect, misery and anguish, so is the democratic rule. Men may make all kinds of rules, but they get back again into despotism. Every man has power to go to hell because by nature man's will is towards self-realisation.

We may have no affinity with these things, but in passing judgement (and we never know when the time for passing judgement may come), we will be criminally unjust judges if we have not a true perspective. After the war it will not be a question of judging the autocrat but of judging the democrat, and the one is as bad as the other unless he is ruled by a power greater than himself.

3. In the Dispensational Scheme
(Ecclesiastes 8:11–17)
(a) Patience of God and Bad (verse 11)
Because sentence against an evil work is not executed speedily, therefore the heart of the sons of men is fully set in them to do evil.

We say, Why does God allow these things? Why does He allow a despot to rule? In this dispensation it is the patient long-suffering of God that is being manifested. God allows men to say what they like and do what they like (see 2 Peter 3:14). Peter says that God is long-suffering, and He is giving us ample opportunity to try whatever line we like both in individual and national life. If God were to end this dispensation now, the human race would have a right to say, You should have waited, there is a type of thing You never let us try.

God is leaving us to prove to the hilt that it cannot be done in any other way than Jesus Christ's way, or the human race would not be satisfied.

(b) Patience of God and Good (verses 12–13)
Though a sinner do evil an hundred times, and his days be prolonged, yet surely I know that it shall be well with them that fear God, which fear before Him: but it shall not be well with the wicked, neither shall he prolong his days, which are as a shadow; because he feareth not before God.

God allows the good to develop itself in the heart of the bad, and Solomon banks on the fact that the man who is rooted and grounded in confidence in God will come out right in the end. Nowadays we have the preaching of expediency: If you tell people that, they will take advantage of it. If the Almighty leaves His open knives around, it is not our business to put on the sheath. The rugged truths of God seem to give licence to men; but do they? The prig notion makes us say certain things in order to terrorise people from doing wrong. But how much better are they if they don't do it? The reward for doing right is not that I get an insurance ticket for heaven, but that I do the right because it is right. Honesty ceases to be the best policy if I am honest for a reason. If any man will live godly, he shall suffer persecution. If a man wants success and a good time in the actual condition of things as they are, let him keep away from Jesus Christ, let him ignore His claims and the heroism of His holiness, there is no commercial value in it. In the final wind up it is the man who has stuck true to God and damned the consequences who will come out the best; whether he has made the best or the worst of himself in this life is another matter.

(c) Preordination of God and Now
(verses 14–15)
There is a vanity which is done upon the earth; that there be just men, unto whom it happeneth according to the work of the wicked; again, there be wicked men, to whom it happeneth according to the work of the righteous: I said that this also is vanity. Then I commended mirth, because a man hath no better thing under the sun than to eat, and to drink, and to be

merry: for that shall abide with him of his labour the days of his life, which God giveth him under the sun.

God's programme for a man is Now, not what he is going to do presently but what he is now. Solomon says your attitude to life as it actually is now, is to remember you are a man or woman, and that you have to live on the earth as a human being and not try to be an angel. It is your relationship to God which fits you to live on the earth in the right way, not necessarily the successful way. Sometimes you will have the worst of it for doing right.

(d) Probation of God and Worry (verse 16)
When I applied mine heart to know wisdom, and to see the business that is done upon the earth: (for also there is that neither day nor night seeth sleep with his eyes).

To-day men's hearts are failing them for fear, not the men in the actual fighting, they are wonderfully sustained; but the business man at home. His relationships involve a great deal more than "now," they involve the presently and his children who are to come after him. How can he have faith in God when he sees the security of the future hauled to bits? Solomon indicates that the wisest thing to do is to build our faith in God and not far-reach so that we have to watch everything and have no room for faith in God, no time to pay attention to how we live in the Now.

(e) Providence of God and Faith (verse 17)
Then I beheld all the work of God, that a man cannot find out the work that is done under the sun: because though a man labour to seek it out, yet he shall not find

it; yea farther; though a wise man think to know it, yet shall he not be able to find it.

The summing up of the whole matter, says Solomon, is that you cannot locate yourself, you are placed in circumstances over which you have no control. You do not choose your own heredity or your own disposition, these things are beyond your control, and yet these are the things which influence you. You may rake the bottom of the universe, but you cannot explain things; they are wild, there is nothing rational about them. We cannot get to the bottom of things; we cannot get behind the before of birth or the after of death; therefore the wise man is the one who trusts the wisdom of God, not his own wits. The amateur providence trusts his wits, and if he has not been knocked out by the hard problems of life, he can say cheap and nasty things; but when once he is hit by the real tragedy of life he will find it is not in the power of human wits to guide him, and he becomes either a man of faith or a fatalist. Faith is trust in a God Whose ways you cannot trace, but whose character you know, and the man of faith hangs on to the fact that He is a God of honour. Fatalism means "my number's up," I have to bow to the power whether I like it or not; I do not know the character of the power, but it is greater than I am and I must submit. In this dispensation we do know the character of God, although we do not know why His providential will should be as it is. Solomon indicates that the only thing to do in the present condition of things is to remain true to God, and God will not only see us through but will see the whole thing out to a perfect explanation. That is the faith of a Christian, and it takes some sticking to.

TIME, DEATH AND TRIFLES
Ecclesiastes 9

If there be good in that I wrought,
Thy hand compelled it, Master, Thine.
Where I have failed to meet Thy thought
I know, through Thee, the blame is mine.
Take not that vision from my ken;
O, whatso'er may spoil or speed,
Help me to need no aid from men,
That I may help such men as need!

Rudyard Kipling

1. The Indiscernible Public Power of God (Ecclesiastes 9:1–2)

2. The Interim Probationary Programme of God (Ecclesiastes 9:3–4)

3. The Invincible Powerful Portion of Death (Ecclesiastes 9:5–6)

4. The Instructive Practical Prudence of Time (Ecclesiastes 9:7–9)

5. The Imperative Performing Practice of Work (Ecclesiastes 9:10)

6. The Incalculable Precarious Preference of Life (Ecclesiastes 9:11–12)

7. The Invidious Petulant Price for Wisdom (Ecclesiastes 9:13–16)

8. The Inveterate Popular Prejudice for Grab (Ecclesiastes 9:17–18)

We are apt to imagine that if we cannot state a thing in words it is of no value to us. What counts in talking and in reading is the atmosphere that is produced and what is opened up that would not be otherwise, There is a literature of knowledge and a literature of power. The former gives us informing stuff and we can say—This is what I have got; by the latter you cannot say what you have got but you are the better for it, your mind and heart are enlarged. We need more than information. The domain of things represented by the literature of power is that which comes with a knowledge of God's Book. One of the great secrets of life is that obedience is the key to spiritual life as curiosity is the key to intellectual life. In the spiritual domain curiosity is not only of no use but is a direct hindrance. When once a man learns that spiritual knowledge can only be gained by obedience, the emancipation of his nature is incalculable

1. The Indiscernible Public Power of God
(Ecclesiastes 9:1–2)
For all this I considered in my heart even to declare all this, that the righteous, and the wise, and their works, are in the hand of God: no man knoweth either love or hatred by all that is before them. All things come alike to all: there is one event to the righteous, and to the wicked; to the good and to the clean, and to the unclean; to him that sacrificeth, and to him that sacrificeth not: as is the good, so is the sinner; and he that sweareth, as he that feareth an oath.

Indiscernible—you cannot discern exactly why the power should take the turn it does. The old divines spoke of a miracle as "the public power of God." God emerges suddenly and does something beyond human power. Our Lord's miracles were cinematograph shows to His disciples of what His Father was always doing (see John 2:1–11). Our Lord never worked a miracle in order to show what He could do; He was not a wonder worker, and when people sought Him on that line, He did nothing (cf. Luke 23:8–9). Solomon is referring to the indiscernible power of God in that He completely mystifies any calculations you may make in life. If you go on the mathematical or the rational line, you will come across something you cannot cal-

culate, something that can only be described as an act of God. You cannot say that because a man is good and has been well brought up and behaves well that he will reach success and prosperity; you will find that bad men who overreach and tyrannise come to prosperity while good men do not (see Psalm 73:1–18).

It is much easier not to look at the facts of life but to take an intellectual view which acts as a searchlight, and has the tyranny of an idea or an intuition. A man's intellectual view reveals what it does and no more, everything looks simple in the light of it; but when we come to the daylight of facts we shall find something that knocks the bottom board out of all our calculations. If you read a book by a philosopher about life it looks as simple as can be, no complications or difficulties; but when you are flung out "into the soup," you find that your simple line of explanation won't work at all. Just when you thought you had found the secret, you find you are off the line.

Fundamentally, not shallowly, life can never be guided by principles. In the Christian domain we make the blunder of trying to guide our life by the principles of Jesus Christ's teaching. The basis of Christianity is not primarily virtue and honesty and goodness, not even holiness, but a personal relationship to God in Jesus Christ which works out all the time by "spontaneous moral originality." Principles are of a lesser order, and if they are applied apart from the life of Jesus Christ they may become anti-Christian. Things cannot be worked out on a logical line, there is always something incalculable. You may think to reach your goal through obedience to a set of principles, but you will find it won't work that road. Solomon says that neither the good man nor the bad man ends where you expect him to. All you can say is that every man has his own setting from a starting-point he knows nothing about. One of the finest and wisest books ever written for young men is Leckie's *Map of Life.* Leckie was not a genius, but a man of intense moral earnestness and a careful intellectual collator as well,

2. The Interim Probationary Programme of God (Ecclesiastes 9:3–4)
This is an evil among all things that are done under the sun, that there is one event unto all: yea, also the heart of the sons of men is full of evil, and madness is in their heart while they live, and after that they go to the dead. For to him that is joined to all the living there is hope: for a living dog is better than a dead lion.

The Bible always states the obvious, and we find it to be the thing we have never looked at. Very few of us see the obvious, consequently when it is stated it strikes us as being original.

"For a living dog is better than a dead lion." "The Lord spake unto Joshua, saying, Moses My servant is dead"—now therefore go to mourning? No—"now therefore arise, go over this Jordan, thou, and all this people, unto the land which I do give to them." The Bible never allows us to waste time over the departed. It does not mean that the fact of human grief is ignored, but the worship of reminiscence is never allowed. "We have to remember the departed and live in the light of them"—the Bible won't have it. "While the child was yet alive, I fasted and wept; for I said, Who can tell whether GOD will be gracious to me, that the child may live? But now he is dead, wherefore should I fast? can I bring him back again?" In the Garden of Gethsemane the disciples went to sleep when they should have watched with their Lord, and when Jesus came He said, "Sleep on now, and take your rest: . . . Arise, let us be going" (RV). That opportunity is lost for ever, you cannot alter it, but arise and go to the next thing. We find this inevitable vanishing all through the Bible, and a man has to "ring out the grief that saps the mind." One of the most deeply ingrained forms of selfishness in human nature is that of misery. The isolation of misery is far more proud than any other form of conceit.

The interim between birth and death is a school training, a programme of which we have not the laying out. We may calculate and say we are going to do this and that, but "ye know not what shall be on the morrow." It is a haphazard life, and we have to bank on God's wisdom, not on our own. It looks as if Solomon were counselling the Bohemian life, and as if Jesus Christ did the same when He said "Therefore I say unto you, Take no thought for your life." A Bohemian is careless about everything, and neither Jesus Christ nor Solomon teaches that. Jesus Christ taught that a man was to be carefully careless about everything saving his relationship to God. The great care of the life, Jesus says, is to make the relationship to God the one care. Most of us are careful about everything saving that.

The life we are living has a programme which we fulfil but about which we know nothing. We have been put into a programme that we have no say in, and we bungle our part by trying to be our own organisers.

There's a divinity that shapes our ends,
Rough-hew them how we will.

3. The Invincible Powerful Portion of Death *(Ecclesiastes 9:5–6)*

For the living know that they shall die: but the dead know not any thing, neither have they any more a reward; for the memory of them is forgotten. Also their love, and their hatred, and their envy, is now perished; neither have they any more a portion for ever in anything that is done under the sun.

There is no further reward in practical existence for a dead man. We must lay our account with the invincible portion of death, it will come every time. Remember that your friend will die and act accordingly, and many a mean thing will wither on your tongue. There is a difference between sensitiveness and impressionableness. A sensitive man never says anything that would sting another, whereas the one we are apt to call sensitive is only impressionable to what stings him. Very few of us are sensitive; we are all impressionable. It is remembering the invincible portion of death that makes things different. Solomon says you cannot bank on insurance, or speculations, or on any kind of calculation; you can bank on only one thing, that your interim of life may at any second be cut short; therefore your only confidence is to remain true to God.

4. The Instructive Practical Prudence of Time *(Ecclesiastes 9:7–9)*

Go thy way, eat thy bread with joy, and drink thy wine with a merry heart; for God now accepteth thy works. Let thy garments be always white; and let thy head lack no ointment. Live joyfully with the wife whom thou lovest all the days of the life of thy vanity, which he hath given thee under the sun, all the days of thy vanity: for that is thy portion in this life. and in thy labour which thou takest under the sun.

"Let thy garments be always white," i.e., live suitably attired to your station in life. Solomon's insistence is on the haphazard. These things—food, sex, money and mother earth, must always have their place in the life of any man of God, and they either make men and women devils or make them what they should be. The man of God uses these things to express his relationship to God; whereas the man who does not know God tries to find his lasting good in the things themselves. Paul in riddling false religion says that it will deny the basis of life, that is, it will teach abstinence from meats and marriage. The practical test of a man's life in Time is how he lives in connection with these things.

The devastations of war are appalling, but there are compensations, and one compensation of this war will be that we shall be driven back to the elemental. Some problems will not be revived again, they are finished; but every man will have a totally new attitude to these things and a new reverence for them. They will have a hold now which the refinement of civilisation had made us lose.

5. The Imperative Performing Practice of Work *(Ecclesiastes 9:10)*

Whatsoever thy hand findeth to do, do it with thy might; for there is no work, nor device, nor knowledge, nor wisdom, in the grave, whither thou goest.

The Bible nowhere teaches us to work for work's sake. That is one of the great bugbears of the anti-Christian movement in the heart of Christianity to-day. It is Work with a capital W in which the worship of Jesus Christ is lost sight of. People will sacrifice themselves endlessly for the work. Perspiration is mistaken for inspiration. Our guidance with regard to work is to remember that its value is in what it does for us. It is difficult not to let ulterior considerations come in— "What's the good of doing this, we are only here for a short time, why should we do it as if it were to last for ever?" Solomon's counsel is—"Whatsoever thy hand attaineth to do by thy strength *that do*" (RV mg). He is not recommending work for work's sake, but because through the drudgery of work the man himself is developed. When you deify work, you apostatise from Jesus Christ. In the private spiritual life of many a Christian it is work that has hindered concentration on God. When work is out of its real relation it becomes a means of evading concentration on God. Carlyle pointed out that the weariness and sickness of modern life is shown in the restlessness of work. When a man is not well he is always doing things, an eternal fidget. Intense activity may be the sign of physical weariness. When a man is healthy his work is so much part of himself that you never know he is doing it; he does it with his might, and that makes no fuss. We lose by the way we do our work the very thing it is intended to bring us.

At the back of all is the one thing God is after, what a man is, not what he does, and Solomon keeps that in view all the time. It is what we are in our relation to things that counts, not what we attain to in them. If you put attainment as the end you may reap a broken heart and find that all your outlay ends in disaster, death cuts it short, or disease, or ruin.

6. The Incalculable Precarious Preference of Life (*Ecclesiastes 9:11–12*)

I returned, and saw under the sun, that the race is not to the swift, nor the battle to the strong, neither yet bread to the wise, nor yet riches to men of understanding, nor yet favour to men of skill; but time and chance happeneth to them all. For man also knoweth not his time: as the fishes that are taken in an evil net, and as the birds that are caught in the snare; so are the sons of men snared in an evil time, when it falleth suddenly upon them.

Life is immensely precarious, haphazard. A Christian does not believe that everything that happens is ordained by God; what he believes is that he has to get hold of God's order no matter what happens in the haphazard. "And we know that to them that love God all things work together for good, even to them that are called according to His purpose" (Romans

8:28 RV). All things are permitted by God, but all things are not appointed by God, they appoint themselves; but God's order abides, and if I maintain my relationship to Him He will make everything that happens work for my good. God on the one hand, myself on the other, and the rush of the haphazard in between will work toward the best.

"The race is not to the swift." The lad who is exceptionally clever at school very often becomes nothing afterwards; he attained too early. No boy has any right to attain too early or mature too quickly. By the time he comes to the age of twenty or thirty the power that ought to mature is not there, he has ripened too soon. The boy who gives the grandest promise does not always become what you expect, while the lad who is stodgy to begin with may come out top. One of the finest commentators on the Bible was an ignorant dunce as a lad, with no promise at all to begin with. There is always an incalculable element in everyone, therefore, Solomon argues, you cannot calculate. The crisis reveals what a man is made of. You cannot say what you would do in circumstances you have never been in because of this incalculable element, and when you are put in new circumstances you may suddenly find forces in yourself you never dreamed were there. You have no idea what is in you either for good or bad; you cannot estimate and say what you will do; therefore, says Solomon, don't bank on calculations.

"For man also knoweth not his time." You never know when your opportunity is going to come. Every man has to go out to sea to break from his moorings, whether by a storm or by a big lifting tide. There is a preference in life you cannot get at. Why does God choose one man and not another? "For promotion cometh neither from the east nor from the west, nor from the south. But God is the judge: He putteth down one, and setteth up another" (Psalm 75:6–7).

7. The Invidious Petulant Price for Wisdom (*Ecclesiastes 9:13–16*)

This wisdom have I seen also under the sun, and it seemed great unto me: There was a little city, and few men within it; and there came a great king against it, and besieged it, and built great bulwarks against it: now there was found in it a poor wise man, and he by his wisdom delivered the city; yet no man remembered that same poor man. Then said I, Wisdom is better than strength: nevertheless the poor man's wisdom is despised, and his words are not heard.

We do not put any price at all on wisdom when we have got what wisdom brings. When we attain success we do not remember the one who gave us the right counsel; the wise man who guided things aright is not taken into account. When a thing is done successfully in the Army or the Navy, it is very rarely the men of the regiment or the crew that are mentioned but only the figure head at the top. Any man with wisdom knows that that kind of preference is conceded, and there is no use losing heart over it. The discerning man understands that it is what lies behind the scenes that accounts for success. In the same way there has often been a remarkably good but obscure woman behind a prominent man who has done great things. Solomon's counsel is to take into account the fact that you cannot expect to be recognised. Remember that your lasting relationship is with God, otherwise you will find heartbreak and disappointment and become cynical.

8. The Inveterate Popular Prejudice for Grab
(Ecclesiastes 9:17–18)

The words of wise men are heard in quiet more than the cry of him that ruleth among fools. Wisdom is better than weapons of war: but one sinner destroyeth much good.

It is difficult to maintain a high standard when you are working in a community which has a lower standard. For example, we are told that the natives here do not understand any treatment but kicking and cursing and if they are not treated in that way will take advantage of you. That may be true, but you will also find that when they see you are allowing yourself to be taken advantage of, they themselves will begin to climb. When we are over-reached most of us get sick and give up. The counsel given by Jesus Christ all through is on the line of abandon.

When a life is taken from the shelter of its ignorance it goes through a stage of transition, often worse than the stage of ignorance, before it comes to real emancipation. Witness the Reformation and the freeing of the slaves. In the transition stage we want to grab things for ourselves and ruin all progress in life. Evolution, like Christian Science, is a hasty conclusion. There may be nine facts which seem to make a thing clear and conclusive, and one fact that contradicts. There is always something that swerves away from the explainable. The only explanation lies in a personal knowledge of God through Jesus Christ, not on the basis of philosophy or of thinking, but on the basis of a vital relationship to Him which works in the actual condition of things as they are. "I am the Way, the Truth, and the Life."

DIFFERENTIATIONS
Ecclesiastes 10

Neither mourn if human creeds be lower than the
    heart's desire!
Thro' the gates that bar the distance comes a gleam
    of what is higher.
Wait till Death has flung them open, when the man
    will make the Maker
Dark no more with human hatreds in the glare of
    deathless fire!

                        Tennyson

1. The Best of Men Are but the Best of Men (Ecclesiastes 10:1–3)
2. The Besetters of Men and the Behaviour of Men (Ecclesiastes 10:4–7)
3. The "Before" of Men Determines the "After" of Men (Ecclesiastes 10:8–10)
4. The "Beyond" of Men Decides the "Breed" of Men (Ecclesiastes 10:11–15)
5. The Beginnings of Mastery Disposes the Mastered (Ecclesiastes 10:16–17)
6. The Bungling of Men Spells the Beggary of Men (Ecclesiastes 10:18–20)

It is one of the sharpest disillusionments to learn that "the best of men are but the best of men," and it takes us some time to learn that it is true. The Apostle Paul brings out the same truth—Don't glory in men; don't think of men more highly than you ought to think. We always know what the other man should be, especially if he is a Christian. We are all lynx-eyed in seeing what other people ought to be. We erect terrific standards, and then criticise men for not reaching them. The standard of Christianity is not that of a man, but of God; and unless God can put His Spirit into a man, that standard can never be reached. According to New Testament wisdom and to Hebrew wisdom, until we are rightly related to God we will always be cruel to other men. Take it in the matter of love: if I am not related to God first my love becomes cruel, because I demand infinite satisfaction from the one I love; I demand from a human being what he or she can never give. There is only one Being Who can satisfy the last aching abyss of the human heart, and that is the Lord Jesus Christ.

1. The Best of Men Are but the Best of Men (Ecclesiastes 10:1–3)

Dead flies cause the ointment of the apothecary to send forth a stinking savour: so doth a little folly him that is in reputation for wisdom and honour. A wise man's heart is at his right hand; but a fool's heart at his left. Yea also, when he that is a fool walketh by the way, his wisdom faileth him, and he saith to everyone that he is a fool.

How many remember that Solomon ruled Israel magnificently for many years? We remember his supreme acts of folly, and Solomon says that is the way human life is summed up. We remember the bad a man has done but not the good. It is possible to blast a man's reputation by raising your shoulders; but you can never blast a man's character. Character is what a man is; reputation is what other people think he is. "A long and splendid possible friendship has often been ruined by the agile cleverness of some men for labels." You meet a man and sum him up in a phrase. There were possibilities of his becoming a friend, but he will never be that now. This kind of clever business ruins the possibility of friendship.

Again we are apt to lose all distinction of right and wrong and to make excuses and say—Oh yes, there is always one fact more. "There is so much good in the worst of us and so much bad in the best of us, that it ill behoves any of us to talk about the rest of us." Although you know that the best of men are but the best of men, it is part of moral calibre to hold true to the highest you know, and to remember that "there is none good save one, even God."

"A wise man's heart is at his right hand; but a fool's heart is at his left." A wise man's heart guides the decisions of his mind; a fool makes decisions of mind and his heart drags after him.

In laying your account with men, whether it be with a government or with a drill-sergeant, remember there is no such being as a perfect man. You are bound to find shortcomings; and beware of the snare of remembering only the bad things a man does. We are all built that way.

2. The Besetters of Men and the Behaviour of Men (Ecclesiastes 10:4–7)

If the spirit of the ruler rise up against thee, leave not thy place; for yielding pacifieth great offences. There is an evil which I have seen under the sun, as an error which proceedeth from the ruler: folly is set in great dignity, and the rich sit in low place. I have seen servants upon horses, and princes walking as servants upon the earth.

Solomon is stating the obvious; most of us are too clever to be obvious. He is dealing with the man who happens to be placed under a providential order of

tyranny. The difficulty of a man's behaviour is the kind of men that beset him as rulers, and Solomon's counsel is amazingly shrewd: Let him say what he likes, it will blow over in time. In practical life it is the providential order of tyranny that embitters men more quickly than anything. We all shirk the counsel of Jesus Christ when He says, in effect, Never look for justice but never cease to give it. If you do look for justice, you will become bitter and cease to be a disciple of Jesus Christ. You are in a providential order of tyranny in which your behaviour is to be determined by your previous relationship to God, that is, your conduct is to be determined by the relationship which reaches furthest back. In the same way if you are the servant of men for their sake you will soon be heartbroken; but if you serve men for the sake of Jesus Christ, nothing can ever discourage you (cf. 2 Corinthians 4:5). Solomon's counsel is to keep your mouth shut if you are under a tyranny where you can gain nothing by expressing yourself. Behave yourself rightly, and if you wait long enough the thing will be put right. After all, the man who loses his temper quickest is the one who finds it quickest. The man you need to beware of is not the man who flares up, but the man who smoulders, who is vindictive and harbours vengeance.

"Folly is set in great dignity, and the rich sit in low place." A ruler who is not a wise man places the fools in dignity through favouritism, and the man who lives at the basis of things and all in between have to be the cat's-paw of the man who has obtained his position through wire-pulling. You can never hold a steady course unless you are rightly related to God first of all.

One of the most difficult things to do is to place men. A man who knows men and can place them rightly is worth his weight in gold, and Solomon points out that such men are rare.

3. The "Before" of Men Determines the "After" of Men (Ecclesiastes 10:8–10)

He that diggeth a pit shall fall into it; and whoso breaketh an hedge, a serpent shall bite him. Whoso removeth stones shall be hurt therewith; and he that cleaveth wood shall be endangered thereby. If the iron be blunt, and he do not whet the edge, then must he put to more strength: but wisdom is profitable to direct.

Many men are determinate, but not deliberate, and sooner or later they have to revise their decisions. The thing that comes after in a man's career is frequently determined by his having gone too hot-headedly into things to begin with. Don't be too earnest in clearing away the hedges. What makes me act determines the result of my action in the record of my life. Earnestness is not everything; I may be an earnest lunatic. We use the phrase "drunk and incapable," but it is just as possible to be sober and incapable. The great thing is to be enthusiastic and capable. Solomon's warning is that earnestness may often cover up an evasion of concentration in a life. John McNeill[29] said about the student of Elisha who lost the axe-head—"If he had been of the modern school, Elisha would have said "Whack awa wi' the stump, man; earnestness is everything." "Solomon points out that earnestness may be the characteristic of a fool. Earnestness in prayer is often put in the place of right relationship to God. If you read the New Testament carefully you do not find that Jesus Christ ever counsels earnestness in prayer, except in Luke 11, and there it is earnestness in connection with importunate prayer on behalf of others. The prayer Jesus Christ counsels is that based on simplicity. "But when ye pray, use not vain repetitions, as the heathen do: for they think that they shall be heard for their much speaking. Be not ye therefore like unto them: for your Father knoweth what things ye have need of before ye ask Him." Prayer is never heard on the ground of earnestness, but only on the ground of the Redemption (see Hebrews 10:19).

4. The "Beyond" of Men Decides the "Breed" of Men *(Ecclesiastes 10:11–15)*

Surely the serpent will bite without enchantment; and a babbler is no better. The words of a wise man's mouth are gracious; but the lips of a fool will swallow up himself. The beginning of the words of his mouth is foolishness: and the end of his talk is mischievous madness. A fool also is full of words: a man cannot tell what shall be; and what shall be after him, who can tell him? The labour of the foolish wearieth every one of them, because he knoweth not how to go to the city.

If you are a wise man, you will lay your account with the fact that you cannot calculate. You cannot say that your charmer will charm the snake, it may sting you first. The before of a man's birth determines his breed. That one man is as good as another is a theory that does not work out in practice. Some men are handicapped before they are born; others are perfectly fit before they are born, their heredity is clear. Breeding counts every time, but if you over-breed you produce genius and lunacy. Breeding counts for nothing in the value of a man in God's sight, it is the heart relationship that counts, and one man cannot judge another. When Jesus Christ came He paid no attention to breeding. In matters of practical living, says Solomon, if you are wise you will watch a man's breeding; but when you estimate men in God's sight, you must esti-

mate from another standpoint, that of their relationship to Him.

5. The Beginnings of Mastery Disposes the Mastered *(Ecclesiastes 10:16–17)*

Woe to thee, O land, when thy king is a child, and thy princes eat in the morning! Blessed art thou, O land, when thy king is the son of nobles, and thy princes eat in due season, for strength, and not for drunkenness!

When rulers eat in the morning they reorganise God's order and are simply shallow Epicureans. The man who masters men merely by his position determines the kind of men he masters. Some men are completely crushed and broken, sulky and taciturn, and their master is to blame. Whereas the influence of one man of integrity over men is incalculable, e.g., Donald Hankey's *Beloved Captain;* and it is a terrible condemnation if a man's influence is without that characteristic. A man's character tells over his head all the time. The mastership of a man who does not defy the ordinances of God is that of worth-ship, he is worthy; whereas men who are mastered by those given to defying the law of God come to an appalling condition.

6. The Bungling of Men Spells the Beggary of Men *(Ecclesiastes 10:18–20)*

By much slothfulness the building decayeth; and through idleness of the hands the house droppeth through. A feast is made for laughter, and wine maketh merry: but money answereth all things. Curse not the king, no not in thy thought; and curse not the rich in thy bedchamber: for a bird of the air shall carry the voice, and that which hath wings shall tell the matter.

"By much slothfulness the building decayeth." Solomon is pointing out that the bungling of men spells the beggary of men. "Whatsoever thy hand findeth to do, do it with thy might." Our version of that too often is— "There's a thing to be done, but why should I do it?" Or, "Why should it be done properly, it is only for a little while?" That line spells beggary. No man if he is wise will be content with a knock-up job.[30]

"Money answereth all things." Although money may cover up defects, yet ultimately it may lead to disaster.

"Curse not the king, no not in thy thought." We cannot think anything without the thought having its consequence. Jesus Christ warns us of this—"With what measure ye mete, it shall be measured unto you" (RV). The basis of life is retribution, but Our Lord allows no room for retaliation.

---

29. John McNeill: late-nineteenth-century Scottish evangelist brought to faith in Christ through the preaching of D. L. Moody.

30. knock-up job: something done hastily, carelessly, or in a slipshod way.

TIMIDITIES OF RATIONALISM
Ecclesiastes 11

Time was I shrank from what was right
From fear of what was wrong,
I would not brave the sacred fight
Because the foe was strong.

But now I cast that finer sense
And surer shame aside;
Such dread of sin was indolence,
Such aim at Heaven was Pride!

Newman

1. The Counsels of Extravagance (Ecclesiastes 11:1)

2. The Confusion of Economy (Ecclesiastes 11:2–4)

3. The Confines of Exposition (Ecclesiastes 11:5–6)

4. The Consciousness of Experience (Ecclesiastes 11:7–8)

5. The Concentration After Expansion (Ecclesiastes 11:9–10)

The boldness of Rationalism is not in what it does, but in the way it criticises. Rationalism is a method of criticism, but when it comes to action the rationalist is amazingly timid. Nothing bold has ever been done in the name of rationalism. In all the big crises of life the rationalist is at a discount. He is great at writing books, at pointing out the futilities of religion, etc., but no rationalist has ever produced the heroism, the adventure, or the nobility that the people and the things he criticised have produced. The reasonable man is, after all, the timid man, when it comes to certain things he refuses to venture.

We hear it said that Jesus Christ taught nothing contrary to common sense: everything Jesus Christ taught was contrary to common sense. Not one thing in the Sermon on the Mount is common sense. The basis of Christianity is neither common sense nor rationalism, it springs from another centre, viz. a personal relationship to God in Christ Jesus in which everything is ventured on from a basis that is not seen. We are told that God expects us to use our "sanctified common sense"; but if we mean that that is Christianity, we will have to come to the conclusion that Jesus Christ was mad. If you go on the economical basis you get into confusion. Rationalism makes us timid, shrewd in criticising, but nothing else. We never do the things that foolish people do.

1. The Counsels of Extravagance
(Ecclesiastes 11:1)

Cast thy bread upon the waters: for thou shalt find it after many days.

Solomon states what Our Lord elaborates in the Sermon on the Mount, viz. that our reason for giving is not to be because men deserve it, but because Christ tells us to give. All through the Old and New Testaments the counsel is on the line of hospitality. As long as we have something to give, we must give. How does civilisation argue? "Does this man deserve that I should give to him?" "If I give that man money, I know what he will do with it." Jesus Christ says, *"Give to him that asketh thee,"* not because he deserves it, but *because I tell you to* (see Matthew 5:42). Some folks are so hyper-conscientious that they are good for nothing. Extravagance is the only line for the religious man. We do not believe this to begin with, we are so completely reasonable and common sense, consequently we base everything on self-realisation instead of on Christ-realisation.

The counsel of extravagance comes out all through the Bible. We are apt to ignore it by the timidity of our reasoning. The one thing Jesus Christ commended was Mary of Bethany's extravagant act. It was not her duty nor was it useful, and yet Our Lord said that wherever His gospel should be preached "that also which this woman hath done shall be spoken of for a memorial of her" (RV). The disciples, who were perfectly reasonable, said, What a waste! Jesus Christ said, "She hath wrought a good work on Me." The true nature of devotion to Jesus Christ must be extravagance.

2. The Confusion of Economy
(Ecclesiastes 11:2–4)

Give a portion to seven, and also to eight; for thou knowest not what evil shall be upon the earth. If the clouds be full of rain, they empty themselves upon the earth: and if the tree fall toward the south, or toward the north, in the place where the tree falleth, there it shall be.

Death transforms nothing. Every view of death outside the Bible view concludes that death is a great transformer. The Bible says that death is a confirmer. Instead of death being the introduction to a second chance, it is the confirmation of the first chance. In dealing with the Bible, bear in mind this point of view.

"Economy is doing without what you want just now in case a time may come when you will want what you don't want now." It is possible to be so economical that you venture nothing. We have deified economy, placed insurance and economy on the throne, consequently we will do nothing on the line of adventure or extravagance. To use the word "economy" in connection with God is to belittle and misunderstand Him. Where is the economy of God in His sunsets and sunrises, in the grass and flowers and trees? God has made a superabounding number of things that are of no use to anyone. How many of us bother our heads about the sunrises and sunsets? Yet they go on just the same. Lavish extravagance to an extraordinary degree is the characteristic of God, never economy. Grace is the over-flowing favour of God. Imagine a man who is in love being economical! The characteristic of a man when he is awake is never that he is calculating and sensible.

Common sense is all very well in the shallow things, but it can never be made the basis of life, it is marked by timidities. We may say wise and subtle things, but if we bank on common sense and rationalism we shall be too timid to do anything. To-day we are so afraid of poverty that we never dream of doing anything that might involve us in being poor. We are out of the running of the mediaeval monks who took on the vow of poverty. Many of us are poor, but none of us chooses to be. These men chose to be poor, they believed it was the only way they could perfect their own inner life. Our attitude is that if we are extravagant a rainy day will come for which we have not laid up. You cannot lay up for a rainy day and justify it in the light of Jesus Christ's teaching. We are not Christians at heart, we don't believe in the wisdom of God, but only in our own. We go in for insurance and economy and speculation, everything that makes us secure in our own wisdom.

3. The Confines of Exposition
(Ecclesiastes 11:5–6)
As thou knowest not what is the way of the spirit, nor how the bones do grow in the womb of her that is with child: even so thou knowest not the works of God who maketh all. In the morning sow thy seed, and in the evening withhold not thine hand: for thou knowest not whether shall prosper, either this or that, or whether they both shall be alike good.

The rationalist demands an explanation of everything. The reason I won't have anything to do with God is because I cannot define Him. If I can define God, I am greater than the God I define. If I can define love and life, I am greater than they are. Solomon indicates that there is a great deal we do not know and cannot define. We have to go on trust in a number of ways, therefore, he says, be careful that you are not too emphatic and dogmatic in your exposition of things.

A Christian is an avowed agnostic. I cannot find God out by my reason, therefore I have to accept the revelation given of Him by Jesus Christ. I do not know anything about God, things look as if He were not good, and yet the revelation given by Jesus Christ is that He is good, and I have to hang in to that revelation in spite of appearances.

"In the morning sow thy seed," i.e., don't bother about the origin of things. Solomon teaches all through the things that Jesus Christ insists on. Don't be careful whether men receive what you give in the right way or the wrong way, see to it that you don't withhold your hand. As long as you have something to give, give, let the consequences be what they may.

There is no possibility of saying a word in favour of a man after death if he did not do things before his death. The wisest thing is to make friends of the mammon of unrighteousness, that when you pass from this life they may receive you into everlasting habitations (see Luke 16:9).

4. The Consciousness of Experience
(Ecclesiastes 11:7–8)
Truly the light is sweet, and a pleasant thing it is for the eyes to behold the sun: Yea, if a man live many years, let him rejoice in them all; but let him remember the days of darkness, for they shall be many. All that cometh is vanity. (RV)

Solomon is stating the practical attitude to things in the midst of the haphazard. You have to live this actual life, he says, with our confidence based on God, and see that you keep your day full of the joy and light of life; enjoy things as they come. When we have a particularly good time, we are apt to say, "Oh well, it can't last long." We expect the worst. When we have one trouble, we expect more. The Bible counsels us to rejoice—"yet let him remember the days of darkness."

The Bible talks about drinking wine when we are glad (see Psalm 104:15); this is different from the modern view. It is bad to drink wine when you are in the dumps. Solomon is amazingly keen that a man should enjoy the pleasant things, remembering that that is why they are here. The universe is meant for enjoyment. ". . . God, who giveth us richly all things to enjoy." "Whatsoever ye do whether ye eat or drink, do all to the glory of God." We argue on the rational line—Don't do this or that because it is wrong. Paul argues in this way: Don't do it, not because it is wrong, but because the man who follows you will stumble if he does it, therefore cut it out, never let him see you do it any more (cf. 1 Corinthians 8:9–13). Solomon's attitude is a safe and sane one, that when a man is rightly related to God he has to see that he enjoys his own life and that others do too.

5. The Concentration after Expansion
(Ecclesiastes 11:9–10)

Rejoice, O young man, in thy youth; and let thy heart cheer thee in the days of thy youth, and walk in the ways of thine heart, and in the sight of thine eyes: but know thou, that for all these things God will bring thee into judgement. Therefore remove sorrow from thy heart, and put away evil from thy flesh: for childhood and youth are vanity.

"For all these things God will bring thee into judgement." "Judgement" means being brought into the arena of your own expansion. It is not that God is an almighty detective hiding round corners to catch and punish you, but that every time you have an expansion of heart or mind in thinking you have to pay for it, and pay for it in an added concentration. There are times when we feel enlarged, we have met someone who has expanded our life; Solomon reminds us that we have to pay for that enlargement, and live up to the limit of the expansion by an added concentration. If we don't, we will come a terrible smash. It is an appalling thing to see a young man with an old head on his shoulders; a young man ought not to be careful but to be full of cheer. "Rejoice, O young man, in thy youth." Solomon is not advocating the sowing of wild oats, but that a man should enter into his life fully and remember that he must pay the price in the right way, not the wrong. When you have an opening up of your nature either in love or religion or adventure, you will have to pay for it in an added concentration. That means you have to bring all your life into keeping with the particular expansion; if you don't, you will become an arrant sentimentalist. To get hold of this truth is a big emancipation.

"Remove sorrow from thy heart, and put away evil from thy flesh." Youth is youth and age is age, and we have no business to require the head of age on the shoulders of youth. One of the affectations before the war was that we should never be enthusiastic about anything. That is not the style of a young man. According to Solomon, his life ought to be full to the last degree of expanding ecstasy, and he counsels him to do right things to the limit of his ability. Be enthusiastic and capable, go into things with all the vigour of life. But be prepared to pay for it. To pay for it means you must concentrate your life on a bigger plan; if you don't, you will become a dreamer. When a man has the vision of a poet or an artist, he has to learn to express himself, to become his own medium. There are more artistic people than artists because folks refuse to do this. Artistic people have art like a severe headache, they never work it out; they spurt out artistic ability, which is of no use to anyone. That is artistic disease, not art. Solomon's counsel is robust and strong—"Let thy heart cheer thee in the days of thy youth, and walk in the ways of thine heart." The young man who cannot enjoy himself is no good, he has a sinister attitude to life. The man who can enjoy himself is not pretending to be what he is not. The best thing to do is to burn your bridges behind you, make things inevitable, and then go ahead.

THE DISSOLVING TABERNACLE
Ecclesiastes 12

1. Lively Youth and Lingering Age (Ecclesiastes 12:1)
2. Luminous Skies and Beclouded Vision (Ecclesiastes 12:2)
3. Lordly Mansion and Tumbling Dwelling (Ecclesiastes 12:3–5)
4. Life's Shapely Instruments and Death's Broken Things (Ecclesiastes 12:6)
5. Languishing Dust and Ever-Living Spirit. (Ecclesiastes 12:7)

We have been shown how to enjoy life. Now we are told of the days when such enjoyment abates. The sparkle of youth will depart. The keen sense of things is diminished; sun, moon and stars are beclouded. This is a chapter of contrasts.

1. Lively Youth and Lingering Age
(Ecclesiastes 12:1)

Remember also thy Creator in the days of thy youth. (RV)

We need a personal knowledge of God through all our life. The time to discover Him for ourselves is in Life's earliest morning—"that from a child thou hast known the holy Scriptures, which are able to make thee wise unto salvation," wrote Paul to Timothy (2 Timothy 3:15). "And ye fathers, provoke not your children to wrath: but nurture them in the chastening and admonition of the Lord" (Ephesians 6:4 RV).

We are so built that in childhood we can more easily come to a knowledge of God in simplicity than in later years. And in those formative years the personal life can be shaped and fitted to God's standard more surely than later on.

In the flower of your days when life is known in its rich fullness, when the natural powers are in undiluted vigour, then make place for God in personal consciousness. The prodigal remembered his Father when he had *spent all*. He should have remembered him, gratefully, and with increasing understanding of his love and care, when his Father was bestowing on him his goods. God gives us all things richly to enjoy, and in youth and early manhood heaps rich precious bounties upon us, God must be remembered then, else we shall grievously hurt Him, and defraud ourselves.

"While the evil days come not"—age with its infirmities is part of our human lot. Of Moses it was written, "His eye was not dim, neither was his natural force abated" (Deuteronomy 34:7). But that was something unusual. There is "An Old Man's Parade" in the Bible, and we see decrepitude and frailty and fear showing their marks on bodily life. Isaac was old and his eyes were dim that he could not see. And Jacob too—"one told Joseph, Behold thy father is sick," and the old man, sitting on the bed, stretched out his hands to bless his grandchildren. It is a pleasant sight to see the old man with his worn-out frame passing on the Divine blessing to those in their youth, and praying "The angel which hath redeemed me from all evil, bless the lads" (Genesis 48:16 RV). We catch glimpses of the same thing in the New Testament: old Zechariah, and Simeon; there is "Paul the aged"; and Peter ready to put off his earthly tabernacle. They had remembered their Creator in the days of their youth, and in their old age He was precious to them.

2. Luminous Skies and Beclouded Vision (*Ecclesiastes 12:2*)
While the sun, or the light, or the moon, or the stars, be not darkened, nor the clouds return after the rain.

There is a loss of the *sparkle* of youth; there is not the same power of recovery after strain. How fascinatingly beautiful this earth can be to the keen vision of youth. The great poets wrote their abiding poems in their early years. It is God's order that the world should be a bright place for bairns. They have the capacity for entering into such natural joys; and it should not be denied them. There is a richer vision for mature minds who have been "born anew" (RV) and seen the Kingdom of God. Milton in his blindness saw rarer beauties than through the opened eyes of his youth.

Only the cynic will despise the loveliness and allurement of youthful days; but the saint will learn that even that bears the fatal hall-mark of "vanity." It too must pass. The happy delights of youth slip through our fingers as we hold them.

3. Lordly Mansion and Tumbling Dwelling (*Ecclesiastes 12:3–5*)
In the day when the keepers of the house shall tremble, and the strong men shall bow themselves, and the grinders cease because they are few, and those that look out of the windows be darkened, and the doors shall be shut in the streets, when the sound of the grinding is low, and he shall rise up at the voice of a bird, and the daughters of music shall be brought low; and when they shall be afraid of that which is high, and fears shall be in the way, and the almond tree shall flourish, and the grasshopper shall be a burden, and desire shall fail: because man goeth to his long home, and the mourners go about the streets.

Man's body is frequently described under the figure of a house. What a lordly house man's body is. We go back to watch its first construction in Genesis 1:27. The artistry of God is upon it all. Our bodies now are damaged by Man's Fall; but even so, how wonderful they are. No wonder we have the injunction, "Glorify God therefore *in your body*" (1 Corinthians 6:20 RV).

Verses 3–4 is a description of Old Age in its frailty. The keepers of the house (arms) and the strong men (legs) are weak and trembling; the grinders cease (teeth) and the windows are darkened (eyesight dimmed), the doors shut (ears are deaf), the grinding low (slow and tedious mastication), the easily startled nerves, and the loss of voice, the inability to climb, and the fear of highway traffic; the whitened hair like the almond tree in blossom, when any work seems a burden, and the failing natural desire, all portray the old man nearing the end of his earthly journey.

4. Life's Shapely Instruments and Death's Broken Things (*Ecclesiastes 12:6*)
Or ever the silver cord be loosed, or the golden bowl be broken, or the pitcher be broken at the fountain, or the wheel broken at the cistern.

The figures here used suggest the beauty and serviceableness of the human organs. The spinal cord as a silver chain; the shapely head as a golden bowl, the tireless heart as a household pitcher in constant use, and the circulatory blood system as a wheel in use at the well, all these show us Life's vital ministry.

Until Death invades and begins to destroy the precious things—the silver cord put out of action, the bowl broken, the pitcher broken, the wheel broken. Here is Death in his fearsome aspect as house-breaker and destroyer. "The last enemy that shall be destroyed is death" (1 Corinthians 15:26). Our Lord "became obedient even unto death" (Philippians 2:8 RV). "But Christ being raised from the dead dieth no more; death hath no more dominion over Him"—nor us either (Romans 6:9).

5. Languishing Dust and Ever-Living Spirit
(Ecclesiastes 12:7)

Then shall the dust return to the earth as it was: and the spirit shall return unto God who gave it.

Man is dust and divinity. "And the LORD God formed man of the dust of the ground, and breathed into his nostrils the breath of life" (Genesis 2:7).

Man is constituted to have affinity with everything on this earth. This is not his calamity, but his peculiar dignity. We do not further our spiritual life in spite of our bodies, but in, and by means of our bodies. (Biblical Psychology)

The dust shall return to the earth, but resurrection means the restoration of the full-orbed life of a man. What is sown a natural body will be raised a spiritual body. "This corruptible must put on incorruption, and this mortal must put on immortality" (1 Corinthians 15:53).

The spirit that returns to God shall find future embodiment. Saints like Paul have had a deep longing to be clothed upon with "our house which is from heaven." Jesus Christ has brought to us His Redemption which affects spirit, soul and body. Already we experience an amazing spiritual renovation through identification with Jesus Christ in His death and resurrection (Romans 6:4). But though we have received "the firstfruits of the Spirit," we are waiting for the "redemption of our body" (Romans 8:23).

We turn to the New Testament for the full word on Man's final form. "The earnest expectation of the creation waiteth for the revealing of the sons of God" (Romans 8:19 RV). For that great hour we hope and long, when we shall pass from beneath the Shade of His Hand into the full Shine of His Face.

The Servant as His Lord

Oswald Chambers

INTRODUCTION

The Servant as His Lord (1959) combines four booklets previously published individually in the "sixpenny series." Over the years, Mrs. Chambers amalgamated a number of smaller books into combined volumes to keep them in print in the most economical format.

Source
This material is from talks and lectures given at League of Prayer[1] meetings, at the Bible Training College[2] and to British Commonwealth soldiers in Egypt during 1916 and 1917.

Publication History
- **The Fighting Chance:** These talks on Romans 8:35–39 were given to a League of Prayer audience in London. They were published as a booklet in 1935.
- **The Soul of a Christian:** OC gave these lectures at the Bible Training College from January 21 through March 25, 1915. The material was published as articles in the *BTC Journal*,[3] October 1934 through March 1935, then as a booklet in 1936.
- **The Saints in the Disaster of Worldliness:** These were talks to British Commonwealth soldiers in Egypt during 1916 and 1917. They were published as articles in *Spiritual Life* magazine: November and December 1937, "The Saints in the Disaster of Worldliness"; June 1938, "Out of the Wreck I Rise" (on Romans 8:37); July 1938, "The Conditions of Spiritual Life" (on Matthew 10:24–42). As a booklet, they were published under the title *The Patience of the Saints* in 1939.
- **The Sacrament of Saints:** These lectures were given in the sermon class OC taught at the Bible Training College, London. They were published as a booklet in 1934, subtitled, "The Making of Saints under the Parable of Bread."

---

1. Pentecostal League of Prayer: founded in London in 1891 by Reader Harris (1847–1909), prominent barrister and friend and mentor of Oswald Chambers.

2. Bible Training College (BTC): a residential school near Clapham Common in southwest London. Sponsored by the League of Prayer; operated from 1911 until it closed in July 1915 because of World War I. Oswald Chambers was principal and main teacher; Biddy Chambers, his wife, was lady superintendent.

3. *Bible Training Course Monthly Journal*: published from 1932 to 1952 by Mrs. Chambers, with help from David Lambert.

FOREWORD

This book has a message for our time. There is much discernment of the state of our age at its closing period. "What is described in the climax is true in every stage till the climax is reached." Jesus Christ foretold tribulation to His followers. But God gives us a fighting chance of winning through to triumph; and there is much here to nourish and guide His saints in their hours of conflict. There is much also about a saint's inner life—the soul of a Christian. The soul is the same in every age. It can be self pervaded, or influenced by Satanic power, or God possessed. There is also a remarkable exposition of the closing verses of Romans 8. We get a glimpse into the deep things of life. And we learn much about the principalities and powers that encircle us, but are not to conquer us. There is a lovely parable of the making of bread used to illustrate the making of saints. And a word about the patience of the saints in a whirl of tumult. The four sections have appeared as separate booklets, but in this form they fuse into one great message, making clear the truth that the Lord's servant may be, and should be, "*as his Lord*."

David Lambert[4]

Yet it was well, and Thou hast said in season,
"As is the Master shall the servant be:"
Let me not slide into the treason,
Seeking an honour which they gave not Thee.

. . . .

Yea, thro' life, death, thro' sorrow and thro' sinning
He shall suffice me, for He hath sufficed:
Christ is the end, for Christ was the beginning,
Christ the beginning, for the end is Christ.

F. W. H. Myers[5]

---

4. David Lambert (1871–1961): Methodist minister, friend of Oswald and Biddy Chambers; assisted Mrs. Chambers with OC publications from 1917 until his death in 1961.
5. F. W. H. Myers (1843–1901): British poet and educator.

CONTENTS

THE FIGHTING CHANCE
Romans 8:35–39

The Mental Field

Who shall separate us from the love of Christ? shall tribulation, or anguish . . . ? (RV)

During the French Revolution little boys who could not much more than walk carried a banner around with the words, "Tremble, tyrants, we are growing" printed on it. That is the aspect I want us to look at. We are not meant to be "carried to heaven on flow'ry beds of ease," we are given the fighting chance, and it is a glorious fight. Jesus Christ came to fit men to fight, He came to make the lame, the halt, the paralysed, the all but sin-damned, into terrors to the prince of this world.

If there is one thing an unsaved man is incapable of doing, it is fighting against the awful powers of sin. He can fight in the physical realm because he has the spirit of lust; but Paul warns that "our wrestling is not against flesh and blood, but against . . . the spiritual hosts of wickedness in the heavenly places" (RV). No man is a match for that warfare unless he is saved by God's grace. "Wherefore take up the whole armour of God. . . ." Fancy telling a man to put on the armour of God while he has a traitor on the inside! A man has to put on the armour of God to fight in when he has had the lustful disposition taken out of him; for what purpose? That he may fight all that comes against him and come off more than conqueror. Have you ever seen Jesus Christ take a man who has been paralysed by sin, paralysed by a wrong past, by a present that makes him say, "I shall never be different"—have you ever seen Jesus Christ take that man and turn him into a fighter, one who can "turn to flight armies of aliens"? That is what Jesus Christ can do by His marvellous salvation; He can put into the man whose energy has been sapped by sin and wrong until he is all but in hell, a life so strong and full that Satan has to flee whenever he meets him. Is there a man here who would not give his right arm, nay, his very life, if God would fit him to fight, and make him more than conqueror over sin and Satan and circumstances? Thank God, He can do it! Oh, let me repeat it, I do not care how defaced you may be morally, how weak and backslidden, I do know that Jesus Christ can make you more than conqueror as you draw on His Resurrection life.

"The fighting chance" exactly describes the way we are made. Take our bodies: we are kept healthy by our capacity to fight, and the stronger the forces within the better is our health. Health simply means a perfect balance between the body and the outer world. The same is true mentally. I continually come across people with rusty "thinkers," they think about their business but about nothing else, and the forces within have become desperately weak; consequently when tribulation comes their minds are confused, and the result is that errors come into the life. If the forces within are strong and healthy they give us warning and enable us to crush in a vice on the threshold of the mind everything that ought not to come there. God can impart to a man the power to select what his mind thinks, the power to think only what is right and pure and true.

If it is a fight in the physical and mental realm is also a fight in the spiritual realm, only tremendously intensified, because when we receive the new life from God, Satan instantly brings all his power to crush it out. But thank God, no matter how the enemy presses He can make us, more than conquerors because the very life of Jesus is imparted to us and we are able to face the devil and sin as He did.

(a) Predicted
In the world ye shall have tribulation: but be of good cheer; I have overcome the world. (John 16:33; see John 17:14–16)

Jesus Christ foretold tribulation; He conveyed His message with a clarion voice to the saints in all ages—"In the world ye shall have tribulation," and the Apostle Paul continually warns us that we have no right to settle on our lees. "For verily, when we were with you, we told you plainly [mg] that we are to suffer affliction; even as it came to pass, and ye know" (1 Thessalonians 3:4 RV). Tribulation means being thronged by severe affliction and trouble; that is what the saints are to expect in this dispensation and not be astonished when it comes. God allows tribulation and anguish to come right to the threshold of our lives in order to prove to us that His life in us is more than a match for all that is against us. When we see the awfulness of evil in this world we imagine there is no room for anything but the devil and wrong; but this

is not so. God restrains the powers of evil. How does He do it? Through the lives of the saints who are pushing the battle everywhere their feet are placed. The devil tackles on the right hand and on the left but they are more than conquerors, they not only go through the tribulation, but are "exceeding joyful" in it.

(b) Portrayed
O Jerusalem, Jerusalem, which killeth the prophets, and stoneth them that are sent unto her![RV] how often would I have gathered thy children together, even as a hen gathereth her chickens under her wings, and ye would not! (Matthew 23:37; see Romans 9:1–3)

Have you ever noticed the examples the New Testament gives of those who go through tribulation? Our Lord Himself and the Apostle Paul. The writer to the Hebrews says, *"Consider him. . . ."* Have you ever considered Jesus Christ's distress over Jerusalem? Do we know anything about that kind of tribulation? There is a difference between the distress that comes to our human minds and the distress of the Holy Ghost through us. Jesus warned that "because iniquity shall abound, the love of many shall wax cold." Why? Because people are not rooted in the right place. No matter how iniquity may abound, or how crushing may be the afflictions that throng around, Jesus Christ can make us more than conquerors while at the same time we taste the anguish of the Holy Ghost.

A great danger besets Christians, and Satan is at the back of it, viz., the danger which makes men and women think that they are God's favourites. No one can monopolise God; it is easy to say that, and yet we seem to think we can. God has no favourites, but when we let Him have His right of way through us He begins to unveil something more of His purposes in our lives. Has God unfolded to you His purpose in your family? in your business? in Battersea?[6] wherever you are? or is tribulation making you wilt? making you swoon for sympathy? making you stagnate? It is an easy business to want to get away from tribulation, but fighting makes us strong, gloriously strong.

Are you saying—"I wonder if I am ever going to get out of these circumstances? if things are ever going to alter for me?" Let God alter you, let Him put within you the life of His Son, and backed by Almighty God, you will not only get the fighting chance, but you will glory in tribulation—the tramp of the conqueror about you. God grant we may let our hearts talk to our minds, and let our minds follow on to know; and we can only know by means of this tribulation-experience.

---

6. Battersea: area of southwest London; location of the League of Prayer headquarters.

When you have to go and see some "big" person, remember to take a deep breath and you will be surprised to find how courageous you feel. Apply that spiritually, when there is tribulation and distress thronging round you, take time and draw in a tremendous draught of the grace of God, and you will find it is a delight to meet it because He makes us more than conquerors in the midst of it all.

The Moral Field
Who shall separate us from the love of Christ? shall . . . persecution? (Romans 8:35)

Morality is not something with which we are gifted, we make morality; it is another word for character. "Except your righteousness" (i.e., your morality) "shall exceed the righteousness of the scribes and Pharisees," said Jesus, "ye shall in no wise enter into the kingdom of heaven" (RV). Morality is not only correct conduct on the outside, but correct thinking within where only God can see. No matter how a man may have been tampered with by Satan, God can re-make him so that in every moral battlefield he can come off more than conqueror . Thank God He does give us the fighting chance! In certain moods we are inclined to criticise God for not [having] made the world like a foolproof machine whereby it would be impossible to go wrong. If God had made men and women like that we would have been of no worth to Him. Jesus Christ by His almighty Redemption makes us of the stuff that can stand the strain.

One afternoon I was watching the birds on the lake in Battersea Park and I got a splendid illustration of persecution. There were all kinds of birds—ducks and seagulls and swans, and some birds not native to our shores. Children were feeding them, and one white duck got hold of a crust. Immediately the other ducks tried to grab it from her, but she swam through her own crowd, easily outwitting them. Then the foreign birds swooped down on her, a new style of enemy, but I never saw rabbit or boy chase and turn with such dexterity as that duck, and over and over again the seagulls struck the water instead of the duck. Then along came the cygnets and tried to pull the duck back by main force and take the crust from her, but the more they tackled, the more dextrous she got, until at last she cleared them all and got complete victory. That is exactly the meaning of persecution—systematic vexation.

(a) Place
And he that was sown upon the rocky places, this is he that heareth the word, and straightway with joy receiveth it; yet hath he not root in himself, but endureth for a while; and when tribulation or persecution ariseth because of the word, straightway he stumbleth. (Matthew 13:20–21 RV)

The first place where you meet persecution is after conversion. I am not using the word "conversion" in the sense of regeneration, but of being in the condition to *receive* something from God (see Acts 26:18). As soon as you turn in the direction of God and receive a word from Him, you will find systematic vexation begin on that particular word—"and when tribulation or persecution ariseth because of the word, straightway he stumbleth." The proof that you have the root of the matter in you is that you easily prevail against persecution. How many of us have turned aside at the very outset, at conversion point, when we first begin to testify, because of persecution? Jesus Christ told us to expect it. I think we are losing sight of the real meaning of testimony; it is not for the sake of others, but for our own sake. It makes us know we have no one to rely on but God.

Persecution is not only met with at the threshold, it increases as we go on in the Christian life. A man may get through persecution from his own crowd, but when it comes to persecution from principalities and powers, that is a domain he knows nothing about. When we are saved and sanctified God does not shield us from any requirement of a son or daughter of His; He lifts His hand off, as it were, and says to the devil "Do your worst": "Ye are of God, little children, and have overcome them: because greater is He that is in you, than he that is in the world" (1 John 4:4); and we find to our delight that we are made more than conquerors. We talk about people being "loved into blessing," but no one is loved into blessing unless he is first lured by that love to a tremendous surgical operation. There must be a radical alteration within before the new life is there which will overcome all that comes against it. Persecution is the thing that tests our Christianity, and it always comes in our own setting; the crowd outside never bothers us. To have brickbats and rotten eggs flung at you is not persecution, it simply makes you feel good and does you no harm at all. But when your own crowd cut you dead and systematically vex you, then says Jesus, "count it all joy." Leap for joy "when men shall hate you, and when they shall separate you from their company, and reproach you, and cast out your name as evil *for the Son of man's sake*"—not for the sake of some crotchety notion of our own.

(b) Profit
Blessed are ye when men shall reproach you, and persecute you, and say all manner of evil against you falsely, for My sake. Rejoice, and be exceeding glad; for great is your reward in heaven. (Matthew 5:11–12 RV; see 2 Corinthians 12:10)

Jesus Christ not only warned that persecution would come, He went further and said that it was profitable to go through persecution. *"Blessed are ye, when men shall . . . persecute you."* The way the world treats me is the exhibition of my inner disposition. "Whosoever maketh himself a friend of the world is the enemy of God." The line where the world ends and Christianity begins alters in every generation. What was worldliness in Paul's day is not worldliness in our day; the line is altering all the time. To-day the world has taken on so many things out of the Church, and the Church has taken on so many things out of the world, that it is difficult to know where you are. Immediately you let the disposition God gives you manifest itself, you are going to be a "speckled bird."[7] "Is mine heritage unto me as a speckled bird of prey?" (RV) asked Jeremiah. No matter how sweet and winsome you may be, you will come across something that positively detests you. "If the world hate you, ye know that it hated Me before it hated you." Do we know anything about it?

Is some discouraged soul saying—"If only God would give me different circumstances"? No one understands your circumstances but God, and He has given you the fighting chance to prove you can be more than conqueror in all these things. Let God lift you out of the broken place, out of the bedraggled place. Let Him put within you the Holy Spirit so that you can face the music of life and become more than conqueror in every place where you have been defeated. Carlyle[8] said of Tennyson that he was always carrying about with him a lump of chaos and turning it into cosmos. That is another way of putting this truth, that we make our own character. God gives us a new disposition, the disposition of His Son; then we have to work out what He has worked in, and the way we react in the circumstances God engineers for us produces character.

Have you ever noticed how God permits the natural virtues to break down? People whose lives have been moral and upright get astounded when these virtues begin to crumble. They have been trying to build up a character on these virtues, and it cannot be done. Natural virtues are not a promise of what we are going to be, but a remnant of what we once were. No natural virtue can come anywhere near the standard Jesus Christ demands. We have to receive the Holy Spirit and let Him bring us to the place where we are so identified with the Death of Jesus that it is "no longer I, but Christ that liveth in me" (RV); and then go on to build up a character on the basis of Jesus Christ's disposition. The Christian life is drawn from first to last, and all in between, from the Resurrection life of the Lord Jesus.

The Material Field
Who shall separate us from the love of Christ? shall . . . nakedness, or peril, or sword? (Romans 8:35)

The Material Field, i.e., things that come to a man's life from the outside—famine, nakedness, peril, sword. The Apostle Paul seems to be never tired of comparing the Christian life to a fight, and a fight against tremendous odds, but always a winning fight. In these verses Paul brings before our contemplation every conceivable battlefield; every manoeuvre and strategy of the enemy is embraced, no phase of his tactics is left out, and in it all he says we are "more than conquerors through Him that loved us." We cannot be *more than* conquerors if there is nothing to fight! Our Lord Himself and the Spirit of God in the Epistles make it very clear that everything that is not of God will try its best to kill His life out of us; yet instead of doing that it makes us all the stronger. The love of God in Christ Jesus is such that He can take the most unfit man—unfit to survive, unfit to fight, unfit to face moral issues—and make him not only fit to survive and to fight, but fit to face the biggest moral issues and the strongest power of Satan, and come off more than conqueror. The love in God in Christ Jesus through the mighty Atonement is such that it can do this for the feeblest, the most sinful man, if he will hand himself over to God.

(a) The Book of Martyrs
Verily, verily, I say unto thee, when thou wast young, thou girdest thyself and walkest whither thou wouldest: but when thou shalt be old, thou shalt stretch forth thy hands, and another shall gird thee, and carry thee whither thou wouldest not. (John 21:18; cf. John 16:2; Luke 10:19)

A martyr is one who is put to death for adherence to principles. Martyrdom is not peculiar to the Christian religion. Men and women who suffer death for adhering to principles are found not only in the Christian religion, but in every religion under heaven, and outside any religion; but the particular type of martyrdom we are referring to is that of those men and women who go to death because of obedience to the principles of the life of Jesus in them.

In 1 Corinthians 4:9, Paul mentions a strange training for the apostles. He says that "God hath set forth us, the apostles, last of all" (i.e., as the last item in the day's play in the theatre) "as men doomed to death, for we are made a spectacle unto the world . . ." (RV); and the writer to the Hebrews, reminding us of

---

7. "speckled bird": a person who stands out as abnormal, odd, or eccentric.

8. Thomas Carlyle (1795–1881): Scottish-born literary figure in nineteenth-century England, a writer, biographer, essayist, historian, and critic.

the witnesses of old, says the same thing: they were "destitute, afflicted, ill treated" (11:36–37 RV). We are apt to say that we are not called to martyrdom to-day, but I think we shall begin to find that we are, and to a crueller martyrdom than that of the early days, which was intense and fierce and then over.

"*. . . or nakedness?*" Nakedness means to be destitute of clothing and shelter, destitute of all sustenance for life. God said to Satan concerning Job—"Behold, all that he hath is in thy hand [RV mg]." That permission has never been withdrawn, and every now and again Satan gets permission from God to play havoc with all our material possessions. "For a man's life consisteth not in the abundance of the things which he possesseth." If our life is in our material possessions, and nakedness, peril and sword tackle and destroy them, where is our faith? But if we bank on the love of God in Jesus Christ He will make us more than conqueror "in all these things." God grant we may put God first. When Mary of Bethany broke the alabaster box of ointment on the feet of Jesus, the disciples were indignant and said, "To what purpose is this waste, for this ointment might have been sold for much and given to the poor." Have you ever noticed how strangely Jesus answered them? "For ye have the poor always with you, and whensoever ye will ye can do them good; but Me ye have not always." Did Jesus mean that He had no care for the poor? That He did not understand what an awful, stinging, grinding thing it is to be poverty-stricken and destitute? No one on earth felt these things more keenly than Jesus did, but He was pointing out that, as His disciples, the great note for our lives is not sympathy with the poor, not an understanding of the needs of men, but an understanding of His point of view.

(b) The Boycott of Mediocrity
Blessed are ye, when men shall hate you, and when they shall separate you from their company, and reproach you, and cast out your name as evil, for the Son of man's sake. (Luke 6:22 RV; cf. 1 Peter 4:4)

"All that would live godly in Christ Jesus shall suffer persecution" (RV), says Paul, and our Lord says the same thing. Men will make you destitute of their society, they will cut you dead, and when they do speak of you, they will speak evil. No man knew this better than the Apostle Paul, and what did he do? He despised being despised! Persecution is systematic vexation, it does not leave you alone, it is something that throngs you; but to be boycotted means to be left alone, destitute of the comrades you used to have—

"they think it strange that ye run not with them to the same excess of riot, speaking evil of you." But they don't know that you carry a wonderful kingdom within, a kingdom full of light and peace and joy no matter how destitute and alone you may be on the outside. That is the wonderful work of the Lord in a man's soul. "Rejoice in that day, and leap for joy."

One of the things I remember during the Welsh Revival[9] was the unspeakable presence of God. It was unlike anything I had ever felt before. You could *feel* the presence of God in the very atmosphere, and tell the districts where it was and where it was not, and I remember coming to the conclusion that if a martyr felt the marvel of that Presence he would not feel the pain. Another thing that struck me was that while many were getting right with God, others were content with the enthusiasm of the presence of God and bringing forth no "fruits meet for repentance." When shall we understand that God's method is repentance first and then the reviving life of God? If revival does not bring forth fruits meet for repentance it will end in riot and ultimately in ruin.

(c) The Big Meaning
Even as it is written, For Thy sake we are killed all the day long; we were accounted as sheep for the slaughter. (Romans 8:36 RV)

Anaesthesis means insensibility to pain, and there is such a thing as spiritual anaesthesis—God put you to sleep while the thing hurts. Some Christians do not seem to know that they are going through things, they are so wonderfully upheld by the life and power of God within, and when you begin to sympathise with them, they look at you in amazement—"Why, what have I been through?" They had never realised that the battle was on. The danger is to get taken up with external tribulations and trials and when we come to the end of the day to say, "Thank God, I have just got through!" Where is "the unsearchable riches of Christ" about that? The grace of God will make us marvellously impervious to all the onslaughts of tribulation and persecution and destitution because we are seated in heavenly places in Christ Jesus and cannot be awakened up to self-pity. God sends His rough weather and His smooth weather, but we pay no attention to either because we are taken up only with the one central thing—the love of God in Christ Jesus.

Where are you placed in your circumstances? Is it tribulation and anguish that are perplexing you? Is it nervous trouble that is overcoming you, the nameless dread that comes from nerves that are all on fire and jangled? I firmly believe there is no type of mental or

---

9. Welsh Revival (1904–05): sweeping evangelism and spiritual renewal that began in Wales and affected churches throughout Britain.

nervous disease over which Jesus Christ cannot make us more than conqueror as we draw on His Resurrection life. Is your battlefield the moral one? Persecution, systematic vexation, in your home because you have got right with God? Persistent ridicule from those you work with because of your obedience to Jesus Christ? Jesus Christ can make you more than conqueror there. Remember, morality is produced by fight, not by dreaming, not by shutting our eyes to facts, but by being made right with God; then we can make our morality exactly after the stamp of Jesus Christ.

The Natural Manoeuvres
For I am persuaded, that neither death, nor life . . . shall be able to separate us from the love of God, which is in Christ Jesus our Lord. (Romans 8:38–39)

Paul has catalogued the things over which we are more than conquerors—tribulation, anguish, persecution, famine, nakedness, peril, sword; now he seems to strike another note, a note of defiance—"for I am persuaded, that neither death, nor life . . . shall be able to separate us from the love of God, which is in Christ Jesus our Lord."

> *He conjures; he marshals before him; he names over in all their greatest horror every conceivable trouble which afflicts the soul of man; he calls them up and he passes them in review before him, and he bids them do their worst, and sets them all at defiance. . . . Life is an infinitely worse thing than death, more terrible, more appalling.*
>
> *Dr. David Smith*[10]

(a) The Great Dread—Death
Death is a great dread. It is easy to say that God is love until death has snatched away your dearest friend, then I defy you to say that God is love unless God's grace has done a work in your soul. Death means extinction of life as we understand it; our dead are gone and have left an aching void behind them. They do not talk to us, we do not feel their touch, and when the bereaved heart cries out, nothing comes back but the hollow echo of its own cry. The heart is raw, no pious chatter, no scientific cant can touch it. It is the physical calamity of death *plus* the thing behind which no man can grasp, that makes death so terrible. We have so taken for granted the comfort that Jesus Christ brings in the hour of death that we forget the awful condition of men apart from that revelation. Do strip your mind and imagination of the idea that we have comfort about the departed apart from the Bible; we have not. Every attempt to comfort a bereaved soul apart from the revelation Jesus Christ brings is a vain speculation. We know nothing about the mystery of death apart from what Jesus Christ tells us; but blessed be the Name of God, what He tells us makes us more than conquerors, so that we can shout the victory through the darkest valley of the shadow that ever a human being can go through.

The Bible reveals that death is inevitable—"and so death passed upon all men" (Romans 5:12). "It is appointed unto men once to die" (Hebrews 9:27). Repeat that over to yourself. It is appointed to every one of us that we are going to cease to be as we are now, and the place that knows us now shall know us no more. We may shirk it, we may ignore it, we may be so full of robust health and spirits that the thought of death never enters, but it is inevitable.

Another thing—the Bible says that a certain class of man is totally indifferent to death, "for there are no pangs in their death" (Psalm 73:4 RV). Over and over again the Bible points out that the wicked man, the Esau-type of man who is perfectly satisfied with life as it is, has not the slightest concern about death— because he is so brave and strong? No, because he is incapable of realising what death means. The powers that press from the natural world have one tendency, and one only, to deaden all communication with God.

One other thing—the Bible says there are those who are intimidated by death, ". . . that through death He might bring to nought him that had the power of death, that is, the devil; and might deliver all them who through fear of death were all their lifetime subject to bondage" (Hebrews 2:14–15 RV). The thought of death is never away from them; it terrorises their days, it alarms their nights. Now read very reverently Hebrews 5:7: "Who . . . having offered up prayers and supplications with strong crying and tears unto Him that was able to save Him from death . . ." Who is that? The Lord Jesus Christ. We cannot begin to fathom this passage; after years of meditation on it we come only to the threshold of realising what Gethsemane represents. Jesus Christ can deliver from the dread of death—"that through death He might bring to nought him that had the power of death, that is, the devil." Death has no terror for the man who is rightly related to God through Jesus Christ. "How blest the righteous when he dies!" Were there any terrors in the passing of the Founder of the League of Prayer?[11] It was a marvellous and glorious translation. "O death, where is thy victory? O death, where is thy

---

10. David Smith (1866–1937): Scottish-born Presbyterian minister, teacher, and author.

11. Founder of the League of Prayer: Reader Harris (1847–1909), prominent British barrister, founded the Pentecostal League of Prayer in 1891; friend and mentor of Oswald Chambers.

sting?"—absolutely nullified, destroyed by the majestic might of the Atonement.

(b) The Greatest Danger—Life

Life is a far greater danger than death. I want to say something, crudely, but very definitely: the Bible nowhere says that men are damned; the Bible says that men are damnable. There is always the possibility of damnation in any life, always the possibility of disobedience; but, thank God, there is also always the possibility of being made "more than conqueror." The possibilities of life are awful. Think—are you absolutely certain that you are not going to topple headlong over a moral precipice before you are three years older? Look back on your life and ask yourself how it was you escaped when you were set on the wrong course—the tiniest turn and you would have been a moral ruin? Disease cut off with a tremendous fell swoop your companions—why did it not cut you off? The men with you in your youth who were so brilliant—where are they now? Out in the gutter some of them, all but damned while they live. Why are you not there? Why am I not there? Oh, it does us good, although it frightens us, to look at the possibilities of life. May God help us to face the issues.

Unless a man's peace and prosperity are based on a right relationship to God, it may end in a sudden and terrible awakening. We never know whether the next moment is going to bring us face to face with green pastures or a hurricane. The Bible reveals that here is a ruling principle at work in this world that hates God, and when we take sides against that principle there is the very devil to face. That is the Apostle Paul's argument here. When we are born again into the heavenly kingdom, then come tribulation and anguish, then come persecution and famine, then come nakedness, peril and sword; then comes life, and then comes death—mocking us with paradoxes and puzzles we cannot explain. The possibilities and perils of life are enormous. It is only when some such considerations get hold of men who are bound up in "a show of things" that they begin to see the need for Jesus Christ's Redemption.

(c) The Greater Deliverance

I have been drawing a very dark picture, you say. I have not. It is not within the power of human tongue or archangel's tongue to state what an awful fact death is, and what a still more awful fact life is. But thank God, there is the greatest deliverance conceivable from all that life may bring and from all that death may bring. Jesus Christ has destroyed the dominion of death, and He can make us fit to face every problem of life, more than conqueror all along the line.

Let God have His way, and He will turn the drama of your life into a doxology, and you will

understand why the Psalmist breaks out with the words, "O that men would praise the LORD for His goodness, and for His wonderful works to the children of men!" Jesus Christ can make the weakest man into a Divine dreadnought, fearing nothing. He can plant within him the life that was in Himself, the life Time cannot touch. "Verily, verily, I say unto you, he that believeth . . . hath everlasting life," that is, the life Jesus had, so that a man can face all the powers of hell with a conqueror's tread. Heroics? No, heroism. Heroics sound all very well on a stage, or on paper, but heroism works in flesh and blood, and Jesus Christ makes us flesh-and-blood dreadnoughts. Not all the power of the enemy can fuss or turn aside the soul that is related to God through the Atonement.

The Supernatural Manoeuvres

For I am persuaded, that neither . . . angels, nor principalities, nor powers . . . shall be able to separate us from the love of God, which is in Christ Jesus our Lord. (Romans 8:38–39)

By the help of God's Spirit I want, for one moment, to lift the veil from the unseen world as the Bible reveals it that we may understand what a marvellous salvation we have; a salvation that keeps us not only from dangers we see and know, not only from sin and all we understand as the works of the devil, but a salvation that keeps us from dangers we know nothing about. Oh, there are tremendous possibilities around us! The Bible reveals that the unseen world has rulers and majesties and tremendous beings with whom man can get into communication and be possessed by, but God pronounces His curse on the man or woman who dares to communicate with them.

(a) Messengers of the Unseen Universe

"Neither . . . angels . . ." The Bible has a great deal to say about angels: there are *Angelic Hosts* (see Matthew 26:53; Hebrews 1:7, 14) and *Angelic Helpers* (see Psalm 91:11–12; Matthew 18:10). When we were taught as children that angels watch around our beds it was not a fairy story we were told, but a revelation fact. The angels are there to guard us, and they watch and guard every blood-bought soul. And there is an *Angelic Hell;* there is no other place for fallen angels (Matthew 25:41; Jude 6; Revelation 20:10). It is never stated that God has provided a place for men who will not come to Him; it is implied with solemn warning that the only place they can go to is that "prepared for the devil and his angels."

The good angels are a host and the bad angels are a host. To-day spiritualism is having tremendous vogue; men and women are getting into communication with departed spirits and putting themselves in league with the unseen powers. If you have got as far as reading fortunes in tea-cups, *stop.* If you have gone as far as telling fortunes by cards, *stop*. I will tell you why—the devil uses these apparently harmless things to create a fearful curiosity in the minds of men and women, especially young men and women, and it may bring them into league with the angelic forces that hate God, into league with the principalities and the rulers of this world's darkness. Never say, "What is the harm in it?" Push it to its logical conclusion and ask— "Where will this end?" You are absolutely safe as long as you remain under the shelter of the Atonement; but if you do not—I don't care what your experiences are—you are absolutely unsafe. At any minute dangers may beset you, terrors and darkness may take hold of you and rack your life with terrific perils.

God grant we may keep as far away from these things as we can. But if in the strange providence of God you find you are near a spiritualist meeting, pray, and keep on your praying, and you will paralyse every power of the medium if he is genuine. No spiritualistic seance can continue if there is a Christian anywhere near who knows how to lay hold of God in prayer; no spirits will communicate. I could tell you wonderful stories of how God's power has worked. Blessed be God; Jesus Christ's salvation makes us more than conqueror over the angelic forces.

(b) Majesties of the Unseen Universe

"nor principalities . . ." A principality is the jurisdiction of a prince. According to the Bible, the kingdoms of this world are under the rule of the prince of this world, viz., Satan (cf. Matthew 4:8–9). A time is coming when they will be taken from him,—"the kingdom of the world is become the kingdom of our Lord, and of His Christ" (RV), but at present they are in his power.

Men say—"I can't help committing sin"; "I can't help doing this thing." Are they right? Perfectly right. You may talk to further orders[12] about a weak will; there is nothing more absurd. It is not the man's weak will; he has got into league with a power stronger than he is, and when once a man gets in league with the prince of this world, I defy all his strength of will to stand before the terrific power of this world's darkness for one second. According to the New Testament, there is such a thing as obsession by unclean, malicious, wicked spirits who will damn and ruin body and soul in hell (cf. Luke 11:21–26). A moral empty heart is the resort of these spirits when a man is off his guard. But if a man has been born again of the Spirit of God and is keeping in the light, he cannot help going right because he is backed by the tremendous power of Almighty God. What does the

Apostle John say?—"the evil one toucheth him not" (RV). What a marvellous certainty! God grant we may be so filled with the Holy Spirit that we listen to His checks along every line. No power can deceive a child of God who keeps in the light with God. I am perfectly certain that the devil likes to deceive us and limit us in our practical belief as to what Jesus Christ can do. There is no limit to what He can do, absolutely none. *"All things are possible to him that believeth*." Jesus says that faith in Him is omnipotent. God grant we may get hold of this truth.

(c) Miracles of the Unseen Universe

"nor powers . . ." The word is the same as that translated "miracles." A miracle is a work done by one who has fuller knowledge and authority than we have. Things that were called miracles a hundred years ago are not thought of as miracles to-day because men have come to a fuller knowledge. The miracles of Jesus were an exhibition of the power of God, that is, they were simply mirrors of what God Almighty is doing gradually and everywhere and all the time; but every miracle Jesus performed had a tremendous lesson behind it. It was not merely an exhibition of the power of God, there was always a moral meaning behind for the individual. That is why God does not heal some people. We are apt to confine life to one phase only, the physical: there are three phases— physical, psychical and spiritual. Whenever Jesus touched the physical domain a miracle happened in the other phases as well. If a miracle is wrought by any other power in the physical it leaves no corresponding stamp of truth in the other domains of soul and spirit. In this dispensation it is not a question of whether God will sovereignly permit us to be delivered from sin, it is His expressed will that we should be delivered from sin; but when it comes to healing it is not a question of God's will, but of His sovereignty, that is, whether the pre-dispensational efficacy of the Atonement is active on our behalf just now. There is no case of healing in the Bible that did not come from a direct intervention of the sovereign touch of God. We make the mistake of putting an abstract truth deduced from the Word of God in the place of God Himself. When God does not heal it is time we got down to close quarters with God and asked Him why. There is a deep lesson behind; we cannot lay down a general law for everyone, we can only find out the reason by going to God.

Our Lord revealed that the public power of Satan would be greater in the days in which we live than ever before. "For there shall arise false Christs, and

---

12. to further orders: ad infinitum; endlessly; of military origin, meaning continuing the present action until one receives different orders.

false prophets, and shall shew great signs and wonders; so as to lead astray, if possible, even the elect" (Matthew 24:24 RV), and the Apostle Paul foretold that there would be "signs and lying wonders . . . according to the working of Satan" (2 Thessalonians 2:9 RV), but we have no need to fear if we are experiencing the salvation of the Lord Jesus. He will banish all the tremendous powers and majesties that have been set against Him: "having put off from Himself the principalities and the powers [RV mg], He made a shew of them openly, triumphing over them in it." According to the Bible, the One who laughs last is God. "He that sitteth in the heavens shall laugh" (Psalm 2:4). The Apostle Paul has embraced every possible phase of the enemy's tactics, and he says we are more than conquerors in them all through Him that loved us.

The Frontier Battle Lines

For I am persuaded, that neither . . . things present, nor things to come, nor powers, nor height, nor depth, nor any other creation [RV mg], shall be able to separate us from the love of God, which is in Christ Jesus our Lord. (Romans 8:38–39)

In these verses Paul does not mention the ordinary trials of life; he mentions the imperilling experiences which thousands have gone through these past years, distress and anguish which hold the eyes too much awake to sleep, tribulation that tears and lacerates everything; but, he says, the love of God is untouched by these experiences. That love renders impotent the strength of our most formidable enemy. Any of the elemental ministries, life, death, things present, things to come, may kill the castles built by human love; may remove and shatter them like an incoming tide, their strength is overwhelming, but they are powerless to touch the love of God in Christ Jesus. When one reads the Apostle Paul, language seems completely beggared in the attempt to express his devotion to Jesus Christ. Faith itself, with Paul, seems to be lost sight of and merged altogether in his personal intimacy with Jesus Christ; his is the very faith of the Son of God, which is not conscious of itself. Remember, this is not meant only for the Apostle Paul, it is for everyone of us. God grant that the Holy Spirit may so kindle all our natural powers, so invade us with the power of God, that we may begin to "comprehend . . . what is the breadth, and length, and depth, and height" of the love of Christ for our souls.

(a) The Infinitely Great

"nor height . . ." For generations the telescope has been made the means of terrifying us instead of bringing God nearer to us. Those who deal with the great secrets of the universe imply that our planet is such a tiny spot in the tremendous universe that it is a piece of stupid conceit on our part to think that God watches over us. And to make our planet the centre where God performed the marvellous drama of His own history of the Incarnation and Atonement is absurd, they say. But watch a simple-minded person, one who is right with God and is not terrified by the reasonings of men, as he looks at the stars and exclaims, "when I consider Thy heavens, the work of Thy fingers, the moon and the stars, which Thou hast ordained; what is man, that Thou are mindful of him?" It is said not in despair, but in adoring wonder. Then watch the man who is not right with God. The sight of the infinitely great to him pushes God right out of it, until God becomes a great first Cause, a remote cold principle. The far-flung battle lines reach beyond the stars to the very throne of God, and deeper down than the deepest depths of hell; they may test and storm, they may spread seas and space, but, says Paul, "I am persuaded that they are not able to separate us from the love of God which is in Christ Jesus our Lord."

(b) The Infinitely Little

"nor depth . . ." Look at the world either through a telescope or a microscope and you will be dwarfed into terror by the infinitely great or the infinitely little. Naturalists tell us that there are no two blades of grass alike, and close inspection of a bee's wing under a microscope reveals how marvellously it is made. What do I read in the Bible? I read that the God of heaven counts the hairs of our heads. Jesus says so. I read that the mighty God watches the sparrows so intimately that not one of them falls on the ground without His notice. I read that the God who holds the seas in the hollow of His hand and guides the stars in their courses, clothes the grass of the field. Through the love of God in Christ Jesus we are brought into a wonderful intimacy with the infinitely great and the infinitely little.

(c) The Infinitely Possible

"nor any other creation . . ." The Apostle Paul knew better than most of us that there are principalities and powers and ordinances behind the seen universe that may at any moment flash forth as an uncanny spiritual "airship," or burst up from the deep as a terrific supernatural "submarine," terrifying us out of our wits. But, he says, no matter what the different creations may be, "I am persuaded that neither . . . height, nor depth, nor any other creation, shall be able to separate us from the love of God, which is in Christ Jesus our Lord." Paul is not boasting, he is speaking from his own absolute certainty that the Cross of Christ has in it the very secret heart of God. We belittle and misrepresent the love of God when we see it merely on the surface. It is easy to think imperially, easy to think

big thoughts and dream big dreams. But Jesus Christ is not big thoughts and big dreams. He is a tremendously big Saviour for little insignificant creatures such as we are. Through the Atonement God Almighty can place you, my poor, weak, timid, sin-tossed brother or sister, where nothing can touch you or harm you. No wonder the Apostle Paul goes down to the lowest depths and climbs to the highest heights, and shouts in triumph—"we are more than conquerors through Him that loved us"!

If this great God is ours, what about our bodies, can He keep them in trim? What about our minds, can He keep our imaginations stayed upon Him so that we are able to say without hysterics—"Therefore will we not fear, though the earth be removed, and though the mountains be carried into the midst of the sea"? Every now and again an attack from the unseen realm may surprise us and take us off our guard, but if we are right with God, what do we find? We find God on guard, and we are amazed and stand back and say, "Why, this is wonderful!"—"Kept by the power of God."

"Who shall separate us from the love of Christ?" At the end of all trials, and when there is no more trial, the love of God is not finished; it still goes on. ". . . having loved His own which were in the world, He loved them unto the end." This is the great theme that keeps the soul of the saint undaunted in courage. It does not matter where a man may get to in the way of tribulation or anguish, none of it can wedge in between and separate him from the love of God in Christ Jesus.

Let me close with a simple illustration. Children are sometimes afraid in the dark, fear gets into their hearts and nerves and they get into a tremendous state; then they hear the voice of mother or father, and all is quietened and they go off to sleep. In our own spiritual experience it is the same; some terror comes down the road to meet us and our hearts are seized with a tremendous fear; then we hear our own name called, and the voice of Jesus saying, "It is I, be not afraid," and the peace of God which passeth understanding takes possession of our hearts.

The Soul of a Christian
Foreword (1936)

There is perennial value in these Talks because they deal with abiding things. The soul of man retains its constituent elements and has to face the same sort of problems. Man needs God, and when he would fain find Him, or be found of Him it is well to know progress may be hindered by blocked roads, by blindness or fear, or unbelief or basic enmity against God. Oswald Chambers had well explored that way to God, and God's way to man, and these Talks are the fruit of that knowledge and experience gained by exploring his own heart and in dealing with his fellows. He says, "All this vast complex of 'me,' which we cannot begin to understand, God knows completely." Every man is "lost" who is content i[n] his native estrangement from his God, till the Holy Spirit is allowed to adjust the repentant and believing heart to God through Christ's Redemption. The second Talk is a mighty discourse on "God's scrutiny of man," as the first might be called "How to become a hilarious saint." These Talks come to grips with us, and some things heard form the speaker's lips years ago have lost none of their power to lay hold on heart and mind and will. They will help men who are in earnest, as Jacob Behmen[13] put it, to become rightly related to eternal righteousness, and God's own wholeness (holiness). It will pay anyone to soak in the message of this book till, by the working of God's Spirit and the surgery of events, he comes to himself, and comes right home to God.

D. L. (David Lambert)

SOUL SATISFACTION

O Lord, Thou hast searched me, and known me. Psalm 139:1

None of them can by any means redeem his brother, nor give to God a ransom for him: (for the redemption of their soul is costly, and must be let alone for ever). Psalm 49:7–8 (RV)

Beware of believing that the human soul is simple, for it is not true. Read Psalm 139, and look into yourself, and you will soon find you are much too complex to touch. Charles Wagner[14] was the apostle of naturalness, "the gospel of temperament"—Be simple! How can anyone who is wide-awake be simple? We befool ourselves into moral imbecility if we believe those who tell us the human soul is simple. As long as we think we understand ourselves we are in a lamentable state of ignorance. The first dose of conviction of sin, or of the realisation of what the Psalmist states, viz., the unfathomable depths of our own souls, will put an end to that ignorance. The only One who can redeem the human soul is the Lord Jesus Christ and He has done it, and the Holy Spirit brings the realisation of this to us experimentally. All this vast complex "me" which we cannot begin to understand, God knows completely, and through the Atonement He invades every part of our personality with His life.

Soul is the responsible expression of the ruling personal spirit, and when the personal spirit is filled with God's Spirit, we have to see that we obey His Spirit and reconstruct another soul. God's Spirit entering my spirit does not become my spirit, but quickens my spirit, and I begin to express a new soul. It is not the nature of the working of the soul that is altered, that remains the same in a regenerate human spirit as in an unregenerate human spirit, but a different driving power expresses itself. When God's Spirit comes into my personal spirit, instantly I am introduced to a life which manifests itself in contradiction to my old way of reasoning and expressing myself, and the consequence is that the life whereby I have affinity with other people is upset and they wonder what is the matter with me, a disturbing element has come in which cannot be estimated. The incoming of the Spirit of God disturbs the reasoning

---

13. Jacob Behmen, also Jakob Bohme (1575–1624): German mystic.14. Charles Wagner (1852–1918): Protestant cleric and writer in Paris; authored *The Simple Life,* published in 1904.

14. Charles Wagner (1852–1918): Protestant cleric and writer in Paris; authored *The Simple Life,* published in 1904.

faculties, and for a while the soul that is born from above (RV mg) is inarticulate, it has no expression; the equilibrium has been upset by the incoming of a totally new spirit into my spirit, and Jesus Christ says, "In your patience ye shall win your souls" (Luke 21:19 RV)—acquire your new soul with patience.

Satisfaction and the demand for satisfaction is a God-given principle in human nature, but it must be satisfaction in the highest. "Blessed are they which do hunger and thirst after righteousness: for they shall be filled."

Naturally

But the natural man receiveth not the things of the Spirit of God: for they are foolishness unto him: neither can he know them, because they are spiritually discerned. (1 Corinthians 2:14)

We preach to men as if they were conscious they were dying sinners, they are not; they are having a good time, and our talk about being born from above (RV mg) is in a domain they know nothing of. We do not need the Holy Spirit to reveal that immorality is wrong, but we do need the Holy Spirit to reveal that the complacency of the natural life has Satan at its basis. Nowadays we have come to the conclusion that a man must be a down-and-out sinner before he needs Jesus Christ to do anything for him; consequently we debase Jesus Christ's salvation to mean merely that He can save the vile and sensual man and lift him into a better life. We quote our Lord's statement that "the Son of Man came to seek and to save that which was lost" (RV) and misinterpret His meaning by limiting "the lost" to those who are lost in our eyes.

The natural man does not want to be born again. If a man's morality is well within his own grasp and he has enough religion to give the right tone to his natural life, to talk about being born again seems utterly needless. The natural man is not in distress, he is not conscious of conviction of sin, or of any disharmony, he is quite contented and at peace. Conviction of sin is the realisation that my natural life is based on a disposition that will not have Jesus Christ. The Gospel does not present what the natural man wants but what he needs, and the Gospel awakens an intense resentment as well as an intense craving. We will take God's blessings and loving-kindnesses and prosperities, but when it comes to the need of having our disposition altered, there is opposition at once. When we come down to close quarters and God's Spirit tells us we must give up the right to ourselves to Jesus Christ and let Him rule, then we understand what Paul meant when he said that "the carnal mind," which resides in the heart, is "enmity against God."

No man can have his state of mind altered without suffering for it in his body, and that is why men do anything to avoid conviction of sin. When a worldly man who is happy, moral and upright, comes in contact with Jesus Christ, his "beauty," i.e., the perfectly ordered completeness of his nature, is destroyed and that man must be persuaded that Jesus Christ has a better kind of life for him otherwise he feels he had better not have come across Him. If I knew nothing about sin before the Holy Spirit came, then why did He come? If I am peaceful and happy and contented and living my life with my morality well within my own grasp, why does the Holy Spirit need to come in and upset the balance and make me miserable and unfit for anything? It is time we asked ourselves these questions. God's Book gives us the answer. Thank God, we are coming to the end of the shallow presentation of Christianity that makes out that Jesus Christ came only to give us peace. Thousands of people are happy without God in this world, but that kind of happiness and peace is on a wrong level. Jesus Christ came to send a sword through every peace that is not based on a personal relationship to Himself. He came to put us right with God that His own peace might reign.

Satanically

But if our gospel be hid, it is hid to them that are lost: in whom the god of this world hath blinded the minds of them which believe not, lest the light of the glorious gospel of Christ, who is the image of God, should shine unto them. (2 Corinthians 4:3–4)

Paul did not say "the lost" were the drunkards and social pariahs, but those "in whom the god of this world hath blinded the minds of them which believe not"—they see nothing whatever in all that Jesus Christ stands for.

If the natural remains united with itself long enough it will lead to a deadly Satanic satisfaction, a blind happiness. The words "diabolical" and "Satanic" do not mean the same. Judas became diabolical: "the devil having already put into the heart of Judas Iscariot, Simon's son, to betray Him" (John 13:2 RV); Peter became "Satanic": "But He turned, and said unto Peter, Get thee behind Me, Satan" (Matthew 16:23). The Bible holds man responsible for the introduction of Satan. Satan is the representative of the devil, and the devil is the adversary of God in the rule of man. When our Lord came face to face with Satan He dealt with him as representing the attitude man takes up in organising his life apart from any consideration of God. For a thing to be Satanic does not mean that it is abominable and immoral; the Satanically-managed man is absolutely self-governed and has no need of God.

When Satan rules the hearts of natural men under the inspiration of the devil, they are not troubled, they are at peace, entrenched in clean worldliness (cf. Psalm 73), and before God can rule a man's kingdom He must first overthrow this false rule. In the parable in Luke 11:21 our Lord says that "when the strong man fully armed" (Satan) "guardeth his own court, his goods" (i.e., the souls of men) "are in peace" (RV); there is no breaking out into sin and wrongdoing. The one thing the prince of this world will guard against is the incoming of Jesus Christ, the "stronger than he," because "he taketh from him his whole armour wherein he trusted" (RV), The coming of Jesus Christ is not a peaceful thing, it is a disturbing, an overwhelming thing. Am I willing to be born into the realm Jesus Christ is in? If so, I must be prepared for chaos straight off in the realm I am in. The rule which has come in between God and man has to be eclipsed, and Jesus Christ's entering in means absolute chaos concerning the way I have been looking at things, a turning of everything upside down. "Think not that I am come to send peace on the earth: I came not to send peace, but a sword" (Matthew 10:34). The old order and the old peace must go, and we cannot get back peace on the old level. Immediately Jesus Christ comes in that peace is gone, and instead there is the sword of conviction. A man does not need the Holy Spirit to tell him that external sins are wrong, ordinary culture and education will do that; but it does take the Holy Spirit to convict us of sin as our Lord defined it. The Holy Spirit is unmistakable in His working, and our Lord said that, "He, when He is come, will convict the world in respect of sin, . . . *because they believe not on Me*" (John 16:8–9 RV). That is the very essence of sin. If once we have allowed Jesus Christ to upset the equilibrium, holiness is the inevitable result, or no peace for ever.

One of the most cunning travesties of Satan is to say that he is the instigator of drunkenness and external sins. Man himself is responsible for doing wrong things, and he does wrong things because of the wrong disposition that is in him. The true blame for sin lies in the wrong disposition, and the cunning of our nature makes us blame Satan when we should blame ourselves. When men go into external sins Satan is probably as much upset as the Holy Ghost, but for a different reason. Satan knows perfectly well that when men go into external sin and upset their lives, they will want another Ruler, a Saviour, a Deliverer; but as long as he can keep them in peace and unity and harmony apart from God he will do so. The Bible reveals that there is a solidarity of sin, a bond of union, that keeps men together known as "the body of sin"; it is the mutual inheritance of the human race (see Romans 5:12). The Bible also reveals that Satan is anxious to keep that solidarity intact, because whenever men break out into immoral conduct, it disintegrates his kingdom. The one other force that disintegrates the solidarity of sin is the Spirit of God. Never have the idea that a worldling is unhappy, a worldling is perfectly happy, as thoroughly happy as a Christian. The persons who are unhappy are the worldlings or the Christians if they are not at one with the principle that binds them. When a worldling is not a worldling at heart, he is miserable; and when a Christian is not a Christian at heart, he is miserable, he carries his religion like a headache instead of something that is worth having. Remember then, the two things that disintegrate Satan's kingdom—breaking out into acts of sin, and conviction by the Spirit of God. This is the solution of a number of moral problems.

The beginning of calamities from the natural standpoint is when our Lord comes across people. The thing that upsets our natural complacency is a touch from our Lord. It may come in a personal interview (as in John 4), but when it comes it is all up instantly with the old order, we can never get it back. Before the Spirit of God can bring peace of mind He has to clear out the rubbish, and before He can do that He has to give us an idea of what rubbish there is.

Spiritually

But God . . . even when we were dead in sins, hath quickened us together with Christ, (by grace ye are saved;) and hath raised us up together, and made us sit together in heavenly places in Christ Jesus. (Ephesians 2:5–6)

If all Jesus Christ came to do was to upset me, make me unfit for my work, upset my friendships and my life, produce disturbance and misery and distress, then I wish He had never come. But that is not all He came to do. He came to lift us up to "the heavenly places" where He is Himself. The whole claim of the Redemption of Jesus is that He can satisfy the last aching abyss of the human soul, not hereafter only, but here and now. Satisfaction does not mean stagnation, it means the knowledge that we have the right type of life for our souls. The hymn has it rightly, "Oh, the peace my Saviour gives!" That peace is the deepest thing a human personality can know, it is almighty. The Apostle Paul emphasises the hilarity of life—"Be not drunk with wine, . . . but be filled with the Spirit." Enthusiasm is the idea, intoxicated with the life of God. The healthy pagan and the healthy saint are the ones described in God's Book as hilarious; all in between are diseased and more or less sick. We have no business to be sick unless it is just a preparatory stage towards something better, when God is nursing us through some spiritual illness; but if it is the main characteristic of the life there is something wrong.

"Blessed are the poor in spirit." The knowledge of our own poverty brings us to the moral frontier where Jesus Christ works; then He says, If you ask God, He will give you the Holy Spirit. "If ye then, being evil, know how to give good gifts unto your children: how much more shall your heavenly Father give the Holy Spirit to them that ask Him?" (Luke 11:13). The Holy Spirit is the One who regenerates us into the kingdom to which Jesus Christ belongs. "Marvel not that I said unto thee, Ye must be born again." The touch that comes is as mysterious as the wind . The

miracle of the creation of Redemption in our soul is that we suddenly feel an insatiable desire for salvation. Our Lord said, "No man can come to Me, except the Father which hath sent Me draw him," and that is the way He draws him. Redemption is the great Reality that is continually creating within us a longing for God.

GOD'S SEARCHING OF A SINCERE SOUL

Intercessory Introspection

Search me, O God, and know my heart: try me, and know my thoughts. . . . (Psalm 139:23–24)

It is far more rare to find a sincere soul than one might suppose. No one but a fool or a sincere soul would ever pray this prayer—"Search me, O God," search me right out to the remotest depths, to the innermost recesses of my thoughts and imaginations; scrutinise me through and through until I know that Thou dost know me utterly, that I may be saved from my own ways and brought into Thy way. Any soul who prays that prayer will be answered.

Psalm 139 states for us the profoundest experience of a soul's life with God. It is a marvellous moment in a man's life when he knows he is explored by God. The introspective tendency in us which makes us want to examine ourselves and know the springs of our thoughts and motives takes the form of prayer with the Psalmist. He speaks of God as the Creator of the vast universe outside him, of His omnipotence and omnipresence, but he does not end there. There is something infinitely more mysterious to the Psalmist than the universe outside him, and that is the mystery of his own soul. "There are mountain-peaks in my soul I cannot climb, ocean depths I cannot fathom; there are possibilities within which terrify me, therefore, O God, search me." That is introspective intercession.

We must live scrutinised by God, and if you want to know what the scrutiny of God is like, listen to Jesus Christ: "for from within, out of the heart of men, evil thoughts proceed . . . ," and then follows a rugged catalogue of things few of us know anything about in conscious life, consequently we are apt to be indignant and resent Jesus Christ's diagnosis—"I have never felt like a murderer, or an adulterer, therefore those things cannot be in me." To talk in that way is proof that we are grossly ignorant of ourselves. If we prefer to trust our ignorant innocence we pass a verdict on the only Master of the human heart there is, we tell Him He does not know what He is talking about. The one right thing to do is to listen to Jesus

Christ and then hand our hearts over to God to be searched and guarded, and filled with the Holy Spirit, then the wonderful thing is that we never need know and never shall know in actual experience the truth of Jesus Christ's revelation about the human heart. But if we stand on our own rights and wisdom at any second an eruption may occur in our personal life and we shall discover to our unutterable horror that what Jesus said is appallingly true.

We have no business to be ignorant about ourselves. If any of us have come to manhood or womanhood with the idea that we have a holy innocence on the inside, we are desperately deluded. There is no human being on earth with an innocence which is not based on ignorance, and if we have come to the stage of life we are now in with the belief that innocence and purity are the same thing, it is because we have paid no attention to what Jesus Christ said. Purity is something that has been tested and tried, and triumphed; innocence has always to be shielded. When the Holy Spirit comes in He brings into the centre of our personal life the very Spirit that was manifested in the life of the Lord Jesus, viz., *Holy* Spirit. Jesus Christ has undertaken through His Redemption to put into us a heart so pure that God Almighty can see nothing to censure in it, and the Holy Spirit searches us not only to make us know the possibilities of iniquity in our heart, but to make us "unblameable in holiness" in His sight.

The great cry to-day is, "Fulfil yourself, work out what is in you." If you do, you will work out your own condemnation. But if you let God deal with what is wrong, let Him "presence you with Divinity," you will be able to work *out* what He works *in,* which is a totally different thing. The cry to realise ourselves is the cry to keep God out. If we do not know the tremendous depths of possible iniquity in our hearts, it is because we have never been scrutinised by the Holy Ghost; but let Him turn His searchlight right down to the inmost recesses, and the best of us are shuddering on our faces before God. When the Holy Ghost does scrutinise us (and He will not do it if we do not want Him to, this is the day of our option; a time is coming when He will do it whether we want Him to or not, when we will be only too glad to creep anywhere out of the sight of God whose eyes search as a flame of fire), He reveals not only a depth of possible iniquity that makes us shudder, but a height of holiness of which we never dreamed. The great mystic work of the Holy Spirit is in the dim regions of our personality where we cannot go: "And I pray God your whole spirit and soul and body be preserved blameless unto the coming of our Lord Jesus Christ" (1 Thessalonians 5:23). "But no man can get there!" Then was the Apostle Paul mad when he said we could be presented "holy and without blemish [RV] and unreproveable in His sight"? No, the Apostle Paul had been to the Cross of Christ and had learned there a secret which made him say—"God forbid that I should glory, save in the cross of our Lord Jesus Christ," because it is by means of His Cross that Jesus Christ can present us faultless before the throne of God. "Do you mean to say that God can bring the winnowing fan of His Spirit and search out my thoughts and imaginations and find nothing deserving of blame?" That is the meaning of the Atonement as far as our practical experience is concerned; no soul gets there saving by the sovereign grace of God. If we have not caught the meaning of the tremendous moral aspect of the Atonement it is because we have never prayed this prayer, "Search me, O God." Are we sincere enough to ask God to search us, and sincere enough to abide by what His searching reveals?

Impeccable Integrity

But if we walk in the light, as He is in the light, . . . the blood of Jesus Christ His Son cleanseth us from all sin. (1 John 1:7)

If that means cleansing from all sin in conscious experience only, may God have mercy on us. A man who has been made obtuse by sin will say he is not conscious of sin. Cleansing from all sin by the blood of Jesus is far deeper than we can be conscious of, it is cleansing from all sin in the sight of God because the disposition of His Son is working out in every particular, not to our consciousness, but deeper than our consciousness. We are not cleansed more and more from all sin, if we walk in the light, as God is in the light, we *are* cleansed from all sin. In our consciousness it works with a keen poignant knowledge of what sin is. The great need to-day amongst those of us who profess sanctification is the patience and ability to work out the holiness of God in every detail of our

lives. When we are first adjusted to God the Holy Spirit works on the big general lines, then He begins to educate us down to the scruple,[15] He makes us sensitive over things we never before thought of. No matter what our experience may be we must beware of the curse of being stationary, we have to go on and on "perfecting holiness in the fear of God."

If you have been making a great profession in your religious life but begin to find that the Holy Spirit is scrutinising you, let His searchlight go straight down, and He will not only search you, He will put everything right that is wrong; He will make the past as though it had never been; He will restore the years the cankerworm hath eaten; He will "blot out the handwriting of ordinances that is against you" (RV); He will put His Spirit within you and cause you to walk in His ways; He will make you pure in the deepest recesses of your personality. Thank God, Jesus Christ's salvation is a flesh-and-blood reality!

Who is going to do all this in us? The Lord Jesus Christ. Let Jesus Christ proclaim His Gospel: we can have the very disposition of Jesus imparted to us, and if we have not got it we will have to tell God the reason why. We have to tell God we don't believe He can do it—there are details of our lives He cannot put right, back tracks He cannot clear up, ramifications of evil He cannot touch. Thank God that is a lie! He can. If God cannot do that we have "followed cunningly devised fables." That is where the fight has to be fought—along the line of what Jesus Christ can do in the human soul. Unless God has searched us and cleansed us and filled us with the Holy Spirit so that we are undeserving of censure in His sight, the Atonement has not been applied to our personal experience.

Are we willing to let God scrutinise us, or are we doing that worst of all things, trying to justify ourselves? People say if they are living up to all the light they have, meaning the light of conscience, they are all right. We may be consciously free of sin, but we are not justified on that account; we may be walking in the light of our conscience, but we are not justified on that account either (cf. 1 Corinthians 4:3–4); we are only justified in the sight of God through the Atonement at work in our inner life. God grant we may let His searching scrutiny go right through us until there is nothing God has not searched. We are far too big for ourselves, infinitely too big. The majority of us try to put ourselves in a bandbox,[16] but we cannot cabin and confine our lives. There is a purpose in every life that is in God's keeping of which we know little, but which He will fulfil if we let Him rightly relate us to Himself.

---

15. down to the scruple: to the smallest item.

16. bandbox: in Chambers' day, a small, round box made to hold neckbands or collars for shirts; metaphorically, something small, narrow, cloistered, self-contained.

THE NEED TO BE A CHRISTIAN

Never confuse personality with consciousness. Personality is the perplexing factor of my self which continually changes and yet remains the same. All we can deal with in psychology is consciousness, but God does not limit our salvation by our consciousness. The need to be a Christian is not simply that Jesus Christ's salvation may work in our conscious life, but that the unconscious realm of our personality may be protected from supernatural powers of which we know nothing. When the Holy Spirit enters into us He brings the marvellous revelation that God guards the unfathomable part of our personality; He goes to the springs of our personal life which we cannot touch, and prevents our being tampered with and bewitched out of God's purpose in Redemption. We belittle and misrepresent the Redemption if we refer it merely to our conscious life. Many spiritual testimonies get as far as—"Once I was that in conscious life, and now I am this, and Jesus did it." Well, thank God for that, but we are much more than we are conscious of, and if Jesus Christ only came to alter our conscious life, then the Redemption is "much ado about nothing." But when we come to examine the New Testament we find that Redemption does infinitely more than alter our conscious life; it safeguards the unconscious realm which we cannot touch. Our conscious experience is simply the doorway into the only Reality there is, viz., the Redemption. We are not only "presenced with Divinity," but protected by Deity in the depths of personality below the conscious realm.

Piratical Invasions from the Unconscious

Part of our personal life is conscious, but the greater part is unconscious, and every now and again the unconscious part emerges into the conscious and upsets us because we do not know where it comes from or where it leads to, and we get afraid of ourselves. There is a great deal more of "me" I do not know than that I do know. No man knows the springs of his motives or of his will; when we begin to examine ourselves we come to the threshold of the unconscious and cannot go any further. The Psalmist realised this when he prayed, "Search me, O God"; explore me to the beginning of my motives. Below the threshold of consciousness is the subconscious part of our personality which is full of mystery. There are forces in this realm which may interfere with us and we cannot control them, it is with this realm that the Spirit of God deals.

An island of the sea is easily explored, yet it may prove to be but the top of a mountain the greater part of which is hidden under the sea, going down to deeper depths than we can fathom. So our personality is infinitely more than we can be conscious of; consequently we must never estimate ourselves by the part we are conscious of, or be so stupid as to say we are only what we are conscious of. We are all in danger of doing this until we come across things in ourselves that surprise us. People say, "Oh, I can't understand myself!" Of course you cannot. "No one else understands me!" Of course they don't; if they did, we would not be worth understanding. There is only one Being Who understands us, and that is our Creator. We must beware of estimating God's salvation by our experience of it. Our experience is a mere indication in conscious life of an almighty salvation which goes far beyond anything we ever can experience.

Have we ever awakened to the fact that there are forces of evil around us greater than we can control? Jesus Christ by His Redemption not only saves us completely, but keeps us oblivious of the awful dangers there are outside: "the evil one toucheth him not" (RV). We are kept where we are unconscious of the need to be kept. Thank God for His safeguarding, for His salvation which keeps us waking and sleeping, conscious and unconscious, in danger and out of it.

There are supernatural powers and agencies that can play with us like toys whenever they choose unless we are garrisoned by God. The New Testament continually impresses this upon us: "For we wrestle not against flesh and blood, but against principalities, against powers, against the rulers of the darkness of this world, against spiritual wickedness in the high places." According to the Bible, spiritualism is not a trick, it is a fact. Man can communicate with beings of a different order from his own; he can put himself into a state of subjectivity in which spirits can appear. A medium commits the great crime psychically because he gives himself over to a force the nature of which he does not know. He does great violence to his own rectitude and tampers with the balance of his sanity by putting himself into league with powers the character of which he does not know. Mediumship, whereby unseen spirits talk to men and women, will destroy the basis of moral sanity because it introduces a man into domains he had better leave alone. Drunkenness and debauchery are child's play compared with the peril of spiritualism. There is something uncannily awful about tampering with these supernatural powers, and in the speeding up of these days the necromantic element is increasing. Be on the look out for the manifestations that are not of God; all have the one sign, they ignore Jesus Christ. Beware of the advice: "Yield, give up your will." No man or woman has any right to yield himself or herself to any impression or any influence; immediately they do they are susceptible to all kinds of supernatural powers. There is only one Being to Whom we must yield, and that is the Lord Jesus Christ. Be sure that it is Jesus Christ to whom you yield, then the whole nature is safeguarded for ever.

Pushing Down God's Barriers

When the Holy Spirit comes in He makes us know that there are things we must remain ignorant of. Beware of entering into competition with the Holy Spirit. When we become curious and pry where we have no business to pry, we are eating of the fruit of the tree of which God said, "Thou shall not eat of it." The spiritualistic trend of to-day is an example of this very thing. Men and women are pushing down God's barriers and coming into contact with forces they cannot control. Unless we hand over the keeping of our personality to God to garrison, there are a hundred and one influences which can come into us which we never can control but which will soon control us. The blight of God rests on a man or woman who dares to take any way of knowing what is hidden other than Jesus Christ's way. He is the only One who is "worthy to open the book." If by intellectual curiosity we push away the barriers God has seen fit to put, we shall experience pain and suffering from which God will not protect us. We cannot play the fool with our bodies and souls and hoodwink God. Certain kinds of moral disobedience produce sicknesses which no physical remedy can touch, the only cure is obedience to Jesus Christ. The barriers are placed by a God who is absolutely holy, and He has told us clearly, "Not that way." If we turn to necromancy even in such seemingly ridiculous ways of telling fortunes in teacups or by cards or planchette, we commit a crime against our own souls, we are probing where we have no right to probe. People say, "There's no harm in it." There is all the harm and the backing up of the devil in it. The only One who can open up the profound mysteries of life is God, and He will do it as He sees we can stand it (cf. Deuteronomy 29:29).

Soul is the expression of the personal spirit in the body, and it is the expression of soul that is either good or bad. What we *do* tells as much as what we are in the final issue. There are two entrances into the soul, viz., the body and the spirit. The body is within our control, the spirit is not, and if our spirit is not under the control of God there is nothing to prevent other spirits communicating through it to the soul and body. It is impossible to guard our spirit, the only One who can guard its entrances is God. If we hand ourselves over to His keeping we shall be kept not only from what

we understand as dangers, but from dangers we have never even imagined. The conscious ring of our life is a mere phase; Jesus Christ did not die to save that only; it is the whole personality that is included in the Redemption. We are safeguarded from dangers we know nothing about. Thank God if the unseen realm does not impinge on you. There are people in whom the walls between the seen and unseen are exceedingly thin and they are constantly being tortured; the salvation of Jesus Christ can save them from it all. We are ill-taught if we look for results only in the earthlies when we pray. A praying saint performs far more havoc among the unseen forces of darkness than we have the slightest notion of.

Perils of Self-Ignorance

Who can understand his errors? cleanse Thou me from secret faults. (Psalm 19:12)

Is there some fault God has been checking you about and you have left it alone? Be careful lest it end in a dominant sin. The errors are silent, they creep in on us, and when we stand in the light of Jesus Christ we are amazed to find the conclusions we have come to. The reason is that we have deluded ourselves. This self-security keeps us entirely ignorant of what we really are, ignorant of the things that make the salvation of Jesus Christ necessary. When we say to ourselves—"Oh well, I am no worse than anyone else," that is the beginning; we shall soon produce blindness to our own defects and entrench ourselves around with a fictitious security. Jesus Christ has no chance whatever with the man who has the silent security of self-ignorance. When he hears anyone speak about deliverance from sin, he is untouched—"I have no need to be delivered." Paul says, "If our gospel be hid, it is hid to those in whom the god of this world hath blinded their minds"—blinded to everything Jesus Christ stands for, and a man is to blame for getting there.

For a man to be at peace in his mind, undisturbed and at unity in himself, is a good thing, because in a united personality there is freedom from self-consciousness; but if that peace and unity are without any consideration of Jesus Christ, it is a peace of death, a peace altogether apart from God, and when the Holy Spirit comes in He comes not as a Comforter, but as a thorough Disturber, and upsets this natural unity. No wonder men will do anything to avoid conviction of sin, anything to keep the searchlight of God out, anything to keep away from morbid introspection. But thank God for the men and women who have come to the end of themselves and who say, "Search me, O God, I cannot live any longer in a vain show," and He will do it. We are driven back every time to our relationship with God; it is the only safe thing.

If the Spirit of God can come into the unconscious part of our personality, the spirit of the devil can come there also. "The devil having now put into the heart of Judas Iscariot" (the personality of Judas) "to betray Him" (John 13:2); and Jesus said of Judas, "Have I not chosen you twelve, and one of you is a devil? He spake of Judas Iscariot the son of Simon" (John 6:70–71). Some people seem to think it is an amazingly clever thing to doubt Jesus Christ; it is an evil thing. Whenever the evil personality of unbelief asked the Lord anything, He never answered; but when the heart cries out, He answers immediately.

"And He, when He is come, will convict . . . of sin"—because men are immoral?—No, *because they believe not on Me*" (John 16:8–9 RV). These words reveal the very essence of sin. Sin is not measured by a creed or social order: sin is measured by a Person, Jesus Christ. When the Holy Spirit comes in He is unmistakable in the direction of His work, He goes direct to the thing that keeps us from believing in Jesus Christ. The work of the Holy Spirit is to make us realise the meaning of the Redemption. As long as we believe it on the outside it does not upset our complacency, but we don't want to be perturbed on the inside. Paul says that some people have a "foolish heart"—"When they knew God, they glorified Him not as God" (Romans 1:21). In actual life they were amazingly shrewd and calculating, but their hearts were foolish towards God. Beware of turning your back on what you know is true because you do not want it to be real. Jesus Christ never says that a man is damned because he is a sinner; the condemnation is when a man sees what Jesus Christ came to do and will not let Him do it. That is the critical moment, "the judgement" (John 3:19 RV), in a man's life.

There are possibilities below the threshold of our life which no one knows but God. We cannot understand ourselves or know the spring of our motives, consequently our examination of ourselves can never be unbiased or unprejudiced. We are only safe in taking an estimate of ourselves from our Creator, not from our own introspection. But although introspection cannot profoundly satisfy us, we must not conclude that introspection is wrong. Introspection is right, because it is the only way we shall discover that we need God. Introspection without God leads to insanity. The people who have no tendency to introspect are described as "dead in trespasses and sins," quite happy, quite contented, quite moral, all they want is easily within their own grasp; but they are dead to the world to which Jesus Christ belongs, and it takes His voice and His Spirit to awaken them. If we estimate our life by the abundance of things which we possess consciously, there will come a drastic awakening one day because we shall have to leave it all at death. We shall have to leave this body, which keeps the personal spirit in conscious life, and go clean through the threshold of consciousness to where we do not know. It is a desperate thing to die if we have only been living in the conscious realm.

These aspects reveal the need to be a Christian as an enormous need. Thank God for the amazing security of His salvation! It keeps us not only in conscious life but from dangers of which we know nothing, unseen and hidden dangers, subtle and desperate.

CHARACTERISTICS OF THE SOUL

The Soul in Sinful Badness—*Working Inwards*

(a) Gross Inquisitiveness
And when the woman saw that the tree was good for food, and that it was a delight to the eyes, and that the tree was to be desired to make one wise, she took of the fruit thereof, and did eat. (Genesis 3:6 RV)

There are some things of which we must be ignorant, because knowledge of them comes in no other way than by disobedience to God. In the life originally designed for Adam it was not intended that he should be ignorant of evil, but that he should know evil through understanding good. Instead, he ate of the fruit of the tree of knowledge of good and evil and thereby knew evil positively and good negatively; consequently none of us knows the order God intended. The knowledge of evil that comes through the Fall has given human nature a bias of insatiable curiosity about the bad, and only when we have been introduced into the Kingdom of God do we know good and evil in the way God constituted man to know them.

If we want to discover things in the material universe we must be intellectually curious; but for finding things out scientifically it does not matter whether a man is good or bad. It is right to be curious about the natural world; if we are not intellectually curious we shall never learn anything. God never encourages laziness. But when we come to the domain Jesus Christ lives in, curiosity is of no avail. The only way to find out things in the moral universe is by obedience.

The philosophy of life is based on the topsy-turvy reasoning of going into things in order to find out about them, which is like saying you have to go into the mud before you can know what clean water is. "I must know the world"—if you do, you will only know good by contrast with evil. Modern teaching implies that we must be grossly experienced before we are of any use in the world. That is not true. Jesus Christ knew good and evil by the life which was in Him, and God intended that man's knowledge of evil should come in the same way as to our Lord, viz., through the rigorous integrity of obedience to God. When a man is convicted of sin he knows how terrific is the havoc sin has wrought in him and he knows with what a mighty salvation he has been visited by God; but it is only by obedience to the Holy Spirit that he begins to know what an awful thing sin is.

A great deal of our social work to-day is a history of moral house-breaking; men and women have gone into work to which God never sent them, consequently their moral and spiritual integrity has been violated. Work is taken up with the absurd deification of pluck—"This thing has got to be done, and I must do it," and they damage their souls in doing it because God is not there to protect. But when a man or woman is called of God, the facts he or she has to face never upset the equilibrium of the life because they are garrisoned by the presence of God. Too often when merely moral men or women go into bad surroundings they become soiled, no matter what their moral standard is; but the men and women who have been made pure by the Holy Ghost are kept like the light, unsullied.

(b) Growing Iniquity
And he said, . . . Hast thou eaten of the tree, whereof I commanded thee that thou shouldest not eat? . . . (Genesis 3:11–12; see Jude 4, 10)

Every child born of natural generation is innocent, but it is the innocence of ignorance. Naturally we are in an impaired state, and when our innocence is turned into knowledge we find to our humiliation how tremendously impaired it is. It is the ignorant innocence of determinedly being without the knowledge of God (Romans 1:18–23). It is safer to trust God's revelation than our own innocence. Jesus Christ is either the supreme Authority on the human heart or He is not worth listening to, and He said: "For from within, out of the heart of men, proceed . . . ," and then comes that very ugly catalogue. Jesus did not say, "Into the human heart these things are injected," but, "from within, out of the heart of men all these evil things proceed." If we trust our innocent ignorance to secure us, it is likely that as life goes on there will come a burst-up from underneath into our conscious life which will reveal to us that we are uncommonly like what Jesus Christ said.

Iniquity means turning out of the straight. Whenever anything begins to turn you out of the straight, stop and get it put right, no matter what else suffers. If you don't, you will grow in iniquity, and if you grow in iniquity you will call iniquity integrity; sensuality spirituality, and ultimately the devil, God. The most terrible verdict on the human soul is that it no longer believes in purity, and no man gets there without being himself to blame. There is such a thing as "Paradise Lost."[17] The gates can never again be opened in this life, they are shut as inevitably as God shuts anything.

(c) Great Independence
And the serpent said unto the woman, Ye shall not surely die: for God doth know that in the day ye eat thereof, then your eyes shall be opened, and ye shall be as God, knowing good and evil. (Genesis 3:4–5 RV; see Genesis 3:22)

Adam was intended by God to take part in his own development by a series of moral choices, to sacrifice his natural life to God by obedience and thereby transform it into a spiritual life. Instead, he deliberately ate of the fruit of the tree of the knowledge of good and evil, and thereby became god over himself (Genesis 3:5). The characteristic of sin is independence of God—"I can look after myself; I know exactly how far to go. I intend to develop my life without God—why shouldn't I?" Whenever we say, "Why shouldn't I?" we tell Jesus Christ to retire and we take our life into our own hands, and instead of working from within and manifesting the beauty of holiness, we work inwards and become more and more self-centred, harder, and more indifferent to external things.

The knowledge of evil that came through the Fall gives a man a broad mind, but instead of instigating him to action it paralyses his action. Men and women whose minds are poisoned by gross experience of evil are marvellously generous with regard to other people's sins; they argue in this way—"To know all is to pardon all." Every bit of their broadmindedness paralyses their power to *do* anything. They know good only by contrast with evil, which is the exact opposite of God's order. When a man knows good and evil in the way God intended he should he becomes intolerant of evil, and this intolerance shows itself in an intense activity against evil. Jesus Christ never tolerated sin for one moment, and when His nature is having its way in us the same intolerance is shown. The marvel of the grace of God is that He can take the strands of evil and twistedness out of a man's mind and imagination

---

17. Dante's *Paradise Lost*, published in 1667.

and make him simple towards God. Restoration through the Redemption of Jesus Christ makes a man simple, and simplicity always shows itself in action. There is nothing simple in the human soul or in human life. The only simple thing is the relationship of the soul to Jesus Christ, that is why the Apostle Paul says, "I fear, lest by any means, . . . your minds should be corrupted from the simplicity that is in Christ."

The Soul in Spiritual Beauty—*Working Outwards*

(a) Golden Ignorance
And the LORD God formed man of the dust of the ground, and breathed into his nostrils the breath of life; and man became a living soul. (Genesis 2:7 see Luke 2:40, 52)

The presentation of true Christian experience brings us face to face with spiritual beauty; a beauty which can never be forced or imitated, because it is a manifestation from within of a simple relationship to God that is being worked out all the time. There is nothing simple saving a man's relation to God in Christ, and that relationship must never be allowed to be complicated. Our Lord's Childhood expresses this spiritual beauty, "And the child grew, and waxed strong, becoming [mg] full of wisdom. . . . And Jesus advanced in wisdom and age [mg]" (RV). The great characteristic of our Lord's life was that of "golden ignorance"; there were things He did not know and that He refused to know. Jesus Christ developed in the way God intended human beings to develop, and He exhibited the kind of life we ought to live when we have been born from above (RV mg). "But," you say, "how am I to live a life like Jesus Christ? I have not the 'golden ignorance' He had; I have a heredity I had no say in, I am not holy nor likely to be." The marvel of the Redemption is that Jesus Christ can put into any man His own hereditary disposition of holiness, and all the standards He gives are based on that disposition. "Marvel not that I said unto thee, Ye must be born from above [RV mg]" (John 3:7). The characteristic of a child is innocence, but remember there is a difference between the innocence of an ordinary child and the innocence of the Babe of Bethlehem. Natural innocence is based on ignorance, and as life goes on things awaken and prove that innocence is not purity, it is not based on an unsullied foundation. Profoundly speaking, a child is not pure, and yet the innocence of a child charms us because it makes visible all that we understand by purity.

(b) Growing Integrity
And the LORD God commanded the man, saying, Of every tree of the garden thou mayest freely eat: but of the tree of the knowledge of good and evil, thou shalt not eat of it: for in the day that thou eatest thereof thou shalt surely die. (Genesis 2:16–17; see 2 Corinthians 11:3)

Integrity means the unimpaired state of anything. The "golden ignorance" manifested in our Lord's Childhood and Boyhood was unimpaired when He reached Manhood and was manifested in a growing integrity. Jesus Christ carried out all that Adam failed to do, and He did it in the simple way of obedience to His Father. It is not the passing of the years that matures the life of the Son of God in us, but obedience. As we obey we find that all the power of God is at our disposal, and we too can grow in spiritual beauty. Are we humble and obedient, learning as Jesus learned, or are we hurrying into experiences we have no right to? If we have to find reasons for doing what we do, we should not do it. The life of a child is one of simple obedience. We grow spiritually by obeying God through the words of Jesus being made spirit and life to us, and by paying attention to where we are, not to whether we are growing or not. We grow spiritually as our Lord grew physically, by a life of simple, unobtrusive obedience. If we do not obey God's Word and pay attention to the circumstances He has engineered for us, we shall not grow in spiritual beauty but will become lop-sided; our integrity will be impaired by something of the nature of inordinate lust. Remember, lust can be spiritual. Lust disputes the throne of God in us—"I have set my mind to this, or that, and I must have it at once." That will lead to gross experience. It means there is some desire, some inordinate affection or imagination we are not bringing into captivity to the obedience of Christ.

The soul in spiritual beauty must be a born-again soul, i.e., something has come into it from without. Luke 1:35 ("wherefore also that which is to be born shall be called holy, the Son of God," RV mg) is the symbol of what happens when the Holy Ghost comes into us, our natural life is made the mother of the Son of God. We have to nourish the life of the Son of God in us, and we do it by bringing our natural life into accordance with His life and transforming it into a spiritual life by obedience.

(c) Grand Invincibility
And I will put enmity between thee and the woman, and between thy seed and her seed: and he shall bruise thy head, and thou shalt bruise his heel. (Genesis 3:15 RV; see Romans 16:19–20)

When we begin our life with God, we wish He would make it impossible for us to go wrong. If God did, our obedience would cease to be of value. When God created man, He put into his hands the free choice of good or evil, and that choice is there still, and the very test develops the character. The basis of life is antagonism in every domain, physical, mental, moral and spiritual, we only maintain health by fighting. Naturally we are not virtuous, but innocently ignorant. Disinclination to sin is not virtue, any more than innocence is purity. The danger is to make a virtue of necessity. It is fighting that produces virtue, moral stability on the inside. Virtue has character at the back of it, it has been tested and tried and has triumphed. Spiritual stability within produces holiness. Our Lord was invincible as a Man: "Who is worthy to open the book? . . . Worthy art Thou to take the book, and to open the seals thereof" (Revelation 5:2, 9 RV). Jesus Christ proved Himself worthy, not only in the domain of God which we do not know, but in the domain of man which we do know. By means of His Redemption Jesus Christ makes us the sons and daughters of God, and we have to "put on the new man," in accordance with the life of the Son of God

formed in us, and as we do we become invincible— "more than conquerors through Him that loved us."

"I would have you wise unto that which is good, and simple unto that which is evil" (RV). The Apostle Paul's counsel fits on exactly with Genesis 3:15 . By obeying the life that was in Him, Jesus Christ manifested the wisdom of the serpent and the harmlessness of the dove . If we know good only by contrast with evil, we shall have the devilishness of the serpent through gross experience. But when we know good and evil in the way Jesus Christ knew them, all our subtle wisdom is on the side of the good and our dove-like nature is towards evil. When we are born again we have to obey the Spirit of God, and as we draw on the life of Jesus and learn to assimilate and carry out what He speaks to us, we shall grow in ignorance of certain things and be alive and alert only to what is God's will for us.

THE TEMPLE OF GOD

Desecration

And Jesus went into the temple, and began to cast out them that sold and them that bought [RV] in the temple, and overthrew the tables of the money-changers. . . . (Mark 11:15; cf. John 2:13–17)

We bring to the New Testament a sentimental conception of our Lord; we think of Him as the "meek and mild and gentle Jesus" and make it mean that He was of no practical account whatever. Our Lord *was* "meek and lowly in heart," yet watch Him in the Temple, meekness and gentleness were not the striking features there. We see instead a terrible Being with a whip of small cords in His hands, overturning the money-changers' tables and driving out men and cattle. Is He the "meek and gentle Jesus" there? He is absolutely terrifying; no one dare interfere with Him. Why could He not have driven them out in a gentler way? Because passionate zeal had eaten Him up, with a detestation of everything that dared to call His Father's honour into disrepute.

"Make not my Father's house an house of merchandise"—the deification of commercial enterprise. Everything of the nature of wrong must go when Jesus Christ begins to cleanse His Father's house.

If you have been laid hold of by the Spirit of God don't think it strange concerning the spring-cleaning God is giving you, and don't clamour for anything because it will have to go. The setting apart of my body by the Holy Ghost for a temple of God is a terror to everything in me that is not of God. Sensuality and sordidness lurk about the bodily temple until

Jesus Christ cleanses it. Sensuality is that which gratifies my particular senses, it is the working of my body in connection with external circumstances whereby I begin to satisfy myself. Sensuality may be unutterably disgusting or it may be amazingly refined, but it is based on the wrong thing and has to go; it can have nothing to do with the temple of God, i.e., with man as God created him.

My body is designed to be a "temple of the Holy Ghost," and it is up to me to stand for the honour of Jesus Christ in my bodily practices. When the Spirit of God comes in, He cleanses the temple and does not let one darling sin lurk. The one thing Jesus Christ insists on in my bodily life is chastity. As individuals we must not desecrate the temple of God by tampering with anything we ought not to tamper with; if we do, the scourge of God will come. Immediately the Spirit of God comes in we begin to realise what it means—everything that is not of God has to be turned clean out. People are surprised and say, "I was told God would give the Holy Spirit to them that ask Him; well, I asked for the Holy Spirit and expected that He would bring me joy and peace, but I have had a terrible time ever since." That is the sign He has come, He is turning out the "money-changers" and the "cattle," i.e., the things that were making the temple into a trafficking place for self-realisation. We soon find why the Gospel can never be welcome. As long as we speak winsomely about the "meek and gentle Jesus," and the beautiful ideas the Holy Spirit produces when He comes in, people are captivated, but that is not the Gospel. The Gospel does away with any other ground to stand on than that of the Atonement. Speak about the peace of heaven and the joy of the Lord, and men will listen to you; but tell them that the Holy Spirit has to come in and turn out their claim to their right to themselves, and instantly there is resentment—"I can do what I like with my body; I can go where I choose." The majority of people are not blackguards and criminals, living in external sin, they are clean-living and respectable, and it is to such that the scourge of God is the most terrible thing because it reveals that the natural virtues may be in idolatrous opposition to God.

"*. . . and the seats of them that sold doves.*" I may not be giving way to sensuality and sordidness, but I may be crooning a dirge of self-pity—doves in a cage are always cooing—"Oh it is so hard for me, you don't know what I have to give up; doing the will of God is such an enormous cost." Consecration by the Spirit of God means merciless dealing with that kind of thing, He has no sympathy with it. How can we be of the slightest use to God if we are always whining about our own condition? The compromise arising from self-pity is quite sufficient to extinguish the whole purpose of God in a life.

"*. . . and would not suffer that any men should carry any vessel through the temple.*" The Spirit of God will not allow me to use my body for my own convenience; the whole limit must be God's. I am not to serve my own ends with my body, I am to serve the ends of Jesus Christ and be a devoted disciple of His. Lust (the spirit of—I must have this thing at once) can have no part or lot in the house of God. So many spend their time in educating themselves for their own convenience—"I want to educate myself, and realise myself." I must not use the temple of God for the convenience of self-love; my body must be preserved from trafficking for myself. One of the hardest scourges of God comes just here.

"*And He taught, saying unto them, Is it not written, My house shall be called of all nations the house of prayer? but ye have made it a den of thieves.*" Have I been doing this? What has my soul been busy with during this past year? What have I been thinking in my mind and imagination? I may have been talking about holiness, but what has it meant to me? Is my body the temple of the Holy Ghost and am I taking care to see that it is? Is my imagination, and reasoning, and thinking regarded as the house of God? or am I making it a house of merchandise—making it more for me and mine? wanting to go through this in order to grasp something for myself? God does not use us as an exhibition of what He can do. Jesus Christ said, "I am . . . the Truth"; therefore the temple of my body must be consecrated to Him. The Temple was to be the house

of prayer for all the nations, and my personal life is to be the same. God will bring some extraordinary people to traffic through our temple. Think how we have trafficked through Him! Natural affinities do not count for anything in the spiritual life, but only the affinities produced by the Spirit of God (cf. 1 John 1:7).

Desolation

O Jerusalem, Jerusalem, thou that killest the prophets, and stonest them which are sent unto thee, how often would I have gathered thy children together, even as a hen gathereth her chickens under her wings, and ye would not! Behold, your house is left unto you desolate. (Matthew 23:37–38)

The historic Temple was twice cleansed by our Lord; then when He came again to Jerusalem He no longer spoke of it as "My Father's house," but, "Behold, your house is left unto you desolate." A terrible pronouncement, and a terrible possibility in our own lives. It is appallingly true that we may get to the place where Jesus can no longer say of us, "My Father's house"; where He can no longer give us the benefit of scourging and cleansing, but can only retire, a weeping Christ, over our wilfulness. "How often would I . . . , and ye would not!" You have spurned and despised every messenger I sent, and now I say unto you, "Ye shall not see Me henceforth, till ye shall say, Blessed is he that cometh in the name of the Lord."

Is yours a desolated life, deserted in soul? Then in plain honesty don't blame your father or mother or anyone in your family; don't blame the fact that you had no education, or that someone thwarted you when you were sixteen, or that you were heartbroken when you were twenty-four, or had a business disaster when you were thirty. These things may be facts, but they are not to the point. Nothing that transpires outside me can make the tiniest difference to me morally unless I choose to let it. The desolation described by Jesus was brought on by the people of God themselves and by them alone. Is God saying to you, "You have spurned and hated and murdered My messengers"? If so, it will be a painful thing for your desolated soul to say—"Blessed is He that cometh in the name of the Lord"—Blessed is the one who stabs and hurts and disillusions me as to where I am.

A sinner who has never been cleansed by the direct act of the Lord may hear the Gospel and receive the Holy Spirit, and He will do all the cleansing. Compare that condition with one who has backslidden, one who had been cleansed by God, but has allowed the traffic to get back, sensuality, self-seeking, self-interest; the "cattle" are all back, the "doves" and the "moneychangers' tables," with a deepened and increased element of thieving. It is no longer making more for me and mine, it is a downright thieving of God's time and opportunities, and God's sacredness in other lives. That is what a spiritual thief does. Such a soul has to come back to God in desolation. It is no use to tell the backslider to receive the Holy Spirit, he cannot; the Holy Spirit will not be received by him; he has to come back to God in desolation. In the parable of the two sons some of the elements in the parables of the lost sheep and the lost coin are missed out—the shepherd goes to seek the lost sheep, and the woman searches for the lost coin; but the father does not go to the far country, the son has to leave the pigs and what pigs eat and come back; and if you have backslidden you will have to do the same. "O Israel, return unto the LORD thy God; for thou hast fallen by thine iniquity. Take with you words, and return unto the LORD: say unto Him, Take away all iniquity, and receive us graciously [mg]" (RV). Take with you words and say, "By mine iniquity have I fallen"—by lust, by worldliness, by self-interest, you know exactly what it is. You have been trying to find comfort here and there and you will never get it; your soul is night, your heart is steel; you have spurned and trodden under and despised God's messengers, and you will only see God when you say, "Blessed is He that cometh in the name of the Lord." Then says God—"I will heal their backsliding, I will love them freely; for mine anger is turned away from him" (Hosea 14:4 RV).

Dedication

Know ye not that ye are the temple of God, and that the Spirit of God dwelleth in you? If any man defile the temple of God, him shall God destroy; for the temple of God is holy, which temple ye are. (1 Corinthians 3:16–17)

Am I prepared to recognise that my body is a temple of the Holy Ghost? You say, "I did not know there were so many things in my life unsuited to the temple of God." Then let God turn them out—"I don't know whether He will." You do. Cannot you tell when Jesus Christ lays His scourge on the back of the thing that should not be there? Never for one moment sympathise with anyone who says, "I don't know how to get to God." There is no one in the world more easy to get to than God. Only one thing prevents us from getting there, and that is the refusal to tell ourselves the truth. Am I prepared to receive the Holy Spirit? prepared to recognise that my body and soul and spirit are meant to be "presenced with Divinity"? Jesus Christ did not live and die to be our Example only, but that He might put us in the place where He is by means of His wonderful Atonement. Reverence your own body and soul and spirit for this one purpose, and reverence everyone else's, for the same purpose.

Dedication means setting apart to some sacred purpose. The historic Temple was to be "the house of prayer for all the nations" (RV), and my body and soul and spirit is to be God's house of prayer, preserved for devotion. I have to realise that my body is the temple of the Holy Ghost, the place where the work of intercession is carried on. Prayer based on the Redemption creates what could not be until the prayer is offered. The Spirit needs the nature of a believer as a shrine in which to offer His intercessions. My personality, as far as I am conscious of it, and a great deal more than I am conscious of, is the shrine of the Holy Ghost. Have I recognised that it is? If I have, I shall be amazingly careful to keep it undefiled for Him. I am responsible before God for conducting my body as the temple of the Holy Ghost. Am I doing it, or is my body dictating to God, telling Him what it must do? If I only want God to keep my body healthy, He never will; I have to govern and rule my body as a temple of the Holy Ghost. "Let not sin therefore reign in your mortal body, that ye should obey it in the lusts thereof." When I become a Christian I have exactly the same body as before, but I have to see that my members which were used as "servants of sin" are now used as "servants of righteousness." The Apostle Paul tells us how it is done; he says, "I keep under my body," I "buffet" it (RV), and make it obey, until bodily senses and spiritual intuitions work together smoothly and naturally. Our bodies are not our shame, but our glory, and if we keep them as a temple of the Holy Ghost we shall find that the life of Jesus will be manifested in our mortal flesh .

We have to recognise that our personal life is meant for Jesus Christ; that we have been designed not for ourselves but for our Lord and Master. "If any man will come after Me, let him deny himself, and take up his cross, and follow Me." How significant is our Lord's insistence on His own Person in relation to human destiny. The modern jargon is all for self-realisation; we educate ourselves for the purpose of self-realisation, we select our friendships for self-realisation purposes. Jesus says, "Whosoever shall lose his life for My sake"—deliberately fling it away—"shall find it" (RV). The one great dominant recognition is that my personal self belongs to Jesus Christ. The counterfeit is giving ourselves as devotees to a cause. Thousands of people are losing their life for the sake of a cause; this is perilously wrong because it is so nearly right. Anything that rouses us to act on the line of principles instead of a relationship to a person fosters our natural independence and becomes a barrier to yielding to Jesus Christ. Have we recognised that our body is a temple of the Holy Ghost, or are we jabbering busybodies, so taken up with Christian work that we have no time for the Christ whose work it is, no time for Him in the morning, no time for Him at night, because we are so keen on doing the things that are called by His Name? What we have to watch to-day is the competition of Causes against devotion to Jesus Christ. One life yielded to God at all costs is worth thousands only touched by God. "Let him . . . take up his cross, and follow Me." What is the cross? The cross is the deliberate recognition of what my personal life is for, viz., to be given to Jesus Christ; I have to take up that cross daily and prove that I am no longer my own. Individual independence has gone, and all that is left is personal passionate devotion to Jesus Christ through identification with His Cross. "And ye are not your own; for ye are [KJV] bought with a price: glorify God therefore in your body" (1 Corinthians 6:19–20 RV).

ARRIVING AT MYSELF

By the Surgery of Providence
But when he came to himself . . . (Luke 15:17 RV)

It is difficult to realise that it is God who arranges circumstances for the whole mass of human beings; we come to find, however, that in the Providence of God there is, as it were, a surgical knife for each one of us individually, because God wants to get at the things that are wrong and bring us into a right relationship to Himself. At first we trust our ignorance and call it innocence; we trust our innocence and call it purity, until God in His mercy surrounds us with providences which act as an alchemy transmuting things and showing us our real relation to ourselves. To say, "Oh, I'm sick of myself," is a sure sign that we are not. When we really are sick of ourselves we will never say so, but will gladly come to the end of ourselves. So long as we say, "I'm tired of myself," it is a sign that we are profoundly interested in ourselves.

(a) The Sin of Self-Importance
Father, give me the portion of thy substance that falleth to me. And he divided unto them his living. (Luke 15:12 RV)

This is a picture of one who has become spiritually independent; the portion of goods from the Father has been received, there has been a real experience of God's grace, but there is the letter "I" about it, a self-assertive determination to carry things out in my own way. The most powerful type of spiritual delusion is produced in this way; it is based on ignorance of what we should do with the substance the Father has given us: we should devote it absolutely to Him. If we forget this we are certainly in danger of the sin of self-importance. It begins with the realisation that God does do His recreating work through us if we are children of His—"Yes, God did use me," you say. God will use anything or anyone (cf. Matthew 7:21–23). Unless there is abandonment to the Lord Jesus self-importance will always be inclined to utilise God's blessing for its own ends. No man can abandon to Jesus Christ without an amazing humiliation to his own self-importance. We are all tremendously important until the Holy Ghost takes us in hand, then we cease to be important and God becomes all-important.

(b) The Sordidness of Self-Indulgence
And not many days after, the younger son gathered all together, and took his journey into a far country; and there he wasted his substance with riotous living. . . . (Luke 15:13 RV)

The soul that has claimed its portion and become spiritually independent may ultimately be degraded into feeding pigs and eating with them. More awful things are said about backsliding than about any other sin. If we do not maintain a walk in accordance with the perception given, we shall fall as degradingly low as we were high before. The depth of degradation is measured by the height of attainment. Don't deal with it on the surface and say, "I'm not built that way, I have none of those sordid tastes." The nature of any dominating lust is that it keeps us from arriving at a knowledge of ourselves. For instance, a covetous man will believe he is very generous. Thank God for the surgery of providence by means of which He deals with these absurdities. The way God brings us to know ourselves is by the kind of people He brings round us. What we see to condemn in others is either the discernment of the Holy Ghost or the reflection of what we are capable of ourselves. We always notice how obtuse other people are before we notice how obtuse we ourselves are. If we see meanness in others, it is because we ourselves are mean[18] (Romans 2:1). If we are inclined to be contemptuous over the fraud in others it is because we are frauds ourselves. We have to see ourselves as God sees us, and when we do it keeps us in the right place—"My God, was I ever like that to Thee? so opinionated

---

18. mean: as used here, something or someone ordinary, common, low, or ignoble, rather than cruel or spiteful.

and conceited, so set on my own ends, so blind to myself?" These things, which are most unpalatable, are true, nevertheless. Beware of any belief which makes you self-indulgent; it comes from the pit however beautiful it sounds. It is an indication of a wrong relationship that does not spring from the attitude of abandon; and we become perverse and remain ignorant of the fact that we need to be guarded by God.

(c) The Sorrow of Self-Introspection
But when he came to himself he said, How many hired servants of my father's have bread enough and to spare, and I perish here with hunger! (Luke 15:17 RV)

There is no pain on earth to equal the pain of wounded self-love. Unrequited love is bad enough, but wounded self-love is the cruellest thing in human life because it shifts the whole foundation of the life. The prodigal son had his self-love wounded; he was full of shame and indignation because he had sunk to such a level. There was remorse, but no repentance yet, no thought of his father.

"I will arise and go to my father, and will say unto him, Father I have sinned against heaven, and in thy sight: I am no more worthy to be called thy son. . . . And he arose, and came to his father." That is repentance. The surgery of Providence had done its work, he was no longer deluded about himself. A repentant soul is never allowed to remain long without being gripped by the love of God.

> *Man, what is this, and why art thou despairing?*
> *God shall forgive thee all but thy despair.*

Let the surgery of providence drive you straight to God. The Spirit of God works from the standpoint of God, i.e., from a standpoint inconceivable to the natural man. The words "miraculous" and "supernatural" are disliked to-day through the influence of modern psychology on spiritual work, i.e., the attempt to define on psychical lines, materialistically psychical lines, how God works in a soul. The surgery of the providence of God will break up all ignorance of ourselves. It is impossible for a human being to guard his unconscious personality, only God can do it. If we have not abandoned to Jesus Christ we are likely to be trapped on every hand by our complete ignorance of ourselves, and panic will result. Panic leads us away from the control of God and leaves us not only beyond our own control but possibly under the control of other forces. The one safeguard is abandonment to the Lord Jesus, receiving His Spirit, and obeying Him.

By the Surprises of Personality
And the glory which Thou gavest Me I have given them; that they may be one, even as We are one. (John 17:22)

(a) My Right to My Individual Self
If any man would come after Me, let him deny himself, and take up his cross, and follow Me. (Matthew 16:24 RV)

The natural is not sinful, neither is it spiritual; the ruling disposition of my personality makes it either sinful or spiritual. The natural life and individuality are practically one and the same. Individuality is the characteristic of a child, it is the natural husk of personality and it is there by God's creation to preserve the personal life; but if individuality does not become transfigured by the grace of God, it becomes objectionable, egotistical and conceited, interested only in its own independence. When natural independence merges into independence of God it becomes sin; and sin isolates and destroys and ultimately damns the personal life. Jesus Christ lays His axe at the root of independence. There is nothing dearer to the heart of the natural man than independence. Wherever there is authority, I go against it in order to show I am independent; I insist on my right to myself, my right to an independent opinion. That spirit does not fit in with Jesus Christ at all. Independence and pride are esteemed by the natural man, but Jesus says, "that which is highly esteemed among men is abomination in the sight of God."

The statements of Jesus about discipleship produce embarrassment in the natural man: "From that time many of His disciples went back, and walked no more with Him" (John 6:66). If we are to be disciples of Jesus Christ, our independent right to our individual self must go, and go altogether. We evade the claims of Jesus by saying they have a mystical meaning and we try to get away from their intensely practical rugged meaning. "If any man would come after Me," said Jesus, "let him deny himself" (RV), i.e., deny his right to his individual self. Our Lord always mentions the most intimate relationships in connection with discipleship, relationships which make our human life what it is by the creation of God, and He implies that any one of these relationships may enter into competition in some form or other with His call, and if they do, He says it must be prompt obedience to Himself. It is not only sin that awakens resentment in the natural heart of man to the claims of Jesus Christ, but individuality which has been abused by the disposition of sin. The Holy Spirit continually urges us to sign away our right to our individual self to Jesus. "Learn of Me," says Jesus, "for I am meek and lowly in heart." How few of us do learn of Him! We cling to our individuality like a drowning man to a straw—"Of course God will recognise my individual peculiarisms and prejudices." Jesus Christ pays attention to one thing only—"If you would be My disciple, deny your right to yourself." Individual peculiarisms are excrescences belonging to the husk of the personality and are the things that produce all the difficulty. When the disposition of sin has been dealt with by identification with the Death of Jesus, the natural individual life still remains. Individuality must be transfigured by the indwelling of the Holy Spirit, and that means a sword going through the natural. Over and over again the Holy Spirit brings us to the place which in evangelical language is called "full surrender." Remember what full surrender is. It is not giving up this thing and that, but the deliberate giving up of my right to my individual self. As long as we are slaves to our ideas of individuality we distort the presentation of our Lord's teaching about discipleship.

(b) The Recognition of My Personal Self
He that findeth his life shall lose it; and he that loseth his life for My sake shall find it. (Matthew 10:39)

We have to recognise that our personal life is meant for Jesus Christ. The modern jargon is for self-realisation—"I must save my life": Jesus Christ says, "whosoever shall lose his life for My sake shall find it." The cross is the deliberate recognition of what our personal self is for, viz., to be given to Jesus, and we take up that cross daily and prove we are no longer our own. Whenever the call is given for abandon to Jesus Christ, people say it is offensive and out of taste. The counterfeit of abandon is that misleading phrase "Christian service." I will spend myself for God, I will do anything and everything but the one thing He asks me to do, viz., give up my right to myself to Him. "But surely Christian service is a right thing?" Immediately we begin to say that, we are off the track. It is the right *Person*, the Lord Jesus Christ, not the right thing: don't stop short of the Lord Himself—"*for My sake.*" The great dominating recognition is that my personal self belongs to Jesus. When I receive the Holy Spirit, I receive not a possible oneness with Jesus Christ, but a real intense oneness with Him. The point is, will I surrender my individual life entirely to Him? It will mean giving up not only bad things, but things which are right and good (cf. Matthew 5:29–30). If you have to calculate what you are willing to give up for Jesus Christ, never say that you love Him. Jesus Christ asks us to give up the best we have got to Him, our right to ourselves. There is only this one crisis, and in the majority of lives it has never been reached, we are brought up to it again and again, and every time we go back. Self-realisation must be renounced in order that Jesus Christ may realise Himself in us.

(c) The Realisation of Christian Self
I indeed baptize you with water unto repentance: but He that cometh after me is mightier than I, whose shoes I am not worthy to bear: He shall baptize you with the Holy Ghost, and with fire. (Matthew 3:11)

This is neither the individual self, nor the personal self, but the Christian self. ". . . that they may be one, even as We are one." How is this oneness to come about? By the baptism of the Holy Ghost and in no other way. When the Spirit of Jesus comes into me He comes into my personal spirit and makes me incandescent with God. The individual peculiarisms are seen no longer but only the manifestation of oneness with God. One person can merge with another person without losing his identity; but an individual remains definitely segregated from every other individual. When the disciples were baptised by the Holy Ghost they became witnesses to Jesus (see Acts 1:8; 4:13). When a man falls in love his personality emerges and he enters into relationship with another personality. Love is not anything for me at all; love is the deliberate giving of myself right out to another, the sovereign preference of my person for another person. The idea, I must have this person for myself, is not love, but lust. Lust counterfeits love in the same way that individuality counterfeits personality. The realisation of the Christian self means that Jesus Christ is manifested in my natural life—not Christian sentiment, but *Christian self.* Individuality is not lost, it is transfigured by identification with the Person of Jesus.

Is there any use in beating about the bush? We call ourselves Christians, what does our Christianity amount to practically? Has it made any difference to my natural individual life? It cannot unless I deliberately give up my right to myself to Jesus, and as His disciple begin to work out the personal salvation He has worked in . Independence must be blasted right out of a saint. God's providence seems to pay no attention whatever to our individual ideas because He is after only one thing—"that they may be one, even as We are one." It may look like a thorough breaking up of the life, but it will end in a manifestation of the Christian self in oneness with God. Sanctification is the work of Christ in me, the sign that I am no longer independent, but completely dependent upon Him. Sin in its essential working is independence of God: personal dependence upon God is the attitude of the Holy Ghost in my soul.

The Saints in the Disaster of Worldliness

Here is the patience of the saints, they that keep the commandments of God, and the faith of Jesus. Revelation 14:12 (RV)

The language of the Book of Revelation is easily misunderstood. For instance, when we use the word "beast" we mean something particularly offensive to our sensibilities; the "beast" in the Book of Revelation is anything but offensive; he is not an immoral beast, socially understood, but a beast from God's standpoint.

The Patience of the Enshrined Life of God
Here is the patience of the saints.

The revelation of God in the Bible works in a twofold way: first the Incarnate Fact, our Lord Jesus Christ; second, the interpretation of that Fact enshrined in the lives of those who are "called to be saints." A saint is one in whom the life of Jesus Christ is formed.

The description given in Revelation 14:9–11 is the description of prosperous worldliness such as has never been seen before, but from God's standpoint it is a moral disaster, and I should say we are very near the type of civilised life that this refers to. What is described in the climax is true in every stage until the climax is reached. After the War[20] this combine of everything, in which it will be impossible to have religion independent of an organisation, or business independent of a federation, will take place.

(a) In the Perversion of Religion
If any man worshippeth the beast and his image, and receiveth a mark on his forehead, or upon his hand . . . (RV)

This is the description of a man who has given the best he has got to the ruling power that gives him what he wants. If he is consecrated entirely there, he will meet with undoubted prosperity. He receives "a mark on his forehead, or upon his hand" (symbols of thought and grasp), a mark of the time in which he lives, cut off from everything other than the present order of things. The worship that should be given to

God is given to "the beast and his image." The saint has to endure, keeping "the word of My patience," maintaining the enshrined life of God in the midst of this perversion of religion. We can always recognise the mark of the beast if we put this one simple test—was it necessary for Jesus Christ to have lived and died to produce that attitude to life?

(b) In the Punishment of Revelation
. . . he also shall drink of the wine of the wrath of God, which is mingled unmixed in the cup of His anger. (Revelation 14:10 RV)

—intoxicated by the elemental wrath of God. The love of God and the wrath of God are obverse sides of the same thing. If we are morally rightly related to God we see His love side, but if we reverse the order and get out of touch with God, we come to a place where we find everything is based on wrath—not that God is angry, like a Moloch,[21] but wrath is inevitable; we cannot get out of it. If we give the best we have got to worldliness we shall one day wake up to the revelation of what we have done and shall experience the wrath of God, mingled with ungovernable despair—"I gave the best I had got, not to God, but to the world, and I can't alter now." This is not only true with individuals, but with the whole of civilised life. Take the good, thoroughgoing, prosperous, worldly business men of any country who have worshipped at the shrine of a pagan worldliness, you will find exactly what Jesus says, their hearts fail them—"men fainting for fear, and for expectation of the things which are coming on the world" (RV). Men who have worshipped mammon have the mark of the beast in thought and grasp, and when the realisation of where they are comes, they "faint for fear." Civilisations will get there; and the panic in any country will be beyond all limits. God is the controller of History.

(c) In the Pain of Recession
and the smoke of their torment ascendeth up for ever and ever. (Revelation 14:11)

---

19. Zeitoun (zay TOON), Egypt: six miles northeast of Cairo; site of a YMCA camp, the Egypt General Mission compound, and, from 1916 to 1919, the Imperial School of Instruction, training base for British, Australian, and New Zealand troops during World War I.

20. the War: World War I (1914–1918).

21. moloch: tyrannical power requiring sacrifice to be appeased.

That is the pictorial way of presenting the atmosphere of the wrath in which civilisations will be found when once God is manifested. When mediaeval artists wanted to portray a crime they usually accompanied the scene with bad weather. According to God's Book, this is not merely pictorial, but a representation of what will actually take place. "The smoke of their torment" refers not only to the physical condition of individuals, but to the terrific disturbance in Nature which is connected with it. Satan is "the prince of the power of the air."

Take the popular idea of Christianity and compare it with the patience of the saints, and you will see where we are. Popular Christianity says, "We must succeed." The Book of Revelation says success cannot be marked, it is impossible. The New Testament conception of spirituality in the world is a forlorn hope always, by God's design. Take the parable of the Sower, which is the key to all the parables, only one-fourth of the seed sown brings forth fruit in this dispensation. We are determined to be successful; the Apostle Paul says we are called upon to be faithful (1 Corinthians 4:1–2). In this dispensation it is a day of humiliation in the lives of the saints, as it was in the life of our Lord. We have to remain steadfastly patient to God through the whole thing.

The Practice of the Expressed Love of God
. . . they that keep the commandments of God.

What are the commandments? "The first of all the commandments is, . . . thou shalt love the Lord thy God with all thy heart, and with all thy soul, and with all thy mind, and with all thy strength: the second is . . . this, Thou shalt love thy neighbour as thyself" (Mark 12:30–31).

(a) Among the Unseemly
"Love . . . doth not behave itself unseemly . . ." *(1 Corinthians 13:4–5 RV).* In prosperous worldliness there is any amount that is unseemly, not from the social standpoint, but from the saint's standpoint. The way worldly sagacity argues is—Pay men back in their own coin, if you have been deceived, deceive in order to get your rights—"an eye for an eye and a tooth for a tooth." You cannot do that if you are a saint. We must practise the expressed love of God and behave among the unseemly as the children of God. There is no test on earth to equal it. There is unseemly laughter at the saint—"Where is your success? What have you done? what is the good of missionary enterprise? what is the use of talking about spiritual things to soldiers?" If the saints are not practising the expression of the love of God, they will be discouraged and give up. Discouragement is "disenchanted egotism"; "I have not got what I wanted, therefore I am not going on, I give it up. I have lost my conceit."

"Love . . . taketh not account of evil . . ." (RV); it does not ignore the fact that there is evil, but it does not take it into calculation. Someone has done us a wrong, and we say, "Now I must be careful. . . ." Our attitude is to be that of the expressed love of God, and if we take the evil into account we cannot express His love. We must deal with that one as God has dealt with us. There is no bigger, stiffer job for a saint than that.

(b) Among the Unspiritual
"Love . . . rejoiceth not in unrighteousness, but rejoiceth with the truth . . ." *(1 Corinthians 13:4, 6 RV).* Prosperous worldliness is unspiritual and those who do not pray and who are not at all holy get on well. There is so much nervous energy spent in spiritual exercises, in giving time to study, that the temptation is to let these things slip. We have to express the love of God and see that we do not become unspiritual among the unspiritual tendencies around us. If you listen to the talk of the day in which we live you find it is sagacious common sense that rules, the spiritual standpoint is taboo, like a fairy-story. The question is, will we maintain the spiritual standpoint, or say, "oh yes, it is rather too high"? We do not need Jesus Christ and the Bible for the ordinary common-sense standpoint, and if in a crisis we act according to common sense we do not express the love of God.

(c) Among the Unshameable
". . . beareth all things, . . . endureth all things" *(1 Corinthians 13:7).* After every phase of a particular type of successful civilised life, we get the anti-conventionalist who tries to develop the unshameable attitude and brags about things. It is called pluck; it is not, it is shamelessness, and it is easy to remain unspiritual before that.

At the basis of every one of these matters, the unseemly, the unspiritual, the unshameable, is something that is right, a strong basis of common sense; but the test for the saint is not common sense, but "Is this what Jesus Christ stood for?" "For I am not ashamed of the Gospel," says the Apostle Paul. If you dare to stand for Jesus Christ and His presentation of things in certain crises, men will separate you from their company, treat you with unutterable contempt. "Blessed are ye," said Jesus, "when men shall hate you, and when they shall separate you from their company, and reproach you, and cast out your name as evil, for the Son of man's sake" (Luke 6:22). We have to express the love of God in the midst of these things.

The Power of the Enshrouded Loyalty to God
. . . and the faith of Jesus.

The faith of Jesus is exhibited in temptation and can be summed up in His own words: "I came . . . not to do mine own will, but the will of Him that sent Me." Jesus remained steadfastly loyal to His Father, and the saint has to keep the faith of Jesus.

(a) Under the Success of Civilisation (Matthew 4:3–4)

In the Temptation the sagacity of Satan is seen from every standpoint—"If Thou art the Son of God, command that these stones become bread" (RV): "Look after men's bodies, feed them and heal them, and you will get men under Your control." Was Satan right? would Jesus Christ have gained the Kingship of men if He had put their needs first? Read John 6:15—"Jesus therefore perceiving that they were about to come and take Him by force, to make Him king, withdrew again into the mountain Himself alone" (RV). It is this temptation which has betaken the Christian Church to-day. We worship Man, and God is looked upon as a blessing machine for humanity. We find it in the most spiritual movements of all. For instance, watch how subtly the missionary call has changed. It is not now the watchword of the Moravian[22] call, which saw behind every suffering heathen the Face of Christ: the need has come to be the call. It is not that Jesus Christ said "Go," but that the heathen will not be saved if we do not go. It is a subtle change that is sagacious, but not spiritual. The need is never the call: the need is the opportunity. Jesus Christ's first obedience was to the will of His Father—"Lo, in the volume of the Book it is written of Me, I delight to do Thy will," and, "As the Father hath sent Me, even so send I you" (RV). The saint has to remain loyal to God in the midst of the machinery of successful civilisation, in the midst of worldly prosperity, and in the face of crushing defeat.

(b) Under the Success of Ceremonialism (Matthew 4:5–7)

"If Thou art the Son of God, cast Thyself down . . ." (RV). "Do some supernatural wonder, use apparatus whereby You will paralyse men's wits and stagger them, and the world will be at Your feet." In the midst of the success of worldliness we get an outburst of spiritualism, of supernaturalism, fire called down from heaven by the authority of the devil, and all kinds of signs and wonders whereby people say, "Lo, here is Christ." Jesus said, "The kingdom of God cometh not with observation." I believe in the Second Coming, but not always in its advocates. They are apt to ignore altogether what Jesus said.

(c) Under the Success of Compromise (Matthew 4:8–10)

"All these things will I give Thee, if Thou wilt fall down and worship me." "Be diplomatic, be wise, compromise in a wise shrewd way and You will get everything under Your own control." That is the kind of thing the peace of the world is based on, we call it "diplomacy." Jesus maintained His faith in God's methods in spite of the temptations which were so sagacious and wise from every standpoint, saving the standpoint of the Spirit of God. The insinuation of putting men's needs first, success first, has entered into the very domain of evangelism, and has substituted "the passion for souls" for "the passion for Christ," and we experience shame when we realise how completely we have muddled the whole thing by not maintaining steadfast loyalty to Jesus Christ.

You will find the things God uses, not to develop you, but to develop the manifestation of God in you, are just the things we are apt to ignore—successful worldliness, other people, trials of our faith—these are the things that either make a saint un-saintly, or give God the chance to exhibit Himself. The most delightful saint is the one who has been chastened through great sorrows. The type of character produced by great sorrows is different from that produced by the pressure of the "mosquito" order of things. The saints are unnoticed, there is no flourish of trumpets about them, nothing self-advertised, but slowly and surely this characteristic comes out—the stamp of a family likeness to Jesus Christ, and men take knowledge of them, that they have been with Jesus.

---

22. The Moravian Mission traces its beginnings to the 1730s, to a Christian community founded by Count Nicholas Zinzendorf.

"OUT OF THE WRECK I RISE"

Nay, in all these things we are more than conquerors through Him that loved us. Romans 8:37

God does not do what false Christianity makes out—keep a man immune from trouble, there is no promise of that; God says, *"I will be with him in trouble."* The moral frontier where Jesus Christ works is the great dominant note in the New Testament, the external manifestation comes later. At present it is the relationship on the inside that is being dealt with—the personal preference of the soul for God, which is the great fruit of Christianity. No matter what actual troubles in the most extreme form get hold of a man's life, not one of them can touch the central citadel, viz., his relationship to God in Christ Jesus.

This is one of the greatest assets of the spiritual aspect of Christianity, and it seems to be coming to the fore just now. Before the War it may have been imaginary to talk about these things in the universal sense but now they are up-to-date in thousands of lives. The "wrecks" are a fact. Mental, moral, physical and spiritual wrecks are all around us to-day. The Apostle Paul is not talking of imaginary sentimental things, but of desperately actual things, and he says we are "more than conquerors" in the midst of them all, super-conquerors, not by our wits or ingenuity, our courage or pluck, or anything other than the fact that not one of them can separate a man from the love of God in Christ Jesus, even though he should go into the "belly of hell." We are inclined to ask God to do the magic business, to perform a miracle which will alter our external circumstances; but if we are ever going to understand what the God whom Jesus Christ presents is like, we have to remember that that is not His first job. The first thing God does is to alter a man's disposition on the inside, and then enable him to deal with the "mess" on the outside. God never coerces a man, he has to take God's way by his own moral choice; we reverse the order and demand of God that He does our work. The tawdry things that have been presented as the findings of Christianity make one impatient.

The Cares of Tribulation
Who shall separate us from the love of Christ? shall tribulation . . . ?

The word "tribulation" has its root in the Latin *tribulum*—a sledge for rubbing out corn; literally, a thing with teeth that tears. Christianity is not prayer meet-

ings and times of fellowship, these are magnificent and essential in certain conditions for the manifestation of the Christian life, but when tribulation is tearing you to bits, they cannot be. Tribulation describes a section of a man's life. Rightly or wrongly, we are exactly in the condition we are in. I am sorry for the Christian who has not some part of his circumstances he wishes was not there! People with psychological "elbows" bring tribulation. Let the tribulations be what they may—exhausting, galling, fatiguing—they are never noble things, "Beelzebub" miseries that buzz over the windows of a man's soul so that he cannot see out—we can be "more than conquerors" in them if we maintain our belief in the relationship God has to us in Christ Jesus.

"To him that overcometh . . ." God does not give us the overcoming life: He gives life to the man who overcomes. If in every case of tribulation, from gnats to the cruelty of the sword, we take the step as if there were no God to assist us, we shall find He is there. The idea is not that we get the victory, but that the Victor has got us. "But thanks be unto God, who always leadeth us in triumph in Christ, and maketh manifest through us the savour of His knowledge in every place" (2 Corinthians 2:14 RV).

The Waters of Anguish
or anguish . . . ? (RV)

"Anguish" comes from a word meaning to press tightly, to strangle, and the idea is not a bit too strong for the things people are going through. They are not sentimental things, but real things, where every bit of a man's life is twisted and wrung out to the last ebb. Can the love of God in Christ hold there, when everything says that God is cruel to allow it, and that there is no such thing as justice and goodness? Shall anguish separate us from the love of God? No, we are more than conquerors in it, not by our own effort but by the fact that the love of God in Christ holds. If we look for God in the physical domain we shall see Him nowhere; if we look for Him in the kingdom on the inside, in the moral relationships, we shall find Him all the time. We lose faith in God when we are hurt in the physical domain and God does not do what we want; we forget that He is teaching us to rely on His love. Watch some people and you will wonder how a human being can support such anguish; yet instead of being full of misery, they are the opposite; they seem to be held by a power that baffles all human intelligence, to have a spiritual energy we know nothing of—what accounts for it? "When thou passest through the waters, I will be with thee; . . . when thou walkest through the fire, thou shalt not be burned." The waters are real, and the fire is real, but Paul claims that the relationship to God holds.

"And ye shall hear of wars and rumours of wars: see that ye be not troubled." When men's hearts are fainting for fear, does Jesus Christ expect us to be undisturbed? how is it to be done? have we to become callous and indifferent, or so worn out that we have not enough vitality to feel things? Jesus Christ means that the relationship He can bring us into with Himself can hold us undisturbed in the midst of every disturbance there is. If there is anything supernatural, that is! Human pluck cannot stand these things, there is a limit. No human being can stand calamity and anguish without going under or getting into a panic. Panic is a sudden terror, our whole being gets into a flutter and we don't know where to turn, we can take a forlorn stand, but it barely stills the panic inside. If we are going to be more than conquerors in calamity, it can only be in the marvellous way by which God "ships in" the supernatural and makes it natural.

The Mutinies of Persecution
or persecution . . . ?

Immediately we get hold of a particular thing in the spiritual domain we are going to be systematically vexed by those who don't intend us to have it; they are set on gibing it out of us, because if we are right, they are wrong. Mutiny, a rise against authority, comes from persecution. There is any amount of weakness in us all, but deep down there is red-handed rebellion against the authority of Jesus Christ—"I'll be damned before I yield." Don't take a poetical view of things that go beyond science. At bottom, sin is red-handed mutiny that requires to be dealt with by the surgery of God—and He dealt with it on Calvary.

The Spectre of Famine
or famine . . . ?

Can a man remain true to the love of God when he is famine-stricken? God does not prevent physical suffering because it is of less moment than what He is after. "And fear not them which kill the body, but are not able to kill the soul" (Matthew 10:28). Famine is a most appalling spectre, it means extreme scarcity. Can I not only believe in the love of God, but be more than conqueror while I am being starved? Either the Apostle Paul is deluded, and Jesus Christ is a deceiver, or some extraordinary thing happens to a man who

can hold on to the love of God when the odds are all against His character.

The Scare of Poverty
or nakedness . . . ?

The scare of poverty is the most effectual onslaught. If we know that obedience to God means absolute poverty, how many of us would go through with it? The scare of poverty will knock the spiritual backbone out of us unless we have the relationship to God that holds. It is easy to fling away what you have, child's play to sell all you have got and have nothing left, the easiest piece of impulse, nothing heroic in it; the thing that is difficult is to remain detached from what you have so that when it goes you do not notice it. That is only possible by the power of the love of God in Christ Jesus.

The Cruelty of the Sword
. . . or peril, or sword?

In every one of "these things" logic is shut up. A logic-monger can silence the man who is suffering with his facts, but suppose the man who is suffering has got hold of Reality and the logic-monger finds he is only "slinging" actualities? Did you ever try to justify God in what He allows? God is not justified unless He can work things out on the line Paul brings out, and we only get there by a moral revolution. The one who deals with the logical rational side has the best of the argument just now though not the best of the facts, and one of the biggest humiliations is that you cannot say a word, you must let the chattermagging[23] go on. You can shut the mouth of the man who has faith in God, but you cannot get away from the fact that he is being kept by God. That is a domain which logic must shut out resolutely until it is realised that logic is an instrument only. A man can go through tribulations which make you hold your breath as you watch him; he goes through things that would knock the wits out of us and make us give way to blasphemy and whimperings. He is not blind or insensitive, yet he goes through in marvellous triumph—what accounts for it? One thing only, the fact that behind it all is the love of God which is in Christ Jesus our Lord. Spiritually, morally, and physically the saint is brought clean through, triumphant, out of the wreck wrought by tribulation, anguish, persecution, famine, nakedness, peril and sword. Whatever may be the experiences of life, whether terrible and devastating or monotonous, it makes no difference, they are all rendered impotent, because they cannot separate us from the love of God, which is in Christ Jesus Our Lord. *"Out of the wreck I rise"* every time.

---

23. chattermagging: jabbering; spouting off; rambling on.

THE CONDITIONS OF SPIRITUAL LIFE
Matthew 10:24–42

Religion is a matter of taste, a matter in which a man's religious life and his actual life do not necessarily agree. In spiritual life that could never be; spiritual life means the real life, and it is significant that whenever Jesus talks about discipleship He speaks of it in actual terms.

"It is enough for the disciple that he be as his Master." At first sight this looks like an enormous honour: to be "as his Master" is marvellous glory—is it? Look at Jesus as He was when He was here, it was anything but glory. He was easily ignorable, saving to those who knew Him intimately; to the majority of men He was "as a root out of a dry ground." For thirty years He was obscure, then for three years He went through popularity, scandal, and hatred; He succeeded in gathering a handful of fishermen as disciples, one of whom betrayed Him, one denied Him, and all forsook Him; and He says, "It is enough for you to be like that." The idea of evangelical success, Church prosperity, civilised manifestation, does not come into it at all. When we fulfil the conditions of spiritual life we become unobtrusively real.

The Dear Sorrows of Spiritual Difference
(Matthew 10:24–26)
A disciple is not above his Master. (RV)

When we become spiritual there is a change in us that our former companions feel but cannot locate; they intuitively sense that something is different, there is something that does not agree with their natural outlook. It is a most embarrassing difference in the closest relationships of life (see Matthew 10:22–23). Our affinity with Jesus Christ does make a difference, it produces sorrow and misunderstandings, things that cannot be explained. But Jesus says, when misunderstandings arise, "Don't be afraid, one day it will be understood how it came about." Meantime we have to lay our account with the sorrows of spiritual difference, but our devotion to Jesus is so intense that no matter what those sorrows are, we are prepared to go through with it.

The Defiant Sagacity of Spiritual Discretion
(Matthew 10:27–28)
What I tell you in the darkness, speak ye in the light. (RV)

There are dark nights in the soul; darkness is the time to listen. If we are to be true to the conditions of spiritual life we must speak not what is expedient, we must speak the truth regarding spiritual realities. The Christianity which is not spiritual says we must by no means offend, or do anything that hurts a Christian brother's feelings. Did Jesus ever offend anyone knowingly? He certainly did (see Matthew 12:1–8); but He never put a stumbling block in anyone's way. The sagacity of spiritual discretion does not mean we have to be obstinate and pig-headed, with a ban of finality[24] about our views, or that we preach what is expedient—"Oh yes, I agree with you, but it is not expedient to say that kind of thing in public." If God has given us the revelation it is not our business to hide our light under a bushel (Matthew 5:15–16). In your sagacity be wise. Don't preach out of natural discretion, but out of spiritual discretion which comes from intimacy with God. The prophet is more powerful than the priest or king, and in our Lord the prophet-element is the great one. Jesus never spoke with the sagacity of a human being, but with the discretion of God. Beware of saying what is expedient from your own common-sense standpoint, especially when it comes to the big truths of God.

The Detailed Security of Spiritual Dependence *(Matthew 10:28–31)*
And be not afraid of them which kill the body, but are not able to kill the soul. (RV)

"Be not afraid of them which kill the body"—leave that alone, but beware of being disobedient to your own spiritual stand before God, because that will kill both body and soul, i.e., make you reprobate. Watch if in the tiniest degree you begin to be afraid. "Now what is going to happen to me physically, in matters of money, in my social circumstances, if I do obey Jesus?" Jesus distinctly says, "Pay no attention to that, beware only of being destroyed both physically and spiritually by disobedience." Whenever we get out of touch with spiritual reality our body instantly suffers. The source of physical strength in spiritual life is different from what it is in natural life. In natural life we draw our strength direct from without; in spiritual life we draw our physical strength, consciously or uncon-

---

24. ban of finality: limitation or curse of having one's mind made up; unwilling to consider new information.

sciously, from communion with God. When that is broken, physical health begins to be destroyed. Jesus says, Your Father, who looks after the sparrows, will care for you, fear not therefore. It is not to be a life of self-interest at all. When God calls us He never gives security; He gives us a knowledge of Himself. We reveal how much we believe in the things Jesus said when we reason like this—"Is this God's will for me? No, it can't be because there is no security." "It is enough for the disciple that he be as his Master." Jesus never had any home of His own, never a pillow on which to lay His head . His poverty was a deliberate choice. We may have to face destitution in order to maintain our spiritual connection with Jesus, and we can only do that if we love Him supremely. Every now and again there is the "last bridge"—"I have gone far enough, I can't go any further." If you are going on with God it is impossible to secure your interests at all. We have to go on in perfect confidence that our Father in heaven knows all about us. Are we prepared to fulfil these conditions when they arise?

The Dreaded Stand of Spiritual Destiny
(Matthew 10:32–33)
Every one therefore who shall confess Me before men . . . (RV)

When I am born from above (RV mg) not only is the Holy Spirit in me, but the Son of God is formed in me (Galatians 4:19), and to "confess" Him means that I allow His disposition to have its way through my bodily life. *". . . him will I also confess before My Father who is in heaven."* Will He? or will He have to say, "There is not one detail of your life that has manifested Me. I have had no chance of looking through your eyes, of working through your hands, or loving through your heart"? The true evangelist is the one whose life in every detail overflows with the mani-

fested life of Jesus (cf. Matthew 7:22–23). The world has a right to say, "Produce your goods." In actual circumstances we can prevent Jesus Christ being hurt if we take the blow, but if we stand on our rights the blow goes back on Him. It is not aggressive doing on our part that wins, but the manifestation that it is the Lamb who breaks the seals . If we stand for Jesus Christ we have to take care to nourish His life in us, to bear His Name; then He says He will confess us before His Father who is in heaven.

The Suffering of Spiritual Discipleship
(Matthew 10:34–39)
I came not to send peace, but a sword. (v. 34)

It never cost a disciple anything to follow Jesus; to talk about cost when you are in love with anyone is an insult. The point of suffering is that it costs other people—fathers, mothers, households; consequently we decline to go on, consideration for others causes us to hold back. If we go on with it, then others will suffer. Have we in effect told Jesus we are not prepared for this? "Obedience to Your call would mean I should get into difficulties with my home, my father, my mother, and I cannot possibly be the means of bringing suffering on them." Jesus says, "If you are going to be My disciples, you must be prepared to." God knows what it costs them, and what it costs you to allow it.

The Solidarity of Spiritual Discipline
(Matthew 10:40–42)
He that receiveth you receiveth Me. . . .

Solidarity means a consolidation or a oneness of interests. Here, the solidarity is between ourselves and God; we deliberately identify ourselves with God's interests in other people. "Inasmuch as ye did it unto one of the least [KJV] of these My brethren, *ye did it unto Me*" (RV).

The Sacrament of Saints

I

I am the living bread which came down out of heaven: if any man eat of this bread, he shall live for ever: yea and the bread which I will give is My flesh, for the life of the world. John 6:51

Why should I start at the plough of my Lord, that maketh deep furrows on my soul? I know He is no idle husband-man, He purposeth a crop.

Samuel Rutherford[25]

Good corn is not bread; if we are compelled to eat corn we will suffer for it. Corn must be ground and mixed and kneaded and baked, and baked sufficiently, before it is fit to be eaten. When the husk is away and the kernel garnered, we are apt to think that all is done; but the process has only just begun. A granary of corn is not bread; people cannot eat handfuls of corn and be nourished, something must be done to the corn first. Apply that illustration to the life of a sanctified saint. The afflictions after sanctification are not meant to purify us, but to make us broken bread in the hands of our Lord to nourish others. Many Christian workers are like Ephraim, "a cake not turned"; they are faddists and cranks, and when they are given out for distribution they produce indigestion instead of giving nourishment.

The Way of the Plough (Matthew 13:18–23)
Hear ye then the parable of the sower. . . . (Matthew 13:18 RV)

It is the plough that prepares the ground for sowing the seed. The hard way through the field is the same soil as the good ground, but it is of no use for growing corn because it has never been ploughed. Apply that to your own soul and to the souls of men. There are lives that are absolutely stupid towards God, they are simply a way for the traffic of their own concerns. We are responsible for the kind of ground we are. No man on earth has any right to be a highroad; every man has the chance of allowing the plough to run through his life. Sorrow or bereavement or conviction of sin, anything that upsets the even, hard way of the life and produces concern, will act as the plough. A man's concern about his eternal welfare witnesses that the plough has begun to go through his self-complacency. The words of our Lord, "Think not that I came

to cast [mg] peace on the earth: I came not to cast [mg] peace, but a sword" (RV), are a description of what happens when the Gospel is preached—upset, conviction, concern and confusion.

The Wildness of the Place (Genesis 3:17–19)
And unto Adam He said, . . . cursed is the ground for thy sake; in sorrow shalt thou eat of it all the days of thy life. . . . (Genesis 3:17)

That is a description of the place where the plough has to go. It was once a holy place, but now it is desecrated and wild. "The heart is deceitful above all things, and it is exceedingly corrupt: who can know it?" (Jeremiah 17:9 RV). The way through the field which has been battered hard by men's feet is an illustration of the human heart. The human heart should be the abode of God's Holy Spirit, but it has been trampled hard by passions until God has no part in it, and the plough has to come into the desecrated place. As workers we must remember this fundamental line. The tendency to-day is to ignore it, to say that men do not need ploughing, they need praising; that the human heart is not bad; that the world is not a wild place. The plough has to come into every place which has been desecrated by the prince of this world, for one purpose—for the seed to be sown.

The Work of Patience
Be not deceived; God is not mocked: for whatsoever a man soweth, that shall he also reap. (Galatians 6:7)

Don't sow the human heart with mingled seed: "thou shalt not sow thy field with two kinds of [RV] seed" (Leviticus 19:19). God's seed will always bring forth fruit if it is put in the right conditions. Man cannot order the seasons or make the seed to grow (cf. Jeremiah 33:20); and as preachers and teachers we are powerless to make saints. Our duty is to put the seed into the right place and leave the rest to God. It would be foolish for a farmer to sow his seed and tell his servants to watch it; he must sow his seed in the right place and then trust in God and Nature, and by and by he will reap his harvest. So all we can do is to sow the seed of the Word of God in the hearts of the hearers. The words our Lord uttered in reference to Himself are true of every seed that is sown—"Except

25. Samuel Rutherford (1600–1661): Scottish minister, Covenanter.

a corn of wheat fall into the ground and die, it abideth alone; but if it die, it bringeth forth much fruit." All Christian work, if it is spiritual, must follow that law, because it is the only way God's fruit can be brought forth.

Be endlessly patient. There is nothing more impertinent than our cross infidelity in God. If He does not make us ploughers and sowers and reapers all at once, we lose faith in Him. Modern evangelism makes the mistake of thinking that a worker must plough his field, sow the seed, and reap the harvest in half-an-hour. Our Lord was never in a hurry with the disciples, He kept on sowing the seed and paid no attention to whether they understood Him or not. He spoke the truth of God, and by His own life produced the right atmosphere for it to grow, and then left it alone, because He knew well that the seed had in it all the germinating power of God and would bring forth fruit after its kind once it was put in the right soil. We are never the same after listening to the truth; we may forget it, but we will meet it again. Sow the Word of God, and everyone who listens will get to God. If you sow vows, resolutions, aspirations, emotions, you will reap nothing but exhaustion ". . . and ye shall sow your seed in vain, for your enemies shall eat it" (Leviticus 26:16); but sow the Word of God, and as sure as God is God, it will bring forth fruit. Human sympathy and human emotions and human hypnotism in preaching are the signs of a spiritual hireling and a thief . Sow emotions, and the human heart will not get beyond you. There are men and women at work for God who steal hearts from God, not intentionally, but because they do not preach the Word of God. They say, "I don't want anyone to think about me"; that should never need to be said. If the thought of ourselves is lurking anywhere as we preach, we are traitors to Jesus Christ. Our duty is to get people through to God. A man may not grasp all that is said, but something in him is intuitively held by it. If you talk truth that is vital to yourself you will never talk over anyone's head. See that you sow the real seed of the Word of God, and then leave it alone.

II

. . . an offering made by fire, of a sweet savour unto the LORD. *Leviticus 2:2*

This Scripture (Leviticus 2), as in fact all Scripture, testifies that service is self-surrender, self-sacrifice. Christ, to satisfy others, was broken; the bread-corn must still be bruised; and the nearer our ministry approaches the measure of His ministry—immeasurably far as we shall ever be behind Him—the more shall we resemble Him, the bruised, the oppressed, the broken One.

Reaping

Corn that has come to fruition must be watched. The enemy of souls, works most havoc in the standing corn. Our Lord told the disciples to pray "the Lord of the harvest, that He send forth labourers into His harvest" (RV), to cut down the corn, i.e., to disciple men and women. God puts in His sickle by the hand of a disciple and cuts us down where we never thought we would have to be cut down. Every sanctified soul is handed over by God to a disciple to be reaped for Him. What do we say to the people who have come into the experience of sanctification— "Thank God, you are all right now"? That is not discipling them. People come in to reap who have no right to reap. We have to let sanctified souls know that they are there to be cut down, to be reaped, to be made into bread to feed the world. We are apt to shout "Hallelujah" when souls enter into sanctification, but it is then that a time of intense care and anxiety begins until these lives are reaped for God. The need is to watch the standing corn, to watch those who are right with God until they are matured and established. Notice the earnest solicitation Paul had for his converts: "My little children, of whom I am again in travail until Christ be formed in you" (RV). The time after sanctification in every soul under our care is an additional concern to us if we are true servants of God. Times of revival have led the Church to rejoicing instead of watching by earnest prayer until these souls are reaped. Never sympathise with a cut-down soul, but rejoice, and teach them to rejoice.

"For what is our hope, or joy, or crown of rejoicing? . . . For ye are our glory and our joy." This is the dividing of the spoil. How many of us are going to hear Jesus Christ say when we stand before Him, "That soul was reaped by you"? Jean MacLean wrote underneath the only photograph she ever had taken, "Spoilt for this world saving as I can win souls to Jesus." She was an obscure, noble missionary and was used by God in untold numbers of lives, she literally reaped them for God.

Threshing

The first description John the Baptist gives of Jesus is that of a Divine Husbandman at work in His threshing-floor (see Matthew 3:12). When corn is stored in the granary we are apt to think that that is the end, but it is only the beginning. Sanctification is a reaping, an end, but also a beginning. Standing corn has to be cut down and go through the processes of reaping, threshing, grinding, mixing and baking before it is good for food; and sanctified souls must be told that their only use is to be reaped for God and made into bread for others. It is time we got away from all our shallow thinking about sanctification. The majority who are introduced into an experience of sanctification remain at the gateway—"saved and sanctified"; but they do not know how to go on, consequently they begin to stagnate. We need to learn that God has a lot to do with a saint after sanctification; our perplexities come because this is not realised. We have to see that as right dividers of the word of truth, we bring this before people.

Beware of being guided by mental or spiritual affinities, let God mix you as He sees fit. Peter thought he knew better than God, but God had to mix Peter with the Gentiles before he became good bread (see Acts 10:9–16).

Grinding

Jesus said that in the lives of the saints there will be tribulation, not difficulties, but tribulation. The great cry of modern enterprise is success; Jesus says we cannot be successful in this age. This is the age of the humiliation of the saints, that means we have to stand true to Jesus Christ while the odds are crushingly against Him all the time.

"Tribulation worketh patience." In the experience of tribulation we are brought to understand what millstones are. Millstones are used to grind the corn to powder, and typify the sacredness of the discipline of life—"No man shall take the mill or the upper millstone to pledge: for he taketh a man's life to pledge" (Deuteronomy 24:6). You have been having a snug time in the granary, then God brings you out and puts you under the millstones, and the first thing that happens is the grinding separation our Lord spoke of—"Blessed are ye when men shall . . . cast out your name as evil for the Son of man's sake." The

other crowd want to have nothing more to do with you, you are crushed for ever out of any resemblance to them. Very few of us know anything about suffering *"For My sake."* When God is putting His saints through the experience of the millstones, we are apt to want to interfere. Hands off! No saint dare interfere in the discipline of the suffering of another saint. God brings these things into our lives for the production of the bread that is to feed the world.

In the East the women sing as they grind the corn between the millstones; and "the sound of the millstones," is music in the ears of God. The worldling does not think it music, but the saint who is being made into bread knows that his Father knows best, and that He would never allow the suffering if He had not some purpose. Ill-tempered people, hard circumstances, poverty, wilful misunderstandings and estrangements, are all millstones. Had Jesus any of these things in His own life? He had a devil in His company for three years; He lived at home with brothers and sisters who did not believe in Him; He was continually thwarted and misunderstood by the Pharisees, and He says, "the disciple is not above his Master." If we have the tiniest element of self-pity in us God dare not put us anywhere near the millstones. When these experiences come, remember God has His eyes on every detail.

Baking

There is a spiritual significance in the methods of preparing the meal offering mentioned in the Book of Leviticus (Ch. 2)—the frying pan, seething in pots, or baking in an oven. Why some people suffer is open and clear to everyone; others are placed in a boiling tumult (watch a porridge pot and you will see what this means), and only God knows what is happening. Others again are placed in fierce, silent ovens, no one knows what is going on, but when they are taken out they are precious to God and man alike. God is producing good food for Himself and for His saints. We all have our special functions, never try to do what someone else is doing; let God make you what He wants you to be. He knows your circumstances and He will alter them when He chooses. Be careful of God's honour as a saint.

III

He that soweth the good seed is the Son of man; and the field is the world; and the good seed, these are the sons of the kingdom. Matthew 13:37–38 (RV)

Be content, ye are His wheat growing in our Lord's field. And if wheat, ye must go under our Lord's threshing instrument, in His barn-floor, and through His sieve, and through His mill to be bruised, as the Prince of your salvation, Jesus, was (Isaiah 53:10), that ye may be found good bread in your Lord's house.

Samuel Rutherford

God sows His saints in the most useless places, according to the judgement of the world. Where they will glorify Him is where God puts His saints, and we are no judge at all of where that is. When we become rightly related to God the likelihood of our being of use to men seems in the eyes of the world to be pathetically crippled. People say, "Don't be so absurd as to go and bury yourself there." We have to let God sacrifice us as He likes, and go where He sends us. Never be deluded into making this statement: "I am here because I am so useful"; say rather, "I am here because God wants me here." The one lodestar of the saint is God Himself, not estimated usefulness.

Blessed Bread
Sacrificed
And He took the five loaves, and the two fishes, and looking up to heaven, He blessed, and brake and gave the loaves to the disciples, and the disciples to the multitude. (Matthew 14:19 RV; cf. Romans 12:1)

God never uses in His service those who are sentimentally devoted to Him; He uses only those who are holy within in heart and holy without in practice. The Book of Leviticus is full of spiritual teaching, and the significance of all the detail is that a servant of God must keep himself unspotted from the world, sternly and guardedly holy, not for his own sake but for the sake of his calling. No man has any right to break the Word of God and feed the people of God unless he is without blemish spiritually through the Atonement. That standard is being blotted out nowadays. "And no man taketh the honour unto himself"— nearly all do, though. Preaching is worthy in God's sight when it costs something, when we are really living out what we preach. The truth of God is to be presented in such a way that it produces saints.

Broken Bread
Suffering
And as they were eating, Jesus took bread, and blessed, and brake it; and He gave to the disciples, and said, Take, eat; this is My body. (Matthew 26:26 RV; cf. 1 Peter 4:19)

Not only does God waste His saints according to the judgements of men, He seems to bruise them most mercilessly. You say, "But it could never be God's will to bruise me": if it pleased the Lord to bruise His own Son, why should He not bruise you? To choose suffering is a disease; but to choose God's will even though it means suffering is to suffer as Jesus did according *to the will of God*.

In the Bible it is never the idealising of the sufferer that is brought out, but the glorifying of God. God always serves Himself out of the saint's personal experience of suffering. If suffering is used to idealise the sufferer there is an aftermath of sickly sentimentality—"What I have gone through!" and God is not glorified. In actual life the true sufferers and the affected sufferers are mixed, and the Spirit of God gets His chance only through the one or two who are so completely effaced by means of identification with the Death of Christ that the thought of what they are going through never affects them. The thing that strikes one about such lives is never the sense of restraint but of inspiration, the feeling that there is unfathomably more behind.

If we are self-willed when God tries to break us and will do anything rather than submit, we shall never be of any use to nourish other souls; we shall only be centres of craving self-pity, discrediting the character of God. Jesus called self-pity Satanic (see Matthew 16:22–23). No one understands a saint but the saint who is nearest the Saviour, and if we accept sympathy from any others, we will end in being traitors to Jesus Christ, because the reflex thought is, "Well, God is dealing hardly with me." The people we have to knit to our souls are not those who sympathise with us, they hinder, because sympathy if it is from a wrong source always enervates, but those who bring us into a fuller realisation of the purpose of God.

Jesus Christ represents the Bread of God broken to feed the world, and the saints are to be broken bread in His hands to satisfy Jesus Christ and His saints. When by the sanctifying power of the grace of God we have been made into bread, our lives are to be offered first of all to Jesus Christ. *"Give Me to drink."* In the Old Testament the first fruits were always offered to God, and that is the symbol for our lives. The saint is meant to satisfy the heart of Jesus first, and then be used to feed His saints. "... and ye shall be My witnesses"—a perfect delight to Me wherever I place you. The saints who satisfy the heart of Jesus make other saints strong and mature for God. The one characteristic of the life is, "In all the world there is none but Thee, my God, there is none but Thee."

The consummation of self-sacrifice is that just as our Lord was made broken bread and poured-out wine for us, so He can make us broken bread and poured-out wine for others; but He cannot do it if there is anything in us that would make us give way to self-pity when He begins to break us. The one mainspring of the life is to be personal, passionate devotion to Jesus Christ.

Beatified Bread
Sovereignty
For I reckon that the sufferings of this present time are not worthy to be compared with the glory which shall be revealed to us-ward.... (Romans 8:18 RV; cf. Ephesians 2:6)

The saints who satisfy the heart of Jesus are the imperial people of God for ever, nothing deflects them, they are super-conquerors, and in the future they will be side by side with Jesus. "He that overcometh, I will give to him to sit down with Me in My throne, even as I also overcame, and sat down with My Father, in His throne" (Revelation 3:21 RV). The glorified Lord will take up His abode with the saint who puts God first in reality, not in sentiment. "We will come unto him, and make Our abode with him." The Triune God abiding with the saint! Jesus Christ is made heavenly bread to us now, and there is a glorious day coming—and is even now in the experience of many of His people—when the nourishment of the life is the same for the saint as for his Lord. "I will come in to him, and will sup with him, and he with Me" (Revelation 3:20).

INTRODUCTION

Source
These lectures were given in the at the Bible Training College,[1] London, from February to June 1915.

Publication History
The lectures were originally published as a book in 1930, subtitled "A Series of Missionary Studies."

In January 1915, Oswald Chambers began teaching a new class at the Bible Training College dealing with "Missionary Matters." Guest lecturers included many noted missionaries, among them, the already legendary C. T. Studd.

In the January 1915 edition of *Tongues of Fire*, the League of Prayer[2] magazine, Chambers noted:

It is with great thanksgiving we record that eight of our students are now in the foreign field on active service, and that six more will be appointed to active foreign service this year. This is all evidence that as soon as a student is ready, God's corner is opened by God, for we undertake to find no sphere of labour for our students, our duty is to see that this house[3] maintains the honour of God and that each student is put into a right spiritual atmosphere and His clearly discerned will always follows.

At the time, Chambers did not know that the College would close in a few months because of World War I and that he and Biddy and Kathleen[4] would be among those thrust out into a new field of service, ministering to soldiers in Egypt[5] through the YMCA.

He did, however, firmly believe that "the call of God is the call according to the nature of God; where we go in obedience to that call depends entirely on the providential circumstances which God engineers."

---

1. The Bible Training College (BTC) was a residential school near Clapham Common in southwest London. It was sponsored by the Pentecostal League of Prayer and operated from 1911 until it closed in July 1915 because of World War I. Oswald Chambers was principal and main teacher; Biddy Chambers, his wife, was lady superintendent.

2. The Pentecostal League of Prayer was founded by Reader Harris in 1891.

3. this house: This is a reference to the Bible Training College (BTC).

4. Kathleen Chambers (1913–1997) was the only child of Oswald and Biddy Chambers.

5. in Egypt: At Zeitoun, six miles northeast of Cairo, was a YMCA camp, the Egypt General Mission compound, and, from 1916 to 1919, the Imperial School of Instruction, a training base for British, Australian, and New Zealand troops for service in World War I.

CONTENTS

FOREWORD

A preface or foreword is scarcely needed to introduce the reader to this treasure-house of thought on missions. Those who have read other books by our friend, Oswald Chambers, know what to expect. A message not for superficial minds and hearts. Those who love to think on the kingdom and whose heart the King has entered will not be disappointed as they read these pages.

These stirring talks were given to the students at the Bible Training College in London, of which Revelation Oswald Chambers was Principal, before he went out to Egypt. The students that heard him are now scattered in many parts of the world, and proving faithful witnesses of Christ.

The twenty-two short chapters are in a sense

Bible-studies, but they are not mere Bible-readings—strings of texts with a moral. They whisper the secret of the burning heart, of the fully surrendered life, of a love that will not let go. The words pulsate with life and are a clarion-call away from idle daydreams to the stern path of duty. One sentence, among many others, specially riveted my attention and sums up the style, the man, and the message:

"In my study am I a wool-gatherer, or like a man looking for his Lord?"

This book will not find casual readers, but the thoughtful reader will want to read it a second time and God will bless the message.

S. M. Zwemer[6]
Princeton, N.J.

THE CALL

1. The Voice of the Nature of God

And I heard the voice of the Lord, saying, Whom shall I send, and who will go for Us? Then I said, Here am I; send me. (Isaiah 6:8 RV)

When we speak of a call we nearly always leave out one essential feature, viz.: the nature of the one who calls. We speak of the call of the sea, the call of the mountains, the call of the great ice barriers. These calls are heard by a few only because the call is the expression of the nature from which the call comes, and can only be heard by those who are attuned to that nature.

The call of God is essentially expressive of the nature of God, it is His own voice. Paul says that "God commendeth His *own* love toward us" (RV), the love that is exactly expressive of His nature. Get that thought with regard to the call of God. Very few of us hear the call of God because we are not in the place to answer; the call does not communicate because we have not the nature of the One Who is calling. In the case of Isaiah, his soul was so attuned because of the tremendous crisis he had passed through, that the call of God was recorded to his amazed soul. God did not

lay a strong compulsion on Isaiah; Isaiah was in the presence of God and he overheard, as it were, the soliloquy of God: "Whom shall I send, and who will go for Us?" and in conscious freedom he replied, "Here am I; send me."

There is a good deal of instruction to be got by watching the faces of people in certain surroundings—by the sea shore, in an art gallery, during music; you can tell at once if they are listening to the call of the thing or simply reflecting themselves. Most of us have no ear for anything but ourselves, anything that is not "me" we cannot hear. We are dead to, and without interest in the finest music, we can yawn in a picture gallery, and be uninspired by a sunrise or a sunset. That is true not only of the soul's denseness to natural beauties, or to music and art and literature, but true with regard to the awakening of the soul to the call of God. To be brought within the zone of God's voice is to be profoundly altered.

The call of God is not the echo of my nature, but expressive of God's nature. The call of God does not consider my affinities or personality. It is a call that I cannot hear as long as I consider my personality or temperament; but immediately I am brought into the

---

condition Isaiah was in, I am in a relationship to God whereby I can hear His call.

There are strands of the call of God providentially at work that you know and no one else does. It is the threading of God's voice for you on some particular line, and it is no use to consult anyone else about it, or to say that other people are dull because they do not hear it. "Immediately I conferred not with flesh and blood." You feel amazed at the sense of God's call, and in your eagerness you talk to someone else about it, and you find that they much prefer to talk about their breakfast. Then comes the danger that you are apt to become contemptuous. Keep that profound relationship between your soul and God.

2. The Vision of the New Life from God

Verily, verily, I say unto thee, Except a man be born again, he cannot see the kingdom of God. (John 3:3)

The power of vision which the new birth gives refers to perception by the personal spirit, and the characteristic of being born from above (RV mg) is that you begin to discern the rule of God. God's rule was there all the time, but true to His nature; now you have received His nature, you can perceive His rule. It is a good thing to mark the times when you feel your personal spirit trembling on the verge of a new vision. It may be during a lecture or in prayer, you nearly see something, then it goes, don't be distressed; it is the evidence of the new life from God. The life given by God is capable of immediately hearing the voice of God's own nature. Unless the nature of God comes into you, said Jesus to Nicodemus, you cannot understand Him; but if His nature comes into you, of course you will hear Him (John 3:3–8). Intuition is the power to sense things without reasoning, and is a better guide than what is stated explicitly; but there is something infinitely more satisfactory—the entrance of the Holy Spirit into a man at new birth enabling him to see the Kingdom of God and to enter into it.

3. The Vocation of the Natural Life for God

But when it pleased God, who separated me from my mother's womb, and called me by His grace, to reveal His Son in me, that I might preach Him among the Gentiles, [RV]. (Galatians 1:15–16)

The call of God is the call according to the nature of God; where we go in obedience to that call depends entirely on the providential circumstances which God engineers. The call of God is not a call to any particular service, although my interpretation of the call may be; the call to service is the echo of my identification with God. My contact with the nature of God has made me realise what I can do for God. Service is the outcome of what is fitted to my nature; God's call is fitted to His nature, and I never hear His call until I have received His nature. When I have received His nature, then His nature and mine work together; the Son of God reveals Himself in me, and I, the natural man, serve the Son of God in ordinary ways, out of sheer downright devotion to Him.

The call to service is the result of my obedience to the realised call of God. Profoundly speaking there is no *call* to service for God; it is my own actual "bit," the overflow of superabounding devotion to God. God does not have to come and tell me what I must do for Him, He brings me into a relationship with Himself wherein I hear His call and understand what He wants me to do, and I do it out of sheer love to Him. To serve God is the deliberate love gift of a nature that has heard the call of God. When people say they have had a call to foreign service, or to any particular sphere of work, they mean that their relationship to God has enabled them to realise what they can do for God. Their natural fitting for service and the call of God is identified as one in them.

The vocation of the natural life for God is stated by Paul—"When it pleased God . . . to reveal His Son in me that I might preach Him *[sacramentally express Him]* among the Gentiles."

THE CALL OF GOD

Unto me . . . was this grace given, to preach unto the Gentiles the unsearchable riches of Christ. Ephesians 3:8 (RV)

1. The Consciousness of the Call (*Jeremiah 1:5; Amos 7:14–15*)

We are apt to forget the mystic, supernatural touch of God which comes with His call. If a man can tell you how the call of God came to him and all about it, it is questionable whether he ever had the call. The call to be a professional man may come in that explicit way, but the call of God is much more supernatural. The realisation of the call of God in a man's life may come as with a sudden thunder-clap or by a gradual dawning, but in whatever way it comes, it comes with the undercurrent of the supernatural, almost the uncanny; it is always accompanied with a glow—something that cannot be put into words. We need to keep the atmosphere of our mind prepared by the Holy Spirit lest we forget the surprise of the touch of God on our lives.

Before I formed thee . . . I knew thee.

There are pre-natal forces of God at work in a man's life which he may be unconscious of for long enough; but at any moment there may break upon him the sudden consciousness of this incalculable, supernatural surprising power that has got hold of his life before he has got hold of it himself.

Another force at work is the prayers of other people. You are born into this world and will probably never know to whose prayers your life is the answer. It may be your own father and mother who have been used by God to dedicate your life to Him before you were born. The prayers may have remained apparently unanswered, but in reality they are answered; and your life should be the answer in actuality. Our lives are the answers not only to the prayers of other people, but to the prayer the Holy Spirit is making for us, and to the prayer of Our Lord Himself. When once you realise this, you will understand why it is that God does not say "By your leave" when He comes into your life.

If we have been getting hard and metallic, untouched spiritually—not backsliding, but getting out of touch with God, we shall find the reason is because we are allowing things to come in between us and the sense of God's call. At any minute God may bring the wind of His Spirit across our life, and we shall realise with a startled mind that the work we have been doing in the meantime is so much rubbish (cf. 1 Corinthians 3:12–13). There is so much self-chosen service; we say—"I think I will do this, and that for God." Unless we work for God in accordance with His supernatural call, we shall meet havoc and disaster and upset. The moment that the consciousness of the call of God dawns on us, we know that it is not a choice of our own at all; the consciousness is that of being held by a power we do not fully know. "*I have chosen him.*" If we are saved and sanctified, we are called to testify to it; but the call to preach is something infinitely other and belongs to a different category. Paul describes it as a *"necessity"*—"Woe is unto me, if I preach not the gospel!"

Then answered Amos . . . I was no prophet, neither was I a prophet's son; but I was an herdman, and a dresser of sycomore trees: And the Lord took me from following the flock, and the Lord said unto me, Go, prophesy unto My people Israel. (Amos 7:14–15 RV)

The only way I can begin to fulfil the call of God is by keeping my convictions out of the way, my convictions as to what I imagine I am fitted for. The fitting goes much deeper down than the natural equipment of a man.

Whenever the call of God is realised, there is the feeling—"I am called to be a missionary." It is a universal feeling because the Holy Spirit sheds abroad the love of God in our hearts, and "God so loved *the world.* . . ." We make a blunder when we fix on the particular location for our service and say—"God called me *there.*" When God shifts the location, the battle comes—will I remain consistent to what I have said I am going to do, or be true to the insurgent call of God, and let Him locate me where He likes? The most seemingly untoward circumstances will be used by God for the men and women He has called. How ever much of wrong or of the devil there may seem to be at work, if a man is called of God, every force will be made to tell for God's purpose in the end. God watches all these things when once a man agrees with His purpose for him, and He will bring not only the conscious life, but all the deeper regions of life which we cannot reach, into harmony with His purpose. If the call of God is there, it is not within the power of untoward things to turn you. Your heart remains, not untouched by them, but unbroken, and you are surprised at yourself—"Why didn't I go under here, and there?" *"I called thee."*

We try to make calls out of our own spiritual consecration, but when we are put right with God, He blights all our sentimental convictions and devotional calls. He brushes them all aside, and rivets us with a passion that is terrific to one thing we had never dreamed of, and in the condition of real communion with God, we overhear Him saying: "Whom shall I send, and who will go for Us?" and for one radiant, flashing moment we see what God wants, and say in conscious freedom—"Here am I; send me."

2. The Character of the Call
(*1 Corinthians 9:16*)

Paul puts out of court the idea that the preaching of the gospel is chosen as the choice of a profession is made. He says it is a necessity laid upon him . He was called to preach, even from his mother's womb, although for years he did not recognise it. Then suddenly the call awakened in him, and he realised that that was what God had been after all the time.

There is no mention of sin in Paul's apprehension, that came after; it was an apprehension of the call of God, a call which "separated" him unto the gospel. I have chosen him, ". . . for I will shew him how many things he must suffer for My name's sake" (RV). God called him in order to use him as broken bread and poured-out wine for others. When once Paul realised God's call and knew the meaning of his life, there was no competitor for his strength. Is there anything competing for our strength in our devotion to the call of God? It is not the devil but the "little foxes, that spoil the vines"—the little annoyances, the little actual things that compete for our strength, and we are not able to pray, things come in between, and our hearts are troubled and our minds disturbed by them. We have forgotten what Jesus said—"As the Father hath sent Me, even so send I you" (RV). Our Lord never allowed anything to disturb Him out of His oneness with the Father; only one thing held Him—"Lo, I am come ... to do Thy will, O God" (RV). With us, there are things that compete for the strength that should be given to God only. Thank God for such places as this Bible Training College where God gives us time to be shut in quietly. He is letting us see how competitors for our strength will knock the consciousness of His call right out.

Have I been forgetting the character of God's call? Has there been a refusal to be made broken bread and poured-out wine? If so, life is consequently being lived on the threshold of conscious devotion and conscious declension. This always happens when I do not realise that it is God Who engineers my circumstances, when I "despise the day of small things." I refuse to see God's hand in the circumstances of the weather that prevented me on such and such a day, I refuse to see God's hand in the routine of my life, and as a result there is no sense of arrestment by God, no being made broken bread and poured-out wine for others, but a dryness and a deadness all through. Prayer has brought no light, studying God's word has brought no comfort. This has nothing to do with the soul's salvation, but with the obliteration of the character of God's call. Let me take a revision and see how in the little things God has not been first, but my notions, my affinities, consideration of my temperament.

If we are not in full conscious allegiance to Our Lord, it has nothing to do with our personal salvation, but with this "broken bread and poured-out wine" aspect of life. God can never make me wine if I object to the fingers He uses to crush me with. If God would only crush me with His own fingers, and say, "Now, My son, I am going to make you broken bread and poured-out wine in a particular way and everyone will know what I am doing. . . ." But when He uses someone who is not a Christian, or someone I particularly dislike, or some set of circumstances which I said I would never submit to, and begins to

make *these* the crushers, I object. I must never choose the scene of my own martyrdom, nor must I choose the things God will use in order to make me broken bread and poured-out wine. His own Son did not choose. God chose for His Son that He should have a devil in His company for three years. We say—I want angels, I want people better than myself, I want everything to be significantly from God, otherwise I cannot live the life, or do the thing properly; I want to be always gilt-edged. Let God do as He likes. If you are ever going to be wine to drink, you must be crushed. Grapes cannot be drunk, grapes are only wine when they have been crushed. I wonder what kind of coarse finger and thumb God has been using to squeeze you, and you have been like a marble and escaped? You are not ripe yet, and if God *had* squeezed you, the wine that came out would have been remarkably bitter. Let God go on with His crushing, because it will work His purpose in the end.

3. The Commission of the Call (*John 20:21; Luke 4:18–19*)

Have we answered God's call in every detail during this Session?[7] Have we really been the "sent" ones of Jesus as He was the sent One of God? We can soon know. What has been competing for our strength?—what kind of things have we objected to? What things have hindered our times of communion, so that we have had to pray about them when we had no business to be in the place where we could notice them? We ought to have been living in John 14:1; but the heart has been troubled, and we have taken account of the evil (RV), consequently we have been less concerned about God's enterprises than about our own. Woe unto me, said Paul, if I do not keep concentrated on this one thing, that I am called of God for His service.

God puts us through discipline, not for our own sake, but for the sake of His purpose and His call. Never debate about anything God is putting you through, and never try to find out why you are going through it. Keep right with God and let Him do what He likes in your circumstances, and you will find He is producing the kind of bread and wine that will be a benefit to others.

---

7. this Session: Lectures given during spring 1915.

THE POINT OF SPIRITUAL HONOUR

I am debtor both to Greeks and to Barbarians. Romans 1:14 (RV)

Do I feel this sense of indebtedness to Christ that Paul felt with regard to every unsaved soul I meet, every unsaved nation? Is it a point of spiritual honour with me that I do not hoard blessings for myself? The point of spiritual honour in my life as a saint is the realisation that I am a debtor to every man on the face of the earth because of the Redemption of the Lord Jesus Christ.

Paul realised that he owed everything to Jesus Christ, and it was in accordance with his sense of spiritual honour that he spent himself to the last ebb to express his indebtedness to Jesus Christ. When a man is indwelt by the Holy Spirit, he never talks in cold logic, he talks in passionate inspiration; and the inspiration behind all Paul's utterances is the fact that he viewed Christ as his Creditor. "For I could wish that myself were accursed from Christ for my brethren. . . ." The great characteristic of Paul's life was that he realised he was not his own; he had been bought with a price, and he never forgot it. His whole life was based on that one thing. Paul sold himself to Christ—"the bondslave of Jesus." For "I determined not to know any thing among you, save Jesus Christ, and Him crucified."

We are apt to have the idea that a man called to the ministry is called to be a different kind of being from other men. According to Jesus Christ, he is called to be the "doormat" of other men; he is their spiritual leader, but never their superior. "Ourselves your servants for Jesus' sake." No matter how men treat me, Paul argues, they will never treat me with the hatred and spite with which I treated Jesus Christ; and as long as there is a human being who does not know Jesus Christ, I am his debtor to serve him until he does. When the realisation comes home that Jesus Christ has served me to the end of all my meanness,[8] my selfishness and sin, then nothing I meet with from others can exhaust my determination to serve men for His sake. I am not to come among men as a superior person, I am to come among men as the love-slave of Jesus Christ, realising that if I am worth anything at all, it is through the Redemption. That is the meaning of being made broken bread and poured-out wine in reality.

I am made all things to all men, that I might by all means save some.

Paul attracted to Jesus all the time, never to himself. He became a sacramental personality, that is, wherever he went Jesus Christ helped Himself to his life (cf. 2 Corinthians 2:14). Many of us are subtly serving our own ends, and Jesus Christ cannot help Himself to our lives; if I am abandoned to Jesus, I have no ends of my own to serve. Paul said, "I know how to be abased" (RV)—I know how to be a "doormat" without resenting it, because the mainspring of his life was devotion to Jesus.

Thank God, when He has saved us, He does give us something to do, some way of expressing our gratitude to Him. He gives us a great noble sense of spiritual honour, the realisation that we are debtors to every man because of the Redemption of Jesus Christ. The sense of our debt to Jesus is so overwhelming that we are passionately concerned for that brother, that friend, those unsaved nations; in relation to them we are the bondslaves of Jesus.

Am I doing anything to enable Jesus Christ to bring His Redemption into actual manifestation in other lives? I can do it only if the Holy Spirit has wrought in me this sense of spiritual honour. When I realise what Jesus Christ has done for me, then I am a debtor to every human being until they know Him too, not for their sake, not because they will otherwise be lost, but because of Jesus Christ's Redemption. Am I willing to sell myself to Jesus, to become simply His bondslave, in order that He may see of the travail of His soul and be satisfied?

The great motive and inspiration of service is not that God has saved and sanctified me, or healed me; all that is a fact, but the great motive of service is the realisation that every bit of my life that is of value I owe to the Redemption; therefore I am a bondslave of Jesus. I realise with joy that I cannot live my own life; I am a debtor to Christ, and as such I can only realise the fulfilment of His purposes in my life. To realise this sense of spiritual honour means I am spoilt for this age, for this life, spoilt from every standpoint but this one, that I can disciple men and women to the Lord Jesus. Paul was a lonely debtor in a world of repudiators. Does your brother repudiate the Redemption of Jesus? Does the net result of your life work appeal to him only on one

---

8. The word mean as used here refers to something or someone ordinary, common, low, or ignoble, rather than cruel or spiteful.

line, the line of Redemption? Does he take no account of you on any other line? Never let anything deter you from spending for other souls every ounce of spiritual energy God gives you. There will be an actual manifestation of the Redemption in lives presently. Whatever you spend of yourself in the fulfilling of your sense of spiritual honour will come back to you in absolute recreation, physical and moral and spiritual.

If any man see his brother sin a sin which is not unto death, he shall ask, and he shall give him life for them that sin not unto death. (1 John 5:16)

Quit praying about yourself, and be spent in vicarious intercession as the bondslave of Jesus. How many souls have we failed to bring through to God because of our crass unbelief in prayer? Jesus Christ places the emphasis on intercessory prayer—"He that believeth on Me, the works that I do shall he do also; and greater works than these shall he do; because I go unto the Father. And whatsoever ye shall ask in My name, that will I do, that the Father may be glorified in the Son. If ye shall ask Me anything in My name, that will I do" (RV). That is reality; that is actuality! The actuality will take place—the almighty interaction of God on other lives in answer to prayer based on Redemption, not to prayer based on human sympathy or human plaintiveness. When we pray on the fundamental basis of the Redemption, our prayers are made efficacious by the personal presence of the Holy Ghost Who makes real *in* us what Jesus did *for* us. How God works in answer to prayer is a mystery that logic cannot penetrate, but that He does work in answer to prayer is gloriously true. We all have faith in God, but is our faith pre-eminent when it comes into contact with actualities? Our part in intercessory prayer is not to enter into the agony of intercession, but to utilise the common-sense circumstances God has placed us in, and the common-sense people He has put us amongst by His providence, to bring them before God's throne and give the Holy Spirit a chance to intercede for them. That is how God is going to sweep the whole world with His saints.

Am I banking in unshaken faith on the Redemption of Jesus Christ? Is it my conviction among men that every man can be presented "perfect in Christ Jesus"? Or do I allow men's sins and wrongs so to obliterate the power of the Redemption that I sink under them? Jesus said—he that believeth on Me, out of him "shall flow rivers of living water," i.e., by active belief in Jesus based on the Redemption, and by prayer and service based on that same Redemption.

VISION, VALLEY, VERITY

Life is not as idle ore,
But iron dug from central gloom,

....

And batter'd by the shocks of doom
To shape and use.

It is always well to go back to the foundation truths revealed in God's word regarding what He expects of the man or woman who wishes to be what He wants. "Called to be saints," that is what God expects.

Thank God for the sight of all you have never yet been. The vision is not an ecstasy or a dream, but a perfect understanding of what God wants, it is the Divine light making manifest the calling of God. You may call the vision an emotion or a desire, but it is something that absorbs you. Learn to thank God for making known His demands. You have had the vision, but you are not there yet by any means. You have seen what God wants you to be but what you are not yet. Are you prepared to have this "iron dug from central gloom" battered into "shape and use?" "Battering" conveys the idea of a blacksmith putting good metal into right useful shape. The batterings of God come in commonplace days and commonplace ways, God is using the anvil to bring us into the shape of the vision. The length of time it takes God to do it depends upon us. If we prefer to loll on the mount of transfiguration, to live on the memory of the vision, we are of no use to live with the ordinary stuff of which human life is made up. We have not to live always in ecstasy and conscious contemplation of God, but to live in reliance on what we saw in the vision when we are in the midst of actualities. It is when we are going through the valley to prove whether we will be the "choice" ones, that most of us turn tail; we are not prepared for the blows which must come if we are going to be turned into the shape of the vision. It does not matter with what the vision is connected, there is always something that corresponds to the valley of humiliation. God gives us the vision, then He takes us down to the valley to batter us into its shape, and it is in the valley that we faint and give way, while all the time God is wanting to get us through to the veritable reality.

Abraham

In Genesis 15:1, we read "After these things the word of the LORD came unto Abram in a vision, saying, Fear not, Abram: I am thy shield, and thy exceeding great reward." After the vision there followed the valley of humiliation, and Abraham went through thirteen years of silence. Genesis 16 is an illustration of the danger of listening to good advice when it is dark instead of waiting for God to send the light. The act of Abraham and Sarah produced a complexity in God's plan all down the ages. The intervening years brought Abraham through his valley of humiliation. During those years of silence all Abraham's self-sufficiency was destroyed, every strand of self-reliance was broken; there was no possibility left of relying on common-sense ways, and when Abraham had exhausted all human strength and wisdom, then God appeared to him. "And when Abram was ninety years old and nine, the LORD appeared to Abram, and said unto him, I am the Almighty God; walk before Me, and be thou perfect" (Genesis 17:1). No vision this time, but Reality. Abraham, after his humiliation, was in a fit state to stand the reward—God Himself. Abraham became a man more sure of God than of anything else.

The one thing for which we are all being disciplined is to know that God is real. As soon as God becomes real, other people become shadows. Nothing that other saints do or say can ever perturb the one who is built on the real God. "In all the world, my God, there is none but thee, there is none but thee."

The danger is to try to anticipate the actual fulfilment of the real vision. On the mount of transfiguration we saw clearly a vision of what God wanted, and we transacted business with God spiritually; then immediately afterwards there was nothing but blank darkness. Remember Isaiah's word—"Who is among you . . . that walketh in darkness, and hath no light? let him trust in the name of the LORD, and stay upon his God." The temptation is to work up enthusiasm, to kindle a fire of our own and walk in the light of it. God's "nothings" are His most positive answers. We have to stay on God and wait. Never try to help God to fulfil His word.

Moses

And it came to pass in those days, when Moses was grown, that he went out unto his brethren, and looked on their burdens. (Exodus 2:11)

That is an indication of the vision of God's purpose for Moses, viz., the deliverance of his brethren. It is a great moment in a man's life when he realises that he has to go a solitary way alone. Moses was "learned in all the wisdom of the Egyptians," a man in a royal setting by the providence of God, and he saw the burden of God's people, and his whole heart and mind was ablaze with the vision that he was the man to deliver them. He *was* the man to deliver his people, but not yet, there was something in the road, and God sent him into the

wilderness to feed sheep for forty years. Imagine what those years must have meant to Moses, realising on the threshold of his manhood the vision of what he was to do; seeing, as no one else could see, the burdens of his people, and feeling in himself the certainty that he was the one to deliver them; how he would ponder over God's ways during those forty years.

Then we read that God appeared to Moses and said—"Come now therefore, and I will send thee unto Pharaoh, that thou mayest bring forth my people the children of Israel out of Egypt" (Exodus 3:10). At first, Moses was certain that he was the one to deliver his people; but forty years have passed since he had the vision, and there is a different characteristic in Moses now. It is no longer the big "I am," but the little "I am." When God came with a renewal of the call, Moses had the quaver of the little "I am"—"Who am I, that I should go?" The little "I am" always sulks when God says Do. And the Almighty's reply to Moses is full of stirring indignation—"I AM THAT I AM" hath sent thee. The big "I am" and the little "I am" have to go until there is no "I am" but God, He must dominate. Let the little "I am" be shrivelled up in God's indignation. Is it not illuminating how God knows where we are, and the kennels we crawl into, no matter how much straw we hide under! He will hunt us up like a lightning flash. No human being knows human beings as God does.

"Behold, there is a place by Me, and thou shalt stand upon a rock" (Exodus 33:21). Moses has come to the Reality of all realities, recognition by God. The place in God's mind for Moses was by Him on the rock, recognised by God as His true yoke fellow. Nothing can deflect the life that has once been placed by God on the rock. After the forty years of humiliation Moses was in a fit state to receive the recognition of God without being unduly lifted up.

"There is a place by Me. . . ." No man ever gets beside God who has not first been beside himself and knocked out of his wits with worry and anxiety about the mess he has made of things. That is the meaning of conviction of sin, the realisation—"What a fool I have been! how wicked and vile! and I ought to have been this and that!"

Moses' experience was of the type in which the certainty is brought home that God has been preparing you for something, and you realise that you have the power potentially to do what He wants. You can recall the perfect reality of the vision, the clear understanding of what God said to you then. You say—"I know He said it, I almost saw Him, it was so real. I know God called me to be a missionary—but it was a long time ago, and I suppose I was mistaken, for look at me now, something in an office." You know you were not mistaken. The call was right, but you were not ready for it. God has to season us, there has to be a time of humiliation before the vision is turned into verity. We have to learn not only how useless we are, but how marvellously mighty God is. "Many are called, but few prove the choice ones."

Think of the enormous leisure of God! He never is in a hurry. We are in such a frantic hurry. We get down before God and pray, then we get up and say, "It is all done now," and in the light of the glory of the vision we go forth to do the thing. But it is not real, and God has to take us into the valley and put us through fires and floods to batter us into shape, until we get into the condition in which He can trust us with the reality of His recognition of us.

Isaiah

In the year that King Uzziah died I saw also the Lord sitting upon a throne, high and lifted up, and His train filled the temple. (Isaiah 6:1)

Isaiah's vision stands for another type of the call of God. In the profound grief of the greatest bereavement of his life, Isaiah saw the Lord, and right on top of the vision came deep and profound dejection on account of his sin and unworthiness. "Woe is me! for I am undone; because I am a man of unclean lips, and I dwell in the midst of a people of unclean lips: for mine eyes have seen the King, the LORD of hosts." The effect of the vision of the holiness of the Lord was to bring home to Isaiah that he was a man of unclean lips; there was deep dejection at his utter unfitness to be anything like what he had seen. Then the live coal from off the altar was laid upon his mouth—the cleansing fire was applied where the sin had been concentrated, and in the communion with God resulting

from his intense spiritual cleansing, Isaiah overheard God say, "Whom shall I send, and who will go for Us?" and from heartbreak and disenchantment to simple humble attachment, he said: "Here am I; send me." Isaiah was made the Representative of God.

Each one of us has a counterpart somewhere in the experiences of these three men of God. In the case of Abraham, the valley of humiliation lasted thirteen years; Moses, forty years; Isaiah, a few minutes. No two of us are alike, each one stands alone before God. Your valley may be a darkness where you have nothing but your duty to guide you, no voice, no thrill, but just steady, plodding duty; or it may be a deep agonising dejection at the realisation of your unfitness and uncleanness and insufficiency. Let God put you on His wheel and whirl you as He likes, and as sure as God is God and you are you, you will turn out exactly in accordance with the vision He gave you. Don't lose heart in the process.

If ever we have had the vision—and all of us probably have had, it may have been when we were little children, or when we were very ill, or after a bereavement—we may try as we like to be satisfied on a lower level, but God will not let us. The goads of God are in, and it is hard to kick against them. Ever since we first had the vision, God has been at work getting us through the valley of humiliation, battering us into the shape of the vision, and over and over again we have tried to get out of God's hands and batter ourselves into our own shape—"Now this is the place I must be in; this is what the vision means." Keep paying the price. Let God see that you are willing to live up to the vision.

OUR LORD'S SURPRISE VISITS

Let your loins be girded about, and your lamps burning; and be ye yourselves like unto men looking for their lord. . . . For in an hour that ye think not the Son of man cometh. Luke 12:35–36, 40 (RV)

The greatest need of the missionary is to be ready to face Jesus Christ at any and every turn, and it is not easy to be ready to do that, whatever our experience of sanctification may be. The great battle all along is not so much against sin, as against being so absorbed in work that we are not ready to face Jesus Christ. The one great need is not to face our beliefs and our creeds, or the question whether we are of any use or not, but to face our Lord. This attitude of being ready to face Him means more and more disentanglement from so-called religious work, and more and more

intense spiritual reality in so-called secular work. The whole meaning of the Christian life from Our Lord's standpoint is to be ready for Him.

The element of surprise is always the note of the life of the Holy Ghost in us. We are born again by the great surprise—"The wind bloweth where it listeth, and thou hearest the voice thereof, but knowest not whence it cometh, and whither it goeth: so is every one that is born of the Spirit" (John 3:8 RV). Men cannot tie up the wind, it blows where it lists; neither can the work of the Holy Spirit be tied up in logical methods. Jesus never comes where we expect Him; if He did, He would not have said "Watch." Be ye also ready: for in an hour when ye think not the Son of man cometh" (RV). Jesus appears in the most illogical connections, where we least expect Him, and the only way a worker can keep true to God amidst the difficulties of work either in this country or in heathen lands is to be ready for His surprise visits. We have not to depend on the prayers of other people, not to look for the sympathy of God's children, but to be ready for the Lord. It is this intense reality of expecting Him at every turn that gives life the attitude of child wonder that Jesus wants it to have. When we are rightly related to God, life is full of spontaneous joyful uncertainty and expectancy—we do not know what God is going to do next; and He packs our life with surprises all the time.

That is the line on which Our Lord always comes, and the line we are apt not to look for Him. It comes home in ways like this: You have prepared a sermon or an address very carefully and feel that God gave you a good time in the delivery of it, but nothing happens. At another time you talk without much consideration, and suddenly there comes the certainty—"Why, that is the Lord! that was said by Him, not by me." Beware of the idea that we can tie the Lord Jesus up by spiritual logic: "This is where He will come, and that is where He will not come." If we are going to be ready for Jesus whenever He comes, we must stop being religious—using religion as a kind of higher culture, and become spiritually real, alert and ready for Him.

Let your loins be girded about.

It is impossible to run in the loose Eastern garments unless they are girt up. The writer to the Hebrews counsels us to "lay aside every weight, and the sin which doth closely cling to us" (RV mg). He is not speaking of inbred sin, but of the circumambient sin, the spirit of the religious age in which we live, which will entangle the feet of the saint and hinder his running the race. Loose, trailing, uninspired thinking about sin will very soon trip us up. Gird up your thinking about sin, about holiness, about the eternal realities and the call of the unseen things. It is amazing to see the unreadiness of even some of the most spiritual people, they are continually clogged and tripped up by the wrong thing. If we are looking to Jesus and avoiding the spirit of the religious age in which we live, and setting our hearts on thinking along Jesus Christ's lines, we shall be called unpractical and dreamy; but when He appears in the burden and the heat of the day, we alone shall be ready. When you meet a man or woman who puts Jesus Christ first, knit that one to your soul.

And your lights burning; and ye yourselves like unto men [looking for their lord, RV].

Am I like a man looking for his Lord where no one sees me but God? In my study, am I a wool-gatherer or like a man looking for his Lord? Am I like a man looking for his Lord in my home, in my contact

with other people—is the lamp of conscience trimmed and burning there? Our Lord does not trim the lamp, we have to, and it is not done once for all, but once and for always, i.e., always now. Conscience in a saint will make him look after his scruples according to the light of God. As servants of God in other lands you will have to go among people whose lives are twisted and perverted by unconscious corruption, but if your conscience is as a lamp trimmed and burning, then the Lord can visit others through you at any second.

Is the lamp of your affections burning clear? If not, you will lose out in that way quicker than in any other. Inordinate affection means that you have allowed convictions to go to the winds. Keep the centre of your heart for Jesus Christ and watch inordinate affection as you would the devil. There is more reason to be found there as to why Christians are not ready for Jesus Christ's surprise visits than anywhere else.

Is the lamp of hope burning bright? "And every man that hath this hope in him purifieth himself." And what a hope it is! "We shall see Him as He is." "Blessed are those servants, whom the Lord when He cometh shall find watching."

Do you imagine that there will be crowds to come up to that standard? Jesus said No, it is one here and one there, always a "little flock." Our Lord is not talking of salvation, but about being His servants. Whenever Jesus got down to His truth, the crowds left Him (see John 6:66). To-day the craze is for crowds.

The one great need for the missionary is to be ready for Jesus Christ, and we cannot be ready unless we have seen Him. We must trust no one, not the finest saint who ever walked this earth, if once he hinders our sight of Jesus. It is Jesus Christ we have to be ready to meet; Jesus Christ for whom we must work.

Readiness implies a light relationship to God and a knowledge of where we are at present. We are so busy telling God where we should like to go. Most of us are waiting for some great opportunity, something that is sensational, then we cry—"Here am I; send me." Whenever Jesus is in the ascendant, in revival times, when the exciting moment comes, we are there; but readiness for God and for His work means that we are ready to do the tiniest thing or the great big thing, it makes no difference. We are so built that we must have sympathy or we will never do our best; but this instinct is apt to be prostituted unless we get burned into our hearts an understanding of what Jesus said: "Lo, I am with you all the days" (RV mg). He is the one Who is surrounding us, listening and sympathising and encouraging. Our audience is God, not God's people, but God Himself. The saint who realises that can never be discouraged, no matter where he goes. The audience of the ready saint is God, He is the arena of all his actions. To know that

God is the One Who sympathises and understands and watches us will bring the ready soul into touch and sympathy with God. What we lack to-day is sympathy with God's point of view. When once we get into sympathy with God, He will bring us into touch with His purposes and with the real needs of men and women.

"Ye shall be My witnesses" (RV). To be a witness of Jesus means that when any duty presents itself we hear His voice just as He heard His Father's voice, and we are ready for it with all the alertness of our love for Him. The knowledge that Jesus expects to do with us as His Father did with Him becomes the closely imbedded conception of our lives. "I can put you where I like, in pleasant duties or in mean[9] ones; you will know that I know where you are because the union is that of My Father and Myself"—"one as We are." That is the only simplicity there is, the simplicity of a heart relationship to Jesus. Beware of believing that the human soul is simple, or that human life

is simple. Our relationship to God in Christ is the only simple thing there is. If the devil succeeds in making this relationship complicated, then the human soul and human life will appear to be simple; whereas in reality they are far too complex for us to touch. That is why Paul said "I fear, lest . . . your minds should be corrupted from the simplicity that is in Christ Jesus." We have to keep that pristine simplicity free from anything like tarnish.

Be ready for the sudden surprise visits of Our Lord, and remember there is no such thing as prominent service and obscure service; it is all the same with God, and God knows better than ourselves what we are ready to do. Think of the time we waste trying to get ready when God gives the call! A ready person never needs to get ready. The bush that burned with fire and was not consumed is the symbol for everything that surrounds the ready saint. Anyone can see an ordinary bush, the ready soul sees it ablaze with God.

THE "GO" OF PREPARATION
Matthew 5:23–24

Nerve us with patience, Lord, to toil or rest,
Toiling at rest on our allotted level,
Unsnared, unscared by world or flesh or devil,
Fulfilling the good will of Thy behest.
Not careful here to hoard, not here to revel,
But waiting for our treasure and our zest
Beyond the fading splendour of the west,
Beyond this deathstruck life and deadlier evil.
Not with the sparrow building here a house,
But with the swallow tabernacling, so
a still to poise alert, to rise and go
On eagle wings, with wing outspeeding wills,
Beyond earth's gourds and past her almond boughs,—
past utmost bound of the everlasting hills.

Preparation is not something suddenly accomplished, but a process steadily maintained. It is easy to imagine that we get to a settled state of experience where we are complete and ready; but in work for God it is always preparation and preparation. Moral preparation comes before intellectual preparation, because moral integrity is of more practical value than any amount of mental insight.

1. Moral Preparation
In writing to the Philippians Paul mentions two "perfections": "not as though I . . . were already *perfect*" (3:12); "Let us therefore, as many as be *perfect* . . ." (3:15). The first refers to the perfection of attainment; the second to the perfection of adjustment to God. When by the experience of sanctification we are in perfect adjustment to God, we can begin to live the perfect life, that is, we can begin to attain. A child is a perfect human being, so is a man; what is the difference? The one is not yet grown, the other is full grown. When we are sanctified, we are perfectly adjusted to God, but we have done nothing yet, we are simply perfectly fit to begin. The whole life is right, undeserving of censure in the sight of God; now we can begin to attain in our bodily life, to prove that we are perfectly adjusted. Somewhere in the metropolis there exists what is probably a unique museum of broken materials used in engineering works. It is a splendidly organised testing laboratory wherein have been held many practical tests upon materials which have failed. The museum is used not only to discover the cause of the breakdown in the material, but also to test substances

---

9. The word mean as used here refers to something or someone ordinary, common, low, or ignoble, rather than cruel or spiteful.

which it is proposed to employ in the construction of buildings and machinery. That is the purpose of such places as this Bible Training College—for testing the material to be used in God's service. Remember, nothing and no one can detect us saving God. We are in the quarry now and God is hewing us out. God's Spirit gathers and marks the stones, then they have to be blasted out of their holdings by the dynamite of the Holy Ghost, to be chiselled and shaped, and then lifted into the heavenly places. God grant that many may go through the quarrying and the chiselling and the placing. Think of the scrutiny of Jesus Christ that each one of us has to face! Think of His eyes fastening on us and pointing us out before God as He says—"Father, that is My work; that is the meaning of Gethsemane, that is the meaning of Calvary. I did all that man's work in him, all that woman's work in her; now You can use them."

(a) Heroism and Sacrifice
If therefore thou art offering thy gift at the altar . . .
(Matthew 5:23 RV)

The Jews were scrupulous over external purity, and if on the way to the Temple to offer his paschal lamb, a man should recollect that he had leaven in his house, he had to hasten back and remove the leaven; and then when he had purged his house, carry his offering to the altar.

The sense of the heroic appeals readily to a young Christian. Take Peter, for instance. Humanly speaking, Peter was attracted to Jesus by his sense of the heroic. When Jesus said "Follow Me," Peter followed at once; it was no cross to him. It would have been a bigger cross not to follow, for the spell of Jesus Christ was on him. We are apt to under-estimate this enthusiastic sense of the heroic. It would be a terrible thing to be incapable of it, a terrible thing to be incapable of making such a declaration as Peter made—"I will lay down my life for Thy sake." Peter meant what he said, but he did not know himself. The scrutiny of our Lord's words brings the tide of enthusiasm suddenly to the test. Many of us have come to the altar for service, but are we willing to bind the sacrifice with cords to the horns of the altar? The altar means fire—burning and purification and insulation for one purpose, to detach us to God. Along with the sense of the heroic, there is a base element of selfishness, a lurking desire to fix the scenery of our own martyrdom. We feel if only we could fix the place and the spectators, we could go all lengths. But God fixes the place.

The illustration Our Lord used in Matthew 5:21–22 is unfamiliar to us, but the application is familiar. He is illustrating the descending scale of wrong tempers of mind. An angry man was in danger of being brought before the rulers for judgement; a contemptuous, disdainful man was regarded in the same way as a blasphemer and was brought before the ruler of the Sanhedrin; the man who gave way to abuse was in danger of being classed with criminals and flung out on the scrap heaps where the fires burned up the rubbish.

(b) Hardship and Sensitiveness
and there rememberest that thy brother hath ought against thee . . .

Not—"there you rake up by a morbid sensitiveness," but—"there you remember," the inference is that it is brought to your conscious mind by the Spirit of God. Never object to the intense sensitiveness of the Holy Spirit in you when He is educating you down to the scruple.[10] When we are first put right with God, it is the great general principles that are at work, then God begins to make the conscience sensitive here and there. Don't quench the Spirit. His checks are so tiny that common sense cannot detect them. If there is a sense of being out of touch with God, then at the peril of your soul you go and ask someone else what you have done wrong, you must go direct to God. The other soul is never so keen as the Spirit of God. When He checks, never debate, but obey at once. It is not a question of having had the law of God put in front of our mind: "This is what you must do and that is what you must not do," and then deliberate disobedience on our part. It is more an instinct of the spirit, an instantaneous feeling, a still small voice which we can easily quench; but if we do quench it, we become soiled, and every time the check comes and we do not heed it, the soiling is deepened. "Grieve not the . . . Spirit." He does not come with a voice like thunder, with strong emphatic utterance—that may come ultimately; but at the beginning His voice is as gentle as a zephyr. At the same time it carries an imperative compulsion—we know the voice must be obeyed.

The "go" of preparation is to let the word of God scrutinise. We are full of the sense of heroic sacrifice, and it seems hard to be reminded of things that happened in the past; but the thing that the Holy Spirit is detecting is that disposition in us that will never work in His service.

Over and over again men have gone into work for God in order to evade concentration on God on these lines. The note of false enthusiasm is the condition of the heathen. The need is made the call; but it is an artificial enthusiasm. No enthusiasm for humanity

---

10. down to the scruple: to the smallest item.

will ever stand the strain that Jesus Christ will put on His workers. Only one thing will stand the strain, and that is the personal relationship to Jesus of a man or woman who has gone through the mill of God's spring-cleaning until there is one purpose only—"I am here for God to use me as He wills."

2. Mental Preparation
(a) Direction by First Impulse
Leave there thy gift before the altar . . .

When God shows you there is something to do, don't be sulky with God; and don't say—"Oh well, I suppose after all God does not want me." Don't affect a heaviness of soul because other missionaries are not what they ought to be; don't criticise the missionary society you belong to. Our Lord's instruction is that you leave your gift and go; take your direction from the conviction He gave you when you first offered yourself to Him. Have nothing to hide from God. If you have, then let God riddle you with His light. If there is sin, *confess* it, not *admit* it. Are you willing to obey your Lord and Master in this particular, no matter what the humiliation may be to your right to yourself?

(b) Departure to the Former Condition
And go thy way . . .

Our Lord's direction is simple—Go back the way you came, and put that thing right. Never put a thing aside because it is insignificant. If you trace it down, the insignificant thing has at the back of it the disposition of my right to myself. Trace a scruple to its base and you find a pyramid; if you deal with the scruple, God will deal with the pyramid. The thing itself may be a detail, it is the disposition behind that is wrong, the refusal to give up your right to yourself—the thing God intends us to do if we are ever going to be disciples. Never discard a conviction; if it is important enough for the Spirit of God to have brought it to your mind, that is the thing He is detecting. You were looking for a great big thing to do, and God is telling you of some tiny thing; but at the back of the tiny thing is the central citadel of obstinacy. "Do you think I am going to humiliate myself? Besides, if I do this thing, it will cause others to stumble." No one will ever stumble because of us if we do what is right and obey what God indicates. Never remain true to a former confession of faith when God's Spirit indicates there is something else for you to do. Go the way indicated by the conviction given you at the altar. It is marvellous what God detects in us for His spring-cleaning!

3. Spiritual Preparation
(a) The Unblameable Attitude in Human Life
first be reconciled to thy brother . . .

"Unblameable" does not mean faultless, but undeserving of censure. Jesus is saying—Have an attitude of mind and temper of spirit to the one who has something against you that makes reconciliation as natural and as easy as breathing. Jesus does not mention the other person. He says—*you* go. There is no question of rights. The stamp of the saint is that he can waive his own rights and obey the Lord Jesus. That is the temper of soul to be in all through, unblameable in our attitude towards one another. Our Lord demands that there be not a trace of resentment even suppressed. A wrong temper of mind is the most blameworthy thing there is. It is not only what we say but what we think that tells.

(b) The Unblameable Attitude in Divine Life
. . . and then come and offer thy gift.

The process is clearly marked by Our Lord: first, the heroic spirit of sacrifice, then the sudden checking by the sensitiveness of the Holy Spirit; the stoppage at the point of conviction, and the going in obedience to God's word; constructing an unblameable attitude of mind and temper to the one with whom we were wrong, and then the glad, simple, unhindered offering of our gift to God.

THE "GO" OF RENUNCIATION

Luke 9:57–62

Braver souls for truth may bleed;
Ask us not of noble deed!
  Small our share in Christ's redemption—
  From His war we claim exemption.
Not for us the cup was drained;
  Not for us the crown of thorn
  On His bleeding brow was borne:
Not for us the spear was stained
  With the blood from out His side,
  Not for us the Crucified.
Let His hands and feet be torn!
  On the list we come but low:
Not for us the cross was taken,
Us no bugle call can waken
  To the combat, soldier fashion.

Missionary enterprise, to be Christian, must be based on the passion of obedience, not on the pathos of pity. The thing that moves us to-day is pity for the multitude; the thing that makes a missionary is the sight of what Jesus did on the Cross, and to have heard Him say "Go." Jesus Christ pays no attention whatever to our sentiment. In the New Testament the emphasis is not on the needs of men, but on the command of Christ, Go ye." The only safeguard in Christian work is to go steadily back to first principles.

1. The Rigour of Rejection (*Luke 9:57–58*)
(a) The Declaration of Dignified Devotion
And there came a scribe [mg "one scribe"—implying a scribe of the ruling class] and said unto Him, Master, I will follow Thee whithersoever Thou goest. (Matthew 8:19 RV)

Any remnant of consciousness that position in society, or profession, is of value to Jesus is rigorously rejected by Our Lord. The first thing we think of is just that very thing—"If that man were saved, what a wonderful influence he would be for Jesus Christ." Any sense that the cause of Christ will be benefited if I give myself to it, or any trace of listening to the suggestion of others that I should be of value in my Lord's service, receives no encouragement from Jesus. The ruggedness of Our Lord's presentation of things strikes us as being very harsh. All He said to this man was—The foxes have holes, and birds of the air have nests; but the Son of man hath not where to lay His head." Our Lord is no respecter of persons. We would have treated this man very differently—"Fancy losing

the opportunity of that man!" "Fancy bringing a north wind about him that froze him and turned him away discouraged!" We do respect persons; we do place confidence in the flesh. We need to go back to the centre of the Christian faith, the Cross of Jesus Christ. It is not a question of education nor of personal qualifications, but of understanding Who Jesus is, and knowing what He has done for us.

What is the test we put first for work at home or abroad? Sentimentally, we put the call of God first, but actually we are inclined to fix on the abilities of certain people. Our Lord pays not the remotest attention to natural abilities or natural virtues; He heeds only one thing—Does that man discern Who I am? does he know the meaning of My Cross? The men and women Jesus Christ is going to use in His enterprises are those in whom He has done everything. Our Lord lays down the conditions of discipleship in Luke 14:26–27, 33, and implies that the only men and women He will use in His building enterprises are those who love Him personally, passionately and devotedly, beyond any of the closest relationships on earth.

(b) The Detection of Discernment
But Jesus did not trust Himself unto them, for that He knew all men, . . . for He Himself knew what was in man. (John 2:24–25 RV)

Always take these words of Jesus into account in interpreting His replies, and you will learn never to apologise for your Lord. Our Lord's attitude to this particular scribe was one of severe discouragement, because He knew what was in him. Jesus Christ's answers are never based on caprice, but on a knowledge of what is in man. The answers of Jesus hurt and offend until there is nothing left to hurt or offend (cf. Matthew 11:6). If we have never been hurt by a statement of Jesus, it is questionable whether we have ever really heard Him speak. Jesus Christ has no tenderness whatever towards anything that is ultimately going to ruin a man for the service of God. If the Spirit of God brings to our mind a word of the Lord that hurts, we may be perfectly certain there is something He wants to hurt to death.

The rigour of rejection leaves nothing but my Lord and myself and a forlorn hope. "Let the hundredfold come or go," says Jesus, "your lodestar must be your relationship to Me, and I have nowhere to lay My head."

(c) The Discouragement of Drastic Discipline
Ye know not what ye ask. Are ye able to drink of the cup that I am about to drink? (Matthew 20:22)

The words of Jesus to the scribe knock the heart out of self-consciousness in service for Jesus, serving Jesus because it pleases one's self. Jesus told him that if he followed Him he would be homeless and possession-less. Do you expect to be a successful worker for Jesus if you are a disciple of His? Then you are doomed to a discouraging disappointment. Our Lord never called us to successful service; He calls us to present Him: "I, if I be lifted up from the earth, will draw all men unto Me." God saves men; we are sent out to present Jesus Christ and His Cross, and to disciple the souls He saves. The reason we do not make disciples is that we are not disciples ourselves, we are out for our own ends.

2. The Rally of Reluctance (*Luke 9:59–60*)
(a) The Solicitation of the Lord
And He said unto another, Follow Me.

Jesus said "Follow Me" to a man who was straightway awakened into a ferment of sensitive apprehension. When the call of God begins to dawn, we are full of "Why," and "But," and "What will happen if I do?" This man did not want to disappoint Jesus, nor to hurt his father. When Jesus called him, he was staggered into sensitive apprehension.

(b) The Sensitiveness of the Loyal
Lord, suffer me first to go and bury my father.

When Jesus calls, there is the ordeal of conflicting loyalties. Probably the most intense discipline we have to go through is that of learning loyalty to God by the path of what looks like disloyalty to our friends. This is stated in its profoundest form in Luke 14:26—"If any man cometh unto Me, and *hateth* not his own father mother, and wife, and children, and brethren, and sisters, yea, and his own life also, he cannot be My disciple" (RV). Learn to estimate the disproportion in your loyalties. A man will put his Lord to open shame before he will be disloyal to a friend. But when any soul learns how to lay down his life for his Friend, Jesus Christ, other people promptly become shadows until they become realities in Him. When a sense of loyalty to father or mother perplexes you, picture Jesus showing to you His pierced hands and feet, and wounded side, and thorn-crowned head, and hear Him say—"Think, what that must have meant to My mother, and it is I Who call you to follow Me." No one could have had a more sensitive love in human relationship than Jesus; and yet He says there are times when love to father and mother must be hatred in comparison to our love for Him. The sense of loyalty to father or mother or friends may easily slander Jesus because it implies that He does not understand our duty to them. If Jesus had been loyal to His earthly mother, He would have been a traitor to His Father's purpose. Obedience to the call of Christ nearly always costs everything to two people—the one who is called, and the one who loves that one. We put sensitive loyalty to relationships in place of loyalty to Jesus; every other love is put first, and He has to take the last place. We will readily give up sin and worldliness, but God calls us to give up the very closest, noblest and most right tie we have, if it enters into competition with His call. Beware of the inclination to dictate to God as to what you will allow to happen if you obey Him.

(c) The Strenuousness of the Leaving
But He said unto him, leave the dead to bury their own dead; but go thou and publish abroad the kingdom of God. (RV)

These words sound stern, but it must be remembered that Jesus spoke them to only one class of men, to the man who realised his duty to his father. There are only too many who are willing to leave father and mother to preach the gospel in other lands. Always keep our Lord's sayings in their setting, and before taking a word of Jesus for yourself, see that yours is a similar case. In a conflict of loyalties, obey Jesus at all costs, and you will find that He will remember your mother, as He remembered His own mother on the Cross.

3. The Renunciation of Reservations (*Luke 9:61–62*)
The blind devotion of the first enthusiasm has to be pulled down into discipline.

(a) The Volunteer of Enthusiasm
And another also said, Lord, I will follow Thee; but . . .

The one who says "Yes, Lord, but . . ." is always the one who is fiercely ready, but never goes. This man had one or two reservations, and one of them was that he wanted a valedictory service.

(b) The Vacillation of Endearments
First suffer me to bid farewell to them that are at my house. (RV)

Beware of the vacillation that comes through thinking of the "Marys" and "Johns" I love at home—my little mission, my church, my native place; it is apt to develop into wanting to fix the scene of your own martyrdom. The exacting call of Jesus leaves no margins of good-byes, because "Good-bye" as it is often used, is pagan, not Christian.

(c) The Voice of Exactitude
No man, having put his hand to the plough, and looking back, is fit for the kingdom of God.

In order to plough a straight furrow, you must look neither at the plough nor behind you, but at the far end of the field ahead. When once the call of God comes, begin to go and never stop going, no matter how many delightful resting places there may be on the way.

Christ's call is "Follow Me." Our attitude ought to be—"Lord, if it be Thou, bid me come unto Thee," and Jesus will say "Come."

THE "GO" OF UNCONDITIONAL IDENTIFICATION
Mark 10:17–24

Then came a slow
And strangling failure. I
Yet felt somehow
A mighty power was brooding, taking shape
Within me; and this lasted till one night
When, as I sat revolving it and more,

A still small voice from without said,
—Seest thou not,

Desponding child, where spring defeat and loss?
Even from thy strength . . .
. . . Know, not for knowing's sake,
But to become a star to men for ever;
Know, for the gain it gets, the praise it brings,
The wonder it inspires, the love it breeds:
Look one step onward, and secure that step!

When the rich young ruler saw Jesus, he wanted to be like Him, he had the master passion to be perfect. Anything less than the desire to be perfect in a profession or calling is humbug, and so in religion. Beware of quibbling over the word "perfection." It does not refer to the full consummation of a man's powers, it simply means perfect fitness for doing the will of God; a perfect adjustment to God until all the powers are perfectly fitted to do His will.

1. The Look and the Loving of the Lord
And Jesus looking upon him . . . (RV)

(a) Who Is the Lord?
This question must be answered by every man—who is ruling me? In our Lord's calling of a disciple He never puts personal holiness in the front, He puts in the front absolute annihilation of my right to myself and unconditional identification with Himself—such a relationship with Him that there is no other relationship on earth in comparison. Luke 14:26 has nothing to do with salvation and sanctification, it has to do with unconditional identification with Jesus. None of us know the absolute "go" of abandon to Jesus until we are in unconditional identification with Him.

Have you ever realised Who the Lord is in your life? The call to service is not the outcome of an experience of salvation and sanctification, there must be the recognition of Jesus Christ as Lord and Master as well as Saviour. "Who say ye that I am?" (RV). That is the abiding test. Jesus Christ makes human destiny depend absolutely on Who men say He is. Membership of His Church is based on that one thing only, a recognition of Who Jesus is and the public confession of it. Any man who knows Who Jesus is has had that revelation from God. "Blessed art thou, Simon-Barjonah: for flesh and blood hath not revealed it unto thee, but My Father which is in heaven. And I also say unto thee, that thou art Peter, and upon this rock I will build My church" (RV). What rock? The rock of the knowledge of Who Jesus is and the confession of it.

"And as He was going forth on His way [mg], there ran one to Him, . . . and asked Him, Good Master, what shall I do that I may inherit eternal life? And Jesus said unto him, Why callest thou Me good? none is good save one, even God" (Mark 10:17–18 RV). "If I am only a good man, it is of no more use to come to Me than to anyone else; but if your coming means that you discern Who I am, then comes the first condition: "If thou wouldest enter into life, keep the commandments" (RV). The rich young ruler had to realise that there is only One Who is good, viz., God; and the only "good thing" from Jesus Christ's point of view is union with that One, with nothing in between, and the steady maintenance of that union.

(b) What Is His Look?
"And Jesus looking upon him loved him" (RV). When Jesus saw the sterling worth and uprightness of the rich young ruler, He loved him. Natural virtues are lovely in the sight of Jesus, because He sees in them remnants of His Father's former handiwork.

Has Jesus ever looked at you? Get rid of your experiences as you ask yourself that question. Experiences may be a barrier to our knowing Jesus; we forget Him in being taken up with what He has done for us. The look of Jesus transforms and transfigures. His look means the heart broken for ever from allegiance to any but Himself. Where you are "soft" with God, is where the Lord has looked upon you; where you are hard and vindictive, insistent on your own way, certain that other people are more likely to be wrong than you, is where whole tracts of your nature have never been transformed by His gaze.

(c) What Is His Love?

The love of Jesus spoils us for every other interest in life save as we can disciple men and women to Him. It is woe to every other ambition when once Christ fixes His love on a man or woman consciously. The love Jesus fixed on this man resulted in the biggest sorrow he ever had—"and he went away sorrowful" (RV).

2. The Lack and Longing of the Loved

(a) What Lack I Yet?

Our Lord instantly presses another penetrating IF—"If thou wouldest be perfect . . ." (RV). Entrance into life is the recognition of Who Jesus is, and we only recognise Him by the power of the Holy Spirit. Unless this recognition of Jesus is put first, we shall present a lame type of Christianity that excludes the type of man represented by this young ruler. In the majority of cases recognition of Who Jesus is comes before conviction of sin. This second "If" is far more searching: "*If thou wouldest be perfect*"—then come the conditions.

Do I really want to be perfect? Do I really desire at all costs to every other interest that God should make me perfect? Can I say with Murray McCheyne[11]—"Lord, make me as holy as You can make a saved sinner"? Is that really the desire of my heart? When we are right with God, He gives us our desires and aspirations. Our Lord had only one desire, and that was to do the will of His Father, and to have this desire is the characteristic of a disciple.

(b) One Thing Thou Lackest

Go, sell that thou hast, and give to the poor . . . and come, follow Me. (RV)

These words mean a voluntary abandoning of riches and a deliberate, devoted attachment to Jesus Christ. We are so desperately wise in our own conceit that we continually make out that Jesus did not mean what He said, and we spiritualise His meaning into thin air. Jesus saw that this man depended on his riches. If He came to you or to me He might not say that, but He would say something that dealt with whatever He saw

we were depending on. "Sell that thou hast," strip yourself of every possession, disengage yourself from all things until you are a naked soul; be a man merely and then give your manhood to God. Reduce yourself until nothing remains but your consciousness of yourself, and then cast that consciousness at the feet of Jesus Christ.

(c) One Right Thing to Do

Our Lord is not talking about salvation, but—If you want to be perfect, those are the conditions; and you need not accept them unless you like, you are at perfect liberty to say—"No, thank you, I am much obliged for being delivered from hell and the abominations of sin, but this is rather too much to expect, I have my own interests in life." Sell all you have, said Jesus, barter it, obliterate it.

Never push an experience you have had into a principle by which to guide others. If you take what Jesus said to this man and make it mean that He taught we were to own nothing, you are evading what He taught, by making it external. Our Lord told the rich young ruler to loosen himself from his property because that was the thing that was holding him. The principle is one of fundamental death to possessions while being careful to use them aright.

Am I prepared to strip myself of what I possess in property, in virtues, in the estimation of others—to count all things to be loss in order to win Christ? I can be so rich in poverty, so rich in the consciousness that I am nobody, that I shall never be a disciple; and I can be so rich in the consciousness that I am somebody that I shall never be a disciple. Am I willing to be destitute even of the sense that I am destitute? It is not a question of giving up outside things, but of making myself destitute to myself, reducing myself to a mere consciousness and giving that to Jesus Christ. I must reduce myself until I am a mere conscious man, fundamentally renounce possessions of all kinds—not to save my soul, only one thing saves a man's soul, absolute reliance on the Lord Jesus—and then give that manhood to Jesus.

"Go thy way, sell . . ." Jesus did not say—Sell all you have and give the proceeds to the deserving poor; nor did He say—Consecrate all you have to My service. Jesus Christ does not claim any of our possessions. One of the most subtle errors is that God wants our possessions. He does not; they are not of any use to Him. He does not want my property, He wants myself. "Sell whatsoever you have and give the proceeds away; but as for you—you come and follow Me."

---

11. Robert Murray McCheyne (1813–1843) was a Scottish minister whose short but intense life left a great impact on Scotland.

3. The Light and Leading of the Life
And thou shalt have treasure in heaven: and come, follow Me.

(a) The Reduction and Renunciation
But when the young man heard the saying, he went away sorrowful: for he was one that had great possessions. (RV)

When he "heard the saying. . . ." When we *hear* a thing is not necessarily when it is spoken, but when we are in a state to listen to it and to understand. Our Lord's statements seem to be so simple and gentle, and they slip unobserved into the subconscious mind.

Then something happens in our circumstances, and up comes one of these words into our consciousness and we *hear* it for the first time, and it makes us reel with amazement. This man, when he heard what Jesus said, understood what He meant, he did not dispute it, he did not argue, he heard it, and he went away expressionless with sorrow. There was no doubt as to what Jesus said, no debate as to what He meant, and it produced in him a sorrow that had no words. He found he had too big an interest in the other scale, and he drooped away from Jesus in sadness, not in rebellion.

(b) The Revelation and the Riches
And thou shalt have treasure in heaven.

It is the trial of our faith that makes us wealthy in heaven. We want the treasure on earth all the time. We interpret answers to prayer on the material plane only, and if God does not answer there, we say He does not answer at all. "Treasure in heaven" is faith that has been tried, otherwise it is only possible gold. "Oh yes, I believe God can do everything." But have I proved that He can do *one* thing? If I have, the next time a trial of faith comes I can go through it smilingly, because of the wealth in my heavenly banking account.

(c) The Regulation and the Road
And come, follow Me. (RV)

"Come, follow Me," not, Find out the way, but—Come. You cannot come if there is any remnant of the wrong disposition in you, because you are sure to want to direct God. "Come unto Me"! these words were spoken to men who had felt the appeal of the Highest, the aspiration, the longing, the master passion to be perfect—"Come unto Me," and I will rest you, stay you, poise you; "take My yoke upon you and learn of Me," and you will discover rest all along the way. "If any man will come after Me, let him deny himself, and take up his cross, and follow Me." The road is the way He went. "I will make the place of My feet glorious." Where is the place of His feet? Among the poor, the sick and sorrowful, among the bad and devil-possessed, among the hypocrites. And He says, "Follow Me—there."

THE "GO" OF SACRAMENTAL SERVICE
Matthew 5:41

Lord, I have fallen again—a human clod!
Selfish I was, and heedless to offend;
Stood on my rights. Thy own child would not send
Away his shreds of nothing for the whole God!
Wretched, to thee who savest, low I bend:
Give me the power to let my rag-rights[12] go
In the great wind that from thy gulf doth blow.

Keep me from wrath, let it seem ever so right:
My wrath will never work thy righteousness.
Up, up the hill, to the whiter than snow-shine,
Help me to climb, and dwell in pardon's light.
I must be pure as thou, or ever less
Than the design of me—therefore incline
My heart to take men's wrongs as thou tak'st mine.

To go the second mile means always do your duty, and a great deal more than your duty, in a spirit of loving devotion that does not even know you have done it. If you are a saint the Lord will tax your walking capacity to the limit. The supreme difficulty is to go the second mile with God, because no one understands why you are being such a fool.

The summing up of Our Lord's teaching is that it is impossible to carry it out unless He has done a supernatural work in us. The Sermon on the Mount is not an ideal, because an ideal must have as its working power the possibility of its realisation in the disposition obsessed by it. "Love your enemies"; "Give to him that asketh thee"; these things have no place in the natural disposition of a man. Jesus Christ is the

---

12. rag rights: self-righteousness; see Isaiah 64:6.

only One Who can fulfil the Sermon on the Mount. We have to face ourselves with the teaching of Jesus, and see that we do not wilt it away. The demands Our Lord makes on His disciples are to be measured by His own character. The Sermon on the Mount is the statement of the working out in actuality of the disposition of Jesus Christ in the life of any man.

Have we really come to the conclusion that if we are ever to be disciples it must be by being made disciples supernaturally? As long as we have the endeavour and the strain and the dead-set purpose of being disciples, it is almost certain we are not. Our Lord's making of a disciple is supernatural; He does not build on any natural capacity. "Ye did not choose Me, but I chose you" (RV). That is always the way the grace of God begins to work, it is a constraint we cannot get away from. We can disobey it, but we cannot generate it. The drawing power is the supernatural grace of God, and we can never trace where that work begins. We have to choose to obey, and He does all the rest. To face ourselves with the standards of Jesus produces not delight, but despair to begin with; but immediately we get to despair we are willing to come to Jesus as paupers and to receive from Him. Despair is the initial gateway to delight in faith.

1. The Dangers of Intensity on Alien Ground

In Our Lord's day the class known as Zealots hated the Roman dominance with an intensity of detestation; they would bow their heads and have their necks severed by the Roman sword rather than obey the tyrant. Just as the early disciples of Jesus were on alien ground politically, so as disciples of the Lord we are on alien ground in this world. The intensity of early devotion to Jesus must make for fanaticism to begin with. An intense person sees nothing, feels nothing, and does nothing unless it be violently. There was a difference between the disciples of John the Baptist and the disciples of Jesus. John taught his disciples asceticism, there was no sociability about him. When Jesus came He was not marked by intense religious zeal in the way everyone else was. External intensities marked the religious age in which Jesus lived, but they did not mark Him. Our Lord did not identify Himself with the cause of the Zealots: but He laid down His life as the Servant of Jehovah. We bring an alien atmosphere to the New Testament. Nowadays many would sum up Jesus as an idle man.

(a) The Direction by Impulse

In the training of the early disciples Our Lord persistently checked impulse, and Peter, the most impulsive of them all, got rebuke after rebuke for obeying impulse. Watch how the Spirit of God checks whenever we obey impulse. His checks always bring a rush of self-conscious foolishness, and instantly we want to vindicate ourselves. Impulse must be disciplined into intuition. There was nothing of the nature of impulse about Our Lord, nor of cold-bloodedness, but a calm strength that was never disturbed by panic. Most of us develop our Christianity along the line of our temperament, not along the line of God. To try and develop Christianity along the line of impulse is an impertinence when viewed alongside the strong Son of God. Some of us are like grasshoppers spiritually. Impulse is a natural trait in natural life, but in spiritual things Our Lord absolutely checks it because it always hinders. Discipleship is built not on natural affinities but entirely on the supernatural grace of God. The one characteristic of discipleship is likeness to Jesus Christ.

(b) The Dissipation of Impressions

All human beings have some kind of affinity for everything God has made. Our Lord deliberately reduces the impressions arising from these natural affinities until He gets the heart established in grace. In Luke 14:26 Our Lord mentions the closest affinities, all of which have been created by God, and yet He says there are times when a man must hate them. Notice how your nature reacts when you listen to some of the stern teaching of the Bible. There is a feeling of outrage, and yet at the same time the certainty that it is right. God's original order was that there should be no sin, therefore every natural affinity could be indulged in; but sin entered in, and consequently when we become disciples the first thing we have to do is to cut off many affinities and live a maimed life. In the Sermon on the Mount Our Lord distinctly teaches the necessity of being maimed (see Matthew 5:29–30). If you are going to be spiritual, says Jesus, you must barter the natural, i.e., sacrifice it. If you say—I do not want to sacrifice the natural for the spiritual; then, says Jesus, you must barter the spiritual. It is not a punishment, but an eternal principle. Be prepared to be maimed, to be a one-eyed faddist, until your heart gets established. It is this dissipation of impressions that makes many a would-be disciple a deserter. Our Lord's statements embrace the whole of the spiritual life from beginning to end, and in verse 48 of Matthew 5, He completes the picture He began to give in verses 29–30—"Ye therefore shall be *perfect*, as your heavenly Father is perfect" (RV).

(c) The Disposition of Interests

The interests of the Son of God and of the disciple are to be identical. How long it takes to manifest that identity depends on the private history of the disciple and his Lord. Our Lord warns His disciples not to cast their pearls before swine. He is inculcating the need to examine carefully what we present of God's truth to others. If Our Lord reduces our affinities and makes us live a maimed life in the meantime, it is at the peril of our spiritual life we try to explain it to others. A false idea of confessing makes us tell secrets that should never be told, they are between God and the soul. There are affinities of heart and of life that are dealt with by God in secret and we must never say a word about them to others. Other people seeing the limitations of the life say—What can there be wrong in this and in that? There is nothing wrong in it, but we know that it is at the peril of our life with God that we touch it. The maimed life and the misunderstood life must go on. Be prepared to be a limited fool in the sight of others, says Jesus, in order to further your spiritual character. We value the understanding of those we love most so much that Jesus has to take the last place. A disciple in the making may often tell Jesus that his father or his mother or his friend or other interests must be heeded first, and the Lord administers no rebuke. The inevitable lesson is learned presently in a way in which it ought never to have had to be learned.

2. The Delays in Identification

Passionate genuine affection for Jesus will lead to all sorts of vows and promises which it is impossible to fulfil. It is an attitude of mind and heart that sees only the heroic. We are called to be unobtrusive disciples, not heroes. When we are right with God, the tiniest thing done out of love to Him is more precious to Him than any eloquent preaching of a sermon. We have introduced into our conception of Christianity heroic notions that come from paganism and not from the teaching of Our Lord. Jesus warned His disciples that they would be treated as nobodies; He never said they would be brilliant or marvellous. We all have a lurking desire to be exhibitions for God, to be put, as it were, in His show room. Jesus does not want us to be specimens, He wants us to be so taken up with Him that we never think about ourselves, and the only impression left on others by our life is that Jesus Christ is having unhindered way.

"Peter . . . walked upon the waters, to come to Jesus" (Matthew 14:29 RV). Walking on water is easy to impulsive pluck, but walking on dry land as a disciple of Jesus Christ is different, Peter walked on the water to go to Jesus, but he followed Him afar off on the land. We do not need the grace of God to stand crises; human nature and our pride will do it. We can buck up and face the music of a crisis magnificently, but it does require the supernatural grace of God to live twenty-four hours of the day as a saint, to go through drudgery as a saint, to go through poverty as a saint. to go through an ordinary, unobtrusive, ignored existence as a saint, unnoted and unnoticeable. The "show business," which is so incorporated into our view of Christian work to-day, has caused us to drift far from Our Lord's conception of discipleship. It is instilled

in us to think that we have to do exceptional things for God; we have not. We have to be exceptional in ordinary things, to be holy in mean streets, among mean people, surrounded by sordid sinners. That is not learned in five minutes.

Jesus took the early disciples in hand to train them, and at the end of three years of intimate companionship with Him, they all forsook Him and fled. Then they came to the end of themselves and all their self-sufficiency, and realised that if ever they were going to be different, it must be by receiving a new Spirit. After the Resurrection, Jesus "breathed on them, and saith unto them, Receive ye the Holy Ghost."

Do we really believe we need another Spirit? Are we basing our religious life on our impulses, on our natural affections, on what other people tell us we are? or are we based on what Jesus wants us to be? Jesus guides us by making us His friends.

"Why cannot I follow Thee even now?" (John 13:37 RV). Determination and devotion, protestations and vows are all born of self-consciousness, and must die out of a disciple. A child never makes vows. We have to be so taken up with Jesus that we are never impudent enough to vow anything. All our vows and resolutions end in denial because we have no power to carry them out. Natural devotion will always deny Jesus Christ somewhere or other. Whenever the grace of God takes hold of a man, he never thinks of vowing anything, he is lost in an amazing devotion which is not conscious.

> *Since mine eyes have looked on Jesus,*
> *I've lost sight of all beside.*

The domination of self-consciousness has to be put to death—"I have vowed, I have promised, and I have consecrated." It all has to go until there is only one "I," the Lord Jesus Christ.

"What is that to thee?" (John 21:22). A disciple is one who minds neither his own business nor any one else's business, but looks steadfastly to Jesus and goes on following Him. We read books about the consecration of other men, but it is as so much scaffolding, it all has to go, and the time comes when there is only one thing left—following Jesus. One of the severest lessons we get comes from our stubborn refusal to see that we must not interfere in other people's lives. It takes a long time to realise the danger of being an amateur providence, i.e., interfering with God's order for others. We see a certain person suffering and we say, "He shall not suffer; I will see that he does not," and we put our hand straight in front of God's permissive will to prevent it, and He has to say, *"What is that to thee?"*

All these things are elements in our identification with Jesus. How long it takes Him to get us identified with Him depends upon us. We cause delays to God by persistently doing things in our own way. He never gets impatient, He waits until everything has fallen away and there is nothing left but identification with Him. To be absolutely centred in Jesus means that all things and all people are welcome alike to me, because they are all arranged for in their times and seasons by my heavenly Father.

3. The Discipline by Instruction in Apprehending Growth

Beware of continually wanting to be thrilled. In the natural world the one who is always wanting experiences of ecstasy and excitement is disappointingly unreliable, and the same is true in the spiritual world. There are unemployables in the spiritual domain, spiritually decrepit people who refuse to do anything unless they are supernaturally inspired.

(a) His Cross
Him they compelled to . . . bear His cross. (Matthew 27:32)

Simon the Cyrenian, in unwillingly fulfilling the instruction given in the Sermon on the Mount, unconsciously points out the lesson to us that we must be identified with the cross of Christ before ever we can carry our own cross.

(b) His Cup
My cup indeed ye shall drink. (Matthew 20:23 RV)

This is not the cup of martyrdom, for Our Lord was not a martyr. We must be identified with the atoning Death of Our Lord before we can be disciples. Many of us want to be disciples, but we do not want to come by way of His atoning Death; we do not want to be compelled to be orthodox to the Cross of Christ, to drink the cup that He drank. But there is no other way. We must be regenerated, supernaturally made all over again, before we can be His disciples.

(c) His Confession
Behold, we go up to Jerusalem. (Luke 18:31)

That is the mightiest word on discipleship that Our Lord ever spoke, for Jerusalem was the place where He reached the climax of His Father's will for Him, and He identifies us with Himself in our going up to our Jerusalem.

We have become so taken up with the idea of being prepared for something in the future that that is the conception we have of discipleship. It is true, but it is also untrue. The attitude of the Christian life is that we must be prepared *now*, this second; this is the time. What we are in relation to Jesus, not what we do or say for Him, gives His heart satisfaction and furthers His Kingdom. "Every one therefore who shall *confess* Me before men . . . ," said Jesus. The word "confess" means that every particle of our nature says the same thing, not our mouth only, but the very make up of our flesh and blood, confesses that Jesus Christ has come in the flesh (cf. 1 John 4:2). It is easy to talk, easy to have fine thoughts; but none of that means being a disciple. Being a disciple is to be something that is an infinite satisfaction to Jesus every minute, whether in secret or in public.

WHAT IS A MISSIONARY?

Yet it was well, and Thou hast said in season
  As is the Master shall the servant be:
Let me not subtly slide into the treason,
  Seeking an honour which they gave not Thee:

Never at even, pillowed on a pleasure,
  Sleep with the wings of aspiration furled,
Hide the last mite of the forbidden treasure,
  Keep for my joys a world within the world.

He as He wills shall solder and shall sunder,
  Slay in a day and quicken in an hour,
Tune Him a chorus from the Sons of Thunder,
  Forge and transform my passion into power.

Ay, for this Paul, a scorn and a reviling,
  Weak as you know him and the wretch you see,

Even in these eyes shall ye behold His smiling,
  Strength in infirmities and Christ in me.

1. The Sure Characteristics (*John 17:18; 20:21–23*)

The great danger in missionary enterprise is that God's call may be effaced by the needs of the people until human sympathy overwhelms altogether the significance of Jesus Christ's sending. "As the Father hath sent Me, even so send I you" (RV). A missionary is a saved and sanctified soul detached to Jesus. The one thing that must not be overlooked is the personal relationship to Jesus Christ and to His point of view; if that is overlooked, the needs are so great, the conditions so perplexing, that every power of mind and heart will fail and falter. We are apt to forget that the great reason for missionary enterprise is not first the elevation of the people; nor first the education of the people; nor even first the salvation of the people, but first and foremost the command of Jesus Christ—"Go ye therefore, and make disciples of all the nations" (RV).

If we are going to remain true to the Bible's conception of a missionary, we must go back to the source—a missionary is one sent by Jesus Christ as He was sent by the Father. The great dominating note is not first the needs of men, but the command of Jesus Christ, consequently the real source of inspiration is always behind, never in front. Today the tendency is to put the inspiration in front; the great ideal is to sweep everything in front of us and bring it all out in accordance with our conception of success. In the New Testament the inspiration is behind, viz., the Lord Jesus Christ Himself. We are called to be true to *Him*, to be faithful to *Him*, to carry out *His* enterprises.

In revising the lives of men and women of God and the history of the Church of God, there is a tendency to say—"How wonderfully astute those men and women were! How perfectly they understood what God wanted of them!" The truth is that the astute mind behind these men and women was not a human mind at all, but the mind of God. We give credit to human wisdom when we should give credit to the Divine guidance of God through childlike people who were foolish enough in the eyes of the world to trust God's wisdom and supernatural equipment, while watching carefully their own steadfast relationship to Him.

The New Testament lays down clearly what the work of the missionary is, it is to disciple all nations according to the command of the Risen Lord. The method of missions is clearly stated in each of the four Gospels. St. Matthew records the farewell command which Jesus gave to His disciples, and that command is to teach, i.e., disciple, all nations; not make converts to our ways of thinking, but make disciples of Jesus. In St. Mark's Gospel the method is defined as preaching the gospel to every creature, accompanied by the power to cast out devils, and to speak with new tongues. In St. Luke's Gospel the method is described as preaching repentance and remission of sins unto all the nations (RV), and in St. John's Gospel the method is described by Our Lord as feeding His sheep and tending His lambs. The methods through which the life-giving truth is to be presented are as varied as the needs and conditions of the nations among whom the missionaries are placed.

Jesus Christ did not say—Go and save souls; the salvation of souls is God's work. Jesus told the disciples to go and teach, disciple, all nations. The salvation of souls comes about through the ministry of God's word and the proclaiming of the Redemption by God's servants; but the command to the missionary is to disciple those who are saved. Every now and again the Church becomes content with seeing people saved. When men get saved, then the disciple's work begins, and the great point about discipling is that you can never make a disciple unless you are one yourself. When the disciples came back from their first mission, they were filled with joy and said—"Lord, even the devils are subject unto us in Thy name," and Jesus said, in effect, "Don't rejoice in successful service, but rejoice that you are rightly related to God through Me." Those who remain true to the call of God are those whose lives are stamped and sealed by God; they have one great purpose underneath, and that is to disciple men and women to Jesus.

2. The Subject Matter (*Luke 24:45–48*)

The subject matter of missions is the Life and Death and Resurrection of Jesus Christ for one purpose—"that repentance and remission of sins should be preached in His name unto all the nations" (RV). The subject matter of missions remains an unchangeable truth, an historic fact, "the Lamb that hath been slain from the foundation of the world" (RV). The Cross as it is manifested in the life of Our Lord is not the cross of a martyr. He came on purpose to die. When once men get away from the teaching of the New Testament, the first thing that happens is that sin is minimised and the meaning of the Cross of Christ departed from. The Cross of Jesus Christ is the historic manifestation of the inherent nature of the Trinity. Through all the ages the perplexity in the minds of men without the Spirit of God arises because the Bible presents something utterly unlike what the natural heart thinks it wants. The natural mind of man thinks of God in a circle, everything is going to evolve and develop in a plain simple way. According to the Bible, things do not go as we expect them to, either in individual life or in history, but always at cross purposes. The symbol of the nature of God is not a circle, complete and self-centred; the symbol of God's nature is the Cross. The end God has in view is entirely different from that arrived at by man's unaided thinking. For instance, the conception that is working like leaven to-day all through missionary enterprise is that we are going to evolve into a circle of brilliant success, and the great conflict that awaits the missionary to-day is the conflict against the evolutionary idea that everything is growing better. The Bible does not look forward to an evolution of mankind; the Bible talks of a *revolution*—"Marvel not that I said unto thee, Ye must be born anew" (RV). We have to get back to the preaching of the Cross, and the remission of sins through the death of Our Lord.

3. The Scriptural Method (*John 21:15–17*)

The method here is described by Our Lord as feeding His lambs and tending His sheep. Continually we get to the place where we see no one as sinful because we do not want to become shepherds. The great challenge is made to the missionary himself; not that people are difficult to get saved, not that backsliders are difficult to reclaim, not that there is callous indifference on the part of people to the message; the challenge is to my faith in my Lord—do I believe He is able? Our Lord seems to come steadily to us in every individual case we meet—*"Believe ye that I am able to do this?"* Whether it be a case of demon possession, bodily upset, mental twist, backsliding, indifference, difference of nationality and thought, the challenge is to me. Do I know my Risen Lord? Do I know the power of His indwelling Spirit? Am I wise enough in God's sight, and foolish enough according to the wisdom of the world, to bank on what Jesus has told me? Or am I abandoning the supernatural position, which is the only one for a missionary, of boundless confidence in Jesus? If we take up any other method, we depart altogether from the scriptural method laid down by Our Lord—"All power is given unto Me. . . . Go ye therefore."

Every time God presents us with a problem in Christian work, He gives us something to match it in our own heart, and if we will let His power work there, we shall go forth with unshakeable confidence in what He can do for any man. If once a man knows in his own life that God can do what Jesus Christ said He could, he can never be put in the place where he will be discouraged. He may be put in the heart of the vilest and most terrible phases of heathenism, but he can never be discouraged, nor can he be defiled, because he has the very nature of God in him and he is kept like the light, unsullied.

4. The Special Persons (*Matthew 16:18*)

Matthew 16:18 is Our Lord's statement as to what constitutes membership in His church—a revelation of Who He is and the public confession of it. No man knows Who Jesus Christ is but by the Spirit of God, and the fact that he knows Who Jesus is and makes confession of it is the bedrock on which Christ builds His Church, according to His own word. The special person called to do missionary work is every person who is a member of the Church of Christ. The call does not come to a chosen few, it is to everyone of us. The special call is to stay at home. The big call remains—"Go ye"; and if I am staying, I have to give God the reason. According to Our Lord, there is not a home church and a foreign church, it is all one great

work, beginning at home and then going elsewhere, "beginning from Jerusalem" (RV). Jerusalem was not the home of the disciples; Jerusalem was the place where Our Lord was rejected. "Begin there," said Jesus. In His first sermon at Nazareth Our Lord said that it was God's way to send His message by strangers before it was accepted, and the history of the Church has proved that it is out of the mouth of strangers that the great awakenings have always come. Take any country that has had the life of God introduced into it, it has never been introduced by those belonging to the country, but always from outside.

In Our Lord's conception all the world is the same to God, and the command to go embraces us all. Missionaries are ordained to preach, trained to teach and to heal, skilled to win savage races for Christ, but every method is to be subordinated to the one great message of the remission of sins through faith in His blood (Romans 3:25–26). Whatever line the missionary takes, whether it be medical or educational, he has only one purpose; one great truth has gripped him and sent him forth and holds him, so that he has nothing else on earth to live for but to proclaim the Death of Christ for the remission of sins. The note of false missionary enterprise leaves out the fundamental purpose of evangelisation and says that civilisation must come first. Robert Moffatt[13] uttered solemn words when he said he little thought he would live to see the day when earnest missionaries would reverse the order of God, when the watchword would be not to evangelise first, but to civilise. Our Lord illustrates this in His parable (see Matthew 13:32). The birds of civilisation come and lodge in the branches of the spiritual tree and men say "Now this is what is to be!" and they have not seen God's purpose at all. If we do not see God's purpose we shall continually be misled by externals.

The thing to watch in all our enterprise for God is lest we should get swamped out of personal relationship to Jesus Christ, the One Who gives us the command—*"Go ye."* "I am made all things to all men," says Paul, "that I might by all means save some." The one dominating purpose and passion at the heart of the missionary is his own personal relationship to Jesus Christ. A missionary is a construction made through the Atonement by the God Who made the universe. It is not a sentiment, it is true, that God spoils a man or woman for any other use in the world saving for one thing only, to win souls to Jesus and to disciple them in His Name. The saddest thing is to see a man or woman who gave great promise of being a power for God in the world, fizzle out like an extinct volcano. The reason of it is that a rational common-

---

13. Robert Moffatt (1795–1883) was a pioneer Scottish missionary to South Africa.

sense explanation of holy things has ruthlessly torn down the great scriptural idea at the heart of the life, consequently the life has withered and become a negligible quantity from God's standpoint.

Thank God for the words of Our Lord—"He that believeth on Me," out of him "shall flow rivers of living water." Always remain true to the Fountainhead.

MISSIONARY MUNITIONS

During the Great War[14] the Minister of Munitions of this country said that everything depended on the workshops of Britain.[15] What was true in the enormous world crisis of war is symbolically true in work for God. But what are the workshops that supply the munitions for God's enterprises? The workshop of missionary munitions is the hidden, personal, worshipping life of the saint.

1. Worshipping as Occasion Serves
(*John 1:48*)
The constant, private habit of the life of the missionary ought to be worshipping as occasion serves, that is the first great essential for fitness. The time will come when no more "fig tree" life is possible; when we are right out in the open and glare of the work, and we shall find ourselves without any value then if we have not been worshipping God as occasion serves. We imagine we should be all right if a big crisis arose; but the crisis only reveals the stuff we are made of, it does not put anything into us. "If God gives the call, of course, I shall rise to the occasion." You will not, unless you have risen to the occasion in the workshop. If you are not the real article before God there, doing the duty that lies nearest, instead of being revealed as fit for God when the crisis comes, you will be revealed as unfit. Crises always reveal character, and we are all ignorant of our true character until it is revealed to us.

If you do not worship as occasion serves at home, you will be of no use in the foreign field; but if you put the worship of God first, and get the revelation of Who God is, then, when the call comes you will be ready for it, because in the unseen life and preparing, and now when the strain comes you are perfectly fit to be relied on by God. Worshipping is greater than work in that it absorbs work.

"And He saith unto him, Verily, verily, I say unto you, Ye shall see the heaven opened, and the angels of God ascending and descending upon the Son of man" (RV). Our Lord is the One in Whom God and man can meet as one. If that has never been learned in our private worshipping life, it will never be realised in active public work. "There is no need for this private worship of God, I cannot be expected to live the sanctified life in the circumstances I am in; there is no time for praying just now, no time for Bible reading; when I get out into the work and the opportunity comes for all that, of course I shall be all right." If you have not been worshipping as occasion serves, you will not only be useless when you get out into service but a tremendous hindrance to those who are associated with you. Imagine a general having ammunition made in a workshop at the back of the trenches! His men would be blown up whilst attempting it. Yet that is what we seem to expect to do in work for God.

2. Ministering as Opportunity Surrounds
(*John 13:14–15*)
Ministering as opportunity surrounds does not mean selecting our surroundings, but being very selectly God's in any haphazard surroundings He may engineer for us. The characteristics we exhibit in our immediate surroundings are an indication of what we shall be like in other circumstances by and by.

"Jesus, knowing that the Father had given all things into His hands, and that He came forth from God and goeth unto God . . ." (RV)—we might have expected the record to go on: "He was transfigured before them"; but we read that the next thing Our Lord did was of the most menial commonplace order—"He took a towel, and girded Himself. . . . Then He . . . began to wash the disciples' feet" (RV). Can we use a towel as Our Lord did? Towels and basins and feet and sandals, all the ordinary sordid things of our lives, reveal more quickly than anything what we are made of. It is not the big occasions that reveal us, but the little occasions.

---

14. The Great War: World War I (1914–1918).

15. Chambers' actual quote in his lecture was: "The first minister of munitions in this Empire has just said: 'You have read appeals for the front, appeals to the workshop, I would almost say at the present moment everything depends on the workshops of Britain. Have you read that anxious tale of the struggle which is now going on in Galicia, read it, read it well, read it intelligently and you will find how much the workshops count in this war.'"

It takes God Incarnate to do the most menial commonplace things properly.

"If I then, the Lord and the Master, have washed your feet, ye also ought to wash one another's feet" (RV). Our Lord did not say: "I have been the means of the salvation of thousands, I have been most successful in My service, now you go and do the same thing"—He said: *"I have washed your feet; you go and wash one another's feet."* We try to get out of it by washing the feet of those who do not belong to our own set—we will wash the heathen's feet, or feet in the slums, but fancy washing my brother's feet, my wife's, my husband's, the feet of the minister of my church! Our Lord said—*"one another's feet."*

Watch the humour of our Heavenly Father. It is seen in the way He brings across our path the type of person who exhibits to us what we have been like to Him. "Now," He says, "show that one the same love that I have shown you." If Jesus Christ has lifted us in love and grace, we must show that love to someone else. It is of no use to say—"Oh, I will do all that when I get out to the field." The only way to produce the munitions for God's enterprises is to minister as opportunity surrounds us now, and God will surround us with ample opportunity of doing to others as He has done to us.

The workshop for missionary munitions on which God draws for His work is the private lives of those who are not only saved and sanctified by Him, but who immediately begin to minister where they are. We read of Peter's wife's mother that when Jesus touched her, "she arose, and ministered unto Him" (RV); a perfect and complete deliverance, and immediate service; there was no interesting convalescent stage. Some people do not like to get saved all of a sudden, they do not like to have their problems solved in a lightning flash, they prefer to be spiritual sponges—and mop up all the sympathy they can. Peter's wife's mother is the type of the life in which God has done His work. In the full and amazing strength of God, she arose and did what lay nearest, and went on as if she had never been ill.

3. Graduating as Obligations Separate (Matthew 11:28–29)

Verse 29—"Take My yoke upon you, and learn of Me," is the graduating course in the training school of Our Lord. Many of us get as far as verse 28—"Come unto Me," then come the obligations which separate us from all else, and we have to enter into the discipline of fellowship. We have to take upon us His yoke, and see that we bow our neck to no other yoke; then when the strain comes, we can go through anything.

"Learn of Me; for I am meek and lowly in heart." We say readily—"Of course Jesus was meek and lowly," but was He? Read the account of the cleansing of the Temple; where is the meek and mild and gentle Jesus there? He "made Himself of no reputation," but when His Father's honour was touched, all was different. The meekness and lowliness of Our Lord is seen in His relationship to His Father; He never murmured at anything His Father brought, and never gave way to self-pity. That is the meekness and lowliness of heart we need to learn, and we shall never learn it unless the Redemption of Our Lord has been at work in us, completely restoring and emancipating us, and getting us into yoke with Him. If we have taken His yoke upon us, we shall never say when things are difficult—"Why should this happen to me?" We shall be meek toward God's dispensations for us as Jesus was meek towards His Father.

"And ye shall find rest unto your souls," you will make the continual discovery of the undisturbedness of heart which is the delight of those who "follow the Lamb whithersoever He goeth."

The workshop of missionary munitions is the temple of the Holy Ghost, our actual bodily lives. "Know ye not that *ye* are the temple of God?"

THE MISSIONARY'S MASTER

To have a master and to be mastered are not the same thing, but diametrically opposed. If I have the idea that I am being mastered, it is a sure proof that I have no master. If I feel I am in subjection to someone, then I may be sure that that someone is not the one I love. To have a master means to have one who is closer than a friend, one whom I know knows me better than I know myself, one who has fathomed the remotest abyss of my heart and satisfied it, one who brings me the secure sense that he has met and solved every perplexity of my mind—that, and nothing less, is to have a master. Jesus Christ is the Master of the missionary. The conception of mastership that we get from human life is totally different from the mastership of Jesus. If I have the idea that I am being mastered by Jesus, then I am far from being in the relationship to Himself He wants me to be in, a relationship where He is easily Master without my conscious knowledge of it, all I am aware of is that I am His to obey.

Our Lord never takes measures to make us obey Him. Our obedience is the outcome of a oneness of spirit with Him through His Redemption. That is why, whenever Our Lord talked about discipleship, He prefaced it with an "IF"—"you do not need to unless you like"; but—"*If* any man will be My disciple, let him deny himself," i.e., "deny his independence, give up his right to himself to Me." Our Lord is not talking about a man's position hereafter, but about being of value to Him in this order of things. Human authority always insists on obedience; Our Lord never does. He makes His standard very clear, and if the relation of the spirit within me is that of love to Him, then I do all He says without any hesitation. If I begin to hesitate and to debate, it is because I love someone else in competition with Him, viz., myself. The only word by which to describe mastership in experience is *love*—"If ye love Me, ye will keep My commandments" (RV).

Obedience to Jesus Christ is essential, but not compulsory; He never insists on being Master. We feel that if only He would insist, we should obey Him. But Our Lord never enforces His "thou shalt's" and "thou shalt not's"; He never takes means to force us to do what He says; He never coerces. In certain moods we wish He would *make* us do the thing, but He will not; and in other moods we wish He would leave us alone altogether, but He will not. If we do not keep His commandments, He does not come and tell us we are wrong, we know it, we cannot get away from it. There is no ambiguity in our mind as to whether what He says is right. Our Lord never says "you *must*," but if we are to be His disciples we know we must. Christianity is not a "sanctified" anything; it is the life of Jesus manifested in our mortal flesh by the miracle of His Redemption, and that will mean that whenever a crisis comes, Jesus is instantly seen to be Master without a moment's hesitation; there is no debate.

"Ye call Me Master and Lord: and ye say well; for so I am"—But *is* He? The great consciousness in the mind of Our Lord is that He is our Master, and we, too, have to come into this consciousness. "Master" and "Lord" have very little place in our spiritual vocabulary; we prefer the words "Saviour" and "Sanctifier" and "Healer." In other words, we know very little about love as Jesus revealed it. It is seen in the way we use the word "obey." Our use of the word implies the submission of an inferior to a superior; obedience in Our Lord's use of the word is the relationship of equals, a son and father. ". . . though He were a Son, yet learned He obedience by the things which He suffered." Our Lord was not a servant of God, He was His Son. The Son's obedience as Redeemer was *because He was* Son, not in order *to be* Son.

1. The Master Touch in Sickness—
The Master Physician
And He touched her hand, and the fever left her; and she arose, and ministered unto Him. (Matthew 8:15 RV)

These words crystallise for us the revelation of Our Lord as the Master Physician. When He touches, there is no convalescence. Unless the missionary is one who has been touched by the Master Physician, his touch may be one of skill but not of supreme healing. When Our Lord is the Master of a disciple, He conveys His effectual touch through him to others.

Touch has more power than even speech to convey the personality. If some people touch us, we feel the worse for it for days; if others touch us, we live a transfigured life for days. That is an experience recognisable by us all, but we may not have realised that it is because the touch conveys the dominating personality behind. A caress from a bad personality is incarnated hypocrisy. It is at grave peril to our own souls that we ignore these subtle indications of warning. When once the barriers that God creates around His children are broken down and His warnings ignored, we shall find that the enemy will break through at the places we have broken down. If we keep in touch with the Master, He will keep us out of touch with badness.

The Master touch of Our Lord breaks the fever of self, and life is profoundly altered. When Our Lord is the Master of a disciple, no matter where he goes, His touch comes through him all the time. She only "touched the hem of His garment." The missionary is, as it were, the hem of His garment, and virtue goes out through the garment's hem to the needy one who touched.

2. The Master Touch in Sightlessness—
The Master Artist
Then touched He their eyes, saying, According to your faith be it done unto you. (Matthew 9:29 RV)

The Master Touch produces sight.

In human sight the thing we soon lose is what Ruskin called "the innocence of the eye." An artist records exactly from this "innocence" of sight, he does not bring in his logical faculties and interfere with what he sees by telling himself what he ought to see. Most of us know what we are looking at, and instead of trusting the "innocence" of sight, we confuse it by trying to tell ourselves what we see. If ever you have been taught by anyone to *see*, you will know what this means. Drummond[16] says that Ruskin taught him to *see*. An artist does not tell us what he sees, he enables us to see; he communicates the unutterable identity of what he sees. It is a great thing to see *with* anyone.

---

16. Henry Drummond (1851–1897) was a Scottish writer and evangelist.

Jesus never tells us what to see, but when His touch is upon our eyes, we know that we see what He is seeing, He restores this pristine innocence of sight. "Except a man be born again, he cannot *see* the kingdom of God."

An artist conveys his personality by means of his medium and creates wonderful things, and if the Master touch has given the missionary his sight, God can do wonderful things through him. Paul was sent by God to *"open [men's] eyes*, and to turn them from darkness to light."

A skilled artist does not need to use more than two or three colours; an amateur requires all the tubes in his box squirted out like a condensed rainbow. The Master Artist used strange things to open blind eyes, e.g., spittle, clay, and water from a pool—but remember *He* used them, and He produced the miracle of sight. The missionary may easily be looked on as one of the despised things, but if Jesus uses him, he will produce sight in men.

3. The Master Touch in Hearing—
The Master Musician
And He touched his ear, and healed him. (Luke 22:51)

When the Master touch comes on the sick or the sightless or the deaf, the miracle of the personality is conveyed at once. Touch conveys the personality to the flesh and to the sight, and sound conveys the personality to the hearing. It is personality that gives to sound, which is un-moral, its moral or immoral character. There is some music, for instance, that you lis-

ten to at the peril of your soul because of the personality behind it. Better by far be unmusical than listen to it. The one who is healed by the Master Musician has the personality of God conveyed to him. When we have been ravished with the wonder of the Master Musician's music, He gives us a badly tuned instrument to put into repair for Him.

4. The Master Touch in Speech—
The Master Speaker
And He took him aside from the multitude . . . and touched his tongue. (Mark 7:33)

This incident is one of many that reveal the unique use of speech by Our Lord. "And looking up to heaven, He sighed, and saith unto him, Ephphatha, that is, Be opened." The tongue was in its right place in Our Lord, He only used it to speak the words of God, He never spoke from His right to Himself. "The words that I say unto you I speak not from Myself: but the Father abiding in Me, doeth His works" (RV). The words Jesus spoke were the exact expression of the thought of God. "And the Word was God."

The Master Speaker, after conveying His life to us by means of His words, turns us loose into a tower of Babel and tells us to speak His messages there. The missionary is one whom Jesus Christ has taken aside from the multitude, and, having put His fingers into his ears and touched his tongue, has sent him straight forth from hearing his Master, with his own tongue loosened and his speech plain, to speak "all the words of this life."

THE MISSIONARY'S WAY

I am the way, and the truth, and the life. John 14:6

However far we may drift, we must always come back to these words of our Lord: "I am the way"—not a road that we leave behind us, but the way itself. Jesus Christ is the way *of God*, not a way that leads to God; that is why He says—"Come unto *Me,*" "abide in *Me.*" "I am . . . the truth," not the truth about God, not a set of principles, but the truth itself. Jesus Christ is the Truth *of God.* "No man cometh unto the Father, but by Me." We can get to God as Creator in other ways, but no man can come to God as Father in any other way than by Jesus Christ (cf. Matthew 11:27). "I am . . . the life." Jesus Christ is the Life *of God* as He is the Way and the Truth of God. Eternal life is not a gift from God, it is the gift of *God Himself.* The life imparted to me by Jesus is the life of God. "He that hath the Son hath the life"; "I am come that they

might have life"; "And this is life eternal, that they should know Thee the only true God" (RV). We have to abide in the *way*; to be incorporated into the *truth*; to be infused by the *life*.

1. The Conditions of the Way
Have this mind in you, which was also in Christ Jesus. (Philippians 2:5)

Paul goes on to state the characteristics of the mind which we are to form, viz., the mind which was in Christ Jesus when He was on this earth, utterly self-effaced and self-emptied; not the mind of Christ when He was in glory. We receive the Spirit of Christ as a gift, but we do not receive His mind, we have to construct that, and this is done in the same way that we construct the natural mind, viz., by the way our disposition reacts when we come in contact with external things. Mind, or soul, is the way the personal spirit expresses itself in the body. We have to lose our own way of thinking and form Jesus Christ's way. "Acquire your soul with patience." It takes time and discipline. When we are regenerated and have the life of the Son of God in us, God engineers our circumstances in order that we may form the mind of Christ.

(a) Of Exaltation
Who, being in the form of God, counted it not a thing to be grasped to be on an equality with God. (RV mg)

Our Lord's exaltation was His equality with the Father. In the Christian life there are stages of experience that are exalted; times when we know what it is to live in the heavenly places in Christ Jesus, when we seem to be more on the mount than anywhere else. But we are not made for the mountain, we are made for the valley; we are made for the actual world, not for the ideal world; but to be so in communion with the ideal that we can work it out in the actual and make it real. There is no life like the life of a missionary for bringing the ideal and the actual together. "Come unto Me, . . . and I will give you rest," said Jesus; "I will bring the ideal and the actual into one."

(b) Of Subordination
But emptied Himself. (RV)

Our Lord annihilated Himself from His former exaltation and took "the form of a servant, being made in the likeness of men; . . . He humbled Himself, becoming obedient even unto death, yea, the death of the cross" (RV). Our Lord by His own choice emptied Himself of all His former glory; and if we are to enter into fellowship with Him, we must deliberately go through the annihilation, not of glory, but of our right to ourselves in every shape and form. Our Lord's former condition was one of absolute equality with God: our former condition is one of absolute independence of God. "Let him deny himself," says Jesus. It is easy to do it in theory, easy to *count* all things but loss. Paul says he not only counted all things but loss, he *"suffered* the loss of all things" that he might win Christ. It is a sad thing to only come the length of counting the loss and say, "Oh yes, I see it will cost me my right to myself, it will cost me the world, it will cost me everything; but I do not intend to experience the loss. These things sound all right in the ideal, but they hit a bit too hard in the actual."

(c) Of Sanctification
"And for their sakes I sanctify Myself." The idea of sanctification as Our Lord here uses it is the separation of holiness to God's use and for God's purpose. Our Lord separated His holy Self to God. This idea of sanctification worked out in a missionary's life

means more than the fact that he is personally identified with his Lord, it means that he deliberately sets apart his sanctified self for God. The experience of sanctification is usually presented as a personal identification with Jesus Christ by which He is made unto us sanctification; the sanctification Our Lord refers to is the sanctification of that sanctification. Beware of the idea of sanctification that makes a man say— "Now I am sanctified I can do what I like." If he does, he is immoral. Even Christ pleased not Himself. If our experience of sanctification ends in pious sentiment, the reason is that it has never dawned on us that we must deliberately set our sanctified selves apart for God's use as Jesus did.

2. The Commission of the Way
As the Father hath sent Me, even so send I you. (John 20:21 RV)

Our Lord's first obedience was not to the needs of men, not to the consideration of where He would be most useful, but to the will of His Father. "Lo, I am come . . . to do Thy will, O God" (RV). And the first obedience of the missionary is to the will of his Lord. "Ye call Me Master and Lord: and ye say well; for so I am"; but does it mean any more to us than the mere saying of it? "If I then, the Lord and the Master, have washed your feet, ye also ought to wash one another's feet" (RV), and we cannot do it by sentiment. It was in the hour when Jesus knew "that the Father had given all things into His hands, and that He came forth from God, and goeth unto God" (RV) that He began to wash the disciples' feet; and it is when we realise our union with Jesus Christ as our Lord and Master that we shall follow His example. It takes God Incarnate to do the meanest duty as it ought to be done. When Jesus touched things that were sordid and ordinary, He transfigured them.

(a) The Witness (John 8:18–19; 15:27)
Just as Our Lord was a witness Who satisfied His Father; so a Christian witness is one who satisfies his Master. "Ye shall be My witnesses" (RV); "not witnesses to what I can do, but witnesses who satisfy Me in any circumstances I put you in. I reckon on you for extreme service, with no complaining on your part and no explanation on Mine." Being a martyr does not necessarily involve being a witness, but being a witness will involve martyrdom.

(b) The Word (John 14:10; 17:8)
Our Lord says that His word was not His own, but His Father's. Jesus never spoke from His right to Himself. "The words that I say unto you, I speak not from [RV] Myself." Jesus Christ is the Word of God in His own Person; He spoke the words of God with

a human tongue, and He has given to His disciples the words the Father gave to Him. The disciple has not only to speak the words of God with his tongue, but to bear the evidence of being a word of the Son, as Jesus was the Word of God. To "confess" Christ means to say, not only with the tongue, but with every bit of our life, that Jesus has come into our flesh. The Son was the exact expression of the Father, and the saint must be an exact expression of the Son.

(c) The Work (John 9:4; 14:12)

"We must work the works of Him that sent Me" (RV). According to Our Lord, the need is never the call. The need is the opportunity; the call is the call of God. The call of God is like the call of the sea, or of the mountains, or of the ice-fields; no one hears those calls who has not the nature of the sea or of the mountains or of the ice-fields in him; and no one hears the call of God who has not the nature of the Almighty in him. If we have received the nature of God then we begin slowly to discern what God wants us to do. Never have the idea that your discernment of the need is the call. The need is the opportunity which will prove whether you are worthy of the call. Because you realise a need you have no right to say— "I must go"; if you are sanctified, you cannot go unless you are sent.

3. The Conflict of the Way

If the world hateth you, ye know that it hath hated Me before it hated you. (John 15:18 RV)

Our Lord told His disciples over and over again that they must lay their account with the hatred of the world.

(a) Of Contrast (Matthew 10:16)

In this verse Our Lord gives the vivid contrast of sheep and wolves, of doves and serpents, and He uses the contrast in a particular connection, viz., that of proclaiming His Gospel.

(b) Of Contumely (Matthew 10:17–20)

If these verses are unfamiliar to us to-day, it is because we are out of the centre of identification with Our Lord's purposes, and are seeking to bring Him into our enterprises; but as surely as we are in fellowship with Him, we shall find the terrible and unpalatable truth expressed in these verses to be a very actual portion.

(c) Of Courage (Matthew 10:22–24)

The courage Our Lord alludes to here is that born in a heart in vivid relationship to Himself, compelling the body to perform the will of God even at the cost of death. Our Lord makes little of physical death, but He makes much of moral and spiritual death.

4. The Consolations of the Way

I will not leave you desolate: I come unto you. (John 14:18 RV)

The consolations of the ways are not the sympathies of human sensibilities, but the great sustainings of the personal Holy Ghost.

(a) Of Love (John 17:26)

The first mighty name for the consolations of the way is love—"that the love wherewith Thou lovedst Me may be in them" (RV). It is the Holy Ghost Who brings this consolation, He sheds abroad the love of God in our hearts, the nature of God as exhibited in Jesus, with its impenetrable reserves. No human being can pump up what is not there. The consolation of love is not that of exquisite human understanding, it is the real nature of God holding the individual life in effectual rectitude and effectual communion in the face of anything that may ever come.

(b) Of Joy (John 15:11)

Joy is not happiness, joy is the result of the perfect ful-filment of the purpose of the life. We never want praise if we have done perfectly what we ought to do; we only want praise if we are not sure whether we have done well. Jesus did not want praise; He did not need it, and He says "that My joy may be in you" (RV). The joy of Jesus Christ was in the absolute self-surrender and self-sacrifice of Himself to His Father, the joy of doing what the Father sent Him to do—"I delight to do Thy will," and that is the joy He prays may be in His disciples. It is not a question of trying to work as Jesus did, but of having the personal presence of the Holy Ghost Who works in us the nature of Jesus. One of the consolations of the way is the fathomless joy of the Holy Ghost manifesting itself in us as it did in the Son of God in the days of His flesh.

(c) Of Peace (John 14:27)

The peace Jesus refers to here is not the peace of a conscience at rest, but the peace that characterised His own life. "My peace I give unto you." His peace is a direct gift through the personal presence of the Holy Ghost.

5. The Consummation of the Way

We will come unto him, and make Our abode with him. (John 14:23)

Jesus says that the relationship between the Father and the Son is to be the relationship between the Father and the Son and the sanctified soul.

(a) Oneness (John 17:22)

"That they may be one, even as We are one." Are we as close to Jesus Christ as that? God will not leave us alone until we are. There is one prayer that God must answer, and that is the prayer of Jesus.

(b) Sovereignty (Matthew 19:28–29)

Peter in his Epistle says that we are to be "a royal priesthood." The sovereignty alluded to by Peter, and by Our Lord in these verses, is ultimately to be a literal sovereignty, as well as a spiritual sovereignty.

(c) Glory (John 17:22)

"The glory which Thou hast given Me I have given unto them" (RV). What was the glory that Jesus had when He was Son of Man? It was not an external glory; Jesus effaced the Godhead in Himself so effectually that men without the Spirit of God despised Him. His glory was the glory of actual holiness, and that is the glory He says He gives to the saint. The glory of the saint is the glory of actual holiness manifested in actual life here and now. There is a glory which the saint is only to behold, "that they may behold My glory, which Thou hast given Me" (John 17:24). What is that glory? "The glory which I had with Thee before the world was." That glory we are not to share, but to behold. The word "glory" here must be understood in the same sense as the word "form" in Philippians 2:6. It refers to the absolute relation of Deity which the Son of God had before He became Incarnate.

The consummation of the missionary's way is centred in John 14:23. "We will come unto him, and make Our abode with him"—the Triune God abiding with the saint.

MISSIONARY PREDESTINATIONS

Isaiah 49:1–2

This passage refers to the whole nation of Israel, to Our Lord Jesus Christ, and to every individual saint.

1. The Election of Perfect Fitness for God

God created the people known as Israel for one purpose, to be the servant of Jehovah until through them every nation came to know Who Jehovah was. The nation created for the service of Jehovah failed to fulfil God's predestination for it; then God called out a remnant, and the remnant failed; then out of the remnant came One Who succeeded, the One Whom we know as the Lord Jesus Christ. The Saviour of the world came of this nation. He is called "the Servant of God" because He expresses exactly the creative purpose of God for the historic people of God. Through that one Man the purpose of God for the individual, for the chosen nation, and for the whole world, is to be fulfilled. It is through Him that we are made "a royal priesthood."

When this election to God in Christ Jesus is realised by us individually, God begins to destroy our prejudices and our parochial notions and to turn us into the servants of His own purpose. The experience of salvation in individual lives means the incoming of this realisation of the election of God. When we are born from above (RV mg), we understand what is incomprehensible to human reason, viz., that the predestinations of God and our infinitesimal lives are made one and the same by Him. From the standpoint of rationalism, that is nonsense; but it is revelation fact. The connection between the election of God and human free will is confusing to our Gentile type of mind, but the connection was an essential element underlying all Hebrew thought. The predestinations of God cannot be experienced by individuals of their own free choice; but when we are born again, the fact that we do choose what has been predestined of God comes to us as a revelation. The rationalist says it is absurd to imagine that the purposes of Almighty God are furthered by an individual life, but it is true. God's predestinations are the voluntary choosing of the sanctified soul. One way in which the realisation works out with us personally is when we say—"The Lord led me here." The detailed guidance of God is a literal truth in the individual lives of saints. Our relation to the election of God is the one thing to be concerned over; consequently the need can never be the call. The call is of God, and the engineering of our circumstances is of God, never on the ground of our usefulness. The call of God relates us to the purpose of God.

The Purpose of the Missionary's Creation
He hath made me. . . . (RV)

The first thing God does with us after sanctification is to "force through the channels of a single heart" the interests of the whole world by introducing into us the nature of the Holy Ghost. The nature of the Holy Ghost is the nature of the Son of God; the nature of the Son of God is the nature of Almighty God, and the nature of Almighty God is focused in John 3:16. When we are born from above (RV mg) the realisation dawns that we are built for God, not for ourselves, "He hath made me." We are brought, by means of new birth, into the individual realisation of God's great purpose for the human race, and all our small, miserable, parochial notions disappear.

If we have been living much in the presence of God, the first thing that strikes us is the smallness of the lives of men and women who do not recognise God. It did not occur to us before, their lives seemed to be broad and generous; but now there seems such a fuss of interests that have nothing whatever to do with God's purpose, and are altogether unrelated to the election of God. It is because people live in the things they possess instead of in their relationship to God, that God at times seems to be cruel. There are a thousand and one interests that God's providential hand has to brush aside as hopelessly irrelevant to His purpose, and if we have been living in those interests, we go with them (cf. Luke 12:15).

"The LORD hath called me from the womb." In this rugged phrase Isaiah declares the creative purpose of God for Israel and Judah. Creation has the opposite meaning to selection. The essential pride of Israel and Judah (and of the Pharisees in Our Lord's day) was that God was obliged to select them because of their superiority to other nations. God did not *select* them: God *created* them for one purpose, to be His bondslaves.

There were no nations until after the flood. After the flood the human race was split up into nations, and God called off one stream of the human race in Abraham, and created a nation out of that one man (see Genesis 12:2, *et seq*). The Old Testament is not a history of the nations of the world, but the history of that one nation. In secular history Israel is disregarded as being merely a miserable horde of slaves, and justly so from the standpoint of the historian. The nations to which the Bible pays little attention are much finer to read about, but they have no importance in the Redemptive purpose of God. His purpose was the creation of a nation to be His bondslave, that through that nation all the other nations should come to know Him. The idea that Israel was a magnificently developed type of nation is a mistaken one. Israel was a despised, and a despisable nation, continually turning away from God into idolatry; but nothing ever altered the purpose of God for the nation. The despised element is always a noticeable element in the purpose of God. When the Saviour of the world came, He came of that despised nation; He Himself was "despised and rejected of men," and in all Christian enterprise there is this same despised element, "things which are despised, hath God chosen."

The realisation by regeneration of the election of God, and of being made thereby perfectly fit for Him, is the most joyful realisation on earth. When we are born from above (RV mg) we *realise* the election of God, our being regenerated does not *create* it. When once we realise that through the salvation of Jesus we are made perfectly fit for God, we understand why Jesus is apparently so ruthless in His claims why He demands such absolute rectitude from the saint: He has given him the very nature of God.

The creative purpose of God for the missionary is to make him His servant, one in whom He is glorified. When once we realise this, all our self-conscious limitations will be extinguished in the extraordinary blaze of what the Redemption means. We have to see that we keep the windows of our soul open to God's creative purpose for us, and not confuse that purpose with our own intentions. Every time we do so, God has to crush our intentions and push them on one side, however it may hurt, because they are on the wrong line. We must beware lest we forget God's purpose for our life.

2. The Election of Perfect Finish for God

God elected a certain nation to be His bondslave, and through that nation a knowledge of His salvation is to come to all the world. The history of that nation is a record of awful idolatry and backsliding, they remained true neither to God's prophets nor to God Himself; but in spite of everything the fulfilment of God's purpose for the nation of His choice is certain. The election of the nation by God was not for the salvation of individuals; the elect nation was to be the instrument of salvation to the whole world. The story of their distress is due entirely to their deliberate determination to use themselves for a purpose other than God's. The beginning of their corruption was their desire to have a king and to be like other nations—"Nay; but we will have a king over us; that we also may be like all the nations; and that our king may judge us, and go out before us, and fight our battles." Whenever Israel sought to use themselves for their own purposes, God smashed those purposes up.

We must be careful not to confuse the predestination of God by making His election include every individual; or to have the idea that because God elected a certain nation through whom His salvation was to come, therefore every individual of that nation is elected to salvation. The history of the elect nation disproves this, but it does not alter God's purpose for the nation. Individuals of the elect nation have to be saved in the same way as individuals of nations that have not been elected. Election refers to the unchangeable purpose of God, not to the salvation of individuals. Each individual has to choose which line of predestination he will take—God's line or the devil's line. Individual position is determined by individual choice, but that is neither here nor there in connection with God's purpose for the human race.

Individuals enter into the realisation of the creative purpose of God for the human race by being born again of the Spirit; but we must not make the predestination of God for the race to include every individual, any more than God's predestination for the elect nation included every individual. Salvation is of universal application, but human responsibility is not done away with.

The purpose of God for man is that he should "glorify God and enjoy Him for ever." Sin has switched the human race off on to another line, but it has not altered God's purpose for the human race in the tiniest degree. The election of the perfect fitness for God of the human race is abiding. It is exhibited in the Man Christ Jesus, and that is the ideal the human race is destined to reach in spite of all that sin and the devil can do—the "measure of the stature of the fulness of Christ." As Son of Man, Jesus Christ mirrors what the human race is to be like on the basis of Redemption. Sin and the devil may do their worst, but God's purpose will only be made manifest all the more gloriously (see Romans 5:12–21).

Preparation of the Missionary's Characteristic
He hath made my mouth like a sharp sword.

The outstanding characteristic of the ancient people of God, of Our Lord Jesus Christ, and of the missionary is the "prophet," or preaching, characteristic. In the Old Testament the prophet's calling is placed above that of king and of priest. It is the lives of the prophets that prefigure the Lord Jesus Christ. The character of the prophet is essential to his work. The characteristic of God's elective purpose in the finished condition of His servant is that of preaching. "It pleased God by the foolishness of preaching to save them that believe."

Notice the emphasis that the New Testament places on "confessing," on "preaching," and on "testifying," all expressive of this perfect finish for God. And notice too that it is this characteristic that Satan attacks. He is at the back of the movement abroad to-day which advocates living a holy life, but "don't talk about it." Men never suffer because they live a godly life; they suffer for their speech. Humanly speaking, if Our Lord had held His tongue, He would not have been put to death. "If I had not come *and spoken* unto them, they had not had sin: but now they have no cloke for their sin."

A saint is made by God, "He ... made me." Then do not tell God He is a bungling workman. We do that whenever we say "I can't." To say "I can't" literally means we are too strong in ourselves to depend on God. "I can't pray in public; I can't talk in the open air." Substitute "I won't," and it will be nearer the truth. The thing that makes us say "I can't" is that we forget that we must rely entirely on the creative purpose of God and on this characteristic of perfect finish for God.

Much of our difficulty comes because we choose our own work—"Oh well, this is what I am fitted for." Remember that Jesus took a fisherman and turned him into a shepherd. That is symbolical of what He does all the time. Indoor work has to do with civilisation; we were created for out-of-door work, both naturally and spiritually. The idea that we have to consecrate our gifts to God is a dangerous one. We cannot consecrate what is not ours (1 Corinthians 4:7). We have to consecrate ourselves, and leave our gifts alone. God does not ask us to do the thing that is easy to us naturally; He only asks us to do the thing we are perfectly fitted to do by grace, and the cross will always come along that line.

3. The Election of Perfect Fittedness to God
Israel is still in the shadow of God's hand, in spite of all her wickedness. God's purposes are always fulfilled, no matter how wide a compass He may permit to be taken first.

The Plan of the Missionary's Concentration
In the shadow of His hand hath He hid me. (RV)

As applied to the saint, this phrase refers to the experience of knowing, not with a sigh, but with deepest satisfaction, that "in all the world there is none but Thee, my God, there is none but Thee." The shadow of God's hand may seem to be the cruellest, most appalling shadow that ever fell on human life, but we shall find what the disciples found—"they feared as they entered the cloud. And suddenly they saw Jesus only with themselves." Never misunderstand the shadow of God's hand. When He puts us there it is assuredly to lead us into the inner meaning of Philippians 3:10—"that I may know Him." The stern discipline that looks like distress and chastisement turns out to be the biggest benediction; it is the shadow of God's hand that keeps us perfectly fitted in Him.

The kindness and the generosity of God is known when once we come under the shadow of His hand. We may kick if we like or fume, and the fingers hurt; but when we stop kicking, the fingers caress. To say "Through the shadow of bereavement I came to know God better," is different from saying, "God took away my child because I loved him too much." That is a lie, and contrary to the God of love Jesus revealed. If there is a dark line in God's face to us, the solution does not lie in saying what is not true to fact, but in bowing our heads and waiting; the explanation is not yet. All that is dark and obscure just now will one day be as radiantly and joyously clear as the truth about God we already know. No wonder our Lord's counsel is, "Fear not!"

THE MISSIONARY GOAL

In natural life we have ambitions and aims which alter as we develop; in the Christian life the goal is given at the beginning, viz., Our Lord Himself. "Till we all come in the unity of the faith, and of the knowledge of the Son of God, unto a perfect man, unto the measure of the stature of the fulness of Christ." We do not start with our idea of what the Christian life should be, we start with Christ, and we end with Christ. Our aims in natural life continually alter as we develop, but development in the Christian life is an increasing manifestation of Jesus Christ.

1. Companionship with His Goal (*Luke 18:31–34*)

Behold, we go up to Jerusalem.

That is not the language of a martyr living beyond His dispensation. Our Lord is not foreseeing with the vision of a highly sensitive nature that His life must end in disaster, He states over and over again that He came on purpose to die. "From that time began Jesus to shew unto His disciples, how that He must go unto Jerusalem, and suffer many things of the elders and chief priests and scribes, and be killed, and the third day be raised up" (Matthew 16:21 RV). The Scriptures leave no room for the idea that Our Lord was a martyr (cf. Luke 24:25–27). Jerusalem stands in the life of our Lord as the place where He reached the climax of His Father's will.

This word of our Lord's is taken as exhibiting the missionary goal, "Behold, we go up to Jerusalem," and unless we go with Him there, we shall have no companionship with Him. The New Testament centres round one Person, the Lord Jesus Christ. We are regenerated into His Kingdom by means of His Cross, and then we go up to our Jerusalem, having His Life as our example. We must be born from above (RV mg) before we can go up to our Jerusalem, and the things He met with on His way will throw a flood of light on the things we shall meet with. Our Jerusalem means the place where we reach the climax of Our Lord's will for us, which is that we may be made one with Him as He is one with the Father. The aim of the missionary is not to win the heathen, not to be useful, but to do God's will. He *does* win the heathen, and he *is* useful, but that is not his aim; his aim is to do the will of his Lord.

2. Considering His Facing of the Way (*Luke 9:51–55*)

He stedfastly set His face to go to Jerusalem.

The set purpose of Our Lord's life was to do the will of His Father; that was His dominating interest all through. He went on His way to Jerusalem unhasting and unresting, not hurrying through the villages where they "did not receive Him, because His face was as though He were going to Jerusalem" (RV); nor loitering in those villages where they welcomed Him. Our danger is to be deflected by the things we meet with on the way to our Jerusalem—"I am so misunderstood and so persecuted here that I must get away; or, this is where I am so useful that I must stay awhile."

Ambition means a set purpose for the attainment of our own ideal, and as such it is excluded from the Kingdom of Our Lord. When the disciples asked "Who then is greatest in the kingdom of heaven?" (RV) Jesus called to Him a little child and said— "Except ye . . . become as little children, ye shall in no wise enter into the kingdom of heaven" (RV). The nature of the kingdom of heaven is revealed in the implicit nature of a child, because a child does not work according to a set ambition, he obeys the simple law of his nature. If we are children of God, the simple law of our nature is the Holy Ghost; His one set purpose is the glorification of Jesus, and He pays no attention to our secular or our religious notions.

Are we entering into competition with the purpose of the Holy Ghost by having purposes and ambitions of our own? As we face the way to our Jerusalem, we must adhere to the set purpose of the Holy Ghost, which is to glorify Jesus. We must never be deflected by the pride of those who reject us because of that purpose, nor be deterred by the prejudices of those in the same way with us. We must consider *Him*, and go up to Jerusalem *with Him*. The "one thing" in the life of the Apostle Paul was not an ambition; it was a set purpose born of the Holy Ghost in him.

3. Comparing His Faring on the Way (*Luke 13:22–35*)

And He went on His way through cities and villages, teaching, and journeying on unto Jerusalem. (Luke 13:22 RV)

Our Lord was not fanatical. Had He been a fanatic, He would have said—"Because I am going up to Jerusalem there is no need to stay in this village or that; I have only one duty, and that is to go up to Jerusalem." Our Lord took plenty of time to do His duty in the cities and villages that He went through on His way up to Jerusalem. Nothing made Him hurry through the villages where He was persecuted, or linger in those where He was blessed.

Verses 31–33. Our Lord met deceit on His way to Jerusalem, but it did not deter Him from His set purpose.

Verses 34–35. Our Lord also realised desperate distress on His way, but nothing caused Him to swerve one hair's breadth from the set purpose of God.

As workers for God we shall meet with deceit and with distress on our way to Jerusalem, for "the disciple is not above his Master." It is true of the Master that "He shall not fail nor be discouraged." In the intimate circle of Our Lord's own disciples there was one whom He called a devil, but He never allowed that to deter or discourage Him.

Various things will make us forget to do our duty, e.g., excess of joy (*see* Acts 12:12). In the excitement of a revival we become so taken up with joy that we forget the home duties and everything else.

4. Contemplating His Findings on the Way (*Luke 17:11–19*)

And it came to pass, as they were on the way to Jerusalem . . . there met Him ten men that were lepers. (RV)

Our Lord met ingratitude on His way to Jerusalem— "Were not the ten cleansed? but where are the nine?" but it did not turn Him from His purpose. We shall meet the same thing on the way to our Jerusalem, there will be people who get blessed and one or two will show gratitude, and the rest gross ingratitude. Never allow this feeling to come in—"Well, I am going to do no more for that one, I did everything I could for him and all I got was gross ingratitude." That sentiment will deflect us from going up to our Jerusalem. We are not here to serve our own purpose; we are here, by the grace of God and by His indwelling Spirit, to glorify our Lord and Master. If He brings us up against callous people, mean, ungrateful, sponging people, we must never turn our faces for one second from our Jerusalem, because that is a temper of mind in which Jesus cannot be glorified.

We have to learn to go the second mile with God. Some of us get played out in the first ten yards because God compels us to go where we cannot see the way, and we think we will wait until we get nearer the big crisis. We can all see the big crisis—"Oh yes, I would like to do that for God"; but what about the obscure duty waiting to be done? If we do not do the walking, steadily and carefully, in the little matters, we shall do nothing when the big crisis comes. We shall flag when there is no vision, no uplift—just the common round, the trivial task; but if we keep our faces steadfastly set towards our Jerusalem, and go there considering Him, it will not be possible for drudgery to damp us.

5. Concerning His Finishing on the Way (*Luke 19:11–28*)

And He added and spake a parable, because He was nigh to Jerusalem.

As Our Lord drew near to His Cross the disciples became more and more perplexed; until at last, at the end of three years of the most intimate contact with Him, they said "What is it that He saith unto us? . . . We know not what He saith" (RV). After the Resurrection, Our Lord breathed on them and said— "Receive ye the Holy Ghost." "And their eyes were opened, and they knew Him." "Then opened He their mind, that they might understand the scriptures" (RV). If we try to get "head first" into what Our Lord teaches, we shall exhibit the same stupidity as the disciples did, until we have received the Holy Spirit and learnt to rely on Him, and to interpret the words of Jesus as He brings them to our mind.

6. Consummating His Fulfilment at the Goal (*Luke 23:33*)

There they crucified Him.

That is what happened to Our Lord when He reached Jerusalem, but that "happening" is the gateway to our salvation. By His death on the Cross, Our Lord made the way for every son of man to come into communion with God. The saints do not end in crucifixion; by the Lord's grace, they end in glory. In the meantime the missionary's watchword is—"Behold, I too go up to Jerusalem."

THE MISSIONARY PROBLEM

1. Scheme of Enterprise

Ask of Me, and I will give thee the nations for thine inheritance, and the uttermost parts of the earth for thy possession. (Psalm 2:8 RV)

The emphasis in this Psalm and all through the Bible is that missionary enterprise is God's thought, not man's. We do not know, apart from the Spirit of God, what God's purpose is. The problems surrounding work in the mission field, and any branch of Christian work, are too big to be coped with by man's intellect alone; yet the humblest saint in communion with God works out God's answer to every problem, for the most part unconsciously to himself. To attempt to understand the problems that are pressing on the shores of Christian work to-day at home and abroad, apart from God, will result in an absolute bewilderment of mind and spirit. It must all come back to one point, a personal relationship to God in Christ Jesus. There is nothing simple in the human soul or in human life; only one thing is simple, and that is the relationship of the individual soul to God, "the simplicity that is in Christ." In work for God it is not sufficient to be awake to the need, to be in earnest, to want to do something; it is necessary to prove from every standpoint, moral, intellectual and spiritual, that the only way to live is in personal relationship to God. It is the individual men and women living a life rooted and grounded in God, who are fulfilling God's purpose in the world.

The great Author and Originator of all missionary enterprise is God, and we must keep in touch with His line. The call to the missionary does not arise out of the discernment of his own mind, or from the sympathy of his own heart, but because behind the face of every distorted, downtrodden heathen, he sees the face of Jesus Christ, and hears His command—"Go ye therefore, and make disciples of all the nations" (RV). The need of the heathen world can only be met by our Risen Lord Who has all power in heaven and in earth, and by our receiving from Him the endurement of power from on high. We have to see that we conserve the energy of regenerating grace planted in us by the Holy Ghost through the Atonement, then wherever we go, the rivers of living water will flow through our lives.

From the very beginning God's work has seemed a forlorn hope, as if He were being worsted; and all the arguments seem to be in favour of working on other lines—the line of education, of healing, and of civilisation. These are the "birds" which come and lodge in the branches, and men are saying that the present manifestation of civilisation is the outcome of Christianity. "*This*," they say, "is Christianity, this is the thing, these educational forces, these healing and civilising forces. This is what missions ought to be doing, not going off on the line of personal sanctification or of devotion to Jesus; we have grown out of all that. We must devote ourselves to the things we can see; we must educate and train these benighted races and introduce our wider, better views, and in that way the Kingdom of God will come in." This is not God's way. God will bring in His Kingdom in His own way. Jesus says that in this dispensation "the kingdom of God cometh not with observation. . . . Behold, the kingdom of God is within you." All these forces of civilisation have been allowed to lodge in the branches of the spiritual tree of Christianity, whilst the Life that makes them possible is not recognised. They receive shelter from that which they are not themselves, and men's eyes are blinded to the real issue. It is astounding how far away men will get when once they leave the humble stand of a life hid with Christ in God.

2. Spiritual Evangelisation

And the heathen shall know that I am the Lord, saith the LORD God, when I shall be sanctified in you before their eyes. (Ezekiel 36:23)

The first purpose of missionary enterprise is evangelistic, and the evangel is that of personal sanctification. A missionary and a Christian ought to be one and the same, and a Christian is one who is united to his Lord by a living union of character. It is easy to rouse enthusiasm along medical, educational and industrial lines, on the ground that wherever Christianity is made known, social development follows. This is true, but all these things are secondary. The first aim of missionary enterprise is the spiritual evangelisation of the people, and the missionary must be united to Jesus Christ by the spiritual bond of sanctification before he can evangelise others. Wherever a Christian is placed, he must work out the sanctified life. We have to beware of the notion that spirituality is something divorced from contact with sordid realities. The one and only test of a spiritual life is in practical reality. When a missionary's life is taken and placed down under the black night of heathenism, there is only one thing that can stand, and that is the sanctification wrought by God—a personal union with Jesus Christ, and the realisation that he is there for one purpose only, to make disciples of Jesus Christ.

If missionary enthusiasm is awakened without missionary knowledge being given, men go out totally unprepared to face the conditions in heathen lands, and every hour of the day they are faced with moral problems that shock every human sensibility. Unless the call of God has been heard, and the mind and nerves are prepared to face these things from God's standpoint, the whole nature fails under the strain, and the result is, either that the missionary returns home broken, or that he sinks down into oblivion on the mission field itself. We have to call ourselves up short in reading missionary books that sweep us off our feet, and see if they tally with God's purpose. It is extraordinary how few of them do. It is the needs of the heathen that are put first, the awfulness of the conditions that prevail in heathen lands. None of this constitutes the call for a missionary. The appeal is based on the command of our Lord—"Go ye therefore, and make disciples of all the nations" (RV). Not—"Go because the conditions of the heathen will be improved"; they will be, but the great motive of the missionary is the command of Jesus Christ for spiritual evangelisation. We have to guard our motive in work for God as jealously as we would guard anything that God actually put into our hand. It needs more courage to face God with our motive in work for Him than it does to face an audience with our message. We have continually to face our own personal sanctification and our motive for service, with the Lord Himself, to let His searchlight come, and to see that we remain true to Him. We are not sent to develop the races, we are sent to preach the gospel to every creature because Our Lord has commanded it, *and for no other reason*. God's purpose is at the back of the whole thing, and His purpose is revealed by His Spirit to sanctified souls only.

To-day people are trying to better Jesus Christ's programme, and are saying that they must first of all look after men's bodies, heal them and teach them, and then evangelise them. This reminds one of the legend which says that the birds decided that whichever of them could fly the highest, should be their king; whereupon the wren perched on the back of the eagle, and when the eagle soared up into the sky, the little wren flew up higher still. Many modern books on missionary enterprise are like the wren on the back of the eagle, they think they can go one better than Jesus Christ, "His teaching was all very well for the beginning stages, but now we can go one better."

Missionary enterprise on the line of education, and healing, and social amelioration is magnificent, but it is secondary, and the danger is to give it the first place. The temptation is more subtle to-day than ever it has been, because the countries of the world are being opened up as never before. It sounds so plausi-ble and right to say—Heal the people, teach them, put them in better surroundings, and then evangelise them; but it is fundamentally wrong. The cry "Civilise first, and then evangelise" has honeycombed itself into missionary work in every land; and it takes the Spirit of God to show where it is in direct opposition to God's line. It is putting men's needs first, and that is the very heart and kernel of the temptation Satan brought to Our Lord. Our Lord's first obedience was not to the needs of men, but to the will of His Father. We must beware of putting anything first that Jesus does not put first. The testimony of missionaries over and over again is to the effect that when once evangelistic work is put in the second place, it is the devil who gets his way, not God. Dr. Moffatt said that civilisation drives away the tiger, but breeds the fox. That was the statement of a man after years of work in the mission field, and with ample opportunity of estimating all the forces at work. The introduction of civilisation, without the emphasis on living the life hid with Christ in God, tends to increase the power of evil because it covers it with a veil of refinement.

"The heathen shall know that I am the LORD . . . when I shall be sanctified *in you* before their eyes." The only reason for a Christian to go out to the mission field is that his own life is hid with Christ in God, and the compulsion of the providence of God outside, working with the imperative call of His Spirit inside, has wedded itself to the command of Jesus— "Go ye therefore, and make disciples of all the nations" (RV). The awakening force spiritually will not come from the civilisation of the West, but from the lives of the lonely, obscure missionaries who have stood true to God, and through whom the rivers of living water have flowed.

3. Supernatural Hope for Missions

Thus saith the LORD, Stand ye in the ways, and see, and ask for the old paths, where is the good way, and walk therein, and ye shall find rest for your souls. (Jeremiah 6:16)

In looking back over centuries of missionary work, the tendency is to say—"This is where that effort failed, and this is where the other failed"; but the real reason for the failure is missed, viz., that God's ideal had been abandoned. If you talk about the need for personal sanctification to an aggressive Christian worker, he will say—"You are a dreamer of dreams, we have to get to work and *do* something"; whereas it is not a question of doing things, but a question of realising deep down until there is no shadow of doubt about it, that if we are going to do anything, it must be by the supernatural power of God, not by our own ingenuity and wisdom. Holiness people are not unpractical, they are the only ones who are building on the great underlying ideal of God. Our business as workers for God is to find out what God's ideal is, to ask ourselves on what line we are doing our duty; whether we are progressing along the line of God's ideal, and working that out, or being caught up in the drift of modern views and evolving away from God's ideal. The Sermon on the Mount is the perpetual standard of measurement for those at work for God, and yet the statements of Jesus Christ are continually being watered down, and even contradicted by many to-day. There is not the slightest use in going to the foreign field to work for God if we are not true to His ideal at home. We should be a disgrace to Him there.

How many of us really live up to all the light we have? If we examine ourselves before God, we will find that we dare not go one step beyond our own crowd, no matter what the Lord says. If we get any new light on God's word, or on His will for our lives, we take on the cringe of the coward—"I wonder if the others have seen that"; or, "Oh well, if they do not do it, I must not." Very few of us walk up to the light we get unless someone else will go with us. For instance, if we notice how often Jesus Christ talks about being persecuted and cast out for His Name's sake, we shall soon see how far we have fallen away from His ideal. Even the most spiritual among us have little of the genius of the Holy Ghost in our lives. We accept the ordinary common-sense ways of doing things without ever examining them in the light of God. When we do begin to re-relate our lives in accordance with God's ideal, we shall encounter the scorn, or the amazement, or the ridicule, or pity of the crowd we belong to. There are books and teachers that tell us that when God is at work in our lives, it will be manifested in ostensible ways of blessing. Jesus says that the ostensible way in which it will work out is the way of ridicule. "As He is, so are we in this world." What we are insisting on is a right relationship to God first, and then the carrying out of work along God's line. Whether our work is a success or a failure has nothing to do with us. Our call is not to successful service, but to faithfulness. Our Lord demands of us a personal watchful relationship to Himself, and the doing of the duty that lies nearest from that standpoint; and whether men recognise it or not, it will tell for eternity whether we are in the home or the foreign field. It depends on our standpoint which line we emphasise. A personal relationship to Jesus Christ first, then from that basis, as much practical work as possible. Unless the missionary is based on a right relationship to God, he will fizzle out in the passing of the years and become a negligible quantity from God's standpoint. The men and women who stand absolutely true to God's ideal are the ones who are telling for God. God has staked His honour on the work of Jesus Christ in the souls of those whom He has saved, and sanctified, and sent.

THE KEY TO THE MISSIONARY PROBLEM

Matthew 9:38

1. The Key to the Master's Orders

Pray ye therefore . . .

The key to the missionary problem is in the hand of God, not of man, and according to Our Lord, the key is prayer, not work, as that word is popularly understood, because work may mean evading spiritual concentration. Our Lord says—*"Pray* ye therefore. . . ."

We are not speaking of the lock which the key has to open, viz., the problems of missionary enterprise, but of the *key* to those problems. That key is put into our hands by Jesus Christ, and it is not a common-sense key. It is not a medical key, nor a civilising key, nor an educational key, not even an evangelical key; the key is prayer. We are challenged straight away by the difference between our view of prayer and Our Lord's view. Prayer to us is not practical, it is stupid, and until we do see that prayer is stupid, that is, stupid from the ordinary natural common-sense point of view, we will never pray. "It is absurd to think that God is going to alter things in answer to prayer!" But that is what Jesus says He will do. It sounds stupid, but it is a stupidity based on His Redemption. The reason that our prayers are not answered is that we are not stupid enough to believe what Jesus says. It is a child, and only a child who has prayer answered; a wise and prudent man does not (cf. Matthew 11:25). We have to be as natural as children in our relationship to Jesus Christ, and He does His work all the time. Jesus Christ is our Master, and He lays down His orders very distinctly—"Pray ye therefore. . . ."

(a) Prayer the Work (John 14:12–14)

We are apt to think of prayer as a common-sense exercise of our higher powers in order to prepare us for work; whereas in the teaching of Jesus, prayer is not to fit us for the "greater works," prayer *is* the work. Prayer is the outcome of our apprehension of the nature of God, the means whereby we assimilate more and more of His mind, and the means whereby He unveils His purposes to us.

(b) Prayer the Fruit (John 15:16)

The way fruit remains is by prayer. Our Lord puts prayer as the means to fruit-producing and fruit-abiding work; but, remember, it is prayer based on His agony, not on our agony. God is not impressed by our earnestness, He nowhere promises to answer prayer because of our agony in intercession, but only on the ground of Redemption. We have "boldness to enter into the holiest *by the blood of Jesus*," and in no other way. We take the crown off Redemption as the ground on which God answers prayer and put it on our own earnestness. Prayer is the miracle of Redemption at work in us, which will produce the miracle of Redemption in the lives of others.

(c) Prayer the Battle (Ephesians 6:11–20)

The armour is for the battle of prayer. "Take up the whole armour of God. . . . Stand therefore, . . ." and then pray. The armour is not to fight in, but to shield us while we pray. Prayer is the battle. The reason we do not pray is that we do not own Jesus Christ as Master, we do not take our orders from Him. The key to the Master's orders is prayer, and where we are when we pray is a matter of absolute indifference. In whatever way God is engineering our circumstances, that is the duty—*pray*.

2. The Key to the Master's Ownership
the Lord of the harvest . . .

According to Our Lord, He owns the harvest, and the harvest is the crisis in innumerable lives all over the world. "Pray ye therefore the Lord of the harvest"— not pray because we are wrought up over the needs of the heathen, nor pray to procure funds for a society, but *pray to the Lord of the harvest*. It is appalling how little attention we pay to what Our Lord says. "As the Father hath sent Me, even so send I you" (RV)—to put in a sickle, to reap. All over the world, there are crises in lives, they are all around us, heathen and Christian, we meet them by the score every day we live; but unless we are set on obeying our Master's orders, we shall never see them. Supposing the crisis comes in my father's life, my brother's life, am I there as a labourer that the harvest may be reaped for Jesus? Jesus said, "Go ye therefore, and make disciples of all the nations"; and we cannot disciple others unless we ourselves are disciples. The evangelical emphasis has too often been: "So many souls saved, thank God, now they are all right." the idea being that we have done this thing for God. It is God who saves men; we have to do the discipling after they are saved.

(a) His Position in His Own World
(Colossians 1:16–18)

Our Lord's position in His own world is that of Creator. From the remotest star to the last grain of sand,

all things were created by Him. His own creatures always recognised Him—"He came unto His own things" (John 1:11 RV mg). They do not recognise our lordship because we have too much of the brute about us; the whole creation is waiting for the revealing of the sons of God (RV).

(b) His Position among His Own People
(John 1:11)

"And they that were His own received Him not" (RV). Jesus is never recognised by any man until the personal crisis of conviction of sin is reached. He is the owner of *the harvest*, not of everyone; they will not have Him until this point of crisis is reached. Jesus Christ owns the harvest which is produced in men by the distress of conviction of sin; and it is this harvest we have to pray that labourers may be thrust out to reap. We may be taken up with the activities of a denomination, or be giving ourselves up to this committee and that, whilst all about us people are ripe unto harvest and we do not reap one of them, but waste our Lord's time in over-energised activities for furthering some cause or denomination.

Jesus Christ is the Lord of the harvest. There are no nations whatever in His outlook, no respect of persons with Him; His outlook is *the world*. How many of us pray without respect of persons, and with respect to one Person only, Jesus Christ?

(c) His Position over His Own Disciples
(John 17:6)

"Thine they were, and Thou gavest them Me." The disciple is Christ's own, and the disciple is not above his Master. He tells us to pray, His Spirit is abroad, and the fields are white already to harvest, but the eyes of all saving His disciples are holden. If for one whole day, quietly and determinedly, we were to give ourselves up to the ownership of Jesus and to obeying His orders, we should be amazed at its close to realise all He had packed into that one day. We say— "Oh, but I have a special work to do." No Christian has a special work to do. A Christian is called to be Jesus Christ's own, one chosen by Him; one who is not above his Master, and who does not dictate to Jesus as to what he intends to do. Our Lord calls to no special work; He calls to Himself. Pray to the Lord of the harvest, and He will engineer your circumstances and thrust you out.

3. The Key to the Master's Option
. . . that He send forth labourers into His harvest. (RV)

The form the prayer is to take is also dictated by the Master—"that He send forth labourers into His harvest." This leaves no room for the "amateur providence" notion which arises out of our neglect to take our orders from Jesus Christ. We must pray to the

Lord of the harvest, and take our orders from Him, and from no one else. The desire to be an amateur providence always arises when Jesus Christ is not recognised as the universal Sovereign.

(a) The Direction of the Work (John 4:35–38)

The "others" who laboured are the prophets and apostles, "and ye are entered into their labours." The great Sower of the seed of the Redemption is the Holy Ghost. The direction of the work is at the option of the Master, not at the choice of the disciple. Mark the significance of the term "labour." We refuse to pray unless we get thrills. May God save us from that counterfeit of true prayer, it is the intensest form of spiritual selfishness. We have to labour, and to labour along the line of His direction. Jesus Christ says—*Pray*. It looks stupid; but when we labour at prayer results happen all the time from His standpoint, because God creates something in answer to, and by means of prayer, that was not in existence before. *"Labour."* It is the one thing we will not do. We will take open-air meetings, we will preach—but labour at prayer! There is nothing thrilling about a labouring man's work, but it is the labouring man who makes the conceptions of the genius possible; and it is the labouring saint who makes the conceptions of his Master possible.

(b) The Disposition of the Worker (Matthew 10:24)

Wherever the providence of God may dump us down, in a slum, in a shop, in the desert,[17] we have to labour along the line of His direction. Never allow this thought—"I am of no use where I am," because you certainly can be of no use where you are not! Wherever He has engineered your circumstances, pray, ejaculate to Him all the time. Impulsive prayer, the prayer that looks so futile, is the thing God heeds more than anything else. Jesus says—"If ye abide in Me, and My words abide in you, ask *whatsoever ye will*, and it shall be done unto you" (RV). Think what an astonishment it will be when the veil is lifted, to find the number of souls that have been reaped for Jesus because our disposition had made Him Master, and we were in the habit of taking our orders from Him. Our Lord in one of His parables reveals that God sows His saints in the places that are most useless according to the judgement of the world; He puts them where He likes. Where God is being glorified is where He puts His saints, and we are no judge of where that is.

(c) The Distinctness of the Way (John 14:6)

The Master says He is the Way; then abide in Him. He says He is the Truth; then believe in Him. He says He is the Life; then live on Him.

Prayer is the answer to every problem there is. How else could Our Lord's command in John 14:1 be fulfilled in our experience? How could we have an untroubled heart if we believed that the heathen who had not heard the Gospel were damned? What would the Redemption of Jesus Christ be worth, of what use would the revelation given in John 3:16 be, if it depended on the laggard laziness of Christians as to whether men are to be saved or not?

We have to live depending on Jesus Christ's wisdom, not on our own. He is the Master, and the problem is His, not ours. We have to use the key He gives us, the key of prayer. Our Lord puts the key into our hands, and we have to learn to pray under His direction. That is the simplicity which He says His Father will bless.

THE KEY TO THE MISSIONARY

Matthew 28:16–20

1. The Universal Sovereignty of Christ

All power is given unto Me in heaven and in earth.

The "all things" of Matthew 11:27 is limited to the revelation of the Father; the "all power" of Matthew 28:18 refers to the absolute sovereign universal power of the Risen Lord. "All power is given unto Me. . . . Go ye therefore, and teach all nations." The basis of the missionary appeal is the authority of Jesus Christ. Our Lord puts Himself as the supreme sovereign Lord over His disciples. He does not say the heathen will be lost if you do not go, but simply—"This is My commandment to you as My disciples—Go and teach all nations." Jesus did not say—"Go into all the world"; or, "Go into the foreign field," but simply—"Go and teach," i.e., "preach and teach out of a living experience of Myself." We are all based on a conception of importance, either our own importance, or the importance of someone else; Jesus tells us to go and

---

17. in the desert: Chambers was speaking to soldiers camped in Egypt.

teach based on the revelation of *His* importance. "All power is given unto *Me*. . . . Go *ye* therefore. . . ."

(a) The Real Solitude with Christ
"Then the eleven disciples went away into Galilee, into a mountain . . ." The disciples had been in intimate fellowship with Jesus, day and night, for three years; they had seen Him go through the unfathomable agony of Gethsemane; they had seen Him put to death on Calvary; they had seen Him after His Resurrection, and now they stand in solitude with Him. If we want to know the universal sovereignty of Christ, we must get into solitude with Him. It is not sufficient for someone else to tell us about Him; we must perceive with our own eyes Who He is, we must know Him for ourselves. Jesus Christ alone is the key to the missionary.

The danger to-day is to make practical work the driving wheel of our enterprises for God. All the intense social work and aggressive movements of our day are apt to be anti-Christian. They are antagonistic to the sovereignty of the Lord Jesus Christ, because they are based on the conception that human ingenuity is going to bring in the Kingdom of God, and Jesus Christ is made of no account.

(b) The Right Spot to Meet Christ
". . . where Jesus had appointed them." "Come unto Me," that is the right spot to meet Jesus Christ. "Come unto Me, all ye that labour and are heavy laden"—and how many missionaries are! We banish these marvellous words of the universal Sovereign of the world to the threshold of an evangelistic after-meeting. They are the words of Jesus to His disciples. He says "Come," and we have deliberately to take time to come. If we do not take time to come, we shall be inclined to call God's messages the devil. We are so busy in work for Him that when He just touches us, down we go, and in our panic we say—"Oh! that must be the devil." It was God. "Despise not thou the chastening of the Lord."

We must get to the place of real solitude with Christ. He is our mountain-height and our sea-calm; He is the recreating power; He is the universal Sovereign. He tells us to consider the lilies; we say—"No, we must consider life." We mistake the mechanism of life for life itself, and that idea has become incorporated into Christian work. In the active work we do for God we do not really believe that Jesus Christ is sovereign Lord; if we did, we should fuss less and build more in faith in Him. We cannot do the Saviour's work by fuss, but only by knowing Him as the supreme sovereign Lord.

(c) The Rectified Sight of Christ
"And when they saw Him, they worshipped Him: but some doubted." It is not the doubt of unbelief, but the

doubt of wonder—"Can it really be so simple as that?" If it is not as simple as that, it is all wrong. When we transacted business with the sovereign Christ, the misgiving in our heart was that it was too simple. The simplicity is the very thing that is of Jesus; anything that is not simple is not of Him. Anything that is complicated is not of His sovereignty, but of our self-interest, our self-will, our self-consideration.

It is a great thing to have our spiritual sight tested by the Celestial Optician, to watch the way in which He rectifies and readjusts our sight. There is one unmistakable witness that Jesus promised us, and that is the gift of His peace. "My peace I give unto you." No matter how complicated the circumstances may be, one moment of contact with Jesus and the fuss is gone, the panic is gone, all the shallow emptiness is gone, and His peace is put in, absolute tranquillity, because of what He says—"All power is given unto Me." Do we look and act as if we believed He had all power in heaven and in earth? What is our actual life like? Is it conducted on the line of John 14:1—an undisturbedness of heart arising out of belief in Jesus? We must remember to take time to worship the Being Whose Name we bear.

2. The Unobtrusive Service of the Commission
Go ye therefore.

These words are simply the introduction to a commission. The unobtrusive service of the commission is outlined in the quiet, almost commonplace statement—"Go your way, remembering what I have told you."

(a) How to Go (Acts 1:8)
There is always the danger of starting up false enthusiasm in missionary work—"Oh yes, I will go, where shall I go?" That is like making a false start in a race and having to go back to the starting point. Our Lord's word "go" simply means "live," and Acts 1:8 describes the "going." Jesus did not say to the disciples—*"Go* into Jerusalem, *go* into Judaea, *go* into Samaria, *go* into the uttermost part of the earth"; but—*"Ye shall be My witnesses"* (RV) in all these places: He undertakes to establish the goings. So many people are obsessed with this idea—"What are you going to *do?*" I hope none of us are going to *do* anything: I hope we are going to *be* what He wants us to be.

In Matthew 28:19 Our Lord does not say—"Go into all the world," but—"Go ye therefore, and teach." He does the engineering. In Acts 1:8 He does not say "Ye shall receive power, and *you shalt go* into Jerusalem"—but—*"Ye shall be My witnesses . . ."* (RV). How the disciples went is described later in the Acts of the Apostles, they went at the point of the sword, persecution arose and scattered them by the providence of God. "How to go" refers to the personal spiritual character of the missionary, not to his feet.

(b) How to Keep Going (John 15:7)

These wonderful words tell us how to keep going in our personal lives, viz., by the words of Jesus. "If ye abide in Me, and My words abide in you." We have continually to pull ourselves up short and recognise the amazing simplicity of Jesus Christ's counsel. The reason we get perplexed is that we do not believe He is Sovereign Lord, we do not believe that He will never forget anything we remember; we conjure up a hundred and one things that we imagine He has forgiven. Instead of praying to the Lord of the harvest to thrust out labourers, we pray—"O Lord, keep my body right; see after this matter and that for me." Our prayers are taken up with our concerns, our own needs, and only once in a while do we pray for what He tells us to. "Ask *whatsoever ye will*, and it shall be done unto you" (RV). We must feed on His word, and that will keep our spiritual life going. Where we are placed is a matter of indifference. God does the engineering, and He sends us out. "Has God given you a special call to this place?" He never does. The place is arranged for by His providence, not by His call.

(c) How to Keep Going till We're Gone (Acts 20:24)

This verse tells us how to keep going till we're gone—firstly, by allowing no afflictions to move us from our confidence in the sovereignty of Jesus Christ; and secondly, by not considering our life dear unto ourselves but only to Jesus Christ for the carrying out of His purposes; and thirdly, by fulfilling the ministry we have received of Him to testify the gospel of the grace of God, then we shall go, all together, like Oliver Wendell Holmes' pony chaise, every part worn out at the same time. That is what happens with a wholesome Christian life.

3. The Unique Sacrament of the Charter
And teach all nations.

That is the central point of the commission—Teach, "make disciples of all the nations" (RV); disciple everyone, not proselytise everyone. There is nothing more objectionable than the spiritual prig. The type for the missionary is God's own Son, and He did not go about button-holing men. There were plenty of promising men in Our Lord's day, one of them came to Jesus and asked what he might do to inherit eternal life, and the words Jesus spoke to him sent him away in heart-breaking discouragement. Our Lord never pleaded, He never cajoled, He never entrapped; He simply spoke the sternest words mortal ears ever

heard, and then left it alone. Our Lord has a perfect understanding that when once His word is heard, it will bear fruit sooner or later.

To-day a number of hysterical and sentimental things are apt to gather round the missionary appeal. The need of the heathen is made the basis of the appeal instead of the authority of Jesus Christ. The need is made the call. It may be good up to a certain point, but it is not the line for the disciples of Jesus Christ. Our Lord did not tell His disciples to gather together and select certain people and send them out. That is what is being done in many places to-day, because we do not take our conception of missionary enterprise from the New Testament. We adapt the New Testament to suit our own ideas; consequently we look on Jesus Christ as One Who assists us in our enterprises. The New Testament idea is that Jesus Christ is the absolute Lord over His disciples.

(a) Administer Your Learning (John 17:17–18)

A disciple must administer to those who are ripe for it what he himself has learned. Jesus Christ is the Lord of the harvest; and the harvest is the critical moment in individual lives that is produced by conviction of sin, and Jesus alone is the judge of when that moment comes.

Many years ago I knew a godly old shepherd in the Highlands, John Cameron. He was so marvellously used by God in his contact with people that whenever he talked to them about their souls they would get saved. One summer John said to me—"If you get permission to talk to my ploughman about his soul, do." Naturally, I said, "Why don't you talk to him yourself?" He replied, "Didn't I say, If you get permission? If you don't know about getting permission, you don't know anything about the Holy Ghost. Do you think I talk to everyone I meet? If I did, I would make God a liar. No, I have to get permission before I talk to a soul."

This ploughman was with John for three years, and they were together every day, bringing the sheep over the hills, and John never once spoke to him about his soul. They would meet people on the hills, and John would talk to them and they would get saved. But he never said a word to the ploughman about spiritual things, until at last one day the ploughman burst out—"For God's sake, talk to me about my soul, or I'll be in hell." So John did talk to him, and the man was wonderfully saved. Then he asked John Cameron why he had not spoken to him before. And John said, "Probably you know why, better than I do—I didn't get permission." Then the ploughman told him this—"When you 'fee'd'[18] me, I knew you

---

18. fee'd: employed; taken on as a worker.

were a religious man, and I said to some of my mates—'If old John talks to me about my soul, I'll let him know what he is doing.'"

So the administering of the word is not ministering it where we think it is needed; the word has to be sown in living touch with the Lord of the harvest, sown in touch with Him in solitude and prayer, and He will bring the folks round—black and white, educated and uneducated, rich and poor. They are all there, "white already to harvest," but most of us are so keen on our own notions that we do not recognise that they are ripe for reaping. If we are in touch with Jesus Christ, He says all the time—This is the moment; this one here, that one there, is ready to be reaped. We say—"Oh, but I want to go and get scores of heathen saved, I do not want to be the means of reaping my brother"; but your brother happens to be the one who is white to harvest. The commission is to teach, to disciple—that is, to administer the word.

(b) Abandon Your Life (John 20:23)

These words refer to the sacrament of an abandoned life, filled with the Holy Ghost, through whom the Sovereign Lord makes His words to be spirit and life. "That was exactly the word I needed, how did you know?" You did not know anything about it, you were living in abandoned devotion to Jesus, and He administered the word through you. It is not done by our wits and ingenuity, by our agony and distress, or by our piety, but entirely by our abandon to Jesus Christ.

(c) Apply Your Loyalty (Revelation 2:10)

These words reveal how to apply our loyalty to our Sovereign Lord in every condition and every circumstance. "Be thou faithful unto death."

The key to the missionary is the absolute Sovereignty of the Lord Jesus Christ. We must get into real solitude with Him, feed our soul on His word, and He will engineer our circumstances. "Consider the lilies how they grow"—they live where they are put, and we have to live where God places us. It is not the going of the feet, but the going of the life in real vital relationship to Jesus Christ. God will bring round a stationary life far more than He can ever bring round a "going" missionary, if the "going" missionary is not one whose life is hid with Christ in God. The goings must be of God. There are a hundred and one things in human life that we cannot control; but Jesus says—"All power is given unto Me in heaven and in earth." Then what are we up to with all our worrying? He says, "Let not your heart be troubled, . . . *believe also in Me.*"

"All power is given unto Me. . . . Go ye therefore." "Go established in Me, and disciple everyone whom I bring around you; I will tell you when they are ripe for it." We shall find that it is not possible to be self-conscious servants of Jesus. We are never of any use to Him in our self-conscious moments; it is in the ordinary times when we are living simply in faith in Him that He gives out the sacrament of His word through us. "He that believeth on Me, . . ." out of him "shall flow rivers of living water."

THE KEY TO THE MISSIONARY MESSAGE
Luke 24:47–49

1. The Remissionary Message of the Missionary

And that repentance and remission of sins should be preached in His name . . . (Luke 24:47)

It is easy to forget that the first duty of the missionary is not to uplift the heathen, not to heal the sick, not to civilise savage races, because all that sounds so rational and so human, and it is easy to arouse interest in it and get funds for it. The primary duty of the missionary is to preach "repentance and remission of sins . . . in His name." The key to the missionary message, whether the missionary is a doctor, a teacher, an industrial worker, or a nurse—the key is the remissionary purpose of Our Lord Jesus Christ's death. The idea of the "missionary" class, the "ministerial" class, the "Christian worker" class has arisen out of our ideas of civilised life, not out of the New Testament faith and order. The New Testament

faith and order is that as Christians we do not cease to do our duty as ordinary human beings, but in addition we have been given the key to the missionary message, viz., the proclaiming of the remissionary purpose of the Life and Death of Our Lord. The other work is to be done so instinctively and naturally that it does not interfere with proclaiming the missionary message. We need to remember that Christians must do all that human beings ought to do, and much more, because they are supernaturally endued, but we must never confound that with what Our Lord has entrusted His servants to do, viz., to go and make disciples (RV).

(a) The Limitless Significance of Christ the Lamb of God (1 John 2:2)

It is possible to take any phase of Our Lord's life, the healing phase, the teaching phase, the saving and sanctifying phase, but there is nothing limitless about any of these. But take this: "the Lamb of God, which taketh away the sin of the world." That is limitless. The key to the missionary message is the limitless significance of Jesus as the propitiation for our sins. A missionary is one who is soaked in the revelation that Jesus Christ is "the propitiation for our sins: and not for ours only, but also for the sins of the whole world." The key to the missionary message is not the kindness of Jesus; not His going about doing good; not His revealing of the Fatherhood of God; but the remissionary aspect of His life and death. This aspect alone has a limitless significance.

(b) The Limitless Significance of Sin Against the Lamb of God (2 Corinthians 5:21)

If the significance of Christ as the propitiation for sins is limitless, the domain to which His propitiation applies is limitless also. Sinfulness against Christ is as limitless as the propitiation. "Therefore, as through one man sin entered into the world, and death through sin; and so death passed upon all men, for that all sinned" (Romans 5:12 RV). We are apt to talk sentimental nonsense about the Universal Fatherhood of God; to knock the bottom board out of Redemption by saying that God is love and of course He will forgive sin. When the Holy Spirit comes, He makes us know that God is *holy* love, and therefore He cannot forgive sin apart from the Atonement; He would contradict His own nature if He did. The only ground on which God can forgive sin and reinstate us in His favour, is through the Cross of Christ, and in no other way.

"Him who knew no sin He made to be sin" (RV). Jesus Christ went through identification with sin, and put away sin on the Cross, so that every man on earth might be freed from sin by the right of His Atonement. God made His own Son to be sin that He might make the sinner a saint—*"that we might become the righteousness of God in Him."* (RV).

The key to the missionary message is not man's views or predilections regarding Redemption, but the revelation given by Our Lord Himself concerning His life and death, "the Son of man came . . . to give His life a ransom for many." When the Holy Ghost comes in, He brings us into touch with the Lord Jesus Himself, and gives us the key to the missionary message, which is not the proclaiming of any particular view of salvation, but the proclaiming of "the Lamb of God, which taketh away the sin of the world." The Holy Ghost sheds abroad the love of God in our hearts, and the love of God is world-wide; there is no patriotism in the missionary message. This does not mean that patriots do not become missionaries, but it does mean that the missionary message is not patriotic. The missionary message is irrespective of all race conditions, it is for the whole world. "God so loved *the world. . . .*"

Sin against Christ the Lamb of God is world-wide, the propitiation of Christ is world-wide, and the missionary's message is world-wide; it is a message not of condemnation, but of remission. "That repentance and remission of sins should be preached in His name unto all the nations" (RV).

The only final thing in the world is the Redemption of Jesus Christ.

(c) The Limitless Significance of the Sermon on Christ (John 1:29)

The significance of the sermon on Christ the Lamb of God is limitless because He is the Lamb *of God*, not of man. "Behold the Lamb of God, which taketh away the sin of the world." The Bible reveals all through that Our Lord bore the sin of the world by *identification*, not by *sympathy*. He came here for one purpose only— to bear away the sin of the world in His own Person on the Cross. He came to redeem men, not to set them a wonderful example. We have to beware of becoming the advocate of a certain view of the limitless. The Redemption avails for everyone—"The Lamb of God, which taketh away the sin of the world," not the sin of those who belong to any particular country, but the sin *of the world*. The words are worthy only of Almighty God's wisdom, not of man's.

2. The Regenerative Magnitude of the Mission

preached in His name among all nations, beginning from [RV] Jerusalem . . .

"These are they which follow the Lamb whithersoever He goeth" (Revelation 14:4). These words form a magnificent commentary on sacramental preaching, i.e., preaching in His name.

(a) The Personal Possession of the Nature of the Lamb of God

Jesus spoke these words to His disciples, and to no one else. To be a disciple means to be a believer in Jesus—one who has given up his right to himself to the ownership of Christ. "You must possess My nature in yourselves," says Jesus, "then go and preach in My Name"—in My nature.

(b) The Powerful Programme of the Naiveté of the Lamb of God

Naiveté means natural simplicity and unreservedness of thought. The Divine simplicity of the phrase— "preached in His name"! It is entirely free from diplomacy in any shape or form. The amazing simplicity of the nature of God is foolish judged by human wisdom; but "the foolishness of God is wiser than men."

The key to the missionary message is the proclamation of this gospel of propitiation for the sins of the whole world. We must be careful lest we become too wise for Jesus and say—"Oh but the people will never understand." We should say—"God knows how to make them understand, therefore we will do what He tells us." If we have got hold of the truth of God for ourselves, we have to give it out and not try to explain it. It is our explanations of God's truth that befog men. Let the truth come out in all its rugged force and strength, and it will take effect in its own way. "That *repentance and remission of sins* should be preached . . ." We are not to preach the doing of good things; good deeds are not to be preached, they are to be performed.

(c) The Particular Place of the Negotiations of the Lamb of God

". . . among all nations, beginning from [RV] Jerusalem." The particular place where Our Lord tells His disciples to begin is where He is not believed in; and we do not need to go to the back of beyond for that. The first place may be inside our own skull, in the intellect that will not believe in Him. If we remain true to Jesus Christ and to His command to preach in His name, it will mean encountering hostility when we come in contact with the culture and wisdom and education that is not devoted to Jesus.

3. The Responsive Martyrdom of the Missionary
. . . And ye are witnesses of these things. (Luke 24:48)

These imperative words are spoken to Jesus Christ's disciples. A witness is one who has deliberately given up his life to the ownership of another, not to a cause, and death will never make him swerve from his allegiance.

(a) The Wonder of Witnessing
"Behold, I send the promise of My Father upon you," and in Acts 1:8 Jesus tells them what the result of the coming of the promise of the Father will be, "Ye shall be My witnesses" (RV). Many a man is prevented from being a witness to Jesus by over-zealousness for His cause. "What are you being trained for? Are you going to be a minister, a deaconess, a missionary? What is the use of all this training?" Bible training and missionary training is not meant to train men for a purpose for which human nature can train itself. Religious institutions start out on the right line of making witnesses to Jesus, then they get swept off on

to the human line and begin to train men for certain things, to train for a cause, or a special enterprise, or for a denomination, and the more these training places are multiplied, the less chance is there of witnesses to Jesus being made. Nowadays we are in danger of reversing Jesus Christ's order. There stands the eternal word of Christ—"As the Father hath sent Me, *even so send I you.*" (RV). Too often a missionary is sent first by a denomination, and secondly by Christ. We may talk devoutly about Jesus in our meetings, but He has to take the last place.

One way in which Satan comes as an angel of light to Christians to-day is by telling them there is no need to use their minds. We *must* use our minds; we must keep the full power of our intellect ablaze for God on any subject that awakens us in our study of His word, always keeping the secret of the life hid with Christ in God. Think of the sweat and labour and agony of nerve that a scientific student will go through in order to attain his end; then think of the slipshod, lazy way we go into work for God.

(b) The Woe of Witnessing
A missionary is one who is wedded to the charter of his Lord and Master. "I determined not to know any thing among you, save Jesus Christ, and Him crucified." It is easier to belong to a coterie and tell what God has done for us, or to become a devotee to Divine healing, or a special type of sanctification. Paul did not say—"Woe is unto me if I do not preach what Jesus Christ has done for me," but—"Woe is unto me, if I preach not the gospel!" Personal experience is a mere illustration that explains the wonderful difference the Gospel has made in us. Our experience is the gateway into the Gospel for us; but it is not the Gospel. This is the Gospel: "that repentance and remission of sins should be preached in His name."

(c) The Worship of Witnessing
Worship is the love offering of our keen sense of the worth-ship of God. True worship springs from the same source as the missionary himself. To worship God truly is to become a missionary, because our worship is a testimony to Him. It is presenting back to God the best He has given to us, publicly not privately. Every act of worship is a public testimony, and is at once the most personally sacred and the most public act that God demands of His faithful ones.

THE LOCK FOR THE MISSIONARY KEY

Romans 10:14–15

1. The Discovered Sense of Responsibility
How then shall they call . . . ?

The awakened sense of responsibility to God for the whole world is seen in the rousing up of the Christian community in sympathy towards missionary enterprise. Within recent years missionary organisation from the human standpoint has almost reached the limit of perfection. But if all this perfection of organisation does is to make men discover a new sense of responsibility without an emphatic basing of everything on Redemption, it will end in a gigantic failure. To-day many are interested in the foreign field because of a passionate interest in something other than the Lord Jesus and His command—"Go ye therefore, and make disciples" (RV). All this organisation ought to mean that we can go ahead as never before; but if once the dethronement of Jesus creeps in, the finest organisation will but perfect the lock which cannot open of itself.

There are wonderful things about light, but there are terrible things also. When once the light of God's Spirit breaks into a heart and life that has been perfectly happy and peaceful without God, it is hell for that one. "If I had not come and spoken unto them, they had not had sin." If we take this aspect of things out of the individual setting and put it into a universal setting, we shall see the reason of the antipathy to foreign missions. It is because light brings confusion and disaster. The light produces hell where before there was peace; it produces pain where before there was death. God's method in the pathway of light is destructive before it is constructive. The missionary is the incarnation of Holy Ghost light, and when he comes all the things of the night tremble. The night of heathenism is being split up, not by the incoming of civilisation, but by the witness of men and women who are true to God.

In this country we know nothing about what Jesus mentions in Matthew 10:34–39, but wherever the missionary brings the evangel of Jesus, he will have to face it. Those who become converts to Jesus have to go through these things literally, they are persecuted and flung out; and unless the missionary knows God and trusts in Him entirely, he will step down to a lower level and compromise, and tell the people they need not do certain things in exactly the way that Jesus indicates. But if he stands true to God, he will preach the truth, at whatever cost to the converts. No nervous system can stand that strain, no sensitiveness of mind can stand that test, nothing but the Holy Ghost can stand it, because He has the mind of God.

2. The Discovered Service of Reasonableness
How shall they believe . . . ?

Never before has there been such an educated and reasonable and intense grasp of all the problems, social and international and personal, as there is today. Everything has been laid at the service of the missionary. The opportunity is one that makes us hold our breath with amazement, and at the same moment sink back—But who has the key? All the forces of civilisation and education and healing are in perfect trim; the fulness of time has come as never before; the only thing that is lacking is the key that fits the lock. To-day the emphasis is on the reasonable aspects of missionary work, the healing, civilising, and educational. These are all admirable, and if the key were used, they would facilitate rapidly our Lord's purpose and make it much easier to get into the heart of the problem; but the danger is that we have forgotten the key. The key is the Lordship of Jesus Christ and His supreme authority.

3. The Discovered Scheme of Representatives
How shall they hear . . . ?

There is nothing more thrilling than the realisation of what is at the disposal of the Christian church to-day. Every element of science, skill and learning has been taxed to its limit to serve the missionary purpose. It is a magnificent scheme, and all of it in order that the world might hear, but *"How shall they hear without a preacher?"* The work that is being done cannot be too highly praised, but it is not preaching. "Woe is unto me, if I preach not the gospel," that was the burning message of the Apostle Paul. In spite of all the perfection of organisation the magnificent equipment and tremendous resolve, the purpose for which the whole thing was started is frequently not fulfilled, and the scheme ends simply as something to be admired. That accounts for the alternation of exaltation and despair. Just when everything seems ripe for God and our hopes are raised to the highest pitch, we are suddenly chilled, because there is no message, nothing to be believed, nothing for the world to hear. Our organisation has enabled us to re-arrange and systematise the problems, but it cannot solve the problems. It is not that the scheme is wrong. What is wrong is that the key has been lost, the Lordship of

Jesus Christ has been forgotten; His supreme authority over the missionary has been ignored, He is not realised as King of kings.

Out of the centre of His own agony in the Garden, Our Lord counsels us to "watch and pray" lest we slip into temptation. Missionary enterprise will reveal more quickly than anything whether we have been caught by the lure of wrong roads to the Kingdom. When we pray "Thy kingdom come," we have to see that we allow the King to have His way in us first, that we ourselves are personally related to Him by sanctification. God's plan is that the truth must die—"Except a corn of wheat fall into the ground and die, it abideth alone . . ." (John 12:24). Christian work, if it is spiritual, has followed that law at home and everywhere, because that is the only way in which it can bring forth God's fruit.

4. The Discovered Source of Reserves
How shall they preach . . . ?

A missionary is one sent by Jesus Christ as the Father sent Him. Our Lord's first obedience was not to the needs of men, but to the will of His Father, and the first great duty of the Christian is not to the needs of his fellow men, but to the will of his Lord. To elevate the heathen, to lift up the down-trodden and oppressed, is magnificent, but it is not the reason for missionary enterprise. The teaching of the New Testament is that we ought to be doing all these things to the best of our ability, but missionary enterprise is another thing. A missionary is one who is fitted with the key to the missionary lock while he pursues the ordinary callings of life.

What is needed to-day is *Christian sociology*, not *sociology Christianised*. One way in which God will reintroduce the emphasis on the Gospel is by bringing into His service men and women who not only understand the problems, but who have learned that the secret of the whole thing is supernatural regeneration, that is, personal holiness wrought by the grace of God.

Jesus Christ came to do what no human being can do, He came to redeem men, to alter their disposition, to plant in them the Holy Spirit, to make them new creatures. Christianity is not the obliteration of the old, but the transfiguration of the old. Jesus Christ did not come to teach men to be holy: He came to make men holy. His teaching has no meaning for us unless we enter into His life by means of His death. The Cross is the great central point. Jesus Christ is not first

a Teacher, He is first a Saviour; and the thing that tells in the long run in the missionary's life is not successful understanding of His teaching, but the realisation in his own personal life of the meaning of the Cross. There is only One Who saves men, and that is God. The missionary is there to proclaim the marvel of that salvation, and what he proclaims becomes a sacrament in himself, he is made the incarnation of what he preaches. The missionary will be put into places where he has to stand alone, because he is being held true to the content of the Gospel as it is in Jesus. There is a loneliness which comes from a defiant heroism which has no element of the Gospel in it.

There is no more wholesome training for the foreign field than doing our duty in the home field. The foreign field is apt to have a glamour over it because it is away somewhere else. There is an inspiration and a sense of the heroic about going to the foreign field—until we get there, and find that the most terrible things we ever touched at home were clean and vigorous compared to the corruption that has to be faced there. Unless the life of a missionary is hid with Christ in God before he begins his work, that life will become exclusive and narrow, it will never become the servant of all men, it will never wash the feet of others. Therefore we come back to the first principle— "The heathen shall know that I am the LORD . . . *when I shall be sanctified in you before their eyes."*

5. The Discovered Supremacy of Redemption
How beautiful are the feet of them that preach the gospel of peace, and bring glad tidings of good things!

Thank God for the countless numbers of individuals who realise that the only Reality is Redemption; that the only thing to preach is the Gospel; that the only service to be rendered is the sacramental service of identification with Our Lord's Death and Resurrection. To preach the Gospel is to proclaim that God saves from sin and regenerates into His Kingdom anyone and everyone who believes on the Lord Jesus. It means even more—it means to disciple all the nations (RV) not only on the authority of Jesus, but on the flesh and blood evidence of entire sanctification in the life of the missionary. "When it pleased God . . . to reveal His Son in me, that I might preach Him among the heathen."

Thus we end where we began, with Our Lord Jesus Christ. He is the First and the Last, and laying His hands on the missionary, He says—"Fear not; I . . . have the keys."

THE KEY TO MISSIONARY DEVOTION

3 John 7

We live in a complex world, amid such a mass of sensibilities and impressionabilities that we are apt to imagine that it is the same with God. It is our complicated rationalism that makes the difficulty. We have to beware of every simplicity saving the simplicity that is in Christ.

The key to missionary devotion is put in our hand at the outset, "For His name's sake they went forth." The key is amazingly simple, as is everything connected with Our Lord. Our difficulties arise when we lose the key, and we lose the key by not being simple.

1. The Domination of the Master Himself (*John 21:15–16*)

The Master dominates, not domineers over, His disciples. His is the domination of holy love. If once, for one moment, we see the Lord, we may fall and slip away, but we shall never rest until we find Him again. The destiny of every human being depends on his relationship to Jesus Christ, it is not on his relationship to life, or on his service or his usefulness, but simply and solely on his relationship to Jesus Christ.

(a) Love for Him
Simon, son of Jonas, lovest thou Me more than these?

The sovereign preference of the disciple's person must be for the Person of the Lord Jesus over every other preference. This preference for Him is first and last against all competition. Love is difficult to define, although simple to know; life is difficult to define, although simple to have. What we obtain we can to a certain extent define; but all we have as a personal inheritance is indefinable. Intellect and logic are instruments, they are not life. The tyranny of the intellectual Napoleon is that he makes out that the intellect is life. Intellect is the expression of life. In the same way, theology is said to be religion; theology is the instrument of religion.

Love cannot be defined. Try and define your love for Jesus Christ, and you will find you cannot do it. Love is the sovereign preference of my person for another person, and Jesus Christ demands that that other person be Himself. That does not mean we have no preference for anyone else, but that Jesus Christ has the sovereign preference; within that sovereign preference come all other loving preferences, down to flowers and animals. The Bible makes no distinction between Divine love and human love, it speaks only of love.

When a disciple is dominated by his love to Jesus Christ, he is not always conscious of Him. It is absurd to think that we have to be conscious all the time of the one we love most. The one we are conscious of is the one we do not love most. A child is not conscious all the time of his love for his mother; it is the crisis that produces the consciousness. When we are getting into the throes of love, we are conscious of it because we are not in love yet. We imagine that we have to take God into our consciousness, whereas God takes us into His consciousness; consequently we are rarely conscious of Him.

(b) Love to Him
Simon, Son of Jonas, lovest thou Me? He saith unto Him, Yea, Lord; Thou knowest that I love Thee.

In verse 15 Our Lord had made a comparison— "Lovest thou Me more than these?" Here He makes no comparison—"Lovest thou Me?" To demand a declaration of love beyond comparison is to risk losing all. A missionary must be dominated by this love beyond compare to the Lord Jesus Christ, otherwise he will be simply the servant of a denomination or a cause, or a seeker for relief from a crushing sorrow in work. Many go into Christian work not for the sake of His Name, but in order to find surcease from their own sorrow; because of unrequited love; or because of a bereavement or a disappointment. Such workers are not dominated by the Master, and they are likely to strew the mission field with failure and sighs, and to discourage those who work with them. There is only one thing stronger than any of these things, and that is love.

(c) Love in Him
He saith unto him the third time, Simon son of Jonas, lovest thou Me?

Our Lord's question elicits the amazed confession of Peter's deepest heart—"Lord, Thou knowest all things; Thou knowest that I love Thee." Peter did not say—Look at this, and that, to confirm it. Love never professes; love confesses. "Peter was grieved because He said unto him the third time. . . ." Our Lord's thrice repeated question revealed to Peter's own soul that there was no one he loved more than Jesus, and in utter amazement as he looks at himself in his grief, he says, "Thou knowest that I love Thee." When once the domination of the Master over the heart of a disciple reaches the depth of that expression, then He entrusts His call to that one—"Feed My sheep."

"*Lovest thou Me? . . . Feed My sheep.*" Our Lord indicated three times over how love to Himself is to be manifested in the life of the lover, viz., in identification with His interests in others. Our Lord does not ask us to die for Him, but to identify ourselves with His interests in other people—not identify *Him* with *our* interests in other people. "Feed My sheep," see that they get nourished in their knowledge of Me.

Paul in 1 Corinthians 13:4–8 gives the charter of love. "Love suffereth long, and is kind; . . . taketh not account of evil. . . . Love never faileth" (RV). The love of God is wrought in us by the Holy Ghost. He sheds abroad the love of God, the nature of God, in our hearts, and that love works efficaciously through us as we come in contact with others. The test of love for Jesus Christ is the practical one, all the rest is sentimental jargon.

2. The Denomination of the Master's Name (Matthew 28:18–20)

"Make disciples of all the nations" (RV). That cannot be done unless Jesus Christ is Who He says He is. The apostolic office is not based on faith, but on love. The two working lines for carrying out Jesus Christ's command are, first, the sovereign preference of our person for the Person of Jesus Christ; and second, the willing and deliberate identification of our interests with Jesus Christ's interests in other people. Ardour must never be mistaken for love, nor the sense of the heroic for devotion to Jesus, nor self-sacrifice for fulfilling a spiritual destiny. It is much easier to follow in the track of the heroic than to remain true to Jesus in drab, mean[19] streets. Human nature unaided by God can do the heroic business; human pride unaided by God can do the self-sacrificing (cf. 1 Corinthians 13:1–3); but it takes the supernatural power of God to keep us as saints in the drab commonplace days. The need can never be the call for missionary enterprise. The need is the opportunity. The call is the commission of Jesus Christ and relationship to His Person. "All power is given unto *Me. . . . Go ye therefore.*" Any work for God that has less than a passion for Jesus Christ as its motive will end in crushing heartbreak and discouragement.

(a) Loyalty to His Character
All power is given unto Me.

Loyalty to the Master's character means that the missionary believes in his Lord's almightiness on earth as well as in heaven, though every common-sense rational fact should declare loudly that He has no more power than a morning mist. If we are going to be loyal to Jesus Christ's character as it is portrayed in the New Testament, we have a tremendously big task on hand. Loyalty to Jesus is the thing that is stuck at to-day. Folk will be loyal to work, to ideals, to anything, but they are not willing to acknowledge loyalty to Jesus Christ.

Christian workers frequently become intensely impatient of this idea of loyalty to Jesus. Our Lord is dethroned more emphatically by Christian workers than by the world. Loyalty to Jesus is the outcome of the indwelling of the personal Holy Spirit working in us the supernatural Redemption of Christ, and keeping us true to His Name when every common-sense fact gives the lie to it. In Psalm 73 the Psalmist says that he nearly lost his faith in God because every rational fact seemed to prove that he had trusted a fiction. There is no test to equal the test of remaining loyal to Jesus Christ's character when the ungodly man is in the ascendant. We are apt to become cynical, and a cynical view is always a distorted view, a view arising out of pique because some personal object is being thwarted.

(b) Loyalty to His Call
Go ye therefore, and make disciples of all the nations. (RV)

Loyalty to the call of Our Lord means not merely that we keep the letter of His command, but that we keep in contact with His nature, i.e., His Name. "Except ye . . . become as little children." The meaning of new birth is receiving His nature. The call of the sea, the call of the mountains, the call of the wild—all these calls are perfectly in accord with the nature of the caller, not necessarily in accord with the nature of the one who listens. Everyone does not hear the call of the sea, only the one who has the nature of the sea in him hears it. The call of the mountains does not come to everyone, only to the one who has the nature of the mountains in him. Likewise the call of God does not come to everyone, it comes only to those who have the nature of God in them. The call of Jesus Christ does not come to everyone, only to those who have His nature. Our loyalty is not to stand by the letter of what Jesus says, but to keep our soul continually open to the nature of the Lord Jesus Christ.

(c) Loyalty to His Commission
Teaching them to observe all things whatsoever I have commanded you.

Loyalty to the commission means, first of all, that the missionary sets himself to find out all that his Lord taught. There is not a greater test for loyal concen-

---

19. The word mean as used here refers to something or someone ordinary, common, low, or ignoble, rather than cruel or spiteful.

tration than that. Jesus did not say—"Teach salvation," or, "teach sanctification"; or," teach Divine healing," but—"Teach whatsoever I have commanded you." There is no room for the specialist or the crank or the fanatic in missionary work. A fanatic is one who has forgotten he is a human being. Our Lord never sent out cranks and fanatics, He sent out those who were loyal to His domination. He sent out ordinary men and women, plus dominating devotion to Himself by the indwelling Holy Ghost. A missionary is not sent by Jesus Christ to do medical work, educational work, industrial work; all that is part of the ordinary duty of life, and a missionary ought to be so equipped that he does these things naturally. But Jesus Christ never sends His disciples to do these things; He sends His disciples to *teach*, to *"make disciples of all the nations"* (RV).

3. The Detachment for the Master (*John 21:18–22*)

This detachment to Jesus is rarely referred to, it means personal attachment to no one and to nothing saving Our Lord Himself. Our Lord did not teach detachment from other things: He taught attachment to Himself. Jesus Christ was not a recluse. He did not cut Himself off from society, He was amazingly in and out among the ordinary things of life; but He was disconnected fundamentally from it all. He was not aloof, but He lived in another world. His life was so social that men called Him a glutton and a winebibber, a friend of publicans and sinners. His detachments were inside towards God. Our external detachments are often an indication of a secret vital attachment to the thing from which we keep away externally. Before we are rightly detached to Jesus Christ, we spend our time keeping ourselves detached from other things, which is a sure sign of a secret affinity with them. When we are really detached to Jesus, He can entrust us with all other things. "Lo, we have left all, and have followed Thee," said Peter, implying—"What shall we get?" Jesus told him that they would get a hundredfold more of all they had given up, once the detachment to Himself had been formed.

(a) The Life Sacrificed

Verily, verily, I say unto thee, When thou wast young, thou girdest thyself, and walkedst whither thou wouldest: but when thou shalt be old, thou shalt stretch forth thy hands, and another shall gird thee, and carry thee whither thou wouldest not.

These words are a description of the nature of internal sacrifice and every unspiritual desire will plead against the undesirability of the sacrifice. "God could never expect me to give up my magnificent prospects and devote my life to the missionary cause." But He happens to have done so. The battle is yours. He says no more, but He waits.

(b) The Life Sacramented

Now this He spake, signifying by what manner of death he should glorify God. And when He had spoken this, He saith unto him, Follow Me. (RV)

Three irrational conclusions—"death," "glorifying God," "following Me," and at His Ascension Jesus disappears. Our Lord never talks on the basis of reason, He talks on the basis of Redemption. What is nonsense rationally is Redemptive Reality. The "Follow Me" spoken three years before had nothing mystical in it, it was an external following; now it is a following in internal martyrdom.

"Sacramented" means that the elements of the natural life are presenced by Divinity as they are broken in God's service providentially. We have to be entirely adjusted into Jesus before He can make us a sacrament. The missionary must be a sacramental personality, one through whom the presence of God comes to others.

(c) The Life Sacred

Jesus saith unto him, If I will that he tarry till I come, what is that to thee? Follow thou Me.

Not only is the life of the missionary sacred to God, but the lives of others are sacred also, and when one tries to pry into another's concerns, he will receive the rebuke of Our Lord—"What is that to thee? *Follow thou Me.*"

HIS!

Thine they were, and Thou gavest them Me. John 17:6

It is this aspect of a disciple's life that is frequently forgotten. We are apt to think of ourselves as our own, of the work as our work. A great point in spiritual nobility has been reached when we can really say, "I am not my own." It is only the noble nature that can be mastered—an unpalatable truth if we are spiritually stiffnecked and stubborn, refusing to be mastered. The Son of God is the Highest of all, yet the characteristic of His life was obedience. We have to learn that God is not meant for us, it is we who are meant for God. Jesus Christ does satisfy the last aching abyss of the human heart, but that must never lead to thinking of God the Father, God the Son, and God the Holy Ghost as an Almighty arrangement for satisfying us. *"Know ye not that . . . ye are not your own?"* It is this realisation that is wrought in us by the Holy Ghost.

His! Does that apply to us? Have we realised that our body is not our own, but His—"the temple of the Holy Ghost"! Have we realised that our heart and affections are not our own, but His? If so, we shall be careful over inordinate affection. Have we realised that all the ambitions of life are His? We are out for one thing only, for Jesus Christ's enterprises. That is the inner secret of the missionary—I know that I am His, and that He is carrying on His enterprises through me; I am His possession and He can do as He likes with me.

Each one has the setting of his own difficulties and temptations, and so it is with the missionary. If we cannot live at home as His, we shall find it much more difficult to live in the foreign field as His; we shall be more likely to make things ours than to remain loyal to Him. If we have been "wobblers" at home, we shall be "wobblers" out there. If we have learned to face ourselves with God at home, we shall face ourselves with God out there. But we have to learn to do it, and it is not easy at the beginning. Where he is placed is a matter of indifference to the missionary; if he maintains his contact with God, out of him will flow rivers of living water. We have the idea that we engineer missionary enterprise; but it is the genius of the Holy Spirit that makes us go." God does not do anything *with* us, only *through* us; consequently the one thing God estimates in His servants is the work of the Holy Spirit.

Jesus Christ is the only One Who has the right to tell us what it means to be His, and in Luke 14:26–33 He is laying down the conditions of discipleship. These conditions are summed up in one astounding

word—*"hate."* "If any man cometh unto Me, and hateth not . . . [i.e., a hatred of every good thing that divides the heart from loyalty to Jesus], he cannot be My disciple" (RV). Every one of the relationships Jesus mentions may be a competitive relationship. We may prefer to be our mother's, or our father's, or our own, and Jesus does not say we cannot be, but He does say—*"he cannot be My disciple,"* he cannot be one over whom Jesus writes the word "Mine."

In verses 28–33 Our Lord is not referring to a cost the disciple has to estimate, but stating that He has estimated the cost. Jesus Christ is not less than a man among men, and He has counted the cost; that is why He makes the conditions so stern. The men who say— "Lord, Lord," are not the ones Jesus takes on His enterprises; He takes only those men in whom He has done everything, they are the ones upon whom He can rely. Many devote themselves to work for God in whom Jesus Christ has done nothing; consequently they bungle His business, run up the white flag to the prince of this world and compromise with him. Jesus says that the only ones He will take on His building and battling enterprises are those who are devoted to Him because He has altered their disposition.

1. The Missionary Watching (*Matthew 26:38*)

"Watch with Me"—with no private point of view of your own; watch entirely with Me. In the early stages of Christian experience, we do not watch *with* Jesus, we watch *for* Him. We do not know how to watch with Jesus in the circumstances of our lives, in the revelation of His word; we have the idea only of His watching with us, answering our problems, helping us. But Jesus says—*"Watch with Me."* How is it possible to watch with One Whom we do not understand? The early disciples did not understand Jesus in the slightest. They had been with Him for three years, they loved Him to the limit of their natural hearts, but they had no idea what He meant when He talked of His Kingdom or of His Cross. Jesus was inscrutable to them on these main points. They could not watch with Him for the simple reason that they did not know what He was after. They could not watch with Him in His Gethsemane, they did not know why He was suffering, and they slept for their own sorrow. Then Jesus gave Himself up, and they all forsook Him, and fled, and when they saw Him put to death on the cross, their hearts were broken. Then after the Resurrection, Jesus came to them and said— "Receive ye the Holy Ghost," and they learned to watch with Him all the rest of their lives.

The real centre of the disciple's devotion is watching with Jesus. When once we have learned to watch with Him, the thought of self is not kept down because it is not there to keep down; self-effacement is complete. Self has been effaced by the deliberate giving up to another self in sovereign preference, and the manifestation of the life in the actual whirl of things is—"I am not my own, but His."

2. The Missionary Waiting (*Revelation 3:10*)
Because thou hast kept the word of My patience.

This is not the patience of pessimism, nor of exhaustion, but the patience of joyfulness because God reigns. It may be illustrated by likening the saint to a bow and arrow in the hand of God. God is aiming at His mark, and He stretches and strains until the saint says—"I cannot stand any more," but God does not heed. He goes on stretching until His purpose is in sight, then He lets fly, and the arrow reaches His mark.

Moses "endured, as seeing Him who is invisible." The vision of God is the source of the patience of a saint. A man with the vision of God is not devoted simply to a cause or a particular issue, but to God Himself. Our Lord sent no one out on the ground of what He had done for them, but only because they had seen Him, and by the power of His Spirit had perceived Who He was. Nothing can daunt the man who has seen Jesus. The one who has only a personal testimony as to what Jesus can do for him may be daunted; but nothing can turn the man who has seen Him. It takes the endurance which comes from a vision of God to go on without seeing results. We are not here for successful service, but to be faithful. Had Jesus any results? Before we go into work for Him we must learn that the disciple is not above his Master. We cannot be discouraged if we belong to Him, for it was said of Him— "He shall not fail nor be discouraged." Discouragement is "disenchanted egotism." "Things are not happening in the way I expected they would, therefore I am going to give it all up." To talk like that is a sure sign that we are not possessed by love for Him, but only by love for ourselves. Discouragement always comes when we insist on having our own way.

3. The Missionary Worshipping
. . . worship God in the spirit. (Philippians 3:3)

Circumcision is the Old Testament symbol for New Testament sanctification. To worship God "in the spirit" is not to worship Him sincerely, in the remote part of our nature; but to worship Him by the power of the Spirit He gives to us. The Holy Spirit never becomes our spirit, He quickens our spirit into oneness with God. Worship is the tryst of sacramental identification with God; we deliberately give back to God the best He has given us that we may be identified with Him in it. "I beseech you, . . . present your bodies a living sacrifice, . . . which is your spiritual worship" (RV mg). Worship of God is the sacramental element in a saint's life. We have to give back to God in worship every blessing He has given us.

4. The Missionary Witnessing (Acts 1:8)
But ye shall receive power, when the Holy Ghost is come upon you: and ye shall be My witnesses. (RV)

The Holy Ghost is the One Who expounds the nature of Jesus to us. When the Holy Ghost comes in, He does infinitely more than deliver us from sin, He makes us one with our Lord. "My witnesses," a satisfaction to Jesus wherever He places us. To be a witness means to live a life of unsullied, uncompromising, and unbribed devotion to Jesus. A true witness is one who lets his light shine in works that exhibit the disposition of Jesus. Our Lord makes the one who is a witness His own possession, He becomes responsible for him. We have to be entirely His, to exhibit His Spirit no matter what circumstances we are in. It is extraordinary to watch God alter things. We have to worship God in the difficult circumstances, and when He chooses, He will alter them in two seconds. If we deliberately sign ourselves as "His," then all that happens is the fulfilment of Our Lord's own words in Matthew 11:28–29: "Come unto Me . . . , and I will give you rest. Take My yoke upon you, and learn of Me; . . . and ye shall find rest unto your souls."

Christ! I am Christ's! and let the name suffice you,
Ay, for me too He greatly hath sufficed;
Lo with no winning words I would entice you,
Paul has no honour and no friend but Christ.

Yea, thro' life, death, thro' sorrow and thro' sinning
He shall suffice me, for He hath sufficed:
Christ is the end, for Christ was the beginning,
Christ the beginning, for the end is Christ.

Workmen of God

The Cure of Souls

Oswald Chambers

INTRODUCTION

Source

The material in *Workmen of God* is from lectures given during March and April 1911 at Speke Hall, Battersea, London—headquarters of the League of Prayer.[1]

Publication History

- As articles: The lectures were published as articles in *Tongues of Fire* magazine from April through November, 1911, and in *God's Revivalist* and *Bible Advocate* magazines, Cincinnati, Ohio, from February through June 1912.

- As a booklet: *The Discipline in the Cure of Souls*, 1915 and 1919, contained the following preface:

  The contents of this little book are the condensed matter of half a dozen addresses given at Speke Hall, Battersea,[2] London, S.W.—Oswald Chambers

- As a book: The material was published as *Workmen of God* in 1937.

From November 1907 to July 1915, Oswald Chambers worked full-time with the Pentecostal League of Prayer in Britain. During the first four years, he traveled throughout the United Kingdom speaking at churches and League meetings. Then, from 1911 to 1915 he served as principal of the Bible Training College[3] (BTC), London, an arm of the League of Prayer.

During Chambers' first year as principal of the BTC,[4] he continued a heavy speaking schedule for the League. In the Thursday night Holiness Meetings leading up to Easter 1911, he taught this series, "How to Work for the Cure of Souls."

The phrase "the cure of souls" likely emerged from Chambers' reading of Dr. P. T. Forsyth (1848–1921), a Congregationalist minister and theologian. Chambers read many of Forsyth's books, valued his insights, and often quoted Forsyth in his lectures and sermons.

In 1915, C. Rae Griffin, a student and friend of Chambers at the Bible Training College, persuaded Oswald to print some of his talks as booklets. The Discipline Series were the first, and these messages were published as a booklet in 1915 with the proceeds going toward Chambers' ensuing work as a chaplain among the troops in Egypt.[5]

---

1. Pentecostal League of Prayer: founded in London in 1891 by Reader Harris (1847–1909), prominent barrister and friend and mentor of Oswald Chambers.

2. Speke Hall, in Battersea, southwest London: location of League of Prayer headquarters.

3. Bible Training College (BTC): residential school near Clapham Common in southwest London sponsored by the League of Prayer; operated from 1911 until it closed in July 1915 because of World War I. Oswald Chambers was principal and main teacher; Biddy Chambers, his wife, was lady superintendent.

4. BTC: Bible Training College.

5. in Egypt: Zeitoun (zay TOON), Egypt, six miles northeast of Cairo; site of a YMCA camp, the Egypt General Mission compound, and, from 1916 to 1919, the Imperial School of Instruction, training base for British, Australian, and New Zealand troops during World War I.

FOREWORD

Another book by Oswald Chambers! I wonder if his eager readers think of him as a writer of mature old age, giving the stored wisdom of a long life in these searching, virile, helpful messages. If so, they are mistaken. The facts are that his books are records of addresses and lectures that he gave during a decade of wonderful public and private ministry, both to students and congregations who were privileged to listen to him between 1907 and 1917. His wife, with God-given wisdom and energy, garnered this precious treasure by taking verbatim reports in shorthand throughout these busy years. Thus, when Oswald Chambers suddenly and unexpectedly died in Egypt in his early forties (during the Great War),[6] he left behind him a wealth of spiritual vitamins, which have ever since been enriching us through his books.

And now this latest book goes forth, at a time when soul-sickness is more than ever rampant. The messages are full of spiritual discernment and diagnosis, and they were first given at Speke Hall, Battersea, when Oswald Chambers was Principal of the Bible Training College at Clapham Common. Those of us who listened to him then, and worked with him, will never forget his forceful challenging statements, and we can never be thankful enough for the inspiration of his life and the blessing that resulted from his teaching.

He had a brilliant intellect, a highly trained disciplined mind and body, and an outstanding gift for teaching; but his great power lay in his consuming devotion to his Lord, in his entire reliance on the Holy Spirit, and in his absolute trust in the revelation of God through the Scriptures.

As these messages now go forth to a still wider circle, may they continually cause many to be wise in winning souls.

Mary R. Hooker[7]
Ridgelands College,
Wimbledon
April 1937

CONTENTS

---

6. The Great War: World War I (1914–1918).

7. Mary R. Hooker (1881–1965): eldest daughter of Reader Harris and a close associate of Oswald and Biddy Chambers; was instrumental in establishing the Bible Training College in 1910; served as president of the League of Prayer and wrote *Adventures of an Agnostic* (1959), a biography of her father, the founder of the League.

Chapter 1

HOW TO WORK FOR THE CURE OF SOULS

And David said, There is none like that; give it me.
1 Samuel 21:9

The setting is known to us all. David is talking about Goliath's sword, and he asks for it, "give it me." We read the passage in Deuteronomy where Moses said to the children of Israel, "the cause that is too hard for you, bring it unto me, and I will hear it" (Deuteronomy 1:17). I want to take these two Old Testament mighty men of God as types of what the worker for God must be like to work for the cure of souls.

With regard to the sword that there is none like it, if you will turn to Hebrews 4:12, you will see how I want to take Goliath's sword and spiritualise it in the hands of a worker for God among the children of men: "For the word of God is living, and active, and sharper than any two-edged sword, and piercing even to the dividing of soul and spirit, of both joints and marrow, and quick to discern the thoughts and intents of the heart" (RV). Now it is quite obvious that if you are not David and are trying to use Goliath's sword, you will do far more harm to yourself than damage to the enemy. You must be in the direct line of succession to David. David and Moses were mighty giants, but we have to be of the same family connection. What is the same family connection in this dispensation? Why, those who are born again of the Spirit of God, and those who are so identified with the Lord Jesus that they have entered into the experience of entire sanctification. When they use the word of God they do not damage themselves, nor hurt other souls; but they do great damage to the kingdom of the devil and bring benefit to the souls of men.

Before we take up the question of the kind of souls we shall have to deal with, we must deal with the worker. Now there are big difficulties in the way. The first difficulty is that we are not dealing with men's bodies. If we were, we could be taught in special schools and colleges, trained and developed in such a way that we should know fairly well how to apply principles to the various ailments of people, because physical ailments have a wonderful likeness to each other. This has led many Christian workers astray, they think that because men's bodies and bodily ailments are alike, and because one cure, carefully and judiciously prescribed by a physician who diagnosed the case aright was successful and can be applied to other cases with similar results, that men's souls can be treated in the same way. But you cannot deal with the human soul and with the ailments and

difficulties of the human soul according to any principle whatever. I think that any of you who have worked for God know this, that immediately you get into the way of using certain verses of Scripture and applying them to those who are seeking new birth, and certain other verses to those seeking sanctification, you will find suddenly that God's Spirit will depart from you and He will not use those verses in your hands any more. The reason is this, that immediately we get wedded to a short-cut in dealing with souls, God leaves us alone.

The first thing I want to lay down for the worker (I am talking about one who really is born again of the Spirit of God and has been entirely sanctified) is that he or she must rely on the Holy Spirit to direct them as to what to say in the case of every soul that comes. Do not rely on your memory, do not remember how you dealt with cases in the past, but recognise and rely on the Holy Spirit that He will bring to your remembrance the particular verse for you to apply at this time. You will find over and over again that God will bring confusion to your methods and will make you apply a text to sanctification which you in your system have said can only be applied to new birth; and He will make you apply a text which you have said can only apply to sanctification to something else, and you will make incessant blunders in work for God if you are not careful and watchful and heedful of the guidance of the Holy Spirit and of His bringing the word of God to your remembrance. Remember, then, that the worker who is rightly related to God must ever rely on the Holy Spirit for guidance in each individual case.

Then I want to apply Moses' statement: "The cause that is too hard for you, bring it unto me." Do you know how to bring your cases to God? We all know how to bring them to one another and how to talk to Christian workers about dealing with souls, but just as there are quack doctors in the medical profession, so there is the same thing in the spiritual domain. Beware of anything that does not fling you straight back in reliance on the Holy Spirit as the most practical factor you know in bringing to your remembrance the word of God and how to apply it.

Then another thing—the worker must live among the facts he has to deal with. Regarding the training of workers, take the highest class we know of, ministers. One of the greatest difficulties in most of our colleges for training ministers, who are supposed to work for the cure of souls, is that they are never taught how to deal with souls. There is hardly a college anywhere for training ministers where the question of dealing with souls is ever mentioned. Ministers will bear me out in this, that everything they have learned they have had to learn out of their own experience. They are trained in everything but how to deal with the facts they have to deal with.

There are two kinds of facts the worker must be amongst—he must go to school among human souls. I mean we must keep ourselves in touch, not with theories, but with people, and never get out of touch with human beings, if we are going to use the word of God skilfully amongst them, and if the Holy Spirit is to apply the word of God through us as workmen needing not to be ashamed. Live among your human facts, and you will find how continually God stirs up your nest. If you are a worker, He will constantly surround you with different kinds of people, with different difficulties, and He will constantly put you to school amongst those facts. He will keep you in contact with human stuff, and human stuff is very sordid; in fact, human stuff is made of just the same stuff as you and I are made of; do not shut yourself away from it. Beware of the tendency to live a life apart and shut away. Get amongst men. Jesus prayed, "I pray not that Thou shouldest take them out of the world, but that Thou shouldest keep them from the evil."

Then there is another series of facts, viz., Bible facts. We have to go to school among human souls, and we have to educate ourselves in Bible facts. A remarkable thing about this Book of God (and I hope, by God's grace, to point this out) is that for every type of human being we come across there is a distinct, clear line laid down here as to the way to apply God's truth to it. The stupid soul, the stubborn soul, the soul that is mentally diseased, the soul that is convicted of sin, the soul with the twisted mind, the sensual soul—everyone of the facts that you meet in your daily walk and business has its counterpart here, and God has a word and a revelation fact with regard to every life you come across.

Let me emphasise these three things again: First, the Christian worker who is right with God must rely every moment on the Holy Spirit when dealing with another soul. Second, the worker must live among human facts, men and women, not theories. Do not let us tell ourselves what men and women are like, let us find out what they are like. One of the greatest mistakes in the world is to tell yourself what a man is like; you do not know what he is like. The only One Who can teach you how to deal with the various specimens around you is the Holy Spirit. The third thing is, ransack this old Book from cover to cover in the most practical way you know—by using a concordance, by re-writing the Psalms, or by any other immediate practical method.

I know it is customary to ridicule certain ways in which some people say God guides them, but I am very chary about ridiculing any methods. For example, it is easy to ridicule this kind of method: "Lord, direct me to a word, I am just going to shut my eyes and open the Book and put my finger on a passage." I say it is easy to ridicule it, yet it is absurd to say that God has not led people in that way; He has. Why I mention these facts is to knock certain theories to pieces. You cannot tie God down to a particular line. You will find that God does use the most extraordinary methods people adopt; only do not take anyone else's way, get to know how God deals with you, and how He deals with others through you in the most practical way.

Keep these three things in mind—reliance on the Holy Spirit of God, keeping in contact with people, and above all, keeping in contact with the revelation facts in God's Book; live amongst them, and ask God how to apply them.

Another thing I want to mention—never believe what people tell you about themselves. There is only one person in a thousand who can actually tell you his or her symptoms; and beware of the people who can tell you where they are spiritually. I mean by that, never be guided by what people tell you; rely on the Spirit of God all the time you are probing them.

Let me read you this in regard to medical treatment—

Recent evidence in the law courts has pointed to a fact which the medical profession holds of great value—the necessity, not only of personal and private interview with a patient, but of the penetrative ability to get at the real facts and symptoms. In other words, successful diagnosis depends on the doctor's acumen in cross-examination. "Cross-examination of a patient is almost always necessary," says an eminent medical man. "They will give me causes, or rather what they think are causes, instead of symptoms. The rich patient is more troublesome in this respect than the poor, for he has had leisure in which to evolve a sort of scheme of his illness, based on 'popular' medical knowledge.

"Patients always colour facts, speaking absolutely instead of relatively. They never tell the truth about the amount of sleep they have had or as to appetite. They frequently say they have had nothing to eat. Casually you find there were two eggs at least for breakfast. A minute or two later they remember stewed steak for dinner. Perhaps the greatest need for cross-examination is that it gives an extended opportunity to the medical man to examine the patient objectively. The most important symptoms are generally those the patient never notices."

If that is true in the medical profession which deals with men's bodies, it is a thousandfold more true about spiritual symptoms when it comes to dealing with a man's soul. Do beware, then, of paying too much attention to the talk of the one that is in trouble, keep your own heart and mind alert on what God is saying to you; get to the place where you will know when the Holy Spirit brings the word of God to your remembrance for that one.

Now there is a wrong use of God's word and a right one. The wrong use is this sort of thing—someone comes to you, and you cast about in your mind what sort of man he is, then hurl a text at him like a projectile, either in prayer or in talking as you deal with him. That is a use of the word of God that kills your own soul and the souls of the people you deal with. The Spirit of God is not in that. Jesus said, "the words I speak unto you, they are spirit, and they are life." "Who also hath made us able ministers of the new testament; not of the letter, but of the spirit: for the letter killeth, but the spirit giveth life." Do remember to keep your soul in unsullied touch with the directions of the Spirit.

Another thing that is very puzzling is this. Probably all of you have had experiences as I have on this line: you listen to clear Bible teaching, unmistakably clear, almost taking people by the hand and leading them straight into the Kingdom of God, but they never come. Another time a man gets up and twists everything, and to your astonishment people are born again. That frequently happened in Water Street Mission in New York, a man who had been wonderfully saved would get up and tell what he had been and what he was now, then others would do the same, and the Spirit of God got hold of the people before you knew where you were, out they came to the altar, and these rough men knelt down and prayed with them and they "struck something," as they say out there, and something "struck them," and they were wonderfully born again.

Now these are facts we have to look at. You cannot put God down to a prescribed method. These souls were real, living, good specimens of what God had done, and the Spirit of God worked through them. I mention that because it confuses a great amount of our reasoning in Christian work; over and over again you will find that some poor, ignorant servant, or artisan, who seems scarcely to know how to put anything together, is used of God mightily in the salvation of souls, and others who have a clear understanding of the whole thing and put the way of salvation ever so clearly, yet nothing happens. So all we can get at is the main methods laid down in God's Book about the worker. Let us ask ourselves, "Do I experimentally know what the salvation of God is? Do I know what entire sanctification means in my own experience?" The worker for God must be in a healthy, vigorous, spiritual condition himself.

I want to say one word of criticism about the choosing of Sunday-school teachers. The way Sunday-school teachers are chosen is that immediately a person gets introduced into the Kingdom of God, they are given a Sunday-school class to teach. When you come to God's way, you will find something very different; immediately a soul gets introduced into the kingdom of God, it has got to do something, but it is something along the line of the new life it has received, obedience and walking in the light, until it is consolidated in the ways of God. Why is this necessary? Because dealing with souls is tenfold more dangerous than dealing with bodies. Unless you are in a healthy, vigorous condition with God, you will catch the disease of the soul you are dealing with instead of helping to cure it. Unless you are out amongst the tremendous facts of God's revelation in the Bible, unless you know how to take breezy walks through that Book, unless you know how to walk up and down that country and take in the air of God's hills and get thoroughly robust and continually change your walk amongst those facts, you are sure to catch the diseases of the souls you are dealing with. So remember, it is absolutely necessary to be like the cedars of Lebanon. Do you know the characteristic of a Lebanon tree? The cedars of Lebanon have such extraordinary power of life that instead of nourishing parasites it kills them, the life within is so strong and so robust that instead of feeding the parasites it chokes them off. God grant that we may be so filled with His life, may flourish as the cedars of Lebanon, so that He can trust us down in all the dark, difficult places amongst the souls of our brother men and be able to pour His tremendous health and power through us.

How sad it is to see men and women who did begin to work for God, and whose work God honoured, slowly fall off. Why? They have caught the disease of death amongst the people they have been dealing with. In the medical profession, particularly doctors who deal with the insane, have continually to be changed, continually shifted. Why? Because they take the diseases and troubles they live amongst, and you will find that God the Holy Ghost has an amazing power of shifting His workers. Some wonder why God keeps shifting them, why He shifts their circumstances; the reason is not only to keep them in touch with the great sphere of work, but to keep their souls alive.

Do remember, then, that it is necessary for the worker to be healthy, and beware of this mistake, that by working for God amongst men, you develop your own Christian life; you do not unless your Christian life is there first. It is so obvious that it needs to be said over again—you cannot develop your own Christian life unless it is there. The advice given that if you work for God you develop your own life often means that if you work for God you get right yourself; you do not, you have to be right with God first.

The next time you deal with a soul at the penitent form, remember it is one thing to tell him to receive the Spirit of God, to recognise and rely on Him, but quite another thing for you to do the same thing. Unless you recognise the Spirit of God, and rely on Him, and expect Him to bring to your remembrance some word that is going to apply in that case, you will be of very little use as an expert soul-curer and for putting people in the way to get right with God.

Then do live among human facts! Thank God He has given the majority of us the surroundings of real, definite, sordid human beings; there is no pretence about them, the people we live among and come in contact with are not theories, they are facts. That is the kind of thing God wants us to keep among.

Then third, see that you get into this Book. I feel more than hungry to see men and women roused up to get hold of this Book and live among its facts, then the Spirit of God will bring to your remembrance how to apply the truth in each case.

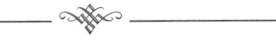

Chapter II

THE WORKER AMONG THE ABNORMAL

For the Son of man is come to seek and to save that which was lost. Luke 19:10

Abnormal means not normal or according to rule, not upright, not good. God's Book says that the whole of the human race is abnormal.

In our first talk we dealt with the Christian worker, and we found that first of all he must have a definite experience in his own life of the marvellous salvation of God. Then that he must learn how to recognise and rely on the Spirit of God in dealing with souls; he must live in the facts of the Bible, and keep in touch with the facts of human life. Now we deal with some of the facts of human life as God's Book reveals them,

I want to notice a very important distinction, viz., that the "lost" from the Bible standpoint are not doomed. The lost, Jesus Christ is seeking for; the doomed are those who rebel against the seeking Saviour. To Jesus Christ, all men are lost, and the worker who is going to work for the cure of souls must have the same outlook. We have to bear this in mind because workers to-day are not taking the standpoint of the Lord Jesus Christ.

In Luke 19 we find a specimen of a lost man. "The Son of man is come to seek and to save that which was lost." Notice the setting of this statement. Zacchaeus was a chief publican and as such he would be possessed of many ill-gotten gains; he was a man of wealth and position, a dishonourable man, but perfectly content with his dishonour. Zacchaeus was not troubled in the tiniest degree, his whole nature towards God was frozen, no sign of life about him. In the far North the thermometer freezes and can record nothing, and it remains frozen until the temperature alters; immediately the temperature alters, then the thermometer registers. This man Zacchaeus was frozen towards God, his conscience did not bother him, he was "lost," quite contented, quite happy, and quite curious. When Jesus Christ came his way, the man's nature unfroze, something began to work at once.

The first thing the worker has to learn is how to bring the Lord Jesus Christ in contact with frozen souls, those who are dead towards God, whose consciences are not the slightest bit disturbed. How is the worker to bring the Lord Jesus Christ across the life that is dead in trespasses and sins and does not know it? By the Holy Spirit and personal experience alone. By personal experience I mean what we have already insisted on: I must know personally what God has done in my soul through Jesus Christ; and I must have learned how to rely on the Holy Spirit, because the Holy Spirit makes Jesus Christ present to all kinds and conditions of men. The majority of people when they come across a nature like Zacchaeus will say he is simply selfish, sordid and indifferent; he is not convicted of sin, it is no use to try and deal with him. That is the attitude we all maintain to the "Zacchaeus" type of man until we learn how to bring Jesus Christ close to him. Whenever Jesus Christ came across men in His day, they knew where they were, and they either rebelled or followed him. They either went away exceeding sorrowful, or they turned with their whole nature towards Him.

The next thing we have to learn by contact with Jesus Christ is this, that if the whole human race—everybody, good, bad and indifferent—is lost, we must have the boundless confidence of Jesus Christ Himself about us, that is, we must know that He can save anybody and everybody. There is a great deal of importance to be attached to this point. Just reflect in your mind and think of some lives you know that are frozen; there is no conviction of sin; they are dishonourable, and they know it; they are abnormal, off the main track altogether, but they are not a bit troubled about it; talk to them about their wrong doing and they are totally indifferent to you. You have to learn how to introduce the atmosphere of the Lord Jesus

Christ around those souls. As soon as you do, something happens. Look what happened to Zacchaeus— "And Zacchaeus stood, and said unto the Lord, Behold, Lord, the half of my goods I give to the poor; and if I have wrongfully exacted aught of any man, I restore fourfold" (RV). Who had been talking to him about his doings? Not a soul. Jesus had never said a word about his evil doings. What awakened him? What suddenly made him know where he was? The presence of Jesus!

Wherever a worker for God goes, the same thing will happen if the Spirit of God is getting His way through that man or woman. If you are right with God in personal experience, saved and sanctified (to use our own technical words), and the Spirit of God is getting His way with you, other people will get to know where they are wrong, and until they learn the reason they will say you are criticising them; but you are perfectly conscious that you have never criticised them. What has happened? This very thing, the Holy Spirit's presence through you has brought the atmosphere that Jesus Christ's presence always brought, and has thawed the ice around their mind and their conscience and they are beginning to be convicted.

Let me insist that the worker must know how to bring every kind and condition of man into contact with Jesus Christ, and the only way that can be done is by reliance on the Holy Spirit and by personal experience. If you are trying to work for God and have no definite experience of your own and do not know how to rely on the Holy Spirit, God grant that you may come to the place where you do know, then wherever you go the atmosphere produced will thaw things around men's consciences and hearts.

Men's minds will always assent that Jesus Christ is right—why? Because Jesus Christ is Incarnate Reason. There is something in Jesus Christ that appeals to every man, no matter what condition he is in. If once Jesus Christ is brought into contact with a man, let that man seem to us dead and indifferent, destitute of anything like goodness—let him come in contact with Jesus Christ by the Holy Spirit, and you will instantly see that he can grasp something about Him in a way we cannot understand unless we know the Holy Spirit.

Jesus Christ always appeals to men's consciences— why? Because He is Incarnate Righteousness. So many people try to explain things about Jesus Christ, but no worker need ever try to do that. You cannot explain things about Jesus Christ, rely on the Holy Spirit and He will explain Jesus to the soul. Let me recommend you to have this boundless confidence in Jesus Christ's power as you go into work for God! If you do not believe practically in your heart that the Lord Jesus Christ can alter and save the man you are talking to, you limit Jesus Christ in that life. You may say, "Oh, yes, Jesus Christ can save you; He can alter the whole

thing and can put His new life within you and make you a new man"; but if *you* do not believe He can do it, you limit God's power in that life, and God holds you responsible. So the first thing the worker must do is to keep his heart always believing in Jesus.

Are you in constant contact with frozen natures in your own family, in your business, in your friendships? You have talked with them, prayed with them, you have done everything you know how, but there is not the slightest sign of conviction of sin, no trouble of conscience or heart. They are not "out-and-out" sinners, but you know that they are "in-and-in" sinners; you know they are wrong and twisted and have things that are not clean, but you cannot make them realise it; they always get away, frozen and untouched. Then bring your own soul face to face with Jesus Christ: "Lord, do *I* believe that Thou canst thaw that man's nature, that woman's nature, until the Holy Spirit has a chance of saving him or her?" That is the first difficulty to be overcome—what state of faith in Jesus Christ have I? Then next ask yourself, Do I believe that the Lord Jesus Christ can take that selfish, sensual, twisted, self-satisfied nature that is all wrong and out of order—do I believe that He can make it perfect in the sight of God? Oh, do let us get back to this tremendous confidence in the Lord Jesus Christ's power! back to reliance on the Holy Spirit, and to remembering that Jesus came to seek the lost.

In the fifteenth chapter of St. Luke's Gospel, our Lord speaks about the joy of finding lost things, and to me there is always this appeal: the Lord wants my eyes to look through; is He looking through them? The Lord wants my brain to think through; is He thinking through it? The Lord wants my hands to work with; is He working with them? The Lord wants my body to live and walk in for one purpose— to go after the lost from His standpoint; am I letting Him walk and live in me?

The worker must see that Jesus Christ has His right of way in him in each particular. Oh, the number of men and women to-day who are working on the line of self-realisation; seeking the training of the mind and of the body—for what purpose? To help them realise themselves! Jesus Christ wants this body so that He can work through it to find those who are out of the way. Do remember that it is the most practical thing on this earth to be a worker for the cure of souls. You have to rely on the Holy Spirit and to live among human facts and Bible facts. Have you, Christian worker, accepted the verdict of Jesus Christ regarding the human race, viz., that they are all lost, and have you got boundless confidence in Jesus Christ, are you perfectly certain that if a soul can only get in contact with Jesus, He can save him absolutely?

I want to give one word of warning to workers for God, especially Sunday-school teachers and preachers of the Gospel—beware of the snare of putting anything first in your mind but Jesus Christ. If you put the needs of your people first, there is something between you and the power of God. Face Jesus Christ steadily, and allow nothing, no work and no person, to come between you and Him. For what purpose? That the Holy Spirit may flow through you in your preaching to the needs of the people around. You will find that people will always distinguish between that kind of message and the message that is spoken out of sympathy with them. There is only one Being Who understands us all and that is the Holy Spirit, and He understands the Lord Jesus Christ too, and if you keep the avenues of your soul open to Him and get your messages from Him and see that you allow nothing to obscure Him, you will find He will locate the people. For every new message you give, God will give you human beings who have been convicted by it, and you will have to deal with them, whether you like it or not; and you will have not only to deal with them, but you will have to take them on your heart before God. God will make you work for the cure of the souls He has wounded by your message. If the wounding has come along His line, the line of the faithful proclamation of His message, He will let you see Him healing that soul through you as a worker, as you rely on

the Holy Spirit. God grant that as we go forth to our varied work we may be filled with the Spirit, and then patiently do the drudgery!

I want to say one other thing that will connect this talk with the next one—the Spirit of God will not work for the cure of some souls without you, and God is going to hold to the account of some of us the souls that have gone un-cured, un-healed, un-touched by Jesus Christ because we have refused to keep our souls open towards Him, and when the sensual, selfish, wrong lives came around we were not ready to present the Lord Jesus Christ to them by the power of the Holy Spirit. Workers for God, let us believe with all our heart these Divine revelations, and never despair of any soul under heaven. If you have a chronic case—I mean by that, someone who is always coming out at every altar call but never getting anywhere, thank God for it. I have found this out, that as far as I am concerned, God uses those chronic seekers as an education to me. It is a tremendous temptation to put them on one side and say, "It is no use dealing with such people." It is! If they keep chronic long enough they will educate you so sufficiently that the Lord will be able to manifest His patience through you as He never could otherwise, and all of a sudden those souls will come into the light.

Chapter III
THE WORKER AMONG THE HARDY ANNUALS

For there are no bands in their death: but their strength is firm. Psalm 73:4

By "hardy annuals" I mean the healthy-minded sinners. We pointed out before that from Jesus Christ's point of view all men are lost, but we have so narrowed and so specialised the term "lost" that we have missed its evangelical meaning; we have made it mean that only the people who are down and out in sin are lost.

In the seventeenth chapter of Acts we see Paul the Pharisee, and the sanctified Apostle of God, face to face with healthy-minded, vigorous pagans. Jesus Christ came in contact with such people over and over again, and you will find that you have to come in contact with them too. They are once-born people, and perfectly content with being once-born. They are usually upright, quite sufficient for themselves morally, very bright and happy, and you seem to feel they have not the slightest need of the Lord Jesus Christ in their lives. That class formed a great setting all round our Lord's life. In the days of His flesh our Lord worked almost exclusively amongst Jews, but

every now and again a Gentile burst through into the inner circle, and Jesus always dealt with him in a totally different manner. Whenever our Lord dealt with a religious Jew there was a serious solemnity about Him, and a serious solemnity about the Jew; but immediately our Lord came in contact with a Greek, He seemed to read the sharp wit of the Greek straightaway and dealt with him accordingly.

In the fifteenth chapter of St. Matthew we read that our Lord departed into the coasts of Tyre and Sidon, the reason being that He wanted to be alone; He had had too much publicity and was trying to get His disciples away. Then a Syrophoenician woman burst through with a request to which Jesus pays no attention, the reason being quite obvious—He wanted to be quiet, and He knew perfectly well that this woman would blaze abroad more than ever what He could do. But her faith was strong, she knew that if she could get hold of the Lord Jesus He would heal her daughter. Watch how our Lord deals with her; He gives her a proverb and she gives Him back a proverb: "It is not meet to take the children's bread and cast it to the dogs." "Yea, Lord: for even the dogs eat of the crumbs which fall from their masters' table" (RV). Her type of mind was foreign to the religious Jews, but Jesus understood her at once, and He praised her for her faith. "O woman, great is thy faith: be it done unto thee even as thou wilt."

The healthy-minded tendency is very strong to-day. It is the explanation of Unitarianism in its shallower aspect; the explanation of the New Thought movement and the Mind Cure movement, of Christian Science; it is the explanation of how people can be quite happy, quite moral, quite upright, without having anything to do with the Lord Jesus Christ. Our Lord describes these people in terms of the once-born, as "lost." The problem for us as workers is, how are we to get these irreligious people who are quite happy and healthy-minded, to the place where they want Jesus?

The Syrophoenician woman came to our Lord at the end of a busy spell, and you will find that these healthy-minded folks will often come across you when you are fagged out and will ask you all kinds of questions. They did of the Apostle Paul—"What would this babbler say? . . . He seemeth to be a setter forth of strange gods: because he preached Jesus and the resurrection" (RV). In writing to the Corinthians, Paul says, "We preach Christ crucified, . . . unto the Greeks foolishness."

Every worker for God has surely come across the type of man that makes him feel foolish; the external life, and internal life as far as you know is quite sterling and upright, and he puts questions to you that bring you to a complete standstill, you cannot answer them, and he succeeds in making you feel amazingly foolish. For instance, you preach that Jesus Christ lived and died and rose again to save men from their sins and to put them right with God; these people have no sin that they are conscious of, you cannot point to a spot in their whole life, they are healthy-minded and happy, but absolutely pagan, and they say, "What was the use of Jesus Christ dying for me? I am all right; I do exactly what I ought to do. I am not a blackguard, I am not a thief, I am not a sinner. Why ever should Jesus Christ die for me?" Unless you are used to it, that line of thing produces a sense of unutterable foolishness in you. How are we to bring the Gospel of Jesus Christ, and our Lord Himself, before a man or woman of that sort?

I want us to look at three types of pagans—Gallio, Herod and Pilate. Gallio was an ordinary pagan, upright and just, and when the Apostle Paul was brought before him he did not care anything about him. "And Gallio cared for none of those things." He said in effect, "I have nothing whatever to do with your religious quarrels, I am not here to decide questions of your law for you." The opponents of Christianity are not weak, they are opponents who are able to ignore us; so the first thing to do is to examine and see what kind of Gospel we are preaching. If you are only preaching before this kind of pagan, upright, righteous and just, but without a spark of religion in him, that Jesus Christ can save sinners, that is not the Jesus Christ he needs. You have to preach the Lord Jesus Christ revealed in God's Word.

The first thing I want to impress on our hearts and minds as workers is this—we must not preach one phase of Christ's work. Jesus said, "I, if I be lifted up from the earth, will draw all men unto Myself" (RV). Have I a pet doctrine I am lifting up? If I have, then these healthy-minded folk will simply heap ridicule on me; but immediately I preach Christ, something happens—the Spirit of God begins to work where I cannot. The first point for us to remember then, is that we must preach Christ, not a pet theory of our own, no matter how right and true it is, no matter how important a doctrine or how really the outcome of our Lord's work; that is not what we have to present, we have to present Jesus Christ. "And Philip . . . preached unto him Jesus" (Acts 8:35).

Paul was able to stand the ridicule, the cultured ridicule, of the Athenian philosophers because he knew Jesus Christ, he knew Him as the greatest, grandest and most worthy Being that was ever on this earth. See that you present the Lord Jesus Christ Himself to your ordinary pagan. The Spirit of God will guide you as you rely on Him to the presentation that is required for each one. Some people present Jesus Christ in packets, they have one packet of verses marked "Salvation," another marked "Sanctification," another marked "The Baptism with the Holy Ghost." The reason they do this is easy to understand—these particular verses have been used mightily in their experience in saving souls, but as we pointed out at the first, immediately we begin to depend on our special prescription the Spirit of God will depart from us. In every case we have to deal with, whether it be the case of a man with a frozen conscience, or a healthy-minded pagan, we have to learn how to rely on the Holy Spirit straightaway—"Lord, this man is healthy, his sense of justice clear, his record clean, but he cares for none of these things; I cannot deal with him." We have to present Jesus Christ in all His power, and rely on the Holy Spirit to deal with him.

There is another type of pagan and he is represented by Herod. Herod is a rare type of pagan, he is obscene; he was bad, unmentionably bad, and you will find that when he saw Jesus Christ face to face he was not the slightest bit troubled. Why? He had heard the voice of God before through John the Baptist, and he had ordered that voice to be silent. Herod is the presentation of the awful possibility of a fixed character, absolutely fixed in immorality. Jesus Christ did not awaken one tremor of conscience in him, he had signed his own death-warrant. When the voice of God came to him in repeated warnings through John the Baptist about the thing that was wrong in his life, he would not listen, he persisted in his badness until he killed all his affinity for God, and when Jesus Christ stood before him he was not an atom troubled. Did you ever notice what is recorded? "Now when Herod saw Jesus, he was exceeding glad"—why? For the same reason that people go to a picture show, they want to see things. We read that Herod questioned Jesus in many words; "but He answered him nothing." "There is a sin unto death"—there is a final apostasy from God, there is a sealed doom on an immortal soul while it lives, where God Almighty cannot awaken one echo of response—"I do not say that he shall pray for it," says John (1 John 5:16).

If you have never faced the question yourself, face it now—you are not as bothered now as you once were, if you are bothered at all, about Jesus Christ's line of things, and you are to blame; there will come a time when you will not be bothered even as much as you are now. Once Herod heard John the Baptist gladly (Mark 6:20). If God has ever pointed out to you in the past the one thing that is wrong in your life, you are to blame if you did not listen. A time will come when all the tremendous presentation of the truth of God will become a farce. God forbid that any worker should ever stand face to face with a son of perdition, with a man or woman who has apostatised from God. There is such a thing as fixity of character, and when one's prayers go out for such an one they are arrested by God, not by the devil, and frozen before they get out of the lips. This is a truth, an awful and terrible truth, but one that people will not listen to.

Another type of pagan is Pilate. Pilate represents the type of pagan who always seeks his own interests; that type is known to us all to-day. People belong to certain churches because it is better for their business; or they shift their membership to other churches because it is more convenient for business. A once-born man, who acts from this point of view is an opportunist. "If it is Jesus Christ's Gospel that is in the ascendancy, then I will use it to serve my own ends." You have to bring that man face to face with Christ, not with your experience, but with Jesus Christ Himself.

Gallio is a type of the ordinary pagan, healthy minded, vigorous, strong and happy. Is it right to be healthy-minded? Of course it is. Is it right to be happy? Of course it is. That is why the new phases of thought we have alluded to are spreading and putting down Christianity. If you can teach a man how to ignore sin, you have him. If you can tell him how to ignore pain successfully and disease and trouble, he will listen to you. If you can tell him how to ignore the possibility of judgement coming on him for wrong-

doing, he will listen to you. If you can show a man how he can be delivered from the torture of sin, delivered from a pain-stricken body, loosened from a bad past, then you have him. Mark you, every one of these points is right; the prince of this world delivers on that line, and so does the Lord Jesus Christ. Watch Jesus Christ's life—the people would take all His blessings, but they would not get rightly related to Him; and our difficulty is in presenting men with Jesus Christ apart from what He can do. How does Jesus Christ teach a man to forget sin? By forgiving him. How does a pagan teach a man to forget sin? "Ignore it, think no more about it, realise yourself!" Can it be done? Of course it can be done. If you will just sin long enough, you will forget how sinful you have been, and is it likely that a man who has forgotten how wrong he has been is going to be willing to face Jesus Christ, who, as soon as He sees him, will flash through him his past wrong? The first thing Jesus Christ does is to open a man's eyes wide to the wrong and then deliver him from it. If anyone here is getting to the place of forgetting sin by ignoring it, the place of healthy-mindedness and happiness without facing the past wrong, that is the characteristic of the pagan; but Jesus will open our eyes wide to see the wrong and will deliver us from it by putting us on another platform.

The Syrophoenician woman wanted the Lord Jesus Christ. She did not care one iota about the disciples, what she wanted was the Lord Jesus Christ. Again we read that certain Greeks came to the disciples saying, "Sir, we would see Jesus." What did those disciples do? They went and told Jesus. Christian worker, when anyone belonging to the healthy pagan type comes to your meeting, whose presence there means "We would see Jesus," what do you do? Try and persuade him? You never will. Remember what Philip and Andrew did—they went and told Jesus. Whenever you get the request, either by presence or by word: "We would see Jesus," don't begin with "firstly, secondly and thirdly," go to Jesus and say, "Lord, these people want to see Thee."

Again we come back to our first points—rely on the Holy Ghost as the most practical Being you ever knew, and live among the facts of God's Word and among human facts, and people will recognise Jesus Christ through you. God grant that every worker may ever remember that the only One Who can touch "the hardy annuals" whom no truth seems to upset, who carry bright, cheerful faces, and no adversity turns them aside, is the Lord Jesus Christ Himself. People say that it is so hard to bring Jesus Christ and present Him before the lives of men to-day. Of course it is, it is so hard that it is impossible except by the power of the indwelling Holy Ghost. A crisis comes in every man's life. The 107th Psalm is a record of people who would not come to God until they were at their wits' end. When they were at their wits' end, then they cried to God and He heard them.

If you go and tell men it is better to be good than bad, they will say, "Yes, that is so, but how are you going to make bad men good?" That is the problem. Unless your religion will go to the lowest and the worst and the most desperate case you know of, your religion is of no use. There are a great many forms of belief which cannot begin to touch the worst of mankind, they can only deal with cultured minds and

hearts. Jesus Christ's religion goes down to the lowest of the low as well as up to the highest of the high, and to all in between. The marvel of Jesus Christ is that He takes facts as they are. He Himself is the answer to every problem of heart and mind and life. The next time you come across a "hardy annual," see that you lay hold of God for that one until Jesus Christ is presented by the power of the Holy Ghost, and then you will see the altered face, the altered attitude, and the altered life.

Chapter IV

THE WORKER AMONG BACKSLIDERS

And on some have mercy with fear; hating even the garment spotted by the flesh. Jude 23 (RV)

The best example of a backslider in the New Testament (the word "backslider" is never used in the New Testament, it is an Old Testament word) is in 2 Timothy 4:10. "For Demas forsook me, having loved this present world" (RV)—he has gone back to where he prefers. Couple with that Jeremiah 2:13, and you will have a good indication of what a backslider is: "For My people have committed two evils; they have forsaken Me the fountain of living waters, and hewed them out cisterns, broken cisterns, that can hold no water." Backsliding is twofold, and the term can only be applied to people in this condition. We use the word very loosely, we apply it to people who are degenerating, to people who have committed sin; but a backslider is neither one nor the other, a backslider is worse than both. He is worse than a person who is degenerating, and worse than a person who has committed sin; he has forsaken God and taken up with something else.

It is customary to talk of Peter as being a backslider when he denied his Lord; what happened to Peter was that he got a revelation of what he was capable of, viz., of denying his Lord with oaths and curses. What were the conditions that led to Peter's fall? He had followed Jesus out of genuine devotion, and in true loyalty of heart to Jesus he had pictured a great many things that might happen, but never in his wildest moment did he imagine that Jesus Christ was tamely going to give Himself up to the powers of the world, and when Peter saw Jesus Christ quietly give Himself right over to the rabble and let them take Him, all Peter's thoughts were turned into confusion, his heart was in despair, and in that condition, he "followed afar off." Then when he was tormented by stinging questions, he suddenly found in himself this awful condition he was totally

ignorant of, a condition that made him deny with oaths and curses that he ever knew Jesus. Remember, Peter belonged to a dispensation we cannot begin to imagine, a dispensation before Jesus Christ died and rose again; but if we do not live in the dispensation Peter lived in, we can understand the people he represents. Peter was loyal-hearted and devoted to Jesus, but grossly ignorant of what he was capable of—quite loyal, but quite ignorant, and in the trying crisis suddenly to his amazement he finds that he is capable of evil that horrifies him.

The way God deals with a backslider, and teaches us to deal with a backslider, is clear enough for us to talk about it now.

Let us first of all examine for ourselves and find out whether in using the word "backslider" we are applying it to the right condition of a man. The backslidden condition is twofold: it is forsaking God and taking up with something else; it is not the condition of a man awakening to the presence of the disposition of sin in himself. A backslider is a man who does know what God's grace is, who does know what sin is, and who does know what deliverance is, but who has deliberately forsaken God and gone back because he loved something else better.

The question is often asked, "Can a Christian sin?" He certainly can, but the sin must be confessed immediately and forgiven, for if a Christian allows an act of sin to go on it will lead him steadily on until he will pervert all the ways of God and hew out a way for himself.

The statement is frequently made that in dealing with a backslider, the worker has to bring him to being born again of the Spirit. A backslider has not to be born again, he is in a much worse condition than a man not born again: he has to have his backslidings healed and be restored. The statements in the Bible about backsliding are very solemn. Backsliding is the most awful crime spiritually; it is forsaking God and hewing out for one's self "broken cisterns, that can hold no water." With a backslider it is not the question of a soul needing to be born again, but a much harder case than a man who has never been born again. Do not get confused because when you have to face backsliders you find you cannot deal with them as you deal with any ordinary sinner. Their hearts are frozen, they are not convicted of sin, they are absolutely dull and dead towards all God wants. They will tell you quite mechanically, "Oh yes, I once knew God, I did experience this and that, but I deliberately stepped aside." The process may be gradual, but the backsliding condition is reached by forsaking God and taking up with something else.

In 2 Peter 2:15 you will find a luminous word for workers—". . . forsaking the right way, they went astray, having followed the way of Balaam the son of Beor, who loved the hire of wrong-doing" (RV). Who was Balaam? A prophet. What was his way? Making a market of his gift. The New Testament speaks in three different ways about Balaam: "the way of Balaam," "the error of Balaam" (Jude 11) and "the teaching of Balaam" (Revelation 2:14 RV). The "way" of Balaam is to make a market of one's gift, presuming on it, putting yourself in God's show-room. "I am here as a specimen of what God can do." Immediately a Christian begins to put himself into the "show business" that is the way towards backsliding. The "error" of Balaam is seeing only the standard of natural morality and never discerning God's ways behind. Immediately a Christian gets into the way of following his own wise common-sense morality, rather than the dictates of the Spirit of God backing the Word of God, he is on the high road to backsliding. Beware how you guide your Christian life and your Christian experience. Are you simply taking the ordinary high standards of the world in your business? Beware, that is an error that leads to backsliding. "Oh, well, they all do it, I must do the same." That is the ordinary standard; if it conflicts in the tiniest degree with the clear standard of God, beware! It is an error that leads to the false doctrine which is the very heart of backsliding, making a judicious mix-up between corrupt worldliness and godliness. That is the way backsliding will begin, it is fixing your eyes on the wrong thing. The "teaching" of Balaam is the corrupting of God's people. Balaam taught Balak to corrupt the people by enticing them to marry the women of Moab. That is the Old Testament incident, but what does it mean? It means trying to compromise between corrupt worldliness and Christian profession. These are three dangerous characteristics pointed out in the New Testament, and they are fruitful in backsliding.

When you come to deal with backsliders, one of the greatest dangers is that they spread their disease more quickly than any other. The presence of one backslider is a peril to a whole community. His or her influence is tenfold worse than a hundred sinners who have never been saved, and the worker for God who begins to deal with a backslider has to learn, first of all, his unutterable powerlessness to touch him.

Let us face the backslider now. Are you going to begin by asking him to receive the Spirit of God? You will have no answer. He may say, "Yes, Lord, I am sorry, please give me the Holy Spirit," but God won't. You won't find one case anywhere on record in the Old or New Testament in which God deals with a backslider along those lines. Let me take as an illustration the parable in the fifteenth chapter of St. Luke. I know this parable is used in many ways, but I want to use it as a picture of the backslider. It is obvious why it is called "The Parable of the Prodigal Son," but it is not called so in the Bible, it is called "The Parable of the Two Sons." One son went away and spent his substance in riotous living, the other son stayed at home. Both are as bad as each other. The spirit of the stay-at-home was every bit as bad as the wild riot of the younger boy who went away.

Did the father send any message to the far country after the younger boy? There is no record of any message being sent. What did the younger boy have to do? He had to do exactly what is recorded in Hosea long before that picture was painted by our Lord—he had to return. Drawn by God? It does not say so. Read the fourteenth chapter of Hosea: "I will heal their backsliding"; but the backslider has to get up first, leave the pigs and what pigs eat, and go back to where he came from. Help granted him? None whatever. Messages from the home country? Not one. Tender touches of God's grace on his life? No. Can you picture that prodigal son returning, a degraded, sunken, sin-stained man, going back in all the cruel, bald daylight? Oh, it is a hard way to go back out of a backslider's hell; a hard, hard way! Every step of it is cruel, every moment is torture. But what happened? Before that younger son had got very far, the father saw him "and ran, and fell on his neck, and kissed him"!

Worker for God among backslidden souls, remember God's way, put the sting, if you can, into the backslider's soul that he may get up and come back to God, and what has he to do? Take with him words and say, "By mine iniquity have I fallen." Did the prodigal son take with him words? He did, he rehearsed them over and over again where he was amongst the pigs—"I will say to my father this and that," he had it all by heart. Does Hosea say the same? He does: Take with you words, and return unto the Lord, and say, "By mine iniquity have I fallen." What does iniquity mean? Unequal dealing, turning out of the way.

Is there a backslider listening to this? Then rouse yourself and go back to God. "But I feel no drawing."

You won't feel any. I do not find one instance in the Bible of God drawing a backslider in the same way that He draws a sinner. The word to the backslider is: *"Return."* "Take with you words, and return unto the LORD: say unto Him, Take away all iniquity" (RV).

Every Christian worker will bear me out in this next statement, that in dealing with a backslider, you are exhausted to the last drop of your energy. When we work with other classes, like those we have been touching on, God seems to supply grace at the very moment; but we need to remember that if in the other cases we need to rely on the Holy Ghost, we need to do so here a thousandfold more.

Intercessory prayer for a backslider is a most instructive but a most trying work for God, and it will teach the worker that prayer is not only making petitions, but that prayer is breathing an atmosphere. The Christian Church nearly always separates those two; when it emphasises the atmosphere of prayer, it forgets the petition; and when it emphasises the petition it is apt to forget the atmosphere, but the two must go together, and you need to be freshly bathed moment by moment in the limpid life of God (if I may use the phrase) as you pray for your backslider. If ever the worker needs wisdom that cometh from above, it is in the moment of dealing with a backslider. How am I going to awaken, how am I going to sting into action, a backslidden soul? How am I going to get that soul to go back?

I said just now that no message was sent to the far country; God sends none, but, worker for God, will you be a message from the Father? Will you so bathe your life in the atmosphere of prayer that when you come in contact with a backslidden soul, it will awaken a remembrance of the Father, awaken a remembrance of what that soul once was? Will you let your life be like a bunch of flowers from the Father's home garden, just awakening for one moment a remembrance of what life once was, and then pass on, and pray and watch, and you will be mightily rewarded by God when you see that poor backslidden soul get up and go back to God, taking with him words and saying, "By mine iniquity have I fallen."

If ever you hear a testimony along this line, "I was a backslider, but, thank God, I am healed now," do call a halt in that soul. Backsliding in the Bible is called by words used for the most shocking immorality. Can you imagine anybody who has been guilty of an awful moral crime talking about it in the glib, off-hand way some people talk about backsliding? When a backslider has been reclaimed by God and brought back, when he has returned and has been met by God, the memory of the past is too tremendously humiliating to be mentioned often, and when it is mentioned the atmosphere of the life is one of deep repentance towards God. Never sympathise with a backslider; do all in your power to goad him to return to God. If you cannot do it in words, do it by living in the atmosphere of God and awakening some remembrance of what he once was.

Another illustration of backsliding is in the twenty-third chapter of Matthew. It is not in reference to a person, but to the city of Jerusalem, but it gives a good picture of the way God deals with backsliders: "O Jerusalem, Jerusalem, which killeth the prophets, and stoneth them that are sent unto her! how often would I have gathered thy children together, even as a hen gathereth her chickens under her wings, and ye would not! Behold, your house is left unto you desolate. For I say unto you, Ye shall not see Me henceforth, till ye shall say, Blessed is He that cometh in the name of the Lord" (RV). "How often would I, . . . and ye would not!"

Oh, if any here should be backsliders, let me counsel you to return to God, and tell Him that you have fallen away from Him by your own unequal doings. Take with you words and tell Him so, let the lash fall, and before you know another thing God will receive you! The prodigal son was all but choked on the bosom of his father before he got half his recital out; but he had to show that he was in earnest, he had to return first, and you must do the same.

Christian worker, if you have someone in your mind who is a backslider, one who did know the grace of God, who did run well but who has compromised, has a name to live but is dead, then God grant you may realise the filling up of "that which is behind of the afflictions of Christ" in intercessory prayer. The backsliders are the most dangerous class under Heaven to touch, and no one but a man or woman who knows how to live bathed moment by moment in the love of God, who knows how to prevail in prayer, ought to touch the case of a backslider. It needs the wisdom that cometh from above, and if you have indeed been led by God to face such a life, do it on God's line. Do not try and bring God around by way of your ignorance; go along the clearly discerned lines that are given in His Word. Get that one to understand, either through his own intelligence or by praying that he must return of his own accord.

"Take with you words, and return unto the LORD" (RV), then God says, "I will heal their backsliding, I will love them freely."

Chapter V
THE WORKER AMONG THE "TWO-FACED"

*Even so ye also outwardly appear righteous unto men,
but within ye are full of hypocrisy and iniquity.
Matthew 23:28*

By "two-faced" I do not mean the kind of character
John Bunyan refers to in his "Mr. Facing both-ways,"
I mean a man guilty of internal hypocrisy. "Two-faced" is simply a figure of speech for double dealing
and falsehood. If you never have taken the trouble to
go through the Bible to see how much God's Word
has to say about the "two-faced," do it, and you will be
surprised. Let me give you one or two passages to
show you that this subject is not isolated or novel, not
something taken because it sounds different from
what is usually taken. It is taken because it describes
a class of folk that are so difficult to deal with that we
rarely hear them mentioned.

> *Beware of false prophets, which come to you in
> sheep's clothing, but inwardly they are ravening
> wolves. (Matthew 7:15)*

> *For there shall arise false Christs, and false
> prophets, and shall shew great signs and wonders;
> so as to lead astray, if possible, even the elect.
> (Matthew 24:24 RV)*

> *Holding a form of godliness, but having denied the
> power thereof: from these also turn away. For of
> these are they that creep into houses, and take cap-
> tive silly women laden with sins, led away by
> divers lusts. (2 Timothy 3:5–6 RV)*

These are simply a few of a number of passages in
the Bible where the Spirit of God and our Lord draw
the portrait of the "two-faced." Let me repeat it, the
"two-faced" are the hardest and most difficult people
to work among. When we face the double-dealing,
two-faced man of God, our hearts sink, our whole
souls are terrified. We must not read the Bible like
children. God requires us to read it as men and
women, spiritual men and women, I mean. There are
things in the Bible that stagger us, things that amaze
and terrify; and the worker for God needs to understand not only the terrors of life around, but the terrors of life as God's Book reveals it.

Let us go back to the incident recorded in
2 Samuel 12. For subtlety, for amazing insight and
sublime courage, Nathan is unequalled; and what a
soul was David to have in his list for God! Would to
God there were more preachers and Christian workers after the stamp of Nathan. David did not even

begin to realise, after a year of the grossest and most
dastardly hypocrisy, that Nathan was brandishing the
sword straight into his own conscience, and only
when David had made his answer and Nathan had
heaved out the strong denunciations of God and
thrust the sword straight home with, "Thou art the
man," did David say, "I have sinned against the
LORD." There was no bungling about Nathan's work.

If you want to know how it was possible for a
mighty man of God like David to have sinned the most
wicked sin possible—I do not refer to adultery or to
murder, but to something infinitely worse, a deep, subtle, inward hypocrisy, tremendous and profound; David
lived it for a year and administered justice while all the
time he was a "whited sepulchre"—you must first allow
God to examine deep down into the possibilities of
your own nature.

Mark how Nathan came to David. "And the LORD
sent Nathan unto David." Be sure, before you face the
hypocrite and the two-faced soul that God has sent you,
and then use all the subtlety you have from the knowledge of your own heart. Any worker who has stood
before God's all-searching eye for five minutes is not
staggered at David's fall. Any heart-sin recorded is possible for any human heart, and why I say that the worker
amongst the "two-faced" will find it the hardest work is
that he has to get his subtlety, his wisdom, not only from
God on High, but from a strange, mighty probing of
his own nature. If the worker for God is going to go all
lengths for God for the cure of souls, he has to allow
God to examine deep down the possibilities of his own
nature. That is why it is hard to deal with the "two-
faced." That is why, Christian worker, God will take you
through disciplines and experiences that are not meant
for your particular life; they are meant to make you
ready for God to send as He sent Nathan. Then you can
use that subtle sword. "Be ye therefore wise as serpents,
and harmless as doves," said our Lord.

One solid year of deep heart-hypocrisy in King
David's life, suddenly faced by Nathan, and watch
how Nathan dealt with it. He used a parable of such
God-given insight that David was blind as to his
meaning. The sword went straight into David's conscience. As soon as David said, "The man that hath
done this is a son of death" (RV mg), "he is worthy of
this and it shall be done," instantly with sublime
courage Nathan said, "Thou art the man." Then came
the denunciations of God.

Worker for God, before you go among the infirm,
the sick, the subtle, the hypocritical, let God deal with

you. A child cannot wield the sword of the Spirit; it must be wielded by one fed on strong meat, one who has been deeply dealt with and examined by God's Spirit, in whom the last springs and possibilities of iniquity and wrong in his own nature have been disclosed to him that he may understand the marvel of God's grace.

Notice what the Apostle Paul did in a similar case. Read his epistle to the Galatians, and see how he dealt with "false brethren"—"And that because of the false brethren privily brought in, who came in privily to spy out our liberty which we have in Christ Jesus, that they might bring us into bondage: to whom we gave place in the way of subjection, no, not for an hour; that the truth of the gospel might continue with you" (2:4–5 RV). "False *brethren*"—mark the phrase, it is not mine, it is Paul's; they were brethren, though two-faced and untrue. What are we to do with them? "To whom we gave place in the way of subjection, no, not for an hour"—why? That our views might be expounded? No. That they might be detected as hypocrites? No. "That the truth of the gospel might continue with you." "Let brotherly love continue." This is perfect love to God; blazing, fiery zeal for God's honour, and mercilessness against God's enemies. There is a time to smite and a time to smile; a time to slay and thrust straight home when the true, sterling worth of your own repentance and the true, sterling worth of God's work of grace in your heart is put to the test.

When these false brethren crept in unawares, cunningly and craftily working against the honour of the Lord Jesus Christ, how did Paul deal with them? He withstood them; but be careful when you deal with false brethren that you are on the Apostle's line. If you dare to touch a false brother and your life has not been riddled through by God's searchlight, beware! If you are going to face false brethren, if you are going to work for the cure of the two-faced souls, if you are going to work so that the thrust of the sword of the Spirit will go straight home to the conscience, be prepared first to be dealt with by God, or else, if you begin to use your suspicions, your carping criticisms instead of God's insight, you may get a reply like this: "Jesus I know, and Paul I know; but who are ye?" Set a thief to catch a thief, that is the method of the world; but when God Almighty sends a worker He sends one whom He has literally turned inside out, in a spiritual sense, one whose disposition He has altered and allowed the man or woman to know what He has done. There is no false knowledge in that worker's life. That worker goes straight for one purpose, the condemnation of the sinner, not to show his discernment, but that he may bring the soul out of its duplicity, out of its hypocrisy, into the light of God. Don't begin to work from your carnal suspicions—how many people mistake carnal suspicions for spiritual discernment! If

God gives you a spirit of discernment, it is all right, there are times when He does, but I would like to warn you—never ask God to give you discernment. I have heard people ask God to give them the spirit of discernment, and I have felt constrained to say, "Lord, lead that soul not into temptation."

If God is going to give you power, Christian worker, to work for the cure of souls in their worst form, among the "two-faced" and the hypocritical, remember, first He will give you such an insight into the possibilities of your own sinfulness, and then such a comprehension of the marvels of His grace and wonderful salvation that you will have all the subtlety Nathan had. You will not be silent, you will speak out. Oh, for more voices to speak out when false doctrines are being taught! Would there were more to stand on the Nathan line, and wield the sword with all the wisdom of God's Spirit into the consciences of men, so that before men could know what they were driving at, the sword would have gone straight home with a "Thou art the man"! Oh, for more of that kind of wisdom! To be right with God, so examined by God, that God can send the blade of the anecdote, or the blade of the parable, straight to the imagination, and while the imagination is busy the sword has gone straight home. Then comes the application without a moment's delay—"Thou art the man," and the cry goes up, "I have sinned against the LORD." Then listen to Nathan's message to David afterwards: "And Nathan said unto David, The LORD also hath put away thy sin; thou shalt not die." What a message!

One more thing, in the multitude of all the talk and all the words nowadays, do not forget the first point—if you are going to work for the cure of souls, you cannot choose the kind of souls you are going to work with, and when God brings you face to face with a two-faced life, an inwardly hypocritical life, then you will understand what the examination of God's Spirit is in you. Then you will understand what it is to be used in God's hands as "a new sharp threshing instrument having teeth." Then you will know what it is for the sword of God to wound and bruise you until you can feel no more, that He may thrust home the sword that will kill the error and save the soul you are driving at. God grant we may understand that working for the cure of souls is not a babe's work; it is a man's work, requiring man's power, grasped and transformed by God Almighty, so that God can get straight through the worker to the man He is waiting for.

The one who stands beside Nathan in the New Testament is John the Baptist. There was no belittling of his message; when he was before Herod there was no trimming down the message to win his favour, no subtle telling a lie against himself for his own vanity. There is more of that done than most people think.

Nathan and John the Baptist came straight from God, and if you come straight from God you have to be spotless; there must be nothing between you and God, Christian worker. John the Baptist came straight from God and talked straight for God. Do you talk straight for God? When the message you have to deliver, brother preacher, strikes straight home, don't water it down just a little. Go straight for God if you come from Him. Neither for fear nor favour alter the message. What happened to John the Baptist? He went straight back to God, minus his head. That was the result of his message.

The Spirit of God discerns more incapacity in workers in dealing with the "two-faced" than in any other way. God grant we may so live under His searchlight that we may come straight from God and talk straight for God. It is easier to be silent than to obey God when you are face to face with a hypocrite, and if you are silent, you will get the applause of men. "When I say unto the wicked, Thou shalt surely die; and thou givest him not warning, nor speakest to warn the wicked from his wicked way, to save his life;

the same wicked man shall die in his iniquity; but his blood will I require at thine hand" (Ezekiel 3:18).

The next time you take a meeting, there may be a man after God's own heart there, but he has got on the line of internal hypocrisy and so may end as a son of perdition: you be faithful! You may have added to your list that day the soul of a David. But if you, seeing him and knowing him, begin to trim your message, God will require that man's blood at your hands. "If thou warn the wicked, and he turn not from his wickedness, nor from his wicked way, he shall die in his iniquity; but thou hast delivered thy soul" (Ezekiel 3:19). Obey God at every price! But mark you, Christian worker, if you obey God, He is going to let you be tried to the point of agony. In dealing with souls, it is easy to dabble in shallow water with the abnormal, it is easy to dabble with the lost, it is easy to dabble with the ordinary, easily comprehended sinners, but when we begin to work with the backsliders and when we are face to face with the internal hypocrites, then we need the subtlety which comes through the Spirit of God, and many draw back. God grant many may go forward!

Chapter VI

THE WORKER AMONG SICK SOULS

The destruction that wasteth at noonday. Psalm 91:6

I wonder if this has been growing clear to you, that we cannot understand the cases we have to deal with. One of the first things a worker for God has to learn by experience is that strangely obvious lesson, that none of us can understand the cases we meet to work with. Then how can we work for the cure of them? Remember the first principles we laid down: By knowing Jesus Christ for ourselves experimentally, and then by relying on the Holy Spirit.

"And I hated all my labour wherein I laboured under the sun" (Ecclesiastes 2:18 RV). These words were written by Solomon, the wisest man that ever lived, and you will find the last summing up of all he says is the statement of a sick soul, not a healthy-minded soul, not a vigorous sunshiny hopeful soul, but exactly the opposite.

We have spoken about the worker for the cure of souls among the "hardy annuals," the hardy sinners, nothing sick about them, they are healthy and happy and wholesome. Now I want to take exactly the opposite kind of people. If our religion is only a religion of cheerfulness for the healthy-minded, it is no good for London, because more than half the people there, a great deal more than half, are not able to be cheerful,

their minds and consciences and bodies are so twisted and tortured that exactly the opposite seems to be their portion. All the talking and preaching about healthy-mindedness, about cheering up and living in the sunshine will never touch that crowd. If all Jesus Christ can do is to tell a man he has to cheer up when he is miserable; if all the worker for God can do is to tell a man he has no business to have the "blues"—I say if that is all Jesus Christ's religion can do, then it is a failure. But the wonder of our Lord Jesus Christ is just this, that you can face Him with any kind of men or women you like, and He can cure them and put them into a right relationship with God.

The New Testament mentions quite a few of these sick souls. We will take two just now—Thomas and Mary Magdalene. Thomas was naturally gloomy, not happy and healthy-minded, that was not the way he was made. He was loyal to Jesus Christ, but he took the "sick" view of life; he always thought the worst was going to happen. You remember that when Lazarus died and Jesus said He was going to Bethany, Thomas said, "Let us also go that we may die with Him." It was no use going to Thomas and preaching the gospel of cheerfulness; you cannot alter facts by saying "Cheer up." What did Jesus Christ do for

Thomas? He brought him into personal contact with Himself and altered him entirely (see John 20:24–29).

Mary Magdalene was another type of the sick soul, tortured and afflicted. It was no use going to Mary and telling her to believe there was no such thing as the devil, no such thing as sin, she was absolutely incapable of taking the first step. What did Jesus Christ do for Mary Magdalene? Help her to be happy when she was miserable? Help her to realise that there was no such thing as demon-possession? No. He turned out the demons and healed her (Luke 8:2).

In the second chapter of Hebrews we read of a great crowd of sick souls who were subject to bondage through fear of death, and Jesus Christ came to deliver them from their bondage; and in 1 Corinthians 11:30 (RV) we read, "For this cause many among you are weak and sickly, and not a few sleep." I have simply run over these cases to show that there is sufficient indication in the Book of God for us to recognise that there are sick souls naturally.

One word about the physical condition of people. There is a threshold to our nerves, that is, a place where the nerves begin to record. Some people's nerves do not record things as quickly as others. Some people have what is called the "misery" threshold of nerves, the threshold where the nerves begin to record is much lower down than it is in other people. Take it in connection with sound, some people can sleep in a tremendous racket, noise makes not the slightest difference to them. The ear gathers up vibrations, and only when those vibrations are quick enough do we hear. If the threshold of our hearing were lower, we should hear anything that makes waves in the atmosphere, we should hear the flowers grow, everything that grows makes a motion in the atmosphere. The majority of us have a threshold that is high up, and we cannot hear unless there is sufficient vibration in the atmosphere. Get a nervous system where the threshold of nerves is low, and life is an abject torture to that one wherever he goes. What is the good of telling him to cheer up? There is a bigger problem there than we can touch. That one is in contact with forces which the majority of us know nothing about; he is tortured by things we never hear, tortured by things we never feel. Such people take a very gloomy view of life; they cannot help it.

When a worker meets a soul like that, what is he going to do—preach the gospel of temperament, "Cheer up and look on the bright side," or preach Jesus Christ? "The gospel of cheerfulness" is a catchword of the day—it may be all very well among people who are naturally cheerful, but what about the folk who cannot be cheerful, who through no fault of their own have bodies where the threshold of their nerves is so low down that life is a misery? Read the second chapter of Hebrews again, and you will find it says that Jesus Christ took on Him not the nature of angels, but—"since then the children are sharers in flesh and blood, He also Himself in like manner partook of the same" (RV). Jesus Christ took on Him a flesh and blood nature with nerves and He knows exactly how the human frame is tuned and how it is tortured. Every Christian worker ought to know how to bring the sick souls, the souls that take the gloomy view, to Jesus Christ. These people will accept all you say about the need to receive His Spirit, but nothing happens; they do not cheer up. How are we going to bring Jesus Christ into contact with them?

If you read Acts 10:38 (RV) you will find Peter says a wonderful thing about Jesus of Nazareth—"how that God anointed Him with the Holy Ghost and with power: who went about doing good, and healing all that were oppressed of the devil." Peter had just awakened to the fact that "God is no respecter of persons," and it is important to notice that he says God anointed *Jesus of Nazareth* with the Holy Ghost and with power. Peter had never preached like that before. When he preached to the Jews he had presented Jesus Christ as being first the Son of God. As soon as he came in contact with the outside crowd who were not Jews, who were not religious, the Spirit of God makes him present Him as Jesus of Nazareth. When men are being led of the Spirit of God, they never preach their convictions.

But I want to notice what it was Peter said Jesus of Nazareth did; He healed "all that were oppressed of the devil." There are only two religions that accept gloom as a fact (I mean by gloom, sin, anguish and misery, the things that make people feel that life is not worth living), viz., Buddhism and Christianity. Every other religion ignores it. This is the age of the gospel of cheerfulness. We are told to ignore sin, ignore the gloomy people, and yet more than half the human race is gloomy. Sum up your own circle of acquaintances, and then draw your inference. Go over the list, and before long you will have come across one who is gloomy, he has a "sick" view of things, and you cannot alter that one. How are you going to get that oppression taken off? Tell him to take so many weeks' holiday by the sea? Take iron pills and tonics? No! Living in the peace and joy of God's forgiveness and favour is the only thing that will brighten up and bring cheerfulness to such an one. Only when God takes a life in hand can there come deliverance from the "blues," deliverance from fits of depression, discouragement and all such moods. The Scriptures are full of admonitions to rejoice, to praise God, to sing aloud for joy; but only when one has a cause to rejoice, to praise, and to sing aloud, can these things truly be done from the heart. In the physical realm the average sick man does not take a very bright view of life, and with the sick in soul true brightness and cheer are an impossibility. Until the soul is cured there is always an underlying dread and fear which steals away the gladness and the "joy unspeakable and full of glory" which God wishes to be the portion of all His children.

In dealing with sick souls, we must remember the Master's way, how He went to the root of the matter. Hear Him as He said, time and again when one was brought to Him for physical healing, "thy sins be forgiven thee." Dig out the "root of bitterness," then there can be no fruit to sour the life and set the nerves on edge.

My brother or sister, if you are a worker for Jesus Christ, He will open your eyes wide to the fact that sin and misery and anguish are not imaginary, they are real. Anguish is as real as joy; fired, jangled and tortured nerves are as real as nerves in order. Low threshold nerves, where everything is an exquisite misery, are as real as high threshold nerves where nothing is misery. Listen to this, they are Luther's own words:

> "I am utterly weary of life. I pray the Lord will come forthwith and carry me hence. Let Him come above all with His last judgement. I will stretch out my neck, the thunder will burst forth and I shall be at rest." And having a necklace of white agates in his hand at the time, he added: "O God, grant that it may come with out delay. I would readily eat up this necklace to-day for the judgement to come to-morrow."
>
> The Electress Dowager one day, when Luther was dining with her, said to him, "Doctor, I wish you may live forty years to come."
>
> "Madame," replied he, "rather than live forty years more, I would give up my chance of Paradise."

That was Luther speaking at the end of his life. What produced the misery? He saw the havoc the Reformation had wrought, he did not see the good, he was too near it.

There was the same thing in Goethe's writings; in 1824 he writes:

> I will say nothing against the course of my existence, but at the bottom it has been nothing but pain and burden, and I can affirm that, during the whole of my seventy-five years, I have not had four weeks of genuine well-being. It has been the perpetual rolling of a rock that must be raised up again.

Robert Louis Stevenson said that three hours out of every five he was insane with misery. John Stuart Mill said that life was not worth living after you were a boy.

This is not fiction, these are human facts. What does Christian Science do—ignores them! New Thought—ignores them! Mind Cure—ignores them! Jesus Christ opens our eyes to these facts, but here comes the difficulty: how am I to get Jesus Christ in contact with these sick souls?

In the first place, will you realise that you do not know how to do it? I want to lay that one principle down very strongly. If you think you know how to present Jesus Christ to a soul, you will never be able to do it. But if you will learn how to rely on the Holy Ghost, believing that Jesus Christ can do it, then I make bold to state that He will do it. If you get your little compartment of texts, and search them out and say, "I know how to deal with this soul," you will never be able to deal with it; but if you realise your absolute helplessness and say, "My God, I cannot touch this life, I do not know where to begin, but I believe that Thou canst do it," then you can do something.

It is wonderful to see Jesus Christ slip His coolness and His balm through fired and jangled nerves, turn out demons, alter the whole outlook and lift the life into a totally new relationship. Have you ever seen Him do that? I have seen Him do it twice in my lifetime, and I will never forget it. While you watch and while you realise the marvellous work of God going on in those gloomy, tortured lives, it is as if you were bathed in the sunlight of the Presence of God in a way you never are until you are face to face with one of these cases that make you realise your own utter helplessness and the power of Jesus Christ.

It was Jesus Christ coming in contact with Thomas that altered his gloom; the disciples' testimony could not do it. "Thomas, we have seen the Lord," and out of the agony of his sick soul, Thomas says, "I cannot, I dare not, believe!" "Except I shall see in His hands the print of the nails, and put my finger into the print of the nails, and put my hand into His side, I will not believe." The testimony of the disciples was not the slightest bit of use, but when Jesus Christ came in contact with Him, all was different. "Then saith He to Thomas, Reach hither thy finger, and see My hands; and reach hither thy hand, and put it into My side; and be not faithless, but believing. Thomas answered and said unto Him, My Lord and my God" (RV).

And Mary Magdalene—what did Jesus Christ do for her? He turned the demons out of her. "Mary that was called Magdalene, from whom seven devils had gone out" (Luke 8:2 RV).

Demon possession means that one body can hold several personalities. Do you believe that? Very few people do nowadays, but it is an awful fact, not only in the New Testament, but outside the New Testament, that one body may be the holder of more than one personality. How much room does thought take up? None. Personality partakes of the nature of thought. How much room does personality take up? None. "And when He was come forth upon the land, there met Him a certain man out of the city, who had demons [ASV]. . . . And Jesus asked him, What is thy name? And he said, Legion; for many demons [ASV] were entered into him" (see Luke 8:27–30 RV). Many devils in one man, the modern man laughs at the idea, but the poor, tortured, demon-possessed man is left alone. Jesus Christ heals him and delivers him of them all.

God grant us the grace so to rely on the Holy Ghost, to so know our ignorance, so to get out of the way with our knowledge, that we will let the Holy Ghost bring the Majestic Christ face to face with the diseased, sick folk we meet. The majority of workers are in the road with their convictions of how God is going to work, there is no real, living, stirring, vital reliance on the Holy Ghost which places straight before the tortured, stricken soul the Mighty Lord Jesus. God grant we may so rely on the Holy Spirit that we may allow Him to introduce through the agony of our intercession—that is the point, through the agony of vicarious intercession—the Living, Mighty Christ! My brother and sister, are you willing to allow Jesus Christ to use every bit of your life to trample on in His way to another soul? Do you know anything about spending one costly drop of blood in vicarious intercession? There is nothing worked in the way of result in answer to prayer that does not cost somebody something. "Who in the days of His flesh, having offered up prayers and supplications with strong crying and tears . . ." (RV). When you meet your sick soul, do you cry awhile and then go home and sleep, instead of taking that soul before God and vicariously interceding until by reliance on the Holy Spirit, Jesus Christ is presented to that darkened, difficult life? Blessed be the Name of God, there is no case too hard for Jesus Christ!

One more thing—what is it produces sick souls? Our emotions are associated with certain things and the value of those things to us lies in the emotion they start. For instance, you have some things in your home that are of no use to anybody on earth, but to you they are enormously valuable. Let something come in and destroy your emotions and associations, and what kind of a world are you in? A world in which suicide is the only outlet. Let some paralysis come and destroy your emotions, all your associated ideas with things, with people, with houses, with friends, with work, and the light is gone out of the sky, the power and the joy out of life, everything is paralysed, and the universe is one black prison-house. What will produce that? Look at the prodigal son. Have you ever dropped the plumb-line down into his heart and tried to fathom one phase only of his cry—"I have sinned against heaven, and in thy sight"? Oh, the agony of the soul that has been paralysed on the inside—the gloom, the darkness, and the shadow! No preaching of the gospel of good cheer will touch that; it is only the great Life-giving, Life-imparting Christ Who can touch it. Oh, my brother or sister, you have lately been brought face to face with some case and you have said, "This is conviction of sin," but you know it is not. You have tried all the Scriptural teaching you know, with no result. You have tried to advocate this thing and that, but no result, and you have been humiliated to the dust before God. Is not this the reason—you have been trying to find out what is wrong? God will never show you what is wrong; that is not your business. What He wants us to do is to bring the case to Him: "Lord, use my intercession as a channel through which Thou canst reach that soul." God grant that we may be so centred in Him that He can use us in that wonderful way.

Chapter VII
THE WORKER AMONG THE STUPID SOULS

Behold, I have played the fool, and have erred exceedingly. 1 Samuel 26:21

This is a statement made by the prophet of the Most High God, and a King of Israel. Before I read some passages from God's Book to show you that the stupid soul is continually brought before the attention of the reader of God's Word, I would like you to notice what the word "stupid" means. It does not mean ignorant, but anything formed or done without reason or judgement. Ignorance is being without knowledge "and the times of this ignorance God winked at ['overlooked,' RV]" (Acts 17:30). Do distinguish between ignorance and stupidity!

Let us look at one or two passages:

And Moses and Aaron gathered the assembly together before the rock, and he said unto them, Hear now, ye rebels; shall we bring you forth water out of this rock? (Numbers 20:10 RV)

Because they provoked his spirit, so that he spake unadvisedly with his lips. (Psalm 106:33)

When any one heareth the word of the kingdom, and understandeth it not, then cometh the evil one, and snatcheth away that which hath been sown in his heart. (Matthew 13:19 RV)

For we ourselves also were sometimes foolish. (Titus 3:3)

For of these are they that creep into houses, and take captive silly women laden with sins, led away by divers lusts, ever learning, and never able to come to the knowledge of the truth. (2 Timothy 3:6–7 RV)

For when by reason of the time ye ought to be teachers, ye have need again that some one teach you the rudiments of the first principles of the oracles of God; and are become such as have need of milk, and not of solid food. (Hebrews 5:12 RV)

My reason for running over these passages is that the truth may sink into our minds that the Bible lays a tremendous emphasis on the fact that there are stupid souls.

Now let us get back to Saul. I know it is not the usual way of summing up Saul, but I want to take him as an illustration of the stupid soul. Read the description of Saul in 1 Samuel 9:2 (RV)—"And [Kish] had a son, whose name was Saul, a choice young man and a goodly: and there was not among the children of Israel a goodlier person than he: from his shoulders and upward he was higher than any of the people." His physique was magnificent, his bodily presence wonderful, but he was amazingly stupid. Samuel was known everywhere, he was such a mighty prophet and man of God, but there were two people who did not know him—a man called Kish and his son Saul; they spent their time breeding asses, and knew nothing whatever about Samuel. Saul actually met Samuel and asked him if he could tell him where the seer was! How did Saul get the first inkling of who Samuel was? Through one of his father's servants. If you are a stupid soul spiritually, do get in touch with a godly servant—in touch with someone who does know the seer! And Samuel said to him, "I am the seer; . . . and in the morning I will let thee go, and will tell thee all that is in thine heart" (RV). Then we read that "God gave him another heart." If Saul had gone on in obedience to God's Word, his life would have fulfilled God's intention; but instead of that, he is a model for all time of a stupid soul.

What are we to do when we come across stupid souls? Ignorant souls we can deal with, they need knowledge; the stupid soul does not need knowledge; the stupid soul needs to have the word of God until it is worried by it. The difficulty is how the worker is to get the word of God into its right place. Jesus Christ says the stupid soul is the one that hears the word and does not understand it. "When any one heareth the word of the kingdom, and understandeth it not . . ." (Matthew 13:19). Does God hold a man culpable for being stupid spiritually? He certainly does. Every case of stupidity recorded in the Bible is

punished by God. How can I get the word of God into a stupid soul? Read 1 Samuel 15, and see how Samuel dealt with Saul. "The commandment of God, why did you not obey that?" Take the Apostle Paul, the very same thing: "O foolish Galatians, who hath bewitched you, that ye should not obey the truth . . . ?" And our Lord's own words: "O foolish men, and slow of heart to believe after [mg] all that the prophets have spoken!" (RV).

This is the time, Christian worker, when you must use the word until you get it wedged in somehow in that stupid soul, until it rankles and worries its way to the soul's salvation or destruction, and there was never a class that will drive a worker closer to God than the stupid soul, they will tax every bit of patience and endurance you have. They always pretend to want to do something—"ever learning, and never able to come to the knowledge of the truth"—why? They would not obey the word they heard, that is the beginning. You remember Samuel asked Saul if he had fulfilled the word of God with regard to the Amalekites, and Saul said he had: "Blessed be thou of the LORD: I have performed the commandment of the LORD. And Samuel said, "What meaneth then this bleating of the sheep in mine ears, and the lowing of the oxen which I hear?" Pretending, that is the first characteristic of the stupid soul. Again in his last agony, when Saul went off on the spiritualistic line, Samuel says the same thing: "Because thou obeyedst not the voice of the LORD."

You will come across the stupid soul in connection with the elementary work of grace, the new birth: "I want to be sanctified, I have done this and that and the other." Well, be perfectly certain they have not; if those things had been done, there would be no "bleating of the sheep," no provision for the lusts of the flesh, none of the laying down of careful lines for the development of things that ought not to be in the Christian life. Is any soul beginning to deceive itself? That is the danger of stupidity; when once it begins to disobey God's Word ever so little, it begins to deceive itself. "Well, God is very hard with me, I did fulfil the word of God, I did what I knew how to." How is the worker going to get the word of God driven straight home? As you wait before God, there is no class for which God will give you passages of Scripture more quickly than for this class, and at your peril you lower the standard of the word of God.

The first thing I want to note with regard to the worker is this, never sympathise with a stupid soul. Sympathise with the sick soul; sympathise with the abnormal soul—sympathy is needed for nearly every soul but the stupid soul, but never sympathise with stupidity in the approach of a soul to God. Watch Samuel, watch Paul and watch our Lord—the word of God, the word of God, the word of God, first second and last; no sympathy, no help, only the word of God.

Have you ever noticed that if a stupid soul hears a word of God too often it may turn again and trample on that word? A man who ultimately became a great power for God, on his own testimony, said that the centre of his life was once full of this kind of stupidity. He was a so-called worker for God for several years, until he came across this verse: "ye are not your own; for ye were bought with a price" (RV), and he said wherever he went that verse kept chiding him; when he read a book he would come across it; when he heard a sermon it would be from that text, until he said, "At last I took my penknife and cut the verse out of every Bible I had." Then the Spirit of God awakened him as to what he had done, and he confessed the whole thing before God and God forgave him his stupidity.

Christian worker, when God gives you a word for a soul who is stupid, keep at it. This is the time when you have to keep using the verse God gives you for a soul: every time you meet him, every time you write to him, every time you talk to him. The only way you will stir up that one out of his stupidity is by driving home the word of God, and presently you will see that stupid soul saved from perdition, if it has not gone as far away from God as Saul, and as far away as many a stupid soul will go for lack of faithful workers. But if you as a worker have one strand of stupidity in you, one characteristic in your life where you are apt to make statements and judgements unreasonably, beware that your message does not become a boomerang. A boomerang is a peculiar weapon so balanced that when you fling it as far from you as you can, it comes back and hits you! God's word is always a boomerang to the worker who uses it if he is not right with Him.

Worker for God, are you quite sure there is no strand of stupidity in you? Are you quite sure you are not in the category of those who are ever learning, but never coming to the knowledge of the truth? Are you facing something about which you are very willing to be stupid? Then the word of God in your hand will come straight back to you when you try to deal with another soul—"Thou art the man." But if you are living rightly yourself, then keep on the line of pressing the word home. Will you just run over in your mind, worker, the stupid souls you have in your Sunday-school class, in your Church services—are you glossing over the word God gave you for them? Hammer at it morning, noon and night; if you cannot get at their ears, get at them by prayer. If it is Luke 11:13, then keep at it until they say, "I wish you would be quiet about Luke 11:13; is there nothing else in the Bible but that verse?" But what about "the bleating of the sheep"? That is what keeps you to your point, and God will never let you get away from it. If a man says he has received the Spirit of God and yet has not gone on with God, there is always a word of God to tell him why, and if you are a worker for God you will be a persistent annoyance and aggravation to that one whenever you meet him, until ultimately he comes to the place where he will praise God for the annoyance. Every worker can give instances of God awakening the stupid soul by persistence on the one point. This is the stern element in Christian work.

How did Jesus Christ deal with the foolishness or the stupidity of the two disciples on the road to Emmaus? These disciples were good, simple souls, honest and true, but they had become stupid, blinded by their own grief, their own point of view. What did Jesus say to them? "O fools, and slow of heart to believe all that the prophets have spoken." The word "fool" is often used in the New Testament, but not always in the same way, here it means literally, "My little imbecile children, when will you believe all that the prophets have spoken?" This is stupidity of a totally different order, a stupidity that Jesus deals with very pointedly, but very patiently. It is a stupidity that has obliterated the interpretation of the word of God because of personal grief and perplexity. Is Jesus Christ coming to you by the Spirit and saying, "My little imbecile child, when will you believe what I say?" Is there any particular thing in your life, Christian worker, that you have become slow of heart to believe? Do not let the stupidity grow. Get the word of God for it. Oh, if there ever was a need, it is for people to search and ransack this Book and get at what God says. How much time have you given to finding out what the Bible has to say? An hour a day? "Oh, I cannot give an hour." Half an hour? "Oh no, I cannot give that." Five minutes? "Yes, I could do that." Well, have you done it? Five minutes a day out of twenty-four hours to find out what the word of God says! No wonder God says, "My people doth not consider."

Never water down the word of God to the understanding of your people. Would that God the Holy Ghost would thunder that through you as He has thundered it through me! Never drag down the word of God to anybody's understanding. Hammer at it, keep at it, and drive at it, till the laziness is taken out of people's hearts and brains and bodies, and they are willing to face what this Book has to say about their condition, and face it with the sterling earnestness they use to see what the newspapers have to say when they are on the hunt for a new situation. God grant we may learn the imperativeness of getting at what the word of God has to say about our particular need, then perhaps we will begin to understand why we have that need.

"The words that I speak unto you, they are spirit, and they are life." The word of God is "a lamp" and "a light," but when people get off on the "stupid" lines, it is all instincts, impressions, vague ideas—"ever learning, and never able to come to the knowledge of the truth." Then is the time when men of reprobate mind creep in and lead astray. There are a number of "creepers" stealing in nowadays, religious "creepers," and they will steal into your soul, my brother and sister, just where you are stupid. Has something been said to you recently from the word of God that has awakened you with a startling realisation to the fact that you have not obeyed God on a certain point?

Then may God bring you face to face with a faithful worker who will bring the same thing to you, whatever it is, until you get through. When the word of God has begun its piercing even to the dividing of soul and spirit, it will have its wonder-working way and heal and re-create and dissipate the stupidity.

Chapter VIII
THE WORKER AND THE PASSION FOR SOULS

To the weak I became weak, that I might gain the weak: I am become all things to all men, that I may by all means save some. 1 Corinthians 9:22 (RV)

You hear people say that Paul showed his wonderful breadth of mind, his culture and generosity, his gentleness and patience, by becoming all things to all men. He did nothing of the sort; he said, "I am become all things to all men" for one purpose only— "that I may by all means save some." He did not say, "I became all things to all men that I might show what a wonderful being I am." There is no thought of himself in the whole matter.

The phrase "a passion for souls" is a dangerous one; a passion for souls may be either a diseased lust or a Divine life. Let me give you a specimen of it as a diseased lust—"Woe unto you, scribes and Pharisees, hypocrites! for ye compass sea and land to make one proselyte; and when he is become so, ye make him twofold more a son of hell than yourselves" (Matthew 23:15 RV). "Proselyte" is a technical word for convert, and our Lord is showing that these Pharisees had a great passion for souls which He stamped as of the devil; and if you read the thirteenth chapter of Acts you will find a remarkable thing occurs—the proselytes became exactly what Jesus Christ said they would, "twofold more a son of hell," far more superstitious and fanatical; the devout women alluded to who persecuted the apostles were proselytes (vv. 43–50). In Revelation 13:11–17, you will find again the passion for souls as a diseased lust. I refer to the beast coming up out of the earth; the consummation of his power was to get the souls of men into one solid mass.

But have we got clearly in our minds what the passion for souls as a Divine life is? Read James 5:19–20 (RV): "My brethren, if any among you do err from the truth, and one convert him; let him know, that he which converteth a sinner from the error of his way shall save a soul from death, and shall cover a multitude of sins." The Apostle is talking to those whom we understand as Christians, "If any among you, my brethren, do err from the truth . . ."

Again, our Lord in speaking to His disciples, used some striking phrases, all of which refer to this passion for souls, in Matthew 4:18–22, He speaks about making them "fishers of men"; in John 21:15–17, He says "Feed My sheep," a striking phrase which has a direct bearing on the right passion for souls: and after the Resurrection He said, "Go ye therefore, and make disciples of all the nations" (Matthew 28:19 RV). I want to take these three phrases as a guide for the worker in regard to this great passion for souls.

There is a telling pathos about the twenty-first chapter of John; all the disciples had forsaken the Shepherd, and Jesus says, "Now never you forsake the flock, you become broken bread and poured-out wine and feed the flock." God grant we may understand that the passion for souls is not a placid, scientifically worked-out thing, it compresses all the energy of heart and brain and body in one consuming drive, day and night from the beginning of life to the end—a consuming, fiery, living passion. That was the characteristic of our Lord's life, and of the lives of all the disciples after Pentecost, and of the life of the Apostle Paul.

Take first of all the phrase "fishers of men." There are one or two significant things about that figure of speech. The early disciples were fishermen, and the Spirit of God seems to point out that their earthly employment was a parable of their Divine vocation. David was a shepherd, he became the shepherd of Israel. Paul was a tent-maker; he was used by God for making men's bodies into tabernacles of the Holy Ghost. I wonder how many of you know what it is to be out all night at sea fishing? I do. Before the early dawn, about three or four in the morning, you feel so amazingly cold and so amazingly indifferent that you don't know whether you care for anything, and there is an exact counterpart of those nights in work for God. Do you know what it is to have a relationship to God so consuming, a personal, passionate devotion to Jesus Christ so powerful that it will stand you in good stead through every cold night, while you are watching and waiting to land men for God? It is those cold nights of waiting, cold nights of praying and of preaching, when, like Gideon's army over again, many leave and forsake and just the few are left, that are the test[ed].

What a marvellous illustration fishing is, especially fishing with the net, and Jesus Christ told the disciples He would make them "fishers of men," catchers of men. Unless we have this divine passion for souls burning in us because of our personal love for Jesus Christ, we will quit the work before we are much older. It is an easy business to be a fisherman when you have all the enthusiasm of the catch, everybody then wants to be a fisherman. Just as everybody comes in with the shout and the "Hallelujah" when revival signs are abroad; but God is wanting those who through long nights, through difficult days of spiritual toil, have been trying to let down their nets to catch the fish. Oh, the skill, the patience, the gentleness and the endurance that are needed for this passion for souls; a sense that men are perishing won't do it; only one thing will do it, a blazing, passionate devotion to the Lord Jesus Christ, an all-consuming passion. Then there is no night so long, no work so hard and no crowd so difficult, but that love will outlast it all.

God grant that we may see that our passion for souls springs from that on which the Moravian Mission[8] founded its enterprise—the fifty-third chapter of Isaiah; behind every heathen face, behind every face besotted with sin, they saw the Face of the Son of God; behind every broken piece of earthenware, they saw Jesus Christ; behind every down-trodden mass of human corruption, they saw Calvary. That was the passion that was their motive. God grant we may get it back again. That is the deep, true, evangelical note for the passion for souls, the consuming passion that transfigures a man's self, that transfigures a woman's self, and makes him or her indeed wise and patient and able fishers of men.

Beware of the people who tell you how to fish! I know a good many people who have tried to learn how to fish from books, but they never did learn. The only way to learn how to fish is to fish! An old sea-captain whom I know very well, who has been a fisherman all his days, told me he met a man who had published a book on how to catch fish. The captain took him out in his boat; they stayed out four hours, but he didn't have enough strength to put one piece of line over the boat, he was too seasick. That was the instructor of how to catch fish!

Beware of the books that tell you how to catch men. Go to Calvary, and let God Almighty deal with you until you understand the meaning of the tremendous cost to our Lord Jesus Christ, and then go out to catch men. God grant we may get away from the instructors on how to catch fish and get out into the fishing business!

Mrs. Howard Hooker[9] pointed out in an address one day that the disciples when Jesus Christ called them were mending their nets, and she made the remark, "The majority of Christian people are always washing and mending their nets; but when Jesus Christ comes along, He tells them to launch out and let them down; it is the only way to catch fish." God grant we may see the aptness of Jesus Christ's words, "I will make you fishers of men." Is there some Sunday-school teacher to whom it has been a cold, cold year in your class, have you gone home every Sunday afternoon with a heart like lead, and have you cried to God, saying, "O God, I have prayed and asked and longed, but not one of these lives can I get for Thee"? God grant if you feel like that, you may go back to Calvary again and again, until the Holy Ghost expounds to you the tremendous, passionate love of the Lord Jesus Christ.

Have you ever noticed one thing about the early disciples, viz., that in every case the choice is the Lord's, not the man's. "Ye have not chosen Me, but I have chosen you." Jesus turned away everyone who came to Him and said, "I want to be Your disciple." Jesus Christ knows the men and women He wants. God grant that His choice may fall on everyone of us, and that we may learn with patience and discipline how He is going to teach us to be patient, to be powerful and to be passionate in His service! Never losing heart, never being discouraged, never being excited over a big catch. Many a worker has rendered himself useless to God by his undue hilarity over a big revival for God. "Notwithstanding in this rejoice not, that the spirits are subject unto you," said Jesus; "but rather rejoice, because your names are written in heaven." God grant we may understand that the mainspring of our passion for souls must be a personal, passionate devotion to the Lord Jesus Christ.

Then the shepherding of the flock. Read John 21, every one of the disciples had forsaken Jesus; the night had got too cold, too dark, their own grief was too overwhelming, and they all forsook Him and fled. Then Jesus came to them in the upper room and imparted to them His Spirit, and now He gives them this commission—"Feed My lambs"; "Tend My sheep"(RV); "Feed My sheep."

Now both the fisherman's art and the shepherd's art sound poetical until you have tried them! I begin to thank God that in my boyhood and early manhood I had to take so many tries at a good many things. I

---

8. Moravian Mission: traces its beginnings to a Christian community founded by Count Nicholas Zinzendorf in the 1730s.
9. Mary R. Hooker

did not like it at the time, but I am thankful now I had to do shepherding in the highlands of Scotland. When you have to carry across your shoulders a dirty old wether and bring it down the mountain-side, you will soon know whether shepherding is poetry or not; you will soon know whether it is not the most taxing, the most exhausting and the most exasperating work; and Jesus uses the illustration for the passion for souls. Quiet, judicious knowing how to do it won't do it; passion alone will do it. One of the grandest men I ever knew was a sheep-farmer, and he told me of his nephew whom he was trying to train as a sheep-farmer (he is now a minister in Canada)—"The boy cannot learn sheep-farming; it must be born in him." That used to be the old shepherd's great theory, that you could not teach a man how to look after sheep unless it was born in him. Jesus Christ drives home the very same truth to the disciples. To whom did He say, "Feed My lambs"? To Peter. Who was Peter? A very wayward sheep. Peter had not only forsaken Jesus Christ, he denied with oaths and curses he ever knew Him, and now that Peter has received the Holy Spirit and is personally, passionately devoted to Jesus Christ, do you think that anybody could have such patience with young converts as Peter? Who was it that wrote, "Tend the flock of God which is among you, exercising the oversight, not of constraint, but willingly, according unto God" (RV)? Peter. Peter had marvellously learned through his own experience how to be patient, how to be tender, how to be full of grateful watchfulness over all the Lord's sheep.

But there is another aspect. When Jesus said, "Feed My sheep," He gave Peter nothing to feed them with. This is a tremendous point. You cannot nourish the flock of God unless you are rightly related to the Shepherd. You may be the mouthpiece for God's truth to the unsaved, but you cannot nourish the flock of God which is among you unless you are rightly related to the Shepherd, unless you are willing to let God use you as broken bread and poured-out wine to feed His sheep. Much-tried Christian worker, you are not understanding what God is putting you through; perhaps this is what He is fitting you for, to teach you how to feed His sheep, to tend the flock of God. Sunday-school teacher, perhaps Jesus Christ is teaching you how He is going to make you broken bread and poured-out wine. Take some time, Christian worker, over your Bible, and see what God has to say about shepherds, about hireling shepherds. This work of feeding and tending sheep is hard work, arduous work, and love for the sheep alone will not do it, you must have a consuming love for the great Shepherd, the Lord Jesus Christ; that is the point I want to leave impressed. Love for men as men will never stand the strain. In order to catch men for the Lord Jesus Christ, you must love Jesus Christ absolutely, beyond

all others. You must have a consuming passion of love, then He will flow through you in a passion of love and yearning and draw men to Himself.

Then, lastly, "make disciples of all the nations" (Matthew 28:19 RV). "Making yourselves ensamples to the flock," says Peter (RV). What does that mean? Be a walking, talking, living example of what you preach, in every silent moment of your life, known and unknown; bear the scrutiny of God, until you prove that you are indeed an example of what He can do, and then "make disciples of all the nations." Now we come to the great, grand idea of the universal and spiritual aspect of the work of a Christian. There is no respect of persons with God, no respect of nations with God—here, there, anywhere and everywhere, wherever God likes to stir up your nest and fling you, disciple all the nations. When souls are born again into the kingdom of God the Church of Christ makes a tremendous rejoicing, as it ought to make, but then what does it do? When God brings souls to you who have been brought into His kingdom by His sovereign work of grace, what have you to do? Disciple them, and the only way you can disciple them is not by making them proselytes of your views, but by teaching them to do what Jesus commanded you to do and you have done. Watch the Apostle Paul's testimony—"who shall bring you into remembrance of *my ways which be in Christ*." How often the Apostle Paul says, when talking to his converts, "Ye are our glory and joy." Sunday-school teacher, can you say, "God has manifested His grace in me, and if you come to the same place He will manifest it in you"? Or, do you have to say, "Do as I say, but not as I do"? Before we can disciple all the nations, we ourselves must be where we want other people to be. Watch again that matchless Apostle's life, the consuming, passionate agony of his soul was for the converts, not for the crowd outside; discipling is the one stamp of that mature Apostle's life. "My little children, of whom I am again in travail until Christ be formed in you" (Galatians 4:19 RV).

Another thing: Sunday-school worker, and Christian worker, and minister, you must be farther on and higher up than those you are leading, and you must be going on all the time. Now we come to the meaning of God's discipling of various workers, of His removing some workers and of putting others over the heads of others. Beware of being stationary! God grant that we may be going on with Him continually so that we can disciple all we come in contact with. When a young convert asks you a question—"Can God deliver me from the disposition of sin?" what will you say? If you cannot answer, "Thank God, He can deliver you," then beware! God may have to remove your candlestick as a teacher, as a worker. How does the Apostle Paul finish that wonderful chapter,

1 Corinthians 9—"I buffet my body, and bring it into bondage: lest by any means, after that I have preached to others, I myself should be rejected" (RV), cast away as reprobate silver. God grant that no Christian worker may fall from the heaven of his usefulness because he refuses to go on with God!

If you have cooled down in your spiritual life, Christian worker, has it not come about that some weeks ago, or some months ago, you were asked a question and you could not answer it, and you ought to have been able to answer it? It was a practical, pointed question about what God could do for a man's soul, or for his body, and you could not answer it, why? Because the side issue of your own life was not clear; and until you make that issue clear, you are left as reprobate silver. You have preached to others? Yes, and God blessed your preaching, but from the second you begin to neglect the side issues of your life, that moment God begins to leave you alone as a worker for Him. God grant you may get back again, all the avenues clearly open to Him, avenues of heart and head and body and soul, back premises and front premises, underground and overhead, and all around, clear and open to God! Then let the questions come from anywhere, questions that touch the head, questions that touch the back record, questions that touch the underneath record—"Can God restore the years the cankerworm hath eaten?" "Can God alter the build of a man's mind?" "Can God destroy laziness out of a man?" I was talking to an elderly minister the other day, and speaking of ministers and Christian workers generally, he said, "The great defect in all branches of Christian work is laziness." The only cure for laziness is to be filled with the life of God to such an overwhelming extent that He can spend you to the last cell of your body, to the last drop of your blood, for His own glory. God grant that the consuming passion for souls for Jesus Christ's sake may get hold of us as never before!

One other thing I want you to notice with regard to this passion for souls. God will put you through many mills that are never meant for you, mills you never would be put through but that He wants to make you good bread for His little ones to eat. Christian worker, you see the meaning now of that hard place you have been in; God wants to make you bread well enough baked until you are His "standard" bread, and then He can break you for the feeble amongst the flock. What is the consuming passion in the Apostle Paul's life? Devotion to the Lord Jesus Christ. "For I could wish that I myself were anathema from Christ for my brethren's sake, my kinsmen according to the flesh" (RV). "And I will most gladly spend and be spent out [mg] for your souls" (RV). Christian worker, have you lost out in that consuming passion? If you are getting cooled down, visit the Cross of the Lord Jesus Christ and ask the Spirit of God to give you insight into its meaning, ask Him that you may understand it in a new way. Then go forth, and—

Measure my life by loss instead of gain;
Not by the wine drunk, but the wine poured forth.

Chapter IX
THE GOD-APPROVED WORKER

Give diligence to present thyself approved unto God, a workman that needeth not to be ashamed, handling aright the word of truth. 2 Timothy 2:15 (RV)

We have been dealing with the worker for the cure of souls, now I want to deal with the prevention which is better than cure. How can a man or woman become a workman approved unto God? Read 1 Timothy 4:16—"Take heed to thyself, and to thy teaching" (RV). If you forget everything else, do not forget that verse. The word "heed" occurs again in Acts 3:5 and 20:28. It means to concentrate, to screw your mind down, fix it, limit it, curb it, confine it, rivet it on yourself and on your teaching. It is a strong word, a powerful word, a word that grips, a rousing word. That is what we have to do if we are going to be workmen approved unto God.

But I want you to notice first of all who is talking and who he is talking to. It is the Apostle Paul talking to Timothy, or writing to Timothy, or sending a message to Timothy. Paul's method was that of apprenticeship, that is always God's method of training workers. In the old days when artists used to have apprentices, they used to put the boy in charge of mixing paints and in between doing this he would watch the artist paint, and slowly bit by bit, doing the hard work and watching the master work, he would learn to "take heed." That was Paul's method. Timothy had a good mother and a godly grandmother, and he was trained spiritually in this apprentice style. If you are going to be a worker for the cure of souls, God will bring you under masters and teachers. That is the method God always uses. He does not use anyone who is undisciplined. Thank God for every worker who was ever placed under apprenticeship!

"Take heed to thyself" (RV). That is not self-realisation; it is self-preparation, and the first thing I want to notice about self-preparation is in chapter 4:13, "Give attendance to reading." The word "reading" does not mean what we understand by reading—opening a book and looking at it; it means what we understand in Scotland by expository preaching. "Listen to that kind of discourse, Timothy, read that kind of manuscript, and when you open your mouth, follow that specimen." What is expository preaching? It is not taking a text out of its setting and using it as a title; it means that the verse is taken in its setting and applied where it is meant to apply. I wonder how many workers are taking heed to their reading in this expository way. I wonder what kind of preacher you delight to listen to? What kind of book you like to read, what kind of instruction you delight to listen to? Paul tells Timothy to take heed, first of all, to this important thing. "Give attendance to reading."

In order to get this more crystallised in our minds, read Nehemiah 8:4–5: "And Ezra the scribe stood upon a pulpit of wood, which they had made for the purpose. . . . And Ezra opened the book in the sight of all the people; (for he was above all the people;) and when he opened it, all the people stood up." That is the God-ordained method of expounding God's Word, and it is as if Paul said to Timothy, "When you read, when you listen and when you teach, remember God's time-honoured method—get upon your pulpit of wood as an official." There are two kinds of official worker—the one who may become a castaway; that is what the Apostle Paul dreaded—"I keep under my body, and bring it into subjection: lest that by any means, when I have preached to others, I myself should be a castaway." The other kind of worker is the one who is an example of what he teaches. But the point to notice here is that the person who expounds God's Word has to be seen of all the people; if his sermons are written, let the people see they are written; if he is reading from the Bible, let the people see that he is; if he is reading someone else's sermon, let him say so. These are not trifling things, they are tremendously important things, and the word "reading" covers them all. "Search after that kind of preacher, Timothy, and listen to him."

Worker for God—and I speak this to myself as well as to you—what do you fasten your mind on when you listen to a preacher, when you read a book? When Jesus Christ said "Thou shalt love the Lord thy God with all thy heart," He did not stop there, He went on to say, "and with all thy soul, and with all thy *mind*, and with all thy strength." Oh, I wish I had time, I would kindle you by telling you of some folks I know who have lifted themselves out of the very

gutter of ignominy and ignorance by sheer grind in the secular callings of life. Would to God we had the same stick-to-it energy in God's line! Many a lad have I known in Scotland who has worked hard day and night to attain a scholarship in secular callings, and are we to be behind them? This word of the Apostle Paul's is used in that connection—"take heed," concentrate, stick at it, fix the mind on it. Give heed to reading, be careful of your self-preparation. God grant that we may be approved unto God by what we build in. When Paul mentions the matter of conversation, he says, "See that your speech is edifying"—good building-up stuff, not sanctimonious talk, but real solid stuff that makes people stronger in the Word of God, stronger in character, stronger in practical life.

Paul says to Timothy another thing, "of these things put them in remembrance, charging them in the sight of the Lord, that they strive not about words, to no profit, to the subverting of them that hear" (RV). And again, "Shun profane babblings: for they will proceed further in ungodliness, and their word will eat as doth a gangrene" (RV). And again, "But foolish and ignorant questionings refuse, knowing that they gender strifes" (RV). "Don't argue! don't enter into controversy at any price." Paul told Timothy not to enter into controversy at any price, and Paul was the arch-controversialist himself! Paul spent most of his days in controversy, and yet he tells Timothy not to argue! But have you read Paul's method of controversy? Paul put himself with amazing courtesy and amazing insight and amazing tenderness into the place of the man he was disputing with. The reason Paul tells Timothy not to argue, and the reason he tells me not to argue, and the reason he tells you not to argue, is that we argue from our own point of view. We argue not for the truth's sake, we argue to prove we are right. God grant that we may learn to take heed lest we get switched off on arguing. Is there some worker for God likely to be twisted and turned aside by battling for the faith? Let me read you some words I have jotted down in my Bible:

Oh, the unmitigated curse of controversy! Oh, the detestable passions that corrections and contradictions kindle up to fury in the proud heart of man! Eschew controversy, my brethren, as you would eschew the entrance to hell itself. Let them have it their way; let them talk; let them write; let them correct you; let them traduce you; let them judge and condemn you; let them slay you. Rather let the truth of God suffer itself, than that love suffer. You have not enough of the divine nature in you to be a controversialist.

Dr. Alexander Whyte[10]

10. Alexander Whyte (1836–1921): Scottish minister who influenced Chambers during Oswald's time at Edinburgh University, 1895–1896.

"Heal me," prays St. Augustine, again and again, "of this lust of mine of always vindicating myself."

Take heed, fix your mind, never be wheedled into controversy. Let the Spirit of God controvert. One of my greatest snares ever since I became a Christian is this very thing. I know what it means, I know the galling humiliation and agony in days that have gone by of wanting to argue the point out, and I know, possibly better than any of you, the inwardness of the point that the Apostle Paul is driving at with Timothy—"Don't do it, Timothy; stop, you will damage your own soul, you will hinder the truth of God, you will bruise the souls you talk to." God grant we may fix and concentrate our minds and take heed to this! Take heed to yourself, take heed how you read, and above all don't argue. Have you learned this, Christian worker, that when any soul begins to discuss the baptism with the Holy Spirit, it is time you got out of the way? they have a controversy with the Holy Ghost, not with you. "Sanctification" is not a man's term; it is God's: "the baptism with the Holy Ghost" is not man's conception, it is God's, and when a soul begins to argue on these matters, remember, worker for God, it is the Holy Spirit they are arguing with, the Word of God they are haggling about. God grant we may not hinder those who are battling their way slowly into the light.

One more thing: Paul tells Timothy to "preach the word; be instant in season, out of season" (2 Timothy 4:2). Watch the setting of that. Timothy was fragile in body physically, Paul is frequently telling him how to take care of his body, and yet here is the Apostle telling this young man who is feeble in body to preach the word in season and out of season, what does he mean? To take every opportunity of preaching the word? He does not mean any such thing; he means "preach the word in season or out of season with regard to yourself, never let your bodily condition hin-

der your preaching." The Apostle Paul is driving at laziness, heart-sloth. God grant we may learn how to be instant in season and out of season, always at it, night and day, whether we feel like it or not. When you come to read deeper down between the lines in the Bible, you will find running all through it the awful curse on laziness and spiritual sloth. Has it come on you mentally, Christian worker? Then may God rouse you up to get to reading, to get to work with your pencil and notebook, in cars and out of cars, behind the counter, anywhere. God grant we may be roused up in the spiritual domain to put energy and vim into our work and never say, "I can't"; "I have no time." Of course you have not, no man worthy of the name ought to have time to give to God, he has to take it from other things until he knows how God values time. Take heed to yourself, and never allow anything to produce laziness and sloth.

And lastly, "Continue in these things; for in doing this thou shalt save both thyself and them that hear thee" (1 Timothy 4:16 RV). There is the charter for the worker, he is to be a pattern. "Let no man despise thy youth" (v. 12). Was Paul telling Timothy to stand up and say, "I know I am only a youngster, but I defy any man to contradict me"? Paul is saying, "Do not let youth be despised in you," and then he tells him to be "an ensample to them that believe, in word, in manner of life, in love, in faith, in purity" (RV). The only way youth can save itself from being despised is by the life being in keeping with the profession, the teaching backed by it, the conversation, the manner of life, the purity, the clean, vigorous, upright manhood; not only a worker sent from God, but an ensample of what God can do. The baptism with the Holy Ghost and fire made the disciples the incarnation of what they taught. God grant that we may be the pattern of what we preach, that we may be workmen approved unto God, rightly dividing the word of truth.

Chapter X

THE HOLY WORKER

But of the rest durst no man join himself to them; . . . and believers were the more added to the Lord. . . . Acts 5:13–14 (RV)

I want to end where I began, with the character of the worker. God grant we may understand the power of a holy worker for God. I don't mean a holiness worker; what we need is *holy* workers—there is a big difference.

"But of the rest durst no man join himself to them; . . . and believers were the more added to the Lord" (RV). Have you caught the contrast?—a holy dread and a holy discipleship, they always go together. The souls who stand true to God are those whom God's Spirit has added.

"And great fear came upon"—the crowd outside? No, "upon the whole church, and upon all that heard these things" (RV). And then a wonderful thing happened—a great benediction fell on the multitude outside, "and believers were the more added to the Lord, multitudes both of men and women."

I want to deal with this holy dread and holy discipleship. "Knowing therefore the terror of the Lord, we persuade men." It is necessary for those of us who are workers for God to allow the Spirit of God to lift the veil sometimes and strike terror through us. We take our salvation and our sanctification too cheaply, without realising that Jesus Christ went through the deep waters of uttermost damnation that we might have it. We read that a great fear came across the members of the early Church: "And great fear came upon the whole church, and upon all that heard these things" (RV)—why? They realised, what we have to realise, that the Pentecostal dispensation produces not only Pentecostal living people, but liars to the Holy Ghost. Look for one moment at Ananias. "But Peter said, Ananias, why hath Satan filled thy heart to lie to the Holy Ghost, and to keep back part of the price of the land?. . . How is it that thou hast conceived this thing in thy heart?" (RV). Read the last verses of chapter 4, "Barnabas . . . having a field, sold it, and brought the money, and laid it at the apostles' feet" (RV). It is probable that indirectly Barnabas was responsible for Ananias. Barnabas had done a wonderful thing and doubtless he was praised for it, and Ananias wanted to equal it. We need to live stedfastly in the presence of God so that when we are praised we don't arouse the spirit of envy, the spirit that makes a man want to do something, not because he loves God, but because he wants to emulate us. Let me ask you who are workers, and let me ask myself, "Why do you work for the salvation of souls? Why do you want to spend and be spent for others?" "Mrs. So-and-so does it and she is my ideal." Beware! "I watched Mr. So-and-so and I want to be like him." Beware! God grant we may see that the great need of every worker is a first-hand acquaintance with Jesus Christ which puts to death the spirit of ambition. Ambition has murder at its heart; our Lord showed His disciples that ambition is impossible in His kingdom, "Except ye . . . become as little children, ye shall in no wise enter into the kingdom of heaven" (RV). Our attitude is to be one of steadfast personal devotion to Jesus Christ, not measuring ourselves by ourselves, and comparing ourselves with ourselves. Among the last words Mr. Reader Harris[11] wrote was this phrase—"Don't imitate." That means far more than mere external imitation, it means in the deep spiritual sense what I am trying to bring before you now—don't try and do something for God because somebody else is doing it. Oh, the amount of instigation in God's work that comes along that line!

Mark one more thing. Peter said to Ananias, "Thou hast not lied unto men, but unto God." Christian worker, how much time are you giving to prayer, to reading your Bible? "Oh, I am giving all the time I can." Be careful that you are not lying to the Holy Ghost. Pentecostal lying begins in this way, dragging down the intense holiness of God which keeps a man right with God in every detail of his life. Let us examine ourselves the next time we say, "I have not time," or, "I give all the time I can to the study of God's Word, I give all the time I can to praying." God grant we may be put on the alert on these lines that we may not be found lying to the Holy Ghost. May these words come with warning and with scrutiny and bring our souls face to face with God.

And now holy discipleship. "But of the rest durst no man join himself to them" (RV). I wonder, Christian worker, if we realise what we are doing when we ask a man to give himself to Jesus Christ, do we know what we are telling him to do? We are telling him to kill for ever his right to himself, we are telling him that he has to be holy, chaste to the last recess of his bodily life. If ever that word needed thundering in Christian work it needs thundering to-day, chastity in bodily life. You cannot have holiness without a chaste physical life. Oh, the sapping of the power of God because of unchaste men and women who preach His Gospel. God grant that the touch of God may startle and amaze any self-indulgent man or woman. May we remember the next time we go forth to speak for God that our bodies are the temples of the Holy Ghost. Immediately we realise this and bind ourselves to those who realise the same truth, God will begin to do His marvels in saving men unto Himself. So many of us are being caught up by the benedictions that fall on the crowd outside. The crowd outside will magnify the power of God, but none of those who are not right with God dare join them. If any Christian worker wants to get the strong grip of iron into his soul and into his work for God, let him read the Acts of the Apostles. The power of those holy workers checked impostors on the right hand and on the left. A Holy Ghost movement always brings impostors, parasites, by the legion. The only safeguard for the Christian worker is, "Holiness unto the Lord." If we are living rightly with God, living holy lives in secret and in public, God puts a wall of fire round about us. Beware of calling anything holiness that is only winsome and sweet to the world. God grant we may never lose the touch of God that produces the holy dread.

---

11. Reader Harris (1847–1909): prominent British barrister, founded the Pentecostal League of Prayer in 1891; friend and mentor of Oswald Chambers.

Now we come to our last point. This holy discipleship will result in multitudes being added to the Lord. "And believers were the more added to the Lord, multitudes both of men and women." Is not that what we want, multitudes added to the Lord? How is it to be done? By captivating addresses? Mrs. Howard Hooker reminded us the other night when speaking of her father, that his preaching was always on the line of sanctification; a great many people could not stand it and consequently went away. It has always been the same and always will be. When once the holiness of God is manifested in human lives and in preaching (and the two go together), these two things happen: a great number durst not join themselves, and multitudes are added to the Lord. Never think that the blessing and benediction of God on the outside crowd is all. It is a mere fringe. Men and women are blessed, their bodies are healed, devils are turned out; but the point is that multitudes of those who believe are added to the Lord.

God grant that we may stand steadfastly true to Him and live this holy life. As we go forth tonight, let us remember Jesus Christ's commission, "All power is given unto Me in heaven and in earth. Go ye therefore and make disciples of [RV] all the nations." As we examine our hearts before God let us renew our covenant with Him.

Notes on Isaiah

Oswald Chambers

INTRODUCTION

Source

The *Notes on Isaiah* are taken from lectures by Oswald Chambers at the Bible Training College in 1912 and 1913.[1]

Publication History

- As articles: This material was first published as thirteen articles in the *Bible Training Course (BTC) Journal*,[2] between April 1941 and March 1944.
- This material has never been published in book form until now.

In January 1912, Oswald Chambers began teaching Isaiah in his biblical theology class at the Bible Training College, London. During the next three years, he covered the Four Great Prophets (Isaiah, Jeremiah, Ezekiel, and Daniel) as part of his Old Testament survey course.

Mrs. Chambers apparently did not take detailed notes of these lectures as she did with other classes. As lady superintendent of the College, she had a myriad of daily responsibilities for students and the college operation. In later terms, she taught her own class in Scripture memory. In May 1913, she gave birth to their only child, Kathleen,[3] making it even more difficult to attend all of Oswald's classes and record the lectures in shorthand.

The fact that Mrs. Chambers' notes were abbreviated most likely led to her decision not to publish them in book form.

---

1. The Bible Training College (BTC) was a residential school near Clapham Common in southwest London. It was sponsored by the League of Prayer and operated from 1911 until it closed in July 1915 because of World War I. Oswald Chambers was principal and main teacher; Biddy Chambers, his wife, was lady superintendent.

2. The *Bible Training Course Journal* was published from 1932 to 1952 by Mrs. Chambers, with help from David Lambert.

3. Kathleen Chambers (1913–1997) was the only child of Oswald and Biddy Chambers.

CONTENTS

FOREWORD

A Series of Notes on the great evangelical Prophet Isaiah by Oswald Chambers begins in this number of the *Journal.* They will extend through this new volume. They are in the nature of a first draft following a very close study of the subject and so are not carried to that completed stage which was probably intended. But gems of great beauty abound in them, and truths of deepest significance for us, as for those of Isaiah's time, are made clear. The Outlines sometimes cover more ground than the comments following exhaust. Lovers of the Word of God will value them and find continual help in searching the Scriptures—that we may find Him.

As a groundwork of his own studies O. C. was able to discern and use the rare scholarship behind such Commentators as Dr. George Adam Smith[4] though he did not accept their "critical" positions, such as the Deutero-Isaiah in chapters 40–66. Here is a note on that very subject. "The Book of Isaiah is the field the Higher Critics have torn up with their hooves; the one reason is an inveterate suspicion of anything to do with belief in the Mind of God. The only mind for the author of the Bible is the Mind of God, and the only Interpreter is the Spirit of God."

Yet he recognised, as I heard him once say, that Dr. G. A. Smith showed a marvellous insight into the moral and spiritual significance of Isaiah's prophecy. Therefore, on occasion, he would quote him and accept some of his illuminating remarks.

We shall find in these Notes deep fundamental things, well worth our careful study and appropriation.

David Lambert[5]

April 1941

---

4. George Adam Smith (1856–1942) was a Scottish Old Testament scholar.

5. David Lambert (1871–1961) was a Methodist minister and friend of Oswald Chambers. He assisted Mrs. Chambers with OC publications from 1917 until his death in 1961.

FROM THE BIBLE TRAINING COURSE MONTHLY JOURNAL
VOL. 10 APRIL–MAY 1941 NOS. 1–2
NOTES ON ISAIAH

INTRODUCTORY

And after that with wonder rose in me
Strange speech of early prophets, and a tale
First learnt and last forgotten, song that fell
With worship from the lonely Israelites,
Simeon and Anna; for these twain as one
Fast by the altar and in the courts of God
Led a long age in fair expectancy.
And all these pointed forward, and I knew
That each was prophet and singer and sire and seer.
That each was priest and mother and maid and king,
With longing for the babe of Nazareth,
For that man-child who should be born and reign.

F. W. H. Myers[6]

First Principle—Holiness as the Law
1. The Unveiled Prophecy at Work in Darkness
    (a) The Vision Glorious (Isaiah 9:6; 11:1–10)
    (b) The Valley of Grovelling (Isaiah 1:27)
    (c) The Vindication of God (saiah 39:6)

Second Principle—Chastisement as the Means
2. The Unveiled Prophecy at Work in Daylight
    (a) When it was Dark (Isaiah 1:28–31)
    (b) When it was Dawn (Isaiah 1:25–27)

Third Principle—Holy Remnant as the Result
    (a) Advent of the Dayspring (Isaiah 2:3)
    (b) Agents of the Deliverance (Isaiah 44:28; 52:13–15)
    (c) Anointed Deliverer in Temporalities (Isaiah 45:1–4)
    (d) Anointed Deliverer in Eternalities (Isaiah 53:1–2)

We have to acquire the habit of brooding on what the prophets uttered. Brooding is exalted, excessive attention.

There is a difference between exegetical interpretation and spiritual interpretation. The danger of spiritual interpretation is that we interpret in the light of our own experience, consequently there can be many spiritual interpretations. When we come to these prophetic visions we come to something we have never experienced. The modern mind won't have it that there is anything supernatural in the visions; the reason for that is an inveterate prejudice against the supernatural; an incurable suspicion which will not allow that the Mind of God is other than the mind of a man. The great inspiring Mind behind the prophets and the apostles is not an ingenious human mind, but the Mind of Almighty God. "For the prophecy came not in old time by the will of man: but holy men of God spake *as they were moved by the Holy Ghost*" (2 Peter 1:21).

The spirit of a man is his personality, his soul is that personality trying to express itself in rational words and ideas. The Spirit of God coming into the prophets and the apostles takes the ideas they have formed by contact with the world and brings them into a new combination of which God alone is the Author. That is why the expression is not the same; individuality is marked, e.g., Isaiah is different from Ezekiel, John from Paul; there is the same Mind behind, but not the same ideas.

Never imagine that the prophets had a perfectly clear plan as to what they prophesied; the Spirit of God made them prophesy infinitely more than they knew. We know so much from the New Testament that the prophets did not know at all. The prophets speak with all the blood and passion of their natures; they do not stand off like a superior authority, they are wrapped up in their prophecy. Notice the identification of the prophet with the life of his time; we gather our spiritual skirts from touching the life of the time we are in. These men did not, they stood for God in every condition of things. The prophets prefigure Jesus Christ in an even more marvellous way than the ritual of the Old Testament.

The Bible is a record of facts that actually occurred and the Spirit of God makes them the symbol of something other which we only discern as we rely on Him. Our own lives illustrate this, as we look back we realise that the incidents have been connected by a Hand behind. We imagine that if we could order the history of our lives according to a mathematical system everything would be all right, but the providence of God makes our lives higgledy-piggledy, twisting round anyhow, the reason being that He is bringing out His purpose in His own way. Leave your life alone; you cannot alter history, and you cannot alter life; see that you

---

6. F. W. H. Myers (1843–1901) was a British poet and educator.

maintain a right attitude to God, let come what will. What we are apt to call interruptions are God's way of introducing us to a new knowledge of Himself.

God will never have us follow Him blindly, He won't amaze us, He won't dazzle us with sudden floods of light. He breaks His revelation bit by bit as we will accept it. The appeal made by Jesus Christ is His character, His truth and His beauty, every man's conscience when he sees Him says, That Man is right. There is nothing of the nature of the superstitious.

The supernatural power of Satan never reasons, it appeals to man's superstition, not to his conscience.

When we begin to work for God there is any amount of crude harsh sternness about us, and we have the word of God for it, but slowly and surely through the discipline of life we begin to come to another aspect of those same statements. When we understand how God is dealing with us, He takes us where we can understand His dealing with the world outside.

FROM THE BIBLE TRAINING COURSE MONTHLY JOURNAL
VOL. 10 JUNE–JULY 1941 NOS. 3–4
NOTES ON ISAIAH

THE PROPHETIC VISION
Isaiah 1

The vision of Isaiah the son of Amoz, which he saw concerning Judah and Jerusalem. . . . Isaiah 1:1

> *Yea, Lord, I know it, teach me yet anew*
> *With what a fierce and patient purity*
> *I must confront the horror of the world.*
> *For very little space on either hand*
> *Parts the sane mind from madness;*
>
> . . . .
>
> *I would I never may be left of thee,*
> *O God, my God, in whatsoever ill;*
> *Be present while thou strikest, thus shall grow*
> *At least a solemn patience with the pain;—*
> *When thou art gone what is there in the world*
> *Seems not dishonoured, desperate with sin?*

F. W. H. Myers

1. God Is Nigh—Personal Relations (Isaiah 1:1)
   Practical Relations (Isaiah 1:4–8)

2. God Is Love—Rousing of Moral Reasonings (Isaiah 1:18)
   Recession from Moral Righteousness (Isaiah 1:21–23)
   Reviving of Mental Repentance (Isaiah 1:24-31)

3. God Is High—Refuge of Religiousness (Isaiah 1:11–15)
   Revolution of Rectitude (Isaiah 1:16–17)

1. God Is Nigh
Whenever the people of God disobey God in any particular, God's judgements are severe. There seems to be a peculiar disproportion about God's judgements: *"My people* doth not consider." God's judgement on wrong is inevitable, but it is not inevitable to the individual; it depends on the individual whether he escapes the judgement. There is no law to make a man go wrong saving himself; there is no law to keep a man right saving himself. There is no such thing as fate; a human being always has the power to do the incalculable thing. There are fatal issues, but not fate. When God's decrees come to pass it is because men will not turn. God's will is supreme, but God never fights against us; it is self-will that fights against God. When the Spirit of God is at work in him a man lets God's will overcome, there is no fight, it is a higher power easily overcoming. If I view anything as inevitable with regard to any human being I am unbeliever. I have no right to have anything less than the hope and the belief of Jesus Christ with regard to the worst and most hopeless of men.

2. God Is Love
When the Bible says "God is love" it means what it says, but remember that the love of God is exhibited on a cruel cross. The love of God cannot make room for sin or self-interest, therefore the appeal of the love of God is not that of kindness and gentleness, but of holiness. If you take the natural view of the love of God you will become atheistic. If God were love according to our natural view of love He ought never to cause us pain, He ought to allow us to be peaceful; but the first thing God does is to cause us pain and to rouse us wide awake. He comes into our lives all along with ideals and truths which annoy and sting us and break up our rest, until He brings us to the one point, that it is only moral and spiritual relationships

which last. That is why God looks cruel judged from the human sentimental standpoint; He loves us so much that He will not prevent us being hurt.

God will never allow any of us to rest in a sleep of conscience, He will reason with us and rouse us, and then He will give us a "clearing house" for conscience. The doctrines of salvation that ignore the love of God as revealed to a man's conscience are false because they do not tell us how our guilty conscience is to be cleansed. The "clearing house" which God grants to us through the atoning blood of Jesus Christ is intercession. We enter into a roused relationship with God through the Atonement, and then we are put in the place where we can repair the damage we have done to other lives. No matter what our spiritual experiences may be, if we are in danger of forgetting what we owe in intercession to the lives we damaged before we got right with God, the Holy Spirit will bring it back to us—"Remember that person, that relationship." Many a life is paralysed because this is not realised—"I know God has forgiven me, I know I am right with God, but every now and again I remember the things I did that damaged other lives." If I put the wrong right with my fellow men, have I become right with God? No, get right with God and He will put you on the way to be right with your fellow men. When people are being roused by the Holy Spirit they always want to confess to you; never allow them to. It is not confession to men that is required but the confession of a guilty conscience to God.

Mental repentance means an altered point of view. Have I altered my point of view with regard to service of God? The Almighty is not going to allow His people to be unconscious hypocrites, He is not going to allow them to pray and worship while all the time their moral nature is asleep. "To what purpose is the multitude of your sacrifices unto Me? saith the LORD." Before any sacrifice or service can be acceptable to God it must be the outcome of a reasoning together with God. Have I ever thought what my salvation and my sanctification mean from God's standpoint?

3. God Is High

Immediately we are born again God puts upon us a condition which was never there before, viz. that of holiness. A born-again soul is condemned to holiness; he is not at liberty to do what he likes but only what God likes, a "bondslave of Jesus"; my relationship to God first, second and third and all the time. The modern note is that we have sinned against this one and that one: every sin we commit against another is a sin against God, and the Bible brings us face to face with God. Can my salvation stand the glaring light of God? Can my relationship with my fellow men stand the light of God? It has got to one day. That is the way the Spirit of God rouses us up to see that there is no refuge in anything or anyone other than Himself. The whole life must be established in God. The one thing that keeps us right is walking in the light of the great High God. We have to be as open and above board in every relationship of our lives as Nature is. The first thing that happens to an artificial religious life is that it wants to be a little out of keeping with the intense purity of Nature.

FROM THE BIBLE TRAINING COURSE MONTHLY JOURNAL
VOL. 10 AUGUST–SEPTEMBER 1941 NOS. 5–6
NOTES ON ISAIAH

THE PAINFUL PATH TO POWER
Isaiah 6

His face is glorious with a beam
Unborrowed from our earthly skies,
The radiance of a heavenly dream
Is on his brow and in his eyes,
And in his breast the unconquered heart
That fails not when his brethren fail,
That sees his earliest friends depart
One after one and doth not quail.
One after one they go, the bold
Companions of his dwindling band,
For under stormy skies and cold
Their march is, through a barren land.
And some their earlier faith deride

(For man is man and seeks his own),
Till the last straggler leaves his side,
And the worn pilgrim walks alone.

This chapter is a record of the experience Isaiah went through before entering on his prophetical ministry. Isaiah is his own remembrancer. It is easy to forget the love of our espousals, to be so taken up with Christian work that we forget after a while what God has done for us. We have to keep the call of God alive, and continually recall to our minds what we are here for. This process will reveal at once whether the soul has had any personal history with God. There is no danger of spiritual retrogression if we will keep in mind the times, one or more, when the Spirit of God has touched us.

God intends us to be reserved over His revelations, but we are rarely allowed to be reserved about ourselves. God can make a man so one with Himself that he never thinks of being reserved because he does not take himself into account. Here Isaiah is being led by the Spirit of God to give his own experience, proving thereby that he is God's man, spoilt for everything else but loyalty to God. The making of a prophet is along this line. The proof that the Spirit of God is at work in me is that I am willing to testify to what God has done; that is always the evidence of a supernatural element at work.

1. The Price of Vision

In the year that king Uzziah died . . . (see 2 Kings 15:1–4; 2 Chronicles 26:16–23)

God's dates are not man's. God seems to pay no attention to our calendars; He has a calendar of His own in which He suddenly surprises a man in the midst of his days. Leave room for God. We expect God only on special days, in particular meetings; that is not God's way. He comes suddenly, at midnight or at noonday. We learn to trace our history by the rare moments in which we find out who we are and where we are tending. There are moments

> Sure, tho' seldom, . . .
> When the spirit's true endowments
> Stand out plainly from its false ones. . . .

Isaiah chronicles his time by these moments.

The history of our soul with God is frequently that of the passing of the hero. Over and over again God removes our friends in order to bring Himself in their place, and that is where we faint and fail and get discouraged. Take it personally—"In the year that the one who stood for God to me died"—"I gave up everything?" "I became ill?" or—"I saw also the Lord"?

My vision of God depends upon the state of my character. Character determines revelation. Before I can say "I saw also the Lord" there must be something corresponding to God in my character. Until I am born again and enter into the Kingdom of God I see only along the line of my prejudices; I need the surgical operation of external events and an internal purification. It must be God first, God second and God third, until the life is faced steadily with God and no one else is of any account. "In all the world there is none but thee, my God, there is none but thee." Let God see that you are willing to live up to the vision; keep paying the price. "I was not disobedient unto the heavenly vision," says the Apostle Paul. Am I obeying the vision, or only beginning to dole out the price of it?

2. The Purging of the Prophet's Perception

I saw also the Lord sitting upon a throne, high and lifted up, and His train filled the temple.

The purpose of the vision is to enable me to see "the arm of the LORD" behind all circumstances (see Isaiah 53:1). God never gives a man the power to say "I see" until his character proves itself worthy of its purification. What hinders the purging of our perception is that we will build our faith on our experiences instead of on the God who gave us the experiences. My experience is the evidence of my faith, never the ground of it, and is meant to reveal to me a God who is bigger than any experience. In the case of Isaiah we are dealing with a prophet in the Presence of God (cf. Revelation 1:17–18). Have I seen also the Lord, and do I know that He is holy?

3. The Platform of the Vision

. . . sitting upon a throne, high and lifted up, and His train filled the temple.

If my worship is consumed in the glory of the Lord till that is the one thing left in my mind, I have come to the right place of vision. In the Old Testament the idea of God's holiness is that of aloofness and separateness, the sublimity of God. No un-holiness can ever stand before God, therefore if God is going to bring man into fellowship with Himself He has to reinstate him in every particular. Anything that belittles or obliterates the holiness of God by a false view of the love of God is untrue to the revelation given by Jesus Christ.

In this prophet we have a marvellous picture of the Atonement.

4. The Presence and the Perfected Praise

Above it stood the seraphims. . . . And one cried unto another, and said, Holy, holy, holy, is the LORD of hosts: the whole earth is full of His glory. (Isaiah 6:2–3)

When the veil is lifted, instead of seeing the Ark, Isaiah sees the Lord; instead of the usual Temple ritual, he hears the praise of sinless beings, and with a rush his own sinfulness and the sin of his people heads itself up on one particular point: "Then said I, Woe is me! for I am undone; because I am a man of unclean lips. . . ." Isaiah went through the crisis of face-to-face contact with God and the effect of the vision of God's holiness was to bring home to him that he was a man of unclean lips, i.e. the expression of his nature was pernicious. He not only confesses his own sin but identifies himself with the sin of his people—"and I dwell in the midst of a people of unclean lips."

Our Lord said "Out of the abundance of the heart the mouth speaketh." But remember when it is that our speech reveals what is in our heart, viz., when we are brought to a sudden crisis and the whole nature expresses itself. The majority of us are much too cunning to express what is in our heart until we are brought to a crisis, then the true state of our heart is out instantly. A crisis will always reveal the condition of our heart because it makes us express ourselves. The Spirit of God convicts us by focusing our mind on one particular point, there is never any vague sense of sin, and if we will yield to His conviction He will lead us down to the disposition of sin underneath. That is always the way God deals with us when we are consciously in His presence.

5. The Process of the Vision
Then flew one of the seraphims unto me, having a live coal in his hand, . . . and he laid it upon my mouth, and said, Lo, this hath touched thy lips; and thine iniquity is taken away, and thy sin purged. (Isaiah 6:6–7)

There is nothing between God and Isaiah now. The fire expiates his guilt at the very spot where he is convicted of his personal sin. Second Corinthians 5:21 ("For He hath made Him to be sin for us, who knew no sin; that we might be made the righteousness of God in Him") states what God makes to transpire in every soul who is identified with Jesus: there is a moral agreement with God's verdict on sin in the Cross and we experience the expiation of our sin through the marvel of His substitution for us on the Cross. All the Old Testament ritual and the presentation of truth by the prophets is blended in one marvellous Personality, the Lord Jesus Christ, and by the "new and living way, which He has consecrated" any one of us can enter into the holiest, with no ceremonial in between, no intermediary—God and my own soul brought face to face in Jesus Christ. The only sacrifice which we as sinners have to bring is a contrite heart, "Nothing in my hands I bring. . . ." What happens then is that the whole life is given over to God for His service. When once the application of the sacrifice of Christ has been made it is the essence of pain to use the life for any other purpose than for Him (see Colossians 1:24). The symbol of the live coal "from off the altar" represents the twofold nature of the substitution of Christ, not only Christ *for* me, but Christ *in* me. This is the key to the Apostle Paul's teaching of identification, not the sacrifice of the body of Christ at a distance, but my identification with that sacrifice so that the Atonement is made efficacious in me and God can indwell me as He indwelt His Son.

6. The Programme after the Vision
God did not address the call to Isaiah; Isaiah overheard God saying, "Whom shall I send, and who will go for Us?" God did not lay a strong compulsion on Isaiah;

Isaiah was in the presence of God and realised that there was nothing else for him to do but say, in conscious freedom, "Here am I; send me." If we will let the Spirit of God bring us face to face with God we too shall hear something akin to what Isaiah heard, the still, small voice of God, and in perfect freedom say, "Here am I; send me." We have to get out of our minds the idea of expecting God to come with compulsion and pleadings. When Our Lord called His disciples there was no irresistible compulsion from outside; the quiet, passionate insistence of His "Follow Me" was spoken to men with every power wide awake.

There is one fact more about Isaiah which must always be borne in mind, and that is he not only heard God's call but he understood the nature of God who gave the call. It is not sufficient to say "God reigns" we must know the nature of the God who reigns. Isaiah stood unperturbed because he knew God. Isaiah had been disillusioned about himself and about the people of God, there is not a single prop left; in this respect he comes nearest to the attitude of Jesus Christ who would not commit Himself to men because "He knew what was in man."

What is true of the great prophets is true in our own little world. After we have had the vision of God and have had a time alone with Him we are plunged straight away into appalling affairs, when either all we have learned is absolutely swamped, or else we emerge exactly in accordance with the vision God gave. God only gives us visions of Himself for one purpose, that we may work them out into character. When once you have had the vision of God, or the experience of sanctification, you will be put into places where everything is as unlike God as the world, the flesh and the devil can make it, and you have to be there not to criticise, but to stand true to God in the centre of it all, and be crushed by the things that are not of God. The natural tendency is to withdraw; when God wants to withdraw His children, *He* does it (see 1 Peter 4:12–13). After God has given us a time of face-to-face contact with Himself and then puts us into tumults, the temptation is to sit down and say "Where is the blessedness I had when first I knew the Lord?" The Spirit of God holds us steady until we learn to know God, and the details of our lives are established before Him, then nothing on the outside can move us. God can rely on the man or woman to whom He has given the vision of Himself. Some of us are rushing on at such a headlong pace in Christian organisation, we want to vindicate God's character in a great revival, but if God did give us a revival we would be the first to forget Him and swing off on some false fire. When once we know Him we can stand wherever He puts us.

FROM THE BIBLE TRAINING COURSE MONTHLY JOURNAL
VOL. 10 OCTOBER–NOVEMBER 1941 NOS. 7–8
NOTES ON ISAIAH

THROUGH THE SHADOW OF AN AGONY COMETH REDEMPTION
Isaiah 8–11

Thou! if thou wast He, who at mid-watch came,
By the starlight, naming a dubious name!
And if, too heavy with sleep—too rash
With fear—O Thou, if that martyr-gash
Fell on Thee coming to take thine own,
And we gave the Cross, when we owed the Throne—
Thou art the Judge. We are bruised thus.
But, the Judgement over, join sides with us!
Thine too is the cause! and not more thine
Than ours, is the work of these dogs and swine,
Whose life laughs through and spits at their creed!
Who maintain Thee in word, and defy Thee in deed!

Robert Browning

It is characteristic of the prophecies of Isaiah that just when he is summing up the sins of the people and you should imagine that God was going to denounce them, there comes a ray of light in the darkness, e.g. Isaiah 9:1–2: "they that dwelt in the land of deep darkness, upon them hath the light shined" (RV mg).

There is a danger in trying to trace out God's way where He has not revealed it. Our experiences of God are simply part of the revelation of God Himself. The great line of God's revelation has never altered, and when individuals and nations leave their experiences and remain true to God, they find the revelation goes on all the time. God did not give a progressive revelation of Himself through the Old Testament: the people progressively grasped the revelation, which is very different. For instance, God knew when He told Abraham to offer up Isaac for a burnt offering that Abraham would interpret it to mean he was to kill his son. God can only reveal His will according to the state of a man's character and his traditional belief. Abraham had to be brought to the last limit of the tradition he held about God before God could give him its right meaning. Abraham had to have his faith purified, i.e., to have it stripped of every tradition he held until he stood face to face with God and understood His mind, and Abraham is the father of the faithful.

Isaiah 9

Isaiah is speaking as he is "moved by the Holy Ghost," and he portrays a character neither he nor anyone else had ever seen. The Mind of God alone knows the Being Isaiah is portraying. The remarkable thing is that when Jesus Christ comes, every one of the things the prophets have been saying fit in with one Personality, the Being whom we know as the Lord Jesus Christ. Isaiah never saw Jesus Christ, he could not have imagined Him, then what inspired him? the very Mind of God (see 1 Peter 2:20).

"The zeal of the LORD of hosts will perform this" (Isaiah 9:7). The meaning of the word "zeal" is a mixture of hot anger and affection. Jealousy in its good sense comes near the meaning, it is that overflow of love that cannot keep still, when men think God has surely done all He will do and can do for an ungrateful race, He visits them in their distress and carries them forward into His desired haven for them. God Almighty is ever gracious in His promises, He does not only fulfil His promises, He over-fulfils them. In our Lord's parable of the two sons, the love of the father for the elder brother staggers religious calculations about the love of God.

Isaiah 10

(See *2 Kings 18–19).* According to Isaiah, the rulers of the people are the expression of the life and ambition of the people. We fix on the mountain-peak characters and say they are to blame, but God holds the people themselves responsible also. The people are never exonerated for having bad rulers; the reason they have bad rulers is that they are bad people. Those who rule the people do not autocratically crush them, the people are their inspirers; they are the rulers the people deserve. The man of God has to vicariously take on himself the suffering under the providential order of tyranny. Isaiah was right in the midst of it all, yet he stood like a rock, perfectly confident in God, and let the onslaught of tyranny do its worst (cf. John 19:10–11).

The paralysing effect of brute force was making the people lose their faith in God. Isaiah found King Ahaz wanting, he found the people of God wanting, but he does not have the idea that the nation is going to hell; he gathers together the remnant that stands true, and the hope persistently crops up, born in him by the Spirit of God, that what God has shown him in vision will yet be fulfilled, and the nation be one with God.

The things dominantly in force to-day are the characteristics of Assyria. Fear is apt to make us atheistic and in our outlook we enthrone the devil, not God. God is behind it all, not a thing happens but He knows all about it. When the tyrannizers crow and think they have the right by their own power, suddenly the message of God comes—"Wherefore it shall come to pass, that when the Lord hath performed His whole work upon mount Zion and on Jerusalem, I will punish the fruit of the stout heart of the king of Assyria, and the glory of his high looks . . ." (Isaiah 10:12).

Isaiah 11

"And the spirit of the LORD shall rest upon Him, . . . and He shall be of quick understanding [mg] in the fear of the LORD" (RV), literally, "He shall draw His breath in the fear of the LORD" (Isaiah 11:2–3). The only way we can breathe the atmosphere of the fear of the Lord is by being born from above (RV mg) of the Spirit of God, then we find that Jesus Christ is our moral open air. The hymn has the idea—

Prayer is the Christian's vital breath,
The Christian's native air. . . .

The Personality Isaiah is describing has definitely clear characteristics, He produces His own atmosphere. Just as sea and mountain air form the open air to our physical life, so Jesus Christ is the moral atmosphere for our spiritual life, and if we try to draw our breath from any other source we instantly get diseased. By prayer and communion with God we live out in God's moral open air, consequently we can live in the cities and amongst the places of men and maintain the life which is in accordance with the Messiah's life Isaiah is referring to—the only thing is that in the practical domain of Christian ethics we forget to do it! The enemy of our souls goes for all he is worth against our praying, against our solitudes with God, he tries to prevent us drawing our breath in the fear of the Lord. The great need is to bring every thought and imagination into captivity to the obedience of Christ until every bit of our nature is reconstructed, and we manifest the reconstruction as we draw on the same Source as the Messiah drew from, viz., God.

Isaiah 11:6–9. Isaiah is forecasting what is going to be through the Redemption: everything that has been touched by the consequences of man's sin will be put absolutely right by God. The point to note is that the mediator in all this is man himself—"For the earnest expectation of the creature waiteth for the manifestation of the sons of God." The order is—For God our worship; for man our service; for the creature our providence through the meditation of holiness. Everything that has partaken of the curse is to be absolutely reinstated by Jesus Christ.

"And the wolf shall dwell with the lamb. . . . They shall not hurt nor destroy in all My holy mountain: for the earth shall be full of the knowledge of the LORD, as the waters cover the sea" (RV). The lower creation was not in antipathy to human beings until they learned to suspect them. This is proved by Darwin's experiments and in isolated experiences such as St. Francis of Assisi.

FROM THE BIBLE TRAINING COURSE MONTHLY JOURNAL
VOL. 10 DECEMBER 1941–JANUARY 1942 NOS. 9–10
NOTES ON ISAIAH

THE TRIBULATION OF NATIONS
Isaiah 13–23

. . . the day of the LORD is at hand. Isaiah 13:6

The Day of the Lord is at hand, at hand:
The storms roll up the sky;
The nations sleep starving on heaps of gold:
All dreamers toss and sigh;
The night is darkest before the morn,
When the pain is the sorest, the child is born,
And the Day of the Lord is at hand.

Charles Kingsley[7]

Every day is somebody's day, not a day that we prepare but a day prepared for us. Herod's "convenient day" came. It dawns quietly and ordinarily like any other day, then suddenly something happens and it is marked as either the blackest or the brightest day. If it is the blackest day it is God bringing you to the place where there streams up over your head the trend of your character unseen before. It is these moments we live for, the rest we trifle away; when they come there is no illusion left, we know as clear as a sunbeam whether we are going "or the right way, the wrong

---

7. Charles Kingsley (1819–1875) was an English cleric and writer.

way, to our triumph or undoing." It depends on what use we make of the doom days whether we are in a right or wrong relationship at the final doomsday. God does not leave a man with a "ghastly smooth life, dead at heart"; God's convicting days are His mercies preparing us for the final Doomsday. God gives doom days to nations as well as to individuals. This dispensation is man's day when he can do exactly as he likes, and we are doing it; we are allowed absolute liberty for a time. If you want a mirror of how God is dealing with the world at large, watch your own private history with Him.

It is necessary to guard our spirit when we read the Bible. For instance, it is possible to credit God with a personal vindictiveness that belongs to the devil; as if God were saying to the nations through Isaiah, "You have withstood Me and slandered Me, you have done everything you could against My people, but now the time has come when I will grind you to powder and obliterate you from off the face of the earth." Or take Our Lord's words, "How can ye escape the damnation of hell?" Who was it spoke them? The One who died on Calvary. Behind the words is an unfathomable sadness that even God Himself cannot save them from perdition. The idea is not that God in great triumphal power is going to ignore every other nation, but rather that through the first-born people of God all the other nations are to come to know Him. It is perilously possible to credit God with our prejudices, even after we are sanctified. We make hell out to be a place for the venting of our spleen, not for the working of the justice of God. God never justifies our spleen.

Isaiah's message needs to come home to us to-day, viz. that God is behind the devil, not the devil behind God; all the great world forces are in front of God, and they cannot do a thing without His permission. To-day we are so emphasising the freedom of the human will that we are forgetting the sovereignty of God, consequently when we come up against the forces at work in the world we are paralysed by fear and get into despair, which we need never have done if we had been built up in faith in God. Never minimise what you don't understand, and never knuckle under to the world forces; stand strong in faith in God—"I don't understand this, but I know God is behind it." Weigh the force and stand true to God at all costs. Too often we rush in where angels fear to tread. Let God place you by His providence where He will, the tendency is to "wobble" out of it—"I would rather stand for God somewhere else." We have the idea that we ought to separate ourselves from the world and its enterprises; that is foreign to Isaiah and to Our Lord (see John 17:15). We are to be *in* the world while not *of* it, and to denounce by lip and life the things that are wrong.

The world forces referred to in these chapters are not foreign to us, they are at our very doors to-day—civilisation, being pushed under the guise of Christianity; communism, socialistic blether full of all kinds of promise; and commercialism, binding every nation under heaven into one. Isaiah faced these forces fearlessly, and we have to do the same. There is no cowardice about Isaiah or about his message. He never lost his faith in God or got discouraged, and when the things he foretold happened, he did not desert the people.

"The Lord hath founded Zion, and in her shall the afflicted of His people take refuge" (Isaiah 14:32 RV). Just as Zion is spoken of as the central place of safety for the nations, so the only safe place for the saint, and it is as safe as God Himself, is the secret place of the Most High, abiding under the shadow of the Almighty (cf. Psalm 125:1–2). The same great majestic note is brought out in Psalm 46—"Therefore will not we fear, though . . ." It is the grand position got from the great God. Behind everything stands God; behind the tumult and the confusion God is bringing out everything according to His will. The great thing about faith in God is that it keeps a man undisturbed in the midst of disturbance. Every now and again God lets loose the hounds of hell all around you, and if you are His child, indwelt by His Spirit, you will experience the truth that Isaiah proclaims, viz. that all the forces outside you are futile because they are less powerful than the indwelling of God (see 1 John 4:4). No matter what may be the clanging of forceful interests all around, the work of God's grace stands true in His servants. Discouragement comes when we say what God will do—that God will always keep me healthy, that He will always be bringing me into the land of Canaan where I will eat honey; well, He won't. God is concerned about only one thing, viz. getting me into a personal relationship with Himself. There is no possibility of discouragement if we will only remember that this is the relationship, not God's blessings, but Himself. Beware of the modern craze for healing, it is Satan's opportunity to switch the saints off the central thing. A thing may have its source in Jesus Christ and yet easily turn traitor to Him once it becomes divorced from Himself. If Satan cannot switch the saints off on false fire, he will switch them off on anything that is less than the central thing. The central thing is the life hid with Christ in God where we can stand by the grace of God where this prophet stood, true to God and to God's aspect of things, letting other things shift as they may. "A man's life consisteth not in the abundance of the things which he possesseth" (Luke 12:15); it consists only in what he is. All our judgements of God, and our mis-judgements, are based on our own point of view, not on Jesus Christ's. Am I cultured in the iron tonic of the Bible? Have I really got incorporated into my faith the certainty that God will never allow anything to last that is not godly?

The whole experiment of the human race from God's standpoint is the overthrow of the devil, not by God—the devil is no match for God—but by man. God is going to overthrow the arrogance of the devil by a being less than Himself, viz. by man, that is why God became Incarnate. There is only one expression of God's attitude to the devil and that is Calvary.

The Spirit of Jesus conflicts with the things we esteem highest. It is impossible to carry out the principles of the Sermon on the Mount and have success. The mark of the beast is here already, and it will grow clearer before the man of sin is revealed (see 2 Thessalonians 2). It is slighting no one to say that prosperity in this order of things along with godliness is impossible, and growingly more impossible.

The destruction of every civilisation there has ever been has come about through a force for which the civilisation had a contempt.

We estimate by what a man possesses; God's only concern is what a man *is*. There is only one thing that will endure and that is personality, no possessions, no pretence, nothing in the way of what men call greatness will last. All the rest is trappings; in their right place, great and good trappings, but Satan wants to keep our minds on them. Holiness in character is the only thing that will remain. Some of us will have a spiritual character so microscopic that it will take the archangels to find it! The majority of us are bound up in the show of things, and when the stern dark lines of God's truth come we say it is harsh. It is the true strain only we cannot hear it aright unless we are where the prophet Isaiah was—standing with God behind the show of things, consequently he is imperturbable, he never got into a panic.

It would be a liberal education to go through the Bible unbiased by convictions. Stop exploiting the Bible to back up a particular doctrine and let the Bible bring you into its own atmosphere and you will find that instruction is clear and emphatic regarding every phase of life there is. If Satan as an angel of light can limit and bind us to our own particular experiences he will succeed in keeping us from an understanding of the Mind of God. The great need for the saint is to get his brains at work on the Word of God, otherwise he will stagnate, no matter how much he may name the Name of God.

(These chapters were not studied in detail, consequently only some brief notes are available.)

FROM THE BIBLE TRAINING COURSE MONTHLY JOURNAL
VOL. 11 APRIL–MAY 1942 NOS. 1–2
NOTES ON ISAIAH

ISAIAH 24–26

1. The Mysterious Inevitableness of Sin (Isaiah 24)

Behold, the LORD maketh the earth empty, and maketh it waste, and turneth it upside down, and scattereth abroad the inhabitants thereof. . . . The earth also is polluted under the inhabitants thereof; because they have transgressed the laws, changed the ordinance, broken the everlasting covenant. (Isaiah 24:1, 5)

The Bible reveals that the material world has been blighted by reason of man's sin. The connection between man's sin and the material universe is indelible, the connection is made by God. The great truth which runs all through God's Book and takes clearer features in the New Testament is that the material universe and the moral universe are from the same Hand. Man was intended by God to govern Nature (see Genesis 1:26); instead, he has infected it with his sin and it has become a partaker of the curse with him, so that "the whole creation groaneth and travaileth in pain together until now."

Men say "We are going to build a holy city on this earth"—you cannot; the earth is infected, it is a diseased chamber, and the holy city will never be on it until God has purged it with fire and taken the epidemic out of it. The Bible says that the holy city is going to come down from above (see Revelation 21:2). God cannot bring in the Millennium by moral renovation, but only by cremation, by burning all the infected rubbish out. Beware of saying that God is too kind and loving to do that; we have to read God's love in the light of His character, and He is absolutely just and holy.

Sin infects matter although it is not in matter, and this has given rise to the old pagan idea that sin is in the flesh. Sin is a disposition which rules human nature, but it is not in human nature. The things Our Lord mentions as proceeding, "from within, out of the heart of men," are all connected with the physical life (see Mark 7:20–23); and when Paul speaks of the outcome of indwelling sin he connects it with the physical life (see Colossians 3:5). We have no standing before God physically, morally or spiritually; the only way we can ever stand before God is through the Atonement. It is truths like this that enable us to understand the meaning of the Cross. Sin has infected the material universe as well as human nature, and both must be cleansed and purged. If I can see how it works in my individual life I will see how it works in the world at large.

We infect all we possess by what we are. This principle is brought out all through. If I indent myself on any place, my study for instance, as being lazy, that place will take its revenge on me every time I enter it by making me feel lazy. The opposite is also true, if I have made my study a place of stern industry it will act upon me as an inspiration every time I go into it. Nearly every man and woman has a blighted place somewhere, blighted not by someone else but by themselves, by their relationship to someone else in that particular place. Where is it you feel most tested physically? You will find it is in the place where you have been peculiarly mean in days gone by. If we are irritable at home it is because we have been in the habit of being mean there, and when we come into the same situation the meanness shows itself in irritability of nerves. There is a great deal said rightly and wrongly about the power of circumstances over a man; circumstances have a stupendous power, but unless we realise that Jesus Christ undertakes for a man's circumstances as well as for the removal of the disposition of sin, we shall never experience all the benefits which come through the Atonement. "Wherefore if any man is in Christ, he is a new creature: the old things are passed away"; not only sin, but the whole old order of things; "behold, they are become new" (RV).

2. The Vision of Resurrection *(Isaiah 25–26)*
The great note of the Bible revelation is not immortality but Resurrection. The doctrine of the Resurrection is that something comes from God Himself direct into the dust of death. Dust is the symbol of death—"Awake and sing, ye that dwell in the dust"

(Isaiah 26:19 RV). A dead body retains the look of life, but touch it, and it is gone; God will bring it the "dew of light [mg] and the earth shall cast forth the dead" (RV). The Resurrection is the manifestation of the direct power of God, not the manifestation of inherent life. The Bible always goes back to God; books about "the implicit promise of immortality" go into vague hopes—"Because I have so many hopes that cannot be realised in this life, it would be unjust if there were no life after death." That is not Christianity; Christianity is centred in the power of God, and the resurrection is the direct work of the sovereign God—nothing between God and a dead body. "Thy dead shall live; my dead bodies shall arise." When the Apostle Paul wants to measure the power of God in our lives he uses the illustration of the resurrection of Jesus Christ from the dead (Romans 8:11; Ephesians 1:19–20, etc.).

To-day people prefer to talk about the implicit promise of immortality rather than the resurrection. Probably the most amazing writer on the theme of immortality was Dr. F. W. H. Myers, he was a poet of the first order and he became a scientist in order to try and prove his intuitions; he wrote a book entitled *Human Personality and the Survival of the Body after Death*. The whole of his argument ends where it begins, in intuition; you cannot prove an implicit intuition. Men try to make out that the idea of the resurrection is something that occurred naturally to the human mind; it is a revelation, granted by God to His own people. "For since by man came death, by man came also the resurrection of the dead" (1 Corinthians 15:21). "He hath swallowed up death for ever. . . . And it shall be said in that day, Lo this is our God; . . . we have waited for Him, we will be glad and rejoice in His salvation" (Isaiah 25:8–9 RV).

"Thou wilt keep him in perfect peace, whose mind [imagination, RV mg] is stayed on Thee: because he trusteth in Thee" (Isaiah 26:3). Undisciplined imagination is the greatest disturber not only of growth in grace, but of spiritual sanity.

FROM THE BIBLE TRAINING COURSE MONTHLY JOURNAL
VOL. 11 JUNE–SEPTEMBER 1942 NOS. 3–6
NOTES ON ISAIAH

ISAIAH 27–29

1. The Day of Jehovah's Judgements (Isaiah 27)

Let him take hold of My strength, that he may make peace with Me. (Isaiah 27:5)

The judgements of God are for another purpose than the vindictive spirit of man would like to make out. It was this that gave Jonah the sulks with the Almighty, and the same spirit is seen in the elder brother—jealous of God's generosity to others. You never find that spirit in the prophets; if there is destruction and death it is for one purpose only, viz., deliverance. God is on the line of salvation, not of damnation; He only damns the damnable things, and Jesus Christ's presentation is that if you identify yourself with the damnable things even God Himself cannot save you; it is a determined dead set against the good and a determined identification with the wrong (cf. Matthew 23:33). When you come in contact with the great destructive sins in other lives, be reverent with what you don't understand; there are elements you know nothing about, and God says "Leave them to Me." Never make a virtue out of necessity; virtue is the overcoming by moral strength an inclination to go the other way.

2. Reiteration by Conscience and Commonplace (Isaiah 28)

He that believeth shall not make haste. (Isaiah 28:16)

Conscience does not shout in thunderclaps, you can easily drown its record, but it goes on, and if you do not heed it for a while because of sensational sinning, as soon as the sensation exhausts itself, back comes the monotonous tick, tick, that nearly drives a man mad. God will never make us listen to Him; we have to will to listen. In the midst of all the excitement the prophet says "he that believeth shall not make haste"—no wonder they ridiculed him! "We have to get on with the negotiations with Assyria and Egypt." Isaiah says when the judgement comes you will find that all your alliances are like a bed that is too short (Isaiah 28:20), a hopeless commonplace annoyance. The punishment of sensational sinners is never sensational but appallingly commonplace, dull, dreary, desperate drudgery. Prison is not man's order, it is God's order for the man who refuses to listen to what he calls the childish platitudes of God and life; he is determined to get rid of the quiet ordinary ways on which God has built human life, then he has to take the commonplace way of prison to bring him back to his senses. Take it in the religious domain, people who are given over to religious excitement cannot stand a solid godly meeting, they must have sensationalism—crowds, speaking in tongues. God never works like that. Beware of sensationalism in every shape and form.

3. God's Performances (Isaiah 29)

Ye turn things upside down! Shall the potter be counted as clay; that the thing made should say of him that made it, He made me not; or the thing framed say of him that framed it, He hath no understanding? (Isaiah 29:16 RV)

In our own day we seem to have come to the conclusion that God has made a number of blunders and we have to put them right; we have private notions of our own which if put down in black and white would prove that we do not believe God is intelligent in allowing the history of the world to go on as it has, in allowing sin and war. We talk about these things as if they were amazing blunders that nearly take God's breath away and we have to do the best we can. We won't see that behind the whole thing is the wisdom of God, that neither bad men nor the devil himself can do one thing without the direct permission of God. "The foolishness of God is wiser than men." God has chosen "the weak things of the world," and men laugh at them. To the crowd we represent Jesus says, "Fear not, little flock, for it is your Father's good pleasure to give you the kingdom." A man who has faith in God is easily ridiculed, then when he comes out into the sun people say, What a cunning man he was, look how he worked it all out. We would rather credit man with an intelligence he never possessed than credit God with intelligence. The astuteness behind all is the Mind of God.

"And in that day shall the deaf hear the words of the book . . ." (Isaiah 29:18)—"that day"—the day in which God manifests His wisdom and turns man's wisdom to nonsense. The result of God's wisdom is a moral result, it is going to be realised to its full extent in what we call the Millennium, but it is manifested now whenever God's wisdom bursts through. All through Isaiah there is the confidence that God is reigning and ruling; the devil likes to make us believe that we are in a losing battle. Nothing of the sort! we have to overcome all the

things that try to obscure God. The rugged truths of Isaiah point out not only the appalling state of the world as it is, but that we have to live a holy life in it by the power of God, not a sequestered life in particular temples or rituals, but real genuine magnificent men and women of God, no matter what the devil or the world or the flesh may do. The only thing God is interested in is *life*, He is not interested in religious forms, and this is what the people had forgotten, they only recognised God in their moribund religious services. God is going to make us worthy of the best saints we have known if we go on with Him (Isaiah 29:22–24).

FROM THE BIBLE TRAINING COURSE MONTHLY JOURNAL
VOL. 11 OCTOBER–DECEMBER 1942 NOS. 7–9
NOTES ON ISAIAH

THE CENTRE OF THE CYCLONE
Isaiah 30

The test of true religion is the knowledge of the character of God. As long as you think of God in the quietness of a religious meeting you will never know God—what kind of God have you got when you are in touch with the wrong, bad, evil things? God's Book reveals that it is right in the midst of the very opposite of God that His blessings occur. The very things which seem to be making for destruction become the revealers of God. It is an easy business to preach peace when you are in health and have everything you want, but the Bible preaches peace when things are in a howling tumult of passion and sin and iniquity; it is in the midst of anguish and terror that we realise who God is and the marvel of what He can do.

1. The Buttresses of a Bungled Building
Therefore this iniquity shall be to you as a breach ready to fall, swelling out in a high wall, whose breaking cometh suddenly at an instant. (Isaiah 30:13)

The trouble is not that the wall has been badly built, but there is too much on the inside and it will burst through no matter what buttresses there are; the real danger comes from within. The supposed buttresses will prove to be breaches—"and he shall break it as a potter's vessel is broken, breaking it in pieces without sparing" (Isaiah 30:14 RV). Your principles may be all right, but if the personal relationship to God is ignored the whole thing will come to the ground. Belief in God will always manifest itself in right principles, but if you put principles first you will end in disbelief in God. Men quote Our Lord's words: "thou shalt love thy neighbour as thyself"; true, but if you build on that you blot God out of His heaven and you end as an atheist where you began as a lover of men. It is the same truth that Jesus enunciated: "... he that gathereth not with Me scattereth." In Luke 14:26–33, where Our Lord is laying down the conditions of discipleship, He implies that He is not less than a man

among men—"I know the kind of building I am going to rear, *I* have counted the cost and only those in whom My work is effective will be taken up into My building and battling enterprises"; consequently there will be no incompleteness, no bursting out from within of what is wrong, in Jesus Christ's building.

2. The Benefit of Building by Belief
And therefore will the LORD wait, that He may be gracious unto you, ... for the LORD is a God of judgement: blessed are all they that wait for Him. (Isaiah 30:18)

God's purpose is not destruction but the bringing out into light and blessing all the nations as well as His own people. Nowadays we have lost the iron tonic of the belief in God behind everything. The Bible view is that God is allowing the devil and sin to do their worst, but behind all the calamities He is working out His purpose. Learn to relate everything in your own life to God, and remember that if things go wrong it is because they must go wrong, but the must is not necessity, it is God. "Things wrong are needful where wrong things abound." If we had made the world would we have made pain? No, we would have ruled pain out. We all pronounce against God and say that pain comes from the devil. The devil knows far too much to allow pain—when he reigns "his goods," i.e. the souls of men, "are in peace." Pain, physical, moral and spiritual pain is the gateway of life every time. The thing that to us is the ugliest blot on the face of Creation God makes to be the angel of the revelation of Himself.

Belief in God's mercy will always be inclined to wobble between sleepy satisfaction that God is indulgent and fretful impatience that He is indifferent. When we become spiritual the thing that comes out more and more clearly is not so much the fact that we have discerned God, but His amazing patience with us in our absurd bungling ways of talking about Him. God never hurries up no matter what men say about

Him, He goes steadily forward, and bit by bit as we follow the light of the Spirit of God we begin to discern His methods.

"For the LORD is a God of judgement: blessed are all they that wait for Him." The only place of confidence is personal trust in God and patient waiting for Him. One of the things we have to unlearn is the idea of judgement which never came from God's Book, viz. the idea that God is vindictive. Our Lord never spoke from personal vindictiveness, He spoke from a knowledge of the eternal principles of God, which are inexorable. To trust in the goodness of God is not enough, it is not eternal and abiding; we have to trust *God,* who is infinitely more than goodness.

3. The Benign Blessing of the Besieged

For the people shall dwell in Zion at Jerusalem: thou shalt weep no more. (Isaiah 30:19)

All through Isaiah is true to his original vision, viz. the survival of the holy remnant. That stands symbolically for the indestructibility of God's purpose, and it will be true historically also, the prevailing of God's purpose notwithstanding all that the devil and sin may do. The danger with us as workers is that we do not stand in the thick of things as the prophets did, we stand aloof from them and are no use in the way God intends us to be. Whatever the circumstances may be we have to stand true for God *there.*

"Ye shall have a song, as in the night . . . and gladness of heart" (Isaiah 30:29). God makes His people sing

where in the eyes of the world it seems ironical to sing—in a besieged city where things are going to ruin, in the suburbs of hell, in the valley of the shadow of death. When you see lives in the midst of turmoil and anguish full of amazing brightness and uncrushable elasticity of faith in God, if you do not know God you will say, "However can they go through it? how is it that they remain undiscouraged and undismayed?" The explanation is the presence of God made real in His promises. Think of the ridiculously legal way we treat the promises; we say to God, "You made this promise now fulfil it." The promise itself is the fulfilment, God's presence is *in* the promise. No one can fulfil a promise but the one who made it. "For all the promises of God in Him are yea, and in Him Amen, unto the glory of God by us" (2 Corinthians 1:20), not "yea and Amen" to faith, but *in Christ Jesus.*

The Book of God is a revelation of God; that means there is no key to its interpretation other than a knowledge of God. Likewise our lives are a series of puzzles and God alone is the answer to them. Unless we discern God in Bible interpretation and in the interpretation of our lives we will come to disaster. God's Book is merciless on sham and pretence, anything that obscures the one real relationship—"In all the world there is none but Thee, my God there is none but Thee." God first, second and third; not refinement, but holiness—a holy God and a holy people and Isaiah cares for nothing else.

FROM The Bible Training Course Monthly Journal
Vol. 11 January–March 1943 Nos. 10–12
Notes on Isaiah

ISAIAH 36–38

1. The Tryst of Faith *(Isaiah 36)*
. . . that the trial of your faith, . . .

All our beliefs unless they have been made ours through suffering, stand helpless immediately we are faced by a healthy pagan. Rabshakeh stands for rationalism, and rationalism can never understand the "Isaiah" element, viz. the impregnable citadel of faith in God. If we obey the "Isaiah" element we are brought where Isaiah is trying to bring these people—"in quietness and in confidence shall be your strength."

Sennacherib, the Assyrian king, has been subduing the fenced cities of Judah, and now he sends this astute man, Rabshakeh, to Jerusalem with a great army, and he struts before the people with all the assurance imag-

inable. We are familiar with Isaiah's method of bringing his message to the people and then making them decide, and Rabshakeh does the same thing (see Isaiah 36:4–10). The most formidable enemy to faith in God is rationalism because there is no answer saving on the spiritual line. When people go down spiritually it is because they have begun to heed the earnestness which quotes the words of God without His Spirit. The first thing always that blinds us is that people are in earnest. If the people had heeded Isaiah and learned to depend upon God for themselves they would have seen through the disguise of Rabshakeh's earnestness.

The trial of faith never comes along a fantastic line, it always comes along a line on which we can be tested. Here, Rabshakeh's counsel made it seem the wisest thing to affiliate with Assyria; the facts he hurls at them are facts. Beware of the talk that sympathises with your bias—no one is unbiased; there is nothing captivates you more quickly. In listening to certain people you feel, "That is the only thing that can be said," they bear you down with an overplus of common sense. If in the face of all the appeals of common sense you remain true to God, that is the "proof of your faith" (RV) which will be found to the glory of God. The nature of faith is that it must be tested; and the trial of faith does not come in fits and starts, it goes on all the time. The one thing that keeps us right with God is the great work of His grace in our hearts. All the prophets had to take part in something they did not understand, and the Christian has to do the same. If we were to say "This is the way God is going to work," it would lead to spiritual pride, to the ban of finality[8] about our views, to imagining that God was on our side. The question for us is, will we so yield to the Spirit of God that we always side with Him? The "trial of your faith" is in order to bring God into the practical details of your life.

2. The Tribulation of Faith *(Isaiah 37)*
. . . being much more precious than gold . . . (RV)

Faith is the trend of the life all through, and everything that is not "hid with Christ in God" is against it. The trial of faith always comes in such a way that it is a perplexity to know what to do. You get advice that sounds wise, it has your welfare in view; everything seems right, and yet there is the feeling that there is an error at the heart of it.

"And Hezekiah received the letter from the hand of the messengers, and read it: and Hezekiah went up unto the house of the LORD, and spread it before the LORD" (Isaiah 37:14). If any letter is not important enough to be spread "before the LORD" it is too small to annoy you. If I have not prayed about things so ridiculously small that I almost blush to mention them, I have not learned the first lesson in prayer.

It is not easy to find your way to God in a sudden crisis unless you have been in the habit of going to God about everything. The thing that rationalism ridicules is not a man praying to God when he is in distress, but a man praying to God when he is not in distress. To the rationalist it is ridiculous to pray to God about everything; behind the ridicule is the devil to keep us from knowing the road when the crisis comes. Hezekiah knew the road. In his prayer (Isaiah 37:16–20) Hezekiah tells God what he knows God knows already. That is the meaning of prayer—I tell

God what I know He knows in order that I may get to know it as He does (cf. Matthew 6:8). It is not true to say that a man learns to pray in calamities, he never does; he calls on God to deliver him, but he does not pray (see Psalm 107:6, 13, 19).

A man only learns to pray when there is no calamity.

3. The Triumph of Faith *(Isaiah 38)*
. . . might be found unto praise and honour and glory at the appearing of Jesus Christ. (1 Peter 1:7)

God's Book is like life, it records facts; we try to be consistent to our theories instead of to God's character. God has a way of bringing in facts which upset a man's doctrines if they stand in the way of God getting at his soul. God does not deal with lives in our way, but in His own way. When we get down to the real issues of life we forget to be consistent to doctrine because we are face to face with God, and those who have been teaching us how to do things have to retire.

"What shall I say? He hath both spoken unto me, and Himself hath done it: I shall go softly ["as in solemn procession," mg] all my years because of the bitterness of my soul. O Lord, by these things men live. . . ." (Isaiah 38:15–16 RV). If you have studied the faces of men and women you will find you can always tell those who have been face to face with danger, it has brought out a dignity of expression and a stateliness, and it is these lives that set the pace for a society that had been going too quickly. It is a benediction for a young life to have to face danger and death, the character is more likely to tell for good ultimately than if it had gone with a skip and jump into life without any realisation of its tremendous depths.

It is perilously easy to conclude that God's honour is bound up with my deliverance; whereas my deliverance is in order to bring me into touch with Reality and not for God's honour at all. If, like Hezekiah, you go through a crisis you find that all the small mean[9] things in your nature disappear, you are face to face with the real issues—your back is to life and your face is to death; then when God brings you through the crisis with your back to death and your face to life, be careful that you don't degenerate into a "small potato." We are apt to think that any one who has faced death and has seen the true issues of life will never become small and mean again, but that is a great fallacy. When we forget to walk in the light of the vision the meanness and selfishness will crop up again. Hezekiah forgot the grand stately processional gait and he degenerated into a childish piece of disgraceful con-

---

8. The "ban of finality" means the limitation or curse of having one's mind made up, to the point of being unwilling to consider new information.

9. The word mean as used here refers to something or someone ordinary, common, low, or ignoble, rather than cruel or spiteful.

duct (see Isaiah 39). If you have had a spiritual awakening, a time of the sense of God's presence and revelation of His word, a crisis you can only account for by God, remember you have to pay for it, if you are to be worth God's trouble—to pay for it by the determination to keep steadily on that line. The crisis in which God was revealed is to be the light of your life when there is no crisis. Keep paying the price; let God see you are willing to live up to the vision.

In a crisis leave everything to God, shut out every voice saving the voice of God and the psalm of your own deliverance; make it your duty to remain true to both these voices.

In the life of a saint tribulation does this supernatural thing—it brings back innocence with experience; in the natural world experience brings cunning and craftiness. We sit down under the tyranny of a devil's lie and say, "I can't undo the past": you cannot, but God can. God can make the past, as far as our spiritual life is concerned, as if it had never been and even in its worst features He can make it bring out the "treasures of darkness."

FROM THE BIBLE TRAINING COURSE MONTHLY JOURNAL
VOL. 12 APRIL–JUNE 1943 NOS.1–3
NOTES ON ISAIAH

THE LORD GOD OMNIPOTENT REIGNETH
Isaiah 40

1. The Voice of Inner Reassurance (Isaiah 40:1–2)

Comfort ye, comfort ye My people, saith your God. (Isaiah 40:1)

A revelation-voice always implies a previous knowledge. God cannot make a revelation to a sinner; He can make a revelation to a backslidden saint, and in order to effect this He sends His Spirit to prepare the way by conviction. This revelation-voice comes to the people of God who are experiencing punishment for their sin; but they have had an experience of God, they have known Him, and in the midst of their tribulation His voice speaks to them.

We cannot imitate God's voice, even when we utter His words. The preacher can never rouse up a backslider; it is only when the Spirit of God has got hold of the preacher and is making the words of God living, that the backslider hears God's voice and awakens. The insistent need in practical Christianity is to rely on the Spirit of God; it is the only way to kill the arrogant impudence of preachers. I look upon a congregation as those whom I have to induce to come to God—and I am made of the same stuff as they are! The only reason for my being in the preacher's place is that I have heard God's voice and He has done something in me which He can for them, and I deliver God's message, knowing that the Spirit will apply it as I rely upon Him. Beware of ignoring the ministry of the Spirit by relying on your sensible knowledge of the people you talk to. The great snare in modern Christian enterprise is this very thing—"Do remember the people you are talking to."

We have to stay true to God and His message, not to our knowledge of the people. We must not consider what the people want but what God wants us to present to them, and as we rely on His Spirit we find God works His marvels in His own way.

"Comfort ye, comfort ye My people, saith your God." Notice the "My," and remember that they were a disobedient people, and yet God is "not ashamed to be called their God." It is not the love of God for a pure saint, but the love of God for a sin-stained people. He might well have been ashamed of them on account of their sin and degradation, but His voice comes in all its amazing wonder—"Speak ye comfortably ["to the heart of," RV mg] to Jerusalem. . . ." It is a wonderful picture of what God does in the Atonement.

2. The Voice of Imminent Reality (Isaiah 40:3–5)

Prepare ye the way of the LORD. . . . And the glory of the LORD shall be revealed. (Isaiah 40:3, 5)

Unless we prepare on the outside in accordance with the inner vision we are not in God's order. John the Baptist prepared the way of the Lord historically, but take it personally—how many valleys have I exalted, and how many mountains have I made low? How many mountains of prejudice have I put out of the way? If we prepare on the outside we enable God to plant His glory there, and the first thing we have to do is to go dead against our ingrained prejudices which put a barrier round about us. If I will *do* in accordance with what God has made me *be*, He will reveal His glory.

3. The Voice of Insistent Reminding *(Isaiah 40:6–8)*

The grass withereth, . . . but the word of our God shall stand for ever. (Isaiah 40:8)

Think of asking these people in their misery and sin to prepare the way of the Lord! No wonder the prophet says, "What shall I cry?" "Cry first," the voice says, "that everything is vanity; don't build your hopes again on anything you can see; don't put your confidence again in men, in alliances with Egypt and Assyria; they all wither as the grass." Then comes the heartening verity—"but the word of our God shall stand for ever." Everything will shift but God and His word. How steadily the Spirit of God warns us not to put our trust in men and women, not even in princes, or in anything or anyone but God and His word. Isaiah is reminding the people of this—"You should by this time have said farewell for ever to confidence in everyone and everything but God." That is what happens in sanctification. It has to be a valediction once and for ever to confidence in anyone but God, then the hundred-fold can be given without any fear of deceiving the heart.

4. The Voice of Infinite Redemption *(Isaiah 40:9–11)*

Behold, the Lord GOD will come with strong hand, and His arm shall rule for Him. (Isaiah 40:10)

Isaiah is not trying to convert the minds of the people, but speaking to their hearts. They have got into despair—"We do not doubt what God can do, but He has wearied of us, and we don't blame Him." Isaiah's message comes to recover to them their lost heritage. What we all need is someone who can make real to us the ideas we had of God but have forgotten; the only

One who can do this for us is the Spirit of God. Isaiah is bringing back to the people first of all the memory of who God is; you cannot have faith in anyone you have forgotten. It is not God's promises we need, it is Himself. "His presence is salvation." Once let that Presence come, and all the inner forces of hope are rallied at once. Isaiah is calling upon them to "hang in" to God— "No matter how challenging facts may be to disprove your faith, remember that you did know God, and that there is good reason for all that has happened." The reason the children of Israel could not see this was that they were not blaming themselves—"We are God's favoured people, the things which have happened are from the devil." No, they are from God. God is using external forces as a scourge to bring back His people to Himself—Holiness as a law; chastisement as a means; a holy remnant as a result. Isaiah calls upon them to exercise unshaken faith in God and in His predicted deliverance of which there seems no likelihood. This profound truth runs all through God's word. It is not faith when you trust in what you see; faith is trusting in what you don't see, hanging in to the God whose character you know though meantime there is no evidence that He is at work on your behalf.

The vision of God's purpose comes from a pure heart, from an acute intellect; the condition is—the inner life right with God. An illiterate old woman with a pure heart has a greater insight into the purposes of God than a prime minister. If the prime minister has a pure heart as well as powerful intellect, then you have a man like Isaiah, a giant for God. The sanctification-metaphysic underlies everything. The opportunity is given to us all to be the choice souls. The God who guides the stars, unhasting and unresting, will as assuredly fulfil what He has promised.

FROM THE BIBLE TRAINING COURSE MONTHLY JOURNAL
VOL. 12 JULY–SEPTEMBER 1943 NOS. 4–6
NOTES ON ISAIAH

"SERVUS SERVORUM DEI"
Isaiah 42

1. Commission for Service

Behold My servant, whom I uphold.

A servant is one who is at the disposal of another—"a servant of the servants of God." Christianity is the deification of this type of service. Jesus Christ Himself is the servant of all— "I am in the midst of you as He that serveth" (RV), and Paul delights to call himself "a bondservant of Jesus" (RV mg). If you want to know

what a servant of God is to be like, read what Isaiah says in this chapter and the following ones about the great Servant, Jesus Christ. The characteristics of the great Servant must be the characteristics of every servant; it is the identification of the servant of God with the immortal characteristics of God Himself.

In service for God we have to be abandoned to Him, let Him put us where He will, whether He blesses us or crushes us with burdens, we have nothing to do with what it costs. God will bring folks round in order to see whether He can put anything on you to bear for them—"I can put the burden of insight on that man, that woman, they have only one interest in life, and that is Myself." Would to God that we would get finished once for all with the experience of being rightly adjusted to God, and let Him begin to send us forth into vicarious service for Him! May God make us understand that if we are in His service He will do exactly what He likes with us. We are not saved and sanctified for ourselves, but for God to crush us with burdens if He chooses. What do we know about filling up that which remains behind of the sufferings of Christ? A servant of Jesus Christ is one who is willing to go to martyrdom for the reality of the Gospel of God.

2. Character of the Servant

He shall not cry, nor lift up, nor cause his voice to be heard in the street. (Isaiah 42:2)

This verse refers to the tone of the servant, self-effaced to such an extent that self is not thought of; nothing sickly or sentimental, but complete self-effacement so that Jesus only is known. The servant is absorbed in Jesus as He was in God. The mark of false service is the self-conscious pride of striving after God's favour. "The Holy Ghost will glorify *Me,*" said Jesus.

"He shall not . . . cause his voice to be heard in the street," i.e., he shall not advertise himself. Nothing is entered into for the sake of self-vindication; just as Our Lord never showed any desire to be found in the right, but only a strong desire that the right of God should have its way. Could we stand the humiliation Jesus stood of having words flung at us without saying "Now I must explain"? Men never heard His voice in the street vindicating Himself, but watch Him in the Temple, with a whip of small cords in His hand driving out the moneychangers; then it was His Father's honour that was at stake.

3. Considerateness of the Service

A bruised reed shall he not break, and the smoking flax shall he not quench.

This verse refers to the quality of the service. The accuser of the brethren comes and says to God, "That man is a broken reed, don't build any hope on him whatever, he is a hindrance and an upset to You; break him." But no, the Lord will bind up the broken reed and make it into a wonderful instrument and discourse sweet music through it. Or Satan insinuates—"That woman is a perfect disgrace to You, she has only one spark of grace among all the fibres of her being, the best thing to do is to stamp out that spark." But no, He will raise it to a flame. The whole conception of the work of a servant of God is to lift up the despairing and the

hopeless. Immediately you start work on God's line He will bring the weak and infirm round you, the surest sign that God is at work is that that is the class who come—the very class we don't want, with the pain and the distress and limitation. We want the strong and robust, and God gathers round us the feeble-minded, the afflicted and weak. Pain in God's service always leads to glory. We want success, God wants glory. Some of us have the notion, till God shakes it out of us, that we are saved and sanctified to have a holy hilarious time before God and among men. Never! We are saved and sanctified to be the servants of men—"ourselves your servants for Jesus' sake."

4. The Creator's Call to the Servant

Thus saith God . . . , He that created the heavens and stretched them out; . . . I the LORD have called thee in righteousness. . . . (Isaiah 42:5–6)

Naturally we never look to Nature for illustrations of the spiritual life, we look at the methods of business men, at man's handiwork. Our Lord drew all His illustrations from His Father's handiwork, He spoke of lilies and trees and grass and sparrows. As Christians we have to feast our souls on the things ignored by practical people. A false spirituality blots Nature right out. The way to keep your spiritual life un-panicky, free from hysterics and fuss, free from flagging and breaking, is to consider the bits of God's created universe you can see *where you are.* Foster your life on God and on His creation and you will find a new use for Nature. Read the life of Jesus—the calm, unhasting, unperturbed majesty of His life is like the majesty of the stars in their courses because both are upheld by the same power. Nothing happens in history or in Nature without God's permission and under His direct control. When the saints say, "God gave us good weather"; "He overruled that disaster for my good"; "He changed the wind"—in the eyes of the world, it is absurd. None of these things happens by chance, they have a distinct permissive purpose behind, and the saint discerns this. Jesus bases everything on what looks ridiculous to the eyes of common sense if God is ignored. Take intercessory prayer—how ridiculous it looks for a being like you or me to pray and expect God to answer: is it? It becomes the sublimest truth when we get hold of these principles.

"To open the blind eyes, to bring out the prisoners from the prison, and them that sit in darkness out of the prison house." That is the "Beulah" of the saints, the land of rest to which the service of men will bring men when it is performed in God's way. The law of God running all through the Bible is that every spiritual nature must be able to reproduce its kind, otherwise it abides alone; not produce the attitude of life, you can do that by your creeds, but produce your own kind. "Go . . . and make

disciples" (RV), said Jesus, and you cannot disciple others unless you are a disciple yourself. God regenerates lives; we disciple those whom He regenerates.

"I am the LORD: *that is My name."* The one test of a saint, which is another name for servant, is that he knows the incommunicable Name.

FROM THE BIBLE TRAINING COURSE MONTHLY JOURNAL
VOL. 12 OCTOBER–DECEMBER 1943 NOS. 7–9
NOTES ON ISAIAH

GOD THE GOAL
Isaiah 45

I am the LORD, *and there is none else; beside Me there is no God. Isaiah 45:5* (RV)

1. "Lo, These Are Parts of His Ways"
Thus saith the LORD *to His anointed, to Cyrus . . .*

God does not work according to His own precedents. To learn this supreme lesson, that God is not concerned about His own precedents, is to keep your soul in the state of a child, humbly depending on God, who will then guide you everywhere. Israel was looking at God's dealings with them in the light of what He had done in the past, forgetting altogether that what God had done in the past proved Him to be the sovereign Lord. Cyrus, the Persian, is not to be taken as a type of Christ, though God says of him "He is My shepherd, and shall perform all My pleasure." Cyrus is an illustration of the sovereignty of God. Behind all his successful campaigns was no "lucky star," or chance, or fortune, but the great fundamental, unshakeable purpose of God. Remember there is a difference between an instrument and a servant; a servant is one who has given up his right to himself to the God whom he proclaims. The term "servant" in this sense is never applied to Cyrus; he is an instrument in God's hands for the deliverance of His people.

2. Ways Past Finding Out
I will give thee the treasures of darkness, and hidden riches of secret places. . . . (Isaiah 45:3)

We often state the character of God in terms of brutal harshness which makes men atheists, while our motive is to glorify Him. Ever remember that "eternal life" is to know God, therefore you cannot expect to know Him in five minutes or forty years. Measure your ultimate delight in God's truth and joy in God by the little bit that is clear to you. There are whole tracts of God's character unrevealed to us as yet, and we have to bow in patience until God is able to reveal the things which look so dark. The danger is lest we make the little bit of truth we do know a pinnacle on which we set

ourselves to judge everyone else. It is perilously easy to make our conception of God like molten lead and pour it into our specially designed mould and then when it is cold and hard, fling it at the heads of the religious people who don't agree with us. The stamp of the saint is not the metallic rapping out of a testimony to salvation and sanctification, but the true humility which shows the fierce purity of God in ordinary human flesh. The purity in your soul burns the wrong in other souls because it is the fierce purity of God, and it was the purity of God in Christ that made people either hate Him or turn to Him. We are so certain that we must be right because we have had the experience of salvation and sanctification; the only sign that you are right is that you are a bondslave of Jesus.

There are depths inaccessible in the Divine nature; mysteries unrevealed in the method of God's procedure. God never reveals anything ahead of moral and spiritual progress. The Christian worker who has never walked in the darkness of God's hand with no light, has never walked with God at all. The principle of walking with God is that it is a walk by faith, not by sight; a walk in the light of Christ, not in the light of dogmatic conviction. Jesus as our example was under the shadow of the hand of God. "If it be possible, let this cup pass from Me." He knew He could have called twelve legions of angels to His rescue, but He did not call one; not one fire of His own did He kindle, not one self-generated effort did He ever make. One of the saddest sights is to see Christians who were true go under through the lassitude of some sorrow. This is where it begins—God brought them under the shadow of His hand, and they said, "This is the devil, I have no business to be in darkness," forgetting that there are things God cannot explain. Our Lord taught over and over again that things will never be explained in this life. We have to get rid of the idea that we are going to be vindicated down here; Jesus was not. The millennium age will be the vindication of the saints; this is the age of their humiliation. The triumphant thing for a saint is to stand true to God in spite of all the odds the world, the flesh and the devil can bring. God's Spirit will lead us away from our limitations and teach us to think the thoughts of God behind the things that contradict them, He will give us the "treasures of darkness." This was true in Isaiah's own life, he was undaunted because he was going on with God, events did not affect him. Along this line we get some idea of the amazing courage of these men of God. God never vindicates His saints in their own lifetime. The place of scrutiny for us to keep our lives faced with the Lord; at the back of all is the love of God which will not let a soul go. If you are a servant of God, He will put you through desert experiences without asking your permission.

FROM THE BIBLE TRAINING COURSE MONTHLY JOURNAL
VOL. 12 JANUARY–MARCH 1944 NOS. 10–12
NOTES ON ISAIAH

OUR IMPLICIT DIFFERENCE WITH GOD
Isaiah 53

Surely He . . . : yet we. . . . Isaiah 53:4

Every heart, saintly or unsaintly, differs from God on the subject of pain. It is an implicit difference, i.e., better felt than expressed. We argue, "Why should there be pain?" "Things have no business to be like this; *this* is what God means. . . ." Whenever pain is mentioned as being God's plan, the innate heart of man rebels—"Surely God does not mean that we are only perfected through suffering?"

1. Vicarious Inspiration

The 53rd chapter of Isaiah stands alone as a great burst of amazing prophecy. The greatest spiritual exposition of the Lord Jesus Christ is not in the New Testament; it is in this chapter, given by a man who lived hundreds of years before Christ was born. If you want to know the characterisation of the Person of Christ you will find it here, sketched by His Father, through the mouth of Isaiah. The prophet Isaiah, more even than the Apostle Paul, interprets the Person of Christ; his is the power of seeing not with the outward eye, but with the inward vision of the spirit. In these latter chapters an alteration comes over Isaiah's picturing of the Servant of Jehovah; it is no longer a personification, but a Person; the great truth dawns on the prophet that it is God Himself in His Servant who is the vicarious Sufferer. It was no mighty monarch who was to come, no great conqueror, but One in the guise of a sufferer. Vicarious suffering is always voluntary.

2. Vicious Indifference
He is despised and rejected of men. (Isaiah 53:3)

When Our Lord came on this earth how many discerned Him? "We needs must love the Highest when we see it"; but the highest is measured by our inner disposition, and when the Son of God, who was The Highest, appeared, men did not love Him; in fact, He was unheeded, despised and rejected. He could easily be unheeded because He did not resent it; He could be treated like the earth under our feet. If we belong to His crowd we shall be despised. Watch how people treat you who don't love Him.

"He was despised, and we esteemed Him not." This is God's picture of how His Servant will appear, not sometimes, but at all times. We will preach what the Apostle Paul never preached; we will preach an exalted Christ: Paul said, "For I determined not to know any thing among you, save Jesus Christ and Him *crucified*." Modern holiness teachers ignore God's method and present what is called the glory side; we have to present the side represented by the Cross. These are all characteristics of this implicit difference; we say, "Surely God does not mean we have to present a despised and neglected and crucified Jesus?" He does. The Spirit of God presents the glorified, exalted Jesus; but the only way that presentation can be made is through the Cross. "I, if I be lifted up from the earth, will draw all men unto Me," said Jesus; He is exalted on the Cross. Where we blunder is in trying to explain the Cross doctrinally while we refuse to do what Jesus told us to do, lift Him up.

We want to present our understanding of how God worked in our own experience, consequently we confuse people. Present Jesus Christ, and the Holy Spirit will do in them what He has done in you. The preaching of the Cross will produce its miraculous result in lives, not what we preach *about* the Cross (see 1 Corinthians 1:21).

When the Bible speaks of the Death of Jesus it is not as the crucifixion of a Nazarene Carpenter, but as the point in history which reveals the nature of God—that He is not sitting on the remote circle of the world in omnipotent indifference, but that He is right at the very heart of things. The symbol for God is not a circle, but a cross, symbolic of supreme suffering and distress.

3. Voluntary Identification

Surely He hath borne our griefs, and carried our sorrows: yet we did esteem Him stricken, smitten of God, and afflicted. (Isaiah 53:4)

The coming of God is always on the line where the devil and sin have ranged themselves—"But where sin abounded, grace did much more abound." The majority of people who have never been touched by affliction see Jesus Christ's death as a thing beside the mark; but when a man is convicted of sin, then for the first time he begins to see something else—"At last I see; I thought He was smitten *of God;* but now I see He was wounded for *my* transgressions. He was bruised for *my* iniquities: the chastisement of *my* peace was upon Him." The hand of God *was* on Him; the reason for His suffering *was* sin; but it was *our* sin, *our* transgression. "Surely He hath borne our griefs": He bore *for* all. We cannot bear *for* anyone, it is impossible. Jesus Christ came weighted with the message of God, but that was not what weighed Him down; the thing that weighed Him down was sin. The only thing that made God's shoulders stoop was sin. He made His own Son *to be sin;* and the Son "put away sin by the sacrifice of *Himself.*"

Jesus Christ's suffering was unique: He knew why He suffered. The sufferings of Jesus are God's inscrutable plan for the carrying out of His Redemptive purpose—"Ought not Christ to have suffered . . . ?" There was nothing of the morbid fanatic about Our Lord: He looked beyond the travail to the joy set before Him, consequently He "endured the cross, despising the shame."

Has the Christian anything like this to go through? Peter talks about suffering when you don't deserve it.

"But if, when ye do well, and suffer for it ye take it patiently, this is acceptable with God." No man can do that unless the Son of God is born in him. Have you ever accepted an undeserved stripe? Suffering unjustly will either produce sympathy with Satan or similarity to Christ. Sympathy with Satan arises from self-pity—"Why should I have to go through this?'

What do we know about filling up "that which is behind of the afflictions of Christ"? Have we ever taken on our shoulders for one second the consequence of the insight the Holy Spirit gives into the corruption of men and women as they are? or is the recoil so desperately offensive that we turn away from it? Insight is an additional burden God places on us. Be careful not to turn your insight into supercilious criticism. Immediately you become spiritual your body becomes the burden-bearer for sins you never committed, so do your nerves. This is the dispensation of the humiliation of the saints; the more you walk in the light with God the more humiliating is your position on earth. It is true God does keep His saints in health, but remember what He does it for, that they may be crushed with burdens. If you take holiness or health as an exhibition of what God has done for you, you will get dry rot in your soul, but pour it out like water on the ground, spend right out to the last drop, and you will find the supply is always there. You can't reserve anything if you are a servant of Jesus Christ. It is the finest saints who are most easily utilised. Every servant of God suffers in his stand for God because of the upheaval that the stand makes in the natural order. The natural has to be sacrificed, that is what it was made for, in order to make it spiritual.

Forgiveness of sin is the great revelation of God, all the rest is slight. We have belittled the meaning of forgiveness of *sin* by making it mean the forgiveness of offences. The only way God can forgive sin is because His Servant "poured out His soul unto death." Have I ever realised that the only way I am forgiven is by the panging depth of suffering God's Servant went through? The consciousness of what sin is comes long after the redemptive processes have been at work. The man who comes to for God for the first time convicted of sins knows nothing about sin; it is the ripest saint who knows what sin is. Our salvation is the outcome of what it cost the Son of God. "He shall see of the travail of His soul, and shall be satisfied."

Notes on Jeremiah

Oswald Chambers

INTRODUCTION

Source

Notes on Jeremiah is from lectures that were part of Oswald Chambers' study of the Four Great Prophets (Isaiah, Jeremiah, Ezekiel, Daniel) in the biblical theology class at the Bible Training College,[1] London, in 1912 and 1913.

Publishing History

- As articles: The lectures were published as articles in the *Bible Training Course (BTC) Journal*,[2] from May 1936 through March 1940.
- As a book: This material has never before been published in book form.

This material covers only the first 29 chapters of Jeremiah. Undoubtedly, Chambers lectured on the entire book, but Mrs. Chambers was unable to take her usual verbatim shorthand notes of the entire series.

In reading these notes, it should be remembered that the lectures were delivered to students with open Bibles in a setting where study of the biblical text was an integral part of the educational process. As always, Chambers' goal in teaching was not imparting knowledge but seeing lives changed by the Holy Spirit of God.

---

1. The Bible Training College (BTC) was a residential school near Clapham Common in southwest London. It was sponsored by the League of Prayer and operated from 1911 until it closed in July 1915 because of World War I. Oswald Chambers was principal and main teacher; Biddy Chambers, his wife, was lady superintendent.

2. The *Bible Training Course Journal* was published from 1932 to 1952 by Mrs. Chambers, with help from David Lambert (1871–1961), a Methodist minister and friend of Oswald Chambers.

CONTENTS

FROM THE BIBLE TRAINING COURSE MONTHLY JOURNAL
VOL. 5 MAY 1936 NO. 2
NOTES ON JEREMIAH

Some valuable comments on the Book of Jeremiah by Oswald Chambers are being prepared for the *Journal* for the coming year. This is instead of the Notes referred to last month. They will appear later. Meanwhile these Notes on Jeremiah will come with inspiration and enlightenment on that great Prophet of God.

JEREMIAH 1

I was not born
Informed and fearless from the first, but shrank
From aught which marked me out apart from men:
I would have lived their life, and died their death
Lost in their ranks, eluding destiny:
I profess no other share
In this selection of my lot, than this
My ready answer to the will of God
Who summons me to be his organ. All
Whose innate strength supports them shall succeed
No better than the sages.

Browning

There is a difference between a personal experience of sanctification and the call of God to be a worker. The latter involves the very mystery that was exhibited in the life of Our Lord, viz. the sanctification of my holy self to God. "For their sakes I sanctify Myself" (John 17:19). Just as Our Lord was made broken bread and poured out wine for us, so the worker is to be made broken bread and poured out wine for others. These great big shadowy prophetic figures are difficult to define, but bring them to the light of Jesus Christ and you will see their meaning. Jesus Christ is the only One Who can throw light on the prophecies of Isaiah, and He is the only One Who throws any kind of light on the acute suffering and amazing misery of this prophet.

We are apt to conceive of a servant of God as being a great strong terrific leader whom nothing ever affects. In Jeremiah the acme of human sensitiveness is sanctified in the service of God. The servant of God is never self-elected, there is always this impelling call of God, and it is always the most unlikely man, the most unlikely woman, God calls.

Jeremiah is not suffering for his own sin, or because he is sensitive; he is suffering because he has seen what Jesus Christ knew better than anyone, that there is a deep moral tragedy at the heart of human beings. Sin is not weakness, it is not disease, it is red-handed rebellion against God, and the magnitude of that rebellion is expressed in the Cross of Christ. If we are going to get near the threshold of what the agony of Our Lord represents, we must get far beyond the individual small mean[3] ideas of our own particular troubles and religious experiences; we must be made to understand what the positive vile evil of the world is in God's sight. We know heart-hunger and soul-despair for ourselves, but have we ever understood what Jesus Christ wanted His disciples to understand when He took them to watch with Him in the Garden?

Very few of us understand why clouds of darkness come. It is God trying to get us into line with the prophets and apostles. It is the Holy Spirit seeking to bring us into the place of vicarious intercession, and we nearly always misunderstand it and say, "I must have sinned," or "I must get out of this, I have got the blues."

"Ah, Lord God! I cannot speak: for I am a child." That is said not in the sense of weakness but—"I don't comprehend, I don't begin to see what the message means; and God said, "Say not, I am a child: for thou shalt go to all that I shall send thee." Jeremiah was not a personality like Elijah or Moses, a great towering leader, he was the exact antipodes. All through his prophecy we shall find that he was a man who would have done anything rather than what God made him do. Every nature brings with it the setting of its own temptation.

In as far as we have ever heard the call of God the recoil of our nature is a staggering from the whole thing. "Who is sufficient for these things?" "But I cannot, I am a child." It is not cowardice or weakness, but the transition moment when the whole life is staggered by the blow of the revelation. Never call it weakness or lack of faith. Jeremiah saw from God's standpoint the positive challenging of God, the Satanic hatred of God, and it meant for him the

---

3. The word mean as used here refers to something or someone ordinary, common, low, or ignoble, rather than cruel or spiteful.

bathing in sorrows the human frame could scarcely stand, but Jeremiah's courage was superb.

It was not the courage of foolhardiness but the courage of a hyper-sensitive man being held by God; he sees the terror of the evil and wrong and knows his own sensitiveness, and yet hears God saying, "Be not afraid." There are people who are fearless and we say they are courageous, but there is no moral virtue in their courage, it is born either of physical or moral obtuseness. Spiritual courage is the high heart that sees the difficulty and faces it. That is the courage that is valuable to God.

FROM THE BIBLE TRAINING COURSE MONTHLY JOURNAL
VOL. 5 JUNE 1936 NO. 3
NOTES ON JEREMIAH

THE DAWNING OF THE ETERNAL WORD

Give me a voice, a cry and a complaining,—
Oh let my sound be stormy in their ears!
Throat that would shout but cannot stay for
  straining.
Eyes that would weep but cannot wait for tears.

Myers[4]

Now the word of the LORD came unto me, saying . . .
Jeremiah 1:4 (RV)

Beware of separating personal spiritual life from historical facts. Spiritual life is not simply the illumination of the Spirit of God in a man, it is much more; spiritual life is based on historical facts, i.e., on the life and statements of Jesus Christ. The great snare is to go off on new things; Jesus said the Holy Spirit will "bring to your remembrance all that I said unto you" (RV). There is always a witness, the word comes, it comes to us from without. How am I to know what God has ordained me for? By His eternal word. We have to stir up our minds and find out what God's purpose is by obeying His word and relying on His Spirit. "My people doth not consider," says God (Isaiah 1:3). Will the word of God come to *me?* Of course it will! Will the Spirit of God see that I fulfil that word? Of course He will! If we will keep in the light with God, our destination is as sure and as established as God, as certain as His throne.

When once you realise the Divine purpose behind your life you will never say again, "I am so weak"; you will know you are, but you will be strong in His strength. The only strength we have is the strength of God, which comes to us from the vision of God and of His power. The time of stress in which there is no vision, no insight, no sensing of the presence of God, is the time to stand firm in faith in God and God will do all the rest. Keep true to God and your development in God's plan is certain.

"I am with thee to deliver thee" (Jeremiah 1:19). This promise to Jeremiah was a marvellous sustaining that never left him (see 15:20). But what would have been the good of that promise if Jeremiah had not come face to face with the Speaker of those words? What good would it have been for Jesus to say, "Lo, I am with you all the days" (RV mg) before His resurrection and appearing to the disciples? The vision of Jesus Himself is granted to a man's spirit; he sees and knows not only what Jesus has done for him but Who his Lord is; then every time His word is recalled there is an incoming of a courage which never can fail. The "Go" of Mark 16:15 was said after the disciples had seen Jesus. We must not only be saved and sanctified, but we must have seen Jesus and heard Him say, "Go ye."

The prophets had to live through this trial of faith in God's word before they uttered it. Jeremiah experienced this personal trial of faith in God. His statements were not the statements of a gramophone—"God will bring everything out all right, I need not care." Jeremiah was in the grip of a dominating purpose that made him care, and with sublime courage he declared God's word all the time. The spirit of God does not put things simply to the intellect; He puts them simply to the heart.

Jeremiah traces his spiritual awakening to God's use of Nature to him (Jeremiah 1:11–12). A prophet sees more than an ordinary man sees. The budding rod of an almond tree would mean to us, Spring is coming; to Jeremiah it meant, Jehovah is awaking. God made the natural thing that Jeremiah saw a symbol to expound His purpose to him; it was a symbolic portrayal of an inner meaning. Nothing can stand a prophet in good stead but what he sees when God opens his eyes.

---

4. F. W. H. Myers (1843–1901): British poet and educator.

The reason men and women are exhausted in life is because they have not realised God's purpose for them; when once they are awakened by the Spirit of God, regenerated by Him, and fitted on to His purpose for them, they will end where God wants them to end.

We are predestined by God to be His sons, but not in spite of ourselves. God has so constituted things that if we refuse to fulfil our predestination everything will tell in contrast to that predestination

(cf. John 8:44). The confusion is to make predestination mean we have no choice at all; we have. Jeremiah had the choice, he nearly made the great refusal and said, No. We have power to disobey; if we had not we should have no power to obey; but we have no power to alter the almighty decrees of God.

Divine sovereignty means that God created man for a Divine purpose. God's destiny for man is by His throne; wrath and confusion is the result for any man who steps aside.

FROM The Bible Training Course Monthly Journal
VOL. 5 JULY 1936 No. 4
NOTES ON JEREMIAH

UNREQUITED LOVE
Jeremiah 2–3

I remember . . . the love of thine espousals. Jeremiah 2:2

God is the "adornment" of His people; but God says, "My people have forgotten Me days without number"; the dead set of their life has been away from God (Jeremiah 2:32). Forgetting as an infirmity of mere consciousness is one thing; but forgetting by steadfastly refusing to recognise is another thing. These people had deliberately turned out of God's way. They were wantoning after some other god than the God Who is holy (2:33).

If we would get used to recognising the anguish and horror in God's heart when His people wanton to worldliness, we should understand better why the prophets of the Old Testament and the apostles of the New Testament use terms of the most disgusting offence known amongst civilised men (see 2:24–25); the words are spoken to those who have forsaken what they know. The thing that shocks us most is not the thing that shocked Jesus most. Social immorality shocks us till we don't know where we are; but what struck the heart of Jesus Christ with horror was immorality against God, pride against Himself (see Luke 16:15).

"They hated Me without a cause." If you are true to God and you come across a man who does not want to be true to God, you will find a growing inveterate hatred and venom that can only end in murder in some way or another. Don't banish the bold, crimson language of the prophets by thinking only of physical murder; anyone who has wronged or tempted or neglected his brother, or has multiplied temptations in the way of God's little ones, is called bloodguilty by the prophets (see 2:34).

"Yet thou saidst, I am innocent." The innocence arising from evil is always like that—"I've done nothing." It is the innocence we are all born with; sooner or later it takes its stand with evil and only knows good by contrast; whereas the innocence arising from the presence of the Spirit of God takes its stand with good and knows evil only by contrast. If we hand our hearts over to God we need never know in experience that what Jesus Christ says of the human heart is true (see Mark 7:20–23). When we have to bolster up our position by reasons and arguments it is a sure sign we are on a rotten foundation, and behind our plausible talk we are at our wits' end working to secure a right position. The instinct that inspires a backslider is on the diplomatic line.

Jeremiah 3:4–5. Jeremiah says these people speak all right but they do evil all the time. The prevailing attitude to-day is the healthy-minded attitude that treats remorse as a disease of the nerves and sin as a mere intellectual nuisance—"Do things; don't give way to absurd self-examination." Jesus Christ stands for the unhindered facing of the world, the flesh and the devil, and an equally unhindered facing of God, and such a facing will always bring a man to the evangelical attitude—"Just as I am." Beware of bracing yourself up to be cheerful when you should be broken up into repentance.

Watch and beware of universal notions that ride rough-shod over intimate things, over suffering, and above all over sin. It is difficult for a spiritually minded person to understand why people are attracted by New Theology, Christian Science, Buddhism. These things attract the semi-cultured people, and it is those people with whom we come in contact; they are removed by position and training from the gross evils of life, and are interested in religious topics and always hunting for some ideal to which they can give their intellectual assent. It is amongst this crowd that most of our work has to be done, and it is where we find the most opposition to God. We do not need a new Gospel; what we need is the old truths re-stated to hit the things that are wrong to-day. If you use the terms of a bygone age and apply them to the sins of bygone days, you don't hit the things that are wrong to-day. Sin was in existence in Jeremiah's day, and in John Wesley's day, and it is in our existence in our day, but in very different guises. To-day we have to fight the Higher Thought teaching, the Mind Cure teaching, Christian Science; the one great objection of all these is to sin. Sin to them is a mere nuisance. It works out along the line that the miraculous is never going to happen—"God cannot make the past as though it had never been"; "God cannot raise the dead"; "God cannot heal the sick; He cannot forgive sin." We have to be amongst them as those who know that God Almighty does the exceptional and the miraculous. It is comparatively easy to do work amongst the submerged tenth, to present Jesus Christ to them, for they flock into the Kingdom of God before the other class. The one safeguard is in a personal attitude to a personal Lord and Saviour.

FROM THE BIBLE TRAINING COURSE MONTHLY JOURNAL
VOL. 5 OCTOBER 1936 NO. 7
NOTES ON JEREMIAH

"LIFE, A FURY SLINGING FLAME"
Jeremiah 4

The great truth underlying calamity is that the truth and the way of God is seen but abandoned because it is too difficult. Unless we understand this we shall misjudge God in His dealings with His people and imagine that He is too stern. In personal life the same truth applies; calamity and disaster always follow when God's way is seen but abandoned because it was difficult. Abandon is not rebellion yet; abandon simply means—"That is a nice vision, but it is not for me." From that moment you begin your chapter of calamities; if you have seen the vision, it *is* for you. Every now and again, not often, but sometimes, God brings us to a point of climax, either as sinners or saints, and it means the Great Divide in our life; we either abandon into worse sordidness spiritually or we become ablaze for the glory of God.

1. Where the Battle's Lost or Won *(Jeremiah 4:1–2)*

"If thou wilt put away thine abominations out of My sight . . ." (Jeremiah 4:1). The battle is lost or won in the secret places of the will with God alone, never first in external circumstances. The battle may take one minute or a year, it depends on you, not on God. The Spirit of God apprehends us till we are obliged to get alone with Him, and until the battle is fought out between ourselves and God we will lose it every time in circumstances. We say, "I will wait until I get into the circumstances and put God to the test," we cannot, we must transact business with God in secret in our own wills. When that is done we can go forth with the smiling certainty that our battle is won, nothing will ever again enthral us on that line. The world, the flesh and the devil have not the slightest power over the man who can rule his own spirit, who has fought the battle out before God and won there. When that is done, the external life is child's play; lose it there, and calamity and disaster and upset are as fatally sure as God's decrees.

2. Where the Bitter Ways Begin *(Jeremiah 4:3–4)*

"Break up your fallow ground, and sow not among thorns" (4:3). Get rid of all your idols, then plough up the ground and sow without the thorns. If God gives you a clear indication in regard to something in your life and what He wants you to do, and you say, "Yes, Lord, I will do it," but you don't proceed to plough up the fallow ground for that purpose and remove the extraneous thing, you will have a cruel conflict. Spiritually every domain of our personal life that comes under apprehension by the Spirit of God is a call to cultivate it for God. We limit God by reminding ourselves of what we have allowed Him to do in the past, and that is why some people are continually going round in a circle spiritually till they get dizzy; they won't break up the new soil of their life for God.

When the secret places of your will before God are revealed you know exactly what you have to do. Let the word of God bore a hole in your self-complacency about the particular thing He has hauled you up about and then put in another word that He brings to you, and you will soon find His dynamite at work. It will come in and blow the bedrock of your obstinacy to splithereens, and never will it occur again in that particular line. In His parable of the sower and the seed our Lord uses the stony ground as indicative of spiritual feignedness, the bedrock of obstinacy has never been blasted to atoms. We are choked by a little thing that has not its root in God, which God condemned and we pathetically wept over but left there. To compromise with anything God has condemned is to be condemned (see John 3:19). To see a thing must be removed and not remove it is to be scorched and withered, by God's decree.

Unless we have taken in secret before God the territory of our own personal life for Him, when the trumpet is sounded and the standard raised in external circumstances (Jeremiah 4:5–6), we shall be swept like chaff before the wind. Never put a thing off and say, "It does not matter, no one sees." No, but they will see you go down like standing corn before the scythe in external circumstances, because you played the traitor to God in secret. If God has revealed anything to you for the tiniest glimmer of a second and you don't obey Him and cultivate that territory for Him, you will go down when the crisis comes. Other people seem to be kept and yet they were not living in the external life quite as well as you; but the point was in secret between you and God, you had only feigned obedience. The explanation of many a calamity is along that line—one fact more in lives which we never guessed at, and when the storm came and the wind blew and the rain beat, the life was not found established on the rock and down it went, the reason being it had not been true in the place of secret testing. The great danger in the time of secret testing is conferring with flesh and blood. Remember, God does not look at people as we look at them; He looks at us where He alone can see, viz. our hearts.

FROM THE BIBLE TRAINING COURSE MONTHLY JOURNAL
VOL. 5 NOVEMBER 1936 NO. 8
NOTES ON JEREMIAH

"WHEN TIME'S A MANIAC SCATTERING DUST"
Jeremiah 4:11–22

The prophecies of Jeremiah are a powerful and timely reminder that human beings are not pathetic babes in the wood, but mutinous people. Ours is not a pathetic separation from God, but a tragic one. It is difficult to get the modern mind to face the dark line that runs all through the Bible; our mood to-day is healthy minded and pathetic and the things in the Bible don't seem to have anything to do with us, but it is good to have the veil lifted and know what we would be like if Jesus Christ had not died. There is a reason in the justice of God for all the dire calamities that happen. If we drink in the atmosphere of religious life round about us, we shall find any amount that is alien to the Bible, such as the aspect of God as a great loving Father, with no power or holiness about Him, and when we come to the stern statements about the Cross of Jesus and the denunciations of sin, we shall have no affinity with them, but we shall preach "smooth things" (Isaiah 30:10).

Although Jeremiah seems to deal in volcanic destructions, a little spring of the clear pure water of life is always revealed that is a great strengthening to God's children. We do live in times of devastation, war and calamities, but those who know God have this consolation, that in and above all these calamities God is working out His purposes absolutely undistressed, and although clouds and darkness are around, they know that the clouds are but the dust of His feet. "The joy of the LORD is your strength," not our joy in God, but the joy *of God;* our strength is in the fact that we know God rules and rejoices.

The Divine sovereignty of God allows Satan liberty and human beings liberty, and the margins of that liberty are known only to God. To remember that the devil is not the power behind God, but a power allowed by God, makes a great difference in our attitude to the happenings of life. Jeremiah points out that all the calamities need never have been participated in by the house of Judah if they had only obeyed God.

It is not a question of Jeremiah saying to Jerusalem, Go and ask God to wash you; he says, "O Jerusalem, wash thine heart from wickedness, that thou mayest be saved" (Jeremiah 4:14). We are always caught up with the trick of asking God to do what we have to do. Never give way to reverie, imaginations, or thinking over which you have no control; to do so is the surest way to slip into a relapse.

God brings us to the point where the fortress of the will is stormed by Him. If we yield, the battle is fought and won; but if we don't keep on the fighting line God has drawn, we shall suffer a relapse and be taken by storm by the very powers we ought to have overcome, e.g., vain imaginings about God, empty moonings, spiritual reveries, spiritual ecstasies, spiritual anythings that we have not gripped up. The call comes strongly, "Wash your heart" and don't allow vain thoughts to lodge in you. Few of us realise the power God has given us to grip on the threshold of the mind as in a vice the things that ought not to be there.

Jeremiah says he can hear voices of calamity—"watchers from a far country," and it will be worse for Judah than for Israel because "She hath been rebellious against Me, saith the LORD" (see 4:15–17).

It is quite easy as a disciple to be in agreement with the Lord over everything but His personal authority. Our Lord bases the final destiny of His disciples on their relationship to His personal authority and to nothing else (cf. Matthew 7:23). Beware of exploiting the Lord to suit your temperament. A true servant of God if he sees we are not submitting to the authority of the Lord Jesus, will produce all kinds of alarms—"I can see "watchers" coming here and there and before you know where you are you will be dragged down." If we say, "You are talking nonsense," we shall go down, caught in the dust and anguish and frantic turmoil of besetting calamity.

Calamities that leave us bitter are deserved somewhere. When disasters choke the heart, and paralyse all goodness, there is one fact more in the past that will explain them. "Thy way and thy doings have procured these things unto thee" (4:18). Infatuation is the affectionate insanity of a wrong relationship allowed.

Paul is strong on this line—he calls it "inordinate affection." God never allows the danger of an infatuation without a tremendous warning, and if we persist we shall go headlong to destruction.

I am pained at my very heart; . . . I cannot hold my peace. (4:19)

Desperate tides of the whole great world's anguish Forced thro' the channels of a single heart.

This is one of the great moments in Jeremiah's life, his identification with God and His point of view is clearly brought out. The same thing is stated in Romans 9:3 and Colossians 1:24. On the human side it seems an utter waste of grief; Jeremiah has agonised over the calamities that are going to overtake God's people because of their rebelliousness, but all his weeping did not alter it; seen from God's standpoint, it is a portrayal of the cost to God in His own heart when His people turn away from Him.

Destruction upon destruction is cried. (4:20)

When calamities are sent for wrong-doing they never stop until they are done. The old superstition that grief never comes single-handed, is based on a great fundamental fact, but the sad thing is that calamities have no business in the life of God's children. If any, knowing better, step aside from God by rebellion, calamities will come exactly like a broken-down mill dam—turmoil after turmoil, destruction after destruction, the only thing to do is to return and get out on to the bank, otherwise destruction is as inevitable as that God is on His throne.

THE BIBLE TRAINING COURSE MONTHLY JOURNAL
VOL. 5 DECEMBER 1936 NO. 9
NOTES ON JEREMIAH

"LO, THERE WAS NO MAN"
Jeremiah 4:23–5:6

Lo, there was no man. . . . Seek . . . , if ye can find a man. Jeremiah 4:25; 5:1

As disciples of Jesus Christ, we must learn to brood on the terrible things revealed in the Bible, and made known to us in Christian service, until the Spirit of God exults in and through us because we have discerned God's meaning. Life is tragic, and we must get out of our glib notions. We drift into the line of good taste and civilised preaching and a winsome personality, and when we come to the truth of the Cross of Christ, we are in a totally other world, and if the

world revealed in the Bible is a true world, most of us live in a fool's paradise. The views expressed in the Bible are always intense, but never exaggerated. They are the statements of what human life is in the sight of God. It is so much easier to do Christian work than to be concentrated on God's point of view. The reason of discouragement is because we do not brood on God's point of view, or take time to understand what the Cross of Christ means. The Cross of Jesus Christ is not a martyrdom, it does not procure salvation; it is the only salvation.

1. The Vision of the Last Man *(Jeremiah 4:23–31)*

I beheld, and, lo, there was no man. (Jeremiah 4:25)

In verses 23–31 Jeremiah tells what he sees in the spirit; he is not piling up metaphors to terrify himself and others. He sees bursting over Judah a visitation of God that convulses the whole earth, and in his brooding and insight before God he sees himself as the "last man." When once you have been scrutinised by the Spirit of God you are the "last man" on earth in your experience—there is no comfort in friendship, no beauty in the earth, no confidence anywhere. It is a terrible stripping to stand face to face with Jesus Christ, everything is consumed. No man can stand before God unless God be in him. The final judgement in individual life is at the Cross of Jesus Christ, and through that Cross can go no benefit, no beauty, no blessing, no health. The Cross is God's last word: at the Cross the prince of this world is judged; at the Cross we are born from above (RV mg), and at the Cross we go through our final judgement. That is why so many workers will end in disaster; we do not want the Cross of Christ, we do not want God's judgement, and when we come face to face with crime we are shocked and slander God because we have never brooded on the facts of life as God reveals them in His Book. The Cross of Christ means that sin must die in us or the life of God must die in us, individually and in the world.

"For thus saith the LORD, The whole land shall be a desolation" (4:27 RV). The basis of life on earth apart from God is chaos. When once we see that all the complacencies of life, of Christian service, are built on chaos that will go into corruption, we shall understand why the Cross of Christ figures what it does. It is not a complete evolution, it is a Cross that knocks everything out saving God's purpose for man. Take it in our own spiritual experience, how much gets through to God? Nothing but our life, no health, no wealth, no possessions, no virtues, only our life, and if we are wedded to the other things we shall end in destruction. No whining and no shirking will ever help us to escape the utter confusion that is at the basis of every bit of human life that has ignored God. There is only one thing that will stand—our soul and God. Beware of being misled by strong individual preachers, strong individual work; if they don't lead to God direct, they may lead to perdition. The moments are rare, but they do come, when God wants us to stand alone with Him, and we get terrified. If once God can get us to stand alone with Him, He can trust us anywhere on earth; but until He gets us there we never can be trusted. We are misled by the idiosyncrasies of great preachers; they put before us fine conceptions, but they do not leave us face to face with God.

2. The Valley of the Lost Man *(Jeremiah 5:1–6)*

Seek . . . , if ye can find a man, if there be any that doeth justly . . . (5:1 RV)

Have you found a man or woman of God on whom you can depend? If you have, you are blind. There is none! Don't glory in man, for the best of men are but the best of men; bank on God alone. We are captivated by strong personalities and if they don't leave us with Jesus Christ they take us to hell. You cannot find a man anywhere on this earth whom you can trust; the only thing you can trust in yourself and in other people is what Jesus Christ has been allowed to do. Many of us win to ourselves, not to Jesus Christ. "The people have no Bible but they have us." It is true, but it is a perilous line. In preaching to the world, Jesus says, "Lift *Me* up." You will never find a man according to God's own heart until you become one yourself, then you can be trusted with the sight, for you won't bank on him.

When you come across these truths you go through the panic of the last Judgement here, but then it won't be in death or the world, the flesh or the devil to turn you. There is nothing to terrify the man who knows Jesus Christ, not only what He can do, but Himself.

From The Bible Training Course Monthly Journal
Vol. 5 January 1937 No. 10
Notes on Jeremiah

MASKED PERILS
Jeremiah 5:7–21

The Bible is not so much a revelation about God as a revelation of God who is adequate to deal with the worst. Holiness is the moral power of God, and the Bible manifests that the moral power of God must act and act until it is everywhere.

1. Debasing Religious Ideals *(Jeremiah 5:7–9)*
These verses are shocking, and are meant to be. This debasing of religious ideals is simply the re-emphasis of the great law of our human nature, viz. that religious emotions die in degradation unless carried out on their own high level. Beware of ever saying to yourself, "God's law is not exactly binding to me, I am under grace." To be under grace should mean that we can fulfil the law of God gracefully.

Loyalty is the outcome of personal devotion to a person, and religious disloyalty grows into us from outside observances that are not the outcome of devotion to God.

2. Disowning Religious Instruction *(Jeremiah 5:11–13)*
The false prophets comforted the people in their vain belief; such prophets become "wind"; they speak from themselves, and the emptiness of their prophecies falls upon their own heads. Jeremiah states that God's omnipotence will not enforce moral truth upon an unwilling mind; there must be an open mind and heart before the truth of God can be received. A scaled mind refuses to be instructed, and a prejudiced mind can only see along the line of its prejudices. Beware of saying, "I will never be in that state of mind." Any state of mind possible to any human being is possible in every human being.

3. The Prophet's Power *(Jeremiah 5:14)*
This great verse reveals God's seal on the prophet who speaks from Him and His judgement of the false prophets who speak from themselves. The voice of God reveals that He is an atmosphere of righteous fire, and as in Isaiah, so in Jeremiah, the tumbling and turmoil in human history is caused everywhere by the consuming fire of God rather than by the futile rage of the devil. In reading history the saint sees that the great presence and power is God, not the devil. That God is a consuming fire means that He burns and burns until there is nothing left to burn.

4. The Providence of Peril *(Jeremiah 5:15–17)*
Hordes of barbarians and powers of worldly dominion are unconscious of God, but God uses them for His own purpose. Nothing happens by chance. When our Lord stood before Pilate He said, "Thou couldest have no power at all against Me, except it were given thee from above" (John 19:11). The tyranny of the Roman Empire over God's people was the providential order of God, and Jesus recognised that this was so, He did not start a revolution, or say, "We must fight against this" (cf. John 18:36). Perils are clear to God's mind alone, but they mean panic to everyone who does not know the mind of God. So here Jeremiah reveals that behind all is God's hand. Never take your participation in the perils of providence unintelligently, but get the mind of God.

5. Purpose in Pain *(Jeremiah 5:18)*
A great snare arises in history and in personal life when we mistake the effects for the cause. In personal life conscience tells us that the cause of calamity lies in a self-indulgent heart. We say, "I don't know why I lost my temper, or why I spoke so hastily." We do know, or we can know. Never mistake the effect of the physical condition for the cause of why we went wrong. We went wrong because the great atmosphere of the fire of God was consuming in us the things that were wrong. They are unrecognised and unrealised, but when the material circumstances come—the world, the flesh and the devil—down we go, and we say, "If only we had been warned we would have stood." But we would not. It is only when conscience has recognised that God is a consuming fire that we stand unperturbed, sure overcomers for God.

In verse 18 Jeremiah reveals that God is a holy God, Who will not allow His people to remain unholy. There is a lesson in every circumstance for the life that is hid with Christ in God which no one else can understand, and which we can only be instructed about from the inside. We learn the marvellous truth that we may become more than conquerors through our right relationship to God over everything that may come against us.

6. The Price of Petulance *(Jeremiah 5:19)*

Serving strange gods in God's house—the inevitable result is that we shall be taken out of God's house and made drudges in the lands of our idols. Self-will in the worship of God will mean a slavery to selfishness that must be destroyed.

7. Persistence in Perversity *(Jeremiah 5:21)*

"Hear now this, O foolish people, and without understanding; which have eyes, and see not; which have ears, and hear not." In the centre of the retina there is one spot where there are no nerves for conveying waves of light. Perversity means a spiritual blind spot. There is one spot at the background of our lives, which, whenever it is faced by God's truths we do not see.

Isaiah and Jeremiah treat spiritual blindness as culpable. The blindness of ignorance and the blindness of perversity are two different things. The blindness of ignorance says, "I do not see that yet." The attitude of the saint is, "I must wait over that before God"—absolutely free from perversity, he has no other end to serve but God's end, which is a coming into more light. Perversity is always back and if it is persisted in it means that God is blotted out of His heaven for us.

FROM THE BIBLE TRAINING COURSE MONTHLY JOURNAL
VOL. 5 FEBRUARY 1937 NO. 11
NOTES ON JEREMIAH

THE CITY OF DREADFUL NIGHT
Jeremiah 5–6

The study of Jeremiah brings us face to face with the great Bible truth that a nation is judged by its ideals rather than by its achievements. This is also true of individual life. "So-and-so is a good man, therefore he is all right"—there are whole areas of pathetic personal sentiment which blot Jesus Christ's standards out of the standards of men.

1. Everybody's Doing It *(Jeremiah 5:25–31)*

The universality of sinning is one of the great facts revealed in God's Book. Unless we see this, we will never understand the need for the Cross of Christ. If it is possible for there to be sin but no sinning, then the Atonement is unnecessary. The terrible truth that the man of sin is born from the bosom of sanctification is one that is always ignored outside God's Book. The sin of a heathen nation never comes anywhere near the sin of what we call a Christian nation.

(a) The Propagation of Super-sinners (5:26–27)

Whenever God talks about sin, He always makes its setting His own people. "For among My people are found wicked men." Jeremiah is talking on the line that they, as the people of God, have fostered super-sinners, the like of which have not been seen on the earth before. To-day there are books known and revered by many which are a cultured snare to get Christians away from the one great standing in Christ Jesus. Sin, blasphemy and perditious acts are only possible in a community God has blessed. I am either producing fruit to the glory of God, or I am turning myself into a son or daughter of perdition. Judas and John are both productions of the Person of the Lord Jesus Christ.

(b) The Prosperity of Sleek Selfishness (5:28–29)

Prosperity that does not spring from a godly motive is the external sign of having forsaken God. That is a charge that touches the very centre of modern philanthropy. We are philanthropic, not because we are godly, but because it is a much more prosperous game; righteousness in God's sight never troubles us. Unless we are rightly related to God, nearly all our works have the sign of the prosperity about them of God having left us alone. God will never allow a child of His to prosper on that line. The one thing that matters is our motive before God.

(c) The Perversity of Successful Sinning (5:30–31)

Perversity is often full of wonder and prosperity before men, but horribly hideous before God. "A wonderful and horrible thing is come to pass in the land; the prophets prophesy falsely, and the priests bear rule by their means" (RV). The prophets prophesy falsely, they prophesy differently from the men of God, and the priests manipulate their work among the people under the direction of the false prophets, "and My people love to have it so," because no holiness is demanded, and Jeremiah asks, "What will ye do in the end thereof?" The most fruitful stock of anti-Christian heresy starts from the worship of healthy-mindedness. This is emphasised again by Paul. Paul will never have the kind of preaching that does not declare the holy demands of a holy God.

That is the thing we detest—that God is holy. Tell us God is loving, but do not tell us He is a holy God; we hate that, and that is the one thing that makes the heart of man rage against Jesus Christ. It is not with the gross, vile sins that you will find the problem, but with the refined, cultured, intellectual living, religious to the last degree. Put the standard of Jesus Christ before that good taste, that good living, good uprightness, and you will begin to see what the profound hatred of man is like against the Lord Jesus Christ. That is the problem we have to face to-day, and we must not live in a fool's paradise.

2. Everybody's Done by It *(Jeremiah 6:1–8)*
Sin swindles, riddles and destroys everything and everybody that touches it.

(a) The Summons to Anyone (6:1)
"If any one of the children of Benjamin hear the summons, let him answer." The summons of God seems to come in the most irresponsible ways and is accompanied by these words, "If any man hear My voice." Whenever God's call enters into your life and mine, it is for us to listen. We have nothing to do as to whether other people have heard it or not. We cannot answer God's call collectively (cf. John 6:68–70). Never get disturbed out of hearing God's voice by saying other people have not heard it.

(b) Surrounding by Antagonism (6:2–6)
When anyone is right with God, there is the fascination of the power and Spirit of God through them that is attractive; it is a beautiful, a fascinating, winsome, wonderful thing, and gets hold of men, good, bad and indifferent, and the devil alike; but if once the individual saint forgets the source from whence it comes, God will curse the beauty. Beware that God's beauty which He puts on you His saint, is not prostituted to a flirtation with God's antagonists.

(c) The Stagnation Anathematized (6:7–8)
Cities are the "cisterns" of the modern world and an illustration of Jeremiah's meaning. It is more difficult and creditable to live a godly life in a village than in a city, because in a village you have everything open and in the city you have everything artificial. A city man is narrow-minded, everything is protected for him. The place where God is most ignored and everything goes on with satisfaction is a city. In the city other things beside spirituality will succeed; in the country the only thing that will prosper is the worship of the God Who loves the earth. The black belief is always produced in the city. In order to make proper changes in a nation's life, you must change the people's wants. Our Lord alters the "want," and consequently the whole life is simplified. We are so given up to material prosperity, the things that are of use, but when the primal sacrifice exhibited in a man like Scott is seen, it has the effect of simplifying the wants of the people for a time.

Verses 8–15. Jeremiah realises that the people cannot hear God's Word, therefore it is vain to speak warning to them, for you can never warn a pleased person. Satisfaction in any shape or form is impregnable to warning; personal uprightness is always alert to the voice of warning.

FROM The Bible Training Course Monthly Journal
Vol. 5 March 1937 No. 12
Notes on Jeremiah

THE CITY OF DREADFUL NIGHT
(Continued)
Jeremiah 6

Therefore I am full of the fury of the LORD. Jeremiah 6:11

Fury means the fundamental wrath of God against sinners, and that wrath is at the basis of everything that is not right, especially in those men and women who have perverted God's way. Jeremiah was a pent-up channel of the fundamental wrath of God, and he says there is no alternative but to pour it out—"I am weary with holding in." There are certain characteristics in people's lives that must mean hell, and about which we must warn them. (cf. Ezekiel 3:17–21). The danger is to mix our personal spite with the fury of the Lord. When his realisation of the fury of the Lord was at its height, Jeremiah let it out; others preferred to preach "peace" symptoms—"saying, Peace, peace; when there is no peace" (Jeremiah 6:14). "They treat the healing of the hurt of My people as a trifling, temperamental matter; there is no such thing as the grace of shame amongst them." The majority of people do not see what is wrong, and the talk of a prophet like Jeremiah is nonsense. We never can face the things that are wrong, apart from God, without getting insane. If sin is a trifling thing and we can preach to the healing of people and bring peace on any other line, then the tragedy of the Cross is a huge blunder. To live a life hid with Christ in God means we see at times what men and women are like without God, from God's standpoint, and it also means vicarious intercession for them, while they look upon us with pity.

1. The Fear of the Past

Thus saith the LORD, Stand ye in the ways and see, and ask for the old paths, where is the good way, and walk therein, and ye shall find rest for your souls. But they said, We will not walk therein. (6:16)

The ideas of men are in connection with what is before us, but the ideas of God are always from the past. The fighting quality of ungodly human nature is the frightened attitude of those who refuse to look back. Have you ever noticed the forced gaiety of a bad person, of someone who has something they want to cover up? The audacity of the whole thing is fundamental fright; it is the fear of the past. "I will do anything you like, but don't let me think about the past." We do not want to be forgiven; we want to forget, because we are cowards.

2. The Fruit of Thoughts

Behold, I will bring evil upon this people, even the fruit of their thoughts. (6:19)

"For as he thinketh in his heart, so is he." "Our thoughts pilot our lives, our actions follow." Our thoughts are like the power of the engines in a steamer; if the pilot on board is in agreement with the engineer, they go steadily in one direction. If my thoughts are right, I am going steadfastly to God's destination for me. We have to guard our fundamental thoughts and be renewed in the spirit of our mind and fitted in to God's purpose.

3. The Fact of the Broken Heart

Your burnt offerings are not acceptable, nor your sacrifices pleasing unto Me. (6:20 RV)

"The sacrifices of God are a broken spirit" (Psalm 51:17)—that of a spirit God has made glad by a great forgiveness. The sign of this kind of broken heart is that the saint is untroubled by storms, and undismayed by bereavement because he is confident in God.

4. The Fundamental Stumblingblock

Therefore thus saith the LORD, Behold, I will lay stumblingblocks before this people. (Jeremiah 6:21)

If there were no holy God, un-holy people would not stumble. What is the line of my thinking—comfort, prosperity, peace? Then God, the holy God, will be a stumbling-block to me. People are departing, not from religious creeds, but from the moral standard of God. That is what the innate rage is against—that God requires us to be holy as He is holy, perfect as He is perfect, pure as He is pure. To-day the tendency has got hold of people, and they do not know where it started from, to discard the standards Jesus Christ erected. The great stumbling-block in modern spiritual life is our Lord Himself in His character, and in the demands the Spirit of God makes. If God would only stop being holy, stop demanding personal holiness, bodily and mental chastity, we would be happy. Yes, but on the way to hell. It is God who puts the stumbling-blocks; they are not there by accident, and the stumbling over them awakens us; if we go on perpetually stumbling, we shall ultimately break our necks. The truth of God always brings us face to face with the standard revealed in our Lord Jesus Christ.

from The Bible Training Course Monthly Journal
VOL. 6 APRIL 1937 NO. 1
Notes on Jeremiah

REPROBATE
Jeremiah 6

They are all grievous revolters. . . . Refuse silver shall men call them, because the LORD hath rejected them. Jeremiah 6:28, 30

1. The Problem of Providence *(Jeremiah 6:22–23)*

Providence is God's oversight and in-ruling of the men on this earth, and men without the Spirit of God alternately disbelieve and hate the providence of God. The natural heart hates God's rule because it is unknown, we do not see what God is driving at, we cannot see why we should be disciplined. When we have the Spirit of God we do not understand what God is doing, but we know God. Faith is the process by which our confidence is built up in a Person Whose character we know, however perplexing the present things may be that He is doing. Fate is super-stitious yielding to a person whose character we do not know and have not the slightest confidence in but have succumbed to. A stoic is a fatalist, he succumbs to an unknown ruling; a saint is one who lives amongst earth's troubles and trials with a passionate joy the stoic knows nothing about. In reading the writings of the stoics we are apt to be misled for a time because they say the same things as Christians, but from a different standpoint.

The truth behind the picture which Jeremiah gives in verse 23 is that the cruelty and mercilessness is not only allowed by God, but is actually being used by Him as a means, and that God is not perplexed as we are by the terror of His providence to those who do not know Him. Providence can never be inter-preted reasonably; it can only be understood super-naturally.

2. The Perils of Panic *(Jeremiah 6:24–26)*

The terror of panic is as certain as God's rule to every man who sides with the corruptible things. God's providential terrors recognise no favourites. If a child of His clings to the edge of a volcano, that child will come to grief as surely as those who do not care for God. The child of God must be *with* the God of ter-ror, then he will be kept till the indignation be over-past, for God can never be shaken (see Hebrews 12:29). If we cling to things that are going to be shaken, then God will not prevent us being shaken

with them, until we learn to let go of everything that He has condemned. We must be burned as fiercely pure as God is pure, and God will not leave us alone until we are. There is a difference between looking at God in the light of "love is God," and seeing Him in the light of "God is love." God is *holy* love, and noth-ing that is corruptible can come anywhere in His presence, it has to be burned and blazed right out of us. Jeremiah's identification with the people is the most wonderful evidence of his vicarious attitude in God's service (see Jeremiah 6:11). The servants of God have to be careful that they do not introduce any personal vindictiveness into the wrath of God, and here though Jeremiah stands with the people who are being swept away by God, he does not slander God by taking the people's point of view. When standing as God's mouthpiece, we must never do what Dante did, put our pet enemies in the hottest places. And when we stand with the people, we must not accept their slander against God. A prophet stands mid-way, not as a mediator, but as a director.

Jeremiah states that there is no refuge anywhere (see 6:25–26)—retreat if you must, but you will retreat into deeper terror. How much of our security and peace is the outcome of the civilised life we live, and how much is built up in faith in God? When a soul stands face to face with God, there is no refuge apart from God, it simply prepares for itself another terrible moment later. Let us take a revision of where our faith is built, is it built on our godly surroundings, on the order of things that has gathered round about us? If it is, when God's providence allows the shattering blow of an enemy to come upon all these things, then we shall be full of fear. When we stand face to face with God, we are at our final judgement—no refuge anywhere, no advice from friends, nothing at all can shelter then, there is nothing but ourselves and God (cf. Romans 8:1). The history of this in a human soul is a wonder-ful way of seeing how God works in the world.

3. The Process of Perfection *(Jeremiah 6:27)*

If God were to manifest Himself suddenly to us we would be His slaves, witless, fascinated off our bal-ance; but He wants us to come to Him with a perfect understanding of Who we are coming to and why. When we trust God we suffer with joy because we know that every bit of God's truth is going to be as gladsome a delight to us as the little bit of truth we already know is. All the terrors of God's processes in history do not alarm us, because the one bit we do know personally about God is so ineffably full of light and joy; therefore we can wait in patience. If a man does not know God suffering makes him a revolter.

4. The Position of the Reprobate *(Jeremiah 6:29–30)*

Every confidence, every love, every devotion that is not based on a personal relationship to God will be reprobate, not only in the experience of the individual, but in the history of the world. God will demonstrate to us in His patient way that if we are building on anything less than Jesus Christ it will prove useless, because we have banked on the wrong thing (see 1 Corinthians 3:10–15; 9:27).

FROM THE BIBLE TRAINING COURSE MONTHLY JOURNAL
VOL. 6 MAY 1937 NO. 2
NOTES ON JEREMIAH

DEGRADED DEVOTION
Jeremiah 7

Therefore will I do unto this house, which is called by My name . . . as I have done to Shiloh. Jeremiah 7:14

To seek a place instead of a Person is the first peril in the spiritual life, and to sentimentalise over places where God has met you is the beginning of spiritual twist. Beware of relying on a principle saving you from moral wrong, for it never can. A personal relationship to a personal Saviour is the only power that can shield the soul from moral peril. The golden rule is, my personal Saviour in every place, not that in certain places I meet my Saviour.

1. A Different Standpoint *(Jeremiah 7:1–2)*
In chapters 4–6 Jeremiah stood in the market-place in Jerusalem and talked moral talk to the people; now he takes his stand at the gates of the temple, and the governing idea of what he says is that reality must be at the back of ritual, or else ritual will land the soul in perdition.

Remember, the temple of God to-day is the human body, and unless its health is based on the worship of God, its very health will prove its perdition. It is not true that bad men get diseased bodies, it is the saints like the Apostle Paul, whose bodies are so frail that they have learned that their physical health is a mere case for God's service through their soul. Consequently when anyone has learned, whether by suffering or by direct intimation from God, that physical health depends on relationship to God, then God can remove them when He likes. A bad man goes on living long after God has departed from him. Self-deception always arises by ignoring the personal relationship to God, a relationship based on the forgiveness of sin and nothing else.

2. A Discriminating Scrutiny *(Jeremiah 7:3)*
Amend your ways and your doings.

Whenever our spiritual insight outstrips our practical doings, we are on dangerous ground, for God never gives genuine illumination apart from practical goodness. The only way to keep right with God is to walk in the light. The pure in heart are the only ones who see God, and no one is pure in heart who has not received absolution from sin through the Atonement. If we are spiritual, God will dry up the fountains of illumination from other sources, and if we seek for illumination elsewhere, as these people did, we shall be led astray. It is quite easy to get insight and illumination and direction elsewhere, there are other forces eager to direct us and to direct us more cheaply, but God's direction can never be bought. When you come up against a spiritual wall, thank God (Isaiah 50:10–11).

3. A Drastic Scathing *(Jeremiah 7:4)*
When there is moral wrong in a man who is susceptibly religious, he will get more and more religious. The more moral rottenness, the more exciting is the appeal. Beware that the excitement of the flesh does not simulate spiritual earnestness, for sensual excess is never so full as when it is devotional. If you are a preacher, beware of being carried away by emotion, by an unbalanced sensibility about something—an appeal to the senses or affections that is not rightly rooted and established in a personal relationship to God; the more rotten that balance gets, the more passionately inspiring is the appeal. Look into your own soul and ask yourself when you prayed most passionately, when you were nearest to God or farthest from

Him? When did your prayers take on the passion that appealed to other people? When you were farthest away, not when you were nearest. When you are nearest to God the flesh has no chance to magnify itself, it is a communion. The stamp of public prayer that Jeremiah condemns and ridicules is the prayer with the impassioned appeal that exactly fits people who want the false prophet. It was because these people had swept away the reality of religion that they had got into this security for sensual sins while they developed ritualistic worship. Our relationship to God is the one thing we have to watch. Beware of fleshly sentiment taking its revenge in making you publicly sincere when you are not profoundly real.

4. A Denouncing Sermon *(Jeremiah 7:7–8)*
To apply Jeremiah's words in our dispensation, read the Sermon on the Mount. Stealing, murder, immorality may never be performed physically, but a vestige of thinking along that line, Jesus says, is as bad in God's sight. Human nature hates God's message that there is a bad tendency inside that has to be plucked out, and

unless it is it will damn us. It is extraordinary that although this truth is insisted on all through the Bible from Genesis to Revelation, it is the one thing we do not believe. It is this underlying thought of God's Redemption that human nature hates.

5. A Degenerate Service *(Jeremiah 7:10–11)*
Will ye . . . come and stand before Me in this house which is called by My name and say, We are delivered, that ye may do all these abominations? (RV)

We never get to a place where we are not liable to do this. We pray to be delivered from a calamity so that we may do what we like. The miracle of forgiveness means the miracle of a holy life. Self-examination is the only exercise for a soul who would remain true to the light of God. It is not the place, and not sanctimonious drivel, or anything less than a personal relationship to Jesus Christ that holds us right. The hardest thing in a saint's life is to maintain a simple belief in Jesus until he realises the one relationship is— my Lord and I; then His joy will be fulfilled in us.

FROM THE BIBLE TRAINING COURSE MONTHLY JOURNAL
VOL. 6 JUNE 1937 NO. 3
NOTES ON JEREMIAH

THE CUP OF THE LORD AND OF DEVILS
Jeremiah 7:16–34

Truth is perished. Jeremiah 7:28

1. Moral Impossibility *(Jeremiah 7:16–20)*
It is a moral impossibility for a godly man to commit a sin, for when a man sins in that degree he is a sinner, not a godly man (1 John 3:9). God's forgiveness is a miracle, and it is the Atonement only that makes it possible.

(a) Prohibited Intercession (7:16)
That there is a sin unto death is a fact revealed in God's Word, and its nature is returning persistence to wrong of which one has been convicted (1 John 5:16). Intercession must never spring from pity, but from the perfect Atonement of our Lord Jesus Christ. To pray for a sinner on the ground of Christ's redemption is not intercession, but a prayer that God will in His mercy bring that man to salvation. Intercession is only possible in the Holy Ghost, and God can never forgive a sinner unless he repents the repentance wrought by the Atonement. Intercession can only be

in the Holy Ghost, i.e. in accordance with the mind of God. The liberty and the hindrance is only known to the child of God.

(b) Provoking Indecencies (7:17–19)
How can God forgive us if we persist in our sins? If God can save us while we persist in doing those things, He ceases to be a God worth worshipping. Sin must be damned, and if we stand with sin we shall be damned too. Jesus Christ's salvation is the destruction of the sinner in the man, not of the man. A spiritual indecency is a compromise with a being less than God that we may prosper. If God calls us to recklessly trust Him, do we still lay hold of something that keeps us in with another power as well in case God fails? If we are going on with God we must stand alone. A man who does the thing that is lawful as a natural man prospers, but if he becomes spiritual and does it, God will curse everything he possesses. Apply this individually and collectively. God will make known to us clearly the impossible tracks of conduct, that we may avoid them.

2. Mental Iniquities *(Jeremiah 7:21–28)*

Mental iniquities on the part of God's children arise when a symbol is separated from the reality it is meant to bring near.

(a) God Careless of Sacrifices (7:21)

In Israel sacrifices were of two kinds—first, the burnt offering wholly consumed on the altar, and second, the peace offering of which only a part was burned, while the rest was eaten at a sacrificial meal by the offerer and his friends. Jeremiah says with scorn, "God says you are welcome to them both." When once religious rites cease to be the expression of spiritual realities, they become a curse.

(b) God Calling for Sanctification (7:22–23)

Commentators have said that sacrifices were not ordained by God—God gave the law and the people introduced the sacrifices. God ordained the sacrifices to be the symbolic expression of spiritual reality, and when the people took away the symbol from the reality God cursed it. "Whosoever shall eat the bread or drink the cup of the Lord unworthily, shall be guilty of the body and the blood of the Lord" (1 Corinthians 11:27 RV)—"unworthily," i.e., separating the symbol from the reality. The more inner corruption, the more strict the adherence to sacrificial systems.

(c) God Concerning Stubbornness (7:24–28)

Jeremiah says that God has been sending prophets to exhort and warn them, but they "will not" to hearken; they listen respectfully enough, but have no intention of obeying; it is a farce. All the counsels of their minds are according to the stubbornness of their own outlook (cf. Ezekiel 33:31–32). God is bent on our obedience; we are bent on earnest pretence. The only way to listen to the voice of God is to obey Him. God will never leave us long without the goad. The goads of God are the words of God, probing us into right roads.

3. Mystic Infidelities *(Jeremiah 7:29–34)*

By mystic infidelities is meant the spiritual sentiments that refuse to wed themselves with God's revealed will. It is the counterpart to spiritualism in spiritual life—communicating with generated sentiments of our own souls instead of bringing every sentiment we have to the bar of the will of God.

(a) Sign of Death (7:29)

The only way to spiritual obedience and reality is the way across the life of nature.

(b) The Sorrows of Degradation (7:30–31)

Every conscious physical possession, mental, moral and spiritual, that has not been disciplined by obedience to God, will drag down the personal life to unfathomable degradations.

(c) Shock of Doom (7:32–34)

Jeremiah says all joy shall be dumb "for the land shall become a waste" (RV). All religion must be spiritual in its essence; bodily beauty, mental beauty, moral or spiritual beauty that has never been brought into subjection to God's law and made spiritual, these very charms will end in a desolation of hell. Immediately we begin to substitute religious ritual for spiritual reality, we will incur in our manner and measure exactly what Jeremiah states here the people of Judah will inherit. Everything has to be turned into spiritual life by a process of obedience. The natural life in a child of God is a lamb for sacrifice, and we have to sacrifice it to the will of God until we turn it into a spiritual thing as Jesus sacrificed His will to the will of His Father.

FROM THE BIBLE TRAINING COURSE MONTHLY JOURNAL
VOL. 6 JULY 1937 NO. 4
NOTES ON JEREMIAH

ETERNAL INSOMNIA
Jeremiah 8

And death shall be chosen. Jeremiah 8:3

Our Lord Jesus used these burning words, "Where their worm dieth not, and the fire is not quenched," in referring to the condition of people who deprive themselves of right judgement by persistently going wrong. (See 2 Thessalonians 2:11). In the prophecies of Jeremiah we have the same great revelation, that eternal issues are involved in temporal living, put in a different connection. If we are going to remain true disciples of Jesus Christ, we will have to remain alien to the day we live in.

1. "The Mills of God Grind Slowly" *(Jeremiah 8:1–3)*

Such terrible suggestions as these verses contain serve as a very wholesome awakening, and bring men to the understanding of the need of Redemption. In God's Book there is sufficient to indicate that there is not only a great deal more than we know, but that the only One Who knows about it is God Himself; and our Lord and the prophets occasionally draw the veil from what is behind the scenes of terror and anguish for lives that deliberately and emphatically reject the messages of God's redemption in this life. Along these lines come God's revelation facts about spiritualism. The Bible calls spiritualism devilish reality. As a Christian, beware of putting any human experience down to superstition until you have been careful to find out what God's Book has to say about it. These soul perils begin in our lives in palmistry, telling fortunes in teacups, or by cards. Curiosity is awakened and increased, and people degenerate their relationship to God into a spiritual séance. Once begin to tread that path, and nothing but God Almighty's grace can save you from the unutterable curse of the crime of spiritualism. That is one thing as Christian workers we have to face in these days. Some men can do a thing with impunity, others are blighted for doing it; the reason being that there is a relationship from which the one has turned back and the other has never known. If a man or woman has known God and turned back, then the corresponding riot of calamity is in proportion; that is why comparing ourselves with ourselves, we do always err from the truth. The one relationship to maintain is the simple one towards God. Keeping that, it is life and peace and joy; outside that, it is terror and anguish wherever you may be found. The measure of my misery when I turn from God is proportioned to my knowledge of Him when I walked with Him.

2. "Yet They Grind Exceeding Small"
(Jeremiah 8:4–7)

The way of the transgressor is hard—until he persists in turning his will to the transgression, then he revels in it—"Why then is this people of Jerusalem slidden back by a perpetual backsliding?"—and now it is not difficult for them to go dead against everything God has said. As in the days of Noah, so all through the Bible, when the signs of the times point to the coming of a great calamity, the majority are merely amused at the fools who believe it. The subject of the Second Coming is the one the average unholy Christian cannot stand, and the tendency is to listen, as the people did in Jeremiah's day, to the false prophets (2 Peter 3:3–6).

3. ". . . With Exactness Grinds He All"
(Jeremiah 8:8–13)

Jeremiah says the pen of the scribes is false; he accuses them of expounding the Word of God in a lying manner, prophesying falsely. We have an exact counterpart to-day. The modern scholar pretends to be expounding the Word of God, but in reality he is writing with a lying pen, he builds his wisdom out of his own rationalism, and takes out of the law of God only what agrees with it.

"The wise men are ashamed, they are dismayed and taken"—those who hold themselves wise shall be dismally deceived in their hopes when the great calamity comes upon the sin-hardened people. The way we get mystically infidel is when we allow sentiments in our spiritual life to be insubordinate to God's written Word, vague speculations which we refuse to pin down to God's law. These develop a sentimental view of God—"God knows how simple our hearts are, and these calamities will never come to us." But God's Word goes through all those sentiments and points out directly where we went astray—there was one point where we would not obey the truth. Isaiah, Jeremiah and Ezekiel all say the same, that it is the prophet and the people together who corrupt one another. Paul says the same to Timothy—"For the time will come when they will not endure the sound doctrine; but, having itching ears, will heap to themselves teachers after their own lusts" (2 Timothy 4:3). It is true to our very doors to-day.

"And they have healed the hurt of the daughter of My people lightly, saying, Peace, peace; when there is no peace" (Jeremiah 8:11). That is the perpetual peril at all times, relieving present pain by a temporal fictitious cure, when what is needed for an effectual cure is a surgical operation.

FROM THE BIBLE TRAINING COURSE MONTHLY JOURNAL
VOL. 6 SEPTEMBER 1937 NO. 6
NOTES ON JEREMIAH

INFATUATION
Jeremiah 8:14–9:8

Infatuation is something that deprives us of right judgement and swings us right off our balance. Look back on your past history with God and you will see where you have been infatuated. The voice that speaks from God's side is balanced by a thousand that speak on the other side. "And for this cause God sendeth them a working of error, that they should believe a lie" (2 Thessalonians 2:11 RV). That is the result of infatuation. Christians individually and collectively become infatuated when they think not of the Lord Jesus Christ as strange to this order in which we live—either He must be crucified or we must take up the cross. We have to face the world and life from God's standpoint, to look at subjects that strike terror to our inmost souls. All Christians are not Christian workers, but those who are called to be workers need the courage of the Holy Ghost to face life from God's standpoint. We have to keep our hearts and minds faced with the awful condition of human life apart from the Cross of Christ. We must get into our souls the iron of God which makes us strong enough to present Jesus Christ to men. A Christian worker does well to hold judgement in abeyance about themselves and about others when there is no genuine shame and repentance. God cannot forgive sin and remain God on any other footing than the atoning death of Jesus Christ.

1. Unreturning Grace *(Jeremiah 8:14–17)*
We looked for peace, but no good came; and for a time of healing, and behold dismay! (8:15 RV)

A surrender to the inevitable disaster of sin without any shame or self-blame is the first seal of doom. The infatuated mood, in which we think we are not to blame for the calamities that come upon us, is very common. Job was in no wise responsible for the calamities that came upon him; but here Jeremiah is stating that the calamities are because of the people's sins. People bow inevitably to their sorrows, but never find out whether they are to blame. It is easy to drift right away from the Bible standpoint and from the cross of Christ by re-accommodating our faith to a spirit that hates Jesus Christ. The majority of us know nothing about shame and repentance, consequently we drift from the central point because we more easily get into sympathy with men than with God, and

this is slander against God. To save the world cost Jesus Christ His life, and if we teach that the world can be saved in any other way we slander God.

These people had generated their infatuated hopes on the preaching of the false prophets. Jesus Christ not only gives us ideals, but He shows us that men are incapable of attaining them, and He came that they might get there by the miracle of His grace. Other teachers never refer to the possibility of our getting there, and it is that kind of teacher we like. Men can never attain the ideal that God demands they shall attain, unless they attain it by regeneration through the cross of Christ; and that never comes in experience but by shame and repentance. Some people seem to be easily morally good, and we say, "Oh, they are all right." If they are all right, the cross of Christ is a farce. If natural virtue and natural goodness are really all right, then the cross is a sham, but immediately we come to see that the characteristics of the new life are based in our experience of shame and repentance we can always recognise these experiences. When we go down amongst men and women, let them be never so bad and degraded, we never can despair because, no matter how bad they may be, we know of a Saviour Who can save them.

2. Unrelieved Grief *(Jeremiah 8:18–22)*
For the hurt of the daughter of My people am I hurt. (8:21)

The people are not sad, they think the prophet has a dose of dyspepsia. Just before the judgement of God the majority of people are happy; they are infatuated. Standing in the courts of the temple Jeremiah is talking to a people battened in prosperity, but the prophet hears what is coming. Have we ever been through anything of that description? Have we ever been touched once with filling up that which is behind of the afflictions of Christ? or are we caught up by the jargon of the modern spirit which is full of adversity to the cross of Jesus Christ? The idea is that if we are in joy and peace we are all right. "Think not that I came to send peace on the earth: I came not to send peace, but a sword" said Jesus (RV).

Verses 21–22 picture the prophet's distress. He can find no comfort for his heart. The reason we do not suffer over other people is that we do not stand where Jeremiah stood. Some of us have a secret delight when people go down, though we do not say so. It crushed the heart out of Jeremiah because he saw them as the people of God.

Jeremiah in the abandon of his grief wishes that he were nothing but a "fountain of tears" day and night because of the infatuated people (9:1). He had to minister to a people who became worse and worse because he ministered to them. It is incorporated into us, unless we are saturated with the Bible idea, that we succeed for God. In the New Testament there is no such notion, only faithfulness to Jesus Christ; success does not lie along His line. God has His own

purposes which we do not know and have not to look for. We have to see that we keep steadfastly faithful to Him. "Their tongue is a deadly arrow; it speaketh deceit" (9:8 RV).

The characteristic of a child of God is that there is no deceit, nothing to hide from God (1 John 1:7). Never trust any man or woman, and never trust yourself, trust only the grace of God. As sure as we put our trust in man, no matter how good, we learn that the human heart is a cunning house of deceit. We all work for our own ends till we get into the light with God; then we have no end to serve, we are without guile. The only way to keep in the light is to remain true to Jesus Christ and not guard ourselves; let Him guard and let Him watch.

FROM THE BIBLE TRAINING COURSE MONTHLY JOURNAL
VOL. 6 NOVEMBER 1937 NO. 8
NOTES ON JEREMIAH

LACHRYMA CHRISTI
Jeremiah 9:9–26

Lachryma Christi is a wine of a sweet taste produced from grapes grown on Mount Vesuvius. The words literally mean "the tears of Christ." The symbolism is perfect to those who understand that the value of human life to God is that it produces the wine that He delights in.

In these studies we are crushing through at all costs the views that have no home whatever in the Bible, and few, as workers, can stand the crushing until they get down to the Bible standpoint, from where they will never be budged again.

1. Desolation *(Jeremiah 9:9–11; Matthew 23:38)*
Our Lord Jesus Christ and the Old Testament prophets are inseparable from one another, for in the Person and the teaching of our Lord all that the prophets taught is in part fulfilled, and will be completely fulfilled.

Desolation wrought by God is the indelible proof that God is God, and a holy God. If we make our abode on the sides of a volcano, desolation may come at any minute. Keep in mind the continual interference of God in human life; that is the mental atmosphere of the Bible. Outside the Bible, people talk about the immanence of God—everything going on quietly and calmly and in order. It goes on tempestuously and crushingly. That is God's order—revolution, around Himself as the central Being.

2. Discernment *(Jeremiah 9:12–16; 1 Corinthians 3:12–15)*
Jeremiah states that wisdom and enlightenment are not to be found among the infatuated people, they have been swept away from right judgement by false prophets who taught that everything develops along a natural rational line. That was the infatuation in Jeremiah's day, and in our own day the proclaimers of the truth of God are in the minority; men won't listen to them.

There are those who say there is no such thing as the supernatural incoming of Jesus Christ, either in history or in the human heart. Our Lord Jesus Christ is not Someone Who has sprung from human nature by evolution: He is Someone Who has come crushing into the human nature by the superb miracle of the Incarnation. The supernatural is the only explanation of our lives if we are right with God, and at any moment God may tumble our lives up as He likes. The question is, Are we willing to let Him? We have to maintain our personal relationship to God in Christ Jesus, no matter what happens. The one thing that is of value to God in a human life is a personal relationship of holiness to God, and every part of physical, mental, moral life and of Christian work that is not so related will be desolated and burnt as rubbish.

3. Dirge *(Jeremiah 9:17–22; Luke 6:24–26)*
The characteristic of life to-day is that the gospel of "Cheer up, look on the bright side," is being preached on all sides. Our Lord says, in effect, that every hap-

piness and peace and well-being that is based on the ignoring of a relationship to God will end in dirges and woes, disasters and terrors. Every now and again God lifts the veil from the eyes of His children and shows us the numbers in our own circle who are absolutely dead to God's standpoint. It is these revelations that bring distress to the soul before God in intercession, and enable us to understand what Paul means when he says, "I . . . fill up on my part that which is lacking of the afflictions of Christ" (Colossians 1:24 RV). We must stand with one camp or the other, we are either with God and the forlorn hope, or with the crowd who are going on without God, whose happiness and joy and prosperity is all fictitious.

4. Disquisition *(Jeremiah 9:23–24; 1 Corinthians 1:20–21)*

The righteousness of God embraces the wise man, the mighty man, the rich man, and brings them into a new standpoint. Apart from God, it is man's wisdom and man's power, and man's cunning commer-

cialism that are gloried in. Think of the wise outlook on life that ignores the supernatural incoming of God in Christ, the supernatural Atonement, and the supernatural works of grace in experimental salvation and sanctification; compared with the shrewd wisdom of the world, these are nought. The wisdom of the wise is based on a rational explanation of everything, but "the foolishness of God is wiser than men." "Hath not God made foolish the wisdom of the world?"

5. Discrimination *(Jeremiah 9:25–26)*

"All the house of Israel are uncircumcised in heart" (RV). They were circumcised by rite, but not in reality, therefore they are classed by Jeremiah with the heathen in this respect that they were devoid of all room for glorying in the sight of God. External religious rites divorced from spiritual reality, all through God's Book, are revealed as the abiding stumbling-block to the real worship of God, whereas they should be a means of grace.

THE BIBLE TRAINING COURSE MONTHLY JOURNAL
VOL. 6 DECEMBER 1937 NO . 9
NOTES ON JEREMIAH

IRRECONCILABLE
Jeremiah 10:1–16

Every man is brutish in his knowledge. Jeremiah 10:14

1. The Paralysis of Aspiring to Nirvana *(Jeremiah 10:1–5)*

Nirvana is a Sanscrit word which means "a blowing out," like a candle. The abiding tendency of the experience in life without a personal knowledge of God is to become more and more convinced that individual life is a delusion. Spiritually it is made to mean that we have to lose ourselves in God. That is never taught in the Bible. Our type of life is the Lord Jesus Christ—a strong, vigorous, intense, separate Personality; He never lost Himself in God; and the one thing that the Holy Spirit does is to develop and increase the value of our personality to God. Verses 1–5 are a warning against idolatry because it leads to nothingness. If once we forget that God is holy, we will be inclined to pay attention to premonitions, to fatalistic notions. Jeremiah says, Have nothing to do with such things (10:2). Beware of every profession of wisdom that takes a line that leads away from the God whom Jesus Christ revealed.

"Be not afraid of them" (10:5). We have to be shaken out of everything that awakens fear till we do

not fear anything. "Therefore will we not fear, though . . ." (RV). A great part of our life is given over to fetishness, to our own ideas and conceptions, and we are terrified out of our wits by things we could name. God's purpose is to get us to the place where Jesus was—unafraid, unafraid of death or of anything that is less than God. "For where your treasure is, there will your heart be also." Unless our hearts are rooted and grounded in God, there are a thousand and one things that will awaken terror. Beware of everything that defaces your faith in God, and learn to welcome the manifestation of God that enables you to efface yourself in devotion to Him.

2. The Progress of Alone to the Alone *(Jeremiah 10:6–11)*

The "aloneness" of God is a doctrine continually stated in the Bible. The Bible does not say that Nature is God, nor does it state anywhere that all will be absorbed into God. The Bible view of God is not being accepted to-day; we do not think of God as the Being presented in the Bible, our actions prove we do not; the things we are haunted by prove we do not; the way we don't trust Him proves we do not. To have the conception clearly in our souls that God is a transcendent God must be wrought in us by the Holy Ghost. God created everything and upholds all things by the word of His power, and His nature is discerned by His handiwork, but that is a different thing from saying God is all. God breathes into us the Holy Spirit Who energises our spirit, and we become eternally never God, but God's lovers (see Romans 5:5). The Apostle Paul states that men are without excuse when they worship God's work as God (Romans 1:25).

Jeremiah 10:7–9. An idol, says Jeremiah, is itself "a doctrine of vanities." Paul states exactly the same truth for his dispensation, and it is the same to-day. To worship a work of God is blasphemy. "For that they exchanged the truth of God for a lie" (Romans 1:25 RV). The ungodly disposition in a man makes him worship beings or things or ideas in order to render them powerless, and the same idea is apt to creep into the worship of God amongst Christians if not watched—"God will never let this or that come to me; I am a favourite of His." Jesus Christ's life is an illustration as to how God will deal with us, He will not shield us from the world, the flesh or the devil, they are allowed to do their worst because God has staked His all on what He has done in us (see John 16:33; 1 John 4:4). Trials and tribulations are trumpet calls to the witnesses to God. Beware lest Satan steals a march[5] when the tribulations begin.

Paul emphasises the fact that God is a sovereign Being, not a sentimental blessing. The Bible instils iron into our nature, it leaves none of the weak, sentimental things we hold in such esteem. The Bible is packed full of the most stern truths, yet it is anything but pessimistic. The Hebrew Scriptures know nothing about overwhelming sadness, they are optimistic. The modern Christian mind is not nourished with the Bible, it is nourished with conceptions that ignore Jesus Christ.

3. The Providence of Almighty God
(Jeremiah 10:12–16)

"Almighty God" means that there is no one or thing or force mightier. If you have ever been given the tiniest inkling of the meaning of what God said to Abraham, "I am God Almighty" (RV)—"El Shaddai," that moment will stand out in your experience infinitely more than your experience of sanctification or any other experience. One moment's realisation that Almighty God is your Father through Jesus Christ, and I defy anything to terrify you again for long. If we realise, what these prophets realised, that nothing can happen without God's permission, we are kept in peace. Worrying is wicked in a Christian. "Let not your heart be troubled." How dare we be troubled if Almighty God Who made the world and everything in it, is our Father? Why should we ignore God by worshipping what He has made, and then giving way to intellectual infidelity and sceptically doubting if He is wise and good at all? "Though He slay me, yet will I trust in Him"—God can do what He likes, I know it is all right, let happen what will.

FROM The Bible Training Course Monthly Journal
Vol. 6 January 1938 No. 10
Notes on Jeremiah

CORRECTION
Jeremiah 10:17–11:8

O Lord, correct me, but with judgement. Jeremiah 10:24

The prayer is for chastening. When God seems to let the calamity fall on a good person, it leads to the salvation of a bad person. This is difficult to put in words. Correction is not for the detection of faults, but in order to make perfect. We cannot be made good as dogs are, our wills must share in the making. God does not make us good in spite of ourselves. The terrors of God arise when God puts His finger on a man or a nation to draw them out of darkness into the light. Those who take God's way of coming into the light will find ultimately nothing but unspeakable joy and peace, life and love.

1. Weeping in Woe but Willing *(Jeremiah 10:17–25)*

The prophecies of Jeremiah, like other truths of God, are addressed to the conscience and the will, not to the intellect or imagination. These verses are Jeremiah's statement about the people coming slowly to understand God's judgements.

---

5. steal a march: to secretly obtain an advantage over an opponent; military: to move troops without the enemy's knowledge.

(a) Violent Exile (10:17–18)

"Gather up thy bundle from the ground" (RV mg). Whatever in us can be or can make an adversary of God, whatever prevents us doing the will of God, must be got rid of. In Jeremiah's day the people continually reverted to idolatry; after the captivity idolatry never appears again; when our Lord came it was the spirit of Pharisaism that He condemned. If we could get into God's presence with any sin remaining, God would not be holy. There must be nothing to hide. Our difficulties arise because we do not realise this. We receive the light, but we won't do what we ought, and God has to come with His inevitable compulsion—"Behold, I will sling out the inhabitants of the land at this time" (RV). We have got to be holy some day, why not be holy now? God will not leave us until He has burnt everything that can be burnt out of us. We hinder Him, that is why He is so long.

(b) Vicarious Experience (10:19–20)

"Truly this is my grief, and I must bear it" (RV). Jeremiah did not stand aloof, he took on him the position of the people before God. The cause of the calamity was that "the shepherds are become brutish" (10:21 RV), i.e., they did not seek wisdom and guidance from God, so they could not deal wisely. No matter how moral we may be, every domain of our life that is not regulated by the direct application of the wisdom of God is brutish in God's sight. What do we teach in our Sunday School classes, our Bible classes? what do we preach to our congregations? Do we teach and preach "brute" wisdom, or the wisdom of God through Jesus Christ? (cf. 1 Corinthians 1:30).

(c) The Voice of Earnestness (10:23–25)

Verse 23—"O Lord, I know that the way of man is not in himself: it is not in man that walketh to direct his steps"—is a confession, not of sin, but of realised condition. Have we ever made that confession in our own souls before God? If we have, we know, and delight to know, that it is not within man's power to arrange the course of his life. The test is, have we the childlike attitude towards God, are we always on the look-out for His supernatural working? Most of us are rationalistic infidels, we never think that God is supernatural at all. We rule out the miraculous and the supernatural because it is not according to the outlook of to-day.

2. Warning in Word, but Wilful (Jeremiah 11:1–8)

The greatest obstruction to the working of God comes from those who give themselves to interpreting the words of God rather than doing them. "The word that came to Jeremiah from the Lord . . ."—to proclaim we must have heard the word first. "and say thou unto them, Thus saith the Lord. . . ." The tendency is strong to let down and say, "God won't be stern, He won't expect you to give up all that." He will. "God does not expect you to walk in the light so that you have nothing to hide," but He does. We must see that we remain true to the revelation we have had, otherwise the condemnation will come on us that came on the false prophets of old. We are here for one purpose—to stand for the revelation of God's truth to the people of God and to sinners. The tendency is to water down God's truth in the case of some darling relationship and say God did not mean what we know He did. We must never shield a person from God's truth; if we do, we put them into the dark and deepen their torture instead of their peace. ". . . which I commanded your fathers in the day that I brought them forth out of the land of Egypt." The first view of God after experiencing His deliverance is the true one, don't modify it. The modification comes in when the testimony partakes of the nature of—"Once I was delivered. . . ." The New Testament bids us walk in the light, not remain in the house of memory and recall. When we were first delivered by God there was no one in the world for us then but Him, is there anybody now? The one great passion of heart and soul and body was for Jesus Christ, is it now? or are we beginning to modify things and make them more plausible and fitting to worldly customs and ideas?

It is one thing to claim a thing, but another thing to enter in on that claim. God wants us to possess. If a man acknowledges God's voice, God will tax the very universe to enable him to obey. To get a glimpse only of what obedience means makes us say it is difficult: obedience is superbly easy because we have Almightiness on our side. Acknowledge God's voice, take the step in the right direction and obey, and you will be backed by omnipotence in every detail.

FROM THE BIBLE TRAINING COURSE MONTHLY JOURNAL
VOL. 6 FEBRUARY 1938 NO. 11
NOTES ON JEREMIAH

MISAPPREHENSION
Jeremiah 11:9–12:6

Let me reason the case with Thee. Jeremiah 12:1 (KJV mg)

Misapprehensions of God arise from not understanding that His way for us is obedience until we discern, not waiting to obey until we know. The only way to know God more fully is to obey what we have discerned, then we shall know something more.

1. Conspiracy against God *(Jeremiah 11:9–13)*

The breach of faith towards the covenant of God is called by God a conspiracy—"the house of Israel and the house of Judah have broken My covenant which I made with their fathers" (11:10). The Bible is the only Book that reveals a solidarity of evil, and this historical record is part of that revelation. In Ephesians 6:11–12 the Apostle Paul refers to the same underlying truth, that evil has not its birth in one man's doing, but that it is diabolically easy for all men to do the wrong thing. If we will obey, we are backed by Omnipotence; but if once we begin to be cunning and suspicious and to doubt, we are backed by a diabolical inspiration as compelling on the wrong side as obedience is on the right. At the back of all are those two powers—God and the devil. When men state they cannot help doing wrong, they speak truly. It is as if all men and devils had met together and conspired against the Lord.

Some such revelation is necessary before we discern what it was made the Cross of Jesus Christ necessary, viz. a solidarity of evil which we know nothing about until we are born again of the Spirit of God. Freedom from guile, from reviling, from threatening (see 1 Peter 2:22–23)—never having any connection with the little steps in evil which connect us with the tremendous solidarity of evil which is a conspiracy against God and all God stands for. Watch every encroaching of suspicion, "Never believe the thing that ought not to be true," because if you do, you find you have a diabolical genius for doing it. Once begin to suspect, and you can suspect like the devil himself. Once imagine that people are beginning to overreach you and you will have a diabolical genius for seeing where they overreach you, and then you will begin to have the same view of God.

2. Condensed against Prayer *(Jeremiah 11:14)*

The Lord will not only not receive any intercession for the covenant-breaking people, but He will not answer their own prayer for deliverance. "For I will not hear them in the time that they cry unto Me for their evil" (RV mg). It is as if God had condensed Himself into adamant. Unless we keep in touch with God by obedience it is possible to pray for a wrong thing. In this case the people have rebelled and do not intend to obey, they only pray because they are suffering, not because they want God's will to be done in them.

3. Contempt for Holiness *(Jeremiah 11:15–17)*

"What hath My beloved to do in Mine house, seeing she hath wrought lewdness with many?" (11:15). A contempt for holiness is the outcome of preferring to listen in order to intellectually comprehend, combined with a stubborn refusal to obey (see Acts 7:51).

4. Conspiracy against Jeremiah *(Jeremiah 11:18–23)*

The prophet had not known they had devised devices against him, but he says "the LORD gave me knowledge of it" (RV). Our Lord told His disciples that their oneness with Him would be recognised in the fact that they would be persecuted and hated as He was (John 15:18–20). Fellowship with Jesus Christ means disaster in the eyes of the wisdom of the world.

5. Controversy with God *(Jeremiah 12:1–4)*

The enmity which Jeremiah experienced from the people of Anathoth, his native place, causes him to expostulate with God and to demand that they be cut off out of the land—"pull them out like sheep for the slaughter." Think how easy it is to get into that mood!

6. Cumulative Adversity *(Jeremiah 12:5–6)*

The Lord reproves Jeremiah for his outburst of impatience by telling him he must patiently endure worse. The bittersweet drop in the prophet's cup had not yet been tasted, for he was to find that not only his own townsmen, but his own brethren and the house of his father, had dealt treacherously with him. A simple thing to have faith in God, isn't it! It means steadfastly enduring, as seeing Him Who is invisible, and letting God work out His ways through you.

"My Lord and I" is a very beautiful sentiment, but before we know it as a living experience we have to fight our way through all the contradicting things to the un-afraid, simple life that trusts in God.

FROM THE BIBLE TRAINING COURSE MONTHLY JOURNAL
VOL. 6 MARCH 1938 NO. 12
NOTES ON JEREMIAH

PROGRESSIVE REALISATION
Jeremiah 12:7–17

I will return, and have compassion on them. Jeremiah 12:15

Jeremiah begins to realise his own messages; he has experienced the correcting wounds of God, and it has had a very illuminating effect upon him. Few suffer more seriously in character than the men and women who for one reason or another are exempt from frank, honest criticism. That privileged lot is cruel in the extreme.

Progressive realisation does not mean that God reveals Himself by inches, but that we realise His revelation of Himself by inches as we obey.

1. Not a Divine Rescript but a Human Revolt *(Jeremiah 12:7–13)*

Jeremiah realises that the sufferings and the judgements that are about to fall on the people of God are not a Divine rescript (i.e., an edict or decree), but the result of that people's revolt.

Mine heritage is become unto me as a lion in the forest: she hath uttered her voice against Me; therefore I have hated her. (12:8 RV)

God is expounding to Jeremiah, and through Jeremiah, and through to all time, if His people disobey and rebel, the result of God's way of ordering things is inevitable. It is not a Divine edict, but the way God has constituted things. When self-realisation is accepted as the law of self, it becomes the enemy of the life of God.

"Is mine heritage unto me as a speckled bird of prey?" (RV). This is not a picture of a saint living a holy life in the world; it is the picture of a saint who is leaving God and going into the world, with the result that the birds of prey, i.e., those who have never recognised God, are tearing that life to bits, and God does not protect it. That is the thing that staggered Jeremiah. God is bringing him to see the reason: the people have rebelled against Him. If I backslide, I take some of the glorious plumage of the heritage of God with me, and as it gets bedraggled I am torn to pieces by the people who never knew Jesus Christ.

"Many shepherds have destroyed My vineyard . . . No man layeth it to heart" (RV). God would have been "a wall of fire round about and . . . the glory in the midst" if they had been obedient. The difference between God as a consuming fire and natural fire is just this, that the further you get away from God the more fiercely you feel His burnings, but when you are close to Him, you will find it is a glorious protection.

2. The Divine Event to Which the Whole World Tends *(Jeremiah 12:14–17)*

Thus saith the LORD against all mine evil neighbours, . . . Behold, I will pluck them up from off their land. (12:14 RV)

God is behind the devil; He is watching, and sees when the devil begins to gloat and attempt to interfere. An evil man or the devil himself can never hurt a backslider other than by God's permission.

"I will return, and have compassion on them" (12:15). That judgement and mercy are two phases of the same thing is part of the progressive realisation that men and women get as they walk in the light. The house of life has God at the back door and the front, if we bar both doors against Him, He will burst them open in mercy with a hurricane. When havoc is round about, men slander God, but havoc is the great presence of God working His own purposes. Everything is havoc but God and the man.

"If they will diligently learn the ways of My people, . . . then shall they be built up in the midst of My people" (12:16 RV). God created the people known as Israel for one purpose, to be His servants until through them every nation came to know God. Through every period they turned away from that preordained purpose because they wanted to be like other nations. This is the reason of all the judgements that paralysed Jeremiah.

The truth about God is Jesus Christ—light, life and love. Whatever is dark to us will, by means of our obedience, become as clear as the truth which we have made ours by obedience. The bit we do know is the most glorious, unfathomable delight conceivable, and that is going to be true about everything to do with God and us. The process is continual obedience.

This world is for redemption, not for progress, and a Christian is one who has been taken into that secret by the personal experience of Redemption. It is a continual revelation centring round one thing, the Cross of God in Jesus Christ, and the characteristic is that we have to be crucified too, and live only the life "hid with Christ in God."

FROM THE BIBLE TRAINING COURSE MONTHLY JOURNAL
VOL. 7 APRIL 1938 NO. 1
NOTES ON JEREMIAH

DEFACEMENT
Jeremiah 13:1–17

. . . before He cause darkness . . . Jeremiah 13:16

When a man is afraid of God the only right thing for him to do is to run straight to God and not wait to dress himself. The further we get away from God the more we want to dress ourselves up in prayer, etc., but if we fly, just as we are, God will take us and remove the unclean thing.

1. Outward Perishing and Inward Corrupting *(Jeremiah 13:1–11)*

Behold, the girdle was marred, it was profitable for nothing. . . . After this manner will I mar the pride of Judah, and the great pride of Jerusalem. (13:7, 9)

God created His chosen people for one purpose, not to be like other nations, but to be His servant until through them every nation should come to know Who Jehovah is. Israel continually "backed out" of God's purpose for them.

"And, behold, the girdle was marred." The marring of the girdle has reference to the inward moral state of the people; the captivity has to do with the external state of the people. God did not send Israel into captivity, they put themselves there. They corrupted themselves inwardly first, they became as a dirty girdle—"This evil people . . . shall even be as this girdle, which is profitable for nothing" (RV). The purpose of God in the captivity was to remove those who were evil from His people, preserving the remnant. The physical disappearance of the people is foretold in Leviticus 26; they perished outwardly because they had been corrupted inwardly. The inward corruption did not take place during the exile, but before; and because of the inward corruption they were taken into captivity.

Verse 11 is a wonderful revelation of the heart of God towards His people—"that they might be unto Me for a people, and for a name, and for a praise, and for a glory [the counterpart of this verse is Deuteronomy 26:18–19, and this purpose is the explanation of the stern indignation of God against the stubbornness that seemed to thwart it]: but they would not hear." The Babylonish captivity put an end to idolatry for ever. When Our Lord came the people were guilty of Pharisaism. The characteristic of Pharisaism in Our Lord's day was an intense hatred of idolatry (cf. Luke 11:24–26).

Spiritually when an individual builds his confidence on anything less than God inevitably there will be a perishing of the ground of confidence. Experience is the door to a life. The wonderful thing about real living experience is that it is never referred to as past, but merely as the entrance into what is now enjoyed. Beware of building your faith on your experience of God's grace instead of on God Who makes the experience possible. "Ye seek Me," said Jesus, "not because ye saw signs, but because ye ate of the loaves and were filled" (RV). "Put men's bodies first, feed them, heal them, educate them, then they will make You King." Perfectly true, but the devil's truth that has gone forth to-day as an angel of light. Instead of God's ways being put first, every other thing is put first.

2. Inward Dissipation and Outward Degeneration *(Jeremiah 13:12–17)*

Thus saith the LORD, Behold, I will fill all the inhabitants of this land . . . with drunkenness. (cf. Psalm 60:3)

There is a difference in the way God deals with a disobedient child of His and the way He deals with a man who is going on his course without realising what he is doing. The prophets always make God take the responsibility for the destructions that come across His disobedient children.

"Give glory to the LORD your God." There are always one or two in the midst of a corrupt people who will listen to God's voice. Repentance is never given to crowds of people, but to individuals in the crowd. "If any man will hear My voice . . ." These prophets while they proclaim the judgements of God always present the pleading of God with individuals. Never succumb to believing in an inevitable fate, but fly to God, then you will never know the darkness or the judgements on sin (cf. John 3:19). Judgement comes because of conscious rejection or conscious neglect. If we see and do not obey, there will be the wandering in the shadows, by God's decree. There is always a way back to God, and that is to fly as you are, not as you want to be.

"But if ye will not hear it, my soul shall weep in secret for your pride" (Jeremiah 13:17 RV). Jeremiah expresses the deep vicarious grief that is always welling up in him and makes him such a type of Our Lord (see Luke 13:34). To realise that it is possible for everyone to be in the light and experiencing the love of God, keeps us close to God's heart in intercession for those who will not heed.

FROM THE BIBLE TRAINING COURSE MONTHLY JOURNAL
VOL. 7 MAY 1938 NO. 2
NOTES ON JEREMIAH

THE SILENT SACRED LAND
Jeremiah 13:18–27

Wherefore come these things upon me? Jeremiah 13:22

To some people every day brings fresh causes to disbelieve God and to others new opportunities of praising and knowing God. This is not because the one is in physical health and the other not, but because one has a moral twist and the other has not. Disbelief in God is never only intellectual, it is moral.

1. Ashes of Roses
Sit ye down low [mg]: for your headtires are come down, even your beautiful crown [mg]. . . . Judah is carried away captive all of it. (13:18–19 RV)

We have to be "kings and priests unto God," but when once our bodies or our circumstances slip away from the rule of God in and through us there is "the fading flower of his glorious beauty" (Isaiah 28:1 RV). When we cease to *do* the will of God and begin to suffer it like stoics, instantly our "country" goes from us—"even the crown of your glory" (RV).

> *One might almost fill a large flower bed with plants arranged according to their cold-resisting powers, so that on each morning of late autumn and early winter we could see how much frost there had been the night before by the plants that had suffered.*
>
> E. K. Robinson

There is no virtue, no holiness, no life apart from the one Life, that can stand the frosted air of the world, the flesh and the devil and be more than conqueror. Jeremiah is revealing that if the life of the Son of God is not in us everything will fade and pass into ashes; when His life is in us there is no fading of any flower or beauty (cf. Isaiah 42:3).

2. Accomplishment of Ruin
The cities of the South are shut up, and there is none to open them. (13:19 RV)

Apart from the manifestation of the life of the Son of God in us all strongholds of natural virtues will sink into ruin. The Spirit of God puts corruption on natural virtues and excellencies because they belong to the man and the life of old. The Spirit of God never patches up our natural virtues, He never takes them and makes them more noble. He reconstructs us by re-creation until we are in the image of Jesus Christ.

3. Aspects of Realisation
Where is the flock that was given thee, thy beautiful flock? (13:20)

Learn to watch what God has put the sentence of death on, first in His Word, and then in personal experience. The life of the Son of God in us is the only thing that has no sentence of death on it. If we remain true to His life in us these disasters will be impossible because His Life is incorruptible.

4. Anguish of Rigour
. . . shall not sorrows take hold of thee, as of a woman in travail? (13:21 RV)

In stating the bondage of a turncoat from God's ways the Bible applies terms of the greatest ruggedness (cf. 2 Peter 2:22). God reveals the truth that the meanest[6] elements in personal life exercise tyranny over men who used to be a great power for God.

5. Ashamed in Retreat
. . . thy heels suffer violence. (Jeremiah 13:22 RV)

---

6. The word mean as used here refers to something or someone ordinary, common, low, or ignoble, rather than cruel or spiteful.

Some sorrows leave a stateliness, but this will be a cowering shame and misery; the people will be driven into captivity like the most degraded of slaves, without even sandals on. Such suffering does not teach obedience, it is the result of deliberate transgression. Shame pulls the house of life into despicable ruin (cf. Luke 15:14–16). There is no refuge for the house of life saving in the Lord Jesus Christ; no refuge in natural goodness, in prayer; not only no refuge but no salvation. The only way in which the house of life is made secure, and more than secure, an amazing beauty, is through the salvation of Jesus Christ. When the Spirit of God comes into us and prepares the way for the forming of the life of the Son of God in us, there is every now and again a great aftermath of inexpressible shame as He throws light on the past. It is more than humility, it is humiliation. Humility is a virtue, the outcome of God's indwelling; humiliation is where the Spirit of God strikes down into the things that have been defying God, till there is nothing left to support them.

6. Anathema to Rebels
Can the Ethiopian change his skin . . .?

The condition of the people is hopeless, habit has become second nature; the day for reformation has gone by. Never trust innocence of outlook in yourself or in other people when the statements of God's word are directly opposite (see Mark 7:21 and Jeremiah 17:19). We continually trust in ourselves and other people until we have learned to have absolute confidence in God. It is difficult when convicted to turn to Jesus Christ; we turn to vowing; but unless we turn to Jesus in obedience and let His life enter in, it is hopeless, for we build again on the same old foundation. "I never could be guilty of that." Yes, you could. The only place of safety is under the shadow of the Almighty. See you don't play hide and seek, but keep up the absolute life of "hide." "Your life is hid with Christ in God"; then there will be immunity from all the things spoken of here but if once through curiosity we begin to go out in speculation or in vagaries of our own, we shall find that God is no respecter of persons.

7. Actual Rejection
Therefore will I scatter them, as the stubble that passeth away. . . . This is thy lot, the portion measured unto thee from Me, saith the LORD. *(13:24–25* RV)

"We are the people of God, it does not matter what our moral character is like." The prophets talked in this way and the people trusted them (cf. 7:4–8).

  "Woe unto thee, O Jerusalem! Thou wilt not be made clean; how long shall it yet be?" (13:27 RV)—a sore, long-lasting purifying judgement time.

FROM THE BIBLE TRAINING COURSE MONTHLY JOURNAL
VOL. 7 JUNE 1938 NO. 3
NOTES ON JEREMIAH

DROUGHT
Jeremiah 14

They come to the pits, and find no water. . . . For that no rain hath been in the land, the plowmen are ashamed. Jeremiah 14:3–4 (RV)

While one desire remains unsatisfied, God is not Lord over all. That means we must quit some desires or else quit God. Most of us bring our desires to God and He has to wither them. When we delight in God He gives us our desires because they are in accordance with His will (see Psalm 37:4). A child goes to its mother about its skin and its toys, and we dare not think there are some things about us not for God to behold. A child of God is like a child of nature. Things that trouble a child are taken to its mother, and things that bother the child of God ought to be taken to God at once. Innocence of knowledge is the charm of a mature life and is like the ignorance of a child. Beware of being a spiritual prig, full of knowledge, instead of having the great innocence of knowledge which is the life of faith.

1. The Destruction that Wasteth at Noonday (*Jeremiah 14:1–9*)
Two things the Bible states are sure for men if they obey God—bread and water (see Isaiah 33:16); that is all God has promised us. Look over the history of civilisations and you will find every disaster has come by taking more. A spiritual application may be made along this line—"a famine . . . of hearing the words of the LORD" strikes every soul that has departed from the living God and dwelt by pleasant spiritual experiences—God's word dead to you, no inspiration about it; prayer dead, spiritual communion dead, you wait and long and pray and nothing happens, every-

thing languishing and dying. You will find if sin has not been the cause, there has been a selfish glutting of your soul on experiences instead of going on to know God Who gave you the experiences. We refuse to eat the old corn of the land, we prefer manna—that God should always do some exceptional thing for us. Spiritual famine and dearth, if it does not start from sin, starts from being a spiritual glutton, dwelling entirely on the experience that God has given us instead of seeing that the experience is but the gateway to the life. Life is the thing we live, experience is the gateway to new phases of life, and if we remain at the gate always we shall die of starvation.

"We have sinned against Thee" (Jeremiah 14:7). There is a difference between a moralist's and a Christian's condemnation of sin. A spiritual Christian always feels the unmitigated horror of the sin of another. A moralist never does, to him it is an occasion to "lambaste" something that is wrong. A Christian knows that the possibilities of every sin ever committed are in him but for the grace of God. The condemnation of sin before we are saved is bitter, intense and proud. After we are saved, the sins of others come upon us with the twofold weight of the possibility of doing the like ourselves, and the possibility of vicarious intercession.

"Why shouldest Thou be . . . as a mighty man that cannot save?" (14:9). Why does not God speak? This is not atheism, but the agony of a human heart getting into the secret of the Cross. The Cross of Jesus Christ is not the cross of a martyr, but the revelation of the essential nature of the Trinity. The most earnest of us deal with the Cross as a thing that is past, it is never past, it is the eternal revelation of Almighty God. Instantly we come face to face with all the possibility of moral development that must come by suffering (cf. Hebrews 5:8).

2. Deceived into the Snare of the Fowler (Jeremiah 14:10–22)

And the LORD said unto me, Pray not for this people for their good. When they fast, I will not hear their cry. . . . (14:11–12 RV)

Jeremiah pleads that the people have been misled by false prophets, but God says—"I sent them not, neither have I commanded them, neither spake I unto them"; they prophesied out of the deceit of their hearts. That does not mean self-deceit, it means deceit which the heart has devised that flattered sinful passions.

"And thou shalt say this word unto them, Let mine eyes run down with tears night and day, and let them not cease" (14:17 RV). God tells Jeremiah to show his own grief to the people.

"Hast Thou utterly rejected Judah? hath Thy soul lothed Zion? . . . Do not abhor us, . . . remember, break not Thy covenant with us" (14:19, 21). In such words the prophet is born again in an agony of grief into a childlike simplicity, pouring out his soul before God. When the mind is born again of grief it loses all reason and becomes like a child, it has nothing to plead, only absolute despair.

FROM THE BIBLE TRAINING COURSE MONTHLY JOURNAL
VOL. 7 JULY 1938 NO. 4
NOTES ON JEREMIAH

SCARCELY SAVED
Jeremiah 16

They shall not be lamented. Jeremiah 16:4

"And if the righteous scarcely be saved, where shall the ungodly and the sinner appear?" (1 Peter 4:18). Heaven must have held its breath several times over the best of us.

1. The Prophet's Vicarious Aloofness (Jeremiah 16:1–9)
Thou shalt not take thee a wife. . . . (16:2)

Vicarious aloofness is all very well in mind, but it is quite another matter to exhibit it in actual life. We must be careful to remember that Jeremiah was a man first and then a prophet, he was not an ascetic. This command to Jeremiah means that every relationship of a man's life, even to the most intimate and God-ordained, must be sacrificed at times to God's will. If we take celibacy as a command of God we make God contradict Himself. Whenever celibacy or poverty are enjoined in the Bible they are enjoined because God wants to express in that crisis a particular message in a particular age. This command is not a principle laid down but a command from God to a prophet.

"All things are lawful, . . . but all things are not expedient," says Paul, i.e., all things are lawful to me as a natural man, but not expedient to me as a spiritual man because I am under a superior command, viz.: a relationship to God. "I don't intend to waive rights, this particular reading and culture is good for me; this particular recreation is a great expansion to my mind, therefore I will do it"—absolutely pagan reasoning from beginning to end. How many of us have begun to realise our privilege of not doing things? The liberty to waive our rights is the great privilege of Christian sanctity. One of the meanest things is to say, "I don't do certain things because it will damage me." Paul's argument is—"I don't do certain things because it will damage someone else" (see 1 Corinthians 8:9–13). "For I could wish that myself were accursed from Christ for my brethren, my kinsmen according to the flesh." Paul there expresses this vicarious attitude, which is characteristic alone of the Spirit of Christ (cf. Exodus 32:32).

2. The Prophetic Visualised Amelioration (*Jeremiah 16:10–15*)

Verse 10 presents the attitude that God is taking unreasonable liberties—"Wherefore hath the LORD pronounced all this great evil against us?" Impregnable self-righteousness will scandalise God ruthlessly. Self-pity is the morbid side of self-righteousness—"Why should this thing fall on me? God is taking liberties with me, I am in the right."

   "Therefore will I cast you forth out of this land into the land that ye have not known, . . . and there shall ye serve other gods day and night" (RV), i.e., "you may serve the gods you have longed so much after as long as you will." God restrains and restrains, warns and warns, overlooks and overlooks; then He begins to bring out embarrassments against us. In the days before you knew God you did any number of things which God overlooked, but try and do them now, and if you persist you will realise what is written in Psalm 106:15— "And He gave them their request; but sent leanness into their soul." "He gave them their request"—all restraint gone. The man who has known what God is like, and what His life is like, but still persists in going against it, will come to a time when God will fling him out to do as he chooses.

3. The Prophetic Visitation Approaching (*Jeremiah 16:16–21*)

For Mine eyes are upon all their ways. . . . (16:17)

The tendency to-day is to put the consequences of sin as the consequences of sin: the consequences of sin have a righteous God behind them. We take the Bible idea out of punishments and say it is the inevitable result. The Bible says that the inevitable result is brought by a personal God, and is not an ordinary moral result. Beware of making punishment the mere result of sin, it arises from the presence of a personal God.

FROM THE BIBLE TRAINING COURSE MONTHLY JOURNAL
VOL. 7 SEPTEMBER 1938 NO. 6
NOTES ON JEREMIAH

THE FOUNTAIN OF LIFE
Jeremiah 17

The LORD, the fountain of living waters. Jeremiah 17:13

The truth of the moment is brought by Jesus into relation with Himself, the Truth. He will not allow us to rest in any detail of truth unless it is rooted in Him, it will turn to a curse instead of blessing. God continually brings us to a willingness for death on every line—death to our wishes, our desires, death to everything that in any degree is going to detach us from the Fountain of Life: we are willing to die to everything, consequently we never die. As long as we side with the thing that is going to be destroyed, we shall be destroyed with it. Every individual has the power to turn the course of life into destruction or into perfection, according to what way he chooses when God reveals the best way.

1. The Eternal Punishment of Sin (*Jeremiah 17:1–4*)

All sin is unpardonable, every sinner is pardonable. God's punishment of sin is eternal, i.e. ageless. "For ye have kindled a fire in My anger which shall burn for ever" (RV). God cannot alter, and as long as there is sin it must be punished. If punishment for sin ceases, God ceases to be God. God loves where He cannot yet forgive, where forgiveness in its full sense is as yet impossible, there is no contact of heart because that which lies between has not even begun to yield to the "besom" of holy destruction.

(a) The Seat of Sin (17:1–2)
The sin of Judah . . . is graven upon the table of their heart.

"The table of their heart" is the inward seat of sin. If sin is graven with a pen of iron upon the human heart, it was also graven with an iron nail in our Lord's hands and feet. Consciousness of sin is the exhaustion of sin, and is as big an alarm to the devil as it is a joy to the Holy Ghost. It is when we are not conscious of sin that condemnation is certain; when it spurts out in wrongs and immoralities, there is a chance for God. "The publicans and the harlots . . ."—the people who explode into all kinds of wrongs and crimes—"go into the kingdom of God before you," said Jesus. The deep condensed pressure of iniquity only shows itself with tremendous force like that when we go on in certain lines of conduct. When Jesus Christ comes on the scene the pressure in the heart bursts out at once (cf. John 15:22).

(b) The Severity of Sanctity (17:3–4)

"I will give thy substance and all thy treasures for a spoil . . ." (RV). We distinguish between sin and the sinner, but the Bible never does. God can never pardon sin, it is impossible: He can forgive the sinner when once the sinner accepts His verdict against sin. If he does not,

the punishment of sin is eternal. Eternal life or eternal death is the quality of the particular type of life a man lives. There is no alteration—God cannot pardon sin, but He instantly receives the sinner when the sinner leaves his sin and comes to Him. The Atonement of the Lord Jesus Christ does not mean that God forgives the sinner and leaves him in his sin; God forgives a man for being a sinner and puts him in the place where he need never be a sinner any more.

Distinction must be made between punishment and suffering. Punishment is not suffering that makes people better; people who are punished are nearly always hardened, as in this case. God often brings a man down to elemental life by punishment for sin in order to save his soul, and through intense physical suffering, either for his own wrongdoing or the wrongdoing of others, he is brought back to elemental life because God is only after one thing, a right relationship to Himself, and He does not care about our physical comforts. Until we are rightly related to Him, God will play ruthless havoc with every comfort and relationship we have.

THE BIBLE TRAINING COURSE MONTHLY JOURNAL
VOL. 7 OCTOBER 1938 No. 7
NOTES ON JEREMIAH

THE FOUNTAIN OF LIFE

(Continued)
Jeremiah 17

2. The Eternal Programme of Sanctity
(Jeremiah 17:5–13)
(a) The Barren Heath

The Bible unvarnishedly speaks of fundamental trust in another as wickedness. "Cursed be the man that trusteth in man, and maketh flesh his arm . . ." Wherever we trust in goodness or nobility instead of in God, we suddenly find ourselves in a howling waste wilderness. The attitude of a godly life is to put no confidence in anything or anyone but God. Not only do we find disillusionment, but we find that God does not allow us teachers or comrades or friends too long. Immediately our teachers or friends begin to wean our trust from Him, there is blighting and upset, followed by separation; until the great secret is learned that when once a man or woman's heart is strong in confidence in God, there is no snare in earthly friendship because the heart is at rest with God, and there are no

areas of desert and wilderness such as are frequently seen in lives.

Jesus Christ brings us into a sanctity where God alone lives. The lives that grow stronger are lives in the desert, deep-rooted in God, and they always remind us of God when we come in contact with them; they never sentimentalise our hearts around them. We can never rest in a man or woman of God, there is always something thorny about them that warns us off, until the man or woman becomes a mere indicator to Jesus Christ. In the Bible we never find the close intimacies of friendship that we find everywhere else. Great men and great women are taken up and dropped, and the one Figure left is Jesus Christ. We do not forget the friends who have helped us, but they have merged us into a better knowledge of Jesus Christ. Every friendship that does not lead to a deeper, better knowledge of God and at the same time make us fundamentally independent of that friendship, is a curse.

(b) The Blighting Hideousness
The heart is deceitful above all things, and desperately wicked: who can know it? (17:9)

The Spirit of God corrupts our natural virtues. If we are naturally pure-minded, naturally good-tempered, naturally loving, we shall find that since we became spiritual God's corruption has been put on everything that was of old, because the natural virtues are not promises of what we are going to be, but remnants of what we were created to be, and the new life re-forms its own virtues. It is the most woeful thing to see people in the service of God depending on what the grace of God never gave them, depending on what they have by the accidents of heredity. Intellectually we nearly always sympathise with pagan virtues, while spiritually God is trying to get us into contact with the real life of the Lord Jesus Christ that cannot be described in terms of natural virtues.

And every virtue we possess, . . .
Is His alone.

In the life of Jesus, the perfectly sinless One, the natural was offered by Him as a sacrifice to God. When we are sanctified the perpetual temptation is to do what Jesus did not do—"Now I am sanctified I can do what I like." I cannot. My natural life and natural gifts are to be turned into a spiritual possession by offering them to God.

"They have forsaken the LORD, the fountain of living waters." We face the problems of life with a pagan intellect and say, "How confusing." The Bible is simple—Holiness unto the LORD and no care for any other thing. The whole of life is meant to exhibit that God is making saints, not civilisations or clever able men and women, but saints.

FROM THE BIBLE TRAINING COURSE MONTHLY JOURNAL
VOL. 7 NOVEMBER 1938 No. 8
NOTES ON JEREMIAH

DIZZINESS
Jeremiah 17:14–18

The human body has a "spirit level" in the head, when that spirit level is disturbed, vertigo or dizziness is the result. There is a "spirit level" spiritually, viz. union with God, and unless that is kept right dizziness and confusion of thought will always happen.

1. Dejection and Derision (*Jeremiah 17:14–15*)
"Reproach hath broken my heart" (cf. Matthew 27:39–44). They reproached Jesus with the truth and He had not a word to say. He died in ignominy and shame, remember. It was not that sinners jeered at Him, but that the people He came to save flung in His teeth the things that He had said. The same thing with Jeremiah—"Behold, they say unto me, Where is the word of the LORD? let it come now," and Jeremiah turned to God in despair. "Oh Lord, bring me not to confusion by leaving these prophecies unfulfilled."

If you stand for God's truth you are sure to experience reproach, and if once you open your mouth to vindicate yourself, you lose everything you were on the point of gaining. Let the ignominy and shame come. "For we also are weak in Him." It is the one thing we won't be—"weak in Him." When Paul said, "I can do all things through Christ which strengtheneth me," they were weak things he spoke about, how to be abased, to be hungry, to suffer need. That is the test of a Christian, the power to descend until you are looked upon as absolute refuse and you have not a word to say any more than your Lord had. Only in that condition see that your faith in God does not fail.

2. Devotion and Depression (*Jeremiah 17:16–17*)
These verses explain why Our Lord said that God's message would only be accepted through strangers (see Luke 4:16–27). A stranger knows nothing whatever about our condition, the consequence is his message goes straight home and conscience says, "That must be the voice of God." A person who knows us dare not say what he knows because immediately he does it is difficult to appear free from personal vindictiveness.

People charged Jeremiah with exhibiting personal spleen—"You have been saying these things and nothing has happened; you simply prophesy because you are vindictive against us." It is easier to be true to conviction than to be true to God. As workers for God we must be identified with God, not with His message.

Another danger of a prophet is the snare the prophet Jonah fell into, and Jeremiah also nearly fell into it. Jonah denounced the people of Nineveh and when God did not carry it out, Jonah was angry with God.

3. Directed Destruction *(Jeremiah 17:18)*
Bring upon them the day of evil. . . .

This is not the utterance of a spiteful, vindictive temperament; it is the statement of a prophet of God Who knows God's truth, and knows also that the saving of himself as a prophet means the destruction of the people whom he loves better than himself. "Destroy them with double destruction," till everything contrary to God has been broken and demolished. This is where Jeremiah is nearest Jesus Christ and farthest from us. "I only want to see the people who are against me humiliated"—that is the spirit of the devil. The spirit of a prophet is—"God must be vindicated, and as a servant of God I will stand alongside the vindication, although it means standing with God against the ones who are dearer to me than life."

FROM THE BIBLE TRAINING COURSE MONTHLY JOURNAL
VOL. 7 DECEMBER 1938 No. 9
NOTES ON JEREMIAH

THE POTTER AND THE CLAY
Jeremiah 17:19–18:10

I do with you as this potter. Jeremiah 18:6

1. The Re-Statement of the Blessed Health *(Jeremiah 17:19–27)*
These verses show that the way of safety appointed to the people lies in keeping one of the fundamental precepts of the Decalogue, viz. the observance of the Sabbath. "Thus saith the LORD; take heed for your life's sake [RV mg], and bear no burden on the sabbath day, nor bring it in by the gates of Jerusalem" (17:21–22). Verses 24–26 describe the blessings which will be brought to the people if they hallow the Sabbath day, and verse 27 describes the curse if it is profaned. Being not under the law but under grace means that we fulfil all the old law easily and a good deal more. With regard to the Sabbath, Jesus said "the Son of man is Lord also of the sabbath." That means we have to remember that Jesus Christ is the Lord of the one day that is His, though we can rob Him of it. When we recognise that the Sabbath day belongs to God, every other day that we give over to Him is our gift. The same with regard to money and possessions. The giving of the tenth is not a sign that it all belongs to God, but a sign that the tenth belongs to God and the rest is ours, and we are held responsible for what we do with it. Our Lord says, "Think not that I came to destroy the law or the prophets: I came not to destroy, but to fulfil" (Matthew 5:17 RV). If we will heed the spirit of God He will always check when we are in danger of turning liberty into license.

2. The Resource of Boundless Holiness *(Jeremiah 18:1–10)*
Every prophecy in Jeremiah begins with a reference to the word of the Lord coming to him. "The word which came to Jeremiah from the LORD, saying, Arise, and go down to the potter's house, and there I will cause thee to hear My words" (18:1–2). The word of Jehovah which came to Jeremiah by suggestion in the potter's house was that God is sovereign in history, He will mould and re-mould until He gets the "vessel" to His mind. And yet God's sovereignty has limitations which He Himself has sovereignly placed in man—the mysterious gift of freedom. With man rests the final issue, not with God.

"O house of Israel, cannot I do with you as this potter? saith the LORD. Behold, as the clay in the potter's hand, so are ye in Mine hand, O house of Israel" (18:6). The illustration God uses is that of a potter dealing with stubborn clay and remodelling it according to his own purpose. The snare of belief in God's sovereignty is to make that sovereignty a logically consistent thing, whereas the sovereignty of God is the free will of God in which two conditions are plainly placed by God Himself, first the holiness of God and second the freedom of man. The truth of God in application is always moral. Jeremiah is bringing the truth in application to these people that they are not going to obtain anything from God unless they maintain a right relationship to Him, and that even if they should be destroyed on the wheel, God's purpose for His covenant people would still come to pass.

God never gives us an answer, He simply puts us on lines where it is possible for the truth to break more and more as we go on.

FROM THE BIBLE TRAINING COURSE MONTHLY JOURNAL
VOL. 7 JANUARY 1939 No. 10
NOTES ON JEREMIAH

EXCELSIOR
Jeremiah 18:11–23

Will a man leave the snow of Lebanon. . . ? Jeremiah 18:14

"Excelsior" means higher still. The conception of these studies is that man must look higher for the source of life and salvation than the experience of life, apart from an experimental knowledge of God, would lead him to look. Once fail from looking at the highest and degeneration begins. It is the early desires that are the highest and best.

1. False Direction *(Jeremiah 18:11–13)*

These people are affecting to be the people of God—"We are the people of God, this is the temple of God; and these prophets" talk is all beside the mark, the prophets we like to listen to are those who prophesy smooth things." Affectation is the attitude of life when there is no life, and the higher the life affected, the deeper the iniquity. Jeremiah is probing straight down to the rottenness at the heart. The early aspirations God stirred in them have gone, and now they simply make God and everything in connection with Him an affectation to go on their own ways. "But they say, . . . we will walk after our own devices, and we will do every one after the stubbornness of his evil heart" (18:12 RV).

2. Forsaken Direction *(Jeremiah 18:14–17)*

"Will a man leave the snow of Lebanon . . . ?" Will a man forsake the very way of his own life when he knows what it is? It is just that obstinacy that makes the problem of individual and national life. "Knowledge is virtue, if only men knew, they would not go wrong," is not true. It is not sufficient to be persuaded a thing is wrong; there is an obstinacy that deliberately takes the law into its own hand and leaves the source of its life. There needs to be a recognition of where the source of life is and a determination to stay at it. Backsliding is the prevailing of human stubbornness after the experimental knowledge of salvation. Backsliding is never spoken of in the Bible as a degenerate tendency, but as a conscious forsaking. "They have caused them to stumble in their ways, in the ancient paths" (RV)—the ways the patriarchs walked in, of time immemorial, a dateless way, the way of always

being in right relationship to God; but they have caused them to stumble out of that way by making sacrifices to vanity. It is no longer "Satisfy us early with Thy mercy" but, "Satisfy us with these other things, we want material prosperity and success." They have forgotten the Source of their life while still maintaining the gesticulations of a life that had been nourished from the mountain-tops of God, but is no longer nourished there. They have found "a way not cast up," a way on which one cannot advance. Once stop looking at the mountain and all prosperity, which is but an effect, vanishes. Never falter by trying to make anything lesser the cause for what is greater; for instance, trying to make health of body the cause for a right spiritual relationship, or material prosperity the cause for worshipping God, and never make obedience the reason that God is blessing you, obedience is the effect of being rightly related to God. Remember our life is maintained from the heights only.

3. Forced Direction *(Jeremiah 18:18–23)*

Then said they, Come and let us devise devices against Jeremiah. . . . And let us not give heed to any of his words. (18:18)

Beware of seeking out inconsistencies in God's children in order to evade obeying God's message yourself. If there comes to you a message on personal holiness, beware of the tendency that puts you on the watch to see if that person is consistent; the reason you watch is that you want to evade obeying God's message. There is an antipathy to the message of holiness which prides itself on being amazingly shrewd, and whenever a man of God is known to fall, there is a sigh of relief—"Well, that saves me, I have always been suspicious about this holy life," and under the affectation of profound sadness there is a glow of relief on the inside. The trick is as old as the garden of Eden.

Verses 19–23. Jeremiah asks God to bring down His vengeance upon the people, he sees that the people he loves can only be touched by the vengeance of God; and yet Jesus said, "The Son of man is not come to destroy men's lives, but to save them." But we must never forget what is Our Lord's definition of life, "a man's life consisteth not," He says, "in the abundance of the things which he possesseth," and devastation and destruction of these things may mean the salvation of the life as Jesus sees it. One of the hardest lessons to learn is that of "hands off" in certain kinds of suffering, because you may be putting yourself in the way of God saving a life. The only way in which the salvation of that life can come may be the very way you have told God you will never allow it to come. The secret is to maintain life from the highest plane—"hid with Christ in God."

FROM THE BIBLE TRAINING COURSE MONTHLY JOURNAL
VOL. 7 FEBRUARY 1939 NO. 11
NOTES ON JEREMIAH

BROKEN POTTERY
Jeremiah 19

A potter's vessel, that cannot be made whole again.
Jeremiah 19:11

There are two sins of spiritual condition that cannot be forgiven; the first is sin against man—spiritual murder, unforgiving dislike; the second is sin against God—shutting God out from worship and everything. Neither of these sins are acts, they are conditions. When a man holds either, God is outside him in every sense, holding to him only by the Creator relationship, and He keeps that hold against the will of the man. The ordinary occurrences of life reveal to us the condition of our hearts and minds—a dislike that will not forgive, that has not the slightest intention of making any excuse. That is a natural condition that cannot be forgiven until a man wishes to turn from it. The great characteristic of the supernatural grace of God is put by Jesus on the line of forgiveness. Forgiveness is not an act, it is the supernatural manifestation of a miracle within us.

In Jeremiah 18 a picture of muddled clay remodelled; in this chapter we have a picture of a made and used vessel smashed into the scrap-heap. "We have Abraham to our father" (Luke 3:8). "My father and mother were spiritual, therefore I am a child of God." We are only children of God by personal regeneration through the Atonement. Children of God are not made by physical creation, but by moral creation. God created His ancient people for one purpose only, to be His servants until the whole world should know Who He is, that purpose will be fulfilled whether His people are on the scrap-heap or not.

1. Jeremiah and the Judicious Minds
(Jeremiah 19:1–2; John 2:13–17)
The attitude of Our Lord to the judicious minds of His day was similar. In the temple precincts judicious minds were without excuse, because they understood what Our Lord was doing. Outside Jerusalem, Our Lord always said, "Don't tell anyone Who I am"; every time He went to Jerusalem He made it clear Who He was.

The presentation of the Gospel of God to sinners is one of love and mercy, but to the house of God one of judgement and truth. When we preach to the crowd outside we lambaste drunkenness and other things, Jesus never did. The stern messages of the Bible are never given to sinners, but to God's people. If we follow the order God gives, we will find John 16:1 is true.

2. Jeremiah and the Judgement Message
(Jeremiah 19:3; 1 Corinthians 3:17)
"They have . . . estranged this place. . . ." They have disowned it as the house of God and made it their own place. "If any man destroyeth the temple of God, him shall God destroy; for the temple of God is holy, which temple ye are" (RV). Our bodies are the temples of the Holy Ghost, we must take care not to estrange "this place."

In the second cleansing of the Temple Our Lord "would not suffer that any man should carry a vessel through the temple," making it a convenience (see Mark 11:15–17). How many of us use our bodily strength as a convenience for ourselves? The appeal nowadays is to rest on Sundays not because it is God's day, but because we shall do our work better in the week. God touches His children's bodies with pain in an extraordinary way (see 1 Peter 4:1); the devil takes care we do not suffer in the flesh as long as we use our bodies for ourselves. We can always escape the purpose of God for our bodily lives. Don't disown your body as a temple of God, but know that whatever happens to your body is under the sovereignty of God.

"*. . . which temple ye are.*" The abode of God is not the abode of God's blessings, but the abode of the blessing God. "We have this treasure in earthen vessels," and the vessel must be broken before the light appears. When God is making our bodies transparent for Himself to shine through we ask Him to patch us up. "No," says God, "I am making a window." He made His Son a bruised and broken vessel *(see* Isaiah 53). When we are bruised we say "That is the devil." Don't despise the chastenings of the Lord. We are God's and God is in us for His glory. We must always take our orders from God's sovereignty, not from our ideas of how God should work.

3. Despising the Justice of God *(Jeremiah 19:4; 1 Corinthians 4:5)*
And have filled this place with the blood of innocents.

In cleansing the temple courts Jesus did not drive out the doves, He asked the owners to take them out. "Judge nothing before the time, until the Lord come." In mind and spirit and heart there are pure affections and ideas born of the Holy Ghost that are being turned into merchandise by us, we use them not for God's glory but for our own ends, and ask God to bless them. The devil will make you judge your sentiments before the Lord appears; don't. The devil will

counterfeit a hyper-conscientiousness for the detecting voice of the Spirit of God. This motive was wrong, that was wrong, he tries to make us rake up things before God. There are times when we are brought under the scrutiny of God and are marvellously conscious of the Lord's presence, that is the moment to judge, that is the crisis of self-revelation. When those moments come, don't despise them.

4. Desecrating the Worship of God *(Jeremiah 19:5; Galatians 5:4)*

They have offered burnt-offerings "which I commanded not." The Apostle Paul is dealing with the same sentiment. When once we begin to choose what we are going to dedicate to God, or to what religious creed or conviction we are going to devote our lives, we are desecrating what God has consecrated. God has told us to worship Him by presenting our bodies to Him. "Present your bodies a living sacrifice, holy, acceptable to God, which is your spiritual worship [RV mg]" (Romans 12:1).

FROM THE BIBLE TRAINING COURSE MONTHLY JOURNAL
VOL. 7 MARCH 1939 NO. 12
NOTES ON JEREMIAH

THE FOOLISHNESS OF GOD
Jeremiah 20

O LORD, . . . every one mocketh me. Jeremiah 20:7

Jeremiah came back to the city and repeated to all the people the message he gave to the elders (Jeremiah 19:14–15). For the first time Jeremiah is designated by his office—"the prophet" (20:2), and the action of Pashur is against him as a prophet for his public utterance. According to the people Pashur was right and Jeremiah a raving fanatic. How we select things out of the Bible! We have forgotten what Paul wrote— "For He was crucified through weakness. . . . For we also are weak in Him" (RV). A Christian is one who can be weak, an abject failure in the eyes of the world. Jeremiah is getting into the throes of this central revelation of God Almighty—the Cross.

1. The Degradation of Divinity *(Jeremiah 20:1–6)*
There comes a time with nations or individuals when they may degrade Divinity and never be bothered again (cf. Mark 6:27; Luke 23:8–9). The despite done to Jeremiah is done to God Almighty (cf. Acts 9:4— "Saul, Saul, why persecutest thou Me?"). Our Lord

identifies His great name with the feeblest of His disciples.

2. The Discipline of Grace *(Jeremiah 20:7–18)*
It takes the grace of God to go through disgrace unspoilt. If Jeremiah's distress makes you condemn him, pass it by; but if, according to the reason of this world, you understand that God's ways are foolishness, you will put Jeremiah's grief and staggered amazement within sight of Gethsemane and Calvary and no one else near. Every problem is faced and fathomed in the prophecies of Jeremiah, that is why he stands nearer to the centre of God's heart than any of the prophets.

(a) Deceived (20:7–8)
"O Lord, Thou hast deceived me, and I was deceived." Jeremiah says in heart-breaking sobs before God "I have been deceived in what I hoped Thou wouldest do." His cry is not the theological argument of a man's mind, he is pouring it all out before God; there is no charge brought against God and no reply from God. I spoke

because the people were reproaching Thy word, and now I see nothing but "derision all the day" (RV).

(b) Distressed (20:9)
Jeremiah is sensitive to the last degree to all the affinities of the people and he speaks out of perplexity—if I determine to keep silent, "then there is in mine heart as it were a burning fire shut up in my bones, and I am weary with forbearing" (RV).

(c) Defamed (20:10)
"I have heard the defaming of many. . . . Denounce, and we will denounce him, say all my familiar friends, they that watch for my halting" (RV). "The people watch for inconsistencies in my life that they may say on that ground I am not preaching Thy truth." To be defamed

means that if you stand for God you will not be able to stand for anything else—"no use since they turned religious."

(d) Devoted (20:11–13)
"But the LORD is with me"—a sudden outburst of the devotion of Jeremiah's heart for God. "For unto Thee have I revealed my cause" (RV). When in communion with God his desires are a delight, he sees and enjoys deliverance. "Sing unto the LORD, praise ye the LORD: for He hath delivered the soul of the needy" (RV).

(e) De Profundis (20:14–17)
It takes the Man of Sorrows to understand where Jeremiah has got to.

FROM THE BIBLE TRAINING COURSE MONTHLY JOURNAL
VOL. 8 APRIL 1939 NO. 1
NOTES ON JEREMIAH

THE FEAR OF GOD
Jeremiah 22

O earth, earth, earth, hear the word of the LORD.

A thing that is unknown and yet known to be, is always formidable. "Perfect love casteth out fear"—but not love in its beginning. To say "Therefore will we not fear, though . . ." (RV) is only possible when the love of God is having its way.

1. Oracle to Royal Jurisdiction *(Jeremiah 22:1–5; Matthew 21:5)*
"Go down to the house of the king. . . ." These verses indicate that every power of human government that can be used by the devil and self-interest can be reclaimed and used by God. On the other hand, everything that is usable by God is abusable by the devil. The sin of the people of God was not that they desired a king, but that they desired a king that they might be "like all the nations" (1 Samuel 8:19–20).

"Behold, thy King cometh unto thee, meek, and riding upon an ass" (RV). These words express in emblem as well as in act the whole of Old Testament prophecy along this line—a meek king, a lowly king, "riding upon an ass," which in Scripture stands for mankind. Our Lord is the only One Who can ride on humanity, "loose" (Mark 11:2). The true King is Jesus Christ Who shall reign not only in spiritual reality but in external visible reality.

2. Oracle of Royal Judgement *(Jeremiah 22:6–19; Matthew 23:38; 25:41)*
"And I will prepare destroyers against thee. . . ." As in the Book of Isaiah, so in Jeremiah, God is revealed as the Controller behind every power of evil; when evil strikes His people it strikes not only by God's permission but under His direct control (cf. Isaiah 37:29; John 19:11). The kings of that time by their godless courses hurried on the threatened destruction. "Weep ye not for the dead, . . . but weep sore for him that goeth away" (Jeremiah 22:10). Jeremiah counsels them not only to bemoan the king being carried away prisoner, but for the forsaken condition of the people.

"Behold, your house is left unto you desolate." Twice before Jesus had said, "My Father's house," the solemn application being that God hands individuals as well as nations over to a desecrated temple which He calls "your house." We need to bear in mind that chaos and wrath are the foundation of the life of every man who does not live in communion with God.

". . . everlasting fire, prepared for the devil and his angels." God's holiness never alters its attitude to devilishness; as long as God endures, He endures as "everlasting fire" to the devil. God is "a consuming fire" and if we side with the devil we shall know His burning. Divine fire as opposed to natural fire, burns the fiercer

the farther you get away from it; when you get nearer to God, His burning becomes a comfort. Condemnation corresponds to light rejected (John 3:19). God always allows the lash to fall more heavily on His own people if once they pervert their knowledge of Him. Never ignore the fact that God is a holy God.

"Shalt thou reign, because thou strivest to excel in cedar?" (Jeremiah 22:15 RV). Kingship does not consist in the erection of royal palaces, but in the administration of right and justice.

Watch the danger of architectural prominence; whenever money which has been given for missionary enterprise goes for the erection of buildings in the name of the Son of Man Who came "to seek and to save that which was lost," starvation comes to God's people. Paul's irony in 1 Corinthians 4:8 brings to light an abiding truth: we are saved to be "kings and priests," but to become kings and priests without the humility of salvation will produce an oppression that is a disgust to the heart of God.

3. Oracle of Retributive Justice *(Jeremiah 22:20–23; John 15:2, 6)*

I spake unto thee in thy prosperity; but thou saidst, I will not hear. . . . (22:21)

Two phases of retributive justice are mentioned in John 15: the quiet removal of a fruitless branch by God (John 15:2); the noisy public removal of a fruitless branch by men (John 15:6). Steadfast maintenance of a relationship to God by private obedience is the only way to bear fruit.

FROM THE BIBLE TRAINING COURSE MONTHLY JOURNAL
VOL. 8 MAY 1939 NO. 2
NOTES ON JEREMIAH

PROPHETS WISE AND OTHERWISE
Jeremiah 23

Mine heart within me is broken because of the prophets. Jeremiah 23:9

1 . The Development of the Prophet

A prophet is one who knows with holy certainty that God's perfect will must eventually overcome all resistance and self-will. In chapter 23 Jeremiah speaks against the accredited leaders of the day and against the professional preachers. All that refers to the prophets of the Old Testament dispensation has a direct application to us, no matter what we think we are. The principles are for all, even the most insignificant of us. A great deal of what we proclaim can never be worked out in experience, but whenever a standard has to be proclaimed we are exonerated or condemned according to the way we carry out those dictates of the Spirit of God. We must be the living incarnation of what we teach or else we are humbugs. Our Lord frequently mentions the prophets. He Himself was a prophet, He came to proclaim the truth of God (cf. Matthew 23:37).

2. The Degeneracy of the Prophet

In chapter 23 Jeremiah points out very clearly how degeneration starts and continues. When an organisation is maintained by pagan methods it becomes aggressive, intolerant and quite unlike anything that takes its standard from Jesus Christ. There may be no trace of this in the individual lives of those belonging to the organisation, they may be truly humble saints. We are apt to say we are battling for God's glory when we are battling for our own organisation; union with Jesus Christ is the one essential.

(a) The Stealer in Messages

"Therefore, behold, I am against the prophets, saith the LORD, that steal My words every one from his neighbour" (23:30). Stealing in this connection does not mean taking what does not belong to us, but persuading ourselves and other people that it never belonged to anyone else. Where did you get your form of testimony from? Have you stolen God's words from your neighbour? The stealer takes the truths from his neighbour and gives them to the people without applying them to himself. The beginning of degeneracy is on that line.

(b) The Strenuous Planner

"Behold, I am against the prophets, saith the LORD, that use [take, RV mg] their tongues and say, He saith" (23:31). Spiritual life produces mental energy, but strenuous mental energy may be the counterfeit of spiritual life. The test is—is the life of God manifested in the personal life of the prophet? When people get to know us, do they find that we are amazingly captious and unlike Our Lord. Jesus said, "By their fruits ye shall know them."

(c) The Scathing of the Motive

"Behold, I am against them that prophesy lying dreams, . . . and cause My people to err by their lies" (23:32 RV). God scathes the motive at the heart of the false prophet. A lie is not necessarily an inaccuracy of speech. If a prophet says, "Of course God does not mean you to live up to that standard," that is a lie which causes God's people to err. If we are not working out in our private lives the messages we are handing out, we are deepening the damnation of our own souls as messengers of God.

3. The Direction of the Prophet
(a) Be Simple and Natural (23:14)

A prophet has no manner or etiquette, he is undecoratedly simple, and must find his own way into the immediate presence of God. You can get at a man in any other calling in life quicker than at a minister, because a minister is apt to be artificial.

(b) Be Sanctified and Natural (23:18)

Jeremiah's personal relationship to God was much more in evidence than the time he gave to prayer. The important direction for right guidance as a worker is to realise the presence of God and your relationship to Him. The majority of us measure our realisation of God's presence by the time we give to prayer—abominable self-righteousness! "They have their reward," said Jesus. Jeremiah lived in relationship to God all the time. The one dominant note of his life was that he was God's man. He stood apart from the Schools of the prophets, and that is why his word came with such a challenge against the prophets.

FROM THE BIBLE TRAINING COURSE MONTHLY JOURNAL
VOL. 8 JUNE 1939 NO. 3
NOTES ON JEREMIAH

RULE OR RUIN
Jeremiah 23

The Lord is our righteousness. Jeremiah 23:6 (RV)

A Christian worker is measured by the words he speaks in the name of God. It is perilously easy to do one of two things, viz. to bind burdens on other people by God's word that we do not understand and have no intention of helping them lift (see Luke 11:46), or to placidly explain away the full purport of the word of God. Our Lord did not scathe sin, He came to save from it. The aftermath of a crooked personal disposition works out in scathing sin (see Luke 9:54).

1. Perils of Power (*Jeremiah 23:1–3; cf. Luke 22:24–27*)

Temporal power is merely the manifestation of a Divine purpose leaving ample room for the prostitution of that power. "But the LORD hardened Pharaoh's heart." When once a man is placed in a position of honour under God's providence and does not maintain a right relationship to God, the very position in which God has put him will harden him away from God. Power we must have, whether we like it or not, but power is a terrible peril unless the life is rooted in God's grace.

Bear in mind the distinction between the results of sin and punishment for sin. Verse 2 refers to the latter—". . . behold, I will visit upon you the evil of your doings, saith the LORD." The inevitable *result* of sin is to destroy the power of knowing it is sin. The *punishment* of sin is that God banishes the sinner from His presence. What is being forgotten to-day is that there is any punishment—"This is simply the result of having made a mistake." The suffering that comes to the children of bad people is the inevitable result of sin, not its punishment; punishment is meted out here or hereafter to the parents who may never suffer in this present life. In this case God interfered with the punishment because they were His people.

"*Ye have scattered My flock, and driven them away . . .*" (23:2). Beware of the possibility of being faced by God at some time with the lives you have been the cause of being driven out.

2. Pearl of Price (*Jeremiah 23:4–8; Matthew 13:45–46*)

These verses are a warning as to the easy way we try to ignore the deep unchangeable purposes of Almighty God. God's purposes are brought about not only by sovereign decrees but by the delightful acquiescence of His people. That is why it takes time. God does not badger us into His will. His will will be done, and the marvel of the grace of God is that the most eager longing we have is for His will.

Any rejoicing before God that is not based on humility is never born of the Spirit of God; rejoicing is made possible by the Atonement only and is wrought by the Holy Spirit. Bit by bit God lets us see what the grace of God covers and atones for. The only attitude a Christian can have is one of absolute humility before God; if we are anything at all in the holy life it is by the grace of God and no other way. The Apostle Paul never forgot what he had been. The deeper we go into the grace of God the more profound is our humility, there is no holiness without humility.

3. Pressure of Pain *(Jeremiah 23:9–15)*

"Mine heart within me is broken. . . ." This is not the despondent crushing on account of sin alluded to in Psalm 51, but a profound inward emotion that staggered the prophet until he became like a drunken man because of God's wrath at the lives of the people. That is the way God works. He takes one or two and makes them understand the condition of things around them, and they have no comrades. When God is bringing a new manifestation of Himself into the world, He burdens someone, and the burden is not a pious affectation. When God begins to favour you with a burden, never try to find out whether anyone else has the same burden. We have our own little difficulties and suffering, but who among us can God take up into the distress of the Holy Ghost when He is bringing in a new manifestation of His purposes? The characteristic of a saint is not—"There are great dangers and perils, I wonder God does not rouse up His people." He won't; He will rouse you. Don't confer with others (Galatians 1:16). It is a great peril to see things, because the pressure of the pain is the beginning of being made broken bread and poured-out wine. Nothing is more abhorrent to God and man than an affected burden. The child of God is a child, and a child's griefs and joys are tremendous, but you can always tell when grief is affected because it fixes our minds on the person instead of rousing us up to realise what God is doing through that person.

FROM THE BIBLE TRAINING COURSE MONTHLY JOURNAL
VOL. 8 JULY 1939 NO. 4
NOTES ON JEREMIAH

HIDDEN ROCKS
Jeremiah 23:9–12

They . . . caused My people Israel to err. Jeremiah 23:13

The phrase "hidden rocks" is used in the Epistle of Jude as illustrating false brethren (*see* Jude 12 RV). At times these "rocks" present themselves in the guise of moods or sentiments. In this chapter Jeremiah is dealing with the false prophets whose peril to the people of God is that they are as rocks unlighted in the way of warning.

1. Masked Perils of Spiritual Service *(Jeremiah 23:9–15)*

False brethren, false moods and false prophets always begin right, and only the Spirit of God is capable of unmasking them.

"Their course is evil, and their force is not right" *(23:10),* literally, "they are valiant in wrong." "Raging waves of the sea, foaming out their own shame," is Jude's description of the same kind of thing in another dispensation. "Yea, in My house have I found their wickedness, saith the LORD" (Jeremiah 23:11). Both prophet and priest who should lead the people the right way, are profane; they desecrate even the house of God by their wickedness.

Every power of personal influence with which God invests a prophet of His, turns into a thronging enticement to evil when that prophet departs from abiding in God. John 15:6 states in the language of Our Lord that lack of fruit means sovereign removal by God. "Wherefore their way shall be unto them as slippery ways in the darkness" (Jeremiah 23:12). The secure places of sanctification and the slippery places are put close together in the Bible. There is no scope to equal the scope of a Christian community for the grossest immorality out of hell. A man or woman who has been right with God and who lets in immorality will end worse than a heathen, there is a genius for doing wrong. "For I will bring evil upon them, . . . saith the LORD" (23:12). The evil does not happen, it is ordered. Abiding in Christ is the only safety.

2. Mighty Power of Spiritual Fellowship *(Jeremiah 23:16–22; cf. Jude 12–13)*

Jeremiah is having revealed to him the corruption of the false prophets of God—"they speak a vision of their own heart, and not out of the mouth of the LORD" (23:16). If the preaching of a servant of God does not make me brace myself up and watch my feet and my ways, one of two things is the reason—either the preacher is unreal, or I hate being better. At some time or other all of us have had a detestation of being better. The rage produced by being faced with a life which in reality is better than our own, awakens either a desire to be like it, or else hatred without cause against that life. "They hated Me without a cause," said Jesus.

These men are—

"without fear." They prophesy continued peace and well-being to the despisers of God. "Ye shall have peace; . . . No evil shall come upon you."

"without water." "For who hath stood in the counsel of the LORD, and hath perceived and heard His word?" Jeremiah implies that none of the prophets have stood in the counsel of the Lord; he himself is there and he knows the Word of the Lord because of the prophetic vision that comes with it. These prophets are not in the counsel of God, there is no "water" (cf. John 7:37–39), no life or liberty or freedom, no lift into the presence of God, because they are not believing in God, they are expounding a theory. "The words that I speak unto you, they are spirit, and they are life." "The words I *speak* . . ."; the devil does the quoting. God makes His Word living by speaking it to you. There is a feeling of deep settled peace when the Holy Ghost brings a word, full of light and illumination, you know better than you can express, "The Lord said that to me." A false worker banks only on the statements of God divorced from communion with God. "God has said that, now stick to it." Never cling to the Word of God in an experience as something separable from God; if you do, the result will be perplexity arising out of a false confidence not rooted in God. The one test is, Am I so abiding in Jesus that every word of His is like the one He did speak? Beware of the obstinacy of belief in a word God spoke once your connection with Him is severed. The obstinacy Jeremiah alludes to is a sensual firmness, "I don't intend to budge." You never find a noble, pure character obstinate; every trace of obstinacy means sensual selfishness somewhere; it is not strength of will, but lack of will.

"without fruit." "I have not sent these prophets, yet they ran." The test that prophets preach from the presence of God is that fruit appears, not in the shape of converts, but in the shape of godly living. "Ye shall know them by their fruits." The test is—How many people stop being mean,[7] being impure, stop committing sin? how many people learn to live rightly? The sign that God is in the word and making it living is the fruit of godliness in the lives of those who speak it and in the lives of their hearers.

The quest of spiritual power while forgetting the uses of such power is an unlighted rock that ends in destruction. Pride submerges itself and becomes piety, but it is just as devilish. Why do I want to be sanctified? Why do I want to understand God's Word? Why do I want to be pure and upright? It is quite possible to covet and put yourself on the quest for high spiritual power and end in "the blackness of darkness." Spiritual power means abiding in the vine until there is nothing but the vine, absolute effacement of myself for Jesus Christ. The false mood will creep in from the submerged part of your life whenever you get the idea that you have to be a written epistle. Of course you have, but you have not to know it! Beware of the idea—"Now I am in God's showroom, I must be careful what to say and do because I am a specimen of His work." The branch knows nothing about the fruit; all the branch knows is that "My Father . . . purgeth it." "I am the Vine," said Jesus, not the root; "I am everything there is; you are the branches."

---

7. The word mean as used here refers to something or someone ordinary, common, low, or ignoble, rather than cruel or spiteful.

FROM THE BIBLE TRAINING COURSE MONTHLY JOURNAL
VOL. 8 SEPTEMBER 1939 No. 6
NOTES ON JEREMIAH

SUBMERGED ROCKS
Jeremiah 23:23–40

I . . . will utterly forget you. Jeremiah 23:39

The greatest perils of the soul are submerged.

1. What the Spirit Speaketh Expressly
(Jeremiah 23:23–27; cf. 1 Timothy 4:1)

We can only detect the express speaking of the Spirit by the same Spirit being in us. We do not naturally rely on the Spirit of God to expound God's word, we use our own intelligence. We think of God as being "somewhere," and we think of the hereafter in terms of space and time. When the Spirit of God expounds the spiritual life He does not deal with locations. "Am I a God at hand, saith the LORD, and not a God afar off?" There is neither "near" nor "far" with God. We have to un-learn our parochial notions about God, viz. the idea that He is interested in our local circumstances; the truth is that God enables us to be interested in Him in our local circumstances.

"I have heard what the prophets have said, that prophesy lies in My name." To "prophesy lies in My name" is to speak a Bible truth about God because it sounds right and then live exactly as if our own common sense were God. All our morality that is not based on a right relationship to God is as "filthy rags" in His sight.

Verse 27—"which think to cause my people to forget My Name . . ."—refers to the fact that the prophets relate their dreams to their fellow-men, not to their fellow-prophets. We hear too much about the "Higher Christian Life,"[8] about entire sanctification, and the baptism of the Holy Ghost; they are experiences wrought by God, to be confessed in His Name. These realities of the soul are closely allied to reticence. Jesus did not say, "everyone who shall *testify of Me*," but, "every one who shall *confess Me* before men . . ." (RV). The glib way in which we rap out our testimony, "Bless God, I am saved and sanctified," is shallow hypocrisy. Watch the one who makes a glowing testimony of Jesus, his speech is chastened into a confession. The confession of what God has done for me is for my own sake, not for the sake of those who listen—"I know that in this matter I have no one to depend upon but God."

2. While "The Spots Sport Expression"
(Jeremiah 23:28–32; cf. 2 Peter 2:13)

A "dream" placed in opposition to "My word," God says, is as "straw" compared with "wheat." The Bible student must be careful to distinguish between the speculations of his own heart and the word of God. The question is not whether we agree with what God's Word says, but, Did God say it? If we agreed with it, we should fathom God. There is a great deal that is obscure in God's Word and it is only revealed as the saint goes on with God.

Verse 29. Jeremiah says that God's word is as fire, and like a hammer that breaks a rock in pieces. There will be nothing left in a man but God's work when He has done with him; He spares not (cf. 1 Corinthians 3:13; Hebrews 4:12).

The practice of these prophets is characterised in three ways: first, stealing the word of God from one another in order to give their utterances the character of Divine oracle, ". . . that steal My words every one from his neighbour" (Jeremiah 23:30)—giving it out as God's message to me; it is not, it is God's word, and the only proof that it is God's message to me is that it is being worked out in my life. Second, they "use their tongues, and say, He saith" (23:31). The reference is to the secret communications of Jehovah. The snare for us to-day is mistaking intense mental effort for inspiration. Speaking in God's Name never fags the speaker. Give the message God gives you and you are re-created. The source of the inspiration is not mental effort, but concentration on God. Third, they feign revelations by means of dreams (23:32). Beware of brooding on the Word of God in a "hot" atmosphere because out of it you will generate a wrong speculation. Be simple and obedient, and the Word of God will open to you as naturally as breathing.

3. And "The Self-Willed Speaketh Evil"
(Jeremiah 23:33–40; cf. 2 Peter 2:14–22)

These terrible words are the New Testament counterpart of what Jeremiah is dealing with in this chapter. ". . . having a heart exercised in covetousness" (2 Peter 2:14 RV). Covetousness means the lust of

---

8. The Higher Christian Life was a concept taught by various groups and organizations that emphasized sanctification and personal holiness.

possessing according to my affinities. In reading God's Word be careful of being guided by affinities instead of by the Holy Spirit. The Holy Spirit makes us face facts for which we have no affinity.

The adversaries of Jeremiah ask in mockery, "What is the burden of the LORD?" (Jeremiah 23:33), and he is told to say that God will avenge the sneer not only on the person, but on his house as well (cf. Matthew 18:6).

Verse 35 is God's instructions to Jeremiah as to how the prophecy is to be spoken of, viz. they are to inquire with reverence, not with ridicule. Why should not other people have revelations from God as well as you? The notion that others are sure to go wrong springs from a wrong disposition. "For ye have perverted the words of the living God" (23:36). Never ridicule the way in which people say God guides them; all you know is that God does not guide you like that, but never ridicule. Never bring in your natural affinities to put you on a superior platform for judging others. God has a thousand ways of guiding, and His way for *you.*

Verse 39 pronounces three terrible results of their mockery—"I will utterly forget you." "I will forsake you." "I will . . . cast you out of My presence."

FROM THE BIBLE TRAINING COURSE MONTHLY JOURNAL
VOL. 8 OCTOBER 1939 NO. 7
NOTES ON JEREMIAH

WHAT WORTH TO GOD?
Jeremiah 24

What seest thou, Jeremiah? Jeremiah 24:3

The estimate a Christian must hold of his own value is what he is worth to God. You cannot judge whether you are right with God by His blessings because "He maketh His sun to rise on the evil and on the good, and sendeth rain on the just and on the unjust." God is not meant to bless us; the vital question is—What am I worth to God? In times of affliction am I giving way to self-pity? am I badgering the throne of God for Him to bless me, or saying "Though He slay me, yet will I wait for Him" (RV)?

1. Prophetic Inward Vision *(Jeremiah 24:1–2)*
"The LORD *shewed me. . . ."*—it was an inward vision, seeing with the eyes of the spirit. In order to understand prophetic language we must have the Spirit which gives the vision, viz. the Spirit of God. The Lord caused Jeremiah to see the vision in the spirit, the place of it is given—"before the temple of the LORD"; and also the time—"after that Nebuchadnezzar king of Babylon had carried away captive Jeconiah . . . to Babylon" (see 2 Kings 24:12).

2. Pictorially Inspired Voice *(Jeremiah 24:2–3)*
The question, "What seest thou, Jeremiah?" is the call for Jeremiah to state clearly to himself what it is he sees. "Behold, two baskets of figs set before the temple of the LORD" (RV)—these symbolise the people as they appear before God. They had been trying to bring wrong things to the altar, and now God is saying He will destroy the evil and wrong out of the nation.

"I beseech you therefore, brethren, by the mercies of God, to present your bodies a living sacrifice, holy, acceptable to God, which is your reasonable service" (Romans 12:1 RV). This verse refers to an abiding law, individually and nationally, viz., we cannot consecrate to God anything that is sinful. We cannot present our bodies "a living sacrifice" to God unless we have been cleansed from sin; He won't have them. The call in this verse is not for sanctification, but for the service of the sanctified. We can never begin to be of worth to God in service until we have been through what is represented in the atoning sacrifice of Our Lord Jesus Christ. That is why the majority of us are of no worth to God. We are of no value to God until we enter into the experience of instantaneous, continuous sanctification, then our "spiritual worship" (RV mg) is the offering of ourselves "a living sacrifice, holy, acceptable to God," and we no more bother about ourselves. God makes the work we do for Him the means of getting us to the place where we are willing to be purified.

3. Interpretation of the Symbol *(Jeremiah 24:4–7)*
"And I will build them, . . . and I will plant them." The "building" and "planting" refer to the spiritual regeneration of the people as well as to restoration to former well-being. "And I will give them an heart to know Me, that I am the LORD: and they shall be My

people, and I will be their God: for they shall return unto Me with their whole heart," so that they may be in truth God's people.

The chastisement of good people comes through their vicarious identification by God with bad people. The prophets Jeremiah and others went into captivity with the people of God. "For whom the Lord loveth He chasteneth." God says, "If you are My children you will stand by and endure the suffering falling on others; remember My eye is upon you, stand true to Me no matter what the providential order of tyranny around you may be."

Many of us are spiritual bastards, we don't endure chastening, we either sulk or we say it is the devil. The time to "follow after peace" (RV) is not when the blessing of God is ostensibly on us, but when the blessing of God is not on us because of the wrongdoing of the crowd we belong to. When the chastisement comes, most of us say, "Well, this is pretty hard lines on me!" Be there in the providence of God as a vicarious sufferer.

FROM THE BIBLE TRAINING COURSE MONTHLY JOURNAL
VOL. 8 NOVEMBER 1939 NO. 8
NOTES ON JEREMIAH

THE DAY OF THE LORD
Jeremiah 25–26

For the LORD hath a controversy with the nations.
Jeremiah 25:31

In the Bible the Day of the LORD is an awful day, a day of the final vindication of goodness and final establishment of righteousness. Judgement is never to be interpreted on the line of personal vindictiveness; from God's standpoint judgement is the grandest fulfilment of His purposes. There is only one triumphant will at the heart of all things, and that will is God's. Every power is under God's control; the devil is *not* behind God (cf. Isaiah 37:29).

1. The Programme of Calamity *(Jeremiah 25:12)*

For "three and twenty years" Jeremiah has been speaking to the people the word of the Lord, "rising up early and speaking; but ye have not hearkened"; and now from news from the outside, they begin to see that what Jeremiah said was true. God's judgements are conditional.

(a) The Breath of Deity (25:1–14; cf. 2 Peter 1:21)
The word of the LORD hath come unto me. (25:3)

The prophets were holy *men,* not mechanisms; they were "moved by the Holy Ghost" to say what they did. Each prophet had a distinct characteristic of his own, they were not all "moved" in the same way. We are not meant to be "channels only," we are infinitely more responsible than "channels." Imagination in a prophet is the power to see in the spirit what the Spirit of God wishes him to see.

(b) The Book of Doom (25:15–26)
Take the cup of the wine of this fury at My hand, and cause all the nations, to whom I send thee, to drink it. (25:15)

The figure of a cup is common in Old Testament prophecy and has reference to the Divine chastisement about to be inflicted (cf. Isaiah 51:17–22; Ezekiel 23:31–33; Habakkuk 2:16). Jeremiah 25:16 refers not only to the figure but to its actual fulfilment—"And they shall drink, . . . and be mad, because of the sword that I will send among them." War with its horrors so stupefies the people that they are helpless. In the Bible war is always a judgement of God on His own people. Jeremiah performs the duty commanded by the Lord—"Then took I the cup at the LORD's hand, and made all the nations to drink." Then comes the list of the nations on which the judgement is to fall, beginning with Jerusalem. After all the kings on whom the king of Babylon is to execute judgement have been mentioned, he himself must drink the cup of wrath (25:26).

2. The Prophet and the Peril *(Jeremiah 26)*

Jeremiah continually warned the people that if they did not repent and come up to God's standard for them, He would blight all that they possessed, including Jerusalem and the temple. That was what enraged them against Jeremiah. They said he used his prophetic right to tell an untruth; for, they argued, God would never destroy His own holy city or the Temple in which He was worshipped (26:11). Any position before God based on a foundation other than living in the light of God and depending upon Him, is doomed to destruction. Take it personally, unless we keep in the light with God there is no guarantee that He will not leave us. How much do we depend on God and how much on our surroundings? We continually ask the question, "Hath any of the rulers believed on Him?" (RV) until we see the Lord for ourselves, then we have strength to go "without the camp, bearing His reproach."

Verses 1–2 reveal the underlying secret of Jeremiah—he was under the command of God. "Thus saith the LORD; stand . . . and speak . . . all the words that I command thee . .; keep not back a word" (RV).

Verses 3–11 reveal the prophet's undeflected obedience. "When Jeremiah had made an end of speaking all that the LORD had commanded him . . . , the people laid hold on him, saying, Thou shalt surely die" (RV).

Verses 12–24 reveal the undeterred courage of the prophet in standing for God—there was no defiance about Jeremiah, only superb self-effacement.

Our Lord said, "If My kingdom were of this world, then would My servants fight." There was no "fight" in Jesus, neither is there to be any in His servants; His courage was superbly moral. The same is true of Jeremiah.

FROM THE BIBLE TRAINING COURSE MONTHLY JOURNAL
VOL. 8 DECEMBER 1939 NO. 9
NOTES ON JEREMIAH

THE BURDEN OF THE YOKE
Jeremiah 27

Make thee bonds and yokes, and put them upon thy neck. Jeremiah 27:2

"In the beginning of the reign of Jehoiakim . . . came this word unto Jeremiah from the LORD." It was a supernatural command, not a sensational speculation on the prophet's part. It is perilously easy in this present dispensation to receive the inspiration of the Holy Ghost and yet not be true to God. There is an optimism born not of the Holy Ghost but of man's fancies, whereby he deals with the future and refuses to live a spotlessly holy life in the present. The servants of God are faithful overcomers in the present circumstances, no matter what forces of evil may be abroad. Our Lord always uncovered the controlling disposition of men (cf. Matthew 23:25–27); the true prophets of God did the same, and so do the saints to-day.

God does not act according to His own precedents, therefore logic or a vivid past experience can never take the place of personal faith in a personal God. It is easier to be true to a conviction formed in a vivid religious experience and say, "I will never alter that," than to be true to Christ, because if I am true to Christ, my convictions will have to be altered. Unless the personal experience leads to a life, it will turn us into fossils, instead of being "witnesses unto Me." Some of us are no good unless we are kept in the circumstances in which our convictions were formed, but God is constantly stirring up our nests that we may learn that the only simplicity there is is not the simplicity of a logical belief, but "the simplicity that is in Christ," the maintained simplicity of a relationship with Christ that is never altered in any circumstance.

There is no evidence of immediate opposition to Jeremiah for the simple reason that moral power is greater than physical force; Jeremiah's moral integrity paralysed the people's action. When opposition does strike the servant of God, it is by God's permissive will. As long as men count themselves Christians on any other ground than that they are free from themselves and the identified bond slaves of Jesus Christ, so long will they despitefully use the servants of God.

Jeremiah entered into identification with the judgement of God on the crowd; we separate ourselves from the crowd, what we should separate ourselves from is the wrong disposition of heart. If we bear the yoke of Christ we shall render the power of wrong impotent by living under it in the power of right. The moral power of the Spirit of God is "mighty through God to the pulling down of strong holds"; it works not like leaven, but like dynamite.

The Spirit of God teaches us to bear the yoke of Christ even under the yoke of a tyrant. "Take My yoke upon you, and learn of Me; for I am meek and lowly in heart: and ye shall find rest unto your souls" (Matthew 11:29; cf. Philippians 4:3; 1 Timothy 6:1; Acts 15:10). Wear the yoke of Christ under every other yoke.

FROM THE BIBLE TRAINING COURSE MONTHLY JOURNAL
VOL. 8 JANUARY 1940 NO. 10
NOTES ON JEREMIAH

SEALED ORDERS
Jeremiah 28

And the prophet Jeremiah went his way. Jeremiah 28:11

Sealed orders, from Abraham on, are always a sign from God. Abraham "went out, not knowing whither he went." God does not act according to His own precedents, therefore logic, or a vivid past experience, can never take the place of personal faith in a personal God. Never try to explain God until you have obeyed Him, and never accept an explanation of any way of God which involves what, in your best mood, you would scorn as false and unfair in a man. The only bit of God we understand is the bit we have obeyed. To the intellect it is absurd to call God loving and just, but immediately you obey God you begin to discern that God is a God of absolute love and justice. The discernment is a satisfaction not to your intellect but to your *life*. Never be surprised if there are whole areas of thinking that are not clear, they never will be until you obey (John 7:17).

Jeremiah's words "Amen: The LORD do so" (28:6) are not ironical. Jeremiah was without the lust for self-vindication, he would gladly have been led to see that his prophecy of calamity was wrong. The Apostle Paul exhibits the same marvellous self-effacement as Jeremiah (see Romans 9:3).

We never gain any knowledge by intellectual curiosity, but only as a relationship of simplicity to God is it maintained. In John 9 Our Lord was dealing with religious teachers who had known God's way in the past but they were blind to His ways in the present. Jesus said unto them, "If ye were blind, ye should have no sin: but now ye say, We see; therefore your sin remaineth" (John 9:41). Our Lord's phrase "blind leaders of the blind" was used of those who built their teaching as to how God would act in the future on their knowledge of how He had acted in the past, instead of on a personal knowledge of God. Never come to this conclusion—I am not likely to go wrong, but you are and I must warn you. The duty of every

Christian (and it is the last lesson we learn) is to make room for God to deal with other people direct as He deals with us; we will limit them and try to make everyone in our mould. We have to keep in unbroken touch with God and give every soul the same freedom and liberty before God as God gives us.

"Nevertheless hear thou now this word that I speak in thine ears, and in the ears of all the people" (Jeremiah 28:7). Hananiah would not listen to God's "darkness" (see Jeremiah 28:10–11). Darkness is the time to listen. No silence is so profound as the silence that falls on a soul that has quenched the Spirit of God by concentration on religious convictions. Many a Christian worker who began as a blazing fire for God has become extinguished because he would not walk in the light of the Lord. "Lest that by any means . . . I myself should be a castaway." If the mighty Apostle spake words like these, it behoves us to remember that it is possible for any one of us to be cast away as a servant of God. Our only safety is in concentration on God with nothing between.

When the call of God first comes it is not devotion to God that appeals to us, but the sense of the heroic, it thrills us to give up everything for Jesus. Then when we are led into the wilderness alone, we learn how rarely we live in the light of honesty before God. We talk too much about heroism because the majority of us are only barely honest. There is only one heroic Figure, the Lord Jesus Christ. We take the pattern and print of the crowd we have been brought up with and persuade ourselves that we are there. We have to get out of the complacency of superiority that is apt to come when the grace of God has done anything for us; the most the grace of God succeeds in doing for us is to make us honest. There is only one holiness, the holiness of God, and unless that holiness is imparted to us by direct identification, we are not even honest.

FROM THE BIBLE TRAINING COURSE MONTHLY JOURNAL
VOL. 8 FEBRUARY 1940 NO. 11
NOTES ON JEREMIAH

OTHERWORLDLINESS IN THIS WORLD
Jeremiah 29:1–14

For I know the thoughts that I think toward you, saith the LORD. Jeremiah 29:11

When we are worldlings we are tempted to be spiritual, and in devotional surroundings we are tempted to be worldly. It is the relationship on the inside that produces goodness, not external surroundings. God never safeguards from without, He garrisons from within. Unless this principle is understood, we shall build on a wrong foundation.

1. Divine Order of Degradation *(Jeremiah 29:4; cf. 1 Thessalonians 1:10)*

"*. . . whom I have caused to be carried away captive from Jerusalem unto Babylon*" *(RV)*. The great message of the prophets is that evil and tyranny are there by the permissive will of God, there is never any room for thinking that these things happen by chance (cf. Isaiah 45:7). Never tie God up in His own laws; He is never guided by precedence. If a prophet is more concerned with logic than with loyalty to God, he will always mislead.

"and to wait for His Son from heaven." In the early days of Christianity, as well as in our own day, the providential order of tyranny was a most significant thing, and the great word of the Apostle Paul was to endure it with patience. Some people are so impatient and full of criticism of the present order of things that they tell us Jesus Christ is coming again at once; others are cynical and say, "Where is the promise of His coming?" We have no control whatever over external history; God has, and as saints we have to wait in patience wherever we are placed in the providential order of tyranny.

2. Devoted Obedience in Dust *(Jeremiah 29:5–7; cf. 1 Thessalonians 4:10–11)*

"*Build ye houses, and dwell in them; . . . And seek the peace of the city whither I have caused you to be carried away captive,*" Jeremiah commands the people to obey God's order in the dust and dirt of captivity. When we become rightly related to God we are loosened from everything around us, and the danger is to imagine we have to get out of the world. Our Lord did not pray that His disciples should be taken out of the world, but that they should be kept from the evil. It is nothing but unmitigated cowardice to get out of the world; we have to remain unspotted in the midst of it. "Do you mean to tell me I can live a holy life *there?*" If you cannot, the grace of God is a fiction. External surroundings make no difference to our inner life, but our inner life makes a telling difference on our surroundings. (See Philippians 2:15). A sunbeam may shine in a hovel, but it can never be soiled. Let God engineer your circumstances where He likes, and you will be kept as the light.

3. Declaration of Divine Plans *(Jeremiah 29:8–11; cf. 1 Thessalonians 5:3)*

Jeremiah warns the people against listening to prophets who prophesy falsely—"I have not sent them, saith the LORD." Our problem is not one of proportion: how much worldliness can I live in? but of spiritual insight which will enable me to live a holy life in the midst of worldliness, looking for the fulfilment of God's promises. The man who builds a temple on the slopes of a mountain is a fool; the only thing that is not out of place on a mountain is a cottage, because it does not ape the mountain. With the great towering world all around them God's children are as cottages tucked away in safety, and the word of Our Lord comes, "Be of good cheer; I have overcome the world." The great craze to-day is work: God's word is "wait." Patience means standing under and enduring until the strain is past. The Spirit of God never adopts the tactics of the world. Remain uncrushably true to Jesus Christ wherever the providential order of God places you.

FROM THE BIBLE TRAINING COURSE MONTHLY JOURNAL
VOL. 8 MARCH 1940 NO. 12
NOTES ON JEREMIAH

HOW LONG?
Jeremiah 29:15–32

I know, and am a witness, saith the LORD. *Jeremiah 29:23*

God is bound to destroy sin. Suffering is not the opposite of sin: good is the opposite of sin. Evil is eternally evil, and suffering can never atone for it. Sorrow and confession and self-abasement alone will make up for the evil. Never apologise for God.

1. The Outlook Is the Background of Life
(Jeremiah 29:15–20; 2 Peter 2:15)
The background of personal and of national life determines its outlook. The false prophets had as the background of their life the idea that they were the people of God and He would never punish them.

Verses 15–16. This is the opportunism of temperament, i.e., serving the times in which we live according to our particular temperament and prejudices, upholding those views which are expedient. This danger besets every one of us—"It is expedient not to say certain things"; "preserve your cause by diplomacy." Beware of coming under the curse of Meroz, who came not "to the help of the LORD against the mighty," by judging it expedient to do nothing. We prefer to quote Gamaliel rather than Paul. Gamaliel's advice is not the advice for a Christian; "Who is made to stumble, and I burn not?" (RV) is the Christian attitude.

Verses 17–18. God will make the false prophets a thing to shudder at. The reaction on the sinner of God's destruction of his sin is the realisation of its hideousness; all his complacency goes (cf. Psalm 39:11). Sin must go at all costs. God is ever severe in His handling of His children who will cling to sin through the pride of heredity. The people of Jeremiah's day refused to see this, they did not think God would punish them, and God had to lay His hand upon them until the last possible strand of sin was destroyed.

Verses 19–20. Beware of being misled by affinities for certain aspects of God's truth, it always makes us liable to be deluded. Every movement of the Spirit of God springs from the same source, and the counterfeit is to try and make the effect of one revival the cause of another. To exploit God's word by curiosity instead of relying on the Spirit of God is ever misleading; obedience is the only line of illumination. If you pry into truths before God has engineered the circumstances in which those truths can be obeyed, you will go wrong. A clever exposition is never right, because the Spirit of God is not clever (cf. Matthew 11:25).

2. The Overlook Is the Backing of Life
(Jeremiah 29:21–23; 2 Peter 2:17–22)
. . . which prophesy a lie unto you in My name.

What is overlooked in the programme of a life is at once the measure of its strength and its weakness. These prophets overlooked the fact that Jeremiah was the prophet of God. There were true prophets, but these verses refer to the false ones, and God says that they are growing worse. When God takes His hand off a bad man, He lets the devil do his worst.

2 Peter 2:17–22. These terrible words, rugged and shocking in their intensity, refer to the abiding peril of an official man of God who is not proving himself God's man; he will end in worse corruption than the man who has not an official position. The peril begins whenever I take this attitude—"Remember who I am." There is only one safety, a life hid with Christ. The great need is to be God's servant, not merely His instrument (Matthew 7:21).

3. The Oversight of the Blessed Life
(Jeremiah 29:24–32; 2 Peter 3:11)
That God guards His own is true of the least and the greatest of His children (Matthew 18:6). Jeremiah's life and character is a proof of this. Jeremiah stood fearlessly for God; a servant of God must be unbribed. Neither a prophet nor a poet can be paid for their work; if they are, they become time-servers, and the community to which they belong ought to have the right to turn them out. The prophets in Babylon were doing their best to keep up the heart of the people, and one can understand their indignation with Jeremiah's prophecy. He is told to tell the prophet Shemaiah that he shall not share in the blessing which the Lord will yet bestow upon His people—"because he hath taught rebellion against the LORD."

But how many there are among our ministers, and how many there will be, eager on all questions of the day, frank and friendly and fearless, active and kind, but with very little about them that suggests the powers of the world to come. They die and are mourned, but their places are soon filled and they are forgotten. But men return again and again to the few who have mastered the spiritual secret, whose life has been hid with Christ in God. These are of the same religion, whatever differences there may be in their theology, they are of the old time religion hung to the nails of the Cross.

Robert Murray McCheyne[9]

---

9. Robert Murray McCheyne (1813–1843) was a Scottish minister whose short but intense life left a great impact on Scotland.

Studies in the Sermon on the Mount

Oswald Chambers

INTRODUCTION

Source

Oswald Chambers' talks on the Sermon on the Mount were given at the League of Prayer's[1] annual summer convention in Perth, Scotland, in July 1911; in lectures at the Bible Training College[2] from 1911 to 1915; and in talks to soldiers in Egypt in 1916.

Publication History

- As a study outline: Material on Matthew 5–7 was published in the autumn of 1912, for the fourth session of Oswald Chambers' Bible School correspondence classes—part of his outreach to people who wanted to study the Bible but could not attend the Bible Training College in London.
- As articles: The lectures were published as articles in the July 11 through December 12, 1912, issues of *God's Revivalist* and *Bible Advocate* magazines, in Cincinnati, Ohio.
- As a book: God's Revivalist Press, Cincinnati, Ohio, published *Studies in the Sermon on the Mount* in 1915. In the years after Oswald's death in 1917, Mrs. Chambers continued to revise and republish. A fourth edition was issued in 1929.
- As a booklet: Outlines and summaries of nine talks on Matthew 5–7 were included in the booklet *A Bible Training Course,* published in 1916. An opening note by Oswald Chambers said: "This booklet is comprised of the series of Bible Study subjects taken at Zeitoun, Egypt,[3] with the Australian and New Zealand troops 1916, with marked appreciation."

In July 1911, Oswald and Biddy Chambers journeyed to Perth, Scotland, for the annual summer convention of the League of Prayer. Oswald always enjoyed a visit to Perth, where he had spent his formative boyhood years from ages seven through fifteen.

At the League convention,[4] Oswald spoke at noon for five days (July 17–21) on "God's Making of Christians," from the Sermon on the Mount. Mrs. Chambers took verbatim notes of her husband's messages, as she did on countless occasions during their seven years of marriage. Oswald delivered the same basic material many times, always revised and adapted for each audience.

At a memorial service for Chambers in December 1917, a close friend described Oswald's life as "the finest commentary on the Sermon on the Mount I know."

---

1. The League of Prayer was founded in London by Reader Harris, a friend and mentor of Oswald Chambers, in 1891.

2. The Bible Training College (BTC) was a residential school near Clapham Common in southwest London. It was sponsored by the Pentecostal League of Prayer and operated from 1911 until it closed in July 1915 because of World War I. Oswald Chambers was principal and main teacher; Biddy Chambers, his wife, was lady superintendent.

3. At Zeitoun (zay TOON), six miles northeast of Cairo, was a YMCA camp, the Egypt General Mission compound, and, from 1916 to 1919, the Imperial School of Instruction, a training base for British, Australian, and New Zealand troops during World War I.

4. The Perth Convention was the annual meeting sponsored by the Pentecostal League of Prayer and held in Perth, Scotland.

CONTENTS

FOREWORD

In the Fifth Study the author says—"Jesus tells His disciples to test preachers and teachers by their fruit. There are two tests—one is the fruit in the life of the preacher, and the other is the truth of the doctrine." It is a genuine joy to be able to apply these touchstones of character and teaching to the life and words of Oswald Chambers.

It was the writer's rare privilege to be in the same home with him and to sit under his ministry for a number of months; to see him daily, and to find in him a patient counsellor, an exemplary as well as trustworthy teacher, and a Christ-like friend. The following words are none too vividly descriptive of this modern prophet-teacher:

> *Who never sold the truth to serve the hour,*
> *Nor paltered with eternal God for power,*
> *Who let the turbid stream of rumour flow*
> *Thro' either babbling world high or low;*
> *Whose life is work, whose language rife*
> *With rugged maxims hewn from life,*
> *Who never spoke against a foe.*

And as to the second test proposed—the fruit of the doctrine—will there be found in all the Church of Christ of today one whose records are more weighty with spiritual values? "But," says some simple soul, "I don't understand him." The more is the pity. Leave then the evening newspaper, the book of religious wonder-tales, the high-flown writings watered with adjectives, but empty of thought or power, and read these pages again and again until the truth soaks through to your innermost consciousness. There is about us a flood of profession, but a failure in possession; a torrent of criticism for those who "follow not us," but a trickling rivulet of sound advice to ourselves. To heed the words of our Lord's Sermon on the Mount as interpreted by Oswald Chambers will transform holiness people into holy people, and faithless verbosity into Christian humility. Unto which glorious result God speed the day!

J. F. Knapp[5]
Bible School,
Cincinnati, U. S. A.

---

5. John F. Knapp was the eldest son of Martin Wells Knapp. M. W. Knapp founded God's Bible School in Cincinnati, where Chambers taught from January to July 1907.

Study No. 1

HIS TEACHING AND OUR TRAINING
Matthew 5:1–20

Divine Disproportion (Matthew 5:1–12)
    (a) The "Mines" of God (Matthew 5:1–10;
       cf. Luke 6:20–26)
    (b) The Motive of Godliness (Matthew
       5:11–12)

Divine Disadvantage (Matthew 5:13–16)
    (a) Concentrated Service (Matthew 5:13)
    (b) Conspicuous Setting (Matthew 5:14–16)

Divine Declaration (Matthew 5:17–20)
    (a) His Mission (Matthew 5:17–19)
    (b) His Message (Matthew 5:20)

In order to understand the Sermon on the Mount, it is necessary to have the mind of the Preacher, and this knowledge can be gained by anyone who will receive the Holy Spirit (see Luke 11:13; John 20:22; Acts 19:2). The Holy Ghost alone can expound the teachings of Jesus Christ. The one abiding method of interpretation of the teachings of Jesus is the Spirit of Jesus in the heart of the believer applying His principles to the particular circumstances in which he is placed. "Be ye transformed by the renewing of your mind," says Paul, "that ye may prove", i.e., *make out,* "what is that good, and acceptable, and perfect, will of God.

Beware of placing our Lord as Teacher first instead of Saviour. That tendency is prevalent to-day, and it is a dangerous tendency. We must know Him first as Saviour before His teaching can have any meaning for us, or before it can have any meaning other than that of an ideal which leads to despair. Fancy coming to men and women with defective lives and defiled hearts and wrong mainsprings, and telling them to be pure in heart! What is the use of giving us an ideal we cannot possibly attain? We are happier without it. If Jesus is a Teacher only, then all He can do is to tantalise us by erecting a standard we cannot come anywhere near. But if by being born again from above we know Him first as Saviour, we know that He did not come to teach us only: *He came to make us what He teaches we should be.* The Sermon on the Mount is a statement of the life we will live when the Holy Spirit is having His way with us.

The Sermon on the Mount produces despair in the heart of the natural man, and that is the very thing Jesus means it to do, because immediately we reach the point of despair we are willing to come to Jesus Christ as pau-

pers and receive from Him. "Blessed are the poor in spirit"—that is the first principle of the Kingdom. As long as we have a conceited, self-righteous idea that we can do the thing if God will help us, God has to allow us to go on until we break the neck of our ignorance over some obstacle, then we will be willing to come and receive from Him. The bed-rock of Jesus Christ's Kingdom is poverty, not possession; not decisions for Jesus Christ, but a sense of absolute futility, "I cannot begin to do it." Then, says Jesus, "Blessed are you." That is the entrance, and it takes us a long while to believe we are poor. The knowledge of our own poverty brings us to the moral frontier where Jesus Christ works.

Every mind has two compartments—conscious and subconscious. We say that the things we hear and read slip away from memory; they do not really, they pass into the subconscious mind. It is the work of the Holy Spirit to bring back into the conscious mind the things that are stored in the subconscious. In studying the Bible never think that because you do not understand it, therefore it is of no use. A truth may be of no use to you just now, but when the circumstances arise in which that truth is needed, the Holy Spirit will bring it back to your remembrance. This accounts for the curious emergence of the statements of Jesus; we say, "I wonder where that word came from?" Jesus said that the Holy Spirit would "bring all things to your remembrance, whatsoever I have said unto you." The point is, will I obey Him when He does bring it to my remembrance? If I discuss the matter with someone else the probability is that I will not obey. "Immediately I conferred not with flesh and blood. . . ." Always trust the originality of the Holy Spirit when He brings a word to your remembrance.

Bear in mind the twofold aspect of the mind; there is nothing supernatural or uncanny about it, it is simply the knowledge of how God has made us. It is foolish therefore to estimate only by what you consciously understand at the time. There may be much of which you do not begin to grasp the meaning, but as you go on storing your mind with Bible truth, the Holy Spirit will bring back to your conscious mind the word you need and will apply it to you in your particular circumstances. These three things always work together—moral intelligence, the spontaneous originality of the Holy Spirit and the setting of a life lived in communion with God.

Divine Disproportion *(Matthew 5:1–12)*

Our Lord began His discourse by saying, "Blessed are . . . ," and His hearers must have been staggered by what followed. According to Jesus Christ they were to be blessed in every condition which from earliest childhood they had been taught to regard as a curse. Our Lord was speaking to Jews, and they believed that the sign of the blessing of God was material prosperity in every shape and form, and yet Jesus said, Blessed are you for exactly the opposite: "Blessed are the poor in spirit. . . . Blessed are they that mourn," *et cetera*.

(a) The "Mines" of God *(Matthew 5:1–10; cf. Luke 6:20–26)*

The first time we read the Beatitudes they appear to be simple and beautiful and un-startling statements, and they go unobserved into the subconscious mind. We are so used to the sayings of Jesus that they slip over us unheeded, they sound sweet and pious and wonderfully simple, but they are in reality like spiritual torpedoes that burst and explode in the subconscious mind, and when the Holy Spirit brings them back to our conscious minds we realise what startling statements they are. For instance, the Beatitudes seem merely mild and beautiful precepts for unworldly people and of very little use for the stern world in which we live. We soon find, however, that they contain the dynamite of the Holy Ghost, they explode like a spiritual "mine" when the circumstances of our lives require them to do so, and rip and tear and revolutionise all our conceptions.

The test of discipleship is obedience to the light when these truths are brought to the conscious mind. We do not hunt through the Bible for some precept to obey—Jesus Christ's teaching never leads to making ourselves moral prigs, but we live so in touch with God that the Holy Spirit can continually bring some word of His and apply it to the circumstances we are in. We are not brought to the test until the Holy Spirit brings the word back.

Neither is it a question of applying the Beatitudes literally, but of allowing the life of God to invade us by regeneration, and then soaking our minds in the teaching of Jesus Christ which slips down into the subconscious mind. By and by a set of circumstances will arise when one of Jesus Christ's statements emerges, and instantly we have to decide whether we will accept the tremendous spiritual revolution that will be produced if we do obey this precept of His. If we do obey it, our actual life will become different, and we shall find we have the power to obey if we will. That is the way the Holy Spirit works in the heart of a disciple. The teaching of Jesus Christ comes with astonishing discomfort to begin with, because it is out of all proportion to our natural way of looking at things; but Jesus puts in a new sense of proportion, and slowly we form our way of walking and our conversation on the line of His precepts: Remember that our Lord's teaching applies only to those who are His disciples.

(b) The Motive of Godliness *(Matthew 5:11–12)*

The motive at the back of the precepts of the Sermon on the Mount is love of God. Read the Beatitudes with your mind fixed on God, and you will realise their neglected side. Their meaning in relationship to men is so obvious that it scarcely needs stating, but the Godward aspect is not so obvious. "Blessed are the poor in spirit"—towards God. Am I a pauper towards God? Do I know I cannot prevail in prayer; I cannot blot out the sins of the past; I cannot alter my disposition; I cannot lift myself nearer to God? Then I am in the very place where I am able to receive the Holy Spirit. No man can receive the Holy Spirit who is not convinced he is a pauper spiritually. "Blessed are the meek"—towards God's dispensations. "Blessed are the merciful"—to God's reputation. Do I awaken sympathy for myself when I am in trouble? Then I am slandering God because the reflex thought in people's minds is—How hard God is with that man. It is easy to slander God's character because He never attempts to vindicate Himself. "Blessed are the pure in heart"—that is obviously Godward. "Blessed are the peacemakers"—between God and man, the note that was struck at the birth of Jesus.

Is it possible to carry out the Beatitudes? Never! Unless God can do what Jesus Christ says He can, unless He can give us the Holy Spirit Who will remake us and bear us into a new realm. The essential element in the life of a saint is simplicity, and Jesus Christ makes the motive of godliness gloriously simple, viz., Be carefully careless about everything saving your relationship to Me. The motive of a disciple is to be well-pleasing to God. The true blessedness of the saint is in determinedly making and keeping God first. Herein lies the disproportion between Jesus Christ's principles and all other moral teaching: Jesus bases everything on God-realisation, while other teachers base everything on self-realisation.

There is a difference between devotion to principles and devotion to a person. Jesus Christ never proclaimed a cause; He proclaimed personal devotion to Himself—*"for My sake."* Discipleship is based not on devotion to abstract ideals, but on devotion to a Person, the Lord Jesus Christ, consequently the whole of the Christian life is stamped by originality. Whenever the Holy Spirit sees a chance to glorify Jesus Christ, He will take your whole personality and simply make it blaze and glow with personal passionate devotion to the Lord Jesus. You are no longer devoted to a cause, nor the devotee of a principle, you are the devoted love-slave of the Lord Jesus. No man on earth has that love unless the Holy Ghost has imparted it to him. Men may admire Him and respect Him and reverence Him, but no man can *love* God until the Holy Ghost has shed abroad that love in his heart (see Romans 5:5). The only Lover of the Lord Jesus Christ is the Holy Ghost.

> *Blessed are ye, when men shall revile you, and persecute you, and shall say all manner of evil against you falsely, for My sake.*

Jesus Christ puts all the blessedness of high virtue and rare felicity on the ground of—"for My sake," It is not suffering for conscience' sake, or for convictions' sake, or because of the ordinary troubles of life, but something other than all that—*"for My sake."*

"Blessed are ye, when men shall hate you, and when they shall separate you from their company, and shall reproach you, and cast out your name as evil, for the Son of Man's sake." Jesus did not say—"Rejoice when men separate you from their company because of your own crotchety notions"—but when they reproach you *"for My sake."* When you begin to deport yourself amongst men as a saint, they will leave you absolutely alone, you will be reviled and persecuted. No man can stand that unless he is in love with Jesus Christ; he cannot do it for a conviction or a creed, but he can do it for a Being Whom he loves. Devotion to a Person is the only thing that tells; devotion to death to a Person, not devotion to a creed or a doctrine.

> *Who that one moment has the least descried Him,*
> *Dimly and faintly, hidden and afar,*
> *Doth not despise all excellence beside Him,*
> *Pleasures and powers that are not and that are:—*
>
> *Ay, amid all men bear himself thereafter*
> *Smit with a solemn and a sweet surprise,*
> *Dumb to their scorn and turning on their laughter*
> *Only the dominance of earnest eyes.*

Divine Disadvantage *(Matthew 5:13–16)*

The disadvantage of a saint in the present order of things is that his confession of Jesus Christ is not to be in secret, but glaringly public. It would doubtless be to our advantage from the standpoint of self-realisation to keep quiet, and nowadays the tendency to say—"Be a Christian, live a holy life, but don't talk about it"—is growing stronger. Our Lord uses in illustration the most conspicuous things known to men, viz., salt, light, and a city set on a hill, and He says—"Be like that in your home, in your business, in your church; be conspicuously a Christian for ridicule or respect according to the mood of the people you are with." Again, in Matthew 10:26–28, our Lord

taught the need to be conspicuous proclaimers of the truth and not to cover it up for fear of wolfish men.

(a) Concentrated Service *(Matthew 5:13)*

Not *consecrated* service, but *concentrated*. Consecration would soon be changed into sanctification if we would only concentrate on what God wants. Concentration means pinning down the four corners of the mind until it is settled on what God wants. The literal interpretation of the Sermon on the Mount is child's play; the interpretation by the Holy Spirit is the stern work of a saint, and it requires spiritual concentration.

"Ye are the salt of the earth." Some modern teachers seem to think our Lord said "Ye are the *sugar* of the earth," meaning that gentleness and winsomeness without curative-ness is the ideal of the Christian. Our Lord's illustration of a Christian is salt, and salt is the most concentrated thing known. Salt preserves wholesomeness and prevents decay. It is a disadvantage to be salt. Think of the action of salt on a wound, and you will realise this. If you get salt into a wound, it hurts, and when God's children are amongst those who are "raw" towards God, their presence hurts. The man who is wrong with God is like an open wound, and when "salt" gets in it causes annoyance and distress and he is spiteful and bitter. The disciples of Jesus in the present dispensation preserve society from corruption; the "salt" causes excessive irritation which spells persecution for the saint.

How are we to maintain the healthy, salty tang of saintliness? By remaining rightly related to God through Jesus Christ. In the present dispensation, Jesus says, "The kingdom of God cometh not with observation: . . . for, behold, the kingdom of God is within you." Men are called on to live out His teaching in an age that will not recognise Him, and that spells limitation and very often persecution. This is the day of the humiliation of the saints; in the next dispensation it will be the glorification of the saints, and the Kingdom of God will be outside as well as inside men.

(b) Conspicuous Setting *(Matthew 5:14–16)*

The illustrations our Lord uses are all conspicuous, viz., salt, light, and a city set on a hill. There is no possibility of mistaking them. Salt to preserve from corruption has to be placed in the midst of it, and before it can do its work it causes excessive irritation which spells persecution. Light attracts bats and night-moths, and points out the way for burglars as well as honest people: Jesus would have us remember that men will certainly defraud us. A city is a gathering place for all the human drift-wood that will not work for its own living, and a Christian will have any number of parasites and ungrateful hangers-on. All these considerations form a powerful temptation to make us pretend we are not salt, to make us put our light under a bushel, and cover our city with a fog, but Jesus will have nothing in the nature of covert discipleship.

"Ye are the light of the world." Light cannot be soiled; you may try to grasp a beam of light with the sootiest hand, but you leave no mark on the light. A sunbeam may shine into the filthiest hovel in the slums of a city, but it cannot be soiled. A merely moral man, or an innocent man, may be soiled in spite of his integrity, but the man who is made pure by the Holy Ghost cannot be soiled, he is as light. Thank God for the men and women who are spending their lives in the slums of the earth, not as social reformers to lift their brother men to cleaner sties, but as the light of God, revealing a way back to God. God keeps them as the light, unsullied. If you have been covering your light, uncover it! Walk as children of light. The light always reveals and guides; and men dislike it, and prefer darkness when their deeds are evil (John 3:19–20).

Are we the salt of the earth? Are we the light of the world? Are we allowing God to exhibit in our lives the truth of these startling statements of Jesus Christ?

Divine Declaration *(Matthew 5:17–20)*
(a) His Mission *(Matthew 5:17–19)*
I am come . . . to fulfil.

An amazing word! Our shoes ought to be off our feet and every common-sense mood stripped from our minds when we hear Jesus Christ speak. In Him we deal with God as man, the God-Man, the Representative of the whole human race in one Person. The men of His day traced their religious pedigree back to the constitution of God, and this young Nazarene Carpenter says, *"I am the constitution of God"*; consequently to them He was a blasphemer.

Our Lord places Himself as the exact meaning and fulfilment of all Old Testament prophecies. His mission, He says, is to fulfil the law and the prophets, and He further says that any man who breaks the old laws because they belong to a former dispensation, and teaches men to break them, shall suffer severe impoverishment. If the old commandments were difficult, our Lord's principles are unfathomably more difficult. Our Lord goes behind the old law to the disposition. Everything He teaches is impossible unless He can put into us His Spirit and remake us from within. The Sermon on the Mount is quite unlike the Ten Commandments in the sense of its being absolutely unworkable unless Jesus Christ can remake us.

There are teachers who argue that the Sermon on the Mount supersedes the Ten Commandments, and that, because "we are not under law, but under grace" (RV), it does not matter whether we honour our father and mother, whether we covet, *et cetera*. Beware of statements like this: There is no need nowadays to observe giving the tenth either of money or of time; we are in a new dispensation and everything belongs to God. That, in practical application, is sentimental dust-throwing. The giving of the tenth is not a sign that all belongs to God, but a sign that the tenth belongs to God and the rest is ours, and we are held responsible for what we do with it. To be "not under the law, but under grace" does not mean that we can do as we like. It is surprising how easily we can juggle ourselves out of Jesus Christ's principles by one or two pious sayings repeated sufficiently often. The only safeguard is to keep personally related to God. The secret of all spiritual understanding is to walk in the light, not the light of our convictions, or of our theories, but the light of God (1 John 1:7).

(b) His Message *(Matthew 5:20)*
Think of the most upright man you know, the most moral, sterling, religious man (e.g., Nicodemus was a Pharisee, so was Saul of Tarsus—"blameless" according to the law)—who has never received the Holy Spirit; Jesus says you must exceed him in righteousness. You have to be not only as moral as the most moral man you know, but infinitely more—to be so right in your actions, so pure in your motives, that God Almighty can see nothing to blame in you.

Is it too strong to call this a spiritual torpedo? These statements of Jesus are the most revolutionary statements human ears ever listened to, and it needs the Holy Ghost to interpret them to us; the shallow admiration for Jesus Christ as a Teacher that is taught to-day is of no use.

Who is going to climb that "hill of the LORD"? To stand before God and say—"My hands are clean, my heart is pure"? who can do it? Who can stand in the Eternal light of God and have nothing for God to blame in him? Only the Son of God; and if the Son of God is formed in us by regeneration and sanctification, He will exhibit Himself through our mortal flesh. That is the ideal of Christianity—"that the life also of Jesus might be made manifest in our mortal flesh."

Jesus says our disposition must be right to its depths, not only our conscious motives but our unconscious motives. Now we are beyond our depth. Can God make me pure in heart? Blessed be the Name of God, He can! Can He alter my disposition so that when circumstances reveal me to myself, I am amazed? He can. Can He impart His nature to me until it is identically the same as His own? He can. That, and nothing less, is the meaning of His Cross and Resurrection.

"Except your righteousness shall *exceed. . . .*" The righteousness of the scribes and Pharisees was right, not wrong; that they did other than righteousness is obvious, but Jesus is speaking here of their *righteousness*, which His disciples are to exceed. What exceeds right doing if it be not right being? Right being without right doing is possible if we refuse to enter into relationship with God, but that cannot "exceed the righteousness of the scribes and Pharisees." Jesus Christ's message here is that our righteousness must *"exceed* the righteousness of the scribes and Pharisees" in *doing*—they were nothing in *being*—or we shall never enter into the kingdom of heaven. The monks in the Middle Ages refused to take the responsibilities of life and they shut themselves away from the world; all they wanted was to *be* and not *do*. People to-day want to do the same thing and they cut themselves off from this and that relationship. That does not exceed the righteousness of the scribes and Phar-

isees. If our Lord had meant exceed in *being* only, He would not have used the word "exceed"; He would have said—"Except your righteousness *be otherwise than* . . . " We cannot exceed the righteousness of the most moral man we know on the line of what he *does*, but only on the line of what he *is*.

The teaching of the Sermon on the Mount must produce despair in the natural man; if it does not, it is because he has paid no attention to it. Pay attention to Jesus Christ's teaching and you will soon say, "Who is sufficient for these things?" *"Blessed are the pure in heart."* If Jesus Christ means what He says, where are we in regard to it? "Come unto Me," says Jesus.

Study No. 2
ACTUAL AND REAL
Matthew 5:21–42

The Account with Purity (Matthew 5:21–30)
  (a) Disposition and Deeds (Matthew 5:21–22)
  (b) Temper of Mind and Truth of Manner (Matthew 5:23–26)
  (c) Lust and License (Matthew 5:27–28)
  (d) Direction of Discipline (Matthew 5:29–30)

The Account with Practice (Matthew 5:31–37)
  (a) Speech and Sincerity (Matthew 5:33)
  (b) Irreverent Reverence (Matthew 5:34–36)
  (c) Integrity (Matthew 5:37)

The Account with Persecution (Matthew 5:38–42)
  (a) Insult (Matthew 5:38–39)
  (b) Extortion (Matthew 5:40)
  (c) Tyranny (Matthew 5:41–42)

A man cannot take in anything he has not begun to think about, consequently until a man is born again what Jesus says does not mean anything to him. The Bible is a universe of revelation facts which have no meaning for us until we are born from above; when we are born again we see in it what we never saw before. We are lifted into the realm where Jesus lives and we begin to see what He sees (John 3:3).

By Actual is meant the things we come in contact with by our senses, and by Real that which lies behind, that which we cannot get at by our senses (cf. 2 Corinthians 4:18). The fanatic sees the real only and ignores the actual; the materialist looks at the actual only and ignores the real. The only sane Being who ever trod this earth was Jesus Christ, because in Him the actual and the real were one. Jesus Christ does not

stand first in the actual world, He stands first in the real world; that is why the natural man does not bother his head about Him—"the natural man receiveth not the things of the Spirit of God: for they are foolishness unto him." When we are born from above we begin to see the actual things in the light of the real. We say that prayer alters things, but prayer does not alter actual things nearly so much as it alters the man who sees the actual things. In the Sermon on the Mount our Lord brings the actual and the real together.

The Account with Purity *(Matthew 5:21–30)*
Our Lord in these verses is laying down the principle that if men are going to follow Him and obey His Spirit, they must lay their account with purity. No man can make himself pure by obeying laws. Purity is not a question of doing things rightly, but of the doer on the inside being right. Purity is difficult to define; it is best thought of as a state of heart just like the heart of our Lord Jesus Christ. Purity is not innocence; innocence is the characteristic of a child, and although, profoundly speaking, a child is not pure, yet his innocence presents us with all that we understand by purity. Innocence in a child's life is a beautiful thing, but men and women ought not to be innocent, they ought to be tested and tried and pure. No man is born pure: purity is the outcome of conflict. The pure man is not the man who has never been tried, but the man who knows what evil is and has overcome it. And so with virtue and morality, no one is born virtuous and moral, we are born unmoral. Morality is always the outcome of conflict, not of necessity. Jesus Christ

demands that purity be explicit as well as implicit—that is, my actual conduct, the actual chastity of my bodily life, the actual chastity of my mind, is to be beyond the censure of Almighty God—not beyond the censure of my fellow men, that would produce Pharisaism, I can always deceive the other fellow. Jesus Christ has undertaken by His Redemption to put in me a heart that is so pure that God can see nothing to censure in it. That is the marvel of the Redemption—that Jesus Christ can give me a new heredity, the unsullied heredity of the Holy Spirit, and if it is there, says Jesus, it will work out in actual history.

In Matthew 15, our Lord tells His disciples what the human heart is like—"Out of the heart proceed. . . ." and then follows the ugly catalogue. We say, "I never felt any of those things in my heart," and we prefer to trust our innocent ignorance rather than Jesus Christ's penetration. Either Jesus Christ must be the supreme Authority on the human heart, or He is not worth listening to. If I make conscious innocence the test, I am likely to come to a place where I will find with a shuddering awakening that what Jesus said is true, and I will be appalled at the possibility of evil in me. If I have never been a blackguard, the reason is a mixture of cowardice and the protection of civilised life; but when I am undressed before God I find that Jesus Christ is right in His diagnosis. As long as I remain under the refuge of innocence, I am living in a fool's paradise. There is always a reason to be found in myself when I try to disprove what Jesus says.

Jesus Christ demands that the heart of a disciple be fathomlessly pure, and unless He can give me His disposition, His teaching is tantalising. If all He came to do was to mock me by telling me to be what I know I never can be, I can afford to ignore Him, but if He can give me His own disposition of holiness, then I begin to see how I can lay my account with purity. Jesus Christ is the sternest and the gentlest of Saviours.

The Gospel of God is not that Jesus died for my sins only, but that He gave Himself for me that I might give myself to Him. God cannot accept goodness from me. He can only accept my badness, and He will give me the solid goodness of the Lord Jesus in exchange for it (see 2 Corinthians 5:21).

(a) Disposition and Deeds (Matthew 5:21–22)
Our Lord is using an illustration that was familiar to the disciples. If a man disregarded the common judgement, he was in danger of being brought into an inner court, and if he was contemptuous with that court, he was in danger of the final judgement. Jesus uses this illustration of the ordinary exercise of judgement to show what the disposition of a disciple must be like, viz., that my motive, the place I cannot get at myself, must be right—the disposition behind the

deed, the motive behind the actual occurrence. I may never be angry in deed, but Jesus Christ demands the impossibility of anger in disposition. The motive of my motives, the spring of my dreams, must be so right that right deeds will follow naturally.

In Psalm 139 the Psalmist is realising that he is too big for himself, and he prays "O Lord, explore me, search me out, and see if there be any way of grief in me, trace out the dreams of my dreams, the motives of my motives, make these right, and lead me in the way everlasting." Deliverance from sin is not deliverance from conscious sin only, it is deliverance from sin in God's sight, and He can see down into a region I know nothing about. By the marvellous Atonement of Jesus Christ applied to me by the Holy Spirit, God can purify the springs of my unconscious life until the temper of my mind is unblameable in His sight.

Beware of refining away the radical aspect of our Lord's teaching by saying that God puts something in to counteract the wrong disposition—that is a compromise. Jesus never teaches us to curb and suppress the wrong disposition; He gives us a totally new disposition, He alters the mainspring of action. Our Lord's teaching can be interpreted only by the new Spirit which He puts in; it can never be taken as a series of rules and regulations.

A man cannot imitate the disposition of Jesus Christ: it is either there, or it is not. When the Son of God is formed in me, He is formed in my human nature, and I have to put on the new man in accordance with His life and obey Him; then His disposition will work out all the time. We make character out of our disposition. Character is what we make, disposition is what we are born with; and when we are born again we are given a new disposition. A man must make his own character, but he cannot make his disposition; that is a gift. Our natural disposition is gifted to us by heredity; by regeneration God gives us the disposition of His Son. Jesus Christ is pure to the depths of His motives, and if His disposition can be formed in me, then I begin to see how I can lay my account with purity. "Marvel not that I said unto thee, ye must be born again." If I let God alter my heredity, I will become devoted to Him, and Jesus Christ will have gained a disciple. Many of us who call ourselves Christians are not devoted to Jesus Christ.

Our Lord goes behind the old law to the disposition. Everything He says is impossible unless He can put His Spirit into me and remake me from within, then I begin to see how it can be done. When a man is born from above, he does not need to pretend to be a saint, he cannot help being one. Am I going to be a spiritually real man or a whitewashed humbug? Am I a pauper in spirit or conceited over my own earnestness? We are so tremendously in earnest that we are blinded by our earnestness and never see that God is more in earnest than we are. Thank God for the absolute poverty of spirit that receives from Him all the time.

There is only one way in which as a disciple you will know that Jesus has altered your disposition, and that is by trying circumstances. When circumstances put you to the test, instead of feeling resentment you experience a most amazing change within, and you say, "Praise God, this is an amazing alteration! I know now that God has altered me, because if that had happened to me before I should have been sour and irritable and sarcastic and spiteful, but now there is a well of sweetness in me which I know never came from myself." The proof that God has altered our disposition is not that we persuade ourselves He has, but that we prove He has when circumstances put us to the test. The criticism of Christians is not wrong, it is absolutely right. When a man says he is born again, he is put under scrutiny, and rightly so. If we are born again of the Holy Ghost and have the life of Jesus in us by means of His Cross, we must show it in the way we walk and talk and transact all our business.

(b) Temper of Mind and Truth of Manner (Matthew 5:23–26)

Our Lord in these verses uses another illustration familiar in His day. If a man taking a paschal lamb to the priest as an offering, remembered he had leaven in his house, he had to go back and take out the leaven before he brought his offering. We do not carry lambs to sacrifice nowadays, but the spiritual meaning of the illustration is tremendous, it emphasises the difference between reality and sincerity.

"If when you come to the altar," says Jesus, "there you remember your brother has ought against you, don't say another word to Me, but go and be reconciled to your brother, and then come and offer your gift." Jesus does not mention the other person, He says "*You* go." He does not say, "Go half-way," but "first *go*." There is no question of your rights.

Talk about practical home-coming truth! This hits us where we live. A man cannot stand as a humbug before Jesus Christ for one second. The Holy Spirit makes us sensitive to things we never thought of before. Never object to the intense sensitiveness of the Holy Spirit in you when He is educating you down to the scruple;[6] and never discard a conviction. If it is important enough for the Holy Spirit to have brought it to your mind, that is the thing He is detecting.

The test Jesus gives is not the truth of our manner but the temper of our mind. Many of us are wonderfully truthful in manner but our temper of mind is rotten in God's sight. The thing Jesus alters is the temper of mind.

Jesus says, "If when you come to the altar, there you remember"—not, "there you rake up something by a morbid sensitiveness," (that is where Satan gets hold of embryo Christians and makes them hyper-conscientious), but "there rememberest that thy brother hath ought against thee"; the inference is that the Holy Spirit brings it to your memory, never check it, say "Yes, Lord, I recognise it" and obey Him at once, however humiliating it may be.

It is impossible to do this unless God has altered your temper of mind; but if you are a saint you will find you have no difficulty in doing what otherwise would be an impossible humiliation. The disposition which will not allow the Son of God to rule is the disposition of my claim to my right to myself; that, and not immorality, is the essence of sin: "I will exercise my right to myself in this particular matter," but if my disposition has been altered, I will obey Jesus at all costs.

Watch the thing that makes you snort morally. If you have not had the temper of your mind altered by Jesus Christ, then the Holy Spirit brings something to your remembrance to be put right you will say, "No, indeed, I am not going to make that up when I was in the right and they were in the wrong; they will say, "We knew we would make you say you were sorry!" Unless you are willing to yield your right to yourself on that point absolutely, you need not pray any more, there is a barrier higher than Calvary between you and God. That is the temper of mind in us all until it has been altered. When it has been altered, the other temper of mind is there that makes reconciliation as natural as breathing, and to our astonishment we find we can do what we could not do before. The instant you obey, you find the temper of your mind is real. Jesus Christ makes us real, not merely sincere. The people who are sincere without being real are not hypocrites, they are perfectly earnest and honest, and desirous of fulfilling what Jesus wants, but they really cannot do it, the reason being that they have not received the One Who makes them real, viz., the Holy Spirit.

Jesus Christ brings men to the practical test. It is not that I say I am pure in heart, but that I prove I am by my deeds; I am sincere not only in manner but in the attitude of my mind. All through the Sermon on the Mount the same truth is brought out. "Except your righteousness shall *exceed* the righteousness of the scribes and Pharisees . . ." We have to fulfil all the old law and much more, and the only way it can be done is by letting Jesus alter us within, and by remembering that everything He tells us to do we *can* do. The whole point of our Lord's teaching is, "Obey Me, and you will find you have a wealth of power within."

---

6. down to the scruple: to the smallest item.

(c) Lust and License (Matthew 5:27–28)

Our Lord goes to the root of the matter every time with no apology. Sordid? Frantically sordid, but sin is frantically sordid, and there is no excuse in false modesty, or in refusing to face the music of the devil's work in this life. Jesus Christ faced it and He makes us face it too.

Our natural idea of purity is that it means according obedience to certain laws and regulations, but that is apt to be prudery. There is nothing prudish in the Bible. The Bible insists on purity, not prudery. There are bald shocking statements in the Bible, but from cover to cover the Bible will do nothing in the shape of harm to the pure in heart, it is to the impure in heart that these things are corrupting. If Jesus Christ can only make us prudish, we should be horrified if we had to go and work amongst the moral abominations of heathendom; but with the purity Jesus Christ puts in He can take us where He went Himself, and make us capable of facing the vilest moral corruption unspotted, He will keep us as pure as He is Himself. We are scandalised at social immoralities because our social sense of honour is upset, but are we cut to the heart when we see a man living in pride against God? When the Holy Ghost is at work He puts in new standards of judgement and proportion.

Remember that every religious sentiment that is not carried out on its right level carries with it a secret immorality. That is the way human nature is constituted; whenever you allow an emotion and do not carry it out on its legitimate level, it will react on an illegitimate level. You have no business to harbour an emotion the conclusion of which you see to be wrong. Grip it on the threshold of your mind in a vice of blood and allow it no more way.

God does not give a man a new body when he is saved: his body is the same, but he is given a new disposition. God alters the mainspring; He puts love in the place of lust. What is lust? The impatience of desire—I must have it at once. Love can wait seven years; lust cannot wait two seconds. Esau and his mess of pottage is a picture of lust; Jacob serving for Rachel is a picture of love. In these verses lust is put on the lowest level, but remember that lust runs from the lowest basis of immorality right up to the very height of spiritual life. Jesus Christ penetrates right straight down to the basis of our desires. If ever a man is going to stand where lust never strikes him, it can only be because Jesus has altered his disposition; it is impossible unless Jesus Christ can do what He says He can. A disciple has to be free from the degradation of lust, and the marvel of the Redemption is that Jesus can free him from it. Jesus Christ's claim is that He can do for a man what he cannot do for himself. Jesus does not alter our human nature, it does not need altering: He alters the mainspring. The great marvel of the salvation of Jesus is that He alters heredity. License is the rebellion against all law—"I will do what I like and care for no one"; liberty is the ability to perform the law, there is no independence of God in my make-up.

Do you see how we are growing? The disciples were being taught by Jesus Christ to lay their account with purity. Purity is too deep down for us to get to naturally. The only exhibition of purity is the purity in the heart of our Lord, and that is the purity He implants in us, and He says we will know whether we have that purity by the temper of mind we exhibit when we come up against things which before would have awakened in us lust and self-desire. It is not only a question of possibility on the inside, but of a possibility that shows itself in performance. That is the only test there is—"he that doeth righteousness is righteous" (1 John 3:7).

(d) Direction of Discipline (Matthew 5:29–30)

If God has altered the disposition, where is the need of discipline? and yet in these verses our Lord speaks of very stern discipline, to the parting with the right hand and the eye. The reason for the need of discipline is that our bodies have been used by the wrong disposition, and when the new disposition is put in the old physical case is not taken away, it is left there for us to discipline and turn into an obedient servant to the new disposition (see Romans 6:19).

And if thy right hand offend thee, cut it off, and cast it from thee: for it is profitable for thee that one of thy members should perish, and not that thy whole body should be cast into hell.

What does that mean? It means absolute unflinching sternness in dealing with the right things in yourself that are not the best. "The good is the enemy of the best" in every man, not the bad, but the good that is not good enough. Your right hand is not a bad thing, it is one of the best things you have, but Jesus says if it offends you in developing your spiritual life, and hinders you in following His precepts, cut it off and cast it from you. Jesus Christ spoke rugged truth, He was never ambiguous, and He says it is better to be maimed than damned, better to enter into life lame in man's sight and lovely in God's than to be lovely in man's sight and lame in God's. It is a maimed life to begin with, such as Jesus describes in these verses; otherwise we may look all right in the sight of our fellow men, but be remarkably twisted and wrong in the sight of God.

One of the principles of our Lord's teaching which we are slow to grasp is that the only basis of the spiritual is the sacrifice of the natural. The natural life is neither moral nor immoral, I make it moral or immoral by my ruling disposition. Jesus teaches that the natural life is meant for sacrifice, we can give it as a gift to God, which is the only way to make it spiritual (see Romans 12:1–2). That is where Adam failed: he refused to sacrifice the natural life and make it spiritual by obeying God's voice, consequently he sinned, the sin of taking his right to himself. Why did God make it necessary for the natural to be sacrificed to the spiritual by me? God did not. God's order was that the natural should be transformed into the spiritual by obedience; it was sin that made it necessary for the natural to be sacrificed, which is a very different thing. If you are going to be spiritual, you must barter the natural, sacrifice it. If you say—"I do not want to sacrifice the natural for the spiritual," then, Jesus says, you must barter the spiritual. It is not a punishment, but an eternal principle.

This line of discipline is the sternest that ever struck mankind, there is nothing more heroic or more grand than the Christian life. Spirituality is not a sweet tendency towards piety in people who have not enough life in them to be bad; spirituality is the possession of the life of God which is masculine in its strength, and He will make spiritual the most corrupt, twisted, sin-stained life if He be obeyed. Chastity is strong and fierce, and the man who is going to be chaste for Jesus Christ's sake has a gloriously sterling job in front of him.

When Jesus Christ has altered our disposition, we have to bring our body into harmony with the new disposition, and cause it to exercise the new disposition, and this can only be done by stern discipline, discipline which will mean cutting off a great many things for the sake of our spiritual life. There are some things that to us are as our right hand and eye, yet we dare not use them, and the world that knows us says—"How absurd you are to cut off that, whatever is wrong in a right hand?" and they will call us fanatics and cranks. If a man has never been a crank or a fanatic, it is a pretty sure sign that he has never begun seriously to consider life. In the beginning the Holy Spirit will check us in doing a great many things that may be perfectly right for everyone else but not right for us. No one can decide for another what is to be cut off, and we have no right to use our present limitations to criticise others.

Jesus says we must be prepared to be limited fools in the sight of others, in order to further our spiritual character. If we are willing to give up wrong things only for Jesus Christ, never let us talk about being in love with Him. We say—"Why shouldn't I? there is no harm in it." For pity's sake, go and do it, but remember that the construction of a spiritual character is doomed when once we take that line. Anyone will give up wrong things if he knows how, but are we prepared to give up the best we have for Jesus Christ?

The only right a Christian has is the right to give up his rights.

The Account with Practise *(Matthew 5:31–37)*

Practice means continually doing that which no one sees or knows but ourselves. Habit is the result of practice, by continually doing a thing it becomes second nature. The difference between men is not a difference of personal power, but that some men are disciplined and others are not. The difference is not the degree of mental power but the degree of mental discipline. If we have taught ourselves how to think, we will have mental power *plus* the discipline of having it under control. Beware of impulse. Impulsiveness is the characteristic of a child, but it ought not to be the characteristic of a man, it means he has not disciplined himself. Undeterred impulse is undisciplined power.

Every habit is purely mechanical, and whenever we form a habit it makes a material difference in the brain. The material of the brain alters very slowly, but it does alter, and by repeatedly doing a thing a groove is formed in the material of the brain so that it becomes easier to do it again, until at last we become unconscious of doing it. When we are regenerated we can re-form by the power and the presence of God every habit that is not in accordance with His life. Never form a habit gradually; do it at once, do it sharply and definitely, and never allow a break. We have to learn to form habits according to the dictates of the Spirit of God. The power and the practice must go together. When we fail it is because we have not practised, we have not brought the mechanical part of our nature into line. If we keep practising, what we practise becomes our second nature, and in a crisis we will find that not only does God's grace stand by us, but our own nature also. The practising is ours not God's and the crisis reveals whether or not we have been practising. The reason we fail is not because of the devil, but because of inattention on our part arising from the fact that we have not disciplined ourselves.

Verses 31–32—marriage and money form the elemental constitution of personal and social life. They are the touchstones of reality, and around these two things the Holy Spirit works all the time. Marriage is one of the mountain peaks on which God's thunder blasts souls to hell, or on which His light transfigures human lives in the eternal heavens. Jesus Christ faces fearlessly the question of sin and wrong, and He teaches us to face it fearlessly also. There is no circumstance so dark and complicated, no life so twisted, that He cannot put right. The Bible was not written for babes and fools, it was written for men and women who have to face hell's facts in this life as well as heaven's facts. If Jesus Christ cannot touch those lives that present a smooth face but have a hideous tragedy behind them, what is the good of His salvation? but, bless God, He can. He can alter our disposition, and He can alter the dreams of our dreams until lust no longer dwells in them.

(a) Speech and Sincerity (Matthew 5:33)

Sincerity means that the appearance and the reality are exactly the same. "Remember," says Jesus, "that you stand before the tribunal of God, not of men; practise the right kind of speech and your Father in heaven will back up all that is true. If you have to back it up yourself, it is of the evil one." We ought not to have to call on anyone to back up our word; our word ought to be sufficient; whether men believe us or not is a matter of indifference. We all know men whose word is their bond; there is no need for anyone to back up their word, their character and life are quite sufficient. Refrain your speech until you can convey the sincerity of your mind through it. Until the Son of God is formed in us we are not sincere, not even honest, but when His life comes into us, He makes us honest with ourselves and generous and kind towards others.

There is a snare in being able to talk about God's truth easily because frequently that is where it ends. If we can express the truth well, the danger is that we do not go on to know more. Most of us can talk piously, we have the practice but not the power. Jesus is saying that our conversation should spring from such a basis of His Spirit in us that everyone who listens is built up by it. Unaffected sincerity always builds up; corrupt communication makes us feel mean[7] and narrow. There are men who never say a bad word, yet their influence is devilish. Don't pay attention to the outside of the platter, pay attention to that which is within the platter. Practise the speech that is in accordance with the life of the Son of God in you, and slowly and surely your speech and your sincerity will be in accord.

(b) Irreverent Reverence (Matthew 5:34–36)

In our Lord's day the habit was common, as it is to-day, of backing up ordinary assertions with an appeal to the name of God. Jesus checks that, He says never call on anything in the nature of God to attest what you say, speak simply and truly, realising that truth in a man is the same as truth in God. To call God in as a witness to back up what you say is nearly always a sign that what you are saying is not true. Similarly if you can find reasons for the truth of what you say, it is proof that what you say is not strictly true; if it were, you would never have to find reasons

to prove it. Jesus Christ puts in a truthfulness that never takes knowledge of itself.

Irreverent reverence is something our Lord checks, talking flippantly about those things which ought only to be mentioned with the greatest reverence. I remember an Indian woman who was wonderfully saved, she was an ugly woman but at the pronouncement of the name of Jesus Christ, her face was transfigured, the whole soul of the woman was in reverent adoration of her Lord and Master.

(c) Integrity (Matthew 5:37)

Integrity means unimpaired purity of heart. God can make our words the exact expression of the disposition He has put in. Jesus taught by example and by precept that no man should stand up for his own honour but only for the honour of another. Our Lord was never careful of His own honour, He "made Himself of no reputation." Men called Him a glutton and a winebibber, a madman, devil-possessed, and He never opened His mouth; but immediately they said a word against His Father's honour, He not only opened His mouth, but He said some terrible things (see Mark 11:15–18). Jesus Christ by His Spirit alters our standard of honour, and a disciple will never care what people say of him, but he will care tremendously what people say of Jesus Christ; he realises that his Lord's honour is at stake in his life, not his own honour. What is the thing that rouses you? That is an indication of where you live.

Scandal should be treated as you treat mud on your clothes. If you try and deal with it while it is wet, you rub the mud into the texture, but if you leave it till it is dry you can flick it off with a touch, it is gone without a trace. Leave scandal alone, never touch it.

Let people do what they like with your truth, but never explain it. Jesus never explained anything; we are always explaining, and we get into tangles by not leaving things alone. We need to pray St. Augustine's prayer, "O Lord, deliver me from this lust of always vindicating myself." Our Lord never told His disciples when they made mistakes; they made any number of blunders, but He went on quietly planting the truth and let mistakes correct themselves.

In the matter of praise, when we are not sure of having done well we always like to find out what people think; when we are certain we have done well, we do not care an atom whether folk praise us or not. It is the same with regard to fear, we all know men who say they are not afraid, but the very fact that they say it, proves they are. We have to learn to live on the line of integrity all through.

Another truth we do not sufficiently realise is the influence of what we think over what we say. A man

---

7. The word mean as used here refers to something or someone ordinary, common, low, or ignoble, rather than cruel or spiteful.

may say wonderfully truthful things, but his thinking is what tells. It is possible to say truthful things in a truthful manner and to tell a lie in thinking. I can repeat to another what I heard you say, word for word, every detail scientifically accurate, and yet convey a lie in saying it, because the temper of my mind is different from the temper of your mind when you said it. A lie is not an inexactitude of speech, a lie is in the motive. I may be actually truthful and an incarnate liar. It is not the literal words that count but their influence on others.

Suspicion is always of the devil, and is the cause of people saying more than they need say, and in that aspect it "cometh of evil." If we submit children to a sceptical atmosphere and call in question all they say, it will instil the habit of backing up what is said, "Well, ask him if you don't believe me." Such a thought would never occur to a child naturally, it only occurs when the child has to talk to suspicious people who continually say, "Now I don't know whether what you are saying is true." The child gets the idea that it does not speak the truth unless some one backs it up. It never occurs to a pure honest heart to back up what it says; it is a wounding insult to be met with suspicion, and that is why from the first a child ought never to be submitted to suspicion.

The Account with Persecution (Matthew 5:38–42)

(a) Insult (Matthew 5:38–39)

If a disciple is going to follow Jesus Christ, he must lay his account not only with purity and with practice, but also with persecution. The picture our Lord gives is not familiar to us. In the East, a slap on the cheek is the greatest form of insult, its equivalent with us would be spitting in the face. Epictetus, a Roman slave, said that a slave would rather be thrashed to death than flicked on the cheek. Jesus says, "If any man shall smite thee on thy right cheek, turn to him the other also." The Sermon on the Mount indicates that when we are on Jesus Christ's errands, no time is to be taken in standing up for ourselves. Personal insult will be an occasion in the saint for revealing the incredible sweetness of the Lord Jesus.

The Sermon on the Mount hits where it is meant to hit, and it hits every time. Jesus says, "Whosoever shall smite thee on thy right cheek, as My representative, pay no attention," i.e., show a disposition equivalent to turning the other cheek also. Either Jesus Christ was mad to say such things, or He was the Son of God. Naturally, if a man does not hit back it is because he is a coward; supernaturally, it is the manifestation of the Son of God in him: both have the same appearance outwardly. The hypocrite and the saint are alike in the public eye; the saint exhibits a meekness which is contemptible in the eyes of the world; that is the immense humiliation of being a Christian. Our strength has to be the strength of the

Son of God, and "He was crucified through weakness." Do the impossible, and immediately you do, you know that God alone has made it possible.

These things apply to a disciple of Jesus and to no one else. The only way to interpret the words of God is to let the Holy Spirit interpret them for us. Jesus said that the Holy Spirit would bring back to our remembrance what He has said, and His counsel is: when you come across personal insult you must not only not resent it, but make it an occasion of exhibiting the Son of God.

The secret of a disciple is personal devotion to a Personal Lord, and a man is open to the same charge as Jesus was, viz., that of inconsistency, but Jesus Christ was never inconsistent to God. There is more than one consistency. There is the consistency of a little child, a child is never the same, always changing and developing, a consistent child; and there is the consistency of a brick wall, a petrified consistency. A Christian is to be consistent only to the life of the Son of God in him, not consistent to hard and fast creeds. Men pour themselves into creeds, and God Almighty has to blast them out of their prejudices before they become devoted to Jesus Christ. "The expulsive power of a new affection" is what Christianity supplies. The reality of the life of the Son of God in us must show itself in the appearance of our lives.

The miracle of regeneration is necessary before we can live the Sermon on the Mount. The Son of God alone can live it, and if God can form in us the life of the Son of God as He introduced him into human history, then we can see how we can live it too, and that is Jesus Christ's message—"Marvel not that I said unto thee, Ye must be born again." (Cf. Luke 1:35.)

(b) Extortion (Matthew 5:40)

Another unfamiliar picture to us, but one that had tremendous meaning in our Lord's day. If a man's cloak and coat were taken from him as the result of a lawsuit, he could get back the loan of the coat to sleep in at night. Jesus uses the illustration to point out what we are going to meet with as His disciples. If they extort anything from you while you are in My service, let them have it, but go on with your work. If you are My disciple, says Jesus, you will have no time to stand up for yourself. Never insist on your rights. The Sermon on the Mount is not, Do your duty; but, Do what is not your duty. It is never your duty to "resist not evil," that is only possible to the Son of God in you.

(c) Tyranny (Matthew 5:41–42)

Under the Roman dominance soldiers could compel any one to be a baggage-carrier for a mile. Simon the Cyrenian is a case in point, the Roman soldier compelled him to be baggage-carrier for Jesus Christ. Jesus says, "If you are My disciple, you will always go the second mile, you will always do more than your duty"; there will be none of this spirit—"Oh well, I can't do any more, they have always misunderstood and misrepresented me"; you will go the second mile, not for their sakes, but for Jesus Christ's sake. It would have been a sorry look-out for us if God had not gone the second mile with us. The first thing God requires of a man is to be born from above, then when he goes the second mile for men it is the Son of God in him Who does it. The only right a Christian has is the right not to insist upon his rights. Every time I insist upon my rights I hurt the Son of God. I can prevent the Son of God being hurt if I take the blow myself, but if I refuse to take it, it will go back on Him (cf. Colossians 1:24).

Verse 42 is an arena for theological acrobats, "Give to him that asketh thee, and from him that would borrow of thee turn not thou away." That is the statement either of a madman, or of God Incarnate. We always say we do not know what Jesus Christ means when we know perfectly well He means something which is a blunt impossibility unless He can remake us and make it possible. Jesus brings us with terrific force straight up against the impossible, and until we get to the place of despair we will never receive from Him the grace that enables us to do the impossible and manifest His Spirit.

These statements of Jesus revolutionise all our conceptions of charity. Much of our modern philanthropy is based on the motive of giving to the poor man because he deserves it, or because we are distressed at seeing him poor. Jesus never taught charity from those motives: He said, "Give to him that asketh thee, not because he deserves it, but because I tell you to." The great motive in all giving is Jesus Christ's command. We can always find a hundred and one reasons for not obeying our Lord's commands, because we will trust our reasoning rather than His reason, and our reason does not take God into calculation. How does civilisation argue? "Does this man deserve what I am giving him?" Immediately you talk like that, the Spirit of God says, "Who are you? Do *you* deserve more than other men the blessings you have?"

"Give to him that asketh thee." Why do we always make this mean money? Our Lord makes no mention of money. The blood of most of us seems to run in gold. The reason we make it mean money is because that is where our heart is. Peter said "Silver and gold have I none; but such as I have give I thee." God grant we may understand that the spring of giving is not impulse nor inclination, but the inspiration of the Holy Spirit, I give because Jesus tells me to.

The way Christians wriggle and twist and compromise over this verse springs from infidelity in the ruling providence of our Heavenly Father. We enthrone commonsense as God and say, "It is absurd; if I give to every one that asks, every beggar in the place will be at my door." Try it. I have yet to find the man who obeyed Jesus Christ's command and did not realise that God restrains those who beg. If we try to apply these principles of Jesus Christ's literally, without the indwelling Spirit, there will be no proof that God is with us, but when once we are rightly related to God and are letting the Holy Spirit apply the words to our circumstances, we shall find the restraining hand of God, for if ever God's ruling is seen, it is seen when once a disciple obeys Jesus Christ's commands.

Study No. 3.

INCARNATE WISDOM AND INDIVIDUAL REASON
Matthew 5:43–6:34

Divine Rule of Life (Matthew 5:43–48)
(a) Exhortation (Matthew 5:43–44)
(b) Example (Matthew 5:45)
(c) Expression (Matthew 5:46–48)

Divine Region of Religion (Matthew 6:1–18)
(a) Philanthropy (Matthew 6:1–4)
(b) Prayer (Matthew 6:5–15)
(c) Penance (Matthew 6:16–18)

Divine Reasonings of Mind (Matthew 6:19–24)
(a) Doctrine of Deposit (Matthew 6:19–21)
(b) Doctrine of Division (Matthew 6:22–23)
(c) Doctrine of Detachment (Matthew 6:24)

Divine Reasonings of Faith (Matthew 6:25–34)
(a) Careful Carelessness (Matthew 6:25)
(b) Careful Unreasonableness (Matthew 6:26–29)
(c) Careful Infidelity (Matthew 6:30–32)
(d) Concentrated Consecration (Matthew 6:33–34)

We live in two universes: the universe of commonsense in which we come in contact with things by our senses and the universe of revelation with which we come in contact by faith. The wisdom of God fits the two universes exactly, the one interprets the other.

Jesus Christ is the expression of the Wisdom of God. If we take the common-sense universe and discard the revelation of Jesus Christ we make what He says foolishness, because He talks from the universe of revelation all the time. Jesus Christ lived in the revelation world which we do not see, and until we get into His world we do not understand His teaching at all. In Him we find that the universe of revelation and the universe of common-sense were made one, and if ever they are to be one in us it can only be by receiving the heredity of Jesus, viz., Holy Spirit.

In the common-sense universe the faculty required is intellectual curiosity, but when we enter into the domain from which Jesus Christ talks, intellectual curiosity is ruled out and moral obedience takes the absolute place. "If any man will do His will, he shall know. . . . " If we are going to find out the secrets of the world we live in, we must work at it. God does not encourage laziness. He has given us instruments whereby we are able to explore this universe and we do it entirely by intellectual curiosity; but when we come to the domain which Jesus Christ reveals, no amount of studying or curiosity will avail an atom, our ordinary common-sense faculties are of no use, we cannot see God or taste God, we can dispute with Him, but we cannot get at Him by our senses at all, and common-sense is apt to say there is nothing other than this universe. How are we to get into contact with this other universe to which Jesus Christ belonged and from which He speaks? We come in contact with the revelation facts of God's universe by faith wrought in us by the Spirit of God, then as we develop in understanding, the two universes are slowly made one in us. They never agree outside Jesus Christ.

An understanding of Redemption is not necessary to salvation any more than an understanding of life is necessary before we can be born into it. Jesus Christ did not come to found religion, nor did He come to found civilisation, they were both here before He came; He came to make us spiritually real in every domain. In Jesus Christ there was nothing secular and sacred, it was all real, and He makes His disciples like Himself.

Divine Rule of Life *(Matthew 5:43–48)*
In these verses our Lord lays down a Divine rule which we by His Spirit have to apply to every circumstance and condition of our lives. Our Lord does not make statements which we have to follow literally; if He did we should not grow in grace. In the realm of God it is a spiritual following, and we have to rely upon His Spirit to teach us to apply His statements to the various circumstances in which we find ourselves.

(a) Exhortation *(Matthew 5:43–44)*
Our Lord's exhortation here is to be generous in our behaviour to all men whether they be good or bad. The marvel of the Divine love is that God exhibits His love not only to good people but to bad people. In our Lord's parable of the two sons we can understand the father loving the prodigal son, but he also exhibits his love to the elder brother, to whom we feel a strong antipathy. Beware of walking in the spiritual life according to your natural affinities. We all have natural affinities—some people we like and others we do not; some people we get on well with and others we do not. Never let those likes and dislikes be the rule of your Christian life. "If we walk in the light, as He is in the light, we have fellowship one with another," i.e., God gives us fellowship with people for whom we have no natural affinity.

(b) Example *(Matthew 5:45)*
Woven into our Lord's Divine rule of life is His reference to our Example. Our Example is not a good man, not even a good Christian man, but God Himself. We do not allow the big surprise of this to lay hold of us sufficiently. Jesus nowhere says, "Follow the best example you have, follow Christians, watch those who love Me and follow them"; He says, "Follow your Father which is in heaven—that you may be good men? That you may be loveable to all men?" No, "that ye may be the children of your Father which is in heaven," and that implies a strong family likeness to Jesus Christ. The Example of a disciple is God Almighty and no one less; not the best man you know, nor the finest saint you ever read about, but God Himself.

> *That ye may be the children of your Father . . . in heaven.*

Our Lord's exhortation to us is to love our fellow-men as God has loved us. The love of God is not like the love of a father or a mother, it is the love *of God*. "God commendeth *His own love* toward us" (Romans 5:8 RV). The love of God is revealed in that He laid down His life for His enemies, and Jesus tells us to love our fellow-men as God has loved us. As disciples of Jesus, we are to identify ourselves with God's interests in other people, to show to the other man what God has shown us, and God will give us ample opportunity in our actual lives to prove that we are perfect as our Father in heaven is perfect.

"Ye have heard that it hath been said, Thou shalt love thy neighbour, and hate thine enemy. But I say unto you, Love your enemies." Again I want to emphasise the fact that the teaching of Jesus Christ does not appear at first to be what it is. At first it appears to be beautiful and pious and lukewarm; but before long it becomes a ripping and tearing torpedo which splits to atoms every preconceived notion a man ever had. It takes a long time to get the full force of our Lord's statements. "I say unto you, Love your enemies"—an easy thing to do when you have no enemies; an impossible thing when you have. "Bless them that curse you"—easy when no one is cursing you, but impossible when someone is. "Do good to them that hate you, and pray for them that despitefully use you." It seems easy to do all this when we have no enemies, when no one is cursing or persecuting us; but if we have an enemy who slanders and annoys and systematically vexes us, and we read Jesus Christ's statement "I say unto you, *Love your enemies*"— how are we going to do it? Unless Jesus Christ can remake us within, His teaching is the biggest mockery human ears ever listened to. Talk about the Sermon on the Mount being an ideal! Why, it rends a man with despair—the very thing Jesus means it to do, for when once we realise that we cannot love our enemies, we cannot bless them that curse us, we cannot come anywhere near the standard revealed in the Sermon on the Mount, then we are in a condition to receive from God the disposition that will enable us to love our enemies, to pray for those that despitefully use us, to do good to those that hate us.

"I say unto you, Love your enemies." Jesus does not say, "Love every one." The Bible never speaks vaguely, it always speaks definitely. People speak about loving "mankind," and loving "the heathen"; Jesus says, "Love your enemies." Our Lord does not say, "*Bless* your enemies," He says, "*Love* your enemies." He does not say, "*Love* them that curse you"; He says, "*Bless* them that curse you." "*Do good* to them that hate you"—not *bless* them. He does not say, "*Do good* to them that despitefully use you"; He says, "*Pray for* them that despitefully use you." Each one of these commands is stamped with sheer impossibility to the natural man. If we reverse the order Jesus has given it can be done with strain, but kept in His order I defy any man on earth to be able to do it unless he has been regenerated by God the Holy Ghost. When a man does love his enemies, he knows that God has done a tremendous work in him, and every one else knows it too.

(c) Expression (Matthew 5:46–48)
Christian character is not expressed by good doing, but by God-likeness. It is not sufficient to do good, to do the right thing, we must have our goodness stamped by the image and superscription of God, it is supernatural all through. The secret of a Christian's life is that the supernatural is made natural by the grace of God. The way it is worked out in expression is not in having times of communion with God, but in the practical details of life. The proof that we have

been regenerated is that when we come in contact with the things that create a buzz, we find to our astonishment that we have a power to keep wonderfully poised in the centre of it all, a power we did not have before, a power that is only explained by the Cross of Jesus Christ.

Verse 48 is a re-emphasis of verse 20. The perfection of verse 48 refers to the disposition of God in me—"Ye therefore shall be perfect as your heavenly Father is perfect" (RV), not in a future state, but—"You shall be perfect as your Father in heaven is perfect if you let Me work that perfection in you." If the Holy Spirit has transformed us within, we will not exhibit good human characteristics, but Divine characteristics in our human nature. There is only one type of holiness and that is the holiness of God, and Jesus gives God Almighty as our Example. How many of us have measured ourselves by that standard, the standard of a purity of heart in which God can see nothing to blame?

May this Divine rule of our Lord's bring us to the bar of the standard of Jesus Christ. His claim is measured by these tremendous statements of His. He can take the vilest piece of "broken earthenware," He can take you and me, and can fit us exactly to the expression of the Divine life in us. It is not a question of putting the statements of our Lord in front of us and trying to live up to them, but of receiving His Spirit and finding that we can live up to them as He brings them to our remembrance and applies them to our circumstances.

God grant we may have the courageous range of faith that is required. "Be ye therefore perfect, even as your Father which is in heaven is perfect"—and men will take knowledge of me that I am a good man? Never! If ever it is recorded of me—"What a good man that is," I have been a betrayer somewhere. If we fix our eyes on our own whiteness we shall soon get dry rot in our spiritual life. All our righteousness is "as filthy rags" unless it is the blazing holiness of Jesus in us uniting us with Him until we see nothing but Jesus first, Jesus second, and Jesus third. Then when men take knowledge of us, they will not say that we are good men, that we have a wonderful whiteness, but that Jesus Christ has done something wonderful in us. Always keep at the Source of spiritual blessings—Jesus Christ Himself.

Our Lord says in verse 30, "For it is profitable for thee that one of thy members should perish, and not that thy whole body should be cast into hell," i.e., He is referring to a *maimed* life. In verse 48 He says, "Be ye therefore *perfect,* even as your Father which is in heaven is perfect." Is our Father in heaven maimed? Has He a right arm cut off, a right eye plucked out? In verse 48 Jesus completes the picture He began to give in verse 30. Our Lord's statements embrace the whole of the spiritual life from the beginning to the end. In verses 29–30, He pictures a maimed life: in verse 48 He pictures a full-orbed life of holiness. Holiness means a perfect balance between our disposition and the laws of God. The maimed life is the characteristic at the beginning, and if we have not had that characteristic it is questionable whether we have ever received the Holy Spirit. What the world calls fanaticism is the entrance into Life. We have to begin the life with God as maimed souls; the swing of the pendulum makes us go to the opposite extreme of what we were in the life of the world. We are so afraid of being fanatical; would to God we were as afraid of being "fushionless."[8] We should a thousand times rather be fanatical in the beginning than poor "fushionless" creatures all our lives, limp and useless. May we get to the place where we are willing to cut off the right arm, to pluck out the right eye, to enter into Life hirplers,[9] maimed, having cut off whatever there was need to, however beautiful; and, blessed be the name of God, we shall find that He will bring every life that obeys Him to a full-orbed unity.

Always make allowances for people when they first enter into Life, they have to enter on the fanatical line. The danger is lest they stay too long in the stage of fanaticism. When fanaticism steps over the bounds, it becomes spiritual lunacy. In the beginning of the life in grace we have to limit ourselves all round, in right things as well as wrong; but if when God begins to bring us out of the light of our convictions into the light of the Lord, we prefer to remain true to our convictions, we become spiritual lunatics. Walking in the light of convictions is a necessary stage, but there is a grander, purer, sterner light to walk in, viz., the light of the Lord.

How impatient we are! When we see a life born from above of the Spirit and the necessary limitations and severances and maimings taking place, we will try and do God's work for Him, and God has to rap us sharply over the knuckles and say—"Leave that soul in My care." Always allow for the swing of the pendulum in yourself and in others. A pendulum does not swing evenly at first, it begins with a tremendous swing to one extreme and only gets back to the right balance gradually, and that is how the Holy Spirit brings the grace of God to bear upon our lives. "I do not frustrate the grace of God," says Paul.

Divine Region of Religion *(Matthew 6:1–18)*
In chapter 5, our Lord demands that our disposition be right with Him in our ordinary natural life lived to men; in chapter 6, He deals with the domain of our life lived to God before men. The main idea in the region of religion is, Your eyes on God, not on men.

(a) Philanthropy (Matthew 6:1–4)
It was inculcated, as it were, into the very blood of the Jew to look after the stranger (see Deuteronomy 15:7–8, Leviticus 19:8, 10), and in our Lord's day the Pharisees made a tremendous show of giving; they gave from a play-acting motive, that they might "have glory of men." They would put their money in the boxes in the women's court of the Temple with a great clang which sounded like a trumpet. Jesus tells us not to give in that way, with the motive to be seen of men, to be known as a generous giver, for "Verily I say unto you, They have their reward," that is all there is to it.

Briefly summed up these verses mean: Have no other motive in giving than to please God. In modern philanthropy we are "egged on" with other motives— It will do them good; they need the help; they deserve it. Jesus Christ never brings out that aspect in His teaching; He allows no other motive in giving than to please God. In chapter 5, He says—"Give because I tell you to,—and here, He teaches us not to have mixed motives. It is very penetrating to ask ourselves this question—"What was my motive in doing that kind act?" We will be astounded at how rarely the Holy Spirit gets a chance to fit our motives on to being right with God, we mix our motives with a hundred and one other considerations. Jesus Christ makes it steadily simple—one motive only, your eyes on God; "if you are My disciple, you will never give with any other motive than to please God." The characteristic of Jesus in a disciple is much deeper down than doing good things, it is goodness in motive because the disciple has been made loved by the supernatural grace of God.

"But when thou doest alms, let not thy left hand know what thy right hand doeth," i.e., do good until it is an unconscious habit of the life and you do not know you are doing it, you will be covered with confusion when Jesus Christ detects it. "Lord, when saw we Thee an hungered, and fed Thee? . . . Inasmuch as ye have done it unto one of the least of these My brethren, ye have done it unto Me." That is our Lord's magnanimous interpretation of kind acts that people have never allowed themselves to think anything of. Get into the habit of having such a relationship to God that you do good without knowing you do it, then you will no longer trust your own impulse, or your own judgement, you will trust only the inspiration of the Spirit of God. The mainspring of your motives will be the Father's heart, not your own; the Father's

---

8. fushionless: insipid; lacking energy; mentally or spiritually dull.
9. hirpler: one who walks with a limp or hobble.

understanding, not your own. When once you are rightly related to God, He will use you as a channel through which His disposition will flow.

(b) Prayer (Matthew 6:5–15)

Prayer, says Jesus, is to be looked at in the same way as philanthropy, viz., your eyes on God, not on men. Watch your motive before God; have no other motive in prayer than to know Him. The statements of Jesus about prayer which are so familiar to us are revolutionary. Call a halt one moment and ask yourself—"Why do I pray? What is my motive? Is it because I have a personal secret relationship to God known to no one but myself?"

The Pharisees were obliged to pray so many times a day, and they took care that they happened to be in the midst of the city when the hour for prayer came, and then in an ostentatious manner they would give themselves to prayer. Jesus says, "Thou shalt not be as the hypocrites are, their motive is to be known as praying men, and, verily, they have their reward." Our Lord did not say it was wrong to pray in the corners of the streets, but He did say that the motive "to be seen of men" was wrong. "But thou, when thou prayest, enter into thy closet, and when thou hast shut thy door, pray to thy Father which is in secret," i.e., get a place for prayer where no one imagines that that is what you are doing, shut the door and talk to God in secret. It is impossible to live the life of a disciple without definite times of secret prayer. You will find that the place to enter in is in your business, as you walk along the streets, in the ordinary ways of life, when no one dreams you are praying, and the reward comes openly, a revival here, a blessing there. The Scots have a proverb, "Aye keep a bittie to yersel," and as you go on with God you learn more and more to maintain this secret relationship with God in prayer.

When we pray we give God a chance to work in the unconscious realm of the lives of those for whom we pray, when we come into the secret place it is the Holy Ghost's passion for souls that is at work, not our passion, and He can work through us as He likes. Sects produce a passion for souls; the Holy Spirit produces a passion for Christ. The great dominating passion all through the New Testament is for our Lord Jesus Christ.

Jesus also taught the disciples the prayer of patience. If you are right with God and God delays the manifested answer to your prayer, don't misjudge Him, don't think of Him as an unkind friend an unnatural father, or an unjust judge, but keep at it, your prayer will certainly be answered, for "every one that asketh receiveth." "Men ought always to pray, and not to faint," i.e., not to cave in. "Your heavenly Father will explain it all one day," Jesus says, "He cannot just now because He is developing your character."

In verse 8 Jesus goes to the root of all prayer—"Your Father knoweth what things ye have need of, before ye ask Him." Common-sense says, "Then why ask Him?" Prayer is not getting things from God, that is a most initial stage; prayer is getting into perfect communion with God; I tell Him what I know He knows in order that I may get to know it as He does. Jesus says, "Pray because you have a Father, not because it quietens you, and give Him time to answer." If the life of Jesus is formed in me by regeneration and I am drawing my breath in the fear of the Lord, the Son of God will press forward in front of my common-sense and change my attitude to things.

Most of us make the blunder of depending upon our own earnestness and not on God at all, it is confidence in Jesus that tells (see 1 John 5:14). All our fuss and earnestness, all our gifts of prayer, are not of the slightest use to Jesus Christ, He pays no attention to them. If you have a gift of prayer, may God wither it up until you learn how to get your prayers inspired by God the Holy Ghost. Do we rely on God, or on our own earnestness when we pray? God is never impressed by our earnestness; we are not heard because we are in earnest, but on the ground of Redemption only. We have "boldness to enter into the holiest *by the blood of Jesus,*" and by no other way.

"Your Father knoweth what things ye have need of." "Remember," says Jesus, "your Father is keenly and divinely interested in you, and prayer becomes the 'blether' of a child to his father." We are inclined to take everything and every one seriously saving God; our Lord took nothing and no one seriously but His Father, and He teaches us to be as children before men, but in earnest before our Father in heaven. Notice the essential simplicity of our Lord's teaching all through—right towards God, right towards God.

(c) Penance (Matthew 6:16–18)

Penance means putting ourselves into a strait-jacket for the sake of disciplining our spiritual character. Physical sloth will upset spiritual devotion quicker than anything else. If the devil cannot get at us by enticing to sin, he will get at us by sleeping-sickness spiritually—"Now you cannot possibly get up in the morning to pray, you are working hard all day and you cannot give that time to prayer, God does not expect it of you." Jesus says God does expect it of us. Penance means doing a hardship to the body for the sake of developing the spiritual life. Put your life through discipline but do not say a word about it—"appear not unto men to fast." Jeremy Taylor said that men hang out the sign of the devil to prove there is an angel within, i.e., they wear sad countenances and look tremendously severe in order to prove they are holy. Jesus taught His disciples to be hypocrites, "but thou, when thou fastest, . . . wash thy face," i.e., never allow anyone to imagine you are putting yourself through discipline. If ever we can tell to others the discipline we put ourselves through in order to further our life with God, from that moment the discipline becomes useless. Our Lord counsels us to have a relationship between ourselves and God that our dearest friend on earth never guesses. When you fast, fast to your Father in secret, not before men. Do not make a cheap martyr of yourself, and never ask for pity. If you are going through a time of discipline, pretend you are not going through it—"appear not unto men to fast." The Holy Spirit will apply this to each one of us. There are lines of discipline, lines of limitation, physical and mental and spiritual, and the Holy Spirit will say—"You must not allow yourself this and that." Ostensible external fasts are of no use, it is the internal fasting that counts. Fasting from food may be difficult for some, but it is child's play compared with fasting for the development of God's purpose in your life. Fasting means concentration. Five minutes' heed to what Jesus says and solid concentration on it would bring about transactions with God that would end in sanctification.

> *Be not, as the hypocrites, of a sad countenance: for they disfigure their faces, that they may appear unto men to fast.*

May God destroy for ever "the grief that saps the mind," and the luxury of misery and morbid introspection that men indulge in in order to develop holiness, and may we bear the shining faces that belong to the sons of God. "They looked unto Him, and were radiant" (Psalm 34:5 American Version).

Divine Reasonings of Mind *(Matthew 6:19–24)*

It is a fruitful study to find out what the New Testament says about the mind. The Spirit of God comes through the different writers with the one steady insistence to stir up our minds (e.g., Philippians 2:5; 2 Peter 1:12–13). Satan comes as an "angel of light" to those Christians only whose hearts are right but whose minds are not stirred up. Our Lord in these verses deals with the mind and tells us how we are to think and to reason about things. Unless we learn to think in obedience to the Holy Spirit's teaching, we will drift in our spiritual experience without any thinking at all. The confusion arises when we try to think and to reason things out without the Spirit of God

(a) Doctrine of Deposit (Matthew 6:19–21)

The Holy Spirit teaches us to fasten our thinking upon God; then when we come to deal with property and money and everything to do with the matters of

earth, He reminds us that our real treasure is in heaven . Every effort to persuade myself that my treasure is in heaven is a sure sign that it is not. When my motive has been put right, it will put my thinking right.

"But lay up for yourselves treasures in heaven," i.e., have your banking account in heaven, not on earth; lay up your confidence in God, not in your common-sense. It is the *trial* of your faith that makes you wealthy, and it works in this way: every time you venture out on the life of faith, you will come across something in your actual life which seems to contradict absolutely what your faith in God says you should believe. Go through the trial of faith and lay up your confidence in God, not in your common-sense, and you will gain so much wealth in your heavenly banking account, and the more you go through the trial of faith the wealthier you will become in the heavenly regions, until you go through difficulties smilingly and men wonder where your wealth of trust comes from.

It is a trial of faith all through. The conflict for the Christian is not a conflict with sin, but a conflict over the natural life being turned into the spiritual life. The natural life is not sinful, the disposition that rules the natural life is sinful, and when God alters that disposition, we have to turn the natural life into the spiritual by a steady process of obedience to God, and it takes spiritual concentration on God to do it. If you are going to succeed in anything in this world, you must concentrate on it, practise it, and the same is true spiritually. There are many things you will find you cannot do if you are going to be concentrated on God, things that may be perfectly legitimate and right for others, but not for you if you are going to concentrate on God. Never let the narrowness of your conscience condemn the other man. Maintain the personal relationship, see that you yourself are concentrated on God, not on your convictions or your point of view, but on God. Whenever you are in doubt about a thing, push it to its logical conclusion—"Is this the kind of thing that Jesus Christ is after or the kind of thing Satan is after?" Immediately your decision is made, act on it.

(b) Doctrine of Division (Matthew 6:22–23)

In verse 22, our Lord is using the eye as the symbol of conscience in a man who has been put right by the Holy Spirit. A single[10] eye is essential to correct understanding. One idea runs all through our Lord's teaching—Right with God, first, second and third. If we are born again of the Holy Ghost we do not persuade ourselves that we are right with God, we *are* right with Him because we have been put right by the Holy Spirit. Then if we walk in the light as God is in

---

10. single: pure; unmixed.

the light, that will keep our eye single, and slowly and surely all our actions begin to be put into the right relationship, and everything becomes full of harmony and simplicity and peace.

No one has a single motive unless he has been born from above; we have single ambitions, but not single motives. Jesus Christ is the only One with a single motive, and when His Spirit comes into us the first thing He does is to make us men with a single motive, a single eye to the glory of God. The one motive of Jesus is to turn men into sons of God, and the one motive of a disciple is to glorify Jesus Christ.

If therefore the light that is in thee be darkness, how great is that darkness!"

Darkness is my point of view, my right to myself; light is God's point of view. Jesus Christ made the line of demarcation between light and darkness very definite, the danger is lest this division gets blurred. "Men loved darkness rather than light, because their deeds were evil," said Jesus.

(c) Doctrine of Detachment (Matthew 6:24)
Ye cannot serve God and mammon.

A man of the world says we can; with a little subtlety and wisdom and compromise (it is called diplomacy, or tact), we can serve both. The devil's temptation to our Lord to fall down and worship him, i.e., to compromise, is repeated over and over again in Christian experience. We have to realise that there is a division as high as heaven and as deep as hell between the Christian and the world. "Whosoever therefore would be a friend of the world maketh himself an enemy of God" (RV).

This doctrine of detachment is a fundamental theme of our Lord's and runs all through His teaching. You cannot be good and bad at the same time; you cannot serve God and make your own out of the service; you cannot make "honesty is the best policy" a motive, because immediately you do, you cease to be honest. The riddling the Spirit of God puts a man through is the sternest on earth—"Why are you a student for the ministry, a missionary, a preacher of the Gospel?" There should be one consideration only— to stand right with God, to see that that relationship is the one thing that is never dimmed, then all other things will right themselves. Immediately that relationship is lost sight of, a multitude of motives begin to work and you soon become worn out. Never compromise with the spirit of mammon. When you are right with God, you become contemptible in the eyes of the world. Put into practice any of the teaching of the Sermon on the Mount and you will be treated with amusement at first; then if you persist, the world will get annoyed and will detest you. What will hap-

pen, for instance, if you carry out Jesus Christ's teaching in business? Not quite so much success as you bargained for. This is not the age of the glorification of the saints, but the age of their humiliation. Are you prepared to follow Jesus Christ outside the camp, the special camp to which you belong?

"Ye cannot serve God and mammon. What is mammon? The system of civilised life which organises itself without considering God. We have to stand absolutely true to God's line of things. Thank God for every one who has learned that the dearest friend on earth is a mere shadow compared with Jesus Christ. There must be a dominant, personal, passionate devotion to Him, and only then are all other relationships right (cf. Luke 14:26). Jesus Christ is not teaching ordinary integrity, but supernormal integrity, a likeness to our Father in heaven. In the beginning of our spiritual life we must make allowance for the swing of the pendulum. It is not by accident but by the set purpose of God that in the reaction we go to the opposite extreme of all we were before. God breaks us from the old life violently, not gradually, and only when we are right with Him does He bring us back into the domain of men; we are to be *in* the world, but not of it. When we become mature in godliness God trusts His own honour to us by placing us where the world, the flesh, and the devil may try us, knowing that "greater is He that is in you, than he that is in the world."

Divine Reasonings of Faith (Matthew 6:25–34)
Faith is our personal confidence in a Being Whose character we know, but Whose ways we cannot trace by common-sense. By the reasonings of faith is meant the practical out-working in our life of implicit, determined confidence in God. Common-sense is mathematical; faith is not mathematical, faith works on illogical lines. Jesus Christ places the strongest emphasis on faith, and especially on the faith that has been tried. To have faith tests a man for all he is worth, he has to stand in the common-sense universe in the midst of things which conflict with his faith, and place his confidence in the God Whose character is revealed in Jesus Christ. Jesus Christ's statements reveal that God is a Being of love and justice and truth; the actual happenings in our immediate circumstances seem to prove He is not; are we going to remain true to the revelation that God is good? Are we going to be true to His honour, whatever may happen in the actual domain? If we are, we shall find that God in His providence makes the two universes, the universe of revelation and the universe of common-sense, work together in perfect harmony. Most of us are pagans in a crisis; we think and act like pagans, only one out of a hundred is daring enough to bank his faith in the character of God.

The golden rule for understanding in spiritual matters is not intellect, but obedience. Discernment in the spiritual world is never gained by intellect; in the common-sense world it is. If a man wants scientific knowledge, intellectual curiosity is his guide; but if he wants insight into what Jesus Christ teaches, he can only get it by obedience. If things are dark to us spiritually, it is because there is something we will not do. Intellectual darkness comes because of ignorance; spiritual darkness comes because of something I do not intend to obey.

(a) Careful Carelessness (Matthew 6:25)

Jesus does not say, "Blessed is the man who does not think about anything"; that man is a fool; He says, "Be carefully careless about everything saving one thing, viz., your relationship to God." That means we have to be studiously careful that we are careless about how we stand to self-interest, to food, to clothes, for the one reason only, that we are set on minding our relationship to God. Many people are careless about what they eat and drink, and they suffer for it; they are careless about what they put on, and they look as they have no right to look; they are careless over property, and God holds them responsible for it. Jesus is saying that the great care of the life is to put the relationship to God first and everything else second. Our Lord teaches a complete reversal of all our practical sensible reasonings. Do not make the ruling factor of your life what you shall eat, or what you shall drink, but make zealous concentration on God the one point of your life. The one dominating abandon of the life is concentration on God, consequently every other carelessness is careless in comparison. In Luke 14:26, our Lord lays down the conditions of discipleship, and He says that the first condition is personal, passionate devotion to Himself until every other devotion is hatred in comparison.

"Take no thought for your life. . . ." Immediately we look at these words of our Lord, we find them the most revolutionary of statements. We argue in exactly the opposite way, even the most spiritual of us—"I *must* live, I *must* make so much money, I *must* be clothed and fed." That is how it begins; the great concern of the life is not God, but how we are going to fit ourselves to live. Jesus Christ says, "Reverse the order, get rightly related to Me first, see that you maintain that as the great care of your life, and never put the concentration of your care on the other things." It is a severe discipline to allow the Holy Spirit to bring us into harmony with the teaching of Jesus in these verses.

(b) Careful Unreasonableness (Matthew 6:26–29)

Jesus declares it to be unreasonable for a disciple to be careful of all that the natural man says we must be careful over. "Behold the fowls of the air: for they sow not, neither do they reap, nor gather into barns; yet your heavenly Father feedeth them. Are ye not much better than they? . . . Consider the lilies of the field, how they grow; they toil not, neither do they spin: and yet I say unto you, That even Solomon in all his glory was not arrayed like one of these." Jesus does not use the illustration of the birds and the flowers by accident, He uses it purposely in order to show the utter unreasonableness from His standpoint of being so anxious about the means of living. Imagine the sparrows and blackbirds and thrushes worrying about their feathers! Jesus says they do not trouble about themselves at all, the thing that makes them what they are is not their thought for themselves, but the thought of the Father in heaven. A bird is a hard-working little creature, but it does not work for its feathers, it obeys the law of its life and becomes what it is. Jesus Christ's argument is that if we concentrate on the life He gives us, we will be perfectly free for all other things because our Father is watching the inner life. We have to maintain obedience to the Holy Spirit, Who is the real principle of our life, and God will supply the "feathers," for are we not "much better than they"?

It is useless to mistake careful consideration of circumstances for that which produces character. We cannot produce an inner life by watching the outer all the time. The lily obeys the law of its life in the surroundings in which it is placed, and Jesus says, as a disciple, consider your hidden life with God; pay attention to the Source and God will look after the outflow. Imagine a lily hauling itself out of its pot and saying, "I don't think I look exactly right here." The lily's duty is to obey the law of its life where it is placed by the gardener. "Watch your life with God," says Jesus, "see that that is right and you will grow as the lily." We are all inclined to say, "I should be all right if only I were somewhere else." There is only one way to develop spiritually, and that is by concentrating on God. Don't bother about whether you are growing in grace or whether you are being of use to others, but believe on Jesus and out of you will flow rivers of living water.

"Consider the lilies of the field, how they grow"—they simply *are*. Take the sea and the air, the sun, the stars and the moon, they all *are*, and what a ministration they exert! So often we mar God's designed influence through us by our self-conscious effort to be consistent and useful. It seems unreasonable to expect a man to consider the lilies, yet that is the only way he can grow in grace. Jesus Christ's argument is that the men and women who are concentrated on their Father in heaven are those who are the fittest to do the work of the world. They have no ulterior motive in arranging their circumstances in order to produce a fine character. They know it cannot be done in that way. How are you to grow in the knowledge of God? By remaining where you are, and by remembering that your Father knows where you are and the circumstances

you are in. Keep concentrated on Him and you will grow spiritually as the lily.

"Which of you by taking thought can add one cubit unto his stature?" Jesus is speaking from the implicit domain. How many people are born into the world by taking thought? The springs of natural life cannot be got at by the reasoning of common-sense, and when you deal with the life of God in your soul, Jesus says, "Remember that your growth in grace does not depend on your watching it, but on your concentration on your Father in heaven."

Notice the difference between the illustrations we use in talking of spiritual growth and the illustrations Jesus uses. We take our illustrations from engineering enterprises, from motor-cars and aeroplanes, *et cetera,* things that compel our attention. Jesus Christ took His illustrations from His Father's handiwork, from sparrows and flowers, things that none of us dream of noticing; we are all breathless and passionate and in a hurry. We may think till all is blue,[11] but Jesus says you cannot add one inch to your height in that way. We cannot possibly develop spiritually in any way other than the way He tells us, viz., by concentration on God.

Our Lord's counsel to His disciples is, "Be as the lily and the star." When a man is born from above he is inclined to become a moral policeman, one who unconsciously presents himself as better than other men, an intolerable spiritual prig. Which are the men who influence us most? The men who "buttonhole" us, or the men who live their lives as the stars in the heaven and the lily of the field, perfectly simple and unaffected? These are the lives that mould us, our mothers and wives and friends who are of that order, and that is the order the Holy Ghost produces. If you want to be of use, get rightly related to Jesus Christ and He will make you of use unconsciously every moment you live; the condition is believing on Him.

(c) Careful Infidelity (Matthew 6:30–32)
Suppose Jesus tells you to do something that is an enormous challenge to your common sense, what are you going to do—hang back? If once your nerves are in the habit of doing a thing physically, you will do it every time, until you break the habit deliberately; and the same is true spiritually. Over and over again you will get up to what Jesus wants and turn back every time when it comes to the point, like a man balking a hurdle, until you break the habit and abandon resolutely. Jesus Christ demands of the man who trusts in Him the same reckless sporting spirit that the natural man exhibits in his life. If a man is going to do anything worth while, there are times when he has to risk everything on a leap, and in the spiritual world

Jesus Christ demands that we risk everything we hold by our common-sense and leap into what He says. Immediately we do, we find that what He says fits on as solidly as our common-sense.

Following Jesus Christ is a risk absolutely; we must yield right over to Him, and that is where our infidelity comes in, we will not trust what we cannot see, we will not believe what we cannot trace, then it is all up with our discipleship. The great word of Jesus to His disciples is *Abandon.* When God has brought us into the relationship of disciples, we have to venture on His word; trust entirely to Him and watch that when He brings us to the venture, we take it.

Jesus sums up common-sense carefulness in a man indwelt by the Spirit of God as infidelity. If after you have received the Holy Spirit, you try and put other things first instead of God, you will find confusion. The Holy Spirit presses through and says—"Where does God come in in this new relationship? in this mapped-out holiday? in these new books you are buying?" The Holy Spirit always presses that point until we learn to make concentration on God our first consideration. It is not only wrong to worry, it is real infidelity because it means we do not believe God can look after the little practical details of our lives, it is never anything else that worries us. Notice what Jesus said would choke the word He puts in—the devil? No, the cares of this world. That is how infidelity begins. It is "the little foxes, that spoil the vines," the little worries always. The great cure for infidelity is obedience to the Spirit of God. Refuse to be swamped by the cares of this world, cut out nonessentials and continually revise your relationship to God and see that you are concentrated absolutely on Him. The man who trusts Jesus Christ in a definite practical way is freer than anyone else to do his work in the world. Free from fret and worry, he can go with absolute certainty into the daily life because the responsibility of his life is not on him but on God. If once we accept the revelation of Jesus Christ that God is our Father and that we can never think of anything He will forget, worry becomes impossible.

(d) Concentrated Consecration (Matthew 6:33–34)
Seek ye first the kingdom of God, and His righteousness; and all these things shall be added unto you.

"Seek ye first the kingdom of God"—"But suppose I do, what about this thing and that? who is going to look after me? I would like to obey God, but don't ask me to take a step in the dark." We enthrone commonsense as almighty God and treat Jesus Christ as a spiritual appendage to it. Jesus Christ hits desperately hard at every one of the institutions we bank all

11. till all is blue: until you're exasperated, blue in the face.

our faith on naturally. The sense of property and of insurance is one of the greatest hindrances to development in the spiritual life. You cannot lay up for a rainy day if you are trusting Jesus Christ.

Our Lord teaches that the one great secret of the spiritual life is concentration on God and His purposes. We talk a lot about consecration, but it ends in sentimentalism because there is nothing definite about it. Consecration ought to mean the definite yielding of ourselves over as saved souls to Jesus and concentrating on that. There are things in actual life that lead to perplexity, and we say—"I am in a quandary and I don't know which way to take." "Be renewed in the spirit of your mind," says Paul, concentrate on God, so that you may "make out" what is His will. Concentration on God is of more value than personal holiness. God can do what He likes with the man who is abandoned to Him. God saves us and sanctifies us, then He expects us to concentrate on Him in every circumstance we are in. "Immediately I conferred not with flesh and blood." When in doubt, haul yourself up short and concentrate on God and every time you do, you will find that God will engineer your circumstances and open the way perfectly securely, the condition on your part being that you concentrate on God.

"Seek ye first the kingdom of God, and His righteousness; and all these things shall be added unto you." At the bar of common-sense Jesus Christ's statements are those of a fool; but bring them to the bar of faith and the Word of God, and you begin to find with awe-struck spirit that they are the words of God.

Study No. 4.

CHARACTER AND CONDUCT
Matthew 7:1–12

Christian Characteristics (Matthew 7:1–5)
    (a) The Uncritical Temper (Matthew 7:1)
    (b) The Undeviating Test (Matthew 7:2)
    (c) The Undesirable Truth-teller (Matthew 7:3–5)

Christian Considerateness (Matthew 7:6–11)
    (a) The Need to Discriminate (Matthew 7:6)
    (b) The Notion of Divine Control (Matthew 7:7–10)
    (c) The Necessity for Discernment (Matthew 7:11)

Christian Comprehensiveness (Matthew 7:12)
    (a) The Positive Margin of Righteousness
    (b) The Proverbial Maxim of Reasonableness
    (c) The Principal Meaning of Revelation

"And beside this, giving all diligence, add to your faith virtue. . . ." Peter is writing to those who are the children of God, those who have been born from above, and he says, Add, give diligence, concentrate. "Add" means all that character means. No man is born with character; we make our own character. When a man is born from above a new disposition is given to him, but not a new character; neither naturally nor supernaturally are we born with character. Character is what a man makes out of his disposition as it comes in contact with external things. A man's character cannot be summed up by what he does in spots, but only by what he is in the main trend of his existence.

When we describe a man we fix on the exceptional things, but it is the steady trend of a man's life that tells. Character is that which steadily prevails, not something that occasionally manifests itself. Character is made by things done steadily and persistently, not by the exceptional or spasmodic, that is something God mourns over—"your goodness is as a morning cloud," He says (Hosea 6:4). In Matthew 7 our Lord is dealing with the need to make character.

Christian Characteristics *(Matthew 7:1–5)*
(a) The Uncritical Temper (Matthew 7:1)
Judge not, that ye be not judged.

Criticism is part of the ordinary faculty of a man, he has a sense of humour, i.e., a sense of proportion, he sees where things are wrong and pulls the other fellow to bits; but Jesus says, "As a disciple, cultivate the uncritical temper." In the spiritual domain, criticism is love turned sour. In a wholesome spiritual life there is no room for criticism. The critical faculty is an intellectual one, not a moral one. If criticism becomes a habit it will destroy the moral energy of the life and paralyse spiritual force. The only person who can criticise human beings is the Holy Spirit. No human being dare criticise another human being, because immediately he does he puts himself in a superior position to the one he criticises. A critic must be removed from what he criticises. Before a man can criticise a work of art or a piece of music, his information must be complete, he must stand away from what he criticises as superior to it. No human being can ever take that attitude to another human being; if he does he puts himself in the wrong position and grieves the Holy Spirit. A man who is continually criticised becomes good for nothing, the effect of criticism knocks all the gumption and power out of him. Criticism is deadly in its effect because it divides a man's powers and prevents his being a force for anything. That is never the work of the Holy Ghost. The Holy Ghost alone is in the true position of a critic; He is able to show what is wrong without wounding and hurting.

The temper of mind that makes us lynx-eyed in seeing where others are wrong does not do them any good, because the effect of our criticism is to paralyse their powers, which proves that the criticism was not of the Holy Ghost; we have put ourselves into the position of a superior person. Jesus says a disciple can never stand away from another life and criticise it, therefore He advocates an uncritical temper, "Judge not." Beware of anything that puts you in the place of the superior person.

The counsel of Jesus is to abstain from judging. This sounds strange at first because the characteristic of the Holy Spirit in a Christian is to reveal the things that are wrong, but the strangeness is only on the surface. The Holy Spirit does reveal what is wrong in others, but His discernment is never for purposes of criticism, but for purposes of intercession. When the Holy Spirit reveals something of the nature of sin and unbelief in another, His purpose is not to make us feel the smug satisfaction of a critical spectator, "Well, thank God, I am not like that"; but to make us so lay hold of God for that one that God enables him to turn away from the wrong thing. Never ask God for discernment, because discernment increases your responsibility terrifically; and you cannot get out of it by talking, but only by bearing up the life in intercession before God until God puts him right. "If any man see his brother sin a sin which is not unto death, he shall ask, and He shall give him life for them that sin not unto death" (1 John 5:16). Our Lord allows no room for criticism in the spiritual life, but He does allow room for discernment and discrimination.

If we let these search-lights go straight down to the root of our spiritual life we will see why Jesus says, "Don't judge"; we won't have time to. Our whole life is to be lived so in the power of God that He can pour through us the rivers of living water to others. Some of us are so concerned about the outflow that it dries up. We continually ask, "Am I of any use?" Jesus tells us how to be of use: "Believe in Me, and out of you will flow rivers of living water."

"Judge not, that ye be not judged." If we let that maxim of our Lord's sink into our hearts we will find how it hauls us up. "Judge not"—why, we are always at it! The average Christian is the most penetratingly critical individual, there is nothing of the likeness of Jesus Christ about him. A critical temper is a contradiction to all our Lord's teaching. Jesus says of criticism, "Apply it to yourself, never to anyone else." "Why dost thou judge thy brother? . . . for we shall all stand before the judgement seat of Christ." Whenever you are in a critical temper, it is impossible to enter into communion with God. Criticism makes you hard and vindictive and cruel, and leaves you with the flattering unction that you are a superior person. It is impossible to develop the characteristics of a saint and maintain a critical attitude. The first thing the Holy Spirit does is to give us a spring-cleaning, and there is no possibility of pride being left in a man after that. I never met a man I could despair of after having discerned all that lies in me apart from the grace of God. Stop having a measuring rod for others. Jesus says regarding judging, "Don't; be uncritical in your temper, because in the spiritual domain you can accomplish nothing by criticism." One of the severest lessons to learn to is leave the cases we do not understand to God. There is always one fact more in every life of which we know nothing, therefore Jesus says, "Judge not." We cannot do it once and for all, we have to remember always that this is our Lord's rule of conduct.

(b) The Undeviating Test (Matthew 7:2)

For with what judgement ye judge, ye shall be judged: and with what measure ye mete, it shall be measured to you again.

This statement of our Lord's is not a haphazard guess, it is an eternal law which works from God's throne right down (see Psalm 18:25–26). The measure you mete is measured to you again. Jesus speaks of it here in connection with criticism. If you have been shrewd in finding out the defects of others, that will be exactly the measure meted out to you, people will judge you in the same way. "I am perfectly certain that man has been criticising me." Well, what have you been doing? Life serves back in the coin you pay; you are paid back not necessarily by the same person, but the law holds good—"with what judgement ye judge, *ye shall be judged.*" And it is so with regard to good as well as evil. If you have been generous, you will meet with generosity again; if you mete out criticism and suspicion to others, that is the way you will be treated. There is a difference between retaliation and retribution. According to our Lord, the basis of life is retribution, but He allows no room for retaliation.

In Romans 2, this principle is applied still more definitely, viz.:, I am guilty myself of what I criticise in another. Every wrong I see in you, God locates in me; every time I judge you, I condemn myself. "Therefore thou art inexcusable, O man, whosoever thou art that judgest: for wherein thou judgest another, thou condemnest thyself; for thou that judgest doest the same things." God does not look at the act, He looks at the possibility. We do not believe the statements of the Bible to begin with. For instance, do we believe that what we criticise in another we are guilty of ourselves? We can always see sin in another because we are sinners. The reason we see hypocrisy and fraud and unreality in others is because they are all in our own hearts. The great danger is lest we call carnal suspicion the conviction of the Holy Ghost. When the Holy Ghost convicts men, He convicts for conversion, that men might be converted and manifest other characteristics. We have no right to put ourselves in the place of the superior person and tell others what we see is wrong; that is the work of the Holy Ghost.

The great characteristic of the saint is humility. We realise to the full that all these sins and others would have been manifested in ourselves but for the grace of God, therefore we have no right to judge. Jesus says, "Judge not, because if you do judge, it will be measured to you again exactly as you have judged." Which of us would dare stand before God and say, "My God, judge me as I have judged my fellow men"? We have judged our fellow-men as sinners; if God had judged us like that we would be in hell. God judges us through the marvellous Atonement of Jesus Christ.

(c) The Undesirable Truth-Teller (Matthew 7:3–5)
The kind impudence of the average truth-teller is inspired of the devil when it comes to pointing out the defects of others. The devil is lynx-eyed over the things he can criticise, and we are all shrewd in pointing out the mote in our brother's eye. It puts us in a superior position, we are finer spiritual characters than they. Where do we find that characteristic? In the Lord Jesus? Never! The Holy Ghost works through the saints unbeknown to them, He works through them as light. If this is not understood, you will think the preacher is criticising you all the time. He is not; it is the Holy Spirit in the preacher discerning the wrong in you.

The last curse in our lives as Christians is the person who becomes a providence to us; he is quite certain we cannot do anything without his advice, and if we do not heed it, we are sure to go wrong. Jesus Christ ridiculed that notion with terrific power, "Thou hypocrite, first cast out the beam out of thine own eye; and then shalt thou see clearly to cast out the mote out of thy brother's eye." "Thou hypocrite," literally, "play-actor," one whose reality is not in keeping with his sincerity. A hypocrite is one who plays two parts consciously for his own ends. When we find

fault with other people we may be quite sincere, and yet Jesus says in reality we are frauds.

We cannot get away from the penetration of Jesus Christ. If I see the mote in my brother's eye, it is because I have a beam in my own. It is a most homecoming statement. If I have let God remove the beam from my own outlook by His mighty grace, I will carry with me the implicit sunlight confidence that what God has done for me He can easily do for you, because you have only a splinter, I had a log of wood! This is the confidence God's salvation gives us, we are so amazed at the way God has altered us that we can despair of no one; "I know God can undertake for you, you are only a little wrong, I was wrong to the remotest depths of my mind; I was a mean,[12] prejudiced, self-interested, self-seeking person and God has altered me, therefore I can never despair of you, or of anyone."

These statements of our Lord's save us from the fearful peril of spiritual conceit, "Thank God I am not as other men"; and also make us realise why such a man as Daniel bowed his head in vicarious humiliation and intercession, "I have sinned with Thy people." That call comes every now and again to individuals and to nations.

Christian Considerateness (Matthew 7:6–11)
Consider how God has dealt with you and then consider that it is for you to do likewise.

(a) The Need to Discriminate (Matthew 7:6)
Give not that which is holy unto the dogs, neither cast ye your pearls before swine, lest they trample them under their feet, and turn again and rend you.

Jesus Christ is inculcating the need to examine carefully what we present in the way of God's truth to others. If we present the pearls of God's revelation to unspiritual people, God says they will trample the pearls under their feet; not trample us under their feet, that would not matter so much, but they will trample the truth of God under their feet. These words are not human words, but the words of Jesus Christ, and the Holy Spirit alone can teach us what they mean. There are some truths that God will not make simple. The only thing God makes plain in the Bible is the way of salvation and sanctification, after that our understanding depends entirely on our walking in the light. Over and over again men water down the word of God to suit those who are not spiritual, and consequently the word of God is trampled under the feet of "swine." Ask yourself, "Am I in any way flinging God's truth to unspiritual swine?" "Be careful," Jesus says, "not to give God's holy things to 'dogs,' i.e., a symbol

---

12. The word *mean* as used here refers to something or someone ordinary, common, low, or ignoble, rather than cruel or spiteful.

of the folk outside. Don't cast your holy things before them, nor give the pearls of God's truth to men who are 'swine.'" Paul mentions the possibility of the pearl of sanctification being dragged in the mire of fornication; it comes through not respecting this mighty caution of our Lord. We have no right to talk about some points in our experience. There are times of fellowship between Christians when these pearls of precious rarity get turned over and looked at, but if we flaunt them without the permission of God for the means of converting people, we will find that what Jesus says is true—that they will trample them under their feet.

Our Lord never tells us to confess anything but Himself, "Whosoever . . . shall confess *ME* before men . . ." (Matthew 10:32). Testimonies to the world on the subjective line are always wrong, they are for saints, for those who are spiritual and who understand; but our testimony to the world is our Lord Himself, confess Him, "He saved me, He sanctified me, He put me right with God." It is always easier to be true to our experience than to Jesus Christ. Many a man spurns Jesus Christ in any other phase than that of his particular religious idea. The central truth is not Salvation, nor Sanctification, nor the Second Coming; the central truth is nothing less than Jesus Christ Himself. "I, if I be lifted up from the earth, will draw all men unto Me." Error always comes in when we take something Jesus Christ does and preach it as the truth. It is part of the truth, but if we take it to be the whole truth we become advocates of an idea instead of a Person, the Lord Himself. The characteristic of an idea is that it has the ban of finality.[13] If we are only true to a doctrine of Christianity instead of to Jesus Christ, we drive our ideas home with sledge-hammer blows, and the people who listen to us say, "Well, that may be true"; but they resent the way it is presented. When we follow Jesus Christ the domineering attitude and the dictatorial attitude go and concentration on Jesus comes in.

(b) The Notion of Divine Control (Matthew 7:7–10)

By the simple argument of these verses our Lord urges us to keep our minds filled with the notion of God's control behind everything and to maintain an attitude of perfect trust. Always distinguish between being possessed of the Spirit and forming the mind of Christ. Jesus is laying down rules of conduct for those who have the Spirit. Notion your mind with the idea that God is there. If once the mind is notioned on that line, when we are in difficulties it is as easy as breathing to remember, "Why, my Father knows all

about it!" It is not an effort, it comes naturally. Before, when perplexities were pressing we would go and ask this one and that, now the notion of the Divine control is forming so powerfully in us that we simply go to God about it. We will always know whether the notion is working by the way we act in difficult circumstances. Who is the first one we go to? what is the first thing we do? the first power we rely on? It is the working out of the principle indicated in Matthew 6:25–34, God is my Father, He loves me, I can never think of anything He will forget, why should I worry? Keep the notion strong and growing of the control of God behind all things. Nothing happens in any particular unless God's mind is behind it, so we can rest in perfect confidence. There are times when God cannot lift the darkness, but trust Him. Jesus said God will appear at times like an unkind friend, but He is not; He will appear like an unnatural father, but He is not; He will appear like an unjust judge, but He is not. The time will come when everything will be explained. Prayer is not only asking, it is an attitude of heart that produces an atmosphere in which asking is perfectly natural, and Jesus says, "every one that asketh receiveth."

A man will get from life everything he asks for, because he does not ask for that which his will is not in. If a man asks wealth from life, he will get wealth, or he was playing the fool when he asked. "If ye abide in Me," says Jesus, "and My words abide in you, ye shall ask *what ye will*, and it shall be done unto you." We pray pious blether, our will is not in it, and then we say God does not answer; we never *asked* Him for anything. Asking means that our wills are in what we ask.

You say, "But I asked God to turn my life into a garden of the Lord, and there came the ploughshare of sorrow, and instead of a garden I have been given a wilderness." God never gives a wrong answer. The garden of your natural life had to be turned into ploughed soil before God could turn it into a garden of the Lord. He will put the seed in now. Let God's seasons come over your soul, and before long your life will be a garden of the Lord.

We need to discern that God controls our asking. We bring in what Paul calls "will worship" (Colossians 2:23). Will is the whole man active; there are terrific forces in the will. The man who gains a moral victory by sheer force of will is the most difficult man to deal with afterwards. The profound thing in man is his will, not sin. Will is the essential element in God's creation of man; sin is a perverse disposition which entered into man. At the basis, the human will is one with God; it is covered up with all kinds of

---

13. The "ban of finality" means the limitation or curse of having one's mind made up, to the point of being unwilling to consider new information.

desires and motives, and when we preach Jesus Christ the Holy Spirit excavates down to the basis of the will and the will turns to God every time. We try to attack men's wills; if we lift up Jesus He will push straight to the will. When Jesus talked about prayer He never said, "If the human will turns in that direction. . . ." He put it with the grand simplicity of a child—*Ask.* We bring in our reasoning faculties and say, "Yes, but . . ." Jesus says, "If ye abide in Me, and My words abide in you, ye shall ask *what ye will,* and it shall be done unto you."

(c) The Necessity for Discernment (Matthew 7:11)
If ye then, being evil, know how to give good gifts unto your children, how much more shall your Father which is in heaven give good things to them that ask Him?

But remember that we have to ask things that are in keeping with the God Whom Jesus Christ reveals, things in keeping with His domain. God is not a necromancer, He wants to develop the character of a son of God. We can know "the things of a man" by "the spirit of man which is in him," but "the things of God" can only be spiritually discerned (see 1 Corinthians 2:9–14).

The discernment referred to here is the habitual realisation that every good thing we have has been given to us by the sheer sovereign grace of God. Jesus says, "Have this reasoning incorporated into you: how much have you deserved?" Nothing, everything has been given to us by God. Then may God save us from the mean,[14] accursed, economical notion that we must only help the people who deserve it. One can almost hear the Holy Ghost shout in the heart, "Who are you that talk like that? Did *you* deserve the salvation God has given you? Did *you* deserve to be filled with the Holy Spirit?" All that is done by the sheer sovereign mercy of God. "Then be like your Father in heaven," says Jesus; "be perfect even as He is perfect." "This is My commandment, That ye love one another; as I have loved you." It is not done once and for all, it is a continual steadfast growing habit of the life.

Humility and holiness always go together. Whenever hardness and harshness begin to creep into the personal attitude towards another, we may be certain we are swerving from the light. The preaching must be as stern and true as God's word, never water down God's truth; but when you deal with others never forget that you are a sinner saved by grace, wherever you stand now. If you stand in the fullness of the blessing of God, you stand there by no other right than the sheer sovereign grace of God.

Over and over again we blame God for His neglect of people by our sympathy with them, we may not put it into words but by our attitude we imply that we are filling up what God has forgotten to do. Never allow that idea, never allow it to come into your mind. In all probability the Spirit of God will begin to show us that people are where they are because we have neglected to do what we ought. To-day the great craze is socialism, and men are saying that Jesus Christ came as a social reformer. Nonsense! We are the social reformers; Jesus Christ came to alter us, and we try to shirk our responsibility by putting our work on Him. Jesus alters us and puts us right; then these principles of His instantly make us social reformers. They begin to work straightway where we live, in our relationship to our fathers and mothers, to our brothers and sisters, our friends, our employers, or employees. "Consider how God has dealt with you," says Jesus, "and then consider that you do likewise to others."

Christian Comprehensiveness (Matthew 7:12)
Christian grace comprehends the whole man. "Thou shalt love the Lord thy God with all thy *heart,* and with all thy *soul,* and with all thy *mind,* and with all thy *strength.*" Salvation means not only a pure heart, an enlightened mind, a spirit right with God, but that the whole man is comprehended in the manifestation of the marvellous power and grace of God, body, soul, and spirit are brought into fascinating captivity to the Lord Jesus Christ. An incandescent mantle illustrates the meaning. If the mantle is not rightly adjusted only one bit of it glows, but when the mantle is adjusted exactly and the light shines, the whole thing is comprehended in a blaze of light, and every bit of our being is to be absorbed until we are aglow with the comprehensive goodness of God. "The fruit of the Spirit is in all goodness and righteousness and truth." Some of us have goodness only in spots.

(a) The Positive Margin of Righteousness
The limit to the manifestation of the grace of God in us is our body, and the whole of our body. We can understand the need of a pure heart, of a mind rightly adjusted to God and a spirit indwelt by the Holy Spirit, but what about the body? That is the margin of righteousness in us. We make a divorce between a clear intellectual understanding of truth and its practical outcome. Jesus Christ never made such a divorce; He takes no notice of our fine intellectual conceptions unless their practical outcome is shown in reality.

There is a great snare in the capacity to understand a thing clearly and to exhaust its power by stating it. Overmuch earnestness blinds the life to reality, earnestness becomes our god. We bank on the earnest-

---

14. The word mean as used here refers to something or someone ordinary, common, low, or ignoble, rather than cruel or spiteful.

ness and zeal with which things are said and done, and after a while we find that the reality is not there, the power and presence of God are not being manifested, there are relationships at home, or in business, or in private, that show when the veneer is scratched that we are not real. To say things well is apt to exhaust the power to do them, so that a man has often to curb the expression of a thing with his tongue and turn it into action, otherwise his gift of facile utterance may prevent his doing the things he says.

(b) The Proverbial Maxim of Reasonableness
Therefore all things whatsoever ye would that men should do to you, do ye even so to them.

Our Lord's use of this maxim is positive, not negative. *Do* to others whatsoever ye would that they should do to you—a very different thing from not doing to others what you do not want them to do to you. What would we like other people to do to us? "Well" says Jesus, "do that to them; don't wait for them to do it to you." The Holy Ghost will kindle your imagination to picture many things you would like others to do to you, and this is His way of telling you what to do to them—"I would like people to give me credit for the generous motives I have." Well, give them credit for having generous motives. "I would like people never to pass harsh judgements on me." Well, don't pass harsh judgements on them. "I would like other people to pray for me." Well, pray for them. The measure of our growth in grace is our attitude towards other people. "Thou shalt love thy neighbour as thyself," says Jesus. Satan comes in as an angel of light and says, "But you must not think about yourself."

The Holy Spirit will make you think about yourself, because that is His way of educating you so that you may be able to deal with others. He makes you picture what you would like other people to do to you, and then He says, "Now go and do those things to them." This verse is our Lord's standard for practical ethical conduct. "Whatsoever ye would that men should do to you, do ye even so to them." Never look for right in the other man, but never cease to be right yourself. We always look for justice in this world, but there is no such thing as justice. Jesus says, "Never look for justice, but never cease to give it." The stamp all through our Lord's teaching is that of the impossible unless He can make us all over again, and that is what He came to do. He came to give to man a new heredity to which His teaching applies.

(c) The Principal Meaning of Revelation
Jesus Christ came to make the great laws of God incarnate in human life; that is the miracle of God's grace. We are to be written epistles, "known and read of all men." There is no allowance whatever in the New Testament for the man who says he is saved by grace but who does not produce the graceful goods. Jesus Christ by His Redemption can make our actual life in keeping with our religious profession.

In our study of the Sermon on the Mount it would be like a baptism of light to allow the principles of Jesus Christ to soak right down to our very make-up. His statements are not put up as standards for us to attain; God remakes us, puts His Holy Spirit in us, then the Holy Spirit applies the principles to us and enables us to work them out by His guidance.

Study No. 5.
IDEAS, IDEALS AND ACTUALITY
Matthew 7:13–29

Two Gates, Two Ways (Matthew 7:13–14)
  (a) All Noble Things Are Difficult
  (b) My Utmost for His Highest
  (c) A Stoot Hairt tae a Siae Brae

Test Your Teachers (Matthew 7:15–20)
  (a) Possibility of Pretence (Matthew 7:15)
  (b) Place of Patience (Matthew 7:16)
  (c) Principle of Performance (Matthew 7:17–18)
  (d Power of Publicity (Matthew 7:19–20)

Appearance and Reality (Matthew 7:21–23)
  (a) Recognition of Men (Matthew 7:21)

  (b) Remedy Mongers (Matthew 7:22)
  (c) Retributive Measures (Matthew 7:23)

The Two Builders (Matthew 7:24–29)
  (a) Spiritual Castles (Matthew 7:24)
  (b) Stern Crisis (Matthew 7:25)
  (c) Supreme Catastrophe (Matthew 7:26–27)
  (d) Scriptural Concentration (Matthew 7:28–29)

An idea reveals what it does and no more. When you read a book about life, life looks simple; but when you actually face the facts of life you find they do not come into the simple lines laid down in the book. An idea is like a search-light, it lights up what it does and no more, while daylight reveals a hundred and one facts the search-light had not taken into account. An idea is apt to have a ban of finality about it, we speak of the tyranny of an idea.

An ideal embodies our highest conceptions, but it contains no moral inspiration. To treat the Sermon on the Mount merely as an ideal is misleading. It is not an ideal, it is a statement of the working out of Jesus Christ's disposition in actuality in the life of any man. A man grows ashamed of not being able to fulfil his ideals, and the more upright he is, the more agonising is his conflict; "I won't lower my ideals," he says, "although I can never hope to make them actual." No man is so laboured as the man who has ideals which he cannot carry out. Jesus Christ says to such, "Come unto Me, . . . and I will give you rest," i.e., "I will "stay" you, put something into you which will make the ideal and the actual one." Without Jesus Christ there is an unbridgeable gap between the ideal and the actual; the only way out is a personal relationship to Him. The salvation of God not only saves a man from hell, but alters his actual life.

Two Gates, Two Ways *(Matthew 7:13–14)*
Our Lord continually used proverbs and sayings that were familiar to His hearers, but He put an altogether new meaning to them. Here He uses an allegory that was familiar in His day, and He lifted it by His inspiration to embody His patient warnings.

Always distinguish between warning and threatening. God never threatens; the devil never warns. A warning is a great arresting statement of God's, inspired by His love and patience. This throws a flood of light on the vivid statements of Jesus Christ, such as those in Matthew 23. Jesus is stating the inexorable consequence, "How can ye escape the damnation of hell?" There is no element of personal vindictiveness. Be careful how you picture our Lord when you read His terrible utterances. Read His denunciations with Calvary in your mind.

It is the great patient love of God that gives the warning. "The way of transgressors is hard." Go behind that statement in your imagination and see the love of God. God is amazingly tender, but the way of transgressors cannot be made easy. God has made it difficult to go wrong, especially for His children.

"Enter ye in at the strait gate. . . ." If a man tries to enter into salvation in any other way than Jesus Christ's way, he will find it a broad way, but the end is distress. Erasmus said it took the sharp sword of sorrow, difficulties of every description, heart-breaks and disenchantments, to bring him to the place where he saw Jesus Christ as the altogether lovely One, and, he says, "When I got there I found there was no need to have gone the way I went." There is the broad way

of reasonable self-realisation; but the only way to a personal knowledge of eternal redemption is straight and narrow. Jesus says, "I am the Way."

There is a difference between salvation and discipleship. A man can be saved by God's grace without becoming a disciple of Jesus Christ. Discipleship means a personal dedication of the life to Jesus Christ. Men are "saved; yet so as by fire" who have not been worth anything to God in their actual lives. "Go ye therefore, and *make disciples*" (Matthew 28:19 RV), said Jesus. The teaching of the Sermon on the Mount produces despair only in a man who is not born again. If Jesus came to be a teacher only, He had better have stayed away. What is the use of teaching a human being to be what no human being can be—to be continually self-effaced, to do more than his duty, to be completely disinterested, to be perfectly devoted to God? If all Jesus Christ came to do was to teach men to be that, He is the greatest taunter that ever presented any ideal to the human race. But Jesus Christ came primarily and fundamentally to regenerate men. He came to put into any man the disposition that ruled His own life, and immediately that is given to a man, the teaching of Jesus begins to be possible. All the standards our Lord gives are based on His disposition.

Notice the apparent unsatisfactoriness of the answers of Jesus Christ. He never once answered a question that sprang from a man's head, because those questions are never original, they always have the captious note about them. The man with that type of question wants to get the best of it logically. In Luke 13:23–24, a certain devout man asked Jesus a question, "Lord, are there few that be saved?" and Jesus replied, "Strive to enter in at the strait gate," i.e., "see that your own feet are on the right path." Our Lord's answers seem at first to evade the issue, but He goes underneath the question and solves the real problem. He never answers our shallow questions, He deals with the great unconscious need that makes them arise. When a man asks an original question out of his own personal life, Jesus answers him every time.

(a) All Noble Things Are Difficult
Our Lord warns that the devout life of a disciple is not a dream, but a decided discipline which calls for the use of all our powers. No amount of determination can give me the new life of God, that is a gift; where the determination comes in is in letting that new life work itself out according to Christ's standard. We are always in danger of confounding what we can do with what we cannot do. We cannot save ourselves, or sanctify ourselves, or give ourselves the Holy Spirit; only God can do that. Confusion continually occurs when we try to do what God alone can do, and try to persuade ourselves that God will do what we alone can do. We imagine that God is going to make us

walk in the light; God will not; it is we who must walk in the light. God gives us the power to do it, but we have to see that we use the power. God puts the power and the life into us and fills us with His Spirit, but we have to work it out. "Work out your own salvation," says Paul, not, "work for your salvation," but *"work it out";* and as we do, we realise that the noble life of a disciple is gloriously difficult and the difficulty of it rouses us up to overcome, not faint and cave in. It is always necessary to make an effort to be noble.

Jesus Christ never shields a disciple from fulfilling all the requirements of a child of God. Things that are worth doing are never easy. On the ground of Redemption the life of the Son of God is formed in our human nature and we have to put on the new man in accordance with His life, and that takes time and discipline. "Acquire your soul with patience" (see Luke 21:19). Soul is my personal spirit manifesting itself in my body, the way I reason and think and look at things. Jesus says that a man must lose his soul in order to find it.

We deal with the great massive phases of Redemption—that God saves men by sheer grace through the Atonement, but we are apt to forget that it has to be worked out in practical living amongst men. "Ye are My friends," says Jesus, "therefore lay down your life for Me; not go through the crisis of death, but lay out your life deliberately for Me, take time over it." It is a noble life and a difficult life. God works in us to do His will, only we must do the doing; and if once we start to do what He commands we find we can do it, because we work on the basis of the noble thing God has done for us in Redemption.

(b) My Utmost for His Highest

God demands of us our utmost in working out what He has worked in. We can do nothing towards our redemption, but we must do everything to work it out in actual experience on the basis of regeneration. Salvation is God's "bit," it is complete, we can add nothing to it; but we have to bend all our powers to work out His salvation. It requires discipline to live the life of a disciple in actual things. "Jesus knowing . . . that He was come from God, and went to God, . . . took a towel, . . . and began to wash the disciples' feet." It took God Incarnate to do the ordinary menial things of life rightly, and it takes the life of God in us to use a towel properly. This is Redemption being actually worked out in experience, and we can do it every time because of the marvel of God's grace.

"If ye love Me, ye will keep My commandments" (John 14:15 RV). Jesus makes this the test of discipleship. The motto over our side of the gate of life is— "All God's commands I can obey." We have to do our utmost as disciples to prove that we appreciate God's utmost for us, and never allow "I can't" to creep in.

"Oh, I am not a saint, I can't do that." If that thought comes in, we are a disgrace to Jesus Christ. God's salvation is a glad thing, but it is a holy, difficult thing that tests us for all we are worth. Jesus Christ is bringing many *sons* to glory, and He will not shield us from any of the requirements of sonship. He will say at certain times to the world, the flesh, and the devil, "Do your worst, I know that 'greater is He that is in you, than he that is in the world.'" God's grace does not turn out milksops, but men and women with a strong family likeness to Jesus Christ. Thank God He does give us difficult things to do! A man's heart would burst if there were no way to show his gratitude. "I beseech you therefore, brethren," says Paul, "by the mercies of God, that ye present your bodies a *living sacrifice.*"

(c) A Stoot Hairt tae a Stae Brae

A stoot hairt tae a stae brae (i.e., a strong heart to a difficult hill). The Christian life is a holy life; never substitute the word "happy" for "holy." We certainly will have happiness, but as a consequence of holiness. Beware of the idea so prevalent to-day that a Christian must always be happy and bright, "keep smiling." That is preaching merely the gospel of temperament. If you make the determination to be happy the basis of your Christian life, your happiness will go from you; happiness is not a cause but an effect that follows without striving after it. Our Lord insists that we keep to one point, our eyes fixed on the strait gate and the narrow way, which means pure and holy living.

"Take My yoke upon you, and learn of Me." It seems amazingly difficult to put on the yoke of Christ, but immediately we do put it on, everything becomes easy. In the beginning of the Christian life it seems easier to drift and to say "I can't," but when once we do put on His yoke, we find, blessed be the Name of God, that we have chosen the easiest way after all. Happiness and joy attend, but they are not our aim, our aim is the Lord Jesus Christ, and God showers the hundredfold more on us all the way along.

In order to keep a stout heart to the difficult braes of life, watch continually against worry coming in. *"Let not your heart be troubled,"* is a command, and it means that worrying is sinful. It is not the devil who switches folk off Christ's way, but the ordinary steep difficulties of daily life, difficulties connected with food, and clothing, and situations. The "cares of this world, . . . choke the word," said our Lord. We all have had times when the little worries of life have choked God's word and blotted out His face from us, enfeebled our spirits, and made us sorry and humiliated before Him, even more so than the times when we have been tempted to sin. There is something in us that makes us face temptation to sin with vigour and earnestness, but it requires the stout heart that God gives to meet the cares of this life. I would not give much for the man who had nothing in his life to make him say, "I wish I was not in the circumstances I am in." "In the world ye shall have tribulation: but be of good cheer; I have overcome the world"—"and you will overcome it too, you will win every time if you bank on your relationship to Me." Spiritual grit is what we need.

"Enter ye in at the strait gate." We can only get to heaven through Jesus Christ and by no other way; we can only get to the Father through Jesus Christ, and we can only get into the life of a saint in the same way.

Test Your Teachers *(Matthew 7:15–20)*
In these verses Jesus tells His disciples to test preachers and teachers by their fruit. There are two tests—one is the fruit in the life of the preacher, and the other is the fruit of the doctrine. The fruit of a man's own life may be perfectly beautiful, and at the same time he may be teaching a doctrine which, if logically worked out, would produce the devil's fruit in other lives. It is easy to be captivated by a beautiful life and to argue that therefore what that he teaches must be right. Jesus says, "Be careful, test your teacher by his fruit." The other side is just as true, a man may be teaching beautiful truths and have magnificent doctrine while the fruit in his own life is rotten. We say that if a man lives a beautiful life, his doctrine must be right; not necessarily so, says Jesus. Then again we say because a man teaches the right thing, therefore his life must be right; not necessarily so, says Jesus. Test the doctrine by its fruit, and test the teacher by his fruit. "If the Son therefore shall make you free, ye shall be free indeed," the freedom of the nature will work out.

"By their fruits ye shall know them." You do not gather the vindictive mood from the Holy Ghost; you do not gather the passionately irritable mood from the patience of God; you do not gather the self-indulgent mood and the lust of the flesh in private life from the Spirit of God. God never allows room for any of these moods.

As we study the Sermon on the Mount we find that we are badgered by the Spirit of God from every standpoint in order to bring us into a simplicity of relationship to Jesus Christ. The standard is that of a child depending upon God.

(a) Possibility of Pretence (Matthew 7:15)
Beware of false prophets, which come to you in sheep's clothing, but inwardly they are ravening wolves.

Our Lord here is describing dangerous teachers, and He warns us of those who come clothed in right doctrine, but inwardly their spirit is that of Satan.

It is appallingly easy to pretend. If once our eyes are off Jesus Christ, pious pretence is sure to follow.

First John 1:7 is the essential condition of the life of the saint, "If we walk in the light, *as He is in the light,*" i.e., with nothing folded up, nothing to hide. Immediately we depend upon anything other than our relationship to God, the possibility of pretence comes in, pious pretence, not hypocrisy (a hypocrite is one who tries to live a two-fold life for his own ends and succeeds), but a desperately sincere effort to be right when we know we are not.

We have to beware of pretence in ourselves. It is an easy business to appear to be what we are not. It is easy to talk and to preach, and to preach our actual life to damnation. It was realising this that made Paul say—"I keep under my body, . . . lest that by any means, when I have preached to others, I myself should be a castaway." The more facile the expression in words, the less likely is the truth to be carried out in life. There is a peril for the preacher that the listener has not, the peril of expressing a thing and letting the expression react in the exhaustion of never doing it. That is where fasting has to be exercised—fasting from eloquence, from fine literary finish, from all that natural culture makes us esteem, if it is going to lead us into a hirpling walk with God. "This kind can come forth by nothing, but by prayer and fasting." Fasting is much more than doing without food, that is the least part, it is fasting from everything that manifests self-indulgence. There is a certain mood in us all which delights in frank speaking, but we never intend to do what we say, we are "enchanted but unchanged." The frank man is the unreliable man, much more so than the subtle, crafty man, because he has the power of expressing a thing right out and there is nothing more to it.

(b) Place of Patience (Matthew 7:16)
Ye shall know them by their fruits. Do men gather grapes of thorns, or figs of thistles?

This warning is against over-zealousness on the part of heresy-hunters. Our Lord would have us bide our time. Luke 9:53–55 is a case in point. Take heed that you do not allow carnal suspicion to take the place of the discernment of the Spirit. Fruit and fruit alone is the test. If you see the fruit in a life showing itself in thistles, Jesus says you will know the wrong root is there, for you do not gather thistles from any root but a thistle root; but remember that it is quite possible in winter time to mistake a rose tree for something else, unless you are expert in judging. So there is a place for patience, and our Lord would have us heed this. Wait for the fruit to manifest itself and do not be guided by your own fancy. It is easy to get alarmed and to persuade ourselves that our particular convictions are the standards of Christ, and to condemn every one to perdition who does not agree with us; we are obliged to do it because our convictions have taken the place of God in us. God's Book never tells us to walk in the light of convictions, but in the light of the Lord.

Always distinguish between those who object to your way of presenting the Gospel and those who object to the Gospel itself. There may be many who object to your way of presenting the truth, but that does not necessarily mean that they object to God making them holy. Make a place for patience. Wait before passing your verdict. "Ye shall know them by their fruits." Wrong teaching produces its fruit just as right teaching does if it is given time.

(c) Principle of Performance (Matthew 7:17–18)
Even so every good tree bringeth forth good fruit; but a corrupt tree bringeth forth evil fruit. A good tree cannot bring forth evil fruit, neither can a corrupt tree bring forth good fruit.

If we say we are right with God, the world has a perfect right to watch our private life and see if we are so. If we say we are born again, we are put under scrutiny, and rightly so. If the performance of our life is to be steadily holy, the principle of our life must be holy, i.e., if we are going to bring forth good fruit, we must have a good root. It is possible for an aeroplane to imitate a bird, and it is possible for a human being to imitate the fruit of the Spirit. The vital difference is the same in each: there is no principle of life behind. The aeroplane cannot persist, it can only fly spasmodically; and our imitation of the Spirit requires certain conditions that keep us from the public gaze, then we can get on fairly well. Before we can have the right performance in our life, the inside principle must be right—we must know what it is to be born from above, to be sanctified and filled with the Holy Ghost, then our lives will bring forth the fruit. Fruit is clearly expounded in the Epistles, and it is quite different from the gifts of the Spirit, or from the manifest seal of God on His own word, it is *"the fruit of the Spirit."* Fruit-bearing is always mentioned as the manifestation of an intimate union with Jesus Christ (John 15:1–5).

(d) Power of Publicity (Matthew 7:19–20)
Every tree that bringeth not forth good fruit is hewn down, and cast into the fire. Wherefore by their fruits ye shall know them.

Jesus Christ makes publicity the test; He lived His own life most publicly (John 18:20). The thing that enraged our Lord's enemies was the public manner in which He did things; His miracles were the public manifestation of His power. To-day people are annoyed at public testimony. It is no use saying, "Oh yes, I live a holy life, but I don't say anything about it," for you certainly do not, the two go together. If a thing has its root in the heart of God, it will want to be public, to get out, it must do things in the external and the open, and Jesus not only encouraged this publicity. He insisted upon it. For good or bad, things must be dragged out. "There is nothing covered, that shall not be revealed; and hid, that shall not be known." It is God's law that men cannot hide what they really are. If they are His disciples it will be publicly portrayed. In Matthew 10 Jesus warned His disciples of what would happen when they publicly testified, but, He said, "Don't hide your light under a bushel for fear of wolfish men; be careful only that you don't go contrary to your duty and have your soul destroyed in hell as well as your body. Be wise as serpents, and harmless as doves." Our Lord warns that the man who will not be conspicuous as His disciple will be made to be conspicuous as His enemy. As surely as God is on His throne, the inevitable principle must work, the revealing of what men really are. One of the dangers of the Higher Christian Life movement[15] is this hole-and-corner aspect—secret times alone with God. God drags everything out in the sun. Paul couples sanctification and fornication, meaning that every type of high spiritual emotion that is not worked out on its legitimate level will react on a wrong level. To be in contact with external facts is necessary to health in the natural world, and the same thing is true spiritually. God's spiritual open air is the Bible. The Bible is the universe of revelation facts; if we live there our roots will be healthy and our lives right. It is of no use to say, "I once had an experience"; the point is, where is it now? Pay attention to the Source, and out of you will flow rivers of living water. It is possible to be so taken up with conscious experience in religious life that we are of no use at all.

Appearance and Reality (Matthew 7:21–23)
Our Lord makes the test of goodness not only goodness in intention, but the active carrying out of God's will. Beware of confounding appearance and reality, of judging only by external evidence. God honours His word no matter who preaches it. The men Jesus Christ refers to in verse 21 were instruments, but an instrument is not a servant. A servant is one who has given up his right to himself to the God Whom he proclaims, a witness to Jesus, i.e., a satisfaction to Jesus Christ wherever he goes. The baptism of the Holy

---

15. Higher Christian Life Movements refers to various groups and organizations that emphasized sanctification and personal holiness.

Ghost turns men into the incarnation of what they preach until the appearance and the reality are one and the same. The test of discipleship as Jesus is dealing with it in this chapter is fruit-bearing in godly character, and the disciple is warned not to be blinded by the fact that God honours His word even when it is preached from the wrong motive (cf. Philippians 1:15).

The Holy Spirit is the One Who brings the appearance and the reality into one in us; He does *in* us what Jesus did *for* us. The mighty redemption of God is made actual in our experience by the living efficacy of the Holy Ghost. The New Testament never asks us to *believe* the Holy Spirit, it asks us to *receive* Him; He makes the appearance and the reality one and the same thing. He *works in* our salvation and we have to *work it out*, with fear and trembling lest we forget to. Thank God, He does give us the sporting chance, the glorious risk. If we could not disobey God, our obedience would not be worth anything. The sinless-perfection heresy says that when we are saved we cannot sin; that is a devil's lie. When we are saved by God's grace, God puts into us the possibility of not sinning, and our character from that moment is of value to God. Before we were saved we had not the power to obey, but now He has planted in us on the ground of Redemption the heredity of the Son of God, we have the power to obey, and consequently the power to disobey. The walk of a disciple is gloriously difficult, but gloriously certain. On the ground of the perfect Redemption of Jesus Christ, we find that we can begin now to walk worthily, i.e., with balance. John the Baptist "looking upon Jesus *as He walked, . . . saith, Behold the Lamb of God!*" Walking is the symbol of the ordinary character of a man, no show to keep up, no veneer. "I perceive that is an holy man of God, which passeth by us continually" (2 Kings 4:9).

(a) Recognition of Men (Matthew 7:21)
Not every one that saith unto Me, Lord, Lord, shall enter into the kingdom of heaven; but he that doeth the will of my Father which is in heaven.

Human nature is fond of labels, but a label may be the counterfeit of confession. It is so easy to be branded with labels, much easier in certain stages to wear a ribbon or a badge than to confess. Jesus never used the word *testify;* He used a much more searching word— *confess.* "Whosoever therefore shall confess Me before men, . . ." The test of goodness is confession by doing the will of God. "If you do not confess Me before men" says Jesus, "neither will your heavenly Father confess you." Immediately we confess, we must have a badge, if we do not put one on, other people will. Our Lord is warning that it is possible to wear the label without having the goods; possible for a man to wear the badge of being His disciple when he is not. Labels are all

right, but if we mistake the label for the goods we get confused. If the disciple is to discern between the man with the label and the man with the goods, he must have the spirit of discernment, viz., the Holy Spirit. We start out with the honest belief that the label and the goods must go together, they should do, but Jesus warns that sometimes they get severed, and we find cases where God honours His word although those who preach it are not living a right life. In judging the preacher, He says, judge him by his fruit.

(b) Remedy Mongers (Matthew 7:22)
Many will say to Me in that day, Lord, Lord, have we not prophesied in Thy name? And in Thy name have cast out devils? And in Thy name done many wonderful works?

If we are able to cast out devils and to do wonderful works, surely we are the servants of God? Not at all, says Jesus, our lives must bear evidence in every detail. Our Lord warns here against those who utilise His words and His ways to remedy the evils of men whilst they are disloyal to Himself. "Have we not prophesied in Thy name . . . cast out devils . . . done many wonderful works?"—not one word of confessing Jesus Christ, one thing only, they have preached Him as a remedy. In Luke 10:20 our Lord told the disciples not to rejoice because the devils were subject to them, but to rejoice because they were rightly related to Himself. We are brought back to the one point all the time—an unsullied relationship to Jesus Christ in every detail, private and public.

(c) Retributive Measures (Matthew 7:23)
And then will I profess unto them, I never knew you: depart from Me, ye that work iniquity.

In these solemn words Jesus says He will have to say to some Bible expositors, some prophetic students, some workers of miracles—"Depart from Me, ye that work iniquity." To work iniquity is to twist out of the straight; these men have twisted the ways of God and made them unequal. "I never knew you"—you never had My Spirit, you spoke the truth and God honoured it, but you were never *of* the truth. "Depart from Me," the most appallingly isolating and condemning words that could be said to a human soul.

Only as we rely upon and recognise the Holy Spirit do we discern how this warning of our Lord's works. We are perplexed because men preach the right thing and God blesses the preaching, and yet all the time the Spirit warns—No, no, no. Never trust the best man or woman you ever met; trust the Lord Jesus only. "Lean not unto thine own understanding"; "put not your trust in princes"; put your trust in no one but Jesus Christ. This warning holds good all the way along. Every character will lead away from God if taken as a guide. We are never told to follow in all the footsteps of the saints, but only in so far as they have obeyed God, " . . . who shall bring you into remembrance of my ways *which be in Christ*" (1 Corinthians 4:17). Keep right with God; keep in the light. All our panics, moral, intellectual and spiritual, come on that line. Whenever we take our eyes off Jesus Christ we get startled, "There is another man gone down, I did think he would have stood right." *Look unto Me*," says Jesus.

The Two Builders *(Matthew 7:24–29)*

The emphasis in these verses is laid by our Lord on *hearing* and *doing*. He has given us His disposition, and He demands that we live as His disciples: how are we going to do it? "By hearing My words and doing them," says Jesus. We hear only what we listen for. Have we listened to what Jesus has to say? Have we paid any attention to finding out what He did say? Most of us do not know what He said. If we have only a smattering of religion, we talk a lot about the devil; but what hinders us spiritually is not the devil nearly so much as inattention. We may *hear* the sayings of Jesus Christ, but our wills are left untouched, we never *do* them. The understanding of the Bible only comes from the indwelling of the Holy Spirit making the universe of the Bible real to us.

(a) Spiritual Castles (Matthew 7:24)

We speak of building castles in the air; that is where a castle should be—whoever heard of a castle underground! The problem is how to get the foundation under your castle in the air so that it can stand upon the earth. The way to put foundations under our castles is by paying attention to the words of Jesus Christ. We may read and listen and not make much of it at the time, but by and by we come into circumstances when the Holy Spirit will bring back to us what Jesus said—are we going to obey? Jesus says that the way to put foundations under spiritual castles is by hearing and doing "these sayings of Mine." Pay attention to His words, and give time to doing it. Try five minutes a day with your Bible. The thing that influences us most is not the thing we give most time to, but the thing that springs from our own personal relationship, that is the prime motive that dominates us.

"Ye call Me Master and Lord: and ye say well; for so I am"—but is He? Think of the way we back out of what He says! "I have given you an example, that ye should do as I have done to you." We say it is all very well up to a certain point, and then we abandon it. If we do obey the words of Jesus Christ, we are sure to be called fanatics. The New Testament associates shame with the gospel (see Romans 1:16; 1 Peter 4:12–13).

(b) Stern Crisis (Matthew 7:25)

Our spiritual castles must be conspicuous, and the test of a building is not its fair beauty but its foundations. There are beautiful spiritual fabrics raised in the shape of books and of lives, full of the finest diction and activities, but when the test comes, down they go. They have not been built on the sayings of Jesus Christ, but built altogether in the air with no foundations under them.

"Build up your character bit by bit by attention to My words," says Jesus, then when the supreme crisis comes, you will stand like a rock. The crisis does not come always, but when it does come, it is all up in about two seconds, there is no possibility of pretence, you are unearthed immediately. If a man has built himself up in private by listening to the words of Jesus and obeying them, when the crisis comes it is not his strength of will that keeps him, but the tremendous power of God—"kept by the power of God." Go on building yourself up in the word of God when no one is watching you, and when the crisis comes you will find you will stand like a rock; but if you have not been building yourself up on the word of God, you will go down, however strong your will. All you build will end in disaster unless it is built on the sayings of Jesus Christ; but if you are doing what Jesus told you to do, nourishing your soul on His word, you need not fear the crisis whatever it is.

(c) Supreme Catastrophe (Matthew 7:26–27)

Every spiritual castle will be tested by a three-fold storm—rain, floods and winds: the world, the flesh and the devil, and it will only stand if it is founded on the sayings of Jesus. Every spiritual fabric that is built *with* the sayings of Jesus instead of being founded on them, Jesus calls the building of a foolish man. There is a tendency in all of us to appreciate the sayings of Jesus Christ with our intellects while we refuse to *do* them; then everything we build will go by the board when the test comes. Paul applies this in 1 Corinthians 3:12–13, "Now if any man build upon this foundation gold, silver, precious stones, wood, hay, stubble; every man's work shall be made manifest: for the day shall declare it, because it shall be revealed by fire; and the fire shall try every man's work of what sort it is." All has to be tested by the supreme test.

All that we build will be tested supremely, and it will tumble in a fearful disaster unless it is built on the sayings of Jesus Christ. It is easy to build *with* the sayings of Jesus, to sling texts of Scripture together and build them into any kind of fabric. But Jesus brings the disciple to the test, "You hear My sayings and quote them, but do you *do* them—in your office, in your home life, in your private life?" Notice the repulsion you feel towards anyone who tries to build *with* the sayings of Jesus. Our Lord allows no room for having some compartments holy and others unholy, everything must be radically built on the foundation.

(d) Scriptural Concentration (Matthew 7:28–29)

This summing up is a descriptive note by the Holy Spirit of the way in which the people who heard Jesus Christ were impressed by His doctrine. Its application for us is not, "What would Jesus do?" but, "What did Jesus *say?*" As we concentrate on what He said, we can stake our immortal souls upon His words. It is a question of scriptural concentration, not of sentimental consecration. When Jesus brings something home by His word, don't shirk it, e.g., something your brother has against you (see Matthew 5:23–24), some debt, something that presses—if you shirk that point, you become a religious humbug. The Holy Spirit's voice is as gentle as a zephyr, the merest check; when you hear it do you say, "But that is only a tiny detail, the Holy Spirit cannot mean that, it is much too trivial a thing"? The Holy Spirit does mean that, and at the risk of being thought fanatical you must obey.

When we are beginning to walk in the right way with God, we shall find the spirit of self-vindication will be unearthed; trying to fulfil what Jesus says will bring it to the light. What does it matter what any one thinks of us as long as Jesus Christ thinks we are doing the right thing, as long as we can hear Him say, "Well done, good and faithful servant"?

Notes on Ezekiel

Oswald Chambers

INTRODUCTION

Source

The material in *Notes on Ezekiel* is taken from lectures by Oswald Chambers at the Bible Training College, London,[1] between January and June 1914.

Publication History

- As articles: These notes on the book of Ezekiel were published as articles in the *Bible Training Course (BTC) Journal*,[2] from April 1948 to September 1949.
- As a book: This material was never published in book form.

These lectures were given as part of Oswald Chambers' series on the four great Old Testament prophets—Isaiah, Jeremiah, Ezekiel, and Daniel. The classes on Ezekiel consisted of fifty-four lectures covering all forty-eight chapters of the book.

For unknown reasons, Mrs. Chambers' usually thorough verbatim shorthand notes are incomplete for this series of lectures. The notes published as articles in the *B.T.C. Journal* covered only chapters 1 through 34. Perhaps for that reason, she never published them in book form.

---

1. Bible Training College (BTC): a residential school near Clapham Common in southwest London; sponsored by the League of Prayer; operated from 1911 until it closed in July 1915 because of World War I. Oswald Chambers was principal and main teacher; Biddy Chambers, his wife, was lady superintendent.

2. *Bible Training Course Journal:* published from 1932 to 1952 by Mrs. Chambers, with help from David Lambert.

CONTENTS

PREFATORY REMARKS FROM THE *BIBLE TRAINING COURSE (BTC) JOURNAL*, APRIL–JUNE 1949

AS THEY WERE SPOKEN

The *Journal* Notes on the Prophets have preserved for the present-day the very matter and method of Oswald Chambers' messages as they were given at the Bible Training College. They have about them a spontaneous and explosive quality. Much concentrated thought was given to pondering the Bible words. Then was poured out some intensive teaching based on some portion of that vital Word of God. It was not an analytical treatment of a chapter or a Book but a discernment, given by the Spirit of God, to a child-like mind, of the piercing message of God to His people in every age. That is what makes them so valuable to us who receive them today. They are as fresh and as living as when they were spoken. They reach the nerve-centre of a responsive soul. They stir us to obedience and appropriation and realisation of the truth. We remember them, by this means, those who have had the rule over us, who spake unto us the Word of God; and considering the issue of their life we imitate their faith. Hebrews 13:7.

The *Journal* will continue its ways, as the Lord permits. The Notes on Ezekiel will still appear. Also the striking Sermon Class Notes and other articles.

D. L.[3]

---

3. D. L.: David Lambert (1871–1961), Methodist minister; friend of Oswald and Biddy Chambers. Assisted Mrs. Chambers with OC publications from 1917 until his death in 1961.

NOTES ON EZEKIEL
Ezekiel 1–2

I would choose to see
The brightness of the heavenly things, although
Their lightning-glory leave me blind henceforth
To any earthly glow; and I would hear
But once the voice of God Almighty sweep
In thunder from His throne, although from hence
Mine ear be deaf to the sweet trembling chime
Of this world's music. I had rather stand
A Prophet of my God, with all the thrills
Of trembling, which must shake the heart of one
Who in earth's garments, in the vesture frail
Of flesh and blood, is called to minister
As Seraphs do with fire—than bear the palm
Of any other triumph.

                                        B. M.

In attempting to interpret a Book like Ezekiel we have to bear in mind that it can never be fully interpreted, only the fullness of time and God Himself can interpret it, but we ought not to misunderstand the clear lines on which the interpretation runs.

When we describe the isolation and loneliness of the prophets we are apt to imagine that that is what God expects of us today, but it is not; the isolation of those lonely mighty men of God of Old Testament days belongs to a different order. We are not called upon to live the life of the prophet in this dispensation; the life of the prophet is descriptive of the Church, not of individual Christians. Just as the Old Testament prophets stood alone for God, so the Church of Christ in this dispensation is to stand alone for God. There is no room for the idea that I am a peculiarly isolated individual—"I . . . only am left." Nothing could be more foreign to the New Testament conception. If only every one else were hypocrites it would exalt the sense that I am a lonely servant of God, but it is most humiliating to find there are "seven thousand . . . which have not bowed unto Baal." If you imagine you are called on to be isolated and aloof, the first thing you will do is to get under a juniper tree, refuse to eat or do anything natural, and you will be as free from sanity as from the Spirit of God.

Ezekiel's age at the time of his initiation into the prophetic office would probably be about thirty. Up to the age of thirty life is full of promise, of expectation and ambition; after that age, or what is represented by it, life is now a challenge to you to prove your mettle, the world, the flesh and the devil will test the stuff you are made of.

Prophetic Perception
The heavens were opened, and I saw visions of God.
(Ezekiel 1:1)

"And I saw visions of God." Ezekiel saw what God caused him to see; there was nothing in the nature of hallucination or fairy story about the vision. The full meaning of what Ezekiel is passing through dawns on him when he realises that he is in the presence of God, and he recognises his own insignificance. When the vision came to Isaiah he expressed himself subjectively—"Woe is me! for I am undone; because I am a man of unclean lips." There was nothing of this about Ezekiel, he was altogether taken up with the vision of God.

Have you ever seen God in all His power and majesty? The vision of God and the realisation of who He is, for even a moment, is worth all the experiences of God's grace you ever had. Nothing can turn the soul that has seen God, it is a sheet-anchor for ever, like Moses he endures, "as seeing Him who is invisible." Every other thing may fail, but one thing will last, and that is the vision of God by the illumination of the Holy Spirit.

It was in the fifth year of the captivity that "the word of the LORD came expressly unto Ezekiel the priest . . . and the hand of the LORD was there upon him." The arresting apprehension of God came to Ezekiel in the fifth year of captivity—five years "rusting" in agony of soul before God, aloof and useless. We have to beware lest our impatience makes us infidel; impatience means unbelief in God's providence, and is due to lack of right relationship of the personal life to God. In the first flush of salvation and sanctification there were months, maybe years, of real service and real results, now you are "shut up," and in all probability you are of more use to God because in the early days you estimated by what you could see. Take the majority of Christian workers, what is the one thing they rebel against? Being trained for God— "Let us get into practical work" is the cry, and how much discipline is there? how much do I know of my own soul! how much of God's Book? how much have I learned to live the life "hid with Christ in God"? how much do I know about heart-break? how much about other people being turned into shadows? how much, beyond mere pathetic sentiment, about being made broken bread and poured-out wine in God's hands? What is called practical work is the greatest hindrance in God's dealing with souls. We rush through life and call ourselves practical, we mistake bustle for business, activity for real life, and when the activities stop we go out like vapour, our work is not based on the fundamental energy of God.

"The word of the LORD came *expressly* unto Ezekiel the priest," i.e., enthrallingly and exclusively. There was no thought of Ezekiel saying, "I would like to devote myself to the service of God"; neither did he become a servant of God for surcease from his own sorrow (see Ezekiel 24:18). God used Ezekiel's bereavement, not to develop him, but that he might represent His purposes to the people. We look upon the disciplines of life as though God were trying to emancipate us through them; if we would come into right relationship with God we would hear His call— isolated expressly for one purpose. When God puts a special call on a special person it always means isolation for a time. (Cf. Galatians 1:15–16.) Aloneness must be made an opportunity for God in the life, or Satan gets the victory.

"And when I saw it, I fell upon my face, and I heard a voice of one that spake. And He said unto me, Son of man, stand upon thy feet, and I will speak with thee" (Ezekiel 1:28–2:1) On your face is never the position in which God can speak with you; only when you stand on your feet at God's command, after having been on your face before Him, can God speak with you. The counterfeit of spiritual power does not put a man on his feet, it does not turn him into a son of God, it is merely a vague fanatical influence. To stand on your feet before God is expressive of the realisation that I know what I was created for, viz., for God. We are not here to serve God, but for God; the self-consciousness of being a saint never enters in; "Oh, to be nothing, nothing" means that God made a great blunder in making me.

Commission of the Prophet *(Ezekiel 2:3–5)*

—And it was a terrible commission. "And He said unto me, Son of man, I send thee to the children of Israel, to nations that are rebellious . . ." (RV). A rebellious people can never be thought of as "babes in the wood"—poor distracted people, no vice in them, just been cruelly misled: it is the revelation of anarchy and rebellion. God placed Ezekiel among people who long ago had taken the first wrong step and now they are in captivity, and Ezekiel has to suffer with them that God may press home His message through the bruising of His servant. There is no call of God to be prosperous, but there is a call to be a proclaimer of God's truth to the gates of death. It is the winsome note that men want today—"I don't mind listening as long as you talk about the kindness of God, but don't tell me God damns sin, don't tell me He allows no quarter for lying or for lust." The Gospel awakens an intense craving and an equally intense resentment. The snare of the devil, through God's own servants, comes when they say "Now remember the people." Never water down God's word to suit men's experience. We palliate the truth of God because it offends, while in personal dealing our tendency is to be vindictive and hard. Be possessed with unflinching courage in preaching the truth of God, but when you deal with sinners, remember who you are. God tells Ezekiel to be concentrated on the message He gives him, no matter with what result. The preacher must never be guided by his own natural affinities, that will make him a traitor to the cause of God. God must make His prophets vitally one with His voice—holy man and holy message, one.

NOTES ON EZEKIEL
Ezekiel 3–4

And He said unto me, Son of man, eat that thou findest; eat this roll. . . . Ezekiel 3:1 (RV)

The word of God to Ezekiel was to be a living power in his inmost being. The application of the command to us is that we must appropriate the words of God, and we do it by eating the "Living Bread" ("Except ye eat the flesh of the Son of man and drink His blood, ye have not life in yourselves," John 6:53 RV), and by assimilating the truths that the Word of God abiding in us speaks to us. Fanaticism comes in when we say, "I won't appropriate the words of God, I don't want to be limited to what Jesus Christ says, I must get other

messages." We have to put ourselves in the place where we can appropriate the words of God, that is why we are here—in this College—to appropriate the words of God.

"Then did I eat it" (Ezekiel 3:3). Ezekiel states the simple, stupendous fact that he did what God told him to do. The conception of "swallowing" a word of God has in it the essence of obedience. There is no room for debate when God speaks. Obedience is never the outcome of intellectual discernment, it springs from moral simplicity, keeping in the light of God. "Eat this roll"—an unpalatable thing to do, but

Ezekiel obeyed, "and it was in my mouth as honey for sweetness." Obedience to a word of God always brings an amazing sweetness to the life of the obeyer. Over and over again God brings us up to a word of His, e.g., the conditions of discipleship (Luke 14:26) and we say, "Oh, I couldn't possibly "swallow" that," and we nibble at it and run away from it, and God brings us back to it again and again until we are willing to obey; immediately we obey and appropriate the word it becomes "as honey for sweetness."

"And He said unto me, Son of man, go, get thee unto the house of Israel, and speak with My words unto them. . . . But the house of Israel will not hearken unto thee; for they will not hearken unto Me" (Ezekiel 3:4, 7). The reason Israel so dislike the truths Ezekiel brings to them is because they rebel against the One who sent him—"for all the house of Israel are of an hard forehead and of a stiff heart" (RV). Ezekiel is told to go where God's permissive will seems contrary to His order. This problem runs through the whole Bible. Satan and sin and suffering are plainly and clearly not in God's order, but they are here just as plainly and clearly by His permissive will. An abiding peril in Christian service is the inspiration of sympathy for men springing from the devil, with one object—to slander God's permissive will.

Isaiah, Jeremiah and Ezekiel all base their message on the fact that God is holy and that He demands a holy people. The sins of Israel and Judah can be packed into one phrase—pride of independence, which makes out that God was obliged to select them because of their superiority to other nations. God did not *select* them: He *created* them for one purpose, that they should be His bondslaves until the whole world comes to know Him. The message of the prophets is that although they have forsaken God, it has not altered God. The Apostle Paul emphasises the same truth, that God remains God even when we are unfaithful (see 2 Timothy 2:13). Never interpret God as changing with our changes. He never does; there is no variableness in Him.

"Moreover He said unto me, Son of man, all My words that I shall speak unto thee receive in thine heart, and hear with thine ears" (Ezekiel 3:10). Ezekiel had to receive what he heard before he repeated it; this is imperative in all spiritual development. Reception of God's word implies personal devotion to the One who speaks it. "And go, get thee to them of the captivity. . . ." The insulation of a prophet means internal detachment from everyone saving God, while the life experimentally is in touch with everyone and everything but God. Ezekiel was in captivity in Babylon, among the renegade people of God.

"So the Spirit lifted me up, and took me away, and I went in bitterness, in the heat of my spirit, and the hand of the LORD was strong upon me" (v. 14).

Ezekiel was inspired of God, God's message was blazing in him, and the anger in his spirit against the people was hot and intense—"Wait till I get to the people, I'll tell them what God says"; but when he did get there, God kept him quiet for seven days, all his message gone from him. "Then I came to them of the captivity . . . , and I sat where they sat, and remained there astonished among them seven days" (v. 15) Then his attitude was—"Have I still to give Your message?" God restores him from all possibility of personal resentment, and then repeats the message. There was no fanaticism in Ezekiel. When we begin to work for God we have any number of crude, harsh sternnesses, we have the word of God for the people, but slowly and surely through the discipline of life we begin to be related to a different aspect of the message and can give it free from individual spleen.

"And it came to pass at the end of seven days, that the word of the LORD came unto me, saying, Son of man, I have made thee a watchman unto the house of Israel. . . ." Ezekiel, in common with all the Old Testament prophets, had not to generate his message out of his own individuality, he had simply to obey God. The obedient life is stated for us in Matthew 11:25 and 1 John 1:7, simplicity and single unfoldedness before God. Do I believe in God, or in a wise and understanding way of doing God's work? The message God laid on Ezekiel to deliver found no natural affinity for itself in him; the message was built on a supernatural affinity with God. God mortifies our affinities that limit Him. Like the Apostle Paul, Ezekiel has a "Woe is unto me, if I preach not the gospel"; he had a commission to warn the people of God, not win them, and he was to speak according to God's discretion, not according to his own judgement.

"Thou also, son of man, take thee a tile, and lay it before thee, and pourtray upon it a city, even Jerusalem. . . ." (Ezekiel 4:1 RV). This taking of a tile and drawing on it to portray a city is indicative of what the apostle refers to in 1 Corinthians—"the foolishness of God" (1 Corinthians 1:25). The Church of Jesus Christ has her commission, and just as Ezekiel must have seemed stupid to the people of his day, so the Church of Christ seems ridiculous in the eyes of the wisdom of the world. The Church is commissioned to preach the Gospel, to use no carnal weapons, but to see that her members are otherworldly while in this world. Our Lord came to do His Father's will, that was His first great obedience, and the first great obedience of the Church is to Jesus Christ, our exalted Lord; the temptation is to put man's needs first. The Church is to have affinity with God and with no one else. Salvation is always of God's almighty grace, our work is with individuals, we are to preach the gospel to every creature; the danger is to neglect the individuals God has placed us amongst for other individuals He has not placed us

amongst. The desire for revivals may mean shirking our individual responsibility.

"... so shalt thou bear the iniquity of the house of Israel" (Ezekiel 4:5). Verses 4 through 8 indicate a deeper aspect of Ezekiel's commission, the vicarious aspect. Ezekiel is to personify identification with the justice of God in His punishment of Israel and Judah. The Old Testament prophets never stood aloof from the judgements of God; they identified themselves with the life of their time and vicariously underwent the judgements. We gather our spiritual skirts around us from touching the life of the time we are in; the prophets did not, they stood firm for God in actual conditions. They are a marvellous prefiguring of Our Lord whom it pleased God to bruise. The Son of God

became vicariously identified with sin, and through that identification with sin the Church of God is born in order that she might bear the burden of God's purpose for the whole world. It takes evil to destroy evil; it takes sin to destroy sin—"Him who knew no sin He *made to be sin*" (2 Corinthians 5:21 RV). "He hath . . . *put away sin* by the sacrifice of Himself" (Hebrews 9:26).

Ezekiel 4:13–17 portrays the unclean condition of the people religiously. Remember what ceremonial uncleanness meant to a prophet—"Then said I, Ah Lord GOD! Behold, my soul hath not been polluted . . . ." Our Lord's death on the Cross is the exact fulfilment of this, and the depth and profundity of the horror is indicated for us in the Garden of Gethsemane and on the Cross of Calvary.

ONLY BRIEF SCATTERED NOTES ARE AVAILABLE ON THESE CHAPTERS AND TO THE END OF THE BOOK. [MRS. CHAMBERS' FOOTNOTE IN THE ORIGINAL TEXT.]

EZEKIEL 5–9

As soon as Ezekiel is laid hold of by the Spirit he is told to repeat the message of the other prophets, viz., that judgement is to fall on Jerusalem. Remember, the Temple with its laws and ordinances had been instituted by God and built according to His plan; this explains the antipathy of the people to the message of the prophets—"We are God's chosen people, we have 'chapter and verse' to prove that God established Jerusalem as His own, it is nonsense to say, as the prophets do, that God is going to depart from the Temple and blight and lay low His own people." The people maintain that the judgements of God are not abroad among them; they bank on the notion that they are God's favourites. They had to learn that God champions no man or nation. The people of God were cast off by God because they refused to be His people.

> *This is Jerusalem: . . . Behold, I, even I, am against thee; and I will execute judgements in the midst of thee in the sight of the nations. . . . Thus shall mine anger be accomplished, and I will satisfy my fury upon them. (Ezekiel 5:5, 8, 13 RV)*

The terrible finality of these verses appals us. Whenever in the prophets or in the New Testament we come to statements of the justice of God at work it is always the same—inescapably terrible and full of doom. Viewed apart from the interpretation of the Spirit of God, God's dealings with men and with nations are perplexing. There are certain dark lines in God's face, but the modern man has spectacles so skilfully arranged that those dark lines are not seen—

"Narrow-minded people in other dispensations believed these things, but we know better now." The terrible side of God's character is only realised by us when the truth dawns on us individually that God is no respecter of persons. Beware of tying God up in His own laws and saying He can't do what He says He is going to do. The greatest ingredient in the sovereignty of God is the measure of free will He has given man; but be careful you don't make the sovereignty of God the binding of Almighty God by human logic.

"... *and your idols may be broken and cease*" (Ezekiel 6:6). Idolatry is the outcome not of ignorance, but of perversity. Compare the attitude of the prophets with regard to idolatry with the amazing respect Paul showed to the Athenians who were not idolaters, but men who were feeling after God. Idolatry is never a dumb feeling after God. No nation under heaven ever became idolatrous in order to feel after God; they become idolatrous because they refuse to recognise the Creator. (See Romans 1.) The evolutionary idea that men develop from worshipping idols to worshipping God is absurd; it was the opposite with the people of God—they began with God and ended with idols. That accounts for the mercilessly scathing denunciation of idolatry by all the prophets.

"*Yet will I leave a remnant* . . ." (Ezekiel 6:8). The destructive power of God's judgements is to lead a remnant to the experience of repentance. The Apostle Paul says it is the goodness of God that leads men to repentance—unfortunately it is apt to be only God's destructions that lead to repentance. The goodness of God does lead some men to repentance, but not all, because the effect of wrong-doing is to destroy the power of knowing the wrong and men become self-complacent in their wrong. The signs of repentance are a broken and a contrite heart and weeping eyes before God. The "godly sorrow" which rends the unity of a man's life is one of the rarest treasures of human experience because it brings me, through self-loathing, to recognise the tears God shed over me, in the blood of His Son.

". . . and they shall profane My secret place" (Ezekiel 7:22 RV). Ezekiel is the prophet who points out the nearness of idolatry to the worship of God. Anything that detracts from the holiness of God or from holy human life is an abominable "image of jealousy" in the temple of God. God is there seeing it all; that is the reason He departs. In our day Satan as angel of light is not prevented from placing that image in the bodily temple of the Holy Ghost whenever imaginative or spiritual or intellectual thoughts are not being brought into captivity to the obedience of Christ. That truth applied to us individually means this—once realise that your body is the temple of the Holy Ghost, and you can never again do with success what you once did, the slightest attempt to do so brings a painful realisation of Paul's words in 1 Corinthians 3:17—"If any man destroyeth the temple of God, him shall God destroy" (RV). I have no jurisdiction over my body, there is only one honour at stake, the honour of God. Defiling the temple of the Holy Ghost is the result of my exercising my right to myself; realising this made Paul say, "I buffet my body, and bring it into bondage: lest by any means, after that I have preached to others, I myself should be rejected" (RV).

". . . as I sat in mine house, . . . the hand of the Lord GOD fell there upon me" (Ezekiel 8:1). Ezekiel's abstraction is typical of spiritual concentration—shut out from external things for concentration on the purpose of God. The great need for Christians today is occasional fasting from intellectual and religious and social activities in order to give ourselves wholly to the realisation of some purpose of God. Acts of consecration and devotional exercises leave us much the same; concentration on God never leaves us the same. This place[4] is for concentration on God and on nothing else.

"And it came to pass, while they were smiting, and I was left, that I fell upon my face, and cried, and said, Ah Lord GOD! wilt Thou destroy all the residue of Israel in Thy pouring out of Thy fury upon Jerusalem?" (Ezekiel 9:8 RV). The severity of judgement is not only on men, but enters into the very house of God itself, and Ezekiel finds there is no room for intercession (cf. 1 John 5:16). Intercession must neither spring from blind, compromising human pity, or we shall be in danger of trampling the blood of the Son of God under foot and saying God is vindictive. The wrath of God is never manifested because God is being thwarted. Wrath is the eternal basis of the moral life of fallen man as chaos is the basis of his material life. Wrath and love are both eternal; they are, so to speak, the obverse sides of the revelation of Almighty God. It is the inherent nature of sin to bring condemnation, and the point to be remembered is that God cannot save one man from the consequence of his sin unless there is an Atonement to build him back into relationship with God. When man sinned he fell into wrath and chaos; it is not that God visited it personally on him, it is the way God has constituted things. The love of God is the only inexorable thing there is, it will blaze and burn till He has made everyone as pure as He is Himself, saving the one who determines to side with sin and Satan and abide for ever on the obverse side of the love of God, viz., His wrath. The Bible reveals the power man has to choose to do this.

"For our God is a consuming fire"—an unspeakable comfort to the saint; unmitigated terror to the sinner. God will have nothing in His Presence but holiness. The Incarnation is the very heart of God manifested on the plane of chaos and wrath: God in the Person of His Son came right down to the very last depth of that chaos and wrath, and clothed Himself in the humanity of the race that was powerless to lift itself, and in His own Person He annihilated the wrath till now there is no more condemnation to those who are in Christ Jesus, no more touch of the wrath of God. The Atonement means that Jesus Christ creates us anew into a right relationship with God, not like the former creation, but like the relationship He Himself exhibited—"conformed to the image of His Son."

---

4. This place: the Bible Training College (BTC).

EZEKIEL 10–13

God's Awesomeness (Ezekiel 10)

. . . and the court was full of the brightness of the LORD's glory. (Ezekiel 10:4)

We are too shallow to be afraid of God. All the Hebrew prophets reveal this truth, that there is only one Cause and no "second causes." It requires a miracle of grace before we believe this, consequently we are foolishly fearless, but when the grace of God lifts us into the life of God we fear nothing and no one saving God alone. The "no second causes" truth was ever apparent to Our Lord, e.g., "Thou couldest have no power at all against Me, except it were given thee from above" (John 19:11).

Much discipline of mind and heart is necessary to enable us to believe that one day we shall hear and see the very sounds and sights of war and wrong blending inconceivably in praise. In the final restitution of all things by God hell and the devil himself have a distinct place. Confusion arises when we do not see God as Almighty: "God is not the greatest power, the devil seems to have much more power than God"— to talk like that is proof that I have not come into right relationship with God. To imagine that because I see God is going finally to restore all things to His original purpose therefore I myself am sure to be all right, is a persistent and recurring blunder; and I had better beware lest I suffer from delusion. If my first step has not been one of penitential repentance I will at one time meet the "artillery" of God and down I go, no matter how earnestly I pray and mouth my testimony, for this reason—God will have nothing in His presence but holiness and uprightness and integrity. "Those things will never happen to me, there are circumstances in my case which exonerate," there are not. God's demands are inexorable, only one thing will satisfy Him, and that is speckless, spotless holiness, and He will never let us go until He has brought us there—unless we wrest ourselves out of His hand.

Left Desolate (Ezekiel 11)

and the glory of the LORD went up from the midst of the city. . . . (Ezekiel 11:23)

Left desolate means that the heart of God is stabbed afresh by the pride of His people; the glory of the Lord departing from the city is evidence that God is a holy God. "Behold, your house is left unto you desolate," said our Lord (Matthew 23:38).

It must be borne in mind that the wisdom of the world is foolish only to God, it is not foolish to any other wisdom (see 1 Corinthians 1:20–25). You may often find yourself forced into a box of humiliated silence not because you are being overborne or censoriously sat on, but because the wisdom that is presented to you is so wise and understanding that you have not a word to say against it, and yet you know it is not the view of God. The demand to put the needs of man before the will of God is the outcome of the reasoning of human wisdom—and the wisdom of man is really wisdom, it can give the most satisfactory, sensible, judicious explanation for the course advocated, no human logic can stand against it. The temptation of our Lord centred round one point—"Do God's will in Your own way." The striking thing about our Lord is that He did not do God's will by the findings of His own will, consequently for thirty years He did nothing—nothing but *being*. Had He been a fanatic He would have found a hundred things to do. It is a crucial point in practical spiritual experience when we learn not to be more eager to do God's will than He is for us to do it. Our zeal to serve God may be and often is our insistence on God proving that our way is right; we see what God's will is as we wait before Him, and then we hurry up circumstances in order to do it, and we receive a severe punishment at the hand of God (cf. Genesis 15–16). God will put us in circumstances where we have to take steps of which we do not see the meaning, only on looking back do we discern that it was God's will for us.

Disillusionment (Ezekiel 12)

Nothing is so disastrously enervating as disillusionment, we much prefer our fictions and fairy stories about ourselves, to the stern realisation of what we really are in God's sight. In spiritual life disillusionment generally comes in relation to other people, that is why Paul says, "Wherefore let no one glory in men" (1 Corinthians 3:21 RV) and ". . . not to think of himself more highly than he ought to think" (Romans 12:3). In Ezekiel 12 the disillusionment comes in connection with national life and is in relation to God: the people begin to realise that God is not what they had vainly hoped He was. Ezekiel 12:1–6 forms God's answer to their expectation that He would reinstate the permanence of Jerusalem.

"The word of the LORD also came unto me, saying, Son of man, thou dwellest in the midst of the rebellious house, . . . for they are a rebellious house" (v. 2 RV).

The underlying fact of the antagonism of man's heart with the heart of God must be borne in mind when we consider the sweeping judgements of God symbolised in Ezekiel's conduct. If the antagonism of the heart of man to the holiness of God is not removed, man's imagination will not only picture God wrongly but he will come to know the wrath of God instead of the love of God. "My net also will I spread upon him, and he shall be taken in My snare" (v. 13). It is a terrible truth that many of us go astray until we are afflicted (see Psalm 119:67); we conceive in our pride that "we shall not be moved" and in this stage we dislike and radically disagree with the sterner presentations of God in the Bible, and it is only by the sharp sword of affliction and the profound conviction of the meanness[5] of our pride that we are brought to see God for ourselves and are ready to turn and obey His commands.

Prophetic Opportunism (Ezekiel 13)

Because, even because, they have seduced My people, saying, Peace; and there is no peace. (Ezekiel 13:10 RV)

Prophetic opportunism means preaching the truth of God, but without regard to being consistent with His holiness.

"*Because ye have spoken vanity, and seen lies, therefore, behold, I am against you, saith the Lord GOD*" *(Ezekiel 13:8).* The hostility of the false prophets against God and of God against them is an appalling revelation: God compels the man who will not come into agreement with Him to become His enemy—"Behold, I am against you." The warning in our individual lives comes in this way: in a personal crisis never lean to your own understanding, or as surely as you do, God is silent first, and then comes destruction. If I am spiritual what I have to prove in a crisis is that God is sufficient to guide me in His own way; if I trust to my wits it is all the god I have got, and God will hold me responsible for my fanaticism and delusion. Watch yourself in a wrong mood, a mood when "the bastard self seems in the right," you are as blind as a bat towards God; no moral relationship on earth will touch you as long as you are in that mood— "This thing will I do and hang the consequences." The explanation of that mood is that your mind is blinded by the god of this world.

Ezekiel 13:6–11 states the familiar truth that the revelation of God to me is determined by the state of my character toward God. "With the merciful Thou wilt shew Thyself merciful," says the Psalmist, "and with the perverse Thou wilt shew Thyself froward" (Psalm 18:25–26 RV). If we persist in being stiff-necked toward God, we will find He is stiff-necked toward us; if we show ourselves meek toward God, He will reveal Himself as gentle toward us. Here, God is showing Himself froward with the froward (KJV).

For wholesome holiness remember that God exempts no saint from the law of retribution, viz.: "With what measure ye mete, it shall be measured unto you" (Matthew 7:2 RV). One of the most chastening experiences is to watch how God pays back on our own heads our un-Christian judgement of others. The last possibility of indignation on our part is dead when we realise that we have been paid back in our own coin by the decree of God. Jesus Christ puts it this way—"But if ye forgive not men their trespasses"—and they really are wrongs—"neither will your Father forgive your trespasses."

"And if the prophet be deceived and speaketh a word, I the LORD have deceived that prophet" (Ezekiel 14:9 RV). This verse states that if a prophet gives a response that is not true it confirms the people in their delusion. A true prophet would never answer a disloyal request. In dealing with other people be careful to keep in such touch with God that you are not disloyal in heart yourself; if you are, you will talk to people you have no business to; whereas if you are loyal to God you can't answer some people and they go away with the peculiar certainty that you are a fool. None of us is free from disloyalty unless we are absolutely loyal. We are always on the wrong line when we come to God with a preoccupied mind because a preoccupied mind springs from a disloyal heart: "I don't want to do God's will, what I want is for God to give me permission to do what I want to do." That is disloyalty, and the experience of Psalm 106:15 is the inevitable result—"And He gave them their request; but sent leanness into their soul." In every particular that the heart is disloyal to God, God has to play havoc with our petitions; we are passionately in earnest over them, but God won't answer them because if He does it will ruin us. Loyalty to God means the continual carrying of the cross, the cross which comes from being a disciple whereby we deliberately and emphatically sign away our right to ourselves, our right to be loyal to anything and anyone but God.

---

5. meanness: mean, as used here, something or someone ordinary, common, low, or ignoble, rather than cruel or spiteful.

EZEKIEL 14–37

Son of man, when a land sinneth against Me by committing a trespass, . . . though these three men, Noah, Daniel, and Job were in it, they should deliver but their own souls by their righteousness, saith the Lord GOD. Ezekiel 14:13–14 (RV)

—prerogative wrath. The intense anguish of the godly is that in the final issue they are decreed by God to stand with Him instead of with those who are going the wrong way. It is not, "No matter what happens to the crowd, we will be all right"; the point is that the saint longs, would go through condemnation itself, if only men might be saved. "Yet now, if Thou wilt forgive their sin—; and if not, blot me, I pray Thee, out of Thy book which Thou hast written" (Exodus 32:32). "For I could wish that myself were accursed from Christ for my brethren" (Romans 9:3).

We only see these great truths bit by bit, the peril is to shut up our minds and say there is nothing in them.

For Fruit or Fire (Ezekiel 15)

What is the vine tree more than any tree . . . ? (Ezekiel 15:2)

The vine is of no value if it is not fruitful; trees which are not fruit-bearing are excellent for other purposes, but not so the vine which is fit only for fruit or for fire. "If a man abide not in Me, he is cast forth as a branch, and is withered; and they gather them, and cast them into the fire, and they are burned" (John 15:6 RV). What God burns is not weakness, not imperfection, but perverted goodness. Fruit is the manifestation of the essential nature of the tree, and our human lives are meant to bring forth the fruit of the Spirit, which is, literally, the life of God in me, invading me, producing fruit for His glory. "Herein is My Father glorified, that ye bear much fruit" (John 15:8).

Leaves of a tree are a fruit, but not *the* fruit; they are for the nourishment of the tree itself, that is why in the autumn they push off and sink into the ground where they become disintegrated and are taken into the root again. The fruit proper is never for the tree itself, it is for the husbandman. Woe be to the man who mistakes leaves for fruit! The reason Our Lord cursed the barren fig tree was because it stood as a symbol of leaves being proudly mistaken for fruit. (*See* Matthew 21:31.) When we mistake what we do for the fruit, we are deluded; what tells is not what we do, but what is produced by what we do.

The election of God by creation is an illustration of, though not the same as, "the election of grace." Election by creation means that God created the people known as Israel for one purpose—to be His servants until through them every nation should come to know Him. The "election of grace" is that anyone, Jew or Gentile, can, by God's free grace, enter into relationship with Him in and through our Lord Jesus Christ. The realisation of the election of grace by regeneration, and of being thereby perfectly fitted for glorifying God, is the most joyful realisation.

God's Love Unrequited (Ezekiel 16)

When God speaks of man's turning away from Him, He always uses terms which awaken disgust in us. Abstract terms for sin are never used in the Bible. A remarkable thing about Bible statements is that the language used is always in keeping with the facts—when an ugly fact is dealt with, an ugly word is used. The good taste that glosses over sin is ignored by Jesus (e.g. Mark 7:21–23). The Bible teaches "the morality of truth"; today we reverse the order and talk about that veneered humbug, "the truth of morality," viz., anything that is true is moral. The Bible always speaks in the final analysis.

The terrible picture given in this Chapter, and the ghastly humiliation of it to Ezekiel, has its counterpart in our personal experience when we really see our condition by our first birth as viewed in the sight of God. This is a rare type of conviction of sin—the distress of an "un-refuged" life. When a man gets there, there is only one of two places for him—either suicide or the Cross of Christ. No man can stand before God when once the law of God is made clear to his conscience. Only the Redemption of Jesus can enable a man to stand before God.

Every part of our human nature which is not brought into subjection to the Holy Spirit after experiencing deliverance from sin will prove a corrupting influence. We are not delivered from human nature; human nature was created by God, not by the devil; it is impaired, and enfeebled, but it is not sinful. The first creation retains the remnants of God's handiwork; recreation is the building of a spiritual habitation, "an habitation of God," and all our effort is to be spent in disciplining the natural life in obedience to the new creation (RV mg) wrought in us through the Spirit. If I refuse to make my natural life spiritual by the slow process of obedience, my religious profession becomes a disgusting hypocrisy. Any attempt to build on the natural virtues will ultimately outrage the grace of God, whereas dependence on God means the successful working of God's grace in me. "I do not make void the grace of God," said Paul (RV).

Heredity *v.* Humbug (Ezekiel 18)
. . . the soul that sinneth, it shall die. (Ezekiel 18:4)

These words refer to acts of sin. The principle is inevitable: the wrong things we do, we are whipped for, whether we are sinners or saints. We all have the sneaking idea that we are the favourites of God—"It's all right for me to do this, God will understand." If I as a child of God commit sin, I will be as sternly dealt with as if I were not His child. If a Christian commits a sin he must confess it and accept propitiation, and the degree in which he does not accept propitiation shows itself in a determined, settled gloom which is mistaken for penitence. If I have never been struck through with repentance I am scarcely on the first rung of Christian experience. The luxury of gloom is one of the most spiteful sins against God—I have humiliated myself to myself, and instead of getting right with God on the ground of the Atonement I deny that Jesus Christ does anything, and rummage down to the depths of myself in order to justify myself. Repentance means I accept the absolute forgiveness of God on the ground of the Atonement.

It Is God (Ezekiel 20)
Beware of two things—first, denying free will to God by stating to yourself as Israel and Judah did in their day, that God will only work according to His own precedents; and, second, thinking that God is bound to see you through irrespective of what you are or do. Don't tie God up in your own conceptions, or say too surely you know what God will do. For instance, never say because the devil rules in a certain place that God won't come into it: God will come where He likes. The sovereign purposes of God work out slowly and inexorably, but ever be careful to note where God's sovereignty is at work among men in matters of history and Time, and where it is at work in matters of eternal destiny. Beware of allowing your memory of how God has worked to take the place of present vital moral relationship to Him.

"Then said I, Ah Lord GOD: they say of me, Is he not a speaker of parables?" (v. 49 RV). Ezekiel's words are an indication of the way we always find it difficult to understand what we don't like. Remember, the human heart does not like what God likes until it is made God-like. Re-examine for yourself the teaching in the Bible which you say you don't understand, and see if the reason is not your dislike of what is taught. Beware of an escape of mind that is not true to Bible revelation. The destruction and terrors of God's punishment are as much God's decree as are the peace and joy and prosperity of God. Damnation and salvation are not natural results, they are Divine results.

We can choose the way we take, but we have no control over where that way ends.

The Song of the Sword (Ezekiel 21)
Thus saith the LORD: Say, A sword, a sword, it is sharpened, and also furbished. (Ezekiel 21:9 RV)

"And take . . . the sword of the Spirit, which is the word of God." When I have been using "the sword of the Spirit" in a spirit of indignation against another, it is a terrible experience to find the sword suddenly wrested out of my hand and laid about me personally by God. Let your personal experience of the work of God's Spirit instruct you at the foot of Calvary; let the light of God riddle you through, then you will never use the word of God to another, never turn the light of God on him, without fear and trembling. "For the word of God is living, and active, and sharper than any two-edged sword . . ." (RV). The word of God is the sword that cuts first in me and then in others. The truth of God can never be escaped from by those who utter it—"Thou therefore that teachest another, *teachest thou not thyself?* thou that preachest a man should not steal, *dost thou steal?*"

Liberty *v.* Licence (Ezekiel 23)
. . . they took both one way. (Ezekiel 23:13)

Liberty is the ability to obey the law of God, with the power to live according to its demands; license is the unrestrained impulse to traffic against the law of God. I know nothing about being made "free from the law" until I cease from unintelligently doing what I am told to do because I am told, and do it because there is no need to be told; only then do I do it rightly. Freedom from the law means that there is no independence of God in my make-up. No one is free who does what he likes. "For Christ also pleased not Himself" (RV). The seal of immorality is that I do what I like; the seal of freedom is that I do what God likes. No natural man can keep the law of God, it is only when the Holy Spirit is in him that the ability is there, then he keeps the law of God easily.

If you try and define Divine omnipotence and human free will in intellectual terms, you find language fails because they contradict each other. Every choice a saint makes is a free, untrammelled[6] choice of a human will, and yet in the final analysis it will be found to be in accord with the foreknowledge of God. We say, "I'll do what I like," but the strange thing is we never do, there is always a nemesis, always an incalculable factor to be estimated. To say, "I let God have His way" is a snare, because when I say that I never do, what happens is that in saying it I slip out

---

6. untrammelled: free, unhindered, not entangled.

of my moral responsibility. I am not asked whether or not I will exercise my will, I am obliged to, and when I am born again the regenerating power of God increases my moral responsibility.

Ezekiel 24

I the LORD have spoken it: it shall come to pass, and I will do it; I will not go back, neither will I spare, neither will I repent; according to thy ways, and according to thy doings, shall they judge thee, saith the LORD GOD. (Ezekiel 24:14)

The house of Israel remains for all time God's terrible object lesson of the determined spiritual obstinacy that refuses to be enlightened along any line but that of personal prejudice—"the rebellious house," God calls them (Ezekiel 12:2 RV). In national life and in personal life delusion always arises when a word has been spoken by God and been perverted by prejudice. Beware what you are for and what you are against. Whatever produces obstinacy is never of God. Immediately you are brought into a closeness of relationship to God you will know what obstinacy means. Every time, not sometimes, after the experience of sanctification comes the battle royal, and until the battle is fought out on the plane of holiness we will know nothing about the purpose of God for our life. We have accepted God's blessings, accepted deliverance from what we call sin, but we have never yielded to God, we prefer to stick to our own obstinate way of looking at things. It is possible to step into the dark any time we like, and darkness always comes along the line of obstinacy. If the Holy Spirit is obeyed the stubbornness is blown out, the dynamite of the Holy Ghost blows it out.

Sorrow (Ezekiel 24)

Also the word of the LORD came unto me, saying, Son of man, behold I take away from thee the desire of thine eyes with a stroke: yet neither shalt thou mourn nor weep, neither shall thy tears run down. Sigh, be silent [RV mg]; make no mourning for the dead. . . . (vv. 15–17)

Sorrow is cruel, and must work either delight or death; "godly sorrow" worketh delight *via* repentance; "the sorrow of the world worketh death" *via* sullenness. The sorrow that can be expressed is scarcely worthy of the name, but the sorrow that has one end in God and the other in the inarticulate depths of human experience is worthy of the name. Ezekiel's sorrow sprang from the fact that God took his flesh and blood, his nerves, his affections, to write a sign of warning for His rebellious people. "Thus shall Ezekiel be unto you a sign" (Ezekiel 24:24 RV). How many lives has God got to make a "sign" to me before I believe Him?

"So I spake unto the people in the morning; and at even my wife died; and I did in the morning as I was commanded" (RV). Verse 18 is unequalled for condensed human interests, Divine strength, and superb control. Nowhere in the Bible do we find any of the modern tendency to yelp, or any of the sentimental stuff we get written today. The deep sorrows of human hearts ought never to be touched, never dragged out into poetry and literature, because if the sorrow is real it can never be expressed. The Bible remains on the basis of reality all through; there is nothing enervating in its griefs or in its joys, and it is because we have got so far away from the robust iron tonic of the Bible that we strew the road with sentimentality. We are meant to be men and women of God, not sentimentalists.

There is no honourable escape from the way of sorrow. The *Via Dolorosa* is the way of God; the way of shallow happiness is the way of Satan. Our individual sympathies, whether we realise it or not, either centre around the way of Satan or the way of the Saviour. (Cf. Matthew 16:23.) The last lesson we learn is "hands off" other lives; our hands off that God's hands may be on.

Ezekiel 28

Thus saith the Lord GOD: Because thine heart is lifted up, and thou hast said, I am a god . . . (Ezekiel 28:2 RV)

Pride in its most estimable as well as its most debased form is self-deification; it is not a yielding to temptation from without, but a distinct alteration of relationships within. Watch where you are not willing to give up your self-confident obstinacy in little things, and you will know how much pride there is in your heart, how much you will set your moral teeth against God's providential order—"I won't yield"; "I won't for a second allow anyone to usurp my rights." To that life will come the revelation of God as an enemy. If we have had detected in us any lurking of pride, when are we going to break from it? we will have to break some day, why not now?

". . . and thou hast sinned" (v.16). The committing of sin destroys the power of knowing it is sin, and a man can be perfectly happy on that level. It is possible for a man to sink to the level of being a bad, happy man. The Bible reveals that a man kills *himself* according to the measure of his sinning, "the soul that sinneth, it shall die" (Ezekiel 18:4). I may suffer because of the sins of my progenitors—I am never punished for them; but I shall certainly be punished for my own sins. Before sin is imputed it must be personal. Sin is not a theoretical question, but a practical one. No man is punished because he has an heredity of sin, God deals with that entirely through the death of His Son on the Cross; what He holds me responsible for is

refusing to let Him deliver me. Immediately I see that Jesus Christ can deliver me from the heredity of sin— not acts of sin, but the heredity of sin, which is the inheritance of the whole human race through Adam— and I refuse to let Him, that is the seal of condemnation. But remember I must have seen that that is what He came to do; I must have seen *the* Light, Jesus Christ (John 3:19). It must be a terrible thing to meet a man who deliberately by his own choice has become a disbeliever in Jesus. Dis-belief and un-belief are not the same; dis-belief implies moral perversion. The standard of condemnation is what a man consciously sees and knows. "If I had not come," said Jesus, "and spoken unto them, they had not had sin: but now they have no excuse for their sin" (RV).

... *"and they shall know that I am the LORD, when I shall have executed judgements in her" (Ezekiel 28:22).* There is something purely punitive in God's government of the world; the law has not only to punish the evil-doer, but to vindicate itself. The law must be justified, and it is this aspect of punishment with regard to God and His holy law that men do not like to think about. When God's judgements are abroad they have the most appalling power of isolation about them, every man feels himself isolated before God. God's judgements shake all the shakeable things till there is nothing left as a separate consciousness but identity with God.

Ezekiel 29–30
It shall be the basest of the kingdoms. (Ezekiel 29:15)

Ezekiel uses the same image as Isaiah for the untrustworthiness of Egypt—"because they have been a staff of reed to the house of Israel." ("Behold, thou trustest upon the staff of this bruised reed, even upon Egypt" Isaiah 36:6 RV.) Egypt was to become a crippled, second-rate power, nothing illuminating or inspiriting, only degradation and humiliation. After supreme prosperity, to be punished, not magnificently but by dreary commonplace monotony, is itself the most terrible punishment. When I have done wrong I expect that God must give me a tremendous punishment, instead of that He quietly ignores me. I try to rouse Him by my protestations and prayers, but He pays no attention, then after a while He lifts me up in the most ordinary way and lets me understand my utter insignificance. It is the only way I realise that He is God.

"Thus saith the Lord GOD: I will also destroy the idols" (Ezekiel 30:13 RV). The difference, and it is a fundamental one, in the way the prophets of God treat idolatry and the way natural thoughtful men treat it is that the latter speak of it as a reversion to type; the Bible always speaks of idolatry as a perversion from type, a distinct backsliding. The prophets never deal pitifully with idolatry; the natural man never deals sternly with it. The distinction is vital.

Ezekiel 33–34
"So thou, son of man, I have set thee a watchman unto the house of Israel; therefore hear the word at My mouth, and give them warning from Me" (Ezekiel 33:7 RV). The false prophets stood for the exoneration of the people; the true prophets stood for their condemnation. Today there are those who side with men against God instead of proclaiming the Gospel of God and putting the responsibility of choice on men themselves. The loyalty is to be to God's word. Not, "If you don't do what I tell you, you will be wrong," but, "These are the words of God, and you will meet them again." The peril in preaching does not lie with the hearers, but with the preacher. It is appallingly easy to preach. Every word I have spoken in this place in the name of God, if I have not been living up to its standard myself, will increase and deepen my condemnation before God. A man may be used as the mouthpiece of God, but he must remember he has a personal destiny to fulfil before God. Ezekiel went through his prophetic career unscathed because he fulfilled his own spiritual destiny.

"He heard the sound of the trumpet, and took not warning . . ." (Ezekiel 33:5). God never coerces, and we are not children of God when we do; but God never accommodates His demands to human compromise, and we are disloyal to God's truth if we do. The great point in a man's personal life with God is to agree with God's verdict with no remnant of a desire to vindicate himself. We cannot make God's issue for our life plain when we like, but when it is found out, that is the moment of choice. Watch the moments when the still small voice of God makes an issue regarding God's will clear to your mind—choose what He says and you will enter on a new plane of discipline and delight; don't choose, and you will enter on a plane of amused happy compromise. Moments are not denied us

> *When the spirit's true endowments*
> *Stand out plainly from its false ones,*
> *And apprise it if pursuing*
> *Or the right way or the wrong way*
> *To its triumph or undoing.*

"Should not the shepherds feed the sheep?" (Ezekiel 34:2 RV). In the New Testament the terms "shepherd" and "sheep" are applied not to kings and nations, but to the disciples of Jesus. When Our Lord commissioned Peter He did not tell him to go and save souls, but—"Feed My sheep; tend My lambs"; guard My flock. We have to be careful lest we rebel against the commission to disciple men to Jesus and become energetic proselytisers to our own way of thinking—"but

the shepherds fed themselves, and fed not My sheep" (Ezekiel 34:8 RV). When we stand before God will He say, "Well done, good and faithful servant"? or will He say, "You have not been a shepherd of My sheep, you have fed them for your own interest, exploited them for your own creed"? When a soul gets within sight of Jesus Christ, leave him alone.

Ezekiel 37

The hand of the LORD was upon me, and He . . . set me down in the midst of the valley; and it was full of bones. (Ezekiel 37:1 RV)

The sight of our eyes never gives us realities, only actualities; the vision of the valley of bones was a reality, not an actuality, that is, Ezekiel had it revealed to him in a vision. Our Lord's question to Thomas, "Because thou hast seen Me, hast thou believed?" (John 20:29 RV mg) refers to the abiding difference between actuality and reality. No man ever believes because he sees, every man must believe before he perceives the reality of what he looks at.

"And He said unto me, Son of man, can these bones live?" (Ezekiel 37:3). In dealing with Bible experiences we must ever make allowance for the miraculous, which never contradicts reason, but very often does contradict common sense. The miraculous transcends reason and lifts it into another world than the logical one, consequently spiritual experience is something I have *lived* through, not thought through. The Bible is based on what makes life, life, i.e., on the implicit.

"Again He said unto me, Prophesy over these bones, and say unto them, O ye dry bones, hear the word of the LORD" (v. 4 RV). The Spirit of God makes us reverent with human wrecks. A man lying beneath the wrath of God is not the victim of His neglect. No man is beyond the pale of God's grace if he is still the object of God's wrath, because wrath is the obverse side of God's love.

(No notes are available on the later chapters.)

Bibliography

Complete Works of Oswald Chambers

Approved Unto God, combined volume (1946) includes **Facing Reality**
    Approved Unto God (1936)
    Theme: Christian service; being a worker for God
    Lectures at the Bible Training College
    Facing Reality (1939)
    Theme: Belief
    Messages given at League of Prayer meetings and Bible Training College classes in Britain; talks to British Commonwealth troops in Egypt

As He Walked
    See **Our Brilliant Heritage**

Baffled to Fight Better (1917)
    Theme: Job and the problem of suffering
    Talks to soldiers in Egypt

Biblical Ethics (1947)
    Theme: Christian ethics, morality, philosophy
    Lectures at: The Bible Training College; League of Prayer meetings in Britain; talks to soldiers in Egypt

Biblical Psychology (1912, 1936)
    Theme: Soul, spirit, personality; the origins of man
    Lectures at the Bible Training College

Bringing Sons unto Glory (1944)
    Theme: Studies in the life of Christ, the meaning of His life for us
    Lectures at the Bible Training College and evening classes in London

Called of God (1936)
    Theme: The missionary call
    Selections from **My Utmost for His Highest**

Christian Disciplines (Published in various forms 1907–1968))
    Themes: Divine guidance, suffering, peril, prayer, loneliness, patience
    Talks given in Britain and the U.S.

Conformed to His Image (1950)
    Theme: Christian thinking, faith
    Classes taught at the Bible Training College; sermons and talks in Britain, America and Egypt

Disciples Indeed (1955)
    Themes: Belief, the Bible, the call of God, the character of God, experience, the Holy Spirit, the moral law, personality, personal relationship, prayer, preaching, preparation, redemption, sin, study, the teaching of Jesus, temptation, testimony, thinking, workers for God
    From talks in the Sermon Class at the Bible Training College

Facing Reality
    See **Approved unto God**

The Fighting Chance
    See **The Servant as His Lord**

Gems from Genesis (1989)
    See **Not Knowing Whither** (1934) and **Our Portrait in Genesis** (1957)

God's Workmanship (1953)
    Theme: Practical Christian living
    Lectures and sermons given in England and Egypt, 1910–1917

The Graciousness of Uncertainty
    See **The Love of God**

Grow Up Into Him
    See **Our Brilliant Heritage**

He Shall Glorify Me (1946)
    Theme: Three chapters on the Holy Spirit, then miscellaneous sermons
    Lectures at the Bible Training College; talks to soldiers in Egypt

The Highest Good Later editions include **The Pilgrim's Song Book** and **Thy Great Redemption**
    The Highest Good (1938)
    Theme: Righteousness, morality, ethics
    Lectures from Christian Ethics class at the Bible Training College
    The Pilgrim's Song Book (1940)
    Theme: Psalms 120-128; The Pilgrim Psalms; the Psalms of Ascent
    Talks in Wensleydale District, summer 1915, before leaving for Egypt
    Thy Great Redemption (1937)
    Theme: Redemption
    Lectures given at the Bible Training College

If Thou Wilt Be Perfect (1939)
    Theme: Spiritual philosophy/mystic writers
    Lectures on Biblical Philosophy given at the Bible Training College

If Ye Shall Ask (1937)
    Theme: Prayer
    Lectures given at the Bible Training College; at League of Prayer gatherings in Britain; to British Commonwealth troops in Egypt

Knocking At God's Door (1957), first published as **A Little Book Of Prayers** (1938)
    Theme: A prayer for each day of the year
    Oswald Chambers' personal prayers gleaned from his journals

A Little Book of Prayers
    See **Knocking at God's Door**

The Love of God (1938)
    Theme: Three chapters on the love of God

Two talks on the love of God from Dunoon years; one talk from Egypt
The book includes:
The Ministry of the Unnoticed (1936)
　　Theme: Service in ordinary circumstances
　　Three devotional talks to students at Bible Training College
The Message of Invincible Consolation (1931)
　　Theme: Difficulties, suffering
　　Two talks on 2 Corinthians 4:16–18, given at annual meeting of the League of Prayer
The Making of a Christian (1918, 1935)
　　Theme: New birth, right thinking and living
　　Talks at Bible Training College and in Egypt
Now Is It Possible (1923, 1934)
　　Theme: Holy living, faith, discipleship
　　Three talks given to students at the Bible Training College
The Graciousness of Uncertainty (1938)
　　Theme: Faith, facing the unknown
　　Talk to soldiers in Egypt
The Making of a Christian
　　See **The Love of God**
The Message of Invincible Consolation
　　See **The Love of God**
The Ministry of the Unnoticed
　　See **The Love of God**
The Moral Foundations of Life (1936)
　　Theme: Ethical principles of Christian life
　　Lectures at the Bible Training College
My Utmost for His Highest (U.K. 1927; U.S. 1935)
　　Theme: Practical Christian living; a reading for each day of the year
　　Compiled by Mrs. Chambers from all her notes of Oswald's talks
Notes on Ezekiel (1949)
　　Theme: Abbreviated exposition of Ezekiel 1–34
　　Lectures at the Bible Training College
Notes on Isaiah (1941)
　　Theme: The character of God from Isaiah 1–53
　　Lectures at the Bible Training College
Notes on Jeremiah (1936)
　　Theme: Lessons about God and man from Jeremiah 1–29
　　Lectures at the Bible Training College
Not Knowing Whither (1934)
　　Theme: Faith; facing the unknown; lessons from the life of Abraham, Genesis 12–25
　　Lectures on Genesis at the Bible Training College
Now Is It Possible
　　See **The Love of God**
The Pilgrim's Song Book
　　See **The Highest Good**
Our Portrait in Genesis (1957)
　　Theme: Exposition of Genesis 1–6; 26–37
　　Lectures on Genesis at the Bible Training College
Our Brilliant Heritage, combined volume (1965) includes **Grow Up Into Him** and **As He Walked**
Our Brilliant Heritage (1929)
　　Theme: The Gospel mystery of sanctification
　　Talks to League of Prayer meetings, London
Grow Up Into Him (1931)
　　Theme: Christian habits

Lectures at the Bible Training College
As He Walked (1930)
　　Theme: Christian experience
　　Lectures at the Bible Training College
The Philosophy of Sin (1937)
　　Theme: Studies in the problems of man's moral life
　　Lectures at the Bible Training College
The Place of Help (1935)
　　Theme: Practical Christian living
　　Miscellaneous talks, many in Egypt identified by date and place
The Psychology of Redemption, subtitled Making All Things New (1922; 2d edition, 1930; 3d edition, 1935)
　　Theme: Parallels between the life of Christ and the Christian's life of faith
　　Lectures at the Bible Training College, League of Prayer convention, classes in Egypt
Run Today's Race (1968)
　　Theme: "Seed Thoughts," a sentence for each day
　　Drawn from previously published articles and books
The Sacrament of Saints
　　See **The Servant as His Lord**
The Saints In the Disaster of Worldliness
　　See **The Servant as His Lord**
The Servant as His Lord, combined volume (1959) of four previously published booklets
The Fighting Chance (1935)
　　Theme: Exposition of Romans 8:35–39
　　Talks given to a League of Prayer audience in London
The Soul of a Christian (1936)
　　Theme: Personal relationship with God
　　Lectures at the Bible Training College
The Saints In the Disaster of Worldliness (1939)
　　Theme: Perseverance, patience
　　Lectures to soldiers in Egypt
The Sacrament of Saints (1934)
　　Theme: Being made "broken bread" in the hands of God
　　Lectures in the Sermon Class at the Bible Training College
Shade of His Hand (1924)
　　Theme: "Is Life Worth Living?" Themes from Ecclesiastes
　　Talks to soldiers in Egypt
The Shadow of an Agony (1918)
　　Theme: War, upheaval, facing the tragedies of life
　　Talks to soldiers in Egypt
So Send I You (1930), subtitled, The Secret of the Burning Heart
　　Theme: The call, preparation, service of a missionary;
　　Lectures at the Bible Training College
The Soul of a Christian
　　See **The Servant as His Lord**
Studies In the Sermon on the Mount (1915, 1929)
　　Theme: Study of Matthew 5–7
　　Talks at League of Prayer convention and the Bible Training College
Thy Great Redemption
　　See **The Highest Good**
Workmen of God (1937), subtitled, The Cure of Souls
　　Theme: Dealing with the spiritual conditions of others
　　Talks to a League of Prayer audience in London

Index